DJing For Dummies

Cheat Sheet

What to Take when You're DJing

Pin this list to your door so you never forget the important stuff! Chapter 24 goes into more detail about the things you need.

Records/CDs

Take the right ones, and something to clean them with (see Chapter 3).

Headphones and slipmats

Not all clubs have them. Remember the headphone adaptor too!

MiniDisc recorder (or a blank tape)

Try to record everything you do for reference. MiniDisc is easier.

Demo tapes/CDs/MiniDiscs

You never know when the right person will ask you for a demo.

Tools

A small screwdriver set and some duct-tape can save the night.

Pen and paper

For requests, your drink orders, and giving out and taking phone numbers.

Something to drink (non-alcoholic)

An energy drink will keep you going through the night.

Something to eat

You can devour jelly babies or an energy bar in between mixes.

Car and house keys

Don't laugh – I always forget mine and get locked out.

Business cards

Keep your business cards in your wallet so they're on hand to give out to interested folks.

Chill tape for the ride home

To come down after the high of the best night of your life.

Calculating the Beats Per Minute (BPM) of a Tune

Beats per minute (BPMs) are a way to describe how fast your records are. The name gives it away; the BPM is the number of beats that occur in one minute. Count how many beats play in 30 seconds. If you counted the first beat when you started your watch, subtract 1, then double the result. If you didn't count that first beat, simply double the figure. That's your BPM.

Pitch Change versus Beats Per Minute Change

When you try to beatmatch two different records, knowing the BPM of each tune helps you make an educated guess as to how much to adjust the pitch control (which is what you use to make your tunes' bass beats play at the same speed).

If you don't want to guess, and want to work out the amount to change the pitch control more precisely, use the following formula to work out how much an adjustment on the pitch control will change the original BPM:

(Original BPM × pitch change) / 100 = BPM change

For example, 130 BPM tune with a 5 per cent pitch increase would be:

(130 × 5) / 100 = 6.5 BPM

For more about beatmatching, head to Chapter 12.

For Dummies: Bestselling Book Series for Beginners

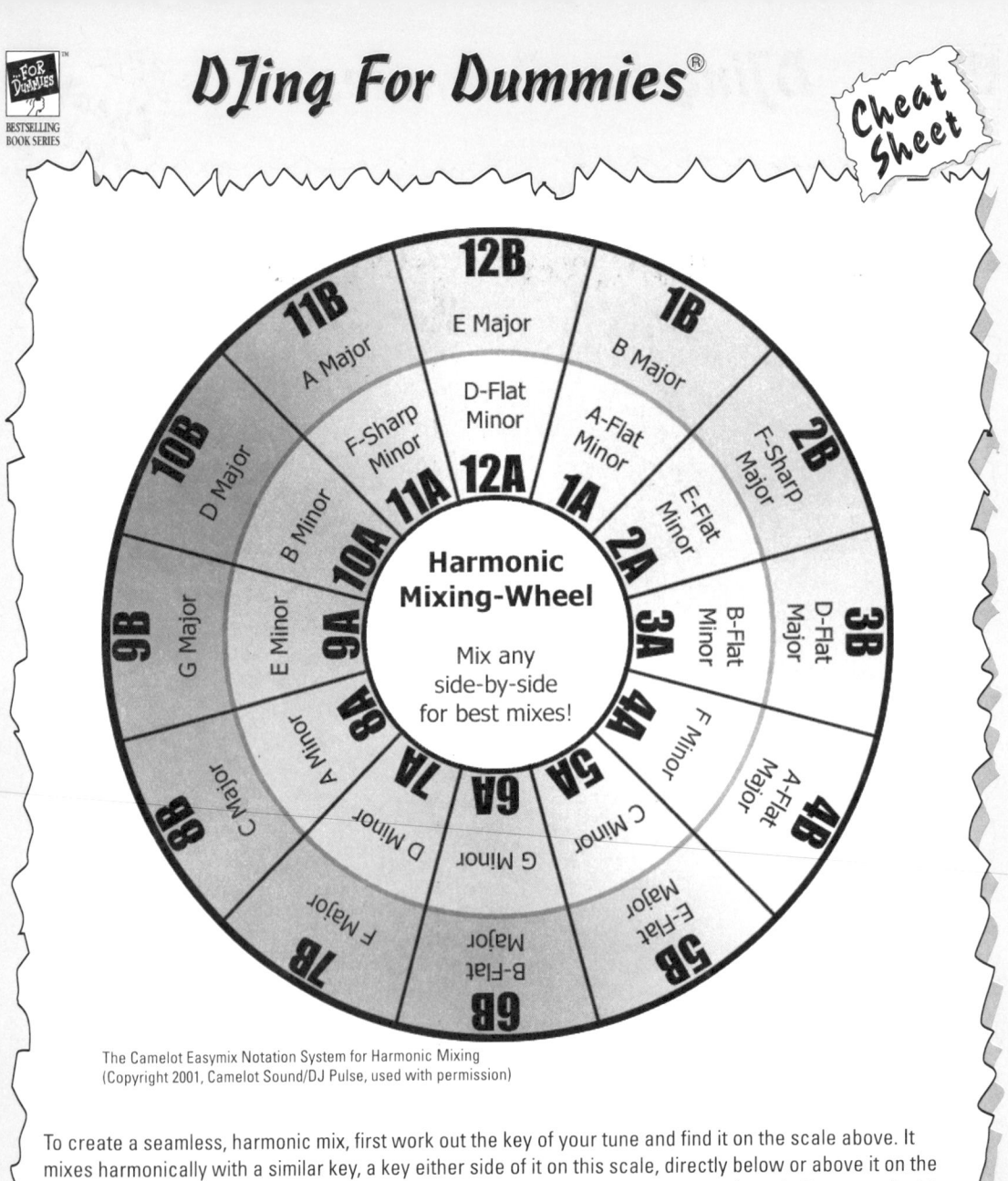

The Camelot Easymix Notation System for Harmonic Mixing
(Copyright 2001, Camelot Sound/DJ Pulse, used with permission)

To create a seamless, harmonic mix, first work out the key of your tune and find it on the scale above. It mixes harmonically with a similar key, a key either side of it on this scale, directly below or above it on the other ring, and to a lesser extent with the keys left and right on the ring below or above it. For example, 1A will mix well with 12A, 2A, and 1B, and will be acceptable to mix with tunes that have a key of 12B and 2B.

For more information about mixing, go to Chapter 14.

Copyright © 2006 John Wiley & Sons, Ltd. All rights reserved. Item 3275-8.
For more information about John Wiley & Sons, call (+44) 1243 779777.

For Dummies: Bestselling Book Series for Beginners

DJing

FOR

DUMMIES®

by John Steventon

John Wiley & Sons, Ltd

DJing For Dummies®
Published by
John Wiley & Sons, Ltd
The Atrium
Southern Gate
Chichester
West Sussex
PO19 8SQ
England

E-mail (for orders and customer service enquires): cs-books@wiley.co.uk

Visit our Home Page on www.wileyeurope.com

Wiley also publishes its books in a variety of electronic formats. Some content that appears in print may not be available in electronic books.

British Library Cataloguing in Publication Data: A catalogue record for this book is available from the British Library.

ISBN-13: 978-0-470-03275-6

Printed and bound in Great Britain by Bell & Bain Ltd, Glasgow.

10 9 8 7 6 5 4

WILEY

About the Author

John Steventon, also known as Recess, was transformed from clubber to wannabe DJ by BBC Radio 1's 1996 'Ibiza Essential Mix'. Fascinated by what he heard, he bought a second-hand pair of turntables, his best friend's record collection, and started to follow the dream of becoming his newest hero, Sasha.

With no other resource available when he first started DJing, John would take notes, writing articles to refer to if ever he felt like he needed help. Joining the Internet revolution meant 15 megabytes of free Web space, and as he'd already written these notes about learning how to DJ, John thought it would be good to share that information with the rest of the world wide web. He created the 'Recess' persona, and expanded the site as his knowledge grew. Originally a small, basic Web site, www.recess.co.uk has grown over the years both in size and reputation to become one of the foremost online resources for learning how to DJ – the place where newbie DJs turn to.

Having developed a career as a TV editor at the same time, now heading up post-production at a TV production company, he has scaled down the time spent DJing in clubs, but Recess is always online to help the new DJ overcome those first few hurdles, and offer advice to those who need that extra bit of reassurance.

John is 31, plays way too much squash and poker, is married to Julie, and they both live together with three cats and a smile on the outskirts of Glasgow, Scotland.

Dedication

This book is dedicated to my Dad, Richard Steventon, who I'm sure would have got a kick out of seeing his son write a book.

And to Julie: my best friend, my wife, my smile; without whom I'd be half a person. You are my lobster.

Author's Acknowledgements

My list of acknowledgments is surprisingly long, but these are the people without whom this book would not have been inspired, created, or nearly as long as it ended up!

Thanks to Graham Joyce, who sold me his record collection and started me on this journey, who got me my first break in a roundabout way, and took me to the place that I eventually met my wonderful wife. My sister, Pamela Tucker, who claims if it wasn't for her, I wouldn't have made friends with Graham and is therefore responsible for everything good in my life! My mum, Mary Steventon for being my Mum and for helping with the text accuracy in this book (even if she had NO idea what it all meant). My uncle, David Steventon, for sowing the seed that maybe people would find my writing interesting; my lovely in-laws, Jim (sorry, 'Sir'), Margaret (the lasagne queen), and Vicki Fleming for entertaining Julie while I spent months writing this book; Carol Wilson for making sure I wasn't signing away the rest of my life; and Lucky, Ziggy, and Ozzy for being my writing companions.

Ian, Jason, Nichol, Al, Gus, Jonny, Dave, Gary, Tony, Iain, and the other poker people for letting me blow off steam until 7 in the morning trying to take their money. All the staff and DJs at what used to be Café Cini in Glasgow where I got my break as a DJ. Paul Crabb for inspiration and distraction (I know, I still can't believe I wrote a book before you!) and Flora Munro for work deflection and a hell of a cup of coffee.

This book wouldn't have had half the info in it if it wasn't for the following people helping me out and kindly granting me permission to reuse images of their gear: David Cross at Ableton, Adam Peck at Gemini, Stephanie Lambley for Vestax images, Sarah Lombard at Stanton, Tara Callahan at Roland, Mike Lohman at Shure, Sarah O'Brien at PPLUK, Carole Love at Pioneer, Grover Knight at Numark, David Haughton at Allen & Heath, Wilfrid at Ortofon, Justin Nelson at NGWave, Ryan Sherr at PCDJ, Laura Johnston at Panasonic, Jeroen

Backx at Freefloat, all at Etymotic, NoiseBrakers, Sony, and Denon, Mark Davis from Harmonic-mixing.com, Yakov V at Mixedinkey.com for his help with the Harmonic Mixing info, everybody on all DJing Internet forums for letting me bug them for the past eight months, all the visitors to my Recess Web site, and everyone else who has touched this book in any way – I can't mention everyone, but thank you all.

And finally, from Wiley, Wejdan Ismail for keeping me afloat, Jason Dunne for giving me the chance to write this book, and believing in this project from the first conversation, and finally Rachael Chilvers, whose support, understanding, and encouragement made it a pleasure to write this book, so that it never felt like *work* and never became something I didn't want to do (and also for laughing at my poor jokes and stories).

Phew . . . let's hope I never win an Oscar!!

Publisher's Acknowledgements

We're proud of this book; please send us your comments through our Dummies online registration form located at www.dummies.com/register/.

Some of the people who helped bring this book to market include the following:

Acquisitions, Editorial, and Media Development

Executive Editor: Jason Dunne

Executive Project Editor: Martin Tribe

Project Editor: Rachael Chilvers

Development Editor: Kelly Ewing

Content Editor: Steve Edwards

Copy Editor: Juliet Booker

Technical Reviewer: Russell Deeks, Associate Editor, *iDJ* magazine

Proofreader: Anne O'Rorke

Special Help: Jennifer Bingham

Cover Photo: © JupiterImages

Cartoons: Rich Tennant, www.the5thwave.com

Composition Services

Project Coordinator: Jennifer Theriot

Layout and Graphics: Carl Byers, Karl Brandt, Denny Hager, Barbara Moore, Barry Offringa, Rashell Smith, Ronald Terry

Proofreader: Jessica Kramer

Indexer: Techbooks

Publishing and Editorial for Consumer Dummies

    Diane Graves Steele, Vice President and Publisher, Consumer Dummies

    Joyce Pepple, Acquisitions Director, Consumer Dummies

    Kristin A. Cocks, Product Development Director, Consumer Dummies

    Michael Spring, Vice President and Publisher, Travel

    Brice Gosnell, Associate Publisher, Travel

    Kelly Regan, Editorial Director, Travel

Publishing for Technology Dummies

    Andy Cummings, Vice President and Publisher, Dummies Technology/General User

Composition Services

    Gerry Fahey, Vice President of Production Services

    Debbie Stailey, Director of Composition Services

Contents at a Glance

Introduction 1

Part I: Stocking Up Your DJ Toolbox 7
Chapter 1: Catching DJ Fever...9
Chapter 2: Starting Off with the Bare Bones 17
Chapter 3: Retro Chic or PC Geek? Buying Records, CDs, and MP3s 31
Chapter 4: Shopping for Equipment.......................................47

Part II: Navigating the Maze: Equipment Essentials 63
Chapter 5: Getting Decked Out with Turntables 65
Chapter 6: Perfecting Your Decks: Slipmats and Needles 85
Chapter 7: Keeping Up with the Techno-Revolution 97
Chapter 8: Stirring It Up with Mixers 117
Chapter 9: Ear-Splitting Advice about Not Splitting Your Ears: Headphones........137
Chapter 10: Letting Your Neighbours Know That You're a DJ: Amplifiers.............147
Chapter 11: Plugging In, Turning On: Set-up and Connections....................157

Part III: The Mix 177
Chapter 12: Grasping the Basics of Mixing 179
Chapter 13: Picking Up on the Beat: Song Structure.....................199
Chapter 14: Mixing Like the Pros...211
Chapter 15: Mixing with CDs 227
Chapter 16: Scratching Lyrical 237

Part IV: Getting Noticed and Playing Live 257
Chapter 17: Building a Foolproof Set 259
Chapter 18: Making a Great Demo..275
Chapter 19: Getting Busy With It: Working as a DJ.......................301
Chapter 20: Facing the Music: Playing to a Live Crowd 313

Part V: The Part of Tens 331
Chapter 21: Ten Resources for Expanding Your Skills and Fan Base......................333
Chapter 22: Ten Answers to DJ Questions You're Too Afraid to Ask....................341

Chapter 23: Ten DJing Mistakes to Avoid 349
Chapter 24: Ten Items to Take with You When DJing 355
Chapter 25: Ten Great Influences on Me 359

Index 365

Table of Contents

Introduction 1

About This Book..1
Conventions Used in This Book 2
Foolish Assumptions 2
How This Book Is Organised...2
    Part I: Stocking Up Your DJ Toolbox 3
    Part II: Navigating the Maze: Equipment Essentials............3
    Part III: The Mix 3
    Part IV: Getting Noticed and Playing Live 3
    Part V: The Part of Tens..4
Icons Used in This Book...4
Where to Go from Here..4

Part 1: Stocking Up Your DJ Toolbox 7

Chapter 1: Catching DJ Fever 9

Discovering the Foundations of DJing....................................9
    Equipping yourself 10
    Making friends with your wallet 10
    Knowing your music 11
    Researching and discovering......................................11
    Connecting your equipment 12
Beatmatching Takes Patience and Practice...........................13
Working as a DJ 14

Chapter 2: Starting Off with the Bare Bones 17

Making a List, Checking It Twice.......................................17
Choosing Your Input Devices 18
    Thinking about turntables (for vinyl DJs).....................18
    Deciding on CD decks 20
    Musing on MP3s and PCs 22
Mixing It Up with Mixers 23
Monitoring Your Music with Headphones 24
Powering Things Up with Amplifiers 25
Figuring Out the Furniture 26
    Considering ergonomics and stability...........................26
    Selecting store-bought stands 27
    Building bricks and the new vibration killers.................27
Locating Your DJ Setup 28

Chapter 3: Retro Chic or PC Geek? Buying Records, CDs, and MP3s 31

Knowing Your Genre's Format Availability 31
    Reflecting on vinyl..32
    Keeping up with CDs...32
Buying Records and CDs 33
    Sizing up vinyl formats 33
    Sussing out CD options...34
    Researching your tunes...36
    Listening to the music 37
    Weighing up the pros and cons of classic anthems
      and new music 38
Byting into MP3s 39
Surfing into Online Record Stores...40
    Knowing where to go 40
    Previewing tracks 41
    Ordering and delivery...41
    Using auction sites 42
Protecting Your Records and CDs..42
    Storing records 42
    Cleaning records, CDs, and the needle............................43
    Repairing vinyl..44
    Fixing warped records and CDs 45
    Repairing CDs 45

Chapter 4: Shopping for Equipment 47

Taking Stock Before You Shop 47
    Trying before you buy 48
    Budgeting your money 48
Buying Brand New..50
    Cruising the high street 50
    Opting for online shopping 52
Buying Second-hand 53
    Scanning newspapers 53
    Dipping into pawn shops..54
    Bidding on auction Web sites 54
Making Sure That Your Kit Works 55
    Checking cables...56
    Testing turntables 56
    Vetting CD decks...58
    Monitoring mixers 59
    Assessing headphones 61
    Sounding out amplifiers and speakers 61

Part II: Navigating the Maze: Equipment Essentials.......63

Chapter 5: Getting Decked Out with Turntables 65
Avoiding Cheap Turntables 65
Motoring in the right direction...66
Watching out for pitch control design..67
Identifying Key Turntable Features 68
Start/Stop 68
On/Off...69
33/45/78 RPM 69
Strobe light..69
Deckplatters 70
Target light 71
Pitch control 72
Counterweight/height adjust..74
Antiskate..74
Removable headshell/cartridge 75
45 RPM adaptor 75
Customising Your Sound with Advanced Turntable Features.................76
Pitch range options...76
Pitch bend and joystick control 77
Tempo reset/Quartz lock...78
Master Tempo/Key Lock..79
Digital display of pitch..79
Adjustable brake for Start/Stop..80
Reverse play..80
Different shaped tonearms..80
Removable cabling 81
Digital outputs 82
Battle or club design 82
Built-in mixer 82
Servicing Your Turntables 83

Chapter 6: Perfecting Your Decks: Slipmats and Needles 85
Sliding with Slipmats 85
Choosing an appropriate slipmat..86
Winning the friction war 87
Getting Groovy with Needles and Cartridges...88
Choosing the Right Needle for Your DJ Style..93
Feeling the Force with Counterweight Settings 94
Nurturing Your Needles...95

Chapter 7: Keeping Up with the Techno-Revolution **97**

Choosing Your Format: Analogue or Digital 97
 My way is the best! 98
 Looking at the pros and cons 99
Choosing a CD Deck That Fits Your Style 104
Looking Into the Future of Vinyl 107
Getting into MiniDisc, MP3s, and PCs 107
 Remembering MiniDisc decks 107
 Wising up to MP3s 108
 Mixing with iPods 110
 Mixing on PC 111
Futureproofing with Live and Traktor 113
 Live 114
 Traktor 115

Chapter 8: Stirring It Up with Mixers **117**

Getting Familiar with Mixer Controls 117
 Inputs 117
 Outputs 118
 Multiple channels 119
 Cross-faders 119
 Channel-faders 122
 Headphone monitoring 123
 EQs and kills 124
 Input VU monitoring 125
 Gain controls 125
 Balance and pan controls 126
 Hamster switch 126
 Punch and transform controls 127
 Effects Send and Return 127
 Built-in effects 127
 Built-in samplers 129
 Built-in beat counters 129
 Beat light indicators 130
 Fader starts 130
Choosing the Right Mixer 131
 The seamless mix DJ 131
 The scratch DJ 132
 The effects DJ 133
 The party/wedding DJ 134
Servicing Your Mixer 135

Chapter 9: Ear-Splitting Advice about Not Splitting Your Ears: Headphones 137

Choosing a Good Set of Headphones 137
    Single-sided, coiled cords..140
    Swivelling earpieces..140
    User-replaceable parts..140
    Stick it to your ears..141
Remembering that the Volume Doesn't Have to Go Up to 11.................142
Using Earplugs...142

Chapter 10: Letting Your Neighbours Know That You're a DJ: Amplifiers 147

Choosing Suitable Amplification.......................................147
    Settling on your home stereo.....................................148
    Purchasing powered speakers....................................149
    Opting for an amplifier and separate speakers 149
    A power margin for error 150
Working with Monitors...152
Positioning Your Monitor...153
Noise Pollution: Keeping an Ear on Volume Levels 154
    Protecting your ears 154
    Keeping the noise down for the people around you.....................155
    Realising that you only need one speaker 155

Chapter 11: Plugging In, Turning On: Set-up and Connections 157

Getting Familiar with Connectors 157
    RCA/Phono connections..158
    XLRs 158
    Quarter-inch jack 159
Setting Up and Connecting the Turntable..........................160
    Deckplatter..160
    Tonearm...161
    Peripherals..164
Plugging In the Mixer...164
    Connecting turntables to a mixer...............................164
    Connecting CD decks to a mixer 166
    Connecting iPods and MP3s to a mixer......................167
    Connecting a computer as an input device 167
    Plugging in your headphones 168
    Connecting effects units to a mixer 169
    Connecting mixer outputs 170
    Connecting a mixer to your home hi-fi 171
    Connecting a mixer to powered speakers...................171

Connecting a mixer to your PC/Mac 172
Connecting your computer to an amplifier....................................173
Troubleshooting Set-up and Connections 173

Part III: The Mix...177

Chapter 12: Grasping the Basics of Mixing 179

Knowing What Beatmatching's All About 179
Understanding BPMs 180
Calculating BPMs..181
Discovering How to Beatmatch..182
Setting up your equipment..182
Locating the first bass beat..183
Starting your records in time..184
Adjusting for errors...187
Knowing which record to adjust 188
Using the Pitch Control 188
Matching the pitch setting 189
Playing too slow or too fast 190
Taking your eyes off the pitch control................................191
Introducing Your Headphones 193
Switching over to headphone control 193
Cueing in your headphones 193
Centre your head with stereo image..................................195
Practising with your headphones 197

Chapter 13: Picking Up on the Beat: Song Structure 199

Why DJs Need Structure...200
Multiplying beats, bars, and phrases..................................200
Hearing the cymbal as a symbol 202
Everything changes...203
Counting on where you are 203
Studying Song Structure...205
Accepting that Every Tune's Different 207
Developing Your Basic Instincts 208
Listening to a Sample Structure 208

Chapter 14: Mixing Like the Pros 211

Perfecting Placement...211
Intros over outros...212
Melodic outro..213
Melodic intro...214
Mixing Breakdowns..215

Controlling the Sound of the Mix 217
  Bringing the cross-fader into play...217
  Discovering the secret of channel-faders.............................218
  Letting you in on a big, curvy secret 219
  Balancing it out with EQs 220
Using Mixing Tricks and Gimmicks...221
  Spinbacks and dead-stops...221
  Power off..222
  A cappella 223
  Cutting in 223
Mixing Different Styles of Music...224
  The wedding/party/rock/pop mix...224
  The R & B mix 225
  Drum and bass, and breakbeat...226

Chapter 15: Mixing with CDs **227**
Navigating the CD..227
  Buttons 228
  Jog dials 229
  Platters..230
Working with the Cue 231
  Locating the cue 232
  Storing the cue...232
  Check the cue 233
  Starting the tune...233
Adjusting the Pitch 233
Taking Advantage of Special Features 235

Chapter 16: Scratching Lyrical **237**
Setting Up the Equipment the Right Way.................................238
  Weighing up needles 239
  Giving slipmats the slip 241
  Touching up mixers...241
  Making the mixer a hamster 241
  Setting the right height..242
Preparing for the Big Push...242
  Wearing out your records 242
  Marking samples..243
  Fixing the hole in the middle 245
Scratching on CD, MP3, and Computer 246
  Scratching on PC 247
  Marking CDs and MP3s...247
Mastering the Technique 248
  Getting hands on 248

Starting from Scratch and Back Again..249
   Scratching without the cross-fader......................................250
   Introducing cross-fader fever 251
   Combining scratches 254
Juggling the Beats 255
   Offsetting 256
   Practice, dedication, and patience....................................256

Part IV: Getting Noticed and Playing Live 257

Chapter 17: Building a Foolproof Set 259

Choosing Tunes to Mix Together 259
   Beatmatching – the next generation 260
   Mixing with care 261
   Getting in tune with harmonic mixing 262
   Keying tunes..266
   Knowing how much to pitch..267
Developing a Style..268
   Easing up on the energy 269
   Changing the key 269
   Increasing the tempo 270
   Avoiding stagnation 272
   Respecting the crowd 272
   Getting your style on tape...273

Chapter 18: Making a Great Demo 275

Preparing to Record the Demo..275
   Programming your set 276
   Picking and arranging the tunes 276
   Bridging the gaps..278
   Practising your set 278
   Setting up to record 279
   Correcting recording levels..281
Looking After Sound Processing...284
   Keeping an even volume..284
   Setting your EQs 286
Performing the Demo..289
   Stay focused 289
   Become a perfectionist..291
   Listen with an open mind 291
Making a Demo CD on Computer 292
   Editing your mix 292
   Burning a CD 295
Sending Off the Mix..298

Chapter 19: Getting Busy With It: Working as a DJ **301**

Marketing Yourself 301
Flood the world with your demo...302
Play for free 304
Offer owners what they want to hear 305
Joining an Agency 305
Research an agency...307
Meet the criteria to join...307
Cut your losses 308
Networking Your Way to Success...309
Sell yourself 309
Make friends...309
Go 'undercover' 310
Marketing Yourself on the Internet 310

Chapter 20: Facing the Music: Playing to a Live Crowd **313**

Investigating the Venue 314
Scoping the club 314
Getting ready to party...317
Preparing to Perform 318
Selecting the set 318
Organising your box..319
Knowing What to Expect at the Club...320
Dealing with nerves..320
Getting used to your tools..320
Working in a loud environment 322
Playing Your Music 322
Reading a crowd 323
Handling requests 324
Taking over from someone else 326
Finishing the night..328

Part V: The Part of Tens *331*

**Chapter 21: Ten Resources for Expanding Your Skills
and Fan Base** **333**

Staying Current with Media 333
Visiting DJ Advice Web Sites...334
Getting Answers through DJ Forums...334
Reading Other Books...335
Getting Hands-On Advice 336
Listening to Other People's Mixes 337
Participating in Competitions..337

Hosting Your Own Night 338
Uploading Podcasts or Hosted Mixes 338
Immerse Yourself in What You Love 339

Chapter 22: Ten Answers to DJ Questions
You're Too Afraid to Ask 341

Do I Need to Talk? 341
What Should I Wear? 342
How Do I Go to the Toilet? 342
Can I Invite My Friends into the DJ Booth? 343
How Do I Remove the Beat, or Vocals? 344
How Do I Choose My DJ Name? 345
Do I Get Free Drinks? (And How Do I Get Drinks from the Bar?) 346
Who Does the Lighting for the Night? 346
Should I Re-set the Pitch to Zero After Beatmatching? 347
What Do I Do if the Record or CD Skips or Jumps? 348

Chapter 23: Ten DJing Mistakes to Avoid 349

Forgetting Slipmats/Headphones 349
Taking the Needle off the Wrong Record 349
Banishing Mixer Setting Problems 350
Getting Drunk when Playing 350
Leaving Records Propped Up 351
Leaning Over the Decks 351
Avoiding Wardrobe Malfunction 352
Spending Too Long Talking to Someone 352
Leaving Your Last Tune Behind 352
Not Getting Paid Before You Leave 352

Chapter 24: Ten Items to Take with You When DJing 355

All the Right Records or CDs 355
Make it Personal with Headphones and Slipmats 356
You're a Star! MiniDisc Recorder (or a Blank Tape) 356
Pack Your Tools and Save the Day 356
Always Be Prepared: Pen and Paper 357
Keep Fuelled with Food and Drink 357
Spread the Music with Demo Tapes and CDs 357
Keep Moving with Car Keys 358
Have Wallet, Will Travel 358
Just Chill: Chill Tape for the Ride Home 358

Chapter 25: Ten Great Influences on Me 359

Renaissance – Disc 1 359
Tonsillitis 360
La Luna: 'To the Beat of the Drum' 360

Ibiza 1996 Radio 1 Weekend...360
The Tunnel Club, Glasgow 361
Jamiroquai – 'Space Cowboy' 362
Jeremy Healy..362
Alice Deejay – 'Better Off Alone' 362
Delirium 'Silence'...363
Sasha and Digweed Miami 2002...364

Index...*365*

Introduction

$\mathcal{P}$eople come to DJing from different places and for different reasons, but they can be split into those who love the music, those who want to make money, and those who think that DJing is cool and want to be famous. You may fall into one, or all three of these categories, but the most important one is loving the music.

If you're a good DJ, and get lucky, you may become rich and famous, but when you're starting off, if you don't love the music, you may become easily bored and impatient with the time and practise you need to invest in your skills, and quit. Even if you do manage to get good at DJing, if you don't love playing and listening to the music, night after night working in clubs will start to feel too much like work. DJing isn't work; it's getting paid to do something you love.

When I started DJing, I already loved the music, but the first time I experienced the true skill of a DJ working a crowd (Sasha, Ibiza 1996) I fell in love with DJing, and knew I wanted to be one. The mechanics of it didn't occur to me until I first stood in front of two turntables and a mixer, all I wanted to do was play other people's music and have control over a crowd.

About This Book

This book is based on my Web site www.recess.co.uk that since 1996 has given new DJs all over the world the information they need to become great DJs. I use a very simple technique for starting off as a DJ, which begins with the basics of starting tunes and matching beats. You can find many other ways to develop your skills, but as they skip the basics, and involve a lot of trial and error and confusion, I've had much more success coaching DJs with my process than I have with any other.

This book isn't only for the *club DJ* who plays electronic dance music (house/trance/progressive/drum and bass/breakbeat, and so on); the *party DJ* (weddings, parties, and also R & B and rock DJs) can find this book just as useful.

The equipment sections and how to use the variety of function options available to you (found in Part I) are relevant to all DJs. Beatmatching and scratching (check out Part III) are complicated subjects but I also cover mixing without beatmatching. Just because different skills are involved doesn't mean that club DJs should skip that part of the book, or that party DJs should rip out the beatmatching and scratching information. Knowledge is skill, and the more skilful you are as a DJ, the better you'll become, and the more work you'll get.

Conventions Used in This Book

Musical terms like *beat structure* are usually described using phrases that, to the uninitiated, can sound like gibberish. So if a boffin has used ten words to describe something, I've tried to put it across in a reader-friendly way.

I call the music you DJ with *tunes* or *tracks*. I've steered away from calling each track a *song* as songs imply vocals, and not all music you play as a DJ will have vocals.

I group CD/turntables/MP3 players and software as *decks* unless I'm writing in specifics. I figured you'd get bored of lines such as 'Go to your turntable/CD/PC/iPod and start the tune. Then go to the other turntable/CD/PC/iPod and put on a different tune'. Repetition is not a good thing. I repeat, repetition is not a good thing.

Foolish Assumptions

I assume that you find lines like the last one amusing. Don't worry; I know that I'm not funny, so I don't try too often. I won't distract you from the subject at hand, but every now and then, something takes over, and I try to be funny and entertaining. I apologise for that now, but after all, a humorous, entertaining approach is what the *For Dummies* series of books is famous for.

Apart from that, this book assumes that you want to be a DJ, that you want to put in the time it takes to get good at it, you love the music, and you won't get fed up when it takes longer than 10 minutes to be the next Sasha/Oakenfold/Tiesto/DJ QBert. I also assume that you don't have vast experience of music theory.

How This Book Is Organised

All *For Dummies* books are put together in a reader-friendly, modular way. You can look at the table of contents, pick a subject, flick to that page, and find the information you need.

The book still has a structure as a whole, like any other book. It starts at the beginning, with choices on what equipment to use, moves onto the process of developing DJ skills, and ends playing live to a crowd of a thousand people. This structure means that you can read it from cover to cover like any book, with you as the main character!

Part I: Stocking Up Your DJ Toolbox

Part I describes the core pieces of equipment that you need in order to be a DJ, the best ways to build your collection of tunes, and has a chapter dedicated to the art of shopping, with advice on shopping in the high street and going online to research and buy your tunes and equipment.

Part II: Navigating the Maze: Equipment Essentials

From a format choice of CD or vinyl or MP3 to how the controls on the mixer work, Part II is all about using, choosing, connecting, and setting up your equipment for DJ use. I wouldn't dare to presume to tell you exactly what to buy, but I do offer advice on what may be most suitable for you and your budget.

Part III: The Mix

The nitty-gritty of DJing. From the basics of beatmatching to the complicated moves demanded by the scratch artist, Part III deals with all the information you need to develop your skills as a DJ. This information is important so spend lots of time with this part, because the chapters describe key techniques that mould and shape you as a DJ.

Part IV: Getting Noticed and Playing Live

After developing your DJ skills, the next step is to get work and show people just how good you are. Part IV gives lots of information on how to sell yourself, how to create a great sounding (and looking) demo, and what to do once you get work. DJing is not simply a case of standing in the DJ booth expecting everyone to love everything you play!

Part V: The Part of Tens

These chapters squeeze in the last tips, tricks, and common sense reminders that ease the way toward you becoming a successful, professional DJ.

Icons Used in This Book

Every now and then, a little *For Dummies* message pops up in the margin of the book. It's there to let you know when something's extra useful, essential for you to remember, may be dangerous to your equipment or technique, or if what follows is technical gobbledegook.

This one's easy: it highlights something you should burn into your memory to help your progress and keep you on the right path on your journey to becoming a great DJ.

Tips are little bits of info that you may not need, but they can help speed up your development, make you sound better, and generally make your life easier as a DJ.

When you're starting out as a DJ, you may need to navigate your way through a number of tricky situations. A few of them end with broken records/needles and CDs, or a damaged reputation as a DJ. Heed the advice when you see this icon, and proceed with caution.

They're unavoidable; words put together by someone else in a small room that mean absolutely nothing. Where possible, I try to translate technical DJing terms into English for you.

Where to Go from Here

Go to the kitchen, make yourself a sandwich, pour a nice cold glass of water or hot pot of coffee, put on some music you love, and jump into Chapter 1 – or whichever chapter takes your fancy! If you want to know about beatmatching, go to Chapter 12; if you want to know how to connect your equipment, go to Chapter 11.

When you feel inspired, put down the book and try out some of the techniques you've read about. If you want to spend 20 minutes DJing just so you can hear the music, but don't want to concentrate on your skills, do it. Your love of the music and DJing is just as important as the mechanics of how you do it, if not more.

You can also jump online and check out the video and audio clips that support this book at www.recess.co.uk. The site that I've used to develop DJs from all over the world is now a resource for this book, just for you. You can drop me a line there, and ask me anything you want to know.

Part I
Stocking Up Your DJ Toolbox

The 5th Wave   By Rich Tennant

"No, I don't want my CDs browned or
toasted – I want them <u>burned</u>."

In this part . . .

Finding the right equipment and music to buy when you start your DJing journey can be a bit of a minefield. These opening chapters take you through the essentials you need to start DJing, and explore the shopping options open to you.

Chapter 1

Catching DJ Fever

. . . .

In This Chapter

▶ Having what it takes to be a DJ

▶ Mechanics and creativity

▶ Reaching the journey's end – the dance floor

. . . .

*T*he journey you take as a DJ – from the very first record you play when you enter the DJ world to the last record of your first set in front of a club filled with people – is an exciting, creative, and fulfilling one, but you need a lot of patience and practice to get there.

DJ turntables, CD players, and mixers are selling so quickly now that they're in danger of outselling guitars and pianos. Hundreds of DJs over the world are on a quest to entertain and play great music. Everyone needs an advantage when they compete with hundreds of like-minded people. Your advantage is knowledge. I can help you with that.

Discovering the Foundations of DJing

DJing is first and foremost about music. The clothes, the cars, the money, and the fame are all very nice, and I'm sure that DJs who get all the attention aren't complaining, but playing the right music and how a crowd reacts is what moulds a DJ. As the DJ, you are in control of everybody's night. As such, you need to be professional, skilful, and knowledgeable about what the crowd wants to hear, and ready to take charge of how much of a good time they're having.

What kind of DJ you become lies in how you choose, use, and respect your DJ tools and skills. Become a student of DJing as well as someone who loves music and performing to a crowd, and your foundations will be rock solid.

Equipping yourself

The equipment you use as a DJ can define you just as much as the music you play. The basic components you need are:

- ✔ **Two input devices.** You can choose from CD players, MP3 players, a PC with DJing software, or the more traditional vinyl turntables. (Head to Chapters 2, 5, 7, and 15 to find out more.)

- ✔ **A mixer.** This box of tricks lets you change from one tune to the other. Different mixers have better control over how you can treat the sound as you mix from tune to tune. (Chapter 8 tells you everything you need to know about mixers.)

- ✔ **A pair of headphones.** Headphones are essential for listening to your next record while one is already playing. (See Chapter 9 for some good advice.)

- ✔ **Amplification.** You have to be heard, and depending on the music you play, you have to be LOUD! (You can find out more in Chapter 10.)

- ✔ **Records/CDs/MP3s.** What's a DJ without something to play? (Take a look at Chapter 3.)

Providing that your wallet is big enough, making the choice between CD and vinyl is no longer a quandary. The functions on a turntable are equally matched by those on a CD player, so the decision comes down to aesthetics, money, and what kind of person you are. You may like the retro feel of vinyl and find that the music you want to play is available on vinyl, or you may like the modern look of CD players or laptops, and prefer the ready availability of MP3s and CDs – it's your choice. Chapters 3, 5, 7, and 15 can help you with your decision.

Making friends with your wallet

DJing costs money. Whether you shop online, or if you go to the high street, the first thing to do is look at your finances. If you've been saving up money for long enough, you may have a healthy budget to spend on your equipment. Just remember, the expense doesn't stop there. Every month new tunes are released, you'll be yearning for music to play and may start to think of buying other items in terms of how many records can you get, instead. I remember saying once '£50 for a shirt? That's 10 records!'

You don't get the personal touch, but shopping online can be cheaper for equipment and music, and if you can't afford new DJ equipment right now, use PC software to develop your skills, and buy the real thing when you can. Flip through to Chapters 4 and 7 for more information.

Knowing your music

Throughout the years I've been helping people to become DJs, one of the most surprising questions I've been asked is: 'I want to be a DJ. Can you tell me what music I should spin?' This question seems ridiculous to me. Picking the genre (or genres) of your music is really important, as you need to love and feel passionate about playing this music for the rest of your DJ career. (Head to Chapter 3 for more on genre and music formats.)

After you've found your musical elixir, start to listen to as much of it as you can. Buy records and CDs, listen to the radio, search the Internet for information on this genre, and discover as much as you can. This groundwork is of help when choosing the records you want to play, when looking for artist's remixes, and is an aid to developing your mixing style. Doing a tiny bit of research before you leap into DJing goes a long way towards helping you understand the facets and building blocks of the music you love. Become a student of trance, a scholar of jungle, and a professor of pop – just make sure that you start treating your music as a tool, and be sure to use that tool like a real craftsman.

Researching and discovering

You know the music you want to play, you've decided on the format that's right for you, you've been saving up for a while; now you need to wade through the vast range of equipment that's available and be sure that you're buying the best DJ setup for the job at hand.

With technology advancing faster than I can write this book, you can easily get lost in the features that are available to you on CD decks, mixers, and turntables. Take as much time as you can to decide on what you want to buy. Go online and do some research, ask others in DJ forums for their thoughts on the equipment you're thinking about buying, and make sure that you're buying something that does what you want it to do, and that any extra features aren't bumping up the price for something you'll never use.

Here's a brief guide to what to look for on each piece of equipment you may look to buy:

- ✔ Proper DJ turntables need a strong motor, a pitch control to adjust the speed the record plays at, a good needle, and sturdy enough construction to handle the vibrations and abuse that DJing dishes out. A home hi-fi turntable won't do, I'm afraid. Check out Chapter 5 for more information.

- ✔ Mixers ideally have 3-band EQs (equalisers) for each input channel, a cross-fader, headphone cue controls, and a good display to show you the level at which the music is sent out of the mixer so you don't blow any speakers accidentally. Chapter 8 goes into more detail on this and other functions on the mixer.

- ✔ CD decks need to be sturdy enough that they won't skip every time the bass drum booms over the speakers. The controls on a CD deck are more important than on a turntable because you can't physically speed up and slow down the CD with your hands. Jog wheels, easy-to-navigate time and track displays, and a pitch bend along with the pitch control are all important core features of a CD turntable. Chapter 15 is dedicated to everything CD-related.

- ✔ Headphones need to be comfortable, sound clear when played at high volume, and cut out a lot of external noise so that you don't have to play them too loud. Your ears are extremely important, so try not to have your headphones at maximum all the time. Chapter 9 is the place to go for guidance on choosing headphones and protecting ears.

- ✔ Volume and sound control are the watchwords for amplification. You don't need a huge amplifier and bass-bins for your bedroom, but similarly, a home hi-fi isn't going to be much use in a town hall. Chapter 10 helps you find the right balance.

Connecting your equipment

After you have all the pieces of your DJ setup, your final task is to put together the jigsaw. Knowing how to connect you equipment isn't just important, it's totally vital. If you don't know what connects to what, and what the ins and outs of your set-up are, you can't troubleshoot when things go wrong. And things do go wrong, at the worst of times.

Eventually, you'll be showing off your DJ skills and someone will ask you to play at a party with your equipment; equipment that you connected up a year ago, with the help of your 4-year-old brother. Think of the soldier who has to assemble a gun from parts to functional in minutes; that's how comfortable you need to be when connecting together the parts of your DJ setup – except you only need to kill 'em on the dance floor. (Chapter 11 tells you all you need to know about connections.)

Beatmatching Takes Patience and Practice

DJing is a combination of mechanical and creative skill. *Beatmatching* (adjusting the speed that two tunes play at so that their bass drum beats constantly play at the same time) is the mechanical aspect that's regarded as the core foundation of the club DJ. Given enough time, patience and practice, anyone can learn these basics. Look to Chapters 12 and 15 to find out more.

After the core skill of beatmatching, what sets a good DJ apart from an okay DJ is his or her creativity. You need another set of building blocks to help you develop your creativity. How you stack up these blocks plays a big part in determining how skilled a DJ you can become:

- ✔ Good sound control is the first building block of your skill and creativity. You need a good ear to gauge if one tune is too loud during a mix, or if you have too much bass playing to the dance floor. This skill is something that develops, and can be honed through experience, but a DJ with a good ear for sound quality is already halfway there. Chapter 14 covers sound control to create a great-sounding mix, and Chapters 18 and 19 have information about controlling the overall sound of your mix when playing live or to tape.

- ✔ A knowledge of the structure of a tune is the second essential building block in your quest to becoming a creative DJ. Knowing how many bars and phrases make up larger sections of tunes is important for creating exciting mixes. In time, DJs develop a sixth sense about how a tune has been made, and what happens in it, so they don't have to rely on pieces of paper, and notes to aid them with their mixes. Chapter 13 takes you through this structure step by step.

- ✔ Although scratching is considered more of a stand-alone skill, you can harness this technique to add a boost of excitement and unpredictability to the mix and is the third building block to creative DJing. Instead of letting a CD or record play at normal speed, the scratch DJ stops it with their hand and plays a short section (called a sample) backwards and forwards to create a unique sound. This also helps with the foundation mechanics of DJing. People are taught to be scared of touching their records, or don't have the gentle touch needed to work with vinyl or a CD controller properly. Scratching soon sorts all that out, leaving no room for excuses. Your dexterity working with your tunes increases tenfold by the time you've developed even the most basic of scratch moves as described in Chapter 16.

It's all about style

Style is the true creative avenue, because it's all down to the music. The order you play your tunes in, changing keys, mixing harmonically, changing genre, increasing the tempo, and creating a roller-coaster ride of power and energy are the reasons that one DJ is better than the other.

Your technique may be a little weak, but if you're playing the right tunes, that can be forgiven. (That's not an excuse to skip the basics though!) The idea is to create a set that tries to elicit emotional and physical reactions from the crowd; in other words, they dance all night, and smile all night.

Working as a DJ

The hardest bit about performance is actually getting the chance to perform. Every job in the entertainment industry is fought over by hundreds of people and you need to come out on top if you want to succeed.

You need to set yourself apart from the competition and make sure that you have the skills to sell yourself. Convince club owners and promoters that you're going to be an asset to their club, and then perform on the night. Here's what you need to do:

- ✔ Demo tapes (or CDs or MiniDiscs) are your window to the world. They are the first way to let people know what you're like as a DJ. Whether it's your friends, your boss, or someone in the industry, a demo is a reflection of you, and you only. Only release your best work, and don't make excuses if it's not good enough. Chapter 18 has the information you need about demos.

- ✔ Market yourself well. Use all avenues described in Chapter 19 to get even the most basic start in a club or pub.

After you've secured any kind of work, your development from beginner to DJ is only half way through. You've spent time creating a good mix in the bedroom, but now, no matter whether you're playing Cream in Liverpool, or the Jones's wedding at the local town hall, you need to pull off a successful night.

Consider the following (all of which are covered in more detail in Chapters 19 and 20):

- ✔ Like anything new, preparation is the key to a successful night. Leave yourself with no surprises, do as much investigation as possible, research the unknown, settle any money matters, make sure that you and the management (or wedding party) are on the same musical playing field, so that all you have to worry about on the night is entertaining the crowd.

✔ Reading the crowd is the most important skill you can develop and you may take weeks, months, even years to master the technique properly. The *tells* you pick up from the body language on the dance floor rival any poker player's. You look at the dance floor and instantly react to how people dance, and what their expressions are, and then compensate for a down-turn in their enjoyment, or build upon it to make it a night to remember.

✔ Because you're the main focal point of the night, you also have to be a people person. You are the representative of the club, and so need to act accordingly. One wrong word to the wrong person, one wrong tune played at the wrong time, or even something as simple as appearing as if you're not enjoying yourself, can rub off on the dance floor, and your job as an entertainer is on thin ice.

Above all, always remember from the bedroom to a bar, from a town hall wedding to the main set at a huge night club in Ibiza, you're here because you want to be a DJ. You love the music, you want to put in the time, you want to entertain people, and you want to be recognised for it.

Chapter 2

Starting Off with the Bare Bones

. . . .

In This Chapter

▶ Discovering a DJ's basic equipment

▶ Getting to know the vital controls and functions

▶ Putting an end to feedback and vibrations

▶ Using the right furniture

. . . .

*Y*ou have lots of options when it comes to choosing and buying your first set of DJ equipment. The amount of money you have to spend is one factor. Any decision you've already come to about using vinyl, CDs, or MP3s to mix with obviously has a huge impact on what you buy (help with that decision is given in Chapter 7), and the music and mixing style you want to adopt also plays a big part in your first DJ setup.

Consider this chapter as a shopping list of equipment you need to be a DJ. Later chapters help guide you towards the best equipment to use, and the most suitable equipment for your budget.

Making a List, Checking It Twice

You need to make sure that you get the appropriate gear for the music you want to play, and like any craftsman, you need to ensure that you get the right set of tools for the job.

Any DJ setup consists of the following basic elements, each of which I describe later in this chapter:

✔ **At least two input devices.** Turntables, CD decks, MP3 players, and even PCs are the common DJ input devices.

✔ **A mixer.** This is used to change the music that comes from the speakers from one input device to the other.

✔ **Headphones.** These plug into the mixer so you can hear the next tune you want to play without anyone else hearing it through the speakers.

↙ **Amplifier.** Without an amplifier (and speakers), the people on the dance floor won't hear any of the great music you've chosen to play.

↙ **Something to put it all on.** You could sit on the floor cross-legged, with everything laid out on the carpet, but it's probably easier to build, buy, or borrow some furniture.

Add to that a few meters of cabling, some understanding neighbours, and a bunch of CDs and records, and your DJ journey can begin.

Choosing Your Input Devices

As a DJ, you can choose from a wide range of current formats:

↙ Vinyl

↙ CD

↙ MiniDisc

↙ MP3 (includes using a PC or Mac)

↙ Whatever else comes along in the future.

Although what to use is technically your choice, depending on the genre of music you want to play, your decision may already have been made for you. (Check out Chapter 3 for information about how genres affect format choices.) The following sections describe each format.

The one thing I'd say before going through your options is that though having only one CD deck and only one turntable may seem like a good idea, it may lead to a lot of confusion, and force your hand in many mix situations. You'll have to mix from vinyl to CD, to vinyl to CD, and so on, losing the option of mixing from one CD to another, or one vinyl tune to another vinyl tune.

If you think you'll primarily be a vinyl DJ, you can gamble and just buy one CD deck (with your two turntables), in hopes that you'll never want to mix from CD to CD, but that's still a risk. Or, if you're planning on just using CDs, you may want to have a turntable, which you can incorporate into your DJ setup, or use it to transfer your vinyl tunes onto CD.

Thinking about turntables (for vinyl DJs)

Turntables are the workhorse of the DJ industry. They've been around in one form or another since the dawn of recorded music, and have been the main-stay in clubs and a vital part of dance music since its conception. A record is a circular piece of hard, but flexible vinyl with a single spiral groove cut into each side that starts on the outer edge and eventually ends up in the centre of the record. This groove contains millions of tiny bumps and variations that contain the music information.

To turn these bumps back into music, the needle (also called a *stylus*, with a diamond tip) sits inside this groove. The record sits on a rotating disc (called a *deckplatter*) so that the needle travels from any particular starting point in the groove and gradually works its way towards the centre. The bumps and variations in the groove cause the needle to vibrate. These vibrations are converted to an electrical signal, which is then sent directly to an amplifier, (or, in a DJ setup, to a mixer), and is then translated into musical sound.

You must use the correct kind of turntable. The one that comes with your parent's hi-fi is unlikely to be suitable for DJing (unless your dad is Fatboy Slim). These record players are meant for playing records in one direction, at a normal speed, and don't have to deal with knocks and vibrations like a DJ turntable must.

The bare minimum requirements for a DJ's turntable are

- ✔ A variable pitch control to adjust the speed of the record (typically through a range of 8–10 per cent faster or slower than normal). Advanced turntables give the option of up to 100 per cent pitch change, but if this is your first turntable, that isn't a vital option right now.

- ✔ A removable *headshell* to use different kinds of DJ-suitable needles and cartridges (see Chapter 6 for more information).

- ✔ A smooth surface to the deckplatter so it will turn under the *slipmat* (a circular piece of felt that sits between the record and the deckplatter See Chapter 6 for more).

- ✔ Enough motor power to keep the turntable spinning under the slipmat if you hold the record stopped with your hand (Chapter 5 has more about different styles of turntable motor, and how the *torque* (power) of the motor can help or hinder your mixing capabilities).

Options such as anti-skate, Stop and Start buttons, target light, dimpled turntable plate with a strobe light, and a solid outer chassis (which helps to prevent vibrations), aren't on the bare essentials list for a turntable to DJ with, but without them, you may find some techniques really difficult! Fortunately, almost all DJ decks come with these functions. (If you're unsure of what any of these features are and want more information, go to Chapter 5, which describes them all in full detail.)

Because of their build quality and strength, the Technics 1200 and 1210 series of turntables have become the industry standard in the DJ booth, although the top-range Vestax turntables have made a considerable dent in Technics'

former monopoly. However, even second-hand Technics and Vestax decks are an expensive piece of kit, so fortunately for the DJ on a budget, DJ turntables by other manufacturers emulate this classic design, such as the Gemini TT02 shown in Figure 2-1).

The advantages of this familiar design are the layout of controls, the counter-weighted tone-arm, and the position and size of the pitch control. The long pitch control running down the right-hand side of the turntable enables the DJ to be a lot more precise when setting the playing speed for the record. Some of the really cheap turntables on the market have very small pitch sliders or knobs, making it harder to change the pitch by the minute amounts sometimes necessary.

Although features have been added, corners have been rounded, and basic designs have been improved upon, this basic design in Figure 2-1 is one you come across most often when choosing a DJ turntable – all around the world.

Figure 2-1:
The Gemini
TT02
turntable.

Deciding on CD decks

Once upon a time you could only play a CD at normal speed, and you had to place your CD players on cotton wool to prevent vibrations. As for finding the right place to start the tune and starting it at the right time, those details lay in the lap of the gods of technology rather than DJ skill.

Fortunately for everyone, the design and technology of CD decks for DJ use has improved incredibly over the years.

As with turntables (see preceding section), when choosing your CD decks, try to avoid standard CD players that are used with a hi-fi, or portable 'Walkman' style CD players. Even if you're not worried about changing the speed of the song, DJ CD decks are a lot easier to control and can take a lot more abuse and vibration than a typical home CD player.

CD decks for DJs should include the following vital functions:

- ✔ Pitch control (the same as with turntables, having a range of at least 8 per cent faster or slower than normal).

- ✔ A set of controls that lets you easily find the song or part of the song you want to play. These controls are either buttons that skip through the CD or the tune, or a *jog wheel*, which is turned clockwise or anti-clockwise to skip through the tune with more precision.

- ✔ A time display that you don't have to squint at to read (especially in the dark!).

Chapter 15 has more detailed descriptions of CD deck functions, and how to use CD decks to mix with instead of vinyl.

Optional basic controls that I strongly suggest include:

- ✔ Pitch bend (to temporarily speed up or slow down the CD without using the pitch control).

- ✔ An anti-skip function built into the CD player (which prevents the CD from skipping from all the bass vibrations in a loud environment).

- ✔ Ability to play CD-RW discs (rewritable CDs that can be made and erased a number of times).

The pitch bend feature isn't necessarily vital on beginner's CD decks, but without it, you'll face a lot of difficulty mixing. And without anti-skip, you have to be careful not to bump your decks or set the bass in the music too high because the CD will most likely skip. Something's 'retro cool' about a record jumping, but when a CD skips, you want to hit the decks with a hammer!

Even though most home CD players can play CD-R (recordable on once only) and CD-RW (multiple recordings) discs nowadays, basic DJ CD decks may not have that feature. With the Internet giving access to a lot of rare music, you'll want your CD decks to play burnt CDs without skipping.

Musing on MP3s and PCs

MP3s are computer music files that have been *compressed* (reduced in size) while still retaining most of the original sound quality. This makes them easy to download and send over the Internet, and they take up very little storage space on computer hard discs and personal *MP3 players* (similar to a Walkman or personal CD player, but a lot smaller). To give you an idea of how this compression helps, my iPod (a popular, fashionable MP3 player) is only 60 gigabytes in size, but it contains enough music so that I wouldn't hear the same tune play for *six weeks*! I'd need over 800 CDs to hold the same amount of music. MP3s are here to stay, and the DJ equipment manufacturers have been quick to realise it. You can burn MP3s to a CD disc as a traditional CD that can play on any CD player, or you can create an MP3 disc, which stores more tunes than a CD, keeping the files in MP3 format. You need a CD deck that can play these MP3 discs.

Although you can plug iPods and any other personal MP3 player into a mixer directly, they aren't used for anything other than the most basic level of DJing. As with turntables and CD players, it's the ability to alter the speed your music plays at that sets apart conventional home equipment from DJ equipment. (Chapter 7 has more information about mixing with personal MP3 players, and Chapter 11 covers connecting an MP3 player to your mixer.)

As MP3s start off as computer files, there are a few different ways to utilise them.

Software

Nowadays, you can find a new wave of DJs who carry only a laptop, headphones, and a couple of cables. *Laptop DJing* is sweeping through the DJ community (for better or for worse). You may need to modify your PC to turn it into a DJing system, but it usually means buying only a new sound card.

The advantage of using your PC to mix is that the software normally contains the entire DJ mixing package. In a series of windows, or one well-designed window, the software gives the user two input players on screen and a mixer. So all you need is a lot of music files and your PC's soundcard connected to an amplifier, and you're a DJ!

MP3s aren't the only file formats that you can play with DJing software. As long as your hard drive is large enough to hold the files, most programs play the majority of common audio formats available today.

The range, complexity, and price of software available to the PC (or Mac) DJ is growing at an extraordinary speed. As processing speed increases and hard drives become larger and cheaper, more titles come onto the market. Traktor by Native Instruments is fast becoming the industry standard, but software such as BPM Studio Pro, PCDJ, Virtual DJ, and MixVibes to mention a few are all available on the market. The Hitsquad Musician Network's Web site (www.hitsquad.com/smm/cat/DJ_MIXING/) holds a lot of shareware versions of this software, and many other titles.

A backlash has emerged against Laptop DJs, similar to when CD DJing took off, putting a lot of vinyl jocks' noses out of joint. The big problem with Laptop DJing is that it lacks performance.

To combat the lack of showmanship when DJing on computer, software companies have designed controllers for the PC and Mac, which help take the mouse-click out of DJing. In my opinion, the software company Ableton (www.ableton.com) is leading the way with its *Live* software. DJing deity Sasha has stopped using vinyl, preferring to use a Mac with the Live software and a controller that helps him create unique DJ sets. (Chapter 7 has more about Live and the other control options when using MP3s on a PC or Mac.)

MP3 DJ decks

MP3 decks can be split into two camps:

- ✔ CD decks that can play MP3 CDs (a CD that has MP3 files burnt to it in MP3 format rather than a normal uncompressed CD files).

- ✔ Players that contain their own internal hard drive, on which you can store tens of thousands of audio files.

Because MP3 decks' design and controls are normally identical to those of CD decks, they have the same basic vital functions as DJ CD decks. However, because an MP3 CD can hold 100 songs and hard-drive systems can hold over 100,000 songs, you need a comprehensive, but easy-to-use, menu system to help you navigate through the massive library quickly.

Mixing It Up with Mixers

The mixer is the glue that keeps the night running smoothly, and the dancers dancing without falling over. The purpose of the *mixer* is to alter the sound that you hear from one input to another without any breaks – creating a seamless transition. Chapter 8 contains detailed information about everything mentioned below and further information about more advanced features on mixers.

The most basic features a mixer must have for DJ use are:

- ✔ **A cross-fader.** On most DJ mixers, the important control that helps to change the sound from one input to another is the *cross-fader*. As you move the *cross-fader* from left to right (or reverse), the sound you hear through the speakers gradually changes from one deck to the other. If you leave the *cross-fader* in the middle, you hear both songs playing at the same time. How you change the music from one song to the other is a massive part of how you're regarded as a DJ.

✔ **At least two input channels.** These should have a switch on each to select a *phono input* (to use turntables) or a *line input* (for everything else).

✔ **Headphone monitoring with Pre Fade Listen (PFL).** PFL (or cue) lets you hear the music through the headphones without it playing through the speakers. This is vital when you want to set the right start point for the next tune, and when you're beatmatching.

✔ **LED indicators to display the sound level inputting and outputting through the mixer.**

✔ **Gain controls.** These are used in conjunction with the input LED indicators, and are extremely important for keeping the overall level (volume) of the mix smooth, creating a professional sound to the mix.

✔ **EQs (equalisers) for the bass, mid, and high sound frequencies.** These three simple controls help you add creativity, and improve the sound quality of the mix, transforming lacklustre transitions from one tune to another into great-sounding, seamless ones.

Budget mixers (around £50) are likely not to have the gain and EQ controls. These aren't 100 per cent necessary if you're a party DJ that doesn't create long, overlapping mixes, but for the sake of around £30 more, you can find a mixer (such as the Numark DM1050) which has everything I recommend at an affordable price range.

With these functions, you have a lot of control over your mixes and can go a long way toward sounding like a pro. A whole range of features and functions can help you adjust and improve your mixes, but they aren't as vital as the six I describe in the preceding list.

Monitoring Your Music with Headphones

Don't underestimate the importance of a really good set of headphones. When you're in the middle of a noisy DJ booth, your headphones are the only way to ensure that the mix is as smooth as your hairstyle.

Though not a major factor when practising DJing in your the bedroom, in the live arena having clear headphones that don't distort when you turn them up really loud is extremely important. If you can't easily, and clearly hear the records you're playing now and want to play next, your mix has the potential to go really wrong, really quickly!

When choosing a good starter set of DJ headphones, concentrate on comfort and sound. Make sure they're soft and nice to wear, and that when you use them, you can hear a good bass thump and the high frequencies are clear. If you get a chance to test them at quite a loud volume, carefully do so (you don't want to damage them, or your ears), just to make sure that they don't distort or that the mid-range frequencies don't drown out the bass beats.

If you choose to buy budget headphones so you can afford better turntables, I have to recommend that you spend your first DJ pay cheque on a good pair of DJ-specific headphones – you'll only encounter problems with poor headphones and may not get any more pay cheques! Check out Chapter 9 for loads more about headphones.

Good headphones are *very* important, and so are your ears. Remember to get quality headphones that won't destroy your ears with a high mid-range, but also remember they don't always have to be at full volume!

Powering Things Up with Amplifiers

The sound signal that comes out of the mixer is barely strong enough to power your headphones, so you need something to increase (amplify) this signal so that it drives some speakers (makes 'em work). You can amplify your music in four different ways (Chapter 10 has more on these options):

- **Buy a separate amplifier and speakers.** This choice can be a bit costly, but it's a great way of doing it.

- **Plug the mixer's output cable into the CD or AUX port in the back of your home stereo (if you have one).** I prefer this method at home because it cuts down on the amount of equipment you need – and money you have to spend – and it means that you already have a built-in tape recorder, or MiniDisc recorder, to record your mixes.

- **Use powered speakers – speakers that contain a built-in amplifier.** Providing that they're sufficiently powerful to let you hear the music loud enough, they will suffice.

A few people I know actually use the powered speakers from their computers. For professional use, my preference is a great monitor by JBL (which is used in DJ booths a lot). I use a pair of Roland powered speakers at home right now as my decks are in a small room that doesn't need a massive amount of amplification. They've got big speakers in them and sound great when turned up loud.

> ✔ **Use the speakers on your Mac or PC.** This approach is pretty much the same as using powered speakers, except that instead of connecting the speakers directly to the mixer, you connect your mixer to a computer's soundcard first. This method has the added bonus of being able to record to your computer anytime, for easy uploading of your mixes to the Internet. (Chapter 11 has guidance on connecting your mixer to a computer.)

Figuring Out the Furniture

Furniture is probably the most overlooked and least thought about aspect of your DJ setup. Some people spend weeks researching the best decks and mixer to buy and completely forget that in the end, they need something to put them on.

Two items of furniture for you to consider are:

✔ Something to put your decks and mixer on

✔ Somewhere to keep your records and discs

Considering ergonomics and stability

When looking for a DJ desk, you need something that's solid enough so the needle doesn't jump and the CD can't skip when your cat breathes on it. Even more important is the height level of your decks and mixer.

If you need to bend down to use your equipment, you'll end up like the Hunchback of Notre Dame after all the hours of practice you'll be putting in. So make sure that your equipment is at a height that enables you to practise with your body erect and your shoulders back, in line with your spine. I have a great friendship with Dr Dan, my chiropractor, due to years of not following my own advice!

Correct ergonomics for any desk (and that includes a DJ 'desk') are that you need not reach, stretch, or bend to use equipment. Ideally, you want to stand tall, with your shoulders back, and your elbows at 90 degrees when DJing. Protect your neck, too, by looking down at the controls, rather than craning your neck downwards like a goose! Although everybody's height is different, these ergonomic principles mean that if you're using something like a computer desk, you probably need to find some bricks or a couple of breezeblocks to raise your decks to a comfortable height.

Selecting store-bought stands

A few desk units are specifically designed for DJ use, with an adjustable height, a flat top for your decks and mixer, and some big cabinets underneath to keep your records in. My concern with keeping everything in the same unit is that if you're flopping all your records around in the cabinet when trying to find a tune, moving 50 records from left to right creates a hell of a wallop – and is likely to skip the needle.

Check out any online DJ store, and you find a great range of DJ desks and stands. Nearly all of them are flat-pack so you need to assemble them yourself – make sure you pack some patience with your screwdriver!

I've found that the king of flat-pack, Ikea, do a great unit (in the 'Billy' range) that your decks can fit on/in – the only problem is that the shelves would never take the weight of 2,000 tunes. (See www.ikea.co.uk.)

I was lucky enough that a unit that my Dad had built in the 1970s, and which everything sits on perfectly, was lying around in my house. The records don't fit in the unit, but I prefer not to keep the records in the same unit anyway.

For my records, I use a hard plastic shelving stand from a DIY shop. It holds about 2,000 records, shows no sign of buckling from the weight, and lets me keep my records standing on their sides. Two reasons why this is important are: flicking through your records is easy, and records warp if left piled on top of each other.

If you do keep your records in a similar shelving unit, make sure the unit is level, and store your records so that the opening is against a wall. I had a terrible accident with Timo Maas's *Ubik* when it dropped out of its sleeve because of a wonky shelving unit – let's just say it's half the record it used to be . . .

Building bricks and the new vibration killers

Another point to consider with your furniture is how to minimise vibrations. Though there's a chance your needles may skip if you're bumped into by a clumsy dancer, the main concern is with speaker vibrations, and feedback, or 'howl round'.

Remember that the purpose of the needle is to translate vibrations from the record groove into sound. Feedback happens when the sound from your speakers reaches the turntable (through sound vibrations), and is re-amplified – which reaches the turntable, and is re-amplified. This re-amplification creates a snowball effect (a re-re-re-re-re-amplification), creating a ringing noise that rapidly gets louder and louder, which is known as *feedback*. It hurts your ears and your speakers, so try to avoid it.

If possible, avoid putting speakers on the same unit that your decks are on, but if you can't avoid that arrangement, try to minimise the vibrations by setting the decks on something that absorbs the vibration. Like in many bedrooms of budding DJs across the world, I used to sit my decks on top of bricks. If you're looking for a classier way of doing the same thing, you can use specially designed 'feet' for your turntables. Made out of metal, they replace the normal rubber feet that are on each corner of the turntable to absorb vibrations more effectively than a brick can.

Isolator feet can be quite expensive (around £90 for 4). A fantastic alternative if you can afford £30, is the Freefloat 'cushion' that you sit the decks on top of (Figure 2-2 shows the Freefloat deck stabiliser). This cushion not only stabilises the decks, but has the added advantage of looking a lot better than some bricks 'borrowed' from a building site!

Figure 2-2:
The Freefloat deck stabiliser.

Locating Your DJ Setup

Where you set up your decks in the bedroom has probably already been decided by the current position of your bed and television, but if you have loads of space to tinker with and can consider positioning yourself anywhere in the room then the main factor is to stay near to your speakers. Chapter 10 has a section on positioning your monitors, but as long as you're within

4 feet of a speaker, you don't have to worry about audio delay or acoustic problems.

One thing that has always amazed me is why bedroom DJs feel the need to set up their decks so that they're facing a wall. Try turning everything around so that you're looking out across the room. This positioning not only helps with visualisation, when you start to imagine yourself playing in a big club, but looks a lot more impressive when your mates come to see you show off your skills. You need to keep the cables tidy so they're not all hanging off the back of the desk, but this aspect gives you a much better feel of being in the DJ booth.

Chapter 3

Retro Chic or PC Geek? Buying Records, CDs, and MP3s

• •

In This Chapter

▶ Looking at how genre affects what format you use

▶ Buying your tunes the smart way

▶ Considering the legalities of MP3s

▶ Caring for your CDs and records

• •

*I*f your decks, mixer, and headphones are the tools you use as a DJ, consider your records, CDs, and MP3s as the nails, screws, and glue that you need in order to perform your best work.

In this chapter, I cover the different formats depending on genre, what to look for when buying your tunes, and how to make sure that your hard-found records and CDs stay in great condition, for as long as possible.

Knowing Your Genre's Format Availability

Though you may dream of being a vinyl DJ, the genre you want to play may force you to be a CD DJ, instead. During the '70s and '80s, this factor wasn't an issue, as music was released across all formats, vinyl, tape, and then CD. But, as records became less popular, and CD became the main way to buy music, the choice of what you can play on vinyl has dropped considerably.

So musical genres can be split into two distinct groups:

▶ Music available on vinyl

▶ Everything else

Reflecting on vinyl

As sales for the home consumer market have fallen over the years, vinyl has been aimed almost exclusively at the club music market because of its long associated history. Music genres such as house, trance, drum and bass, hip-hop, and techno still release the majority of their tunes on vinyl.

Some rock, classical, folk, and country music is still released on vinyl, and a bit of a resurgence is going on in the indie/alternative scene in the UK for 7-inch singles, but when you compare the range of music that's released across all the different genres, only a tiny percentage of it is available on vinyl.

Unreleased music is certainly an area that keeps vinyl alive. Record companies sometimes send a promotional recording (promo, in the business) to DJs in hopes that it will get early exposure and gain popularity at gigs. Promotional copies of music can be like gold dust in the DJ world, and when you start to receive promos on vinyl, you know that you're worth something as a DJ, as vinyl promos become more and more rare.

CDs and MP3s have become more popular for promos because they're cheaper and more convenient to send out than pressing a thousand records. Vinyl is still handed out to the chosen few, however, and you know that you're in a position of reckoning when you're a working DJ who receives promos on vinyl.

As well as releases from some underground, smaller record labels, many bootlegs and unsigned records are still only available in stores on vinyl. These *white label records* are produced for a number of reasons: If the artist hasn't been signed to a proper record label; as a limited pressing released by an artist or band that wants people to hear and use their music (often with a view that a major label will notice, and sign them up); or when a record label wants to release a market taster before committing money and resources to a tune for a major release.

Keeping up with CDs

Hardly any music is released nowadays that isn't available on CD. Dance, rock, folk, classical, country, pop – all waiting for you on a shiny, 12-centimetre disc.

Though promotional and bootleg records aren't always available on CD, and some underground record labels don't release CD versions of their records, this factor isn't a huge problem. The easiest way around this hurdle is just to buy yourself a cheap (but good quality) turntable, buy the tunes you can't get on CD as vinyl, record them to PC, and burn them onto a CD. (For more on buying equipment, see Chapter 4.)

Unfortunately, recording from CD to vinyl doesn't work out quite as cost effectively. As a rock DJ, you find that most of the tunes you want to play are on CD only, so to be a rock DJ that uses vinyl, you need a way to transfer the CDs you want to play onto vinyl. For example, Vestax make a 'vinyl burner' (the VRX-2000), and Vinylium make the Kingston Dub Cutter to add onto a standard Technics turntable. Both of which etch the music into blank 12-inch records, but at around £4,500 for the Dub Cutter and £8,500 for the Vestax, you'd better be making a *lot* of records to get your money's worth.

Buying Records and CDs

CDs and records are expensive, so you need to make sure that you're buying the right music, by the right people, from the right place. Therefore, you need to consider all options when you're about to spend your hard-earned money.

Sizing up vinyl formats

As you may already know, vinyl comes in a number of different sizes, as follows:

- **7-inch singles:** Not as popular as they were a few years ago, 7-inch singles tend to have the main release on the A-side and a different song on the B-side. The A-side may be a specially edited version of the original tune for radio (known as a *radio-edit*), which cuts it down to a minimum length and content, and may remove parts of the tune that you'd really want the crowd to hear. You may also find that you don't like, or don't want to play, the B-side to a crowd of clubbers either.

   7-inch singles are small so they're quite fiddly to work with, and the cut-down version of the main tune on the A-side, and lack of remixes of the tune, mean that they aren't often used by club DJs. However, many northern soul, ska, and reggae DJs still find that the 7-inch is king for releases of their music.

- **LPs:** You'd think that as a vinyl DJ, buying an *LP,* or an album on vinyl, of an artist's music would make good financial sense because all their tracks are included on it. If you're only interested in playing the original recording and aren't going to scratch, then this option isn't that bad.

   Wedding and party DJs who still like to use vinyl can use LPs because the tune on the record is more than likely the one most people are familiar with, and they aren't likely to do any scratching!

The downside to using full-length LP albums is that they're quite hard to use for club DJing due to the amount of space dedicated to each song. With only an inch or two's worth of vinyl available to play the entire track, you may find that the *map of the tune* (see Chapter 13), which is created by the different shading of the black rings, is fairly difficult to see, and the tightly compacted groove is more prone to picking up scratches, pops, and crackles.

✔ **12-inch singles:** These singles are designed and produced with the DJ in mind. Typically, you get two or three *remixes* of the same tune on the one record, offering a lot more choice and versatility with how you play the tune. Remixes are variations of the same tune, sometimes by the producer who created it, or sometimes by other producers who change the sound of the original tune entirely (like Tiesto did to Sarah McLachlan's 'Silence'). The lay out of the record changes from tune to tune, but often, the main mix that the record company feels may be most popular sits on an entire side of a 12-inch single, with the other side left for a couple of remixes.

Though you do find a second, different tune on the B-side of some 12-inch singles, DJs prefer a range of remixes to work with, rather than a second tune that they may not like, which is considered a waste of space.

Sussing out CD options

CD's can come in different sizes, but the 3-inch diameter mini-CD didn't really take off for music sales, and instead found its place as a CD-Rom business card and a gimmick promo. Unlike vinyl, no matter how loud the music has been recorded, the amount you can fit on a CD is restricted to 74 minutes on a 740-megabyte CD and 80 minutes on an 800-megabyte CD.

✔ **CD singles:** CD singles are like the middle ground between a 7-inch single and a 12-inch single. CD singles normally contain the main release of a tune (which may still be a radio-edit), the full mix of a tune (if appropriate), and the B-side that would be on the 7-inch single, but most importantly, they usually contain one or two of the remixes that are found on the 12-inch versions.

Annoyingly, though, they may not contain all the remixes that the 12-inch single has. Perhaps the record company makes a decision to keep the best music only for the DJs using vinyl. Who knows – it certainly is frustrating for the CD-only DJ.

✔ **CD albums:** Albums on CD are similar to LPs in that they give you more songs from the artist, but they only give you one mix (the original) of the tune to play. Size and reliability isn't an issue with CD albums as is the

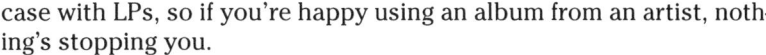

case with LPs, so if you're happy using an album from an artist, nothing's stopping you.

✔ **Compilation CDs and LPs:** For the party or wedding DJ who just needs a load of tunes, unmixed compilation albums with 20 or more individual tunes on them can help build a large music collection.

One compilation CD can contain your entire track list for an evening. Buy two copies of the same CD so that you can mix from one to the other, and you have a record collection for £30 – where the individual tunes together would probably cost you £100!

One point to be careful about when buying compilation CDs is that although they contain the original-mix tunes, the tracks on them might actually be the dreaded radio-edited versions, and not the full length tunes that you want to play.

✔ **Mixed CD albums:** Whether you're looking for pop music, commercial dance music, or happy-hardcore tunes, you may come across a lot of premixed CD albums that contain a whole load of tunes that you'd like to get your hands on.

Using premixed CDs has many problems. The first is an etiquette issue. If a DJ friend has taken the time to hunt down a rare track, and included it on a mix-CD for you, only for you to use that mix-CD one night when DJing, your friend is liable to get pretty angry with you. DJs treasure their music collection, even more so if they spend time hunting down a rare tune, and because you didn't spend any time (or money) sourcing that tune, yet still played it as though you had, you're likely to lose a friend.

The bigger problem with mixed CDs though, is that lifting only one tune out of the original DJ's mix to use in your own set is hard to do because of the overlapping between the intro and outro. Head to Chapter 15 for the ins and outs of mixing with CDs.

The party DJ: Sticking with familiarity

The great thing about being a party DJ is that you only need to play the tunes (and the mixes of the tunes) that everybody knows. Playing a deep house remix of 'Brown Eyed Girl' is probably just going to throw people off the dance floor – so you don't need to spend the time looking for rare mixes of tunes that club DJs do.

Go to a record store, buy a few compilation CDs, bolster your collection up with tunes that aren't on a compilation CD, and you'll have a great set list for a great night.

Researching your tunes

You can find a lot of music on the market, and most of it is bad so you need a way to find the good eggs in the batch – and avoid the bad. Start reading DJ magazines and pay particular attention to the record reviews. You may make a couple of mistakes and go on wild goose chases, but eventually you're likely to find a reviewer with the same taste as you. You can trust what he or she says about a new record so you can pay particular attention to that tune next time you go record shopping. You needn't die by a reviewer's advice, but write-ups are a good place to start.

Try listening to specialist radio shows, such as Pete Tong on Radio 1 (www.bbc.co.uk/radio1, where you can listen again to the show and read the tracklist), with an open mind. Going back and listening to the show again is a really good idea because you can easily get distracted the first time around and miss the little hook in a tune that turns it from okay to wahey! And face facts, sometimes the DJ says the title or artist a bit too fast to catch so you need to hear it again. If you throw a tape into the recorder while listening to the show, or record it to PC, you can always listen to the show again and again.

Eventually, to supplement the advice you get from radio shows, magazines, and Web sites, you may end up standing in front of a huge rack of records, reading the blurb the store has written about a tune, trying to decide whether this tune is one you like or not.

You can supplement what the store writes about a tune by considering the label and artist. When you've bought enough records, listened to enough radio shows, and read enough magazines, you'll start to show an affinity toward certain labels and artists.

If most of the records you like are released on a similar range of labels, always focus on them first. Even the big labels sign a few turkeys, but going back to a familiar label is a good way to thin out a lot of rubbish that gets released.

In addition, artists that you like are obviously a good lead for finding tunes. If you like the last five or six tunes by an artist, you have a good chance of liking the newest one on the rack in front of you, too. But as well as your favourite artists' own work, check out who's done the remixes of their tunes. If you look at other tracks remixed by professional mixers, you may find that although you've never heard of the main artist, you really like the tune, whether it's the original, or the remix.

Eventually, your selection of artists, labels, and remix artists all create links to other labels, re-mixers, and artists that sprawl out like a web of knowledge helping you pick out tunes that you'd never have normally looked at.

Avoiding musical holes

If you're relying on a review or recommendation to pick out a record you've not heard, try listening to as much of the track as you can to make sure that it doesn't have a *'musical hole'* in the middle.

What I mean by a musical hole is that a tune can be beautiful for the first couple of minutes, but then turns to musical mush in the middle. For some ungodly reason, the artist decided to kill everything, and play 20 seconds of a car alarm going off.

This point has further implications if you're buying tunes to play that evening in a club/party. Unless you really trust the person who's recommending the record, be sure to listen to it from start to finish, just so you know that *Merry Christmas* isn't going to suddenly start playing half way through.

And I'm not kidding; I played a record that did that. In the middle of summer. I could have curled up into a ball and cried . . .

The guidance of a knowledgeable guy or gal behind the counter can prove invaluable for getting hold of the latest, greatest tunes, and when you spend enough money (and time) in a specialist record store, the staff there can get to know your tastes, recommend tracks, and start handing over the tunes that they reserve for their preferred customers.

Listening to the music

If you plan to spend £5 to £15 for a record, even if the hype is huge or your trusted reviewer loves it, always listen to it first.

All good record stores have a listening post (a spot in the store with a turntable/CD deck and a pair of headphones for you to listen to records and CDs before buying them), or they have a deck sitting in the back, which, if you ask nicely and look as though you're going to buy something, you can review your music choices on.

Don't feel as if you have to rush listening to the record just because a guy's standing over you, waiting to listen to his records. You're about to spend quite a lot of money so take your time to ensure that you're spending it wisely. Listen to as much of the record as you can, and check for scratches and dirt on the surface of the CD or vinyl – be aware that a lot of people don't know how to treat records properly, especially ones they haven't bought yet (see the section 'Following record store etiquette' later in the chapter).

Following record store etiquette

Unfortunately, some people don't treat records in stores very well. As DJing becomes more popular and mainstream, larger music chains are catering for the growing numbers of DJs. With more people and larger stores, manners, etiquette, and responsibility suffers.

Here's my guide to good record store etiquette (which is not hard to figure, just basic manners), whether you're in a large or small store:

- Use the dedicated 'listening post' record if a copy's available in the rack, rather than opening a shrink-wrapped, unplayed copy.

- Replace records and CDs where you got them from.

- Put the tunes back in the same state you found them (don't bunch them up in the inlays, and clean records if you get them dirty).

- Handle vinyl carefully – remember, you don't own it yet. Now is the time to handle your records like your mum always told you to, by the edges – no fingerprints please.

- Take your time to listen to the tune, but don't take a pile of 20 tunes and monopolise the only listening post in the shop.

- If the turntable at the post is a cheap one, don't think that breaking it or treating it badly doesn't matter.

- Be careful with the needles; most stores would rather remove the listening post than replace a needle.

- Handle headphones with care. Once again, the store may provide cheap headphones, but don't break them just because they're cheap. Be careful with the headband – which can snap if mistreated.

Weighing up the pros and cons of classic anthems and new music

You've grown up with certain tunes, quite possibly the ones that made you want to be a DJ, so obviously you want to own them for yourself to play and mix, which is great. As a beginner, owning records that you're familiar with, love to hear, and that mean a lot to you is a positive thing. Even if your progress with beatmatching and mixing isn't going that well, you still love listening to the music you're playing.

However, you do need to think about what happens when you try to get work as a DJ – how many places are going to be happy for you to play only old tunes? I was lucky. My first DJing gig was called 'A Decade of Anthems', which meant that I could play whatever I wanted, new, or old. But if your sights are set on the big clubs, you may end up spending a lot of money on old tunes that you never play live.

Sure, dropping in a classic tune once in a while during a set in a club is great. Check out the crowd to gauge their reaction to what you're playing (see Chapter 20 for more info on reading the crowd), and ask yourself if they seem like a knowledgeable bunch that would respond to a classic tune. If the answer's yes, try playing a really good, older tune, but be careful, as reading the crowd wrongly can clear a dance floor faster than a night in a curry house!

Then you have the brand spanking new tunes to think about. If you don't have a paying DJ job yet, think hard about the tunes you're buying; don't buy anything *just* because it's the big tune at the moment, or you'll play it once or twice at home, include it in a couple of mix-tapes, and then demote it to the back of the record box because its initial appeal has now completely worn off.

As a working DJ, you need to buy tracks that get frequently played in the clubs. However, if you don't think that you'll ever play a track, even if you're still stuck DJing in the bedroom, don't buy it simply because it's popular.

Of course, you can't know which tunes are going to stand the test of time. Some tracks may surprise you by lasting a while, but if you feel you are compromising your musical integrity by buying a tune, you can bet that you won't be playing it after a month or two. In the end, buy the majority (and I mean 99 per cent) of tunes for your *own* enjoyment, not just for the pulsing masses on the dance floor.

Byting into MP3s

MP3s are a cheap, convenient way to buy your music, but what's the best way to get hold of them and what are the legal implications of using them?

Explaining the legal concept of obtaining and using MP3 tunes is very simple. If you go to somewhere like iTunes to buy and download your MP3s, you're doing so legally. If you use peer-to-peer software to share MP3s, and download a few gigabytes' worth of music without giving any money towards the artist, you're doing so illegally.

As a DJ, you're an artist yourself, and you need to share responsibility with your fellow artists. Imagine this scenario: What if you make it big as a DJ, and release a CD of a mix, thinking, 'Great, now I can afford to feed my wife and kids'. One copy is sold, which is then shared across the Internet. So everyone owns a copy of your hard work, but you have only 15p to show for all your effort. I bet you'd be unhappy.

One of the arguments made for file sharing is that people who make music make so much money in the first place that they shouldn't care about this loss of revenue. If you're talking about Metallica, maybe it is relevant to your argument, but music theft is still just as illegal.

Take an example of (imaginary) new producer, 'DJ Steve' who's just released his first single. Suddenly, the single's a smash hit, and DJs all over the world are downloading his track to play in nightclubs, but he doesn't have a strong financial foundation to absorb such a loss of revenue. All this time, you're getting paid to play his music that you didn't pay for in a club, while he starves . . . Okay, maybe I'm being a little heavy handed here, but as a DJ who gets paid to play, you'll be treading on very thin ground by playing stolen music, both legally and morally.

The governing of MP3s for DJ use has been the cause for many discussions in previous years. In the United Kingdom, a new Digital DJ Licence has been produced by an organisation called PPL (Phonographic Performance Limited, the UK record industry collecting society) to allow DJs to legally copy sound recordings onto a computer for use when DJing in clubs. At time of writing this legislation is yet to be finalised and enforced, but the PPL proposal is that if you use a laptop, iPod, MP3 player, or other hard-disk based piece of DJ equipment to DJ with, then you need to take out the Digital DJ Licence (at a proposed cost of £200 a year). See www.ppluk.com for more.

This extraordinarily complicated subject requires more page space than I have available to cover fully. Go to Phonographic Performance Limited's Web site (www.ppluk.com) or contact their Performer Services Helpdesk on 020 7534 1131 to make sure that you're legal in the UK.

Surfing into Online Record Stores

The Internet's a wonderful thing. I've found everything from poker chips to a house online. For the DJ hunting for rare records, the Internet is a treasure trove. In the years before the Internet, the poor DJ would trudge from store to store, and hunt through the *Yellow Pages* trying to track down a few elusive records. Now, all you have to do is boot up, sign on, and surf for it!

Knowing where to go

Specialist Web sites like Hard to Find Records (www.htfr.com), Juno Records (www.juno.co.uk), and Replay Records (www.replayrecords.com) carry huge back catalogues and all the latest tunes. Don't pass by the commercial Web sites, such as Tower Records (www.towerrecords.com), HMV (www.hmv.co.uk), Virgin (www.virginmegastores.com), and the all-encompassing

Amazon (www.amazon.com) if you're looking for some tunes, especially the more commercial and popular tracks.

Using the Internet as a store front is an exceptionally convenient way to see records, and as a result, hundreds of online stores are on the Net. If you search on the Internet for online record stores in your country, you find a host of Web sites selling a range of music not that far from where you live. If you can't find what you're looking for, start searching more widely on the Web. Most online record stores post to anywhere in the world, so you have to wait only a day or two for your goodies but make sure that you know your currency conversions!

Prices are usually a little cheaper than the high street store, too, because online retailers don't have as high overheads. You may miss out on the personal touch from the people behind the counter when you compare shopping online with going into your local, specialist record shop, but you can get over this downside by ensuring that you do your research first.

Previewing tracks

Nearly all specialist online stores let you play MP3s or Real Audio versions of the tracks they sell, so you can preview the tune before buying. Although the older tunes in the catalogue may not be available to preview, this way is a lot easier than standing in line at a record store waiting for your turn at the listening post to hear the latest tunes!

Preview MP3s are encoded with a low setting and are sometimes only 1-minute (or less) sections taken from the record. The lower quality and brief listening-time lets you preview the tune well enough, but doesn't run the risk of you using the download to DJ with instead of buying the tune. As you don't get to hear the entire tune, you may be running the risk of the record going somewhere strange (see the earlier sidebar about musical holes), but you won't have a problem if you've researched the tune and heard it before on a radio show or in a club.

Ordering and delivery

With every online store, whether you're browsing for shoes, garden furniture, rucksacks, or iPod accessories, getting reliable customer service for buying and receiving items is the most important aspect of the store. If you find you have difficulty buying a record because you can't navigate the site well enough, you won't return to it or buy anything. If delivery takes a long time, is too expensive, or heaven forbid, the store sends you the wrong item, you'll think twice before returning to that store.

With many online stores, if you order enough, delivery is free. Even when you do have to pay a postage cost, the overall cost of what you're buying online can amount to what you would have paid in the store anyway. And by the time you add on money for petrol and parking, or a train fare, and consider the time spent looking for the record in a store, you're probably happier to wait a day or two for the record to arrive. Shopping online is a convenient and relaxing way to buy your records and CDs.

Using auction sites

Sites such as eBay are a great resource to find tunes that you thought were long gone. As with buying anything online, however, try to make sure that the records (and CDs) are in proper, playable condition. Be sure that:

- You don't get ripped off by postage
- The seller has good feedback
- You get some kind of assurance that the guy *does* actually have the record (I've been stung that way before, unfortunately).

Protecting Your Records and CDs

You may have the best DJ set-up in the world, the best turntables, needles, amplifier, mixer, effects units, and CD players ever made, but if your records and CDs are scratched and dirty, they'll sound just as bad on top-quality equipment as they would on basic equipment.

Storing records

How you store your records when you're not playing them is extremely important for keeping them clean and protecting them from getting scratches.

Put your records back in the inner and outer sleeves properly, and if possible store the record so that the opening doesn't point upwards. If you do have the opening pointing up, all the dust and dirt that floats through the air gravitates toward the record (due to static electricity, but mostly gravity) and your tunes get dirty without your ever taking the vinyl out of its sleeve!

If you have the patience, go one step further by rotating the inner sleeve by 90 degrees inside the main sleeve, so even if dirt and dust did get into the main sleeve, the opening of the inner sleeve is on the other side, and dust can't get in to dirty the record.

Cleaning records, CDs, and the needle

Think of your records and CDs as you do your teeth. If you can prevent damage occurring by cleaning them before and after use, they'll last a lot longer, and you won't have that feeling of doom when everything starts to go wrong. (I'm a hypocrite by the way, I hate going to the dentist, and always wait for toothache . . .)

- **CDs.** CDs are easy to clean. A soft, lint-free cloth, wiped in a straight line from the center out, removes any dust on the disc. If you've spilt orange juice on the CD, you may want to give it a clean by wiping the CD (in the same direction) with weak soapy water. Rinse the CD carefully and then pat it dry with a soft cloth. Water may have entered into the disc sandwich, but if you play it in a CD player for 10 minutes, the moisture gets spun out (you won't damage your CD player as long as you've patted it dry first).

  Try to stay clear of CD cleaning machines, which clean the CD in a circular motion. Cleaning them in that way is not recommended; always wipe from the center of the CD outwards in a straight line.

  Prevention is the best cure, so always return your CDs to the CD case or wallet after use. Don't be lazy and leave your used CDs lying around the DJ booth, which risks getting beer and cigarette ash dropped on to your hard-found music.

- **Records.** Various cleaning solutions are available for keeping your records sparkling, and a few promise that if you clean the record once with the solution, you'll never need to clean it again. Some people swear by using lighter fluid to clean the record, others say that alcohol or soapy water (rinsed *very* well afterwards) works wonders.

  I find that a wipe with a carbon fibre brush (designed for this purpose) in a circular motion round the record before and after playing is more than enough. In truth though, in the middle of a darkened DJ booth, a quick wipe with your T-shirt is probably the best your record can look forward to!

- **Needle.** The reason you need to be so careful about keeping your record clean is because of the friction caused by the needle travelling through the record groove which creates heat (up to 150 degrees centigrade). Any dirt in the groove gets welded onto the side of the needle and gouges its way through the walls of the groove, which has been made soft by the 150-degree heat. This chain of events (and leaving your records on your bed) is the major cause of all the pops and crackles that can appear on your beloved records.

Repairing vinyl

If one of your tunes has a scratch that makes the needle jump, you're probably better off looking for a new copy. But, if you really want to try to salvage it, you can try a technique with a sewing needle, before throwing the record in the bin. I was taught this about 18 years ago by a friend who scratched my Van Halen album, and it's stuck with me ever since (though the friend wasn't so lucky . . .)

I emphasise that this method is a last resort option. All you need is a sewing needle, a magnifying glass, and a lot of care and patience to do this without ruining your record even more. Here's what you do:

1. **Play the record to locate the exact position of the scratch and look closely at whether the needle jumps forward or backward.**

   If the needle jumps to a previous part of the record, the scratch runs from right to left. If it skips to a part you've not heard yet, the scratch goes from left to right across the record.

2. **Take the record off the turntable and place it on top of a soft, protective cloth on a flat surface.**

   In a well-lit room, look through the magnifying glass to see where the scratch is on the record.

   Now pick up the sewing needle – you need a small one. (You may want to wind some tape around the needle so that you can hold it more securely.)

3. **Drag the sewing needle along the groove from one or two centimetres in front of the scratch to one or two centimetres behind it.**

   Drag in the opposite direction to the scratch. If the needle jumps backward when you're playing the record, you need to drag the sewing needle in an anticlockwise direction. (And if it jumps to a point later in the tune, drag it in a clockwise direction.)

   While dragging the needle along the groove, apply a little pressure as you start, increasing to a moderate pressure as you reach the scratch, and then releasing the pressure for the next couple of centimetres. Any reduction in audio quality is less noticeable by a gradual change in pressure. You may have to go through five or six groove lines to cover the entire scratch.

   Note: If you're at all clumsy, this method isn't for you.

   Instead of carefully dragging through a needle, some DJs simply press down pretty hard on the turntable's cartridge while slowly playing the record through the scratch to achieve a similar effect. If the scratch isn't too deep, this technique can repair it. However, if the scratch is too deep, it can just make things worse, so it's a bit of a lottery really!

Fixing warped records and CDs

Your records and CDs can become pliable under heat, which can cause them to warp. Vinyl can also warp just through stress, so your records are likely to warp when left at a strange angle with weight on them. Some compounds in vinyl and CDs aren't affected by heat, making repairs quite difficult, but if they were unplayable anyway, you may want to try the following method, which was first adopted for vinyl, but works just as well for CDs that become pliable under heat.

1. **Clean the record.**

2. **Place the record between two clean sheets of glass.**

   Make sure that the vinyl and the glass are completely clean before doing this, or you may fix the warp only to find that you've scratched the record!

3. **Warm up the record when it's inside the glass sandwich by using a hairdryer or leaving it out in the sun.**

   The hair dryer is better because you can work out how long and how hot you need to get the glass in order for this technique to work. You can't be too sure how much heat the sun gives off (I live in Scotland, and the sun's not that hot there!) so you can't guarantee replicating the same temperature using the sun when treating other warped records.

4. **No matter how you heat it up, after it's warm, apply an even weight on the glass over the record and leave it for a few days.**

5. **Come back to it and see if the record's flat again.**

Another similar method involves putting the record in the oven to generate the heat. I tried it once. The results weren't pretty . . . Be careful with how much heat you apply; too much, and the record will look like Dali made it.

If you want to test out fixing warped vinyl before having a go on your precious records, go to a second-hand record store, and search for (or ask for) a couple of warped records that you can use as test cases. After you've perfected the technique with them, you can fix your own records.

Repairing CDs

Record stores carry many products that you can use to protect your CDs from scratches in the first place, or repair them if they've been scratched. Just don't try to be smart like me and use Brasso to clean the CD. That idea doesn't work too well . . .

Some people swear by fluids and gizmos which remove part of the protective surface of the CD to smooth out the scratches. I'd be very careful using this approach though: you don't want to run the risk of removing too much of the surface – your CD player may not be too happy playing thin CDs.

If you've accidentally cracked one of your CDs, and you don't want to buy (or can't find) a replacement copy, you may still be able to play the CD.

Parts of the CD that are cracked are probably unplayable (and remember, a CD plays from the inside-out) but the rest of it may still be okay. Be careful though, if the cracks are too plentiful, when you play the CD, it may disintegrate.

Some audio-ripping software has an advanced error correction built into it, which may let you archive broken discs before throwing them in the bin – but in the end, you may find that buying a new copy of the CD is easier.

Chapter 4

Shopping for Equipment

. . . .

In This Chapter

▶ Trying out the right gear for you, and sticking to your budget

▶ Making the choice between high street and the Internet

▶ Choosing to buy new versus second-hand

▶ Checking that your kit works properly

. . . .

You've soul searched, and you've read ample magazines (and books, I hope!) and browsed enough Web sites to last you a lifetime on the subject, so now you're ready to take the plunge into buying equipment.

Buying equipment used to be straightforward. Your choice was limited to one specialist shop, a bit out of town, that would sell DJ gear. The guy running it would be a bit shifty, and you'd always leave feeling ripped off and dirty.

The situation has now changed. With so much competition in the DJ equipment market, stores can't afford to put off the buyer, and with attractive package deals, free postage, and good support, the days of the prickly, aloof salesman are long gone.

Taking Stock Before You Shop

People who have a dream don't want to listen to advice from others telling them to think carefully before spending their money. And, if you feel as excited as I did when I got my first DJ setup then I may not be able to convince you that doing so is important – but I will try. Before you take the padlock off your piggy bank, simply consider this piece of preparation – you need to be positive that you know exactly what you're going to buy with the money you've budgeted.

Trying before you buy

Before you even consider opening your wallet to buy your dream setup, try to find out whether you can go anywhere to use some DJ equipment first. Some stores let you demo their kit before buying, but that idea's not really what you're after, because you want to spend a good amount of time trying it out.

Ideally, you want to use the setup of a friend who has a couple of turntables and CD decks, with loads of records and CD's ready for you to rifle through and have fun with. You get an idea of the equipment you need and how it works, but more importantly, you'll probably develop an affinity for one medium or another, which is a lot of help when choosing between CD and vinyl.

Finding someone with a good DJ set-up isn't as unlikely as you may think, because if you're interested in becoming a DJ, you probably know someone who is one already. But what if you don't know anyone who is willing, or has the equipment to let you practise on? You can try looking for a recording studio with DJ decks, or renting some equipment, but the drawback of that (apart from needing to spend money) is that you need to bring your own records/CDs, and you may not have built a huge collection yet!

The friendlier DJ equipment stores let you demo some of their equipment if you look as if you're going to buy it, but not many of them have a room in the back with a full DJ setup for you to try out your skills. By all means ask the store for a prolonged demo, but don't hold your breath.

After you've taken the opportunity to try out your skills, and you're still sure that DJing is right for you, now's the time to blow the dust off your wallet, and go shopping.

Budgeting your money

How much money you have and how you spend it vastly alters the choice of equipment available for you to buy, including whether you opt for new or second-hand. A wide range of equipment is on the market, and I highlight the popular manufacturers in this section, but remember, they're not the only ones out there!

If you buy cheap turntables or CD decks that don't play at a constant speed or skip when there are too many bass vibrations even the best mixer in the world can't fix that. A basic mixer may be very basic, but is still sufficient when you're developing your initial skills as a DJ. It's far cheaper to upgrade your basic mixer to a better one than it is to upgrade two turntables from basic to professional.

Knowing why to try

The important thing about using someone else's setup before you part with your cash is that you have a chance to find out whether you're going to enjoy being a DJ. You won't become a DJ within an hour on the decks, but you will know if you love DJing as much as you thought you would, and if you find out that it's not as easy as you thought, you may want to postpone buying equipment, and use computer software while deciding whether you've really got the knack and patience to be a DJ.

In each budget level below, I mention the turntable or CD deck first, and then tell you to worry about the mixer. You need to be thinking in the same way when shopping. Spend as much money as you can on the players and then spend what's left on a mixer.

- **£200+.** You can buy a very basic mixer and a basic set of turntables or CD decks within this budget. If you have only £200, I believe that your best option is to pick up basic Numark, Stanton, or Gemini turntables/CD decks second-hand. You can discover how to mix on these decks, but if they are very basic, and have had a lot of use, they may not be the most reliable decks in the world, meaning that they may eventually hold back your progress – so you'll want to start saving now to be able to buy better ones after a few months.

- **£400+.** For around £400, you can get new, intermediate level turntables or CD decks by the same manufacturers as above and others such as Kam, Citronic, and American DJ. If you're buying CD decks, the ones in this price bracket come with a better range of functions than the basic models, and you get a more reliable, strong motor if you buy turntables. You won't have much money left after the decks though, so you may still have to buy a very basic mixer.

- **£800+.** By the time you've got £800 to spend on your DJ setup, I hope that you took my advice about trying out DJing on someone else's equipment first! Spending a large sum of money on something that you may never have done before – and you aren't 100 per cent sure that you're going to love DJing – is questionable, even when you do take into account your equipment's potential re-sale value. That said, you can get some intermediate level turntables/CD decks and a good mixer, or you can get top level decks (my preference is Numark's high-end range of turntables, Technics 1210 turntables, or good Pioneer or Vestax CD decks) and a slightly better than basic mixer – I suggest the ones made by companies such as Numark, Gemini, and Stanton.

> ✔ **$1,500+.** Budgets that stretch to £1,500+ open up the world to you. I prefer the top of the range turntables or CD decks from Technics, Vestax, Pioneer, and Denon, which can cost between £700 and £2,000 for two. And my choice of mixers are by Pioneer, Rane, and Allen and Heath, which cost you between £500 and £1,500. If you're spending that amount of money on DJ kit, though, I assume that you're upgrading, or you've been using someone else's equipment for long enough to know that this isn't a gamble, and you have what it takes to be a DJ.

If you're about to spend six month's worth of hard-saved money on the equipment, make sure that you've got some left to spend on all the records and CDs you want to play on them. I spent about £40 per month on records when I first started DJing, but that soon ballooned to hundreds, so consider how this hobby can affect the rest of your lifestyle.

Buying Brand New

Buying your decks and mixer brand new has many advantages. As well as having the choice of the latest, greatest gear, your equipment comes to you untouched and working perfectly. If any problems crop up, the stores should replace faulty kit, and if your equipment fails after the end of their returns policy, you have the backup of a manufacturer's warranty to sort out anything that goes wrong. Not that anything ever goes wrong, of course . . .

The obvious downside to buying your DJ gear new is the price. But, with high-street stores and online stores competing with each other, driving prices ever lower, if you hunt long enough, and are patient, you can find some great deals.

Resale value is the other downside to buying new. Consider a pair of Technics 1210 MkII turntables. Brand new, they cost around £700, but second-hand, you can find them for £400 or less, which is a considerable loss. If you buy a second-hand pair of 1210's, you can sell them for the same amount of money in five year's time. Other brands don't always hold their value so well.

Cruising the high street

Fortunately, DJing became a mainstream hobby a couple of years ago. Everyone wants to be a DJ, so DJ shops have smartened up their stores and selling styles. Most cities now have at least one place that sells DJ equipment, and if you're in a large city, you can find a few of them, all competing for your money.

Trying before you buy and cry

I learnt a hard lesson regarding not trying before buying, and being too heavily influenced by a magazine review. I was trying to choose between two very popular mixers and had read that although one of them had better features, the controls weren't laid out very well, and were difficult to use (especially in the dark) because they were crammed too close together. I stood in the shop staring at both of the mixers, and didn't have the sense (or this book) to think to ask to try them both (even just to twiddle the knobs). I bought the more expensive, better featured one of course, and assumed that the guy in the magazine must have fat hands.

The first time I accidentally hit the wrong switch the magazine review came crashing back into my mind! There's nothing like the silence of accidentally switching over to the line input to make you really regret some choices.

A high-street store offers three things you won't get anywhere else.

✔ The chance to *use* a range of different equipment

✔ The personal touch of being able ask a sales rep questions

✔ Immediate gratification

A range of different equipment

The ability for you to have even a quick demo on the equipment in the shop sets local stores apart from online stores, and gives you the chance to compare many different pieces of kit.

You may have read in magazines and books that one style of turntable is better than another, or that single CD decks are better than twin units, but until you are able to stand in front of them, touch them, and use them, you won't be certain yourself. Second guessing your choice after spending a whole load of cash on your kit based only on a review is not ideal.

The personal touch

There's no doubt about it. Getting face-to-face, immediate advice from someone and being able to hold a conversation about what you want and need is extremely helpful when you're buying equipment. The guys (or gals) you're talking to at your local DJ store have sold a lot of kit in their time and typically really know their stuff.

You need to be happy that you've made the right choice with your purchase, especially if you're spending a month's worth of wages. A salesperson wants to make a sale, that much is true, but he or she still wants to help you buy the right equipment so you'll come back to that shop for more when you need it.

Immediate gratification

I don't know if having immediate gratification is important to you, but it sure is for me. If I buy something, I want it now. I want to be able to take it away with me and use it as soon as I get home.

If the piece of equipment I want is only a small amount extra in a shop, and if I'm really jazzed about getting it, I'd much rather go into a shop, buy it, and take it home there and then, than have to sit at home the next day hoping that every car that drives past the house is the delivery dude.

Opting for online shopping

Whether you use a shop that also sells online or an online reseller that doesn't actually hold any stock, you can expect dramatic price drops from online stores. With so many Web sites trying to get your business, a bit of patience and comparison can save you money.

Most sites have fantastic customer support and are really good at answering customers' questions via e-mail. However, the drawback to online shopping is that you can't have a face-to-face conversation and get answers immediately to your myriad questions. Although some Web sites offer live Web-chat or telephone assistance to try to get around this hurdle, they can't compete with you being able to walk around a store with a salesperson.

Ironically, even though an Internet store can seem faceless and anonymous, their after-sales customer service is usually as good if not better than high-street stores. An online shop is only as good as its reputation, and when shoppers start writing bad things, other people listen. The DJ community is a tight-knit one, and online stores need to avoid causing ill feelings, word of which can then spread like wildfire.

In addition to great customer service and attractive prices, Internet stores enable you to build your own package in an attempt to lure you away from high-street stores. A *package* is where the store offers you the turntables (or CD decks) and a mixer together at a reduced price. High-street shops typically can't mix-and-match packages quite so freely due to stock limitations. They can order other equipment in for you, but if you have to wait anyway, you may as well go online and get it cheaper!

Whether they physically hold the stock or not, Internet stores have access to every piece of kit available, which opens up the possibility to get any combination of turntable or CD deck and mixer you can think of. With access to an equally large range of headphones, amplifiers, cables, needles, and so on, the choice and price you can get online if you already know what you want to buy is really attractive.

A number of manufacturers sell their own combinations of decks and mixer and aim them at beginner DJs. In my opinion, Numark's DJ in a Box and Gemini's Scratch Master package are affordable, convenient ways to buy basic kit on a small budget. The downside to these packages is that you may outgrow it when your DJ skills demand more functions to help you work with the music. The safest option is to arm yourself with research and build your own package.

Many people are going into the high-street DJ store and asking all the right questions, finding out the best equipment for their use, and then buying it all online through a cheaper store. There's no rule against it, just morals, and a little dent in your karma. (My Karma ran over my Dogma a long time ago though.) And if your local high-street store goes out of business, who are you going to talk to then?

Buying Second-hand

The advantage of buying your DJ gear second-hand is that you get a better standard of equipment for your money. Rather than you having to buy a basic set of decks and mixer brand new, you can afford a better second-hand set.

The disadvantage is that you don't know how well the kit has been treated. You can find some key things to look out for when buying second-hand later in this chapter because you can never be too sure that the turntables haven't spent the last 10 years of their use being drowned in beer and cigarette ash!

You can use three different places to source your second-hand equipment:

- ✔ Classified adverts in newspapers and shop windows
- ✔ Pawn shops
- ✔ Auction Web sites

Scanning newspapers

Newspaper classified sections have been hit pretty hard by auction Web sites over recent years, with less items being entered for sale. Fortunately, because not as many people look at newspaper second-hand sections anymore, there's less of a chance that someone else spots and buys your dream DJ setup before you do. Also, because items in newspapers are normally sold at a fixed price or a 'nearest offer', you can secure the item immediately, rather than needing to enter a bidding war!

Items sold in the classified section are probably quite local to you, too. You can save a little money by picking up what you're buying rather than having to pay for postage, and you can take a look at the equipment first, and see it working before handing over your money.

I'm getting all grown-up on you now, to warn you about the dangers of going to strangers' houses – be careful. Always let someone know where you're going, and try to take someone with you just in case the seller starts to raise the price, which can make the situation confrontational, and even aggressive.

Dipping into pawn shops

Take advantage of people (DJs!) who have fallen on hard times and go looking in a pawn shop. Over the past 10 years, a new wave of second-hand stores have appeared that have transformed the traditional murky pawn shop into a modern shop that rivals many high-street stores. They often have better displays, a large selection to choose from, and a few even have expert salespeople who can help you with any questions you have.

Some second-hand shops aren't really set up for you to check out the equipment before you buy, but I strongly suggest that you request to see as much of the equipment in working order as possible. I went to buy a mixer from a pawn shop once, and asked to see it working before I paid for it. They plugged it in, turned it on, and a nice plume of smoke came out the back. So, I went somewhere else, quickly. (See the later section 'Making Sure That Your Kit Works'.)

Bidding on auction Web sites

Auction sites are the new way to sell everything in your house that isn't nailed to the floor. You find using them is a great way to get a bargain, and the seller/buyer rating systems give you a relatively safe way to buy (or sell) your equipment. You need a little patience to get the best deal, but as long as you know what you want before you start looking, you can find some great deals.

Check out these popular auction Web sites as a start:

- ✔ eBay (www.ebay.co.uk)
- ✔ uBid (www.ubid.com)
- ✔ QXL (www.qxl.co.uk)
- ✔ eBid (www.ebid.co.uk)

Although the feedback/rating systems on auction sites are a great way to tell how reputable a seller is, use caution when you're looking to part with your money.

When buying on an Internet auction site, you need to worry about two basic things:

 ✔ The seller won't send the goods to you after you've paid

 ✔ The seller hasn't been accurate in the item description

Looking at the rating of a seller gives you an idea of whether you need to worry about not receiving your goods after payment. Take time to check out what's been written about a seller, and if you're not convinced that they've sold enough to warrant you dealing with them, be extremely wary before handing over a whole load of cash!

Don't feel bad about emailing the seller to ask any questions that aren't covered in the item's description. Ask him or her to confirm the working order of the equipment, its general condition, and if they're prepared to accept responsibility for items that don't work correctly upon arrival with you. In the unlikely event of the seller 'bending the truth' with the item description, email evidence proves invaluable if you need to make an official complaint about them to the auction site.

The last point you need to consider when ordering anything from online auction sites is the postage and packaging costs. Two decks and a mixer need a lot of protection to survive being loaded into the back of a van in a cardboard box. You may think the postage costs are quite high, but the mountains of bubble wrap and foam required may be inflating the costs of carriage. Some sellers may try to make extra money by boosting the price of postage, so if you suspect anyone of attempting this practice on you, send a quick email asking them to include a receipt for the cost of postage.

Making Sure That Your Kit Works

If you're given the opportunity to try out the equipment before buying second-hand, try to be as thorough as possible, testing and checking all moving parts and any controls known to be vulnerable to malfunction.

Listen to the voice inside your head; your first impressions are nearly always correct. If you look at the equipment and can see that it's well kept, in a clean environment, chances are you'll find no problems. If it's dirty, dented, and scraped, and kept in the damp basement of a messy teenager, give the equipment a thorough test, described in the following sections, before you part with your cash! (Rubber gloves are optional . . .)

Checking cables

Wiggle all cables and check all connections. On turntables, mixers, amplifiers, and headphones, make sure that you move the cables around and listen out for connection problems. You know if you have a problem because you hear crackling sounds, or the music cuts out entirely for a moment.

Testing turntables

The first thing to check out on a turntable is the accuracy of the motor. (Chapter 5 covers everything you need to know about the workings of turntables.) The red light that shines onto the dots on the side of the turntable platter is a strobe light and helps you to check if the motor fluctuates in speed when it's playing (see Figure 4-1). To test this, set the pitch control to 0, and look at how the dots on the side of the turntable move.

At 0 pitch on Technics decks, for example, the row of dots second from the bottom should appear completely stationary; at +6 per cent, the top row of dots should appear stationary. If the dots move a little, you may be able to adjust the motor to fix this. If the dots move erratically, speeding up, then slowing down, and then going in the opposite direction, and so on, the motor has a major problem.

Figure 4-1: The power switch on a turntable, with the strobe light underneath it shining onto the calibration dots on the deckplatter.

Assuming that you're happy with the motor at the four calibration speeds (shown in Figure 4-1, next to the control: -3.3, 0, +3.3, and +6 per cent), start to move the pitch control smoothly from 0 pitch into the + (faster) region. As you increase the pitch, the second row of dots on the side of the turntable start to turn from right to left, and as you increase the pitch fader even more, the dots start to move faster and faster. This change in the dots should indicate a smooth increase in speed; if the increase is erratic, you have something wrong with the pitch control or the motor. Repeat this method for the slower pitch region.

As you check how the pitch control affects the speed of the turntable, try to notice how the fader feels as you move it. If you start to feel that it's sticking in places and is hard to move (apart from 0 pitch, when it clicks into place), the pitch fader is probably really dirty. You can buy degreaser spray that cleans out dirty faders, but start to ask questions about how well the turntable was maintained and why the kit is in such a state of disrepair.

The last thing to check on the motor is that the 45 and 33 buttons do their job. A few people have forgotten to check this, only to get the deck home and find that the turntable only plays at 45, no matter how hard they hit the 33 button with a hammer.

If you have the time, lift off the deckplatter (the bit that turns around with the record on it) so you can take a look underneath. If that area is really dirty, then you may find that the motor is dirty, too. Ask whether you can unscrew the cover and take a look at the motor if this is the case – although you may annoy the person who's selling the turntable with this rather invasive request.

Take a look at the deckplatter while you've got it in your hands, and make sure that it's not warped or bent. Place it on a flat surface, and make sure that the platter makes contact with the surface all the way round. If (heaven forbid) you're looking at belt-driven decks, take a look at the belt too, which is located under the deckplatter. Check carefully for signs of stretching or damage. Belts are easily replaceable, and don't cost much, but damage and wear indicates that the turntable has had a lot of use over time.

Finally, examine the *tonearm* (the arm that holds the needle over the record). The biggest problem you may find is a wobbly tonearm assembly. If the seller is a chatty chappy, you may have already found out how the decks were used. If he (or she) used them in clubs and took them to the clubs in cases, be extra vigilant when checking the tonearm. Though a turntable case is a nice sturdy item, it doesn't actually offer much protection for the tonearm, which is the most delicate part of the turntable.

You have two basic ways to check the tonearm for damage. In both cases, if the tonearm has a height adjustment control, make sure that it's locked (see Chapter 5 if you want to know more about the height adjustment feature):

✔ **Wiggle it.** Be very gentle, but try moving the assembly. Does it move while you wiggle it? If it does, it's likely to be damaged.

✔ **Float the tonearm.** This method is the more precise way to check for damage to the bearings in the tonearm assembly. You may want to remove the needle from the cartridge, just in case you get this bit wrong; even better, ask whoever you're buying from to do this check.

With the antiskate control (which is sometimes used to cancel out the pull of the tone-arm towards the centre of the record) set to 0, turn the counterweight (the weight on the back of the tonearm) so that the tone-arm floats in mid air. (For more information on how to do this check out Chapter 11.)

Move the tonearm toward the middle of the record, and once there, start to increase the antiskate control. As the antiskate is increased, the tone-arm starts to move back toward its resting place. If it doesn't move, or if it jams in one place, you're tonearm assembly is likely to have serious and expensive problems.

If the turntable's tonearm fails either test, run for the hills. The repair job for this fault is very expensive and troublesome, and not one you should undertake yourself.

While you're looking at the tonearm, have a quick peek at the needle and cartridge. Needles can be replaced, but you may not want to pay for a new one so soon, so if it's bent, or squashed, ask for a little money off the price. On the cartridge, look at the wires that connect into the headshell. Check for signs of corrosion or loose connections.

If you're willing to buy decks that have been quite heavily used, you may want to think about getting them serviced. A good technician can usually get everything back to normal again, but that comes at a price, so be warned that the cost of repair added to the cost of the deck may just cost the same as a new turntable!!

Vetting CD decks

Checking how the pitch control affects the playback speed on CD decks is harder than on a turntable, because you don't have a visual reference like the strobe light on a turntable. However, CD decks don't tend to suffer from the same motor problems as turntables, so you really only need to check that the pitch control and pitch bend functions work properly and are free of dirt.

Here are a few tips for checking out CD decks:

✔ Make sure that the pitch control increases and decreases the speed of the tune in a constant, smooth way and that the pitch bend buttons temporarily change the pitch when you press them, and the pitch of the tune returns quickly to the set pitch when you release the buttons.

✔ Try to use every function on the CD unit. If you researched the CD deck well enough before choosing to buy it, you probably know what functions to expect. To be on the safe side, bring a checklist for that particular model and make sure that they all work.

✔ Inspect the CD loading system. If the CD deck loads with a tray, make sure that it's not bent, that no bits are missing, and that it goes in and out smoothly. If the CD slots directly into the deck, try inserting a CD a few times, and make sure that the deck doesn't spit your CD back at you. (Although, maybe it just doesn't like the music you're playing . . .) If the CD deck uses a top loading method to accept the CD, make sure that the deck closes properly, and as with the other loading methods, ensure that the CD plays properly once it's in there!

✔ If the CD deck has a good antiskip function (which prevents the CD from skipping when there's a lot of vibrations), get a demonstration of that working properly. Ask the seller to do this demo, rather than thumping it with your fist a couple of times. Make sure that you're satisfied with the anti-skip, and that it does actually prevent the CD from skipping when faced with vibrations.

Monitoring mixers

Make sure that you get a chance to see the mixer turned on, and in action – you don't want to get it home and see smoke pouring out of it! (Turn to Chapter 8 for more on mixers.)

Before you play anything through the mixer, connect the turntables/CD decks to the mixer and listen. If you can hear any kind of electrical hum from the equipment or through the speakers, turn off the decks, so only the mixer is on, and if you can still hear a loud hum, firstly ask the seller if this noise is normal, and then check the connections (especially the earth connection) for any problems. The noise may be a harmless operational hum given off by the mixer, but if you're not convinced that this sound's good, it probably isn't!

After you've listened to the mixer with nothing playing through it, put on a record/CD and check that all the controls do what they're supposed to. The *master level*, the *gain control*, the *EQs*, the *channel faders*, the *cross fader*, the *booth controls*, and *effects section* (all of which are mentioned in Chapter 8); absolutely everything needs to be checked for each channel on the mixer.

Listen for any signal (sound) dropout or any crackling sounds as you turn knobs and move faders.

When checking the faders, pay particular attention to the cross fader. The cross fader should have a smooth fluid motion from one side to the other, and you need to check for faults in the fader's control of the audio.

The first thing to listen for is any crackling as you move the fader from one side to the other, but more importantly, listen for any music 'bleeding in' from the other channel. If you're playing music into channel 1, and nothing is playing on channel 2, move the cross fader over to channel 2, where you'd expect it to be silent. If you can still hear channel 1 playing faintly while you should have silence, you've got a problem with the cross fader.

Depending on the mixer you're looking at, you may still want to buy it, and if the mixer has a user-replaceable cross fader, ask the seller to knock off some money so you can buy a new one. A worn cross fader may be a sign of extensive wear and tear to the mixer, but then again, it may just be a worn cross fader after months of use by a scratch DJ. Go with your instincts.

If you have headphones and a microphone available, try them out with the mixer. Turn the cables of the headphones and microphone around while they're plugged in and listen for any loose connections causing the signal to cut out.

Use all the headphone cue controls, making sure that you get a good, clear sound from each channel, and if the headphone section includes a headphone mix or split cue, test them to make sure that you don't have signal cut out here either. Plug in the microphone and check that the controls and the inputs are clear of any crackles, and if the mixer has a *talk-over* function, which dips the level (volume) of the music so you can be heard talking over it, be sure that it works properly.

For mixer outputs, you probably see a *Master Out*, a *Record Out*, and if you're looking at a good mixer, a *Booth Out* or *Zone Out* (these outputs are described in Chapter 5). Test all three of the outputs through the amplifier, and make sure that there are no breaks in signal when you wiggle the wires.

The Line/Phono switches are often overlooked when people are checking out a second-hand mixer. Ensure that the switch from Line to Phono for each channel works without crackling, and check for silence when you switch to either Line or Phono when they don't have an input. For example, if you have turntables plugged into the mixer, when you switch to LINE; make sure that you can't still hear the turntable playing.

If the mixer has any other features mentioned in Chapter 5, such as BPM counters, cross fader curve adjusts, punch buttons or hamster switches, check that they all work, too.

Assessing headphones

If the gear you're buying includes headphones, listen carefully to them at varying volumes. Move the cable around to make sure that you don't hear any breaks in the signal, and check the connection of the cable to the mixer to ensure that it's securely fitted to the ear pieces, and if you move around a lot that you don't lose sound.

Turn the volume up in the headphones for a few seconds. Be careful not to play the music so loud that you may damage your hearing, but still try to play the sound at a volume loud enough to check if the music distorts. Distortion can naturally occur on headphones when played too loud, but they need to take a lot of volume before starting to sound fuzzy.

Sounding out amplifiers and speakers

Lastly, look at the amplifier and speakers (if provided) in the same way you did the mixer and headphones (see previous section, and Chapter 10). Check that you don't get a loud hum coming through the speakers, check that all the controls are working properly on the amplifier, and make sure that the speakers don't distort at moderate sound levels. As always, give the cables a little wiggle, and check that the connections don't crackle or that the signal cuts out.

If the speakers are in an open cabinet that lets you view the *drivers* (another name for the actual speaker), then inspect them for tears, dents, or even stains. If the cone on the speaker is ripped or badly dented, this damage can cause the music to start distorting really quickly, and may fail completely if you play the music too loud, so don't even consider buying them. If you see stains, liquid may have got inside the speaker, which as well as weakening the speaker cone, may be well on its way to corroding cables and circuit boards inside.

Part II
Navigating the Maze: Equipment Essentials

The 5th Wave   By Rich Tennant

"It's my mixer that sets me apart from other DJs."

In this part . . .

You need to make an informed decision about which equipment is best for you and your DJing style and, more importantly, how it all works when you get it home! Part II covers the features and functions of turntables, mixers, headphones, and amplifiers, as well as explaining the different designs of needles and cartridges for turntables, and the wonders of slipmats.

To wrap up this part of the book, Chapter 11 is dedicated to how to set up and connect all of your equipment, and how to troubleshoot the connections if something goes wrong.

Chapter 5

Getting Decked Out with Turntables

In This Chapter
▶ Finding out about the basic parts of a turntable
▶ Keeping up to date with new innovations
▶ Caring for your turntables

*A*ll turntables are equal in that they play records, but, like most things in life, some are better than others. In this chapter, I go through the functions you need to look for when purchasing a turntable.

Avoiding Cheap Turntables

Deciding what turntable to buy and use is largely based on your budget. When you do go shopping, don't go for the cheapest option so that you can save a little money. Investing in a better quality turntable puts you straight on the road to becoming a quality DJ. Actually, maybe reversing the point makes this clearer; the worse your turntable, the harder it is to become a good DJ.

The main things to watch out for on cheap turntables are that they tend to have belt-driven motors rather than direct drive motors (see the following section), and they often skimp on essential DJ features such as removable headshells, counterweighted tone arms, and long pitch sliders.

Spend as much money as you can on the turntable – only then think about purchasing the rest of your equipment. Great decks remain great decks no matter what mixer and headphones you use, but not even the best mixer or the clearest headphones can solve the problems inherent with cheap, belt-driven decks.

Motoring in the right direction

Belt-driven decks do seem like an attractive option when you're looking to become a DJ because they're so much cheaper than their direct-drive big brothers. Of course, some people claim that their belt-drive decks are fine to mix with, scratch with, and so on, and I'm sure that they think they are. But the first time these folks use a good direct-drive deck, they change their minds and (reluctantly) accept that they've been thinking only with their wallets and have been fooling themselves. (A few people still stand by their belt-driven decks, but they're either stubborn as a mule, or have super-human powers of adaptability.)

Belt-driven turntables

Inside a belt-driven turntable is a small motor with a rubber band linking it to the underside of the *deckplatter* (the part you put the record on). This makes the method of turning a record similar to how turning the front cog with your bike pedals makes the back wheel turn. This method of powering the turntable means that there isn't much *torque* (power to the turntable), meaning that the deckplatter often grinds to a halt when you hold the record stopped.

The other downside is that the speed the turntable plays at can fluctuate, speeding up and slowing down. When you're trying to match the beats of two records (*beatmatching*, described in Chapter 12), the fluctuation of speed makes keeping the bass beats playing at the same time, for anything over 10 seconds, extremely difficult. You may blame your own beatmatching skills rather than realising it's the turntable's fault.

Direct-drive turntables

Direct-driven turntables are a better option than belt-driven ones. Where belt-driven turntables have a rubber band transferring power from the motor to the deckplatter, which then spins around a centre spindle, in direct-drive turntables the centre spindle *is* the motor (so it *drives* the motor *directly*).

The improved power (torque) of the direct-drive method means start-up times of well under half a second, and the power from the motor is more than enough to keep the turntable spinning under the slipmat when you're preparing to start a tune or doing complicated scratches.

The turntable speed is solid and reliable on a direct-drive turntable. Though you can get pitch wobbles around the 0 pitch mark (see the sidebar 'The Bermuda Pitch Zone exists'), you can be confident that any beatmatching errors are your errors, not the fault of a weak transfer of power through a rubber band. You may regard this fact as a double-edged sword – but the moment you realise you can't make excuses and blame your performance on bad turntables, your DJing skills start to improve!

Short-term gains, long-term pains

If you're happy doing things the hard way, you may find that at least one good thing comes out of learning to DJ on belt-driven turntables. In the short term, you'll become an extremely accurate, attentive DJ when beatmatching.

I've found that beginner DJs who start by using top of the range turntables from Technics, Vestax, and Numark can have a really easy time. The motor is so powerful and reliable that they don't need to worry about speed fluctuations throwing off their beatmatching skills. When these DJs have to use a poorer set of turntables at a party early on in their DJ development, they may find that their concentration and levels of attention aren't as good as those DJs who were forced to develop on bad decks and may have difficulty keeping their beats matched because they're not used to the bad deck problems.

I must stress, however, that eventually, the good DJs develop attention and accuracy just through time spent practising, developing their own skills – no matter what turntable they

use – so this isn't an excuse to buy cheap, belt-driven decks.

One club that I DJ'd at in the past developed a problem with their turntables due to a 'customer' of the club spilling beer over them. While they were getting repaired, the club owner decided to hire a pair of belt-driven turntables. Due to the heat of the club, the belts started to stretch, causing the decks to be even worse at holding their pitch, which made beatmatching extremely difficult.

Fortunately, I was used to decks that played in this way as one of the pubs that I'd worked at had decks with motor problems, which felt just like shoddy belt-driven decks and really used to annoy me. From using those decks frequently, I developed the intuition and concentration to hear beats slipping out of time before they were noticeable to the dance floor, and wasn't too fazed by such a problem when it happened in the club that night.

The other DJ wasn't quite so lucky . . .

Watching out for pitch control design

Watch out for cheap turntables that use a small (two-inch/five-centimetre) pitch fader or rotary knob to adjust the pitch of the record. You won't often find either on direct drive decks, but super-cheap belt driven decks sometimes have them. These pitch faders are too small to make the fine adjustments needed to keep the beats of your records playing in time, and makes beatmatching insanely difficult.

Look at the standard design of a turntable (the Technics 1210 in Figure 5-1) and notice the large pitch control down the side of the deck that lets you make minute adjustments to the pitch. Make sure that the turntable you buy is based on a similar design.

Identifying Key Turntable Features

A DJ turntable has many key features. Some of them are similar in function to a home hi-fi's record player, but added functionality to these controls and designs is what truly separates a DJ turntable from a hi-fi's record player. This section covers what these features do so that you not only buy the correct turntables, but also know how to make use of them.

Start/Stop

Automatic hi-fi record players start turning when you lift the needle onto the record, and only stop turning when you take the needle off and replace the arm on the rest, or when the needle gets to the end of the record and automatically returns to the rest.

This isn't helpful for the DJ – you need manual control of how the motor starts and stops. You sometimes need to stop the turntable, but still leave the needle at a specific place on the record. This is usually when you've taken time to find the place to start the record from (the *cue* point) but don't want to start the tune for a couple of minutes. The Start/Stop button gives full control over how and when the turntable starts and stops.

Pressing Stop when the record is playing is a great DJ technique too (see the end of Chapter 14).

On/Off

The On/Off switch on a DJ turntable is normally on the bottom-left corner of the deck, next to the Start/Stop button. The switch is raised above the deck-platter, and the strobe light is positioned underneath (see the later sections in the chapter for information about the deckplatter and strobe light). Though used mostly for the mundane task of turning the turntable on and off; you can also use it creatively in the mix (described in Chapter 14).

You may find that the On/Off switch on Technics decks has a tendency to get very loose after a bit of use and abuse. Loosening can lead to all kinds of accidental *power-offs* if you brush against it by mistake and turn off the power. With the release of the MkIII version of the 1210 turntable, Technics recessed the power switch into the holder to reduce the risk of such an accident.

33/45/78 RPM

There's nothing particularly special about the RPM (revolutions per minute) button on your DJ deck; when you press 33 and the pitch control is set to 0, the record makes 33 revolutions in one minute, and when at 45, the record revolves 45 times in one minute.

If you don't know what speed your turntable should be set to, look at the record label or cover, which tells you whether to play it at 33 or 45 RPM. Or simply try listening to it. If you're playing Barry White, and it sounds like the Chipmunks, you're playing the record too fast; try pressing the 33 button!

Older record players also have a separate setting for 78 RPM, but most modern records aren't pressed at 78 RPM anymore, so it isn't included as a standard control. If you do have an antique 78 RPM vinyl you'd like to play, some turntables have a sneaky hidden setting: When you press the 33 and 45 buttons together, the turntable plays at 78 RPM.

Strobe light

The strobe light is the soft red light at the side of the turntable (normally bottom left corner, integrated as part of the On/Off switch). It's not just a pretty red light, it's a strobe light that you use to calibrate the motor on the turntable (expensive home record players also have a strobe light).

Look at the little dots that go around the side of the *deckplatter*. On Technics turntables, if you play the turntable with the pitch set to 0, the second row of dots from the bottom should appear to be still. If these dots move left or right, the motor isn't playing at exactly 33 or 45 revolutions per minute (RPM) and the motor may have a problem. Each of the four lines of dots represents a different pitch range, as Figure 5-2 shows.

You find more information on using the strobe light for checking the turntable motor in Chapter 4.

Deckplatters

The *deckplatter* is the part of the turntable that spins round and is what the slipmat and the record sit on. Home hi-fis have a rubber mat firmly glued onto the platter, which is useless for DJing with, because the deckplatter needs to be made of smooth metal to let the slipmat slip (see Chapter 6 for what a slipmat is and how to make it slip better).

When you buy Technics decks, they come with a thick rubber mat sitting on top of the deckplatter, which fortunately, isn't glued down. If your decks came with a similar thick rubber mat on top of the metal deckplatter, simply lift it off, exposing the deckplatter, and keep the rubber mat somewhere safe. I find down the back of the wardrobe is a safe enough place.

Figure 5-2:
The strobe light on a Technics 1210.

Target light

Like your health, you don't really think about this little pop-up light called the *target light*, or miss it until you don't have it. Bizarrely, a couple of turntables on the market don't have target lights, or offer it only as an add-on option. It may be a small, simple feature, but it's also absolutely vital.

The target light (shown in Figure 5-3) sits on the edge of the deckplatter and shines a light along the grooves of the record where the needle traces, enabling you to see the grooves more clearly. Why do you want one? Apart from letting you see where the needle is (or where you'd like to put it), if you take a look at a record under good light, you can see groups of different shaded rings on the record. These rings are the map of the tune; the darker rings are the quieter parts, and the lighter rings are the louder parts.

You may not think that you need a target light much when you're DJing in the comfort of your 100-watt bedroom light bulb, but when you're standing in a darkened, smoke-filled DJ booth, this tiny light is your beacon for perfect mixing!

Figure 5-3:
The target
light on a
Technics
1210. A
helpful little
fella.

Pitch control

The pitch control adjusts the rate at which the turntable turns. If you move the pitch control into the + area (towards you on a standard DJ turntable), the record plays faster; and if you move the pitch control towards the – area (away from you), the record plays slower.

Different turntables have different ranges, but you typically find that pitch ranges are between 8 or 12 per cent in either direction. Technics 1210 MkII decks only give you + and – 8 (see the later section 'Customising Your Sound with Advanced Turntable Features' for information on turntables with increased pitch ranges).

Although the record plays faster the more you increase the pitch control, it is called a *pitch control*, not a speed control, so the more you increase the speed, the higher the pitch of the music gets. So you may start to beatmatch two tunes you think will sound great together, but when you increase the pitch on one of the tunes, the two tunes may sound out of tune, like your dad singing in the shower along with the radio. See the section 'Master Tempo/Key Lock' later in the chapter for one way around this issue (and take the batteries out of the radio to stop your dad singing in the shower).

The numbers

The numbers on the pitch control can be confusing. These numbers do not refer to BPMs (beats per minute, the usual measurement of tempo) of the music you're playing, but rather a percentage difference of the speed of the turntable. The only time the numbers correlate exactly with the BPM is if the tune you're playing has a BPM of 100. If you move the control to 1 per cent, you increase the pitch by 1 per cent of 100, which is 1; and would be the same for the other numbers (5 per cent would be 5 BPM and so on).

As you're unlikely to play a tune with exactly 100 BPM, you need to understand that the pitch control affects the BPM in percentage change. If you're playing a 150-BPM tune and decrease the pitch to –1 per cent, then the tune now plays at 148.5 BPM. A 130-BPM tune with the pitch set to +5.5 per cent increases by 7.15 BPM – so you can assume that tune now plays 'around' 137 BPM, and match other tunes to it accordingly. (The mathematical calculation for this is on the Cheat Sheet inside the front cover of the book.)

So this percentage reference is useful when you're beatmatching; trying to match two tunes that were recorded at different speeds. For instance, you're playing a tune at 135 BPM, and you know that the next tune you want to play in the mix has been recorded at 140 BPM. This 5 BPM difference is around 3.5 per cent of 140 BPM, so to get the 140 BPM tune to play at 135, you have to move the pitch fader down to -3.5 to get you in a 'ball-park' area of the correct pitch (3.5 per cent is actually 4.9 BPM, but it's close enough). All it takes after that is a little fine tuning of the pitch, and you'll have the tune beat-matched really quickly.

The Bermuda Pitch Zone exists

The decks that I learnt on used to change the pitch the wrong way for a 1 per cent region; if I moved the pitch fader to +1 per cent, the music slowed down, and the music would speed up if I moved the pitch fader into the − region. Fortunately, after the +/−1 per cent area, the pitch control would go back to normal – otherwise, I'd have gone mad!

Even my Technics 1210s suffer from this problem, but not as pronounced as with the decks I learnt on. The 1210s just hover around 0 pitch between +/−0.5 per cent, and then go back to normal again.

Fortunately, the problem has been noticed, and rectified by turntable manufacturers. First by Vestax, and then Technics on their 1210 MkIII, so the pitch fader is now completely smooth, with no click point as you pass through 0 pitch to cause this problem

You can find ways to 'hack' your turntables to disable the quartz lock feature that is the cause of the problem, but you'll have to search on the Internet for these hacks because I don't want this book to create an epidemic of broken turntables!

However, the pitch control isn't an exact science. The difference that even 1 millimetre of change can make to the speed of your record is enough to throw off your beatmatching; even though the fader sits somewhere near the 2 per cent area, you may actually be playing at 2.2 per cent, and that 0.2 per cent can make a huge dent in your beatmatching skills, so use your ears, and listen to what the beat is doing, rather than only relying on the numbers on the pitch control.

Digital turntables with a little LCD display that give you a readout of what you set the pitch to let you be more exact with your pitch fader, but the numbers on an analogue fader should be seen only as a general reference, and not taken as read.

Accuracy

The other problem with the pitch control is that through time, its accuracy starts to shift, so when you set the pitch to 4.5 per cent, the turntable is actually only running at 4 per cent. But even worse, is the area around the 0 pitch mark on the turntable (what I like to call the 'Bermuda Pitch Zone', because it's easy to get lost in there for days!). On problem decks, when you set the pitch control to 0 pitch, the control clicks into place, and locks into 0 per cent pitch. When you move the pitch control away from the 0 pitch click point, the motor sometimes has trouble knowing which way you're moving the pitch fader, and does the opposite of where you're setting the control, or sometimes belligerently remaining at 0 pitch for a short distance either side of the click point.

Counterweight/height adjust

The *counterweight* is a metal weight that rotates on the back of the tonearm, which, when turned anticlockwise to add weight, increases the down pressure of the needle on the record, making it less likely to skip when you're moving the record back and forth, either to find the start point of a record (the *cue*), or when scratching. Chapter 11 has detailed information on calibrating and using the counterweight properly.

The higher you set the tonearm, the steeper the angle at which the needle points down into the groove, exerting even more down-force, making it even less likely to skip. A lot of scratch DJs adopt this setting to give increased needle stability. Be careful though, if you've set your tonearm height to the top, and the counterweight on at full, you'll wear out your records and your needles really fast.

You may have read about or heard of DJs who like to put the counterweight on back to front, to get a little more down pressure onto the needle; this action is very bad for your needle and your records, damaging and wearing them out too quickly. For the scratch DJ who accepts accelerated wear as part of the consequence of scratching, this is fine. But as a beatmatching, mixing DJ, never put on more weight than is suggested by the needle manufacturer. If you need to add that much weight, chances are your technique is wrong, your needles are already damaged or dirty, or you're using the wrong needle altogether (these issues are covered in Chapter 6).

Antiskate

When a record plays forwards, the needle in the groove is pulled in toward the centre of the record (a *centripetal* force). *Antiskate* cancels out this pull by adding an equal force that pulls the needle out toward the outer edge of the record, keeping the needle in the middle of the groove with no sideways force to wear out the walls of the groove.

Although antiskate helps to keep the home listener's vinyl copies of Mozart in pristine condition, it is often redundant for the DJ. As a DJ, you don't only play the record forwards; between scratching and back cueing, you also do your fair share of playing the tune backwards. When you play a record backwards, the force that normally pulls the needle into the centre of the record when playing forwards is now pulling out toward the edge of the record (it's become a *centrifugal* force). If an antiskate setting is already pulling the record out to the edge, there's more force than normal acting on the needle, making it even *more* likely to jump out of the groove. For this reason, most DJs tend to leave antiskate set to 0.

Removable headshell/cartridge

This feature is a key step up from the basic, home record players that just have a moulded headshell. The needle on these record players may still be replaceable, but because the needle plugs into a moulded mount on the end of the tonearm, you are stuck using that needle and can't choose a needle better suited for DJing.

The needle you use is very important depending on the style of DJing you do. DJs who want to scratch need to set up their needles for maximum stability, and beatmatching DJs need to ensure that they get the best sound and versatility from their needles and cartridges. Therefore, being able to change the needle design and the headshell, for example from a standard Technics design to an all-in-one headshell, and adjust the angle at which the needle points into the groove, is an important factor for achieving these requirements. (See Chapter 6 for more on the different designs of headshells, needles, and cartridges.)

From a practical point of view, removable headshells can be a life-saver if you damage a needle during a set in a club. If something happens to the needle on the turntable, and you have a spare headshell to hand, instead of fiddling around trying to remove the needle from the cartridge to replace it (in a dark, loud DJ booth, while under pressure to get the next tune ready to mix it in) you can whip off the headshell containing the damaged needle, and screw on a new one, all within five seconds.

45 RPM adaptor

In the days before CD and hard-disc jukeboxes, 45 RPM, 7-inch singles were crammed into a jukebox. These records were produced with an extra large hole in the middle (25 millimetres in diameter, compared to 5 millimetres on 33 RPM LPs) so that they can be mechanically moved from the rack and sat securely on the unit that played the record in the jukebox. Because the singles used in jukeboxes were the same as those on sale to the public, a 25-millimetre adaptor was placed onto the centre spindle to increase its diameter so the record could be played properly on home turntables with only a 5-millimetre centre spindle.

Now relegated to a recess in the top-left corner of the turntable, this shiny piece of metal has become (virtually) obsolete due to the demise of traditional jukebox records. However, if you play older records (ska/northern soul stuff especially), or newer reggae/ragga 7-inch singles, you'll find that you may still need to use this adaptor on some of those records.

Customising Your Sound with Advanced Turntable Features

The basic features on a turntable enable you to play a record, and change the playing speed. For most DJs, that's more than enough. But for some, gadgets, buttons, and switches all go hand-in-hand with creativity and individuality, so they look to turntables with enhanced features to create their own sound and mix style.

When you look at the gadgets and controls on your turntables, just bear one thing in mind – where are you going to be DJing? If you only ever intend to make mix tapes and run your own parties (on your own equipment), then feel free to sneer and ignore this warning, but if you're planning on playing in clubs, have a quick think about how much you use these add-ons, and the likelihood of them being available on the clubs' set-up.

This argument is similar to the one about relying on beat counters to develop your beatmatching skills (see Chapter 8). The advanced functions such as reverse play, quartz lock, digital displays, and pitch bend/controls with 50 per cent variance are all useful, adding a nice dimension to your mixes when at home, but as 97 per cent of clubs still use Technics 1210s (with nothing more than a pitch control that's a bit wonky around 0 pitch and a rock-steady motor), ask yourself if your advanced turntable DJ skills will travel well to these clubs. If you can only mix well on advanced turntables, you're in for a tough time when you can't use any.

I'm not saying don't get turntables with advanced features on them. I'm not even going to lie and say that you'll never work in a club with these features (some clubs are beginning to replace the older 1210 MkII turntables with more advanced Vestax decks as they realise technology is advancing, and so reinvest in better equipment), but in the same vein as beat counters, don't rely on these advanced features to make you a good DJ.

Pitch range options

Once upon a time, your choice of pitch range was limited to 8 per cent faster or slower (unless you opened up, and started screwing around with the innards of the turntable); that was when Technics 1200/1210s ruled the roost. But things have moved on. Now 12 per cent pitch variance has become a standard on many turntables, but advances in pitch control mean that the DJ can have 50 per cent pitch variance on offer, or more!

Simplicity is reliability

I believe that the Technics 1200 and 1210 MkII turntables have gained popularity over the years in no small part because they're extremely reliable. They're reliable because there's very little in them to go wrong – just a motor, a few electronics to control the power and speed of the motor, and the audio output.

Adding extra features to turntables can increase the chance of breakdown and malfunction.

However, in my opinion, manufacturers such as Gemini, Vestax, and Numark have proven that turntables can be elevated to another level of functionality by offering the DJ extra creativity (for a price), while ensuring a long life-span for the equipment by increasing reliability and build quality.

You aren't likely to play a tune at 50 per cent that often, but you're certain to want to play a tune faster than 8 per cent. Some scratch, funk, and drum-and-bass DJs like to over-pitch their tunes, making them sound completely different. (Try to steer away from using tunes with vocals when you do this though, because the vocalist will sound as if they've been inhaling helium!)

Sliding the pitch control up or down to 50 per cent at the end of a tune is a good technique to use (sparingly) to get from one tune to another, but increased pitch options are more about offering the DJ another level of creativity than about everyday use.

Pitch bend and joystick control

Pitch bend was first introduced on CD decks. Instead of speeding up or slowing down the turntable by pushing the record, spinning the spindle, or touching the side of the deck, you get two buttons on the turntable, or a joystick, which control small bursts of speed. When the + or – pitch bend buttons or controls are used, the turntable speeds up or slows down by a small amount. When released, the deck returns to your original speed setting.

CD DJs who are used to using buttons instead of their hands to control the speed bumps on their tunes, welcome these controls when they first use vinyl. You still need to set the pitch control, and start the record at the right time, but if you're more familiar using buttons to correct the speed of CDs, the concept and the technique of using the turntable's pitch bend is the same, making the migration from CD to vinyl all that bit easier for the CD DJ.

Predictability

Pitch bend controls give you a consistently smooth and predictable increase and decrease in turntable speed; you can't say the same about your fingers!

The knack of adjusting the speed of the record with your hands is something that you pick up after a few hours, but sometimes you come across a record that feels stiff to move, or flies away too fast, and turns a lot faster than you thought, almost spinning out of control as you try to speed it up. The constant, definite change that you always have to hand, as you press the pitch bend buttons, no matter what record you use, means that your mixing is easier, quicker, and sounds better. See Chapter 12 for how and why you need these bursts of power to get the bass beats back in time.

Cleaner records

Pitch bend is also a good alternative to pushing or slowing down the tune with your fingers because it protects your records from excessive finger prints and grime. As a DJ, you're actively encouraged to touch your records, but developing a method that keeps your records as clean as possible is still a good thing.

When you're considering buying turntables with pitch bend, try to see the feature in action first. Some turntables have a really clumsy control over the speed boost/lag, and can _zip_ up the speed of your tune by too much too fast, sometimes rendering the control pointless because you can never make small enough adjustments to get the bass beats back in time.

Tempo reset/Quartz lock

Earlier in this chapter, I described the 'Bermuda Pitch Zone', which is where the pitch control goes a little wonky through the 0 pitch range on turntables that _click_ into place when set to 0. To get around this problem, turntable manufacturers started to make turntables with _clickless_ pitch faders that glide through the 0 pitch area, moving smoothly all the way through the entire pitch range. The problem with a clickless fader, though, is that you can't be sure when you're at exactly 0 pitch anymore. Some turntables still show a green light as you pass 0, but a better option is the quartz lock or tempo reset button, which resets the pitch to 0 pitch, no matter where you set the pitch control.

Some people use this quartz lock almost like a pitch bend when the record is playing too fast. Hit the button once to slow the tune down temporarily and then again to bring the tune back to the speed you set it at. This technique is a bit hit and miss, though, and not as accurate as a pitch bend, or using your hands. I like to use it if I've slowed a record right down by 50 per cent (or more) to really drag out the last couple of beats of a breakdown to instantly return to 0 pitch rather than an acceleration as the slider is moved. The downside to this is if you were playing the tune at 5 per cent before the slow down, because the tune will now be playing at 0 per cent, 5 per cent slower than before.

Master Tempo/Key Lock

Master Tempo, first available as an add-on to turntables by a company called Vinyl Touch, then available on Pioneer CD decks, and now an option on a number of advanced, digital turntables, enables you to change the speed of a tune, but not its pitch.

Remember, the pitch control isn't just a speed control. As you increase or decrease the pitch control, the pitch of the music gets higher or lower as a consequence of the tune playing faster or slower. Pressing the Master Tempo button means that you can affect only the speed, leaving the pitch of the music as it was recorded.

I like the design of the *Key Lock* on the Numark TTX1 that takes this technique a step further. You can use the pitch control to select whatever pitch setting you want the tune to play at, press the Key Lock button, and then adjust the music tempo while retaining your original pitch setting. Or for even greater control over this, I recommend the Gemini PDT6000, which has two faders on the right-hand side of the turntable, one for pitch adjustments (speed) and another called *Key Adjustment*, a setup that enables you to change the pitch of the tune without changing the tempo.

All of these controls can be quite temperamental, though. With the Master Tempo, or Key Lock turned on, if the pitch of the deck is set to more than 4 or 5 per cent, you can sometimes get digital noise added to the music, making the track sound as if it's playing underwater. Tunes with strong vocals tend to suffer the worst from this problem, whereas simple, musical tracks can withstand quite a large change.

You won't find any hard and fast rules for using the Master Tempo and Key Lock features, so you simply need to keep experimenting to work out how far you can push each of your tunes.

Digital display of pitch

The pitch control is an essential tool on a turntable, but its analogue nature means that you can't be 100 per cent sure that when you set the pitch to 3.5 per cent, the pitch has actually changed by 3.5 per cent. Sometimes, the smallest pitch change is all that's needed to make the beats of two tunes play at the same time; with a pitch fader that has no display, you have to guess whether the pitch changes at all when you move the fader by only a millimetre.

A digital display on the turntable shows you exactly where you've set the pitch, and whether you've increased or decreased the pitch by a small enough amount to make the beats play in time. This info helps you mix with confidence, taking away some of the guesswork that comes with analogue pitch controls.

Adjustable brake for Start/Stop

Traditionally, when you press Stop on the turntable, the record stops in about half a second. Some decks enable you to adjust the brake, which changes the time that the record takes to stop, giving you more control if you decide to use *Stop* as a mixing technique (see Chapter 14).

The half-second Stop option is really nice, but even prolonging that to about 1 bar of music (which equals 4 beats) can add another dimension to the mix, or you can set a really long brake time, and emulate the power-off.

In some instances, you can tighten the brake up so much, that when you press Stop, the record plays backwards! This tip is a really good trick on turntables that don't have a reverse play function but that do enable you to easily and quickly alter the brake.

On some turntables though, you have to unscrew the turntable to get to the screw that controls the brake adjustments. Carrying out this manoeuvre obviously isn't very convenient when you're in the middle of a mix, so if you think that your mixing style would benefit from using different brake speeds through a mix, I suggest that you take a look at something like the Gemini PT6000, which has the brake control as a knob next to the pitch control.

Reverse play

Instead of adjusting the brake to make the turntable play backwards on basic-feature turntables, advanced turntables sometimes have a handy little button (sometimes located next to the pitch control) that does exactly the same thing.

Simply press the Reverse button, and the deck plays backwards. You get a *slow-down-to-stop, start-up* delay as you do this operation, but if your timing's right when pressing this button, it sounds great.

CD decks give you the option of instantly reversing the direction of the music, rather than needing to account for this delay as the record changes direction. See Chapter 15 for information on reverse play with CDs and other CD features.

Different shaped tonearms

For years, the standard shape of the tonearm on a turntable was *S* shape. The S-shape creates a variety of different forces upon the needle as it's pulled into the centre of the record: A tracking force, an inside force, and a vertical force, which not only adds to the wear on the record, but due to so many different forces, you can understand why the needle jumps out of the groove when scratching. In the late 90s, Vestax pioneered the *ASTS* straight tonearm for DJs, which only has the tracking force affecting the needle. By cancelling out some of the lateral forces, the turntable achieves maximum stability, and the needle is less likely to skip out of the groove when you're in the middle of a really complicated, frantic scratch move.

The straight tonearm isn't aimed at only the scratch DJ, though. The reduction in forces acting on the needle in the groove means that you get a lot less wear on the vinyl, your records last and sound good for much longer, and the needle is less likely to pop out of the groove when you're trying to locate the start (*cue*) point in the record.

A lot of turntables come with only an S-shape or only a straight tonearm, but some decks from companies such as Numark now include both styles, in an interchangeable format, so you can change the design of tonearm as often as you change your socks.

Also, you find that modification companies can change the standard S-shape tonearm on your turntable into a straight tonearm, and can create a fixture similar to the headshell joint that enables you to easily swap from one design to the other, depending on your mood (or more likely, style of mixing that day).

Removable cabling

For years, turntables came with the *RCA cables* (you may know them as *phono cables*) hard-wired into the electronic gubbins inside the casing. This set-up meant that any damage to the cables (normally caused by dropping something onto the cables, or even worse, the deck itself) involved opening up the casing and re-soldering the connections (if possible) or sending your precious turntable off to a repairman.

When equipment manufacturers realised that this procedure was problematic for DJs, they started to make turntables with RCA plugs on the back, just like the inputs on the mixer. These turntables now have removable cables that you plug between the turntable and the mixer, and if anything happens to damage the cables, they are easy to replace. The new design can also prevent further damage to your turntable because if something is dropped on the cable, instead of the tug on the cable pulling the turntable onto the floor, the RCA plugs may act as a shock release, unplugging themselves through the force on the cable, saving the turntable from damage.

Chapter 11 has more about preventing these kinds of cable accidents in the first place and how to connect the RCA cables and the ground wire from the turntables to the mixer.

Digital outputs

As well as addressing the mechanics of the cabling on the back of the turntable, manufacturers also looked at the range and quality of output connections that they offer to the technology driven DJ. Not content with the analogue signal sent through the RCA outputs, digital outputs such as USB and S/PDIF are now on offer for you to connect to a mixer or PC with a similar input. I describe these connections in more detail in Chapter 11.

Battle or club design

Look into the history of DJing, and you see that club DJs have the turntables positioned as per the manufacturers' expectations, but scratch DJs turn them around 90 degrees, anticlockwise. The reason that scratch DJs turn their decks around is so that the needle is clear of their hands as they move like lightning from deck to mixer to the other deck, and back again, all in the blink of an eye.

Although this position means that the Start/Stop button, the power control, and the pitch fader have also moved by 90 degrees, this factor hasn't been a problem for the scratch DJ because for years, there hasn't been any alternative, forcing them to adapt. But companies such as Numark and Vestax saw a gap in the turntable market, and have designed turntables with Start/Stop switches at both corners, and pitch faders that can be moved from one side of the deck to the other, all of which give the scratch DJ more control over the layout and the ease of use of his or her tools.

If you're a beatmatching DJ with no interest in scratching, turning up to a club that has the turntables set up with this 'vertical alignment' for scratch DJs can be extremely annoying. It's not as easy to access the pitch control, it's a bit harder to take the needle on and off the record, and simply isn't as comfortable to beatmatch with the turntables set up like this. Some time spent using turntables with this orientation soon gets you over this hurdle, so when you research a venue you're due to play in, be sure to look at how the turntables are aligned, and put in any required practice at home with this set-up if need be.

Built-in mixer

Okay, I'm going out on a limb here: I believe that the Vestax QFO (Figure 5-4) is the ultimate in advanced scratch turntables. Suggested, tested, and tweaked by DJ QBert (a famous scratch DJ), this turntable is a feature-packed single deck aimed at performance scratch DJs, with a built-in mixer for performing scratches, reverse play, quartz lock, and a straight tonearm. But best of all, you can take off two of the feet, put a strap on the remaining two feet, and wear it like a guitar!

Figure 5-4:
The Vestax
QFO
turntable.

How practical the QFO is as a turntable for everyday use (especially at the cost of £750) is questionable, but if you're looking for the ultimate turntable gadget, then this is it.

Servicing Your Turntables

Make your turntables last as long as possible by showing them a little bit of care and attention from time to time. You can find information all over the Internet for fixing various broken parts on your decks, but a little cleaning and lubrication can keep the gremlins at bay.

As a general rule for all your equipment, when you're not using it, keep it covered. With turntables, if you have plastic lids for them, put those back on when you're not using the decks. If you keep the decks in flight cases, put the lid back on. If you have neither of these, put a clean bed-sheet (or something soft, clean, and lintfree) over the decks when they're not used, to catch any dust before it gets a chance to settle on your faders, motor, and tonearm.

  ✔ **Motor:** If you keep the motor properly lubricated, it can run smoothly for years. All you need to do is remove the deckplatter and put a small drop of sewing machine oil on the centre spindle. Use lubricating oil such as sewing machine oil rather than covering the entire insides of your deck with a silicon coating such as WD-40 spray!

After you've lubricated the motor, replace the platter, and spin it round with your hand. You can use the turntable immediately, as long as you didn't pour half a can of oil all over the inner workings of the deck.

✓ **Tonearm:** You need a can of compressed air, and a can of degreasing lubricant to thoroughly clean and lubricate the tonearm assembly (the degreaser dissolves any dirt you can't clean by hand). Don't worry if you think that this method is expensive, you're going to need it for your mixer, too (see Chapter 8).

Cover the rest of your equipment with a sheet you don't mind getting dusty, and then spray the tonearm assembly with the compressed air to remove any surface dust (the sheet is so you don't just move the dust from one deck to another). Spray the grease dissolver over the bearings in the tonearm to remove any ground-in dirt and to lubricate the bearings. If you can't find a degreaser with built-in lubricant, use a needle dipped in oil to lubricate each of the bearings in turn.

✓ **Faders:** Similar to the cross-fader on the mixer, use a can of compressed air to blow any dirt out of the pitch fader. Use a cleaning lubricant to dissolve any dirt residue in the fader if you think that you have a problem, but using the compressed air is usually adequate to clean the fader.

✓ **Headshell:** If you ever suffer from signal dropout from the cartridge (which is when the music starts to break up and cut out), use a pencil, or a pin to clean any dirt off the contacts. I've heard of DJs licking the contact points on the headshell and the cartridge to try to clean off any dirt but, as well as being disgusting, your saliva (mixed with the beer you've been drinking) ends up damaging the contacts in the long run.

Check that the screws holding the cartridge are tight, that the needle is clean of any dirt build-up, and that it sits securely inside the cartridge.

✓ **Under the platter:** If your turntable comes with a removable deckplatter, lift it off, and wipe around the underside with a lint-free cloth, and make sure to pick up any dust or dirt that may get trapped underneath. Using the spray can of air may be a bad idea because you can blow the dust further inside the deck chassis. Although a little dirt may not cause a problem with the electronics, it's not a good idea to keep forcing more and more dust than normal inside the turntable.

Chapter 6

Perfecting Your Decks: Slipmats and Needles

In This Chapter

▶ Understanding what slipmats are for

▶ Making sure that your slipmats slip

▶ Knowing the differences in needle designs

▶ Picking the right needle and cartridge for your DJing style

▶ Prolonging the life of your needles (and records)

*W*hen choosing a turntable to DJ with, Chapter 5 encourages you to look for one with a good pitch control, adjustable tonearm, strong motor, and a solid design. These characteristics can set the DJ deck apart from the home hi-fi record player.

However, you still need to look at two more areas before your turntable is a true DJ tool: slipmats, and what types of needles and cartridges to use.

Sliding with Slipmats

As well as acting as an antistatic device, the slipmat is a key factor in transforming your new turntables from just a really good pair of record players to fully functional DJ decks.

The *slipmat* is the same shape and size of a 12-inch record, and sits between the record and the *deckplatter* (the part of the turntable that rotates to make the record rotate). Slipmats are normally made out of felt, and if you've taken my advice in Chapter 5 about making sure that your turntables have a smooth, metal deckplatter, you find that the low friction between the felt and the metal keeps the deckplatter turning underneath the record when you hold it in a stopped position. This simple function of the slipmat is extremely important when you want to start a record playing at an exact time, and is essential for successful beatmatching.

If the deckplatter has stopped turning underneath the record, when you let go of the record to start playing again, it can take almost a second to get up to full speed again, meaning you've started the record later that you'd planned. With the slipmat helping the deckplatter continue to turn under the stopped record, the record takes little or no time to get to full speed, and your records start exactly when you want them to.

This friction-free slip is also essential for the scratch DJ so that he or she can move the record backwards and forwards easily, without the drag and inertia of the full weight of the deckplatter moving back and forth with the record.

The setup you want to achieve with the slipmat goes like this:

✔ The deckplatter (the part with the bumps on the side that turns round) is at the very bottom.

✔ The slipmat goes on top of that

✔ The record is then placed directly onto the slipmat

When you first buy your turntables, they may come with a thick, heavy rubber mat on the deckplatter with the slipmats placed on top of them. *Please* remove this big rubber mat so you have the same setup as previously described. If you leave the rubber mat on, the slipmat won't slip over the thick heavy rubber, and the deckplatter will grind to a halt when you try to hold it stopped.

Choosing an appropriate slipmat

The two design concepts that affect how well your slipmat slips are its thickness and weight, and what kind of design is printed on it.

The best slipmat is made from a smooth, compacted felt, and is thin and light. If the slipmat is too thick and heavy, and the felt too rough (or too fluffy), the extra friction drags on the deckplatter, making it turn a lot slower under a stopped record, or making it stop completely.

The image you have printed on the slipmat can be a great expression of your personality. Search any online record store, and you find a whole load of slipmats with different logos, designs, photos, and colours printed on them. Slipmats like these are great to look at, but try to steer away from cheap versions that are covered in print because, depending on what they use to print onto the slipmats, it may stick to the record and cause drag problems, or the design can wear off and look bad, and may actually harm your records.

My first set of slipmats came second-hand (as did the turntables), and the print had started to come away and go slightly brittle, which ended up scratching some of my beloved tunes. I got around this problem by turning the mat upside-down, so the logo was in contact with the deckplatter, and the felt touching the record. This method had the added bonus of reducing the friction even more, and made the slipmat a lot more . . . slippy.

Winning the friction war

When you hold your record still, the power of the motor (known as *torque*) directly affects how easily the deckplatter continues to turn underneath. If you have a weak motor or (gasp), you chose belt-driven turntables (see Chapter 5 for more on choosing a turntable) the turntable may have a hard time keeping the deckplatter turning even with the best friction-killing slipmats. Even on the better turntables, such as Technics and Vestax, if the slipmats are too thick and rough, they can drag and pull on the turntable, slowing it down. I've experienced this problem in a few clubs that had old, big, thick woolly slipmats.

In both these cases, the solution is to reduce the friction between the slipmat and the deckplatter. You can buy commercial products such as Flying Carpets, which you put between the slipmat and the deckplatter, but you can first try out a couple of home remedies using wax paper and cardboard that I discuss shortly.

If you do find that your turntables grind to a halt when you hold the record stopped, before adding something else to reduce the friction, take a look at your technique. You don't need to press down hard on the record to hold it stopped, just rest one or two fingers towards the outer edge and that should be enough. Too much pressure adds resistance, stopping the deckplatter turning.

In the end, if you have a good pair of slipmats on a turntable and a good motor, that's all you need to keep the turntable turning while you're mixing or scratching. In case you were wondering, I use the Technics slipmats that came with my 1210 turntables, and a light touch.

Wax paper

Wax paper placed between the slipmat and the deckplatter is a great way of reducing friction and resistance. If you don't want to go out and buy wax paper for this purpose, take a look through your records and look at the inner sleeves that protect them. You may find a sleeve made out of wax paper.

Older records (such as in your parents' record collection) are most likely to use wax-paper inner sleeves. Either ask your parents if you can swap one of their wax sleeves for a paper one from your collection (that you no longer wish to protect with an inner sleeve), or go to a record fair or second-hand store, and look for a cheap record that has a wax paper sleeve. All you care about is that the sleeve isn't creased and is in good condition, it doesn't matter what the actual record is, so go for a cheap one. Although, if you choose wisely, you may be able to give the record to your mum for Mother's Day!

Here's how to make a friction-killer:

1. **Place the wax paper/inner sleeve on a flat cutting surface.**

   Carpets, dining room tables, and the hood of your car are all suggestions of surfaces NOT to use.

2. **Using your existing slipmat as a template and a sharp utility knife as a cutting tool, cut a 12-inch (30-centimetre) circle out of the wax paper.**

3. **Mark the centre of your cut-out by putting a pen through the centre of the slipmat, then cut a tiny hole at that point for the centre spindle on the turntable to go through.**

4. **Place this wax cut-out between the deckplatter and the slipmat, and try it out.**

   You'll find that the record slips more easily now.

Cardboard cut-out

Another option for fighting friction is to reduce the surface area that slips.

Take a piece of thin cardboard, cut it into a 6-inch (15-centimetre) diameter circle, poke a hole through the middle, and place that between the slipmat and the deckplatter.

Be careful with your choice of cardboard because if it's too thick, the record may be unstable when you hold the outer edge to stop the record, causing the needle to jump.

This cardboard circle reduces the surface area of the slipmat that's in contact with the deckplatter, and because cardboard creates a lot less friction than the felt of the slipmat, the records slip more easily. You may even want to try cutting out a 12-inch (30-centimetre) circle.

Getting Groovy with Needles and Cartridges

The *needle* is the part on the turntable that sits in the groove of the record. As the record plays, the groove causes vibrations in the needle, which the cartridge translates into electrical signals, which are then sent from the turntable to the mixer, and you hear music. This is how the groove makes you groove.

You need to know what the different kinds of needle and cartridge are, and how to pick the correct ones for your DJing style. The needles you use as a DJ are a lot stronger than the ones you find in home turntables because they need to take a fair bit of abuse. *Back cueing* (playing the record backwards while trying to find the place to start), scratching, the inevitable *whoops* when you rip the needle right across the record, and repeatedly taking the needle off and placing it somewhere else on the record with a thump can all take a toll on even the most robust of needles.

Along with strength, you also want to demand good sound quality from your needles and cartridges. You need them to pick up the solid bass melodies and bass beats and still give you the crisp high frequencies from the records.

The good news is that any needle and cartridge designed for DJs can go on any turntable. You don't have to use Stanton needles and cartridges on Stanton turntables; you don't have to use the Technics headshell that comes with Technics turntables. Manufacturers of DJ turntables have been smart enough to design a universal connection from the cartridge to the tonearm, so that you can use any cartridge on any turntable. This flexibility stands assuming that you've not just bought a basic, cheap, hi-fi turntable with an all-in-one, moulded tonearm and cartridge, or gone for a high-end design that uses different connections. Figure 6-1 shows the back of some cartridges with the same connection.

Figure 6-1:
The same
connection
on the back
of different
cartridges.

Your cartridge and needle considerations come in pairs (fitting, because you usually buy them in pairs). Firstly, there are two main designs for how the cartridge eventually attaches to the tonearm, and then there are two different styles of needle that you have to decide on:

✔ **Headshells with the cartridge and needle screwed on:** This design is the one that nearly always accompanies your turntables when you buy them. This doesn't mean it's a poor design, it's just the design that covers all bases. One of the most popular and enduring scratch DJ needle setups is a Shure M44-7 needle and cartridge attached to this headshell, and the Stanton 500AL (see Figure 6-2) is found in clubs and bedrooms all over the land.

The top of the cartridge is screwed to the headshell, and the needle plugs into the cartridge (the needle is the front, white part shown in Figure 6-3). Four coloured cables make the electrical connection from the cartridge to the headshell, which then plugs into the tonearm to make the final connection.

Figure 6-2:
A Technics
headshell
with
Stanton
500AL
attached.

Figure 6-3:
A dis-
assembled
needle and
cartridge
with a
Technics
headshell.

✔ **Built-in headshell:** This design does away with the separate headshell; instead, the cartridge, which is the main body of this unit, plugs directly into the tonearm. The needle is still separate, and easily removed and replaced, but the sleek all-in-one design makes this cartridge a very attractive part of your turntable.

Many people mistakenly believe that this all-in-one design isn't suitable for scratch DJs, but this isn't so. To name only two, the Numark CC-1, pictured in Figure 6-4, is the 'signature model' of the Scratch Perverts, and the Ortofon Concorde QBert was developed through DJ Qbert (both world-class scratch DJs).

However, this style of needle and cartridge does have a strong link in clubs for the beatmixing DJ. As well as commonly using elliptical-shaped needles, which produce better sound quality than their spherical cousins (I go into this in more detail next), this design makes seeing where the needle is on the record a lot easier.

Figure 6-4:
The Numark
Carl Cox
needle and
cartridge.

After you've decided on the design of your needles and cartridges, the next thing you have to think about is whether to buy elliptical or spherical needles for your carts. A lot of manufacturers supply both shapes for the same cart, and you can get them for both the designs mentioned previously, so the choice is down to your preference rather than availability.

✔ **Spherical:** A spherical needle has a rounded tip that only makes contact with the straight sides of the groove, so the contact between the needle and the groove is extremely small (see Figure 6-5). This means that the sound quality is reduced because the needle isn't picking the amount of bumps and variations from the groove that it could if it were making contact with a larger area.

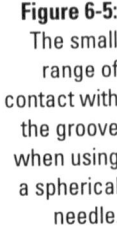
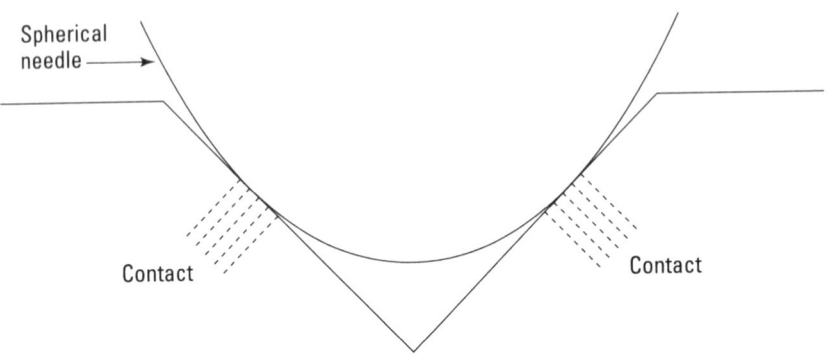

Figure 6-5:
The small
range of
contact with
the groove
when using
a spherical
needle.

Spherical
needle

Contact

Contact

The small contact area compromises sound quality, but also means that the *tracking force* (the force created between the needle and the sides of the groove) is incredibly strong, so the needle puts up a fight against jumping out of the groove when scratching or finding a start point on the record. However, the concentration of the tracking force means that the record wears down more quickly.

✔ **Elliptical:** Elliptical needles make more contact with the sides of the groove because of their cone shape (shown in Figure 6-6); therefore, producing much better sound quality because they can pick up more information from the groove. However, the trade-off for this increased sound quality is that the tracking force is now spread out over a larger surface area, making the needle a bit more sensitive, and prone to getting knocked out of the groove. What this spread of tracking force means to a beatmixing DJ is that you can't be as rough when working with your records during a mix, making them unsuitable for advanced scratching by most people (though simple scratching like baby scratching should be fine).

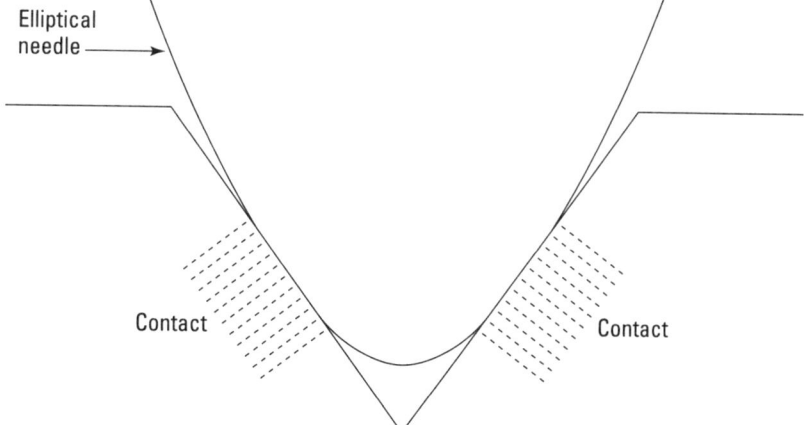

Figure 6-6:
The larger range of contact with the groove when using an elliptical needle.

Choosing the Right Needle for Your DJ Style

Scratch DJs and beatmixing DJs demand different features from their needles. A scratch DJ is more concerned that the needle stays glued into the groove than about sound quality, so a spherical needle that creates a lot of tracking force is more suitable. Headshell mounted carts such as the Ortofon GT and the Shure M447 are both popular, but the built-in headshell carts like the Ortofon Concorde QBert are also popular with scratch DJs.

Beatmixing DJs are more concerned with sound quality, though they do still demand that the needle stays in the groove. Fortunately, because this kind of DJ isn't too rough when working with the vinyl, elliptical needles are a great choice because they give the sound quality desired while preserving the life of the DJ's records.

Ortofon have a vast range of pro carts designed for mixing, and in my experience, Stanton's Groovemaster, Numark's CC-1, and Shure's M35X all offer great sound quality and long life for your records.

The last thing to say about needles is that if you're buying new turntables, find out if they come supplied with needles and cartridges. Most stores include the basic Stanton 500AL cartridge and needle set with turntables, but do check – never assume. Imagine this scenario: You're waiting excitedly for your decks to be delivered, but then find out that needles and carts haven't been included, so you have to wait before you can use them – and all because you forgot to check when you ordered them.

Feeling the Force with Counterweight Settings

The counterweight affects the tracking force of the needle in the groove. The heavier the counterweight, the stronger the force, so the more secure the needle in the groove is – but the quicker your records wear out.

In Chapter 11, I describe how to set up your tonearm properly for DJ use, to add the correct amount of tracking force with the counterweight. How much counterweight you add on the tonearm is dictated firstly by the needle manufacturers. The documentation you receive with the needles and cartridges tells you the suggested tracking force, and suggested tonearm height for the needles you've bought. However, some of these figures aren't aimed toward DJ use, and are actually calculated for the greatest longevity of your records.

As a brief guide for you, here are the most popular counterweight settings for common DJ needles:

Needle	Counterweight (in grammes)
Stanton 500AL II, Stanton Discmaster II, Stanton 605SK	2–5
Shure M44-7, Shure Whitelabel	1.5–3
Numark CC-1	3–6
Ortofon Concorde DJ S	2–4
Ortofon Concorde Night-Club S	2–5

If you find that the needle still skips when you're scratching or trying to find the start point of the record, first check your technique. If you're quite rough as you move the record with your hands, may be *you're* the one making the needle jump out of the groove. You don't have to be forceful to move the record; you can move it back and forth just as quickly with a light, fluid motion as with a harsh, rough, jerky movement. When you push and pull the record, follow the curve of the record, rather than pushing and pulling in a straight line. This 'straight line' force is a common cause of the needle popping out of the groove.

If you think that the needle is jumping because not enough weight is on it, try gradually increasing the counterweight until the needle stops skipping. Take your time and increase the counterweight by small amounts each time, and when the needle does stay securely in the groove, try taking a little weight back off again; you'll probably find it's still okay.

Though vinyl is designed to be long-lasting and not wear out too quickly, if you find you've had to use the full counterweight on the needle to keep it from jumping out the groove, you must understand that the record and the needle will wear more quickly than usual because of the added tracking force.

Nurturing Your Needles

Knowing when you need to change your needles requires a mix of professional help and general knowledge. The only way to truly know if your needles are worn out and in need of replacement is to look at them through a microscope. Not many people have a microscope sitting next to their turntables, so you may want to do a bit of research now and get in touch with some of the specialist stores in your area to see if they can check your needles for you. A few DJ stores may offer this service, but the high-end audio equipment stores are the ones that can help you, or guide you toward someone who can.

However, you can look for the following simple things yourself:

- Is the needle picking up lots of dirt from the record?
- If you play a quiet part in a record, the next time you play it, does it pop and crackle?
- Do the high frequencies (especially the hi-hat cymbal sounds that normally play in between bass drum beats) sound fuzzy?
- Have you had your needles longer than a year, and used them nearly every day for a couple of hours?
- Do you simply think that they need replacing?

If you can answer yes to half of these questions, especially the last one, then the chances are you need to replace your needles. If you're using relatively cheap needles such as Stanton 500ALs, you may simply want to trust your gut instinct and buy some new needles. But, if you're using something like the Ortofon Night-Club E, which cost £45 each, if you answered yes to these questions, get them checked out first by a professional – rather than immediately going out to spend £90 on a pair of new needles.

Because you plan to DJ with these needles, their lifespan is inevitably somewhat shortened, but you can do a couple of things to extend their usefulness:

- ✔ **Keep your records clean.** You'd think that if Mr Diamond and Mr Dust got into a fight with each other, Mr Diamond would win. Unfortunately, that's not the case with your diamond-tipped needle and the dust in the groove of you record.

  If you consider that by the time you play three or four records, the needle has travelled through over a couple of miles' worth of record groove, if a piece of dirt is constantly grinding away on the diamond tip, the needle's going to wear down much more quickly than if it were playing on a clean record.

- ✔ **Keep the weight down.** The more counterweight you add, the quicker the needle wears down. It's as simple as that.

Your needles and your cartridges are literally the first point of contact for the music you're playing. Take care of your needles, and make sure that you replace them when they're worn. No matter how good the rest of your equipment is, if your needles aren't picking up all the information they should from the record, your music won't sound as good as it can.

There's a saying in the television business that I keep repeating when I'm editing: that you can only make poop from poop. It's exactly the same with your needles; bad sound in equals bad sound out. Enough said.

Chapter 7

Keeping Up with the Techno-Revolution

In This Chapter

▶ Looking at the blurry line between analogue and digital formats

▶ Understanding what CD deck styling means for the DJ

▶ Mixing with MiniDisc, MP3s, and iPods

▶ Introducing the big boys on the block of mixing software

Kane and Abel, the Capulets and the Montagues, Apple and Microsoft, Britney and Christina; throughout time, history and literature have told of the wars between two similar sides. Wars that exist because of what the two sides have in common, not because of how different they are. When CD decks first came onto the scene, vinyl purists all over the world cried foul. CDs were seen as a great threat to the vinyl DJ and DJs started to take sides between the standard vinyl method of DJing, and the CD upstart (and to a great extent, CD has won a fair share of battles, if not the war).

With MP3 and laptop DJing becoming more and more popular, CD and vinyl formats have both come under threat, but with technology evolving at an incredibly fast rate, the reasons for choosing one format over another become more and more blurry.

This chapter covers the major differences between CD and vinyl, and what the MP3 new kid has to offer.

Choosing Your Format: Analogue or Digital

In brief, digital audio is better than analogue audio – but that doesn't necessarily mean it sounds better.

Analogue audio (which you encounter as a DJ when you use vinyl) playing from the right sound system may sound *warmer* (more pleasant with a feeling of depth and warmth) than a CD playing through a stereo, but the fragility of vinyl, which suffers from cracks, pops, skips, and jumps through time is a flaw that (in my opinion) gives digital audio an edge over analogue audio.

Digital music doesn't have the same risks attached. The only time a CD sounds different is when you use a different sound system. A CD never wears out, it never degrades, and, as long as you take care to prevent deep scratches on the surface of the disc, you never need to worry about the CD skipping or jumping.

MP3s and MiniDiscs are different again. To keep the digital file sizes small, both of these formats are heavily compressed, so they lose a lot of audio information in their creation. How good the music sounds relies on the compression setting. If the music has been too heavily compressed, it can sound as if it's been recorded underwater, because too many audio frequencies have been removed to keep the file size small (see the section 'Wising up to MP3s' later in this chapter for more information on how different amounts of compression affects sound quality). For some people, with the correct compression setting, the convenience of the small file sizes (and disc size for MiniDisc) is an acceptable trade off against audio quality when compared to analogue vinyl.

My way is the best!

For the DJ, audio quality isn't normally the ammunition (or defence) used when arguing over the best format to use. The arguments that you hear put across concern:

- ✔ Versatility
- ✔ Cost
- ✔ Aesthetics

Versatility and cost are related to each other:

- ✔ Vinyl DJs say that CDs aren't good because it costs too much to buy a CD deck that lets you scratch, and for the beatmatching DJ, you're just pressing buttons on CDs, and there's no showmanship in that.

- ✔ CD DJs say that turntables aren't good because you pay a lot of money for something that just plays the record, with no effects, no loop function, and the needle has a tendency to skip and jump.

- ✔ MP3 DJs who use computers to DJ with scoff at both of them for wasting time carrying around records and CDs while they can store an entire music collection on the hard drive of a laptop or Apple Powerbook.

Because each of the formats come up with different ways of doing the same thing that the others do, the defining line between each of them gets more and more blurred. Not counting monetary considerations, DJing format decisions all come down to personal choice, the genre of music you play, and more likely, how cool you think you look using the equipment (the basis of the aesthetics argument).

Looking at the pros and cons

If you compare a record and a CD (a real CD from a store, not an MP3 burnt to a CD-R) and you can afford to buy any equipment on the market, you find that the strengths of the argument advising you to make the choice of one format over the other are limited. The following sections cover a few of the cases to be heard when arguing for CD or vinyl.

Vinyl is analogue, and therefore uncompressed, which makes records better than CDs

Vinyl devotees have a theory that your emotional response to music is affected by the sound frequencies discarded when converting music to CD (these are the frequencies that make vinyl sound *warmer*). I agree that sometimes you can feel a loss of warmth when playing the CD version of a tune at home when compared to the vinyl version of the same recording, but I think that this loss stems more from the quality of the CD player, the speakers, and the turntable than from how the CD was created.

Because you play your music at 100 decibels through a really loud and probably compressed sound system, as a DJ, this argument about losing the emotional audio frequencies doesn't actually hold up, as they wouldn't actually make it through the PA system and onto the dance floor. Good clubs set up the sound system to give the best possible sound for the format you're using, but most clubs you encounter (especially as you climb up the DJ career ladder) have a preset sound no matter what you play. It's up to you to adjust the EQs (equalisers) on the mixer (see Chapter 8) to try to compensate for this.

If you're lucky, the club you're working in may let you tweak the amplifier's EQ settings to make the dance floor sound how you'd like it. (Check out Chapter 20 for guidance on tweaking.)

Vinyl uses something called the RIAA equalisation curve (the specification for the correct playback of vinyl records, established by the Recording Industry Associate of America) to boost the high frequencies and kill the bass frequency to fit the audio data on the vinyl. This compression is deciphered by the mixer (which is why you need to plug into the *phono* inputs on the mixer – see Chapter 8 for more), which converts the audio back to the original sound. So although analogue audio can contain the entire frequency range of the original sound, it's not *strictly* true that vinyl is an uncompressed format.

You can't scratch with CDs

The fact that you can't scratch with CDs used to be true, but if you have the money for good CD decks it isn't true any longer. See Chapters 15 and 16 for a more detailed answer.

Some tunes are only available on vinyl

Some tunes come only on vinyl, but this fact isn't something that should force you into using a format you're unhappy with. For the CD DJ, the simplest way to get around the problem is to buy a turntable, record the tune to your computer, and burn it to CD.

All you need is a good quality, direct-drive turntable that plays accurately at 0 pitch (refer to Chapter 5), a good set of needles, and a computer with a soundcard and CD burner (see the later section 'Mixing on PC'), and you can convert all your records to CD. You may even want to incorporate the turntable into your DJ setup for some variation!

If you have lots of vinyl that you're transferring onto CD and you have a BPM (beats per minute) counter on your mixer, set the BPM for each different genre to the same reading (125 for house, 135 for trance, and so on) as you record them. This way, when you play back tunes with a similar genre from CD, beatmatching is really easy, because you won't have to change the speed of your tunes by much (if at all) in order to match the beats. (Check out Chapter 12 for more about beatmatching.)

Turntables and records are heavy and cumbersome

Turntables are solid and heavy for a good reason; if they weren't, the needle would skip with all the booming bass you're playing through the club's sound system.

Having lugged around a couple of bags and boxes filled with vinyl to clubs, I'll concede that a wallet with 100 CDs inside, or an iPod, is a lot lighter than the equivalent amount of tunes on vinyl, but I could do with losing a few pounds anyway, and see 'night club weight training' as a booster to my gym activities.

On an affectation level, I'm embarrassed to say that I feel really cool walking into clubs with two big boxes filled with records. *Everyone* I pass in the crowd knows I'm the DJ (and if they don't, I make sure to bash their knees with the record boxes a couple of times). If you walk into a club with a little wallet filled with 100 CDs, the crowd may think that you're just there to read the meter!

I was kidding about the boxes and the knees. I'd never do that . . .

Turntables don't have built-in effects

Until CD players included built-in effects, this point was never an issue. If you wanted effects, you'd buy a separate effects processor like the Pioneer EFX-1000 or you'd get a mixer with built-in effects. Personally, I'd much rather have the effects on the mixer than on the turntable or CD player, I like to be able to think of the DJ booth as 'playback' (turntables/CD decks and so on) and 'control' (the mixer) areas – and having both playback and control on one unit can throw my (sometimes limited) concentration.

However, my opinions aside, loop controls, and multiple *cue points* (places to start playing from) make CD decks incredibly versatile, and do make them better than a single turntable, giving the DJ the ability to remix a tune directly from the CD deck (see Chapter 15 for more on these functions).

You can't see the music on CD

The great thing about vinyl is that all the different shades of grey and black rings on the record let you see where you are in the tune. If you look closely at the changes between the darkness of the rings, you can work out how long it will be until the breakdown, chorus, and so on, and you'll know when to start your mix accordingly.

As a CD (which is just a shiny disc without shading information) just spins around inside the deck, you have to take the time to discover the structure of your tunes, and read the time display, remembering when things happen in the tune to be able to mix properly on CD. Or you did, until recently . . .

Manufacturers realised that this issue was a big flaw for the beatmatching DJ, and have started to show a representation of the music's waveform on read-outs of CD decks (see Figure 7-1). The waveform is larger for loud parts, and smaller for quiet parts, so you can tell by the dips and troughs when the tune is about to change to a quieter or louder part of the tune. You still need to know the structure of the tune, and the waveform is more of a ball-park reference than a precise guide, but it's transformed mixing on CD from blind memory of a tune structure to a visual trigger of your memory.

Figure 7-1:
The peaks and troughs show the quieter and louder parts of the tune.

Turntables are more expensive than CD decks

Whether turntables are more expensive than CD decks is a bit of a grey area. I've found that one of the most expensive vinyl-only turntables is the Technics SL-1210M5G, which is around £450; and one of the highest models of CD deck is the Pioneer CDJ-1000MkIII, which costs £760. However, if you look at the cost in comparison to what features are included, turntables can be a lot more expensive than CD decks.

A £100 turntable will probably be belt-driven, have a weak motor, won't hold the pitch very well, will most likely cause feedback when played too loud due to the thin plastic body, and you'll probably get fed up with it in a year or so. On the other hand, if you spend £100 on a CD deck like the Gemini CDJ-01, in my opinion, you'll have got yourself a deck that gives you a reliable pitch control with pitch bend and a loop function (though the antiskip may not be great). These basic functions on a basic CD deck give you more control over your mix than a cheap, belt-driven turntable ever could.

If you have £200 to spend, you find that the features on the CD decks you look at outclass what's on a turntable of the same price. Although the turntable you can afford now has a high *torque* (power), direct-drive motor like the Numark TT500, and may offer a pitch bend and large ranges of pitch variance (sometimes over 50 per cent faster or slower), I still don't think that a turntable competes with a CD deck in the same price range.

For £200, you can afford twin CD decks, so you'd only have to pay £200 to get both of the input devices, instead of paying £400 for two turntables! Or I would recommend that you get something similar to the Numark AXIS 9, with loads of built-in effects, multiple cue points, a beat counter, seamless looping, *and* the chance to do some scratching on CD, too!

If you compare the £450 Technics SL-1210-Mk5G mentioned previously to a CD deck in a similar price range, you find that the turntable is still beaten hands down on features. For £450, you can get the Numark CDX CD player, and this thing rocks! It's built like a turntable, with a massive 12-inch (30 centimetre) platter on top so you can work with the CD as if it's a 12-inch record. It has built-in effects, MP3 playback and 3,000 programmable cue points (where the tune starts from).

So, if you want to compare top prices, CD decks are more expensive, but you get a lot more for your buck. To properly compare CDs and vinyl though you need to spend those bucks! (Refer to Chapter 4 for more on buying and budgeting for equipment.)

You lack aesthetic performance when using CDs

As the design, control, and versatility of CD decks becomes closer to the turntable, the argument about the lack of aesthetic performance is now shifting to be aimed at the laptop DJ, but aesthetics are still the big consideration when choosing to go digital or analogue.

Hunting for it, falling in love with it

Sometimes, you find a record that you work with, bond with, fall in love with, and think of it as your own, with an odd jealousy raising its head when you hear another DJ playing *your* song. This situation happened to me when a tune called 'Silence' by Delirium was released (a great trance tune with Sarah McLachlan's vocals). I heard the Tiesto remix of it somewhere, and dedicated whatever time it took to find this record on vinyl, even though it was already available as a low-quality illegal MP3 recorded from a radio show.

After a day trawling through the record stores in Glasgow, I eventually found it at a tiny record store, and played it as much as I could. It was great to play it week after week and see the enthusiasm of the dance floor grow each time I played it. Eventually, the clubbers saw the same

thing in the tune that I did, people started requesting it, and I had to play it two or three times a night.

A month later, the tune really took off, DJs were happily downloading illegal MP3s of it, the mainstream charts got hold of it, clubs and the radio played the tune to death, and I think that I actually mourned the loss of something I truly felt I'd discovered and owned. I don't think any of that would have happened to me if I'd just downloaded it from the net and burnt it to CD. The work and time I put into finding a tune I loved really paid off.

You'll be pleased to know that I still play it from time to time, and it's one of the only tunes that has got me dancing and singing in the DJ booth.

You can navigate the tune on CD just as well as you can with vinyl and you can scratch just as well as the best of them – as long as you're using top range CD decks – yet, the sight of a DJ lifting a record out of its sleeve, cleaning it on his or her T-shirt, and placing the needle on the record can still send out a 'this is a true DJ' message to some club owners; one that pressing buttons on a CD deck never could.

Whether that's right or wrong, you do get the feeling that mixing with vinyl is more of a skill than mixing with CDs. Strangely, the risk that exists when starting the record by hand, which may cause an error in your mix, or that the needle may skip, seems to be a selling point to some clubs compared to the cold, calculated ease of starting a tune on CD.

Personal pride

The best vinyl DJs fall in love with their records, and this love is generated partly by the work they need to put in to find them, and own them. To have a vinyl recording of a cherished new tune can mean you've worked hard to track down an elusive copy of the record, or you're a DJ of a standard that gets on a DJ promo mailing list. Either way, it takes talent or dogged perseverance to own this new piece of music on vinyl.

A CD or MP3 DJ could boot up their computer, jump online, download the same tune illegally, and immediately have access to any other music the heart could desire.

Understanding how technology has blurred the line

The early CD decks were based on the domestic CD player, and though they added a pitch control and a jog wheel to search through the tunes, they weren't complicated animals at all. This fuelled the vinyl DJs reluctance to accept that CDs may take over one day, and also meant that CD decks were only used by 'early adopters' who put up with their limitations, and tendency for the CD to skip when subjected to bass vibration.

Since those offerings, technology has improved the CD deck not only to compete with vinyl in all areas, but also lead the way in functionality and creativity. Pitch bend, master tempo, scratching, seamless looping, hot cues, mixing between two tunes on the same CD, and holding an entire collection of MP3s on one CD disc have all blurred the line between vinyl and CD.

Times have shifted incredibly fast over the past few years (even over the time it's taken to write this book) to generate more of a widespread acceptance of CD DJing. Judge Jules (one of the biggest UK DJs) has stated that he no longer uses vinyl, and will only use CD DJ decks when playing in clubs. I have always called myself a 'vinyl dinosaur' and thought that I'd never use CD decks, but after a visit to Ibiza (which included the chance to see Jules play at Eden) and the research into what CD decks can do in order to be able to write this chapter, I now have two Pioneer CDJ1000's sitting happily next to my Technics 1210 turntables. (So it doesn't need to be an either/or situation.)

This theft of music is a major problem in the music industry as a whole, not only DJing. Music is stolen through peer-to-peer networks and illegal download sites, and the money needed to keep producing music isn't being generated. So illegal download DJs are ultimately shooting themselves in the foot, because soon there won't be any good music to download. See Chapter 3 for more on the legalities of downloading MP3s.

The DJ may be the only person in the club who knows how special the fact is that they're playing the next big tune on vinyl, but it really is something to get excited about, and personal pride in your work is what keeps you going through the ups and downs of DJing.

Choosing a CD Deck That Fits Your Style

Two factors affect what kind of CD decks you use as a DJ, – money (see Chapter 4), and your DJing style (scratch DJ/beatmatching DJ/wedding DJ, and so on).

Although a lot of beatmatching DJs like to introduce some scratching into their sets to add another layer to their skills, having a facility to scratch on their CD decks isn't a prerequisite. If you're starting out as a beatmatching

DJ, and you're buying your first set of CD decks, you probably just want to get the basics of beatmatching correct before you start to think about adding in new tricks such as scratching to your mixes.

Still, you need to think about some of the important functions that come on a CD deck for you to beatmatch properly. A pitch control to at least +/– 8 per cent is vital, as is a pitch bend adjuster to temporarily affect the speed of the tune without needing to change where you've set the pitch control. Easy to use controls for finding what track you want to play and where you want to start it from (called the *cue*), and a clear time displays are important so you don't waste time wondering where you are on the CD. The design of the CD deck isn't so important to the beatmatching DJ. Twin CD decks and single CD decks are both viable options for the beatmatching DJ.

Twin CD

Twin CD decks are split into two halves. The top part is a control panel, with two sets of time displays, playback and cue controls, a pitch slider and pitch bend, and a jog wheel for each CD player.

These controls let the beatmatching DJ find the right place in the track, start it playing, set the pitch controls to match the beats, set any loop options, return to the cue point, start the tune with a press of a button, and adjust the speed briefly with the pitch bend if the beats aren't properly matched. (See Chapter 15 for more on pitch controls, and more info about mixing on CD.)

The controller is linked by a control cable to the other half of the unit; two CD players that use a 'tray' system (like a home CD player) to take the CDs in and out.

Twin CD with built-in mixer

You can find a few twin CD decks out there like the Numark CD MIX series that take this design one step further, and instead of a separate twin CD unit and a mixer, everything comes together as one piece of equipment. This design is good on paper, but as the mixer that's included with this kind of setup (especially in the case of the CD MIX) is quite basic, you'll be limiting yourself in creativity by going down this route.

This design is fantastic for the party/wedding DJ, who only uses the mixer to set the volumes of both the CD players, and performs a very simple, very quick mix from one CD to the other. But because the mixer is quite basic, (especially with the lack of EQ controls) it doesn't give you full control over the sound of the mix. Although this style may seem suitable when you start as a beatmatching DJ, you'll eventually yearn for a new mixer. The problem is that although you can send the outputs of the CD decks to another mixer, you're still stuck with the entire CD and original mixer lumped together in a big box of plastic and metal. The mixer will always be part of your set-up, whether you use it or not.

Single CD

Single CD decks don't tend to use the tray design that the twin units use. Older CD decks used a top-loading design, where the top of the deck was hinged, opening up for you to insert the CD, but the newer CD decks use a slot on the front of the unit, which automatically takes in and 'spits out' the CD using motors (similar to the CD player you may have on your car stereo).

The controls on offer on single CD decks are similar to the twin units, except the pitch slider may be a lot longer (which offers you finer control), the jog wheel is bigger, and you may have a host of other controls to enhance your mixes such as loops, reverse play, sample banks, and hot-cues (see Chapter 15).

The ease of use for cueing the track by working with the large jog wheel instead of pressing search buttons, and the extra functions mentioned above, all come together to give the beatmatching CD DJ a lot of creativity.

Single CD decks take up a lot more room, and although they can be mounted and raised above the turntables to save space, they usually sit flat next to the turntables, increasing the horizontal space needed for your DJ setup.

Scratch DJs and CD decks

Innovations in CD technology have now given the scratch DJ an avenue to scratch on CD. But if you want to be able to scratch well on a CD, it does come at a price.

The main thing that affects how well you're going to be able to scratch on the CD deck is the size of the jog wheel used to perform the scratch. Scratch DJs need large jog wheels that they can scratch on as if it's a normal record. This means that the jog wheels on twin CD decks, which are sprung, and only turn 90 degrees left and right, aren't suitable for the scratch DJ.

I've found that single CD decks with relatively small jog wheels, although still used by scratch DJs, make it a lot harder to perform complicated scratches. I prefer the pro level CD decks that come with a large jog wheel, such as the affordable Stanton C.304, or the more expensive Pioneer CDJ-1000MKIII and Denon DN-S3500.

CD decks that use motorised deckplatters instead of jog wheels such as the Denon just mentioned, the Technics SL-DZ1200, and the Pioneer CDJ-1000MKIII (which doesn't have a motorised platter) are becoming the standard for scratch DJs due to their similarity to vinyl turntables.

Looking Into the Future of Vinyl

So where does all this innovation of CD decks leave vinyl? Many say vinyl has been on its way out since CD decks first appeared, but it still hasn't curled up its toes and left us just yet. The reason for that is pretty much the same reason why club owners may choose a vinyl DJ over a CD DJ: Falling in love with everything about vinyl is easy.

Vinyl DJs prefer the hands on approach to vinyl rather than pressing buttons; they get off on the kudos of being the person who knows how to DJ with vinyl, and as the technology with CDs improves, the only concession these DJs will make is to add CD decks to their vinyl setup, and become a fuller, more well-rounded DJ that way, but they'd never replace their trusty turntables.

But how much longer vinyl stays mainstream is another question, though. Big name DJs are swearing off vinyl and going totally CD, some clubs and pubs only have CD decks now, (so the vinyl jocks can't get a foot in the door), and in some sad cases, you find turntables being used only as somewhere to sit a pile of CDs.

Getting into MiniDisc, MP3s, and PCs

The battle between digital and analogue isn't a two horse race anymore. CD is definitely vinyl's main threat, MiniDiscs may have fallen a few fences back, but MP3s played on computers are coming up fast in the outside lane!

Remembering MiniDisc decks

MiniDisc DJ decks were pitched against CD decks for a while in the late 1990s, sharing an almost identical design to the twin CD decks that were available. They don't really deserve to be relegated to a place in the DJ history books just yet though. There was nothing wrong with them; they were actually a lot more versatile than CD decks, because you could use one of the players as a recorder and the other as a player, set multiple cue points and edit the tunes and track lists at will, but as CDs had already won the home playback race by then, and the cost of burning music to CDs was plummeting, MiniDisc never became a serious rival.

Hybrid turntables let you have it all

The CD versus vinyl argument has had the wind blown out of it through the release of *hybrid* turntables, which play CDs *and* vinyl, both from the same unit.

The turntables do come at a price (between £500 and £700), but Numark and Gemini have both brought out hybrid turntables that let you use the deckplatter like a giant jog wheel to control CDs as if they were vinyl, and when you want to play a record, you can do so on the same piece of equipment. Packed with effects and features, if the DJ can afford the price that these and future hybrid turntables demand, the days of the separate turntable and CD player may soon be coming to an end.

The future need for MiniDisc, apart from being used at the odd wedding or by a party DJ, is probably as a recording medium. Take a personal MiniDisc recorder with you when you're DJing, plug it into the record out of a mixer, you have an ideal medium for recording your sets.

Although MiniDisc is still more convenient than taking a CD burner into a DJ booth to record your set, if you record a fantastic mix to MiniDisc, you still have to play it into the PC in real time (if you recorded 60 minutes, you have to play, and wait 60 minutes for the recording to stop) and probably through an analogue feed, which may affect the sound quality. However, ripping a 60-minute set from a CD or recording to an MP3 recorder are both far quicker, and sometimes better sound quality than MiniDisc (depending on your compression setting).

In a time of iPods and MP3 players, the lack of connectivity to instantly drag a recorded mix from MiniDisc to computer to CD will always hold MiniDiscs back from being a more popular recording format for the DJ and home market.

Wising up to MP3s

As the Internet plays a larger part in our lives, changing the way we receive our music, our movies, and our television, MP3 has firmly taken hold as the way to listen to and buy music. Available throughout the Internet on pay sites (and, unfortunately, illegal sites), MP3s are a quick and cost effective way to get your music, and with iPods becoming a style icon, MP3 is the fashionable way to listen to music.

On a typical CD, you can fit only 74 minutes of CD quality music. If you burn your MP3s onto a CD at 192 Kbps (kilobits per second) stereo (the best trade-off for sound quality versus file size) you can get over 500 minutes worth of good quality music stored onto CD. If taking a wallet filled with CDs to a club changes the horizon for vinyl DJs, just think what MP3 CDs could mean! You can walk into a club with a pair of headphones and two CD discs filled with hundreds of MP3s, and be a DJ!

MP3s are able to cut the file sizes down by compression, throwing away sound frequencies that don't make much of an impact on the sound quality of the music. This method is perfectly acceptable to a lot of people, and with a good pair of headphones on your iPod (I use the Shure E2c ear buds in case you were wondering) you soon get used to this drop in audio quality, and your brain adjusts to accept this level as the standard sound of the music.

In addition, MP3s are a convenient and cheap way to buy your music. iTunes is a fantastic place to go for music because you can buy single tracks from albums that you like instead of buying the entire album. Spending 99p on the only track you want rather than spending £15 on the entire album saves a lot of money.

For a similar approach aimed more towards the DJ, download sites such as Audiojelly (www.audiojelly.com) and DJ Download (www.djdownload.com) work in the same way as iTunes and have a large range of dance tunes available.

Promos

Back in the heydays of vinyl, a great deal of secrecy was behind promotional music from record companies. Mailing lists were like a secret cult to try to get your name on; jealousy, pride, mistrust, and lies were all born out of the desire to try to get your name on one of these record lists so you could receive the latest club tunes pre-release and get your hands on them before anyone else did.

Now though, MP3 versions of new tunes, as well as CDs from companies like PromoOnly (www.promoonly.com), are distributed to DJs for promotional use. Unfortunately, this has opened the floodgates for people to get access to new music illegally. Record companies send out MP3 tasters of tunes, leaving the vinyl pressings to the chosen few, and all it takes is for one person to grab hold of one of these, encode it to MP3, post it on the Net, and the whole world can download it, burn it to CD, and play it in a club that night.

This is literally putting record labels out of business, but unfortunately, the companies are stuck between a rock and a hard place. If they don't send out promos, no one knows how good their new tune is. If they do, people steal the music and the record label doesn't make any money.

The cons of using MP3s

The major downside to MP3 though is the sound quality. A 1minute, CD quality recording, (a 16-bit stereo wave file, sampled at 44.1 kHz (kilohertz)) is around 10 Mb (megabytes) in size. A 1-minute, 128 Kbps (kilobits per second) stereo MP3 is around 1 Mb in size, and that 9 Mb of difference does impact the sound quality, whether you can hear it or not.

Those missing 9 Mb of information have a huge effect on how the music sounds in a club. The low, sub-bass frequencies and the high frequencies are the main casualties of MP3 encoding, and they're responsible for the clarity of the music, but more importantly, the sub-bass is what makes your whole body shake as the bass beats thump.

Sub-woofer amplifiers and careful attention to EQ settings can emulate this sub-bass information from what frequencies are left, but this emulation is still nowhere near to the original bass on a record or CD.

The end result of using highly compressed MP3s in a big club is that the sound can have a muddy, thin sound to it, missing the warmth and depth that makes music so good to listen to at such high volumes. Highly compressed MP3s can be harder to EQ (alter the bass, high, and mid frequencies) properly, and the bad sound can enter the crowd's sub-conscious, so they feel that you're not as good as other DJs, even if your skills are just the same.

Mixing with iPods

Until recently, mixing with Apple's iPod MP3 players used to be a simple case of plugging the headphone outputs of two iPods into a mixer, using the click wheel on the iPod to find, cue, and start a tune, and then using the cross-fader on a mixer to change from iPod to iPod. This was OK if you were just a party DJ, changing simply from one tune to the other without beat matching, but it was useless for the club DJ.

Spotting a gap in the market, Numark saw that DJs wanted to use iPods, and designed the iDJ mixer. With the release of the iDJ2, you can adjust the pitch (which changes the speed) of the tunes playing from your iPod, and you only need one iPod to play from, saving you money, and the hassle of needing two iTunes libraries on your computer. With the option to add hard drives (using the USB (Universal Serial Bus) connection) and memory sticks, the iDJ2 allows DJs to play two tunes from one iPod at the same time, scratch the music, and see the music as a waveform on a large LCD screen. In my opinion, this shows that Numark excel because they listen to what DJs need, and release good kit in response.

Mixing on PC

Mixing on your PC and laptop DJing used to be confined to the bedroom and to some very innovative DJs. Both these types of people were looked upon as a bit mad, and would sometimes suffer from PC gremlins at inopportune moments. As software and hardware developments marry into the massive availability of music on MP3, the biggest problem with laptop DJing in a night-club right now is convincing the club owner to let you do it.

Due to a handful of disadvantages, such as the fact that performing with a PC or Mac lacks the excitement of using vinyl (ten times worse than with CD decks!), problems connecting and fitting equipment into the DJ booth, and the fear that your laptop may crash halfway through a mix because of the heat, sweat, and beer, you can find that clubs are reluctant to let the PC DJ show their skills.

Fortunately, the flipside of this is that the convenience of DJing from a laptop means that pubs and parties are starting to embrace this new technology, for better or for worse. Recently, I've seen more and more pubs where the only music setup they have is an Apple PowerBook or a laptop sitting in the corner of the bar, hooked into the amplifier. Whether they're simply playing music out of iTunes with cross-fade turned on, or playing out pre-mixed sets from the hard drive, replacing the DJ with a computer and reclaiming the space means that DJs are starting to be measured in gigahertz and version numbers rather than skill, knowledge, and (importantly) pay cheques.

Fortunately, clubs still recognise the need for someone to adapt and control the night, and don't seem to have tried to get away with this particular modus operandi yet. But already, you can find that a lot of real DJs out there are losing work due to the boss and his automix laptop at the end of the bar.

Software only

Although most DJ software comes with hardware controllers, the mouse and the keyboard can be used to control your mix just as well.

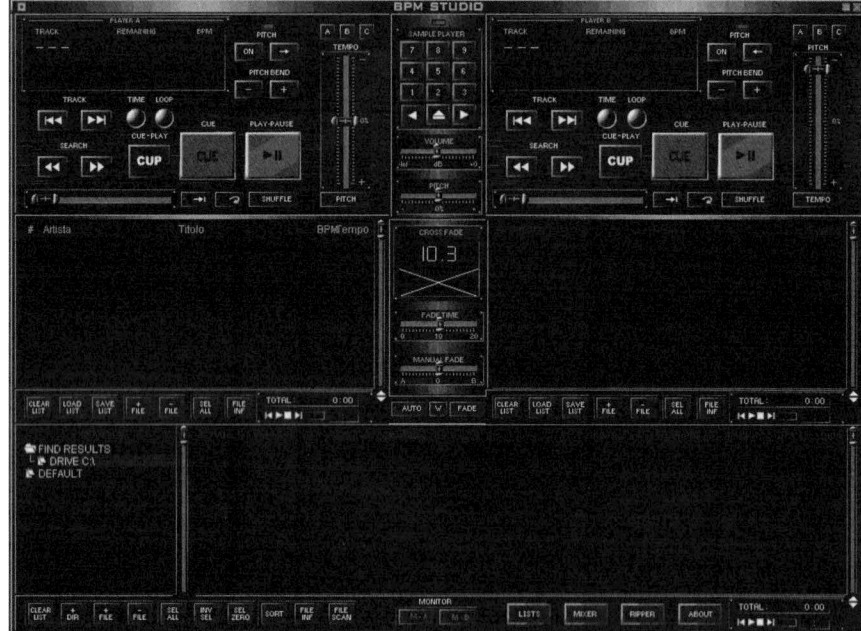

Figure 7-2: A screenshot from Alcatech's BPM Studio DJ software.

I've found that most programs, such as BPM Studio (see Figure 7-2), Virtual DJ 3, PCDJ, Pioneer's new DJS software, and Traktor all contain the three major areas for DJing; playback control, file library, and the mixer. How each of these titles lets you control these three areas is what separates one from the other, but they're usually laid out in a similar way, only the graphics and functionality differ:

- ✔ The controls are laid out in a similar fashion to the controls on a twin CD player. All the normal playback, cue, and pitch controls are there for you to adjust using mouse clicks and keyboard strokes.

- ✔ The library is where you load in the tunes (from CD, or MP3 files on the hard drive, and so on) to play in the mix.

- ✔ The mixer is how you change from one tune to the other. Depending on what software you buy, the mixer may be very simple and simply a means to change from one tune to the other, or a very complicated one that gives you full control over the mix, and the sound of the mix.

- ✔ Other features like BPM (beats per minute) counters, loop controls, wave displays, effects, and sample banks are all unique in design and how they're used to the particular title of software.

The actual mix from track to track is almost identical to using CD decks (see Chapter 15 for more detailed information on mixing with CD). The mixing process goes like this:

1. **Load a track into the onscreen player you wish to use.**

2. **Find, and set a cue point for the start of the track.**

3. **Play the track, and set the pitch using the onscreen pitch fader.**

4. **Return to the cue point, then press 'Play' to start the track playing when you want it to start.**

5. **Use the pitch bend buttons to get the beats to play in time if they start to drift apart.**

6. **When you wish to mix from track to track, press 'Auto Mix' if that's an option to perform a preset length of mix from track to track or, to control the mix properly, drag the onscreen cross-fader from one side to the other.**

The mixer

The mixer is normally where software is let down. The more complicated and powerful the software that you buy, the better control you have over the tunes and the sound of the mix. Effects, beat counters, and Master Tempo are very useful, but if you don't have full control over the mix from one tune to the other, you won't be able to realise your full creative potential in the first place. Make sure that you can change the volume of each tune you play independently, and can change the EQ of each track separately.

Hardware controllers

To make controlling the playback of the tunes a lot easier, and also make DJing with the PC look a lot more like conventional DJing, hardware controllers are available to control the software. These controllers can be quite expensive though, and sometimes don't include hardware to emulate the mixer, so you still have to use the keyboard/mouse to mix from one track to the other.

Each software title has a range of different controllers that you can use with their programs, so check out their Web sites before buying the software to see what's available to you.

Futureproofing with Live and Traktor

Nearly all software DJ solutions emulate a twin CD set-up like BPM Studio. This is great for mixing from one tune to the other, but Live by Ableton (for Mac OS and PC Windows) uses more of a sequencer approach to put together the mix, taking mixing on PC (or Mac) a step further by allowing the DJ to remix any of the tunes live, during the mix.

Live

Live has been designed to be used through each stage of the musical process; so you create the music, and then perform that creation to the crowd as a DJ. The software is so versatile that the DJ using Live can remix the tunes 'on-the-fly', live to the crowd and add MIDI (musical instrument digital interface) controllable instruments to the mix, to create a completely unique remix, and a DJ set that nobody else has ever heard, or may ever hear again.

You need to do a fair bit of prep-work before you can beatmatch with Live, which is one argument that some people have against using it to DJ with. Instead of having a pitch control to affect the speed of your tracks, Live uses a *warp* function that helps to change the tempo of the tune. The warped songs in Live are linked to the program's internal BPM clock, so changing the BPM of a tune from 135 BPM to 138 BPM is effortless, and takes no time at all during a performance. For this technique to *be* effortless, you need to give the software reference points to know how to adjust a tune's BPM quickly, and in Live, these are called *warp markers,* which you add to the waveform display in the Live software.

The set-up process sounds quite complicated, but it's not. If you ripped your entire CD collection into Live for a mix, you would need to take a little time to analyse the tracks, and prepare each of the songs with warp markers in order for Live to be able to change the BPM when you're beatmatching.

Many people accuse Live DJs of cheating, lacking the skill to beatmatch, and say that sets performed on Live are preconceived, and no better than a mix tape played through the sound system. Sasha, John Digweed, and Gabriel & Dresden are typical of the DJs that use Live: they've all proven that they're already masters of their craft, and use Live to expand their creativity, rather than cheat the DJ skills. Because the beatmatching is essentially done for you by Live, the DJ is left to focus more on what tunes they want to mix, how the mixes between tunes are put together, and create the effects and track layering that build up a unique sound to the mix.

A whole host of controllers and options are available for whatever stage of the music process you use Live for, so you aren't faced with a DJ staring at an iMac, clicking a mouse. With audio interfaces and controllers for making music, and mixer and output interfaces to control Live for DJ performances, no one can be accused of lacking in aesthetics when using a computer with Live and a few controllers attached to it.

Sasha has fully embraced Live for DJing, using a custom-designed controller (which he's called 'The Maven') and (currently) an iMac G5. With other big name DJs also getting the Live bug, it seems that Ableton's Live software looks to become one of the industry standards for computer DJing. Check out www.ableton.com for more information.

Traktor

For DJs who still prefer a bit more control over the music they use, Traktor by Native Instruments is definitely emerging as a leader. The interface is similar to the other software titles (like BPM Studio and PCDJ), but Traktor takes everything to a new level. By offering four players (instead of two on some other titles), you can mix four tracks at the same time, or *drop in* samples (play sections of other tunes or sound clips) over an existing mix and transform an ordinary tune into something spectacular that no one has ever heard before.

Where the mixer has been the letdown on some of the other software titles, Traktor really has this part of the interface licked. With an initial design based on the fantastic Allen & Heath Xone:92 mixer, the mixer section of Traktor already offers you everything you need to control the sound of the mix. But Traktor takes it a step further by letting you switch individual channels on the mixer so their EQ sections emulate the Pioneer DJM-600 and Ecler Nuo4! Traktor truly caters for the fussy DJ who prefers a certain sound to the mix and can be left frustrated by the sound control of other software titles.

With a host of controllers to make the DJing experience a performance as well as something technically fascinating, Traktor is sure to find a place as the cream of the DJ emulation systems.

Chapter 8

Stirring It Up with Mixers

· ·

In This Chapter

▶ Finding out about the mixer's most common features

▶ Looking at the advanced options available

▶ Choosing the right mixer for your DJ style

▶ Keeping your mixer in tip-top condition

· ·

Mixers are a very demanding breed of animal. They come with many functions and features, and can manipulate the music in many ways, but in the end, mixers only do what *you* tell them to do.

This chapter explains how the vital controls on a mixer function and how they relate to your DJ mixing style. Understanding that much sets you on your way to buying the right mixer.

Getting Familiar with Mixer Controls

In your journey as a DJ, you'll come across a vast range of mixers. Some you may already know about, and some you won't ever have seen before. If you understand what the features are on a mixer, and how to use them, you need never accidentally press the wrong button and cut out the sound.

Well, maybe *never* is too strong a word . . .

Inputs

The common DJ mixer accepts three different input methods:

✔ **Phono** inputs for turntables.

✔ **MIC** inputs for microphones.

✔ **Line** inputs for everything else.

Some digital mixers also have USB and Firewire inputs to connect digital sources (such as CD, MiniDisc, and PC inputs) and keep the music playing at the best possible quality. For information on how to connect these, and the standard inputs mentioned above, head to Chapter 11.

Records are recorded in a special way in order to fit all the information onto the vinyl. The mixer needs to translate the signal it receives from the turntable in a completely different way to a CD player or any other device, and it is the *phono input* that is used for this translation.

All other equipment (CD players, MiniDisc players, MP3 players, the audio output from your computer and DVD player and so on) sends out a Line signal to the mixer. When you want to use any of these, you use the *Line input* on the mixer.

Both input channels on a two-channel mixer have a line and a phono input connection. This means that you can connect two turntables and two CD players to a two-channel mixer, and use the Line/Phono switch that selects whether to use the CD player or turntable input for either channel.

As well as accepting playback devices like turntables and CD players, most mixers also have *XLR* or ¼-inch *jack inputs* for connecting a microphone. There's usually a separate volume and *EQ (equaliser) control* (to affect the bass, mid, or high frequencies in your voice) so that you can sound great speaking to the crowd.

Outputs

Basic mixers usually have two outputs, with the better ones having at least three outputs.

- ✔ **Master Out** is connected to an amplifier. The LED display on the mixer relates to how strong a music signal you're sending to the amplifier. The stronger the signal, the less you have to turn up the amplifier. Too strong a signal though, and you may cause the sound to distort because the amplifier can't process it properly.

- ✔ **Record Out** is for sending music to a recording device. The output LEDs on the mixer have no bearing on how strong a signal you send to a recording device (tape recorder, CD recorder, PC, and so on) through this connection. Only the *channel-faders* (the vertical faders) and the *gain control* (which changes how strong a signal comes in from the turntables or CD players) affect the level of signal you send to a recording device.

✔ **Booth Out** is for sending to a separate speaker in the DJ booth so that you can hear the music too! This is vital in a large club where the main speakers are far away. The delay in sound between those speakers and your ears can make beatmatching very difficult.

For more on each of these outputs, and how to connect them to their intended recipients, check out Chapter 11.

Multiple channels

Although you can have two turntables and two CD players plugged into a two channel mixer and flick from Line to Phono, having a dedicated channel for each input is more convenient.

You also need more than two channels on your mixer if you want to use three CDs or three turntables because you can't plug a turntable into the Line input, and you can't plug a CD deck into the Phono input on a mixer. You can buy a converter that changes a phono signal into a line signal, so you can have one turntable in the phono input, and another in the line input of one channel, but it's a lot of trouble, expense, and potential confusion.

A mixer with three or four inputs can cater to most DJs' needs, and if you need more than four channels to use all your equipment, I'd be more worried about the electricity bills than where to plug it all in!

Cross-faders

The *cross-fader* (see Figure 8-1) is a simple horizontal slider that enables you to change the output of the mixer from one input device to another – from what you're currently playing to music playing into another channel of the mixer. The cross-fader is a lot like the control on your shower that lets you adjust how much hot and cold water comes out. You can have only cold, only hot, and many, many different combinations in between.

Figure 8-1:
A cross-fader on a mixer.

After you've towelled off thoroughly, go to your DJ setup. *Tune A* plays into Channel 1 on a two-channel mixer (and is usually the turntable or CD deck positioned on the left side of the mixer) and *Tune B* plays into Channel 2 (on the right-hand side of the mixer).

With the cross-fader positioned to the far left, you only hear *Tune A*. When the cross-fader is all the way to the right, all you hear is *Tune B*.

However, the cross-fader comes into its own when it's anywhere in between. If the cross-fader is in the middle, the output of the mixer is both *Tune A* and *Tune B*, and if the cross-fader is to the left of middle, you can hear more of *Tune A* than *Tune B* (and vice versa).

How much louder *Tune A* is than *Tune B* is dictated by something called *the cross-fader curve*. The cross-fader curve controls how quickly one tune gets louder as the other one gets quieter when you move the cross-fader from side to side. The following figures show some common cross-fader curves you'll encounter. Figure 8-2 shows a simple cross-fader curve.

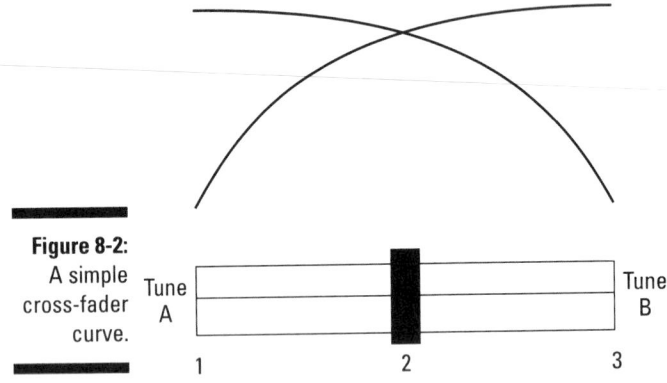

Figure 8-2:
A simple cross-fader curve.

✔ At Position 1 marked on the cross-fader, Channel 1 is at full, Channel 2 is silent.

✔ By Position 2, both tunes are playing at around 90 per cent of their loudest volume.

✔ By Position 3, Channel 2 is at its loudest, and Channel 1 is silent.

The cross-fader curve in Figure 8-3 helps to stop both your tunes blaring out of the speakers simultaneously at near to full volume.

- ✔ At Position 1, Channel 1 is full, Channel 2 is off.

- ✔ At Position A, Channel 1 is still full; Channel 2 is starting to come in (playing at about 10 per cent of its full volume by this stage).

- ✔ At Position 2, both tunes are at 80 per cent of their normal volume.

- ✔ By Position B, Channel 2 is now playing at full volume, and Channel 1 is playing at 10 per cent volume.

- ✔ And by Position 3, Channel 2 is playing at full volume, with Channel 1 silent.

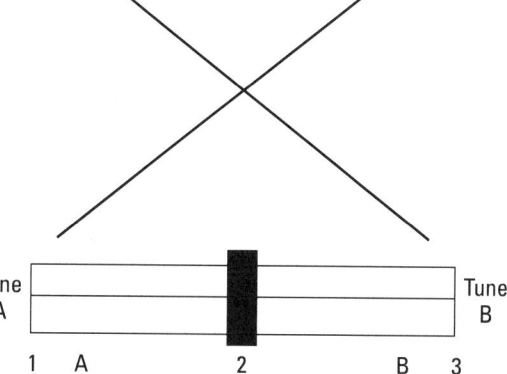

Figure 8-3:
A faster
cut-in on the
cross-fader
curve.

Although this curve is similar to the first example, the straight line in the 'curve' gradually brings in one tune while removing the other one, whereas the swooping curve in the first example kept the tunes playing together for longer at a higher volume level.

Figure 8-4 shows the cross-fader curve preferred by many scratch DJs due to the speed at which the second tune can be *cut in* (made audible) at full volume.

- ✔ Position 1 shows Channel 1 playing full, Channel 2 is off.

- ✔ At Position A, both channels are playing full volume, and it only took a small amount of cross-fader movement to get there.

- ✔ This situation stays constant until Position B.

- ✔ At position 3, Channel 2 is full, and Channel 1 has been removed.

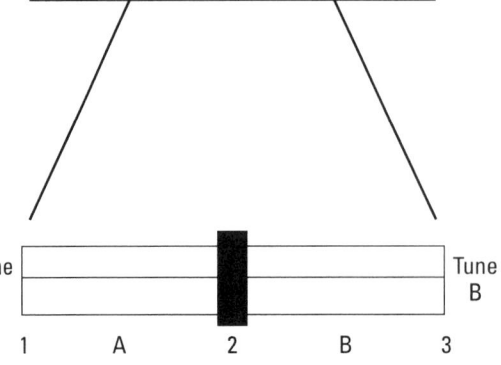

Figure 8-4:
The more
immediate
'Scratch'
curve for
the cross-
fader.

You can also get a straight X-shape curve, which fades one tune out while bringing the other tune in at exactly the same ratio throughout the move. If *Tune A* is playing at 10 per cent, *Tune B* is at 90 per cent – if *Tune A* is at 73 per cent, *Tune B* plays at 27 per cent, and so on. (That's likely to be the *cross-fader curve* of your shower control, too.)

A number of mixers come with just one kind of cross-fader curve, but most mid- to high-range mixers have a way to change the cross-fader curve by selecting pre-defined curves with a switch, or with a control that enables you to create any kind of curve you like.

Channel-faders

Channel-faders are the *up and down* faders that control how loud the music comes out of the mixer when the cross-fader is all the way over to one side, allowing the full power of a channel to play.

Taking another visit to your bathroom, think of channel-faders like the taps on the bathroom shower. Even though the water mixer (the cross-fader) is set to only let out cold water, if you don't turn on the cold tap, nothing comes out. So although the cross-fader lets you mix hot and cold water to the perfect temperature through the showerhead, the channel-faders control how much hot and how much cold water is available to mix together in the first place.

Getting back into the DJ booth then, the ability to vary the volume of the two channels, as well as mixing with the cross-fader gives incredibly precise control over the mix. If you use the channel-faders in conjunction with the cross-fader to their extremes, you get the kind of curve shown in Figure 8-5.

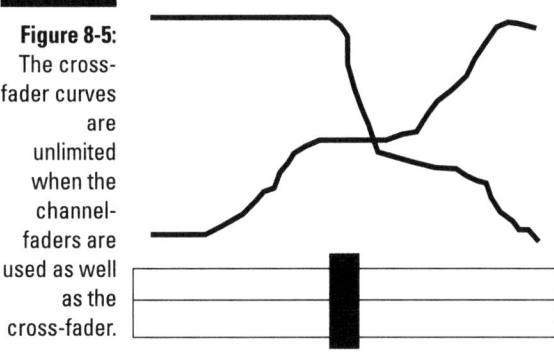

Figure 8-5:
The cross-fader curves are unlimited when the channel-faders are used as well as the cross-fader.

Chapter 15 covers how to use your channel-faders to help your mixes sound really professional.

Headphone monitoring

The headphone section on the mixer is simple, but extremely important. Plug your headphones into the quarter-inch jack socket (if you're using a mini-jack, which is on the end of your iPod headphones, you need a converter from the mini jack to quarter-inch jack to do this). Use the headphone volume control (which doesn't need to be set to full, please) along with the cue controls to listen to individual channels on your mixer (or a few of them together at the same time).

Headphone cue controls can be split into two functions:

- ✔ Choosing what plays into your headphones.
- ✔ Controlling how you hear the music in your headphones.

Each channel on the mixer has a *Cue* or *PFL* (pre-fade listen) button assigned to it. When you press it, you can listen to the music in that channel without having to play it through the main speakers. This function means that you can listen to any combination of any of the channels on the mixer at any one time. You can listen to Channel 1 on its own or with Channel 2 playing at the same time — or have Channels 1, 2, 3, and 4 all playing in the headphones. That might not sound very good, though.

For beatmatching DJs, headphones are used to find the start point of the next tune you want to play (called the *cue*), and they're also used to make sure that the beats of both tunes are playing at the same time. This is called beatmatching, and it is the fundamental concept of DJing. Go to Chapter 12 to discover how the headphones are used to enable the DJ to do this, and how the following ways of listening to music in the headphones can give you more control over the beatmatching process:

- ✔ **Headphone Mix** enables you to play both tunes in stereo in your headphones, and a mini cross-fader or rotary knob gives you control over how loud each tune plays over the other (exactly like a cross-fader, except for your headphones). This function is especially useful because you can check how the two tunes sound playing together before letting the dance floor hear, and check that the beats of both tunes really are playing in time.

- ✔ **Split Cue** sends one selected channel into the left earpiece of the headphones, and another one into the right earpiece (as if you are listening to one tune in the headphones and have one ear to the dance floor). This feature is a lifesaver when you don't have a monitor (speaker) in the DJ booth and the delay in sound from the dance floor speakers makes it hard to check if the bass beats are playing at the same time.

EQs and kills

The *EQ controls* on a mixer enable you to increase or decrease three broad musical frequency bands: high, mid, and low. The amount of change is measured in decibels (abbreviated as *dB*), and although mixers let you increase the EQ bands by +12 dB or more, the amount they take out is actually of more importance to the DJ.

A *cut* setting on an EQ *pot* (a professional term for any rotary knob) removes the EQ frequency band from the tune completely. So when you cut the bass from a tune, all you hear is the tinny *hi-hats* (the *tchsss tchsss* sound made by the cymbals on a drum kit) and the *mid-range* (which carries the vocals and main melody of a tune).

The difference between an EQ pot and a kill switch is that an EQ enables the DJ to vary the amount of frequency cut out, from just a little to the entire band, whereas a kill switch instantly removes the bass frequency at the push of a button, and then puts it back in when pressed again. No grey areas here!

EQs on a mixer serve two purposes. Firstly, they let you make the tune you're playing sound great; if the bass is too loud through the speakers, you can reduce it using the Bass EQ, and if the music sounds a little too shrill, reducing the high and mid controls can fix the problem.

But apart from sound processing, EQs are essential for the *seamless mix* DJ who wants the transition (mix) between tunes to be as unnoticeable as possible. If you get a chance to study DJs such as Paul Oakenfold, Tiesto, and Sasha closely, you can see just how much they use the EQs to aid their mixes. Chapter 14 has a whole section dedicated to using EQs to create seamless mixes, and Chapter 20 has a section about adjusting the overall sound from the mixer with EQs.

Input VU monitoring

Your mixer has a VU display to show the strength of the signal going *out* of the mixer, and an important enhancement of this feature is the option of checking the strength of the signal coming *in* to the mixer.

The normal output display is two lines of LED lights, one showing the strength of the left hand side of the stereo music, the other showing the right hand side. Some mixers offer the DJ an option to change this display into the left line of LEDs showing the input strength of Channel 1, and the right line displaying Channel 2's input strength. Or, in the case of mixers like Pioneer's DJM-600, a separate line of LEDs next to each channel's EQ controls shows the strength of the input signal – leaving the Master Output display to always show how strong a signal you're sending out of the mixer.

Gain controls

Gain controls are wrongly seen by many as just another volume control. Don't regard them as a way to affect the volume coming *out* of the mixer, look at them as a way to affect the music coming *in* to the mixer.

If the input level LED for Channel 1 is at 0 dB, occasionally flashing into the red +3 dB area, and Channel 2's LEDs show that its input signal is well below 0 dB, you use the gain control to increase the input level of Channel 2 to match Channel 1. If you mix from Channel 1 to Channel 2 without matching the input levels, you'll notice a drop in volume even with both channel-faders set to full. If you can get this level right at the input stage, rather than worrying about it at the output stage when it's too late, you're using the gain control correctly.

Gain control is especially important for scratch DJs, who need to be able to *max out* their channel-faders (put them up to full) and have confidence that the volume of both tracks are identical.

If your bass EQ is set to *cut*, or *kill* when checking the channel's input level, it can appear a lot weaker than it really is. When you then bring the bass frequencies back into the music, your speakers won't be very happy with you, because you'll be playing far too loudly, and may damage your equipment (or at the very least, your reputation!). For a detailed description on how to match the input levels to create an even volume to the mix, head to Chapter 17.

Balance and pan controls

The *balance control* alters which speaker the sound comes from. When the control is to the left, music only comes out of the left speaker, the reverse for the right-hand side, and when the control is in the middle, music comes out through both speakers, much like the balance on your home stereo.

However, some mixers have balance controls (sometimes called *pan* controls) on each channel rather than having a control that affects the mixer's Master Output. Why do you want balance controls on each channel? Sometimes (for example), if you have one channel panned all the way to the left, and another all the way to the right, and bring the cross-fader into the middle, the effect of having one tune playing in one ear, and another in the other ear can sound really good (if you've chosen the right tunes and both bass beats are playing at the same time). This feature works well with plain beats, especially if you constantly change the balance settings during the mix.

Hamster switch

Mixers used by scratch DJs often have a *hamster switch*, which simply reverses the control of the cross-fader (but the channel-faders remain the same). So instead of hearing Channel 1 when the cross-fader is all the way to the left, you now hear Channel 2, and vice versa.

This is useful from a body mechanics point of view. You can perform some of the scratch moves (such as the crab and the twiddle, described in Chapter 16) faster if the cross-fader is 'bounced' off the thumb (which is a quarter of the way along the cross-fader slot) and the end of the cross-fader slot to cut the music in and out very quickly. Some moves are quite uncomfortable for a lot of DJs because the standard mixer set-up means twisting their wrists, so the hamster switch sets the mixer to make these moves a lot easier, and more comfortable to perform.

In case you're wondering, it's not called a hamster switch because a hamster chewed through the cables to reverse the control (which crossed my mind). It's named after The Bullet Proof Scratch Hamsters who used to connect the decks up to the mixer the wrong way round in order to reverse the normal channel and cross-fader set-up.

Punch and transform controls

If you have the cross-fader completely on Channel 2 (what I call *closed off* onto Channel 2), pressing the *punch button* changes the output to Channel 1 until released. Note, however, that some mixers don't take account of where you leave the channel-faders, only where you set the gain controls, so make sure you set those gain controls properly, otherwise you may experience a huge drop (or rise) in volume when you punch in the other channel!

Transform controls were designed as an advancement to the technique of *cutting* a mixer's channel in and out of the mix (quickly hearing it, then not hearing it) using the Line/Phono switch. When using turntables, flick this switch over to Line and the music cuts out (for CD, flick it to Phono). The problem is that you often hear a clicking or popping sound when you switch, so Transform controls were designed to do the same thing, but won't pop or click when you use them. (If nothing is playing through the other channel, the punch button *punches in* silence in much the same way as this transform control.)

Effects Send and Return

The *Effects Send and Return* enables you to send just one channel from the mixer to be processed by an external effects processor (like the Pioneer EFX-1000, for example), to add whatever groovy effects you want, then it's returned in the blink of an eye for you to use it in the mix. All the while, the other channels on the mixer are unaffected. A detailed description of how the Send and Return inputs and outputs connect to an effects processor is in Chapter 11. I cover the kinds of effects available in the following section, but check out www.recess.co.uk for a run down of different effects processors available.

Built-in effects

Although some mixers offer sound effects such as sirens and horns, I don't really mean this type of effect. Rather than having to use an external effects processor, mixers like the Pioneer DJM-600 have built-in effects such as flanger, echo, delay, transform, pitch, loop, and reverb assignable (able to add the effect) to each channel or the Master Output. These additions are a great way of making the music sound different to how it was originally recorded.

The most common effects you find on mixers are:

- **Delay** repeats a selected part of the tune while the rest of the tune is still playing. Especially useful for repeating musical hooks in quieter parts of tracks or for doubling-up bass beats to play three bass beats where only two would normally play.

- **Echo** is similar to the Delay feature, except the music fades away when repeating to create an echo effect. Useful again in quieter parts of the tune (or at the very end of your DJ set).

- **Auto Pan** automatically changes sounds back and forth between left and right speakers.

- **Auto Transformer** cuts the entire sound in and out at a speed you set. I love using this to create a stuttering effect as the music builds up or during a scratch (see Chapter 16 for how to manually perform a *Transform*).

- **Filter** manipulates the sound frequencies of the music to alter its *tonal quality* by removing then replacing a range of frequencies. The filter isn't the same as using the EQs on the mixer to kill and replace frequencies though, because a specific sound is also added to it.

  If you've ever been to the beach and held a shell to your ear to hear the sea, you'll recognise that the sweeping effect added to the music while the filter removes and replaces the music is much the same as the resonation of ambient sound you hear from the shell – as if the shell had a tiny DJ crab inside it, playing music . . .

  The filter effect doesn't always sweep in and out. Certain filters enable you to select a certain range of frequencies, add the resonating filter effect, then keep the music in that same state until the filter is turned off, or altered.

- **Flanger** makes a 'swooshy' sound like playing music through a jet engine while it climbs and falls, while retaining the full frequency range (and usually boosting the bass frequencies) of the music. The most over-used effect ever (but really cool the first time you use it!).

- **Reverb** adds reverberation to the music so that it sounds as if you're playing in a massive hall. Turn it up to full, and the sound is like listening to music in the toilets at a club.

- **Pitch Shifter** can change the pitch of the music. Useful to try to match the pitch of another tune, but mixers vary in their ability to do this.

You may encounter other built-in effects, as well, of course. This list of effects is taken from the Pioneer DJM-600 that I use.

Built-in samplers

Samplers are available as external machines (often in combination with an effects processor), but a *built-in sampler* is great because it enables you to take a short vocal sample or a few bars of beats from a tune and extend or introduce a mix by playing these samples.

An example of where this feature has been used is in the 1990s song 'Nighttrain' by Kadoc. At the very beginning of the record, James Brown says 'All aboard, the Nighttrain'. By recording that vocal sample into the sampler, and playing it way before you start the mix, you create anticipation of what's yet to come. I used to do this as a scratch (see Chapter 16 for how), but the sampler made this a lot easier and simpler to do.

The better samplers have loop controls on them, where the sample you take is looped seamlessly over and over again, meaning you can really extend the mix. A good use of this technique is to record four bars of beats into the sampler and loop them to extend the outro of a tune, or to add beats over a breakdown to keep the energy of the dance floor going.

Built-in beat counters

Beat counters give you a visual display of how many beats in a minute there are in the tune you're playing. Two channel mixers with built-in beat counters have a counter for each channel. Multiple channel mixers can have a counter for each channel, or two counters that you can assign (choose to use) to any channel you like. By comparing the BPMs (beats per minute) of two tunes using the beat counter, you know how much to speed up or slow down the next tune to match the BPM of the one currently playing, which is the basis of beatmatching. (See Figure 8-6 for an example of a built-in beat counter.)

A beat counter that displays the BPM to one decimal point (for example, 132.7 BPM) is more accurate than one that only shows whole numbers. If one tune is playing at 131.6 BPM and another is playing at 132.4, and the counter simply rounds up and down those figures to show them both as 132 BPM, it's actually wrong by 0.8 BPM, which is a huge difference when beatmatching.

Beat counters can be a real help to the beginner to let them understand what's happening with the beats, and tune their ear to gauge when a tune is running too fast or too slow, but they can also be a real hindrance. If you're going to refer to a beat counter as you develop your beatmatching skills, you need the discipline *not* to rely on it. Otherwise, the first time you stand behind a mixer that doesn't have a beat counter (which is going to be quite often in clubs), and are expected to beatmatch using just your ears, you'll find it very hard and possibly get into a lot of trouble!

Figure 8-6: A built-in beat counter on the Pioneer DJM600.

Beat light indicators

Similar to beat counters, in that they help beatmatching by giving you a visual representation of the bass beat, *beat light indicators* are little LED lights that flash in time with the beat of the tune. By looking at the lights of two tunes flashing together (or not together), you can tell if the beats are playing at the same time.

Beat light indicators are very nice to watch in the dark, but personally, I think that they're next to useless when compared to your ears.

Fader starts

Found mostly when you use a Pioneer mixer in conjunction with Pioneer CDJ decks, the *fader start* control enables you to start a CD playing simply by moving the cross-fader, rather than having to go to all the trouble of pressing Play. Sarcasm aside, the fader start is a fantastic feature for doing some basic forward scratches with.

For normal mixing though, I'd still rather press Play on the CD deck and then move the fader for the smooth fade, or move the fader into the middle and then press Play for the instant start. But the fader start can be useful if both of your hands are taken up using the EQs to make the mix sound as smooth as possible, and (like me) the CD decks are the furthest away on your DJ set-up, meaning you have to move and reach to start the CD.

Choosing the Right Mixer

Different mixers suit different kinds of DJs. If you're looking to spend a lot of money on your mixer, make sure that you're buying one with the right functions on it depending on your mixing style:

- ✔ **The seamless mix DJ** needs a mixer that helps every mix sound perfect by controlling the sound levels and the sound frequencies of each tune during the mix.

- ✔ **The scratch DJ** needs to chop and change from track to track using a slick cross-fader on the mixer.

- ✔ **The effects DJ** isn't content with the sound of the tunes as the original producers intended, and wants the option to add a series of different sounds and effects to the music, making a new sound unique to that performance.

- ✔ **The wedding DJ** uses a mixer as a means to change between a wide range of different styles of music.

The seamless mix DJ

The *club* or *house* mixer is used by house DJs, trance DJs, drum-and-bass DJs, anyone who wants full control of how the music sounds when they're mixing, to create the best transition from one tune to another. So another name for this type of DJ is a *seamless mix* DJ.

If you're a seamless mix DJ, the important extra features you need on your mixer are:

- ✔ EQs to fully control the sound of each tune, with the ability to cut or kill the frequencies to help tidy up the mix.

- ✔ Multiple channels so that you can use more than two CD decks, MP3 players, or turntables at the same time.

✔ Headphone monitoring, which needs to be as comprehensive as possible, with headphone mix, and ideally split cue for when no DJ booth monitor is available.

✔ Easy-to-use (and see) metering that shows the input level strength as well as the mixer's output level.

✔ Beat counters and built-in effects, though not essential, are a great tool for the seamless DJ.

The *house* mixer can be quite large, and has the controls spread out to remove the risk of accidentally pressing something if the mixer controls were crammed together.

The scratch DJ

Although the mixers used by the seamless mix DJ can be used by scratch DJs, *battle mixers* are mixers designed specifically for scratching. With only two channels, they make good use of space to allow the DJ unobstructed control of the channel-faders, and of a robust, fluid cross-fader.

Although by no means essential, extra controls such as punch and transform buttons, along with hamster switches and cross-fader curve controls, are becoming standard tools for the scratch DJ. You can find built-in effects and BPM counters on a lot of scratch mixers, though I think that I'd fall over if I had to use all that lot, and scratch at the same time!

The design of the battle mixer is as important as the features it offers (see Figure 8-7). Because the most important controls on a scratch mixer are the cross-fader and the channel-faders, these three controls take up a lot of space and are kept clear of any obstructions. To this end, the headphone input is located on the front of the mixer (often along with the cross-fader curve adjust) so it's not poking up from the mixer, where you're going to smack it with your hands one day! Screws are handily recessed into the face plate, too; if you've ever caught your hand on a ragged screw when moving quickly from deck to mixer, the blood all over the mixer has shown you exactly why!

The most important part of any battle mixer is the cross-fader and how it performs. Because you make a lot of fast movements with the fader when scratching, any resistance on the cross-fader is not a good thing, so you need to have as slick and fluid a cross-fader as possible, and a few mixers, such as the DJM-909, take this feature to a new level by offering a control to adjust the *feel* (how stiff it is) of the fader while you're scratching.

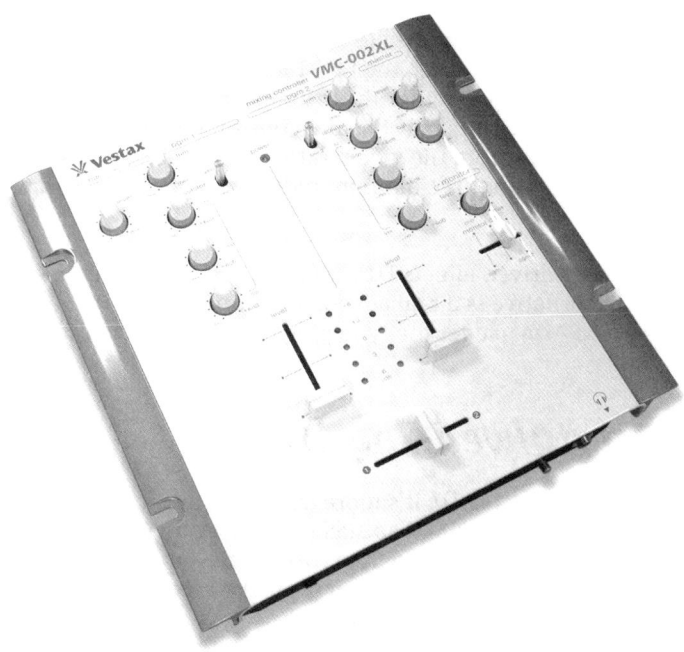

Figure 8-7:
The Vestax
VMX-002XL.
Note the
headphone
input on the
front
(bottom
right).

Scratching is incredibly taxing on a cross-fader, so it needs to be durable and replaceable (or at least cleanable until you can afford a new cross-fader). New designs of non-contact, optical, and magnetic cross-faders from manufacturers such as Rane and Stanton are increasing the lifespan, durability, and ease of use of the cross-fader. But don't worry, the standard cross-fader on a battle mixer is good enough for developing the basic skills.

The effects DJ

The EQs and design of the club mixer mentioned for the seamless DJ are perfect for the *effects DJ*, although frequently, the effects DJ demands more than the built-in effects available on the club mixer.

In this case, the *send and return* function on the mixer (see the section 'Effects Send and Return' earlier in this chapter on this function), is especially important. This function enables you to send individual channels to an effects processor and add whatever effects you want, without having to effect the entire output of the mixer.

Manufacturers like Pioneer design their top range equipment to work together in harmony to make life easier for the effects DJ, as is the case with the CDJ-1000 CD decks, the EFX-1000 effects processor, and the DJM-800 mixer. By connecting together these items, the effects DJ can create effects, set start and loop points on CDs, and control how they're started, mixed, and effected solely from the mixer, rather than needing to work all the different controls on three different pieces of equipment during an important mix.

For the gadget-driven effects DJ with a hundred things happening at the same time, this alternative is a real advantage (until the day Pioneer release a Human-Third-Arm gadget that you plug into your belly button . . .).

The party/wedding DJ

As a *party and wedding DJ*, it's more about the music you play rather than the way you mix it together, and as such, you don't need an expensive, feature-laden mixer. If you have more than two CD players or turntables, then multiple channels can be useful, but you normally have a simple set-up.

EQ controls on the microphone are important to help to sharpen your voice as you talk over the music, enabling you to control the evening with clarity. It goes without saying, that the microphone you use should be a good quality one in the first place. One of the workhorse microphones that (in my opinion) you'll never go wrong buying is the Shure SM58; it sounds great, is simple to connect, and it's almost indestructible (though please don't try to prove me wrong).

Controlling the sound using EQs when mixing from tune to tune to make it seamless isn't such an important feature for the party DJ compared to the seamless DJ. However, EQs can help remove some bass or add some high frequencies when you're trying to overcome bad sound in different sizes of hall. A *global EQ* on the amp, which just affects the entire sound output, is probably enough, but you can also consider the option to change the sound for each tune played.

Built-in beat counters are all but redundant, because the party set list has wide-ranging BPMs. From Tom Jones' 'Delilah' at 64 BPM to Ricky Martin's 'Livin' La Vida Loca' at 178 BPM, the BPM variance is so large, that there's no way you can try to beatmatch them!

As to built-in effects, apart from using the reverb effect on your voice when speaking to the people on the dance floor, they won't be of much use at a party. Although I'd love to hear a flanger effect running through 'Build me up Buttercup'. . .

Servicing Your Mixer

Although your turntable or CD player is the piece of equipment with the most moving mechanical parts, the piece that's most likely to suffer from problems first – if you don't keep it clean and treat it well – is your mixer.

You need to look at two things in order to keep your mixer in proper working condition. Clean all the dust away from the rotary controls, and clean and lubricate the faders.

You need the following tools to clean your mixer properly:

- ✔ A can of compressed air
- ✔ Lubricant
- ✔ A screwdriver

Follow these steps to clean your mixer:

1. **If you can pull the knobs off the rotary controls on the mixer, take them all off at the same time, place them next to the mixer, and lay them out in the order that they've come off, so that you can replace each knob on its respective control.**

2. **After you remove all the knobs, spray around each of the controls with the compressed air to blow away any dust that may be lodged in them.** You may also want to wipe the mixer carefully with a lint-free cloth to remove any stubborn dust particles after spraying.

3. **If you have a mixer that enables you remove the channel-faders as well as the cross-fader, use a screwdriver to take out the faders one at a time (so you don't mix up where they should be replaced).** After you have the faders out of the mixer, blow the compressed air into every crevice in the fader to get out any dirt and dust. Then spray the fader with a lubricant, and replace it back into the mixer.

Some lubricants also clean the faders by dissolving any dirt that may have worked its way deep into the fader, which causes crackles and sound *bleeding* (hearing the music quietly when it should be silent). However, sometimes your faders still make crackle noises, are too stiff, and start to malfunction, in which case you can buy replacement faders from your preferred DJ store.

4. **If your mixer doesn't have removable channel-faders, and they sound crackly, try spraying first compressed air and then cleaning lubricant into slot in the mixer where the channel-fader pokes through.** However, you may be too late, and may not be able to reverse the damage yourself, meaning you'll have to send the mixer off to get repaired – or more likely, buy a new mixer.

Keep your mixer covered when not in use, and remove any dirt build-up before it gets the chance to find its way into sensitive areas. Keep your mixer clean and free of dirt, and give the faders a quick lubrication every couple of months so that your mixer lasts for years.

Chapter 9

Ear-Splitting Advice about Not Splitting Your Ears: Headphones

In This Chapter

▶ Knowing what makes a good set of headphones

▶ Stopping to think about headphone and amplifier volumes

▶ Protecting your ears when faced with excessive volumes

*T*he funny thing about headphones is that they're probably the most important part of your DJ setup because you can't mix properly without them, but, strangely, many DJs treat them as an afterthought.

The only time I've ever really panicked in the DJ booth was when I couldn't hear clearly through the cheap headphones I was using. I couldn't hear any bass, couldn't hear how the beats were playing together, and was effectively mixing 'blind' (or should that be 'deaf'?). If you've followed the same cheap path that I did, when you do start to demand more from your headphones, put some thought into what you need, and don't just get caught up in current fashion trends.

And no, your iPod headphones won't do. . .

Choosing a Good Set of Headphones

As you advance your DJ skills, you start to become aware of all the things that are holding you back from progressing. Cheap decks and a basic mixer are nearly always the first things to be upgraded, but consider what your current headphones sound like. Can you hear a good, solid bass thump? Or are the mid-range frequencies drowning out the rest of the music? Better headphones will improve your beatmatching a lot faster than a new mixer can.

The following six factors can help you when deciding what to buy:

- **Weight/Comfort**. Ideally, you're looking for headphones that are light-weight so they don't hurt your ears when they've been sat on your head for a couple of hours. That's not to say that lightest is best, though. If the headphones are too light, they may fall off when you lean forward to look down at the mixer, or they may be so light that they don't sit tightly over your ears, letting in a lot of external noise as a consequence.

  Because you may be wearing them for four hours at a time, the ear cups need to be soft and sit comfortably on your ears. The headphone band that joins the two ear pieces needs to be comfortable when worn on your head in a normal position, but still be just as comfortable when you twist the band backward to free one of your ears to hear the monitor (speaker) in the DJ booth.

- **Closed-back**. *Closed-back headphones* like those shown in Figure 9-1 have the outer parts of the ear cups sealed, so they don't let as much external sound through to your ears. This enables you to clearly hear the next tune you want to play in the headphones while in the DJ booth, where you get a lot of background noise coming from the dance floor.

  The best style of headphones are closed back and sit nice and tight on your ears, a bit like ear mufflers, but with speakers inside!

Figure 9-1:
Technics
headphones
with the
closed back
design to
the earcups.

✔ **Wide frequency response**. At school, you were probably taught your hearing ranged from 20 Hz (the deep, deep bass sounds) to 20,000 Hz (really high, hissy sounds). In reality, your hearing is probably closer to 20 Hz to 16,000Hz, although children and dogs can hear up to 20,000 Hz.

Quality DJ headphones can typically cover the frequencies from 5 Hz to 30,000 Hz so they cover the bass and sub-bass ranges all the way through to the stuff only really dogs and sound engineers can hear!

✔ **Low impedance.** If you don't know anything about impedance, it's okay, you don't need to, but it's all about electrical resistance. You only need to know to try to match the impedance of your headphones as closely as possible to the impedance of the mixer you use. A large mismatch can lead to distortion, unwanted noise, and sometimes a drop in the maximum volume your headphones can play at (all things you really don't need when DJing).

Fortunately, most DJ equipment manufacturers are well aware of this issue and design their equipment within the same impedance range. This isn't something to lose a night's sleep about, but impedance can play a big part in the quality of the sound you hear if you hugely mismatch it.

✔ **High sound pressure level**. *Sound pressure level* is just a way to describe how loud your headphones (and speakers in general) can play at. You want your headphones to be able to play loud to let you cope with noisy DJ booths, but as always, please remember you don't have to turn up your headphones too loud (see 'Remembering that the Volume Doesn't Have to Go Up to 11' later in this chapter).

Have a realistic budget when upgrading your headphones. If your current pair only cost £10, you won't benefit much by getting another pair for £30. Save up some more money and start looking to spend around £100 on a set of Sony, Sennheiser, Technics, or Pioneer headphones, which I think are the market leaders. Don't be fooled by fashion. Few people care that you have the latest, best-looking headphones. And to be honest, no one (apart from fellow DJs) is going to care about your headphones anyway, they only care about the music!

Realising no one cares about headphones

I remember one night when Alex P did a guest spot at a club I had a residency at, and the other DJ (Dave Armstrong) and I were left wandering through the club, feeling a bit bored whilst waiting for him to finish (because remember, DJs don't dance). At this time, the new Sony MDR-V700 DJ headphones had just come out, and they were the fashionable choice of the discerning DJ – including the two of us.

Thinking we were being really cool and funny, we both put on our headphones, and wandered around the club, talking to people we passed, and had a bit of a laugh. I look back at the image now of two guys with matching headphones on their heads in the middle of a nightclub, with Dave trying to chat up all the girls, and I cringe. I think that Dave pulled in the end though.

These considerations play a major role in deciding what headphones you eventually buy, but other features are available that may yet swing your decision from one pair to another.

Single-sided, coiled cords

Coiled cords are the curly ones that you sometimes see guitarists use (Brian May from Queen uses a coiled guitar lead). By coiling the cable, manufacturers are able to offer a lot more length to the DJ without the danger of a dangling, long, straight cable that can bunch up on the floor and trip you up. Single-sided cables are attached to only one earpiece, and the cable travels from one ear-cup to the other through the headband.

Only after spending an evening in the DJ booth with a pair of headphones that don't have single-sided cabling, do you realise why this simple design is so important. By the end of the night's mixing, after repeatedly putting on and taking off your headphones, putting them down, picking them up, dropping them under the decks, and so on – you'll have spun the cable round enough to almost strangle yourself as the two cables twist around your neck. A single-sided cord has nothing to wrap around, and stays out of the way, keeping you breathing happily for the rest of the evening.

A single-sided, coiled cord, such as the one on the Technics RPDJ1210 headphones that I use, is perfect for giving you a long, coiled cable, which allows you to move around in the DJ booth, and the single-sided cord means that you don't end up garrotting yourself by the end of the night!

Swivelling earpieces

Sometimes the headband on the headphones can feel slightly uncomfortable when you pull one of the ear cups back behind your ear to listen to the live sound. Swivelling ear cups mean that you can pull the ear cup behind your ear, but the headband stays across the middle of your head.

This setup is advantageous not only because of comfort, but because it also reduces the stress on the headband. Cheap, plastic headphones (like the cheap ones I started with) can snap after being twisted backwards too many times.

User-replaceable parts

Sennheiser's HD25 and HD25SP headphones are designed to be completely modular, with each piece user-replaceable. This design means that you need never stress about these headphones breaking or malfunctioning. Provided you have the spare parts in your DJ bag, all you have to do is replace the broken part, and keep on mixing.

Having been in the position where someone wrenched the cable out of my headphones one evening when they stood on them (my fault for leaving them on the floor) the opportunity to instantly replace the cable would have been fantastic. (I had to mix with only one ear working for the rest of the night).

Stick it to your ears

Figure 9-2 shows an example of a 'stick' headphone that has only one ear-cup. By wedging the cup between your shoulder and your ear, you can cut out more external sound, and hear the music a bit clearer through the one ear-piece. However, I still prefer traditional headphones, which let you do exactly the same thing, and still give you the choice of hearing the music in stereo – and you won't end up with a strained neck from craning it to one side. DJs such as Fatboy Slim and David Morales have used this style of headphone with great success, and their heads don't loll to one side, so absolutely nothing is wrong with this design.

Figure 9-2:
The Stanton
DJ Pro 3000
STK 'Stick'
headphones.

Remembering that the Volume Doesn't Have to Go Up to 11

Please forgive the Spinal Tap reference (watch *This is Spinal Tap* if you don't understand the 'Up to 11' reference!), but the only person that knows you're playing the headphones at full volume is you – you can't show off to anyone, as no one else can hear. Playing your headphones at full volume harms you and your mixing more than it'll make you look cool. You don't need music to be loud to enjoy it, and you certainly don't need to look forward to wearing hearing aids in your future.

As a drummer from age 10 who also used to go to loud rock concerts, a clubber who used to go to clubs at least four times a week (and dance right next to the speaker, because it was somewhere to keep the drinks!), and a DJ from age 21 through to the current day, I've always surrounded myself with loud music. I pay the price for that now by having a constant ringing in my ears (something called *tinnitus*). Although it doesn't affect what I hear, you don't want to wake up in the middle of the night and just hear a ringing in your ears, believe me. Do everything you can to protect your ears. You are *not* invincible.

In addition to causing irreversible ear damage, if you play the music in your headphones too loud, you'll find mixing a lot harder. Beatmatching (see Chapter 12) is easier when you find the perfect level to listen to the headphones, while the amp is still blaring out at 130 dB.

When *beatmatching*, you need to listen to two tunes at the same time to work out if their bass beats are playing at the same time. The most common technique (single ear monitoring) involves listening to one tune in one ear through the headphones and the other tune in the other ear from the speakers or monitor in the DJ booth. Playing one tune so that it plays louder than the other makes it harder to concentrate on the bass drums from both tunes.

For more information on the single ear monitoring technique, and guidance on how to check that you've set the levels (volumes) of both the amplifier and the headphones correctly, go to Chapter 12.

Using Earplugs

Earplugs can make a world of difference to your future hearing, and the quality of your mixing. I encourage you to use earplugs when practising in the bedroom so you'll be used to using them when it comes to DJing in a club. I only wear one earplug during a mix, protecting the ear that listens to the music from the monitor, but I always keep another on hand to pop in my other ear when not in the mix.

Remember, the decibel level in a club can be upwards of 100 decibels (decibels, abbreviated as *dB*, are a way of calculating how loud sound is) and as a DJ who gets work four or five times a week (if you're lucky) you're exposed to this level more often than any clubber. So, although I recommend using one ear plug in your ear open to the monitor when you're mixing, I strongly suggest that you plug the other one in when you're not.

Even though during a mix, I don't have an earplug in my headphone monitoring ear, that ear benefits from the protection given to the other ear. Because the earplug reduces the loudness of the music that enters the ear that's open to the monitor, you can reduce the volume at which the headphones are playing. If you didn't lower the volume of the headphones, it would be harder to concentrate on the music from the monitor, making it harder to beatmatch.

Even though you're standing next to a really good quality monitor, the noise levels and acoustic sound inside a club still make hearing specific parts of a tune quite difficult. Maybe you want to hear a subtle change in the melody, or you want to hear the hi-hat cymbals as they change, or you just want to hear the bass drum beats stand out from the rest of the tune. You can sometimes have difficulty picking out these parts with the combination of sound from the dance floor and the monitor, and you may (wrongly) consider turning up the monitor in the DJ booth to try to hear the music better.

You experience this difficulty because the sound waves from the dance floor and from your monitor in the booth mix together, making it harder for you to pick out and concentrate on the parts of the song you need to. Using an earplug means that the sound waves have to travel through the foam before they get into your ear, so the music sounds a lot clearer. Wearing an earplug is like running a brush through tangled hair. It's much easier to separate the hair if it's been brushed (or filtered in the earplug case), and pick only the parts you'd like to concentrate on. (Just make sure that the person whose hair you're stroking is happy with this!)

The basic foam earplugs that you get from the chemist cost about £1 for three pairs and aren't designed specifically for listening to music. They're designed more for getting to sleep when the person sleeping next to you is doing an impression of a sawmill. They do a very good job at cutting out high volume levels but aren't good at retaining the quality of the music (they don't really let through the high frequencies so they're like sending the person with tangled hair to get it all cut off to fix the problem).

If you think that the cheap foam earplugs still aren't letting you hear what you need to hear in the music, you have two options – buy more expensive ear plugs off the shelf or get some professionally made for you:

✔ **Off the shelf:** You can find lots of great designs for earplugs that try to maintain the quality of the sound that enters your ears. To mention only one, *Hocks Noisebrakers* (shown in Figure 9-3) embrace the laws of physics to bounce the sound coming into the earplug back out again, which has the effect of not letting anything over 80 dB into your ears, without sacrificing the quality of what you're listening to. They cost about £15, so are a step up in price from the basic foam ones, but they do work well, and save your ears while still making it easier to mix.

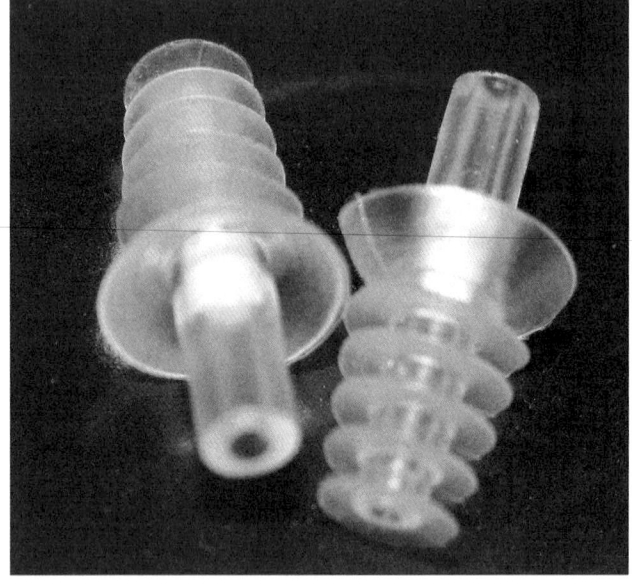

Figure 9-3:
Hocks
Noise-
brakers
earplugs.

✔ **Custom made:** Custom-made ear plugs from companies such as Etymotic and Advanced Communication Solutions (ACS) are costly (around £165 for the ACS ER-15s), but they have a superior ability to maintain sound quality while reducing the volume level. An impression is made of your ear cavity in order to make an earplug that fits snugly into your ears, and your ears only (see Figure 9-4).

For more information about earplugs, check out www.earplugstore.com.

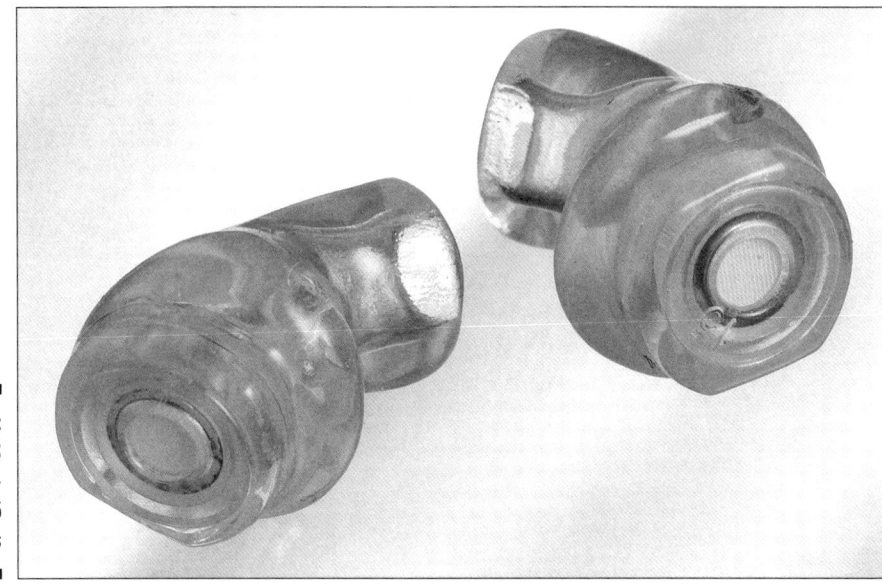

Figure 9-4:
ACS
custom-
made ER-15
earplugs

Chapter 10

Letting Your Neighbours Know That You're a DJ: Amplifiers

In This Chapter

▶ Choosing the right amplification for your wallet and environment

▶ Getting to grips with connecting it all up

▶ Keeping the sound down to save your hearing, and your neighbours' sanity

*E*ach stage of the DJ equipment chain is vital. Without the amplifier and speakers, you'd be the only person to hear how good a DJ you are. In this chapter, I cover the various methods of amplification, the best way to connect and place your speakers, and how to play at a volume that won't get you ejected from the neighbourhood.

Choosing Suitable Amplification

Not only do you need to choose a method of amplification that's suitable to the size of room you're playing in, but also for the size of your wallet – which are both important factors. The key word here is *suitable*. If you're just in your bedroom practising at a moderate volume, you won't have much need of a £3,000, 1,000-watt amplifier and set of speakers, so save your money!

The different ways you can amplify the signal from the mixer so you can hear it through speakers are via:

✔ **Your home stereo.** For the bedroom DJ who has a good-sounding stereo with a spare input to plug the mixer into. This is the method I use in my practice room.

✔ **Powered speakers (each speaker has a built-in amplifier).** If you don't have a home stereo, or the one you have doesn't have a spare input, powered speakers are perfect as an all-in-one solution.

✔ **A separate amplifier and speakers.** This combination is the best choice if you have a large room/hall/club that you need to fill with music.

Settling on your home stereo

Your *home stereo* (or *hi-fi*) is probably the easiest and cheapest route to go down when you're just playing in the bedroom for practise because you probably already own one. As long as you have a spare input channel on your hi-fi, and you can position the speakers somewhere near to your DJ setup to get a good sound from them, your home stereo is a very good option. Though a hi-fi may not be as loud as a separate amplifier, if you're playing in a modest-sized bedroom, it should be more than loud enough.

Don't sneer at the idea of using a hi-fi. They can have great sound quality, produce very loud volumes, and probably have a built-in tape or MiniDisc recorder to record your mix sessions.

If you get the chance to buy a new hi-fi for this use, search for one that has a manual graphic equaliser on it, rather than relying on some pre-set nonsense about 'Hall', 'Big Hall', 'Stadium', and 'Bread Bin,' to approximate the different sounds that those areas would make. If you plan to use the hi-fi as a tape recorder, full control of the sound on your stereo is especially important (see Chapter 18 for guidance on making great sounding tapes), and a manual equaliser lets you adjust the sound to your taste, by controlling a range of different sound frequencies individually. Even if that means another £20, you won't regret your choice. Hi-fis with pre-set EQs (equalisers) are great for domestic, easy listening at home. You're a DJ – you're far from domesticated.

The hi-fi also needs a spare input on the back of it to plug in your mixer. If you only have CD and Phono inputs on the back, and you already have a CD player plugged into the hi-fi, you'll need to unplug the CD player, and plug in your mixer each time you want to use your decks. (If you don't know why the Phono input is off-limits, refer to Chapter 8.) Try to pick a hi-fi with a separate AUX (auxiliary) input to plug your mixer into.

The length of the cable between the hi-fi unit and the speakers can also affect your choice of purchase. For example, I have a Sony hi-fi with less than a metre's worth of speaker cable between the base unit and each of the speakers. I have no plans to use it with my decks, but the length of cable provided is useless for DJ use because I can't get the speakers either side of the decks without needing to sit the base unit on top of my mixer!

Purchasing powered speakers

If you don't have an amplifier or don't want to tie up an input on your hi-fi with your mixer, *powered speakers* (also knows as *active monitors*) are a good alternative. Powered speakers are the same as normal speakers, except that they don't use a separate amplifier; each speaker has its own, built-in amplifier so you can connect the output from your mixer directly to the speakers.

Each speaker needs to be connected to a power supply, so make sure that wherever you intend to sit them, you have a power point close by. If at all possible, to maintain audio quality, don't cross the power cable over any of the audio cables, as this may cause electrical interference. You probably won't have any problems if you do, but if you can get into the habit of properly laying the cables between two pieces of equipment now, you'll know to keep the speaker cable away from power leads if you're ever connecting a lot of speakers and amplifiers for a party or club night because the volumes involved may reveal electrical interference.

Powered monitors are very popular in the DJ booth, especially if the mixer doesn't have a booth control. The volume control for this monitor is usually situated somewhere accessible on the side or back of the cabinet, which is perfect for the DJ to turn it up or down whenever needed. Powered monitors in the DJ booth also don't tie up an entire amplifier for the sake of one speaker, making good financial sense.

For bedroom use, powered speakers can range in quality (and price) from budget monitors, such as those by Ion and Numark that cost about £40 a pair and have an acceptable sound (though to my mind they're lacking a bit in bass thump), to great-sounding powered speakers such as those made by Behringer, Alesis, and JBL, which can cost £300–600 a pair or even £6,000 for a pair of RCF 4PRO7001 concert-quality active speakers. You may need a friendly bank manager for those ones though!

Good quality, surround-sound powered speakers used with computers can sometimes be an option too.

Opting for an amplifier and separate speakers

An amplifier powering separate speakers can be overkill in the bedroom. 500 watts of music is more than you may need even in a large hall, so if you buy a high-rated amplifier and speakers, and turn up the volume to full, don't be surprised if your neighbours come knocking on the door!

Both the amplifier and the speaker have a power rating, which is measured in *watts* (abbreviated as *W*). The higher the number of watts, the louder you can play the music. Generally speaking, the rating on the back of your *amp* (short for amplifier) tells you the maximum sustained output that the amp can produce. On speakers, however, you may see two ratings, the *average* and the *peak* rating. The average rating (also known as *RMS*) refers to the maximum *sustained* output that your speakers can handle. The peak rating refers to how much power they can handle momentarily without risk of damage.

In non-tekky talk, think about a trampoline. How low the membrane on a trampoline is to the ground when you're standing still on it would be the *average* rating, it's happy at this level, and nothing's really going to go wrong with it. When you start jumping on the trampoline, as you land, the membrane gets a lot closer to the ground momentarily. How close it can get to the ground before suffering damage is the *peak* rating of your trampoline . . .

The peak value is always higher than the average value, and is why manufacturers like to print the peak in their documentation – it makes the speaker look more powerful.

When matching up an amplifier for use with your speakers, make sure that the power of the amplifier is less than the average rating of the speakers, which is much safer. No matter how loud the amp goes, it shouldn't be able to blow the speaker this way. If you *do* want to choose an amp that's more powerful than the average output of the speaker, make sure not to buy an amp that's more powerful than the peak rating of the speaker. Even if you make a promise to yourself that you'll never turn the amp up to 10, you can't say the same for your friends, or cat.

A power margin for error

Choosing the rating of the amps and speakers, especially when considering a lot of power for a hall, or club setup, takes a little forethought and margin for error.

If you are looking to buy a setup that would give you 200 watts of power, the best option isn't actually to go out and buy a 200-watt amplifier, and speakers with an average rating of 200 watts. Even buying two 100-watt amplifiers to make up a total of 200 watts of sound so that if one of the amps blew you'd still have 100 watts of sound available, isn't the ideal way to set up your sound system.

The preferred way to set up this amount of power is to buy three amplifiers, and three sets of speakers, and run them all at two-thirds of their output level. Running two amplifiers at full volume all the time isn't the best way to keep them working for a long time. Three amps at two-thirds of their power run happily for a long time. And even if one of them did blow, you'd still only lose one-third of the power, instead of all, or half of the power in the other two examples.

Although 2 x 100 W amplifiers give around the same power as a single 200 W amplifier, a 200 W unit is not twice as powerful as the 100W unit – it's just more powerful. To double the amount of power you have to increase the power of the amplifier tenfold. Table 10-1 is a general guide to the room size, occupancy, and power rating you may need for different situations. This guide isn't a set-in-stone rule, and you may want more than suggested to give you a little 'headroom' of power, in case you want to go louder.

Table 10-1	Amplifier Power Needed for Different Room Sizes
Room and Occupancy	*Power Needed*
Empty(ish) bedroom (you, your bed, your decks, and the cat)	20–40 watts
Full(ish) bedroom (a few friends came for a visit)	40–60 watts
Big room or small, half-full hall (back room in a pub)	80–150 watts
Large hall, half full (local Scout hall, and so on)	150–300 watts
Large hall, lots of people (phew, they came!)	500–800 watts

You may have noticed from the selection suggested that the number of people in the room affects the amount of power you need. People are very greedy. Not only do they raid your fridge for beer and food, but their bodies also absorb a lot of the audio frequencies, robbing some of the volume from the room. The more people that turn up, the louder you have to play the music to be heard at the same volume! The good thing is that even though you have to turn up the sound a bit, the soaking of the stray sound waves by the crowd actually improves the sound on the dance floor.

But as well as counting the people on the dance floor, when you're choosing the amount of amplification for an event, take a look at what's around you; the décor and the floor are just as important as the size and capacity of the room. A room with wooden floors and wooden walls reflects the audio waves around the room, making the music sound a lot louder than it's actually coming out of the speakers. Inversely, a room with carpet flooring that has big, thick curtains in it, is going to absorb a lot of the sound waves, so you may need a touch more power.

If you want to know how to connect multiple sets of speakers into your amplifiers (which is essential knowledge for club systems and some mobile DJs), check out www.recess.co.uk.

Working with Monitors

Good monitors are an important part of the DJ booth. Whether you have a dedicated speaker that you can control independently without affecting what is playing to the dance floor, or if your monitor is another speaker attached to the main amplifier, the booth monitor can make the difference to your night going well, or going to you-know-where.

Your booth monitor is your link to what's really happening on the dance floor. Without hearing the exact audio that's coming from the mixer and the moment it comes from the mixer, you'll have a really hard time beatmatching. In the bedroom, the 'dance floor' sound and the music you hear in the monitor are the same thing (usually because they *are* the same thing), but in a club, the two sounds are a bit different.

The booth monitor is like your health. You don't miss it until you don't have it anymore. It not only lets you gauge how the music sounds playing to the dance floor, but also helps with the accuracy of your beatmatching.

The speakers on the dance floor are probably only 10–20 metres away from the DJ booth, and they're sure to be loud enough for you to hear them. But volume doesn't have much to do with how long the sound takes to get from the mixer to the speakers and then to your ears. The speed of sound is 330 metres per second. If the speakers are 20 metres away, the sound takes around $\frac{1}{16}$th of a second to get to you. In music, this fraction of a second is an extraordinarily long piece of time, and though it seems like a tiny delay, the delay is enough to throw your beatmatching out of time and make you sound like a complete amateur.

This is where the DJ booth monitor comes in. The monitor is often a pair of speakers either side of the DJ, but in some cases, is just a single speaker positioned to the left or right of the DJ. The monitor right next to your ears cuts the audio delay from $\frac{1}{16}$th of a second to $\frac{1}{256}$th of a second (if it's a metre away), which is more than acceptable.

Positioning Your Monitor

Unless you live in a mansion, you're unlikely to have to deal with any delay from your speakers in the bedroom to where you have your decks set up. If you do live in an oversized room that's causing delay similar to working in a club, ask *butler* to bring one of the speakers closer to you. Sarcasm aside, if bringing a speaker closer to you isn't an option, then you can hook up a separate booth monitor (maybe a powered speaker) to play right next to your DJ set-up, or you can add another pair of speakers to your existing set-up, and place them next to your homemade DJ booth.

The key to positioning the monitor is to put it in the right place that helps you to mix as well as you can. You need to make sure that you can hear the music clearly, with as much clarity as possible, and also position it in the best place to counteract any audio delay, and audio spillage from the dance floor.

The perfect position for a monitor in the DJ booth is 1–2 metres from the mixer, slightly in front of you, at head height, and with the speaker turned in to point directly at you. Assuming that your speaker has the *bass driver* (the big speaker) at the bottom, and the *tweeter* (which plays the high frequencies) at the top, this position is perfect for getting the best sound quality from your monitor.

If the monitor is too high, the bass driver dominates the tweeter, drowning out a lot of the high frequencies from the music. If the monitor is too low, aimed at your waist, the bass may sound unclear, compounded by the dominating high-frequency tweeter that would be at head height. Turning the monitor on its side so both the tweeter and bass driver are at the same height helps to prevent either eventuality.

The monitor needs to be close enough to counteract any delay from the dance floor, and also overpower any music from the dance floor that may still be heard in the DJ booth. If the speaker can be kept close, and facing you, it gives you the best clarity. Too far away, and you may find it harder to pick out a solid bass thump or the crisp hi-hats and snare drum that are used as reference when beatmatching (see Chapter 12).

For your bedroom setup, you may not have as much room, or control over where you can put the speakers. The two things to keep the same as in the club DJ booth are that the speakers are in front of you, and pointing toward your ears, and that you try not to set the speakers on the same piece of furniture that your decks are on. If the vibrations from the speaker cause the turntable to vibrate, you generate feedback. If you're using CDs, you may cause the CD player to skip with the bass vibrations.

Noise Pollution: Keeping an Ear on Volume Levels

Many reasons come to mind as to why you shouldn't play your music loud all the time, but hearing damage (which is covered in Chapter 9), neighbour relations, and the quality of your mixes are paramount.

Protecting your ears

Keeping the volume of your monitor at the lowest functional level protects your ears, and reduces any risk of distortion from the headphones or the monitor when you aren't playing everything at full power (which causes the sound to lose quality and makes it hard to concentrate on).

One of the most popular ways to match the bass beats of two records is to use a technique called *single-ear monitoring*. This technique is when you have one ear open to the music from the monitor, playing the *live* sound from the amplifier, and the other ear has one of the headphone cups on, listening to the *cued* song that you wish to play next. (For more information on this, check out Chapter 12.)

Getting spooked into turning down the bass

When I still lived at home with my mum, I had a huge setup in my bedroom, with six 100-watt speakers dotted around the room, which was on the ground floor of the house (no wonder with all that noise!). I used to spend hours playing my tunes, working out new mixes, having fun, and improving my skills. I didn't always play the music really loud, and I hardly ever played it at full volume, but I had a huge subwoofer that made a hell of a thump every time the bass drum pounded away.

Eventually, my next-door neighbour got fed up with feeling the vibrations of the beats through the floor in his house – 30 feet away! Because a dual-car garage linked the houses, the vibrations travelled through the foundations of my house and into his house. All this disturbance led to him banging on the window of my room for 10 minutes, getting increasingly frustrated at waiting for me to turn around and notice him. When I eventually did turn round, and saw a (less than happy) face staring in through the window, it scared the heck out of me! I thought it was a ghost against the window. I turned the bass down after that fright.

The volume of the music that comes into your head from the monitor needs to match the volume at which the headphones are playing into your other ear. Due to the proximity of the headphone to your ear, this is about perceived volume rather than trying to match the actual decibel level coming from that amp – because to do so would make you go deaf.

You only have to play the monitor loud enough to drown out the music from the dance floor, which helps the accuracy of your beatmatching. You may be surprised at how little it takes. After you've reached that level, try not to increase the volume, even if you're really digging the music!

Keeping the noise down for the people around you

Keeping the music at a sensible level so that you don't go deaf or harm your mixing skills is important, but you also have your sense of social responsibility to think of. Not only may the rest of the people in your flat, house, or building start to get a little irked with you when you play the pounding bass beats at full volume for hours at a time, but the people in the surrounding houses may soon get fed up with the dull thudding noise coming from your house.

Realising that you only need one speaker

When you're DJing at home, you really only need the one speaker, and that's the one you use for the 'live ear' when using single ear monitoring to beatmatch, (your equivalent of a DJ booth monitor).

When I realised the bass of my subwoofer was deeply annoying to the neighbours, I put switches onto all of my speakers, so I was able to leave only the monitor speaker running. This meant that I could play the music just as loud as before, but because only one speaker was playing, the volume that other people could hear (and the bass thump, because I'd turned off the subwoofer) was a lot lower.

Light switches aren't meant to be used as controls for sound outputs, so do some research to see if the switch you're thinking of using would add too much resistance to the signal from the amplifier to the speaker, even when it's just passing through the circuit. This resistance may only cause a drop in sound quality or volume, but in the worst case it may break your amplifier.

Chapter 11

Plugging In, Turning On: Set-up and Connections

....

In This Chapter

▶ Setting up and connecting your turntables properly for DJ use

▶ Connecting everything to your mixer, and your mixer to everything

▶ Troubleshooting why you're not hearing what you should be hearing

....

*Y*ou've spent a heap of cash on your new turntables, CD decks, and a mixer, bought an amplifier loud enough to deafen the back row in a stadium, and everything's turned on, ready to go – except you can't hear anything.

You simply have to check that everything has been set up correctly and follow the chain of inputs and outputs to see that all your equipment is plugged into the right place.

Getting Familiar with Connectors

Before you connect your equipment together, getting familiar with the connections you're using is a good idea. The most common connection types you come across are *RCA* (also called *Phono*), *XLR*, and ¼-inch jacks (also known as *TRS*). In order for music to play in stereo, you mostly encounter two of each of these for connecting your equipment. One cable and connector carries what you hear out of the left speaker; the other carries what you hear out of the right speaker. Quarter-inch jack plugs are also available as a single, stereo connector (as seen at the end of your headphones).

Some turntables, CD decks, and mixers have started using digital connections to keep audio quality at maximum. *USB* (universal serial bus) and Firewire are connections you'll have seen before on computers, and along with *S/PDIF* (Sony/Philips Digital Interface Format) these digital connections send both sides of the stereo sound through one cable, which is then interpreted and separated back into stereo music by whatever you're plugging into.

It's not always the clubber's fault

Blaming an accident on the customers of the clubs that you play in is quite easy, but as a DJ, you have to be careful of doing things that can break connections yourself. I remember one evening playing at a bar and I had the lid of the record box neatly balanced on the DJ booth. I knocked it with my hand, it fell down the back, bounced onto the cables coming out of the mixer, pulled out the Master Output cable, and plunged the place into silence for about three minutes while I tried to work out what I'd done. Thank goodness I worked there as a barman; otherwise they'd have thrown me out on my ear for being so careless!

RCA/Phono connections

RCA connections are also known as Phono connections, but I call them RCA to stop any confusion with the Phono/Line terminology for inputs on the back of the mixer.

RCAs are the most common connections you'll use as inputs and outputs to your DJ mixer. They come in pairs, one for each side of the stereo signal and each of them is a different colour. The left signal cable is usually white, though it can be yellow or black, but the right-hand side of the audio signal is always red. This makes remembering which cable plugs into where easy. Simply remember that Red = Right.

XLRs

Used for amplifier connections and microphones, XLRs are the preferred connection for professional audio equipment because they're capable of reducing interference when using long cables, and because they lock into place so they can't accidentally pop out if a drunken clubber falls on them.

XLR connections (see Figure 11-1) come in two different flavours:

- ✔ **Balanced** XLRs are used in professional audio equipment. When the connectors from the mixer and to the input of the amplifier are *wired up* (the individual wires are attached to the connector) so that they're balanced, this cancels out any unwanted electrical interference.

- ✔ **Unbalanced** XLRs are more common as a *pro-sumer* (a mixture of professional and consumer) connection. An unbalanced XLR simply passes the audio signal through the cable, and any unwanted electrical or radio interference that's picked up by a long cable remains, playing through the speakers or to your recording device.

XLR microphone (*mic*) inputs and *master outputs* on DJ mixers are often compatible with cables and connectors that are both balanced and unbalanced, but it's best to check the specifications of the equipment you use if you're unsure of the connections when buying a new microphone, amplifier, or mixer.

Quarter-inch jack

A ¼-inch jack (also known as a TRS jack), is what you find at the end of your DJ headphones (though not the one on the end of your iPod headphones, that is a *3.5-millimetre* jack). Quarter-inch jacks also come in balanced and unbalanced varieties. Balanced connectors are mono, so you need two of them, but an unbalanced connector can carry a stereo signal, so only needs one cable and jack plug. If you need to know whether the jack you're holding in your hand is mono or stereo, look at the black bands on the tip; one band means it's mono, two bands mean it's a stereo jack, as shown in Figure 11-2.

Figure 11-1: Two XLR connectors, one for the left, the other for the right.

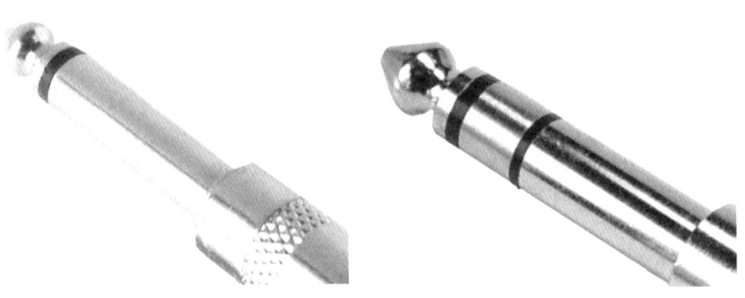

Figure 11-2:
Left: A mono quarter-inch jack (TRS) connector.
Right: A stereo quarter-inch jack connector.

Setting Up and Connecting the Turntable

CD decks, MiniDisc decks, and MP3 players aren't particularly complicated to set up. Plug them in using RCA cables (see the relevant sections later in this chapter) and turn them on. Turntables are slightly more complicated creatures, with three different elements to be set up:

- Deckplatter
- Tonearm
- Peripherals

Deckplatter

The deckplatter (the part of the turntable that rotates) is an easy part of the turntable to deal with. If you're using direct-drive turntables, all you have to do is make sure that you've removed the thick rubber mat that may have come with the turntable, then place the slipmat directly on top of the deckplatter and the record sits on top of the slipmat.

If you've just bought brand new belt-driven turntables, you may find that the belt hasn't been linked between the motor and the deckplatter. Carefully lift off the deckplatter, and look underneath; if the belt isn't linked to the motor, it is probably taped to the underside of the deckplatter. Stretch the belt between the motor's capstan (the bit of the motor that turns) and the underside of the deckplatter. If in doubt, check the manual for instructions!

Tonearm

The tonearm holds the needle. If the tonearm is poorly set up, the needle can jump out of the groove when you're trying to find the cue point (discussed in Chapter 12). Worse than that though, a poorly set up tonearm can permanently damage the needle and your records.

The tonearm may require adjustment in three different ways:

- ✔ Counterweight
- ✔ Height
- ✔ Antiskate

Counterweight

The *counterweight* controls how much down-force is applied to the needle to keep it in the groove. The amount to add is suggested by the manufacturer of the needles and cartridges that you're using (Chapter 6 tells you more about needles and cartridges, and has a table of common counterweight settings).

Because the counterweight can add lots of weight when fully screwed on, or make the tonearm point to the sky when it's almost hanging off the back, the key to achieving your desired setting begins with a technique known as *floating the tonearm* (Figure 11-3 shows the correct, floating position, notice how it is completely parallel to the deckplatter, pointing neither up, nor down). To float your tonearm, follow these steps:

1. **Remove any records from the turntable, and the needle protector from the needle if it has one.**

2. **Starting on one of the turntables, carefully lift the tonearm off its rest towards the middle of the deckplatter.**

3. **Gently hold onto the finger-lift on the headshell with your left hand (so the needle doesn't crash down onto the slip-mat), and turn the counterweight clockwise so that it starts to move towards the back end of the tone arm.**

4. **As you move the weight backwards, frequently check to see if there has been a shift in weight from the tonearm pointing downward, to pointing upward.**

5. **Find the setting for the counterweight where the needle floats in mid air, not pointing up, nor dropping down to the slipmat, as shown in Figure 11-3.**

Figure 11-3:
The
tonearm
perfectly
balanced,
with the
needle
removed
from the
cartridge
to avoid
damage.

6. **After you've found the floating point, return the tonearm to its rest and use the tonearm clamp to lock it into place.**

7. **Now hold the silver part of the counterweight, and use two fingers to grip the black ring on the front of the weight. The ring, which has numbers on it, turns independently to the rest of the counterweight.**

8. **Turn the black ring until the line pointing down from the number 0 lines up with the line on the tone arm beneath it.**

   Take a look at Figure 11-4, which shows you how to control the black ring.

The tonearm is now set to the floating position and has *been zeroed.* If your needle manufacturer suggests that you add three grams of counterweight onto the tonearm, turn the entire counterweight anticlockwise (so the black ring also turns) until the number 3 on the black ring lines up with the mark below it on the tonearm.

Height

There are two reasons why you may need to alter the height of the tonearm. The technical reason is that the tonearm must always be perfectly parallel to the deckplatter, and because some cartridges are bigger than others, you use the height adjustment to compensate for this. The other reason is if you're a scratch DJ. Scratch DJs use the raised tonearm height to add even more down-force to the needle, reducing the chances of it jumping out of the groove.

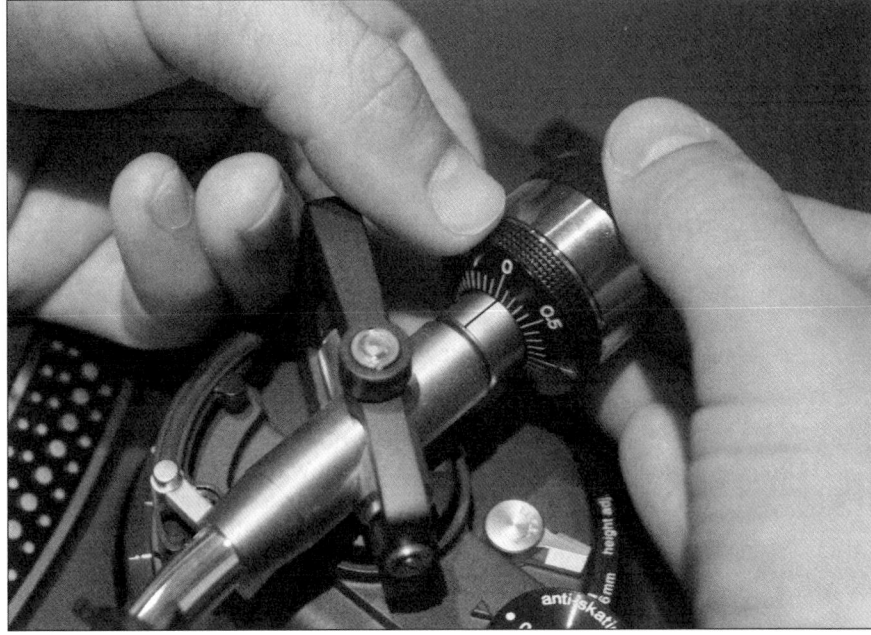

Figure 11-4:
One hand supports the back of the counter-weight, while the other rotates only the numbered ring.

The height adjustment on most decks is a ring at the bottom of the tonearm assembly, which raises or lowers the tonearm as it turns clockwise or anti-clockwise. A small mark on the assembly shows you how much height you've added, and unless you're a scratch DJ, your best bet is to follow the height suggested by the makers of the needle and cartridge you're using.

When you're altering the height of the tonearm, set the tonearm in the tonearm rest with the clamp on to hold it in place, or remove the needle from the cartridge. Otherwise, one wrong move, and the needle can bounce across the record/slipmat/deckplatter, and get damaged.

Look out for the lock switch on the tonearm – without releasing this lock, you can't change the height, and if you try to force the ring, thinking it's stuck, you may do permanent damage to the tonearm assembly. Also be aware that when left in an unlocked position, the tonearm moves slightly, and may fool you into thinking that you've damaged the tonearm.

Antiskate

Antiskate prevents wear on records by adding a force pulling the needle towards the outer edge of the record to counteract an inward force when a record is playing forwards.

As a DJ, though, you won't simply play records forwards. When you're trying to find a starting point (called the *cue*) you play the record backwards and forwards, and if you're a scratch DJ, you play the record backwards just as much as you play it forwards. Because an outward force is exerted on the needle when a record is played backwards, the outward pull of antiskate is exaggerated and can cause the needle to jump, so it's best to leave the anti-skate set to 0. (Chapter 5 has more about antiskate.)

Peripherals

The last items to attend to when setting up your turntables are the feet and the lids. Keeping the lids attached to the turntables when you're mixing is a bad idea; they get in the way and you may knock them, causing the needle to jump. Don't be lazy, take them on and off each time you use your decks.

The rubber feet on your turntables don't act as mere vibration dampeners. Because the feet screw in, adjusting how tightly they're attached to the turntable affects the height of each of the four corners of the turntable, which is ideal when compensating for the badly built DIY furniture that your decks sit on. Grab a spirit level if you want to be precise, and adjust the feet to make sure that your decks are level. If they're not level, the needles could skip.

Plugging In the Mixer

The first time you take a look at the back of a mixer, it can look quite daunting with all the different inputs and outputs, but after you've plugged in a couple of pieces of equipment, you find out just how simple it is back there. For more information on mixers and any functions you may be unsure of that are mentioned in this section, refer to Chapter 8.

Connecting turntables to a mixer

Turntables are unique in their connection, as they're the only item of DJ equipment that plugs into the Phono input on the mixer, and they have a thin ground wire (also called an *earth*) connection that needs to be connected to prevent electrical hum and static from the turntables.

Connection is simple:

1. **Take the two RCA cables that come out the back of the turntable and plug them into the Phono input on the mixer.**

   The RCA outputs of the turntable and the inputs on the back of the mixer are coloured, and are nearly always red and white. Remember, the red

RCA is the right-hand side of the music signal, and white is the left-hand side (see the earlier section 'RCA/Phono connections').

If your turntable uses detachable cables, make sure you connect the RCA cables to the correct colours on the turntable outputs as well as the mixer inputs.

2. **After you've connected the cables properly, set the switch for the channel you've just plugged into to *Phono* (not *Line*).**

3. **Connect the ground (earth) wire.** Take a good look at the back of your deck. If you bought a DJ turntable and you can't see a ground wire there, don't assume that the deck doesn't need one. If you bought your decks second-hand, the last person who used the decks may not have realised how important it was, and cut it off!

Fortunately, you don't have the same hunt for *where* to plug the ground wire. All but the cheapest, nastiest mixers have a ground point on the back of the mixer, normally a thumb screw that you use to cinch the ground wires from both turntables between a washer on the screw and the body of the mixer (as shown in Figure 11-5).

Be sure that you have a secure connection for both turntables to this ground point by checking that the metal ends of the wires make connection with the ground point's metal washer or screw. You'll know if your turntables haven't been properly grounded, because you'll hear static or a really nasty, loud hum playing through the speakers.

Figure 11-5: Two ground wires screwed to the back of the mixer.

Some turntables include digital outputs (mentioned in the 'Getting familiar with connectors' section earlier in the chapter) as well as the traditional analogue RCA outputs. When these digital connections are used in conjunction with a digital mixer (like the Pioneer DJM-800) the audio quality is pristine and suffers very little noise or interference.

Connecting CD decks to a mixer

CD decks, along with anything else that uses a Line signal to connect to the mixer, usually use RCA outputs that connect to the mixer's *Line* RCA inputs. If you only use two CD decks, plug them into the Line inputs on the mixer.

If however, you're combining CD decks and turntables, it's a good idea to connect them in the same way they're arranged in front of you. Suppose that you arrange your equipment in this order:

Turntable 1 – CD 1 – Mixer – CD 2 – Turntable 2

The easiest set-up is to connect turntable 1 to channel 1, CD 1 to channel 2, CD 2 to channel 3, and turntable 2 to channel 4 on the mixer. Connecting to the channels on the mixer in the same order as the equipment causes less confusion about what channel controls what equipment. Just make sure that you switch the Line/Phono switch to Line for the CD decks and Phono for turntables.

You can have this same set-up with only two channels on the mixer. Plug turntable 1 into the *phono* input on channel 1, and CD 1 into the *line* input on channel 1. Then plug turntable 2 into *phono* on channel 2, and CD2 into *line* on channel 2. The only danger here is that you need to remember to switch the appropriate channel from phono to line (or vice versa) to use the right piece of equipment. Also, you won't be able to mix from turntable 1 to CD 1 or turntable 2 to CD 2 because even though they're different machines, they're both playing into the same channel.

Before deciding on an arrangement and what channel to use for what equipment, take a look at what the mixer suggests you connect to what channel. On the Pioneer DJM-600 that I use, Channel 1 and Channel 2 are suggested for CD decks that have the *player control* feature, which starts the CD playing when the cross-fader is moved (so you don't need to press play on the CD). I prefer using Channels 1 and 4 for CD decks though, and as I don't take advantage of the player control for my CDJ1000's, that's okay by me.

CD decks can also make use of digital connections mentioned at the beginning of this chapter. As the CD music is digital (rather than analogue vinyl), maintaining the music signal as digital with digital inputs on a mixer keeps sound quality at maximum.

Connecting iPods and MP3s to a mixer

Unless you're using one of the Numark iDJ mixers specifically designed for mixing with iPods, you need to use a cable that converts the output of your iPod (or any other MP3 player) to two RCA plugs. You can get a cable that's based on the dock connector of the iPod that splits into two RCA plugs (this is how a lot of people play their iPods through a home hi-fi) but without that, and for most of the other MP3 players, you need a cable that splits the headphone output into two RCA plugs.

You can buy these cables from most electronic spares stores, or simply type '*3.5 mm stereo jack to RCA*' into any search engine, or eBay (www.ebay.co.uk), and you'll find one for about £5. Just make sure that the jack on the end of the cable you go for is stereo (it'll have two black bands on the tip), and is 3.5 millimetre, otherwise, it won't fit into the MP3 player's headphone output.

As with the CD decks, simply plug the RCAs from this cable into the *Line* input on the back of the mixer, making sure that the channel you use for this input on the mixer is switched over to Line.

Because headphone outputs are normally weaker than a typical *Line* output, you may have to set your MP3 player to a high volume, or increase the gain on the mixer by more than normal in order to keep the volume of the MP3 music similar to the rest of your inputs (CDs, turntables, and so on).

Connecting a computer as an input device

Laptops and PCs are becoming a bigger part of DJing. Computers used to be simple recording and editing devices used to add effects and edit out any bad parts of the mix, but now they're used as input devices. The software you use should detail any special connection instructions in order to properly set up the computer to enable it for DJ use – always refer to the manual first.

To connect the outputs of the computer to the mixer so that you can mix the computer music with another source (CD players, turntables, and so on) you use the *soundcard* on the computer. The soundcard processes the digital music data, and converts it to a Line signal to be sent to the mixer (the reverse also happens, see 'Connecting a Mixer to the PC/Mac' later in the chapter).

If you have a soundcard with RCA outputs, this connection is simple. Using a cable with two RCA connectors on each end, connect the RCA outputs of the computer's soundcard to the RCA *Line* inputs on the mixer. If there is a 3.5-millimetre jack output on the soundcard, you'll need the RCA to stereo 3.5-millimetre lead mentioned in the previous section 'Connecting iPods and MP3s to a mixer'.

If you're using a laptop or have a computer with a very basic soundcard, you may notice that the only audio connections you have are a headphone output and a microphone input. You can use the headphone output as long as you have the RCA to 3.5-millimetre jack cable, but you may want to be able to record *in* to the computer. In which case, you need to look at a new soundcard.

Fortunately, a wide range of analogue to digital USB and Firewire converters (common computer input connections) are available to buy. Edirol (shown in Figure 11-6), Alesis, Behringer, and a whole host of other makes have products at varying prices (and quality) which let you solve the problem of not having a soundcard, or a good enough soundcard on your computer.

Plugging in your headphones

Plugging in your headphones is as simple as finding the hole marked 'headphone' on your mixer, and plugging them in, but I want to mention it here so that I can bring up the use of 3.5-millimetre adaptors. These adaptors let you convert headphones with a small jack (like your iPod headphones, but please, *not* your iPod headphones, they're not suitable for DJing) into the big, 6.35-millimetre (¼ inch) size that your mixer needs.

Figure 11-6:
The Edirol audio to USB by Roland with analogue inputs and outputs connected to a USB connection.

Your headphone jack isn't a headphone rest

Please don't get into the habit of hooking your headphones over the headphone jack when you're not using them. A club I worked in had the mixer at an angle, and also had very little room in the DJ booth, allowing hardly any room to put anything down. So, when I wasn't using my headphones, I'd hook them over the headphone jack; which seemed sensible to me. That was until I aimed a bit high, and hit the power switch with the head band from the headphones, plummeting the club into silence, and I almost blew a speaker when I turned the mixer on without turning the volume down . . . oops. Hooking headphones over the jack connection can cause damage to both the mixer and the headphones, which may lead to sound problems (the headphones may 'cut out' and go silent).

Some mixers have the headphone input on top of the mixer; others have it on the closest side to you, or even both. Choose your input and plug in. Simple.

Connecting effects units to a mixer

You can connect effects units to the mixer in two ways:

✔ **Between the mixer and the amplifier:** Direct connection is the most basic, and easiest way to connect your effects unit. Take the Master Output of your mixer (two RCAs) and plug them into the Line input on the effects unit. Then, take the output of the effects unit (still two RCAs) and plug them into the input of the amplifier.

The drawback to this method of connection is that the entire audio signal will be effected by the effects unit; you won't be able to play one channel from the mixer *clean* (without effects) while the other one gets a whole load of crazy effects applied to it.

✔ **With *Send and Return* connections:** You can send music from an individual channel on the mixer to an effects unit using the Send and Return option. Using this means that you can apply an effect to only one channel, leaving other channels to play unaffected through the speakers.

The signal from the mixer can be sent to (and returned from) the effects processor in two different ways:

• If the effects processor can accept multiple inputs, you can use a mixer with a separate Send and Return for each of the channels. Controls on the effects processor (and sometimes on the mixer) let you choose what channel on the mixer to apply the effect to. With the correct controls, any number of channels can be 'effected' while any number of channels can be 'un-effected'. This method is by far the most versatile approach to using an effects processor, but does tend to require a large mixing desk instead of a compact DJ mixer.

- Some DJ-specific mixers with multiple channels may have only one pair of Send and Return connections but have a control on the mixer that assigns what channels are sent. The DJM-600 that I use lets you send any one of the four channels, or the entire Master Output to an effects unit, so though it's not quite as versatile as the option to include or exclude any number of channels, it can still give you clean audio from one channel while 'effecting' another, which is good enough for me.

The connections for send and return vary, but on the DJM600, it's a pair of mono ¼-inch jacks for each direction. One pair connects from *send* on the mixer to the input of the effects unit, then another pair connects from the effects unit to *return* on the mixer. You may find some units use RCAs for this purpose or stereo ¼-inch jacks, so take a close look at your mixer and the effects unit so that you know what cables you need.

Connecting mixer outputs

After you have all the inputs connected to the mixer you need to look at how to connect your mixer to an amplifier in order to hear the music, and maybe also connect to a recording device (tape, MiniDisc, CD, PC, and so on) so that you can capture the moments of greatness you'll achieve in the mix.

Your mixer has two (or sometimes three) outputs:

- ✔ **Master Out** is the connection to use when connecting to an amplifier. Using a stereo RCA cable, connect one end to the Master Out on the mixer, and the other end to an input on the amplifier. If the amp has more than one input channel, and you're also sending items like a TV, PlayStation, or another CD player to it, you may want to add sticky labels to change the normal 'Input 1, Input 2' labels that'll be on the amp, to help you remember what channel lets you hear what.

More expensive, professional mixers may use a second Master Output that uses XLR connections rather than RCA connections.

The Master Out is affected by the *Master Level Control* on the mixer, so if you turn that down, the volume of the music from the mixer reduces.

- ✔ **Record Out** is reserved for *recording devices* (tape, MiniDisc, CD, PC, or any other recording format you're using). The reasons you use this output rather than the Master Out, are because:

  - The Master Out is probably going to an amp anyway

- You get a slight reduction in output level for the Record Output, in order to avoid distortion or clipping of the sound when recording

- The Record Out bypasses the Master Level Control, so if you turn the Master Output down (maybe to take a phone call), the music level you send to the recording device won't change.

Like the Master Output, connect the Record Outputs to the recorder's inputs using a stereo RCA cable, making sure to continue to plug the red RCA output to the red RCA input, and the white output to the white input. (For information on how to set the record levels on your tape recorder, see Chapter 18.)

✔ **Booth Output** on the mixer is fed into a separate amplifier and speaker in the DJ booth (known as the *Booth Monitor*). (Chapter 9 has important information about setting the volume of the Booth Monitor and the headphones to allow you to mix properly.)

The connection is the same as Record Out and Master Out; connect one end of a stereo RCA cable to the Booth Output on the mixer, and the other end to the Booth Monitor's input.

Connecting a mixer to your home hi-fi

Connecting to your home stereo (hi-fi) is similar to connecting to an ampli-fier. The connection is made using a stereo RCA cable from the Master Output on the mixer to the hi-fi – but you need to pay attention to the input you choose to use on the hi-fi. On the back of a hi-fi, you probably see some of these inputs: Line, CD, TV, DVD, Aux, and if you have an old (or really good) hi-fi, a Phono input too.

If your CD deck is already connected to the hi-fi, you connect your TV through the TV input, and the DVD input is used too, you'll be left with Aux or Phono. Use the Aux input for the mixer. Even though the music you're play-ing may be coming from turntables as a Phono signal, by the time that signal plays through a mixer the signal has been transformed into a Line level signal.

Of course, if you don't have a CD player or TV plugged into the hi-fi, you can use the TV and CD channels, too, as long as you stay away from the Phono input (which is meant for direction connection from a record player). Remember to set the switches on the front of the hi-fi to the correct input.

Connecting a mixer to powered speakers

Sometimes, powered speakers only have a jack input (like the headphone input on your mixer), so check if you need to buy an RCA (the output from your mixer) to jack cable for each of the speakers (left and right).

You can find more information on using amplifiers, powered speakers, and home hi-fis to play your music in Chapter 10.

Connecting a mixer to your PC/Mac

Whether you're using the computer as an amplifier, or if you plan to record the mix to edit it or upload it to the Internet, the connection between your computer and your mixer is similar to all the other equipment you'll connect. Connect the output from the mixer to the input on the computer's soundcard (see 'Connecting a computer as an input device' earlier in the chapter for detailed information on the connections and what a soundcard is used for). Use the Record Output if you're only using the computer for recording, and the Master Output if using the computer as an amplifier (this frees up the Record Output for a recording device).

If your soundcard came with instructions and software for setting up the computer to be able to accept a Line input, please refer to the manual carefully. If it's a Windows controlled soundcard, you can use the *Volume Control Properties* to activate the Line input. Follow these steps to active it:

1. **Double click on the volume icon in the taskbar to open the Volume Control window.**

2. **On the Volume Control window, choose Options (top left) then Properties from the drop down menu.**

3. **In the Properties window that opens, check the 'Adjust Volume for Recording' option.**

4. **Scroll down the list of devices under 'Show the following volume controls' and make sure that LINE IN is selected, then click OK.**

   After clicking 'ok', you'll see that the Record Control window replaces the Volume Control window.

5. **Check the box marked 'Select' underneath LINE IN, ensure the *balance* is set to the middle, and set the volume fader to about ¾ of the way up.**

6. **Open up the software you plan to use to record the output from the mixer, and play some music to check if you're receiving music from the mixer.**

You may want to turn off any other recording inputs (de-select them in the Record Control) or mute other playback devices in the Volume Control Window (by selecting Mute) to make sure that Windows system sounds or sounds from other programs aren't accidentally combined with the sound from your mixer. Nothing's worse than being halfway through a great mix only to have Homer Simpson say 'D'oh!' over the mix when you get an e-mail. Come to think of it, that might be quite cool . . .

Connecting your computer to an amplifier

Fortunately, connecting your computer to an amplifier (if you're using software to mix MP3s for example) is a lot simpler. Follow these steps to connect up your computer to your amplifier:

1. **Look back at the preceding section for connecting a mixer to the computer. Open the Volume Control window, and locate the Volume and Wave controls. Make sure that both of the faders are at least at 75 per cent, that neither of the *mute* check boxes are selected, and the balance controls are both in the middle.**

2. **Connect the output on the soundcard to the input channel on your amp you wish to use.** Again, if your amplifier has a Phono input, please steer clear of this. You are sending a Line signal from the PC to the amp, so you need to use one of the Line inputs.

3. **If your soundcard is controlled by a different piece of software than the Windows Volume Control, check that all settings are correct for outputting from the soundcard.**

Troubleshooting Set-up and Connections

Sometimes, you're sure that you have everything plugged into the right place, you've turned everything on, everything's playing, but you just can't hear anything. Take a look through the following list of troubleshooting issues, and see whether one of these solutions can answer your connection and turntable set-up problems.

Why do my needles keep jumping when cueing?

If you're having a problem with your needles jumping around, try working through these possible solutions:

✔ Refer to manufacturer guidelines on where to set the height and counterweight of your tonearm. If you're given a range of numbers to set the counterweight to (between 3 and 5 grams for example), set the counterweight to the lowest number first, then gradually increase the weight until the needle stops skipping.

✔ Check the settings provided with the needle and cart for the height of the tonearm, and make sure that it's completely parallel to the record. If you need to set the weight or height to more than the recommended amount, your technique or needles could be at fault:

- Make sure that you're cueing the record back and forth in the curved direction of the record. If you push and pull horizontally, rather than in a curve, this action may make the needle jump.

- Old, worn needles are more prone to skipping.

One of the turntables sounds really bad, it's distorting, and the high frequencies sound fuzzy.

The first thing to do is to look at your needles. Are the needles caked in dirt? (Carefully remove the dirt from around them.) Are they really old? (Replace them.) Are they inserted into the cartridge properly? (Check, and re-insert them.)

If you think it's a malfunction, try swapping the headshell from one turntable to another or try swapping the needle from one headshell to the other. In case you have a connection problem rather than a needle or headshell problem, try swapping round the turntable connections to the mixer.

I hear a really strange humming noise coming from my turntables.

The ground wire may not be connected. Make sure that it's securely attached to the earth/ground connector on the back of the mixer.

Everything's connected, a record (or CD) is playing, but I can't hear any music through the amplifier.

Ask yourself the following questions:

✔ Are the LEDs on the mixer flashing up and down to show that the mixer is receiving some music? If not, there's currently no signal.

✔ Have you used the correct inputs on the mixer for your CD players or turntables and set the Line/Phono switches accordingly? (Line for CD, Phono for turntables.)

✔ If you're currently playing one channel of music, have you made sure that the cross-fader is on that side, and the channel-fader it up at least to 75 per cent, and if the cross-fader has an assign function to control any of the channels, is it switched to control the correct channel?

✔ If the mixer LEDs are flashing, have you made sure that you've connected the mixer's Master Output to a Line input on the amplifier?

✔ If the amplifier has the capability for multiple inputs, have you made sure that you've set the input switch or button to the correct input?

✔ Are the Master Level and the Input Level on the amplifier set at a point where you should hear music?

✔ Are the speakers connected?

✔ Have you tried connecting something else to the amplifier to check that it isn't a problem with the amplifier, or the input channel you're using?

I can hear the music from the amp now, but I can't hear anything through the headphones.

Try the following steps:

✔ Firstly, check that you have your headphones plugged in, turned up, and switched to monitor the correct channel.

✔ Try turning all the headphone cue switches on. If you can hear music now, you were pressing the wrong cue button, or you've connected your equipment to a channel you didn't intend.

✔ Plug your headphones into another piece of equipment with a head-phone socket (such as the amplifier) to make sure that this problem isn't a malfunction with your headphones.

Why is everything distorting badly when I play a CD?

Check if you've inserted the outputs of your CD decks into the Phono inputs of the mixer by accident. This causes distortion. Plug into the Line input.

Why is everything really quiet when using my turntables, even when everything is turned up to maximum?

Make sure that you've plugged your turntables into the Phono input. If you've put them into the Line input, they'll be very quiet.

Everything sounds nice through the mixer, but distorts through the amp.

Ask yourself the following questions:

✔ Have you turned up the input level on the amp too high? Turn it down a bit; see if that helps.

✔ How strong a level are you sending out of the mixer? Take a look at where the LEDs on the mixer are flashing; try not to play the music above + 5 dB on the scale, as it may cause some nasty distortion.

✔ Have you plugged into the Phono inputs of the amplifier by accident? Change the connections to plug into the Line inputs.

Music is happily playing through the mixer, but I can't get any music into the PC.

Try the following steps:

- ✔ Make sure that the speakers on your computer are turned on and all volume controls (including the computer's) are turned up.

- ✔ Check the connections and ensure that you've plugged the output from the mixer to the Line input of the soundcard. You may find a *Mic* input right next to the Line input, so double check that you didn't plug into the wrong place when you were fumbling behind the PC.

- ✔ Check the meters on the recording software. They will be bouncing up and down if they're receiving a signal or will sit at 0 if not.

- ✔ Check the Record Control (which you can access through the volume control icon on the taskbar). Double check that Line input has been selected, and that the input level is set to at least 75 per cent.

- ✔ Have a quick read of the manual that came with the software and the soundcard to see if you need to do something special.

The meters are flashing like mad in the software, I'm able to record what's going in, but nothing is coming back out of the PC.

Check that you've connected the Line Out from the soundcard and not plugged into the Mic or Line In by accident.

Check the Volume Control found in the task bar. Make sure that you haven't accidentally checked the *mute* box thinking it was the *select* box from the Record Control (I do this all the time).

Why doesn't my recording device seem to record anything when connected directly to the mixer?

Have a look at your connection. There's a good chance that you didn't connect the Record Output to the Line In on the recorder.

If that isn't the case, ask yourself three questions:

- ✔ Did you accidentally use the Booth Output to send to the recording device, but turned the Booth Output volume off? If so, switch the cables over to Record Out, which is preferable to turning up the booth output.

- ✔ Is the input level control on the recording device switched to accept the Line input, and turned up to an appropriate level?

- ✔ Does your recording device need to be in *Record mode* in order to register any input? This isn't a common case on home tape and MiniDisc recorders, but on a lot of professional equipment, if a CD/DAT/MiniDisc is in the machine, you need to press the Record button on its own to get the device into record mode (the machine only starts recording when Record and Play are pressed together), which tells the electronics to accept a signal in rather than just play a signal out.

Part III
The Mix

The 5th Wave   By Rich Tennant

"He's taught me all I know about scratching."

In this part . . .

DJ skills are two-fold. Beatmatching is the core skill of the electronic dance music DJ – all DJs who play this genre of music need this skill. Chapter 12 in this part tells you all you need to know about beatmatching.

The second part of your DJ skills are the most important, and apply to all genres of music – choosing the tunes to play, the order to play them, and how and when to mix between them.

If you want to add another layer of creativity and performance to the mix, scratching is covered in Chapter 16, with guidance on how to start your journey as a creative DJ or a dedicated scratch turntablist.

Chapter 12

Grasping the Basics of Mixing

In This Chapter

▶ Discovering the essence of club DJing

▶ Working out the tempo of your records – beats per minute

▶ Finding the first beat of the record with confidence

▶ Starting your records so the beats play in time

▶ Using the pitch setting to match tempos of records

▶ Getting to grips with headphone cueing techniques

*D*Js play music. They play music that people want to dance to, and play music that keeps them on the dance floor. As a DJ, if you can't do that simple thing, you're not going to be a big hit with the crowd.

Club DJs employ a technique called *beatmatching*, which makes the bass drum beats of two different records play at the same time. That way, when they change from one record to another, the people on the dance floor don't have to adjust their dancing rhythm.

In this chapter, you discover all the tools and skills you need to beatmatch. The secret of successful beatmatching is simple: good concentration and lots of practise – no special tricks required. The great news is that once you've made the investment of devoting your time and concentration to mastering beatmatching, the skill sticks to you like glue.

Knowing What Beatmatching's All About

Matching beats is a very simple concept, but it's the core skill of every club DJ. Although certain kinds of music don't lend themselves to beatmatching (rock music, for example) if you want to play in a club where the DJ is expected to beatmatch records to mix them together, you'd better develop the skill!!

Practice makes perfect

Practice makes a huge difference when developing your beatmatching skills. If you practise for two hours a night, you should be 75 per cent as good as anyone else at beatmatching by the end of one week – it's the last 25 per cent, perfecting it, that takes time to develop.

As you become more comfortable with your records and turntables, you'll probably take a month or so before you get the beats matched quickly without having to rush it or 'guess' in order to start the mix before the other record runs out.

You may take months, maybe even years to achieve perfect beatmatching and be confident that 99 per cent of the time, you have the beats matched accurately and that they stay locked together for the duration of the mix. Just remember that during all that time spent practising, you get to listen to the music *you* love and the music *you* want to hear.

Through the course of a night, a DJ gradually makes the music play faster and faster until it reaches what I call the *sweet spot*. This sweet spot occurs when the bass beat from the music matches the speed of the heart beats of the people dancing. This speed can be anything between 130 and 145 beats per minute for most club music, but can be more depending on the music genre.

When the speeds of the pounding bass beats and the thumping heartbeats get closer and closer, the combination of pulsating rhythms begins to do strange things to the body and emotions of the people on the dance floor. This euphoric moment is commonly signified by a *hands in the air* moment on the dance floor. It makes me sweat a bit, but that's just me . . .

Importantly, even if you consider this phenomenon as some kind of voodoo mind control, you need to understand that you have to play at a tempo where people are comfortable dancing, are really enjoying themselves, and the night has a great energy to it.

Understanding BPMs

Beats per minute (BPMs) are a way to describe how fast (known as the *tempo*) your records are. The name gives it away; the BPM is the number of beats that occur in one minute.

As a *very broad* generality, house music has a BPM between 110 and 130 BPM, trance music ranges mostly between 130 and 145, and hard-house and happy hardcore can be well in excess of that.

Calculating BPMs

When you try to beatmatch two different records, knowing the BPM of each tune helps you make an educated guess about how much to adjust the *pitch control* (which is what you use to change the speed of your tunes).

You can adopt two main approaches for counting BPMs:

✔ **Use a beat counter.** A beat counter is a useful DJ backup tool that automatically calculates and displays the BPM of the tune for you. Stand-alone counters that calculate the BPM of what you're listening to in the headphones, or that you plug the individual channels into, cost between £70 and £200. If you're thinking about BPM counters, and you haven't chosen your mixer yet, it makes good financial sense to look at a mixer with built-in BPM counters. Instead of buying a basic mixer and an expensive BPM counter, the combined money lets you afford a really good mixer with built-in BPM counters.

✔ **Calculate the BPM yourself.** The free approach. It doesn't take long, and is easy to do. Set the tune to 0 pitch and get a stopwatch ready. Hit start, and count how many bass beats you hear for 30 seconds. If you counted a beat as you started the watch, subtract one and double the figure – that calculates the beats per minute for that track.

For example, if you counted 67 beats in 30 seconds and counted a beat as you hit start, the BPM would be 66 x 2 = 132. If you counted 60.5 beats in 30 seconds, and started counting after you started the stop watch, the BPM would be 60.5 x 2 = 121 BPM.

You can count the beats for an entire minute of course, but you'll probably find that the difference between the 30 second and 60 second count isn't noticeable enough to warrant doing it for longer.

If you can get into a routine of calculating the BPMs of your records as you buy them, you'll always be on top of your calculations.

Don't count your life away

I used to spend a full minute calculating the BPM because I wanted to be sure that I was *really* accurate. Eventually, I figured that by the time I'd counted 120 records, an extra hour of my life was used up for no real reason! I'd rather have spent that hour mixing.

After you've been DJing for a few months, you find you don't have to worry about knowing exact BPMs any more. After a while, you'll not only develop the skill to tell instantly if a tune is faster or slower than the one playing, but you'll also develop a memory of the general tempo of your records before you play them and won't need to refer to calculations.

Discovering How to Beatmatch

Your choice of format doesn't matter – CD, vinyl, MP3, or anything else – the mechanics of beatmatching are the same. It's just the controls that are different.

Vinyl DJing is the skill that's most easily transferable to other formats, so as I take you through how to match beats, I reference using turntables. Chapter 15 covers the mechanics of using CD equipment, and most DJ computer programs emulate the controls on CD equipment, so Chapter 15 is also relevant to computer DJs.

Setting up your equipment

A few basic settings and requirements can help you master the fundamentals of mixing comfortably:

✔ Make sure that your DJ setup is switched on and hooked into an amplifier (check out Chapter 11 for more on connecting up). Don't worry about headphones for now; you get to them later.

✔ Use two copies of the same record (preferably something that has a simple, constant beat from the very beginning). The reason for using two copies of the same record is that when both pitch controls on the turntables are at 0 (known as the *green light* area), they both play at exactly the same BPM. This fact means that you don't have to worry about one tune playing faster than the other, and makes getting to grips with starting your records and keeping them in time a lot easier.

✔ Set your mixer so that you can hear both records at the same time and at the same volume. (Typically, this requirement means moving the cross fader into the middle, and setting both of the vertical channel faders to maximum, with the gain and EQ (equaliser) controls set the same on both channels). The reason you set the mixer to hear both records at the same time is so that you only have to worry about working with the tunes – you don't waste time and concentration trying to adjust the controls on the mixer. This method may sound messy while you're starting out, and your dog may leave the room, but don't worry – you'll move on to proper mixing soon, and the dog needs some exercise.

Locating the first bass beat

Every journey begins with a step, and every beatmatch begins with a beat. To start with, find a tune with a solid, clear bass beat right from the beginning. (In a perfect world, all records would start with a constant bass beat, making beatmatching a lot easier.)

Whether you've chosen a record with the beat at the beginning, or if you've picked a record that has its first beat 45 seconds in, the following points can help you locate the first bass beat so that the needle is *cued up* (ready to play) at the very instant the first beat is about to play:

- **Listening for the beat:** The first option is to simply start the record from the beginning and wait until you hear the first beat. Place your finger on the record to stop it playing when you hear the first beat, and play it backwards by hand. As you play the record backwards, you hear the part of the record you've just heard playing in reverse. (Don't be overly concerned about revealing any Satanic messages when doing this; dance music doesn't tend to contain any.) If you use a tune that starts with a beat from the very beginning, the last thing you hear playing backwards is the first beat. The instant that beat goes silent is where you want to leave the needle.

- **Winding to the beat:** If you're impatient or in a rush, you can turn the record around really fast with your finger until your hear the *'brrrrrrrrrrp'* noise of beats playing really fast, then play the record backwards until you find the very first of those beats.

- **Looking for the beat:** Take a close look at a record, and you can see a lot of different shades of grey and black rings (the target light on your deck shows up this shading). The darker parts of the record means that it doesn't have as much information cut into the groove and is likely to not contain a beat. Look at the beginning of the record where the rings change from dark to light – the lighter shaded area contains more sound information, and is probably where the beat starts. Place the needle where the dark and light rings join. If you can hear the beat, spin the record backwards until the beats stop, if you still hear the introduction, play the record forwards until you find the first beat.

    If you have a *wave display* on your CD decks, which has a series of peaks and troughs to show the louder and quieter parts of the tune, refer to your wave display to find where the big peaks begin – that's likely to be where the beats start. (For more on CD deck functions, check out Chapter 15.)

No matter how you choose to locate it, make sure that the needle is waiting patiently at the very beginning of that first beat, press stop, and get ready to start your tunes!

'For an Angel' – for a new DJ

For years, I've used the same record when helping people develop their DJ skills: Paul Van Dyk's 'For an Angel'. It's quite an old tune now and, to be honest, my two copies of it are getting extremely worn (especially at the beginning). The reason I love to use this track is that it has really clear, solid-sounding bass drums throughout, and the bass beats start at the very beginning.

Starting your records in time

When you're happy with finding the first beat on the record, go to the other turntable and get ready to start. (I'm left handed so I seem to always start on the left.)

1. **Place your finger on the outer inch of the vinyl.**

   Notice I didn't say *press* – just place your finger, you only need a little pressure.

2. **Press the Start button.**

   Due to the wonder of slipmats, the turntable turns underneath the record while you're still holding it (if it doesn't, shame on you for buying cheap equipment).

   Now the easy part.

3. **Take your finger off the record.**

   Glorious music should now flood through your speakers.

4. **While the record is playing, listen to it.** Don't simply *hear* it – take a moment to really listen to what's happening (this is called *listening with an active ear*). Really concentrate on listening to the bass drums.

   You should pick up that the bass drum has two different sounds. One of them is just a bass drum on its own, and the other one is normally the bass drum combined with another sound (sometimes a *clap* – or a snap sounding drum called a *snare drum*). Listen – notice the difference in emphasis between the first beat of the bass drum (represented by X in my DJ beat notation that follows) and the second beat of the bass drum (represented by XO to show that's X combined with another sound):

   X   XO   X   XO   X   XO   X   XO

5. **When you're comfortable with the sounds of the beat, move over to the other turntable, check that the pitch control is at 0, press Start on the turntable, and hold the record still while the deckplatter turns underneath it.**

   The first beat that you've located on your tune and are ready to start from is normally the bass drum on its own. What you're about to try is starting this first beat at the same time as the tune that's currently playing through speakers also plays a bass beat on its own.

   Have a listen again. Make sure that you know what bass beat sound you want to start on. At this early stage, you may find that counting the beats in your head is helpful: '1 – 2, 1 – 2, 1 – 2,' or '*bass – snare, bass – snare, bass – snare*'

   The record is poised, ready to go; the deckplatter is still spinning underneath; you're now sure that you know the sound of the beat you want to start on.

6. **So let go.**

Chances are, one of three things happen.

- ✔ **You get it right first time – both beats are playing at the same time.** Well done! Give it a few more goes to make sure that you've really got the knack.

- ✔ **In your haste, you let go too early and the two bass beats sound like a galloping horse when they play together.** Don't worry, it's easily done. Take the needle off, find that first beat again, and have another go.

- ✔ **You're over-cautious, wait too long, start the tune too late, and the beats sound like a trainwreck together.** Again, very easily done. Just go back to the first beat and try it again.

Deciphering drum patterns

Although most house/club music follows a pounding bass beat, not all dance music has this simple and basic rhythm. Drum patterns are as varied as the music they accompany, ranging from a simple bass/snare beat to the complicated patterns of drum and bass and jungle. Different music genres are often distinguished as much by their drum pattern as by the music.

The drum pattern alone is enough to be able to recognise breakbeat, R&B, or 2-step garage.

If you're interested in finding out more about drumming and drum patterns, I heartily recommend *Drumming For Dummies* (Wiley) by Jeff Strong.

The good news is that a small timing error may not be all your fault. Before you get too frustrated at not getting your records to start in time, check out a couple of external factors:

- ✔ **Give a little push.** You may find that waiting too long happens more often than not, which is common and happens to the best DJs. The good news is that the delay may be nothing to do with when you let go of the record but more to do with the motor in the turntable.

  In your attempt to start the beats in time, even though the slipmat was doing its job, and the deckplatter was still turning underneath the record, if you just lifted your finger off the record to start it playing, the motor can still take a fraction of a second to get the turntable up to full speed.

  The more powerful the turntable's motor, the quicker it gets up to speed, but even the best of decks can introduce a tiny delay. (All you CD DJs are allowed a smug smile at this point.)

  To get around motor lag, don't just let go of the record, give it a gentle push, too. How much of a push you have to give the record is just as much a knack as starting it at the right time, but like everything else with beatmatching, you'll get the knack with practice.

- ✔ **Make sure that you've really got that beat!** The other common cause of not starting the beat in time is not having the needle at the very beginning of the first beat.

  To get used to finding exactly where the beat is, play a couple of inches duration of the record backwards and forwards through the needle, as if you were scratching slowly. The record will make a *Boom – woomp – boom – woomp* noise as you rock it back and forth.

  If you perform this rocking (scratching) motion at the same time as the other tune plays its bass beats, you'll find your timing for when you eventually release the record improves. Scratch forward when the other tune only plays a bass beat, and backwards as the other tune plays the bass and snare beat. Then, when you eventually start the tune, all you have to do is let go (rather than pull the record back again).

  This rocking motion can also help if you've chosen a record which has a first bass beat that isn't a solid thump playing on its own with no other music. With all the noise around you in a DJ booth, you can have difficulty hearing that first beat if it isn't a solid *Thump*. By rocking the beat back and forth through the needle, you're giving your brain more information to help it pick out the bass sound from all the other noise.

  Try this rocking technique a few times as you practise starting the record in time. You'll be amazed at how quickly you get used to *working the vinyl* (a fancy-pants way of saying using and touching the record). Your parents may have told you never to touch records and to treat them with care, which is right for their Beethoven LPs, but not for DJing. Moving the needle off and on the record, finding the first beat and starting it playing at the right time all go toward making you more comfortable with your DJ tools.

Adjusting for errors

When you make a timing error starting the beats, starting over again is perfect when you're developing your skills, but it isn't how experienced DJs deal with errors. Try starting the beat again – but from now on, if you make a timing error, use the following methods to bring the records *back in time* (make the bass beats play at the same time):

✔ **Starting too soon:** If you started the new record too early and its bass beats are playing before the bass beats on the tune that you're trying to match the beats to, you need to temporarily slow the new record down a little to get it in time. Lightly place your finger on the dimpled ring running around the side of the spinning turntable to add a little friction.

This added friction slows the speed at which the turntable turns and eventually slows the record down enough so that the beats play at the same time. When the beats now play in time, take your finger off the dimples to return the record to normal speed. The amount of pressure to add to the dimples takes a little getting used to, and if you're ticklish, try not to giggle – it doesn't look professional!

✔ **Starting too late:** When you start the record too late, and the beats on the new tune play after the one you're trying to match, you can try a couple of methods to speed up the record. One of them is to tightly grab the turntable's *center spindle* that pokes through the record with your thumb and middle finger and turn that around to make the turntable turn faster than normal.

Another (my preferred method) is to place your finger lightly on the label at around the 6 o'clock position, and push that round to help the record play faster.

Do try to be gentle when making these timing adjustments. If you press down too hard on the side of the turntable, it will grind to a halt! Or if you push the label around too hastily, you may knock the needle out of the groove, or zip forward through the tune by 20 seconds!

Nerves and carelessness don't mix

I remember my first night playing live in front of real people (eek!). I was so nervous that when I tried to speed up the record by pushing the label, my hand slipped and I ripped the needle right across the record (which is why I now start at the six o'clock position, nowhere near the needle!).

Fortunately, you tend to only do this kind of thing once . . . it's incredible how quickly you learn from a mistake like that!

You can use another method to fix a starting error, which involves temporarily increasing or decreasing the pitch control to alter the speed of the tune, then, when the beats are back in time, returning the pitch control to where it was originally set. However, if you don't return the pitch control to exactly where you moved it from, the beats start to drift apart and play out of time. The only time you're guaranteed to return the pitch back to the correct place is if it was originally set to 0 pitch, because the pitch control clicks into place or lights up green when at 0 pitch. However, 99 per cent of the time, you won't have set the tunes anywhere near 0 pitch originally.

Experiment with all the methods and find the one that you're most comfortable with. Importantly, you need to find the error adjustment method that suits you the best, giving you consistent, positive results.

Knowing which record to adjust

When you need to alter the speed of a tune to make the beats go back in time, you almost always adjust the tune that isn't playing through the speakers yet – the *cued track*, which you normally listen to in your headphones. If you were to speed up or slow down the *live* track that people can hear, they'll start shouting 'Sack the DJ!' (a phrase that strikes fear into the heart of any DJ). If both tunes are playing through the speakers when you're in the middle of mixing one tune into the other, adjust the quieter of the two tunes.

There are cases (usually a tune with a constant note playing) where speeding up or slowing down the quieter tune sounds terrible because of the pitch 'speed-bump' to the notes playing, but practice will give you the experience to know which one to change.

Using the Pitch Control

After you're comfortable starting your records in time (see the previous section 'Starting your records in time'), the next step in beatmatching is to follow the same process, using the same records, but this time, one of the records starts off playing at a different speed to the other one so you can get used to working with the pitch control.

At this stage of getting to grips with beatmatching, the advantage of using the same two records as in the first exercise is that you can compare the pitch controls to help you match the turntable speeds. The downside is that you still play the same tune over and over. Don't worry, you'll move on to other tunes soon.

Matching the pitch setting

The pitch slider on a turntable (and CD and MiniDisc decks) is numbered to show the percentage increase/decrease of the turntable rotation, and therefore the percentage change of the original BPM of the tune. On Technics 1210 MkII turntables, the pitch slider is 0 when in the middle, + 8 when moved closest to you, and -8 when moved away from you to the furthest point (this assumes you don't have your turntables sideways for scratching – see Chapter 16).

The numbers on the pitch control are *not* how many BPMs you may add or subtract. If you play a 130 BPM tune and set the pitch control to +4, you're not adding 4BPM, you're adding four per cent to the original BPM. Four per cent of 130 is 5.2, which means the 130 BPM tune now plays at 135.2 BPM.

Here's an example of how to calculate where to set the pitch control on the *cued track* (the track you've lined up to play next) in order for it to match the *live track* that's currently playing through the speakers to the crowd:

- ✔ **The live track is a 130 BPM track with its pitch set to +2 per cent.** This data means that the record is running at around 132.5 BPM (2 per cent of 130 BPM is 2.6, which I round down to 2.5 BPM).

- ✔ **The cued track is 138 BPM.** You therefore need to take around 5.5 BPM off this record to make it close in BPM to the live track. Because it's best to deal in rough estimates with the first adjustment to the pitch control (see 'Taking your eyes off the pitch control' later in this chapter), this BPM drop means taking the pitch control down to around -4 per cent to slow it down enough.

Following that simple piece of maths, you're very close to matching the beats of both tunes, and only have to fine-tune the pitch setting to get the bass beats to play perfectly in time.

Rather than read theory on how to use the pitch control, go back to your turntables, and try to following method with the same identical tunes:

- ✔ Slide the pitch control on your live track to about +3 per cent. (The numbers on Technics turntables go up in twos, so set the pitch slider between 2 and 4 if you have one of these.)

- ✔ Start the *cued* track (remember, this is still set to 0 pitch and is an identical tune to the one you've just set to +3 per cent) on the bass beat and you'll notice that the beats start to drift apart and play out of time very quickly.

✔ Fortunately, you can cheat by looking at the other pitch control. Because you can see that the other tune is set to +3 per cent, you know that you need to set the pitch on this identical tune to the +3 per cent mark in order to get the records running at the same speed. After you change the pitch, have another shot at starting the beats in time.

This is all just for practise – when you use different tunes, you won't have the visual guide of looking at the pitch control on the other turntable to know whether you need to speed up or slow down the new tune. You may get lucky and set the pitch exactly the first time, but you'll probably find that the beats start to drift apart after 10 seconds or so, because even though you've moved the pitch control to the +3 per cent mark, the pitch control may not be totally accurate.

At this point, things start to get a little tricky. You need to be able to tell whether the cued track is running too fast or too slow in order to make the beats play in time again. You work this status out by listening to the sound that the bass drums make together.

Playing too slow or too fast

Knowing when a tune is playing too fast or too slow is *by far the hardest part of DJing*. This question is the one that I most commonly get asked, and the hardest thing for a lot of new DJs to figure out. If you can hear that a record is slipping out of time before anyone else can and if you can react to it and fix it before anyone hears it, you'll be as good at beatmatching as any top-class DJ.

The reason people new to DJing have difficulty making this judgement is that they haven't spent the time to train their ears to listen out for the audio clues that provide the answer. These audio clues are *B'loom* and *l'Boom*. Spend time practising the following method, and listen to, and concentrate on the sound that plays when a tune is running too fast or running too slow.

In order to be able to tell whether your cued track is playing too slow or too fast, you need to change your mixer setting so that the live track's channel fader is set to about three-quarters of the volume of the cued track's channel.

You've made this change because you need to identify when the cued track's bass beat hits. If both tracks played at full volume, you wouldn't know what beat was playing first (especially because at the moment they're currently both the same tune!). Having one louder than the other helps you distinguish one from the other.

I've discovered that the best way to describe what to listen for is by using onomatopoeic words (words that you can associate with sounds): *l'Boom* and *B'loom*. (Please bear with me here . . . I haven't gone mad.)

Simply, when the cross fader is in the middle, the cued tune is beating away at full volume: *Boom Boom Boom Boom . . .*

The live tune is playing quieter than the cued track; instead of sounding like a loud *Boom*, it's a softer *loom* sound: *loom loom loom loom*. (Honestly, bear with me, it does makes sense when you put this into practice.)

So the two sounds you hear that let you know whether to speed up or slow down the cued track are:

- ✔ **B'loom:** When the louder tune (in this case, the cued tune) runs too fast, you hear its beat first – and the sound you hear is: *B'loom, B'loom, B'loom, B'loom.*

- ✔ **l'Boom:** When the cued tune is too slow and plays after the live track, it sounds like: *l'Boom, l'Boom, l'Boom, l'Boom.*

Being able to hear the sounds of both bass drum beats with all the rest of the music playing takes a fair bit of concentration, but spend a little time practising and you'll realise that I'm not as mad as I sound.

Go back to your decks and start trying to match the pitch settings. Listen carefully to the sound that the bass drums are making. Listen especially for *l'Boom* or *B'loom*, and try to work out whether your cued track is running too slow or too fast.

If you got it wrong and have slowed down a track that was already running too slow, that's okay! Just remember the sound that you heard that made you think that it was running too fast and re-associate that with running too slow.

This technique takes practice, and you may want to adopt a trial-and-error approach for a while. Go back to 0 pitch on both of the records, slow one of them down, and listen to the sound the bass beats make – then speed one up, listen to *that* sound, and take note of the difference.

Taking your eyes off the pitch control

When you're used to hearing the different sounds that a record makes when it's running too fast or too slow, the next step is to adjust the pitch control without looking at where the other turntable's pitch control is set, using only your ears as your guide.

Using the same identical records, increase the pitch control on the live record but this time with something covering the reading, so you know that it's increased, but you can't cheat by looking at where the pitch control is set to. A bit childish I know, but you're cheating days are done.

To match the pitch control on the cued turntable to this new setting, I consider four different ranges of adjustment:

✔ Large, rough adjustments to get somewhere close

✔ Medium adjustments (about 1 – 2 per cent on the pitch slider) to get closer

✔ Small adjustments (about ¼ of 1 per cent) to finalise it

✔ Minute adjustments (millimetres) for fine tuning during the mix

For example:

✔ If the cued record starts to run too slow immediately, speed it up by about 4 per cent.

✔ If it then runs a little too fast, but not as fast as before, reduce the pitch by about 1 per cent.

✔ If it's now taking about 10 seconds to run noticeably too slow, increase the pitch by about ¼ of 1 per cent.

✔ If you're almost there, but after 20 seconds you start to hear '*B'loom*' (the louder, cued record is running too fast) – slow down the record by the tiniest amount. Nudging the pitch control to move by only a millimetre is sometimes all that it takes.

Practising happy

Always think about the fact that you're spending the time practising because you want to be a DJ – and you want to be a DJ because, as well as a lot of other things, DJing really is a heck of a lot of fun.

If you start to get a little frustrated as you try to develop any of your beatmatching skills, take a step back, get a glass of water (anything stronger may inflame matters!), and come back to your set-up with one thought in mind – to have fun. Don't tape yourself, don't try to be something you're not, don't sweat it. Just play some music and smile like you mean it!

Introducing Your Headphones

When you start the record and set the pitch control (see the preceding section), you can play both records through the amplifier at the same time and listen to the live sound to find out whether you managed to get the beats in time. Sadly, you don't get that option when mixing to tape, or to an audience, so I think that it's time to take the stabilisers off and start to work out if the beats are *in sync* (play at the same time) through your headphones from now on. Your neighbours and dog will thank you for this.

Switching over to headphone control

In order to start making best use of the headphones, your mixer needs to be set up so that no matter what you do with the cued track, you only hear the live track playing through the amplifier's speakers, and you only start to hear the cued track playing through the speakers when you move the cross fader toward the cued track's channel.

Set your mixer to these settings:

- ✔ Cross fader all the way over to the live track's side.
- ✔ Headphone cue switched to the cued track.
- ✔ Gain controls and EQ settings on both channels set identically (so both records play at the same volume, with the same amount of bass/mid/ high frequencies playing).
- ✔ Both channel faders at maximum.

The last setting is for ease of use while you're developing your skills, as this, along with the EQ and Gain settings, maintains an identical playout volume for both identical records. As you get better as a DJ, you'll find that setting the channel faders to maximum can cause volume problems. (See Chapter 14 for more information.)

If you are unsure of how any of these settings affect the sound through your mixer, or for detailed explanations of the different cueing options, refer to Chapter 8.

Cueing in your headphones

Making the pitch adjustments to the cued track in the headphones while listening to the live track through the speakers is not an easy thing to do at first. *Cueing* in your headphones (finding where you want to start in a track and also setting the pitch control during the beatmatching process) is another key skill of beatmatching that once gained, stays with you forever. Think of the following techniques as a bit like patting your head and rubbing your tummy, or juggling four chainsaws. Though not quite as dangerous.

Cueing with single ear monitoring

The most popular way to cue in the headphones is called *single-ear monitoring*. Quite simply, one ear is covered by the headphones playing the cued track, and the other ear is left clear to listen to the live track through the main speakers. This way, you can hear both tracks and compare them in your head.

Cueing with headphone mix

A *headphone mix* can be used as an extension to *single-ear monitoring*, or it can be used with both ears of the headphones on to check that the beats are playing in time.

When *single-ear monitoring* with the cued track playing at a good volume in your headphones, the headphone mix lets you play the live track quietly over it (what I call *bleeding in*) so you can hear the *B'loom, l'Boom* bass beat clues (see the earlier section 'Playing too slow or too fast') in the ear with your headphones on.

With the cued track playing louder, if you hear *B'loom*, the cued track is running too fast, if you hear *l'Boom*, your cued track is running too slow. When you get half way through the mix, and the cued track is now the louder tune through the speakers too, you may wish to swap the headphone cue controls so that the cued track becomes the live track and is now the quieter one, and the old live track now plays louder in the headphones (and becomes the cued track). This now means that when you hear *B'loom*, the tune you are mixing out of (which is now the cued track) is running too fast, and when you hear *l'Boom*, it's running too slow – which is the opposite of when you started the mix.

Apart from helping to spot the *l'Boom* and *B'loom* indicators, the other advantage of a headphone mix is that you can do a trial mix with both ears of your headphones on before letting anyone hear it. Some records just don't play well with others, and listening to a mix first in your headphones can be a great safety net for preventing a poor choice of tunes to mix together.

You may even find that you're happier with both ears of the headphones on when checking the beats are in line. The *B'loom* and *l'Boom* indicators may be easier to hear through both ears, rather than single ear monitoring.

If you are going to check the beats and maybe even perform the mix with both of your ears inside the headphones, periodically take them off, just so you can hear the music playing to the dance floor. You may think that you're performing the best mix in the world, when in reality, the people on the dance floor can only hear distortion and noise.

Headphone mix isn't a vital option on the mixer, but every little bit helps – especially when beginning!

Cueing with split cue

Another headphone monitoring option is *split cue* where one ear of the headphones plays the cued signal and the other ear plays the live signal.

This technique is almost identical to single ear monitoring (see the earlier section), where one ear is in headphones and one ear open to the live sound, except that the live sound is a lot clearer through headphones than from the speakers on the dance floor.

Centre your head with stereo image

Listening to two tunes at the same time, and comparing if their bass beats are playing together takes a lot of concentration. Your brain isn't normally in situations where it needs to listen and react to two things at the same time, and it tries to shut one of them out, so listening to two tunes at the same time may take some getting used to. The trick to getting this method right is how you set the volume in your headphones.

Loss of hearing aside, the main reason to keep your headphones set to a sensible volume is that you need to match the volume to what's playing in your *other* ear.

When you put your headphones on both ears to listen to music, you notice that the music seems to be playing in the middle of your head. This sensation is known as the *stereo image* and is the voodoo magic of stereo sound (see Figure 12-1).

If you monitor the live and cued track using single ear monitoring, the perfect volume to set your headphones to is when you've created a similar *stereo image* in your head between the live speakers and the headphone. (Or if you use split cue, match the volume in one ear of the headphones to the other ear – the same principle applies here.)

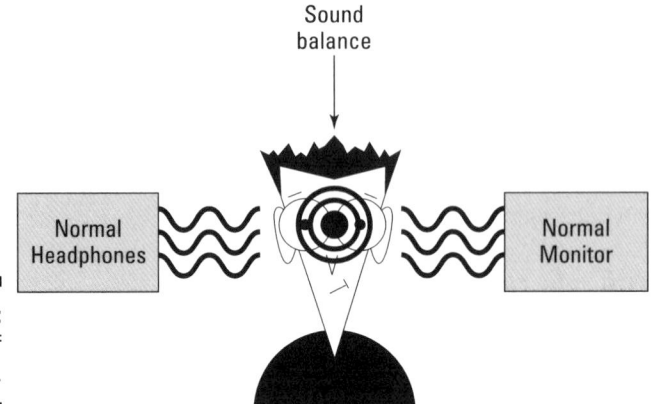

Figure 12-1:
The joy of
stereo.

If the headphone or the loudspeaker is louder than the other, it becomes the
more dominant sound, throwing off the balance of the stereo image so that
your brain finds concentrating on both records much harder to do. Figure
12-2 gives you an idea of this imbalance.

Figure 12-2:
When the
loudspeaker
is louder,
the music
ends up off
centre.
When the
headphone
is too loud,
the stereo
image is off
centre in
the other
direction.
The stereo
image is
perfect
when both
volumes are
the same.

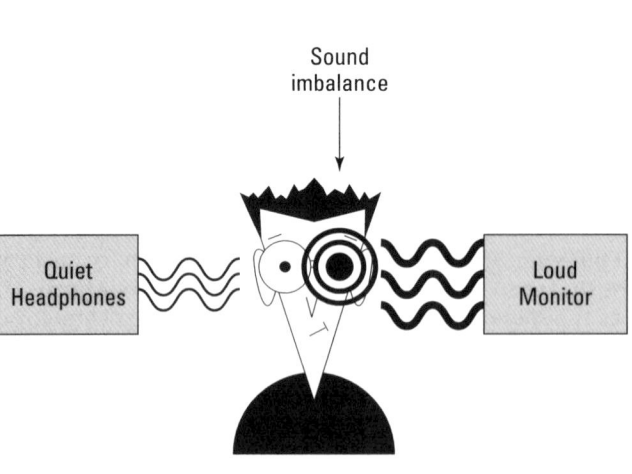

This technique can be adopted in reverse and is why you turn up the TV volume when you're being nagged at home – when the TV is louder, it's harder to hear the nagger!

When listening to two copies of the same record, you really get the chance to feel what I'm on about in regards to stereo image. Set both records to 0 pitch, start them playing at the same time (you're great at that now I trust) and adjust the headphone volume louder and quieter. Close your eyes and listen where the sound appears in your head. When you have a balance of volume between the live speaker and the headphone, the music creates a near perfect stereo image in the middle of your head.

You won't often have the need to mix the same tune into itself (check out Chapter 14 for examples of good reasons why you might though) and when you play different tunes, they won't create a perfect stereo sound in your head. However, the bass beat is the key. Even though the rest of the tune is different, all you need in order to create a stereo image in your head to concentrate on is the bass beat.

If you're having difficulty concentrating on the bass beats, or if the tune you're playing doesn't have a solid '*BOOM BOOM BOOM BOOM*' bass beat, listen to the snare beat instead (the clapping/snapping sound that normally follows the bass drum). The snare drum is a sharper, clearer sound that some people find they can more easily pick out from the rest of the tune.

Practising with your headphones

There's no right or wrong method for cueing in your headphones. The headphone cueing section on your home mixer can have an enormous effect on your cueing style, as does the room or club you're playing in. I suggest that you practise how to beatmatch with single ear monitoring first as it's the most common technique, but choose the method you prefer and make sure that you're 100 per cent happy with it.

Knowing how to use all three kinds of headphone cueing makes you a well-rounded DJ. If you can only mix using single ear monitoring for example, the first time you play in a club that doesn't have a monitor in the DJ booth, and you get a delay that's caused by the distance between the main speakers and the DJ booth, you're going to struggle. If you're faced with that occasion and if the mixer has the option, if you know how to mix with a split cue in the headphones, you're prepared for such a problem.

To get used to using your headphones to monitor your tunes, go back to your DJ setup and if you haven't already, set the mixer so you can hear the live track through the speakers and the cued track through your headphones.

Go back to the basics of starting the record (as the section 'Locating the first bass beat', earlier in the chapter, describes), and match the pitch settings of the two identical records, all the time listening to the cued track in your headphones and the live track through the speakers.

When you're confident with cueing in the headphones and can comfortably tell if the beats are in time this way, you can start creating long mixes without the beats of the tunes drifting apart, and can spend more time creating impressive, professional-sounding mixes.

Chapter 13

Picking Up on the Beat: Song Structure

In This Chapter

▶ Understanding how songs are constructed

▶ Introducing beats, bars, and phrases – and a certain sheep

▶ Working out where you are in a tune

▶ Relying on your memory and instincts

▶ Trying it out on a sample structure

*B*eing a good DJ means getting yourself a split personality. So one half of you plays great tunes, in the perfect order; and the other half of you creates the perfect mix from tune to tune.

You need more than straightforward beatmatching to create the perfect mix. How you adjust the EQs (equalisers) and overall sound level changes the dynamics of a mix, but the most important factor is choosing which parts of your tunes to mix over each other.

Your knowledge of beat structures kicks in at this stage. Starting from the simple bar, which grows into a phrase, which blossoms into a verse; songs are mapped out in an extraordinarily ordinary fashion.

When you crack the code of how a tune is constructed, your instincts take over, you don't need to think, and you can effortlessly create smooth transitions through your set that gets you praise for your skills.

For further guidance and information on understanding beat structures listen to the audio files on my Web site (www.recess.co.uk) that accompanies this book.

Why DJs Need Structure

The simplest of mixes involves playing the introduction of a new tune over the last part (the *outro*) of the tune you wish to mix out of. In order to start this mix in time, the DJ needs to know when the outro is about to start. By analysing how beats and bars are put together to make up verses, choruses, introductions and outros (all of which are described in detail in the section 'Studying Song Structure' later in the chapter) you won't miss a beat.

Knowledge of beat structure is vital for all kinds of DJs. Whether your style is to create minute-long, seamless transitions from tune to tune, or you simply start one tune as another ends, an understanding of how a tune is put together enables you to mix without any risk of gaps in bass drum beats, drops in the fun and energy of the night, or even worse – silence.

For more information on how different parts of tunes overlap to alter the sound and energy of the mix, check out Chapter 14.

Multiplying beats, bars, and phrases

Just as a wall is constructed from hundreds of bricks layered on top of each other, and then added to other walls to make a house, the beats in a tune are grouped together, and added to further groups, and these groups are joined together to make larger structures, all of which are part of a bigger whole – the song. But before you start looking at how walls make a house (or how verse and choruses make a tune) you need to know how a wall is built – or a chorus is created – out of beats and bars. If you can count to four, you can easily deal with beat structure, because the building blocks of nearly all tunes you'll encounter are grouped into fours:

- ✔ Four beats to a bar
- ✔ Four bars to a phrase
- ✔ Four phrases to a verse (normally)

Although typically made up of four phrases, the length of a verse can change depending on the decision of the songwriter.

The easiest way to explain how four beats become a bar, and four bars become a phrase is with song lyrics. Unfortunately, I'd have to pay a lot of money if I wanted to use the lyrics to a recent, famous song, so I use the nursery rhyme 'Baa, Baa, Black Sheep' to show how the *magic number 4* multiplies beats into bars and phrases.

To demonstrate the principle that you get four beats to a bar, look at the first line of the nursery rhyme, which is 'Baa, baa, black sheep', and lasts one baa (sorry, *Bar*) in length. Each one of these words is sung on a different beat of the bar, and the first word has more emphasis than the next three.

The drum beat that accompanies this bar follows a basic pattern of 'Bass' – 'Bass/Snare' (check out Chapter 12 for more), as you can see in the following:

Beat 1 – *Baa* (bass drum)

Beat 2 – *baa* (bass drum and snare)

Beat 3 – *black* (bass drum)

Beat 4 – *sheep* (bass drum and snare)

Moving further into the nursery rhyme, this first bar is the first of the four bars that make up the first *phrase*:

Bar 1 – *Baa, baa, black sheep,*
Bar 2 – *Have you any wool?*
Bar 3 – *Yes sir, yes sir,*
Bar 4 – *Three bags full.*

This first phrase is grouped together with three others to create 16 lines (and therefore 16 bars) and create a full *section*.

Baa, baa, black sheep,
Have you any wool?
Yes sir, yes sir,
Three bags full. (End of Phrase 1 – 4 lines/bars in length)

One for the master,
One for the dame,
And one for the little boy
Who lives down the lane. (End of Phrase 2 – rhyme is 8 bars to here)

Baa, baa, black sheep,
Have you any wool?
Yes sir, yes sir,
Three bags full. (End of Phrase 3 – rhyme is 12 bars to here)

One to mend the jerseys
One to mend the socks
And one to mend the holes in
the little girls' frocks. (End of Phrase 4 – total rhyme duration is 16 bars)

Take another look at the 16 lines in the nursery rhyme. Although four different *phrases* make up the entire rhyme, the first two and the second two phrases can be grouped together as two different parts of the rhyme. Both halves start with the identical '*Baa, baa, black sheep, have you any wool, yes sir, yes sir, three bags full*' phrase, but the next phrase is different.

You find the same principle in music; the second half of a verse may sound very similar to the first half, but in the final, fourth phrase, the sounds, drums, and energy of any vocals or instruments increases to let you know that you're approaching the end of the entire verse rather than the end of the first half.

Hearing the cymbal as a symbol

Not all songs have lyrics to follow that let you know where you are in the tune. Even though music without lyrics sometimes has a change of the melody through the different phrases, you may need a little more guidance to help you pinpoint your position. If you've just dropped the needle, or started the CD at a random point in a record with a view to starting a mix, you need to know how to work out where you are in a 4-phrase (16-bar) pattern.

Luckily for DJs, record producers are very kind people, and tend to leave *end-of-phrase markers* (commonly cymbal crashes) at or after the end of phrases.

The four phrases given in the '*Baa, Baa, Black Sheep*' example have three key, different types of endings:

- ✔ The end of the first and third phrase (probably identical)
- ✔ The end of the second phrase (the halfway point)
- ✔ The end of the fourth phrase *(the most powerful)*

The end of the first and third phrase is likely to have a cymbal crash as a simple punctuation point to the end (often on the fourth beat of the fourth bar), but nothing too special.

The end of the second phrase, the halfway point, has a little more to it, because that first half exists as a discreet part of the story. This ending probably has a small change to the drums, such as a mini drum roll, and end with a cymbal crash on the fourth beat, or the first beat of the next (ninth) bar.

The end of the fourth phrase is the important one. This *end-of-phrase marker* lets you know that the tune is about to move on to a new section, from a verse to a chorus, a chorus to a breakdown, or a breakdown to a verse, and so on. It is similar to the halfway marker, but more pronounced and powerful. The drum roll is longer, the vocals have more depth, and the energy is a lot higher.

Everything changes

Markers at the end of each phrase are common in some genres of music, but don't rely on this fact; markers at the end of Phrases 1 and 3 aren't always provided. Knowing your tunes inside out really helps you at this stage.

If the tune has lyrics, then recognising the lyric cues for the end of phrases – when you've listened to the tune enough times – is relatively easy.

For a tune without lyrics, listen to how it changes from phrase to phrase, even without these end-of-phrase marker points. The main hook may start over, the melody may have a key change, another instrument may be introduced, another drum sound or synthesised sound may be added, or you may pick up on a general *shift* in the volume or power of the music made by the addition of filters/compressors, a feeling to the music rather than something that you can actually hear and define.

Clever producers try to bend the rules, and play with what we expect to hear, but in most tunes out there, *something* changes, or is added every four bars.

Counting on where you are

Start one of your tunes playing, listen to it, and try to hear how the beats build into bars, bars build into phrases, phrases into halves of verses like the nursery rhyme, and then how the verse moves into the next part.

To help you get to grips with this, start from the very first bass beat, and as the music plays, count along with the beats, as shown in Figure 13-1:

Figure 13-1: Counting along with the beats.

BAR	1				2				3				4			
BEAT	1	2	3	4	1	2	3	4	1	2	3	4	1	2	3	4
SAY	ONE	two	three	four	TWO	two	three	four	THREE	two	three	four	FOUR	two	three	four

Count the bar number as the first beat of the bar. The point of counting this way is simply so that you know which bar you're on.

Remember that the first beat of the bar has more emphasis to it, so when you're counting the beats, put more energy into saying the first number '*ONE two three four – TWO two three four*', and so on. At the end of the first phrase (four bars) of the tune that you're playing, listen to what happens. On beat 4 of the fourth bar, or beat 1 of the next bar, you're likely to hear a cymbal crash, or some kind of sound that acts as the end of the phrase. The marker sound for this first phrase is likely to be the same for all the first phrases of a section throughout the rest of the tune.

Carry on counting and listening to how each phrase ends, and take special care to compare how each of the phrases end, and how this indicates where you are in the 16 bars.

Keep listening to the entire tune because the opening section (the intro) may only be eight bars long. As you listen to the rest of the tune, use your knowledge of phrase lengths, and remember the different end-of-phrase marker styles to help you decide what makes up the intro, verse, and the chorus, all of which I describe in detail in the following section 'Studying Song Structure'.

Don't forget to be an active listener, (really listen to what's playing, rather than sitting back and enjoying the music) and concentrate on the sounds that you're hearing: drums, vocal samples (an '*Oh yeah*' at the end of a bar is a good indicator!), changes in melodies or the bass line, any strange whoosh or other electronic noises – any of these sounds can be the markers that the songwriter has left, to let you know where you are in the tune.

When you've cracked the beats/bars/phrases formula of how a tune is put together, when you can identify the different end-of-phrase markers, and when you've developed these instincts to be able to tell when the music is about to change, you find that you no longer need to count out beats and bars.

I can't stress strongly enough that you should try to move away from *counting beats* as quickly as possible. Developing a reliance on beat counting in order to mix well can stifle your creativity and may end in disaster. Not only do you risk looking like 'Rain Man' when you count the beats and bars as they roll by, but if something happens to throw your concentration, and you don't know where you are in the tune, the potential to create a nightmare mix is too big. Dedicate the time and concentration to develop the memory and the skill that enable you to listen to a track halfway through and know where you are within one or two phrases.

Studying Song Structure

The people on the dance floor aren't really interested in how songs are made, although they do anticipate and respond to the different parts of the music – just as you need to, too. As a DJ, you have to know when the tune is playing a verse, a chorus, or a breakdown – even if there aren't any lyrics. Combined with knowledge about how beats and bars are grouped together to make verses and choruses, you'll have all the information you need to create seamless, error-free, professional-sounding mixes.

Introductions, verses, choruses, breakdowns, and outros (the end of the tune) are the different groups of bars and phrases that go together to create an entire tune:

- ✔ **Introduction (or intro):** The part at the very beginning of the tune before the main tune starts. It can be as long, or as short as a piece of string but usually consists of a multiple of 8 bars in length, with normally a change or addition of instrument or sound every 4 bars. At the end of the intro, and audio clue (build up, drum roll or cymbal crash sound) is included letting you know that it's about to end.

  The most DJ-friendly intro lasts for at least 16 bars, and is made up of just drum beats for the first 8 of them. The second set of 8 bars may start to introduce music such as the bass line to the tune. This type of intro is extremely useful for the seamless, beatmatching DJ – Chapter 14 tells you why, and how to deal with different types of intros.

- ✔ **Verse:** In tunes with lyrics, each verse usually has different lyrics. If the tune has no lyrics, it's harder to discern, and though it may contain the main musical *hook* (the part of the tune that you hum in the shower), it won't be too powerful and energetic. In most cases, the verse lasts for 16 bars, and is split into two sets of 8 bars where the melody repeats itself, but builds up through to the end of the 16th bar.

- ✔ **Chorus:** The part in the tune that normally has the same lyrics each time its heard. In tunes without lyrics, this is the most energetic, catchy, and powerful part of the tune. The chorus is usually based around the melodic *hook* of the tune. It's shorter and more powerful than the verse at only 8 bars (two phrases), and lifts the energy of the track (and the dance floor). You may find that a *marker cymbal* is included to crash between the two phrases, and it has a build-up out of the second phrase.

Even music without lyrics still has a verse and chorus. What you find is that the main *hook* (the catchy part) that runs through the tune is quite subdued in one part, and then powerful, energetic, and obvious in another part. The subdued section is the verse of the tune, and the more powerful *full-on* section is the chorus.

✔ **Breakdown:** The part where you can have a little rest. It's a transition/ bridge from the end of the chorus to the beginning of the next part.

If a breakdown is included very early on in the track, it's likely to be quite short, and is known as a mini-breakdown. It can be 8 bars long or as short as 4 bars.

To create a nice bridge out of the chorus and back into the next verse, breakdowns tend to be less powerful. The bass drums drop out, and the bass melodies and a reduced version of the hook to the tune (the catchy melody that repeats a lot) plays. The last bar has a build-up, like the end of a chorus or verse, and you may hear an indicator on the last beat of the bar, or the first beat of the next bar, to let you know that it's changed to a new part.

The main breakdown probably lasts twice the duration of any mini-breakdown already in the tune, but is typically 16 bars in length. It follows the same sound design as the mini-breakdown, but has longer to get in and out, probably has less sounds and instruments to begin with, and includes a crescendo (a build-up, like a drum roll with the instruments getting louder and faster) for the last 2 bars or entire last phrase.

✔ **Outro:** The part you listen to before the next song starts. Chances are that the last major element before the outro is a chorus. This chorus either repeats until the end (which is a DJ-unfriendly fade out) or you have a DJ-friendly outro.

The best kind of outro is actually a reverse of the intro. The intro starts with just beats, introduces the bass line, and then starts the tune. If, after the last chorus, the music distils into just the drums, the bass melody, and a cut-down version of the main melody for 8 bars, and then the next 8 bars are the drums and maybe the bass melody, you have 16 bars on hand that make mixing into the next tune easy (head to Chapter 14).

Outros can last for a *long* time, though. Every 8 bars, another element may be stripped off, until all you have is the hi-hat and the snare drum. Rather than a waste of vinyl (or bytes), this type of outro is extremely useful if you like to create long, over-lapped mixes.

These main blocks of the song are linked together by repetition, and yet even more repetition. The next verse and chorus tend to be much the same as the first two. If lyrics are used in the song, different verses have different sets of lyrics, but the chorus probably won't change. Although the structure, melody, and patterns remain the same, the music may introduce new sounds or effect processing to the original verse/chorus to create a new *depth* to the tune (changing the sound slightly gives the listener a feeling of progression through the tune).

As the breakdown drops the energy of the tune to its lowest point, a lot of songwriters like to follow it with a chorus – the most energetic part of the tune. Once again, more instruments and sounds may be introduced to give the chorus a slightly newer feel.

Depending on how long the tune is, the main breakdown may be followed by more verses, choruses, and mini-breakdowns.

Accepting that Every Tune's Different

We'd soon get bored listening to tunes that were designed to the same structure, even if the music was all different.

In music production, altering the length of an intro, adding extra verses or choruses or changing their length, adding breakdowns and mini-breakdowns, and extending outros are all part of what makes a tune unique when still following the basic *four beats to a bar, four bars to a phrase* structure.

The brain is an incredible organ. When you listen to a track with an active ear, after three or four run throughs, your brain remembers the basic structure of the tune, and then relies on triggers (such as the markers, vocals, or even just looking at the different shades of rings on the record) that help you remember the structure of that track along with the 1,000 other tracks in your collection.

The trick to getting your brain to work for you is to listen to your music a lot. You can't expect to know the structure of a tune immediately; you need to listen to it a few times. Practising your mixing skills gives you the opportunity to get to know your tunes, but I recommend copying your tracks to an iPod/tape/MiniDisc/CD so that you can listen to your music at any time.

Always listen with an active ear to the structure, the melody, the hook, and the lyrics. Your brain stores all this information in your subconscious, calling upon these memories and your knowledge of how a tune is constructed from bars and phrases, ensuring that you never get confused during the mix.

Developing Your Basic Instincts

Your memory and instincts for your music develop in the same way as they do when you drive a car. When driving, you don't have to think '*Accelerate . . . foot off a little . . . steer . . . straighten up . . . brake . . . clutch . . . check mirror . . . change to third . . . clutch . . . change to second . . . accelerate*', and so on, you just do it. You develop your instincts as a driver through practice and experience. It's exactly the same with DJing.

You know that the first beat of the bar is emphasised, you know that the melody or line of a lyric is likely to start on the first beat of a bar, and from listening to the tune, you know the kind of *end-of-phrase markers* that a certain tune uses at the end of a phrase, at the end of half a phrase, and when it's about to change to another element like a verse or chorus.

In the *Baa, Baa, Black Sheep* example given in the earlier section 'Multiplying beats, bars, and phrases', when you hear '*Have you any wool?*', your instincts tell you that you're in the second bar of either Phrase 1 or Phrase 3, because you know the lyrics so well.

The lyrics in the phrase that follows tells you what half of the verse you're in, so if the next phrase begins '*One for the master*', you know that you're only in Phrase 2 – but if you hear '*One to mend the jerseys*', you know that it's Phrase 4.

However, try to listen for the different end-of-phrase marker that can tell you if you're just halfway through the verse, or about to enter a new part of the tune so you don't have to rely on remembering a vast range of lyrics. Songs without lyrics are exactly the same, except you have to listen for the changes in music and instruments, rather than the changes of lyrics.

Listening to a Sample Structure

After you know how beats become bars, and bars multiply like rabbits (or sheep for that matter!) to become verses and choruses, the best thing you can do is to go through the structure of an entire tune, and then describe each part in a bit more detail.

In my Web site to accompany this book (www.recess.co.uk), you find a section that contains some audio examples. When you finish reading this chapter, I recommend that you download one of the tunes. Listen to it, and try to hear not only what happens to mark the change from the larger parts of the tune, but also what happens every four and eight bars. The following structure may help you discern the structure of the sample tune:

- ✔ **Intro:** 16 bars
- ✔ **Verse 1:** 16 bars (4 phrases)
- ✔ **Chorus 1:** 8 bars (2 phrases)
- ✔ **Mini breakdown:** 8 bars
- ✔ **Verse 2:** 16 bars (4 phrases)
- ✔ **Chorus 2:** 8 bars (2 phrases)
- ✔ **Breakdown:** 16 bars
- ✔ **Chorus 3:** 8 bars (2 phrases)
- ✔ **Verse 3:** 16 bars (4 phrases)
- ✔ **Chorus 4:** 8 bars (2 phrases)
- ✔ **Chorus 5:** 8 bars (2 phrases)
- ✔ **Outro:** 16 bars

Chapter 14

Mixing Like the Pros

In This Chapter

▶ Selecting the best placement points in your tunes

▶ Using your mixer's controls to their full potential

▶ Reaching the next level of beatmatching

▶ Mixing tips for different genres

*I*n this chapter, you build on your beatmatching skills (refer to Chapter 12) so that you can mix the tunes at the correct point, and use the controls on the mixer to make the transition from tune to tune as smooth and skilful as possible. The mixing techniques in this chapter take time, experimentation, and practice to get right before you can use them creatively. Understand the core concepts, but don't be bound by them, and discover the moments when breaking the rules is a good thing.

Recording your practice sessions when experimenting with the following techniques can be useful. In the heat of the moment, you may think that something didn't work, but when you listen back, it actually turned out great! Try anything, and if it sounds good to you – others may like it, too.

Check out my Web site (`www.recess.co.uk`) that accompanies this book for examples of the techniques mentioned throughout the chapter.

Perfecting Placement

From Van Halen to Van Morrison, Silicon Soul to Soul to Soul, most tunes that you play follow the basic building blocks described in Chapter 13; four beats to a bar, four bars to a phrase, and multiples of eight bars to a *section* (a section is an entire intro, verse, chorus, and so on, and typically lasts for eight or sixteen bars). One tune may have more choruses than another, or a longer intro, monster length breakdowns or extended outros, but this structure knowledge makes creating the perfect mix easier for you.

The perfect mix begins with *perfect placement*. Placement is simply the choice of what parts of the tunes you mix over each other. Perfect placement occurs when both tunes start or end a section at the same time – not only are the beats of both tunes matched, but their structural changes match too. If the tune you want to mix out of (Tune A) is about to change from a chorus to its outro, an example of perfect placement would be to start the new tune (Tune B) so that its change from intro to verse happens on the exact beat that Tune A changed.

Intros over outros

If Tune A has a 16-bar outro, and Tune B has a 16-bar intro, simply overlapping the intro and outro is an option, but often intros and outros have no melody and are just a simple bass drum and *hi-hats* (the 'tchsss' sounding cymbal sound). Sixteen bars of that though can sound dull, unprofessional, and boring. Figure 14-1 shows an example of a better sounding transition, where Tune A has two 8-bar choruses before the outro. You can create an overlap with the 16-bar intro of Tune B playing over the two choruses (marked Chorus 1 and Chorus 2) of Tune A. Then the outro of Tune A plays over the verse of Tune B.

In all the figures in this chapter, numbers in italics mean that the tune is at a lower volume, and numbers change size as the music fades in or out (gets gradually louder or quieter). Bold numbers mean playing at normal volume.

Figure 14-1:
16-bar intro
of *Tune B*
playing over
the last two
choruses of
Tune A.

Tune A:	**Chorus 1** | **Chorus 2** |	**16-bar outro**	
Bars	**12345678**|**12345678**|	*12345678*|*12345678*	|
Tune B:	**16-bar intro**	| **Verse**	
Bars	*12345678*|*12345678*|	**12345678**|**12345678**	|

If both tunes had vocals in the chorus and verse, ending the vocal on Tune A, then Tune B's vocals starting instantly may seem a little too quick. In this case, create a little rest, or an anticipation of what's to come. To introduce this pause, start Tune B at the end of Chorus 1, at the start of Chorus 2. This later starting point creates an 8-bar rest while the outro of Tune A mixes with the intro of Tune B, and then the verse of Tune B begins (see Figure 14-2).

Figure 14-2:
The outro
of Tune A
mixes with
the intro of
Tune B.

Tune A:	Chorus 1	Chorus 2	16-bar outro	
Bars	1 2 3 4 5 6 7 8	1 2 3 4 5 6 7 8	1 2 3 4 5 6 7 8	*1 2 3 4 5 6 7 8*
Tune B:		16-bar intro		Verse
Bars		*1 2 3 4 5 6 7 8* 1 2 3 4 5 6 7 8	1 2 3 4 5 6 7 8	1 2 3 4 5 6 7 8

Ideally, the outro of Tune A or the intro of Tune B is more than just plain drum beats. A bass melody or subtle background noise is enough to keep interest going in this mix for 8 bars. A 4-bar *rest* is better if there are only drum beats.

Melodic outro

Not all tunes have pounding bass beats from start to finish. Some have moody, beatless, melodic outros that sound great over an intro with a strong beat.

In Figure 14-2, the intro was slowly faded up to sneak into the mix. However, if you want to keep a constant beat going by mixing 16 bars of beat intro over 16 bars of beatless melodic outro, you have to start Tune B so that it instantly plays at full volume.

If *Tune B* has a good build-up out of the intro, and into the verse, you can keep *Tune A*'s outro playing at near to full volume until the end, then fade it out on the very last beat before *Tune B*'s verse starts (check out Figure 14-3).

Figure 14-3:
Tune B's
beat intro
mixes over
Tune A's
beatless
melodic
outro.

Tune A:	Chorus 2	16-bar melodic outro	(Tune A has now ended)	
Bars	1 2 3 4 5 6 7 8	1 2 3 4 5 6 7 8 1 2 3 4 5 6 7 8		
Tune B:		16-bar bass beat intro	Verse	
Bars		1 2 3 4 5 6 7 8 1 2 3 4 5 6 7 8	1 2 3 4 5 6 7 8 1 2 3 4 5 6 7 8	

Mixing beat intros over beatless melodic outros means you can't afford to make a starting error – you have to start the beat precisely in time. Spend lots of time practising starting records so they're instantly heard to develop the confidence to start the beats on time, every time, without needing any error correction. (If you need to go back to the basics of starting tunes, check out Chapter 12). Waiting one or two beats to check that you're in time, and then quickly moving the cross-fader to the middle (or worse, fading in the beats) makes the mix sound terrible, unprofessional, and usually ruins it (and your reputation). This technique is a lot easier for CD DJs who only need to press a button.

If you're not confident with the instant start or don't want to mix the full 16 bars of intro over outro, start the beats of Tune B at the beginning of Chorus 2 (8 bars before the outro of Tune A begins) to make sure that your timing is immaculate. Then move the cross-fader to the middle after 8 bars, as Tune A hits the outro (see Figure 14-4). You can also slowly mix in the beats using the EQs (equalisers) through Chorus 2 to smooth the transition (see 'Balancing it out with EQs' later in the chapter).

Figure 14-4:
Using the cross-fader to fade out Tune A's outro over the verse of Tune B.

Tune A:	**Chorus 2**	**16-bar outro**	
Bars	1 2 3 4 5 6 7 8 | 1 2 3 4 5 6 7 8	| 1 2 3 4 5 6 7 8 *(very quiet, if not out completely)*	
Tune B:	**16-bar intro**		**Verse**
Bars	| 1 2 3 4 5 6 7 8 | 1 2 3 4 5 6 7 8 | 1 2 3 4 5 6 7 8		

Melodic intro

The reverse of melodic outros is a bit tougher, because mixing an intro with no beats means that with no drums to keep time, when the beats in *Tune B* eventually start, you risk them playing at a completely different time to the beats from *Tune A*.

If the intro has a melody or a very soft rhythm, concentrate on that. Tapping your feet with this rhythm can help to keep your concentration. Practise this mix as much as you can, as when you do it live, all the noise and distraction in the DJ booth can mean that you end up with a train wreck of a mix!

Mixing Breakdowns

You don't have to play a tune from the very beginning to the very end. Mixing two breakdowns over each other, or an intro over a breakdown can sound great, and lets you shorten a really long tune. (Chapter 13 has more on breakdowns and mini-breakdowns.) Here are a few combinations to try:

✔ **Breakdown over breakdown:** No matter whether your breakdowns are 8-bars or 16-bars long, if both are the same length, start *Tune B's* breakdown as *Tune A's* breakdown starts, then gradually fade and EQ out *Tune A* so all that's left is *Tune B's* breakdown that's about to build up into the beats again. (See Figure 14-5.)

✔ **Mini-breakdowns:** As breakdowns are normally at least halfway through a tune, you may not want to start *Tune B* at that point, as it'll cut out so much of the tune. Have a listen through the track, an 8-bar mini-breakdown may be in the first half of *Tune B*, probably after the first chorus, or it may be right after the intro, used as a way to emphasise the start of the main tune. In which case, try this (See Figure 14-6):

Figure 14-5:
Two breakdowns mix over each other to skilfully introduce the new tune.

Tune A:		Breakdown	
Bars		1 2 3 4 5 6 7 8	1 2 3 4
Tune B:		Breakdown	Verse/Chorus
Bars		*1 2 3 4 5 6 7 8*	1 2 3 4 5 6 7 8	1 2 3 4 5 6 7 8	1 2 3 4 5 6 7 8

Figure 14-6:
A mini-breakdown introduces a new tune early on rather than halfway through.

Tune A:		Breakdown	
Bars		1 2 3 4 5 6 7 8	*1 2 3 4 5 6 7 8*
Tune B:		Mini-Breakdown	Verse/Chorus
Bars		1 2 3 4 5 6 7 8	1 2 3 4 5 6 7 8	1 2 3 4 5 6 7 8

✔ If you start *Tune B* 8 bars earlier so that you mix out halfway through *Tune A*'s breakdown, you add a feel of urgency and pace to the mix (See Figure 14-7):

✔ **Beat Intro over breakdown:** This method, shown in Figure 14-8, is identical to starting a *beat intro* over a *melodic outro* (see Figure 14-3). You need the confidence to start Tune B with the cross-fader open to carry the beats through the breakdown. However, because this is a natural breakdown in Tune A, you can fade in Tune B's beats if you use the EQs to kill the bass before starting the fade (see 'Controlling the Sound of the Mix' later in the chapter for information on EQs). The hi-hats from Tune A keep a rhythm going and you can quickly bring the bass in halfway through the breakdown. How well this method works and how good it sounds greatly depend on the tunes that you're using.

In that example, if you're still not confident starting the beats with an open cross-fader, start Tune B in the same place, wait until the end of the eighth bar, then quickly move the cross-fader to the middle. A sudden introduction of beats can sometimes sound a bit jarring however, so you can try killing the bass and gradually fading Tune B in over the first 8 bars of Tune A's breakdown.

Figure 14-7:
By not letting Tune A finish its breakdown before mixing fully into Tune B, you achieve a great sense of urgency.

Tune A:		16-bar Breakdown		(last 8 bars	
Bars		1 2 3 4 *5 6 7 8*		are silent)	
Tune B:		Mini-Breakdown		Verse/Chorus	
Bars		*1 2 3* 4 5 6 7 8		1 2 3 4 5 6 7 8	1 2 3 4 5 6 7 8

Figure 14-8:
Beats from Tune B start instantly as Tune A enters its breakdown.

Tune A:		Breakdown	
Bars		1 2 3 4 5 6 7 8	1 2 3 4 5 *6 7 8*	
Tune B:		16-bar intro		Verse/Chorus	
Bars		1 2 3 4 5 6 7 8	1 2 3 4 5 6 7 8	1 2 3 4 5 6 7 8	1 2 3 4 5 6 7 8

These examples are the simplest, most basic placement principles to take into consideration when mixing your tunes. You can mix your tunes in thousands of different ways depending on where you start *Tune B* from, and where in *Tune A* you start the mix. Change where you start Tune B backward or forward by 8 or 16 bars, experiment with how soon or late to mix out of Tune A.

Listen to your tunes with an active ear for all the audio clues and markers (refer to Chapter 13) that let you work out the best places to mix in and out of your tunes.

Controlling the Sound of the Mix

After you've mastered the mechanics of beatmatching and know the best places to mix in and out of your tunes, your true creativity comes from controlling the sound of the mix. The cross-fader, the channel-faders, and the EQ controls on your mixer are the salt and lemon to your tequila, the candlelight to your dinner, and the chocolate to your chilli; they all add extra zest and finesse to the mix. (I'm not kidding – add a little chocolate to your chilli – it's lovely.)

Bringing the cross-fader into play

How fast you move the cross-fader from one tune to another can dramatically alter the power of a mix. Smoothly moving from one tune to the other over the course of 16 bars can be very subtle. Chopping back and forth from tune to tune adds a sense of immediacy, which can be really powerful at the right moment. These methods work with the right tunes, but if all you do is whip the fader across quickly for each mix, you'll come across as a DJ who can't hold the beats matched for a long time and needs to mix out quickly.

Don't forget that every mix has two halves. You're not only bringing in a new tune, the old tune still needs to be taken out. Apply the same care and attention when moving the cross-fader to fully mix out of a track, as you do when mixing in the new track.

A cross-fader move that lasts four beats or less is hard to get wrong, just time the move from one side to the other to last four beats (you'll be at the halfway point by the second beat). Moves that last longer than four beats need a bit more of a pattern and control to them.

The way to approach longer mixes is to move the cross-fader so that the increases occur on the hi-hat *tchsss* sound in between the bass drums. This method helps to hide the increase in volume from the new track, and makes taking out the old tune less noticeable. The *cymbal crashes* and *build-ups* are great places to hide larger moves of the cross-fader. When something from either tune adds impact, move the cross-fader a further distance than the move before. If you suddenly hear the mix starting to sound messy, move the cross-fader back a bit, and let the music play for a bar without any increase (provided you have time in the tunes to do so).

You can also use crescendos and temporary bass beat drop-outs to disguise your cross-fader moves. A *crescendo* is a fancy way of saying *build-up*. A four-beat crescendo is over quite quickly, so you may want to have the two tunes mixed together for a couple of phrases beforehand with the cross-fader still favouring Tune A (the outgoing tune). Then during the four beats of the crescendo, move the cross-fader over so that the new tune is dominant, and the old tune is playing in the background. When to finish the mix is up to you.

The opposite is just as appropriate. Instead of a build-up, the last four beats of a phrase may have no bass drum beat. Instead of playing the new tune lightly in the background, keep it silent, then just as the last beat of Tune A's anti-build-up plays (at the end of the phrase), quickly move the cross-fader over to the new tune. Moving the cross-fader all the way over in one beat can be an incredibly powerful mix, or you can move the cross-fader so that it favours the new tune (about three-quarters of the way across) and kill the bass on the outgoing tune to keep it subtly playing in the background (see the section 'Balancing it out with EQs' for info on EQ control).

Discovering the secret of channel-faders

Channel-faders are lonely little fellows. Lots of DJs put them up to full and leave them there forever. But these vertical faders have a secret, undercover role that many DJs don't tap in to.

The primary role of the channel-fader is to work in conjunction with the gain control to control how loud the music from a channel plays out of the mixer. (If you're unsure of how to make this adjustment, check out Chapter 8.) With the input levels matched for both channels, you need to decide where to set the channel-faders when you want the tunes to play at their loudest.

DJs quite commonly set up their mixer so that the channel-fader needs to be set to its highest point (sometimes marked 10) for this optimum play out volume. For scratch DJs, this setting is correct, and very important so that they can just flick up the fader to be at full volume, but for beatmatching DJs who try to keep the volume of the mix a smooth constant from start to finish, this isn't the best way to set up the mixer.

The best way to set up your mixer is so that your channel-faders are set at three-quarters of the way to maximum (around 7 if your fader is marked from 0–10). Using this technique means that when you mix in the next tune, if the tune is a bit too quiet even though the levels looked correct, you can quickly raise the channel-fader to compensate for the lack of volume.

Letting you in on a big, curvy secret

Cross-fader curves affect how much one tune gets louder and the other one gets quieter as the cross-fader is moved from side to side (you can find examples of cross-fader curves in Chapter 8). However, sometimes the curve isn't subtle enough for a smooth, seamless mix and can cause the two tunes to play too loudly over each other, sounding messy and unprofessional. So you need to find a way to gain more control over the output of each tune during the mix. The channel-faders release you from the strict constraints of the cross-fader curve.

For a simple mix that gives you precise control over each tune's volume try the following:

1. **Set the channel-fader on the new tune (Tune B) to one-quarter of its loudest point.**

2. **When you're ready to start mixing in the new tune, move the cross-fader into the middle, following the techniques described in the section 'Bringing the cross-fader into play' earlier in this chapter.**

3. **Start to raise Tune B's channel-fader, continuing to increase it in time with the hi-hats.**

4. **Keep an eye on the output meters, and an ear on the sound of the mix, and as the Tune B gets louder, slowly lower the channel-fader of the outgoing tune (Tune A) until the Tune B is dominant, and Tune A is playing at a volume that is best for that moment in the mix (likely to be similar to where the channel-fader was when you started Tune B).**

5. **When you want to fully mix out Tune A, move the cross-fader all the way over to Tune B's side.**

How you change the positions of the channel-faders, and the time you take to do so, is up to you. You can simply raise one fader while lowering the other, or wait for the Tune B's channel-fader to be halfway up before you start lowering Tune A's fader. Make the adjustments depending on your own personal style, the output levels and what sounds best with the two tunes you're using.

If you prefer, you can leave the cross-fader in the middle (or turn it off if you have that function) to bypass the cross-fader function all together. This option gives you ultimate control over the individual volumes of your tunes during the mix. The only difference to the previous method is that you start with the channel-fader at 0 for the incoming tune (Tune B), and end with the channel-fader at 0 for the outgoing tune (Tune A).

Balancing it out with EQs

As with channel-faders, *EQs* have multiple roles. The first role is sound control; affecting how the music sounds on tape or to the dance floor. You can also use EQs to add some variation and spice to a tune. Check out the section 'Cutting in' later in this chapter. But their most useful role is in smoothing the sound of the mix. Good EQ control can't do anything about a poor choice of tunes to mix together, but great EQ control can turn a passable mix into an incredible one.

Smoothing a transition with the bass EQ

The bass EQ is the one that you use most to create an even sound through the mix. When both tunes play with their bass at full, even if one tune is quieter than the other, the bass drums are too powerful and the bass melodies combine to sound messy.

The simplest but most effective technique is to *kill* the bass (reduce it to or near to, its lowest point) on the incoming tune when you start to mix it in, and when you want to make this tune the dominant one, increase the bass EQ at the same time as decreasing the bass EQ on the tune that you are mixing out of. This manoeuvre means that the amount of bass you hear through the speakers stays the same; the bass is simply coming from a different tune.

With the right tunes, taking your time over this swap can create a subtle, unnoticeable mix. Or, swapping the EQs in one beat can cause a *hands in the air* moment to emphasise a change in key (see Chapter 17), a change in the power of the mix, a change in genre, or to introduce the bass line from a tune that you know the crowd will love.

Taking the edge off with the mid-range and high-end

Despite the fact that the high frequencies aren't as loud and obvious as the bass frequencies, they're just as important in controlling the sound of the mix. Two sets of loud hi-hats playing over each other can sound just as bad as two sets of bass drums and bass melodies. The technique is exactly the same as the bass EQ, except you don't need to cut the high EQ nearly as much. For example, on my Pioneer DJM-600 mixer, I find that the twelve o'clock position is normally the best place to leave the EQ for normal play-out. When I want to cut out the high EQ to help the sound of the mix, I only need to move the knob to around the ten o'clock position (rather than the seven o'clock position for the bass EQ).

As the mid EQ covers a larger range of frequencies, how much you use this technique depends on the tunes you're playing. You may not need to swap over the mid EQs if there isn't a noticeable clash of sounds, or you may even find that rather than cutting the mid EQ, you want to boost it. Sometimes, when the outgoing tune is playing quieter, I boost the mid-range to play just those frequencies louder than normal. If you have a melody or sound repeating in the background of the tune, this emphasis can lengthen and strengthen the mix.

Always keep an eye on the meters and an ear on the sound of the mix while you're swapping any EQs. Strive to keep an even sound as the two tunes play over each other. If one tune is too loud, or both tunes have too much bass or high frequency, you may create a cacophony of noise.

Using Mixing Tricks and Gimmicks

Tricks and gimmicks are great to use once in a while as they add surprise, and a little pizzazz to your mix. Avoid over using them, however, because the listener may think that you only use them because you can't mix between tunes properly. They're best used as transitions in to a new *chapter* of the mix, an increase in energy, a change in genre, a key change, or even just a change in tempo.

With each technique, experiment with how long you take to move the cross-fader and where the cross-fader is positioned when you start the trick. Start by setting the cross-fader so that you can't hear the next tune until the start of the move, then find out what it sounds like if you have the cross-fader in the middle when you start the move. Give thought to volume control as well because some of these tricks really don't like to be performed with the channel-fader at maximum – you may deafen the dance floor, and can blow a speaker!

Spinbacks and dead-stops

Try out a technique called a *spinback* – abbreviated *SB* in Figure 14-9. Beatmatch and start a mix between two tunes with perfect placement (see 'Perfecting Placement' at the beginning of the chapter) so that the tune you want to mix out of (Tune A) ends a section as Tune B (the new tune) begins the first phrase of a section. On the very last beat before this change, place your finger on Tune A and spin the record back, sharply. As the tune spins backwards, close the cross-fader over to Tune B within one beat, as shown in Figure 14-9:

Figure 14-9:
The
spinback is
performed
on the
fourth beat
of the fourth
bar, then
instantly
mixes into
Tune B.

| Bar 1 | Bar 2 | Bar 3 | Bar 4 | Bar 1
Tune A: |**1 2 3 4**|**1 2 3 4**|**1 2 3 4**|**1 2 3** *SB*|*SILENT*
Tune B: |*1 2 3 4*|*1 2 3 4*|*1 2 3 4*|*1 2 3 4* | **1 2 3 4**

To perform a *dead-stop*, instead of spinning the record back in the example above, press the Start/Stop button on Tune A (the one you're mixing out of). This action makes the tune stop playing in about one beat (unless your decks have a function to change the 'brake speed' and you've set it to last longer). As with the spinback, move the cross-fader over to Tune B by the time it plays the first beat of the new section (so the move only lasts one beat).

Power off

A *power off* is when you turn off the power to the turntable (normally located bottom left with the red strobe light underneath it). When you turn off the turntable, it gradually gets slower and slower, until it stops.

Power off is a great trick in the DJ booth if you have good lights, and some-one who knows how to use them. Ask your partner-in-mayhem to kill the lights at the same time as you do the power off. Chances are, everyone will think '*Power Cut!!*'. After a few seconds, slam in the next tune at the most powerful point, at full volume, as the lighting jock floods the dance floor with as much light as possible. This trick takes the dance floor by surprise, and – you hope – really jazzes them up. It's very clichéd, but at the right time, works a treat.

A cappella

If you have an instrumental track that you think would sound better with something else over the top of it, look for an *a cappella*, a separate vocal track without any instruments behind it.

The problem with using vocals is that you need the vocal to be sung in the same key as the instrumental you want to play it over, otherwise it sounds out of tune. This makes speeches and other spoken words a great alternative. I have a copy of JFK's inaugural speech that I love to mix over long instrumental tracks. The line 'Ask not what your country can do for you' is an incredible introduction into the most powerful parts of a tune.

Don't get so involved in your new creation that you forget to mix in the next track. Your blend of a 'Learn Italian' lesson over a great instrumental may be going down really well, but if you run out of time to beatmatch and mix in the next tune, you've wasted your time.

A third input device (CD/turntable/laptop) in your set-up lets you play the a cappella over the instrumental, beatmatch the next tune, and start the mix with the a cappella playing the whole time. You can also use an audio program to pre-mix the creation on computer, burning it to CD to play later. However, the spontaneous performance side of the live new mix is often what makes it special.

Cutting in

Cutting in beats from another tune gets its roots from *beatjuggling* (see Chapter 16). The idea is to beat match two tunes, and move the cross-fader between them to temporarily *cut in* beats from one tune over the other. In the right hands, this method can be incredibly fast and complicated. Figure 14-10 shows a basic, slow pattern (underlined numbers are the beats you can hear):

Figure 14-10:
Various beats from Tune B are 'cut in' to Tune A to add power and a new feel to the tune.

```
           | Bar 1 | Bar 2 | Bar 3 | Bar 4 | Bar 1 |
Tune A:   |1 2 3 4|1 2 3 4|1 2 3 4|1 2 3 4|1 2 3 4|
Tune B:   |1 2 3 4|1 2 3 4|1 2 3 4|1 2 3 4|1 2 3 4|
```

You don't have to move the cross-fader all the way over when cutting in beats, you can go three-quarters of the way across so that you can still hear the original tune. I find placing a finger at the three-quarter point helps this, because you can just bounce the cross-fader off your finger – it stops the cross-fader getting any further than three-quarters of the way across, no matter how fast or hard you cut in the other tune.

A variation on cutting in beats is *cutting out* frequencies of the tune. Dropping the power out of the bass for the last bar of a phrase before it changes to a new element can be extremely effective, and using it when the crowd is extremely excitable and energetic can blow the roof off the club. Which is no mean feat if you're in the basement!

Mixing Different Styles of Music

Some genres of music don't rely on rules like beatmatching and perfect place-ment in order to get from tune to tune. The music is more important than the mix, but making the transition from one tune to another does take a special skill. You still need these techniques as a beatmatching DJ; you may need these skills to change genres, take over from someone else, or change the feel of the mix.

The wedding/party/rock/pop mix

In many ways, the transition between tunes is a lot harder for the wedding/party/rock/pop DJ. A beatmatching DJ has the safety net of simply matching the beats, and then fading between tunes, with no fade out, no sudden start, no change in tempo, and no drastic genre change. The wedding/party DJ needs to work with all these issues.

The important part of this mix is where in the new tune you start. Tunes like 'Brown Eyed Girl' by Van Morrison (a wedding favourite) that have a power-ful, instant start are great to work with. As the outgoing tune is fading out, start the opening bass melody of 'Brown Eyed Girl' at full volume, then quickly fade out the outgoing tune within one or two beats. You can wait for a natural fade at the end of a track, or if you don't want to wait that long, fade the outgoing song down to about 50 per cent of its current volume, then start the new track at full volume.

If you want to mix a house tune with pounding bass beats into a track you can't beatmatch out of, the technique is still the same. Because house tracks tend to have long, beat-only intros, start them later, when the main tune kicks in.

Looking deeper at the technique, you have to work out how much you need to fade out a tune before starting the next one, and when to start the next tune. Some tunes sound fine when you start them at the beginning of the out-going tune's bar – some sound better on the third or fourth beat of the bar. Practice and experience in listening to, and playing, your tunes lets you develop the skill, and an instinct for how best to mix your tunes.

Of course, not all records have a powerful point in the tune that you'd like to start from. For instance, maybe you want to play a slow track, so people can smooch and dance closer (and you can run to the bathroom or the bar). The mix out of the last track is the same as with the 'Brown Eyed Girl' track, but instead of an immediate, full-volume start on the new track, it may sound better if you took a full bar (four beats) to go from quiet to full volume, and create a smooth, swelling fade-up of 'Wonderful Tonight', for example.

Another option is to talk during the mix. Your tales of the buffet, drink promos, and comments about the mother-of-the bride's inappropriate dancing can all be used to cover a mix.

The trick is to control the volume of the music as you speak into the microphone; keep the music low enough so that you can be heard, but loud enough so that it doesn't sound like a monologue from you. Listen to how radio DJs talk over the beginning of songs that they play. They know when the tune changes from intro to the main song and time their chatter to coincide; get to know your tunes so you can do the same thing. Perform a simple cross-fade between the two tunes, speaking over the mix to hide the transition, and stop waffling just as the main tune starts. Chapter 22 has more information about talking into a microphone.

The R & B mix

R & B doesn't tend to have the long, luxurious intros that house and trance music has, so the tunes often have a very good opening bar that you can use to mix over the last tune much like the party DJ mix. In addition, R & B often kills bass beats for the last bar of a phrase, making this point perfect for mixing in the new tune, because otherwise the complicated, bass-heavy drums fight with each other.

R & B does have scope for beatmatching if you have tunes with similar beat patterns, but R & B works best when the beatmatch mix is as short as possible. Using the new tune, a short baby scratch (see Chapter 16) in time with the beats on the outgoing tune, then starting the new tune playing from a powerful point is an excellent way to mix when you can't match beats.

Drum and bass, and breakbeat

Drum and bass, and breakbeat are both genres that tend to follow the four beats to a bar structure that house/trance follows, so you're normally able to follow the basic principles of placement mentioned in the earlier section 'Perfecting Placement'. However, the beats in the bars are a lot more complicated, so if you're trying to beatmatch breakbeat or drum and bass, it can help to focus on the snare sounds instead of the bass drums.

A huge phenomenon in drum and bass circles over the past few years has been the *double drop*, an extension of breakdown mixing. All genres can benefit from this technique. Beatmatch and start a mix so that two tunes are about to hit a breakdown (also called a *drop*) at the same time – the drop on either tune may be the main breakdown, or a shorter one earlier or later in the tune. The key is to mix them together so they both come *out* of their drops at the same time, after which you keep both tunes audible, playing through the speakers. So if you're mixing an 8-bar drop into a 16-bar drop, be sure to start the 8-bar drop halfway through the longer one.

Tune selection is vital for creating a good sounding double-drop. Don't perform it with just any two tunes – they need to have a complementary rhythm and key, and you need to pay special attention to volume and EQ control on both tunes to avoid a messy sound. Experiment with the tunes you use, and the drops in the tune you use for the double-drop. Performed well, this live re-mix when playing two tunes over each other sounds really powerful.

Chapter 15

Mixing with CDs

. . . .

In This Chapter

▶ Locating the right tune and cue point using different CD deck controls

▶ Starting the CD and making pitch corrections

▶ Trying out additional CD deck features

. . . .

*T*he great thing about mixing with CDs is that the only way the beats of two tunes can drift out of time is if you haven't correctly set the pitch. When the pitch is right and the beats are in sync, all you have to worry about is the mix, not dodgy motors on cheap turntables.

Chapter 12 is written with the vinyl DJ in mind. This chapter discusses the controls on CD decks and how CD DJs use them to do the same thing as the vinyl DJ, then take mixing to another level of creativity.

Navigating the CD

No matter what format you use to DJ with – CD, MP3, vinyl, and so on – the basic concepts of beatmatching remain the same: find a precise starting point (the *cue*), set the pitch control so that the beats of your tunes play at the same speed, and start the new tune so that the beats play at the same time as the other tune. The choice you make about what format to use only affects the mechanics of *how* you go about each stage.

Vinyl is an easy format to use to find the cue – simply pick the right side of the record, look at the groove, place the needle near to where you want to start, then play the record backwards and forwards to find the precise cue point. The hardest part of vinyl DJing is starting the record so the beats play in time with the beats on the other tune.

CD DJing is completely opposite to vinyl DJing. After you've found the correct cue point, it's extremely easy to start the tune in time; all you need to do is press the start button in time with the other beats. Locating the precise cue however, is a bit more difficult. Finding the cue on a CD means locating the right track on the CD, *scanning* (fast-forward or rewinding) through the track to find the general area you want to start from, then *fine tuning* the cue by playing the CD forwards or backwards by the smallest of amounts.

Although this doesn't sound particularly difficult, remember that you don't have a visual reference other than the time display to know where (or when) you're in the tune in order to set the cue. *Wave displays*, which have a series of peaks and troughs to show the louder and quieter parts of the tune, can help with this problem, but you only find them on the more expensive CD decks such as the Pioneer CDJ1000MkIII (check out Chapter 7 for more information, and a picture).

Keep the inlay covers or written tracklists with your CDs (don't just print on the CD itself though – reading when the CD's spinning inside the CD player is rather hard!) If you put all your CDs together in a case, this makes it easier to read the track names and numbers, and saves you time and frustration when trying to find the track you want to play next in the mix.

Different CD decks have slightly different sets of controls to find the cue, using one, or (more commonly) a mixture of the following designs:

- ✔ Buttons
- ✔ Jog dials
- ✔ Platters

Buttons

CD decks with very basic controls use only buttons to navigate the CD. One pair of + and – buttons are used to go through the track numbers on the CD to locate the correct tune to play. A second pair is used for searching through the CD, and for fine tuning the *cue* point.

The longer you hold down search buttons, the faster the CD plays in either direction. If you just tap the search button, the CD plays frame by frame (a frame is the smallest time change that the CD deck can give you), which enables you to locate the exact cue.

Repeatedly tapping the search button makes the music play in slow-mo, but because the CD deck repeats each frame you stop on over and over again until you move on, the sound you hear is like a broken CD. This digital noise can initially lead to difficulty in hearing where you are in the tune, making it hard to set a precise cue. Listen out for a change in the sound that's playing; when the sound has more bass to it, you're likely to be on the bass drum. (Your cue is likely to be one of the bass drums in the tune – see Chapter 12.)

Using buttons to find the cue is quite laborious and takes patience and a good memory of the tune to do quickly. However, developing the knack for finding the cue this way doesn't take long, and although the cheaper, budget CD decks tend to use only buttons, as long as you can find the precise cue when you need to, nothing's wrong with this basic design.

Jog dials

The Jog dial on a twin CD deck is between 3–5 inches in diameter, and is normally made of two parts, an outer ring and an inner disc (see Figure 15-1).

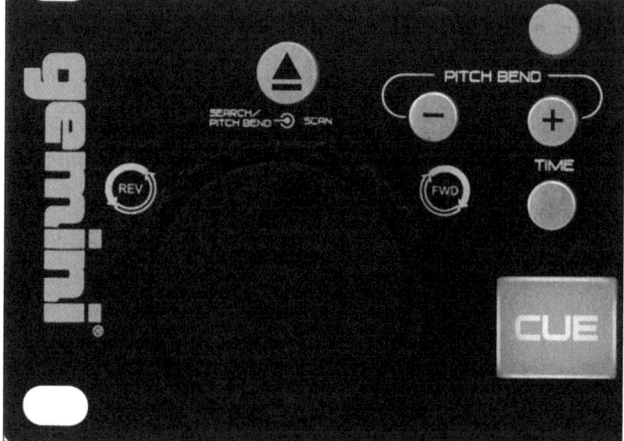

Figure 15-1: The jog dial on a twin CD deck.

CD decks with jog dials still usually use buttons to find the track you want to play on the CD, but a sprung outer ring on the dial replaces the search button on the cheaper decks to find the general area in the tune you want to start from. How far you turn the ring left or right changes how fast the tune searches backwards or forwards. When released, the ring returns to the centre position, playing the music at the speed you set with the pitch control.

An inner disc inside the outer, sprung ring makes fine-tuning the cue a lot easier. Most CD decks are designed so that their inner disc gives a little click as it turns, with each click representing a frame in the music. By spinning this disc backwards and forwards quickly, you can play the music in slow-mo, then turn the disc slower to play the music slower to find the exact frame. When scanning through the track frame by frame, you do still hear a digital repetition of the frame you are on, so this still takes concentration, a knack, and a good ear to hear properly.

The jog dial on a twin CD deck is small and quite fiddly to use, but the ease of use of the centre disc makes finding a precise cue a lot easier than just pressing buttons. Single CD decks that use a sprung jog dial tend to have much larger dials because the top of the deck has more room – and this increased workspace makes fine-tuning the cue easier.

Platters

Digital turntables, which act and have controls almost identical to vinyl turntables, have revolutionised CD DJing. CD decks used to try to keep up with, and emulate turntables, but the introduction of *platters* now means CD decks have matched, and surpassed, the functionality of the vinyl turntable.

You have a choice of motorised, rotating platters (as found on the Technics SLDZ1200 and Denon DN-S3500 – see Figure 15-2) and manual platters (as with the Pioneer CDJ1000MkIII that I use), which only turn and affect the music when you touch the platter. You can find the cue in the same way as a vinyl DJ, by controlling the CD just like a record on a turntable, spinning the platter back and forth to find the general area of the tune. But more importantly, when locating the cue, these decks emulate the exact sound you'd hear if you were using vinyl rather than the stuttering, digital, broken CD sound on other CD decks.

You can still use track Skip and Search buttons to locate the general area in a specific tune, but you then use the platter to fine-tune the cue point like you would with a record on a turntable, playing it backwards and forwards until you find the exact place.

Figure 15-2:
The Denon
DNS3500
platter.

Working with the Cue

Finding the cue, storing it to the CD deck, being able to immediately and accurately return to it time and time again, edit it, and reset it, are not only all vital functions, but also make the CD deck more advanced than vinyl turntables. After you locate and store a cue, you never have any doubt that when you return to the cue and press Play on the CD deck, you'll start at the exact same place time and time again (until you change the set cue point of course).

The four steps to properly work with the *cue* are:

1. **Locate the cue.**
2. **Store the cue.**
3. **Check the cue**
4. **Start the tune from the cue.**

Locating the cue

No matter what controls your CD deck has, you need to locate the precise cue. If you often start from similar parts of the track, take a note of what the time display reads and write that info next to the track title on the inlay sleeve.

Some CD decks (like the CDJ1000s) have memory cards that can save the cue points that you set on your CDs. This means that you can return to a previously stored cue almost immediately after you pop the CD into the deck.

If you haven't written down the cue time, or your CD deck doesn't save cue points, you need to search for a desired cue. Here's how to use the controls to find the cue:

1. **Use the Search controls to get close to where you want to set the cue, and if the tune doesn't automatically start playing when you release the search control, press Play so that you can hear the music playing as normal.**

2. **When you're near to the cue point, press Play again to pause the music, then use the Jog controls (buttons, dials, or platters) to slowly go through the tune to find the exact start point of a the first bass drum of a bar or phrase, or whatever piece of music you want to start from.**

When fine-tuning the cue, if you want to start on a bass drum, you'll hear the sound change to have more bass frequencies as the drum hits. Experiment with setting the cue before, or on this sound, to see how this affects your timing when you press play. It may only be 100th of a second difference, but it can make *all* the difference between starting beats in time, or slightly out of time.

Storing the cue

After you've found your cue point, you need to store that position to the CD deck. On some CD decks, when the CD is in Pause mode and you've located the exact cue, you simply need to press Play to set the cue point and if you ever need to return to it, just press the cue button again. Pioneer CD decks are different in that you press the Cue button to store the cue when you've found it. Interestingly, the Denon DNS3500 CD decks have a button that lets you choose between either of those methods, so you can set the cue in the way that's most familiar to you. Read the manual that comes with your CD decks so you know what method you should use to store the cue.

Check the cue

Press Play, and if you find that you haven't set the cue accurately enough, press the Cue button to return to the cue. Use the jog controls to find the correct cue, and then set the a new cue by pressing Play or Cue when in Pause mode (depending on your CD decks).

After you've found and successfully stored the cue, you need to return the CD to that cue, ready to start the tune in the mix. This usually means pressing the Cue button. If you paused the CD as you pressed Cue, the CD may return and pause. If the CD was playing at the time you pressed Cue, it'll return to cue and continue playing.

If you're in Pause mode on a Pioneer CD deck, pressing Cue resets the cue to the point where you paused the CD instead of returning to the set cue, so it needs to be in Play mode to return to the cue. You won't make this mistake too often, but it may take a little time to get used to.

Starting the tune

Starting tracks for beatmatching on CD is a lot easier than on vinyl. Listen to the bass beat from the other tune, try to block out the rest of the music and focus on the boom from the bass; almost like meditation. When you are at *one* with the beat, and are at the best part of the tune to start, press the Play button, and you should start the bass beats in sync with the other tune. Pressing the button exactly on the beat takes practice, but it's nowhere near as hard as starting tunes on a turntable.

If you prefer starting tunes like vinyl, CD decks with motorised platters let you do this. You simply find the cue point, hold the platter still, then let go, or give a little push to start the tune.

Adjusting the Pitch

As with vinyl DJing, locating the cue and starting the tune in time is only part of beatmatching. The other important part is using the pitch control to adjust the speed to make the bass beats of the new tune in the mix play at the same time as the one currently playing through the speakers.

The good news is that the pitch slider on CD decks acts in exactly the same way as on a turntable (refer to Chapter 5). They may have improvements, such as adjusting the range from 4 per cent to 100 per cent or more, but the principle is the same: moving it towards you (into the + area) makes the tune play faster; away from you (the – area) makes the tune play slower. (Check out Chapter 12 for more on the basics of using pitch control when mixing.)

If the pitch control is set slightly too fast or too slow and the beats start to drift, you can't push the CD like a piece of vinyl (even if you could, the CD would skip). So *pitch bend* controls are on hand to get the tracks back in time. These controls may be different depending on the CD decks you're using:

- ✔ **Buttons:** Normally found on twin CD decks rather than single decks, two buttons, one marked '+' and one marked '–' temporarily speed up or slow down the tune when you press them. The longer (and sometimes harder) you press the button, the greater the pitch bend you achieve. When you let go of the button, the CD returns to the speed you originally set with the pitch control.

- ✔ **Small jog ring:** Found on a number of twin CD decks, there's usually a button or switch that changes the function of the sprung outer ring from 'search' to 'pitch-bend'. You turn the jog ring to the right to go slightly faster, and to the left to go slower. How far left or right you turn the ring affects how large a pitch bend you get. When you return the ring to the centre position, the CD plays at the set pitch again

- ✔ **Large jog wheel:** Depending on your CD deck, the large jog wheel may work in exactly the same way as the small jog ring above. In the case of the expensive CD decks with platters, you can temporarily adjust the speed that the tune plays at as if it was a piece of vinyl.

  With vinyl, if you need the record to run faster you can make the record turn faster, or if you need to slow it down, you add some resistance to the side of the deck. It's exactly the same with the DNS3500 and the SLDZ1200, push the platter to play it faster, or run your finger along the side to slow it.

  The Pioneer CDJ1000 uses a ring around the edge of the platter as a pitch bend. Turn it clockwise to speed up the tune, or anticlockwise to slow it down. Importantly, it's only when the ring moves that any change happens to the CD and the speed the ring is moved at directly affects the amount of pitch bend. So quickly spinning the ring forward or back by a couple of inches is normally all it takes to get the beats back in sync.

No matter what method you use to adjust the pitch error, remember to change the pitch control to reflect your adjustment. If you needed to briefly slow down the tune, make sure that you reduce the pitch control slightly, and increase it if you needed to speed up. Otherwise, because you haven't set the speed of the tunes exactly in time, you'll need to keep using the pitch bend to get the beats back in time.

Taking Advantage of Special Features

Given that scratching on CD seemed impossible a few years ago, yet now most professional CD decks offer this function, guessing what future possibilities may be in store for the CD deck is exciting. For the present though, CD decks have more creative control than a regular, vinyl turntable, offering features such as the following:

- **Master tempo:** *Master tempo* on a CD deck is the same as on a turntable (refer to Chapter 5). This function allows you to speed up or slow down a tune without changing the key that the music was recorded in. So if you play Barry White and *pitch him up* (speed up the tune) by 16 per cent, he still sounds like Barry, whereas decks without Master Tempo make him sound like a chipmunk.

- **Hot Cues:** Normally labeled *1, 2, 3* or *A, B, C*, these are extra cue points that can be set *on-the-fly*, which means that you don't have to stop or pause the CD in order to set them. Doing so takes a little hand/ear coordination, but setting and then returning to these cue points is very simple.

  You can use hot-cues to jump around the CD, instantly playing different parts of a tune, or even jump to a cue set in another track on the CD! Repeatedly pressing the same Cue button lets you play the same part over and over, returning to that cue point each time you press the button.

- **Loop:** The *loop* function plays a discreet part of a tune from an *in point* (that you can set anywhere in the tune) to an *out point* (that you also need to set). When you hit the Loop button, the music plays from in to out, then in to out over and over again, until you stop the loop. You can use this creatively to keep a good part of a track repeating, or you can use it as a safety net. If you haven't had time to set up the next track in the mix yet and you're approaching the end of a tune, you can repeat a section of the end of the tune, giving you the time to set up and mix in a new tune. (This shouldn't ever happen, but sometimes, you spend too long talking to the wrong person, and run out of record.)

Looping intros and outros, or sections of a tune can extend the mix, and subtly remix the tune to make something different, or looping part of a buildup to extend it adds variety to the mix. If the build-up is a drum-roll, edit the length of the loop so it gets shorter and shorter; the shorter the loop gets, the more frantic the breakdown sounds and you can work the crowd into a frenzy before finally ending the loop or hitting a hot-cue button and crashing back into the powerful beats of the tune.

✔ **Sample banks:** Similar to the loop function, instead of setting in and out points to play, you can record a section of the music into *sample banks* (memory contained on the CD deck) to play back as and when you like.

You can use the stored samples in as many ways as you can think of. They can be looped, played on their own, and, on some CD decks, they can also play over the CD that the sample was taken from, letting you remix a track or mix into another tune on the same CD! The creative possibilities are endless.

✔ **Reverse:** *Reverse* play is possible, and a nice gimmick with vinyl, but CD decks give you a lot more control. For starters, you can choose whether you want the CD to go into reverse just like a turntable or instantly. If a record is at 0 pitch at 33 revs per minute (rpm), the record needs to slow down from 33 rpm to 0, and then accelerate from 0 to 33 rpm in reverse. Some CD decks offer the same de-acceleration and acceleration sound, but also the choice to instantly reverse the tune without any delay. The Denon DNS3500 gives an incredible level of control over reverse playback.

The extras available on CD decks mount up with each release. Built-in effects, scratching, MP3 playback, advanced reverse play, visual displays for the track's waveform, and more – to go through each feature and their best uses would take up the rest of this book!

If you're unsure about what your CD deck can do, or the best way to utilise the functions, read the manual, go to clubs to see them used in action, and look at the manufacturers' Web sites; they may have video clips of their gear in action.

Or just toss the manual under the bed and experiment for a while. Then after you're thoroughly confused, try to find that manual again . . .

Chapter 16

Scratching Lyrical

. . . .

In This Chapter

▶ Ensuring your gear is up to scratch

▶ Marking your records properly

▶ Scratching on vinyl, CD, MP3, and computer

▶ Lending you a helping hand with basic scratching

. . . .

Scratching is a specialised skill that takes a lot of practice and patience to master. When you've taken the time to develop the skill, half the people you know will drop their jaws in amazement at what you're doing, while the other half will open their mouths just as wide – and yawn.

Whether you go on to develop the crab, the flare, or the twiddle is up to you, but if you can master the baby scratch, the forward scratch, and the cut, even if you consider yourself only a beatmatching, mixing DJ, you'll be adding another weapon to your arsenal of knowledge.

Scratching techniques get you used to working with vinyl. When you've grasped the basics you develop a feel for how much pressure you need to apply (very little) in order to hold the record still while the deckplatter is turning, you're able to wind the record back and forth without the needle flying off, and you develop solid, stable hands when holding the record stopped, ready to start it.

The Web site that accompanies this book has audio and video clips to support the information contained in this chapter, because most of the techniques are better shown rather than described. Be sure to logon to check that you're happy with what you're doing (see www.recess.co.uk).

Setting Up the Equipment the Right Way

Anyone who has used equipment that was poorly configured or wasn't suitable for scratching will show the emotional scars as proof that you can't afford to get the set-up wrong.

If you're using CDs to scratch with, you don't need to set up much on the CD decks, apart from maybe the resistance of the platter (see Chapters 7 and 15) and switching the CD deck to vinyl mode in order to create the right 'scratch' sounds.

For traditional, turntable scratch DJs, I mention a few of the basic, but vital requirements that your turntables need to be suitable for DJing in Chapter 5. Turntables built for mixing share many of the same characteristics as those used for scratching. Powerful, direct-drive motors are essential, and an adjustable tonearm, removable headshells, and sturdy design are also crucial.

However, how you set up the needles, the orientation of the turntable, and how you plug in to your mixer are just as important as the make and model of turntable that you're using.

A big factor for scratching DJs is the positioning of the decks. Instead of setting them up as the manufacturer intended (tonearm and pitch fader on the right-hand side), scratch DJs rotate the entire turntable, 90 degrees anticlockwise, so that the tonearm and pitch control are farthest away from the DJ.

The traditional set-up only gives the DJ around 100 degrees of the record's circumference to work with (shown in Figure 16-1, top), so the DJ can only pull the record back so far before hitting the needle, which would knock it out of the groove. Rotating the turntable by 90 degrees gives the DJ 250 degrees of vinyl to work with (shown in Figure 16-1, bottom), making scratching that much easier.

Weighing up needles

The most popular needle for scratching over the years has been the Shure M44-7, shown in Figure 16-2, though the DMC Championships (where scratch DJs compete to be the best) recently insisted that all contestants used carts and needles from the Ortofon range, to create fairness among all contestants. Check out Chapter 6 for information on what makes a needle good for scratch use.

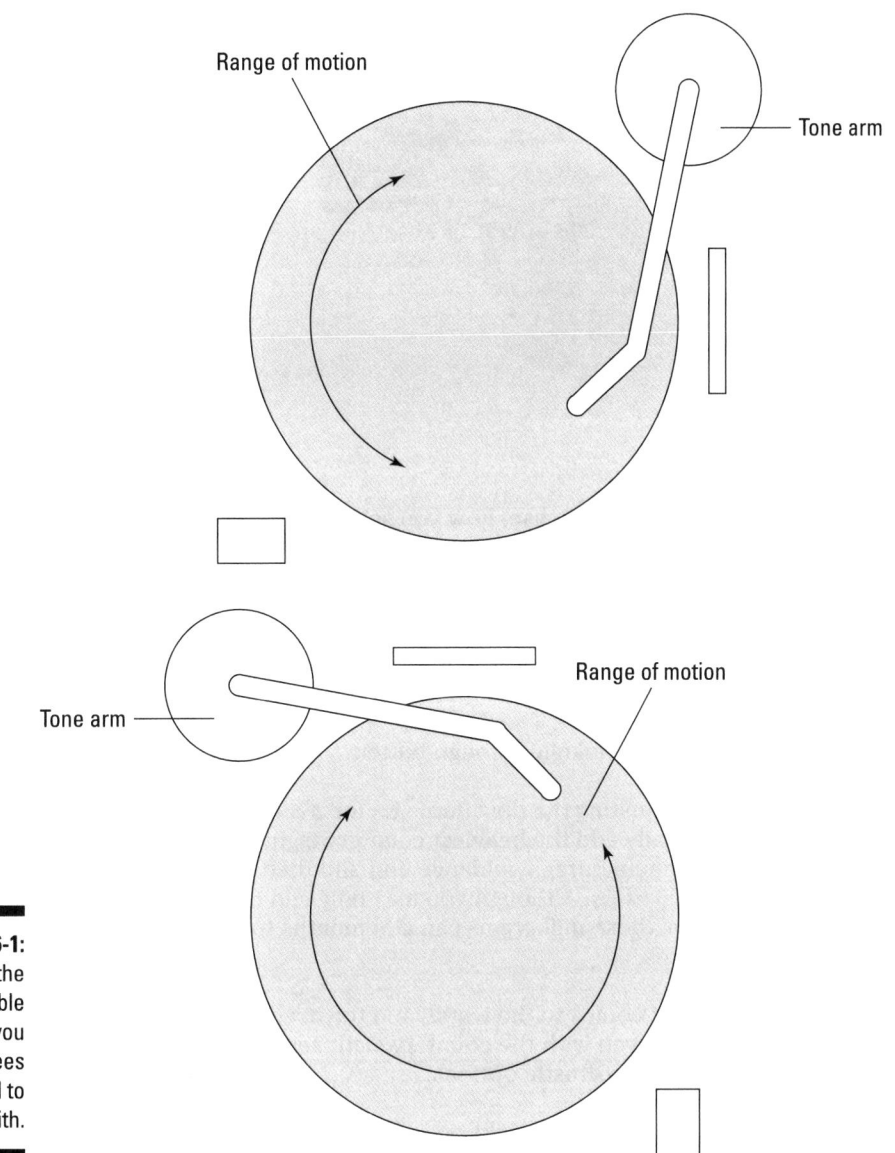

Figure 16-1:
Rotating the
turntable
gives you
250 degrees
of vinyl to
work with.

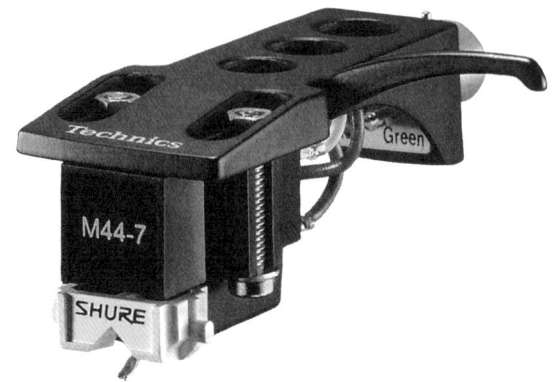

Figure 16-2:
The Shure
M44-7
needle and
cartridge.

No matter what you use, how you set up the needle and the counterweight can drastically affect the stability of the needle. You don't want the needle jumping out of the groove when you're performing a tough scratch.

The two ways to control the stability of your needle are through the down-force acting on the needle, and the angle that it 'digs' into the groove. Simply set the needle so that it angles into the groove by 10 degrees and it'll stick to the groove like glue. The downside, though, is that the needle wears out the groove like a hot knife through butter.

If you're adjusting the downforce on the needle to control stability, don't automatically add the heaviest counterweight available. Try to take the needle manufacturer's guidance first and then add weight gradually if the needle still skips. Although you may only end up a couple of milligrams off maximum, those milligrams can add months to the lifespan of your needle and records.

If the worst comes to the worst, and the needle still flies when you're trying to scratch, even with the counterweight set to maximum, you can try a couple of more drastic options:

- ✔ Put the counterweight on backwards so the black ring (with numbers on it) points away from the tonearm. As the back end of the counterweight isn't tapered, it has more bulk, which adds more weight.

- ✔ Raise the height of the tonearm so the sharper angle makes the needle point down into the groove, creating more downforce. Don't put it too high though, otherwise the front of the cartridge rubs against the record.

- ✔ The last, and most destructive option is to create extra downforce to the cartridge by adding a weight, such as a coin or Blutack, stuck onto the headshell. Doing this may help keep the needle in the groove, but you'll wear out your records and needles quicker than your wallet can buy them! Having to put extra force on the needle probably means that your technique is at fault rather than the set-up of your needle. See section 'Mastering the Technique' later in this chapter for a word on proper hand technique.

As a final note, keep your needles and records clean at all times to reduce the possibility of foreign objects gouging holes in the record or making the needle less stable. Chapter 6 covers methods for cleaning and caring for your needles and records.

Giving slipmats the slip

As a scratch DJ, your slipmats should be slippery enough so that they don't resist or drag when you're scratching, yet still have enough grip so they won't skid during a scratch, or when you let go of the record to play it. (Check out Chapter 6 for everything you need to know about slipmats.)

Touching up mixers

Chapter 8 covers the vital functions needed for a scratch mixer, but you can make a couple of further improvements yourself. Firstly, take a look at your cross-fader. Make sure that you keep it lubricated so that it moves smoothly, without unwanted resistance.

Secondly, secure the faders and cross-faders. The parts that you touch to move the faders do have a tendency to fly off if you're a bit rough with them. Pull them off, and put a piece of paper over the metal protrusion that sticks out to make it thicker, and then put the knob back on. The knob will now be wedged and harder to knock off, solving any flying knob problems!

Making the mixer a hamster

When the mixer is connected *hamster style* (the normal set-up is reversed, so channel 1 plugs into channel 2, and channel 2 plugs into channel 1) or a hamster switch is activated, this set-up reverses the normal cross-fader function so that the opposite channel plays to the side that the cross-fader points to. If you normally move to the left to hear channel 1 and right for channel 2, you'll now move to the right for channel 1 and the left for channel 2. Many DJs prefer this because it's a more natural and comfortable way to work.

Setting the right height

The height level of your decks and mixer can affect how well you scratch. Adjust the height of your set-up so that your elbow is higher than your hand, which is a commonly adopted position for scratching, but experiment with what height is best for you.

Preparing for the Big Push

You can't scratch if you don't have anything to scratch with. You need to find a section of a tune (called a *sample*), which you'll use when scratching. For most scratches, this sample is not very long, a few seconds at most, and normally around a second in duration. There's no rule on what to use as your sample, but vocal samples, drums, beeps, and brass stabs can all sound great in the right hands.

There's no limit to what record you can use to take your sample from either. Seven-inch and 12-inch LPs have grooves that are a bit too compact to scratch with properly, so 12-inch singles are more common, but if you can find a sample, can mark the record correctly, and have the technique to scratch well with it, don't let anyone tell you that you're wrong.

You don't even need to pick dance records. Classical tunes, spoken word records, rock, folk, and country – they all have the potential to have that two second sample that sounds great as a scratch. I had a 'Teach Yourself Spanish' record that I used a couple of times for its strange vocal sounds.

The best records for scratching are specifically designed *battle breaks* with scratch-friendly samples. Although these records may only have ten short samples on an entire side, each sample is repeated at the same point on the circumference of the vinyl. This configuration means that if the needle skips out of the groove into the groove next to it, you'll be at the exact same point in the sample, and no one will know any different (unless the needle jumped by an inch into another sample).

Wearing out your records

Between the increased downforce into the groove and the repetition of the needle passing back and forth over the same part of the record, the record inevitably suffers wear and tear.

However, as audio fidelity isn't essential with scratching, unlike straight mixing, wear only becomes a problem if the record is damaged and starts to skip, or if the sample starts to sound too fuzzy. Keep your needles and records clean, and don't use more weight than you need, and your tunes will still last a long time.

Marking samples

Scratch DJs need to locate the sample on a record quickly, and be able to return to it accurately over and over again. With a combination of markers on the vinyl locating the exact groove where the sample starts, and marks on the label to easily return to the beginning of that sample, hunting for the sample is easy.

The first thing you need to do is locate the specific point in a specific groove on a record that contains the sample you're going to scratch and mark it so you can return to it quickly.

One of the most popular ways to mark the start of the sample is to use a small sticker on the vinyl. I use the little numbered stickers that you get with video tapes, as they're small and the numbers come in useful for remembering what sample to use next (check out Figure 16-3). Every DJ has a different kind of sticker they like using, so find one that you like, and *stick with it.*

Figure 16-3:
A record with various numbered stickers marking samples.

Mark the groove to the left of the sample so that it's not in the way when you're performing the scratch. Here's how:

1. **Find the sample on the record and press Stop on the turntable with the needle at the *very* beginning of the sample.**

2. **Place a sticker very lightly (so it's not stuck) right in front of the needle. Then slowly turn the record with your hand so it plays in the forwards direction.**

   Turning the record pushes the sticker out of the way, into the groove *to the left of* the sample (if it goes to the right, try again, but when you place the sticker in front of the needle, offset it to the left slightly).

3. **Check that you're in the right place by gently rocking the record back and forth, then press down on the sticker to make it stick to the groove next to the start of the sample.**

The drawback to marking the record in this manner is that if you want to play the entire track, a great big sticker is in the way!

If you think that you'll want to play the record in full, try using a *chinagraph* pencil (a white, wax-based pencil) to lightly draw a line (or an arrow, whatever you want) directly onto the vinyl. Be sure not to press down too heavily, or the wax from the pencil gets in the grooves and is just as troublesome as the sticker. Ultraviolet pens (you need to remember a UV light though so you can read it later!) are good alternatives to the chinagraph, as are silver pens (but you still need to watch that the pen doesn't fill up the groove). Eventually, the pen marks do wear off, but as long as you catch the wear in time, and reapply your marker, you shouldn't need to worry.

If you're using a battle-breaks record with multiple versions of the same samples through the record, you don't need to mark the record itself – you can just draw a big fat line on the label of the record (see Figure 16-4). This line refers to the start of every sample (because they all start at the point on the record's circumference).

Think of the record as a clock face. The idea is to draw a line on the label so that when it's pointing in a particular direction (twelve o'clock and nine o'clock are best) you know that you're at the beginning of the sample. Use something small and straight (a cassette box is perfect), draw a line from the centre spindle to the outer edge of the record's label to point to whatever clock number you'd like. Then make the line more noticeable by using a thick marker, or adding a sticker that protrudes over the *blank grooves* at the end of the record (the smooth, silent part of the record, next to the label).

Figure 16-4:
Drawing a
line on a
record label.

If you prefer to have a sticker on the outer edge of the record instead of a line from the centre of the record, follow the same principle, placing the sticker at the nine or twelve o'clock position to point out the start of all the samples. You can use this technique along with a sticker marking the specific groove to make sure that you can find the sample quickly, and return to it easily.

Fixing the hole in the middle

You can easily blame a jumpy needle on having too little counterweight, but sometimes the jumping is due to the record having too large a hole in the middle. A wide hole can be so loose that the centre spindle bangs off the edges of the hole, and bounces the needle out of the groove. The easiest way to fix this problem is to pass an inch-long (2.5 centimetre) piece of tape through the hole, sticking equal halves of it to either side of the label. When you've stuck enough pieces of tape at different positions through the hole, the diameter reduces, solving the problem.

Sometimes the hole is too small so that the record won't fit over the centre spindle properly (either not at all, or it's way too tight, causing the turntable to slow down when you try to hold the record still). When I am unfortunate to get a record that's too tight, all I do is get a small piece of sandpaper, roll it up into a cylinder, put it through the hole in the record, then holding the sandpaper, spin the record round it. Do this action a couple of times, and the hole opens up a bit.

The sandpaper method can be dangerous. If you spin the record too long, you will make the hole too big, and have to tape it up. Or, if you're really unlucky, and are a bit heavy handed, you may cause small cracks in the record.

Scratching on CD, MP3, and Computer

The fact that you can't scratch with CDs used to be true, scratch artists simply weren't able to perform on this format. Sure, the manuals with some CD decks said that if you 'play around' with the jog wheel, you can create interesting 'scratch effects'. But they weren't kidding anyone; scratching as we know it, wasn't available to the CD DJ until recently.

Now, CD decks including the (quite expensive) Denon DN-S3500, Pioneer CDJ-1000, and Technics SL-DZ1200, as well as more affordable CD decks from Numark, Gemini, and Stanton, all let you scratch just as much as you can with vinyl.

All these 'scratch' CD decks have large jog wheels, or deckplatters similar to turntables that are motorised to spin round like a record, or a static control that affects the music only when you move it to perform a scratch. (See Chapter 15 for a more detailed description of CD jog wheels and deckplatters.)

Different decks have different styles, feel, and design to their scratching controls, along with how well they are able to emulate the sound of a record scratching when moving very fast. The Technics CD deck has a large, motorised rotating deckplatter, which has grooves cut into it to make the giant deckplatter feel even more like vinyl, whereas the Pioneer CDJ1000s that I use have a smaller control that only turns when you move it. These are all major factors when you come to make your choice of CD deck for scratching.

You're not just limited to the platter and ability to sound just like a vinyl turntable during the scratch, as these decks have other attributes that allow them to compete with vinyl for scratching: multiple sample banks and cue point controls, built-in effects, instant reverse play, and more, all make the CD deck incredibly versatile to scratch with compared to traditional vinyl.

These effects and controls have removed some of the art and skill from scratching that we associate with vinyl, but they have evolved the creative process of scratching to a completely new, technology driven level. Even though the fundamental basics of scratching are the same on a vinyl turn-table or a CD deck, the skills are slightly different for either format (you can be rougher on CD decks for a start, as you don't need to worry about a needle jumping out of the groove) making direct comparison and competition between the two less and less relevant.

Scratching on PC

In my view, the leading software titles that let you scratch with your PC files are Final Scratch, DigiScratch, and Serato.

With these titles, the hardware controller has been taken to a new level. Instead of using a custom-built control unit like the Hercules with Virtual DJ 3, or something like the DAC3 controller for PCDJ, you just use your existing turntable that hooks into a box of tricks (hardware that is essentially just a soundcard in a box), which then plugs into the PC to control the files through software on the computer.

The key though, is the special vinyl that comes with the package that you use to scratch with. Instead of using ordinary records, the vinyl provided contains a control code (which in the case of DigiScratch, they refer to as *time-code*, a series of blips that refer to time). As you move the vinyl back and forth, the control code is interpreted by the hardware box, which then sends the control information to the computer. This means that when you move the record backwards, the computer file plays backwards; when you play forwards, really fast, the file plays forwards, really fast. The computer contains the files for you to load up, and set cue point for, but it's still your hands, your turntable, and your skill that controls the scratching.

The different software and hardware titles available to scratch with offer you slightly different control options, as well as different lengths of 'lag-time' spent to interpret the control code. Try to get a demo on the scratch software you'd like to use before going out and buying it to make sure that you're happy.

Marking CDs and MP3s

When scratching on MP3 using time-coded vinyl, marking your sample is relatively easy. The software interface takes care of a lot of the cueing of the sample, and as you're using vinyl, you can mark the label with a line to return to the start of a sample (see the earlier section 'Marking samples').

As marking the actual CD isn't possible, the jog dial or display on scratch CD decks have markers that you use to point to the start of the sample. It seems as if they've thought of everything . . .

Mastering the Technique

Technique is everything. If you develop a smooth, flowing – yet still ultra fast – control over the vinyl, you're more likely to keep the needle glued into the groove. With CD decks, you still need a fluid motion to create a great scratch, but you don't need to worry about popping the needle out of the groove. If you spend the time to develop the dexterity and the coordination needed to scratch with either hand on either of your decks and move the cross-fader independently, you're well on your way to becoming a world-class DJ.

Getting hands on

Vinyl is really sensitive, and even with the extra counterweight pressure, the new needles, the proper hole size, and the slippy mats, if you have a hand like a baby elephant, you're going to make that needle fly!

You need to develop the correct *hand* technique. Things to bear in mind are that although you're dealing with a lot of quick direction changes, try to be smooth; don't jerk the record back and forth. When performed in succession, too many rough jerky movements will pop the needle out the groove.

When you scratch the record, try to move it back and forth following the curve of the record. If you try to pull the record back and forth in a straight line, you're adding a lot of sideways pulling and pushing pressure, which when released, may be enough to jump the needle out of the groove.

As well as hand technique, you need to develop a knowledge of what changes the sound of the scratch, (not including external effects processors). The five key ways to make a sample sound different when scratching are:

- ✔ **Location.** You may have found a nice sample on a record, but you still have full control over what part of the sample you play. Just because the sample has someone saying *scratch*, doesn't mean that you have to play that full word. You may choose only to scratch with the *sc* part of the word, or maybe trying a scribble scratch on the *tch* part sounds unique, and matches what you want to do perfectly.

  Changing where in the sample you scratch by just a couple of millimetres (or a tenth of a second) can make the difference between a good sound and a great sound.

- ✔ **Direction.** Nearly all samples sound incredibly different when played backwards as opposed to forwards, and if you're not too sure about the sound of your scratch, you may find that scratching the record in the other direction improves the sound immensely.

✔ **Speed.** The speed that any sample moves can alter your scratch from a low, rumbling, guttural sound to a high-pitched, shrill, chirpy sound. So don't fall into the trap of scratching at the same speed all the time. Change it up mid-scratch from a fast-forward motion to a slow backwards move, mix up the speed during a move (see 'The tear' scratch section later) and listen out for how the speed you scratch the record at can alter the power of your scratch.

✔ **Audibility.** How loud you can hear the sample playing, or if you can hear it at all, is important. Although the cross-fader is the main control for whether you can hear the sample or not, don't forget about the channel-fader.

You can scratch using the channel-fader instead of the cross-fader, and you can use the channel-fader to set how loud you hear the scratch, which adds an extra dimension to the scratch. Gradually fading out the scratch using only the cross-fader is difficult, but when used on its own or in conjunction with the cross-fader, the channel-fader can give you that extra level of audio control.

✔ **EQ.** Using the EQ (equaliser) to adjust the amount of bass, mid, or treble present can change a shrill sounding scratch into a muddy, dark sounding one; in the middle of a scratch if you like.

Unless you have four hands, scratching, using the cross-fader, the channel-fader, and the EQ control all at the same time is hard, but with practice and patience, you'll be amazed at how fast you can move from control to control.

Starting from Scratch and Back Again

Try the following scratches on their own first, without playing anything on the other *deck* (CD/vinyl/MP3 and so on). Then when you're happy, choose a tune with a slow beat to play on the other deck, and scratch over that beat. You don't have to use a beat-only tune, but scratching over melodies and vocals may sound messy and confusing.

Check my Web site at www.recess.co.uk for audio files and movie clips of the scratch if you're unsure of what it should sound or look like.

For all these scratches, I give guidance on what direction you should scratch in, and what cross-fader action you may need, but as you get used to each scratch, adjust how quickly you do the scratch, what part of the sample you're scratching from, and how much of it you play.

Scratching without the cross-fader

The three scratches I discuss in this section help you develop the hand control to work with the vinyl (or CD deckplatter control) properly. Plus they're the building blocks of all the scratches that follow in the section 'Introducing cross-fader fever.' Even though they're simple moves, mastering them is very important. You don't need to use the cross-fader for these three scratches so leave it in the middle position, with the channel-fader at full.

The baby scratch

The baby scratch is the first scratch for you to try out as it is by far the simplest, easiest scratch to attempt. This one is for anyone who comes to your house, and says 'can I have a go?' It may also be how you broke the needle on your dad's turntable when you were 9 years old . . .

The baby scratch is just a forward movement followed immediately by a backward movement. Both directions are audible throughout the scratch (which is why you don't need the cross-fader on this scratch). If the sample you're using is someone singing 'Hey!', then the sound would be like:

Hey *(forwards)* – yeH *(backwards)* – Hey . . . yeH . . . Hey . . . yeH . . .

To start scratching to the beat of another tune, perform the forward motion on the first beat of the bar and the backward motion on the second beat:

Beats: 1   2   3   4   1   2   3   4
Scratch: Hey yeH Hey yeH Hey yeH Hey yeH

When you're comfortable matching the *1, 2, 3, 4* beats of the bar with *'Hey, yeH, Hey, yeH'*, (two full baby scratches), speed up the scratch so that you're going forwards and backwards on each beat (which make a four full baby scratches):

Beats:
1   2   3   4   1   2   3   4
Scratch:
Hey-yeH Hey-yeH Hey-yeH Hey-yeH Hey-yeH Hey-yeH Hey-yeH Hey-yeH

The scribble scratch

The scribble scratch is similar to the baby scratch, except the amount that the record moves backwards and forwards is tiny, and there's a lot more scratches to the beat, let alone the bar!

By tensing the wrist and forearm, while pressing down on the record with one finger, the muscles leading to your finger vibrate, causing the record to move backwards and forwards really quickly. If you think that you can generate enough speed without needing to tense your muscles, just move the record back and forth as fast as you can.

No matter what your technique is, you want to make the amount of vinyl passing under the needle as small as possible (less than a centimetre is best).

The tear

The tear is also similar to the baby scratch, except that instead of two sounds, the scratch is split into three. The cross-fader is still left *open* (you can hear the sound) for the duration of the scratch, but introducing a change in the backward speed creates the third part of the scratch.

The forward *stroke* (move) is the same as the baby scratch, but the first half of the backstroke is fast and the second half of the stroke is half that pace.

Practise changing the speed of the *backstroke* first to help you get used to the change in tempo, and then try adding the forward stroke to the two-part backward stroke.

Introducing cross-fader fever

The scratches described in this section involve using the cross-fader. Before you go any further, find where the *cut-in* point on the cross-fader is. The cut in point is how far you have to move the cross-fader before the appropriate channel can be heard. Depending on the cross-fader curve , this point can be a few millimetres of movement, or you may need to get the cross-fader into the middle before hearing the scratch at full volume. (Chapter 8 has more information on cross-fader curves and cut-in points.)

The forward scratch

The forward scratch gives you the perfect start to using the cross-fader. Using exactly the same movement as in the baby scratch, start with the cross-fader past the cut-in point, so that you can hear the forward movement, then just before you move the record back, close the cross-fader so that the back stroke can't be heard.

When you're used to cutting off the back stroke of the baby scratch, start to scratch to the beat. With the '*Hey!*' example, you match the *1, 2, 3, 4* beat of the bar with *Hey, Hey, Hey, Hey:*

Beats:	1	2	3	4	1	2	3	4
Scratch:	Hey	Hey	Hey	Hey	Hey	Hey	Hey	Hey

The backward scratch

As you may have guessed, *the backward scratch* is exactly the same as the forward scratch, except that this time you hear only the back stroke of the baby scratch. So, you hear '*yeh, yeh, yeh, yeh*' as you scratch to the four beats of the bar:

Beats:	1	2	3	4	1	2	3	4
Scratch:	yeh	yeh	yeh	yeh	yeh	yeh	yeh	yeh

Or you can use it in the off-beat, which is where it would be naturally if you were performing a baby scratch:

Beats:	1	2	3	4	1	2	3	4
Scratch:		yeh		yeh	yeh	yeh	yeh	yeh	yeh

The cut

The cut is when you play the sample at normal speed and direction, but only play parts of it. I used to love doing this scratch with the James Brown 'All Aboard' sample at the beginning of Kadoc's 'Nightrain'. It would sound something like '*All, (pause) All All A All-Aboard*':

Beats:	1	2		3	4	1	2		3	4
Scratch:	All	*(rest)*		All	All	A	All	Aboard	*(rest)*	*(rest)*

After I had scratched with it for a while over another tune, I would just let the sample play, the tune would kick in, and the mix was done. Which shows that scratching and mixing aren't mutually exclusive.

To perform this scratch, position the sample so that it's right behind the needle. On a particular point in the other tune, (at the start of a bar in my Kadoc example) move the cross-fader in and let the record run. When you want the sample to stop, close the cross-fader, wind the record back to the beginning of the sample, and let it run again.

The trick is to make sure that you get the sample wound back to the correct place in time. This is the perfect time to mark a line on the record label, so that when it's pointing at twelve o'clock, you know that you're at the start of the sample (see the earlier section 'Marking samples').

The chop

The *chop* is very similar to the cut, except that instead of playing the record at normal pace, you control how fast the sample plays. By varying how fast

Your thumb isn't only for hitch-hiking

Opening and closing the cross-fader fast becomes more and more difficult the faster you try to move it. When you do feel limited, use your thumb as a spring to return the cross-fader to the closed position.

If you have a small distance to travel to the cut-in point on the cross-fader, rest your thumb at that point, but angle your thumb so that it leans toward the closed position. Using your middle (or ring) finger, tap the cross-fader so it bounces off your thumb, and returns to the closed position, which is a lot quicker. This is a lot easier to do if your mixer is set up *hamster style* (see the section 'Making the mixer a hamster').

you play parts of the sample, you can create some strange melodies to accompany what you're scratching over.

And of course, the *reverse chop* (and *reverse cut*) is when the fader is open for the back stroke rather than the forward stroke.

The chirp

The chirp is where hand co-ordination starts to become essential. Start the scratch with the cross-fader open, but just as you hear the sample play, smoothly (though quickly) close off the cross-fader. For the back stroke, do the exact opposite; as you move the record backwards, open the cross-fader.

With the right sample, the right speed of scratch, and movement of the cross-fader, this technique creates a bird-like whistling, or *chirp* noise.

The transformer

The *transformer* is another simple scratch that helps you with the timing of your cross-fader moves, and also develops co-ordination between your hands.

To get used to the transformer, play the sample forwards so that it lasts one bar's length (a couple of seconds), then backwards for one bar. You can play for longer or shorter if you wish, but keeping the move to one bar gives you limits to work for now that you can expand on when you get good at the transformer.

As you play the sample, open and close the cross-fader on each of the beats of the bar. As you do so, you hear the sample split into four parts playing forwards, and four parts of the sample playing backwards. When you're happy, double the speed that you cut the music in and out with, then if you think that you can move the cross-fader fast enough, double it again, so that you're opening and closing the cross-fader 16 times for a bar.

Flares

The *flare scratch* takes the sample, and cuts it into two by quickly closing and re-opening the cross-fader. The scratch starts with the cross-fader open, which closes halfway through the sample, and then opens again. If the sample you're scratching is just someone saying *scratch*, then you would hear *scr tch*.

When the cross-fader is closed off quickly, it makes a clicking sound. In the preceding *scr tch* example, chopping the sample into two takes one movement, one click, and is called a *one click forward flare*.

Crab scratch

To get used to the cross-fader action for a *crab scratch*, click your fingers. Now instead of just your middle finger clicking off your thumb, click all four of your fingers across your thumb, starting off with the pinkie. This is the crab action, except with the cross-fader knob between your fingers and thumb.

Place your thumb as a spring to the cross-fader in the same way that you used it for the transformer scratch. As your fingers bounce the cross-fader off your thumb, the sample is cut into four, really quickly.

You may find this move easier to perform with your mixer set-up in a hamster style because you'll be bouncing the fader off the side of the fader slot and your thumb, but with practise, the move can be performed both ways.

Twiddle scratch

The *twiddle scratch* is the precursor to the crab scratch. Instead of using all four fingers to perform the crab scratch, only two are used to *twiddle* the cross-fader, which produces a slightly more constant rhythm to the scratch than the crab.

Combining scratches

When you're familiar with these fundamentals, start combining them to create strings of different scratches over the beat.

Start off simply, by switching from one scratch to another. Try changing a baby scratch to a forward scratch, or a forward scratch to a reverse scratch.

Here are a few more ideas:

✔ **Transforming with transformers:** Adding transforms to any of your scratches is a great way to change up the sound of some of the basic moves. Add a transform to a forward scratch, so that you *transform* the forward movement, but still don't hear any of the back stroke. Or add a transform to a tear to really test you coordination!

✔ **Adding flare:** Add a flare, or a crab to my *All Aboard* example for the cut scratch, which adds a stutter effect to part of it.

There are many combinations of how to move the record, how to move the cross-fader, and the speed to do it all in. Check out my Web site (`www.recess.co.uk`) for a few more ideas on how to mix up the fundamentals.

Juggling the Beats

Beatjuggling is a great skill and one that when mastered, earns you a lot of respect from your peers.

Using two records (they don't have to be identical, but it helps) with just a drum beat, a new beat is created using a combination of all the scratch fundamentals from tune to tune, while also winding back the sample to the beginning of the beat.

Properly marking your records is incredibly important here, as you won't have the time to listen in headphones to how you're cueing up the tune to start it again. You need to rely on spotting the line at twelve o'clock, and have faith that you're at the start of the sample.

Much as you would if you were juggling with balls, start off simply:

1. **With two identical records, cue them so that they both play from the exact same point.**

2. **Play one bar of the drum beat on one record, then move the cross-fader over to the other record, and play a bar on that record.**

3. **While that bar is playing, wind the first record back to the start of the bar, and when the second record has finished its first bar, start the first record again.**

This method means that you play the same bar of drums over and over again, which may sound easy, but believe me, it isn't. You can get easily flustered, get the timing wrong for the start of the bar, and make a pig's ear of something so simple-sounding.

When you're happy with a using the whole bar, halve the time that one record plays before switching over. Then when you're really confident, start to play the beat so that the first beat plays from the first record, the second beat from the second record, but wind back the beats, so you only hear the first two beats of the bar play.

Offsetting

By the time you can swap from beat to beat comfortably, you'll want to create more complicated drum beats. Offsetting one of the records is a great and simple way to start. Begin by starting one of the tunes half a beat later, so instead of a simple *Bass Snare Bass Snare* for the four beats of the bar, you now have *BassBass SnareSnare BassBass SnareSnare* in the exact same amount of time. The first bass is from the first tune, and the second one is from the second tune.

Leaving the cross-fader in the middle creates that run of beats, but closing the cross-fader off to one of the beats temporarily starts to chop it up a lot more.

Beats:	1		2		3		4	1		2		3		4
Sounds:	**B1**	B2	**S1**	S2	**B1**		**S1**	S2	B2	**S1**	S2	**B1**	B2	**S1**

(Where the B is Bass, S is Snare, **Bold** is Deck 1 and normal is Deck 2.)

This method is only the tip of the iceberg for cutting up the beat. The faster you cut between tracks, the different offset beats, and the different lengths of the beats you have to work with can all come together to make a really complicated beat. And that's not even thinking about cymbals, hi-hats, and drum rolls!

Practice, dedication, and patience

Practice, dedication, and patience should make up your personal mantra for beatjuggling (and scratching as a whole). Record knowledge and manual dexterity are extremely important, but you need to be fluent and *tight* with the beats. You need to keep your scratch moves fluid and in keeping with the rhythm of what you're scratching over, and if you're beatjuggling, the beat you make needs to flow as though a drummer were playing it – that way, you'll earn respect for your skills.

Part IV
Getting Noticed and Playing Live

The 5th Wave   By Rich Tennant

MIXING THE FIRST "RUDE AUDIENCE" CD

"I laid down a general shuffling sound, over dubbed with periodic coughing, some muted talking files, and an awesome ringing mobile phone loop."

In this part . . .

One morning you'll wake up and realise that you're meant for more in this world than DJing in front of your cat (and annoying the neighbours). You may sound great when played through a home stereo or iPod, but the time when you play to a packed hall or a club filled with like-minded people is when you really spread your wings as a DJ.

This part of the book leads you through making the perfect demo mix, trying to secure work, and then what to do when you're standing in the DJ booth with a thousand people in front of you wanting you to give them the best night of their lives.

This is DJing.

Chapter 17

Building a Foolproof Set

....

In This Chapter

▶ Driving the rhythm

▶ Selecting the right key for harmonic mixing

▶ Developing a style all of your own

....

*A*fter you've taken a look at the different ways you can mix your tunes together (refer to Chapters 12, 14, and 16), you need to start examining the tunes you're using in the mix.

As well as looking a bit closer at why a tune can mix well with one tune but not another, this chapter covers developing your own style when DJing, rather than simply replicating all those who have come before you. No one's saying that following the same fundamentals as other DJs is wrong, but if you can think about what you're trying to do with the order of the tunes in your mix, you'll be a lot better DJ than the one who mixes Tune A with Tune B just because they sound good together.

Choosing Tunes to Mix Together

The tunes you select, and the order you play them in are just as important as the method you use to get from tune to tune. The best technical mix in the world can sound terrible if the tunes don't play well together and boredom can set in if you stick to the same sound, genre, and the same energy level (pace and the power of the music) all night.

In order to get a feel for what kind of tunes mix well with each other, you need to consider the core differences that make tunes different from one another (other than the melody and vocals and so on). The main differences are the driving rhythm, the key the tunes are recorded in, and the tempo a tune was originally recorded at.

Beatmatching – the next generation

Matching the pounding bass beats of your tunes is one thing, and after you get the knack, playing bass drums together is relatively simple and sounds good. However, the core *driving rhythm* is another rhythm that you need to consider and listen out for in the tunes.

A track is made up of the *backing track* (the drums, bass line, and any rhythmic, electronic sounds), and the main melody and/or vocals. The backing track is the driving force to the tune, and has a rhythm of its own that is separate to the pounding bass beats. A great example of this is the '*duggadugga duggadugga duggadugga duggadugga*' driving rhythm in Donna Summer's 'I Feel Love'.

If what follows sounds a little childish, that's because it is. I remember it from school, so thanks to Mr Galbraith for making this concept stick!

When beatmatching bass drum beats, you only have to worry about the solid '*thump thump thump*' of the tunes playing over each other. Now you need to listen out for the four driving rhythms: *Ta*, *Ta-te*, *Ta-te-ta*, and *Ta-fe-te-te*. These can be added to each other to make more complicated rhythms, but when two of them mix with other (from two different tunes) you need to be aware of how they may sound, and when considering what tunes to use in the mix, give thought to how well one core rhythm will play over another.

You get four beats to the bar. Each of the driving rhythm fundamentals occur on the beat (so you get four of each to a bar):

Ta – (sounds like '*Baa*' in the line 'Baa, Baa, Black Sheep'):

Beat	1	2	3	4	1	2	3	4
Rhythm	Ta	Ta	Ta	Ta	Ta	Ta	Ta	Ta
Word	Baa	Baa	Baa	Baa	Baa	Baa	Baa	Baa

Ta is just a single sound on each beat of the bar.

Ta-te – (sounds like '*Have you*' in the line 'Have you any wool'):

Beat	1	2	3	4	1	2	3	4
Rhythm	Ta-te	Ta-te	Ta-te	Ta-te	Ta-te	Ta-te	Ta-te	Ta-te
Word	Have you	Have you	Have you	Have you	Have you	Have you	Have you	Have you

Ta-te is two sounds of equal length to each beat (though often one can be emphasised, making it more powerful than the other).

Sometimes, you don't hear the *ta* part of the beat, and just hear the second, *te* portion; known as an *offbeat*. This simple offbeat is a favourite bass rhythm for a lot of producers who want a powerful, stripped down sound to the tune.

Ta-te ta (it's like saying 'Lemonade' on each beat):

Beat	1	2	3	4	1	2	3	4
Rhythm	Ta-te ta	Ta-te ta	Ta-te ta	Ta-te ta	Ta-te ta	Ta-te ta	Ta-te ta	Ta-te ta
Word	Lemonade	Lemonade	Lemonade	Lemonade	Lemonade	Lemonade	Lemonade	Lemonade

Ta-te ta is very similar to *ta-te*, except that instead of two equal sounds, you get two quick sounds (which take up the same time as *ta* in the *ta-te* rhythm) followed by one sound that lasts as long as the *te* half of *ta-te*. Splitting the *ta-te ta* rhythm into two, the halves are *ta-te* and *ta* (*Lemon* and *ade*). 'Lemon' is said very quickly, and it lasts the same duration as 'ade'.

The *ta-te-ta* rhythm is one of my favourites, it sounds great repeated on its own or when used to break up any of the other driving rhythms.

Ta-fe-te-te (like saying 'Mississippi' on each beat of the bar):

Beat	1	2	3	4	1	2	3	4
Rhythm	Ta-fe-te-te	Ta-fe-te-te	Ta-fe-te-te	Ta-fe-te-te	Ta-fe-te-te	Ta-fe-te-te	Ta-fe-te-te	Ta-fe-te-te
Word	Mississippi	Mississippi	Mississippi	Mississippi	Mississippi	Mississippi	Mississippi	Mississippi

Four equal sounds to each beat give a powerful, hypnotic rhythm to the tune. This sound is the '*duggadugga*' rhythm I mentioned earlier for 'I Feel Love'. It adds a lot of energy to a bass melody, and if a filter or a flanger effect is added to this rhythm (see Chapter 8), it leaves the dance floor in a trance.

Mixing with care

Mixing between similar driving rhythms can be a bit tricky. *Ta-fe-te-te* mixes in beautifully to another *Ta-fe-te-te* in the right hands, but if you don't have the tunes precisely beatmatched, the four sounds fall in between each other, giving eight very messy sounds. The same goes for *Ta-te ta*, you need good beatmatching skills to mix two of these sounds together (or mix *Ta-te ta* into *Ta-fe-te-te*).

Though *ta* and *ta-te* are simpler and easier to beatmatch, they tend to be strong bass lines, and because they're so strong, they don't always mix well. If the rhythm of one tune is *ta*, and the other is the offbeat *te* (that is, you don't hear the *ta* from *ta-te*), unless the *ta* note from one tune and the *te* from the other tune are very similar, the mix can sound strange, and out of tune.

Mixing *ta* or *ta-te* rhythms (including the offbeat part of *ta-te*) with either of the more complicated rhythms (*ta-te ta* and *ta-fe-te-te*) is a solution to this problem. However, this method will eventually stifle your creativity. If you need to go from a complicated driving rhythm to a simple one, then back again to a complicated one in order to progress through a mix, you will break up the flow of the set. That's why spending time to refine your beatmatching skills is important, so that you're happy mixing complicated driving rhythms.

Mixing from one driving rhythm to another can add a change in the power of the set. Going from a *ta* core rhythm to *ta-te ta* can make the mix sound faster and more intense, even if the beats per minute (BPMs) are still the same.

Changing from *ta-fe-te-te* to the offbeat version of *ta-te* (only the *te* part) is an incredibly effective way of making the mix sound darker by simplifying and concentrating the sound from a frantic, four sound rhythm to a single sounding, simple, basic rhythm. When coupled with a key change (see the later in this chapter 'Changing the key'), the effect can lift the roof off!

The same driving rhythm principles apply to the hi-hat pattern (the *tchsss*-sounding cymbals). Though most tunes tend to use an open hi-hat sound played in between each bass drum beat (the offbeat *te*), be careful when the patterns get more complicated. If you try to mix two *ta-fe-te-te* hi-hat patterns together, and get the beatmatching wrong, it'll sound dreadful.

Getting in tune with harmonic mixing

Your beatmatching may be perfect (see Chapter 12), your volume control may be spot on (see Chapter 14), and you've chosen two tunes with complimentary driving rhythms, but sometimes two tunes sound out of tune with each other. *Harmonic mixing* comes in at this point, and is the final step for creating truly seamless mixes. Harmonic mixing isn't an essential step of the mixing ladder by any means, it's something you may think about only one out of every five mixes, but if you want to create long, flowing, seamless mixes, harmonic mixing certainly plays a very important part.

Every song with a melody has a musical key, and instruments and vocals play and sing their notes based around this musical key (and is why you hear people say 'I'll sing this in C Minor'). This kind of key may not unlock any real doors, but it does unlock vast chasms of creativity for you. DJs like Sasha, Oakenfold, John Digweed, and many others have all harnessed harmonic mixing to create smooth, controlled mixes that add an extra level of depth and skill to their styles.

Most DJs first approach harmonic mixing by accident, and then try to improve through trial and error. Trial and error is extremely important. Blindly following the musical rules that follow in this section of what key mixes into what is a bad idea. Like counting beats in Chapter 13, knowing how the key affects how well tunes mix together is important. More important is developing an ear for what sounds good when mixed together, rather than referring to a piece of paper, or rule that you read in an incredibly informative book.

However, we all need a little backup, and somewhere to turn to if we're unsure what to do next. Which is where the principle of *key notations* comes in, and you have the choice of two systems to help you understand.

Brace yourself here, the terminology surrounding key notations may seem like a foreign language, but don't worry, it's not something to be scared of.

Traditional key notation

In the Western world, music has 24 different keys; 12 major, and 12 minor (whether they're major or minor depends on the notes that are used to create that key), which is known as the *traditional key notation* system. Each key mixes perfectly with four keys, and mixes to an acceptable level with two other keys, as shown in Table 17-1.

Table 17-1		Harmonic Song Key Combinations		
Key of Song Playing	*Tonic*	*Perfect Fourth (Sub-Dominant)*	*Perfect Fifth (Dominant)*	*Relative Minor*
C Major	C Major	F Major	G Major	A Minor
Db Major	Db Major	Gb Major	Ab Major	Bb Minor
D Major	D Major	G Major	A Major	B Minor
Eb Major	Eb Major	Ab Major	Bb Major	C Minor
E Major	E Major	A Major	B Major	Db Minor
F Major	F Major	Bb Major	C Major	D Minor
Gb Major	Gb Major	B Major	Db Major	Eb Minor
G Major	G Major	C Major	D Major	E Minor
Ab Major	Ab Major	Db Major	Eb Major	F Minor
A Major	A Major	D Major	E Major	Gb Minor

(continued)

Table 17-1 *(continued)*

Key of Song Playing	Tonic	Perfect Fourth (Sub-Dominant)	Perfect Fifth (Dominant)	Relative Minor
Bb Major	Bb Major	Eb Major	F Major	G Minor
B Major	B Major	E Major	Gb Major	Ab Minor
C Minor	C Minor	F Minor	G Minor	Eb Major
Db Minor	Db Minor	Gb Minor	Ab Minor	E Major
D Minor	D Minor	G Minor	A Minor	F Major
Eb Minor	Eb Minor	Ab Minor	Bb Minor	Gb Major
E Minor	E Minor	A Minor	B Minor	G Major
F Minor	F Minor	Bb Minor	C Minor	Ab Major
Gb Minor	Gb Minor	B Minor	Db Minor	A Major
G Minor	G Minor	C Minor	D Minor	Bb Major
Ab Minor	Ab Minor	Db Minor	Eb Minor	B Major
A Minor	A Minor	D Minor	E Minor	C Major
Bb Minor	Bb Minor	Eb Minor	F Minor	Db Major
B Minor	B Minor	E Minor	Gb Minor	D Major

It's okay, no need to start worrying; calculating which keys combine best with each other is actually very simple. In Table 17-1, look at C Major, then look at the keys written next to it. It obviously mixes with a tune with the same key as its own (known as the *tonic*), but it also mixes beautifully with the three keys next to it, F Major, G Major, and A Minor. However, as C Major works really well with A Minor, you can also incorporate the keys that A Minor works well with. These key combinations from A Minor are acceptable rather than perfect, you have to judge for yourself whether they match well enough for what you're trying to do (which is why it's important to use your ears).

This chart is kind of mind blowing though, and is not easy to read. The minor/major thing is a bit confusing if you don't have any musical experience, and working out what mixes into what can take a while. Fortunately, Mark Davis at www.harmonic-mixing.com developed the Camelot Sound Easymix System, which takes the confusion out of working out what key mixes with what.

The Camelot Sound Easymix System

The *Camelot Sound Easymix System* is an alternative approach that addresses the confusing layout and label names of the traditional key notation system (see Table 17-1). With the Camelot system each key is given a *keycode*; a number from 1 to 12 and a letter (A for Minor, and B for Major). Then all the keys are arranged as a tidy clock face, as shown on the Cheat Sheet at the front of the book.

The keys that mix harmonically are identical to the traditional notation, but rather than looking at a confusing table, you only need to look at the keycode for the key of the tune that you're playing, then look to the left and right and directly above or below, depending on whether the key you're referring to is on the inner or outer ring of the diagram.

So if your tune is 12B (E Major), you can mix it with a tune with the same key, with 11B, 1B from the same major family, but you can also mix it perfectly with 12A from the minor ring, and you can get a nice result mixing into 11A and 1A tunes.

Mixing tunes with compatible keys works perfectly if you play all your tunes at 0 pitch, and never change their speed, or if you have CD decks or turntables with a Master Tempo control that doesn't change the pitch as you change the speed. But when you change the speed on normal CD decks and turntables, the pitch of the tune changes too, and the original key starts to change into a new one. When using the Camelot Sound Easymix System, for every 6 per cent you change the pitch, you need to change the keycode by 7 numbers according to their system (see the Cheat Sheet).

So if you have a 3B tune, and pitch it up to 6 per cent, it's no longer a 3B tune, it's now a 10B tune. Or if you pitch down by 6 per cent, it becomes an 8B tune. Move round the circle by 7 segments to see for yourself. A 6 per cent pitch change means that the 3B tune is no longer suited to 4B, 2B, 3A, 4A, and 2A. For a good harmonic mix, you need to choose tunes with a keycode of 11B, 9B, 10A, 11A, or 9A (when *they* are playing at a similar speed too).

How accurate the eventual keycode ends up for these adjustments depends entirely on how accurate your turntables are. Use the calibration dots on the side of the turntable to see if it truly is running at 6 per cent. (Refer to Chapter 5.)

Harmonic mixing is a vast concept that can be bent/twisted/broken or ignored at will, and the extreme concepts of which could take up ten of these books. If you want to delve deeper into the theory of harmonic mixing, I strongly suggest taking a visit to DJ Prince's Web site, which is dedicated purely to harmonic mixing, so visit www.djprince.no when the mood strikes.

Keying tunes

Both the traditional and Camelot notation systems may sound helpful, and believe it or not, are very simple and easy to understand, but one thing is still missing: How do you determine the key of the tune you're currently playing?

The three different ways to work out the key of a tune are:

✔ **Review online databases:** DJ forums and Web sites across the Internet offer huge databases of song keys. The people who created the Camelot Easymix system have a subscription-based database at www.harmonic-mixing.com, and forums like www.tranceaddict.com/forums have huge posts dedicated to the keys of tunes old and new.

✔ **Use your ears:** Figuring out the key by ear is by far the hardest amount of work, taking patience, a good ear for music, and a fair bit of musical theory knowledge.

  1. Play the tune at 0 pitch on the turntable/CD player.

  2. Then use a piano/keyboard or a computer-generated tone, to go through all 12 notes on the scale, as shown in Figure 17-1.

  3. The note that sounds the best, and melts into the music is the 'root key' (the C in C Major, and so on).

Finding whether the key is minor or major takes the whole thing to another level of complication, and if you want to go into that in detail, you need to start looking at musical theory books. Check out books like *Guitar For Dummies*, 2nd Edition, by Mark Phillips and John Chappell and *Piano For Dummies* by Blake Neely (both published by Wiley), as they explain this theory in a way that's easy to understand.

I'm a drummer at heart, and have zero musical theory knowledge so the way I was taught how to gauge minor/major by ear is that if the music sounds striking, bold, and solid, it's likely to be a major key. If the music evokes emotion, and tugs at your heart strings, it's likely (though not guaranteed) to be minor.

If you don't want to delve too deeply into musical theory, you can work out the root of the key and be happy with that knowledge, then simply use trial and error to find the best tunes to mix with. This isn't much better than trial and error *without* knowledge of the root key, but it's a step closer to harmonic mixing – and sometimes, a step is all it takes to be great.

Though it's hard work, and takes a lot of musical knowledge, working out the key (or just the root key) yourself is good because as you listen to the tunes, and find out the key, you develop an appreciation for what to listen to, and will eventually develop an ear to judge which tunes match together without the need to refer to a list of suitable tunes, or a notation like the Camelot Easymix system.

✔ **Software:** Computer programs are available that do all the work for you to work out the key. One of these programs, 'Mixed in Key', analyses each of your wave and MP3 files and calculates what key they're recorded in according to the Camelot system (see the earlier section 'The Camelot Sound Easymix System'). The program is surprisingly accurate, extremely effective, and a free version is available from www.MixedInKey.com.

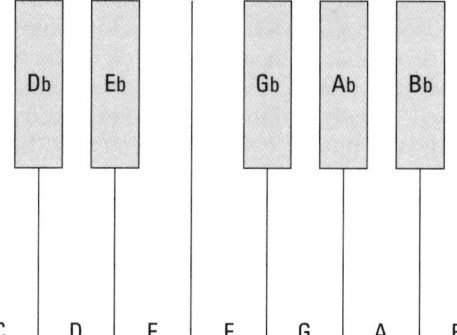

Figure 17-1:
The 12 notes on a piano scale.

When you've worked out what key your tune is in, write a little note on the record sleeve or next to the track name on the CD case. That way, finding a tune that mixes harmonically is made easy.

Knowing how much to pitch

Your turntables or CD decks may offer you an 8 per cent pitch range, or may let you go faster or slower by 100 per cent, but unless you have a special use for going really fast or slow, if you go much over 5 per cent pitch, the majority of music may start to sound strange to the ears of the people on the dance floor. If you have a Master Tempo control on your decks, you can play the music as fast or slow as you like, and the pitch won't change, just the speed, so if you activate that control, you'll never need to worry about taking things *too far*.

The ear and the brain can account for 5 per cent pitch difference to the original and still consider the music as *normal* sounding, but as you get past that guide number, the more you risk the listener thinking that something's not right.

How far you can push the pitch of a tune (without Master Tempo) depends entirely on the tune itself, and the genre of music you're playing. I've got loads of instrumental tunes that I happily pitch up to 12 per cent and no one notices, but I'd never go past 5 per cent with most vocal tracks. Many genres can be transformed into something new by *cranking up* the pitch. A DJ I know used to play a 33 RPM house record at 45 RPM because it changed it into a great sounding drum and bass tune (though I don't think that there were any vocals on that track).

Like everything else in DJing, no hard and fast rule exists, but if you find yourself straying too far past 5 per cent, it's important to stop, and ask yourself whether the tune still sounds okay. The reason you need to increase (or decrease) the pitch by so much may be because you may be crossing genres, trying to mix a smooth house track into a trance track for example. Although the structure, the key, the driving rhythm, and the pitch of the tune may all sound fine, from a genre point of view, ask yourself if these tunes really play well next to each other. Like the bully and the weird kid at school, just because two tunes fit together like jigsaw pieces, it doesn't mean that they're meant to go together. They may be from different jigsaw puzzles!

Developing a Style

The tunes you pick to play and the way you mix them come together to define your DJ style. Your style can, and should be, pliable depending on what club you're playing in and what kind of music is expected of you.

If like me, you came to DJing because you were inspired by another DJ or a music genre as a whole, you'll already have a basic style before you even start to think about one. However, try not to simply be a copycat of your favourite DJ. Listen to as many DJs as you can for inspiration, then put everything you've picked up from other DJs into a big pot, give it a stir, add in your own creative ideas that have been spawned from listening to these DJs, and hopefully, you have that little twist to your style that makes you different from other DJs.

Your style may also change from what you play in the bedroom and hand out on tapes, to what you play in a club. You may be a trance fiend in the bedroom, but the club you work at demands commercial dance music, so you have to tone down the music you play. This fact doesn't pigeonhole you as a commercial dance DJ, it's quite the opposite. You're actually a well-rounded DJ; you can play top trance in the biggest clubs in the land, or play commercial tunes and tailor your set list to a mainstream crowd.

If you're at 100 per cent where do you go?

I always think back to a guy called Martin Woods, my old squash coach. One thing I learnt from him (apart from some terrible language on court) was that if I hit everything as hard as possible all the time, I'd never have a way to change my game apart from slowing it down, which would make me predictable and boring. So, he advised me to hit the ball at about 90 per cent of power for most of the rallies, so I could inject pace and energy when I knew it was time to add pressure, or slow it down and change my game to keep my opponent guessing.

The genre of music you play doesn't define how you put it together though. Between key changes, tempo changes, energy changes, and genre changes, you can put together your own unique style, but which is still aimed at the people you're playing for – the crowd in front of you.

Easing up on the energy

If all you do is play music at full pace, full power all the time, the only thing you can do is slow down, or reduce the energy. But if you're almost at full energy, waiting to give something else when the time's right, even if that's for long periods, you'll be a DJ in control of the crowd or listener.

You'll want to be at 100 per cent power often through your set, but don't stagnate at that level and become stale. At least look to undulate the power of your tunes from start to finish, if not the tempo. Changing the driving rhythm (see the section 'Beatmatching – the next generation' earlier in the chapter) is a great way to alter the power.

When playing live, try to take the crowd through different levels of emotions. Take them from cheering and smiling, to a little more intense, eyes closed and hands in the air, and then back to cheering and bouncing up and down on the dance floor. If you can put together a musical experience instead of choosing 20 tunes just because they mix well with each other, you'll be more creative, be able to work the crowd, and hopefully be regarded as a great DJ.

Changing the key

Looking at the notation system discussed in the earlier section 'The Camelot Sound Easymix System', when you're mixing in key, you have the choice to change key by working your way around the circle provided by this system, and by moving from the inner ring to the outer ring.

Getting a backhanded compliment

I once lost out on getting the big, main-set Saturday night slot in a club because 'You'd only try to take the crowd somewhere special, we just want a DJ who plays random tunes and lets the crowd decide how happy they are'. I was annoyed at the time, missing out on the bigger slot, but looking back on it, it was one hell of a compliment. It meant everything I was striving to do was noticed by the management. Even if they did lack the sense to use that for the good of the club.

But harmonic mixing isn't just a way to let you mix in the next tune seamlessly, you can use key changes to step up the power of the night, or take the set into a more intense, dramatic level.

If you're trying to get a bit more moody and serious with the mix, lowering the key of the mix using a simple offbeat bass melody, or a rugged sounding *Ta-fe-te-te* driving rhythm (see the earlier section 'Beatmatching – the next generation' for an explanation) can really take the mix into a deep, intense place that's like saying to the crowd 'Come with me . . . I'm going to take you somewhere for the next twenty minutes'.

When you want to come up for air from a deep place, I find that changing up in key so that the notes are higher in pitch makes the mix sound brighter, happier, and full of renewed energy. If you've spent a long time in the set playing dark, complicated trance or hard house tunes, a simple offbeat driving rhythm that changes the mix up in key can be like a strong espresso in the morning – it gives the mix, and the crowd a burst of energy, and leads you into a new part of your mix.

Increasing the tempo

If the first tune you used in a mix was set to play at 130 BPM (beats per minute) and you beatmatched all the tunes that followed precisely, the entire set would play at 130 BPM and bore the pants off the dance floor.

The normal progression of a set is to have an upward trend in BPM from start to finish, with little speed bumps to slow the pace down by one or two BPM for a couple of tunes but then rev it all up again, which can work really well. Slowing down the set slightly can add energy, rather than kill it.

If you have a BPM counter on your mixer (refer to Chapter 12), play a premixed CD by one of you favourite DJs through it, and watch the counter gradually move up through the set, and look for these little tempo-speed-bumps, too.

The easiest way to increase the pace is to gradually increase the pitch fader through a series of tunes. If you have the patience (and length of tune to allow it), at the end of every two bars, move the pitch fader by a small amount (about 2 or 3 millimetres). Spread out through enough tunes, you can get to the perfect BPM you want to play at.

Be careful when moving the pitch control because if you do it too quickly, the people on the floor will hear the music get higher in pitch (remember, it's not just a speed control, it also changes the pitch of the music). Those of you who have decks with a Master Tempo need not worry about this problem. When you change the pitch control with Master Tempo turned on, the tempo of the music increases (or decreases), but the pitch stays the same, and as long as you still take some time over the change (about 15 seconds per BPM), no one consciously registers the speed increase.

Jumps

If you don't have the patience to stand over the tune and move the pitch control in small amounts, you can use the breakdowns and other changes in the tune to boost, or *jump*, the pitch by around half a per cent. Use the first beat of the bar on the new phrase to jump up the pitch control. How much you can increase it, and whether you can spread this move over a couple of bars rather than the entire track, depends on the tune that you're playing.

Using your brain

A few years ago, I heard a great breakbeat tune called 'Symmetry C' by Brainchild that Oakenfold used as a way to step up energy, if not tempo. So, I wondered how well it would work as a tempo change tool, too. One night, I'd increased the BPM to about 133 by the gradual method, at which point the floor was packed and happy as I'd been playing lots of music they knew and liked. But I wanted to take the mix up a gear.

Instead of playing faster and heavier music from the same genre, which would eventually lead to boredom, I used 'Symmetry C' as a bridge. As it had a swelling, beatless intro, I didn't even need to beatmatch it in; I just faded up over the outro of the last tune. I didn't play it for long, but it meant that I was able to jump from 133 to about 138 in one step. Over the course of the next two or three tunes, everyone went nuts without knowing why!

Or if you're planning to instantly jump the pitch as the tune hits the break-down, do it between the last beat of the phrase and the first beat of the breakdown. You're best doing this with tunes that don't have a strong melody to the breakdown and it takes practice and experimentation to get it right.

Genre changes

If the beat structure of a new, faster tune is different from the one that's currently playing, telling whether the tempo has changed can be hard, but you can use this to your advantage. Switching from house to R & B or from trance to breakbeat (and eventually back again) can be an extremely effective, and unnoticeable way of speeding up the mix

Avoiding stagnation

When you think enough about the music you play and the order and style you play it in, you start to fall in love with a few mixes. I've fallen into this trap a few times, repeating the same series of mixes week after week, or night after night. (This is especially common in warm-up sets, when you can wrongly assume that people don't care about what, or how you mix).

The downsides to repeating mixes are

✔ A mix that works in one club to one set of people won't automatically work the next night, to a different set of people

✔ Regulars to the club recognise the mix, and you appear uncreative

✔ You're going through the motions, the fun and excitement has gone

Because of the amount of time you've spent practising, you should have a sixth sense about the range of mixes that are available to you. For the sake of your development, the people on the dance floor, and the tunes in your box that never get to see the light of day, don't stick to the same transitions.

Respecting the crowd

Developing your own style is extremely important, but you still need to respect the crowd you're playing to especially when trying to get work. It's one of those Catch 22 situations that you can't avoid; how do you get experience if you need experience to get a job that gives you the experience? If you're a famous DJ, your style can be anything you want. Almost like the emperor's new clothes, some folks will love what you're doing no matter what you do or what you play.

But, when you're trying to build up your reputation, or just starting off, you need to be careful about pushing the crowd past their comfort level. If you're playing in a club where they're used to loads of scratching, samples dropped in all the time, and some pretty freaky choices of tunes, then you're okay, the crowd will like what you're doing, and if you're any good, you'll earn their respect. Hopefully, someone will notice you, and you'll get on the next rung of the ladder.

If you're working in a more commercial club though, and you try to do exactly the same strange, odd-sounding moves from the DJ booth, you may look up and find 200 people staring blankly at you, only to pause to let the tumble-weed roll past them. In this instance, tone your style down to what the audience probably expects; a smooth, constant beat for them to dance to, with not many challenging tunes or mix techniques.

This action may sound like selling out, and for many it is, but ask yourself if you'd rather be a poor artist or a paid DJ who can afford the time and money to develop in the right places at the right time, and has the ambition to do so!

Getting your style on tape

When you make a demo to show off your skills, your style is entirely up to you (head to Chapter 18 to find out more about making a demo). Your demo is a reflection of who you are, and what you want to do. Let it rip, show off how good you are at scratching, use your six turntables past their potential, and create the most awe inspiring mix anyone has ever heard.

You need to have a goal when you make a demo like this, though. Have a game plan when you show off this taster as your DJ style. If you're sending it to clubs, and the feedback you get is that it's too full on, send another one back to them that's been toned down a bit. But carry on handing out demos to your friends that are mixed in the way *you* want to mix them.

Adapt to get work, and then start to incorporate your own style, but never give up on what truly makes you want to DJ in your own time. If you compromise too far in one direction, you may never come back!

Chapter 18

Making a Great Demo

In This Chapter

▶ Putting together a list of tunes to be proud of

▶ Making sure that there's a point to the mix

▶ Setting the levels and EQs for perfect sound

▶ Staying focused and being a perfectionist

▶ Recording to computer and burning CDs

▶ Getting noticed

*Y*ou've spent a long time developing your skills as a DJ. Now you have to let people out there know how good you are by making a demo of your best mix.

Your demo reflects you in every way. You won't have the benefit of standing next to the club owner to explain that at 15 minutes and 20 seconds into your mix the cat jumped onto the decks, which caused the needle to jump, threw your concentration, and that's why the mix sounds awful.

You can't send in a sloppy looking (and sounding) CD and expect them to think that you're a professional, and you must let this taster be your best work. Your demo tape or CD marks you as a good DJ, or a bad DJ. So you'd better make it sound great.

Preparing to Record the Demo

The most important aspects of your demo are that the sound is well recorded, the music is mixed together well, and it doesn't seem as if you've just thrown together 20 tunes to make up 90 minutes of tape (or 74 minutes of CD) with no real thought. Your demo must show that you have a vision of how to progress a mix from start to finish.

Your first demo will probably be made in your bedroom, but in time, you can become comfortable enough with your skills as a DJ to tape a live set, and hand that out to people.

Programming your set

Which tunes to put on a demo tape and how to progress from start to finish is up to you and your DJing style. Some DJs like to make their demos emulate the pro-mixed CDs that they own; start off with a sample from a movie, or some ambient sound effects, mix into the first tune that also has a quiet introduction, then build up the mix for the next 90 minutes. Others prefer just to put on the first tune with a pounding beat, hit start, and take it from there, no need for a gentle introduction for these guys!

Progressive and trance DJs are more likely to be the ones who use the gradual introduction into a mix, as it does set up a mood for the next 90 minutes, and is probably what they've heard other DJs do. House DJs are about the rhythm and the musicality of what they play, so starting off with the bass beat and bass melody or a strong vocal with the beats coming in 16 bars later (see Chapter 13) is a really powerful way to start for this style of DJ.

The quality and style of your demo is a reflection of *you* as a DJ. If you make a demo that copies DJ Tiesto from start to finish, but when left to create your own DJ set, it's not as controlled and flowing as his, what are you going to be like when you first stand in the DJ booth? If someone hires you because you faithfully copied Tiesto's latest mix as your demo, you'll soon be found out that you can't mix without the benefit of plagiarism after the fifth week in a row of playing the same set!

The last thing to think about before rifling through your record box is showing what sort of music you can play. If you plan to send in a demo to a drum and bass club, adding some epic trance to the mix isn't very relevant. And if you want to send a mix to a house, or commercial club with a view to be the DJ from start to finish, you'll probably want to create your set so that you start off with some relaxed house music, move up in tempo and energy, and finish off with tunes that you know will make the crowd lose their minds on the dance floor.

Picking and arranging the tunes

In the months (or weeks if you're a natural) you've spent getting to grips with DJing, you should have developed a few mixes from tune to tune that you're really happy with, and give you goose bumps when you perform them. (There's no shame in taking pride in what you do. If you do a mix that makes you smile, there's a fair chance everyone else will smile, too!) If you have six or seven of these individual mixes between two tunes, that gives you 12–14 tunes to work with for your demo. Assuming that each track lasts about 4 minutes, you have just under an hour's worth of music to play.

Depending on the range of music in your DJ box, no doubt some of these tracks differ slightly in style, and others won't mix into any of the other 14 tracks in your current playlist. However, you still have a record box (or CD wallet) brimming with records that you love to play, so start considering some of these as the *glue tunes* that hold your mix together.

 From the 14 tunes you know you want to use in your demo, you can create a *map* of the mix by arranging them in order in front of you. If for example, your current playlist contains two gentle house tracks, two light, chart dance tracks, four vocal house tracks, two uplifting American house tracks, and four trance tracks, you may want to play them in the following order:

✔ Gentle house

✔ Vocal house

✔ Uplifting American house

✔ Chart (popular, mainstream) club tunes

✔ Trance

The order gives the mix a progression of power from beginning to end. This playlist is very simple and basic in structure, and certainly isn't right for a lot of music styles, DJs, and clubs you may apply for, but the idea of progressing through a mix, rather than throwing songs into the mix because you think that they may mix well, is crucial to showing your overall DJ skills, rather than just your beatmatching skills.

Chapter 17 has more information on creating an undulating set list and details how you dip the energy of the night by playing a slightly less powerful tune in between two energetic ones and how to change tempo and so on. But before you make your first tape, try to develop a solid understanding of progressing the mix – then you can start experimenting with the order that you play your tunes in, varying the amount of energy in the mix just like a roller-coaster going up and down.

Bridging the gaps

Take a look in your record box and hunt for the *glue tunes* that'll help you progress from one level of energy or genre to the next. Sometimes, you find a glue tune that mixes perfectly, is the perfect genre, and perfectly increases the energy enough to be a great transition into next track. Sometimes, the two tunes you're trying to bridge between are actually poorly thought out, and have such a large divide in pace and style between them that you'd be unwise to keep forcing that mix (what I call *crowbarring* in a tune).

Be careful if you plan to use mix techniques like spinbacks, dead stops, or even fade outs (refer to Chapter 14) to get around any problems of tunes mixing together. They can be used incredibly effectively, and can add a level of excitement (and energy) to the mix, but if performed poorly, or at the wrong time (or too many times), they can sound as if you've used them because you couldn't mix from one tune to the other. Your skills as a DJ are on show in your demo, so these techniques may actually work against you.

Don't simply include tunes to bridge the gap between your original tracks because they're musical glue. You want to use them because you really like playing them, and really want to include these tunes in the mix. Don't ever add a tune into the mix only with the purpose of bridging from one tune to another. Whether it's a vocal sample, a movie clip, or just another tune from the box, you need to be happy that this tune reflects on you as a DJ – because you chose it, and you put it in the mix.

With these bridge tunes added to the tracks you originally picked, you should end up with a full mix close to the length of tape (90 minutes or 60 minutes) or CD (74 minutes) that you plan to send out.

Practising your set

After you've chosen all your tunes, and you've decided on the order that you think they play best in, the time has come for you to practise your set in stages before trying to perform it all in one go.

Throwing a tape into the recorder so that you can listen back to your test mixes is a sensible idea. It's funny how a lot of mixes can sound good when you do them, but when you listen back to the tape, the mix can sound really rushed, and amateurish, or alternatively may even sound better than you thought.

Feel free to experiment at this stage with how you mix your tunes together. If you think that a mix between two particular tunes can be slightly better, trust your instincts and look at ways to improve what you're currently trying to do. Ask yourself the following questions about your mix:

✔ If you change the mix transition between tunes by 4, 8, or 16 bars, does that make a difference?

✔ If you start the new tune 16 bars later, does everything fall into place?

✔ Are you using the EQ (equaliser) controls with enough subtlety through the mix to create the seamless mix you're looking for?

✔ One last time, are you sure that the order of your tunes in the mix is the best ?

Address each possibility and create a mix that is the best you can do.

If you take a long time to put together and play a good 70–90 minute mix, that's not an issue. When you started putting the mix together, you were unlikely to be able to play it perfectly in front of an audience. Therefore, a perfect mix probably wasn't an accurate reflection of your abilities at that point, and practising your set does have several major benefits:

✔ When you practise your set to perfection, you put out your best work for people to listen to.

✔ Playing the set over and over again and analysing how to make it better is the best way to develop the skills needed to spot a bad mix, and know how to improve or fix it.

✔ Each time you practise the set, your beatmatching and knowledge of beat structure through repetition increases incredibly.

✔ Creating a set you're excited about, that has a purpose other than general practice, and uses tunes you love listening to, removes any boredom factor, and your skills develop without you realising it!

Practise your set until you're completely comfortable playing it. Reaching the stage where you know the mix points and starting cue points like the back of your hand is important, as is being happy with all the EQ settings and strange volume anomalies that may occur (see the later section 'Looking After Sound Processing').

Setting up to record

Before you can start to record your demo, you need to set up your equipment to ensure the best possible sound quality. Two factors can affect your sound quality:

✔ You need a good quality tape (or CD/PC) recorder that you know how to work, which can faithfully record your mix without failing on you, chewing up the tape, or cutting out halfway through.

✔ You need to be familiar with your mixer and know how to control the sound output on it.

Avoiding poor quality recordings

The only thing less appealing than a tape with train wreck mixing and a poor choice of music, is one that's badly recorded. Always keep in mind that no matter who you send your tape to, whether it's your best friend, your mother, or Paul Oakenfold, this tape demonstrates your skills as a DJ. If it's badly recorded, you instantly lose points, and will be dubbed as unprofessional!

Tape versus CD for demos

From a functional point of view, these days you should really make a demo CD of your mix rather than a tape. The sound quality is far better for starters, but the ability to skip tracks to the next mix instantly on CD, rather than messing around with the fast-forward button makes CD the preferred format.

To cover all eventualities, if you have the time (and the money for the increased cost) I'd advise creating tapes and CDs. Why would you want to reduce the options of how someone can listen to your mix? When you send both formats, you show that you have an understanding for what people want, and you show consideration and thought toward those you're trying to get work from, because they may not have a tape player or CD player where they'll be listening to the demo (a car for instance).

Don't hand out tapes you know are bad

Years ago, I had a stereo that had a problem with the recording heads that would temporarily drop the high frequencies from the music. I was so excited at being a DJ, and I really wanted to make sure that all my friends had tapes of me DJing. Everybody would politely take these tapes from me, but one day I went to a friend's house, and saw my 'Recession' mix tape sitting next to the stereo with Sellotape over the record-prevent tabs. When I asked him about it, he said that although he liked the mix, after listening to it once, he'd got fed up with the sound problems, and figured that he'd rather have a recording of Pete Tong from the radio instead. That really hurt, but it taught me a valuable lesson.

Cassette tapes need to be recorded properly in order to sound good. Different makes of tapes have different tolerances to the amount of signal they can handle (how loud you play the music from the mixer to the tape recorder). The packaging on the tape tells you the perfect range (in decibels).

Always be sure to work within the tolerance that the tape can accept. If you play too loud, the sound distorts; too quiet a signal, and you get a lot of tape hiss, which loses the clarity and brightness of the sound of the music.

Although a CD plays at a quiet volume on a stereo if under-recorded, you shouldn't have any problems with the recording quality from these low level recordings. Set the levels on your CD (or computer) recorder too loud though, and you suffer from digital clipping, which isn't a nice noise at all. The music just cuts out and pops when recorded too loud. A little bit of *clipping* on CD sounds a lot worse than a little bit of distortion on a cassette tape.

MiniDisc and DAT for demos

MiniDisc is a great digital format to record to. With MP3 players becoming more popular as playback devices, in my opinion the future for MiniDisc lies more in its recording performance than the playback of pre-recorded or downloaded music.

The audio quality of MiniDisc is good enough for you to make multiple, great sounding copies of your mix. If you only record to audio tape, you have to make copies of the tape (called *making another generation*, which vastly reduces the sound quality of the new tape), or keep performing your mix each time you want to send your tape somewhere new – and as much as you love the music, that will eventually feel like a drag, and you won't enjoy per-forming that mix as much anymore.

DAT (digital audio tape) is the professional format used to record music, and can often be used as a final master of a recording made in the recording studio. As it's seen as specialised, professional equipment, very few people own DAT players, so you'll be wasting your time (and money, DAT tapes are expensive) sending DATs to clubs and bars. As with MiniDisc, if you have access to DAT recorders, use a DAT as a master recording of your mix, and make your duplications from it.

Correcting recording levels

In order to make sure that the CDs and tapes you record hit the proper balance between enough volume to prevent tape hiss with no risk of sound distortion – your recorder needs to have some kind of record level indicator.

This indicator is usually very similar to the output VU meter on your mixer; a set of two lines of LEDs that are different colours (green, yellow, and then red) depending on how strong the signal is. The meter should be laid out so that any music you play over a certain level (sometimes when it hits +3 decibels) makes the red LEDs start to flash. If your tape can accept up to +8 decibels as an input strength, and you set the record level to a normal maximum of +3 decibels, if the music spikes by 2 decibels because of an unexpected loud part of the record, you're still within the recording limits of your equipment (as the signal is only +5 decibels, which is still 3 decibels under the recording limits).

If you set the record level so that it's almost hitting the +8 decibel mark for the normal playback of your records, when this musical spike occurs, the level is now +10 decibels, and you will distort the recording.

Limiters

Limiters are used to clamp down on any peaks in level, helping to prevent distortion. If you do have a limiter on your home recorder, it will probably have a very harsh attack, so if the music does peak, the limiter immediately reduces the overall level of the music by 2 or 3 decibels. This dip can be very noticeable on the recording, and sounds as though you've crashed down on the output level on the mixer by accident.

Some professional limiters are really good, and can be used as a great safety net for unexpected peaks in the music signal, but I still recommend that you concentrate on setting the record levels correctly in the first place, so you don't lose some quality and clarity when the limiter kicks in.

Matching the levels

The best way to control the audio levels being recorded is to make sure that when the music is playing at its loudest point, the mixer's output level meter is set to display the same as the tape (or CD recorder) input level meter. This way, you can look at the output LEDs on the mixer showing +3 decibels, and be happy that the tape recorder is recording the music at +3 decibels, too.

Lining up your equipment

Setting your equipment so that everything you look at shows the same value is known as *lining up* your equipment. This alignment is all done by playing a *reference tone* through the mixer. A reference tone is a constant sine wave playing at 1 kilohertz.

A constant tone is preferable because you can be exact about metering the precise signal level. When you play music to line up the equipment, the LEDs are erratic, and flash up and down to show the different changes in the signal level. A constant tone is just that; constant. The level (and the LEDs) change only if you move the faders on the mixer, or the input control on the recorder.

The process of lining up equipment using tone is as follows:

1. **If you haven't got your own reference tone, download one from my Web site (www.recess.co.uk), and transfer it to CD or MP3.**

2. **Even if you use turntables, find a CD or MP3 player to plug into your mixer, and play this tone into one of the channels.**

3. **If you need to press a switch or button to see the input level coming into the mixer, do so now (see Chapter 8 for information on input levels).**

4. **Use the gain controls on the mixer to adjust the gain so that the input level of the tone shows +3 decibels on the input level LEDs.**

   This adjustment may mean increasing, or reducing the gain control. If you're playing the reference tone out of the headphones of an MP3 player, the signal may be weaker than normal; if so, turn the volume up on the MP3 player as well as the gain control to make sure that the input level is at +3 decibels.

5. **Set the channel-fader for this channel to the maximum position you would set it when playing a tune normally.**

   For scratch DJs, this setting is normally right up to the top. For beat-mixing DJs, I always recommend setting your *maximum point* to three-quarters of the way up (refer to Chapter 14 for why).

6. **If you need to switch the display LEDs back to display the Master Output level, do so now.**

7. **Use the Master Level control-fader to make the LEDs for the output of the mixer display +3 decibels.**

   After you've made this adjustment, any changes you make to the gain control on the input channel are mirrored by the readout of the mixer. If you reduce the gain on the reference tone to only 0 decibels, you will notice that the Master Level output LEDs also drop down to 0 decibels.

8. **If you've just tried adjusting the gain to a 0 decibel setting as suggested in Step 7, return the gain (and therefore the Master Level) to +3 decibels.**

9. **Set the recording level on the tape recorder.**

   Setting this level is simply a case of increasing (or decreasing) the input control so the LEDs display +3 decibels on the recorder.

The +3dB level is used only to line up your equipment and make the LED displays show the same thing. If you want a +6dB output to the recording device, increase the gain control on the channel input to +6dB, and you'll see the Master Level Output display and the display on the recording equipment now show +6dB.

The Master Output Level control doesn't affect the strength of the signal sent out of the Record Outputs. If you reduce the Master Level Control so the meters only show +3dB in the preceding example, you're still sending +6dB out of the mixer to the recording device. As long as you make sure that the input levels of your different input channels match +6 decibels, and the Master Output level is used as a visual reference to be sure that the signal level doesn't exceed or fall too far from +6 decibels, you're then able to prevent any noticeable volume changes from one track to the next.

Unfortunately, this precise guide on how to line up your equipment only works properly if your recording equipment has a record level control. If you send the music into a home-style hi-fi with a preset record level, you may have to spend a lot of time trying to find the proper output level from your mixer through trial and error in order to create good quality recordings.

Looking After Sound Processing

When you come to look after the sound of your mix, you have two major considerations; keeping an even volume between tunes, and the EQs.

Keeping an even volume

Keeping a smooth volume to your mix is almost as important as keeping the bass beats in time. A drop in volume from tune to tune when they're both playing their loudest parts sounds very amateurish, and must be avoided at all cost.

As you have lined up the equipment (see the preceding section) properly, volume control is a simple process. You need to use the gain controls and the input level meters on your mixer to match the input levels of your tunes.

If you don't have input level meters on your mixer, you'll find keeping the volume of your tunes in the mix the same is a lot harder. What you can do is put both ears of the headphones on, and quickly switch from hearing each tune through them, if you hear a drop in volume from one tune to the next, use the gain controls to increase or decrease the level of the *incoming* tune (the tune you're about to mix in) until they both sound about the same.

If you don't have gain controls on your mixer, I recommend saving up to buy a new one, quickly! In Chapter 14, I mention the importance of setting the channel-faders to three-quarters of the way up rather than all the way up. This is of extreme benefit to the people without gain controls, because if a tune you've just mixed in doesn't sound as loud as the one you're mixing out of, you still have some headroom (the other quarter of the way up on the channel-fader) to increase how loud the new tune plays. With practice, and patience, you'll eventually develop the knack to catch these changes before anyone else can hear them.

Assuming that you have a mixer with gain controls and input level meters, making sure that all your tunes play out at a similar volume through the duration of the mix is very simple. Here's how:

1. **Before you press record, with the EQs for bass, mid, and high frequencies set to the position for perfect sound to come out from the mixer (see the next section 'Setting your EQs), start a tune and look at the input level LED display on the mixer (you may need to press a button or switch to do this).**

2. **Use the gain control to set the input level to your preferred point.**

   (I usually suggest that the meter should light up the first red LEDs (sometimes at the +3 decibel point), and maybe make the next set light up from time to time, but not constantly. Your settings depend on the mixer you use and what you're recording to).

3. **After you have pressed record and started the first tune playing, pick out the next tune, and play it through the headphones with the EQs set to the optimum play out position.**

4. **Use the gain control to set the input level LEDs on the new tune so that they're as close as possible to the current tune you're playing through the speakers.**

When the channel-faders are both set to the same level, both tunes should play out of the mixer at the same volume. Unless:

- ✔ **You forget to set the EQs to the optimum play out level before checking the input level LEDs, which gives an artificial reading.** If the bass has been killed (when mixing out of the last tune for instance) and you don't reset it to neutral (which is hopefully 0), when you check the new tune's input level, the reduced bass will cause it to have a lot less signal strength than it should. So if, for example, you'd set the gain control to make the input LED's match the +3 decibels of the other tune, when you finally realise the bass has been cut, and put it back in, the tune may now play with a +8 decibel signal strength. Get into the routine of resetting the EQs after every mix so you don't fall into this trap.

- ✔ **Your tunes have a bass beat and rhythm, which, although sounding fine, over-powers the rest of the tune, showing a false 'high' reading.** So although the LEDs show an input strength of +3 decibels, the tune actually sounds *weak* (reduced volume and power) compared to the other tunes in the mix.

The only way to get around this problem is to get to know your tunes. If this problem happens once in practice, take a note (or make a note on the record sleeve) to remind you that that tune needs the gain to be set a little higher, or the bass level killed slightly to allow you to raise the gain in order to match the volume with the rest of the mix.

Cross-fader curves also have a part to play in the volume of a mix. Check out Chapter 8 for information about how the cross-fader curve affects the volume during a mix between two tunes, but if the curve allows both tunes to play at full volume at the same time, the overall output level increases, and may cause the sound to distort on tape or clip on CD (see Figure 18-1). The two ways around this problem are to use a cross-fader curve that has a slight dip in the middle to compensate for the boost of two tunes playing together at full volume (see the section in Chapter 8 about cross fader curves – especially Figure 8-2 and 8-3), or use the channel-faders to dip the tunes slightly through the mix, then return them to full when the mix is almost over. More information on using channel-faders to enhance the mix is in Chapter 14.

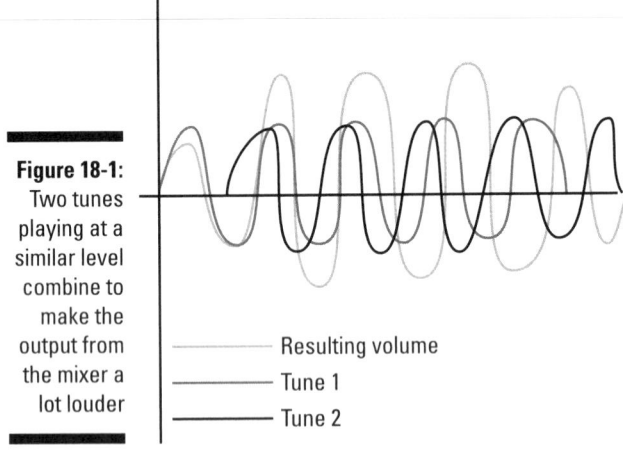

Figure 18-1:
Two tunes playing at a similar level combine to make the output from the mixer a lot louder

——— Resulting volume

——— Tune 1

——— Tune 2

Setting your EQs

Different recorders (and tapes) react in different ways to how you set the EQs (equalisers) on your mixer. Some have a tendency to record too much bass, others can record too much mid-range or high frequencies of the tunes.

As well as any problems caused by your recording equipment, you also have to consider how you have setup the EQs on your amplifier. If you have the bass set very high on your amp (or stereo) you probably have the bass EQs on the mixer set lower than normal. With this setting, the recordings you make sound *a bit thin* (a description of a sound that's lacking in bass).

The best way of making sure that you select the best EQ settings for your recording is to start off with a blank sheet. The first thing to do is set all the EQs on the mixer to their neutral point. This point is normally marked with a 0, or is the halfway point on the control (for rotary knobs, this means setting the EQ so that it's pointing to the twelve o'clock position on a clock face.) In this way, the music that you're sending out of the mixer isn't being affected by the EQ controls, and each of the three frequency bands (bass, mid, and high) remains exactly as the artist intended.

However, different mixers process sound slightly differently. Some cheap mixers need to have the bass and high frequencies increased slightly, with the mid-range reduced in order to make the tune sound right. If you have a good pair of headphones, use them to gauge the audio quality from the mixer and use the EQs to set the sound of the music so it sounds good to you.

Obviously, different tunes need their EQs tweaked in order to make the bass, or high frequencies stand out a little more in the mix. Different tunes also have different sounding bass drums, and you may want to use the mid and bass EQs to try to match the strength of the bass beat as you go through the mix. You may need to try a couple of different tunes to find a general setting for the EQs to make the music sound best.

Testing, testing

To check the frequency settings of the music coming out of the mixer and on to tape, simply make a test recording. Listen to the recording on a tape recorder (or CD player) other than the one you've used to record it with. I find that car stereos play music back very faithfully (although, not the bass thumping, body shaking one that Darren has in his pimped-out ride). If the music sounds fine in the car (especially when compared to pre-recorded tapes and CDs that you normally play in the car) then you can be 95 per cent sure that you've set up the EQs and levels on your mixer (and recorder) to allow the mix to be recorded properly.

If the recording doesn't sound right, and you need to add a little more bass, look to the recording unit first before adjusting the mixer. If your tape recorder has recording EQs that you can adjust, increase the bass slightly, and do another test recording. If your recorder doesn't have EQ controls, you need to adjust the EQs on the mixer in order to make the music sound as good as possible on tape.

The reason you change the EQs on the recorder first is because as a DJ, you use the EQs more as a mixing tool than as a sound processing tool. See Chapter 14 for more information on how to use the EQs to enhance your mixes, but the key here is that if you have to boost the bass by 6 decibels (most controls go to about 12 decibels) in order to make the music sound good on tape, when you mix in another tune with elevated bass frequencies, you risk the danger of your mixer not being able to process that combined, high-bass signal well enough, and the sound quality of your mix suffers.

Sound engineers take the time to EQ instruments and vocals precisely, but hardly move the EQs away from those settings after they've been set. As a DJ, you'll be constantly changing the EQs as you mix, so knowing that each control just needs to be returned to 0 to make the tune sound normal, greatly benefits the sound processing and speed of your mixes.

Setting EQs on the recorder or the mixer may take a little time to get right, but helps the music you put on tape sound the best it can.

Adjusting the amplifier

You change the EQ settings on your amplifier depending on your circumstances. You may be recording the music through your home hi-fi, which also acts as your amplifier, so the EQ settings you make to improve the recording also affect the sound from the hi-fi (amplifier).

If you're using a separate recorder from the amplifier though, concentrating on the sound that goes from the mixer into the recorder is more important than adjusting the amp. After you've set up the sound to make the perfect recording to tape or CD, you can then go to your amplifier and tweak the frequencies to give you the best sound you'd like to hear from the speakers.

Changing the EQs for the amp first is a waste of time and makes concentrating on generating the best EQs for the tape recording a lot harder. If you set the EQs for the amp first and then find that you have to increase the bass EQ on the mixer to get a perfect recording, the bass through the amp is now going to be too high, and you have to re-adjust it, and probably the mid and high frequencies, too. You may also feel reluctant to alter the beautiful sound you've created through the amplifier and sacrifice the sound quality of your recording.

Only you know how you like to hear the music through the amp, but the basic guideline is for the sound to have a clear, solid bass beat, (but not so much that the bass frequencies take over the rest of the tune, which may make it sound *muddy*), the mid range shouldn't be so high that it dominates the bass frequencies, and the high frequencies should be set so that you can hear the hi-hat cymbals playing crisply over the bass and mid frequencies.

Performing the Demo

You've chosen a good order for your tunes that make up the demo, you've set all the recording controls to get the best sound possible, and you've practised the set so that you actually dream about how the tunes are put together. Now take the final step and record your demo.

Press the record button on the CD/tape/MiniDisc/DAT/computer, (let tapes run for about five seconds to make sure that you're past the blank leader tape at the very beginning) then take a deep breath – it's for real this time – and start the mix. An hour and a half later, you'll either have gold dust or fertiliser sitting in the recording device.

If it's the latter, make a cup of coffee, compose yourself, and do it again, and again, and again – until you get it right. You don't need to get too annoyed with yourself if you mess the demo up (though messing up right at the end of your mix *is* especially frustrating). Remember that the professional DJs who actually mix on their CDs (rather than using computer software to do it for them) have been doing this DJing lark a lot longer than you have, and are (for the time being) just plain better than you.

The pros also have the option to stop when they make an error, then start again from where they left off, and piece everything together in the recording studio. If you record directly to audio tape, or even CD and MiniDisc, you need to perform the entire set from start to finish without getting anything wrong. If you record your mix to a computer, you can edit out the bad parts, and repair your errors by stopping and starting.

You're cheating yourself out of an invaluable process of improving your DJing if you use a computer to tidy up your mixes when you're starting out. Each time you go through your set, whether you complete it or not, you're expanding your skills, and getting one step closer to how good your idols are. If you just stop and restart the mix between two tunes after an error when recording to computer, it amounts to nothing more than shortcutting.

If you do like taking shortcuts though, head to the section 'Making a Demo CD on Computer' later in this chapter to find out more about re-editing your mix on computer.

Stay focused

If you have to run through your set three or four times (or more) before you create a recording that you're happy with, maintain your composure, stay focused on what you're trying to do, and try not to get frustrated and angry by any mistakes you make.

You can do a few simple things to help keep your head in the game.

- Arrange your records in the order you plan to play them in, so you don't have to hunt through the record box to find the next tune, run out of time, and mess up the mix.

- Wipe off any dust from the records, and check for any build-up of grime on the needles. You don't want to be halfway through the mix and see a fluff ball tracking in front of one of your needles; the sound quality suffers, and the needle may skip.

- Have something to eat before you start recording. Low blood sugar is the number one cause of snapped records in my DJ room. I get really grumpy and easily frustrated when I'm hungry, and (reluctantly) admit to throwing one or two records into a wall after a bad mix on an empty stomach.

- Keep some water on hand. Hunger can sometimes be thirst in disguise. Keep yourself properly hydrated so you don't start to feel tired and worn out.

- If you mess up a mix after getting one hour through it, take a ten-minute break, go for a walk, clear your head, and come back to the mix ready to have another go. This break not only takes out any boredom factor that may lead to impatience, but also gives your ears a rest from the music playing out from the amp.

- Go to the toilet before you start. Needing to pee during a set not only makes you rush a mix so you can run off to the smallest room, but you may be in there a while, and miss the next mix. Be sensible and go before you start the mix. Just remember to wash your hands, please.

DJing made me put on weight

I thought I'd be smart about not getting hungry when I recorded. I used to keep a bag of Jelly Babies with me when DJing at home, or in clubs, just in case I got a drop in my sugar levels, and needed a quick jolt. A bag of Jelly Babies per night makes your waistline grow incredibly fast. Couple that with more time spent DJing than on the squash court, and it's no wonder my waistline grew! (It's all better now, getting married made me care about fitting back into my kilt.)

Become a perfectionist

No matter how long you take to get the mix right, get the mix right. Keep in mind that your demo can be passed to anybody. You never know who may hear your work, and have an influence on your career.

Therefore, the demo has got to be perfect in your eyes. Never, ever utter the words 'That'll do'. If you want to be a bedroom DJ for the rest of your life, then fine, it probably will do. But if you have even a pinch of ambition in you, start again. Even if you miss out one beat, or have a picky problem with the levels, re-do the mix. To make an error is acceptable; not to improve because of your errors, or fix them, should be completely unacceptable to you. Get to a stage that when you hear demos by DJs who don't care as much as you do, you can take pride in being more of a professional than them.

If the demo is for submission to a competition or a job, remember that you're up against tens of thousands of budding DJs. Decks are almost outselling guitars; *everyone* wants to be a DJ. Now do you get how important it is to be perfect? (On tape at least.)

Listen with an open mind

When you listen back to your mix to gauge how your performance sounds, judge it with an open mind. Things to look out for are any noticeable drops in volume through the tune transitions, distortion on the tape, any *galloping horse* bass drum beats when beatmatching, noticeable pitch bends when you speed up (or slow down) a tune to get it back in time, poor EQ control, and choosing the wrong time to mix from one tune to another.

However, don't fall into the trap of over-criticism when you listen to the mix. Knowing exactly when a mix happens and exactly what to listen to can make you develop blindness to the overall sound of the mix, and because you hear the transition, automatically assume that it's a bad mix. I actively encourage you to listen to the mix with a critic's ear, but also listen to it with a passive listener's ear. If the mix was performed well, and still sounds great, is it really that bad, and is there really a way to make the transition seamless?

Come back to that same mix in a couple of months' time, when you don't have every second of it fresh in your mind, and I'm sure that you'll like it more than you do now. The chance that your opinion may change with the passage of time is not an excuse to let poorly beatmatched or poorly conceived mixes enter into your demo, but also don't beat yourself up trying to create a seamless mix that isn't possible.

Making a Demo CD on Computer

Recording your demo to computer can make your demo a lot more versatile. You can add CD track marks precisely where you would like them to be, you can edit a 'best of' taster mix to go before or after the main mix, and (although not encouraged) by recording to computer, you can edit out your fluffs (mistakes).

Once you have successfully connected your mixer to the computer (refer to Chapter 11), and have set up the software to process the incoming music at the correct recording level (refer to the manual that comes with your software) you need to set the quality of your recording.

CD quality sound is 44.1 kilohertz (or 44100 hertz) 16 bit (binary notation), stereo (multiple sound) and you can change the audio recording quality to this setting using your recording software (even with the basic Windows Sound Recorder system). If you record the mix at a lower sample or bit rate, you can still transfer the mix onto CD, but the quality of the recording won't be as good and the computer may need to re-process the audio first in order for the music to be playable on CD.

CD audio quality takes up about 100 megabytes for every ten minutes you record, so make sure that your hard drive has at least twice the space you require. Some software records to a virtual *cache* first, taking up space on the hard drive, but needs the same amount of space again to save the file.

With the record levels set correctly (see the manual for your software) and sample rates all set, all you need to do is press Record on the software, start your mix, press Stop when you've finished it and save it to the hard drive.

Editing your mix

Using a computer to edit out any poor performance for your demo isn't conducive to improving your mixing skills. Don't get into the cheating habit.

For re-editing your mix you need software that's a bit more sophisticated than the Windows Sound Recorder. For PC, I use Adobe Audition, NGWave, or Pro Tools. On the Mac, I use Apple Soundtrack, Pro Tools, and Audacity to edit, effect, and save the mixes to different formats. There are hundreds of different software audio editors available. You may even have one installed with your CD burner software. Have a look through your program folder on your PC/Mac before spending any money on some expensive software.

Here's how to fix a mix if you make errors while performing it:

1. **When you record your mix to computer and make an error, press Stop on the software, and save the file.**

2. **Call this file something recognisable like 'Mix Part 1' and save it to a new folder, keeping your work organised and tidy.**

3. **Assuming that you got the mix between two tunes wrong, work out if this happened because you set the pitch of the incoming tune incorrectly, and if so, adjust the pitch on that tune.** (Only change the pitch on the incoming tune, not the one that was already playing through the speakers, because if you change the pitch on the playing tune, the beats (and pitch of the tune) won't match the saved file, where you left off.)

4. **With the file saved, and any pitch setting errors corrected, move the needle or skip the CD about 30 seconds before you're due to start the mix.** Press Record on the PC, press Start on the CD/turntable, and continue with the mix as though you'd never stopped.

If you make any more errors, save the file each time you stop as a sequential number (Mix Part 2, Mix Part 3, and so on). If you mess up the same mix again between the two tunes, you don't need to save that file, just stop, and start again, and save that part of the mix when it's finally right.

After you've completed the mix, albeit split into three or four different files, you need to start putting the mix back together again.

The software or even computer you use may be different from what I'm about to describe, but the principle remains the same:

1. **Open up the Mix Part 1 file (the first file) and play it.**

   A visual representation of the music (a symmetrical group of peaks and troughs called the *waveform* – see Figure 18-2) appears on screen to help you navigate the file. Usually there's a time indicator bar that moves along the waveform as the music plays to let you know where in the music is currently playing.

2. **Find an appropriate point on Mix Part 1 to stop.**

   This point would probably be before you started mixing into the next tune and it's best to stop playback at the beginning of a phrase (see Chapter 13 if you're unsure what a phrase is). Zoom in to the waveform tight enough to see the different peaks as each bass beat hits. When you've zoomed in close enough, you should easily be able to position the time indicator at the exact point the first bass beat of the first bar of a phrase hits.

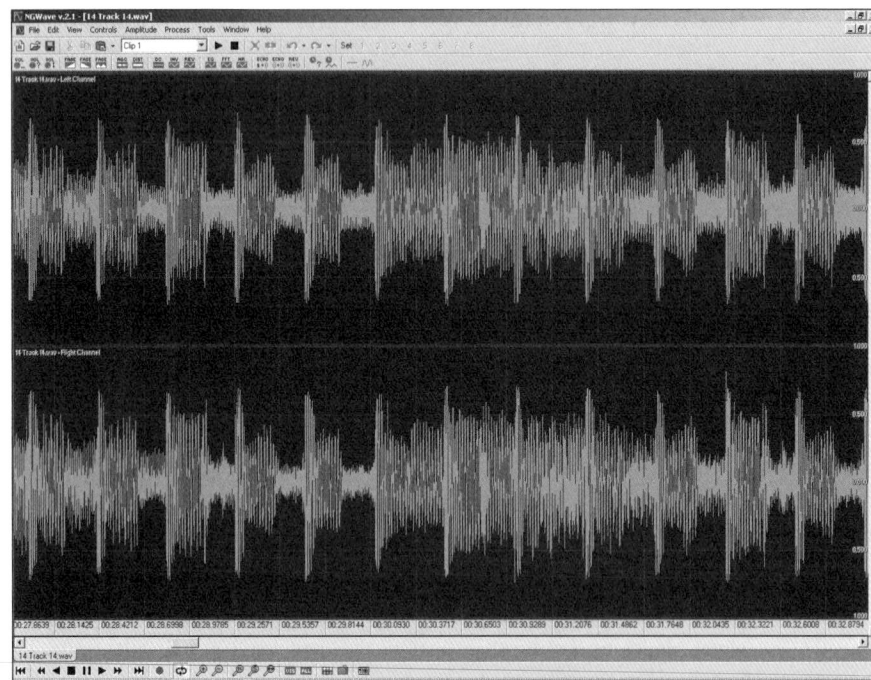

Figure 18-2:
The
waveform
displayed on
NGWave.

3. **Open up the Mix Part 2 file in another window.**

4. **Because you've started Mix Part 2 before the error in Mix Part 1, this overlap means you can find the identical point in Mix Part 2 that you stopped Mix Part 1 at.**

   If you know the tunes well, and stopped Mix Part 1 at the beginning of a phrase, this operation doesn't take too long. You need to zoom in to the waveform again to be able to get the time indicator to exactly the same position in the music that Mix Part 1 has been left at.

5. **Select Mix Part 2's waveform from where you set the time indictor, to the end of the waveform (in Adobe Audition, you just click and drag from the indicator all the way to the right-hand side of the waveform).**

6. **Copy this selection of the waveform to the clipboard (normally just by pressing Ctrl+C, (or CMD+C on a Mac) or choosing Edit then Copy from the menu bar).**

7. **Change the window back to the Mix Part 1 waveform and write down the time that the time indicator is currently sitting at, so you can easily check your edit point.**

8. **Without moving the time indicator on Mix Part 1, paste the file from the clipboard onto the waveform (choose Edit then Paste, or press Ctrl+V (or CMD+V)).**

   This stage may vary according to the software you're using, but the essence is that you're pasting Mix Part 2 over Mix Part 1 from the point where you left the time indicator, so you shouldn't have any noticeable repetition, or cut in music, and the music should continue as though nothing has ever happened.

9. **Set the time indicator to the time you wrote down, and listen to the join between the two parts of the mix.**

   The join should sound completely normal. If it doesn't, undo the paste of Mix Part 2 (Ctrl Z, CMD+Z or Edit, Undo), check where you set your time indicators and have another go.

10. **Repeat this process for all the mix parts you had to make in order to get the end of the mix without any errors, and save this file as 'Master Mix'.**

   You now have one file made up of all your changes that sounds as though you've never done anything wrong.

If you made beatmatching errors, volume or EQ control mistakes, or anything else went wrong in the mix, you can patch it all up by using this editing method.

When saving the file, save it as a Wave file (WAV) (or as an AIFF for Mac) and be sure to check that the save settings are the same as the record settings (44.1 KHz, 16 bit, Stereo). You may also want to save the file as an MP3 or any other audio format you'd like. Saving as an MP3 at 192 Kbps (kilobits per second) gives you great quality at a massively reduced file size compared to the CD quality WAV or AIFF files, and is perfect for uploading to the Internet for others to listen to.

Burning a CD

After you save your final mix as a WAV or AIFF file, you can burn the mix to CD. Depending on your operating system, you can probably just insert a blank CD into your CD recorder, *drag* the WAV or AIFF file onto the CD icon on your computer, and follow the prompts to burn an audio CD (rather than a data CD, which won't play in a normal CD player).

Or, if you have designated software to control your CD burner (like Toast for a Mac, or Nero for a PC) you can customise the information that's burnt with the CD. It's normally this software that enables you to split the one large file up so that instead of one long track burnt to CD, you have a different track on the CD for each tune you used in your mix, without any audio gap between these tracks.

Creating a track-split CD

If you want to increase your professionalism stakes by a point or two, make sure to create a mix CD that's split into individual tracks. Not only does this method make your mix seem a lot more professional, but this presentation means that the people you send the CD out to can easily scan through the CD to listen to just the transitions between tunes to gauge how good you are as a DJ, rather than listening to the entire CD or trying to scan through one long, 74-minute track on CD to find your mix points.

You can split a CD in two ways:

- **The hardest way:** You can create a CD with multiple tracks by using your audio editing software (see the section 'Editing your mix'). The software gives you a time code for the music, and this code is essential to doing this method properly. The time code is a precise measurement for working out where you are in the tune. The measurement is normally shown as hours, minutes, seconds, and thousands of a second (HH:MM:SS:DDD). Here's how to do it the hard way:

  1. If your first tune (out of 15) starts at 0:00:00:000 and you want the second track on the CD to start at 0:04:15:150, then save the mix from 00:00:00:000 to 00:04:15:150 as an individual file.

  2. If track two ends at 0:09:35:223, save the mix from 0:04:15:151 (notice that it's one thousandth of a second ahead of the last cut point) to 0:09:35:223 as another separate file.

  3. Go through this process for the whole mix so that you now have 15 individual WAV files that make up your mix. Give the files numbers when saving them not titles, which makes life easier when you come to keeping them in the correct order.

  4. With each file saved in sequence (1, 2, 3, 4, 5, 6, 7, 8, 9, and so on) use your CD burning software to add each of the files to the list of files to be burnt to the CD (in numerical order).

  5. Set the gap between each track to 0 seconds. You may have to refer to the manual for how to make this setting. If you don't set the gap to 0 seconds, and it remains at the default setting (normally 2 seconds), you will get a two second gap between each of your tracks, which won't sound like a proper DJ mix and will end up being filed – in the trash can!

6. After you've added all the tracks and set the gap in between each track, simply burn the disc to CD and listen back to it to make sure that you've split all the individual tracks up properly, without gaps or blips in sound caused by getting the time-codes wrong.

✔ **The simplest way:** Create a track split CD by using the built-in track splitting functions on software such as Nero Burning Rom, Dart Pro, and Sonic Foundry. Each piece of software has a way of marking where you'd like to add track split points, without having to physically split up the wave file itself.

As long as you remember to set the gap between each of the tracks to 0 seconds, the finished CD is neatly split into all your chosen tracks, without the danger of missing 1,000th of a second that may cause a *blip* in the sound.

The process is almost the same as splitting the file into 15 (or however many tracks you used) separate files. The software normally shows a waveform of the music (see Figure 18-2), which you play through from start to finish, adding markers to the waveform as you review it. You don't need to play the track in real time from start to finish, you can skip ahead, back, play slowly, and so on, all in aid of finding the exact point you'd like to add the track split marker.

Check the manual that came with your software for more detailed instructions on how to make CDs with individual split tracks.

Mix CDs you find in shops tend to put track splits at the end, or halfway through a mix, but when the club owner hits *Next* on the CD player, he'll skip past your DJing skills. So for a demo, you may want to put them before each of the mixes start, so that the club owner can just skip forward to hear how you perform each of the transitions.

Creating a transition only mix

If you've recorded your mix to computer, and you have enough space left at the end of your CD, you may want to include a *transition only* version of your demo. As some club promoters may only care about how you mix from tune to tune, and can get enough of a sense of how you've programmed your set by only listening to the highlights, or maybe just don't care, you can help your cause by including a series of audio tracks that just contain the 30 seconds (approximately) of time spent mixing from one tune to another.

Before you begin, you need to work out if you have enough space on the CD to include a highlights mix. On a 14-track mix, the highlights probably take up to 7–10 minutes of CD space. So if your mix is longer than 65 minutes, you may have to edit this taster down to a bare minimum.

Open up your Master WAV or AIFF file, and for each mix, select the start of a phrase before the mix starts, until the very end of a phrase after you've completed the mix. Save each of these ranges of the mix to an individual WAV file, from phrase start to phrase finish for each transition of the mix. You should end up with twelve different files to cover the 14-track mix.

If you've accurately selected each of the transitions at the exact beginning and end of a phrase, you should be able to copy and paste them all into one long file in your audio editor. This instantly creates a highlight mix, which shouldn't jump from track to track (unless you increased (or decreased) the pitch of a tune in the middle of it, so the end is faster than the beginning. In which case, you'll just have to make do with a 'jump-cut' in which the transition version suddenly gets faster).

This taster mix may sound a bit quick, and if you have the space on the CD, you may want to extend the length of time given to some (or all) of the highlights. However, if the manager only cares about the transition, and you can still keep the beats pounding and uninterrupted, brevity may actually be rewarded.

Sending Off the Mix

After you've created your demo tape/CD/MiniDisc, the final stage is to create a *package* that sells you properly, and make sure that whoever receives it knows where it came from, even it the demo gets separated from the rest of the package items you send in the padded envelope. (See Chapter 19 for more info on where to send your demo.)

To create a selling package, you may wish to include a brief CV along with the demo, covering your experience as a DJ, the styles of music you mix, whether you drive, how old you are, where you live, whether you DJ with vinyl, CD, or MP3s on a laptop, if you are comfortable speaking through a microphone, and a quick paragraph explaining why you've applied to them for work, and why it would be mutually beneficial for you to be their DJ.

If you don't look like a monster, popping in a photograph to include in the package is a good idea, too. If you can show how presentable you are, they're more likely to consider you, and if you're good looking, they may not even listen to the mix, and just hire you based on how the ladies (or guys) will fawn over you!

Decide whether you want to send in multiple formats of the mix. Obviously, a tape, a CD, and a MiniDisc version of your mix covers nearly all the bases, and you won't be faced with the excuse of 'I didn't have a MiniDisc player to listen to your demo, sorry' – but this can get costly when you're sending out loads of demos. So if you can, send a CD and a tape. If not, just send a CD.

Include a track list of your mix, and indicate key moments in the demo if it's not split into separate tracks. If you've added a highlights mix at the end of the CD, be sure to make that plainly obvious. If the people listening to the mix don't know that it's been specially edited for their convenience, they may wonder what it is (and be amazed at how fast you can mix from tune to tune).

I can't stress enough the importance of following this piece of advice: Clearly write your name, your phone number, and your e-mail address on every piece of paper or plastic, every cover, CD, tape, MiniDisc, photograph, inlay sleeve, and covering letter that you send out with your demo.

If you can print the label on your CD, make it a nice design, but make sure your details show up clearly. Add stickers to your tapes, make sure that you type up your CV, and include your contact details on *everything* – keep it clear, keep it neat, and remember, the devil's in the detail, get your phone number and email address right!

Chapter 19

Getting Busy With It: Working as a DJ

In This Chapter

▶ Marketing yourself the smart way

▶ Dealing with DJ agencies

▶ Schmoozing your way into the DJ booth

*W*hen you start off as a DJ, the hardest thing you do is mastering how to beatmatch. Now that you're a great DJ, the next hurdle to overcome is getting yourself that first DJing job.

You've put together a demo CD or tape; you love it, your cat loves it, your mum loves it, and even your best friend can't pick any holes in it. So now's the time to put it to good use – selling yourself as a DJ.

This chapter provides you with advice and guidance on how to approach bars and clubs for work, gives you a pep talk about persistence, and though I can't guarantee that you'll get any work, this chapter should fill you up with ideas and enthusiasm for the task at hand.

You have three main ways to get ahead, and get work:

✔ Market yourself

✔ Join an agency

✔ Network

Marketing Yourself

Self-promotion is the key to success. No one else does the work for you. Sure, when you make it as a big DJ, you can farm the hassle onto other people, but when you're starting off, you need to promote yourself diligently and single-mindedly. The same unfaltering perseverance and determination that kept you going through any difficulties you had when developing your DJing skills are exactly what you need to effectively sell yourself.

Flood the world with your demo

You should have a pile of tapes or CDs that are properly labelled with your name on them and a tracklist together with an accompanying CV (and photo), packaged up ready to be delivered to the clubs and pubs you want to work at. If you've not got that far yet, check out Chapter 18 for advice on making a good demo.

Include a covering note in each of your demo packages, specifically tailored to the bar or club you're trying to get work from. Do your research; if it's a club that plays different genres of music each night, mention which night you think you'd be best for. Or, if your taste and music collection is suitable for a range of their nights, let them know that you're a versatile DJ. Be as specific as you can; nothing's worse than being on the receiving end of a vague letter that simply says, 'I want to be DJ, here's my CD, I hope you can help'.

Show them that you know their establishment, tell them what you can add if they hire you, promoting the fact that you're a focused, professional DJ with a goal of working at their club.

Handing over your demo

By far the best approach when submitting your demo is to hand it in personally. Bars are easy as they're open for most of the day and night, so ask to speak to the manager or bar manager and hand over your demo. Ask them if they'd mind listening to your demo, and tell them you'll be back in a week to see if they like it. Be polite and friendly when speaking with them, no matter how long the conversation lasts, and whether or not they're polite and friendly in return.

If no management is available, don't be tempted to just leave it with the bar staff, come back another day when you may have a chance of meeting someone who can help.

Clubs can be a little harder when trying to get hold of someone of responsibility, as when they're open, these people are either preparing for the night ahead, or dealing with all the nuances of running a club. Even if you have to return to a club a few times, striking up conversations with the bar staff or stewards to find what's the best time to come back with your demo is well worth the effort. And as long as you're polite, and don't take up too much of their time, your demo shouldn't end up in the bin.

Knowing where to send your demo

Do some research in the areas you're going to spread around your demo so you know all the best places to apply to. Don't just stick to the places you go to on a Friday night, have a look around the entire city, and make a list of all the appropriate pubs and clubs that may be interested in your skills.

Choose clubs and pubs that play the music you're playing. If you're a drum and bass DJ, don't bother sending a tape into a commercial dance club, and if you're an R & B DJ, you're wasting your time by sending a demo tape into an underground jungle club.

If you're in a city with enough variety of bars, no doubt they'll demand the same qualities in a DJ as a club would. This news is good for you though, as by now you're a professional sounding, club-ready DJ.

If you live in a small town with no bars or clubs that play your kind of music, you'll need to develop some wanderlust. Look to the nearest city or large town to where you live for clubs that play the music you want to play. Don't try to force your music on people who don't want to listen. But at the same time, don't give up. Don't feel that a brick wall has been placed in front of you that you can't get around. You just need to go to neighbouring towns and cities and dedicate yourself to spending a lot of time there instead.

Geography of a club: How far is too far?

You may want to try for global or national domination, but if you can't get to the club, what's the point? If you do live 500 miles from a club you're sending your demo to, have a think about how you're going to get there, and if it's financially viable to travel that distance. If you're only going to get £100 for a night's work, consider how much you're willing to *pay to play* by catching a train/plane to get there, then staying overnight in a hotel as you can't get back.

Or, it may be you've booked a two-week holiday to Ibiza in the hope that you can get a spot in a pub or club out there for one or two nights. Send out a whole load of tapes to places you think might let you play a few weeks in advance (or months) before you travel, take some tunes with you, and follow up your submission personally. If you're spending the money to go there anyway, why not give it a bash?

At this early stage in your career, the problem of getting a gig 500 miles away is unlikely to occur, but try to think about every eventuality now, so that you're not surprised when it happens.

Following up

When you're sure that the bars and clubs have your demo, follow up with a friendly phone call about a week after you sent it. If someone is kind enough to take your call, ask politely if they've received your demo. If they have, ask them what they thought of it, and hang on every word they say as they criticise your performance. Thank them for their time, and their honesty, and if they don't want to use you, ask if you can send in another demo that reflects their comments.

If they haven't received your demo, tell them that you'll send in another one by the next post. Amend your cover letter to include the name of the person you spoke to, and include a line about chatting to them on the phone.

If you suffer from phone phobia, get over it. Don't be scared of phoning clubs and bars. You've nothing to lose in a phone call, and everything to gain.

Handling rejection

You can't afford to have a fear of rejection. You need to put yourself out there, and hope people like you. Different club owners and promoters reject you in different ways; some take the time out to say no, some just don't get back in touch.

If they don't respond, keep sending demos until they do get back in touch – remember, persistence is key. If they do respond, but don't want to hire you, then hopefully they told you the reason why they didn't like the demo. If they comment on something you didn't realise, and you agree with it, fix the problem and send off a new demo. They may say 'I was actually just being polite before', but perhaps the time you've taken to make another demo reflecting their comments may show them how serious you are about working for them.

 The knack is to keep trying until they either take you on, or tell you to stop sending in demos because they don't like you! You have to be very strong minded because the rejection letters will come flooding in, and a lot of them won't be polite, but if you have the skills, you'll find someone, somewhere, sometime, who'll give you a chance.

Every time you start to wonder if this way truly is an effective form of selling yourself, think of John Digweed. He got his big break when he sent a demo to Renaissance, and he's now one of the most well-known DJs in the world.

Play for free

Play for free are three little words that can get you very far. Ask yourself this question, would you rather play for free, or not play at all? As you try to get work, getting your foot in the door is more important than getting paid.

When you send off or hand in your demo, offer the bar/club one or two free nights of your services to let them see how good you are. You're more than likely to get the chance of a warm-up slot from one or two places if you offer to play for free, prove you have the skills to be a good DJ, and agree to play music suitable for a warm-up set (see Chapter 20 for tips on what to play in a warm-up set).

Offer owners what they want to hear

If you've been to a club, for research or a night out, you should already have an idea of what rocks the night, and what kills the night.

In your covering letter that accompanies your demo, mention all the things that make the club strong, and give an indication of what you can do to make it even better. I'd stop short of criticising the club and telling them what they're bad at though, use positive language, and make them feel that choosing you is a good thing.

And tell them you'll make them lots of money. Club owners like that . . .

Joining an Agency

Joining a DJ agency can be a good way of spreading the word about your skills. What role they play depends largely on how good and how famous you are as a DJ.

You have your choice of several different types of agencies:

- ✔ **Artist management:** Catering for famous, established, pro DJs that are in high demand rather than newbies trying to get a break, or even the regular DJ at a small club, these agencies are less about hand holding and advice, and are more about making sure nights go smoothly, money is paid on time, and that the high profile DJs on their books are well publicised, and booked solidly. As managers, these agencies deal with the publicity, bookings, travel, accommodation, and so on, the only thing that the DJ needs to worry about is the music and maintaining a good reputation, which is the promotion that keeps the bookings coming in.

  Any booking fees payable to the DJ are paid to the management, who take a percentage cut (usually between 10 and 15 per cent) before passing the rest onto the DJ. The less bookings the DJ has, the less money the agency makes, so making sure that the DJs on their roster are reliable, booked solidly, and getting paid is in their best interest.

✔ **Local agencies:** Large towns and cities have DJ agencies that cater for the clubs, bars, function rooms, wedding parties, and any reason someone may want a DJ. Although fame won't be as large an issue, a strong track record of playing a lot of gigs is a necessity for these agencies to sign you up.

A DJ agency has a pool of DJs that go to bars and clubs requesting a DJ. Local agencies take a similar percentage cut of the booking fee as the artist management agencies. As the DJs on their books don't have fame to sell themselves, these agencies work hard for their cut.

✔ **Internet agencies:** A new wave of Internet DJ agencies help you with promoting yourself, rather than finding work for you. They don't actively seek out work on your behalf, but clubs and bars come to them requesting a DJ, and the agency passes on your details to the club. Reputable Internet agencies have a large dossier of clubs who request DJs on their roster, and are able to prove a large *hit-rate* for their DJs working at clubs.

In many cases, you pay a yearly subscription to the Internet agency, rather than handing over a percentage of what you earn. This is an extremely controversial concept, and opinions are very strong on both sides as to whether you should pay upfront to try to find work.

Paying upfront: For and against

Whether you should pay upfront before an agency gets you work is cause for a lot of heated discussion. One side of the argument is that you should only need to pay if the agency gets you work, and the agency should take a cut from the booking. That approach is used by most *bricks and mortar* agencies, which have a staff of representatives visiting clubs. The club promoter pays the agency directly, who then pass the money (minus a cut) onto you.

Because most Internet agencies are actually just middlemen that let you promote yourself to their contacts, they have no way of telling if you have been hired, or if you've been paid. Relying on you to declare all the nights you've worked

through agency contacts becomes an unworkable proposition, hence the request to pay for their services upfront.

The obvious risk with paying up front is that you pay the money to the agency, and they don't get you any work. Until Internet agencies get a stronger track record, my suggestion is to exhaust every possibility under the sun and work as hard as you can to get work under your own steam before approaching an Internet agency. If you're still finding it hard to get work, and you're sure your skills aren't letting you down, do a *lot* of background research into Internet agencies and what they do, and tread very carefully before parting with any money.

Research an agency

Before joining any agency, take a look at any testimonials that may be on their Web site, and if you get the chance, get in touch with the DJs and clubs to check that the agency is genuine. Some unscrupulous people out there do make up information to try to seem more professional, so do as much research as you can and post questions on DJ *forums* (communities where DJs go to chat about their work – Chapter 21 has a list of forums).

Alarm bells should ring if the agency's Web site has no recent testimonials from DJs, if DJs mentioned don't respond to your e-mails, if the agency forces you into a contract longer than a year, or if you discover any hidden charges.

Contact the people in charge of running the agency. Even though they may sound fierce in their literature when they mention trying to contact them, they have to show you due care and attention. You need to be sure that you'll get a service for the money that you're looking to invest in their help. If they aren't polite, helpful, and professional at the beginning of your relationship with them, run like the wind!

The cut of your booking fee that an agency demands varies. If the cut is larger than 10–15 per cent, find out if you get an extra service for that extra money, and if you don't, think hard about whether you want to hand over that extra money for nothing.

Finally, when you're happy to sign on the dotted line with an agency, show the contract to a lawyer first, just in case you missed something.

Meet the criteria to join

DJ agencies have a reputation to uphold, and as such, they do have some strict criteria that you must meet before they sign you up. Pro agencies for the famous DJ tend to *headhunt* the DJ. When someone gains a reputation for drawing a crowd, and has become a well-known DJ, these agencies *swoop in* and offer to add the DJ to their roster.

Although local and Internet agencies may have restrictions on age limits and where you live, the one constant you find is that you need to have had experience before these agencies will take you onto their books. If you've gained experience under your own steam, made your own contacts, and developed them to gain you work then you show the talent needed to secure work, and the determination and mindset needed to be a professional in the DJing business.

Many agencies won't add you to their DJ roster based purely on a demo CD. They can't take the risk that the DJ may have taken months to perfect that one mix, or that they've used a computer program to *touch up* a sloppy performance. But apart from this, the difference between playing in the bedroom without any pressure and playing in a club in front of a thousand clubbers in a room with a bad sound system is huge. Nerves and comfort aren't an issue in the bedroom, but the first time you play live in a club, you'll be nervous and in alien surroundings as a DJ. If you make a mistake because you're wet behind the ears, it won't reflect well on you, or the agency promoting you.

The music you play as a DJ may change the kind of agencies that you approach. Some agencies only work with wedding/party DJs, while others only represent club DJs, and won't accept a wedding DJ onto their books.

When you approach an agency that represents a vast range of DJ styles, let them know at the outset what kind of music you play best. Even if you have a wide range from R & B to hard house, you need to let the agency know whether you have the music (or desire) to spend an evening playing Frank Sinatra and Neil Diamond tracks at a retirement party.

If you do have the patience to be a workhorse DJ who plays anything just to get ahead, let them know that you'll play anything, anywhere; and in time, hope that you've earned their trust so they start putting you in clubs where you can play the music you want. The downside to the workhorse approach is the amount of bowling alleys that you may have to play Britney Spears' tunes in.

Cut your losses

It's hard work trying to get on an agency's roster. Be persistent, but also be aware of when you're making the wrong move. I spent a long time trying to get involved with an agency in my area. When I finally tracked down the guy who ran it, we just didn't click, and when he found out that I already had work and I wasn't willing to drop it to join his agency, it ended as a very short phone call.

Depending on the contacts you build up through networking (see the next section), and the kind of places and size of clubs you want to play at, you may never need the services of an agency. I have never been on an agency roster. That's not because I don't want to (or from a lack of trying), but is simply because the contacts I've made through networking have been helpful in getting me work.

Networking Your Way to Success

Get used to the phrase: 'It's not what you know, it's who you know.' Everyone you talk to about your quest to find work eventually says it.

Networking can range from a simple *meet and greet* with a club or bar owner when you hand over your demo, to meeting people who introduce you to more people, and eventually getting work from those connections.

Sell yourself

Attitude and presentation can go a long way in this industry. If you can convince a club or bar owner that you'd actually be good to have around, either because you seem like a reliable kind of person or because you're well dressed and attractive enough to be eye candy for the public, then you've already given yourself a step up the ladder.

Some genres of music promote and thrive on the aloof *too cool for you* style of DJ, but it's not something I'd recommend you do, or want to adopt myself.

Make friends

Going straight to a club owner and asking for work is a ballsy move. If they say no, you may have blown your chances of working for them. If you befriend the bar staff and the DJ, who may then recommend you for a small DJing spot, you may get a lot more luck.

 How you develop your relationship with people is down to your personality. If you think you're the type who can strike up a friendship with a DJ in a pub, and use that friendship to get somewhere, by all means go for it. Just realise that the DJ will peg you for a DJ wannabe from the moment you even glance at his/her records and the turntables. Don't pretend that's not why you're there, but unless you think it's worthwhile pushing it, play it cool, and hold off the hard sell for a while, making friends with the DJ.

Getting to know bar staff, particularly senior bar staff can be another good avenue to get into the club, even as a warm-up DJ. Again, you need to take some time, become a regular, get to know them and the club well, and when you're happy that you can start to push your luck, hand over a tape, and see what becomes of it.

Beginning my journey

My journey began when I was a barman in a pub in Glasgow called Café Cini. Before the DJs arrived, a tape would play at low level through the sound system. After a couple of months of working behind the bar, I slipped one of my tapes into the machine.

Luckily Pauline, the manageress, liked the tape and asked who did it. When she found out it was me, she offered me a 1-hour warm up before the DJ arrived (paid in Irn Bru). This spot led to an hour during the main part of the night (more Irn Bru), and then became a night of my own for

money (which I spent on Irn Bru), and expanded on from there (as did my waistline due to all that Irn Bru!).

One of the other DJs who had just opened up his own club offered me a warm-up spot, giving me my first piece of club experience. From there, I met another DJ who was giving up his Friday night residency at a club, and suggested, with his recommendation, that I should get in touch with the owners to take over.

So from a basic bar job, my DJ career began. It can be that easy for you too.

Go 'undercover'

Getting a foot in the door when you're already inside is easy! Insider knowledge is the best advantage you can have. A bar job in a club or pub you want to work in is an excellent way of selling yourself surreptitiously. You can subtly spread word of your skills, and repeatedly let people hear your demo until they realise that they like you, and want to put you in the booth. By the time they grasp your true agenda, it's too late, they're already happy to have hired you as the DJ!

Marketing Yourself on the Internet

Creating the best Web site in the world won't get you any work on its own, but a Web site that backs you up as a professional DJ goes a long way to impressing those who choose to check it out.

As well as hosting your latest mix and a DJ CV for future employers, your site can also promote the nights you work to other people. If you establish a good following that you can keep up to date through your Web site, and almost guarantee a club that a certain number of people will turn up, your case for working at the club is sweetened by the guaranteed door money they will receive.

With the creation of Web sites like www.myspace.com, you don't even need to have your own Web site anymore, and can instantly get in touch with all your *friends* to let them know where and when you're playing next. You can use WYSIWYG (*what you see is what you get*) layout editors to spruce up your profile, but with some HTML knowledge and creativity, you can create a vibrant, well-laid out and informative profile that sells you just as well as a personal Web site.

The only downside to a MySpace profile page compared to your own site is simply the professionalism of the Web URL. I think that as a Web URL, www.recess.co.uk looks more professional than www.myspace.com/dj_recess.

For a more dedicated DJ approach to the Web sites your profile is viewed on, check out sites like www.djpassion.co.uk, www.djpromoter.com, www.mydjspace.net and www.myclubbingspace.com.

Some DJ profile sites are linked to venues that use the DJs who submit profiles, others on the Internet are enhanced forums and Internet radio stations. But as long as they're free, sign up and promote yourself as much as you can through all possible avenues.

Internet forums are a great way to promote yourself and find out what's going on in the music world. Chapter 21 has a list of the best forums on the Internet. The discussion forum for this book is located at www.djrecess.co.uk/php.

Chapter 20

Facing the Music: Playing to a Live Crowd

In This Chapter

▶ Knowing what to expect from the venue

▶ Being prepared for all eventualities

▶ Reading a crowd, and reacting to their reactions

▶ Dealing with requests, with tact

▶ Ending the night just right

*Y*ou're ready. You've practised for months, your friends know how good you are, you've sent your demo to bars and clubs to let them know how good you are, and now's your chance to show hundreds of people on the dance floor just how good you are. Stepping out of the bedroom and into a club's DJ booth is a big leap, so you have a few things to consider.

I've always said that this leap is like driving a car. You spend ages with a driving instructor who teaches you how to pass your test, and then once you're on your own in the real world, making decisions for yourself, you learn how to drive. As a new DJ, you spend a year or more in your bedroom perfecting your technique and building knowledge about your music, and only when you get out into the real world and find work do you develop the skills to become a true DJ.

The difference between DJing in the bedroom and in a club is crowd control, knowing what people want to hear and being able to adapt to how they're reacting to the music you're playing. Knowing when to move up from one genre to another, or when to increase the energy of the mix is something that comes with experience and practice, but the most important skill you develop is the ability to lose yourself and love what you're doing while simultaneously reading the crowd's reaction to the music you're playing.

Investigating the Venue

Nothing's scarier than the unknown. Investigate the club or hall you're booked to play well in advance. If you're putting on your own night in a club, you only have to worry about getting people to turn up! If you've been asked to play a party or wedding in the local town hall, you need to find out what you're expected to play, what equipment you need to take, and start memorising the bride and groom's names!

Scoping the club

No matter whether this is your first ever set in a club, or if you're an established DJ, do your homework. Set up a meeting with the club owner, manager, or promoter to discuss a few things. If you can't set up a meeting, try to go to the club on a similar night to the one you've been booked for (the same night a week before is perfect), listen to the music that's being played, and watch the crowd's reaction. (See 'Reading a crowd' later in the chapter.)

When you're doing some investigation at the club, try to strike up a conversation with the bar staff and the toilet attendants (if the club has them). As they hear everything that's said, and everything that's played through a night, they can sometimes be a better wealth of knowledge than the club promoter for the music that works best, the kind of people who go there, and the general mood and patterns of the people who frequent the club.

When you're the warm-up DJ

If you've been asked to do the warm-up set before the main DJ comes on, ask the promoter/manager if they have any limitations to what kind of music you can play. If you're working in a house/trance club, the promoter may want you to play lighter, well-known musical tunes to warm up the crowd, so the main DJ can progress from soft to hard when they arrive.

The warm-up set is extremely important to the club, and your career. If you treat this gig as a throwaway hour and a half where what you mix doesn't matter, the customers at the club won't get warmed up, and you won't be asked to return. Although the music may be softer than you normally play at home, suppress your musical snobbery and realise that playing whatever you've been asked to is really important, so you can keep your foot in the door and hope that they'll eventually let you play the main set where you can show them what you're capable of.

When you're playing the main set

As the main set DJ, you have fewer constraints, but you still need to find out whether the club has a music policy. They may have a limit as to how fast you can play and limit you to playing certain genres (perhaps they'd rather you didn't play the harder stuff in trance clubs, or death metal in rock clubs).

You may think that you're there to play the latest, greatest underground tunes, but maybe the guy you're replacing just played hard, loud music all the time, and the club is looking for a change. When a club goes through a tough period, they tend to opt for a change in music policy, and that normally involves following whatever is the most popular, fashionable music at the time. So if you've been brought into a club that used to play hard dance music and is now trying to move away from that, you may find that the club asks you to throw in some R & B through the first part of the set, then some really commercial, popular dance music in the main part of the set.

Every set may be your big break. So swallow your pride, and realise that for every five commercial tunes you play, you'll be able to play one or two that people haven't heard yet, but which you know will be massive. But don't push your luck! Research the music scene, read magazines, listen to other DJ mixes, and listen to suitable radio shows, and you'll develop an ear to pick tunes that eventually become popular. You won't have to gamble with what you play, you'll know that you're playing the *next big thing*.

Provided this doesn't annoy the management, when you pick the right tunes that launch from underground to mainstream, the club owner and promoter will recognise that you know your stuff, and will hopefully start to respect your musical knowledge and give you a little more musical wriggle room.

When you're replacing a DJ

If you're replacing a DJ, finding out why is important. When you've been asked to fill the role, you don't want to end up making the same kind of mistakes as the last guy. Ask the promoter what led to their dismissal and if they were doing something wrong.

I was lucky enough to be invited to watch a DJ that I was replacing play the week before he was fired, so I was able to hear for myself what was going wrong. I had to tell the promoter what I thought he was doing wrong though, and how I'd do it better as a test of my DJ skills, but fortunately, I passed his test!

You may find that the DJ has been doing everything perfectly, but that a personality clash has led to their dismissal or resignation, in which case, put on a smile and remember what the DJ was doing that worked.

Minding the other details

Discuss money terms well before you turn up to play your set. Different clubs, nights, and locations change how much you can charge. You're DJing for the love of music and the opportunity, not the financial gain, but it doesn't hurt to get something in writing that states how much you'll get, and when you're going to get paid!

While you're investigating the club, try to get a sneaky peak inside the DJ booth. If you've managed to secure a meeting when the club is closed, take your time to look around the booth and take a note of the equipment that's in it, and where everything is located.

The main things to check are which mixer, turntables, and CD decks they use; whether a booth monitor is provided inside the DJ booth; where you put your records/CDs; and where the amplifiers are.

If a monitor isn't supplied, you can ask about getting one, but unless you're a famous DJ that the club can make loads of money out of, they probably won't agree to your request. If you don't have a monitor, you need to work out the best way to get around the audio delay.

If you're unsure of how to use any of the controls in the club's DJ booth, do some research before you turn up on the night for your set. If the mixer has functions that you'd like to use, but don't know how, finding out how is very important. The first time I used a DJM-500 mixer, I had no idea how to work the effects on it, and was banging the yellow button with no result. I didn't find out how to use it properly until I got home and read about it.

If you use bottom-of-the-range twin CD decks at home, and you're faced with top-of-the-range single CD decks at the club, go online or ask someone you know who has those decks, to make sure that you're happy using them on the night.

Most clubs still cater for the vinyl DJ and tend to use the industry standard Technics 1210s, but if they're innovative, and use turntables with extra features like the Vestax, Gemini, and Numark range, a quick read over an online manual gives you all the knowledge you need to properly use them.

As much as we'd all love to use our own turntables, mixers, and CD decks, there aren't many clubs that let you take your own kit. In the right club, with a friendly manager, you may be able to take along your own mixer if you're working the entire night. CD decks and turntables are normally off-limits to change, but you can always ask. You may want to wait until you've developed a good relationship with the club, and have proven yourself before asking about tearing apart the DJ booth!

Blowing speakers by proxy

I know from experience that you need to be very careful when swapping over equipment. I used to take my own mixer to a club, as theirs was quite basic. Unfortunately, the cables weren't marked well, and when I plugged them back into their mixer at the end of the night, I didn't do it right. The next night, the unknowing DJ turned on all the amps, and almost blew out most of the speakers due to the electrical *pop* my incorrect connections created.

Getting ready to party

Houses and town halls aren't designed to be makeshift clubs, so you need to do a little more investigation to make sure that you're well prepared for playing at these venues.

If you decide to have a party in your house so that you can impress your friends with your skills, the only things you have to worry about are the neighbours, keeping enough ice in the fridge, and where to set up.

If you hire a hall to play at, you need to think about suitable amplification (refer to Chapter 10), lights, and something more substantial than the kitchen table to set up on. If you're inviting 200 people to the town hall, think about security; you may need a few big fellas there, just in case things get out of hand.

Whether the party's at your house or in a hired hall, music policy isn't an issue, as you decide what to play. You still need to react to how the people at the party respond to what you're playing, though. Don't be bullheaded and persevere with music that they aren't enjoying just because you want to play it.

If you're booked to play at someone else's party, be it a birthday party, leaving night, or wedding, they can give you an indication of what they expect you to play. If it's someone who knows that you're a DJ, but doesn't know that you specialise in drum and bass, you may want to let them know, so they don't expect Britney Spears and Destiny's Child, but actually get old Roni Size and Goldie tracks, instead.

Unless you're told otherwise, don't expect them to provide any equipment. You'll be lucky if there's even a table for you to set your equipment up on. So arranging suitable amplification and lighting is down to you, and you'll need to use your own DJ set-up. Visit the venue you've been booked to play at well in advance. Someone who works there should be able to tell you the most popular place to set up your make shift DJ booth, and when you see the hall, you can work out how much amplification you need.

Preparing to Perform

Baden Powell wasn't wrong about the value of preparation. When your set looms only hours away, try to think of everything before you play, so you're not faced with any big surprises.

Selecting the set

From your music policy discussions with the club owner or organiser of the party, you should know what music you're able to play for your set. With this in mind, you can flick through your collection and pick out the tunes you're most likely to play that night.

Now go back into your collection and pick out the same amount again. There's nothing wrong with taking loads of records with you. If you have the space, use it. Longing for a record that you haven't put in is a bad thing, but reaching for that tune – the one that you'd otherwise have left at home – and using it to win over a tough crowd can only be a good thing.

Predetermined set lists

Trying to work out the entire set from start to finish before you get to a club isn't a good idea. Even if the club owner has given you a music policy to stay within, you still need to tailor the music for the people on the dance floor.

If you decide before your set to play light house music for the first two hours but the club is packed after an hour, demanding more energetic music, you have the choice of playing the other hour of house music (which may bore the people out of the club) or skipping directly to the music that they want to hear – only to worry about the extra hour of music you have to fill up at the end of the night.

Some forethought about your tunes can help if you're taking over from another DJ. Think about your opening tunes so that you can settle in easily, but don't get tunnel vision and think of only one or two openers. Have enough tunes with you to cover many eventualities; one tune if it's a bit low key, another if the dance floor is going wild, and another if it's in between, in the bizarre transitional phase.

Checkpoint tunes

If you don't like the idea of a completely off-the-cuff set but don't want to create a start to finish set list, use key tunes for your set, like checkpoints that you pass as you increase the energy and the tempo of the night. If the checkpoints are tunes that people love to hear, you can use them as markers to help you map out your set from start to finish.

Providing you practise enough with your collection, you should be able to choose from a lot of tunes that you can mix in and out of the checkpoint tunes, all of which in turn mix in to another large number of good tunes. Keep your eye on the dance floor, and try to estimate when you think that you're going to change the pace or energy again, and work towards putting in the next key tune to move the mix to another level.

But remember, on every journey, you sometimes need to take a detour. Even with a skeleton framework of tunes to link your mix, you still need to be flexible and react to the crowd (see the section 'Reading the crowd' later in this chapter).

Organising your box

You don't have to organise your tunes alphabetically or by genre if you don't want to, but by having an order to the chaos of your record box or CD wallet, you make finding that elusive track when you need it most much easier. You have a couple or organisational options:

- **By genre:** If you're doing a set that requires you to play multiple genres, or multiple subgenres of music, grouping each genre together in the record box or CD wallet makes good sense. Especially as most of these genres relate to a specific point in the night (for instance R & B at the beginning, then vocal house, then commercial dance, then trance, then progressive house), grouping these genres together makes navigating your way through the set more manageable.

- **Multiple boxes/bags:** If you have a few boxes and bags that you take with you, have one for each genre or power level in the night, splitting your boxes so that all the beginning of the night tunes are in one box, and all the main set tunes are in another box. This way, you won't have to wade through two boxes crammed with 120 records (or CD wallets with thousands of tunes) to find a specific track.

Laziness has its value . . . at last!

I'm quite lazy as a DJ when it comes to arranging tunes. I pick them out from anywhere, but always replace them at the front of the box. But this method means that the tunes I play most often are always at the front of the box. Before I set off for a night though, when I look through the tunes that I think that I might play, I put the

ones I'm 90 per cent sure to include at the front of the box, the ones I'd play only if I thought the crowd was the type to respond are next, and then ones I'd only play in an emergency, or if the night was going *so* well that I can play anything, go right at the back.

Knowing What to Expect at the Club

Getting to a club early lets you plan your evening properly, gives you time to get used to the equipment, chat to the bar staff and promoter about what kind of night they think that it's going to be, and steady any nerves that may have developed.

Dealing with nerves

Unless you're a rock, you will get nervous on the first night you play. If you're lucky, your nerves will subside with time, to be replaced by nervous excitement. I believe that the moment you stop getting that excited feeling in your stomach before playing a set, you should take stock, and ask yourself if you still love what you're doing, or just going through the motions.

You may be tempted, but try not to turn to alcohol as a way to get over your nerves, even if it is free. You want to be as clear headed as possible when you're playing. Dutch courage is not courage, it's a mask. Your nervousness reduces after a few good mixes anyway, but be aware of this feeling, and use it as a reminder that what you're doing is important, and your fear of messing up is borne of your desire to be a great DJ.

Getting used to your tools

If you get the chance to visit the club before playing the set, as a customer or when meeting the promoter, take my advice and look at the equipment in the DJ booth to give you the chance of reading up on any items that you've never used before (see the earlier section 'Minding the other details').

Take the opportunity of turning up at the club early and throwing on a couple of tunes to get used to the equipment. If you've only read how to use something new in a manual, this time is great for working through anything you're unsure of.

Setting the levels and EQ

As well as getting used to the equipment, you can figure out how the sound comes across in the club, and hopefully change it to your liking. There's a long night ahead of you. If you don't like the sound, it'll be even longer!

Put on a record you know really well, with all the EQs set to twelve o'clock (this is the *flat* position on your mixer, where no frequency has been added or cut by any amount). Turn the music up loud and stand at various parts of the dance floor. Don't only stand in front of the massive bass speakers, where you'll be shaken to pieces by the vibrations, move around, from the outskirts of the dance floor to the centre, and in front of the booth.

During your journey around the dance floor, listen to the sound in each position. If the different areas of the club are covered by multiple amps and EQs, ask if you can change them to suit the sound that you prefer. If only one amp and EQ is available for the entire dance floor, you have to stand in the middle and set the best sound for that position. There's nothing more you can do.

If the club won't let you touch the sound system's EQs, you need to use the EQs on the mixer instead, which isn't the best option, but is still better than leaving the club sounding shrill, with no bass in it. The tune that you use to check the sound should be your benchmark tune. Use this tune to set the EQs, and then match everything that follows to your benchmark.

Don't forget that people suck up sound vibrations. Our clothes, our skin, and our big gangly bones all absorb sound frequencies. This fact means that you have to set the mixer to play louder as the club gets busier and you'll also find a lot of the bass frequencies disappear into the crowd's greedy bellies.

Every once in a while (probably when you need a pee), jump onto the dance floor and have a quick listen to how the music sounds. If you can hear too much conversation rather than music, of if your ears start shimmering with the amount of mid range, cross your legs and adjust the EQs so it sounds better – then go to the bathroom during the next track.

Setting the monitor

Not only do you need a monitor in the DJ booth, but you also need to set the level to create a virtual stereo image between the music in your headphones, and the music playing from the monitor. (If you have no idea what I'm on about, see Chapter 12.)

Pop in an ear plug (honestly, I strongly recommend that you use an ear plug in your *live* ear – refer to Chapter 9) and set the level so that you can hear everything clearly, but the music isn't so loud that you're eardrums are quivering. I've heard people talk about *tiring* the ear – who knows what that means – but if you play music too loud, for too long, you do find that concentrating on the music blaring out at you is hard and you'll end up with permanent hearing damage.

If the club doesn't have a monitor, I hope you found that out when you went for a visit to the club, and have spent the past week practising like a mad DJ to get around the problem.

Working in a loud environment

This job may be the first time that you play in a volume level louder than your home stereo, so use the opportunity of turning up early to get used to all the differences that a club's volume may throw at you.

Nothing prepares you for the feeling of the beat thumping through your body when DJing. When you're in a club as a clubber it's a cool feeling, but as a DJ, if the beat is slightly delayed to what you're hearing through the monitor or the headphones, you can find the timing a little disconcerting at first.

It's not all bad live though. A club's sound system can be very forgiving for small beatmatching errors. The heavy sub bass can be so thick sounding, that a slight *l'Boom* or *B'loom* (see Chapter 12 if you've no idea at all what I'm on about) is easily hidden. With good headphones, you can hear this small timing error before anyone can tell on the dance floor.

The music sounds different, too. The sound system in a club doesn't have the full fidelity of your headphones, with the sub-bass sometimes overpowering the bass and mid-range melodies, so you find that some mixes that don't work quite as well on tape work fine played live with the right EQ controls (using kills to minimise any key or melody mismatches).

Playing Your Music

You've investigated, discovered, and prepared until you're blue in the face. You've been a polite DJ and turned up as early as possible (even if it is just to give you the chance to sit in the bathroom). Your night's about to begin.

Reading a crowd

If this night is your first time playing to a crowd of people you don't know, the main difference you notice is how much thought you start to put into your tunes in order to keep people on the dance floor.

In time, you will become a body language expert, looking at the reactions of the people on the floor as they throw their hands in the air and dance like there's no tomorrow – or throw their hands up in the air in disgust.

First, think about how *you* react when you're at a club. When you're enjoying yourself, what do you do? If you're the type of clubber who grins from ear to ear, and throws your hands in the air, and you're playing the kind of music that makes you want to do that, look for this kind of response from the people on the dance floor. When you're bored, and listless, how do you react? Look into people's eyes. If they're staring into the distance, or at the floor, or if they're dancing with no real thought or energy, they've gone to a happy place, waiting for something to change. It's up to you to make that change.

Don't base your readings on just the people in front of you. Look through the crowd. If you get a chance to go for a wander, walk around and look at how people are responding to the music. A glum face isn't a good thing to see. Fifteen glum faces are a kick up the backside that should make you play something better.

Just ask . . . if you dare

The relationship you've developed with the toilet attendant and bar staff can really help you out. They're a great source of information on how well you're doing, and how the night is going.

In one club that I worked at, the toilet attendant knew everything that was going on. If the people who came in to use the facilities were having a good night, he'd be quick to feed that info back to me, and if he heard tales that something's not quite right with the music, I'd know before it was too late. Never before or since has a visit to the bathroom been so enlightening.

If you want, you can just ask someone how they're enjoying their night, either personally or collectively, over the microphone. If you get a collective groan, or even worse, silence, change it, quickly. If you get cheers, whoops, and hands in the air, keep it going, you're doing well.

Progress the set

DJing is not a race. You won't win anything for playing all the newest, best, and biggest tunes in the first 30 minutes, you'll lose everyone on the dance floor. You'll wear them out, they'll become bored with the same sound, and as you won't have any big tunes left, the people on the floor will get bored with the rest of the set. If you resort to repeating tunes, they've already heard them, so they aren't as excited. Your light shone brightly, but not for long enough.

Use the checkpoint tunes (see the earlier section 'Checkpoint tunes') as a way to pepper the set with good tunes, and to move the set on in energy and tempo. But don't just arbitrarily decide to change things. Always keep an eye on how the people on the dance floor are reacting to what you're playing. If the dance floor isn't busy enough, if the wrong kinds of people are dancing, or if the alcohol level hasn't kicked in yet, playing slightly heavier music may empty the dance floor. Or if you don't change the pace soon, your set will start to sound dull and monotonous, and people will start to haemorrhage off the dance floor.

Test the waters. If you can't obviously tell by the reaction of the people on the dance floor, take things a little harder bit by bit (maybe lessen it from time to time) to see what kind of stuff they're responding to, then stick with that level until your crowd reading reveals that the time has come to move up (or down) a gear.

Handling requests

I deal with requests with the following considerations:

- Was I going to play the tune they've asked for anyway? If so, I'm happy to say yes when they ask, and let them know when it'll be on.

- How polite were they about it? Manners go a long way. I'm not saying I'd play *anything* if someone was polite enough, but bad manners make me less likely to play something. *Please* and *thank you* don't take any time or effort to say, and they can get you so far in this world.

No matter what you consider when someone asks for a record (this includes how good looking they are) remember that they've paid money to get into the club and are expecting to be entertained, so at least let them down gently.

If you don't want to play the tune they've asked for, either because you don't have it, or it's not the right time to play that tune, say the following, depending on how hopeful you want to leave them:

✔ 'I've left it at home, sorry.'

✔ 'I'll take a look, but I *think* that I've left it at home . . . sorry.'

Requests as a warm-up DJ

The warm-up set can be difficult for requests. The owner/promoter has told you to play lighter tunes that everyone knows, not too hard and not the latest, biggest tracks. Halfway through the set, a couple of people ask you to play the big tunes of the moment, or as I once got 'asked', *'Play some heavy stuff I can dance to, this stuff sucks.'*

Herein lies a couple of problems. The place isn't near full, the promoter has strongly said no to playing those tunes, but they're the customer, and they've paid to be entertained. This situation is why I stress the importance of talking to the owner/promoter when you get offered the job, to iron out these possible problems (see the earlier section 'When you're the warm-up DJ'). Maybe this is exactly why they have a music policy; to weed out the kind of people that just want to dance at full speed on an empty dance floor.

Requests as the main DJ

Playing the main set in a club removes a lot of restrictions to what you can play. The main problem with requests is when someone asks for a tune that you don't like, don't have, or isn't appropriate for that point in the night.

This situation can arise if someone doesn't realise the kind of club they've gone to. The amount of times I've asked to play an R & B track in a trance club amazes me, but usually this request is prefaced by '*I was dragged here by my friends and don't like this music, so . . .* '

Friendly lighting jocks and bouncers can sometimes step in and take the role of a mediator in passing on requests. This option saves you from entering into a three-minute argument with someone over a tune that you're not willing to play and then end up missing the next mix.

Requests as a party DJ

As a club DJ, you have some licence to say no to people when they ask for tunes, as you got the job because you have a superior knowledge about the music, but as a party DJ, you have to appear at the mercy of the people you're playing for, whether you follow through with their request or not.

However, a few occasions can crop up when you'd say no to a request, if you don't have that particular song, or if it wouldn't go down well at all.

Don't beat yourself up

You're in control of everybody's night as the DJ, and with that, comes quite a lot of pressure. This pressure can make you flustered, and can lead to panic if things start to go wrong. In the bedroom, if you make a mistake, it doesn't matter, as you can start the mix again and no one will know any different. In a club, if you make a mistake, it means a lot more.

If your last mix was a disaster, be hard on yourself by all means as you're a perfectionist, and should have done better, but don't let one mistake spoil the rest of your set. Not everyone hears errors, no matter how bad they are. A lot of people aren't as tuned in to the music as you are, or they're having too good a time to care. Watch for reactions, if the people on the floor start chanting '*Sack the DJ*, you know that you've made a boo-boo, but if they're still smiling and dancing, don't beat yourself up over something that didn't matter.

If you're working at a wedding, and the dance floor has all the grandparents on it, dropping the latest gangsta rap or nu metal tune may be a bit of a mistake. Or if you're a rock DJ, and everyone's going nuts for the 1980s Bon Jovi/Van Halen set you're currently playing, agreeing to play one request for White Zombie may not prove to be the best decision you made all night.

Taking over from someone else

The warm-up DJs have a hard life; they turn up, play for an hour and a half to get the crowd in the mood, then someone pushes them out of the way and finishes the job they started. When you're the person doing the pushing, pause and pay attention to what was happening before you entered the DJ booth.

Aim to get into the club at least 15 minutes before you start so that you can listen to the end of the warm-up DJs set. This time gives you a chance to gauge how the crowd is responding to the music, and also avoids you repeating a tune that has only just been played. Ask the warm-up DJ as many questions about the crowd's reaction to the music already played, and how he or she feels the night is going to continue based on their experience so far.

Check the set-up

Checking the set-up is extremely important. Look at what the DJ is using. If he or she is only using CDs, and you're about to use the turntables, quickly check the turntables and the settings on the mixer to make sure that the previous DJ hasn't disconnected, broken, or switched off something that will end up causing you problems.

Look at how the DJ is mixing, too. If they're only using the channel-faders, look at the cross-fader. If the mixer has assignable switches, the DJ may have switched off the cross-fader, so it has no control over the mix.

Gauge the mood

Use your body language skills to judge what mood the crowd is in before deciding how to start your set. If the club is busy, with pent-up energy, and the warm-up DJ has been getting loads of requests for more upbeat tunes, use that to your advantage by instantly changing up from light, warm-up music to something a lot newer, faster, and harder. That change adds an instant boost to the crowd. Bear in mind though, not to blow your entire set trying to take the crowd even higher, only to run out of tunes to play.

If the people are still tentatively moving onto the dance floor, be a bit more gradual about the change in music. Do start to move on from what has been played before, but do it gradually to keep the people on the dance floor.

Play with momentum

If you're taking over from someone who's already playing fast, powerful tunes, you have a choice; you can mix out of their last tune in a smooth, seamless, unnoticeable mix, announce your arrival with a change in tempo/genre/key/volume or try something like a dead stop, spinback, or power off if you really want to let people know that you're taking over. (Check out Chapters 14 and 16 for more on these techniques.)

A cacophony of sound

The very first time I played live, the warm-up guy before me had turned off the cross-fader and used the channel-faders on their own. The problem was, I forgot to turn the cross-fader back on, and as I needed to mix with the headphones on both ears because the DJ booth didn't have a monitor, it ended in disaster. I put on the headphones, set the input level for both channels, pressed the cue switches so both tunes played in my headphones, then raised the channel-fader to full, and slowly moved the cross-fader from left to right.

As the headphones were over both ears, I didn't hear that when I raised the channel-fader, the new tune crashed in at full volume over the other tune, and when I moved the cross-fader from left to right, nothing happened; both tunes continued to play over each other at full volume.

I'd let the mix go on for so long that the beats had started to drift apart, but I didn't think that mattered as the outgoing tune was quiet, then silent. Or so I thought. I took my headphones off, and only after a brief moment of panic at the terrible noise coming from the speakers was it obvious what had happened. I slammed the channel-fader on the outgoing tune to zero and hung my head in shame. But, the lesson here is that no one else noticed! I couldn't believe it. The only thing I can think is that because it was in a pub, not everyone was there for the music.

Playing too much, too soon

Although not always a mistake, slamming in a really heavy tune when only 20 people are on the dance floor is a dangerous gamble. I heard a DJ make a terrible mistake when the warm-up was still playing light vocal house as the dance floor was only just beginning to fill up. Instead of gently coaxing more people onto the dance floor with a steady increase in pace and energy, the new DJ tried an instant, dramatic change using an older, classic tune 'Born Slippy' by Underworld. It's a great tune at the right time, but straight on the back of light, musical house music, the change was way too much, and the 20 people who *had* made it to the dance floor quickly left, leaving an empty, desolate dance floor for him to panic about.

My preference is to use a basic, simple sounding tune. Something that's just drums and a powerful, offbeat bass melody coming out of a quite frantic tune is a good way to change the power without changing the tempo (described in Chapter 17 as an offbeat only *ta-te* into a *ta fe te te*). I can then build the set back up to a fuller feel in my own time, rather than carrying on with the same sound as the other DJ, which the crowd will soon tire of.

Change the music

One of the most interesting things I've ever had to do was take over from a heavy metal DJ. Changing from Iron Maiden to David Morales is not a natural thing to do! I used a simple fade out with an instant start of the next tune, which isn't a particularly hard mix, but choosing the right tune to start with is important. The tune I used, 'Needin' U' by David Morales, was a simple, recognisable tune with the offbeat simple bass line I mentioned above, and it worked very well.

Finishing the night

After a successful night in the DJ booth, putting on the last tune and letting it run out can be hard – you just want to keep playing all night long. Have a think about how you want to finish your set about an hour before you finish.

How busy the club is determines how you end the set. If the club is still packed, keep playing great tunes until the end, then try to finish with the best tune you can think of. I love finishing with BT's 'Believer' because it's an energetic, musical track that finishes with 'I'm a believer . . ..' echoing into silence. This ending is so much better than simply fading out the last record.

Some clubs request that you tone down the energy and pace of the music towards the end of the night or when the dance floor starts to get quieter, so people aren't hyper as they leave the club. I think that sells the club and the clubbers short a bit – you need to play the most suitable music for the people who are there from start to finish.

Respect the licensing laws for the club you're playing in; you don't want them to lose their licence just because you wanted to squeeze in one more track. Even if people are screaming for another track, don't take the law into your own hands and play another one. That's a sure route to not being asked back next week! The owner/promoter will probably hang over you towards the end of the night to make sure that you stop anyway, so don't push your luck.

The last things to do as you finish your night are to pack up all your records, disconnect any tape or mini disc recorders you've used to record your set, put everything in a safe place, then find the person with your money!

If you're working through an agency, your payment gets sorted through them, so you only need to say your goodbyes, and leave with the knowledge that you've had another successful night. Otherwise, you have to play what I call *hunt the money-man*. You may have to look in some strange places, but you'll eventually find the person who pays you. Unless you've something better to do, don't leave their sight until you get paid. In full.

While you're still in the club, have a last word with the bar staff and the toilet attendant to find out how they felt the night went. Always listen to feedback. If they say something you don't agree with, that's fine, but remember it, and look out for it next time, in the unlikely event that they know better than you.

Part V
The Part of Tens

"Pull the Tchaikovsky out of your mix, dude. Too many people are breaking into 'Swan Lake'."

In this part . . .

The Part of Tens is a regular feature in all *For Dummies* books. Short and snappy, these chapters are the really fun ones!

From how to go to the toilet in the middle of a DJ set, to where to go to find out more information on DJing, the nuggets of information in the final chapters of this book aren't as much the icing on the cake – more the knife to cut the cake!

Chapter 21

Ten Resources for Expanding Your Skills and Fan Base

In This Chapter

▶ Knowing where to go for more information

▶ Discovering tuition that may be available to you

▶ Exposing yourself (musically)

*T*he skills you're developing are the strong foundations that lead you to become a good DJ. Unfortunately, you can't rest on your laurels. Your skills and reputation need constant bolstering, and the following ten resources keep you ahead of the scene and boost your reputation so that people know who you are when you're playing, and will seek you out.

Your thirst for knowledge should never end. The moment you think that you know it all, you start going backwards. Keep up with new equipment, keep an eye on the scene so you can start to read drifting music tastes, and share as much information as you can with other DJs.

Staying Current with Media

TV, radio, DVD, magazines, and the Internet are all incredible resources for your development as a DJ.

Magazines (and their supporting Web sites) dedicated to DJ culture, equipment, and music always keep you up to date. Music reviews and DJ charts in magazines can be invaluable as long as you trust the DJ or reviewer's opinions and they keep you ahead of DJs who think that going to a club once a month is enough.

I'm on the mailing list for *Night* magazine that's dedicated to news about new clubs opening, new sound installations, and all the juicy information that you usually only hear about a couple of months after decisions have been made. If you can find out about a new club development in your area before the other DJs, you can get a head start and send off a demo to the developers before the other DJs know about it.

Radio shows are great ways of hearing new music. Most of them announce what tracks they're playing regularly (or have a Web site that updates with a track list). BBC Radio 1 is an unbelievable resource for new music. If you're outside the UK, check out (www.bbc.co.uk/radio1) and look for Pete Tong and Judge Jules' shows.

TV programmes that interview DJs who play music you love, have features on equipment and culture, and reviews about the clubs that play your style of music can give you insight into how you need to develop in order to progress in an ultra-competitive market.

DVDs and videos that show you how to DJ can be a great help. Sometimes you need to see a technique to fully understand it (which is why my Web site www.recess.co.uk has video clips of most techniques). Inspirational footage or video clips of your favourite DJ hosted online (do a search through www.youtube.com) can light a fire under you to make you more determined to become a DJ as well as show you a whole host of new skills.

Visiting DJ Advice Web Sites

Ten years ago, the Internet had a dearth of information about DJing, with only a couple of Web sites trying to shed light on *how* to be a DJ.

Since then, many sites have sprung up with different ways of explaining how to DJ. Apart from my own Web site (www.recess.co.uk), the best Web sites on the Internet for club mixing are www.djmandrick.com (a great site about how to beatmatch), www.djprince.no for incredibly detailed information about harmonic mixing, and www.i-dj.co.uk, the Web site for International DJ magazine, which keeps you up to date on the music scene and new equipment.

Getting Answers through DJ Forums

DJ forums are a great place to post any questions that are troubling you, and are also a fantastic way to get involved with a good community that listens to your mixes and gives you brutally honest feedback to help you with your development. Create a screen name (go for an anonymous one, so that you can post those embarrassing questions without fear of personal ridicule), and visit forums like:

- ✔ www.djforums.com/forums A huge community with advice on technique, a classified section, mix submissions, advice for mobile DJs, and a lot more.

- ✔ www.i-dj.co.uk/messageboard This is the forum for *I-DJ* magazine, which has loads of subsections and a lot of members on hand to help you out. Nearly all magazines have their own forum, so check out the homepage of your favourite magazine to see if it has a community you'd like to join.

- ✔ www.tranceaddict.com/forums Though the name suggests the site is only for trance DJs, it's actually for all kinds of electronic dance music. A friendly, fun community with a great thread for DJs to post pictures of their own DJ equipment set-up. Humour, advice, and guidance are all on hand here.

- ✔ www.djchat.com/boards The forums mentioned above are primarily for the club/electronic dance music DJ. DJChat.com has over 21,000 members, but more importantly, deals with all different types of DJing, from country, to Christian, to karaoke, to Latin music.

Most users on forums are polite and helpful but to minimise any flaming (abuse), try to post into the correct section, check your spelling, and be polite – also, do a quick search to check that someone hasn't already posted your question.

You'll find me on any of the preceding forums or on the forum on my own Web site (www.djrecess.co.uk/php) as Recess or DJ Recess.

Reading Other Books

I'm hurt that you'd think of reading another book after this one.

On a serious note, of the other books out there on the market on DJing, by far the best one to buy, in my opinion, is *How to be a DJ* by Chuck Fresh (Premier Press). The book covers every aspect of becoming a DJ, and is aimed at every kind of DJ, from wedding to radio to club DJing. But the best thing is how it's written: he's very friendly, he doesn't patronise you, and doesn't spend the whole time swearing and trying to be cool.

Beware of some of the e-books and guides available in the back of DJ magazines or online. Although many of them are genuine and very helpful, others are a complete waste of time and money or, as I've found, are rip-offs of my Web site! Post a request on a DJ forum (see the previous section for ideas on where to go) for a review of a particular guide, just to be sure.

Getting Hands-On Advice

If you have the money, and want hands-on advice on all aspects of DJing, then academies like DJ Academy (www.djacademy.org.uk) SubBass DJ Academy (www.subbassdj.com), and Point Blank Music College (www.pointblank london.com) in the UK, or Norcal DJMPA (www.norcaldjmpa.com) and Scratch DJ (www.scratch-dj.com) in the US are the most popular. As courses cost money (out of your own pocket), do some research into a course before signing up for it, to ensure that any money you spend will be money well spent, rather than thrown away.

Universities and colleges have also realised that there's an avenue for teaching DJs, with the formation in the UK of the *National Certificate in Music Technology, DJ & Mixing* course. Covering beatmatching, scratching, studio production, computer technology, sound creation and more, these courses, like the private DJ Academies, can teach you a lot about DJing and related industries, but have the added advantage of keeping your mum off your back, because you can tell her you're at college, learning a skill.

The benefit of formal training is that you have the continuity of someone who's there to correct you when you're doing something wrong, who makes you practise (rather than you drifting off to play your PlayStation), and most importantly, someone who you can ask questions when you're unsure what to do.

Courses can show you the mechanics of how to mix, and they provide information on the other aspects of DJing (sound production, accountancy, promotion, and so on) but what they *can't* teach you is how to be a DJ in a more esoteric sense. What do I mean by *esoteric*? That DJing is partly developed and absorbed into your knowledge not by the process of someone telling you what to do, but through time spent practising, through experience, confidence, failure, trial and error, and simply by listening to your tunes. If you do a course, you still need the same amount of time practising and developing to grow into your talent and truly become a great DJ.

Listening to Other People's Mixes

When you listen to different genres and different DJs on the radio, the Internet, or in a club, you open your eyes to different techniques. No matter how good or bad the performance, you always gain something from listening to any kind of mix, including music you haven't heard before.

Listening to a bad mix is just as helpful as hearing a good one. If you can recognise what makes a bad mix bad, you can listen out for those same things in your own mixes (such as bad tune selection, poor beatmatching, and sloppy volume or EQ control) and work on making your mixes top notch.

Participating in Competitions

You can hand out as many demos as you like, but sometimes you need a few more strings to your bow so that you can spread the word about your DJ prowess. Take a look at magazines, the Internet, and what's on in your local area to see if any DJ *battles* or competitions are on the horizon that provide the perfect opportunity for you to show off your skills.

Due to its very nature, club DJing is quite hard to put into a proper competition format without becoming a competition for how many tunes you can play in your 15-minute slot. However, *Bedroom DJ* competitions invite unknown DJs to send in a full-length mix on CD or tape and are a strong avenue to propel DJs careers. James Zabiela and Yousef both got noticed because of wins in *Muzik* magazine.

For scratch DJs, you don't get a better opportunity than the DMC Scratching Championships to show off your *mad skillz*. You'll be up against really tough competition, but hopefully the experience and the chance to meet top level DJs will improve your career prospects.

If you can't face any competitions or the rejection of not making the final of a magazine competition, look for clubs and bars that have an *open booth* night, where DJs take half-hour slots to play music and impress the people on the floor. If you're good, you'll be noticed.

Hosting Your Own Night

If you can't find anyone to let you work on a Friday night in their club, the solution's simple. Put on your own night. You may have to settle for a town hall somewhere, or a Tuesday night in a dingy club, but if you can get enough people to turn up to a night you run, if you organise it well, and if you make it a complete success (which means no one gets hurt!), word will spread and you may get headhunted (in the good way). Even if the night doesn't generate any direct interest from a club owner or promoter, you'll have a very strong section on your DJing CV to show people you're driven and serious about becoming a DJ.

Promotion is the key. Get as many friends, and friends of friends along as you can. If you can run the night with another DJ, all the better; that's two sets of friends you can get into the club. Hand out flyers (without littering or getting arrested), wander around a few pubs to get more people to come along, run an Internet site promoting the event, and do everything you can to try to get as many people to come as possible.

Make sure that everyone knows what music to expect, try to get a group of *ringers* (people specifically invited for the task) who'll dance on the floor no matter what you play, and don't forget to read the crowd and play music that they want to hear. If you only play *your* set all night, and don't try to entertain the people that have come to see you, you'll find a dramatic drop in numbers the next time you play.

Under-eighteen discos and running a night in scout halls and town halls are a good idea, but can be fraught with logistical problems. Most often, the problems involve alcohol and security, so be careful if you're trying to run a night without professional help – be sure that you're on the right side of the law.

Uploading Podcasts or Hosted Mixes

As disc space and bandwidth gets cheaper and cheaper, more Web sites (such as www.djpassion.co.uk, www.djmixtape.net, and www.mydjspace.net to mention only three of the hundreds available) give you the choice to upload and promote your set for anyone across the world to download (and sometimes cast judgement on).

You find many different podcasting directories out there, from iTunes to www.blogging.com and www.podcast.com. Each one has a slightly different requirement on how to upload and set up the podcast, so I recommend that you visit the Web site of the directory you wish to use, and follow their tutorials to get your podcast . . . cast.

Immerse Yourself in What You Love

The most obvious resource for your development is visiting the clubs that you love. In the same way that listening to as many mixes as possible can help your development, so can going to as many clubs as possible. Clubs with music other than the genre you play can teach you a lot, but your best development comes from going to clubs that play the music you love.

Split yourself in two. Be the DJ who absorbs what's happening, recognising how the DJ is working (or alienating) the crowd, and take everything you can from a good DJ and absorb the good things into your own skills. But also, spend time on the dance floor as a normal clubber. Dance like a mad person, feel the music, let the bass flood through your body, and don't stop smiling the whole time.

This is what you want to make other people do – experience and recognise a good night when you're on the dance floor, and then look for yourself in the crowd next time you play live.

Chapter 22

Ten Answers to DJ Questions You're Too Afraid to Ask

In This Chapter

▶ Leaving your post and keeping your cool

▶ Modifying the mood by customising the music and lighting

▶ Making a good impression – picking your DJ name, and dressing for success

*T*his chapter covers miscellaneous FAQs. The following ten questions are the most popular *sheepish* questions I've been asked over the past decade, and although I answer many questions in this book, these two handfuls don't really fit in anywhere else, and are perfect as a Part of Tens chapter.

What kind of DJ you are, and where you're playing at, can generate a different answer to a lot of the following questions. Where applicable, I split the answer into Club DJ and Party DJ (which covers weddings, parties, bowling alleys, anywhere that's all about fun and entertainment).

Do I Need to Talk?

Whether you need to address your audience when you're DJing is a really good question. A lot of people become DJs because they love the music, and love mixing it together, but many of them don't figure that they'll ever have to use a microphone and speak to the audience. In short, yes, you need to talk.

The mechanics of using a microphone are simple enough. Put the microphone very close to your mouth, and as you speak, reduce the channel-fader of the music that's currently playing, so you can be heard over it. When you're not talking, move the microphone away from your mouth (so you're not heard breathing at 100 decibels), and raise the channel-fader back to normal. You could be raising and lowering the fader many times in one sentence, but as long as you do it quickly, and with confidence, it's okay.

You may have a *talk-over* button on your mixer that does the same thing. The drop in volume of the music can be a bit sudden though, so if the sound isn't right, forget about it, and use the channel-faders instead.

If you want to run a party or wedding night well, you need to get used to talking to people on the dance floor. You may be asked to introduce the bride and groom or announce that the buffet is open, so you need to be comfortable, clear, and confident when you speak through the microphone. If you're a shy type, just become an actor, and put on your DJ voice. If you think that your voice is a bit dull, add a little *radio DJ* inflection to your voice while you're talking to the party goers. This may sound a bit forced to you, but they won't know any better (and, let's be honest, probably won't be listening). No one wants to hear the DJ announce the buffet with nerves in their voice; they may wonder what you did to the potato salad!

What Should I Wear?

If you're a club DJ, the question of what to wear is easily answered by taking your lead from the dress code of the club you're playing and picking a comfortable version of that. I tend to wear a black T-shirt, fawn coloured jeans, and Timberlands when I'm DJing. The T-shirt keeps me cool and comfortable in a hot DJ booth, and the colour of the jeans tends to fit in with most clubs' dress code. If you're doing the whole set on your feet for six hours, choose comfortable shoes.

Famous DJs can wear what they want. As they become icons though, their fashion sense can be held to scrutiny, so expect their black T-shirts to be made by a top fashion label.

If you're a wedding DJ, remember that everyone else at the wedding has made an effort. I'm not saying to turn up in a frock, tux, or a kilt (though it *would* probably be appreciated), but turn up smart, with a pressed shirt and trousers.

You're probably charging a lot of money for your service, and the reason you can charge this amount is because you're a professional DJ. Be professional and turn up smart and smiling.

How Do I Go to the Toilet?

Now for that certain unmentionable matter of going to the toilet. Let's just say – quickly.

If you can, try to *go* before you go. If you're nervous, you may be hopping on and off of the lavatory anyway, but try to make sure that any visits to the toilet are quick, and won't involve a long time sitting down (if you get what I mean).

If you're a club DJ and the pressure mounts, put on a long record, ask a *trusted* friend or a bouncer to stand by the decks then get in and out as fast as you can. By trusted, I mean someone who won't think that he or she can take over while you're gone.

As a wedding DJ, however, you may be on your own. If the pressure mounts so to speak, first try to hold it in until the buffet break (if you get one). If you can't, quickly make friends with a waiter or girl/guy who you think that you can trust to look after your decks, or just make a break for it – and get back as quick as you can. Just remember to wash your hands, please.

No matter what type of DJ you are, the tune you put on to cover your comfort break is quite important. It has to be long enough to cover your absence, have little chance of skipping or jumping while you're gone, and not be too repetitive (so the crowd doesn't get bored with it).

Worst case scenario for blokes involves you peeing into a beer bottle. It's not nice.

Can I Invite My Friends into the DJ Booth?

Whether you invite your friends into the DJ booth very much depends on what kind of place you're working at. If you take your girlfriend/boyfriend with you to a party as your *DJ Assistant* to make your life easier by getting drinks and taking requests, it's probably welcomed. If you're in a club, however, and your other half sits grumpily behind you in the DJ booth, takes up space, and gets in everybody's way, the club manager may eventually ask her or him to leave the booth.

Your friends will just want to have a laugh in the DJ booth and will probably end up ripping the needle off the record, or pressing Stop on the CD decks *for a lark*. If you got your friends into the club for free, make them pay their way by spending most of their time on the dance floor, having the time of their lives, keeping the night looking like a huge success.

How Do I Remove the Beat, or Vocals?

How you go about removing the beat or vocals from a track is a tricky one. For an entire tune, you can't. Sometimes, you can remove enough of the frequencies from a sample (a small section) of music so that it sounds clean enough for you to play over something else.

A friend of mine, in a band called Pacifica, did this with a sample from Blondie's 'Heart of Glass'. He used that guitar riff as the hook to a tune he'd released ('Lost in Translation'), and halfway through, he wanted to use the 'Ooo ooo – aa aa' vocal sample. Unfortunately, even the cleanest sounding part of Heart of Glass still has drums and a bass melody over it. Eventually, with patience and a good engineer using compressors, expanders, filters, EQs (equalisers), and a little voodoo magic, the sample was cleaned up for use in the song.

The danger with EQing out the music from a sample is that by removing the frequencies that make the drum sounds and music, you also remove the frequencies that make up the vocal sample. So when you cut the high frequencies to remove the high-hats cymbals, you also remove all the *sibilance* (the *ssssss* sounds like a snake makes) from the vocal. The same applies to the bass and mid frequencies.

As a result of sharing frequencies between the vocal and the music track, it's impossible to remove all music from an entire song, leaving only the vocal. If you hear a vocal version of a tune, it's an *a cappella* (vocals with no accompanying music) released by the artist, or maybe someone has recorded a very good imitation of the vocals, and used that, hoping no one could tell the difference.

You can, however, remove only the vocals. This method is by no means perfect, but it may work for you. When music is recorded, the standard procedure is that the instruments are *panned* left and right into a stereo signal, but the vocals remain centered in the middle. With computer software (in my opinion Cool Edit is really good for this process) you can remove everything that's in the centre pan (the vocals), leaving only the stereo music information.

This doesn't give you perfect results (you certainly won't have a clean, CD-quality audio track that you can play on its own), but you may end up with something that you can add your own sounds to, using this stripped tune as a foundation for a new creation. Some tunes work better than others with this method, and like everything else in DJing, it takes a lot of time and practice to get right.

How Do I Choose My DJ Name?

When you come to choose your DJ name, the first thing to ask yourself is whether your real name is good enough or if you want to be DJ 'Something'. Pete Tong, Paul Oakenfold, Paul Van Dyk, Erik Morillo, David Morales, John Digweed – they've all got *real* names instead of 'DJ Tong' or 'J to the D' and so on.

However, you may decide that your name isn't powerful enough to be displayed on a billboard (here's hoping), or perhaps you're looking for anonymity. In which case you can create a full name pseudonym (such as Bob Sinclar – real name Christophe LeFriant) or come up with a DJ name, in DJ 'Something' format, or just one name. That's why I came up with Recess, because I figured John Steventon wouldn't look that good on the back of a bus.

When trying to pick a name, think of what you do, who you are, what you play, how you play, what your other interests are, what your real name is – and see how you can mutate that to a good DJ name.

Or, if you're lazy, or looking for inspiration, check out the Web site called Quiz Meme (www.quizmeme.com) where you type your name, and it spits out a DJ name for you. I typed in John Steventon, and got DJ Flowing Cranny. I typed in Recess – and got DJ Vinyl Artist; so it must be right!

Another way to come up with a name is to mutate words. Think of ten words that you'd use to describe yourself or your music, and consider if they (or any derivations of them) would be good. For example, if you're a deep house DJ who likes to fish you might come up with DJ Deep Lure, which could then be mutated into DJ D'Allure. Or not . . .

However, how you're commonly known is still one of the most personal ways to create your DJ name. Nicknames are a great start, but if, like in my case, you were called something stupid like 'butter' at school, you may want to explore other avenues. Alexander Coe had the easiest name change in the world, and is now one of the most famous DJs on the planet – he could've chosen Xander, Zander, Alex Coe, or anything else as his DJ name, but instead, he chose Sasha (which is the Russian derivation of the similar Aleksandr), and that worked out very well for him!

In my case, Recess is bit of both. My initials are J.R.C.S. and I dropped the J to leave RCS, which I mutated to Recess. (JRCS reads too much like jerks . . .)

Do I Get Free Drinks? (And How Do I Get Drinks from the Bar?)

If you're a club DJ, try to negotiate whether you get free drinks when you first speak to the owner/promoter about working at their club. The worst they can say is no, and it saves any future embarrassment.

If you're well enough known as a DJ, you can submit a *rider* (a condition of the job) before you get to the club, demanding a case of Bud and a bag of green Jelly Babies to be in the booth for when you start, but for local clubs, and lesser known DJs, you probably find that you only get a free drink when the bar manager comes into the booth for a chat.

If you're a party DJ and you're lucky, the father of the bride, or birthday girl or boy, may offer you a drink halfway through the night when they're having a really good time, and at their happiest point – but don't count on it.

At clubs, leaving the DJ booth to head to the bar for a drink is usually a big no-no. If you don't get free drinks at a club, and no one's available to go to the bar for you, you'll probably have to go thirsty until a glass collector or bar staff come along that you can ask to get a drink for you. But take a bottle of water (or whatever you think is better for you) just in case no one's kind enough to offer.

At pubs, parties, and weddings, popping to the bar to buy a drink is normally okay, and if the staff know that you're the DJ (believe me, some don't) you'll probably get served really quickly.

Who Does the Lighting for the Night?

Regarding the question of who does the lighting for the night, wedding and party DJs tend to bring their own lights, as well as amps and DJing equipment and they control the lights. When choosing lights, you may want to go for ones that have sensors in them to make them move and flash based on the sound of music (no, not the film). With these, all you need to do is set everything up, and the lights take care of themselves. The other option is to get a compact control unit with different preset patterns to make the lights move and flash in different orders (though usually still in time with the music).

As far as clubs are concerned, I've worked in a few that had a similar pre-set lighting arrangement, except that they tend to have more lights than the wedding or party setup. However, most of the places I've worked in (and been to as a clubber) had a separate *lighting jock* to control the lights.

The difference that a good or bad lighting jock can make is almost as important as the music you play. Creative use of strobe lights, *gobos* (the rotating flashing lights), and intricate laser shows along with the new wave of *VJs* (video jockeys) who use machines like the Pioneer DVJ-X1 to create incredible displays with video images, can really enhance the clubbing experience for the crowd.

If you strike up a good relationship with the lighting jock, and let them know anything peculiar about the tunes you're playing that may help them work in harmony with your mix, the two of you can eventually build an incredible show together that feels like an orchestrated event. Or you can just ask him or her to get your drinks for you . . . it's your choice.

Should I Re-set the Pitch to Zero After Beatmatching?

Do you reset the pitch to 0 after beatmatching one tune with another? No.

The two main reasons why you beatmatch tunes when mixing are

- ✔ To keep a constant, pounding bass beat for the clubbers to dance to.
- ✔ To play the music at a pace that matches the speed of the clubbers' beating hearts.

If you decide that 135 BPM (beats per minute) is the perfect pace at which to play your music, and you put on a tune that plays at 130 BPM when set at 0 pitch, you need to raise the pitch control to about 4 per cent in order to get it to play at 135 BPM.

Setting the pitch control back to 0 after you've beatmatched and mixed the two tunes together will not only sound terrible as the pitch of the music lowers (unless you're using decks with *master tempo*, which keeps the pitch the same no matter how fast you play the tune) but now the tune will be playing at a speed that's way below the pace of the clubbers' heartbeats. They'll have to dance slower, and you will kill the energy of the night.

The result is even worse the other way round. Imagine that you've had to reduce the tempo of a 140 BPM tune to –4 per cent. When you speed the track up by resetting the pitch to 0, you'll tire everyone out by the end of the tune, as it's now playing at 140 BPM to a dance floor that's used to grooving at only 135 BPM!

Fluctuations in BPM as you progress through a two-hour set can be useful (refer to Chapter 17), but when you're beatmatching, you'll probably find that the only time you'll ever play a tune at 0 per cent pitch is at the very beginning of the night when you play your first tune.

What Do I Do if the Record or CD Skips or Jumps?

You're a professional DJ. Be professional about getting around what to do if the record or CD skips or jumps. A jump on a record isn't too bad, as at least it's just a repeat of 1 or 2 seconds of music that plays through the PA, but if a CD skips, it's a nasty sound, and you need to do something, instantly.

If you can't just skip to the next track on the CD, hit the *Search* button on the CD deck to advance 5 or 10 seconds past the part that's skipping (lower the channel-fader at the same time to hide what you're doing).

With a record, the best thing to do is to lower the channel-fader to about 25 per cent of normal playout volume and *knock* the needle forward through the record by half a centimetre or so. Yes, this method won't sound too good, and yes, you may damage your record, but your record's already damaged if it's skipping, and it already doesn't sound good because it's repeating itself!

Prevent this sort of occurrence happening by cleaning your records or CDs before playing them (head to Chapters 5 and 7 for more on caring for your music collection).

I like to cue up the next track almost instantly after mixing into a track for this very reason, as then I have the next tune sitting there, ready to mix in quickly if something goes wrong. If you wait until the end of a track to cue up the next one, you'll have nothing to do an emergency mix with if needs be. Sure, the mix won't sound great, but how does that compare to how the music currently sounds?

Everything you ever do, DJing or otherwise, involves skill and knowledge, but also how you cope under pressure. If you can fix a catastrophe like a damaged CD with composure and professionalism, you show all those around you that you're in control, and meant to be where you are – in the DJ booth, as a professional DJ.

Chapter 23

Ten DJing Mistakes to Avoid

In This Chapter

▶ Avoiding mistakes that make you look and sound unprofessional

▶ Leaving for the night with all your tunes, and all your money

*T*he ten common mistakes described in this chapter are exactly that: common. A couple of them may never happen to you, but, unfortunately, some may happen too often. I haven't made all the mistakes in this chapter. Most of them, yes. But not all.

What's important about the mistakes you make (in DJing or just life in general) is that you learn from them. Make sure that you don't do them again, or at the very least, make sure that you know how to cope with the consequences . . . such as the sound of silence in a club.

Forgetting Slipmats/Headphones

Forgetting your slipmats (which is an easy thing to do) is not too much of a big deal as most clubs have their own set, but if you fail to bring your headphones, the club is unlikely to have a spare pair of quality headphones lying around for forgetful DJs to use.

Check out Chapter 24 and the Cheat Sheet at the front of the book for a checklist of ten things that you need to take with you when DJing.

Taking the Needle off the Wrong Record

Taking the needle off the wrong record is exactly the same as pressing Stop or Eject on the wrong CD player. I guarantee that at some stage in your DJ career, you'll make the same mistake. Hopefully, you'll be in the sanctuary of your own bedroom, where only the cat can judge you on your error.

If you're unfortunate enough to make this mistake when DJing live in a club, put the needle back on (carefully, don't throw it back on the record in a mad panic), or quickly press Play on the CD deck. If you ejected the CD, press Play on the other deck, and quickly move the cross-fader over to that channel.

Next, allocate blame. It's probably easier to blame the sound system. You never know, someone in the crowd may be gullible enough to believe you! Then squat down to hide in the DJ booth for a couple of minutes, and wait for the abuse to die down.

Banishing Mixer Setting Problems

Mixers are now available with an increasing number of functions, which unfortunately means that the chance of you forgetting to change these settings increases, too.

Leaving assign controls set to the wrong channel is easily done, so when you move the cross-fader, you're fading into silence (or the wrong tune). Bass kills are often unwittingly left on during a mix, only dawning on you halfway through the tune that the bass is missing. And effects like flanger or echo can easily be left on because you're focusing your attention on the next tune (or the girl/boy on the dance floor). A lapse of concentration is all it takes to ruin a good mix (and sometimes your night) – so concentrate!

Getting Drunk when Playing

You need to be fully in control of your equipment but you won't be able to do that if you've had too many beers or tequilas back there in the DJ booth. Having a couple of alcoholic drinks for Dutch courage is all very well but being so plied with booze that you can't even see the mixer in front of you and can't mix properly is not going to be considered very professional.

I've heard tales of DJs guzzling a case of Bud before going behind the decks, but unless you have a liver the size of a small house, if you must drink, just make it a couple, then stick to water.

Leaving Records Propped Up

If you have to leave your records *poking out* at an angle from your record box to know where the next few tunes you'd like to play are that's okay, but removing a record from its sleeve, and propping it up against a speaker (or similar) is a bad idea. Eventually, you or someone else will bump into the speaker/desk, and the record will drop to the floor, snapping in half (which is an extremely effective way of getting you out of this habit, though!)

Cutting corners in this way breeds laziness and disrespect for your records. As a DJ, your records (and CDs) are the most important things in the world to you – don't risk damaging them by being lazy.

Leaning Over the Decks

As the DJ, you're the *host* of the evening, and you're allowed to show or receive some appreciation (handshakes and kisses on the cheeks being the best way). Just make sure you're appreciated a little to the left of the decks so that you don't bump into the decks or hit something on the mixer.

Copy-cat rip

I saw a great photo in DJ magazine a few years ago of Sasha leaning across the decks so that someone from the dance floor could light his cigarette. Back in the days when I did smoke (it's not big, it's not clever, and it *will* kill you) I thought this look was so cool, I'd try to do the same.

Not only did I receive some friendly abuse from the lighting guy while I waited for someone to oblige with a match, when I did lean over the decks, my T-shirt got caught on the needle on the record, ripping it right off. (The needle that is, not the T-shirt.) Fortunately, it was the cued record rather than the one playing to the dance floor, but it was further compounded by me dropping the lit cigarette onto the turntable because I was so flustered by what I'd just done.

Avoiding Wardrobe Malfunction

Avoiding a wardrobe malfunction is harder than you think. From jeans that are cut too low (so when you bend over to pick up a record, everyone can see your butt-cleavage) to ladies wearing a white bra under a black top so the UV lights show off their glowing chests, you'd be surprised what can go wrong.

Hats, scarves, ponchos, and false beards will all eventually get tangled up in your equipment, or fall onto the decks. Wearing costumes (think Elvis costumes, gorilla outfits, or Tarzan wraps) seem like a good idea in principle, but try to have a quick practice wearing them before you start mixing; your furry paws or rhinestone cuffs may turn your mixing into a nightmare.

Spending Too Long Talking to Someone

Stay professional: don't spend so long talking to a friend, potential employer or member of the opposite sex that you don't have enough time to properly cue up and mix in the next track. Even if you do have enough time to cue up the tune, don't rush the mix just so that you can go back to talking to them. And whatever you do, don't spend so long talking to someone that the record runs out completely. Unless of course you want to get fired.

Leaving Your Last Tune Behind

If you're just doing part of the night, and someone is taking over from you, chances are, you finished your set on a really good tune, so you don't want to leave it behind. Wait until the next DJ has mixed out of your last tune, then pick up your record/CD, pack your bags, and leave the booth. If you're pulled away by someone, ask the DJ to put your tune to one side, and say that you'll pick it up later – at least that way he or she won't walk off with it by accident.

Not Getting Paid Before You Leave

After a night rocking the crowd, don't leave the club before you've been paid in full. Don't fall for excuses such as 'I don't have my cheque book', or 'I don't have it all here, can I give you half now, and the rest next time?' I've fallen for this in the past (both times with club promoters who I thought I could trust).

Every case is different, and you should know how much you can push and stand your ground with the club promoter/owner/bride and groom to demand payment. The safest thing to do is to agree on the amount before you set foot into the DJ booth (preferably on paper, signed by both of you). That way, you can be very persistent about making sure that you get all the money you're due.

If you don't agree on an amount before playing though, good luck to you . . .

Chapter 24

Ten Items to Take with You When DJing

. . . .

In This Chapter

▶ Tooling up for the job of DJing

▶ Remembering things to keep you going through the night

▶ Getting home and calming yourself down

. . . .

From the obvious items like your records and headphones, to the less obvious matter of taking a drink and something to make a recording of your mix, the ten items described in this chapter are everything you need for a successful night on the decks.

You may want to tear out the Cheat Sheet at the front of the book and keep this list taped to the back of your door, or next to your car keys, so that you can check it over before you leave the house. (And take the list with you, so you know to bring everything back with you!)

All the Right Records or CDs

You may have thousands of records or CDs in your collection. Make sure that you're taking the right ones with you. Checking for one last time that you've picked up the right box or CD wallet won't hurt! Also take a carbon brush to clean your records, and a soft cloth for CDs.

Make it Personal with Headphones and Slipmats

Have a last check to make sure that your headphones still work, and that you take any adaptors needed to make them work. If you use headphones that you can repair with spare parts (like the Sennheiser HD25s), take your bag of tools and spares.

Put your slipmats between some records in the record box so they stay flat and undamaged. Just remember to take them back at the end of the night!

Using your own slipmats prevents any problems with fluffy, thick, dirty slipmats that a club may use. You'll have become accustomed to how slippy your own slipmats are on a set of Technics 1210s. Basic slipmats on a club's set of decks may create a lot of drag, and even worse, may damage your records due to dirt and crusted beer spillages.

You're a Star! MiniDisc Recorder (or a Blank Tape)

Make the most of every opportunity by recording yourself in the mix, which is especially helpful at the start of your career. You'll benefit dramatically as you can study your performance and improve on it. If a club doesn't have any means to record the mix (check beforehand), take along a MiniDisc recorder (or similar) so you can take away evidence that you rocked the crowd!

Pack Your Tools and Save the Day

Any real man knows that the only tools you need are WD-40 and duct tape. But, if you want to get fancy, throw some differing size and shaped screwdrivers into a bag too, as you never know when you may need a Phillips head screwdriver to save the day.

Always Be Prepared: Pen and Paper

Not just for taking phone numbers of good-looking clientele, you need a pen and paper for taking requests, sending drinks orders to the bar, and swapping phone numbers with people who want to book you.

Keep Fuelled with Food and Drink

Unfortunately, you're not there to have a picnic, you've got a job to do. But, take some sustenance to keep you going in case your body needs fuel.

Contrary to popular belief, you don't have to put vodka into your Red Bull or Irn-Bru 32. Keep one or two cans of your chosen energy drink with you, and if you start to flag halfway through the night, drink one for the caffeine fix.

Be warned though, that some people don't react well to the sudden hit of caffeine. So trying one in the middle of a set, in front of a 1,000 people is not the best time to see if your body likes caffeine and guarana!

In addition to an energy drink, you also need to take something to eat in case you get hungry. Hunger leads to bad moods, and bad moods can make you lose your concentration, and you won't be as attentive to the crowd's needs. Popping wine gums and jelly babies gives you a quick sugar fix, and they contain almost no fat.

Eating an energy bar gives you a better range of nutrients (though a larger fat content) and fills you up for longer, but does run the risk of tasting like cardboard.

Spread the Music with Demo Tapes and CDs

Nothing beats someone asking for a mix tape/CD of your work after hearing you play in a club. Nothing's worse than not having one with you. Take a few copies of your most recent mix (check out Chapter 18 for tips on how to create the best sounding, and best looking CD or tape) and hand them out with a big smile on your face.

A few examples of your best work are also really handy if someone wants to book you for a night somewhere. If you give them a great mix to take away, they won't forget about you – just remember to include your phone number!

Keep Moving with Car Keys

You're not going to get far without your car keys. I've spent many an evening standing at the boot of the car, head in hands in disbelief that I left my keys behind again! Okay if you're just leaving your house, but not okay if they're in your jacket pocket, in the locked-up club that you've just played at.

Have Wallet, Will Travel

You never know when you'll need a little cash, either for taxis home as you left your car keys behind, or just to go grab some chow after your set.

If you have a few business cards, keep them in your wallet, on hand to give out when you need to do some self promotion.

Just Chill: Chill Tape for the Ride Home

Sometimes, I finish my set at four o'clock in the morning, and am in no mood to keep the buzz going by listening to more pumping tunes on the way home. So, I keep a copy of the soundtrack to the film 'The Big Blue' in my car for such occasions.

It contains some of the most fantastic pieces of music I've heard in a long time. My wife Julie worries about it sending me to sleep on the drive home, but all it does is take the edge off the natural high I've got from an evening of energy and musical rapture (but it doesn't do much about the caffeine rush I have due to one too many of those energy drinks!).

I recommend the film too . . .

Chapter 25

Ten Great Influences on Me

In This Chapter

▶ Recognising what's influenced me over the years

▶ Losing faith, then gaining it back again

*Y*our influences are very personal: look at the music you listen to, the people you meet, and the places you go as key points in your career. With these influences, you should be able to make a map of how you developed as a DJ. This chapter describes my journey.

Renaissance – Disc 1

As a key point in my DJ life, *Renaissance – Disc 1* was my first introduction to real dance music. Until I heard this mix by Sasha and Digweed, I thought that dance music was the acid scene, and pop acts such as Snap releasing repetitive, obvious music. Up until I heard this disc, all I listened to was Van Halen, Mr Big, Bon Jovi, and Peter Gabriel. (I think that I've just come out musically.)

Since I first heard it, I've always had a copy of this mix to hand. I had it on tape on my Walkman while mowing lawns, a CD in the car when driving to college, a MiniDisc in my pocket looking for a job, and an iPod strapped to my arm as I go to the gym before work.

Individually, the tunes on the mix are powerful, well-made pieces of work, but the way they were mixed to create a 74-minute journey has always affected me, and I think that the skill it involves is the reason I've always strived to create a seamless mix that has a start, a middle, and an end – rather than just 20 tunes thrown together because they sound nice.

Tonsillitis

You may consider tonsillitis an odd choice as an influence, but as I lay in bed, ill for a week, falling in and out of consciousness, with only the radio to keep me from delirium, I was able to hear music that I'd never heard before.

I'd never heard of a guy called Pete Tong, and at six o'clock on a Friday night, his show started, and my eyes were opened to so many different genres of dance music. From trance, to drum and bass, to American house, I lay in bed, struggling to stay awake. I'd never listened to Radio 1 other than during the day and never listened during weekends, so the Essential Selection, Trevor Nelson, Dave Pearce, and the Essential Mix all opened my eyes to more than just the same Renaissance CD I'd been listening to over and over again.

What started off as an accident because I was too ill to stand up and change the station on the radio (or turn on the TV) ended up as a Friday night ritual; me, Pete Tong, a piece of paper, and a tape recorder.

La Luna: 'To the Beat of the Drum'

I couldn't dance, I had long hair, and I wasn't dressed very well. I spent most of the night a bit lost, standing on the stairs while everyone had fun, but what I do remember is that the very first piece of music I heard as I walked in to my first dance club was La Luna's 'To the Beat of the Drum'.

The piece of music was really simple, but seeing the reaction of the people in the club, feeling the bass drum vibrating through my body, and hearing dance music at this volume, in this atmosphere, for the first time unlocked something in me that left the Van Halen and Bon Jovi CDs unplayed for the next seven or eight years!

(A haircut and better clothes followed almost immediately.)

Ibiza 1996 Radio 1 Weekend

Every summer since 1995, BBC Radio 1 has gone to Ibiza to broadcast from the best clubs on the White Isle. This event has become a solid part of Radio 1's programming, but for me, they've never done better than the 2:00–4:00

a.m. slot at Amnesia in July 1996. I can honestly say that the reason I became a DJ was because of the 90 minutes I could fit on tape of Sasha in the mix. So if you want anyone to blame, give him a call!

As far as a DJ set is concerned, Sasha's set was a step forward from the Renaissance mix I'd heard over and over again. As it was in a live situation, there was an obvious gearing of the set list to working the crowd rather than appealing to a home listener on CD, and it showed me the magic of DJing – that DJing was about more than just playing other people's records.

What sold this mix to me, and still gives me goose bumps when I listen to it (which I am right now in case you're wondering) was at around the halfway point, after playing some really strong, energetic, pounding tunes, he played 'Inner City Life' by Goldie. While still keeping the energy and the tempo of the mix at a similar level, Sasha was able to completely change the dynamic of the mix with just this one tune. It was like having a rest – without having a rest! The mix of 'Inner City Life' that he played was like a roller coaster of power itself. Frantic beats followed by a long breakdown with a gorgeous voice singing over it and a simple, melodic piano hook, and then an energy dipping outro, which ended as beats and electric noises.

Bringing the power back into the mix using the snare beats of a tune called 'Yummy' by Agh was the turning point for the real power of the mix, the crowd went wild, and I can't say I've heard a mix since that's affected me as much.

The Tunnel Club, Glasgow

The Tunnel Club in Glasgow was like my home for six or seven years. It still exists now, in a slightly tamer version of its past, and became an R & B club, but it still holds incredible memories for me.

The three things I'll take away from that club are the smell of dry ice and Red Bull that blasted into your face as you entered the club, the constant quality level of DJs and music that they played every weekend, and that I met my wife Julie there – dancing with friends on the other side of the floor.

Julie's support, advice, and ability to smile politely when I'm boring her with new music, and new ways to mix from tune to tune has kept me going for the past ten years. As it was due to the Tunnel that we met, I can hold the club responsible for my current happiness, and position to write this book.

Jamiroquai – 'Space Cowboy'

Jamiroquai's 'Space Cowboy' was the first time I'd ever heard an original tune remixed to be something better in my eyes. I didn't know much about Jamiroquai, but did know 'Space Cowboy' when they released it as a single. I thought it was okay, but at the time, didn't like the change in sound and style from verse to chorus. Then David Morales gave the tune an overhaul. His remix of 'Space Cowboy' is always in my record box (mostly unplayed unfortunately), and is always in my top ten favourite tune list.

Listening to this track was the first time I'd been able to compare the original to a remix and understand the elements needed to change a song from a good original recording to a dance remix, and have the structure and sounds that would work perfectly on the dance floor.

Jeremy Healy

Jeremy Healy was the first DJ I heard that put a lot more performance into the mix than just playing the records. I first heard him do a hot mix on the Essential Selection, where he was using his tune 'Stamp' to scratch with, and then saw him at the Tunnel, where he spent the entire time scratching, dropping samples of other records in, and making the most of the time, space, and records he had available.

DJing is still seen by many as just *playing other people's records* and the only skill that's needed is the 20 seconds you take to mix from one track to another. Healy proved that a lot more can be done during the tune to make the mix and the performance unique to that DJ.

Alice Deejay – 'Better Off Alone'

Not all my influences have been positive ones.

I found this tune, 'Better Off Alone' by Alice Deejay, when it was just an instrumental by DJ Jurgen. It has a lovely little hook in it, and sounds great. I played it a lot, and got a good response in the pubs and clubs whenever I played it.

The problem was, someone got hold of it, and put a vocal over it, changing the dynamic and sound of the track from something that was an interesting musical piece to commercial *cheese*. Unfortunately, everyone liked it, and as I preferred the original tune, I automatically disliked this vocal version, because it managed to turn a good track that I liked to play, to a bad track I hated playing.

But that issue was the key. I still had to play it. The places I worked at demanded a high amount of commercial tracks on the playlist to offset any unknown, more underground sounding tracks (ironically, the track was classed as underground before getting the vocal).

This track, and several others to come, taught me that sometimes you have to play what the club and the clubbers want. Until you become a DJ with the renown and power of Tiesto, Sasha, or Oakenfold, you have to follow the club's guidelines. At the beginning, DJing is all about keeping people happy, and making enough money to eat. If I'd refused to play that track, I'd have been asked not to return as the DJ, and I knew that the right thing to do was just keep playing the tune until the appeal wore off.

Delirium 'Silence'

In Chapter 7, I write about falling in love with the tune 'Silence' by Delirium, playing it as often as I could, and how it still means a lot to me to listen to. But I see this tune as a double-edged sword. I see this tune as the turning point in my DJing career, when it all went a bit sour. This tune wasn't directly responsible, but after 'Silence' was such a success, the market was flooded with records that were very simple, obvious, bland melodies with some woman singing over them.

Obviously, records of this sort had been released for years before 'Silence', but the success of 'Silence' opened the gates for money-grabbers who figured they could release a weak record with vocals and make some money. Which they did. Not all of them were bad; some really good vocal tracks came out of this wave. But many producers missed the point that 'Silence' was such a big success because the music was really good, and stood well on its own, but more importantly, Sarah McLachlan's voice was haunting, unique, and perfectly matched to the music, and a club atmosphere.

Ultimately, this crossover commercialisation of the dance scene drove the good music away. The people who were buying these records started to go to the clubs that would normally play less commercial music, and they started to demand to hear what they knew. Club owners, reacting to a new voice, seeing the rise in profits with the new batch of clubbers, happily agreed. This move drove the music I loved playing deeper and deeper underground to a point that it was hard to get work playing it.

The problem with commercial trends is that by their very nature they move from fad to fad. Eventually, as each new track sounded more like the old one, the novelty of this music wore off, and the clubbers moved away to R & B and nu metal. This meant that the clubs who'd abandoned their old music policy needed to readjust.

Some clubs started to play heavier and heavier music, would let people into the clubs that they wouldn't have in the past, or changed their music scene completely (like The Tunnel's move to R & B). This left music (and the club scene as a whole as I saw it) in a state of flux, leaving me a bit concerned for my future as a DJ, and for the music I loved to play.

Sasha and Digweed Miami 2002

My last key influential music moment in this chapter is the Radio 1 Essential Mix that Sasha and Digweed did in April 2002 at the Winter Music Conference in Miami, USA.

Though I'd drifted away from the scene for over a year by the time I heard this mix in late 2003, I did still have a soft spot in my heart for this pairing – I still thanked them for the reason I started to listen to dance music in the first place. A friend had this mix on his iPod, and I asked if I could have a copy, just to hear what was going on.

Two hours later, I realised that my assumptions and prejudices about music and how the dance scene had ended up after its hyper-commercialisation were wrong in a global view. I felt as if I was being musically reborn.

The mix was incredibly well thought out, some of the tunes in the mix were amazing (the mix from Adam Dived 'Headfirst' to Solid Session's 'Janeiro' almost blew the speakers in my car I played it so loud!) and this mix was the key that marked my return to this music, and to DJing – and is the reason why I'm here, writing this book.

Thanks for reading it.

Good luck.

Index

• *Symbols and Numerics* •

3.5-millimetre adaptor, 168
3.5-millimetre jack, 159, 167
7-inch singles, 33
12-inch singles, 34

• *A* •

a cappella (mixing technique), 223
Ableton (Live software), 23, 113–115
academies, DJ, 336
active monitor, 149
adaptor, 3.5-millimetre, 168
Adobe Audition (software), 292, 294
Advanced Communication Solutions (ACS)
    earplugs, 144, 145
agency
  artist management, 305
  booking fee, 305, 306, 307
  criteria to join, 307–308
  Internet, 306
  local, 306
  paying upfront, 306
  researching, 307
Agh (*Yummy*), 361
AIFF file, 295, 298
air, compressed, 84, 135
albums, 33–35
Alcatech (BPM Studio), 23, 112
Alesis
  connectors, 168
  speakers, 149
Allen and Heath mixers, 50, 115
Amazon (Web site), 41
American DJ (equipment manufacturer), 49
amplifiers
  choosing, 147–152
  computer connection to, 173
  connecting mixer to, 170
  description, 25–26
  EQ settings, 288

home stereo, 147, 148
power rating, 150–151
powered speakers, 147–148, 149
room size, power needed by, 151
testing, 61
troubleshooting, 174–175
antiskate function, turntable, 19, 58, 74,
    163–164
antiskip function, CD decks, 21, 59
Apple Soundtrack (software), 292
Armstrong, Dave (DJ), 139
artist management, 305
auction sites, 42, 54–55
Audacity (software), 292
audience
  reading a crowd, 323–324
  requests, 324–326
  talking to, 341–342
audio delay, 152, 153
audio formats, 22
Audiojelly (Web site), 109
audio-ripping software, 46
Auto Pan (mixer effect), 128
Auto Transformer (mixer effect), 128
Aux input, home stereo, 171

• *B* •

baby scratch, 250
back cueing, 89
backing track, 260
backward scratch, 252
backwards play, in beatmatching, 183
balance control, mixer, 126
bars
  counting, 203–204
  number in phrase, 200–201
  number of beats in, 200–201
bass beat, locating, 183
bass driver, 153
bass, killing, 220
bathroom breaks, 342–343

battle breaks, 242, 244
battle mixer, 132–133
BBC Radio 1, 334, 360, 364
beat
  counting, 203–204
  cut in, 223–224
  locating first bass, 183
  number in bar, 200–201
  removing from track, 344
  rocking back and forth, 186
  structure, 199–209
beat counter
  mixer, 129–130, 181
  stand-alone, 181
beat light indicators, mixer, 130
beatjuggling
  cutting in beats, 223
  description, 255–256
  offsetting, 256
  practice, 256
beatmatching
  audio cues (B'loom and l'Boom), 190–191,
    194
  beats per minute calculation, 181–182
  with belt-driven turntable, 66, 67
  booth monitor, 152
  on CD, 233
  description, 13, 179–180, 260–261
  with direct-drive turntable, 66
  equipment setup, 182
  errors, adjusting for, 187–188
  headphone use with, 123–124, 193–197
  with Live software, 114
  locating first bass beat, 183
  mixer settings, 193
  motor lag, 186
  pitch control, 191–192, 347–348
  pitch setting, matching, 189–191
  practice, 180, 192
  rocking beat back and forth, 186
  single-ear monitoring, 142, 154–155
  slipmats for, 86
  starting records in time, 184–186
  sweet spot, 180
beatmatching DJs
  CD decks for, 104–105
  channel-fader setup, 218–219

needle choice, 91, 93, 94
  scratching by, 104–105
beats per minute (BPMs), 100, 180–182
Bedroom DJ competitions, 337
Behringer
  connectors, 168
  speakers, 149
Bermuda Pitch Zone, 73
Better Off Alone (Deejay), 362–363
bleeding, 60, 136, 194
blogging.com (Web site), 339
booking fees, 305, 306, 307
books, as resources, 335–336
Booth Out, mixer output, 60, 119, 171
bootlegs, 32
BPM Studio (Alcatech), 23, 112
BPMs (beats per minute), 100, 180–182
Brainchild (*Symmetry C*), 271
brake, for Start/Stop, 80
brake speed, 222
breakbeat, mixing, 226
breakdown
  description, 206
  double-drop mixing, 226
  end-of-phrase marker, 203
  mixing, 215–216
Brown Eyed Girl (Morrison), 224
brush, carbon fibre, 43, 355
budgeting, 48–50
build-ups, 218
Bullet Proof Scratch Hamsters, 127
burning a CD, 295–298

• *C* •

cables
  checking, 56
  control, 105
  Master Output, 158
  RCA, 81
  RCA to 3.5-millimetre jack, 168
  removable, 81
  speaker, 148
cache, virtual, 292
Camelot Sound Easymix System, 265
capstan, 160
carbon fibre brush, 43, 355

cardboard cut-out, to reduce friction, 88
cartridge, 75, 89–94
cassette tapes, demo, 281
CD
    burning, 295–298
    cleaning, 43
    cue checking, 233
    cue location, 227–229, 232
    cue storage, 232
    demo, 280–281
    demo on computer, 292–298
    formats, 34–35
    music available on, 32
    pros and cons of format, 99–104
    quality of sound, 292
    repairing, 45–46
    scanning, 228
    scratching, 238
    skips/jumps, 348
    track-split, 296–297
    warped, fixing, 45
CD deck. *See also* CD deck features
    controls, 21
    cost, 49–50, 102
    improvements in, 20–21, 104
    MP3 CDs, 23
    for scratch DJ, 106
    scratching on, 246–247
    single, 106
    slot-loading, 106
    testing, 58–59
    top-loading, 106
    tray system, 105
    twin, 105
CD deck features. *See also* CD deck
    antiskip function, 21, 59
    built-in effects, 101
    buttons, 228–229, 234
    hot cues, 235
    jog dial, 229–230, 234
    loop, 235
    Master Tempo, 235
    pitch blend, 234
    pitch control, 234
    pitch slider, 233–234
    platters, 230–231
    player control, 166

    reverse play, 236
    sample banks, 236
    wave display, 101, 228
CD-R/CD-RW discs, 21
channel-faders
    cleaning, 135–136
    mixer, 122–123, 218–219
    settings for beatmatching, 193
Chappell, John (*Guitar For Dummies*), 266
chinagraph pencil, 244
chirp (scratching technique), 253
chop (scratching technique), 252
chorus, 203, 205
Citronic (equipment manufacturer), 49
classified sections, newspaper, 53–54
cleaning machine, CD, 43
clothing, 342, 352
club
    equipment, 316, 320–322
    giving demo to, 302–304
    investigating the venue, 314–316
    location of, 303
    visiting, 339
club DJ, iPod mixing, 110
club music, bass beat, 185
competition, 238, 337
compilations, 35
compressed air, 84, 135
compression, 22, 109
computer
    amplifier connection, 173
    CD demo on, 292–298
    hardware controllers, 113, 247
    keying tunes with, 267
    laptop DJing, 22–23, 111–113
    mix editing, 292–295
    mixer connection, 167–168, 172–173
    mixing on PC, 111–113
    scratching on, 247
    software, 111–113
    sound files, 295
    soundcard, 167–168, 172, 176
    troubleshooting set-up and connections, 175–176
connections
    CD deck to mixer, 166
    computer as input device, 167–168

connections *(continued)*
  computer to amplifier, 173
  digital, 157
  effects units to mixer, 169–170
  Firewire, 157, 168
  headphones, 168–169
  iPods and MP3s to mixer, 167
  mixer outputs, 170–171
  mixer to home hi-fi, 171
  mixer to PC/Mac, 172–173
  pro-sumer, 158
  quarter-inch jack, 159–160
  RCA/Phono, 158
  Send and Return, 169–170
  S/PDIF (Sony/Philips Digital Interface
    Format), 157
  tonearm, 161–164
  troubleshooting, 173–176
  turntable, 160–164
  turntable to mixer, 164–166
  USB (universal serial bus), 157, 168
  XLR, 118, 158–159
constant tone, 282
control cable, 105
control code, 247
cords, headphone, 140
counterweight
  description, 74
  for scratching, 240
  settings, 94–95, 161–162, 173
crab scratch, 254
creativity, developing, 13
crescendo, 218
cross-fader
  cleaning, 135–136
  curves, 120–122, 219, 286
  cutting in, 224
  hamster switch, 126
  mixer, 23–24, 59, 60, 119–122
  mixing, use in, 217–218
  offsetting, 256
  scratching, use in, 133, 251–254
  securing, 241
  settings for beatmatching, 193
crowbarring, 278
crowd, reading, 15
cue
  checking, 233
  hot, 235

locating on CD, 227–229, 232
  on-the-fly setting, 235
  storing, 232
Cue button
  CD deck, 232, 233, 235
  mixer, 123
cue points, multiple, 101
cut (scratching technique), 252
cut setting, 124
cutting in, 223–224
cutting out, 224
cymbal crash, 202, 204, 205, 218

DAC3 controller, 247
Dart Pro (software), 297
DAT (digital audiotape), demo on, 281
dead-stop, 222
decibels, 143
deckplatter, 19, 66, 70, 84, 160
Deejay, Alice (*Better Off Alone*), 362–363
degreaser, 84
Delay (mixer effect), 128
Delirium (*Silence*), 103, 363
demo
  CD, 280–281, 292–298
  DAT (digital audiotape), 281
  editing mix, 292–295
  EQ settings, 286–288
  gaps, bridging, 278
  handing over, 302–303
  MiniDisc, 281
  perfect, 291
  performance, 289–291
  picking and arranging tunes, 276–277
  practising your set, 278–279
  preparing to record, 275–284
  programming your set, 276
  recording levels, correcting, 281–284
  sending off, 298–299
  setting up to record, 279–281
  sound processing, 284–288
  style, showing off, 273
  taking with you when DJing, 357–358
  tapes, 14, 281
  track-split, 296–297
  transition only, 297–298

volume, 284–286
where to send, 303
Denon
    DN-S3500 (CD deck), 106, 230–232, 236, 246
    turntable, 50
desk, DJ, 26–27
DigiScratch (software), 247
digital audiotape (DAT), demo on, 281
digital DJ Licence, 40
Digweed, John (DJ), 114, 262, 359, 364
distortion, 175
Dived, Adam (*Headfirst*), 364
DJ Academy, 336
DJ Danger icon, 4
DJ Download (Web site), 109
DJ in a Box (Numark), 53
DJ Prince (Web site), 265
DJ Speak icon, 4
djchat.com (Web site), 335
djforums.com (Web site), 335
djmandrick.com (Web site), 334
djmixtape.net (Web site), 338
djpassion.co.uk (Web site), 311, 338
djprince.no (Web site), 334
djpromoter.com (Web site), 311
djrecess.co.uk (Web site), 152, 311, 335
DJS software (Pioneer), 112
DMC Championships, 238, 337
double drop (mixing technique), 226
downloading MP3s, 104
drinks, 346
drivers, 61
drop, 226
drop in samples, 115
drum
    bass, 184, 197
    pattern, 185
    snare, 184, 197
drum and bass, mixing, 226
drum-and-bass DJ, 131
Drumming For Dummies (Strong), 185

• E •

earpieces, headphone, 140
earplugs, 142–145, 322
earplugstore.com (Web site), 144
eBay (Web site), 42, 54, 167

eBid (Web site), 54
Echo (mixer effect), 128
Ecler Nuo4!, 115
Edirol connectors, 168
effects DJ, mixer for, 133–134
Effects Send and Return, 127
effects unit, connecting to mixer, 169–170
electrical interference, 149
end-of-phrase markers, 202–203, 208
energy, 269
EQ (equaliser)
    amplifier, 288
    balancing with, 220–221
    global, 134
    high, 220–221
    home stereo, 148
    mid, 221
    mixer, 24, 118, 124–125, 286–288
    recorder, 288
    settings at club venue, 321
    settings for beatmatching, 193
    smoothing transition with bass, 220
    test recording, 287–288
    use in scratching, 249
EQ pot, 124
equipment. *See also specific items*
    amplifiers, 25–26
    basic components, 10, 17–18
    CD decks, 20–21
    club, 316, 320–322
    connecting, 12
    furniture, 26–28
    headphones, 24–25
    input devices, 18–23
    location, 28–29
    mixers, 18–23, 23–24
    MP3 players, 22–23
    research on, 11
    speakers, 25–26
    to take when DJing, 355–358
    turntables, 18–20
    what to look for, 12
equipment, shopping for
    auction Web sites, 54–55
    budgeting, 48–50
    from high-street store, 50–52
    new, 50–53
    newspaper classified sections, 53–54
    online, 52–53

equipment, shopping for *(continued)*
  packages, 52
  pawn shops, 54
  second-hand, 53–55
  testing equipment, 55–61
  trying before buying, 48, 49, 51, 55
ergonomics, 26
error correction, in audio-ripping software, 46
etiquette, record store, 38
Etymotic (earplug maker), 144

• *F* •

fader start control, mixer, 130–131
faders
  mixer, 59–60
  securing, 241
  servicing, 84
Fatboy Slim (DJ), 141
feedback, 27–28
file sharing, 39–40
Filter (mixer effect), 128
Final Scratch (software), 247
Firewire connection, 118, 157, 168
Flanger (mixer effect), 128
flare scratch, 254
floating, tonearm, 161–162
focus, maintaining, 289–290
For an Angel (Van Dyk), 184
format, analogue versus digital, 97–104
forums, DJ, 266, 307
forward scratch, 251
Freefloat deck stabiliser, 28
frequency response, 139
Fresh, Chuck (*How to be a DJ*), 335
friction
  adding to adjust for timing error, 187
  reduction with cardboard cut-out, 88
  reduction with wax paper, 87–88
  slipmats and, 87
friends
  in DJ booth, 343
  networking with, 309
full-on section, 205
furniture
  desk, 26–27
  ergonomics, 26

stability, 26
vibrations, minimising, 27–28

 • *G* •

Gabriel & Dresden (DJs), 114
gain controls
  mixer, 24, 125–126, 284–285
  settings for beatmatching, 193
Gemini CDJ-01 (CD deck), 102
Gemini Scratch Master package, 53
Gemini turntable
  cost, 49
  hybrid, 108
  Key Adjustment feature, 79
  PT6000, 80
  reliability of, 77
  TT02, 20
genre, format availability, 31–33
glue tunes, 277, 278
Goldie (*Inner City Life*), 361
graphic equaliser, home stereo, 148
green light area, 182
ground wire, 164, 174
Guitar For Dummies (Phillips and
  Chappell), 266

• *H* •

hamster style, 241, 253
hamster switch, mixer, 126–127
hands in the air moment, 180, 220
Hard to Find Records (Web site), 40
hardware controllers, 113, 247
harmonic mixing, 262–265
harmonic-mixing.com (Web site), 264, 266
Headfirst (Dived), 364
headphone monitoring
  headphone mix, 124, 194–195
  practicing, 197–198
  single ear, 194
  split cue, 195
headphones
  beatmatching, use in, 193–197
  choosing, 25, 137–141
  closed-back, 138
  comfort, 138

connecting to mixer, 168–169
cords, 140
cost, 139
cue controls, 60, 123–124
cueing in, 193–195
earpieces, swiveling, 140
forgetting, 349
frequency response, 139
impedance, 139
importance of, 24, 25
iPod, 123, 159
mixer, 123–124
monitoring mixer with Pre Fade Listen
    (PFL), 24
practicing with, 197–198
replaceable parts, 140–141
resting on headphone jack, 169
sound pressure level, 139
stereo image, 195–197
stick, 141
taking personal when DJing, 356
testing, 61
troubleshooting, 175
upgrading, 139
volume, 142
weight, 138
headshell, 19, 75, 84, 90
Healy, Jeremy (DJ), 362
hearing damage, 142, 322
Hercules, 247
hi-fi, 148, 171
hi-hats, 124, 212, 218, 220
Hitsquad Musician Network (Web site), 23
HMV (Web site), 40
Hocks Noisebrakers (earplugs), 144
home stereo, 25, 147, 148, 171
hook, 205
hosting your own night, 338
house DJ, 131
house mixer, 131–132
house music
  bass beat, 185
  beats per minute (BPMs), 180
How to be a DJ (Fresh), 335
humming noise, from turntable, 174

• I •

I Feel Love (Summer), 260, 261
Ibiza, 360–361
icons, used in text, 4
iDJ mixer (Numark), 110–111
i-dj.co.uk (Web site), 334, 335
Ikea (Web site), 27
impedance, 139
Inner City Life (Goldie), 361
input channels, mixer, 24
input devices
  CD decks, 20–21
  formats, 18
  MP3 players, 22–23
  turntables, 18–20
input level meter, mixer, 282, 284–285
instincts, developing, 208
interference, electrical, 149
Internet
  auction sites, 54–55
  DJ agencies, 306
  marketing yourself on, 310–311
  online record stores, 40
  stores, 52–53
intros
  description, 205
  looping, 235
  melodic, 214
  mixing beat intro over breakdown, 216
  over outros, 212–213
Ion powered speaker, 149
iPod
  connection to mixer, 167
  headphones, 109, 123
  mixing with, 110–111
iTunes, 39, 109, 111

• J •

Jamiroquai (*Space Cowboy*), 362
Janeiro (Solid Session), 364
JBL speakers, 149
jog dial/wheel, CD deck, 21, 106, 229–230,
    234

Jules, Judge (DJ), 104, 334
jump, 271–272
Juno Records (Web site), 40

• K •

Kam (equipment manufacturer), 49
Key Adjustment, 79
key change, 269–270
Key Lock (turntable feature), 79
key notation, 263–264
keycode, 265
kill switch, 124

• L •

La Luna (*To the Beat of the Drum*), 360
laptop DJing, 22–23, 111–113
leader tape, 289
lighting, 346–347
limiters, 282
line input, mixer, 24, 117–118
Line RCA input, 166
Line switch, mixer, 60
Line/Phono switch, mixer, 166
listening
   with an active ear, 184
   with open mind, 291
   to other people's mixes, 337
listening post, record store, 37, 38
Live software (Ableton), 23, 113–115
loop function, CD deck, 235
LPs, 33–34, 35
lubrication, 83–84, 136

• M •

magazines, 333–334
map
   mix, 277
   tune, 34
marker, end-of-phrase, 202–203, 208
marketing
   agencies, joining, 305–308
   demo, 302–303
   following up, 304
   Internet, 310–311
   networking, 309–310
   playing for free, 304–305
   rejection, handling, 304
   self-promotion, 301–302
marking
   CDs, 247
   MP3s, 247
   samples, 243–245
Master Level, mixer control, 170, 171, 283
Master Out, mixer output, 60, 118, 169, 170
Master Output Level control, 283, 284
Master Tempo
   CD deck, 235, 267, 271
   turntable feature, 79
maximum sustained output, speaker, 150
May, Brian (guitarist), 140
McLachlan, Sarah (recording artist), 103
melodic intros, 214
melodic outros, 213–214
MIC input, mixer, 117–118
microphone, mixer, 60
MIDI (musical instrument digital interface),
   114
mid-range, 124
mini-breakdown, 206, 215
MiniDisc, 107–108, 281, 356
mini-jack, 123
mistakes, DJing, 349–353
MixedInKey.com (Web site), 267
mixer. *See also* mixer connections; mixer
      features
   battle, 132–133
   choosing correct, 131–135
   cost, 24, 49–50
   for effects DJ, 133–134
   EQ settings, 286–288
   hamster style, 241, 253
   height, 241
   house, 131–132
   mistakes, avoiding, 350
   outputs, 170–171
   for party/wedding DJ, 134–135
   for scratching, 132–133, 241
   for seamless mix DJ, 131–132
   servicing, 135–136
   settings for beatmatching, 193
   setup for beatmatching, 182
   software, 112, 113
   testing, 59–60
   troubleshooting, 174

in turntable, 82–83
in twin CD deck, 105
mixer connections. *See also* mixer
 CD deck to mixer, 166
 computer to mixer, 167–168
 effects units to mixer, 169–170
 headphones, 168–169
 iPods and MP3s to mixer, 167
 mixer to home hi-fi, 171
 mixer to PC/Mac, 172–173
 mixer to powered speakers, 171–172
 Send and Return, 169–170
 turntable to mixer, 164–166
mixer features. *See also* mixer
 balance control, 126
 beat counter, 129–130, 181
 beat light indicators, 130
 channel-faders, 122–123
 channels, multiple, 119
 cross-faders, 119–122
 description, 23–24
 effects, built-in, 127–128
 Effects Send and Return, 127, 133
 EQ (equaliser), 124–125
 fader start, 130–131
 gain controls, 125–126, 284–285
 hamster switch, 126–127
 headphone, 123–124
 input level meters, 284–285
 inputs, 117–118
 outputs, 118–119
 pan control, 126
 punch button, 127
 samplers, built-in, 129
 talk-over button, 342
 transform controls, 127
 VU display, 125
mixing
 beat intro over breakdown, 216
 breakbeat, 226
 breakdown over breakdown, 215
 with CDs, 227–236
 channel-fader use, 218–219
 cross-fader use, 217–218
 drum and bass, 226
 EQ control, 220–221
 harmonic, 262–265
 intros over outros, 212–213
 melodic intro, 214

 melodic outro, 213–214
 mini-breakdowns, 215
 R&B mix, 225
 speeches/spoken words, 223, 225
 volume control, 219–220
 wedding/party/rock/pop mix, 224–225
mixing tricks and gimmicks
 a cappella, 223
 cutting in, 223–224
 dead stop, 222
 experimenting with, 221
 power off, 222
 spinback, 221–222
MixVibes, 23
monitor
 active, 149
 audio delay and, 152, 153
 booth, 171, 321–322
 importance of, 152
 positioning, 153
 powered, 149
Morales, David (DJ), 141
Morrison, Van (*Brown Eyed Girl*), 224
motor, turntable
 choosing, 66–67
 friction, 87
 servicing, 83–84
 testing, 56–57
MP3
 availability, 108
 compression, 109
 cons of using, 110
 DJ decks, 23
 DJ use of, 39–40
 download sites, 109
 files, 22, 109
 from online record stores, 40–42
 player, 22, 167
 previewing, 41
 promos, 109–110
 scratching on, 247
 software, 22–23
 sound quality, 110
music
 buying, 33–42
 CD formats/options, 34–35
 classic anthems and new tracks, 38–39
 listening to, 37
 MP3, 39–40

music *(continued)*
  previewing, 41
  researching, 36–37
  vinyl formats, 33–34
musical hole, 37
musical instrument digital interface (MIDI), 114
Muzik magazine, 337
myclubbingspace.com (Web site), 311
mydjspace.net (Web site), 311, 338
myspace.com (Web site), 311

• *N* •

name, choosing DJ, 345
National Certificate in Music Technology, DJ & Mixing (course), 336
Native Instruments (Traktor), 22, 115
needle
  abuse, 89
  for beatmixing DJ, 91, 93, 94
  cleaning, 43
  connection, 89–91
  counterweight, 240
  counterweight settings, 94–95
  downforce adjustment, 240
  elliptical, 93
  extending lifespan of, 96
  function of, 88
  headshell cartridge, 75
  jump, 44
  with new turntable, 94
  for scratching, 90, 91, 93, 238, 240–241
  sewing, 44
  skipping, 95, 173, 174
  spherical, 92–93
  tracking force, 93, 94
  troubleshooting, 174
  turntable, 58
  when to replace, 95–96
Neely, Blake (*Piano For Dummies*), 266
Nero (software), 295, 297
nerves, dealing with, 320
networking, 309–310
newspaper classified sections, 53–54
NGWave (software), 292, 294
Night (magazine), 334
noise pollution, 154–155
Norcal DJMPA (academy), 336

notation, traditional key, 263–264
Numark
  CC-1 needle, 91, 92, 94
  CD deck, 102, 105
  DM1050 mixer, 24
  iDJ mixer, 110–111
  powered speaker, 149
Numark turntable
  for beatmatching, 67
  cost, 49
  hybrid, 108
  Key Lock feature, 79
  reliability of, 77
  for scratch DJ, 82
  tonearm style, 81
  TT500, 102

• *O* •

Oakenfold (DJ), 262, 271
offbeat, 261–262
offsetting, 256
oil, lubricating, 83–84
online shopping, 40–42, 52–53
On/Off switch, turntable, 69
onomatopoeic words, 191
open booth night, 337
Ortofon needles, 91, 93–94, 96, 238
output level meter, mixer, 282
outros
  description, 206
  intros over, 212–213
  looping, 235
  melodic, 213–214

• *P* •

package, equipment, 52
pan controls, mixer, 126
party/wedding DJ
  CD deck for, 105
  compilation CD, 35
  mixing, 134–135, 224–225
  requests, handling, 325–326
pawn shops, 54
payment, 316, 329, 352–353
PCDJ (software), 23, 112, 247
peak rating, speaker, 150

peer-to-peer networks, 39, 104
pencil, chinagraph, 244
pens, ultraviolet, 244
performance
  clothing, 342
  on club equipment, 318, 320–322
  demo, 289–291
  finishing the night, 328–329
  items to take when DJing, 355–358
  in loud environment, 322
  main set, 315
  momentum, 327–328
  nerves, dealing with, 320
  preparation, 318–320
  reading a crowd, 323–324
  as replacement DJ, 315
  requests, handling, 324–326
  talking to audience, 341–342
  venue, investigating, 314–318
  as warm-up DJ, 314, 325, 326
Performer Services Helpdesk, 40
PFL (Pre Fade Listen) button, 24, 123
Phillips, Mark (*Guitar For Dummies*), 266
phono cables, 81
Phono connection, 158
Phono input, mixer, 24, 117–118, 164–165
Phono switch, mixer, 60
Phonographic Performance Limited (PPL), 40
phrase
  end-of-phrase marker, 202–203, 205
  number in verse, 200–202
  number of bars in, 200–201
Piano For Dummies (Neely), 266
Pioneer CD decks, 102, 106, 228, 230, 246
Pioneer DJS software, 112
Pioneer EFX-1000 (processor), 101, 134
Pioneer mixers
  cost, 50
  DJM-600, 115, 128, 130, 220
  DJM-800, 134, 166, 170
Pioneer turntables, 49–50
pitch, 267–268
pitch bend
  CD deck, 21, 77–78, 105, 234
  computer software, 113
pitch control
  adjusting for timing error, 188
  adjusting without looking, 191–192
  CD decks, 21, 58–59, 105, 234

digital display, 79
  jump, 271–272
  resetting after beatmatching, 347–348
  settings, matching, 189–191
pitch control, turntable
  accuracy, 73
  description, 19–20
  design, 67
  numbers, 72–73
  setup, 182
  testing, 56–57
pitch fader
  computer software, 113
  turntable, 57, 73, 78
pitch range options, turntable, 76–77
Pitch Shifter (mixer effect), 128
pitch slider
  CD deck, 106, 233–234
  turntable, 189
placement
  beat intro over breakdown, 216
  breakdown over breakdown, 215
  bridging gaps, 278
  intros over outros, 212–213
  melodic intro, 214
  melodic outro, 213–214
  mini-breakdowns, 215
  perfecting, 211–214
  picking and arranging tunes, 276–277
platters, CD deck, 230–231
player control feature, CD deck, 166
podcast.com (Web site), 339
podcasts, 338–339
Point Blank Music College, 336
power off (mixing technique), 222
power rating, 150
PowerBook, Apple, 111
PPL (Phonographic Performance Limited), 40
practice, 180, 192, 256, 278–279
Pre Fade Listen (PFL) button, 24, 123
preparation, as key to success, 14
Pro Tools (software), 292
programming your set, for demo, 276
PromoOnly (Web site), 109
promos, 32, 109
pro-sumer connection, 158
punch button, 127

• Q •

QBert (DJ), 91
quarter-inch jack, 159–160
quartz lock, 78
quizmeme.com (Web site), 345
QXL (Web site), 54

• R •

radio shows, 334
radio-edit, 33
Rane mixer, 50
R&B mix, 225
RCA cables, 81
RCA connection
   computer soundcard, 167–168
   computer to mixer, 167–168
   general, 158
   iPod and MP3 player to mixer, 167
   mixer outputs, 170–171
   turntable to mixer, 164–166
RCA plugs, 81
Real Audio, 41
re-amplification, 27–28
Recess (DJ), 345
recess.co.uk (Web site), 1, 5
record level indicator, 281–282
Record Out, mixer output, 60, 118, 170–171
record store
   etiquette, 38
   listening post, 37, 38
   online, 40–42
recorder
   EQ settings, 288
   MiniDisc, 108, 356
   quality, 280
   record level, 281–282
   troubleshooting, 176
Recording Industry Association of America (RIAA), 99
recording, test, 287–288
records
   blank grooves, 244
   cleaning, 43
   fixing the hole in the middle, 245–246
   formats, 33–34
   listening to, 37
   marking samples, 243–245
   mistakes with, 351
   physical description, 18–19
   repairing vinyl, 44
   shading on, 183
   storing, 27, 42–43
   warped, fixing, 45
   wear, 95, 240, 241, 242–243
   white label, 32
reference tone, 282, 283
rejection, handling, 304
Remember icon, 4
remix, 34
Renaissance–Disc 1 (mix), 359
Replay Records (Web site), 40
requests, 324–326
resources for skill expansion
   books, 335–336
   club visiting, 339
   competition participation, 337
   DJ forums, 334–335
   hands-on advice, 336
   hosting your own night, 338
   listening to mixes, 337
   media, 333–334
   uploading podcasts or hosted mixes, 338–339
   Web sites, advice, 334
Reverb (mixer effect), 128
reverse chop, 253
reverse cut, 253
reverse play
   CD deck, 236
   turntable feature, 80
rhythm, driving, 260–262
RIAA (Recording Industry Association of America), 99
room size, power needs for, 151
RPM (revolutions per minute) button, 69

• S •

sample, 242
sample banks, CD deck, 236
sampler, built-in, 129
sandpaper, 246

Sasha (DJ), 114–115, 262, 345, 359, 364
scratch DJ
  CD deck, 106
  channel-fader setup, 218
  gain control use by, 125
  mixer for, 132+133
  needle set-up, 90, 91, 93
  slipmats for, 86
  tonearm height, 162–163
  turntables for, 82, 238
Scratch DJ (academy), 336
Scratch Master package (Gemini), 53
Scratch Perverts (DJ), 91
scratching
  battle break use, 242, 244
  on CD, 246–247
  on computer, 247
  description, 13, 237
  equipment setup, 238–242
  mastering, 248–249
  mixer, 241
  MP3, 247
  needles for, 238, 240–241
  record wear, 240, 241, 242–243
  sample, finding, 242
  sample, marking, 243–245
  slipmats for, 241
scratching technique
  baby scratch, 250
  backward scratch, 252
  chirp, 253
  chop, 252
  combining scratches, 254–255
  crab scratch, 254
  cut, 252
  flare scratch, 254
  forward scratch, 251
  hand technique, 248
  mastering, 248–249
  reverse chop, 253
  reverse cut, 253
  scribble scratch, 250–251
  tear, 251
  transformer, 253
  twiddle scratch, 254
scribble scratch, 250–251
seamless mix, 125
seamless mix DJ, 131–132

search buttons, CD deck, 106, 230
section, 211
Send and Return connections, 169–170
send and return function, mixer, 127, 133
Sennheiser headphones, 140–141, 356
Serato (software), 247
set. *See also* set building
  bridging gaps, 278
  checkpoint tunes, 319
  demo, 276–279
  lists, predetermined, 318
  picking and arranging tunes, 276–277
  practising, 278–279
  programming, 276
set building. *See also* set
  beatmatching, 260–261
  energy, 269
  genre changes, 272
  harmonic mixing, 262–265
  jumps, 271–272
  key changing, 269–270
  keying tunes, 266–267
  mixing, 261–262
  pitch, 267–268
  stagnation, avoiding, 272
  style, developing, 268–273
  tempo, increasing, 270–272
  tune choice, 259–268
set-up. *See also* connections
  deckplatter, 160
  tonearm, 161–164, 173–174
  troubleshooting, 173–176
  turntable, 160–164
Shure
  E2c ear buds, 109
  needles, 90, 93–94, 238, 240
Silence (Delirium), 103, 363
sine wave, 282
single-ear monitoring, 142,
    154–155, 194
singles, 33–34
Skip button, CD deck, 230
skipping, needle, 95, 173, 174
slipmat
  cardboard cut-out to reduce friction, 88
  choosing appropriate, 86–87
  description, 19, 85–86
  forgetting, 349

slipmat *(continued)*
  friction and, 87–88
  for scratching, 241
  taking personal when DJing, 356
  wax paper to reduce friction, 87–88
software
  Adobe Audition, 292, 294
  Apple Soundtrack, 292
  Audacity, 292
  audio-ripping, 46
  Dart Pro, 297
  DigiScratch, 247
  DJ, 22–23, 111–113
  DJS, 112
  Final Scratch, 247
  Live, 23, 113–115
  mixer, 112, 113
  MP3, 22–23
  Nero, 295, 297
  NGWave, 292, 294
  PCDJ, 23, 112, 247
  peer-to-peer sharing, 39
  Pro Tools, 292
  Serato, 247
  Sonic Foundry, 297
  Toast, 295
  Virtual DJ 3, 23, 112, 247
Solid Session *(Janeiro)*, 364
song structure
  bars, 200–201
  beats, 200–201
  breakdown, 203, 206
  chorus, 203, 205
  counting beats, 203–204
  cymbal crash, 202, 204, 205
  differences in, 207
  importance for DJs, 200
  introduction, 205
  listening to sample, 208–209
  marker, end-of-phrase, 202–203, 208
  outro, 206
  phrases, 200–202
  section, 211
  studying, 205–207
  verse, 200–202, 205
Sonic Foundry (software), 297
Sony MDR-V700 DJ headphones, 139
Sony/Philips Digital Interface Format
    (S/PDIF), 157

sound
  control, importance of, 13
  distortion, 175
  noise pollution, 154–155
  speed of, 152
  warmth, 99
sound pressure level, 139
soundcard, computer, 22, 172, 176
Space Cowboy (Jamiroquai), 362
S/PDIF (Sony/Philips Digital Interface
    Format), 157
speakers
  bass driver, 153
  booth monitor, 152–153
  cable, 148
  computer, 26
  cost, 149
  drivers, 61
  home stereo, 25, 148
  mixer connection to, 171–172
  positioning, 28–29
  power rating, 150–151
  powered, 25, 147–148, 149, 171–172
  room size, power needed by, 151
  testing, 61
  tweeter, 153
speeches/spoken words, mixing in, 223,
    225
spinback, 221–222
split cue (headphone monitoring), 195
Split Cue (mixer function), 124
stagnation, avoiding, 272
stands, 27
Stanton
  C.304 (CD deck), 106
  Discmaster II (needle), 94
  DJ Pro 3000 STK 'Stick' headphones, 141
  500AL II (needle), 94
  500AL (needle), 90, 94, 96
  Groovemaster (needle), 94
  605SK (needle), 94
  turntable, 49
starting error, in beatmatching, 187–188
Start/Stop button, turntable, 68, 80
stereo, home, 25, 147, 148, 171
stereo image, 195–197
stick headphone, 141
stickers, for marking samples, 244–245
storage, of records, 42–43

strobe light, turntable, 56, 69–70
Strong, Jeff (*Drumming For Dummies*), 185
style
  crowd, respect for, 272–273
  developing, 268–273
  energy, 269
  importance of, 14
  jumps, 271–272
  key changing, 269–270
  stagnation, avoiding, 272
  on tape, 273
  tempo, increasing, 270–272
stylus, 19
SubBass DJ Academy, 336
subwoofer, 154
Summer, Donna (*I Feel Love*), 260, 261
sweet spot, 180
Symmetry C (Brainchild), 271

• *T* •

talk-over function, mixer, 60
target light, turntable, 19, 71
tear, 251
Technics RPDJ1210 headphones, 138, 140
Technics SL-DZ1200 (CD deck), 106, 230, 246
Technics turntable
  for beatmatching, 67
  cost, 20, 49–50
  deckplatter, 70
  Kingston Dub Cutter, 33
  pitch control, 72
  quality of, 19–20
  reliability of, 77
  SL-1210M5G, 102
  slipmats, 87
  strobe light, 69–70
  1210 models, 19, 50, 68–71, 76–77, 189
tells, 15
tempo
  beats per minute (BPMs), 180–182
  feel for, 182
  increasing, 270–272
  reset, 78
test recording, 287–288
testing equipment
  amplifiers, 61
  before buying, 48, 49, 51, 55

cables, 56
CD decks, 58–59
headphones, 61
mixers, 59–60
speakers, 61
turntables, 56–58
theft of music, 104
Tiesto (DJ), 276
time code, 247
time display, CD deck, 21, 105
time indicator, recording software, 293–295
timing error, adjusting for, 187
tinnitus, 142
Tip icon, 4
To the Beat of the Drum (La Luna), 360
Toast (software), 295
tonal quality, 128
tone, lining up equipment using, 282–283
tonearm
  antiskate setting, 163–164
  cartridge connection to, 89
  counterweight, 74, 94–95, 161–162, 173
  floating, 161–162
  height, 58, 74, 162–163, 174
  servicing, 84
  set-up and connection, 161–164
  shapes, 80–81
  testing, 57–58
  troubleshooting, 173–174
Tong, Pete (radio show host), 36, 334, 360
tonsillitis, of author, 360
tools, 356
torque, turntable, 66, 87, 102
Tower Records (Web site), 40
track split marker, 297
tracking force, 93, 94
Traktor (Native Instruments), 22, 112, 115
trance DJ, 131
trance music, 180
tranceaddict.com (Web site), 266, 335
transform controls, 127
transformer (scratching technique), 253
transition only mix, 297–298
triggers, 207
troubleshooting, set-up and connections, 173–176
TRS jack, 159–160

tunes
  bridge, 278
  checkpoint, 319
  choosing for mix, 259–268
  glue, 277, 278
  keying, 266–267
  organising, 319
  picking and arranging, 276–277
  pitch, 267–268
  set lists, predetermined, 318
  structure of, 13
Tunnel Club, Glasgow, 361
turntable. *See also* turntable features
  belt-driven, 66–67, 160
  brands, 19–20
  cheap, avoiding, 65–67
  connection to mixer, 164–166
  cost, 49–50, 102
  description, 18–19
  digital, 230
  direct-driven, 66
  feet for, 28
  humming noise from, 174
  hybrid, 108
  motor, 56–57, 66, 67, 83
  peripherals, 164
  reliability of, 77
  requirements for, 19
  rotating 90 degrees, 238, 239
  for scratch DJs, 238
  servicing, 83–84
  stylus, 19
  testing, 56–58
  torque, 66
  troubleshooting, 173–174
  weight, 100
turntable features. *See also* turntable
  adaptor, 45 rpm, 75
  antiskate, 19, 58, 74, 163–164
  brake, 80
  cabling, removable, 81
  cartridge, 75
  counterweight, 74
  deckplatter, 70, 160
  description, 19, 20
  digital outputs, 82
  headshell, 75
  height adjust, 74
  Key Lock, 79

Master Tempo, 79
mixer, built-in, 82
needles, 88–96
On/Off switch, 69
outputs, 82
pitch bend, 77–78
pitch control, 19–20, 56–57, 67, 72–73, 79
pitch range, 76
quartz lock, 78
reverse play, 80
RPM button, 69
rubber mat, 86
for scratch DJs, 82
slipmats, 85–88
Start/Stop button, 68, 80
strobe light, 69–70
target light, 71
tempo reset, 78
tonearm, 57–58, 80–81, 161–164,
    173–174
tweeter, 153
twiddle scratch, 254

• U •

uBid (Web site), 54
ultraviolet pens, 244
underground record labels, 32
USB input, mixer, 118
USB (universal serial bus) connection, 157,
    168

• V •

Van Dyk, Paul (*For an Angel*), 184
verse
  hook, 205
  lyrics of, 205
  phrases in, 200–202
Vestax
  mixer, 133
  vinyl burner, 33
Vestax turntable
  for beatmatching, 67
  in clubs, 76
  cost, 19–20, 49–50
  mixer, built-in, 82–83
  pitch fader, 73

reliability of, 77
for scratch DJ, 82
tonearm style, 81
vibrations, minimising, 27–28
vinyl
formats, 33–34
future of, 107
music available on, 32
personal pride in, 103–104
promos on, 32, 109
pros and cons of format, 99–104
recording from CD to, 33
repairing, 44
RIAA equalisation curve, 99
tune availability on, 100
turntables for, 18–20
wear on, 95
Vinyl Touch turntable, 79
Vinylium (Kingston Dub Cutter), 33
Virgin (Web site), 40
Virtual DJ 3 (software), 23, 112, 247
vocals, removing from track, 344
volume
control, 219–220
headphone, 142
keeping even, 284–286
Volume Control, Windows, 172–173, 176
VU display, mixer, 125, 282

• *W* •

warp function, Live software, 114
warped records, fixing, 45
watts, 150
WAV files, 295, 296, 298
wave display, CD deck, 183, 228
waveform, 101, 293–295
wax paper, to reduce friction, 87–88
WD-40 spray, 84
Web site
Ableton, 23, 115
Amazon, 41
auction, 54–55
Audiojelly, 109
BBC, 334
blogging.com, 339
DJ Academy, 336
DJ advice, 334
DJ Download, 109

DJ Prince, 265
djchat.com, 335
djforums.com, 335
djmandrick.com, 334
djmixtape.net, 338
djpassion.co.uk, 311, 338
djprince.no, 334
djpromoter.com, 311
djrecess.co.uk, 152, 311, 335
earplugstore.com, 144
eBay, 42, 54, 167
eBid, 54
Hard to Find Records, 40
harmonic-mixing.com, 264, 266
Hitsquad Musician Network, 23
HMV, 40
i-dj.co.uk, 334, 335
Ikea, 27
Juno Records, 40
MixedInKey.com, 267
myclubbingspace.com, 311
mydjspace.net, 311, 338
myspace.com, 311
Norcal DJMPA, 336
online shopping, 52–53
podcast.com, 339
PPL, 40
PromoOnly, 109
quizmeme.com, 345
QXL, 54
Radio 1, 36
recess.co.uk, 1, 5
Replay Records, 40
Scratch DJ, 336
SubBass DJ Academy, 336
Tower Records, 40
tranceaddict.com, 266, 335
uBid, 54
Virgin, 40
youtube.com, 334
wedding/party DJ
CD deck for, 105
compilation CD, 35
mixing, 134–135, 224–225
requests, handling, 325–326
white label records, 32
whoops, 89
Windows Sound Recorder system, 292
Woods, Martin (squash coach), 269

• X •

XLR connections, 118, 158–159

• Y •

Yousef (DJ), 337
youtube.com (Web site), 334
Yummy (Agh), 361

• Z •

Zabiela, James (DJ), 337
Zone Out, mixer output, 60

FOR DUMMIES®

Do Anything. Just Add Dummies

UK editions

0-7645-7027-7

0-470-02921-8

0-7645-7054-4

PERSONAL FINANCE

0-7645-7023-4

0-470-02860-2

0-7645-7039-0

BUSINESS

0-7645-7018-8

0-7645-7025-0

0-7645-7026-9

Answering Tough Interview
Questions For Dummies
(0-470-01903-4)

Arthritis For Dummies
(0-470-02582-4)

Being the Best Man
For Dummies
(0-470-02657-X)

British History
For Dummies
(0-470-03536-6)

Building Confidence
For Dummies
(0-470-01669-8)

Buying a Home on a Budget
For Dummies
(0-7645-7035-8)

Buying a Property in Eastern
Europe For Dummies
(0-7645-7047-1)

Children's Health
For Dummies
(0-470-02735-5)

Cognitive Behavioural Therapy
For Dummies
(0-470-01838-0)

CVs For Dummies
(0-7645-7017-X)

Diabetes For Dummies
(0-7645-7019-6)

Divorce For Dummies
(0-7645-7030-7)

eBay.co.uk For Dummies
(0-7645-7059-5)

European History
For Dummies
(0-7645-7060-9)

Gardening For Dummies
(0-470-01843-7)

Genealogy Online
For Dummies
(0-7645-7061-7)

Golf For Dummies
(0-470-01811-9)

Hypnotherapy For Dummies
(0-470-01930-1)

Irish History For Dummies
(0-7645-7040-4)

Marketing For Dummies
(0-7645-7056-0)

Neuro-linguistic Programming
For Dummies
(0-7645-7028-5)

Nutrition For Dummies
(0-7645-7058-7)

Parenting For Dummies
(0-470-02714-2)

Pregnancy For Dummies
(0-7645-7042-0)

Retiring Wealthy For Dummies
(0-470-02632-4)

Rugby Union For Dummies
(0-470-03537-4)

Small Business Employment
Law For Dummies
(0-7645-7052-8)

Starting a Business on
eBay.co.uk For Dummies
(0-470-02666-9)

Su Doku For Dummies
(0-470-01892-5)

The GL Diet For Dummies
(0-470-02753-3)

Thyroid For Dummies
(0-470-03172-7)

UK Law and Your Rights
For Dummies
(0-470-02796-7)

Wills, Probate and Inheritance
Tax For Dummies
(0-7645-7055-2)

Winning on Betfair
For Dummies
(0-470-02856-4)

Available wherever books are sold. For more information or to order direct go to www.wiley.com or call 0800 243407 (Non UK call +44 1243 843296)

FOR DUMMIES®

Do Anything. Just Add Dummies

HOBBIES

0-7645-5232-5

0-7645-6847-7

0-7645-5476-X

Also available:

Art For Dummies
(0-7645-5104-3)
Aromatherapy For Dummies
(0-7645-5171-X)
Bridge For Dummies
(0-471-92426-1)
Card Games For Dummies
(0-7645-9910-0)
Chess For Dummies
(0-7645-8404-9)

Improving Your Memory
For Dummies
(0-7645-5435-2)
Massage For Dummies
(0-7645-5172-8)
Meditation For Dummies
(0-471-77774-9)
Photography For Dummie
(0-7645-4116-1)
Quilting For Dummies
(0-7645-9799-X)

EDUCATION

0-7645-7206-7

0-7645-5581-2

0-7645-5422-0

Also available:

Algebra For Dummies
(0-7645-5325-9)
Algebra II For Dummies
(0-471-77581-9)
Astronomy For Dummies
(0-7645-8465-0)
Buddhism For Dummies
(0-7645-5359-3)
Calculus For Dummies
(0-7645-2498-4)

Forensics For Dummies
(0-7645-5580-4)
Islam For Dummies
(0-7645-5503-0)
Philosophy For Dummies
(0-7645-5153-1)
Religion For Dummies
(0-7645-5264-3)
Trigonometry For Dummie
(0-7645-6903-1)

PETS

0-470-03717-2

0-7645-8418-9

0-7645-5275-9

Also available:

Labrador Retrievers
For Dummies
(0-7645-5281-3)
Aquariums For Dummies
(0-7645-5156-6)
Birds For Dummies
(0-7645-5139-6)
Dogs For Dummies
(0-7645-5274-0)
Ferrets For Dummies
(0-7645-5259-7)

Golden Retrievers
For Dummies
(0-7645-5267-8)
Horses For Dummies
(0-7645-9797-3)
Jack Russell Terriers
For Dummies
(0-7645-5268-6)
Puppies Raising & Training
Diary For Dummies
(0-7645-0876-8)

FOR DUMMIES®

The easy way to get more done and have more fun

FOR DUMMIES

Helping you expand your horizons and achieve your potential

INTERNET

The Internet FOR DUMMIES

0-7645-8996-2

Blogging FOR DUMMIES

0-471-77084-1

Creating Web Pages FOR DUMMIES

0-7645-7327-6

Also available:

eBay.co.uk
For Dummies
(0-7645-7059-5)

Dreamweaver 8
For Dummies
(0-7645-9649-7)

Web Design
For Dummies
(0-471-78117-7)

Everyday Internet
All-in-One Desk Reference
For Dummies
(0-7645-8875-3)

Creating Web Pages
All-in-One Desk Reference
For Dummies
(0-7645-4345-8)

DIGITAL MEDIA

Digital Photography FOR DUMMIES

0-7645-9802-3

iPod & iTunes FOR DUMMIES

0-471-74739-4

Digital SLR Cameras & Photography FOR DUMMIES

0-7645-9803-1

Also available:

Digital Photos, Movies, &
Music GigaBook
For Dummies
(0-7645-7414-0)

Photoshop CS2
For Dummies
(0-7645-9571-7)

Podcasting
For Dummies
(0-471-74898-6)

Blogging
For Dummies
(0-471-77084-1)

Digital Photography
All-In-One Desk Reference
For Dummies
(0-7645-7328-4)

Windows XP Digital Music
Dummies
(0-7645-7599-6)

COMPUTER BASICS

PCs FOR DUMMIES

0-7645-8958-X

Laptops FOR DUMMIES

0-470-05432-8

Windows XP FOR DUMMIES

0-7645-7326-8

Also available:

Office XP 9 in 1
Desk Reference
For Dummies
(0-7645-0819-9)

PCs All-in-One Desk
Reference For Dummies
(0-471-77082-5)

Pocket PC For Dummies
(0-7645-1640-X)

Upgrading & Fixing PCs
For Dummies
(0-7645-1665-5)

Windows XP All-in-One De
Reference For Dummies
(0-7645-7463-9)

Macs For Dummies
(0-470-04849-2)

Essentials of Physiology

FOURTH EDITION

Lauralee Sherwood

West Virginia University

BROOKS/COLE
CENGAGE Learning

Australia • Brazil • Japan • Korea • Mexico • Singapore • Spain • United Kingdom • United States

Essentials of Physiology, **Fourth Edition**
Lauralee Sherwood

Publisher: Yolanda Cossio

Acquisitions Editor: Yolanda Cossio

Development Editor: Suzannah Alexander

Assistant Editor: Alexis Glubka

Editorial Assistant: Joshua Taylor

Media Editor: Alexandria Brady

Marketing Manager: Tom Ziolkowski

Marketing Assistant: Elizabeth Wong

Marketing Communications Manager: Linda Yip

Content Project Manager: Michelle Clark

Design Director: Rob Hugel

Art Director: John Walker

Print Buyer: Paula Vang

Rights Acquisitions Specialist: Don Schlotman

Production Service: Graphic World, Inc.

Text Designer: Jeanne Calabrese

Photo Researcher: Bill Smith Group

Text Researcher: Sarah D'Stair

Copy Editor: Graphic World, Inc.

Illustrator: Graphic World, Inc.

Cover Designer: Denise Davidson

Cover Image: © Patrik Giardino/Getty Images

Compositor: Graphic World, Inc.

Library of Congress Control Number: 2010932981

International Edition:

ISBN-13: 978-0-8400-6237-6

ISBN-10: 0-8400-6237-0

Cengage Learning International Offices

Asia
www.cengageasia.com
tel: (65) 6410 1200

Latin America
www.cengage.com.mx
tel: (52) 55 1500 6000

Australia/New Zealand
www.cengage.com.au
tel: (61) 3 9685 4111

UK/Europe/Middle East/Africa
www.cengage.co.uk
tel: (44) 0 1264 332 424

Brazil
www.cengage.com.br
tel: (55) 11 3665 9900

Represented in Canada by Nelson Education, Ltd.
tel: (416) 752 9100 / (800) 668 0671
www.nelson.com

India
www.cengage.co.in
tel: (91) 11 4364 1111

Cengage Learning is a leading provider of customized learning solutions with office locations around the globe, including Singapore, the United Kingdom, Australia, Mexico, Brazil, and Japan. Locate your local office at: **www.cengage.com/global**

For product information: **www.cengage.com/international**
Visit your local office: **www.cengage.com/global**
Visit our corporate website: **www.cengage.com**

"AVAILABILITY OF RESOURCES MAY DIFFE BY REGION. Check with your local Cengage Learn ing representative for details."

Printed in China by China Translation & Printing Services Limited
1 2 3 4 5 6 7 14 13 12 11 10

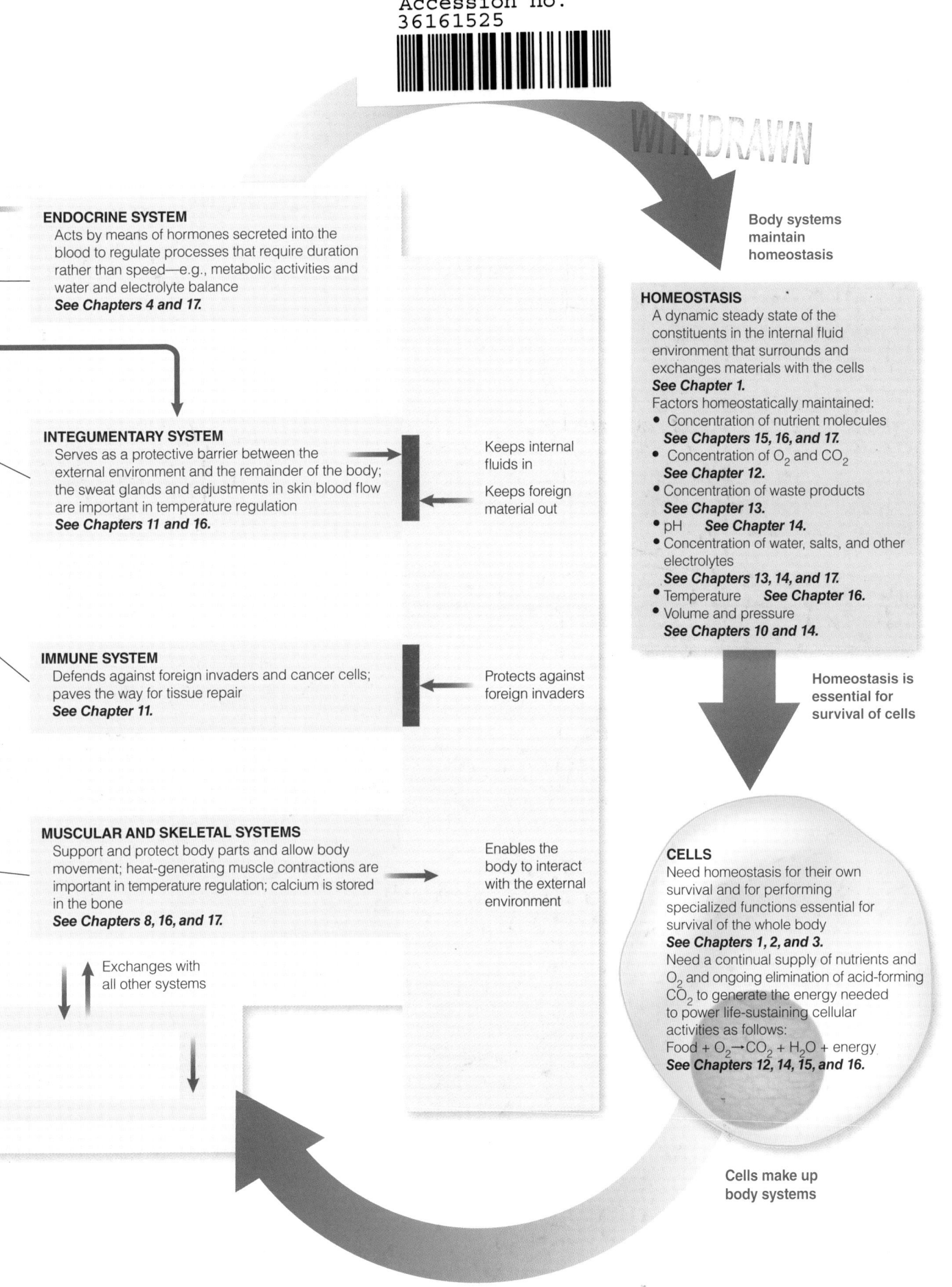

ENDOCRINE SYSTEM
Acts by means of hormones secreted into the blood to regulate processes that require duration rather than speed—e.g., metabolic activities and water and electrolyte balance
See Chapters 4 and 17.

INTEGUMENTARY SYSTEM
Serves as a protective barrier between the external environment and the remainder of the body; the sweat glands and adjustments in skin blood flow are important in temperature regulation
See Chapters 11 and 16.

Keeps internal fluids in

Keeps foreign material out

IMMUNE SYSTEM
Defends against foreign invaders and cancer cells; paves the way for tissue repair
See Chapter 11.

Protects against foreign invaders

MUSCULAR AND SKELETAL SYSTEMS
Support and protect body parts and allow body movement; heat-generating muscle contractions are important in temperature regulation; calcium is stored in the bone
See Chapters 8, 16, and 17.

Enables the body to interact with the external environment

Exchanges with all other systems

Body systems maintain homeostasis

HOMEOSTASIS
A dynamic steady state of the constituents in the internal fluid environment that surrounds and exchanges materials with the cells
See Chapter 1.
Factors homeostatically maintained:
- Concentration of nutrient molecules
  See Chapters 15, 16, and 17.
- Concentration of O_2 and CO_2
  See Chapter 12.
- Concentration of waste products
  See Chapter 13.
- pH   *See Chapter 14.*
- Concentration of water, salts, and other electrolytes
  See Chapters 13, 14, and 17.
- Temperature   *See Chapter 16.*
- Volume and pressure
  See Chapters 10 and 14.

Homeostasis is essential for survival of cells

CELLS
Need homeostasis for their own survival and for performing specialized functions essential for survival of the whole body
See Chapters 1, 2, and 3.
Need a continual supply of nutrients and O_2 and ongoing elimination of acid-forming CO_2 to generate the energy needed to power life-sustaining cellular activities as follows:
Food + $O_2 \rightarrow CO_2 + H_2O$ + energy
See Chapters 12, 14, 15, and 16.

Cells make up body systems

SUCCEED in your course with these easy-to-use online tools

Save time, learn more, and improve your grade
CengageNOW™

Get the grade you want and study in less time NOW. This easy-to-use online resource helps you learn difficult physiology concepts through self-paced learning modules that include tutorials, interactive quizzes, and animations. *Personalized Study Plans*, generated by pre- and post-tests, help you focus on the topics you still need to master. Also included are an interactive eBook and easy-to-navigate online physiology tutorials that guide you through realistic and technologically sophisticated two- and three-dimensional animations. (See below.) To purchase, enter ISBN: 978-1-111-47393-8 at **www.cengagebrain.com**.

AVAILABLE WITHIN CENGAGENOW:

Master key concepts and prepare for exams
Online Physiology Tutorials™

Easy-to-navigate and visually exciting, these online physiology tutorials help you understand various body functions including secretion, synapses and neuronal integration, heart, respiratory mechanics, and swallowing. These dynamic tutorials guide you through two- and three-dimensional animations, images, interactive exercises, and quizzing to help you master difficult-to-visualize physiology processes.

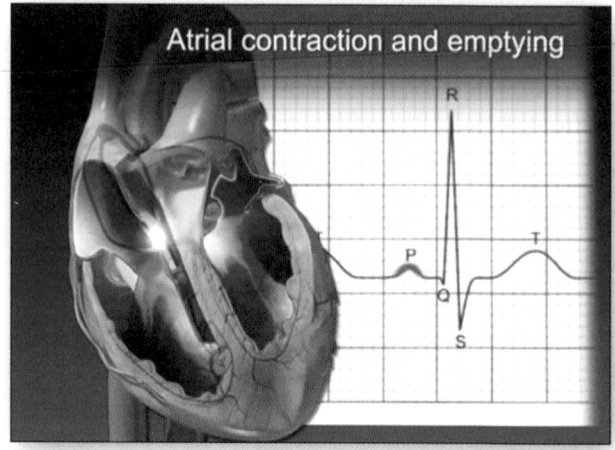

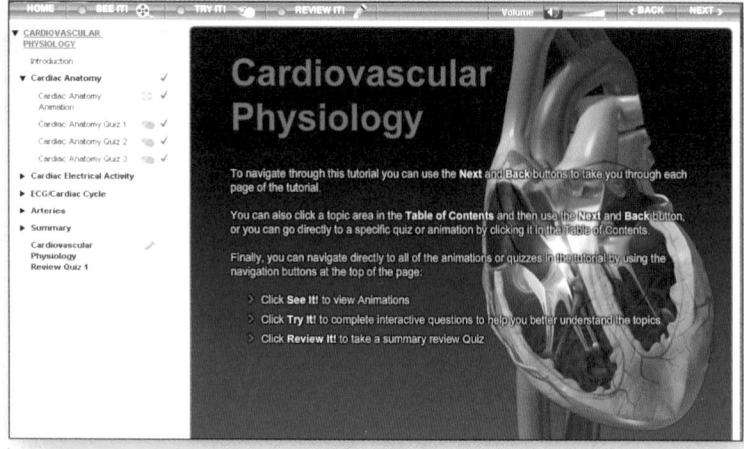

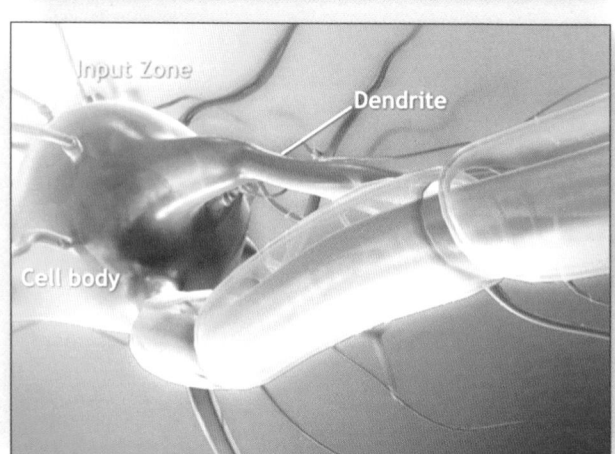

Essentials of Physiology

FOURTH EDITION

To my family,
in celebration of the continuity of life,
with memories of the past,
joys of the present,
and expectations of the future:

My parents,
Larry (in memoriam) and Lee Sherwood

My husband,
Peter Marshall

My daughters and "sons,"
Melinda and Mark Marple
Allison Tadros and Bill Krantz

My grandchildren,
Lindsay Marple
Emily Marple
Alexander Tadros
Lauren Krantz

Brief Contents

1 Introduction to Physiology and Homeostasis 1

2 Cell Physiology 20

3 The Plasma Membrane and Membrane Potential 46

4 Principles of Neural and Hormonal Communication 76

5 The Central Nervous System 114

6 The Peripheral Nervous System: Afferent Division and Special Senses 150

7 The Peripheral Nervous System: Efferent Division 190

8 Muscle Physiology 208

9 Cardiac Physiology 244

10 The Blood Vessels and Blood Pressure 278

11 The Blood and Body Defenses 316

12 The Respiratory System 366

13 The Urinary System 404

14 Fluid and Acid–Base Balance 442

15 The Digestive System 464

16 Energy Balance and Temperature Regulation 508

17 The Endocrine System 526

18 The Reproductive System 578

Appendix A
The Metric System A-1

Appendix B
A Review of Chemical Principles A-3

Appendix C
Storage, Replication, and Expression of Genetic Information A-18

Appendix D
The Chemistry of Acid-Base Balance A-30

Appendix E
Answers to End-of-Chapter Objective Questions, Points to Ponder, and Clinical Considerations A-38

Glossary G-1

Index I-1

Contents

1 Introduction to Physiology and Homeostasis 1

Introduction to Physiology 1
Physiology focuses on mechanisms of action. 1
Structure and function are inseparable. 1
Levels of Organization in the Body 1
The chemical level: Various atoms and molecules make up the body. 2
The cellular level: Cells are the basic units of life. 2
The tissue level: Tissues are groups of cells of similar specialization. 3
The organ level: An organ is a unit made up of several tissue types. 4
The body system level: A body system is a collection of related organs. 5
The organism level: The body systems are packaged together into a functional whole body. 5
Concept of Homeostasis 5
Body cells are in contact with a privately maintained internal environment. 5
Body systems maintain homeostasis, a dynamic steady state in the internal environment. 7

BEYOND THE BASICS
Stem-Cell Science and Tissue Engineering: The Quest to Make Defective Body Parts Like New Again 8

Homeostatic Control Systems 11
Homeostatic control systems may operate locally or bodywide. 11
Negative feedback opposes an initial change and is widely used to maintain homeostasis. 11
Positive feedback amplifies an initial change. 14
Disruptions in homeostasis can lead to illness and death. 15

**Chapter in Perspective:
Focus on Homeostasis** 15

Review Exercises 15
Objective Questions 15
Essay Questions 16
Points to Ponder 16
Clinical Consideration 17

2 Cell Physiology 20

Observations of Cells 21
An Overview of Cell Structure 21
The plasma membrane bounds the cell. 22
The nucleus contains the DNA. 22
The cytoplasm consists of various organelles, the cytoskeleton, and the cytosol. 23
Endoplasmic Reticulum and Segregated Synthesis 23
The rough ER synthesizes proteins for secretion and membrane construction. 23
The smooth ER packages new proteins in transport vesicles. 23
Golgi Complex and Exocytosis 24
Transport vesicles carry their cargo to the Golgi complex for further processing. 24
The Golgi complex packages secretory vesicles for release by exocytosis. 25
Lysosomes and Endocytosis 26
Lysosomes digest extracellular material brought into the cell by phagocytosis. 26
Lysosomes remove worn out organelles. 27
Peroxisomes and Detoxification 27
Peroxisomes house oxidative enzymes that detoxify various wastes. 27
Mitochondria and ATP Production 28
Mitochondria are enclosed by two membranes. 29
Mitochondria play a major role in generating ATP. 29
The cell generates more energy in aerobic than in anaerobic conditions. 32
The energy stored within ATP is used for synthesis, transport, and mechanical work. 35
Cytosol: Cell Gel 35

BEYOND THE BASICS
Aerobic Exercise: What For and How Much? 36

The cytosol is important in intermediary metabolism, ribosomal protein synthesis, and nutrient storage. 36
Cytoskeleton: Cell "Bone and Muscle" 37
Microtubules help maintain asymmetric cell shapes and play a role in complex cell movements. 37

Microfilaments are important to cellular contractile systems and as mechanical stiffeners. **39**

Intermediate filaments are important in cell regions subject to mechanical stress. **41**

Chapter in Perspective:
Focus on Homeostasis 41

Review Exercises **42**
Objective Questions **42**
Essay Questions **42**
Points to Ponder **43**
Clinical Consideration **43**

3 The Plasma Membrane and Membrane Potential 46

Membrane Structure and Functions 47

The plasma membrane is a fluid lipid bilayer embedded with proteins. **47**

The lipid bilayer forms the basic structural barrier that encloses the cell. **49**

The membrane proteins perform various specific membrane functions. **49**

BEYOND THE BASICS
Cystic Fibrosis: A Fatal Defect in Membrane Transport 50

The membrane carbohydrates serve as self-identity markers. **51**

Cell-to-Cell Adhesions 51

The extracellular matrix serves as biological "glue." **51**

Some cells are directly linked by specialized cell junctions. **52**

Overview of Membrane Transport 54

Lipid-soluble substances of any size and small water-soluble substances can permeate the plasma membrane without assistance. **54**

Active forces use energy to move particles across the membrane but passive forces do not. **54**

Unassisted Membrane Transport 54

Particles that can permeate the membrane diffuse passively down their concentration gradient. **54**

Ions that can permeate the membrane also move passively along their electrical gradient. **56**

Osmosis is the net diffusion of water down its own concentration gradient. **56**

Tonicity refers to the effect the concentration of nonpenetrating solutes in a solution has on cell volume. **58**

Assisted Membrane Transport 59

Carrier-mediated transport is accomplished by a membrane carrier changing its shape. **60**

Facilitated diffusion is passive carrier-mediated transport. **62**

Active transport is carrier-mediated and uses energy to move a substance against its concentration gradient. **62**

With vesicular transport, material is moved into or out of the cell wrapped in membrane. **64**

Membrane Potential 66

Membrane potential is a separation of opposite charges across the plasma membrane. **66**

Membrane potential is due to differences in the concentration and permeability of key ions. **66**

Chapter in Perspective:
Focus on Homeostasis 71

Review Exercises **72**
Objective Questions **72**
Essay Questions **73**
Points to Ponder **73**
Clinical Consideration **73**

4 Principles of Neural and Hormonal Communication 76

Introduction to Neural Communication 77

Nerve and muscle are excitable tissues. **77**

Membrane potential becomes less negative during depolarization and more negative during hyperpolarization. **77**

Electrical signals are produced by changes in ion movement across the plasma membrane. **78**

Graded Potentials 78

The stronger a triggering event, the larger the resultant graded potential. **78**

Graded potentials spread by passive current flow. **79**

Graded potentials die out over short distances. **80**

Action Potentials 80

During an action potential, the membrane potential rapidly, transiently reverses. **81**

Marked changes in membrane permeability and ion movement lead to an action potential. **81**

The Na^+–K^+ pump gradually restores the concentration gradients disrupted by action potentials. **84**

Action potentials are propagated from the axon hillock to the axon terminals. **84**

Once initiated, action potentials are conducted throughout a nerve fiber. **86**

The refractory period ensures one-way propagation of action potential. **87**

Action potentials occur in all-or-none fashion. **89**

The strength of a stimulus is coded by the frequency of action potentials. **89**

Myelination increases the speed of conduction of action potentials. **89**

Synapses and Neuronal Integration 91

Synapses are junctions between presynaptic and postsynaptic neurons. **91**

A neurotransmitter carries the signal across a synapse. **92**

Some synapses excite, whereas others inhibit, the postsynaptic neuron. **92**

Each neurotransmitter–receptor combination always produces the same response. **93**

Neurotransmitters are quickly removed from the synaptic cleft. 94

The grand postsynaptic potential depends on the sum of the activities of all presynaptic inputs. 94

Some neurons secrete neuromodulators in addition to neurotransmitters. 96

Drugs and diseases can modify synaptic transmission. 96

Neurons are linked through complex converging and diverging pathways. 97

Intercellular Communication and Signal Transduction 97

Communication among cells is largely orchestrated by extracellular chemical messengers. 97

Extracellular chemical messengers bring about cell responses primarily by signal transduction. 99

Some extracellular chemical messengers open chemically gated receptor-channels. 99

Most extracellular chemical messengers activate second-messenger pathways via G-protein-coupled receptors. 99

Introduction to Hormonal Communication 100

Hormones are classified chemically as hydrophilic or lipophilic. 100

The mechanisms of synthesis, storage, and secretion of hormones vary according to their chemical differences. 100

Hydrophilic hormones dissolve in the plasma; lipophilic hormones are transported by plasma proteins. 102

Hormones generally produce their effect by altering intracellular proteins. 102

Hydrophilic hormones alter preexisting proteins via second-messenger systems. 102

BEYOND THE BASICS
Programmed Cell Suicide: A Surprising Example of a Signal Transduction Pathway 104

By stimulating genes, lipophilic hormones promote synthesis of new proteins. 106

Comparison of the Nervous and Endocrine Systems 106

The nervous system is "wired," and the endocrine system is "wireless." 107

Neural specificity is due to anatomic proximity, and endocrine specificity is due to receptor specialization. 107

The nervous and endocrine systems have their own realms of authority but interact functionally. 108

Chapter in Perspective: Focus on Homeostasis 108

Review Exercises 109
Objective Questions 109
Essay Questions 109
Points to Ponder 110
Clinical Consideration 111

5 The Central Nervous System 114

Organization and Cells of the Nervous System 115

The nervous system is organized into the central nervous system and the peripheral nervous system. 115

The three functional classes of neurons are afferent neurons, efferent neurons, and interneurons. 116

Glial cells support the interneurons physically, metabolically, and functionally. 117

Protection and Nourishment of the Brain 119

The delicate CNS is well protected. 120

The brain depends on constant delivery of oxygen and glucose by the blood. 120

Overview of the Central Nervous System 120

BEYOND THE BASICS
Strokes: A Deadly Domino Effect 121

Cerebral Cortex 122

The cerebral cortex is an outer shell of gray matter covering an inner core of white matter. 123

The four pairs of lobes in the cerebral cortex are specialized for different activities. 123

The parietal lobes accomplish somatosensory processing. 123

The primary motor cortex located in the frontal lobes controls the skeletal muscles. 125

The higher motor areas are also important in motor control. 127

Different regions of the cortex control different aspects of language. 127

The association areas of the cortex are involved in many higher functions. 128

The cerebral hemispheres have some degree of specialization. 129

An electroencephalogram is a record of postsynaptic activity in cortical neurons. 129

Basal Nuclei, Thalamus, and Hypothalamus 130

The basal nuclei play an important inhibitory role in motor control. 131

The thalamus is a sensory relay station and is important in motor control. 131

The hypothalamus regulates many homeostatic functions. 132

Emotion, Behavior, and Motivation 132

The limbic system plays a key role in emotion. 132

The limbic system and higher cortex participate in controlling basic behavioral patterns. 132

Motivated behaviors are goal directed. 133

Norepinephrine, dopamine, and serotonin are neurotransmitters in pathways for emotions and behavior. 133

Learning and Memory 134

Learning is the acquisition of knowledge as a result of experiences. 134

Memory is laid down in stages. 134

Short-term memory and long-term memory involve different molecular mechanisms. 135

Memory traces are present in multiple regions of the brain. 135

Cerebellum 136

The cerebellum is important in balance and in planning and executing voluntary movement. 136

Brain Stem 138

The brain stem is a vital link between the spinal cord and the higher brain regions. 138

Sleep is an active process consisting of alternating periods of slow-wave and paradoxical sleep. 138

The sleep–wake cycle is controlled by interactions among three neural systems. 140

The function of sleep is unclear. 140

Spinal Cord 140

The spinal cord extends through the vertebral canal and is connected to the spinal nerves. 140

The white matter of the spinal cord is organized into tracts. 140

Spinal nerves carry both afferent and efferent fibers. 141

The spinal cord is responsible for the integration of many basic reflexes. 141

Chapter in Perspective:
Focus on Homeostasis 145

Review Exercises 145
Objective Questions 145
Essay Questions 146
Points to Ponder 146
Clinical Consideration 147

6 The Peripheral Nervous System: Afferent Division and Special Senses 150

Receptor Physiology 151

Receptors have differential sensitivities to various stimuli. 151

A stimulus alters the receptor's permeability, leading to a graded receptor potential. 152

Receptor potentials may initiate action potentials in the afferent neuron. 152

Receptors may adapt slowly or rapidly to sustained stimulation. 153

Visceral afferents carry subconscious input, whereas sensory afferents carry conscious input. 153

Each somatosensory pathway is "labeled" according to modality and location. 154

Acuity is influenced by receptive field size. 154

Perception is the conscious awareness of surroundings derived from interpretation of sensory input. 155

Pain 155

Stimulation of nociceptors elicits the perception of pain plus motivational and emotional responses. 155

The brain has a built-in analgesic system. 156

Eye: Vision 156

The eye is a fluid-filled sphere enclosed by three specialized tissue layers. 156

BEYOND THE BASICS
Acupuncture: Is It for Real? 157

The amount of light entering the eye is controlled by the iris. 157

The eye refracts the entering light to focus the image on the retina. 158

Accommodation increases the strength of the lens for near vision. 160

Light must pass through several retinal layers before reaching the photoreceptors. 162

Phototransduction by retinal cells converts light stimuli into neural signals. 162

Rods provide indistinct gray vision at night, whereas cones provide sharp color vision during the day. 167

Color vision depends on the ratios of stimulation of the three cone types. 167

The sensitivity of the eyes can vary markedly through dark and light adaptation. 168

Visual information is separated before reaching the visual cortex. 168

The thalamus and visual cortex elaborate the visual message. 169

Visual input goes to other areas of the brain not involved in vision perception. 171

Ear: Hearing and Equilibrium 171

Sound waves consist of alternate regions of compression and rarefaction of air molecules. 171

The external ear plays a role in sound localization. 173

The tympanic membrane vibrates in unison with sound waves in the external ear. 173

The middle ear bones convert tympanic membrane vibrations into fluid movements in the inner ear. 173

The cochlea contains the organ of Corti, the sense organ for hearing. 174

Hair cells in the organ of Corti transduce fluid movements into neural signals. 175

Pitch discrimination depends on the region of the basilar membrane that vibrates. 175

Loudness discrimination depends on the amplitude of vibration. 177

Deafness is caused by defects in either conduction or neural processing of sound waves. 178

The vestibular apparatus is important for equilibrium by detecting position and motion of the head. 178

Chemical Senses: Taste and Smell 181

Taste receptor cells are located primarily within tongue taste buds. 181

Taste discrimination is coded by patterns of activity in various taste bud receptors. 183

The olfactory receptors in the nose are specialized endings of renewable afferent neurons. 183

Various parts of an odor are detected by different olfactory receptors and sorted into "smell files." 183

Odor discrimination is coded by patterns of activity in the olfactory bulb glomeruli. 185

The olfactory system adapts quickly. 185

Chapter in Perspective:
Focus on Homeostasis   185

Review Exercises   186
Objective Questions   186
Essay Questions   186
Points to Ponder   187
Clinical Consideration   187

7   The Peripheral Nervous System: Efferent Division   190

Autonomic Nervous System   191
An autonomic nerve pathway consists of a two-neuron chain.   191
Parasympathetic postganglionic fibers release acetylcholine; sympathetic ones release norepinephrine.   192
The sympathetic and parasympathetic nervous systems dually innervate most visceral organs.   192
The adrenal medulla is a modified part of the sympathetic nervous system.   196
Several receptor types are available for each autonomic neurotransmitter.   196
Many regions of the CNS are involved in the control of autonomic activities.   197
Somatic Nervous System   197
Motor neurons supply skeletal muscle.   197
Motor neurons are influenced by many areas of the CNS involved in motor control.   197
Neuromuscular Junction   198
Motor neurons and skeletal muscle fibers are chemically linked at neuromuscular junctions.   198
ACh is the neuromuscular junction neurotransmitter.   198
Acetylcholinesterase ends ACh activity at the neuromuscular junction.   200
The neuromuscular junction is vulnerable to several chemical agents and diseases.   201

BEYOND THE BASICS
Botulinum Toxin's Reputation Gets a Facelift   203

Chapter in Perspective:
Focus on Homeostasis   204

Review Exercises   204
Objective Questions   204
Essay Questions   205
Points to Ponder   205
Clinical Consideration   205

8   Muscle Physiology   208

Structure of Skeletal Muscle   209
Skeletal muscle fibers are striated by a highly organized internal arrangement.   209

Myosin forms the thick filaments.   210
Actin is the main structural component of the thin filaments.   210
Molecular Basis of Skeletal Muscle Contraction   212
During contraction, cycles of cross-bridge binding and bending pull the thin filaments inward.   212
Ca^{2+} is the link between excitation and contraction.   213
Contractile activity far outlasts the electrical activity that initiated it.   218
Skeletal Muscle Mechanics   218
Whole muscles are groups of muscle fibers bundled together and attached to bones.   218
Muscle tension is transmitted to bone as the contractile component tightens the series-elastic component.   219
The two primary types of contraction are isotonic and isometric.   219
The velocity of shortening is related to the load.   220
Contractions of a whole muscle can be of varying strength.   220
The number of fibers contracting within a muscle depends on the extent of motor unit recruitment.   220
The frequency of stimulation can influence the tension developed by each muscle fiber.   221
Twitch summation results from a sustained elevation in cytosolic Ca^{2+}.   222
There is an optimal muscle length at which maximal tension can be developed.   223
Skeletal Muscle Metabolism and Fiber Types   224
Muscle fibers have alternate pathways for forming ATP.   224
Increased O_2 consumption is necessary to recover from exercise.   225
There are three types of skeletal muscle fibers, based on differences in ATP splitting and synthesis.   225
Muscle fibers adapt considerably in response to the demands placed on them.   226

BEYOND THE BASICS
Are Athletes Who Use Steroids to Gain Competitive Advantage Really Winners or Losers?   227

Control of Motor Movement   228
Multiple neural inputs influence motor unit output.   228
Muscle receptors provide afferent information needed to control skeletal muscle activity.   229
Smooth and Cardiac Muscle   231
Smooth muscle cells are small and unstriated.   231
Smooth muscle cells are turned on by Ca^{2+}-dependent phosphorylation of myosin.   234
Multiunit smooth muscle is neurogenic.   235
Single-unit smooth muscle cells form functional syncytia.   236
Single-unit smooth muscle is myogenic.   236
Gradation of single-unit smooth muscle contraction differs from that of skeletal muscle.   237
Smooth muscle can still develop tension when stretched.   238
Smooth muscle is slow and economical.   239
Cardiac muscle blends features of both skeletal and smooth muscle.   239

Chapter in Perspective:
Focus on Homeostasis 239

Review Exercises 240
Objective Questions 240
Essay Questions 240
Points to Ponder 241
Clinical Consideration 241

9 Cardiac Physiology 244

Anatomy of the Heart 245
The heart is positioned in the middle of the thoracic cavity. 245
The heart is a dual pump. 246
Pressure-operated heart valves ensure that blood flows in the right direction through the heart. 248
The heart walls are composed primarily of cardiac muscle fibers. 249
Cardiac muscle fibers are interconnected by intercalated discs and form functional syncytia. 249
Electrical Activity of the Heart 250
Cardiac autorhythmic cells display pacemaker activity. 250
The sinoatrial node is the normal pacemaker of the heart. 251
The spread of cardiac excitation is coordinated to ensure efficient pumping. 252
The action potential of cardiac contractile cells shows a characteristic plateau. 254
Ca^{2+} entry from the ECF induces a larger Ca^{2+} release from the sarcoplasmic reticulum. 255
A long refractory period prevents tetanus of cardiac muscle. 256
The ECG is a record of the overall spread of electrical activity through the heart. 256
Different parts of the ECG record can be correlated to specific cardiac events. 257
The ECG can be used to diagnose abnormal heart rates, arrhythmias, and damage of heart muscle. 259
Mechanical Events of the Cardiac Cycle 259
The heart alternately contracts to empty and relaxes to fill. 260
Two normal heart sounds are associated with valve closures. 262
Turbulent blood flow produces heart murmurs. 262
Cardiac Output and Its Control 263
Cardiac output depends on the heart rate and the stroke volume. 263
Heart rate is determined primarily by autonomic influences on the SA node. 263
Stroke volume is determined by the extent of venous return and by sympathetic activity. 265
Increased end-diastolic volume results in increased stroke volume. 265
Sympathetic stimulation increases the contractility of the heart. 266
In heart failure, the contractility of the heart decreases. 267

Nourishing the Heart Muscle 268
The heart receives most of its own blood supply through the coronary circulation during diastole. 268
Atherosclerotic coronary artery disease can deprive the heart of essential oxygen. 269

BEYOND THE BASICS
Atherosclerosis: Cholesterol and Beyond 272

Chapter in Perspective:
Focus on Homeostasis 273

Review Exercises 274
Objective Questions 274
Essay Questions 274
Points to Ponder 275
Clinical Consideration 275

10 The Blood Vessels and Blood Pressure 278

Patterns and Physics of Blood Flow 279
To maintain homeostasis, reconditioning organs receive blood flow in excess of their own needs. 279
Blood flow through a vessel depends on the pressure gradient and vascular resistance. 280
The vascular tree consists of arteries, arterioles, capillaries, venules, and veins. 282
Arteries 282
Arteries serve as rapid-transit passageways to the organs and as a pressure reservoir. 282

BEYOND THE BASICS
From Humors to Harvey: Historical Highlights in Circulation 283

Arterial pressure fluctuates in relation to ventricular systole and diastole. 284
Blood pressure can be measured indirectly by using a sphygmomanometer. 285
Mean arterial pressure is the main driving force for blood flow. 287
Arterioles 287
Arterioles are the major resistance vessels. 287
Local control of arteriolar radius is important in determining the distribution of cardiac output. 289
Local metabolic influences on arteriolar radius help match blood flow with the organs' needs. 289
Local histamine release pathologically dilates arterioles. 290
The myogenic response of arterioles to stretch helps tissues autoregulate their blood flow. 290
Local heat application dilates arterioles and cold application constricts them. 291
Extrinsic sympathetic control of arteriolar radius is important in regulating blood pressure. 291
The medullary cardiovascular control center and several hormones regulate blood pressure. 292

Capillaries 292

Capillaries are ideally suited to serve as sites of exchange. 292

Water-filled capillary pores permit passage of small, water-soluble substances. 295

Interstitial fluid is a passive intermediary between blood and cells. 295

Diffusion across the capillary walls is important in solute exchange. 296

Bulk flow across the capillary walls is important in extracellular fluid distribution. 297

The lymphatic system is an accessory route by which interstitial fluid can be returned to the blood. 299

Edema occurs when too much interstitial fluid accumulates. 300

Veins 301

Veins serve as a blood reservoir, as well as passageways back to the heart. 301

Venous return is enhanced by several extrinsic factors. 302

Blood Pressure 305

Blood pressure is regulated by controlling cardiac output, total peripheral resistance, and blood volume. 306

The baroreceptor reflex is an important short-term mechanism for regulating blood pressure through immediate effects on the heart and blood vessels. 307

Hypertension is a serious national public-health problem, but its causes are largely unknown. 308

Orthostatic hypotension results from transient inadequate sympathetic activity. 310

Circulatory shock can become irreversible. 310

Chapter in Perspective: Focus on Homeostasis 311

Review Exercises 312
Objective Questions 312
Essay Questions 312
Points to Ponder 313
Clinical Consideration 313

11 The Blood and Body Defenses 316

Plasma 317

The hematocrit represents the packed cell volume; plasma accounts for the rest of the volume. 317

Plasma water is a transport medium for many inorganic and organic substances. 317

Many of the functions of plasma are carried out by plasma proteins. 318

Erythrocytes 319

The structure of erythrocytes is well suited to their main function of O_2 transport in the blood. 319

The bone marrow continuously replaces worn-out erythrocytes. 320

Erythropoiesis is controlled by erythropoietin from the kidneys. 320

Anemia can be caused by a variety of disorders. 321

Polycythemia is an excess of circulating erythrocytes. 322

Blood types depend on surface antigens on erythrocytes. 322

Platelets and Hemostasis 324

Platelets are cell fragments shed from megakaryocytes. 324

Hemostasis prevents blood loss from damaged small vessels. 324

Vascular spasm reduces blood flow through an injured vessel. 324

Platelets aggregate to form a plug at a vessel tear or cut. 325

Clot formation results from a triggered chain reaction involving plasma clotting factors. 326

Fibrinolytic plasmin dissolves clots. 328

Inappropriate clotting produces thromboembolism. 328

Hemophilia is the primary condition that produces excessive bleeding. 329

Leukocytes 329

Leukocytes primarily function as defense agents outside the blood. 329

Pathogenic bacteria and viruses are the major targets of the immune system. 329

There are five types of leukocytes. 329

Leukocytes are produced at varying rates depending on the changing needs of the body. 331

Immune responses may be either innate and nonspecific or adaptive and specific. 332

Innate Immunity 333

Inflammation is a nonspecific response to foreign invasion or tissue damage. 333

Inflammation is an underlying culprit in many common, chronic illnesses. 336

Nonsteroidal and anti-inflammatory drugs and glucocorticoids suppress the inflammation response. 337

Interferon transiently inhibits multiplication of viruses in most cells. 337

Natural killer cells destroy virus-infected cells and cancer cells on first exposure to them. 337

The complement system punches holes in microorganisms. 337

Adaptive Immunity: General Concepts 339

Adaptive immune responses include antibody-mediated immunity and cell-mediated immunity. 339

An antigen induces an immune response against itself. 339

B Lymphocytes: Antibody-Mediated Immunity 340

Antigens stimulate B cells to convert into plasma cells that produce antibodies. 340

Antibodies are Y shaped and classified according to properties of their tail portion. 340

Antibodies largely amplify innate immune responses to promote antigen destruction. 341

Clonal selection accounts for the specificity of antibody production. 342

Selected clones differentiate into active plasma cells and dormant memory cells. 343

BEYOND THE BASICS
Vaccination: A Victory Over Many Dreaded
Diseases   345

T Lymphocytes: Cell-Mediated Immunity   345
T cells bind directly with their targets.   345
The three types of T cells are cytotoxic, helper, and
   regulatory.   346
Cytotoxic T cells secrete chemicals that destroy target
   cells.   346
Helper T cells secrete chemicals that amplify the activity of
   other immune cells.   347
T lymphocytes respond only to antigens presented to them by
   antigen-presenting cells.   348
The major histocompatibility complex is the code for self-
   antigens.   349
The immune system is normally tolerant of self-antigens.   351
Immune surveillance against cancer cells involves an interplay
   among immune cells and interferon.   352

Immune Diseases   354
Immunodeficiency diseases result from insufficient immune
   responses.   354
Allergies are inappropriate immune attacks against harmless
   environmental substances.   354

External Defenses   357
The skin consists of an outer protective epidermis and an
   inner, connective tissue dermis.   358
Specialized cells in the epidermis produce keratin and melanin
   and participate in immune defense.   359
Protective measures within body cavities discourage pathogen
   invasion into the body.   359

Chapter in Perspective:
Focus on Homeostasis   360

Review Exercises   361
Objective Questions   361
Essay Questions   362
Points to Ponder   362
Clinical Consideration   363

12   The Respiratory System   366

Respiratory Anatomy   367
The respiratory system does not participate in all steps of
   respiration.   367
The respiratory airways conduct air between the atmosphere
   and the alveoli.   368
The gas-exchanging alveoli are thin-walled, inflatable air sacs
   encircled by pulmonary capillaries.   369
The lungs occupy much of the thoracic cavity.   371
A pleural sac separates each lung from the thoracic wall.   371

Respiratory Mechanics   371
Interrelationships among pressures inside and outside the
   lungs are important in ventilation.   371
The transmural pressure gradient normally stretches the lungs
   to fill the larger thoracic cavity.   372

Flow of air into and out of the lungs occurs because of cyclic
   changes in intra-alveolar pressure.   373
Airway resistance influences airflow rates.   375
Airway resistance is abnormally increased with chronic
   obstructive pulmonary disease.   376
Elastic behavior of the lungs is a result of elastic connective
   tissue and alveolar surface tension.   379
Pulmonary surfactant decreases surface tension and
   contributes to lung stability.   379
The lungs normally operate about "half full."   380
Alveolar ventilation is less than pulmonary ventilation because
   of dead space.   382

Gas Exchange   384
Gases move down partial pressure gradients.   384
Oxygen enters and CO_2 leaves the blood in the lungs passively
   down partial pressure gradients.   384
Factors other than the partial pressure gradient influence the
   rate of gas transfer.   385
Gas exchange across the systemic capillaries also occurs down
   partial pressure gradients.   386

Gas Transport   387
Most O_2 in the blood is transported bound to
   hemoglobin.   387
The P_{O_2} is the primary factor determining the percent
   hemoglobin saturation.   388
Hemoglobin promotes the net transfer of O_2 at both the
   alveolar and the tissue levels.   389
Factors at the tissue level promote the unloading of O_2 from
   hemoglobin.   390
Hemoglobin has a higher affinity for carbon monoxide than
   for O_2.   391
Most CO_2 is transported in the blood as bicarbonate.   392
Various respiratory states are characterized by abnormal
   blood-gas levels.   393

BEYOND THE BASICS
Effects of Heights and Depths on the Body   394

Control of Respiration   395
Respiratory centers in the brain stem establish a rhythmic
   breathing pattern.   395
The magnitude of ventilation is adjusted in response to three
   chemical factors: P_{O_2}, P_{CO_2}, and H^+.   396
Decreased arterial P_{O_2} increases ventilation only as an
   emergency mechanism.   397
Carbon dioxide–generated H^+ in the brain is normally the main
   regulator of ventilation.   398
Adjustments in ventilation in response to changes in arterial H^+
   are important in acid–base balance.   399
During apnea, a person "forgets to breathe."   399

Chapter in Perspective:
Focus on Homeostasis   400

Review Exercises   400
Objective Questions   400
Essay Questions   400
Points to Ponder   401
Clinical Consideration   401

13 The Urinary System 404

Kidneys: Functions, Anatomy, and Basic Processes 405

The kidneys perform a variety of functions aimed at maintaining homeostasis. 405

The kidneys form the urine; the rest of the urinary system carries the urine to the outside. 406

The nephron is the functional unit of the kidney. 406

The three basic renal processes are glomerular filtration, tubular reabsorption, and tubular secretion. 408

Glomerular Filtration 410

Glomerular capillary blood pressure is the major force that causes glomerular filtration. 411

Changes in the GFR result primarily from changes in glomerular capillary blood pressure. 412

The kidneys normally receive 20% to 25% of the cardiac output. 413

Tubular Reabsorption 414

Tubular reabsorption is tremendous, highly selective, and variable. 414

Tubular reabsorption involves transepithelial transport. 414

An active Na^+–K^+ ATPase pump in the basolateral membrane is essential for Na^+ reabsorption. 415

Aldosterone stimulates Na^+ reabsorption in the distal and collecting tubules. 416

Atrial natriuretic peptide inhibits Na^+ reabsorption. 418

Glucose and amino acids are reabsorbed by Na^+-dependent secondary active transport. 419

In general, actively reabsorbed substances exhibit a tubular maximum. 419

Glucose is an example of an actively reabsorbed substance that is not regulated by the kidneys. 419

Phosphate is an example of an actively reabsorbed substance that is regulated by the kidneys. 421

Active Na^+ reabsorption is responsible for the passive reabsorption of Cl^-, H_2O, and urea. 421

In general, unwanted waste products are not reabsorbed. 422

Tubular Secretion 422

Hydrogen ion secretion is important in acid–base balance. 422

Potassium ion secretion is controlled by aldosterone. 422

Organic anion and cation secretion helps efficiently eliminate foreign compounds from the body. 423

Urine Excretion and Plasma Clearance 424

Plasma clearance is the volume of plasma cleared of a particular substance per minute. 425

If a substance is filtered but not reabsorbed or secreted, its plasma clearance rate equals the GFR. 425

If a substance is filtered and reabsorbed but not secreted, its plasma clearance rate is always less than the GFR. 425

If a substance is filtered and secreted but not reabsorbed, its plasma clearance rate is always greater than the GFR. 425

The kidneys can excrete urine of varying concentrations depending on the body's state of hydration. 427

The medullary vertical osmotic gradient is established by countercurrent multiplication. 428

Vasopressin-controlled, variable H_2O reabsorption occurs in the final tubular segments. 429

Renal failure has wide-ranging consequences. 434

Urine is temporarily stored in the bladder, from which it is emptied by micturition. 434

BEYOND THE BASICS
Dialysis: Cellophane Tubing or Abdominal Lining as an Artificial Kidney 436

Chapter in Perspective: Focus on Homeostasis 437

Review Exercises 438
Objective Questions 438
Essay Questions 439
Points to Ponder 439
Clinical Consideration 439

14 Fluid and Acid–Base Balance 442

Balance Concept 443

The internal pool of a substance is the amount of that substance in the ECF. 443

To maintain stable balance of an ECF constituent, its input must equal its output. 443

Fluid Balance 444

Body water is distributed between the ICF and the ECF compartments. 444

The plasma and interstitial fluid are similar in composition, but the ECF and ICF differ markedly. 444

Fluid balance is maintained by regulating ECF volume and osmolarity. 445

Control of ECF volume is important in the long-term regulation of blood pressure. 445

Control of salt balance is primarily important in regulating ECF volume. 446

Controlling ECF osmolarity prevents changes in ICF volume. 447

BEYOND THE BASICS
A Potentially Fatal Clash: When Exercising Muscles and Cooling Mechanisms Compete for an Inadequate Plasma Volume 448

During ECF hypertonicity, the cells shrink as H_2O leaves them. 449

During ECF hypotonicity, the cells swell as H_2O enters them. 449

No water moves into or out of cells during an ECF isotonic fluid gain or loss. 450

Control of water balance by means of vasopressin is important in regulating ECF osmolarity. 450

Vasopressin secretion and thirst are largely triggered simultaneously. 451

Acid–Base Balance   452

Acids liberate free hydrogen ions, whereas bases accept them.   452

The pH designation is used to express [H⁺].   453

Fluctuations in [H⁺] alter nerve, enzyme, and K⁺ activity.   454

Hydrogen ions are continually added to the body fluids as a result of metabolic activities.   454

Chemical buffer systems minimize changes in pH by binding with or yielding free H⁺.   456

Chemical buffer systems act as the first line of defense against changes in [H⁺].   457

The respiratory system regulates [H⁺] by controlling the rate of CO_2 removal.   457

The respiratory system serves as the second line of defense against changes in [H⁺].   457

The kidneys help maintain acid–base balance by adjusting their rate of H⁺ excretion, HCO_3^- excretion, and NH_3 secretion.   458

The kidneys are a powerful third line of defense against changes in [H⁺].   459

Acid–base imbalances can arise from either respiratory dysfunction or metabolic disturbances.   459

**Chapter in Perspective:
Focus on Homeostasis**   460

Review Exercises   461
Objective Questions   461
Essay Questions   461
Points to Ponder   461
Clinical Consideration   461

15   The Digestive System   464

General Aspects of Digestion   465

The digestive system performs four basic digestive processes.   465

The digestive tract and accessory digestive organs make up the digestive system.   466

The digestive tract wall has four layers.   467

Regulation of digestive function is complex and synergistic.   467

Receptor activation alters digestive activity through neural reflexes and hormonal pathways.   470

Mouth   471

The oral cavity is the entrance to the digestive tract.   471

The teeth are responsible for chewing.   471

Saliva begins carbohydrate digestion, is important in oral hygiene, and facilitates speech.   472

Salivary secretion is continuous and can be reflexly increased.   472

Digestion in the mouth is minimal; no absorption of nutrients occurs.   473

Pharynx and Esophagus   473

Swallowing is a sequentially programmed all-or-none reflex.   473

During the oropharyngeal stage of swallowing, food is prevented from entering the wrong passageways.   473

The pharyngoesophageal sphincter keeps air from entering the digestive tract during breathing.   473

Peristaltic waves push food through the esophagus.   474

The gastroesophageal sphincter prevents reflux of gastric contents.   474

Esophageal secretion is entirely protective.   475

Stomach   475

The stomach stores food and begins protein digestion.   475

Gastric filling involves receptive relaxation.   475

Gastric storage takes place in the body of the stomach.   476

Gastric mixing takes place in the antrum of the stomach.   476

Gastric emptying is controlled by factors in the duodenum.   476

Emotions can influence gastric motility.   477

The stomach does not actively participate in vomiting.   477

Gastric digestive juice is secreted by glands located at the base of gastric pits.   478

Hydrochloric acid activates pepsinogen.   478

Pepsinogen is activated to pepsin, which initiates protein digestion.   480

Mucus is protective.   480

Intrinsic factor is essential for absorption of vitamin B_{12}.   480

Multiple regulatory pathways influence the parietal and chief cells.   481

Control of gastric secretion involves three phases.   481

Gastric secretion gradually decreases as food empties from the stomach into the intestine.   482

The gastric mucosal barrier protects the stomach lining from gastric secretions.   482

Carbohydrate digestion continues in the body of the stomach; protein digestion begins in the antrum.   483

The stomach absorbs alcohol and aspirin but no food.   483

**BEYOND THE BASICS
Ulcers: When Bugs Break the Barrier**   484

Pancreatic and Biliary Secretions   485

The pancreas is a mixture of exocrine and endocrine tissue.   485

The exocrine pancreas secretes digestive enzymes and an aqueous alkaline fluid.   485

Pancreatic exocrine secretion is regulated by secretin and CCK.   486

The liver performs various important functions, including bile production.   487

Bile is continuously secreted by the liver and is diverted to the gallbladder between meals.   488

Bile salts are recycled through the enterohepatic circulation.   488

Bile salts aid fat digestion and absorption.   489

Bile salts are the most potent stimulus for increased bile secretion; CCK promotes gallbladder emptying.   490

Bilirubin is a waste product excreted in the bile.   490

Small Intestine   491

Segmentation contractions mix and slowly propel the chyme.   491

The migrating motility complex sweeps the intestine clean between meals.   492

The ileocecal juncture prevents contamination of the small intestine by colonic bacteria.   493

Small-intestine secretions do not contain any digestive enzymes.   493

The small-intestine enzymes complete digestion within the brush-border membrane.   493

The small intestine is remarkably well adapted for its primary role in absorption.   494

The mucosal lining experiences rapid turnover.   496

Energy-dependent Na^+ absorption drives passive H_2O absorption.   496

Digested carbohydrates and proteins are both absorbed by secondary active transport and enter the blood.   497

Digested fat is absorbed passively and enters the lymph.   497

Vitamin absorption is largely passive.   499

Iron and calcium absorption is regulated.   499

Most absorbed nutrients immediately pass through the liver for processing.   499

Extensive absorption by the small intestine keeps pace with secretion.   499

Diarrhea results in loss of fluid and electrolytes.   499

Large Intestine   500

The large intestine is primarily a drying and storage organ.   500

Haustral contractions slowly shuffle the colonic contents back and forth.   500

Mass movements propel feces long distances.   500

Feces are eliminated by the defecation reflex.   500

Constipation occurs when the feces become too dry.   501

Large-intestine secretion is entirely protective.   501

The colon contains myriad beneficial bacteria.   501

The large intestine absorbs salt and water, converting the luminal contents into feces.   501

Intestinal gases are absorbed or expelled.   501

Overview of the Gastrointestinal Hormones   502

**Chapter in Perspective:
Focus on Homeostasis**   502

Review Exercises   503
Objective Questions   503
Essay Questions   504
Points to Ponder   504
Clinical Consideration   505

16   Energy Balance and Temperature Regulation   508

Energy Balance   509

Most food energy is converted into heat in the body.   509

The metabolic rate is the rate of energy use.   510

Energy input must equal energy output to maintain a neutral energy balance.   511

Food intake is controlled primarily by the hypothalamus.   511

Obesity occurs when more kilocalories are consumed than are burned up.   515

People suffering from anorexia nervosa have a pathological fear of gaining weight.   516

Temperature Regulation   516

Internal core temperature is homeostatically maintained at 100°F (37.8°C).   516

Heat input must balance heat output to maintain a stable core temperature.   517

Heat exchange takes place by radiation, conduction, convection, and evaporation.   517

Sweating is a regulated evaporative heat-loss process.   518

The hypothalamus integrates a multitude of thermosensory inputs.   518

Shivering is the primary involuntary means of increasing heat production.   519

The magnitude of heat loss can be adjusted by varying the flow of blood through the skin.   519

The hypothalamus simultaneously coordinates heat-production and heat-loss mechanisms.   520

During a fever, the hypothalamic thermostat is "reset" at an elevated temperature.   520

**BEYOND THE BASICS
The Extremes of Cold and Heat Can Be Fatal**   521

**Chapter in Perspective:
Focus on Homeostasis**   522

Review Exercises   522
Objective Questions   522
Essay Questions   523
Points to Ponder   523
Clinical Consideration   523

17   The Endocrine System   526

General Principles of Endocrinology   527

Hormones exert a variety of regulatory effects throughout the body.   527

The effective plasma concentration of a hormone is normally regulated by changes in its rate of secretion.   528

The plasma concentration of a hormone is influenced by its rate of excretion.   529

Endocrine disorders result from hormone excess or deficiency or decreased target-cell responsiveness.   530

The responsiveness of a target cell can be varied by regulating the number of hormone-specific receptors.   530

Hypothalamus and Pituitary   531

The pituitary gland consists of anterior and posterior lobes.   531

The hypothalamus and posterior pituitary act as a unit to secrete vasopressin and oxytocin.   531

Most anterior pituitary hormones are tropic.   534

Hypothalamic releasing and inhibiting hormones help regulate anterior pituitary hormone secretion.   536

Target-gland hormones inhibit hypothalamic and anterior pituitary hormone secretion via negative feedback. **538**

Endocrine Control of Growth **538**

Growth depends on GH but is influenced by other factors. **539**

GH is essential for growth, but it also directly exerts metabolic effects not related to growth. **539**

GH exerts its growth-promoting effects indirectly by stimulating insulin-like growth factor. **539**

GH, through IGF, promotes growth of soft tissues by stimulating hyperplasia and hypertrophy. **539**

Bone grows in thickness and in length by different mechanisms, both stimulated by GH. **540**

GH secretion is regulated by two hypophysiotropic hormones. **540**

Abnormal GH secretion results in aberrant growth patterns. **542**

Pineal Gland and Circadian Rhythms **542**

The suprachiasmatic nucleus is the master biological clock. **542**

Melatonin helps keep the body's circadian rhythm in time with the light–dark cycle. **543**

BEYOND THE BASICS
Tinkering with Our Biological Clocks **544**

Thyroid Gland **545**

The major cells that secrete thyroid hormone are organized into colloid-filled follicles. **545**

Thyroid hormone is synthesized and stored on the thyroglobulin molecule. **545**

To secrete thyroid hormone, the follicular cells phagocytize thyroglobulin-laden colloid. **547**

Most of the secreted T_4 is converted into T_3 outside the thyroid. **547**

Thyroid hormone is the main determinant of the basal metabolic rate and exerts other effects. **547**

Thyroid hormone is regulated by the hypothalamus–pituitary–thyroid axis. **547**

Abnormalities of thyroid function include both hypothyroidism and hyperthyroidism. **548**

A goiter develops when the thyroid gland is overstimulated. **549**

Adrenal Glands **549**

Each adrenal gland consists of a steroid-secreting cortex and a catecholamine-secreting medulla. **550**

The adrenal cortex secretes mineralocorticoids, glucocorticoids, and sex hormones. **550**

The major effects of mineralocorticoids are on Na^+ and K^+ balance and blood pressure homeostasis. **551**

Glucocorticoids exert metabolic effects and play a key role in adaptation to stress. **551**

Cortisol secretion is regulated by the hypothalamus–pituitary–adrenal cortex axis. **552**

The adrenal cortex secretes both male and female sex hormones in both sexes. **552**

The adrenal cortex may secrete too much or too little of any of its hormones. **553**

The adrenal medulla consists of modified sympathetic postganglionic neurons. **554**

Epinephrine reinforces the sympathetic nervous system and exerts additional metabolic effects. **555**

Integrated Stress Response **555**

The stress response is a generalized pattern of reactions to any situation that threatens homeostasis. **555**

The multifaceted stress response is coordinated by the hypothalamus. **557**

Activation of the stress response by chronic psychosocial stressors may be harmful. **557**

Endocrine Pancreas and Control of Fuel Metabolism **557**

Fuel metabolism includes anabolism, catabolism, and interconversions among energy-rich organic molecules. **557**

Because food intake is intermittent, nutrients must be stored for use between meals. **558**

The brain must be continuously supplied with glucose. **558**

Metabolic fuels are stored during the absorptive state and mobilized during the postabsorptive state. **560**

The pancreatic hormones, insulin and glucagon, are most important in regulating fuel metabolism. **561**

Insulin lowers blood glucose, fatty acid, and amino acid levels and promotes their storage. **562**

The primary stimulus for increased insulin secretion is an increase in blood glucose concentration. **563**

The symptoms of diabetes mellitus are characteristic of an exaggerated postabsorptive state. **564**

Insulin excess causes brain-starving hypoglycemia. **566**

Glucagon in general opposes the actions of insulin. **567**

Glucagon secretion is increased during the postabsorptive state. **567**

Insulin and glucagon work as a team to maintain blood glucose and fatty acid levels. **567**

Epinephrine, cortisol, and GH also exert direct metabolic effects. **567**

Parathyroid Gland and Control of Calcium Metabolism **568**

Plasma Ca^{2+} must be closely regulated to prevent changes in neuromuscular excitability. **568**

Parathyroid hormone raises free plasma Ca^{2+} levels by its effects on bone, kidneys, and intestine. **569**

Bone continuously undergoes remodeling. **569**

Mechanical stress favors bone deposition. **569**

PTH raises plasma Ca^{2+} by withdrawing Ca^{2+} from the bone bank. **570**

PTH acts on the kidneys to conserve Ca^{2+} and eliminate PO_4^{3-}. **570**

PTH indirectly promotes absorption of Ca^{2+} and PO_4^{3-} by the intestine. **571**

The primary regulator of PTH secretion is plasma concentration of free Ca^{2+}. **571**

Calcitonin lowers plasma Ca^{2+} concentration but is not important in the normal control of Ca^{2+} metabolism. **571**

Vitamin D is actually a hormone that increases calcium absorption in the intestine. **571**

Disorders in Ca²⁺ metabolism may arise from abnormal levels of PTH or vitamin D.   **572**

Chapter in Perspective: Focus on Homeostasis   573

Review Exercises   **574**
Objective Questions   **574**
Essay Questions   **574**
Points to Ponder   **575**
Clinical Consideration   **575**

18   The Reproductive System   *578*

Uniqueness of the Reproductive System   579

Unique among body systems, the reproductive system does not contribute to homeostasis but exerts other important effects.   **579**
The reproductive system includes the gonads, reproductive tract, and accessory sex glands, all of which are different in males and females.   **579**
Reproductive cells each contain a half set of chromosomes.   **580**
Gametogenesis is accomplished by meiosis, resulting in genetically unique sperm and ova.   **581**
The sex of an individual is determined by the combination of sex chromosomes.   **583**
Sexual differentiation along male or female lines depends on the presence or absence of masculinizing determinants.   **583**

Male Reproductive Physiology   585

The scrotal location of the testes provides a cooler environment essential for spermatogenesis.   **585**
The testicular Leydig cells secrete masculinizing testosterone.   **585**
Spermatogenesis yields an abundance of highly specialized, mobile sperm.   **587**
Throughout their development, sperm remain intimately associated with Sertoli cells.   **589**
LH and FSH from the anterior pituitary control testosterone secretion and spermatogenesis.   **589**
GnRH activity increases at puberty.   **590**
The reproductive tract stores and concentrates sperm and increases their fertility.   **591**
The accessory sex glands contribute the bulk of the semen.   **591**
Prostaglandins are ubiquitous, locally acting chemical messengers.   **592**

Sexual Intercourse Between Males and Females   593

The male sex act is characterized by erection and ejaculation.   **593**
Erection is accomplished by penis vasocongestion.   **593**
Ejaculation includes emission and expulsion.   **595**
Orgasm and resolution complete the sexual response cycle.   **595**
Volume and sperm content of the ejaculate vary.   **595**
The female sexual cycle is similar to the male cycle.   **595**

BEYOND THE BASICS
Environmental "Estrogens": Bad News for the Reproductive System   **596**

Female Reproductive Physiology   597

Complex cycling characterizes female reproductive physiology.   **597**
The steps of gametogenesis are the same in both sexes, but the timing and outcome differ sharply.   **598**
The ovarian cycle consists of alternating follicular and luteal phases.   **599**
The follicular phase is characterized by the development of maturing follicles.   **601**
The luteal phase is characterized by the presence of a corpus luteum.   **601**
The ovarian cycle is regulated by complex hormonal interactions.   **603**
Cyclic uterine changes are caused by hormonal changes during the ovarian cycle.   **607**
Oral contraceptives prevent ovulation.   **608**
Pubertal changes in females are similar to those in males.   **608**
Menopause is unique to females.   **608**
The oviduct is the site of fertilization.   **609**
The blastocyst implants in the endometrium through the action of its trophoblastic enzymes.   **610**
The placenta is the organ of exchange between maternal and fetal blood.   **612**
Hormones secreted by the placenta play a critical role in maintaining pregnancy.   **614**
Maternal body systems respond to the increased demands of gestation.   **616**
Changes during late gestation prepare for parturition.   **616**
Scientists are closing in on the factors that trigger the onset of parturition.   **616**
Parturition is accomplished by a positive-feedback cycle.   **618**
Lactation requires multiple hormonal inputs.   **620**
Breast-feeding is advantageous to both the infant and the mother.   **621**
The end is a new beginning.   **622**

Chapter in Perspective: Focus on Homeostasis   623

Review Exercises   **623**
Objective Questions   **623**
Essay Questions   **624**
Points to Ponder   **624**
Clinical Consideration   **624**

A   The Metric System   A-1

B   A Review of Chemical Principles   A-3

Chemical Level of Organization in the Body   A-3
Atoms   A-3
Elements and atomic symbols   A-3
Compounds and molecules   A-3
Atomic number   A-3
Atomic weight   A-4
Chemical Bonds   A-4
Electron shells   A-4
Bonding characteristics of an atom and valence   A-4
Ions; ionic bonds   A-5
Covalent bonds   A-5
Nonpolar and polar molecules   A-6
Hydrogen bonds   A-7
Chemical Reactions   A-7
Balanced equations   A-7
Reversible and irreversible reactions   A-7
Catalysts; enzymes   A-8
Molecular and Formula Weight and the Mole   A-8
Solutions, Colloids, and Suspensions   A-8
Solutions   A-9
Electrolytes versus nonelectrolytes   A-9
Measures of concentration   A-9
Colloids and suspensions   A-9
Inorganic and Organic Chemicals   A-10
Distinction between inorganic and organic chemicals   A-10
Monomers and polymers   A-10
Acids, Bases, and Salts   A-10
Acids and bases   A-10
Salts; neutralization reactions   A-11
Functional Groups of Organic Molecules   A-11
Carbohydrates   A-11
Chemical composition of carbohydrates   A-11
Types of carbohydrates   A-11
Lipids   A-12
Simple lipids   A-12
Complex lipids   A-13
Proteins   A-13
Chemical composition of proteins   A-13
Peptide bonds   A-14
Levels of protein structure   A-14
Hydrolysis and denaturation   A-16
Nucleic Acids   A-16
High-Energy Biomolecules   A-17

C   Storage, Replication, and Expression of Genetic Information   A-18

Deoxyribonucleic Acid and Chromosomes   A-18
Functions of DNA   A-18
Structure of DNA   A-18
Genes in DNA   A-18
Packaging of DNA into chromosomes   A-18
Complementary Base Pairing, Replication, and Transcription   A-19
DNA replication   A-19
DNA transcription and messenger ribonucleic acid   A-20
Translation and Protein Synthesis   A-22
Triplet code; codon   A-22
Ribosomes   A-23
tRNA and anticodons   A-24
Steps of protein synthesis   A-24
Energy cost of protein synthesis   A-24
Polyribosomes   A-24
Control of gene activity and protein transcription   A-24
Cell Division   A-26
Mitosis   A-26
Meiosis   A-27
Mutations   A-27

D   The Chemistry of Acid–Base Balance   A-30

Dissociation Constants for Acids   A-30
The Logarithmic Nature of pH   A-30
Chemical Buffer Systems   A-30
Henderson–Hasselbalch Equation   A-31
Respiratory Regulation of Hydrogen Ion Concentration   A-31
Renal Regulation of Hydrogen Ion Concentration   A-32
Acid–Base Imbalances   A-34

E   Answers to End-of-Chapter Objective Questions, Points to Ponder, and Clinical Considerations   A-38

Glossary   G-1

Index   I-1

Preface

Goals, Philosophy, and Theme

Even though I started teaching physiology in the mid-1960s, today I still am awestruck at the miraculous intricacies and efficiency of body function. No machine can perform even a portion of natural body function as effectively. My goal in writing physiology textbooks is not only to help students learn about how the body works but also to share my enthusiasm for the subject matter. Most of us, even infants, have a natural curiosity about how our bodies work. When a baby first discovers it can control its own hands, it is fascinated and spends many hours manipulating them in front of its face. By capitalizing on students' natural curiosity about themselves, I try to make physiology a subject they can enjoy learning.

Even the most tantalizing subject can be difficult to comprehend if not effectively presented, however. Therefore, this book has a logical, understandable format with an emphasis on how each concept is an integral part of the entire subject. Too often, students view the components of a physiology course as isolated entities; by understanding how each component depends on the others, a student can appreciate the integrated functioning of the human body. The text focuses on the mechanisms of body function from cells to systems and is organized around the central theme of homeostasis—how the body meets changing demands while maintaining the internal constancy necessary for all cells and organs to function.

Essentials of Physiology is a carefully condensed version of my *Human Physiology: From Cells to Systems. Essentials of Physiology* is of manageable length and depth while providing scientifically sound coverage of the fundamental concepts of physiology and incorporating pedagogical features that make it interesting and comprehensible.

Because this book is intended as an introduction and, for most students, may be their only exposure to a formal physiology text, all aspects of physiology receive broad coverage. Materials were selected for inclusion on a "need-to-know" basis, so the book is not cluttered with unnecessary detail. Instead, content is restricted to relevant information needed to understand basic physiologic concepts.

No assumptions regarding prerequisite courses have been made. Since anatomy is not a prerequisite course, enough relevant anatomy is integrated within the text to make the inseparable relation between structure and function meaningful. Furthermore, new pedagogical features have been added to make this fourth edition even more approachable by students with limited background.

New information based on recent discoveries has been included in all chapters. Students can be assured of the timeliness and accuracy of the material presented. This edition is the most extensive revision yet, taking into account new discoveries in the field as well as clarifying, modifying, and simplifying as needed. Some controversial ideas and hypotheses are presented to illustrate that physiology is a dynamic, changing discipline.

This text is designed to promote understanding of the basic principles and concepts of physiology rather than memorization of details. The text is written in simple, straightforward language, and every effort has been made to ensure smooth reading through good transitions, logical reasoning, and integration of ideas throughout the text.

Text Features and Learning Aids

Implementing the homeostasis theme

A unique, easy-to-follow, pictorial homeostatic model showing the relationship among cells, systems, and homeostasis is developed in the introductory chapter. Each chapter begins with a specially tailored version of this model, accompanied by a brief description emphasizing how the body system considered in the chapter functionally fits in with the body as a whole. This opening feature orients students to the homeostatic aspects of the material that follows. At the close of each chapter, **Chapter in Perspective: Focus on Homeostasis** helps students put into perspective how the part of the body just discussed contributes to homeostasis. This closing feature, the opening homeostatic model, and the introductory comments work together to facilitate students' comprehension of the interactions and interdependency of body systems, even though each system is discussed separately.

Pedagogical illustrations

Anatomic illustrations, schematic representations, step-by-step descriptions within process-oriented figures, photographs, tables, and graphs complement and reinforce the written material. Flow diagrams are used extensively to help students integrate the written information. In the flow diagrams, lighter and darker shades of the same color denote a decrease or increase in a controlled variable, such as blood pressure or the concentration of blood glucose. Physical entities, such as body structures and chemicals, are distinguished visually from actions. Icons of physical entities are incorporated into the flow diagrams.

Also, integrated color-coded combinations of a figure with a table help students better visualize what part of the body is responsible for what activities. For example, anatomic depiction of the brain is integrated with a table of the functions of the major brain components, with each component shown in the same color in the figure and the table.

A unique feature of this book is that people depicted in the various illustrations are realistic representatives of a cross-section of humanity (they were drawn from photographs of real people). Sensitivity to various races, sexes, and ages should enable all students to identify with the material being presented.

Analogies

Many analogies and frequent references to everyday experiences are included to help students relate to the physiology concepts presented. These useful tools have been drawn in large part from my over four decades of teaching experience. Knowing which areas are likely to give students the most difficulty, I have tried to develop links that help them relate the new material to something with which they are already familiar.

Pathophysiology and clinical coverage
Another effective way to keep students' interest is to help them realize they are learning worthwhile and applicable material. Because many students using this text will have health-related careers, frequent references to pathophysiology and clinical physiology demonstrate the content's relevance to their professional goals. Clinical Note icons flag clinically relevant material, which is integrated throughout the text.

Boxed feature

An in-depth boxed feature, **Beyond the Basics**, is incorporated within each chapter. These boxes expose students to high-interest information on such diverse topics as stem cell research, acupuncture, exercise physiology, new discoveries regarding common diseases such as strokes, historical perspectives, and body responses to new environments such as those encountered in deep-sea diving.

Feedforward statements as subsection titles

Instead of traditional short topic titles for each major subsection (for example, "Heart valves"), feedforward statements alert students to the main point of the subsection to come (for example, "Pressure-operated heart valves ensure that blood flows in the right direction through the heart"). These headings also break up large concepts into smaller, more manageable pieces for the student, and as an added bonus, the listing of these headings in the **Contents** at the beginning of the book serves as a set of objectives for each chapter.

Key terms and word derivations
Key terms are defined as they appear in the text. Because physiology is laden with new vocabulary words, many of which are rather intimidating at first glance, word derivations are provided to enhance understanding of new words.

Review and Self-Evaluation Tools in the Text

The **Study Card** presents the major points of each chapter in concise, section-by-section bulleted lists, including cross-references for page numbers, figures, and tables. With this summary design students can review more efficiently by using both written and visual information to focus on the main concepts before moving on.

The **Review Exercises** at the end of each chapter include a variety of question formats for students to self-test their knowledge and application of the facts and concepts presented. A **Points to Ponder** section features thought-provoking problems that encourage students to analyze what they have learned, and the **Clinical Consideration**, a mini case history, challenges them to apply their knowledge to a patient's specific symptoms. Answers and explanations for these exercises are found in Appendix E and online, as described in the following sections.

Appendixes and glossary
The appendixes are designed for the most part to help students who need to brush up on some foundation materials or who need additional resources.

■ *Appendix A,* **The Metric System**, is a conversion table between metric measures and their English equivalents.

■ Most undergraduate physiology texts have a chapter on chemistry, yet physiology instructors rarely teach basic chemistry concepts. Knowledge of chemistry beyond that introduced in secondary schools is not required for understanding this text. Therefore, I provide instead *Appendix B,* **A Review of Chemical Principles,** as a handy reference for students who need an introduction or a brief review of basic chemistry concepts that apply to physiology.

■ Likewise, *Appendix C,* **Storage, Replication, and Expression of Genetic Information**, serves as a reference for students or as assigned material if the instructor deems appropriate. It includes a discussion of DNA and chromosomes, protein synthesis, cell division, and mutations.

■ The chemical details of acid–base balance are omitted from the text proper but are included in *Appendix D,* **The Chemistry of Acid–Base Balance**, for those students who have the background and need for a more chemically oriented approach to this topic.

■ *Appendix E,* **Answers to End-of-Chapter Objective Questions, Points to Ponder, and Clinical Considerations**, provides answers to all objective learning activities and explanations for the Points to Ponder and Clinical Consideration.

- The **Glossary,** which offers a way to review the meaning of key terminology, includes phonetic pronunciations of the entries.

New to the Fourth Edition

This edition has undergone numerous revisions to make the book as current, relevant, and accessible to students as possible. Every aspect of the text has been upgraded as the following examples illustrate. For a detailed list of all changes, contact your Cengage Learning sales representative.

Extensive new art

Over 90% of the art has been upgraded in this edition, with more three-dimensional art; many conceptually redesigned new figures to enhance student understanding; brighter, more contemporary, and more visually appealing colors; and more consistent style throughout. New to this edition, icons of physical entities are incorporated into flow diagrams to aid students in learning what structures are involved in specific actions. Also, more process-oriented figures with integrated step-by-step descriptions are provided, allowing visually oriented students to review processes through figures.

New figures to this edition include the following examples:

- Figure 5-10, Cortical pathway for speaking a word seen or heard

- Figure 6-2, Magnitude of receptor potential, frequency of action potentials in afferent fiber, and rate of neurotransmitter release at afferent terminals as a function of stimulus strength

- Figure 8-22, Arrangement of thick and thin filaments in a smooth muscle cell in relaxed and contracted states (including cellular blow ups of filament arrangement and sliding), and Figure 8-23, Activated myosin cross bridge in smooth muscle

- Figure 17-24, Location and structure of the pancreas and cell types in the islets of Langerhans

- Figure 18-10, Comparison of mitotic and meiotic divisions producing spermatozoa and eggs from germ cells

Examples of extensively revised, newly conceptualized figures to enhance understanding include the following:

- Figure 2-12, Oxidative phosphorylation at the mitochondrial inner membrane

- Figure 3-17, Symport of glucose

- Figure 4-7, Permeability changes and ion fluxes during an action potential

- Figure 6-19, Phototransduction, further retinal processing, and initiation of action potentials in the visual pathway

- Figure 9-13, Electrocardiogram waveforms in lead II and electrical status of the heart associated with each waveform

Following are examples of a new and a revised table:

- Table 7-2, Properties of Autonomic Receptor Types (new)

- Table 10-1, Features of Blood Vessels (now with new art comparing the structure of blood vessel types incorporated into the table)

Updated content

Timely material has been incorporated throughout as the following examples illustrate:

- Added current information to the boxed feature *Stem Cell Science and Tissue Engineering: The Quest to Make Defective Body Parts Like New Again* regarding induced pluripotent stem cells, organ printing, and new federal policy regarding use of embryonic stem cells (Chapter 1)

- Updated the ionic mechanism for the cardiac pacemaker potential, including the role of funny channels (Chapter 9)

- Expanded coverage of adipokines and introduced distinction between visceral fat and subcutaneous fat (Chapter 16)

- Revised discussion of pro-opiomelanocortin to reflect new understanding of differential processing of this molecule by anterior pituitary corticotropes, skin keratinocytes, hypothalamic appetite-suppressing neurons, and brain endorphin-producing neurons (Chapter 17)

- Expanded and updated presentation of the acrosome reaction and penetration of sperm through the corona radiata and zona pellucida, including the role of ZP3. Added the underlying molecular mechanism for block to polyspermy (Chapter 18)

Clearer, more concise coverage

I look at every edition with fresh eyes for opportunities to make the writing as clear, concise, and relevant for the readers as possible, as the following changes in one chapter (Chapter 3) exemplify:

- Mentioned that some drugs target ion channels, for example, Ca^{2+} blockers, and noted that more than 60 genetic mutations in channels have been linked to human diseases

- Added definitions of solution, solvent, solute, and concentration immediately prior to coverage of diffusion down concentration gradients

- Reworked the section on osmosis, osmotic pressure, and tonicity for improved clarity and flow. Added a new figure for tonicity and osmotic water movement

- Compared the similarities and differences between channels and carriers

- Further distinguished between primary and secondary active transport, moved coverage of secondary active transport from a later chapter to this chapter and expanded the discussion to include symport (cotransport) and antiport (countertransport or exchange), and extensively revised all accompanying figures

Organization

There is no ideal organization of physiologic processes into a logical sequence. In the sequence I chose, most chapters build on material presented in immediately preceding chapters, yet each chapter is designed to stand on its own, allowing the instructor flexibility in curriculum design. This flexibility is facilitated by cross-references to related material in other chapters. The cross-references let students quickly refresh their memory of material already learned or proceed, if desired, to a more in-depth coverage of a particular topic.

The general flow is from introductory background information to cells to excitable tissue (nerve and muscle) to organ systems, with logical transitions from one chapter to the next. For example, Chapter 8, "Muscle Physiology," ends with a discussion of cardiac (heart) muscle, which is carried forward in Chapter 9, "Cardiac Physiology." Even topics that seem unrelated in sequence, such as Chapter 11, "Blood and Body Defenses," and Chapter 12, "The Respiratory System," are linked together, in this case by ending Chapter 11 with a discussion of respiratory defense mechanisms.

Several organizational features warrant specific mention. The most difficult decision in organizing this text was placement of the endocrine material. There is merit in placing the chapters on the nervous and the endocrine (hormone-secreting) systems in close proximity because they are the body's two major regulatory systems. However, discussing details of the endocrine system immediately after the nervous system would disrupt the logical flow of material related to excitable tissue. In addition, the endocrine system cannot be covered in the depth its importance warrants if it is discussed before students have the background to understand this system's roles in maintaining homeostasis.

My solution to this dilemma is Chapter 4, "Principles of Neural and Hormonal Communication." This chapter introduces the underlying mechanisms of neural and hormonal action before the nervous system and specific hormones are mentioned in later chapters. It contrasts how nerve cells and endocrine cells communicate with other cells in carrying out their regulatory actions. Building on the different modes of action of nerve and endocrine cells, the last section of this chapter compares, in a general way, how the nervous and endocrine systems differ as regulatory systems. Chapter 5 then begins with the nervous system, providing a good link between Chapters 4 and 5. Chapters 5, 6, and 7 are devoted to the nervous system. Specific hormones are introduced in appropriate chapters, such as hormonal control of the heart and blood vessels in maintaining blood pressure in Chapters 9 and 10 and hormonal control of the kidneys in maintaining fluid balance in Chapters 13 and 14. The body's processing of absorbed energy-rich nutrient molecules is largely under endocrine control, providing a link from digestion (Chapter 15) and energy balance (Chapter 16) to the endocrine chapter (Chapter 17). The endocrine chapter pulls together the source, functions, and control of specific endocrine secretions and serves as a summarizing and unifying capstone for homeostatic body function. Finally, building on the hormones that control the gonads (testes and ovaries) introduced in the endocrine chapter, the last chapter, Chapter 18, diverges from the theme of homeostasis to focus on reproductive physiology.

Besides the novel handling of hormones and the endocrine system, other organizational features are unique to this book. For example, unlike other physiology texts, the skin is covered in the chapter on defense mechanisms of the body (Chapter 11), in consideration of the skin's recently recognized immune functions. Departure from traditional groupings of material in sev-

eral important instances has permitted more independent and more integrated coverage of topics that are frequently omitted or buried within chapters concerned with other subject matter. For example, a separate chapter (Chapter 14) is devoted to fluid balance and acid–base regulation, topics often tucked within the kidney chapter. Another example is the grouping of the autonomic nervous system, motor neurons, and the neuromuscular junction in an independent chapter (Chapter 7) on the efferent division of the peripheral nervous system, which serves as a link between the nervous system chapters and the muscle chapter (Chapter 8). Energy balance and temperature regulation are also grouped into an independent chapter (Chapter 16).

Although there is a rationale for covering the various aspects of physiology in the order given here, it is by no means the only logical way of presenting the topics. Because each chapter is able to stand on its own, especially with the cross-references provided, instructors can vary the sequence of presentation at their discretion. Some chapters may even be omitted, depending on the students' needs and interests and the time constraints of the course.

Ancillaries for Instructors

Human Physiology CourseMate™
Interested in a simple way to complement your text and course content with study and practice materials? Cengage Learning's Human Physiology CourseMate brings course concepts to life with interactive learning, study, and exam preparation tools that support the printed textbook. Watch student comprehension soar as your class works with the printed textbook and the textbook-specific website. The Human Physiology CourseMate goes beyond the book to deliver what you need!

CengageNOW™
CengageNOW is an online teaching and learning resource that gives you more control in less time and delivers better outcomes—NOW. CengageNOW offers all of your teaching and learning resources in one intuitive program organized around the essential activities you perform for class—lecturing, creating assignments, grading, quizzing, and tracking student progress and performance. CengageNOW provides students access to an integrated e-book, interactive tutorials, active figures, videos, stunning new animations (including 3D), and other multimedia tools that help students to get the most out of your course.

Instructor PowerPoints
Each chapter includes main points, art, and photos from the text conveniently preloaded into PowerPoint slides.

Online Instructor's Manual
The Instructor's Manual—available online—contains suggestions for using all components available with the text, in addition to source lists of learning aids, film and software resources, relevant websites, and additional organization guidance for instructors.

Electronic Test Bank

The Test Bank includes thousands of questions in a variety of formats for each text chapter. Also available in ExamView®.

Ancillaries for Students

CengageNOW™

CengageNOW is an easy-to-use online resource that helps students study in less time to get the grade they want—NOW. Class-tested and student-praised, CengageNOW offers a variety of features that support course objectives and interactive learning. Helping students to be better prepared for class and learn difficult physiology concepts, this web-based resource offers self-paced learning modules with tutorials, interactive quizzes, and animations. With a Personalized Study Plan including pre- and post-tests, animations, and interactive exercises, students can focus on difficult topics in which they need help most.

The animations help bring to life some of the physiologic processes most difficult to visualize, enhancing the understanding of complex sequences of events. Better than ever, the collection of animations has been expanded to include some new, more integrative, realistic, and technologically sophisticated animations.

Acknowledgments

I gratefully acknowledge the many people who helped with the first three editions of the *Essentials of Physiology* textbook as well as with the seven editions of the Sherwood, *Human Physiology: From Cells to Systems* textbook on which the *Essentials* version is based.

In addition to the 162 reviewers who carefully evaluated the forerunner books for accuracy, clarity, and relevance, I express sincere appreciation to the following individuals who served as reviewers for this edition:

Ahmmed Ally, Massachusetts College of Pharmacy and Health Sciences

Deborah Barry, Mountwest Community & Technical College

Linda Collins, University of Tennessee at Chattanooga

Gibril O. Fadika, Hampton University

Michael S. Finkler, Indiana University–Kokomo

Eric Hall, Rhode Island College

Dean Lauritzen, City College of San Francisco

David Thomson, Brigham Young University

Also, I am grateful to the users of the textbook who have taken time to send helpful comments.

I have been fortunate to work with a highly competent, dedicated team from Brooks/Cole. It has been a source of comfort and inspiration to know that so many people have been working diligently in so many ways to bring this book to fruition.

Yolanda Cossio, Publisher, deserves warm thanks for her vision, creative ideas, leadership, and ongoing helpfulness. Yolanda was a strong advocate for making this the best edition yet. Yolanda's decisions were guided by what is best for the instructors and students who will use the textbook. On a personal note, I appreciated her concern and caring when I had surgery during the development process of the book. Thanks also to Editorial Assistants Brandusa Radoias, Kristina Chiapella, and Joshua Taylor who trafficked paperwork and coordinated many tasks for Yolanda during the development process.

I appreciate the efforts of Developmental Editor Suzannah Alexander for facilitating the development process, which proceeded on schedule with no problems or surprises. I am especially grateful for the time she spent talking me through the steps I needed to take to submit the art manuscript entirely electronically for the first time in my over 20 years of authorship.

I am grateful for the creative insight of Brooks/Cole Senior Art Director John Walker, who oversaw the overall artistic design of the text and found the dynamic cover image that simultaneously depicts motion, strength, grace, and agility. The new art style for this edition was developed by Suzannah Alexander to ensure that the visual aspects of the text are aesthetically pleasing, consistent, contemporary, and meaningful.

The technology-enhanced learning tools in the media package were updated under the guidance of Managing Media Editor Shelley Ryan and Technology Project Manager Alex Brady. Assistant Editor Alexis Glubka oversaw the development of the multiple hard-copy components of the ancillary package, making sure it was a cohesive whole. A hearty note of gratitude is extended to all of them.

On the production side, I would like to thank Content Project Manager Michelle Clark, who closely monitored every step of the production process while simultaneously overseeing the complex production process of multiple books. I felt confident knowing that she was making sure that everything was going according to plan. I also thank Rights Acquisitions Specialist Don Schlotman for tracking down permissions for the art and other copyrighted materials incorporated in the text, an absolutely essential task. With everything finally coming together, Print Buyer Paula Vang oversaw the manufacturing process, coordinating the actual printing of the book.

No matter how well a book is conceived, produced, and printed, it would not reach its full potential as an educational tool without being efficiently and effectively marketed. Marketing Manager Tom Ziolkowski, Marketing Assistant Elizabeth Wong, and Marketing Communications Manager Linda Yip played the lead roles in marketing this text, for which I am most appreciative.

Brooks/Cole also did an outstanding job in selecting highly skilled vendors to carry out particular production tasks. First and foremost, it has been my personal and professional pleasure to work with two very capable Production Editors at Graphic World: Carol O'Connell, who smoothed out the inevitable bumps in the beginning of the production process, and Laura Sullivan, who took over midstream when Carol moved to another position and helped bring the book to conclusion without missing a beat. In their competent hands lay the responsibility of seeing that all art, typesetting, page layout, and other related details got done right and in a timely fashion.

Finally, my love and gratitude go to my family for the sacrifices in family life as this edition was being developed and produced. I want to thank my husband, children, grandchildren, and mother for their patience and understanding during the times I was working on the book instead of being there with them or for them. My husband, Peter Marshall, deserves special appreciation and recognition for assuming extra responsibilities while I was working on the book. I could not have done this, or any of the preceding books, without his help, support, and encouragement.

Thanks to all!

Lauralee Sherwood

Essentials of Physiology

FOURTH EDITION

During the minute that it will take you to read this page:

Your eyes will convert the image from this page into electrical signals (nerve impulses) that will transmit the information to your brain for processing.

Your heart will beat 70 times, pumping 5 liters (about 5 quarts) of blood to your lungs and another 5 liters to the rest of your body.

Approximately 150 million old red blood cells will die and be replaced by newly produced ones.

More than 1 liter of blood will flow through your kidneys, which will act on the blood to conserve the "wanted" materials and eliminate the "unwanted" materials in the urine. Your kidneys will produce 1 ml (about a thimbleful) of urine.

Your digestive system will be processing your last meal for transfer into your bloodstream for delivery to your cells.

Besides receiving and processing information such as visual input, your brain will provide output to your muscles to help maintain your posture, move your eyes across the page as you read, and turn the page as needed. Chemical messengers will carry signals between your nerves and muscles to trigger appropriate muscle contraction.

You will breathe in and out about 12 times, exchanging 6 liters of air between the atmosphere and your lungs.

Your cells will consume 250 ml (about a cup) of oxygen and produce 200 ml of carbon dioxide.

You will use about 2 calories of energy derived from food to support your body's "cost of living," and your contracting muscles will burn additional calories.

Introduction to Physiology and Homeostasis

CHAPTER AT A GLANCE

Introduction to Physiology
Definition of physiology
Relationship between structure and function

Levels of Organization in the Body
Cells as the basic units of life
Organizational levels of tissues, organs, systems, and organisms

Concept of Homeostasis
Significance of the internal environment
Necessity of homeostasis
Factors that are homeostatically maintained
Contributions of each body system to homeostasis

Homeostatic Control Systems
Components of a homeostatic control system

Introduction to Physiology

The activities described on the preceding page are a sampling of the processes that occur in our bodies all the time just to keep us alive. We usually take these life-sustaining activities for granted and do not really think about "what makes us tick," but that's what physiology is about. **Physiology** is the study of the functions of living things. Here, we focus on how the human body works.

Physiology focuses on mechanisms of action.

Two approaches are used to explain events that occur in the body: one emphasizing the *purpose* of a body process and the other the underlying *mechanism* by which this process occurs. In response to the question "Why do I shiver when I am cold?" one answer would be "to help my body warm up, because shivering generates heat." This approach, which explains body functions in terms of meeting a bodily need, emphasizes *why* body processes occur. Physiologists, however, explain *how* processes occur in the body. They view the body as a machine whose mechanisms of action can be explained in terms of cause-and-effect sequences of physical and chemical processes— the same types of processes that occur throughout the universe. A physiologist's explanation of shivering is that when temperature-sensitive nerve cells detect a fall in body temperature, they signal the area in the brain responsible for temperature regulation. In response, this brain area activates nerve pathways that ultimately bring about involuntary, oscillating muscle contractions (that is, shivering).

Structure and function are inseparable.

Physiology is closely related to **anatomy,** the study of the structure of the body. Physiological mechanisms are made possible by the structural design and relationships of the various body parts that carry out each of these functions. Just as the functioning of an automobile depends on the shapes, organization, and interactions of its various parts, the structure and function of the human body are inseparable. Therefore, as we tell the story of how the body works, we provide sufficient anatomic background for you to understand the function of the body part being discussed.

Levels of Organization in the Body

We now turn to how the body is structurally organized into a total functional unit, from the chemical level to the whole body (● Figure 1-1). These levels of organization make possible life as we know it.

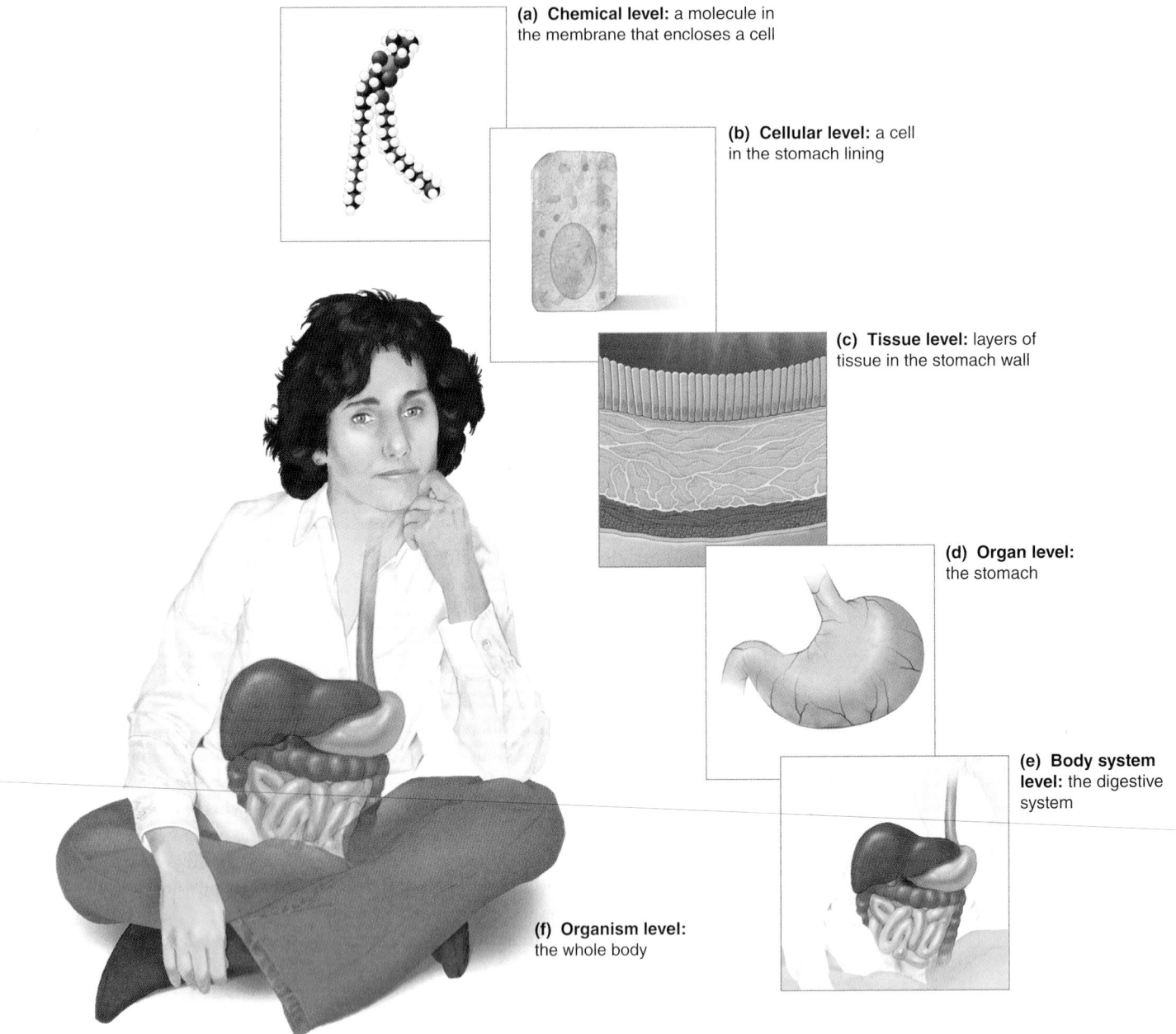

● FIGURE 1-1 Levels of organization in the body, showing an example for each level.

(a) **Chemical level:** a molecule in the membrane that encloses a cell

(b) **Cellular level:** a cell in the stomach lining

(c) **Tissue level:** layers of tissue in the stomach wall

(d) **Organ level:** the stomach

(e) **Body system level:** the digestive system

(f) **Organism level:** the whole body

The chemical level: Various atoms and molecules make up the body.

Like all matter, both living and nonliving, the human body is a combination of specific *atoms,* which are the smallest building blocks of matter. The most common atoms in the body—oxygen (O_2), carbon, hydrogen, and nitrogen—make up approximately 96% of the total body chemistry. These common atoms and a few others combine to form the *molecules* of life, such as proteins, carbohydrates, fats, and nucleic acids (genetic material, such as deoxyribonucleic acid, or DNA). These important atoms and molecules are the inanimate raw ingredients from which all living things arise. (See Appendix B for a review of this chemical level.)

The cellular level: Cells are the basic units of life.

The mere presence of a particular collection of atoms and molecules does not confer the unique characteristics of life. Instead, these nonliving chemical components must be arranged and packaged in precise ways to form a living entity. The **cell,** the fundamental unit of both structure and function in a living being, is the smallest unit capable of carrying out the processes associated with life. Cell physiology is the focus of Chapter 2.

An extremely thin, oily barrier, the *plasma membrane,* encloses the contents of each cell and controls movement of materials into and out of the cell. Thus, the cell's interior contains a combination of atoms and molecules that differs from the mixture of chemicals in the environment surrounding the cell.

Given the importance of the plasma membrane and its associated functions for carrying out life processes, Chapter 3 is devoted entirely to this structure.

Organisms are independent living entities. The simplest forms of independent life are single-celled organisms such as bacteria and amoebas. Complex multicellular organisms, such as trees and humans, are structural and functional aggregates of trillions of cells (*multi* means "many"). In the simpler multicellular forms of life—for example, a sponge—the cells of the organism are all similar. However, more complex organisms, such as humans, have many kinds of cells, such as muscle cells, nerve cells, and gland cells.

Each human organism begins when an egg and sperm unite to form a single new cell, which multiplies and forms a growing mass through myriad cell divisions. If cell multiplication were the only process involved in development, all the body cells would be essentially identical, as in the simplest multicellular life-forms. However, during development of complex multicellular organisms such as humans, each cell also **differentiates,** or becomes specialized to carry out a particular function. As a result of cell differentiation, your body is made up of about 200 specialized types of cells.

BASIC CELL FUNCTIONS All cells, whether they exist as solitary cells or as part of a multicellular organism, perform certain basic functions essential for their own survival. These basic cell functions include the following:

1. Obtaining food (nutrients) and O_2 from the environment surrounding the cell.

2. Performing chemical reactions that use nutrients and O_2 to provide energy for the cells, as follows:

$$\text{Food} + O_2 \rightarrow CO_2 + H_2O + \text{energy}$$

3. Eliminating to the cell's surrounding environment carbon dioxide (CO_2) and other by-products, or wastes, produced during these chemical reactions.

4. Synthesizing proteins and other components needed for cell structure, for growth, and for carrying out particular cell functions.

5. Largely controlling the exchange of materials between the cell and its surrounding environment.

6. Moving materials internally from one part of the cell to another, with some cells also being able to move themselves through their surrounding environment.

7. Being sensitive and responsive to changes in the surrounding environment.

8. In the case of most cells, reproducing. Some body cells, most notably nerve cells and muscle cells, lose the ability to reproduce soon after they are formed. This is the reason strokes, which result in lost nerve cells in the brain, and heart attacks, which bring about death of heart muscle cells, can be so devastating.

Cells are remarkably similar in the ways they carry out these basic functions. Thus, all cells share many common characteristics.

SPECIALIZED CELL FUNCTIONS In multicellular organisms, each cell also performs a specialized function, which is usually a modification or elaboration of a basic cell function. For example, by taking special advantage of their protein-synthesizing ability, the gland cells of the digestive system secrete digestive enzymes that break down ingested food; **enzymes** are specialized proteins that speed up particular chemical reactions in the body.

Each cell performs these specialized activities in addition to carrying on the unceasing, fundamental activities required of all cells. The basic cell functions are essential for survival of individual cells, whereas the specialized contributions and interactions among the cells of a multicellular organism are essential for survival of the whole body.

Just as a machine does not function unless all its parts are properly assembled, the cells of the body must be specifically organized to carry out the life-sustaining processes of the body as a whole, such as digestion, respiration, and circulation. Cells are progressively organized into tissues, organs, body systems, and finally the whole body.

The tissue level: Tissues are groups of cells of similar specialization.

Cells of similar structure and specialized function combine to form **tissues,** of which there are four *primary types:* muscle, nervous, epithelial, and connective (● Figure 1-2). Each tissue consists of cells of a single specialized type, along with varying amounts of extracellular material (*extra* means "outside of").

■ **Muscle tissue** consists of cells specialized for contracting, which generates tension and produces movement. There are three types of muscle tissue: *skeletal muscle,* which moves the skeleton; *cardiac muscle,* which pumps blood out of the heart; and *smooth muscle,* which controls movement of contents through hollow tubes and organs, such as movement of food through the digestive tract.

■ **Nervous tissue** consists of cells specialized for initiating and transmitting electrical impulses, sometimes over long distances. These electrical impulses act as signals that relay information from one part of the body to another. Such signals are important in communication, coordination, and control in the body. Nervous tissue is found in the brain, spinal cord, nerves, and special sense organs.

■ **Epithelial tissue** consists of cells specialized for exchanging materials between the cell and its environment. Any substance that enters or leaves the body proper must cross an epithelial barrier. Epithelial tissue is organized into two general types of structures: epithelial sheets and secretory glands. *Epithelial sheets* are layers of tightly joined cells that cover and line various parts of the body. For example, the outer layer of the skin is epithelial tissue, as is the lining of the digestive tract. In general, epithelial sheets serve as boundaries that separate the body from its surroundings and from the contents of cavities that open to the outside, such as the digestive tract lumen. (A **lumen** is the cavity within a hollow organ or tube.) Only selective transfer of materials is possible between regions separated by an epithelial barrier. The type and extent of controlled exchange vary, depending on the location and function of the epithelial tissue. For example, the skin can exchange little between the body and the surrounding environment, making it a protective barrier. By contrast, the epithelial cells lining the small intestine of the digestive tract are specialized for absorbing nutrients that have come from outside the body.

Glands are epithelial tissue derivatives specialized for secreting. **Secretion** is the release from a cell, in response to appropriate stimulation, of specific products that have been produced by the cell. There are two categories of glands: exocrine and endocrine (● Figure 1-3). **Exocrine glands** secrete through ducts to the outside of the body (or into a cavity that opens to the outside) (*exo* means "external"; *crine* means "secretion"). Examples are sweat glands and glands that secrete digestive juices. **Endocrine glands** lack ducts and release their secretory products, known as *hormones,* internally into the blood (*endo* means "internal"). For example, the pancreas secretes insulin into the blood, which transports this hormone to its sites of action throughout the body. Most cell types depend on insulin for taking up glucose (sugar).

■ **Connective tissue** is distinguished by having relatively few cells dispersed within an abundance of extracellular material. As its name implies, connective tissue connects, supports, and anchors various body parts. It includes such diverse structures as the loose connective tissue that attaches epithelial tissue to underlying structures; tendons, which attach skeletal muscles to bones; bone, which gives the body shape, support, and protection; and blood, which transports materials from one part of the body to another. Except for blood, the cells within connective tissue produce specific structural molecules that they release into the extracellular spaces between the cells. One such molecule is the rubber band–like protein fiber *elastin;* its presence facilitates the stretching and recoiling of structures such as the lungs, which alternately inflate and deflate during breathing.

Organ:
Body structure that integrates different tissues and carries out a specific function

Stomach

Epithelial tissue
protection, secretion, absorption

Connective tissue
structural support

Muscle tissue
movement

Nervous tissue
communication, coordination, control

● **FIGURE 1-2 The stomach as an organ made up of all four primary tissue types.**

Muscle, nervous, epithelial, and connective tissue are the primary tissues in a classical sense; that is, each is an integrated collection of cells with the same specialized structure and function. The term *tissue* is also often used, as in clinical medicine, to mean the aggregate of various cellular and extracellular components that make up a particular organ (for example, lung tissue or liver tissue).

The organ level: An organ is a unit made up of several tissue types.

Organs consist of two or more types of primary tissue organized together to perform a particular function or functions. The stomach is an example of an organ made up of all four pri-

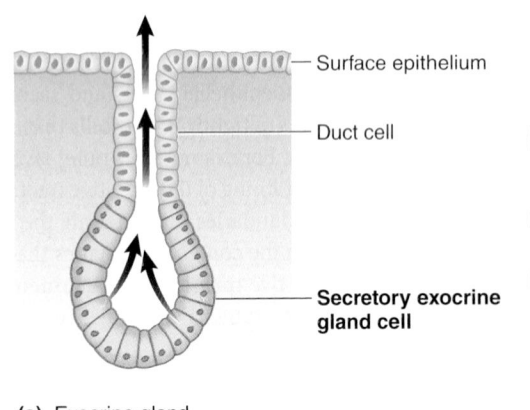
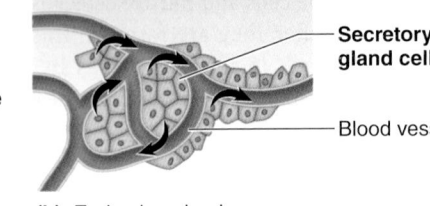

● **FIGURE 1-3 Exocrine and endocrine glands.** (a) Exocrine gland cells release their secretory product through a duct to the outside of the body (or to a cavity in communication with the outside). (b) Endocrine gland cells release their secretory product (a hormone) into the blood.

Surface epithelium

Duct cell

Secretory exocrine gland cell

(a) Exocrine gland

Surface epithelium

Secretory endocrine gland cell

Blood vessel

(b) Endocrine gland

mary tissue types (see ● Figure 1-2). The tissues of the stomach function collectively to store ingested food, move it forward into the rest of the digestive tract, and begin the digestion of protein. The stomach is lined with epithelial tissue that restricts the transfer of harsh digestive chemicals and undigested food from the stomach lumen into the blood. Epithelial gland cells in the stomach include exocrine cells, which secrete protein-digesting juices into the lumen, and endocrine cells, which secrete a hormone that helps regulate the stomach's exocrine secretion and muscle contraction. The wall of the stomach contains smooth muscle tissue, whose contractions mix ingested food with the digestive juices and push the mixture out of the stomach and into the intestine. The stomach wall also contains nervous tissue, which, along with hormones, controls muscle contraction and gland secretion. Connective tissue binds together all these various tissues.

The body system level: A body system is a collection of related organs.

Groups of organs are further organized into **body systems.** Each system is a collection of organs that perform related functions and interact to accomplish a common activity essential for survival of the whole body. For example, the digestive system consists of the mouth, pharynx (throat), esophagus, stomach, small intestine, large intestine, salivary glands, exocrine pancreas, liver, and gallbladder. These digestive organs cooperate to break food down into small nutrient molecules that can be absorbed into the blood for distribution to all cells.

The human body has 11 systems: circulatory, digestive, respiratory, urinary, skeletal, muscular, integumentary, immune, nervous, endocrine, and reproductive (● Figure 1-4). Chapters 4 through 18 cover the details of these systems.

The organism level: The body systems are packaged together into a functional whole body.

Each body system depends on the proper functioning of other systems to carry out its specific responsibilities. The whole body of a multicellular organism—a single, independently living individual—consists of the various body systems structurally and functionally linked as an entity that is separate from its surrounding environment. Thus, the body is made up of living cells organized into life-sustaining systems.

Currently, researchers are hotly pursuing several approaches for repairing or replacing tissues or organs that can no longer adequately perform vital functions because of disease, trauma, or age-related changes. (See the boxed feature on pp. 8–9, ◗ Beyond the Basics. Each chapter has a similar boxed feature that explores in greater depth high-interest, tangential information on such diverse topics as environmental impact on the body, benefits of exercise, ethical issues, discoveries regarding common diseases, and historical perspectives.)

We next focus on how the different body systems normally work together to maintain the internal conditions necessary for life.

Concept of Homeostasis

If each cell has basic survival skills, why can't the body cells live without performing specialized tasks and being organized according to specialization into systems that accomplish functions essential for the whole organism's survival? The cells in a multicellular organism cannot live and function without contributions from the other body cells because most cells are not in direct contact with the external environment. The **external environment** is the surrounding environment in which an organism lives. A single-celled organism such as an amoeba obtains nutrients and O_2 directly from its immediate external surroundings and eliminates wastes back into those surroundings. A muscle cell or any other cell in a multicellular organism has the same need for life-supporting nutrient and O_2 uptake and waste elimination, yet the muscle cell is isolated from the external environment surrounding the body. How can it make vital exchanges with the external environment with which it has no contact? The key is the presence of a watery **internal environment.** The internal environment is the fluid that surrounds the cells and through which they make life-sustaining exchanges.

Body cells are in contact with a privately maintained internal environment.

The fluid collectively contained within all body cells is called **intracellular fluid (ICF).** The fluid outside the cells is called **extracellular fluid (ECF).** Note that the ECF is outside the cells but inside the body. Thus, the ECF is the internal environment of the body: You live in the external environment; your cells live within the body's internal environment.

ECF is made up of two components: the **plasma,** the fluid portion of the blood, and the **interstitial fluid,** which surrounds and bathes the cells (*inter* means "between"; *stitial* means "that which stands") (● Figure 1-5).

No matter how remote a cell is from the external environment, it can make life-sustaining exchanges with its own surrounding fluid. In turn, particular body systems accomplish the transfer of materials between the external environment and the internal environment so that the composition of the internal environment is appropriately maintained to support the life and functioning of the cells. For example, the digestive system transfers the nutrients required by all body cells from the external environment into the plasma. Likewise, the respiratory system transfers O_2 from the external environment into the plasma. The circulatory system distributes these nutrients and O_2 throughout the body. Materials are thoroughly mixed and exchanged between the plasma and the interstitial fluid across the capillaries, the smallest and thinnest of the blood vessels. As a result, the nutrients and O_2 originally obtained from the external environment are delivered to the interstitial fluid, from which the body cells pick up these needed supplies. Similarly, wastes produced by the cells are released into the interstitial fluid, picked up by the plasma, and transported to the organs that specialize in eliminating these wastes from the internal environment to the external environment. The lungs remove CO_2 from the plasma, and the kidneys remove other wastes for elimination in the urine.

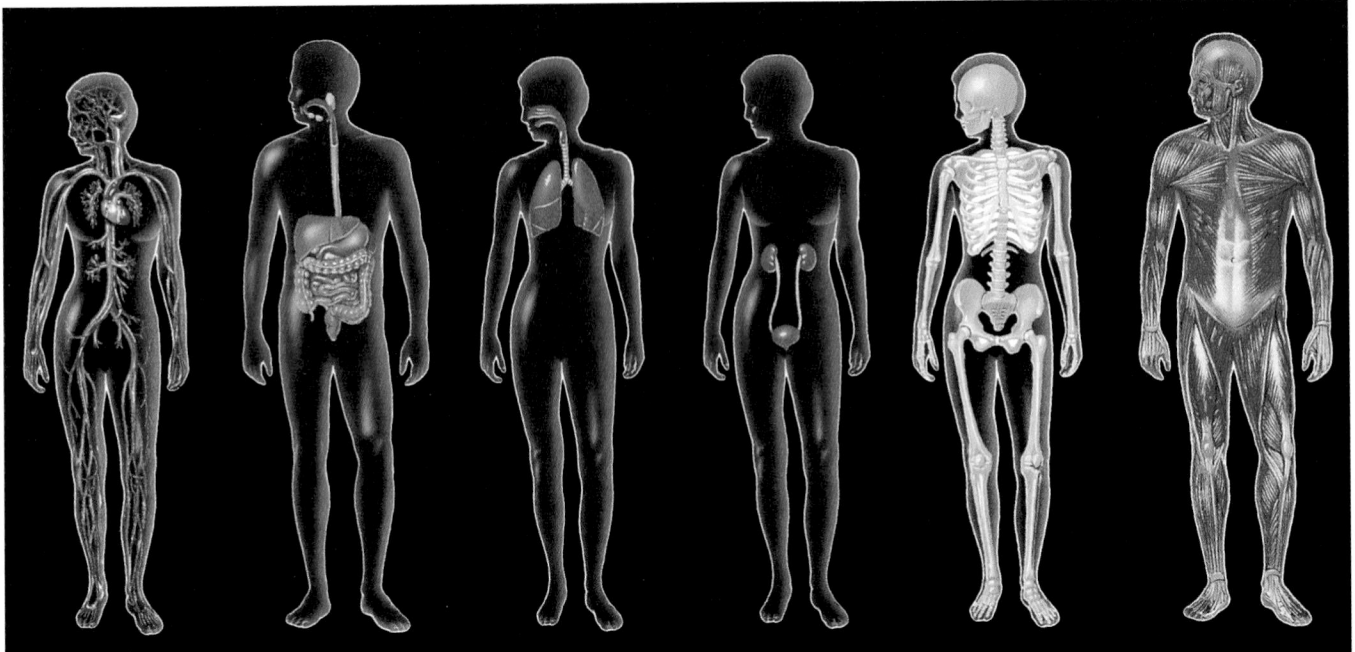

Circulatory system
heart, blood vessels, blood

Digestive system
mouth, pharynx, esophagus, stomach, small intestine, large intestine, salivary glands, exocrine pancreas, liver, gallbladder

Respiratory system
nose, pharynx, larynx, trachea, bronchi, lungs

Urinary system
kidneys, ureters, urinary bladder, urethra

Skeletal system
bones, cartilage, joints

Muscular system
skeletal muscles

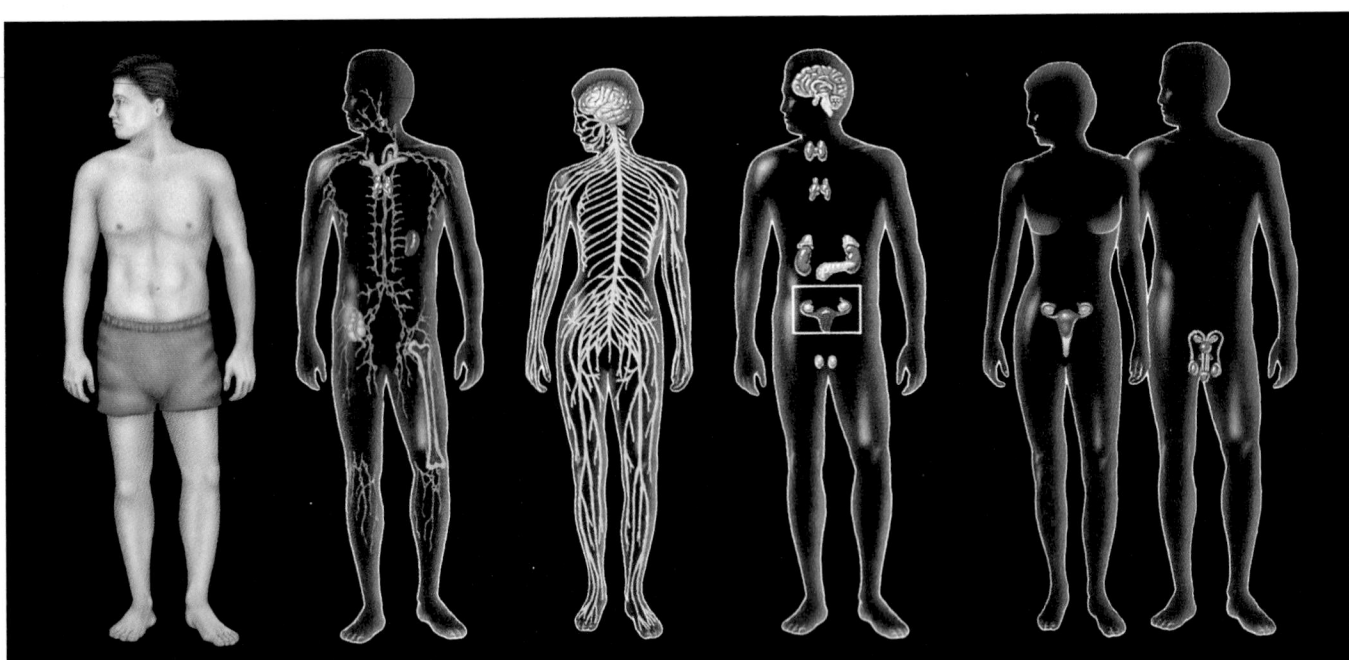

Integumentary system
skin, hair, nails

Immune system
lymph nodes, thymus, bone marrow, tonsils, adenoids, spleen, appendix, and, not shown, white blood cells, gut-associated lymphoid tissue

Nervous system
brain, spinal cord, peripheral nerves, and, not shown, special sense organs

Endocrine system
all hormone-secreting tissues, including hypothalamus, pituitary, thyroid, adrenals, endocrine pancreas, gonads, kidneys, pineal, thymus, and, not shown, parathyroids, intestine, heart, skin, adipose tissue

Reproductive system
Male: testes, penis, prostate gland, seminal vesicles, bulbourethral glands, associated ducts

Female: ovaries, oviducts, uterus, vagina, breasts

● **FIGURE 1-4 Components of the body systems.**

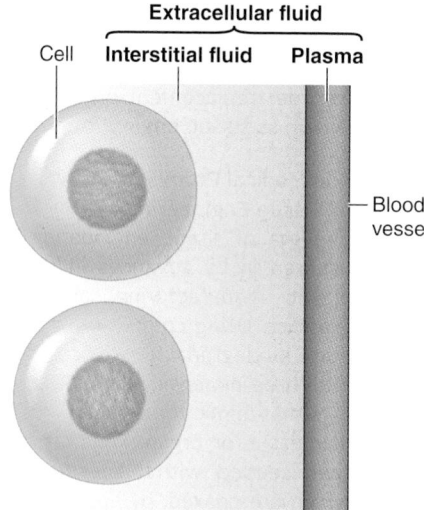

● **FIGURE 1-5 Components of the extracellular fluid (internal environment).**

Thus, a body cell takes in essential nutrients from its watery surroundings and eliminates wastes into these same surroundings, just as an amoeba does. The main difference is that each body cell must help maintain the composition of the internal environment so that this fluid continuously remains suitable to support the existence of all body cells. In contrast, an amoeba does nothing to regulate its surroundings.

Body systems maintain homeostasis, a dynamic steady state in the internal environment.

Body cells can live and function only when the ECF is compatible with their survival; thus, the chemical composition and physical state of this internal environment must be maintained within narrow limits. As cells take up nutrients and O_2 from the internal environment, these essential materials must constantly be replenished. Likewise, wastes must constantly be removed from the internal environment so that they do not reach toxic levels. Other aspects of the internal environment important for maintaining life, such as temperature, also must be kept relatively constant. Maintenance of a relatively stable internal environment is termed **homeostasis** (*homeo* means "the same"; *stasis* means "to stand or stay").

The functions performed by each body system contribute to homeostasis, thereby maintaining within the body the environment required for the survival and function of all cells. Cells, in turn, make up body systems. This is the central theme of physiology and of this book: *Homeostasis is essential for the survival of each cell, and each cell, through its specialized activities as part of a body system, helps maintain the internal environment shared by all cells* (● Figure 1-6).

The internal environment must be kept relatively stable, but this does not mean that its composition, temperature, and other characteristics are absolutely unchanging. Both external and internal factors continuously threaten to disrupt homeostasis. When any factor starts to move the internal environment away from optimal conditions, the body systems initiate appropriate counterreactions to minimize the change. For example, exposure to a cold environmental temperature (an external factor) tends to reduce the body's internal temperature. In response, the temperature control center in the brain initiates compensatory measures, such as shivering, to raise body temperature to normal. By contrast, production of extra heat by working muscles during exercise (an internal factor) tends to raise the body's internal temperature. In response, the temperature control center brings about sweating and other compensatory measures to reduce body temperature to normal.

Thus, homeostasis is not a rigid, fixed state but a dynamic steady state in which the changes that do occur are minimized by compensatory physiological responses. The term *dynamic* refers to each homeostatically regulated factor being marked by continuous change, whereas *steady state* implies that these changes do not deviate far from a constant, or steady, level. This situation is comparable to the minor steering adjustments you make as you drive a car along a straight stretch of highway. Small fluctuations around the optimal level for each factor in the internal environment are normally kept, by carefully regulated mechanisms, within the narrow limits compatible with life.

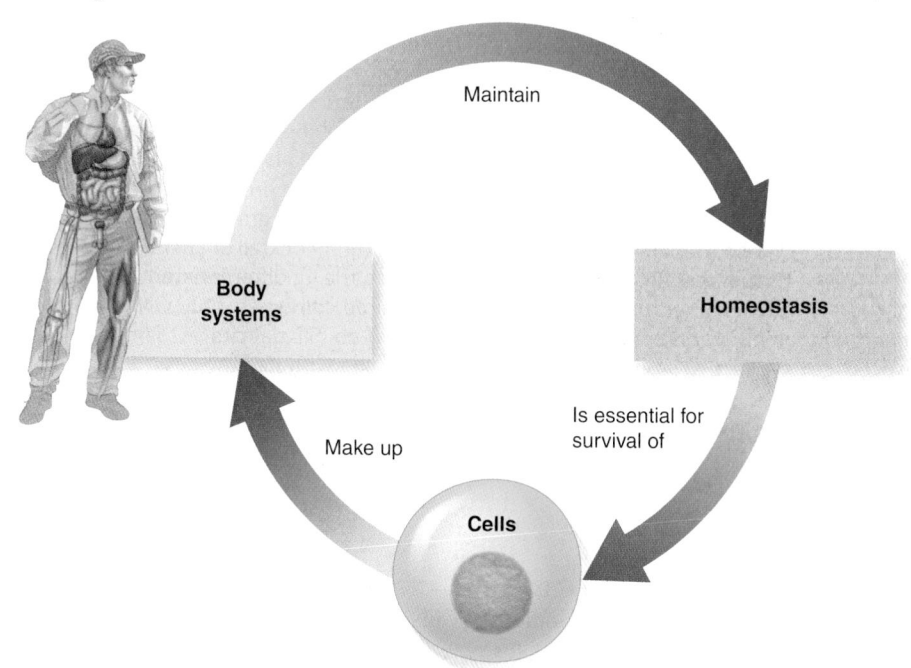

● **FIGURE 1-6 Interdependent relationship of cells, body systems, and homeostasis.** Homeostasis is essential for the survival of cells, cells make up body systems, and body systems maintain homeostasis. This relationship serves as the foundation for modern-day physiology.

Beyond the Basics

Stem-Cell Science and Tissue Engineering: The Quest to Make Defective Body Parts Like New Again

Liver failure, stroke, paralyzing spinal-cord injury, diabetes mellitus, damaged heart muscle, arthritis, extensive burns, a cancerous breast, an arm mangled in an accident: Although our bodies are remarkable and normally serve us well, sometimes a body part is defective, injured beyond repair, or lost in such situations. In addition to the loss of quality of life for affected individuals, the cost of treating patients with lost, permanently damaged, or failing organs accounts for about half of the total health-care expenditures in the United States. Ideally, when the body suffers an irreparable loss, new, permanent replacement parts would be substituted to restore normal function and appearance. Fortunately, this possibility is moving rapidly from the realm of science fiction to the reality of scientific progress.

The Medical Promise of Stem Cells

Stem cells offer exciting medical promise for repairing or replacing organs that are diseased, damaged, or worn out. **Stem cells** are versatile cells that are not specialized for a specific function but can divide to give rise to highly specialized cells while maintaining a supply of new stem cells. Two categories of stem cells are being explored: embryonic stem cells and tissue-specific stem cells from adults. **Embryonic stem cells (ESCs)** result from the early divisions of a fertilized egg. These undifferentiated cells ultimately give rise to all mature, specialized cells of the body, while simultaneously self-renewing. ESCs are *pluripotent,* meaning they have the potential to generate any cell type in the body if given the appropriate cues.

During development, the undifferentiated ESCs give rise to many partially differentiated **tissue-specific stem cells,** each of which becomes committed to generating the highly differentiated, specialized cell types that compose a particular tissue. For example, tissue-specific muscle stem cells give rise to specialized muscle cells. Some tissue-specific stem cells remain in adult tissues, where they serve as a continual source of new specialized cells to maintain or repair structure and function in that particular tissue. Tissue-specific stem cells have even been found in adult brain and muscle tissue. Even though mature nerve and muscle cells cannot reproduce themselves, to a limited extent, adult brains and muscles can grow new cells throughout life by means of these persisting stem cells. However, this process is too slow to keep pace with major losses, as in a stroke or heart attack. Some investigators are searching for drugs that might spur a person's own tissue-specific stem cells into increased action to make up for damage or loss of that tissue—a feat that is not currently feasible.

More hope is pinned on nurturing stem cells outside the body for possible transplant into the body. In 1998, for the first time, researchers succeeded in isolating ESCs and maintaining them indefinitely in an undifferentiated state in culture. With **cell culture,** cells isolated from a living organism continue to thrive and reproduce in laboratory dishes when supplied with appropriate nutrients and supportive materials.

The medical promise of ESCs lies in their potential to serve as an all-purpose material that can be coaxed into whatever cell types are needed to patch up the body. Studies in the last decade demonstrate that these cells have the ability to differentiate into particular cells when exposed to the appropriate chemical signals. As scientists gradually learn to prepare the right cocktail of chemical signals to direct the undifferentiated cells into the desired cell types, they will have the potential to fill deficits in damaged or dead tissue with healthy cells. Scientists even foresee the ability to grow customized tissues and eventually whole, made-to-order replacement organs, a process known as **tissue engineering.**

The Medical Promise of Tissue Engineering

The era of tissue engineering is being ushered in by advances in cell biology, plastic manufacturing, and computer graphics. Using computer-aided designs, pure, biodegradable plastics are shaped into three-dimensional molds or scaffoldings that mimic the structure of a particular tissue or organ. The plastic mold is then "seeded" with the desired cell types, which are coaxed, by applying appropriate nourishing and stimulatory chemicals, into multiplying and assembling into the desired body part. After the plastic scaffolding dissolves, only the newly generated tissue remains, ready to be implanted into a patient as a permanent, living replacement part.

More recently, some investigators are experimenting with *organ printing.* Based on the principle used in desktop printers, organ printing involves computer-aided layer-by-layer deposition of "biological ink." Biological ink consists of cells, scaffold materials, and supportive growth factors that are simultaneously printed in thin layers in a highly organized pattern based on the anatomy of the organ under construction. Fusion of these living layers forms a three-dimensional structure that mimics the body part the printed organ is designed to replace.

What about the source of cells to seed the plastic mold or print the organ? The immune system is programmed to attack foreign cells, such as invading bacteria or cells transplanted into the body from another individual. Such an attack brings about rejection of transplanted cells unless the transplant recipient is treated with *immunosuppressive drugs* (drugs that suppress the immune system's attack on the transplanted material). An unfortunate side effect of these drugs is the

---

HOMEOSTATICALLY REGULATED FACTORS Many factors of the internal environment must be homeostatically maintained. They include the following:

1. *Concentration of nutrients.* Cells need a constant supply of nutrient molecules for energy production. Energy, in turn, is needed to support life-sustaining and specialized cell activities.

2. *Concentration of O_2 and CO_2.* Cells need O_2 to carry out energy-yielding chemical reactions. The CO_2 produced during these reactions must be removed so that acid-forming CO_2 does not increase the acidity of the internal environment.

reduced ability of the patient's immune system to defend against potential disease-causing bacteria and viruses. To prevent rejection by the immune system and avoid the necessity of lifelong immunosuppressive drugs, tissue engineers could use appropriate specialized cells harvested from the recipient if these cells were available. However, because of the very need for a replacement part, the patient often does not have any appropriate cells for seeding or printing the replacement. This is what makes ESCs potentially so exciting. Through genetic engineering, these stem cells could be converted into "universal" seed cells that would be immunologically acceptable to any recipient; that is, they could be genetically programmed to not be rejected by any body.

Here are some of the tissue engineers' early accomplishments and future predictions:

- Engineered skin patches are being used to treat victims of severe burns.
- Laboratory-grown cartilage and bone graft substitutes are already in use.
- Lab-grown bladders were the first organs successfully implanted in humans.
- Heart-muscle patches are being developed for repairing damaged hearts.
- Progress has been made on building artificial heart valves and teeth.
- Tissue-engineered scaffolding to promote nerve regeneration is being tested in animals.
- Progress has been made on growing two complicated organs, the liver and the pancreas.
- Engineered joints will be used as living, more satisfactory alternatives to the plastic and metal devices used as replacements today.
- Ultimately, complex body parts such as arms and hands will be produced in the laboratory for attachment as needed.

Tissue engineering thus holds the promise that damaged body parts can be replaced with the best alternative, a laboratory-grown version of "the real thing."

Ethical Concerns and Political Issues

Despite this potential, ESC research is fraught with controversy because of the source of these cells: They are isolated from discarded embryos from abortion clinics and in-vitro fertility ("test-tube baby") clinics. Opponents of using ESCs are morally and ethically concerned because embryos are destroyed in the process of harvesting these cells. Proponents argue that these embryos were destined to be destroyed anyway—a decision already made by the parents of the embryos—and that these stem cells have great potential for alleviating human suffering. Thus, ESC science has become inextricably linked with stem-cell politics as public policy makers, scientists, and bioethicists attempt to balance a host of ethical issues against the tremendous potential clinical application of ESC research.

Until U.S. President Barack Obama took office, federal policy prohibited use of public funding to support research involving human embryos, so the scientists who isolated cultured ESCs relied on private money. During the 2009 election, where a candidate stood on ESC science became a hot campaign issue. One of the first directives newly elected President Obama made was to permit federal support for ESC research.

The Search for Noncontroversial Stem Cells

Some researchers have been searching for alternative ways to obtain stem cells. Some are exploring the possibility of using tissue-specific stem cells from adult tissues as a substitute for pluripotent ESCs. Until recently, most investigators believed these adult stem cells could give rise only to the specialized cells of a particular tissue. However, although these partially differentiated adult stem cells do not have the complete developmental potential of ESCs, they have been coaxed into producing a wider variety of cells than originally thought possible. To name a few examples, provided the right supportive environment, stem cells from the brain have given rise to blood cells, bone-marrow stem cells to liver and nerve cells, and fat-tissue stem cells to bone, cartilage, and muscle cells. Thus, researchers may be able to tap into the more limited but still versatile developmental potential of adult tissue–specific stem cells. Although ESCs hold greater potential for developing treatments for a broader range of diseases, adult stem cells are more accessible than ESCs, and their use is not controversial. For example, researchers dream of being able to take fat stem cells from a person and transform them into a needed replacement knee joint. However, interest in these cells is dwindling because they have failed to live up to expectations in recent scientific studies.

Long-running political setbacks have inspired still other scientists to search for new ways to obtain the more versatile ESCs for culturing new cell lines without destroying embryos. For example, one group of researchers has successfully turned back the clock on adult mouse skin cells, converting them to their embryonic state, by inserting key regulatory genes active only in early embryos. These reprogrammed cells, called **induced pluripotent stem cells (iPSCs),** have the potential to differentiate into any cell type in the body. By using iPSCs from a person's own body, scientists could manipulate these patient-specific, genetically matched cells for treating the individual, thus avoiding the issue of transplant rejection. Currently one big problem precluding the use of iPSCs is that the viruses used to insert the genes can cause cancer. Researchers are now looking for safer ways to shunt adult cells back to their embryonic state.

Whatever the source of the cells, stem-cell research promises to revolutionize medicine. According to the Centers for Disease Control's National Center for Health Statistics, an estimated 3000 Americans die every day from conditions that may in the future be treatable with stem cell derivatives.

---

3. *Concentration of waste products.* The end products of some chemical reactions have a toxic effect on body cells if these wastes are allowed to accumulate.

4. *pH.* Changes in the pH (relative amount of acid; see pp. 453 and A-30) of the ECF adversely affect nerve cell function and wreak havoc with the enzyme activity of all cells.

5. *Concentrations of water, salt, and other electrolytes.* Because the relative concentrations of salt (NaCl) and water in the ECF influence how much water enters or leaves the cells, these concentrations are carefully regulated to maintain the proper volume of the cells. Cells do not function normally when they are swollen or shrunken. Other electrolytes (chemicals that form

ions in solution and conduct electricity; see pp. A-5 and A-9) perform a variety of vital functions. For example, the rhythmic beating of the heart depends on a relatively constant concentration of potassium (K^+) in the ECF.

6. *Volume and pressure.* The circulating component of the internal environment, the plasma, must be maintained at adequate volume and blood pressure to ensure bodywide distribution of this important link between the external environment and the cells.

7. *Temperature.* Body cells function best within a narrow temperature range. If cells are too cold, their functions slow down too much; if they get too hot, their structural and enzymatic proteins are impaired or destroyed.

BODY SYSTEM CONTRIBUTIONS TO HOMEOSTASIS The 11 body systems contribute to homeostasis in the following important ways (● Figure 1-7):

1. The *circulatory system* (heart, blood vessels, and blood) transports materials such as nutrients, O_2, CO_2, wastes, electrolytes, and hormones from one part of the body to another.

2. The *digestive system* (mouth, esophagus, stomach, intestines, and related organs) breaks down dietary food into small nutrient molecules that can be absorbed into the plasma for distribution to the body cells. It also transfers water and electrolytes from the external environment into the internal environment. It eliminates undigested food residues to the external environment in the feces.

3. The *respiratory system* (lungs and major airways) gets O_2 from and eliminates CO_2 to the external environment. By adjusting the rate of removal of acid-forming CO_2, the respiratory system is also important in maintaining the proper pH of the internal environment.

4. The *urinary system* (kidneys and associated "plumbing") removes excess water, salt, acid, and other electrolytes from the plasma and eliminates them in the urine, along with waste products other than CO_2.

5. The *skeletal system* (bones and joints) provides support and protection for the soft tissues and organs. It also serves as a storage reservoir for calcium (Ca^{2+}), an electrolyte whose plasma concentration must be maintained within narrow limits. Together with the muscular system, the skeletal system enables the body and its parts to move. Furthermore, the bone marrow—the soft interior portion of some types of bone—is the ultimate source of all blood cells.

6. The *muscular system* (skeletal muscles) moves the bones to which the skeletal muscles are attached. From a purely homeostatic view, this system enables a person to move toward food or away from harm. Furthermore, the heat generated by muscle contraction helps maintain body temperature. In addition, because skeletal muscles are under voluntary control, a person can use them to accomplish myriad other movements by choice. These movements, which range from the fine motor skills required for delicate needlework to the powerful movements involved in weight lifting, are not necessarily directed toward maintaining homeostasis.

7. The *integumentary system* (skin and related structures) serves as an outer protective barrier that prevents internal fluid from being lost from the body and foreign microorganisms from entering. This system is also important in regulating body temperature. The amount of heat lost from the body surface to the external environment can be adjusted by controlling sweat production and by regulating the flow of warm blood through the skin.

8. The *immune system* (white blood cells and lymphoid organs) defends against foreign invaders such as bacteria and viruses and against body cells that have become cancerous. It also paves the way for repairing or replacing injured or worn-out cells.

9. The *nervous system* (brain, spinal cord, nerves, and sense organs) is one of the body's two major regulatory systems. In general, it controls and coordinates body activities that require swift responses. It is especially important in detecting changes in the external environment and initiating reactions to them. Furthermore, it is responsible for higher functions that are not entirely directed toward maintaining homeostasis, such as consciousness, memory, and creativity.

10. The *endocrine system* (all hormone-secreting glands) is the other major regulatory system. In contrast to the nervous system, the endocrine system in general regulates activities that require duration rather than speed, such as growth. It is especially important in controlling the blood concentration of nutrients and, by adjusting kidney function, controlling the volume and electrolyte composition of the ECF.

11. The *reproductive system* (male and female gonads and related organs) is not essential for homeostasis and therefore is not essential for survival of the individual. It is essential, however, for perpetuating the species.

As we examine each of these systems in greater detail, always keep in mind that the body is a coordinated whole even though each system provides its own special contributions. It is easy to forget that all body parts actually fit together into a functioning, interdependent whole body. Accordingly, each chapter begins with a figure and discussion that focus on how the body system to be described fits into the body as a whole. In addition, each chapter ends with a brief review of the homeostatic contributions of the body system. As a further tool to help you keep track of how all the pieces fit together, ● Figure 1-7 is duplicated on the inside front cover as a handy reference.

Also be aware that the functioning whole is greater than the sum of its separate parts. Through specialization, cooperation, and interdependence, cells combine to form an integrated, unique, single living organism with more diverse and complex capabilities than are possessed by any of the cells that make it up. For humans, these capabilities go far beyond the processes needed to maintain life. A cell, or even a random combination of cells, obviously cannot create an artistic masterpiece or design a spacecraft, but body cells working together permit those capabilities in an individual.

Now that you have learned what homeostasis is and how the functions of different body systems maintain it, let us look at the regulatory mechanisms by which the body reacts to changes and controls the internal environment.

Homeostatic Control Systems

A **homeostatic control system** is a functionally interconnected network of body components that operate to maintain a given factor in the internal environment relatively constant around an optimal level. To maintain homeostasis, the control system must be able to (1) detect deviations from normal in the internal environmental factor that needs to be held within narrow limits, (2) integrate this information with any other relevant information, and (3) make appropriate adjustments in the activity of the body parts responsible for restoring this factor to its desired value.

Homeostatic control systems may operate locally or bodywide.

Homeostatic control systems can be grouped into two classes—intrinsic and extrinsic controls. **Intrinsic,** or **local, controls** are built into or are inherent in an organ (*intrinsic* means "within"). For example, as an exercising skeletal muscle rapidly uses up O_2 to generate energy to support its contractile activity, the O_2 concentration within the muscle falls. This local chemical change acts directly on the smooth muscle in the walls of the blood vessels supplying the exercising muscle, causing the smooth muscle to relax so that the vessels dilate, or open widely. As a result, increased blood flows through the dilated vessels into the exercising muscle, bringing in more O_2. This local mechanism helps maintain an optimal level of O_2 in the fluid immediately around the exercising muscle's cells.

Most factors in the internal environment are maintained, however, by **extrinsic,** or **systemic, controls,** which are regulatory mechanisms initiated outside an organ to alter the organ's activity (*extrinsic* means "outside of"). Extrinsic control of the organs and body systems is accomplished by the nervous and endocrine systems, the two major regulatory systems. Extrinsic control permits coordinated regulation of several organs toward a common goal; in contrast, intrinsic controls serve only the organ in which they occur. Coordinated, overall regulatory mechanisms are crucial for maintaining the dynamic steady state in the internal environment as a whole. For example, to restore blood pressure to the proper level when it falls too low, the nervous system acts simultaneously on the heart and blood vessels throughout the body to increase blood pressure to normal.

Negative feedback opposes an initial change and is widely used to maintain homeostasis.

To stabilize physiological factors being regulated, homeostatic control mechanisms operate primarily on the principle of negative feedback to resist change. In **negative feedback,** a change in a homeostatically controlled factor triggers a response that seeks to restore the factor to normal by moving the factor in the opposite direction of its initial change. That is, a corrective adjustment opposes the original deviation from the normal desired level.

A common example of negative feedback is control of room temperature. Room temperature is a **controlled variable,** a factor that can vary but is held within a narrow range by a control system. In our example, the control system includes a thermostat, a furnace, and all their electrical connections. The room temperature is determined by the activity of the furnace, a heat source that can be turned on or off. To switch on or off appropriately, the control system as a whole must "know" what the *actual* room temperature is, "compare" it with the *desired* room temperature, and "adjust" the output of the furnace to bring the actual temperature to the desired level. A thermometer in the thermostat provides information about the actual room temperature. The thermometer is the **sensor,** which monitors the magnitude of the controlled variable. The sensor typically converts the original information regarding a change into a "language" the control system can "understand." For example, the thermometer converts the magnitude of the air temperature into electrical impulses. This message serves as the input into the control system. The thermostat setting provides the desired temperature level, or **set point.** The thermostat acts as an **integrator,** or **control center:** It compares the sensor's input with the set point and adjusts the heat output of the furnace to bring about the appropriate response to oppose a deviation from the set point. The furnace is the **effector,** the component of the control system commanded to bring about the desired effect. These general components of a negative-feedback control system are summarized in ● Figure 1-8a. Carefully examine this figure and its key; the symbols and conventions introduced here are used in comparable flow diagrams throughout the text.

Let us look at a typical negative-feedback loop. For example, if the room temperature falls below the set point because it is cold outside, the thermostat, through connecting circuitry, activates the furnace, which produces heat to raise the room temperature (● Figure 1-8b). Once the room temperature reaches the set point, the thermometer no longer detects a deviation from that point. As a result, the activating mechanism in the thermostat and the furnace are switched off. Thus, the heat from the furnace counteracts, or is "negative" to, the original fall in temperature. If the heat-generating pathway were not shut off once the target temperature was reached, heat production would continue and the room would get hotter and hotter. Overshooting the set point does not occur, because the heat "feeds back" to shut off the thermostat that triggered its output. Thus, a negative-feedback control system detects a change away from the ideal value in a controlled variable, initiates mechanisms to correct the situation, and then shuts itself off. In this way, the controlled variable does not drift too far above or below the set point.

What if the original deviation is a rise in room temperature above the set point because it is hot outside? A heat-producing furnace is of no use in returning the room temperature to the desired level. An opposing control system involving an air conditioner is needed to reduce the room temperature. In this case, the thermostat, through connecting circuitry, activates the air conditioner, which cools the room air, the opposite effect from that of the furnace. In negative-feedback fashion, once the set

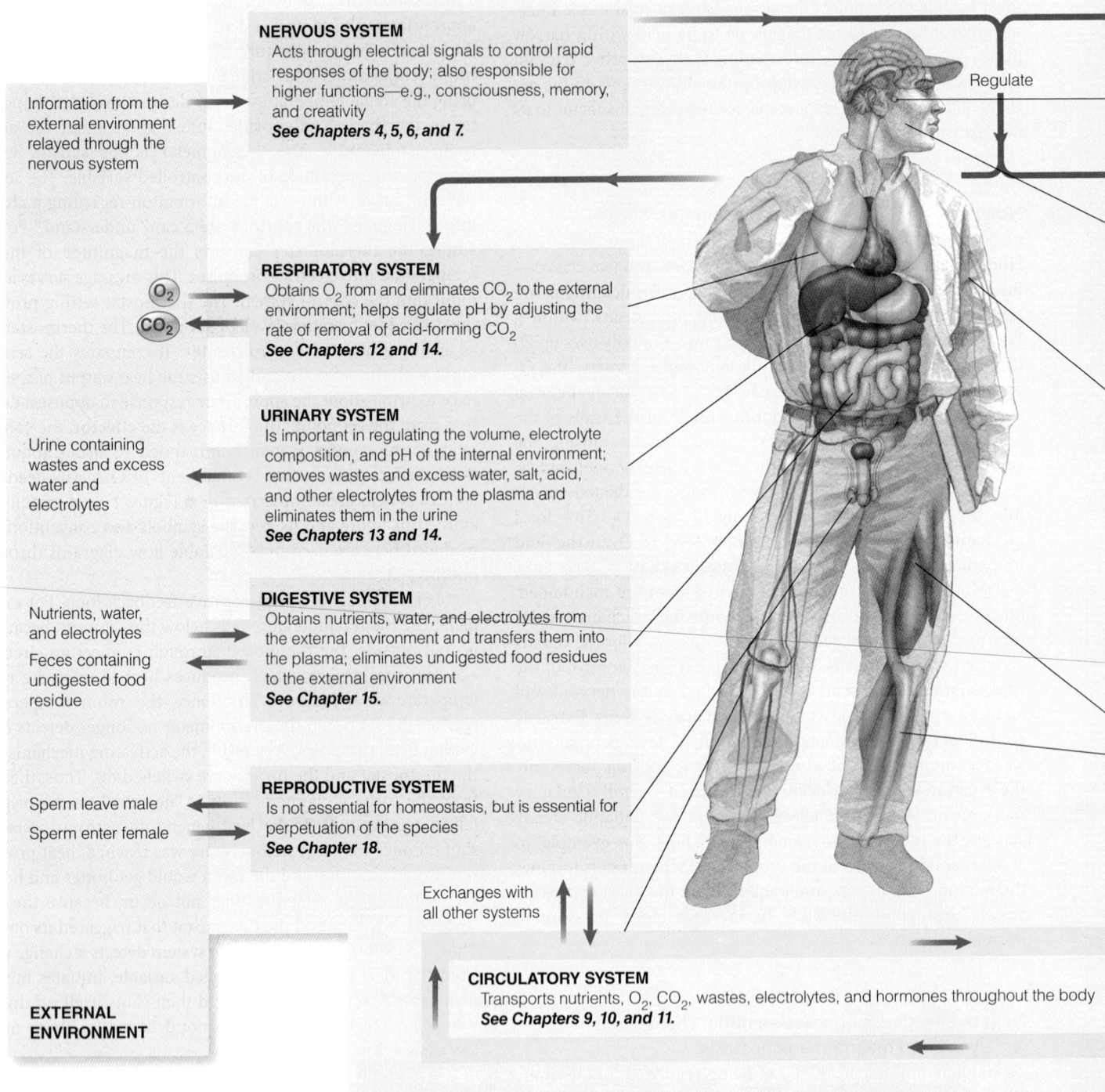

BODY SYSTEMS
Made up of cells organized according to specialization to maintain homeostasis
See Chapter 1.

NERVOUS SYSTEM
Acts through electrical signals to control rapid responses of the body; also responsible for higher functions—e.g., consciousness, memory, and creativity
See Chapters 4, 5, 6, and 7.

Information from the external environment relayed through the nervous system

Regulate

O_2
CO_2

RESPIRATORY SYSTEM
Obtains O_2 from and eliminates CO_2 to the external environment; helps regulate pH by adjusting the rate of removal of acid-forming CO_2
See Chapters 12 and 14.

URINARY SYSTEM
Is important in regulating the volume, electrolyte composition, and pH of the internal environment; removes wastes and excess water, salt, acid, and other electrolytes from the plasma and eliminates them in the urine
See Chapters 13 and 14.

Urine containing wastes and excess water and electrolytes

DIGESTIVE SYSTEM
Obtains nutrients, water, and electrolytes from the external environment and transfers them into the plasma; eliminates undigested food residues to the external environment
See Chapter 15.

Nutrients, water, and electrolytes

Feces containing undigested food residue

REPRODUCTIVE SYSTEM
Is not essential for homeostasis, but is essential for perpetuation of the species
See Chapter 18.

Sperm leave male

Sperm enter female

Exchanges with all other systems

EXTERNAL ENVIRONMENT

CIRCULATORY SYSTEM
Transports nutrients, O_2, CO_2, wastes, electrolytes, and hormones throughout the body
See Chapters 9, 10, and 11.

● **FIGURE 1-7 Role of the body systems in maintaining homeostasis.**

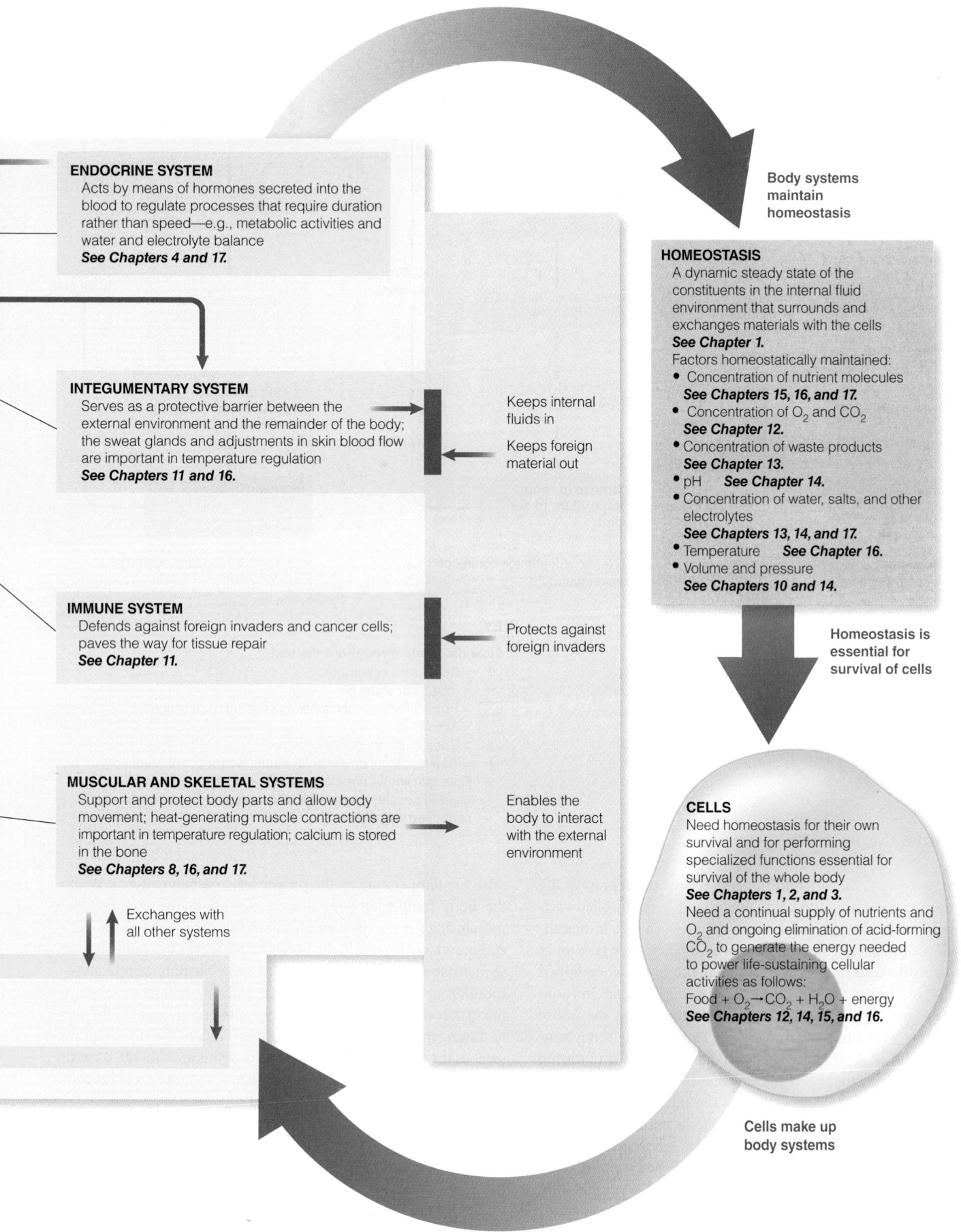

ENDOCRINE SYSTEM

Acts by means of hormones secreted into the blood to regulate processes that require duration rather than speed—e.g., metabolic activities and water and electrolyte balance
See Chapters 4 and 17.

INTEGUMENTARY SYSTEM

Serves as a protective barrier between the external environment and the remainder of the body; the sweat glands and adjustments in skin blood flow are important in temperature regulation
See Chapters 11 and 16.

Keeps internal fluids in

Keeps foreign material out

IMMUNE SYSTEM

Defends against foreign invaders and cancer cells; paves the way for tissue repair
See Chapter 11.

Protects against foreign invaders

MUSCULAR AND SKELETAL SYSTEMS

Support and protect body parts and allow body movement; heat-generating muscle contractions are important in temperature regulation; calcium is stored in the bone
See Chapters 8, 16, and 17.

Enables the body to interact with the external environment

Exchanges with all other systems

Body systems maintain homeostasis

HOMEOSTASIS

A dynamic steady state of the constituents in the internal fluid environment that surrounds and exchanges materials with the cells
See Chapter 1.
Factors homeostatically maintained:
- Concentration of nutrient molecules
  See Chapters 15, 16, and 17.
- Concentration of O_2 and CO_2
  See Chapter 12.
- Concentration of waste products
  See Chapter 13.
- pH   *See Chapter 14.*
- Concentration of water, salts, and other electrolytes
  See Chapters 13, 14, and 17.
- Temperature   *See Chapter 16.*
- Volume and pressure
  See Chapters 10 and 14.

Homeostasis is essential for survival of cells

CELLS

Need homeostasis for their own survival and for performing specialized functions essential for survival of the whole body
See Chapters 1, 2, and 3.
Need a continual supply of nutrients and O_2 and ongoing elimination of acid-forming CO_2 to generate the energy needed to power life-sustaining cellular activities as follows:
Food + $O_2 \rightarrow CO_2 + H_2O$ + energy
See Chapters 12, 14, 15, and 16.

Cells make up body systems

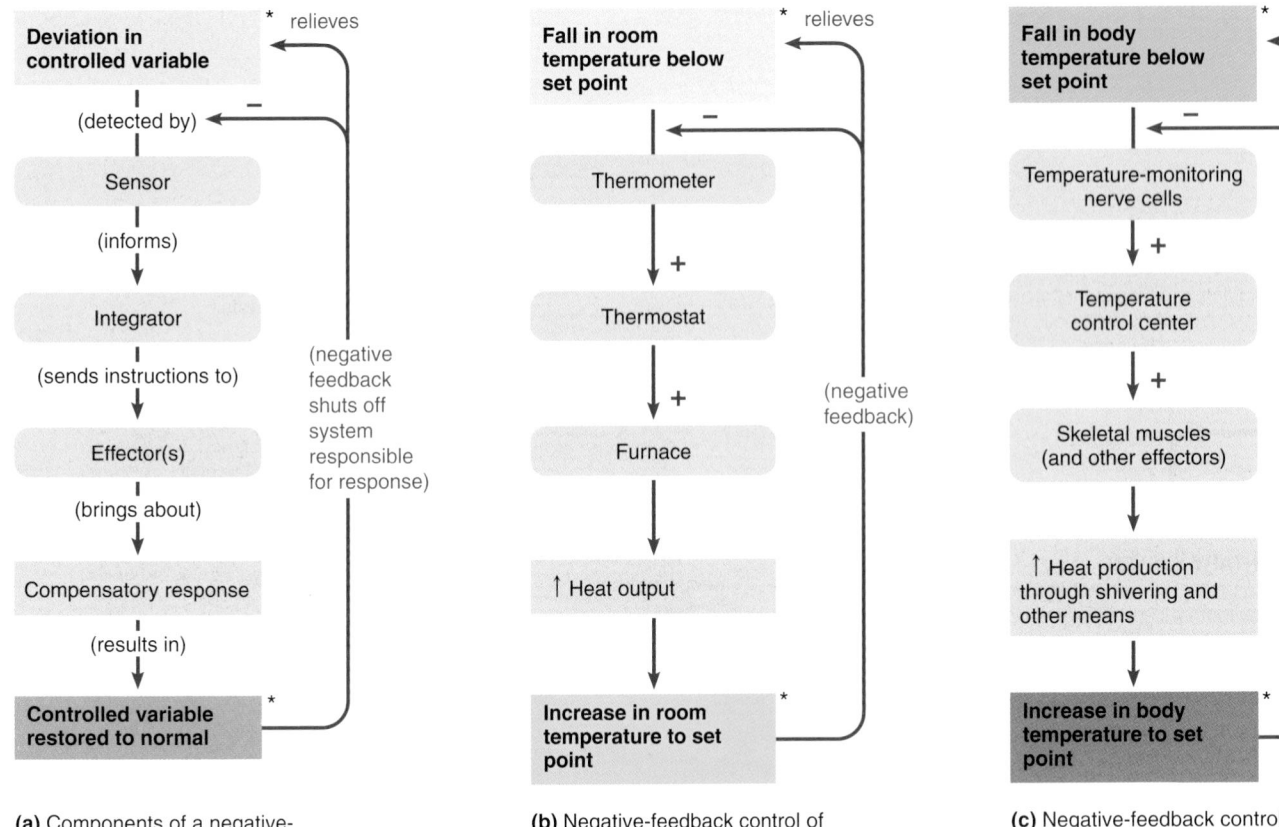

(a) Components of a negative-feedback control system

(b) Negative-feedback control of room temperature

(c) Negative-feedback control of body temperature

KEY

Flow diagrams throughout the text
- **+** = Stimulates or activates
- **–** = Inhibits or shuts off
- ⬭ = Physical entity, such as body structure or a chemical
- ▭ = Actions
- | = Compensatory pathway
- | = Turning off of compensatory pathway (negative feedback)
- * Note that lighter and darker shades of the same color are used to denote, respectively, a decrease or an increase in a controlled variable.

● **FIGURE 1-8 Negative feedback.**

point is reached, the air conditioner is turned off to prevent the room from becoming too cold. Note that if the controlled variable can be deliberately adjusted to oppose a change in one direction only, the variable can move in an uncontrolled fashion in the opposite direction. For example, if the house is equipped only with a furnace that produces heat to oppose a fall in room temperature, no mechanism is available to prevent the house from getting too hot in warm weather. However, the room temperature can be kept relatively constant through two opposing mechanisms, one that heats and one that cools the room, despite wide variations in the temperature of the external environment.

Homeostatic negative-feedback systems in the human body operate in the same way. For example, when temperature-monitoring nerve cells detect a decrease in body temperature below the desired level, these sensors signal the temperature control center in the brain, which begins a sequence of events that ends in responses, such as shivering, that generate heat and

raise the temperature to the proper level (● Figure 1-8c). When the body temperature reaches the set point, the temperature-monitoring nerve cells turn off the stimulatory signal to the skeletal muscles. As a result, the body temperature does not continue to increase above the set point. Conversely, when the temperature-monitoring nerve cells detect a rise in body temperature above normal, cooling mechanisms such as sweating are called into play to lower the temperature to normal. When the temperature reaches the set point, the cooling mechanisms are shut off. As with body temperature, opposing mechanisms can move most homeostatically controlled variables in either direction as needed.

Positive feedback amplifies an initial change.

In negative feedback, a control system's output is regulated to resist change so that the controlled variable is kept at a relatively steady set point. With **positive feedback,** by contrast, the output enhances or amplifies a change so that the controlled variable continues to move in the direction of the initial change. Such action is comparable to the heat generated by a furnace triggering the thermostat to call for even *more* heat output from the furnace so that the room temperature would continuously rise.

Because the major goal in the body is to maintain stable, homeostatic conditions, positive feedback does not occur nearly as often as negative feedback. Positive feedback does play an important role in certain instances, however, as in the birth of a baby. The hormone oxytocin causes powerful contractions of the uterus (womb). As the contractions push the baby against the cervix (the exit from the uterus), the resultant stretching of the cervix triggers a sequence of events that brings about the release of even more oxytocin, which causes even stronger uterine contractions, triggering the release of more oxytocin, and so on. This positive-feedback cycle does not stop until the baby is finally born. Likewise, all other normal instances of positive-feedback cycles in the body include some mechanism for stopping the cycle.

Disruptions in homeostasis can lead to illness and death.

 Despite control mechanisms, when one or more of the body's systems malfunction, homeostasis is disrupted, and all cells suffer because they no longer have an optimal environment in which to live and function. Various pathophysiological states develop, depending on the type and extent of the disruption. The term **pathophysiology** refers to the abnormal functioning of the body (altered physiology) associated with disease. When a homeostatic disruption becomes so severe that it is no longer compatible with survival, death results.

Chapter in Perspective: Focus on Homeostasis

In this chapter, you learned what homeostasis is: a dynamic steady state of the constituents in the internal fluid environment (the extracellular fluid) that surrounds and exchanges materials with the cells. Maintenance of homeostasis is essential for survival and normal functioning of cells. Each cell, through its specialized activities, contributes as part of a body system to the maintenance of homeostasis.

This relationship is the foundation of physiology and the central theme of this book. We have described how cells are organized according to specialization into body systems. How homeostasis is essential for cell survival and how body systems maintain this internal constancy are the topics covered in the rest of this book. Each chapter concludes with this capstone feature to facilitate your understanding of how the system under discussion contributes to homeostasis, as well as of the interactions and interdependency of the body systems.

REVIEW EXERCISES

Objective Questions (Answers on p. A-38)

1. Which of the following activities is *not* carried out by every cell in the body?
   a. obtaining oxygen and nutrients
   b. performing chemical reactions to acquire energy for the cell's use
   c. eliminating wastes
   d. largely controlling exchange of materials between the cell and its external environment
   e. reproducing
2. Which of the following is the proper progression of the levels of organization in the body?
   a. chemicals, cells, organs, tissues, body systems, whole body
   b. chemicals, cells, tissues, organs, body systems, whole body
   c. cells, chemicals, tissues, organs, whole body, body systems
   d. cells, chemicals, organs, tissues, whole body, body systems
   e. chemicals, cells, tissues, body systems, organs, whole body

3. Cells in a multicellular organism have specialized to such an extent that they have little in common with single-celled organisms. (*True or false?*)
4. Cell specializations are usually a modification or elaboration of one of the basic cell functions. (*True or false?*)
5. The four primary types of tissue are _____, _____, _____, and _____.
6. The term ___ refers to the release from a cell, in response to appropriate stimulation, of specific products that have been synthesized largely by the cell.
7. _____ glands secrete through ducts to the outside of the body, whereas _____ glands release their secretory products, known as _____, internally into the blood.
8. _____ controls are inherent to an organ, whereas _____ controls are regulatory mechanisms initiated outside an organ that alter the activity of the organ.

9. Match the following:

___ 1. circulatory system
___ 2. digestive system
___ 3. respiratory system
___ 4. urinary system
___ 5. muscular and skeletal systems
___ 6. integumentary system
___ 7. immune system
___ 8. nervous system
___ 9. endocrine system
___ 10. reproductive system

(a) obtains oxygen and eliminates carbon dioxide
(b) supports, protects, and moves body parts
(c) controls, via hormones it secretes, processes that require duration
(d) acts as the transport system
(e) removes wastes and excess water, salt, and other electrolytes
(f) perpetuates the species
(g) obtains nutrients, water, and electrolytes
(h) defends against foreign invaders and cancer
(i) acts through electrical signals to control the body's rapid responses
(j) serves as an outer protective barrier

Essay Questions

1. Define physiology.
2. What are the basic cell functions?
3. Distinguish between the external environment and the internal environment. Distinguish between the intracellular fluid (ICF) and the extracellular fluid (ECF). Discuss the relationship between the internal environment and the ECF. What fluid compartments make up the ECF?
4. Define homeostasis.
5. Describe the interrelationships among cells, body systems, and homeostasis.
6. What factors must be homeostatically maintained?
7. Define and describe the components of a homeostatic control system.
8. Compare negative and positive feedback.

POINTS TO PONDER

(Explanations on p. A-38)

1. Considering the nature of negative-feedback control and the function of the respiratory system, what effect do you predict that a decrease in carbon dioxide (CO_2) in the internal environment would have on how rapidly and deeply a person breathes?

2. Would the oxygen (O_2) levels in the blood be (a) normal, (b) below normal, or (c) elevated in a patient with severe pneumonia, resulting in impaired exchange of O_2 and CO_2 between the air and blood in the lungs? Would the CO_2 levels in the same patient's blood be (a) normal, (b) below normal, or (c) elevated? Because CO_2 reacts with water to form carbonic acid, would the patient's blood (a) have a normal pH, (b) be too acidic, or (c) not be acidic enough (that is, be too alkaline), assuming that other compensatory measures have not yet had time to act?

3. The hormone insulin enhances the transport of glucose (sugar) from the blood into most body cells. Its secretion is controlled by a negative-feedback system between the concentration of glucose in the blood and the insulin-secreting cells. Therefore, which of the following statements is correct?
   a. A decrease in blood glucose concentration stimulates insulin secretion, which in turn further lowers blood glucose concentration.
   b. An increase in blood glucose concentration stimulates insulin secretion, which in turn lowers blood glucose concentration.
   c. A decrease in blood glucose concentration stimulates insulin secretion, which in turn increases blood glucose concentration.
   d. An increase in blood glucose concentration stimulates insulin secretion, which in turn further increases blood glucose concentration.
   e. None of the preceding is correct.

4. Given that most AIDS victims die from overwhelming infections or rare types of cancer, what body system do you think HIV (the AIDS virus) impairs?

5. Body temperature is homeostatically regulated around a set point. Given your knowledge of negative feedback and homeostatic control systems, predict whether narrowing or widening of the blood vessels of the skin will occur when a person exercises strenuously. (*Hints:* Muscle contraction generates heat. Narrowing of the vessels supplying an organ decreases blood flow through the organ, whereas vessel widening increases blood flow through the organ. The more warm blood flowing through the skin, the greater is the loss of heat from the skin to the surrounding environment.)

(Explanation on p. A-38)

Jennifer R. has the "stomach flu" that is going around campus and has been vomiting profusely for the past 24 hours. Not only has she been unable to keep down fluids or food, but she has also lost the acidic digestive juices secreted by the stomach that are normally reabsorbed back into the blood farther down the digestive tract. In what ways might this condition threaten to disrupt homeostasis in Jennifer's internal environment? That is, what homeostatically maintained factors are moved away from normal by her profuse vomiting? What body systems respond to resist these changes?

Chapter 1

Introduction to Physiology (p. 1)

■ Physiology is the study of body functions.

■ Physiologists explain body function in terms of the mechanisms of action involving cause-and-effect sequences of physical and chemical processes.

■ Physiology and anatomy are closely interrelated because body functions highly depend on the structure of the body parts that carry them out.

Levels of Organization in the Body (pp. 1–5)

■ The human body is a complex combination of specific atoms and molecules.

■ These nonliving chemicals are organized in a precise way to form cells, the smallest entities capable of carrying out life processes. Cells are the body's structural and functional living building blocks. *(Review Figure 1-1.)*

■ The basic functions performed by each cell for its own survival include (1) obtaining O₂ and nutrients, (2) performing energy-generating chemical reactions, (3) eliminating wastes, (4) synthesizing proteins and other cell components, (5) controlling movement of materials between the cell and its environment, (6) moving materials throughout the cell, (7) responding to the environment, and (8) reproducing.

■ In addition to its basic functions, each cell in a multicellular organism performs a specialized function.

■ Cells of similar structure and specialized function combine to form the four primary tissues of the body: muscle, nervous, epithelial, and connective. *(Review Figure 1-2.)*

■ Glands are derived from epithelial tissue and specialized for secretion. Exocrine glands secrete through ducts to the body surface or into a cavity that communicates with the outside; endocrine glands secrete hormones into the blood. *(Review Figure 1-3.)*

■ Organs are combinations of two or more types of tissues that act together to perform one or more functions. An example is the stomach. *(Review Figure 1-2.)*

■ Body systems are collections of organs that perform related functions and interact to accomplish a common activity essential for survival of the whole body. An example is the digestive system. *(Review Figure 1-4.)*

■ Body systems combine to form the organism, or whole body.

Concept of Homeostasis (pp. 5–10)

■ The fluid inside the cells of the body is intracellular fluid (ICF); the fluid outside the cells is extracellular fluid (ECF).

■ Because most body cells are not in direct contact with the external environment, cell survival depends on maintaining a relatively stable internal fluid environment with which the cells directly make life-sustaining exchanges.

■ The ECF serves as the body's internal environment. It consists of the plasma and the interstitial fluid. *(Review Figure 1-5.)*

■ Homeostasis is the maintenance of a dynamic steady state in the internal environment.

■ The factors of the internal environment that must be homeostatically maintained are its (1) concentration of nutrients; (2) concentration of oxygen and carbon dioxide; (3) concentration of waste products; (4) pH; (5) concentrations of water, salt, and other electrolytes; (6) volume and pressure; and (7) temperature. *(Review Figure 1-7.)*

■ The functions performed by the 11 body systems are directed toward maintaining homeostasis. These functions ultimately depend on the specialized activities of the cells that make up the system. Thus, homeostasis is essential for each cell's survival, and each cell contributes to homeostasis. *(Review Figures 1-6 and 1-7.)*

Homeostatic Control Systems (pp. 11–15)

■ A homeostatic control system is a network of body components working together to maintain a controlled variable in the internal environment relatively constant near an optimal set point despite changes in the variable.

■ Homeostatic control systems can be classified as (1) intrinsic (local) controls, which are inherent compensatory responses of an organ to a change, and (2) extrinsic (systemic) controls, which are responses of an organ triggered by factors external to the organ, namely, by the nervous and endocrine systems.

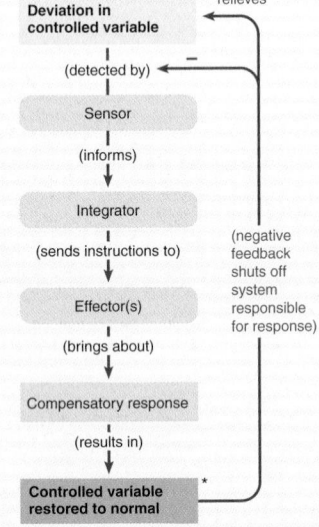

■ Both intrinsic and extrinsic control systems generally operate on the principle of negative feedback: A change in a controlled variable triggers a response that drives the variable in the opposite direction of the initial change, thus opposing the change. *(Review Figure 1-8.)*

(a) Components of a negative-feedback control system

■ In positive feedback, a change in a controlled variable triggers a response that drives the variable in the same direction as the initial change, thus amplifying the change. Positive feedback is uncommon in the body but is important in several instances, such as during childbirth.

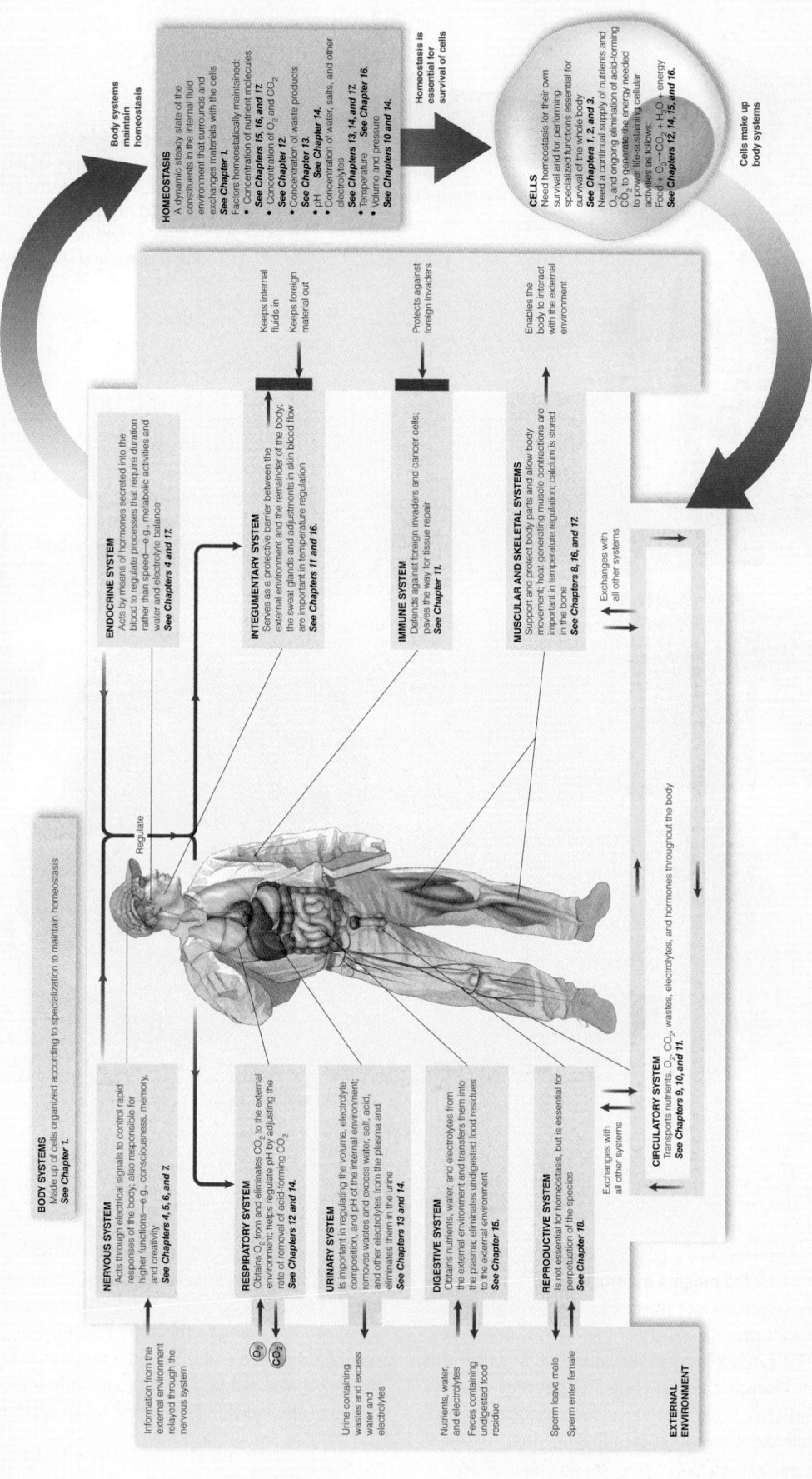

BODY SYSTEMS
Made up of cells organized according to specialization to maintain homeostasis
See Chapter 1.

Body systems maintain homeostasis

HOMEOSTASIS
A dynamic steady state of the constituents in the internal fluid environment that surrounds and exchanges materials with the cells
See Chapter 1.
Factors homeostatically maintained:
• Concentration of nutrient molecules
  See Chapters 15, 16, and 17.
• Concentration of O_2 and CO_2
  See Chapter 12.
• Concentration of waste products
  See Chapter 13.
• pH *See Chapter 14.*
• Concentration of water, salts, and other electrolytes
  See Chapters 13, 14, and 17.
• Temperature *See Chapter 16.*
• Volume and pressure
  See Chapters 10 and 14.

Homeostasis is essential for survival of cells

CELLS
Need homeostasis for their own survival and for performing specialized functions essential for survival of the whole body
See Chapters 1, 2, and 3.
Need a continual supply of nutrients and O_2 and ongoing elimination of acid-forming CO_2 to generate energy needed to power life-sustaining cellular activities as follows:
Food + $O_2 \rightarrow CO_2 + H_2O$ + energy
See Chapters 12, 14, 15, and 16.

Cells make up body systems

NERVOUS SYSTEM
Acts through electrical signals to control rapid responses of the body; also responsible for higher functions—e.g., consciousness, memory, and creativity
See Chapters 4, 5, 6, and 7.

RESPIRATORY SYSTEM
Obtains O_2 from and eliminates CO_2 to the external environment; helps regulate pH by adjusting the rate of removal of acid-forming CO_2
See Chapters 12 and 14.

URINARY SYSTEM
Is important in regulating the volume, electrolyte composition, and pH of the internal environment; removes wastes and excess water, salt, acid, and other electrolytes from the plasma and eliminates them in the urine
See Chapters 13 and 14.

DIGESTIVE SYSTEM
Obtains nutrients, water, and electrolytes from the external environment and transfers them into the plasma; eliminates undigested food residues to the external environment
See Chapter 15.

REPRODUCTIVE SYSTEM
Is not essential for homeostasis, but is essential for perpetuation of the species
See Chapter 18.

ENDOCRINE SYSTEM
Acts by means of hormones secreted into the blood to regulate processes that require duration rather than speed—e.g., metabolic activities and water and electrolyte balance
See Chapters 4 and 17.

Regulate

INTEGUMENTARY SYSTEM
Serves as a protective barrier between the external environment and the remainder of the body; the sweat glands and adjustments in skin blood flow are important in temperature regulation
See Chapters 11 and 16.

Keeps internal fluids in
Keeps foreign material out

IMMUNE SYSTEM
Defends against foreign invaders and cancer cells; paves the way for tissue repair
See Chapter 11.

Protects against foreign invaders

MUSCULAR AND SKELETAL SYSTEMS
Support and protect body parts and allow body movement; heat-generating muscle contractions are important in temperature regulation; calcium is stored in the bone
See Chapters 8, 16, and 17.

Enables the body to interact with the external environment

Exchanges with all other systems

CIRCULATORY SYSTEM
Transports nutrients, O_2, CO_2, wastes, electrolytes, and hormones throughout the body
See Chapters 9, 10, and 11.

Information from the external environment relayed through the nervous system

O_2
CO_2

Urine containing wastes and excess water and electrolytes

Nutrients, water, and electrolytes
Feces containing undigested food residue

Sperm leave male
Sperm enter female

Exchanges with all other systems

EXTERNAL ENVIRONMENT

Body Systems

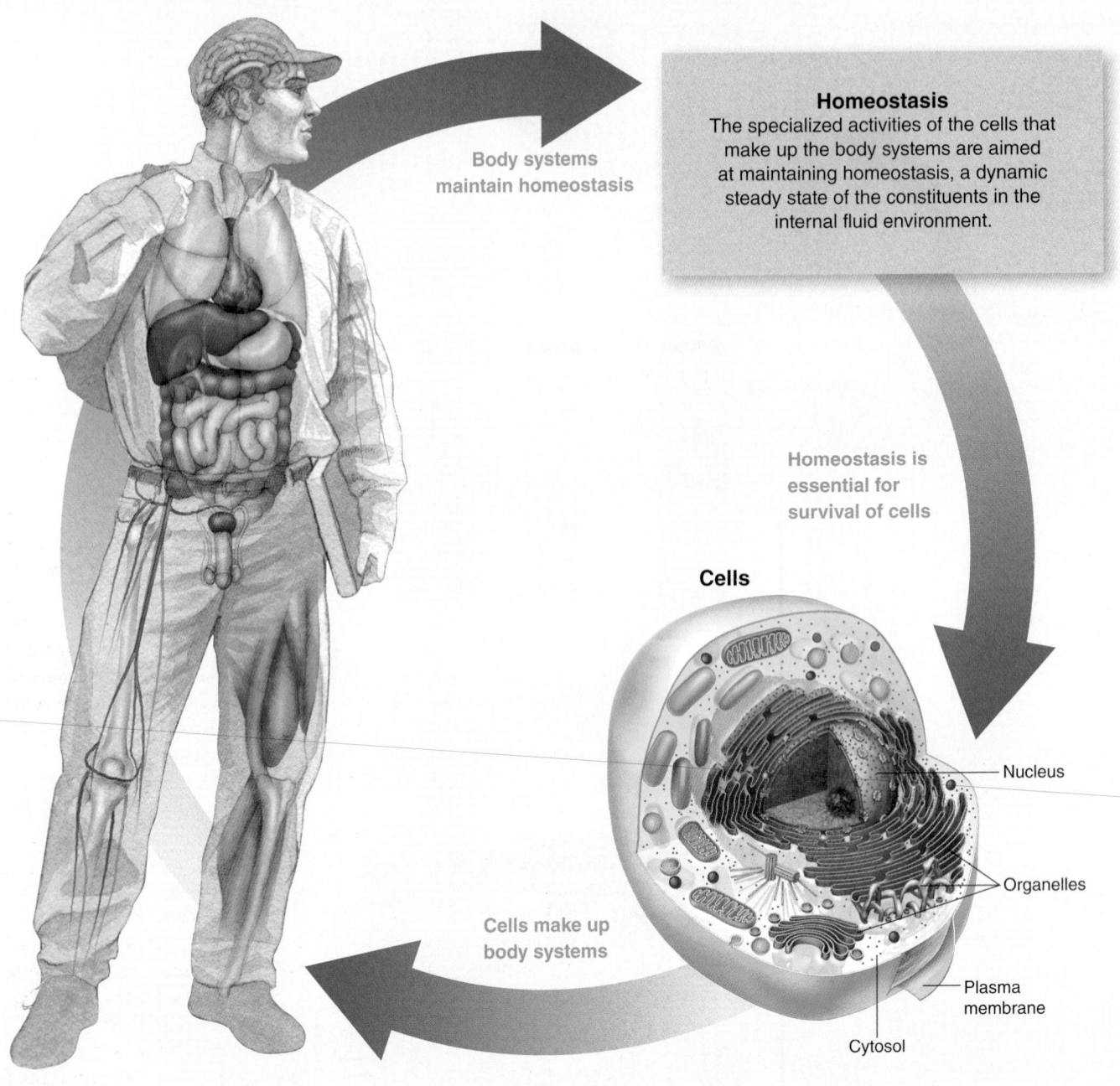

Body systems maintain homeostasis

Homeostasis
The specialized activities of the cells that make up the body systems are aimed at maintaining homeostasis, a dynamic steady state of the constituents in the internal fluid environment.

Homeostasis is essential for survival of cells

Cells

Nucleus

Organelles

Plasma membrane

Cytosol

Cells make up body systems

Cells are the highly organized, living building blocks of the body. A cell has three major parts: the **plasma membrane,** which encloses the cell; the **nucleus,** which houses the cell's genetic material; and the **cytoplasm.** The cytoplasm consists of the cytosol, organelles, and cytoskeleton. The *cytosol* is a gel-like liquid within which the organelles and cytoskeleton are suspended. *Organelles* are discrete, well-organized structures that carry out specialized functions. The *cytoskeleton* is protein scaffolding that extends throughout the cell and serves as the cell's "bone and muscle."

Through the coordinated action of these components, every cell performs certain basic functions essential to its own survival and a specialized task that helps maintain homeostasis. Cells are organized according to their specialization into body systems that maintain the stable internal environment essential for the whole body's survival. All body functions ultimately depend on the activities of the individual cells that make up the body.

Cell Physiology

CHAPTER AT A GLANCE

Observations of Cells

An Overview of Cell Structure

Endoplasmic Reticulum and
Segregated Synthesis
Rough endoplasmic reticulum
Smooth endoplasmic reticulum

Golgi Complex and Exocytosis
Role of the Golgi complex
Secretion by exocytosis

Lysosomes and Endocytosis
Role of lysosomes
Endocytosis

Peroxisomes and Detoxification

Mitochondria and ATP Production
Glycolysis
Role of mitochondria: citric acid cycle and
    oxidative phosphorylation
Generation of ATP in aerobic and
    anaerobic conditions
Uses of ATP

Cytosol: Cell Gel
Importance of cytosol

Cytoskeleton: Cell "Bone and Muscle"
Role of microtubules, microfilaments, and
    intermediate filaments

Observations of Cells

Although the same chemicals that make up living cells are found in nonliving matter, researchers have not been able to organize these chemicals into living cells in a laboratory. Life stems from the unique and complex organization and interactions of these inanimate chemicals within the cell. Cells, the smallest living entities, are the living building blocks for the immensely complicated whole body. Thus, cells are the bridge between chemicals and humans (and all other living organisms). By probing deeper into the molecular structure and organization of the cells that make up the body, modern physiologists are unraveling many of the broader mysteries of how the body works.

The cells that make up the human body are so small they cannot be seen by the unaided eye. The smallest visible particle is 5 to 10 times larger than a typical human cell, which averages about 10 to 20 micrometers (μm) in diameter (1 μm = 1 millionth of a meter). About 100 average-sized cells lined up side by side would stretch a distance of only 1 mm (1 mm = one-thousandth of a meter; 1 m = 39.37 in.). (See Appendix A for a comparison of metric units and their English equivalents. This appendix also provides a visual comparison of the size of cells in relation to selected structures.)

Until the microscope was invented in the middle of the 17th century, scientists did not know that cells existed. With the development of better light microscopes in the early 19th century, they learned that all plant and animal tissues consist of individual cells. The cells of a hummingbird, a human, and a whale are all about the same size. Larger species have more cells, not larger cells. These early investigators also discovered that cells are filled with a fluid that, given the microscopic capabilities of the time, appeared to be a rather uniform, soupy mixture believed to be the elusive "stuff of life." In the 1940s, when researchers first employed electron microscopes to observe living matter, they began to realize the great diversity and complexity of the internal structure of cells. (Electron microscopes are about 100 times more powerful than light microscopes.) Now that scientists have even more sophisticated microscopes, biochemical techniques, cell culture technology, and genetic engineering, the concept of the cell as a microscopic bag of formless fluid has given way to our current understanding of the cell as a complex, highly organized, compartmentalized structure.

An Overview of Cell Structure

The trillions of cells in a human body are classified into about 200 types based on specific variations in structure and function. Yet despite their diverse structural and functional specializations, different cells share many features. Most human cells have three major subdivisions: the *plasma membrane,* which encloses the cells; the *nucleus,* which contains the cell's genetic material; and the *cytoplasm,* the portion of the cell's interior not occupied by the nucleus (● Figure 2-1). Here, we provide an overview of each subdivision, and then we focus primarily on the cytoplasm in this chapter. The plasma membrane and nucleus are described in further detail later.

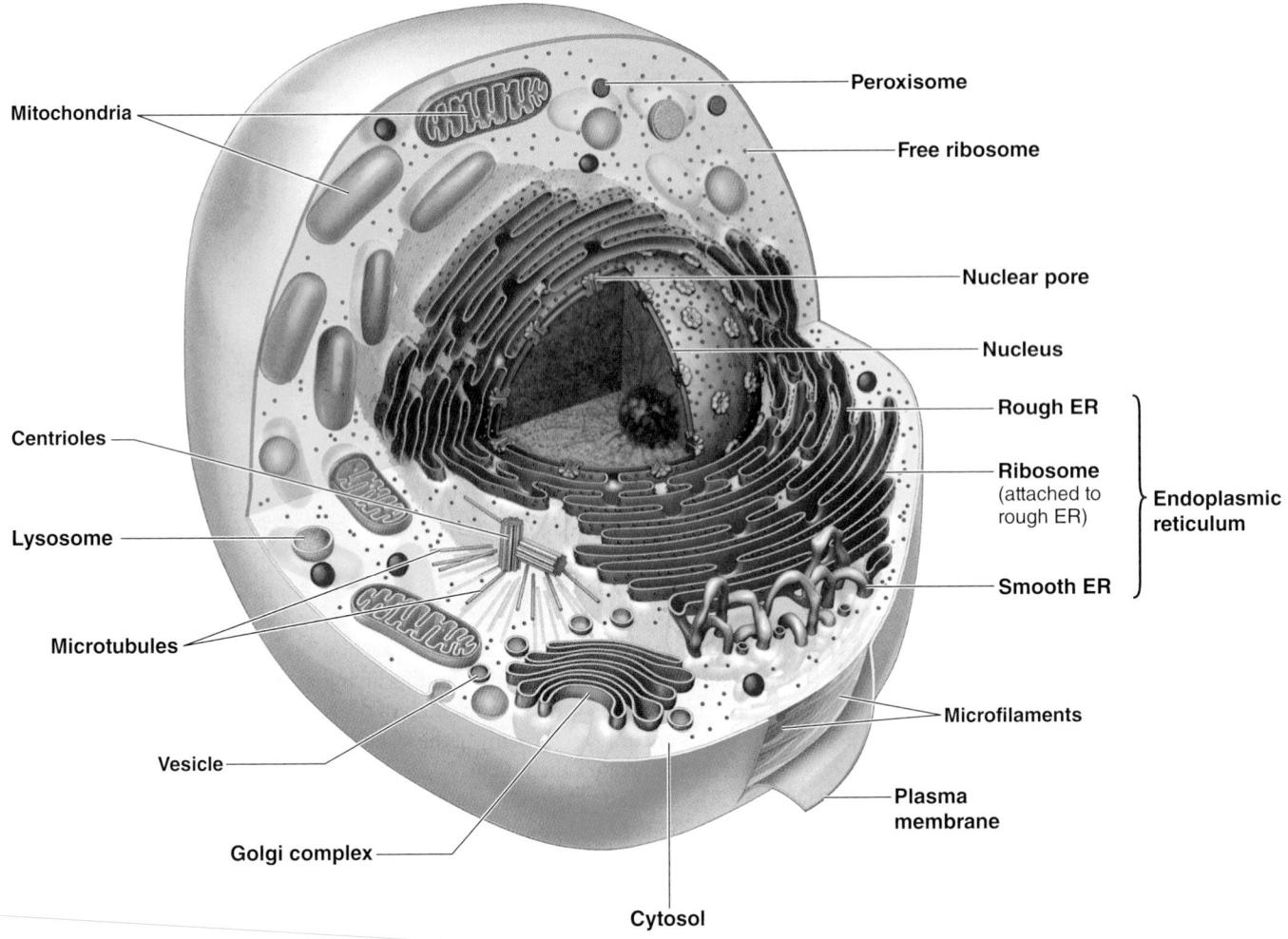

Peroxisome

Free ribosome

Nuclear pore

Nucleus

Rough ER

Ribosome
(attached to
rough ER)

Endoplasmic
reticulum

Smooth ER

Mitochondria

Centrioles

Lysosome

Microtubules

Vesicle

Golgi complex

Microfilaments

Plasma
membrane

Cytosol

● FIGURE 2-1 Diagram of cell structures visible under an electron microscope.

The plasma membrane bounds the cell.

The **plasma membrane** is a thin membranous structure that encloses each cell and is composed mostly of lipid (fat) molecules and studded with proteins. This barrier separates the cell's contents from its surroundings; it keeps the *intracellular fluid (ICF)* within the cells from mingling with the *extracellular fluid (ECF)* outside the cells. The plasma membrane is not simply a mechanical barrier to hold in the contents of a cell; its proteins selectively control movement of molecules between the ICF and the ECF. The plasma membrane can be likened to the gated walls that enclosed ancient cities. Through this structure, the cell controls the entry of nutrients and other needed supplies and the export of products manufactured within, while at the same time guarding against unwanted traffic into or out of the cell. The plasma membrane is discussed thoroughly in Chapter 3.

The nucleus contains the DNA.

The two major parts of the cell's interior are the nucleus and the cytoplasm. The **nucleus,** which is typically the largest single organized cell component, can be seen as a distinct spherical structure, usually located near the center of the cell. It is surrounded by a double-layered membrane, the **nuclear envelope,** which

separates the nucleus from the rest of the cell. The nuclear envelope is pierced by many **nuclear pores** that allow necessary traffic to move between the nucleus and the cytoplasm.

The nucleus houses the cell's genetic material, **deoxyribonucleic acid (DNA),** which has two important functions: (1) directing protein synthesis and (2) serving as a genetic blueprint during cell replication. DNA provides codes, or instructions, for directing synthesis of specific structural and enzymatic proteins within the cell. By specifying the kinds and amounts of proteins that are produced, the nucleus indirectly governs most cell activities and serves as the cell's control center.

Three types of **ribonucleic acid (RNA)** play roles in protein synthesis. First, DNA's genetic code for a particular protein is transcribed into a **messenger RNA (mRNA)** molecule, which exits the nucleus through the nuclear pores. Within the cytoplasm, mRNA delivers the coded message to *ribosomes,* which "read" the code and translate it into the appropriate amino acid sequence for the designated protein being synthesized. **Ribosomal RNA (rRNA)** is an essential component of ribosomes. **Transfer RNA (tRNA)** delivers the appropriate amino acids within the cytoplasm to their designated site in the protein under construction.

Besides providing codes for protein synthesis, DNA serves as a genetic blueprint during cell replication to ensure that the cell produces additional cells just like itself, thus continuing the identical type of cell line within the body. Furthermore, in the reproductive cells (eggs and sperm), the DNA blueprint passes on genetic characteristics to future generations. (See Appendix C for further details of DNA and RNA function and protein synthesis.)

The cytoplasm consists of various organelles, the cytoskeleton, and the cytosol.

The **cytoplasm** is that portion of the cell interior not occupied by the nucleus. It contains a number of discrete, specialized *organelles* (the cell's "little organs") and the *cytoskeleton* (a scaffolding of proteins that serve as the cell's "bone and muscle") dispersed within the *cytosol* (a complex, gel-like liquid).

Organelles are distinct, highly organized structures that perform specialized functions within the cell. On average, nearly half of the total cell volume is occupied by organelles. Each organelle is a separate compartment within the cell that is enclosed by a membrane similar to the plasma membrane. Thus, the contents of an organelle are separated from the surrounding cytosol and from the contents of other organelles. Nearly all human cells contain five main types of organelles—the *endoplasmic reticulum, Golgi complex, lysosomes, peroxisomes,* and *mitochondria.* Organelles are like intracellular "specialty shops." Each is a separate internal compartment that contains a specific set of chemicals for carrying out a particular cellular function. This compartmentalization permits chemical activities that would not be compatible with one another to occur simultaneously within the cell. For example, the enzymes that destroy unwanted proteins in the cell operate within the protective confines of the lysosomes without the risk of destroying essential cell proteins. Organelles are similar in all cells, although some variations occur depending on the specialized capabilities of each cell type. Just as each organ plays a role essential for survival of the whole body, each organelle performs a specialized activity necessary for survival of the whole cell.

The **cytoskeleton** is an interconnected system of protein fibers and tubes that extends throughout the cytosol. This elaborate protein network gives the cell its shape, provides for its internal organization, and regulates its various movements.

The remainder of the cytoplasm not occupied by organelles and cytoskeleton consists of the **cytosol** ("cell liquid"). The cytosol is a semiliquid, gel-like mass. Many of the chemical reactions that are compatible with one another are conducted in the cytosol. (For clarification, the ICF encompasses all fluid inside the cell, including that within the cytosol, the organelles, and the nucleus.)

In this chapter, we examine each of the cytoplasmic components in more detail, concentrating first on the organelles.

Endoplasmic Reticulum and Segregated Synthesis

The **endoplasmic reticulum (ER)** is an elaborate fluid-filled membranous system distributed extensively throughout the cytosol. It is primarily a protein- and lipid-producing factory.

Two distinct types of ER—rough and smooth—can be distinguished. The **rough ER** consists of stacks of relatively flattened interconnected sacs, whereas the **smooth ER** is a meshwork of tiny interconnected tubules (● Figure 2-2). Even though these two regions differ considerably in appearance and function, they are connected to each other. In other words, the ER is one continuous organelle with many interconnected channels. The relative amount of rough and smooth ER varies among cells, depending on the activity of the cell.

The rough ER synthesizes proteins for secretion and membrane construction.

The outer surface of the rough ER membrane is studded with small particles that give it a "rough" or granular appearance under a light microscope. These particles are **ribosomes,** which are rRNA–protein complexes that synthesize proteins under the direction of nuclear DNA (see ● Figure C-7, p. A-25). The mRNA carries the genetic message from the nucleus to the ribosome "workbenches" where protein synthesis takes place (see p. A-23). Not all ribosomes in the cell are attached to the rough ER. Unattached or "free" ribosomes are dispersed throughout the cytosol.

The rough ER, in association with its ribosomes, synthesizes and releases various new proteins into the ER lumen, the fluid-filled space enclosed by the ER membrane. These proteins serve one of two purposes: (1) Some proteins are destined for export to the cell's exterior as secretory products, such as protein hormones or enzymes, and (2) other proteins are used in constructing new plasma membrane or other cell structures, such as lysosomes. The plasma membrane consists mostly of proteins and lipids (fats). The membranous wall of the ER also contains enzymes essential for the synthesis of the lipids needed to produce new membrane.

After being released into the ER lumen, a new protein cannot pass out through the ER membrane and therefore becomes permanently separated from the cytosol as soon as it has been synthesized. In contrast to the rough ER ribosomes, free ribosomes synthesize proteins that are used within the cytosol. In this way, newly produced molecules that are destined for export out of the cell or for synthesis of new membrane or other cell components (those synthesized by the ER) are physically separated from those that belong in the cytosol (those produced by the free ribosomes).

How do the molecules newly synthesized within the ER lumen get to their destinations if they cannot pass out through the ER membrane? They do so through the action of the smooth ER.

The smooth ER packages new proteins in transport vesicles.

The smooth ER does not contain ribosomes, so it is "smooth." Lacking ribosomes, it is not involved in protein synthesis. Instead, it serves other purposes that vary in different cell types.

In most cells, the smooth ER is rather sparse and serves primarily as a central packaging and discharge site for molecules to be transported from the ER. Newly synthesized pro-

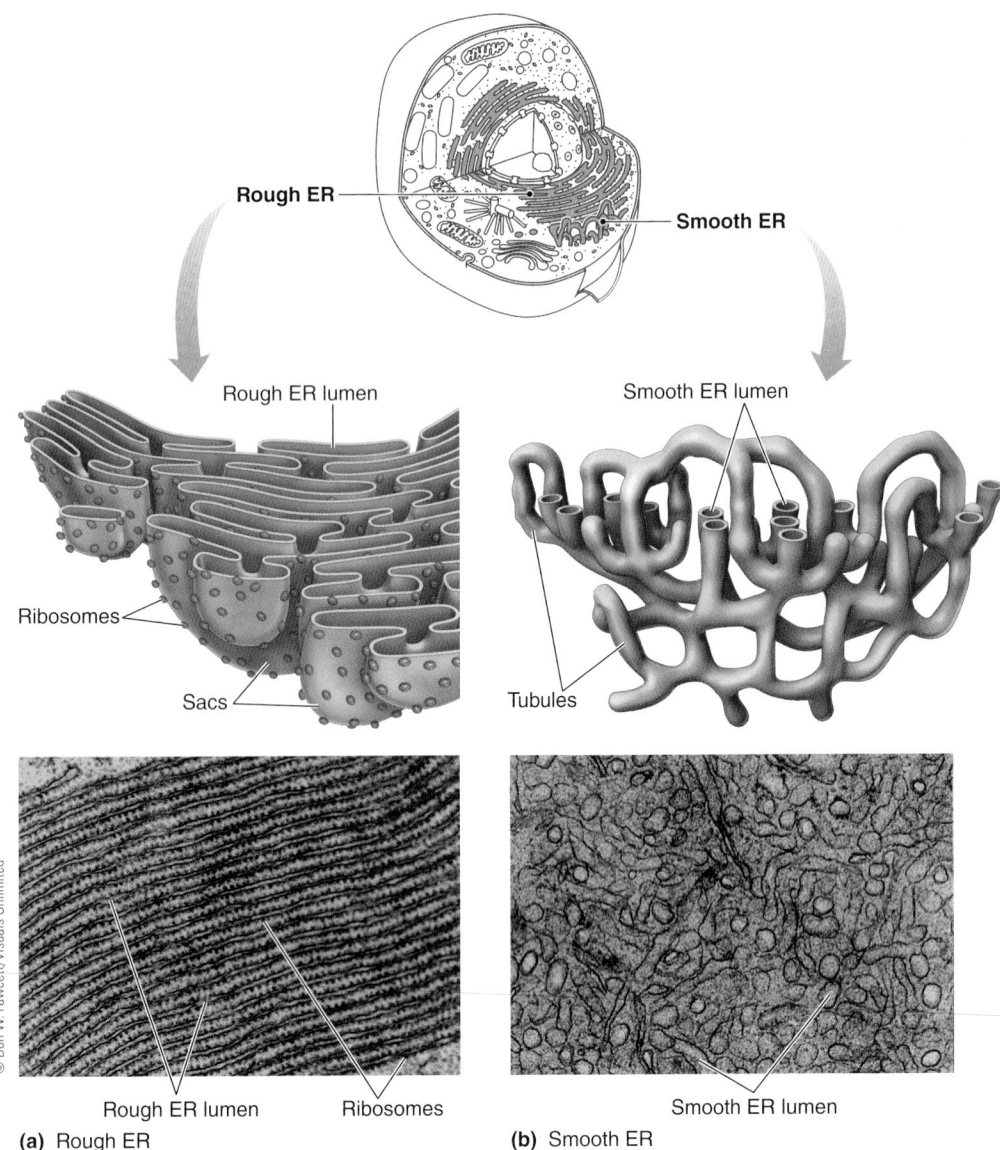

Rough ER

Smooth ER

Rough ER lumen

Smooth ER lumen

Ribosomes

Sacs

Tubules

Rough ER lumen   Ribosomes

Smooth ER lumen

(a) Rough ER

(b) Smooth ER

© Don W. Fawcett/Visuals Unlimited

● **FIGURE 2-2 Endoplasmic reticulum (ER).** (a) Diagram and electron micrograph of the rough ER, which consists of stacks of relatively flattened interconnected sacs studded with ribosomes. (b) Diagram and electron micrograph of the smooth ER, which is a meshwork of tiny interconnected tubules. The rough ER and smooth ER are connected, making one continuous organelle.

Golgi Complex and Exocytosis

The **Golgi complex** is closely associated with the ER. Each Golgi complex consists of a stack of flattened, slightly curved, membrane-enclosed sacs (● Figure 2-4). Note that the flattened sacs are thin in the middle but have dilated, or bulging, edges. The number of Golgi complexes varies, depending on the cell type. Some cells have only one Golgi stack, whereas cells highly specialized for protein secretion may have hundreds of stacks.

Transport vesicles carry their cargo to the Golgi complex for further processing.

Most newly synthesized molecules that have just budded off from the smooth ER enter a Golgi stack. When a transport vesicle reaches a Golgi stack, the vesicle membrane fuses with the membrane of the sac closest to the center of the cell. The vesicle membrane opens up and becomes integrated into the Golgi membrane, and the contents of the vesicle are released to the interior of the sac (see ● Figure 2-3).

These newly synthesized raw materials from the ER travel by means of vesicle formation through the layers of the Golgi stack, from the innermost sac closest to the ER to the outermost sac near the plasma membrane. During this transit, two important, interrelated functions take place:

1. *Processing the raw materials into finished products.* Within the Golgi complex, the "raw" proteins from the ER are modified into their final form, for example, by having a carbohydrate attached.

2. *Sorting and directing the finished products to their final destinations.* The Golgi complex is responsible for sorting and segregating products according to their function and destination, such as products to be secreted to the cell's exterior or to be used for constructing new cell components.

teins and lipids move within the continuous lumen from the rough ER to gather in the smooth ER. Portions of the smooth ER then "bud off" (that is, balloon outward on the surface and then are pinched off), forming **transport vesicles** that enclose the new molecules in a spherical capsule derived from the smooth ER membrane (● Figure 2-3). (A **vesicle** is a fluid-filled, membrane-enclosed intracellular cargo container.) Transport vesicles move to the Golgi complex, described in the next section, for further processing of their cargo.

In contrast to the sparseness of the smooth ER in most cells, some specialized types of cells have an extensive smooth ER, which has additional responsibilities. For example, muscle cells have an elaborate, modified smooth ER known as the *sarcoplasmic reticulum,* which stores calcium used in the process of muscle contraction (see p. 214).

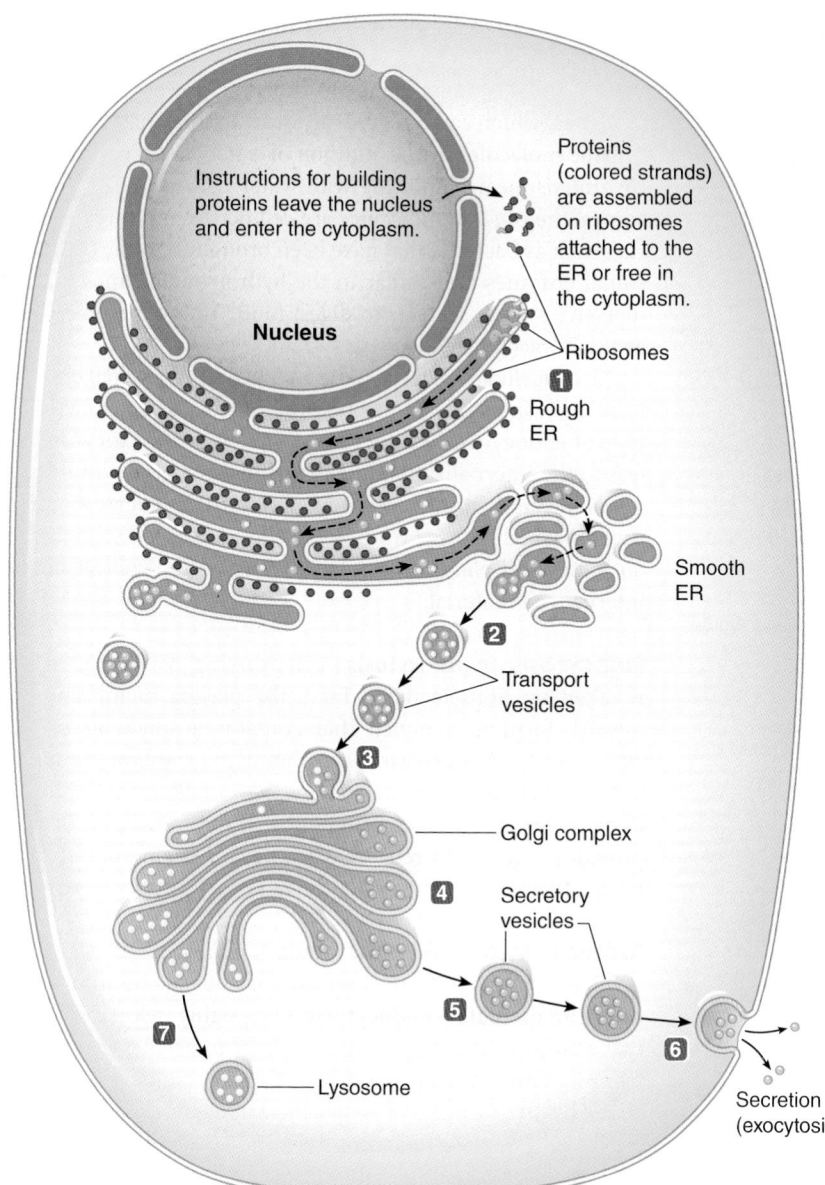

Instructions for building proteins leave the nucleus and enter the cytoplasm.

Proteins (colored strands) are assembled on ribosomes attached to the ER or free in the cytoplasm.

Nucleus

Ribosomes

1

Rough ER

Smooth ER

2

Transport vesicles

3

Golgi complex

4

Secretory vesicles

5

7

6

Lysosome

Secretion (exocytosis)

1 The rough ER synthesizes proteins to be secreted to the exterior or to be incorporated into plasma membrane or other cell components.

2 The smooth ER packages the secretory product into transport vesicles, which bud off and move to the Golgi complex.

3 The transport vesicles fuse with the Golgi complex, open up, and empty their contents into the closest Golgi sac.

4 The newly synthesized proteins from the ER travel by vesicular transport through the layers of the Golgi complex, which modifies the raw proteins into final form and sorts and directs the finished products to their final destination by varying their wrappers.

5 Secretory vesicles containing the finished protein products bud off the Golgi complex and remain in the cytosol, storing the products until signaled to empty.

6 On appropriate stimulation, the secretory vesicles fuse with the plasma membrane, open, and empty their contents to the cell's exterior. Secretion has occurred by exocytosis, with the secretory products never having come into contact with the cytosol.

7 Lysosomes also bud from the Golgi complex.

● FIGURE 2-3 **Overview of the secretion process for proteins synthesized by the endoplasmic reticulum.** Note that the secretory product never comes into contact with the cytosol.

The Golgi complex packages secretory vesicles for release by exocytosis.

How does the Golgi complex sort and direct finished proteins to the proper destinations? Finished products collect within the dilated edges of the Golgi complex's sacs. The edge of the outermost sac then pinches off to form a membrane-enclosed vesicle containing a selected product. For each type of product to reach its appropriate site of function, each distinct type of vesicle takes up a specific product before budding off (like a particular piece of mail being placed in an envelope). Vesicles with their selected cargo destined for different sites are wrapped in membranes containing different surface proteins (like addresses on envelopes) that can "dock" lock-and-key fashion and unload their cargo only at the proper destinations within the cell (similar to being delivered only to the appropriate house address). Once a vesicle has docked at the targeted membrane, the two membranes completely fuse; then the vesicle opens up and empties its contents at this designated site.

As an example, let us look at secretory cells. Secretion refers to release to the cell's exterior, on appropriate stimulation, of a product produced by the cell (see p. 4). Specialized secretory cells include endocrine cells that secrete protein hormones, and digestive gland cells, which secrete digestive enzymes. In secretory cells, numerous large **secretory vesicles,** which contain proteins to be secreted, bud off from the Golgi stacks. Secretory vesicles store the secretory proteins until the cell is stimulated by a specific signal that indicates a need for release of that particular secretory product. On the appropriate signal, a vesicle moves to the cell's periphery, fuses with the plasma membrane, opens, and empties its contents to the outside (● Figures 2-3 and 2-5a). This mechanism—release to the exterior of substances originating within the cell—is referred to as

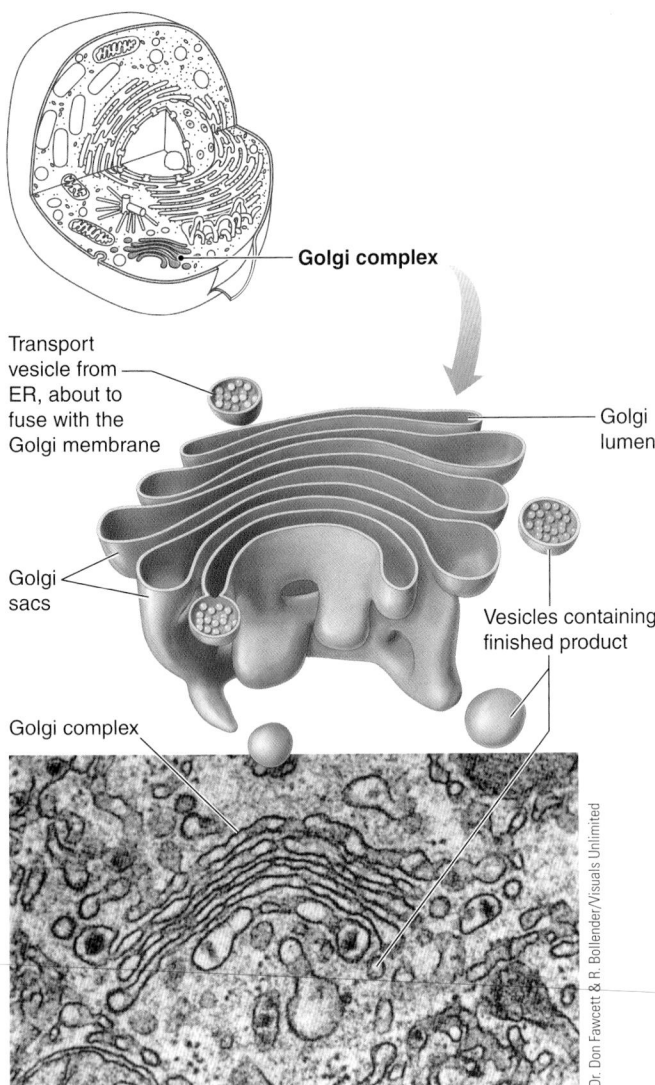

Golgi complex

Transport vesicle from ER, about to fuse with the Golgi membrane

Golgi lumen

Golgi sacs

Vesicles containing finished product

Golgi complex

Dr. Don Fawcett & R. Bollender/Visuals Unlimited

● **FIGURE 2-4 Golgi complex.** Diagram and electron micrograph of a Golgi complex, which consists of a stack of slightly curved, membrane-enclosed sacs. The vesicles at the dilated edges of the sacs contain finished protein products packaged for distribution to their final destination.

exocytosis (*exo* means "out of"; *cyto* means "cell"). Exocytosis is the primary mechanism for accomplishing secretion. Secretory vesicles fuse only with the plasma membrane and not with any of the internal membranes that enclose organelles, thereby preventing fruitless or even dangerous discharge of secretory products into the organelles.

Lysosomes and Endocytosis

Lysosomes are small, membrane-enclosed organelles that break down organic molecules (*lys* means "breakdown"; *some* means "body"). Instead of having a uniform structure, as is characteristic of all other organelles, lysosomes vary in size and shape, depending on the contents they are digesting. Most commonly, lysosomes are small oval or spherical bodies (● Figure 2-6). On average, a cell contains about 300 lysosomes.

Lysosomes digest extracellular material brought into the cell by phagocytosis.

A lysosome contains about 40 different powerful **hydrolytic enzymes,** which catalyze **hydrolysis,** reactions that break down organic molecules by the addition of water (H_2O) at a bond site (*hydrolysis* means "splitting with water"; see p. A-16). In lysosomes, the organic molecules are cell debris and foreign material, such as bacteria, that have been brought into the cell. Lysosomal enzymes are similar to the hydrolytic enzymes that the digestive system secretes to digest food. Thus, lysosomes serve as the intracellular "digestive system."

Extracellular material to be attacked by lysosomal enzymes is brought into the cell through the process of phagocytosis, a type of endocytosis. **Endocytosis,** the reverse of exocytosis, refers to the internalization of extracellular material within a cell (*endo* means "within") (see ● Figure 2-5b). Endocytosis can be accomplished in three ways—*pinocytosis, receptor-mediated endocytosis,* and *phagocytosis*—depending on the contents of the internalized material.

PINOCYTOSIS In **pinocytosis** ("cell drinking"), a droplet of ECF is taken up nonselectively. First, the plasma membrane dips inward, forming a pouch that contains a small bit of ECF (● Figure 2-7a). The plasma membrane then seals at the surface of the pouch, trapping the contents in a small, intracellular **endocytic vesicle.** Besides bringing ECF into a cell, pinocytosis provides a means to retrieve extra plasma membrane that has been added to the cell surface during exocytosis.

RECEPTOR-MEDIATED ENDOCYTOSIS Unlike pinocytosis, which involves the nonselective uptake of the surrounding fluid, **receptor-mediated endocytosis** is a highly selective process that enables cells to import specific large molecules that it needs from its environment. Receptor-mediated endocytosis is triggered by the binding of a specific target molecule such as a protein to a surface membrane receptor specific for that molecule (● Figure 2-7b). This binding causes the plasma membrane at that site to pocket inward and then seal at the surface, trapping the bound molecule inside the cell. Cholesterol complexes, vitamin B_{12}, the hormone insulin, and iron are examples of substances selectively taken into cells by receptor-mediated endocytosis.

Unfortunately, some viruses can sneak into cells by exploiting this mechanism. For instance, flu viruses and HIV, the virus that causes AIDS (see p. 348), gain entry to cells via receptor-mediated endocytosis. They do so by binding with membrane receptors normally designed to trigger the internalization of a needed molecule.

PHAGOCYTOSIS During **phagocytosis** ("cell eating"), large multimolecular particles are internalized. Most body cells perform pinocytosis, many carry out receptor-mediated endocytosis, but only a few specialized cells are capable of phagocytosis, the most notable being certain types of white blood cells that play an important role in the body's defense mechanisms. When a white blood cell encounters a large particle, such as a bacterium or tissue debris, it extends surface projections known as **pseu-**

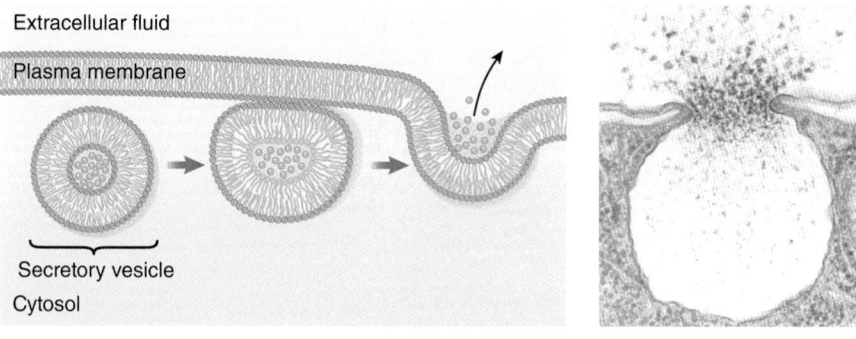

(a) Exocytosis: A secretory vesicle fuses with the plasma membrane, releasing the vesicle contents to the cell exterior. The vesicle membrane becomes part of the plasma membrane.

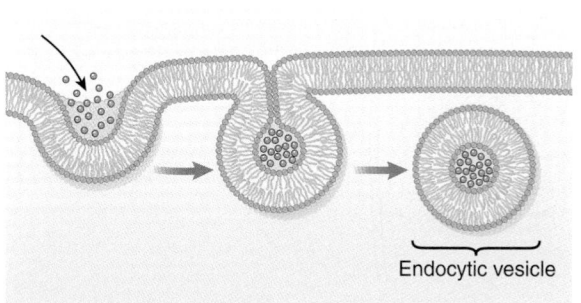
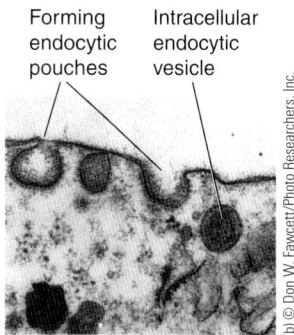

(b) Endocytosis: Materials from the cell exterior are enclosed in a segment of the plasma membrane that pockets inward and pinches off as an endocytic vesicle.

● **FIGURE 2-5 Exocytosis and endocytosis.** Diagram and electron micrographs of (a) exocytosis and (b) endocytosis.

dopods ("false feet") that surround or engulf the particle and trap it within an internalized vesicle (● Figure 2-7c). A lysosome fuses with the membrane of the phagocytic vesicle and releases its hydrolytic enzymes into the vesicle, where they safely attack the bacterium or other trapped material without damaging the remainder of the cell. The enzymes largely break down the engulfed material into raw ingredients, such as amino acids, glucose, and fatty acids, that the cell can use.

Lysosomes remove worn out organelles.

Lysosomes can also fuse with aged or damaged organelles to remove these useless parts of the cell. This selective self-digestion makes way for new replacement parts. In most cells, all organelles are renewable.

Clinical Note Some individuals lack the ability to synthesize one or more of the lysosomal enzymes. The result is massive accumulation within the lysosomes of the compound normally digested by the missing enzyme. Clinical manifestations often accompany such disorders, because the engorged lysosomes interfere with normal cell activity. The nature and severity of the symptoms depend on the type of substance accumulating, which in turn depends on what lysosomal enzyme is missing. Among these so-called *storage diseases* is **Tay-Sachs disease,** which is characterized by abnormal accumulation of complex molecules found in nerve cells. As the accumulation continues, profound symptoms of progressive nervous-system degeneration result.

Peroxisomes and Detoxification

Peroxisomes are membranous organelles that produce and decompose hydrogen peroxide (H_2O_2) in the process of degrading potentially toxic molecules (*peroxi* refers to hydrogen peroxide). Typically, several hundred small peroxisomes about one-third to one-half the average size of lysosomes are present in a cell (see ● Figure 2-6).

Peroxisomes house oxidative enzymes that detoxify various wastes.

Peroxisomes are similar to lysosomes in that they are membrane-enclosed sacs containing enzymes. However, unlike the lysosomes, which contain hydrolytic enzymes, peroxisomes house several powerful oxidative enzymes. **Oxidative enzymes,** as the name implies, use oxygen (O_2), in this case to strip hydrogen from certain organic molecules. This reaction helps detoxify various wastes produced within the cell or foreign toxic compounds that have entered the cell, such as alcohol consumed in beverages. Peroxisomes form H_2O_2 from molecular O_2

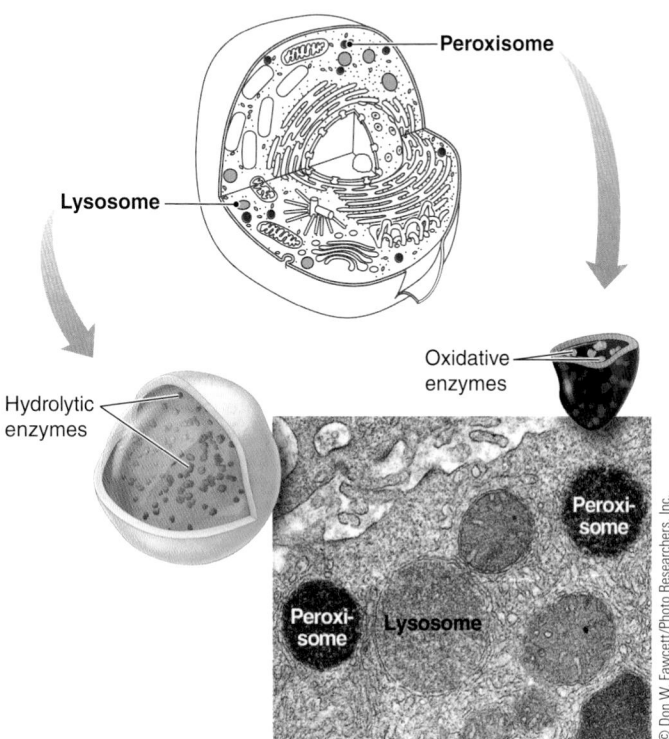

● **FIGURE 2-6 Lysosomes and peroxisomes.** Diagram and electron micrograph of lysosomes, which contain hydrolytic enzymes, and peroxisomes, which contain oxidative enzymes.

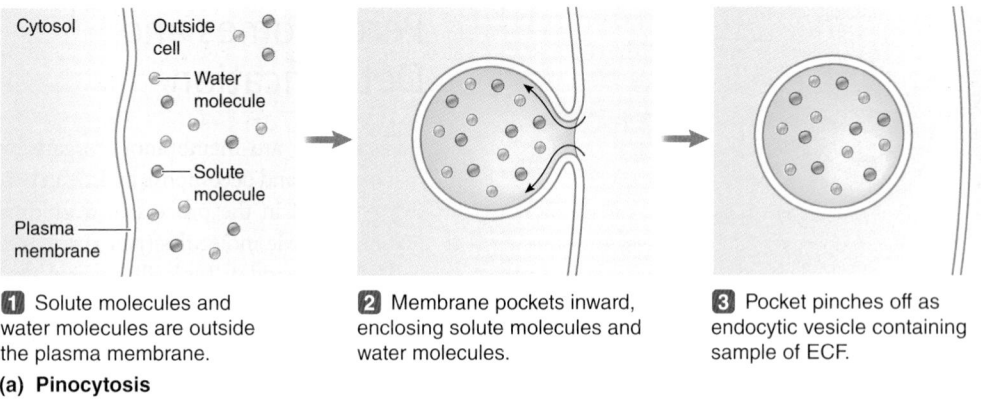

1 Solute molecules and water molecules are outside the plasma membrane.

2 Membrane pockets inward, enclosing solute molecules and water molecules.

3 Pocket pinches off as endocytic vesicle containing sample of ECF.

(a) Pinocytosis

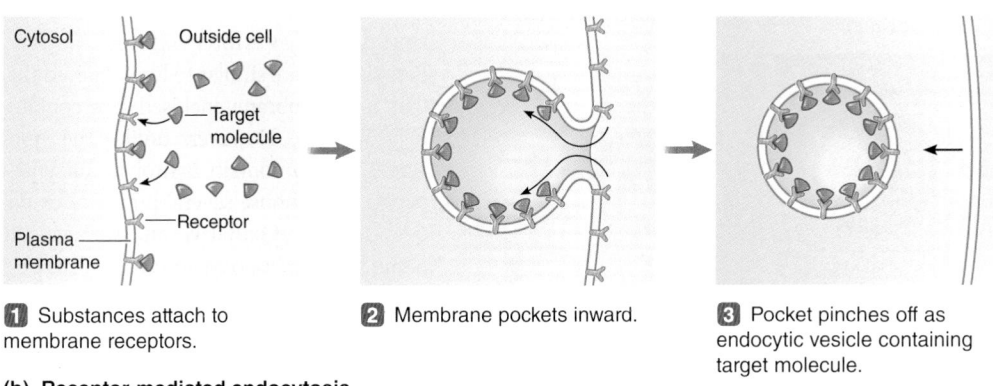

1 Substances attach to membrane receptors.

2 Membrane pockets inward.

3 Pocket pinches off as endocytic vesicle containing target molecule.

(b) Receptor-mediated endocytosis

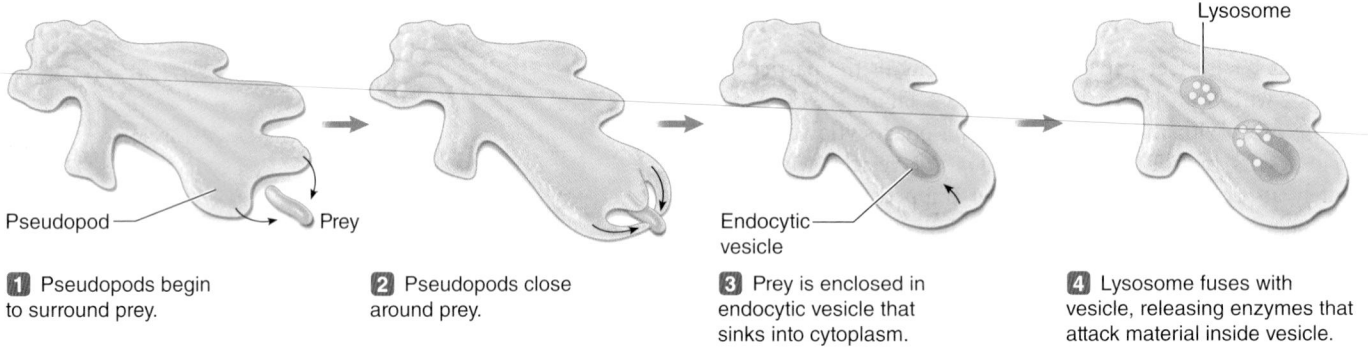

1 Pseudopods begin to surround prey.

2 Pseudopods close around prey.

3 Prey is enclosed in endocytic vesicle that sinks into cytoplasm.

4 Lysosome fuses with vesicle, releasing enzymes that attack material inside vesicle.

(c) Phagocytosis

● **FIGURE 2-7 Forms of endocytosis.** (a) Pinocytosis: The surface membrane dips inward to form a pouch and then seals the surface, forming an intracellular endocytic vesicle that nonselectively internalizes a bit of extracellular fluid. (b) Receptor-mediated endocytosis: When a large molecule such as a protein attaches to a specific surface receptor, the membrane pockets inward and then pinches off to selectively internalize the molecule in an endocytic vesicle. (c) Phagocytosis: White blood cells internalize multimolecular particles such as bacteria or old red blood cells by extending pseudopods that wrap around and seal in the targeted material. A lysosome fuses with and degrades the vesicle contents.

and the hydrogen atoms stripped from the toxic molecule. H_2O_2 is destructive if allowed to accumulate, but peroxisomes contain an enzyme that decomposes potent H_2O_2 into harmless H_2O and O_2.

Mitochondria and ATP Production

Mitochondria are the energy organelles, or "power plants," of the cell; they extract energy from the nutrients in food and transform it into a usable form for cell activities. Mitochondria generate about 90% of the energy that cells—and, accordingly, the whole body—need to survive and function. A single cell may contain as few as a hundred or as many as several thousand mitochondria, depending on the energy needs of each particular cell type. In some cell types, the mitochondria are densely compacted into the regions of the cell that use the most energy. For example, mitochondria are packed between the contractile units in the muscle cells of the heart.

Mitochondria are enclosed by two membranes.

Mitochondria are rod-shaped or oval structures. Each mitochondrion is enclosed by a double membrane—a smooth outer membrane that surrounds the mitochondrion itself, and an inner membrane that forms a series of infoldings or shelves called **cristae,** which project into an inner cavity filled with a gel-like solution known as the **matrix** (● Figure 2-8). The two membranes are separated by a narrow intermembrane space. The cristae contain proteins that ultimately are responsible for converting much of the energy in food into a usable form. The generous folds of the inner membrane greatly increase the surface area available for housing these important proteins. The matrix consists of a concentrated mixture of hundreds of different dissolved enzymes that prepare nutrient molecules for the final extraction of usable energy by the cristae proteins.

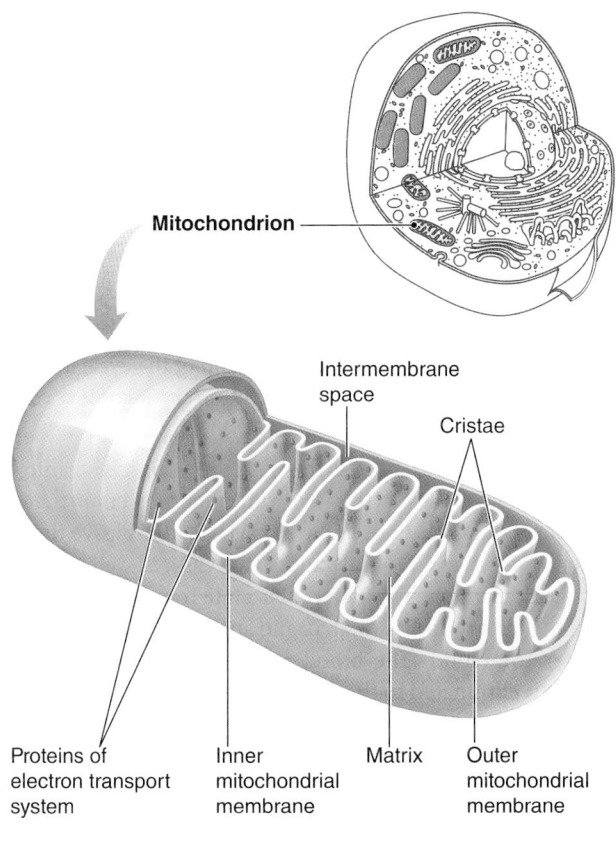

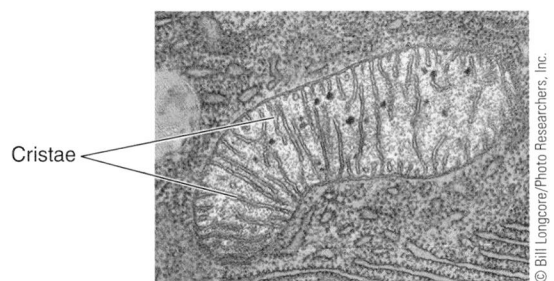

● **FIGURE 2-8 Mitochondrion.** Diagram and electron micrograph of a mitochondrion. Note that the outer membrane is smooth while the inner membrane forms folds known as cristae that extend into the matrix. An intermembrane space separates the outer and inner membranes. The electron transport proteins embedded in the cristae are ultimately responsible for converting much of the energy of food into a usable form.

Mitochondria play a major role in generating ATP.

The source of energy for the body is the chemical energy stored in the carbon bonds of ingested food. Body cells are not equipped to use this energy directly. Instead, the cells must extract energy from food nutrients and convert it into a form they can use—namely, the high-energy phosphate bonds of **adenosine triphosphate (ATP),** which consists of adenosine with three phosphate groups attached (*tri* means "three"; see p. A-17). When a high-energy bond such as that binding the terminal phosphate to adenosine is split, a substantial amount of energy is released. ATP is the universal energy carrier—the common energy "currency" of the body. Cells can "cash in" ATP to pay the energy "price" for running the cell machinery. To obtain immediate usable energy, cells split the terminal phosphate bond of ATP, which yields adenosine diphosphate (ADP)—adenosine with two phosphate groups attached (*di* means "two")—plus inorganic phosphate (P_i) plus energy:

$$ATP \xrightarrow{\text{splitting}} ADP + P_i + \text{energy for use by the cell}$$

In this energy scheme, food can be thought of as the "crude fuel" and ATP as the "refined fuel" for operating the body's machinery. The food is digested, or broken down by the digestive system into smaller absorbable units that can be transferred from the digestive tract lumen into the blood (see Chapter 15). For example, dietary carbohydrates are broken down primarily into glucose, which is absorbed into the blood. No usable energy is released during the digestion of food. When delivered to the cells by the blood, the nutrient molecules are transported across the plasma membrane into the cytosol. (Details of how materials cross the membrane are covered in Chapter 3.)

We now turn attention to the steps involved in ATP production within the cell and the role of the mitochondria in these steps. **Cellular respiration** refers collectively to the intracellular reactions in which energy-rich molecules are broken down to form ATP, using O_2 and producing carbon dioxide (CO_2) in the process. In most cells, ATP is generated from the sequential dismantling of absorbed nutrient molecules in three stages: *glycolysis* in the cytosol, the *citric acid cycle* in the mitochondrial matrix, and *oxidative phosphorylation* at the mitochondrial inner membrane (● Figure 2-9). (Muscle cells use an additional cytosolic pathway for immediately generating energy at the onset of exercise; see p. 224.) We use glucose as an example to describe these stages.

GLYCOLYSIS Among the thousands of enzymes in the cytosol are the those responsible for **glycolysis,** a chemical process involving 10 sequential reactions that break down a six-carbon sugar molecule, glucose, into two pyruvate molecules, each with three carbons (*glyc* means "sweet"; *lysis* means "breakdown") (● Figure 2-10). During this process, two hydrogens are released and transferred to two NADH molecules for later use. (You will learn more about NADH shortly.) Some energy from the broken chemical bonds of glucose is used directly to convert ADP into ATP. However, glycolysis is not efficient in terms of energy extraction: The net yield is only two molecules of ATP per glucose molecule processed. Much of the energy originally contained in the glucose molecule is still locked in the chemical

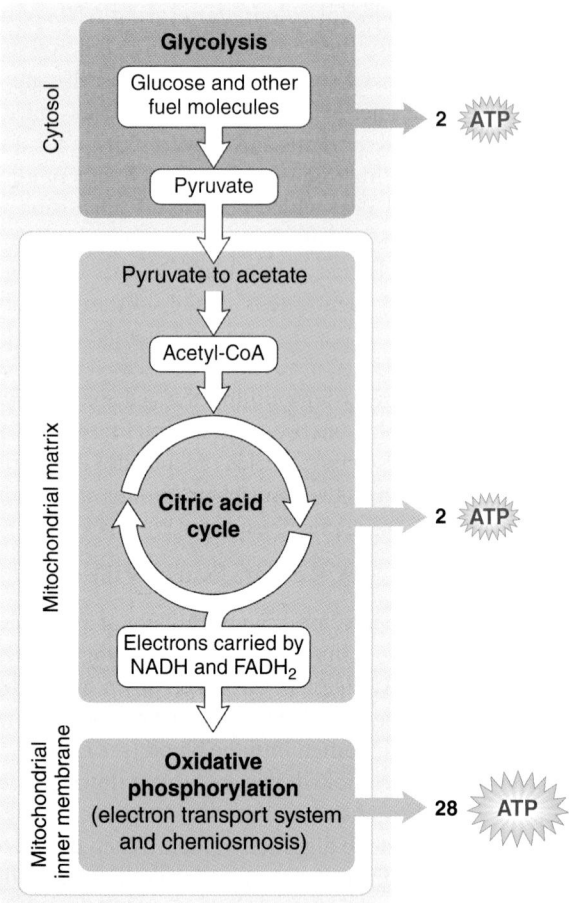

Glycolysis

Glucose and other fuel molecules

Cytosol

2 ATP

Pyruvate

Pyruvate to acetate

Acetyl-CoA

Citric acid cycle

Mitochondrial matrix

2 ATP

Electrons carried by NADH and FADH₂

Oxidative phosphorylation (electron transport system and chemiosmosis)

Mitochondrial inner membrane

28 ATP

● FIGURE 2-9 **Stages of cellular respiration.** The three stages of cellular respiration are glycolysis, the citric acid cycle, and oxidative phosphorylation.

bonds of the pyruvate molecules. The low-energy yield of glycolysis is not enough to support the body's demand for ATP. This is where the mitochondria come into play.

CITRIC ACID CYCLE The pyruvate produced by glycolysis in the cytosol is selectively transported into the mitochondrial matrix.

Cytosol

Glycolysis → ATP

Pyruvate to acetate

Citric acid cycle → ATP

Oxidative phosphorylation → ATP

One 6-carbon glucose molecule

Ten separate steps

2 NAD⁺ → 2 NADH

2 ADP + 2 Pᵢ → 2 ATP

Two 3-carbon pyruvate molecules

● FIGURE 2-10 **Glycolysis in the cytosol.** Glycolysis splits glucose (six carbons) into two pyruvate molecules (three carbons each), with a net yield of two ATP plus two NADH (available for further energy extraction by the electron transport system).

Here, one of its carbons is enzymatically removed in the form of CO_2 and later eliminated from the body as an end product, or waste (● Figure 2-11). Also, another hydrogen is released and transferred to another NADH. The two-carbon molecule remaining after the breakdown process, acetate, combines with coenzyme A (CoA), a derivative of pantothenic acid (a B vitamin), to produce the compound acetyl-CoA.

Acetyl-CoA then enters the **citric acid cycle,** a cyclical series of eight biochemical reactions that are catalyzed by the enzymes of the mitochondrial matrix. This cycle of reactions can be compared to one revolution around a Ferris wheel, except that the molecules themselves are not physically moved around in a cycle. On the top of the Ferris wheel, acetyl-CoA, a two-carbon molecule, enters a seat already occupied by oxaloacetate, which has four carbons. These two molecules link to form a six-carbon citrate molecule (at intracellular pH, citric acid exists in an ionized form, citrate), and the trip around the citric acid cycle begins. (This cycle is alternatively known as the **Krebs cycle,** in honor of its principal discoverer, or the **tricarboxylic acid cycle,** because citrate contains three carboxylic acid groups.) At each step in the cycle, matrix enzymes modify the passenger molecule to form a slightly different molecule (shown in ● Figure 2-11). These molecular alterations have the following important consequences:

1. Two carbons are "kicked off the ride"—released one at a time from six-carbon citrate, converting it back into four-carbon oxaloacetate, which is now available at the top of the cycle to pick up another acetyl-CoA for another revolution through the cycle.

2. The released carbon atoms, which were originally present in the acetyl-CoA that entered the cycle, are converted into two molecules of CO_2. Note that two carbon atoms enter the cycle in the form of acetyl-CoA and two carbon atoms leave the cycle in the form of two CO_2 molecules. This CO_2, as well as the CO_2 produced during the formation of acetate from pyruvate, passes out of the mitochondrial matrix and subsequently out of the cell to enter the blood. The blood carries the CO_2 to the lungs, where it is eliminated to the atmosphere through breathing. The oxygen used to make CO_2 from these released carbons is derived from the molecules involved in the reactions, not from free molecular oxygen supplied by breathing.

3. Hydrogens are also "bumped off" during the cycle at four of the chemical conversion steps. The key purpose of the citric acid cycle is to produce these hydrogens for entry into the electron transport system in the inner mitochondrial membrane. The hydrogens are transferred to two different hydrogen carrier molecules— **nicotinamide adenine dinucleotide (NAD⁺),** a derivative of the B vitamin niacin, and **flavine adenine dinucleotide (FAD),** a derivative of the B vitamin riboflavin. The transfer of hydrogen converts these compounds

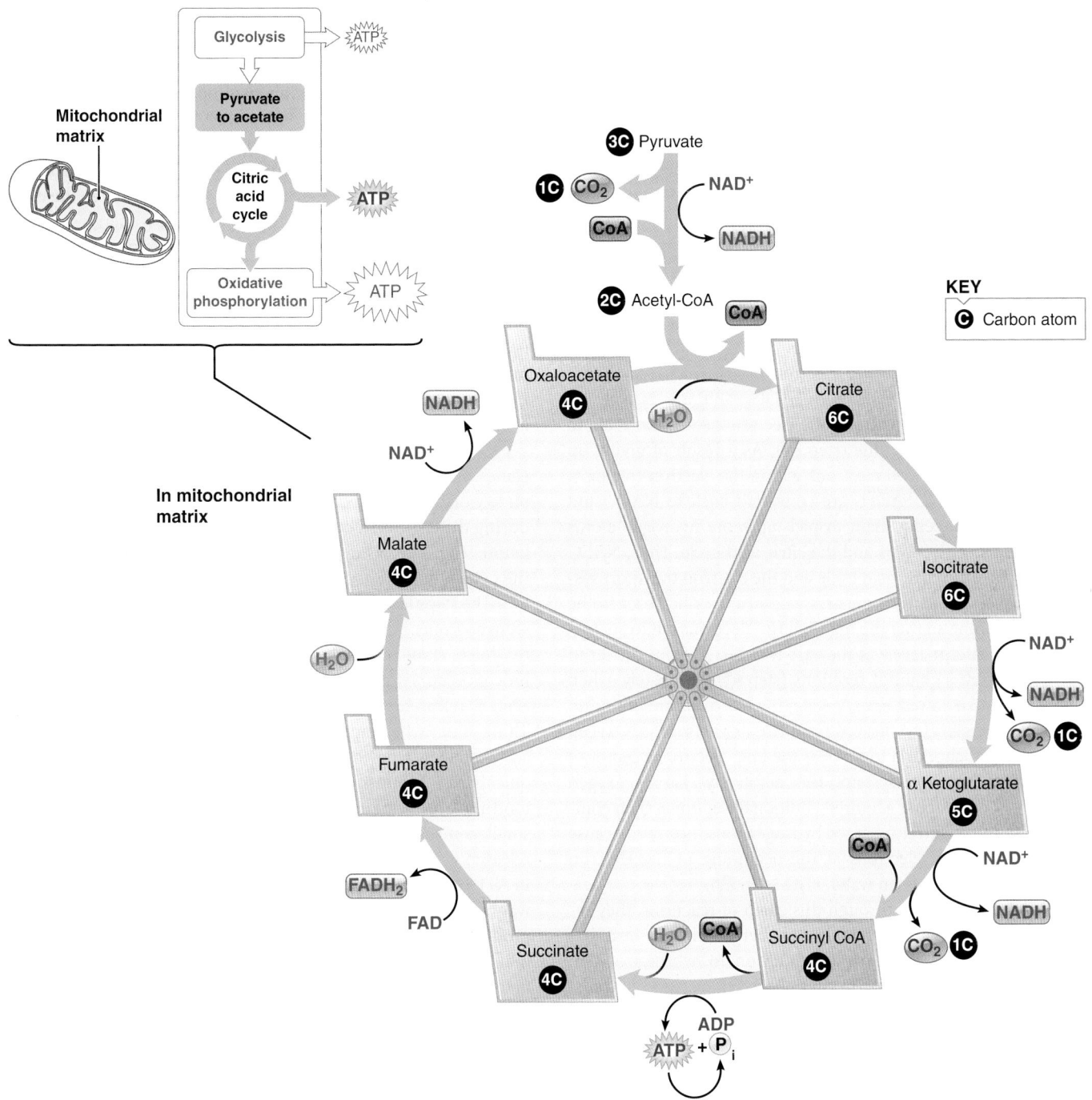

● FIGURE 2-11 **Citric acid cycle in the mitochondrial matrix.** The two carbons entering the cycle by means of acetyl-CoA are eventually converted to CO_2, with oxaloacetate, which accepts acetyl-CoA, being regenerated at the end of the cyclical pathway. The hydrogens released at specific points along the pathway bind to the hydrogen carrier molecules NAD^+ and FAD for further processing by the electron transport system. One molecule of ATP is generated for each molecule of acetyl-CoA that enters the citric acid cycle, for a total of two molecules of ATP for each molecule of processed glucose.

to NADH and $FADH_2$, respectively. Three NADH and one $FADH_2$ are produced for each turn of the citric acid cycle.

4. One more molecule of ATP is produced for each molecule of acetyl-CoA processed. Because each glucose molecule is converted into two acetate molecules, fueling two turns of the citric acid cycle, two more ATP molecules are produced from each glucose molecule.

So far, the cell still does not have much of an energy profit. However, the citric acid cycle is important in preparing the hydrogen carrier molecules for their entry into the final stage, oxidative phosphorylation, which produces far more energy than the sparse amount of ATP produced by the cycle itself.

OXIDATIVE PHOSPHORYLATION Considerable untapped energy is still stored in the released hydrogens, which contain electrons at high energy levels. **Oxidative phosphorylation** refers to the process by which ATP is synthesized using the energy released by electrons as they are transferred to O_2. This process involves two groups of proteins, both located at the inner mitochondrial membrane: the *electron transport system* and *ATP synthase.*

The "big payoff" in energy capture begins when NADH and $FADH_2$ enter the electron transport system. The **electron transport system** consists of a series of protein complexes that contain electron carriers (● Figure 2-12). As the electron transport system begins, the high-energy electrons are extracted from the hydrogens held in NADH and $FADH_2$ and are transferred through a series of steps from one electron-carrier molecule to another in an assembly line (step **1**). As a result of giving up hydrogen ions (H^+) and electrons within the electron transport system, NADH and $FADH_2$ are converted back to NAD^+ and FAD (step **2**), freeing them to pick up more hydrogen atoms released during glycolysis and the citric acid cycle. Thus, NAD^+ and FAD link the citric acid cycle and the electron transport system. The electron carriers are arranged in a specific order in the inner membrane so that the high-energy electrons fall to successively lower energy levels as they are transferred from carrier to carrier through a chain of reactions (step **3**). Ultimately, when they are in their lowest energy state, the electrons are bound to molecular oxygen (O_2) derived from the air we breathe. Oxygen enters the mitochondria to serve as the final electron acceptor of the electron transport system. This negatively charged oxygen (negative because it has acquired additional electrons) then combines with the positively charged hydrogen ions (positive because they have donated electrons at the beginning of the electron transport system) to form water, H_2O (step **4**).

As electrons move through this chain of reactions, they release free energy. Part of the released energy is lost as heat, but some is harnessed by the mitochondrion to synthesize ATP. Energy released during the transfer of electrons is used to transport hydrogen ions (H^+) across the inner mitochondrial membrane from the matrix to the space between the inner and the outer mitochondrial membranes, known as the *intermembrane space* (step **5**). As a result, hydrogen ions are more heavily concentrated in the intermembrane space than in the matrix. This H^+ gradient generated by the electron transport system (step **6**) supplies the energy that drives ATP synthesis by the membrane-bound mitochondrial enzyme ATP synthase.

ATP synthase consists of several connected components, including a headpiece located in the matrix and other components embedded in the inner membrane. Because H^+ ions are more heavily concentrated in the intermembrane space than in the matrix, they have a strong tendency to flow back into the matrix through the inner membrane via channels located within the ATP synthase complexes (step **7**). This flow of H^+ ions activates ATP synthase and powers ATP synthesis by the headpiece, a process called **chemiosmosis.** Passage of H^+ ions through the channel makes the headpiece spin like a top (step **8**), similar to the flow of water making a waterwheel turn.

As a result of the changes in its shape and position as it turns, the headpiece is able to sequentially pick up ADP and P_i, combine them, and release the ATP product (step **9**).

Oxidative phosphorylation encompasses the entire process by which ATP synthase synthesizes ATP by phosphorylating (adding a phosphate to) ADP using the energy released by electrons as they are transferred to O_2 by the electron transport system. The harnessing of energy into a useful form as the electrons tumble from a high-energy state to a low-energy state can be likened to a power plant converting the energy of water tumbling down a waterfall into electricity.

When activated, ATP synthase provides a rich yield of 28 more ATP molecules for each glucose molecule processed (● Figure 2-13). Approximately 2.5 ATP are synthesized as a pair of electrons released by NADH travels through the entire electron transport system to oxygen. The shorter pathway followed by an electron pair released from $FADH_2$ (see ● Figure 2-12) synthesizes about 1.5 ATP. This means a total of 32 molecules of ATP are produced when a glucose molecule is completely dismantled in cellular respiration: 2 during glycolysis, 2 during the citric acid cycle, and 28 during oxidative phosphorylation. The ATP is transported out of the mitochondrion into the cytosol for use as the cell's energy source.

The steps leading to oxidative phosphorylation might at first seem an unnecessary complication. Why not just directly oxidize, or "burn," food molecules to release their energy? When this process occurs outside the body, all energy stored in a food molecule is released explosively in the form of heat (● Figure 2-14). Think about what happens when a marshmallow you're roasting accidentally catches on fire. The burning marshmallow gets hot quickly as a result of the rapid oxidation of sugar. In the body, food molecules are oxidized within the mitochondria in many small, controlled steps so that their chemical energy is gradually released in small quantities that can be more efficiently captured in ATP bonds and stored in a form that is useful to the cell. In this way, much less of the energy is converted to heat. The heat that is produced is not completely wasted energy; it is used to help maintain body temperature, with any excess heat being eliminated to the environment.

The cell generates more energy in aerobic than in anaerobic conditions.

The cell is a more efficient energy converter when O_2 is available (● Figure 2-15). In an **anaerobic** ("lack of air," specifically "lack of O_2") condition, the degradation of glucose cannot proceed beyond glycolysis, which takes place in the cytosol and yields only two molecules of ATP per molecule of glucose. The untapped energy of the glucose molecule remains locked in the bonds of the pyruvate molecules, which are eventually converted to lactate if they do not enter the pathway that ultimately leads to oxidative phosphorylation.

When sufficient O_2 is present—an **aerobic** ("with air" or "with O_2") condition—mitochondrial processing (that is, the citric acid cycle in the matrix and the electron transport system and ATP synthase at the inner membrane) harnesses enough energy to generate 30 more molecules of ATP, for a total net yield of 32 ATPs per molecule of glucose processed. (For a description

1 The high-energy electrons extracted from the hydrogens in NADH and $FADH_2$ are transferred from one electron-carrier molecule to another.

2 The NADH and $FADH_2$ are converted to NAD^+ and FAD, which frees them to pick up more hydrogen atoms released during glycolysis and the citric acid cycle.

3 The high-energy electrons fall to successively lower energy levels as they are transferred from carrier to carrier through the electron transport system.

4 The electrons are passed to O_2, the final electron acceptor of the electron transport system. This oxygen, now negatively charged because it has acquired additional electrons, combines with H^+ ions, which are positively charged because they donated electrons at the beginning of the electron transport system, to form H_2O.

5 As electrons move through the electron transport system, they release free energy. Part of the released energy is lost as heat, but some is harnessed by the mitochondrion to transport H^+ across the inner mitochondrial membrane from the matrix to the intermembrane space at Complexes I, III, and IV.

6 As a result, H^+ ions are more heavily concentrated in the intermembrane space than in the matrix. This H^+ gradient supplies the energy that drives ATP synthesis by ATP synthase.

7 Because of this gradient, H^+ ions have a strong tendency to flow into the matrix across the inner membrane via channels within the ATP synthase complexes.

8 This flow of H^+ ions activates ATP synthase and powers ATP synthesis by the headpiece, a process called **chemiosmosis**. Passage of H^+ ions through the channel makes the headpiece spin like a top.

9 As a result of changes in its shape and position as it turns, the headpiece picks up ADP and P_i, combines them, and releases the ATP product.

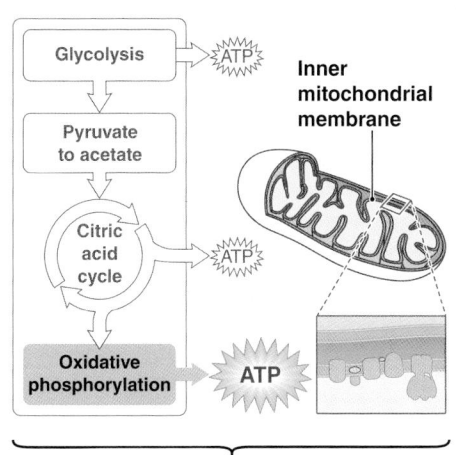

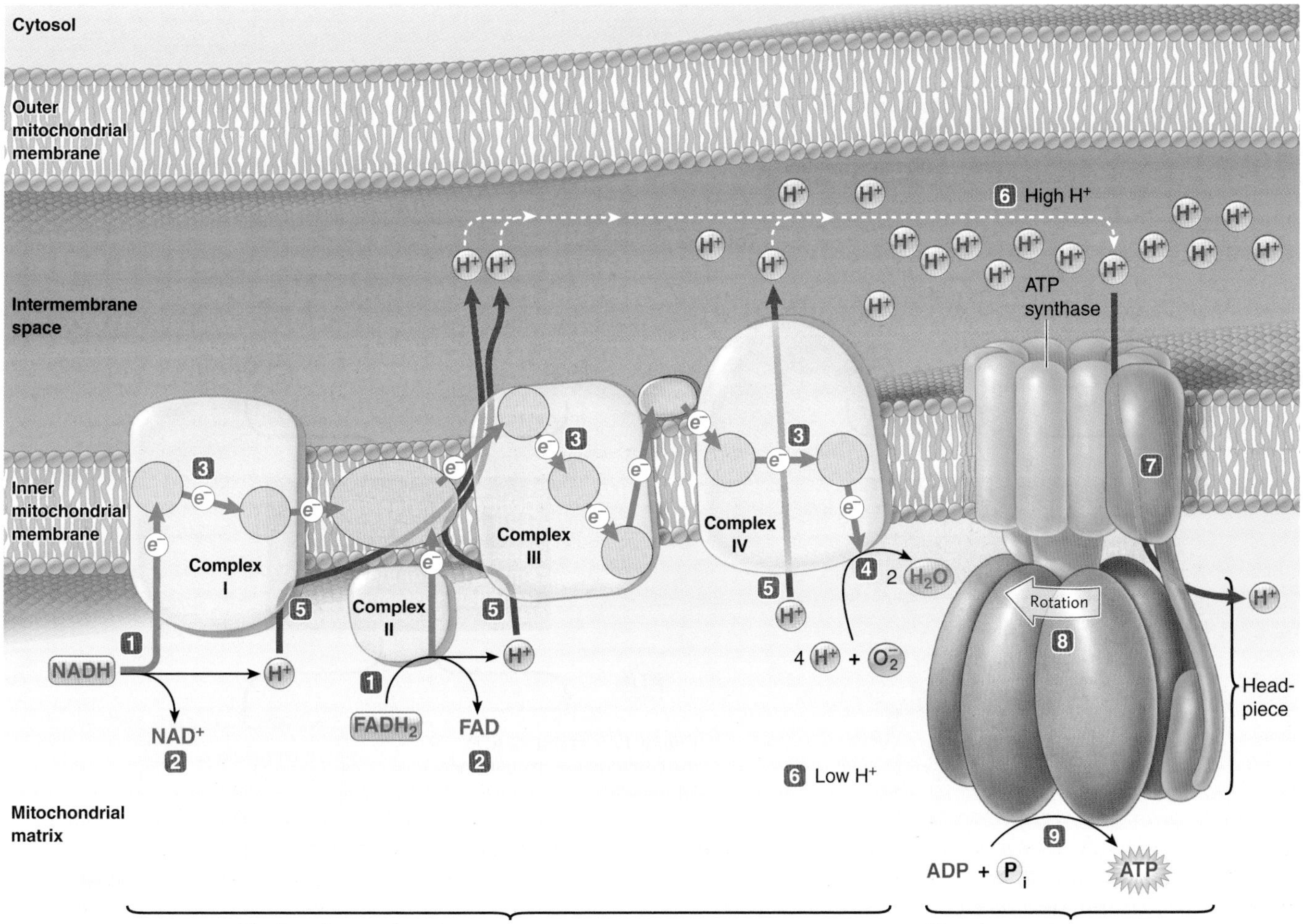

Electron tranport system
Electrons flow through a series of electron carriers from high-energy to low-energy levels; the energy released builds an H^+ gradient across the inner mitochondrial membrane.

Chemiosmosis
ATP synthase catalyzes ATP synthesis using energy from the H^+ gradient across the membrane.

Oxidative phosphorylation

● **FIGURE 2-12 Oxidative phosphorylation at the mitochondrial inner membrane.** Oxidative phosphorylation involves the electron transport system (steps 1–6) and chemiosmosis by ATP synthase (steps 7–9). The electron transport system consists of a series of electron carriers (pink circles) associated with four large protein complexes (in light green).

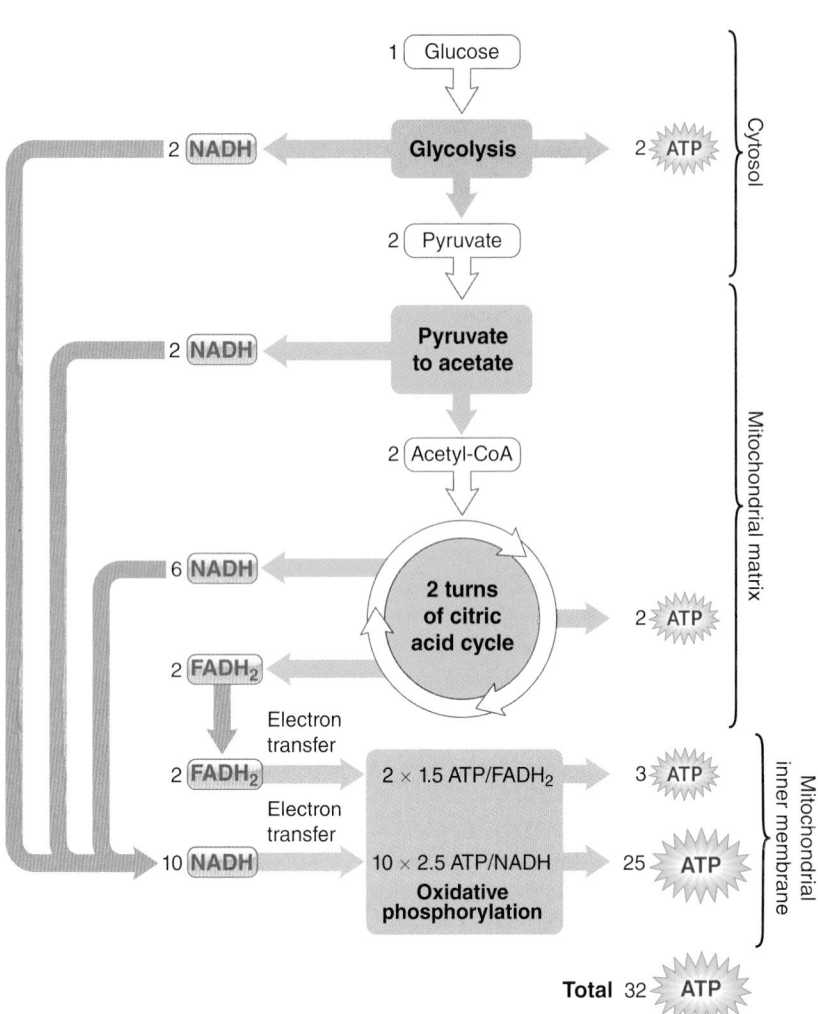

● FIGURE 2-13 **Summary of ATP production from the complete oxidation of one molecule of glucose.** The total of 32 ATP assumes that electrons carried by each NADH yield 2.5 ATP and those carried by each FADH₂ yield 1.5 ATP during oxidative phosphorylation.

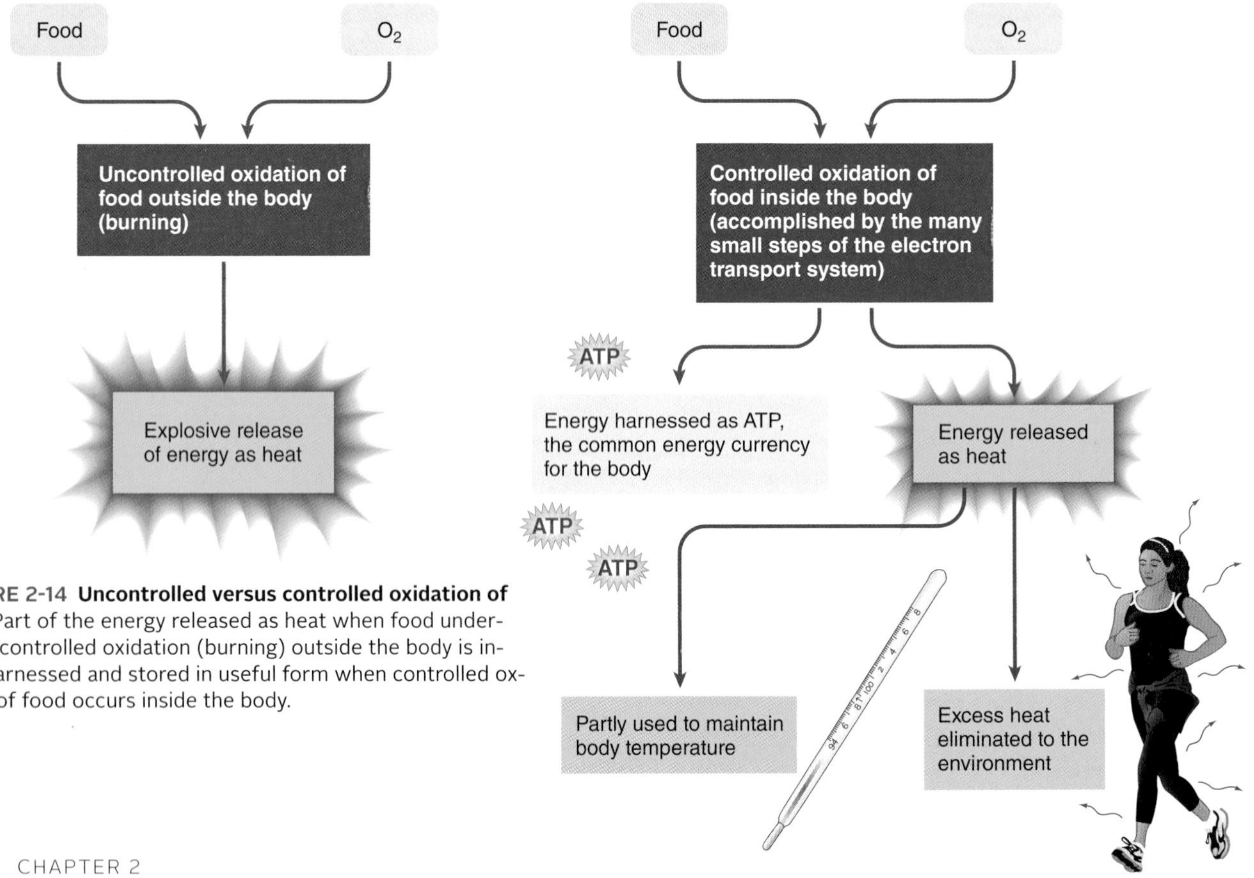

● FIGURE 2-14 **Uncontrolled versus controlled oxidation of food.** Part of the energy released as heat when food undergoes uncontrolled oxidation (burning) outside the body is instead harnessed and stored in useful form when controlled oxidation of food occurs inside the body.

Food   O₂

Uncontrolled oxidation of food outside the body (burning)

Explosive release of energy as heat

Food   O₂

Controlled oxidation of food inside the body (accomplished by the many small steps of the electron transport system)

ATP

Energy harnessed as ATP, the common energy currency for the body

ATP

ATP

Energy released as heat

Partly used to maintain body temperature

Excess heat eliminated to the environment

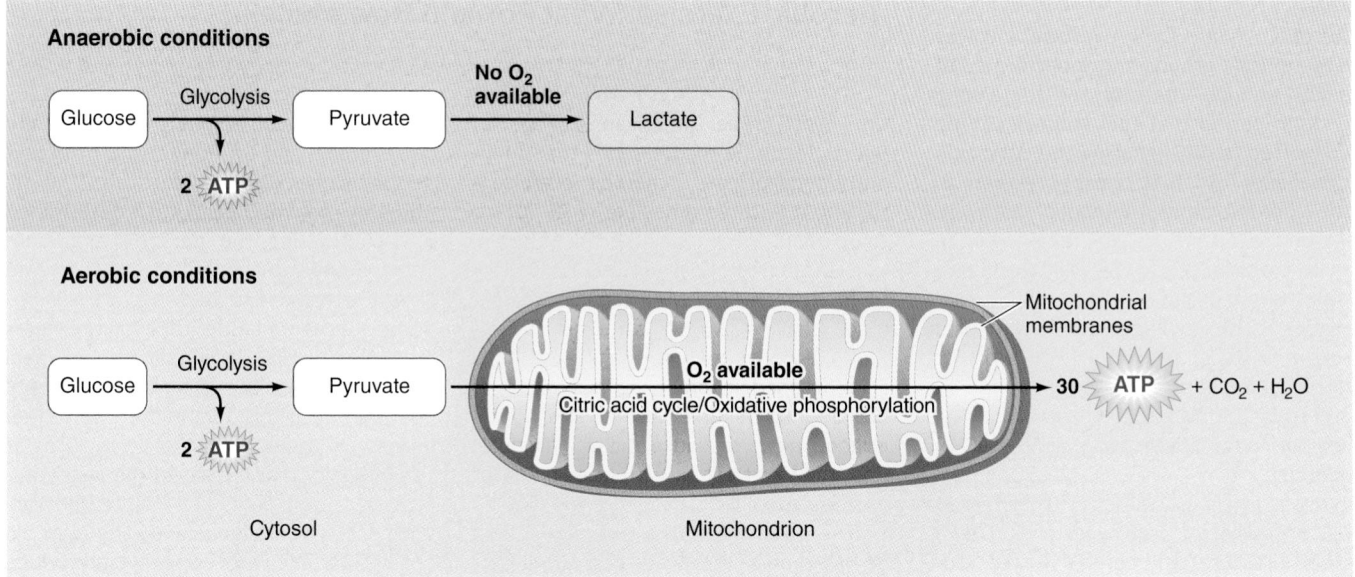

Anaerobic conditions

Glucose → [Glycolysis] → Pyruvate → [No O_2 available] → Lactate

2 ATP

Aerobic conditions

Glucose → [Glycolysis] → Pyruvate → [Citric acid cycle/Oxidative phosphorylation, O_2 available] → 30 ATP + CO_2 + H_2O

2 ATP

Mitochondrial membranes

Cytosol   Mitochondrion

● **FIGURE 2-15 Comparison of energy yield and products under anaerobic and aerobic conditions.** In anaerobic conditions, only 2 ATP are produced for every glucose molecule processed, but in aerobic conditions a total of 32 ATP are produced per glucose molecule.

of aerobic exercise, see the boxed feature on p. 36, ❿ Beyond the Basics.) The overall reaction for the oxidation of food molecules to yield energy during cellular respiration is as follows:

$$\text{Food} + \underset{\substack{\text{(necessary} \\ \text{for oxidative} \\ \text{phosphorylation)}}}{O_2} \rightleftharpoons \underset{\substack{\text{(produced} \\ \text{primarily} \\ \text{by the citric} \\ \text{acid cycle)}}}{CO_2} + \underset{\substack{\text{(produced by} \\ \text{the electron} \\ \text{transport} \\ \text{system)}}}{H_2O} + \underset{\substack{\text{(produced} \\ \text{primarily by} \\ \text{ATP synthase)}}}{\text{ATP}}$$

Glucose, the principal nutrient derived from dietary carbohydrates, is the fuel preference of most cells. However, nutrient molecules derived from fats (fatty acids) and, if necessary, from proteins (amino acids) can also participate at specific points in this overall chemical reaction to eventually produce energy. Amino acids are usually used for protein synthesis rather than energy production, but they can be used as fuel if insufficient glucose and fat are available (see Chapter 16).

Note that the oxidative reactions within the mitochondria generate energy, unlike the oxidative reactions controlled by the peroxisome enzymes. Both organelles use O_2, but they do so for different purposes.

The energy stored within ATP is used for synthesis, transport, and mechanical work.

Once formed, ATP is transported out of the mitochondria and is then available as an energy source in the cell. Cell activities that require energy expenditure fall into three main categories:

1. *Synthesis of new chemical compounds,* such as protein synthesis by the ER. Some cells, especially cells with a high rate of secretion and cells in the growth phase, use up to 75% of the ATP they generate just to synthesize new chemical compounds.

2. *Membrane transport,* such as the selective transport of molecules across the kidney tubules during the process of urine formation. Kidney cells can expend as much as 80%

of their ATP currency to operate their selective membrane-transport mechanisms.

3. *Mechanical work,* such as contraction of the heart muscle to pump blood or contraction of skeletal muscles to lift an object. These activities require tremendous quantities of ATP.

As a result of cell energy expenditure to support these various activities, large quantities of ADP are produced. These energy-depleted molecules enter the mitochondria for "recharging" and then cycle back into the cytosol as energy-rich ATP molecules after participating in oxidative phosphorylation. In this recharging–expenditure cycle, a single ADP/ATP molecule may shuttle between mitochondria and cytosol thousands of times per day. On average a person recycles the equivalent of his or her body weight of ATP every day.

The high demands for ATP make glycolysis alone an insufficient, as well as inefficient, supplier of power for most cells. Were it not for the mitochondria, which house the metabolic machinery for oxidative phosphorylation, the body's energy capability would be limited. However, glycolysis does provide cells with a sustenance mechanism that can produce at least some ATP under anaerobic conditions. Skeletal muscle cells in particular take advantage of this ability during short bursts of strenuous exercise, when energy demands for contractile activity outstrip the body's ability to bring adequate O_2 to the exercising muscles to support oxidative phosphorylation.

Having completed our discussion of the organelles, we now turn to the cytosol.

Cytosol: Cell Gel

Occupying about 55% of the total cell volume, the cytosol is the semiliquid portion of the cytoplasm that surrounds the organelles. Its nondescript appearance under an electron microscope

Aerobic ("with O₂") **exercise** involves large muscle groups and is performed at a low enough intensity and for a long enough period that fuel sources can be converted to ATP by using the citric acid cycle and oxidative phosphorylation as the predominant metabolic pathway. Aerobic exercise can be sustained from 15 to 20 minutes to several hours at a time. Short-duration, high-intensity activities, such as weight training and the 100-meter dash, which last for a matter of seconds and rely solely on energy stored in the muscles and on glycolysis, are forms of **anaerobic** ("without O₂") **exercise.**

Inactivity is associated with increased risk of developing both hypertension (high blood pressure) and coronary artery disease (blockage of the arteries that supply the heart). The American College of Sports Medicine recommends that an individual participate in aerobic exercise a minimum of three times per week for 20 to 60 minutes to reduce the risk of hypertension and coronary artery disease and to improve physical work capacity. Recent studies have shown the same health benefits are derived whether the exercise is accomplished in one long stretch or is broken into multiple shorter stints. This is good news, because many individuals find it easier to stick with brief bouts of exercise sprinkled throughout the day.

The intensity of the exercise should be based on a percentage of the individual's maximal capacity to work. The easiest way to establish the proper intensity of exercise and to monitor intensity levels is by checking the heart rate. The estimated maximal heart rate is determined by subtracting the person's age from 220. Significant benefits can be derived from aerobic exercise performed between 70% and 80% of maximal heart rate. For example, the estimated maximal heart rate for a 20-year-old is 200 beats per minute. If this person exercised three times per week for 20 to 60 minutes at an intensity that increased the heart rate to 140 to 160 beats per minute, the participant should significantly improve his or her aerobic work capacity and reduce the risk of cardiovascular disease.

---

gives the false impression that the cytosol is a liquid mixture of uniform consistency, but it is actually a highly organized, gel-like mass with differences in composition and consistency from one part of the cell to another.

The cytosol is important in intermediary metabolism, ribosomal protein synthesis, and nutrient storage.

Three general categories of activities are associated with the cytosol: (1) enzymatic regulation of intermediary metabolism, (2) ribosomal protein synthesis, and (3) storage of fat, carbohydrate, and secretory vesicles.

ENZYMATIC REGULATION OF INTERMEDIARY METABOLISM The term **intermediary metabolism** refers collectively to the large set of chemical reactions inside the cell that involve the degradation, synthesis, and transformation of small organic molecules such as simple sugars, amino acids, and fatty acids. These reactions are critical for ultimately capturing the energy used for cell activities and for providing the raw materials needed to maintain the cell's structure, function, and growth. Intermediary metabolism occurs in the cytoplasm, with most of it being accomplished in the cytosol. The cytosol contains thousands of enzymes involved in intermediary biochemical reactions.

RIBOSOMAL PROTEIN SYNTHESIS Also dispersed throughout the cytosol are the free ribosomes, which synthesize proteins for use in the cytosol itself. In contrast, recall that the rough ER ribosomes synthesize proteins for secretion and for construction of new cell components.

STORAGE OF FAT, GLYCOGEN, AND SECRETORY VESICLES Excess nutrients not immediately used for ATP production are converted in the cytosol into storage forms that are readily visible under a light microscope. Such nonpermanent masses of stored

material are known as **inclusions.** Inclusions are not surrounded by membrane, and they may or may not be present, depending on the type of cell and the circumstances. The largest and most important storage product is fat. Small fat droplets are

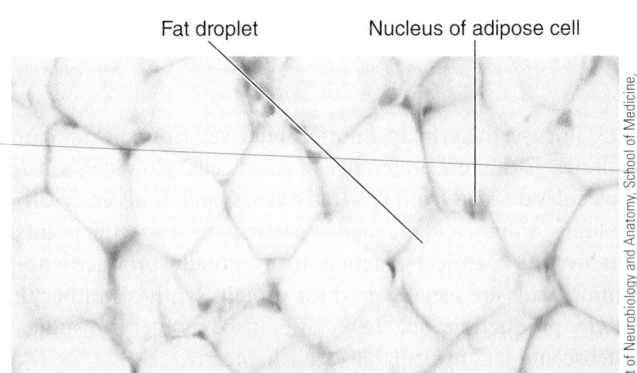

(a) Fat storage in adipose cells

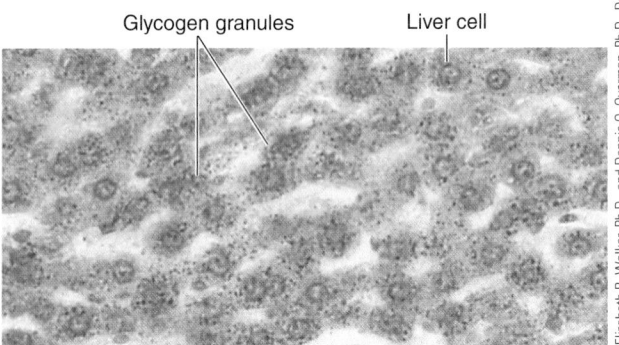

(b) Glycogen storage in liver cells

● **FIGURE 2-16 Inclusions.** (a) Light micrograph showing fat storage in adipose cells. A fat droplet occupies almost the entire cytosol of each cell. (b) Light micrograph showing glycogen storage in liver cells. The red-stained granules throughout the cytosol of each liver cell are glycogen deposits.

present within the cytosol in various cells. In **adipose tissue,** the tissue specialized for fat storage, stored fat molecules can occupy almost the entire cytosol, where they merge to form one large fat droplet (● Figure 2-16a). The other visible storage product is **glycogen,** the storage form of glucose, which appears as clusters or granules dispersed throughout the cell (● Figure 2-16b). Cells vary in their ability to store glycogen, with liver and muscle cells having the greatest stores. When food is not available to provide fuel for the citric acid cycle and electron transport system, stored glycogen and fat are broken down to release glucose and fatty acids, respectively, which can feed the mitochondrial energy-producing machinery. An average adult human stores enough glycogen to provide energy for about a day of normal activities and typically has enough fat stored to provide energy for two months.

Secretory vesicles that have been processed and packaged by the ER and Golgi complex also remain in the cytosol, where they are stored until signaled to empty their contents to the outside. In addition, transport and endocytic vesicles move through the cytosol.

Cytoskeleton: Cell "Bone and Muscle"

Different cell types in the body have distinct shapes, structural complexities, and functional specializations. These unique characteristics are maintained by the cytoskeleton, an elaborate protein scaffolding dispersed throughout the cytosol that acts as the "bone and muscle" of the cell by supporting and organizing the cell components and controlling their movements.

The cytoskeleton has three distinct elements: (1) *microtubules,* (2) *microfilaments,* and (3) *intermediate filaments* (● Figure 2-17). These elements are structurally linked and functionally coordinated to provide certain integrated functions for the cell. These functions, along with the functions of all other components of the cytoplasm, are summarized in ▲ Table 2-1.

Microtubules help maintain asymmetric cell shapes and play a role in complex cell movements.

Microtubules are the largest of the cytoskeletal elements. They are slender, long, hollow, unbranched tubes composed primarily of **tubulin,** a small, globular, protein molecule (see ● Figure 2-17a). Microtubules position many of the cytoplasmic organelles, such as the ER, Golgi complex, lysosomes, and mitochondria. They are also essential for maintaining the shape of asymmetric cells, such as nerve cells, whose elongated axons may extend up to a meter in length from where the cell body originates in the spinal cord to where

the axon ends at a muscle (● Figure 2-18a). Along with specialized intermediate filaments, microtubules stabilize this asymmetric axonal extension.

Microtubules also play an important role in some complex cell movements, including (1) transport of secretory vesicles or other materials from one region of the cell to another, (2) movement of specialized cell projections such as cilia and flagella, and (3) distribution of chromosomes during cell division through formation of a mitotic spindle. Let us examine each of these roles.

VESICLE TRANSPORT Axonal transport provides a good example of the importance of an organized system for moving secretory vesicles. In a nerve cell, specific chemicals are released from the terminal end of the elongated axon to influence a muscle or another structure that the nerve cell controls. These chemicals are largely produced within the cell body where the nuclear DNA blueprint, endoplasmic reticular factory, and Golgi packaging and distribution outlet are located. If they had to diffuse on their own from the cell body to a distant axon terminal, it would take the chemicals about 50 years to get there—obviously an impractical solution. Instead, the microtubules that extend from the beginning to the end of the axon provide a "highway" for vesicular traffic along the axon.

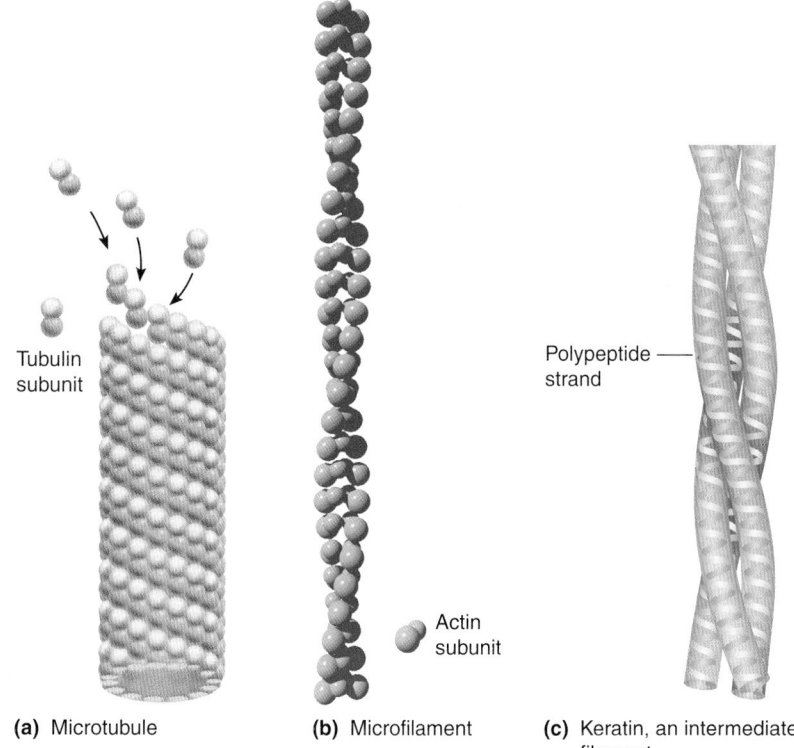

Tubulin subunit

Actin subunit

Polypeptide strand

(a) Microtubule **(b)** Microfilament **(c)** Keratin, an intermediate filament

● **FIGURE 2-17 Components of the cytoskeleton.** (a) A microtubule, the largest of the cytoskeletal elements, is a long, hollow tube formed by two slightly different variants of globular-shaped tubulin molecules. (b) Most microfilaments, the smallest of the cytoskeletal elements, consist of two chains of actin molecules wrapped around each other. (c) The intermediate filament keratin, found in skin, is made of three polypeptide strands wound around one another. The composition of intermediate filaments, which are intermediate in size between microtubules and microfilaments, varies among cell types.

Cytoplasm Component	Structure	Function
Organelles		
Endoplasmic reticulum	Extensive, continuous membranous network of fluid-filled tubules and flattened sacs, partially studded with ribosomes	Manufactures products for secretion and forms new plasma membrane and other cell components
Golgi complex	Sets of stacked, flattened membranous sacs	Modifies, packages, and distributes newly synthesized proteins
Lysosomes	Membranous sacs containing hydrolytic enzymes	Serve as cell's "digestive system," destroying foreign substances and cellular debris
Peroxisomes	Membranous sacs containing oxidative enzymes	Perform detoxification activities
Mitochondria	Rod- or oval-shaped bodies enclosed by two membranes, with the inner membrane folded into cristae that project into an interior matrix	Act as energy organelles; are a major site of ATP production; contain enzymes for the citric acid cycle, proteins of the electron transport system, and ATP synthase
Cytosol		
Intermediary metabolism enzymes	Enzymes dispersed within the cytosol	Facilitate intracellular reactions involving degradation, synthesis, and transformation of small organic molecules
Transport, secretory, and endocytic vesicles	Transiently formed, membrane-enclosed products synthesized within or engulfed by the cell	Transport or store products being moved within, out of, or into the cell, respectively
Inclusions	Glycogen granules, fat droplets	Store excess nutrients
Cytoskeleton		As an integrated whole, the cell's "bone and muscle"
Microtubules	Long, slender, hollow tubes composed of tubulin molecules	Maintain asymmetric cell shapes and coordinate complex cell movements, specifically serving as highways for transport of secretory vesicles within a cell, serving as the main structural and functional component of cilia and flagella, and forming a mitotic spindle during cell division
Microfilaments	Intertwined helical chains of actin molecules; microfilaments composed of myosin molecules are also present in muscle cells	Play a vital role in various cellular contractile systems, including muscle contraction and amoeboid movement; serve as mechanical stiffeners for microvilli
Intermediate filaments	Irregular, threadlike proteins	Help resist mechanical stress

Molecular motors are the transporters. A molecular motor is a protein that attaches to the particle to be transported and then uses energy harnessed from ATP to "walk" along the microtubule, with the particle riding "piggyback" (*motor* means "movement"). *Kinesin,* the molecular motor that carries secretory vesicles to the end of the axon, consists of two "feet," a stalk, and a fanlike tail (see ● Figure 2-18a). The tail binds to the secretory vesicle to be moved, and the feet swing forward one at a time, as if walking, using the tubulin molecules as stepping-stones (see ● Figure 2-18b).

A different molecular motor, *dynein,* carries vesicles containing debris in the opposite direction up the microtubule for degradation by lysosomes in the nerve cell body.

MOVEMENT OF CILIA AND FLAGELLA Microtubules are also the dominant structural and functional components of cilia and flagella. These specialized motile protrusions from the cell surface

allow a cell to move materials across its surface (in the case of a stationary cell) or to propel itself through its environment (in the case of a motile cell). **Cilia** (meaning "eyelashes"; singular, *cilium*) are short, tiny, hairlike protrusions usually found in large numbers on the surface of a ciliated cell. **Flagella** (meaning "whips"; singular, *flagellum*) are long, whiplike appendages; typically, a cell has one or a few flagella at most. Even though they project from the surface of the cell, cilia and flagella are both intracellular structures—they are covered by the plasma membrane.

Cilia beat or stroke in unison in a given direction, much like the coordinated efforts of a rowing team. In humans, ciliated cells line the respiratory tract and the oviduct of the female reproductive tract. The coordinated stroking of the thousands of respiratory cilia help keep foreign particles out of the lungs by sweeping outward dust and other inspired (breathed-in) particles (● Figure 2-19). In the female reproductive tract, the

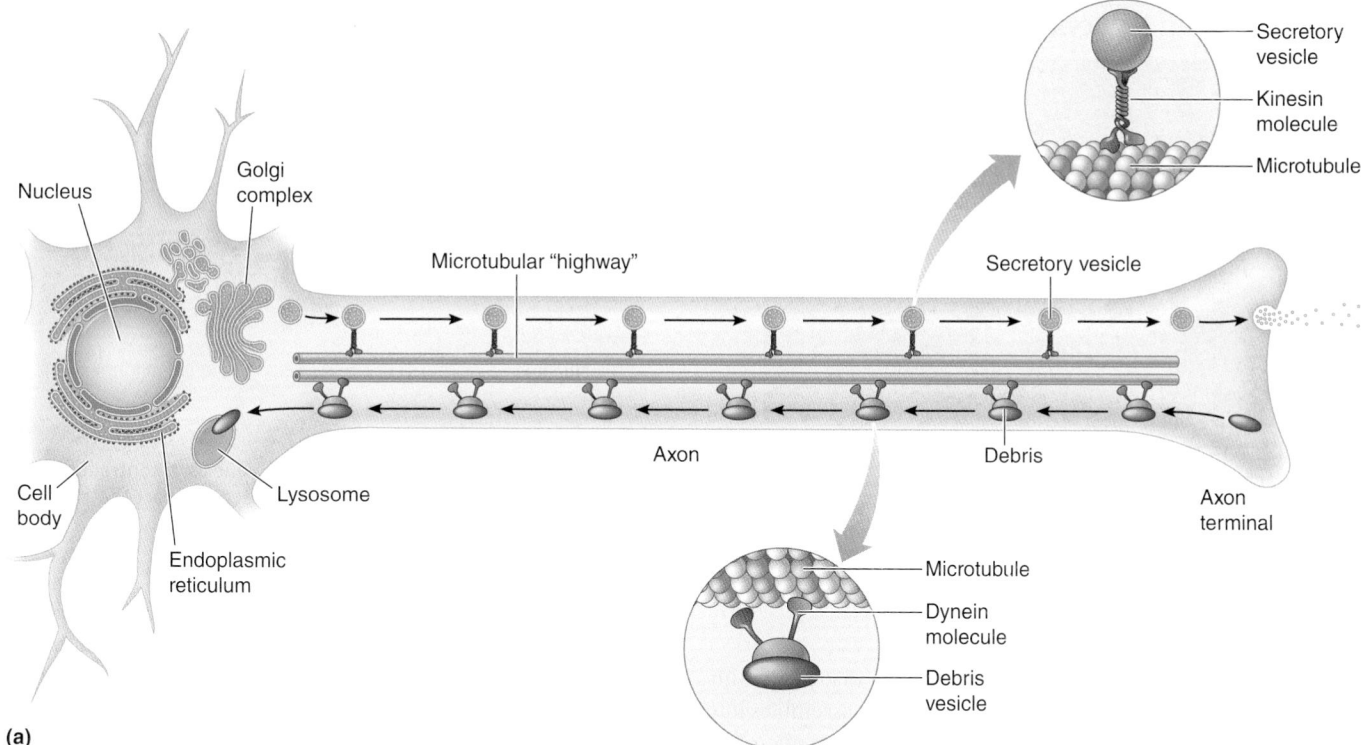

(a)

● FIGURE 2-18 **Two-way vesicular axonal transport along the microtubular "highway" in a nerve cell facilitated by molecular motors.** (a) Secretory vesicles are transported from the site of production in the cell body along a microtubular "highway" to the terminal end for secretion. Vesicles containing debris are transported in the opposite direction for degradation in the cell body. The top enlargement depicts kinesin, a molecular motor, carrying a secretory vesicle down the microtubule by using its "feet" to "step" on one tubulin molecule after another. The bottom enlargement depicts another molecular motor, dynein, transporting debris up the microtubule. (b) How a kinesin molecule "walks" by alternately attaching and releasing its "feet" as it cyclically swings the rear foot ahead of the front foot.

(b)

sweeping action of the cilia lining the oviduct draws the egg (ovum), released from the ovary during ovulation, into the oviduct and then guides it toward the uterus (womb). The only human cells that have a flagellum are sperm (see ● Figure 18-6, p. 589). The whiplike motion of the flagellum or "tail" enables a sperm to move through its environment, which is crucial for maneuvering into position to fertilize the female ovum.

FORMATION OF THE MITOTIC SPINDLE Cell division involves two discrete but related activities: *mitosis* (nuclear division), which depends on microtubules, and *cytokinesis* (cytoplasmic division), which depends on microfilaments and is described in the next section. During **mitosis,** the DNA-containing chromosomes of the nucleus are replicated, resulting in two identical sets. These duplicate sets of chromosomes are separated and drawn apart to opposite sides of the cell so that the genetic material is evenly distributed in the two halves of the cell (see p. A-26).

The replicated chromosomes are pulled apart by a cellular apparatus called the **mitotic spindle,** which is transiently assembled from microtubules only during cell division (see ● Figure C-10, p. A-28). The microtubules of the mitotic spindle are formed by the **centrioles,** a pair of short cylindrical structures that lie at right angles to each other near the nucleus (see ● Figure 2-1). As part of cell division, the centrioles first dupli-

cate themselves; then, the new centriole pairs move to opposite ends of the cell and form the spindle apparatus between them through a precisely organized assemblage of microtubules.

Clinical Note

Some anticancer drugs prevent cancer cells from reproducing by interfering with the microtubules that ordinarily pull the chromosomes to opposite poles during cell division.

Microfilaments are important to cellular contractile systems and as mechanical stiffeners. **Microfilaments** are the smallest elements of the cytoskeleton. The most obvious microfilaments in most cells are those composed of **actin,** a protein

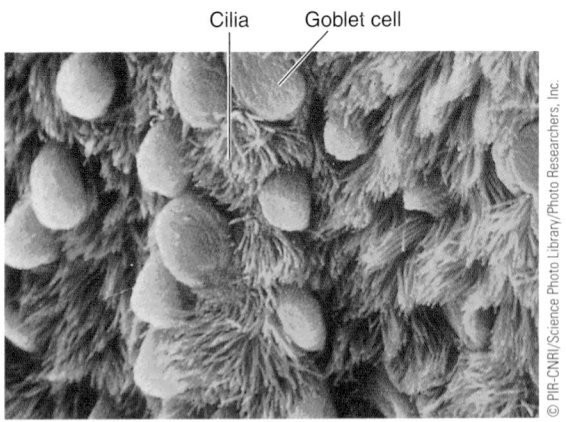

Cilia   Goblet cell

© PIR-CNRI/Science Photo Library/Photo Researchers, Inc.

● **FIGURE 2-19 Cilia in the respiratory tract.** Scanning electron micrograph of cilia on cells lining the human respiratory tract. The respiratory airways are lined by goblet cells, which secrete a sticky mucus that traps inspired particles, and epithelial cells that bear numerous hairlike cilia. The cilia all beat in the same direction to sweep inspired particles up and out of the airways.

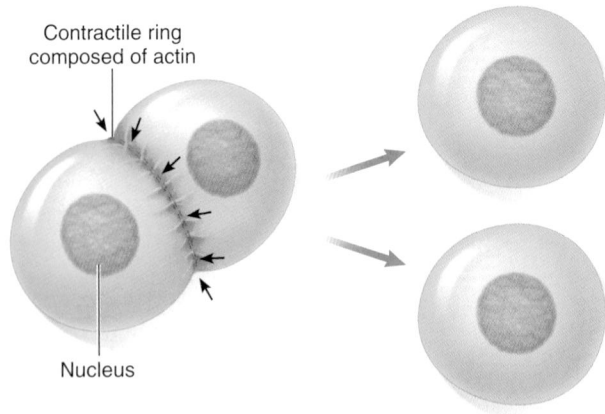

Contractile ring composed of actin

Nucleus

● **FIGURE 2-20 Cytokinesis.** During cytokinesis, a contractile ring composed of actin filaments tightens, squeezing apart the two duplicate cell halves formed by mitosis.

molecule that has a globular shape similar to that of tubulin. Unlike tubulin, which forms a hollow tube, actin assembles into two strands, which twist around each other to form a microfilament (see ● Figure 2-17b). In muscle cells, the protein **myosin** forms a different kind of microfilament (see ● Figure 8-4, p. 212). In most cells, myosin is not as abundant and does not form such distinct filaments.

Microfilaments serve two functions: (1) They play a vital role in various cell contractile systems, and (2) they act as mechanical stiffeners for several specific cell projections.

MICROFILAMENTS IN CELL CONTRACTILE SYSTEMS The most obvious, best-organized, and most clearly understood cell contractile system is that found in muscle. Muscle contains an abundance of actin and myosin microfilaments, which bring about muscle contraction through the ATP-powered sliding of actin microfilaments in relation to stationary myosin microfilaments. Myosin is a molecular motor that has heads that walk along the actin microfilaments, pulling them inward between the myosin microfilaments. Microfilament sliding and force development are triggered by a complex sequence of electrical, biochemical, and mechanical events initiated when the muscle cell is stimulated to contract (see Chapter 8 for details).

Nonmuscle cells may also contain musclelike assemblies. Some of these microfilament contractile systems are transiently assembled to perform a specific function when needed. A good example is the contractile ring that forms during **cytokinesis,** the process by which the two halves of a dividing cell separate into two new daughter cells, each with a full complement of chromosomes. The ring consists of a beltlike bundle of actin filaments located just beneath the plasma membrane in the middle of the dividing cell. When this ring of fibers contracts and tightens, it pinches the cell in two (● Figure 2-20).

Complex actin-based assemblies are also responsible for most cell locomotion. Four types of human cells are capable of moving on their own—sperm, white blood cells, fibroblasts

(connective tissue cells that form scars), and skin cells. Flagella propel sperm. The other motile cells move via **amoeboid movement,** a cell-crawling process that depends on the activity of their actin filaments, in a mechanism similar to that used by amoebas to maneuver through their environment. When crawling, the motile cell forms fingerlike pseudopods at the "front" or leading edge of the cell in the direction of the target. For example, the target that triggers amoeboid movement might be the proximity of food in the case of an amoeba or a bacterium in the case of a white blood cell (see ● Figure 2-7c, p. 28). Pseudopods are formed as a result of the organized assembly and disassembly of branching actin networks. During amoeboid movement, actin filaments continuously grow at the cell's leading edge through the addition of actin molecules at the front of the actin chain. This filament growth pushes that portion of the cell forward as a pseudopod protrusion. Simultaneously, actin molecules at the rear of the filament are being disassembled and transferred to the front of the line. Thus, the filament does not get any longer; it stays the same length but moves forward through the continuous transfer of actin molecules from the rear to the front of the filament in what is termed a *treadmilling* fashion. The cell attaches the advancing pseudopod to surrounding connective tissue and at the same time detaches from its older adhesion site at the rear. The cell uses the new adhesion site at the leading edge as a point of traction to pull the bulk of its body forward through cytoskeletal contraction.

White blood cells are the most active crawlers in the body. These cells leave the circulatory system and travel by amoeboid movement to areas of infection or inflammation, where they engulf and destroy microorganisms and cellular debris. Amazingly, it is estimated that the total distance traveled collectively per day by all your white blood cells while they roam the tissues in their search-and-destroy tactic would circle Earth twice.

MICROFILAMENTS AS MECHANICAL STIFFENERS Besides their role in cellular contractile systems, actin filaments serve as mechanical supports or stiffeners for several cellular extensions, of which the most common are microvilli. **Microvilli** are micro-

Microvilli

● **FIGURE 2-21 Microvilli in the small intestine.** Scanning electron micrograph showing microvilli on the surface of a small-intestine epithelial cell.

Dr. R. G. Kessel & Dr. R. H. Kardon/Visuals Unlimited

scopic, nonmotile, hairlike projections from the surface of epithelial cells lining the small intestine and kidney tubules (● Figure 2-21). Their presence greatly increases the surface area available for transferring material across the plasma membrane. In the small intestine, the microvilli increase the area available for absorbing digested nutrients. In the kidney tubules, microvilli enlarge the absorptive surface that salvages useful substances passing through the kidney so that these materials are saved for the body instead of being eliminated in the urine. Within each microvillus, a core consisting of parallel linked actin filaments forms a rigid mechanical stiffener that keeps these valuable surface projections intact.

Intermediate filaments are important in cell regions subject to mechanical stress.

Intermediate filaments are intermediate in size between microtubules and microfilaments—hence their name. The proteins that compose the intermediate filaments vary among cell types, but in general they appear as irregular, threadlike molecules. These proteins form tough, durable fibers that play a central role in maintaining the structural integrity of a cell and in resisting mechanical stresses externally applied to a cell.

Intermediate filaments are tailored to suit their structural or tension-bearing role in specific cell types. For example, skin cells contain irregular networks of intermediate filaments made of the protein **keratin** (see ● Figure 2-17c). These intracellular filaments connect with the extracellular filaments that tie adjacent cells together, creating a continuous filamentous network that extends throughout the skin and gives it strength. When surface skin cells die, their tough keratin skeletons persist, forming a protective, waterproof outer layer. Hair and nails are also keratin structures.

Chapter in Perspective: Focus on Homeostasis

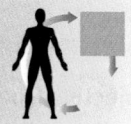

The ability of cells to perform functions essential for their own survival, as well as specialized tasks that help maintain homeostasis within the body, ultimately depends on the successful, cooperative operation of the intracellular components. For example, to support life-sustaining activities, all cells must generate energy, in a usable form, from nutrient molecules. Energy is generated intracellularly by chemical reactions in the cytosol and mitochondria.

In addition to being essential for basic cell survival, the organelles and cytoskeleton participate in many cells' specialized tasks that contribute to homeostasis. Here are several examples:

- Both nerve and endocrine cells release protein chemical messengers (neurotransmitters in nerve cells and hormones in endocrine cells) that are important in regulatory activities aimed at maintaining homeostasis. For example, neurotransmitters stimulate the respiratory muscles, which accomplish life-sustaining exchanges of oxygen and carbon dioxide between the body and the atmosphere through breathing. These protein chemical messengers are all produced by the endoplasmic reticulum and Golgi complex and are released by exocytosis from the cell when needed.
- The ability of muscle cells to contract depends on their highly developed cytoskeletal microfilaments sliding past one another. Muscle contraction is responsible for many homeostatic activities, including (1) contracting the heart muscle, which pumps life-supporting blood throughout the body; (2) contracting the muscles attached to bones, which enables the body to procure food; and (3) contracting the muscle in the walls of the stomach and intestine, which moves the food along the digestive tract so that ingested nutrients can be progressively broken down into a form that can be absorbed into the blood for delivery to the cells.
- White blood cells help the body resist infection by making extensive use of lysosomal destruction of engulfed particles as they police the body for microbial invaders. These white blood cells are able to roam the body by means of amoeboid movement, a cell-crawling process accomplished by coordinated assembly and disassembly of actin, one of their cytoskeletal components.

As we begin to examine the various organs and systems, keep in mind that proper cell functioning is the foundation of all organ activities.

REVIEW EXERCISES

Objective Questions (Answers on p. A-38)

1. The barrier that separates and controls movement between the cell contents and the extracellular fluid is the _____.

2. The chemical that directs protein synthesis and serves as a genetic blueprint is _____, which is found in the _____ of the cell.

3. The cytoplasm consists of _____, which are discrete specialized, intracellular compartments, a gel-like mass known as _____, and an elaborate protein scaffolding called the _____.

4. Transport vesicles from the _____ fuse with and enter the _____ for modification and sorting.

5. The *(what kind of)* _____ enzymes within the peroxisomes primarily detoxify various wastes produced within the cell or foreign compounds that have entered the cell.

6. The universal energy carrier of the body is _____.

7. The largest cells in the human body can be seen by the unaided eye. *(True or false?)*

8. Amoeboid movement is accomplished by the coordinated assembly and disassembly of microtubules. *(True or false?)*

9. Using the answer code on the right, indicate which type of ribosome is being described:
   ___ 1. synthesizes proteins used to construct new cell membrane
   ___ 2. synthesizes proteins used intracellularly within the cytosol
   ___ 3. synthesizes secretory proteins such as enzymes or hormones

   (a) free ribosome
   (b) rough ER-bound ribosome

10. Using the answer code on the right, indicate which form of energy production is being described:
    ___ 1. takes place in the mitochondrial matrix
    ___ 2. produces H_2O as a by-product
    ___ 3. results in a rich yield of ATP
    ___ 4. takes place in the cytosol
    ___ 5. processes acetyl CoA
    ___ 6. takes place in the mitochondrial inner-membrane cristae
    ___ 7. converts glucose into two pyruvate molecules
    ___ 8. uses molecular oxygen
    ___ 9. is accomplished by the electron transport system and ATP synthase

    (a) glycolysis
    (b) citric acid cycle
    (c) oxidative phosphorylation

Essay Questions

1. What are a cell's three major subdivisions?
2. State an advantage of organelle compartmentalization.
3. List the five major types of organelles.
4. Describe the structure of the endoplasmic reticulum, distinguishing between rough and smooth. What is the function of each?
5. Compare exocytosis and endocytosis. Define *secretion, pinocytosis, receptor-mediated endocytosis,* and *phagocytosis.*
6. Which organelles serve as the intracellular "digestive system"? What type of enzymes do they contain? What functions do these organelles serve?
7. Compare lysosomes with peroxisomes.
8. Distinguish among *cellular respiration, oxidative phosphorylation,* and *chemiosmosis.*
9. Describe the structure of mitochondria, and explain their role in cellular respiration.
10. Distinguish between the oxidative enzymes found in peroxisomes and those found in mitochondria.
11. Cells expend energy on what three categories of activities?
12. List and describe the functions of each component of the cytoskeleton.

(Explanations on p. A-39)

1. Let's consider how much ATP you synthesize in a day. Assume that you consume 1 mole of O_2 per hour or 24 moles per day (a mole is the number of grams of a chemical equal to its molecular weight; see p. A-8). About 6 moles of ATP are produced per mole of O_2 consumed. The molecular weight of ATP is 507. How many grams of ATP do you produce per day at this rate? Given that 1000 g equal 2.2 pounds, how many pounds of ATP do you produce per day at this rate? (This is under relatively inactive conditions!)

2. The stomach has two types of exocrine secretory cells: *chief cells,* which secrete an inactive form of the protein-digesting enzyme *pepsinogen,* and *parietal cells,* which secrete *hydrochloric acid (HCl)* that activates pepsinogen. Both cell types have an abundance of mitochondria for ATP production—the chief cells need energy to synthesize pepsinogen, and the parietal cells need energy to transport hydrogen ions (H^+) and chloride ions (Cl^-) from the blood into the stomach lumen. Only one of these cell types also has an extensive rough endoplas-mic reticulum and abundant Golgi stacks. Would this type be the chief cells or the parietal cells? Why?

3. The poison *cyanide* acts by binding irreversibly to one component of the electron transport system, blocking its action. As a result, the entire electron transport process comes to a screeching halt, and the cells lose more than 94% of their ATP-producing capacity. Considering the types of cell activities that depend on energy expenditure, what would be the consequences of cyanide poisoning?

4. Why do you think a person is able to perform anaerobic exercise (such as lifting and holding a heavy weight) only briefly but can sustain aerobic exercise (such as walking or swimming) for long periods? (*Hint:* Muscles have limited energy stores.)

5. One type of the affliction *epidermolysis bullosa* is caused by a genetic defect that results in production of abnormally weak keratin. Based on your knowledge of the role of keratin, what part of the body do you think would be affected by this condition?

(Explanation on p. A-39)

Kevin S. and his wife have been trying to have a baby for the past three years. On seeking the help of a fertility specialist, Kevin learned that he has a hereditary form of male sterility involving nonmotile sperm. His condition can be traced to defects in the cytoskeletal components of the sperm's flagella. As a result of this finding, the physician suspected that Kevin also has a long history of recurrent respiratory tract disease. Kevin confirmed that indeed he has had colds, bronchitis, and influenza more frequently than his friends. Why would the physician suspect that Kevin probably had a history of frequent respiratory disease based on his diagnosis of sterility due to nonmotile sperm?

Chapter 2

Observations of Cells (p. 21)

■ The complex organization and interaction of the chemicals within a cell confer the unique characteristics of life. The cell is the smallest unit capable of carrying out life processes.

■ Cells are the living building blocks of the body. The structure and function of a multicellular organism ultimately depend on the structural and functional capabilities of its cells. *(Review Table 2-1, p. 38.)*

■ Cells are too small for the unaided eye to see.

■ Using early microscopes, investigators learned that all plant and animal tissues consist of individual cells.

■ Scientists now know that a cell is a complex, highly organized, compartmentalized structure.

An Overview of Cell Structure (pp. 21–23)

■ Cells have three major subdivisions: the plasma membrane, the nucleus, and the cytoplasm. *(Review Figure 2-1.)*

■ The plasma membrane encloses the cell and separates the intracellular fluid (ICF) and extracellular fluid (ECF).

■ The nucleus contains deoxyribonucleic acid (DNA), the cell's genetic material.

■ Three types of ribonucleic acid (RNA) play a role in the protein synthesis coded by DNA: messenger RNA, ribosomal RNA, and transfer RNA.

■ The cytoplasm consists of cytosol, a complex gel-like mass laced with organelles and a cytoskeleton.

■ Organelles are highly organized structures that serve a specific function. They are bound by a membrane that separates the organelle's contents from the surrounding cytosol. There are five major organelles: the endoplasmic reticulum (ER), Golgi complex, lysosomes, peroxisomes, and mitochondria. *(Review Figure 2-1 and Table 2-1, p. 38.)*

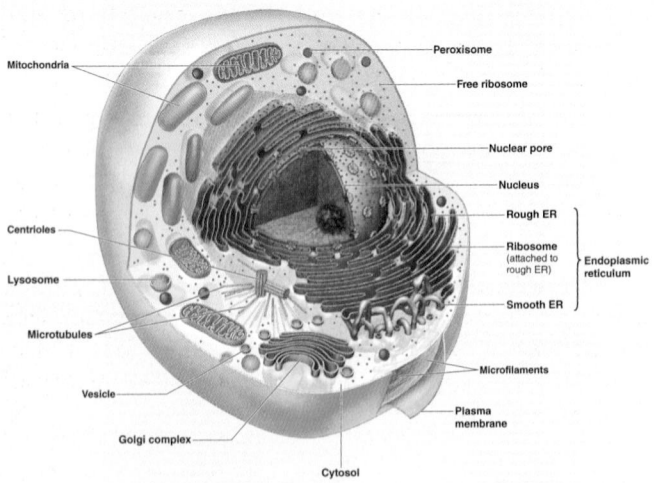

Endoplasmic Reticulum and Segregated Synthesis (pp. 23–24)

■ The ER is a single, complex membranous network that encloses a fluid-filled lumen.

■ The primary function of the ER is to synthesize proteins and lipids that are either (1) secreted to the exterior of the cell, such as enzymes and hormones, or (2) used to produce new cell components, particularly plasma membrane.

■ The two types of ER are rough ER (flattened interconnected sacs studded with ribosomes) and smooth ER (interconnected tubules with no ribosomes). *(Review Figure 2-2.)*

■ The rough ER ribosomes synthesize proteins, which are released into the ER lumen, where they are separated from the cytosol. Also entering the lumen are lipids produced within the membranous walls of the ER.

■ Synthesized products move from the rough ER to the smooth ER, where they are packaged and discharged as transport vesicles. Transport vesicles are formed as a portion of the smooth ER "buds off." *(Review Figure 2-3.)*

Golgi Complex and Exocytosis (pp. 24–26)

■ Transport vesicles move to and fuse with the Golgi complex, which consists of a stack of separate, flattened, membrane-enclosed sacs. *(Review Figures 2-3 and 2-4.)*

■ The Golgi complex serves a twofold function: (1) to modify into finished products the newly synthesized molecules delivered to it in crude form from the ER, and (2) to sort, package, and direct molecular traffic to appropriate intracellular and extracellular destinations.

■ The Golgi complex of secretory cells packages proteins to be exported from the cell in secretory vesicles that are released by exocytosis on appropriate stimulation. *(Review Figures 2-3 and 2-5a.)*

Lysosomes and Endocytosis (pp. 26–27)

■ Lysosomes are membrane-enclosed sacs that contain powerful hydrolytic (digestive) enzymes. *(Review Figure 2-6.)*

■ Serving as the intracellular "digestive system," lysosomes destroy foreign materials such as bacteria that have been internalized by the cell and demolish worn-out cell parts to make way for replacement parts.

■ Extracellular material is brought into the cell by endocytosis for attack by lysosomal enzymes. *(Review Figure 2-5b.)* The three forms of endocytosis are pinocytosis (nonselective uptake of ECF; "cell drinking"), receptor-mediated endocytosis (selective import of a specific large molecule), and phagocytosis (engulfment of a large multimolecular particle; "cell eating"). *(Review Figure 2-7.)*

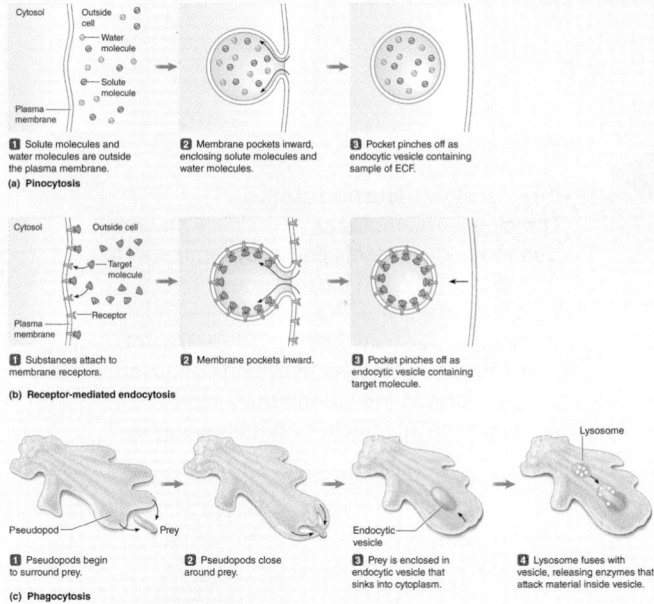

1 Solute molecules and water molecules are outside the plasma membrane.

2 Membrane pockets inward, enclosing solute molecules and water molecules.

3 Pocket pinches off as endocytic vesicle containing sample of ECF.

(a) Pinocytosis

1 Substances attach to membrane receptors.

2 Membrane pockets inward.

3 Pocket pinches off as endocytic vesicle containing target molecule.

(b) Receptor-mediated endocytosis

1 Pseudopods begin to surround prey.

2 Pseudopods close around prey.

3 Prey is enclosed in endocytic vesicle that sinks into cytoplasm.

4 Lysosome fuses with vesicle, releasing enzymes that attack material inside vesicle.

(c) Phagocytosis

Peroxisomes and Detoxification (pp. 27–28)

■ Peroxisomes are small membrane-enclosed sacs containing powerful oxidative enzymes. *(Review Figure 2-6.)*

■ They carry out particular oxidative reactions that detoxify various wastes and toxic foreign compounds that have entered the cell. During these detoxification reactions, peroxisomes generate potent hydrogen peroxide (H_2O_2), which they decompose into harmless water and oxygen.

Mitochondria and ATP Production (pp. 28–35)

■ The rod-shaped mitochondria are enclosed by two membranes, a smooth outer membrane and an inner membrane that forms a series of shelves, the cristae, which project into an interior gel-filled cavity, the matrix. *(Review Figure 2-8.)*

■ Mitochondria are the energy organelles of the cell. They efficiently convert the energy in food molecules to the usable energy stored in ATP molecules. Cells use ATP as an energy source for synthesis of new chemical compounds, for membrane transport, and for mechanical work.

■ *Cellular respiration* refers collectively to the intracellular reactions in which energy-rich molecules are broken down to form ATP, using oxygen (O2) and producing carbon dioxide (CO2) in the process. Cellular respiration includes the sequential dismantling of nutrient molecules and subsequent ATP production in three stages: (1) glycolysis in the cytosol, (2) the citric acid cycle in the mitochondrial matrix, and (3) oxidative phosphorylation at the mitochondrial inner membrane. *(Review Figure 2-9.)*

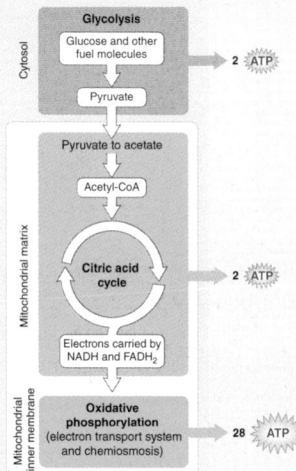

Glycolysis

Glucose and other fuel molecules

Pyruvate

2 ATP

Pyruvate to acetate

Acetyl-CoA

Citric acid cycle

2 ATP

Electrons carried by NADH and FADH₂

Oxidative phosphorylation (electron transport system and chemiosmosis)

28 ATP

■ *Oxidative phosphorylation* includes the electron transport system and chemiosmosis by ATP synthase. The electron transport system extracts high-energy electrons from hydrogens released during nutrient breakdown during glycolysis and the citric acid cycle and transfers them to successively lower energy levels. The free energy released during this process is used to create a hydrogen ion (H^+) gradient across the mitochondrial inner membrane. The flow of H^+ down this gradient activates ATP synthase, an enzyme that synthesizes ATP in a process called chemiosmosis. *(Review Figures 2-10 through 2-13.)*

■ A cell is more efficient at converting food energy into ATP when O2 is available. Without O2 (an anaerobic condition), a cell can produce only 2 molecules of ATP for every glucose molecule processed by glycolysis. With O2 (an aerobic condition), the mitochondrial processes can yield another 30 molecules of ATP for every glucose molecule processed (2 from the citric acid cycle and 28 from oxidative phosphorylation). *(Review Figures 2-13 and 2-15.)*

Cytosol: Cell Gel (pp. 35–37)

■ The cytosol contains the enzymes involved in intermediary metabolism and the ribosomal machinery essential for synthesis of these enzymes, as well as other cytosolic proteins.

■ Many cells store unused nutrients within the cytosol in the form of glycogen granules or fat droplets. These nonpermanent masses of stored material are called inclusions. *(Review Figure 2-16.)*

■ Also present in the cytosol are various secretory, transport, and endocytic vesicles.

Cytoskeleton: Cell "Bone and Muscle" (pp. 37–41)

■ The cytoskeleton, which extends throughout the cytosol, serves as the "bone and muscle" of the cell. *(Review Table 2-1, p. 38.)*

■ The three types of cytoskeletal elements—microtubules, microfilaments, and intermediate filaments—each consist of different proteins and perform various roles. *(Review Figure 2-17.)*

■ Microtubules, made of tubulin, maintain asymmetric cell shapes, serve as highways for intracellular transport by molecular motors, are the main component of cilia and flagella, and make up the mitotic spindle. *(Review Figures 2-18 and 2-19.)*

■ Microfilaments, made of actin in most cells, are important in various cellular contractile systems, including amoeboid movement and muscle contraction. They also serve as mechanical stiffeners for microvilli. *(Review Figures 2-20 and 2-21.)*

■ Intermediate filaments are irregular, threadlike proteins that help cells resist mechanical stress. Different proteins make up intermediate filaments in various cell types. Intermediate filaments are especially abundant in skin cells, where they are composed of keratin.

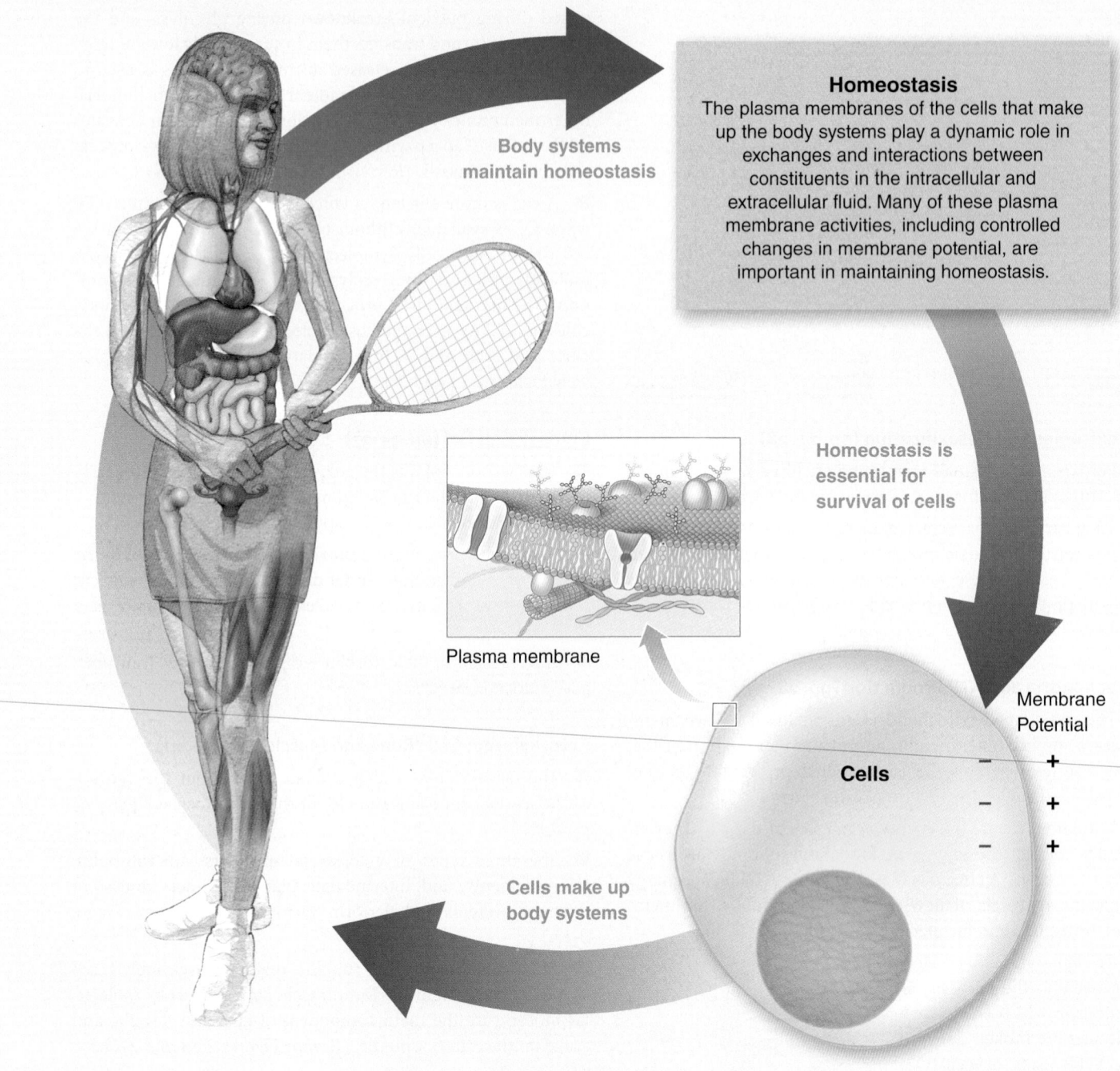

Body Systems

Body systems
maintain homeostasis

Homeostasis
The plasma membranes of the cells that make up the body systems play a dynamic role in exchanges and interactions between constituents in the intracellular and extracellular fluid. Many of these plasma membrane activities, including controlled changes in membrane potential, are important in maintaining homeostasis.

Homeostasis is essential for survival of cells

Plasma membrane

Membrane Potential

− +
− +
− +

Cells

Cells make up body systems

All cells are enveloped by a **plasma membrane,** a thin, flexible, lipid barrier that separates the contents of the cell from its surroundings. To carry on life-sustaining and specialized activities, each cell must exchange materials across this membrane with the homeostatically maintained internal fluid environment that surrounds it. This discriminating barrier contains specific proteins, some of which enable selective passage of materials. Other membrane proteins are receptor sites for interaction with specific

chemical messengers in the cell's environment. These messengers control many cell activities crucial to homeostasis.

Cells have a **membrane potential,** a slight excess of negative charges lined up along the inside of the membrane and a slight excess of positive charges on the outside. The specialization of nerve and muscle cells depends on the ability of these cells to alter their potential on appropriate stimulation.

The Plasma Membrane and Membrane Potential

CHAPTER AT A GLANCE

Membrane Structure and Functions
Trilaminar appearance
Membrane composition; fluid mosaic model
Functions of membrane components

Cell-to-Cell Adhesions
Extracellular matrix
Specialized cell junctions: desmosomes, tight junctions, and gap junctions

Overview of Membrane Transport
Influence of lipid solubility and size of particle
Active versus passive transport

Unassisted Membrane Transport
Diffusion down concentration gradients
Movement along electrical gradients
Osmosis; tonicity

Assisted Membrane Transport
Carrier-mediated transport
Vesicular transport

Membrane Potential
Definition of potential
Ionic basis of resting membrane potential

Membrane Structure and Functions

To survive, every cell must maintain a specific composition of its contents unique for that cell type despite the remarkably different composition of the extracellular fluid (ECF) surrounding it. This difference in fluid composition inside and outside a cell is maintained by the **plasma membrane,** the extremely thin layer of lipids and proteins that forms the outer boundary of every cell and encloses the intracellular contents. Besides acting as a mechanical barrier that traps needed molecules within the cell, the plasma membrane helps determine the cell's composition by selectively permitting specific substances to pass between the cell and its environment. The plasma membrane controls the entry of nutrient molecules and the exit of secretory and waste products. In addition, it maintains differences in ion concentrations inside and outside the cell, which are important in the membrane's electrical activity. The plasma membrane also participates in the joining of cells to form tissues and organs. Finally, it plays a key role in enabling a cell to respond to changes, or signals, in the cell's environment; this ability is important in communication among cells. No matter what the cell type, these common membrane functions are crucial to the cell's survival, to its ability to perform specialized homeostatic activities, and to its ability to coordinate its functions with those of other cells. Many of the functional differences among cell types are due to subtle variations in the composition of their plasma membranes, which in turn enable different cells to interact in different ways with essentially the same ECF environment.

The plasma membrane is a fluid lipid bilayer embedded with proteins.
The plasma membrane of every cell consists mostly of lipids and proteins plus small amounts of carbohydrate. It is too thin to be seen under an ordinary light microscope, but with an electron microscope it appears as a trilaminar structure consisting of two dark layers separated by a light middle layer (*tri* means "three"; *lamina* means "layer") (● Figure 3-1). The specific arrangement of the molecules that make up the plasma membrane is responsible for this "sandwich" appearance.

The most abundant membrane lipids are phospholipids, with lesser amounts of cholesterol. An estimated 1 billion phospholipid molecules are present in the plasma membrane of a typical human cell. **Phospholipids** have a polar (electrically charged; see p. A-6) head containing a negatively charged phosphate group and two nonpolar (electrically neutral) fatty acid chain tails (● Figure 3-2a). The polar end is hydrophilic (meaning "water loving") because it can interact with water molecules, which are also polar; the nonpolar end is hydrophobic (meaning "water fearing") and will not mix with water. In water, phospholipids self-assemble into a **lipid bilayer,** a double layer of lipid molecules (*bi* means "two") (● Figure 3-2b). The hydrophobic tails bury themselves in the center of the bilayer away from the water, and the hydrophilic heads line up on both sides in contact with the water. The outer surface of the bilayer is exposed

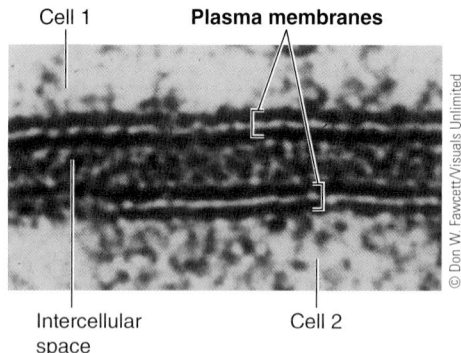

Cell 1   **Plasma membranes**

Intercellular space   Cell 2

© Don W. Fawcett/Visuals Unlimited

● **FIGURE 3-1 Trilaminar appearance of a plasma membrane in an electron micrograph.** Depicted are the plasma membranes of two adjacent cells. Note that each membrane appears as two dark layers separated by a light middle layer.

to ECF, whereas the inner surface is in contact with the intracellular fluid (ICF) (● Figure 3-2c).

The lipid bilayer is fluid, not rigid, with a consistency more like liquid cooking oil than solid shortening. The phospholipids, which are not held together by strong chemical bonds, are constantly moving. They can twirl, vibrate, and move around within their own half of the bilayer, exchanging places millions of times a second. This phospholipid movement largely accounts for membrane fluidity.

Cholesterol contributes to both the fluidity and the stability of the membrane. Cholesterol molecules are tucked between the phospholipid molecules, where they prevent the fatty acid chains from packing together and crystallizing, a process that would drastically reduce membrane fluidity. Through their spatial relationship with phospholipid molecules, cholesterol molecules also help stabilize the phospholipids' position.

Because of its fluidity, the plasma membrane has structural integrity but at the same time is flexible, enabling the cell to change shape. For example, muscle cells change shape as they contract, and red blood cells must change shape considerably as they squeeze their way single file through the capillaries, the narrowest blood vessels.

Membrane proteins are inserted within or attached to the lipid bilayer (● Figure 3-3). Some of these proteins extend through the entire thickness of the membrane, whereas others stud only the outer or inner surface. The plasma membrane has about 50 times more lipid molecules than protein molecules. However, proteins account for nearly half of the membrane's mass because they are much larger than lipids. The fluidity of the lipid bilayer enables many membrane proteins to float freely like "icebergs" in a moving "sea" of lipid. This view of membrane structure is known as the **fluid mosaic model,** in reference to the membrane fluidity and the ever-changing mosaic pattern of the proteins embedded in the lipid bilayer. (A mosaic is a surface decoration made by inlaying small pieces of variously colored tiles to form patterns or pictures.)

A small amount of **membrane carbohydrate** is located on the outer surface of cells, "sugar coating" them. Short carbohydrate chains protrude like tiny antennas from the outer surface, bound primarily to membrane proteins and, to a lesser extent, to lipids (● Figure 3-3).

This proposed structure accounts for the trilaminar appearance of the plasma membrane. When stains are used to help visualize the plasma membrane under an electron microscope (as in ● Figure 3-1), the two dark lines represent the hydrophilic polar regions of the lipid and protein molecules that

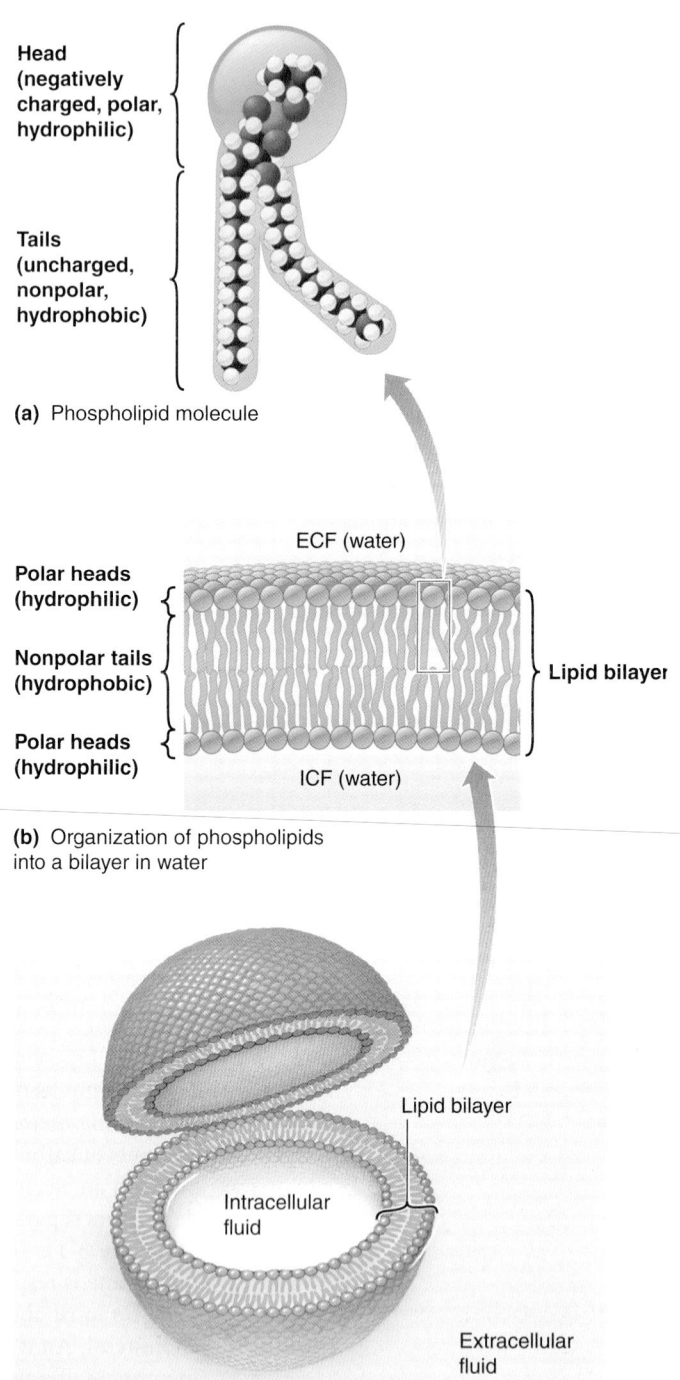

Head (negatively charged, polar, hydrophilic)

Tails (uncharged, nonpolar, hydrophobic)

(a) Phospholipid molecule

ECF (water)

Polar heads (hydrophilic)

Nonpolar tails (hydrophobic)

Polar heads (hydrophilic)

ICF (water)

Lipid bilayer

(b) Organization of phospholipids into a bilayer in water

Lipid bilayer

Intracellular fluid

Extracellular fluid

(c) Separation of ECF and ICF by the lipid bilayer

● **FIGURE 3-2 Structure and organization of phospholipid molecules in a lipid bilayer.** (a) Phospholipid molecule. (b) In water, phospholipid molecules organize themselves into a lipid bilayer with the polar heads interacting with the polar water molecules at each surface and the nonpolar tails all facing the interior of the bilayer. (c) An exaggerated view of the plasma membrane enclosing a cell, separating the ICF from the ECF.

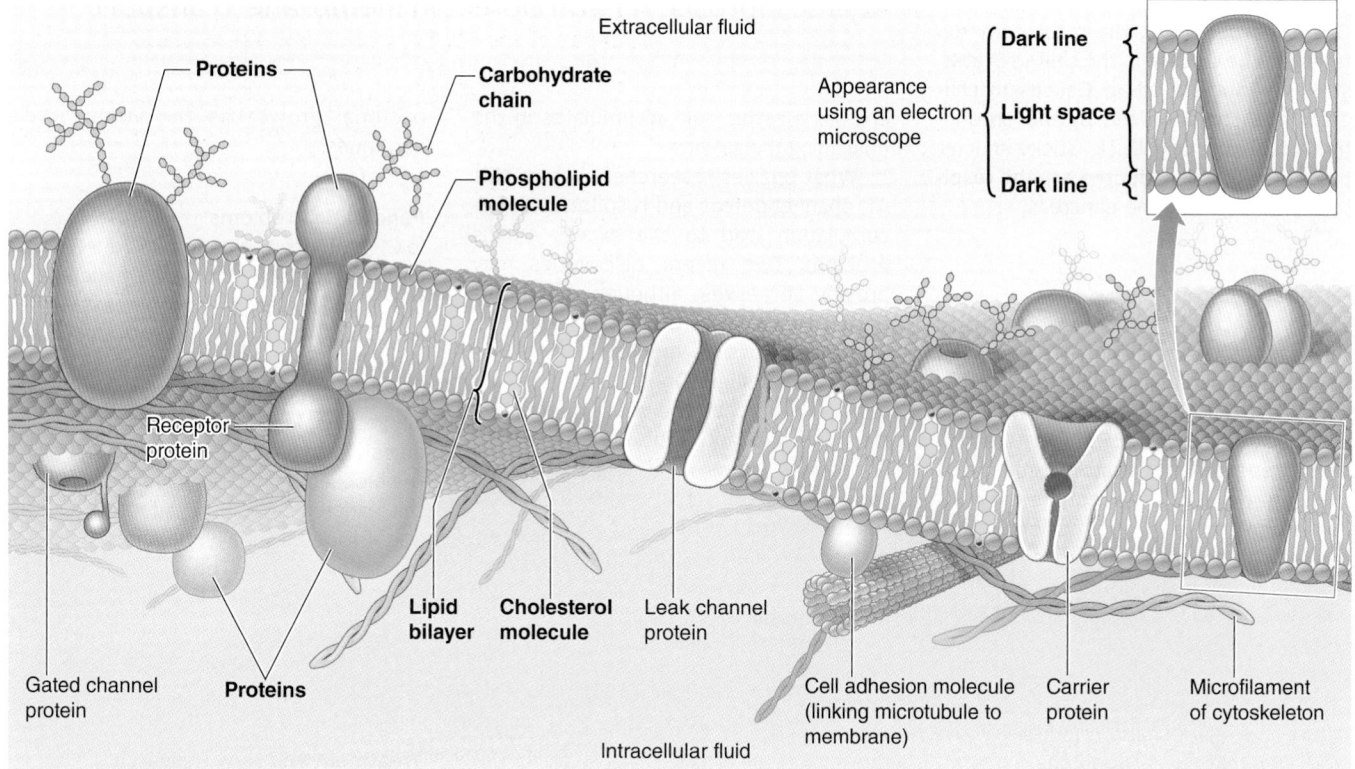

Extracellular fluid

Proteins

Carbohydrate chain

Phospholipid molecule

Appearance using an electron microscope
Dark line
Light space
Dark line

Receptor protein

Gated channel protein

Proteins

Lipid bilayer

Cholesterol molecule

Leak channel protein

Cell adhesion molecule (linking microtubule to membrane)

Carrier protein

Microfilament of cytoskeleton

Intracellular fluid

● FIGURE 3-3 **Fluid mosaic model of plasma membrane structure.** The plasma membrane is composed of a lipid bilayer embedded with proteins. Some proteins extend through the thickness of the membrane or are partially submerged in the membrane, while others are loosely attached to the surface of the membrane. Short carbohydrate chains attach to proteins or lipids on the outer surface only.

have taken up the stain. The light space between corresponds to the poorly stained hydrophobic core formed by the nonpolar regions of these molecules.

The different components of the plasma membrane carry out a variety of functions. The lipid bilayer forms the primary barrier to diffusion, the proteins perform most of the specific membrane functions, and the carbohydrates play an important role in "self-recognition" processes and cell-to-cell interactions. We now examine the functions of these membrane components in more detail.

The lipid bilayer forms the basic structural barrier that encloses the cell.

The lipid bilayer serves three important functions:

1. It forms the basic structure of the membrane. The phospholipids can be visualized as the "pickets" that form the "fence" around the cell.

2. Its hydrophobic interior is a barrier to passage of water-soluble substances between the ICF and the ECF. Water-soluble substances cannot dissolve in and pass through the lipid bilayer. By means of this barrier, the cell can maintain different mixtures and concentrations of solutes (dissolved substances) inside and outside the cell.

3. It is responsible for the fluidity of the membrane.

The membrane proteins perform various specific membrane functions.

Different types of membrane proteins serve the following specialized functions:

1. Some proteins span the membrane to form water-filled pathways, or **channels,** through the lipid bilayer (● Figure 3-3). Water-soluble substances small enough to enter a channel can pass through the membrane by this means without coming into direct contact with the hydrophobic lipid interior. Channels are highly selective. The small diameter of channels prevents particles larger than 0.8 nm (40-billionths of an inch) in diameter from entering. Only small ions can fit through channels. Furthermore, a given channel selectively admits particular ions. For example, only sodium ions (Na^+) can pass through Na^+ channels, and only potassium ions (K^+) can pass through K^+ channels. This channel selectivity is due to specific arrangements of chemical groups on the interior surfaces of the channels. Some channels are **leak channels** that are always open, thus permitting unregulated passage of their selected ion. Others are **gated channels** that may be open or closed to their specific ion as a result of changes in channel shape (that is, opening or closing of gates) in response to controlling mechanisms, described later. Therefore, passage through a gated channel is regulated. Cells vary in the number, kind, and activity of channels they have. Some drugs target channels, such as *calcium (Ca^{2+}) channel blockers* that are

Cystic Fibrosis: A Fatal Defect in Membrane Transport

Cystic fibrosis (CF), the most common fatal genetic disease in the United States, strikes 1 in every 2000 Caucasian children. It is characterized by the production of abnormally thick, sticky mucus. Most dramatically affected are the respiratory airways and the pancreas.

Respiratory Problems

The presence of thick, sticky mucus in the respiratory airways makes it difficult to get adequate air in and out of the lungs. Also, because bacteria thrive in the accumulated mucus, CF patients suffer from repeated respiratory infections. They are especially susceptible to *Pseudomonas aeruginosa,* an "opportunistic" bacterium that is often present in the environment but usually causes infection only when some underlying problem handicaps the body's defenses. Gradually, the involved lung tissue becomes scarred (fibrotic), making the lungs harder to inflate. This complication increases the work of breathing beyond the extra effort required to move air through the clogged airways.

Underlying Cause

CF is caused by one of several genetic defects that lead to production of a flawed version of a protein known as *cystic fibrosis transmembrane conductance regulator (CFTR).* CFTR normally forms the chloride (Cl^-) channels in the plasma membrane. With CF, the defective CFTR gets "stuck" in the endoplasmic reticulum–Golgi system, which normally manufactures and processes this product and then ships it to the plasma membrane (see pp. 23–24). That is, in CF patients, the mutated version of CFTR is only partially processed and never makes it to the cell surface. The resultant absence of CFTR protein in the plasma membrane makes the membrane impermeable to Cl^-. Because Cl^- transport across the membrane is closely linked to Na^+ transport, cells lining the respiratory airways cannot absorb NaCl (salt) prop-

erly. As a result, salt accumulates in the fluid lining the airways.

What puzzles researchers is how this Cl^- channel defect and resultant salt accumulation lead to the excess mucus problem. Two recent discoveries may provide an answer, although these proposals remain to be proven and research into other possible mechanisms continues to be pursued. One group of investigators found that the airway cells produce a natural antibiotic, *defensin,* which normally kills most inhaled airborne bacteria. It turns out that defensin cannot function properly in a salty environment. Bathed in the excess salt associated with CF, the disabled antibiotic cannot rid the lungs of inhaled bacteria. This leads to repeated infections. One of the outcomes of the body's response to these infections is production of excess mucus, which serves as a breeding ground for more bacterial growth. The cycle continues as the lung-clogging mucus accumulates and lung infections become more frequent. To make matters worse, the excess mucus is especially thick and sticky, making it difficult for the normal ciliary defense mechanisms of the lungs to sweep up the bacteria-laden mucus (see pp. 38 and 359). The mucus is thick and sticky because it is underhydrated (has too little water), a problem linked to the defective salt transport.

The second study found an additional complicating factor in the CF story. These researchers demonstrated that CFTR appears to serve a dual role as a Cl^- channel and as a membrane receptor that binds to and destroys *P. aeruginosa* (and perhaps other bacteria). Because CFTR is absent from the airway cell membranes of CF patients, *P. aeruginosa* is not cleared from the airways as usual. Besides causing infection, these bacteria trigger the airway cells to produce unusually large amounts of abnormal, thick, sticky mucus. This mucus promotes more

bacterial growth as the vicious cycle continues.

Pancreatic Problems

In CF patients, the pancreatic duct, which carries secretions from the pancreas to the small intestine, becomes plugged with thick mucus. Because the pancreas produces enzymes important in the digestion of food, malnourishment eventually results. In addition, as the pancreatic digestive secretions accumulate behind the blocked duct, fluid-filled cysts form in the pancreas, with the affected pancreatic tissue gradually degenerating and becoming fibrotic. The name *cystic fibrosis* aptly describes long-term changes that occur in the pancreas and lungs as the result of a single genetic flaw in CFTR.

Treatment and New Research Directions

Treatment consists of physical therapy to help clear the airways of the excess mucus and antibiotic therapy to combat respiratory infections, plus special diets and administration of supplemental pancreatic enzymes to maintain adequate nutrition. Despite this supportive treatment, most CF victims do not survive beyond their 30s, with most dying from lung complications.

Having identified the genetic defect responsible for most CF cases, investigators are hopeful of developing a means to correct or compensate for the defective gene. Another potential cure being studied is development of drugs that induce the mutated CFTR to be "finished off" and inserted in the plasma membrane. Furthermore, several promising new drug therapies, such as a mucus-thinning aerosol drug that can be inhaled, offer hope of reducing the number of lung infections and extending the life span of CF victims until a cure can be found.

widely used in the management of high blood pressure and abnormal heart rhythms. More than 60 genetic mutations in channels have been linked to human diseases. (To learn how a specific channel defect can lead to a devastating disease, see the accompanying boxed feature, ❱ Beyond the Basics.)

2. Other proteins that span the membrane are **carrier,** or **transport, molecules;** they transfer across the membrane specific substances that are unable to cross on their own. The means by which carriers accomplish this transport is described later. Each carrier can transport only a particular

molecule (or ion) or group of closely related molecules. Cells of different types have different kinds of carriers. As a result, they vary as to which substances they can selectively transport across their membranes. For example, thyroid gland cells are the only cells to use iodine. Appropriately, only the plasma membranes of thyroid gland cells have carriers for iodine, so only these cells can transport iodine from the blood into the cell interior.

3. Other proteins, located on the inner membrane surface, serve as **docking marker acceptors;** they bind lock-and-key fashion with the docking marker proteins of secretory vesicles (see p. 25). Secretion is initiated as stimulatory signals trigger fusion of the secretory vesicle membrane with the inner surface of the plasma membrane through interactions between these matching labels. The secretory vesicle subsequently opens up and empties its contents to the outside by exocytosis.

4. Some proteins located on either the inner or the outer cell surface function as **membrane-bound enzymes** that control specific chemical reactions. Cells are specialized in the types of membrane-bound enzymes they have. For example, a specialized area of the outer plasma membrane surface of skeletal muscle cells contains an enzyme that destroys the chemical messenger responsible for triggering muscle contraction, thus allowing the muscle to relax.

5. Many proteins on the outer surface are **receptors,** sites that "recognize" and bind with specific molecules in the cell's environment. This binding initiates a series of membrane and intracellular events (to be described later) that alter the activity of the particular cell. In this way, chemical messengers in the blood, such as water-soluble hormones, influence only the specific cells that have receptors for a given messenger. Even though every cell is exposed to the same messenger via the circulating blood, a given messenger has no effect on cells lacking receptors for this specific messenger. To illustrate, the anterior pituitary gland secretes into the blood thyroid-stimulating hormone (TSH), which attaches only to the surface of thyroid gland cells to stimulate secretion of thyroid hormone. No other cells have receptors for TSH, so only thyroid cells are influenced by TSH despite its widespread distribution.

6. Still other proteins are **cell adhesion molecules (CAMs).** Many CAMs protrude from the outer membrane surface and form loops or hooks by which cells grip one another or grasp the connective tissue fibers between cells. Thus, these molecules help hold the cells within tissues and organs together. Other CAMs protrude from the inner membrane surface and connect to the intracellular cytoskeletal scaffolding.

7. Finally, still other proteins on the outer membrane surface, especially in conjunction with carbohydrates, are important in the cells' ability to recognize "self" (that is, cells of the same type).

The membrane carbohydrates serve as self-identity markers.

The short carbohydrate chains on the outer membrane surface serve as self-identity markers that enable cells to identify and interact with one another in the following ways:

1. Different cell types have different markers. The unique combination of sugar chains projecting from the surface membrane proteins serves as the "trademark" of a particular cell type, enabling a cell to recognize others of its own kind. These carbohydrate chains play an important role in recognition of "self" and in cell-to-cell interactions. Cells can recognize other cells of the same type and join to form tissues. This is especially important during embryonic development. If cultures of embryonic cells of two different types, such as nerve cells and muscle cells, are mixed, the cells sort themselves into separate aggregates of nerve cells and muscle cells.

2. Carbohydrate-containing surface markers are also involved in tissue growth, which is normally held within certain limits of cell density. Cells do not "trespass" across the boundaries of neighboring tissues; that is, they do not overgrow their own territory. The exception is the uncontrolled spread of cancer cells, which have been shown to bear abnormal surface carbohydrate markers.

Cell-to-Cell Adhesions

In multicellular organisms such as humans, the plasma membrane not only is the outer boundary of all cells but also participates in cell-to-cell adhesions. These adhesions bind groups of cells together into tissues and package them further into organs. The life-sustaining activities of the body systems depend not only on the functions of the individual cells of which they are made but also on how these cells live and work together in tissue and organ communities.

At least in part, similar cells organize into appropriate groupings by means of the carbohydrate markers on the membrane surface. Once arranged, cells are held together by three different means: (1) CAMs, (2) the extracellular matrix, and (3) specialized cell junctions. You're already familiar with CAMs. We now examine the extracellular matrix and then specialized junctions.

The extracellular matrix serves as biological "glue."

Tissues are not made up solely of cells, and many cells within a tissue are not in direct physical contact with neighboring cells. Instead, they are held together by a biological "glue" called the **extracellular matrix (ECM).** The ECM is an intricate meshwork of fibrous proteins embedded in a watery, gel-like substance composed of complex carbohydrates. The watery gel, usually called the interstitial fluid (see p. 5), provides a pathway for diffusion of nutrients, wastes, and other water-soluble traffic between the blood and the tissue cells. The three major types of protein fibers woven through the gel are collagen, elastin, and fibronectin.

1. **Collagen** forms flexible but nonelastic fibers or sheets that provide tensile strength (resistance to longitudinal stress). Collagen is the most abundant protein in the body, making up nearly half of the total body protein by weight.

2. **Elastin** is a rubbery protein fiber most plentiful in tissues that must easily stretch and then recoil after the stretching force is removed. It is found, for example, in the lungs, which stretch and recoil as air moves in and out of them.

3. **Fibronectin** promotes cell adhesion and holds cells in position. Reduced amounts of this protein have been found within certain types of cancerous tissue, possibly accounting for cancer cells' inability to adhere well to one another; instead, they tend to break loose and metastasize (spread elsewhere in the body).

The ECM is secreted by local cells present in the matrix. The relative amount of ECM compared to cells varies greatly among tissues. For example, the ECM is scant in epithelial tissue but is the predominant component of connective tissue. Most of this abundant matrix in connective tissue is secreted by **fibroblasts** ("fiber formers"). The exact composition of the ECM also varies for different tissues, thus providing distinct local environments for the various cell types in the body. In some tissues, the matrix becomes highly specialized to form such structures as cartilage or tendons or, on appropriate calcification, the hardened structures of bones and teeth.

Some cells are directly linked by specialized cell junctions.

In tissues where the cells lie close to one another, CAMs provide some tissue cohesion as they "Velcro" adjacent cells together. In addition, some cells within given types of tissues are directly linked by one of three types of specialized cell junctions: (1) *desmosomes* (adhering junctions), (2) *tight junctions* (impermeable junctions), or (3) *gap junctions* (communicating junctions).

DESMOSOMES **Desmosomes** act like "spot rivets" that anchor together two adjacent but nontouching cells. A desmosome consists of two components: (1) a pair of dense, buttonlike cytoplasmic thickenings known as *plaques* located on the inner surface of each of the two adjacent cells; and (2) strong filaments that contain a type of CAM, extend across the space between the two cells, and attach to the plaque on both sides (● Figure 3-4). These intercellular filaments bind adjacent plasma membranes together so that they resist being pulled apart. Thus, desmosomes are adhering junctions. They are the strongest cell-to-cell connections and are most abundant in tissues that are subject to considerable stretching, such as those found in the skin, the heart, and the uterus.

Furthermore, intermediate cytoskeletal filaments, such as tough keratin filaments in the skin (see p. 41), stretch across the interior of these cells and attach to the desmosome plaques located on opposite sides of the cells' interior. This arrangement forms a continuous network of strong fibers throughout the tissue, both through and between cells, much like a continuous line of people firmly holding hands. This interlinking fibrous network reduces the chances of the tissue being torn when stretched.

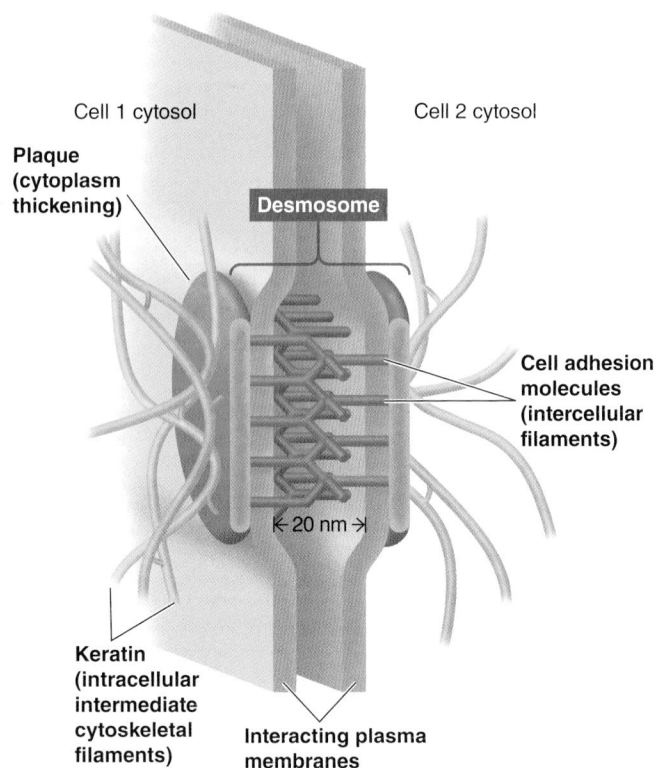

● **FIGURE 3-4 Desmosome.** Desmosomes are adhering junctions that spot-rivet cells, anchoring them together in tissues subject to considerable stretching.

TIGHT JUNCTIONS At **tight junctions,** adjacent cells bind firmly with each other at points of direct contact to seal off the passageway between the two cells. Tight junctions are found primarily in sheets of epithelial tissue, which cover the surface of the body and line its internal cavities. All epithelial sheets are highly selective barriers between two compartments with considerably different chemical compositions. For example, the epithelial sheet lining the digestive tract separates the food and potent digestive juices within the inner cavity (lumen) from the blood vessels on the other side. It is important that only completely digested food particles and not undigested food particles or digestive juices move across the epithelial sheet from the lumen to the blood. Accordingly, the lateral (side) edges of adjacent cells in the epithelial sheet are joined in a tight seal near their luminal border by "kiss" sites, at which strands of proteins known as *occludins* on the outer surfaces of the two interacting plasma membranes fuse directly (● Figure 3-5). These tight junctions are impermeable and thus prevent materials from passing between the cells. Passage across the epithelial barrier, therefore, must take place *through* the cells, not *between* them. This traffic across the cell is regulated by channel and carrier

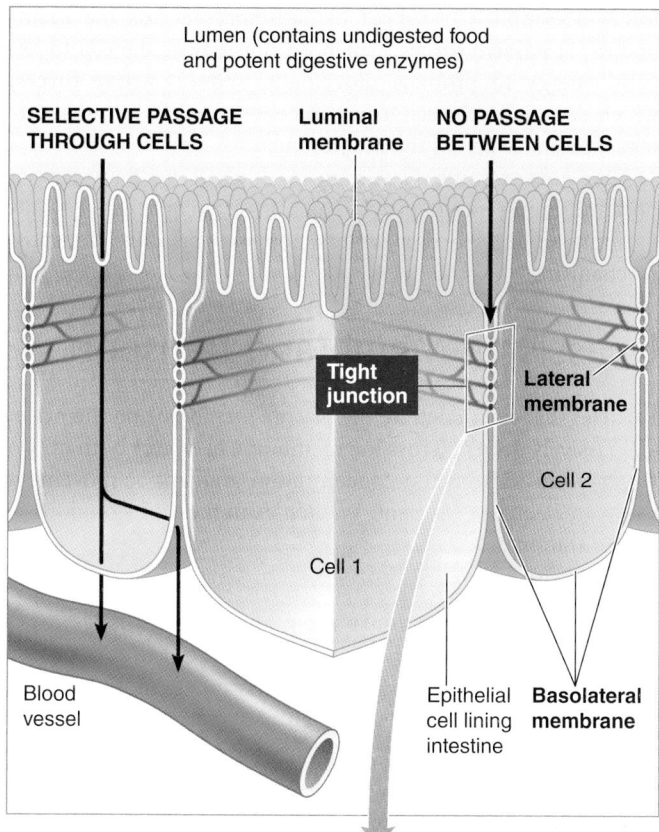

Lumen (contains undigested food and potent digestive enzymes)

SELECTIVE PASSAGE THROUGH CELLS **Luminal membrane** **NO PASSAGE BETWEEN CELLS**

Tight junction

Lateral membrane

Cell 2

Cell 1

Blood vessel

Epithelial cell lining intestine

Basolateral membrane

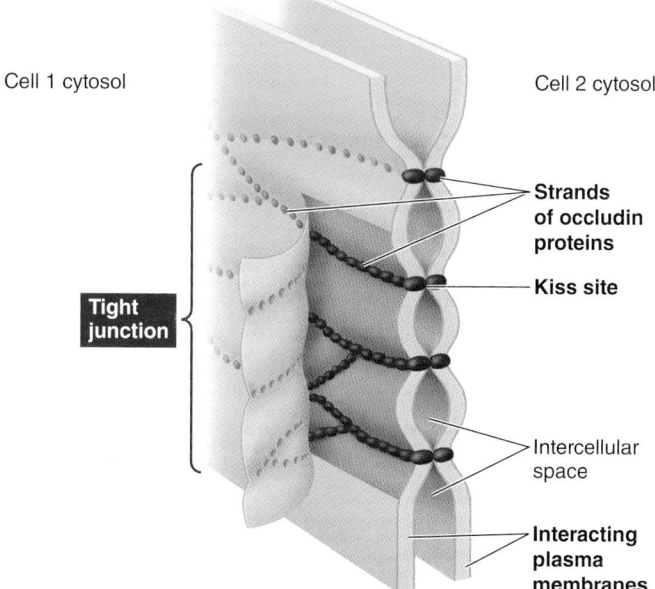

Cell 1 cytosol

Cell 2 cytosol

Tight junction

Strands of occludin proteins

Kiss site

Intercellular space

Interacting plasma membranes

● **FIGURE 3-5 Tight junction.** Tight junctions are impermeable junctions that join the lateral edges of epithelial cells near their luminal borders, thus preventing movement of materials between the cells. Only regulated passage of materials can occur through these cells, which form highly selective barriers that separate two compartments of highly different chemical composition.

proteins. If the cells were not joined by tight junctions, uncontrolled exchange of molecules could take place between the compartments by means of unpoliced traffic through the spaces between adjacent cells. Tight junctions thus prevent undesirable leaks within epithelial sheets.

GAP JUNCTIONS At a **gap junction,** as the name implies, a gap exists between adjacent cells, which are linked by small, connecting tunnels formed by connexons. A **connexon** is made up of six protein subunits (called *connexins*) arranged in a hollow tubelike structure that extends through the thickness of the plasma membrane. Two connexons, one from each of the plasma membranes of two adjacent cells, extend outward and join end to end to form a connecting tunnel between the two cells (● Figure 3-6). Gap junctions are communicating junctions. The small diameter of the tunnels permits small, water-soluble particles to pass between the connected cells but precludes passage of large molecules, such as vital intracellular proteins. Ions and small molecules can be directly exchanged between interacting cells through gap junctions without ever entering the ECF.

Gap junctions are especially abundant in cardiac muscle and smooth muscle. In these tissues, movement of ions (charge-carrying particles) through gap junctions transmits electrical activity throughout an entire muscle mass. Because this electrical activity brings about contraction, the presence of gap junctions enables synchronized contraction of a whole muscle mass, such as the pumping chamber of the heart.

Gap junctions are also found in some nonmuscle tissues, where they permit unrestricted passage of small nutrient mol-

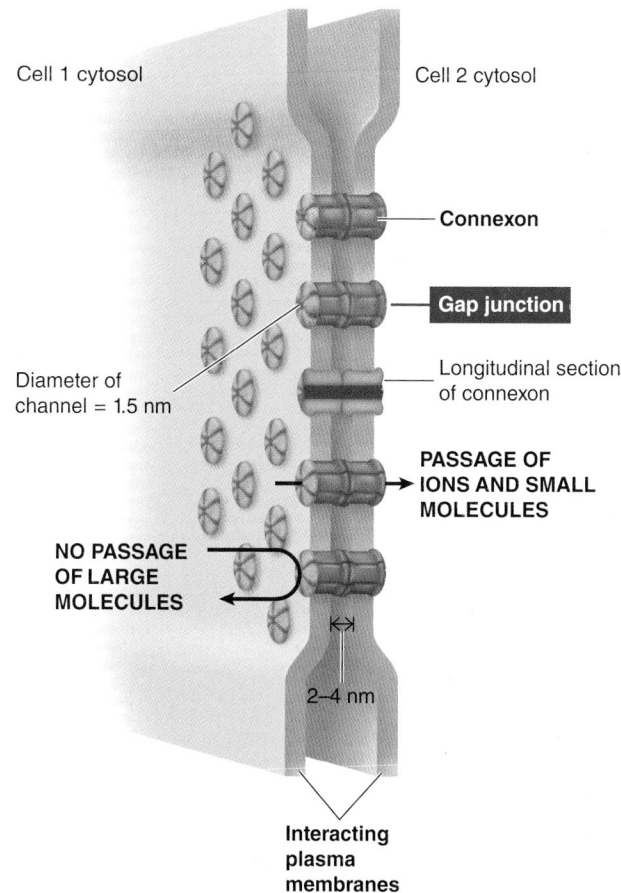

Cell 1 cytosol

Cell 2 cytosol

Connexon

Gap junction

Longitudinal section of connexon

Diameter of channel = 1.5 nm

PASSAGE OF IONS AND SMALL MOLECULES

NO PASSAGE OF LARGE MOLECULES

2–4 nm

Interacting plasma membranes

● **FIGURE 3-6 Gap junction.** Gap junctions are communicating junctions made up of connexons, which form tunnels that permit movement of charge-carrying ions and small molecules between two adjacent cells.

ecules between cells. For example, glucose, amino acids, and other nutrients pass through gap junctions to a developing egg cell from surrounding cells within the ovary, thus helping the egg stockpile these essential nutrients.

Gap junctions also are avenues for the direct transfer of small signaling molecules from one cell to the next. Such transfer permits cells connected by gap junctions to communicate with each other directly. This communication provides one mechanism by which cooperative cell activity is coordinated. In the next chapter, we examine other means by which cells "talk to each other."

We now turn to the topic of membrane transport, focusing on how the plasma membrane selectively controls what enters and exits the cell.

Overview of Membrane Transport

Anything that passes between a cell and the surrounding ECF must be able to penetrate the plasma membrane. If a substance can cross the membrane, the membrane is **permeable** to that substance; if a substance cannot pass, the membrane is **impermeable** to it. The plasma membrane is **selectively permeable:** It permits some particles to pass through while excluding others.

Lipid-soluble substances of any size and small water-soluble substances can permeate the plasma membrane without assistance.

Two properties of particles influence whether they can permeate the plasma membrane without assistance: (1) the relative solubility of the particle in lipid and (2) the size of the particle. Highly lipid-soluble particles can dissolve in the lipid bilayer and pass through the membrane. Uncharged or nonpolar molecules, such as oxygen (O_2), carbon dioxide (CO_2), and fatty acids, are highly lipid soluble and readily permeate the membrane. Charged particles (ions such as Na^+ and K^+) and polar molecules (such as glucose and proteins) have low lipid solubility but are very soluble in water. The lipid bilayer is an impermeable barrier to particles poorly soluble in lipid. For water-soluble (and thus lipid-insoluble) ions less than 0.8 nm in diameter, the protein channels are an alternative route for passage across the membrane. Only ions for which specific channels are available and open can permeate the membrane.

Particles that have low lipid solubility and are too large for channels cannot permeate the membrane on their own. Yet some of these particles, for example, glucose, must cross the membrane for the cell to survive and function. (Most cells use glucose as their fuel of choice to produce adenosine triphosphate, or ATP.) Cells have several means of assisted transport to move particles across the membrane that must enter or leave the cell but cannot do so unaided, as you will learn shortly.

Active forces use energy to move particles across the membrane but passive forces do not.

Even if a particle can permeate the membrane because of its lipid solubility or its ability to fit through a channel, some force is needed to move it across the membrane. Two general types of forces accomplish transport of substances across the membrane: (1) **passive forces,** which do not require the cell to expend energy to produce movement, and (2) **active forces,** which do require the cell to expend energy (ATP) in transporting a substance across the membrane.

We now examine the various methods of membrane transport, indicating whether each is an unassisted or assisted means of transport and whether each is a passive- or active-transport mechanism.

Unassisted Membrane Transport

Particles that can penetrate the plasma membrane on their own are passively driven across the membrane by one or both of two forces: diffusion down a concentration gradient or movement along an electrical gradient. We first examine diffusion down a concentration gradient.

Particles that can permeate the membrane diffuse passively down their concentration gradient.

All molecules and ions are in continuous random motion at temperatures above absolute zero as a result of thermal (heat) energy. This motion is most evident in liquids and gases, where the individual molecules (or ions) have more room to move before colliding with another molecule. Each molecule moves separately and randomly in any direction. As a consequence of this haphazard movement, the molecules often collide, bouncing off one another in different directions like billiard balls striking.

SIMPLE DIFFUSION **Solutions** are homogeneous mixtures containing a relatively large amount of one substance called the **solvent** (the dissolving medium, which in the body is water) and smaller amounts of one or more dissolved substances called **solutes.** The **concentration** of a solution refers to the amount of solute dissolved in a specific amount of solution. The greater the concentration of solute molecules (or ions), the greater the likelihood of collisions. Consequently, molecules within a particular space tend to become evenly distributed over time. Such uniform spreading out of molecules due to their random intermingling is known as **simple diffusion,** or **diffusion** for short (*diffusere* means "to spread out").

To illustrate simple diffusion, in ● Figure 3-7a, the concentration of the solute in a solution differs between area A and area B. Such a difference in concentration between two adjacent areas is called a **concentration gradient** (or **chemical gradient**). Random molecular collisions will occur more frequently in area A because of its greater concentration of solute molecules. For this reason, more molecules will bounce from area A into area B than in the opposite direction. In both areas, individual molecules will move randomly and in all directions, but the net movement of molecules by diffusion will be from the area of higher concentration to the area of lower concentration.

NET DIFFUSION The term **net diffusion** refers to the difference between two opposing movements. If 10 molecules move from area A to area B while 2 molecules simultaneously move from B

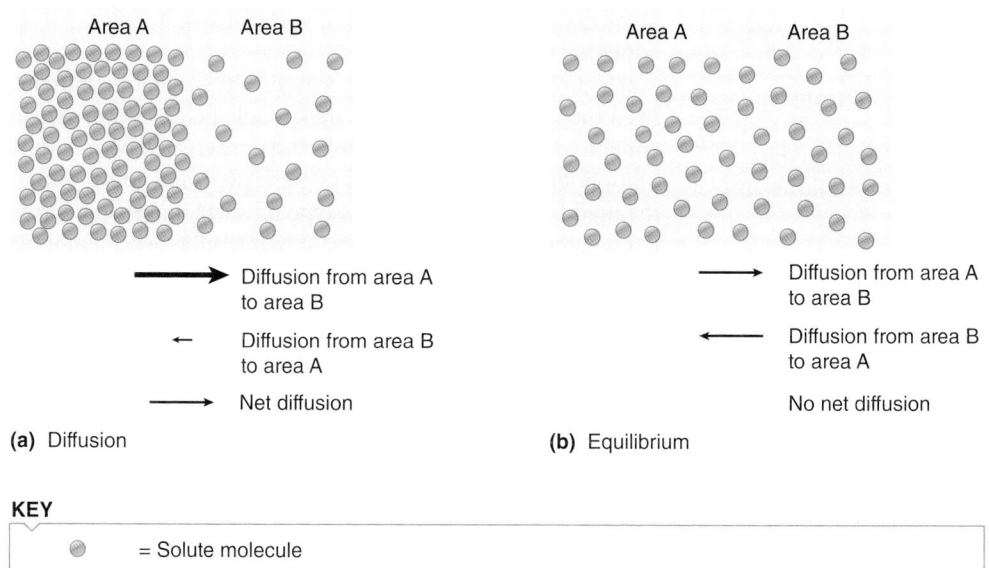

Diffusion from area A
to area B

← Diffusion from area B
to area A

Net diffusion

(a) Diffusion

Diffusion from area A
to area B

← Diffusion from area B
to area A

No net diffusion

(b) Equilibrium

KEY

⬤	= Solute molecule

Net diffusion = Diffusion from area A to area B minus diffusion from area B to area A

→
← : Differences in arrow length, thickness, and direction represent the relative magnitude of molecular movement in a given direction

● **FIGURE 3-7 Diffusion.** (a) Diffusion down a concentration gradient. (b) No concentration gradient and no net diffusion.

to A, the net diffusion is 8 molecules moving from A to B. Molecules will spread in this way until the substance is uniformly distributed between the two areas and a concentration gradient no longer exists (● Figure 3-7b). At this point, even though movement is still taking place, no net diffusion is occurring because the opposing movements exactly counterbalance each other; that is, they are in **equilibrium.** Movement of molecules from area A to area B will be exactly matched by movement of molecules from B to A.

What happens if a plasma membrane separates different concentrations of a substance? If the substance can permeate the membrane, net diffusion of the substance will occur through the membrane down its concentration gradient from the area of high concentration to the area of low concentration until the concentration gradient is abolished, unless there's some opposing force (● Figure 3-8a). No energy is required for this movement, so it is a passive means of membrane transport. The process of diffusion is crucial to the survival of every cell and plays an important role in many specialized homeostatic activities. As an example, O_2 is transferred across the lung membrane by diffusion. The blood carried to the lungs is low in O_2, having given up O_2 to the body tissues for cell metabolism. The air in the lungs, in contrast, is high in O_2 because it is continuously exchanged with fresh air during breathing. Because of this concentration gradient, net diffusion of O_2 occurs from the lungs into the blood as blood flows through the lungs. Thus, as blood leaves the lungs for delivery to the tissues, it is high in O_2.

If the membrane is impermeable to the substance, no diffusion can take place across the membrane, even though a concentration gradient may exist (● Figure 3-8b). For example, because the plasma membrane is impermeable to the vital intracellular proteins, they are unable to escape from the cell, even though they are in greater concentration in the ICF than in the ECF.

FICK'S LAW OF DIFFUSION Several factors, in addition to the concentration gradient, influence the rate of net diffusion across a membrane. The effects of these factors collectively make up Fick's law of diffusion (▲ Table 3-1). Note that the larger the surface area available, the greater the rate of diffusion it can accommodate. Various strategies are used throughout the body for increasing the membrane surface area across which diffusion and other types of transport take place. For example, absorption of nutrients in the small intestine is enhanced by the presence of microvilli, which greatly increase the available absorptive surface in contact with the nutrient-rich contents of the small intestine lumen (see p. 40). Conversely, abnormal loss of membrane surface area decreases the rate of net diffusion. For example, in *emphysema,* O_2 and CO_2 exchange between air and blood in the lungs is reduced because the walls of the air sacs break down, resulting in less surface area available for diffusion of these gases.

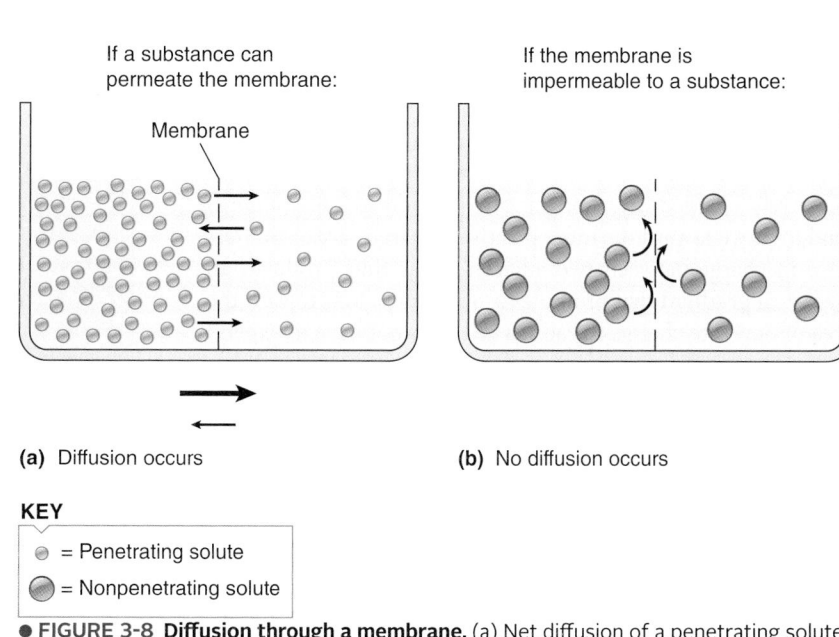

If a substance can permeate the membrane:

Membrane

If the membrane is impermeable to a substance:

(a) Diffusion occurs

(b) No diffusion occurs

KEY

⊝ = Penetrating solute

⬤ = Nonpenetrating solute

● **FIGURE 3-8 Diffusion through a membrane.** (a) Net diffusion of a penetrating solute across the membrane down a concentration gradient. (b) No diffusion of a nonpenetrating solute through the membrane despite the presence of a concentration gradient.

Factors Influencing the Rate of Net Diffusion of a Substance across a Membrane (Fick's Law of Diffusion)

Factor	Effect on Rate of Net Diffusion
↑ Concentration gradient of substance	↑
↑ Surface area of membrane	↑
↑ Lipid solubility	↑
↑ Molecular weight of substance	↓
↑ Distance (thickness)	↓

Also note that the greater the distance, the slower the rate of diffusion. Accordingly, membranes across which diffusing particles must travel are normally relatively thin, such as the membranes separating air and blood in the lungs. Thickening of this air–blood interface (as in *pneumonia,* for example) slows exchange of O_2 and CO_2. Furthermore, diffusion is efficient only for short distances between cells and their surroundings. It becomes an inappropriately slow process for distances of more than a few millimeters. To illustrate, it would take months or even years for O_2 to diffuse from the surface of the body to the cells in the interior. Instead, the circulatory system provides a network of tiny vessels that deliver and pick up materials at every "block" of a few cells, with diffusion accomplishing short local exchanges between blood and surrounding cells.

Ions that can permeate the membrane also move passively along their electrical gradient.

In addition to their concentration gradient, movement of ions (electrically charged particles that have either lost or gained an electron; see p. A-5) is affected by their electrical charge. Ions with like charges (those with the same kind of charge) repel each other, and ions with opposite charges attract each other. If a relative difference in charge exists between two adjacent areas, positively charged ions *(cations)* tend to move toward the more negatively charged area and negatively charged ions *(anions)* tend to move toward the more positively charged area. A difference in charge between two adjacent areas thus produces an **electrical gradient** that promotes movement of ions toward the area of opposite charge. Because a cell does not have to expend energy for ions to move into or out of it along an electrical gradient, this method of membrane transport is passive. When an electrical gradient exists between the ICF and the ECF, only ions that can permeate the plasma membrane can move along this gradient.

Both an electrical and a concentration (chemical) gradient may be acting on a particular ion at the same time. The net effect of simultaneous electrical and concentration gradients on this ion is called an **electrochemical gradient.** Later in this chapter, you will learn how electrochemical gradients contribute to the electrical properties of the plasma membrane.

Osmosis is the net diffusion of water down its own concentration gradient.

Water molecules can readily permeate the plasma membrane. Even though water molecules are strongly polar, they are small enough to slip through momentary spaces created between the phospholipid molecules' tails as they sway and move within the lipid bilayer. However, this type of water movement across the membrane is relatively slow. In many cell types, membrane proteins form **aquaporins,** which are channels specific for the passage of water (*aqua* means "water"). This avenue greatly increases membrane permeability to water. Different cell types vary in their density of aquaporins and thus in their water permeability. About a billion water molecules can pass in single file through an aquaporin channel in a second. The driving force for net movement of water across the membrane is the same as for any other diffusing molecule, namely, its concentration gradient. The term *concentration* usually refers to the density of the solute in a given volume of water. It is important to recognize, however, that adding a solute to pure water in essence decreases the water concentration. In general, one molecule of a solute displaces one molecule of water.

Compare the water and solute concentrations in the two containers in ● Figure 3-9. The container in Figure 3-9a is full of pure water, so the water concentration is 100% and the solute concentration is 0%. In Figure 3-9b, solute has replaced 10% of the water molecules. The water concentration is now 90%, and the solute concentration is 10%—a lower water concentration and a higher solute concentration than in Figure 3-9a. Note that as the solute concentration increases, the water concentration decreases correspondingly. We now examine what happens if pure water is separated from a solution by a membrane permeable to water but not to the solute.

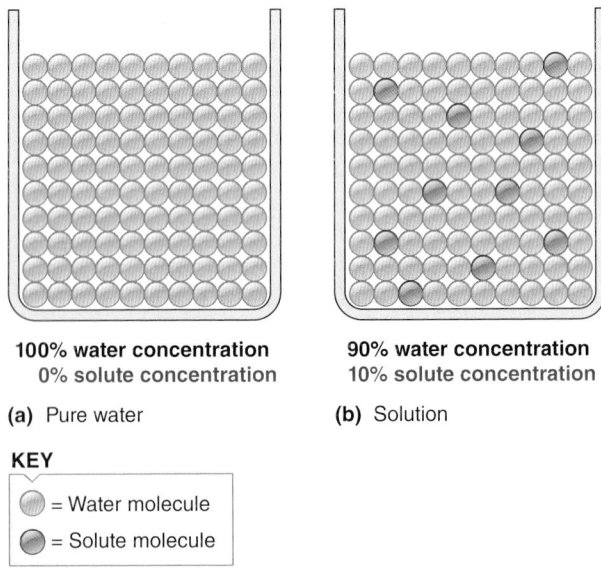

100% water concentration
0% solute concentration

(a) Pure water

90% water concentration
10% solute concentration

(b) Solution

KEY

= Water molecule

= Solute molecule

● FIGURE 3-9 **Relationship between solute and water concentration in a solution.**

MOVEMENT OF WATER WHEN A SELECTIVELY PERMEABLE MEMBRANE SEPARATES PURE WATER FROM A SOLUTION OF A NONPENETRATING SOLUTE If as in ● Figure 3-10 pure water (side 1) and a solution containing a nonpenetrating solute (side 2) are separated by a selectively permeable membrane that permits passage of water but not of solute, water will move passively down its own concentration gradient from the area of higher water concentration (lower solute concentration) to the area of lower water concentration (higher solute concentration). This net diffusion of water down its concentration gradient through a selectively permeable membrane is known as **osmosis.** Because solutions are always referred to in terms of concentration of solute, *water moves by osmosis to the area of higher solute concentration.* Despite the impression that the solutes are "pull-ing," or attracting, water, osmosis is nothing more than diffusion of water down its own concentration gradient across the membrane.

Osmosis occurs from side 1 to side 2, but the concentrations between the two compartments can never become equal. No matter how dilute side 2 becomes because of water diffusing into it, it can never become pure water, nor can side 1 ever acquire any solute. Therefore, does net diffusion of water (osmosis) continue until all the water has left side 1? No. As the volume expands in side 2, a difference in hydrostatic pressure between the two sides is created, and it opposes osmosis. **Hydrostatic (fluid) pressure** is the pressure exerted by a standing, or stationary, fluid on an object—in this case, the membrane (*hydro* means "fluid"; *static* means "standing"). The hydrostatic pressure exerted by the larger volume of fluid on side 2 is greater than the hydrostatic pressure exerted on side 1. This difference in hydrostatic pressure tends to push fluid from side 2 to side 1.

The **osmotic pressure** of a solution (a "pulling" pressure) is a measure of the tendency for osmotic flow of water into that solution because of its relative concentration of nonpenetrating solutes and water. Net movement of water by osmosis continues until the opposing hydrostatic pressure (a "pushing" pressure) exactly counterbalances the osmotic pressure. The magnitude of the osmotic pressure is equal to the magnitude of the opposing hydrostatic pressure necessary to completely stop osmosis. The greater the concentration of nonpenetrating solute → the lower the concentration of water → the greater the drive for water to move by osmosis from pure water into the solution → the greater the opposing pressure required to stop the osmotic flow → the greater the osmotic pressure of the solution. Therefore, a solution with a high concentration of nonpenetrating solute exerts greater osmotic pressure than a solution with a lower concentration of nonpenetrating solute does.

Osmotic pressure is an indirect measure of solute concentration, expressed in units of pressure. A more direct means of expressing solute concentration is the **osmolarity** of a solution, which is a measure of its total solute concentration given in terms of the *number* of particles (molecules or ions). Osmolarity is expressed in *osmoles per liter* (or *Osm*), the number of moles of solute particles in 1 L of solution (see p. A-9). The osmolarity of body fluids is typically expressed in *milliosmoles per liter* (*mOsm;* 1/1000 of an osmole) because the solutes in body fluids are too dilute to conveniently use the osmole unit. Because osmolarity depends on the number, not the nature, of particles, any mixture of particles can contribute to the osmolarity of a solution. The normal osmolarity of body fluids is 300 mOsm.

Thus far in our discussion of osmosis, we have considered movement of water when pure water is separated from a solution by a membrane permeable to water but not to nonpenetrating solutes. However, in the body, the plasma membrane separates the ICF and the ECF, and both of these contain solutes, some that can and others that cannot penetrate the membrane. Let us compare the results of water movement when solutions of differing osmolarities are separated by a selectively permeable membrane that permits movement of water and only some solutes.

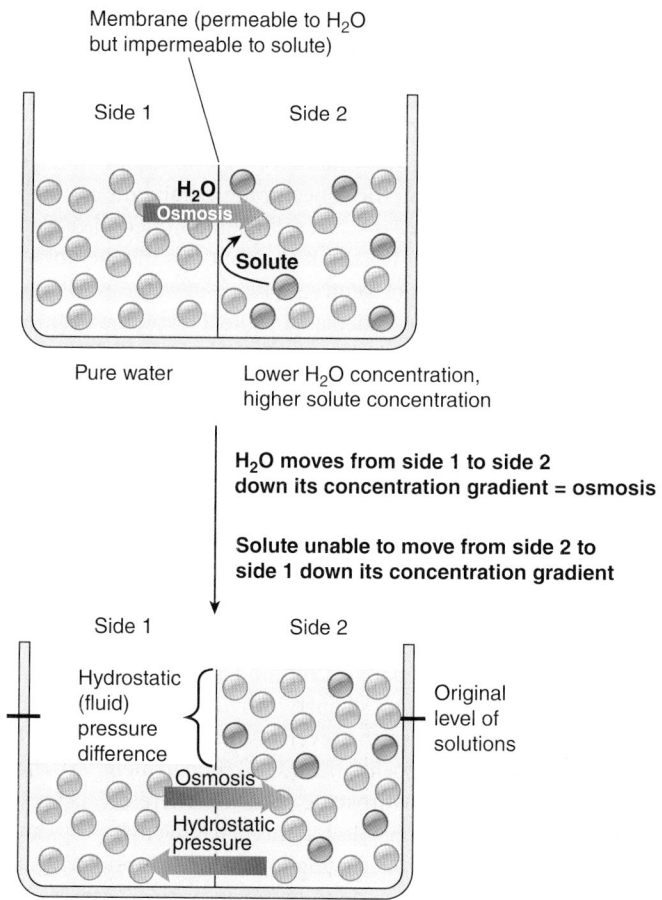

● FIGURE 3-10 **Osmosis when pure water is separated from a solution containing a nonpenetrating solute.**

MOVEMENT OF WATER AND SOLUTE WHEN A MEMBRANE SEPA-RATES UNEQUAL SOLUTIONS OF A PENETRATING SOLUTE Assume that solutions of *unequal* concentration of *penetrating* solute (differing osmolarities) are separated by a membrane that is permeable to both water and solute (● Figure 3-11). In this situation, the solute moves down its own concentration gradient in the opposite direction of the net water movement. The movement continues until both solute and water are evenly distributed across the membrane. With all concentration gradients gone, net movement ceases. The final volume of each side when no further net movement occurs is the same as at the onset. Water and solute molecules merely exchange places between the two sides until their distributions are equalized; that is, an equal number of water molecules move from side 1 to side 2 as solute molecules move from side 2 to side 1. Therefore, solutes that can penetrate the plasma membrane do not contribute to osmotic differences between the ICF and the ECF and do not affect cell volume.

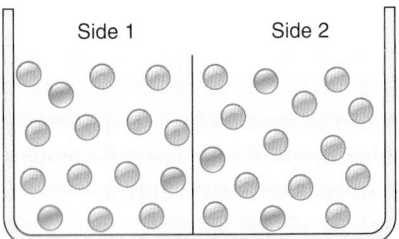

Membrane (permeable to both H_2O and solute)

Side 1   Side 2

H_2O

Solute

Higher H_2O concentration, lower solute concentration

Lower H_2O concentration, higher solute concentration

H_2O moves from side 1 to side 2 down its concentration gradient

Solute moves from side 2 to side 1 down its concentration gradient

Side 1   Side 2

- Water concentrations equal
- Solute concentrations equal
- No further net diffusion
- Equilibrium exists
- No change in volume of the two sides

KEY

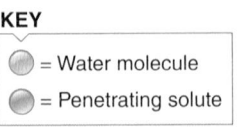

= Water molecule

= Penetrating solute

● **FIGURE 3-11 Movement of water and a penetrating solute un-equally distributed across a membrane.**

MOVEMENT OF WATER WHEN A MEMBRANE SEPARATES EQUAL AND UNEQUAL SOLUTIONS OF A NONPENETRATING SOLUTE If solutions of *equal* concentration of *nonpenetrating* solute (the same osmolarities) are separated by a membrane that is permeable to water but impermeable to the solute, no concentration differences will exist and thus no net movement of water will occur across the membrane. Of course, the solute will not move because the membrane is impermeable to it and no concentration gradient exists for it. This is the usual situation in body fluids. Body cells normally do not experience any net gain (swelling) or loss (shrinking) of volume, because the concentration of nonpenetrating solutes in the ECF is normally carefully regulated (primarily by the kidneys) so that the ECF osmolarity is the same as the osmolarity within the cells. Intracellular osmolarity is normally 300 mOsm, and all intracellular solutes are assumed to be nonpenetrating.

Now assume that solutions of *unequal* concentration of *nonpenetrating* solute (differing osmolarities) are separated by a membrane that is permeable to water but impermeable to the solute (● Figure 3-12). Osmotic movement of water across the membrane is driven by the difference in osmotic pressure of the two solutions. At first, the concentration gradients are identical to those in ● Figure 3-11. Net diffusion of water takes place from side 1 to side 2, but the solute cannot cross the membrane down its concentration gradient. As a result of water movement alone, the volume of side 2 increases while the volume of side 1 correspondingly decreases. Loss of water from side 1 increases the solute concentration on side 1, whereas addition of water to side 2 reduces the solute concentration on that side. If the membrane is free to move so that side 2 can expand without an opposing hydrostatic pressure developing, eventually the concentrations of water and solute on the two sides of the membrane become equal and net diffusion of water ceases. This situation is similar to what happens across plasma membranes in the body. Within the slight range of changes in ECF osmolarity that occur physiologically, if water moves by osmosis into the cells, their plasma membranes normally accommodate the increase in cell volume with no significant change in hydrostatic pressure inside the cells. Likewise, in the reverse situation, if water moves by osmosis out of the cells, the ECF compartment expands without a change in its hydrostatic pressure. Therefore, osmosis is the major force responsible for the net movement of water into or out of cells, without having to take hydrostatic pressure into consideration. At the endpoint, when osmosis ceases, the volume has increased on the side that originally had the higher solute concentration and the volume has decreased on the side with the lower solute concentration. Therefore, osmotic movement of water across the plasma membrane always results in a change in cell volume, and cells, especially brain cells, do not function properly when they swell or shrink.

Tonicity refers to the effect the concentration of nonpenetrating solutes in a solution has on cell volume.

The **tonicity** of a solution is the effect the solution has on cell volume—whether the cell remains the same size, swells, or shrinks—when the solution surrounds the cell. The tonicity of

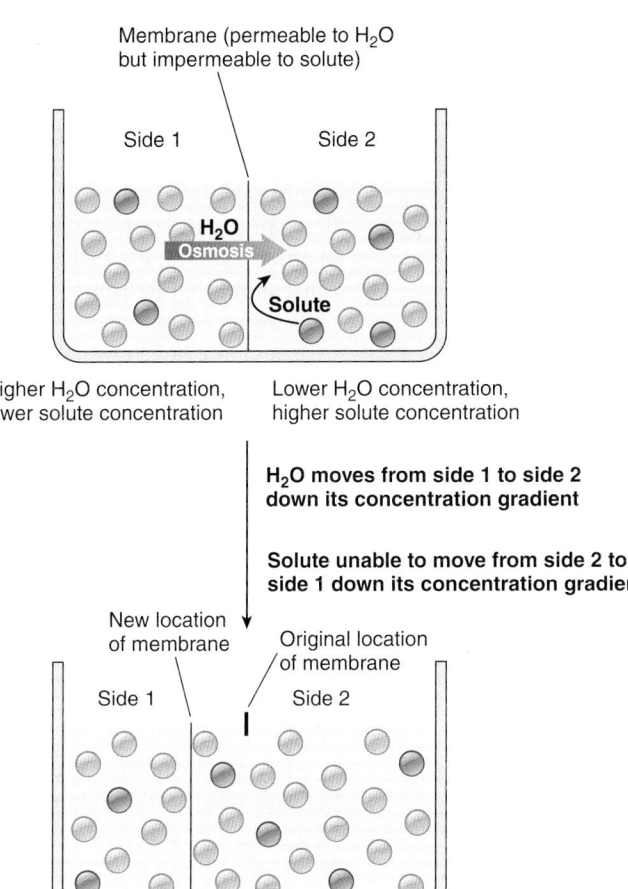

Membrane (permeable to H₂O but impermeable to solute)

Side 1   Side 2

H_2O
Osmosis

Solute

Higher H₂O concentration, lower solute concentration

Lower H₂O concentration, higher solute concentration

H₂O moves from side 1 to side 2 down its concentration gradient

Solute unable to move from side 2 to side 1 down its concentration gradient

New location of membrane

Original location of membrane

Side 1   Side 2

- **Water concentrations equal**
- **Solute concentrations equal**
- **Osmosis ceases; equilibrium exists**
- **Volume of side 1 has decreased and volume of side 2 has increased**

KEY

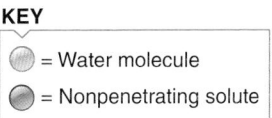 = Water molecule

= Nonpenetrating solute

● **FIGURE 3-12 Osmosis in the presence of an unequally distributed nonpenetrating solute.**

a solution has no units and is a reflection of its concentration of nonpenetrating solutes relative to the cell's concentration of nonpenetrating solutes. (By contrast, the osmolarity of a solution is a measure of its total concentration of both penetrating and nonpenetrating solutes expressed in units of osmoles per liter.) The easiest way to demonstrate this phenomenon is to place red blood cells in solutions with varying concentrations of a nonpenetrating solute (● Figure 3-13).

Normally, the plasma in which red blood cells are suspended has the same osmotic activity as the fluid inside these cells, so the cells maintain a constant volume. An **isotonic solution** (*iso* means "equal") has the same concentration of nonpenetrating solutes as normal body cells do. When a cell is bathed in an isotonic solution, no water enters or leaves the cell by osmosis, so cell volume remains constant. For this reason, the ECF is normally maintained isotonic so that no net diffusion of water occurs across the plasma membranes of body cells.

If red blood cells are placed in a dilute or **hypotonic solution** (*hypo* means "below"), a solution with a below-normal concentration of nonpenetrating solutes (and therefore a higher concentration of water), water enters the cells by osmosis. Net gain of water by the cells causes them to swell, perhaps to the point of rupturing or *lysing*. If, in contrast, red blood cells are placed in a concentrated or **hypertonic solution** (*hyper* means "above"), a solution with an above-normal concentration of nonpenetrating solutes (and therefore a lower concentration of water), the cells shrink as they lose water by osmosis. When a red blood cell decreases in volume, its surface area does not decrease correspondingly, so the cell assumes a *crenated,* or spiky, shape (● Figure 3-13c). Because cells change volume when surrounded by fluid that is not isotonic, it is crucial that the concentration of nonpenetrating solutes in the ECF quickly be restored to normal should the ECF become hypotonic (as with ingesting too much water) or hypertonic (as with losing too much water through severe diarrhea). (See pp. 447–452 for further details about the important homeostatic mechanisms that maintain the normal concentration of nonpenetrating solutes in the ECF.) For the same reason, fluids injected intravenously should be isotonic to prevent unwanted movement of water into or out of the cells. For example, isotonic saline (0.9% NaCl solution) is used as a vehicle for delivering drugs intravenously or for expanding plasma volume without impacting the cells.

Assisted Membrane Transport

All the kinds of transport we have discussed thus far—diffusion down concentration gradients, movement along electrical gradients, and osmosis—produce net movement of solutes capable of permeating the plasma membrane because of their lipid solubility (nonpolar molecules of any size) or their ability to fit through channels (selected ions and water). Poorly lipid-soluble polar molecules that are too big for channels, such as proteins, glucose, and amino acids, cannot cross the plasma membrane on their own no matter what forces are acting on them. This impermeability ensures that large, polar intracellular proteins stay in the cell where they belong and can carry out their life-sustaining functions—for example, serving as metabolic enzymes.

However, because poorly lipid-soluble molecules cannot cross the plasma membrane on their own, the cell must provide mechanisms for deliberately transporting these types of molecules into or out of the cell as needed. For example, the cell must usher in essential nutrients, such as glucose for energy and amino acids for the synthesis of proteins, and transport out metabolic wastes and secretory products, such as water-soluble protein hormones. Furthermore, passive diffusion alone cannot always account for the movement of ions. Some ions move through the membrane passively in one direction and actively in the other direction. Cells use two different mechanisms to accomplish these selective transport processes: *carrier-mediated transport* for transfer of small water-soluble substances across the membrane and *vesicular transport* for movement of large molecules and multimolecular particles between the ECF and the ICF. We examine each of these methods of assisted membrane transport in turn.

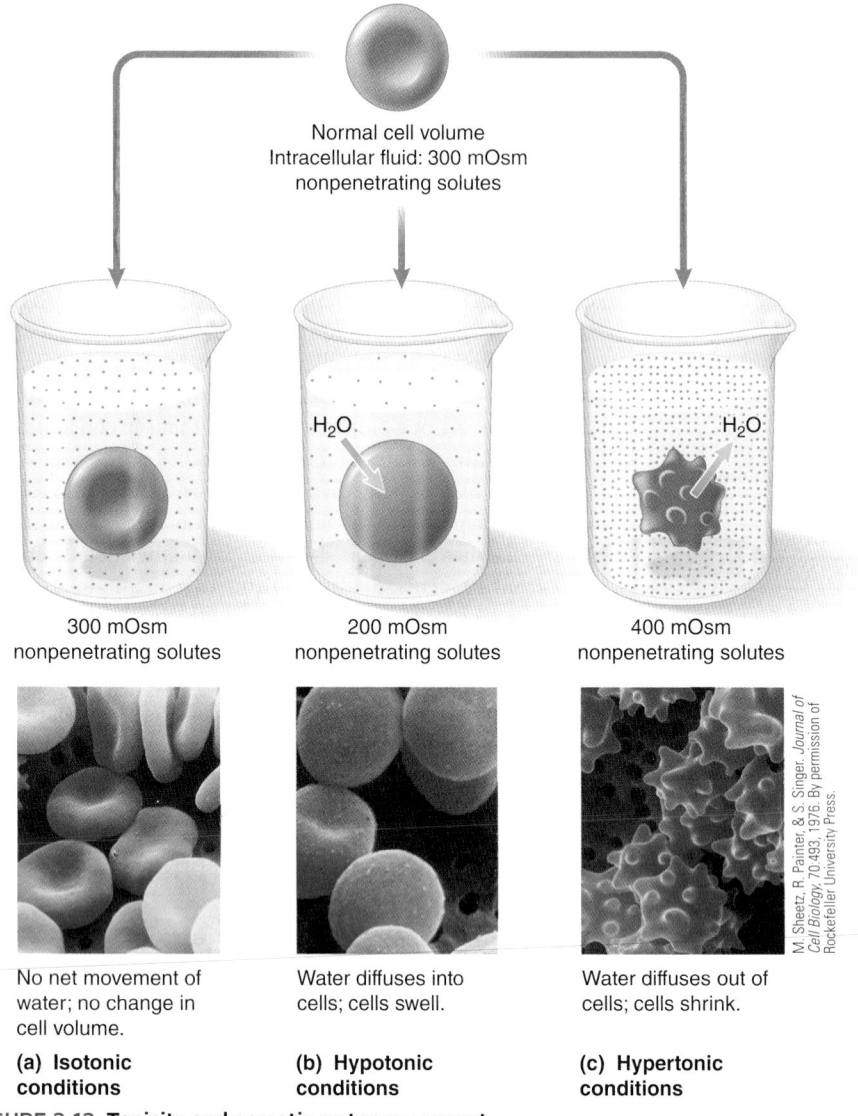

Normal cell volume
Intracellular fluid: 300 mOsm
nonpenetrating solutes

H₂O

H₂O

300 mOsm
nonpenetrating solutes

200 mOsm
nonpenetrating solutes

400 mOsm
nonpenetrating solutes

M. Sheetz, R. Painter, & S. Singer. *Journal of Cell Biology,* 70:493, 1976. By permission of Rockefeller University Press.

No net movement of
water; no change in
cell volume.

Water diffuses into
cells; cells swell.

Water diffuses out of
cells; cells shrink.

**(a) Isotonic
conditions**

**(b) Hypotonic
conditions**

**(c) Hypertonic
conditions**

● **FIGURE 3-13 Tonicity and osmotic water movement.**

Carrier-mediated transport is accomplished by a membrane carrier changing its shape.

A carrier protein spans the thickness of the plasma membrane and can change its conformation (shape) so that specific binding sites within the carrier are alternately exposed to the ECF and the ICF. ● Figure 3-14 shows how this **carrier-mediated transport** works. Step **1** shows the carrier open to the ECF. The molecule to be transported attaches to a carrier's binding site on one side of the membrane—in this case, on the ECF side (step **2**). Then the carrier changes shape, exposing the same site to the other side of the membrane (step **3**). Having been moved in this way from one side of the membrane to the other, the bound molecule detaches from the carrier (step **4**). Next, the carrier reverts to its original shape (back to step **1**).

Both channels and carriers are proteins that span the plasma membrane and serve as selective avenues for movement of water-soluble substances across the membrane, but there are notable differences between them: (1) Only ions fit through the narrow channels, whereas small polar molecules such as glucose are transported across the membrane by carriers.

(2) Channels can be open or closed, but carriers are always "open for business" (although the number and kinds of carriers in the plasma membrane can be regulated). (3) When open for traffic, channels are open at both sides of the membrane at the same time, permitting continuous, rapid movement of ions between the ECF and the ICF through these nonstop passageways. By contrast, carriers are never open to both the ECF and the ICF simultaneously. They must change shape to alternately pick up passenger molecules on one side and drop them off on the other side, a time-consuming process. Whereas a carrier may move up to 5000 particles per second across the membrane, 5 million ions may pass through an open channel in 1 second.

Carrier-mediated transport systems display three important characteristics that determine the kind and amount of material that can be transferred across the membrane: *specificity, saturation,* and *competition.*

1. Specificity. Each carrier protein is specialized to transport a specific substance or, at most, a few closely related chemical compounds. For example, amino acids cannot bind to glucose carriers, although several similar amino acids may be able to use the same carrier. Cells vary in the types of carriers they have, thus permitting transport selectivity among cells.

2. Saturation. A limited number of carrier binding sites are available within a particular plasma membrane for a specific substance. Therefore, the amount of a substance carriers can transport across the membrane in a given time is limited. This limit is known as the **transport maximum (T_m)**. Until the T_m is reached, the number of carrier binding sites occupied by a substance and, accordingly, the substance's rate of transport across the membrane are directly related to its concentration. The more of a substance available for transport, the more transported. When the T_m is reached, the carriers are saturated (all binding sites are occupied) and the rate of the substance's transport across the membrane is maximal. Further increases in the substance's concentration are no longer accompanied by corresponding increases in the rate of transport (● Figure 3-15).

As an analogy, consider a ferry boat that can carry at most 100 people across a river during one trip in an hour. If 25 people are on hand to board the ferry, 25 will be transported

● FIGURE 3-14 **Model for facilitated diffusion, a passive form of carrier-mediated transport.**

1 Carrier protein takes conformation in which solute binding site is exposed to region of higher concentration.

ECF — Solute molecule to be transported
— Carrier protein
Plasma membrane — Binding site
ICF

Concentration gradient
(High)
(Low)

Direction of transport

4 Transported solute is released and carrier protein returns to conformation in step 1.

2 Solute molecule binds to carrier protein.

3 Carrier protein changes conformation so that binding site is exposed to region of lower concentration.

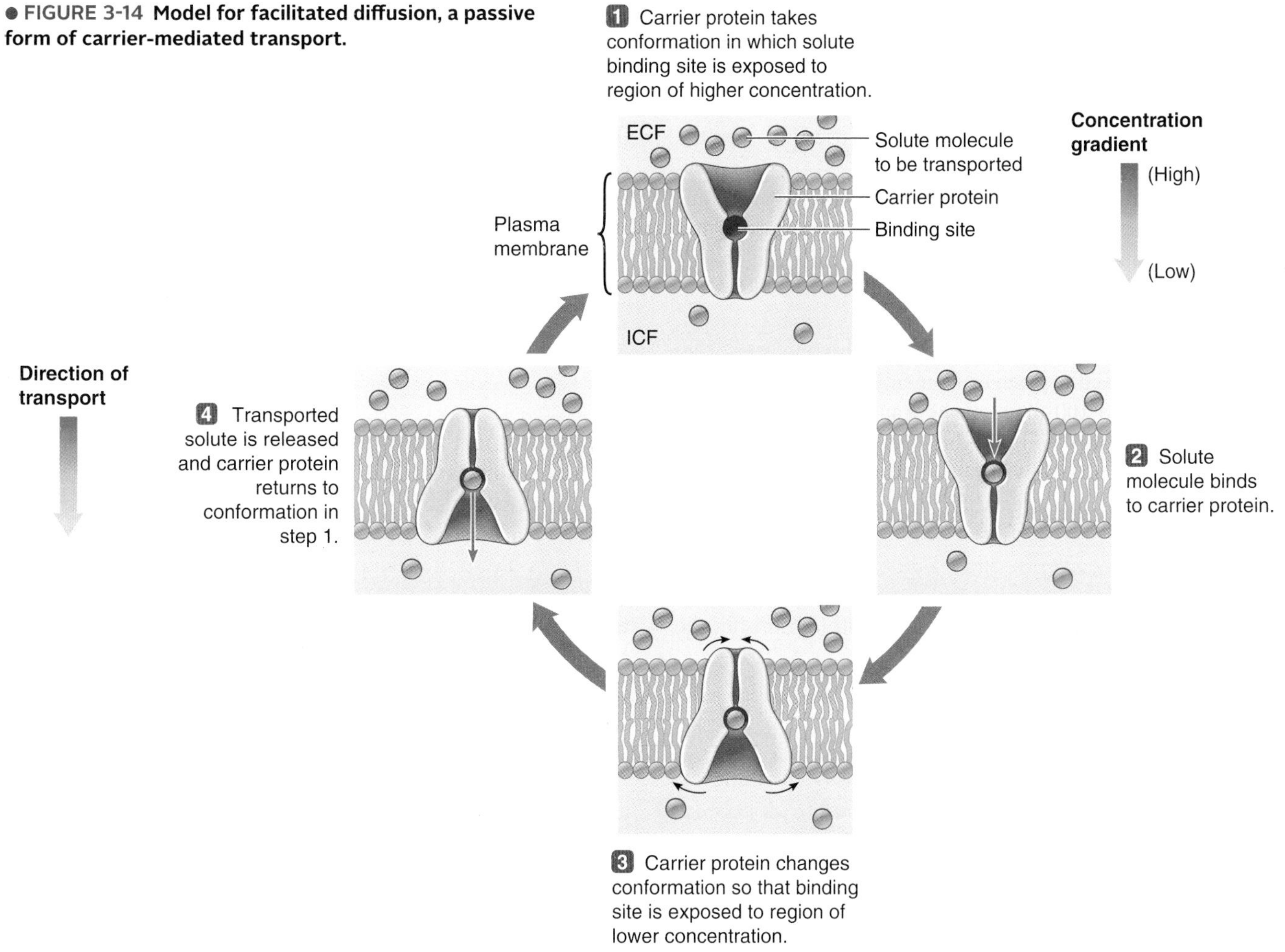

that hour. Doubling the number of people on hand to 50 will double the rate of transport to 50 people that hour. Such a direct relationship will exist between the number of people waiting to board (the concentration) and the rate of transport until the ferry is fully occupied (its T_m is reached). Even if 150 people are waiting to board, only 100 can be transported per hour.

Saturation of carriers is a critical rate-limiting factor in the transport of selected substances across the kidney membranes during urine formation and across the intestinal membranes during absorption of digested foods. Furthermore, it is sometimes possible to regulate the rate of carrier-mediated transport by varying the affinity (attraction) of the binding site for its passenger or by varying the number of binding sites. For example,

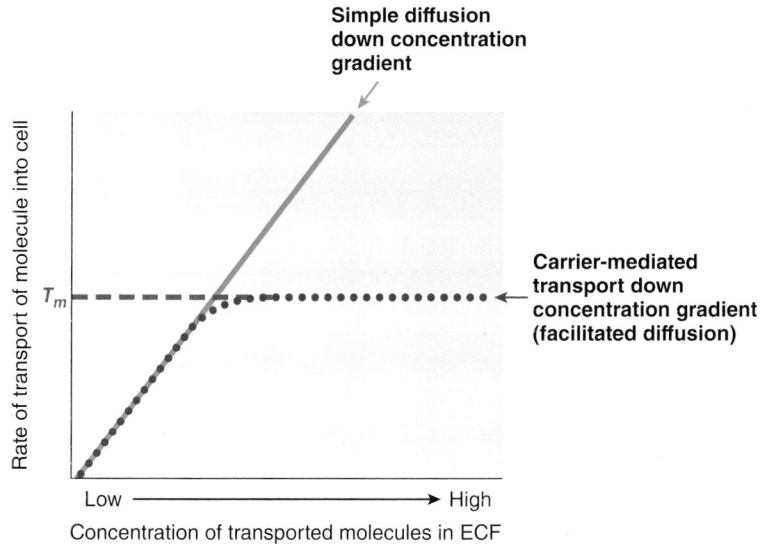

Simple diffusion down concentration gradient

Rate of transport of molecule into cell

T_m

Carrier-mediated transport down concentration gradient (facilitated diffusion)

Low ——————→ High
Concentration of transported molecules in ECF

● FIGURE 3-15 **Comparison of carrier-mediated transport and simple diffusion down a concentration gradient.** With simple diffusion of a molecule down its concentration gradient, the rate of transport of the molecule into the cell is directly proportional to the extracellular concentration of the molecule. With carrier-mediated transport of a molecule down its concentration gradient, the rate of transport of the molecule into the cell is directly proportional to the extracellular concentration of the molecule until the carrier is saturated, at which time the rate of transport reaches the transport maximum (T_m). After T_m is reached, the rate of transport levels off despite further increases in the ECF concentration of the molecule.

the hormone insulin greatly increases the carrier-mediated transport of glucose into most cells of the body by promoting an increase in the number of glucose carriers in the cell's plasma membrane. Deficient insulin action *(diabetes mellitus)* drastically impairs the body's ability to take up and use glucose as the primary energy source.

3. Competition. Several closely related compounds may compete for a ride across the membrane on the same carrier. If a given binding site can be occupied by more than one type of molecule, the rate of transport of each substance is less when both molecules are present than when either is present by itself. To illustrate, assume the ferry has 100 seats (binding sites) that can be occupied by either men or women. If only men are waiting to board, up to 100 men can be transported during each trip; the same holds true if only women are waiting to board. If both men and women are waiting to board, however, they will compete for the available seats. Fifty of each might make the trip, although the total number of people transported will still be the same, 100 people. In other words, when a carrier can transport two closely related substances, such as the amino acids glycine and alanine, the presence of both diminishes the rate of transfer for either.

Facilitated diffusion is passive carrier-mediated transport.

Carrier-mediated transport takes two forms, depending on whether energy must be supplied to complete the process: facilitated diffusion (not requiring energy) and active transport (requiring energy). **Facilitated diffusion** uses a carrier to facilitate (assist) the transfer of a particular substance across the membrane "downhill" from high to low concentration. This process is passive and does not require energy because movement occurs naturally down a concentration gradient. **Active transport,** however, requires the carrier to expend energy to transfer its passenger "uphill" against a concentration gradient, from an area of lower concentration to an area of higher concentration. An analogous situation is a car on a hill. To move the car downhill requires no energy; it will coast from the top down. Driving the car uphill, however, requires the use of energy (generated by the burning of gasoline).

The most notable example of facilitated diffusion is the transport of glucose into cells. Glucose is in higher concentration in the blood than in the tissues. Fresh supplies of this nutrient are regularly added to the blood by eating and by using reserve energy stores in the body. Simultaneously, the cells metabolize glucose almost as rapidly as it enters from the blood. As a result, a continuous gradient exists for net diffusion of glucose into the cells. However, glucose cannot cross plasma membranes on its own because it is not lipid soluble and is too large to fit through a channel. Without glucose carrier molecules (called *glucose transporters,* or *GLUTs;* see p. 562) to facilitate membrane transport of glucose, cells would be deprived of their preferred source of fuel.

The binding sites on facilitated diffusion carriers can bind with their passenger molecules when exposed on either side of the membrane. As a result of thermal energy, these carriers undergo spontaneous changes in shape, alternately exposing

their binding sites to the ECF or the ICF. After picking up the passenger on one side, when the carrier changes its conformation, it drops off the passenger on the opposite side of the membrane. Because passengers are more likely to bind with the carrier on the high-concentration side than on the low-concentration side, the net movement always proceeds down the concentration gradient from higher to lower concentration (see ● Figure 3-14). As is characteristic of all types of mediated transport, the rate of facilitated diffusion is limited by saturation of the carrier binding sites—unlike the rate of simple diffusion, which is always directly proportional to the concentration gradient (see ● Figure 3-15).

Active transport is carrier-mediated and uses energy to move a substance against its concentration gradient.

Active transport also uses a carrier protein to transfer a specific substance across the membrane, but in this case the carrier transports the substance uphill *against* its concentration gradient. Active transport comes in two forms. In **primary active transport,** energy is *directly* required to move a substance against its concentration gradient; the carrier splits ATP to power the transport process. In **secondary active transport,** energy is required in the entire process, but it is *not directly* used to produce uphill movement. That is, the carrier does not split ATP; instead, it moves a molecule uphill by using "secondhand" energy stored in the form of a Na^+ concentration gradient. This gradient is built up by primary active transport of Na^+ by a different carrier. Let us examine each process in more detail.

PRIMARY ACTIVE TRANSPORT In primary active transport, energy in the form of ATP is required to vary the affinity of the binding site when it is exposed on opposite sides of the plasma membrane. In contrast, in facilitated diffusion, the affinity of the binding site is the same when exposed to either the outside or the inside of the cell.

With primary active transport, the binding site has a greater affinity for its passenger (always an ion) on the low-concentration side as a result of *phosphorylation* (attachment of phosphate) of the carrier on this side (● Figure 3-16, step **1**). The carrier acts as an enzyme that has ATPase activity, which means it splits the terminal phosphate from an ATP molecule to yield adenosine diphosphate (ADP) and inorganic phosphate plus free energy (see p. 29). The phosphate group then attaches to the carrier, increasing the affinity of its binding site for the ion. As a result, the ion to be transported binds to the carrier on the low-concentration side (step **2**). In response to this binding, the carrier changes its conformation so that the ion is now exposed to the high-concentration side of the membrane (step **3**). The change in carrier shape reduces the affinity of the binding site for the passenger, so the ion is released on the high-concentration side. Simultaneously, the change in shape is accompanied by *dephosphorylation;* that is, the phosphate group detaches from the carrier (step **4**). The carrier then returns to its original conformation (step **5**). Thus, ATP energy is used in the phosphorylation–dephosphorylation cycle of the carrier. It alters the affinity of the carrier's binding sites on opposite sides

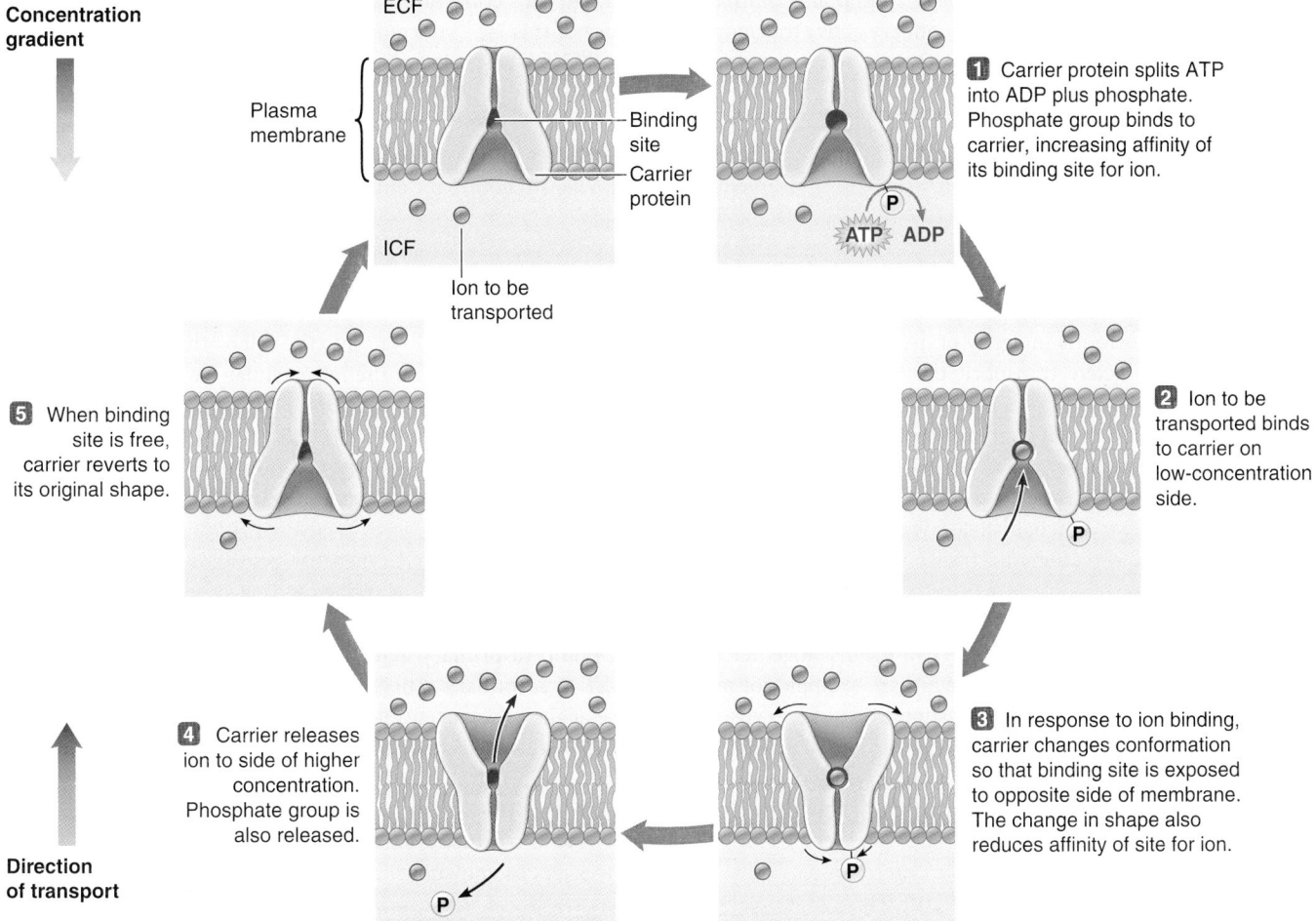

Concentration gradient

ECF

Plasma membrane

Binding site

Carrier protein

ICF

Ion to be transported

Direction of transport

1 Carrier protein splits ATP into ADP plus phosphate. Phosphate group binds to carrier, increasing affinity of its binding site for ion.

ATP → ADP

2 Ion to be transported binds to carrier on low-concentration side.

3 In response to ion binding, carrier changes conformation so that binding site is exposed to opposite side of membrane. The change in shape also reduces affinity of site for ion.

4 Carrier releases ion to side of higher concentration. Phosphate group is also released.

5 When binding site is free, carrier reverts to its original shape.

● **FIGURE 3-16 Model for active transport.** The energy of ATP is required in the phosphorylation–dephosphorylation cycle of the carrier to transport the molecule uphill from a region of low concentration to a region of high concentration.

of the membrane so that transported ions are moved uphill from an area of low concentration to an area of higher concentration. These active-transport mechanisms are often called **"pumps,"** analogous to water pumps that require energy to lift water against the downward pull of gravity.

Primary active-transport pumps all move positively charged ions, namely, Na^+, K^+, hydrogen ion (H^+), or Ca^{2+}, across the membrane. The simplest primary active-transport systems pump a single type of passenger. For example, the Ca^{2+} pump in the plasma membrane transports Ca^{2+} out of the cell, keeping the Ca^{2+} concentration in the cytosol low. These Ca^{2+} transporters are particularly abundant in the plasma membrane of neuron (nerve cell) terminals that store chemical messengers (neurotransmitters) in secretory vesicles (see p. 92). An electrical signal in a neuron terminal triggers the opening of Ca^{2+} channels in the terminal's plasma membrane. Entry of Ca^{2+} down its concentration gradient through these open channels promotes the secretion of neurotransmitter by exocytosis of the secretory vesicles. By keeping the intracellular Ca^{2+} concentration low, the active Ca^{2+} pump helps maintain a large concentration gradient for the entry of secretion-inducing Ca^{2+} from the ECF into the neuron terminal.

Na^+–K^+ PUMP   More complicated primary active-transport mechanisms involve the transfer of two different passengers in opposite directions. The most important example is a sequentially active **Na^+–K^+ ATPase pump** (**Na^+–K^+ pump** for short) found in the plasma membrane of all cells. This carrier transports Na^+ out of the cell, concentrating it in the ECF, and picks up K^+ from the outside, concentrating it in the ICF. No direct exchange occurs of Na^+ for K^+, however. The Na^+–K^+ pump moves three Na^+ out of the cell for every two K^+ it pumps in. (To appreciate the magnitude of active Na^+–K^+ pumping that takes place, consider that a single nerve cell membrane contains perhaps 1 million Na^+–K^+ pumps capable of transporting about 200 million ions per second.)

The Na^+–K^+ pump plays three important roles:

1. It establishes Na^+ and K^+ concentration gradients across the plasma membrane of all cells; these gradients are critically important in the ability of nerve and muscle cells to generate electrical signals essential to their functioning (a topic discussed more thoroughly later).

2. It helps regulate cell volume by controlling the concentrations of solutes inside the cell and thus minimizing osmotic effects that would induce swelling or shrinking of the cell.

3. The energy used to run the Na$^+$–K$^+$ pump also indirectly serves as the energy source for secondary active transport, a topic to which we now turn our attention.

SECONDARY ACTIVE TRANSPORT With secondary active transport, the carrier does not directly split ATP to move a substance against its concentration gradient. Instead, the movement of Na$^+$ into the cell down its concentration gradient (established by the ATP-splitting Na$^+$–K$^+$ pump) drives the uphill transport of another solute by a secondary active-transport carrier. This is efficient, because Na$^+$ must be pumped out anyway to maintain the electrical and osmotic integrity of the cell.

In secondary active transport, the transfer of the solute across the membrane is always coupled (occurs together) with the transfer of the Na$^+$ that supplies the driving force. Secondary active transport carriers have two binding sites: one for the solute being moved and one for Na$^+$. Secondary active transport occurs by two mechanisms—symport and antiport—depending on the direction the transported solute moves in relation to Na$^+$ movement. In **symport** (also called **cotransport**), the solute and Na$^+$ move through the membrane in the same direction, that is, into the cell (*sym* means "together"; *co* means "with"). Glucose and amino acids are examples of molecules transported by symport in intestinal and kidney cells. We discuss the importance of these carriers in more detail shortly. In **antiport** (also known as **countertransport** or **exchange**), the solute and Na$^+$ move through the membrane in opposite directions, that is, Na$^+$ into and the solute out of the cell (*anti* means "opposite"; *counter* means "against"). For example, cells exchange Na$^+$ and H$^+$ by means of antiport. This carrier plays an important role in maintaining the appropriate pH inside the cells (a fluid becomes more acidic as its H$^+$ concentration rises).

Let us examine Na$^+$ and glucose symport in more detail as an example of secondary active transport. Unlike most cells of the body, the intestinal and kidney cells actively transport glucose by moving it uphill from low to high concentration. The intestinal cells transport this nutrient from the intestinal lumen into the blood, concentrating it there, until none is left in the lumen to be lost in the feces. The kidney cells save this nutrient for the body by transporting it out of the fluid that is to become urine, moving it against a concentration gradient into the blood. The symport carriers that transport glucose against its concentration gradient from the lumen in the intestine and kidneys are distinct from the glucose facilitated-diffusion carriers that transport glucose down its concentration gradient into most cells.

Here, we focus specifically on the symport carrier that cotransports Na$^+$ and glucose in intestinal epithelial cells. This carrier, known as the **sodium and glucose cotransporter** or **SGLT,** is located in the luminal membrane (the membrane facing the intestinal lumen) (● Figure 3-17). The Na$^+$–K$^+$ pump in these cells is located in the basolateral membrane (the membrane on the side of the cell opposite the lumen and along the lateral edge of the cell below the tight junction; see ● Figure 3-5, p. 53). More Na$^+$ is present in the lumen than inside the cells because the energy-requiring Na$^+$–K$^+$ pump transports Na$^+$ out of the cell at the basolateral membrane, keeping the intra-

cellular Na$^+$ concentration low (● Figure 3-17, step **1**). Because of this Na$^+$ concentration difference, more Na$^+$ binds to the SGLT when it is exposed to the lumen than when it is exposed to the ICF. Binding of Na$^+$ to this carrier increases its affinity for glucose, so glucose binds to the SGLT when it is open to the lumen side where glucose concentration is low (step **2a**). When both Na$^+$ and glucose are bound to it, the SGLT changes shape and opens to the inside of the cell (step **2b**). Both Na$^+$ and glucose are released to the interior—Na$^+$ because of the lower intracellular Na$^+$ concentration and glucose because of the reduced affinity of the binding site on release of Na$^+$ (step **2c**). The movement of Na$^+$ into the cell by this cotransport carrier is downhill because the intracellular Na$^+$ concentration is low, but the movement of glucose is uphill because glucose becomes concentrated in the cell.

The released Na$^+$ is quickly pumped out by the active Na$^+$–K$^+$ transport mechanism, keeping the level of intracellular Na$^+$ low. The energy expended in this process is not used directly to run the SGLT because phosphorylation is not required to alter the affinity of the binding site to glucose. Instead, the establishment of a Na$^+$ concentration gradient by the Na$^+$–K$^+$ pump (a primary active-transport mechanism) drives the SGLT (a secondary active-transport mechanism) to move glucose against its concentration gradient.

The glucose carried across the luminal membrane into the cell by secondary active transport then moves passively out of the cell by facilitated diffusion across the basolateral membrane and into the blood (step **3**). This facilitated diffusion, which moves glucose down its concentration gradient, is mediated by a passive GLUT identical to the one that transports glucose into other cells, but in intestinal and kidney cells it transports glucose out of the cell. The difference depends on the direction of the glucose concentration gradient. In the case of intestinal and kidney cells, the glucose concentration is higher inside the cells.

Before leaving the topic of carrier-mediated transport, think about all the activities that rely on carrier assistance. All cells depend on carriers for the uptake of glucose and amino acids, which serve as the major energy source and the structural building blocks, respectively. Na$^+$–K$^+$ pumps are essential for generating cellular electrical activity and for ensuring that cells have an appropriate intracellular concentration of osmotically active solutes. Primary and secondary active transport are used extensively to accomplish the specialized functions of the nervous and digestive systems, as well as those of the kidneys and all types of muscle.

With vesicular transport, material is moved into or out of the cell wrapped in membrane.

The special carrier-mediated transport systems embedded in the plasma membrane selectively transport ions and small polar molecules. But how do large polar molecules, such as the protein hormones secreted by endocrine cells, or even multimolecular materials, such as the bacteria ingested by white blood cells, leave or enter the cell? These materials are unable to cross the plasma membrane, even with assistance: They are much too big for channels, and no carriers exist for them (they would not even fit into a carrier molecule). These large particles are transferred between

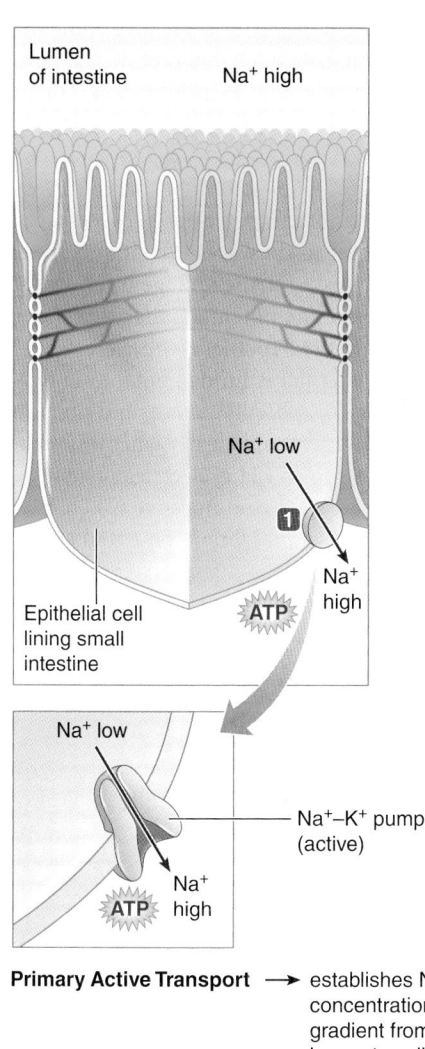

Lumen of intestine — Na⁺ high

Na⁺ low

1 Na⁺ low → Na⁺ high

ATP

Epithelial cell lining small intestine

Na⁺ low

Na⁺–K⁺ pump (active)

Na⁺ high

ATP

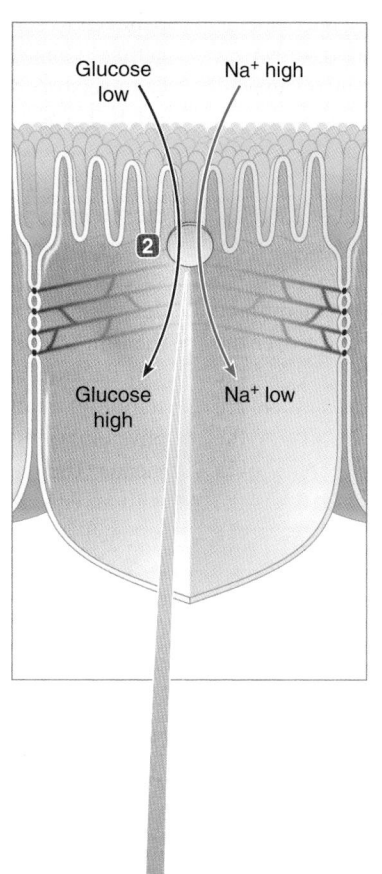

Glucose low — Na⁺ high

2

Glucose high — Na⁺ low

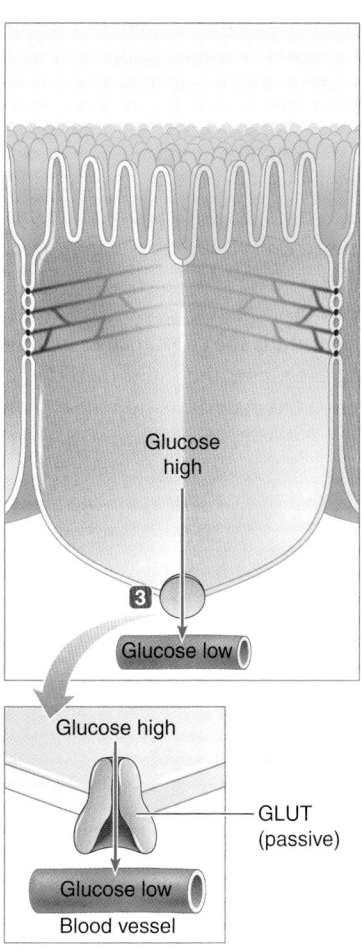

Glucose high

3 Glucose low

Glucose high

GLUT (passive)

Glucose low

Blood vessel

Primary Active Transport → establishes Na⁺ concentration gradient from lumen to cell, which drives → **Secondary Active Transport** → creating glucose concentration gradient from cell to blood used for → **Facilitated Diffusion**

1 Na⁺–K⁺ pump uses energy to drive Na⁺ *uphill* out of cell.

2 SGLT uses Na⁺ concentration gradient to simultaneously move Na⁺ *downhill* and glucose *uphill* from lumen into cell.

3 GLUT passively moves glucose *downhill* out of cell into blood.

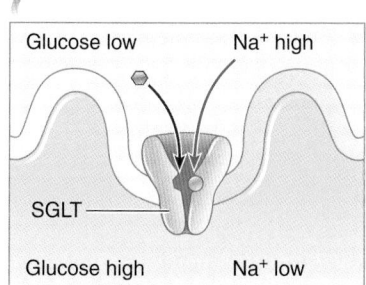

Glucose low — Na⁺ high

SGLT

Glucose high — Na⁺ low

2a Binding of Na⁺ on luminal side, where Na⁺ concentration is higher, increases affinity of SGLT for glucose. Therefore, glucose also binds to SGLT on luminal side, where glucose concentration is lower.

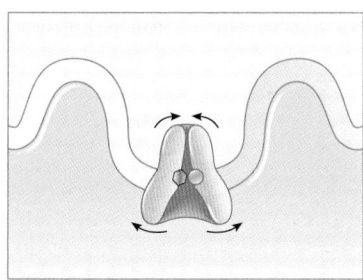

2b When both Na⁺ and glucose are bound, SGLT changes shape, opening to cell interior.

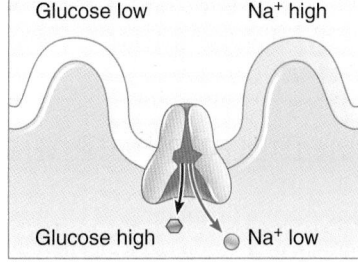

Glucose low — Na⁺ high

Glucose high — Na⁺ low

2c SGLT releases Na⁺ to cell interior, where Na⁺ concentration is lower. Because affinity of SGLT for glucose decreases on release of Na⁺, SGLT also releases glucose to cell interior, where glucose concentration is higher.

● **FIGURE 3-17 Symport of glucose.** Glucose is transported across intestinal and kidney cells against its concentration gradient by means of secondary active transport mediated by the sodium and glucose cotransporter (SGLT) at the cells' luminal membrane.

the ICF and the ECF not by crossing the membrane but by being wrapped in a membrane-enclosed vesicle, a process known as **vesicular transport.** Vesicular transport requires energy expenditure by the cell, so this is an active method of membrane transport. Energy is needed to accomplish vesicle formation and vesicle movement within the cell. Transport into the cell in this manner is termed *endocytosis,* whereas transport out of the cell is called *exocytosis* (see ● Figure 2-5, p. 27).

ENDOCYTOSIS To review, in **endocytosis** the plasma membrane surrounds the substance to be ingested and then fuses over the surface, pinching off a membrane-enclosed vesicle so that the engulfed material is trapped within the cell. Recall that there are three forms of endocytosis, depending on the nature of the material internalized: *pinocytosis* (nonselective uptake of a sample of ECF), *receptor-mediated endocytosis* (selective uptake of a large molecule), and *phagocytosis* (selective uptake of a multimolecular particle) (see ● Figure 2-7, p. 28).

EXOCYTOSIS In **exocytosis,** almost the reverse of endocytosis occurs. A membrane-enclosed secretory vesicle formed within the cell fuses with the plasma membrane and then opens up and releases its contents to the exterior. Protein hormones and enzymes are secreted by this means.

In some cells, endocytic vesicles bypass the lysosomes where they are normally degraded and instead travel to the opposite side of the cell, where they release their contents by exocytosis. This provides a pathway to shuttle large intact molecules through the cell. Such vesicular traffic is one means by which materials are transferred through the thin cells lining the capillaries, across which exchanges are made between the blood and the surrounding tissues.

Our discussion of membrane transport is now complete; ▲ Table 3-2 summarizes the pathways by which materials can pass between the ECF and the ICF. Cells are differentially selective in what enters or leaves because they have varying numbers and kinds of channels, carriers, and mechanisms for vesicular transport. Large polar molecules (too large for channels and not lipid soluble) that have no special transport mechanisms are unable to permeate.

The selective transport of K^+ and Na^+ is responsible for the electrical properties of cells. We turn our attention to this topic next.

Membrane Potential

The plasma membranes of all living cells have a membrane potential, or are polarized electrically.

Membrane potential is a separation of opposite charges across the plasma membrane.

The term **membrane potential** refers to a separation of opposite charges across the membrane or to a difference in the relative number of cations and anions in the ICF and ECF. Recall that opposite charges tend to attract each other and like charges tend to repel each other. Work must be performed (energy ex-

pended) to separate opposite charges after they have come together. Conversely, when oppositely charged particles have been separated, the electrical force of attraction between them can be harnessed to perform work when the charges are permitted to come together again. This is the basic principle underlying electrically powered devices. A separation of charges across the membrane is called a membrane potential because separated charges have the potential to do work. Potential is measured in volts (the same unit used for the voltage in electrical devices), but because the membrane potential is relatively low, the unit used is the **millivolt (mV; 1/1000 of a volt).**

Because the concept of potential is fundamental to understanding much of physiology, especially nerve and muscle physiology, it is important to understand clearly what this term means. The membrane in ● Figure 3-18a is electrically neutral; with an equal number of positive (+) and negative (−) charges on each side of the membrane, no membrane potential exists. In ● Figure 3-18b, some of the positive charges from the right side have been moved to the left. Now the left side has an excess of positive charges, leaving an excess of negative charges on the right. In other words, opposite charges are separated across the membrane, or the relative number of positive and negative charges differs between the two sides. A membrane potential now exists. The attractive force between the separated charges causes them to accumulate in a thin layer along the outer and inner surfaces of the plasma membrane (● Figure 3-18c). These separated charges represent only a fraction of the total number of charged particles (ions) present in the ICF and ECF, however, and most fluid inside and outside the cells is electrically neutral (● Figure 3-18d). The electrically balanced ions can be ignored, because they do not contribute to membrane potential. Thus, an almost insignificant fraction of the total number of charged particles present in the body fluids is responsible for the membrane potential.

Note that the membrane itself is not charged. The term *membrane potential* refers to the difference in charge between the wafer-thin regions of ICF and ECF lying next to the inside and outside of the membrane, respectively. The magnitude of the potential depends on the number of opposite charges separated: The greater the number of charges separated, the larger the potential. Therefore, in ● Figure 3-18e, membrane B has more potential than A and less potential than C.

Membrane potential is due to differences in the concentration and permeability of key ions.

All cells have membrane potential. The cells of *excitable tissues*—namely, nerve cells and muscle cells—have the ability to produce rapid, transient changes in their membrane potential when excited. These brief fluctuations in potential serve as electrical signals. The constant membrane potential present in the cells of nonexcitable tissues and those of excitable tissues when they are at rest—that is, when they are not producing electrical signals—is known as the **resting membrane potential.** Here, we concentrate on the generation and maintenance of the resting membrane potential; in later chapters, we examine the changes that take place in excitable tissues during electrical signaling.

Method of Transport	Substances Involved	Energy Requirements and Force Producing Movement	Limit to Transport
Simple Diffusion			
Diffusion through the lipid bilayer	Nonpolar molecules of any size (e.g., O_2, CO_2, fatty acids)	Passive; molecules move down aconcentration gradient (from high to low concentration)	Continues until the gradient is abolished (no further net movement)
Diffusion through a protein channel	Specific small ions (e.g., Na^+, K^+, Ca^{2+}, Cl^-)	Passive; ions move down an electrochemical gradient through open channels (from high to low concentration and by attraction of the ion to an area of opposite charge)	Continues until the concentration and electrical gradients exactly counterbalance each other (no further net movement)
Osmosis	Water only	Passive; water moves down its own concentration gradient (to an area of lower water concentration, i.e., higher solute concentration)	Continues until the concentration difference is abolished, until it is stopped by an opposing hydrostatic pressure, or until the cell is destroyed
Carrier-Mediated Transport			
Facilitated diffusion	Specific small polar molecules for which a carrier is available (e.g., glucose)	Passive; molecules move down a concentration gradient (from high to low concentration)	Displays a *transport maximum* (T_m); the carriers can become saturated
Primary active transport	Specific cations for which carriers are available (e.g., Na^+, K^+, H^+, Ca^{2+})	Active; ions move against a concentration gradient (from low to high concentration); requires ATP	Displays a T_m; the carriers can become saturated
Secondary active transport (symport or antiport)	Specific small polar molecules and ions for which coupled transport carriers are available (e.g., glucose, amino acids for symport; some ions for antiport)	Active; substances move against a concentration gradient (from low to high concentration); driven directly by a Na^+ gradient established by the ATP-requiring primary pump. In symport, the cotransported molecule and driving ion move in the same direction; in antiport, the transported solute and driving ion move in opposite directions	Displays a T_m; the coupled transport carriers can become saturated
Vesicular Transport			
Endocytosis			
Pinocytosis	Small volume of ECF	Active; the plasma membrane dips inward and pinches off at the surface, forming an internalized vesicle	Control is poorly understood
Receptor-mediated endocytosis	Specific large polar molecule (e.g., protein)	Active; the plasma membrane dips inward and pinches off at the surface, forming an internalized vesicle	Necessitates binding to a specific receptor on the membrane surface
Phagocytosis	Multimolecular particles (e.g., bacteria, cellular debris)	Active; the cell extends pseudopods that surround the particle, forming an internalized vesicle	Necessitates binding to a specific receptor on the membrane surface
Exocytosis	Secretory products (e.g., hormones, enzymes), as well as large molecules that pass through the cell intact	Active; an increase in cytosolic Ca^{2+} induces fusion of a secretory vesicle with the plasma membrane; the vesicle opens up and releases its contents to the outside	Secretion is triggered by specific neural or hormonal stimuli

The unequal distribution of a few key ions between the ICF and the ECF and their selective movement through the plasma membrane are responsible for the electrical properties of the membrane. In the body, electrical charges are carried by ions. The ions primarily responsible for the generation of the resting membrane potential are Na^+, K^+, and large, negatively charged (anionic) intracellular proteins, written as A^-. Other ions (calcium, magnesium, and chloride, to name a few) do not contribute directly to the

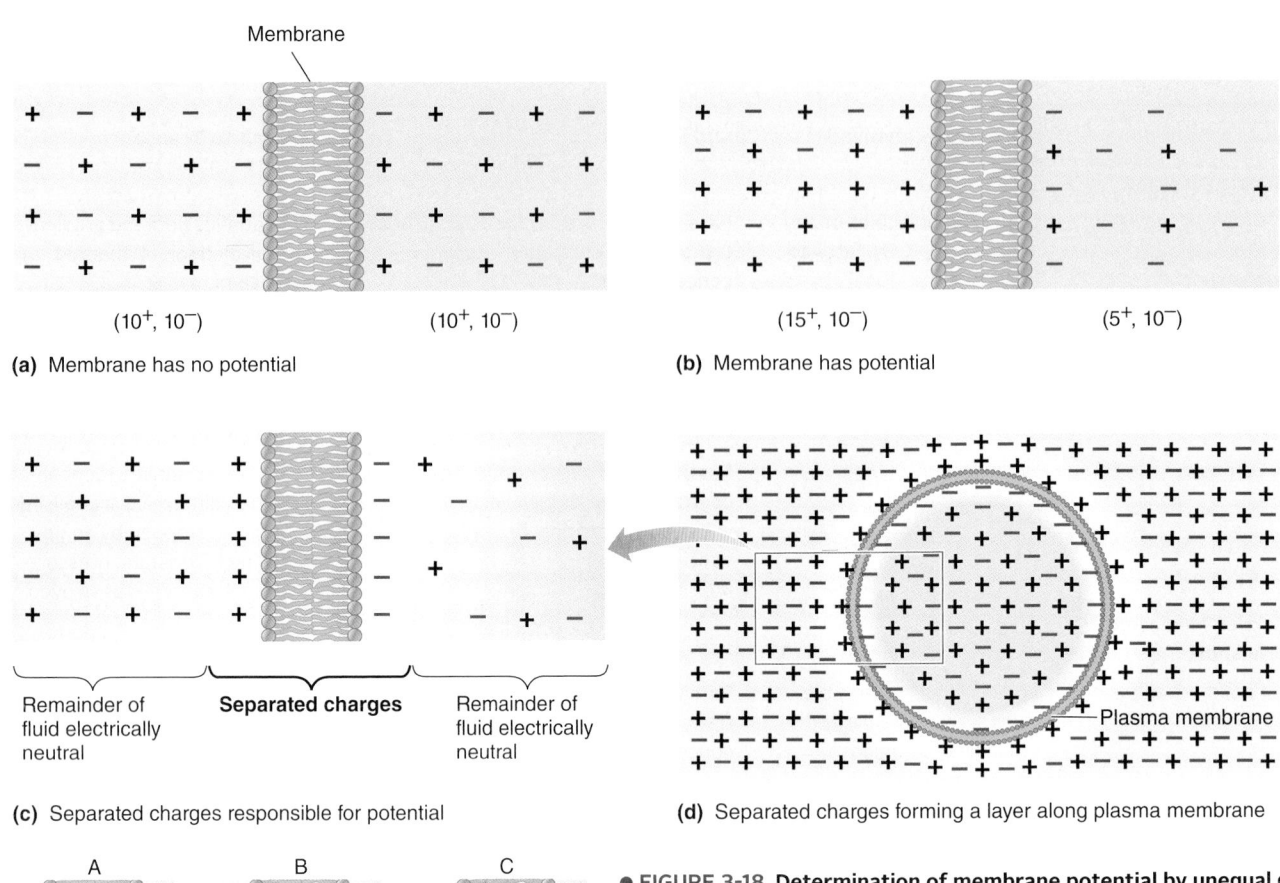

(a) Membrane has no potential

(b) Membrane has potential

(c) Separated charges responsible for potential

Remainder of fluid electrically neutral

Separated charges

Remainder of fluid electrically neutral

(d) Separated charges forming a layer along plasma membrane

Plasma membrane

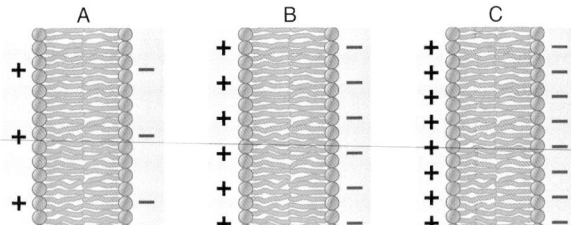

A   B   C

(e) Magnitude of potential: membrane B has more potential than membrane A and less potential than membrane C

● **FIGURE 3-18 Determination of membrane potential by unequal distribution of positive and negative charges across the membrane.**
(a) When the positive and negative charges are equally balanced on each side of the membrane, no membrane potential exists. (b) When opposite charges are separated across the membrane, membrane potential exists. (c) The unbalanced charges responsible for the potential accumulate in a thin layer along opposite surfaces of the membrane. (d) The vast majority of the fluid in the ECF and ICF is electrically neutral. The unbalanced charges accumulate along the plasma membrane. (e) The greater the separation of charges across the membrane, the larger the potential.

resting electrical properties of the plasma membrane in most cells, even though they play other important roles in the body.

The concentrations and relative permeabilities of the ions critical to membrane electrical activity are compared in ▲ Table 3-3. Note that *Na$^+$ is more concentrated in the ECF and K$^+$ is more concentrated in the ICF.* These concentration differences are maintained by the Na$^+$–K$^+$ pump at the expense of energy. Because the plasma membrane is virtually impermeable to A$^-$, these large, negatively charged proteins are found only inside the cell. After they have been synthesized from amino acids transported into the cell, they remain trapped within the cell.

In addition to the active carrier mechanism, Na$^+$ and K$^+$ can passively cross the membrane through protein channels specific for them. It is usually much easier for K$^+$ than for Na$^+$ to get through the membrane because the membrane typically has many more leak channels always open for passive K$^+$ traffic than channels open for passive Na$^+$ traffic. At resting potential

▲ Table 3-3 Concentration and Permeability of Ions Responsible for Membrane Potential in a Resting Nerve Cell

Ion	Extracellular Concentration*	Intracellular Concentration*	Relative Permeability
Na$^+$	150	15	1
K$^+$	5	150	25–30
A$^-$	0	65	0

*Concentration expressed in millimoles per liter, mM

in a nerve cell, the membrane is typically about 25 to 30 times more permeable to K^+ than to Na^+.

Armed with knowledge of the relative concentrations and permeabilities of these ions, we can analyze the forces acting across the plasma membrane. We consider (1) the direct contributions of the Na^+–K^+ pump to membrane potential, (2) the effect that the movement of K^+ alone would have on membrane potential, (3) the effect of Na^+ alone, and (4) the situation that exists in the cells when both K^+ and Na^+ effects are taking place concurrently. Remember throughout this discussion that *the concentration gradient for K^+ will always be outward* and *the concentration gradient for Na^+ will always be inward,* because the Na^+–K^+ pump maintains a higher concentration of K^+ inside the cell and a higher concentration of Na^+ outside the cell. Also, note that because K^+ and Na^+ are both cations (positively charged), *the electrical gradient for both of these ions will always be toward the negatively charged side of the membrane.*

EFFECT OF THE Na^+–K^+ PUMP ON MEMBRANE POTENTIAL The Na^+–K^+ pump transports three Na^+ out for every two K^+ it transports in. Because Na^+ and K^+ are both positive ions, this unequal transport separates charges across the membrane, with the outside becoming relatively more positive and the inside becoming relatively more negative as more positive ions are transported out than in. However, this active-transport mechanism only separates enough charges to generate a small membrane potential. Most of the membrane potential results from the passive diffusion of K^+ and Na^+ down concentration gradients. Thus, the main role of the Na^+–K^+ pump in producing membrane potential is indirect, through its critical contribution to maintaining the concentration gradients directly responsible for the ion movements that generate most of the potential.

EFFECT OF THE MOVEMENT OF K^+ ALONE ON MEMBRANE POTENTIAL: EQUILIBRIUM POTENTIAL FOR K^+ Consider a hypothetical situation characterized by (1) the concentrations that exist for K^+ and A^- across the plasma membrane, (2) free permeability of the membrane to K^+ but not to A^-, and (3) no potential as yet present. The concentration gradient for K^+ would tend to move these ions out of the cell (● Figure 3-19). Because the membrane is permeable to K^+, these ions would readily pass through, carrying their positive charge with them, so more positive charges would be on the outside. At the same time, negative charges in the form of A^- would be left behind on the inside, similar to the situation shown in ● Figure 3-18b. (Remember that A^- cannot diffuse out, despite a tremendous concentration gradient.) A membrane potential would now exist. Because an electrical gradient would also be present, K^+ would be attracted toward the negatively charged interior and repelled by the positively charged exterior. Thus, two opposing forces would now be acting on K^+: the concentration gradient tending to move K^+ out of the cell and the electrical gradient tending to move these same ions into the cell.

Initially, the concentration gradient would be stronger than the electrical gradient, so net movement of K^+ out of the cell would continue and the membrane potential would increase. As more K^+ moved out of the cell, however, the opposing electrical gradient would become stronger as the outside became increasingly positive and the inside increasingly negative. Net outward movement would gradually be reduced as the strength of the electrical gradient approached that of the concentration gradient. Finally, when these two forces exactly balanced each other (that is, when they were in equilibrium), no further net movement of K^+ would occur. The potential that would exist at this equilibrium is known as the **equilibrium potential for K^+** (E_{K^+}). At this point, a large concentration gradient for K^+ would still exist, but no more net movement of K^+ out of the cell would occur down this concentration gradient because of the exactly equal opposing electrical gradient (● Figure 3-19).

The membrane potential at E_{K^+} is -90 mV. By convention, *the sign always designates the polarity of the excess charge on the inside of the membrane.* A membrane potential of -90 mV means that the potential is of a magnitude of 90 mV, with the inside being negative relative to the outside. A potential of $+90$ mV would have the same strength, but the inside would be more positive than the outside.

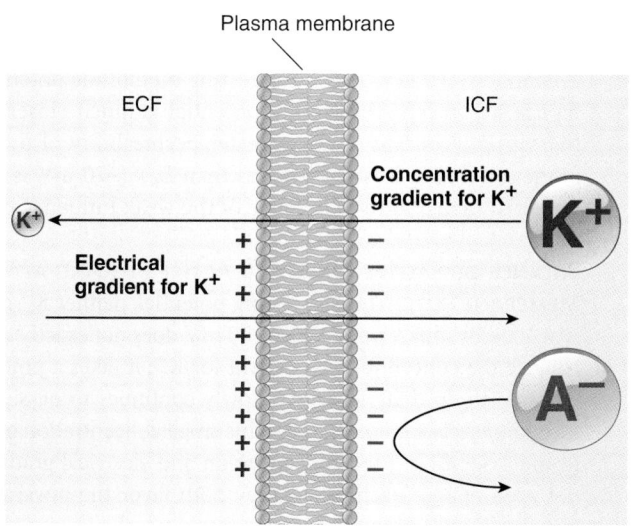

Plasma membrane

ECF — ICF

Concentration gradient for K^+

K^+

Electrical gradient for K^+

A^-

$E_{K^+} = -90$ mV

● **FIGURE 3-19 Equilibrium potential for K^+.**

1 The concentration gradient for K^+ tends to move these ions out of the cell.

2 The outside of the cell becomes more positive as K^+ ions move to the outside down their concentration gradient.

3 The membrane is impermeable to the large intracellular protein anion (A^-). The inside of the cell becomes more negative as K^+ ions move out, leaving behind A^-.

4 The resulting electrical gradient tends to move K^+ into the cell.

5 No further net movement of K^+ occurs when the inward electrical gradient exactly counterbalances the outward concentration gradient. The membrane potential at this equilibrium point is the equilibrium potential for K^+ (E_{K^+}) at -90 mV.

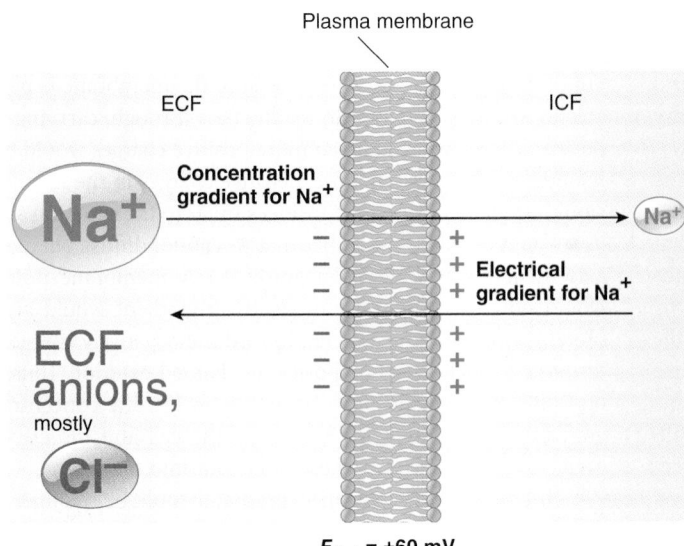

Plasma membrane

ECF

ICF

Na⁺

Concentration gradient for Na⁺

Na⁺

Electrical gradient for Na⁺

ECF anions, mostly

Cl⁻

$E_{Na^+} = +60$ mV

● **FIGURE 3-20 Equilibrium potential for Na⁺.**

1 The concentration gradient for Na⁺ tends to move these ions into the cell.

2 The inside of the cell becomes more positive as Na⁺ ions move to the inside down their concentration gradient.

3 The outside becomes more negative as Na⁺ ions move in, leaving behind in the ECF unbalanced negatively charged ions, mostly Cl⁻.

4 The resulting electrical gradient tends to move Na⁺ out of the cell.

5 No further net movement of Na⁺ occurs when the outward electrical gradient exactly counterbalances the inward concentration gradient. The membrane potential at this equilibrium point is the equilibrium potential for Na⁺ (E_{Na^+}) at +60 mV.

EFFECT OF MOVEMENT OF Na⁺ ALONE ON MEMBRANE POTENTIAL: EQUILIBRIUM POTENTIAL FOR Na⁺   A similar hypothetical situation could be developed for Na⁺ alone (● Figure 3-20). The concentration gradient for Na⁺ would move these ions into the cell, producing a buildup of positive charges on the interior of the membrane and leaving negative charges unbalanced outside (primarily in the form of chloride, Cl⁻; Na⁺ and Cl⁻—that is, salt—are the predominant ECF ions). Net inward movement would continue until equilibrium was established by the development of an opposing electrical gradient that exactly counterbalanced the concentration gradient. At this point, given the concentrations for Na⁺, the **equilibrium potential for Na⁺** (**E_{Na^+}**) would be +60 mV. In this case, the inside of the cell would be positive, in contrast to the equilibrium potential for K⁺. The magnitude of E_{Na^+} is somewhat less than that for E_{K^+} (60 mV compared to 90 mV) because the concentration gradient for Na⁺ is not as large (see Table 3-3); thus, the opposing electrical gradient (membrane potential) is not as great at equilibrium.

CONCURRENT K⁺ AND Na⁺ EFFECTS ON RESTING MEMBRANE POTENTIAL   Neither K⁺ nor Na⁺ exists alone in the body fluids, so equilibrium potentials are not present in body cells. They exist only in hypothetical or experimental conditions. In a living cell, the effects of both K⁺ and Na⁺ must be taken into account. *The greater the permeability of the plasma membrane for a given ion, the greater the tendency for that ion to drive the membrane potential toward the ion's own equilibrium potential.* Because the membrane at rest is 25 to 30 times more permeable to K⁺ than to Na⁺, K⁺ passes through more readily than Na⁺; thus, K⁺ influences the resting membrane potential to a much greater extent than Na⁺ does. Recall that K⁺ acting alone would establish an equilibrium potential of −90 mV. The membrane is somewhat permeable to Na⁺, however, so some Na⁺ enters the cell in a limited attempt to reach its equilibrium potential. This Na⁺ entry neutralizes, or cancels, some of the potential that would have been produced by K⁺ alone if Na⁺ were not present.

To better understand this concept, assume that each separated pair of charges in ● Figure 3-21 represents 10 mV of potential. (This is not technically correct, because in reality many separated charges must be present to account for a potential of 10 mV.) In this simplified example, nine separated pluses and minuses, with the minuses on the inside, represent the E_{K^+} of −90 mV. Superimposing the slight influence of Na⁺ on this K⁺-dominated membrane, assume that two Na⁺ enter the cell down the Na⁺ concentration and electrical gradients. (Note that the electrical gradient for Na⁺ is now inward in contrast to the outward electrical gradient for Na⁺ at E_{Na^+}. At E_{Na^+}, the inside of the cell is positive as a result of the inward movement of Na⁺ down its concentration gradient. In a resting nerve cell, however, the inside is negative because of the dominant influence of K⁺ on membrane potential. Thus, both the concentration and the electrical gradients now favor the inward movement of Na⁺.) The inward movement of these two positively charged Na⁺ neutralizes some of the potential established by K⁺, so now only seven pairs of charges are separated and the potential is −70 mV. This is the resting membrane potential of a typical nerve cell. The resting potential is much closer to E_{K^+} than to E_{Na^+} because of the greater permeability of the membrane to K⁺, but it is slightly less than E_{K^+} (−70 mV is a lower potential than −90 mV) because of the weak influence of Na⁺.

BALANCE OF PASSIVE LEAKS AND ACTIVE PUMPING AT RESTING MEMBRANE POTENTIAL   At resting potential, neither K⁺ nor Na⁺ is at equilibrium. A potential of −70 mV does not exactly counterbalance the concentration gradient for K⁺; it takes a potential of −90 mV to do that. Thus, K⁺ slowly continues to passively exit through its leak channels down this small concentration gradient. In the case of Na⁺, the concentration and electrical gradients do not even oppose each other; they both favor the inward movement of Na⁺. Therefore, Na⁺ continually leaks inward down its electrochemical gradient, but only slowly, because of its low permeability, that is, because of the scarcity of Na⁺ leak channels.

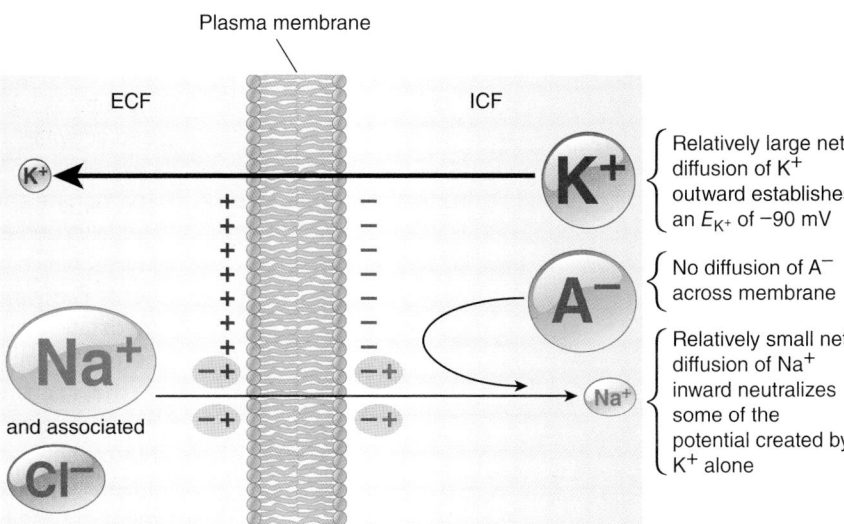

1. The Na⁺–K⁺ pump actively transports Na⁺ out of and K⁺ into the cell, keeping the concentration of Na⁺ high in the ECF and the concentration of K⁺ high in the ICF.

2. Given the concentration gradients that exist across the plasma membrane, K⁺ tends to drive membrane potential to the equilibrium potential for K⁺ (−90 mV), whereas Na⁺ tends to drive membrane potential to the equilibrium potential for Na⁺ (+60 mV).

3. However, K⁺ exerts the dominant effect on resting membrane potential because the membrane is more permeable to K⁺. As a result, resting potential (−70 mV) is much closer to E_{K^+} than to E_{Na^+}.

4. During the establishment of resting potential, the relatively large net diffusion of K⁺ outward does not produce a potential of −90 mV because the resting membrane is slightly permeable to Na⁺ and the relatively small net diffusion of Na⁺ inward neutralizes (in gray shading) some of the potential that would be created by K⁺ alone, bringing resting potential to −70 mV, slightly less than E_{K^+}.

5. The negatively charged intracellular proteins (A⁻) that cannot cross the membrane remain unbalanced inside the cell during the net outward movement of the positively charged ions, so the inside of the cell is more negative than the outside.

Relatively large net diffusion of K⁺ outward establishes an E_{K^+} of −90 mV

No diffusion of A⁻ across membrane

Relatively small net diffusion of Na⁺ inward neutralizes some of the potential created by K⁺ alone

Resting membrane potential = −70 mV

● FIGURE 3-21 **Effect of concurrent K⁺ and Na⁺ movement on establishing the resting membrane potential.**

Such leaking goes on all the time, so why doesn't the intracellular concentration of K⁺ continue to fall and the concentration of Na⁺ inside the cell progressively increase? The reason is that the Na⁺–K⁺ pump counterbalances the rate of passive leakage. At resting potential, this pump transports back into the cell essentially the same number of potassium ions that have leaked out and simultaneously transports to the outside the sodium ions that have leaked in. At this point, no net movement of any ions takes place, because all passive leaks are exactly balanced by active pumping. Because the active pump offsets the passive leaks, the concentration gradients for K⁺ and Na⁺ remain constant. Thus, the Na⁺–K⁺ pump not only is initially responsible for the Na⁺ and K⁺ concentration differences across the membrane but also maintains these differences.

As just discussed, the magnitude of these concentration gradients, together with the difference in permeability of the membrane to these ions, accounts for the magnitude of the membrane potential. Because the concentration gradients and permeabilities for Na⁺ and K⁺ remain constant in the resting state, the resting membrane potential established by these forces remains constant.

SPECIALIZED USE OF MEMBRANE POTENTIAL IN NERVE AND MUSCLE CELLS Nerve and muscle cells have developed a specialized use for membrane potential. They can rapidly and transiently alter their membrane permeabilities to the involved ions in response to appropriate stimulation, thereby bringing about fluctuations in membrane potential. The rapid fluctuations in potential are responsible for producing nerve impulses in nerve cells and for triggering contraction in muscle cells.

These activities are the focus of the next five chapters. Even though all cells display a membrane potential, its significance in other cells is uncertain, although changes in membrane potential of some secretory cells, such as insulin-secreting cells, have been linked to their level of secretory activity.

Chapter in Perspective: Focus on Homeostasis

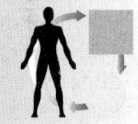

All cells of the body must obtain vital materials, such as nutrients and O₂, from the surrounding ECF; they must also eliminate wastes to the ECF and release secretory products, such as chemical messengers and digestive enzymes. Thus, transport of materials across the plasma membrane between the ECF and the ICF is essential for cell survival, and the constituents of the ECF must be homeostatically maintained to support these life-sustaining exchanges.

Many cell types use membrane transport to carry out their specialized activities geared toward maintaining homeostasis. Here are several examples:

1. Absorption of nutrients from the digestive tract lumen involves the transport of these energy-giving molecules across the membranes of the cells lining the tract.

2. Exchange of O₂ and CO₂ between air and blood in the lungs involves the transport of these gases across the membranes of the cells lining the air sacs and blood vessels of the lungs.

3. Urine is formed by the selective transfer of materials between the blood and the fluid within the kidney tubules across the membranes of the cells lining the tubules.
4. The beating of the heart is triggered by cyclic changes in the transport of Na^+, K^+, and Ca^{2+} across the heart cells' membranes.
5. Secretion of chemical messengers such as neurotransmitters from nerve cells and hormones from endocrine cells involves the transport of these regulatory products to the ECF on appropriate stimulation.

In addition to providing selective transport of materials between the ECF and the ICF, the plasma membrane contains receptors for binding with specific chemical messengers that regulate various cell activities, many of which are specialized activities aimed toward maintaining homeostasis. For example, the hormone vasopressin, which is secreted in response to a water deficit in the body, binds with receptors in the plasma membrane of a specific type of kidney cell. This binding triggers the cells to conserve water during urine formation by promoting the insertion of additional aquaporins (water channels) in the plasma membrane of these cells, thus helping alleviate the water deficit that initiated the response.

All living cells have a membrane potential, with the cell's interior being slightly more negative than the fluid surrounding the cell when the cell is electrically at rest. The specialized activities of nerve and muscle cells depend on these cells' ability to change their membrane potential rapidly on appropriate stimulation. The transient, rapid changes in potential in nerve cells serve as electrical signals or nerve impulses, which provide a means to transmit information along nerve pathways. This information is used to accomplish homeostatic adjustments, such as restoring blood pressure to normal when signaled that it has fallen too low.

Rapid changes in membrane potential in muscle cells trigger muscle contraction, the specialized activity of muscle. Muscle contraction contributes to homeostasis in many ways, including the pumping of blood by the heart and the movement of food through the digestive tract.

REVIEW EXERCISES

Objective Questions (Answers on p. A-39)

1. The nonpolar tails of the phospholipid molecules bury themselves in the interior of the plasma membrane. (*True or false?*)
2. Cells shrink when in contact with a hypertonic solution. (*True or false?*)
3. Channels are open to both sides of the membrane at the same time, but carriers are open to only one side of the membrane at a time. (*True or false?*)
4. Through its unequal pumping, the Na^+–K^+ pump is directly responsible for separating sufficient charges to establish a resting membrane potential of –70 mV. (*True or false?*)
5. At resting membrane potential, there is a slight excess of _____ (*positive/negative*) charges on the inside of the membrane, with a corresponding slight excess of _____ (*positive/negative*) charges on the outside.
6. Using the answer code on the right, indicate which membrane component is responsible for the function in question:
   ___ 1. channel formation
   ___ 2. barrier to passage of water-soluble substances
   ___ 3. receptor sites
   ___ 4. membrane fluidity
   ___ 5. recognition of "self"
   ___ 6. membrane-bound enzymes
   ___ 7. structural boundary
   ___ 8. carriers

   (a) lipid bilayer
   (b) proteins
   (c) carbohydrates

7. Using the answer code on the right, indicate the direction of net movement in each case:
   ___ 1. simple diffusion
   ___ 2. facilitated diffusion
   ___ 3. primary active transport
   ___ 4. Na^+ during symport or antiport
   ___ 5. transported solute during symport or antiport
   ___ 6. water with regard to the water concentration gradient during osmosis
   ___ 7. water with regard to the solute concentration gradient during osmosis

   (a) movement from high to low concentration
   (b) movement from low to high concentration

8. Using the answer code on the right, indicate the type of cell junction described:
   ___ 1. adhering junction
   ___ 2. impermeable junction
   ___ 3. communicating junction
   ___ 4. made up of connexons, which permit passage of ions and small molecules between cells
   ___ 5. consisting of interconnecting fibers, which spot-rivet adjacent cells
   ___ 6. formed by an actual fusion of proteins on the outer surfaces of two interacting cells
   ___ 7. important in tissues subject to mechanical stretching
   ___ 8. important in synchronizing contractions within heart and smooth muscle by allowing spread of electrical activity between the cells composing the muscle mass
   ___ 9. important in preventing passage between cells in epithelial sheets that separate compartments of two different chemical compositions

   (a) gap junction
   (b) tight junction
   (c) desmosome

Essay Questions

1. Describe the fluid mosaic model of membrane structure.
2. What are the functions of the three major types of protein fibers in the extracellular matrix?
3. What two properties of a particle influence whether it can permeate the plasma membrane?
4. List and describe the methods of membrane transport. Indicate what types of substances are transported by each method, and state whether each means of transport is passive or active and unassisted or assisted.
5. Explain what effect an increase in surface area would have on the rate of net diffusion across a membrane. Explain what effect an increase in thickness would have on the rate of net diffusion across a membrane.
6. State three important roles of the Na^+–K^+ pump.
7. Describe the contribution of each of the following to establishing and maintaining membrane potential: (a) the Na^+–K^+ pump, (b) passive movement of K^+ across the membrane, (c) passive movement of Na^+ across the membrane, and (d) the large intracellular anions.

POINTS TO PONDER

(Explanations on p. A-39)

1. A solution may have the same osmolarity as normal body fluids yet not be isotonic. Explain why.
2. Assume that a membrane permeable to Na^+ but not to Cl^- separates two solutions. The concentration of sodium chloride on side 1 is higher than on side 2. Which of the following ionic movements would occur?
   a. Na^+ would move until its concentration gradient is dissipated (until the concentration of Na^+ on side 2 is the same as the concentration of Na^+ on side 1).
   b. Cl^- would move down its concentration gradient from side 1 to side 2.
   c. A membrane potential, negative on side 1, would develop.
   d. A membrane potential, positive on side 1, would develop.
   e. None of the preceding is correct.
3. Compared to resting potential, would the membrane potential become more negative or more positive if the membrane were more permeable to Na^+ than to K^+?
4. Which of the following methods of transport is being used to transfer the substance into the cell in the accompanying graph?

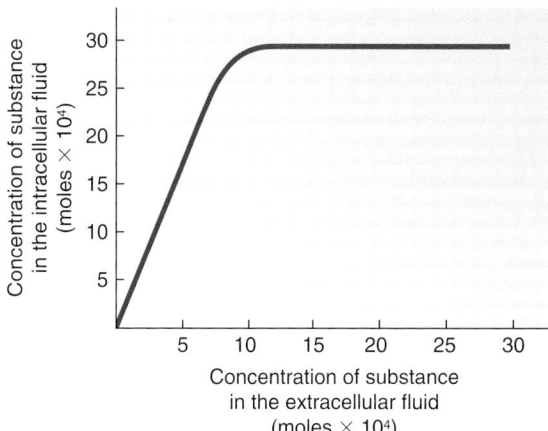

a. diffusion down a concentration gradient
b. osmosis
c. facilitated diffusion
d. active transport
e. vesicular transport
f. it is impossible to tell with the information provided

5. Colostrum, the first milk that a mother produces, contains an abundance of antibodies, large protein molecules. These maternal antibodies help protect breast-fed infants from infections until the babies are capable of producing their own antibodies. By what means would you suspect these maternal antibodies are transported across the cells lining a newborn's digestive tract into the bloodstream?

CLINICAL CONSIDERATION

(Explanation on p. A-40)

When William H. was helping victims following a devastating earthquake in a region that was not prepared to swiftly set up adequate temporary shelter, he developed severe diarrhea. He was diagnosed as having *cholera,* a disease transmitted through unsanitary water supplies that have been contaminated by fecal material from infected individuals.

The toxin produced by cholera bacteria causes Cl^- channels in the luminal membranes of the intestinal cells to open, thereby increasing the secretion of Cl^- from the cells into the intestinal tract lumen. By what mechanisms would Na^+ and water be secreted into the lumen in conjunction with Cl^- secretion? How does this secretory response account for the severe diarrhea that is characteristic of cholera?

Chapter 3

Membrane Structure and Functions (pp. 47–51)

■ All cells are bounded by a plasma membrane, a thin lipid bilayer that is interspersed with proteins and has carbohydrates attached on the outer surface.

■ The appearance of the plasma membrane in an electron microscope as a trilaminar structure (two dark lines separated by a light interspace) is produced by the arrangement of its molecules. The phospholipids orient themselves to form a bilayer with a hydrophobic interior (light interspace) sandwiched between hydrophilic outer and inner surfaces (dark lines). (Review Figures 3-1 through 3-3.)

■ The lipid bilayer forms the structural boundary of the cell, serving as a barrier for water-soluble substances and being responsible for the fluid nature of the membrane. Cholesterol molecules tucked between the phospholipids contribute to the fluidity and stability of the membrane.

■ According to the fluid mosaic model of membrane structure, the lipid bilayer is embedded with proteins. (Review Figure 3-3.) Membrane proteins, which vary in type and distribution among cells, serve as (1) channels for passage of small ions across the membrane, (2) carriers for transport of specific substances into or out of the cell, (3) docking marker acceptors where secretory vesicles dock and release their contents, (4) membrane-bound enzymes that govern specific chemical reactions, (5) receptors for detecting and responding to chemical messengers that alter cell function, and (6) cell adhesion molecules that help hold cells together and are a structural link between the plasma membrane and the intracellular cytoskeleton.

■ Membrane carbohydrates on the outer surface of the cell serve as self-identity markers. (Review Figure 3-3.) They are important in recognition of "self" in cell-to-cell interactions such as tissue formation and tissue growth.

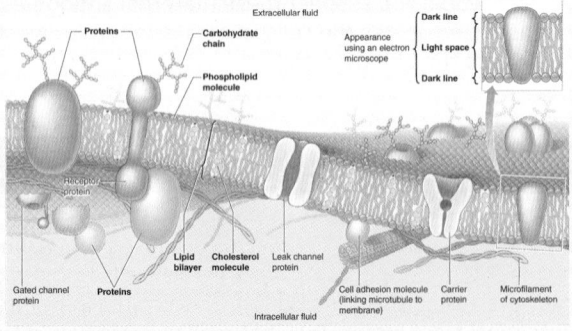

Cell-to-Cell Adhesions (pp. 51–54)

■ The extracellular matrix (ECM) serves as a biological "glue" between the cells of a tissue. The ECM consists of a watery, gel-like substance interspersed with three major types of protein fibers: collagen (provides tensile strength), elastin (permits stretch and recoil), and fibronectin (promotes cell adhesion).

■ Many cells are further joined by specialized cell junctions, of which there are three types: desmosomes, tight junctions, and gap junctions.

■ Desmosomes serve as adhering junctions to hold cells together mechanically and are especially important in tissues subject to a great deal of stretching. (Review Figure 3-4.)

■ Tight junctions actually fuse cells together, preventing the passage of materials between cells and thereby permitting only regulated passage of materials through the cells. These impermeable junctions are found in the epithelial sheets that separate compartments with very different chemical compositions. (Review Figure 3-5.)

■ Gap junctions are communicating junctions between two adjacent, but not touching, cells. They form small tunnels that permit exchange of ions and small molecules between the cells. Such movement of ions plays a key role in the spread of electrical activity to synchronize contraction in heart and smooth muscle. (Review Figure 3-6.)

Overview of Membrane Transport (p. 54)

■ Materials can pass between the extracellular fluid (ECF) and the intracellular fluid (ICF) by unassisted and assisted means.

■ Transport mechanisms may also be passive (the particle moves across the membrane without the cell expending energy) or active (the cell expends energy to move the particle across the membrane). (Review Table 3-2, p. 67.)

Unassisted Membrane Transport (pp. 54–59)

■ Nonpolar (lipid-soluble) molecules of any size cross the membrane unassisted by dissolving in and passively moving through the lipid bilayer down concentration gradients. (Review Figures 3-7 and 3-8.) Small ions can traverse the membrane unassisted by passively moving down electrochemical gradients through open protein channels specific for the ion. (Review Figure 3-3.)

■ In osmosis, water moves passively down its own concentration gradient across a selectively permeable membrane to an area of higher concentration of nonpenetrating solutes. Penetrating solutes do not have an osmotic effect. (Review Figures 3-9 through 3-12.)

■ The *osmolarity* of a solution is a measure of its total number of solute particles, both penetrating and nonpenetrating, both molecules and ions, per liter. The *osmotic pressure* of a solution is the pressure that must be applied to the solution to completely stop osmosis. The *tonicity* of a solution refers to the effect the solution has on cell volume and depends on the solution's relative concentration of nonpenetrating solutes compared to the concentration of nonpenetrating solutes in the cell it surrounds. *(Review Figure 3-13.)*

Assisted Membrane Transport (pp. 59–66)

■ In carrier-mediated transport, small polar molecules and selected ions are transported across the membrane by specific membrane carrier proteins. Carriers open to one side of the membrane, where a passenger binds to a binding site specific for it, and then change shape so that the binding site is exposed to the opposite side of the membrane, where the passenger is released. Carrier-mediated transport may be passive, and move the particle down its concentration gradient *(facilitated diffusion)*, or active, and move the particle against its concentration gradient *(active transport)*. Carriers exhibit a transport maximum (T_m) when saturated. *(Review Figures 3-14 through 3-16.)*

■ There are two forms of active transport: primary active transport and secondary active transport. *Primary active transport* requires the direct use of ATP to drive the pump. *(Review Figure 3-16.)* One of the most important examples of primary active transport is the Na^+–K^+ pump, which concentrates Na^+ in the ECF and K^+ in the ICF. It pumps three Na^+ out of the cell for every two K^+ it pumps in. *Secondary active transport* is driven by a Na^+ concentration gradient established by a primary active-transport system. There are two types of secondary active transport: symport (or cotransport) and antiport (or countertransport or exchange). In *symport,* both the cotransported solute and the driving ion (Na^+) are moved in the same direction (both moving into the cell), with the cotransported solute moving uphill and the driving ion moving downhill. *(Review Figure 3-17.)* In *antiport,* the coupled solute and the driving ion are moved in opposite directions (the solute moving out of and Na^+ moving into the cell), with the solute moving uphill and the driving ion moving downhill.

■ Large polar molecules and multimolecular particles can leave or enter the cell by being wrapped in a piece of membrane to form vesicles that can be internalized (endocytosis) or externalized (exocytosis). *(Review Figures 2-5 and 2-7.)*

■ Cells are differentially selective in what enters or leaves because they possess varying numbers and kinds of channels, carriers, and mechanisms for vesicular transport.

■ Large polar molecules (too large for channels and not lipid soluble) for which there are no special transport mechanisms are unable to cross the membrane.

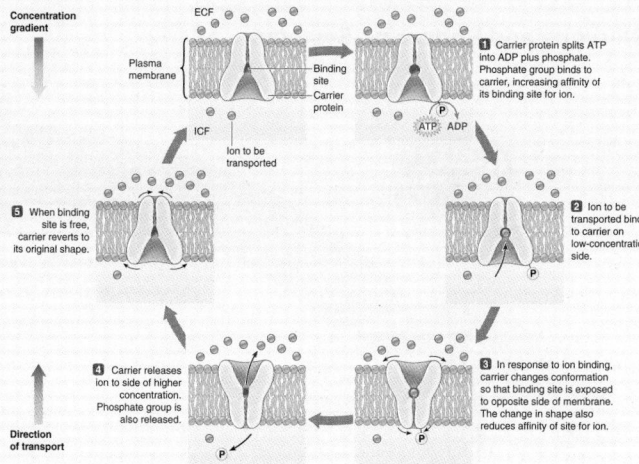

Membrane Potential (pp. 66–71)

■ All cells have a membrane potential, which is a separation of opposite charges across the plasma membrane. *(Review Figure 3-18.)*

■ The Na^+–K^+ pump makes a small direct contribution to membrane potential because it transports more Na^+ out than K^+ in. However, the primary role of the Na^+–K^+ pump is to actively maintain a greater concentration of Na^+ outside the cell and a greater concentration of K^+ inside the cell. These concentration gradients tend to passively move K^+ out of the cell and Na^+ into the cell. *(Review Table 3-3 and Figures 3-19 and 3-20.)*

■ Because the resting membrane is 25 to 30 times more permeable to K^+ than to Na^+, substantially more K^+ leaves the cell than Na^+ enters, resulting in an excess of positive charges outside the cell. This leaves an unbalanced excess of negative charges, in the form of large protein anions ($A-$), trapped inside the cell. *(Review Table 3-3 and Figure 3-21.)*

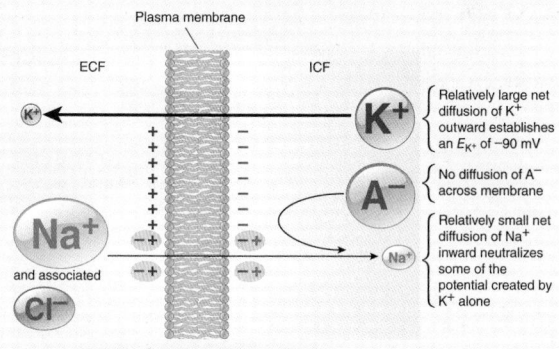

■ When the resting membrane potential of -70 mV is achieved, no further net movement of K^+ and Na^+ takes place, because any further leaking of these ions down their concentration gradients is quickly reversed by the Na^+–K^+ pump.

Nervous and Endocrine Systems

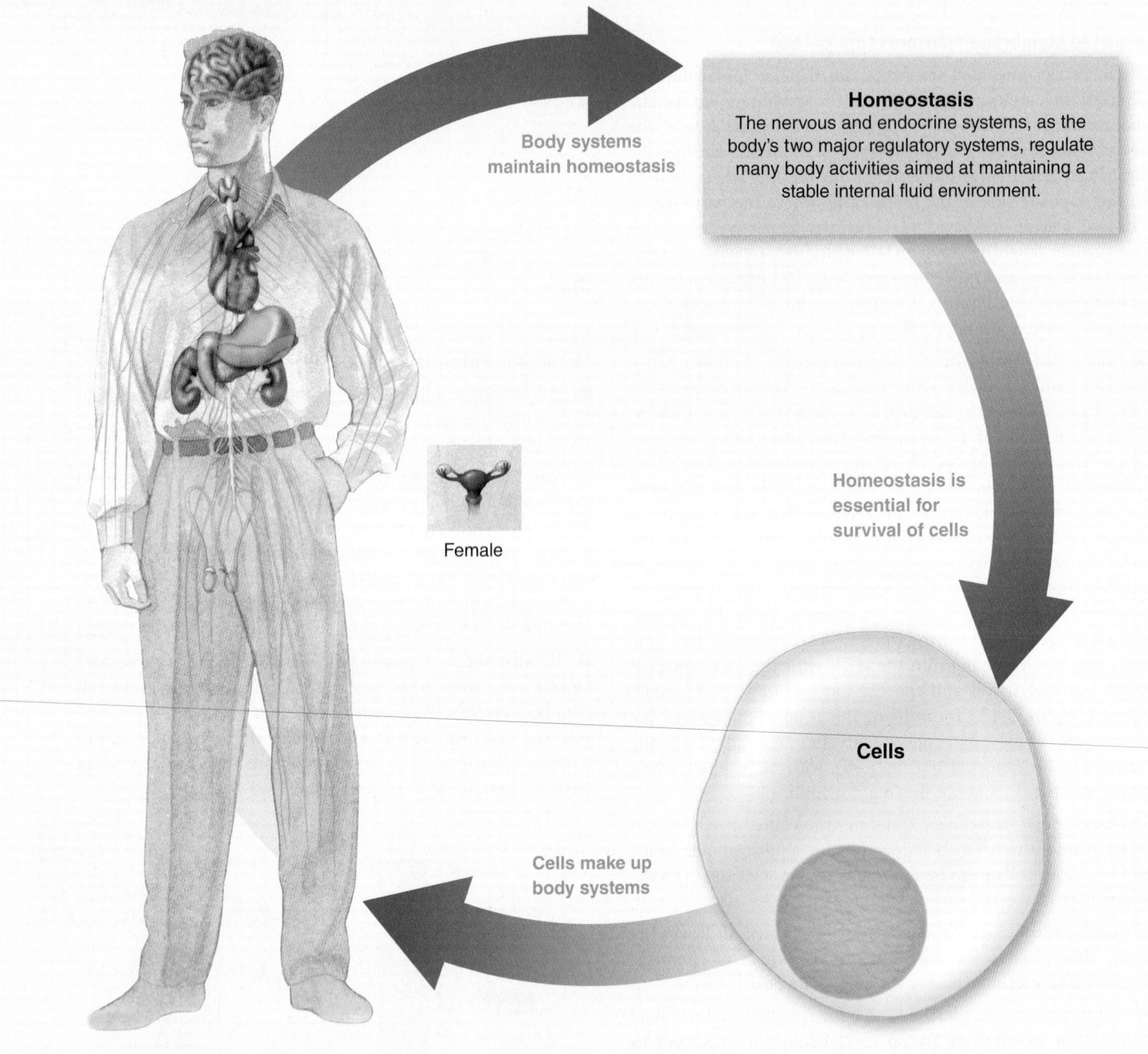

Body systems maintain homeostasis

Homeostasis
The nervous and endocrine systems, as the body's two major regulatory systems, regulate many body activities aimed at maintaining a stable internal fluid environment.

Homeostasis is essential for survival of cells

Female

Cells

Cells make up body systems

To maintain homeostasis, cells must work in a coordinated fashion toward common goals. The two major regulatory systems of the body that help ensure life-sustaining coordinated responses are the nervous and endocrine systems. **Neural communication** is accomplished by means of nerve cells, or neurons, which are specialized for rapid electrical signaling and for secreting neurotransmitters, short-distance chemical messengers that act on nearby target organs. The nervous system exerts rapid control over most of the body's muscles and exocrine secretions. **Hormonal communication** is accomplished by hormones, which are long-distance chemical messengers secreted by the endocrine glands into the blood. The blood carries the hormones to distant target sites, where they regulate processes that require duration rather than speed, such as metabolic activities, water and electrolyte balance, and growth.

Principles of Neural and Hormonal Communication

CHAPTER AT A GLANCE

Introduction to Neural Communication

Graded Potentials

Grading of graded potentials

Spread of graded potentials

Action Potentials

Changes in membrane potential during an action potential

Changes in membrane permeability and ion movement during an action potential

Propagation of action potentials; contiguous conduction

Refractory period

All-or-none law

Role of myelin; saltatory conduction

Synapses and Neuronal Integration

Events at a synapse; role of neurotransmitters

Excitatory and inhibitory synapses

Grand postsynaptic potential; summation

Convergence and divergence

Intercellular Communication and Signal Transduction

Types of cell-to-cell communication

Signal transduction

Introduction to Hormonal Communication

Classification of hormones according to solubility characteristics

Comparison of the synthesis, storage, secretion, and transport of peptide and steroid hormones

Mechanism of hydrophilic hormone action via second-messenger systems

Mechanism of lipophilic hormone action via activation of genes

Comparison of the Nervous and Endocrine Systems

Introduction to Neural Communication

All body cells display a membrane potential, which is a separation of positive and negative charges across the membrane, as discussed in the preceding chapter (see pp. 66–71). This potential is related to the uneven distribution of sodium (Na^+), potassium (K^+), and large intracellular protein anions between the intracellular fluid (ICF) and the extracellular fluid (ECF) and to the differential permeability of the plasma membrane to these ions.

Nerve and muscle are excitable tissues.

The constant membrane potential present when a cell is electrically at rest, that is, not producing electrical signals, is referred to as the *resting membrane potential*. Two types of cells, *neurons (nerve cells)* and *muscle cells,* have developed a specialized use for membrane potential. They can undergo transient, rapid fluctuations in their membrane potentials, which serve as electrical signals.

Nerve and muscle are considered **excitable tissues** because they produce electrical signals when excited. Neurons use these electrical signals to receive, process, initiate, and transmit messages. In muscle cells, these electrical signals initiate contraction. Thus, electrical signals are critical to the function of the nervous system and all muscles. In this chapter, we examine how neurons undergo changes in potential to accomplish their function. Muscle cells are discussed in later chapters.

Membrane potential becomes less negative during depolarization and more negative during hyperpolarization.

Before you can understand what electrical signals are and how they are created, you must become familiar with several terms used to describe changes in potential, which are graphically represented in ● Figure 4-1:

1. **Polarization.** Charges are separated across the plasma membrane, so the membrane has potential. Any time membrane potential is other than 0 millivolts (mV), in either the positive or the negative direction, the membrane is in a state of polarization. Recall that the magnitude of the potential is directly proportional to the number of positive and negative charges separated by the membrane and that the sign of the potential (+ or −) always designates whether excess positive or excess negative charges are present, respectively, on the inside of the membrane. At resting potential, the membrane is polarized at −70 mV in a typical neuron (see p. 70).

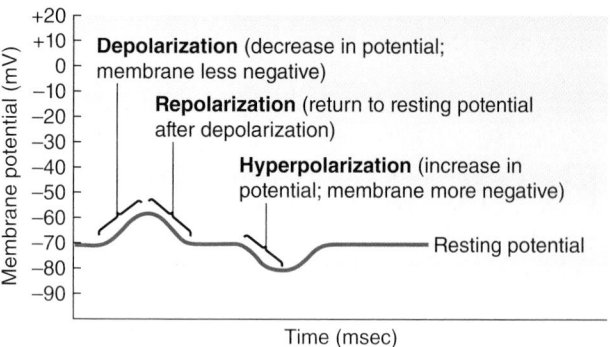

+20
+10
0
−10
−20
−30
−40
−50
−60
−70
−80
−90

Membrane potential (mV)

Depolarization (decrease in potential; membrane less negative)

Repolarization (return to resting potential after depolarization)

Hyperpolarization (increase in potential; membrane more negative)

Resting potential

Time (msec)

● FIGURE 4-1 **Types of changes in membrane potential.**

2. Depolarization. The membrane becomes less polarized; the inside becomes less negative than at resting potential, with the potential moving closer to 0 mV (for example, a change from −70 to −60 mV); fewer charges are separated than at resting potential. This term also refers to the inside even becoming positive as it does during an action potential (a major type of electrical signal) when the membrane potential reverses itself (for example, becoming +30 mV).

3. Repolarization. The membrane returns to resting potential after having been depolarized.

4. Hyperpolarization. The membrane becomes more polarized; the inside becomes more negative than at resting potential, with the potential moving even farther from 0 mV (for instance, a change from −70 to −80 mV); more charges are separated than at resting potential.

One possibly confusing point should be clarified. On the device used for recording rapid changes in potential, during a depolarization, when the inside becomes less negative than at resting, this *decrease* in the magnitude of the potential is represented as an *upward* deflection. By contrast, during a hyperpolarization, when the inside becomes more negative than at resting, this *increase* in the magnitude of the potential is represented by a *downward* deflection.

Electrical signals are produced by changes in ion movement across the plasma membrane.

Changes in membrane potential are brought about by changes in ion movement across the membrane. For example, if the net inward flow of positively charged ions increases compared to the resting state (such as more Na^+ moves in), the membrane depolarizes (becomes less negative inside). By contrast, if the net outward flow of positively charged ions increases compared to the resting state (such as more K^+ moves out), the membrane hyperpolarizes (becomes more negative inside).

Changes in ion movement are brought about by changes in membrane permeability in response to triggering events. A **triggering event** triggers a change in membrane potential by altering membrane permeability and consequently altering ion flow across the membrane. These ion movements redistribute charge across the membrane, causing membrane potential to fluctuate.

Because the water-soluble ions responsible for carrying charge cannot penetrate the plasma membrane's lipid bilayer,

these charges can cross the membrane only through channels specific for them or by carrier-mediated transport. Membrane channels may be either *leak channels* or *gated channels*. As described in Chapter 3, leak channels, which are open all the time, permit unregulated leakage of their specific ion across the membrane through the channels. Gated channels, in contrast, have gates that can be open or closed, permitting ion passage through the channels when open and preventing ion passage through the channels when closed. Gate opening and closing occurs in response to a triggering event that causes a change in the conformation (shape) of the protein that forms the gated channel. There are four kinds of gated channels, depending on the factor that causes the channel to change shape: (1) **voltage-gated channels** open or close in response to changes in membrane potential, (2) **chemically gated channels** change shape in response to binding of a specific extracellular chemical messenger to a surface membrane receptor, (3) **mechanically gated channels** respond to stretching or other mechanical deformation, and (4) **thermally gated channels** respond to local changes in temperature (heat or cold).

There are two basic forms of electrical signals: (1) *graded potentials*, which serve as short-distance signals, and (2) *action potentials*, which signal over long distances. We next examine these types of signals in more detail, beginning with graded potentials, and then explore how neurons use these signals to convey messages.

Graded Potentials

Graded potentials are local changes in membrane potential that occur in varying grades or degrees of magnitude or strength. For example, membrane potential could change from −70 to −60 mV (a 10-mV graded potential) or from −70 to −50 mV (a 20-mV graded potential).

The stronger a triggering event, the larger the resultant graded potential.

Graded potentials are usually produced by a specific triggering event that causes gated ion channels to open in a specialized region of the excitable cell membrane. The resultant ion movement produces the graded potential, which most commonly is a depolarization resulting from net Na^+ entry. The graded potential is confined to this small, specialized region of the total plasma membrane.

The magnitude of the initial graded potential (that is, the difference between the new potential and the resting potential) is related to the magnitude of the triggering event: *the stronger the triggering event, the larger the resultant graded potential.* Here's why, using gated channels that permit net Na^+ entry as a common example: The stronger the triggering event is, the more gated channels open. As more gated channels open, more positive charges in the form of Na^+ enter the cell. The more positive charges that enter the cell, the less negative (more depolarized) the inside becomes at this specialized region. This depolarization is the graded potential. Therefore, the stronger the triggering event is, the larger the graded potential produced.

Also, the duration of the graded potential varies, depending on how long the triggering event keeps the gated channels open. *The longer the duration of the triggering event, the longer the duration of the graded potential.*

Graded potentials spread by passive current flow.

When a graded potential occurs locally in a nerve or muscle cell membrane, the rest of the membrane remains at resting potential. The temporarily depolarized region is called an *active area*. Note from ● Figure 4-2 that, inside the cell, the active area is relatively more positive than the neighboring *inactive areas* that are still at resting potential. Outside the cell, the active area is relatively less positive than adjacent inactive areas. Because of this difference in potential, electrical charges, which are carried by ions, passively flow between the active and the adjacent resting regions on both the inside and the outside of the membrane. Any flow of electrical charges is called a **current.** By convention, the direction of

current flow is always expressed as the direction in which the positive charges are moving (● Figure 4-2c). Inside the cell, positive charges flow through the ICF away from the relatively more positive depolarized active region toward the more negative adjacent resting regions. Outside the cell, positive charges flow through the ECF from the more positive adjacent inactive regions toward the relatively more negative active region. Ion movement (that is, current) is occurring *along* the membrane between regions next to each other on the same side of the membrane. This flow is in contrast to ion movement *across* the membrane through ion channels or by means of carriers.

As a result of local current flow between an active depolarized area and an adjacent inactive area, the potential changes in the previously inactive area. Because positive charges have flowed simultaneously into the adjacent inactive area on the inside and out of this area on the outside, the adjacent area is now more

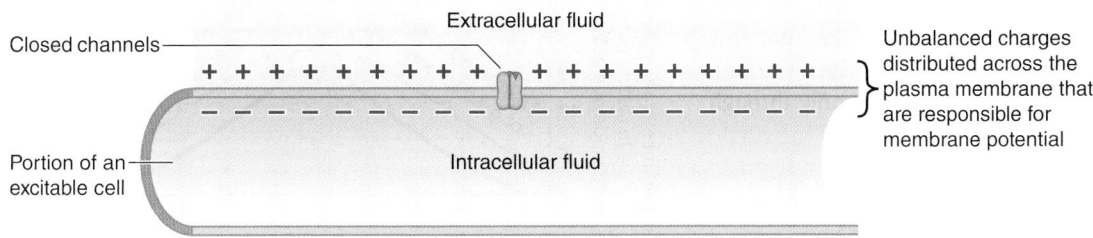

(a) Entire membrane at resting potential

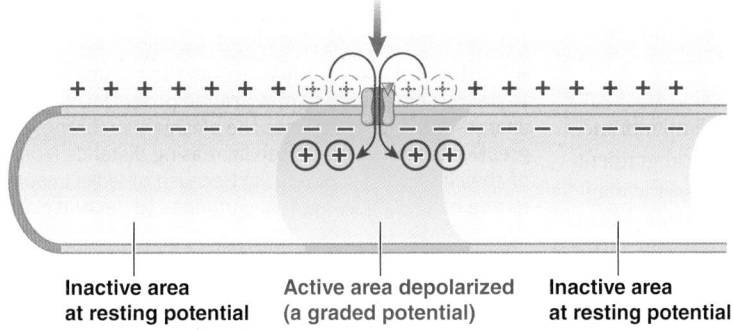

(b) Inward movement of Na⁺ depolarizes membrane, producing a graded potential

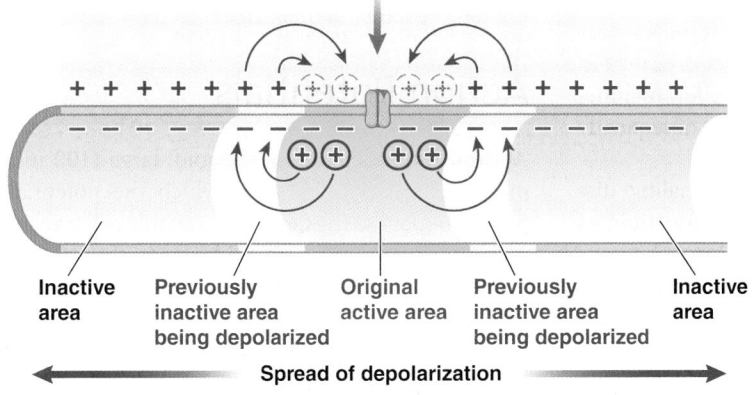

(c) Depolarization spreads by local current flow to adjacent inactive areas, away from point of origin

● FIGURE 4-2 **Current flow during a graded potential.** (a) The membrane of an excitable cell at resting potential. (b) A triggering event opens ion channels, usually leading to net Na⁺ entry that depolarizes the membrane at this site. The adjacent inactive areas are still at resting potential. (c) Local current flows between the active and the adjacent inactive areas, resulting in depolarization of the previously inactive areas. In this way, the depolarization spreads away from its point of origin.

positive (or less negative) on the inside than before and less positive (or more negative) on the outside (● Figure 4-2c). Stated differently, the previously inactive adjacent area has been depolarized, so the graded potential has spread. This area's potential now differs from that of the inactive region immediately next to it on the other side, inducing further current flow at this new site, and so on. In this manner, current spreads in both directions away from the initial site of the change in potential.

The amount of current that flows between two areas depends on the difference in potential between the areas and on the resistance of the material through which the charges are moving. **Resistance** is the hindrance to electrical charge movement. The *greater* the difference in potential, the *greater* the current flow; by contrast, the *lower* the resistance, the *greater* the current flow. *Conductors* have low resistance, providing little hindrance to current flow. Electrical wires and the ICF and ECF are all good conductors, so current readily flows through them. *Insulators* have high resistance and greatly hinder movement of charge. The plastic surrounding electrical wires has high resistance, as do body lipids. Thus, current does not flow directly through the plasma membrane's lipid bilayer. Current, carried by ions, can move across the membrane only through ion channels.

Graded potentials die out over short distances.

The passive current flow between active and adjacent inactive areas is similar to the means by which current is carried through electrical wires. We know from experience that current leaks out of an electrical wire with dangerous results unless the wire is covered with an insulating material such as plastic. (People can get an electric shock if they touch a bare wire.) Likewise, current is lost across the plasma membrane as charge-carrying ions in the form of K^+ leak out through the "uninsulated" parts of the membrane, that is, by diffusing outward down their electrochemical gradient through open leak channels. Because of this current loss, the magnitude of the local current—and thus the magnitude of the graded potential—progressively diminishes the farther it moves from the initial active area (● Figure 4-3a). Another way of saying this is that the spread of a graded potential is *decremental* (gradually decreases) (● Figure 4-3b). Note that in this example the magnitude of the initial change in potential is 15 mV (a change from the resting state of −70 to −55 mV); the change in potential decreases as it moves along the membrane to a potential of 10 mV (from −70 to −60 mV) and continues to diminish the farther it moves away from the initial active area until there is no longer a change in potential. In this way, local currents die out within a few millimeters from the initial site of change in potential and consequently can function as signals for only very short distances.

Although graded potentials have limited signaling distance, they are critically important to the body's function, as explained in later chapters. The following are all graded potentials: *postsynaptic potentials, receptor potentials, end-plate potentials, pacemaker potentials,* and *slow-wave potentials.* These terms are unfamiliar to you now, but you will become well acquainted with them as we continue discussing nerve and muscle physiology. We are including this list here because it is the

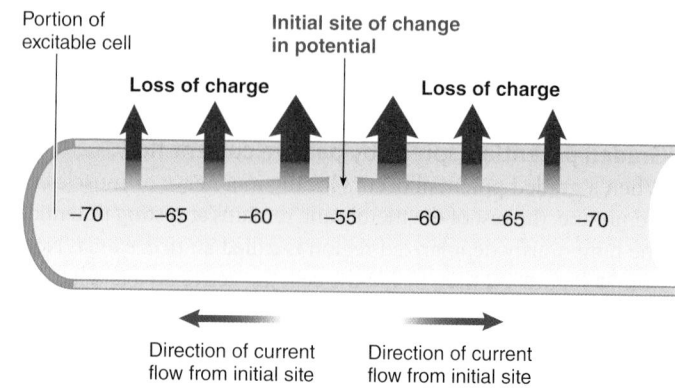

* Numbers refer to the local potential in mV at various points along the membrane.

(a) Current loss across the membrane

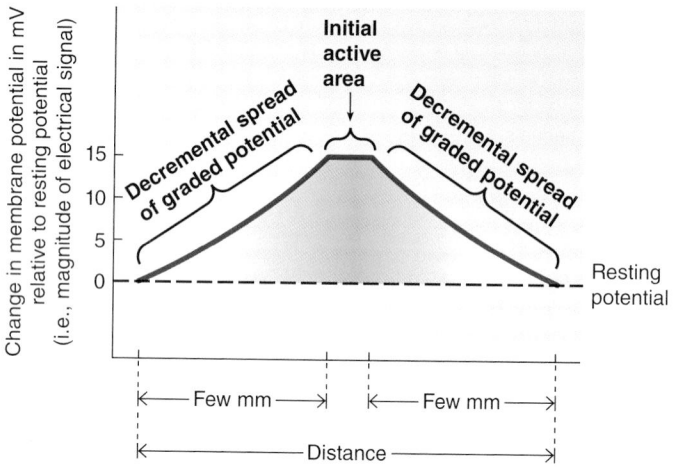

(b) Decremental spread of graded potentials

● **FIGURE 4-3 Current loss across the plasma membrane leading to decremental spread of a graded potential.** (a) Leakage of charge-carrying ions across the plasma membrane results in progressive loss of current with increasing distance from the initial site of the change in potential. (b) Because of leaks in current, the magnitude of a graded potential continues to decrease as it passively spreads from the initial active area. The potential dies out altogether within a few millimeters of its site of initiation.

only place all these types of graded potentials are listed together. For now it's enough to say that most excitable cells produce one of these types of graded potentials in response to a triggering event. In turn, graded potentials can initiate action potentials, the long-distance signals, in an excitable cell.

Action Potentials

Action potentials are brief, rapid, large (100 mV) changes in membrane potential during which the potential actually reverses so that the inside of the excitable cell transiently becomes more positive than the outside. As with a graded potential, a single action potential involves only a small portion of the total excitable cell membrane. Unlike graded potentials, however, action potentials are conducted, or propagated, throughout the entire membrane *nondecrementally;* that is, they do not diminish in strength as they travel from their site of initiation throughout the remainder of the cell membrane. Thus, action potentials can serve as faithful long-distance signals.

Think about the neuron that causes the muscle cells in your big toe to contract (see ● Figure 4-8, p. 85). If you want to wiggle your big toe, commands are sent from your brain down your spinal cord to initiate an action potential at the beginning of this neuron, which is located in the spinal cord. The action potential travels all the way down the neuron's long axon, which runs through your leg to terminate on your big-toe muscle cells. The signal does not weaken or die off, being instead preserved at full strength from beginning to end.

Let us now consider the changes in potential during an action potential, and the permeability and ion movements responsible for generating this change in potential, before we see how action potentials spread throughout the cell membrane without diminishing.

During an action potential, the membrane potential rapidly, transiently reverses.

If a graded potential is large enough, it can initiate an action potential before the graded change dies off. (Later you will discover how this initiation is accomplished for the various types of graded potentials.) Typically, the region of the excitable membrane where graded potentials are produced in response to a triggering event does not undergo action potentials. Instead, passive current flow from the region where a graded potential is taking place depolarizes adjacent portions of the membrane where action potentials can occur.

Depolarization from the resting potential of −70 mV proceeds slowly until it reaches a critical level known as **threshold potential,** typically between −50 and −55 mV (● Figure 4-4). At threshold potential, an explosive depolarization takes place. A recording of the potential at this time shows a sharp upward deflection as the potential rapidly reverses itself so that the in-

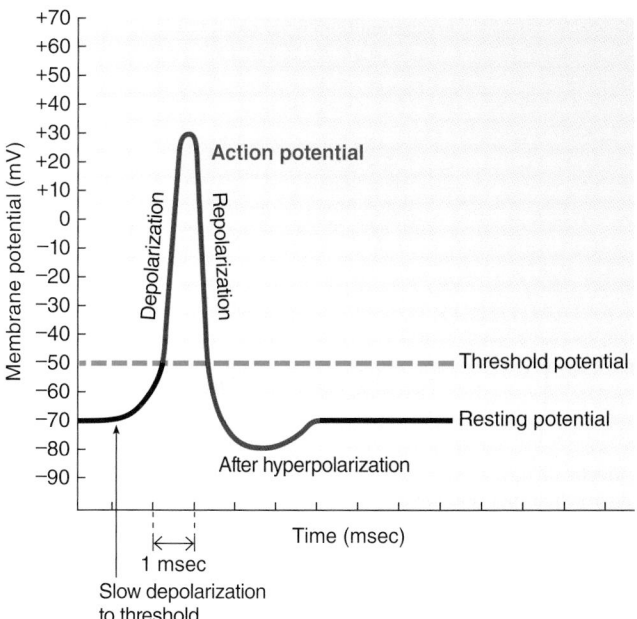

● **FIGURE 4-4 Changes in membrane potential during an action potential.**

side of the cell becomes positive compared to the outside. Peak potential is usually +30 to +40 mV, depending on the excitable cell. Just as rapidly, the membrane repolarizes, dropping back to resting potential. Often, the forces that repolarize the membrane push the potential too far, causing a brief **after hyperpolarization,** during which the inside of the membrane briefly becomes even more negative than normal (for example, −80 mV) before the resting potential is restored.

The action potential is the entire rapid change in potential from threshold to peak and then back to resting. Unlike the variable duration of a graded potential, the duration of an action potential is always the same in a given excitable cell. In a neuron, an action potential lasts for only 1 msec (0.001 second). It lasts longer in muscle, with the duration depending on the muscle type. Often an action potential is referred to as a **spike** because of its spikelike recorded appearance. Alternatively, when an excitable membrane is triggered to undergo an action potential, it is said to **fire.** Thus, the terms *action potential, spike,* and *firing* all refer to the same phenomenon of rapid reversal of membrane potential. If the initial triggered depolarization does not reach threshold potential, no action potential takes place. Thus, threshold is a critical all-or-none point. Either the membrane is depolarized to threshold and an action potential takes place, or threshold is not reached in response to the depolarizing event and no action potential occurs.

Marked changes in membrane permeability and ion movement lead to an action potential.

How is the membrane potential, which is usually maintained at a constant resting level, altered to such an extent as to produce an action potential? Recall that K^+ makes the greatest contribution to the establishment of the resting potential, because the membrane at rest is considerably more permeable to K^+ than to Na^+ (see p. 70). During an action potential, marked changes in membrane permeability to Na^+ and K^+ take place, permitting rapid fluxes of these ions down their electrochemical gradients. These ion movements carry the current responsible for the potential changes that occur during an action potential. Action potentials take place as a result of the triggered opening and subsequent closing of two specific types of channels: voltage-gated Na^+ channels and voltage-gated K^+ channels.

VOLTAGE-GATED Na^+ AND K^+ CHANNELS Voltage-gated membrane channels consist of proteins that have many charged groups. The electrical field (potential) surrounding the channels can distort the channel structure as charged portions of the channel proteins are electrically attracted or repelled by charges in the fluids around the membrane. Unlike most membrane proteins, which remain stable despite fluctuations in membrane potential, voltage-gated channel proteins are especially sensitive to voltage changes. Small distortions in shape induced by changes in potential can cause the channels to change their conformation. Here, again, is an example of how subtle changes in structure can profoundly influence function.

The voltage-gated Na^+ channel has two gates: an activation gate and an inactivation gate (● Figure 4-5). The *activation gate*

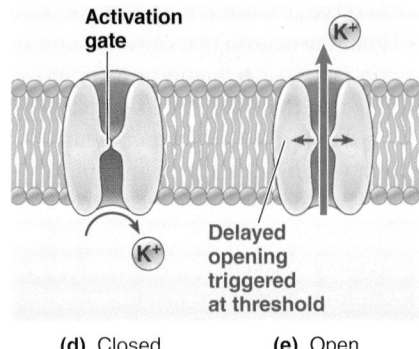

VOLTAGE-GATED SODIUM CHANNEL

VOLTAGE-GATED POTASSIUM CHANNEL

(a) Closed but capable of opening

(b) Open (activated)

(c) Closed and not capable of opening (inactivated)

(d) Closed

(e) Open

● FIGURE 4-5 **Conformations of voltage-gated sodium and potassium channels.**

guards the channel interior by opening and closing like a sliding door. The *inactivation gate* consists of a ball-and-chain-like sequence of amino acids at the channel opening facing the ICF. This gate is open when the ball is hanging free on the end of its chain and closed when the ball binds to the channel opening, thus blocking the opening. Both gates must be open to permit passage of Na^+ through the channel, and closure of either gate prevents passage. This voltage-gated Na^+ channel can exist in three conformations: (1) *closed but capable of opening* (activation gate closed, inactivation gate open, ● Figure 4-5a); (2) *open,* or *activated* (both gates open, ● Figure 4-5b); and (3) *closed and not capable of opening,* or *inactivated* (activation gate open, inactivation gate closed, ● Figure 4-5c). The channel moves through these various conformations as a result of voltage changes that take place during an action potential, as described shortly. When the action potential is over and the membrane has returned to resting potential, the channel reverts back to its "closed but capable of opening" conformation.

The voltage-gated K^+ channel is simpler. It has only an activation gate, which can be either closed (● Figure 4-5d) or open (● Figure 4-5e). These voltage-gated Na^+ and K^+ channels exist in addition to the Na^+–K^+ pump and the leak channels for these ions (described in Chapter 3).

CHANGES IN PERMEABILITY AND ION MOVEMENT DURING AN ACTION POTENTIAL At resting potential (−70 mV), all voltage-gated channels for both Na^+ and K^+ are closed, with the activation gates of the Na^+ channels being closed and their inactivation gates being open; that is, the voltage-gated Na^+ channels are in their "closed but capable of opening" conformation. Therefore, Na^+ and K^+ cannot pass through these voltage-gated channels at resting potential. However, because many K^+ leak channels and few Na^+ leak channels are present, the resting membrane is 25 to 30 times more permeable to K^+ than to Na^+.

When current spreads passively from an adjacent site already depolarized (such as from a site undergoing a graded potential) into a new region still at resting potential, the new region of membrane starts to depolarize toward threshold. This depolarization causes the activation gates of some voltage-gated Na^+ channels in the new region to open so that both gates of these activated channels are now open. Because both the concentration

and the electrical gradients for Na^+ favor its movement into the cell, Na^+ starts to move in. The inward movement of positively charged Na^+ depolarizes the membrane further, opening even more voltage-gated Na^+ channels and allowing more Na^+ to enter, and so on, in a positive-feedback cycle (● Figure 4-6).

At threshold potential, Na^+ permeability, which is symbolized as P_{Na^+}, increases explosively as the membrane swiftly becomes about 600 times more permeable to Na^+ than to K^+. Each channel is either closed or open and cannot be partially open. However, the delicately poised gating mechanisms of the various voltage-gated Na^+ channels are jolted open by slightly different voltage changes. During the early depolarizing phase, more and more Na^+ channels open as the potential progressively decreases. At threshold, enough Na^+ gates have opened to set off the positive-feedback cycle that rapidly causes the remaining Na^+ gates to open. Now Na^+ permeability dominates the membrane, in contrast to the K^+ domination at resting potential. Thus, at threshold Na^+ rushes into the cell,

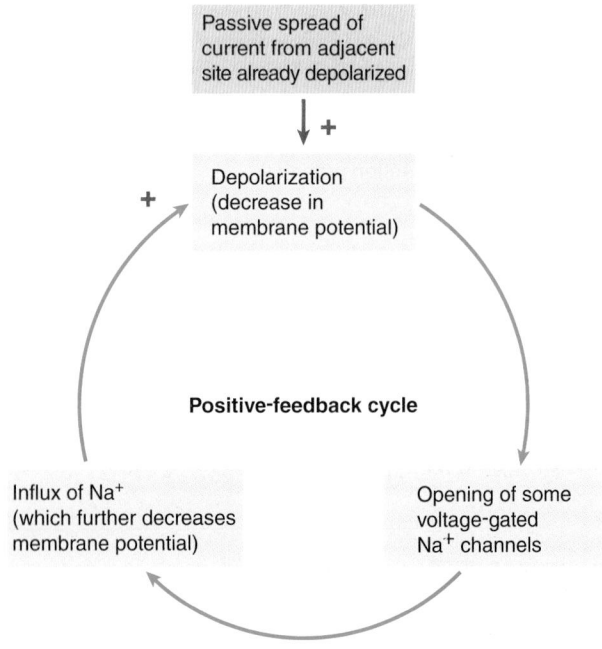

● FIGURE 4-6 **Positive-feedback cycle responsible for opening Na^+ channels at threshold.**

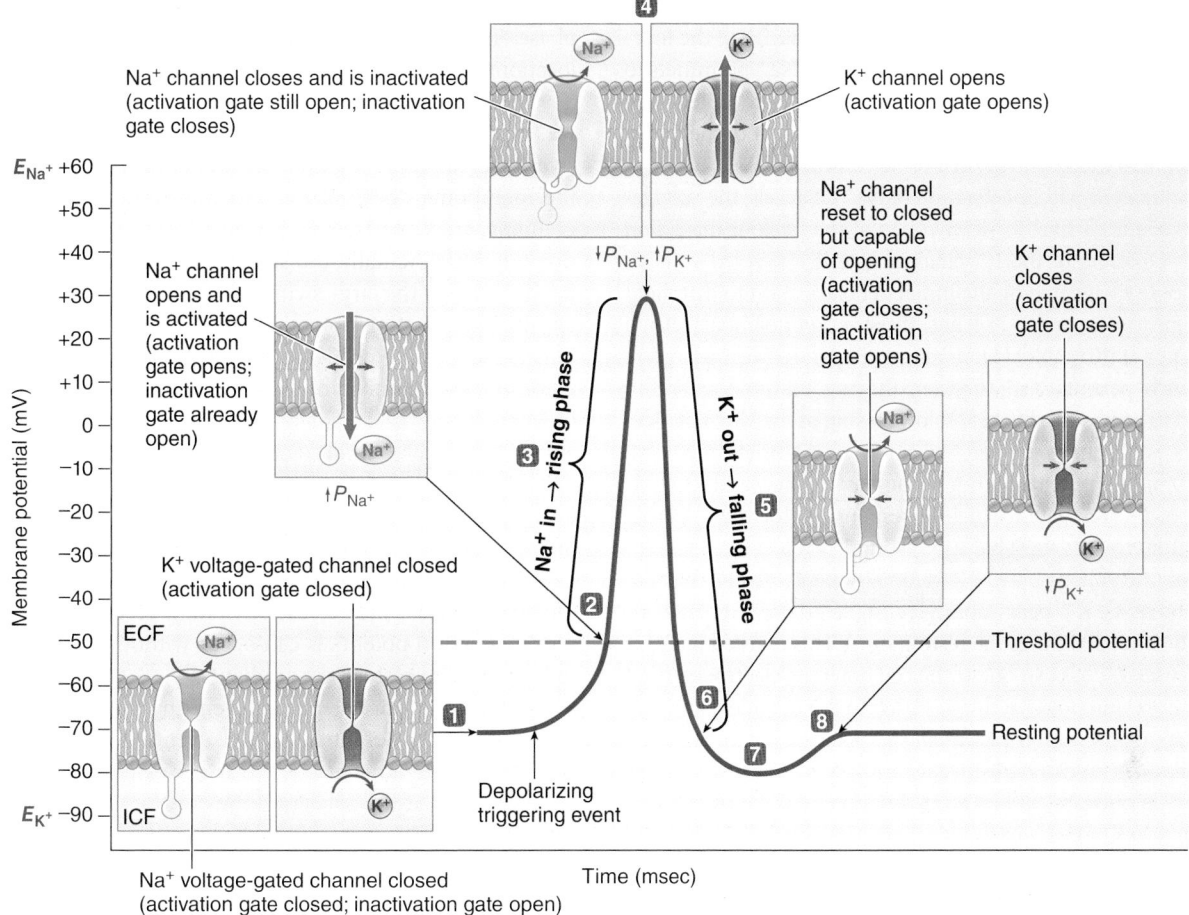

Na⁺ channel closes and is inactivated (activation gate still open; inactivation gate closes)

K⁺ channel opens (activation gate opens)

E_{Na^+} +60

+50

+40

Na⁺ channel opens and is activated (activation gate opens; inactivation gate already open)

+30

+20

+10

0

−10

−20

K⁺ voltage-gated channel closed (activation gate closed)

−30

−40

−50

ECF

Na⁺ in → rising phase

↑P_{Na^+}

↓P_{Na^+}, ↑P_{K^+}

Na⁺ channel reset to closed but capable of opening (activation gate closes; inactivation gate opens)

K⁺ channel closes (activation gate closes)

↓P_{K^+}

K⁺ out → falling phase

Threshold potential

−60

−70

−80

E_{K^+} −90

ICF

↑P_{Na^+}

Depolarizing triggering event

Resting potential

Time (msec)

Na⁺ voltage-gated channel closed (activation gate closed; inactivation gate open)

1 Resting potential: all voltage-gated channels closed.

2 At threshold, Na⁺ activation gate opens and P_{Na^+} rises.

3 Na⁺ enters cell, causing explosive depolarization to +30 mV, which generates rising phase of action potential.

4 At peak of action potential, Na⁺ inactivation gate closes and P_{Na^+} falls, ending net movement of Na⁺ into cell. At the same time, K⁺ activation gate opens and P_{K^+} rises.

5 K⁺ leaves cell, causing its repolarization to resting potential, which generates falling phase of action potential.

6 On return to resting potential, Na⁺ activation gate closes and inactivation gate opens, resetting channel to respond to another depolarizing triggering event.

7 Further outward movement of K⁺ through still-open K⁺ channel briefly hyperpolarizes membrane, which generates after hyperpolarization.

8 K⁺ activation gate closes, and membrane returns to resting potential.

● **FIGURE 4-7 Permeability changes and ion fluxes during an action potential.**

rapidly eliminating the internal negativity and even making the inside of the cell more positive than the outside in an attempt to drive the membrane potential to the Na⁺ equilibrium potential (which is +60 mV; see p. 70). The potential reaches +30 mV, close to the Na⁺ equilibrium potential. The potential does not become any more positive, because, at the peak of the action potential, the Na⁺ channels start to close to the inactivated state and P_{Na^+} starts to fall to its low resting value (● Figure 4-7).

What causes the Na⁺ channels to close? When the membrane potential reaches threshold, two closely related events take place

in the gates of each Na⁺ channel. First, the activation gates are triggered to *open rapidly* in response to the depolarization, converting the channel to its open (activated) conformation. Surprisingly, the conformational change that opens the channel also allows the inactivation gate's ball to bind to the channel opening, thereby physically blocking the mouth of the channel. However, this closure process takes time, so the inactivation gate *closes slowly* compared to the rapidity of channel opening (see ● Figure 4-5c). Meanwhile, during the 0.5-msec delay after the activation gate opens and before the inactivation gate closes, both gates are open and Na^+ rushes into the cell through these open channels, bringing the action potential to its peak. Then the inactivation gate closes, membrane permeability to Na^+ plummets to its low resting value, and further Na^+ entry is prevented. The channel remains in this inactivated conformation until the membrane potential has been restored to its resting value.

Simultaneous with inactivation of Na^+ channels, the voltage-gated K^+ channels start to slowly open at the peak of the action potential. Opening of the K^+ channel gate is a delayed voltage-gated response triggered by the initial depolarization to threshold (see ● Figures 4-5e and 4-7). Thus, three action potential–related events occur at threshold: (1) rapid opening of the Na^+ activation gates, which permits Na^+ to enter, moving the potential from threshold to its positive peak; (2) slow closing of the Na^+ inactivation gates, which halts further Na^+ entry after a brief time delay, thus keeping the potential from rising any further; and (3) slow opening of the K^+ gates, which is responsible for the potential plummeting from its peak back to resting.

When the voltage-gated K^+ channels open at the peak of the action potential, K^+ permeability (designated $P_{K}+$) greatly increases to about 300 times the resting $P_{Na}+$. This marked increase in $P_{K}+$ causes K^+ to rush out of the cell down its electrochemical gradient, carrying positive charges back to the outside. Note that at the peak of the action potential, the positive potential inside the cell tends to repel the positive K^+ ions, so the electrical gradient for K^+ is outward, unlike at resting potential. Of course, the concentration gradient for K^+ is always outward. The outward movement of K^+ rapidly restores the negative resting potential.

To review (● Figure 4-7), *the rising phase of the action potential* (from threshold to $+30$ mV) *is due to Na^+ influx* (Na^+ entering the cell) induced by an explosive increase in $P_{Na}+$ at threshold. The *falling phase* (from $+30$ mV to resting potential) *is brought about by K^+ efflux* (K^+ leaving the cell) caused by the marked increase in $P_{K}+$ occurring simultaneously with inactivation of the Na^+ channels at the peak of the action potential.

As the potential returns to resting, the changing voltage shifts the Na^+ channels to their "closed but capable of opening" conformation, with the activation gate closed and the inactivation gate open. Now the channel is reset, ready to respond to another triggering event. The newly opened voltage-gated K^+ channels also close, so the membrane returns to the resting number of open K^+ leak channels. Typically, the voltage-gated K^+ channels are slow to close. As a result of this persistent increased permeability to K^+, more K^+ may leave than is necessary to bring the potential to resting. This slightly excessive K^+ efflux makes the interior of the cell transiently even more negative than resting potential, causing the after hyperpolarization. When the voltage-gated K^+ channels all close, the membrane returns to resting potential, where it remains until another triggering event alters the gated Na^+ and K^+ channels.

The Na^+–K^+ pump gradually restores the concentration gradients disrupted by action potentials.

At the completion of an action potential, the membrane potential has been restored to its resting condition, but the ion distribution has been altered slightly. Na^+ entered the cell during the rising phase, and a comparable amount of K^+ left during the falling phase. The Na^+–K^+ pump restores these ions to their original locations in the long run, but not after each action potential.

The active pumping process takes much longer to restore Na^+ and K^+ to their original locations than it takes for the passive fluxes of these ions during an action potential. However, the membrane does not need to wait until the concentration gradients are slowly restored before it can undergo another action potential. Actually, the movement of relatively few Na^+ and K^+ ions causes the large swings in membrane potential that occur during an action potential. Only about 1 out of 100,000 K^+ ions present in the cell leaves during an action potential, while a comparable number of Na^+ ions enter from the ECF. The movement of this extremely small proportion of the total Na^+ and K^+ during a single action potential produces dramatic 100 mV changes in potential (between -70 and $+30$ mV) but only infinitesimal changes in the ICF and ECF concentrations of these ions. Much more K^+ is still inside the cell than outside, and Na^+ is still predominantly an extracellular cation. Consequently, the Na^+ and K^+ concentration gradients still exist, so repeated action potentials can occur without the pump having to keep pace to restore the gradients.

Were it not for the pump, even tiny fluxes accompanying repeated action potentials would eventually "run down" the concentration gradients so that further action potentials would be impossible. If the concentrations of Na^+ and K^+ were equal between the ECF and the ICF, changes in permeability to these ions would not bring about ion fluxes, so no change in potential would occur. Thus, the Na^+–K^+ pump is critical to maintaining the concentration gradients in the long run. However, it does not have to perform its role between action potentials, nor is it directly involved in the ion fluxes or potential changes that occur during an action potential.

Action potentials are propagated from the axon hillock to the axon terminals.

A single action potential involves only a small patch of the total surface membrane of an excitable cell. But if action potentials are to serve as long-distance signals, they cannot be merely isolated events occurring in a limited area of a nerve or muscle cell membrane. Mechanisms must exist to conduct or spread the action potential throughout the entire cell membrane. Furthermore, the signal must be transmitted from one cell to the next (for example, along specific nerve pathways). To explain these mechanisms, we begin with a brief look at neuronal structure. Then we examine how an action potential (nerve impulse) is conducted throughout a neuron before we turn to how the signal is passed to another cell.

A single **neuron** typically consists of three basic parts—the *cell body,* the *dendrites,* and the *axon*—although the structure varies depending on the location and function of the neuron. The nucleus and organelles are housed in the **cell body,** from which numerous extensions known as **dendrites** typically project like antennae to increase the surface area available for receiving signals from other neurons (● Figure 4-8). Some neurons have up to 400,000 dendrites, which carry signals *toward*

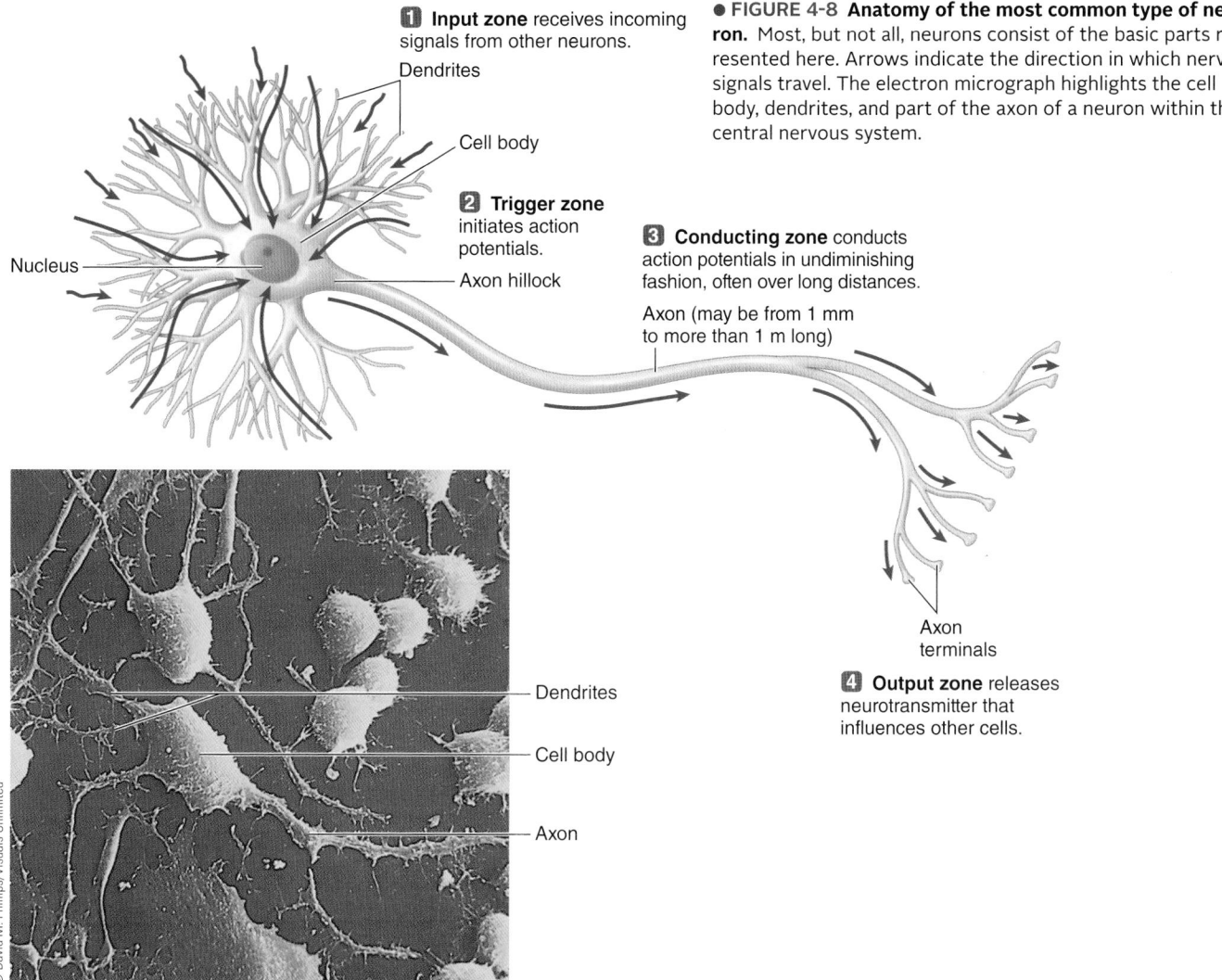

1 **Input zone** receives incoming signals from other neurons.

Dendrites

Cell body

2 **Trigger zone** initiates action potentials.

Nucleus

Axon hillock

3 **Conducting zone** conducts action potentials in undiminishing fashion, often over long distances.

Axon (may be from 1 mm to more than 1 m long)

Axon terminals

4 **Output zone** releases neurotransmitter that influences other cells.

● FIGURE 4-8 **Anatomy of the most common type of neuron.** Most, but not all, neurons consist of the basic parts represented here. Arrows indicate the direction in which nerve signals travel. The electron micrograph highlights the cell body, dendrites, and part of the axon of a neuron within the central nervous system.

Dendrites

Cell body

Axon

© David M. Phillips/Visuals Unlimited

the cell body. In most neurons, the plasma membrane of the dendrites and cell body contains protein receptors that bind chemical messengers from other neurons. Therefore, the dendrites and cell body are the neuron's *input zone,* because these components receive and integrate incoming signals. This is the region where graded potentials are produced in response to triggering events, in this case, incoming chemical messengers.

The **axon,** or **nerve fiber,** is a single, elongated, tubular extension that conducts action potentials *away from* the cell body and eventually terminates at other cells. The first portion of the axon plus the region of the cell body from which the axon leaves are known collectively as the **axon hillock** or **initial segment.** The axon hillock is the neuron's *trigger zone,* because it is the site where action potentials are triggered, or initiated, by the graded potential if it is of sufficient magnitude. The action potentials are then conducted along the axon from the axon hillock to what is typically the highly branched ending at the **axon terminals.** These terminals release chemical messengers that simultaneously influence numerous other cells with which they come into close association. Functionally, therefore, the axon is the *conducting zone* of the neuron, and the axon terminals constitute its *output zone.* (The major exceptions to this typical

neuronal structure and functional organization are neurons specialized to carry sensory information, a topic described in a later chapter.)

Axons vary in length from less than a millimeter in neurons that communicate only with neighboring cells to longer than a meter in neurons that communicate with distant parts of the nervous system or with peripheral organs. For example, the axon of the neuron innervating your big toe must traverse the distance from the origin of its cell body within the spinal cord in the lower region of your back all the way down your leg to your toe.

Action potentials can be initiated only in portions of the membrane with abundant voltage-gated Na^+ channels that can be triggered to open by a depolarizing event. Typically, regions of excitable cells where graded potentials take place do not undergo action potentials because voltage-gated Na^+ channels are sparse there. Therefore, sites specialized for graded potentials do not undergo action potentials, even though they might be considerably depolarized. However, before dying out, graded potentials can trigger action potentials in adjacent portions of the membrane by bringing these more sensitive regions to threshold through local current flow spreading from the site of the graded potential. In a typical neuron, for example, graded potentials are generated in the dendrites and cell body in response to incoming chemical signals. If these graded potentials have sufficient magnitude by the time they have spread to the axon hillock, they initiate an action potential at this trigger zone. The axon hillock has the lowest threshold in the neuron because of its high density of voltage-gated Na^+ channels.

Once initiated, action potentials are conducted throughout a nerve fiber.

Once an action potential is initiated at the axon hillock, no further triggering event is necessary to activate the remainder of the nerve fiber. The impulse is automatically conducted throughout the neuron without further stimulation by one of two methods of propagation: *contiguous conduction* or *saltatory*

conduction. Here, we discuss contiguous conduction. Saltatory conduction is discussed later.

Contiguous conduction involves the spread of the action potential along every patch of membrane down the length of the axon (*contiguous* means "touching" or "next to in sequence"). This process is illustrated in ● Figure 4-9, which represents a longitudinal section of the axon hillock and the portion of the axon immediately beyond it. The membrane at the axon hillock is at the peak of an action potential. The inside of the cell is positive in this active area, because Na^+ has already rushed in here. The remainder of the axon, still at resting potential and negative inside, is considered inactive. For the action potential to spread from the active to the inactive areas, the inactive areas must somehow be depolarized to threshold. This depolarization is accomplished by

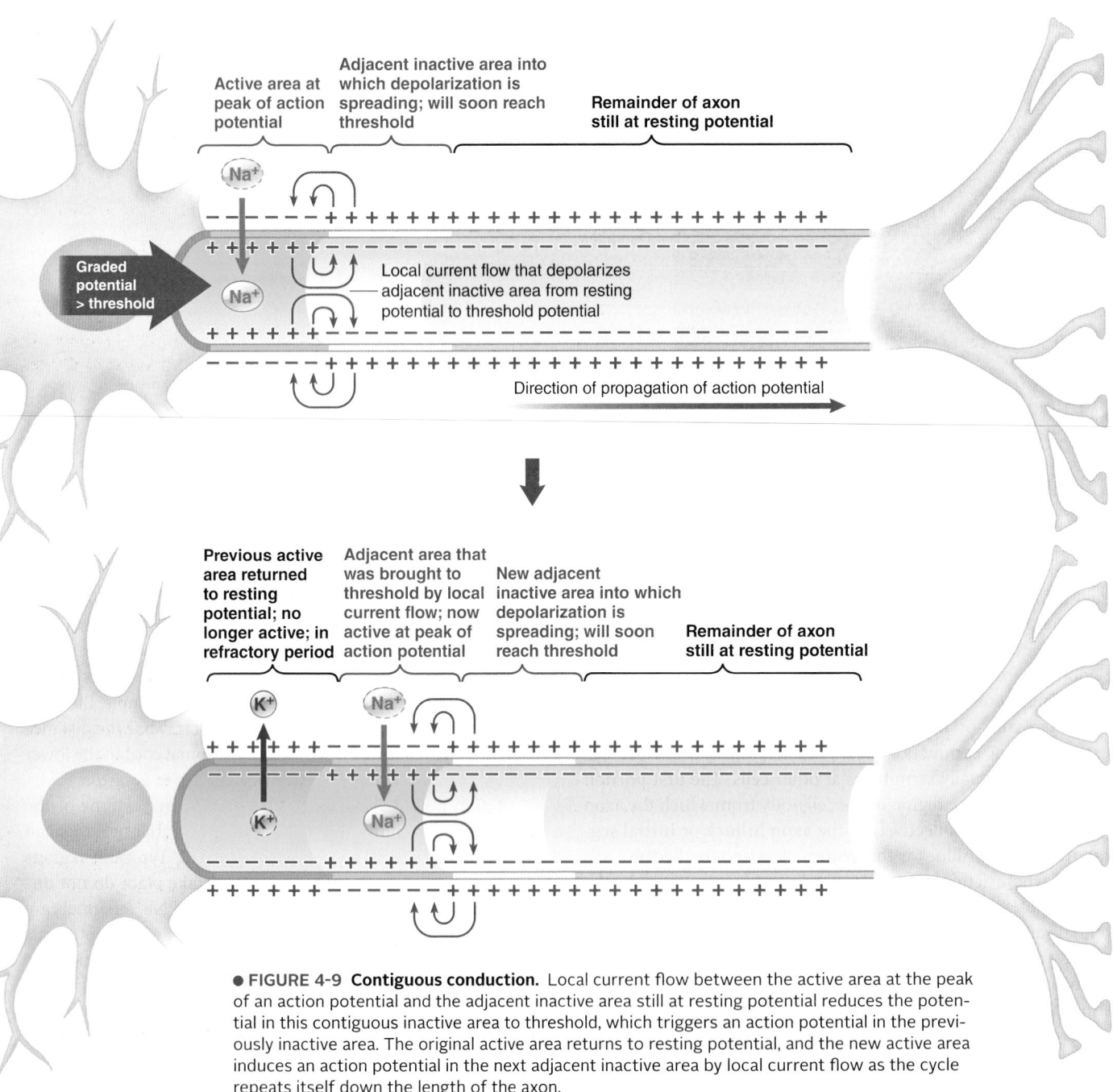

● **FIGURE 4-9 Contiguous conduction.** Local current flow between the active area at the peak of an action potential and the adjacent inactive area still at resting potential reduces the potential in this contiguous inactive area to threshold, which triggers an action potential in the previously inactive area. The original active area returns to resting potential, and the new active area induces an action potential in the next adjacent inactive area by local current flow as the cycle repeats itself down the length of the axon.

local current flow between the area already undergoing an action potential and the adjacent inactive area, similar to the current flow responsible for the spread of graded potentials. Because opposite charges attract, current can flow locally between the active area and the neighboring inactive area on both the inside and the outside of the membrane. This local current flow in effect neutralizes or eliminates some of the unbalanced charges in the inactive area; that is, it reduces the number of opposite charges separated across the membrane, reducing the potential in this area. This depolarizing effect quickly brings the involved inactive area to threshold, at which time the voltage-gated Na^+ channels in this region of the membrane are all thrown open, leading to an action potential in this previously inactive area. Meanwhile, the original active area returns to resting potential as a result of K^+ efflux.

Beyond the new active area is another inactive area, so the same thing happens again. This cycle repeats itself in a chain reaction until the action potential has spread to the end of the axon. *Once an action potential is initiated in one part of a neuron's cell membrane, a self-perpetuating cycle is initiated so that the action potential is propagated along the rest of the fiber automatically.* In this way, the axon is like a firecracker fuse that needs to be lit at only one end. Once ignited, the fire spreads down the fuse; it is not necessary to hold a match to every separate section of the fuse. Therefore, a new action potential can be initiated in two ways, in both cases involving passive spread of current from an adjacent site already depolarized. An action potential is initiated in the axon hillock in the first place by depolarizing current spreading from a graded potential in the cell body and dendrites. During propagation of the action potential down the axon, each new action potential is initiated by depolarizing local current flow spreading from the preceding site undergoing an action potential.

Note that the original action potential does not travel along the membrane. Instead, it triggers an identical new action potential in the bordering area of the membrane, with this process being repeated along the axon's length. An analogy is the "wave" at a stadium. Each section of spectators stands up (the rising phase of an action potential) and then sits down (the falling phase) in sequence one after another as the wave moves around the stadium. The wave, not individual spectators, travels around the stadium. Similarly, new action potentials arise sequentially down the axon. Each new action potential is a fresh local event that depends on induced permeability changes and electrochemical gradients that are virtually identical down the length of the axon. Therefore, the last action potential at the end of the axon is identical to the original one, no matter how long the axon is. In this way, action potentials can serve as long-distance signals without attenuation or distortion.

This nondecremental propagation of an action potential contrasts with the decremental spread of a graded potential, which dies out over a short distance because it cannot regenerate itself. ▲ Table 4-1 summarizes the differences between graded potentials and action potentials, some of which we have yet to discuss.

The refractory period ensures one-way propagation of action potential.

What ensures the one-way propagation of an action potential away from the initial site of activation? Note from ● Figure 4-10 that once the action potential has been regenerated at a new

▲ Table 4-1 Comparison of Graded Potentials and Action Potentials

Property	Graded Potentials	Action Potentials
Triggering events	Stimulus, combination of neurotransmitter with receptor, or inherent shifts in channel permeability	Depolarization to threshold, usually through passive spread of depolarization from an adjacent area undergoing a graded potential or an action potential
Ion movement producing a change in potential	Net movement of Na^+, K^+, Cl^-, or Ca^{2+} across the plasma membrane by various means	Sequential movement of Na^+ into and K^+ out of the cell through voltage-gated channels
Coding of the magnitude of the triggering event	Graded potential change; magnitude varies with the magnitude of the triggering event	All-or-none membrane response; magnitude of the triggering event is coded in the frequency rather than the amplitude of action potentials
Duration	Varies with the duration of the triggering event	Constant
Magnitude of the potential change with distance from the initial site	Decremental conduction; magnitude diminishes with distance from the initial site	Propagated throughout the membrane in an undiminishing fashion; self-regenerated in neighboring inactive areas of the membrane
Refractory period	None	Relative, absolute
Summation	Temporal, spatial	None
Direction of potential change	Depolarization or hyperpolarization	Always depolarization and reversal of charges
Location	Specialized regions of the membrane designed to respond to the triggering event	Regions of the membrane with an abundance of voltage-gated channels

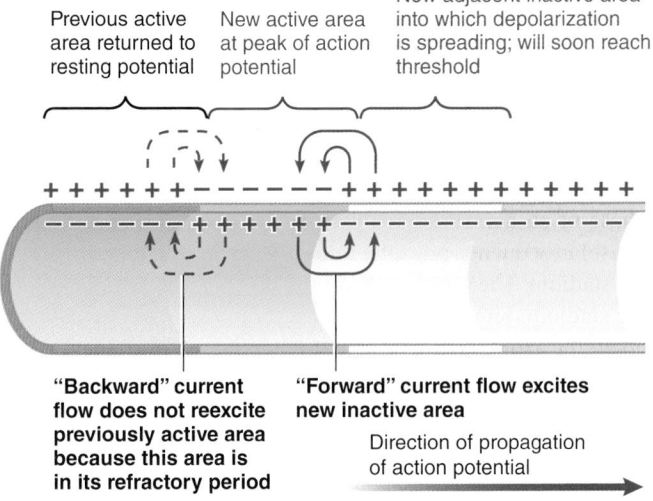

Previous active area returned to resting potential

New active area at peak of action potential

New adjacent inactive area into which depolarization is spreading; will soon reach threshold

+ + + + + — — — — — — + + + + + + + + + + +

— — — — — + + + + + — — — — — — — — — —

"Backward" current flow does not reexcite previously active area because this area is in its refractory period

"Forward" current flow excites new inactive area

Direction of propagation of action potential

● **FIGURE 4-10 Value of the refractory period.** The refractory period prevents "backward" current flow. During an action potential and slightly afterward, an area cannot be restimulated by normal events to undergo another action potential. Thus, the refractory period ensures that an action potential can be propagated only in the forward direction along the axon.

neighboring site (now positive inside) and the original active area has returned to resting (again negative inside), the proximity of opposite charges between these two areas is conducive to local current flow in the backward direction, as well as in the forward direction into as-yet-unexcited portions of the membrane. If such backward current flow were able to bring the

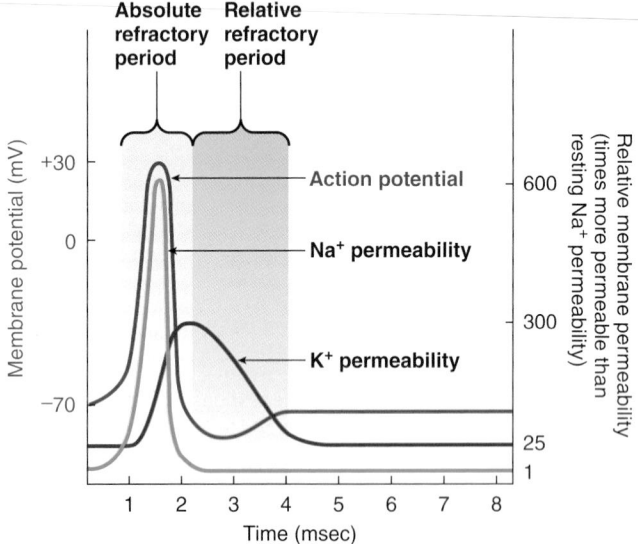

● **FIGURE 4-11 Absolute and relative refractory periods.** During the absolute refractory period, the portion of the membrane that has just undergone an action potential cannot be restimulated. This period corresponds to the time during which the Na⁺ gates are not in their resting conformation. During the relative refractory period, the membrane can be restimulated only by a stronger stimulus than is usually necessary. This period corresponds to the time during which the K⁺ gates opened during the action potential have not yet closed, coupled with lingering inactivation of some voltage-gated Na⁺ channels.

previous active area to threshold again, another action potential would be initiated here, which would spread both forward and backward, initiating still other action potentials, and so on. But if action potentials were to move in both directions, the situation would be chaotic, with numerous action potentials bouncing back and forth along the axon until the neuron eventually fatigued. Fortunately, neurons are saved from this fate of oscillating action potentials by the **refractory period,** during which a new action potential cannot be initiated by normal events in a region that has just undergone an action potential.

Because of the changing status of the voltage-gated Na⁺ and K⁺ channels during and after an action potential, the refractory period has two components: the *absolute refractory period* and the *relative refractory period* ● Figure 4-11). When a particular patch of axonal membrane is undergoing an action potential, it cannot initiate another action potential, no matter how strong the depolarizing triggering event is. This period when a recently activated patch of membrane is completely refractory (meaning "stubborn" or "unresponsive") to further stimulation is known as the **absolute refractory period.** Once the voltage-gated Na⁺ channels are triggered to open at threshold, they cannot open again in response to another depolarizing triggering event, no matter how strong, until they pass through their "closed and not capable of opening" conformation and then are reset to their "closed and capable of opening" conformation when resting potential is restored. Accordingly, the absolute refractory period lasts the entire time from threshold, through the action potential, and until return to resting potential. Only then can the voltage-gated Na⁺ channels respond to another depolarization with an explosive increase in P_{Na^+} to initiate another action potential. Because of the absolute refractory period, one action potential must be over before another can be initiated at the same site. Action potentials cannot overlap or be added one on top of another "piggyback" fashion.

Following the absolute refractory period is a **relative refractory period,** during which a second action potential can be produced only by a triggering event considerably stronger than usual. The relative refractory period occurs after the action potential is completed because of a twofold effect. First, the voltage-gated Na⁺ channels that opened during the action potential do not all reset at once when resting potential is reached. Some take a little longer to be restored to their capable of opening conformation. As a result, fewer voltage-gated Na⁺ channels are in a position to be jolted open in response to another depolarizing triggering event. Second, the voltage-gated K⁺ channels that opened at the peak of the action potential are slow to close. During this time, the resultant less-than-normal Na⁺ entry in response to another triggering event is opposed by K⁺ still leaving through its slow-to-close channels during the after hyperpolarization. Thus, a greater depolarizing triggering event than normal is needed to offset the persistent hyperpolarizing outward movement of K⁺ and bring the membrane to threshold during the relative refractory period.

By the time the original site has recovered from its refractory period and is capable of being restimulated by normal current flow, the action potential has been propagated in the forward direction only and is so far away that it can no longer influence the original site. Thus, *the refractory period ensures the one-way propagation of the action potential down the axon away from the initial site of activation.*

Action potentials occur in all-or-none fashion.

If any portion of the neuronal membrane is depolarized to threshold, an action potential is initiated and relayed along the membrane in an undiminished fashion. Furthermore, once threshold has been reached, the resultant action potential always goes to maximal height. The reason for this effect is that the changes in voltage during an action potential result from ion movements down concentration and electrical gradients, and these gradients are not affected by the strength of the depolarizing triggering event. A triggering event stronger than necessary to bring the membrane to threshold does not produce a larger action potential. However, a triggering event that fails to depolarize the membrane to threshold does not trigger an action potential at all. Thus, *an excitable membrane either responds to a triggering event with a maximal action potential that spreads nondecrementally throughout the membrane or does not respond with an action potential at all.* This property is called the **all-or-none law.**

The all-or-none concept is analogous to firing a gun. Either the trigger is not pulled sufficiently to fire the bullet (threshold is not reached), or it is pulled hard enough to elicit the full firing response of the gun (threshold is reached). Squeezing the trigger harder does not produce a greater explosion. Just as it is not possible to fire a gun halfway, it is not possible to cause a halfway action potential.

The threshold phenomenon allows some discrimination between important and unimportant stimuli or other triggering events. Stimuli too weak to bring the membrane to threshold do not initiate action potentials and therefore do not clutter up the nervous system by transmitting insignificant signals.

The strength of a stimulus is coded by the frequency of action potentials.

How is it possible to differentiate between two stimuli of varying strengths when both stimuli bring the membrane to threshold and generate action potentials of the same magnitude? For example, how can we distinguish between touching a warm object and touching a hot object if both trigger identical action potentials in a nerve fiber relaying information about skin temperature to the central nervous system (CNS)? The answer partly lies in the *frequency* with which the action potentials are generated. A stronger stimulus does not produce a *larger* action potential, but it does trigger a greater *number* of action potentials per second. For an illustration, see ● Figure 10-31, p. 308, in which changes in blood pressure are coded by corresponding changes in the frequency of action potentials generated in the neurons monitoring blood pressure.

In addition, a stronger stimulus in a region causes more neurons to reach threshold, increasing the total information sent to the CNS. For example, lightly touch this page with your finger and note the area of skin in contact with the page. Now, press down more firmly and note that a larger surface area of skin is in contact with the page. Therefore, more neurons are brought to threshold with this stronger touch stimulus.

Once initiated, the velocity, or speed, with which an action potential travels down the axon depends on whether the fiber is myelinated or not. Contiguous conduction occurs in unmyelinated fibers. In this case, as you just learned, each action potential initiates an identical new action potential in the next contiguous (bordering) segment of the axon membrane so that every portion of the membrane undergoes an action potential as this electrical signal is conducted from the beginning to the end of the axon. A faster method of propagation, saltatory conduction, takes place in myelinated fibers. We show next how a myelinated fiber compares with an unmyelinated fiber and then how saltatory conduction compares with contiguous conduction.

Myelination increases the speed of conduction of action potentials.

Myelinated fibers are axons covered with myelin, a thick layer composed primarily of lipids, at regular intervals along their length (● Figure 4-12a). Because the water-soluble ions responsible for carrying current across the membrane cannot permeate this myelin coating, it acts as an insulator, just like plastic around an electrical wire, to prevent leakage of current across the myelinated portion of the membrane. Myelin is not actually a part of the neuron but consists of separate myelin-forming cells that wrap themselves around the axon in jelly-roll fashion. These myelin-forming cells are **Schwann cells** in the peripheral nervous system (PNS) (● Figure 4-12b) (the nerves running between the CNS and the various regions of the body), and **oligodendrocytes** in the CNS (the brain and spinal cord) (● Figure 4-12c). Each patch of lipid-rich myelin consists of multiple layers of the myelin-forming cell's plasma membrane (predominantly the lipid bilayer) as the cell repeatedly wraps itself around the axon. Between the myelinated regions, at the **nodes of Ranvier,** the axonal membrane is bare and exposed to the ECF. Current can flow across the membrane only at these bare spaces to produce action potentials. Voltage-gated Na^+ and K^+ channels are concentrated at the nodes, whereas the myelin-covered regions are almost devoid of these special passageways (● Figure 4-12d). By contrast, an unmyelinated fiber has a high density of these voltage-gated channels along its entire length. As you now know, action potentials can be generated only at portions of the membrane furnished with an abundance of these channels.

The distance between the nodes is short enough that local current can flow between an active node and an adjacent inactive node before dying off. When an action potential occurs at one node, local current flow between this node and the oppositely charged adjacent resting node reduces the adjacent node's potential to threshold so that it undergoes an action potential, and so on. Consequently, in a myelinated fiber, the impulse "jumps" from node to node, skipping over the myelinated sections of the axon; this process is called **saltatory conduction** (*saltare* means "to jump or leap"). Saltatory conduction propagates action potentials more rapidly than contiguous conduction does, because the action potential does not have to be

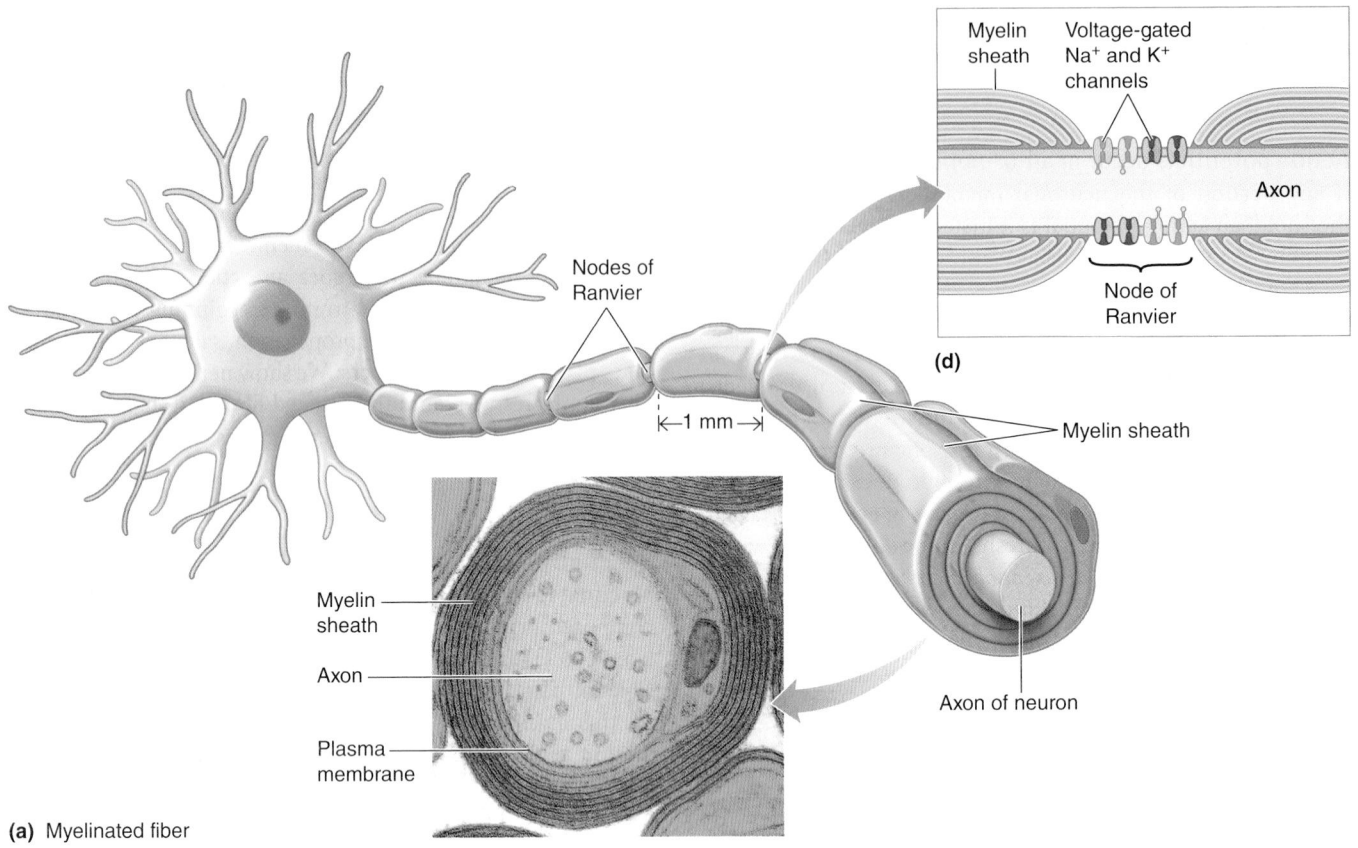

(a) Myelinated fiber

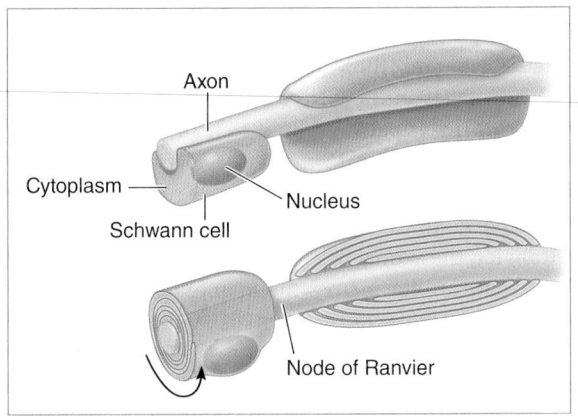

(b) Schwann cells in peripheral nervous system

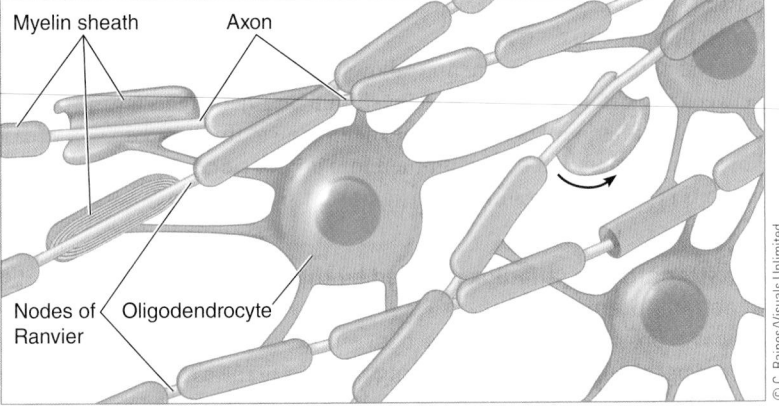

(c) Oligodendrocytes in central nervous system

● **FIGURE 4-12 Myelinated fibers.** (a) A myelinated fiber is surrounded by myelin at regular intervals. The intervening bare, unmyelinated regions are known as nodes of Ranvier. The electron micrograph shows a myelinated fiber in cross section at a myelinated region. (b) In the peripheral nervous system, each patch of myelin is formed by a separate Schwann cell that wraps itself jelly-roll fashion around the nerve fiber. (c) In the central nervous system, each of the several processes ("arms") of a myelin-forming oligodendrocyte forms a patch of myelin around a separate nerve fiber. (d) Voltage-gated channels can be seen concentrated at a node of Ranvier in this longitudinal section.

regenerated at myelinated sections but must be regenerated within every section of an unmyelinated axonal membrane from beginning to end. Myelinated fibers conduct impulses about 50 times faster than unmyelinated fibers of comparable size. You can think of myelinated fibers as the "superhighways" and unmyelinated fibers as the "back roads" of the nervous system when it comes to the speed with which information can be transmitted. Thus, the most urgent types of information are transmitted via myelinated fibers, whereas nerve pathways carrying less urgent information are unmyelinated.

Multiple sclerosis (MS) is a pathophysiologic condition in which nerve fibers in various locations throughout the nervous system lose their myelin. MS is an autoimmune disease (*auto* means "self"; *immune*

means "defense against") in which the body's defense system erroneously attacks the myelin sheath surrounding myelinated nerve fibers. Loss of myelin slows transmission of impulses in the affected neurons. A hardened scar known as a *sclerosis* (meaning "hard") forms at the multiple sites of myelin damage. These scars interfere with and can eventually block the propagation of action potentials in the underlying axons. The symptoms of MS vary considerably, depending on the extent and location of the myelin damage.

You have now seen how an action potential is propagated along the axon. But what happens when an action potential reaches the end of the axon?

Synapses and Neuronal Integration

When the action potential reaches the axon terminals, they release a chemical messenger that alters the activity of the cells on which the neuron terminates. A neuron may terminate on one of three structures: a muscle, a gland, or another neuron. Therefore, depending on where a neuron terminates, it can cause a muscle cell to contract, a gland cell to secrete, another neuron to convey an electrical message along a nerve pathway, or some other function. When a neuron terminates on a muscle or a gland, the neuron is said to **innervate,** or supply, the structure. The junctions between the nerves and the muscles and glands that they innervate are described later. For now, we concentrate on the junction between two neurons—a **synapse** (*synapsis* means "juncture"). (Sometimes the term *synapse* is used to describe a junction between any two excitable cells, but we reserve this term for the junction between two neurons.)

Synapses are junctions between presynaptic and postsynaptic neurons.

Typically, a synapse involves a junction between an axon terminal of one neuron, known as the *presynaptic neuron,* and the dendrites or cell body of a second neuron, known as the *postsynaptic neuron.* (*Pre* means "before," and *post* means "after"; the presynaptic neuron lies before the synapse, and the postsynaptic neuron lies after the synapse.) The dendrites and, to a lesser extent, the cell body of most neurons receive thousands of synaptic inputs, which are axon terminals from many other neurons. Some neurons in the CNS receive as many as 100,000 synaptic inputs (● Figure 4-13).

The anatomy of one of these thousands of synapses is shown in ● Figure 4-14. The axon terminal of the **presynaptic neuron,** which conducts its action potentials *toward* the synapse, ends in a slight swelling, the **synaptic knob.** The synaptic knob contains **synaptic vesicles,** which store a specific chemical messenger, a **neurotransmitter** that has been synthesized and packaged by the presynaptic neuron. The synaptic knob comes close to, but does not touch, the **postsynaptic neuron,** whose action potentials are propagated *away from* the synapse. The space between the presynaptic and the postsynaptic neurons, the **synaptic cleft,** is too wide for the direct spread of current from one cell to the other and therefore prevents action potentials from electrically passing between the neurons.

Instead, an action potential in the presynaptic neuron alters the postsynaptic neuron's potential by chemical means. Synapses operate in one direction only; that is, the presynaptic neuron brings about changes in the membrane potential of the postsynaptic neuron, but the postsynaptic neuron does not directly influence the potential of the presynaptic neuron. The reason for this becomes readily apparent when you examine the events that occur at a synapse.

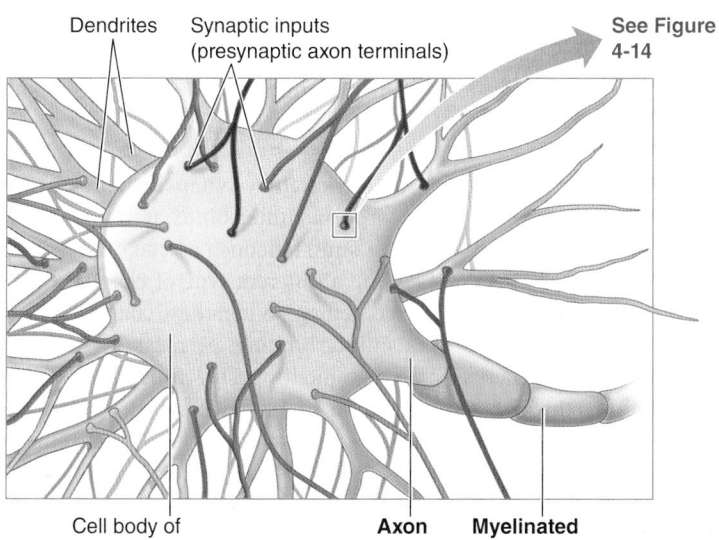

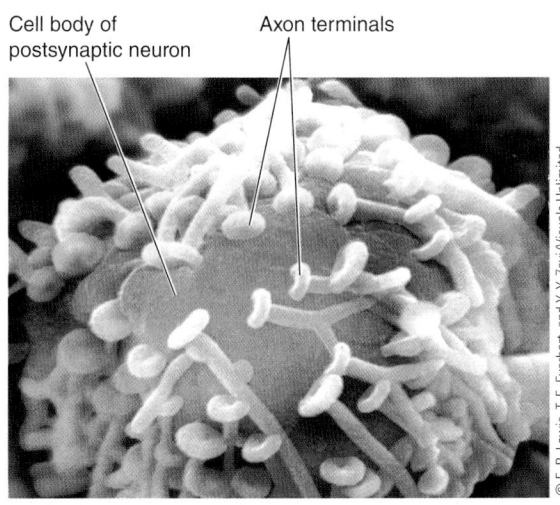

● FIGURE 4-13 **Synaptic inputs (presynaptic axon terminals) to the cell body and dendrites of a single postsynaptic neuron.** The drying process used to prepare the neuron for the electron micrograph has toppled the presynaptic axon terminals and pulled them away from the postsynaptic cell body.

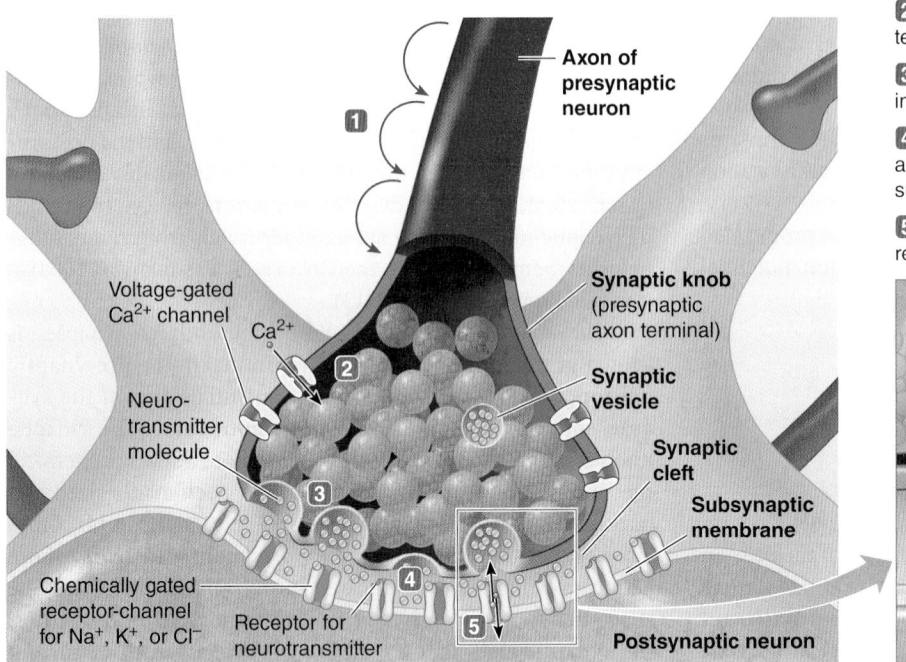

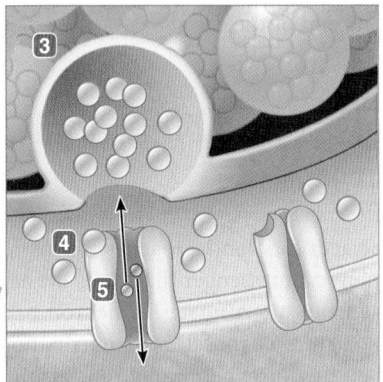

1 Action potential reaches axon terminal of presynaptic neuron.

2 Ca^{2+} enters synaptic knob (presynaptic axon terminal).

3 Neurotransmitter is released by exocytosis into synaptic cleft.

4 Neurotransmitter binds to receptors that are an integral part of chemically gated channels on subsynaptic membrane of postsynaptic neuron.

5 Binding of neurotransmitter to receptor-channel opens that specific channel.

● **FIGURE 4-14** **Structure and function of a single synapse.** The numbered steps designate the sequence of events that take place at a synapse. The blowup depicts the release by exocytosis of neurotransmitter from the presynaptic axon terminal and its subsequent binding with receptors specific for it on the subsynaptic membrane of the postsynaptic neuron.

A neurotransmitter carries the signal across a synapse.

When an action potential in a presynaptic neuron has been propagated to the axon terminal (● Figure 4-14, step 1), this local change in potential triggers the opening of voltage-gated calcium (Ca^{2+}) channels in the synaptic knob. Because Ca^{2+} is more highly concentrated in the ECF (see p. 63), this ion flows into the synaptic knob through the open channels (step 2). Ca^{2+} promotes the release of a neurotransmitter from some synaptic vesicles into the synaptic cleft (step 3). The release is accomplished by exocytosis (see p. 26). The released neurotransmitter diffuses across the cleft and binds with specific protein receptors on the **subsynaptic membrane,** the portion of the postsynaptic membrane immediately underlying the synaptic knob (*sub* means "under") (step 4). These receptors are an integral part of specific ion channels. These combined receptor and channel units are appropriately known as **receptor-channels.** Binding of neurotransmitter to the receptor-channels causes the channels to open, changing the ion permeability of the postsynaptic neuron (step 5). These are chemically gated channels, in contrast to the voltage-gated channels responsible for the action potential and for Ca^{2+} influx into the synaptic knob. Because the presynaptic terminal releases the neurotransmitter and the subsynaptic membrane of the postsynaptic neuron has receptor-channels for the neurotransmitter, the synapse can operate only in the direction from presynaptic to postsynaptic neuron.

Some synapses excite, whereas others inhibit, the postsynaptic neuron.

Each presynaptic neuron typically releases only one neurotransmitter; however, different neurons vary in the neurotransmitter they release. On binding with their subsynaptic receptor-channels, different neurotransmitters cause different ion permeability changes. There are two types of synapses, depending on the resultant permeability changes: *excitatory synapses* and *inhibitory synapses.*

EXCITATORY SYNAPSES At an **excitatory synapse,** the receptor-channels to which the neurotransmitter binds are nonspecific cation channels that permit simultaneous passage of Na^+ and K^+ through them. (These are a different type of channel from those you have encountered before.) When these channels open in response to neurotransmitter binding, permeability to both these ions is increased at the same time. How much of each ion diffuses through an open cation channel depends on their electrochemical gradients. At resting potential, both the concentration and the electrical gradients for Na^+ favor its movement into the postsynaptic neuron, whereas only the concentration gradient for K^+ favors its movement outward. Therefore, the permeability change induced at an excitatory synapse results in the movement of a few K^+ ions out of the postsynaptic neuron, while a larger number of Na^+ ions simultaneously enter this neuron. The result is net movement of positive ions into the cell.

This makes the inside of the membrane slightly less negative than at resting potential, thus producing a *small depolarization* of the postsynaptic neuron.

Activation of one excitatory synapse can rarely depolarize the postsynaptic neuron enough to bring it to threshold. Too few channels are involved at a single subsynaptic membrane to permit adequate ion flow to reduce the potential to threshold. This small depolarization, however, does bring the membrane of the postsynaptic neuron closer to threshold, increasing the likelihood that threshold will be reached (in response to further excitatory input) and that an action potential will occur. That is, the membrane is now more excitable (easier to bring to threshold) than when at rest. Accordingly, the change in postsynaptic potential occurring at an excitatory synapse is called an **excitatory postsynaptic potential,** or **EPSP** (● Figure 4-15a).

INHIBITORY SYNAPSES At an **inhibitory synapse,** binding of a neurotransmitter with its receptor-channels increases the permeability of the subsynaptic membrane to either K⁺ or chloride (Cl⁻), depending on the synapse. The resulting ion movements

bring about a *small hyperpolarization* of the postsynaptic neuron—that is, greater internal negativity. In the case of increased P_{K^+}, more positive charges leave the cell via K⁺ efflux, leaving more negative charges behind on the inside. In the case of increased P_{Cl^-}, because the concentration of Cl⁻ is higher outside the cell, negative charges enter the cell in the form of Cl⁻ ions. In either case, this small hyperpolarization moves the membrane potential even farther from threshold (● Figure 4-15b), lessening the likelihood that the postsynaptic neuron will reach threshold and undergo an action potential. That is, the membrane is now less excitable (harder to bring to threshold by excitatory input) than when it is at resting potential. The membrane is said to be inhibited under these circumstances, and the small hyperpolarization of the postsynaptic cell is called an **inhibitory postsynaptic potential,** or **IPSP.**

Note that EPSPs and IPSPs are produced by opening of chemically gated channels, unlike action potentials, which are produced by opening of voltage-gated channels.

Each neurotransmitter–receptor combination always produces the same response.

Many chemicals serve as neurotransmitters (▲ Table 4-2). Even though neurotransmitters vary from synapse to synapse, the same neurotransmitter is always released at a particular synapse. Furthermore, at a given synapse, binding of a neurotransmitter with its appropriate subsynaptic receptor-channels always leads to the same change in permeability and resultant change in potential of the postsynaptic membrane. That is, the response to a given neurotransmitter–receptor combination is always the same; the combination does not generate an EPSP under one circumstance and an IPSP under another. Some neurotransmitters (for example, *glutamate,* the most common excitatory neurotransmitter in the brain) typically bring about EPSPs, whereas others (for example, *gamma-aminobutyric acid,* or *GABA,* the brain's main inhibitory neurotransmitter) always produce IPSPs. Still other neurotransmitters (for example, *norepinephrine*) can produce EPSPs at one synapse and IPSPs at a different synapse, because different permeability changes occur in response to the binding of this same neurotransmitter to different postsynaptic neurons. Yet the response at a given norepinephrine-influenced synapse is always either excitatory or inhibitory.

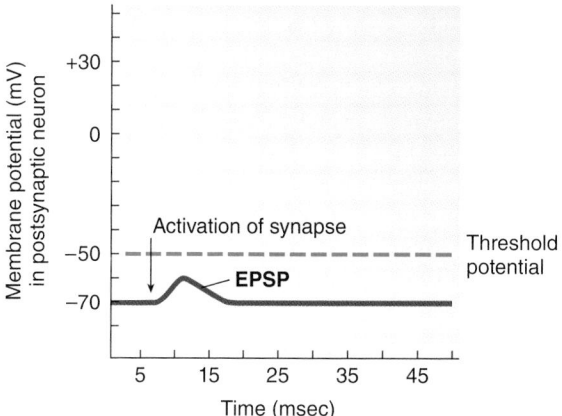

(a) Excitatory synapse

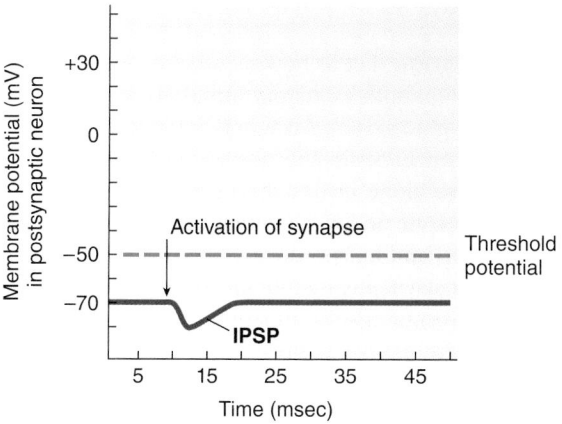

(b) Inhibitory synapse

● **FIGURE 4-15 Postsynaptic potentials.** (a) An excitatory postsynaptic potential (EPSP) brought about by activation of an excitatory presynaptic input brings the postsynaptic neuron closer to threshold potential. (b) An inhibitory postsynaptic potential (IPSP) brought about by activation of an inhibitory presynaptic input moves the postsynaptic neuron farther from threshold potential.

▲ Table 4-2 **Some Common Neurotransmitters**

Acetylcholine	Histamine
Dopamine	Glycine
Norepinephrine	Glutamate
Epinephrine	Aspartate
Serotonin	Gamma-aminobutyric acid (GABA)

Neurotransmitters are quickly removed from the synaptic cleft.

As long as the neurotransmitter remains bound to the receptor-channels, the alteration in membrane permeability responsible for the EPSP or IPSP continues. For the postsynaptic neuron to be ready to receive additional messages from the same or other presynaptic inputs, the neurotransmitter must be inactivated or removed from the postsynaptic cleft after it has produced the appropriate response in the postsynaptic neuron; that is, the postsynaptic "slate" must be "wiped clean." Thus, after combining with the postsynaptic receptor-channel, chemical transmitters are removed and the response is terminated.

Several mechanisms can remove the neurotransmitter: It may diffuse away from the synaptic cleft, be inactivated by specific enzymes within the subsynaptic membrane, or be actively taken back up into the axon terminal by transport mechanisms in the presynaptic membrane. The method employed depends on the particular synapse.

 Some drugs work by interfering with removal of specific neurotransmitters from synapses. For example, **selective serotonin reuptake inhibitors (SSRIs),** as their name implies, selectively block the reuptake of *serotonin* into presynaptic axon terminals, thereby prolonging the action of this neurotransmitter at synapses that use this messenger. SSRIs, such as *Prozac* and *Paxil,* are prescribed to treat depression, which is characterized by a deficiency of serotonin, among other things. Serotonin is involved in neural pathways that regulate mood and behavior.

The grand postsynaptic potential depends on the sum of the activities of all presynaptic inputs.

EPSPs and IPSPs are graded potentials. Unlike action potentials, which behave according to the all-or-none law, graded potentials can be of varying magnitude, have no refractory period, and can be summed (added on top of one another). What are the mechanisms and significance of summation?

The events that occur at a single synapse result in either an EPSP or an IPSP at the postsynaptic neuron. But if a single EPSP is inadequate to bring the postsynaptic neuron to threshold and an IPSP moves it even farther from threshold, how can an action potential be initiated in the postsynaptic neuron? The answer lies in the thousands of presynaptic inputs that a typical neuronal cell body receives from many other neurons. Some of these presynaptic inputs may be carrying sensory information from the environment; some may be signaling internal changes in homeostatic balance; others may be transmitting signals from control centers in the brain; and still others may arrive carrying other bits of information. At any given time, any number of these presynaptic neurons (probably hundreds) may be firing and thus influencing the postsynaptic neuron's level of activity. The total potential in the postsynaptic neuron, the **grand postsynaptic potential (GPSP),** is a composite of all EPSPs and IPSPs occurring around the same time.

The postsynaptic neuron can be brought to threshold by either *temporal summation* or *spatial summation.* To illustrate these methods of summation, we examine the possible interac-

tions of three presynaptic inputs—two excitatory inputs (Ex1 and Ex2) and one inhibitory input (In1)—on a hypothetical postsynaptic neuron (● Figure 4-16). The recording shown in the figure represents the potential in the postsynaptic cell. Bear in mind during our discussion of this simplified version that many thousands of synapses are actually interacting in the same way on a single cell body and its dendrites.

TEMPORAL SUMMATION Suppose that Ex1 has an action potential that causes an EPSP in the postsynaptic neuron. After this EPSP has died off, if another action potential occurs in Ex1, an EPSP of the same magnitude takes place before dying off (● Figure 4-16a). Next, suppose that Ex1 has two action potentials in close succession (● Figure 4-16b). The first action potential in Ex1 produces an EPSP in the postsynaptic membrane. While the postsynaptic membrane is still partially depolarized from this first EPSP, the second action potential in Ex1 produces a second EPSP. Because graded potentials do not have a refractory period, the second EPSP can add to the first, bringing the membrane to threshold and initiating an action potential in the postsynaptic neuron. EPSPs can add together or sum because an EPSP lasts longer than the action potential that caused it. The presynaptic neuron (Ex1) can recover from its refractory period following the first action potential and have a second action potential, causing a second EPSP in the postsynaptic neuron, before the first EPSP is finished.

The summing of several EPSPs occurring very close together in time because of successive firing of a single presynaptic neuron is known as **temporal summation** (*tempus* means "time"). In reality, up to 50 EPSPs might be needed to bring the postsynaptic membrane to threshold. Each action potential in a single presynaptic neuron triggers the emptying of a certain number of synaptic vesicles. The amount of neurotransmitter released and the resultant magnitude of the change in postsynaptic potential are thus directly related to the frequency of presynaptic action potentials. One way in which the postsynaptic membrane can be brought to threshold, then, is through rapid, repetitive excitation from a single persistent input.

SPATIAL SUMMATION Let us now see what happens in the postsynaptic neuron if both excitatory inputs are stimulated simultaneously (● Figure 4-16c). An action potential in either Ex1 or Ex2 produces an EPSP in the postsynaptic neuron; however, neither of these alone brings the membrane to threshold to elicit a postsynaptic action potential. But simultaneous action potentials in Ex1 and Ex2 produce EPSPs that add to each other, bringing the postsynaptic membrane to threshold, so an action potential does occur. The summation of EPSPs originating simultaneously from several presynaptic inputs (that is, from different points in "space") is known as **spatial summation.** A second way to elicit an action potential in a postsynaptic cell, therefore, is through concurrent activation of several excitatory inputs. Again, in reality, up to 50 simultaneous EPSPs are required to bring the postsynaptic membrane to threshold.

Similarly, IPSPs can undergo both temporal and spatial summation. As IPSPs add together, however, they progressively move the potential farther from threshold.

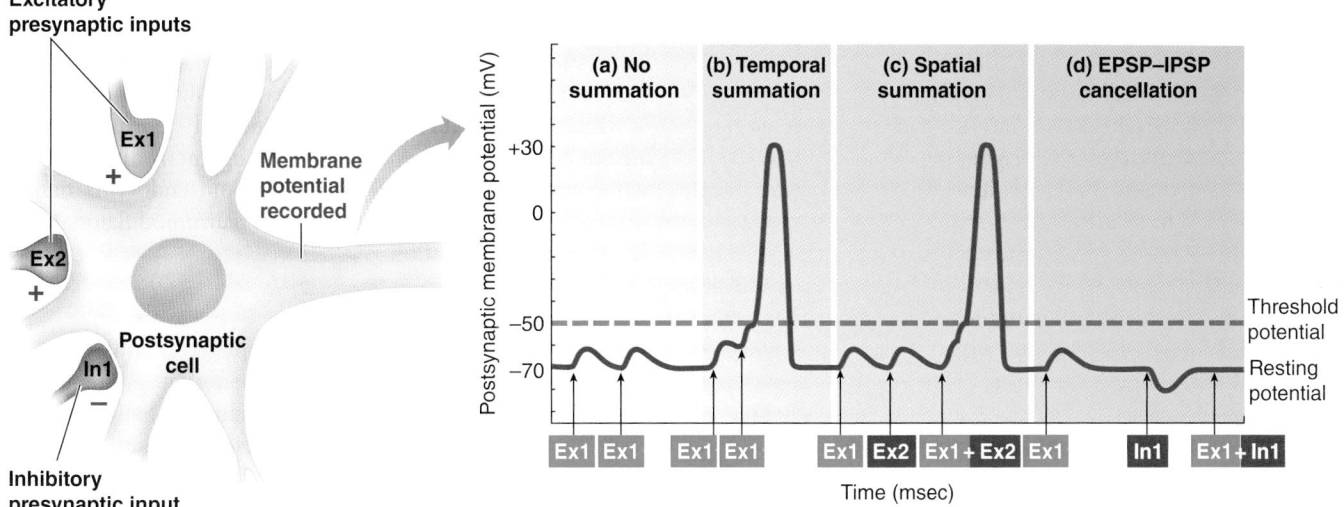

(a) If an excitatory presynaptic input (Ex1) is stimulated a second time after the first EPSP in the postsynaptic cell has died off, a second EPSP of the same magnitude will occur.

(b) If, however, Ex1 is stimulated a second time before the first EPSP has died off, the second EPSP will add on to, or sum with, the first EPSP, resulting in *temporal summation*, which may bring the postsynaptic cell to threshold.

(c) The postsynaptic cell may also be brought to threshold by *spatial summation* of EPSPs that are initiated by simultaneous activation of two (Ex1 and Ex2) or more excitatory presynaptic inputs.

(d) Simultaneous activation of an excitatory (Ex1) and inhibitory (In1) presynaptic input does not change the postsynaptic potential, because the resultant EPSP and IPSP cancel each other out.

● **FIGURE 4-16 Determination of the grand postsynaptic potential by the sum of activity in the presynaptic inputs.** Two excitatory (Ex1 and Ex2) and one inhibitory (In1) presynaptic inputs terminate on this hypothetical postsynaptic neuron. The potential of the postsynaptic neuron is being recorded. For simplicity in the figure, summation of two EPSPs brings the postsynaptic neuron to threshold, but in reality many EPSPs must sum to reach threshold.

CANCELLATION OF CONCURRENT EPSP AND IPSP If an excitatory and an inhibitory input are simultaneously activated, the concurrent EPSP and IPSP more or less cancel each other out. The extent of cancellation depends on their respective magnitudes. In most cases, the postsynaptic membrane potential remains close to resting potential (● Figure 4-16d).

IMPORTANCE OF POSTSYNAPTIC NEURONAL INTEGRATION The magnitude of the GPSP depends on the sum of activity in all presynaptic inputs and, in turn, determines whether or not the postsynaptic neuron will undergo an action potential to pass information on to the cells on which the neuron terminates. The following oversimplified real-life example demonstrates the benefits of this neuronal integration. The explanation is not completely accurate technically, but the principles of summation are accurate.

Assume for simplicity's sake that urination is controlled by a postsynaptic neuron that innervates the urinary bladder. When this neuron fires, the bladder contracts. (Actually, voluntary control of urination is accomplished by postsynaptic integration at the neuron controlling the external urethral sphincter rather than the bladder itself.) As the bladder fills with urine and becomes stretched, a reflex is initiated that ultimately produces EPSPs in the postsynaptic neuron responsible for causing bladder contraction. Partial filling of the bladder does not cause

enough excitation to bring the neuron to threshold, so urination does not take place. That is, action potentials do not occur frequently enough in presynaptic neuron Ex1, which fires reflexly in response to the degree of bladder stretching, to generate EPSPs close enough together in the postsynaptic neuron to bring the latter to threshold (● Figure 4-16a). As the bladder progressively fills, the frequency of action potentials progressively increases in presynaptic neuron Ex1, leading to more rapid formation of EPSPs in the postsynaptic neuron. Thus, the frequency of EPSP formation arising from Ex1 activity signals the postsynaptic neuron of the extent of bladder filling. When the bladder becomes sufficiently stretched that the Ex1-generated EPSPs are temporally summed to threshold, the postsynaptic neuron undergoes an action potential that stimulates bladder contraction (● Figure 4-16b).

What if the time is inopportune for urination to take place? Presynaptic inputs originating in higher levels of the brain responsible for voluntary control can produce IPSPs at the bladder postsynaptic neuron (In1 in ● Figure 4-16d). These "voluntary" IPSPs in effect cancel out the "reflex" EPSPs triggered by stretching of the bladder. Thus, the postsynaptic neuron remains at resting potential and does not have an action potential, so the bladder is prevented from contracting and emptying even though it is full.

What if a person's bladder is only partially filled, so that the presynaptic input from this source (Ex1) is insufficient to bring the postsynaptic neuron to threshold to cause bladder contraction, yet the individual needs to supply a urine specimen for laboratory analysis? The person can voluntarily activate another excitatory presynaptic neuron originating in higher brain levels (Ex2 in ● Figure 4-16c). The "voluntary" EPSPs arising from Ex2 activity and the "reflex" EPSPs arising from Ex1 activity are spatially summed to bring the postsynaptic neuron to threshold. This achieves the action potential necessary to stimulate bladder contraction, even though the bladder is not full.

This example illustrates the importance of postsynaptic neuronal integration. Each postsynaptic neuron in a sense "computes" all the input it receives and "decides" whether to pass the information on (that is, whether threshold is reached and an action potential is transmitted down the axon). In this way, neurons serve as complex computational devices, or integrators. The dendrites function as the primary processors of incoming information. They receive and tally the signals from all presynaptic neurons. Each neuron's output in the form of frequency of action potentials to other cells (muscle cells, gland cells, or other neurons) reflects the balance of activity in the inputs it receives via EPSPs or IPSPs from the thousands of other neurons that terminate on it. Each postsynaptic neuron filters out information that is not significant enough to bring it to threshold and does not pass it on. If every action potential in every presynaptic neuron that impinges on a particular postsynaptic neuron were to cause an action potential in the postsynaptic neuron, the neuronal pathways would be overwhelmed with trivia. Only if an excitatory presynaptic signal is reinforced by other supporting signals through summation will the information be passed on. Furthermore, interaction of EPSPs and IPSPs provides a way for one set of signals to offset another, allowing a fine degree of discrimination and control in determining what information will be passed on.

Some neurons secrete neuromodulators in addition to neurotransmitters.

In addition to secreting classical neurotransmitters that act rapidly to bring about a change in the potential of a postsynaptic neuron (an EPSP or an IPSP), some neurons co-secrete larger molecules known as **neuropeptides** from distinctly different vesicles in the axon terminal at the same time that the neurotransmitter is released. Most neuropeptides function as **neuromodulators** that do not cause the formation of EPSPs or IPSPs but instead act slowly to bring about long-term changes that subtly *modulate* (that is, depress or enhance) the action of the synapse. The neuronal receptors to which neuromodulators bind are not located on the subsynaptic membrane, and they do not directly alter membrane permeability and potential. Neuromodulators may act at either presynaptic or postsynaptic sites. For example, a neuromodulator may influence the level of an enzyme involved in the synthesis of a neurotransmitter by a presynaptic neuron, or it may alter the sensitivity of the postsynaptic neuron to a particular neurotransmitter by causing long-term changes in the number of subsynaptic receptors for the neurotransmitter.

Thus, neuromodulators delicately fine-tune the synaptic response. Whereas neurotransmitters are involved in rapid communication between neurons, neuromodulators are involved with more long-lasting events, such as learning and motivation.

Interestingly, the synaptically released neuromodulators include many substances that also have distinctly different roles as hormones released into the blood from endocrine tissues. Therefore, some hormones also act as neuromodulators to influence synaptic function.

Drugs and diseases can modify synaptic transmission.

 Most drugs that influence the nervous system function by altering synaptic mechanisms. Synaptic drugs may block an undesirable effect or enhance a desirable effect. Possible drug actions include (1) altering the synthesis, storage, or release of a neurotransmitter; (2) modifying neurotransmitter interaction with the postsynaptic receptor; (3) influencing neurotransmitter reuptake or destruction; and (4) replacing a deficient neurotransmitter with a substitute transmitter.

You already learned about SSRIs. As another example, the socially abused drug **cocaine** blocks the reuptake of the neurotransmitter *dopamine* at presynaptic terminals. It does so by binding competitively with the dopamine reuptake transporter, which is a protein molecule that picks up released dopamine from the synaptic cleft and shuttles it back to the axon terminal. With cocaine occupying the dopamine transporter, dopamine remains in the synaptic cleft longer than usual and continues to interact with its postsynaptic receptors. The result is prolonged activation of neural pathways that use this chemical as a neurotransmitter, especially pathways that play a role in feelings of pleasure. In essence, when cocaine is present, the neural switches in the pleasure pathway are locked in the "on" position.

Cocaine is addictive because the involved neurons become *desensitized* to the drug. After the postsynaptic cells are incessantly stimulated for an extended time, they can no longer transmit normally across synapses without increasingly larger doses of the drug. Specifically, with prolonged use of cocaine, the number of dopamine receptors in the brain is reduced in response to the glut of the abused substance. As a result of this desensitization, the user must steadily increase the dosage of the drug to get the same "high," or sensation of pleasure, a phenomenon known as *drug tolerance*. When the cocaine molecules diffuse away, the sense of pleasure evaporates, because the normal level of dopamine activity no longer "satisfies" the overly needy demands of the postsynaptic cells for stimulation. Cocaine users reaching this low become frantic and profoundly depressed. Only more cocaine makes them feel good again. But repeated use of cocaine often modifies responsiveness to the drug; the user no longer derives pleasure from the drug but suffers unpleasant *withdrawal symptoms* once its effect has worn off. The user typically becomes **addicted** to the drug, compulsively seeking it out, first to experience the pleasurable sensations and later to avoid the negative withdrawal symptoms. Cocaine is abused by millions who have become addicted to its mind-altering properties, with devastating social and economic effects.

Synaptic transmission is also vulnerable to neural toxins, which may cause nervous system disorders by acting at either presynaptic or postsynaptic sites. For example, **tetanus toxin** prevents the release of the neurotransmitter GABA from inhibitory presynaptic inputs terminating at neurons that supply skeletal muscles. Unchecked excitatory inputs to these neurons result in uncontrolled muscle spasms. These spasms occur especially in the jaw muscles early in the disease, giving rise to the common name of *lockjaw* for this condition. Later, they progress to the muscles responsible for breathing, at which point death occurs.

Many other drugs and diseases influence synaptic transmission, but as these examples illustrate, any site along the synaptic pathway is vulnerable to interference.

Neurons are linked through complex converging and diverging pathways.

Two important relationships exist between neurons: convergence and divergence. A given neuron may have many other neurons synapsing on it. Such a relationship is known as **convergence** (● Figure 4-17). Through converging input, a single cell is influenced by thousands of other cells. This single cell, in turn, influences the level of activity in many other cells by divergence of output. The term **divergence** refers to the branching of axon terminals so that a single cell synapses with and influences many other cells.

Note that a particular neuron is postsynaptic to the neurons converging on it but presynaptic to the other cells at which it terminates. Thus, the terms *presynaptic* and *postsynaptic* refer only to a single synapse. Most neurons are presynaptic to one group of neurons and postsynaptic to another group.

An estimated 100 billion neurons and 10^{14} (100 quadrillion) synapses are found in the brain alone! A single neuron may be connected to between 5000 and 10,000 other neurons. When you consider the vast and intricate interconnections possible among these neurons through converging and diverging pathways, you can begin to imagine the complexity of the wir-

ing mechanism of our nervous system. Even the most sophisticated computers are far less complex than the human brain. The "language" of the nervous system—that is, all communication among neurons—is in the form of graded potentials, action potentials, neurotransmitter signaling across synapses, and other nonsynaptic forms of chemical chatter. All activities for which the nervous system is responsible—every sensation, every command to move a muscle, every thought, every emotion, every memory, every spark of creativity—depend on the patterns of electrical and chemical signaling among neurons along these complexly wired neural pathways.

A neuron communicates with the cells it influences by releasing a neurotransmitter, but this is only one means of intercellular ("between cell") communication. We now consider all the ways by which cells can "talk" with one another.

Intercellular Communication and Signal Transduction

Coordination of the diverse activities of cells throughout the body to accomplish life-sustaining and other desired responses depends on the ability of cells to communicate with one another.

Communication among cells is largely orchestrated by extracellular chemical messengers.

Intercellular communication can take place either directly or indirectly (● Figure 4-18). *Direct* intercellular communication involves physical contact between the interacting cells:

1. *Through gap junctions.* The most intimate means of intercellular communication is through gap junctions, the minute tunnels that bridge the cytoplasm of neighboring cells in some types of tissues. Through gap junctions, small ions and molecules are directly exchanged between interacting cells without ever entering the ECF (see p. 53).

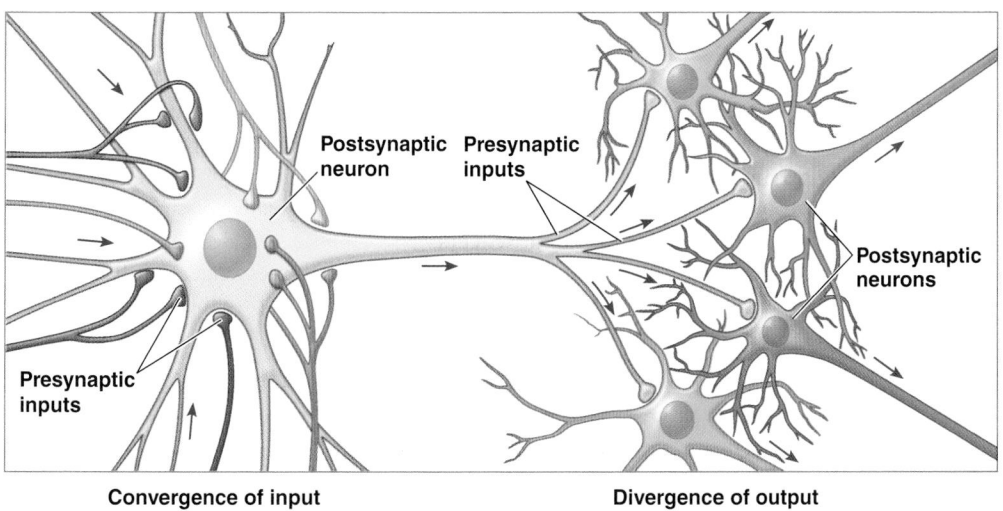

Convergence of input
(one cell is influenced
by many others)

Divergence of output
(one cell influences
many others)

● FIGURE 4-17 **Convergence and divergence.** Arrows indicate the direction in which information is being conveyed.

Postsynaptic neuron
Presynaptic inputs
Postsynaptic neurons
Presynaptic inputs

DIRECT INTERCELLULAR COMMUNICATION

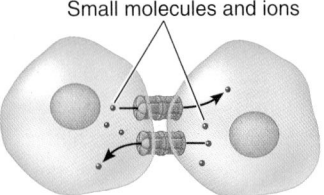

(a) Gap junctions

(b) Transient direct linkup of cells' surface markers

INDIRECT INTERCELLULAR COMMUNICATION VIA EXTRACELLULAR CHEMICAL MESSENGERS

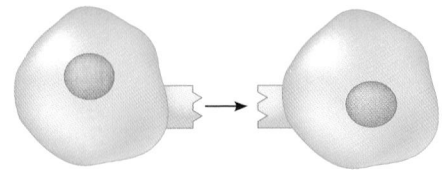

(c) Paracrine secretion

(d) Neurotransmitter secretion

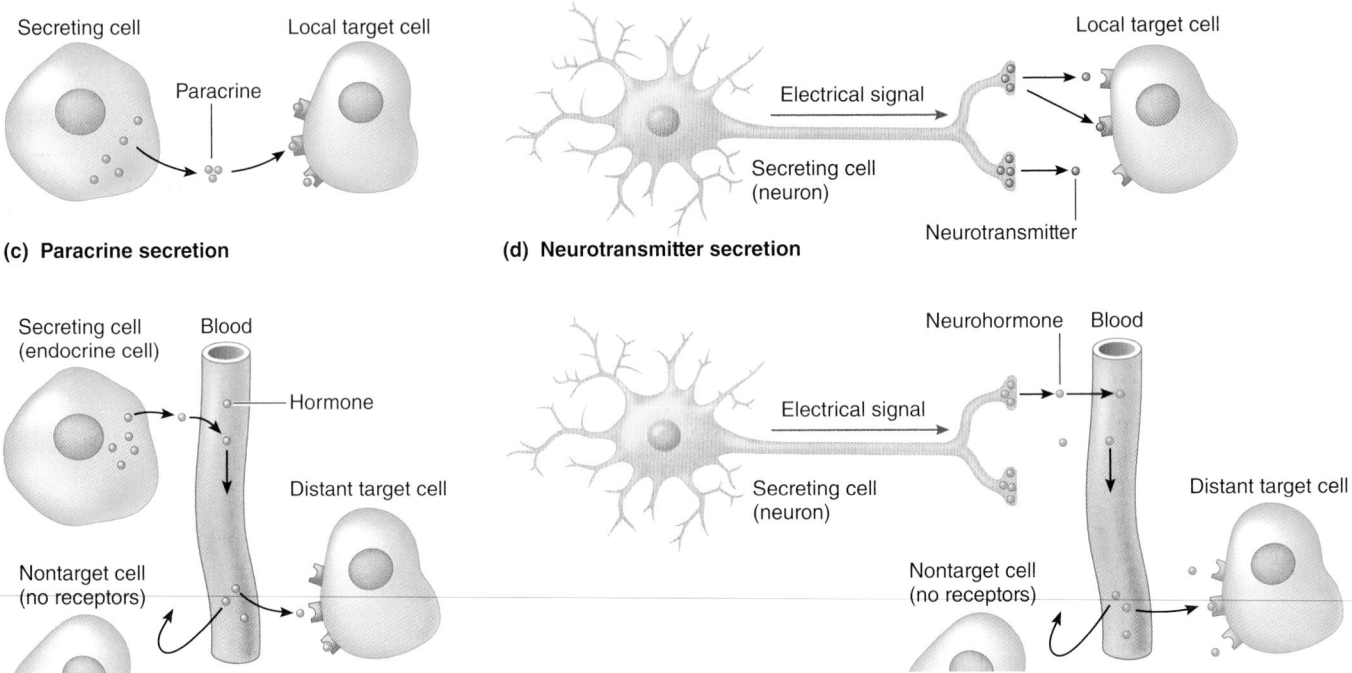

(e) Hormonal secretion

(f) Neurohormone secretion

● **FIGURE 4-18 Types of intercellular communication.** Gap junctions and transient direct linkup of cells by means of complementary surface markers are both means of direct communication between cells. Paracrines, neurotransmitters, hormones, and neurohormones are all extracellular chemical messengers that accomplish indirect communication between cells. These chemical messengers differ in their source and the distance they travel to reach their target cells.

2. *Through transient direct linkup of surface markers.* Some cells, such as those of the immune system, have specialized markers on the surface membrane that allow them to directly link with certain other cells that have compatible markers for transient interactions. This is how the cell-destroying immune cells of the body's defense system specifically recognize and selectively destroy only undesirable cells, such as cancer cells, while leaving the body's own healthy cells alone.

The most common means by which cells communicate with one another is *indirectly* through **extracellular chemical messengers** or **signal molecules,** of which there are four types: *paracrines, neurotransmitters, hormones,* and *neurohormones.* In each case, a specific chemical messenger, the signal molecule, is synthesized by specialized controlling cells to serve a designated purpose. On being released into the ECF by appropriate stimulation, these extracellular chemical messengers act on

other particular cells, the messenger's **target cells,** in a prescribed manner. To exert its effect, an extracellular chemical messenger must bind with target cell receptors specific for it. These receptors are specialized plasma membrane proteins (see p. 51). Different cell types have distinct combinations of receptors, allowing them to react individually to various regulatory chemical messengers.

The four types of chemical messengers differ in their source and the distance to and means by which they get to their site of action.

1. Paracrines are local chemical messengers whose effect is exerted only on neighboring cells in the immediate environment of their site of secretion. Because paracrines are distributed by simple diffusion within the interstitial fluid, their action is restricted to short distances. They do not gain entry to the blood in any significant quantity because they are rapidly inactivated by locally existing enzymes. One example of a paracrine is *histamine,* which is released from a specific type of connective tissue cell during an inflammatory response within an invaded or injured tissue (see p. 333). Among other things, histamine dilates (opens more widely) the blood vessels in the vicinity to increase blood flow to the tissue. This action brings additional blood-borne combat supplies into the affected area.

2. As you just learned, neurons communicate directly with the cells they innervate (their target cells) by releasing *neurotransmitters,* which are short-range chemical messengers, in response to electrical signals (action potentials). Like paracrines, neurotransmitters diffuse from their site of release across a narrow extracellular space to act locally on an adjoining target cell, which may be another neuron, a muscle, or a gland. Neurons themselves may carry electrical signals long distances (the length of the axon), but the chemical messenger released at the axon terminal acts at short range—just across the synaptic cleft.

3. Hormones are long-range chemical messengers specifically secreted into the blood by endocrine glands in response to an appropriate signal. The blood carries the messengers to other sites in the body, where they exert their effects on their target cells some distance from their site of release. Only the target cells of a particular hormone have membrane receptors for binding with this hormone. Nontarget cells are not influenced by any blood-borne hormones that reach them.

4. Neurohormones are hormones released into the blood by *neurosecretory neurons.* Like ordinary neurons, neurosecretory neurons can respond to and conduct electrical signals. Instead of directly innervating target cells, however, a neurosecretory neuron releases its chemical messenger, a neurohormone, into the blood on appropriate stimulation. The neurohormone is then distributed through the blood to distant target cells. Thus, like endocrine cells, neurosecretory neurons release blood-borne chemical messengers, whereas ordinary neurons secrete short-range neurotransmitters into a confined space. In the future, the general term *hormone* will tacitly include both blood-borne hormonal and neurohormonal messengers.

In every case, extracellular chemical messengers are released from one cell type and interact with other target cells to bring about a desired effect in the target cells. We now turn to how these chemical messengers cause the right cellular response.

Extracellular chemical messengers bring about cell responses primarily by signal transduction.

The term **signal transduction** refers to the process by which incoming signals (instructions from extracellular chemical messengers) are conveyed into the target cell, where they are transformed into the dictated cellular response. Binding of the extracellular chemical messenger amounts to a signal for the cell to get a certain job done. During signal transduction, the extracellular signal is transduced, or changed into a form necessary to modify intracellular activities to accomplish the desired outcome. (A *transducer* is a device that receives energy from one system and transmits it in a different form to another system. For example, your radio receives radio waves sent out from

the broadcast station and transmits these signals in the form of sound waves that can be detected by your ears.)

Signal transduction occurs by different mechanisms, depending on the messenger and the receptor type. Lipid-soluble extracellular chemical messengers, such as cholesterol-derived steroid hormones, gain entry into the cell by dissolving in and passing through the lipid bilayer of the target cell's plasma membrane. Thus, these extracellular chemical messengers bind to receptors inside the target cell to initiate the desired intracellular response themselves, usually by changing gene activity. By contrast, water-soluble extracellular chemical messengers cannot gain entry to the target cell because they are poorly soluble in lipid and cannot dissolve in the plasma membrane. The major water-soluble extracellular messengers are protein hormones delivered by the blood and neurotransmitters released from nerve endings. These messengers signal the cell to perform a given response by first binding with surface membrane receptors specific for that given messenger. This binding triggers a sequence of intracellular events that controls a particular cellular activity, such as membrane transport, secretion, metabolism, or contraction.

Despite the wide range of possible responses, binding of an extracellular messenger (also known as the **first messenger**) to its matching surface membrane receptor brings about the desired intracellular response primarily by two general means: (1) by *opening or closing chemically gated receptor-channels* or (2) by *activating second-messenger pathways via G-protein-coupled receptors.* Because of the universal nature of these events, let us examine each more closely.

Some extracellular chemical messengers open chemically gated receptor-channels.

Some extracellular messengers carry out the assigned task by opening or closing specific chemically gated receptor-channels to regulate movement of particular ions across the membrane. In this case, *the receptor itself serves as an ion channel.* When the appropriate extracellular messenger binds to the receptor-channel, the channel opens. An example is the opening of chemically gated receptor-channels in the subsynaptic membrane in response to neurotransmitter binding (see ● Figure 4-14). The resultant small, short-lived movement of given charge-carrying ions across the membrane through these open channels generates electrical signals—in this example, EPSPs and IPSPs.

Most extracellular chemical messengers activate second-messenger pathways via G-protein-coupled receptors.

Most extracellular chemical messengers that cannot enter their target cells do not act on chemically gated receptor-channels to bring about the desired intracellular response. Instead, these first messengers issue their orders by triggering a "Psst, pass it on" process, activating intracellular second-messenger pathways via binding with G-protein-coupled receptors.

The **second-messenger pathway** is initiated by binding of the first messenger (alias the extracellular chemical messenger, alias the signal molecule) to a surface membrane receptor specific for it. In this pathway, *the receptor is coupled with a G pro-*

tein, appropriately called a **G-protein-coupled receptor,** which snakes through the membrane (see ● Figure 4-20). Binding of the first messenger to the receptor activates the **G protein,** which is a membrane-bound intermediary that shuttles along the membrane to alter the activity of a nearby membrane protein called the **effector protein.** Once altered, the effector protein leads to an increased concentration of an intracellular messenger, known as the **second messenger.** The second messenger relays the orders through a series of biochemical reactions inside the cell that cause a change in the shape and function of designated proteins. These activated, designated proteins accomplish the cellular response dictated by the first messenger. Such a chain of reactions leading to a desired effect is called a **cascade.** The intracellular pathways activated by a second messenger are remarkably similar among different cells despite the diversity of ultimate responses. The variability in response depends on the specialization of the cell, not on the mechanism used.

 About half of all drugs prescribed today act on G-protein-coupled receptors. These receptors participate in some way in most body functions, so they are important targets for a variety of drugs used to treat diverse disorders. For example, they include drugs used to reduce high blood pressure, to treat congestive heart failure, to suppress stomach acid, to open airways in asthmatics, to ease symptoms of enlarged prostate, to block histamine-induced allergic responses, to relieve pain, and to treat hormone-dependent cancers.

Second-messenger pathways are widely used throughout the body, including being the key means by which most water-soluble hormones ultimately bring about their effects. Let us now turn our attention to hormonal communication, where we examine one of the most common second-messenger pathways (the cyclic adenosine monophosphate or cAMP second-messenger pathway) in more detail.

Introduction to Hormonal Communication

Endocrinology is the study of homeostatic chemical adjustments and other activities accomplished by hormones, which are secreted into the blood by endocrine glands. Earlier we described the underlying molecular and cellular mechanisms of the nervous system—electrical signaling within neurons and chemical transmission of signals between neurons. We now focus on the molecular and cellular features of hormonal action and compare the similarities and differences in how neurons and endocrine cells communicate with other cells in carrying out their regulatory actions.

Hormones are classified chemically as hydrophilic or lipophilic.

Hormones fall into two distinct chemical groups based on their solubility properties: *hydrophilic* and *lipophilic* hormones. Hormones can also be classified according to their biochemical structure (namely, *peptides, amines,* and *steroids*) as follows (▲ Table 4-3):

1. **Hydrophilic** ("water-loving") **hormones** are highly water soluble and have low lipid solubility. Most hydrophilic hormones are peptide or protein hormones consisting of specific amino acids arranged in a chain of varying length. The shorter chains are peptides, and the longer ones are proteins. For convenience, we refer to this entire category as **peptides.** Insulin from the pancreas is a peptide hormone. The **amines** are so called because they are amino acid derivatives. The amine hormones include one type of hydrophilic hormone (catecholamines) and one type of lipophilic hormone (thyroid hormone). *Catecholamines* are derived from the amino acid tyrosine and are largely secreted by the adrenal medulla. The adrenal gland consists of an inner adrenal medulla surrounded by an outer adrenal cortex. (You will learn more about the location and structure of the endocrine glands and the functions of specific hormones in later chapters.) Epinephrine is the major catecholamine hormone.

2. **Lipophilic** ("lipid-loving") **hormones** have high lipid solubility and are poorly soluble in water. Lipophilic hormones include thyroid hormone and the steroid hormones. *Thyroid hormone,* as its name implies, is secreted exclusively by the thyroid gland; it is an iodinated tyrosine derivative. Even though catecholamines and thyroid hormone are both derived from tyrosine, they behave differently because of their solubility properties. **Steroids** are neutral lipids derived from cholesterol. They include hormones secreted by the adrenal cortex, such as cortisol, and the sex hormones (testosterone in males and estrogen in females) secreted by the reproductive organs.

Minor differences in chemical structure among hormones within each category often result in profound differences in biological response. For example, in ● Figure 4-19, note the subtle difference between the steroid hormone testosterone, the male sex hormone responsible for inducing the development of masculine characteristics, and the steroid hormone estradiol, a form of estrogen, which is the feminizing female sex hormone.

The solubility properties of a hormone determine (1) how the hormone is processed by the endocrine cell, (2) how the hormone is transported in the blood, and (3) how the hormone exerts its effects at the target cell. We first consider the different ways in which these hormone types are processed at their site of origin, the endocrine cell, before comparing their means of transport and their mechanisms of action.

The mechanisms of synthesis, storage, and secretion of hormones vary according to their chemical differences.

Because of their chemical differences, the means by which the various types of hormones are synthesized, stored, and secreted differ.

PROCESSING OF HYDROPHILIC PEPTIDE HORMONES Peptide hormones are synthesized and secreted by the same steps used for manufacturing any protein that is exported from a cell (see ● Figure 2-3, p. 25). From the time peptide hormones are synthesized until they are secreted, they are always segregated from intracellular proteins within membrane-enclosed compartments. Here is a brief outline of these steps:

| Properties | Peptides | AMINES | | Steroids |
		Catecholamines	Thyroid Hormone	
Solubility	Hydrophilic	Hydrophilic	Lipophilic	Lipophilic
Structure	Chains of specific amino acids	Tyrosine derivative	Iodinated tyrosine derivative	Cholesterol derivative
Synthesis	In the rough endoplasmic reticulum; packaged in the Golgi complex	In the cytosol	In the colloid within the thyroid gland (see p. 545)	Stepwise modification of cholesterol molecules in various intracellular compartments
Storage	Large amounts in secretory granules	In secretory granules	In the colloid	Not stored; the cholesterol precursor is stored in lipid droplets
Secretion	Exocytosis of granules	Exocytosis of granules	Endocytosis of the colloid	Simple diffusion
Transport in blood	As a free hormone	Half bound to plasma proteins	Mostly bound to plasma proteins	Mostly bound to plasma proteins
Receptor site	Surface of the target cell	Surface of the target cell	Inside the target cell	Inside the target cell
Mechanism of action	Activation of a second-messenger pathway to alter the activity of pre-existing proteins that produce the effect	Activation of a second-messenger pathway to alter the activity of pre-existing proteins that produce the effect	Activation of specific genes to make new proteins that produce the effect	Activation of specific genes to make new proteins that produce the effect
Hormones of this type	Most hormones	Hormones from the adrenal medulla	Hormones from thyroid follicular cells	Hormones from the adrenal cortex and gonads and some placental hormones

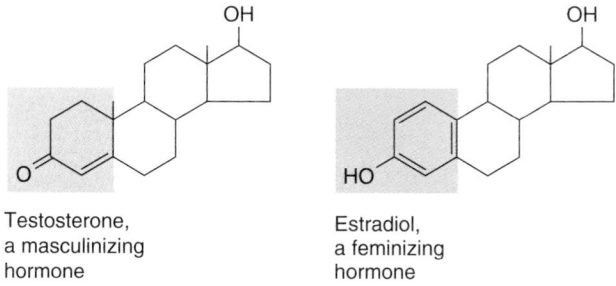

Testosterone, a masculinizing hormone

Estradiol, a feminizing hormone

● **FIGURE 4-19 Comparison of two steroid hormones, testosterone and estradiol.**

1. Large precursor proteins, or **preprohormones,** are synthesized by ribosomes on the rough endoplasmic reticulum (ER). They then migrate to the Golgi complex in membrane-enclosed transport vesicles that pinch off from the smooth ER.

2. During their journey through the ER and Golgi complex, the preprohormones are pruned to active hormones.

3. The Golgi complex packages the finished hormones into secretory vesicles that are pinched off and stored in the cytoplasm until an appropriate signal triggers their secretion.

4. On appropriate stimulation, the secretory vesicles fuse with the plasma membrane and release their contents to the out-

side by exocytosis (see p. 26). The blood then picks up the secreted hormones for distribution.

PROCESSING OF LIPOPHILIC STEROID HORMONES All steroidogenic (steroid-producing) cells perform the following steps to produce and release their hormonal product:

1. Cholesterol is the common precursor for all steroid hormones.

2. Synthesis of the various steroid hormones from cholesterol requires a series of enzymatic reactions that modify the basic cholesterol molecule—for example, by varying the type and position of side groups attached to the cholesterol framework. Each conversion from cholesterol to a specific steroid hormone requires the help of particular enzymes limited to certain steroidogenic organs. Thus, each steroidogenic organ can produce only the steroid hormone or hormones for which it has a complete set of appropriate enzymes. For example, a key enzyme necessary for producing cortisol is found only in the adrenal cortex, so no other steroidogenic organ can produce this hormone.

3. Unlike peptide hormones, steroid hormones are not stored. Once formed, the lipid-soluble steroid hormones immediately diffuse through the steroidogenic cell's lipid plasma membrane to enter the blood. Only the hormone precursor cholesterol is

stored in significant quantities within steroidogenic cells. Accordingly, the rate of steroid hormone secretion is controlled entirely by the rate of hormone synthesis. In contrast, peptide hormone secretion is controlled primarily by regulating the release of presynthesized stored hormone.

4. Following their secretion into the blood, some steroid hormones, as well as thyroid hormone, undergo further interconversions within the blood or other organs, where they are changed into more potent or different hormones.

The adrenomedullary catecholamines and thyroid hormone have unique synthetic and secretory pathways that are described when we address each of these hormones specifically in the endocrine chapter, Chapter 17.

Hydrophilic hormones dissolve in the plasma; lipophilic hormones are transported by plasma proteins.

All hormones are carried by the blood, but they are not all transported in the same manner:

■ The hydrophilic peptide hormones simply dissolve in the blood.

■ Lipophilic steroids and thyroid hormone, which are poorly soluble in water, cannot dissolve to any extent in the watery blood. Instead, most lipophilic hormones circulate to their target cells reversibly bound to plasma proteins in the blood. Some plasma proteins carry only one type of hormone, whereas others, such as albumin, indiscriminately pick up any "hitchhiking" hormone.

Only the small, unbound, freely dissolved fraction of a lipophilic hormone is biologically active (that is, free to cross capillary walls and bind with target cell receptors to exert an effect). The bound form of steroid and thyroid hormones provides a large reserve of these lipophilic hormones that can be used to replenish the active free pool. To maintain normal endocrine function, the magnitude of the small, free, effective pool, rather than the total blood concentration of a particular lipophilic hormone, is monitored and adjusted.

 *Clinical Note* The chemical properties of a hormone dictate not only the means by which blood transports it but also the way in which it can be artificially introduced into the blood for therapeutic purposes. Because the digestive system does not secrete enzymes that can digest steroid and thyroid hormones, hormones such as the sex steroids contained in birth control pills can, when taken orally, be absorbed intact from the digestive tract into the blood. No other type of hormones can be taken orally, because protein-digesting enzymes would attack and convert them into inactive fragments. Therefore, these hormones must be administered by nonoral routes; for example, insulin deficiency is typically treated with daily injections of insulin.

Next, we examine how the hydrophilic and lipophilic hormones vary in their mechanisms of action at their target cells.

Hormones generally produce their effect by altering intracellular proteins.

To induce their effect, hormones must bind with target cell receptors specific for them. Each interaction between a particular hormone and a target cell receptor produces a highly characteristic response that differs among hormones and among different target cells influenced by the same hormone. Both the location of the receptors within the target cell and the mechanism by which binding of the hormone with the receptors brings about a response vary, depending on the hormone's solubility characteristics.

LOCATION OF RECEPTORS FOR HYDROPHILIC AND LIPOPHILIC HORMONES Hormones can be grouped into two categories based on the primary location of their receptors:

1. The hydrophilic peptides and catecholamines, which are poorly soluble in lipid, cannot pass through the lipid membrane barriers of their target cells. Instead, they bind with specific receptors on the *outer plasma membrane surface* of the target cell.

2. The lipophilic steroids and thyroid hormone easily pass through the surface membrane to bind with specific receptors located *inside* the target cell.

GENERAL MEANS OF HYDROPHILIC AND LIPOPHILIC HORMONE ACTION Even though hormones cause a wide variety of responses, they ultimately influence their target cells by altering the cell's proteins in one of two major ways:

1. Surface-binding hydrophilic hormones function largely by *activating second-messenger pathways* within the target cell. This activation directly *alters the activity of preexisting intracellular proteins,* usually enzymes, to produce the desired effect.

2. Lipophilic hormones function mainly *by activating specific genes* in the target cell to cause *formation of new intracellular proteins,* which in turn produce the desired effect. The new proteins may be enzymatic or structural.

Let us examine the two major mechanisms of hormonal action (activation of second-messenger pathways and activation of genes) in more detail.

Hydrophilic hormones alter preexisting proteins via second-messenger systems.

Most hydrophilic hormones (peptides and catecholamines) bind to G-protein-coupled surface membrane receptors and produce their effects in their target cells by acting through a second-messenger pathway to alter the activity of preexisting proteins. There are two major second-messenger pathways: One uses **cyclic adenosine monophosphate** (**cyclic AMP,** or **cAMP**) as a second messenger, and the other employs Ca^{2+} in this role. Both pathways use a G protein, which is found on the inner surface of the plasma membrane, as an intermediary between the receptor and the effector protein (● Figure 4-20). An inactive G protein consists of a complex of alpha (α), beta (β), and gamma (γ) subunits. When an appropriate extracellular messenger (a first messenger) binds with its receptor, the receptor attaches to the associated G protein, activating the G protein. Different G proteins are activated in response to binding of various first messengers to their respective surface receptors. Once activated, the α subunit breaks away from the G-protein complex and moves along the inner surface of the

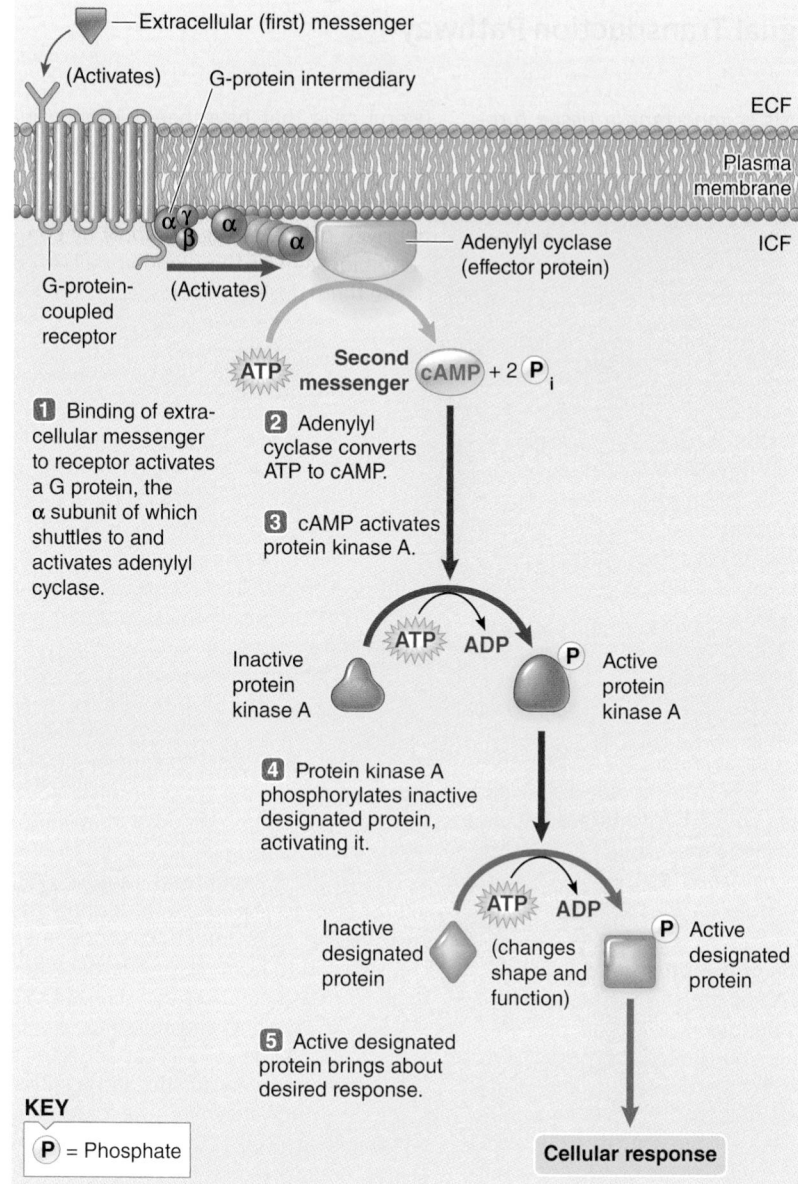

1 Binding of extra-cellular messenger to receptor activates a G protein, the α subunit of which shuttles to and activates adenylyl cyclase.

2 Adenylyl cyclase converts ATP to cAMP.

3 cAMP activates protein kinase A.

4 Protein kinase A phosphorylates inactive designated protein, activating it.

5 Active designated protein brings about desired response.

KEY

P = Phosphate

● **FIGURE 4-20 Mechanism of action of hydrophilic hormones via activation of the cyclic AMP second-messenger pathway.**

plasma membrane until it reaches an effector protein. An effector protein is either an enzyme or an ion channel within the membrane. The α subunit links up with the effector protein and alters its activity. Researchers have identified more than 300 different receptors that convey instructions of extracellular messengers through the membrane to effector proteins by means of G proteins. Different second-messenger pathways influence different effector proteins. We next examine the cAMP pathway in more detail as an example of what happens after an effector protein is activated.

cAMP SECOND-MESSENGER PATHWAY Cyclic AMP is the most widely used second messenger. In the following description of the cAMP pathway, the numbered steps correlate to the numbered steps in ● Figure 4-20. When the appropriate extracellular messenger binds to its surface membrane receptor and activates the associated G protein, the G protein in turn activates

the effector protein, in this case, the enzyme **adenylyl cyclase** (step **1**), which is located on the cytoplasmic side of the plasma membrane. Adenylyl cyclase converts intracellular adenosine triphosphate (ATP) to cAMP by cleaving off two of the phosphates (step **2**). (This is the same ATP used as the common energy currency in the body.) Acting as the intracellular second messenger, cAMP triggers a preprogrammed series of biochemical steps within the cell to bring about the response dictated by the first messenger. To begin, cAMP activates a specific intracellular enzyme, **protein kinase A** (step **3**). Protein kinase A, in turn, *phosphorylates* (transfers a phosphate group from ATP to) a designated preexisting intracellular protein, such as an enzyme important in a particular metabolic pathway. Phosphorylation causes the protein to change its shape and function, thereby activating it (step **4**). This activated protein brings about the target cell's ultimate response to the first messenger (step **5**). For example, the activity of a particular enzymatic protein that regulates a specific metabolic event may be increased or decreased.

Note that in this signal transduction pathway the steps involving the extracellular first messenger, the receptor, the G-protein complex, and the effector protein occur *in the plasma membrane* and lead to activation of the second messenger. The extracellular messenger cannot enter the cell to "personally" deliver its message to the proteins that carry out the desired response. Instead, it initiates membrane events that activate an intracellular second messenger, cAMP. The second messenger then triggers a chain reaction of biochemical events *inside the cell* that leads to the cellular response.

Different types of cells have different proteins available for phosphorylation and modification by protein kinase A. Therefore, a *common second messenger such as cAMP can cause widely differing responses in different cells,* depending on what proteins are modified. Cyclic AMP can be thought of as a molecular "switch" that can "turn on" (or "turn off") different cell events, depending on the kinds of protein activity ultimately modified in the various target cells. The type of proteins altered by a second messenger depends on the unique specialization of a particular cell type. This can be likened to being able to either illuminate or cool a room depending on whether the wall switch you flip on is wired to a device specialized to shed light (a chandelier) or one specialized to create air movement (a ceiling fan). In the body, the variable responsiveness once the switch is turned on results from genetically programmed differences in the sets of proteins within different cells. For example, depending on its cellular location, activating the cAMP pathway can modify heart rate in the heart, stimulate the formation of female sex hormones in the ovaries, break down stored glucose in the liver, control water conservation during urine formation in the kid-

Programmed Cell Suicide: A Surprising Example of a Signal Transduction Pathway

pathways triggered by the binding of an extracellular chemical messenger to a cell's surface membrane receptor are aimed at promoting proper functioning, growth, survival, or reproduction of the cell. But every cell also has an unusual built-in pathway that, if triggered, causes the cell to commit suicide by activating intracellular protein-snipping enzymes, which slice the cell into small, disposable pieces. Such intentional, programmed cell death is called **apoptosis.** (This term means "dropping off," in reference to the dropping off of cells that are no longer useful, much as autumn leaves drop off trees.) Apoptosis is a normal part of life—individual cells that have become superfluous or disordered are triggered to self-destruct for the greater good of maintaining the whole body's health.

Roles of Apoptosis

Here are examples of the vital roles played by this intrinsic sacrificial program:

■ *Predictable self-elimination of selected cells is a normal part of development.* Certain unwanted cells produced during development are programmed to kill themselves as the body is sculpted into its final form. During the development of a female, for example, apoptosis deliberately removes the embryonic ducts capable of forming a male reproductive tract. Likewise, apoptosis carves fingers from a mitten-shaped developing hand by eliminating the weblike membranes between them.

■ *Apoptosis is important in tissue turnover in the adult body.* Optimal functioning of most tissues depends on a balance between controlled production of new cells and regulated cell self-destruction. This balance maintains the proper number of cells in a given tissue while ensuring a controlled supply of fresh cells that are at their peak of performance.

■ *Programmed cell death plays an important role in the immune system.* Apoptosis provides a means to remove cells infected with harmful viruses. Furthermore, infection-fighting white blood cells that have finished their prescribed function and are no longer needed execute themselves.

■ *Undesirable cells that threaten homeostasis are typically culled from the body by apoptosis.* Included in this hit list are aged cells, cells that have suffered irreparable damage by exposure to radiation or other poisons, and cells that have somehow gone awry. Many mutated cells are eliminated by this means before they become fully cancerous.

Comparison of Apoptosis and Necrosis

Apoptosis is not the only means by which a cell can die, but it is the neatest way. Apoptosis is a controlled, intentional, tidy way of removing individual cells that are no longer needed or that pose a threat to the body. The other form of cell death, **necrosis** (meaning "making dead"), is uncontrolled, accidental, messy murder of useful cells that have been severely injured by an agent external to the cell, as by a physical blow, oxygen deprivation, or disease. For example, heart muscle cells deprived of their oxygen supply by complete blockage of the blood vessels supplying them during a heart attack die as a result of necrosis (see p. 271).

Even though necrosis and apoptosis both result in cell death, the steps involved are different. In necrosis the dying cells are passive victims, whereas in apoptosis the cells actively participate in their own deaths. In necrosis, the injured cell cannot pump out Na^+ as usual. As a result, water streams in by osmosis, causing the cell to swell and rupture. Typically, in necrosis the insult that prompted cell death injures many cells in the vicinity, so many neighboring cells swell and rupture together. Release of intracellular contents into the surrounding tissues initiates an inflammatory response at the damaged site (see p. 333). Unfortunately, this inflammatory response may harm healthy neighboring cells.

By contrast, apoptosis targets individual cells for destruction, leaving the surrounding cells intact. A condemned cell signaled to commit suicide detaches itself from its neighbors and then shrinks instead of swelling and bursting. As its lethal weapon, the suicidal cell activates a cascade of normally inactive intracellular protein-cutting enzymes, the **caspases,** which kill the cell from within. The unleashed caspases act like molecular scissors to systematically dismantle the cell.

---

neys, create simple memory traces in the brain, or cause perception of a sweet taste by a taste bud. (See the boxed feature on pp. 104–105, ▶ Beyond the Basics, for a description of a surprising signal-transduction pathway—one that causes a cell to kill itself.)

After the response is completed and the first messenger is removed, the α subunit rejoins the β and γ subunits to restore the inactive G-protein complex. Cyclic AMP and the other participating chemicals are inactivated so that the intracellular message is "erased" and the response can be terminated. Otherwise, once triggered, the response would go on indefinitely until the cell ran out of necessary supplies.

Many hydrophilic hormones use cAMP as their second messenger. A few use intracellular Ca^{2+} in this role. In other cells, the second messenger is still unknown. Remember that activation of second messengers is a universal mechanism employed by various other extracellular messengers in addition to hydrophilic hormones.

AMPLIFICATION BY A SECOND-MESSENGER PATHWAY Several remaining points about receptor activation and the ensuing events merit attention. First, considering the number of steps in a second-messenger relay chain, you might wonder why so many cell types use the same complex system to accomplish such a range of functions. The multiple steps of a second-messenger pathway are actually advantageous because the cascading (multiplying) effect of these pathways greatly amplifies the initial signal. *Amplification* means that the output of a system is greater than the input. Using the cAMP pathway as an example, binding of one extracellular messenger molecule to a receptor activates several adenylyl cyclase molecules (let us arbitrarily say 10), each of which activates many (in our hypothetical ex-

Snipping protein after protein, they chop up the nucleus, disassembling its life-essential deoxyribonucleic acid (DNA); break down the internal shape-holding cytoskeleton; and finally fragment the cell itself into disposable membrane-enclosed packets (see accompanying photo). Importantly, the contents of the dying cell remain wrapped by plasma membrane throughout the entire self-execution process, thus avoiding the spewing of potentially harmful intracellular contents characteristic of necrosis. No inflammatory response is triggered, so no neighboring cells are harmed. Instead, cells in the vicinity swiftly engulf and destroy the apoptotic cell fragments by phagocytosis. The breakdown products are recycled for other purposes as needed. The tissue as a whole has continued to function normally while the targeted cell has unobtrusively killed itself.

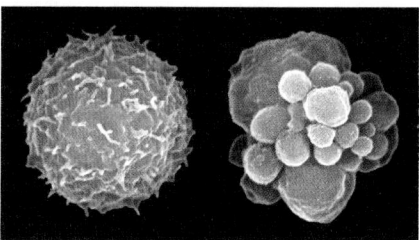

A normal cell (left) and a cell undergoing apoptosis (right).

Control of Apoptosis

If every cell contains caspases, what normally keeps these powerful self-destructive enzymes under control (that is, in inactive form) in cells that are useful to the body and deserve to live? Likewise, what activates the death-wielding caspase cascade in unwanted cells destined to eliminate themselves? Given the importance of these life-or-death decisions, it is not surprising that multiple pathways tightly control whether a cell is "to be or not to be." A cell normally receives a constant stream of "survival signals," which reassure the cell that it is useful to the body, that all is right in the internal environment surrounding the cell, and that everything is in good working order within the cell. These signals include tissue-specific growth factors, certain hormones, and appropriate contact with neighboring cells and the extracellular matrix. These extracellular survival signals trigger intracellular pathways that block activation of the caspase cascade, thus restraining the cell's death machinery. Most cells are programmed to commit suicide if they do not receive their normal reassuring survival signals. With the usual safeguards removed, the lethal protein-snipping enzymes are unleashed. For example, withdrawal of growth factors or detachment from the extracellular matrix causes a cell to promptly execute itself.

Furthermore, cells display "death receptors" in their plasma membrane that receive specific extracellular "death signals," such as a particular hormone or a specific chemical messenger from white blood cells. Activation of death pathways by these signals can override the life-saving pathways triggered by the survival signals. The death-signal transduction pathway swiftly ignites the internal apoptotic machinery, driving the cell to its own demise. Likewise, the self-execution machinery is set in motion when a cell suffers irreparable intracellular damage. Thus, some signals block apoptosis, and others promote it. Whether a cell lives or dies depends on which of these competing signals dominates at any given time. Although all cells have the same death machinery, they vary in the specific signals that induce them to commit suicide.

Considering that every cell's life hangs in delicate balance at all times, it is not surprising that faulty control of apoptosis—resulting in either too much or too little cell suicide—appears to participate in many major diseases. Excessive apoptotic activity is believed to contribute to the brain cell death associated with Alzheimer's disease, Parkinson's disease, and stroke, as well as to the premature demise of important infection-fighting cells in AIDS. Conversely, too little apoptosis most likely plays a role in cancer. Evidence suggests that cancer cells fail to respond to the normal extracellular signals that promote cell death. Because these cells neglect to die on cue, they grow in unchecked fashion, forming a chaotic, out-of-control mass.

Apoptosis is currently one of the hottest topics of investigation in the field. Researchers are scrambling to sort out the multiple factors involved in the signal transduction pathways controlling this process. Their hope is to find ways to tinker with the apoptotic machinery and thus discover badly needed new therapies for treating various big killers.

---

ample, let us say 100) cAMP molecules. Each cAMP molecule then acts on a single protein kinase A, which phosphorylates and thereby influences many (again, let's say 100) specific proteins, such as enzymes. Each enzyme, in turn, is responsible for producing many (perhaps 100) molecules of a particular product, such as a secretory product. The result of this cascade, with one event triggering the next in sequence, is a tremendous amplification of the initial signal. In our hypothetical example, one extracellular messenger molecule has been responsible for inducing a yield of 10 million molecules of a secretory product. In this way, very low concentrations of hormones and other chemical messengers can trigger pronounced cell responses.

REGULATION OF RECEPTORS Although membrane receptors are links between extracellular first messengers and intracellular second messengers in the regulation of specific cellular activities, the receptors themselves are also often subject to regulation. In many instances, receptor number and affinity (attraction of a receptor for its chemical messenger) can be altered, depending on the circumstances. For example, a chronic elevation in blood insulin levels leads to a reduction in the number of insulin receptors, thus lessening the responsiveness of this hormone's target cells to its high levels.

Many diseases can be linked to malfunctioning receptors or to defects in the ensuing signal-transduction pathways. For example, defective receptors are responsible for *Laron dwarfism*. In this condition, the person is abnormally short, despite having normal levels of growth hormone, because the tissues cannot respond normally to growth hormone. This is in contrast to the more usual type of dwarfism in which the person is abnormally short because of growth hormone deficiency.

Having examined the means by which hydrophilic hormones alter their target cells, we now focus on the mechanism of lipophilic hormone action.

By stimulating genes, lipophilic hormones promote synthesis of new proteins.

All lipophilic hormones (steroids and thyroid hormone) bind with intracellular receptors and primarily produce effects in their target cells by activating specific genes that cause the synthesis of new proteins, as summarized in ● Figure 4-21.

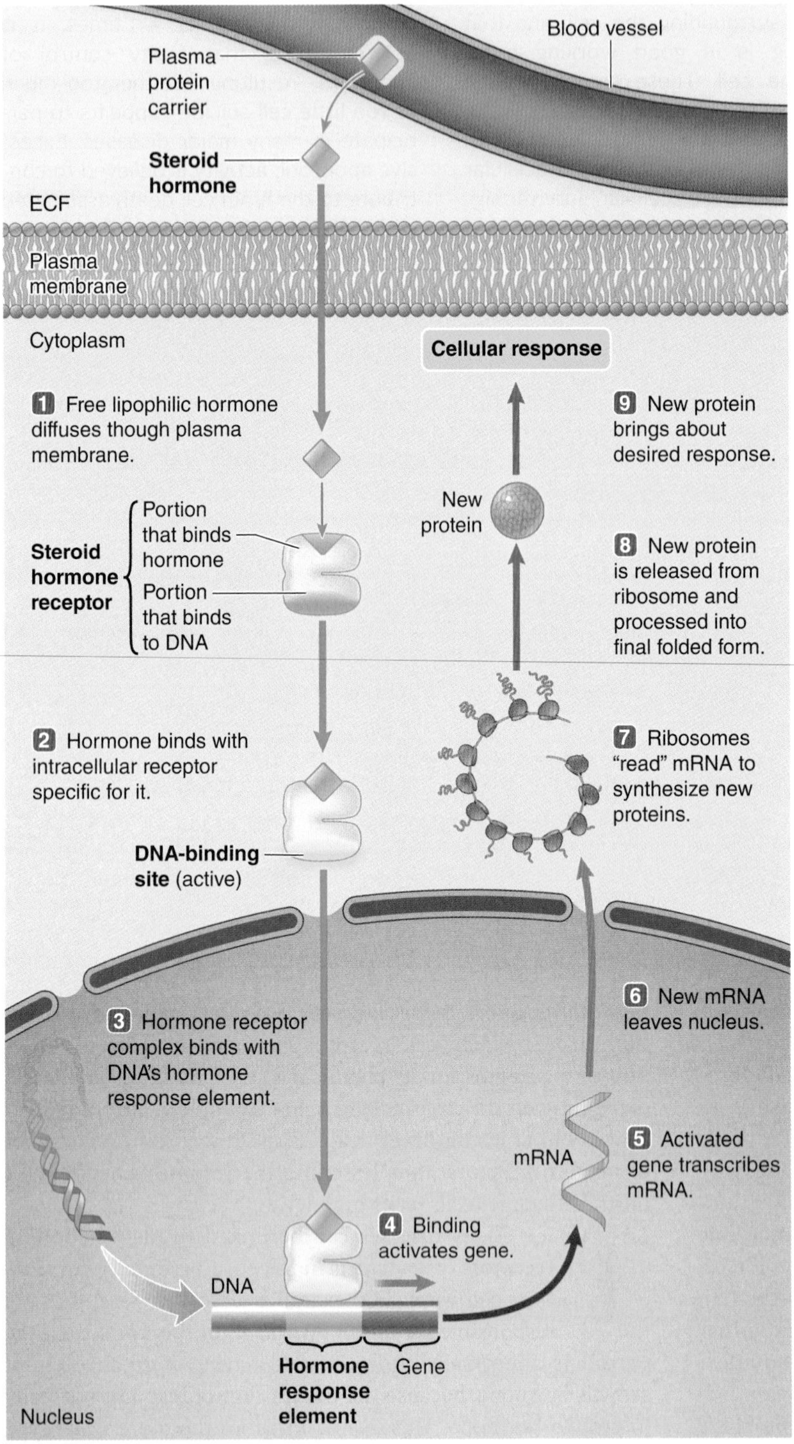

Free lipophilic hormone (hormone not bound with its plasma–protein carrier) diffuses through the plasma membrane of the target cell (step **1**) and binds with its specific receptor inside the cell, either in the cytoplasm or in the nucleus (step **2**). Each receptor has a specific region for binding with its hormone and another region for binding with DNA. The receptor cannot bind with DNA unless it first binds with the hormone. Once the hormone is bound to the receptor, the hormone receptor complex binds with DNA at a specific attachment site on the DNA known as the **hormone response element (HRE)** (step **3**). Different steroid hormones and thyroid hormone, once bound with their respective receptors, attach at different HREs on DNA. For example, the estrogen receptor complex binds at DNA's *estrogen response element*.

Binding of the hormone receptor complex with DNA "turns on" or activates a specific gene within the target cell (step **4**). This gene contains a code for synthesizing a given protein. The code of the activated gene is transcribed into complementary messenger ribonucleic acid (mRNA) (step **5**). The new mRNA leaves the nucleus and enters the cytoplasm (step **6**), where it binds to ribosomes, the "workbenches" that mediate the assembly of new proteins. Here, mRNA directs the synthesis of the designated new proteins according to the DNA code in the activated genes (step **7**). The newly synthesized protein, either enzymatic or structural, is released from the ribosome (step **8**) and produces the target cell's ultimate response to the hormone (step **9**). By means of this mechanism, different genes are activated by different lipophilic hormones, resulting in different biological effects.

Next, we compare the similarities and differences between neural and hormonal responses at the system level.

Comparison of the Nervous and Endocrine Systems

The nervous and endocrine systems are the two main regulatory systems of the body. The **nervous system** swiftly transmits electrical impulses to the skeletal muscles and the exocrine glands that it innervates. The **endocrine system** secretes hormones into the blood for delivery to distant sites of action. Although these two systems differ in many respects, they have much in common (▲ Table 4-4). They both alter their target cells (their sites of action) by releasing chemical messengers (neurotransmitters in the case of neurons, hormones in the case of endocrine cells) that bind with specific receptors of the target cells. This

1 Free lipophilic hormone diffuses though plasma membrane.

2 Hormone binds with intracellular receptor specific for it.

3 Hormone receptor complex binds with DNA's hormone response element.

4 Binding activates gene.

5 Activated gene transcribes mRNA.

6 New mRNA leaves nucleus.

7 Ribosomes "read" mRNA to synthesize new proteins.

8 New protein is released from ribosome and processed into final folded form.

9 New protein brings about desired response.

● **FIGURE 4-21 Mechanism of action of lipophilic hormones via activation of genes.**

Property	Nervous System	Endocrine System
Anatomic Arrangement	A "wired" system: a specific structural arrangement exists between neurons and their target cells, with structural continuity in the system	A "wireless" system: endocrine glands are widely dispersed and not structurally related to one another or to their target cells
Type of Chemical Messenger	Neurotransmitters released into the synaptic cleft	Hormones released into the blood
Distance of Action of the Chemical Messenger	Short distance (diffuses across the synaptic cleft)	Long distance (carried by the blood)
Specificity of Action on the Target Cell	Dependent on the close anatomic relationship between neurons and their target cells	Dependent on the specificity of target cell binding and responsiveness to a particular hormone
Speed of Response	Generally rapid (milliseconds)	Generally slow (minutes to hours)
Duration of Action	Brief (milliseconds)	Long (minutes to days or longer)
Major Functions	Coordinates rapid, precise responses	Controls activities that require long duration rather than speed

binding triggers the cellular response dictated by the regulatory system.

Now let us examine the anatomic distinctions between these two systems and the different ways in which they accomplish specificity of action.

The nervous system is "wired," and the endocrine system is "wireless."

Anatomically, the nervous and endocrine systems are quite different. In the nervous system, each neuron terminates directly on its specific target cells; that is, the nervous system is "wired" into highly organized, distinct anatomic pathways for transmission of signals from one part of the body to another. Information is carried along chains of neurons to the desired destination through action potential propagation coupled with synaptic transmission. In contrast, the endocrine system is a "wireless" system in that the endocrine glands are not anatomically linked with their target cells. Instead, the endocrine chemical messengers are secreted into the blood and delivered to distant target sites. In fact, the components of the endocrine system itself are not anatomically interconnected; the endocrine glands are scattered throughout the body (see ● Figure 17-1, p. 528). These glands constitute a system in a functional sense, however, because they all secrete hormones and many interactions take place among various endocrine glands.

Neural specificity is due to anatomic proximity, and endocrine specificity is due to receptor specialization.

As a result of their anatomic differences, the nervous and endocrine systems accomplish specificity of action by distinctly different means. Specificity of neural communication depends on neurons having a close anatomic relationship with their target cells, so each neuron has a very narrow range of influence. A neurotransmitter is released only to specific adjacent target cells and then is swiftly inactivated or removed before it can enter the blood. The target cells for a particular neuron have receptors for the neurotransmitter, but so do many other cells in other locations, and they could respond to this same mediator if it were delivered to them. For example, the entire system of neurons (called motor neurons) supplying your skeletal muscles uses the same neurotransmitter, *acetylcholine (ACh),* and all your skeletal muscles bear complementary ACh receptors (see Chapter 8). Yet you can wiggle your big toe without influencing any of your other muscles because ACh can be discretely released from the motor neurons specifically wired to the muscles controlling your toe. If ACh were indiscriminately released into the blood, as are hormones, all the skeletal muscles would simultaneously respond by contracting, because they all have identical receptors for ACh. This does not happen because of the precise wiring patterns that provide direct lines of communication between motor neurons and their target cells.

This specificity sharply contrasts to the way specificity of communication is built into the endocrine system. Because hormones travel in the blood, they reach virtually all tissues. Yet only specific target cells can respond to each hormone. Specificity of hormonal action depends on specialization of target cell receptors. For a hormone to exert its effect, the hormone must first bind with receptors specific for it that are located only on or in the hormone's target cells. Target cell receptors are highly selective in their binding function. A receptor recognizes a specific hormone because a portion of its conformation matches a unique portion of its binding hormone in "lock-and-key" fashion. Binding of a hormone with target cell receptors initiates a reaction that culminates in the hormone's final effect. The hormone cannot influence any other cells because nontarget cells lack the right binding receptors. Likewise, a given target cell has receptors that are "tuned" to recognize only one or a few of the many hormones that circulate in its vicinity. Other signals pass by without effect because the cell has no receptors for them.

The nervous and endocrine systems have their own realms of authority but interact functionally.

The nervous and endocrine systems are specialized for controlling different types of activities. In general, the nervous system governs the coordination of rapid, precise responses. It is especially important in the body's interactions with the external environment. Neural signals in the form of action potentials are rapidly propagated along neuronal fibers, resulting in the release at the axon terminal of a neurotransmitter that must diffuse only a microscopic distance to its target cell before a response is effected. A neurally mediated response is not only rapid but brief; the action is quickly halted as the neurotransmitter is swiftly removed from the target site. This permits ending the response, almost immediately repeating the response, or rapidly initiating an alternate response as circumstances demand (for example, the swift changes in commands to muscle groups needed to coordinate walking). This mode of action makes neural communication extremely rapid and precise. The target tissues of the nervous system are the muscles and glands, especially exocrine glands, of the body.

The endocrine system, in contrast, is specialized to control activities that require duration rather than speed, such as regulating organic metabolism; maintaining water and electrolyte balance; promoting smooth, sequential growth and development; and controlling reproduction. The endocrine system responds more slowly to its triggering stimuli than the nervous system does for several reasons. First, the endocrine system must depend on blood flow to convey its hormonal messengers over long distances. Second, hormones typically have a more complex mechanism of action at their target cells than neurotransmitters do; thus, they require more time before a response occurs. The ultimate effect of some hormones cannot be detected until a few hours after they bind with target cell receptors. Also, because of the receptors' high affinity for their respective hormone, the hormones often remain bound to receptors for some time, thus prolonging their biological effectiveness. Furthermore, unlike the brief, neurally induced responses that stop almost immediately after the neurotransmitter is removed, endocrine effects usually last for some time after the hormone's withdrawal. Neural responses to a single burst of neurotransmitter release usually last only milliseconds to seconds, whereas the alterations that hormones induce in target cells range from minutes to days or, in the case of growth-promoting effects, even a lifetime. Thus, hormonal action is relatively slow and prolonged, making endocrine control particularly suitable for regulating metabolic activities that require long-term stability.

Although the endocrine and nervous systems have their own areas of specialization, they are intimately interconnected functionally. Some neurons do not release neurotransmitters at synapses but instead end at blood vessels and release their chemical messengers (neurohormones) into the blood, where these chemicals act as hormones. A given messenger may even be a neurotransmitter when released from a nerve ending and a hormone when secreted by an endocrine cell. An example is *norepinephrine* (see p. 555). The nervous system directly or indirectly controls the secretion of many hormones (see Chapter 17). At the same time, many hormones act as neuromodulators, altering synaptic effectiveness and thereby influencing the excitability of the nervous system. The presence of certain key hormones is even essential for the proper development and maturation of the brain during fetal life. Furthermore, in many instances the nervous and endocrine systems both influence the same target cells in supplementary fashion. For example, these two major regulatory systems both help regulate the circulatory and digestive systems. Thus, many important regulatory interfaces exist between the nervous and the endocrine systems.

In the next three chapters, we concentrate on the nervous system. We examine the endocrine system in more detail in later chapters. Throughout the text, we continue to point out the numerous ways in which these two regulatory systems interact so that the body is a coordinated whole, even though each system has its own realm of authority.

Chapter in Perspective: Focus on Homeostasis

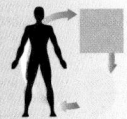

To maintain homeostasis, cells must communicate so that they work together to accomplish life-sustaining activities. To bring about desired responses, the two major regulatory systems of the body, the nervous system and the endocrine system, must communicate with the target cells they are controlling. Neural and hormonal communication is therefore critical in maintaining a stable internal environment, as well as in coordinating nonhomeostatic activities.

Neurons are specialized to receive, process, encode, and rapidly transmit information from one part of the body to another. The information is transmitted over intricate neuronal pathways by propagation of action potentials along the neuron's length, as well as by chemical transmission of the signal from neuron to neuron at synapses and from neuron to muscles and glands through other neurotransmitter–receptor interactions at these junctions.

Collectively, the neurons make up the nervous system. Many activities controlled by the nervous system are geared toward maintaining homeostasis. Some neuronal electrical signals convey information about changes to which the body must rapidly respond to maintain homeostasis—for example, information about a fall in blood pressure. Other neuronal electrical signals swiftly convey messages to muscles and glands stimulating appropriate responses to counteract these changes—for example, adjustments in heart and blood vessel activity that restore blood pressure to normal when it starts to fall. Furthermore, the nervous system directs many activities not geared toward maintaining homeostasis, many of which are subject to voluntary control, such as playing basketball or browsing on the Internet.

The endocrine system secretes hormones into the blood, which carries these chemical messengers to distant target cells where they bring about their effect by changing the activity of enzymatic or structural proteins within these cells. Through its relatively slow-acting hormonal messengers, the endocrine system generally regulates activities that require duration rather than speed. Most of these activities are directed toward maintaining homeostasis. For example, hormones help maintain the proper concentration of nutrients in the internal environment by directing chemical reactions involved in the cellular uptake, storage, release, and use of these molecules. Also, hormones help maintain the proper water and electrolyte balance in the internal environment. Unrelated to homeostasis, hormones direct growth and control most aspects of the reproductive system.

Together, the nervous and the endocrine systems orchestrate a range of adjustments that help the body maintain homeostasis in response to stress. Likewise, these systems work in concert to control the circulatory and digestive systems, which carry out many homeostatic activities.

REVIEW EXERCISES

Objective Questions (Answers on p. A-40)

1. Conformational changes in channel proteins brought about by voltage changes are responsible for opening and closing the gates for Na^+ and K^+ during the generation of an action potential. (*True or false?*)
2. The Na^+-K^+ pump restores the membrane to resting potential after it reaches the peak of an action potential. (*True or false?*)
3. Following an action potential, there is more K^+ outside the cell than inside because of the efflux of K^+ during the falling phase. (*True or false?*)
4. Postsynaptic neurons can either excite or inhibit presynaptic neurons. (*True or false?*)
5. Second-messenger pathways ultimately bring about the desired cell response by inducing a change in the shape and function of particular designated intracellular proteins. (*True or false?*)
6. Each steroidogenic organ has all the enzymes necessary to produce any steroid hormone. (*True or false?*)
7. The one-way propagation of action potentials away from the original site of activation is ensured by the _____.
8. The _____ is the site of action potential initiation in most neurons because it has the lowest threshold.
9. A junction in which the electrical activity in one neuron influences the electrical activity in another neuron by means of a neurotransmitter is called a _____.
10. The neuronal relationship in which synapses from many presynaptic inputs act on a single postsynaptic cell is called _____, whereas the relationship in which a single presynaptic neuron synapses with and thereby influences the activity of many postsynaptic cells is known as _____.
11. A common membrane-bound intermediary between the receptor and the effector protein within the plasma membrane is the _____.
12. Using the answer code on the right, indicate which potential is being described:
    ___ 1. behaves in all-or-none fashion
    ___ 2. has a magnitude of potential change that varies with the magnitude of the triggering event
    ___ 3. spreads decrementally away from the original site
    ___ 4. spreads nondecrementally throughout the membrane
    ___ 5. serves as a long-distance signal
    ___ 6. serves as a short-distance signal

    (a) graded potential
    (b) action potential

13. Using the answer code on the right, indicate which characteristics apply to peptide and steroid hormones:
    ___ 1. are hydrophilic
    ___ 2. are lipophilic
    ___ 3. are synthesized by the endoplasmic reticulum
    ___ 4. are synthesized by modifying cholesterol
    ___ 5. include epinephrine from the adrenal medulla
    ___ 6. include cortisol from the adrenal cortex
    ___ 7. bind to plasma proteins
    ___ 8. bind to intracellular receptors
    ___ 9. bind to surface membrane receptors
    ___ 10. activate genes to promote synthesis of new proteins
    ___ 11. act via a second messenger to alter preexisting proteins
    ___ 12. are secreted into the blood by endocrine glands and carried to distant target sites

    (a) peptide hormones
    (b) steroid hormones
    (c) both peptide and steroid hormones
    (d) neither peptide nor steroid hormones

Essay Questions

1. What are the two types of excitable tissue?
2. Define the following terms: polarization, depolarization, hyperpolarization, repolarization, resting membrane potential, threshold potential, action potential, refractory period, and all-or-none law.
3. Compare the four kinds of gated channels in terms of the factor that opens or closes them.
4. Describe the permeability changes and ion fluxes that occur during an action potential.
5. Compare contiguous and saltatory conduction.
6. Compare the events that occur at excitatory and inhibitory synapses.
7. Compare temporal and spatial summation.
8. List and describe the types of intercellular communication.
9. Define signal transduction.
10. Distinguish between first and second messengers.
11. Describe the sequence of events in the cAMP second-messenger pathway.
12. Compare the nervous and endocrine systems.

(Explanations on p. A-40)

1. Which of the following would occur if a neuron were experimentally stimulated simultaneously at both ends?
   a. The action potentials would pass in the middle and travel to the opposite ends.
   b. The action potentials would meet in the middle and then be propagated back to their starting positions.
   c. The action potentials would stop as they met in the middle.
   d. The stronger action potential would override the weaker action potential.
   e. Summation would occur when the action potentials met in the middle, resulting in a larger action potential.

2. Assume you touched a hot stove with your finger. Contraction of the biceps muscle causes flexion (bending) of the elbow, whereas contraction of the triceps muscle causes extension (straightening) of the elbow. What pattern of postsynaptic potentials would you expect to be initiated as a reflex in the cell bodies of the neurons controlling these muscles to pull your hand away from the painful stimulus: excitatory postsynaptic potentials (EPSPs) or inhibitory postsynaptic potentials (IPSPs)?

   Now assume your finger is being pricked to obtain a blood sample. The same withdrawal reflex would be initiated. What pattern of postsynaptic potentials would you voluntarily produce in the neurons controlling the biceps and triceps to keep your arm extended despite the painful stimulus?

3. Compare the expected changes in membrane potential of a neuron simulated with a *subthreshold stimulus* (a stimulus not sufficient to bring a membrane to threshold), a *threshold stimulus* (a stimulus just sufficient to bring the membrane to threshold), and a *suprathreshold stimulus* (a stimulus larger than that necessary to bring the membrane to threshold).

4. Assume presynaptic excitatory neuron A terminates on a postsynaptic cell near the axon hillock and presynaptic excitatory neuron B terminates on the same postsynaptic cell on a dendrite located on the side of the cell body opposite the axon hillock. Explain why rapid firing of presynaptic neuron A could bring the postsynaptic neuron to threshold through temporal summation, thus initiating an action potential, whereas firing of presynaptic neuron B at the same frequency and the same magnitude of EPSPs may not bring the postsynaptic neuron to threshold.

5. Two classes of drugs that block different receptors are among those used to treat high blood pressure. (1) *Angiotensin receptor blockers (ARBs)* block binding of angiotensin to its receptors on the cells of the adrenal cortex that secrete a salt-conserving hormone, aldosterone. Aldosterone acts on the kidneys to conserve salt (specifically Na^+, with Cl^- following along the resulting electrical gradient) during urine formation. Salt accounts for more than 90% of the osmotic (water-holding) activity of the ECF, including the plasma. (2) β_1-*adrenergic receptor blockers* block binding of epinephrine to its receptors in the heart. Epinephrine, a hormone secreted by the adrenal medulla, increases the rate and strength of contraction of the heart. Explain how each of these drugs lowers blood pressure.

(Explanation on p. A-40)

Becky N. was apprehensive as she sat in the dentist's chair awaiting the placement of her first silver amalgam (the "filling" in a cavity in a tooth). Before preparing the tooth for the amalgam by drilling away the decayed portion of the tooth, the dentist injected a local anesthetic in the nerve pathway supplying the region. As a result, Becky, much to her relief, did not feel any pain during the drilling and filling procedure. Local anesthetics block voltage-gated Na^+ channels. Explain how this action prevents the transmission of pain impulses to the brain.

Chapter 4

Introduction to Neural Communication (pp. 77–78)

■ Nerve and muscle cells are excitable tissues because they can rapidly alter their membrane permeabilities and undergo transient membrane potential changes when excited. These rapid changes in potential serve as electrical signals.

■ Compared to resting potential, a membrane becomes depolarized when the magnitude of its negative potential is reduced (becomes less negative) and hyperpolarized when the magnitude of its negative potential is increased (becomes more negative). *(Review Figure 4-1.)*

■ Changes in potential are brought about by triggering events that alter membrane permeability, in turn leading to changes in ion movement across the membrane.

■ The two kinds of potential change are (1) graded potentials, the short-distance signals, and (2) action potentials, the long-distance signals. *(Review Table 4-1, p. 87.)*

Graded Potentials (pp. 78–80)

■ A graded potential, usually a depolarization, occurs in a small, specialized region of an excitable cell membrane. The site undergoing a potential change is designated an active area. *(Review Figure 4-2.)*

■ The magnitude of a graded potential varies directly with the magnitude of the triggering event.

■ Graded potentials spread decrementally by local current flow between the active area and the adjacent inactive areas and die out over a short distance. *(Review Figures 4-2 and 4-3.)*

Action Potentials (pp. 80–91)

■ During an action potential, depolarization of the membrane to threshold potential triggers sequential changes in permeability caused by conformational changes in voltage-gated Na^+ and K^+ channels. *(Review Figures 4-4 through 4-7.)*

■ These permeability changes bring about a brief reversal of membrane potential, with Na^+ influx causing the rising phase (from -70 to +30 mV) followed by K^+ efflux causing the falling phase (from peak back to resting). *(Review Figure 4-7.)*

■ Before an action potential returns to resting, it regenerates an identical new action potential in the area next to it by means of current flow that brings the previously inactive area to threshold. This self-perpetuating cycle continues until the action potential spreads undiminished throughout the cell membrane.

■ There are two types of action potential propagation: (1) contiguous conduction in unmyelinated fibers, in which the action potential spreads along every portion of the membrane, and (2) the more rapid, saltatory conduction in myelinated fibers, in which the impulse jumps from one node of Ranvier to the next over sections of the fiber covered with insulating myelin. *(Review Figures 4-9 and 4-12.)*

■ The Na^+–K^+ pump gradually restores the ions that moved during propagation of the action potential to their original location, thus maintaining the concentration gradients.

■ It is impossible to restimulate the portion of the membrane where the impulse has just passed until it has recovered from its refractory period, ensuring the one-way propagation of action potentials. *(Review Figures 4-10 and 4-11.)*

■ Either action potentials occur maximally in response to stimulation, or they do not occur (all-or-none law).

■ Variable strengths of stimuli are coded by varying the frequency of action potentials, not their magnitude, in an activated nerve fiber.

Synapses and Neuronal Integration (pp. 91–97)

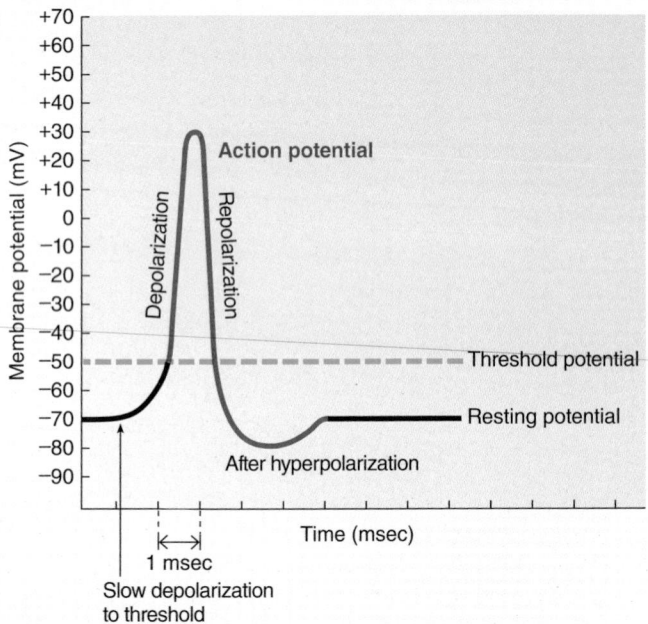

■ One neuron directly interacts with another neuron primarily through a synapse. *(Review Figures 4-13 and 4-14.)*

■ Most neurons have four functional parts: *(Review Figure 4-8.)*

1. The dendrite and cell body region (the input zone) is the postsynaptic component that binds with and responds to neurotransmitters released from other neurons.

2. The axon hillock (the trigger zone) is where action potentials are initiated because it has an abundance of voltage-gated Na^+ channels and thus reaches threshold first in response to an excitatory graded potential change.

3. The axon, or nerve fiber (the conducting zone), conducts action potentials in undiminished fashion from the axon hillock to the axon terminals.

4. The axon terminal (the output zone) serves as the presynaptic component, releasing a neurotransmitter that influences other postsynaptic cells in response to action potential propagation down the axon.

■ Released neurotransmitter combines with receptor-channels on the postsynaptic neuron. (Review Figure 4-14.) (1) If nonspecific cation channels that permit passage of both Na^+ and K^+ are opened, the resultant ionic fluxes cause an EPSP, a small depolarization that brings the postsynaptic cell closer to threshold. (2) If either K^+ or Cl^- channels are opened, the likelihood that the postsynaptic neuron will reach threshold is diminished when an inhibitory postsynaptic potential (IPSP), a small hyperpolarization, is produced. (Review Figure 4-15.)

■ If the dominant activity is in its excitatory inputs, the postsynaptic cell is likely to be brought to threshold and have an action potential. This can be accomplished by (1) temporal summation (EPSPs from a single, repetitively firing, presynaptic input occurring so close together in time that they add together) or (2) spatial summation (adding of EPSPs occurring simultaneously from several presynaptic inputs). (Review Figure 4-16.) If inhibitory inputs dominate, the postsynaptic potential is brought farther than usual from threshold. If excitatory and inhibitory activity to the postsynaptic neuron is balanced, the membrane remains close to resting.

■ Despite the range of neurotransmitters, each synapse always releases the same neurotransmitter to produce a given response when combined with a particular receptor. (Review Table 4-2.)

■ Synaptic pathways between neurons are incredibly complex due to convergence of neuronal input and divergence of its output. Usually, many presynaptic inputs converge on a single neuron and jointly control its level of excitability. This same neuron diverges to synapse with and influence the excitability of many other cells. (Review Figure 4-17.)

Intercellular Communication and Signal Transduction (pp. 97–100)

■ Intercellular communication is accomplished directly via (1) gap junctions or (2) transient direct linkup of cells' complementary surface markers. (Review Figure 4-18.)

■ More commonly, cells communicate indirectly with one another to carry out various coordinated activities by dispatching extracellular chemical messengers, which act on particular target cells to bring about the desired response. The four types of extracellular chemical messengers differ in their source and in the distance and means by which they get to their site of action: (1) paracrines (local chemical messengers), (2) neurotransmitters (short-range chemical messengers released by neurons), (3) hormones (long-range chemical messengers secreted into the blood by endocrine glands), and (4) neurohormones (long-range chemical messengers secreted into the blood by neurosecretory neurons). (Review Figure 4-18.)

■ Transfer of the signal carried by the extracellular messenger into the cell for execution is known as signal transduction.

■ An extracellular chemical messenger that cannot gain entry to the cell, such as a protein hormone (the first messenger), triggers the desired cellular response by binding to the target cell membrane and either (1) opening receptor-channels or (2) activating an intracellular second-messenger pathway via G-protein-coupled receptors. (Review Figures 4-14 and 4-20.)

Introduction to Hormonal Communication (pp. 100–106)

■ Hormones are secreted by endocrine glands into the blood, which transports them to specific target sites where they control a particular function by altering protein activity within the target cells.

■ Hormones are grouped into two categories based on their solubility differences: (1) hydrophilic (water-soluble) hormones, which include peptides (most hormones) and catecholamines (secreted by the adrenal medulla), and (2) lipophilic (lipid-soluble) hormones, which include steroid hormones (the sex hormones and those secreted by the adrenal cortex) and thyroid hormone. (Review Table 4-3.)

■ Hydrophilic peptide hormones are synthesized and packaged for export by the endoplasmic reticulum–Golgi complex, stored in secretory vesicles, and released by exocytosis on appropriate stimulation. They dissolve freely in the blood for transport to their target cells.

■ At their target cells, hydrophilic hormones bind with surface membrane receptors, triggering a chain of intracellular events by means of a second-messenger pathway that ultimately alters preexisting cell proteins, usually enzymes, leading to the target cell's response to the hormone. (Review Figure 4-20.) Through this cascade of reactions, the initial signal is greatly amplified.

■ Steroids are synthesized by modifications of stored cholesterol through enzymes specific for each steroidogenic tissue. Steroids are not stored in the endocrine cells. Being lipophilic, they diffuse out through the lipid membrane barrier as soon as they are synthesized. Control of steroids is directed at their synthesis.

■ Lipophilic steroids and thyroid hormone are both transported in the blood largely bound to carrier plasma proteins, with only free, unbound hormone being biologically active.

■ Lipophilic hormones readily cross the lipid membrane barriers of their target cells and bind with receptors inside the cell. Once the hormone binds with the receptor, the hormone receptor complex binds with DNA and activates a gene, which leads to the synthesis of new enzymatic or structural intracellular proteins that carry out the hormone's effect on the target cell. (Review Figure 4-21.)

Comparison of the Nervous and Endocrine Systems (pp. 106–108)

■ The nervous and endocrine systems are the two main regulatory systems of the body. (Review Table 4-4.) The nervous system is anatomically "wired" to its target organs, whereas the "wireless" endocrine system secretes blood-borne hormones that reach distant target organs.

■ Specificity of neural action depends on the anatomic proximity of the neurotransmitter-releasing neuronal terminal to its target organ. Specificity of endocrine action depends on specialization of target cell receptors for a specific circulating hormone.

■ In general, the nervous system coordinates rapid responses, whereas the endocrine system regulates activities that require duration rather than speed.

**Nervous System
(Central Nervous System)**

Homeostasis
The nervous system, as one of the body's two major regulatory systems, regulates many body activities aimed at maintaining a stable internal fluid environment.

Body systems
maintain homeostasis

Homeostasis is
essential for
survival of cells

Cells

Cells make up
body systems

The **nervous system** is one of the two major regulatory systems of the body; the other is the endocrine system. The three basic functional types of neurons—afferent neurons, efferent neurons, and interneurons—form a complex interactive network of excitable cells. Ninety percent of the cells of the nervous system are nonexcitable glial cells, which interact extensively both structurally and functionally with neurons. The **central nervous system (CNS),** which consists of the brain and spinal cord, receives input about the external and internal environment from the afferent neurons. The CNS sorts and processes this input and then initiates appropriate directions in the efferent neurons, which carry the instructions to glands or muscles to bring about the desired response—some type of secretion or movement. Many of these neurally controlled activities are directed toward maintaining homeostasis. In general, the nervous system acts by means of its electrical signals (action potentials) to control the rapid responses of the body.

CHAPTER AT A GLANCE

Organization and Cells of the Nervous System

Central and peripheral nervous systems

Three classes of neurons

Glial cells

Protection and Nourishment of the Brain

Meninges; cerebrospinal fluid

Blood–brain barrier

Brain's dependence on oxygen and glucose delivery

Overview of the Central Nervous System

Cerebral Cortex

Cortical structure

Sensory perception

Motor control

Language ability

Association areas

Cerebral specialization

Basal Nuclei, Thalamus, and Hypothalamus

Emotion, Behavior, and Motivation

Limbic system

Emotion

Motivated behaviors

Neurotransmitters for emotions and behavior

Learning and Memory

Knowledge acquisition

Memory stages

Mechanisms of short-term and long-term memory; consolidation

Parts of brain involved in memory; declarative and procedural memories; working memory

Cerebellum

Brain Stem

Components and functions of the brain stem

Consciousness; sleep–wake cycle

Spinal Cord

Anatomy of the Spinal Cord

Spinal Reflexes

5

The Central Nervous System

Organization and Cells of the Nervous System

The way humans act and react depends on complex, organized, discrete neuronal processing. Many basic life-supporting neuronal patterns, such as those controlling respiration and circulation, are similar in all individuals. However, there must be subtle differences in neuronal integration between someone who is a talented composer and someone who cannot carry a tune or between someone who is a math wizard and someone who struggles with long division. Some differences in the nervous systems of individuals are genetically endowed. The rest, however, are due to environmental encounters and experiences. When the immature nervous system develops according to its genetic plan, an overabundance of neurons and synapses is formed. Depending on external stimuli and the extent to which these pathways are used, some are retained, firmly established, and even enhanced, whereas others are eliminated.

 Clinical Note A case in point is **amblyopia** (lazy eye), in which the weaker of the two eyes is not used for vision. A lazy eye that does not get appropriate visual stimulation during a critical developmental period will almost completely and permanently lose the power of vision. The functionally blind eye itself is normal; the defect lies in the lost neuronal connections in the brain's visual pathways. However, if the weak eye is forced to work by covering the stronger eye with a patch during the sensitive developmental period, the weaker eye will retain full vision.

The maturation of the nervous system involves many instances of "use it or lose it." Once the nervous system has matured, modifications still occur as we continue to learn from our unique set of experiences. For example, the act of reading this page is somehow altering the neuronal activity of your brain as you (it is hoped) tuck the information away in your memory.

The nervous system is organized into the central nervous system and the peripheral nervous system.

The nervous system is organized into the **central nervous system (CNS),** consisting of the brain and spinal cord, and the **peripheral nervous system (PNS),** consisting of nerve fibers that carry information between the CNS and the other parts of the body (the periphery) (● Figure 5-1). The PNS is further subdivided into afferent and efferent divisions. The **afferent division** carries information *to* the CNS, apprising it of the external environment and providing status reports on internal activities being regulated by the nervous system (*a* is from *ad,* meaning "toward," as in *advance; ferent* means "carrying"; thus, *afferent* means "carrying toward"). Instructions *from* the CNS are transmitted via the **efferent division** to **effector organs**—the muscles or glands that carry out the orders to bring about the desired effect (*e* is from *ex,* meaning "from," as in *exit;* thus, *efferent* means "carrying from"). The efferent nervous system is divided into the **somatic nervous system,** which consists of the fibers of the motor neurons that supply the skeletal muscles; and the **autonomic nervous system,** which consists of fibers that innervate smooth muscle, cardiac muscle, and glands. The latter system is further subdivided into the **sympathetic nervous system** and the **parasympathetic nervous system,** both of which innervate most of the organs supplied by the autonomic system. In addition to the CNS and PNS, the **enteric nervous system** is an extensive nerve network in the wall of the digestive tract. Digestive activities are controlled by the autonomic nervous system and the enteric nervous system, as well as by hormones. The enteric nervous system can act independently of the rest of the nervous system but is also influenced by autonomic fibers that terminate on the enteric neurons. Sometimes the enteric nervous system is considered a third component of the autonomic nervous system, one that supplies the digestive organs only.

It is important to recognize that all these "nervous systems" are really subdivisions of a single, integrated nervous system. These subdivisions are based on differences in the structure, location, and functions of the various diverse parts of the whole nervous system.

The three functional classes of neurons are afferent neurons, efferent neurons, and interneurons.

Three functional classes of neurons make up the nervous system: *afferent neurons, efferent neurons,* and *interneurons.* The afferent division of the PNS consists of **afferent neurons,** which are shaped differently from efferent neurons and interneurons (● Figure 5-2). At its peripheral ending, a typical afferent neuron has a **sensory receptor** that generates action potentials in response to a particular type of stimulus. (This stimulus-sensitive afferent neuronal receptor should not be confused with the special protein receptors that bind chemical messengers and are found in the plasma membrane of all

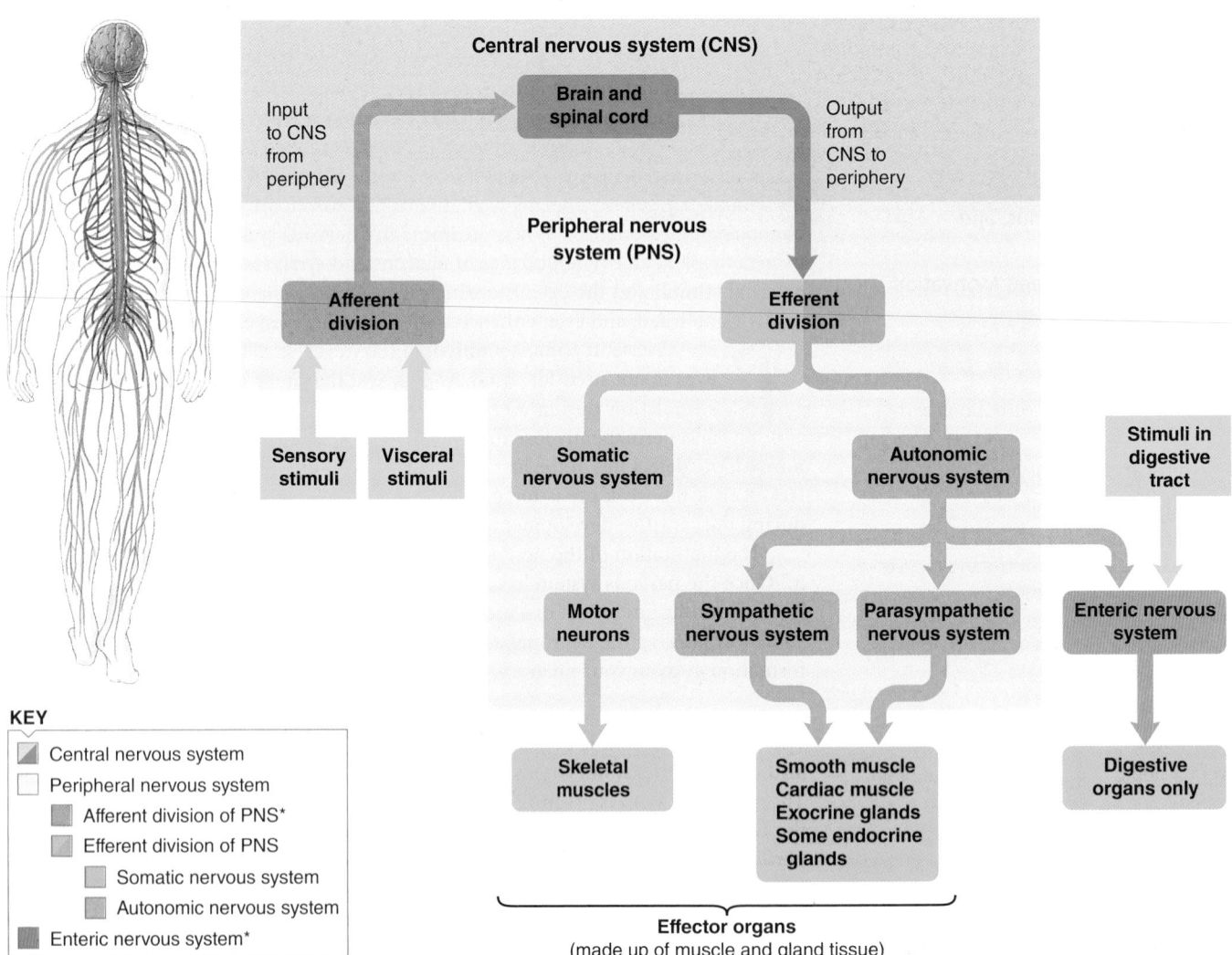

● **FIGURE 5-1 Organization of the nervous system.** *The afferent division of the PNS and the enteric nervous system are not shown in the human figure. Afferent fibers travel within the same nerves as efferent fibers but in the opposite direction. The enteric nervous system lies entirely within the wall of the digestive tract.

cells.) The afferent neuron cell body, which is devoid of dendrites and presynaptic inputs, is adjacent to the spinal cord. A long *peripheral axon,* commonly called the *afferent fiber,* extends from the receptor to the cell body, and a short *central axon* passes from the cell body into the spinal cord. Action potentials are initiated at the receptor end of the peripheral axon in response to a stimulus and are propagated along the peripheral axon and the central axon toward the spinal cord. The terminals of the central axon diverge and synapse with other neurons within the spinal cord, thus disseminating information about the stimulus. Afferent neurons lie primarily within the PNS. Only a small portion of their central axon endings projects into the spinal cord to relay signals from the periphery to the CNS.

Efferent neurons also lie primarily in the PNS. Efferent neuron cell bodies originate in the CNS, where many centrally located presynaptic inputs converge on them to influence their outputs to the effector organs. Efferent axons (*efferent fibers*) leave the CNS to course their way to the muscles or glands they innervate, conveying their integrated output for the effector organs to put into effect. (An autonomic nerve pathway consists of a two-neuron chain between the CNS and the effector organ.)

About 99% of all neurons are **interneurons,** which lie entirely within the CNS. The human CNS is estimated to have more than 100 billion interneurons. As their name implies, interneurons lie between the afferent and the efferent neurons and are important in integrating peripheral information to peripheral responses (*inter* means "between"). For example, on

receiving information through afferent neurons that you are touching a hot object, appropriate interneurons signal efferent neurons that transmit to your hand and arm muscles the message, "Pull the hand away from the hot object!" The more complex the required action, the greater the number of interneurons interposed between the afferent message and the efferent response. In addition, interconnections between interneurons themselves are responsible for the abstract phenomena associated with the "mind," such as thoughts, emotions, memory, creativity, intellect, and motivation. These activities are the least understood functions of the nervous system.

Glial cells support the interneurons physically, metabolically, and functionally.

About 90% of the cells within the CNS are not neurons but **glial cells** or **neuroglia.** Despite their large numbers, glial cells occupy only about half the volume of the brain, because they do not branch as extensively as neurons do.

Unlike neurons, glial cells do not initiate or conduct nerve impulses. However, they do communicate with neurons and among themselves by means of chemical signals. For much of the time since the discovery of glial cells in the 19th century, scientists thought these cells were passive "mortar" that physically supported the functionally important neurons. In the last decade, however, the varied and important roles of these dynamic cells have become apparent. Glial cells help support the neurons both physically and metabolically. They also homeostatically maintain the composition of the specialized extracellular environment surrounding the neurons within the narrow limits optimal for normal neuronal function. Furthermore, they actively modulate (depress or enhance) synaptic function and are considered nearly as important as neurons to learning and memory. There are four major types of glial cells in the CNS—*astrocytes, oligodendrocytes, microglia,* and *ependymal cells*—each with specific roles (● Figure 5-3).

ASTROCYTES Named for their starlike shape (*astro* means "star"; *cyte* means "cell") (● Figure 5-4), **astrocytes** are the most abundant glial cells. They fill several critical functions:

1. As the main "glue" (*glia* means "glue") of the CNS, astrocytes hold the neurons together in proper spatial relationships.

2. Astrocytes serve as a scaffold that guides neurons to their proper final destination during fetal brain development.

3. These glial cells induce the small blood vessels (capillaries) of the brain to undergo the anatomic and functional changes that establish the blood–brain barrier, a highly selective barricade between the blood and the brain that we soon describe in greater detail.

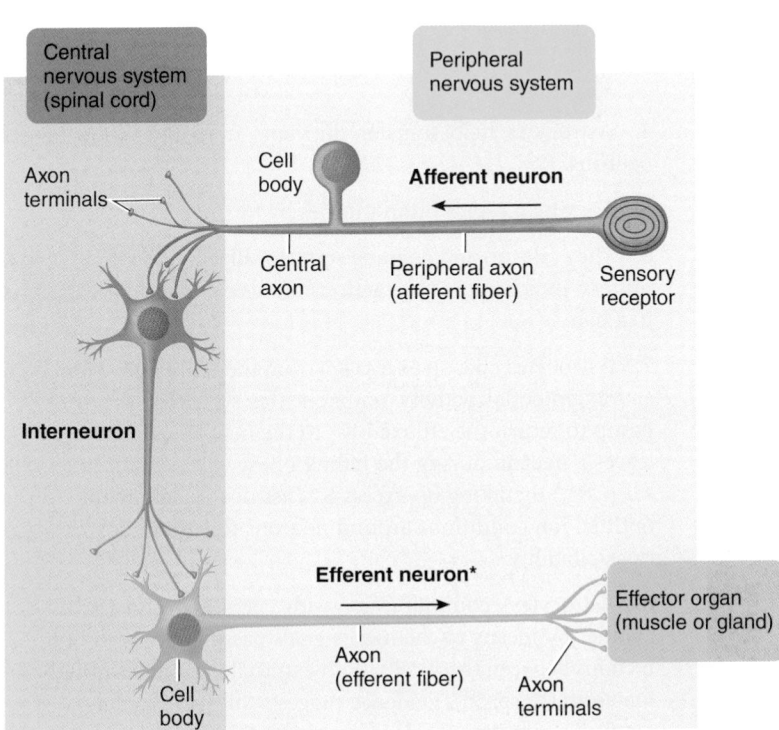

* Efferent autonomic nerve pathways consist of a two-neuron chain between the CNS and the effector organ.

● **FIGURE 5-2 Structure and location of the three functional classes of neurons.** Efferent autonomic nerve pathways consist of a two-neuron chain between the CNS and the effector organ.

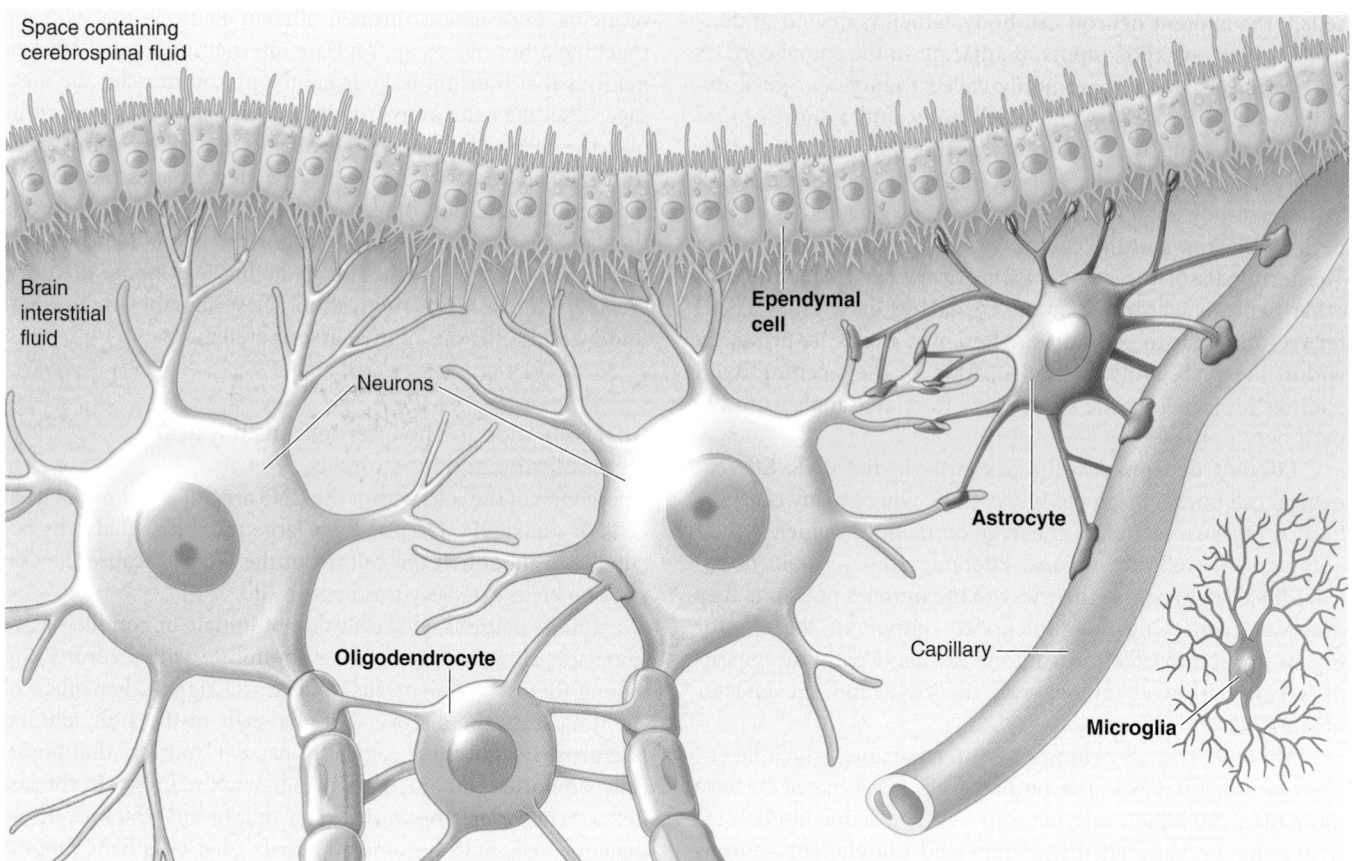

● FIGURE 5-3 **Glial cells of the central nervous system.** The glial cells include the astrocytes, oligodendrocytes, microglia, and ependymal cells.

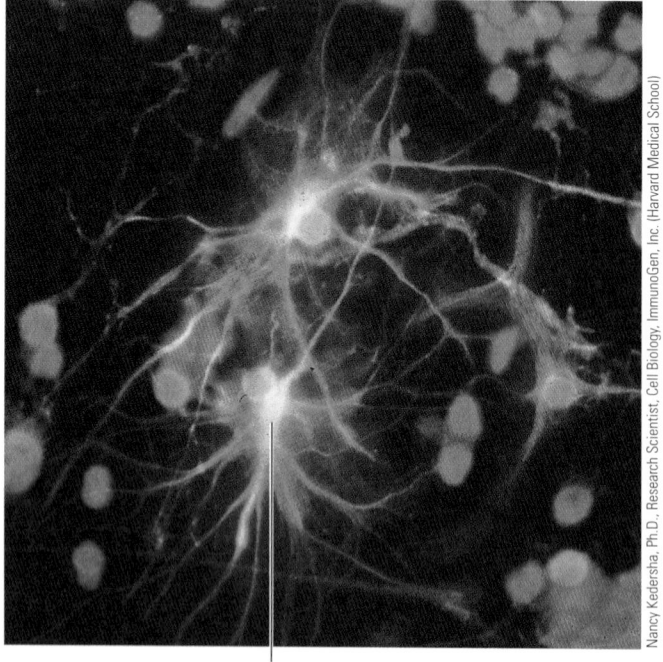

Astrocyte

● FIGURE 5-4 **Astrocytes.** Note the starlike shape of these astrocytes, which have been grown in tissue culture.

4. Astrocytes help transfer nutrients from the blood to the neurons.

5. They help repair brain injuries by forming neural scars.

6. They take up and degrade some locally released neurotransmitters, thus bringing the actions of these chemical messengers to a halt.

7. Astrocytes take up excess K^+ from the brain ECF when high action potential activity outpaces the ability of the Na^+–K^+ pump to return the effluxed K^+ to the neurons. (Recall that K^+ leaves a neuron during the falling phase of an action potential; see p. 84.) By taking up excess K^+, astrocytes help maintain the optimal ion conditions around neurons to sustain normal neural excitability.

8. Astrocytes communicate with neurons and with one another by means of chemical signals passing locally in both directions between these cells, both extracellularly and through gap junctions (see p. 53). Evidence suggests this two-directional chatter plays an important role in synaptic transmission and the brain's processing of information. As examples, via chemical signals astrocytes can share information about action potential activity in nearby neurons, affect neuronal excitability, coordinate and integrate synaptic activity among networks of neurons working to-

gether, and promote the formation of new synapses. Some neuroscientists suggest that synapses should be considered "three-party" junctures involving the glial cells and the presynaptic and postsynaptic neurons. This point of view is indicative of the increasingly important role being placed on astrocytes in synapse function. Thus, astrocytes have come a long way from their earlier reputation as "support staff" for neurons; these glial cells might turn out to be the "board members" commanding the neurons.

OLIGODENDROCYTES **Oligodendrocytes** form the insulative myelin sheaths around axons in the CNS. An oligodendrocyte has several elongated projections, each of which wraps jelly-roll fashion around a section of an interneuronal axon to form a patch of myelin (see ● Figure 4-12c, p. 90, and ● Figure 5-3). Late in fetal life, oligodendrocytes begin secreting *nerve-growth-inhibiting proteins,* such as the chemical messenger dubbed *Nogo.* Scientists speculate that nerve-growth inhibitors normally serve as "guardrails" to keep new nerve endings from straying outside their proper paths. The growth-inhibiting action of oligodendrocytes may thus stabilize the enormously complex structure of the CNS.

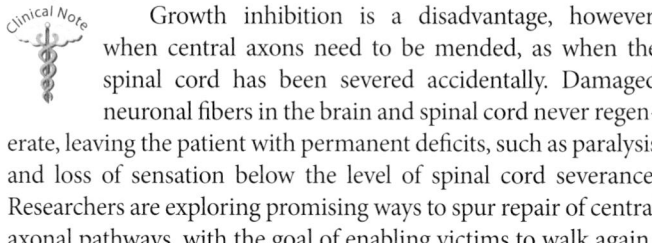 Growth inhibition is a disadvantage, however, when central axons need to be mended, as when the spinal cord has been severed accidentally. Damaged neuronal fibers in the brain and spinal cord never regenerate, leaving the patient with permanent deficits, such as paralysis and loss of sensation below the level of spinal cord severance. Researchers are exploring promising ways to spur repair of central axonal pathways, with the goal of enabling victims to walk again.

By contrast, Schwann cells, the myelin-forming cells of the PNS, form a *regeneration tube* and secrete *nerve-growth-enhancing proteins* that respectively guide and promote regrowth of damaged peripheral axons, as long as the cell body and dendrites remain intact (that is, as long as the neuron is still alive). Successful fiber regeneration permits the return of sensation and movement at some time after peripheral nerve injuries, although regeneration is not always successful.

MICROGLIA **Microglia** are the immune defense cells of the CNS, where they remain stationary until activated by an infection or injury. When trouble occurs in the CNS, microglia become highly mobile and move toward the affected area to remove any foreign invaders or tissue debris by phagocytosis (see p. 26). Activated microglia also release destructive chemicals for assault against their target.

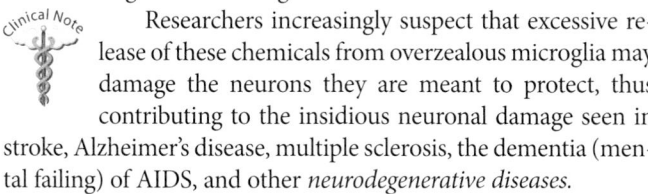 Researchers increasingly suspect that excessive release of these chemicals from overzealous microglia may damage the neurons they are meant to protect, thus contributing to the insidious neuronal damage seen in stroke, Alzheimer's disease, multiple sclerosis, the dementia (mental failing) of AIDS, and other *neurodegenerative diseases.*

EPENDYMAL CELLS **Ependymal cells** line the internal, fluid-filled cavities of the CNS. As the nervous system develops embryonically from a hollow neural tube, the original central cavity of this tube is maintained and modified to form the ventricles and central canal. The four **ventricles** are interconnected

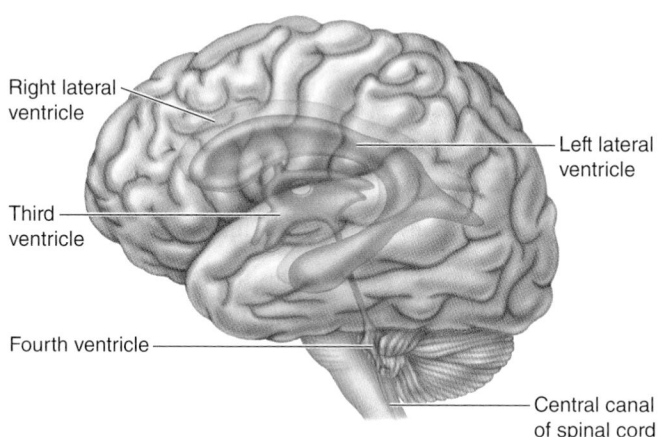

● **FIGURE 5-5 The ventricles of the brain.**

chambers within the brain that are continuous with the narrow, hollow **central canal** through the middle of the spinal cord (● Figure 5-5). The ependymal cells lining the ventricles help form cerebrospinal fluid, a topic to be discussed shortly.

Ependymal cells also have a different role: They serve as neural stem cells with the potential of forming not only other glial cells but new neurons as well (see p. 8). The traditional view has long held that new neurons are not produced in the mature brain. Then, in the late 1990s, scientists discovered that new neurons are produced in a specific part of the hippocampus, a structure important for learning and memory (see p. 135). Neurons in the rest of the brain are considered irreplaceable. But the discovery that ependymal cells are precursors for new neurons suggests that the adult brain has more potential for repairing damaged regions than previously assumed. Currently, no evidence shows that the brain spontaneously repairs itself following neuron-losing insults such as head trauma, strokes, and neurodegenerative diseases. Apparently, most brain regions cannot activate this mechanism for replenishing neurons, probably because the appropriate "cocktail" of supportive chemicals is not present. Researchers hope that probing into why these ependymal cells are dormant and how they might be activated will lead to the possibility of unlocking the brain's undeveloped capacity for self-repair.

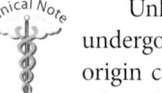 Unlike neurons, glial cells do not lose the ability to undergo cell division, so most brain tumors of neural origin consist of glial cells **(gliomas).** Neurons themselves do not form tumors because they are unable to divide and multiply. Brain tumors of non-neural origin are of two types: (1) those that metastasize (spread) to the brain from other sites and (2) **meningiomas,** which originate from the meninges, the protective membranes covering the CNS. We next examine the meninges and other means by which the CNS is protected.

Protection and Nourishment of the Brain

Central nervous tissue is delicate. Because of this characteristic, and because damaged nerve cells cannot be replaced, this fragile, irreplaceable tissue must be well protected.

The delicate CNS is well protected.

Four major features help protect the CNS from injury:

1. It is enclosed by hard, bony structures. The **cranium (skull)** encases the brain, and the **vertebral column** surrounds the spinal cord.

2. Three protective and nourishing membranes, the **meninges,** lie between the bony covering and the nervous tissue.

3. The brain "floats" in a special cushioning fluid, the **cerebrospinal fluid (CSF).** CSF circulates throughout the ventricles and central canal, as well as over the entire surface of the brain and spinal cord in a space between the meningeal layers. CSF has about the same density as the brain itself, so the brain is essentially suspended in this special fluid environment. The major function of CSF is to be a shock-absorbing fluid to prevent the brain from bumping against the interior of the hard skull when the head is subjected to sudden, jarring movements.

4. A highly selective **blood–brain barrier (BBB)** regulates exchanges between the blood and the brain, thus limiting access of blood-borne materials into the vulnerable brain tissue. Throughout the body, materials can be exchanged between the blood and the interstitial fluid only across the walls of capillaries. Capillary walls are formed by a single layer of cells. The holes or pores usually present between the cells making up a capillary wall permit rather free exchange across capillaries elsewhere. However, the cells that form the walls of a brain capillary are joined by tight junctions (see p. 52). These impermeable junctions seal the capillary wall so that nothing can be exchanged across the wall by passing between the cells. The only permissible exchanges occur through the capillary cells themselves. Only selected, carefully regulated exchanges can be made across this barrier. Thus, transport across brain capillary walls *between* the wall-forming cells is *anatomically prevented* and transport *through* the cells is *physiologically restricted.* Together, these mechanisms constitute the BBB. Astrocytes induce formation of the BBB by signaling the cells that form the brain capillaries to "get tight" and by promoting the production of specific carrier proteins and ion channels that regulate the transport of selected substances through these capillary cells.

By strictly limiting exchange between the blood and the brain, the BBB protects the delicate brain from chemical fluctuations in the blood. For example, even if the K^+ level in the blood is doubled, little change occurs in the K^+ concentration of the fluid bathing the central neurons. This is beneficial because alterations in interstitial fluid K^+ would be detrimental to neuronal function. Also, the BBB minimizes the possibility that potentially harmful blood-borne substances might reach the central neural tissue. It further prevents certain circulating hormones that could act as neurotransmitters from reaching the brain, where they could produce uncontrolled nervous activity. On the negative side, the BBB limits the use of drugs for the treatment of brain and spinal cord disorders, because many drugs cannot penetrate this barrier.

The brain depends on constant delivery of oxygen and glucose by the blood.

Even though many substances in the blood never come in contact with the brain tissue, the brain depends more than any other tissue on a constant blood supply. Unlike most tissues, which can resort to anaerobic metabolism to produce ATP in the absence of O_2 for at least short periods (see p. 32), the brain cannot produce ATP without O_2. Also in contrast to most tissues, which can use other sources of fuel for energy production in lieu of glucose, the brain normally uses only glucose but does not store any of this nutrient. Because of its high rate of demand for ATP, under resting conditions the brain uses 20% of the O_2 and 50% of the glucose consumed in the body. Therefore, the brain depends on a continuous, adequate blood supply of O_2 and glucose. Although it constitutes only 2% of body weight, the brain receives 15% of the blood pumped out by the heart.

 Brain damage results if this organ is deprived of its critical O_2 supply for more than 4 to 5 minutes or if its glucose supply is cut off for more than 10 to 15 minutes. The most common cause of inadequate blood supply to the brain is a stroke. (See the accompanying boxed feature, ▶ Beyond the Basics, for details.)

Overview of the Central Nervous System

The CNS consists of the brain and spinal cord. The estimated 100 billion neurons in your brain are assembled into complex networks that enable you to (1) subconsciously regulate your internal environment by neural means, (2) experience emotions, (3) voluntarily control your movements, (4) perceive (be consciously aware of) your own body and your surroundings, and (5) engage in other higher cognitive processes such as thought and memory. The term **cognition** refers to the act or process of "knowing," including both awareness and judgment.

No part of the brain acts in isolation from other brain regions, because networks of neurons are anatomically linked by synapses and neurons throughout the brain communicate extensively with one another by electrical and chemical means. However, neurons that work together to ultimately accomplish a given function tend to be organized within a discrete location. Therefore, even though the brain operates as a whole, it is organized into regions. The parts of the brain can be grouped in various ways based on anatomic distinctions, functional specialization, and evolutionary development. We use the following grouping:

1. Brain stem

2. Cerebellum

3. Forebrain

    a. Diencephalon

        (1) Hypothalamus

        (2) Thalamus

    b. Cerebrum

        (1) Basal nuclei

        (2) Cerebral cortex

Beyond the Basics

Strokes: A Deadly Domino Effect

The most common cause of brain damage is a **cerebrovascular accident (CVA or stroke).** When a cerebral (brain) blood vessel is blocked by a clot (which accounts for more than 80% of strokes) or ruptures, the brain tissue supplied by that vessel loses its vital O_2 and glucose supply. The result is damage and usually death of the deprived tissue. New findings show that neural damage (and the subsequent loss of neural function) extends well beyond the blood-deprived area as a result of a neurotoxic effect that leads to the death of additional nearby cells. The initial blood-deprived cells die by necrosis (unintentional cell death), but the doomed neighbors undergo apoptosis (deliberate cell suicide; see p. 104). In a process known as **excitotoxicity,** the initial O_2-starved cells release excessive amounts of glutamate, a common excitatory neurotransmitter. The excitatory overdose of glutamate from the damaged brain cells binds with and overexcites surrounding neurons. Specifically, glutamate binds with excitatory receptors that function as calcium (Ca^{2+}) channels. As a result of toxic activation of these receptor-channels, they remain open for too long, permitting too much Ca^{2+} to rush into the affected neighbor-

ing neurons. This elevated intracellular Ca^{2+} triggers these cells to self-destruct. Cell-damaging free radicals (see p. 270) are produced during this process. Adding to the injury, researchers speculate that the Ca^{2+} apoptotic signal may spread from these dying cells to abutting healthy cells through gap junctions, cell-to-cell conduits that allow Ca^{2+} and other small ions to diffuse freely between cells (see p. 53). This action kills even more neuronal victims. Thus, most neurons that die following a stroke are originally unharmed cells that commit suicide in response to the chain of reactions unleashed by the toxic release of glutamate from the initial site of O_2 deprivation.

Until the last decade, physicians could do nothing to halt the inevitable neuronal loss following a stroke, leaving patients with an unpredictable mix of neural deficits. Treatment was limited to rehabilitative therapy after the damage was already complete. In recent years, armed with new knowledge about the underlying factors in stroke-related neuronal death, the medical community has been seeking ways to halt the cell-killing dom-

ino effect. The goal is to limit the extent of neuronal damage and thus minimize or even prevent clinical symptoms such as paralysis. In the early 1990s, doctors started administering clot-dissolving drugs within the first 3 hours after the onset of a stroke to restore blood flow through blocked cerebral vessels. Clot busters were the first drugs used to treat strokes, but they are only the beginning of new stroke therapies. Other methods are under investigation to prevent adjacent neurons from succumbing to the neurotoxic release of glutamate. These include blocking the Ca^{2+} receptor-channels that initiate the death-wielding chain of events in response to glutamate, halting the apoptosis pathway that results in self-execution, and blocking the gap junctions that permit the Ca^{2+} death messenger to spread to adjacent cells. These tactics hold much promise for treating strokes, which are the most common cause of adult disability and the third leading cause of death in the United States. However, to date, no new neuroprotective drugs have been found that do not cause serious side effects.

The order in which these components are listed generally represents both their anatomic location (from bottom to top) and their complexity and sophistication of function (from the least specialized, oldest evolutionary level to the newest, most specialized level).

A primitive nervous system consists of comparatively few interneurons interspersed between afferent and efferent neurons. During evolutionary development, the interneuronal component progressively expanded, formed more complex interconnections, and became localized at the head end of the nervous system, forming the brain. Newer, more sophisticated layers of the brain were added on to the older, more primitive layers. The human brain represents the present peak of development.

The *brain stem,* the oldest region of the brain, is continuous with the spinal cord (▲ Table 5-1 and ● Figure 5-6b). It consists of the midbrain, pons, and medulla. The brain stem controls many life-sustaining processes, such as respiration, circulation, and digestion, common to all vertebrates. These processes are

often referred to as vegetative functions, meaning functions performed unconsciously or involuntarily. With the loss of higher brain functions, these lower brain levels, in conjunction with appropriate supportive therapy such as providing adequate nourishment, can still sustain the functions essential for survival, but the person has no awareness or control of that life, a condition sometimes described as "being a vegetable."

Attached at the top rear portion of the brain stem is the *cerebellum,* which is concerned with maintaining proper position of the body in space and subconscious coordination of motor activity (movement). The cerebellum also plays a key role in learning skilled motor tasks, such as a dance routine.

On top of the brain stem, tucked within the interior of the cerebrum, is the *diencephalon.* It houses two brain components: the *hypothalamus,* which controls many homeostatic functions important in maintaining stability of the internal environment; and the *thalamus,* which performs some primitive sensory processing.

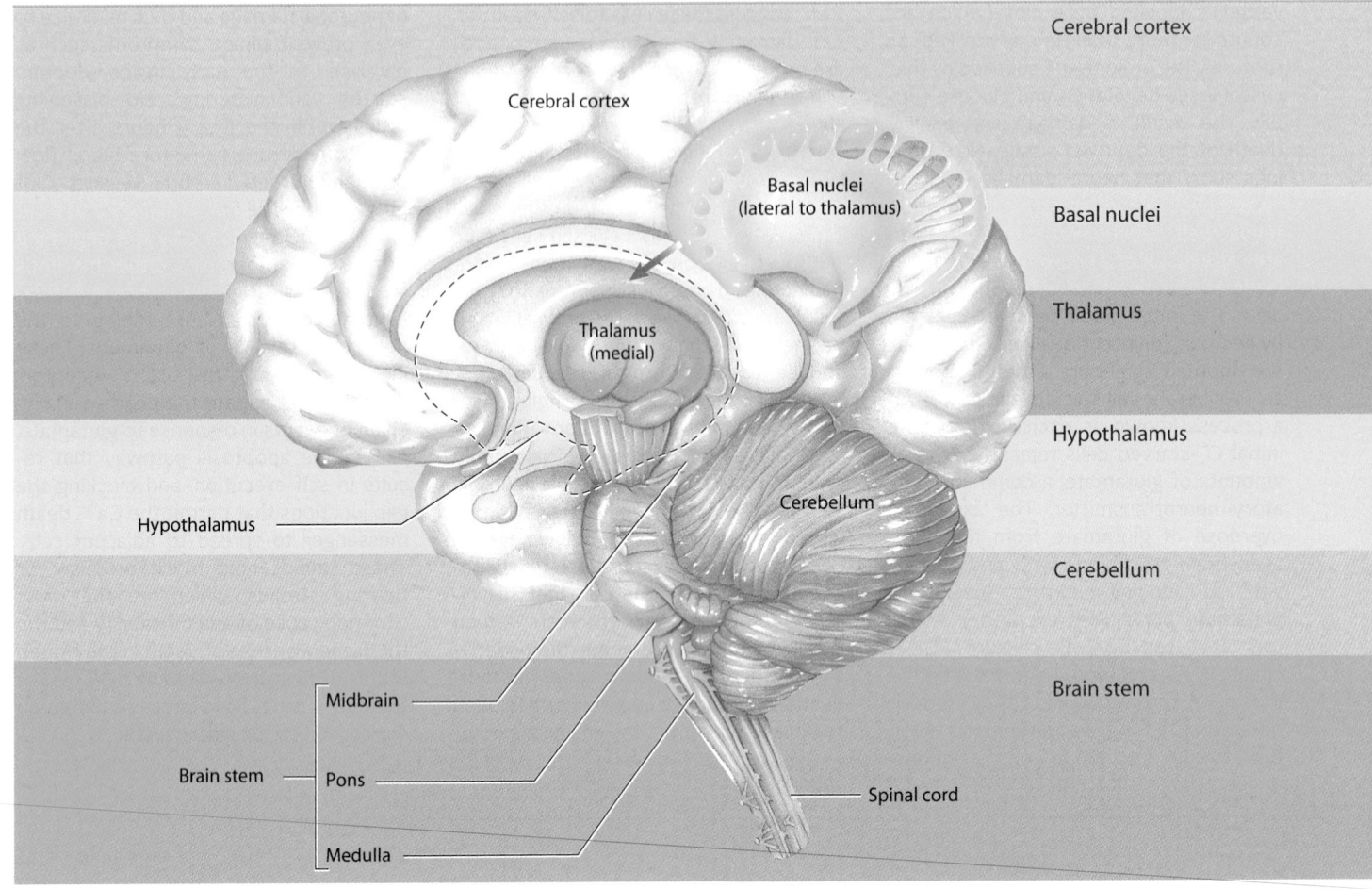

Brain Component

Cerebral cortex

Basal nuclei

Thalamus

Hypothalamus

Cerebellum

Brain stem

Using an ice cream cone as an analogy, on top of this "cone" of lower brain regions is the *cerebrum,* whose "scoop" gets progressively larger and more highly convoluted (that is, has tortuous ridges delineated by deep grooves or folds) the more evolutionarily advanced the vertebrate species is. The cerebrum is most highly developed in humans, where it constitutes about 80% of the total brain weight. The outer layer of the cerebrum is the highly convoluted *cerebral cortex,* which caps an inner core that houses the *basal nuclei.* The myriad convolutions of the human cerebral cortex give it the appearance of a much-folded walnut (● Figure 5-6a). In more ancestral mammal groups, the cortex is smooth. Without these surface wrinkles, the human cortex would take up to three times the area it does and, thus, would not fit like a cover over the underlying structures. The increased neural circuitry housed in the extracerebral cortical area not found in less highly developed species is responsible for many of our unique human abilities. The cerebral cortex plays a key role in the most sophisticated neural functions, such as voluntary initiation of movement, final sensory perception (the brain's interpretation of the body and its surroundings based on sensory input), conscious thought, language, personality traits, and other factors we associate with the mind or intellect. It is the highest, most complex, integrating area of the brain.

Each of these regions of the CNS is now discussed in turn, starting with the highest level, the cerebral cortex, and moving down to the lowest level, the spinal cord.

Cerebral Cortex

The **cerebrum,** by far the largest portion of the human brain, is divided into two halves, the right and left **cerebral hemispheres** (● Figure 5-6a). They are connected to each other by the **corpus callosum,** a thick band consisting of an estimated 300 million neuronal axons that connect the two hemispheres (● Figure 5-6b; also see ● Figure 5-12, p. 130). The corpus callosum is the body's "information superhighway." The two hemispheres communicate and cooperate with each other by means of constant information exchange through this neural connection.

Major Functions

1. Sensory perception
2. Voluntary control of movement
3. Language
4. Personality traits
5. Sophisticated mental events, such as thinking, memory, decision making, creativity, and self-consciousness

1. Inhibition of muscle tone
2. Coordination of slow, sustained movements
3. Suppression of useless patterns of movement

1. Relay station for all synaptic input
2. Crude awareness of sensation
3. Some degree of consciousness
4. Role in motor control

1. Regulation of many homeostatic functions, such as temperature control, thirst, urine output, and food intake
2. Important link between nervous and endocrine systems
3. Extensive involvement with emotion and basic behavioral patterns
4. Role in sleep–wake cycle

1. Maintenance of balance
2. Enhancement of muscle tone
3. Coordination and planning of skilled voluntary muscle activity

1. Origin of majority of peripheral cranial nerves
2. Cardiovascular, respiratory, and digestive control centers
3. Regulation of muscle reflexes involved with equilibrium and posture
4. Reception and integration of all synaptic input from spinal cord; arousal and activation of cerebral cortex
5. Role in sleep–wake cycle

The cerebral cortex is an outer shell of gray matter covering an inner core of white matter.

Each hemisphere is composed of a thin outer shell of *gray matter,* the **cerebral cortex,** covering a thick central core of *white matter* (see ● Figure 5-12). Several other masses of gray matter that collectively constitute the basal nuclei are located deep within the white matter. Throughout the entire CNS, **gray matter** consists mostly of densely packaged neuronal cell bodies and their dendrites, as well as most glial cells. Bundles or tracts of myelinated nerve fibers (axons) constitute the **white matter;** its white appearance is due to the lipid composition of the myelin. The gray matter can be viewed as the "computers" of the CNS and the white matter as the "wires" that connect the computers to one another. Integration of neural input and initiation of neural output take place at synapses within the gray matter. The fiber tracts in the white matter transmit signals from one part of the cerebral cortex to another or between the cortex and the other regions of the CNS. Such communication between different areas of the cortex and elsewhere facilitates integration of their activity. This integration is essential for even a relatively simple task such as picking a flower. Vision of the flower is received by one area of the cortex, reception of its fragrance takes place in another area, and movement is initiated by still another area. More subtle neuronal responses, such as appreciation of the flower's beauty and the urge to pick it, are poorly understood but undoubtedly involve extensive interconnection of fibers among different cortical regions.

The four pairs of lobes in the cerebral cortex are specialized for different activities.

We now consider the locations of the major functional areas of the cerebral cortex. Throughout this discussion, keep in mind that even though a discrete activity is ultimately attributed to a particular region of the brain, no part of the brain functions in isolation. Each part depends on complex interplay among numerous other regions for both incoming and outgoing messages.

The anatomic landmarks used in cortical mapping are specific deep folds that divide each half of the cortex into four major lobes: the *occipital, temporal, parietal,* and *frontal lobes* (● Figure 5-7). Look at the basic functional map of the cortex in ● Figure 5-8a during the following discussion of the major activities attributed to various regions of these lobes.

The **occipital lobes,** located posteriorly (at the back of the head), carry out the initial processing of visual input. Auditory (sound) sensation is initially received by the **temporal lobes,** located laterally (on the sides of the head) (● Figure 5-8a and b). You will learn more about the functions of these regions in Chapter 6 when we discuss vision and hearing.

The parietal lobes and frontal lobes, located on the top of the head, are separated by a deep infolding, the **central sulcus,** which runs roughly down the middle of the lateral surface of each hemisphere. The **parietal lobes** lie to the rear of the central sulcus on each side, and the **frontal lobes** lie in front of it. The parietal lobes are primarily responsible for receiving and processing sensory input. The frontal lobes are responsible for three main functions: (1) voluntary motor activity, (2) speaking ability, and (3) elaboration of thought. We next examine the role of the parietal lobes in sensory perception and then turn to the functions of the frontal lobes in more detail.

The parietal lobes accomplish somatosensory processing.

Sensations from the surface of the body, such as touch, pressure, heat, cold, and pain, are collectively known as **somesthetic sensations** (*somesthetic* means "body feelings") . The means by which afferent neurons detect and relay information to the CNS about these sensations are covered in Chapter 6 when we explore the afferent division of the PNS in detail. Within the CNS, this information is **projected** (transmitted along specific neural pathways to higher brain levels) to the **somatosensory cortex.** The somatosensory cortex is located in the front portion of each parietal lobe immediately behind the central sulcus (● Figures 5-8a and 5-9a). It is the site for initial cortical processing and perception of both somesthetic and proprioceptive input. **Proprioception** is the awareness of body position.

Each region within the somatosensory cortex receives somesthetic and proprioceptive input from a specific area of the body. This distribution of cortical sensory processing is depicted in ● Figure 5-9b. Note that on this **sensory homunculus**

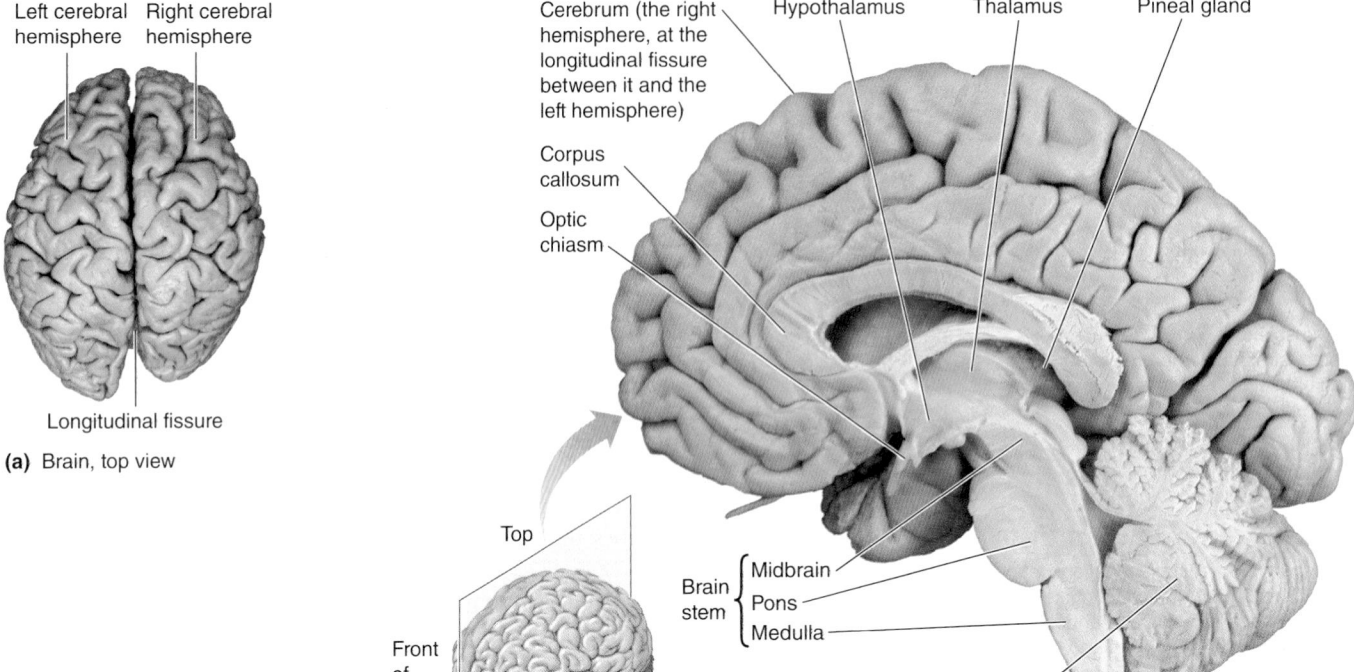

Left cerebral hemisphere   **Right cerebral hemisphere**

Longitudinal fissure

(a) Brain, top view

Cerebrum (the right hemisphere, at the longitudinal fissure between it and the left hemisphere)

Corpus callosum

Optic chiasm

Hypothalamus   Thalamus   Pineal gland

Top

Front of brain

Brain stem { Midbrain / Pons / Medulla

Cerebellum

(b) Brain, sagittal view

● **FIGURE 5-6 Brain of a human cadaver.** (a) Top view of the brain. Note that the deep longitudinal fissure divides the cerebrum into the right and left cerebral hemispheres. (b) Sagittal view of the right half of the brain. All major brain regions are visible from this midline interior view. The corpus callosum is a neural bridge between the two cerebral hemispheres.

Photo: Mark Nielsen, Department of Biology, University of Utah

(*homunculus* means "little man") the different parts of the body are not equally represented. The size of each body part in this homunculus indicates the relative proportion of the somatosensory cortex devoted to that area. The exaggerated size of the face, tongue, hands, and genitalia indicates the high degree of sensory perception associated with these body parts.

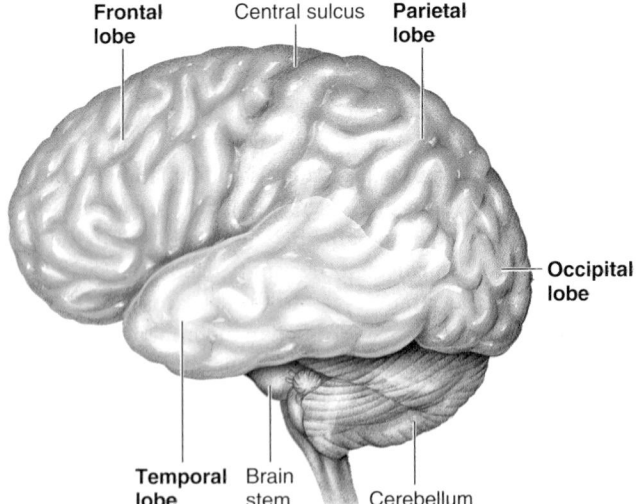

Frontal lobe   Central sulcus   **Parietal lobe**

Occipital lobe

Temporal lobe   Brain stem   Cerebellum

● **FIGURE 5-7 Cortical lobes.** Each half of the cerebral cortex is divided into the occipital, temporal, parietal, and frontal lobes, as depicted in this lateral view of the brain.

The somatosensory cortex on each side of the brain mostly receives sensory input from the opposite side of the body, because most ascending pathways that carry sensory information up the spinal cord cross over to the opposite side before eventually terminating in the cortex. Thus, damage to the somatosensory cortex in the left hemisphere produces sensory deficits on the right side of the body, whereas sensory losses on the left side are associated with damage to the right half of the cortex.

Simple awareness of touch, pressure, temperature, or pain is detected by the thalamus, a lower level of the brain, but the somatosensory cortex goes beyond mere recognition of sensations to fuller sensory perception. The thalamus makes you aware that something hot versus something cold is touching your body, but it does not tell you where or of what intensity. The somatosensory cortex localizes the source of sensory input and perceives the level of intensity of the stimulus. It also is capable of spatial discrimination, so it can discern shapes of objects being held and can distinguish subtle differences in similar objects that come into contact with the skin.

The somatosensory cortex, in turn, projects this sensory input via white matter fibers to adjacent higher sensory areas for even further elaboration, analysis, and integration of sensory information. These higher areas are important in perceiving complex patterns of somatosensory stimulation—for example, simultaneous appreciation of the texture, firmness, temperature, shape, position, and location of an object you are holding.

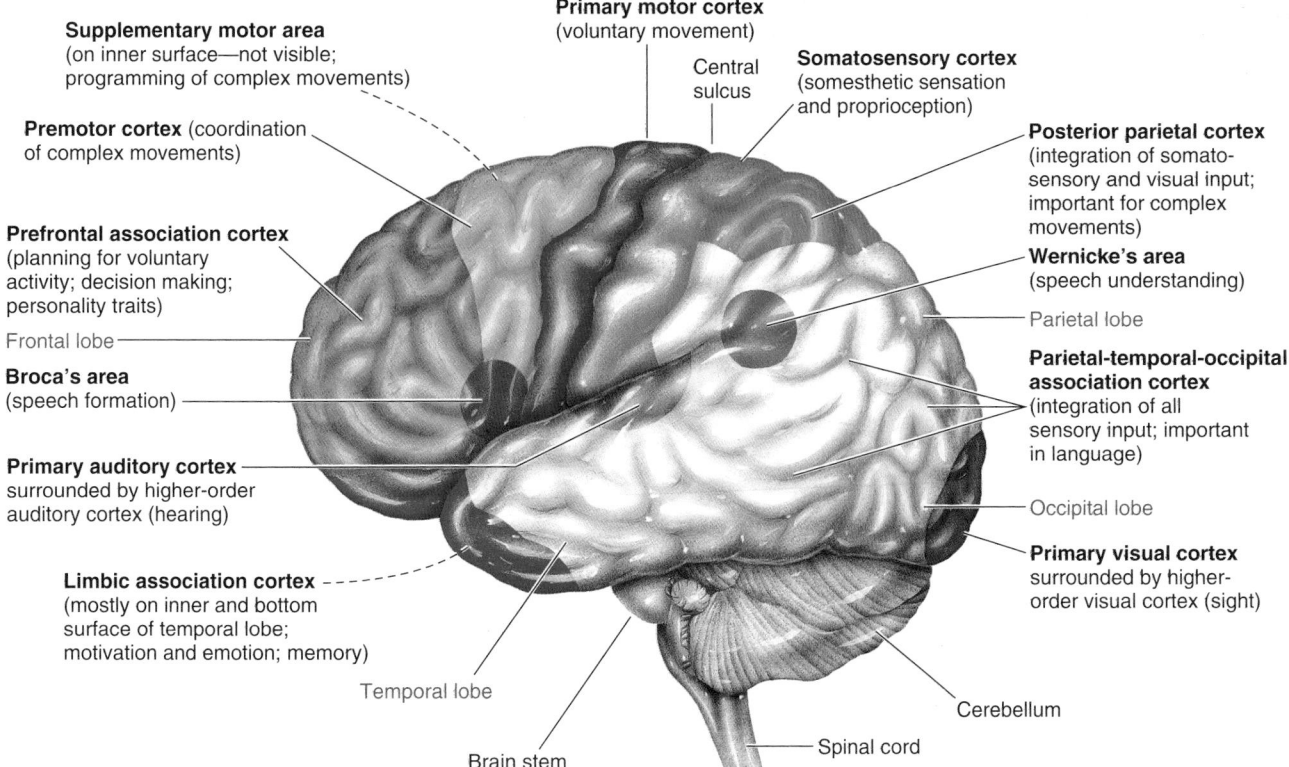

Supplementary motor area
(on inner surface—not visible;
programming of complex movements)

Premotor cortex (coordination
of complex movements)

Prefrontal association cortex
(planning for voluntary
activity; decision making;
personality traits)

Frontal lobe

Broca's area
(speech formation)

Primary auditory cortex
surrounded by higher-order
auditory cortex (hearing)

Limbic association cortex
(mostly on inner and bottom
surface of temporal lobe;
motivation and emotion; memory)

Temporal lobe

Brain stem

Primary motor cortex
(voluntary movement)

Central
sulcus

Somatosensory cortex
(somesthetic sensation
and proprioception)

Posterior parietal cortex
(integration of somato-
sensory and visual input;
important for complex
movements)

Wernicke's area
(speech understanding)

Parietal lobe

Parietal-temporal-occipital
association cortex
(integration of all
sensory input; important
in language)

Occipital lobe

Primary visual cortex
surrounded by higher-
order visual cortex (sight)

Cerebellum

Spinal cord

(a) Regions of the cerebral cortex responsible for various functions

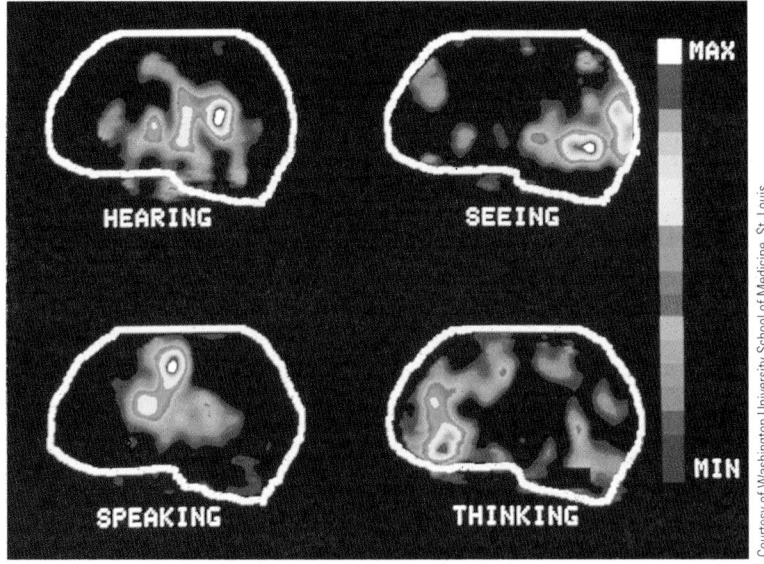

HEARING

SEEING

MAX

SPEAKING

THINKING

MIN

(b) Regions of increased blood flow during different tasks

● **FIGURE 5-8 Functional areas of the cerebral cortex.** (a) Various regions of the cerebral cortex are primarily responsible for various aspects of neural processing, as indicated in this lateral view of the brain. (b) Different areas of the brain "light up" on positron-emission tomography (PET) scans as a person performs different tasks. PET scans detect the magnitude of blood flow in various regions of the brain. Because more blood flows into a particular region of the brain when it is more active, neuroscientists can use PET scans to "take pictures" of the brain at work on various tasks.

The primary motor cortex located in the frontal lobes controls the skeletal muscles.

The area in the rear portion of the frontal lobe immediately in front of the central sulcus and next to the somatosensory cortex is the **primary motor cortex** (see ● Figures 5-8a and 5-9a). It confers voluntary control over movement produced by skeletal muscles. As in sensory processing, the motor cortex on each side of the brain primarily controls muscles on the opposite side of the body. Neuronal tracts originating in the motor cortex of the left hemisphere cross over before passing down the spinal cord to terminate on efferent motor neurons that trigger skeletal muscle contraction on the right side of the body. Accordingly, damage to the motor cortex on the left side of the brain produces paralysis on the right side of the body; the converse is also true.

Stimulation of different areas of the primary motor cortex brings about movement in different regions of the body. Like the sensory homunculus for the somatosensory cortex, the **motor homunculus,** which depicts the location and relative amount of motor cortex devoted to output to the muscles of each body part,

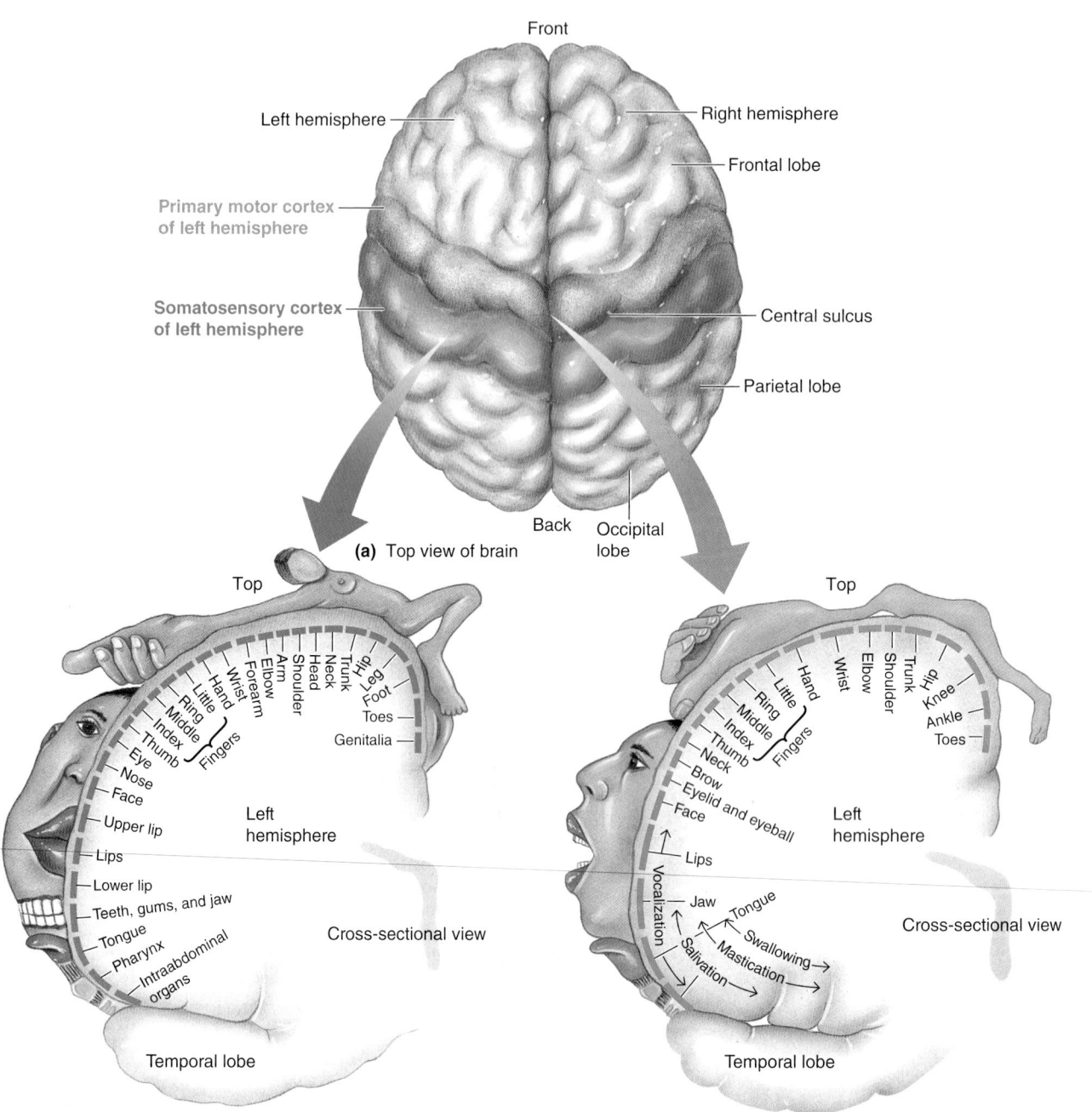

Front

Left hemisphere

Right hemisphere

Frontal lobe

Primary motor cortex of left hemisphere

Somatosensory cortex of left hemisphere

Central sulcus

Parietal lobe

Back

Occipital lobe

(a) Top view of brain

Top

Hip
Leg
Trunk
Neck
Head
Shoulder
Arm
Elbow
Forearm
Wrist
Hand
Little
Ring
Middle
Index
Thumb
Eye
Nose
Face

Foot
Toes
Genitalia

Fingers

Upper lip
Lips
Lower lip
Teeth, gums, and jaw
Tongue
Pharynx
Intraabdominal organs

Left hemisphere

Cross-sectional view

Temporal lobe

(b) Sensory homunculus

Top

Trunk
Shoulder
Elbow
Wrist
Hand
Little
Ring
Middle
Index
Thumb
Neck
Brow
Eyelid and eyeball
Face

Hip
Knee
Ankle
Toes

Fingers

Lips
Jaw
Tongue
Swallowing
Mastication
Salivation
Vocalization

Left hemisphere

Cross-sectional view

Temporal lobe

(c) Motor homunculus

● **FIGURE 5-9 Somatotopic maps of the somatosensory cortex and the primary motor cortex.** (a) Top view of cerebral hemispheres showing the somatosensory cortex and the primary motor cortex. (b) Sensory homunculus showing the distribution of sensory input to the somatosensory cortex from different parts of the body. The distorted graphic representation of the body parts indicates the relative proportion of the somatosensory cortex devoted to reception of sensory input from each area. (c) Motor homunculus showing the distribution of motor output from the primary motor cortex to different parts of the body. The distorted graphic representation of the body parts indicates the relative proportion of the primary motor cortex devoted to controlling skeletal muscles in each area.

is distorted (● Figure 5-9c). The fingers, thumbs, and muscles important in speech, especially those of the lips and tongue, are grossly exaggerated, indicating the fine degree of motor control these body parts have. Compare this to how little brain tissue is devoted to the trunk, arms, and lower extremities, which are not capable of such complex movements. Thus, the extent of representation in the motor cortex is proportional to the precision and complexity of motor skills required of the respective part.

The higher motor areas are also important in motor control.

Even though signals from the primary motor cortex terminate on the efferent neurons that trigger voluntary skeletal muscle contraction, the motor cortex is not the only region of the brain involved with motor control. First, lower brain regions and the spinal cord control involuntary skeletal muscle activity, such as in maintaining posture. Some of these same regions play an important role in monitoring and coordinating voluntary motor activity that the primary motor cortex has set in motion. Second, although fibers originating from the motor cortex can activate motor neurons to bring about muscle contraction, the motor cortex itself does not *initiate* voluntary movement. The motor cortex is activated by a widespread pattern of neuronal discharge, the **readiness potential,** which occurs about 750 msec before specific electrical activity is detectable in the motor cortex. Three higher motor areas of the cortex are involved in this voluntary decision-making period. These higher areas, which all command the primary motor cortex, include the *supplementary motor area,* the *premotor cortex,* and the *posterior parietal cortex* (see ● Figure 5-8a). Furthermore, a subcortical region of the brain, the *cerebellum,* plays an important role in planning, initiating, and timing certain kinds of movement by sending input to the motor areas of the cortex.

The three higher motor areas of the cortex and the cerebellum carry out different, related functions that are all important in programming and coordinating complex movements that involve simultaneous contraction of many muscles. Even though electrical stimulation of the primary motor cortex brings about contraction of particular muscles, no purposeful coordinated movement can be elicited, just as pulling on isolated strings of a puppet does not produce any meaningful movement. A puppet displays purposeful movements only when a skilled puppeteer manipulates the strings in a coordinated manner. In the same way, these four regions (and perhaps other areas as yet undetermined) develop a **motor program** for the specific voluntary task and then "pull" the appropriate pattern of "strings" in the primary motor cortex to produce the sequenced contraction of appropriate muscles that accomplishes the desired complex movement.

The **supplementary motor area** lies on the medial (inner) surface of each hemisphere in front of the primary motor cortex. It plays a preparatory role in programming complex sequences of movement. Stimulation of various regions of this motor area brings about complex patterns of movement, such as opening or closing the hand. Lesions here do not result in paralysis, but they do interfere with performance of more complex, useful integrated movements.

The **premotor cortex,** located on the lateral surface of each hemisphere in front of the primary motor cortex, is important in orienting the body and arms toward a specific target. To command the primary motor cortex to produce the appropriate skeletal muscle contraction for accomplishing the desired movement, the premotor cortex must be informed of the body's momentary position in relation to the target. The premotor cortex is guided by sensory input processed by the **posterior parietal cortex,** a region that lies in back of the primary somatosensory cortex. These two higher motor areas have many anatomic interconnections and are closely related functionally. When either of these areas is damaged, the person cannot process complex sensory information to accomplish purposeful movement in a spatial context; for example, the person cannot successfully manipulate eating utensils.

Even though these higher motor areas command the primary motor cortex and are important in preparing for execution of deliberate, meaningful movement, researchers cannot say that voluntary movement is actually initiated by these areas. This pushes the question of how and where voluntary activity is initiated one step further. Probably no single area is responsible; undoubtedly, numerous pathways can ultimately bring about deliberate movement.

Think about the neural systems called into play, for example, during the simple act of picking up an apple to eat. Your memory tells you the fruit is in a bowl on the kitchen counter. Sensory systems, coupled with your knowledge based on past experience, enable you to distinguish the apple from the other kinds of fruit in the bowl. On receiving this integrated sensory information, motor systems issue commands to the exact muscles of the body in the proper sequence to enable you to move to the fruit bowl and pick up the targeted apple. During execution of this act, minor adjustments in the motor command are made as needed, based on continual updating provided by sensory input about the position of your body relative to the goal. Then there is the issue of motivation and behavior. Are you reaching for the apple because you are hungry (detected by a neural system in the hypothalamus) or because of a more complex behavioral scenario (for example, you started to think about food because you just saw someone eating on television)? Why did you choose an apple rather than a banana when both are in the fruit bowl and you like the taste of both, and so on? Thus, initiating and executing purposeful voluntary movement actually include a complex neuronal interplay that involves output from the motor regions guided by integrated sensory information and ultimately depends on motivational systems and elaboration of thought. All this plays against a background of memory stores from which you can make meaningful decisions about desirable movements.

Different regions of the cortex control different aspects of language.

Unlike the sensory and motor regions of the cortex, which are present in both hemispheres, in most people the areas of the brain responsible for language ability are found in only one hemisphere—the left hemisphere. **Language** is a complex form of communication in which written or spoken words symbolize objects and convey ideas. It involves the integration of two distinct capabilities—namely, *expression* (speaking ability) and *comprehension*—each of which is related to a specific area of the cortex. The primary areas of cortical specialization for language are Broca's area and Wernicke's area. **Broca's area,** which governs speaking ability, is located in the left frontal lobe in close association with the motor areas of the cortex that control the muscles necessary for speaking (see ● Figures 5-8a, 5-8b, and 5-10). **Wernicke's area,** located in the left cortex at the juncture of the parietal, temporal, and occipital lobes, is concerned with language comprehension. It plays a critical role in understanding both spoken and written messages. Furthermore, it is responsible for formulating coherent patterns of speech that are transferred via a bundle of fibers to Broca's area, which in turn controls the act of speaking. Wernicke's area receives input from the visual cortex in the occipital lobe, a pathway important in reading comprehension and in describing objects seen, as well as from the auditory cortex in the temporal lobe, a pathway essential for understanding spoken words. Precise interconnecting pathways between these localized cortical areas are involved in the various aspects of speech.

Because various aspects of language are localized in different regions of the cortex, damage to specific regions of the brain can result in selective disturbances of language. Damage to Broca's area results in a failure of word formation, although the patient can still understand the spoken and written word. Such people know what they want to say but cannot express themselves. Even though they can move their lips and tongue, they cannot establish the proper motor command to say the desired words. In contrast, patients with a lesion in Wernicke's area cannot understand words they see or hear. They can speak fluently, but their perfectly spoken words make no sense. They cannot attach meaning to words or choose appropriate words to convey their thoughts. Such language disorders caused by damage to specific cortical areas are known as **aphasias,** most of which result from strokes. Aphasias should not be confused with **speech impediments,** which are caused by a defect in the mechanical aspect of speech, such as weakness or incoordination of the muscles controlling the vocal apparatus.

Dyslexia, another language disorder, is a difficulty in learning to read because of inappropriate interpretation of words. The problem arises from developmental abnormalities in connections between the visual and the language areas of the cortex or within the language areas themselves; that is, the person is born with "faulty wiring" within the language-processing system. The condition is in no way related to intellectual ability.

The association areas of the cortex are involved in many higher functions.

The motor, sensory, and language areas account for only about half of the total cerebral cortex. The remaining areas, called **association areas,** are involved in higher functions. There are three association areas: (1) the *prefrontal association cortex,* (2) the *parietal–temporal–occipital association cortex,* and (3) the *limbic association cortex* (see ● Figure 5-8a). At one time, the association areas were called "silent" areas, because stimulation does not produce any observable motor response or sensory perception. (During brain surgery, typically the patient remains awake and only local anesthetic is used along the cut scalp. This is possible because the brain itself is insensitive to pain. Before cutting into this precious, nonregenerative tissue, the neurosurgeon explores the exposed region with a tiny stimulating electrode. The patient is asked to describe what

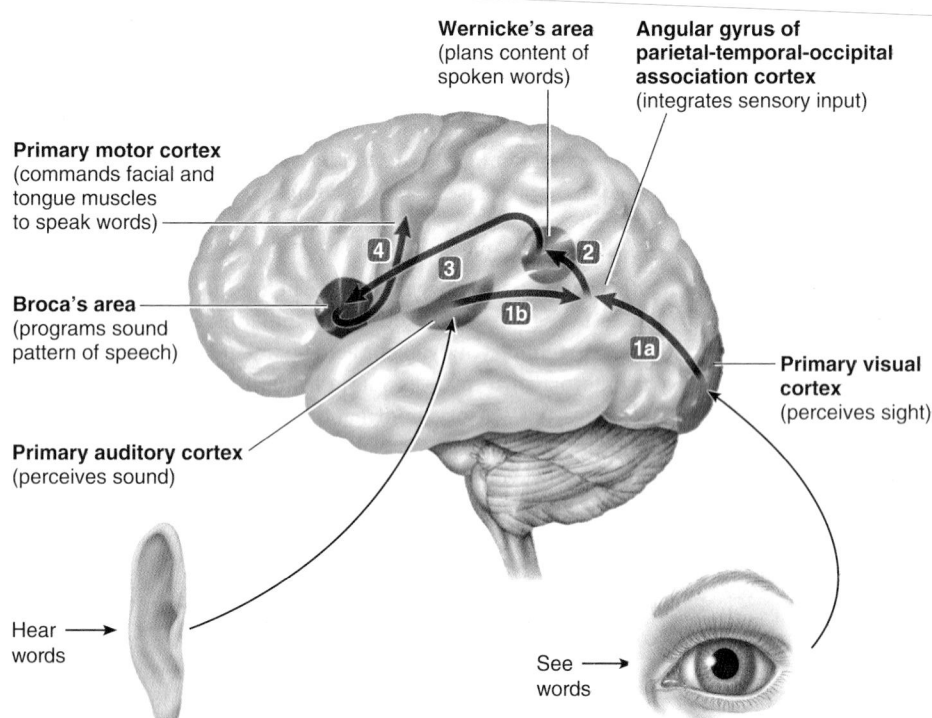

Wernicke's area (plans content of spoken words)

Angular gyrus of parietal-temporal-occipital association cortex (integrates sensory input)

Primary motor cortex (commands facial and tongue muscles to speak words)

Broca's area (programs sound pattern of speech)

Primary auditory cortex (perceives sound)

Primary visual cortex (perceives sight)

Hear words

See words

1a To speak about something seen, the brain transfers the visual information from the primary visual cortex to the angular gyrus of the parietal-temporal-occipital association cortex, which integrates inputs such as sight, sound, and touch.

1b To speak about something heard, the brain transfers the auditory information from the primary auditory cortex to the angular gyrus.

2 The information is transferred to Wernicke's area, where the choice and sequence of words to be spoken are formulated.

3 This language command is then transmitted to Broca's area, which translates the message into a programmed sound pattern.

4 This sound program is conveyed to the precise areas of the primary motor cortex that activate the appropriate facial and tongue muscles for causing the desired words to be spoken.

● **FIGURE 5-10 Cortical pathway for speaking a word seen or heard.** The arrows and numbered steps show the pathway used to speak about something seen or heard. Similarly, appropriate muscles of the hand can be commanded to write the desired words.

happens with each stimulation—the flick of a finger, a prickly feeling on the bottom of the foot, nothing? In this way, the surgeon can ascertain the appropriate landmarks on the neural map before making an incision.)

The **prefrontal association cortex** is the front portion of the frontal lobe just ahead of the premotor cortex. This is the part of the brain that "brainstorms" or thinks (see ● Figure 5-8b). Specifically, the roles attributed to this region are (1) planning for voluntary activity, (2) decision making (that is, weighing consequences of future actions and choosing among options for various social or physical situations), (3) creativity, and (4) personality traits. To carry out these highest of neural functions, the prefrontal cortex is the site of operation of *working memory,* where the brain temporarily stores and actively manipulates information used in reasoning and planning. You will learn more about working memory later. Stimulating the prefrontal cortex does not produce any observable effects, but deficits in this area change personality and social behavior.

The **parietal–temporal–occipital association cortex** lies at the interface of the three lobes for which it is named. In this strategic location, it pools and integrates somatic, auditory, and visual sensations projected from these three lobes for complex perceptual processing. It enables you to "get the complete picture" of the relationship of various parts of your body with the external world. For example, it integrates visual information with proprioceptive input to let you place what you are seeing in proper perspective, such as realizing that a bottle is in an upright position despite the angle from which you view it (that is, whether you are standing up, lying down, or hanging upside down from a tree branch).

The **limbic association cortex** is located mostly on the bottom and adjoining inner portion of each temporal lobe. This area is concerned primarily with motivation and emotion and is extensively involved in memory.

The cortical association areas are all interconnected by bundles of fibers within the cerebral white matter. Collectively, the association areas integrate diverse information for purposeful action.

The cerebral hemispheres have some degree of specialization.

The cortical areas described thus far appear to be equally distributed in both the right and the left hemispheres, except for the language areas, which are found only on one side, usually the left. The left side is also most commonly the dominant hemisphere for fine motor control. Thus, most people are right handed, because the left side of the brain controls the right side of the body. Furthermore, each hemisphere is somewhat specialized in the types of mental activities it carries out best. The **left cerebral hemisphere** excels in logical, analytical, sequential, and verbal tasks, such as math, language forms, and philosophy. In contrast, the **right cerebral hemisphere** excels in nonlanguage skills, especially spatial perception and artistic and musical talents. The left hemisphere tends to process information in a fine-detail, fragmentary way, while the right hemisphere views the world in a big-picture, holistic way. Normally, the two hemispheres share so much information that they complement each other, but in many individuals the skills associated with one hemisphere are more strongly developed. Left cere-bral hemisphere dominance tends to be associated with "thinkers," whereas right hemispheric skills dominate in "creators."

An electroencephalogram is a record of postsynaptic activity in cortical neurons.

Extracellular current flow arising from electrical activity within the cerebral cortex can be detected by placing recording electrodes on the scalp to produce a graphic record known as an **electroencephalogram,** or **EEG.** These "brain waves" for the most part are not due to action potentials but instead represent the momentary collective postsynaptic potential activity (that is, excitatory postsynaptic potentials, or EPSPs, and inhibitory postsynaptic potentials, or IPSPs) (see p. 93) in the cell bodies and dendrites located in the cortical layers under the recording electrode.

Electrical activity can always be recorded from the living brain, even during sleep and unconscious states, but the waveforms vary, depending on the degree of activity in the cerebral cortex. Often the waveforms appear irregular, but sometimes distinct patterns in the wave's amplitude and frequency can be observed. A dramatic example of this is illustrated in ● Figure 5-11, in which the EEG waveform recorded over the occipital (visual) cortex changes markedly in response to simply opening and closing the eyes.

The EEG has three major uses:

1. The EEG is often used as a *clinical tool in the diagnosis of cerebral dysfunction.* Diseased or damaged cortical tissue often gives rise to altered EEG patterns. One of the most common neurological diseases accompanied by a distinctively abnormal EEG is **epilepsy.** Epileptic seizures occur when a large collection of neurons undergo abnormal, synchronous action potentials that produce stereotypical, involuntary spasms and alterations in behavior.

2. The EEG is also used in the *legal determination of brain death.* Even though a person may have stopped breathing and the heart may have stopped pumping blood, it is often possible to restore and maintain respiratory and circulatory activity if resuscitative measures are instituted soon enough. Yet because the brain is susceptible to O_2 deprivation, irreversible brain damage may occur before lung and heart function can be reestablished, resulting in the paradoxical situation of a dead brain in a living body. The determination of whether a comatose patient being maintained by artificial respiration and other supportive measures is alive or dead has important medical, legal, and social implications. The need for viable organs for modern transplant surgery has made

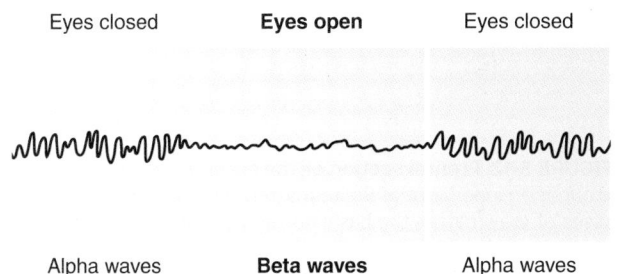

● **FIGURE 5-11 Replacement of an alpha rhythm on an EEG with a beta rhythm when the eyes are opened.**

the timeliness of such life-or-death determinations of utmost importance. Physicians, lawyers, and Americans in general have accepted the notion of brain death—that is, a brain that is not functioning, with no possibility of recovery—as the determinant of death under such circumstances. The most widely accepted indication of brain death is a flat EEG.

3. The EEG is also used to *distinguish various stages of sleep,* as described later in this chapter.

We now shift our attention to the **subcortical regions** of the brain, which interact extensively with the cortex in the perfor-

mance of their functions (*subcortical* means "under the cortex"). These regions include the *basal nuclei,* located in the cerebrum, and the *thalamus* and *hypothalamus,* located in the diencephalon.

Basal Nuclei, Thalamus, and Hypothalamus

The **basal nuclei** (also known as **basal ganglia**) consist of several masses of gray matter located deep within the cerebral white matter (▲ Table 5-1 and ● Figure 5-12). In the CNS, a

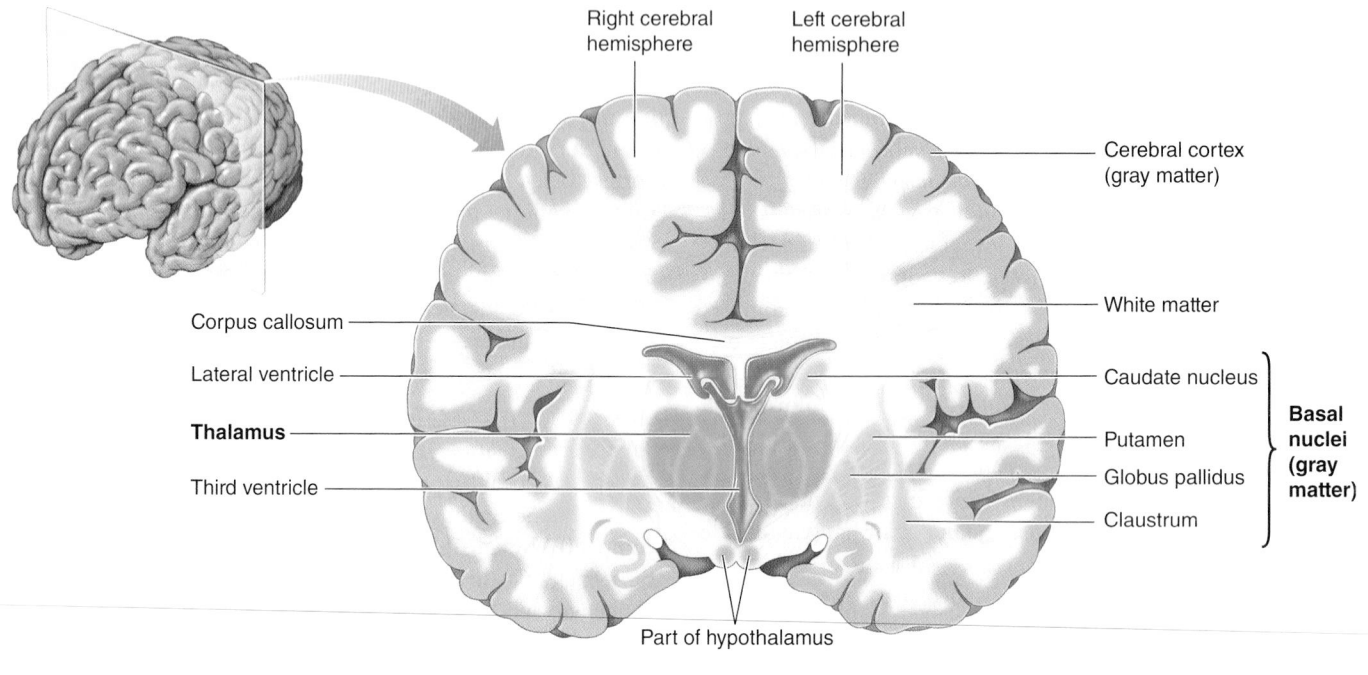

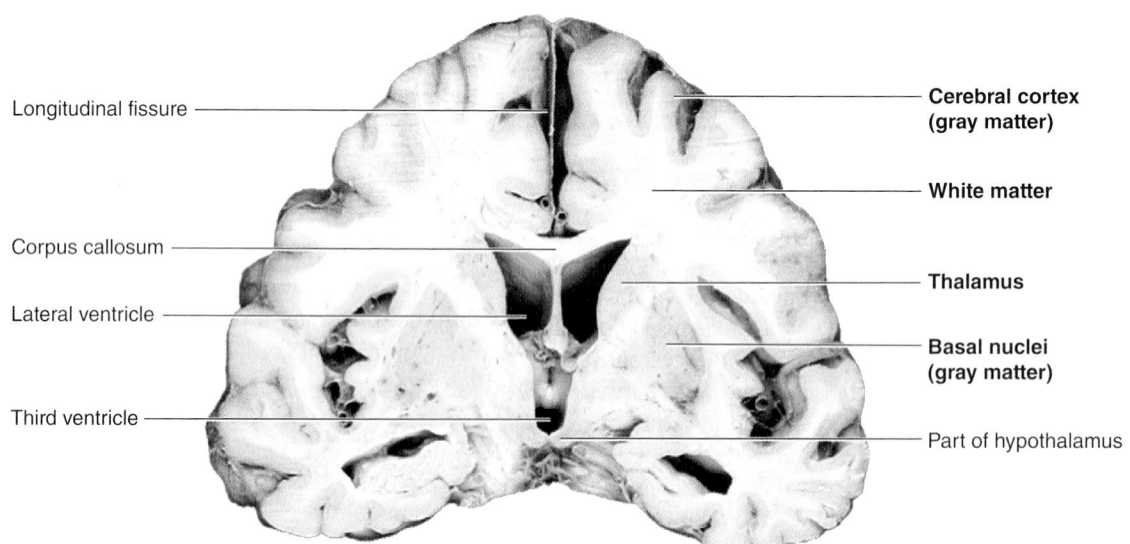

● FIGURE 5-12 **Frontal section of the brain.** The cerebral cortex, an outer shell of gray matter, surrounds an inner core of white matter. Deep within the cerebral white matter are several masses of gray matter, the basal nuclei. The ventricles are cavities in the brain through which the cerebrospinal fluid flows. The thalamus forms the walls of the third ventricle. For comparison, the colors used for these brain components are the same as those used in the lateral view depicted in Table 5-1, p. 122. Also, compare this frontal section of a cadaver brain with the sagittal section of a cadaver brain in Figure 5-6, p. 124.

nucleus (plural, **nuclei**) is a functioning group of neuron cell bodies.

The basal nuclei play an important inhibitory role in motor control.

The basal nuclei play a complex role in controlling movement. In particular, they are important in (1) inhibiting muscle tone throughout the body (proper muscle tone is normally maintained by a balance of excitatory and inhibitory inputs to the neurons that innervate skeletal muscles), (2) selecting and maintaining purposeful motor activity while suppressing useless or unwanted patterns of movement, and (3) helping monitor and coordinate slow, sustained contractions, especially those related to posture and support. The basal nuclei do not directly influence the efferent motor neurons that bring about muscle contraction but act instead by modifying ongoing activity in motor pathways.

Clinical Note The importance of the basal nuclei in motor control is evident in **Parkinson's disease (PD).** This condition is associated with a gradual destruction of neurons that release the neurotransmitter dopamine in the basal nuclei. Because the basal nuclei lack enough dopamine to exert their normal roles, three types of motor disturbances characterize PD: (1) increased muscle tone, or rigidity; (2) involuntary, useless, or unwanted movements, such as *resting tremors* (for example, hands rhythmically shaking, making it difficult or impossible to hold a cup of coffee); and (3) slowness in initiating and carrying out different motor behaviors. People with PD find it difficult to stop ongoing activities. If sitting down, they tend to remain seated, and if they get up, they do so slowly. The standard treatment for PD is the administration of *levodopa (L-dopa),* a precursor of dopamine. Dopamine itself cannot be given because it is unable to cross the BBB, but L-dopa can enter the brain from the blood. Once inside the brain, L-dopa is converted into dopamine, thus substituting for the deficient neurotransmitter.

The thalamus is a sensory relay station and is important in motor control.

Deep within the brain near the basal nuclei is the **diencephalon,** a midline structure that forms the walls of the third ventricular cavity, one of the spaces through which CSF flows (see ● Figure 5-5, p. 119). The diencephalon consists of two main parts, the *thalamus* and the *hypothalamus* (see ▲ Table 5-1 and ● Figures 5-6b, 5-12, and 5-13).

The **thalamus** serves as a "relay station" for preliminary processing of sensory input. All sensory input synapses in the thalamus on its way to the cortex. The thalamus screens out insignificant signals and routes the important sensory impulses to appropriate areas of the somatosensory cortex, as well as to other regions of the brain. Along with the brain stem and cortical association areas, the thalamus helps direct attention to stimuli of interest. For example, parents can sleep soundly through the noise of outdoor traffic but become instantly aware of their baby's slightest whimper. The thalamus is also capable of crude awareness of various sensations but cannot distinguish their location or intensity. Some degree of consciousness resides here as well. Finally, the thalamus plays an important role in motor control by positively reinforcing voluntary motor behavior initiated by the cortex.

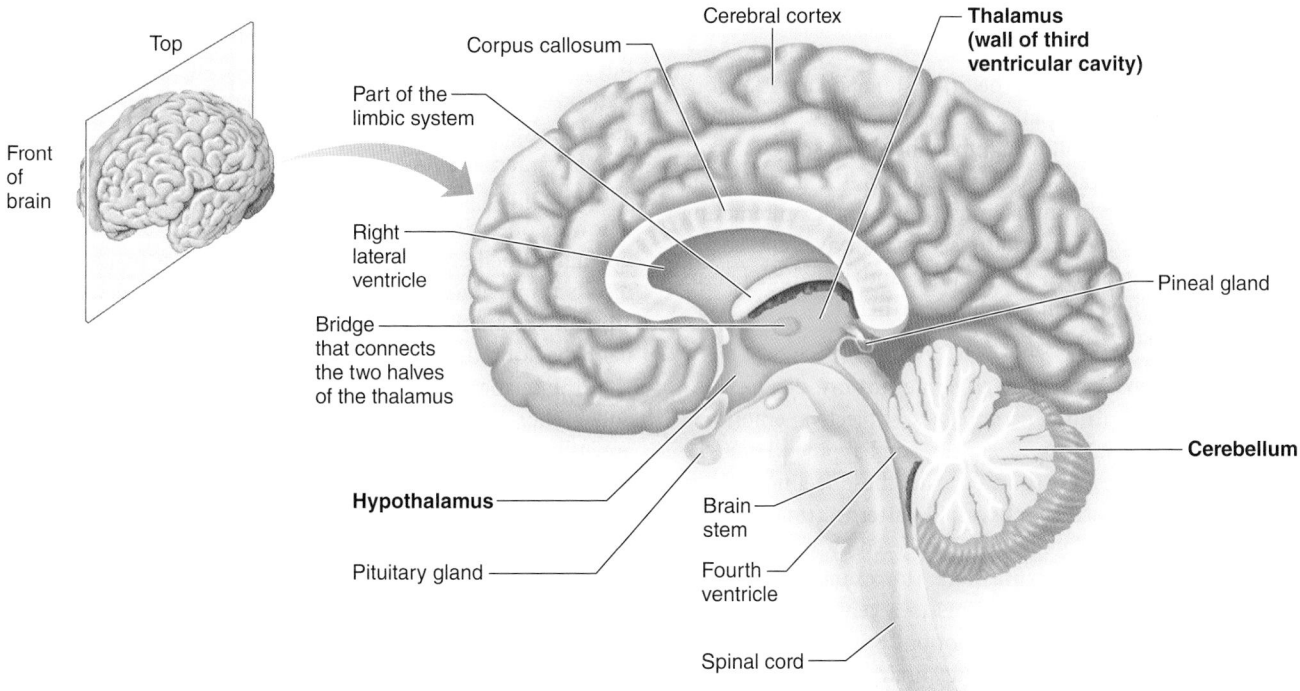

● FIGURE 5-13 **Location of the thalamus, hypothalamus, and cerebellum in sagittal section.**

The hypothalamus regulates many homeostatic functions.
The **hypothalamus** is a collection of specific nuclei and associated fibers that lie beneath the thalamus. It is an integrating center for many important homeostatic functions and is an important link between the autonomic nervous system and the endocrine system. Specifically, the hypothalamus (1) controls body temperature; (2) controls thirst and urine output; (3) controls food intake; (4) controls anterior pituitary hormone secretion; (5) produces posterior pituitary hormones; (6) controls uterine contractions and milk ejection; (7) serves as a major autonomic nervous system coordinating center, which in turn affects all smooth muscle, cardiac muscle, and exocrine glands; (8) plays a role in emotional and behavioral patterns; and (9) participates in the sleep–wake cycle.

The hypothalamus is the brain area most involved in directly regulating the internal environment. For example, when the body is cold, the hypothalamus initiates internal responses to increase heat production (such as shivering) and to decrease heat loss (such as constricting the skin blood vessels to reduce the flow of warm blood to the body surface, where heat could be lost to the external environment). Other areas of the brain, such as the cerebral cortex, act more indirectly to regulate the internal environment. For example, a person who feels cold is motivated to voluntarily put on warmer clothing, close the window, turn up the thermostat, and so on. Even these voluntary behavioral activities are strongly influenced by the hypothalamus, which, as a part of the limbic system, functions with the cortex in controlling emotions and motivated behavior. We now turn to the limbic system and its functional relations with the higher cortex.

Emotion, Behavior, and Motivation

The **limbic system** is not a separate structure but a ring of forebrain structures that surround the brain stem and are interconnected by intricate neuron pathways (● Figure 5-14). It includes portions of each of the following: the lobes of the cerebral cortex (especially the limbic association cortex), the basal nuclei, the thalamus, and the hypothalamus. This complex interacting network is associated with emotions, basic survival and sociosexual behavioral patterns, motivation, and learning. Let us examine each of these brain functions further.

The limbic system plays a key role in emotion.
The concept of **emotion** encompasses subjective emotional feelings and moods (such as anger, fear, and happiness) plus the overt physical responses associated with these feelings. These responses include specific behavioral patterns (for example, preparing for attack or defense when angered by an adversary) and observable emotional expressions (for example, laughing, crying, or blushing). Evidence points to a central role for the limbic system in all aspects of emotion. Stimulating specific regions of the limbic system during brain surgery produces vague subjective sensations that the patient may describe as joy, satisfaction, or pleasure in one region and discouragement, fear, or anxiety in another. For example, the **amygdala,** on the inte-

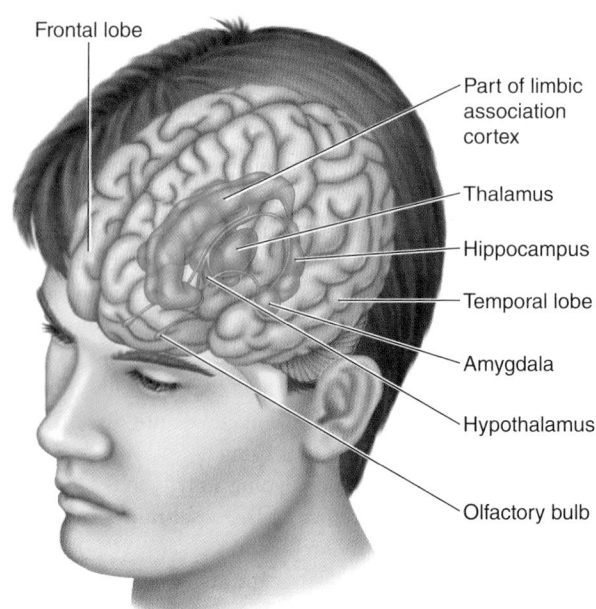

● **FIGURE 5-14 Limbic system.** This partially transparent view of the brain reveals the structures composing the limbic system.

rior underside of the temporal lobe (● Figure 5-14), is especially important in processing inputs that give rise to the sensation of fear. In humans and to an undetermined extent in other species, higher levels of the cortex are also crucial for conscious awareness of emotional feelings.

The limbic system and higher cortex participate in controlling basic behavioral patterns.
Basic inborn behavioral patterns controlled at least in part by the limbic system include those aimed at individual survival (attack, searching for food) and those directed toward perpetuating the species (sociosexual behaviors conducive to mating). In experimental animals, stimulating the limbic system brings about complex and even bizarre behaviors. For example, stimulation in one area can elicit responses of anger and rage in a normally docile animal, whereas stimulation in another area results in placidity and tameness, even in an otherwise vicious animal. Stimulation in yet another limbic area can induce sexual behaviors such as copulatory movements.

The relationships among the hypothalamus, limbic system, and higher cortical regions regarding emotions and behavior are still not well understood. Apparently the extensive involvement of the hypothalamus in the limbic system governs the involuntary internal responses of various body systems in preparation for appropriate action to accompany a particular emotional state. For example, the hypothalamus controls the increase of heart rate and respiratory rate, elevation of blood pressure, and diversion of blood to skeletal muscles that occur in anticipation of attack or when angered. These preparatory changes in the internal state require no conscious control.

In executing complex behavioral activities such as attacking, fleeing, or mating, the individual (humans and other animals) must interact with the external environment. Higher cortical mechanisms are called into play to connect the limbic system and hypothalamus with the outer world so that appropriate overt behaviors are manifested. At the simplest level, the cortex provides the neural mechanisms necessary for implementing the appropriate skeletal muscle activity required to approach or avoid an adversary, participate in sexual activity, or display emotional expression.

Higher cortical levels also can reinforce, modify, or suppress basic behavioral responses so that actions can be guided by planning, strategy, and judgment based on an understanding of the situation. Even if you are angry at someone and your body is internally preparing for attack, you can usually judge whether an attack is appropriate and can consciously suppress the external manifestation of this basic emotional behavior. Thus, the higher levels of the cortex, particularly the prefrontal and limbic association areas, are important in conscious learned control of innate behavioral patterns. Using fear as an example, exposure to an aversive experience calls two parallel tracks into play for processing this emotional stimulus: a fast track in which the lower-level amygdala plays a key role and a slower track mediated primarily by the higher-level prefrontal cortex. The fast track permits a rapid, rather crude, instinctive response ("gut reaction") and is essential for the "feeling" of being afraid. The slower track involving the prefrontal cortex permits a more refined response to the aversive stimulus based on a rational analysis of the current situation compared to stored past experiences. The prefrontal cortex formulates plans and guides behavior, suppressing amygdala-induced responses that may be inappropriate for the situation at hand.

Motivated behaviors are goal directed.

An individual tends to reinforce behaviors that have proved gratifying and to suppress behaviors that have been associated with unpleasant experiences. Certain regions of the limbic system have been designated as **"reward"** and **"punishment" centers,** because stimulation in these respective areas gives rise to pleasant or unpleasant sensations. When a self-stimulating device is implanted in a reward center, an experimental animal will self-deliver up to 5000 stimulations per hour and will continue self-stimulation in preference to food, even when starving. When the device is implanted in a punishment center, animals will avoid stimulation at all costs. Reward centers are found most abundantly in regions involved in mediating the highly motivated behavioral activities of eating, drinking, and sexual activity.

Motivation is the ability to direct behavior toward specific goals. Some goal-directed behaviors are aimed at satisfying specific identifiable physical needs related to homeostasis. **Homeostatic drives** represent the subjective urges associated with specific bodily needs that motivate appropriate behavior to satisfy those needs. As an example, the sensation of thirst accompanying a water deficit in the body drives an individual to drink to satisfy the homeostatic need for water. However, whether water, a soft drink, or another beverage is chosen as the thirst quencher is unrelated to homeostasis. Much human behavior does not depend on purely homeostatic drives related to simple

tissue deficits such as thirst. Human behavior is influenced by experience, learning, and habit, shaped in a complex framework of unique personal gratifications blended with cultural expectations.

Norepinephrine, dopamine, and serotonin are neurotransmitters in pathways for emotions and behavior.

The underlying neurophysiological mechanisms responsible for the psychological observations of emotions and motivated behavior largely remain a mystery, although the neurotransmitters *norepinephrine, dopamine,* and *serotonin* all have been implicated. Norepinephrine and dopamine, both chemically classified as *catecholamines* (see p. 100), are known transmitters in the regions that elicit the highest rates of self-stimulation in animals equipped with do-it-yourself devices. Numerous **psychoactive drugs** affect moods in humans, and some of these drugs have been shown to influence self-stimulation in experimental animals. For example, increased self-stimulation is observed after the administration of drugs that increase catecholamine synaptic activity, such as *amphetamine,* an "upper" drug. Amphetamine stimulates the release of dopamine from dopamine-secreting neurons.

Although most psychoactive drugs are used therapeutically to treat various mental disorders, others, unfortunately, are abused. Many abused drugs act by enhancing the effectiveness of dopamine in the "pleasure" pathways, thus initially giving rise to an intense sensation of pleasure. As you have already learned, an example is cocaine, which blocks the reuptake of dopamine at synapses (see p. 96).

 Depression is among the psychiatric disorders associated with defects in limbic system neurotransmitters. (As a distinction, *psychiatric disorders* involve abnormal activity in specific neurotransmitter pathways in the absence of detectable brain lesions, whereas *neurological disorders* are associated with specific lesions of the brain and may or may not involve abnormalities in neurotransmission. Examples of neurological disorders include PD and Alzheimer's disease.) A functional deficiency of serotonin, norepinephrine, or both is implicated in depression, a disorder characterized by a pervasive negative mood accompanied by a generalized loss of interests, an inability to experience pleasure, and suicidal tendencies. All effective antidepressant drugs increase the available concentration of these neurotransmitters in the CNS. *Prozac,* the most widely prescribed drug in American psychiatry, is illustrative. It blocks the reuptake of released serotonin, thus prolonging serotonin activity at synapses (see p. 94). Serotonin and norepinephrine are synaptic messengers in the limbic regions of the brain involved in pleasure and motivation, suggesting that the pervasive sadness and lack of interest (no motivation) in depressed patients are related at least partly to deficiencies or decreased effectiveness of these neurotransmitters.

Researchers are optimistic that as understanding of the molecular mechanisms of mental disorders is expanded in the future, many psychiatric problems can be corrected or better managed through drug intervention, a hope of great medical significance.

Learning and Memory

In addition to their involvement in emotion and basic behavioral patterns, the limbic system and higher cortex are involved in learning and memory. The cerebellum also plays a key role in some types of learning and memory, as you will see as we examine these processes.

Learning is the acquisition of knowledge as a result of experiences.

Learning is the acquisition of knowledge or skills as a consequence of experience, instruction, or both. Rewards and punishments are integral parts of many types of learning. If an animal is rewarded on responding in a particular way to a stimulus, the likelihood increases that the animal will respond in the same way again to the same stimulus as a consequence of this experience. Conversely, if a particular response is accompanied by punishment, the animal is less likely to repeat the same response to the same stimulus. When behavioral responses that give rise to pleasure are reinforced or those accompanied by punishment are avoided, learning has taken place. Housebreaking a puppy is an example. If the puppy is praised when it urinates outdoors but scolded when it wets the carpet, it will soon learn the acceptable place to empty its bladder. Thus, learning is a change in behavior that occurs as a result of experiences. It highly depends on the organism's interaction with its environment. The only limits to the effects that environmental influences can have on learning are the biological constraints imposed by species-specific and individual genetic endowments.

Memory is laid down in stages.

Memory is the storage of acquired knowledge for later recall. Learning and memory form the basis by which individuals adapt their behavior to their particular external circumstances. Without these mechanisms, it would be impossible for individuals to plan for successful interactions and to intentionally avoid predictably disagreeable circumstances.

The neural change responsible for retention or storage of knowledge is known as the **memory trace.** Generally, concepts, not verbatim information, are stored. As you read this page, you are storing the concept discussed, not the specific words. Later, when you retrieve the concept from memory, you will convert it into your own words. It is possible, however, to memorize bits of information word by word.

Storage of acquired information is accomplished in at least two stages: short-term memory and long-term memory (▲ Table 5-2). **Short-term memory** lasts for seconds to hours, whereas **long-term memory** is retained for days to years. The process of transferring and fixing short-term memory traces into long-term memory stores is known as **consolidation.**

A recently developed concept is that of **working memory,** or what has been called "the erasable blackboard of the mind." Working memory temporarily holds and interrelates various pieces of information relevant to a current mental task. Through your working memory, you briefly hold and process data for immediate use—both newly acquired information and related, previously stored knowledge that is transiently brought forth into working memory—so that you can evaluate the incoming data in context. This integrative function is crucial to your ability to reason, plan, and make judgments. By comparing and manipulating new and old information within your working memory, you can comprehend what you are reading, carry on a conversation, calculate a restaurant tip in your head, find your way home, and know that you should put on warm clothing if you see snow outside. In short, working memory enables people to string thoughts together in a logical sequence and plan for future action.

COMPARISON OF SHORT-TERM AND LONG-TERM MEMORY Newly acquired information is initially deposited in short-term memory, which has a limited capacity for storage. Information in short-term memory has one of two eventual fates. Either it is soon for-

▲ Table 5-2 Comparison of Short-Term and Long-Term Memory

Characteristic	Short-Term Memory	Long-Term Memory
Time of storage after acquisition of new information	Immediate	Later; must be transferred from short-term to long-term memory through consolidation; enhanced by practice or recycling of information through short-term mode
Duration	Lasts for seconds to hours	Retained for days to years
Capacity of storage	Limited	Very large
Retrieval time (remembering)	Rapid retrieval	Slower retrieval, except for thoroughly ingrained memories, which are rapidly retrieved
Inability to retrieve (forgetting)	Permanently forgotten; memory fades quickly unless consolidated into long-term memory	Usually only transiently unable to access; relatively stable memory trace
Mechanism of storage	Involves transient modifications in functions of preexisting synapses, such as altering the amount of neurotransmitter released	Involves relatively permanent functional or structural changes between existing neurons, such as the formation of new synapses; synthesis of new proteins plays a key role

gotten (for example, forgetting a telephone number after you have looked it up and finished dialing), or it is transferred into the more permanent long-term memory mode through *active practice* or *rehearsal.* The recycling of newly acquired information through short-term memory increases the likelihood that the information will be consolidated into long-term memory. (Therefore, when you cram for an exam, your long-term retention of the information is poor!) This relationship can be likened to developing photographic film. The originally developed image (short-term memory) will rapidly fade unless it is chemically fixed (consolidated) to provide a more enduring image (long-term memory). Sometimes only parts of memories are fixed while other parts fade away. Information of interest or importance to the individual is more likely to be recycled and fixed in long-term stores, whereas less important information is quickly erased.

The storage capacity of the long-term memory bank is much larger than the capacity of short-term memory. Different informational aspects of long-term memory traces seem to be processed, codified, and then stored with other memories of the same type; for example, visual memories are stored separately from auditory memories. This organization facilitates future searching of memory stores to retrieve desired information. For example, in remembering a woman you once met, you may use various recall cues from different storage pools, such as her name, her appearance, the fragrance she wore, an incisive comment she made, or the song playing in the background.

Stored knowledge is of no use unless it can be retrieved and used to influence current or future behavior. Because long-term memory stores are larger, it often takes longer to retrieve information from long-term memory than from short-term memory. *Remembering* is the process of retrieving specific information from memory stores; *forgetting* is the inability to retrieve stored information. Information lost from short-term memory is permanently forgotten, but information in long-term storage is often forgotten only temporarily. For example, you may be transiently unable to remember an acquaintance's name and then have it suddenly "come to you" later.

Some forms of long-term memory involving information or skills used daily are essentially never forgotten and are rapidly accessible, such as knowing your own name or being able to write. Even though long-term memories are relatively stable, stored information may be gradually lost or modified over time unless it is thoroughly ingrained by years of practice.

 AMNESIA Occasionally, individuals suffer from a lack of memory that involves whole portions of time rather than isolated bits of information. This condition, known as **amnesia**, occurs in two forms. The most common form, *retrograde* (meaning "going backward") *amnesia,* is the inability to recall recent past events. It usually follows a traumatic event that interferes with electrical activity of the brain, such as a concussion or stroke. If a person is knocked unconscious, the content of short-term memory is essentially erased, resulting in loss of memory about activities that occurred within about the last half hour before the event. Severe trauma may interfere with access to recently acquired information in long-term stores as well.

Anterograde (meaning "going forward") *amnesia,* conversely, is the inability to consolidate memory in long-term storage for later retrieval. It is usually associated with lesions of the medial portions of the temporal lobes, which are generally considered critical regions for memory consolidation. People suffering from this condition may be able to recall things they learned before the onset of their problem, but they cannot establish new permanent memories. New information is lost as quickly as it fades from short-term memory. In one case study, the person could not remember where the bathroom was in his new home but still had total recall of his old home.

Short-term memory and long-term memory involve different molecular mechanisms.

Despite a vast amount of psychological data, only a few tantalizing scraps of physiological evidence concerning the cellular basis of memory traces are available. Obviously, some change must take place within the neural circuitry of the brain to account for the altered behavior that follows learning. A single memory does not reside in a single neuron but rather in changes in the pattern of signals transmitted across synapses within a vast neuronal network.

Different mechanisms are responsible for short-term and long-term memory, as follows:

1. Short-term memory involves transient modifications in the function of preexisting synapses, such as a temporary change in the amount of neurotransmitter released in response to stimulation or temporary increased responsiveness of the postsynaptic cell to the neurotransmitter within affected nerve pathways.

2. Long-term memory storage, in contrast, requires the activation of specific genes that control synthesis of proteins, needed for lasting structural or functional changes at specific synapses. Thus, long-term memory storage involves rather permanent physical changes in the brain. Examples of such changes include the formation of new synaptic connections or permanent changes in pre- or postsynaptic membranes.

Memory traces are present in multiple regions of the brain.

Another question besides the "how" of memory is the "where" of memory. What parts of the brain are responsible for memory? There is no single "memory center" in the brain. Instead, the neurons involved in memory traces are widely distributed throughout the subcortical and cortical regions of the brain. The regions of the brain most extensively implicated in memory include the hippocampus and associated structures of the medial temporal lobes, the limbic system, the cerebellum, and the prefrontal cortex, as well as other areas of the cerebral cortex.

THE HIPPOCAMPUS AND DECLARATIVE MEMORIES The **hippocampus,** the elongated, medial portion of the temporal lobe that is part of the limbic system (see ● Figure 5-14), plays a vital role in short-term memory involving the integration of various related stimuli and is crucial for consolidation into long-term memory. The hippocampus is believed to store new long-term memories only temporarily and then transfer them to other cortical sites for more permanent storage. The sites for long-term storage of various types of memories are only beginning to be identified by neuroscientists.

The hippocampus and surrounding regions play an especially important role in **declarative memories**—the "what" memories of specific people, places, objects, facts, and events that often result after only one experience and that can be declared or verbalized in a statement such as "I saw the Statue of Liberty last summer" or conjured up in a mental image. Declarative memories involve conscious recall.

 People with hippocampal damage are profoundly forgetful of facts critical to daily functioning. Declarative memories typically are the first to be lost. Extensive damage in the hippocampus is evident in patients with **Alzheimer's disease (AD)** during autopsy. The condition is characterized by extracellular neuritic plaques and intracellular neurofibrillary tangles, both of which are especially abundant in the hippocampus. A *neuritic* (or *senile*) *plaque* is an abnormal deposit of a waxy, fibrous protein known as *beta amyloid* surrounded by degenerating dendritic and axonal nerve endings. Beta amyloid is toxic to neurons. *Neurofibrillary tangles* are dense bundles of abnormal cytoskeletal filaments that accumulate in the cell body of an affected neuron and interfere with its vital axonal transport system (see p. 37), further contributing to the neuron's demise. Acetylcholine-secreting neurons that terminate in the hippocampus and cerebral cortex are particularly affected. Neuron death and loss of synaptic communication are responsible for the ensuing dementia. AD accounts for about two thirds of the cases of *senile dementia* (diminution of mental abilities in old age). In the earliest stages of AD, only short-term memory is impaired, but as the disease progresses, even firmly entrenched long-term memories, such as recognition of family members, are lost. Higher mental abilities gradually deteriorate as the patient loses the ability to read, write, and calculate. Language ability and speech are often impaired. In later stages, AD victims are unable to feed, dress, and groom themselves.

THE CEREBELLUM AND PROCEDURAL MEMORIES The cerebellum and relevant cortical regions play an essential role in the "how to" **procedural memories** involving motor skills gained through repetitive training, such as memorizing a particular dance routine. The cortical areas important for a given procedural memory are the specific motor or sensory systems engaged in performing the routine. For example, different groups of muscles are called into play to tap dance than those needed to execute a dive. In contrast to declarative memories, which are consciously recollected from previous experiences, procedural memories can be brought forth without conscious effort. For example, an ice skater during a competition typically performs best by "letting the body take over" the routine instead of thinking about exactly what needs to be done next.

 The distinct localization in different parts of the brain of declarative and procedural memory is apparent in people who have temporal or limbic lesions.

They can perform a skill, such as playing a piano, but the next day they have no recollection of having done so.

THE PREFRONTAL CORTEX AND WORKING MEMORY The major orchestrator of the complex reasoning skills associated with *working memory* is the prefrontal association cortex. The prefrontal cortex serves as a temporary storage site for holding relevant data online and is largely responsible for the so-called executive functions involving manipulation and integration of this information for planning, juggling competing priorities, problem solving, and organizing activities. Researchers have identified different storage bins in the prefrontal cortex, depending on the nature of the current relevant data. For example, working memory involving spatial cues is in a prefrontal location distinct from working memory involving verbal cues or cues about an object's appearance. One recent fascinating proposal suggests that a person's intelligence may be determined by the capacity of working memory to temporarily hold and relate a variety of relevant data.

Cerebellum

The **cerebellum** is a highly folded, baseball-sized part of the brain that lies underneath the occipital lobe of the cortex and is attached to the back of the upper portion of the brain stem (see ▲ Table 5-1, p. 122, and ● Figures 5-6b, p. 124, and 5-13, p. 131).

The cerebellum is important in balance and in planning and executing voluntary movement.

More individual neurons are found in the cerebellum than in the entire rest of the brain, indicative of the importance of this structure. The cerebellum consists of three functionally distinct parts with different roles concerned primarily with subconscious control of motor activity (● Figure 5-15). Specifically, the different parts of the cerebellum perform the following functions:

1. The **vestibulocerebellum** is important for maintaining balance and controls eye movements.

2. The **spinocerebellum** enhances muscle tone and coordinates skilled, voluntary movements. This brain region is especially important in ensuring the accurate timing of various muscle contractions to coordinate movements involving multiple joints. For example, the movements of your shoulder, elbow, and wrist joints must be synchronized even during the simple act of reaching for a pencil. When cortical motor areas send messages to muscles for executing a particular movement, the spinocerebellum is informed of the intended motor command. This region also receives input from peripheral receptors that inform it about the body movements and positions that are actually taking place. The spinocerebellum essentially acts as "middle management," comparing the "intentions" or "orders" of the higher centers with the "performance" of the muscles and then correcting any "errors" or deviations from the intended movement. The spinocerebellum even seems able to predict the position of a body part in the next fraction of a second during

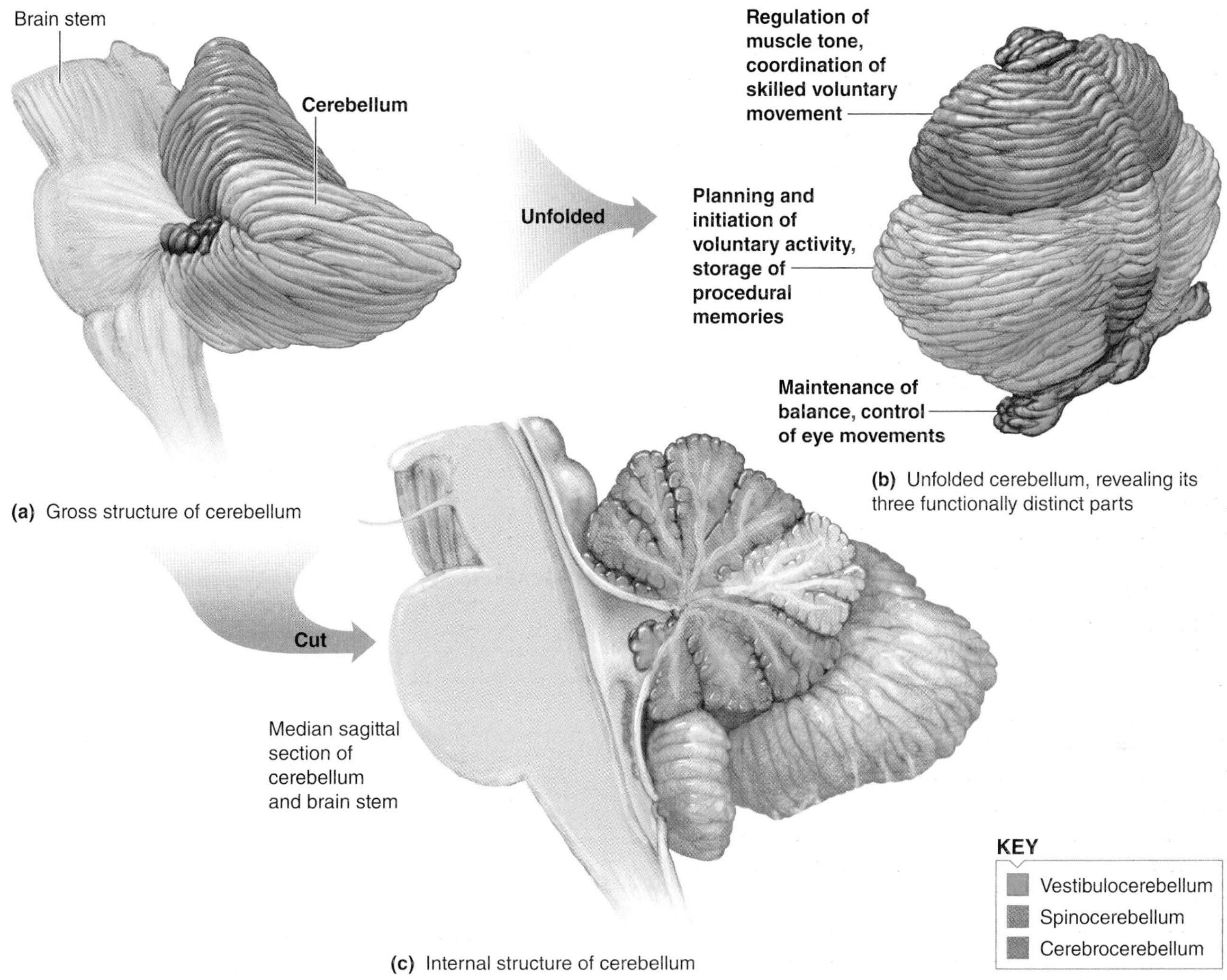

Brain stem

Cerebellum

(a) Gross structure of cerebellum

Regulation of
muscle tone,
coordination of
skilled voluntary
movement

Unfolded

Planning and
initiation of
voluntary activity,
storage of
procedural
memories

Maintenance of
balance, control
of eye movements

(b) Unfolded cerebellum, revealing its
three functionally distinct parts

Cut

Median sagittal
section of
cerebellum
and brain stem

KEY

Vestibulocerebellum
Spinocerebellum
Cerebrocerebellum

(c) Internal structure of cerebellum

● **FIGURE 5-15 Cerebellum.**

a complex movement and to make adjustments accordingly. If you are reaching for a pencil, for example, this region "puts on the brakes" soon enough to stop the forward movement of your hand at the intended location rather than letting you overshoot your target. These ongoing adjustments, which ensure smooth, precise, directed movement, are especially important for rapidly changing (phasic) activities such as typing, playing the piano, or running.

3. The **cerebrocerebellum** plays a role in planning and initiating voluntary activity by providing input to the cortical motor areas. This is also the cerebellar region that stores procedural memories.

 All the following symptoms of cerebellar disease result from a loss of these functions: poor balance; "drunken sailor" gait with wide stance and unsteady walking; rhythmic, oscillating eye movements; reduced muscle tone but no paralysis; inability to perform rapid alternating movements smoothly; and inability to stop and start skeletal muscle action quickly. The latter gives rise to an *intention tremor* characterized by oscillating to-and-fro movements of a limb as it approaches its intended destination. A person with cerebellar

damage who tries to pick up a pencil may overshoot the pencil and then rebound excessively, repeating this to-and-fro process until success is finally achieved. No tremor is observed except in performing intentional activity, in contrast to the resting tremor associated with disease of the basal nuclei, most notably PD.

The cerebellum and basal nuclei both monitor and adjust motor activity commanded from the motor cortex, and like the basal nuclei, the cerebellum does not directly influence the efferent motor neurons. Although they perform different roles (for example, the cerebellum enhances muscle tone, whereas the basal nuclei inhibit it), both function indirectly by modifying the output of major motor systems in the brain. The motor command for a particular voluntary activity arises from the motor cortex, but the actual execution of that activity is coordinated subconsciously by these subcortical regions. To illustrate, you can voluntarily decide you want to walk, but you do not have to consciously think about the specific sequence of movements you have to perform to accomplish this intentional act. Accordingly, much voluntary activity is actually involuntarily regulated.

You will learn more about motor control when we discuss skeletal muscle physiology in Chapter 8. For now, we move on to the remaining part of the brain, the brain stem.

Brain Stem

The **brain stem** consists of the **medulla, pons,** and **midbrain** (see ▲ Table 5-1 and ● Figure 5-6b).

The brain stem is a vital link between the spinal cord and the higher brain regions.

All incoming and outgoing fibers traversing between the periphery and the higher brain centers must pass through the brain stem, with incoming fibers relaying sensory information to the brain and outgoing fibers carrying command signals from the brain for efferent output. Most of these fibers synapse within the brain stem for important processing. Thus, the brain stem is a critical connecting link between the rest of the brain and the spinal cord.

The functions of the brain stem include the following:

1. Most of the 12 pairs of **cranial nerves** arise from the brain stem. With one major exception, these nerves supply structures in the head and neck with both sensory and motor fibers. They are important in sight, hearing, taste, smell, sensation of the face and scalp, eye movement, chewing, swallowing, facial expressions, and salivation. The major exception is cranial nerve X, the **vagus nerve.** Instead of innervating regions in the head, most branches of the vagus nerve supply organs in the thoracic and abdominal cavities. The vagus is the major nerve of the parasympathetic nervous system.

2. Collected within the brain stem are neuronal clusters or **"centers"** that control heart and blood vessel function, respiration, and many digestive activities. An example is the respiratory control center.

3. The brain stem helps regulate muscle reflexes involved in equilibrium and posture.

4. A widespread network of interconnected neurons called the **reticular formation** runs throughout the entire brain stem and into the thalamus. This network receives and integrates all incoming sensory synaptic input. Ascending fibers originating in the reticular formation carry signals upward to arouse and activate the cerebral cortex (● Figure 5-16). These fibers compose the **reticular activating system (RAS),** which controls the overall degree of cortical alertness and is important in the ability to direct attention. In turn, fibers descending from the cortex, especially its motor areas, can activate the RAS.

5. The centers that govern sleep traditionally have been considered to be housed within the brain stem, although recent evidence suggests that the hypothalamus plays a key role too.

We now examine sleep and the other states of consciousness in further detail.

Sleep is an active process consisting of alternating periods of slow-wave and paradoxical sleep.

The term **consciousness** refers to subjective awareness of the external world and self, including awareness of the private inner world of one's own mind—that is, awareness of thoughts, percep-

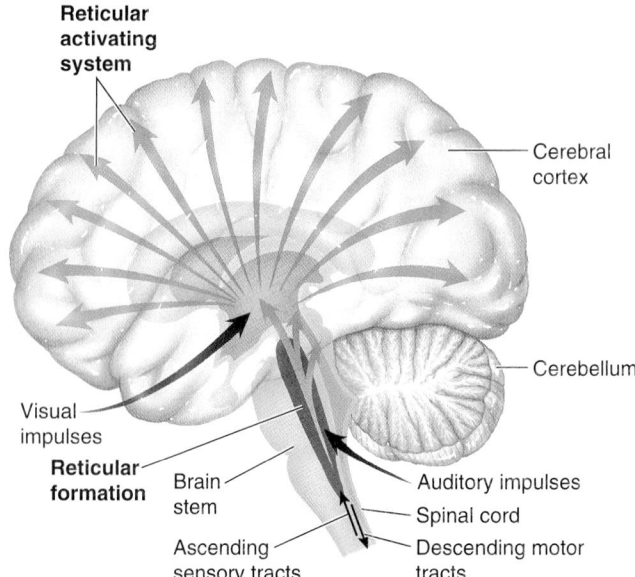

● **FIGURE 5-16 The reticular activating system.** The reticular formation, a widespread network of neurons within the brain stem (in red), receives and integrates all synaptic input. The reticular activating system, which promotes cortical alertness and helps direct attention toward specific events, consists of ascending fibers (in blue) that originate in the reticular formation and carry signals upward to arouse and activate the cerebral cortex.

tions, dreams, and so on. Even though the final level of awareness resides in the cerebral cortex and a crude sense of awareness is detected by the thalamus, conscious experience depends on the integrated functioning of many parts of the nervous system. The cellular and molecular basis underlying consciousness is one of the greatest unanswered questions in neuroscience.

The following states of consciousness are listed in decreasing order of arousal level, based on the extent of interaction between peripheral stimuli and the brain:

- maximum alertness
- wakefulness
- sleep (several types)
- coma

Maximum alertness depends on attention-getting sensory input that "energizes" the RAS and subsequently the activity level of the CNS as a whole. At the other extreme, **coma** is the total unresponsiveness of a living person to external stimuli, caused either by brain stem damage that interferes with the RAS or by widespread depression of the cerebral cortex, such as accompanies O_2 deprivation.

The **sleep–wake cycle** is a normal cyclic variation in awareness of surroundings. In contrast to being awake, sleeping people are not consciously aware of the external world, but they do have inward conscious experiences such as dreams. Furthermore, they can be aroused by external stimuli, such as an alarm going off.

Sleep is an active process, not just the absence of wakefulness. The brain's overall level of activity is not reduced during sleep. During certain stages of sleep, O_2 uptake by the brain is even increased above normal waking levels.

Comparison of Slow-Wave and Paradoxical Sleep

	TYPE OF SLEEP	
Characteristic	Slow-Wave Sleep	Paradoxical Sleep
EEG	Displays slow waves	Similar to the EEG of an alert, awake person
Motor activity	Considerable muscle tone; frequent shifting	Abrupt inhibition of muscle tone; no movement
Heart rate, respiratory rate, and blood pressure	Regular	Irregular
Dreaming	Rare (mental activity is an extension of waking-time thoughts)	Common
Arousal	Sleeper is easily awakened	Sleeper is hard to arouse but apt to wake up spontaneously
Percentage of sleeping time	80%	20%
Other important characteristics	Has four stages; sleeper must pass through this type of sleep first	Rapid eye movements

There are two types of sleep, characterized by different EEG patterns and different behaviors: *slow-wave sleep* and *paradoxical,* or *REM, sleep* (▲ Table 5-3).

EEG PATTERNS DURING SLEEP **Slow-wave sleep** occurs in four stages, each displaying progressively slower EEG waves of higher amplitude (hence, "slow-wave" sleep) (● Figure 5-17). At the onset of sleep, you move from the light sleep of stage 1 to the deep sleep of stage 4 of slow-wave sleep during a period of 30 to 45 minutes; then you reverse through the same stages in the same amount of time. A 10- to 15-minute episode of **paradoxical sleep** punctuates the end of each slow-wave sleep cycle. Paradoxically, your EEG pattern during this time abruptly becomes similar to that of a wide-awake, alert individual, even though you are still asleep (hence, "paradoxical" sleep) (● Figure 5-17). After the paradoxical episode, the stages of slow-wave sleep repeat. You cyclically alternate between the two types of sleep throughout the night. In a normal sleep cycle, you always pass through slow-wave sleep before entering paradoxical sleep. Brief periods of wakefulness occasionally occur.

BEHAVIORAL PATTERNS DURING SLEEP In addition to distinctive EEG patterns, the two types of sleep are distinguished by behavioral differences. It is difficult to pinpoint exactly when an individual drifts from drowsiness into slow-wave sleep. In this type of sleep, the person still has considerable muscle tone and often shifts body position. Respiratory rate, heart rate, and blood pressure remain regular. During this time, the sleeper can be easily awakened and rarely dreams. The mental activity associated with slow-wave sleep is less visual than dreaming. It is more conceptual and plausible—like an extension of waking-time thoughts concerned with everyday events—and it is less likely to be recalled.

The behavioral pattern accompanying paradoxical sleep is marked by abrupt inhibition of muscle tone throughout the body. The muscles are completely relaxed, with no movement taking place except in the eye muscles. Paradoxical sleep is

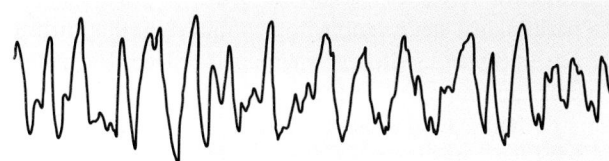

Slow-wave sleep, stage 4

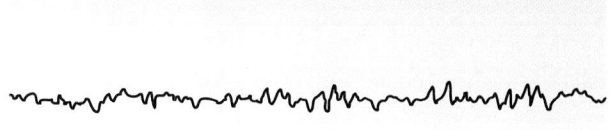

Paradoxical sleep

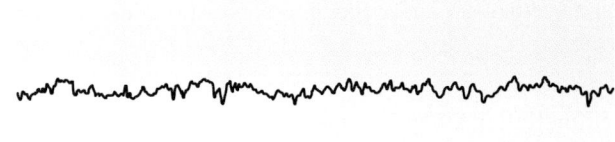

Awake, eyes open

● **FIGURE 5-17** **EEG patterns during types of sleep.** Note that the EEG pattern during paradoxical sleep is similar to that of an alert, awake person, whereas the pattern during slow-wave sleep displays distinctly different waves.

characterized by *rapid eye movements,* hence the alternative name, **REM sleep.** Heart rate and respiratory rate become irregular, and blood pressure may fluctuate. Another characteristic of REM sleep is dreaming. The rapid eye movements are not related to "watching" the dream imagery. The eye movements are driven in a locked, oscillating pattern uninfluenced by dream content.

Brain imaging of volunteers during REM sleep shows heightened activity in the higher-level visual processing areas and limbic system (the seat of emotions), coupled with reduced activity in the prefrontal cortex (the seat of reasoning). This pattern of activity lays the groundwork for the characteristics of dreaming: internally generated visual imagery reflecting activation of the person's "emotional memory bank" with little guidance or interpretation from the complex thinking areas. As a result, dreams are often charged with intense emotions, a distorted sense of time, and bizarre content that is uncritically accepted as real, with little reflection about all the strange happenings.

The sleep–wake cycle is controlled by interactions among three neural systems.

The sleep–wake cycle, as well as the various stages of sleep, is due to the cyclic interplay of three neural systems: (1) an **arousal system,** which is commanded by a specialized group of neurons in the hypothalamus that continuously fire on their own and keep you awake by stimulating the RAS in the brain stem unless these neurons are inhibited by the slow-wave sleep center; (2) a **slow-wave sleep center** in the hypothalamus that brings on slow-wave sleep by inhibiting the arousal system; and (3) a **paradoxical sleep center** in the brain stem that turns off slow-wave sleep and switches to paradoxical sleep. The patterns of interaction among these three neural regions, which bring about the fairly predictable cyclical sequence between being awake and passing alternately between the two types of sleep, are the subject of intense investigation, yet the underlying molecular mechanisms remain poorly understood.

The normal cycle can easily be interrupted, with the arousal system more readily overriding the sleep systems than vice versa; that is, it is easier to stay awake when you are sleepy than to fall asleep when you are wide awake. The arousal system can be activated by afferent sensory input (for example, a person has difficulty falling asleep when it is noisy) or by input descending to the brain stem from higher brain regions. Intense concentration or strong emotional states, such as anxiety or excitement, can keep a person from falling asleep, just as motor activity, such as getting up and walking around, can arouse a drowsy person.

The function of sleep is unclear.

Even though humans spend about a third of their lives sleeping, why sleep is needed largely remains a mystery. Sleep is not accompanied by a reduction in neural activity (that is, the brain cells are not "resting"), as once was suspected, but rather by a profound *change* in activity.

One widely accepted proposal holds that sleep provides "catch-up" time for the brain to restore biochemical or physiological processes that have progressively degraded during wakefulness. Another leading theory is that sleep is necessary to allow the brain to "shift gears" to accomplish the long-term structural and chemical adjustments necessary for learning and memory. These theories are not mutually exclusive. Sleep might serve multiple purposes.

Little is known about the brain's need for cycling between the two types of sleep, although a specified amount of paradoxical sleep appears to be required. Individuals experimentally deprived of paradoxical sleep for a night or two by being aroused every time the paradoxical EEG pattern appeared suffered hallucinations and spent proportionally more time in paradoxical sleep during subsequent undisturbed nights, as if to make up for lost time.

We have completed our discussion of the brain and now shift our attention to the other component of the CNS, the spinal cord.

Spinal Cord

The **spinal cord** is a long, slender cylinder of nerve tissue that extends from the brain stem. It is about 45 cm (18 in.) long and 2 cm in diameter (about the size of your thumb).

The spinal cord extends through the vertebral canal and is connected to the spinal nerves.

Exiting through a large hole in the base of the skull, the spinal cord is enclosed by the protective vertebral column as it descends through the vertebral canal (● Figure 5-18). Paired **spinal nerves** emerge from the spinal cord through spaces formed between the bony, winglike arches of adjacent vertebrae. The spinal nerves are named according to the region of the vertebral column from which they emerge (● Figure 5-19): There are 8 pairs of *cervical (neck) nerves* (namely, C1 to C8), 12 *thoracic (chest) nerves,* 5 *lumbar (abdominal) nerves,* 5 *sacral (pelvic) nerves,* and 1 *coccygeal (tailbone) nerve.*

During development, the vertebral column grows about 25 cm longer than the spinal cord. Because of this differential growth, segments of the spinal cord that give rise to various spinal nerves are not aligned with the corresponding intervertebral spaces. Most spinal nerve roots must descend along the cord before emerging from the vertebral column at the corresponding space. The spinal cord itself extends only to the level of the first or second lumbar vertebra (about waist level), so the nerve roots of the remaining nerves are greatly elongated to exit the vertebral column at their appropriate space (● Figure 5-19b).

The white matter of the spinal cord is organized into tracts.

Although there are some slight regional variations, the cross-sectional anatomy of the spinal cord is generally the same throughout its length (● Figure 5-20). In contrast to the brain, where the gray matter forms an outer shell capping an inner white core, the gray matter in the spinal cord forms an inner butterfly-shaped region surrounded by the outer white matter. As in the brain, the cord gray matter consists primarily of neuronal cell bodies and their dendrites, as well as glial cells. The white matter is organized into **tracts,** which are bundles of nerve fibers (axons of long interneurons) with a similar function. The bundles are grouped into columns that extend the length of the cord. Each of these tracts begins or ends within a particular area of the brain, and each transmits a specific type of information. Some are **ascending** (cord to brain) **tracts** that transmit to the brain signals derived from afferent input. Others

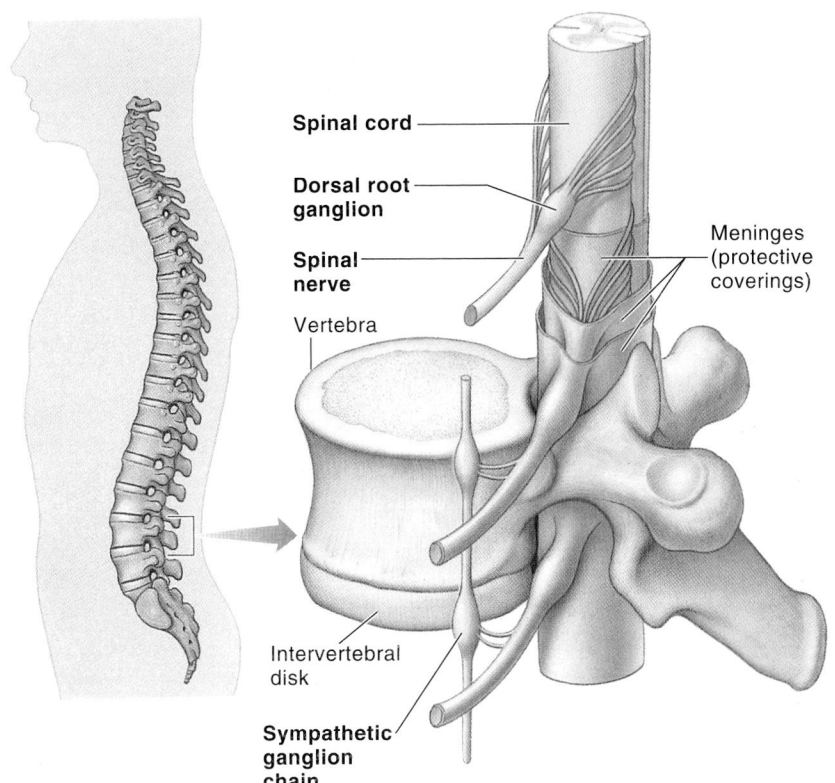

Spinal cord

Dorsal root ganglion

Spinal nerve

Vertebra

Meninges (protective coverings)

Intervertebral disk

Sympathetic ganglion chain

● **FIGURE 5-18 Location of the spinal cord relative to the vertebral column.**

ons in the CNS are called tracts.) The individual fibers within a nerve generally do not have any direct influence on one another. They travel together for convenience, just as many individual telephone lines are carried within a telephone cable yet any particular phone connection can be private without interference or influence from other lines in the cable.

The 31 pairs of spinal nerves and the 12 pairs of cranial nerves that arise from the brain stem constitute the PNS. After they emerge, the spinal nerves progressively branch to form a vast network of peripheral nerves that supply the tissues. Each segment of the spinal cord gives rise to a pair of spinal nerves that ultimately supplies a particular region of the body with both afferent and efferent fibers. Thus, the location and extent of sensory and motor deficits associated with spinal-cord injuries can be clinically important in determining the level and extent of the cord injury.

Each spinal nerve carries sensory fibers from a particular region on the body surface. Spinal nerves also carry fibers that branch off to supply internal organs, and sometimes pain originating from one of these organs is "referred" to the corresponding surface region supplied by the same spinal nerve. **Referred pain** originating in the heart, for example, may appear to come from the left shoulder and arm. The mechanism responsible for referred pain is not completely understood. Inputs arising from the heart presumably share a pathway to the brain in common with inputs from the left upper extremity. The higher perception levels, being more accustomed to receiving sensory input from the left arm than from the heart, may interpret the input from the heart as having arisen from the left arm.

are **descending** (brain to cord) **tracts** that relay messages from the brain to efferent neurons. Because various types of signals are carried in different tracts within the spinal cord, damage to particular areas of the cord can interfere with some functions, whereas other functions remain intact.

Spinal nerves carry both afferent and efferent fibers.

Spinal nerves connect with each side of the spinal cord by a *dorsal root* and a *ventral root* (● Figure 5-20). Afferent fibers carrying incoming signals from peripheral receptors enter the spinal cord through the **dorsal root.** The cell bodies for the afferent neurons at each level are clustered together in a **dorsal root ganglion.** (A collection of neuronal cell bodies located outside the CNS is called a *ganglion,* whereas a functional collection of cell bodies within the CNS is referred to as a *nucleus* or a *center.*) The cell bodies for the efferent neurons originate in the gray matter and send axons out through the **ventral root.** Therefore, efferent fibers carrying outgoing signals to muscles and glands exit through the ventral root.

The dorsal and ventral roots at each level join to form a spinal nerve that emerges from the vertebral column (● Figure 5-20). A spinal nerve contains both afferent and efferent fibers traversing between a particular region of the body and the spinal cord. Note the relationship between a *nerve* and a *neuron.* A **nerve** is a bundle of peripheral neuronal axons, some afferent and some efferent, enclosed by a connective tissue covering and following the same pathway. A nerve does not contain a complete nerve cell, only the axonal portions of many neurons. (By this definition, there are no nerves in the CNS! Bundles of ax-

The spinal cord is responsible for the integration of many basic reflexes.

The spinal cord is strategically located between the brain and the afferent and efferent fibers of the PNS; this location enables the spinal cord to fulfill its two primary functions: (1) serving as a link for transmission of information between the brain and the remainder of the body and (2) integrating reflex activity between afferent input and efferent output without involving the brain. This type of reflex activity is called a *spinal reflex.*

A **reflex** is any response that occurs automatically without conscious effort. There are two types of reflexes: (1) **Simple,** or **basic, reflexes** are built-in, unlearned responses, such as pulling the hand away from a burning hot object, and (2) **acquired,** or **conditioned, reflexes** are a result of practice and learning, such as a pianist striking a particular key on seeing a given note on the music staff. The musician reads music and plays the notes automatically, but only after considerable conscious training effort.

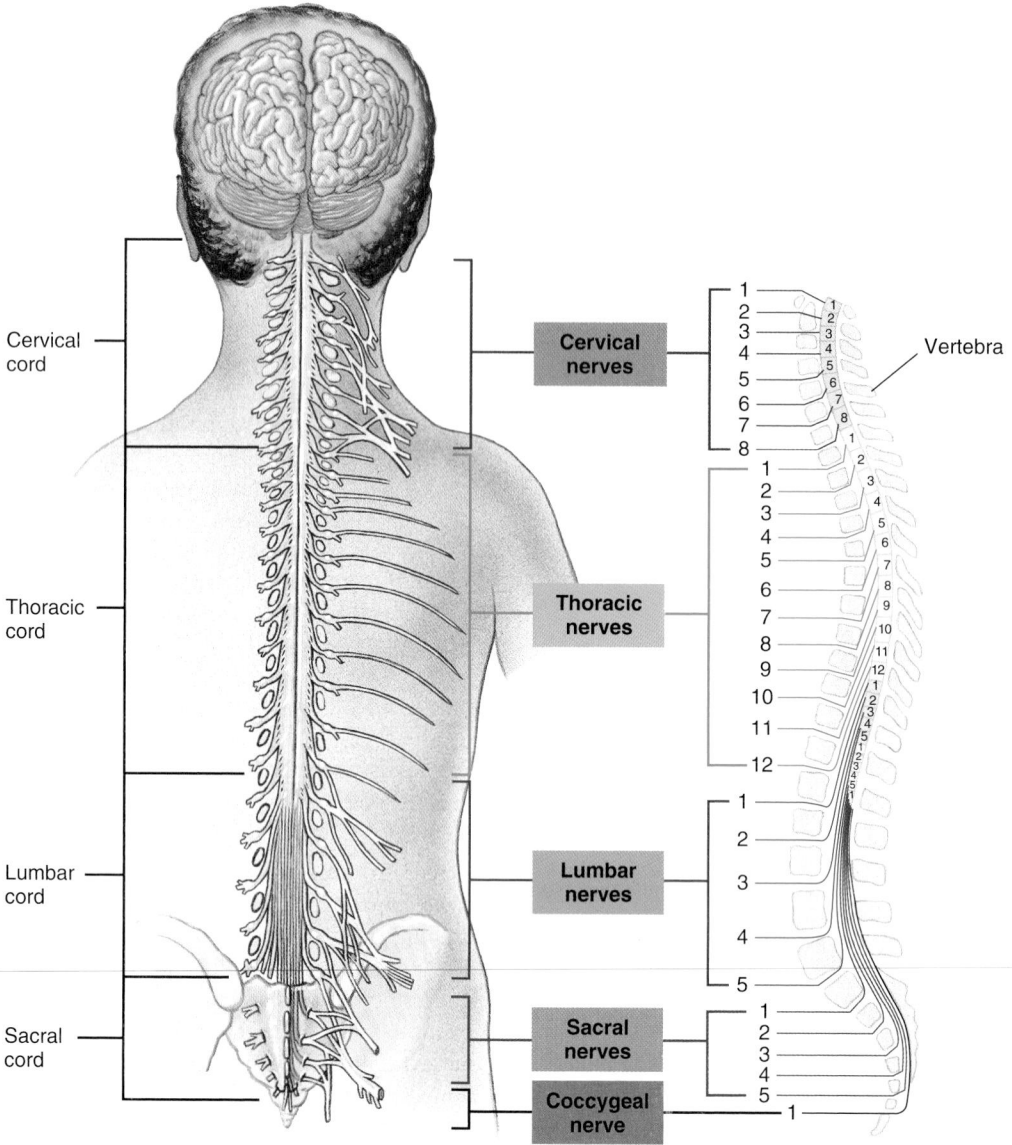

Cervical cord

Thoracic cord

Lumbar cord

Sacral cord

Cervical nerves — 1 2 3 4 5 6 7 8

Vertebra

Thoracic nerves — 1 2 3 4 5 6 7 8 9 10 11 12

Lumbar nerves — 1 2 3 4 5

Sacral nerves — 1 2 3 4 5

Coccygeal nerve — 1

(a) Posterior view of spinal cord

(b) Lateral view of spinal cord

● FIGURE 5-19 **Spinal nerves.** The 31 pairs of spinal nerves are named according to the region of the vertebral column from which they emerge. Because the spinal cord is shorter than the vertebral column, spinal nerve roots must descend along the cord before emerging from the vertebral column at the corresponding intervertebral space, especially those beyond the level of the first lumbar vertebra (L1). (a) Posterior view of the brain, spinal cord, and spinal nerves (on the right side only). (b) Lateral view of the spinal cord and spinal nerves emerging from the vertebral column.

REFLEX ARC The neural pathway involved in accomplishing reflex activity is known as a **reflex arc,** which typically includes five basic components:

1. sensory receptor
2. afferent pathway
3. integrating center
4. efferent pathway
5. effector

The **sensory receptor** (*receptor* for short) responds to a **stimulus,** which is a detectable physical or chemical change in the environment of the receptor. In response to the stimulus, the receptor produces an action potential that is relayed by the **afferent pathway** to the **integrating center** (usually the CNS) for processing. The spinal cord and brain stem integrate basic reflexes, whereas higher brain levels usually process acquired reflexes. The integrating center processes all information available to it from this receptor, as well as from all other inputs, and then "makes a decision" about the appropriate response. The instructions from the integrating center are transmitted via the **efferent pathway** to the **effector**—a muscle or gland—that carries out the desired response. Unlike conscious behavior, in which any one of numerous responses is possible, a re-

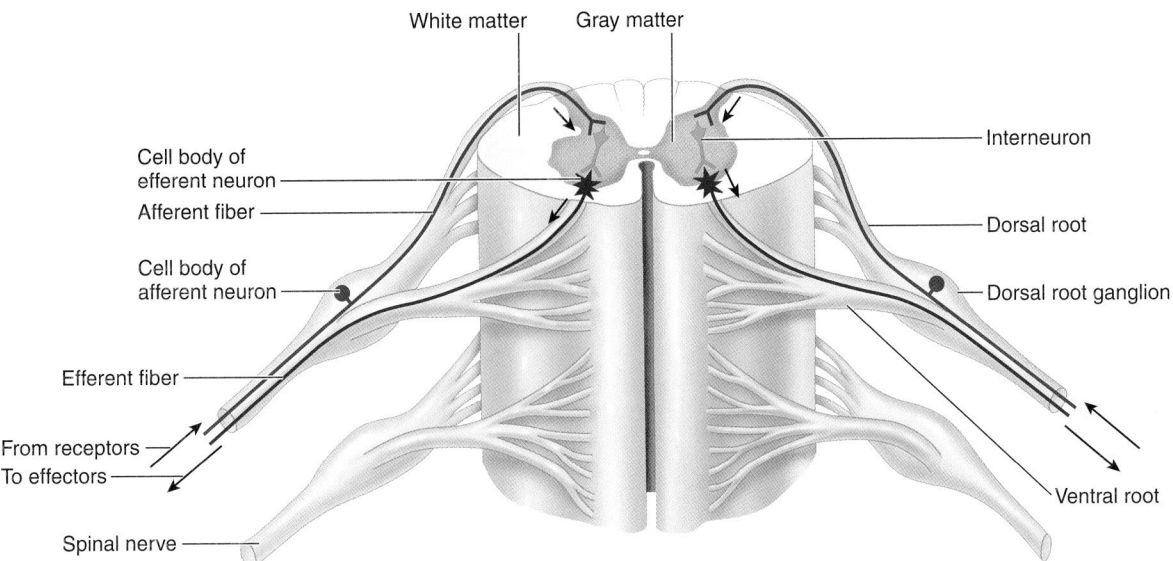

White matter   Gray matter

Cell body of
efferent neuron

Afferent fiber

Cell body of
afferent neuron

Efferent fiber

From receptors
To effectors

Spinal nerve

Interneuron

Dorsal root

Dorsal root ganglion

Ventral root

● **FIGURE 5-20 Spinal cord in cross section.** The afferent fibers enter through the dorsal root, and the efferent fibers exit through the ventral root. Afferent and efferent fibers are enclosed together within a spinal nerve.

flex response is predictable, because the pathway is always the same.

Stretch Reflex A basic **spinal reflex** is one integrated by the spinal cord; that is, all components necessary for linking afferent input to efferent response are present within the spinal cord. The simplest reflex is the **stretch reflex,** in which an afferent neuron originating at a stretch-detecting receptor in a skeletal muscle terminates directly on the efferent neuron supplying the same skeletal muscle to cause it to contract and counteract the stretch. In this reflex, the integrating center is the single synapse within the spinal cord between the afferent and the efferent pathways. The output of this system (whether or not the muscle contracts in response to passive stretch) depends on the extent of summation of EPSPs at the cell body of the efferent neuron arising from the frequency of afferent input (determined by the extent of stretch detected by the receptor). Integration in this case simply involves summation of EPSPs from a single source. (You will learn more about the role of this reflex in Chapter 8.) The stretch reflex is a **monosynaptic** ("one synapse") **reflex,** because the only synapse in the reflex arc is the one between the afferent neuron and the efferent neuron. All other reflexes are **polysynaptic** ("many synapses"), because interneurons are interposed in the reflex pathway and, therefore, a number of synapses are involved. The withdrawal reflex is an example of a polysynaptic basic spinal reflex.

Withdrawal Reflex When a person touches a hot stove (or receives another painful stimulus), a withdrawal reflex is initiated to withdraw from the painful stimulus (● Figure 5-21). The skin has different receptors for warmth, cold, light touch, pressure, and pain. Even though all information is sent to the CNS by way of action potentials, the CNS can distinguish among various stimuli because different receptors and consequently different afferent pathways are activated by different stimuli.

When a receptor is stimulated enough to reach threshold, an action potential is generated in the afferent neuron. The stronger the stimulus is, the greater the frequency of action potentials generated and propagated to the CNS. Once the afferent neuron enters the spinal cord, it diverges to synapse with the following interneurons (the letters correspond to those in ● step **3** of Figure 5-21).

1. An excited afferent neuron stimulates excitatory interneurons that in turn stimulate the efferent motor neurons supplying the biceps (3a), the muscle in the arm that flexes (bends) the elbow joint, pulling the hand away from the hot stove.

2. The afferent neuron also stimulates inhibitory interneurons that inhibit the efferent neurons supplying the triceps (3b) to prevent it from contracting. The triceps is the muscle that extends (straightens out) the elbow joint. When the biceps contracts to flex the elbow, it would be counterproductive for the triceps to contract. Therefore, built into the withdrawal reflex is inhibition of the muscle that antagonizes (opposes) the desired response. This type of connection involving stimulation of the nerve supply to one muscle and simultaneous inhibition of the nerves to its antagonistic muscle is known as **reciprocal innervation.**

3. The afferent neuron stimulates still other interneurons that carry the signal up the spinal cord to the brain via an ascending pathway (3c). Only when the impulse reaches the sensory area of the cortex is the person aware of the pain, its location, and the type of stimulus. Also, when the impulse reaches the brain, the information can be stored as memory, and the person can start thinking about the situation—how it happened, what to do about it, and so on. All this activity at the conscious level is beyond the basic reflex.

As with all spinal reflexes, the brain can modify the withdrawal reflex. Impulses may be sent down descending pathways to the efferent motor neurons supplying the involved muscles to

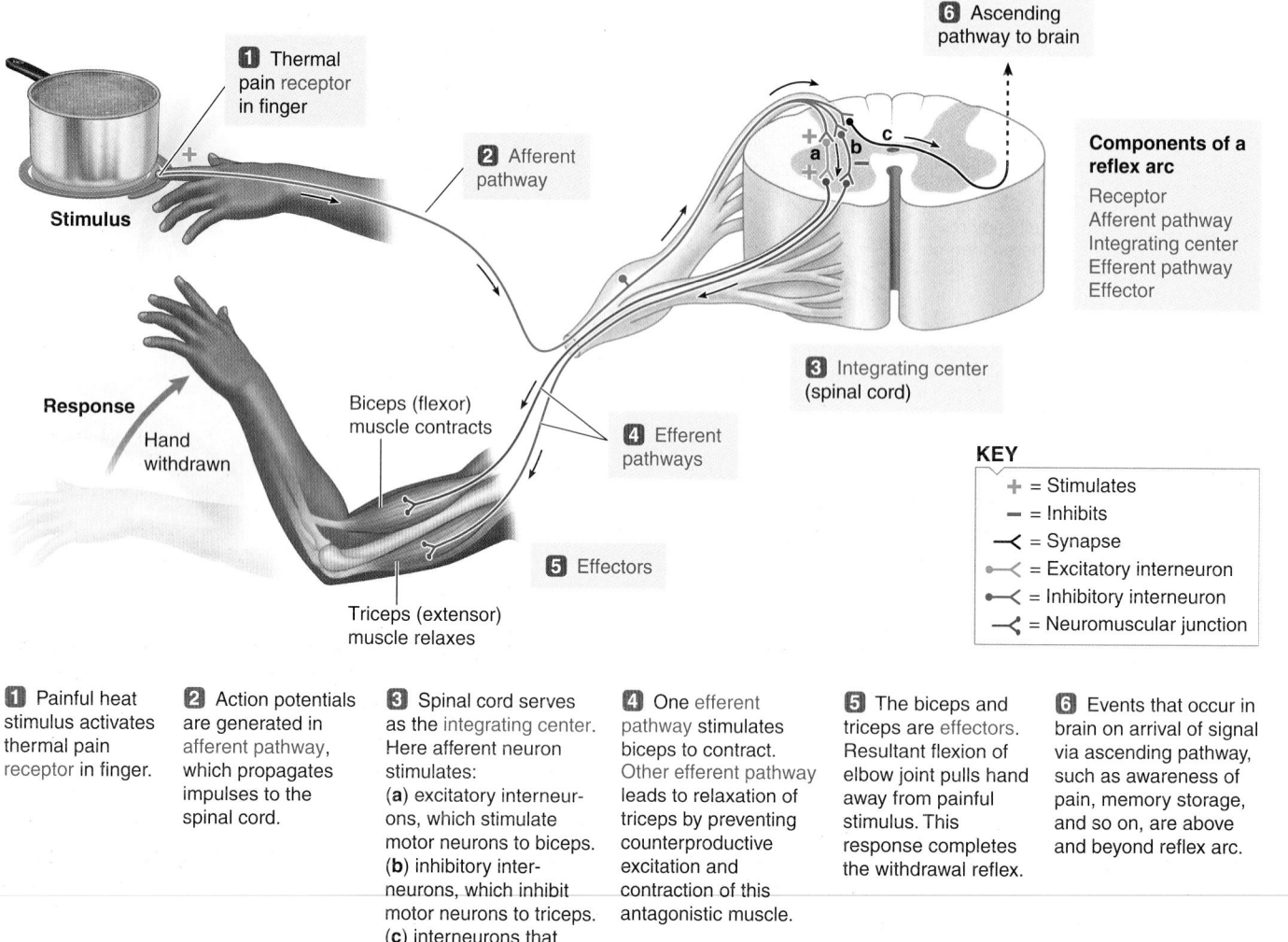

1 Thermal pain receptor in finger

2 Afferent pathway

6 Ascending pathway to brain

Components of a reflex arc
Receptor
Afferent pathway
Integrating center
Efferent pathway
Effector

Stimulus

3 Integrating center (spinal cord)

Response

Hand withdrawn

Biceps (flexor) muscle contracts

4 Efferent pathways

5 Effectors

Triceps (extensor) muscle relaxes

KEY
+ = Stimulates
− = Inhibits
= Synapse
= Excitatory interneuron
= Inhibitory interneuron
= Neuromuscular junction

1 Painful heat stimulus activates thermal pain receptor in finger.

2 Action potentials are generated in afferent pathway, which propagates impulses to the spinal cord.

3 Spinal cord serves as the integrating center. Here afferent neuron stimulates:
(**a**) excitatory interneurons, which stimulate motor neurons to biceps.
(**b**) inhibitory interneurons, which inhibit motor neurons to triceps.
(**c**) interneurons that are part of ascending pathway to brain.

4 One efferent pathway stimulates biceps to contract. Other efferent pathway leads to relaxation of triceps by preventing counterproductive excitation and contraction of this antagonistic muscle.

5 The biceps and triceps are effectors. Resultant flexion of elbow joint pulls hand away from painful stimulus. This response completes the withdrawal reflex.

6 Events that occur in brain on arrival of signal via ascending pathway, such as awareness of pain, memory storage, and so on, are above and beyond reflex arc.

● **FIGURE 5-21 The withdrawal reflex.**

override the input from the receptors, actually preventing the biceps from contracting despite the painful stimulus. When your finger is being pricked to obtain a blood sample, pain receptors are stimulated, initiating the withdrawal reflex. Knowing that you must be brave and not pull your hand away, you can consciously override the reflex by sending IPSPs via descending pathways to the motor neurons supplying the biceps and EPSPs to those supplying the triceps. The activity in these efferent neurons depends on the sum of activity of all their synaptic inputs. Because the neurons supplying the biceps are now receiving more IPSPs from the brain (voluntary) than EPSPs from the afferent pain pathway (reflex), these neurons are inhibited and do not reach threshold. Therefore, the biceps is not stimulated to contract and withdraw the hand. Simultaneously, the neurons to the triceps are receiving more EPSPs from the brain than IPSPs via the reflex arc, so they reach threshold, fire, and consequently stimulate the triceps to contract. Thus, the arm is kept extended despite the painful stimulus. In this way, the withdrawal reflex has been voluntarily overridden.

OTHER REFLEX ACTIVITY Besides protective reflexes (such as the withdrawal reflex) and simple postural reflexes, basic spinal reflexes mediate emptying of pelvic organs (for example, urination). All spinal reflexes can be voluntarily overridden, at least temporarily, by higher brain centers.

Not all reflex activity involves a clear-cut reflex arc, although the basic principles of a reflex (that is, an automatic response to a detectable change) are present. Pathways for unconscious responsiveness digress from the typical reflex arc in two general ways:

1. *Responses at least partly mediated by hormones.* A particular reflex may be mediated solely by either neurons or hormones or may involve a pathway using both.

2. *Local responses that do not involve either nerves or hormones.* For example, the blood vessels in an exercising muscle dilate because of local metabolic changes, thereby increasing blood flow to match the active muscle's metabolic needs.

Chapter in Perspective: Focus on Homeostasis

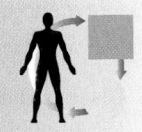

To interact in appropriate ways with the external environment to stay alive, such as in acquiring food, and to make the internal adjustments necessary to maintain homeostasis, the body must be informed about any changes taking place in the external and the internal environment and must be able to process this information and send messages to various muscles and glands to accomplish the desired results. The nervous system, one of the body's two major regulatory systems, plays a central role in this life-sustaining communication. The central nervous system (CNS), which consists of the brain and spinal cord, receives information about the external and the internal environment by means of the afferent peripheral nerves. After sorting, processing, and integrating this input, the CNS sends directions, by means of efferent peripheral nerves, to bring about appropriate muscular contractions and glandular secretions.

With its swift electrical signaling system, the nervous system is especially important in controlling the rapid responses of the body. Many neurally controlled muscular and glandular activities are aimed toward maintaining homeostasis. The CNS is the main site of integration between afferent input and efferent output. It links the appropriate response to a particular input so that conditions compatible with life are maintained in the body. For example, when informed by the afferent nervous system that blood pressure has fallen, the CNS sends appropriate commands to the heart and blood vessels to increase the blood pressure to normal. Likewise,

when informed that the body is overheated, the CNS promotes secretion of sweat by the sweat glands, among other cooling responses Evaporation of sweat helps cool the body to normal temperature. Were it not for this processing and integrating ability of the CNS, maintaining homeostasis in an organism as complex as a human would be impossible.

At the simplest level, the spinal cord integrates many basic protective and evacuative reflexes that do not require conscious participation, such as withdrawing from a painful stimulus and emptying of the urinary bladder. In addition to serving as a more complex integrating link between afferent input and efferent output, the brain is responsible for the initiation of all voluntary movement, complex perceptual awareness of the external environment, self-awareness, language, and abstract neural phenomena such as thinking, learning, remembering, consciousness, emotions, and personality traits. All neural activity—from the most private thoughts to commands for motor activity, from enjoying a concert to retrieving memories from the distant past—is ultimately attributable to propagation of action potentials along individual nerve cells and chemical transmission between cells.

During evolutionary development, the nervous system has become progressively more complex. Newer, more complicated, and more sophisticated layers of the brain have been piled on top of older, more primitive regions. Mechanisms for governing many basic activities necessary for survival are built into the older parts of the brain. The newer, higher levels progressively modify, enhance, or nullify actions coordinated by lower levels in a hierarchy of command; they also add new capabilities. Many of these higher neural activities are not aimed at maintaining life, but they add immeasurably to the quality of being alive.

REVIEW EXERCISES

Objective Questions (Answers on p. A-41)

1. The major function of the CSF is to nourish the brain. (*True or false?*)
2. In emergencies when O_2 supplies are low, the brain can perform anaerobic metabolism. (*True or false?*)
3. Damage to the left cerebral hemisphere brings about paralysis and loss of sensation on the left side of the body. (*True or false?*)
4. The hands and structures associated with the mouth have a disproportionately large share of representation in both the sensory and the motor cortexes. (*True or false?*)
5. The left cerebral hemisphere specializes in artistic and musical ability, whereas the right side excels in verbal and analytical skills. (*True or false?*)
6. The process of transferring and fixing short-term memory traces into long-term memory stores is known as _____.
7. Afferent fibers enter through the _____ root of the spinal cord, and efferent fibers leave through the _____ root.

8. Match the following:
   - ___ 1. consists of nerves carrying information between the periphery and the CNS
   - ___ 2. consists of the brain and spinal cord
   - ___ 3. is the division of the PNS that transmits signals to the CNS
   - ___ 4. is the division of the PNS that transmits signals from the CNS
   - ___ 5. supplies skeletal muscles
   - ___ 6. supplies smooth muscle, cardiac muscle, and glands

   (a) somatic nervous system
   (b) autonomic nervous system
   (c) central nervous system
   (d) peripheral nervous system
   (e) efferent division
   (f) afferent division

9. Using the answer code on the right, indicate which neurons are being described (a characteristic may apply to more than one class of neurons):
   ___ 1. have a receptor at peripheral endings
   ___ 2. lie entirely within the CNS
   ___ 3. lie primarily within the PNS
   ___ 4. innervate muscles and glands
   ___ 5. have a cell body devoid of presynaptic inputs
   ___ 6. is the predominant type of neuron
   ___ 7. is responsible for thoughts, emotions, memory, etc.

   (a) afferent neurons
   (b) efferent neurons
   (c) interneurons

Essay Questions

1. Discuss the function of each of the following: astrocytes, oligodendrocytes, ependymal cells, microglia, cerebrospinal fluid, and blood–brain barrier.
2. Compare the composition of white and gray matter.
3. Draw and label the major functional areas of the cerebral cortex, indicating the functions attributable to each area.
4. Discuss the function of each of the following parts of the brain: thalamus, hypothalamus, basal nuclei, limbic system, cerebellum, and brain stem.
5. Define *somesthetic sensations* and *proprioception*.
6. What is an electroencephalogram?
7. Discuss the roles of Broca's area and Wernicke's area in language.
8. Compare short-term and long-term memory.
9. What is the reticular activating system?
10. Compare slow-wave and paradoxical (REM) sleep.
11. Draw and label a cross section of the spinal cord.
12. List the five components of a basic reflex arc.
13. Distinguish between a monosynaptic and a polysynaptic reflex.

POINTS TO PONDER

(Explanations on p. A-41)

1. Special studies designed to assess the specialized capacities of each cerebral hemisphere have been performed on "split-brain" patients. In these people, the corpus callosum—the bundle of fibers that links the two halves of the brain—has been surgically cut to prevent the spread of epileptic seizures from one hemisphere to the other. Even though no overt changes in behavior, intellect, or personality occur in these patients, because both hemispheres individually receive the same information, deficits are observable with tests designed to restrict information to one brain hemisphere at a time. One such test involves limiting a visual stimulus to only half of the brain. Because of a crossover in the nerve pathways from the eyes to the occipital cortex, the visual information to the right of a midline point is transmitted to only the left half of the brain, whereas visual information to the left of this point is received by only the right half of the brain. A split-brain patient presented with a visual stimulus that reaches only the left hemisphere accurately describes the object seen, but when a visual stimulus is presented to only the right hemisphere, the patient denies having seen anything. The right hemisphere does receive the visual input, however, as demonstrated by nonverbal tests. Even though a split-brain patient denies having seen anything after an object is presented to the right hemisphere, the patient can correctly match the object by picking it out from among several objects, usually to the patient's surprise. What is your explanation of this finding?

2. Which of the following symptoms are most likely to occur as the result of a severe blow to the back of the head?
   a. paralysis
   b. hearing impairment
   c. visual disturbances
   d. burning sensations
   e. personality disorders

3. The hormone insulin enhances the carrier-mediated transport of glucose into most of the body's cells but not into brain cells. The uptake of glucose from the blood by neurons does not depend on insulin. Knowing the brain's need for a continuous supply of blood-borne glucose, predict the effect that insulin excess would have on the brain.

4. Give examples of conditioned reflexes you have acquired.

5. Under what circumstances might it be inadvisable to administer a clot-dissolving drug to a stroke victim?

(Explanation on p. A-41)

Julio D., who had recently retired, was enjoying an afternoon of playing golf when suddenly he experienced a severe headache and dizziness. These symptoms were quickly followed by numbness and partial paralysis on the upper right side of his body, accompanied by an inability to speak. After being rushed to the emergency room, Julio was diagnosed as having suffered a stroke. Given the observed neurological impairment, what areas of his brain were affected?

Chapter 5

Organization and Cells of the Nervous System (pp. 115–119)

■ The nervous system consists of the central nervous system (CNS), which includes the brain and spinal cord, and the peripheral nervous system (PNS), which includes the nerve fibers carrying information to (afferent division) and from (efferent division) the CNS. (*Review Figure 5-1.*)

■ Three functional classes of neurons—afferent neurons, efferent neurons, and interneurons—compose the excitable cells of the nervous system. (*Review Figure 5-2.*) (1) Afferent neurons inform the CNS about conditions in both the external and the internal environment. (2) Efferent neurons carry instructions from the CNS to effector organs, namely, muscles and glands. (3) Interneurons are responsible for integrating afferent information and formulating an efferent response, as well as for all higher mental functions associated with the "mind."

■ Glial cells are nonexcitable cells in the CNS that physically, metabolically, and functionally support the neurons. The four types of glial cells are astrocytes (which serve as the main "glue" of the CNS and chemically communicate with and assist neurons), oligodendrocytes (which form myelin in the CNS), microglia (which are immune defense cells in the CNS), and ependymal cells (which line the internal cavities of the CNS, form cerebrospinal fluid, or CSF, and serve as neural stem cells). (*Review Figures 5-3 and 5-4.*)

Protection and Nourishment of the Brain (pp. 119–120)

■ The brain is provided with several protective devices, which is important because neurons cannot divide to replace damaged cells. (1) The brain is wrapped in three layers of protective membranes—the meninges—and is further surrounded by a hard, bony covering. (2) CSF flows within and around the brain to cushion it against physical jarring. (3) The blood–brain barrier protects the brain against chemical injury by limiting access of blood-borne substances to the brain.

■ The brain depends on a constant blood supply for delivery of O2 and glucose because it cannot generate ATP in the absence of either of these substances.

Overview of the Central Nervous System (pp. 120–122)

■ The parts of the brain from the lowest, most primitive level to the highest, most sophisticated level are the brain stem, cerebellum, hypothalamus, thalamus, basal nuclei, and cerebral cortex. (*Review Table 5-1 and Figure 5-6.*)

Cerebral Cortex (pp. 122–130)

■ The cerebral cortex is the outer shell of gray matter that caps an underlying core of white matter. The cortex itself consists primarily of neuronal cell bodies, dendrites, and glial cells. The white matter consists of bundles of nerve fibers that interconnect various areas. (*Review Figure 5-12, p. 130.*)

■ Ultimate responsibility for many discrete functions is localized in particular regions of the cortex as follows: (1) the occipital lobes house the visual cortex, (2) the auditory cortex is in the temporal lobes, (3) the parietal lobes are responsible for reception and perceptual processing of somatosensory (somesthetic and proprioceptive) input, and (4) voluntary motor movement is set into motion by the motor areas in the frontal lobes. (*Review Figures 5-7 through 5-9.*)

■ Language ability depends on the integrated activity of two primary language areas—Broca's area and Wernicke's area—typically located only in the left cerebral hemisphere. (*Review Figures 5-8 and 5-10.*)

■ The association areas are regions of the cortex not specifically assigned to processing sensory input or commanding motor output or language ability. These areas provide an integrative link between diverse sensory information and purposeful action; they also play a key role in higher brain functions such as memory and decision making. The association areas include the prefrontal association cortex, the parietal–temporal–occipital association cortex, and the limbic association cortex. (*Review Figure 5-8.*)

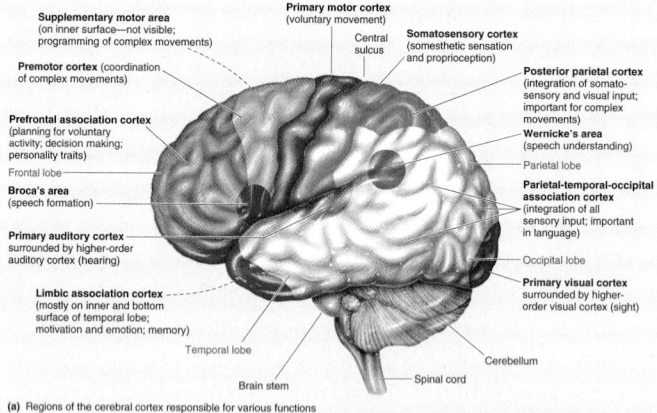

(a) Regions of the cerebral cortex responsible for various functions

Basal Nuclei, Thalamus, and Hypothalamus (pp. 130–132)

■ The subcortical brain structures include the basal nuclei, thalamus, and hypothalamus. (*Review Figures 5-12 and 5-13 and Table 5-1, p. 122.*)

■ The basal nuclei inhibit muscle tone; coordinate slow, sustained postural contractions; and suppress useless patterns of movement.

■ The thalamus is a relay station for preliminary processing of sensory input. It also accomplishes a crude awareness of sensation and some degree of consciousness.

The hypothalamus regulates body temperature, thirst, urine output, and food intake; extensively controls the autonomic nervous system and endocrine system; and is part of the limbic system.

Emotion, Behavior, and Motivation (pp. 132–133)

The limbic system, which includes portions of the hypothalamus and other structures that encircle the brain stem, plays an important role in emotion, basic behavioral patterns, motivation, and learning. (Review Figure 5-14.)

Emotion refers to subjective feelings and moods and the physical responses associated with these feelings.

Basic behavioral patterns triggered by the limbic system are aimed at survival (such as attack) and perpetuation of the species (such as mating behavior). Higher cortical centers can reinforce, modify, or suppress these basic behaviors.

Motivation is the ability to direct behavior toward specific goals.

Learning and Memory (pp. 134–136)

Learning refers to acquiring knowledge or skills as a result of experience, instruction, or both. Memory is storage of acquired knowledge for later recall and use.

There are two types of memory: (1) a short-term memory with limited capacity and brief retention, coded by modification of activity at preexisting synapses, and (2) a long-term memory with large storage capacity and enduring retention, involving relatively permanent structural or functional changes, such as the formation of new synapses between existing neurons. Enhanced protein synthesis underlies these long-term changes. (Review Table 5-2.)

The hippocampus plays a key role in consolidation, the transfer of short-term memory to long-term memory.

The hippocampus and associated structures are especially important in declarative, or "what," memories of specific objects, facts, and events. The cerebellum and associated structures are especially important in procedural, or "how to," memories of motor skills gained through repetitive training.

The prefrontal association cortex is the site of working memory, which temporarily holds currently relevant data—both new information and knowledge retrieved from memory stores—and manipulates and relates them to accomplish the higher-reasoning processes of the brain.

Cerebellum (pp. 136–137)

The cerebellum, attached at the back of the brain stem beneath the cortex, consists of three functionally distinct parts. (Review Figure 5-15.)

The vestibulocerebellum helps maintain balance and controls eye movements. The spinocerebellum enhances muscle tone and helps coordinate voluntary movement, especially fast, phasic motor activities. The cerebrocerebellum plays a role in initiating voluntary movement and in storing procedural memories.

Brain Stem (pp. 138–140)

The brain stem is an important link between the spinal cord and the higher brain levels.

The brain stem is the origin of the cranial nerves. It also contains centers that control cardiovascular, respiratory, and digestive function; regulates postural muscle reflexes; controls the overall degree of cortical alertness via the reticular activating system; and plays a key role in the sleep–wake cycle. (Review Figure 5-16.)

Consciousness is the subjective awareness of the external world and self. The states of consciousness, in decreasing order of arousal level, are (1) maximum alertness, (2) wakefulness, (3) several types of sleep, and (4) coma.

Sleep is an active process, not just the absence of wakefulness. While sleeping, a person cyclically alternates between slow-wave sleep and paradoxical (REM) sleep. (Review Table 5-3.) Slow-wave sleep is characterized by slow waves on the EEG and little change in behavior pattern from the waking state except for not being consciously aware of the external world. Paradoxical, or REM, sleep is characterized by an EEG pattern similar to that of an alert, awake individual; rapid eye movements, dreaming, and abrupt changes in behavior pattern occur. (Review Figure 5-17.)

The leading theories of why we need sleep are for (1) restoration and recovery and (2) memory consolidation.

Spinal Cord (pp. 140–144)

Extending from the brain stem, the spinal cord descends through a canal formed by surrounding protective vertebrae. (Review Figures 5-18 and 5-19.)

The spinal cord has two functions. (1) It is the neuronal link between the brain and the PNS. All communication up and down the spinal cord is located in ascending and descending tracts in the cord's outer white matter. (2) It is the integrating center for spinal reflexes, including some basic protective and postural reflexes and those involved with the emptying of the pelvic organs. (Review Figures 5-20 and 5-21.)

The basic reflex arc includes a receptor, an afferent pathway, an integrating center, an efferent pathway, and an effector. (Review Figure 5-21.)

The centrally located gray matter of the spinal cord contains the interneurons interposed between the afferent input (which comes in through the dorsal root) and the efferent output (which leaves through the ventral root), as well as the cell bodies of efferent neurons. (Review Figure 5-20.)

A nerve is a bundle of peripheral neuronal axons, both afferent and efferent, wrapped in connective tissue and following the same pathway. Spinal nerves supply specific body regions and are attached to the spinal cord in paired fashion throughout its length. (Review Figures 5-18, 5-19 and 5-20.)

The 31 pairs of spinal nerves and the 12 pairs of cranial nerves that arise from the brain stem constitute the PNS. (Review Figure 5-19.)

Nervous System
(Peripheral Nervous System)

Body systems
maintain homeostasis

Homeostasis
The nervous system, as one of the body's two major regulatory systems, regulates many body activities aimed at maintaining a stable internal fluid environment.

Homeostasis is essential for survival of cells

Cells

Cells make up body systems

The nervous system, one of the two major regulatory systems of the body, consists of the central nervous system (CNS), composed of the brain and spinal cord, and the **peripheral nervous system (PNS),** composed of the afferent and efferent fibers that relay signals between the CNS and the periphery (other parts of the body). The **afferent division** of the PNS detects, encodes, and transmits peripheral signals to the CNS, thus informing the CNS about the internal and the external environment. This afferent input to the controlling centers of the CNS is essential in maintaining homeostasis. To make appropriate adjustments in effector organs via efferent output, the CNS has to "know" what is going on. Afferent input is also used to plan for voluntary actions unrelated to homeostasis.

The Peripheral Nervous System: Afferent Division and Special Senses

CHAPTER AT A GLANCE

Receptor Physiology
Receptor types
Receptor potentials; receptor adaptation
Labeled lines for afferent input
Acuity; receptive field
Perception

Pain
Receptors and mechanisms of pain
Built-in analgesic system

Eye: Vision
Anatomy of eye
Light
Refractive structures; accommodation
Phototransduction; retinal processing
Comparison of rod and cone vision; color vision
Dark and light adaptation
Visual pathways; cortical visual processing

Ear: Hearing and Equilibrium
Anatomy of ear
Sound waves
Roles of the external ear and middle ear
Sound transduction by the organ of Corti
Pitch, timbre, and loudness discrimination
Auditory pathway
Vestibular apparatus

Chemical Senses: Taste and Smell
Taste Receptors
Taste transduction and discrimination
Olfactory receptors
Olfactory transduction and discrimination

Receptor Physiology

The peripheral nervous system (PNS) consists of nerve fibers that carry information between the central nervous system (CNS) and the other parts of the body. The afferent division of the PNS sends information about the external and internal environment to the CNS.

A **stimulus** is a change detectable by the body. Stimuli exist in various energy forms, or **modalities,** such as heat, light, sound, pressure, and chemical changes. Afferent neurons have **sensory receptors** (*receptors* for short) at their peripheral endings that respond to stimuli in both the external world and the internal environment. (Though both are called *receptors,* stimulus-sensitive sensory receptors are distinctly different from the plasma-membrane protein receptors that bind with extracellular chemical messengers; see p. 51.) Because the only way afferent neurons can transmit information to the CNS about stimuli is via action potential propagation, receptors must convert these other forms of energy into electrical signals. Stimuli bring about graded potentials known as **receptor potentials** in the receptor. The conversion of stimulus energy into a receptor potential is known as **sensory transduction.** Receptor potentials in turn trigger action potentials in the afferent fiber.

Receptors have differential sensitivities to various stimuli.

Each type of receptor is specialized to respond to one type of stimulus, its **adequate stimulus.** For example, receptors in the eye are sensitive to light, receptors in the ear to sound waves, and heat receptors in the skin to heat energy. Because of this differential sensitivity of receptors, we cannot see with our ears or hear with our eyes. Some receptors can respond weakly to stimuli other than their adequate stimulus, but even when activated by a different stimulus, a receptor still gives rise to the sensation usually detected by that receptor type. As an example, the adequate stimulus for eye receptors (photoreceptors) is light, to which they are exquisitely sensitive, but these receptors can also be activated to a lesser degree by mechanical stimulation. When hit in the eye, a person often "sees stars," because the mechanical pressure stimulates the photoreceptors.

TYPES OF RECEPTORS ACCORDING TO THEIR ADEQUATE STIMULUS Depending on the type of energy to which they ordinarily respond, receptors are categorized as follows:

- **Photoreceptors** are responsive to visible wavelengths of light.

- **Mechanoreceptors** are sensitive to mechanical energy. Examples include skeletal muscle receptors sensitive to stretch, the receptors in the ear containing fine hairs that are bent as a result of sound waves, and blood pressure–monitoring baroreceptors.

- **Thermoreceptors** are sensitive to heat and cold.

- **Osmoreceptors** detect changes in the concentration of solutes in the extracellular fluid (ECF) and the resultant changes in osmotic activity (see p. 57).

- **Chemoreceptors** are sensitive to specific chemicals. Chemoreceptors include the receptors for taste and smell, as well as those located deeper within the body that detect O_2 and CO_2 concentrations in the blood or the chemical content of the digestive tract.

- **Nociceptors,** or **pain receptors,** are sensitive to tissue damage such as cutting or burning.

Some sensations are compound sensations in that their perception arises from central integration of several simultaneously activated primary sensory inputs. For example, the perception of wetness comes from touch, pressure, and thermal receptor input; there is no such thing as a "wetness receptor."

USES FOR INFORMATION DETECTED BY RECEPTORS The information detected by receptors is conveyed via afferent neurons to the CNS, where it is used for various purposes:

- Afferent input is essential for the control of efferent output, both for regulating motor behavior in accordance with external circumstances and for coordinating internal activities directed at maintaining homeostasis. At the most basic level, afferent input provides information (of which the person may or may not be consciously aware) for the CNS to use in directing activities necessary for survival. On a broader level, we could not interact successfully with our environment or with one another without sensory input.

- Processing of sensory input by the reticular activating system in the brain stem is critical for cortical arousal and consciousness (see p. 138).

- Central processing of sensory information gives rise to our perceptions of the world around us.

- Selected information delivered to the CNS may be stored for future reference.

- Sensory stimuli can have a profound impact on our emotions. The smell of just-baked apple pie, the sensuous feel of silk, the sight of a loved one, the sound of someone sharing bad news—sensory input can gladden, sadden, arouse, calm, anger, frighten, or evoke a range of other emotions.

We next examine how adequate stimuli initiate action potentials that ultimately are used for these purposes.

A stimulus alters the receptor's permeability, leading to a graded receptor potential.

A receptor may be either (1) a specialized ending of the afferent neuron or (2) a separate receptor cell closely associated with the peripheral ending of the neuron. Stimulation of a receptor alters its membrane permeability, usually by causing nonspecific cation channels to open. The means by which this permeability change takes place is individualized for each receptor type. Because the electrochemical driving force is greater for sodium

(Na^+) than for other small cations at resting potential, the predominant effect is an inward flux of Na^+, which depolarizes the receptor membrane. This local depolarization, the receptor potential, is a graded potential. As is true of all graded potentials, the stronger the stimulus, the greater the permeability change and the larger the receptor potential (see p. 78). Also, receptor potentials have no refractory period, so summation in response to rapidly successive stimuli is possible. Because the receptor region has few to no voltage-gated Na^+ channels and thus has a high threshold, action potentials do not take place at the receptor itself. For long-distance transmission, the receptor potential must be converted into action potentials that can be propagated along the afferent fiber.

Receptor potentials may initiate action potentials in the afferent neuron.

If a receptor potential is large enough, it may trigger an action potential in the afferent neuron membrane next to the receptor. Depending on the type of receptor, the depolarized receptor brings about depolarization of this adjacent membrane, either by local current flow or by releasing a depolarizing chemical messenger. If the resulting ionic flux in this adjacent membrane is big enough to bring this region to threshold, voltage-gated Na^+ channels open here, triggering an action potential that is conducted along the afferent fiber to the CNS.

Note that the initiation site of action potentials in an afferent neuron differs from the site in an efferent neuron or interneuron. In the latter two types of neurons, action potentials are initiated at the axon hillock located at the start of the axon next to the cell body (see p. 85). By contrast, action potentials are initiated at the peripheral end of an afferent nerve fiber next to the receptor, a long distance from the cell body (● Figure 6-1).

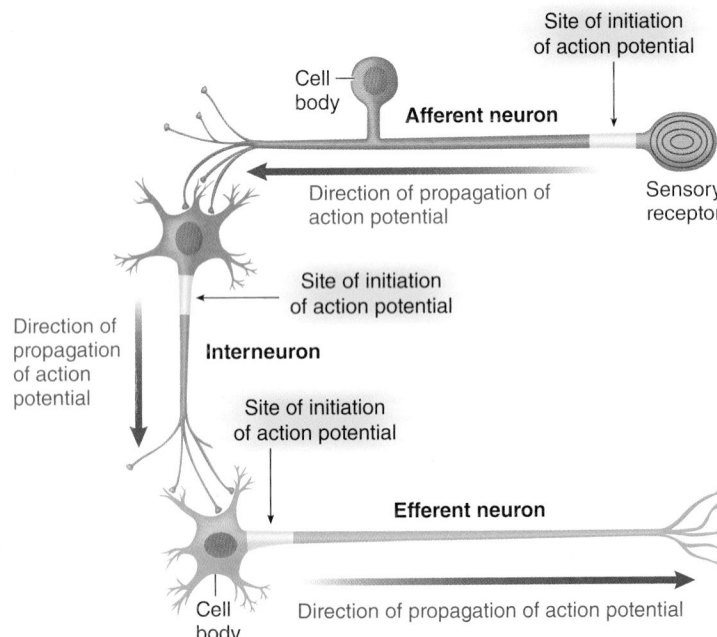

● **FIGURE 6-1 Comparison of the initiation site of an action potential in the three types of neurons.**

The intensity of the stimulus is reflected by the magnitude of the receptor potential. The larger the receptor potential, the greater the frequency of action potentials generated in the afferent neuron (● Figure 6-2). A larger receptor potential cannot bring about a larger action potential (because of the all-or-none law), but it can induce more rapid firing of action potentials (see p. 89). The more rapidly an afferent fiber fires, the more neurotransmitter it releases. This neurotransmitter influences the next cell in the neural pathway, passing on information about stimulus strength. Stimulus strength is also reflected by the size of the area stimulated. Stronger stimuli usually affect larger areas, so correspondingly more receptors respond. For example, a light touch does not activate as many pressure receptors in the skin as does a more forceful touch applied to the same area. Stimulus intensity is therefore distinguished both by the frequency of action potentials generated in the afferent neuron and by the number of receptors and thus afferent fibers activated within the area.

Receptors may adapt slowly or rapidly to sustained stimulation.

Stimuli of the same intensity do not always bring about receptor potentials of the same magnitude from the same receptor. Some receptors can diminish the extent of their depolarization despite sustained stimulus strength, a phenomenon called **adaptation.** Subsequently, the frequency of action potentials generated in the afferent neuron decreases. That is, the receptor "adapts" to the stimulus by no longer responding to it to the same degree.

TYPES OF RECEPTORS ACCORDING TO THEIR SPEED OF ADAPTATION Depending on their speed of adaptation, receptors are classified as *tonic receptors* or *phasic receptors*. **Tonic receptors** do not adapt or adapt slowly (● Figure 6-3a). These receptors are useful when it is valuable to maintain information about a stimulus. Examples of tonic receptors are muscle stretch receptors, which monitor muscle length, and joint proprioceptors, which measure the degree of joint flexion. To maintain posture and balance, the CNS must continually get information about the degree of muscle length and joint position. It is important, therefore, that these receptors do *not* adapt to a stimulus but continue to generate action potentials to relay this information to the CNS.

Phasic receptors, in contrast, are rapidly adapting receptors. The receptor quickly adapts by no longer responding to a maintained stimulus. Some phasic receptors respond with a slight depolarization called the

off response when the stimulus is removed (● Figure 6-3b). Phasic receptors are useful when it is important to signal a change in stimulus intensity rather than to relay status quo information. Many *tactile (touch) receptors* that signal changes in pressure on the skin surface are phasic receptors. Because these receptors adapt rapidly, you are not continually conscious of wearing your watch, rings, and clothing. When you put something on, you soon become accustomed to it because of these receptors' rapid adaptation. When you take the item off, you are aware of its removal because of the off response.

Visceral afferents carry subconscious input, whereas sensory afferents carry conscious input.

Action potentials generated by receptors in afferent fibers in response to stimuli are propagated to the CNS. Afferent information about the internal environment, such as blood pressure and the concentration of CO_2 in the body fluids, never reaches the level of conscious awareness, but this input is essential for determining the appropriate efferent output to maintain homeostasis. The incoming pathway for information derived from

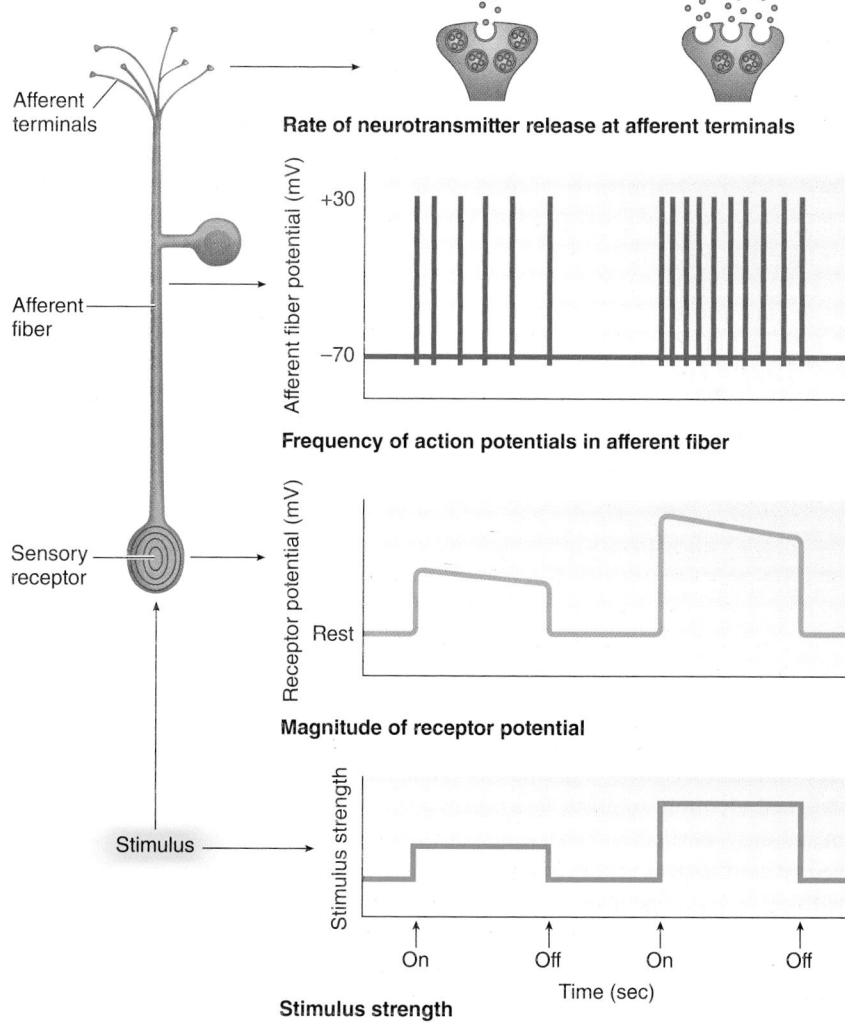

● FIGURE 6-2 **Magnitude of receptor potential, frequency of action potentials in afferent fiber, and rate of neurotransmitter release at afferent terminals as a function of stimulus strength.**

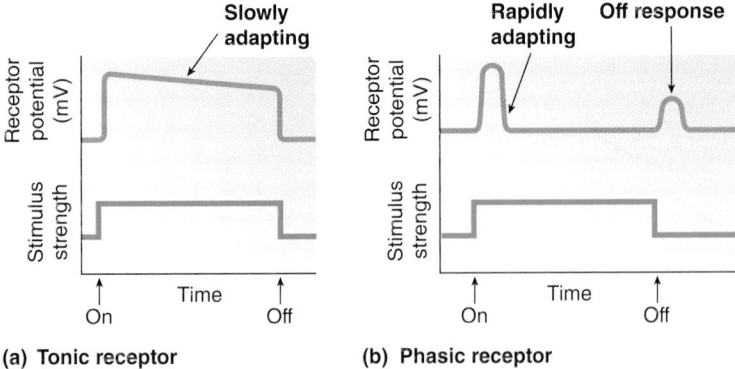

(a) Tonic receptor **(b) Phasic receptor**

● **FIGURE 6-3 Tonic and phasic receptors.** (a) A tonic receptor does not adapt or adapts slowly to a sustained stimulus and thus provides continuous information about the stimulus. (b) A phasic receptor adapts rapidly to a sustained stimulus and often exhibits an off response when the stimulus is removed. Thus, the receptor signals changes in stimulus intensity rather than relaying status quo information.

the internal viscera (the organs in the body cavities, such as the abdominal cavity) is called a **visceral afferent.** Even though mostly subconscious information is transmitted via visceral afferents, people do become aware of pain signals arising from viscera. Afferent input derived from receptors located at the body surface or in the muscles or joints typically reaches the level of conscious awareness. This input is known as *sensory information,* and the incoming pathway is considered a **sensory afferent.** Sensory information is categorized as (1) **somatic** (body sense) **sensation** arising from the body surface, including *somesthetic sensation* from the skin and *proprioception* from the muscles, joints, skin, and inner ear (see p. 123), or (2) **special senses,** including *vision, hearing, equilibrium, taste,* and *smell.* Final processing of sensory input by the CNS not only is essential for interaction with the environment for basic survival (for example, food procurement and defense from danger) but also adds immeasurably to the richness of life.

Each somatosensory pathway is "labeled" according to modality and location.

On reaching the spinal cord, afferent information has two possible destinies: (1) it may become part of a reflex arc, bringing about an appropriate effector response, or (2) it may be relayed upward to the brain via ascending pathways for further processing and possible conscious awareness. Pathways conveying conscious somatic sensation, the **somatosensory pathways,** consist of discrete chains of neurons, or **labeled lines,** synaptically interconnected in a particular sequence to accomplish progressively more sophisticated processing of the sensory information. A particular sensory modality detected by a specialized receptor type is sent over a specific afferent and ascending pathway (a neural pathway committed to that modality) to excite a defined area in the somatosensory cortex. That is, a particular sensory input is **projected** to a specific region of the cortex. Thus, different types of incoming information are kept separated within specific labeled lines between the periphery and the cortex. In this way, even though all information is propagated to the CNS via the same type of signal (action po-

tentials), the brain can decode the type and location of the stimulus. ▲ Table 6-1 summarizes how the CNS is informed of the type (what), location (where), and intensity (how much) of a stimulus.

Acuity is influenced by receptive field size.

Each somesthetic sensory neuron responds to stimulus information only within a circumscribed region of the skin surface surrounding it; this region is called its **receptive field.** The size of a receptive field varies inversely with the density of receptors in the region; the more closely receptors of a particular type are spaced, the smaller the area of skin each monitors. The smaller the receptive field in a region, the greater its **acuity** or **discriminative ability.** Compare the tactile discrimination in your fingertips with that in your calf by "feeling" the same object with both. You can sense more precise information about the object with your richly innervated fingertips because the receptive fields there are small; as a result, each neuron signals information about small, discrete portions of the object's surface. An estimated 17,000 tactile mechanoreceptors are present in the fingertips and palm of each hand. In contrast, the skin over the calf is served by relatively few sensory endings with larger receptive fields. Subtle differences within each large receptive field cannot be detected (● Figure 6-4). The distorted cortical representation of various body parts in the sensory homunculus (see p. 123) corresponds precisely with the innervation density; more cortical space is allotted for sensory reception from areas with smaller receptive fields and, accordingly, greater tactile discriminative ability.

▲ Table 6-1 Coding of Sensory Information

Stimulus Property	Mechanism of Coding
Type of stimulus (stimulus modality)	Distinguished by the type of receptor activated and the specific pathway over which this information is transmitted to a particular area of the cerebral cortex
Location of stimulus	Distinguished by the location of the activated receptor field and the pathway subsequently activated to transmit this information to the area of the somatosensory cortex representing that particular location
Intensity of stimulus (stimulus strength)	Distinguished by the frequency of action potentials initiated in an activated afferent neuron and by the number of receptors (and afferent neurons) activated

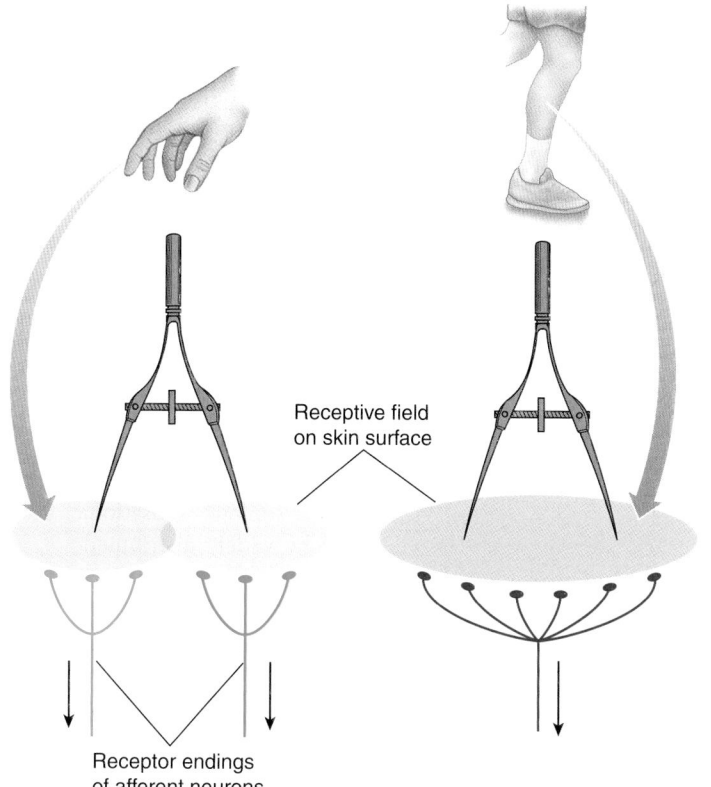

Receptive field
on skin surface

Receptor endings
of afferent neurons

Two receptive fields stimulated by
the two points of stimulation:
Two points felt

Only one receptive field stimulated
by the two points of stimulation
the same distance apart as in (a):
One point felt

(a) Region with small receptive fields

(b) Region with large receptive field

● FIGURE 6-4 **Comparison of discriminative ability of regions with small versus large receptive fields.** The relative tactile acuity of a given region can be determined by the *two-point threshold-of-discrimination test*. If the two points of a pair of calipers applied to the surface of the skin stimulate two different receptive fields, two separate points are felt. If the two points touch the same receptive field, they are perceived as only one point. By adjusting the distance between the caliper points, we can determine the minimal distance at which the two points can be recognized as two rather than one, which reflects the size of the receptive fields in the region. With this technique, it is possible to plot the discriminative ability of the body surface. The two-point threshold ranges from 2 mm in the fingertip (enabling a person to read Braille, where the raised dots are spaced 2.5 mm apart) to 48 mm in the poorly discriminative skin of the calf of the leg.

Perception is the conscious awareness of surroundings derived from interpretation of sensory input.

Perception is our conscious interpretation of the external world as created by the brain from a pattern of nerve impulses delivered to it from receptors. Is the world, as we perceive it, reality? The answer is a resounding no. Our perception is different from what is really "out there"—for several reasons. First, humans have receptors that detect only a limited number of existing energy forms. We perceive sounds, colors, shapes, textures, smells, tastes, and temperature but are not informed of magnetic forces, polarized light waves, radio waves, or X-rays because we do not have receptors to respond to the latter energy forms. What is not detected by receptors, the brain will never know. Second, the information channels to our brains are not

high-fidelity recorders. During precortical processing of sensory input, some features of stimuli are accentuated and others are suppressed or ignored. Third, the cerebral cortex further manipulates the data, comparing the sensory input with other incoming information, as well as with memories of past experiences to extract the significant features—for example, sifting out a friend's words from the hubbub of sound in a school cafeteria. In the process, the cortex often fills in or distorts the information to abstract a logical perception; that is, it "completes the picture." Other species, equipped with different types of receptors, sensitivities, and neural processing perceive a markedly different world from what we perceive.

Having completed our general discussion of receptor physiology, we now examine one important somatic sensation in greater detail—pain.

Pain

Pain is primarily a protective mechanism meant to bring to conscious awareness tissue damage that is occurring or is about to occur. Because of their value to survival, nociceptors (pain receptors) do not adapt to sustained or repetitive stimulation. Storage of painful experiences in memory helps us avoid potentially harmful events in the future.

Stimulation of nociceptors elicits the perception of pain plus motivational and emotional responses.

Unlike other somatosensory modalities, the sensation of pain is accompanied by motivated behavioral responses (such as withdrawal or defense), as well as emotional reactions (such as crying or fear). Also, unlike other sensations, the subjective perception of pain can be influenced by other past or present experiences (for example, heightened pain perception accompanying fear of the dentist or lowered pain perception in an injured athlete during a competitive event).

 All nociceptors can be sensitized by the presence of *prostaglandins,* which greatly enhance the receptor response to noxious stimuli (that is, it hurts more when prostaglandins are present). Prostaglandins are a special group of fatty acid derivatives that are cleaved from the lipid bilayer of the plasma membrane and act locally where released (see p. 592). Tissue injury, among other things, can lead to the local release of prostaglandins. These chemicals act on the nociceptors' peripheral endings to lower their threshold for activation. Aspirin-like drugs inhibit the synthesis of prostaglandins, accounting at least in part for the **analgesic** (pain-relieving) properties of these drugs.

FAST AND SLOW AFFERENT PAIN FIBERS Pain impulses originating at nociceptors are transmitted to the CNS via one of two types of afferent fibers. Different types of nociceptors respond to different painful stimuli. Signals arising from nociceptors that respond to mechanical damage such as cutting or to thermal damage such as burning are transmitted over small, myelinated fibers at rates of up to 30 m/sec (the **fast pain pathway**). Impulses from nociceptors that respond to chemicals released into the ECF from damaged tissue are carried by small, unmyelinated fibers at a slower rate of 12 m/sec (the **slow pain pathway**). Think about the last time you cut or burned your finger. You undoubtedly felt a sharp twinge of pain at first, with a more diffuse, disagreeable pain commencing shortly thereafter. Pain typically is perceived initially as a brief, sharp, prickling sensation that is easily localized; this is fast pain originating from specific mechanical or heat nociceptors. This feeling is followed by a dull, aching, poorly localized sensation that persists and is more unpleasant; this slow pain is activated for a prolonged time because of the persistence of released chemicals at the site long after removal of the mechanical or thermal stimulus that caused the tissue damage.

 Interestingly, the peripheral receptors of the slow pain pathway fibers are activated by **capsaicin**, the ingredient in hot chili peppers that gives them their fiery zing. (In addition to binding with pain receptors, capsaicin binds with heat receptors—hence the burning sensation when eating hot peppers.) Ironically, local application of capsaicin can reduce clinical pain, most likely by overstimulating and damaging the nociceptors with which it binds.

HIGHER-LEVEL PROCESSING OF PAIN INPUT The afferent pain fibers synapse with specific interneurons in the spinal cord from which the signal is transmitted to the brain for perceptual processing. One of the pain neurotransmitters released from these afferent pain terminals is **substance P,** which is unique to pain fibers. When the pain signal reaches the brain, processing by the somatosensory cortex localizes the pain, whereas other cortical areas participate in other conscious components of the pain experience, such as deliberation about the incident. The limbic system is especially important in perceiving the unpleasant aspects of pain.

The brain has a built-in analgesic system.

In addition to the chain of neurons connecting peripheral nociceptors with higher CNS structures for pain perception, the CNS contains a built-in pain-suppressing or **analgesic system** that suppresses transmission in the pain pathways as they enter the spinal cord. This analgesic system suppresses pain largely by blocking the release of substance P from afferent pain-fiber terminals.

The analgesic system depends on the presence of **opiate receptors**. People have long known that **morphine,** a component of the opium poppy, is a powerful analgesic. Researchers considered it unlikely that the body has been endowed with opiate receptors only to interact with chemicals derived from a flower. They therefore began to search for the substances that normally bind with these opiate receptors. The result was the discovery of **endogenous opiates** (morphinelike substances)— the **endorphins, enkephalins,** and **dynorphin**—which are important in the body's natural analgesic system. These endogenous opiates serve as analgesic neurotransmitters; they are released from the descending analgesic pathway and bind with opiate receptors on the afferent pain-fiber terminal. This binding suppresses the release of substance P, blocking further

transmission of the pain signal. Morphine binds to these same opiate receptors, which largely accounts for its analgesic properties. Morphine (and likely the endogenous opiates) also acts centrally to suppress pain.

It is not clear how this natural pain-suppressing mechanism is normally activated. Factors known to modulate pain include exercise, stress, and acupuncture. Researchers believe that endorphins are released during prolonged exercise and presumably produce the "runner's high." Some types of stress also induce analgesia. It is sometimes disadvantageous for a stressed organism to display the normal reaction to pain. For example, when two male lions are fighting for dominance of the group, withdrawing, escaping, or resting when injured would mean certain defeat. (See the accompanying boxed feature, ◗ Beyond the Basics, for an examination of how acupuncture relieves pain.)

This completes our discussion of somatic sensation. Whereas somatic sensation is detected by widely distributed receptors that provide information about the body's interactions with the environment in general, each of the special senses has highly localized, extensively specialized receptors that respond to unique environmental stimuli. The special senses include vision, hearing, equilibrium, taste, and smell, to which we now turn our attention, starting with vision.

Eye: Vision

For **vision,** the eyes capture the patterns of illumination in the environment as an "optical picture" on a layer of light-sensitive cells, the *retina,* much as a nondigital camera captures an image on film. Just as film can be developed into a visual likeness of the original image, the coded image on the retina is transmitted through the steps of visual processing until it is finally consciously perceived as a visual likeness of the original image.

The eye is a fluid-filled sphere enclosed by three specialized tissue layers.

Each **eye** is a spherical, fluid-filled structure enclosed by three layers. From outermost to innermost, these are (1) the *sclera/ cornea,* (2) the *choroid/ciliary body/iris,* and (3) the *retina* (● Figure 6-5b). Most of the eyeball is covered by a tough outer layer of connective tissue, the **sclera,** which forms the visible white part of the eye (● Figure 6-5a).

Anteriorly, the outer layer consists of the transparent **cornea,** through which light rays pass into the interior of the eye. The middle layer underneath the sclera is the highly pigmented **choroid,** which contains many blood vessels that nourish the retina. The choroid layer becomes specialized anteriorly to form the ciliary body and iris, which we describe shortly. The innermost coat under the choroid is the **retina,** which consists of an outer pigmented layer and an inner nervous-tissue layer. The latter contains the *rods* and *cones,* the photoreceptors that convert light energy into nerve impulses. Like the black walls of a photographic studio, the pigment in the choroid and retina absorbs light after it strikes the retina to prevent reflection or scattering of light within the eye.

Acupuncture: Is It for Real?

It sounds like science fiction. How can a needle inserted in the hand relieve a toothache? **Acupuncture analgesia (AA),** the technique of relieving pain by inserting and manipulating threadlike needles at key points, has been practiced in China for more than 2000 years but is relatively new to Western medicine and still remains controversial in the United States.

Brief History

Traditional Chinese teaching holds that disease can occur when the normal patterns of flow of healthful energy (called *qi;* pronounced "chee") just under the skin become disrupted, with acupuncture being able to correct this imbalance and restore health. Many Western scientists have been skeptical because, until recently, the phenomenon could not be explained on the basis of any known, logical, physiologic principles, although a tremendous body of anecdotal evidence in support of the effectiveness of AA existed in China. In Western medicine, the success of acupuncture was considered a placebo effect. The term *placebo effect* refers to a chemical or technique that brings about a desired response through the power of suggestion or distraction rather than through any direct action.

Because the Chinese were content with anecdotal evidence for the success of AA, this phenomenon did not come under close scientific scrutiny until the last several decades, when European and American scientists started studying it. As a result of these efforts, an impressive body of rigorous scientific investigation supports the contention that AA really works (that is, by a physiologic rather than a placebo or psychological effect). In controlled clinical studies, 55% to 85% of patients were helped by AA. Pain relief was reported by only 30% to 35% of placebo controls (people who thought they were receiving proper AA treatment but in whom needles were inserted in the wrong places or not deep enough). Furthermore, its mechanisms of action have become apparent. Indeed, more is known about the underlying physiologic mechanisms of AA than about those of many conventional medical techniques, such as gas anesthesia.

Mechanism of Action

The overwhelming body of evidence supports the *acupuncture endorphin hypothesis* as the primary mechanism of AA's action. According to this hypothesis, acupuncture needles activate specific afferent nerve fibers, which send impulses to the CNS. Here, the incoming impulses cause analgesia by blocking pain transmission at both the spinal-cord and the brain level through use of endogenous opiates. Several other neurotransmitters, such as serotonin and norepinephrine, as well as cortisol, the major hormone released during stress, are implicated as well. (Pain relief in placebo controls is believed to occur as a result of placebo responders subconsciously activating their own built-in analgesic system.)

Acupuncture in the United States

In the United States, AA has not been used in mainstream medicine, even by physicians who have been convinced by scientific evidence that the technique is valid. AA methodology has traditionally not been taught in U.S. medical colleges, and the techniques take time to learn. Also, using AA is more time-consuming than prescribing drugs. Western physicians who have been trained to use drugs to solve most pain problems are generally reluctant to scrap their known methods for an unfamiliar, time-consuming technique. However, acupuncture is gaining favor as an alternative treatment for relief of chronic pain, especially because analgesic drugs can have troublesome side effects. After decades of being spurned by most of the U.S. medical community, acupuncture started gaining respectability following a 1997 report issued by an expert panel convened by the National Institutes of Health (NIH). This report, based on an evaluation of published scientific studies, concluded that acupuncture is effective as an alternative or adjunct to conventional treatment for many kinds of pain and nausea. Now that acupuncture has been sanctioned by NIH and thus been made scientifically legitimate, some medical insurers have taken the lead in paying for this treatment, and some of the nation's medical schools are beginning to incorporate the technique into their curricula. However, most licensed acupuncture practitioners are nonphysicians who have specialized in acupuncture training and oriental medicine at one of the nearly 60 nationally accredited acupuncture schools.

The interior of the eye consists of two fluid-filled cavities, separated by an elliptical **lens,** all of which are transparent to permit light to pass through the eye from the cornea to the retina. The larger posterior cavity between the lens and the retina contains a clear, jellylike substance, the **vitreous humor.** The vitreous humor helps maintain the spherical shape of the eyeball. The anterior cavity between the cornea and the lens contains a clear, watery fluid, the **aqueous humor.** The aqueous humor carries nutrients for the cornea and lens, both of which lack a blood supply. Blood vessels in these structures would impede the passage of light to the photoreceptors.

The aqueous humor is produced by a capillary network within the **ciliary body,** a specialized anterior derivative of the choroid layer. This fluid drains into a canal at the edge of the cornea and eventually enters the blood (● Figure 6-6).

Clinical Note If the aqueous humor is not drained as rapidly as it forms (for example, because of a blocked drainage canal), the excess accumulates in the anterior cavity, causing the pressure to rise within the eye. This condition is known as **glaucoma.** The excess aqueous humor pushes the lens backward into the vitreous humor, which in turn pushes against the inner neural layer of the retina. This compression causes retinal and optic nerve damage that can lead to blindness if the condition is not treated.

The amount of light entering the eye is controlled by the iris.

Not all light passing through the cornea reaches the light-sensitive photoreceptors because of the presence of the iris, a thin, pigmented smooth muscle that forms a visible ringlike

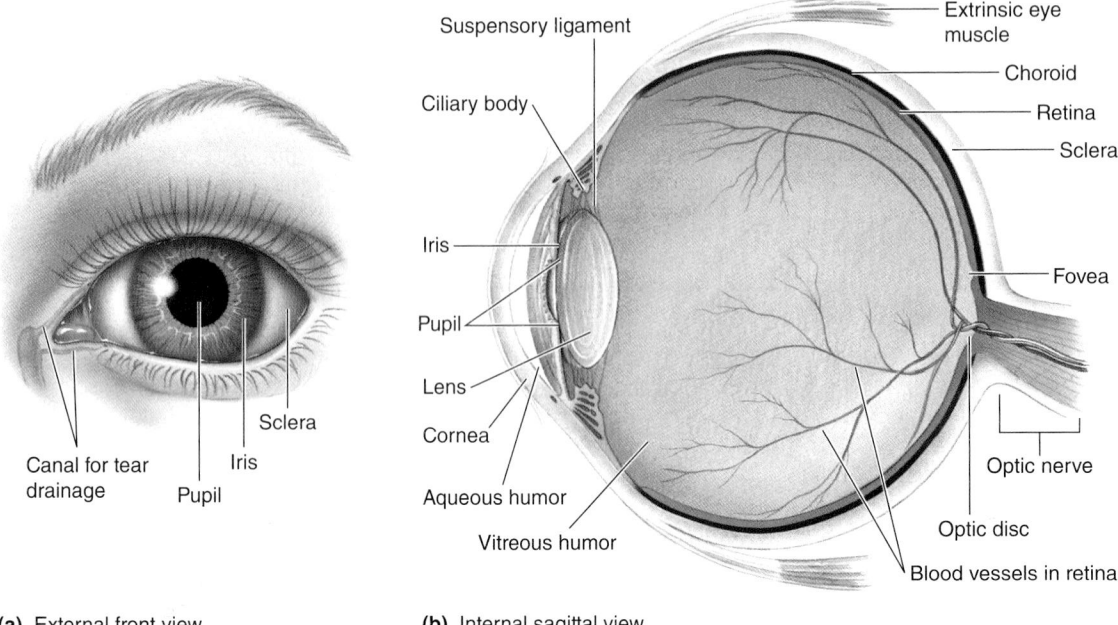

(a) External front view
(b) Internal sagittal view

● FIGURE 6-5 **Structure of the eye.**

structure within the aqueous humor (see ● Figure 6-5a and b). The pigment in the iris is responsible for eye color. The varied flecks, lines, and other nuances of the iris are unique for each individual, making the iris the basis of the latest identification technology. Recognition of iris patterns by a video camera that captures iris images and translates the landmarks into a computerized code is more foolproof than fingerprinting or even DNA testing.

The round opening in the center of the iris through which light enters the interior portions of the eye is the **pupil.** The size of this opening can be adjusted by variable contraction of the iris smooth muscles to admit more or less light as needed, much as the diaphragm controls the amount of light entering a camera. Iris muscles, and thus pupillary size, are controlled by the autonomic nervous system. Parasympathetic stimulation causes pupillary constriction, whereas sympathetic stimulation causes pupillary dilation.

The eye refracts the entering light to focus the image on the retina.

Light is a form of electromagnetic radiation that travels in wavelike fashion. The distance between two wave peaks is known as the *wavelength* (● Figure 6-7). The wavelengths in the electromagnetic spectrum range from 10^{-14} m (quadrillionths of a meter, as in the extremely short cosmic rays) to 10^4 m (10 km, as in long radio waves). The photoreceptors in the eye

● FIGURE 6-6 **Formation and drainage of the aqueous humor.** The aqueous humor is formed by a capillary network in the ciliary body, drains into a canal, and eventually enters the blood.

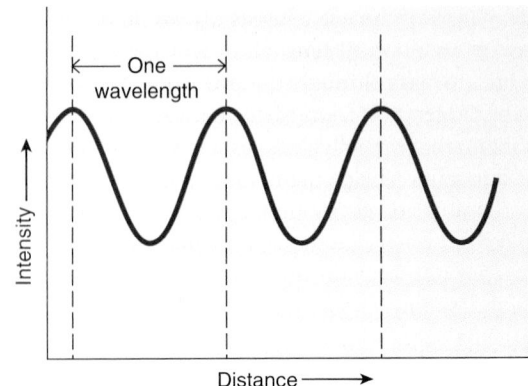

● FIGURE 6-7 **Properties of an electromagnetic wave.** A wavelength is the distance between two wave peaks. The intensity is the amplitude of the wave.

are sensitive only to wavelengths between 400 and 700 nanometers (nm; billionths of a meter). Thus, **visible light** is only a small portion of the total electromagnetic spectrum. Light of different wavelengths in this visible band is perceived as different color sensations. The shorter visible wavelengths are sensed as violet and blue; the longer wavelengths are interpreted as orange and red (see ● Figure 6-20, p. 167).

In addition to having variable wavelengths, light energy varies in intensity; that is, the amplitude, or height, of the wave (● Figure 6-7). Dimming a bright red light does not change its color; it just becomes less intense or less bright.

Light waves *diverge* (radiate outward) in all directions from every point of a light source. The forward movement of a light wave in a particular direction is known as a **light ray.** Divergent light rays reaching the eye must be bent inward to be focused

back into a point (the **focal point**) on the light-sensitive retina and provide an accurate image of the light source (● Figure 6-8).

PROCESS OF REFRACTION Light travels faster through air than through other transparent media such as water and glass. When a light ray enters a medium of greater density, it is slowed down (the converse is also true). The course of direction of the ray changes if it strikes the surface of the new medium at any angle other than perpendicular (● Figure 6-9). The bending of a light ray is known as **refraction.** With a curved surface such as a lens, the greater the curvature, the greater is the degree of bending and the stronger the lens. When a light ray strikes the curved surface of any object of greater density, the direction of refraction depends on the angle of the curvature (● Figure 6-10). A **convex surface** curves outward (like the outer surface

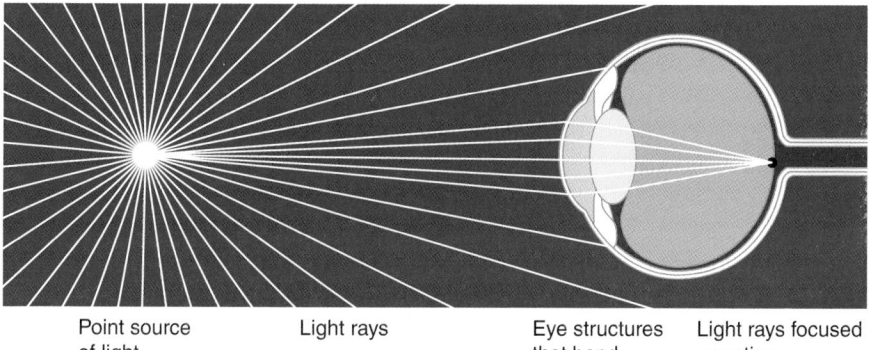

Point source of light Light rays Eye structures that bend light rays Light rays focused on retina

● FIGURE 6-8 **Focusing of diverging light rays.** Diverging light rays must be bent inward to be focused.

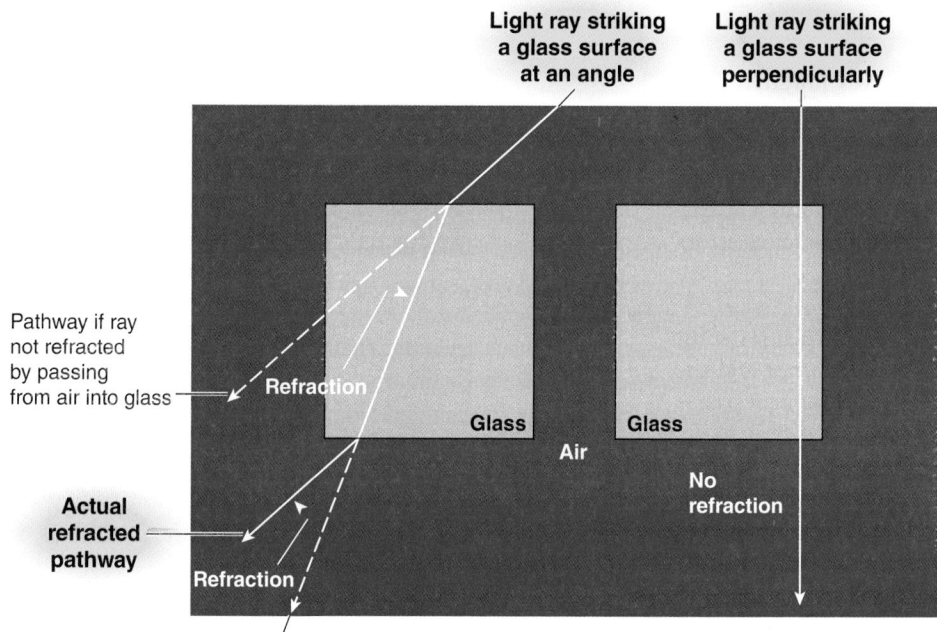

● FIGURE 6-9 **Refraction.** A light ray is bent (refracted) when it strikes the surface of a medium of different density from the one in which it had been traveling (for example, moving from air into glass) at any angle other than perpendicular to the new medium's surface. Thus, the pencil in the glass of water appears to bend. What is happening, though, is that the light rays coming to the camera (or your eyes) are bent as they pass through the water, then the glass, and then the air. Consequently, the pencil appears distorted.

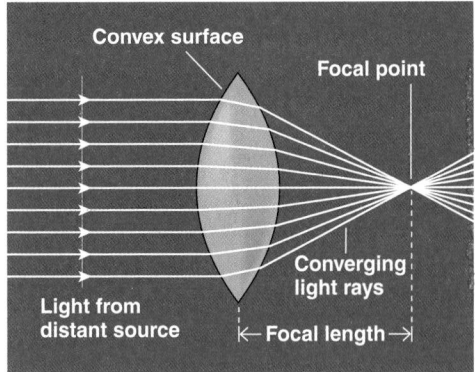

(a) Convex lens

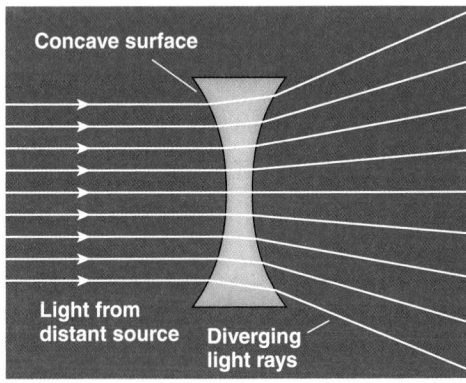

(b) Concave lens

● **FIGURE 6-10 Refraction by convex and concave lenses.** (a) A lens with a convex surface converges the rays (brings them closer together). (b) A lens with a concave surface diverges the rays (spreads them farther apart).

of a ball), whereas a **concave surface** curves inward (like a cave). Convex surfaces converge light rays, bringing them closer together. Because convergence is essential for bringing an image to a focal point, refractive surfaces of the eye are convex. Concave surfaces diverge light rays (spread them farther apart). A concave lens is useful for correcting certain refractive errors of the eye, such as nearsightedness.

THE EYE'S REFRACTIVE STRUCTURES The two structures most important in the eye's refractive ability are the *cornea* and the *lens*. The curved corneal surface, the first structure light passes through as it enters the eye, contributes most extensively to the eye's total refractive ability because the difference in density at the air–cornea interface is greater than the differences in density between the lens and the fluids surrounding it. In **astigmatism,** the curvature of the cornea is uneven, so light rays are unequally refracted. The refractive ability of a person's cornea remains constant, because the curvature of the cornea never changes. In contrast, the refractive ability of the lens can be adjusted by changing its curvature as needed for near or far vision.

Rays from light sources more than 20 feet away are considered parallel by the time they reach the eye. Light rays originating from near objects are still diverging when they reach the eye. For a given refractive ability of the eye, the diverging rays of a near source come to a focal point a greater distance behind the lens

than the parallel rays of a far source come to a focal point (● Figure 6-11a and b). However, in a particular eye, the distance between the lens and the retina always remains the same. Therefore, a greater distance beyond the lens is not available for bringing near objects into focus. Yet for clear vision, the refractive structures of the eye must bring both near and far light sources into focus on the retina. If an image is focused before it reaches the retina or is not yet focused when it reaches the retina, it will be blurred (● Figure 6-12). To bring both near and far light sources into focus on the retina (that is, in the same distance), a stronger lens must be used for the near source (● Figure 6-11c). Let us see how the strength of the lens can be adjusted as needed.

Accommodation increases the strength of the lens for near vision.

The ability to adjust the strength of the lens is known as **accommodation.** The strength of the lens depends on its shape, which in turn is regulated by the ciliary muscle. The **ciliary muscle** is part of the ciliary body, an anterior specialization of the choroid layer. The ciliary body has two major components: the ciliary

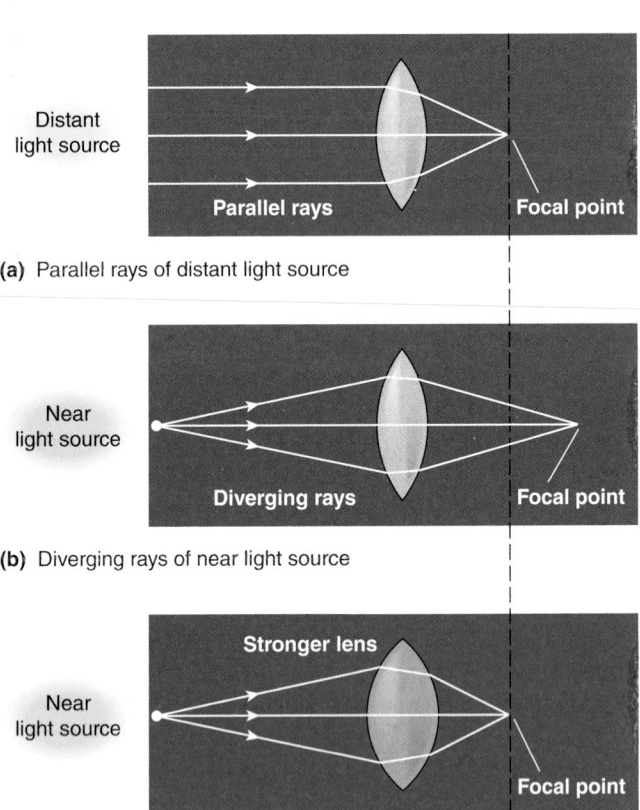

(a) Parallel rays of distant light source

(b) Diverging rays of near light source

(c) Stronger lens needed to focus near light source

● **FIGURE 6-11 Focusing of distant and near sources of light.** (a) The rays from a distant (far) light source (more than 20 feet from the eye) are parallel by the time the rays reach the eye. (b) The rays from a near light source (less than 20 feet from the eye) are still diverging when they reach the eye. A lens of a given strength takes a longer distance to bend the diverging rays from a near light source into focus than to bend the parallel rays from a distant light source into focus. (c) To focus both distant and near light sources in the same distance (the distance between the lens and the retina), a stronger lens must be used for the near source.

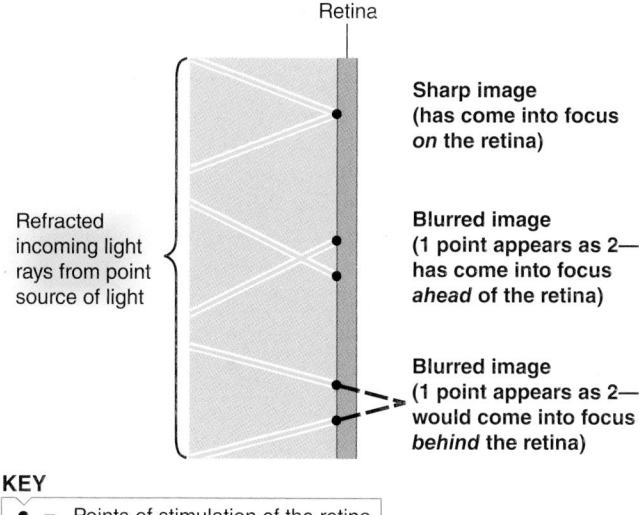

Retina

Refracted incoming light rays from point source of light

Sharp image (has come into focus *on* the retina)

Blurred image (1 point appears as 2— has come into focus *ahead* of the retina)

Blurred image (1 point appears as 2— would come into focus *behind* the retina)

KEY

● = Points of stimulation of the retina

● FIGURE 6-12 **Comparison of images that do and do not come into focus on the retina.**

muscle and the capillary network that produces the aqueous humor (see ● Figure 6-6). The ciliary muscle is a circular ring of smooth muscle attached to the lens by **suspensory ligaments** (● Figure 6-13a).

When the ciliary muscle is relaxed, the suspensory ligaments are taut, and they pull the lens into a flattened, weakly refractive shape (● Figure 6-13b). As the muscle contracts, its circumference decreases, slackening the tension in the suspensory ligaments (● Figure 6-13c). When the suspensory ligaments are not pulling on the lens, it becomes more spherical because of its inherent elasticity. The greater curvature of the more rounded lens increases its strength, further bending light rays. In the normal eye, the ciliary muscle is relaxed and the lens is flat for far vision but the muscle contracts to let the lens become more convex and stronger for near vision. The ciliary muscle is controlled by the autonomic nervous system, with sympathetic stimulation causing its relaxation and parasympathetic stimulation causing its contraction.

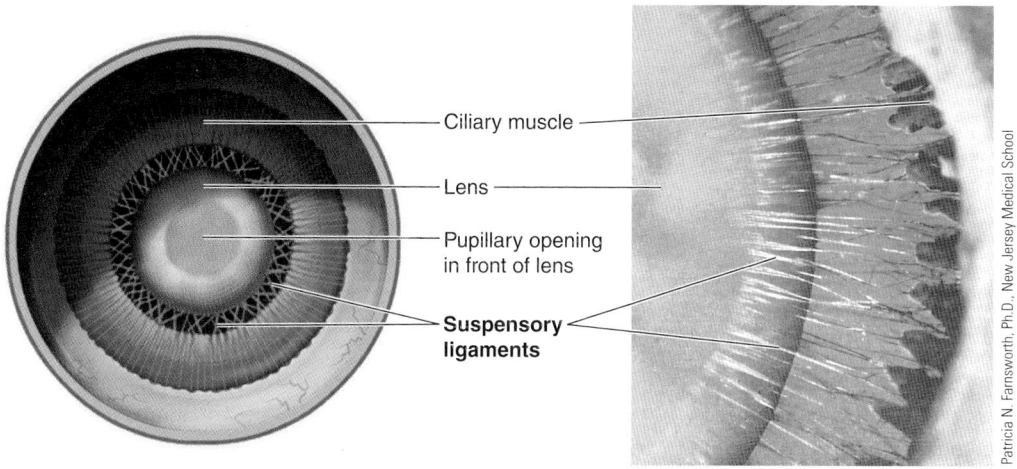

Ciliary muscle

Lens

Pupillary opening in front of lens

Suspensory ligaments

(a) Anterior view of suspensory ligaments extending from ciliary muscles to lens

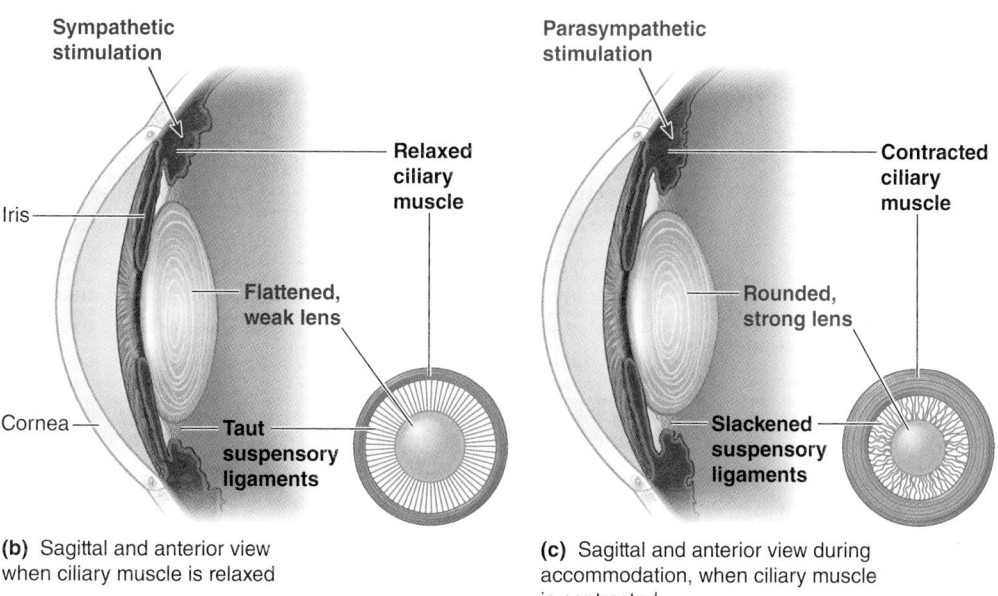

Sympathetic stimulation

Parasympathetic stimulation

Iris

Cornea

Relaxed ciliary muscle

Flattened, weak lens

Taut suspensory ligaments

Contracted ciliary muscle

Rounded, strong lens

Slackened suspensory ligaments

(b) Sagittal and anterior view when ciliary muscle is relaxed

(c) Sagittal and anterior view during accommodation, when ciliary muscle is contracted

● FIGURE 6-13 **Mechanism of accommodation.** (a) Suspensory ligaments extend from the ciliary muscle to the outer edge of the lens. (b) When the ciliary muscle is relaxed, the suspensory ligaments are taut, putting tension on the lens so that it is flat and weak. (c) When the ciliary muscle is contracted, the suspensory ligaments become slack, reducing the tension on the lens and allowing it to assume a stronger, rounder shape because of its elasticity.

The lens is made up of about 1000 layers of cells that destroy their nucleus and organelles during development so that the cells are perfectly transparent. Lacking DNA and protein-synthesizing machinery, mature lens cells cannot regenerate or repair themselves. Cells in the center of the lens are in double jeopardy. Not only are they oldest, but they also are farthest from the aqueous humor, the lens's nutrient source. With advancing age, these nonrenewable central cells die and become stiff. With loss of elasticity, the lens can no longer assume the spherical shape required to accommodate for near vision. This age-related reduction in accommodative ability, **presbyopia,** affects most people by middle age (45 to 50 years), requiring them to resort to corrective lenses for near vision (reading).

The normally transparent elastic fibers in the lens occasionally become opaque so that light rays cannot pass through, a condition known as a **cataract.** The defective lens can be surgically removed and vision can be restored by an implanted artificial lens or by compensating eyeglasses.

Other common vision disorders are *nearsightedness (myopia)* and *farsightedness (hyperopia).* In a normal eye **(emmetropia)** (● Figure 6-14a), a far light source is focused on the retina without accommodation, whereas the strength of the lens is increased by accommodation to bring a near source into focus. In **myopia** (● Figure 6-14b, part 1), because the eyeball is too long or the lens is too strong, a near light source is brought into focus on the retina without accommodation (even though accommodation is normally used for near vision), whereas a far light source is focused in front of the retina and is blurry. Thus, a myopic individual has better near vision than far vision, a condition that can be corrected by a concave lens (● Figure 6-14b, part 2). With **hyperopia** (● Figure 6-14c, part 1), either the eyeball is too short or the lens is too weak. Far objects are focused on the retina only with accommodation, whereas near objects are focused behind the retina even with accommodation and, accordingly, are blurry. Thus, a hyperopic individual has better far vision than near vision, a condition that can be corrected by a convex lens (● Figure 6-14c, part 2). Instead of using corrective eyeglasses or contact lenses, many people are now opting to compensate for refractive errors with laser eye surgery (such as LASIK) to permanently change the shape of the cornea.

Light must pass through several retinal layers before reaching the photoreceptors.

The major function of the eye is to focus light rays from the environment on the rods and cones, the photoreceptor cells of the retina. The photoreceptors then transform the light energy into electrical signals for transmission to the CNS.

The receptor-containing portion of the retina is actually an anatomic extension of the CNS, not a separate peripheral organ. During embryonic development, the retinal cells "back out" of the nervous system, so the retinal layers, surprisingly, are facing backward! The neural portion of the retina consists of three layers of excitable cells (● Figure 6-15): (1) the outermost layer (closest to the choroid) containing the **rods** and **cones,** whose light-sensitive ends face the choroid (away from the incoming light); (2) a middle layer of **bipolar cells** and associated interneurons; and (3) an inner layer of **ganglion cells.** Axons of the ganglion cells join to form the **optic nerve,** which leaves the retina slightly off center. The point on the retina at which the optic nerve leaves and through which blood vessels pass is the **optic disc** (see ● Figure 6-5b). This region is often called the **blind spot;** no image can be detected in this area because it has no rods and cones (● Figure 6-16). We are normally not aware of the blind spot, because central processing somehow "fills in" the missing spot. You can discover the existence of your own blind spot by a simple demonstration (● Figure 6-17).

Light must pass through the ganglion and bipolar layers before reaching the photoreceptors in all areas of the retina except the fovea. In the **fovea,** which is a pinhead-sized depression located in the exact center of the retina (see ● Figure 6-5b), the bipolar and ganglion cell layers are pulled aside so that light strikes the photoreceptors directly. Because of this feature, and because only cones (which have greater acuity or discriminative ability than the rods) are found here, the fovea is the point of most distinct vision. Thus, we turn our eyes so that the image of the object at which we are looking is focused on the fovea. The area immediately surrounding the fovea, the **macula lutea,** also has a high concentration of cones and fairly high acuity (see ● Figure 6-16). Macular acuity, however, is less than that of the fovea because of the overlying ganglion and bipolar cells in the macula.

Macular degeneration is the leading cause of blindness in the Western Hemisphere. This condition is characterized by loss of photoreceptors in the macula lutea in association with advancing age. Its victims have "doughnut" vision. They suffer a loss in the middle of their visual field, which normally has the highest acuity, and are left with only the less distinct peripheral vision.

Phototransduction by retinal cells converts light stimuli into neural signals.

Photoreceptors (rod and cone cells) consist of three parts (● Figure 6-18a):

1. An *outer segment,* which lies closest to the eye's exterior, facing the choroid. It detects the light stimulus.

2. An *inner segment,* which lies in the middle of the photoreceptor's length. It contains the metabolic machinery of the cell.

3. A *synaptic terminal,* which lies closest to the eye's interior, facing the bipolar cells. It varies its rate of neurotransmitter release, depending on the extent of dark or light exposure detected by the outer segment.

The outer segment, which is rod shaped in rods and cone shaped in cones (● Figure 6-18a and c), consists of stacked, flattened, membranous discs containing an abundance of light-sensitive **photopigments.** Each retina contains more than 125 million photoreceptors, and more than 1 billion photopigments may be packed into the outer segment of each photoreceptor.

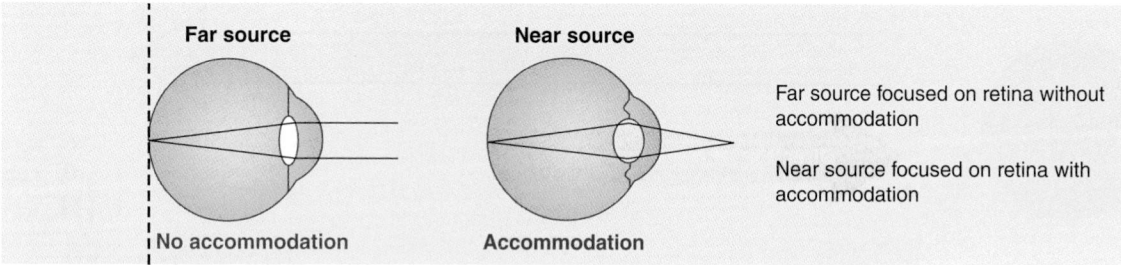

(a) Normal eye (Emmetropia)

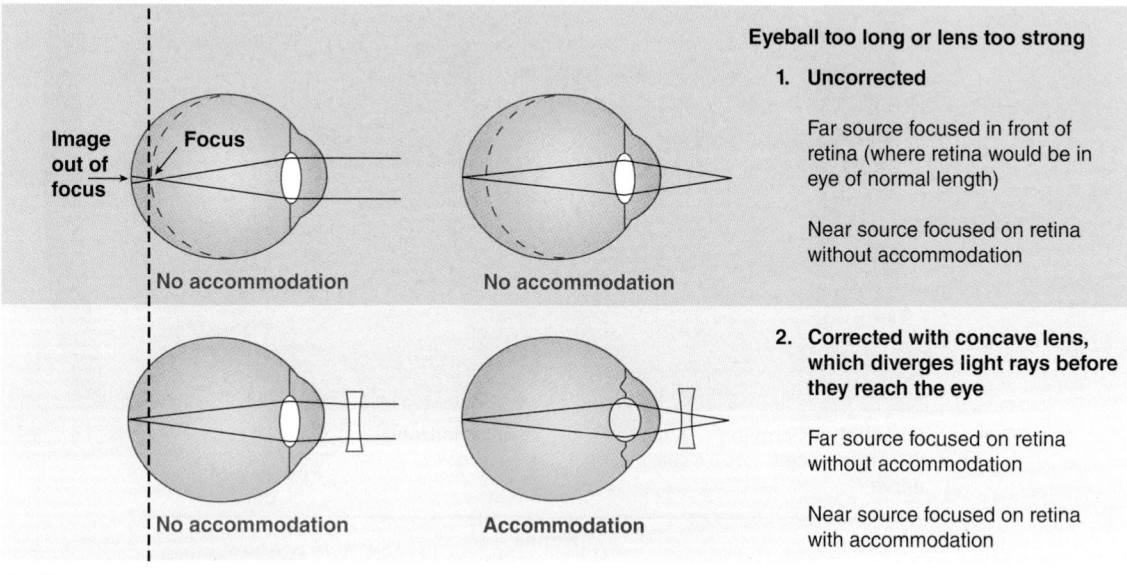

(b) Nearsightedness (Myopia)

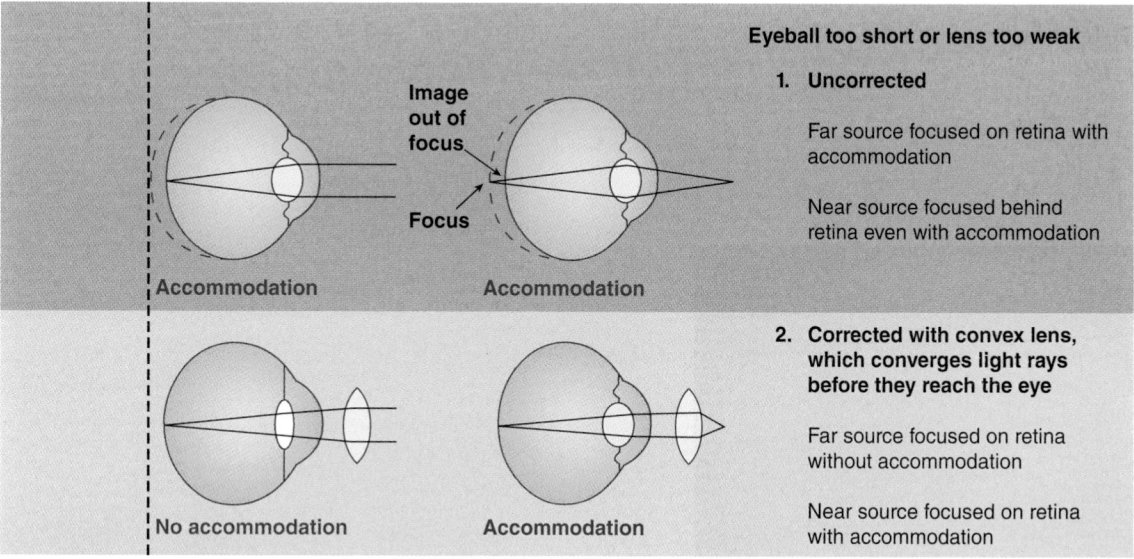

(c) Farsightedness (Hyperopia)

● **FIGURE 6-14 Emmetropia, myopia, and hyperopia.** This figure compares far vision and near vision (a) in the normal eye with (b) nearsightedness and (c) farsightedness in both their (1) uncorrected and (2) corrected states. The vertical dashed line represents the normal distance of the retina from the cornea, that is, the site at which an image is brought into focus by the refractive structures in a normal eye.

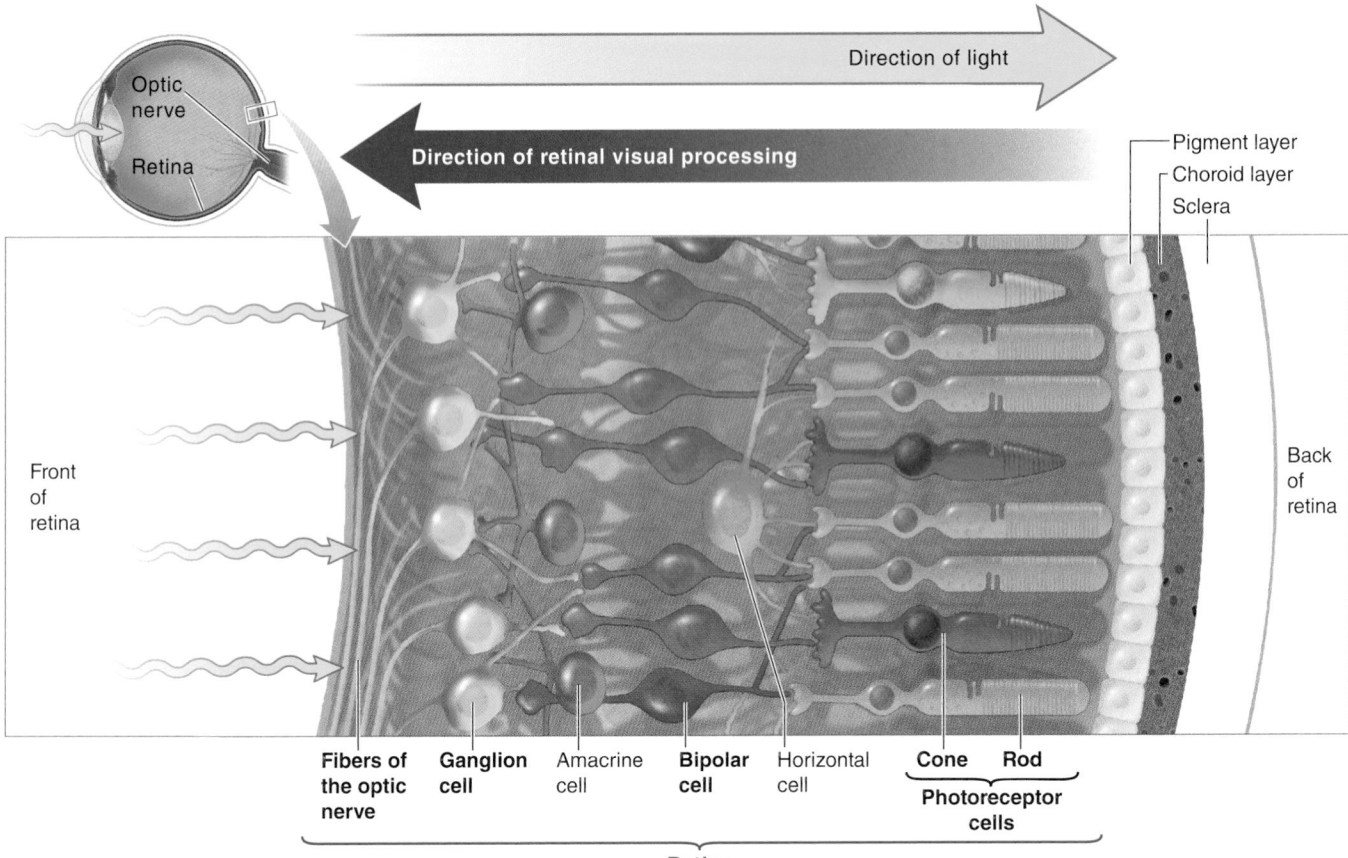

Direction of light

Direction of retinal visual processing

Optic nerve

Retina

Front of retina

Pigment layer
Choroid layer
Sclera

Back of retina

Fibers of the optic nerve | Ganglion cell | Amacrine cell | Bipolar cell | Horizontal cell | Cone | Rod

Photoreceptor cells

Retina

● FIGURE 6-15 **Retinal layers.** The retinal visual pathway extends from the photoreceptor cells (rods and cones, whose light-sensitive ends face the choroid away from the incoming light) to the bipolar cells to the ganglion cells. The horizontal and amacrine cells act locally for retinal processing of visual input.

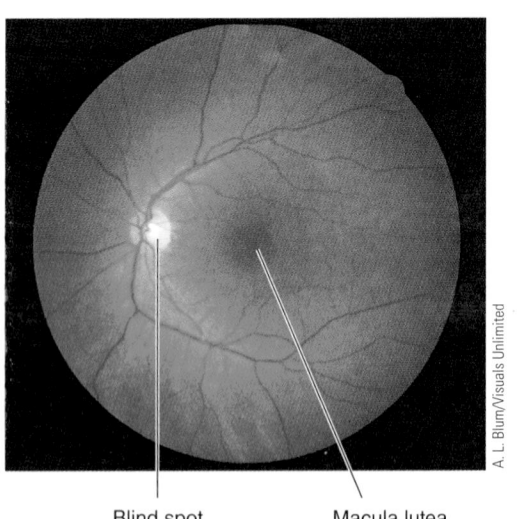

A. L. Blum/Visuals Unlimited

Blind spot   Macula lutea

● FIGURE 6-16 **View of the retina seen through an ophthalmo-scope.** With an ophthalmoscope, a lighted viewing instrument, it is possible to view the optic disc (blind spot) and macula lutea within the retina at the rear of the eye.

● FIGURE 6-17 **Demonstration of the blind spot.** Find the blind spot in your left eye by closing your right eye and holding the book about 4 in. from your face. While focusing on the cross, gradually move the book away from you until the circle vanishes from view. At this time, the image of the circle is striking the blind spot of your left eye. You can similarly locate the blind spot in your right eye by closing your left eye and focusing on the circle. The cross will disappear when its image strikes the blind spot of your right eye.

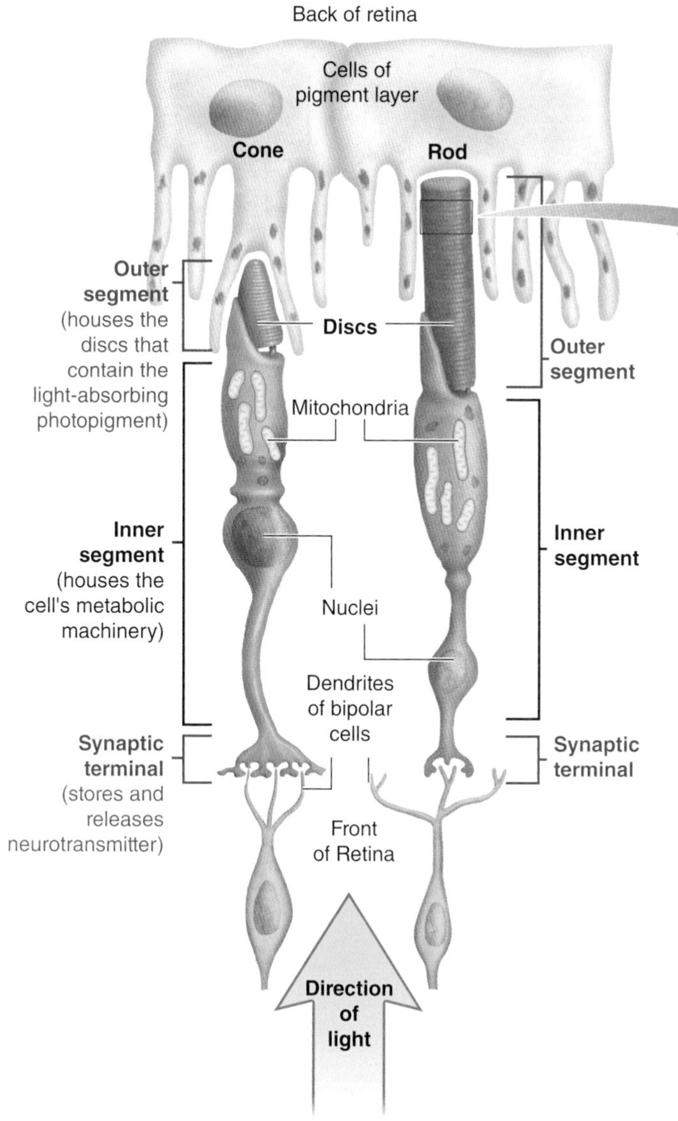

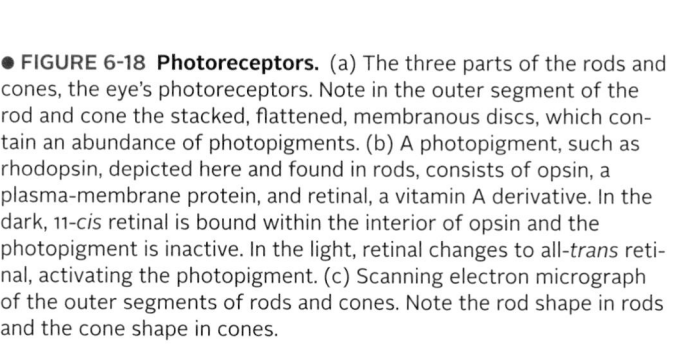

(a) Structure of rods and cones

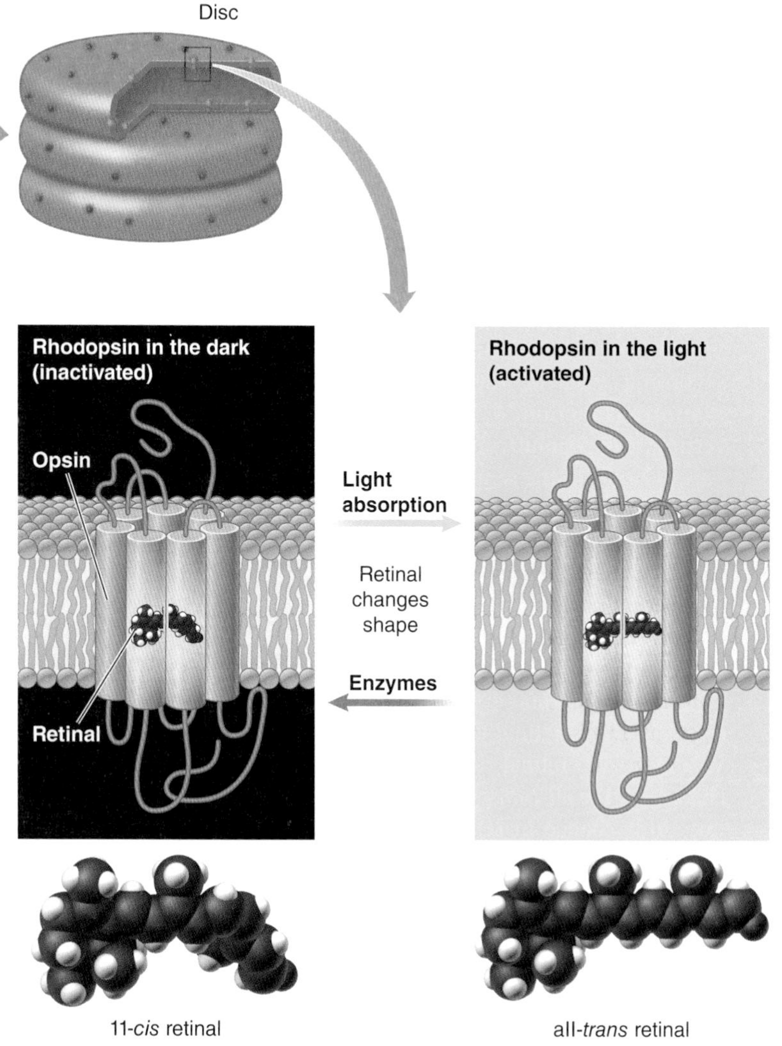

Back of retina

Cells of pigment layer

Cone   Rod

Outer segment (houses the discs that contain the light-absorbing photopigment)

Discs

Mitochondria

Outer segment

Inner segment (houses the cell's metabolic machinery)

Nuclei

Inner segment

Dendrites of bipolar cells

Synaptic terminal (stores and releases neurotransmitter)

Synaptic terminal

Front of Retina

Direction of light

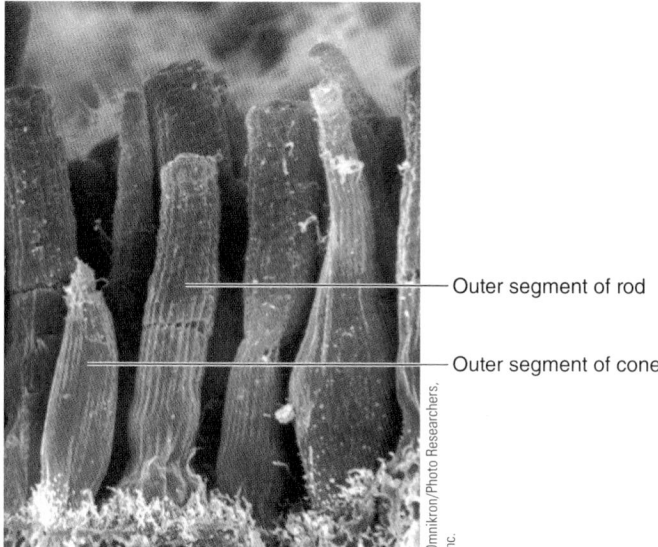

Disc

Rhodopsin in the dark (inactivated)

Opsin

Retinal

Light absorption →

Retinal changes shape

← Enzymes

Rhodopsin in the light (activated)

11-*cis* retinal   all-*trans* retinal

(b) Photopigment rhodopsin in the dark and light

Outer segment of rod

Outer segment of cone

Omnikron/Photo Researchers, Inc.

(c) Outer segments of rods and cones

● **FIGURE 6-18 Photoreceptors.** (a) The three parts of the rods and cones, the eye's photoreceptors. Note in the outer segment of the rod and cone the stacked, flattened, membranous discs, which contain an abundance of photopigments. (b) A photopigment, such as rhodopsin, depicted here and found in rods, consists of opsin, a plasma-membrane protein, and retinal, a vitamin A derivative. In the dark, 11-*cis* retinal is bound within the interior of opsin and the photopigment is inactive. In the light, retinal changes to all-*trans* retinal, activating the photopigment. (c) Scanning electron micrograph of the outer segments of rods and cones. Note the rod shape in rods and the cone shape in cones.

Photopigments undergo chemical alterations when activated by light. Through a series of steps, this light-induced change and the subsequent activation of the photopigment bring about a receptor potential in the photoreceptor that ultimately leads to the generation of action potentials in ganglion cells, which transmit this information to the brain for visual processing.

A photopigment consists of two components: **opsin,** a protein in the disc plasma membrane, and **retinal,** a derivative of vitamin A. Retinal is the light-absorbing part of the photopigment. **Phototransduction,** the process of converting light stimuli into electrical signals, is basically the same for all photoreceptors. We use rods as an example, but the same events take place in cones, except that they preferentially absorb light in different parts of the visible spectrum.

The photopigment in rods is **rhodopsin.** Retinal exists in different conformations in the dark and light. In the dark, it exists as 11-*cis* retinal (● Figure 6-18b). When 11-*cis* retinal absorbs light, it changes to the all-*trans* retinal conformation. This change in retinal's shape activates rhodopsin. In an unusual twist, the Na$^+$ channels of a photoreceptor are open in the absence of stimulation, that is, in the dark. The resultant passive inward Na$^+$ leak, the so-called *dark current*, depolarizes the photoreceptor. The depolarized photoreceptor releases neurotransmitter in the dark. Activation of rhodopsin on light exposure leads to closure of the Na$^+$ channels, stopping the depolarizing Na$^+$ leak and thereby causing hyperpolarization—an unusual receptor potential—in the outer segment (● Figure 6-19). Thus, photoreceptors are *inhibited by their adequate stimulus* (hyperpolarized by light) and *excited in the absence of stimulation* (depolarized by darkness). The receptor potential, which is graded in accordance with the light intensity, passively spreads to the synaptic terminal, where the potential change decreases the release of neurotransmitter from the photoreceptor.

Photoreceptors synapse with bipolar cells, the next layer of excitable cells in the retina. The membrane potential of bipolar cells is influenced by the neurotransmitter released from the photoreceptors. Bipolar cells, similar to photoreceptors, display graded potentials. Some

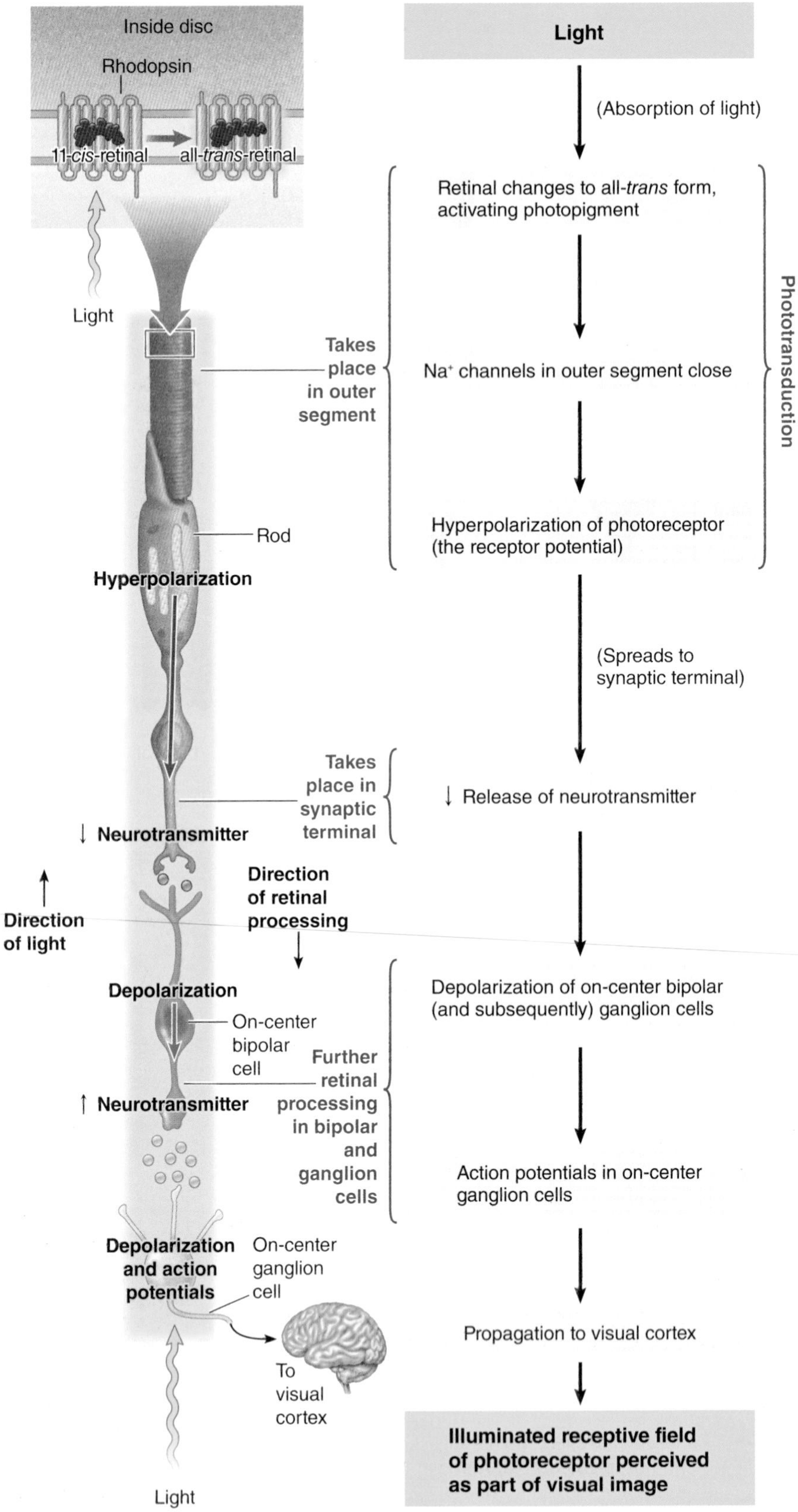

● FIGURE 6-19 **Phototransduction, further retinal processing, and initiation of action potentials in the visual pathway.** Events occurring in the retina and visual pathway in response to a light stimulus.

types of bipolar cells (*on-center cells* excited by light in the center of their receptive field) are "turned on" or depolarized by this reduction in neurotransmitter. (Other bipolar cells, the *off-center cells,* are excited by light in the periphery of their receptive field, adding to the complexity of retinal visual processing.) When on-center bipolar cells depolarize, they increase their neurotransmitter release at the ganglion cells. If ganglion cells are brought to threshold by bipolar cell activity, they undergo action potentials. Thus, action potentials do not originate until the ganglion cells, the first neurons in the chain that must propagate the visual message over a long distance to the brain. Neural messages sent to the visual cortex by the ganglion cells depend on the pattern of light striking the photoreceptors to which they are "wired" via the intervening bipolar cells. As the firing rates of the different ganglion cells change in response to the changing pattern of illumination on the retina, as detected by the photoreceptors, the brain is informed about the rapidity and extent of change in contrast within the visual image.

After the light signal has been passed on to the bipolar cells, the short-lived active form of the photopigment quickly dissociates into opsin and retinal. The retinal is converted back into its 11-*cis* form. In the dark, enzyme-mediated mechanisms rejoin opsin and this recycled retinal to restore the photopigment to its original inactive conformation (see ● Figure 6-18b).

Rods provide indistinct gray vision at night, whereas cones provide sharp color vision during the day.

The retina contains 20 times more rods than cones (120 million rods compared to 6 million cones per eye). Cones are most abundant in the macula lutea in the center of the retina. From this point outward, the concentration of cones decreases and the concentration of rods increases. Rods are most abundant in the periphery. We have examined the similar way in which phototransduction takes place in rods and cones. Now we focus on the differences between these photoreceptors (▲ Table 6-2).

Rods have high sensitivity, so they can respond to the dim light of night. Cones, by contrast, have lower sensitivity to light, being activated only by bright daylight. Thus, rods are specialized for night vision and cones for day vision.

The pathways by which cones are "wired" to the other retinal neuronal layers confer high acuity (sharpness, or the ability to distinguish between two nearby points). Thus, cones provide sharp vision with high resolution for fine detail during the day. By contrast, the wiring pathways of rods provide low acuity, so you can see at night with your rods but at the expense of distinctness.

Cones provide color vision; rods provide vision in shades of gray. There are four photopigments, one in the rods and one in each of three types of cones—**blue, green,** and **red cones.** Each of the four photopigments absorbs different wavelengths of light in the visible spectrum to varying degrees. Rods absorb all visible wavelengths to some degree. Each type of cone absorbs light best in a particular color range, namely, blue, green, or red (● Figure 6-20). Because the photopigments in the three types of cones each respond selectively to a different part of the visible light spectrum, the brain can compare the responses of the three cone types, making color vision in daylight possible. In contrast, the

▲ Table 6-2 Properties of Rod Vision and Cone Vision

Rods	Cones
120 million per retina	6 million per retina
More numerous in the periphery	Concentrated in the fovea
High sensitivity	Low sensitivity
Night vision	Day vision
Low acuity	High acuity
Vision in shades of gray	Color vision

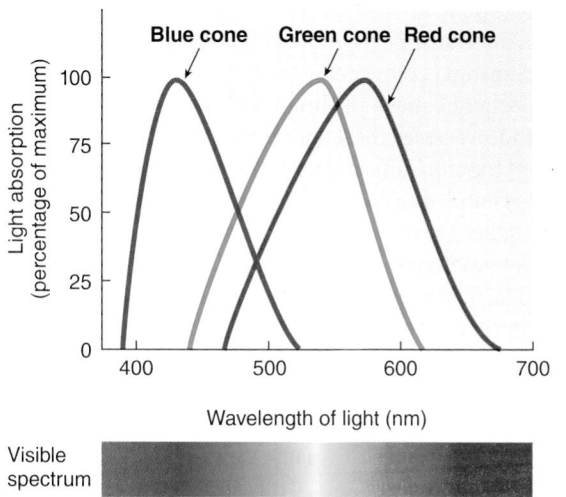

● FIGURE 6-20 **Sensitivity of the three types of cones to different wavelengths.**

brain cannot discriminate among various wavelengths when using visual input from the rods. The rhodopsin in every rod responds in the same way to a given wavelength, so no comparison among rod inputs is possible. Therefore, rods provide vision at night only in shades of gray by detecting different intensities, not different colors. We now examine color vision in further detail.

Color vision depends on the ratios of stimulation of the three cone types.

Vision depends on stimulation of photoreceptors by light. Certain objects in the environment, such as the sun, fire, and lightbulbs, emit light. But how do you see objects such as chairs, trees, and people, which do not emit light? The pigments in various objects selectively absorb particular wavelengths of light transmitted to them from light-emitting sources, and the unabsorbed wavelengths are reflected from the objects' surfaces. These reflected light rays enable you to see the objects. An object perceived as blue absorbs the longer red and green wavelengths of light and reflects the shorter blue wavelengths, which can be absorbed by the photopigment in the eyes' blue cones, thereby activating them.

Each cone type is most effectively activated by a particular wavelength of light in the range of color indicated by its name. However, cones also respond in varying degrees to other wavelengths (● Figure 6-20). **Color vision,** the perception of the many colors of the world, depends on the three cone types' various *ratios of stimulation* in response to different wavelengths. A wavelength perceived as blue does not stimulate red or green cones but excites blue cones maximally. (The percentage of maximal stimulation for red, green, and blue cones, respectively, is 0:0:100.) The sensation of yellow, in comparison, arises from a stimulation ratio of 83:83:0; that is, red and green cones are each stimulated 83% of maximum, while blue cones are not excited. The ratio for green is 31:67:36, and so on, with various combinations giving rise to the sensation of all the different colors. White is a mixture of all wavelengths of light, whereas black is the absence of light.

The extent to which each of the cone types is excited is coded and transmitted in separate parallel pathways to the brain. A distinct color vision center in the primary visual cortex in the occipital lobe of the brain (see ● Figure 5-8, p. 125) combines and processes these inputs to generate the perception of color, taking into consideration the object in comparison with its background. The concept of color is therefore in the mind of the beholder. Most of us agree on what color we see because we have the same types of cones and use similar neural pathways for comparing their output. Occasionally, however, individuals lack a particular cone type, so their color vision is a product of the differential sensitivity of only two types of cones, a condition known as **color blindness.** Not only do color-defective individuals perceive certain colors differently, but they are also unable to distinguish as many varieties of colors (● Figure 6-21). For example, people with certain color defects cannot distinguish between red and green. At a traffic light, they can tell which light is "on" by its intensity, but they must rely on the position of the bright light to know whether to stop or go.

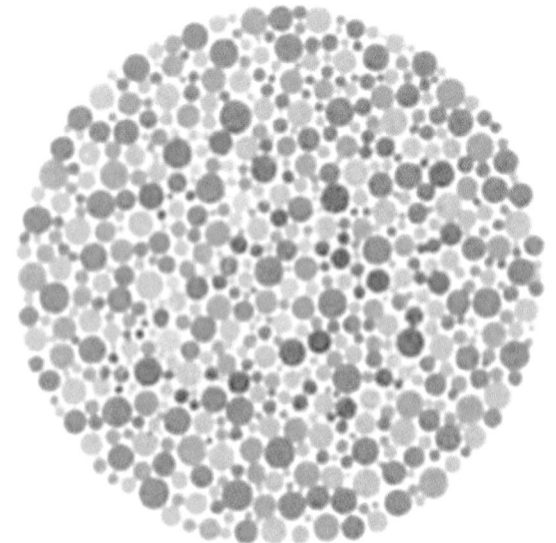

● **FIGURE 6-21 Color blindness chart.** People with red–green color blindness cannot detect the number 29 in this chart.

The sensitivity of the eyes can vary markedly through dark and light adaptation.

The eyes' sensitivity to light depends on the amount of light-responsive photopigment present in the rods and cones. When you go from bright sunlight into darkened surroundings, you cannot see anything at first, but gradually you begin to distinguish objects as a result of the process of **dark adaptation.** Breakdown of photopigments during exposure to sunlight tremendously decreases photoreceptor sensitivity. In the dark, the photopigments broken down during light exposure are gradually regenerated. As a result, the sensitivity of your eyes gradually increases so that you begin to see in the darkened surroundings. However, only the highly sensitive, rejuvenated rods are "turned on" by the dim light.

Conversely, when you move from the dark to the light (for example, leaving a movie theater and entering bright sunlight), at first your eyes are very sensitive to the dazzling light. With little contrast between lighter and darker parts, the entire image appears bleached. As some of the photopigments are rapidly broken down by the intense light, the sensitivity of the eyes decreases and normal contrasts can again be detected, a process known as **light adaptation.** The rods are so sensitive to light that enough rhodopsin is broken down in bright light to essentially "burn out" the rods; that is, after the rod photopigments have already been broken down by the bright light, they no longer can respond to the light. Therefore, only the less sensitive cones are used for day vision.

Our eyes' sensitivity can change as much as 1 million times as they adjust to various levels of illumination through dark and light adaptation. These adaptive measures are also enhanced by pupillary reflexes that adjust the amount of available light permitted to enter the eye.

 Because retinal is a derivative of vitamin A, adequate amounts of this nutrient must be available for synthesis of photopigments. **Night blindness** occurs as a result of dietary deficiencies of vitamin A. Although photopigment concentrations in both rods and cones are reduced in this condition, there is still enough cone photopigment to respond to the intense stimulation of bright light, except in the most severe cases. However, even modest reductions in rhodopsin content can decrease the sensitivity of rods so much that they cannot respond to dim light. The person can see in the day using cones but cannot see at night because the rods are no longer functional. Thus, carrots are "good for your eyes" because they are rich in vitamin A.

Visual information is separated before reaching the visual cortex.

The field of view that can be seen without moving the head is known as the **visual field.** Because of the pattern of wiring between the eyes and the visual cortex, the left half of the cortex receives information only from the right half of the visual field as detected by both eyes, and the right half receives input only from the left half of the visual field of both eyes.

As light enters the eyes, light rays from the left half of the visual field fall on the right half of the retina of both eyes (the medial or inner half of the left retina and the lateral or outer half of the right retina) (● Figure 6-22a). Similarly, rays from the right half of the visual field reach the left half of each retina (the lateral half of the left retina and the medial half of the right retina). Each optic nerve exiting the retina carries information from both halves of the retina it serves. This information is separated as the optic nerves meet at the **optic chiasm** located underneath the hypothalamus (*chiasm* means "cross") (see ● Figure 5-6b, p. 124). Within the optic chiasm, the fibers from the medial half of each retina cross to the opposite side, but those from the lateral half remain on the original side. The re-organized bundles of fibers leaving the optic chiasm are known as **optic tracts.** Each optic tract carries information from the lateral half of one retina and the medial half of the other retina. Therefore, this partial crossover brings together, from the two eyes, fibers that carry information from the same half of the visual field. Each optic tract, in turn, delivers to the half of the brain on its same side information about the opposite half of the visual field.

Clinical Note A knowledge of these pathways can facilitate di-agnosis of visual defects arising from interruption of the visual pathway at various points (● Figure 6-22b).

Before we move on to how the brain processes visual information, take a look at ▲ Table 6-3, which summa-rizes the functions of the various components of the eyes.

The thalamus and visual cortex elaborate the visual message.

The first stop in the brain for information in the visual pathway is the thalamus (● Figure 6-22a). It separates information re-ceived from the eyes and relays it via fiber bundles known as **optic radiations** to different zones in the visual cortex located in the occipital lobes (see Figure 5-8a, p. 125). Each zone processes different aspects of the visual stimulus (for example, form, movement, color, and depth). This sorting process is no small task, because each optic nerve contains more than a million fibers carrying information from the photoreceptors in one retina. This is more than all the afferent fibers carrying so-matosensory input from all other regions of the body! Research-ers estimate that hundreds of millions of neurons occupying about 40% of the cortex participate in visual processing, com-pared to 8% devoted to touch perception and 3% to hearing.

DEPTH PERCEPTION Although each half of the visual cortex re-ceives information simultaneously from the same part of the visual field as received by both eyes, the messages from the two eyes are not identical. Each eye views an object from a slightly different vantage point, even though the overlap is tremendous. The overlapping area seen by both eyes at the same time is known as the **binocular** ("two-eyed") field of vision, which is important for **depth perception.** The brain uses the slight dis-

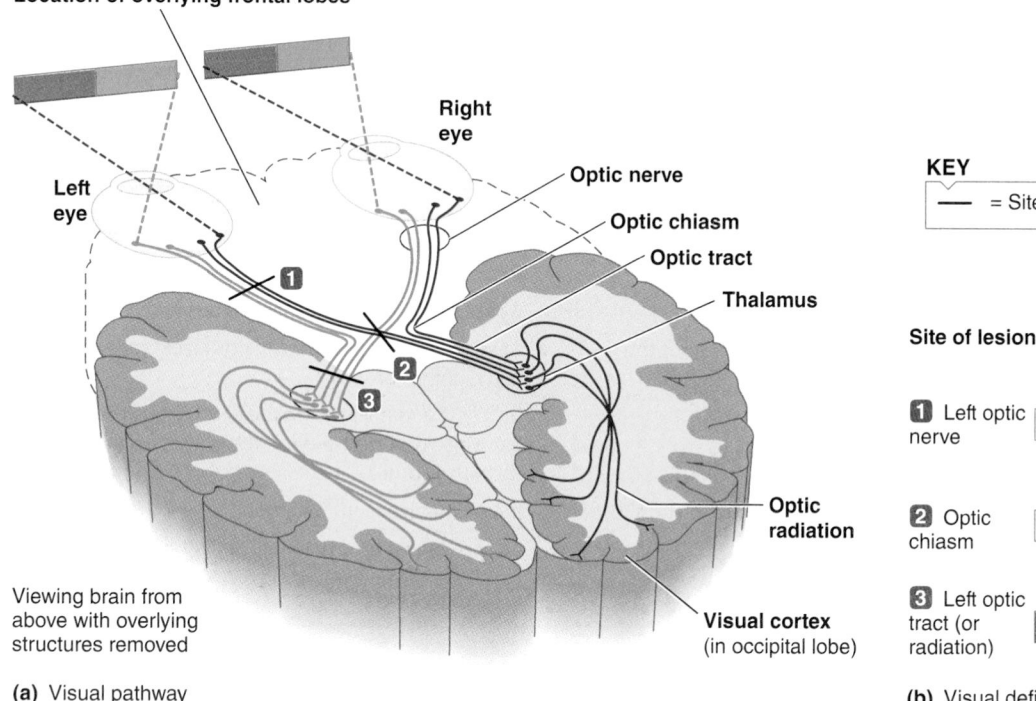

Location of overlying frontal lobes

Left eye

Right eye

Optic nerve

Optic chiasm

Optic tract

Thalamus

Optic radiation

Viewing brain from above with overlying structures removed

Visual cortex (in occipital lobe)

(a) Visual pathway

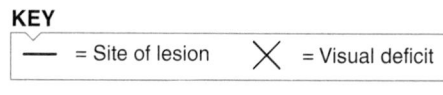

KEY

—— = Site of lesion   ✕ = Visual deficit

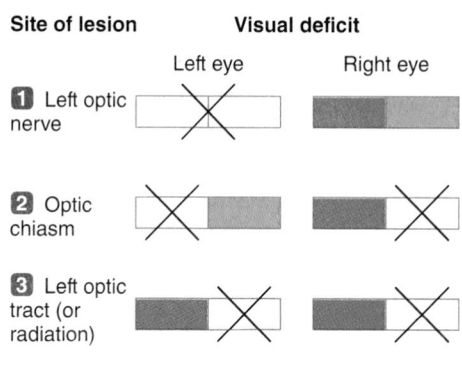

Site of lesion	Visual deficit	
	Left eye	Right eye
1 Left optic nerve		
2 Optic chiasm		
3 Left optic tract (or radiation)		

(b) Visual deficits with specific lesions in visual pathway

● FIGURE 6-22 **The visual pathway and visual deficits associated with lesions in the path-way.** (a) Note that the left half of the visual cortex in the occipital lobe receives information from the right half of the visual field of both eyes (in green), and the right half of the cortex re-ceives information from the left half of the visual field of both eyes (in red). (b) Each visual defi-cit illustrated is associated with a lesion at the corresponding numbered point of the visual path-way in part (a).

Structure (in alphabetical order)	Location	Function
Aqueous Humor	Anterior cavity between the cornea and the lens	A clear, watery fluid that is continually formed and carries nutrients to the cornea and lens
Bipolar Cells	Middle layer of nerve cells in the retina	Important in retinal processing of a light stimulus
Blind Spot	Point slightly off-center on the retina where the optic nerve exits; lacks photoreceptors (also known as the *optic disc*)	Route for passage of the optic nerve and blood vessels
Choroid	Middle layer of the eye	Pigmented to prevent scattering of light rays in the eye; contains blood vessels that nourish the retina; anteriorly specialized to form the ciliary body and iris
Ciliary Body	Specialized anterior derivative of the choroid layer; forms a ring around the outer edge of the lens	Produces the aqueous humor and contains the ciliary muscle
Ciliary Muscle	Circular muscular component of the ciliary body; attached to the lens by means of suspensory ligaments	Important in accommodation
Cones	Photoreceptors in the outermost layer of the retina	Responsible for high acuity, color, and day vision
Cornea	Anterior, clear, outermost layer of the eye	Contributes most extensively to the eye's refractive ability
Fovea	Exact center of the retina	Region with the greatest acuity
Ganglion Cells	Inner layer of nerve cells in the retina	Important in retinal processing of a light stimulus; form the optic nerve
Iris	Visible pigmented ring of muscle within the aqueous humor	Varies the size of the pupil by variable contraction; responsible for eye color
Lens	Between the aqueous humor and the vitreous humor; attaches to the ciliary muscle by suspensory ligaments	Provides variable refractive ability during accommodation
Macula Lutea	Area immediately surrounding the fovea	Has high acuity because of the abundance of cones
Optic Disc	(See entry for *blind spot*)	
Optic Nerve	Leaves each eye at the optic disc (blind spot)	First part of the visual pathway to the brain
Pupil	Anterior round opening in the middle of the iris	Permits variable amounts of light to enter the eye
Retina	Innermost layer of the eye	Contains the photoreceptors (rods and cones)
Rods	Photoreceptors in the outermost layer of the retina	Responsible for high-sensitivity, black-and-white, and night vision
Sclera	Tough outer layer of the eye	Protective connective tissue coat; forms the visible white part of the eye; anteriorly specialized to form the cornea
Suspensory Ligaments	Suspended between the ciliary muscle and the lens	Important in accommodation
Vitreous Humor	Between the lens and the retina	Jellylike substance that helps maintain the spherical shape of the eye

parity in the information received from the two eyes to estimate distance, allowing you to perceive three-dimensional objects in spatial depth. Some depth perception is possible using only one eye, based on experience and comparison with other cues. For example, if your one-eyed view includes a car and a building and the car is larger, you correctly interpret that the car must be closer to you than the building is.

HIERARCHY OF VISUAL CORTICAL PROCESSING Within the cortex, visual information is first processed in the primary visual cortex and then is sent to surrounding higher-level visual areas for even more complex processing and abstraction. Each level of cortical visual neurons has increasingly greater capacity for abstraction of information built up from the increasing convergence of input from lower-level neurons. In this way, the cortex transforms the dotlike pattern of photoreceptors stimulated to varying degrees by varying light intensities in the retinal image into information about position, orientation, movement, contour, and length. Other aspects of visual information, such as depth perception and color perception, are processed simultaneously. How and where the entire image is finally put together is still unresolved. Only when these separate bits of processed information are integrated by higher visual regions is a reassembled picture of the visual scene perceived. This is similar to the blobs of paint on an artist's palette versus the finished portrait; the separate pigments do not represent a portrait of a face until they are appropriately integrated on a canvas.

Visual input goes to other areas of the brain not involved in vision perception.

Not all fibers in the visual pathway terminate in the visual cortex. Some are projected to other regions of the brain for purposes other than direct vision perception. Examples of nonsight activities dependent on input from the rods and cones include (1) contribution to cortical alertness and attention (for example, you get drowsy in a dimly lit room), (2) control of pupil size (for example, your pupils constrict in bright light), and (3) control of eye movements (for example, input from your photoreceptors is used to guide contraction of your external eye muscles to enable you to read this page). Each eye is equipped with a set of six **external eye muscles** that position and move the eye so that it can better locate, see, and track objects. Eye movements are among the fastest, most discretely controlled movements of the body.

About 3% of the eyes' ganglion cells are not involved in visual processing. Instead, they make **melanopsin,** a light-sensitive pigment that plays a key role in setting the body's "biological clock" to march in step with the light–dark cycles (see p. 543).

We next shift our attention from the eyes to the ears.

Ear: Hearing and Equilibrium

Each **ear** consists of three parts: the *external,* the *middle,* and the *inner ear* (● Figure 6-23). The external and middle portions of the ear transmit airborne sound waves to the fluid-filled inner ear, amplifying sound energy in the process. The inner ear houses two sensory systems: the cochlea, which contains the receptors for conversion of sound waves into nerve impulses, making hearing possible, and the vestibular apparatus, which is necessary for the sense of equilibrium.

Sound waves consist of alternate regions of compression and rarefaction of air molecules.

Hearing is the neural perception of sound energy. Hearing involves two aspects: the identification of the sounds (what) and their localization (where). We first examine the characteristics of sound waves and then explore how the ears and brain process sound input to accomplish hearing.

Sound waves are traveling vibrations of air. They consist of regions of high pressure, caused by compression of air molecules, alternating with regions of low pressure, caused by rarefaction of the molecules (● Figure 6-24a). Any device capable of producing such a disturbance pattern in air molecules is a source of sound. A simple example is a tuning fork. When a tuning fork is struck, its prongs vibrate. As a prong of the fork moves in one direction (● Figure 6-24b), air molecules ahead of it are pushed closer to-

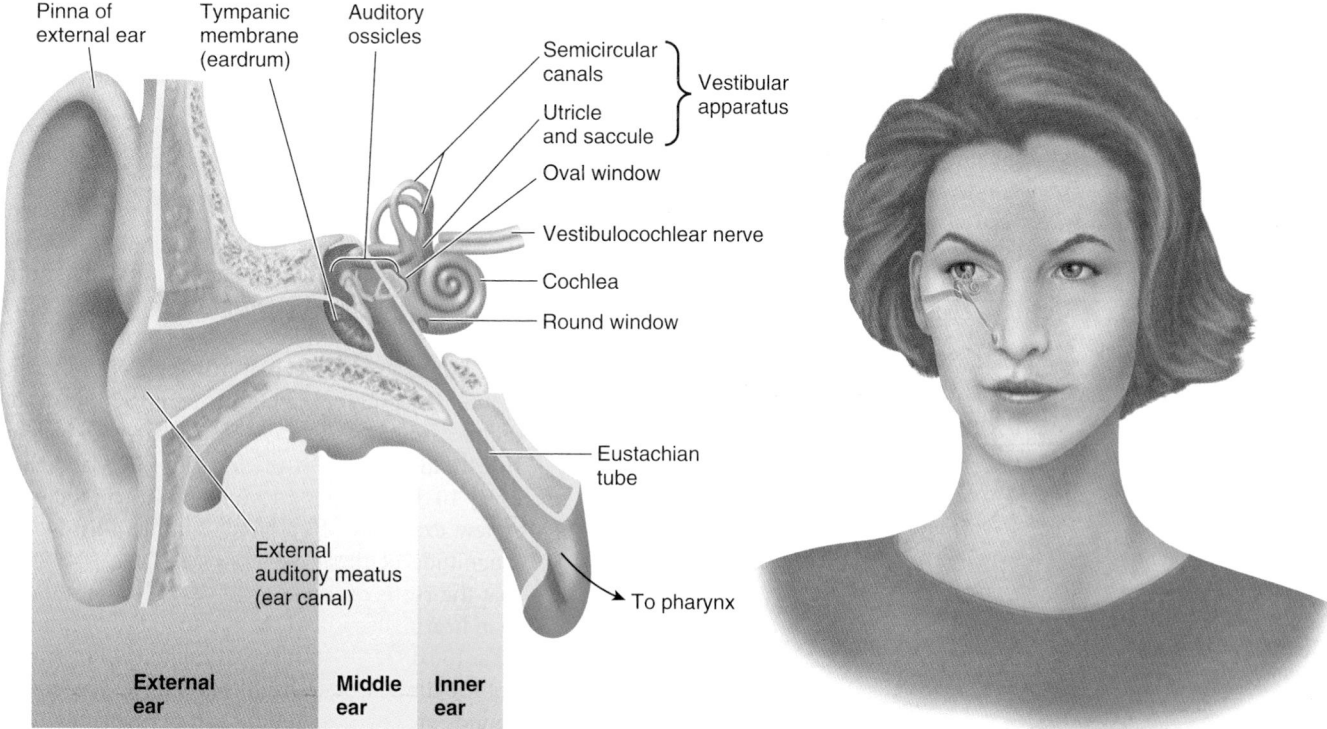

● FIGURE 6-23 **Anatomy of the ear.**

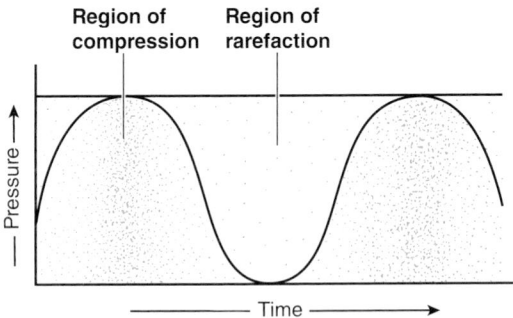

(a) Sound waves

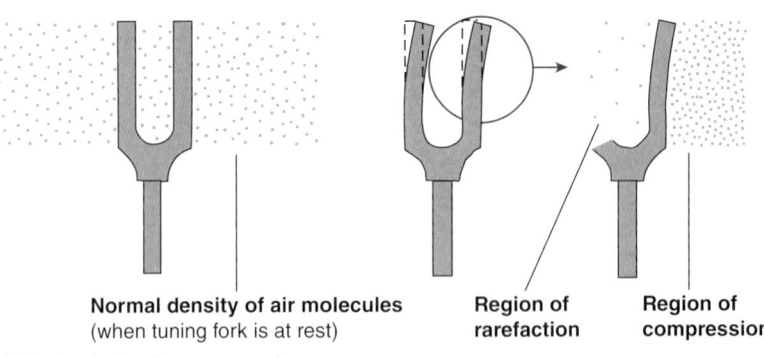

Normal density of air molecules
(when tuning fork is at rest)

Region of
rarefaction

Region of
compression

(b) Tuning fork setting up sound waves

● FIGURE 6-24 **Formation of sound waves.** (a) Sound waves are alternating regions of compression and rarefaction of air molecules. (b) A vibrating tuning fork sets up sound waves, as the air molecules ahead of the advancing arm of the tuning fork are compressed while the molecules behind the arm are rarefied. (c) Disturbed air molecules bump into molecules beyond them, setting up new regions of air disturbance more distant from the original source of sound. In this way, sound waves travel progressively farther from the source, even though each air molecule travels only a short distance when it is disturbed. The sound wave dies out when the last region of air disturbance is too weak to disturb the region beyond it.

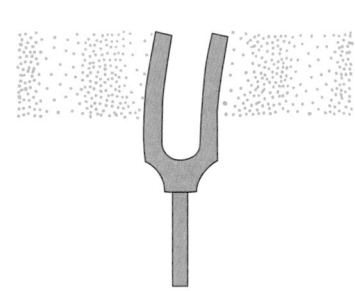
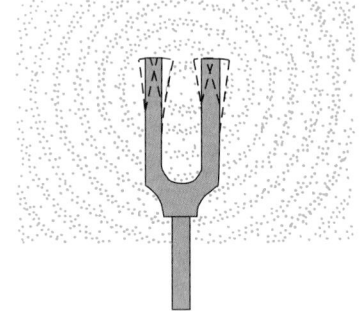

(c) Sound waves traveling from source

gether, or compressed, increasing the pressure in this area. Simultaneously, as the prong moves forward, the air molecules behind the prong spread out, or are rarefied, lowering the pressure in that region. As the prong moves in the opposite direction, an opposite wave of compression and rarefaction is created. Even though individual molecules are moved only short distances as the tuning fork vibrates, alternating waves of compression and rarefaction spread out considerable distances in a rippling fashion. Disturbed air molecules disturb other molecules in adjacent regions, setting up new regions of compression and rarefaction, and so on (● Figure 6-24c). Sound energy gradually dissipates as sound waves travel farther from the original sound source; it finally dies out when the last sound wave is too weak to disturb the air molecules around it. Sound waves can also travel through media other than air, such as water. They do so less efficiently, however;

greater pressure is needed to cause movements of fluid than movements of air.

Sound is characterized by its pitch (tone), intensity (loudness), and timbre (quality) (● Figure 6-25):

■ The **pitch,** or **tone,** of a sound (for example, whether it is a C or a G note) is determined by the *frequency* of vibrations. The greater the frequency of vibration, the higher the pitch. Human ears can detect sound waves with frequencies from 20 to 20,000 cycles per second, or **hertz (Hz),** but are most sensitive to frequencies between 1000 and 4000 Hz.

■ The **intensity,** or **loudness,** of a sound depends on the *amplitude* of the sound waves, or the pressure differences between a high-pressure region of compression and a low-pressure region of rarefaction. Within the hearing range, the greater the amplitude, the louder the sound. Human ears can detect a wide range of sound intensities, from the slightest whisper to the painfully loud takeoff of a jet. Loudness is measured in **decibels (dB),** which are a logarithmic measure of intensity compared with the faintest sound that can be heard—the **hearing threshold.** Because of the logarithmic relationship, every 10 dB indicates a 10-fold increase in loudness. A few examples of common sounds illustrate the magnitude of these increases (▲ Table 6-4). Note that the rustle of leaves at 10 dB is 10 times louder than hearing threshold but the sound of a jet taking off at 150 dB is 1 quadrillion (1 million billion) times, not 150 times, louder than the faintest audible sound. Sounds greater than 100 dB can permanently damage the sensitive sensory apparatus in the cochlea.

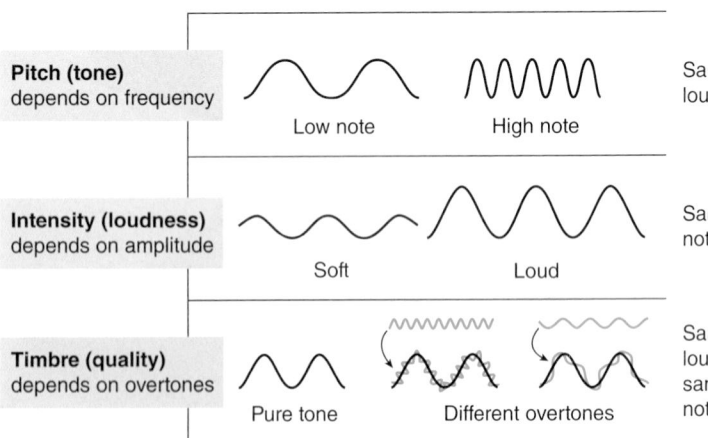

● FIGURE 6-25 **Properties of sound waves.**

Sound	Loudness in decibels (dB)	Comparison to faintest audible sound (hearing threshold)
Rustle of Leaves	10 dB	10 times louder
Ticking of Watch	20 dB	100 times louder
Whispering	30 dB	1000 times louder
Normal Conversation	60 dB	1 million times louder
Food Blender, Lawn Mower, or Hair Dryer	90 dB	1 billion times louder
Loud Rock Concert or Ambulance Siren	120 dB	1 trillion times louder
Takeoff of Jet	150 dB	1 quadrillion times louder

The **timbre,** or **quality,** of a sound depends on its *overtones,* which are additional frequencies superimposed on the fundamental pitch or tone. A tuning fork has a pure tone, but most sounds lack purity. For example, complex mixtures of overtones impart different sounds to different instruments playing the same note (a *C* note on a trumpet sounds different from *C* on a piano). Overtones are likewise responsible for characteristic differences in voices. Timbre enables the listener to distinguish the source of sound waves, because each source produces a different pattern of overtones. Thanks to timbre, you can tell whether it is your mother or girlfriend calling on the telephone before you say the wrong thing.

The external ear plays a role in sound localization.

The specialized receptor cells for sound are located in the fluid-filled inner ear. Airborne sound waves must therefore be channeled toward and transferred into the inner ear, compensating for the loss in sound energy that naturally occurs as sound waves pass from air into water. This function is performed by the external ear and the middle ear.

The **external ear** (see ● Figure 6-23) consists of the *pinna* (ear), *external auditory meatus* (ear canal), and *tympanic membrane* (eardrum). The **pinna,** a prominent skin-covered flap of cartilage, collects sound waves and channels them down the ear canal. The ear canal tunnels through the temporal bone from the exterior to the **tympanic membrane,** a thin membrane that separates the external ear and the middle ear.

Because of its shape, the pinna partially shields sound waves that approach the ear from the rear and thus helps a person distinguish whether a sound is coming from directly in front or behind. Sound localization for sounds approaching from the right or left depends on the sound wave reaching the ear closer to the sound source slightly before it arrives at the farther ear. The auditory cortex integrates all these cues to determine the location of the sound source. It is difficult to localize sound with only one ear.

The tympanic membrane vibrates in unison with sound waves in the external ear.

The tympanic membrane, which is stretched across the entrance to the middle ear, vibrates when struck by sound waves. The alternating higher- and lower-pressure regions of a sound wave cause the exquisitely sensitive eardrum to bow inward and outward in unison with the wave's frequency.

For the membrane to be free to move as sound waves strike it, the resting air pressure on both sides of the tympanic membrane must be equal. The outside of the eardrum is exposed to atmospheric pressure that reaches it through the ear canal. The inside of the eardrum facing the middle ear cavity is also exposed to atmospheric pressure via the **eustachian (auditory) tube,** which connects the middle ear to the **pharynx** (back of the throat) (see ● Figure 6-23). The eustachian tube is normally closed, but it can be pulled open by yawning, chewing, and swallowing. Such opening permits air pressure within the middle ear to equilibrate with atmospheric pressure so that pressures on both sides of the tympanic membrane are equal. During rapid external pressure changes (for example, during air flight), the eardrum bulges painfully as the pressure outside the ear changes while the pressure in the middle ear remains unchanged. Opening the eustachian tube by yawning allows the pressure on both sides of the tympanic membrane to equalize, relieving the pressure distortion as the eardrum "pops" back into place.

Infections originating in the throat sometimes spread through the eustachian tube to the middle ear. The resulting fluid accumulation in the middle ear not only is painful but also interferes with sound conduction across the middle ear.

The middle ear bones convert tympanic membrane vibrations into fluid movements in the inner ear.

The **middle ear** transfers the vibrating movements of the tympanic membrane to the fluid of the inner ear. This transfer is facilitated by a movable chain of three small bones, or **ossicles** (the **malleus, incus,** and **stapes**), that extend across the middle ear (● Figure 6-26a). The first bone, the malleus, is attached to the tympanic membrane, and the last bone, the stapes, is attached to the **oval window,** the entrance into the fluid-filled cochlea. As the tympanic membrane vibrates in response to sound waves, the chain of bones is set into motion at the same frequency, transmitting this frequency of movement from the tympanic membrane to the oval window. The resulting pressure on the oval window with each vibration produces wavelike

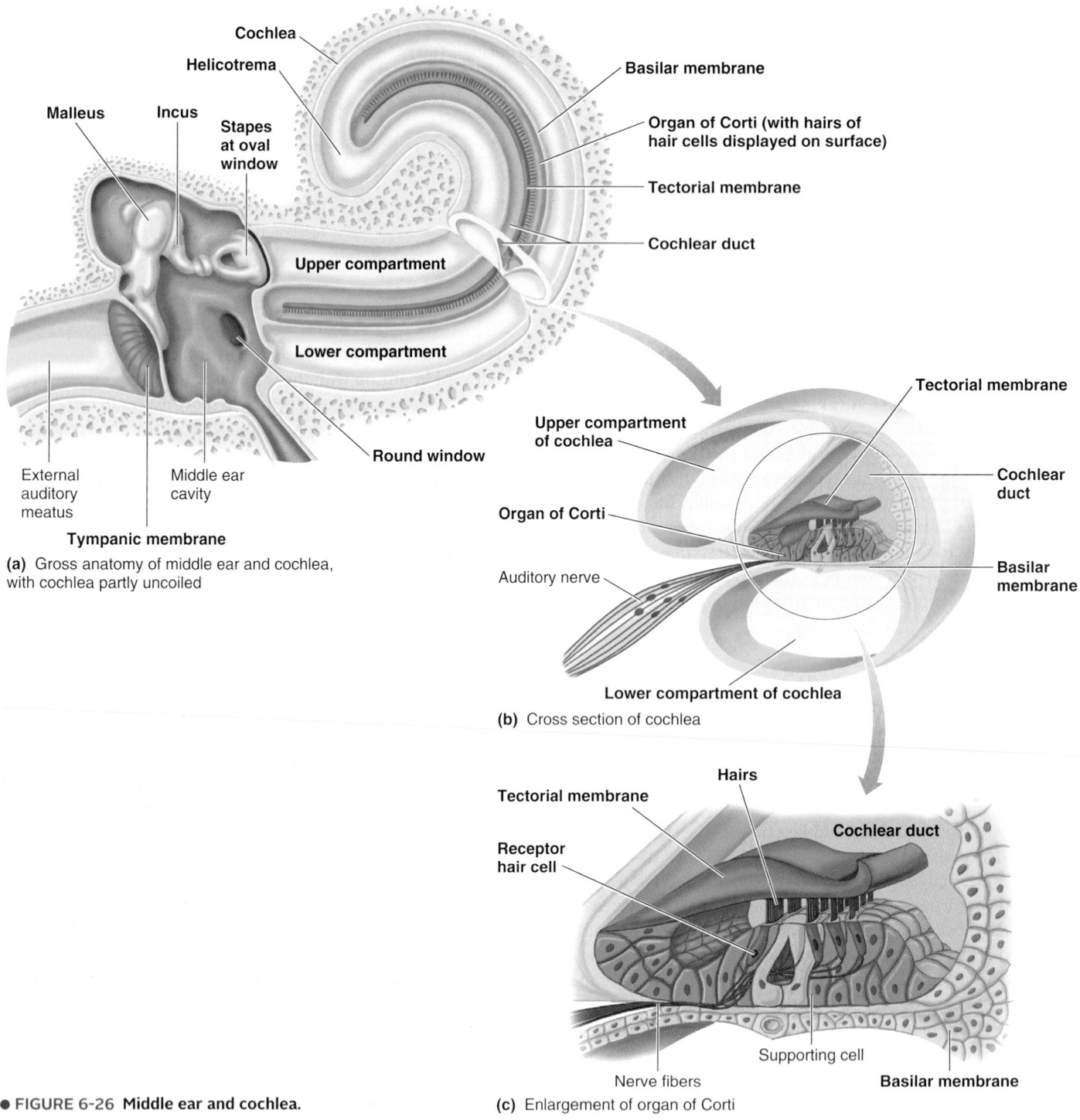

Malleus **Incus** **Stapes at oval window**

Cochlea

Helicotrema

Basilar membrane

Organ of Corti (with hairs of hair cells displayed on surface)

Tectorial membrane

Cochlear duct

Upper compartment

Lower compartment

Round window

External auditory meatus

Middle ear cavity

Tympanic membrane

(a) Gross anatomy of middle ear and cochlea, with cochlea partly uncoiled

Upper compartment of cochlea

Organ of Corti

Auditory nerve

Tectorial membrane

Cochlear duct

Basilar membrane

Lower compartment of cochlea

(b) Cross section of cochlea

Hairs

Tectorial membrane

Receptor hair cell

Cochlear duct

Nerve fibers

Supporting cell

Basilar membrane

(c) Enlargement of organ of Corti

● FIGURE 6-26 **Middle ear and cochlea.**

movements in the inner ear fluid at the same frequency as the original sound waves. Recall that it takes greater pressure to set fluid in motion than needed to move air, but the ossicular system amplifies the pressure of the airborne sound waves sufficiently to produce fluid movements in the inner ear. The mechanical arrangement of the ossicles increases the force exerted on the oval window by 20 times what it would be if the airborne sound wave struck the oval window directly.

The cochlea contains the organ of Corti, the sense organ for hearing.

The pea-sized, snail-shaped **cochlea,** the "hearing" portion of the inner ear, is a coiled tubular system lying deep within the temporal bone (*cochlea* means "snail") (see ● Figure 6-23). It is easier to understand the functional components of the cochlea by "uncoiling" it, as shown in ● Figure 6-26a. The cochlea is divided throughout most of its length into three fluid-filled longitudinal compartments. A blind-ended **cochlear duct,** which constitutes the middle compartment, tunnels lengthwise through the center of the cochlea, not quite reaching its end. The upper compartment is sealed from the middle ear cavity by the oval window, to which the stapes is attached. Another small membrane-covered opening, the **round window,** seals the lower compartment from the middle ear. The region beyond the tip of the cochlear duct where the fluid in the upper and lower compartments is continuous is called the **helicotrema.** The **basilar membrane** forms the floor of the cochlear duct, separating it from the lower compartment. The basilar membrane is especially important because it bears the **organ of Corti,** the sense organ for hearing.

Hair cells in the organ of Corti transduce fluid movements into neural signals.

The organ of Corti, which rests on top of the basilar membrane throughout its full length, contains 15,000 **auditory hair cells** that are the receptors for sound (● Figure 6-26c). Protruding from the surface of each hair cell are about 100 hairs. Hair cells generate neural signals when their surface hairs are mechanically deformed by fluid movements in the inner ear. These hairs contact the **tectorial membrane,** an awninglike projection overhanging the organ of Corti throughout its length (● Figure 6-26b and c).

The pistonlike action of the stapes against the oval window sets up pressure waves in the upper compartment. Because fluid is incompressible, pressure is dissipated in two ways as the stapes causes the oval window to bulge inward: (1) displacement of the round window and (2) deflection of the basilar membrane (● Figure 6-27a). In the first of these pathways, the pressure wave pushes the fluid forward in the upper compartment, around the helicotrema, and into the lower compartment, where it causes the round window to bulge outward into the middle ear cavity to compensate for the pressure increase. As the stapes rocks backward and pulls the oval window outward toward the middle ear, the fluid shifts in the opposite direction, displacing the round window inward. This pathway does not result in sound reception; it just dissipates pressure.

Pressure waves of frequencies associated with sound reception take a "shortcut" (● Figure 6-27a). Pressure waves in the upper compartment are transferred into the cochlear duct and then through the basilar membrane into the lower compartment. Transmission of pressure waves through the basilar membrane causes this membrane to move up and down, or vibrate, in synchrony with the pressure wave. Because the organ of Corti rides on the basilar membrane, the hair cells also move up and down. The hairs of these receptor cells are bent back and forth when the oscillating basilar membrane shifts their position in relationship to the tectorial membrane with which they are in contact (● Figure 6-28). This back-and-forth mechanical deformation of the hairs alternately opens and closes mechanically gated cation channels (see p. 78) in the hair cell, resulting in alternating depolarizing and hyperpolarizing potential changes—the receptor potential—at the same frequency as the original sound stimulus. Like photoreceptors, hair cells do not

undergo action potentials. Instead, graded potential changes in the hair cells lead to changes in the rate of action potentials in the afferent nerve fibers that make up the **auditory (cochlear) nerve,** which conducts the impulses to the brain. These neural signals are perceived by the brain as sound sensations (● Figure 6-29). The neural pathway between the organ of Corti and the auditory cortex in the temporal lobe of the brain (see Figure 5-8a, p. 125) involves several synapses en route, the most notable of which are in the brain stem and the thalamus. The brain stem uses the auditory input for alertness and arousal. The thalamus sorts and relays the signals upward.

Unlike the visual pathways, auditory signals from each ear are transmitted to both temporal lobes because the fibers partially cross over in the brain stem. For this reason, a disruption of the auditory pathways on one side beyond the brain stem does not affect hearing in either ear to any extent.

The primary auditory cortex appears to perceive discrete sounds, whereas the surrounding higher-order auditory cortex integrates the separate sounds into a coherent, meaningful pattern. Think about the complexity of the task accomplished by your auditory system. When you are at a concert, your organ of Corti responds to the simultaneous mixture of the instruments, the applause and hushed talking of the audience, and the background noises in the theater. You can distinguish these separate parts of the many sound waves reaching your ears and can pay attention to those of importance to you.

Pitch discrimination depends on the region of the basilar membrane that vibrates.

Pitch discrimination (that is, the ability to distinguish among various frequencies of incoming sound waves) depends on the shape and properties of the basilar membrane, which is narrow and stiff at its oval window end and wide and flexible at its helicotrema end (see ● Figure 6-27b). Different regions of the basilar membrane naturally vibrate maximally at different frequencies; that is, each frequency displays a peak vibration at a different position along the membrane. The narrow end nearest the oval window vibrates best with high-frequency pitches, whereas the wide end nearest the helicotrema vibrates maximally with low-frequency tones (see ● Figure 6-27c). The pitches in between are sorted out precisely along the length of the membrane from higher to lower frequency. As a sound wave of a particular frequency is set up in the cochlea by oscillation of the stapes, the wave travels to the region of the basilar membrane that naturally responds maximally to that frequency. The energy of the pressure wave is dissipated with this vigorous membrane oscillation, so the wave dies out at the region of maximal displacement.

The hair cells in the region of peak vibration of the basilar membrane undergo the most mechanical deformation and accordingly are the most excited. You can think of the organ of Corti as a piano with 15,000 keys (represented by the 15,000 hair cells) rather than the usual 88 keys. Each hair cell is "tuned" to an optimal sound frequency, determined by its location on the organ of Corti. Different sound waves promote maximal movement of different regions of the basilar membrane and

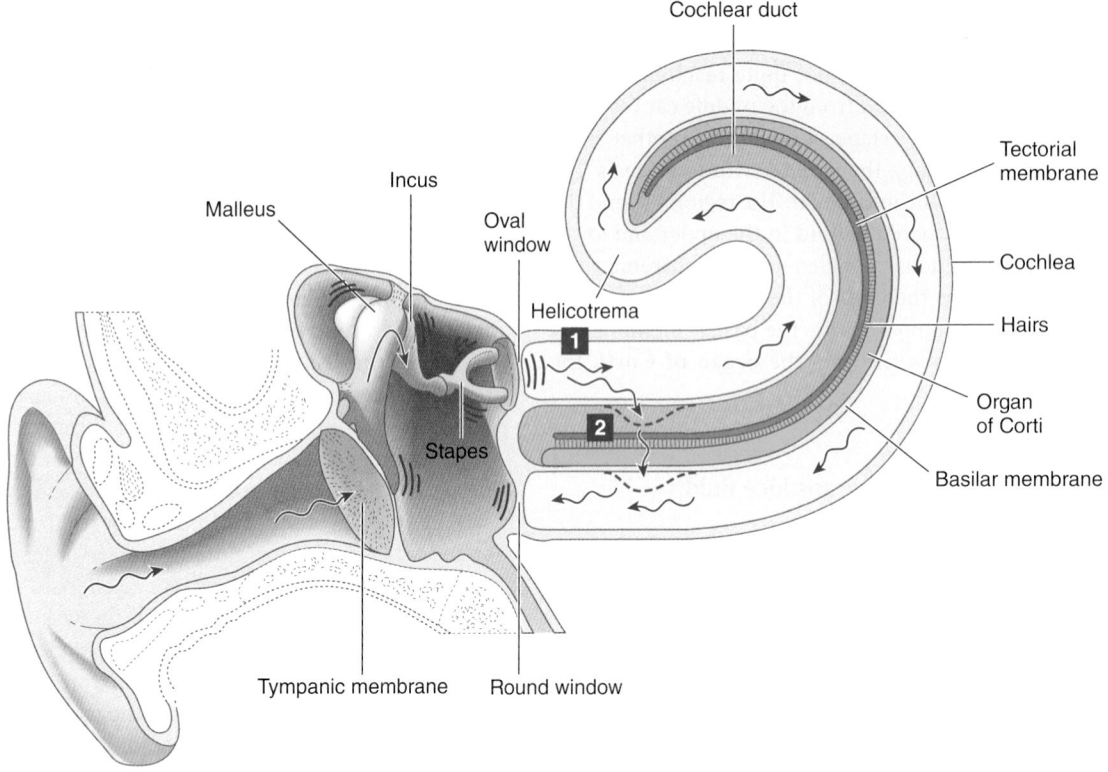

Fluid movement within the cochlea set up by vibration of the oval window follows two pathways:

Pathway 1: Through the upper compartment, around the helicotrema, and through the lower compartment, causing the round window to vibrate. This pathway just dissipates sound energy.

Pathway 2: A "shortcut" from the upper compartment through the basilar membrane to the lower compartment. This pathway triggers activation of the receptors for sound by bending the hairs of hair cells as the organ of Corti on top of the vibrating basilar membrane is displaced in relation to the overlying tectorial membrane.

(a) Fluid movement in cochlea

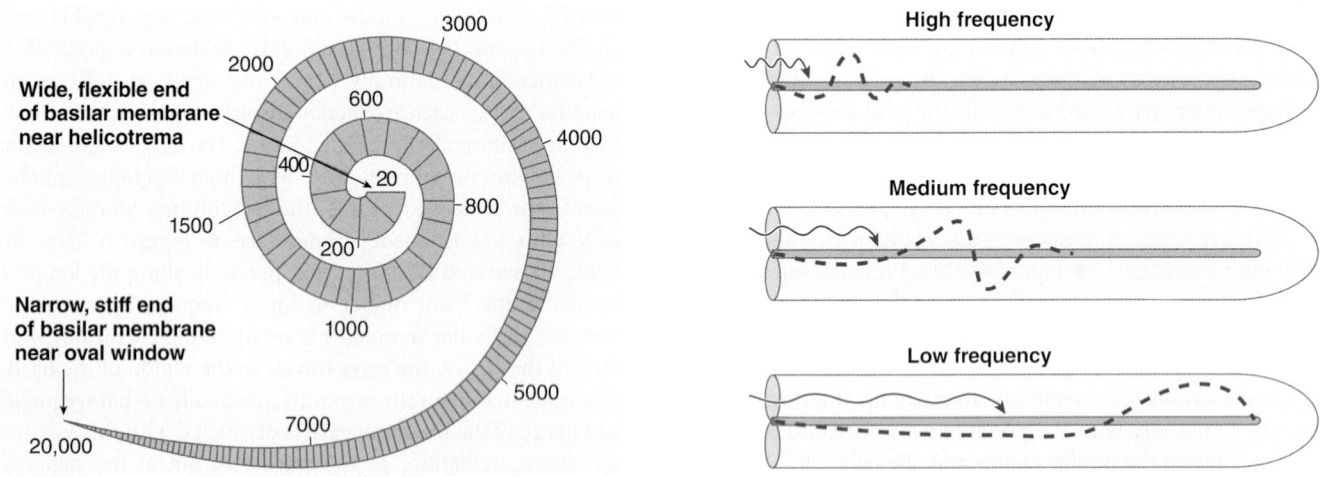

The numbers indicate the frequencies of sound waves in cycles per second (hertz) with which different regions of the basilar membrane maximally vibrate.

(b) Basilar membrane, partly uncoiled

(c) Basilar membrane, completely uncoiled

● **FIGURE 6-27 Transmission of sound waves.** (a) Fluid movement within the cochlea set up by vibration of the oval window follows two pathways, one dissipating sound energy and the other initiating the receptor potential. (b) Different regions of the basilar membrane vibrate maximally at different frequencies. (c) The narrow, stiff end of the basilar membrane nearest the oval window vibrates best with high-frequency pitches. The wide, flexible end of the basilar membrane near the helicotrema vibrates best with low-frequency pitches.

The hairs from the hair cells of the basilar membrane contact the overlying tectorial membrane. These hairs are bent when the basilar membrane is deflected in relation to the stationary tectorial membrane. This bending of the hair cells' hairs opens mechanically gated channels, leading to ion movements that result in a receptor potential.

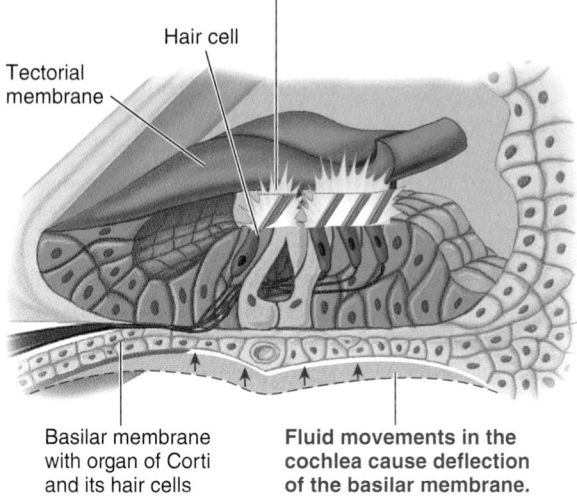

Hair cell

Tectorial membrane

Basilar membrane with organ of Corti and its hair cells

Fluid movements in the cochlea cause deflection of the basilar membrane.

● FIGURE 6-28 **Bending of hairs on deflection of the basilar membrane.**

thus activate differently tuned hair cells (that is, different sound waves "strike" different "piano keys"). This information is propagated to the CNS, which interprets the pattern of hair cell stimulation as a sound of a particular frequency.

Overtones of varying frequencies cause many points along the basilar membrane to vibrate simultaneously but less intensely than the fundamental tone, enabling the CNS to distinguish the timbre of the sound (**timbre discrimination**).

Loudness discrimination depends on the amplitude of vibration.

Intensity (loudness) discrimination depends on the amplitude of vibration. As sound waves originating from louder sound sources strike the eardrum, they cause it to vibrate more vigorously (that is, bulge in and out to a greater extent) but at the same frequency as a softer sound of the same pitch. The greater tympanic membrane deflection translates into greater basilar membrane movement in the region of peak responsiveness, causing greater bending of the hairs in this region. The CNS interprets this greater hair bending as a louder sound. Thus, pitch discrimination depends on "where" the basilar membrane maximally vibrates and loudness discrimination depends on "how much" this place vibrates.

The auditory system is so sensitive and can detect sounds so faint that the distance of basilar membrane deflection is comparable to only a fraction of the diameter of a hydrogen atom, the smallest of atoms. No wonder very loud sounds (for example, the sounds of a typical rock concert) can set up such violent vibrations of the basilar membrane that irreplaceable hair cells are actually sheared off or permanently distorted, leading to partial hearing loss (● Figure 6-30).

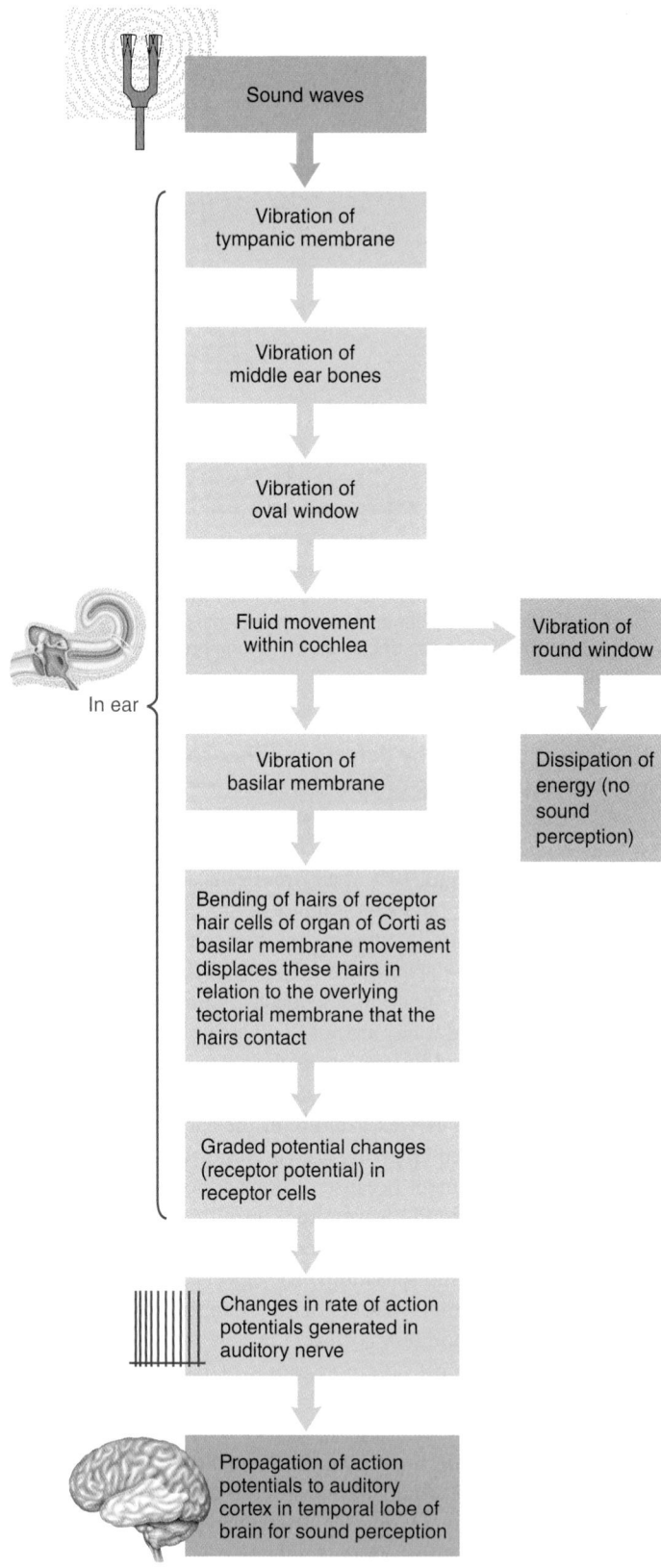

Sound waves

In ear

Vibration of tympanic membrane

Vibration of middle ear bones

Vibration of oval window

Fluid movement within cochlea → Vibration of round window → Dissipation of energy (no sound perception)

Vibration of basilar membrane

Bending of hairs of receptor hair cells of organ of Corti as basilar membrane movement displaces these hairs in relation to the overlying tectorial membrane that the hairs contact

Graded potential changes (receptor potential) in receptor cells

Changes in rate of action potentials generated in auditory nerve

Propagation of action potentials to auditory cortex in temporal lobe of brain for sound perception

● FIGURE 6-29 **Pathway for sound transduction.**

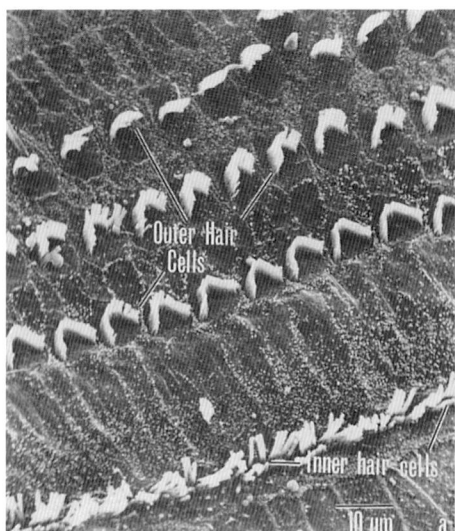

(a) Normal hair cells

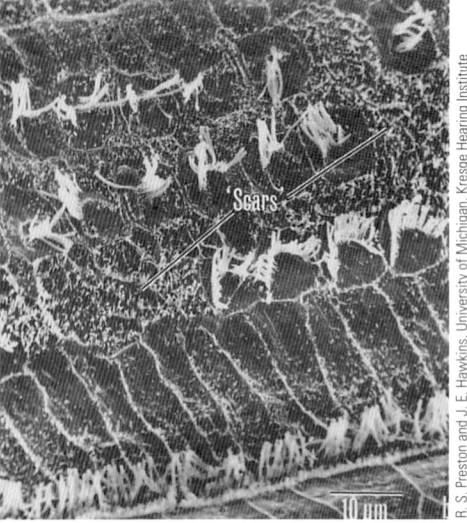

(b) Damaged hair cells

R. S. Preston and J. E. Hawkins, University of Michigan, Kresge Hearing Institute

● **FIGURE 6-30 Loss of hair cells caused by loud noises.** The scanning electron micrographs show portions of the organ of Corti, with its three rows of outer hair cells and one row of inner hair cells, from the inner ear of (a) a normal guinea pig and (b) a guinea pig after a 24-hour exposure to noise at 120 decibels SPL (sound pressure level), a level approached by loud rock music.

Deafness is caused by defects in either conduction or neural processing of sound waves.

Clinical Note

Loss of hearing, or **deafness,** may be temporary or permanent, partial or complete. Hearing loss, which affects about 10% of all Americans, is the second most common physical disability in the United States. Deafness is classified into two types—*conductive deafness* and *sensorineural deafness*—depending on the part of the hearing mechanism that fails to function adequately. **Conductive deafness** occurs when sound waves are not adequately conducted through the external and middle portions of the ear to set the fluids in the inner ear in motion. Possible causes include physical blockage of the ear canal with earwax, rupture of the eardrum, middle ear infections with accompanying fluid accumulation, or restriction of ossicular movement because of bony adhesions. In **sensorineural deafness,** sound waves are transmitted to the inner ear, but they are not translated into nerve signals that are interpreted by the brain as sound sensations. The defect can lie in the organ of Corti, in the auditory nerves or, rarely, in the ascending auditory pathways or auditory cortex.

One of the most common causes of partial hearing loss, **neural presbycusis,** is a degenerative, age-related process that occurs as hair cells "wear out" with use. Over time, exposure to even ordinary modern-day sounds eventually damages hair cells so that, on average, adults have lost more than 40% of their cochlear hair cells by age 65. Unfortunately, partial hearing loss caused by excessive exposure to loud noises is affecting people at younger ages than in the past because we live in an increasingly noisy environment. Currently, more than 28 million Americans have some degree of hearing loss, and this number is expected to climb to 78 million by 2030. According to one study, an estimated 5 million children between 6 and 19 years of age in the United States already have some hearing damage resulting from amplified music and other noise pollution. Hair cells that process high-frequency sounds are the most vulnerable to destruction.

The vestibular apparatus is important for equilibrium by detecting position and motion of the head.

In addition to its cochlear-dependent role in hearing, the inner ear has another specialized component, the **vestibular apparatus,** which provides information essential for the sense of equilibrium and for coordinating head movements with eye and postural movements (● Figure 6-31). **Equilibrium** is the sense of body orientation and motion. The vestibular apparatus consists of two sets of structures lying within a tunneled-out region of the temporal bone near the cochlea—the *semicircular canals* and the *otolith organs.*

The vestibular apparatus detects changes in position and motion of the head. As in the cochlea, all components of the vestibular apparatus contain fluid. Also, similar to the organ of Corti, the vestibular components each contain hair cells that respond to mechanical deformation triggered by specific movements of the fluid. Unlike information from the auditory system, much of the information provided by the vestibular apparatus does not reach the level of conscious awareness.

ROLE OF THE SEMICIRCULAR CANALS The **semicircular canals** detect rotational or angular acceleration or deceleration of the head, such as when starting or stopping spinning, somersaulting, or turning the head. Each ear contains three semicircular canals arranged three-dimensionally in planes that lie at right angles to each other. The receptor hair cells of each semicircular canal are situated on top of a ridge located in a swelling at the base of the canal (● Figure 6-31a and b). The hairs are embedded in an overlying, caplike, gelatinous layer, the **cupula,** which protrudes into the fluid within this swelling. The cupula sways in the direction of fluid movement, much like seaweed leaning in the direction of the prevailing tide.

Acceleration or deceleration during rotation of the head in any direction causes fluid movement in at least one of the semicircular canals because of their three-dimensional arrangement. As you start to move your head, the bony canal and the ridge of hair cells embedded in the cupula move with your head. Initially, however, the fluid within the canal, not being attached to your skull, does not move in the direction of the rotation but lags behind because of its inertia. (Because of inertia, a resting object remains at rest and a moving object continues to move in the same direction unless the object is acted on by some external force that induces change.) When the fluid is

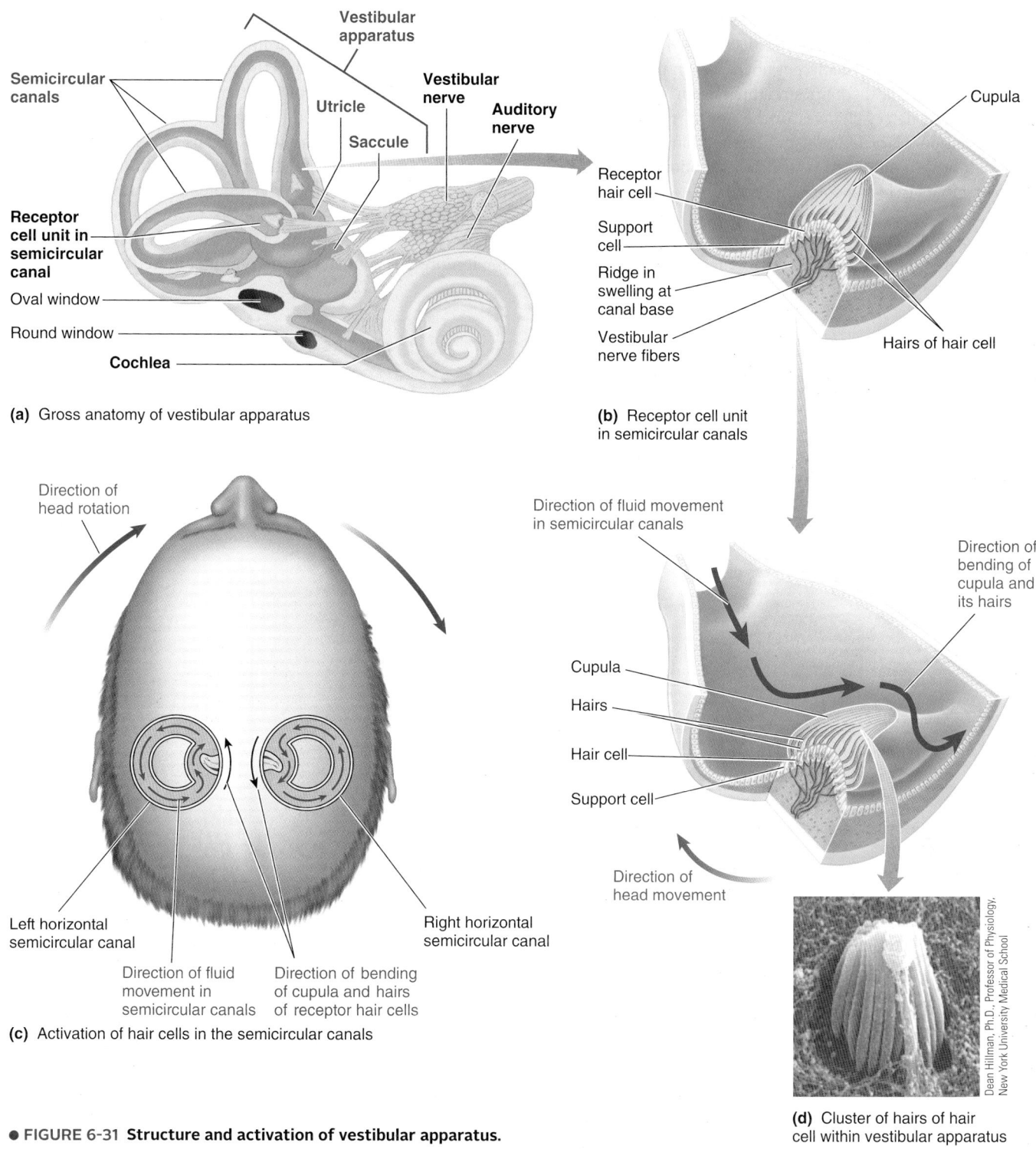

(a) Gross anatomy of vestibular apparatus

(b) Receptor cell unit in semicircular canals

(c) Activation of hair cells in the semicircular canals

(d) Cluster of hairs of hair cell within vestibular apparatus

● FIGURE 6-31 **Structure and activation of vestibular apparatus.**

left behind as you start to rotate your head, the fluid that is in the same plane as the head movement is in effect shifted in the opposite direction from the movement (similar to your body tilting to the right as the car in which you are riding suddenly turns to the left) (● Figure 6-31c). This fluid movement causes the cupula to lean in the opposite direction from the head movement, bending the sensory hairs embedded in it. If your head movement continues at the same rate in the same direc-

tion, the fluid catches up and moves in unison with your head so that the hairs return to their unbent position. When your head slows down and stops, the reverse situation occurs. The fluid briefly continues to move in the direction of the rotation while your head decelerates to a stop. As a result, the cupula and its hairs are transiently bent in the direction of the preceding spin, which is opposite to the way they were bent during acceleration. Bending the hairs in one direction increases the rate of firing in afferent fibers within the **vestibular nerve,** whereas bending in the opposite direction decreases the frequency of action potentials in these afferent fibers. When the fluid gradually comes to a halt, the hairs straighten again. Thus, the semicircular canals detect changes in the rate of rotational movement (rotational acceleration or deceleration) of your head. They do not respond when your head is motionless or when it is moving in a circle at a constant speed.

ROLE OF THE OTOLITH ORGANS The **otolith organs** provide information about the position of the head relative to gravity (that is, static head tilt) and detect changes in the rate of linear motion (moving in a straight line regardless of direction). The otolith organs, the **utricle** and the **saccule,** are saclike structures housed within a bony chamber situated between the semicircular canals and the cochlea (● Figure 6-31a). The hairs of the receptor hair cells in these sense organs also protrude into an overlying gelatinous sheet, whose movement displaces the hairs and results in changes in hair cell potential. Many tiny crystals of calcium carbonate—the **otoliths** ("ear stones")—are suspended within the gelatinous layer, making it heavier and giving it more inertia than the surrounding fluid (● Figure 6-32a).

● FIGURE 6-32 **Structure and activation of utricle.**

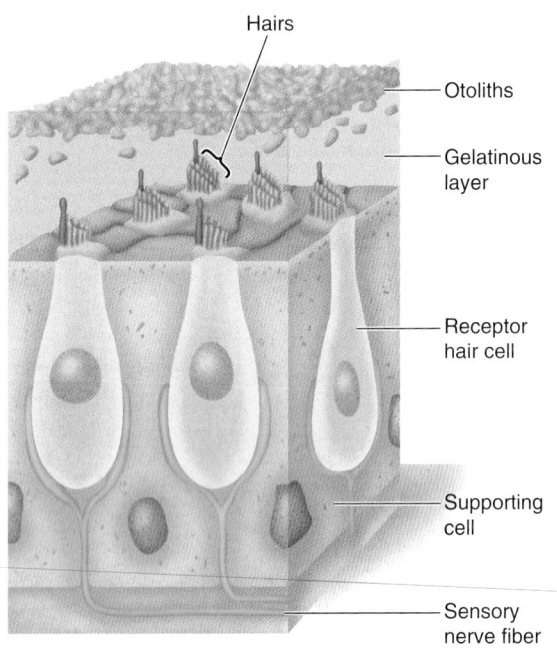

(a) Receptor cell unit in utricle

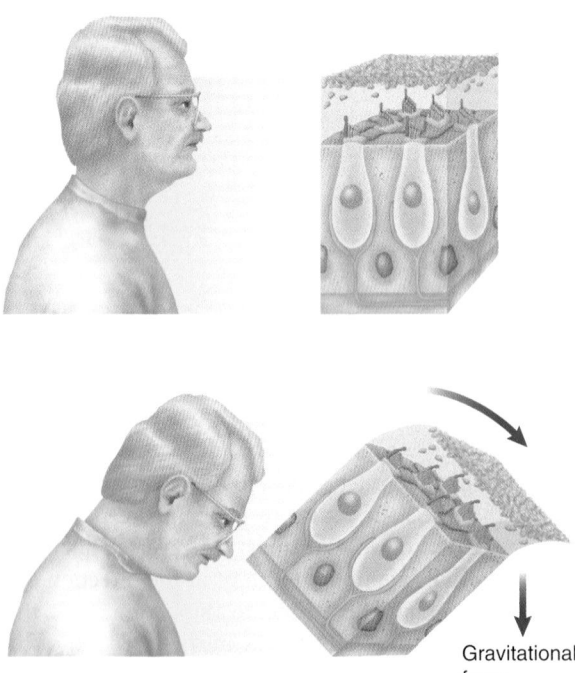

(b) Activation of utricle by change in head position

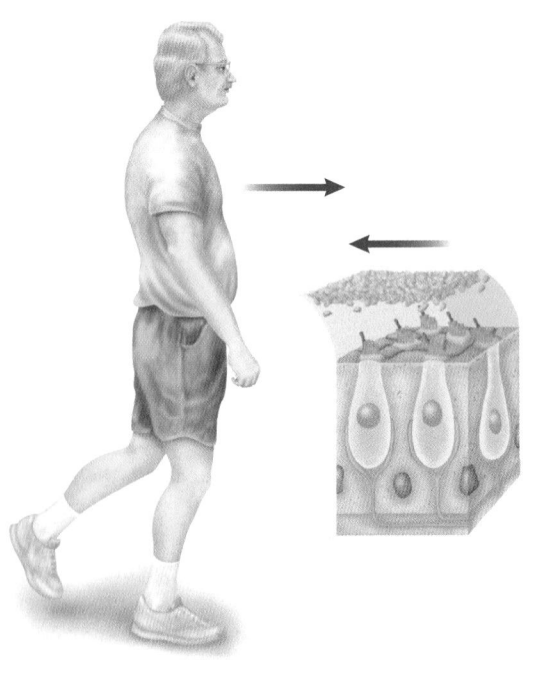

(c) Activation of utricle by horizontal linear acceleration

When a person is in an upright position, the hairs within the utricle are oriented vertically and the saccule hairs are lined up horizontally.

Let us look at the *utricle* as an example. Its otolith-embedded, gelatinous mass shifts positions and bends the hairs in two ways:

1. When you tilt your head in any direction so that it is no longer vertical (that is, when your head is not straight up and down), the hairs are bent in the direction of the tilt because of the gravitational force exerted on the top-heavy gelatinous layer (● Figure 6-32b). This bending produces depolarizing or hyperpolarizing receptor potentials depending on the tilt of your head. The CNS thus receives different patterns of neural activity depending on head position with respect to gravity.

2. The utricle hairs are also displaced by any change in horizontal linear motion (such as moving straight forward, backward, or to the side). As you start to walk forward (● Figure 6-32c), the top-heavy otolith membrane at first lags behind the fluid and hair cells because of its greater inertia. The hairs are thus bent to the rear, in the opposite direction of the forward movement of your head. If you maintain your walking pace, the gelatinous layer soon catches up and moves at the same rate as your head so that the hairs are no longer bent. When you stop walking, the otolith sheet continues to move forward briefly as your head slows and stops, bending the hairs toward the front. Thus, the hair cells of the utricle detect horizontally directed linear acceleration and deceleration, but they do not provide information about movement in a straight line at constant speed.

The saccule functions similarly to the utricle, except that it responds selectively to tilting of the head away from a horizontal position (such as getting up from bed) and to vertically directed linear acceleration and deceleration (such as jumping up and down or riding in an elevator).

Signals arising from the various components of the vestibular apparatus are carried through the vestibulocochlear nerve to the **vestibular nuclei,** a cluster of neuronal cell bodies in the brain stem, and to the cerebellum. Here, the vestibular information is integrated with input from the eyes, skin surface, joints, and muscles for (1) maintaining balance and desired posture; (2) controlling the external eye muscles so that the eyes remain fixed on the same point, despite movement of the head; and (3) perceiving motion and orientation. Some people, for poorly understood reasons, are especially sensitive to particular motions that activate the vestibular apparatus and cause symptoms of dizziness and nausea; this sensitivity is called **motion sickness.**

▲ Table 6-5 summarizes the functions of the major components of the ear.

Chemical Senses: Taste and Smell

Unlike the eyes' photoreceptors and the ears' mechanoreceptors, the receptors for taste and smell are chemoreceptors, which generate neural signals on binding with particular chemicals in their environment. The sensations of taste and smell in association with food intake influence the flow of digestive juices and affect appetite. Furthermore, stimulation of taste or smell receptors induces pleasurable or objectionable sensations and signals the presence of something to seek (a nutritionally useful, good-tasting food) or to avoid (a potentially toxic, bad-tasting substance). Thus, the chemical senses provide a "quality-control" checkpoint for substances available for ingestion. In lower animals, smell also plays a major role in finding direction, in seeking prey or avoiding predators, and in sexual attraction to a mate. The sense of smell is less sensitive in humans and less important in influencing our behavior (although millions of dollars are spent annually on perfumes and deodorants to make us smell better and thereby be more socially attractive). We first examine the mechanism of taste (**gustation**) and then turn our attention to smell (**olfaction**).

Taste receptor cells are located primarily within tongue taste buds.

The chemoreceptors for **taste** sensation are packaged in taste buds, about 10,000 of which are present in the oral cavity and throat, with the greatest percentage on the upper surface of the tongue. A **taste bud** consists of about 50 long, spindle-shaped *taste receptor cells* packaged with *supporting cells* in an arrangement like slices of an orange (● Figure 6-33). Each taste bud has a small opening, the **taste pore,** through which fluids in the mouth come into contact with the surface of its receptor cells. **Taste receptor cells** are modified epithelial cells with many surface folds, or microvilli, that protrude slightly through the taste pore, greatly increasing the surface area exposed to the oral contents (see p. 40). The plasma membrane of the microvilli contains receptor sites that bind selectively with chemical molecules in the environment. Only chemicals in solution—either ingested liquids or solids that have been dissolved in saliva—can attach to receptor cells and evoke the sensation of taste.

Most receptors are carefully sheltered from direct exposure to the environment, but the taste receptor cells, because of their task, often come into contact with potent chemicals. Unlike the eye or ear receptors, which are irreplaceable, taste receptors have a life span of about 10 days. Epithelial cells surrounding the taste

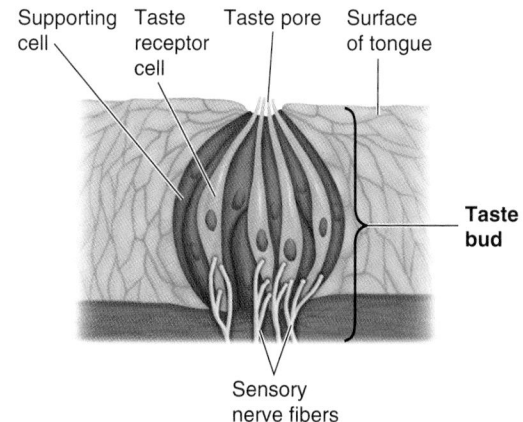

● **FIGURE 6-33 Structure of a taste bud.** The receptor cells and supporting cells of a taste bud are arranged like slices of an orange.

Structure	Location	Function
External Ear		**Collects and transfers sound waves to the middle ear**
Pinna (ear)	Skin-covered flap of cartilage located on each side of the head	Collects sound waves and channels them down the ear canal; contributes to sound localization
External auditory meatus (ear canal)	Tunnels through the temporal bone from the pinna to the tympanic membrane	Directs sound waves to the tympanic membrane
Tympanic membrane (eardrum)	Thin membrane that separates the external ear and the middle ear	Vibrates in synchrony with sound waves that strike it, setting middle ear bones in motion
Middle Ear		**Transfers vibrations of the tympanic membrane to fluid in the cochlea**
Malleus, incus, and stapes	Movable chain of bones that extends across the middle ear cavity; the malleus attaches to the tympanic membrane, and the stapes attaches to the oval window	Oscillate in synchrony with tympanic membrane vibrations and set up wavelike movements in cochlea fluid at the same frequency
Inner Ear: Cochlea		**Houses the sensory system for hearing**
Oval window	Thin membrane at the entrance to the cochlea; separates the middle ear from the upper compartment of the cochlea	Vibrates in unison with movement of the stapes, to which it is attached; oval window movement sets cochlea fluid in motion
Upper and lower compartments of the cochlea	Snail-shaped tubular system that lies deep within the temporal bone	Contain fluid that is set in motion by oval window movement driven by the oscillation of middle ear bones
Cochlear duct	Blind-ended tubular compartment that tunnels through the center of the cochlea between the upper and the lower compartments	Houses the basilar membrane and organ of Corti
Basilar membrane	Forms the floor of the cochlear duct	Vibrates in unison with fluid movements; bears the organ of Corti, the sense organ for hearing
Organ of Corti	Rests on top of the basilar membrane throughout its length	Contains auditory hair cells, the receptors for sound, which undergo receptor potentials when their hairs are bent as a result of fluid movement in the cochlea
Tectorial membrane	Stationary membrane that overhangs the organ of Corti and contacts the surface hairs of the receptor hair cells	Serves as the stationary site against which the hairs of the receptor cells are bent and undergo receptor potentials as the vibrating basilar membrane moves in relation to this overhanging membrane
Round window	Thin membrane that separates the lower compartment of the cochlea from the middle ear	Vibrates in unison with fluid movements to dissipate pressure in the cochlea; does not contribute to sound reception
Inner Ear: Vestibular Apparatus		**Houses sensory systems for equilibrium and provides input essential for maintaining posture and balance**
Semicircular canals	Three semicircular canals arranged three-dimensionally in planes at right angles to each other near the cochlea	Detect rotational or angular acceleration or deceleration
Utricle	Saclike structure in a bony chamber between the cochlea and the semicircular canals	Detects changes in head position away from vertical and horizontally directed linear acceleration and deceleration
Saccule	Lies next to the utricle	Detects changes in head position away from horizontal and vertically directed linear acceleration and deceleration

bud differentiate first into supporting cells and then into receptor cells to constantly renew the taste bud components.

Binding of a taste-provoking chemical, a **tastant,** with a receptor cell alters the cell's ionic channels to produce a depolarizing receptor potential that in turn initiates action potentials in afferent nerve fibers with which the receptor cell synapses. Signals in these sensory inputs are conveyed via synaptic stops in the brain stem and thalamus to the **cortical gustatory area,** a region in the parietal lobe adjacent to the "tongue" area of the somatosensory cortex, where the taste is perceived. Taste signals are also sent to the hypothalamus and limbic system to add affective dimensions, such as whether the taste is pleasant or unpleasant, and to process behavioral aspects associated with taste and smell.

Taste discrimination is coded by patterns of activity in various taste bud receptors.

We can discriminate among thousands of taste sensations, yet all tastes are varying combinations of five **primary tastes:** *salty, sour, sweet, bitter,* and *umami.* Umami, a meaty or savory taste, has recently been added to the list of primary tastes. These primary taste sensations are elicited by the following stimuli:

■ **Salty taste** is stimulated by chemical salts, especially NaCl (table salt).

■ **Sour taste** is caused by acids. The citric acid content of lemons, for example, accounts for their distinctly sour taste.

■ **Sweet taste** is evoked by the particular configuration of glucose. From an evolutionary perspective, we crave sweet foods because they supply necessary calories in a readily usable form. However, other organic molecules with similar structures but no calories, such as saccharin, aspartame, sucralose, and other artificial sweeteners, can interact with "sweet" receptor binding sites.

■ **Bitter taste** is elicited by a more chemically diverse group of tastants than the other taste sensations. For example, alkaloids (such as caffeine, nicotine, strychnine, morphine, and other toxic plant derivatives), as well as poisonous substances, all taste bitter, presumably as a protective mechanism to discourage ingestion of these potentially dangerous compounds.

■ **Umami taste,** which was first identified and named by a Japanese researcher, is triggered by amino acids, especially glutamate. The presence of amino acids, as found in meat, for example, is a marker for a desirable, nutritionally protein-rich food. This taste pathway is also responsible for the distinctive taste of the flavor additive monosodium glutamate (MSG), which is especially popular in Asian dishes.

Salty and sour tastants bring about receptor potentials in taste buds by directly affecting membrane channels, whereas the other three categories of tastants act by binding to G-protein-coupled receptors and activating second-messenger pathways to bring about receptor potentials (see p. 99).

Each receptor cell responds in varying degrees to all five primary tastes but is generally preferentially responsive to one of the taste modalities. The richness of fine taste discrimination beyond the primary tastes depends on subtle differences in the stimulation patterns of all taste buds in response to various substances, similar to the variable stimulation of the three cone types that gives rise to the range of color sensations.

Taste perception is also influenced by information derived from other receptors, especially odor. When you temporarily lose your sense of smell because of swollen nasal passageways during a cold, your sense of taste is also markedly reduced, even though your taste receptors are unaffected by the cold. Other factors affecting taste include temperature and texture of the food, as well as psychological factors associated with past experiences with the food. How the gustatory cortex accomplishes the complex perceptual processing of taste sensation is not yet known.

The olfactory receptors in the nose are specialized endings of renewable afferent neurons.

The **olfactory** ("smell") **mucosa,** a 3 cm^2 patch of mucosa in the ceiling of the nasal cavity, contains three cell types: *olfactory receptor cells, supporting cells,* and *basal cells* (● Figure 6-34). The supporting cells secrete mucus, which coats the nasal passages. The basal cells are precursors for new olfactory receptor cells, which are replaced about every 2 months. The sense of **smell** depends on the **olfactory receptor cells** detecting odors, or scents. An olfactory receptor cell is an afferent neuron whose receptor portion lies in the olfactory mucosa in the nose and whose afferent axon traverses into the brain. The axons of the olfactory receptor cells collectively form the **olfactory nerve.**

The receptor portion of an olfactory receptor cell consists of an enlarged knob bearing several long cilia that extend like a tassel to the surface of the mucosa. These cilia contain the binding sites for attachment of **odorants,** molecules that can be smelled. To be smelled, a substance must be (1) sufficiently volatile (easily vaporized) that some of its molecules can enter the nose in the inspired air and (2) sufficiently water soluble that it can dissolve in the mucus coating the olfactory mucosa. As with taste receptors, molecules must be dissolved to be detected by olfactory receptors.

Various parts of an odor are detected by different olfactory receptors and sorted into "smell files."

The human nose contains 5 million olfactory receptors, of which there are 1000 types. During smell detection, an odor is "dissected" into various components. Each receptor responds to only one discrete component of an odor rather than to the whole odorant molecule. Accordingly, each of the various parts of an odor is detected by one of the thousand different receptors, and a given receptor can respond to a particular odor component shared by different scents. Compare this to the three cone types for coding color vision and the taste buds that respond differentially to only five primary tastes to accomplish coding for taste discrimination.

Odorants act through G-protein-coupled receptors and second-messenger pathways to trigger receptor potentials. Binding of an appropriate scent signal to an olfactory receptor brings about a depolarizing receptor potential that generates

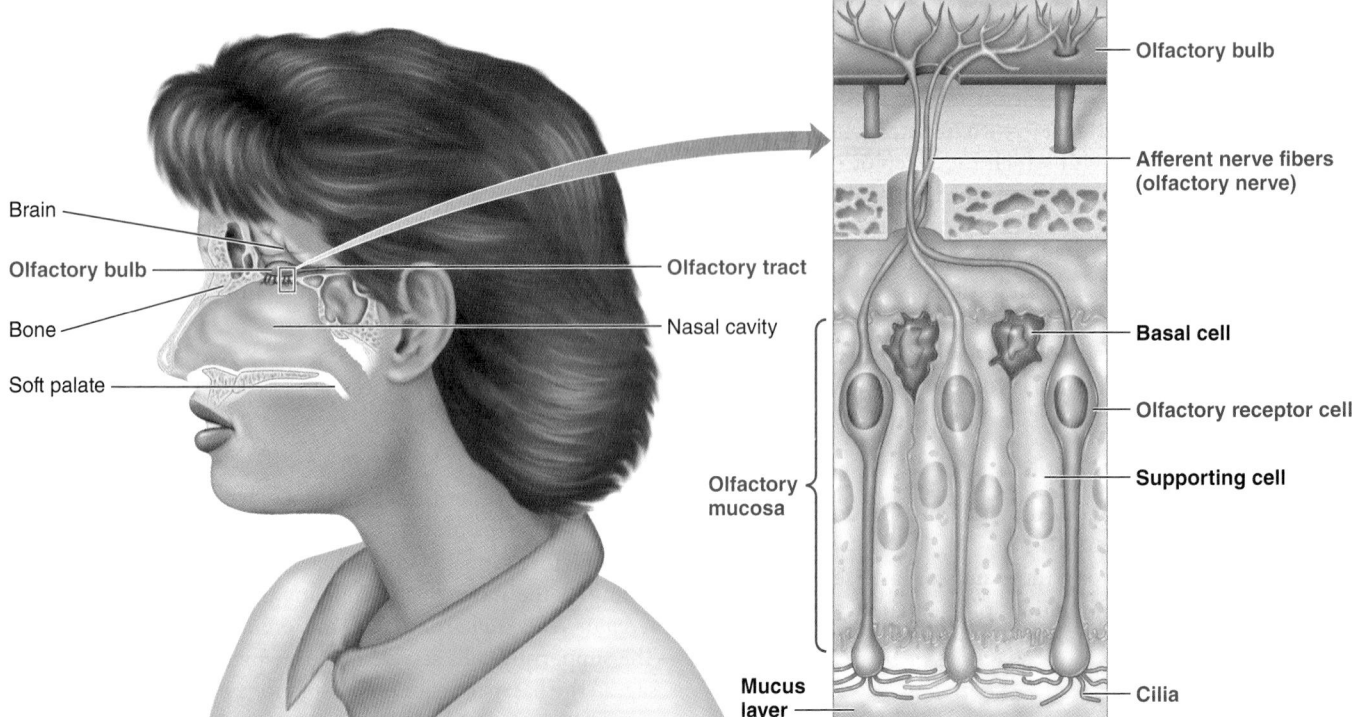

● FIGURE 6-34 **Location and structure of the olfactory receptor cells.**

action potentials in the afferent fiber. The frequency of the action potentials depends on the concentration of the stimulating chemical molecules.

The afferent fibers arising from the receptor endings in the nose pass through tiny holes in the flat bone plate separating the olfactory mucosa from the overlying brain tissue (● Figure 6-34). They immediately synapse in the **olfactory bulb,** a complex neural structure containing several layers of cells that are functionally similar to the retinal layers of the eye. The twin olfactory bulbs, one on each side, are about the size of small grapes (see ● Figure 5-14, p. 132). Each olfactory bulb is lined by small, ball-like neural junctions known as **glomeruli** (meaning "little balls") (● Figure 6-35). Within each glomerulus, the terminals of receptor cells carrying information about a particular scent component synapse with the next cells in the olfactory pathway, the **mitral cells.** Because each glomerulus receives signals only from receptors that detect a particular odor component, the glomeruli serve as "smell files." The separate components of an odor are sorted into different glomeruli, one component per file. Thus, the glomeruli, which are the first relay station in the brain for process-

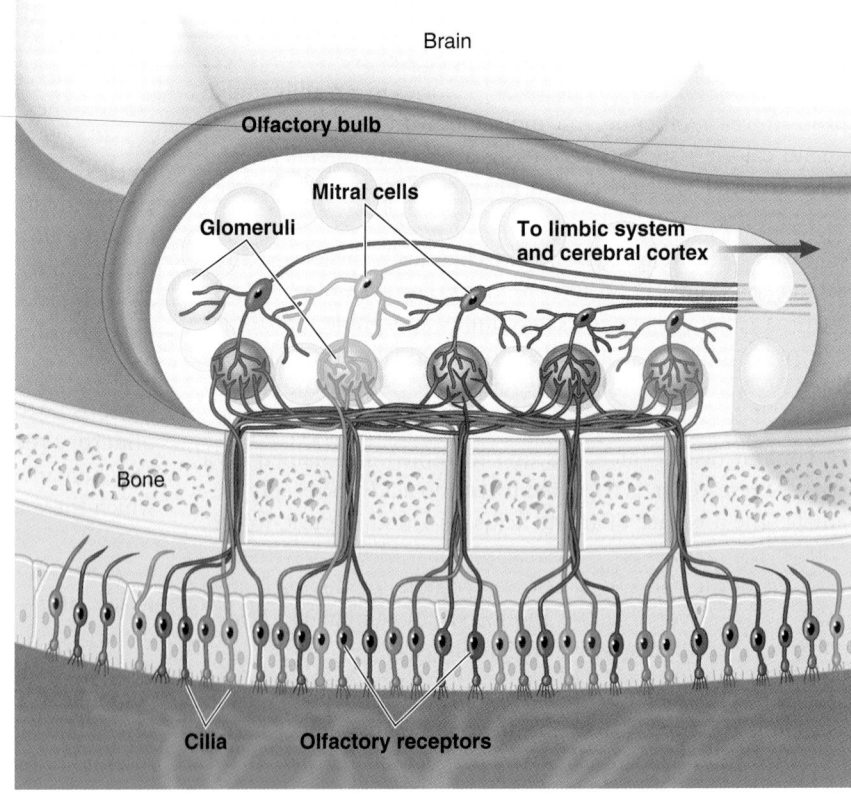

● FIGURE 6-35 **Processing of scents in the olfactory bulb.** Each of the glomeruli lining the olfactory bulb receives synaptic input from only one type of olfactory receptor, which, in turn, responds to only one discrete component of an odorant. Thus, the glomeruli sort and file the various components of an odoriferous molecule before relaying the smell signal to the mitral cells and higher brain levels for further processing.

ing olfactory information, play a key role in organizing scent perception.

The mitral cells on which the olfactory receptors terminate in the glomeruli refine the smell signals and relay them to the brain for further processing. Fibers leaving the olfactory bulb travel in two routes:

1. A subcortical route going primarily to regions of the limbic system, especially the lower medial sides of the temporal lobes (considered the **primary olfactory cortex**). This route, which includes hypothalamic involvement, permits close coordination between smell and behavioral reactions associated with feeding, mating, and direction orienting.

2. A route through the thalamus to the cortex. As with other senses, the cortical route is important for conscious perception and fine discrimination of smell.

Odor discrimination is coded by patterns of activity in the olfactory bulb glomeruli.

Because each odorant activates multiple receptors and glomeruli in response to its various odor components, odor discrimination is based on different patterns of glomeruli activated by various scents. In this way, the cortex can distinguish more than 10,000 scents. This mechanism for sorting out and distinguishing odors is very effective. A noteworthy example is our ability to detect methyl mercaptan (garlic odor) at a concentration of 1 molecule per 50 billion molecules in the air. This substance is added to odorless natural gas to enable us to detect potentially lethal gas leaks. Despite this impressive sensitivity, humans have a poor sense of smell compared to other species. By comparison, dogs' sense of smell is hundreds of times more sensitive than that of humans. Bloodhounds, for example, have about 4 billion olfactory receptor cells compared to our 5 million such cells, accounting for bloodhounds' superior scent-sniffing ability.

The olfactory system adapts quickly.

Although the olfactory system is sensitive and highly discriminating, it is also quickly adaptive. Sensitivity to a new odor diminishes rapidly after a short period of exposure to it, even though the odor source continues to be present. This reduced sensitivity does not involve receptor adaptation, as researchers thought for years; actually, the olfactory receptors themselves adapt slowly. It apparently involves some sort of adaptation process in the CNS. Adaptation is specific for a particular odor, and responsiveness to other odors remains unchanged.

Chapter in Perspective: Focus on Homeostasis

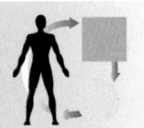

To maintain a life-sustaining stable internal environment, the body must constantly make adjustments to compensate for myriad external and internal factors that continuously threaten to disrupt homeostasis, such as external exposure to cold or internal acid production. Many of these adjustments are directed by the nervous system, one of the body's two major regulatory systems. The central nervous system (CNS), the integrating and decision-making component of the nervous system, must continuously be informed of "what's happening" in both the internal and the external environment so that it can command appropriate responses in the organ systems to maintain the body's viability. In other words, the CNS must know what changes are taking place before it can respond to these changes.

The afferent division of the peripheral nervous system (PNS) is the communication link by which the CNS is informed about the internal and external environment. The afferent division detects, encodes, and transmits peripheral signals to the CNS for processing. Afferent input is necessary for arousal, perception, and determination of efferent output.

Afferent information about the internal environment, such as the CO_2 level in the blood, never reaches the level of conscious awareness, but this input to the controlling centers of the CNS is essential for maintaining homeostasis. Afferent input that reaches the level of conscious awareness, called *sensory information,* includes somesthetic and proprioceptive sensation (body sense) and special senses (vision, hearing, equilibrium, taste, and smell).

The body sense receptors are distributed over the entire body surface, as well as throughout the joints and muscles. Afferent signals from these receptors provide information about what's happening directly to each specific body part in relation to the external environment (that is, the "what," "where," and "how much" of stimulatory inputs to the body's surface and the momentary position of the body in space). In contrast, each special sense organ is restricted to a single site in the body. Rather than provide information about a specific body part, a special sense organ provides a specific type of information about the external environment that is useful to the body as a whole. For example, through their ability to detect, extensively analyze, and integrate patterns of illumination in the external environment, the eyes and visual processing system enable you to see your surroundings. The same integrative effect could not be achieved if photoreceptors were scattered over your entire body surface, as are touch receptors.

Sensory input (both body sense and special senses) enables a complex multicellular organism such as a human to interact in meaningful ways with the external environment in procuring food, defending against danger, and engaging in other behavioral actions geared toward maintaining homeostasis. In addition to providing information essential for interactions with the external environment for basic survival, the perceptual processing of sensory input adds immeasurably to the richness of life, such as enjoyment of a good book, concert, or meal.

Objective Questions (Answers on p. A-41)

1. Conversion of the energy forms of stimuli into electrical energy by the receptors is known as _____.
2. The type of stimulus to which a particular receptor is most responsive is called its _____.
3. All afferent information is sensory information. *(True or false?)*
4. During dark adaptation, rhodopsin is gradually regenerated to increase the sensitivity of the eyes. *(True or false?)*
5. An optic nerve carries information from the lateral and medial halves of the same eye, whereas an optic tract carries information from the lateral half of one eye and the medial half of the other. *(True or false?)*
6. Displacement of the round window generates neural impulses perceived as sound sensations. *(True or false?)*
7. Hair cells in different regions of the organ of Corti are activated by different tones. *(True or false?)*
8. Each taste receptor responds to just one of the five primary tastes. *(True or false?)*
9. Rapid adaptation to odors results from adaptation of the olfactory receptors. *(True or false?)*
10. Match the following:
    ___ 1. is the layer that contains photoreceptors
    ___ 2. marks the point from which the optic nerve leaves the retina
    ___ 3. forms the white part of the eye
    ___ 4. is the colored diaphragm of muscle that controls the amount of light entering the eye
    ___ 5. contributes the most to the eye's refractive ability
    ___ 6. supplies nutrients to the lens and cornea
    ___ 7. produces the aqueous humor
    ___ 8. has adjustable refractive ability
    ___ 9. is the portion of the retina with greatest acuity

    (a) aqueous humor
    (b) fovea
    (c) cornea
    (d) retina
    (e) lens
    (f) optic disc or blind spot
    (g) iris
    (h) ciliary body
    (i) sclera

11. Using the answer codes on the right, indicate which properties apply to taste and/or smell:
    ___ 1. Receptors are separate cells that synapse with terminal endings of afferent neurons.
    ___ 2. Receptors are specialized endings of afferent neurons.
    ___ 3. Receptors are regularly replaced.
    ___ 4. Specific chemicals in the environment attach to special binding sites on the receptor surface, leading to a depolarizing receptor potential.
    ___ 5. There are two processing pathways: a limbic system route and a cortical route.
    ___ 6. Five receptor types are used.
    ___ 7. A thousand receptor types are used.
    ___ 8. Information from receptor cells is filed and sorted by neural junctions called glomeruli.

    (a) applies to taste
    (b) applies to smell
    (c) applies to both taste and smell

Essay Questions

1. List and describe the receptor types according to their adequate stimulus.
2. Compare tonic and phasic receptors.
3. Explain how acuity is influenced by receptive field size.
4. Compare the fast and slow pain pathways.
5. Describe the built-in analgesic system of the brain.
6. Describe the process of phototransduction.
7. Compare the functional characteristics of rods and cones.
8. What are sound waves? What is responsible for the pitch, intensity, and timbre of a sound?
9. Describe the function of each of the following parts of the ear: pinna, ear canal, tympanic membrane, ossicles, oval window, and various parts of the cochlea. Include a discussion of how sound waves are transduced into action potentials.
10. Discuss the functions of the semicircular canals, the utricle, and the saccule.
11. Describe the location, structure, and activation of the receptors for taste and smell.
12. Compare the processes of color vision, hearing, taste, and smell discrimination.

(Explanations on p. A-41)

1. Patients with certain nerve disorders are unable to feel pain. Why is this disadvantageous?
2. Ophthalmologists often instill eye drops in their patients' eyes to bring about pupillary dilation, which makes it easier for the physician to view the eye's interior. The iris contains two sets of smooth muscle, one circular (the muscle fibers run in a circle around the pupil) and the other radial (the fibers radiate outward from the pupil like bicycle spokes). Remember that a muscle fiber shortens when it contracts. Parasympathetic stimulation causes contraction of the circular muscle; sympathetic stimulation causes contraction of the radial muscle. In what way would the drug in the eye drops affect autonomic nervous system activity in the eye to cause the pupils to dilate?
3. A patient complains of not being able to see the right half of the visual field with either eye. At what point in the patient's visual pathway does the defect lie?
4. Explain how middle ear infections interfere with hearing. Of what value are the "tubes" that are sometimes surgically placed in the eardrums of patients with a history of repeated middle ear infections accompanied by chronic fluid accumulation?
5. Explain why your sense of smell is reduced when you have a cold, even though the cold virus does not directly adversely affect the olfactory receptor cells.

CLINICAL CONSIDERATION

(Explanation on p. A-42)

Suzanne J. complained to her physician of bouts of dizziness. The physician asked her whether by "dizziness" she meant feeling lightheaded, as if she were going to faint (a condition known as *syncope*) or feeling that she or surrounding objects in the room were spinning around (a condition known as *vertigo*). Why is this distinction important in the differential diagnosis of her condition? What are some possible causes of each of these symptoms?

Chapter 6

Receptor Physiology (pp. 151–155)

■ The afferent division of the PNS carries information about the internal and external environment to the CNS.

■ Sensory receptors are specialized peripheral endings of afferent neurons. *(Review Figure 6-1.)* Each type of receptor (photoreceptor, mechanoreceptor, thermoreceptor, osmoreceptor, chemoreceptor, or nociceptor) responds to its adequate stimulus (a change in the energy form, or modality, to which it is responsive), translating the energy form of the stimulus into electrical signals.

■ A stimulus typically brings about a graded, depolarizing receptor potential by opening nonspecific cation channels, which leads to net Na^+ entry. Receptor potentials, if of sufficient magnitude, ultimately generate action potentials in the afferent fiber next to the receptor. These action potentials self-propagate along the afferent fiber to the CNS. *(Review Figure 6-1.)* The strength of the stimulus determines the magnitude of the receptor potential, which in turn determines the frequency of action potentials generated. *(Review Figure 6-2 and Table 6-1.)*

■ The magnitude of the receptor potential is also influenced by the extent of receptor adaptation, which is a reduction in receptor potential despite sustained stimulation. (1) Tonic receptors adapt slowly or do not adapt and thus provide continuous information about the stimuli they monitor. (2) Phasic receptors adapt rapidly and often exhibit off responses, thereby providing information about changes in the energy form they monitor. *(Review Figure 6-3.)*

■ Visceral afferent information remains mostly subconscious. Sensory afferent information reaches the level of conscious awareness, including (1) somatic sensation (somesthetic sensation and proprioception) and (2) special senses.

■ Discrete labeled-line pathways lead from the receptors to the CNS so that information about the type and location of stimuli can be deciphered by the CNS. *(Review Table 6-1.)*

■ The term *receptive field* refers to the area surrounding a receptor within which the receptor can detect stimuli. The acuity, or discriminative ability, of a body region varies inversely with the size of its receptive fields. *(Review Figure 6-4.)*

■ Perception is the conscious interpretation of the external world that the brain creates from sensory input. What the brain perceives from its input is an abstraction and not reality. The only stimuli that can be detected are those for which receptors are present. Also, as sensory signals ascend through progressively more complex processing, some of the information may be suppressed, whereas other parts of it may be enhanced.

Pain (pp. 155–156)

■ Painful experiences are elicited by nociceptors responding to noxious mechanical, thermal, or chemical stimuli and consist of two components: the perception of pain coupled with emotional and behavioral responses to it.

■ Pain signals are transmitted over two afferent pathways: a fast pathway that carries sharp, prickling pain signals and a slow pathway that carries dull, aching, persistent pain signals.

■ Afferent pain fibers terminate in the spinal cord on ascending pathways that transmit the signal to the brain for processing. Descending pathways from the brain sometimes use endogenous opiates to suppress the release of substance P, a pain-signaling neurotransmitter from the afferent pain-fiber terminal. Thus, these descending pathways can block further transmission of the pain signal and serve as a built-in analgesic system.

Eye: Vision (pp. 156–171)

■ Light is a form of electromagnetic radiation, with visible light being only a small band in the total electromagnetic spectrum. *(Review Figures 6-7 and 6-20, p. 167.)*

■ The eye houses the light-sensitive photoreceptors essential for vision—the rods and cones found in its retinal layer. *(Review Figures 6-5, 6-15, and 6-18 and Table 6-3, p. 170.)*

■ The iris controls the size of the pupil to adjust the amount of light permitted to enter the eye.

■ The cornea and lens are the primary refractive structures that bend incoming light rays to focus the image on the retina. The cornea contributes most to the total refractive ability of the eye. The strength of the lens can be adjusted through action of the ciliary muscle to accommodate for differences in near and far vision. *(Review Figures 6-8 through 6-14.)*

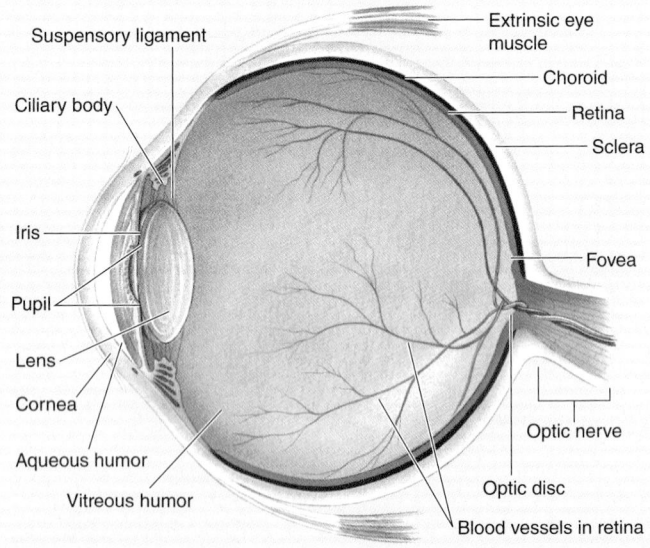

Suspensory ligament · Ciliary body · Iris · Pupil · Lens · Cornea · Aqueous humor · Vitreous humor · Extrinsic eye muscle · Choroid · Retina · Sclera · Fovea · Optic nerve · Optic disc · Blood vessels in retina

(b) Internal sagittal view

■ Rods and cones have three parts: a photopigment-containing outer segment, a metabolically specialized inner segment, and a neurotransmitter-secreting synaptic terminal. *(Review Figures 6-15, 6-18, and 6-19.)*

■ Rods and cones secrete neurotransmitter in the dark. They are activated when their photopigments differentially absorb various wavelengths of light. Photopigments consist of opsin, a membrane protein, and retinal, a vitamin A derivative. The photopigment in rods is rhodopsin. During phototransduction, light absorption by retinal causes a biochemical change in the photopigment that, through a series of steps, brings about a hyperpolarizing receptor potential in the outer segment that leads to decreased neurotransmitter release from the synaptic terminal. Further retinal processing by bipolar and ganglion cells eventually converts this light-induced signal into a change in the rate of action potential propagation in the visual pathway leaving the retina. *(Review Figures 6-18 and 6-19.)*

■ Cones display high acuity but can be used only for day vision because of their low sensitivity to light. Different ratios of stimulation of three cone types by variable wavelengths of light lead to color vision. *(Review Figure 6-20 and Table 6-2.)*

■ Rods provide only indistinct vision in shades of gray, but because they are very sensitive to light, they can be used for night vision. *(Review Table 6-2.)*

■ The visual message is transmitted via a complex crossed and uncrossed pathway to the visual cortex in the occipital lobe of the brain for perceptual processing. *(Review Figure 6-22.)*

Ear: Hearing and Equilibrium (pp. 171–181)

■ The ear performs two unrelated functions: (1) hearing, which involves the external ear, middle ear, and cochlea of the inner ear, and (2) sense of equilibrium, which involves the vestibular apparatus of the inner ear. The ear receptor cells located in the inner ear—the hair cells in the cochlea and vestibular apparatus—are mechanoreceptors. *(Review Table 6-5, p. 182, and Figure 6-23.)*

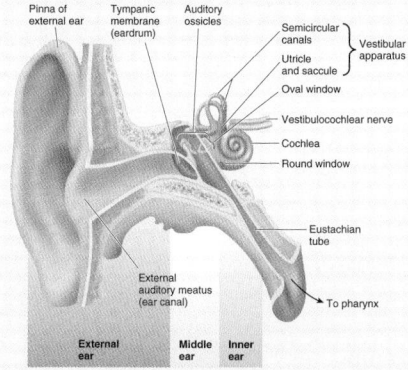

■ Hearing depends on the ear's ability to convert airborne sound waves into mechanical deformations of auditory hair cells, thereby initiating neural signals. Sound waves consist of high-pressure regions of compression alternating with low-pressure regions of rarefaction of air molecules. The pitch (tone) of a sound is determined by the frequency of its waves, the loudness (intensity) by the amplitude of the waves, and the timbre (quality) by its characteristic overtones. *(Review Figures 6-24 and 6-25 and Table 6-4.)*

■ Sound waves are funneled through the ear canal to the tympanic membrane, which vibrates in sync with the waves. Middle ear bones bridging the gap between the tympanic membrane and the inner ear amplify the tympanic movements and transmit them to the oval window, whose movement sets up traveling waves in the cochlear fluid. *(Review Figures 6-26 and 6-27.)*

■ These waves, which are at the same frequency as the original sound waves, set the basilar membrane in motion. Various regions of this membrane selectively vibrate more vigorously in response to different frequencies of sound. The narrow, stiff end of the basilar membrane near the oval window vibrates best with high-frequency pitches, and the wide, flexible end near the helicotrema vibrates best with low-frequency pitches. *(Review Figure 6-27.)*

■ On top of the basilar membrane are the receptive hair cells of the organ of Corti, whose hairs are bent as the basilar membrane is deflected up and down in relation to the overhanging stationary tectorial membrane, which the hairs contact. *(Review Figures 6-26 and 6-28.)*

■ Pitch discrimination depends on which region of the basilar membrane naturally vibrates maximally with a given frequency. Loudness discrimination depends on the amplitude of the vibrations. Hair bending in the region of maximal basilar membrane vibration is transduced into neural signals that are transmitted to the auditory cortex in the temporal lobe of the brain for sound perception. *(Review Figure 6-29.)*

■ The vestibular apparatus in the inner ear consists of (1) the semicircular canals, which detect rotational acceleration or deceleration in any direction, and (2) the utricle and the saccule, which collectively detect changes in the rate of linear movement in any direction and provide information important for determining head position in relation to gravity. Neural signals are generated in response to the mechanical deformation of vestibular hair cells by specific movement of fluid and related structures within these vestibular sense organs. *(Review Figures 6-31 and 6-32.)*

Chemical Senses: Taste and Smell (pp. 181–185)

■ Taste and smell are chemical senses. In both cases, attachment of specific dissolved molecules to binding sites on the receptor membrane causes receptor potentials that, in turn, set up neural impulses signaling the presence of the chemical.

■ Taste receptors are housed in taste buds on the tongue; olfactory receptors are located in the olfactory mucosa in the upper part of the nasal cavity. *(Review Figures 6-33 and 6-34.)*

■ Both sensory pathways include two routes: one to the limbic system for emotional and behavioral processing and one to the cortex for conscious perception and fine discrimination.

■ Taste and olfactory receptors are continuously renewed, unlike visual and hearing receptors, which are irreplaceable.

■ The five primary tastes are salty, sour, sweet, bitter, and umami (a meaty, "amino acid" taste). Taste discrimination beyond the primary tastes depends on the patterns of stimulation of the taste buds, each of which responds in varying degrees to the different primary tastes.

■ There are 1000 types of olfactory receptors, each of which responds to only one discrete component of an odor, an odorant. The afferent signals arising from the olfactory receptors are sorted according to scent component by the glomeruli within the olfactory bulb. Odor discrimination depends on the patterns of activation of the glomeruli. *(Review Figure 6-35.)*

**Nervous System
(Peripheral Nervous System)**

Body systems
maintain homeostasis

Homeostasis
The nervous system, as one of the body's two
major control systems, regulates many body
activities aimed at maintaining a stable
internal fluid environment.

Homeostasis is
essential for
survival of cells

Cells

Cells make up
body systems

The nervous system, one of the two major regulatory systems of the body, consists of the central nervous system (CNS), composed of the brain and spinal cord, and the **peripheral nervous system (PNS),** composed of the afferent and efferent fibers that relay signals between the CNS and the periphery (other parts of the body).

Once informed by the afferent division of the PNS that a change in the internal or the external environment is threatening homeostasis, the CNS makes appropriate adjustments to maintain homeostasis. The CNS makes these adjustments by controlling the activities of effectors (muscles and glands), transmitting signals *from* the CNS to these organs through the **efferent division** of the PNS.

CHAPTER AT A GLANCE

Autonomic Nervous System
Anatomy and neurotransmitters of autonomic fibers
Dominance patterns of sympathetic and parasympathetic systems
Autonomic receptor types
CNS control of autonomic activity

Somatic Nervous System
Motor neurons
Control of somatic activity

Neuromuscular Junction
Events at the neuromuscular junction
Role of acetylcholine
Role of acetylcholinesterase
Influence of specific chemical agents and diseases

The Peripheral Nervous System: Efferent Division

Autonomic Nervous System

The efferent division of the peripheral nervous system (PNS) is the communication link by which the central nervous system (CNS) controls muscles and glands, the effector organs that carry out the intended effects or actions (typically contraction or secretion, respectively). The CNS regulates these effectors by initiating action potentials in the cell bodies of efferent neurons whose axons terminate on these organs. Cardiac muscle, smooth muscle, most exocrine glands, some endocrine glands, and adipose tissue (fat) are innervated by the **autonomic nervous system,** the involuntary branch of the peripheral efferent division. Skeletal muscle is innervated by the **somatic nervous system,** the branch of the efferent division subject to voluntary control. Much of this efferent output is directed toward maintaining homeostasis. The efferent output to skeletal muscles is also directed toward voluntarily controlled nonhomeostatic activities, such as riding a bicycle. (Many effector organs are also subject to hormonal control or to intrinsic control; see p. 11.)

How many different neurotransmitters would you guess are released from the various efferent neuronal terminals to elicit essentially all neurally controlled effector organ responses? Only two: acetylcholine and norepinephrine. Acting independently, these neurotransmitters bring about such diverse effects as salivary secretion, bladder contraction, and voluntary motor movements. These effects are a prime example of how the same chemical messenger may cause different responses in various tissues, depending on specialization of the effector organs.

An autonomic nerve pathway consists of a two-neuron chain.
Each autonomic nerve pathway extending from the CNS to an innervated organ is a two-neuron chain (● Figure 7-1). The cell body of the first neuron in the series is located in the CNS. Its axon, the **preganglionic fiber,** synapses with the cell body of the second neuron, which lies within a ganglion. (Recall that a ganglion is a cluster of neuronal cell bodies outside the CNS.) The axon of the second neuron, the **postganglionic fiber,** innervates the effector organ.

The autonomic nervous system has two subdivisions—the **sympathetic** and the **parasympathetic nervous systems** (● Figure 7-2). Sympathetic nerve fibers originate in the thoracic (chest) and lumbar (abdominal) regions of the spinal cord (see p. 140). Most sympathetic preganglionic fibers are very short, synapsing with cell bodies of postganglionic neurons within ganglia that lie in a **sympathetic ganglion chain** located along either side of the spinal cord (see ● Figure 5-18, p. 141). Long postganglionic fibers originate in the ganglion chain and end on the effector organs. Some preganglionic fibers pass through the ganglion chain without synapsing. Instead, they end later in sympathetic **collateral ganglia** about halfway between the CNS and the innervated organs, with postganglionic fibers traveling the rest of the distance.

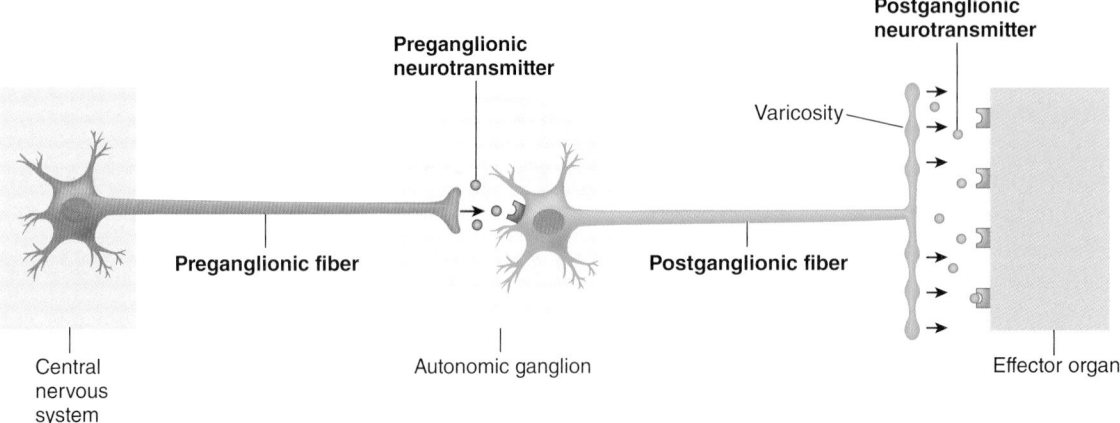

● FIGURE 7-1 Autonomic nerve pathway.

Parasympathetic preganglionic fibers arise from the cranial (brain) and sacral (lower spinal cord) areas of the CNS. These fibers are longer than sympathetic preganglionic fibers because they do not end until they reach **terminal ganglia** that lie in or near the effector organs. Very short postganglionic fibers end on the cells of an organ itself.

Parasympathetic postganglionic fibers release acetylcholine; sympathetic ones release norepinephrine.

Sympathetic and parasympathetic preganglionic fibers release the same neurotransmitter, **acetylcholine (ACh),** but the postganglionic endings of these two systems release different neurotransmitters (the neurotransmitters that influence the autonomic effectors). Parasympathetic postganglionic fibers release ACh. Accordingly, they, along with all autonomic preganglionic fibers, are called **cholinergic fibers.** Most sympathetic postganglionic fibers, in contrast, are called **adrenergic fibers** because they release **noradrenaline,** commonly known as **norepinephrine.**

Postganglionic autonomic fibers do not end in a single terminal swelling like a synaptic knob. Instead, the terminal branches of autonomic fibers have numerous swellings, or **varicosities,** that simultaneously release neurotransmitter over a large area of the innervated organ rather than on single cells (see ● Figures 7-1 and 8-26, p. 238). Because of this diffuse release of neurotransmitter, and because any resulting change in electrical activity is spread throughout a smooth or cardiac muscle mass via gap junctions (see p. 53), autonomic activity typically influences whole organs instead of discrete cells.

The sympathetic and parasympathetic nervous systems dually innervate most visceral organs.

Afferent information coming from the viscera (internal organs) usually does not reach the conscious level (see p. 153). Examples of visceral afferent information include input from the baroreceptors that monitor blood pressure and input from the chemoreceptors that monitor the protein or fat content of ingested food. This input is used to direct the activity of the autonomic efferent neurons. Autonomic efferent output regulates visceral activities such as circulation and digestion. Like vis-

ceral afferent input, autonomic efferent output operates outside the realm of consciousness and voluntary control.

Most visceral organs are innervated by both sympathetic and parasympathetic nerve fibers (● Figure 7-3). Innervation of a single organ by both branches of the autonomic nervous system is known as **dual innervation** (*dual* means "pertaining to two"). ▲ Table 7-1 summarizes the major effects of these autonomic branches. Although the details of this array of autonomic responses are described more fully in later chapters that discuss the individual organs involved, you can consider several general concepts now. As you can see from the table, the sympathetic and parasympathetic nervous systems generally exert opposite effects in a particular organ. Sympathetic stimulation increases the heart rate, whereas parasympathetic stimulation decreases it; sympathetic stimulation slows movement within the digestive tract, whereas parasympathetic stimulation enhances digestive motility. Note that both systems increase the activity of some organs and reduce the activity of others.

Rather than memorize a list such as in Table 7-1, it is better to logically deduce the actions of the two systems by first understanding the circumstances under which each system dominates. Usually, both systems are partially active; that is, some level of action potential activity exists in both the sympathetic and the parasympathetic fibers supplying a particular organ. This ongoing activity is called **sympathetic** or **parasympathetic tone.** Under given circumstances, activity of one division can dominate the other. *Sympathetic dominance* to a particular organ exists when the sympathetic fibers' rate of firing to that organ increases above tone level, coupled with a simultaneous decrease below tone level in the parasympathetic fibers' frequency of action potentials to the same organ. The reverse situation is true for *parasympathetic dominance.* The balance between sympathetic and parasympathetic activity can be shifted separately for individual organs to meet specific demands (for example, sympathetically induced dilation of the pupil in dim light; see p. 158), or a more generalized, widespread discharge of one autonomic system in favor of the other can be elicited to control bodywide functions. Massive widespread discharges take place more often in the sympathetic system. The value of

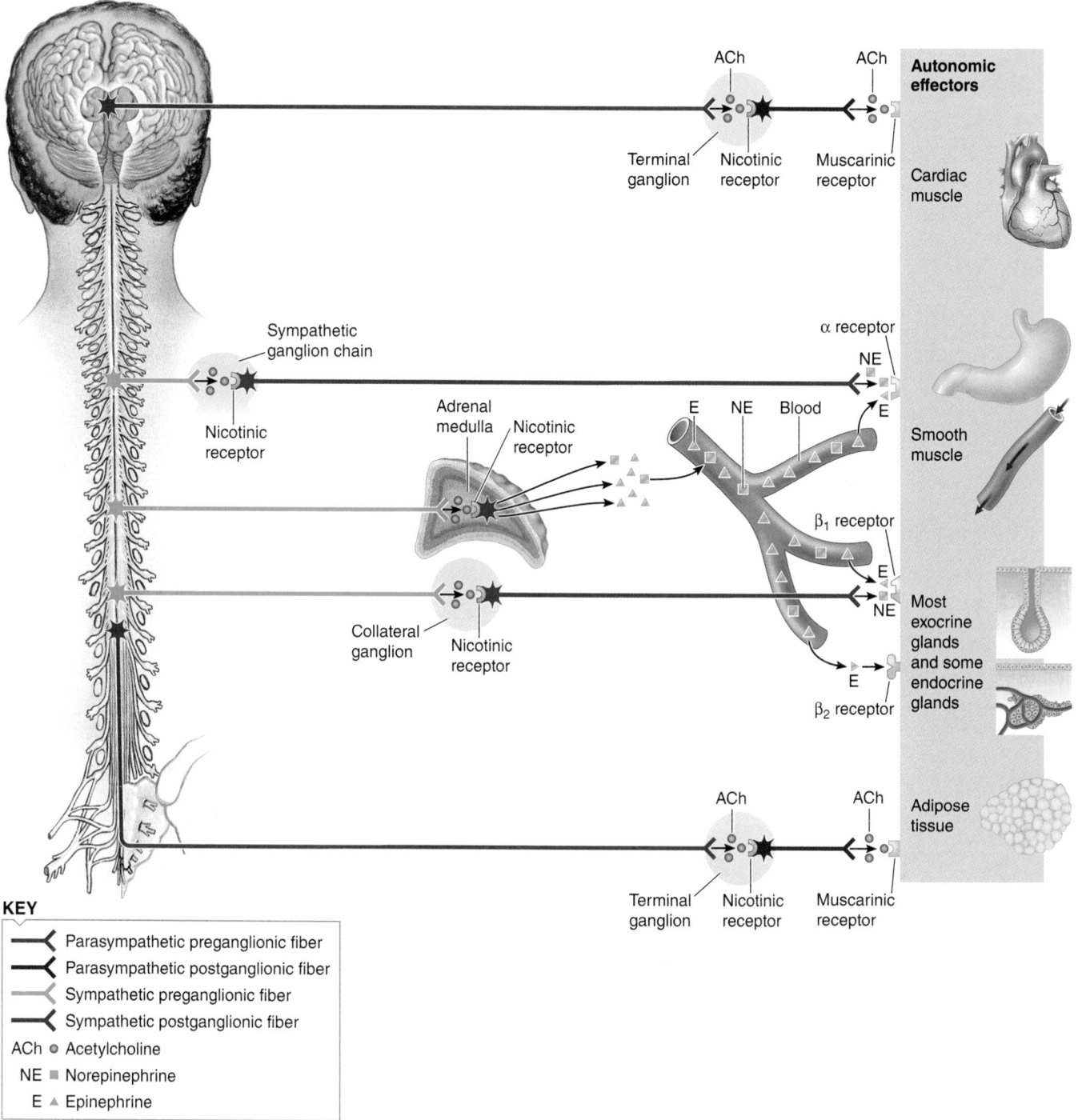

KEY

⟨	Parasympathetic preganglionic fiber
◀	Parasympathetic postganglionic fiber
⟨	Sympathetic preganglionic fiber
◀	Sympathetic postganglionic fiber
ACh ●	Acetylcholine
NE ■	Norepinephrine
E ▲	Epinephrine

● **FIGURE 7-2 Autonomic nervous system.** The sympathetic nervous system, which originates in the thoracic and lumbar regions of the spinal cord, has short cholinergic (acetylcholine-releasing) preganglionic fibers and long adrenergic (norepinephrine-releasing) postganglionic fibers. The parasympathetic nervous system, which originates in the brain and sacral region of the spinal cord, has long cholinergic preganglionic fibers and short cholinergic postganglionic fibers. In most instances, sympathetic and parasympathetic postganglionic fibers innervate the same effector organs. The adrenal medulla is a modified sympathetic ganglion, which releases epinephrine (E) and norepinephrine (NE) into the blood. Nicotinic cholinergic receptors are located in the autonomic ganglia and adrenal medulla and respond to acetylcholine (ACh) released by all autonomic preganglionic fibers. Muscarinic cholinergic receptors are located at the autonomic effectors and respond to ACh released by parasympathetic postganglionic fibers. α_1-, α_2-, β_1-, and β_2-adrenergic receptors are variably located at the autonomic effectors and differentially respond to NE released by sympathetic postganglionic fibers and to E released by the adrenal medulla.

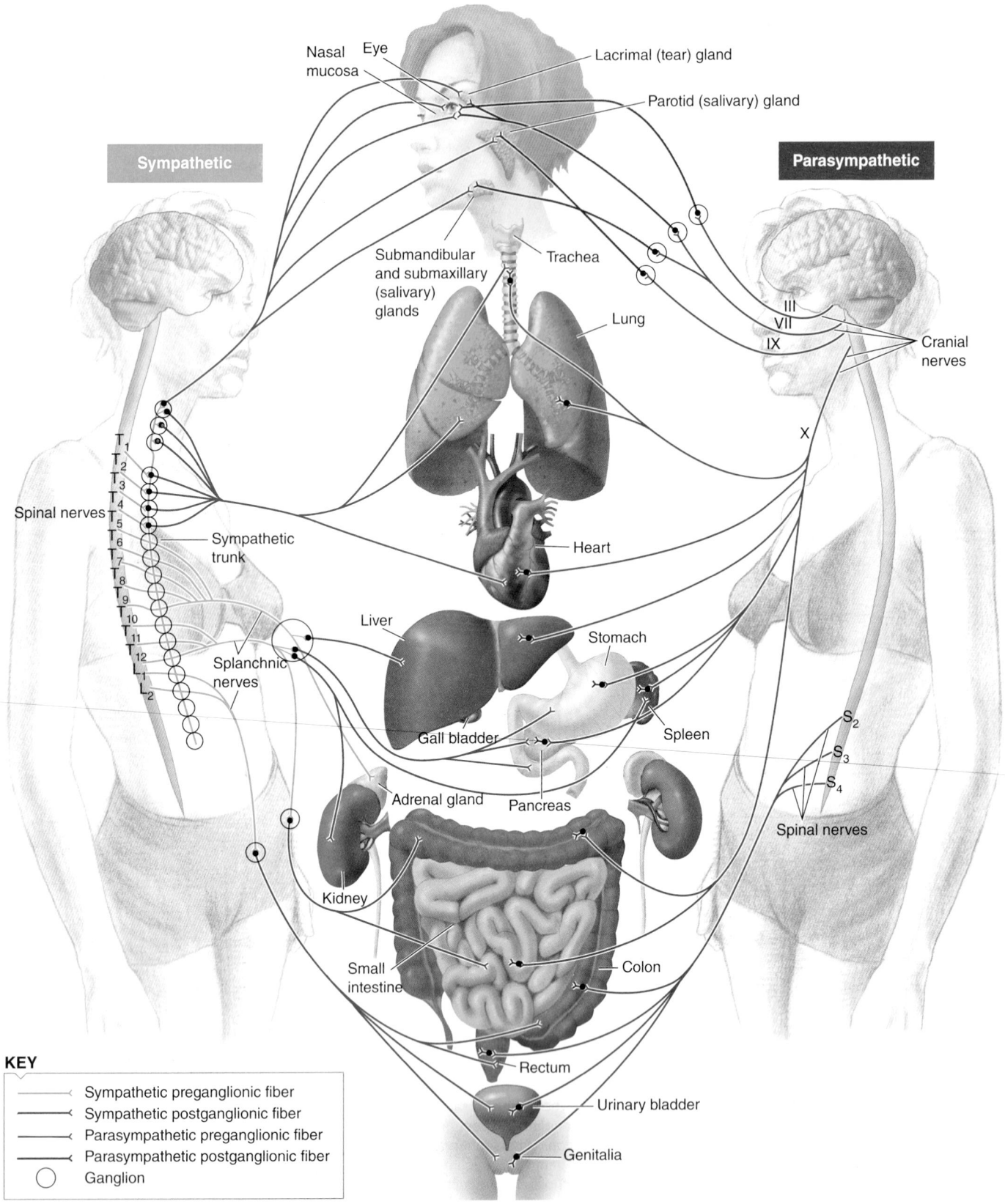

Sympathetic

Parasympathetic

Nasal mucosa Eye Lacrimal (tear) gland
Parotid (salivary) gland

Submandibular and submaxillary (salivary) glands Trachea

Lung

III
VII
IX

Cranial nerves

X

Spinal nerves

T₁
T₂
T₃
T₄
T₅
T₆
T₇
T₈
T₉
T₁₀
T₁₁
T₁₂
L₁
L₂

Sympathetic trunk

Heart

Liver

Stomach

Splanchnic nerves

Gall bladder Spleen

S₂
S₃
S₄

Spinal nerves

Adrenal gland Pancreas

Kidney

Small intestine

Colon

Rectum

Urinary bladder

Genitalia

KEY

—< Sympathetic preganglionic fiber
—< Sympathetic postganglionic fiber
—< Parasympathetic preganglionic fiber
—< Parasympathetic postganglionic fiber
○ Ganglion

● **FIGURE 7-3 Structures innervated by the sympathetic and parasympathetic nervous systems.**

Organ	Effect of Sympathetic Stimulation	Effect of Parasympathetic Stimulation
Heart	Increases heart rate and increases force of contraction of the whole heart	Decreases heart rate and decreases force of contraction of the atria only
Blood Vessels	Constricts	Dilates vessels supplying the penis and the clitoris only
Lungs	Dilates the bronchioles (airways)	Constricts the bronchioles
Digestive Tract	Decreases motility (movement)	Increases motility
	Contracts sphincters (to prevent forward movement of tract contents)	Relaxes sphincters (to permit forward movement of tract contents)
	Inhibits digestive secretions	Stimulates digestive secretions
Urinary Bladder	Relaxes	Contracts (emptying)
Eye	Dilates the pupil	Constricts the pupil
	Adjusts the eye for far vision	Adjusts the eye for near vision
Liver (glycogen stores)	Glycogenolysis (glucose is released)	None
Adipose Cells (fat stores)	Lipolysis (fatty acids are released)	None
Exocrine Glands		
Exocrine pancreas	Inhibits pancreatic exocrine secretion	Stimulates pancreatic exocrine secretion (important for digestion)
Sweat glands	Stimulates secretion by sweat glands important in cooling the body	Stimulates secretion by specialized sweat glands in the armpits and genital area
Salivary glands	Stimulates a small volume of thick saliva rich in mucus	Stimulates a large volume of watery saliva rich in enzymes
Endocrine Glands		
Adrenal medulla	Stimulates epinephrine and norepinephrine secretion	None
Endocrine pancreas	Inhibits insulin secretion	Stimulates insulin secretion
Genitals	Controls ejaculation (males) and orgasm contractions (both sexes)	Controls erection (penis in males and clitoris in females)
Brain Activity	Increases alertness	None

massive sympathetic discharge is clear, considering the circumstances during which this system usually dominates.

TIMES OF SYMPATHETIC DOMINANCE The sympathetic system promotes responses that prepare the body for strenuous physical activity in emergency or stressful situations, such as a physical threat from the outside. This response is typically referred to as a **"fight-or-flight"** response because the sympathetic system readies the body to fight against or flee from the threat. Think about the body resources needed in such circumstances. The heart beats more rapidly and more forcefully, blood pressure is elevated by generalized constriction (narrowing) of the blood vessels, respiratory airways dilate (open wide) to permit maximal airflow, glycogen (stored sugar) and fat stores are broken down to release extra fuel into the blood, and blood vessels supplying skeletal muscles dilate. All these responses are aimed at providing increased flow of oxygenated, nutrient-rich blood to the skeletal muscles in anticipation of strenuous physical activity. Furthermore, the pupils dilate and the eyes adjust for far vision, letting the person visually assess the entire threatening scene. Sweating is promoted in anticipation of excess heat production by the physical exertion. Be-

cause digestive and urinary activities are not essential in meeting the threat, the sympathetic system inhibits these activities.

TIMES OF PARASYMPATHETIC DOMINANCE The parasympathetic system dominates in quiet, relaxed situations. Under such nonthreatening circumstances, the body can be concerned with its own "general housekeeping" activities, such as digestion. The parasympathetic system promotes such **"rest-and-digest"** bodily functions while slowing down those activities that are enhanced by the sympathetic system. For example, the heart does not need to beat rapidly and forcefully when the person is in a tranquil setting.

ADVANTAGE OF DUAL AUTONOMIC INNERVATION What is the advantage of dual innervation of organs with nerve fibers whose actions oppose each other? It enables precise control over an organ's activity, like having both an accelerator and a brake to control the speed of a car. If an animal suddenly darts across the road as you are driving, you could eventually stop if you just took your foot off the accelerator, but you might stop too slowly to avoid hitting the animal. If you simultaneously apply the brake as you lift up on the accelerator, however, you can come to a more rapid, controlled stop. In a similar manner, a sympathetically accelerated heart rate could gradually be reduced to normal following a stressful situation by decreasing the firing rate in the cardiac sympathetic nerve (letting up on the accelerator). However, the heart rate can be reduced more rapidly by simultaneously increasing activity in the parasympathetic supply to the heart (applying the brake). Indeed, the two divisions of the autonomic nervous system are usually reciprocally controlled; increased activity in one division is accompanied by a corresponding decrease in the other.

We now turn to the adrenal medulla, a unique endocrine component of the sympathetic nervous system.

The adrenal medulla is a modified part of the sympathetic nervous system.

The two *adrenal glands* lie above the kidneys, one on each side (*ad* means "next to"; *renal* means "kidney"). The adrenal glands are endocrine glands, each with an outer portion, the *adrenal cortex,* and an inner portion, the *adrenal medulla* (see pp. 550 and 554–555). The **adrenal medulla** is a modified sympathetic ganglion that does not give rise to postganglionic fibers. Instead, on stimulation by the preganglionic fiber that originates in the CNS, it secretes hormones into the blood (see ● Figure 7-2). Not surprisingly, the hormones are identical or similar to postganglionic sympathetic neurotransmitters. About 20% of the adrenal medullary hormone output is norepinephrine, and the remaining 80% is the closely related **epinephrine (adrenaline).** These hormones, in general, reinforce activity of the sympathetic nervous system.

Several receptor types are available for each autonomic neurotransmitter.

Because each autonomic neurotransmitter and medullary hormone stimulates activity in some tissues but inhibits activity in others, the particular responses must depend on specialization of the tissue cells rather than on properties of the chemicals themselves. Responsive tissue cells have one or more of several types of plasma membrane receptor proteins for these chemical messengers. Binding of a neurotransmitter to a receptor induces the tissue-specific response.

CHOLINERGIC RECEPTORS Researchers have identified two types of ACh (cholinergic) receptors—*nicotinic* and *muscarinic*—on the basis of their response to particular drugs. Nicotinic receptors are activated by the tobacco plant derivative nicotine, whereas muscarinic receptors are activated by the mushroom poison muscarine. **Nicotinic receptors** are found on the postganglionic cell bodies in all autonomic ganglia. These receptors respond to ACh released from both sympathetic and parasympathetic preganglionic fibers. **Muscarinic receptors** are found on effector cell membranes (smooth muscle, cardiac muscle, and glands). They bind with ACh released from parasympathetic postganglionic fibers.

ADRENERGIC RECEPTORS The two major classes of adrenergic receptors for norepinephrine and epinephrine are **alpha (α)** and **beta (β) receptors,** which are further subclassified into α_1 and α_2 and into β_1 and β_2 **receptors,** respectively (▲ Table 7-2). These various receptor types are distinctly distributed among sympathetically controlled effector organs as follows:

- α_1 receptors are present on most sympathetic target tissues.
- α_2 receptors are located mainly on digestive organs.
- β_1 receptors are restricted to the heart.
- β_2 receptors are found on smooth muscles of arterioles and bronchioles (small blood vessels and airways).

Different receptor types also have different affinities (attraction) for norepinephrine and epinephrine:

▲ Table 7-2 Properties of Autonomic Receptor Types

Receptor Type	Neurotransmitter Affinity	Effector(s) with This Receptor Type	Effect on Effector
Nicotinic	ACh from autonomic preganglionic fibers	All autonomic postganglionic cell bodies and the adrenal medulla	Excitatory
	ACh from motor neurons	Motor end plates of skeletal muscle fibers	Excitatory
Muscarinic	ACh from parasympathetic postganglionic fibers	Cardiac muscle, smooth muscle, and most exocrine and some endocrine glands	Excitatory or inhibitory, depending on the effector
α_1	Greater affinity for norepinephrine (from sympathetic postganglionic fibers) than for epinephrine (from the adrenal medulla)	Most sympathetic target tissues	Excitatory
α_2	Greater affinity for norepinephrine than for epinephrine	Digestive organs	Inhibitory
β_1	Equal affinity for norepinephrine and for epinephrine	Heart	Excitatory
β_2	Affinity for epinephrine only	Smooth muscles of arterioles and bronchioles	Inhibitory

- α receptors of both subtypes have a greater attraction for norepinephrine than for epinephrine.
- β_1 receptors have about equal affinities for norepinephrine and epinephrine.
- β_2 receptors bind only with epinephrine.

Activation of α_1 receptors usually brings about an excitatory response in the effector organ—for example, arteriolar constriction caused by increased contraction of smooth muscle in the walls of these blood vessels. Activation of α_2 receptors, in contrast, brings about an inhibitory response in the effector, such as decreased smooth muscle contraction in the digestive tract. Stimulation of β_1 receptors, which are found only in the heart, causes an excitatory response, namely, increased rate and force of cardiac contraction. The response to β_2 receptor activation is generally inhibitory, such as arteriolar or bronchiolar dilation caused by relaxation of the smooth muscle in the walls of these tubular structures. As a quick rule of thumb, activation of the subscript "1" versions of adrenergic receptors leads to excitatory responses and activation of the subscript "2" versions leads to inhibitory responses.

 AUTONOMIC AGONISTS AND ANTAGONISTS Drugs are available that selectively alter autonomic responses at each of the receptor types. An **agonist** binds to the neurotransmitter's receptor and causes the same response as the neurotransmitter would. An **antagonist,** by contrast, binds with the receptor, preventing the neurotransmitter from binding and causing a response, yet the antagonist itself produces no response. Thus, an agonist mimics the neurotransmitter's response and an antagonist blocks the neurotransmitter's response. Some of these drugs are only of experimental interest, but others are important therapeutically. For example, *atropine* blocks the effect of ACh at muscarinic receptors but does not affect nicotinic receptors. Because ACh released at both parasympathetic and sympathetic preganglionic fibers combines with nicotinic receptors, blockage at nicotinic synapses would knock out both these autonomic branches. By acting selectively to interfere with ACh action only at muscarinic junctions, which are the sites of parasympathetic postganglionic action, atropine blocks parasympathetic effects but does not influence sympathetic activity. Doctors use this principle to suppress salivary and bronchial secretions before surgery and thus reduce the risk of a patient inhaling these secretions into the lungs.

Likewise, drugs that act selectively at α- and β-adrenergic receptor sites to either activate or block specific sympathetic effects are widely used. Following are several examples. *Salbutamol* selectively activates β_2-adrenergic receptors at low doses, making it possible to dilate the bronchioles in the treatment of asthma without undesirably stimulating the heart (which has mostly β_1 receptors). By contrast, *metoprolol* selectively blocks β_1-adrenergic receptors and is prescribed to treat high blood pressure because it decreases the amount of blood the heart pumps into the blood vessels. Metoprolol does not affect β_2 receptors and so has no effect on the bronchioles.

Many regions of the CNS are involved in the control of autonomic activities.

Messages from the CNS are delivered to cardiac muscle, smooth muscle, and glands via the autonomic nerves, but what regions of the CNS regulate autonomic output?

- Some autonomic reflexes, such as urination, defecation, and erection, are integrated at the spinal-cord level, but all these spinal reflexes are subject to control by higher levels of consciousness.
- The medulla within the brain stem is the region most directly responsible for autonomic output. Centers for controlling cardiovascular, respiratory, and digestive activity via the autonomic system are located there.
- The hypothalamus plays an important role in integrating the autonomic, somatic, and endocrine responses that automatically accompany various emotional and behavioral states. For example, the increased heart rate, blood pressure, and respiratory activity associated with anger or fear are brought about by the hypothalamus acting through the medulla.
- Autonomic activity can also be influenced by the prefrontal association cortex through its involvement with emotional expression characteristic of the individual's personality. An example is blushing when embarrassed, which is caused by dilation of blood vessels supplying the skin of the cheeks. Such responses are mediated through hypothalamic–medullary pathways.

▲ Table 7-3 summarizes the main distinguishing features of the sympathetic and parasympathetic nervous systems.

Somatic Nervous System

Motor neurons supply skeletal muscle.

Motor neurons, whose axons constitute the somatic nervous system, supply skeletal muscles and bring about movement (*motor* means "movement"). The cell bodies of almost all motor neurons are within the spinal cord. The only exception is that the cell bodies of motor neurons supplying muscles in the head are in the brain stem. Unlike the two-neuron chain of autonomic nerve fibers, the axon of a motor neuron is continuous from its origin in the CNS to its ending on skeletal muscle. Motor-neuron axon terminals release ACh, which brings about excitation and contraction of the innervated muscle cells. Motor neurons can only stimulate skeletal muscles, in contrast to autonomic fibers, which can either stimulate or inhibit their effector organs. Inhibition of skeletal muscle activity can be accomplished only within the CNS through inhibitory synaptic input to the dendrites and cell bodies of the motor neurons supplying that particular muscle.

Motor neurons are influenced by many areas of the CNS involved in motor control.

The only way any other parts of the nervous system can influence skeletal muscle activity is by acting on motor neurons. Motor-neuron dendrites and cell bodies are influenced by many converging presynaptic inputs, both excitatory and inhibitory.

Feature	Sympathetic System	Parasympathetic System
Origin of Preganglionic Fiber	Thoracic and lumbar regions of the spinal cord	Brain and sacral region of the spinal cord
Origin of Postganglionic Fiber (location of ganglion)	Sympathetic ganglion chain (near the spinal cord) or collateral ganglia (about halfway between the spinal cord and the effector organs)	Terminal ganglia (in or near the effector organs)
Length of Fibers	Short preganglionic fibers and long postganglionic fibers	Long preganglionic fibers and short postganglionic fibers
Effector Organs Innervated	Cardiac muscle, almost all smooth muscle, most exocrine glands, and some endocrine glands	Cardiac muscle, most smooth muscle, most exocrine glands, and some endocrine glands
Neurotransmitter Released	Preganglionic: ACh	Preganglionic: ACh
	Postganglionic: norepinephrine	Postganglionic: ACh
Types of Receptors for Neurotransmitter	For preganglionic neurotransmitter: nicotinic	For preganglionic neurotransmitter: nicotinic
	For postganglionic neurotransmitter: α_1, α_2, β_1, and β_2	For postganglionic neurotransmitter: muscarinic
Dominance	In emergency ("fight-or-flight") situations during which the body prepares for strenuous physical activity	In quiet, relaxed ("rest-and-digest") situations during which the body promotes "general housekeeping" activities such as digestion

Some of these inputs are part of spinal reflex pathways originating with peripheral sensory receptors. Others are part of descending pathways originating within the brain. Areas of the brain that exert control over skeletal muscle movements include the motor regions of the cortex, the basal nuclei, the cerebellum, and the brain stem (see pp. 125–127, 131, 136–138, and 222).

The somatic system is under voluntary control, but much of skeletal muscle activity involving posture, balance, and stereotypical movements is subconsciously controlled. You may decide you want to start walking, but you do not have to consciously bring about the alternate contraction and relaxation of the involved muscles because these movements are involuntarily coordinated by lower brain centers.

 The cell bodies of motor neurons may be selectively destroyed by **poliovirus.** The result is paralysis of the muscles innervated by the affected neurons. **Amyotrophic lateral sclerosis (ALS),** also known as **Lou Gehrig's disease,** is the most common motor-neuron disease. This incurable condition is characterized by degeneration and eventual death of motor neurons. The underlying cause is uncertain. The result is gradual loss of motor control, progressive paralysis, and finally, death within 3 to 5 years of onset.

Before turning to the junction between a motor neuron and the muscle cells it innervates, we pull together in table form two groups of information we have been examining in this and preceding nervous system chapters. ▲ Table 7-4 summarizes the features of the two branches of the efferent division of the PNS: the autonomic nervous system and the somatic nervous system. ▲ Table 7-5 compares the three functional types of neurons: afferent neurons, efferent neurons, and interneurons.

Neuromuscular Junction

Motor neurons and skeletal muscle fibers are chemically linked at neuromuscular junctions.

An action potential in a motor neuron is rapidly propagated from the cell body within the CNS to the skeletal muscle along the large myelinated axon (efferent fiber) of the neuron. As the axon approaches a muscle, it divides and loses its myelin sheath. Each of these axon terminals forms a special junction, a **neuromuscular junction,** with one of the many muscle cells that compose the whole muscle (● Figure 7-4). Each branch innervates only one muscle cell; therefore, each muscle cell has only one neuromuscular junction. A single muscle cell, called a **muscle fiber,** is long and cylindrical. Within a neuromuscular junction, the axon terminal splits into multiple fine branches, each of which ends in an enlarged knoblike structure called the **terminal button.** The entire axon terminal ending (all the fine branches with terminal buttons) fits into a shallow depression, or groove, in the underlying muscle fiber. This specialized underlying portion of the muscle cell membrane is called the **motor end plate** (● Figure 7-4).

ACh is the neuromuscular junction neurotransmitter.

Nerve and muscle cells do not come into direct contact at a neuromuscular junction. The space, or cleft, between these two structures is too large for electrical transmission of an impulse between them (that is, an action potential cannot "jump" that far). Just as at a neuronal synapse (see p. 91), a chemical messenger carries the signal between a terminal button and the muscle fiber. This neurotransmitter is ACh.

▲ Table 7-4 Comparison of the Autonomic Nervous System and the Somatic Nervous System

Feature	Autonomic Nervous System	Somatic Nervous System
Site of Origin	Brain or spinal cord	Spinal cord for most; those supplying muscles in the head originate in the brain
Number of Neurons from Origin in CNS to Effector Organ	Two-neuron chain (preganglionic and post-ganglionic)	Single neuron (motor neuron)
Organs Innervated	Cardiac muscle, smooth muscle, and glands	Skeletal muscle
Type of Innervation	Most effector organs dually innervated by the two antagonistic branches of this system (sympathetic and parasympathetic)	Effector organs innervated only by motor neurons
Neurotransmitter at Effector Organs	May be ACh (parasympathetic terminals) or norepinephrine (sympathetic terminals)	Only ACh
Effects on Effector Organs	Stimulation or inhibition (antagonistic actions of two branches)	Stimulation only (inhibition is possible only centrally through inhibitory postsynaptic potentials on dendrites and the cell body of the motor neuron)
Type of Control	Involuntary control	Voluntary control, although much activity is subconsciously coordinated
Higher Centers Involved in Control	Spinal cord, medulla, hypothalamus, and prefrontal association cortex	Spinal cord, motor cortex, basal nuclei, cerebellum, and brain stem

RELEASE OF ACh AT THE NEUROMUSCULAR JUNCTION Each terminal button contains thousands of vesicles that store ACh. Propagation of an action potential to the axon terminal (● Figure 7-5, step **1**, p. 202) triggers the opening of voltage-gated calcium (Ca^{2+}) channels in all of its terminal buttons (see p. 78). We focus on one terminal button, but the same events take place concurrently at all terminal buttons of a given neuromuscular junction. When Ca^{2+} channels open, Ca^{2+} diffuses into the terminal button from its higher extracellular concentration (step **2**), which in turn causes the release of ACh by exocytosis from several hundred of the vesicles into the cleft (step **3**).

FORMATION OF AN END-PLATE POTENTIAL The released ACh diffuses across the cleft and binds with specific chemically gated receptor-channels, which are specialized membrane proteins unique to the motor end-plate portion of the muscle fiber membrane (● Figure 7-5, step **4**). (These cholinergic receptors are of the nicotinic type.) Binding with ACh causes these receptor-channels to open. They are nonspecific cation channels that permit both sodium (Na^+) and potassium (K^+) ions, but no anions, traffic through them (step **5**). Because the permeability of the end-plate membrane to Na^+ and K^+ on opening of these channels is essentially equal, the relative movement of these ions through the channels depends on their electrochemical driving forces. Recall that at resting potential the net driving force for Na^+ is much greater than that for K^+ because the resting potential is much closer to the K^+ than to the Na^+ equilibrium potential. Both the concentration and the electrical gradients for Na^+ are inward, whereas the outward concentration gradient for K^+ is almost, but not quite, balanced by the opposing inward electrical gradient. As a result, when ACh triggers the opening of these channels, considerably more Na^+ moves inward than K^+ moves outward, depolarizing the motor end plate. This potential change is called the **end-plate potential (EPP).** It is a graded potential similar to an excitatory postsynaptic potential (EPSP; see p. 93), except that an EPP is considerably larger.

INITIATION OF AN ACTION POTENTIAL The motor end-plate region itself does not have a threshold potential, so an action potential cannot be initiated at this site. However, an EPP brings about an action potential in the rest of the muscle fiber as follows: The neuromuscular junction is usually in the middle of the long, cylindrical muscle fiber. When an EPP takes place, local current flow occurs between the depolarized end plate and the adjacent, resting cell membrane in both directions (● Figure 7-5, step **6**), opening voltage-gated Na^+ channels and thus reducing the potential to threshold in the adjacent areas (step **7**). The subsequent action potential initiated at these sites propagates throughout the muscle fiber membrane by contiguous conduction (step **8**) (see p. 86). The spread runs in both directions, away from the motor end plate toward both ends of the fiber. This electrical activity triggers contraction of the muscle fiber. Thus, by means of ACh, an action potential in a motor neuron brings about an action potential and subsequent contraction in the muscle fiber.

Unlike synaptic transmission, an EPP is normally large enough to cause an action potential in the muscle cell. Therefore, one-to-one transmission of an action potential typically occurs at a neuromuscular junction; one action potential in a nerve cell triggers one action potential in a muscle cell that it innervates. Other comparisons of neuromuscular junctions with synapses can be found in ▲ Table 7-6, p. 203.

| Feature | Afferent Neuron | EFFERENT NEURON | | Interneuron |
		Autonomic Nervous System	Somatic Nervous System	
Origin, Structure, and Location	Receptor at the peripheral ending; elongated peripheral axon travels in the peripheral nerve; cell body located in the dorsal root ganglion; short central axon enters the spinal cord	Two-neuron chain; first neuron (preganglionic fiber) originates in the CNS and terminates on a ganglion; second neuron (postganglionic fiber) originates in the ganglion and terminates on the effector organ	Cell body of the motor neuron in the spinal cord; long axon travels in the peripheral nerve and terminates on the effector organ	Lies entirely within the CNS; some cell bodies originate in the brain, with long axons traveling down the spinal cord in descending pathways; some originate in the spinal cord, with long axons traveling up the cord to the brain in ascending pathways; others form short local connections
Termination	Interneurons*	Effector organs (cardiac muscle, smooth muscle, glands)	Effector organs (skeletal muscle)	Other interneurons and efferent neurons
Function	Carries information about the external and the internal environment to the CNS	Carries instructions from the CNS to the effector organs	Carries instructions from the CNS to the effector organs	Processes and integrates afferent input; initiates and coordinates efferent output; is responsible for thought and other higher mental functions
Convergence of Input on the Cell Body	No (only input is through receptor)	Yes	Yes	Yes
Effect of Input to the Neuron	Can only be excited (through a receptor potential induced by a stimulus; must reach threshold for an action potential)	Can be excited or inhibited (through EPSPs** and IPSPs** at the first neuron; must reach threshold for an action potential)	Can be excited or inhibited (through EPSPs and IPSPs; must reach threshold for an action potential)	Can be excited or inhibited (through EPSPs and IPSPs; must reach threshold for an action potential)
Site of Action Potential Initiation	First excitable portion of the membrane adjacent to the receptor	Axon hillock	Axon hillock	Axon hillock
Divergence of Output	Yes	Yes	Yes	Yes
Effect of Output on Effector Organ	Only excites	Postganglionic fiber excites or inhibits	Only excites	Excites or inhibits

*Except in the stretch reflex, where afferent neurons terminate on efferent neurons.
**EPSPs: excitatory postsynaptic potentials; IPSPs: inhibitory postsynaptic potentials.

Acetylcholinesterase ends ACh activity at the neuromuscular junction.

To ensure purposeful movement, a muscle cell's response to stimulation by its motor neuron must be switched off promptly when there is no longer a signal from the motor neuron. The muscle cell's electrical response is turned off by an enzyme in the motor end-plate membrane, **acetylcholinesterase (AChE),** which inactivates ACh.

As a result of diffusion, many of the released ACh molecules come into contact with and bind to receptor-channels on the surface of the motor end-plate membrane. However, some of the ACh molecules bind with AChE, which is also at the end-plate surface. Being quickly inactivated, this ACh never contributes to the EPP. The ACh that does bind with receptor-channels does so briefly (for about 1 millionth of a second) and then detaches. Some of the detached ACh molecules quickly

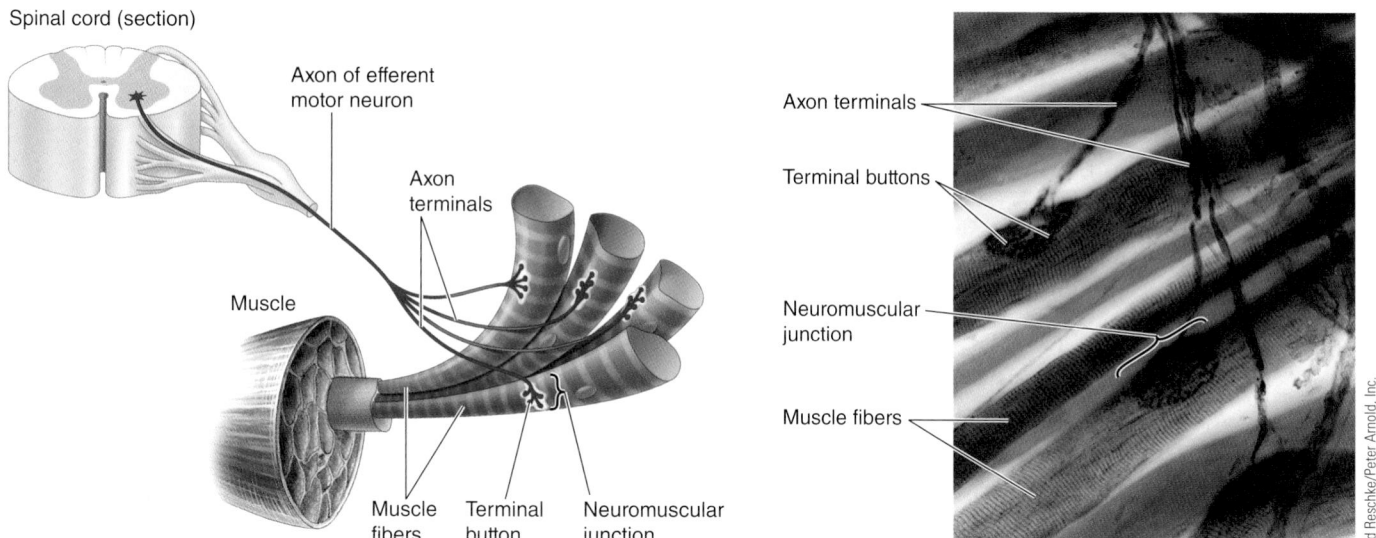

Spinal cord (section)

Axon of efferent motor neuron

Axon terminals

Muscle

Axon terminals

Terminal buttons

Neuromuscular junction

Muscle fibers

Ed Reschke/Peter Arnold, Inc.

Muscle fibers · Terminal button · Neuromuscular junction

● **FIGURE 7-4 Motor neuron innervating skeletal muscle cells.** The cell body of a motor neuron originates in the ventral gray matter of the spinal cord. The axon (somatic efferent fiber) exits through the ventral root and travels through a spinal nerve to the skeletal muscle it innervates. When the axon reaches a skeletal muscle, it divides into many axon terminals, each of which forms a neuromuscular junction with a single muscle cell (muscle fiber). The axon terminal within a neuromuscular junction further divides into fine branches, each of which ends in an enlarged terminal button. Note that the muscle fibers innervated by a single axon terminal are dispersed throughout the muscle but for simplicity are grouped together in this figure.

rebind with receptor-channels, keeping these end-plate channels open, but some randomly contact AChE instead and are inactivated (● Figure 7-5, step **9**). As this process repeats, more ACh is inactivated until all of it has been removed from the cleft within a few milliseconds after its release. ACh removal ends the EPP, so the remainder of the muscle cell membrane returns to resting potential. Now the muscle cell can relax. Or, if sustained contraction is essential for the desired movement, another motor-neuron action potential leads to the release of more ACh, which keeps the contractile process going. By removing contraction-inducing ACh from the motor end plate, AChE permits the choice of allowing relaxation to take place (no more ACh released) or keeping the contraction going (more ACh released), depending on the body's momentary needs.

The neuromuscular junction is vulnerable to several chemical agents and diseases.

Clinical Note Several chemical agents and diseases affect the neuromuscular junction by acting at different sites in the transmission process, as the following examples illustrate.

BLACK WIDOW SPIDER VENOM CAUSES EXPLOSIVE RELEASE OF ACh The venom of black widow spiders exerts its deadly effect by triggering explosive release of ACh from the storage vesicles, not only at neuromuscular junctions but at all cholinergic sites. All cholinergic sites undergo prolonged depolarization, the most harmful result of which is respiratory failure. Breathing is accomplished by alternate contraction and relaxation of skeletal muscles, particularly the diaphragm. Respiratory paralysis occurs as a result of prolonged depolarization of the diaphragm. During this so-called *depolarization block,* the voltage-gated Na^+ channels are trapped in their inactivated state (see p. 82). This depolarization block prohibits the initiation of new action potentials and resultant contraction of the diaphragm. As a consequence, the victim cannot breathe.

BOTULINUM TOXIN BLOCKS RELEASE OF ACh Botulinum toxin, in contrast, exerts its lethal blow by blocking the release of ACh from the terminal button in response to a motor-neuron action potential. *Clostridium botulinum* toxin causes **botulism,** a form of food poisoning. When this toxin is consumed, it prevents muscles from responding to nerve impulses. Death is due to respiratory failure caused by inability to contract the diaphragm. Botulinum toxin is one of the most lethal poisons known; ingesting less than 0.0001 mg can kill an adult human. (See the boxed feature on p. 203, ❱ Beyond the Basics, to learn about a surprising new wrinkle in the botulinum toxin story.)

CURARE BLOCKS ACTION OF ACh AT RECEPTOR-CHANNELS Other chemicals interfere with neuromuscular junction activity by blocking the effect of released ACh. The best-known example is the antagonist **curare,** which reversibly binds to the ACh receptor-channels on the motor end plate. Unlike ACh, however, curare does not alter membrane permeability, nor is it inactivated by AChE. When curare occupies ACh receptor-channels, ACh cannot combine with and open these channels

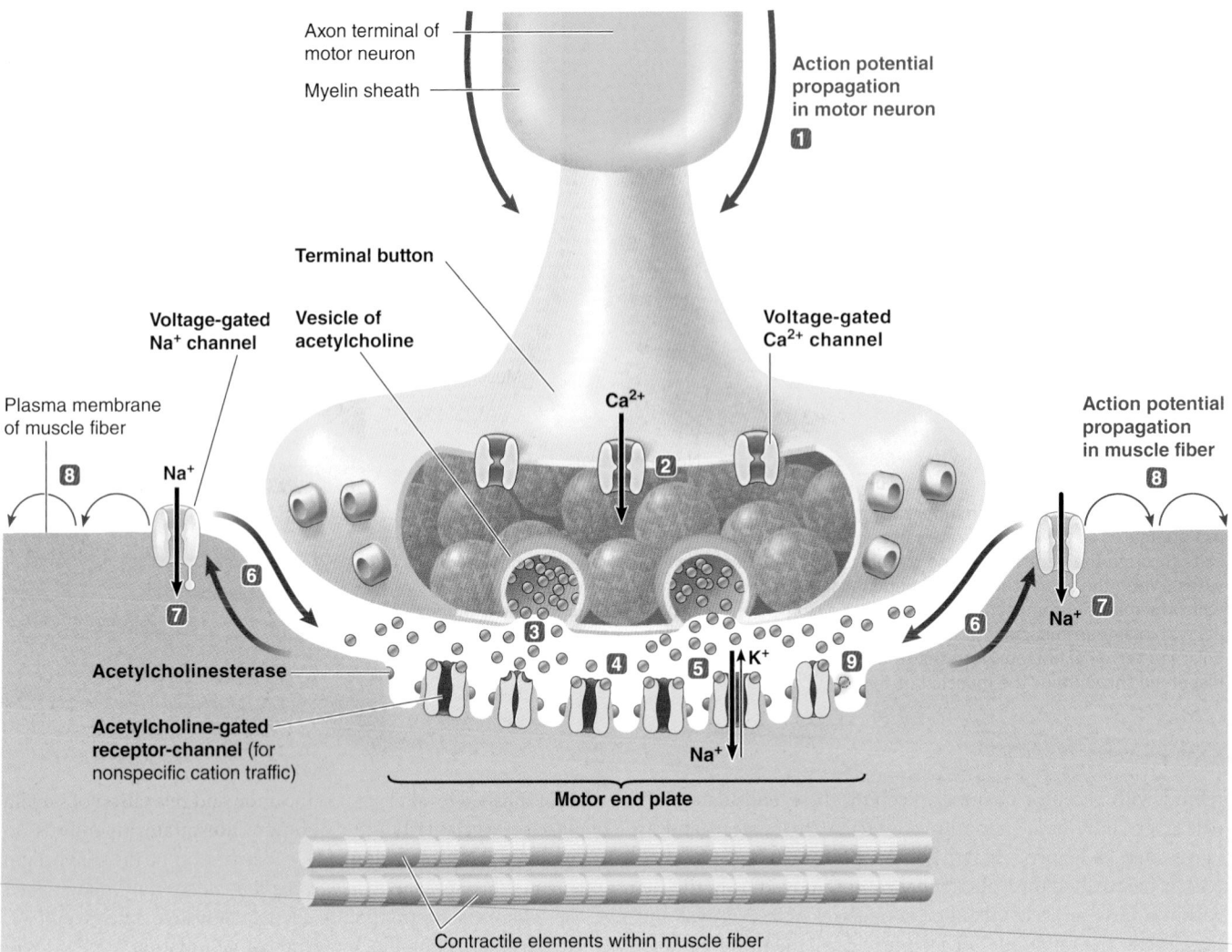

Axon terminal of
motor neuron

Myelin sheath

Action potential
propagation
in motor neuron
1

Terminal button

Voltage-gated
Na⁺ channel

Vesicle of
acetylcholine

Voltage-gated
Ca²⁺ channel

Plasma membrane
of muscle fiber

Ca^{2+}

Action potential
propagation
in muscle fiber
8

8

Na^+

2

Na^+

6

7

3

K^+

9

7

Acetylcholinesterase

4

5

6

Acetylcholine-gated
receptor-channel (for
nonspecific cation traffic)

Na^+

Motor end plate

Contractile elements within muscle fiber

1 An action potential in a motor neuron is propagated to the axon terminal (terminal button).

2 This local action potential triggers the opening of voltage-gated Ca^{2+} channels and the subsequent entry of Ca^{2+} into the terminal button.

3 Ca^{2+} triggers the release of acetylcholine (ACh) by exocytosis from a portion of the vesicles.

4 ACh diffuses across the space separating the nerve and muscle cells and binds with receptor-channels specific for it on the motor end plate of the muscle cell membrane.

5 This binding brings about the opening of these nonspecific cation channels, leading to a relatively large movement of Na^+ into the muscle cell compared to a smaller movement of K^+ outward.

● FIGURE 7-5 **Events at a neuromuscular junction.**

6 The result is an end-plate potential. Local current flow occurs between the depolarized end plate and the adjacent membrane.

7 This local current flow opens voltage-gated Na^+ channels in the adjacent membrane.

8 The resultant Na^+ entry reduces the potential to threshold, initiating an action potential, which is propagated throughout the muscle fiber.

9 ACh is subsequently destroyed by acetylcholinesterase, an enzyme located on the motor end-plate membrane, terminating the muscle cell's response.

to permit the ionic movement responsible for an EPP. Consequently, because muscle action potentials cannot occur in response to nerve impulses to these muscles, paralysis ensues. When enough curare is present to block a significant number of ACh receptor-channels, the person dies from respiratory paralysis caused by inability to contract the diaphragm. In the past, some peoples used curare as a deadly arrowhead poison.

ORGANOPHOSPHATES PREVENT INACTIVATION OF ACh **Organophosphates** are a group of chemicals that modify neuromuscular junction activity in yet another way—namely, by irreversibly inhibiting AChE. Inhibition of AChE prevents the inactivation of released ACh. Death from organophosphates is also due to respiratory failure because the diaphragm cannot repolarize and return to resting conditions, then be

Beyond the Basics

Botulinum Toxin's Reputation Gets a Facelift

The powerful toxin produced by *Clostridium botulinum* causes the deadly food poisoning botulism. Yet this dreaded, highly lethal poison has been put to use as a treatment for alleviating specific movement disorders and, more recently, has been added to the list of tools that cosmetic surgeons use to fight wrinkles.

During the last several decades, botulinum toxin, marketed in therapeutic doses as *Botox,* has offered welcome relief to people with painful, disruptive neuromuscular diseases known categorically as **dystonias.** These conditions are characterized by spasms (excessive, sustained, involuntarily produced muscle contractions) that result in involuntary twisting or abnormal postures, depending on the body part affected. For example, painful neck spasms that twist the head to one side result from *spasmodic torticollis* (*tortus* means "twisted"; *collum* means "neck"), the most common dystonia. The problem is believed to arise from too little inhibitory input compared to excitatory input to the motor neurons that supply the affected muscle. The reasons for this imbalance in motor-neuron input are unknown. The end result of excessive motor-neuron activation is sustained, disabling contraction of the muscle supplied by the overactive motor neurons. Fortunately, injecting minuscule amounts of botulinum toxin into the affected muscle causes a reversible, partial paralysis of the muscle. Botulinum toxin interferes with the release of muscle-contraction-causing ACh from the overactive motor neurons at the neuromuscular junctions in the treated muscle. The goal is to inject just enough botulinum toxin to alleviate the troublesome spasmodic contractions but not enough to eliminate the normal contractions needed for ordinary movements. The therapeutic dose is considerably less than the amount of toxin needed to induce even mild symptoms of botulinum poisoning. Botulinum toxin is eventually cleared away, so its muscle-relaxing effects wear off after 3 to 6 months, at which time the treatment must be repeated.

The first dystonia for which Botox was approved as a treatment by the U.S. Food and Drug Administration (FDA) was *blepharospasm* (*blepharo* means "eyelid"). In this condition, sustained and involuntary contractions of the muscles around the eye nearly permanently close the eyelids.

Botulinum toxin's potential as a treatment option for cosmetic surgeons was accidentally discovered when physicians noted that injections used to counter abnormal eye muscle contractions also smoothed the appearance of wrinkles in the treated areas. It turns out that frown lines, crow's feet, and furrowed brows are caused by facial muscles that have become overactivated, or permanently contracted, as a result of years of performing certain repetitive facial expressions. By relaxing these muscles, botulinum toxin temporarily smoothes out these age-related wrinkles. Botox now has FDA approval as an antiwrinkle treatment. The agent is considered an excellent alternative to facelift surgery for combating lines and creases. This treatment is among the most rapidly growing cosmetic procedures in the United States, especially in the entertainment industry and in high-fashion circles. However, as with its therapeutic use to treat dystonias, the costly injections of botulinum toxin must be repeated every 3 to 6 months to maintain the desired effect in appearance. Furthermore, Botox does not work against the fine, crinkly wrinkles associated with years of excessive sun exposure, because these wrinkles are caused by skin damage, not by contracted muscles.

▲ Table 7-6 **Comparison of a Synapse and a Neuromuscular Junction**

Similarities	Differences
Both consist of two excitable cells separated by a narrow cleft that prevents direct transmission of electrical activity between them.	A synapse is a junction between two neurons. A neuromuscular junction exists between a motor neuron and a skeletal muscle fiber.
Axon terminals store chemical messengers (neurotransmitters) that are released by the Ca^{2+}-induced exocytosis of storage vesicles when an action potential reaches the terminal.	One-to-one transmission of action potentials occurs at a neuromuscular junction, whereas one action potential in a presynaptic neuron cannot by itself bring about an action potential in a postsynaptic neuron. An action potential in a postsynaptic neuron occurs only when summation of EPSPs brings the membrane to threshold.
Binding of the neurotransmitter with receptor-channels in the membrane of the cell underlying the axon terminal opens the channels, permitting ionic movements that alter the membrane potential of the cell.	A neuromuscular junction is always excitatory (an EPP); a synapse may be excitatory (an EPSP) or inhibitory (an IPSP).
The resultant change in membrane potential is a graded potential.	Inhibition of skeletal muscles cannot be accomplished at the neuromuscular junction; this can occur only in the CNS through IPSPs at dendrites and the cell body of the motor neuron.

stimulated to contract again to bring in a fresh breath of air. These toxic agents are used in some pesticides and military nerve gases.

MYASTHENIA GRAVIS INACTIVATES ACh RECEPTOR-CHANNELS

Myasthenia gravis, a disease involving the neuromuscular junction, is characterized by extreme muscular weakness (*myasthenia* means "muscular weakness"; *gravis* means "severe"). It is an autoimmune (meaning "immunity against self") condition, in which the body erroneously produces antibodies against its own motor end-plate ACh receptor-channels. Thus, not all released ACh molecules can find a functioning receptor-channel with which to bind. As a result, AChE destroys much of the ACh before it ever has a chance to interact with a receptor-channel and contribute to the EPP.

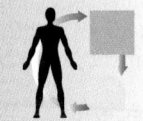

Chapter in Perspective: Focus on Homeostasis

The nervous system, along with the other major regulatory system, the endocrine system, controls most muscle contractions and gland secretions. Whereas the afferent division of the PNS detects and carries information to the CNS for processing and decision making, the efferent division of the PNS carries directives from the CNS to the effector organs (muscles and glands), which carry out the intended response. Much of this efferent output is directed toward maintaining homeostasis.

The autonomic nervous system, which is the efferent branch that innervates smooth muscle, cardiac muscle, and glands, plays a major role in the following homeostatic activities, among others:

- regulating blood pressure
- controlling digestive juice secretion and digestive tract contractions that mix ingested food with the digestive juices
- controlling sweating to help maintain body temperature

The somatic nervous system, the efferent branch that innervates skeletal muscle, contributes to homeostasis by stimulating the following activities:

- skeletal muscle contractions that enable the body to move in relation to the external environment, contributing to homeostasis by moving the body toward food or away from harm
- contractions that accomplish breathing to maintain appropriate levels of oxygen and carbon dioxide in the body
- shivering, which is important in maintaining body temperature

In addition, efferent output to skeletal muscles accomplishes many movements that are not aimed at maintaining a stable internal environment but nevertheless enrich our lives and enable us to engage in activities that contribute to society, such as dancing, building bridges, or performing surgery.

REVIEW EXERCISES

Objective Questions (Answers on p. A-42)

1. Sympathetic preganglionic fibers begin in the thoracic and lumbar segments of the spinal cord. (*True or false?*)
2. Action potentials are transmitted on a one-to-one basis at both a neuromuscular junction and a synapse. (*True or false?*)
3. The sympathetic nervous system
   a. is always excitatory.
   b. innervates only tissues concerned with protecting the body against challenges from the outside environment.
   c. has short preganglionic and long postganglionic fibers.
   d. is part of the afferent division of the PNS.
   e. is part of the somatic nervous system.
4. Acetylcholinesterase
   a. is stored in vesicles in the terminal button.
   b. combines with receptor-channels on the motor end plate to bring about an end-plate potential.
   c. is inhibited by organophosphates.
   d. is the chemical transmitter at the neuromuscular junction.
   e. paralyzes skeletal muscle by strongly binding with acetylcholine (ACh) receptor-channels.
5. The two divisions of the autonomic nervous system are the _____ nervous system, which dominates in "fight-or-flight" situations, and the _____ nervous system, which dominates in "rest-and-digest" situations.
6. The _____ is a modified sympathetic ganglion that does not give rise to postganglionic fibers but instead secretes hormones similar or identical to sympathetic postganglionic neurotransmitters into the blood.
7. Using the answer code on the right, identify the autonomic neurotransmitter being described:
   ____ 1. is secreted by all preganglionic fibers
   ____ 2. is secreted by sympathetic postganglionic fibers
   ____ 3. is secreted by parasympathetic postganglionic fibers
   ____ 4. is secreted by the adrenal medulla
   ____ 5. is secreted by motor neurons
   ____ 6. binds to muscarinic or nicotinic receptors
   ____ 7. binds to α or β receptors

   (a) acetylcholine
   (b) norepinephrine

8. Using the answer code on the right, indicate which type of efferent output is being described:

_____ 1. is composed of two-neuron chains
_____ 2. innervates cardiac muscle, smooth muscle, and glands
_____ 3. innervates skeletal muscle
_____ 4. consists of the axons of motor neurons
_____ 5. exerts either an excitatory or an inhibitory effect on its effector organs
_____ 6. dually innervates its effector organs
_____ 7. exerts only an excitatory effect on its effector organs

(a) characteristic of the somatic nervous system
(b) characteristic of the autonomic nervous system

Essay Questions

1. What is the advantage of dual innervation of many organs by both branches of the autonomic nervous system?
2. Distinguish among the following types of receptors: nicotinic receptors, muscarinic receptors, α_1 receptors, α_2 receptors, β_1 receptors, and β_2 receptors.
3. What regions of the CNS regulate autonomic output?
4. Describe the sequence of events that occurs at a neuromuscular junction.
5. Discuss the effect each of the following has at the neuromuscular junction: black widow spider venom, botulinum toxin, curare, myasthenia gravis, and organophosphates.

POINTS TO PONDER

(Explanations on p. A-42)

1. Explain why epinephrine, which causes arteriolar constriction (narrowing) in most tissues, is often administered in conjunction with local anesthetics.
2. Would skeletal muscle activity be affected by atropine (see p. 197)? Why or why not?
3. Considering that you can voluntarily control the emptying of your urinary bladder by contracting (preventing emptying) or relaxing (permitting emptying) your external urethral sphincter, a ring of muscle that guards the exit from the bladder, of what type of muscle is this sphincter composed and what branch of the nervous system supplies it?
4. The venom of certain poisonous snakes contains α-bungarotoxin, which binds tenaciously to ACh receptor sites on the motor end-plate membrane. What would the resultant symptoms be?
5. Explain how destruction of motor neurons by poliovirus or amyotrophic lateral sclerosis can be fatal.

CLINICAL CONSIDERATION

(Explanation on p. A-42)

Christopher K. experienced chest pains when he climbed the stairs to his fourth-floor office or played tennis but had no symptoms when not physically exerting himself. His condition was diagnosed as *angina pectoris* (*angina* means "pain"; *pectoris* means "chest"), heart pain that occurs whenever the blood supply to the heart muscle cannot meet the muscle's need for oxygen delivery. This condition usually is caused by narrowing of the blood vessels supplying the heart by cholesterol-containing deposits. Most people with this condition do not have any pain at rest but experience bouts of pain whenever the heart's need for oxygen increases, such as during exercise or emotionally stressful situations that increase sympathetic nervous activity. Christopher obtains immediate relief of angina attacks by promptly taking a vasodilator drug such as *nitroglycerin,* which relaxes the smooth muscle in the walls of his narrowed heart vessels. Consequently, the vessels open more widely and more blood can flow through them. For prolonged treatment, his doctor has indicated that Christopher will experience fewer and less severe angina attacks if he takes a β_1-blocker drug, such as *metoprolol,* regularly. Explain why.

Chapter 7

Autonomic Nervous System (pp. 191–197)

■ The CNS controls muscles and glands by transmitting signals to these effector organs through the efferent division of the PNS.

■ There are two types of efferent output: the autonomic nervous system, which is under involuntary control and supplies cardiac and smooth muscle—as well as most exocrine and some endocrine glands—and the somatic nervous system, which is subject to voluntary control and supplies skeletal muscle. (Review Tables 7-4, p. 187, and 7-5, p. 200.)

■ The autonomic nervous system consists of two subdivisions—the sympathetic and parasympathetic nervous systems. (Review Figures 7-2 and 7-3 and Tables 7-1 and 7-3.)

■ An autonomic nerve pathway consists of a two-neuron chain. The preganglionic fiber originates in the CNS and synapses with the cell body of the postganglionic fiber in a ganglion outside the CNS. The postganglionic fiber ends on the effector organ. (Review Figures 7-1 through 7-3 and Table 7-3.)

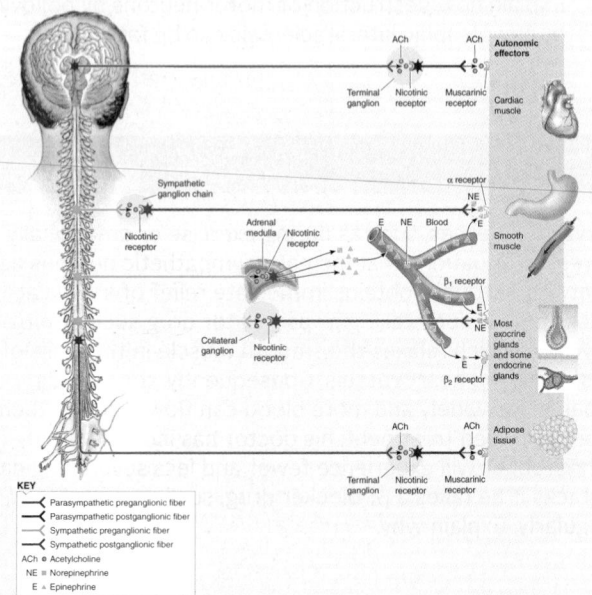

■ All preganglionic fibers and parasympathetic postganglionic fibers release acetylcholine (ACh). Sympathetic postganglionic fibers release norepinephrine. (Review Figure 7-2 and Table 7-3.)

■ Postganglionic fibers have numerous swellings, or varicosities, that simultaneously release neurotransmitter over a large area of the innervated organ. (Review Figures 7-1 and 8-26, p. 238.)

■ The adrenal medulla, an endocrine gland, is a modified sympathetic ganglion that secretes the hormones epinephrine and to a lesser extent norepinephrine into the blood in response to stimulation by the sympathetic preganglionic fiber that innervates it. (Review Figure 7-2.)

■ The same neurotransmitter elicits different responses in different tissues. Thus, the response depends on specialization of the tissue cells, not on the properties of the messenger. (Review Table 7-2.)

■ Tissues innervated by the autonomic nervous system possess one or more of several receptor types for the postganglionic chemical messengers (and for the related adrenomedullary hormone epinephrine). Cholinergic receptors include nicotinic and muscarinic receptors; adrenergic receptors include α_1, α_2, β_1, and β_2 receptors. (Review Figure 7-2 and Tables 7-2 and 7-3.)

■ A given autonomic fiber either excites or inhibits activity in the organ it innervates. (Review Tables 7-1 and 7-2.)

■ Most visceral organs are innervated by both sympathetic and parasympathetic fibers, which in general produce opposite effects in a particular organ. Dual innervation of organs by both branches of the autonomic nervous system permits precise control over an organ's activity. (Review Figure 7-3 and Table 7-1.)

■ The sympathetic system dominates in emergency or stressful ("fight-or-flight") situations and promotes responses that prepare the body for strenuous physical activity. The parasympathetic system dominates in quiet, relaxed ("rest-and-digest") situations and promotes body-maintenance activities such as digestion. (Review Tables 7-1 and 7-3.)

■ Visceral afferent input is used by the CNS to direct appropriate autonomic output to maintain homeostasis. Autonomic activities are controlled by multiple areas of the CNS, including the spinal cord, medulla, hypothalamus, and prefrontal association cortex.

▲ Table 7-2 Properties of Autonomic Receptor Types

Receptor Type	Neurotransmitter Affinity	Effector(s) with This Receptor Type	Effect on Effector
Nicotinic	ACh from autonomic preganglionic fibers	All autonomic postganglionic cell bodies and the adrenal medulla	Excitatory
	ACh from motor neurons	Motor end plates of skeletal muscle fibers	Excitatory
Muscarinic	ACh from parasympathetic postganglionic fibers	Cardiac muscle, smooth muscle, and most exocrine and some endocrine glands	Excitatory or inhibitory, depending on the effector
α_1	Greater affinity for norepinephrine (from sympathetic postganglionic fibers) than for epinephrine (from the adrenal medulla)	Most sympathetic target tissues	Excitatory
α_2	Greater affinity for norepinephrine than for epinephrine	Digestive organs	Inhibitory
β_1	Equal affinity for norepinephrine and for epinephrine	Heart	Excitatory
β_2	Affinity for epinephrine only	Smooth muscles of arterioles and bronchioles	Inhibitory

Somatic Nervous System (pp. 197–198)

■ The somatic nervous system consists of the axons of motor neurons, which originate in the spinal cord or brain stem and end on skeletal muscle. *(Review Figure 7-4 and Table 7-4.)*

■ ACh, the neurotransmitter released from a motor neuron, stimulates muscle contraction.

■ Motor neurons are the common pathway by which various regions of the CNS exert control over skeletal muscle activity. The areas of the CNS that influence skeletal muscle activity by acting through the motor neurons are the spinal cord, motor regions of the cortex, basal nuclei, cerebellum, and brain stem.

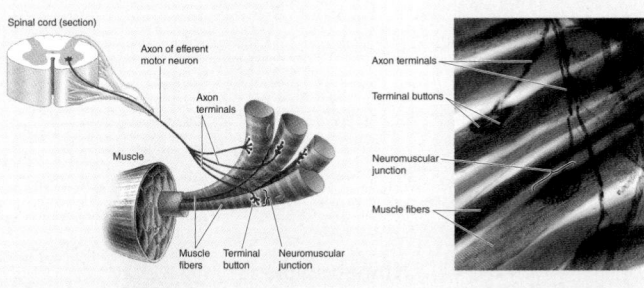

▲ Table 7-4 Comparison of the Autonomic Nervous System and the Somatic Nervous System

Feature	Autonomic Nervous System	Somatic Nervous System
Site of Origin	Brain or spinal cord	Spinal cord for most; those supplying muscles in the head originate in the brain
Number of Neurons from Origin in CNS to Effector Organ	Two-neuron chain (preganglionic and post-ganglionic)	Single neuron (motor neuron)
Organs Innervated	Cardiac muscle, smooth muscle, and glands	Skeletal muscle
Type of Innervation	Most effector organs dually innervated by the two antagonistic branches of this system (sympathetic and parasympathetic)	Effector organs innervated only by motor neurons
Neurotransmitter at Effector Organs	May be ACh (parasympathetic terminals) or norepinephrine (sympathetic terminals)	Only ACh
Effects on Effector Organs	Stimulation or inhibition (antagonistic actions of two branches)	Stimulation only (inhibition is possible only centrally through inhibitory postsynaptic potentials on dendrites and the cell body of the motor neuron)
Type of Control	Involuntary control	Voluntary control, although much activity is subconsciously coordinated
Higher Centers Involved in Control	Spinal cord, medulla, hypothalamus, and pre-frontal association cortex	Spinal cord, motor cortex, basal nuclei, cerebellum, and brain stem

Neuromuscular Junction (pp. 198–204)

■ When a motor neuron reaches a muscle, it branches into axon terminals. Each axon terminal forms a neuromuscular junction with a single muscle cell (fiber). The axon terminal splits into multiple fine branches, each of which ends in an enlarged terminal button. *(Review Figure 7-4 and Table 7-6.)*

■ The specialized region of the muscle cell membrane underlying the axon terminal complex is called the motor end plate. Because these structures do not make direct contact, signals are passed between a terminal button and a muscle fiber by chemical means. *(Review Figure 7-5.)*

■ An action potential in the axon terminal causes the release of ACh from its storage vesicles in the terminal button. The released ACh diffuses across the space separating the nerve and muscle cells and binds to special receptor-channels on the underlying motor end plate. This binding triggers the opening of these nonspecific cation channels. The subsequent ion movements depolarize the motor end plate, producing the end-plate potential (EPP). *(Review Figure 7-5.)*

■ Local current flow between the depolarized end plate and the adjacent muscle cell membrane brings these adjacent areas to threshold, initiating an action potential that is propagated throughout the muscle fiber. This muscle action potential triggers muscle contraction. *(Review Figure 7-5.)*

■ Membrane-bound acetylcholinesterase (AChE) in the motor end plate inactivates ACh, ending the EPP and, subsequently, the action potential and resultant contraction. *(Review Figure 7-5.)*

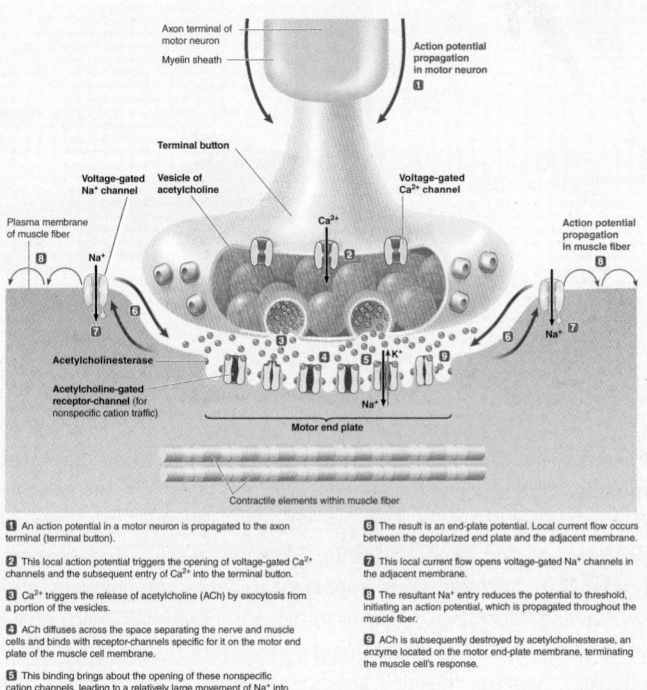

1 An action potential in a motor neuron is propagated to the axon terminal (terminal button).

2 This local action potential triggers the opening of voltage-gated Ca²⁺ channels and the subsequent entry of Ca²⁺ into the terminal button.

3 Ca²⁺ triggers the release of acetylcholine (ACh) by exocytosis from a portion of the vesicles.

4 ACh diffuses across the space separating the nerve and muscle cells and binds with receptor-channels specific for it on the motor end plate of the muscle cell membrane.

5 This binding brings about the opening of these nonspecific cation channels, leading to a relatively large movement of Na⁺ into the muscle cell compared to a smaller movement of K⁺ outward.

6 The result is an end-plate potential. Local current flow occurs between the depolarized end plate and the adjacent membrane.

7 This local current flow opens voltage-gated Na⁺ channels in the adjacent membrane.

8 The resultant Na⁺ entry reduces the potential to threshold, initiating an action potential, which is propagated throughout the muscle fiber.

9 ACh is subsequently destroyed by acetylcholinesterase, an enzyme located on the motor end-plate membrane, terminating the muscle cell's response.

Muscular System

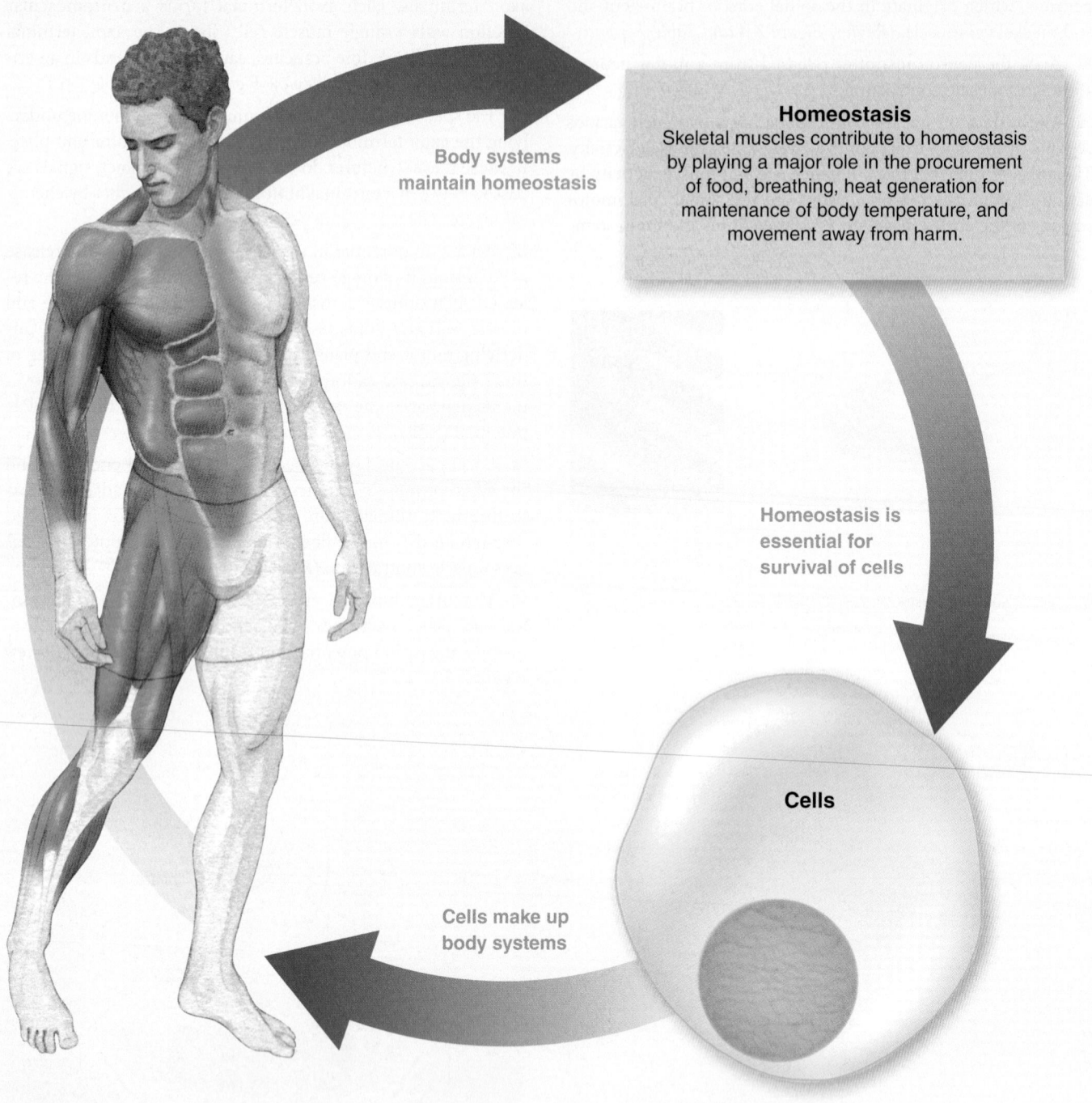

Body systems maintain homeostasis

Homeostasis
Skeletal muscles contribute to homeostasis by playing a major role in the procurement of food, breathing, heat generation for maintenance of body temperature, and movement away from harm.

Homeostasis is essential for survival of cells

Cells

Cells make up body systems

Muscles are the contraction specialists of the body. **Skeletal muscle** attaches to the skeleton. Contraction of skeletal muscles moves bones to which they are attached, allowing the body to perform various motor activities. Skeletal muscles that support homeostasis include those important in acquiring, chewing, and swallowing food and those essential for breathing. Also, heat-generating muscle contractions are important in regulating temperature. Skeletal muscles are further used to move the body away from harm. Finally, skeletal muscle contractions are impor-

tant for nonhomeostatic activities, such as dancing or operating a computer.

The body has two other muscle types. **Smooth muscle** is found in the walls of hollow organs and tubes. Controlled contraction of smooth muscle regulates movement of blood through blood vessels, food through the digestive tract, air through respiratory airways, and urine to the exterior. **Cardiac muscle** is found only in the walls of the heart, whose contraction pumps life-sustaining blood throughout the body.

Muscle Physiology

CHAPTER AT A GLANCE

Structure of Skeletal Muscle
Levels of organization in muscle
Thick- and thin-filament composition

Molecular Basis of Skeletal Muscle Contraction
Sliding filament mechanism
Excitation–contraction coupling

Skeletal Muscle Mechanics
Gradation of contraction: recruitment, summation, and length–tension relationship
Isotonic and isometric contractions
Load–velocity relationship

Skeletal Muscle Metabolism and Fiber Types
Pathways supplying ATP
Muscle fatigue
Excess postexercise oxygen consumption
Muscle fiber types

Control of Motor Movement
Inputs influencing motor-neuron output
Local reflexes, muscle spindles, and Golgi tendon organs

Smooth and Cardiac Muscle
Multiunit and single-unit smooth muscle
Myogenic activity
Factors modifying smooth muscle activity; gradation of smooth muscle contraction
Cardiac muscle

Structure of Skeletal Muscle

Muscle comprises the largest group of tissues in the body, accounting for approximately half of the body's weight. By moving specialized intracellular components, muscle cells can develop tension and shorten, that is, contract. Through their highly developed ability to contract, groups of muscle cells working together within a muscle can produce movement and do work. Controlled contraction of muscles allows (1) purposeful movement of the whole body or parts of the body (such as walking or waving your hand), (2) manipulation of external objects (such as driving a car or moving a piece of furniture), (3) propulsion of contents through hollow internal organs (such as circulation of blood or movement of a meal through the digestive tract), and (4) emptying the contents of certain organs to the external environment (such as urination or giving birth).

Recall that the three types of muscle are *skeletal, cardiac,* and *smooth* (see p. 3). Although these muscle types are structurally and functionally distinct, they can be classified in two ways according to common characteristics (● Figure 8-1). First, muscles are categorized as *striated* (skeletal and cardiac muscle) or *unstriated* (smooth muscle), depending on whether alternating dark and light bands, or striations (stripes), can be seen when the muscle is viewed under a light microscope. Second, muscles are categorized as *voluntary* (skeletal muscle) or *involuntary* (cardiac and smooth muscle), depending on whether they are innervated by the somatic nervous system and subject to voluntary control or are innervated by the autonomic nervous system and not subject to voluntary control, respectively (see p. 191). Although skeletal muscle is categorized as voluntary, because it can be consciously controlled, much skeletal muscle activity is also subject to subconscious, involuntary regulation, such as that related to posture, balance, and stereotypical movements like walking.

Most of this chapter is a detailed examination of the most abundant and best understood muscle, skeletal muscle. Skeletal muscles make up the muscular system. We begin with a discussion of skeletal muscle structure and then examine how it works from the molecular level, through the cell level, and finally to the whole muscle. The chapter concludes with a discussion of the unique properties of smooth and cardiac muscle in comparison to skeletal muscle. Smooth muscle appears throughout the body systems as a component of hollow organs and tubes. Cardiac muscle is found only in the heart.

Skeletal muscle fibers are striated by a highly organized internal arrangement.
A single skeletal muscle cell, known as a **muscle fiber,** is relatively large, elongated, and cylinder shaped. A skeletal muscle consists of a number of muscle fibers lying parallel to one another and bundled together by connective tissue (● Figure 8-2a). The fibers usually extend the entire length of the muscle.

A skeletal muscle fiber contains numerous **myofibrils,** which are cylindrical intracellular structures that extend the entire length of the muscle fiber (● Figure 8-2b). Myofibrils are specialized contractile elements that constitute 80% of the volume of the

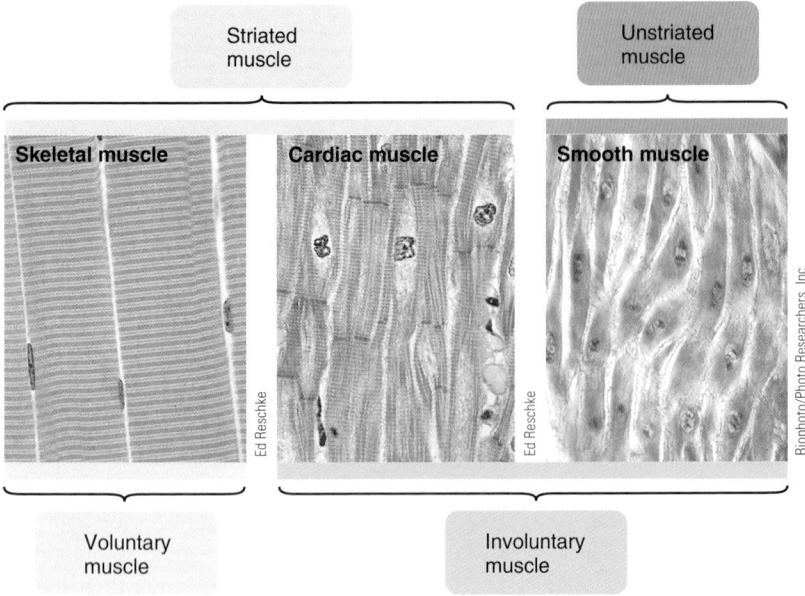

Striated muscle

Skeletal muscle   Cardiac muscle

Unstriated muscle

Smooth muscle

Ed Reschke   Ed Reschke   Biophoto/Photo Researchers, Inc.

Voluntary muscle

Involuntary muscle

● **FIGURE 8-1 Categorization of muscle.**

muscle fiber. Each myofibril consists of a regular arrangement of highly organized cytoskeletal elements—the thick and the thin filaments (● Figure 8-2c). The **thick filaments** are special assemblies of the protein *myosin,* whereas the thin filaments are made up primarily of the protein *actin* (● Figure 8-2d). The levels of organization in a skeletal muscle can be summarized as follows:

Whole muscle →	muscle fiber →	myofibril →	thick and thin filaments →	myosin and actin
(an organ)	(a cell)	(a specialized intracellular structure)	(cytoskeletal elements)	(protein molecules)

Viewed with an electron microscope, a myofibril displays alternating dark bands (the A bands) and light bands (the I bands) (● Figure 8-3a). The bands of all the myofibrils lined up parallel to one another collectively produce the striated or striped appearance of a skeletal muscle fiber visible under a light microscope (● Figure 8-3b). Alternate stacked sets of thick and thin filaments that slightly overlap one another are responsible for the A and I bands (see ● Figure 8-2c).

An **A band** is made up of a stacked set of thick filaments along with the portions of the thin filaments that overlap on both ends of the thick filaments. The thick filaments lie only within the A band and extend its entire width; that is, the two ends of the thick filaments within a stack define the outer limits of a given A band. The lighter area within the middle of the A band, where the thin filaments do not reach, is the **H zone.** Only the central portions of the thick filaments are found in this region. A system of supporting proteins holds the thick filaments together vertically within each stack. These proteins can be seen as the **M line,** which extends vertically down the middle of the A band.

An **I band** consists of the remaining portion of the thin filaments that do not project into the A band. Visible in the middle of each I band is a dense, vertical **Z line.** The area between two Z lines is called a **sarcomere,** which is the functional unit of skeletal muscle. A **functional unit** of any organ is the smallest component that can perform all functions of that organ. Accordingly, a sarcomere is the smallest component of a muscle fiber that can contract. The Z line is a flat, cytoskeletal disc that connects the thin filaments of two adjoining sarcomeres. Each relaxed sarcomere consists of one whole A band and half of each of the two I bands located on either side. An I band contains only thin filaments from two adjacent sarcomeres but not the entire length of these filaments.

With an electron microscope, fine **cross bridges** can be seen extending from each thick filament toward the surrounding thin filaments in the areas where the thick and thin filaments overlap (see ● Figure 8-2c). To give you an idea of the magnitude of these filaments, a single muscle fiber may contain an estimated 16 billion thick and 32 billion thin filaments, all arranged in a precise pattern within the myofibrils.

Not shown in the figure, single strands of a giant, highly elastic protein known as **titin** extend in both directions from the M line along the length of the thick filament to the Z lines at opposite ends of the sarcomere. Titin, the largest protein in the body, contributes extensively to a muscle's elasticity, the ability to spring back to its resting length after having been stretched.

Myosin forms the thick filaments.

Each thick filament has several hundred myosin molecules packed together in a specific arrangement. A **myosin** molecule is a protein consisting of two identical subunits, each shaped somewhat like a golf club (● Figure 8-4a). The protein's tail ends are intertwined around each other like golf-club shafts twisted together, with the two globular heads projecting out at one end. The two halves of each thick filament are mirror images made up of myosin molecules lying lengthwise in a regular, staggered array, with their tails oriented toward the center of the filament and their globular heads protruding outward at regular intervals (● Figure 8-4b). These heads form the cross bridges between thick and thin filaments. Each cross bridge has two sites crucial to the contractile process: (1) an actin binding site and (2) a myosin ATPase (ATP-splitting) site.

Actin is the main structural component of the thin filaments.

Thin filaments consist of three proteins: *actin, tropomyosin,* and *troponin* (● Figure 8-5). **Actin** molecules, the primary structural proteins of the thin filament, are spherical. The backbone of a thin filament is formed by actin molecules joined into two strands and twisted together, like two intertwined strings of pearls. Each actin molecule has a special binding site for attaching with a myosin cross bridge. By a mechanism to be described shortly, binding of myosin and actin at the cross bridges leads

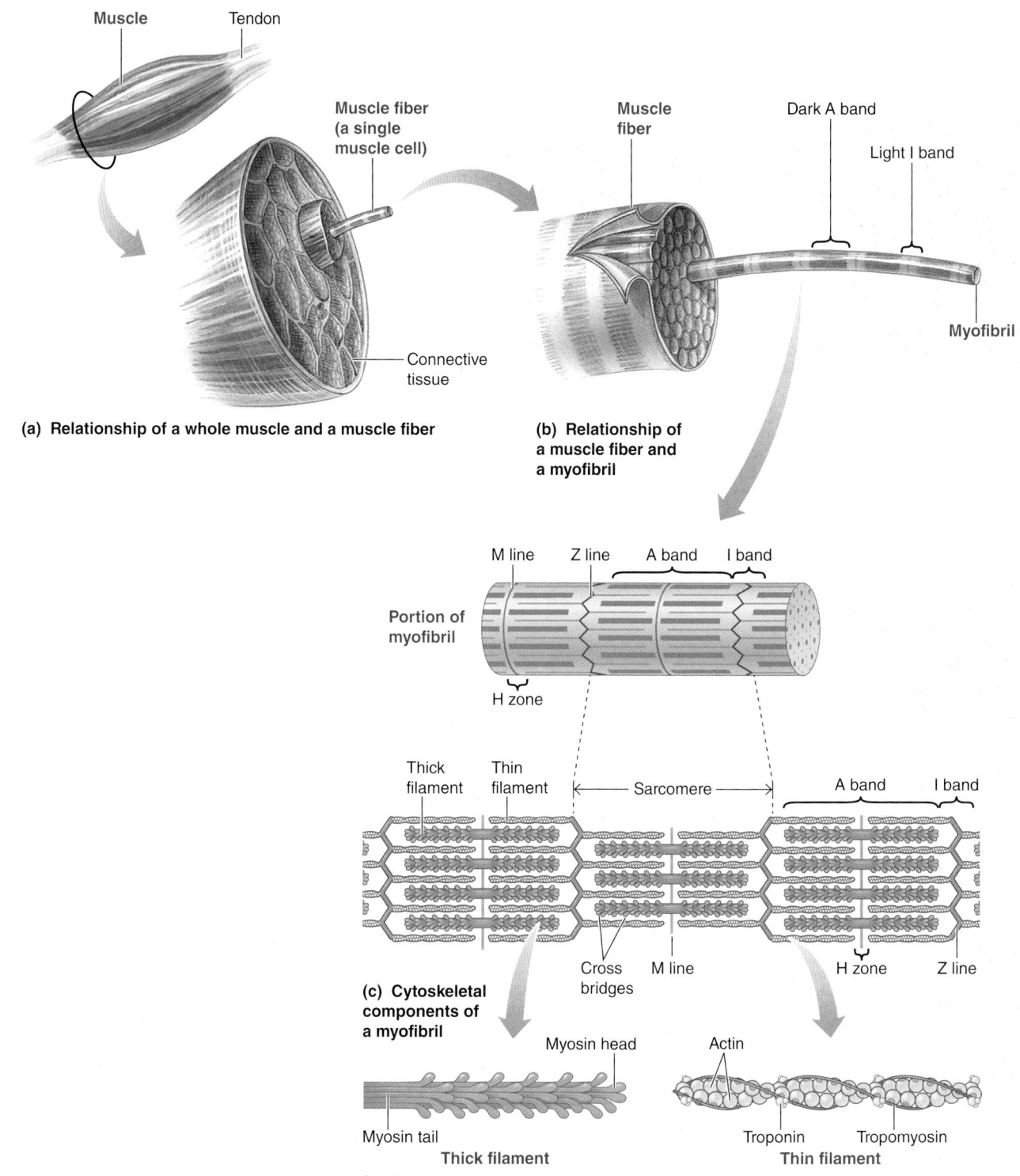

(a) Relationship of a whole muscle and a muscle fiber

(b) Relationship of a muscle fiber and a myofibril

(c) Cytoskeletal components of a myofibril

Thick filament

Thin filament

(d) Protein components of thick and thin filaments

● FIGURE 8-2 Levels of organization in a skeletal muscle.

to contraction of the muscle fiber. Myosin and actin are not unique to muscle cells, but these proteins are more abundant and more highly organized in muscle cells (see pp. 39–40).

In a relaxed muscle fiber, contraction does not take place; actin cannot bind with cross bridges because of the way the two other types of protein—tropomyosin and troponin—are positioned within the thin filament. **Tropomyosin** molecules are threadlike proteins that lie end to end alongside the groove of the actin spiral. In this position, tropomyosin covers the actin sites that bind with the cross bridges, blocking the interaction that leads to muscle contraction. The other thin-filament component, **troponin,** is a protein complex made of three subunits: one binds to tropomyosin, one binds to actin, and a third can bind with calcium (Ca^{2+}).

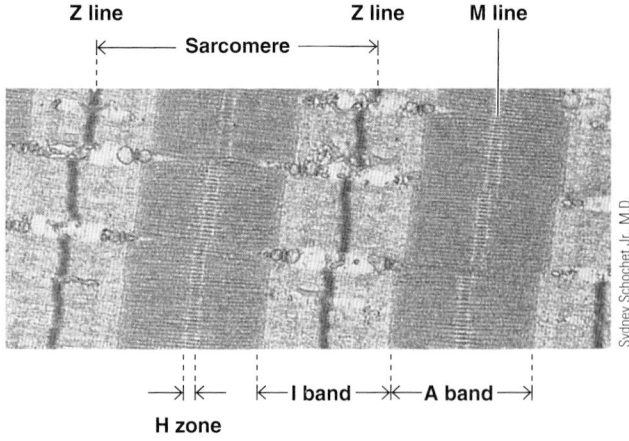

Z line   **Z line**   **M line**

←—— Sarcomere ——→

→|← →|← |←—I band—→|←—A band—→|

H zone

(a) Electron micrograph of a myofibril

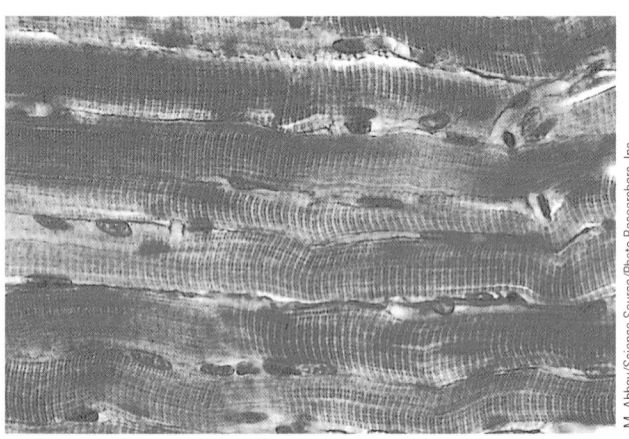

(b) Low-power light micrograph of skeletal muscle fibers

● **FIGURE 8-3 Microscope view of skeletal muscle components.** (a) Note the A and I bands. (b) Note the striated appearance.
Source: (a) Reprinted with permission from Sydney Schochet Jr., M.D., Professor, Department of Pathology, School of Medicine, West Virginia University, *Diagnostic Pathology of Skeletal Muscle and Nerve,* Fig. 1-13 (Stamford, CT: Appleton & Lange, 1986).

When troponin is not bound to Ca^{2+}, this protein stabilizes tropomyosin in its blocking position over actin's cross-bridge binding sites (● Figure 8-6a). When Ca^{2+} binds to troponin, the shape of this protein is changed in such a way that tropomyosin slips away from its blocking position (● Figure 8-6b). With tropomyosin out of the way, actin and myosin can bind and interact at the cross bridges, resulting in muscle contraction.

Molecular Basis of Skeletal Muscle Contraction

Several important links in the contractile process remain to be discussed. How does cross-bridge interaction between actin and myosin bring about muscle contraction? How does a muscle action potential trigger this contractile process? What is the source of the Ca^{2+} that physically repositions troponin and tropomyosin to permit cross-bridge binding? We turn our attention to these topics in this section.

During contraction, cycles of cross-bridge binding and bending pull the thin filaments inward.

Cross-bridge interaction between actin and myosin brings about muscle contraction by means of the sliding filament mechanism.

SLIDING FILAMENT MECHANISM The thin filaments on each side of a sarcomere slide inward over the stationary thick filaments toward the A band's center during contraction (● Figure 8-7). As they slide inward, the thin filaments pull the Z lines to which they are attached closer together, so the sarcomere shortens. As all sarcomeres throughout the muscle fiber's length shorten simultaneously, the entire fiber shortens. This is the **sliding fila-**

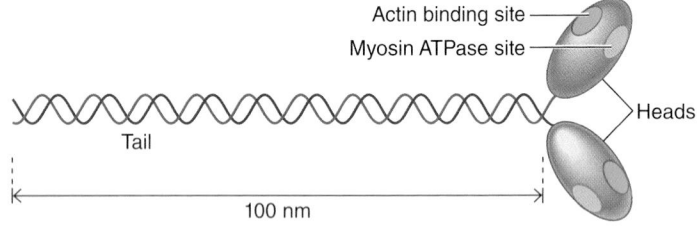

Actin binding site
Myosin ATPase site
Heads
Tail
100 nm

(a) Myosin molecule

● **FIGURE 8-4 Structure of myosin molecules and their organization within a thick filament.** (a) Each myosin molecule consists of two identical, golf-club–shaped subunits with their tails intertwined and their globular heads, each of which contains an actin binding site and a myosin ATPase site, projecting out at one end. (b) A thick filament is made up of myosin molecules lying lengthwise parallel to one another. Half are oriented in one direction, and half are in the opposite direction. The globular heads, which protrude at regular intervals along the thick filament, form the cross bridges.

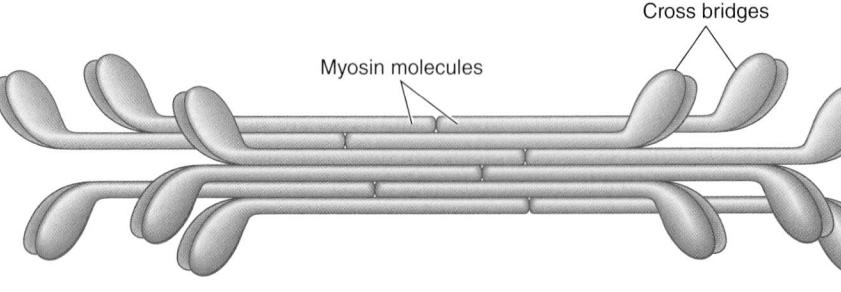

Cross bridges
Myosin molecules

(b) Thick filament

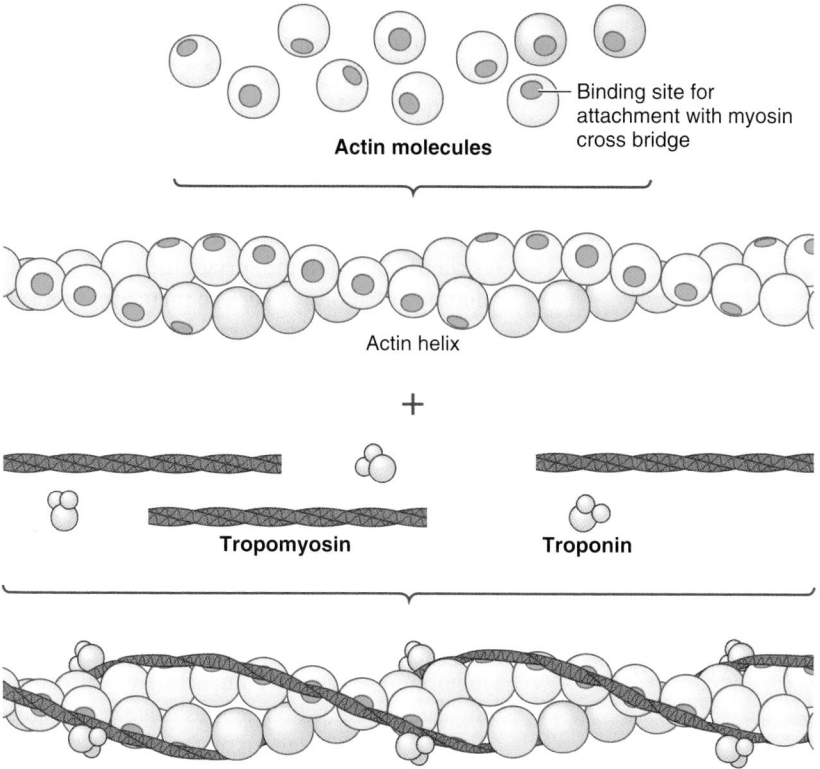

Actin molecules

Binding site for attachment with myosin cross bridge

Actin helix

+

Tropomyosin   Troponin

Thin filament

● **FIGURE 8-5 Composition of a thin filament.** The main structural component of a thin filament is two chains of spherical actin molecules that are twisted together. Troponin molecules (which consist of three small, spherical subunits) and threadlike tropomyosin molecules are arranged to form a ribbon that lies alongside the groove of the actin helix and physically covers the binding sites on actin molecules for attachment with myosin cross bridges. (The thin filaments shown here are not drawn in proportion to the thick filaments in Figure 8-4. Thick filaments are two to three times larger in diameter than thin filaments.)

ment mechanism of muscle contraction. The H zone, in the center of the A band where the thin filaments do not reach, becomes smaller as the thin filaments approach each other when they slide more deeply inward. The I band, which consists of the portions of the thin filaments that do not overlap with the thick filaments, narrows as the thin filaments further overlap the thick filaments during their inward slide. The thin filaments themselves do not change length during muscle fiber shortening. The width of the A band remains unchanged during contraction because its width is determined by the length of the thick filaments, and the thick filaments do not change length during the shortening process. Note that neither the thick nor the thin filaments decrease in length to shorten the sarcomere. Instead, contraction is accomplished by the thin filaments from the opposite sides of each sarcomere sliding closer together between the thick filaments.

POWER STROKE During contraction, with the troponin and tropomyosin "chaperones" pulled out of the way by Ca^{2+}, the myosin cross bridges from a thick filament can bind with the actin molecules in the surrounding thin filaments. Let us concentrate on a single cross-bridge interaction (● Figure 8-8a). The two myosin heads of each myosin molecule act independently, with only one head attaching to actin at a given time.

When myosin and actin make contact at a cross bridge, the bridge changes shape, bending inward as if it were on a hinge and "stroking" toward the center of the sarcomere, like the stroking of a boat oar. This **power stroke** of a cross bridge pulls inward the thin filament to which it is attached. A single power stroke pulls the thin filament inward only a small percentage of the total shortening distance. Repeated cycles of cross-bridge binding and bending complete the shortening.

At the end of one cross-bridge cycle, the link between the myosin cross bridge and the actin molecule breaks. The cross bridge returns to its original shape and binds to the next actin molecule behind its previous actin partner. The cross bridge bends again to pull the thin filament in farther and then detaches and repeats the cycle. Repeated cycles of cross-bridge power strokes successively pull in the thin filaments, much like pulling in a rope hand over hand.

Because of the way myosin molecules are oriented within a thick filament (● Figure 8-8b), all cross bridges stroke toward the center of the sarcomere so that all surrounding thin filaments on each end of the sarcomere are pulled inward simultaneously. The cross bridges do not all stroke in unison, however. At any time during contraction, part of the cross bridges are attached to the thin filaments and are stroking while others are returning to their original conformation in preparation for binding with another actin molecule. Thus, some cross bridges are "holding on" to the thin filaments, whereas others "let go" to bind with new actin. Were it not for this asynchronous cycling of the cross bridges, the thin filaments would slip back toward their resting position between strokes.

How does muscle excitation switch on this cross-bridge cycling? The term **excitation–contraction coupling** refers to the series of events linking muscle excitation (the presence of an action potential in a muscle fiber) to muscle contraction (cross-bridge activity that causes the thin filaments to slide closer together to produce sarcomere shortening). We now turn to excitation–contraction coupling.

Ca^{2+} is the link between excitation and contraction.

Skeletal muscles are stimulated to contract by release of acetylcholine (ACh) at neuromuscular junctions between motorneuron terminal buttons and muscle fibers. Recall that binding of ACh with the motor end plate of a muscle fiber brings about permeability changes in the muscle fiber, resulting in an action potential that is conducted over the entire surface of the muscle cell membrane (see p. 199). Two membranous structures within the muscle fiber play an important role in linking this excitation to contraction—*transverse tubules* and the *sarcoplasmic reticulum*. Let us examine the structure and function of each.

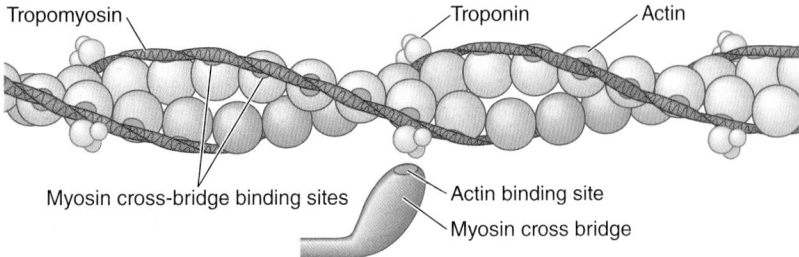

Tropomyosin — Troponin — Actin

Myosin cross-bridge binding sites — Actin binding site — Myosin cross bridge

(a) Relaxed

1 No excitation.

2 No cross-bridge binding because cross-bridge binding site on actin is physically covered by troponin–tropomyosin complex.

3 Muscle fiber is relaxed.

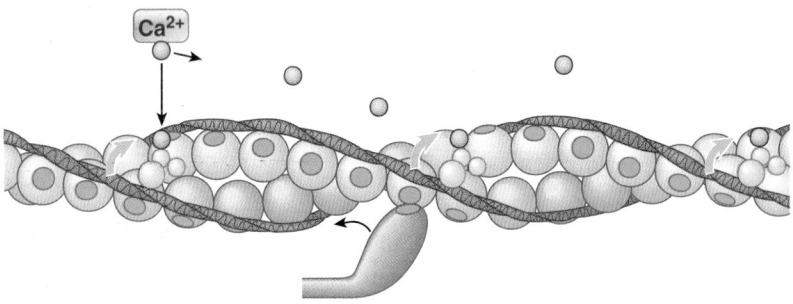

Ca^{2+}

(b) Excited

1 Muscle fiber is excited and Ca^{2+} is released.

2 Released Ca^{2+} binds with troponin, pulling troponin–tropomyosin complex aside to expose cross-bridge binding site.

3 Cross-bridge binding occurs.

4 Binding of actin and myosin cross bridge triggers power stroke that pulls thin filament inward during contraction.

● **FIGURE 8-6 Role of calcium in turning on cross bridges.**

SPREAD OF THE ACTION POTENTIAL DOWN THE TRANSVERSE TUBULES At each junction of an A band and I band, the surface membrane dips into the muscle fiber to form a **transverse tubule (T tubule),** which runs perpendicularly from the surface of the muscle cell membrane into the central portions of the muscle fiber (● Figure 8-9). Because the T tubule membrane is continuous with the surface membrane, an action potential on the surface membrane spreads down into the T tubule, rapidly transmitting the surface electrical activity into the interior of the fiber. The presence of a local action potential in the T tubules leads to permeability changes in a separate membranous network within the muscle fiber, the sarcoplasmic reticulum.

RELEASE OF Ca^{2+} FROM THE SARCOPLASMIC RETICULUM The **sarcoplasmic reticulum** is a modified endoplasmic reticulum (see p. 24) that consists of a fine network of interconnected membrane-enclosed compartments surrounding each myofibril like a mesh sleeve (● Figure 8-9). This membranous network encircles the myofibril throughout its length but is not continuous. Separate segments of sarcoplasmic reticulum are wrapped around each A band and each I band. The ends of each segment expand to form saclike regions, the **lateral sacs,** which are separated from the adjacent T tubules by a slight gap. The lateral sacs store Ca^{2+}. Spread of an action potential down a T tubule triggers the opening of Ca^{2+}-release channels in the adjacent lateral sacs on each side. Ca^{2+} is released into the cytosol from the lateral sacs through all these open Ca^{2+}-release channels. By slightly

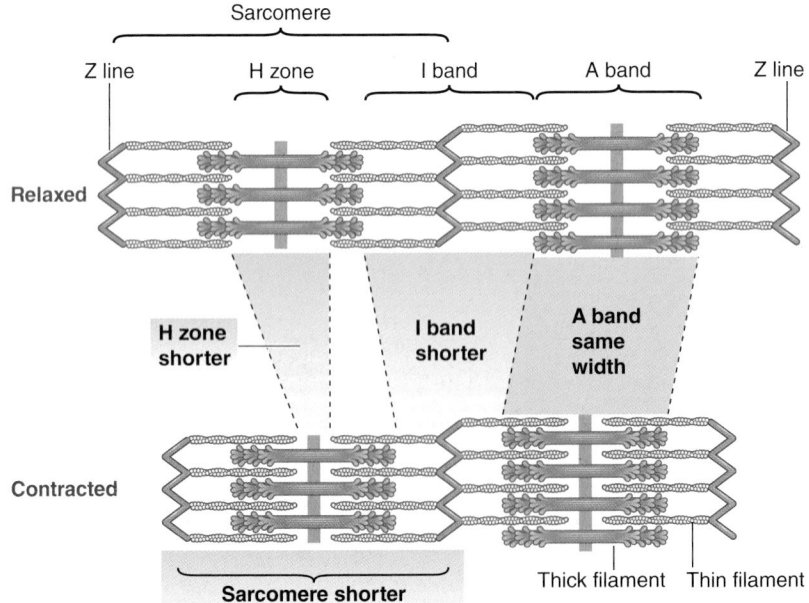

● **FIGURE 8-7 Changes in banding pattern during shortening.** During muscle contraction, each sarcomere shortens as the thin filaments slide closer together between the thick filaments so that the Z lines are pulled closer together. The width of the A bands does not change as a muscle fiber shortens, but the I bands and H zones become shorter.

Actin molecules in thin myofilament

1 Binding: Myosin cross bridge binds to actin molecule.

Myosin cross bridge

Z line

2 Power stroke: Cross bridge bends, pulling thin myofilament inward.

3 Detachment: Cross bridge detaches at end of power stroke and returns to original conformation.

4 Binding: Cross bridge binds to more distal actin molecule; cycle repeats.

(a) Single cross-bridge cycle

(b) All cross-bridge stroking directed toward center of thick filament

● **FIGURE 8-8 Cross-bridge activity.** (a) During each cross-bridge cycle, the cross bridge binds with an actin molecule, bends to pull the thin filament inward during the power stroke, and then detaches and returns to its resting conformation, ready to repeat the cycle. (b) The power strokes of all cross bridges extending from a thick filament are directed toward the center of the thick filament.

repositioning the troponin and tropomyosin molecules, this released Ca^{2+} exposes the binding sites on the actin molecules so that they can link with the myosin cross bridges at their complementary binding sites. Excitation–contraction coupling is summarized in ● Figure 8-10.

ATP-POWERED CROSS-BRIDGE CYCLING Recall that a myosin cross bridge has two special sites, an actin binding site and an ATPase site (see ● Figure 8-4a). The latter is an enzymatic site that can bind the energy carrier *adenosine triphosphate (ATP)* and split it into *adenosine diphosphate (ADP)* and *inorganic phosphate (P_i)*, yielding energy in the process. The breakdown of ATP occurs on the myosin cross bridge before the bridge ever links with an actin molecule (● Figure 8-11, step **1**). The ADP and P_i remain tightly bound to the myosin, and the generated energy is stored within the cross bridge to produce a high-energy form of myosin. To use an analogy, the cross bridge is "cocked" like a gun, ready to be fired when the trigger is pulled. When the muscle fiber is excited, Ca^{2+} pulls the troponin–tropomyosin complex out of its blocking position so that the energized (cocked) myosin cross bridge can bind with an actin molecule (step **2a**). This contact between myosin and actin "pulls the trigger," causing the cross-bridge bending that produces the power stroke (step **3**). Researchers have not found the mechanism by which the chemical energy released

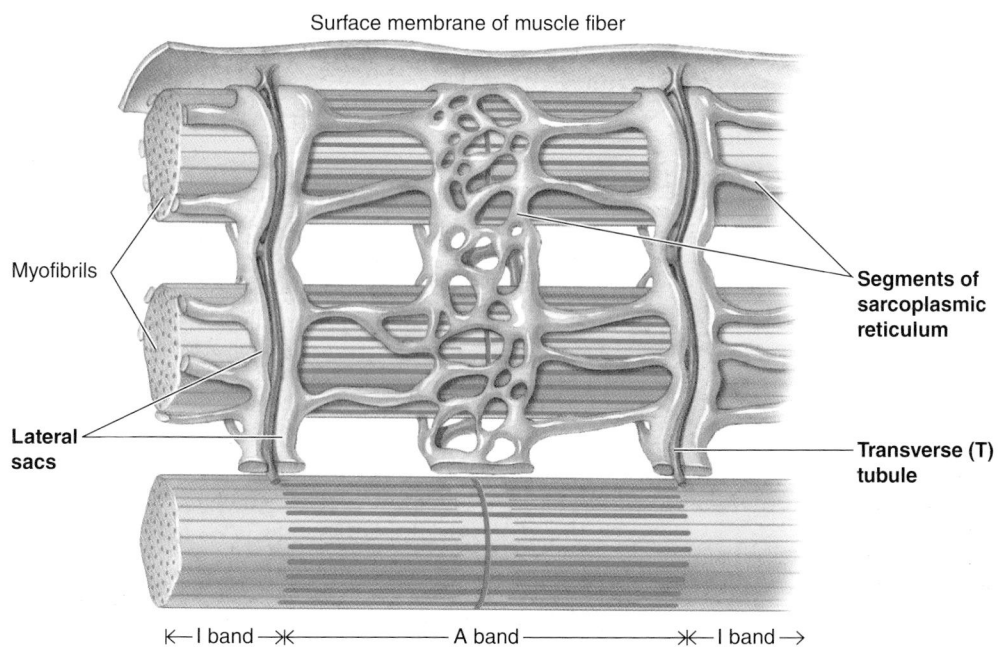

Surface membrane of muscle fiber

Myofibrils

Lateral sacs

Segments of sarcoplasmic reticulum

Transverse (T) tubule

←I band→ ←————A band————→ ←I band→

● **FIGURE 8-9 The transverse (T) tubules and sarcoplasmic reticulum in relationship to the myofibrils.** The T tubules are membranous, perpendicular extensions of the surface membrane that dip deep into the muscle fiber at the junctions between the A and the I bands of the myofibrils. The sarcoplasmic reticulum is a fine, membranous network that runs longitudinally and surrounds each myofibril, with separate segments encircling each A band and I band. The ends of each segment are expanded to form lateral sacs that lie next to the adjacent T tubules.

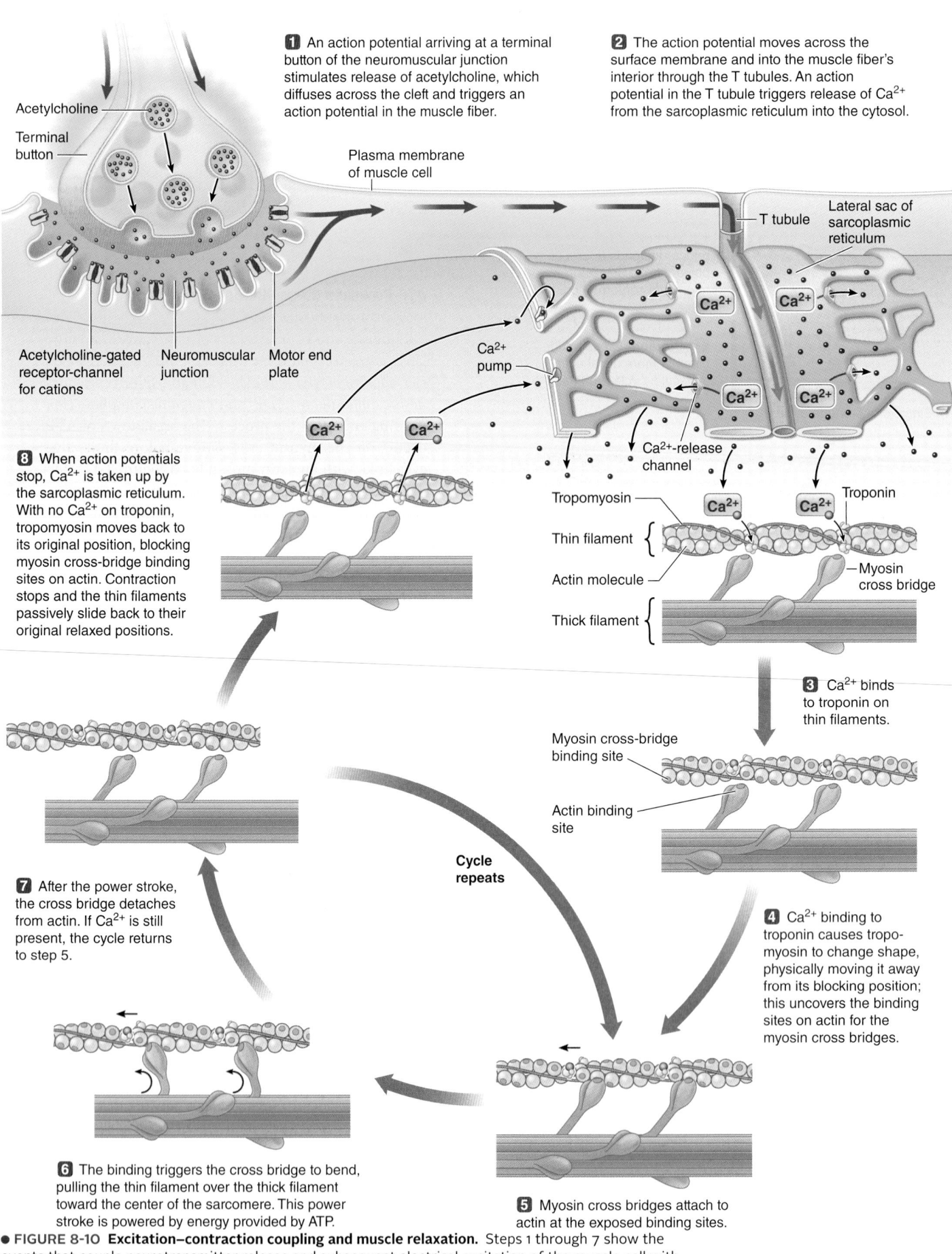

1 An action potential arriving at a terminal button of the neuromuscular junction stimulates release of acetylcholine, which diffuses across the cleft and triggers an action potential in the muscle fiber.

2 The action potential moves across the surface membrane and into the muscle fiber's interior through the T tubules. An action potential in the T tubule triggers release of Ca^{2+} from the sarcoplasmic reticulum into the cytosol.

Acetylcholine

Terminal button

Plasma membrane of muscle cell

T tubule

Lateral sac of sarcoplasmic reticulum

Acetylcholine-gated receptor-channel for cations

Neuromuscular junction

Motor end plate

Ca^{2+} pump

Ca^{2+}

Ca^{2+}

Ca^{2+}

Ca^{2+}

Ca^{2+}

Ca^{2+}-release channel

8 When action potentials stop, Ca^{2+} is taken up by the sarcoplasmic reticulum. With no Ca^{2+} on troponin, tropomyosin moves back to its original position, blocking myosin cross-bridge binding sites on actin. Contraction stops and the thin filaments passively slide back to their original relaxed positions.

Ca^{2+}

Ca^{2+}

Tropomyosin

Thin filament

Actin molecule

Thick filament

Ca^{2+}

Ca^{2+}

Troponin

Myosin cross bridge

3 Ca^{2+} binds to troponin on thin filaments.

Myosin cross-bridge binding site

Actin binding site

Cycle repeats

7 After the power stroke, the cross bridge detaches from actin. If Ca^{2+} is still present, the cycle returns to step 5.

4 Ca^{2+} binding to troponin causes tropomyosin to change shape, physically moving it away from its blocking position; this uncovers the binding sites on actin for the myosin cross bridges.

6 The binding triggers the cross bridge to bend, pulling the thin filament over the thick filament toward the center of the sarcomere. This power stroke is powered by energy provided by ATP.

5 Myosin cross bridges attach to actin at the exposed binding sites.

● **FIGURE 8-10 Excitation–contraction coupling and muscle relaxation.** Steps 1 through 7 show the events that couple neurotransmitter release and subsequent electrical excitation of the muscle cell with muscle contraction. At step 7, if calcium (Ca^{2+}) is still present, the cross-bridge cycle returns to step 5 for another power stroke. If Ca^{2+} is no longer present as a consequence of step 8, relaxation occurs.

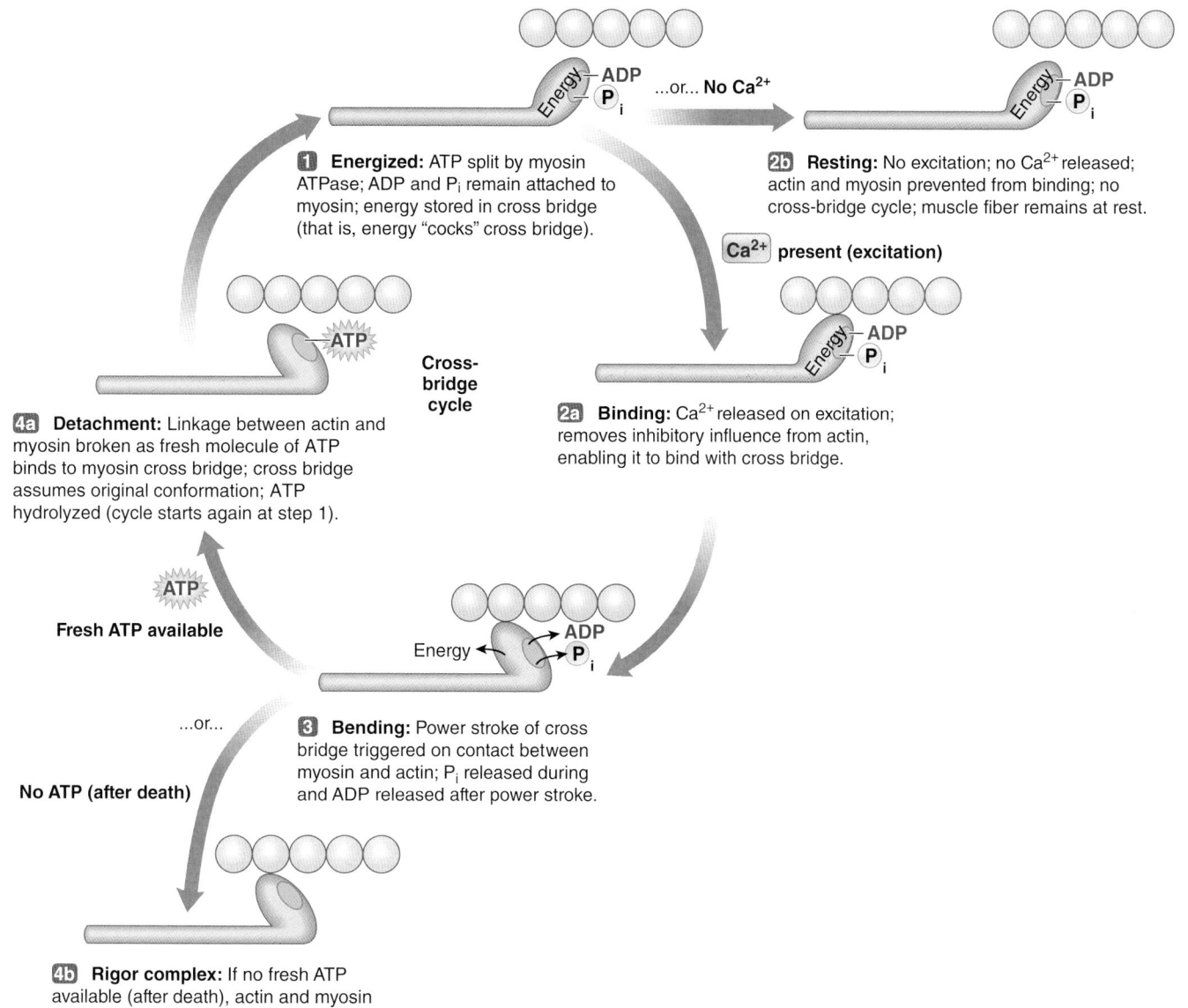

1 **Energized:** ATP split by myosin ATPase; ADP and P_i remain attached to myosin; energy stored in cross bridge (that is, energy "cocks" cross bridge).

...or... **No Ca^{2+}**

2b **Resting:** No excitation; no Ca^{2+} released; actin and myosin prevented from binding; no cross-bridge cycle; muscle fiber remains at rest.

Ca^{2+} **present (excitation)**

Cross-bridge cycle

4a **Detachment:** Linkage between actin and myosin broken as fresh molecule of ATP binds to myosin cross bridge; cross bridge assumes original conformation; ATP hydrolyzed (cycle starts again at step 1).

2a **Binding:** Ca^{2+} released on excitation; removes inhibitory influence from actin, enabling it to bind with cross bridge.

Fresh ATP available

...or...

No ATP (after death)

3 **Bending:** Power stroke of cross bridge triggered on contact between myosin and actin; P_i released during and ADP released after power stroke.

4b **Rigor complex:** If no fresh ATP available (after death), actin and myosin remain bound in rigor complex.

● FIGURE 8-11 **Cross-bridge cycle.**

from ATP is stored within the myosin cross bridge and then translated into the mechanical energy of the power stroke. P_i is released from the cross bridge during the power stroke. After the power stroke is complete, ADP is released.

When the muscle is not excited and Ca^{2+} is not released, troponin and tropomyosin remain in their blocking position so that actin and the myosin cross bridges do not bind and no power stroking takes place (step **2b**).

When P_i and ADP are released from myosin following contact with actin and the subsequent power stroke, the myosin ATPase site is free for attachment of another ATP molecule. The actin and myosin remain linked at the cross bridge until a fresh molecule of ATP attaches to myosin at the end of the power stroke. Attachment of the new ATP molecule permits detachment of the cross bridge, which returns to its unbent form, ready to start another cycle (step **4a**). The newly attached ATP is then split by myosin ATPase, energizing the myosin cross bridge again (step **1**). On binding with another actin molecule,

the energized cross bridge again bends, and so on, successively pulling the thin filament inward to accomplish contraction.

Clinical Note **RIGOR MORTIS** Note that fresh ATP must attach to myosin to permit the cross-bridge link between myosin and actin to break at the end of a cycle, even though the ATP is not split during this dissociation process. The need for ATP in separating myosin and actin is amply shown in **rigor mortis.** This "stiffness of death" is a generalized locking in place of the skeletal muscles that begins 3 to 4 hours after death and completes in about 12 hours. Following death, the cytosolic concentration of Ca^{2+} begins to rise, most likely because the inactive muscle cell membrane cannot keep out extracellular Ca^{2+} and perhaps because Ca^{2+} leaks out of the lateral sacs. This Ca^{2+} moves troponin and tropomyosin aside, letting actin bind with the myosin cross bridges, which were already charged with ATP before death. Dead cells cannot produce any more ATP, so actin and myosin, once bound, cannot detach, because they lack fresh ATP. The thick and thin filaments thus stay linked by the immobilized cross bridges, leaving dead muscles stiff (● Figure 8-11, step **4b**). During the next several days, rigor mortis gradually subsides as the proteins involved in the rigor complex begin to degrade.

RELAXATION How is relaxation normally accomplished in a living muscle? Just as an action potential in a muscle fiber turns on the contractile process by triggering release of Ca^{2+} from the lateral sacs into the cytosol, the contractile process is turned off and **relaxation** occurs when Ca^{2+} is returned to the lateral sacs when local electrical activity stops. The sarcoplasmic reticulum has an energy-consuming carrier, a Ca^{2+}-ATPase pump, which actively transports Ca^{2+} from the cytosol and concentrates it in the lateral sacs (see ● Figure 8-10). Recall that the end-plate potential and resultant muscle-fiber action potential stop when the membrane-bound enzyme acetylcholinesterase removes ACh from the neuromuscular junction (see p. 200). When a local action potential is no longer in the T tubules to trigger release of Ca^{2+}, the ongoing activity of the Ca^{2+} pump returns released Ca^{2+} back into the lateral sacs. Removing cytosolic Ca^{2+} lets the troponin–tropomyosin complex slip back into its blocking position, so actin and myosin can no longer bind at the cross bridges. The thin filaments, freed from cycles of cross-bridge attachment and pulling, return passively to their resting position. The muscle fiber has relaxed.

How long does the contractile activity initiated by an action potential last in response to a single action potential before relaxation occurs?

Contractile activity far outlasts the electrical activity that initiated it.

A single action potential in a skeletal muscle fiber lasts only 1 to 2 msec. The onset of the resulting contractile response lags behind the action potential because the entire excitation–contraction coupling must occur before cross-bridge activity begins. In fact, the action potential is over before the contractile apparatus even becomes operational (● Figure 8-12).

Time is also needed for generating tension within the muscle fiber by means of the sliding interactions between the thick and the thin filaments through cross-bridge activity. The time from contraction onset until peak tension develops—**contraction time**—averages about 50 msec, although this time varies depending on the type of muscle fiber. The contractile response does not end until the lateral sacs have taken up all Ca^{2+} released in response to the action potential. This reuptake of Ca^{2+} is also time-consuming. Even after Ca^{2+} is removed, it takes time for the filaments to return to their resting positions. The time from peak tension until relaxation is complete—the **relaxation time**—usually lasts another 50 msec or more. Consequently, the entire contractile response to a single action potential may last 100 msec or more; this is much longer than the duration of the action potential that initiated it (100 msec compared to 1 to 2 msec). This fact is important in the body's ability to produce muscle contractions of variable strength, as you will discover in the next section.

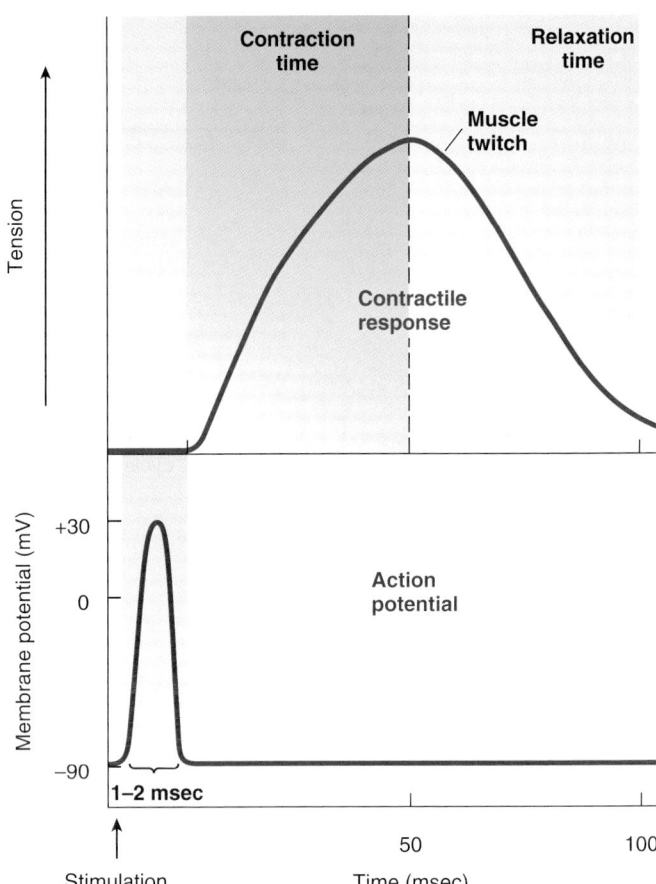

● FIGURE 8-12 **Relationship of an action potential to the resultant muscle twitch.** The duration of the action potential is not drawn to scale but is exaggerated. Note that the resting potential of a skeletal muscle fiber is –90 millivolts (mV), compared to a resting potential of –70 mV in a neuron.

Skeletal Muscle Mechanics

Thus far, we have described the contractile response in a single muscle fiber. In the body, groups of muscle fibers are organized into whole muscles. We now turn to the contraction of whole muscles.

Whole muscles are groups of muscle fibers bundled together and attached to bones.

Each person has about 600 skeletal muscles, which range in size from the delicate external eye muscles that control eye movements and contain only a few hundred fibers to the large, powerful leg muscles that contain several hundred thousand fibers.

Each muscle is sheathed by connective tissue that penetrates from the surface into the muscle to envelop each individual fiber and divide the muscle into columns or bundles. The connective tissue extends beyond the ends of the muscle to form tough, collagenous **tendons** that attach the muscle to bones. A tendon may be quite long, attaching to a bone some distance from the fleshy part of the muscle. For example, some of the muscles involved in finger movement are in the forearm, with long tendons extending down to attach to the bones of the fingers. (You can readily see these tendons move on the top of your hand when you wiggle your fingers.) This arrangement permits greater dexterity; the fingers would be thicker and more awkward if all the muscles used in finger movement were actually in the fingers.

Muscle tension is transmitted to bone as the contractile component tightens the series-elastic component.

Tension is produced internally within the sarcomeres, considered the **contractile component** of the muscle, as a result of cross-bridge activity and thus the sliding of filaments. However, the sarcomeres are not attached directly to the bones. Instead, the tension generated by these contractile elements must be transmitted to the bone via the connective tissue and tendons before the bone can be moved. Connective tissue and tendon, as well as the intracellular titin, have a certain degree of passive elasticity. These noncontractile tissues are called the **series-elastic component** of the muscle; they behave like a stretchy spring placed between the internal tension-generating elements and the bone that is to be moved against an external load (● Figure 8-13). Shortening of the sarcomeres stretches the series-elastic component. Muscle tension is transmitted to the bone by this tightening of the series-elastic component. This force applied to the bone moves the bone against a load. By mechanisms to be described shortly, the amount of tension generated by a muscle can be graded or of varying strengths. In other words, you can vary the force you exert by the same muscle, depending on whether you are picking up a piece of paper, a book, or a 50-pound weight.

A muscle is typically attached to at least two bones across a joint by means of tendons that extend from each end of the muscle. When the muscle shortens during contraction, the position of the joint is changed as one bone is moved in relation to the other—for example, *flexion* (bending) of the elbow joint by contraction of the biceps muscle and *extension* (straightening) of the elbow by contraction of the triceps (● Figure 8-14). The end of the muscle attached to the more stationary part of the skeleton is called the **origin,** and the end attached to the skeletal part that moves is the **insertion.**

The two primary types of contraction are isotonic and isometric.

Not all muscle contractions shorten muscles and move bones. For a muscle to shorten during contraction, the tension developed in the muscle must exceed the forces that oppose movement of the bone to which the muscle's insertion is attached. In the case of elbow flexion, the opposing force, or **load,** is the weight of an object being lifted. When you flex your elbow without lifting any external object, there is still a load, albeit a minimal one—the weight of your forearm being moved against the force of gravity.

There are two primary types of contraction, depending on whether the muscle changes length during contraction. In an **isotonic contraction,**

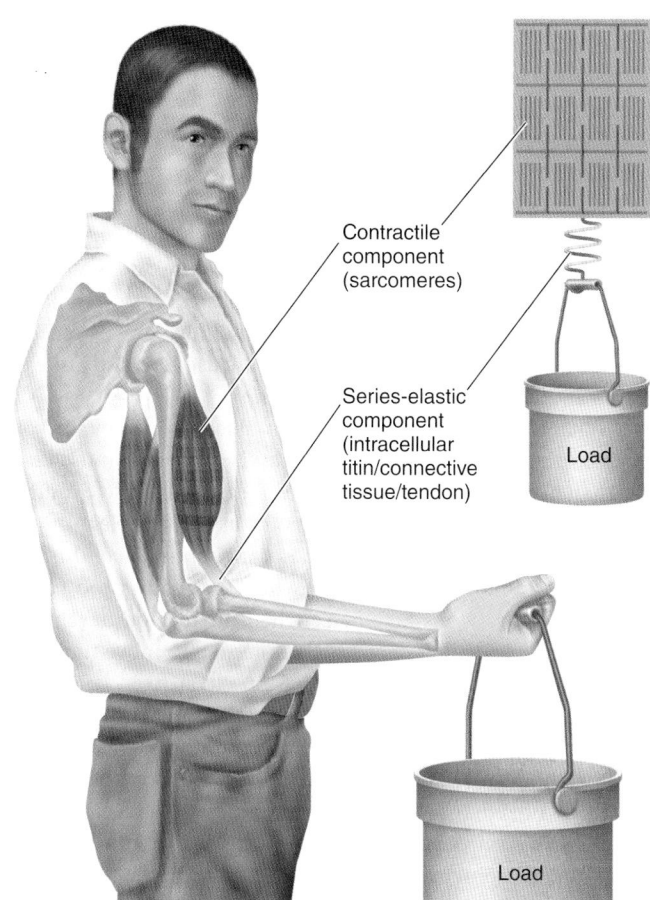

● **FIGURE 8-13 Relationship between the contractile component and the series-elastic component in transmitting muscle tension to bone.** Muscle tension is transmitted to the bone by means of the stretching and tightening of the muscle's intracellular titin, elastic connective tissue, and tendon (collectively the series-elastic component) as a result of sarcomere shortening brought about by cross-bridge cycling (the contractile component).

muscle tension remains constant as the muscle changes length (*isotonic* means "constant tension"). In an **isometric contraction,** the muscle is prevented from shortening, so tension develops at constant muscle length (*isometric* means "constant length"). The same internal events occur in both isotonic and isometric contractions: Muscle excitation turns on the tension-

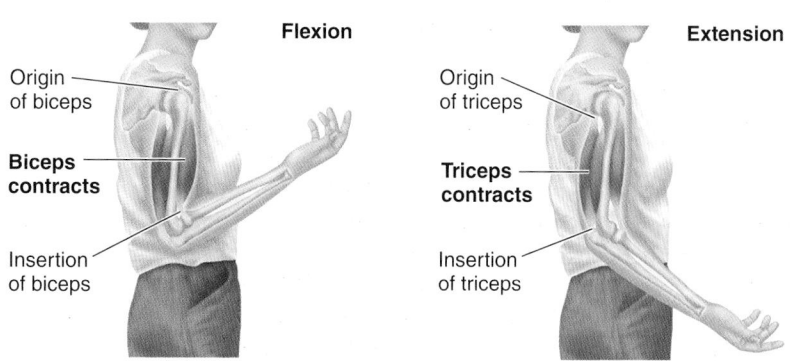

● **FIGURE 8-14 Flexion and extension of the elbow joint.**

generating contractile process, the cross bridges start cycling, and filament sliding shortens the sarcomeres, which stretches the series-elastic component to exert force on the bone at the site of the muscle's insertion.

Considering your biceps as an example, assume you are going to lift an object. When the tension developing in your biceps becomes great enough to overcome the weight of the object in your hand, you can lift the object, with the whole muscle shortening in the process. Because the weight of the object does not change as it is lifted, the muscle tension remains constant throughout the period of shortening. This is an *isotonic contraction*. Isotonic contractions are used for body movements and for moving external objects.

What happens if you try to lift an object too heavy for you (that is, if the tension you can develop in your arm muscles is less than needed to lift the load)? In this case, the muscle cannot shorten and lift the object but remains at constant length despite the development of tension, so an *isometric contraction* occurs. In addition to occurring when the load is too great, isometric contractions take place when the tension developed in the muscle is deliberately less than needed to move the load. In this case, the goal is to keep the muscle at fixed length although it can develop more tension. These submaximal isometric contractions are important for maintaining posture (such as keeping the legs straight while standing) and for supporting objects in a fixed position (such as holding a beverage between sips). During a given movement, a muscle may shift between isotonic and isometric contractions. For example, when you pick up a book to read, your biceps muscle undergoes an isotonic contraction while you are lifting the book, but the contraction becomes isometric as you stop to hold the book in front of you.

CONCENTRIC AND ECCENTRIC ISOTONIC CONTRACTIONS There are actually two types of isotonic contraction—*concentric* and *eccentric*. In both, the muscle changes length at constant tension. With **concentric contractions,** however, the muscle shortens, whereas with **eccentric contractions** the muscle lengthens because it is being stretched by an external force while contracting. With an eccentric contraction, the contractile activity is resisting the stretch. An example is lowering a load to the ground. During this action, the muscle fibers in the biceps are lengthening but are still contracting in opposition to being stretched. This tension supports the weight of the object.

OTHER CONTRACTIONS The body is not limited to pure isotonic and isometric contractions. Muscle length and tension often vary throughout a range of motion. Think about pulling back a bow and arrow. The tension of your biceps muscle continuously increases to overcome the progressively increasing resistance as you stretch the bow. At the same time, the muscle progressively shortens as you draw the bow farther back. Such a contraction occurs at neither constant tension nor constant length.

Some skeletal muscles do not attach to bones at both ends but still produce movement. For example, the tongue muscles are not attached at the free end. Isotonic contractions of the tongue muscles maneuver the free, unattached portion of the tongue to facilitate speech and eating. A few skeletal muscles are completely unattached to bone and actually prevent movement. These are the voluntarily controlled rings of skeletal muscles, known as **sphincters,** that guard the exit of urine and feces from the body by isotonically contracting.

The velocity of shortening is related to the load.

The load is also an important determinant of the **velocity,** or speed, of shortening. During a concentric contraction, the greater the load, the lower the velocity at which a single muscle fiber (or a constant number of contracting fibers within a muscle) shortens. The speed of shortening is maximal when there is no external load, progressively decreases with an increasing load, and falls to zero (no shortening—isometric contraction) when the load cannot be overcome by maximal tension. You have often experienced this load–velocity relationship. You can lift light objects requiring little muscle tension quickly, whereas you can lift heavy objects only slowly, if at all. This relationship between load and shortening velocity is a fundamental property of muscle, presumably because it takes the cross bridges longer to stroke against a greater load.

Now let us examine the means by which muscle tension can be graded or varied.

Contractions of a whole muscle can be of varying strength.

A single action potential in a muscle fiber produces a brief, weak contraction called a **twitch,** which is too short and too weak to be useful and normally does not take place in the body. Muscle fibers are arranged into whole muscles, where they function cooperatively to produce contractions of variable grades of strength stronger than a twitch. Two primary factors can be adjusted to accomplish gradation of whole-muscle tension: (1) *the number of muscle fibers contracting within a muscle* and (2) *the tension developed by each contracting fiber*. We discuss each of these factors in turn.

The number of fibers contracting within a muscle depends on the extent of motor unit recruitment.

The greater the number of fibers contracting, the greater the total muscle tension. Therefore, larger muscles consisting of more muscle fibers can generate more tension than smaller muscles with fewer fibers can.

Each whole muscle is innervated by a number of different motor neurons. When a motor neuron enters a muscle, it branches, with each axon terminal supplying a single muscle fiber (● Figure 8-15). One motor neuron innervates a number of muscle fibers, but each muscle fiber is supplied by only one motor neuron. When a motor neuron is activated, all the muscle fibers it supplies are stimulated to contract simultaneously. This team of concurrently activated components—one motor neuron plus all the muscle fibers it innervates—is called a **motor unit.** The muscle fibers that compose a motor unit are dispersed throughout the whole muscle; thus, their simultaneous contraction results in an evenly distributed, although weak,

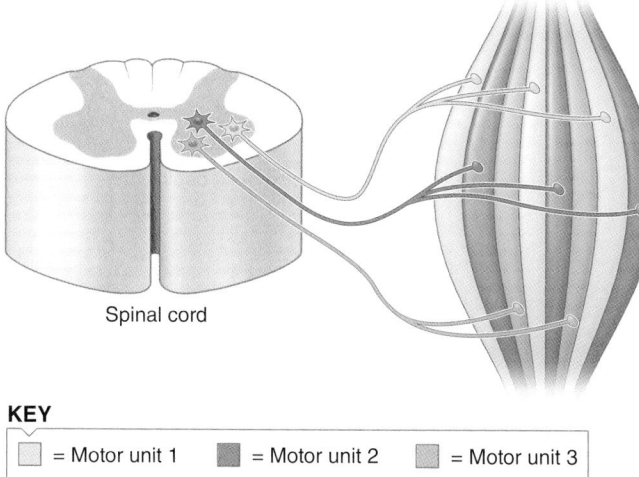

KEY

▢ = Motor unit 1   ▪ = Motor unit 2   ▪ = Motor unit 3

● **FIGURE 8-15 Motor units in a skeletal muscle.**

contraction of the whole muscle. Each muscle consists of numerous intermingled motor units. For a weak contraction of the whole muscle, only one or a few of its motor units are activated. For stronger and stronger contractions, more and more motor units are recruited, or stimulated to contract simultaneously, a phenomenon known as **motor unit recruitment.**

How much stronger the contraction will be with the recruitment of each additional motor unit depends on the size of the motor unit (that is, the number of muscle fibers controlled by a single motor neuron). The number of muscle fibers per motor unit and the number of motor units per muscle vary widely, depending on the specific function of the muscle. For muscles that produce precise, delicate movements, such as external eye muscles and hand muscles, a single motor unit may contain as few as a dozen muscle fibers. Because so few muscle fibers are involved with each motor unit, recruitment of each additional motor unit adds only a small increment to the whole muscle's strength of contraction. These small motor units allow fine control over muscle tension. In contrast, in muscles designed for powerful, coarsely controlled movement, such as those of the legs, a single motor unit may contain 1500 to 2000 muscle fibers. Recruitment of motor units in these muscles results in large incremental increases in whole-muscle tension. More powerful contractions occur at the expense of less precisely controlled gradations. Thus, the number of muscle fibers participating in the whole muscle's total contractile effort depends on the number of motor units recruited and the number of muscle fibers per motor unit in that muscle.

To delay or prevent **fatigue** (inability to maintain muscle tension at a given level) during a sustained contraction involving only a portion of a muscle's motor units, as is necessary in muscles supporting the weight of the body against the force of gravity, **asynchronous recruitment** of motor units takes place. The body alternates motor unit activity, like shifts at a factory, to give motor units that have been active an opportunity to rest while others take over. Changing of the shifts is carefully coordinated, so the sustained contraction is smooth rather than jerky. Asynchronous recruitment is possible only for submaxi-

mal contractions, during which only some of the motor units must maintain the desired level of tension. During maximal contractions, when all muscle fibers must participate, it is impossible to alternate motor unit activity to prevent fatigue. This is one reason you cannot support a heavy object as long as a light one.

The frequency of stimulation can influence the tension developed by each muscle fiber.

Whole-muscle tension depends not only on the number of muscle fibers contracting but also on the tension developed by each contracting fiber. Various factors influence the extent to which tension can be developed. These factors include the following:

1. Frequency of stimulation
2. Length of the fiber at the onset of contraction
3. Extent of fatigue
4. Thickness of the fiber

We now examine the effect of frequency of stimulation; we discuss the other factors in later sections.

TWITCH SUMMATION AND TETANUS Even though a single action potential in a muscle fiber produces only a twitch, contractions with longer duration and greater tension can be achieved by repeated stimulation of the fiber. Let us see what happens when a second action potential occurs in a muscle fiber. If the muscle fiber has completely relaxed before the next action potential takes place, a second twitch of the same magnitude as the first occurs (● Figure 8-16a). The same excitation–contraction events take place each time, resulting in identical twitch responses. If, however, the muscle fiber is stimulated a second time before it has completely relaxed from the first twitch, a second action potential causes a second contractile response, which is added in "piggyback" fashion on top of the first twitch (● Figure 8-16b). The two twitches from the two action potentials add together, or sum, to produce greater tension in the fiber than that produced by a single action potential. This **twitch summation** is similar to temporal summation of excitatory postsynaptic potentials (EPSPs) at the postsynaptic neuron (see p. 94).

Twitch summation is possible only because the duration of the action potential (1 to 2 msec) is much shorter than the duration of the resulting twitch (100 msec). Once an action potential has been initiated, a brief refractory period occurs during which another action potential cannot be initiated (see p. 88). It is therefore impossible to achieve summation of action potentials. The membrane must return to resting potential and recover from its refractory period before another action potential can occur. However, because the action potential and refractory period are over long before the resulting muscle twitch is completed, the muscle fiber may be restimulated while some contractile activity still exists to produce summation of the mechanical response.

If the muscle fiber is stimulated so rapidly that it does not have a chance to relax at all between stimuli, a smooth, sus-

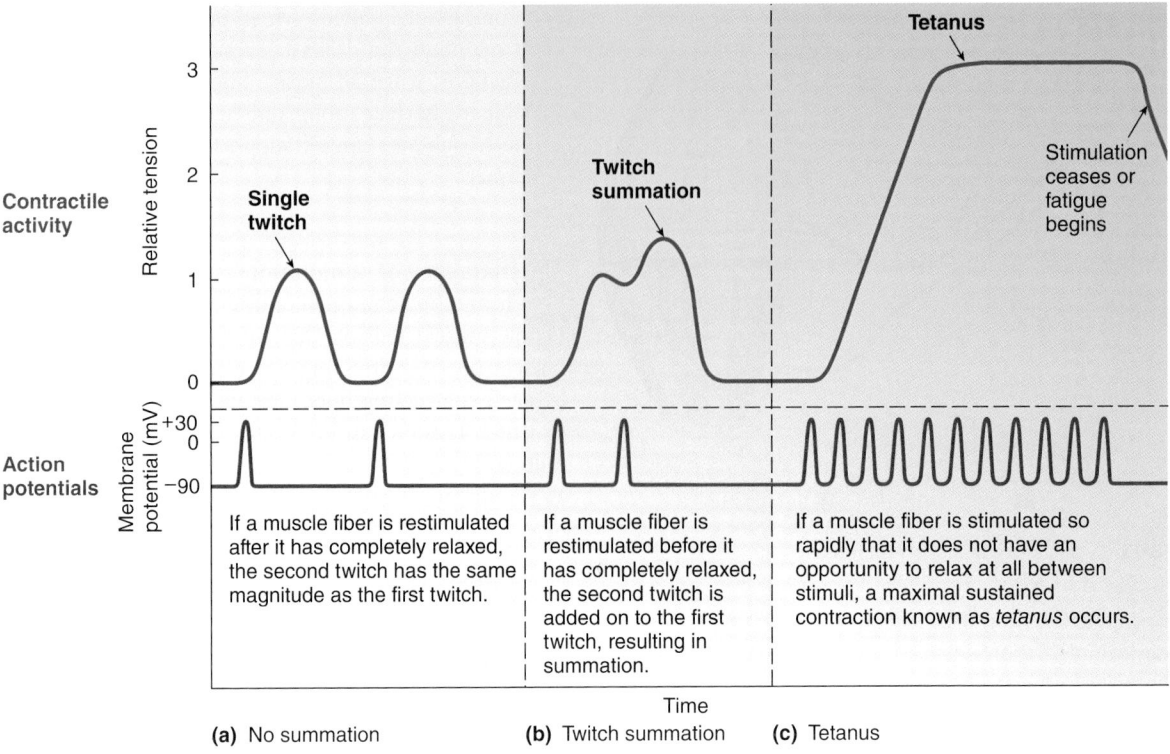

Single twitch

Twitch summation

Tetanus

Stimulation ceases or fatigue begins

Contractile activity

Action potentials

Relative tension

Membrane potential (mV)

+30
0
−90

If a muscle fiber is restimulated after it has completely relaxed, the second twitch has the same magnitude as the first twitch.

If a muscle fiber is restimulated before it has completely relaxed, the second twitch is added on to the first twitch, resulting in summation.

If a muscle fiber is stimulated so rapidly that it does not have an opportunity to relax at all between stimuli, a maximal sustained contraction known as *tetanus* occurs.

Time

(a) No summation **(b)** Twitch summation **(c)** Tetanus

● **FIGURE 8-16 Twitch summation and tetanus.**

tained contraction of maximal strength known as **tetanus** occurs (● Figure 8-16c). A tetanic contraction is usually three to four times stronger than a single twitch. (Don't confuse this normal physiologic tetanus with the disease tetanus; see p. 97.)

Twitch summation results from a sustained elevation in cytosolic Ca²⁺.

What is the mechanism of twitch summation and tetanus at the cell level? The tension produced by a contracting muscle fiber increases as a result of greater cross-bridge cycling. As the frequency of action potentials increases, the resulting tension development increases until a maximum tetanic contraction is achieved. Enough Ca^{2+} is released in response to a single action potential to interact with all the troponin within the cell. As a result, all cross bridges are free to participate in the contractile response. How, then, can repetitive action potentials bring about a greater contractile response? The difference depends on how long enough Ca^{2+} is available. The cross bridges remain active and continue to cycle as long as enough Ca^{2+} is present to keep the troponin–tropomyosin complexes away from the cross-bridge binding sites on actin. Each troponin–tropomyosin complex spans a distance of seven actin molecules. Thus, binding of Ca^{2+} to one troponin molecule leads to the uncovering of only seven cross-bridge binding sites on the thin filament.

As soon as Ca^{2+} is released in response to an action potential, the sarcoplasmic reticulum starts pumping Ca^{2+} back into the lateral sacs. As the cytosolic Ca^{2+} concentration subsequently declines, less Ca^{2+} is present to bind with troponin, so some of the troponin–tropomyosin complexes slip back into

their blocking positions. Consequently, not all cross-bridge binding sites remain available to participate in the cycling process during a single twitch induced by a single action potential. Because not all cross bridges find a binding site, the resulting contraction during a single twitch is not of maximal strength.

If action potentials and twitches occur far enough apart in time for all released Ca^{2+} from the first contractile response to be pumped back into the lateral sacs between the action potentials, an identical twitch response will occur as a result of the second action potential. If, however, a second action potential occurs and more Ca^{2+} is released while the Ca^{2+} that was released in response to the first action potential is being taken back up, the cytosolic Ca^{2+} concentration remains high and might even be elevated further. This prolonged availability of Ca^{2+} in the cytosol permits more of the cross bridges to continue participating in the cycling process for a longer time. As a result, tension development increases correspondingly. As the frequency of action potentials increases, the duration of elevated cytosolic Ca^{2+} concentration increases, and contractile activity likewise increases until a maximum tetanic contraction is reached. With tetanus, the maximum number of cross-bridge binding sites remain uncovered so that cross-bridge cycling, and consequently tension development, is at its peak.

Because skeletal muscle must be stimulated by motor neurons to contract, the nervous system plays a key role in regulating contraction strength. The two main factors subject to control to accomplish gradation of contraction are the *number of motor units stimulated* and the *frequency of their stimulation*. The areas of the brain that direct motor activity combine tetanic contractions and precisely timed shifts of asynchronous motor unit recruitment to execute smooth rather than jerky contractions.

Additional factors not directly under nervous control also influence the tension developed during contraction. Among these is the length of the fiber at the onset of contraction, to which we now turn our attention.

There is an optimal muscle length at which maximal tension can be developed.

A relationship exists between the length of the muscle before the onset of contraction and the tetanic tension that each contracting fiber can subsequently develop at that length. Every muscle has an **optimal length** (l_o) at which maximal force can be achieved during a tetanic contraction beginning at that length. That is, more tension can be achieved during tetanus when beginning at l_o than can be achieved when the contraction begins with the muscle longer or shorter than l_o. This **length–tension relationship** can be explained by the sliding filament mechanism of muscle contraction.

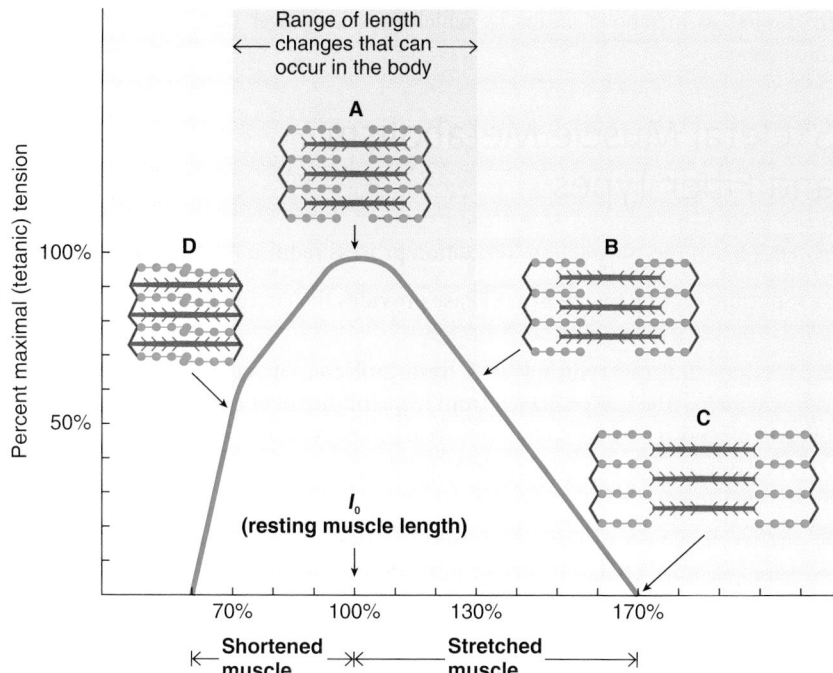

● FIGURE 8-17 **Length–tension relationship.** Maximal tetanic contraction can be achieved when a muscle fiber is at its optimal length (l_o) before the onset of contraction, because this is the point of optimal overlap of thick-filament cross bridges and thin-filament cross-bridge binding sites (point A). The percentage of maximal tetanic contraction that can be achieved decreases when the muscle fiber is longer or shorter than l_o before contraction. When it is longer, fewer thin-filament binding sites are accessible for binding with thick-filament cross bridges, because the thin filaments are pulled out from between the thick filaments (points B and C). When the fiber is shorter, fewer thin-filament binding sites are exposed to thick-filament cross bridges because the thin filaments overlap (point D). Also, further shortening and tension development are impeded as the thick filaments become forced against the Z lines (point D). In the body, the resting muscle length is at l_o. Furthermore, because of restrictions imposed by skeletal attachments, muscles cannot vary beyond 30% of their l_o in either direction (the range screened in light green). At the outer limits of this range, muscles still can achieve about 50% of their maximal tetanic contraction.

CONTRACTILE ACTIVITY AT OPTIMAL LENGTH

At l_o, when maximum tension can be developed (point A in ● Figure 8-17), the thin filaments optimally overlap the regions of the thick filaments where the cross bridges are located. At this length, a maximal number of cross bridges and actin molecules are accessible to each other for cycles of binding and bending. The central region of thick filaments, where the thin filaments do not overlap at l_o, lacks cross bridges; only myosin tails are found here.

CONTRACTILE ACTIVITY AT LENGTHS GREATER

THAN l_o At greater lengths, as when a muscle is passively stretched (point B), the thin filaments are pulled out from between the thick filaments, decreasing the number of actin sites available for cross-bridge binding; that is, some of the actin sites and cross bridges no longer "match up," so they "go unused." When less cross-bridge activity can occur, less tension can develop. In fact, when the muscle is stretched to about 70% longer than its l_o (point C) the thin filaments are completely pulled out from between the thick filaments, preventing cross-bridge activity; consequently, no contraction can occur.

CONTRACTILE ACTIVITY AT LENGTHS LESS THAN l_o If a muscle is

shorter than l_o before contraction (point D), less tension can be developed for two main reasons:

1. The thin filaments from the opposite sides of the sarcomere become overlapped, which limits the opportunity for the cross bridges to interact with actin.

2. The ends of the thick filaments become forced against the Z lines, so further shortening is impeded.

LIMITATIONS ON MUSCLE LENGTH The extremes in muscle length that prevent development of tension occur only under experimental conditions, when a muscle is removed and stimulated at various lengths. In the body, the muscles are positioned so that their relaxed length is approximately at l_o; thus, they can achieve near-maximal tetanic contraction most of the time. Because attachment to the skeleton imposes limitations, a muscle cannot be stretched or shortened more than 30% of its resting (optimal) length, and usually it deviates much less than 30% from normal length. Even at the outer limits (130% and 70% of l_o), the muscles still can generate half their maximum tension.

The factors we have discussed thus far that influence how much tension a contracting muscle fiber can develop—the frequency of stimulation and the muscle length at the onset of contraction—can vary from contraction to contraction. Other determinants of muscle fiber tension—the metabolic capability of the fiber relative to resistance to fatigue and the thickness of the fiber—do not vary from contraction to contraction but depend on the fiber type and can be modified over time. We consider these other factors as we shift our attention from muscle mechanics to metabolic means by which muscles power these movements.

Skeletal Muscle Metabolism and Fiber Types

Three steps in the contraction–relaxation process require ATP:

1. Splitting of ATP by myosin ATPase provides the energy for the power stroke of the cross bridge.

2. Binding (but not splitting) of a fresh molecule of ATP to myosin lets the bridge detach from the actin filament at the end of a power stroke so that the cycle can be repeated. This ATP is later split to provide energy for the next stroke of the cross bridge.

3. Active transport of Ca^{2+} back into the lateral sacs of the sarcoplasmic reticulum during relaxation depends on energy derived from the breakdown of ATP.

Muscle fibers have alternate pathways for forming ATP.

Because ATP is the only energy source that can be directly used for these activities, for contractile activity to continue, ATP must constantly be supplied. Only limited stores of ATP are immediately available in muscle tissue, but three pathways supply additional ATP as needed during muscle contraction: (1) transfer of a high-energy phosphate from creatine phosphate to ADP, (2) oxidative phosphorylation (the electron transport system and chemiosmosis), and (3) glycolysis.

CREATINE PHOSPHATE **Creatine phosphate** is the first energy storehouse tapped at the onset of contractile activity. Like ATP, creatine phosphate contains a high-energy phosphate group, which can be donated directly to ADP to form ATP. A rested muscle contains about five times as much creatine phosphate as ATP. Thus, most energy is stored in muscle in creatine phosphate pools. At the onset of contraction, when the meager reserves of ATP are rapidly used, more ATP is quickly formed by the transfer of energy and phosphate from creatine phosphate to ADP. Because only one enzymatic reaction is involved in this energy transfer, ATP can be formed rapidly (within a fraction of a second) by using creatine phosphate.

Thus, creatine phosphate is the first source for supplying additional ATP when exercise begins. Muscle ATP levels actually remain fairly constant early in contraction, but creatine phosphate stores become depleted. In fact, short bursts of high-intensity contractile effort, such as high jumps, sprints, or weight lifting, are supported primarily by ATP derived at the expense of creatine phosphate. Other energy systems do not have a chance to become operable before the activity is over. Creatine phosphate stores typically power the first minute or less of exercise.

OXIDATIVE PHOSPHORYLATION If the energy-dependent contractile activity is to continue, the muscle shifts to the alternate pathways of oxidative phosphorylation and glycolysis to form ATP. These multistepped pathways require time to pick up their rates of ATP formation to match the increased demands for energy, time provided by the immediate supply of energy from the one-step creatine phosphate system.

Oxidative phosphorylation takes place within the muscle mitochondria if sufficient oxygen (O_2) is present (see p. 32). Although it provides a rich yield of 32 ATP molecules for each glucose molecule processed, oxidative phosphorylation is relatively slow because of the number of steps involved.

During light exercise (such as walking) to moderate exercise (such as jogging or swimming), muscle cells can form enough ATP through oxidative phosphorylation to keep pace with the modest energy demands of the contractile machinery for prolonged periods. To sustain ongoing oxidative phosphorylation, the exercising muscles depend on delivery of adequate O_2 and nutrients to maintain their activity. Activity that can be supported in this way is **aerobic** ("with O_2") or **endurance-type exercise.**

GLYCOLYSIS There are respiratory and cardiovascular limits to how much O_2 can be delivered to a muscle. That is, the lungs and heart can pick up and deliver just so much O_2 to exercising muscles. Furthermore, in near-maximal contractions, the powerful contraction almost squeezes closed the blood vessels that course through the muscle, severely limiting O_2 availability to the muscle fibers. Even when O_2 is available, the relatively slow oxidative phosphorylation system may not be able to produce ATP rapidly enough to meet the muscle's needs during intense activity. A skeletal muscle's energy consumption may increase up to 100-fold when going from rest to high-intensity exercise. When O_2 delivery or oxidative phosphorylation cannot keep pace with the demand for ATP formation as the intensity of exercise increases, the muscle fibers rely increasingly on glycolysis to generate ATP (see p. 29). The chemical reactions of **glycolysis** yield products for ultimate entry into the oxidative phosphorylation pathway, but glycolysis can also proceed alone in the absence of further processing of its products by oxidative phosphorylation. During glycolysis, a glucose molecule is broken down into two **pyruvate** molecules, yielding two ATP molecules in the process. Pyruvate can be further degraded by oxidative phosphorylation to extract more energy. However, glycolysis alone has two advantages over the oxidative phosphorylation pathway: (1) glycolysis can form ATP in the absence of O_2 (operating *anaerobically,* that is, "without O_2"), and (2) it can proceed more rapidly than oxidative phosphorylation. Although glycolysis extracts considerably fewer ATP molecules from each nutrient molecule processed, it can proceed so much more rapidly that it can outproduce oxidative phosphorylation over a given period if enough glucose is present. Activity that can be supported in this way is **anaerobic** or **high-intensity exercise.**

LACTATE PRODUCTION Even though anaerobic glycolysis provides a means of performing intense exercise when O_2 delivery or the oxidative phosphorylation capacity is exceeded, using this pathway has two consequences. First, large amounts of nutrient fuel must be processed, because glycolysis is less efficient than oxidative phosphorylation in converting nutrient energy into the energy of ATP. (Glycolysis yields a net of 2 ATP molecules for each glucose molecule degraded, whereas the oxidative phosphorylation pathway can extract 32 molecules of ATP from each glucose molecule.) Muscle cells can store limited quantities of glucose in the form of glycogen, but anaerobic glycolysis rapidly depletes the muscle's glycogen supplies. Second, when the end product of anaerobic glycolysis, pyruvate, cannot be further processed by the oxidative phosphorylation pathway, it is converted to **lactate.** Lactate accumulation has been implicated in the muscle soreness that occurs during the time that intense exercise is actually taking place. (The delayed-onset pain and stiffness that begin the day after unaccustomed muscular exertion, however, are probably caused by reversible structural damage.) Furthermore, lactate (lactic acid) picked up by the blood produces the metabolic acidosis accompanying intense exercise.

Researchers believe that both depletion of energy reserves and fall in muscle pH caused by lactate accumulation play a role in the onset of muscle fatigue, when an exercising muscle can no longer respond to stimulation with the same degree of contractile activity. Therefore, anaerobic, high-intensity exercise can be sustained for only a short duration, in contrast to the body's prolonged ability to sustain aerobic, endurance-type activities.

Increased O_2 consumption is necessary to recover from exercise.

A person continues to breathe deeply and rapidly for some time after exercising. The need for elevated O_2 uptake during recovery from exercise (**excess postexercise oxygen consumption, or EPOC**) is due to various factors. The best known is repayment of an **oxygen deficit** incurred during exercise, when contractile activity was being supported by ATP derived from nonoxidative sources such as creatine phosphate and anaerobic glycolysis. During exercise, the creatine phosphate stores of active muscles are reduced, lactate may accumulate, and glycogen stores may be tapped; the extent of these effects depends on the intensity and duration of the activity. The biochemical transformations that restore the energy systems all need O_2, which is provided by the sustained increase in respiratory activity after exercise has stopped.

Part of EPOC is not directly related to repayment of energy stores but instead results from a general metabolic disturbance following exercise. For example, secretion of epinephrine, a hormone that increases O_2 consumption by the body, is elevated during exercise. Until the circulating level of epinephrine returns to its preexercise state, O_2 uptake is increased above normal. Furthermore, body temperature rises several degrees Fahrenheit during exercise. A rise in temperature speeds up O_2-consuming chemical reactions. Until body temperature returns to preexercise levels, the increased speed of these chemical reactions partly accounts for EPOC.

We have been looking at the contractile and metabolic activities of skeletal muscle fibers in general. However, not all skeletal muscle fibers use these mechanisms to the same extent.

We next examine the types of muscle fibers based on their speed of contraction and how they are metabolically equipped to generate ATP.

There are three types of skeletal muscle fibers, based on differences in ATP splitting and synthesis.

Classified by their biochemical capacities, there are three major types of muscle fibers (▲ Table 8-1):

1. **Slow-oxidative (type I) fibers**
2. **Fast-oxidative (type IIa) fibers**
3. **Fast-glycolytic (type IIx) fibers**

As their names imply, the two main differences among these fiber types are their speed of contraction (slow or fast) and the type of enzymatic machinery they primarily use for ATP formation (oxidative or glycolytic).

FAST VERSUS SLOW FIBERS Fast fibers have higher myosin ATPase (ATP-splitting) activity than slow fibers do. The higher the ATPase activity, the more rapidly ATP is split and the faster the rate at which energy is made available for cross-bridge cycling. The result is a fast twitch, compared to the slower twitches of those fibers that split ATP more slowly. Thus, two factors determine the speed with which a muscle contracts: the load (load–velocity relationship) and the myosin ATPase activity of the contracting fibers (fast or slow twitch).

OXIDATIVE VERSUS GLYCOLYTIC FIBERS Fiber types also differ in ATP-synthesizing ability. Those with a greater capacity to form ATP are more resistant to fatigue. Some fibers are better equipped for oxidative phosphorylation, whereas others rely primarily on anaerobic glycolysis for synthesizing ATP. Because oxidative phosphorylation yields considerably more ATP from each nutrient molecule processed, it does not readily deplete energy stores. Furthermore, it does not result in lactate accumulation. Oxidative types of muscle fibers are therefore more resistant to fatigue than glycolytic fibers are.

Other related characteristics distinguishing these three fiber types are summarized in Table 8-1. As you would expect, the oxidative fibers, both slow and fast, contain an abundance of mitochondria, the organelles that house the enzymes involved in oxidative phosphorylation. Because adequate oxygenation is essential to support this pathway, these fibers are richly supplied with capillaries. Oxidative fibers also have high myoglobin content. **Myoglobin,** which is similar to hemoglobin, can store small amounts of O_2, but more importantly, it increases the rate of O_2 transfer from the blood into muscle fibers. Myoglobin not only helps support oxidative fibers' O_2 dependency but also gives them a red color, just as oxygenated hemoglobin produces the red color of arterial blood. Accordingly, these muscle fibers are called **red fibers.**

In contrast, the fast fibers specialized for glycolysis contain few mitochondria but have a high content of glycolytic enzymes instead. Also, to supply the large amounts of glucose needed for glycolysis, they contain a lot of stored glycogen. Because the glycolytic fibers need relatively less O_2 to function, they have

▲ Table 8-1   Characteristics of Skeletal Muscle Fibers

Characteristic	TYPE OF FIBER		
	Slow Oxidative (Type I)	Fast Oxidative (Type IIa)	Fast Glycolytic (Type IIx)
Myosin–ATPase Activity	Low	High	High
Speed of Contraction	Slow	Fast	Fast
Resistance to Fatigue	High	Intermediate	Low
Oxidative Phosphorylation Capacity	High	High	Low
Enzymes for Anaerobic Glycolysis	Low	Intermediate	High
Mitochondria	Many	Many	Few
Capillaries	Many	Many	Few
Myoglobin Content	High	High	Low
Color of Fiber	Red	Red	White
Glycogen Content	Low	Intermediate	High

only a meager capillary supply compared with the oxidative fibers. The glycolytic fibers contain little myoglobin and therefore are pale in color, so they are sometimes called **white fibers.** (The most readily observable comparison between red and white fibers is the dark and white meat in poultry.)

GENETIC ENDOWMENT OF MUSCLE FIBER TYPES   In humans, most muscles contain a mixture of all three fiber types; the percentage of each type is largely determined by the type of activity for which the muscle is specialized. Accordingly, a high proportion of slow-oxidative fibers are found in muscles specialized for maintaining low-intensity contractions for long periods without fatigue, such as the muscles of the back and legs that support the body's weight against the force of gravity. A preponderance of fast-glycolytic fibers are found in the arm muscles, which are adapted for performing rapid, forceful movements such as lifting heavy objects.

The percentage of these various fibers not only differs among muscles within an individual but also varies considerably among individuals. Athletes genetically endowed with a higher percentage of the fast-glycolytic fibers are good candidates for power and sprint events, whereas those with a greater proportion of slow-oxidative fibers are more likely to succeed in endurance activities such as marathon races.

Of course, success in any event depends on many factors other than genetic endowment, such as the extent and type of training and the level of dedication. Indeed, the mechanical and metabolic capabilities of muscle fibers can change a lot in response to the patterns of demands placed on them. Let us see how.

Muscle fibers adapt considerably in response to the demands placed on them.

Different types of exercise produce different patterns of neuronal discharge to the muscle involved. Depending on the pattern of neural activity, long-term adaptive changes occur in the muscle fibers, enabling them to respond most efficiently to the types of demands placed on the muscle. Two types of changes can be induced in muscle fibers: changes in their oxidative capacity and changes in their diameter.

IMPROVEMENT IN OXIDATIVE CAPACITY   Regular aerobic endurance exercise, such as long-distance jogging or swimming, promotes metabolic changes within the oxidative fibers, which are the ones primarily recruited during aerobic exercise. For example, the number of mitochondria and the number of capillaries supplying blood to these fibers both increase. Muscles so adapted can use O_2 more efficiently and therefore can better endure prolonged activity without fatiguing. However, they do not change in size.

MUSCLE HYPERTROPHY   The actual size of the muscles can be increased by regular bouts of anaerobic, short-duration, high-intensity resistance training, such as weight lifting. The resulting muscle enlargement comes primarily from an increase in diameter (**hypertrophy**) of the fast-glycolytic fibers called into play during such powerful contractions. Most fiber thickening results from increased synthesis of myosin and actin filaments, which permits a greater opportunity for cross-bridge interaction and consequently increases the muscle's contractile strength. The resultant bulging muscles are better adapted to activities that require intense strength for brief periods, but endurance has not been improved.

INFLUENCE OF TESTOSTERONE   Men's muscle fibers are thicker, and accordingly, their muscles are larger and stronger than those of women, even without weight training, because of the actions of testosterone, a steroid hormone secreted primarily in males. Testosterone promotes the synthesis and assembly of myosin and actin. This fact has led some athletes, both males and females, to the dangerous practice of taking this or closely related steroids to increase their athletic performance. (To explore this topic further, see the accompanying boxed feature, ▶ Beyond the Basics.)

MUSCLE ATROPHY   At the other extreme, if a muscle is not routinely used, its actin and myosin content decreases, its fibers become smaller, and the muscle accordingly **atrophies** (decreases in mass) and becomes weaker. For example, atrophy occurs when a muscle is not used for a long period, as when a cast or brace must be worn or during prolonged bed confinement.

We have now completed our discussion of all the determinants of whole-muscle tension in a skeletal muscle, which are summarized in ▲ Table 8-2. Next, we examine the central and

Beyond the Basics

Are Athletes Who Use Steroids to Gain Competitive Advantage Really Winners or Losers?

The testing of athletes for drugs, and the much publicized exclusion from competition of those found to be using substances outlawed by sports federations, have stirred considerable controversy. One such group of drugs is **anabolic androgenic steroids** (*anabolic* means "buildup of tissues," *androgenic* means "male producing," and *steroids* are a class of hormone). These agents are closely related to testosterone, the natural male sex hormone, which is responsible for promoting the increased muscle mass characteristic of males.

Although their use is outlawed (possessing anabolic steroids without a prescription became a federal offense in 1991), these agents are taken by many athletes who specialize in power events such as weight lifting and sprinting in the hopes of increasing muscle mass and, accordingly, muscle strength. Both male and female athletes have resorted to using these substances in an attempt to gain a competitive edge. Bodybuilders also take anabolic steroids. Furthermore, although most players deny using these agents, experts believe these performance enhancers are widely used in professional sports such as baseball, football, basketball, competitive cycling, and hockey. There are an estimated 1 million anabolic steroid abusers in the United States. Compounding the problem, underground chemists recently created new synthetic performance-enhancing steroids undetectable by standard drug tests. Unfortunately, use of anabolic steroids has spread into our nation's high schools and even younger age groups. Recent studies indicate that 10% of male and 3% of female high school athletes use banned steroids. The manager of the steroid abuse hotline of the National Steroid Research Center reports having calls for help from abusers as young as 12 years old.

Studies have confirmed that steroids can increase muscle mass when used in large amounts and coupled with heavy exercise. One reputable study demonstrated an average 8.9-pound gain of lean muscle in bodybuilders who used steroids during a 10-week period. Anecdotal evidence suggests that some steroid users have added as much as 40 pounds of muscle in a year.

The adverse effects of these drugs, however, outweigh any benefits derived.

In females, who normally lack potent androgenic hormones, anabolic steroid drugs not only promote "male-type" muscle mass and strength but also "masculinize" the users in other ways, such as by inducing growth of facial hair and by lowering the voice. More important, in both males and females, these agents adversely affect the reproductive and cardiovascular systems and the liver, may have an impact on behavior, and may be addictive.

Adverse Effects on the Reproductive System

In males, testosterone secretion and sperm production by the testes are normally controlled by hormones from the anterior pituitary gland. In negative-feedback fashion, testosterone inhibits secretion of these controlling hormones so that a constant circulating level of testosterone is maintained. The anterior pituitary is similarly inhibited by androgenic steroids taken as a drug. As a result, because the testes do not receive their normal stimulatory input from the anterior pituitary, testosterone secretion and sperm production decrease and the testes shrink. This hormone abuse also may set the stage for cancer of the testes and prostate gland.

In females, inhibition of the anterior pituitary by androgenic drugs suppresses the hormonal output that controls ovarian function. The result is failure to ovulate, menstrual irregularities, and decreased secretion of "feminizing" female sex hormones. Their decline diminishes breast size and other female characteristics.

Adverse Effects on the Cardiovascular System

Use of anabolic steroids induces cardiovascular changes that increase the risk of developing atherosclerosis, which in turn is associated with an increased incidence of heart attacks and strokes (see p. 269). Among these adverse cardiovascular effects are (1) a reduction in high-density lipoproteins (HDL), the "good" cholesterol carriers that help remove cholesterol from the body, and (2) elevated blood pressure. Animal studies have also demonstrated damage to the heart muscle itself.

Adverse Effects on the Liver

Liver dysfunction is common with high steroid intake because the liver, which normally inactivates steroid hormones and prepares them for urinary excretion, is overloaded by the excess steroid intake. The incidence of liver cancer is also increased.

Adverse Effects on Behavior

Although the evidence is still controversial, anabolic steroid use appears to promote aggressive, even hostile behavior—the so-called 'roid rages.

Addictive Effects

A troubling new concern is the addiction to anabolic steroids of some who abuse these drugs. In a survey using anonymous, self-administered questionnaires, 57% of steroid users qualified as being addicted. This apparent tendency to become chemically dependent on steroids is alarming because the potential for adverse effects on health increases with long-term, heavy use, the kind of use that would be expected from someone hooked on the drug.

Thus, for health reasons, without even taking into account the legal and ethical issues, people should not use anabolic steroids. However, the problem appears to be worsening. Currently, the international black market for anabolic steroids is estimated at $1 billion per year.

Other Cheating Ways to Build Muscle Mass

Athletes seeking an artificial competitive edge have resorted to other illicit measures besides taking anabolic steroids, such as using human growth hormone or related compounds in the hopes of spurring muscle buildup. More worrisome, scientists predict the next illicit frontier will be gene doping. **Gene doping** refers to gene therapy aimed at improving athletic performance, such as by promoting production of naturally occurring muscle-building chemicals (for example, *insulin-like growth factor*) or by blocking production of *myostatin,* a natural body chemical that puts the brakes on muscle growth. Because these chemicals occur naturally in the body, detection of gene doping will be a challenge.

Number of Fibers Contracting

Number of motor units recruited*

Number of muscle fibers per motor unit

Number of muscle fibers available to contract
(size of muscle)

Tension Developed by Each Contracting Fiber

Frequency of stimulation (twitch summation, tetanus)*

Length of fiber at onset of contraction (length–tension relationship)

Extent of fatigue

   Duration of activity

   Type of fiber (fatigue-resistant oxidative, fatigue-prone glycolytic)

Thickness of fiber

   Pattern of neural activity (hypertrophy, atrophy)

   Amount of testosterone (larger fibers in males than females)

*Factors controlled to accomplish gradation of contraction.

---

local mechanisms involved in regulating the motor activity performed by these muscles.

Control of Motor Movement

Particular patterns of motor unit output govern motor activity, ranging from simply maintaining posture and balance; to stereotypical movements, such as walking; to highly skilled movements, such as gymnastics. Control of any motor movement, regardless of its level of complexity, depends on converging input to the motor neurons of specific motor units. The motor neurons in turn trigger contraction of the muscle fibers within their respective motor units.

Multiple neural inputs influence motor unit output.

Three levels of input to the motor neurons control their output to the muscle fibers they innervate:

1. *Input from afferent neurons.* This input, usually through intervening interneurons, occurs at the level of the spinal cord—that is, spinal reflexes (see p. 143).

2. *Input from the primary motor cortex.* Fibers originating from neuronal cell bodies known as **pyramidal cells** within the primary motor cortex (see p. 125) descend directly without synaptic interruption to terminate on motor neurons in the spinal cord. These fibers make up the **corticospinal** (or **pyramidal**) **motor system.**

3. *Input from the brain stem as part of the multineuronal motor system.* The pathways composing the **multineuronal** (or **extrapyramidal**) **motor system** include synapses that involve many

regions of the brain (*extra* means "outside of"; *pyramidal* refers to the pyramidal system). The final link in multineuronal pathways is the brain stem, especially the reticular formation (see p. 138), which in turn is influenced by motor regions of the cortex, the cerebellum, and the basal nuclei. In addition, the motor cortex itself is interconnected with the thalamus, as well as with premotor and supplementary motor areas; these are all part of the multineuronal system.

The only brain regions that directly influence motor neurons are the primary motor cortex and brain stem; the other involved brain regions indirectly regulate motor activity by adjusting motor output from the motor cortex and brain stem. Numerous complex interactions take place among these various brain regions. (See Chapter 5 for further discussion of the specific roles of these brain regions.)

Spinal reflexes involving afferent neurons are important in maintaining posture and in executing basic protective movements, such as the withdrawal reflex. The corticospinal system primarily mediates performance of fine, discrete, voluntary movements of the hands and fingers, such as those required for doing intricate needlework. Premotor and supplementary motor areas, with input from the cerebrocerebellum, plan the voluntary motor command that is issued to the appropriate motor neurons by the primary motor cortex through this descending system (see p. 127). The multineuronal system, in contrast, primarily regulates overall body posture involving involuntary movements of large muscle groups of the trunk and limbs. The corticospinal and multineuronal systems show considerable complex interaction and overlapping of function. To voluntarily manipulate your fingers to do needlework, for example, you subconsciously assume a particular posture of your arms that lets you hold your work.

 Some inputs converging on motor neurons are excitatory, whereas others are inhibitory. Coordinated movement depends on an appropriate balance of activity in these inputs. The following types of motor abnormalities result from defective motor control:

■ If an inhibitory system originating in the brain stem is disrupted, muscles become hyperactive because of the unopposed activity in excitatory inputs to motor neurons. This condition, characterized by increased muscle tone and augmented limb reflexes, is known as **spastic paralysis.**

■ In contrast, loss of excitatory input, such as that accompanies destruction of descending excitatory pathways exiting the primary motor cortex, brings about **flaccid paralysis.** In this condition, the muscles are relaxed and the person cannot voluntarily contract muscles, although spinal reflex activity is still present. Damage to the primary motor cortex on one side of the brain, as with a stroke, leads to flaccid paralysis on the opposite half of the body (**hemiplegia,** or paralysis of one side of the body). Disruption of all descending pathways, as in traumatic severance of the spinal cord, produces flaccid paralysis below the level of the damaged region—**quadriplegia** (paralysis of all four limbs) in upper-spinal-cord damage and **paraplegia** (paralysis of the legs) in lower-spinal-cord injury.

- Destruction of motor neurons—either their cell bodies or the efferent fibers—causes flaccid paralysis and lack of reflex responsiveness in the affected muscles.

- Damage to the cerebellum or basal nuclei results not in paralysis but in uncoordinated, clumsy activity and inappropriate patterns of movement. These regions normally smooth out activity initiated voluntarily.

- Damage to higher cortical regions involved in planning motor activity results in the inability to establish appropriate motor commands to accomplish desired goals.

Muscle receptors provide afferent information needed to control skeletal muscle activity.

Coordinated, purposeful skeletal muscle activity depends on afferent input from various sources. At a simple level, afferent signals indicating that your finger is touching a hot stove trigger reflex contractile activity in appropriate arm muscles to withdraw the hand from the injurious stimulus. At a more complex level, if you are going to catch a ball, the motor systems of your brain must program sequential motor commands that will move and position your body correctly for the catch, using predictions of the ball's direction and rate of movement provided by visual input. Many muscles acting simultaneously or alternately at different joints are called into play to shift your body's location and position rapidly while maintaining your balance. To appropriately program muscle activity, your CNS must know the starting position of your body. Furthermore, it must be constantly informed about the progression of movement it has initiated so that it can make adjustments as needed. Your brain receives this information, which is known as *proprioceptive input* (see p. 123), from receptors in your eyes, joints, vestibular apparatus, and skin, as well as from the muscles themselves.

You can demonstrate your joint and muscle proprioceptive receptors in action by closing your eyes and bringing the tips of your right and left index fingers together at any point in space. You can do so without seeing where your hands are, because your brain is informed of the position of your hands and other body parts at all times by afferent input from the joint and muscle receptors.

Two types of muscle receptors—*muscle spindles* and *Golgi tendon organs*—monitor changes in muscle length and tension. Muscle length is monitored by muscle spindles; changes in muscle tension are detected by Golgi tendon organs. Both these receptor types are activated by muscle stretch, but they convey different types of information. Let us see how.

MUSCLE SPINDLE STRUCTURE **Muscle spindles,** which are distributed throughout the fleshy part of a skeletal muscle, consist of collections of specialized muscle fibers known as **intrafusal fibers,** which lie within spindle-shaped connective tissue capsules parallel to the "ordinary" **extrafusal fibers** (*fusus* means "spindle") (● Figure 8-18). Unlike an ordinary extrafusal skeletal muscle fiber, which contains contractile elements (myofibrils) throughout its entire length, an intrafusal fiber has a noncontractile central portion, with the contractile elements being limited to both ends.

Each muscle spindle has its own private efferent and afferent nerve supply. The efferent neuron that innervates a muscle spindle's intrafusal fibers is known as a **gamma motor neuron,** whereas the motor neurons that supply the extrafusal fibers are called **alpha motor neurons.** Two types of afferent sensory endings terminate on the intrafusal fibers and serve as muscle spindle receptors, both of which are activated by stretch. Together they detect changes in the length of the fibers during stretching, as well as the speed with which it occurs. Muscle spindles play a key role in the stretch reflex.

STRETCH REFLEX Whenever a whole muscle is passively stretched, its muscle spindle intrafusal fibers are likewise stretched, increasing the firing rate in the afferent nerve fibers whose sensory endings terminate on the stretched spindle fibers. The afferent neuron directly synapses on the alpha motor neuron that innervates the extrafusal fibers of the same muscle, resulting in contraction of that muscle (● Figure 8-19a, steps **1** and **2**). This monosynaptic **stretch reflex** (see p. 143) is a local negative-feedback mechanism to resist any passive changes in muscle length so that optimal resting length can be maintained.

The classic example of the stretch reflex is the **patellar tendon,** or **knee-jerk, reflex** (● Figure 8-20). The extensor muscle of the knee is the *quadriceps femoris,* which forms the front portion of the thigh and is attached just below the knee to the tibia (shinbone) by the *patellar tendon.* Tapping this tendon with a rubber mallet passively stretches the quadriceps muscle, acti-

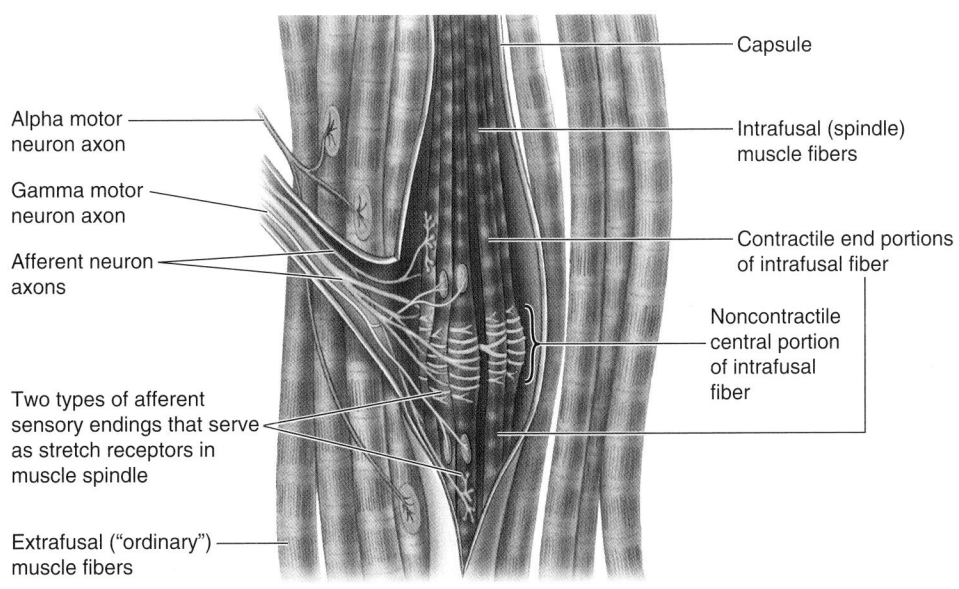

Alpha motor neuron axon

Gamma motor neuron axon

Afferent neuron axons

Two types of afferent sensory endings that serve as stretch receptors in muscle spindle

Extrafusal ("ordinary") muscle fibers

Capsule

Intrafusal (spindle) muscle fibers

Contractile end portions of intrafusal fiber

Noncontractile central portion of intrafusal fiber

● **FIGURE 8-18 Muscle spindle.**

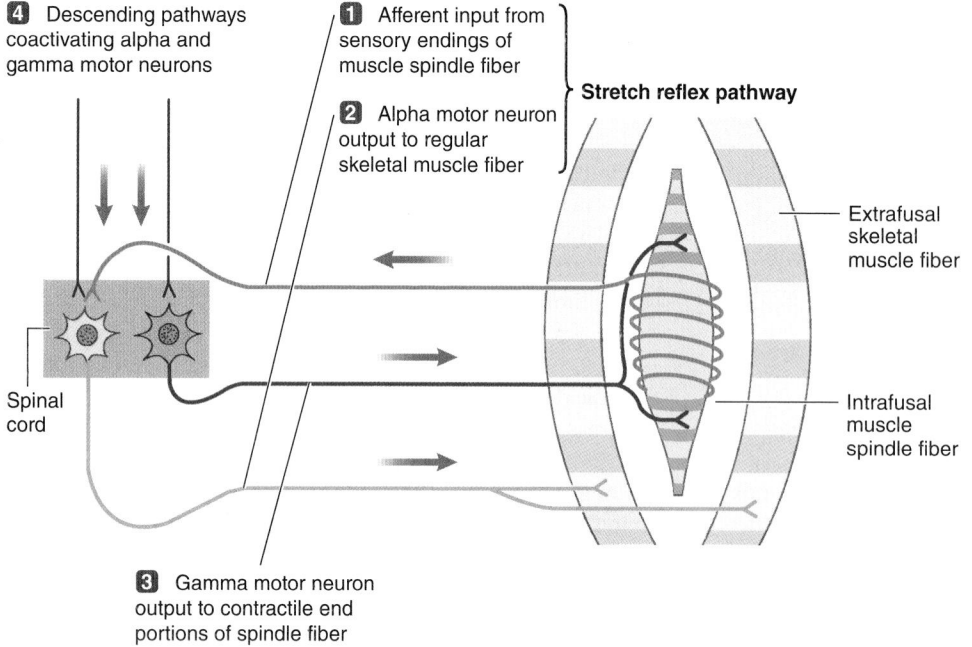

4 Descending pathways coactivating alpha and gamma motor neurons

1 Afferent input from sensory endings of muscle spindle fiber

2 Alpha motor neuron output to regular skeletal muscle fiber

Stretch reflex pathway

Extrafusal skeletal muscle fiber

Intrafusal muscle spindle fiber

Spinal cord

3 Gamma motor neuron output to contractile end portions of spindle fiber

(a) Pathways involved in monosynaptic stretch reflex and coactivation of alpha and gamma motor neurons

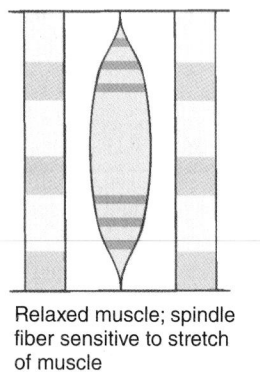

Relaxed muscle; spindle fiber sensitive to stretch of muscle

(b) Relaxed muscle

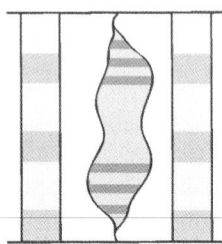

Contracted muscle in hypothetical situation of no spindle coactivation; slackened spindle fiber not sensitive to stretch of muscle

(c) Contracted muscle with no spindle coactivation

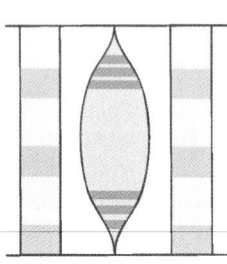

Contracted muscle in normal situation of spindle coactivation; contracted spindle fiber sensitive to stretch of muscle

(d) Contracted muscle with spindle coactivation

● **FIGURE 8-19 Muscle spindle function.**

The primary purpose of the stretch reflex is to resist the tendency for your extensor muscles to passively stretch as a result of gravitational forces when you are standing upright. Whenever your knee joint tends to buckle because of gravity, your quadriceps muscle is stretched. The resulting enhanced contraction of this extensor muscle brought about by the stretch reflex quickly straightens out the knee, keeping your leg extended so that you remain standing.

COACTIVATION OF GAMMA AND ALPHA MOTOR NEURONS Gamma motor neurons initiate contraction of the muscular end regions of intrafusal fibers (see ● Figure 8-19a, step **3**). This contractile response is too weak to have any influence on whole-muscle tension, but it does have an important localized effect on the muscle spindle itself. If there were no compensating mechanisms, shortening of the whole muscle by alpha-motor-neuron stimulation of extrafusal fibers would slacken the spindle fibers so that they would be less sensitive to stretch and therefore not as effective as muscle length detectors (see ● Figure 8-19b and c). **Coactivation** (simultaneous stimulation) of the gamma-motor-neuron system along with the alpha-motor-neuron system during reflex and voluntary contractions (see ● Figure 8-19a, step **4**) takes the slack out of the spindle fibers as the whole muscle shortens, letting these receptor structures maintain their high sensitivity to stretch over a range of muscle lengths (see ● Figure 8-19d). When gamma-motor-neuron stimulation triggers simultaneous contraction of both end muscular portions of an intrafusal fiber, the noncontractile central portion is pulled in opposite directions, tightening this region and taking out the slack. Whereas the extent of alpha-motor-neuron activation depends on the intended strength of the motor response, the extent of simultaneous gamma-motor-neuron activity to the same muscle depends on the anticipated distance of shortening.

GOLGI TENDON ORGANS In contrast to muscle spindles, which lie within the belly of the muscle, Golgi tendon organs are in the tendons of the muscle, where they can respond to changes in

vating its spindle receptors. The resulting stretch reflex brings about contraction of this extensor muscle, causing the knee to extend and raise the foreleg in the well-known knee-jerk fashion.

This test is routinely done as a preliminary assessment of nervous system function. A normal knee jerk indicates that a number of neural and muscular components—muscle spindle, afferent input, motor neurons, efferent output, neuromuscular junctions, and the muscles themselves—are functioning normally. It also indicates an appropriate balance of excitatory and inhibitory input to the motor neurons from higher brain levels. Muscle jerks may be absent or depressed with loss of higher-level excitatory inputs, or they may be greatly exaggerated with loss of inhibitory input to the motor neurons from higher brain levels.

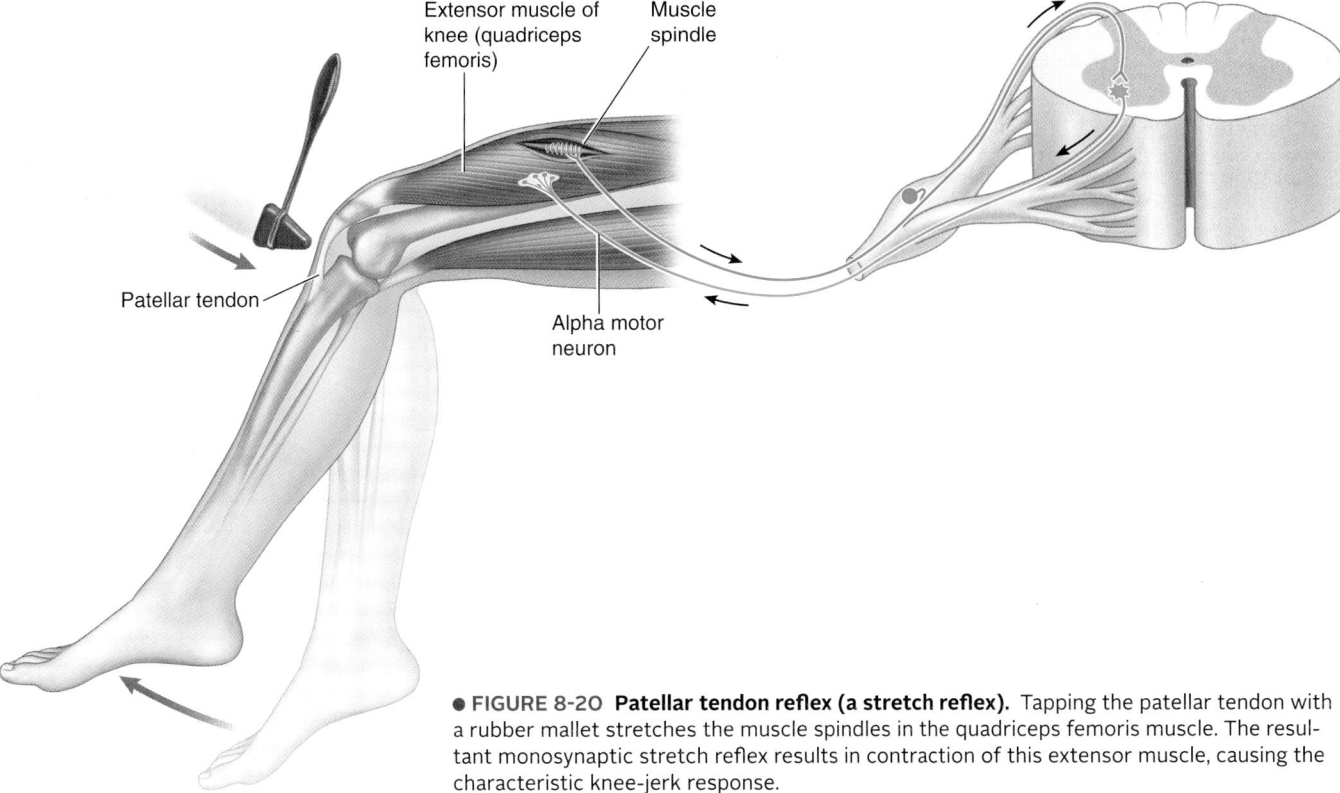

Extensor muscle of
knee (quadriceps
femoris)

Muscle
spindle

Patellar tendon

Alpha motor
neuron

● **FIGURE 8-20 Patellar tendon reflex (a stretch reflex).** Tapping the patellar tendon with a rubber mallet stretches the muscle spindles in the quadriceps femoris muscle. The resultant monosynaptic stretch reflex results in contraction of this extensor muscle, causing the characteristic knee-jerk response.

the muscle's tension rather than to changes in its length. Because several factors determine the tension developed in the whole muscle during contraction (for example, frequency of stimulation or length of muscle at the onset of contraction), it is essential that motor control systems be apprised of the tension actually achieved so that adjustments can be made if necessary.

Golgi tendon organs consist of endings of afferent fibers entwined within bundles of collagen (connective tissue) fibers that make up the tendon. When the extrafusal muscle fibers contract, the resulting pull on the tendon tightens the collagen bundles, which in turn increase the tension exerted on the bone to which the tendon is attached. In the process, the entwined Golgi organ afferent receptor endings are stretched, causing the afferent fibers to fire; the frequency of firing is directly related to the tension developed. This afferent information is sent to the brain for processing. Much of this information is used subconsciously for smoothly executing motor activity, but unlike afferent information from the muscle spindles, afferent information from the Golgi tendon organ reaches the level of conscious awareness. You are aware of the tension within a muscle but not of its length.

Scientists once thought the Golgi tendon organ triggered a protective spinal reflex that halted further contraction and brought about sudden reflex relaxation when the muscle tension became great enough, thus helping prevent damage to the muscle or tendon from excessive, tension-developing muscle contractions. Scientists now believe, however, that this receptor is a pure sensor and does not initiate any reflexes. Other unknown mechanisms are apparently involved in inhibiting further contraction to prevent tension-induced damage.

Having completed our discussion of skeletal muscle, we now examine smooth and cardiac muscle.

Smooth and Cardiac Muscle

The two other types of muscle—smooth muscle and cardiac muscle—share some basic properties with skeletal muscle, but each also displays unique characteristics (▲ Table 8-3). The three muscle types all have a specialized contractile apparatus made up of thin actin filaments that slide relative to stationary thick myosin filaments in response to a rise in cytosolic Ca^{2+} to accomplish contraction. Also, they all directly use ATP as the energy source for cross-bridge cycling. However, the structure and organization of fibers within these muscle types vary, as do their mechanisms of excitation and the means by which excitation and contraction are coupled. Furthermore, important distinctions occur in the contractile response itself. We spend the rest of this chapter highlighting unique features of smooth and cardiac muscle as compared with skeletal muscle, saving more detailed discussion of their function for chapters on organs containing these muscle types.

Smooth muscle cells are small and unstriated.

Most smooth muscle cells are found in the walls of hollow organs and tubes. Their contraction exerts pressure on and regulates the forward movement of the contents of these structures.

Both smooth and skeletal muscle cells are elongated, but in contrast to their large, cylindrical skeletal muscle counterparts, smooth muscle cells are spindle shaped and smaller. Also unlike

	TYPE OF MUSCLE			
Characteristic	Skeletal	Multiunit Smooth	Single-Unit Smooth	Cardiac
Location	Attached to skeleton	Large blood vessels, small airways, eye, and hair follicles	Walls of hollow organs in digestive, reproductive, and urinary tracts and in small blood vessels	Heart only
Function	Movement of the body in relation to the external environment	Varies with the structure involved	Movement of the contents within hollow organs	Pumps blood out of the heart
Mechanism of Contraction	Sliding filament mechanism	Sliding filament mechanism	Sliding filament mechanism	Sliding filament mechanism
Innervation	Somatic nervous system (alpha motor neurons)	Autonomic nervous system	Autonomic nervous system	Autonomic nervous system
Level of Control	Under voluntary control; also subject to subconscious regulation	Under involuntary control	Under involuntary control	Under involuntary control
Initiation of Contraction	Neurogenic	Neurogenic	Myogenic (pacemaker potentials, slow-wave potentials)	Myogenic (pacemaker potentials)
Role of Nervous Stimulation	Initiates contraction; accomplishes gradation	Initiates contraction; contributes to gradation	Modifies contraction; can excite or inhibit; contributes to gradation	Modifies contraction; can excite or inhibit; contributes to gradation
Modifying Effect of Hormones	No	Yes	Yes	Yes
Presence of Thick Myosin and Thin Actin Filaments	Yes	Yes	Yes	Yes
Striated by Orderly Arrangement of Filaments	Yes	No	No	Yes
Presence of Troponin and Tropomyosin	Yes	Tropomyosin only	Tropomyosin only	Yes
Presence of T Tubules	Yes	No	No	Yes
Level of Development of Sarcoplasmic Reticulum	Well developed	Poorly developed	Poorly developed	Moderately developed
Cross Bridges Turned on by Ca²⁺	Yes	Yes	Yes	Yes

Characteristic	TYPE OF MUSCLE			
	Skeletal	Multiunit Smooth	Single-Unit Smooth	Cardiac
Source of Increased Cytosolic Ca²⁺	Sarcoplasmic reticulum	Extracellular fluid and sarcoplasmic reticulum	Extracellular fluid and sarcoplasmic reticulum	Extracellular fluid and sarcoplasmic reticulum
Site of Ca²⁺ Regulation	Troponin in thin filaments	Myosin in thick filaments	Myosin in thick filaments	Troponin in thin filaments
Mechanism of Ca²⁺ Action	Physically repositions the troponin–tropomyosin complex to uncover actin cross-bridge binding sites	Chemically brings about phosphorylation of myosin cross bridges so that they can bind with actin	Chemically brings about phosphorylation of myosin cross bridges so that they can bind with actin	Physically repositions the troponin–tropomyosin complex
Presence of Gap Junctions	No	Yes (few)	Yes	Yes
ATP used Directly by the Contractile Apparatus	Yes	Yes	Yes	Yes
Myosin ATPase Activity (Speed of Contraction)	Fast or slow, depending on type of fiber	Very slow	Very slow	Slow
Means by Which Gradation Is Accomplished	Varying number of motor units contracting (motor unit recruitment) and frequency at which they're stimulated (twitch summation)	Varying number of muscle fibers contracting and varying cytosolic Ca²⁺ concentration in each fiber by autonomic and hormonal influences	Varying cytosolic Ca²⁺ concentration through myogenic activity and influences of the autonomic nervous system, hormones, mechanical stretch, and local metabolites	Varying length of fiber (depending on the extent of filling of heart chambers) and varying cytosolic Ca²⁺ concentration through autonomic, hormonal, and local metabolite influence
Clear-Cut Length–Tension Relationship	Yes	No	No	Yes

skeletal muscle cells, a single smooth muscle cell does not extend the full length of a muscle. Instead, groups of smooth muscle cells are typically arranged in sheets (● Figure 8-21a).

A smooth muscle cell has three types of filaments: (1) thick myosin filaments, which are longer than those in skeletal muscle; (2) thin actin filaments, which contain tropomyosin but lack troponin; and (3) filaments of intermediate size, which do not directly participate in contraction but are part of the cytoskeletal framework that supports the cell shape. Smooth muscle filaments do not form myofibrils and are not arranged in the sarcomere pattern found in skeletal muscle. Thus, smooth muscle cells do not show the banding or striation of skeletal muscle, hence the term *smooth* for this muscle type.

Lacking sarcomeres, smooth muscle does not have Z lines as such but has **dense bodies** containing the same protein constituent found in Z lines (● Figure 8-21b). Dense bodies are positioned throughout the smooth muscle cell, as well as at-

tached to the internal surface of the plasma membrane. Dense bodies are held in place by a scaffold of intermediate filaments. The actin filaments are anchored to the dense bodies. Considerably more actin is present in smooth muscle cells than in skeletal muscle cells, with 10 to 15 thin filaments for each thick myosin filament in smooth muscle compared to 2 thin filaments for each thick filament in skeletal muscle. The thick- and thin-filament contractile units are oriented slightly diagonally from side to side within the smooth muscle cell in an elongated, diamond-shaped lattice, rather than running parallel with the long axis as myofibrils do in skeletal muscle (● Figure 8-22a). Relative sliding of the thin filaments past the thick filaments during contraction causes the filament lattice to shorten and expand from side to side. As a result, the whole cell shortens and bulges out between the points where the thin filaments are attached to the inner surface of the plasma membrane (● Figure 8-22b).

Unlike in skeletal muscle, myosin molecules are arranged in a smooth-muscle thick filament so that cross bridges are present along the entire filament length (that is, there is no bare portion in the center of a smooth-muscle thick filament). As a result, the surrounding thin filaments can be pulled along the thick filaments for longer distances than in skeletal muscle. Also dissimilar to skeletal muscle (in which all thin filaments surrounding a thick filament are pulled toward the center of the stationary thick filament), the myosin proteins in smooth-muscle thick filaments are organized so that half of the surrounding thin filaments are pulled toward one end of the stationary thick filament and the other half are pulled in the opposite direction (● Figure 8-22b).

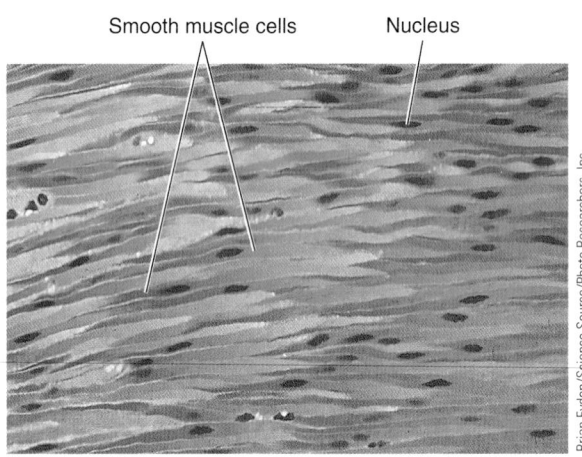

(a) Low-power light micrograph of smooth muscle cells

Smooth muscle cells | Nucleus

Brian Eyden/Science Source/Photo Researchers, Inc.

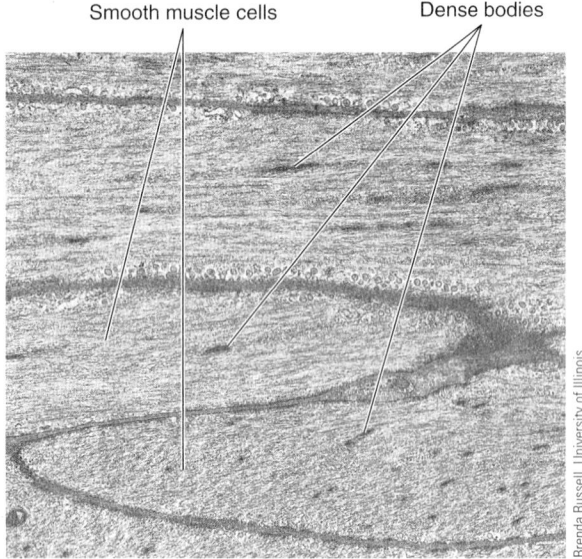

Smooth muscle cells | Dense bodies

Brenda Russell, University of Illinois

(b) Electron micrograph of smooth muscle cells
● **FIGURE 8-21 Microscopic view of smooth muscle cells.**
(a) Note the spindle shape. (b) Note the presence of dense bodies and lack of banding.

Smooth muscle cells are turned on by Ca^{2+}-dependent phosphorylation of myosin.

The thin filaments of smooth muscle cells do not contain troponin, and tropomyosin does not block actin's cross-bridge binding sites. What, then, prevents actin and myosin from binding at the cross bridges in the resting state, and how is cross-bridge activity switched on in the excited state? Smooth muscle myosin can interact with actin only when it is *phosphorylated* (that is, has phosphate from ATP attached to it) at its light chain. The **light chain** is a "necklace" of proteins attached to the head of a myosin molecule, near the "neck" region. During excitation, the increased smooth muscle Ca^{2+} binds with **calmodulin,** an intracellular protein structurally similar to troponin. This Ca^{2+}–calmodulin complex initiates a chain of biochemical events that results in phosphorylation of the myosin light chain. This phosphate on the myosin light chain is in addition to the phosphate accompanying ADP on the myosin cross-bridge ATPase site during the energy cycle (● Figure 8-23). Phosphorylated myosin then binds with actin so that cross-bridge cycling can begin. Therefore, smooth muscle is triggered to contract by a rise in cytosolic Ca^{2+} similar to what happens in skeletal muscle. However, in smooth muscle, Ca^{2+} ultimately turns on the cross bridges by inducing a *chemical* change in myosin in the *thick* filaments (phosphorylation), whereas in skeletal muscle it exerts its effects by causing a *physical* change at the *thin* filaments

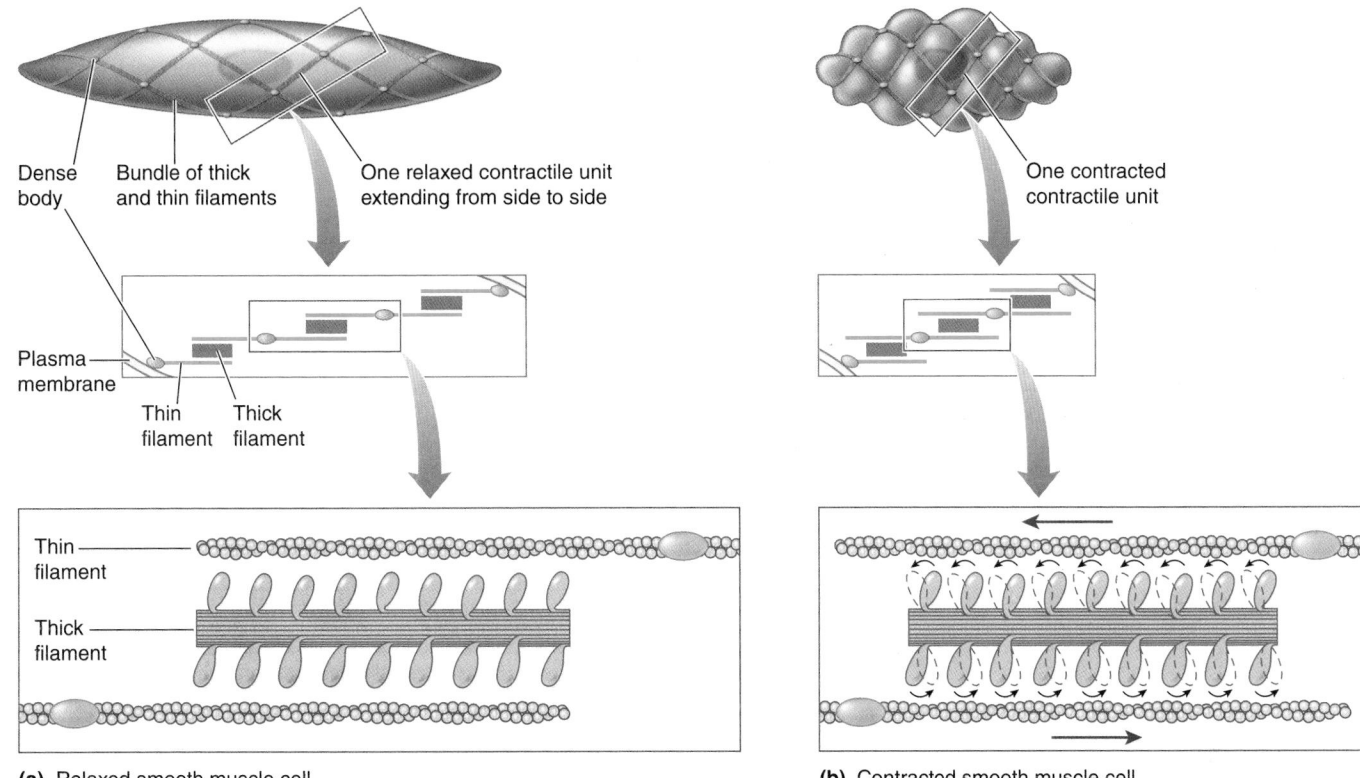

Dense body

Bundle of thick and thin filaments

One relaxed contractile unit extending from side to side

One contracted contractile unit

Plasma membrane

Thin filament

Thick filament

Thin filament

Thick filament

(a) Relaxed smooth muscle cell

(b) Contracted smooth muscle cell

● FIGURE 8-22 **Arrangement of thick and thin filaments in a smooth muscle cell in relaxed and contracted states.**

(moving troponin and tropomyosin from their blocking positions) (● Figure 8-24).

The means by which cytosolic Ca^{2+} concentration increases in smooth muscle cells to turn on the cross bridges also differs from that for skeletal muscle. A smooth muscle cell has no T tubules and a poorly developed sarcoplasmic reticulum. The increased cytosolic Ca^{2+} that triggers contraction comes from two sources: Most Ca^{2+} enters down its concentration gradient from the extracellular fluid (ECF) when surface-membrane Ca^{2+} channels open. The entering Ca^{2+} triggers the opening of Ca^{2+} channels in the sarcoplasmic reticulum so that small additional amounts of Ca^{2+} are released intracellularly from this meager source. Because smooth muscle cells are so much smaller in diameter than skeletal muscle fibers, most Ca^{2+} entering from the ECF can influence cross-bridge activity, even in the central portions of the cell, without requiring an elaborate T tubule–sarcoplasmic reticulum mechanism.

Relaxation in smooth muscle is accomplished by removal of Ca^{2+} as it is actively transported out across the plasma membrane, or back into the sarcoplasmic reticulum, depending on its source. When Ca^{2+} is removed, myosin is dephosphorylated (the phosphate is removed) and can no longer interact with actin, so the muscle relaxes.

We still have not addressed the question of how smooth muscle becomes excited to contract; that is, what opens the Ca^{2+} channels in the plasma membrane? Smooth muscle is grouped into two categories—*multiunit* and *single-unit smooth*

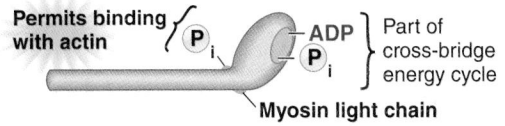

Permits binding with actin

P_i

ADP

P_i

Part of cross-bridge energy cycle

Myosin light chain

● FIGURE 8-23 **Activated myosin cross bridge in smooth muscle.**

muscle—based on differences in how the muscle fibers become excited. Let us compare these two types of smooth muscle.

Multiunit smooth muscle is neurogenic.

Multiunit smooth muscle exhibits properties partway between those of skeletal muscle and those of single-unit smooth muscle. As the name implies, a multiunit smooth muscle consists of multiple discrete units that function independently of one another and must be separately stimulated by nerves to undergo action potentials and contract, similar to skeletal muscle motor units. Thus, contractile activity in both skeletal muscle and multiunit smooth muscle is **neurogenic** ("nerve produced"). That is, contraction in these muscle types is initiated only in response to stimulation by the nerves supplying the muscle. Whereas skeletal muscle is innervated by the voluntary somatic nervous system (motor neurons), multiunit (as well as single-unit) smooth muscle is supplied by the involuntary autonomic nervous system.

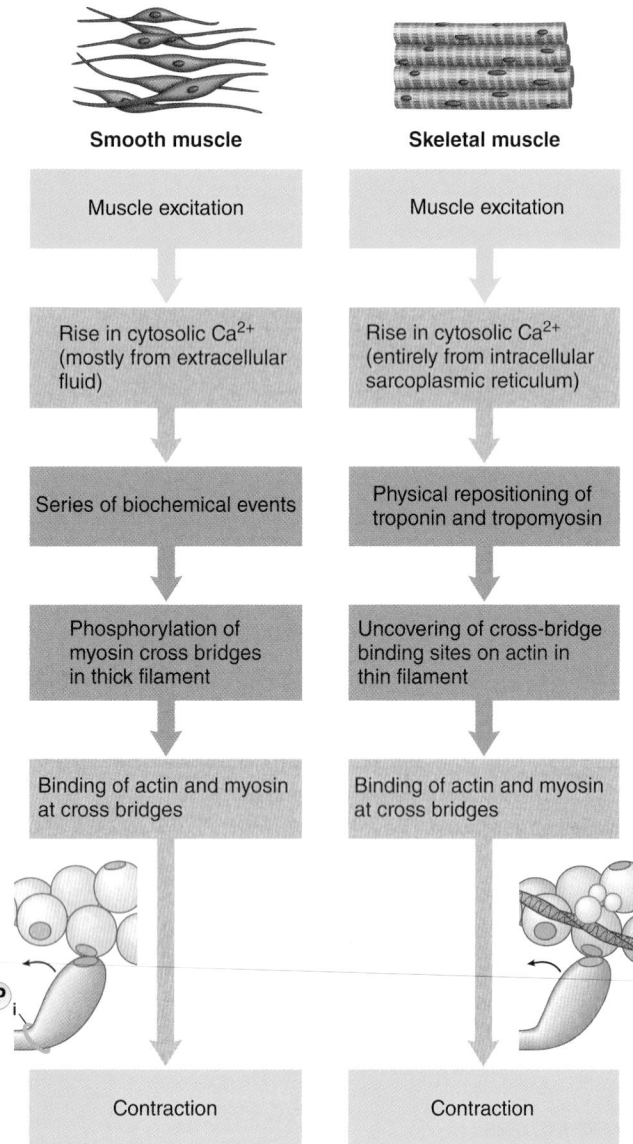

Smooth muscle

Muscle excitation

↓

Rise in cytosolic Ca²⁺ (mostly from extracellular fluid)

↓

Series of biochemical events

↓

Phosphorylation of myosin cross bridges in thick filament

↓

Binding of actin and myosin at cross bridges

↓

Contraction

Skeletal muscle

Muscle excitation

↓

Rise in cytosolic Ca²⁺ (entirely from intracellular sarcoplasmic reticulum)

↓

Physical repositioning of troponin and tropomyosin

↓

Uncovering of cross-bridge binding sites on actin in thin filament

↓

Binding of actin and myosin at cross bridges

↓

Contraction

● **FIGURE 8-24 Comparison of the role of calcium in bringing about contraction in smooth muscle and skeletal muscle.**

Multiunit smooth muscle is found (1) in the walls of large blood vessels; (2) in small airways to the lungs; (3) in the muscle of the eye that adjusts the lens for near or far vision; (4) in the iris of the eye, which alters the pupil size to adjust the amount of light entering the eye; and (5) at the base of hair follicles, contraction of which causes "goose bumps."

Single-unit smooth muscle cells form functional syncytia.

Most smooth muscle is **single-unit smooth muscle,** alternatively called **visceral smooth muscle,** because it is found in the walls of the hollow organs or viscera (for example, the digestive, reproductive, and urinary tracts and small blood vessels). The term *single-unit smooth muscle* derives from the muscle fibers that make up this type of muscle becoming excited and contracting as a single unit. The muscle fibers in single-unit smooth muscle are electrically linked by gap junctions (see p. 53). When an action potential occurs anywhere within a sheet of single-unit smooth

muscle, it is quickly propagated via these special points of electrical contact throughout the entire group of interconnected cells, which then contract as a single, coordinated unit. Such a group of interconnected muscle cells that function electrically and mechanically as a unit is known as a **functional syncytium** (plural, *syncytia; syn* means "together"; *cyt* means "cell").

Thinking about the role of the uterus during labor can help you appreciate the significance of this arrangement. Muscle cells composing the uterine wall act as a functional syncytium. They repetitively become excited and contract as a unit during labor, exerting a series of coordinated "pushes" that eventually deliver the baby. Independent, uncoordinated contractions of individual muscle cells in the uterine wall could not exert the uniformly applied pressure needed to expel the baby.

Single-unit smooth muscle is myogenic.

Single-unit smooth muscle is **self-excitable,** so it does not require nervous stimulation for contraction. Clusters of specialized cells within a functional syncytium display spontaneous electrical activity; that is, they can undergo action potentials without any external stimulation. In contrast to the other excitable cells we have been discussing (such as neurons, skeletal muscle fibers, and multiunit smooth muscle), the self-excitable cells of single-unit smooth muscle do not maintain a constant resting potential. Instead, their membrane potential inherently fluctuates without any influence by factors external to the cell. Two major types of spontaneous depolarizations displayed by self-excitable cells are *pacemaker potentials* and *slow-wave potentials.*

PACEMAKER POTENTIALS With **pacemaker potentials,** the membrane potential of specialized muscle cells gradually depolarizes on its own because of shifts in passive ionic fluxes accompanying automatic changes in channel permeability (● Figure 8-25a). When the membrane has depolarized to threshold, an action potential is initiated. After repolarizing, the membrane potential again depolarizes to threshold, cyclically continuing in this manner to repetitively self-generate action potentials.

Self-excitable smooth muscle pacemaker cells are specialized to initiate action potentials, but they are not equipped to contract. Only a few of all the cells in a functional syncytium are noncontractile, pacemaker cells. Most smooth muscle cells are specialized to contract but cannot self-initiate action potentials. However, once an action potential is initiated by a self-excitable pacemaker cell, it is conducted to the remaining contractile, nonpacemaker cells of the functional syncytium via gap junctions, so the entire group of connected cells contracts as a unit without any nervous input. Such nerve-independent contractile activity initiated by the muscle itself is called **myogenic activity** ("muscle-produced" activity), in contrast to the neurogenic activity of skeletal muscle and multiunit smooth muscle.

SLOW-WAVE POTENTIALS **Slow-wave potentials** are spontaneous, gradually alternating depolarizing and hyperpolarizing swings in potential (● Figure 8-25b) brought about by un-

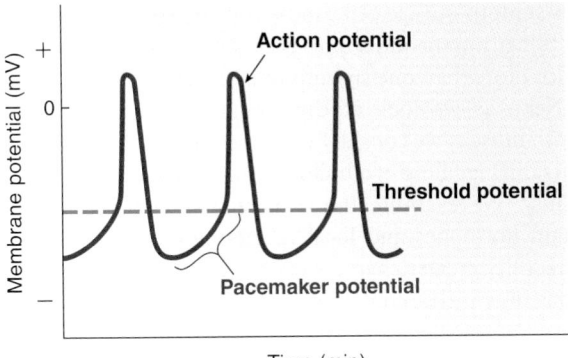

(a) Pacemaker potential

(b) Slow-wave potential

● **FIGURE 8-25 Self-generated electrical activity in smooth muscle.** (a) With pacemaker potentials, the membrane gradually depolarizes to threshold periodically without any nervous stimulation. These regular depolarizations cyclically trigger self-induced action potentials. (b) In slow-wave potentials, the membrane gradually undergoes self-induced depolarizing and hyperpolarizing swings in potential. A burst of action potentials occurs if a depolarizing swing brings the membrane to threshold.

known mechanisms. They occur only in smooth muscle of the digestive tract. Slow-wave potentials are initiated by specialized clusters of nonmuscle pacemaker cells within the digestive tract wall and spread to the adjacent smooth muscle cells via gap junctions. The potential is moved farther from threshold during each hyperpolarizing swing and closer to threshold during each depolarizing swing. If threshold is reached, a burst of action potentials occurs at the peak of a depolarizing swing. These action potentials bring about myogenically induced contraction. Threshold is not always reached, however, so the oscillating slow-wave potentials can continue without generating action potentials and contractile activity. Whether threshold is reached depends on the starting point of the membrane potential at the onset of its depolarizing swing. The starting point, in turn, is influenced by neural and local factors typically associated with meals (see Chapter 15 for further detail). We have now discussed all the means by which excitable tissues can be brought to threshold. ▲ Table 8-4 summarizes the different triggering events that can initiate action potentials in various excitable tissues.

Gradation of single-unit smooth muscle contraction differs from that of skeletal muscle.

Single-unit smooth muscle differs from skeletal muscle in the way contraction is graded. Gradation of skeletal muscle contraction is entirely under neural control, primarily involving motor unit recruitment and twitch summation. In single-unit smooth muscle, gap junctions ensure that an entire smooth muscle mass contracts as a single unit, making it impossible to vary the number of muscle fibers contracting. Only the tension of the fibers can be modified to achieve varying strengths of contraction of the whole organ. The portion of cross bridges activated and the tension subsequently developed in single-unit smooth muscle can be graded by varying the cytosolic Ca^{2+}

▲ Table 8-4 Various Means of Initiating Action Potentials in Excitable Tissues

Method of Depolarizing the Membrane to Threshold Potential	Type of Excitable Tissue Involved	Description of This Triggering Event
Summation of EPSPs (see p. 94)	Efferent neurons and interneurons	Temporal or spatial summation of slight depolarizations (EPSPs) of the dendrite and cell body end of the neuron brought about by changes in channel permeability in response to binding of an excitatory neurotransmitter with surface membrane receptors
Receptor Potential (see p. 152)	Afferent neurons	Typically a depolarization of the afferent neuron's receptor initiated by changes in channel permeability in response to the neuron's adequate stimulus
End-Plate Potential (see p. 199)	Skeletal muscle	Depolarization of the motor end plate brought about by changes in channel permeability in response to binding of the neurotransmitter ACh with receptors on the end-plate membrane
Pacemaker Potential (see p. 236)	Smooth muscle and cardiac muscle	Gradual depolarization of the membrane on its own because of shifts in passive ionic fluxes accompanying automatic changes in channel permeability
Slow-Wave Potential (see p. 236)	Smooth muscle in digestive tract only	Gradual alternating depolarizing and hyperpolarizing swings in potential initiated by associated nonmuscle self-excitable cells; the depolarizing swing may or may not reach threshold

concentration. A single excitation in smooth muscle does not cause all cross bridges to switch on, in contrast to skeletal muscles, where a single action potential triggers release of enough Ca^{2+} to permit all cross bridges to cycle. As Ca^{2+} concentration increases in smooth muscle, more cross bridges are brought into play and greater tension develops.

SMOOTH MUSCLE TONE Many single-unit smooth muscle cells have sufficient levels of cytosolic Ca^{2+} to maintain a low level of tension, or **tone,** even in the absence of action potentials. A sudden drastic change in Ca^{2+}, such as accompanies a myogenically induced action potential, brings about a contractile response superimposed on the ongoing tonic tension.

OTHER FACTORS INFLUENCING SMOOTH MUSCLE ACTIVITY Besides self-induced action potentials, several other factors such as (1) autonomic neurotransmitters, (2) mechanical stretch, (3) certain hormones, and (4) local metabolites can influence contractile activity and the development of tension in smooth muscle cells by altering their cytosolic Ca^{2+} concentration. Thus, smooth muscle is subject to more external influences than skeletal muscle is, even though smooth muscle can contract on its own and skeletal muscle cannot.

MODIFICATION OF SMOOTH MUSCLE ACTIVITY BY THE AUTONOMIC NERVOUS SYSTEM Smooth muscle is typically innervated by both branches of the autonomic nervous system. In single-unit smooth muscle, this nerve supply does not *initiate* contraction, but it can *modify* the rate and strength of contraction, either enhancing or retarding the inherent contractile activity of a given organ. Recall that the isolated motor end-plate region of a skeletal muscle fiber interacts with ACh released from a single axon terminal of a motor neuron. In contrast, the receptors that bind with autonomic neurotransmitters are dispersed throughout the entire surface membrane of a smooth muscle cell. Smooth muscle cells are sensitive to varying degrees and in varying ways to autonomic neurotransmitters, depending on the cells' distribution of cholinergic and adrenergic receptors (see p. 196).

Each terminal branch of a postganglionic autonomic fiber travels across the surface of one or more smooth muscle cells, releasing neurotransmitter from the vesicles within its multiple varicosities (bulges) as an action potential passes along the terminal (● Figure 8-26). The neurotransmitter diffuses to the many receptors specific for it on the cells underlying the terminal. Thus, in contrast to the discrete one-to-one relationship at motor end plates, a given smooth muscle cell can be influenced by more than one type of neurotransmitter, and each autonomic terminal can influence more than one smooth muscle cell.

Next, as we look at the length–tension relationship in smooth muscle, we consider the effect of mechanical stretch (as occurs during filling of a hollow organ) on smooth muscle contractility. We examine the extracellular chemical influences (certain hormones and local metabolites) on smooth muscle contractility in later chapters when we discuss regulation of the various organs that contain smooth muscle.

Smooth muscle can still develop tension when stretched.

The relationship between the length of the muscle fibers before contraction and the tension that can be developed on a subsequent contraction is less closely linked in smooth muscle than in skeletal muscle. The range of lengths over which a smooth muscle fiber can develop near-maximal tension is greater than the range for skeletal muscle. Smooth muscle can still develop considerable tension even when stretched up to 2.5 times its resting length, for two reasons. First, in contrast to skeletal muscle, in which the resting length is at l_o, in smooth muscle the resting (nonstretched) length is much shorter than at l_o. Therefore, smooth muscle can be stretched considerably before reaching its l_o. Second, the thin filaments still overlap the longer thick filaments even in the stretched-out position, so crossbridge interaction and tension development can still take place. In contrast, when skeletal muscle is stretched only three fourths longer than its resting length, the thick and thin filaments are completely pulled apart and can no longer interact (see ● Figure 8-17, p. 223).

The ability of a considerably stretched smooth muscle fiber to still develop tension is important, because the smooth muscle fibers within the wall of a hollow organ are progressively stretched as the volume of the organ's contents expands. Consider the urinary bladder as an example. Even though the muscle fibers in the urinary bladder are stretched as the bladder

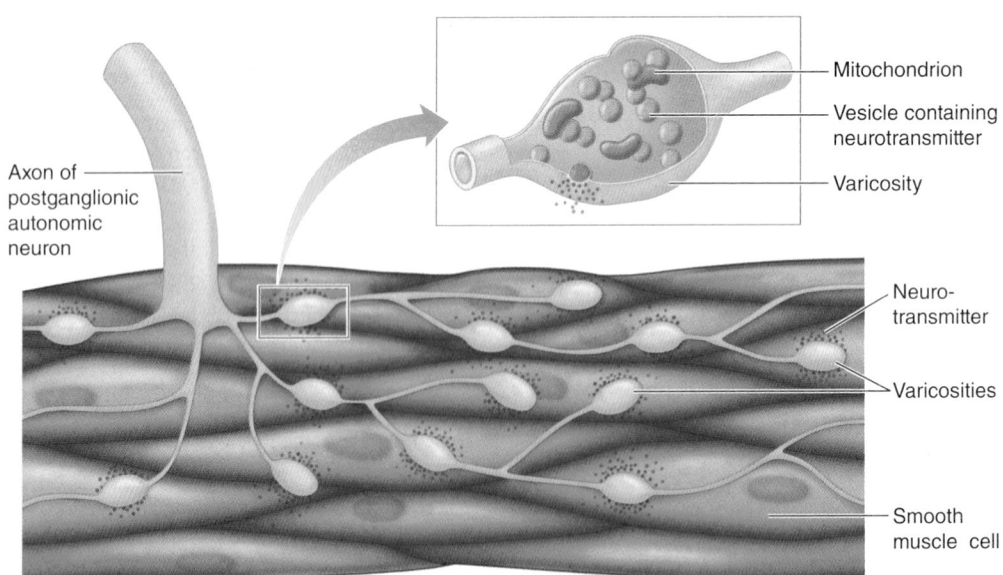

● **FIGURE 8-26 Innervation of smooth muscle by autonomic postganglionic nerve terminals.**

gradually fills with urine, they still maintain their tone and can even develop further tension in response to inputs that regulate bladder emptying. If considerable stretching prevented tension development, as in skeletal muscle, a filled bladder would not be capable of contracting to empty. Smooth muscle fibers can contract to half their normal length, enabling hollow organs to dramatically empty their contents; thus, smooth-muscled viscera can easily accommodate large volumes but can empty to practically zero volume. This length range in which smooth muscle normally functions (anywhere from 0.5 to 2.5 times the normal length) is greater than the limited length range within which skeletal muscle remains functional.

Smooth muscle is slow and economical.

A smooth muscle contractile response proceeds more slowly than a skeletal muscle twitch. ATP splitting by myosin ATPase is slower in smooth muscle, so cross-bridge activity and filament sliding occur about 10 times more slowly in smooth muscle than in skeletal muscle. A single smooth muscle contraction may last as long as 3 seconds (3000 msec), compared to the maximum of 100 msec for a single contractile response in skeletal muscle. Smooth muscle also relaxes more slowly because of slower Ca^{2+} removal. Slowness should not be equated with weakness, however. Smooth muscle can generate the same contractile tension per unit of cross-sectional area as skeletal muscle, but it does so more slowly and at considerably less energy expense. Because of slow cross-bridge cycling during smooth muscle contraction, cross bridges stay attached for more time during each cycle, compared with skeletal muscle; that is, the cross bridges "latch onto" the thin filaments for a longer time each cycle. This **latch phenomenon** enables smooth muscle to maintain tension with comparatively less ATP consumption because each cross-bridge cycle uses up one molecule of ATP. Smooth muscle is therefore an economical contractile tissue, making it well suited for long-term sustained contractions with little energy consumption and without fatigue. In contrast to the rapidly changing demands placed on your skeletal muscles as you maneuver through and manipulate your external environment, your smooth muscle activities are geared for long-term duration and slower adjustments to change. Because of its slowness and the less ordered arrangement of its filaments, smooth muscle has often been mistakenly viewed as a poorly developed version of skeletal muscle. Actually, smooth muscle is just as highly specialized for the demands placed on it. It is an extremely adaptive, efficient tissue.

Cardiac muscle blends features of both skeletal and smooth muscle.

Cardiac muscle, found only in the heart, shares structural and functional characteristics with both skeletal and single-unit smooth muscle. Like skeletal muscle, cardiac muscle is striated, with its thick and thin filaments highly organized into a regular banding pattern. Cardiac thin filaments contain troponin and tropomyosin, which constitute the site of Ca^{2+} action in switching on cross-bridge activity, as in skeletal muscle. Also like skeletal muscle, cardiac muscle has a clear length–tension relation-ship. Like the oxidative skeletal muscle fibers, cardiac muscle cells have lots of mitochondria and myoglobin. They also have T tubules and a moderately well-developed sarcoplasmic reticulum.

As in smooth muscle, Ca^{2+} enters the cytosol from both the ECF and the sarcoplasmic reticulum during cardiac excitation. Ca^{2+} entry from the ECF triggers release of Ca^{2+} intracellularly from the sarcoplasmic reticulum. Like single-unit smooth muscle, the heart displays pacemaker (but not slow-wave) activity, initiating its own action potentials without any external influence. Cardiac cells are interconnected by gap junctions that enhance the spread of action potentials throughout the heart, just as in single-unit smooth muscle. Also similarly, the heart is innervated by the autonomic nervous system, which, along with certain hormones and local factors, can modify the rate and strength of contraction.

Unique to cardiac muscle, the cardiac fibers are joined in a branching network, and the action potentials of cardiac muscle last much longer before repolarizing. Further details and the importance of cardiac muscle's features are addressed in the next chapter.

Chapter in Perspective: Focus on Homeostasis

Skeletal muscles comprise the muscular system itself. Cardiac muscle and smooth muscle are part of organs that make up other body systems. Cardiac muscle is found only in the heart, which is part of the circulatory system. Smooth muscle is found in the walls of hollow organs and tubes, including the blood vessels in the circulatory system, airways in the respiratory system, bladder in the urinary system, stomach and intestines in the digestive system, and tubular components of the reproductive system, an example being the uterus in females.

Contraction of skeletal muscles accomplishes movement of body parts in relation to one another and movement of the whole body in relation to the external environment. Thus, these muscles permit you to move through and manipulate your external environment. At a general level, some of these movements are aimed at maintaining homeostasis, such as moving the body toward food or away from harm. Examples of more specific homeostatic functions accomplished by skeletal muscles include chewing and swallowing food for further breakdown in the digestive system into usable energy-producing nutrient molecules (the mouth and throat muscles are all skeletal muscles) and breathing to obtain O_2 and get rid of carbon dioxide (the respiratory muscles are all skeletal muscles). Contracting skeletal muscles also are the major source of heat production in maintaining body temperature. The skeletal muscles further accomplish many nonhomeostatic activities that enable us to work and play—for example, operating a piece of equipment or riding a bicycle—so that we can contribute to society and enjoy ourselves.

All other systems of the body, except the immune (defense) system, depend on their nonskeletal muscle components to enable them to accomplish their homeostatic functions. For example, contraction of cardiac muscle in the heart pushes life-sustaining blood forward into the blood vessels, and contraction of smooth muscle in the stomach and intestines pushes ingested food through the digestive tract at a rate appropriate for the digestive juices secreted along the route to break down the food into usable units.

REVIEW EXERCISES

Objective Questions (Answers on p. A-42)

1. When an action potential in a muscle fiber is completed, the contractile activity initiated by the action potential stops. *(True or false?)*
2. The velocity at which a muscle shortens depends entirely on the ATPase activity of its fibers. *(True or false?)*
3. When a skeletal muscle is maximally stretched, it can develop maximal tension on contraction, because the actin filaments can slide in a maximal distance. *(True or false?)*
4. A pacemaker potential always initiates an action potential. *(True or false?)*
5. A slow-wave potential always initiates an action potential. *(True or false?)*
6. Smooth muscle can develop tension even when considerably stretched, because the thin filaments still overlap with the long, thick filaments. *(True or false?)*
7. A(n) _____ contraction is an isotonic contraction in which the muscle shortens, whereas the muscle lengthens in a(n) _____ isotonic contraction.
8. _____ motor neurons supply extrafusal muscle fibers, whereas intrafusal fibers are innervated by _____ motor neurons.
9. Which of the following provide(s) direct input to alpha motor neurons? *(Indicate all correct answers.)*
   a. primary motor cortex
   b. brain stem
   c. cerebellum
   d. basal nuclei
   e. spinal reflex pathways
10. Which of the following is *not* involved in bringing about muscle relaxation?
   a. reuptake of Ca^{2+} by the sarcoplasmic reticulum
   b. no more ATP
   c. no more action potential
   d. removal of ACh at the end plate by acetylcholinesterase
   e. filaments sliding back to their resting position

11. Match the following (with reference to skeletal muscle):
   ___ 1. Ca^{2+}
   ___ 2. T tubule
   ___ 3. ATP
   ___ 4. lateral sacs of the sarcoplasmic reticulum
   ___ 5. myosin
   ___ 6. troponin–tropomyosin complex
   ___ 7. actin

   (a) cyclically binds with the myosin cross bridges during contraction
   (b) has ATPase activity
   (c) supplies energy for the power stroke of a cross bridge
   (d) rapidly transmits the action potential to the central portion of the muscle fiber
   (e) stores Ca^{2+}
   (f) pulls the troponin–tropomyosin complex out of its blocking position
   (g) prevents actin from interacting with myosin when the muscle fiber is not excited

12. Using the answer code at the right, indicate what happens in the banding pattern during contraction:
   ___ 1. thick myofilament
   ___ 2. thin myofilament
   ___ 3. A band
   ___ 4. I band
   ___ 5. H zone
   ___ 6. sarcomere

   (a) remains the same size during contraction
   (b) decreases in length (shortens) during contraction

Essay Questions

1. Describe the levels of organization in a skeletal muscle.
2. What produces the striated appearance of skeletal muscles? Describe or draw the arrangement of thick and thin filaments that gives rise to the banding pattern.
3. What is the functional unit of skeletal muscle?
4. Describe the composition of thick and thin filaments.
5. Describe the sliding filament mechanism of muscle contraction. How do cross-bridge power strokes bring about shortening of the muscle fiber?
6. Compare the excitation–contraction coupling process in skeletal muscle with that in smooth muscle.
7. Compare isotonic and isometric contractions.
8. How can gradation of skeletal muscle contraction be accomplished?
9. What is a motor unit? Compare the size of motor units in finely controlled muscles with those specialized for coarse, powerful contractions. Describe motor unit recruitment.
10. Explain twitch summation and tetanus.

11. How does a skeletal muscle fiber's length at the onset of contraction affect the strength of the subsequent contraction?
12. Describe the role of each of the following in powering skeletal muscle contraction: ATP, creatine phosphate, oxidative phosphorylation, and glycolysis. Distinguish between aerobically and anaerobically supported exercise.
13. Compare the three types of skeletal muscle fibers.
14. What are the roles of the corticospinal system and multineuronal system in controlling motor movement?
15. Describe the structure and function of muscle spindles and Golgi tendon organs.

16. Distinguish between multiunit and single-unit smooth muscle.
17. Differentiate between neurogenic and myogenic muscle activity.
18. How can smooth muscle contraction be graded?
19. Compare the contractile speed and relative energy expenditure of skeletal muscle with that of smooth muscle.
20. In what ways is cardiac muscle functionally similar to skeletal muscle and to single-unit smooth muscle?

POINTS TO PONDER

(Explanations on p. A-42)

1. Why does regular aerobic exercise provide more cardiovascular benefit than weight training does? (*Hint:* The heart responds to the demands placed on it in a way similar to that of skeletal muscle.)
2. Put yourself in the position of the scientists who discovered the sliding filament mechanism of muscle contraction by considering what molecular changes must be involved to account for the observed alterations in the banding pattern during contraction. If you were comparing a relaxed and a contracted muscle fiber under an electron microscope (see ● Figure 8-3a, p. 212), how could you determine that the thin filaments do not change in length during muscle contraction? You cannot see or measure a single thin filament at this magnification. (*Hint:* What landmark in the banding pattern represents each end of the thin filament? If these landmarks are the same distance apart in a relaxed and contracted fiber, then the thin filaments must not change in length.)
3. What type of off-the-snow training would you recommend for a competitive downhill skier versus a competitive cross-country skier? What adaptive skeletal muscle changes would you hope to accomplish in the athletes in each case?
4. When the bladder is filled and the micturition (urination) reflex is initiated, the nervous system supply to the bladder promotes contraction of the bladder and relaxation of the external urethral sphincter, a ring of muscle that guards the exit from the bladder. If the time is inopportune for bladder emptying when the micturition reflex is initiated, the external urethral sphincter can be voluntarily tightened to prevent urination even though the bladder is contracting. Using your knowledge of the muscle types and their innervation, of what types of muscle are the bladder and the external urethral sphincter composed, and what branch of the efferent division of the peripheral nervous system supplies each of these muscles?
5. Three-dimensionally, the thin filaments are arranged hexagonally around the thick filaments in a skeletal muscle fiber. Cross bridges project from each thick filament in all six directions toward the surrounding thin filaments. Each thin filament, in turn, is surrounded by three thick filaments. Sketch this geometric arrangement of thick and thin filaments in cross section.

CLINICAL CONSIDERATION

(Explanation on p. A-43)

Jason W. is waiting impatiently for the doctor to finish removing the cast from his leg, which Jason broke the last day of school 6 weeks ago. Summer vacation is half over, and he hasn't been able to swim, play baseball, or participate in any of his favorite sports. When the cast is finally off, Jason's excitement gives way to concern when he sees that the injured limb is noticeably smaller in diameter than his normal leg. What explains this reduction in size? How can the leg be restored to its normal size and functional ability?

Chapter 8

Study Card

Structure of Skeletal Muscle (pp. 209–212)

■ Muscles, contraction specialists, can develop tension, shorten, produce movement, and accomplish work.

■ The three types of muscle are categorized in two ways according to common characteristics: (1) Skeletal muscle and cardiac muscle are striated, whereas smooth muscle is unstriated. (2) Skeletal muscle is voluntary, whereas cardiac muscle and smooth muscle are involuntary. *(Review Figure 8-1 and Table 8-3, pp. 232–233.)*

■ Skeletal muscles are made up of bundles of long, cylindrical muscle cells called muscle fibers, wrapped in connective tissue.

■ Muscle fibers are packed with myofibrils, each myofibril consisting of alternating, slightly overlapping stacked sets of thick and thin filaments. This arrangement leads to a skeletal muscle fiber's striated microscopic appearance, which consists of alternating dark A bands and light I bands. A sarcomere, the area between two Z lines, is the functional unit of skeletal muscle. *(Review Figures 8-2 and 8-3.)*

■ Thick filaments consist of the protein myosin. Cross bridges made up of the myosin molecules' globular heads project from each thick filament toward the surrounding thin filaments. *(Review Figures 8-2 and 8-4.)*

■ Thin filaments consist primarily of the protein actin, which can bind and interact with the myosin cross bridges to bring about contraction. In the resting state, two other proteins, tropomyosin and troponin, lie across the surface of the thin filament to prevent this cross-bridge interaction. *(Review Figures 8-2 and 8-5.)*

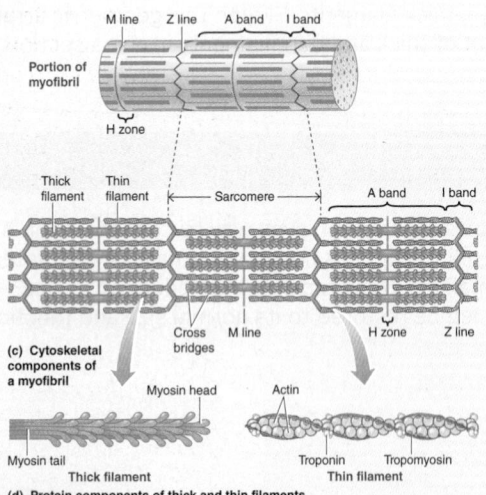

Molecular Basis of Skeletal Muscle Contraction (pp. 212–218)

■ Excitation of a skeletal muscle fiber by its motor neuron brings about contraction through a series of events that results in the thin filaments sliding closer together between the thick filaments. *(Review Figure 8-7.)*

■ This sliding filament mechanism of muscle contraction is switched on by Ca^{2+} release from the lateral sacs of the sarcoplasmic reticulum in response to the spread of a muscle fiber action potential into the central portions of the fiber via the T tubules. *(Review Figures 8-9 and 8-10.)*

■ Released Ca^{2+} binds to troponin, slightly repositioning tropomyosin to uncover actin's cross-bridge binding sites. *(Review Figures 8-6 and 8-10.)*

■ Binding of actin to a myosin cross bridge triggers cross-bridge stroking, powered by energy stored in the myosin head from prior splitting of ATP by myosin ATPase. During a power stroke, the cross bridge bends toward the thick filament's center, "rowing" in the thin filament to which it is attached. *(Review Figures 8-8, 8-10, and 8-11.)*

■ When a fresh ATP attaches to the cross bridge, myosin and actin detach, the cross bridge returns to its original shape, and the cycle is repeated. Repeated cycles of cross-bridge activity slide the thin filaments inward step by step. *(Review Figures 8-8 and 8-11.)*

■ When the action potential ends, the lateral sacs actively take up the Ca^{2+}, troponin and tropomyosin slip back into their blocking position, and relaxation occurs. *(Review Figure 8-10.)*

■ The entire contractile response lasts about 100 times longer than the action potential. *(Review Figure 8-12.)*

Skeletal Muscle Mechanics (pp. 218–224)

■ Tension is generated within a muscle by the contractile component (sarcomere shortening brought about by cross-bridge cycling). To move the bone to which the muscle's insertion is attached, this internal tension is transmitted to the bone as the contractile component stretches and tightens the muscle's series-elastic component (intracellular titin, connective tissue, and tendon). *(Review Figure 8-13.)*

■ The two primary types of muscle contraction—isometric (constant length) and isotonic (constant tension)—depend on the relationship between muscle tension and the load (the weight of an object being lifted). (1) If tension is less than the load, the muscle cannot shorten and lift the object but remains at constant length (an isometric contraction). (2) If the tension exceeds the load, the muscle can shorten and lift the object, maintaining constant tension while shortening (isotonic contraction).

■ The velocity, or speed, of shortening is inversely proportional to the load.

■ Gradation of whole-muscle contraction can be accomplished by (1) varying the number of muscle fibers contracting within the muscle and (2) varying the tension developed by each contracting fiber. *(Review Table 8-2, p. 228.)*

■ The number of fibers contracting depends on (1) the size of the muscle (the number of muscle fibers present), (2) the extent of motor unit recruitment (how many motor neurons supplying the muscle are active), and (3) the size of each motor unit (how many muscle fibers are activated simultaneously by a single mo-

242

tor neuron). A motor unit is a motor neuron plus all of the muscle fibers it innervates. (Review Figure 8-15 and Table 8-2.)

■ Two variable factors that affect fiber tension are (1) frequency of stimulation, which determines the extent of twitch summation, and (2) length of the fiber before the onset of contraction (length–tension relationship). (Review Table 8-2.)

■ Twitch summation is the increase in tension accompanying repetitive stimulation of a muscle fiber. After undergoing an action potential, the muscle cell membrane recovers from its refractory period and can be restimulated while some contractile activity triggered by the first action potential remains so that the twitches induced by the two rapidly successive action potentials sum. If the muscle fiber is stimulated so rapidly that it does not have a chance to start relaxing between stimuli, a smooth, sustained maximal contraction known as tetanus occurs. (Review Figure 8-16.)

■ The tension also depends on the length of the fiber at the onset of contraction. Maximal opportunity for cross-bridge interaction occurs at optimal length (l_o) (the resting muscle length) because of optimal overlap of thick and thin filaments, so the greatest tension can develop. Less tension can develop at shorter or longer lengths. (Review Figure 8-17.)

Skeletal Muscle Metabolism and Fiber Types (pp. 224–228)

■ Three pathways furnish the ATP needed for muscle contraction and relaxation: (1) the transfer of high-energy phosphates from stored creatine phosphate to ADP, providing the first source of ATP at the onset of exercise; (2) oxidative phosphorylation, which efficiently extracts large amounts of ATP from nutrients if enough O_2 is available to support this system; and (3) glycolysis, which can synthesize ATP in the absence of O_2 but uses large amounts of stored glycogen and produces lactate in the process.

■ The three types of skeletal muscle fibers are classified by the pathways they use for ATP synthesis (oxidative or glycolytic) and the rapidity with which they split ATP and subsequently contract (slow twitch or fast twitch): (1) slow-oxidative fibers, (2) fast-oxidative fibers, and (3) fast-glycolytic fibers. (Review Table 8-1.)

Control of Motor Movement (pp. 228–231)

■ Control of motor movement depends on activity in the three types of presynaptic inputs that converge on the motor neurons supplying various muscles: (1) spinal reflex pathways, which originate with afferent neurons; (2) the corticospinal (pyramidal) motor system, which originates in the primary motor cortex and is concerned with discrete, intricate movements of the hands; and (3) the multineuronal (extrapyramidal) motor system, which originates in the brain stem and is involved with postural adjustments and involuntary movements of the trunk and limbs. The final motor output from the brain stem is influenced by the cerebellum, basal nuclei, and cerebral cortex.

■ Establishment and adjustment of motor commands depend on continuous afferent input, especially feedback about changes in muscle length (monitored by muscle spindles) and muscle tension (monitored by Golgi tendon organs). (Review Figure 8-18.)

■ When a whole muscle is stretched, the stretch of its muscle spindles triggers the stretch reflex, which results in reflex con-

traction of that muscle. This reflex resists any passive changes in muscle length. (Review Figures 8-19 and 8-20.)

Smooth and Cardiac Muscle (pp. 231–239)

■ Smooth muscle cells are spindle shaped and smaller than skeletal muscle fibers. The thick and thin filaments of smooth muscle are oriented diagonally in a diamond-shaped lattice instead of running longitudinally, so the fibers are not striated. (Review Figures 8-21 and 8-22.)

■ In smooth muscle, cytosolic Ca^{2+}, which enters from the ECF and is also released from sparse intracellular stores, activates cross-bridge cycling by initiating a series of biochemical reactions that result in phosphorylation of the light chains of the myosin cross bridges to enable them to bind with actin. (Review Figures 8-23 and 8-24.)

■ Multiunit smooth muscle is neurogenic, requiring stimulation of individual muscle fibers by its autonomic nerve supply to trigger contraction.

■ Single-unit smooth muscle is myogenic; it can initiate its own contraction without any external influence, as a result of spontaneous depolarization to threshold potential by a few specialized, self-excitable noncontractile cells within a functional syncytium. The two major types of spontaneous potential changes displayed by self-excitable cells are (1) pacemaker potentials (spontaneous drift to threshold potential, displayed in most single-unit smooth muscle) and (2) slow-wave potentials (spontaneous alternating depolarizing and hyperpolarizing swings in potential, occurring only in digestive tract smooth muscle). When threshold is reached and an action potential is initiated, this electrical activity spreads by means of gap junctions to the surrounding contractile cells within the functional syncytium, so the entire sheet of smooth muscle becomes excited and contracts as a unit. (Review Figure 8-25 and Table 8-4.)

■ The level of tension in single-unit smooth muscle depends on the level of cytosolic Ca^{2+}. Some single-unit smooth muscle cells have sufficient cytosolic Ca^{2+} to maintain a low level of tension known as tone, even in the absence of action potentials.

■ The autonomic nervous system (Review Figure 8-26), as well as hormones and local metabolites, can modify the rate and strength of contractions by altering cytosolic Ca^{2+} concentration.

■ Smooth muscle does not have a clear-cut length—tension relationship. Unlike skeletal muscle, it can develop tension when considerably stretched.

■ Smooth muscle contractions are slow and energy efficient, enabling this type of muscle to economically sustain long-term contractions without fatigue. This economy, coupled with single-unit smooth muscle's ability to exist at various lengths with little change in tension, makes single-unit smooth muscle ideally suited for its task of forming the walls of hollow organs that can distend.

■ Cardiac muscle is found only in the heart. It has highly organized striated fibers, like skeletal muscle. Like single-unit smooth muscle, some specialized, self-excitable cardiac muscle fibers can generate action potentials, which spread throughout the heart with the aid of gap junctions. (Review Table 8-3.)

Circulatory System (Heart)

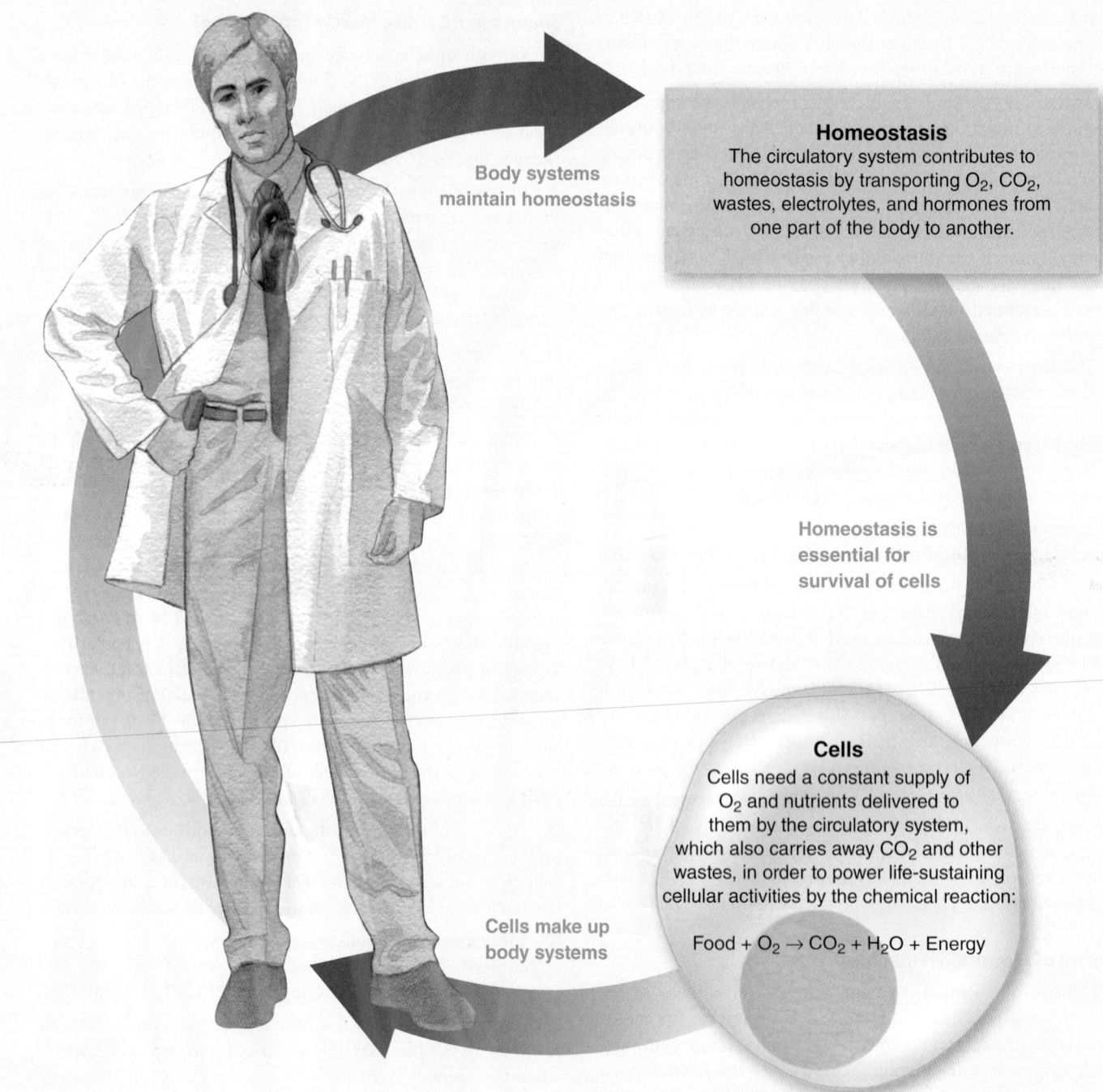

Body systems maintain homeostasis

Homeostasis
The circulatory system contributes to homeostasis by transporting O_2, CO_2, wastes, electrolytes, and hormones from one part of the body to another.

Homeostasis is essential for survival of cells

Cells
Cells need a constant supply of O_2 and nutrients delivered to them by the circulatory system, which also carries away CO_2 and other wastes, in order to power life-sustaining cellular activities by the chemical reaction:

Food + O_2 → CO_2 + H_2O + Energy

Cells make up body systems

To maintain homeostasis, essential materials such as O_2 and nutrients must continually be picked up from the external environment and delivered to the cells and waste products must continually be removed. Furthermore, excess heat generated by muscles must be transported to the skin where it can be lost from the body surface to help maintain body temperature. Homeostasis also depends on the transfer of hormones, which are important regulatory chemical messengers, from their site of production to their site of action. The circulatory system, which contributes to homeostasis by serving as the body's transport system, consists of the heart, blood vessels, and blood.

All body tissues constantly depend on the life-supporting blood flow the heart provides them by contracting or beating. The heart drives blood through the blood vessels for delivery to the tissues in sufficient amounts, whether the body is at rest or engaging in vigorous exercise.

Cardiac Physiology

CHAPTER AT A GLANCE

Anatomy of the Heart
Location of the heart
The heart as a dual pump
Heart valves
Heart walls; cardiac muscle

Electrical Activity of the Heart
Pacemaker activity
Spread of cardiac excitation
Action potential of cardiac contractile
    cells
Cardiac refractory period
Electrocardiography

Mechanical Events of the Cardiac Cycle
Electrical, pressure, and volume
    relationships during diastole and
    systole
Heart sounds

Cardiac Output and Its Control
Determinants of cardiac output
Control of heart rate
Control of stroke volume

Nourishing the Heart Muscle
Coronary circulation
Coronary artery disease

Anatomy of the Heart

From just days following conception until death, the beat goes on. Throughout an average human life span, the heart contracts about 3 billion times, never stopping except for a fraction of a second to fill between beats. Within about 3 weeks after conception, the heart of the developing embryo starts to function. It is the first organ to become functional. At this time, the human embryo is only a few millimeters long, about the size of a capital letter on this page.

Why does the heart develop so early, and why is it so crucial throughout life? It is this important because the circulatory system is the body's transport system. A human embryo, having little yolk available as food, depends on promptly establishing a circulatory system that can interact with the mother's circulation to pick up and distribute to the developing tissues the supplies so critical for survival and growth. Thus begins the story of the circulatory system, which continues throughout life to be a vital pipeline for transporting materials on which the cells of the body absolutely depend.

The **circulatory system** has three basic components:

1. The **heart** is the pump that imparts pressure to the blood to establish the pressure gradient needed for blood to flow to the tissues. Like all liquids, blood flows down a pressure gradient from an area of higher pressure to an area of lower pressure. This chapter focuses on cardiac physiology (*cardia* means "heart").

2. The **blood vessels** are the passageways through which blood is directed and distributed from the heart to all parts of the body and subsequently returned to the heart. The smallest of the blood vessels are designed for rapid exchange of materials between the surrounding tissues and the blood within the vessels (see Chapter 10).

3. **Blood** is the transport medium within which materials being transported long distances in the body, such as O_2, CO_2, nutrients, wastes, electrolytes, and hormones, are dissolved or suspended (see Chapter 11).

Blood travels continuously through the circulatory system to and from the heart through two separate vascular (blood vessel) loops, both originating and terminating at the heart (● Figure 9-1). The **pulmonary circulation** consists of a closed loop of vessels carrying blood between the heart and the lungs (*pulmo* means "lung"). The **systemic circulation** is a circuit of vessels carrying blood between the heart and the other body systems. Each of these vascular loops forms a figure "8." The pulmonary circulation simultaneously loops through the right lung and the left lung; the systemic circulation simultaneously loops through the upper half and the lower half of the body.

The heart is positioned in the middle of the thoracic cavity.

The heart is a hollow, muscular organ about the size of a clenched fist. It lies in the **thoracic** (chest) **cavity** about midline between the **sternum** (breastbone) anteriorly and the **vertebrae** (backbone) posteriorly. Place your hand over your heart. People usually put their hand on the left side of the chest, even though the heart is actually in

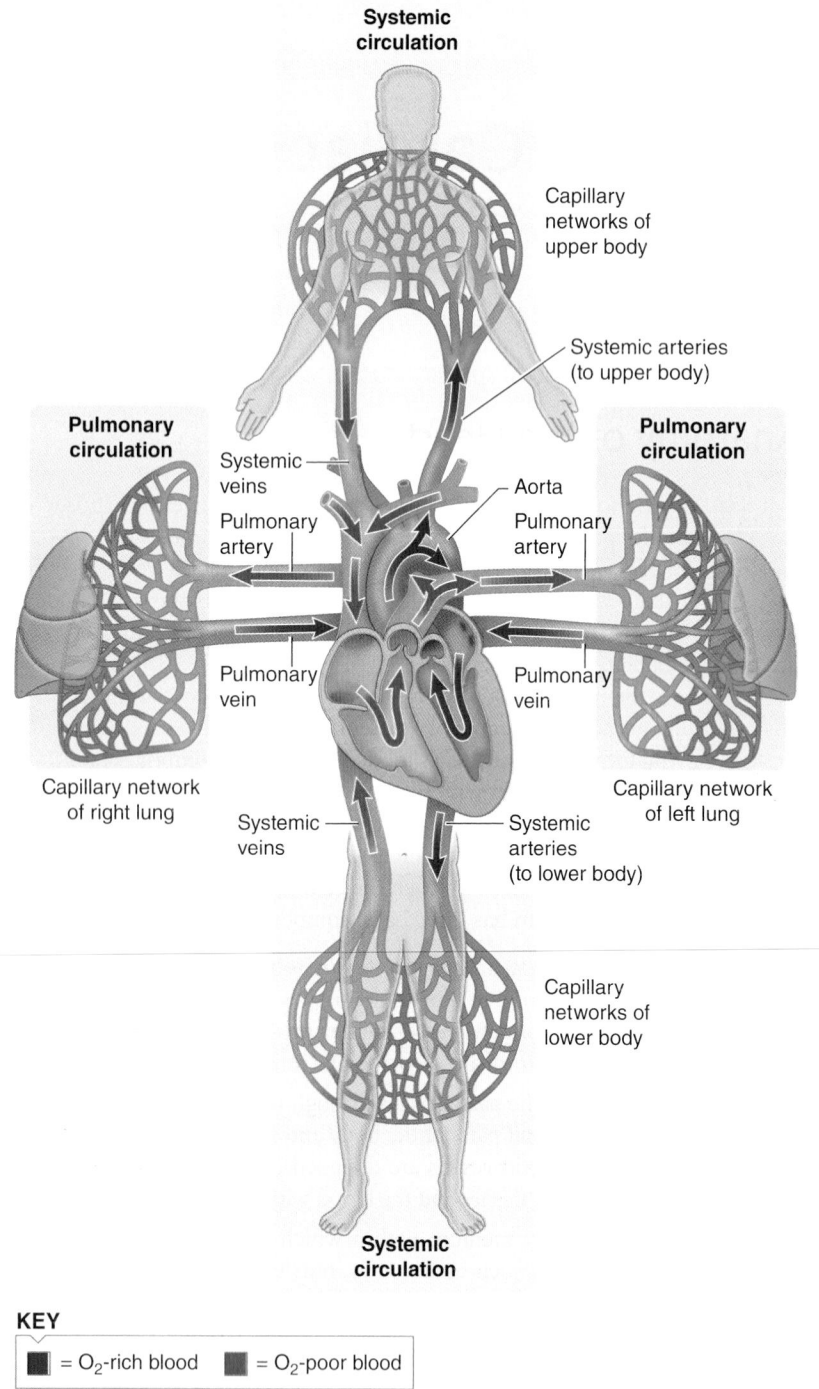

Systemic circulation

Capillary networks of upper body

Systemic arteries (to upper body)

Pulmonary circulation

Systemic veins

Pulmonary artery

Aorta

Pulmonary artery

Pulmonary circulation

Pulmonary vein

Pulmonary vein

Capillary network of right lung

Capillary network of left lung

Systemic veins

Systemic arteries (to lower body)

Capillary networks of lower body

Systemic circulation

KEY

■ = O₂-rich blood   ■ = O₂-poor blood

● **FIGURE 9-1 Pulmonary and systemic circulation in relation to the heart.** The circulatory system consists of two separate vascular loops: the pulmonary circulation, which carries blood between the heart and the lungs, and the systemic circulation, which carries blood between the heart and the organ systems. Each of these loops forms a figure "8," with the pulmonary circulation simultaneously supplying the right and left lungs and the systemic circulation simultaneously supplying the upper and lower parts of the body.

the middle of the chest. The heart has a broad **base** at the top and tapers to a pointed tip, the **apex,** at the bottom. It is situated at an angle under the sternum so that its base lies predominantly to the right and the apex lies to the left of the sternum. When the heart beats forcefully, the apex thumps against the inside of the chest wall on the left side. Because we are aware of

the beating heart through the apex beat on the left side of the chest, we tend to think—erroneously—that the entire heart is on the left.

Clinical Note The heart's position between two bony structures, the sternum and the vertebrae, makes it possible to manually drive blood out of the heart when it is not pumping effectively. Rhythmically depressing the sternum compresses the heart between the sternum and the vertebrae so that blood is squeezed out into the blood vessels, maintaining blood flow to the tissues. Often, this *external cardiac compression,* which is part of **cardiopulmonary resuscitation (CPR),** is a lifesaving measure until appropriate therapy can restore the heart to normal function.

The heart is a dual pump.

Even though anatomically the heart is a single organ, the right and left sides of the heart function as two separate pumps. The heart is divided into right and left halves and has four chambers, an upper and a lower chamber within each half (● Figure 9-2a). The upper chambers, the **atria** (singular, *atrium*), receive blood returning to the heart and transfer it to the lower chambers, the **ventricles,** which pump blood from the heart. The vessels that return blood from the tissues to the atria are **veins,** and those that carry blood away from the ventricles to the tissues are **arteries.** The two halves of the heart are separated by the **septum,** a continuous muscular partition that prevents blood mixing from the two sides of the heart. This separation is extremely important, because the right side of the heart receives and pumps O₂-poor blood, whereas the left side of the heart receives and pumps O₂-rich blood.

THE COMPLETE CIRCUIT OF BLOOD FLOW Let us look at how the heart functions as a dual pump by tracing a drop of blood through one complete circuit (● Figure 9-2a and b). Blood

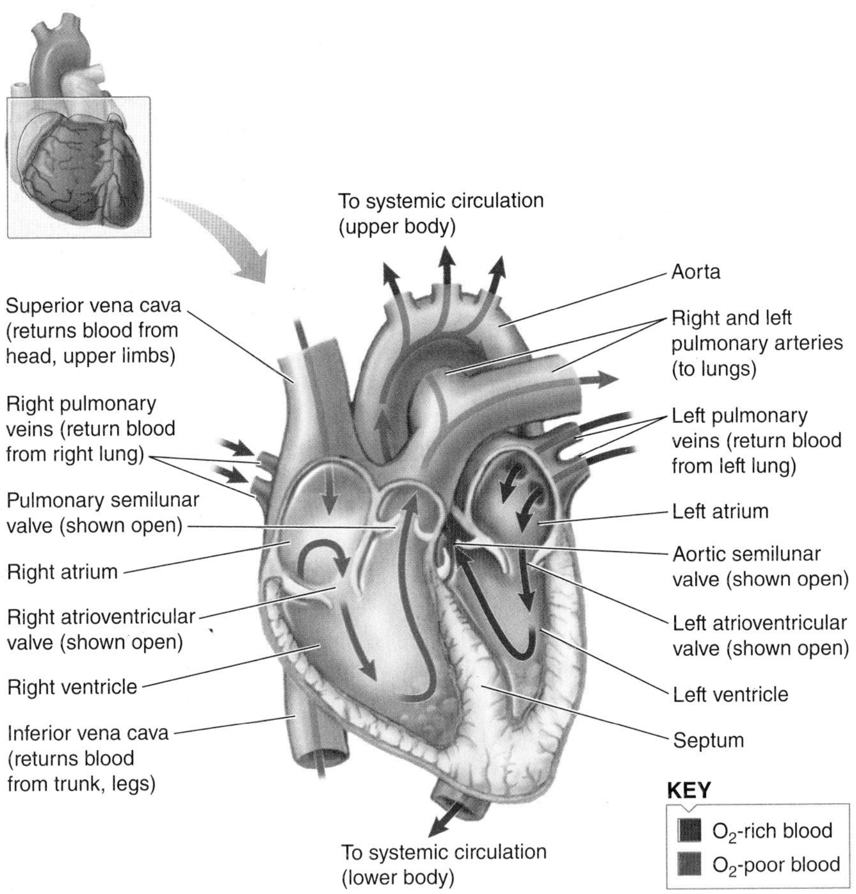

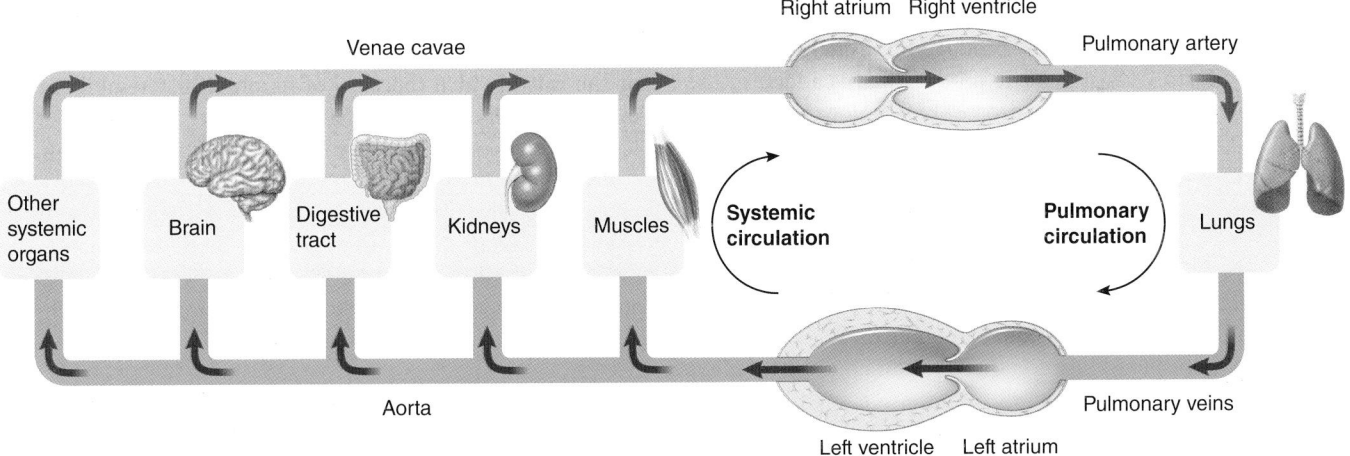

(a) Blood flow through the heart

Superior vena cava (returns blood from head, upper limbs)

Right pulmonary veins (return blood from right lung)

Pulmonary semilunar valve (shown open)

Right atrium

Right atrioventricular valve (shown open)

Right ventricle

Inferior vena cava (returns blood from trunk, legs)

To systemic circulation (upper body)

Aorta

Right and left pulmonary arteries (to lungs)

Left pulmonary veins (return blood from left lung)

Left atrium

Aortic semilunar valve (shown open)

Left atrioventricular valve (shown open)

Left ventricle

Septum

To systemic circulation (lower body)

KEY

■ O₂-rich blood
■ O₂-poor blood

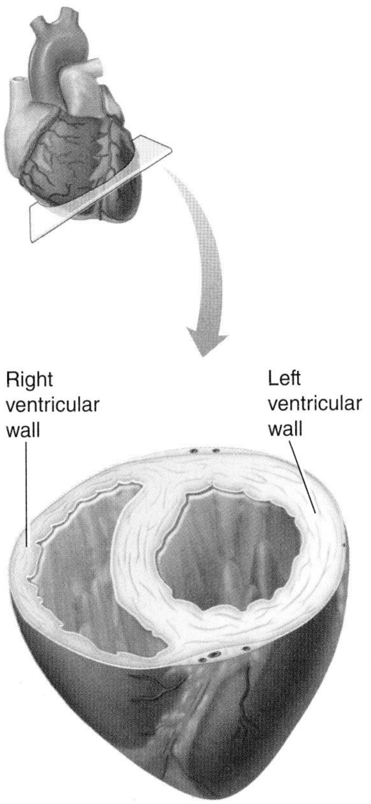

(c) Thickness of right and left ventricles

Right ventricular wall

Left ventricular wall

Right atrium   Right ventricle

Pulmonary artery

Venae cavae

Systemic circulation

Pulmonary circulation

Lungs

Other systemic organs

Brain

Digestive tract

Kidneys

Muscles

Aorta

Pulmonary veins

Left ventricle   Left atrium

(b) Dual pump action of the heart

● **FIGURE 9-2 Blood flow through and pump action of the heart.** (a) The arrows indicate the direction of blood flow. To illustrate the direction of blood flow through the heart, all of the heart valves are shown open, which is never the case. The right side of the heart receives O₂-poor blood from the systemic circulation and pumps it into the pulmonary circulation. The left side of the heart receives O₂-rich blood from the pulmonary circulation and pumps it into the systemic circulation. (b) Note the parallel pathways of blood flow through the systemic organs. (The relative volume of blood flowing through each organ is not drawn to scale.) (c) Note that the left ventricular wall is thicker than the right wall.

returning from the systemic circulation enters the right atrium via two large veins, the **venae cavae**, one returning blood from above and the other returning blood from below heart level. The drop of blood entering the right atrium has returned from the body tissues, where O_2 has been taken from it and CO_2 has been added to it. This partially deoxygenated blood flows from the right atrium into the right ventricle, which pumps it out through the **pulmonary artery.** This artery immediately forms two branches, one going to each of the two lungs. Thus, the *right side of the heart receives blood from the systemic circulation and pumps it into the pulmonary circulation.*

Within the lungs, the drop of blood loses its extra CO_2 and picks up a fresh supply of O_2 before being returned to the left atrium via the **pulmonary veins** coming from both lungs. This O_2-rich blood returning to the left atrium subsequently flows into the left ventricle, the pumping chamber that propels the blood to all body systems except the lungs; that is, *the left side of the heart receives blood from the pulmonary circulation and pumps it into the systemic circulation.* The single large artery carrying blood away from the left ventricle is the **aorta.** Major arteries branch from the aorta to supply the various organs of the body.

In contrast to the pulmonary circulation, in which all the blood flows through the lungs, the systemic circulation may be viewed as a series of parallel pathways. Part of the blood pumped out by the left ventricle goes to the muscles, part to the kidneys, part to the brain, and so on (● Figure 9-2b). Thus, the output of the left ventricle is distributed so that each part of the body receives a fresh blood supply. Accordingly, the drop of blood we are tracing goes to only one of the systemic organs. Tissue cells within the organ take O_2 from the blood and use it to oxidize nutrients for energy production; in the process, the tissue cells form CO_2 as a waste product that is added to the blood (see pp. 3 and 35). The drop of blood, now partially depleted of O_2 content and increased in CO_2 content, returns to the right side of the heart, which again will pump it to the lungs. One circuit is complete.

COMPARISON OF THE RIGHT AND LEFT PUMPS Both sides of the heart simultaneously pump equal amounts of blood. The volume of O_2-poor blood being pumped to the lungs by the right side of the heart soon becomes the same volume of O_2-rich blood being delivered to the tissues by the left side of the heart. The pulmonary circulation is a low-pressure, low-resistance system, whereas the systemic circulation is a high-pressure, high-resistance system. Pressure is the force exerted on the vessel walls by the blood pumped into them by the heart. Resistance is the opposition to blood flow, largely caused by friction between the flowing blood and the vessel wall. Even though the right and left sides of the heart pump the same amount of blood, the left side works harder, because it pumps an equal volume of blood at a higher pressure into a higher-resistance and longer system. Accordingly, the heart muscle on the left side is thicker than the muscle on the right side, making the left side a stronger pump (● Figure 9-2a and c).

Pressure-operated heart valves ensure that blood flows in the right direction through the heart.

Blood flows through the heart in one fixed direction—from veins, to atria, to ventricles, to arteries. The presence of four one-way heart valves ensures this unidirectional flow of blood. The valves are positioned so that they open and close passively because of pressure differences, similar to a one-way door (● Figure 9-3). A forward pressure gradient (that is, a greater pressure behind the valve) forces the valve open, much as you open a door by pushing on one side of it, whereas a backward pressure gradient (that is, a greater pressure in front of the valve) forces the valve closed, just as you apply pressure to the opposite side of the door to close it. Note that a backward gradient can force the valve closed but cannot force it to swing open in the opposite direction; that is, heart valves are not like swinging, saloon-type doors.

AV VALVES BETWEEN THE ATRIA AND THE VENTRICLES Two of the heart valves, the **right** and **left atrioventricular (AV) valves,** are positioned between the atrium and the ventricle on the right and the left sides, respectively (● Figure 9-4a). These valves let blood flow from the atria into the ventricles during ventricular filling (when atrial pressure exceeds ventricular pressure) but prevent the backflow of blood from the ventricles into the atria during ventricular emptying (when ventricular pressure greatly exceeds atrial pressure). If the rising ventricular pressure did not force the AV valves to close as the ventricles contracted to empty, much of the blood would inefficiently be forced back into the atria and veins instead of being pumped into the arteries. The right AV valve is also called the **tricuspid valve** (*tri* means "three") because it consists of three cusps or leaflets (● Figure 9-4b). Likewise, the left AV valve, which has two cusps, is often called the **bicuspid valve** (*bi* means "two") or the **mitral valve** (because of its physical resemblance to a miter, or a bishop's traditional hat).

The edges of the AV valve leaflets are fastened by tough, thin cords of tendinous-type tissue, the **chordae tendineae**, which prevent the valve from *everting* (that is, from being forced by the high ventricular pressure to open in the opposite direction into the atria). These cords extend from the edges of each cusp and attach to small, nipple-shaped **papillary muscles,** which pro-

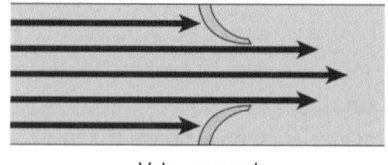

Valve opened

When pressure is greater behind the valve, it opens.

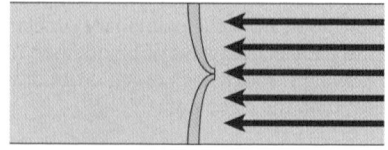

Valve closed; does not open in opposite direction

When pressure is greater in front of the valve, it closes. Note that when pressure is greater in front of the valve, it does not open in the opposite direction; that is, it is a one-way valve.

● **FIGURE 9-3 Mechanism of valve action.**

trude from the inner surface of the ventricular walls (*papilla* means "nipple"). When the ventricles contract, the papillary muscles also contract, pulling downward on the chordae tendineae. This pulling exerts tension on the closed AV valve cusps to hold them in position, much like tethering ropes hold down a hot-air balloon. This action helps keep the valve tightly sealed in the face of a strong backward pressure gradient (● Figure 9-4c).

SEMILUNAR VALVES BETWEEN THE VENTRICLES AND THE MAJOR ARTERIES The other two heart valves, the **aortic** and **pulmonary valves,** lie at the juncture where the major arteries leave the ventricles (● Figure 9-4a). They are known as **semilunar valves** because they have three cusps, each resembling a shallow half-moon-shaped pocket (*semi* means "half"; *lunar* means "moon") (● Figure 9-4b). These valves are forced open when the left and right ventricular pressures exceed the pressure in the aorta and pulmonary artery, respectively, during ventricular contraction and emptying. Closure results when the ventricles relax and ventricular pressures fall below the aortic and pulmonary artery pressures. The closed valves prevent blood from flowing from the arteries back into the ventricles from which it has just been pumped.

Now let us turn to the portion of the heart that actually generates the forces responsible for blood flow, the cardiac muscle within the heart walls.

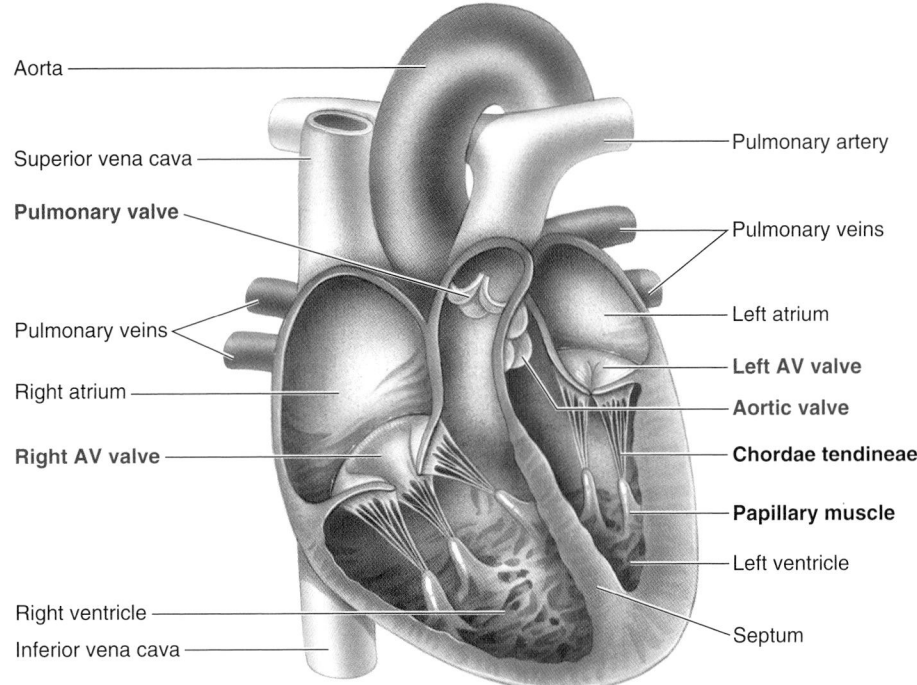

(a) Location of the heart valves in a longitudinal section of the heart

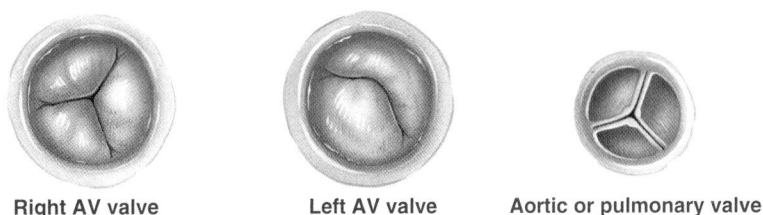

Right AV valve   Left AV valve   Aortic or pulmonary valve

(b) Heart valves in closed position, viewed from above

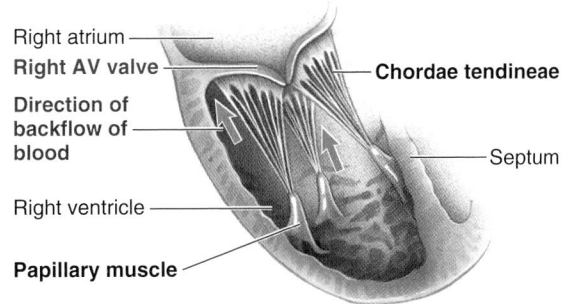

(c) Prevention of eversion of AV valves

● FIGURE 9-4 **Heart valves.**

The heart walls are composed primarily of cardiac muscle fibers.

The heart wall has three distinct layers:

■ A thin, inner layer, the **endothelium,** a unique type of epithelial tissue that lines the entire circulatory system

■ A middle layer, the **myocardium,** which is composed of cardiac muscle and constitutes the bulk of the heart wall (*myo* means "muscle")

■ A thin, external layer, the **epicardium,** that covers the heart (*epi* means "on")

Cardiac muscle fibers are interconnected by intercalated discs and form functional syncytia.

The individual cardiac muscle cells are interconnected to form branching fibers, with adjacent cells joined end to end at specialized structures called **intercalated discs.** Two types of membrane junctions are present within an intercalated disc: desmosomes and gap junctions (● Figure 9-5). A *desmosome,* a type of adhering junction that mechanically holds cells together, is particularly abundant in tissues such as the heart that are subject to considerable mechanical stress (see p. 52). At intervals along the intercalated disc, the opposing membranes

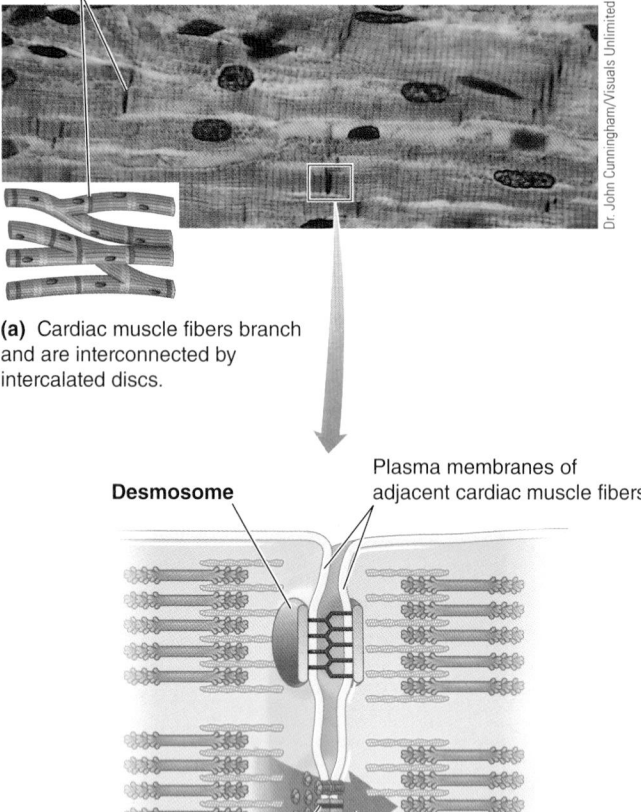

Intercalated discs

(a) Cardiac muscle fibers branch and are interconnected by intercalated discs.

Dr. John Cunningham/Visuals Unlimited

Desmosome

Plasma membranes of adjacent cardiac muscle fibers

Gap junction

Action potential

Intercalated disc

(b) Intercalated discs contain two types of membrane junctions: mechanically important desmosomes and electrically important gap junctions.

● **FIGURE 9-5 Organization of cardiac muscle fibers.** Adjacent cardiac muscle cells are joined end to end by intercalated discs, which contain two types of specialized junctions: desmosomes, which mechanically hold the cells together, and gap junctions, which permit action potentials to spread from one cell to adjacent cells.

approach each other closely to form *gap junctions,* which are areas of low electrical resistance that allow action potentials to spread from one cardiac cell to adjacent cells (see p. 53). Some specialized cardiac muscle cells can generate action potentials without any nervous stimulation. When one of the cardiac cells spontaneously undergoes an action potential, the electrical impulse spreads to all the other cells that are joined by gap junctions in the surrounding muscle mass so that they become excited and contract as a single, functional syncytium (see p. 236). The atria and the ventricles each form a *functional syncytium* and contract as separate units. The synchronous contraction of the muscle cells that make up the walls of each of these chambers produces the force needed to eject the enclosed blood.

No gap junctions join the atrial and ventricular contractile cells; furthermore, the atria and the ventricles are separated by electrically nonconductive fibrous tissue that surrounds and

supports the valves. However, an important, specialized conduction system facilitates and coordinates transmission of electrical excitation from the atria to the ventricles to ensure synchronization between atrial and ventricular pumping.

Because of both the syncytial nature of cardiac muscle and the conduction system between the atria and the ventricles, an impulse spontaneously generated in one part of the heart spreads throughout the entire heart. Therefore, unlike skeletal muscle, where graded contractions can be produced by varying the number of muscle cells contracting within the muscle (recruitment of motor units), either all cardiac muscle fibers contract or none do. A "halfhearted" contraction is not possible. Cardiac contraction is graded by varying the strength of contraction of all the cardiac muscle cells. You will learn more about this process later.

Building on this foundation of heart structure, we next explain how action potentials are initiated and spread throughout the heart. We follow this with a discussion of how this electrical activity brings about coordinated pumping of the heart.

Electrical Activity of the Heart

Contraction of cardiac muscle cells to eject blood is triggered by action potentials sweeping across the muscle cell membranes. The heart contracts, or beats, rhythmically as a result of action potentials that it generates by itself, a property called **autorhythmicity** (*auto* means "self"). There are two specialized types of cardiac muscle cells:

1. **Contractile cells,** which are 99% of the cardiac muscle cells, do the mechanical work of pumping. These working cells normally do not initiate their own action potentials.

2. In contrast, the **autorhythmic cells,** the small but extremely important remainder of the cardiac cells, do not contract but instead are specialized for initiating and conducting the action potentials responsible for contraction of the working cells.

Cardiac autorhythmic cells display pacemaker activity.

In contrast to nerve and skeletal muscle cells, in which the membrane remains at constant resting potential unless the cell is stimulated, the cardiac autorhythmic cells do not have a resting potential. Instead, they display *pacemaker activity;* that is, their membrane potential slowly depolarizes, or drifts, between action potentials until threshold is reached, at which time the membrane fires or has an action potential. An autorhythmic cell membrane's slow drift to threshold is called the **pacemaker potential** (● Figure 9-6; see also p. 236). A unique voltage-gated channel found only in cardiac autorhythmic cells plays a key role in producing the pacemaker potential. Voltage-gated channels typically open when the membrane becomes less negative (depolarizes), but these unusual channels open when the potential becomes more negative (hyperpolarizes) at the end of repolarization from the previous action potential. Because of this unusual behavior, they are sometimes called **funny channels.**

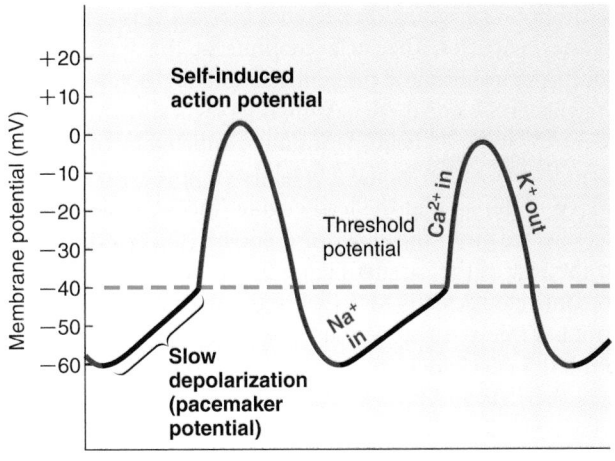

● FIGURE 9-6 Pacemaker activity of cardiac autorhythmic cells. The pacemaker potential (slow, self-induced depolarization to threshold) is largely caused by Na⁺ entry through unique funny channels that open in response to hyperpolarization at the end of the previous action potential. Once threshold is reached, the rising phase of the action potential is the result of Ca²⁺ entry on opening of Ca²⁺ channels, whereas the falling phase is the result of K⁺ exit on opening of K⁺ channels.

When one action potential ends and the funny channels open, the resultant depolarizing net inward Na⁺ movement starts immediately moving the pacemaker cell's potential toward threshold once again. Once threshold is reached, the rising phase of the action potential occurs in response to opening of voltage-gated Ca²⁺ channels and the resulting entry of Ca²⁺, in contrast to nerve and skeletal muscle cells where Na⁺ entry rather than Ca²⁺ entry swings the potential in the positive direction. The falling phase occurs as usual by K⁺ leaving the pacemaker cell as a result of opening of voltage-gated K⁺ channels. Through repeated cycles of drift and fire, these autorhythmic cells cyclically initiate action potentials, which then spread throughout the heart to trigger rhythmic beating without any nervous stimulation.

The sinoatrial node is the normal pacemaker of the heart.

The specialized noncontractile cardiac cells capable of autorhythmicity lie in the following specific sites (● Figure 9-7):

1. The **sinoatrial node (SA node)**, a small, specialized region in the right atrial wall.

2. The **atrioventricular node (AV node)**, a small bundle of specialized cardiac muscle cells located at the base of the right atrium near the septum.

3. The **bundle of His,** a tract of specialized cells that originates at the AV node and enters the septum between the ventricles. Here, it divides to form the right and left bundle branches that travel down the septum, curve around the tip of the ventricular chambers, and travel back toward the atria along the outer walls.

4. **Purkinje fibers,** small terminal fibers that extend from the bundle of His and spread throughout the ventricular myocardium much like small twigs of a tree branch.

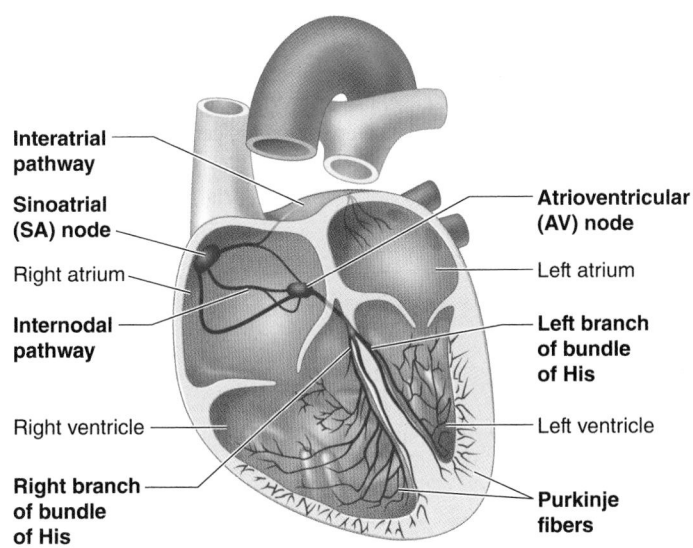

(a) Specialized conduction system of the heart

(b) Spread of cardiac excitation

● FIGURE 9-7 Specialized conduction system of the heart and spread of cardiac excitation. An action potential initiated at the SA node first spreads throughout both atria. Its spread is facilitated by two specialized atrial conduction pathways, the interatrial and internodal pathways. The AV node is the only point where an action potential can spread from the atria to the ventricles. From the AV node, the action potential spreads rapidly throughout the ventricles, hastened by a specialized ventricular conduction system consisting of the bundle of His and Purkinje fibers.

NORMAL PACEMAKER ACTIVITY Because these various autorhythmic cells have different rates of slow depolarization to threshold, the rates at which they are normally capable of generating action potentials also differ (▲ Table 9-1). The heart cells with the fastest rate of action potential initiation are localized in the SA node. Once an action potential occurs in any cardiac muscle cell, it is propagated throughout the rest of the myocardium via gap junctions and the specialized conduction system. Therefore, the SA node, which normally has the fastest rate of autorhythmicity, at 70 to 80 action potentials per minute, drives the rest of the heart at this rate and thus is known as the **pacemaker** of the heart. That is, the entire heart becomes excited, triggering the contractile cells to contract and the heart to beat at the pace or rate set by SA node autorhythmicity, normally at 70 to 80 beats per minute. The other autorhythmic tissues cannot assume their own naturally slower rates, because they are activated by action potentials originating in the SA node before they can reach threshold at their own, slower rhythm.

The following analogy shows how the SA node drives the rest of the heart at its own pace. Suppose a train has 100 cars, 3 of which are engines capable of moving on their own; the other 97 cars must be pulled (● Figure 9-8a). One engine (the SA node) can travel at 70 miles per hour (mph) on its own, another engine (the AV node) at 50 mph, and the last engine (the Purkinje fibers) at 30 mph. If all these cars are joined, the engine that can travel at 70 mph will pull the rest of the cars at that speed. The engines that can travel at lower speeds on their own will be pulled at a faster speed by the fastest engine and therefore cannot assume their own slower rate as long as they are being driven by a faster engine. The other 97 cars (nonautorhythmic, contractile cells), being unable to move on their own, will likewise travel at whatever speed the fastest engine pulls them.

 ABNORMAL PACEMAKER ACTIVITY If for some reason the fastest engine breaks down (SA node damage), the next-fastest engine (the AV node) takes over and the entire train travels at 50 mph; that is, if the SA node becomes nonfunctional, the AV node assumes pacemaker activity (● Figure 9-8b).

If impulse conduction becomes blocked between the atria and the ventricles, the atria continue at the typical rate of 70 beats per minute, and the ventricular tissue, not being driven by the faster SA nodal rate, assumes its own, slower autorhythmic rate of about 30 beats per minute, initiated by the Purkinje fibers. This situation is like a breakdown of the second engine (the AV node) so that the lead engine (the SA node) becomes disconnected from the slow third engine (the Purkinje fibers) and the rest of the cars (● Figure 9-8c). The lead engine (and cars connected directly to it; that is, the atrial cells) continues at 70 mph while the rest of the train proceeds at 30 mph. This **complete heart block** occurs when the conducting tissue between the atria and the ventricles is damaged (as, for example, during a heart attack) and becomes nonfunctional. A ventricular rate of 30 beats per minute will support only a very sedentary existence; in fact, the patient usually becomes comatose.

When a person has an abnormally low heart rate, as in SA node failure or heart block, an **artificial pacemaker** can be used. Such an implanted device rhythmically generates impulses that spread throughout the heart to drive both the atria and the ventricles at the typical rate of 70 beats per minute.

Occasionally, an area of the heart, such as a Purkinje fiber, becomes overly excitable and depolarizes more rapidly than the SA node. (The slow engine suddenly goes faster than the lead engine; see ● Figure 9-8d). This abnormally excitable area, an **ectopic focus,** initiates a premature action potential that spreads throughout the rest of the heart before the SA node can initiate a normal action potential (*ectopic* means "out of place"). An occasional abnormal impulse from a ventricular ectopic focus produces a **premature ventricular contraction (PVC).** If the ectopic focus continues to discharge at its more rapid rate, pacemaker activity shifts from the SA node to the ectopic focus. The heart rate abruptly becomes greatly accelerated and continues this rapid rate for a variable period until the ectopic focus returns to normal. Such overly irritable areas may be associated with organic heart disease, but more frequently they occur in response to anxiety, lack of sleep, or excess caffeine, nicotine, or alcohol consumption.

We now turn to how an action potential, once initiated, is conducted throughout the heart.

The spread of cardiac excitation is coordinated to ensure efficient pumping.

Once initiated in the SA node, an action potential spreads throughout the rest of the heart. For efficient cardiac function, the spread of excitation should satisfy three criteria:

1. *Atrial excitation and contraction should be complete before the onset of ventricular contraction.* Complete ventricular filling requires that atrial contraction precede ventricular contraction. During cardiac relaxation, the AV valves are open, so venous blood entering the atria continues to flow directly into the ventricles. Almost 80% of ventricular filling occurs by this means before atrial contraction. When the atria do contract, more blood is squeezed into the ventricles to complete ventricular filling. Ventricular contraction then occurs to eject blood from the heart into the arteries.

▲ Table 9-1 Normal Rate of Action Potential Discharge in Autorhythmic Tissues of the Heart

Tissue	Action Potentials per Minute*
SA node (normal pacemaker)	70–80
AV node	40–60
Bundle of His and Purkinje fibers	20–40

*In the presence of parasympathetic tone; see pp. 192 and 265.

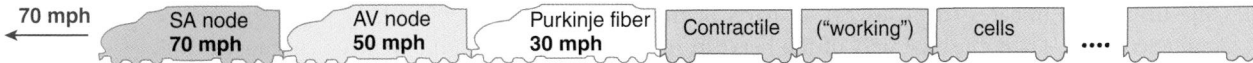

(a) Normal pacemaker activity: Whole train will go **70 mph** (heart rate set by SA node, the fastest autorhythmic tissue).

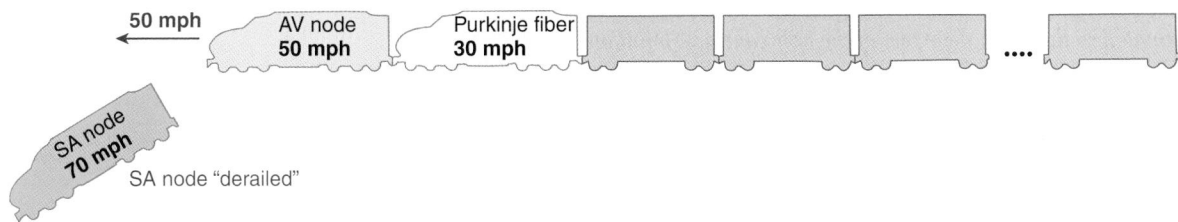

(b) Takeover of pacemaker activity by AV node when the SA node is nonfunctional: Train will go **50 mph** (the next fastest autorhythmic tissue, the AV node, will set the heart rate).

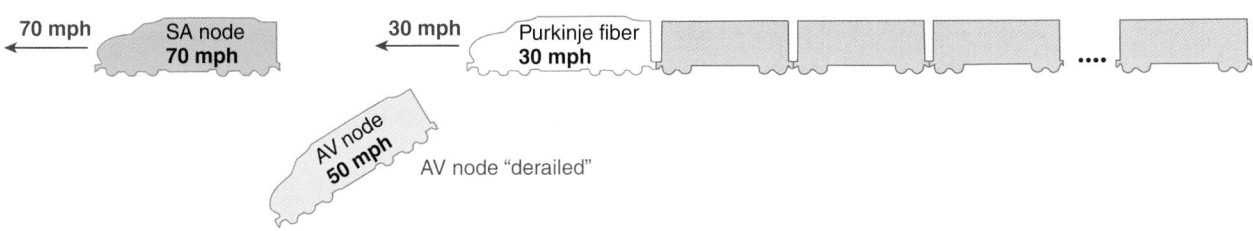

(c) Takeover of ventricular rate by the slower ventricular autorhythmic tissue in complete heart block: First part of train will go **70 mph**; last part will go **30 mph** (atria will be driven by SA node; ventricles will assume own, much slower rhythm).

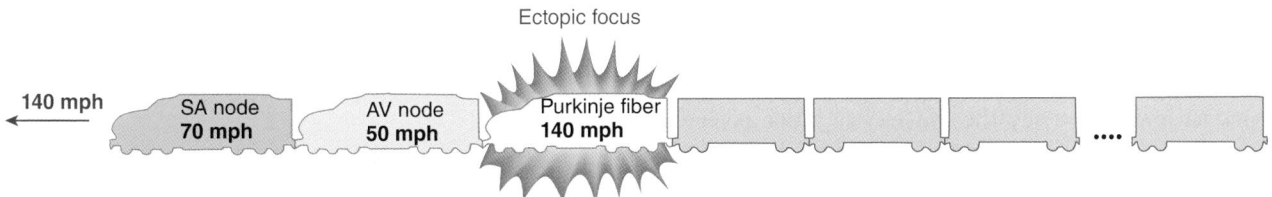

(d) Takeover of pacemaker activity by an ectopic focus: Train will be driven by ectopic focus, which is now going faster than the SA node (the whole heart will be driven more rapidly by an abnormal pacemaker).

● **FIGURE 9-8 Analogy of pacemaker activity.** In complete heart block (c), when ventricular rate is taken over by the slower ventricular autorhythmic tissue, the atrial rate (not shown) is still driven by the SA node.

If the atria and ventricles were to contract simultaneously, the AV valves would close immediately because ventricular pressures would greatly exceed atrial pressures. The ventricles have thicker walls and, accordingly, can generate more pressure. Atrial contraction would be unproductive because the atria could not squeeze blood into the ventricles through closed valves. Therefore, to ensure complete filling of the ventricles—to obtain the remaining 20% of ventricular filling that occurs during atrial contraction—the atria must become excited and contract before ventricular excitation and contraction.

2. *Excitation of cardiac muscle fibers should be coordinated to ensure that each heart chamber contracts as a unit to pump efficiently.* If the muscle fibers in a heart chamber became excited and contracted randomly rather than contracting simultaneously in a coordinated fashion, they would be unable to eject

blood. A smooth, uniform ventricular contraction is essential to squeeze out the blood. As an analogy, assume you have a basting syringe full of water. If you merely poke a finger here or there into the rubber bulb of the syringe, you will not eject much water. However, if you compress the bulb in a smooth, coordinated fashion, you can squeeze out the water.

 In a similar manner, contraction of isolated cardiac muscle fibers is not successful in pumping blood. Such random, uncoordinated excitation and contraction of the cardiac cells is known as **fibrillation.** Fibrillation of the ventricles is more serious than atrial fibrillation. Ventricular fibrillation rapidly causes death, because the heart cannot pump blood into the arteries. This condition can often be corrected by electrical defibrillation, in which a strong electrical current is applied on the chest wall. When this current

reaches the heart, it stimulates (depolarizes) all parts of the heart simultaneously. Usually the first part of the heart to recover is the SA node, which takes over pacemaker activity, again initiating impulses that trigger the synchronized contraction of the rest of the heart.

3. *The pair of atria and pair of ventricles should be functionally coordinated so that both members of the pair contract simultaneously.* This coordination permits synchronized pumping of blood into the pulmonary and systemic circulation.

The normal spread of cardiac excitation is carefully orchestrated to ensure that these criteria are met and the heart functions efficiently, as follows (see ● Figure 9-7b).

ATRIAL EXCITATION An action potential originating in the SA node first spreads throughout both atria, primarily from cell to cell via gap junctions. In addition, several poorly delineated, specialized conduction pathways speed up conduction of the impulse through the atria.

■ The *interatrial pathway* extends from the SA node within the right atrium to the left atrium. Because this pathway rapidly transmits the action potential from the SA node to the pathway's termination in the left atrium, a wave of excitation can spread across the gap junctions throughout the left atrium at the same time as excitation is similarly spreading throughout the right atrium. This ensures that both atria become depolarized to contract simultaneously.

■ The *internodal pathway* extends from the SA node to the AV node. The AV node is the only point of electrical contact between the atria and the ventricles; in other words, because the atria and the ventricles are structurally connected by electrically nonconductive fibrous tissue, the only way an action potential in the atria can spread to the ventricles is by passing through the AV node. The internodal conduction pathway directs the spread of an action potential originating at the SA node to the AV node to ensure sequential contraction of the ventricles following atrial contraction.

CONDUCTION BETWEEN THE ATRIA AND THE VENTRICLES The action potential is conducted relatively slowly through the AV node. This slowness is advantageous because it allows time for complete ventricular filling. The impulse is delayed about 100 msec (the **AV nodal delay**), which enables the atria to become completely depolarized and to contract, emptying their contents into the ventricles, before ventricular depolarization and contraction occur.

VENTRICULAR EXCITATION After the AV nodal delay, the impulse travels rapidly down the septum via the right and left branches of the bundle of His and throughout the ventricular myocardium via the Purkinje fibers. This highly organized conduction system is specialized for rapid propagation of action potentials. Its presence hastens and coordinates the spread of ventricular excitation to ensure that the ventricles contract as a unit.

Although this system carries the action potential rapidly to a large number of cardiac muscle cells, it does not terminate on every cell. The impulse quickly spreads from the excited cells to the rest of the ventricular muscle cells by means of gap junctions.

Because the ventricular mass is so much larger than the atrial mass, the ventricular conduction system is crucial for hastening the spread of excitation in the ventricles. Purkinje fibers can transmit an action potential six times faster than the ventricular syncytium of contractile cells could. If the entire ventricular depolarization process depended on cell-to-cell spread of the impulse via gap junctions, the ventricular tissue immediately next to the AV node would become excited and contract before the impulse had even passed to the heart apex. This, of course, would not allow efficient pumping. Rapid conduction of the action potential down the bundle of His and its swift, diffuse distribution throughout the Purkinje network lead to almost simultaneous activation of the ventricular myocardial cells in both ventricular chambers, which ensures a single, smooth, coordinated contraction that can efficiently eject blood into the systemic and pulmonary circulations at the same time.

The action potential of cardiac contractile cells shows a characteristic plateau.

The action potential in cardiac contractile cells, although initiated by the nodal pacemaker cells, varies considerably in ionic mechanisms and shape from the SA node potential (compare ● Figures 9-6 and 9-9). Unlike the membrane of autorhythmic cells, the membrane of contractile cells remains essentially at rest, about −90 millivolts (mV), until excited by electrical activity propagated from the pacemaker. Once the membrane of a ventricular myocardial contractile cell is excited, the membrane potential rapidly reverses to a positive value of +30 mV as a result of activation of voltage-gated Na^+ channels and Na^+ subsequently rapidly entering the cell, as it does in other excitable cells undergoing an action potential (see p. 82). Unique to the cardiac contractile cells, however, the membrane potential is maintained close to this peak positive level for several hundred milliseconds, producing a *plateau phase* of the action potential. In contrast, the short action potential of neurons and skeletal muscle cells lasts 1 to 2 msec. Whereas the rising phase of the action potential is brought about by activation of comparatively "fast" Na^+ channels, this plateau is maintained primarily by activation of relatively "slow" voltage-gated Ca^{2+} channels in the cardiac contractile cell membrane. These channels open in response to the sudden change in voltage during the rising phase of the action potential. Opening of these Ca^{2+} channels results in a slow, inward diffusion of Ca^{2+}, because Ca^{2+} is in greater concentration in the extracellular fluid (ECF). This continued influx of positively charged Ca^{2+} prolongs the positivity inside the cell and is primarily responsible for the plateau part of the action potential. The rapid falling phase of the action potential results from inactivation of the Ca^{2+} channels and opening of voltage-gated K^+ channels. As in other excitable cells, the cell returns to resting potential as K^+ rapidly leaves the cell.

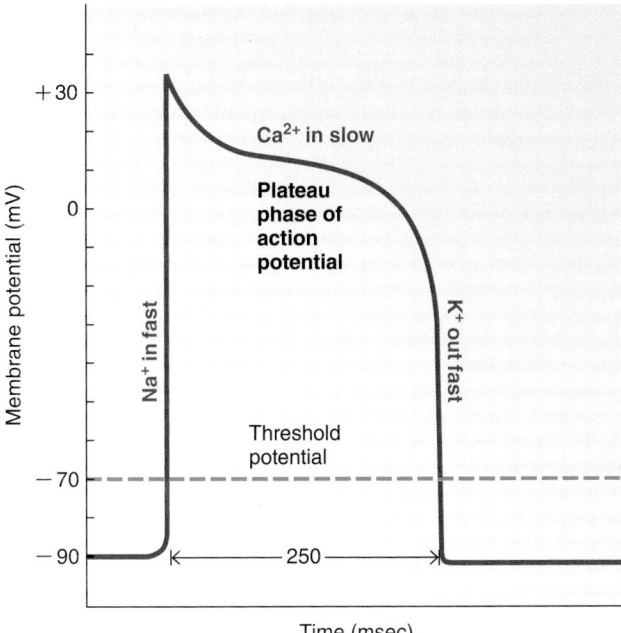

● **FIGURE 9-9 Action potential in contractile cardiac muscle cells.** The action potential in cardiac contractile cells differs considerably from the action potential in cardiac autorhythmic cells (compare with Figure 9-6). The rapid rising phase of the action potential in contractile cells is the result of Na⁺ entry on opening of fast Na⁺ channels at threshold. The unique plateau phase is the result of prolonged Ca²⁺ entry on opening of slow Ca²⁺ channels. The rapid falling phase is the result of K⁺ exit on opening of K⁺ channels.

Let us now see how this action potential brings about contraction.

Ca²⁺ entry from the ECF induces a much larger Ca²⁺ release from the sarcoplasmic reticulum.

In cardiac contractile cells, the slow Ca²⁺ channels lie primarily in the transverse (T) tubules. As you just learned, these voltage-gated channels open during a local action potential. Thus, unlike in skeletal muscle, Ca²⁺ diffuses into the cytosol from the ECF across the T tubule membrane during a cardiac action potential. This entering Ca²⁺ triggers the opening of nearby Ca²⁺-release channels in the adjacent lateral sacs of the sarcoplasmic reticulum (see p. 214). By means of this action, termed **Ca²⁺-induced Ca²⁺ release,** Ca²⁺ entering the cytosol from the ECF induces a much larger release of Ca²⁺ into the cytosol from the intracellular stores (● Figure 9-10). The resultant increase in cytosolic Ca²⁺ turns on the contractile machinery. Ninety percent of the Ca²⁺ needed for muscle contraction comes from the sarcoplasmic reticulum. This extra supply of Ca²⁺, coupled with the slow Ca²⁺ removal processes, is responsible for the long period of cardiac contraction, which lasts about three times longer than the contraction of a single skeletal muscle fiber (300 msec compared to 100 msec). This increased contractile time ensures adequate time to eject the blood.

As in skeletal muscle, the role of Ca²⁺ within the cytosol is to bind with the troponin–tropomyosin complex and physically pull it aside to allow cross-bridge cycling and contraction (● Figure 9-10). However, unlike skeletal muscle, in which suf-

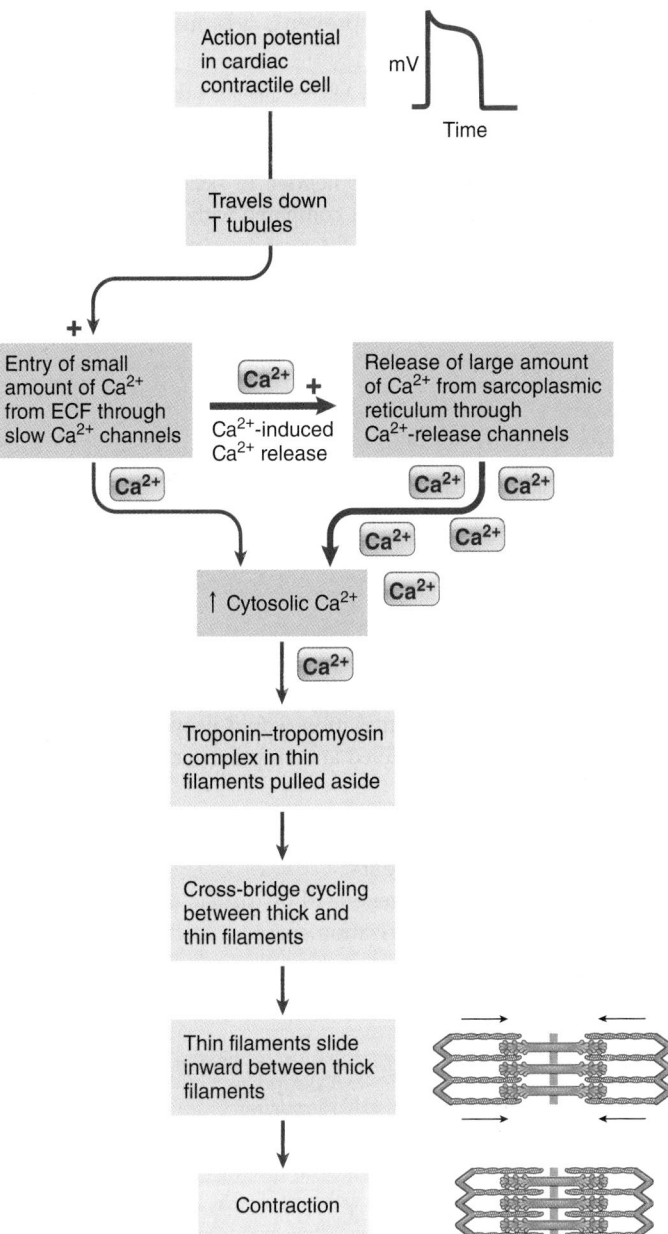

● **FIGURE 9-10 Excitation–contraction coupling in cardiac contractile cells.**

ficient Ca²⁺ is always released to turn on all the cross bridges, in cardiac muscle the extent of cross-bridge activity varies with the amount of cytosolic Ca²⁺. As we will show, various regulatory factors can alter the amount of cytosolic Ca²⁺.

Removal of Ca²⁺ from the cytosol by energy-dependent mechanisms in both the plasma membrane and the sarcoplasmic reticulum restores the blocking action of troponin and tropomyosin, so contraction ceases and the heart muscle relaxes.

 Some drugs alter cardiac function by influencing Ca²⁺ movement across the myocardial cell membranes. For example, Ca²⁺-channel blocking agents, such as *verapamil,* block Ca²⁺ entry during an action potential, reducing the force of cardiac contraction. Other drugs, such as *digitalis,* increase cardiac contractility by causing accumulation of cytosolic Ca²⁺.

A long refractory period prevents tetanus of cardiac muscle.

Like other excitable tissues, cardiac muscle has a refractory period. During the refractory period, a second action potential cannot be triggered until an excitable membrane has recovered from the preceding action potential. In skeletal muscle, the refractory period is very short compared with the duration of the resulting contraction, so the fiber can be restimulated before the first contraction is complete to produce summation of contractions. Rapidly repetitive stimulation that does not let the muscle fiber relax between stimulations results in a sustained, maximal contraction known as *tetanus* (see ● Figure 8-16, p. 222).

In contrast, cardiac muscle has a long refractory period that lasts about 250 msec because of the prolonged plateau phase of the action potential. This is almost as long as the period of contraction initiated by the action potential; a cardiac muscle fiber contraction averages about 300 msec (● Figure 9-11). Consequently, cardiac muscle cannot be restimulated until contraction is almost over, precluding summation of contractions and tetanus of cardiac muscle. This is a valuable protective mechanism, because pumping of blood requires alternate periods of contraction (emptying) and relaxation (filling). A prolonged tetanic contraction would prove fatal: The heart chambers could not be filled and emptied again.

The ECG is a record of the overall spread of electrical activity through the heart.

The electrical currents generated by cardiac muscle during depolarization and repolarization spread into the tissues around the heart and are conducted through the body fluids. A small part of this electrical activity reaches the body surface, where it can be detected using recording electrodes. The record produced is an **electrocardiogram, or ECG.** (Alternatively, the abbreviation **EKG** is often used, from the ancient Greek word *kardia,* instead of the Latin *cardia,* for "heart.")

Remember three important points when considering what an ECG represents:

1. An ECG is a recording of that part of the electrical activity present in body fluids from the cardiac impulse that reaches the body surface, not a direct recording of the actual electrical activity of the heart.

2. The ECG is a complex recording representing the *overall* spread of activity throughout the heart during depolarization and repolarization. It is not a recording of a *single* action potential in a single cell at a single point in time. The record at any given time represents the sum of electrical activity in all the cardiac muscle cells, some of which may be undergoing action potentials while others may not yet be activated. For example, immediately after the SA node fires, the atrial cells are undergoing action potentials while the ventricular cells are still at resting potential. At a later point, the electrical activity will have spread to the ventricular cells while the atrial cells will be repolarizing. Therefore, the overall pattern of cardiac electrical activity varies with time as the impulse passes throughout the heart.

3. The recording represents comparisons in voltage detected by electrodes at two points on the body surface, not the actual potential. For example, the ECG does not record a potential when the ventricular muscle is either completely depolarized or completely repolarized; both electrodes are "viewing" the same potential, so no difference in potential between the two electrodes is recorded.

The exact pattern of electrical activity recorded from the body surface depends on the orientation of the recording electrodes. Electrodes may be loosely thought of as "eyes" that "see" electrical activity and translate it into a visible recording, the ECG record. Whether an upward or downward deflection is recorded is determined by the way the electrodes are oriented with respect to the current flow in the heart. For example, the spread of excitation across the heart is "seen" differently from the right arm, from the left leg, or from a recording directly over the heart. Even though the same electrical events are occurring in the heart, different waveforms representing the same electrical activity result when this activity is recorded by electrodes at different points on the body.

To provide standard comparisons, ECG records routinely consist of 12 conventional electrode systems, or leads. When an electrocardiograph machine is connected between recording electrodes at two points on the body, the specific arrangement of each pair of connections is called a **lead.** The 12 leads each record electrical activity in the heart from different locations—six different electrical arrangements from the limbs and six chest leads at various sites around the heart. To provide a common basis for comparison and for recognizing deviations from normal, the same 12 leads are routinely used in all ECG recordings (● Figure 9-12).

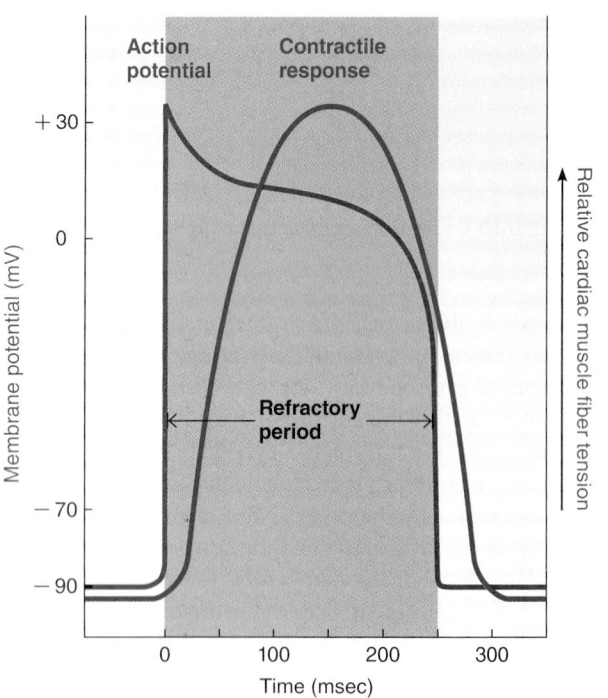

● **FIGURE 9-11 Comparison of the duration of an action potential and the refractory period to the duration of the contractile response in cardiac muscle.**

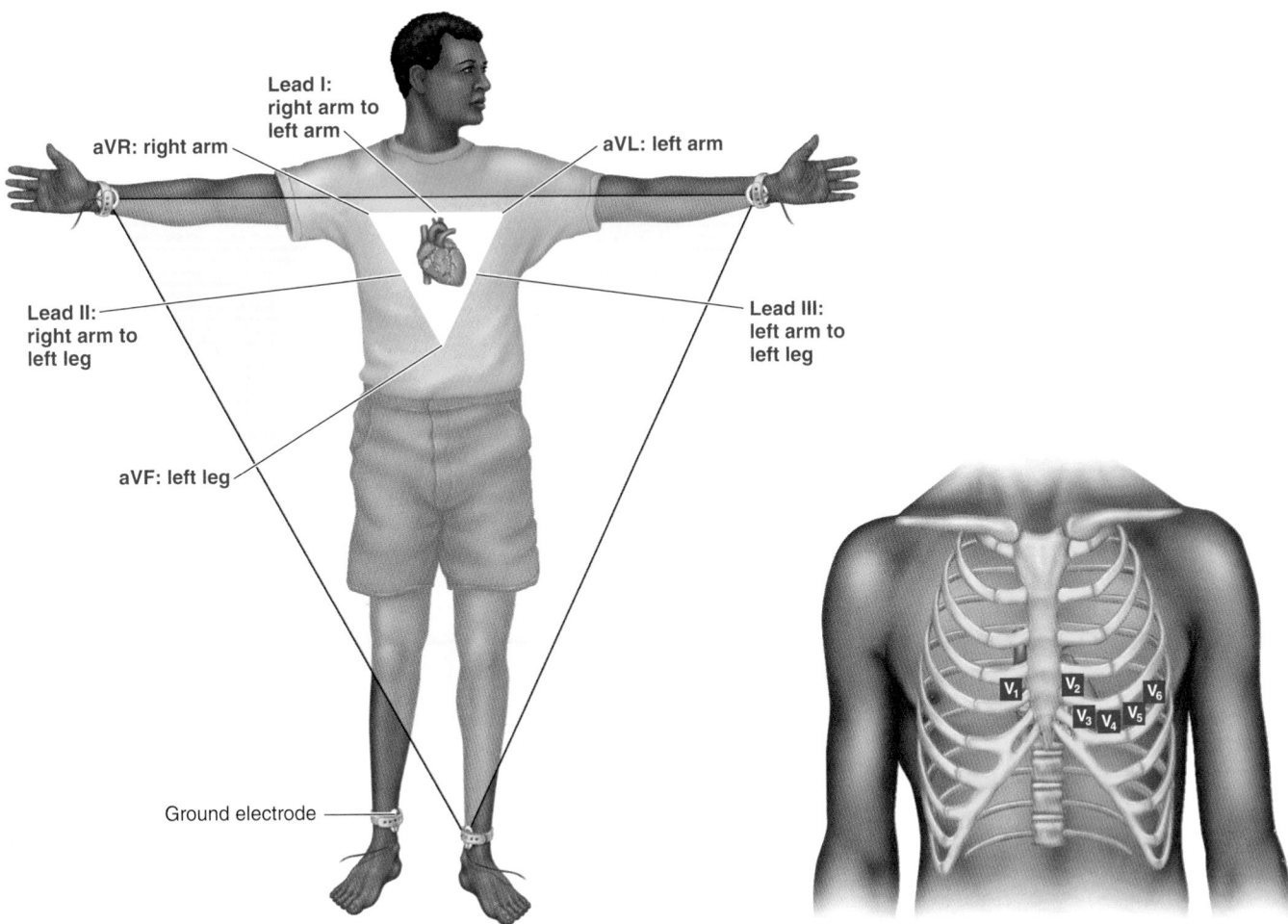

(a) Limb leads

(b) Chest leads

● FIGURE 9-12 **Electrocardiogram leads.** (a) The six limb leads include leads I, II, III, aVR, aVL, and aVF. Leads I, II, and III are bipolar leads because two recording electrodes are used. The tracing records the *difference* in potential between the two electrodes. For example, lead I records the difference in potential detected at the right arm and left arm. The electrode placed on the right leg serves as a ground and is not a recording electrode. The aVR, aVL, and aVF leads are unipolar leads. Even though two electrodes are used, only the actual potential under one electrode, the exploring electrode, is recorded. The other electrode is set at zero potential and serves as a neutral reference point. For example, the aVR lead records the potential reaching the right arm in comparison to the rest of the body. (b) The six chest leads, V_1 through V_6, are also unipolar leads. The exploring electrode mainly records the electrical potential of the cardiac musculature immediately beneath the electrode in six different locations surrounding the heart.

Different parts of the ECG record can be correlated to specific cardiac events.

A normal ECG has three distinct waveforms: the P wave, the QRS complex, and the T wave (● Figure 9-13). (The letters only indicate the orderly sequence of the waves. The inventor of the technique just started in midalphabet when naming the waves.)

- The **P wave** represents atrial depolarization.
- The **QRS complex** represents ventricular depolarization.
- The **T wave** represents ventricular repolarization.

These shifting waves of depolarization and repolarization bring about alternating contraction and relaxation of the heart, respectively.

The following points about the ECG record should also be noted:

1. Firing of the SA node does not generate enough electrical activity to reach the body surface, so no wave is recorded for SA nodal depolarization. Therefore, the first recorded wave, the P wave, occurs when the wave of depolarization spreads across the atria.

2. In a normal ECG, no separate wave for atrial repolarization is visible. The electrical activity associated with atrial repolarization normally occurs simultaneously with ventricular depolarization and is masked by the QRS complex.

3. The P wave is smaller than the QRS complex, because the atria have a smaller muscle mass than the ventricles and consequently generate less electrical activity.

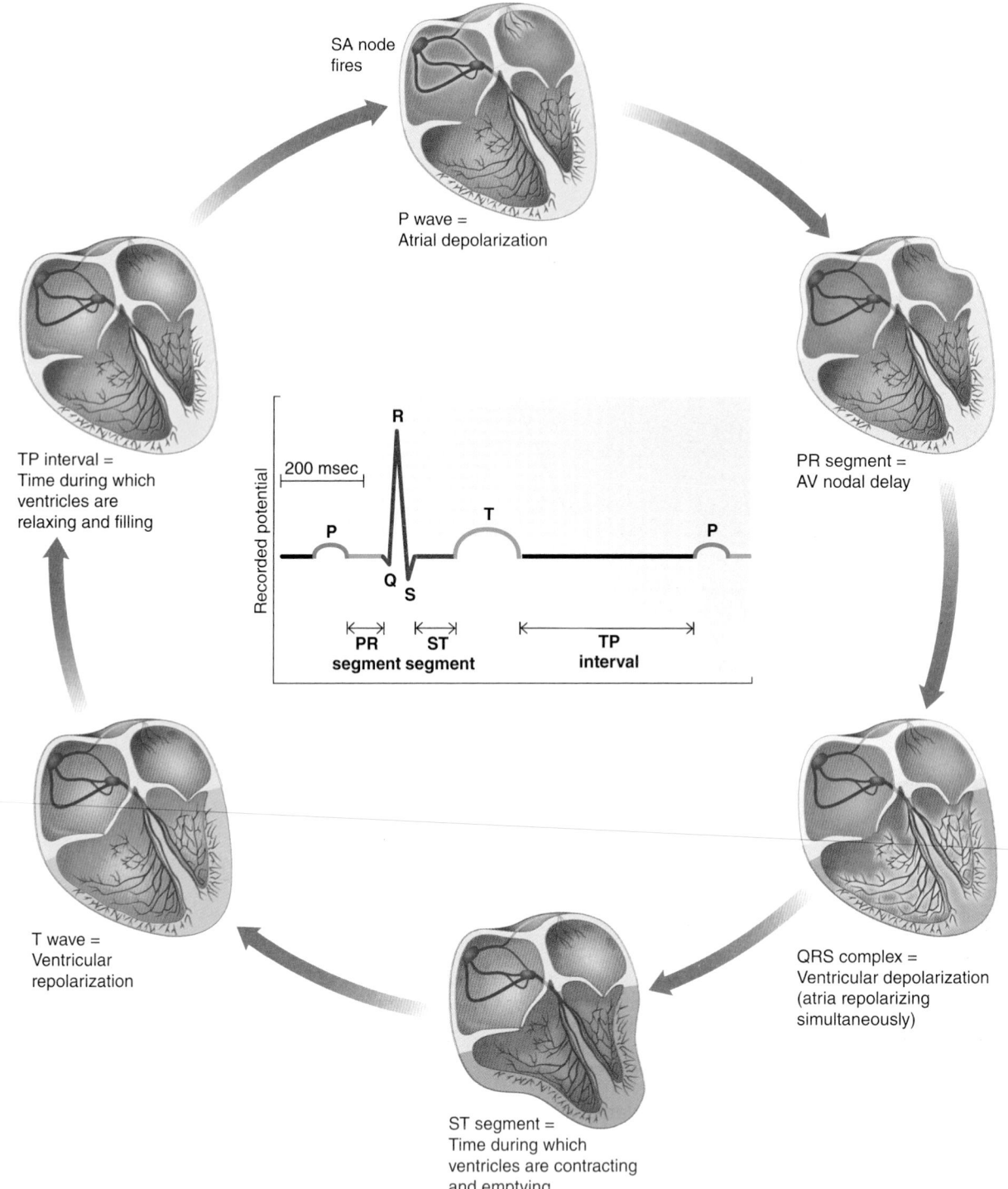

SA node fires

P wave = Atrial depolarization

PR segment = AV nodal delay

QRS complex = Ventricular depolarization (atria repolarizing simultaneously)

ST segment = Time during which ventricles are contracting and emptying

T wave = Ventricular repolarization

TP interval = Time during which ventricles are relaxing and filling

Recorded potential

200 msec

R

P

Q S

T

P

PR segment

ST segment

TP interval

● FIGURE 9-13 **Electrocardiogram waveforms in lead II and electrical status of the heart associated with each waveform.**

4. At the following three points in time, no net current flow is taking place in the heart musculature, so the ECG remains at baseline:

   a. *During the AV nodal delay.* This delay is represented by the interval of time between the end of P and the onset of QRS; this segment of the ECG is known as the **PR segment.** (It is called the "PR segment" rather than the "PQ segment" because the Q deflection is small and sometimes absent, whereas the R deflection is the dominant wave of the complex.) Current is flowing through the AV node, but the magnitude is too small for the ECG electrodes to detect.

   b. *When the ventricles are completely depolarized and the cardiac contractile cells are undergoing the plateau phase of their action potential before they repolarize,* represented by the **ST segment.** This segment lies between QRS and T; it coincides with the time during which ventricular activation is complete and the ventricles are contracting and emptying. Note that the ST segment is *not* a record of cardiac contractile activity. The ECG is a measure of the electrical activity that triggers the subsequent mechanical activity.

c. *When the heart muscle is completely repolarized and at rest and ventricular filling is taking place,* after the T wave and before the next P wave. This period is called the **TP interval.**

The ECG can be used to diagnose abnormal heart rates, arrhythmias, and damage of heart muscle.

Clinical Note Because electrical activity triggers mechanical activity, abnormal electrical patterns are usually accompanied by abnormal contractile activity of the heart. Thus, evaluation of ECG patterns can provide useful information about the status of the heart. The main deviations from normal that can be found through an ECG are (1) abnormalities in rate, (2) abnormalities in rhythm, and (3) cardiac myopathies (● Figure 9-14).

ABNORMALITIES IN RATE The heart rate can be determined from the distance between two consecutive QRS complexes on the calibrated paper used to record an ECG. A rapid heart rate of more than 100 beats per minute is called **tachycardia** (*tachy* means "fast"), whereas a slow heart rate of fewer than 60 beats per minute is called **bradycardia** (*brady* means "slow").

ABNORMALITIES IN RHYTHM *Rhythm* refers to the regularity or spacing of the ECG waves. Any variation from the normal rhythm and sequence of excitation of the heart is termed an **arrhythmia.** It may result from ectopic foci, alterations in SA node pacemaker activity, or interference with conduction. For example, with *complete heart block* the SA node continues to govern atrial depolarization, but the ventricles generate their own impulses at a rate slower than that of the atria. On the ECG, the P waves exhibit a normal rhythm. The QRS and T waves also occur regularly but more slowly than the P waves and independently of P wave rhythm. Because atrial activity and ventricular activity are not synchronized, waves for atrial repolarization may appear, no longer masked by the QRS complex.

CARDIAC MYOPATHIES Abnormal ECG waves are also important in recognizing and assessing **cardiac myopathies** (damage of the heart muscle). **Myocardial ischemia** is inadequate delivery of oxygenated blood to the heart tissue. Actual death, or **necrosis,** of heart muscle cells occurs when a blood vessel supplying that area of the heart becomes blocked or ruptured. This condition is **acute myocardial infarction,** commonly called a **heart attack.** Abnormal QRS waveforms appear when part of the heart muscle becomes necrotic. In addition to ECG changes, because damaged heart muscle cells release character-

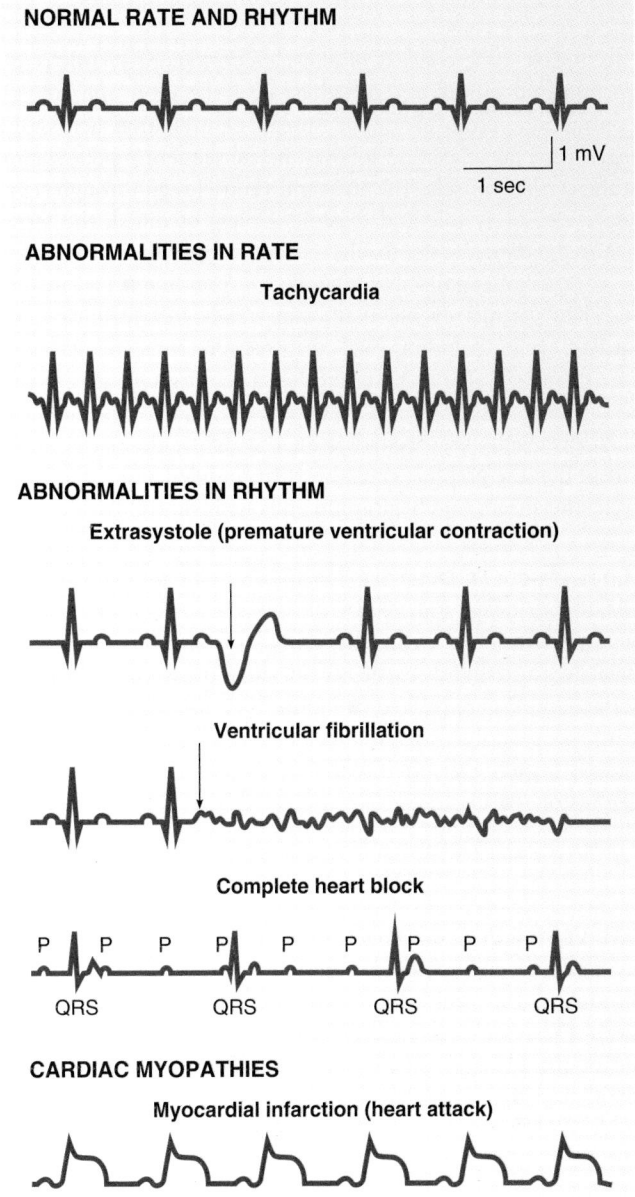

● FIGURE 9-14 **Representative heart conditions detectable through electrocardiography.**

istic enzymes into the blood, the level of these enzymes in the blood provides a further index of the extent of myocardial damage.

Mechanical Events of the Cardiac Cycle

The mechanical events of the cardiac cycle—contraction, relaxation, and the resultant changes in blood flow through the heart—are brought about by the rhythmic changes in cardiac electrical activity.

The heart alternately contracts to empty and relaxes to fill.

The cardiac cycle consists of alternate periods of **systole** (contraction and emptying) and **diastole** (relaxation and filling). Contraction results from the spread of excitation across the heart, whereas relaxation follows the subsequent repolarization of the cardiac muscle. The atria and ventricles go through separate cycles of systole and diastole. Unless qualified, the terms *systole* and *diastole* refer to what is happening with the ventricles.

The following discussion and corresponding ● Figure 9-15 correlate various events that occur concurrently during the cardiac cycle, including ECG features, pressure changes, volume changes, valve activity, and heart sounds. Only the events on the left side of the heart are described, but keep in mind that identical events are occurring on the right side of the heart, except that the pressures are lower. To complete one full cardiac cycle, our discussion begins and ends with ventricular diastole.

MIDVENTRICULAR DIASTOLE During most of ventricular diastole, the atrium is still also in diastole. Because of the continuous inflow of blood from the venous system into the atrium, atrial pressure slightly exceeds ventricular pressure even though both chambers are relaxed (● Figure 9-15, point **1**). Because of this pressure differential, the AV valve is open, and blood flows directly from the atrium into the ventricle throughout ventricular diastole (● Figure 9-15, heart a). As a result of this passive filling, the ventricular volume slowly continues to rise even before atrial contraction takes place (point **2**).

LATE VENTRICULAR DIASTOLE Late in ventricular diastole, the SA node reaches threshold and fires. The impulse spreads throughout the atria, which appears on the ECG as the P wave (point **3**). Atrial depolarization brings about atrial contraction, raising the atrial pressure curve (point **4**) and squeezing more blood into the ventricle. The excitation–contraction coupling process takes place during the short delay between the P wave and the rise in atrial pressure. The corresponding rise in ventricular pressure (point **5**) that occurs simultaneously with the rise in atrial pressure results from the additional volume of blood added to the ventricle by atrial contraction (point **6** and heart b).

END OF VENTRICULAR DIASTOLE Ventricular diastole ends at the onset of ventricular contraction. By this time, atrial contraction and ventricular filling are completed. The volume of blood in the ventricle at the end of diastole is known as the **end-diastolic volume (EDV)** (point **7**), which averages about 135 ml. No more blood will be added to the ventricle during this cycle. Therefore, the end-diastolic volume is the maximum amount of blood that the ventricle will contain during this cycle.

VENTRICULAR EXCITATION AND ONSET OF VENTRICULAR SYSTOLE After atrial excitation, the impulse travels through the AV node and specialized conduction system to excite the ventricle. Simultaneously, the atria are contracting. By the time ventricular activation is complete, atrial contraction is already over. The QRS complex represents this ventricular excitation (point **8**), which induces ventricular contraction. The ventricular pressure curve sharply increases shortly after the QRS complex, signaling the onset of ventricular systole (point **9**). As ventricular contraction begins, ventricular pressure immediately exceeds atrial pressure. This backward pressure differential forces the AV valve closed (point **9**).

ISOVOLUMETRIC VENTRICULAR CONTRACTION After ventricular pressure exceeds atrial pressure and the AV valve has closed, to open the aortic valve, the ventricular pressure must continue to increase until it exceeds aortic pressure. Therefore, after the AV valve closes and before the aortic valve opens, the ventricle briefly remains a closed chamber (point **10**). Because all valves are closed, no blood can enter or leave the ventricle during this time, which is termed the period of **isovolumetric ventricular contraction** (*isovolumetric* means "constant volume and length") (heart c). Because no blood enters or leaves the ventricle, the ventricular chamber stays at constant volume, and the muscle fibers stay at constant length (point **11**), while ventricular pressure continues to rise.

VENTRICULAR EJECTION When ventricular pressure exceeds aortic pressure (point **12**), the aortic valve is forced open and ejection of blood begins (heart d). The amount of blood pumped out of each ventricle with each contraction is called the **stroke volume (SV).** The aortic pressure curve rises as blood is forced into the aorta from the ventricle faster than blood is draining off into the smaller vessels at the other end (point **13**). The ventricular volume decreases substantially as blood is rapidly pumped out (point **14**). Ventricular systole includes both isovolumetric ventricular contraction and ventricular ejection.

END OF VENTRICULAR SYSTOLE The ventricle does not empty completely during ejection. Normally, only about half the blood within the ventricle at the end of diastole is pumped out during the subsequent systole. The amount of blood left in the ventricle at the end of systole when ejection is complete is the **end-systolic volume (ESV)** (point **15**), which averages about 65 ml. This is the least amount of blood that the ventricle will contain during this cycle.

The difference between the volume of blood in the ventricle before contraction and the volume after contraction is the amount of blood ejected during the contraction, that is, EDV − ESV = SV. In our example, the end-diastolic volume is 135 ml, the end-systolic volume is 65 ml, and the stroke volume is 70 ml.

VENTRICULAR REPOLARIZATION AND ONSET OF VENTRICULAR DIASTOLE The T wave signifies ventricular repolarization at the end of ventricular systole (point **16**). When the ventricle repolarizes and starts to relax, ventricular pressure falls below aortic pressure and the aortic valve closes (point **17**). Closure of the aortic valve produces a disturbance or notch on the aortic pressure curve (point **18**). No more blood leaves the ventricle during this cycle, because the aortic valve has closed.

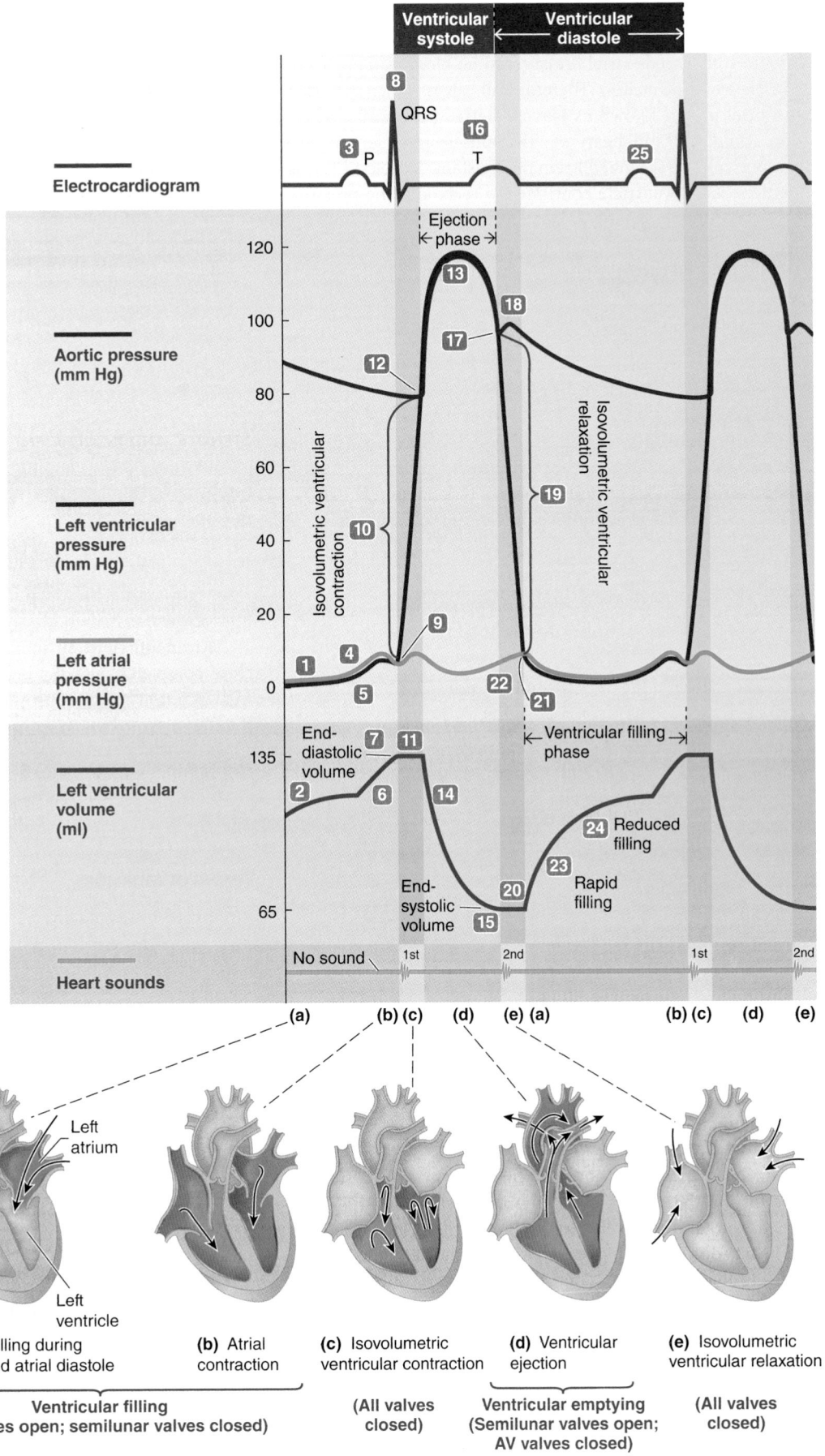

● **FIGURE 9-15 Cardiac cycle.** This graph depicts various events that occur concurrently during the cardiac cycle. Follow each horizontal strip across to see the changes that take place in the electrocardiogram; aortic, ventricular, and atrial pressures; ventricular volume; and heart sounds throughout the cycle. The last half of diastole, one full systole and diastole (one full cardiac cycle), and another systole are shown for the left side of the heart. Follow each vertical strip downward to see what happens simultaneously with each of these factors during each phase of the cardiac cycle. See the text (pp. 260 and 262) for a detailed explanation of the numbered points. The sketches of the heart illustrate the flow of O_2-poor (dark blue) and O_2-rich (dark pink) blood in and out of the ventricles during the cardiac cycle.

Electrocardiogram

Aortic pressure (mm Hg)

Left ventricular pressure (mm Hg)

Left atrial pressure (mm Hg)

Left ventricular volume (ml)

Heart sounds

Ventricular systole | Ventricular diastole

QRS
P   T

Ejection phase

Isovolumetric ventricular contraction

Isovolumetric ventricular relaxation

End-diastolic volume

Ventricular filling phase

Reduced filling

Rapid filling

End-systolic volume

No sound   1st   2nd   1st   2nd

Right atrium — Left atrium

Right ventricle — Left ventricle

(a) Passive filling during ventricular and atrial diastole

(b) Atrial contraction

(c) Isovolumetric ventricular contraction

(d) Ventricular ejection

(e) Isovolumetric ventricular relaxation

Ventricular filling (AV valves open; semilunar valves closed)

(All valves closed)

Ventricular emptying (Semilunar valves open; AV valves closed)

(All valves closed)

ISOVOLUMETRIC VENTRICULAR RELAXATION When the aortic valve closes, the AV valve is not yet open, because ventricular pressure still exceeds atrial pressure, so no blood can enter the ventricle from the atrium. Therefore, all valves are again closed for a brief period known as **isovolumetric ventricular relaxation** (point **19** and heart e). The muscle fiber length and chamber volume (point **20**) remain constant. No blood leaves or enters as the ventricle continues to relax and the pressure steadily falls.

VENTRICULAR FILLING When ventricular pressure falls below atrial pressure, the AV valve opens (point **21**) and ventricular filling occurs again. Ventricular diastole includes both isovolumetric ventricular relaxation and ventricular filling.

Atrial repolarization and ventricular depolarization occur simultaneously, so the atria are in diastole throughout ventricular systole. Blood continues to flow from the pulmonary veins into the left atrium. As this incoming blood pools in the atrium, atrial pressure rises continuously (point **22**). When the AV valve opens at the end of ventricular systole, blood that accumulated in the atrium during ventricular systole pours rapidly into the ventricle (heart a again). Ventricular filling thus occurs rapidly at first (point **23**) because of the increased atrial pressure resulting from the accumulation of blood in the atria. Then ventricular filling slows down (point **24**) as the accumulated blood has already been delivered to the ventricle. During this period of reduced filling, blood continues to flow from the pulmonary veins into the left atrium and through the open AV valve into the left ventricle. During late ventricular diastole, when the ventricle is filling slowly, the SA node fires again, and the cardiac cycle starts over (point **25**).

When the body is at rest, one complete cardiac cycle lasts 800 msec, with 300 msec devoted to ventricular systole and 500 msec taken up by ventricular diastole. Significantly, much of ventricular filling occurs early in diastole during the rapid-filling phase. During times of rapid heart rate, diastole length is shortened more than systole length is. This greatly reduces the time available for ventricular relaxation and filling. However, because much ventricular filling is accomplished during early diastole, filling is not seriously impaired during periods of increased heart rate, such as during exercise.

Two normal heart sounds are associated with valve closures.

Two major heart sounds normally can be heard with a stethoscope during the cardiac cycle. The **first heart sound** is low-pitched, soft, and relatively long, sounding like "lub." The **second heart sound** has a higher pitch and is shorter and sharper, sounding like "dup." Thus, one normally hears "lub-dup-lub-dup-lub-dup . . . ." The first heart sound is associated with closure of the AV valves, whereas the second sound is associated with closure of the semilunar valves (see the "Heart sounds" line at the bottom of the chart in ● Figure 9-15). Opening of valves does not produce any sound.

Because the AV valves close at the onset of ventricular contraction, when ventricular pressure first exceeds atrial pressure,

the first heart sound signals the onset of ventricular systole (● Figure 9-15, point **9**). The semilunar valves close at the onset of ventricular relaxation, as the left and right ventricular pressures fall below the aortic and pulmonary artery pressures, respectively. The second heart sound, therefore, signals the onset of ventricular diastole (point **17**).

Turbulent blood flow produces heart murmurs.

 Abnormal heart sounds, or **murmurs,** are usually (but not always) associated with cardiac disease. Blood normally flows in a *laminar* fashion; that is, layers of the fluid slide smoothly over one another (*lamina* means "layer"). Laminar flow does not produce any sound. When blood flow becomes turbulent, however, a sound can be heard (● Figure 9-16).

STENOTIC AND INSUFFICIENT VALVES The most common cause of turbulence is valve malfunction, either a stenotic or an insufficient valve. A **stenotic valve** is a stiff, narrowed valve that does not open completely. Blood must be forced through the constricted opening at tremendous velocity, resulting in turbulence that produces an abnormal whistling sound similar to the sound produced when you force air rapidly through narrowed lips to whistle.

An **insufficient,** or **incompetent, valve** is one that cannot close completely, usually because the valve edges are scarred and do not fit together properly. Turbulence is produced when blood flows backward through the insufficient valve and collides with blood moving in the opposite direction, creating a swishing or gurgling murmur. An insufficient heart valve is often called a **leaky valve,** because it lets blood leak back through when the valve should be closed.

TIMING OF MURMURS The valve involved and the type of defect can usually be detected by the *location* and *timing* of the murmur. Each heart valve can be heard best at a specific location on the chest. Noting where a murmur is loudest helps the diagnostician tell which valve is involved.

The "timing" of the murmur refers to the part of the cardiac cycle during which the murmur is heard. Recall that the first

(a) Laminar flow (does not create any sound)

(b) Turbulent flow (can be heard)

● **FIGURE 9-16 Comparison of laminar and turbulent flow.**

heart sound signals the onset of ventricular systole and the second heart sound signals the onset of ventricular diastole. Thus, a murmur between the first and the second heart sounds ("lub-murmur-dup—lub-murmur-dup") is a **systolic murmur.** A **diastolic murmur,** in contrast, occurs between the second and the first heart sounds ("lub-dup-murmur—lub-dup-murmur"). The sound of the murmur characterizes it as either a stenotic (whistling) murmur or an insufficient (swishy) murmur. Armed with these facts, one can determine the cause of a valvular murmur (▲ Table 9-2). As an example, a whistling murmur (denoting a stenotic valve) occurring between the first and the second heart sounds (denoting a systolic murmur) indicates stenosis in a valve that should be open during systole. It could be either the aortic or the pulmonary semilunar valve through which blood is being ejected. Identifying which of these valves is stenotic is accomplished by finding where the murmur is best heard.

The main concern with a heart murmur is not the murmur itself but the harmful circulatory results of the defect.

Cardiac Output and Its Control

Cardiac output (CO) is the volume of blood pumped by *each ventricle* per minute (not the total amount of blood pumped by the heart). During any period, the volume of blood flowing through the pulmonary circulation is the same as the volume flowing through the systemic circulation. Therefore, the cardiac output from each ventricle normally is the same, although minor variations may occur on a beat-to-beat basis.

Cardiac output depends on the heart rate and the stroke volume.

The two determinants of cardiac output are *heart rate* (beats per minute) and *stroke volume* (volume of blood pumped per beat or stroke). The average resting heart rate is 70 beats per minute, established by SA node rhythmicity; the average resting stroke volume is 70 ml per beat, producing an average cardiac output of 4900 ml per minute, or close to 5 L per minute:

$$\text{Cardiac output} = \text{heart rate} \times \text{stroke volume}$$
$$= 70 \text{ beats/min} \times 70 \text{ ml/beat}$$
$$= 4900 \text{ ml/min} \cong 5 \text{ L/min}$$

Because the body's total blood volume averages 5 to 5.5 liters, each half of the heart pumps the equivalent of the entire blood volume each minute. In other words, each minute the right ventricle normally pumps 5 liters of blood through the lungs and the left ventricle pumps 5 liters through the systemic circulation. At this rate, each half of the heart would pump about 2.5 million liters of blood in just 1 year. Yet this is only the resting cardiac output; during exercise, cardiac output can increase to 20 to 25 liters per minute (and even more in trained athletes).

How can cardiac output vary so tremendously, depending on the demands of the body? You can readily answer this question by thinking about how your own heart pounds rapidly (increased heart rate) and forcefully (increased stroke volume) when you engage in strenuous physical activities (when you need increased cardiac output). Thus, regulation of cardiac output depends on the control of both heart rate and stroke volume, topics that we discuss next.

Heart rate is determined primarily by autonomic influences on the SA node.

The SA node is normally the pacemaker of the heart because it has the fastest spontaneous rate of depolarization to threshold. When the SA node reaches threshold, an action potential is initiated that spreads throughout the heart, inducing the heart to contract, or have a "heartbeat." This happens about 70 times per minute, setting the average heart rate at 70 beats per minute.

The heart is innervated by both divisions of the autonomic nervous system, which can modify the rate (as well as the strength) of contraction, even though nervous stimulation is not required to initiate contraction. The parasympathetic nerve to the heart, the *vagus nerve,* primarily supplies the atrium, especially the SA and AV nodes. Parasympathetic innervation of the ventricles is sparse. The cardiac sympathetic nerves also

▲ Table 9-2 Type and Timing of Murmur Associated with Various Heart Valve Disorders

Pattern Heard with Stethoscope	Type of Valve Defect	Timing of Murmur	Valve Disorder
Lub-Whistle-Dup	Stenotic	Systolic	*Stenotic semilunar valve.* A whistling systolic murmur signifies that a valve that should be open during systole (a semilunar valve) does not open completely.
Lub-Dup-Whistle	Stenotic	Diastolic	*Stenotic AV valve.* A whistling diastolic murmur signifies that a valve that should be open during diastole (an AV valve) does not open completely.
Lub-Swish-Dup	Insufficient	Systolic	*Insufficient AV valve.* A swishy systolic murmur signifies that a valve that should be closed during systole (an AV valve) does not close completely.
Lub-Dup-Swish	Insufficient	Diastolic	*Insufficient semilunar valve.* A swishy diastolic murmur signifies that a valve that should be closed during diastole (a semilunar valve) does not close completely.

supply the atria, including the SA and AV nodes, and richly innervate the ventricles. Parasympathetic and sympathetic stimulation have the following specific effects on the heart.

EFFECT OF PARASYMPATHETIC STIMULATION ON THE HEART

■ Parasympathetic stimulation decreases the SA node's rate of spontaneous depolarization, prolonging the time required to drift to threshold. Therefore, the SA node reaches threshold and fires less frequently, decreasing the heart rate (● Figure 9-17).

■ Parasympathetic stimulation decreases the AV node's excitability, prolonging transmission of impulses to the ventricles even longer than the usual AV nodal delay.

■ Parasympathetic stimulation of the atrial contractile cells shortens the plateau phase of the action potential by reducing the slow inward current carried by Ca^{2+}. As a result, atrial contraction is weakened.

■ The parasympathetic system has little effect on ventricular contraction because of the sparseness of parasympathetic innervation to the ventricles.

Thus, the heart is more "leisurely" under parasympathetic influence—it beats less rapidly, the time between atrial and ventricular contraction is stretched out, and atrial contraction is weaker. These actions are appropriate, considering that the parasympathetic system controls heart action in quiet, relaxed situations when the body is not demanding enhanced cardiac output.

EFFECT OF SYMPATHETIC STIMULATION ON THE HEART

In contrast, the sympathetic nervous system, which controls heart action in emergency or exercise situations that require greater blood flow, "revs up" the heart.

■ The main effect of sympathetic stimulation on the SA node is to speed up depolarization so that threshold is reached more rapidly. This swifter drift to threshold under sympathetic influence permits more frequent action potentials and a correspondingly faster heart rate (● Figure 9-17).

■ Sympathetic stimulation of the AV node reduces the AV nodal delay by increasing conduction velocity.

■ Similarly, sympathetic stimulation speeds up spread of the action potential throughout the specialized conduction pathway.

■ In the atrial and ventricular contractile cells, both of which have many sympathetic nerve endings, sympathetic stimulation increases contractile strength so that the heart beats more forcefully and squeezes out more blood. This effect is produced by increasing Ca^{2+} permeability through prolonged opening of the slow Ca^{2+} channels. The resultant enhanced Ca^{2+} influx strengthens contraction by intensifying Ca^{2+} participation in excitation–contraction coupling.

The overall effect of sympathetic stimulation on the heart, therefore, is to improve its effectiveness as a pump by increasing heart rate, decreasing the delay between atrial and ventricular contraction, decreasing conduction time throughout the heart, and increasing the force of contraction.

KEY

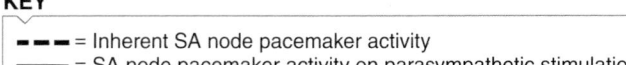

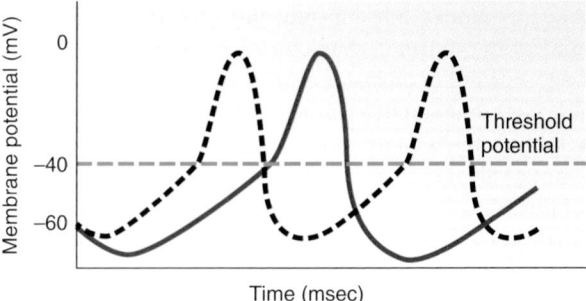

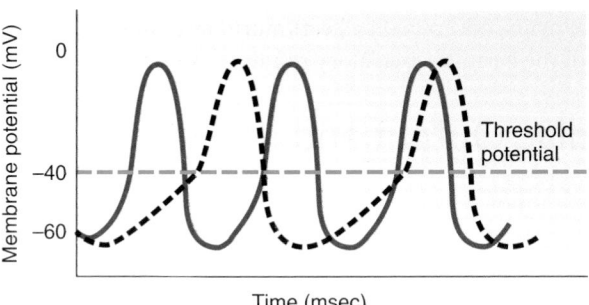

(a) Autonomic influence on SA node potential

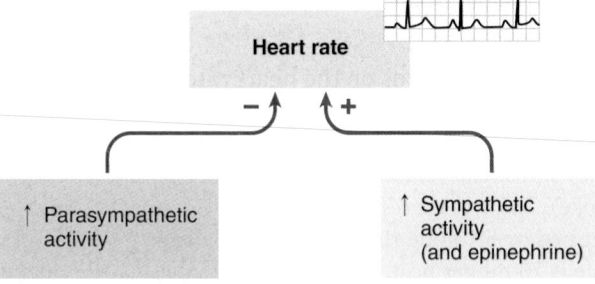

(b) Control of heart rate by autonomic nervous system

● **FIGURE 9-17 Autonomic control of SA node activity and heart rate.** (a) Parasympathetic stimulation decreases the rate of SA nodal depolarization so that the membrane reaches threshold more slowly and has fewer action potentials, whereas sympathetic stimulation increases the rate of depolarization of the SA node so that the membrane reaches threshold more rapidly and has more frequent action potentials. (b) Because each SA node action potential ultimately leads to a heartbeat, increased parasympathetic activity decreases the heart rate, whereas increased sympathetic activity increases the heart rate.

CONTROL OF HEART RATE

Thus, as is typical of the autonomic nervous system, parasympathetic and sympathetic effects on heart rate are antagonistic (oppose each other). At any given moment, heart rate is determined largely by the balance between inhibition of the SA node by the vagus nerve and stimulation by the cardiac sympathetic nerves. Under resting conditions, parasympathetic discharge dominates because acetylcholine (the parasympathetic neurotransmitter) suppresses sympathetic activity by inhibiting the release of norepinephrine (the sympathetic neurotransmitter) from neighboring sympathetic nerve endings. If all autonomic nerves to the heart were blocked, the resting heart rate would increase from its average value of 70 beats per minute to about 100 beats per minute, which is the inherent rate of the SA node's spontaneous discharge when not subjected to any nervous influence. (We use 70 beats per minute as the normal rate of SA node discharge because this is the average rate under normal resting conditions when parasympathetic activity dominates.) The heart rate can be altered beyond this resting level in either direction by shifting the balance of autonomic nervous stimulation. Heart rate is speeded up by simultaneously increasing sympathetic and decreasing parasympathetic activity; heart rate is slowed by a concurrent rise in parasympathetic activity and decline in sympathetic activity. The relative level of activity in these two autonomic branches to the heart in turn is primarily coordinated by the *cardiovascular control center* in the brain stem.

Although autonomic innervation is the primary means by which heart rate is regulated, other factors affect it as well. The most important is epinephrine, a hormone secreted into the blood from the adrenal medulla on sympathetic stimulation. Epinephrine acts in a manner similar to norepinephrine to increase heart rate, thus reinforcing the direct effect that the sympathetic nervous system has on the heart.

Stroke volume is determined by the extent of venous return and by sympathetic activity.

The other component besides heart rate that determines cardiac output is stroke volume, the amount of blood pumped out by each ventricle during each beat. Two types of control influence stroke volume: (1) *intrinsic control* related to the extent of venous return and (2) *extrinsic control* related to the extent of sympathetic stimulation of the heart. Both factors increase stroke volume by increasing the strength of heart contraction (● Figure 9-18). Let us examine each of these mechanisms in detail.

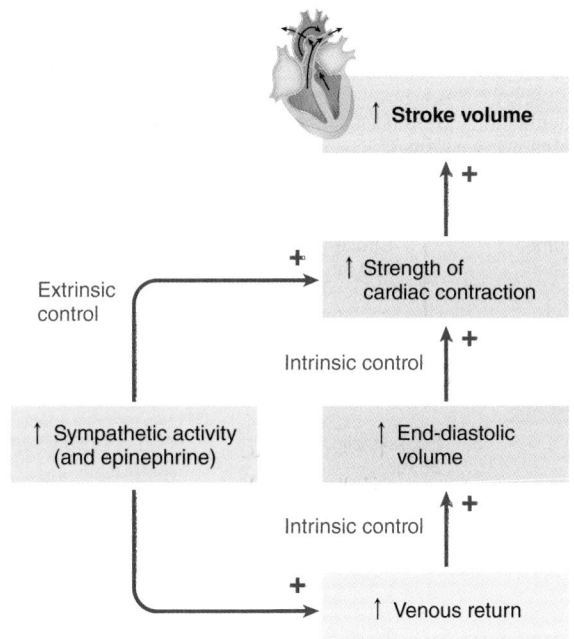

● **FIGURE 9-18 Intrinsic and extrinsic control of stroke volume.**

Increased end-diastolic volume results in increased stroke volume.

Intrinsic control of stroke volume, which refers to the heart's inherent ability to vary stroke volume, depends on the direct correlation between end-diastolic volume (EDV) and stroke volume. As more blood returns to the heart, the heart pumps out more blood, but the relationship is not quite as simple as might seem, because the heart does not eject all the blood it contains. This intrinsic control depends on the length–tension relationship of cardiac muscle, which is similar to that of skeletal muscle. For skeletal muscle, the resting muscle length is approximately the optimal length (l_o) at which maximal tension can be developed during a subsequent contraction. When the skeletal muscle is longer or shorter than l_o, the subsequent contraction is weaker (see ● Figure 8-17, p. 213). For cardiac muscle, the resting cardiac muscle fiber length is less than l_o. Therefore, the length of cardiac muscle fibers normally varies along the ascending limb of the length–tension curve. An increase in cardiac muscle fiber length, by moving closer to l_o, increases the contractile tension of the heart on the following systole (● Figure 9-19).

Unlike in skeletal muscle, the length–tension curve of cardiac muscle normally does not operate at lengths that fall within the region of the descending limb. That is, within physiologic limits, cardiac muscle does not get stretched beyond its l_o to the point that contractile strength diminishes with further stretching.

FRANK–STARLING LAW OF THE HEART What causes cardiac muscle fibers to vary in length before contraction? Skeletal muscle length can vary before contraction because of the positioning of the skeletal parts to which the muscle is attached, but cardiac muscle is not attached to any bones. The main determinant of cardiac muscle fiber length is the degree of diastolic filling. An analogy is a balloon filled with water—the more water you put in, the larger the balloon becomes, and the more it is stretched. Likewise, the greater the diastolic filling, the larger the EDV, and the more the heart is stretched. The more the heart is stretched, the longer the initial cardiac fiber before contraction. The increased length results in a greater force on the subsequent cardiac contraction and thus in a greater stroke volume. This intrinsic relationship between EDV and stroke volume is known as the **Frank–Starling law of the heart.** Stated simply, the law says that the heart normally pumps out during systole the volume of blood returned to it during diastole; increased venous return results in increased stroke volume. In ● Figure 9-19, assume that EDV increases from point A to point B. You can see that this increase in EDV is accompanied by a corresponding increase in stroke volume from point A^1 to point B^1.

ADVANTAGES OF THE CARDIAC LENGTH–TENSION RELATIONSHIP The built-in relationship matching stroke volume with venous return has two important advantages. First, one of the most important functions of this intrinsic mechanism is equalizing output between the right and the left sides of the heart so that blood pumped out by the heart is equally distributed between

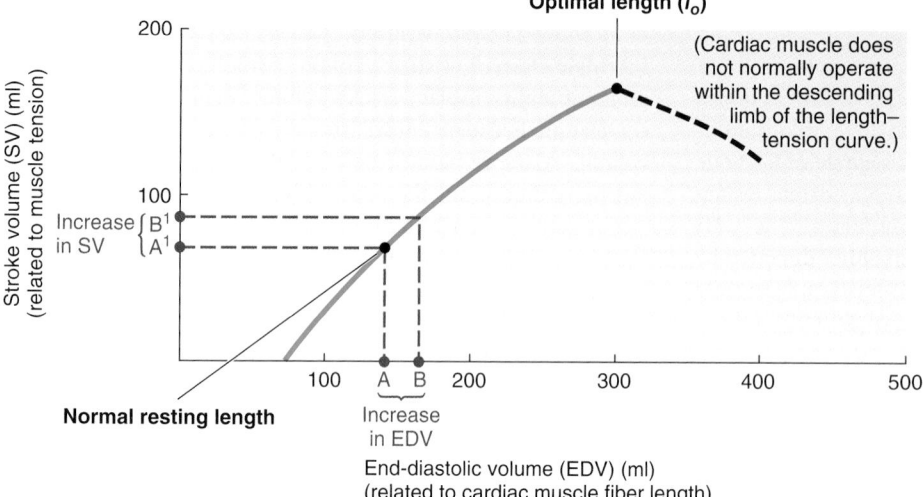

● **FIGURE 9-19 Intrinsic control of stroke volume, or the Frank–Starling curve.** The cardiac muscle fiber's length, which is determined by the extent of venous filling, is normally less than the optimal length (l_o) for developing maximal tension. Therefore, an increase in end-diastolic volume (that is, an increase in venous return), by moving the cardiac muscle fiber length closer to l_o, increases the contractile tension of the fibers on the next systole. A stronger contraction squeezes out more blood. Thus, as more blood is returned to the heart and the end-diastolic volume increases, the heart automatically pumps out a correspondingly larger stroke volume.

the pulmonary and the systemic circulation. If, for example, the right side of the heart ejects a larger stroke volume, more blood enters the pulmonary circulation, so venous return to the left side of the heart increases accordingly. The increased EDV of the left side of the heart causes it to contract more forcefully, so it too pumps out a larger stroke volume. In this way, output of the two ventricular chambers is kept equal. If such equalization did not happen, too much blood would be dammed up in the venous system before the ventricle with the lower output.

Second, when a larger cardiac output is needed, such as during exercise, venous return is increased through action of the sympathetic nervous system and other mechanisms to be described in the next chapter. The resulting increase in EDV automatically increases stroke volume correspondingly. Because exercise also increases heart rate, these two factors act together to increase the cardiac output so that more blood can be delivered to the exercising muscles.

Sympathetic stimulation increases the contractility of the heart.

In addition to intrinsic control, stroke volume is subject to **extrinsic control** by factors originating outside the heart, the most important of which are actions of the cardiac sympathetic nerves and epinephrine. Sympathetic stimulation and epinephrine enhance the heart's **contractility,** which is the strength of contraction at any given EDV. In other words, on sympathetic stimulation the heart contracts more forcefully and squeezes out a greater percentage of the blood it contains, leading to more complete ejection. This increased

contractility results from the increased Ca^{2+} influx triggered by norepinephrine and epinephrine. The extra cytosolic Ca^{2+} lets the myocardial fibers generate more force through greater cross-bridge cycling than they would without sympathetic influence. Normally, the EDV is 135 ml and the end-systolic volume (ESV) is 65 ml for a stroke volume of 70 ml (● Figure 9-20a). Under sympathetic influence, for the same EDV of 135 ml, the ESV might be 35 ml and the stroke volume 100 ml (● Figure 9-20b). In effect, sympathetic stimulation shifts the Frank–Starling curve to the left (● Figure 9-21). Depending on the extent of sympathetic stimulation, the curve can be shifted to varying degrees, up to a maximal increase in contractile strength of about 100% greater than normal.

Sympathetic stimulation increases stroke volume not only by strengthening cardiac contractility but also by enhancing venous return (see ● Figure 9-20c). Sympathetic stimulation constricts the veins, which squeezes more blood forward from the veins to the heart, increasing the EDV and subsequently increasing stroke volume even further.

SUMMARY OF FACTORS AFFECTING STROKE VOLUME AND CARDIAC OUTPUT The strength of cardiac muscle contraction and, accordingly, stroke volume can thus be graded by (1) varying the initial length of the muscle fibers, which in turn depends on the

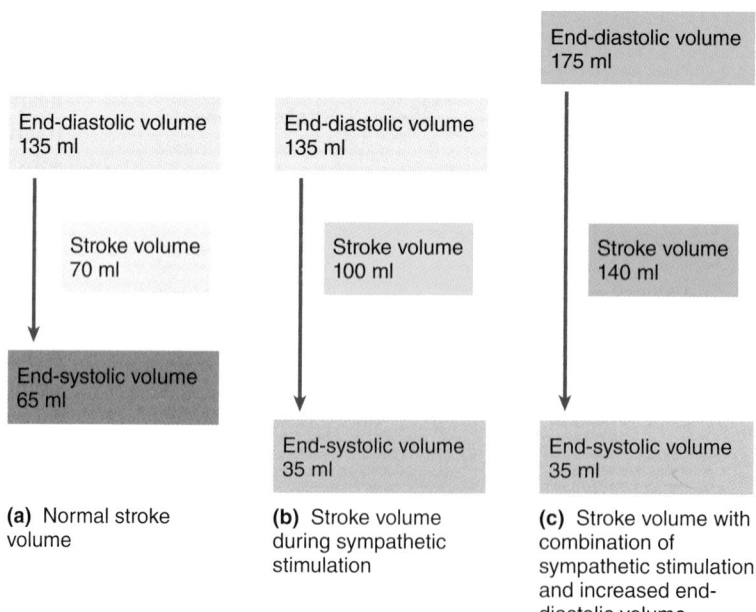

(a) Normal stroke volume

(b) Stroke volume during sympathetic stimulation

(c) Stroke volume with combination of sympathetic stimulation and increased end-diastolic volume

● **FIGURE 9-20 Effect of sympathetic stimulation on stroke volume.**

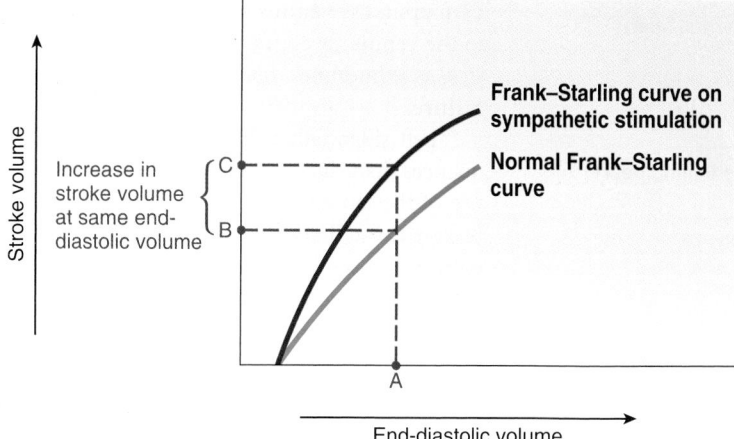

● FIGURE 9-21 **Shift of the Frank–Starling curve to the left by sympathetic stimulation.** For the same end-diastolic volume (point A), a larger stroke volume (from point B to point C) is pumped out on sympathetic stimulation as a result of increased contractility of the heart. The Frank–Starling curve is shifted to the left by variable degrees, depending on the extent of sympathetic stimulation.

degree of ventricular filling before contraction (intrinsic control), and (2) varying the extent of sympathetic stimulation (extrinsic control) (see ● Figure 9-18). This is in contrast to gradation of skeletal muscle, in which twitch summation and recruitment of motor units produce variable strength of muscle contraction. These mechanisms do not apply to cardiac muscle. Here, twitch summation is impossible because of the long refractory period. Recruitment of motor units is not possible, because the heart muscle cells are arranged into functional syncytia where all contractile cells become excited and contract with every beat, instead of into distinct motor units that can be discretely activated.

All the factors that determine cardiac output by influencing heart rate or stroke volume are summarized in ● Figure 9-22. Note that sympathetic stimulation increases cardiac output by increasing both heart rate and stroke volume. Sympathetic activity to the heart increases, for example, during exercise when the working skeletal muscles need increased delivery of O_2-laden blood to support their high rate of ATP consumption.

We next examine how a failing heart cannot pump out enough blood, and then we turn to the final section of this chapter, which focuses on how the heart muscle is nourished.

In heart failure, the contractility of the heart decreases.

 Heart failure is the inability of the cardiac output to keep pace with the body's demands for supplies and removal of wastes. Either one or both ventricles may progressively weaken and fail. When a failing ventricle cannot pump out all the blood returned to it, the veins behind the failing ventricle become congested with blood. Heart failure may occur for a variety of reasons, but the two most common are (1) damage to the heart muscle as a result of a heart attack or impaired circulation to the cardiac muscle and (2) prolonged pumping against a chronically elevated blood pressure. Heart failure presently affects almost 5 million Americans, nearly 50% of whom will die within 5 years of diagnosis. About 500,000

new cases are diagnosed annually, with these numbers expected to rise as the population ages.

PRIME DEFECT IN HEART FAILURE The prime defect in heart failure is a decrease in cardiac contractility; that is, weakened cardiac muscle cells contract less effectively. The intrinsic ability of the heart to develop pressure and eject a stroke volume is reduced so that the heart operates on a lower length–tension curve (● Figure 9-23a). The Frank–Starling curve shifts downward and to the right such that, for a given EDV, a failing heart pumps out a smaller stroke volume than a normal healthy heart.

COMPENSATORY MEASURES FOR HEART FAILURE In the early stages of heart failure, two major compensatory measures help restore stroke volume to normal. First, sympathetic activity to the heart is reflexly increased, which increases heart contractility toward normal (● Figure 9-23b). Sympathetic stimulation can help compensate only for a limited time, however, because the heart becomes less responsive to prolonged sympathetic stimulation. Second, when cardiac output is reduced, the kidneys, in a compensatory attempt to improve their reduced blood flow, retain extra salt and water in the body during urine formation to expand the blood volume. The increase in circulating blood volume increases the EDV. The resultant stretching of the cardiac muscle fibers enables the weakened heart to pump out a normal stroke volume (● Figure 9-23b). The heart is now

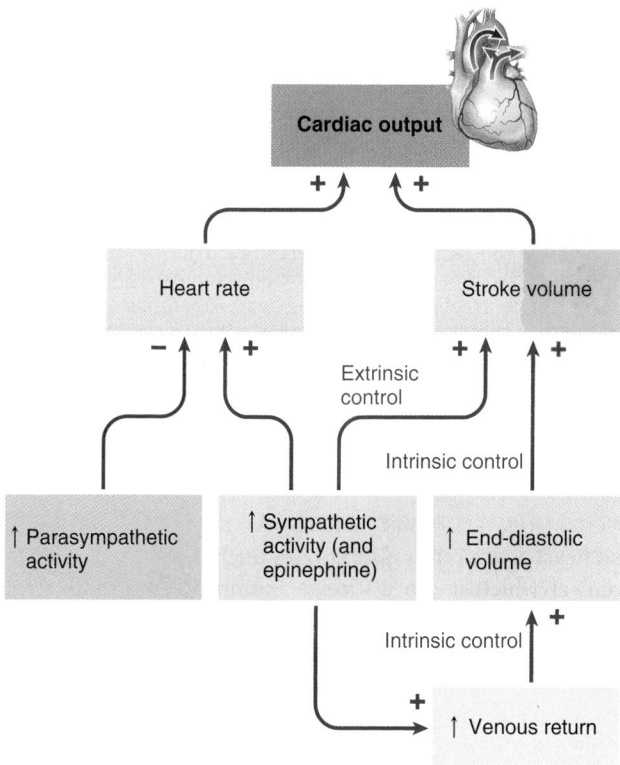

● FIGURE 9-22 **Control of cardiac output.** Because cardiac output equals heart rate times stroke volume, this figure is a composite of Figure 9-17b (control of heart rate) and Figure 9-18 (control of stroke volume).

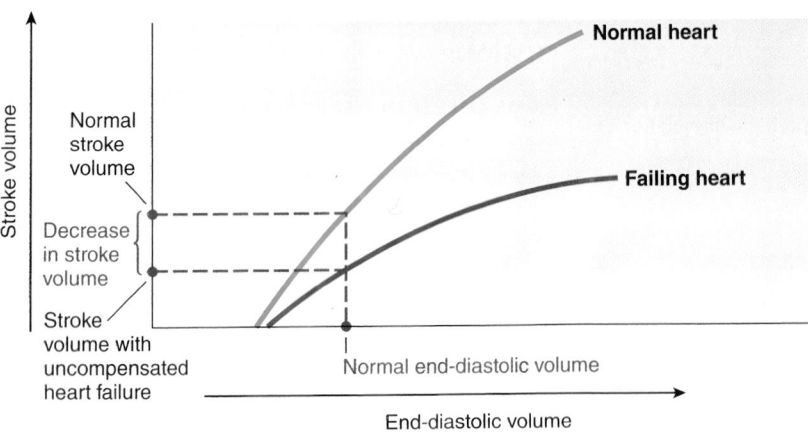

(a) Reduced contractility in a failing heart

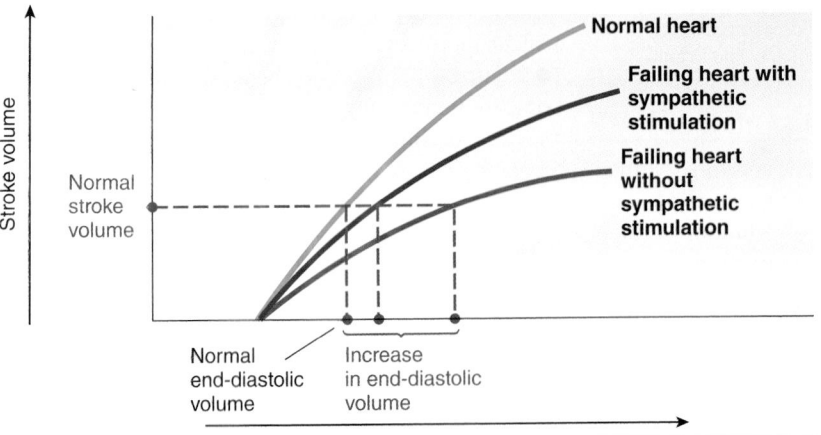

(b) Compensation for heart failure

● **FIGURE 9-23 Compensated heart failure.** (a) The Frank–Starling curve shifts downward and to the right in a failing heart. Because its contractility is decreased, the failing heart pumps out a smaller stroke volume at the same end-diastolic volume than a normal heart does. (b) During compensation for heart failure, reflex sympathetic stimulation shifts the Frank–Starling curve of a failing heart to the left, increasing the contractility of the heart toward normal. A compensatory increase in end-diastolic volume as a result of blood volume expansion further increases the strength of contraction of the failing heart. Operating at a longer cardiac muscle fiber length, a compensated failing heart is able to eject a normal stroke volume.

pumping out the blood returned to it but is operating at a greater cardiac muscle fiber length.

DECOMPENSATED HEART FAILURE As the disease progresses and heart contractility deteriorates further, the heart reaches a point at which it can no longer pump out a normal stroke volume (that is, it cannot pump out all the blood returned to it) despite compensatory measures. At this point, the heart slips from compensated heart failure into a state of decompensated heart failure. Now the cardiac muscle fibers are stretched to the point that they are operating in the descending limb of the length–tension curve. *Forward failure* occurs as the heart fails to pump an adequate amount of blood forward to the tissues because the stroke volume becomes progressively smaller. *Backward failure* occurs simultaneously as blood that cannot enter and be pumped out by the heart continues to

dam up in the venous system. The congestion in the venous system is the reason this condition is sometimes termed **congestive heart failure.**

Left-sided failure has more serious consequences than right-sided failure. Backward failure of the left side leads to pulmonary edema (excess tissue fluid in the lungs) because blood dams up in the lungs. This fluid accumulation in the lungs reduces exchange of O_2 and CO_2 between the air and the blood in the lungs, reducing arterial oxygenation and elevating levels of acid-forming CO_2 in the blood. In addition, one of the more serious consequences of left-sided forward failure is an inadequate blood flow to the kidneys, which causes a twofold problem. First, vital kidney function is depressed; second, the kidneys retain even more salt and water in the body during urine formation as they try to expand the plasma volume even further to improve their reduced blood flow. Excessive fluid retention worsens the already existing problems of venous congestion.

Treatment of congestive heart failure therefore includes measures that reduce salt and water retention and increase urinary output, as well as drugs that enhance the contractile ability of the weakened heart—digitalis, for example.

Nourishing the Heart Muscle

Cardiac muscle cells contain an abundance of mitochondria, the O_2-dependent energy organelles. Up to 40% of the cell volume of cardiac muscle cells is occupied by mitochondria, indicative of how much the heart depends on O_2 delivery and aerobic metabolism to generate the energy necessary for contraction (see p. 32).

The heart receives most of its own blood supply through the coronary circulation during diastole.

Although all the blood passes through the heart, the heart muscle cannot extract O_2 or nutrients from the blood within its chambers for two reasons. First, the watertight endothelial lining does not permit blood to pass from the chamber into the myocardium. Second, the heart walls are too thick to permit diffusion of O_2 and other supplies from the blood in the chamber to the individual cardiac cells. Therefore, like other tissues of the body, heart muscle must receive blood through blood vessels, specifically via the **coronary circulation.** The coronary arteries branch from the aorta just beyond the aortic valve (see ● Figure 9-26, p. 271), and the coronary veins empty into the right atrium.

The heart muscle receives most of its blood supply during diastole. Blood flow to the heart muscle cells is substantially reduced during systole for two reasons: (1) the contracting myocardium compresses the major branches of the coronary arteries and (2) the open aortic valve partially blocks the entrance to the coronary vessels. Thus, about 70% of coronary arterial flow occurs during diastole, driven by the aortic blood pressure, with only 30% occurring during systole, driven by ventricular contraction.

This limited time for coronary blood flow becomes especially important during rapid heart rates, when diastolic time is much reduced. Just when increased demands are placed on the heart to pump more rapidly, it has less time to provide O_2 and nourishment to its own musculature to accomplish the increased workload.

Nevertheless, under normal circumstances, the heart muscle receives adequate blood flow to support its activities—even during exercise, when the rate of coronary blood flow increases up to five times its resting rate. Extra blood is delivered to the cardiac cells primarily by vasodilation, or enlargement, of the coronary vessels, which lets more blood flow through them, especially during diastole. Coronary blood flow is adjusted primarily in response to changes in the heart's O_2 requirements. When cardiac activity increases and the heart thus needs more O_2, local chemical changes induce dilation of the coronary blood vessels, allowing more O_2-rich blood to flow to the more active cardiac cells to meet their increased O_2 demand. This matching of O_2 delivery to O_2 needs is crucial, because heart muscle depends on oxidative processes to generate energy. The heart cannot get enough ATP through anaerobic metabolism.

Atherosclerotic coronary artery disease can deprive the heart of essential oxygen.

 Adequacy of coronary blood flow is relative to the heart's O_2 demands at any moment. In the normal heart, coronary blood flow increases correspondingly as O_2 demands rise. With coronary artery disease, coronary blood flow may not be able to keep pace with rising O_2 needs. The term **coronary artery disease (CAD)** refers to pathological changes within the coronary artery walls that diminish blood flow through these vessels. A given rate of coronary blood flow may be adequate at rest but insufficient in physical exertion or other stressful situations.

CAD is the underlying cause of about 50% of all deaths in the United States. CAD can cause myocardial ischemia and possibly lead to a heart attack by three mechanisms: (1) profound vascular spasm of the coronary arteries, (2) formation of atherosclerotic plaques, and (3) thromboembolism. We discuss each in turn.

VASCULAR SPASM **Vascular spasm** is an abnormal spastic constriction that transiently narrows the coronary vessels. Vascular spasms are associated with the early stages of CAD and are most often triggered by exposure to cold, physical exertion, or anxiety. The condition is reversible and usually does not last long enough to damage the cardiac muscle.

When too little O_2 is available in the coronary vessels, the endothelium (blood vessel lining) releases *platelet-activating factor (PAF)*. PAF, which exerts a variety of actions, was named for its first discovered effect, activating platelets. Among its other effects, PAF, once released from the endothelium, diffuses to the underlying vascular smooth muscle and causes it to contract, bringing about vascular spasm.

DEVELOPMENT OF ATHEROSCLEROSIS **Atherosclerosis** is a progressive, degenerative arterial disease that leads to occlusion (gradual blockage) of affected vessels, reducing blood flow through them. Atherosclerosis is characterized by plaques forming beneath the vessel lining within arterial walls. An **atherosclerotic plaque** consists of a lipid-rich core covered by an abnormal overgrowth of smooth muscle cells, topped off by a collagen-rich connective tissue cap. As the plaque forms, it bulges into the vessel lumen (● Figure 9-24).

Although all the contributing factors have not yet been identified, in recent years investigators have sorted out the following complex sequence of events in the gradual development of atherosclerosis:

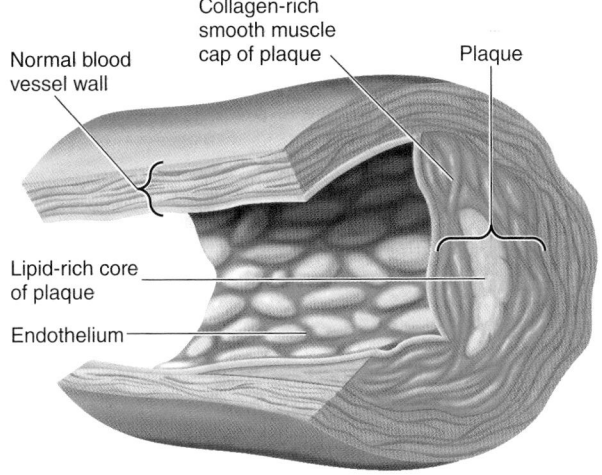

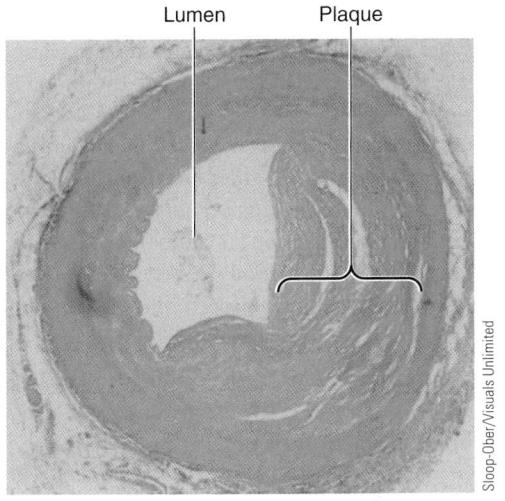

● **FIGURE 9-24 Atherosclerotic plaque in a coronary vessel.**

1. Atherosclerosis starts with injury to the blood vessel wall, which triggers an *inflammatory response* that sets the stage for plaque buildup. Normally, inflammation is a protective response that fights infection and promotes repair of damaged tissue (see p. 333). However, when the cause of the injury persists within the vessel wall, the sustained, low-grade inflammatory response over a course of decades can insidiously lead to arterial plaque formation and heart disease. Plaque formation likely has many causes. Suspected artery-abusing agents that may set off the vascular inflammatory response include oxidized cholesterol, free radicals, high blood pressure, homocysteine, chemicals released from fat cells, or even bacteria and viruses that damage blood vessel walls. The most common triggering agent appears to be oxidized cholesterol. (For further discussion of the role of cholesterol and other factors in the development of atherosclerosis, see the boxed feature on pp. 272–273, ❱ Beyond the Basics.)

2. Typically, the initial stage of atherosclerosis is characterized by accumulation beneath the endothelium of excessive amounts of *low-density lipoprotein (LDL),* the so-called bad cholesterol, in combination with a protein carrier. As LDL accumulates within the vessel wall, this cholesterol product becomes oxidized, primarily by oxidative wastes produced by the blood vessel cells. These wastes are **free radicals,** unstable electron-deficient particles that are highly reactive and cause cell damage by snatching electrons from other molecules.

3. In response to the presence of oxidized LDL or other irritants, the endothelial cells produce chemicals that attract *monocytes,* a type of white blood cell, to the site. These immune cells trigger a local inflammatory response.

4. Once they leave the blood and enter the vessel wall, monocytes settle down permanently, enlarge, and become large phagocytic cells called *macrophages.* Macrophages voraciously phagocytize (see p. 26) the oxidized LDL until these cells become so packed with fatty droplets that they appear foamy under a microscope. Now called *foam cells,* these engorged macrophages accumulate beneath the vessel lining and form a visible *fatty streak,* the beginning of an atherosclerotic plaque.

5. Thus, the earliest stage of a plaque is accumulation beneath the endothelium of a cholesterol-rich deposit. The disease progresses as smooth muscle cells within the blood vessel wall migrate from the muscular layer of the blood vessel to a position on top of the lipid accumulation, just beneath the endothelium. This migration is triggered by chemicals released at the inflammatory site. At their new location, the smooth muscle cells continue to divide and enlarge, producing *atheromas,* which are benign (noncancerous) tumors of smooth muscle cells within the blood vessel walls. Together the lipid-rich core and overlying smooth muscle form a maturing plaque.

6. As it continues to develop, the plaque progressively bulges into the lumen of the vessel. The protruding plaque narrows the opening through which blood can flow.

7. Further contributing to vessel narrowing, oxidized LDL inhibits release of *nitric oxide* from the endothelial cells. Nitric oxide is a local chemical messenger that relaxes the underlying layer of normal smooth muscle cells within the vessel wall. Relaxation of these smooth muscle cells dilates the vessel. Because of reduced nitric oxide release, vessels damaged by developing plaques cannot dilate as readily as normal.

8. A thickening plaque also interferes with nutrient exchange for cells located within the involved arterial wall, leading to degeneration of the wall in the vicinity of the plaque. The damaged area is invaded by *fibroblasts* (scar-forming cells), which form a collagen-rich connective tissue cap over the plaque. (The term *sclerosis* means "excessive growth of fibrous connective tissue," hence the term *atherosclerosis* for this condition characterized by atheromas and sclerosis, along with abnormal lipid accumulation.)

9. In the later stages of the disease, Ca^{2+} often precipitates in the plaque. A vessel so afflicted becomes hard and cannot distend easily.

THROMBOEMBOLISM AND OTHER COMPLICATIONS OF ATHEROSCLEROSIS Atherosclerosis attacks arteries throughout the body, but the most serious consequences involve damage to the vessels of the brain and heart. In the brain, atherosclerosis is the prime cause of strokes, whereas in the heart it brings about myocardial ischemia and its complications. The following are potential complications of coronary atherosclerosis:

■ *Angina pectoris.* Gradual enlargement of protruding plaque continues to narrow the vessel lumen and progressively diminishes coronary blood flow, triggering increasingly frequent bouts of transient myocardial ischemia as the ability to match blood flow with cardiac O_2 needs becomes more limited. Although the heart cannot normally be "felt," pain is associated with myocardial ischemia. Such cardiac pain, known as **angina pectoris** (meaning "pain of the chest"), can be felt beneath the sternum and is often referred to (or appears to come from) the left shoulder and down the left arm (see p. 141). The symptoms of angina pectoris recur whenever cardiac O_2 demands become too great in relation to the coronary blood flow—for example, during exertion or emotional stress. The ischemia associated with the characteristically brief angina attacks is usually temporary and reversible and can be relieved by rest, taking vasodilator drugs such as *nitroglycerin,* or both. Nitroglycerin brings about coronary vasodilation by being metabolically converted to nitric oxide, which in turn relaxes the vascular smooth muscle.

■ *Thromboembolism.* The enlarging atherosclerotic plaque can break through the weakened endothelial lining that covers it, exposing blood to the underlying collagen in the collagen-rich connective tissue cap of the plaque. Foam cells release chemicals that can weaken the fibrous cap of a plaque by breaking down the connective tissue fibers. Plaques with thick fibrous caps are considered stable because they are not likely to rupture. However, plaques with thinner fibrous caps are unstable because they are likely to rupture and trigger clot formation.

Blood platelets (formed elements of the blood involved in plugging vessel defects and in clot formation) normally do not adhere to smooth, healthy vessel linings. However, when platelets contact collagen at the site of vessel damage, they stick to the site and help promote the formation of a blood clot. Furthermore, foam cells produce a potent clot promoter. Such an abnormal clot attached to a vessel wall is called a **thrombus.** The thrombus may enlarge gradually until it completely blocks the vessel at that site, or the continued flow of blood past the thrombus may break it loose. As it heads downstream, such a freely floating clot, or **embolus,** may completely plug a smaller vessel (● Figure 9-25). Thus, through **thromboembolism,** atherosclerosis can result in a gradual or sudden occlusion of a coronary vessel (or any other vessel).

■ *Heart attack.* When a coronary vessel is completely plugged, the cardiac tissue served by the vessel soon dies from O_2 deprivation and a heart attack occurs, unless the area can be supplied with blood from nearby vessels.

The extent of the damaged area during a heart attack depends on the size of the blocked vessel: The larger the vessel occluded, the greater the area deprived of blood supply. As ● Figure 9-26 illustrates, a blockage at point A in the coronary circulation would cause more extensive damage than a blockage at point B would. Because there are only two major coronary arteries, complete blockage of either one of these main branches results in extensive myocardial damage. Left coronary artery blockage is most devastating because this vessel supplies blood to 85% of the cardiac tissue.

A heart attack has four possible outcomes: immediate death, delayed death from complications, full functional recovery, or recovery with impaired function (▲ Table 9-3).

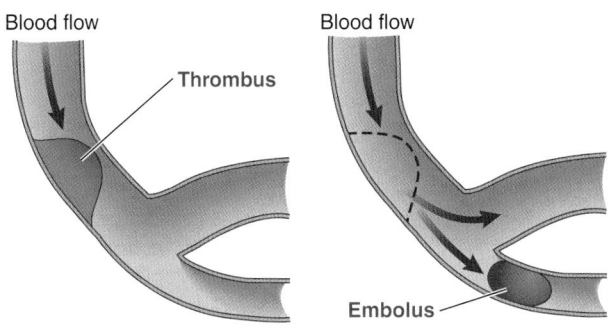

(a) Thrombus   **(b)** Embolus

● **FIGURE 9-25 Consequences of thromboembolism.** (a) A thrombus may enlarge gradually until it completely occludes the vessel at that site. (b) A thrombus may break loose from its attachment, forming an embolus that may completely occlude a smaller vessel downstream.

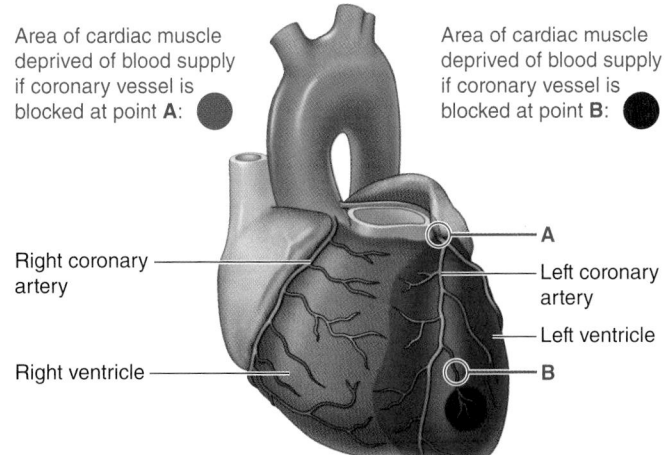

● **FIGURE 9-26 Extent of myocardial damage as a function of the size of the occluded vessel.**

▲ Table 9-3 Possible Outcomes of Acute Myocardial Infarction (Heart Attack)

Immediate Death	Delayed Death from Complications	Full Functional Recovery	Recovery with Impaired Function
Acute cardiac failure because the heart is too weak to pump effectively to support body tissues	Fatal rupture of the dead, degenerating area of the heart wall	Replacement of the damaged area with a strong scar, accompanied by enlargement of the remaining normal contractile tissue to compensate for the lost cardiac musculature	Persistence of permanent functional defects, such as bradycardia or conduction blocks, caused by destruction of irreplaceable autorhythmic or conductive tissues
Fatal ventricular fibrillation from damage to specialized conducting tissue or from O_2 deprivation	Slowly progressing congestive heart failure because the weakened heart cannot pump out all the blood returned to it		

Beyond the Basics

Atherosclerosis: Cholesterol and Beyond

The cause of atherosclerosis is still not entirely clear. Certain high-risk factors have been associated with an increased incidence of atherosclerosis and coronary heart disease. Included among them are genetic predisposition, obesity, advanced age, smoking, hypertension, lack of exercise, high blood concentrations of C-reactive protein, elevated levels of homocysteine, infectious agents, and most notoriously, elevated cholesterol levels in the blood.

Sources of Cholesterol

The body has two sources of cholesterol: (1) dietary intake of cholesterol, with animal products such as egg yolk, red meats, and butter being especially rich in this lipid (animal fats contain cholesterol, whereas plant fats typically do not), and (2) manufacture of cholesterol by cells, especially liver cells.

"Good" versus "Bad" Cholesterol

Actually, it is not the total blood cholesterol level but the amount of cholesterol bound to various plasma protein carriers that is most important to the risk of developing atherosclerotic heart disease. Because cholesterol is a lipid, it is not very soluble in blood. Most cholesterol in the blood is attached to specific plasma protein carriers in the form of lipoprotein complexes, which are soluble in blood. The two major lipoproteins are named for their density of protein as compared to cholesterol: **high-density lipoproteins (HDL),** which contain the most protein and least cholesterol, and **low-density lipoproteins (LDL),** which have less protein and more cholesterol.

Cholesterol carried in LDL complexes has been termed "bad" cholesterol, because cholesterol is transported *to* the cells, including those lining the blood vessel walls, by LDL. The propensity toward developing atherosclerosis substantially increases with elevated levels of LDL. The presence of oxidized LDL within an arterial wall is a major trigger for the inflammatory process that leads to the development of atherosclerotic plaques (see p. 270).

In contrast, cholesterol carried in HDL complexes has been dubbed "good" cholesterol, because HDL removes cholesterol *from* the cells and transports it to the liver for partial elimination from the body. HDL not only removes excess cholesterol from the tissues but also helps protect against the formation of atherosclerotic plaques by inhibiting oxidation of LDL. Furthermore, recent research suggests that HDL has anti-inflammatory action, helps stabilize atherosclerotic plaques so that they are less prone to rupture, and reduces clot formation, all actions that counter the progressive development of atherosclerosis. The risk of atherosclerosis is inversely related to the concentration of HDL in the blood; that is, elevated levels of HDL are associated with a low incidence of atherosclerotic heart disease.

Some other factors known to influence atherosclerotic risk can be related to HDL levels; for example, cigarette smoking lowers HDL, whereas regular exercise raises HDL.

Cholesterol Uptake by Cells

Unlike most lipids, cholesterol is not used as metabolic fuel by cells. Instead, it is an essential component of plasma membranes. In addition, a few special cell types use cholesterol as a precursor for the synthesis of secretory products, such as steroid hormones and bile salts. Although most cells can synthesize some of the cholesterol needed for their own plasma membranes, they cannot manufacture sufficient amounts and therefore must rely on supplemental cholesterol being delivered by the blood.

Cells accomplish cholesterol uptake from the blood by synthesizing receptor proteins specifically capable of binding LDL and inserting these receptors into the plasma membrane. When an LDL particle binds to one of the membrane receptors, the cell engulfs the particle by receptor-mediated endocytosis, receptor and all (see p. 26). Within the cell, lysosomal enzymes break down the LDL to free the cholesterol, making it available to the cell for synthesis of new cellular membrane. The LDL receptor, which is also freed within the cell, is recycled back to the surface membrane.

If too much free cholesterol accumulates in the cell, both the synthesis of LDL receptor proteins (so that less cholesterol is taken up) and the cell's own cholesterol synthesis (so that less new cholesterol is made) are shut down. Faced with a cholesterol shortage, in contrast, the cell makes more LDL receptors so that it can engulf more cholesterol from the blood.

Maintenance of Blood Cholesterol Level and Cholesterol Metabolism

Maintaining a constant blood-borne cholesterol supply to the cells involves an interaction between dietary cholesterol and synthesis of cholesterol by the liver. When the amount of dietary cholesterol is increased, hepatic (liver) synthesis of cholesterol is turned off because cholesterol in the blood directly inhibits a hepatic enzyme essential for cholesterol synthesis. Thus, as more cholesterol is ingested, less is produced by the liver. Conversely, when cholesterol intake from food is reduced, the liver synthesizes more of this lipid because the inhibitory effect of cholesterol on the crucial hepatic enzyme is removed. In this way, the blood concentration of cholesterol is maintained at a fairly constant level despite changes in cholesterol intake; thus, it is difficult to significantly reduce cholesterol levels in the blood by decreasing cholesterol intake.

HDL transports cholesterol to the liver. The liver secretes cholesterol, as well as cholesterol-derived bile salts, into the bile. Bile enters the intestinal tract, where bile salts participate in the digestive process. Most of the secreted cholesterol and bile salts are subsequently reabsorbed from the intestine into the blood to be recycled to the liver. However, the cholesterol and bile salts not reclaimed by absorption are eliminated in the feces and lost from the body.

Thus, the liver has a primary role in determining total blood cholesterol levels, and the interplay between LDL and HDL determines the traffic flow of cholesterol between the liver and the other cells. Whenever these mechanisms are altered, blood cholesterol levels may be affected in such a way as to influence the individual's predisposition to atherosclerosis.

Varying the intake of dietary fatty acids may alter total blood cholesterol levels by influencing one or more of the mechanisms involving cholesterol balance. The blood cholesterol level tends to be raised by ingesting saturated fatty acids found predominantly in animal fats because these fatty acids stimulate cholesterol synthesis and inhibit its conversion to bile salts. In contrast, ingesting polyunsaturated fatty acids, the predominant fatty acids of most plants, tends to reduce blood cholesterol levels by enhancing elimination of both cholesterol and cholesterol-derived bile salts in the feces.

Risk Factors besides Cholesterol

Despite the strong links between cholesterol and heart disease, more than half of all patients with heart attacks have a normal cholesterol profile and no other well-established risk factors. Clearly, other factors are involved in the development of coronary artery disease in these people. These same factors may also contribute to development of atherosclerosis in people with unfavorable cholesterol levels. The following are among the leading other possible risk factors:

- Elevated blood levels of the amino acid **homocysteine** have recently been implicated as a strong predictor for heart disease, independent of the person's cholesterol or lipid profile. Homocysteine is formed as an intermediate product during metabolism of the essential dietary amino acid *methionine.* Investigators believe homocysteine contributes to atherosclerosis by promoting proliferation of vascular smooth muscle cells, an early step in development of this artery-clogging condition. Furthermore, homocysteine appears to damage endothelial cells and may cause oxidation of LDL, both of which can contribute to plaque formation. Three B vitamins—*folic acid, vitamin B_{12},* and *vitamin B_6*—all play key roles in pathways that clear homocysteine from the blood. Therefore, these B vitamins are all needed to keep blood homocysteine at safe levels.

- People with elevated levels of **C-reactive protein,** a blood-borne marker of inflammation, have a higher risk for developing coronary artery disease. In one study, people with a high level of C-reactive protein in their blood were three times more likely to have a heart attack over the next 10 years than those with a low level of this inflammatory protein. Because inflammation plays a crucial role in the development of atherosclerosis, anti-inflammatory drugs, such as aspirin, help prevent heart attacks. Furthermore, aspirin protects against heart attacks through its role in inhibiting clot formation.

- Accumulating data suggest that an infectious agent may be the underlying culprit in a significant number of cases of atherosclerotic disease. Among the leading suspects are respiratory-infection-causing *Chlamydia pneumoniae,* cold-sore-causing herpes virus, and gum-disease-causing bacteria. Importantly, if a link between infections and coronary artery disease can be confirmed, antibiotics may be added to the regimen of heart disease prevention strategies.

As you can see, the relationships among atherosclerosis, cholesterol, and other factors are far from clear. Much research on this complex disease is currently in progress because the incidence of atherosclerosis is so high and its consequences are potentially fatal.

Chapter in Perspective: Focus on Homeostasis

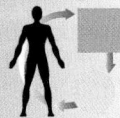

Survival depends on continual delivery of needed supplies to all body cells and on ongoing removal of wastes generated by the cells. Furthermore, regulatory chemical messengers, such as hormones, must be transported from their production site to their action site, where they control a variety of activities, most of which are directed toward maintaining a stable internal environment. Finally, to maintain normal body temperature, excess heat produced during muscle contraction must be carried to the skin, where the heat can be lost from the body surface.

The circulatory system contributes to homeostasis by serving as the body's transport system. It provides a way to rapidly move materials from one part of the body to another. Without the circulatory system, materials would not get quickly enough to where they need to be to support life-sustaining activities. For example, O_2 would take months to years to diffuse from the body surface to internal organs, yet through the heart's swift pumping action the blood can pick up and deliver O_2 and other substances to all the cells in a few seconds.

The heart is a dual pump that continuously circulates blood between the lungs, where O_2 is picked up, and the other body tissues, which use O_2 to support their energy-generating chemical reactions. As blood is pumped through the various tissues, other substances besides O_2 are exchanged between the blood and the tissues. For example, the blood picks up nutrients as it flows through the digestive organs, and other tissues remove nutrients from the blood as it flows through them. Even excess heat is transported by the blood from exercising muscles to the skin surface, where it is lost to the external environment.

Although all the body tissues constantly depend on the life-supporting blood flow provided to them by the heart, the heart itself is quite an independent organ. It can take care of many of its own needs without any outside influence. Contraction of this magnificent muscle is self-generated through a carefully orchestrated interplay of changing ionic permeabilities. Local mechanisms within the heart ensure that blood flow to the cardiac muscle normally meets the heart's need for O_2. In addition, the heart has built-in capabilities to vary its strength of contraction, depending on the amount of blood returned to it. The heart does not act entirely autonomously, however. It is innervated by the autonomic nervous system and is influenced by the hormone epinephrine, both of which can vary heart rate and contractility, depending on the body's needs for blood delivery. Furthermore, as with all tissues, the cells that make up the heart depend on the other body systems to maintain a stable internal environment in which they can survive and function.

Objective Questions (Answers on p. A-43)

1. Adjacent cardiac muscle cells are joined end to end at specialized structures known as _____, which contain two types of membrane junctions: _____ and _____.

2. The heart lies in the left half of the thoracic cavity. (*True or false?*)

3. The only point of electrical contact between the atria and the ventricles is the fibrous tissue that surrounds and supports the heart valves. (*True or false?*)

4. The atria and the ventricles each act as a functional syncytium. (*True or false?*)

5. Which of the following is the proper sequence of cardiac excitation?
   a. SA node → AV node → atrial myocardium → bundle of His → Purkinje fibers → ventricular myocardium
   b. SA node → atrial myocardium → AV node → bundle of His → ventricular myocardium → Purkinje fibers
   c. SA node → atrial myocardium → ventricular myocardium → AV node → bundle of His → Purkinje fibers
   d. SA node → atrial myocardium → AV node → bundle of His → Purkinje fibers → ventricular myocardium

6. What percentage of ventricular filling is normally accomplished before atrial contraction begins?
   a. 0%
   b. 20%
   c. 50%
   d. 80%
   e. 100%

7. Sympathetic stimulation of the heart _____
   a. increases the heart rate.
   b. increases the contractility of the heart muscle.
   c. shifts the Frank–Starling curve to the left.
   d. does both (a) and (b).
   e. does all of the above.

8. Match the following:
   ___ 1. receives O$_2$-poor blood from the venae cavae
   ___ 2. prevent backflow of blood from the ventricles to the atria
   ___ 3. pumps O$_2$-rich blood into the aorta
   ___ 4. prevent backflow of blood from the arteries into the ventricles
   ___ 5. pumps O$_2$-poor blood into the pulmonary artery
   ___ 6. receives O$_2$-rich blood from the pulmonary veins

   (a) AV valves
   (b) semilunar valves
   (c) left atrium
   (d) left ventricle
   (e) right atrium
   (f) right ventricle

9. Circle the correct choice in each instance to complete the statement: The first heart sound is associated with closing of the (*AV/semilunar*) valves and signals the onset of (*systole/diastole*), whereas the second heart sound is associated with closing of the (*AV/semilunar*) valves and signals the onset of (*systole/diastole*).

10. Circle the correct choice in each instance to complete the statements: During ventricular filling ventricular pressure must be (*greater than/less than*) atrial pressure, whereas during ventricular ejection ventricular pressure must be (*greater than/less than*) aortic pressure. Atrial pressure is always (*greater than/less than*) aortic pressure. During isovolumetric ventricular contraction and relaxation, ventricular pressure is (*greater than/less than*) atrial pressure and (*greater than/less than*) aortic pressure.

Essay Questions

1. What are the three basic components of the circulatory system?

2. Trace a drop of blood through one complete circuit of the circulatory system.

3. Describe the location and function of each of the four heart valves. What is the role of the chordae tendineae and that of papillary muscles?

4. What are the three layers of the heart wall? Describe the distinguishing structural features of cardiac muscle cells.

5. What are the two specialized types of cardiac muscle cells?

6. Why is the SA node the pacemaker of the heart?

7. Describe the normal spread of cardiac excitation. What is the significance of the AV nodal delay? Why is the ventricular conduction system important?

8. Compare the changes in membrane potential associated with an action potential in a nodal pacemaker cell with those in a myocardial contractile cell. What is responsible for the plateau phase?

9. Why is tetanus of cardiac muscle impossible? Why is this inability advantageous?

10. Draw and label the waveforms of a normal ECG. What electrical event does each component of the ECG represent?

11. Describe the mechanical events (that is, pressure changes, volume changes, valve activity, and heart sounds) of the cardiac cycle. Correlate the mechanical events of the cardiac cycle with the changes in electrical activity.

12. Distinguish between a stenotic and an insufficient valve.

13. Define the following: end-diastolic volume, end-systolic volume, stroke volume, heart rate, and cardiac output.

14. Discuss autonomic nervous system control of heart rate.

15. Describe the intrinsic and extrinsic control of stroke volume.

16. How is the heart muscle provided with blood? Why does the heart receive most of its own blood supply during diastole?

17. What are the pathological changes and consequences of coronary artery disease?

18. Distinguish between "good" cholesterol and "bad" cholesterol.

(Explanations on p. A-43)

1. The stroke volume ejected on the next heartbeat after a premature ventricular contraction (PVC) is usually larger than normal. Can you explain why? (*Hint:* At a given heart rate, the interval between a PVC and the next normal beat is longer than the interval between two normal beats.)

2. Trained athletes usually have lower resting heart rates than normal (for example, 50 beats per minute in an athlete compared to 70 beats per minute in a sedentary individual). Considering that the resting cardiac output is 5000 ml per minute in both trained athletes and sedentary people, what is responsible for the bradycardia of trained athletes?

3. During fetal life, because of the tremendous resistance offered by the collapsed, nonfunctioning lungs, the pressures in the right half of the heart and pulmonary circulation are higher than those in the left half of the heart and systemic circulation, a situation that reverses after birth. Also in the fetus, a vessel called the **ductus arteriosus** connects the pulmonary artery and aorta as these major vessels both leave the heart. The blood pumped out by the heart into the pulmonary circulation is shunted from the pulmonary artery into the aorta through the ductus arteriosus, bypassing the nonfunctional lungs. What force is driving blood to flow in this direction through the ductus arteriosus?

At birth, the ductus arteriosus normally collapses and eventually degenerates into a thin, ligamentous strand. On occasion, this fetal bypass fails to close properly at birth, leading to a patent (open) ductus arteriosus. In what direction would blood flow through a patent ductus arteriosus? What possible outcomes would you predict might occur as a result of this blood flow?

4. Through what regulatory mechanisms can a transplanted heart, which does not have any innervation, adjust cardiac output to meet the body's changing needs?

5. There are two branches of the bundle of His, the right and left bundle branches, each of which travels down its respective side of the ventricular septum (see ● Figure 9-7, p. 251). Occasionally, conduction through one of these branches becomes blocked (so-called *bundle-branch block*). In this case, the wave of excitation spreads out from the terminals of the intact branch and eventually depolarizes the whole ventricle, but the normally stimulated ventricle completely depolarizes a considerable time before the ventricle on the side of the defective bundle branch. For example, if the left bundle branch is blocked, the right ventricle will be completely depolarized two to three times more rapidly than the left ventricle. How would this defect affect the heart sounds?

(Explanation on p. A-44)

In a physical exam, Rachel B.'s heart rate was rapid and very irregular. Furthermore, her heart rate, determined directly by listening to her heart with a stethoscope, exceeded the pulse rate taken concurrently at her wrist. Such a difference in heart rate and pulse rate is called a *pulse deficit.* No definite P waves could be detected on Rachel's ECG. The QRS complexes were normal in shape but occurred sporadically. Given these findings, what is the most likely diagnosis of Rachel's condition? Explain why the condition is characterized by a rapid, irregular heartbeat. Would cardiac output be seriously impaired by this condition? Why or why not? What accounts for the pulse deficit?

Chapter 9

Anatomy of the Heart (pp. 245–250)

■ The circulatory system is the transport system of the body.

■ The three basic components of the circulatory system are the heart (the pump), the blood vessels (the passageways), and the blood (the transport medium).

■ The heart is positioned midline in the thoracic cavity at an angle, with its wide base lying toward the right and its pointed apex toward the left.

■ The heart is basically a dual pump that provides the driving pressure for blood flow through the pulmonary circulation (between the heart and the lungs) and systemic circulation (between the heart and the other body systems). (*Review Figures 9-1 and 9-2.*)

■ The heart has four chambers: Each half of the heart consists of an atrium, or venous input chamber, and a ventricle, or arterial output chamber. The right atrium receives O_2-poor blood from the systemic circulation and the right ventricle pumps it into the pulmonary circulation. The left atrium receives O_2-rich blood from the pulmonary circulation and the left ventricle pumps it into the systemic circulation. (*Review Figures 9-1, 9-2, and 9-4.*)

■ Four heart valves direct blood in the right direction and keep it from flowing in the other direction. The right and left atrioventricular (AV) valves direct blood from the atria to the ventricles during diastole and prevent backflow of blood from the ventricles to the atria during systole. The aortic and pulmonary semilunar valves direct blood from the ventricles to the aorta and pulmonary artery, respectively, during systole and prevent backflow of blood from these major vessels to the ventricles during diastole. (*Review Figures 9-3 and 9-4.*)

■ The branching cardiac muscle fibers are interconnected by intercalated discs, which contain (1) desmosomes that hold the cells together mechanically and (2) gap junctions that permit spread of action potentials between cells joined together as a functional syncytium. Because the muscle fibers in each chamber of the heart act as a functional syncytium, each chamber contracts as a coordinated unit to ensure efficient pumping. (*Review Figure 9-5.*)

Electrical Activity of the Heart (pp. 250–259)

■ The heart is self-excitable, initiating its own rhythmic contractions. Autorhythmic cells are 1% of the cardiac muscle cells; they do not contract but are specialized to initiate and conduct action potentials. The other 99% of cardiac cells are contractile working cells that contract in response to the spread of an action potential initiated by autorhythmic cells.

■ Autorhythmic cells display a pacemaker potential, a self-induced, slow depolarization to threshold potential, resulting largely from Na^+ entry on opening of unique funny channels in response to hyperpolarization at the end of the previous action potential. The rising phase of the action potential results from Ca^{2+} entry on opening of Ca^{2+} channels at threshold. The falling phase results from K^+ exit on opening of K^+ channels at the peak of the action potential. (*Review Figure 9-6.*)

■ The cardiac impulse starts at the SA node, the heart's pacemaker, which has the fastest rate of spontaneous depolarization to threshold. (*Review Table 9-1 and Figures 9-7 and 9-8.*)

■ Once initiated, the action potential spreads throughout the right and left atria, partially facilitated by specialized conduction pathways but mostly by cell-to-cell spread of the impulse through gap junctions. (*Review Figure 9-7.*)

■ The impulse passes from the atria into the ventricles through the AV node, the only point of electrical contact between these chambers. The action potential is delayed briefly at the AV node, ensuring that atrial contraction precedes ventricular contraction to allow complete ventricular filling. (*Review Figure 9-7.*)

■ The impulse then travels rapidly down the interventricular septum via the bundle of His and rapidly disperses throughout the myocardium by means of the Purkinje fibers. The rest of the ventricular cells are activated by cell-to-cell spread of the impulse through gap junctions. (*Review Figure 9-7.*)

■ Thus, the atria contract as a single unit, followed after a brief delay by a synchronized ventricular contraction.

■ The action potentials of cardiac contractile cells exhibit a prolonged positive phase, or plateau, accompanied by a prolonged period of contraction, which ensures adequate ejection time. This plateau is primarily the result of activation of slow Ca^{2+} channels. (*Review Figure 9-9.*)

■ Ca^{2+} entry though the slow Ca^{2+} channels in the T tubules triggers a much larger release of Ca^{2+} from the sarcoplasmic reticulum within the cardiac contractile cell. This Ca^{2+}-induced Ca^{2+} release leads to cross-bridge cycling and contraction. (*Review Figure 9-10.*)

■ Because a long refractory period occurs in conjunction with this prolonged plateau phase, summation and tetanus of cardiac

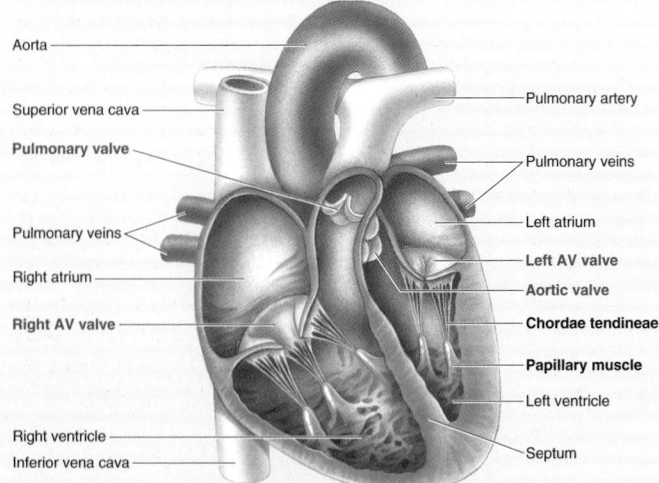

Aorta

Superior vena cava

Pulmonary valve

Pulmonary veins

Right atrium

Right AV valve

Right ventricle

Inferior vena cava

Pulmonary artery

Pulmonary veins

Left atrium

Left AV valve

Aortic valve

Chordae tendineae

Papillary muscle

Left ventricle

Septum

(a) Location of the heart valves in a longitudinal section of the heart

muscle are impossible, ensuring the alternate periods of contraction and relaxation essential for pumping of blood. (*Review Figure 9-11.*)

■ The spread of electrical activity throughout the heart can be recorded from the body surface. In this electrocardiogram (ECG), the P wave represents atrial depolarization; the QRS complex, ventricular depolarization; and the T wave, ventricular repolarization. (*Review Figures 9-12 through 9-14.*)

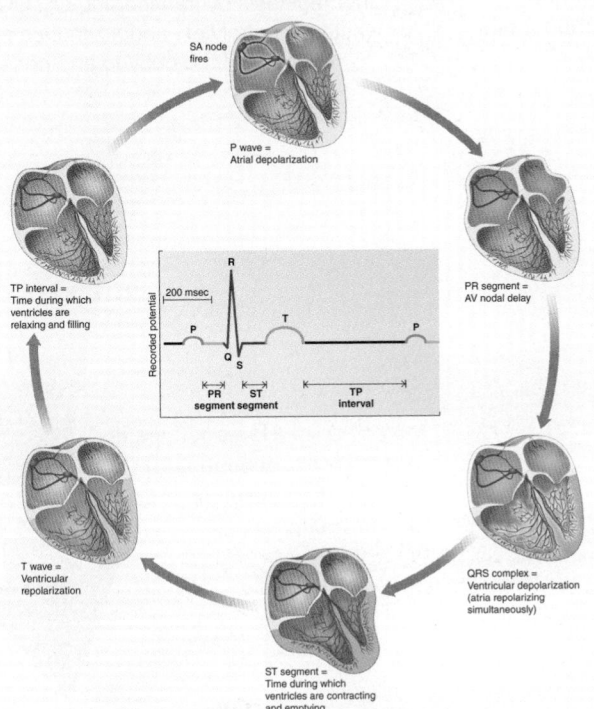

SA node
fires

P wave =
Atrial depolarization

PR segment =
AV nodal delay

TP interval =
Time during which
ventricles are
relaxing and filling

200 msec

PR
segment

ST
segment

TP
interval

QRS complex =
Ventricular depolarization
(atria repolarizing
simultaneously)

T wave =
Ventricular
repolarization

ST segment =
Time during which
ventricles are contracting
and emptying

Mechanical Events of the Cardiac Cycle (pp. 259–263)

■ The cardiac cycle consists of three important events (*Review Figure 9-15*):

1. The generation of electrical activity as the heart autorhythmically depolarizes and repolarizes (*Review Figure 9-13.*)

2. Mechanical activity consisting of alternate periods of systole (contraction and emptying) and diastole (relaxation and filling), which are initiated by the rhythmic electrical cycle.

3. Directional flow of blood through the heart chambers, guided by valve opening and closing induced by pressure changes generated by mechanical activity.

■ The atrial pressure curve remains low throughout the entire cardiac cycle, with only minor fluctuations (normally varying between 0 and 8 mm Hg). The aortic pressure curve remains high the entire time, with moderate fluctuations (normally varying between a systolic pressure of 120 mm Hg and a diastolic pressure of 80 mm Hg). The ventricular pressure curve fluctuates dramatically, because ventricular pressure must be below the low atrial pressure during diastole to allow the AV valve to open for filling and, to force the aortic valve open to allow emptying, it must be above the high aortic pressure during systole. Therefore, ventricular pressure normally varies

from 0 mm Hg during diastole to slightly more than 120 mm Hg during systole. During the periods of isovolumetric ventricular contraction and relaxation, ventricular pressure is above the low atrial pressure and below the high aortic pressure, so all valves are closed and no blood enters or leaves the ventricles. (*Review Figure 9-15.*)

■ The end-diastolic volume (EDV) is the volume of blood in the ventricle when filling is complete at the end of diastole. The end-systolic volume (ESV) is the volume of blood remaining in the ventricle when ejection is complete at the end of systole. The stroke volume (SV) is the volume of blood pumped out by each ventricle each beat. (*Review Figure 9-15.*)

■ Valve closing gives rise to two normal heart sounds. The first heart sound is caused by closing of the AV valves and signals the onset of ventricular systole. The second heart sound results from closing of the aortic and pulmonary valves at the onset of diastole. (*Review Figure 9-15.*)

■ Defective valve function produces turbulent blood flow, which is audible as a heart murmur. Abnormal valves may be either stenotic and not opening completely or insufficient and not closing completely. (*Review Figure 9-16 and Table 9-2.*)

Cardiac Output and Its Control (pp. 263–268)

■ Cardiac output (CO), the volume of blood ejected by each ventricle each minute, is determined by heart rate times stroke volume. (*Review Figure 9-22.*)

■ Heart rate is varied by altering the balance of parasympathetic and sympathetic influence on the SA node. Parasympathetic stimulation slows the heart rate, and sympathetic stimulation speeds it up. (*Review Figure 9-17.*)

■ Stroke volume depends on (1) the extent of ventricular filling, with an increased end-diastolic volume resulting in a larger stroke volume by means of the length–tension relationship (Frank–Starling law of the heart, a form of intrinsic control), and (2) the extent of sympathetic stimulation, with increased sympathetic stimulation resulting in increased contractility of the heart, that is, increased strength of contraction and increased stroke volume at a given end-diastolic volume (extrinsic control). (*Review Figures 9-18 through 9-21.*)

Nourishing the Heart Muscle (pp. 268–273)

■ Cardiac muscle is supplied with oxygen and nutrients by blood delivered to it by the coronary circulation, not by blood within the heart chambers.

■ Most coronary blood flow occurs during diastole, because during systole the contracting heart muscle compresses the coronary vessels.

■ Coronary blood flow is normally varied to keep pace with cardiac oxygen needs.

■ Coronary blood flow may be compromised by atherosclerotic plaques, which can lead to ischemic heart disease ranging in severity from mild chest pain on exertion to fatal heart attacks. (*Review Figures 9-24 through 9-26 and Table 9-3.*)

Cardiovascular System
(Blood Vessels)

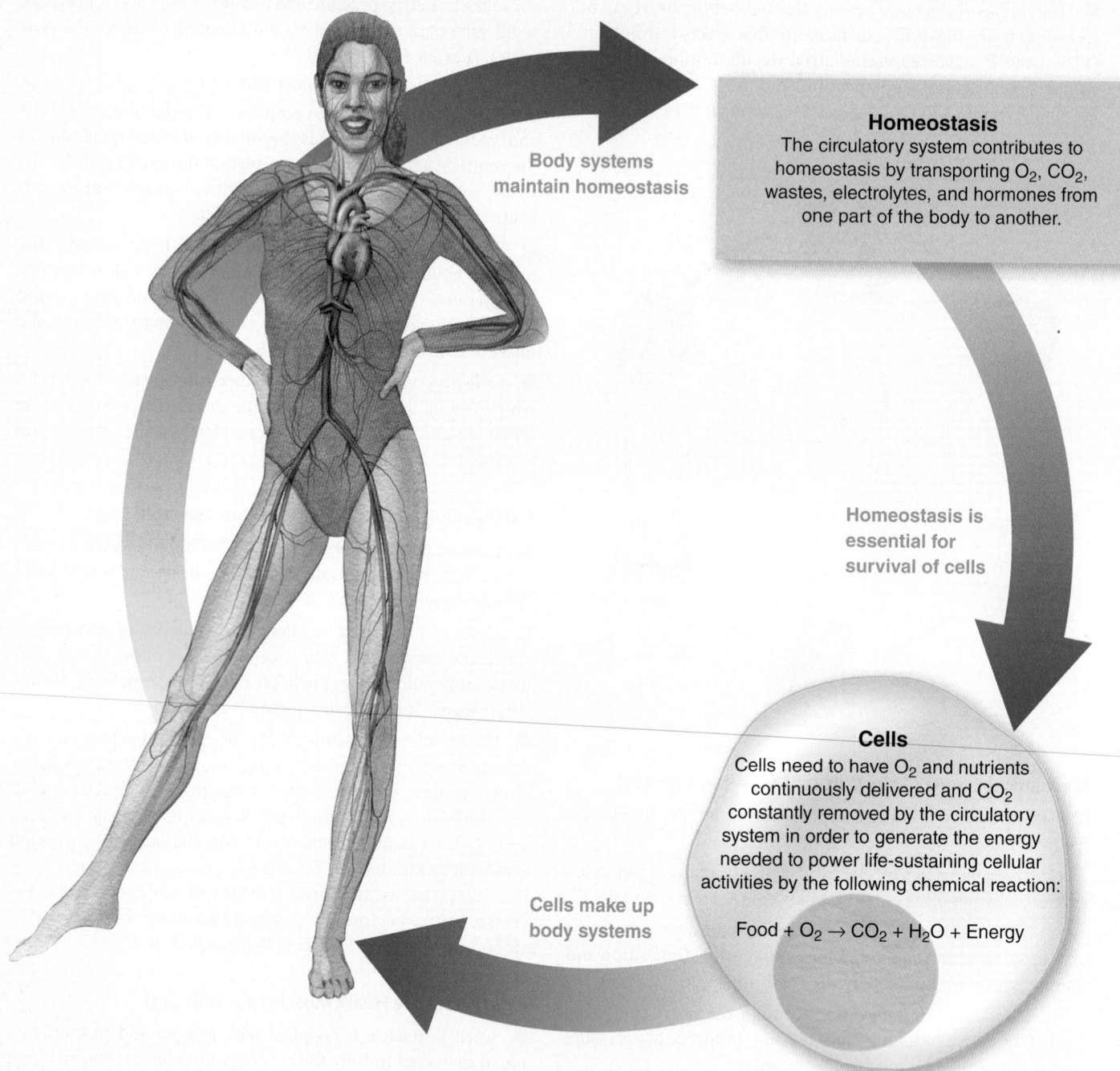

Body systems maintain homeostasis

Homeostasis
The circulatory system contributes to homeostasis by transporting O_2, CO_2, wastes, electrolytes, and hormones from one part of the body to another.

Homeostasis is essential for survival of cells

Cells
Cells need to have O_2 and nutrients continuously delivered and CO_2 constantly removed by the circulatory system in order to generate the energy needed to power life-sustaining cellular activities by the following chemical reaction:

Food + O_2 → CO_2 + H_2O + Energy

Cells make up body systems

The **circulatory system** contributes to homeostasis by serving as the body's transport system. The blood vessels transport and distribute blood pumped through them by the heart to meet the body's needs for O_2 and nutrient delivery, waste removal, and hormonal signaling. The highly elastic **arteries** transport blood from the heart to the organs and serve as a pressure reservoir to continue driving blood forward when the heart is relaxing and filling. The **mean arterial blood pressure** is closely regulated to ensure adequate blood delivery to the organs. The amount of blood that flows through a given organ depends on the caliber (internal diameter) of the highly muscular **arterioles** that supply the organ. Arteriolar caliber is subject to control so that flow to particular organs can be variably adjusted to best serve the body's needs at the moment. The thin-walled **capillaries** are the actual site of exchange between blood and surrounding tissue cells. The highly distensible **veins** return blood from the organs to the heart and serve as a blood reservoir.

The Blood Vessels and Blood Pressure

CHAPTER AT A GLANCE

Patterns and Physics of Blood Flow
Reconditioning organs
Flow, pressure, and resistance relationships
Blood vessel types

Arteries
Passageways to the tissues
Role as a pressure reservoir
Arterial pressure

Arterioles
Major resistance vessels
Control of arteriolar radius
Role in distributing cardiac output
Role in maintaining arterial blood pressure

Capillaries
Sites of exchange
Diffusion across the capillary wall
Bulk flow across the capillary wall
Formation and function of lymph
Edema

Veins
Passageways to the heart
Role as a blood reservoir
Venous return

Blood Pressure
Factors influencing mean arterial pressure
Baroreceptor reflex
Hypertension
Hypotension; circulatory shock

Patterns and Physics of Blood Flow

Most body cells are not in direct contact with the external environment, yet these cells must make exchanges with this environment, such as picking up O_2 and nutrients and eliminating wastes. Furthermore, chemical messengers must be transported between cells to accomplish integrated activity. To achieve these long-distance exchanges, cells are linked with one another and with the external environment by vascular (blood vessel) highways. Blood is transported to all parts of the body through a system of vessels that brings fresh supplies to the vicinity of all cells while removing their wastes.

To review, all blood pumped by the right side of the heart passes through the pulmonary circulation to the lungs for O_2 pickup and CO_2 removal. The blood pumped by the left side of the heart into the systemic circulation is distributed in various proportions to the systemic organs through a parallel arrangement of vessels that branch from the aorta (● Figure 10-1). This arrangement ensures that all organs receive blood of the same composition; that is, one organ does not receive "leftover" blood that has passed through another organ. Because of this parallel arrangement, blood flow through each systemic organ can be independently adjusted as needed.

In this chapter, we first examine some general principles regarding blood flow patterns and the physics of blood flow. Then we turn our attention to the roles of the various types of blood vessels through which blood flows. We end by discussing how blood pressure is regulated to ensure adequate delivery of blood to the tissues.

To maintain homeostasis, reconditioning organs receive blood flow in excess of their own needs.

Blood is constantly "reconditioned" so that its composition remains relatively constant despite an ongoing drain of supplies to support metabolic activities and despite the continual addition of wastes from the tissues. Organs that recondition the blood normally receive much more blood flow than is necessary to meet their basic metabolic needs, so they can adjust the extra blood to achieve homeostasis. For example, large percentages of the cardiac output are distributed to the digestive tract (to pick up nutrient supplies), to the kidneys (to eliminate metabolic wastes and adjust water and electrolyte composition), and to the skin (to eliminate heat). Blood flow to the other organs—heart, skeletal muscles, and so on—is solely for filling these organs' metabolic needs and can be adjusted according to their level of activity. For example, during exercise, additional blood is delivered to the active muscles to meet their increased metabolic needs.

Because reconditioning organs—digestive organs, kidneys, and skin—receive blood flow in excess of their own needs, they can withstand temporary reductions in blood flow much better than other organs can that do not have this extra margin of blood supply. The brain in particular suffers irreparable damage when transiently

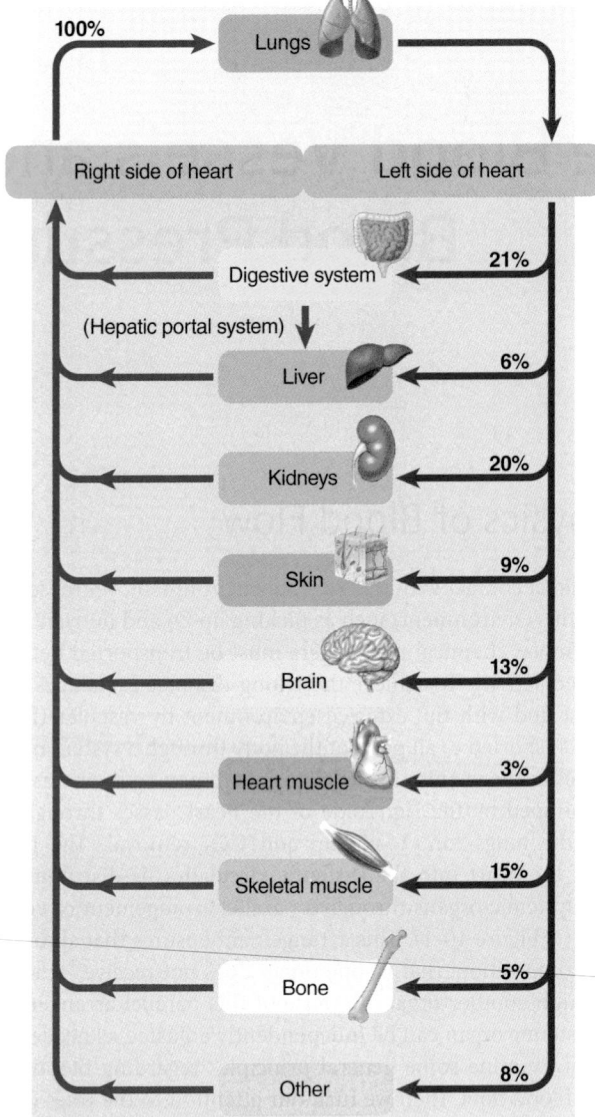

● FIGURE 10-1 Distribution of cardiac output at rest. The lungs receive all the blood pumped out by the right side of the heart, whereas the systemic organs each receive some of the blood pumped out by the left side of the heart. The percentage of pumped blood received by the various organs under resting conditions is indicated. This distribution of cardiac output can be adjusted as needed.

deprived of blood supply. After only 4 minutes without O_2, permanent brain damage occurs. Therefore, constant delivery of adequate blood to the brain, which can least tolerate disrupted blood supply, is a high priority in the overall operation of the circulatory system.

In contrast, the reconditioning organs can tolerate significant reductions in blood flow for quite a long time, and often do. For example, during exercise some of the blood that normally flows through the digestive organs and kidneys is diverted to the skeletal muscles. Likewise, to conserve body heat, blood flow through the skin is markedly restricted during exposure to cold.

Later in the chapter, you will see how distribution of cardiac output is adjusted according to the body's current needs. For now, we concentrate on the factors that influence blood flow through a given blood vessel.

Blood flow through a vessel depends on the pressure gradient and vascular resistance.

The **flow rate** of blood through a vessel (that is, the volume of blood passing through per unit of time) is directly proportional to the pressure gradient (as the pressure gradient increases, flow rate increases) and inversely proportional to vascular resistance (as resistance increases, flow rate decreases):

$$F = \Delta P/R$$

where

F = flow rate of blood through a vessel
ΔP = pressure gradient
R = resistance of blood vessel

PRESSURE GRADIENT The **pressure gradient** is the difference in pressure between the beginning and the end of a vessel. Blood flows from an area of higher pressure to an area of lower pressure down a pressure gradient. Contraction of the heart imparts pressure to the blood, which is the main driving force for flow through a vessel. Because of frictional losses (resistance), the pressure drops as blood flows throughout the vessel's length. Accordingly, pressure is higher at the beginning than at the end of the vessel, establishing a pressure gradient for forward flow of blood through the vessel. The greater the pressure gradient forcing blood through a vessel, the greater the flow rate through that vessel (● Figure 10-2a). Think of a garden hose attached to a faucet. If you turn on the faucet slightly, a small stream of water flows out of the end of the hose, because the pressure is slightly greater at the beginning than at the end of the hose. If you open the faucet all the way, the pressure gradient increases tremendously so that water flows through the hose faster and spurts from the end of the hose. Note that the *difference* in pressure between the two ends of a vessel, not the absolute pressures within the vessel, determines flow rate (● Figure 10-2b).

RESISTANCE The other factor influencing flow rate through a vessel is **resistance**, which is a measure of the hindrance or opposition to blood flow through the vessel, caused by friction between the moving fluid and the stationary vascular walls. As resistance to flow increases, it is more difficult for blood to pass through the vessel, so flow rate decreases (as long as the pressure gradient remains unchanged). When resistance increases, the pressure gradient must increase correspondingly to maintain the same flow rate. Accordingly, when the vessels offer more resistance to flow, the heart must work harder to maintain adequate circulation.

Resistance to blood flow is (1) directly proportional to viscosity of the blood, (2) directly proportional to vessel length, and (3) inversely proportional to vessel radius, which is by far the most important:

$$R \propto \eta L/r^4$$

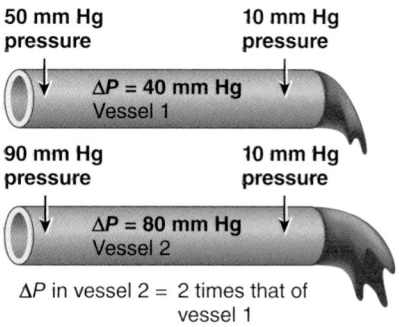

50 mm Hg pressure   10 mm Hg pressure

$\Delta P = 40$ mm Hg
Vessel 1

90 mm Hg pressure   10 mm Hg pressure

$\Delta P = 80$ mm Hg
Vessel 2

ΔP in vessel 2 = 2 times that of vessel 1

Flow in vessel 2 = 2 times that of vessel 1

Flow $\propto \Delta P$

(a) Comparison of flow rate in vessels with a different ΔP

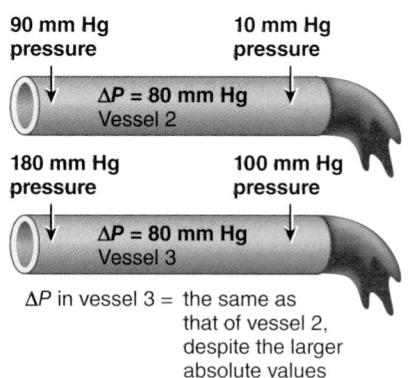

90 mm Hg pressure   10 mm Hg pressure

$\Delta P = 80$ mm Hg
Vessel 2

180 mm Hg pressure   100 mm Hg pressure

$\Delta P = 80$ mm Hg
Vessel 3

ΔP in vessel 3 = the same as that of vessel 2, despite the larger absolute values

Flow in vessel 3 = the same as that of vessel 2

Flow $\propto \Delta P$

(b) Comparison of flow rate in vessels with the same ΔP

● **FIGURE 10-2 Relationship of flow to the pressure gradient in a vessel.** (a) As the difference in pressure (ΔP) between the two ends of a vessel increases, the flow rate increases proportionately. (b) Flow rate is determined by the *difference* in pressure between the two ends of a vessel, not the magnitude of the pressures at each end.

where

η = viscosity
L = vessel length
r = vessel radius

Viscosity refers to the friction developed between the molecules of a fluid as they slide over each other during flow of the fluid. The greater the viscosity, the greater the resistance to flow. In general, the thicker a liquid, the more viscous the liquid. For example, molasses flows more slowly than water because molasses has greater viscosity. Blood viscosity is determined primarily by the number of circulating red blood cells. Normally, this factor is relatively constant and not important in controlling

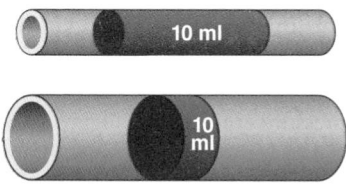

10 ml

10 ml

(a) Comparison of contact of a given volume of blood with the surface area of a small-radius vessel and a large-radius vessel

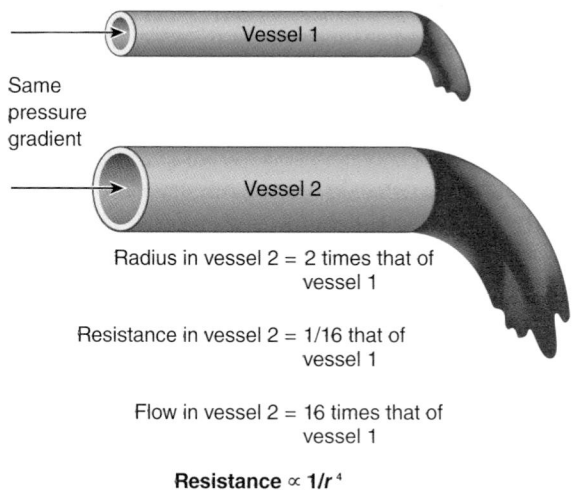

Vessel 1

Same pressure gradient

Vessel 2

Radius in vessel 2 = 2 times that of vessel 1

Resistance in vessel 2 = 1/16 that of vessel 1

Flow in vessel 2 = 16 times that of vessel 1

Resistance $\propto 1/r^4$
Flow $\propto r^4$

(b) Influence of vessel radius on resistance and flow

● **FIGURE 10-3 Relationship of resistance and flow to the vessel radius.** (a) The smaller-radius vessel offers more resistance to blood flow, because the blood "rubs" against a larger surface area. (b) Doubling the radius decreases the resistance to 1/16th and increases the flow 16 times, because the resistance is inversely proportional to the fourth power of the radius.

resistance. Occasionally, however, blood viscosity and resistance to flow are altered by an abnormal number of red blood cells. When excessive red blood cells are present, blood flow is more sluggish than normal.

Because blood "rubs" against the lining of the vessels as it flows past, the greater the vessel surface area in contact with the blood, the greater the resistance to flow. Surface area is determined by both the length and the radius of the vessel. At a constant radius, the longer the vessel, the greater the surface area and the greater the resistance to flow. Because vessel length remains constant in the body, it is not a variable factor in the control of vascular resistance.

Therefore, the major determinant of resistance to flow is the vessel's radius. Fluid passes more readily through a large vessel than through a smaller vessel. The reason is that a given volume of blood comes into contact with more of the surface area of a small-radius vessel than of a larger-radius vessel, resulting in greater resistance (● Figure 10-3a).

Furthermore, a slight change in the radius of a vessel brings about a notable change in flow, because, as can be noted in the preceding equation for *R*, resistance is inversely proportional to the fourth power of the radius (multiplying the radius by itself four times; $R \propto 1/r^4$). Thus, doubling the radius reduces the resistance to 1/16th its original value ($r^4 = 2 \times 2 \times 2 \times 2 = 16$; $R \propto 1/16$) and therefore increases flow through the vessel 16-fold (at the same pressure gradient) (● Figure 10-3b). The converse is also true: Only 1/16th as much blood flows through a vessel at the same driving pressure when its radius is halved. Importantly, the radius of arterioles can be regulated and is the most important factor in controlling resistance to blood flow throughout the vascular circuit.

The significance of the relationships among flow, pressure, and resistance, as largely determined by vessel radius, become even more apparent as we embark on a voyage through the vessels in the next section.

The vascular tree consists of arteries, arterioles, capillaries, venules, and veins.

The systemic and pulmonary circulations each consist of a closed system of vessels (● Figure 10-4). (For the history leading up to the conclusion that blood vessels form a closed system, see the accompanying boxed feature, ❱ Beyond the Basics.) These vascular loops each consist of a continuum of different blood vessel types that begins and ends with the heart, as described here.

Looking specifically at the systemic circulation, **arteries,** which carry blood from the heart to the organs, branch into a "tree" of progressively smaller vessels, with the various branches delivering blood to different regions of the body. When a small artery reaches the organ it is supplying, it branches into numerous **arterioles.** The volume of blood flowing through an organ can be adjusted by regulating the caliber (internal diameter) of the organ's arterioles.

Arterioles branch further within the organs into **capillaries,** the smallest of vessels, across which all exchanges are made with surrounding cells. Capillary exchange is the entire purpose of the circulatory system; all other activities of the system are directed toward ensuring an adequate distribution of replenished blood to capillaries for exchange with all cells. Capillaries rejoin to form small **venules,** which further merge to form small **veins** that leave the organs. The small veins progressively unite to form larger veins that eventually empty into the heart.

The arterioles, capillaries, and venules are collectively referred to as the **microcirculation,** because they are only visible through a microscope. The microcirculatory vessels are all located within the organs. The pulmonary circulation consists of the same vessel types, but all the blood in this loop goes between the heart and the lungs. If all of the vessels in the body were strung end to end, they could circle the circumference of Earth twice!

In discussing the vessel types in this chapter, we refer to their roles in the systemic circulation, starting with systemic arteries.

Arteries

The consecutive segments of the vascular tree are specialized to perform specific tasks (▲ Table 10-1).

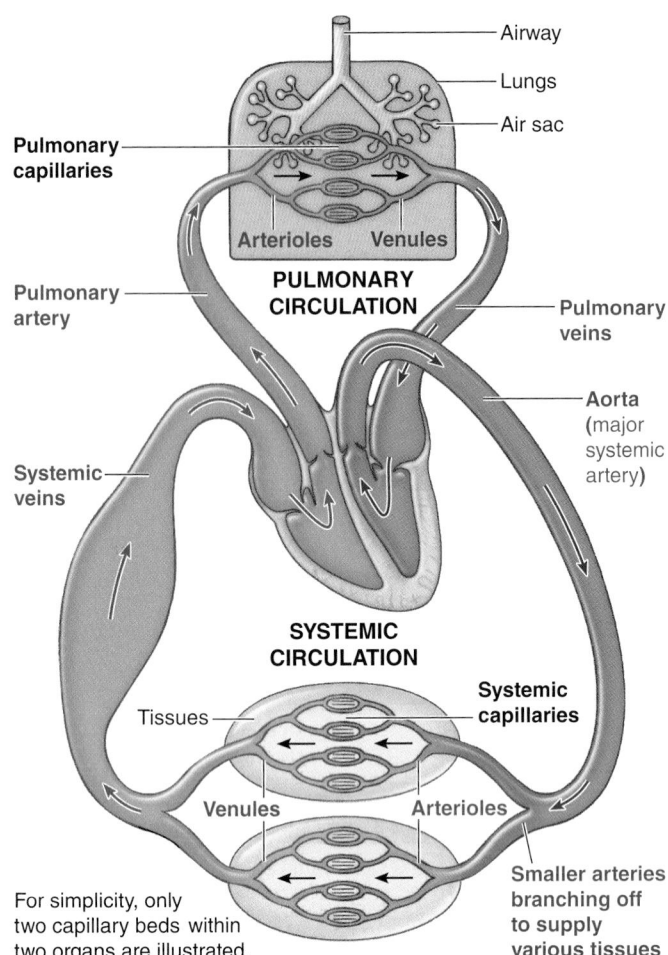

● FIGURE 10-4 **Basic organization of the cardiovascular system.** Arteries progressively branch as they carry blood from the heart to the organs. A separate small arterial branch delivers blood to each of the various organs. As a small artery enters the organ it is supplying, it branches into arterioles, which further branch into an extensive network of capillaries. The capillaries rejoin to form venules, which further unite to form small veins that leave the organ. The small veins progressively merge as they carry blood back to the heart.

Arteries serve as rapid-transit passageways to the organs and as a pressure reservoir.

Arteries are specialized (1) to serve as rapid-transit passageways for blood from the heart to the organs (because of their large radius, arteries offer little resistance to blood flow) and (2) to act as a **pressure reservoir** to provide the driving force for blood when the heart is relaxing.

Let us expand on the role of the arteries as a pressure reservoir. The heart alternately contracts to pump blood into the arteries and then relaxes to refill with blood from the veins. When the heart is relaxing and refilling, no blood is pumped out. However, capillary flow does not fluctuate between cardiac systole and diastole; that is, blood flow is continuous through the capillaries supplying the organs. The driving force for the continued flow of blood to the organs during cardiac relaxation is provided by the elastic properties of the arterial walls.

All vessels are lined with an *endothelium,* a single layer of smooth, flat endothelial cells, that is continuous with the

Beyond the Basics

Today even grade-school children know that blood is pumped by the heart and continually circulates throughout the body in a system of blood vessels. Furthermore, people accept without question that blood picks up O_2 in the lungs from the air we breathe and delivers it to the various organs. This common knowledge was unknown for most of human history, however. Even though the function of blood was described as early as the fifth century BC, our modern concept of circulation did not develop until AD 1628, more than 2000 years later, when William Harvey published his now classical study on the circulatory system.

Ancient Greeks believed everything material in the universe consisted of just four elements: earth, air, fire, and water. Extending this view to the human body, they thought these four elements took the form of four "humors": *black bile* (representing earth), *blood* (representing air), *yellow bile* (representing fire), and *phlegm* (representing water). According to the Greeks, disease resulted when one humor was out of normal balance with the rest. The "cure" was logical: To restore normal balance, drain off whichever humor was in excess. Because the easiest humor to drain off was the blood, bloodletting became standard procedure for treating many illnesses—a practice that persisted well into the Renaissance (which began in the 1300s and extended into the 1600s).

Although the ancient Greeks' notion of the four humors was erroneous, their concept of the necessity of balance within the body was remarkably accurate. As we now know, life depends on homeostasis, maintenance of the proper balance among all elements of the internal environment.

Aristotle (384–322 BC), a biologist as well as a philosopher, was among the first to correctly describe the heart at the center of a system of blood vessels. However, he thought the heart was both the seat of intellect (the brain was not identified as the seat of intellect until more than a century later) and a furnace that heated the blood. He considered this warmth the vital force of life, because the body cools quickly at death. Aristotle also erroneously theorized that breathing ventilated the "furnace," with air serving as a cooling agent. Aristotle could observe with his eyes the arteries and veins in cadavers but did not have a microscope with which to observe capillaries. (The microscope was not invented until the 17th century.) Thus, he did not think arteries and veins were directly connected.

In the third century BC, Erasistratus, a Greek many consider the first "physiologist," proposed that the liver used food to make blood, which the veins delivered to the other organs. He believed the arteries contained air, not blood. According to his view, *pneuma* (meaning "air"), a living force, was taken in by the lungs, which transferred it to the heart. The heart transformed the air into a "vital spirit" that the arteries carried to the other organs.

Galen (AD 130–206), a prolific, outspoken, dogmatic Roman physician, philosopher, and scholar, expanded on the work of Erasistratus and others who had preceded him. Galen further elaborated on the pneumatic theory. He proposed three fundamental members in the body, from lowest to highest: liver, heart, and brain. Each was dominated by a special *pneuma,* or "spirit." (In Greek, *pneuma* encompassed the related ideas of "air," "breath," and "spirit.") Like Erasistratus, Galen believed that the liver made blood from food, taking on a "natural" or "physical" spirit (*pneuma physicon*) in the process. The newly formed blood then proceeded through veins to organs. The natural spirit, which Galen considered a vapor rising from the blood, controlled the functions of nutrition, growth, and reproduction. Once its spirit supply was depleted, the blood moved in the opposite direction through the same venous pathways, returning to the liver to be replenished. When the natural spirit was carried in the venous blood to the heart, it mixed with air that was breathed in and transferred from the lungs to the heart. Contact with air in the heart transformed the natural spirit into a higher-level spirit, the "vital" spirit (*pneuma zotikon*). The vital spirit, which was carried by the arteries, conveyed heat and life throughout the body. The vital spirit was transformed further into a yet higher "animal" or "psychical" spirit (*pneuma psychikon*) in the brain. This ultimate spirit regulated the brain, nerves, feelings, and so on. Thus, according to Galenic theory, the veins and arteries were conduits for carrying different levels of pneuma, and no direct connection existed between veins and arteries. The heart was not involved in moving blood but instead was the site where blood and air mixed. (We now know that blood and air meet in the lungs for the exchange of O_2 and CO_2.)

Galen was one of the first to understand the need for experimentation, but unfortunately, his impatience and his craving for philosophical and literary fame led him to expound comprehensive theories that were not always based on the time-consuming collection of evidence. Even though his assumptions about bodily structure and functions often were incorrect, his theories were convincing because they seemed a logical way of pulling together what was known at the time. Furthermore, the sheer quantity of his writings helped establish him as an authority. His writings remained the anatomic and physiologic "truth" for nearly 15 centuries, throughout the Middle Ages and well into the Renaissance. So firmly entrenched was Galenic doctrine that people who challenged its accuracy risked their lives by being declared secular heretics.

Not until the Renaissance and the revival of classical learning did independent-minded European investigators begin to challenge Galen's theories. Most notably, the English physician William Harvey (1578–1657) revolutionized the view of the roles played by the heart, blood vessels, and blood. Through careful observations, experimentation, and deductive reasoning, Harvey was the first to correctly identify the heart as a pump that repeatedly moves a small volume of blood forward in one fixed direction in a circular path through a closed system of blood vessels (the *circulatory system*). He also correctly proposed that blood travels to the lungs to mix with air (instead of air traveling to the heart to mix with blood). Even though he could not see physical connections between arteries and veins, he speculated on their existence. Not until the discovery of the microscope later in the century was the existence of these connections, capillaries, confirmed, by Marcello Malpighi (1628–1694).

Feature	VESSEL TYPE			
	Arteries	Arterioles	Capillaries	Veins
Number	Several hundred*	Half a million	Ten billion	Several hundred*
Special Features	Thick, highly elastic, walls; large radii*	Highly muscular, well-innervated walls; small radii	Very thin walled; large total cross-sectional area	Thin walled; highly distensible; large radii*
Functions	Passageway from the heart to organs; pressure reservoir	Primary resistance vessels; determination of distribution of cardiac output	Site of exchange; determination of distribution of ECF between plasma and interstitial fluid	Passageway to the heart from organs; blood reservoir
Structure				

Endothelium

Elastin fibers

Smooth muscle

Elastin fibers

Connective tisssue coat (mostly collagen fibers)

Venous valve

Endothelium

Smooth muscle; elastin fibers

Connective tisssue coat (mostly collagen fibers)

Large artery   Arteriole   Capillary   Large vein

Relative Thickness of Layers in Wall

Endothelium
Elastin fibers
Smooth muscle
Collagen fibers

*These numbers and special features refer to the large arteries and veins, not to the smaller arterial branches or venules.

endothelial lining of the heart. A thick wall made up of smooth muscle and connective tissue surrounds the arteries' endothelial lining (▲ Table 10-1). Arterial connective tissue contains an abundance of two types of connective tissue fibers: *collagen fibers,* which provide tensile strength against the high, driving pressure of blood ejected from the heart, and *elastin fibers,* which give the arterial walls elasticity so that they behave much like a balloon.

As the heart pumps blood into the arteries during ventricular systole, a greater volume of blood enters the arteries from the heart than leaves them to flow into the arterioles because these smaller vessels have a greater resistance to flow than the arteries do. The highly elastic arteries expand to temporarily hold this excess volume of ejected blood, storing some of the pressure energy imparted by cardiac contraction in their stretched walls—just as a balloon expands to accommodate the extra volume of air

you blow into it (● Figure 10-5a). When the heart relaxes and temporarily stops pumping blood into the arteries, the stretched arterial walls passively recoil, like an inflated balloon that is released. This recoil exerts pressure on the blood in the arteries during diastole. The pressure pushes the excess blood contained in the arteries into the vessels downstream, ensuring continued blood flow to the organs when the heart is relaxing and not pumping blood into the system (● Figure 10-5b).

Arterial pressure fluctuates in relation to ventricular systole and diastole.

Blood pressure, the force exerted by the blood against a vessel wall, depends on the volume of blood contained within the vessel and the **compliance,** or **distensibility,** of the vessel walls

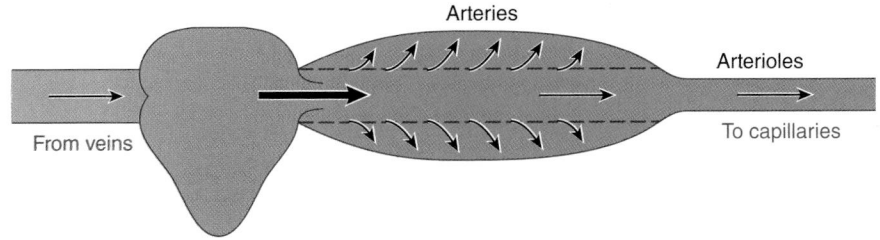

(a) Heart contracting and emptying

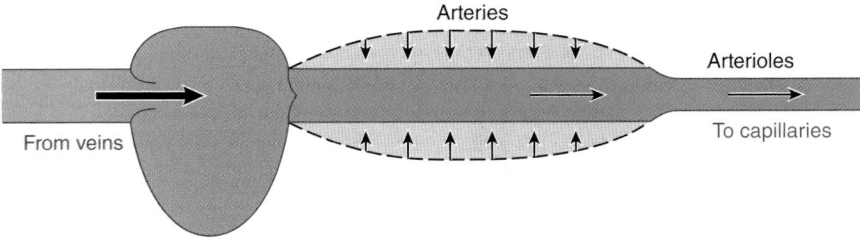

(b) Heart relaxing and filling

● FIGURE 10-5 **Arteries as a pressure reservoir.** Because of their elasticity, arteries act as a pressure reservoir. (a) The elastic arteries distend during cardiac systole as more blood is ejected into them than drains off into the narrow, high-resistance arterioles downstream. (b) The elastic recoil of arteries during cardiac diastole continues driving the blood forward when the heart is not pumping.

(how easily they can be stretched). If the volume of blood entering the arteries were equal to the volume of blood leaving the arteries during the same period, arterial blood pressure would remain constant. This is not the case, however. During ventricular systole, a stroke volume of blood enters the arteries from the ventricle, while only about one third as much blood leaves the arteries to enter the arterioles. During diastole, no blood enters the arteries, while blood continues to leave, driven by elastic recoil. The maximum pressure exerted in the arteries when blood is ejected into them during systole, the **systolic pressure,** averages 120 mm Hg. The minimum pressure within the arteries when blood is draining off into the rest of the vessels during diastole, the **diastolic pressure,** averages 80 mm Hg. Although ventricular pressure falls to 0 mm Hg during diastole, arterial pressure does not fall to 0 mm Hg, because the next cardiac contraction refills the arteries before all the blood drains off (● Figure 10-6; also see ● Figure 9-15, p. 261).

In clinical practice, arterial blood pressure is expressed as systolic pressure over diastolic pressure, with desirable blood pressure being 120/80 (read "120 over 80") mm Hg or slightly less.

When you palpate (feel with your fingers) an artery lying close to the surface of the skin (such as at your wrist or neck), you can feel the artery expand as the pressure rises during systole when blood is ejected into the arterial system by the left ventricle. What you feel when you "take a pulse" is the difference between systolic and diastolic pressures; you don't feel anything during diastole, but you feel the surge in pressure during systole. This pressure difference is known as the **pulse pressure.** When blood pressure is 120/80, pulse pressure is 40 mm Hg (120 minus 80 mm Hg). Because the pulse can be felt each time the ventricles pump blood into the arteries, the pulse rate is a measure of the heart rate.

Blood pressure can be measured indirectly by using a sphygmomanometer.

The changes in arterial pressure throughout the cardiac cycle can be measured directly by connecting a pressure-measuring device to a needle inserted in an artery. However, it is more convenient and reasonably accurate to measure the pressure indirectly with a **sphygmomanometer,** an externally applied inflatable cuff attached to a pressure gauge. When the cuff is wrapped around the upper arm and then inflated with air, the pressure of the cuff is transmitted through the tissues to the underlying brachial artery, the main vessel carrying blood to the forearm (● Figure 10-7a). The technique involves balancing the pressure in the cuff against the pressure in the artery. When cuff pressure is greater than the pressure in the vessel, the vessel is pinched closed so that no blood flows through it. When blood pressure is greater than cuff pressure, the vessel is open and blood flows through.

During the determination of blood pressure, a stethoscope is placed over the brachial artery at the inside bend of the elbow just below the cuff. No sound can be detected either when blood is not flowing through the vessel or when blood is flowing in the normal, smooth laminar flow (see p. 262). Turbulent blood flow, in contrast, creates vibrations that can be heard. The sounds heard when determining blood pressure are distinct from the heart sounds associated with valve closure heard when listening to the heart with a stethoscope.

At the onset of a blood pressure determination, the cuff is inflated to a pressure greater than systolic blood pressure so that the brachial artery collapses. Because the externally applied

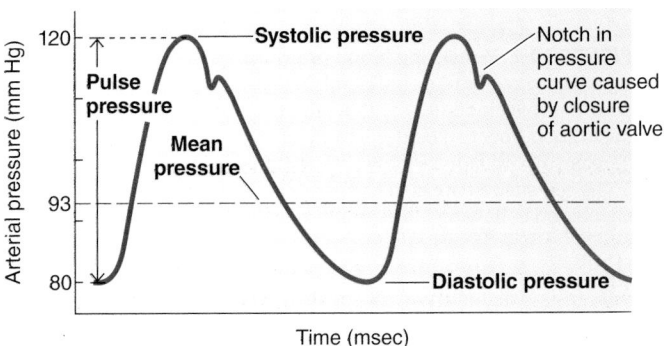

● FIGURE 10-6 **Arterial blood pressure.** The systolic pressure is the peak pressure exerted in the arteries when blood is pumped into them during ventricular systole. The diastolic pressure is the lowest pressure exerted in the arteries when blood is draining off into the vessels downstream during ventricular diastole. The pulse pressure is the difference between systolic and diastolic pressure. The mean pressure is the average pressure throughout the cardiac cycle.

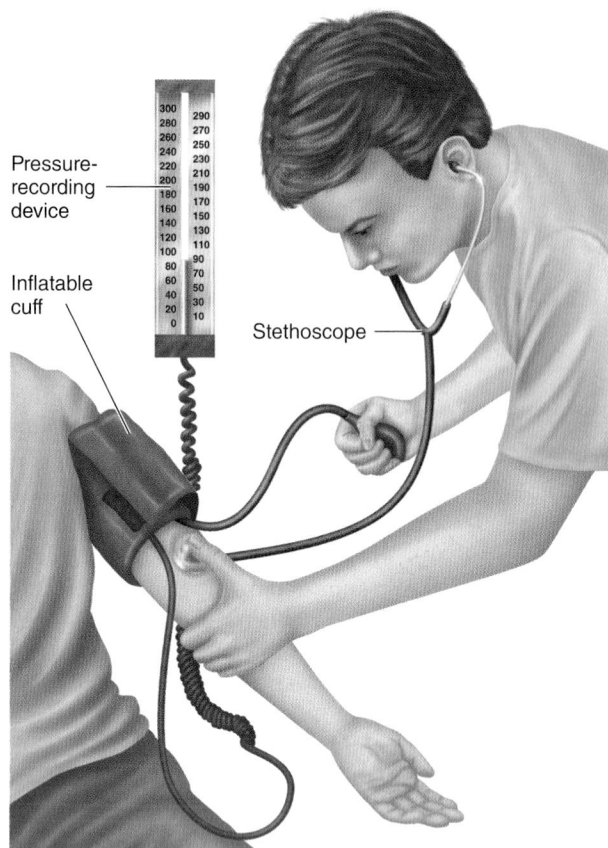

(a) Use of a sphygmomanometer in determining blood pressure

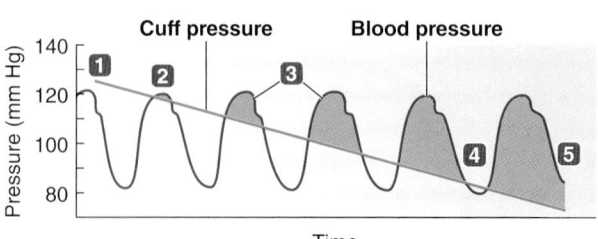

When blood pressure is 120/80:

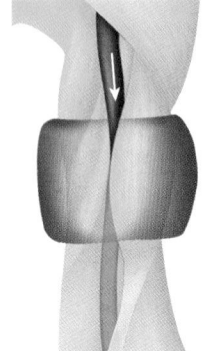

When cuff pressure is greater than 120 mm Hg and exceeds blood pressure throughout the cardiac cycle:

No blood flows through the vessel.

1 No sound is heard because no blood is flowing.

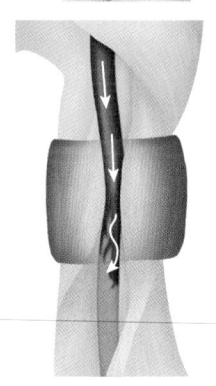

When cuff pressure is between 120 and 80 mm Hg:

Blood flow through the vessel is turbulent whenever blood pressure exceeds cuff pressure.

2 The first sound is heard at peak systolic pressure.

3 Intermittent sounds are produced by turbulent spurts of flow as blood pressure cyclically exceeds cuff pressure.

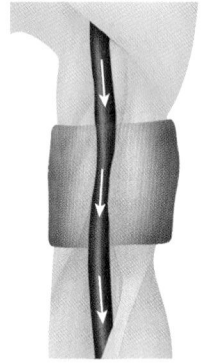

When cuff pressure is less than 80 mm Hg and is below blood pressure throughout the cardiac cycle:

Blood flows through the vessel in smooth, laminar fashion.

4 The last sound is heard at minimum diastolic pressure.

5 No sound is heard thereafter because of uninterrupted, smooth, laminar flow.

● FIGURE 10-7 **Measuring blood pressure.** (a) The pressure in the sphygmomanometer (inflatable cuff) can be varied to prevent or permit blood flow in the underlying brachial artery. Turbulent blood flow can be detected with a stethoscope, whereas smooth laminar flow and no flow are inaudible. (b) The red shaded areas in the graph are the times during which blood is flowing in the brachial artery.

(b) Blood flow through the brachial artery in relation to cuff pressure and sounds

pressure is greater than the peak internal pressure, the artery remains completely pinched closed throughout the entire cardiac cycle; no sound can be heard because no blood is passing through (● Figure 10-7b, point **1**). As air in the cuff is slowly released, the pressure in the cuff is gradually reduced. When the cuff pressure falls to just below the peak systolic pressure, the artery transiently opens a bit when the blood pressure reaches this peak. Blood escapes through the partially occluded artery for a brief interval before the arterial pressure falls below the cuff pressure and the artery collapses again. This spurt of blood is turbulent, so it can be heard. Thus, the highest cuff pressure at which the *first sound* can be heard indicates the *systolic pressure* (point **2**). As the cuff pressure continues to fall, blood intermittently spurts through the artery and produces a sound with each subsequent cardiac cycle whenever the arterial pressure exceeds the cuff pressure (point **3**).

When the cuff pressure finally falls below diastolic pressure, the brachial artery is no longer pinched closed during any part of the cardiac cycle, and blood can flow uninterrupted through the vessel (point **5**). With the return of nonturbulent blood flow, no further sounds can be heard. Therefore, the lowest cuff pressure at which the *last sound* can be detected indicates the *diastolic pressure* (point **4**).

Mean arterial pressure is the main driving force for blood flow.

The **mean arterial pressure** is the *average pressure* driving blood forward into the tissues throughout the cardiac cycle. Contrary to what you might expect, mean arterial pressure is not the halfway value between systolic and diastolic pressure (for example, with a blood pressure of 120/80, mean pressure is not 100 mm Hg). The reason is that arterial pressure remains closer to diastolic than to systolic pressure for a longer portion of each cardiac cycle. At resting heart rate, about two thirds of the cardiac cycle is spent in diastole and only one third in systole. As an analogy, if a race car traveled 80 miles per hour (mph) for 40 minutes and 120 mph for 20 minutes, its average speed would be 93 mph, not the halfway value of 100 mph.

Similarly, a good approximation of the mean arterial pressure can be determined using the following formula:

$$\text{Mean arterial pressure} = \text{diastolic pressure} + 1/3 \text{ pulse pressure}$$

At 120/80,

$$\text{Mean arterial pressure} = 80 + (1/3)\,40 = 93 \text{ mm Hg}$$

The mean arterial pressure, not the systolic or diastolic pressure, is monitored and regulated by blood pressure reflexes described later in the chapter.

Because arteries offer little resistance to flow, only a negligible amount of pressure energy is lost in them because of friction. Therefore, arterial pressure—systolic, diastolic, pulse, or mean—is essentially the same throughout the arterial tree (● Figure 10-8).

Blood pressure exists throughout the entire vascular tree, but when discussing a person's "blood pressure" without qualifying which blood vessel type is being referred to, the term is tacitly understood to mean the pressure in the arteries.

Arterioles

When an artery reaches the organ it is supplying, it branches into numerous arterioles within the organ.

Arterioles are the major resistance vessels.

Arterioles are the main resistance vessels in the vascular tree because their radius is small enough to offer considerable resistance to flow. (Even though capillaries have a smaller radius than arterioles, you will see later how collectively the capillaries do not offer as much resistance to flow as the arterioles do.) In contrast to the low resistance of the arteries, the high degree of arteriolar resistance causes a marked drop in mean pressure as blood flows through these small vessels. On average, the pressure falls from 93 mm Hg, the mean arterial pressure (the pressure of the blood entering the arterioles), to 37 mm Hg, the pressure of the blood leaving the arterioles and entering the capillaries (● Figure 10-8). This decline in pressure helps establish the pressure differential that encourages the flow of blood from the heart to the various organs downstream. Arteriolar resistance also converts the pulsatile systolic-to-diastolic pressure swings in the arteries into the nonfluctuating pressure present in the capillaries.

The radius (and, accordingly, the resistances) of arterioles supplying individual organs can be adjusted independently to accomplish two functions: (1) to variably distribute the cardiac output among the systemic organs, depending on the body's momentary needs, and (2) to help regulate arterial blood pressure. Before considering how such adjustments are important in accomplishing these two functions, we discuss the mechanisms involved in adjusting arteriolar resistance.

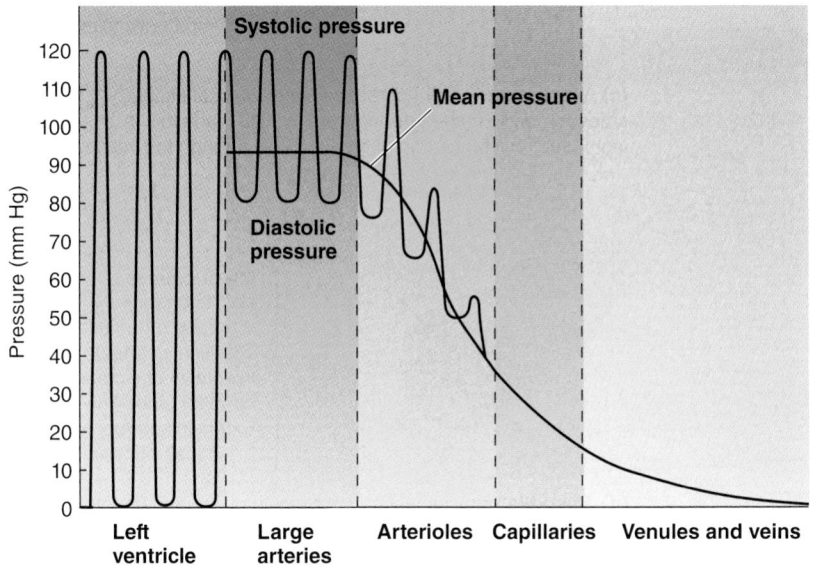

● FIGURE 10-8 **Pressures throughout the systemic circulation.** Left ventricular pressure swings from a low pressure of 0 mm Hg during diastole to a high pressure of 120 mm Hg during systole. Arterial blood pressure, which fluctuates between a peak systolic pressure of 120 mm Hg and a low diastolic pressure of 80 mm Hg each cardiac cycle, is of the same magnitude throughout the large arteries. Because of the arterioles' high resistance, the pressure drops precipitously and the systolic-to-diastolic swings in pressure are converted to a nonpulsatile pressure when blood flows through the arterioles. The pressure continues to decline but at a slower rate as blood flows through the capillaries and venous system.

VASOCONSTRICTION AND VASODILATION Unlike arteries, arteriolar walls contain little elastic connective tissue. However, they do have a thick layer of smooth muscle that is richly innervated by sympathetic nerve fibers (see ▲ Table 10-1). The smooth muscle is also sensitive to many local chemical changes, to a few circulating hormones, and to mechanical stretch. The smooth muscle layer runs circularly around the arteriole (● Figure 10-9a), so when the smooth muscle layer contracts, the vessel's circumference (and its radius) becomes smaller, increasing resistance and decreasing flow through that vessel. **Vasoconstriction** is the term applied to such narrowing of a vessel (● Figure 10-9c). In contrast, the term **vasodilation** refers to enlargement in the circumference and radius of a vessel as a result of its smooth muscle layer relaxing (● Figure 10-9d). Vasodilation leads to decreased resistance and increased flow through that vessel.

VASCULAR TONE Arteriolar smooth muscle normally displays a state of partial constriction known as **vascular tone,** which establishes a baseline of arteriolar resistance (● Figure 10-9b) (see p. 238). Two factors are responsible for vascular tone. First, arteriolar smooth muscle has considerable myogenic activity; that is, it shows self-induced contractile activity independent of any neural or hormonal influences (see p. 236). Second, the sympathetic fibers supplying most arterioles continually release norepinephrine, which further enhances vascular tone.

This ongoing tonic activity makes it possible to either increase or decrease the level of contractile activity to accomplish vasoconstriction or vasodilation, respectively. Were it not for tone, it would be impossible to reduce the tension in an arteriolar wall to accomplish vasodilation; only varying degrees of vasoconstriction would be possible.

A variety of factors can influence the level of contractile activity in arteriolar smooth muscle, thereby substantially changing resistance to flow in these vessels. The factors that cause arteriolar vasoconstriction or vasodilation fall into two categories: local (intrinsic) controls, which are important in determining the distribution of cardiac output, and extrinsic controls, which are important in blood pressure regulation. We look at each of these controls in turn.

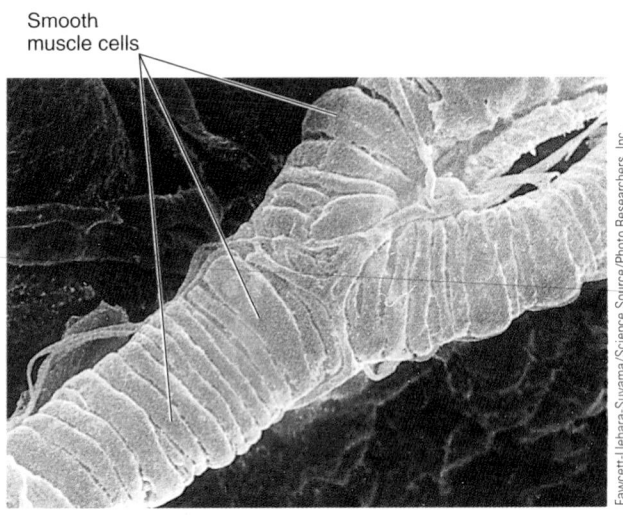

Smooth muscle cells

Fawcett-Uehara-Suyama/Science Source/Photo Researchers, Inc.

(a) Scanning electron micrograph of an arteriole showing how the smooth muscle cells run circularly around the vessel wall

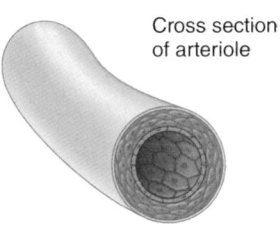

Cross section of arteriole

(b) Normal arteriolar tone

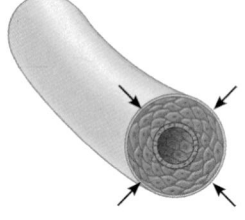

Major causes:
Local control:
↑ Oxygen (O₂) and other local chemical changes indicative of decreased need for blood flow
Extrinsic control:
↑ Sympathetic stimulation

(c) Vasoconstriction (increased contraction of circular smooth muscle in the arteriolar wall, which leads to increased resistance and decreased flow through the vessel)

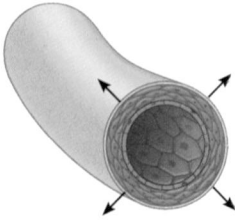

Major causes:
Local control:
↓ O₂ and other local chemical changes indicative of increased need for blood flow
Extrinsic control:
↓ Sympathetic stimulation

(d) Vasodilation (decreased contraction of circular smooth muscle in the arteriolar wall, which leads to decreased resistance and increased flow through the vessel)

● **FIGURE 10-9 Arteriolar vasoconstriction and vasodilation.**

Local control of arteriolar radius is important in determining the distribution of cardiac output.

The fraction of the total cardiac output delivered to each organ is not always constant; it varies, depending on the demands for blood at the time. The amount of the cardiac output received by each organ is determined by the number and caliber of the arterioles supplying that area. Recall that $F = \Delta P/R$. Because blood is delivered to all organs at the same mean arterial pressure, the driving force for flow is identical for each organ. Therefore, differences in flow to various organs are determined by differences in the extent of vascularization and by differences in the resistance offered by the arterioles supplying each organ. From moment to moment, the distribution of cardiac output can be varied by differentially adjusting arteriolar resistance in the various vascular beds.

As an analogy, consider a pipe carrying water, with several adjustable valves located throughout its length (● Figure 10-10). Assuming that water pressure in the pipe is constant, differences in the amount of water flowing into a beaker under each valve depend entirely on which valves are open and to what extent. No water enters beakers under closed valves (high resistance), and more water flows into beakers under valves that are opened completely (low resistance) than into beakers under valves that are only partially opened (moderate resistance).

Similarly, more blood flows to areas whose arterioles offer the least resistance to its passage. During exercise, for example, not only is cardiac output increased, but also, because of vasodilation in skeletal muscle and in the heart, a greater percentage of the pumped blood is diverted to these organs to support their increased metabolic activity. Simultaneously, blood flow to the digestive tract and kidneys is reduced as a result of arteriolar vasoconstriction in these organs. Only the blood supply to the brain remains remarkably constant no matter what the person is doing, be it vigorous physical activity, intense mental concentration, or sleep. Although total blood flow to the brain remains constant, new imaging techniques demonstrate that regional blood flow varies within the brain in close correlation with local neural activity patterns (see Figure 5-8b, p. 125).

Local (intrinsic) controls are changes within an organ that alter the radius of the vessels and hence adjust blood flow through the organ by directly affecting the smooth muscle of the organ's arterioles. Local influences may be either chemical or physical. Local chemical influences on arteriolar radius include (1) local metabolic changes and (2) histamine release. Local physical influences include (1) myogenic response to stretch and (2) local application of heat or cold. Let us examine the role and mechanism of each of these local influences.

Local metabolic influences on arteriolar radius help match blood flow with the organs' needs.

The most important local chemical influences on arteriolar smooth muscle are related to metabolic changes within a given organ. The influence of these local changes on arteriolar radius is important in matching blood flow through an organ with the organ's metabolic needs. Local metabolic controls are especially important in skeletal muscle and in the heart, the organs whose metabolic activity and need for blood supply normally vary most.

ACTIVE HYPEREMIA Arterioles lie within the organ they are supplying and can be acted on by local factors within the organ. During increased metabolic activity, such as when a skeletal muscle is contracting during exercise, local concentrations of several of the organ's chemicals change. For example, the local O_2 concentration decreases as the actively metabolizing cells use up more O_2 to support oxidative phosphorylation for ATP production (see p. 32). This and other local chemical changes (such as increased CO_2) produce local arteriolar dilation by triggering relaxation of the arteriolar smooth muscle in the vicinity. Local arteriolar vasodilation then increases blood flow to that particular area. This increased blood flow in response to enhanced tissue activity is called **active hyperemia** (*hyper* means "above normal"; *emia* means "blood"). When cells are more active metabolically, they need more blood to bring in O_2 and nutrients and to remove metabolic wastes.

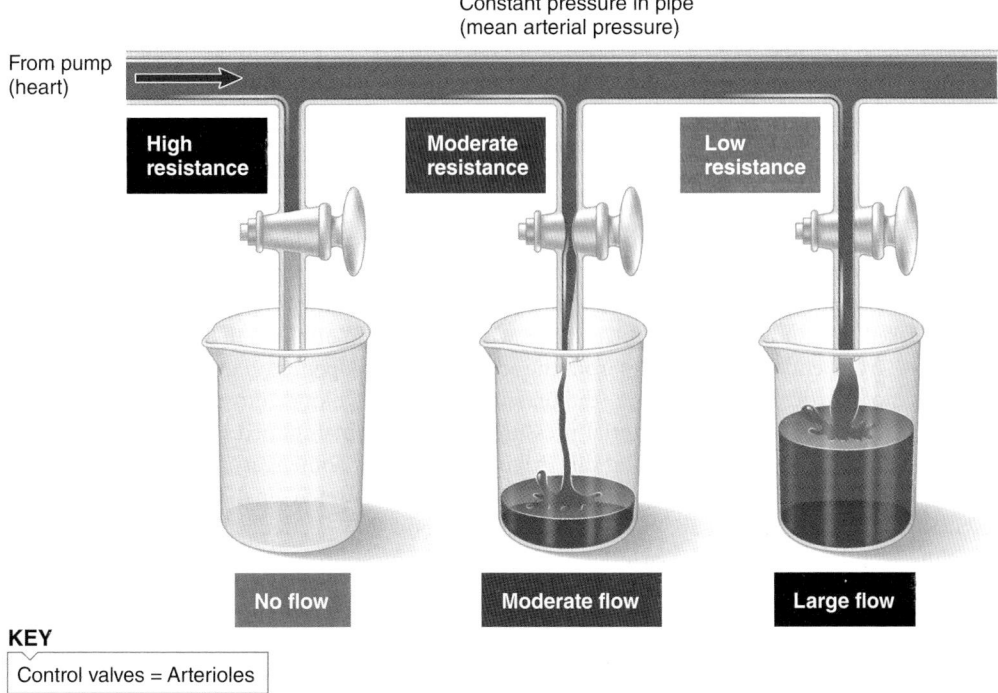

KEY

Control valves = Arterioles

● FIGURE 10-10 **Flow rate as a function of resistance.**

Conversely, when an organ, such as a relaxed muscle, is less active metabolically and thus has reduced needs for blood delivery, the resultant local chemical changes (for example, increased local O_2 concentration) bring about local arteriolar vasoconstriction and a subsequent reduction in blood flow to the area. Local metabolic changes can thus adjust blood flow as needed without involving nerves or hormones.

ENDOTHELIAL DERIVED VASOACTIVE PARACRINES The local chemical changes that bring about these "selfish" local adjustments in arteriolar caliber to match a tissue's blood flow with its needs do not act directly on vascular smooth muscle to change its contractile state. Instead, endothelial cells, the single layer of specialized epithelial cells that line the lumen of all blood vessels, release paracrines (locally acting chemical messengers; see p. 98) in response to chemical changes in the cells' environment (such as a reduction in O_2). These vasoactive ("acting on vessels") paracrines act on the underlying smooth muscle to alter its state of contraction, thus locally regulating arteriolar caliber.

Among the best studied of these vasoactive paracrines is **nitric oxide (NO),** which brings about local arteriolar vasodilation by causing relaxation of arteriolar smooth muscle in the vicinity. NO is a small, highly reactive, short-lived gas molecule that once was known primarily as a toxic air pollutant. Yet studies have revealed an astonishing number of biological roles for NO, which is produced in many tissues besides endothelial cells. NO is one of the body's most important messenger molecules, as shown by the range of functions identified for this chemical and listed in ▲ Table 10-2. As you can see, most areas of the body are influenced by this versatile intercellular messenger molecule.

Endothelial cells release other important paracrines besides NO. As an example, **endothelin** causes arteriolar smooth muscle contraction and is one of the most potent vasoconstrictors yet identified. Still other chemicals, released from the endothelium in response to chronic changes in blood flow to an organ, trigger long-term vascular changes that permanently influence blood flow to a region. For instance, **vascular endothelial growth factor (VEGF)** stimulates new vessel growth, a process known as **angiogenesis.**

Local histamine release pathologically dilates arterioles.

Histamine is another local chemical mediator that influences arteriolar smooth muscle, but it is not released in response to local metabolic changes and is not derived from endothelial cells. Although histamine normally does not participate in controlling blood flow, it is important in certain pathological conditions.

 Histamine is synthesized and stored within special connective tissue cells in many organs and in certain types of circulating white blood cells. When organs are injured or during allergic reactions, histamine is released and acts as a paracrine in the damaged region (see p. 333). By promoting relaxation of arteriolar smooth muscle, histamine is the major cause of vasodilation in an injured area. The resultant increase in blood flow into the area

▲ Table 10-2 Functions of Nitric Oxide

- Causes relaxation of arteriolar smooth muscle. By means of this action, NO plays an important role in controlling blood flow through the tissues and in maintaining mean arterial blood pressure.
- Dilates the arterioles of the penis and clitoris, thus serving as the direct mediator of erection of these reproductive organs. Erection is accomplished by rapid engorgement of these organs with blood.
- Is used as chemical warfare against bacteria and cancer cells by macrophages, large phagocytic cells of the immune system.
- Interferes with platelet function and blood clotting at sites of vessel damage.
- Serves as a novel type of neurotransmitter in the brain and elsewhere.
- Plays a role in the changes underlying memory.
- By promoting relaxation of digestive-tract smooth muscle, helps regulate peristalsis, a type of contraction that pushes digestive tract contents forward.
- Relaxes the smooth muscle cells in the airways of the lungs, helping keep these passages open to facilitate movement of air in and out of the lungs.
- Modulates the filtering process involved in urine formation.
- Directs blood flow to O_2-starved tissues.

produces the redness and contributes to the swelling seen with inflammatory responses (see Chapter 11 for further details).

The myogenic response of arterioles to stretch helps tissues autoregulate their blood flow.

Arteriolar smooth muscle is influenced by locally acting physical factors in addition to local chemical influences. Local physical influences include stretch and temperature changes, with the myogenic response to stretch being the most important physiologically.

Arteriolar smooth muscle responds to being passively stretched by myogenically increasing its tone via vasoconstriction, thereby acting to resist the initial passive stretch. Conversely, a reduction in arteriolar stretching decreases myogenic vessel tone by promoting vasodilation. The extent of passive stretch varies with the volume of blood delivered to the arterioles from the arteries, which depends on the mean arterial pressure (the pressure that drives blood into the arterioles). Mean arterial pressure is normally maintained within narrow limits, but if this driving pressure for some reason becomes abnormal, the myogenic response to stretch enables a tissue to resist changes in its own blood flow secondary to changes in mean arterial pressure by making appropriate adjustments in arteriolar radius. This process, known as **autoregulation,** helps keep tissue blood flow fairly constant despite rather wide deviations in mean arterial driving pressure (*auto* means "self"). For example, when mean arterial pressure falls (such as because of hemorrhage or a weakened heart), the driving force is reduced, so blood flow to organs decreases. Because less blood is flowing through the arterioles, they are not stretched as much as normal. The arterioles respond to this reduced stretch by vasodilating. The increased flow through the vasodilated arterioles helps restore tissue blood flow toward normal despite the reduced driving pressure.

Local heat application dilates arterioles and cold application constricts them.

The effect of temperature changes on arterioles can be exploited clinically. Heat application, by causing localized arteriolar vasodilation, is a useful therapeutic agent for promoting increased blood flow to an area. Conversely, applying ice packs to an inflamed area produces vasoconstriction, which reduces swelling by counteracting histamine-induced vasodilation.

This completes our discussion of the local control of arteriolar radius. Now let us shift attention to extrinsic control of arteriolar radius.

Extrinsic sympathetic control of arteriolar radius is important in regulating blood pressure.

Extrinsic control of arteriolar radius includes both neural and hormonal influences, the effects of the sympathetic nervous system being the most important. Sympathetic nerve fibers supply arteriolar smooth muscle everywhere in the systemic circulation except in the brain. Recall that a certain level of ongoing sympathetic activity contributes to vascular tone. Increased sympathetic activity produces generalized arteriolar vasoconstriction, whereas decreased sympathetic activity leads to generalized arteriolar vasodilation. These widespread changes in arteriolar resistance bring about changes in mean arterial pressure because of their influence on total peripheral resistance, as follows.

INFLUENCE OF TOTAL PERIPHERAL RESISTANCE ON MEAN ARTERIAL PRESSURE To find the effect of changes in arteriolar resistance on mean arterial pressure, the formula $F = \Delta P/R$ applies to the entire circulation as well as to a single vessel:

■ *F.* Looking at the circulatory system as a whole, flow *(F)* through all the vessels in either the systemic or the pulmonary circulation is equal to the cardiac output.

■ *ΔP.* The pressure gradient (ΔP) for the entire systemic circulation is the mean arterial pressure. (ΔP equals the difference in pressure between the beginning and the end of the systemic circulatory system. The beginning pressure is the mean arterial pressure as the blood leaves the left ventricle at an average of 93 mm Hg. The end pressure in the right atrium is 0 mm Hg. Therefore, ΔP = 93 minus 0 = 93 mm Hg, which is equivalent to the mean arterial pressure.)

■ *R.* The total resistance *(R)* offered by all the systemic peripheral vessels together is the **total peripheral resistance.** By far the greatest percentage of the total peripheral resistance is due to arteriolar resistance, because arterioles are the primary resistance vessels.

Therefore, for the entire systemic circulation, rearranging

$$F = \Delta P/R$$

to

$$\Delta P = F \times R$$

gives us the equation

Mean arterial pressure (MAP) =
cardiac output (CO) × total peripheral resistance (TPR)

Thus, the extent of total peripheral resistance offered collectively by all the systemic arterioles influences the mean arterial pressure immensely. A dam provides an analogy to this relationship. At the same time a dam restricts the flow of water downstream, it increases the pressure upstream by elevating the water level in the reservoir behind the dam. Similarly, generalized, sympathetically induced vasoconstriction reflexly reduces blood flow downstream to the organs while elevating the upstream mean arterial pressure, thereby increasing the main driving force for blood flow to all the organs.

These effects seem counterproductive. Why increase the driving force for flow to the organs by increasing arterial blood pressure while reducing flow to the organs by narrowing the vessels supplying them? In effect, the sympathetically induced arteriolar responses help maintain the appropriate driving pressure head (that is, the mean arterial pressure) to all organs. The extent to which each organ actually receives blood flow is determined by local arteriolar adjustments that override the sympathetic constrictor effect. If all arterioles were dilated, blood pressure would fall substantially, so there would not be an adequate driving force for blood flow. An analogy is the pressure head for water in the pipes in your home. If the water pressure is adequate, you can selectively obtain satisfactory water flow at any of the faucets by turning the appropriate handle to the open position. If the water pressure in the pipes is too low, however, you cannot obtain satisfactory flow at any faucet, even if you turn the handle to the maximally open position. Tonic sympathetic activity thus constricts most vessels (with the exception of those in the brain) to help maintain a pressure head on which organs can draw as needed through local mechanisms that control arteriolar radius.

No vasoconstriction occurs in the brain. It is important that cerebral arterioles are not reflexly constricted by neural influences, because brain blood flow must remain constant to meet the brain's continuous need for O_2, no matter what is going on elsewhere in the body. Cerebral vessels are almost entirely controlled by local mechanisms that maintain a constant blood flow to support a constant level of brain metabolic activity. In fact, reflex vasoconstrictor activity in the remainder of the cardiovascular system is aimed at maintaining an adequate pressure head for blood flow to the vital brain.

Thus, sympathetic activity contributes in an important way to maintaining mean arterial pressure, ensuring an adequate driving force for blood flow to the brain at the expense of organs that can better withstand reduced blood flow. Other organs that really need additional blood, such as active muscles (including active heart muscle), obtain it through local controls that override the sympathetic effect.

LOCAL CONTROLS OVERRIDING SYMPATHETIC VASOCONSTRICTION Skeletal and cardiac muscles have the most powerful local control mechanisms with which to override generalized sympathetic vasoconstriction. For example, if you are pedaling a bicycle, the increased activity in the skeletal muscles of your legs brings about an overriding local, metabolically induced vasodilation in those particular muscles, despite the generalized sympathetic vasoconstriction that accompanies exercise. As a result, more blood flows through your leg muscles but not through your inactive arm muscles.

NO PARASYMPATHETIC INNERVATION TO ARTERIOLES Arterioles have no significant parasympathetic innervation, with the exception of the abundant parasympathetic vasodilator supply to the arterioles of the penis and clitoris. The rapid, profuse vasodilation induced by parasympathetic stimulation in these organs (by means of promoting release of NO) is largely responsible for accomplishing erection. Vasodilation elsewhere is produced by decreasing sympathetic vasoconstrictor activity below its tonic level. When mean arterial pressure rises above normal, reflex reduction in sympathetic vasoconstrictor activity accomplishes generalized arteriolar vasodilation to help bring the driving pressure down toward normal.

The medullary cardiovascular control center and several hormones regulate blood pressure.

The main region of the brain that adjusts sympathetic output to the arterioles is the **cardiovascular control center** in the medulla of the brain stem. This is the integrating center for blood pressure regulation (described in further detail later in this chapter). Several other brain regions also influence blood distribution, the most notable being the hypothalamus, which, as part of its temperature-regulating function, controls blood flow to the skin to adjust heat loss to the environment.

In addition to neural reflex activity, several hormones extrinsically influence arteriolar radius. These hormones include the major adrenal medullary hormone epinephrine, which generally reinforces the sympathetic nervous system in most organs, as well as vasopressin and angiotensin II, which are important in controlling fluid balance. Vasopressin is primarily involved in maintaining water balance by regulating the amount of water the kidneys retain for the body during urine formation (see p. 430). Angiotensin II is part of a hormonal pathway, the *renin–angiotensin–aldosterone system,* which is important in regulating the body's salt balance. This pathway promotes salt conservation during urine formation and leads to water retention because salt exerts a water-holding osmotic effect in the ECF (see p. 416). Thus, both these hormones play important roles in maintaining the body's fluid balance, which in turn is an important determinant of plasma volume and blood pressure.

In addition, both vasopressin and angiotensin II are potent vasoconstrictors. Their role in this regard is especially crucial during hemorrhage. A sudden loss of blood reduces the plasma volume, which triggers increased secretion of both these hormones to help restore plasma volume. Their vasoconstrictor effect also helps maintain blood pressure despite abrupt loss of plasma volume. (The functions and control of these hormones are discussed more thoroughly in later chapters.)

This completes our discussion of the various factors that affect total peripheral resistance, the most important of which are controlled adjustments in arteriolar radius. These factors are summarized in ● Figure 10-11.

We now turn to the next vessels in the vascular tree, the capillaries.

Capillaries

Capillaries, the sites for exchange of materials between blood and tissue cells, branch extensively to bring blood within the reach of essentially every cell.

Capillaries are ideally suited to serve as sites of exchange.

There are no carrier-mediated transport systems across capillaries, with the exception of those in the brain that play a role in the blood–brain barrier (see p. 120). Materials are exchanged across capillary walls mainly by diffusion.

FACTORS THAT ENHANCE DIFFUSION ACROSS CAPILLARIES Capillaries are ideally suited to enhance diffusion, in accordance with Fick's law of diffusion (see p. 55). They minimize diffusion distances while maximizing surface area and time available for exchange, as follows:

1. Diffusing molecules have only a short distance to travel between blood and surrounding cells because of the thin capillary wall and small capillary diameter, coupled with the proximity of every cell to a capillary. This short distance is important because the rate of diffusion slows down as the diffusion distance increases.

   a. Capillary walls are very thin (1 μm in thickness; in contrast, the diameter of a human hair is 100 μm). Capillaries consist of only a single layer of flat endothelial cells—essentially the lining of the other vessel types (see ▲ Table 10-1, p. 284). No smooth muscle or connective tissue is present.

   b. Each capillary is so narrow (7 μm average diameter) that red blood cells (8 μm diameter) have to squeeze through in single file (● Figure 10-12). Consequently, plasma contents either are in direct contact with the inside of the capillary wall or are only a short diffusing distance from it.

   c. Researchers estimate that because of extensive capillary branching, scarcely any cell is farther than 0.01 cm (4/1000 in.) from a capillary.

2. Because capillaries are distributed in such incredible numbers (estimates range from 10 billion to 40 billion capillaries), a tremendous total surface area is available for exchange (an estimated 600 m^2). Despite this large number of capillaries, at any point in time these microscopic sized vessels contain only 5% of the total blood volume (250 ml out of a total of 5000 ml). As a result, a small volume of blood is exposed to an extensive sur-

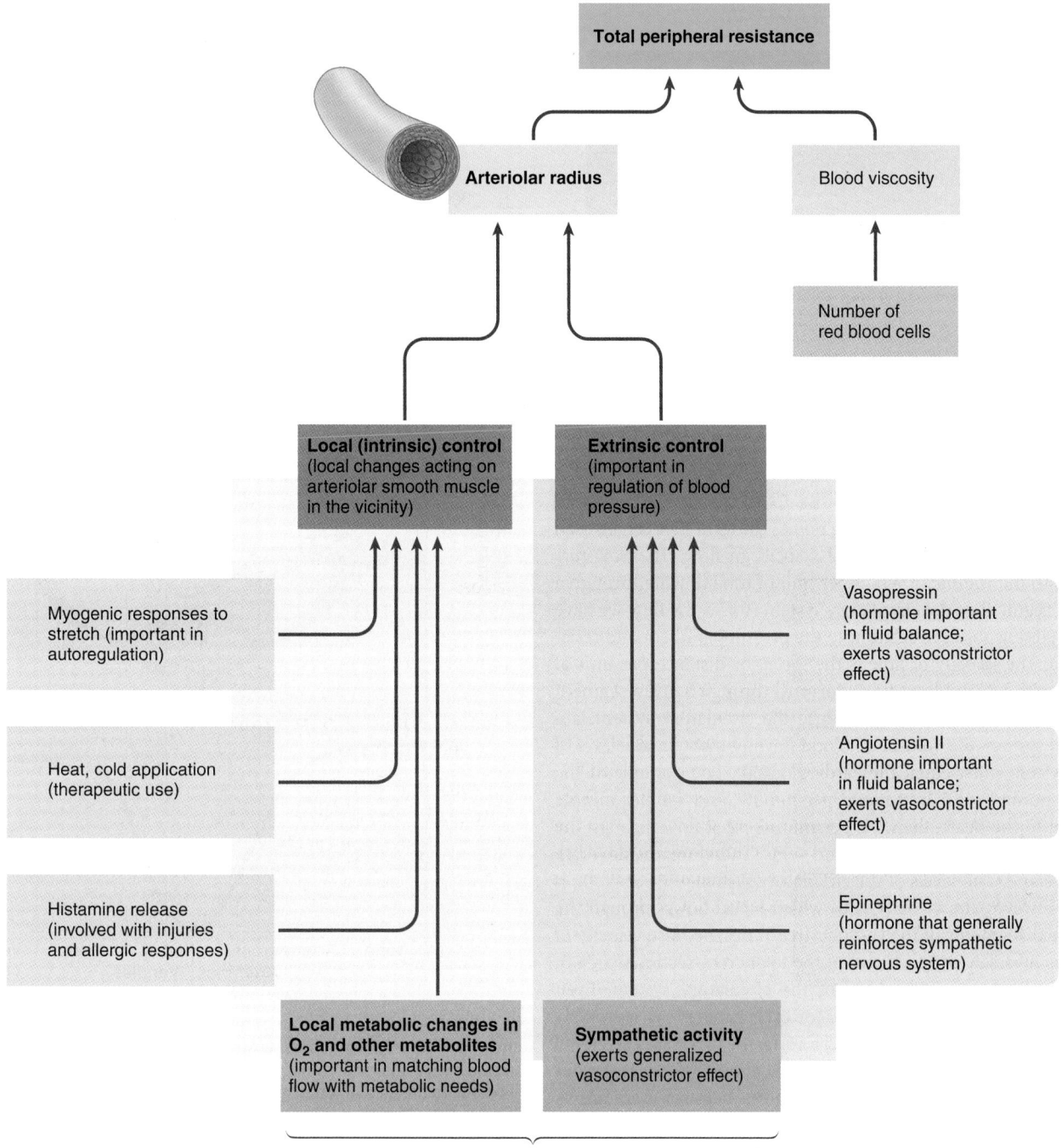

● FIGURE 10-11 **Factors affecting total peripheral resistance.** The primary determinant of total peripheral resistance is the adjustable arteriolar radius. Two major categories of factors influence arteriolar radius: (1) local (intrinsic) control, which is primarily important in matching blood flow through a tissue with the tissue's metabolic needs and is mediated by local factors acting on the arteriolar smooth muscle, and (2) extrinsic control, which is important in regulating blood pressure and is mediated primarily by sympathetic influence on arteriolar smooth muscle.

face area. If all capillary surfaces were stretched out in a flat sheet and the volume of blood contained within the capillaries was spread over the top, this would be roughly equivalent to spreading a half pint of paint over the floor of a high school gymnasium. Imagine how thin the paint layer would be!

3. Blood flows more slowly in the capillaries than elsewhere in the circulatory system. The extensive capillary branching is responsible for this slow velocity of blood flow through the capillaries. Let us see why blood slows down in the capillaries.

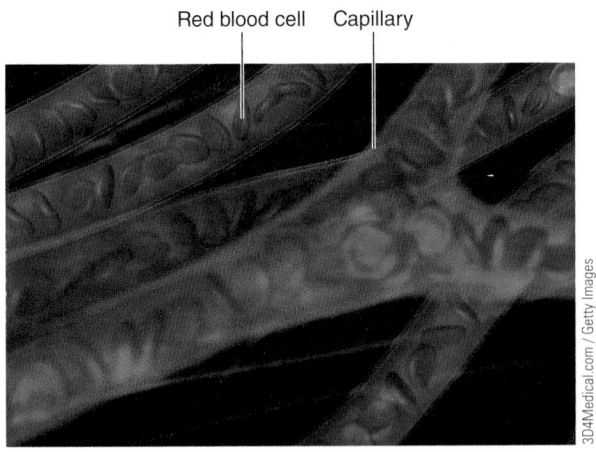

Red blood cell   Capillary

● FIGURE 10-12 **Capillary bed.** The capillaries are so narrow that red blood cells must pass through the capillary bed in single file.

SLOW VELOCITY OF FLOW THROUGH CAPILLARIES First, we need to clarify a potentially confusing point. The term *flow* can be used in two contexts—flow rate and velocity of flow. The *flow rate* refers to the *volume* of blood per unit of time flowing through a given segment of the circulatory system (this is the flow we have been talking about in relation to the pressure gradient and resistance). The *velocity of flow* is the *speed,* or distance per unit of time, with which blood flows forward through a given segment of the circulatory system. Because the circulatory system is a closed system, the volume of blood flowing through any level of the system must equal the cardiac output. For example, if the heart pumps out 5 L of blood per minute, and 5 L per minute return to the heart, then 5 L per minute must flow through the arteries, arterioles, capillaries, and veins. Therefore, the flow rate is the same at all levels of the circulatory system.

However, the velocity with which blood flows through the different segments of the vascular tree varies, because velocity of flow is inversely proportional to the total cross-sectional area of all vessels at any given level of the circulatory system. Even though the cross-sectional area of each capillary is extremely small compared to that of the large aorta, the total cross-sectional area of all capillaries added together is about 750 times greater than the cross-sectional area of the aorta because there are so many capillaries. Accordingly, blood slows considerably as it passes through the capillaries (● Figure 10-13). This slow velocity allows adequate time for exchange of nutrients and metabolic end products between blood and tissue cells, which is the sole purpose of the entire circulatory system. As the capillaries rejoin to form veins, the total cross-sectional area is again reduced, and the velocity of blood flow increases as blood returns to the heart.

As an analogy, consider a river (the arterial system) that widens into a lake (the capillaries) and then narrows into a river again (the venous system) (● Figure 10-14). The flow rate is the same throughout the length of this body of water; that is, identical volumes of water are flowing past all points along the bank of the river and lake. However, the velocity of flow is slower in the wide lake than in the narrow river because the identical volume of water, now spread out over a larger cross-sectional area, moves forward a shorter distance in the wide lake than in the

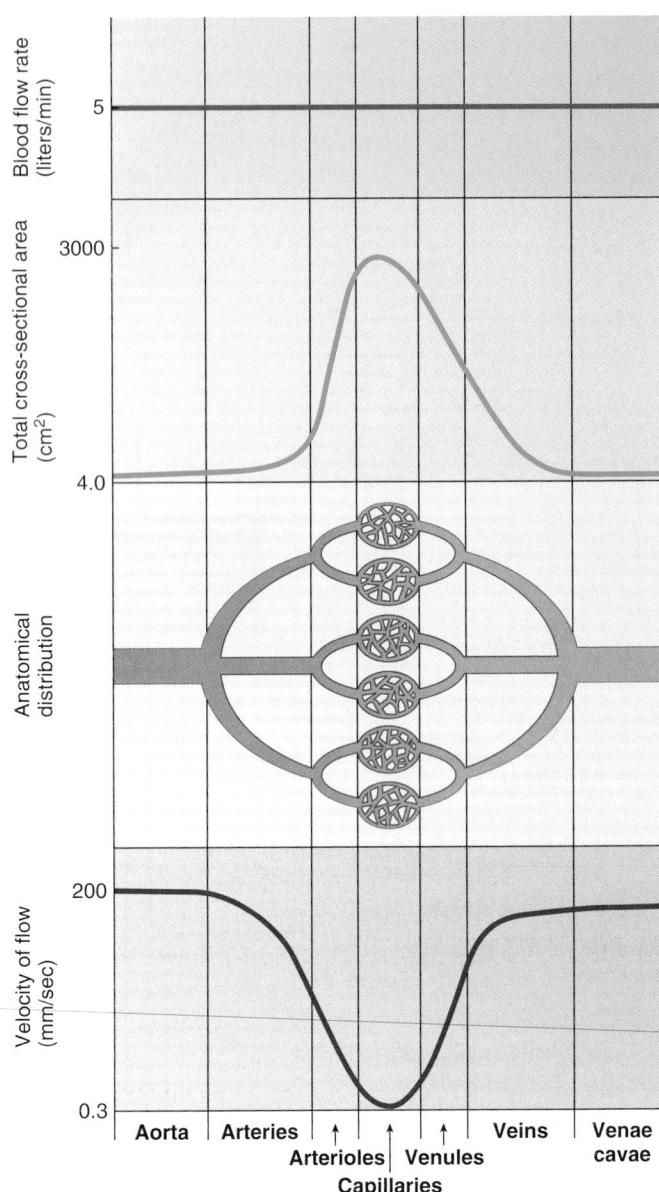

● FIGURE 10-13 **Comparison of blood flow rate and velocity of flow in relation to total cross-sectional area.** The blood flow rate (*red curve*) is identical through all levels of the circulatory system and is equal to the cardiac output (5 L per minute at rest). The velocity of flow (*purple curve*) varies throughout the vascular tree and is inversely proportional to the total cross-sectional area (*green curve*) of all the vessels at a given level. Note that the velocity of flow is slowest in the capillaries, which have the largest total cross-sectional area.

narrow river during a given period. You could readily observe the forward movement of water in the swift-flowing river, but the forward motion of water in the lake would be unnoticeable.

Also, because of the capillaries' tremendous total cross-sectional area, the resistance offered by all capillaries is lower than that offered by all arterioles, even though each capillary has a smaller radius than each arteriole. For this reason, the arterioles contribute more to total peripheral resistance. Furthermore, arteriolar caliber (and, accordingly resistance) is subject to control, whereas capillary caliber cannot be adjusted.

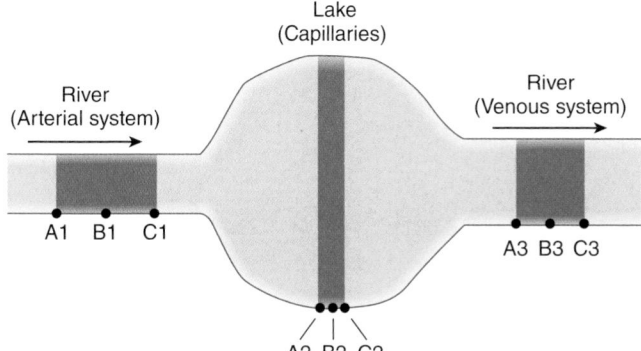

● **FIGURE 10-14 Relationship between total cross-sectional area and velocity of flow.** The three dark blue areas represent equal volumes of water. During 1 minute, this volume of water moves forward from points A to points C. Therefore, an identical volume of water flows past points B1, B2, and B3 during this minute; that is, the flow rate is the same at all points along the length of this body of water. However, during that minute the identical volume of water moves forward a shorter distance in the wide lake (A2 to C2) than in the narrower river (A1 to C1 and A3 to C3). Thus, velocity of flow is slower in the lake than in the river. Similarly, velocity of flow is slower in the capillaries than in the arterial and venous systems.

Water-filled capillary pores permit passage of small, water-soluble substances.

Diffusion across capillary walls also depends on the walls' permeability to the materials being exchanged. The endothelial cells forming the capillary walls fit together like a jigsaw puzzle, but the closeness of the fit varies considerably among organs, as the following examples illustrate:

■ At the tightest extreme, the endothelial cells in brain capillaries are joined by tight junctions (see p. 52). These junctions prevent passage of materials between these cells and thus constitute part of the protective blood–brain barrier (see p. 120).

■ In most capillaries (for example, in skeletal muscle and in lung tissue), the endothelial cells are closely but not tightly joined, and narrow, water-filled **pores** exist at the junctions between these cells (● Figure 10-15). Small, water-soluble substances such as ions, glucose, and amino acids can readily pass through the pores, but large, water-soluble materials such as plasma proteins are kept from passing through. Lipid-soluble substances, such as O_2 and CO_2, can readily pass through the endothelial cells themselves by dissolving in the lipid bilayer barrier of the plasma membrane surrounding the cells.

■ In addition to having the narrow pores between endothelial cells, the leakier capillaries of the kidneys and intestines have larger holes known as **fenestrations** (*fenestra* means "window") that extend through the thickness of the endothelial cells themselves. These through-the-cell passageways are important in the rapid movement of fluid across the capillaries in these organs during the formation of urine and during the absorption of a digested meal, respectively.

For convenience, in the future we lump the between-cell pores and the through-the-cell fenestrations into the single category of *capillary pores.*

Scientists traditionally considered the capillary wall a passive sieve, like a brick wall with permanent gaps in the mortar acting as pores. Recent studies, however, suggest that endothelial cells can actively change to regulate capillary permeability; that is, in response to appropriate signals, the "bricks" can readjust themselves to vary the size of the holes between them. Thus, the degree of leakiness does not necessarily remain constant for a given capillary bed. For example, histamine increases capillary permeability by triggering contractile responses in endothelial cells to widen the intercellular gaps. This is not a muscular contraction, because no smooth muscle cells are present in capillaries; it is the result of an actin–myosin contractile apparatus in the nonmuscular capillary endothelial cells. Because of these enlarged pores, the affected capillary wall is leakier. As a result, normally retained plasma proteins escape into the surrounding tissue, where they exert an osmotic effect. Along with histamine-induced vasodilation, the resulting additional local fluid retention contributes to inflammatory swelling.

Vesicular transport also plays a limited role in the passage of materials across the capillary wall. Large non-lipid-soluble molecules, such as protein hormones that must be exchanged between blood and surrounding tissues, are transported from one side of the capillary wall to the other in endocytic–exocytic vesicles (see p. 66).

Interstitial fluid is a passive intermediary between blood and cells.

Exchanges between blood and tissue cells are not made directly. Interstitial fluid, the true internal environment in immediate contact with the cells, acts as the go-between. Only 20% of the ECF circulates as plasma. The remaining 80% consists of interstitial fluid, which bathes all cells in the body. Cells exchange materials directly with interstitial fluid, with the type and extent of exchange being governed by the properties of cellular plasma membranes. Movement across the plasma membrane may be either passive (that is, by diffusion down electrochemical gradients or by carrier-mediated facilitated diffusion) or active (that is, by carrier-mediated active transport or by vesicular transport) (see ▲ Table 3-2, p. 67).

In contrast, exchanges across the capillary wall between the plasma and the interstitial fluid are largely passive. The only transport across this barrier that requires energy is the limited vesicular transport. Because capillary walls are highly permeable, exchange is so thorough that the interstitial fluid takes on essentially the same composition as incoming arterial blood, with the exception of the large plasma proteins that usually do not escape from the blood. Therefore, when we speak of exchanges between blood and tissue cells, we tacitly include interstitial fluid as a passive intermediary.

Exchanges between blood and surrounding tissues across the capillary walls are accomplished in two ways: (1) passive diffusion down concentration gradients, the primary mechanism for exchanging individual solutes, and (2) bulk flow, a process that fills the different function of determining the distribution of the ECF volume between the vascular and the in-

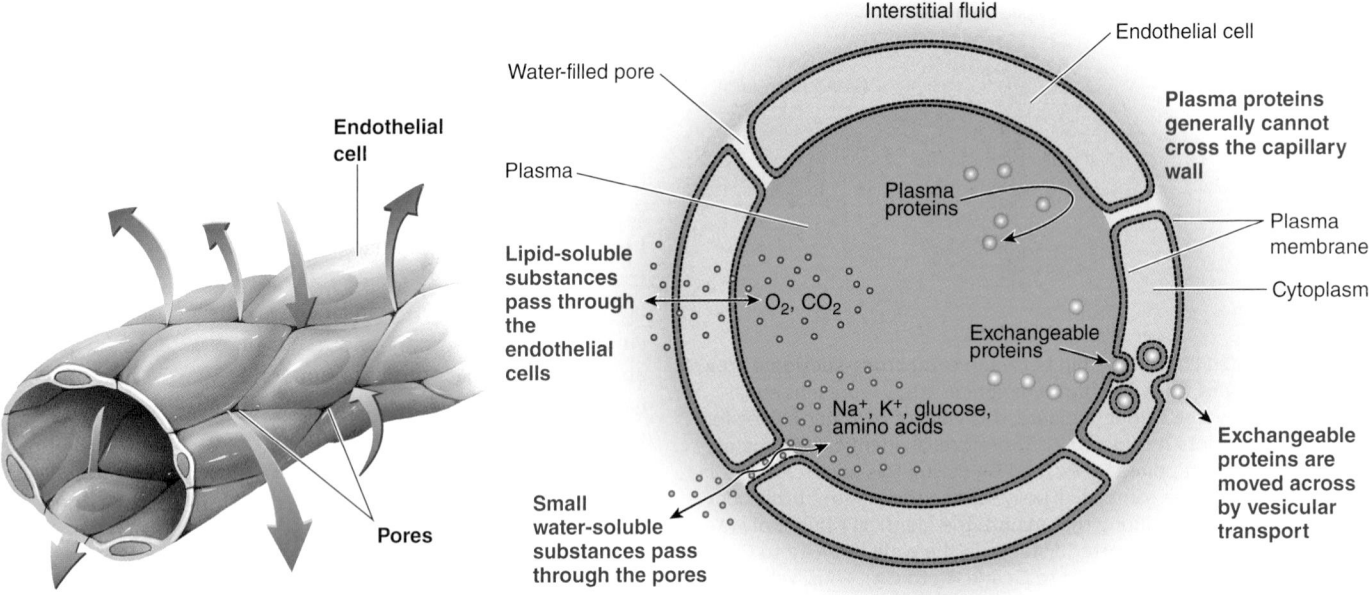

(a) Typical capillary
            (b) Transport across a typical capillary wall

● FIGURE 10-15 **Exchanges across a capillary wall.** (a) Slitlike gaps between adjacent endothelial cells form pores within the capillary wall. (b) As depicted in this cross section of a capillary wall, small water-soluble substances are exchanged between the plasma and the interstitial fluid by passing through the water-filled pores, whereas lipid-soluble substances are exchanged across the capillary wall by passing through the endothelial cells. Proteins to be moved across are exchanged by vesicular transport. (The space between the interior and the exterior layers of the endothelial cell is exaggerated to show vesicular transport.) Plasma proteins generally cannot escape from the plasma across the capillary wall.

terstitial fluid compartments. We now examine each of these mechanisms in more detail, starting with diffusion.

Diffusion across the capillary walls is important in solute exchange.

Because most capillary walls have no carrier-mediated transport systems, solutes cross primarily by diffusion down concentration gradients. The chemical composition of arterial blood is carefully regulated to maintain the concentrations of individual solutes at levels that promote each solute's movement in the appropriate direction across the capillary walls. The reconditioning organs continuously add nutrients and O_2 and remove CO_2 and other wastes as blood passes through them. Meanwhile, cells constantly use up supplies and generate metabolic wastes. As cells use up O_2 and glucose, the blood constantly brings in fresh supplies of these vital materials, maintaining concentration gradients that favor the net diffusion of these substances from blood to cells. Simultaneously, ongoing net diffusion of CO_2 and other metabolic wastes from cells to blood is maintained by the continual production of these wastes at the cell level and by their constant removal by the circulating blood (● Figure 10-16).

Because the capillary wall does not limit the passage of any constituent except plasma proteins, the extent of exchanges for each solute is independently determined by the magnitude of its concentration gradient between blood and surrounding cells. As cells increase their level of activity, they use up more O_2 and

produce more CO_2, among other things. This creates larger concentration gradients for O_2 and CO_2 between these cells and blood, so more O_2 diffuses out of the blood into the cells and more CO_2 proceeds in the opposite direction, to help support the increased metabolic activity.

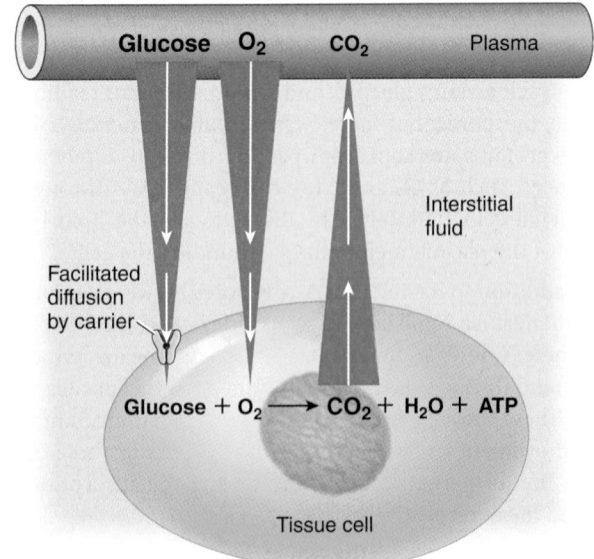

● FIGURE 10-16 **Independent exchange of individual solutes down their own concentration gradients across the capillary wall.**

Bulk flow across the capillary walls is important in extracellular fluid distribution.

The second means by which exchange is accomplished across capillary walls is bulk flow. A volume of protein-free plasma actually filters out of the capillary, mixes with the surrounding interstitial fluid, and then is reabsorbed. This process is called **bulk flow** because the various constituents of the fluid (water and all solutes) are moving in bulk, or as a unit, in contrast to the discrete diffusion of individual solutes down concentration gradients.

The capillary wall acts like a sieve, with fluid moving through its water-filled pores. When pressure inside the capillary exceeds pressure on the outside, fluid is pushed out through the pores in a process known as **ultrafiltration.** Most plasma proteins are retained on the inside during this process because of the pores' filtering effect, although a few do escape. Because all other constituents in plasma are dragged along as a unit with the volume of fluid leaving the capillary, the filtrate is essentially a protein-free plasma. When inward-driving pressures exceed outward pressures across the capillary wall, net inward movement of fluid from the interstitial fluid into the capillaries takes place through the pores, a process known as **reabsorption.**

FORCES INFLUENCING BULK FLOW Bulk flow occurs because of differences in the hydrostatic and the colloid osmotic pressures between plasma and interstitial fluid. Even though pressure differences exist between plasma and surrounding fluid elsewhere in the circulatory system, only the capillaries have pores that let fluids pass through. Four forces influence fluid movement across the capillary wall (● Figure 10-17):

1. **Capillary blood pressure** (P_C) is the fluid or hydrostatic pressure exerted on the inside of the capillary walls by blood. This pressure tends to force fluid *out of* the capillaries into the interstitial fluid. By the level of the capillaries, blood pressure has dropped substantially because of frictional losses in pressure in the high-resistance arterioles upstream. On average, the hydrostatic pressure is 37 mm Hg at the arteriolar end of a tissue capillary (compared to a mean arterial pressure of 93 mm Hg). It de-

clines even further, to 17 mm Hg, at the capillary's venular end because of further frictional loss coupled with the exit of fluid through ultrafiltration along the capillary's length (see ● Figure 10-8, p. 287).

2. **Plasma-colloid osmotic pressure** (π_P) is a force caused by colloidal dispersion of plasma proteins (see p. A-9); it encourages fluid movement *into* the capillaries. Because plasma proteins remain in the plasma rather than entering the interstitial fluid, a protein concentration difference exists between the plasma and the interstitial fluid. Accordingly, a water concentration difference also exists between these two regions. Plasma has a higher protein concentration and a lower water concentration than interstitial fluid does. This difference exerts an osmotic effect that tends to move water from the area of higher water concentration in interstitial fluid to the area of lower water concentration (or higher protein concentration) in plasma (see p. 57). The other plasma constituents do not exert an osmotic effect, because they readily pass through the capillary wall, so their concentrations are equal in plasma and interstitial fluid. Plasma-colloid osmotic pressure averages 25 mm Hg.

3. **Interstitial fluid hydrostatic pressure** (P_{IF}) is the fluid pressure exerted on the outside of the capillary wall by interstitial fluid. This pressure tends to force fluid *into* the capillaries. The value of this pressure varies among tissues and is either at, slightly above, or slightly below atmospheric pressure. For purposes of illustration, we will say it is 1 mm Hg.

4. **Interstitial fluid–colloid osmotic pressure** (π_{IF}) is another force that does not normally contribute significantly to bulk flow. The small fraction of plasma proteins that leak across the capillary walls into the interstitial spaces are normally returned to the blood by the lymphatic system. Therefore, the protein concentration in the interstitial fluid is extremely low, and the interstitial fluid–colloid osmotic pressure is essentially zero. If plasma proteins pathologically leak into the interstitial fluid, however, as they do when histamine widens the capillary pores during tissue injury, the leaked proteins exert an osmotic effect that tends to promote movement of fluid *out of* the capillaries into the interstitial fluid.

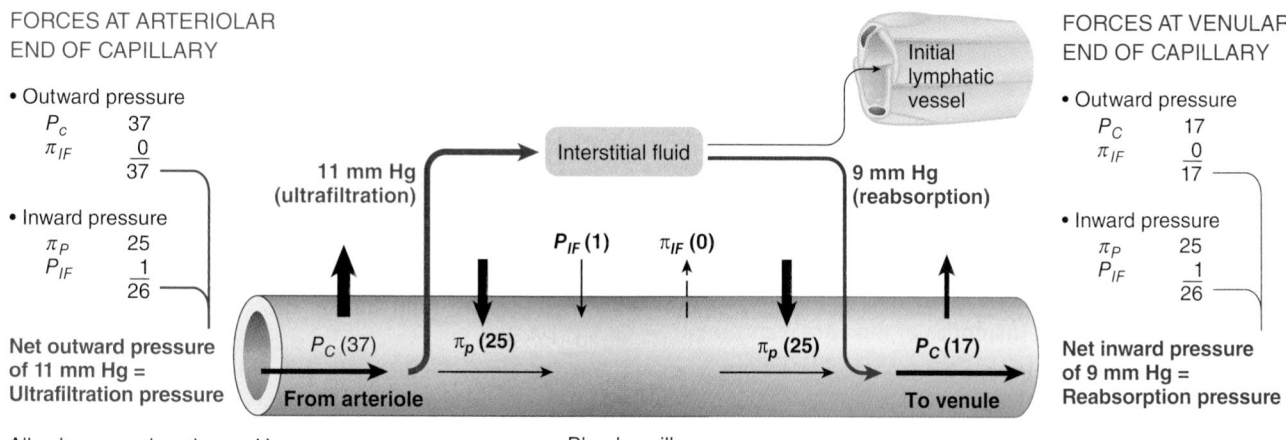

All values are given in mm Hg.

● **FIGURE 10-17 Bulk flow across the capillary wall.** Ultrafiltration occurs at the arteriolar end and reabsorption occurs at the venule end of the capillary as a result of imbalances in the physical forces acting across the capillary wall.

Therefore, the two pressures that tend to force fluid out of the capillary are capillary blood pressure and interstitial fluid–colloid osmotic pressure. The two opposing pressures that tend to force fluid into the capillary are plasma-colloid osmotic pressure and interstitial fluid hydrostatic pressure. Now let us analyze the fluid movement that occurs across a capillary wall because of imbalances in these opposing physical forces (● Figure 10-17).

NET EXCHANGE OF FLUID ACROSS THE CAPILLARY WALL Net exchange at a given point across the capillary wall can be calculated using the following equation:

$$\text{Net exchange pressure} = \underset{\text{(outward pressure)}}{(P_C + \pi_{IF})} - \underset{\text{(inward pressure)}}{(\pi_P + P_{IF})}$$

A positive net exchange pressure (when the outward pressure exceeds the inward pressure) represents an ultrafiltration pressure. A negative net exchange pressure (when the inward pressure exceeds the outward pressure) represents a reabsorption pressure.

At the arteriolar end of the capillary, the outward pressure totals 37 mm Hg, whereas the inward pressure totals 26 mm Hg, for a net outward pressure of 11 mm Hg. Ultrafiltration takes place at the beginning of the capillary as this outward pressure gradient forces a protein-free filtrate through the capillary pores.

By the time the venular end of the capillary is reached, the capillary blood pressure has dropped but the other pressures have remained essentially constant. At this point, the outward pressure has fallen to a total of 17 mm Hg, whereas the total inward pressure is still 26 mm Hg, for a net inward pressure of 9 mm Hg. Reabsorption of fluid takes place as this inward pressure gradient forces fluid back into the capillary at its venular end.

Ultrafiltration and reabsorption, collectively known as *bulk flow*, are thus the result of a shift in the balance between the passive physical forces acting across the capillary wall. No active forces or local energy expenditures are involved in the bulk exchange of fluid between the plasma and the surrounding interstitial fluid. With only minor contributions from the interstitial fluid forces, ultrafiltration occurs at the beginning of the capillary because capillary blood pressure exceeds plasma-colloid osmotic pressure, whereas by the end of the capillary, reabsorption takes place because blood pressure has fallen below osmotic pressure.

It is important to realize that we have taken "snapshots" at two points—at the beginning and at the end—in a hypothetical capillary. Actually, blood pressure gradually diminishes along the length of the capillary so that progressively diminishing quantities of fluid are filtered out in the first half of the vessel and progressively increasing quantities of fluid are reabsorbed in the last half (● Figure 10-18).

ROLE OF BULK FLOW Bulk flow does not play an important role in the exchange of individual solutes between blood and tissues, because the quantity of solutes moved across the capillary wall by bulk flow is extremely small compared to the larger transfer

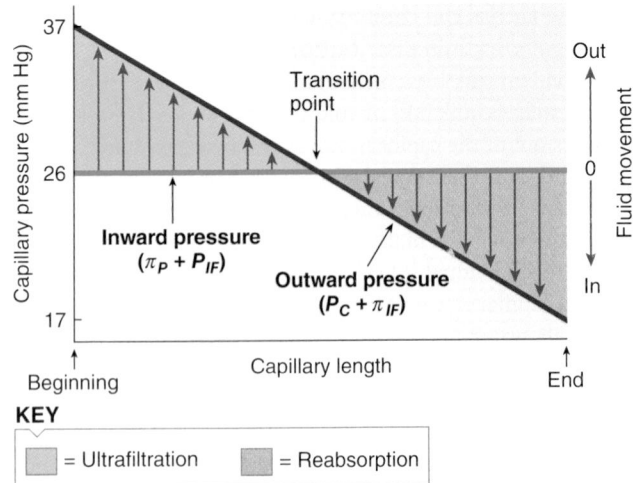

KEY

☐ = Ultrafiltration ☐ = Reabsorption

● **FIGURE 10-18 Net filtration and net reabsorption along the vessel length.** The inward pressure ($\pi_P + P_{IF}$) remains constant throughout the length of the capillary, whereas the outward pressure ($P_C + \pi_{IF}$) progressively declines throughout the capillary's length due to a gradual decrease in P_C. In the first half of the vessel, where the declining outward pressure still exceeds the constant inward pressure, progressively diminishing quantities of fluid are filtered out *(upward red arrows)*. In the last half of the vessel, progressively increasing quantities of fluid are reabsorbed *(downward blue arrows)* as the declining outward pressure falls farther below the constant inward pressure.

of solutes by diffusion. The composition of the fluid filtered out of the capillary is essentially the same as the composition of the fluid that is reabsorbed. Thus, ultrafiltration and reabsorption are not important in the exchange of nutrients and wastes. Bulk flow is extremely important, however, in regulating the distribution of ECF between the plasma and the interstitial fluid. Maintenance of proper arterial blood pressure depends in part on an appropriate volume of circulating blood. If plasma volume is reduced (for example, by hemorrhage), blood pressure falls. The resultant lowering of capillary blood pressure alters the balance of forces across the capillary walls. Because the net outward pressure is decreased while the net inward pressure remains unchanged, extra fluid is shifted from the interstitial compartment into the plasma as a result of reduced filtration and increased reabsorption. The extra fluid soaked up from the interstitial fluid provides additional fluid for the plasma, temporarily compensating for the loss of blood. Meanwhile, reflex mechanisms acting on the heart and blood vessels (described later) also come into play to help maintain blood pressure until long-term mechanisms, such as thirst (and its satisfaction) and reduction of urinary output, can restore the fluid volume to completely compensate for the loss.

Conversely, if the plasma volume becomes overexpanded, as with excessive fluid intake, the resulting rise in capillary blood pressure forces extra fluid from the capillaries into the interstitial fluid, temporarily relieving the expanded plasma volume until the excess fluid can be eliminated from the body by long-term measures, such as increased urinary output.

These internal fluid shifts between the two ECF compartments occur automatically and immediately whenever the balance of forces acting across the capillary walls is changed; they provide a temporary mechanism to help keep plasma volume fairly constant. In the process of restoring plasma volume to an appropriate level, interstitial fluid volume fluctuates, but it is more important that plasma volume be kept constant to ensure that the circulatory system functions effectively.

The lymphatic system is an accessory route by which interstitial fluid can be returned to the blood.

Even under normal circumstances, slightly more fluid is filtered out of the capillaries into the interstitial fluid than is reabsorbed from the interstitial fluid back into the plasma. On average, the net ultrafiltration pressure starts at 11 mm Hg at the beginning of the capillary, whereas the net reabsorption pressure only reaches 9 mm Hg by the vessel's end (see ● Figure 10-17). Because of this pressure differential, on average more fluid is filtered out of the first half of the capillary than is reabsorbed in its last half. The extra fluid filtered out as a result of this filtration–reabsorption imbalance is picked up by the **lymphatic system**. This extensive network of one-way vessels provides an accessory route by which fluid can be returned from the interstitial fluid to the blood. The lymphatic system functions much like a storm sewer that picks up and carries away excess rainwater so that it does not accumulate and flood an area.

PICKUP AND FLOW OF LYMPH Small, blind-ended terminal lymph vessels known as **initial lymphatics** permeate almost every tissue of the body (● Figure 10-19a). The endothelial cells forming the walls of initial lymphatics slightly overlap like shingles on a roof, with their overlapping edges being free instead of attached to the surrounding cells. This arrangement creates one-way, valvelike openings in the vessel wall. Fluid pressure on the outside of the vessel pushes the innermost edge of a pair of overlapping edges inward, creating a gap between the edges (that is, opening the valve). This opening permits interstitial fluid to enter (● Figure 10-19b). Once interstitial fluid enters a lymphatic vessel, it is called **lymph**. Fluid pressure on the inside forces the overlapping edges together, closing the valves so that lymph does not escape. These lymphatic valvelike openings are larger than the pores in blood capillaries. Consequently, large particles in the interstitial fluid, such as escaped plasma proteins and bacteria, can gain access to initial lymphatics but are excluded from blood capillaries.

Initial lymphatics converge to form larger and larger **lymph vessels,** which eventually empty into the venous system near where the blood enters the right atrium (● Figure 10-20a). Because there is no "lymphatic heart" to provide driving pressure, you may wonder how lymph is directed from the tissues toward the venous system in the thoracic cavity. Lymph flow is accomplished by two mechanisms. First, lymph vessels beyond the initial lymphatics are surrounded by smooth muscle, which contracts rhythmically as a result of myogenic activity. When this muscle is stretched because the vessel is distended with lymph, the muscle inherently contracts more forcefully, pushing the lymph through the vessel. This intrinsic "lymph pump" is the major force for propelling lymph. Stimulation of lymphatic smooth muscle by the sympathetic nervous system further in-

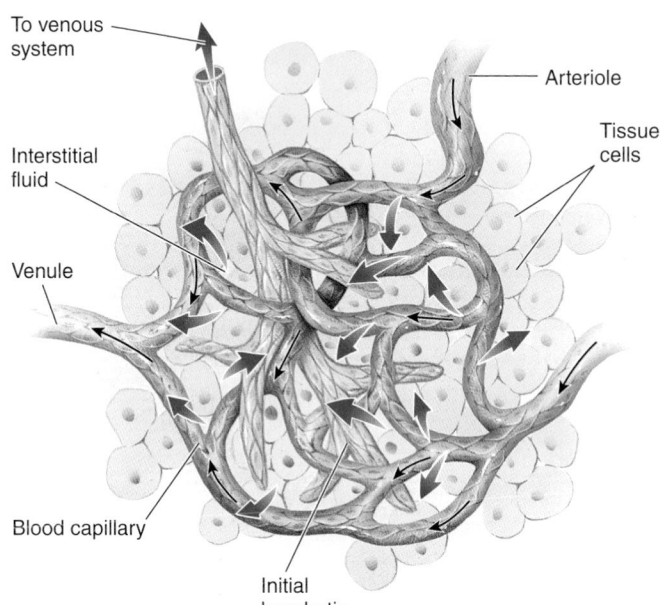

(a) Relationship between initial lymphatics and blood capillaries

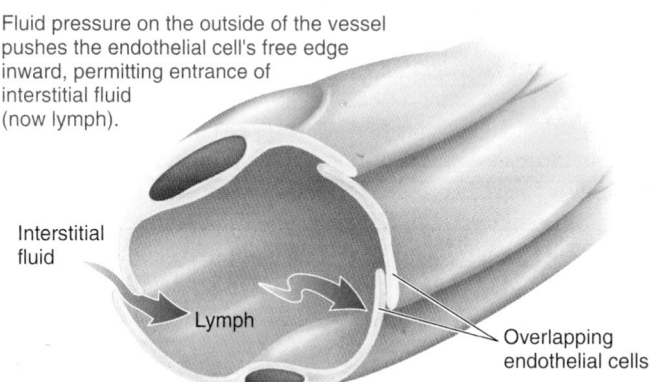

Fluid pressure on the outside of the vessel pushes the endothelial cell's free edge inward, permitting entrance of interstitial fluid (now lymph).

Fluid pressure on the inside of the vessel forces the overlapping edges together so that lymph cannot escape.

(b) Arrangement of endothelial cells in an initial lymphatic

● **FIGURE 10-19 Initial lymphatics.** (a) Blind-ended initial lymphatics pick up excess fluid filtered by blood capillaries and return it to the venous system. The blue arrows show fluid filtering out of and reentering the capillaries, with some fluid entering the initial lymphatic instead. (b) Note that the overlapping edges of the endothelial cells create valvelike openings in the vessel wall.

creases the pumping activity of the lymph vessels. Second, because lymph vessels lie between skeletal muscles, contraction of these muscles squeezes the lymph out of the vessels. One-way valves spaced at intervals within the lymph vessels direct the flow of lymph toward its venous outlet in the chest.

FUNCTIONS OF THE LYMPHATIC SYSTEM Here are the most important functions of the lymphatic system:

■ *Return of excess filtered fluid.* Normally, capillary filtration exceeds reabsorption by about 3 liters per day (20 liters filtered, 17 liters reabsorbed) (● Figure 10-20b). Yet the entire blood volume is only 5 liters, and only 2.75 liters of that is plasma. (Blood cells make up the rest of the blood volume.) With an

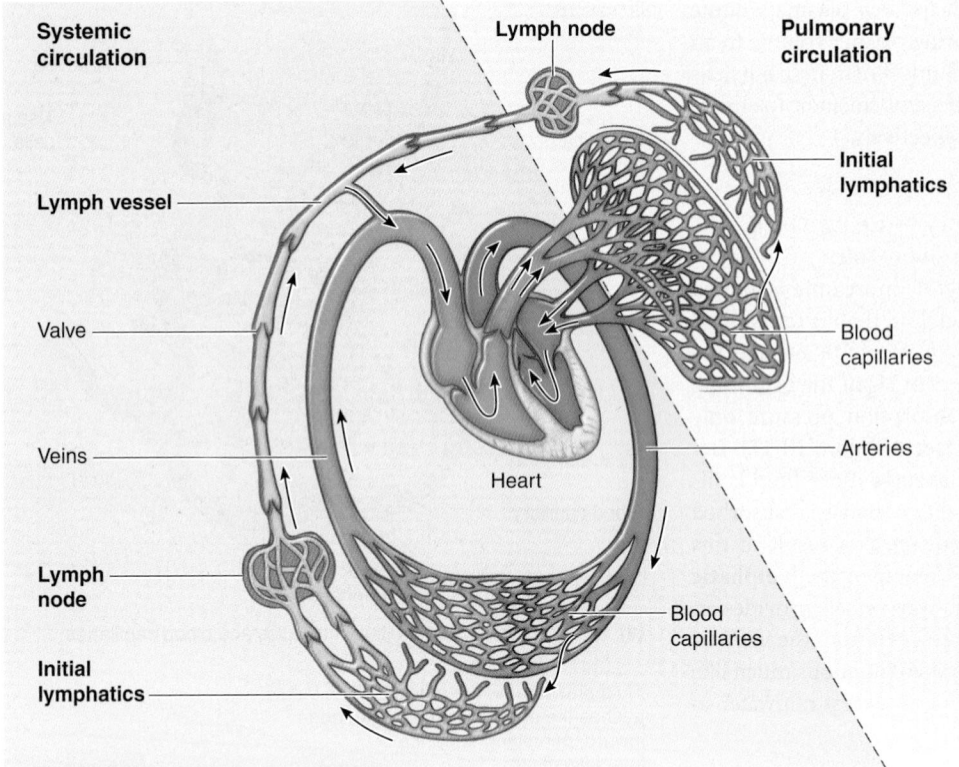

(a) Relationship of lymphatic system to circulatory system

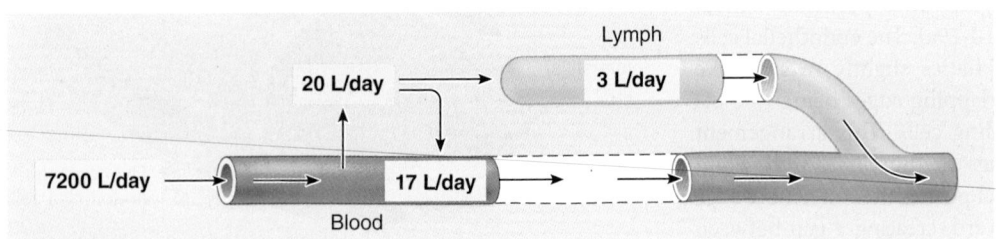

(b) Comparison of blood flow and lymph flow per day

● **FIGURE 10-20 Lymphatic system.** (a) Lymph empties into the venous system near its entrance to the right atrium. (b) Lymph flow averages 3 liters per day, whereas blood flow averages 7200 liters per day.

■ *Transport of absorbed fat.* The lymphatic system is important in the absorption of fat from the digestive tract. The end products of the digestion of dietary fats are packaged by cells lining the digestive tract into fatty particles that are too large to gain access to the blood capillaries but can easily enter the initial lymphatics (see Chapter 15).

■ *Return of filtered protein.* Most capillaries permit leakage of a small amount of plasma proteins during filtration. These proteins cannot readily be reabsorbed back into the blood capillaries but can easily gain access to the initial lymphatics. If the proteins were allowed to accumulate in the interstitial fluid rather than being returned to the circulation via the lymphatics, the interstitial fluid–colloid osmotic pressure (an outward pressure) would progressively increase while the plasma-colloid osmotic pressure (an inward pressure) would progressively fall. As a result, filtration forces would gradually increase and reabsorption forces would gradually decrease, resulting in progressive accumulation of fluid in the interstitial spaces at the expense of loss of plasma volume.

average cardiac output, 7200 liters of blood pass through the capillaries daily under resting conditions (more when cardiac output increases). Even though only a small fraction of the filtered fluid is not reabsorbed by the blood capillaries, the cumulative effect of this process being repeated with every heartbeat results in the equivalent of more than the entire plasma volume being left behind in the interstitial fluid each day. Obviously, this fluid must be returned to the circulating plasma, and this task is accomplished by the lymph vessels. The average rate of flow through the lymph vessels is 3 liters per day, compared with 7200 liters per day through the circulatory system.

■ *Defense against disease.* The lymph percolates through **lymph nodes** located en route within the lymphatic system. Passage of this fluid through the lymph nodes is an important aspect of the body's defense mechanism against disease. For example, bacteria picked up from the interstitial fluid are destroyed by special phagocytes within the lymph nodes (see Chapter 11).

Edema occurs when too much interstitial fluid accumulates.

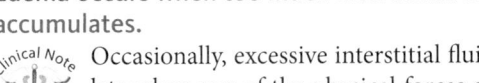

Occasionally, excessive interstitial fluid does accumulate when one of the physical forces acting across the capillary walls becomes abnormal for some reason. Swelling of the tissues because of excess interstitial fluid is known as **edema.** The causes of edema can be grouped into four categories:

1. *A reduced concentration of plasma proteins* decreases π_P. Such a drop in the major inward pressure lets excess fluid filter out, whereas less-than-normal amounts of fluid are reabsorbed; hence, extra fluid remains in the interstitial spaces. Edema can be caused by a decreased concentration of plasma proteins in several ways: excessive loss of plasma proteins in the urine, from kidney disease; reduced synthesis of plasma proteins, from liver disease (the liver synthesizes almost all plasma proteins); a diet deficient in protein; or significant loss of plasma proteins from large burned surfaces.

2. *Increased permeability of the capillary walls* allows more plasma proteins than usual to pass from the plasma into the surrounding interstitial fluid—for example, via histamine-induced widening of the capillary pores during tissue injury or allergic reactions. The resultant fall in π_P decreases the effective inward pressure, whereas the resultant rise in π_{IF} caused by excess protein in the interstitial fluid increases the effective outward force. This imbalance contributes in part to the localized edema associated with injuries (for example, blisters) and allergic responses (for example, hives).

3. *Increased venous pressure,* as when blood dams up in the veins, is accompanied by increased P_C. Because the capillaries drain into the veins, damming of blood in the veins leads to a "backlog" of blood in the capillaries because less blood moves out of the capillaries into the overloaded veins than enters from the arterioles. The resultant elevation in outward hydrostatic pressure across the capillary walls is largely responsible for the edema seen with congestive heart failure (see p. 268). Regional edema can also occur because of localized restriction of venous return. An example is the swelling often occurring in the legs and feet during pregnancy. The enlarged uterus compresses the major veins that drain the lower extremities as these vessels enter the abdominal cavity. The resultant damming of blood in these veins raises blood pressure in the capillaries of the legs and feet, which promotes regional edema of the lower extremities.

4. *Blockage of lymph vessels* produces edema because the excess filtered fluid is retained in the interstitial fluid rather than returned to the blood through the lymphatics. Protein accumulation in the interstitial fluid compounds the problem through its os-

motic effect. Local lymph blockage can occur, for example, in the arms of women whose major lymphatic drainage channels from the arm have been blocked as a result of lymph node removal during surgery for breast cancer. More widespread lymph blockage occurs with *filariasis,* a mosquito-borne parasitic disease found predominantly in tropical coastal regions. In this condition, small, threadlike filaria worms infect the lymph vessels, where their presence prevents proper lymph drainage. The affected body parts, particularly the scrotum and extremities, become grossly edematous. The condition is often called *elephantiasis* because of the elephant-like appearance of the swollen extremities (● Figure 10-21).

Whatever the cause of edema, an important consequence is reduced exchange of materials between blood and cells. As excess interstitial fluid accumulates, the distance between blood and cells across which nutrients, O_2, and wastes must diffuse increases, so the rate of diffusion decreases. Therefore, cells within edematous tissues may not be adequately supplied.

Veins

The venous system completes the circulatory circuit. Blood leaving the capillary beds enters the venous system for transport back to the heart.

Veins serve as a blood reservoir, as well as passageways back to the heart.

Veins have a large radius, so they offer little resistance to flow. Furthermore, because the total cross-sectional area of the venous system gradually decreases as smaller veins converge into progressively fewer but larger vessels, blood flow speeds up as blood approaches the heart.

In addition to serving as low-resistance passageways to return blood from the tissues to the heart, systemic veins also serve as a *blood reservoir.* Because of their storage capacity, veins are often called **capacitance vessels.** Veins have thinner walls with less smooth muscle than arteries do. Also, in contrast to arteries, veins have little elasticity, because venous connective tissue contains considerably more collagen fibers than elastin fibers (see ▲ Table 10-1, p. 284). Unlike arteriolar smooth muscle, venous smooth muscle has little inherent myogenic tone. Because of these features, veins are highly distensible, or stretchable, and have little elastic recoil. They easily distend to accommodate additional volumes of blood with only a small increase in venous pressure. Arteries stretched by an excess volume of blood recoil because of the elastin fibers in their walls, driving the blood forward. Veins containing an extra volume of blood simply stretch to accommodate the additional blood without tending to recoil. In this way veins serve as a **blood reservoir;** that is, when demands for blood are low, the veins can store extra blood in reserve because of their passive distensibility. Under resting conditions, the veins contain more than 60% of the total blood volume (● Figure 10-22).

When the stored blood is needed, such as during exercise, extrinsic factors (soon to be described) reduce the capacity of

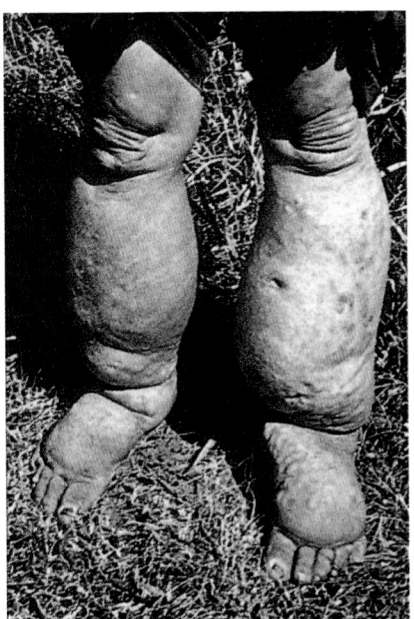

● **FIGURE 10-21 Elephantiasis.** This tropical condition is caused by a mosquito-borne parasitic worm that invades the lymph vessels. As a result of the interference with lymph drainage, the affected body parts, usually the extremities, become grossly edematous, appearing elephant-like.

© Fred Marsik/Visuals Unlimited

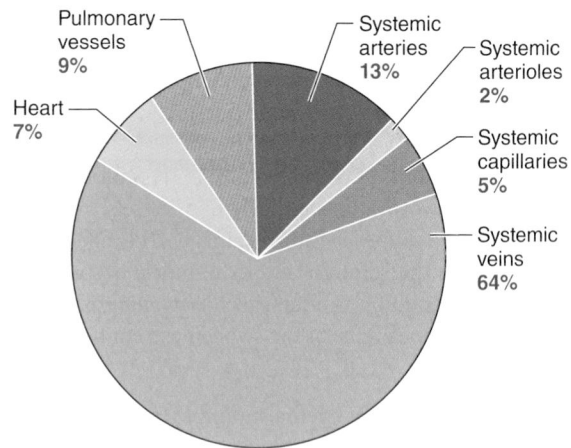

● FIGURE 10-22 **Percentage of total blood volume in different parts of the circulatory system.**

Pulmonary vessels 9%
Systemic arteries 13%
Systemic arterioles 2%
Heart 7%
Systemic capillaries 5%
Systemic veins 64%

the venous reservoir and drive the extra blood from the veins to the heart so that it can be pumped to the tissues. Increased venous return leads to an increased cardiac stroke volume, in accordance with the Frank–Starling law of the heart (see p. 265). In contrast, if too much blood pools in the veins instead of being returned to the heart, cardiac output is abnormally diminished. Thus, a delicate balance exists among the capacity of the veins, the extent of venous return, and the cardiac output. We now turn our attention to the factors that affect venous capacity and contribute to venous return.

Venous return is enhanced by several extrinsic factors.

Venous capacity (the volume of blood that the veins can accommodate) depends on the distensibility of the vein walls (how much they can stretch to hold blood) and the influence of any externally applied pressure squeezing inwardly on the veins. At a constant blood volume, as venous capacity increases, more blood remains in the veins instead of being returned to the heart. Such venous storage decreases the effective circulating blood volume, the volume of blood being returned to and pumped out of the heart. Conversely, when venous capacity decreases, more blood is returned to the heart and is subsequently pumped out. Thus, changes in venous capacity directly influence the magnitude of venous return, which in turn is an important (although not the only) determinant of effective circulating blood volume. The effective circulating blood volume is also influenced short term by passive shifts in bulk flow between the vascular and the interstitial fluid compartments and long term by factors that control total ECF volume, such as salt and water balance.

The term **venous return** refers to the volume of blood per minute entering each atrium from the veins. Recall that the magnitude of flow through a vessel is directly proportional to the pressure gradient. Much driving pressure imparted to the blood by cardiac contraction has been lost by the time the blood reaches the venous system because of frictional losses along the way, especially during passage through the high-resistance arterioles. By the time the blood enters the venous system, blood pressure averages only 17 mm Hg (see ● Figure 10-8, p. 287). However, because atrial pressure is near 0 mm Hg, a small but adequate driving pressure still exists to promote the flow of blood through the large-radius, low-resistance veins.

Clinical Note If atrial pressure becomes pathologically elevated, as in the presence of a leaky AV valve, the venous-to-atrial pressure gradient is decreased, reducing venous return and causing blood to dam up in the venous system. Elevated atrial pressure, among other more common causes, thus can lead to congestive heart failure (see p. 268).

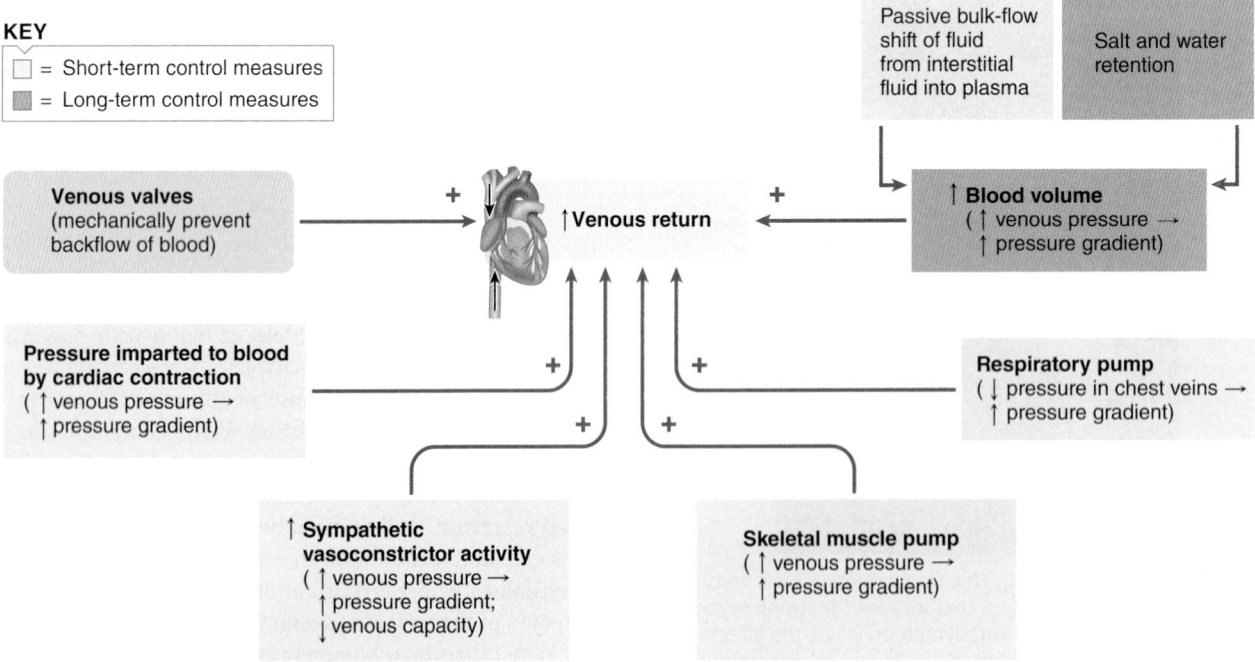

KEY
□ = Short-term control measures
▓ = Long-term control measures

Passive bulk-flow shift of fluid from interstitial fluid into plasma

Salt and water retention

Venous valves (mechanically prevent backflow of blood)

↑**Venous return**

↑ **Blood volume** (↑ venous pressure → ↑ pressure gradient)

Pressure imparted to blood by cardiac contraction (↑ venous pressure → ↑ pressure gradient)

Respiratory pump (↓ pressure in chest veins → ↑ pressure gradient)

↑ **Sympathetic vasoconstrictor activity** (↑ venous pressure → ↑ pressure gradient; ↓ venous capacity)

Skeletal muscle pump (↑ venous pressure → ↑ pressure gradient)

● FIGURE 10-23 **Factors that facilitate venous return.**

In addition to the driving pressure imparted by cardiac contraction, four other factors enhance venous return: sympathetically induced venous vasoconstriction, skeletal muscle activity, the effect of venous valves, and respiratory activity (● Figure 10-23). Most of these secondary factors affect venous return by influencing the pressure gradient between the veins and the heart. We examine each in turn.

EFFECT OF SYMPATHETIC ACTIVITY ON VENOUS RETURN Veins are not very muscular and have little inherent tone, but venous smooth muscle is abundantly supplied with sympathetic nerve fibers. Sympathetic stimulation produces venous vasoconstriction, which modestly elevates venous pressure; this, in turn, increases the pressure gradient to drive more of the stored blood from the veins into the right atrium, thus enhancing venous return. Veins normally have such a large radius that the moderate vasoconstriction from sympathetic stimulation has little effect on resistance to flow. Even when constricted, veins still have a relatively large radius and are still low-resistance vessels.

It is important to recognize the different outcomes of vasoconstriction in arterioles and veins. Arteriolar vasoconstriction immediately *reduces* flow through these vessels because of their increased resistance (less blood can enter and flow through a narrowed arteriole), whereas venous vasoconstriction immediately *increases* flow through these vessels because of their decreased capacity (narrowing of veins squeezes out more of the blood already in the veins, increasing blood flow through these vessels).

Increased venous return leads to increased cardiac output because of the increase in end-diastolic volume. Sympathetic stimulation of the heart also increases cardiac output by increasing the heart rate and increasing the heart's contractility (see p. 264 and p. 266). As long as sympathetic activity remains elevated, as during exercise, the heart pumps out more blood than usual for use by the exercising muscles.

EFFECT OF SKELETAL MUSCLE ACTIVITY ON VENOUS RETURN Many large veins in the extremities lie between skeletal muscles, so muscle contraction compresses the veins. This external venous compression decreases venous capacity and increases venous pressure, in effect squeezing fluid in the veins forward toward the heart (● Figure 10-24). This pumping action, known as the **skeletal muscle pump,** is another way extra blood stored in the veins is returned to the heart during exercise. Increased muscular activity pushes more blood out of the veins and into the heart.

The skeletal muscle pump also counters the effect of gravity on the venous system. Let us see how.

COUNTERING THE EFFECTS OF GRAVITY ON THE VENOUS SYSTEM The average pressures mentioned thus far for various regions of the vascular tree are for a person in the horizontal position. When a person is lying down, the force of gravity is uniformly applied, so it need not be considered. When a person stands up, however, gravitational effects are not uniform. In addition to the usual pressure from cardiac contraction, vessels below heart level are subject to pressure from the weight of the column of blood extending from the heart to the level of the vessel (● Figure 10-25).

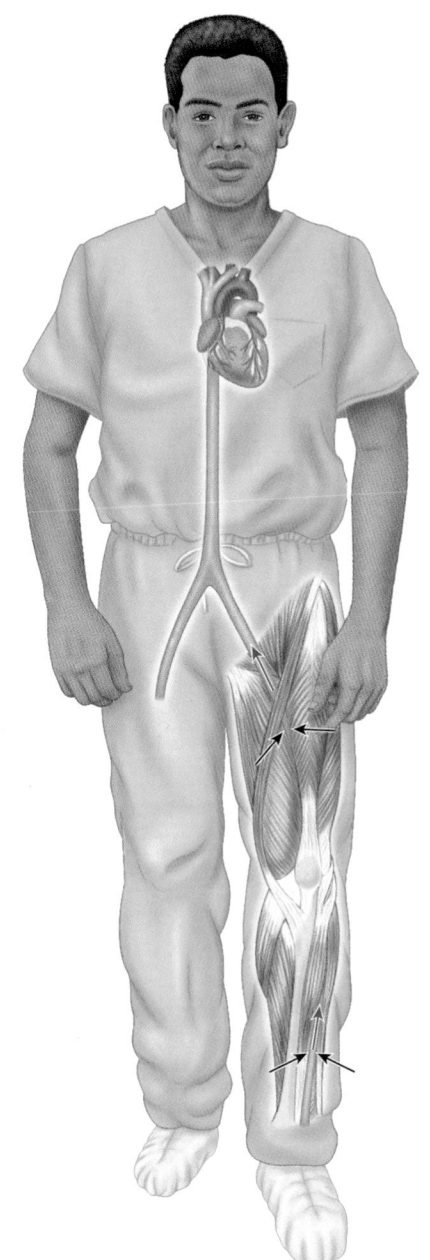

● FIGURE 10-24 **Skeletal muscle pump enhancing venous return.**

This increased pressure has two important consequences. First, the distensible veins yield under the increased hydrostatic pressure, further expanding so that their capacity is increased. Even though the arteries are subject to the same gravitational effects, they are not nearly as distensible and do not expand like the veins. Much of the blood entering from the capillaries tends to pool in the expanded lower-leg veins instead of returning to the heart. Because venous return is reduced, cardiac output decreases and the effective circulating volume shrinks. Second, the marked increase in capillary blood pressure resulting from the effect of gravity causes excessive fluid to filter out of capillary beds in the lower extremities, producing localized edema (that is, swollen feet and ankles).

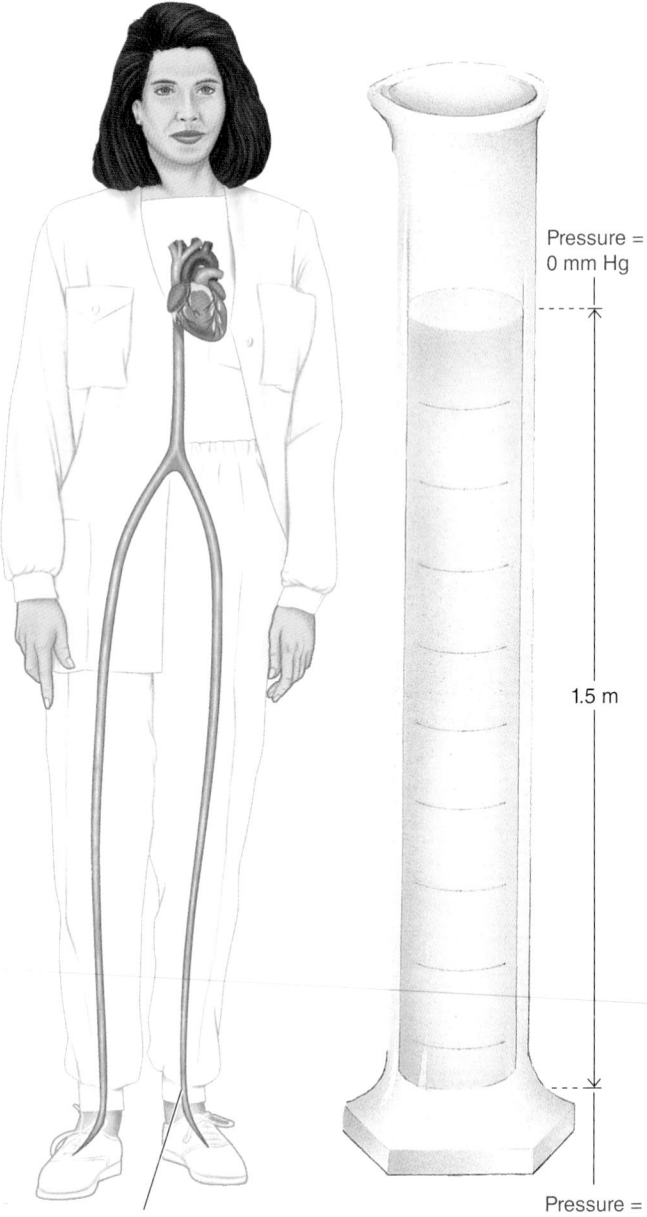

Pressure = 0 mm Hg

1.5 m

Pressure = 90 mm Hg

Pressure = 100 mm Hg

90 mm Hg caused by gravitational effect

10 mm Hg caused by pressure imparted by cardiac contraction

● FIGURE 10-25 Effect of gravity on venous pressure. In an upright adult, the blood in the vessels extending between the heart and the foot is equivalent to a 1.5-m column of blood. The pressure exerted by this column of blood as a result of the effect of gravity is 90 mm Hg. The pressure imparted to the blood by the heart has declined to about 10 mm Hg in the lower-leg veins because of frictional losses in preceding vessels. Together, these pressures produce a venous pressure of 100 mm Hg in the ankle and foot veins. The capillaries in the region are subjected to these same gravitational effects.

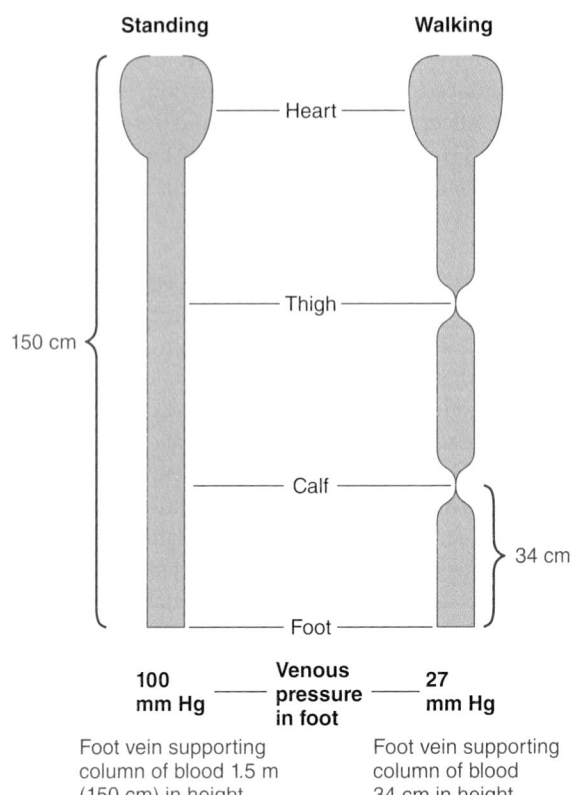

Standing		Walking
	Heart	
150 cm	Thigh	
	Calf	
		34 cm
	Foot	

100 mm Hg	Venous pressure in foot	27 mm Hg
Foot vein supporting column of blood 1.5 m (150 cm) in height		Foot vein supporting column of blood 34 cm in height

● FIGURE 10-26 Effect of contraction of the skeletal muscles of the legs in counteracting the effects of gravity. Contraction of skeletal muscles (as in walking) completely empties given vein segments, interrupting the column of blood that the lower veins must support.

Two compensatory measures normally counteract these gravitational effects. First, the resultant fall in mean arterial pressure that occurs when a person moves from a lying-down to an upright position triggers sympathetically induced venous vasoconstriction, which drives some of the pooled blood forward. Second, the skeletal muscle pump "interrupts" the column of blood by completely emptying given vein segments intermittently so that a particular portion of a vein is not subjected to the weight of the entire venous column from the heart to that portion's level (● Figure 10-26; also see ● Figure 10-24). Reflex venous vasoconstriction cannot completely compensate for gravitational effects without skeletal muscle activity. When a person stands still for a long time, therefore, blood flow to the brain is reduced because of the decline in effective circulating volume, despite reflexes aimed at maintaining mean arterial pressure. Reduced flow of blood to the brain, in turn, leads to fainting, which returns the person to a horizontal position, eliminating the gravitational effects on the vascular system and restoring effective circulation. For this reason, it is counterproductive to try to hold upright someone who has fainted. Fainting is a remedy to the problem, not the problem itself.

Because the skeletal muscle pump facilitates venous return and helps counteract the detrimental effects of gravity on the circulatory system, when you are working at a desk, it's a good idea to get up periodically and, when you are on your feet, to move around. The mild muscular activity "gets the blood moving." It is further recommended that people who must be on their feet for long periods use elastic stockings that apply a continuous gentle external compression, similar to the effect of

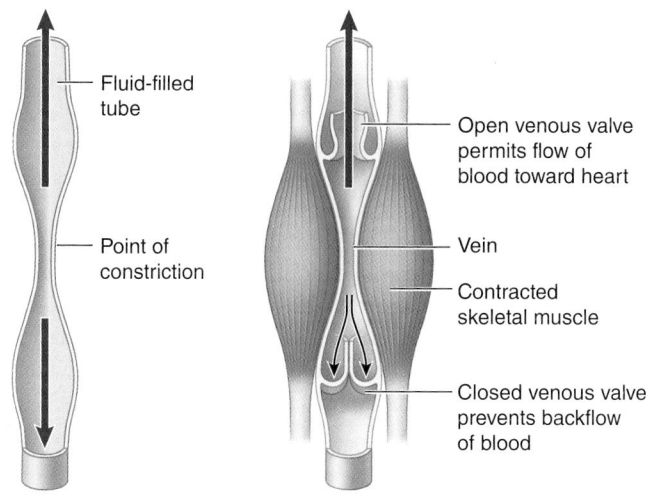

(a) Fluid moving in both directions on squeezing a fluid-filled tube

(b) Action of venous valves, permitting flow of blood toward heart and preventing backflow of blood

● **FIGURE 10-27 Function of venous valves.** (a) When a tube is squeezed in the middle, fluid is pushed in both directions. (b) Venous valves permit the flow of blood only toward the heart.

skeletal muscle contraction, to further counter the effect of gravitational pooling of blood in the leg veins.

EFFECT OF VENOUS VALVES ON VENOUS RETURN Venous vasoconstriction and external venous compression both drive blood toward the heart. Yet if you squeeze a fluid-filled tube in the middle, fluid is pushed in both directions from the point of constriction (● Figure 10-27a). Then why isn't blood driven backward, as well as forward, by venous vasoconstriction and the skeletal muscle pump? Blood can only be driven forward because the large veins are equipped with one-way valves spaced at 2 to 4 cm intervals; these valves let blood move forward toward the heart but keep it from moving back toward the tissues (● Figure 10-27b).

 **Varicose veins** occur when the venous valves become incompetent and can no longer support the column of blood above them. People predisposed to

this condition usually have inherited an overdistensibility and weakness of their vein walls. Aggravated by frequent, prolonged standing, the veins become so distended as blood pools in them that the edges of the valves can no longer meet to form a seal. Varicosed superficial leg veins become visibly overdistended and tortuous. Contrary to what might be expected, chronic pooling of blood in the pathologically distended veins does not reduce cardiac output, because there is a compensatory increase in total circulating blood volume. Instead, the most serious consequence of varicose veins is the possibility of abnormal clot formation in the sluggish, pooled blood. Particularly dangerous is the risk that these clots may break loose and block small vessels elsewhere, especially the pulmonary capillaries.

EFFECT OF RESPIRATORY ACTIVITY ON VENOUS RETURN As a result of respiratory activity, the pressure within the chest cavity averages 5 mm Hg less than atmospheric pressure (that is, is subatmospheric). As the venous system returns blood to the heart from the lower regions of the body, it travels through the chest cavity, where it is exposed to this subatmospheric pressure. Because the venous system in the limbs and abdomen is subject to normal atmospheric pressure, an externally applied pressure gradient exists between the lower veins (at atmospheric pressure) and the chest veins (at less than atmospheric pressure). This pressure difference moves blood from the lower veins to the chest veins, promoting increased venous return (● Figure 10-28). This mechanism of facilitating venous return is called the **respiratory pump** because it results from respiratory activity. Increased respiratory activity, as well as the effects of the skeletal muscle pump and venous vasoconstriction, enhances venous return during exercise.

Blood Pressure

Mean arterial pressure is the blood pressure that is monitored and regulated in the body, not the arterial systolic or diastolic pressure, the pulse pressure, or the pressure in any other part of the vascular tree. Routine blood pressure measurements record the arterial systolic and diastolic pressures, which can be used as a yardstick for assessing mean arterial pressure.

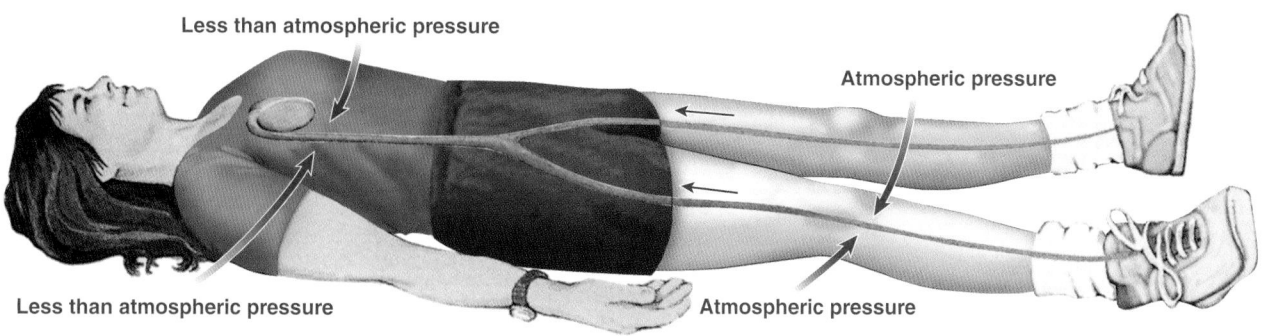

● **FIGURE 10-28 Respiratory pump enhancing venous return.** As a result of respiratory activity, the pressure surrounding the chest veins is lower than the pressure surrounding the veins in the extremities and abdomen. This establishes an externally applied pressure gradient on the veins, which drives blood toward the heart.

Blood pressure is regulated by controlling cardiac output, total peripheral resistance, and blood volume.

Mean arterial pressure is the main driving force for propelling blood to the tissues. This pressure must be closely regulated for two reasons. First, it must be high enough to ensure sufficient driving pressure; without this pressure, the brain and other organs will not receive adequate flow, no matter what local adjustments are made in the resistance of the arterioles supplying them. Second, the pressure must not be so high that it creates extra work for the heart and increases the risk of vascular damage and possible rupture of small blood vessels.

DETERMINANTS OF MEAN ARTERIAL PRESSURE Elaborate mechanisms involving the integrated action of the various components of the circulatory system and other body systems are vital in regulating this all-important mean arterial pressure (● Figure 10-29). Remember that the two determinants of mean arterial pressure are cardiac output and total peripheral resistance:

$$\text{Mean arterial pressure} = \text{cardiac output} \times \text{total peripheral resistance}$$

(Do not confuse this equation, which indicates the factors that *determine* the mean arterial pressure, namely, the magnitude of both cardiac output and total peripheral resistance, with the equation used to *calculate* mean arterial pressure, namely, mean arterial pressure = diastolic pressure + 1/3 pulse pressure.)

Recall that a number of factors, in turn, determine cardiac output and total peripheral resistance (see ● Figure 9-22, p. 267; ● Figure 10-11, p. 293; and ● Figure 10-23, p. 302). Thus, you can quickly appreciate the complexity of blood pressure regulation. Let us work through ● Figure 10-29, reviewing all the factors that affect mean arterial pressure. Even though we have covered all these factors before, it is useful to pull them together. The numbers in the text correspond to the numbers in the figure.

■ Mean arterial pressure depends on cardiac output and total peripheral resistance (**1** on ● Figure 10-29).

■ Cardiac output depends on heart rate and stroke volume **2**.

■ Heart rate depends on the relative balance of parasympathetic activity **3**, which decreases heart rate, and sympathetic activity (including epinephrine throughout this discussion) **4**, which increases heart rate.

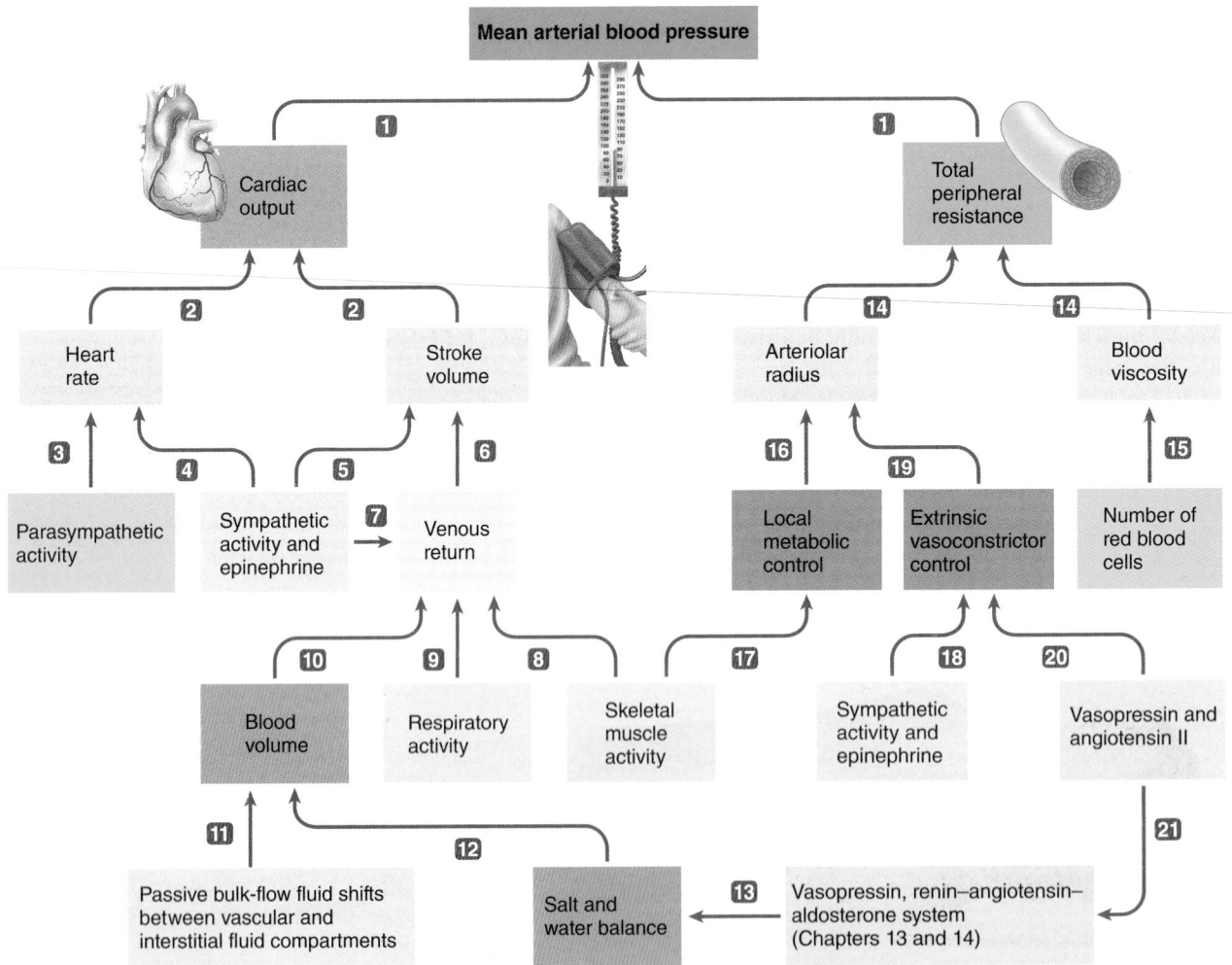

● **FIGURE 10-29 Determinants of mean arterial blood pressure.** Note that this figure is basically a composite of Figure 9-22, p. 267, "Control of cardiac output"; Figure 10-11, p. 293, "Factors affecting total peripheral resistance"; and Figure 10-23, p. 302, "Factors that facilitate venous return." See the text for a discussion of the numbers.

- Stroke volume increases in response to sympathetic activity **5** (extrinsic control of stroke volume).

- Stroke volume also increases as venous return increases **6** (intrinsic control of stroke volume according to the Frank–Starling law of the heart).

- Venous return is enhanced by sympathetically induced venous vasoconstriction **7**, the skeletal muscle pump **8**, and the respiratory pump **9**.

- The effective circulating blood volume also influences how much blood is returned to the heart **10**. The blood volume depends in the short term on the size of passive bulk-flow fluid shifts between the plasma and the interstitial fluid across the capillary walls **11**. In the long term, the blood volume depends on salt and water balance **12**, which are hormonally controlled by the renin–angiotensin–aldosterone system and vasopressin, respectively **13**.

- The other major determinant of mean arterial blood pressure, total peripheral resistance, depends on the radius of all arterioles, as well as blood viscosity **14**. The main factor determining blood viscosity is the number of red blood cells **15**. However, arteriolar radius is the more important factor determining total peripheral resistance.

- Arteriolar radius is influenced by local (intrinsic) metabolic controls that match blood flow with metabolic needs **16**. For example, local changes that take place in active skeletal muscles cause local arteriolar vasodilation and increased blood flow to these muscles **17**.

- Arteriolar radius is also influenced by sympathetic activity **18**, an extrinsic control mechanism that causes arteriolar vasoconstriction **19**, to increase total peripheral resistance and mean arterial blood pressure.

- Arteriolar radius is also extrinsically controlled by the hormones vasopressin and angiotensin II, which are potent vasoconstrictors **20** as well as being important in salt and water balance **21**.

Altering any of the pertinent factors that influence blood pressure changes blood pressure, unless a compensatory change in another variable keeps the blood pressure constant. Blood flow to any given organ depends on the driving force of the mean arterial pressure and on the degree of vasoconstriction of the organ's arterioles. Because mean arterial pressure depends on the cardiac output and the degree of arteriolar vasoconstriction, if the arterioles in one organ dilate, the arterioles in other organs must constrict to maintain an adequate arterial blood pressure. An adequate pressure is needed to provide a driving force to push blood not only to the vasodilated organ but also to the brain, which depends on a constant blood supply. Thus, the cardiovascular variables must be continuously juggled to maintain a constant blood pressure despite organs' varying needs for blood.

SHORT-TERM AND LONG-TERM CONTROL MEASURES Mean arterial pressure is constantly monitored by **baroreceptors** (pressure sensors) within the circulatory system. When deviations from normal are detected, multiple reflex responses are initiated to return mean arterial pressure to its normal value. *Short-term* (within seconds) adjustments are made by alterations in cardiac output and total peripheral resistance, mediated by means of autonomic nervous system influences on the heart, veins, and arterioles. *Long-term* (requiring minutes to days) control involves adjusting total blood volume by restoring normal salt and water balance through mechanisms that regulate urine output and thirst (see Chapters 13 and 14). The size of the total blood volume, in turn, has a profound effect on cardiac output and mean arterial pressure. Let us now turn to the short-term mechanisms involved in ongoing regulation of this pressure.

The baroreceptor reflex is an important short-term mechanism for regulating blood pressure through immediate effects on the heart and blood vessels.

Any change in mean arterial pressure triggers an autonomically mediated **baroreceptor reflex** that influences the heart and blood vessels to adjust cardiac output and total peripheral resistance in an attempt to restore blood pressure toward normal. Like any reflex, the baroreceptor reflex includes a receptor, an afferent pathway, an integrating center, an efferent pathway, and effector organs.

The most important receptors involved in the moment-to-moment regulation of blood pressure, the **carotid sinus** and **aortic arch baroreceptors,** are mechanoreceptors sensitive to changes in mean arterial pressure. These baroreceptors are strategically located (● Figure 10-30) to provide critical information about arterial blood pressure in the vessels leading to the brain (the carotid sinus baroreceptor) and in the major arterial trunk before it gives off branches that supply the rest of the body (the aortic arch baroreceptor).

The baroreceptors constantly provide information about mean arterial pressure; in other words, they continuously generate action potentials in response to the ongoing pressure within the arteries. When mean arterial pressure increases, the receptor potential of these baroreceptors increases, thus increasing the rate of firing in the corresponding afferent neurons. Conversely, a decrease in the mean arterial pressure slows the rate of firing generated in the afferent neurons by the baroreceptors (● Figure 10-31).

The integrating center that receives the afferent impulses about the state of mean arterial pressure is the *cardiovascular control center,* located in the medulla within the brain stem. The efferent pathway is the autonomic nervous system. The cardiovascular control center alters the ratio between sympathetic and parasympathetic activity to the effector organs (the heart and blood vessels). To review how autonomic changes alter arterial blood pressure, study ● Figure 10-32, which summarizes the major effects of parasympathetic and sympathetic stimulation on the heart and blood vessels.

Let us fit all the pieces of the baroreceptor reflex together by tracing the reflex activity that compensates for an elevation or fall in arterial blood pressure. If for any reason mean arterial pressure rises above normal (● Figure 10-33a), the carotid sinus and aortic arch baroreceptors increase the rate of firing in their

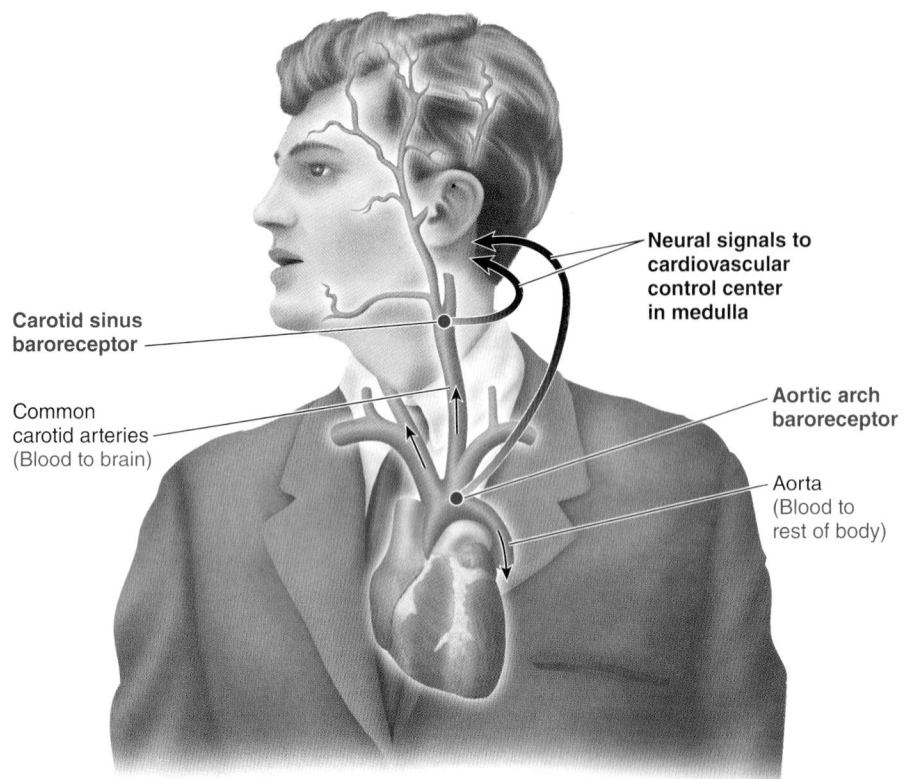

Carotid sinus
baroreceptor

Common
carotid arteries
(Blood to brain)

Neural signals to
cardiovascular
control center
in medulla

Aortic arch
baroreceptor

Aorta
(Blood to
rest of body)

● **FIGURE 10-30 Location of the arterial baroreceptors.** The arterial baroreceptors are strategically located to monitor the mean arterial blood pressure in the arteries that supply blood to the brain (cartoid sinus baroreceptor) and to the rest of the body (aortic arch baroreceptor).

respective afferent neurons. On being informed by increased afferent firing that the blood pressure has become too high, the cardiovascular control center responds by decreasing sympathetic and increasing parasympathetic activity to the cardiovascular system. These efferent signals decrease heart rate, decrease stroke volume, and produce arteriolar and venous vasodilation, which in turn lead to a decrease in cardiac output and a decrease in total peripheral resistance, with a subsequent fall in blood pressure back toward normal.

Conversely, when blood pressure falls below normal (● Figure 10-33b), baroreceptor activity decreases, inducing the

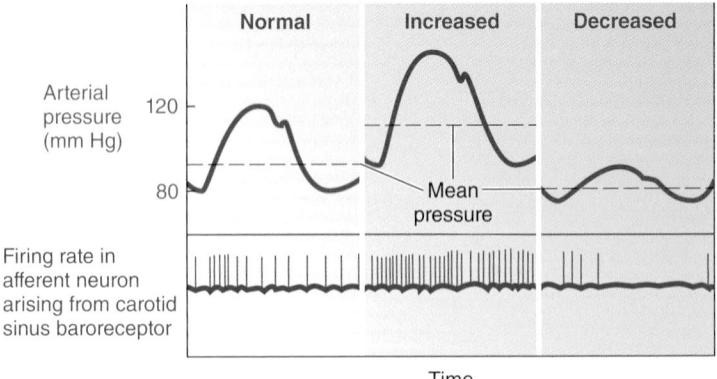

● **FIGURE 10-31 Firing rate in the afferent neuron from the carotid sinus baroreceptor in relation to the magnitude of mean arterial pressure.**

cardiovascular center to increase sympathetic cardiac and vasoconstrictor nerve activity while decreasing its parasympathetic output. This efferent pattern of activity leads to an increase in heart rate and stroke volume, coupled with arteriolar and venous vasoconstriction. These changes increase both cardiac output and total peripheral resistance, raising blood pressure back toward normal.

Despite these control measures, sometimes blood pressure is not maintained at the appropriate level. We next examine blood pressure abnormalities.

Hypertension is a serious national public-health problem, but its causes are largely unknown.

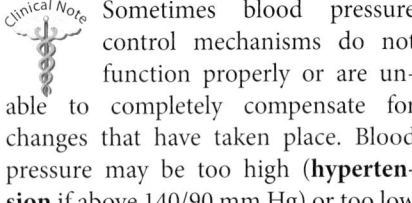 Sometimes blood pressure control mechanisms do not function properly or are unable to completely compensate for changes that have taken place. Blood pressure may be too high (**hypertension** if above 140/90 mm Hg) or too low (**hypotension** if below 100/60 mm Hg). Hypotension in its extreme form is *circulatory shock*. We first examine hypertension, which is by far the most common of blood pressure abnormalities, and then conclude this chapter with a discussion of hypotension and shock.

There are two broad classes of hypertension, secondary hypertension and primary hypertension, depending on the cause. A definite cause for hypertension can be established in only 10% of cases. Hypertension that occurs secondary to another known primary problem is called **secondary hypertension.** For example, when the elasticity of the arteries is reduced by the loss of elastin fibers or the presence of calcified atherosclerotic plaques (see p. 270), arterial pressure is chronically increased by this "hardening of the arteries." Likewise, hypertension occurs if the kidneys are diseased and unable to eliminate the normal salt load. Salt retention induces water retention, which expands the plasma volume and leads to hypertension.

The underlying cause is unknown in the remaining 90% of hypertension cases. Such hypertension is known as **primary (essential** or **idiopathic) hypertension.** Primary hypertension is a catchall category for blood pressure elevated by a variety of unknown causes rather than by a single disease entity. People show a strong genetic tendency to develop primary hypertension, which can be hastened or worsened by contributing factors such as obesity, stress, smoking, or dietary habits.

Whatever the underlying defect, once initiated, hypertension appears to be self-perpetuating. Constant exposure to elevated blood pressure predisposes vessel walls to the development of atherosclerosis, which further raises blood pressure.

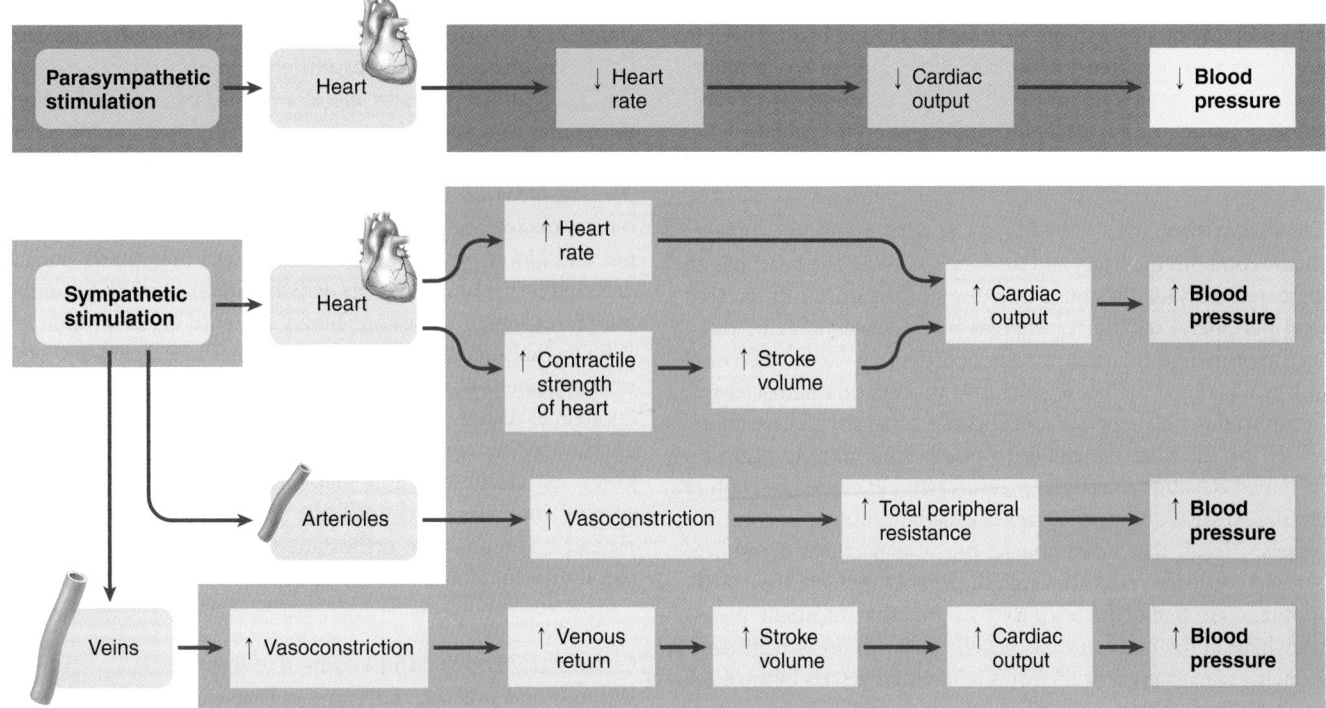

● FIGURE 10-32 **Summary of the effects of the parasympathetic and sympathetic nervous systems on factors that influence mean arterial blood pressure.**

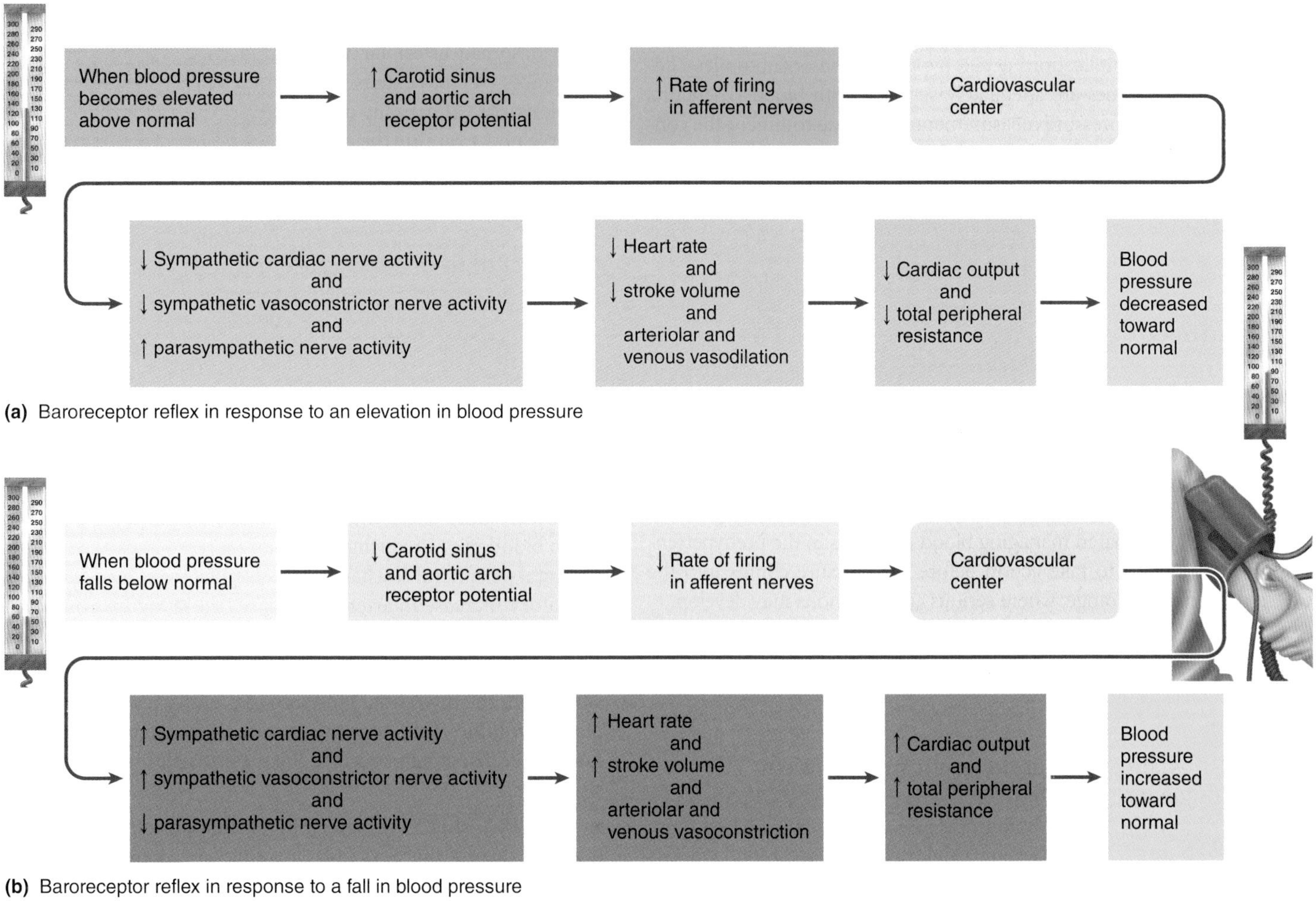

(a) Baroreceptor reflex in response to an elevation in blood pressure

(b) Baroreceptor reflex in response to a fall in blood pressure

● FIGURE 10-33 **Baroreceptor reflexes to restore blood pressure to normal.**

ADAPTATION OF BARORECEPTORS DURING HYPERTENSION The baroreceptors do not respond to bring the blood pressure back to normal during hypertension because they adapt, or are "reset," to operate at a higher level. In the presence of chronically elevated blood pressure, the baroreceptors still function to regulate blood pressure, but they maintain it at a higher mean pressure.

COMPLICATIONS OF HYPERTENSION Hypertension imposes stresses on both the heart and the blood vessels. The heart has an increased workload because it is pumping against an increased total peripheral resistance, whereas blood vessels may be damaged by the high internal pressure, particularly when the vessel wall is weakened by the degenerative process of atherosclerosis. Complications of hypertension include congestive heart failure caused by the heart's inability to pump continuously against a sustained elevation in arterial pressure, strokes caused by rupture of brain vessels, and heart attacks caused by rupture of coronary vessels. (Recall that heart attacks can also occur as a result of blocked coronary vessels through thromboembolism; see p. 270). Spontaneous hemorrhage caused by bursting of small vessels elsewhere in the body may also occur but with less serious consequences; an example is the rupture of blood vessels in the nose, resulting in nosebleeds. Another serious complication of hypertension is renal failure caused by progressive impairment of blood flow through damaged renal blood vessels. Furthermore, retinal damage from changes in the blood vessels supplying the eyes may result in progressive loss of vision.

Until complications occur, hypertension is symptomless, because the tissues are adequately supplied with blood. Therefore, unless blood pressure measurements are made routinely, the condition can go undetected until a precipitous complicating event occurs. When you become aware of these potential complications of hypertension and consider that one third of all adults in America are estimated to have chronic elevated blood pressure, you can appreciate the magnitude of this national health problem.

PREHYPERTENSION In its recent guidelines, the National Institutes of Health identified **prehypertension** as a new category for blood pressures in the range between normal (120/80) and hypertension (140/90). Blood pressures in the prehypertension range can usually be reduced by appropriate dietary and exercise measures, whereas those in the hypertension range typically must be treated with blood pressure medication in addition to changing health habits. The goal in managing blood pressures in the prehypertension range is to take action before the pressure climbs into the hypertension range, where serious complications may develop.

We now examine the other extreme, hypotension, looking first at transient orthostatic hypotension, then at the (more serious) circulatory shock.

Orthostatic hypotension results from transient inadequate sympathetic activity.

Hypotension, or low blood pressure, occurs either when there is a disproportion between vascular capacity and blood volume (in essence, too little blood to fill the vessels) or when the heart is too weak to drive the blood.

The most common situation in which hypotension occurs transiently is orthostatic hypotension. **Orthostatic (postural) hypotension** results from insufficient compensatory responses to the gravitational shifts in blood when a person moves from a horizontal to a vertical position, especially after prolonged bed rest. When a person moves from lying down to standing up, pooling of blood in the leg veins from gravity reduces venous return, decreasing stroke volume and thus lowering cardiac output and blood pressure. This fall in blood pressure is normally detected by the baroreceptors, which initiate immediate compensatory responses to restore blood pressure to its proper level. When a long-bedridden patient first starts to rise, however, these reflex compensatory adjustments are temporarily lost or reduced because of disuse. Sympathetic control of the leg veins is inadequate, so when the patient first stands up, blood pools in the lower extremities without sufficient compensatory responses coming into play to counter the gravity-induced fall in blood pressure. The resultant orthostatic hypotension and decrease in blood flow to the brain cause dizziness or actual fainting.

Circulatory shock can become irreversible.

When blood pressure falls so low that adequate blood flow to the tissues can no longer be maintained, the condition known as **circulatory shock** occurs. Circulatory shock may result from (1) extensive loss of blood volume as through hemorrhage; (2) failure of a weakened heart to pump blood adequately; (3) widespread arteriolar vasodilation triggered by vasodilator substances (such as extensive histamine release in severe allergic reactions); or (4) neurally defective vasoconstrictor tone.

We now examine the compensations for shock, using hemorrhage as an example. It is an important example that pulls together many of the principles discussed in this chapter.

COMPENSATIONS OF SHOCK Following severe loss of blood, the resultant reduction in circulating blood volume leads to a decrease in venous return and a subsequent fall in cardiac output and arterial blood pressure. Compensatory measures immediately attempt to maintain adequate blood flow to the brain by increasing blood pressure toward normal, followed by longer-range measures aimed at restoring plasma volume and replacing lost red blood cells, as follows:

■ In the short term, the baroreceptor reflex response to the fall in blood pressure brings about an increase in cardiac output and total peripheral resistance, which collectively lead to a compensatory increase in arterial pressure (see ● Figure 10-33).

■ The original fall in arterial pressure is accompanied by a fall in capillary blood pressure, which results in immediate fluid shifts from the interstitial fluid into the capillaries to expand the plasma volume. This response is sometimes termed *autotransfusion*, because it helps restore the plasma volume as a transfusion does.

■ This ECF shift is enhanced by plasma protein synthesis by the liver during the next few days following hemorrhage. The plasma proteins exert a colloid osmotic pressure that helps retain extra fluid in the plasma.

■ Urinary output is reduced, thereby conserving water that normally would have been lost from the body. This additional fluid retention helps expand the reduced plasma volume. Expansion of plasma volume further augments the increase in cardiac output brought about by the baroreceptor reflex. Reduction in urinary output results from decreased renal blood flow caused by compensatory renal arteriolar vasoconstriction. The reduced plasma volume also triggers increased secretion of the hormone vasopressin and activation of the salt- and water-conserving renin–angiotensin–aldosterone hormonal pathway, which further reduces urinary output.

■ Increased thirst is stimulated by the fall in plasma volume that occurs with hemorrhage. The resultant increased fluid intake helps restore plasma volume.

■ Over a longer course (a week or more), lost red blood cells are replaced through increased red blood cell production triggered by a reduction in O_2 delivery to the kidneys (see p. 320 for further details).

IRREVERSIBLE SHOCK Compensatory mechanisms are often not enough to counteract substantial fluid loss. Even if they can maintain an adequate blood pressure level, the short-term measures cannot continue indefinitely. Ultimately, fluid volume must be replaced from the outside through drinking, transfusion, or a combination of both. Blood supply to the kidneys, digestive tract, skin, and other organs can be compromised to maintain blood flow to the brain only so long before organ damage begins to occur. A point may be reached at which blood pressure continues to drop rapidly because of tissue damage, despite vigorous therapy. This condition is often termed *irreversible shock,* in contrast to *reversible shock,* which can be corrected by compensatory mechanisms and effective therapy.

Chapter in Perspective: Focus on Homeostasis

Homeostatically, the blood vessels are passageways to transport blood to and from the cells for O_2 and nutrient delivery, waste removal, distribution of fluid and electrolytes, elimination of excess heat, and hormonal signaling, among other things. Cells soon die if deprived of their blood supply; brain cells succumb within 4 minutes. Blood is constantly recycled and reconditioned as it travels through the various organs via the vascular highways. Hence, the body needs only a small volume of blood to maintain the appropriate chemical composition of the entire internal fluid environment on which the cells depend for their survival. For example, O_2 is continually picked up by blood in the lungs and constantly delivered to all the body cells.

The smallest blood vessels, the capillaries, are the actual site of exchange between blood and surrounding cells. Capillaries bring homeostatically maintained blood within 0.01 cm of every cell in the body; this proximity is critical, because beyond a few centimeters materials cannot diffuse rapidly enough to support life-sustaining activities. O_2 that would take months to years to diffuse from the lungs to all the cells of the body is continuously delivered to the "doorstep" of every cell, where diffusion can efficiently accomplish short local exchanges between capillaries and surrounding cells. Likewise, hormones must be rapidly transported through the circulatory system from their sites of production in endocrine glands to their sites of action in other parts of the body. These chemical messengers could not diffuse nearly rapidly enough to their target organs to effectively exert their controlling effects, many of which are aimed toward maintaining homeostasis.

The rest of the circulatory system is designed to transport blood to and from the capillaries. The arteries and arterioles distribute blood pumped by the heart to the capillaries for life-sustaining exchanges to take place, and the venules and veins collect blood from the capillaries and return it to the heart, where the process is repeated.

Objective Questions (Answers on p. A-44)

1. In general, the parallel arrangement of the vascular system enables each organ to receive its own separate arterial blood supply. *(True or false?)*
2. More blood flows through the capillaries during cardiac systole than during diastole. *(True or false?)*
3. The capillaries contain only 5% of the total blood volume at any point in time. *(True or false?)*
4. The same volume of blood passes through the capillaries in a minute as passes through the aorta, even though blood flow is much slower in the capillaries. *(True or false?)*
5. Because capillary walls have no carrier transport systems, all capillaries are equally permeable. *(True or false?)*
6. Because of gravitational effects, venous pressure in the lower extremities is greater when a person is standing up than when the person is lying down. *(True or false?)*
7. Which of the following functions is or are attributable to arterioles? *(Indicate all correct answers.)*
   a. produce a significant decline in mean pressure, which helps establish the driving pressure gradient between the heart and the organs
   b. serve as the site of exchange of materials between blood and surrounding tissue cells
   c. act as the main determinant of total peripheral resistance
   d. determine the pattern of distribution of cardiac output
   e. help regulate mean arterial blood pressure
   f. convert the pulsatile nature of arterial blood pressure into a smooth, nonfluctuating pressure in the vessels farther downstream
   g. act as a pressure reservoir
8. Using the answer code on the right, indicate whether the following factors increase or decrease venous return:
   ___ 1. sympathetically induced venous vasoconstriction   (a) increases venous return
   ___ 2. skeletal muscle activity   (b) decreases venous return
   ___ 3. gravitational effect on the venous system   (c) has no effect on venous return
   ___ 4. respiratory activity
   ___ 5. increased atrial pressure associated with a leaky AV valve
9. Using the answer code on the right, indicate what kind of compensatory changes occur in the factors in question to restore blood pressure to normal in response to hypotension resulting from severe hemorrhage:
   ___ 1. rate of afferent firing generated by the carotid sinus and aortic arch baroreceptors   (a) increased
   ___ 2. sympathetic output by the cardiovascular center   (b) decreased   (c) no effect
   ___ 3. parasympathetic output by the cardiovascular center
   ___ 4. heart rate
   ___ 5. stroke volume
   ___ 6. cardiac output
   ___ 7. arteriolar radius
   ___ 8. total peripheral resistance
   ___ 9. venous radius
   ___ 10. venous return
   ___ 11. urinary output
   ___ 12. fluid retention within the body
   ___ 13. fluid movement from interstitial fluid into plasma across the capillaries

Essay Questions

1. Compare blood flow through reconditioning organs and through organs that do not recondition the blood.
2. Discuss the relationships among flow rate, pressure gradient, and vascular resistance. What is the major determinant of resistance to flow?
3. Describe the structure and major functions of each segment of the vascular tree.
4. How do the arteries serve as a pressure reservoir?
5. Describe the indirect technique of measuring arterial blood pressure by means of a sphygmomanometer.
6. Define *vasoconstriction* and *vasodilation.*
7. Discuss the local and extrinsic controls that regulate arteriolar resistance.
8. What is the primary means by which individual solutes are exchanged across capillary walls? What forces produce bulk flow across capillary walls? Of what importance is bulk flow?
9. How is lymph formed? What are the functions of the lymphatic system?
10. Define *edema,* and discuss its possible causes.
11. How do veins serve as a blood reservoir?
12. Compare the effect of vasoconstriction on the rate of blood flow in arterioles and veins.
13. Discuss the factors that determine mean arterial pressure.
14. Review the effects on the cardiovascular system of parasympathetic and sympathetic stimulation.
15. Differentiate between secondary hypertension and primary hypertension. What are the potential consequences of hypertension?
16. Define circulatory shock. What are its consequences and compensations? What is irreversible shock?

(Explanations on p. A-44)

1. During coronary bypass surgery, a piece of vein is often removed from the patient's leg and surgically attached within the coronary circulatory system so that blood detours, through the vein, around an occluded coronary artery segment. Why must the patient wear, for an extended period after surgery, an elastic support stocking on the limb from which the vein was removed?

2. Assume a person has a blood pressure recording of 125/77.
   a. What is the systolic pressure?
   b. What is the diastolic pressure?
   c. What is the pulse pressure?
   d. What is the mean arterial pressure?
   e. Would any sound be heard when the pressure in an external cuff around the arm was 130 mm Hg? *(Yes or no?)*
   f. Would any sound be heard when cuff pressure was 118 mm Hg?
   g. Would any sound be heard when cuff pressure was 75 mm Hg?

3. A classmate who has been standing still for several hours working on a laboratory experiment suddenly faints. What is the probable explanation? What would you do if the person next to him tried to get him up?

4. A drug applied to a piece of excised arteriole causes the vessel to relax, but an isolated piece of arteriolar muscle stripped from the other layers of the vessel fails to respond to the same drug. What is the probable explanation?

5. Explain how each of the following antihypertensive drugs would lower arterial blood pressure.
   a. drugs that block α_1-adrenergic receptors (for example, phentolamine) (*Hint:* Review adrenergic receptors on p. 196.)
   b. drugs that block β_1-adrenergic receptors (for example, metoprolol)
   c. drugs that directly relax arteriolar smooth muscle (for example, hydralazine)
   d. diuretic drugs that increase urinary output (for example, furosemide)
   e. drugs that block release of norepinephrine from sympathetic endings (for example, guanethidine)
   f. drugs that act on the brain to reduce sympathetic output (for example, clonidine)
   g. drugs that block Ca^{2+} channels (for example, verapamil)
   h. drugs that interfere with the production of angiotensin II (for example, captopril)
   i. drugs that block angiotensin receptors (for example, losartan)

CLINICAL CONSIDERATION

(Explanation on p. A-45)

Li-Ying C. has just been diagnosed as having hypertension secondary to a *pheochromocytoma*, a tumor of the adrenal medulla that secretes excessive epinephrine. Explain how this condition leads to secondary hypertension by describing the effect that excessive epinephrine would have on various factors that determine arterial blood pressure.

Chapter 10

Patterns and Physics of Blood Flow (pp. 279–282)

■ Materials can be exchanged among various parts of the body and with the external environment by means of the blood vessel network that transports blood to and from all organs. (*Review Figure 10-1.*)

■ Organs that replenish nutrient supplies and remove metabolic wastes from the blood receive a greater percentage of the cardiac output than is warranted by their metabolic needs. These "reconditioning" organs can better tolerate reductions in blood supply than can organs that receive blood solely for meeting their own metabolic needs. The reconditioning organs are the digestive organs, kidneys, and skin.

■ The brain is especially vulnerable to reductions in its blood supply. Therefore, maintaining adequate flow to this vulnerable organ is a high priority in circulatory function.

■ The flow rate of blood through a vessel (in volume per unit of time) is directly proportional to the pressure gradient and inversely proportional to the resistance. The higher pressure at the beginning of a vessel is established by the pressure imparted to the blood by cardiac contraction. The lower pressure at the end is the result of frictional losses as flowing blood rubs against the vessel wall. (*Review Figure 10-2.*)

■ Resistance, the hindrance to blood flow through a vessel, is influenced most by the vessel's radius. Resistance is inversely proportional to the fourth power of the radius, so small changes in radius profoundly influence flow. As the radius increases, resistance decreases and flow increases, and vice versa. (*Review Figure 10-3.*)

■ Blood flows in a closed loop between the heart and the organs. The arteries transport blood from the heart throughout the body. The arterioles regulate the amount of blood that flows through each organ. The capillaries are the actual site where materials are exchanged between blood and surrounding tissue cells. The veins return blood from the tissue level back to the heart. (*Review Figure 10-4 and Table 10-1.*)

Arteries (pp. 282–287)

■ Arteries are large-radius, low-resistance passageways from the heart to the organs.

■ Arteries also serve as a pressure reservoir. Because of their elasticity, owing to their abundant elastin fibers, arteries expand to accommodate the extra volume of blood pumped into them by cardiac contraction and then recoil to continue driving the blood forward when the heart is relaxing. (*Review Table 10-1 and Figure 10-5.*)

■ Systolic pressure (average 120 mm Hg) is the peak pressure exerted by the ejected blood against the vessel walls during cardiac systole. Diastolic pressure (average 80 mm Hg) is the minimum pressure in the arteries when blood is draining off into the vessels downstream during cardiac diastole. When blood pressure is 120/80, pulse pressure (the difference between systolic and diastolic pressures) is 40 mm Hg. (*Review Figures 10-6 and 10-7.*)

■ The average driving pressure throughout the cardiac cycle is the mean arterial pressure, which can be estimated using the following formula: mean arterial pressure = diastolic pressure + 1/3 pulse pressure. (*Review Figure 10-8.*)

Arterioles (pp. 287–292)

■ Arterioles are the major resistance vessels. Their high resistance produces a large drop in mean pressure between the arteries and the capillaries. This decline enhances blood flow by contributing to the pressure differential between the heart and the organs. (*Review Figure 10-8.*)

■ Arterioles have a thick layer of circular smooth muscle, variable contraction of which alters arteriolar caliber and resistance. (*Review Table 10-1.*) Tone, a baseline of contractile activity, is maintained in arterioles at all times. Arteriolar vasodilation (expansion of arteriolar caliber above tonic level) decreases resistance and increases blood flow through the vessel, whereas vasoconstriction (narrowing of the vessel) increases resistance and decreases flow. (*Review Figure 10-9.*)

■ Arteriolar caliber is subject to two types of control mechanisms: local (intrinsic) controls and extrinsic controls.

■ Local controls primarily involve local chemical changes associated with changes in the level of metabolic activity in an organ, such as local changes in O_2, which cause the release of vasoactive paracrines from the endothelial cells in the vicinity. Examples include vasodilating nitric oxide and vasoconstricting endothelin. These vasoactive mediators act on the underlying arteriolar smooth muscle to bring about an appropriate change in the caliber of the arterioles supplying the organ. By adjusting the resistance to blood flow, the local control mechanism adjusts blood flow to the organ to match the momentary metabolic needs of the organ. (*Review Figures 10-9 through 10-11 and Table 10-2.*)

■ Arteriolar caliber can be adjusted independently in different organs by local control factors. Such adjustments are important in variably distributing cardiac output.

■ Other local influences include (1) histamine release, which is important in inflammatory and allergic reactions; (2) myogenic response to stretch, which resists changes in the distending force exerted across the vessel wall by blood-pressure driven changes in blood flow; and (3) local application of heat or cold, which is important therapeutically.

■ Extrinsic control is accomplished primarily by sympathetic and to a lesser extent by hormonal influence over arteriolar smooth muscle. Extrinsic controls are important in maintaining mean arterial pressure. Arterioles are richly supplied with sympathetic nerve fibers, whose increased activity produces generalized vasoconstriction and a subsequent increase in total peripheral resistance, thus increasing mean arterial pressure. Decreased sympathetic activity produces generalized arteriolar vasodilation, which lowers mean arterial pressure. These extrinsically controlled adjustments of arteriolar caliber help maintain the appropriate pressure head for driving blood forward to the tissues. Most arterioles are not supplied by parasympathetic nerves. (*Review Figure 10-11.*)

■ Hormones that extrinsically influence arteriolar radius are epinephrine, vasopressin, and angiotensin II, all of which cause generalized arteriolar vasoconstriction.

Capillaries (pp. 292–301)

■ The thin-walled, small-radius, extensively branched capillaries are ideally suited to serve as sites of exchange between blood and surrounding tissue cells. Anatomically, the surface area for exchange is maximized and diffusion distance is minimized in the capillaries. Furthermore, because of their large total cross-sectional area, the velocity of blood flow through capillaries (in distance per unit of time) is relatively slow, providing adequate time for exchanges to take place. (*Review Figures 10-12 through 10-14 and Table 10-1, p. 284.*)

■ Two types of passive exchanges—diffusion and bulk flow—take place across capillary walls.

■ Individual solutes are exchanged primarily by diffusion down concentration gradients. Lipid-soluble substances pass directly through the single layer of endothelial cells lining a capillary, whereas water-soluble substances pass through water-filled pores between the endothelial cells. Plasma proteins generally do not escape. (*Review Figures 10-15 and 10-16.*)

■ Imbalances in physical pressures acting across capillary walls are responsible for bulk flow of fluid through the pores. (1) Fluid is forced out of the first portion of the capillary (ultrafiltration), where outward pressures (mainly capillary blood pressure) exceed inward pressures (mainly plasma-colloid osmotic pressure). (2) Fluid is returned to the capillary along its last half, when outward pressures fall below inward pressures. The reason for the shift in balance down the capillary's length is the continuous decline in capillary blood pressure while the plasma-colloid osmotic pressure remains constant. Bulk flow is responsible for the distribution of ECF between plasma and interstitial fluid. (*Review Figures 10-8, 10-17, and 10-18.*)

■ Normally, slightly more fluid is filtered than is reabsorbed. The extra fluid, any leaked proteins, and bacteria in the tissue are picked up by the lymphatic system. Bacteria are destroyed as lymph passes through lymph nodes on the way to being returned to the venous system. (*Review Figures 10-17, 10-19, and 10-20.*)

Veins (pp. 301–305)

■ Veins are large-radius, low-resistance passageways through which blood returns from the organs to the heart. In addition, the thin-walled, highly distensible veins, as capacitance vessels, can passively stretch to store a larger volume of blood and therefore act as a blood reservoir. The capacity of veins to hold blood can change markedly with little change in venous pressure. At rest, the veins contain more than 60% of the total blood volume. (*Review Table 10-1 and Figure 10-22.*)

■ The primary force that produces venous flow is the pressure gradient between the veins and the atrium (that is, what remains of the driving pressure imparted to the blood by cardiac contraction). (*Review Figures 10-8 and 10-23.*)

■ Venous return is enhanced by sympathetically induced venous vasoconstriction and by external compression of the veins from contraction of surrounding skeletal muscles, both of which drive blood out of the veins. These actions help counter the effects of gravity on the venous system. (*Review Figures 10-23 through 10-26.*)

■ One-way venous valves ensure that blood is driven toward the heart and kept from flowing back toward the tissues. (*Review Figure 10-27.*)

■ Venous return is also enhanced by the respiratory pump. Respiratory activity produces a less-than-atmospheric pressure in the chest cavity, thus establishing an external pressure gradient that encourages flow from the lower veins that are exposed to atmospheric pressure to the chest veins that empty into the heart. (*Review Figures 10-23 and 10-28.*)

Blood Pressure (pp. 305–311)

■ Regulation of mean arterial pressure depends on control of its two main determinants, cardiac output and total peripheral resistance. (*Review Figure 10-29.*) Control of cardiac output, in turn, depends on regulation of heart rate and stroke volume (*review Figure 9-22, p. 267*), whereas total peripheral resistance is determined primarily by the degree of arteriolar vasoconstriction (*review Figure 10-11*).

■ Short-term regulation of blood pressure is accomplished mainly by the baroreceptor reflex. Carotid sinus and aortic arch baroreceptors continuously monitor mean arterial pressure. When they detect a deviation from normal, they signal the medullary cardiovascular center, which responds by adjusting autonomic output to the heart and blood vessels to restore the blood pressure to normal. (*Review Figures 10-30 through 10-33.*)

■ Long-term control of blood pressure involves maintaining proper plasma volume through the kidneys' control of salt and water balance. (*Review Figure 10-29.*)

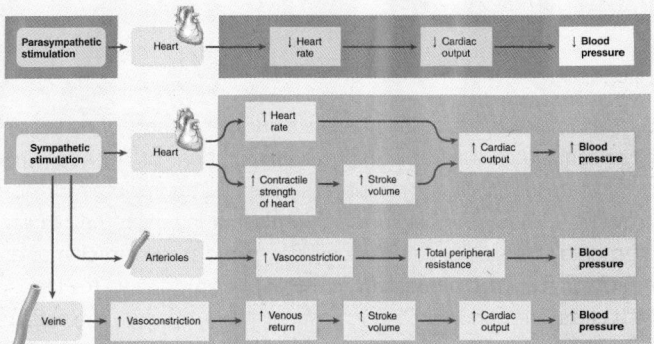

**Blood; Immune System;
Integumentary System (Skin)**

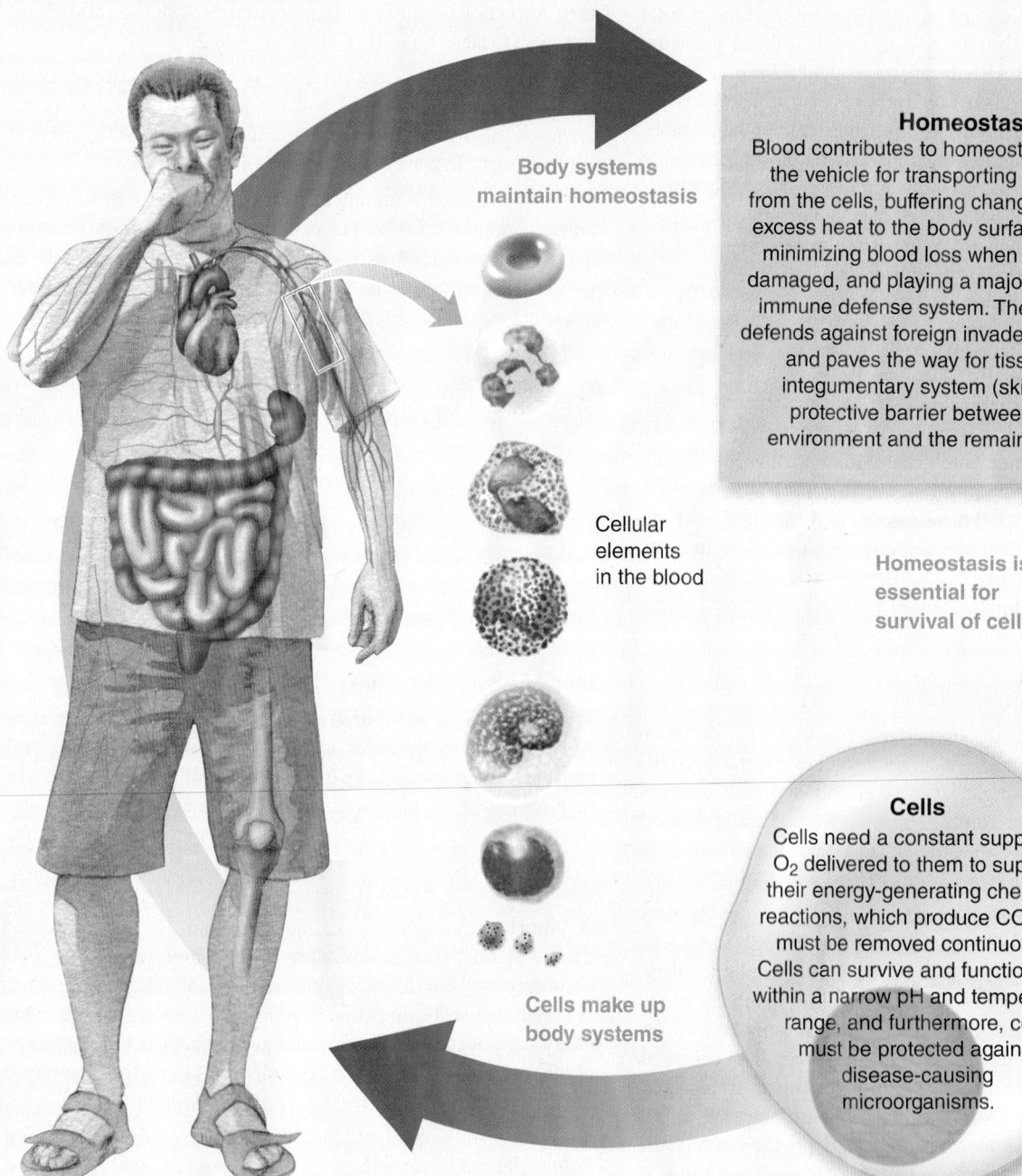

**Body systems
maintain homeostasis**

**Cellular
elements
in the blood**

**Cells make up
body systems**

Homeostasis
Blood contributes to homeostasis by serving as the vehicle for transporting materials to and from the cells, buffering changes in pH, carrying excess heat to the body surface for elimination, minimizing blood loss when a blood vessel is damaged, and playing a major role in the body's immune defense system. The immune system defends against foreign invaders and cancer cells and paves the way for tissue repair. The integumentary system (skin) serves as a protective barrier between the external environment and the remainder of the body.

**Homeostasis is
essential for
survival of cells**

Cells
Cells need a constant supply of O_2 delivered to them to support their energy-generating chemical reactions, which produce CO_2 that must be removed continuously. Cells can survive and function only within a narrow pH and temperature range, and furthermore, cells must be protected against disease-causing microorganisms.

Blood is the vehicle for long-distance, mass transport of materials between the cells and the external environment or between the cells themselves. Such transport is essential for maintaining homeostasis. Blood consists of a liquid **plasma** in which the cellular elements are suspended. Among the blood's cellular elements, **erythrocytes (red blood cells, or RBCs)** transport O_2 in the blood. **Platelets** are important in hemostasis, the stopping of bleeding from an injured vessel. **Leukocytes (white blood cells, or WBCs)** are part of a complex, multifaceted internal defense system, the **immune system.** They are transported in the blood to sites of injury or of invasion by disease-causing microorganisms. The immune system indirectly contributes to homeostasis by helping maintain the health of organs that directly contribute to homeostasis. The **integumentary system** (skin) is an outer protective barrier that prevents the loss of internal fluids and resists penetration by external agents.

The Blood and Body Defenses

CHAPTER AT A GLANCE

Plasma
Hematocrit
Composition and functions of plasma
Plasma proteins

Erythrocytes
Structure and function of erythrocytes
Erythropoiesis

Platelets and Hemostasis
Platelet structure and function
Hemostasis

Leukocytes
Bacteria and viruses as targets of the immune system
Types and functions of leukocytes

Innate Immunity
Inflammation
Interferon
Natural killer cells
Complement system

Adaptive Immunity: General Concepts

B Lymphocytes: Antibody-Mediated Immunity
Plasma cells; antibodies
Clonal selection theory
Memory cells

T Lymphocytes: Cell-Mediated Immunity
Cytotoxic, helper, and regulatory T cells
Antigen-presenting cells
Major histocompatibility complex; self-antigens
Tolerance
Immune surveillance against cancer

Immune Diseases

External Defenses
Structure and function of skin
Protective measures within body cavities

Plasma

The hematocrit represents the packed cell volume; plasma accounts for the rest of the volume.

Blood represents about 8% of total body weight and has an average volume of 5 liters in women and 5.5 liters in men. It consists of three types of specialized cellular elements, *erythrocytes (red blood cells), leukocytes (white blood cells),* and *platelets (thrombocytes),* suspended in the complex liquid *plasma* (● Figure 11-1 and ▲ Table 11-1). Erythrocytes and leukocytes are both whole cells, whereas platelets are cell fragments.

The constant movement of blood as it flows through the blood vessels keeps the cellular elements rather evenly dispersed within the plasma. However, if you put a sample of whole blood in a test tube and treat it to prevent clotting, the heavier cells slowly settle to the bottom and the lighter plasma rises to the top. This process can be speeded up by centrifuging, which quickly packs the cells in the bottom of the tube (● Figure 11-1). Because more than 99% of the cells are erythrocytes, the **hematocrit,** or **packed cell volume,** essentially represents the percentage of erythrocytes in the total blood volume. The hematocrit averages about 42% for women and slightly higher, 45%, for men. Plasma accounts for the remaining volume. Accordingly, the average volume of plasma in the blood is about 58% for women and 55% for men. White blood cells and platelets, which are colorless and less dense than red cells, are packed in a thin, cream-colored layer, the *buffy coat,* on top of the packed red cell column. They are less than 1% of the total blood volume.

Let us first consider the properties of the largest portion of the blood, the plasma, before turning our attention to the cellular elements.

Plasma water is a transport medium for many inorganic and organic substances.

Plasma, being a liquid, consists of 90% water. Plasma water is a medium for materials being carried in the blood. Many inorganic and organic substances are dissolved in the plasma. Plasma also carries heat generated metabolically within tissues to the surface of the skin, where heat energy not needed to maintain body temperature is eliminated to the environment.

Inorganic constituents account for about 1% of plasma weight. The most abundant electrolytes (ions) in the plasma are Na^+ and Cl^-, the components of common salt. Smaller amounts of HCO_3^-, K^+, Ca^{2+}, and other ions are present. The most notable functions of these ions are their roles in membrane excitability, osmotic distribution of fluid between the extracellular fluid (ECF) and the cells, and buffering of pH changes; these functions are discussed elsewhere.

The most plentiful organic constituents by weight are the plasma proteins, which make up 6% to 8% of plasma weight. We examine them more thoroughly in the next

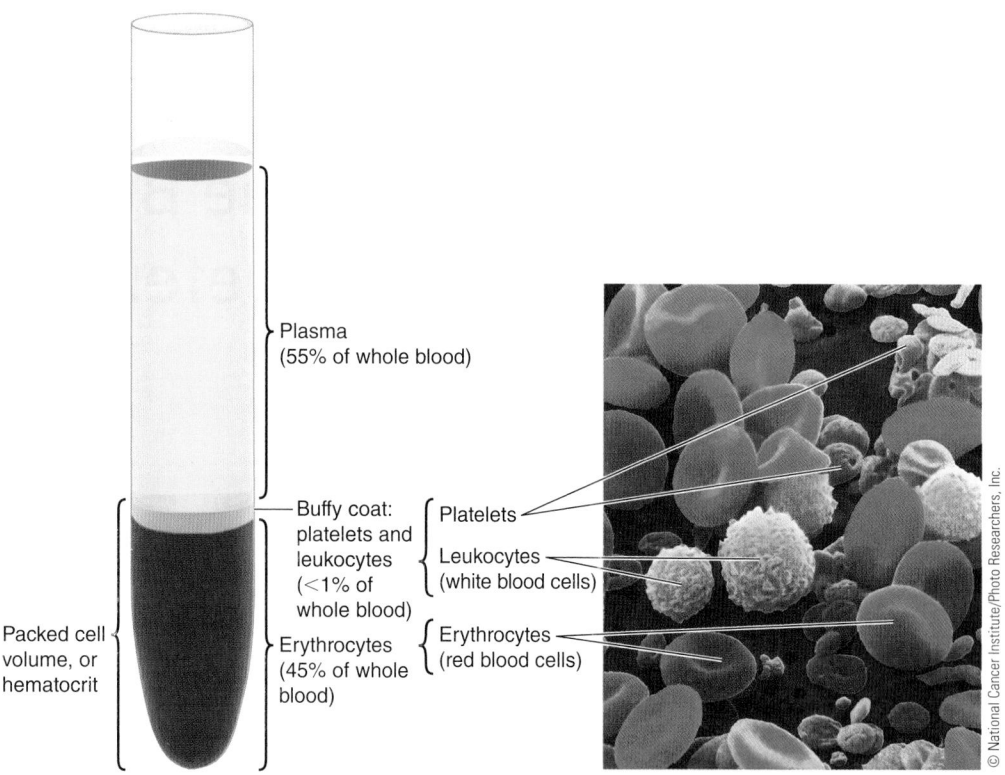

● FIGURE 11-1 **Hematocrit and types of blood cells.** The values given are for men. The average hematocrit for women is 42%, with plasma occupying 58% of the blood volume. Note the biconcave shape of the erythrocytes.

section. The remaining small percentage of plasma consists of other organic substances, including nutrients (such as glucose, amino acids, lipids, and vitamins), waste products (creatinine, bilirubin, and nitrogenous substances such as urea), dissolved gases (O_2 and CO_2), and hormones. Most of these substances are merely being transported in the plasma. For example, endocrine glands secrete hormones into the plasma, which transports these chemical messengers to their sites of action.

Many of the functions of plasma are carried out by plasma proteins.

Plasma proteins are the one group of plasma constituents that are not along just for the ride. These important components normally stay in the plasma, where they perform

▲ Table 11-1 Blood Constituents and Their Functions

Constituent	Functions
Plasma	
Water	Acts as transport medium; carries heat
Electrolytes	Play a role in membrane excitability; distribute fluid osmotically between ECF and ICF; buffer pH changes
Nutrients, wastes, gases, and hormones	Are transported in blood; blood CO_2 plays a role in acid–base balance
Plasma proteins	Exert an osmotic effect important in the distribution of ECF between the vascular and the interstitial compartments; buffer pH changes; transport many substances; include clotting factors, inactive precursor molecules, and antibodies
Cellular Elements	
Erythrocytes	Transport O_2 and CO_2 (mainly O_2)
Leukocytes	
Neutrophils	Engulf bacteria and debris
Eosinophils	Attack parasitic worms; play a role in allergic reactions
Basophils	Release histamine, which is important in allergic reactions, and heparin, which helps clear fat from the blood
Monocytes	Are in transit to become tissue macrophages
Lymphocytes	
B lymphocytes	Produce antibodies
T lymphocytes	Produce cell-mediated immune responses
Platelets	Contribute to hemostasis

many valuable functions. Here are the most important of these functions, which are elaborated on elsewhere in the text:

1. Unlike other plasma constituents that are dissolved in the plasma water, plasma proteins are dispersed as a colloid (see p. A-9). Furthermore, because they are the largest of the plasma constituents, plasma proteins usually do not exit through the narrow pores in the capillary walls to enter the interstitial fluid. By their presence as a colloidal dispersion in the plasma and their absence in the interstitial fluid, plasma proteins establish an osmotic gradient between the blood and the interstitial fluid. This colloid osmotic pressure is the primary force preventing excessive loss of plasma from the capillaries into the interstitial fluid and thus helps maintain plasma volume (see p. 297).

2. Plasma proteins are partially responsible for plasma's capacity to buffer changes in pH (see p. 456).

3. Some plasma proteins bind substances that are poorly soluble in plasma for transport in the plasma. Examples of substances carried by plasma proteins include cholesterol (see p. 272) and thyroid hormone (see p. 102).

4. Many of the factors involved in the blood-clotting process are plasma proteins (see p. 326).

5. Some plasma proteins are inactive, circulating precursor molecules, which are activated as needed by specific regulatory inputs. For example, the plasma protein *angiotensinogen* is activated to *angiotensin*, which plays an important role in regulating salt balance in the body (see p. 417).

6. One specific group of plasma proteins are *antibodies*, or *immunoglobulins*, which are crucial to the body's defense mechanism (see p. 340).

Plasma proteins are synthesized by the liver, with the exception of antibodies, which are produced by lymphocytes, one of the types of white blood cells.

Erythrocytes

Each milliliter of blood on average contains about 5 billion **erythrocytes (red blood cells,** or **RBCs),** commonly reported clinically in a **red blood cell count** as 5 million cells per cubic millimeter (mm^3).

The structure of erythrocytes is well suited to their main function of O_2 transport in the blood.
The shape and content of erythrocytes are ideally suited to carry out their primary function, namely, transporting O_2.

ERYTHROCYTE STRUCTURE Two anatomic features of erythrocytes contribute to the efficiency with which they transport O_2. First, erythrocytes are flat, disc-shaped cells indented in the middle on both sides, like a doughnut with a flattened center instead of a hole (that is, they are biconcave discs) (● Figure 11-1). This unique shape provides a larger surface area for diffusion of O_2 from the plasma across the membrane into the erythrocyte than a spherical cell of the same volume would.

Second, the most important anatomic feature that enables RBCs to transport O_2 is the hemoglobin they contain.

HEMOGLOBIN'S TRANSPORT CAPACITY Hemoglobin is found only in red blood cells. A **hemoglobin** molecule has two parts: (1) the **globin** portion, a protein made up of four highly folded polypeptide chains, and (2) four iron-containing, nonprotein groups known as **heme groups,** each of which is bound to one of the polypeptides (● Figure 11-2). Each of the four iron atoms can combine reversibly with one molecule of O_2; thus, each hemoglobin molecule can pick up four O_2 passengers in the lungs. Because O_2 is poorly soluble in the plasma, 98.5% of the O_2 carried in the blood is bound to hemoglobin (see p. 387).

Hemoglobin is a pigment (that is, it is naturally colored). Because of its iron content, it appears reddish when combined with O_2 and bluish when deoxygenated. Thus, fully oxygenated arterial blood is red, and venous blood, which has lost some of its O_2 load at the tissue level, has a bluish cast.

In addition to carrying O_2, hemoglobin can combine with the following:

1. *Carbon dioxide (CO_2).* Hemoglobin helps transport this gas from the tissue cells back to the lungs (see p. 392).

2. *The acidic hydrogen-ion portion (H^+) of ionized carbonic acid,* which is generated at the tissue level from CO_2. Hemoglobin buffers this acid so that it minimally alters the pH of the blood (see p. 456).

3. *Carbon monoxide (CO).* This gas is not normally in the blood, but if inhaled, it preferentially occupies the O_2-binding sites on hemoglobin, causing CO poisoning (see p. 391).

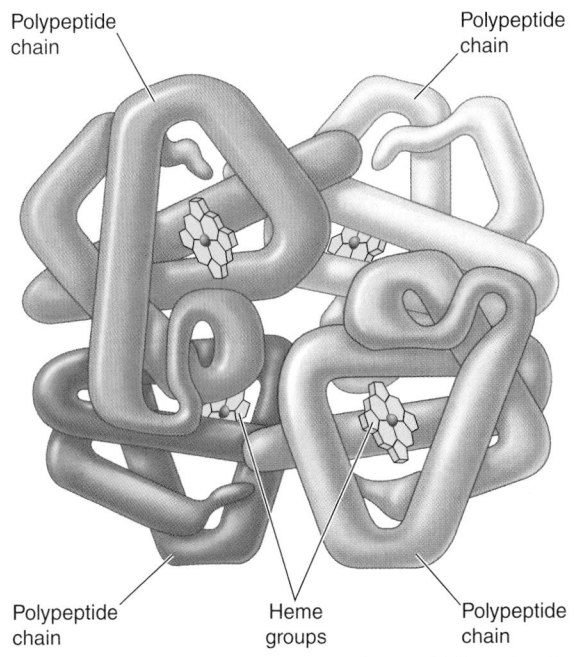

● **FIGURE 11-2 Hemoglobin molecule.** A hemoglobin molecule consists of four highly folded polypeptide chains (the globin portion) and four iron-containing heme groups. The red sphere in the center of each heme represents iron.

4. *Nitric oxide (NO).* In the lungs, the vasodilator nitric oxide binds to hemoglobin. This NO is released at the tissues, where it relaxes and dilates the local arterioles (see p. 290). Vasodilation helps ensure that the O_2-rich blood can make its vital rounds and helps stabilize blood pressure.

Therefore, hemoglobin plays the key role in O_2 transport while contributing significantly to CO_2 transport and the pH-buffering capacity of blood. Furthermore, by toting along its own vasodilator, hemoglobin helps deliver the O_2 it is carrying.

LACK OF NUCLEUS AND ORGANELLES   To maximize its hemoglobin content, a single erythrocyte is stuffed with more than 250 million hemoglobin molecules, excluding almost everything else. (That means each RBC can carry more than 1 billion O_2 molecules.) Red blood cells contain no nucleus or organelles. During the cell's development, these structures are extruded to make room for more hemoglobin. Thus, an RBC is mainly a plasma membrane–enclosed sac full of hemoglobin.

Ironically, even though erythrocytes are the vehicles for transporting O_2 to all other tissues of the body, for energy production erythrocytes themselves cannot use the O_2 they are carrying. Lacking the mitochondria that house the enzymes for oxidative phosphorylation, erythrocytes must rely entirely on glycolysis for ATP formation (see p. 29).

The bone marrow continuously replaces worn-out erythrocytes.

Each of us has a total of 25 trillion to 30 trillion RBCs streaming through our blood vessels at any given time (100,000 times more in number than the entire U.S. population). Yet these vital gas-transport vehicles are short lived and must be replaced at the average rate of 2 million to 3 million cells per second.

ERYTHROCYTES' SHORT LIFE SPAN   The price erythrocytes pay for their generous content of hemoglobin to the exclusion of the usual specialized intracellular machinery is a short life span. Without DNA, RNA, and ribosomes, red blood cells cannot synthesize proteins for cell repair, growth, and division or for renewing enzyme supplies. Equipped only with initial supplies synthesized before they extrude their nucleus and organelles, RBCs survive an average of only 120 days, in contrast to nerve and muscle cells, which last a person's entire life. During its short life span of 4 months, each erythrocyte travels about 700 miles as it circulates through the vasculature.

As a red blood cell ages, its nonreparable plasma membrane becomes fragile and prone to rupture as the cell squeezes through tight spots in the vascular system. Most old RBCs meet their final demise in the **spleen,** because this organ's narrow, winding capillary network is a tight fit for these fragile cells. The spleen lies in the upper left part of the abdomen. In addition to removing most of the old erythrocytes from circulation, the spleen has a limited ability to store healthy erythrocytes in its pulpy interior, is a reservoir for platelets, and contains an abundance of lymphocytes, a type of white blood cell.

ERYTHROPOIESIS   Because erythrocytes cannot divide to replenish their own numbers, the old ruptured cells must be replaced by new cells produced in an erythrocyte factory—the **bone marrow**—which is the soft, highly cellular tissue that fills the internal cavities of bones. The bone marrow normally generates new red blood cells, a process known as **erythropoiesis,** at a rate to keep pace with the demolition of old cells.

In children, most bones are filled with **red bone marrow** capable of blood cell production. As a person matures, however, fatty **yellow bone marrow** incapable of erythropoiesis gradually replaces red marrow, which remains only in a few isolated places, such as the sternum (breastbone), ribs, pelvis, and upper ends of the long limb bones. These are sites where bone marrow is extracted for examination or for use in bone marrow transplants.

Red marrow not only produces RBCs but also is the ultimate source for leukocytes and platelets. Undifferentiated **pluripotent stem cells,** the source of all blood cells, reside in the red marrow, where they continuously divide and differentiate to give rise to each of the types of blood cells (see ● Figure 11-13, p. 332). The different types of immature blood cells, along with the stem cells, are intermingled in the red marrow at various stages of development. Once mature, the blood cells are released into the rich supply of capillaries that permeate the red marrow. Regulatory factors act on the *hemopoietic* ("blood-producing") red marrow to govern the type and number of cells generated and discharged into the blood. Of the blood cells, the mechanism for regulating RBC production is the best understood. We consider it next.

Erythropoiesis is controlled by erythropoietin from the kidneys.

Because O_2 transport in the blood is the erythrocytes' main function, you might logically suspect that the primary stimulus for increased erythrocyte production would be reduced O_2 delivery to the tissues. You would be correct, but low O_2 levels do not stimulate erythropoiesis by acting directly on the red bone marrow. Instead, reduced O_2 delivery to the kidneys stimulates them to secrete the hormone **erythropoietin** into the blood, and this hormone in turn stimulates erythropoiesis by the bone marrow (● Figure 11-3). This increased erythropoietic activity elevates the number of circulating RBCs, thereby increasing O_2-carrying capacity of the blood and restoring O_2 delivery to the tissues to normal. Once normal O_2 delivery to the kidneys is achieved, erythropoietin secretion is turned down until needed again. In this way, erythrocyte production is normally balanced against destruction or loss of these cells so that O_2-carrying capacity in the blood stays fairly constant.

When you donate blood, your circulating erythrocyte supply is replenished in less than a week. In severe loss of RBCs, as in hemorrhage or abnormal destruction of young circulating erythrocytes, the rate of erythropoiesis can be increased to more than six times the normal level.

 SYNTHETIC ERYTHROPOIETIN   Researchers have identified the gene that directs erythropoietin synthesis, so this hormone can now be produced in a laboratory.

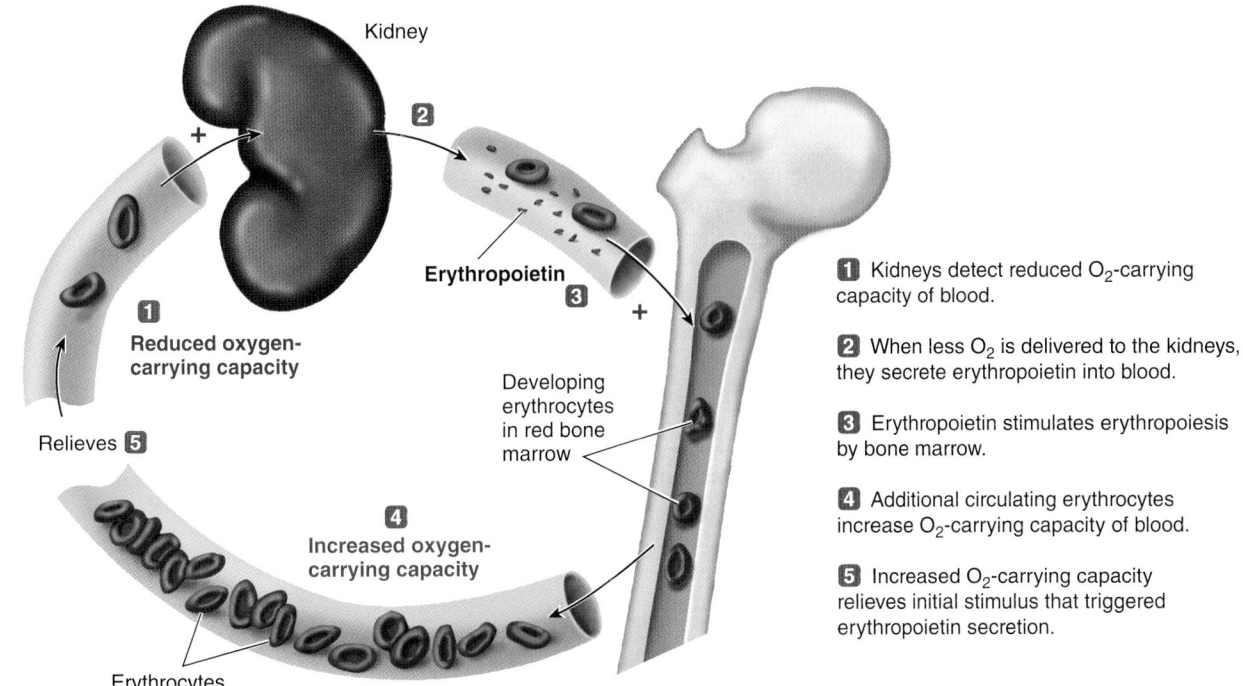

Kidney

Erythropoietin

1 Reduced oxygen-carrying capacity

Relieves **5**

4 Increased oxygen-carrying capacity

Erythrocytes

Developing erythrocytes in red bone marrow

1 Kidneys detect reduced O_2-carrying capacity of blood.

2 When less O_2 is delivered to the kidneys, they secrete erythropoietin into blood.

3 Erythropoietin stimulates erythropoiesis by bone marrow.

4 Additional circulating erythrocytes increase O_2-carrying capacity of blood.

5 Increased O_2-carrying capacity relieves initial stimulus that triggered erythropoietin secretion.

● **FIGURE 11-3 Control of erythropoiesis.**

Laboratory-produced erythropoietin (Epogen, Procrit) has currently become biotechnology's single-biggest moneymaker, with sales exceeding $1 billion annually. This hormone is often used to boost RBC production in patients with suppressed erythropoietic activity, such as those with kidney failure or those undergoing chemotherapy for cancer. (Chemotherapy drugs interfere with the rapid cell division characteristic of both cancer cells and developing RBCs.)

Anemia can be caused by a variety of disorders.

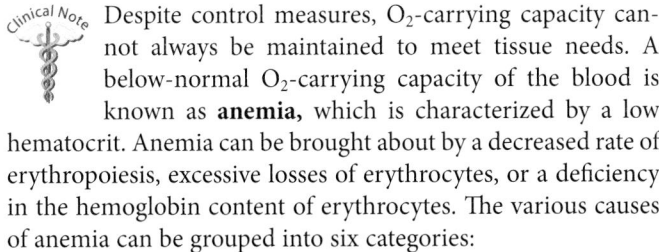

Despite control measures, O_2-carrying capacity cannot always be maintained to meet tissue needs. A below-normal O_2-carrying capacity of the blood is known as **anemia,** which is characterized by a low hematocrit. Anemia can be brought about by a decreased rate of erythropoiesis, excessive losses of erythrocytes, or a deficiency in the hemoglobin content of erythrocytes. The various causes of anemia can be grouped into six categories:

1. Nutritional anemia is caused by a dietary deficiency of a factor needed for erythropoiesis. The production of RBCs depends on an adequate supply of essential raw ingredients, some of which are not synthesized in the body but must be provided by dietary intake. For example, *iron deficiency anemia* occurs when not enough iron is available for synthesizing hemoglobin.

2. Pernicious anemia is caused by an inability to absorb enough ingested vitamin B_{12} from the digestive tract. Vitamin B_{12} is essential for normal RBC production and maturation. It is abundant in various foods and thus is rarely deficient in the diet. The problem is a deficiency of *intrinsic factor,* a special substance secreted by the lining of the stomach (see p. 480).

Vitamin B_{12} can be absorbed from the intestinal tract only when this nutrient is bound to intrinsic factor.

3. Aplastic anemia is caused by failure of the bone marrow to produce enough RBCs, even though all ingredients necessary for erythropoiesis are available. Reduced erythropoietic capability can be caused by destruction of red marrow by toxic chemicals (such as benzene), heavy exposure to radiation (fallout from a nuclear bomb explosion, for example, or excessive exposure to X-rays), invasion of the marrow by cancer cells, or chemotherapy for cancer. The destructive process may selectively reduce the marrow's output of erythrocytes, or it may also reduce the productive capability for leukocytes and platelets. The anemia's severity depends on the extent to which erythropoietic tissue is destroyed; severe losses are fatal.

4. Renal anemia may result from kidney disease. Because erythropoietin from the kidneys is the primary stimulus for promoting erythropoiesis, inadequate erythropoietin secretion by diseased kidneys leads to insufficient RBC production.

5. Hemorrhagic anemia is caused by losing a lot of blood. The loss can be either acute, such as a bleeding wound, or chronic, such as excessive menstrual flow.

6. Hemolytic anemia is caused by the rupture of too many circulating erythrocytes. **Hemolysis,** the rupture of RBCs, occurs either because otherwise normal cells are induced to rupture by external factors, as in the invasion of RBCs by *malaria* parasites, or because the cells are defective, as in sickle cell disease. **Sickle cell disease** is the best-known example among various hereditary abnormalities of erythrocytes that make these cells fragile. It affects about 1 in 650 African Americans. Sickle cell disease is caused by a genetic mutation that changes a single amino acid in the 146-long amino acid chain that makes up a hemoglobin polypeptide. This defective type of hemoglobin joins together to form rigid chains that make the RBC stiff and unnaturally shaped, like a crescent or sickle (● Figure 11-4). Unlike normal erythrocytes, these deformed RBCs tend to clump together. The resultant "logjam" blocks blood flow through small vessels, leading to pain and tissue damage at the affected site. Furthermore, the defective erythrocytes are fragile and prone to rupture, even as young cells, as they travel through the narrow splenic capillaries. Despite an accelerated rate of erythropoiesis triggered by the constant excessive loss of RBCs, production may not be able to keep pace with the rate of destruction, and anemia may result.

Polycythemia is an excess of circulating erythrocytes.

Polycythemia, in contrast to anemia, is characterized by too many circulating RBCs and an elevated hematocrit. There are two general types of polycythemia, depending on the circumstances that trigger the excess RBC production: primary polycythemia and secondary polycythemia.

Primary polycythemia is caused by a tumorlike condition of the bone marrow in which erythropoiesis proceeds at an excessive, uncontrolled rate instead of being subject to the normal erythropoietin regulatory mechanism. The RBC count may reach 11 million cells/mm^3 (normal is 5 million cells/mm^3), and the hematocrit may be as high as 70% to 80% (normal is 42% to 45%). No benefit is derived from the extra O_2-carrying capacity of the blood, because O_2 delivery is more than adequate with normal RBC numbers. Inappropriate polycythemia has harmful effects, however. The excessive number of red cells increases blood's viscosity up to five to seven times normal (that is, makes the blood "thicker"), causing the blood to flow sluggishly, which may actually reduce O_2 delivery to the tissues (see p. 281). The increased viscosity also increases the total peripheral resistance, which may elevate the blood pressure, thus increasing the workload of the heart, unless blood-pressure control mechanisms can compensate (see ● Figure 10-11, p. 293).

Secondary polycythemia, in contrast, is an appropriate erythropoietin-induced adaptive mechanism to improve the blood's O_2-carrying capacity in response to a prolonged reduction in O_2 delivery to the tissues. It occurs normally in people living at high altitudes, where less O_2 is available in the air, or in people for whom O_2 delivery to the tissues is impaired by chronic lung disease or cardiac failure. The price paid for improved O_2 delivery is an increased viscosity of the blood.

We next shift attention to blood types, which depend on special markers on the surface membrane of erythrocytes.

Blood types depend on surface antigens on erythrocytes.

An **antigen** is a large, complex molecule that triggers a specific immune response against itself when it gains entry to the body. For example, antigens are found on the surface of foreign cells such as bacterial invaders. Certain types of white blood cells recognize antigens and produce specific antibodies against them. An **antibody** binds with the specific antigen against which it is produced and leads to the antigen's destruction by various means. Thus, the body rejects cells bearing antigens that do not match its own. You will learn more about these immune responses later in this chapter when we turn to body defenses. For now, we focus on the special antigen–antibody reaction that forms the basis of different blood types.

ABO BLOOD TYPES The surface membranes of human erythrocytes contain inherited antigens that vary depending on blood type. Within the major blood group system, the **ABO system,** the erythrocytes of people with type A blood contain A antigens, those with type B blood contain B antigens, those with type AB blood have both A and B antigens, and those with type O blood do not have any A or B red blood cell surface antigens.

Antibodies against erythrocyte antigens not present on the body's own erythrocytes begin to appear in human plasma after a baby is about 6 months of age. Accordingly, the plasma of type A blood contains anti-B antibodies, type B blood contains anti-A antibodies, no antibodies related to the ABO system are present in type AB blood, and both anti-A and anti-B antibodies are present in type O blood (▲ Table 11-2). Typically, one would expect antibody production against A or B antigen to be induced only if blood containing the alien antigen were injected into the body. However, high levels of these antibodies are found in the plasma of people who have never been exposed to a different type of blood. Consequently, these were considered naturally occurring antibodies, that is, produced without any known exposure to the antigen. Scientists now know that people are routinely exposed at an early age to small amounts of

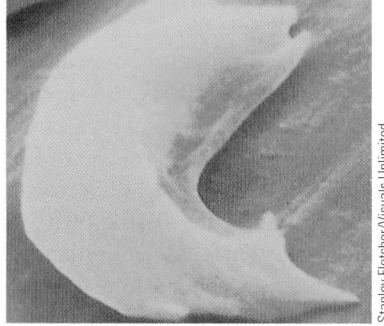

● **FIGURE 11-4 Sickle-shaped red blood cell.**

Stanley Fletcher/Visuals Unlimited.

▲ Table 11-2 **ABO Blood Types**

Blood Type	Antigens on Erythrocytes	Antibodies in Plasma
A	A	Anti-B
B	B	Anti-A
AB	A and B	No antibodies
O	No antigens	Both anti-A and anti-B

A- and B-like antigens associated with common, harmless intestinal bacteria. Antibodies produced against these foreign antigens coincidentally also interact with a nearly identical antigen for a foreign blood group, even on first exposure to it.

TRANSFUSION REACTION If a person is given blood of an incompatible type, two antigen–antibody interactions take place. By far, the more serious consequences arise from the effect of the antibodies in the recipient's plasma on the incoming donor erythrocytes. The effect of the donor's antibodies on the recipient's erythrocyte-bound antigens is less important unless a large amount of blood is transfused, because the donor's antibodies are so diluted by the recipient's plasma that little red blood cell damage takes place in the recipient.

Antibody interaction with an erythrocyte-bound antigen may result in agglutination (clumping) or hemolysis (rupture) of the attacked red blood cells. Agglutination and hemolysis of donor red blood cells by antibodies in the recipient's plasma can lead to a sometimes fatal **transfusion reaction** (● Figure 11-5). Agglutinated clumps of incoming donor cells can plug small blood vessels. In addition, one of the most lethal consequences of mismatched transfusions is acute kidney failure caused by the release of large amounts of hemoglobin from ruptured donor erythrocytes. If the free hemoglobin in the plasma rises above a critical level, it will precipitate in the kidneys and block the urine-forming structures, leading to acute kidney shutdown.

UNIVERSAL BLOOD DONORS AND RECIPIENTS Because type O individuals have no A or B antigens, their erythrocytes will not be attacked by either anti-A or anti-B antibodies, so they are considered **universal donors.** Their blood can be transfused into people of any blood type. However, type O individuals can receive only type O blood, because the anti-A and anti-B antibodies in their plasma will attack either A or B antigens in incoming blood. In contrast, type AB individuals are called **universal recipients.** Lacking both anti-A and anti-B antibodies, they can accept donor blood of any type, although they can donate blood only to other AB people. Because their erythrocytes have both A and B antigens, their cells would be attacked if transfused into individuals with antibodies against either of these antigens.

The terms *universal donor* and *universal recipient* are misleading, however. In addition to the ABO system, many other erythrocyte antigens and plasma antibodies can cause transfusion reactions, the most important of which is the Rh factor.

RH BLOOD-GROUP SYSTEM People who have the **Rh factor** (an erythrocyte antigen first observed in rhesus monkeys, hence the designation Rh) are said to have *Rh-positive* blood, whereas those lacking the Rh factor are considered *Rh-negative.* In contrast to the ABO system, no naturally occurring antibodies develop against the Rh factor.

Anti-Rh antibodies are produced only by Rh-negative individuals when (and if) such people are first exposed to the foreign Rh antigen present in Rh-positive blood. A subsequent transfusion of Rh-

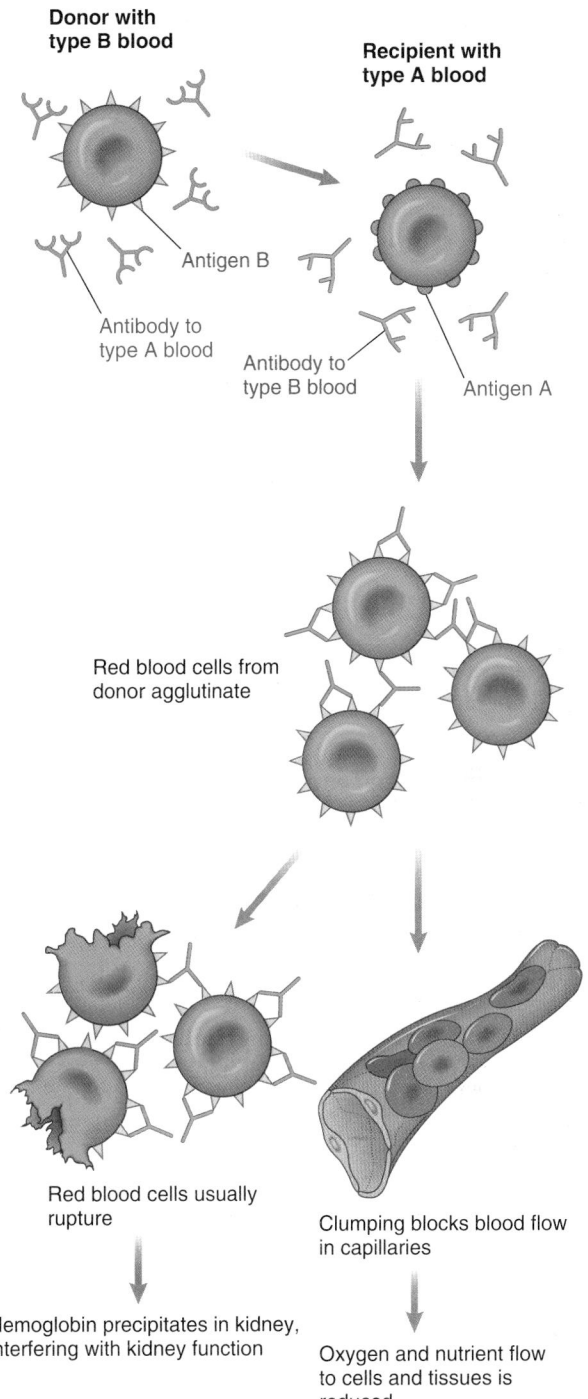

● **FIGURE 11-5 Transfusion reaction.** This transfusion reaction results from type B blood being transfused into a recipient with type A blood.

positive blood could produce a transfusion reaction in such a sensitized Rh-negative person. Rh-positive individuals, in contrast, never produce antibodies against the Rh factor that they themselves possess. Therefore, Rh-negative people should be given only Rh-negative blood, whereas Rh-positive people can safely receive either Rh-negative or Rh-positive blood. The Rh factor is of particular medical importance when an Rh-negative mother develops antibodies against the erythrocytes of an Rh-positive fetus she is carrying, a condition known as **erythro-**

blastosis fetalis, or **hemolytic disease of the newborn.** Because the fetal bone marrow cannot put out mature erythrocytes as fast as the rate of erythrocyte destruction by the maternal antibodies, it releases immature precursors of erythrocytes known as erythroblasts ("erythrocyte formers"), hence the name of the condition. (See the Clinical Consideration on p. 363 for further discussion of this disorder.)

Except in extreme emergencies, it is safest to individually cross-match blood before a transfusion is undertaken even though the ABO and Rh typing is already known, because there are approximately 23 other minor human erythrocyte antigen systems, with hundreds of subtypes. Compatibility is determined by mixing the red blood cells from the potential donor with plasma from the recipient. If no clumping occurs, the blood is considered an adequate match for transfusion.

We next examine platelets, another type of cellular element present in the blood.

Platelets and Hemostasis

An average of 250 million platelets are normally present in each milliliter of blood (range of 150,000 to 350,000/mm³).

Platelets are cell fragments shed from megakaryocytes.

Platelets, or **thrombocytes,** are not whole cells but small cell fragments shed from the outer edges of extraordinarily large bone marrow–bound cells known as **megakaryocytes** (● Figure 11-6). A single megakaryocyte typically produces about 1000 platelets. Megakaryocytes are derived from the same undifferentiated stem cells that give rise to the erythrocytic and leukocytic cell lines (see ● Figure 11-13, p. 332). Platelets are essentially detached vesicles containing pieces of megakaryocyte cytoplasm wrapped in plasma membrane.

Platelets remain functional for an average of 10 days, at which time they are removed from circulation by tissue macro-

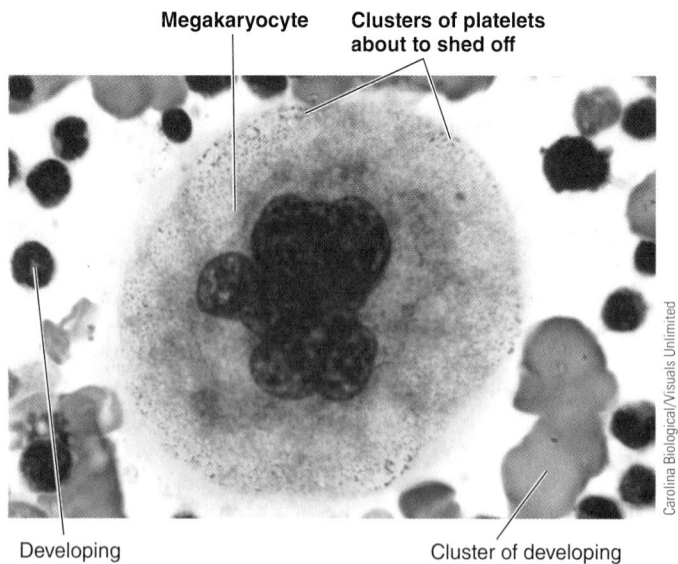

● **FIGURE 11-6 A megakaryocyte forming platelets.**

Megakaryocyte · Clusters of platelets about to shed off · Developing leukocyte · Cluster of developing erythrocytes · Carolina Biological/Visuals Unlimited

phages (large phagocytic cells), especially those in the spleen and liver, and are replaced by newly released platelets from the bone marrow. The hormone **thrombopoietin,** produced by the liver, increases the number of megakaryocytes in the bone marrow and stimulates each megakaryocyte to produce more platelets as needed.

Because platelets are cell fragments, they lack nuclei. However, they have organelles and cytosolic enzyme systems for generating energy and synthesizing secretory products, which they store in numerous granules dispersed throughout the cytosol. Furthermore, platelets contain high concentrations of actin and myosin, which enable them to contract. Their secretory and contractile abilities are important in hemostasis, a topic to which we now turn.

Hemostasis prevents blood loss from damaged small vessels.

Hemostasis is the arrest of bleeding from a broken blood vessel—that is, the stopping of hemorrhage (*hemo* means "blood"; *stasis* means "standing"). For bleeding to take place from a vessel, there must be a break in the vessel wall and the pressure inside the vessel must be greater than the pressure outside it to force blood out through the defect.

The small capillaries, arterioles, and venules are often ruptured by minor traumas of everyday life; such traumas are the most common source of bleeding, although we often are not even aware that any damage has taken place. The body's inherent hemostatic mechanisms normally are adequate to seal defects and stop blood loss through these small microcirculatory vessels.

 The rarer occurrence of bleeding from medium to large vessels usually cannot be stopped by the body's hemostatic mechanisms alone. Bleeding from a severed artery is more profuse and therefore more dangerous than venous bleeding, because the outward driving pressure is greater in the arteries (that is, arterial blood pressure is higher than venous pressure). First-aid measures for a severed artery include applying external pressure to the wound that is greater than the arterial blood pressure to temporarily halt the bleeding until the torn vessel can be surgically closed. Hemorrhage from a traumatized vein can often be stopped simply by elevating the bleeding body part to reduce gravity's effects on pressure in the vein (see p. 303). If the accompanying drop in venous pressure is not enough to stop the bleeding, mild external compression is usually adequate.

Hemostasis involves three major steps: (1) *vascular spasm,* (2) *formation of a platelet plug,* and (3) *blood coagulation (clotting).* Platelets play a pivotal role in hemostasis. They obviously play a major part in forming a platelet plug, but they also contribute significantly to the other two steps.

Vascular spasm reduces blood flow through an injured vessel.

A cut or torn blood vessel immediately constricts. The underlying mechanism is unclear but is thought to be an intrinsic response triggered by a paracrine released locally from the inner lining (endothelium) of the injured vessel (see p. 282). This constriction, or **vascular spasm,** slows blood flow through the defect and thus minimizes blood loss. Also, as the opposing endothelial surfaces of the vessel are pressed together by this initial vascular spasm, they become sticky and adhere to each other, further sealing off the damaged vessel. These physical measures alone cannot completely prevent further blood loss, but they minimize blood flow through the break in the vessel until the other hemostatic measures can actually plug the hole.

Platelets aggregate to form a plug at a vessel tear or cut.

Platelets normally do not stick to the smooth endothelial surface of blood vessels, but when this lining is disrupted because of vessel injury, platelets adhere to the exposed *collagen,* which is a fibrous protein in the underlying connective tissue (see p. 52 and p. 284). This adhesion prevents these platelets from being swept forward in the circulation. This layer of stuck platelets forms the foundation of a hemostatic **platelet plug** at the site of the defect. Collagen activates the bound platelets. Activated platelets quickly reorganize their actin cytoskeletal elements to develop spiky processes, which help them adhere to the collagen and to other platelets. Activated platelets also release sev-

eral important chemicals from their storage granules. Among these chemicals is *adenosine diphosphate (ADP),* which activates other nearby circulating platelets and causes their surfaces to become sticky so that they adhere to the first layer of aggregated platelets. These newly aggregated platelets release more ADP, which causes more platelets to pile on, and so on; thus, a plug of platelets is rapidly built up at the defect site in a positive-feedback fashion (● Figure 11-7).

Given the self-perpetuating nature of platelet aggregation, why does the platelet plug not continue to develop and expand over the surface of the adjacent normal vessel lining? A key reason is that ADP and other chemicals released by the activated platelets stimulate the release of *prostacyclin* and *nitric oxide* from the adjacent normal endothelium. Both these chemicals profoundly inhibit platelet aggregation. Thus, the platelet plug is limited to the defect and does not spread to the nearby undamaged vascular tissue (● Figure 11-7).

The aggregated platelet plug not only physically seals the break in the vessel but also performs three other important roles. (1) The actin–myosin complex within the aggregated platelets contracts to compact and strengthen what was originally a fairly loose plug. (2) The platelet plug releases several

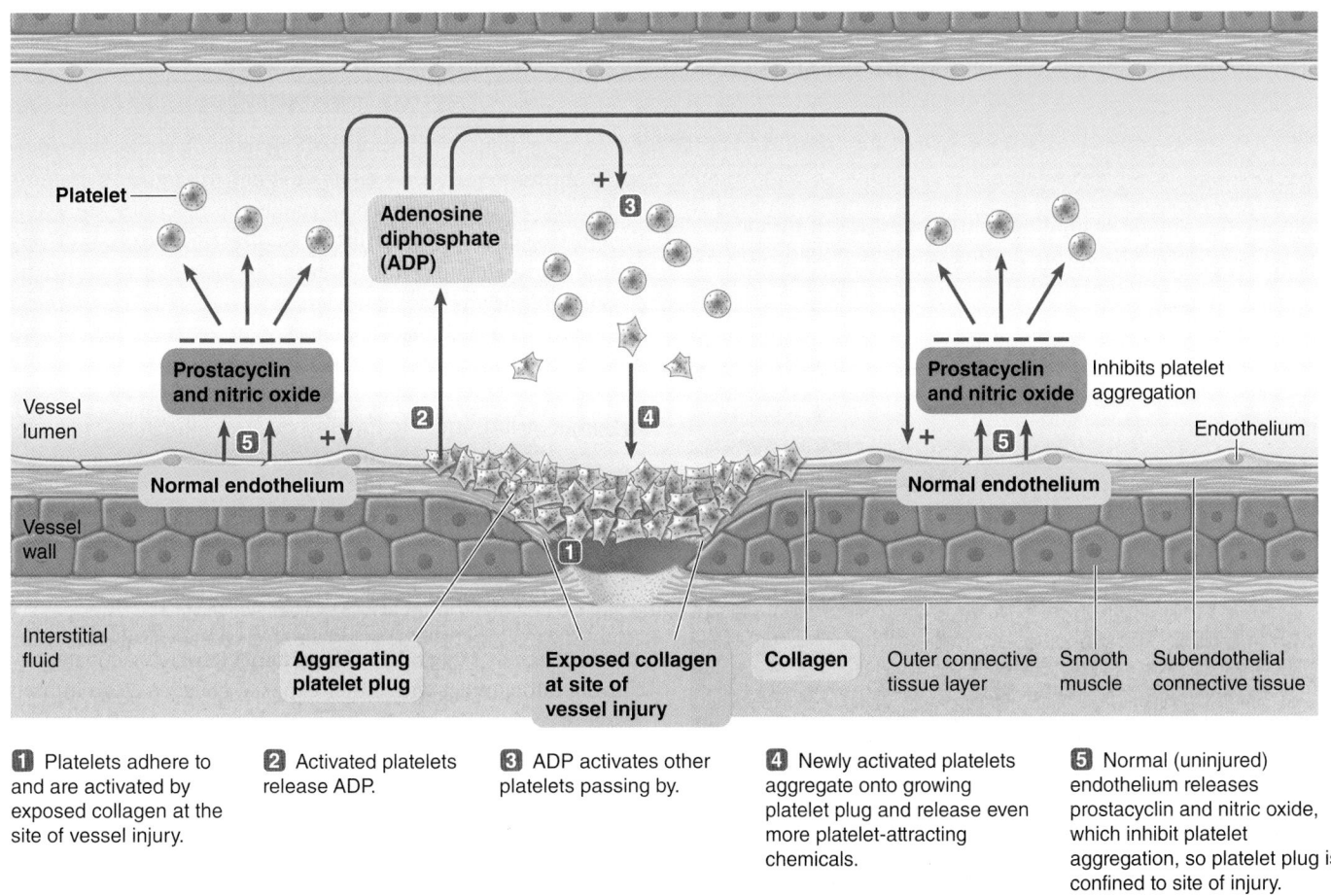

1 Platelets adhere to and are activated by exposed collagen at the site of vessel injury.

2 Activated platelets release ADP.

3 ADP activates other platelets passing by.

4 Newly activated platelets aggregate onto growing platelet plug and release even more platelet-attracting chemicals.

5 Normal (uninjured) endothelium releases prostacyclin and nitric oxide, which inhibit platelet aggregation, so platelet plug is confined to site of injury.

● **FIGURE 11-7 Formation of a platelet plug.** Platelets aggregate at a vessel defect through a positive-feedback mechanism involving release of adenosine diphosphate (ADP) (and other chemicals not shown) from platelets, which stick to exposed collagen at the site of the injury. Platelets are prevented from aggregating at the adjacent normal vessel lining by ADP promoting the release of prostacyclin and nitric oxide from the undamaged endothelial cells.

powerful vasoconstrictors that induce profound constriction of the affected vessel to reinforce the initial vascular spasm. (3) The platelet plug releases other chemicals that enhance blood coagulation, the next step of hemostasis. Although the platelet-plugging mechanism alone is often enough to seal the myriad minute tears in capillaries and other small vessels that occur many times daily, larger holes in vessels require the formation of a blood clot to completely stop the bleeding.

Clot formation results from a triggered chain reaction involving plasma clotting factors.

Blood coagulation, or **clotting,** is the transformation of blood from a liquid into a solid gel. Formation of a clot on top of the platelet plug strengthens and supports the plug, reinforcing the seal over a break in a vessel. Furthermore, as blood in the vicinity of the vessel defect solidifies, it can no longer flow. Clotting is the body's most powerful hemostatic mechanism. It is required to stop bleeding from all but the most minute defects.

CLOT FORMATION The ultimate step in clot formation is the conversion of **fibrinogen,** a large, soluble plasma protein produced by the liver and normally always present in the plasma, into **fibrin,** an insoluble, threadlike molecule. This conversion into fibrin is catalyzed by the enzyme **thrombin** at the site of the injury. Fibrin molecules adhere to the damaged vessel surface, forming a loose, netlike meshwork that traps blood cells, including aggregating platelets. The resulting mass, or **clot,** typically appears red because of the abundance of trapped RBCs, but the foundation of the clot is formed of fibrin derived from the plasma (● Figure 11-8). Except for platelets, which play an important role in ultimately bringing about the conversion of fibrinogen to fibrin, clotting can take place in the absence of all other blood cells.

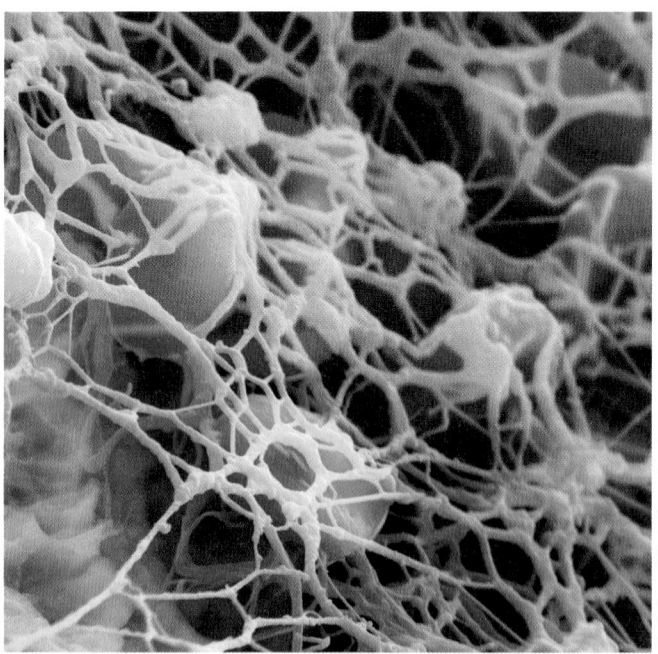

● **FIGURE 11-8 Erythrocytes trapped in the fibrin meshwork of a clot.**

Because thrombin converts the ever-present fibrinogen molecules in the plasma into a blood-stanching clot, thrombin must normally be absent from the plasma except in the vicinity of vessel damage. Otherwise, blood would always be coagulated— a situation incompatible with life. How can thrombin normally be absent from the plasma yet be readily available to trigger fibrin formation when a vessel is injured? The solution lies in thrombin's existence in the plasma in the form of an inactive precursor called **prothrombin.** What converts prothrombin into thrombin when blood clotting is desirable? This conversion involves the clotting cascade.

THE CLOTTING CASCADE Yet another activated plasma clotting factor, **factor X,** converts prothrombin to thrombin; factor X itself is normally present in the blood in inactive form and must be converted into its active form by still another activated factor, and so on. Altogether, 12 plasma clotting factors participate in essential steps that lead to the final conversion of fibrinogen into a stabilized fibrin mesh (● Figure 11-9). These factors are designated by roman numerals in the order in which the factors were discovered, not the order in which they participate in the clotting process.[1] Most of these clotting factors are plasma proteins synthesized by the liver. Normally, they are always present in the plasma in an inactive form, such as fibrinogen and prothrombin. In contrast to fibrinogen, which is converted into insoluble fibrin strands, prothrombin and the other precursors, when converted to their active form, act as proteolytic (protein-splitting) enzymes. These enzymes activate another specific factor in the clotting sequence. Once the first factor in the sequence is activated, it in turn activates the next factor, and so on, in a series of sequential reactions known as the **clotting cascade,** until thrombin catalyzes the final conversion of fibrinogen into fibrin. Several of these steps require the presence of plasma Ca^{2+} and *platelet factor 3 (PF3),* a chemical secreted by the aggregated platelet plug. Thus, platelets also contribute to clot formation.

INTRINSIC AND EXTRINSIC PATHWAYS The clotting cascade may be triggered by the *intrinsic pathway* or the *extrinsic pathway:*

■ The **intrinsic pathway** precipitates clotting within damaged vessels, as well as clotting of blood samples in test tubes. All elements necessary to bring about clotting by means of the intrinsic pathway are present in the blood. This pathway, which involves seven separate steps (shown in blue in ● Figure 11-9), is set off when **factor XII (Hageman factor)** is activated by coming into contact with either exposed collagen in an injured vessel or a foreign surface such as a glass test tube. Remember that exposed collagen also initiates platelet aggregation. Thus, formation of a platelet plug and the chain reaction leading to clot formation are simultaneously set in motion when a vessel is damaged.

---

[1]The term *factor VI* is no longer used. What once was considered a separate factor VI has now been determined to be an activated form of factor V.

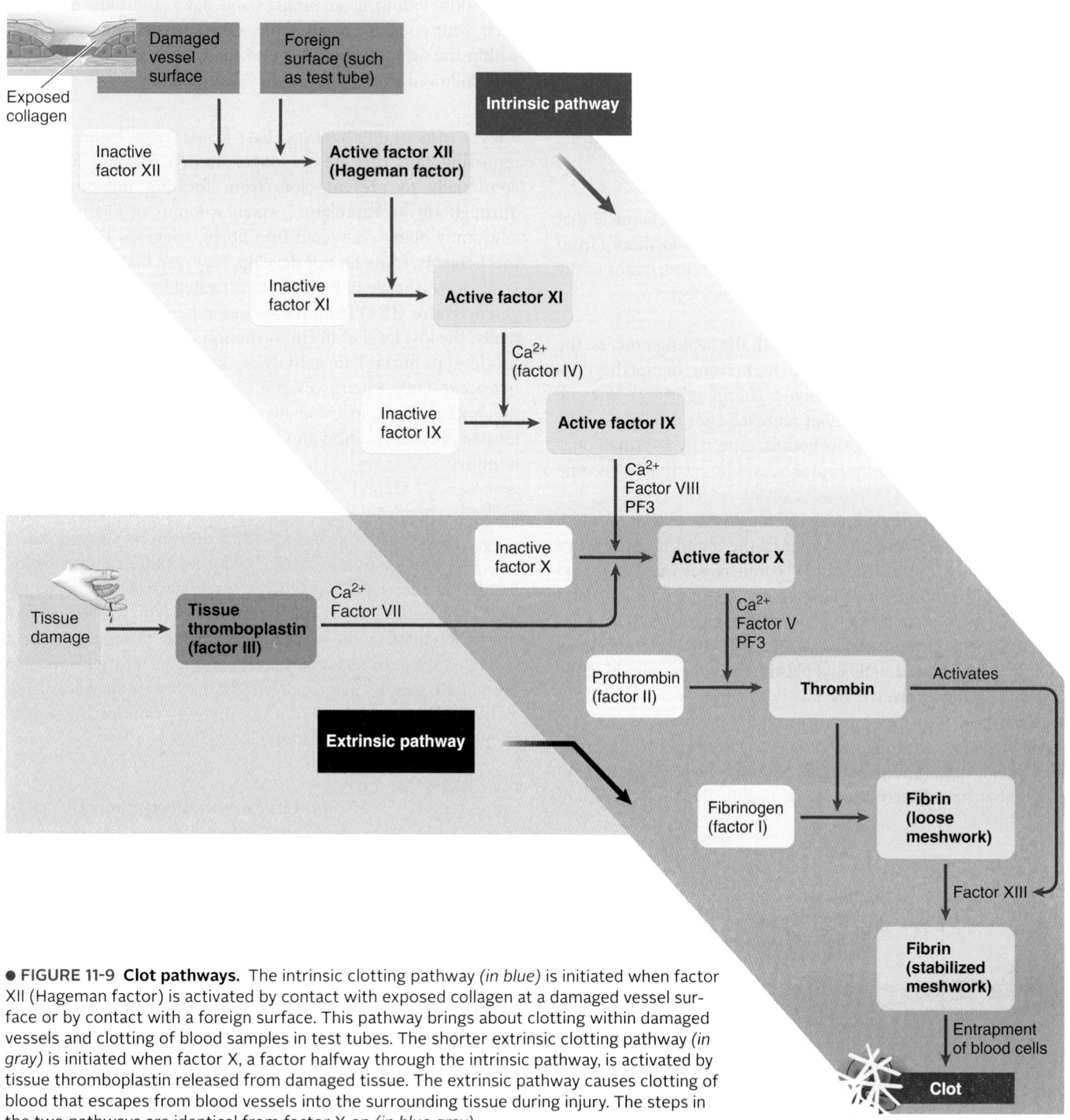

● FIGURE 11-9 Clot pathways. The intrinsic clotting pathway *(in blue)* is initiated when factor XII (Hageman factor) is activated by contact with exposed collagen at a damaged vessel surface or by contact with a foreign surface. This pathway brings about clotting within damaged vessels and clotting of blood samples in test tubes. The shorter extrinsic clotting pathway *(in gray)* is initiated when factor X, a factor halfway through the intrinsic pathway, is activated by tissue thromboplastin released from damaged tissue. The extrinsic pathway causes clotting of blood that escapes from blood vessels into the surrounding tissue during injury. The steps in the two pathways are identical from factor X on *(in blue gray)*.

■ The **extrinsic pathway** takes a shortcut and requires only four steps (shown in gray in ● Figure 11-9). This pathway, which requires contact with tissue factors external to the blood, initiates clotting of blood that has escaped into the tissues. When a tissue is traumatized, it releases a protein complex known as **tissue thromboplastin.** Tissue thromboplastin directly activates factor X, thereby bypassing all preceding steps of the intrinsic pathway. From this point on, the two pathways are identical.

The intrinsic and extrinsic mechanisms usually operate simultaneously. When tissue injury involves rupture of vessels, the intrinsic mechanism stops blood in the injured vessel, and the extrinsic mechanism clots blood that escaped into the tissue before the vessel was sealed off. Typically, clots are fully formed in 3 to 6 minutes.

CLOT RETRACTION Once a clot is formed, contraction of the platelets trapped within the clot shrinks the fibrin mesh, pulling the edges of the damaged vessel closer together. During **clot retraction,** fluid is squeezed from the clot. This fluid, which is essentially plasma minus fibrinogen and other clotting precursors that have been removed during the clotting process, is called **serum.**

Fibrinolytic plasmin dissolves clots.

A clot is not meant to be a permanent solution to vessel injury. It is a transient device to stop bleeding until the vessel can be repaired.

VESSEL REPAIR The aggregated platelets secrete a chemical that helps promote the invasion of fibroblasts ("fiber formers") from the surrounding connective tissue into the wounded area of the vessel. Fibroblasts form a scar at the vessel defect.

CLOT DISSOLUTION Simultaneous with the healing process, the clot, which is no longer needed to prevent hemorrhage, is slowly dissolved by a fibrinolytic (fibrin-splitting) enzyme called **plasmin.** If clots were not removed after they performed their hemostatic function, the vessels, especially the small ones that regularly endure tiny ruptures, would eventually become obstructed by clots.

Plasmin, like the clotting factors, is a plasma protein produced by the liver and present in the blood in an inactive precursor form, **plasminogen.** Plasmin is activated in a fast cascade of reactions involving many factors, among them factor XII (Hageman factor), which also triggers the chain reaction leading to clot formation (● Figure 11-10). When a clot is rapidly being formed, activated plasmin becomes trapped in the clot and later dissolves it by slowly breaking down the fibrin meshwork.

Phagocytic white blood cells gradually remove the products of clot dissolution. You have observed the slow removal of blood that has clotted after escaping into the tissue layers of

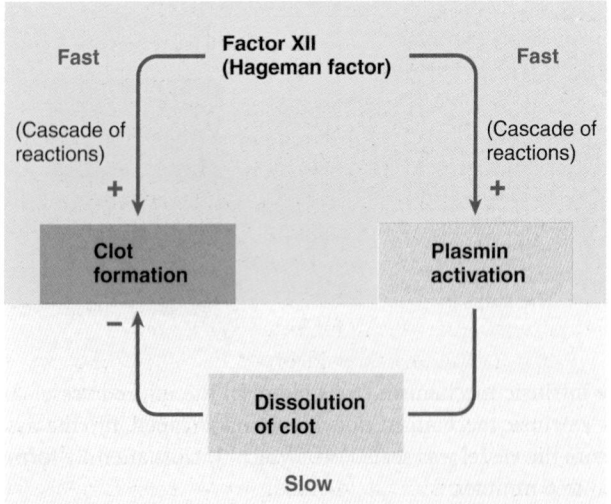

● **FIGURE 11-10 Role of factor XII in clot formation and dissolution.** Activation of factor XII (Hageman factor) simultaneously initiates a fast cascade of reactions that result in clot formation and a fast cascade of reactions that result in plasmin activation. Plasmin, which is trapped in the clot, subsequently slowly dissolves the clot. This action removes the clot when it is no longer needed after the vessel has been repaired.

your skin following an injury. The black-and-blue marks of such bruised skin result from deoxygenated clotted blood within the skin; this blood is eventually cleared by plasmin action, followed by the phagocytic "cleanup crew."

PREVENTING INAPPROPRIATE CLOT FORMATION In addition to removing clots that are no longer needed, plasmin functions continually to prevent clots from forming inappropriately. Throughout the vasculature, small amounts of fibrinogen are constantly being converted into fibrin, triggered by unknown mechanisms. Clots do not develop, however, because the fibrin is quickly disposed of by plasmin activated by **tissue plasminogen activator (tPA)** from the tissues, especially the lungs. Normally, the low level of fibrin formation is counterbalanced by a low level of fibrinolytic activity, so inappropriate clotting does not occur. Only when a vessel is damaged do additional factors precipitate the explosive chain reaction that leads to more extensive fibrin formation and results in local clotting at the site of injury.

 Genetically engineered tPA and other similar chemicals that trigger clot dissolution are frequently used to limit damage to cardiac muscle during heart attacks. Administering a clot-busting drug within the first hours after a clot has blocked a coronary (heart) vessel often dissolves the clot in time to restore blood flow to the cardiac muscle supplied by the blocked vessel before the muscle dies of O_2 deprivation. In recent years, tPA and related drugs have also been used successfully to promptly dissolve a stroke-causing clot within a cerebral (brain) blood vessel, minimizing loss of irreplaceable brain tissue after a stroke (see p. 121).

Inappropriate clotting produces thromboembolism.

 Despite protective measures, clots occasionally form in intact vessels. Abnormal or excessive clot formation within blood vessels—what has been dubbed "hemostasis in the wrong place"—can compromise blood flow to vital organs. The body's clotting and anticlotting systems normally function in a check-and-balance manner. Acting in concert, they permit prompt formation of "good" blood clots, thus minimizing blood loss from damaged vessels, while preventing "bad" clots from forming and blocking blood flow in intact vessels. An abnormal intravascular clot attached to a vessel wall is known as a **thrombus,** and freely floating clots are called **emboli** (singular, *embolus*). An enlarging thrombus narrows and can eventually completely occlude the vessel in which it forms. By entering and completely plugging a smaller vessel, a circulating embolus can suddenly block blood flow (see ● Figure 9-25, p. 271).

Several factors, acting independently or simultaneously, can cause *thromboembolism:* (1) Roughened vessel surfaces associated with atherosclerosis can lead to thrombus formation (see p. 270). (2) Imbalances in the clotting–anticlotting systems can trigger clot formation. (3) Slow-moving blood is more apt to clot, probably because small quantities of fibrin accumulate in the stagnant blood, for example, in blood pooled in varicosed leg veins (see p. 305). (4) Widespread clotting is occasionally triggered by release of tissue thromboplastin into the blood from large amounts of traumatized tissue. Similar widespread clotting can occur in **septicemic shock,** in which bacteria or their toxins initiate the clotting cascade.

Anticoagulant drugs are sometimes given to prevent thromboembolism in people with conditions that make them more prone to the development of clots. For example, *heparin,* which must be injected, accelerates the action of a normal blood-borne inhibitor of thrombin, halting this clot promoter. *Warfarin* (Coumadin), which can be taken orally, interferes with vitamin K's action. Vitamin K, commonly known as the blood-clotting vitamin, is essential for normal clot formation.

Hemophilia is the primary condition that produces excessive bleeding.

 In contrast to inappropriate clot formation in intact vessels, the opposite hemostatic disorder is failure of clots to form promptly in injured vessels, resulting in life-threatening hemorrhage from even relatively mild traumas. The most common cause of excessive bleeding is **hemophilia,** which is caused by a deficiency of one of the factors in the clotting cascade.

People with a platelet deficiency, in contrast to the more profuse bleeding that accompanies defects in the clotting mechanism, continuously develop hundreds of small, confined hemorrhagic areas throughout the body tissues as blood leaks from tiny breaks in the small blood vessels before coagulation takes place. Platelets normally are the primary sealers of these ever-occurring minute ruptures. In the skin of a platelet-deficient person, the diffuse capillary hemorrhages are visible as small, purplish blotches, giving rise to the term **thrombocytopenia purpura** ("the purple of thrombocyte deficiency") for this condition. (Recall that *thrombocyte* is another name for *platelet.*)

Vitamin K deficiency can also cause a bleeding tendency because of incomplete activation of vitamin K–dependent clotting factors.

Leukocytes

Leukocytes (white blood cells, or **WBCs)** are the mobile units of the body's immune defense system. **Immunity** is the body's ability to resist or eliminate potentially harmful foreign materials or abnormal cells. The first line of defense against foreign invaders is the epithelial barriers that surround the outer surface of the body (the skin) and line the body cavities (such as the digestive tract and lungs) that are in contact with the external environment. These epithelial barriers are not part of the immune system. We discuss their roles in the body's overall defense mechanisms after examining the immune system in detail.

Leukocytes and their derivatives, along with a variety of plasma proteins, make up the **immune system,** an internal defense system that recognizes and either destroys or neutralizes materials that are not "normal self," either foreign materials that have entered the body or abnormal cells that have arisen within the body. Specifically, the immune system:

1. defends against invading **pathogens** (disease-producing microorganisms such as bacteria and viruses).

2. functions as a "cleanup crew" that removes worn-out cells (such as aged red blood cells) and tissue debris (for example, tissue damaged by trauma or disease), paving the way for wound healing and tissue repair.

3. identifies and destroys abnormal or mutant cells that arise in the body. This function, termed *immune surveillance,* is the primary internal-defense mechanism against cancer.

Leukocytes primarily function as defense agents outside the blood.

To carry out their functions, leukocytes largely use a "seek out and attack" strategy; that is, they go to sites of invasion or tissue damage. The main reason WBCs are in the blood is for rapid transport from their site of production or storage to wherever they are needed. Unlike erythrocytes, leukocytes are able to exit the blood by assuming amoeba-like behavior to wriggle through narrow capillary pores and crawl to assaulted areas (see ● Figure 11-14, p. 334). As a result, the immune system's effector cells are widely dispersed throughout the body and can defend in any location.

Pathogenic bacteria and viruses are the major targets of the immune system.

The primary foreign enemies against which the immune system defends are bacteria and viruses. Comparing their relative sizes, if an average bacterium were the size of a pitcher's mound, a virus would be the size of a baseball. **Bacteria** are nonnucleated, single-celled microorganisms self-equipped with all the machinery essential for their own survival and reproduction. Pathogenic bacteria that invade the body cause tissue damage and produce disease largely by releasing enzymes or toxins that physically injure or functionally disrupt affected cells and organs. The disease-producing power of a pathogen is known as its **virulence.**

In contrast to bacteria, **viruses** are not self-sustaining cellular entities. They consist only of nucleic acids (genetic material—DNA or RNA) enclosed by a protein coat. Because they lack cellular machinery for energy production and protein synthesis, viruses cannot carry out metabolism and reproduce unless they invade a **host cell** (a body cell of the infected individual) and take over the cell's biochemical facilities for their own uses. Not only do viruses sap the host cell's energy resources, but the viral nucleic acids also direct the host cell to synthesize proteins needed for viral replication.

When a virus becomes incorporated into a host cell, the body's own defense mechanisms may destroy the cell because they no longer recognize it as a "normal self" cell. Other ways in which viruses can lead to cell damage or death are by depleting essential cell components, dictating that the cell produce substances toxic to the cell, or transforming the cell into a cancer cell.

There are five types of leukocytes.

Leukocytes lack hemoglobin (in contrast to erythrocytes), so they are colorless (that is, "white") unless specifically stained for microscopic visibility. Unlike erythrocytes, which are of uniform structure, identical function, and constant number, leukocytes vary in structure, function, and number. There are five types of circulating leukocytes—neutrophils, eosinophils, basophils, monocytes, and lymphocytes—each with a characteristic structure and function. They are all somewhat larger than erythrocytes.

GRANULOCYTES AND AGRANULOCYTES The five types of leukocytes fall into two main categories, depending on the appearance of their nuclei and the presence or absence of granules in their cytoplasm when viewed microscopically (● Figure 11-11). Neutrophils, eosinophils, and basophils are categorized as **polymorphonuclear** (meaning "many-shaped nucleus") **granulocytes** (meaning "granule-containing cells"). Their nuclei are segmented into several lobes of varying shapes, and their cytoplasm contains an abundance of membrane-enclosed granules. The three types of granulocytes are distinguished on the basis of the varying affinity of their granules for dyes: *eosinophils* have an affinity for the red dye eosin, *basophils* preferentially take up a basic blue dye, and *neutrophils* are neutral, showing no dye preference. Monocytes and lymphocytes are known as **mononuclear** (meaning "single nucleus") **agranulocytes** (meaning "cells lacking granules"). Both have a single, large, nonsegmented nucleus and few granules. *Monocytes* are the larger of the two and have an oval or kidney-shaped nucleus. *Lymphocytes,* the smallest of the leukocytes, characteristically have a large spherical nucleus that occupies most of the cell.

FUNCTIONS AND LIFE SPANS OF LEUKOCYTES The following are the functions and life spans of the granulocytes:

■ **Neutrophils** are phagocytic specialists. They engulf and destroy bacteria intracellularly (see ● Figure 2-7c, p. 28). As a further assault, neutrophils can also act like "suicide bombers," undergoing an unusual type of programmed cell death in which they which use vital cellular materials to prepare a web of fibers dubbed *neutrophil extracellular traps (NETs),* which they release into the ECF on their death. These fibers contain bacteria-killing chemicals, enabling NETs to trap and then destroy bacteria extracellularly. Neutrophils invariably are the first defenders on the scene of bacterial invasion. Furthermore, they scavenge to clean up debris. As might be expected in view of these functions, an increase in circulating neutrophils typically accompanies acute bacterial infections.

■ **Eosinophils** are specialists of another type. An increase in circulating eosinophils is associated with allergic conditions (such as asthma and hay fever) and with internal parasite infestations (for example, worms). Eosinophils obviously cannot engulf a larger parasitic worm, but they do attach to the worm and secrete substances that kill it.

■ **Basophils** are the least numerous and most poorly understood of the leukocytes. They are quite similar structurally and functionally to *mast cells,* which never circulate in the blood but instead are dispersed in connective tissue throughout the body. Both basophils and mast cells synthesize and store *histamine* and *heparin,* powerful chemical substances that can be released on appropriate stimulation. Histamine release is important in allergic reactions, whereas heparin speeds up removal of fat particles from the blood after a fatty meal. Heparin can also prevent clotting of blood samples drawn for clinical analysis and is used extensively as an anticoagulant drug, but whether it plays a physiologic role as an anticoagulant is still debated.

Once released into the blood from the bone marrow, a granulocyte usually stays in transit in the blood for less than a day before leaving the blood vessels to enter the tissues, where it survives another 3 to 4 days unless it dies sooner in the line of duty.

By comparison, the functions and life spans of the agranulocytes are as follows:

■ **Monocytes,** like neutrophils, become professional phagocytes. They emerge from the bone marrow while still immature and circulate for only a day or two before settling down in various tissues throughout the body. At their new residences, monocytes continue to mature and greatly enlarge, becoming the large tissue phagocytes known as **macrophages** (*macro* means "large"; *phage*

Leukocytes					Erythrocyte	Platelets
Polymorphonuclear granulocytes			Mononuclear agranulocytes			
Neutrophil	Eosinophil	Basophil	Monocyte	Lymphocyte		
60%–70%	1%–4%	0.25%–0.5%	2%–6%	25%–33%	Erythrocyte concentration = 5 billion/ ml blood	Platelet concentration = 250 million/ ml blood
Differential WBC count (percentage distribution of types of leukocytes)						
Leukocyte concentration = 7 million/ml blood					RBC count = 5,000,000/mm³	Platelet count = 250,000/mm³
WBC count = 7000/mm³						

● FIGURE 11-11 Normal blood cellular elements and typical human blood cell count.

Leukocyte concentration = 7 million/ml blood

WBC count = $7000/mm^3$

RBC count = $5,000,000/mm^3$

Platelet count = $250,000/mm^3$

means "eater"). A macrophage's life span may range from months to years unless it is destroyed sooner while performing its phagocytic activity. A phagocytic cell can ingest only a limited amount of foreign material before it succumbs.

■ **Lymphocytes** provide immune defense against targets for which they are specifically programmed. There are two types of lymphocytes, B and T lymphocytes (B and T cells), which look alike. **B lymphocytes** produce antibodies, which circulate in the blood and are responsible for *antibody-mediated,* or *humoral, immunity.* An antibody binds with and marks for destruction (by phagocytosis or other means) the specific kinds of foreign matter, such as bacteria, that induced production of the antibody. **T lymphocytes** do not produce antibodies; instead, they directly destroy their specific target cells by releasing chemicals that punch holes in the victim cell, a process called *cell-mediated immunity.* The target cells of T cells include body cells invaded by viruses and cancer cells.

Lymphocytes live for about 100 to 300 days. Only a small part of the total lymphocytes are in transit in the blood at any given moment. Most continually recycle among the blood, lymph, and lymphoid tissues. **Lymphoid tissues,** such as the lymph nodes and tonsils, are lymphocyte-containing tissues that produce, store, or process lymphocytes (● Figure 11-12).

Leukocytes are produced at varying rates depending on the changing needs of the body.

All leukocytes ultimately originate from common precursor undifferentiated pluripotent stem cells in the bone marrow that give rise to erythrocytes and platelets (● Figure 11-13). The cells destined to become leukocytes eventually differentiate into various committed cell lines and proliferate under the influence of appropriate stimulating factors. Granulocytes and monocytes are produced only in the bone marrow, which releases these mature leukocytes into the blood. Lymphocytes are originally derived from precursor cells in the bone marrow, but most new lymphocytes actually come from lymphocyte colonies already in the lymphoid tissues originally populated by cells derived from bone marrow.

The total number of leukocytes normally ranges from 5 million to 10 million cells per milliliter of blood, with an average of 7 million/ml, expressed as an average **white blood cell count** of 7000/mm³. Leukocytes are the least numerous of the blood cells (about 1 white blood cell for every 700 red blood cells), not because fewer are produced but because they are merely in transit while in the blood. Normally, about two thirds of the circulating leukocytes are granulocytes, mostly neutrophils, whereas one third are agranulocytes, predominantly lymphocytes (see ● Figure 11-11). However, the total number of white cells and the percentage of each type may vary considerably to meet changing defense needs. Depending on the type and extent of assault the body is combating, different types of leukocytes are selectively produced at varying rates. Chemical messengers arising from invaded or damaged tissues or from activated leukocytes themselves govern the rates of production of the various leukocytes. Specific messengers analogous to erythropoietin direct the differentiation and proliferation of

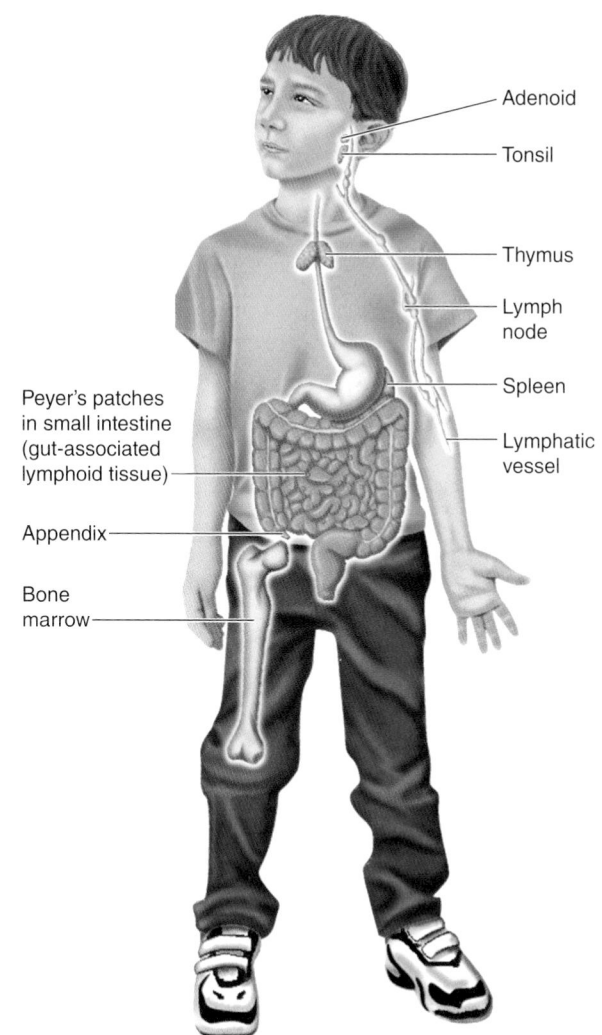

● **FIGURE 11-12 Lymphoid tissues.** The lymphoid tissues, which are dispersed throughout the body, produce, store, or process lymphocytes.

each cell type. Some of these messengers have been identified and can be produced in the laboratory; an example is **granulocyte colony–stimulating factor,** which stimulates increased replication and release of granulocytes, especially neutrophils, from the bone marrow. Marketed under the name Neulasta, this synthetic agent is a powerful new therapeutic tool that can be used to bolster defense and thus decrease the incidence of infection in cancer patients being treated with chemotherapy drugs, which suppress all rapidly dividing cells, including hemopoietic cells in the bone marrow, as well as the targeted cancer cells.

 ABNORMALITIES IN LEUKOCYTE PRODUCTION Even though levels of circulating leukocytes may vary, changes in these levels are normally controlled and adjusted according to the body's needs. However, abnormalities in leukocyte production can occur that are not subject to control; that is, either too few or too many WBCs can be produced. The bone marrow can greatly slow down or even stop production of white blood cells when it is exposed to certain toxic chemical agents (such as benzene and anticancer

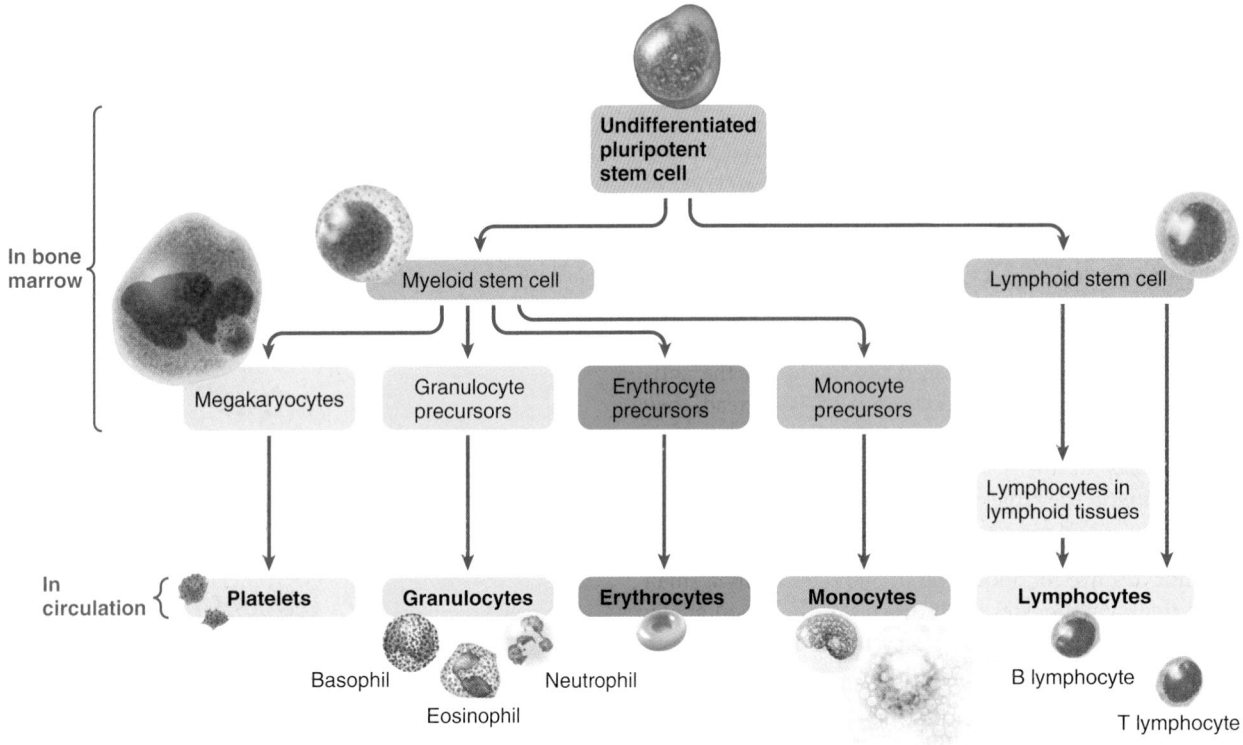

● **FIGURE 11-13 Blood cell production (hemopoiesis).** All the blood cell types ultimately originate from the same undifferentiated pluripotent stem cells in the red bone marrow.

drugs) or to excessive radiation. The most serious consequence is the reduction in professional phagocytes (neutrophils and macrophages), which greatly reduces the body's defense capabilities against invading microorganisms. The only defense still available when the bone marrow fails is the immune capabilities of the lymphocytes produced by the lymphoid tissues.

Surprisingly, one of the major consequences of **leukemia,** a cancerous condition that involves uncontrolled proliferation of WBCs, is inadequate defense capabilities against foreign invasion. In leukemia, the WBC count may reach as high as 500,000/ mm³, compared with the normal 7000/mm³, but because most of these cells are abnormal or immature, they cannot perform their normal defense functions. Another devastating consequence of leukemia is displacement of the other blood cell lines in the bone marrow. This results in anemia because of a reduction in erythropoiesis and in internal bleeding because of a deficit of platelets. Consequently, overwhelming infections or hemorrhage are the most common causes of death in leukemic patients.

We now turn to the two major components of the immune system's response to foreign invaders and other targets—innate and adaptive immune responses. In the process, we further examine the roles of each type of leukocyte.

Immune responses may be either innate and nonspecific or adaptive and specific.

Protective immunity is conferred by the complementary actions of two separate but interdependent components of the immune system: the innate immune system and the adaptive, or acquired, immune system. The responses of these two systems differ in timing and in the selectivity of the defense mechanisms.

The **innate immune system** encompasses the body's *nonspecific* immune responses that come into play immediately on exposure to a threatening agent. These nonspecific responses are inherent (innate or built-in) defense mechanisms that nonselectively defend against foreign or abnormal material of any type, even on initial exposure to it. Such responses provide a first line of internal defense against a range of threats, including infectious agents, chemical irritants, and tissue injury from mechanical trauma and burns. Everyone is born with essentially the same innate immune-response mechanisms, although there are some subtle genetic differences. The **adaptive,** or **acquired, immune system,** in contrast, relies on *specific* immune responses selectively targeted against a particular foreign material to which the body has already been exposed and has had an opportunity to prepare for an attack aimed discriminatingly at the enemy. The adaptive immune system thus takes considerably more time to mount and takes on specific foes. The innate and adaptive immune systems work in harmony to contain, and then eliminate, harmful agents.

INNATE IMMUNE SYSTEM The components of the innate system are always on guard, ready to unleash a limited, rather crude repertoire of defense mechanisms at any and every invader. Of the immune effector cells, the neutrophils and macrophages— both phagocytic specialists—are especially important in innate defense. Several groups of plasma proteins also play key roles, as you will see shortly. The various nonspecific immune responses are set in motion in response to generic molecular patterns associated with threatening agents, such as the carbohydrates typically found in bacterial cell walls but not found in human cells. The responding phagocytic cells are studded with plasma membrane proteins known as **toll-like receptors (TLRs),** which recognize these pathogen-associated molecular patterns. TLRs have been dubbed the "eyes of the innate immune system" because these immune sensors recognize and bind with the unique, telltale pathogen markers, allowing the effector cells of the innate system to "see" pathogens as distinct from "self" cells. A TLR's recognition of a pathogen triggers the phagocyte to engulf and destroy the infectious microorganism. Moreover, activation of the TLR induces the phagocytic cell to secrete chemicals, some of which contribute to inflammation, an important innate response to microbial invasion.

The innate mechanisms give us all a rapid but limited and nonselective response to unfriendly challenges of all kinds, much like medieval guardsmen lashing out with brute-force weapons at any enemy approaching the walls of the castle they are defending. Innate immunity largely contains and limits the spread of infection. These nonspecific responses are important for keeping the foe at bay until the adaptive immune system, with its highly selective weapons, can be prepared to take over and mount strategies to eliminate the villain.

ADAPTIVE IMMUNE SYSTEM The responses of the adaptive, or acquired, immune system are mediated by the B and T lymphocytes. Each B and T cell can recognize and defend against only one particular type of foreign material, such as one kind of bacterium. Among the millions of B and T cells in the body, only the ones specifically equipped to recognize the unique molecular features of a particular infectious agent are called into action to discriminatingly defend against this agent. This specialization is similar to modern, specially trained military personnel called into active duty to accomplish a specific task. The chosen lymphocytes multiply, expanding the pool of specialists that can launch a highly targeted attack against the invader.

The adaptive immune system is the ultimate weapon against most pathogens. The repertoire of activated and expanded B and T cells is constantly changing in response to the various pathogens encountered. Thus, the adaptive immune system adapts to wage battle against the specific pathogens in each person's environment. The targets of the adaptive immune system vary among people, depending on the types of immune assaults each individual meets. Furthermore, this system acquires an ability to more efficiently eradicate a particular foe when rechallenged by the same pathogen in the future. It does so by establishing a pool of memory cells as a result of an encounter with a given pathogen so that, when later exposed to the same agent, it can more swiftly defend against the invader.

We examine in more detail the innate immune responses before looking more closely at adaptive immunity.

Innate Immunity

Innate defenses include the following:

1. *Inflammation,* a nonspecific response to tissue injury in which the phagocytic specialists—neutrophils and macrophages—play a major role, along with supportive input from other immune cell types

2. *Interferon,* a family of proteins that nonspecifically defend against viral infection

3. *Natural killer cells,* a special class of lymphocyte-like cells that spontaneously and nonspecifically lyse (rupture) and thereby destroy virus-infected host cells and cancer cells

4. The *complement system,* a group of inactive plasma proteins that, when sequentially activated, bring about destruction of foreign cells by attacking their plasma membranes

We discuss each of these in turn, beginning with inflammation.

Inflammation is a nonspecific response to foreign invasion or tissue damage.

The term **inflammation** refers to an innate, nonspecific series of highly interrelated events set into motion in response to foreign invasion, tissue damage, or both. The goal of inflammation is to bring to the invaded or injured area phagocytes and plasma proteins that can (1) isolate, destroy, or inactivate the invaders; (2) remove debris; and (3) prepare for subsequent healing and repair. The overall inflammatory response is remarkably similar no matter what the triggering event (bacterial invasion, chemical injury, or mechanical trauma), although some subtle differences may be evident, depending on the injurious agent or the site of damage. The following sequence of events typically occurs during inflammation. As an example, we use bacterial entry into a break in the skin (● Figure 11-14).

DEFENSE BY RESIDENT TISSUE MACROPHAGES When bacteria invade through a break in the external barrier of skin, macrophages already in the area immediately begin phagocytizing the foreign microbes, defending against infection during the first hour or so, before other mechanisms can be mobilized. Resident macrophages also secrete chemicals such as *chemotaxins* and *cytokines* that exert various immune responses, as will be described shortly (● Figure 11-14, step **1**).

LOCALIZED VASODILATION Almost immediately on microbial invasion, arterioles within the area dilate, increasing blood flow to the site of injury. This localized vasodilation is mainly induced by **histamine** released from mast cells in the area of tissue damage (the connective tissue–bound "cousins" of circulating basophils) (step **2**). Increased local delivery of blood brings to the site more phagocytic leukocytes and plasma proteins, both crucial to the defense response.

INCREASED CAPILLARY PERMEABILITY Released histamine also increases the capillaries' permeability by enlarging the capillary pores (the spaces between the endothelial cells) so that plasma

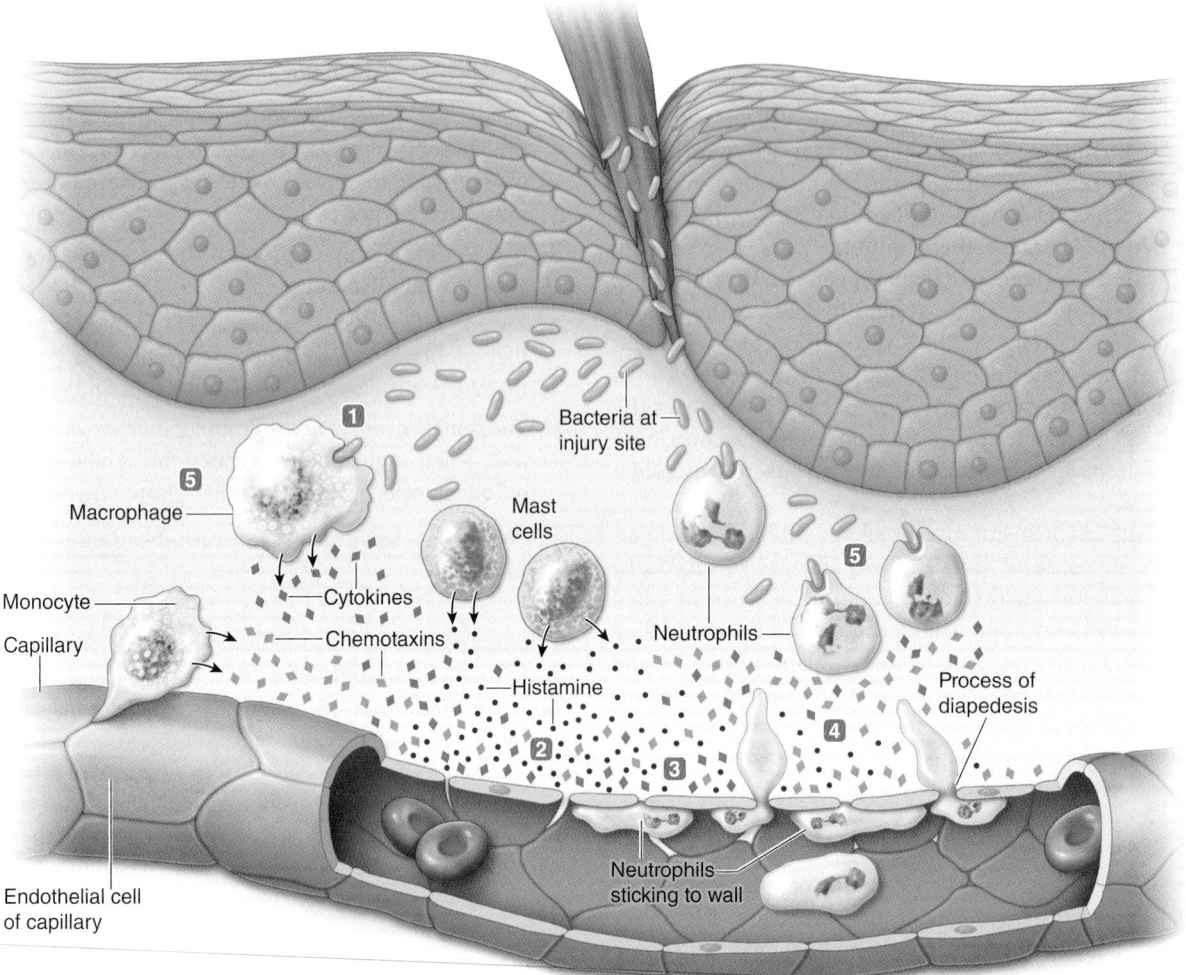

| **1** A break in the skin introduces bacteria, which reproduce at the wound site. Activated resident macrophages engulf the pathogens and secrete cytokines and chemotaxins. | **2** Activated mast cells release histamine. Histamine dilates local blood vessels and widens the capillary pores. | **3** The blood vessel wall becomes sticky, causing neutrophils and monocytes to attach. | **4** Chemotaxins attract neutrophils and monocytes, which squeeze out between cells of the blood vessel wall, a process called diapedesis, and migrate to the infection site. | **5** Monocytes enlarge into macrophages. Newly arriving macrophages and neutrophils engulf the pathogens and destroy them. |

● **FIGURE 11-14 Steps producing inflammation.** Chemotaxins released at the site of damage attract phagocytes to the scene. Note the leukocytes emigrating from the blood into the tissues by assuming amoeba-like behavior and squeezing through the capillary pores, a process known as *diapedesis*. Mast cells secrete vessel-dilating, pore-widening histamine. Macrophages secrete cytokines that exert multiple local and systemic effects.

proteins normally prevented from leaving the blood can escape into the inflamed tissue (see p. 295).

LOCALIZED EDEMA Accumulation of leaked plasma proteins in the interstitial fluid raises the local interstitial fluid–colloid osmotic pressure. Furthermore, the increased local blood flow elevates capillary blood pressure. Because both these pressures tend to move fluid out of the capillaries, these changes favor enhanced ultrafiltration and reduced reabsorption of fluid across the involved capillaries. The end result of this shift in fluid balance is localized edema (see p. 301). Thus, the familiar swelling that accompanies inflammation is the result of histamine-induced vascular changes. Likewise, the other well-known gross manifestations of inflammation, such as redness and heat, are largely caused by the enhanced flow of warm arterial blood to the damaged tissue (*inflammare* means "to set on fire"). Pain is caused both by local distension within the swollen tissue and by the direct effect of locally produced substances on the receptor endings of afferent neurons that supply the area. These observable characteristics of the inflammatory process (swelling, redness, heat, and pain) are coincidental to the primary purpose of the vascular changes in the injured area—to increase the number of leukocytic phagocytes and crucial plasma proteins in the area (● Figure 11-15).

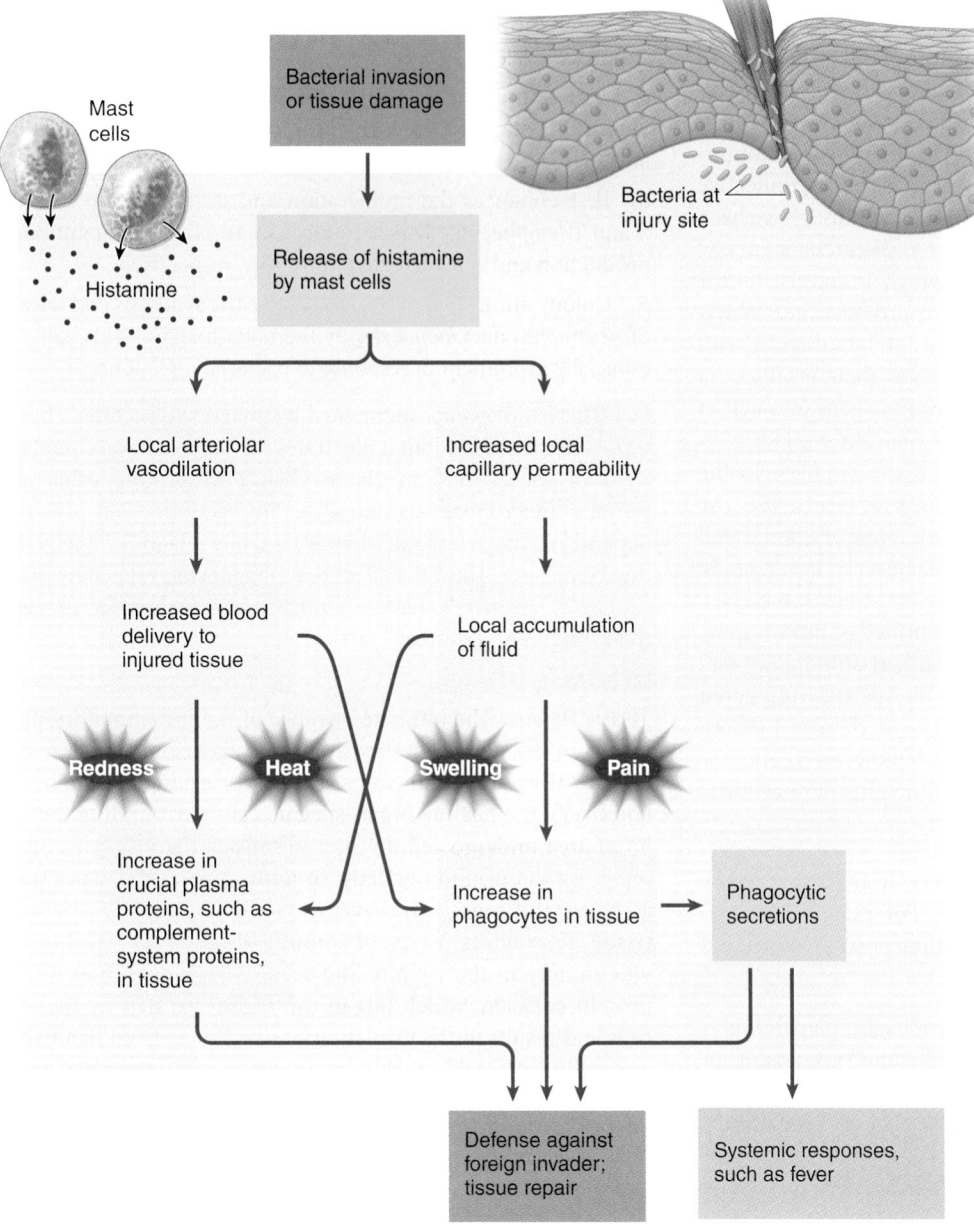

● FIGURE 11-15 **Gross manifestations and outcomes of inflammation.**

slower-commencing but longer-lasting increase in monocyte production also occurs, making available larger numbers of these macrophage precursor cells (step **5**).

MARKING OF BACTERIA FOR DESTRUCTION BY OPSONINS Obviously, phagocytes must be able to distinguish between normal cells and foreign or abnormal cells before accomplishing their destructive mission. Otherwise, they could not selectively engulf and destroy only unwanted materials. First, as you have already learned, phagocytes, by means of their TLRs, recognize and subsequently engulf infiltrators that have standard bacterial cell wall components not found in human cells. Second, foreign particles are deliberately marked for phagocytic ingestion by being coated with chemical mediators generated by the immune system. Such body-produced chemicals that make bacteria more susceptible to phagocytosis are known as **opsonins** (*opsonin* means "to prepare for eating"). The most important opsonins are antibodies and one of the activated proteins of the complement system. An opsonin enhances phagocytosis by linking the foreign cell to a phagocytic cell. This link ensures that the bacterial victim does not have a chance to "get away" before the phagocyte can perform its lethal attack.

EMIGRATION OF LEUKOCYTES Blood-borne neutrophils and monocytes stick to the endothelial lining in response to released cytokines (see ● Figure 11-14, **3**). Leukocytes can emigrate from the blood into the tissues by behaving like amoebas (see p. 40): wriggling through the capillary pores and then crawling toward the injured area (step **4**). The phagocytic cells are attracted to **chemotaxins,** chemical mediators released at the site of damage (*taxis* means "attraction"). Within an hour after injury, the area is teeming with leukocytes that have left the vessels. Once neutrophils or monocytes leave the bloodstream, they never recycle back to the blood.

LEUKOCYTE PROLIFERATION Within a few hours after onset of the inflammatory response, the number of neutrophils in the blood may increase up to four to five times that of normal. A

LEUKOCYTIC DESTRUCTION OF BACTERIA Neutrophils and macrophages clear the inflamed area of infectious and toxic agents, as well as tissue debris, by both phagocytic and nonphagocytic means; this clearing action is the main function of the inflammatory response.

Phagocytes eventually die from the accumulation of toxic by-products from foreign particle degradation or from inadvertent release of destructive lysosomal chemicals into the cytosol. The **pus** that forms in an infected wound is a collection of these phagocytic cells, both living and dead; necrotic (dead) tissue liquefied by lysosomal enzymes released from the phagocytes; and bacteria.

MEDIATION OF THE INFLAMMATORY RESPONSE BY PHAGOCYTE-SECRETED CHEMICALS Microbe-stimulated phagocytes release many chemicals that function as mediators of inflammation. All chemicals other than antibodies that leukocytes secrete are collectively called **cytokines.** Macrophages, monocytes, neutrophils, a type of T cell called a helper T cell, and some nonimmune cells such as fibroblasts (fiber-formers in the connective tissue) all secrete cytokines. More than 100 cytokines have been identified, and the list continues to grow as researchers unravel the complicated chemical means by which immune effector cells communicate with one another to coordinate their activities. Unlike antibodies, cytokines do not interact directly with the antigen (foreign material) that induces their production. Instead, cytokines largely spur other immune cells into action to help ward off the invader. Cytokines typically act locally as paracrines on cells in the vicinity, but some circulate in the blood to exert endocrine effects at distant sites (see p. 98). The cytokines released by phagocytes induce a range of interrelated immune activities, varying from local responses to the systemic manifestations that accompany microbe invasion. Some cytokines have names related to their first identified or most important function, examples being specific *colony-stimulating factors.* Other cytokines are designated as specific numbered *interleukins,* such as interleukin 1 (IL-1), interleukin 2 (IL-2), and so on (*interleukin* means "between leukocytes"). The following are among the most important functions of phagocytic secretions:

1. Some of the chemicals, which are very destructive, directly kill microbes by nonphagocytic means. For example, macrophages secrete *nitric oxide (NO),* a multipurpose chemical that is toxic to nearby microbes (see p. 290).

2. Several chemicals released by macrophages, namely *interleukin 1 (IL-1), interleukin 6 (IL-6),* and *tumor necrosis factor (TNF)* collectively act to bring about a diverse array of effects locally and throughout the body, all of which are geared toward defending the body against infection or tissue injury. They promote inflammation and are largely responsible for the systemic manifestations accompanying an infection.

3. The same trio of cytokines function together as **endogenous pyrogen (EP),** which induces the development of fever (*endogenous* means "from within the body"; *pyro* means "fire" or "heat"; *gen* means "production"). This response occurs especially when the invading organisms have spread into the blood. Endogenous pyrogen causes release within the hypothalamus of *prostaglandins,* locally acting chemical messengers that "turn up" the hypothalamic "thermostat" that regulates body temperature. The function of the resulting elevation in body temperature in fighting infection remains unclear. Fever is a common systemic manifestation of inflammation, suggesting the raised temperature plays an important beneficial role in the overall inflammatory response, as supported by recent evidence. Higher temperatures appear to augment phagocytosis, increase the rate of the many enzyme-dependent inflammatory activities, and interfere with bacterial multiplication. Resolving the controversial issue of whether a fever can be beneficial is extremely important, given the widespread use of drugs that suppress fever.

4. TNF stimulates release of *histamine* from mast cells in the vicinity. Histamine, in turn, promotes the local vasodilation and increased capillary permeability of inflammation.

5. IL-1 enhances the proliferation and differentiation of both *B* and *T lymphocytes,* which, in turn, are responsible for antibody production and cell-mediated immunity, respectively.

6. Colony-stimulating factors stimulate the synthesis and release of *neutrophils* and *monocytes* by the bone marrow. This effect is especially prominent in response to bacterial infections.

This list of events augmented by phagocyte-secreted chemicals is not complete, but it illustrates the diversity and complexity of responses these mediators elicit. Furthermore, other important macrophage–lymphocyte interactions that do not depend on the release of chemicals from phagocytic cells are described later. Thus, the effect that phagocytes, especially macrophages, ultimately have on microbial invaders far exceeds their "engulf and destroy" tactics.

TISSUE REPAIR The ultimate purpose of the inflammatory process is to isolate and destroy injurious agents and to clear the area for tissue repair. In some tissues (for example, skin, bone, and liver), the healthy organ-specific cells surrounding the injured area undergo cell division to replace the lost cells, often repairing the wound perfectly. In nonregenerative tissues such as nerve and muscle, however, lost cells are replaced by **scar tissue.** Fibroblasts, a type of connective tissue cell, start to divide rapidly in the vicinity and secrete large quantities of the protein collagen, which fills in the region vacated by the lost cells and results in the formation of scar tissue. Even in a tissue as readily replaceable as skin, scars sometimes form when complex underlying structures, such as hair follicles and sweat glands, are permanently destroyed by deep wounds.

Inflammation is an underlying culprit in many common, chronic illnesses.

Acute (short-term) inflammatory responses serve a useful purpose for eliminating pathogens from the body, but scientists are increasingly becoming aware that chronic (long-term), low-grade inflammation may be a unifying theory for many chronic diseases. Chronic inflammation occurs when the triggering agent persists long term, either because it is not entirely eliminated or because it is constantly present or continually renewed. Chronic inflammation has an important role in Alzheimer's disease, atherosclerosis and coronary artery disease, asthma, obesity, possibly cancer, and a host of other health problems. Collectively, these conditions are responsible for the majority of morbidity (illness) and mortality (death). Reining in this underlying inflammatory process could have a huge impact on the quality and quantity of life for much of the world's population.

Nonsteroidal anti-inflammatory drugs and glucocorticoids suppress inflammation.

Many drugs can suppress the inflammatory process; the most effective are the *nonsteroidal anti-inflammatory drugs*, or *NSAIDs* (aspirin, ibuprofen, and related compounds) and *glucocorticoids* (drugs similar to the steroid hormone cortisol, which is secreted by the adrenal cortex; see p. 551). For example, aspirin interferes with the inflammatory response by decreasing histamine release, thus reducing pain, swelling, and redness. Furthermore, aspirin reduces fever by inhibiting production of prostaglandins, the local mediators of endogenous pyrogen–induced fever.

Glucocorticoids, which are potent anti-inflammatory drugs, suppress almost every aspect of the inflammatory response. In addition, they destroy lymphocytes within lymphoid tissue and reduce antibody production. These therapeutic agents are useful for treating undesirable immune responses, such as allergic reactions (for example, poison ivy rash and asthma) and the inflammation associated with arthritis. However, by suppressing inflammatory and other immune responses that localize and eliminate bacteria, such therapy also reduces the body's ability to resist infection. For this reason, glucocorticoids should be used discriminatingly.

Now let us shift from inflammation to interferon, another component of innate immunity.

Interferon transiently inhibits multiplication of viruses in most cells.

Interferon is released from virus-infected cells and briefly provides nonspecific resistance to viral infections by transiently interfering with replication of the same or unrelated viruses in other host cells. In fact, interferon was named for its ability to "interfere" with viral replication.

ANTIVIRAL EFFECT OF INTERFERON When a virus invades a cell, the cell synthesizes and secretes interferon in response to being exposed to viral nucleic acid. Once released into the ECF from a virus-infected cell, interferon binds with receptors on the plasma membranes of healthy neighboring cells or even distant cells that it reaches through the blood, signaling these cells to prepare for possible viral attack. Interferon thus acts as a "whistle-blower," forewarning healthy cells of potential viral attack and helping them prepare to resist. Interferon does not have a direct antiviral effect; instead, it triggers the production of virus-blocking enzymes by potential host cells. When interferon binds with these other cells, they synthesize enzymes that can break down viral messenger RNA (see p. 22) and inhibit protein synthesis. Both these processes are essential for viral replication. Although viruses are still able to invade these forewarned cells, the pathogens cannot govern cellular protein synthesis for their own replication (● Figure 11-16).

The newly synthesized inhibitory enzymes remain inactive within the tipped-off potential host cell unless it is actually invaded by a virus, at which time the enzymes are activated by the presence of viral nucleic acid. This activation requirement protects the cell's own messenger RNA and protein-synthesizing machinery from unnecessary inhibition by these enzymes should viral invasion not occur. Because activation can take place only during a limited time span, this is a short-term defense mechanism.

Interferon is released nonspecifically from any cell infected by any virus and, in turn, can induce temporary self-protective activity against many different viruses in any other cells that it reaches. Thus, it provides a general, rapidly responding defense strategy against viral invasion until more specific but slower-responding immune mechanisms come into play.

ANTICANCER EFFECTS OF INTERFERON Interferon exerts anticancer, as well as antiviral, effects. It markedly enhances the actions of cell-killing cells—the *natural killer cells,* the component of innate immunity we describe next, and a special type of T lymphocyte, *cytotoxic T cells*—which attack and destroy both virus-infected cells and cancer cells. Furthermore, interferon itself slows cell division and suppresses tumor growth.

Natural killer cells destroy virus-infected cells and cancer cells on first exposure to them.

Natural killer (NK) cells are naturally occurring, lymphocyte-like cells that nonspecifically destroy virus-infected cells and cancer cells by releasing chemicals that directly lyse (rupture) the membranes of such cells on first exposure to them. Their mode of action and major targets are similar to those of cytotoxic T cells, but the latter can fatally attack only the specific types of virus-infected cells and cancer cells to which they have been previously exposed. Furthermore, after exposure cytotoxic T cells require a maturation period before they can launch their lethal assault. NK cells provide an immediate, nonspecific defense against virus-invaded cells and cancer cells before the more specific and abundant cytotoxic T cells become functional.

The complement system punches holes in microorganisms.

The **complement system** is another defense mechanism brought into play nonspecifically in response to invading organisms. This system can be activated in two ways:

1. By exposure to particular carbohydrate chains present on the surfaces of microorganisms but not found on human cells, a nonspecific innate immune response

2. By exposure to antibodies produced against a specific foreign invader, an adaptive immune response

The system derives its name from its ability to "complement" the action of antibodies; it is the primary mechanism activated by antibodies to kill foreign cells. The complement system destroys cells by forming *membrane attack complexes* that punch holes in the victim cells. In addition to bringing about direct lysis of the invader, the complement cascade reinforces general inflammatory tactics.

FORMATION OF THE MEMBRANE ATTACK COMPLEX In the same mode as the clotting and anticlotting systems, the complement system consists of plasma proteins that are produced by the

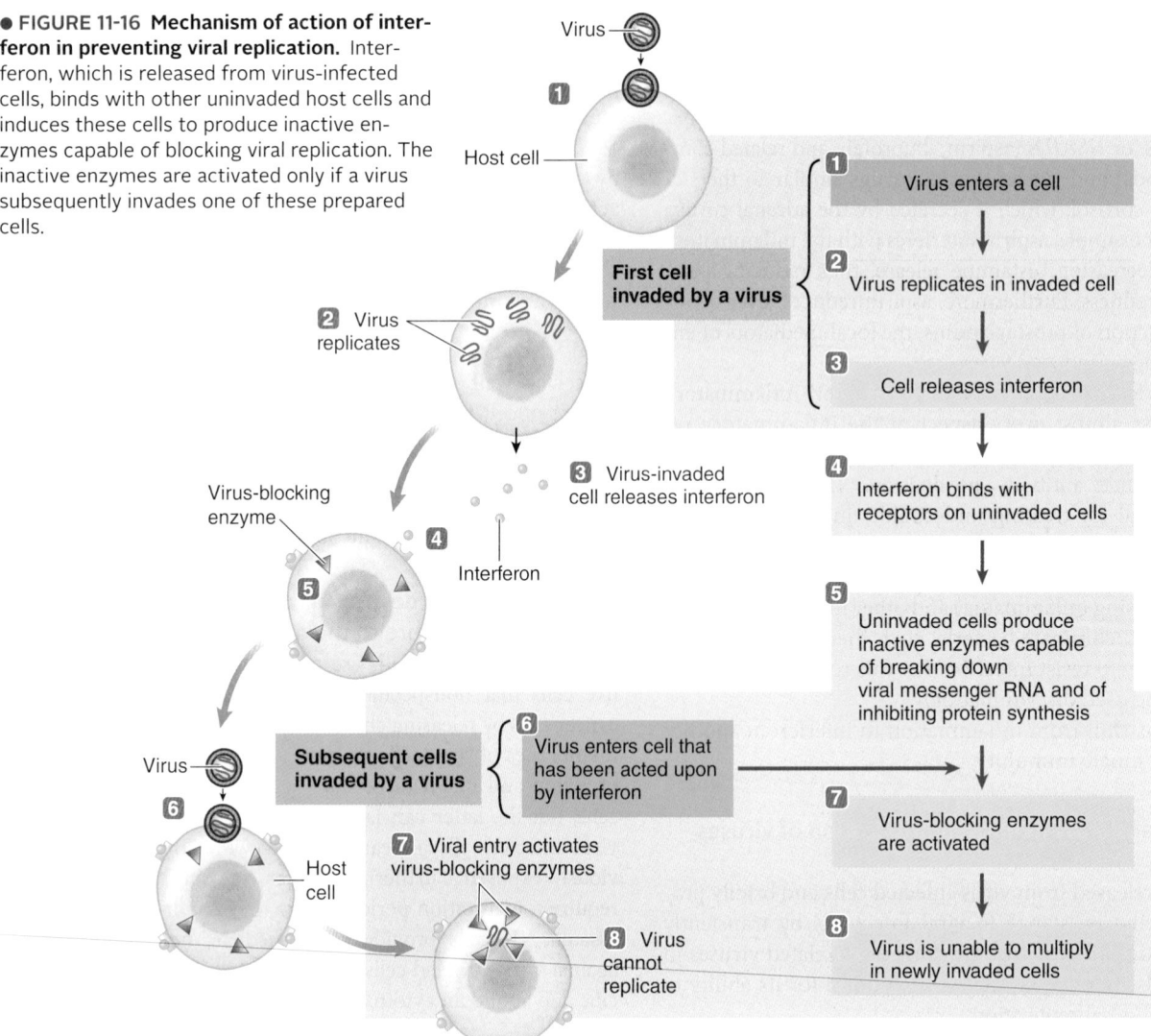

● **FIGURE 11-16 Mechanism of action of interferon in preventing viral replication.** Interferon, which is released from virus-infected cells, binds with other uninvaded host cells and induces these cells to produce inactive enzymes capable of blocking viral replication. The inactive enzymes are activated only if a virus subsequently invades one of these prepared cells.

First cell invaded by a virus

1 Virus enters a cell

2 Virus replicates in invaded cell

3 Cell releases interferon

4 Interferon binds with receptors on uninvaded cells

5 Uninvaded cells produce inactive enzymes capable of breaking down viral messenger RNA and of inhibiting protein synthesis

Subsequent cells invaded by a virus

6 Virus enters cell that has been acted upon by interferon

7 Virus-blocking enzymes are activated

8 Virus is unable to multiply in newly invaded cells

Virus

Host cell

2 Virus replicates

Virus-blocking enzyme

Interferon

3 Virus-invaded cell releases interferon

Virus

Host cell

7 Viral entry activates virus-blocking enzymes

8 Virus cannot replicate

---

liver and circulate in the blood in inactive form. Once the first component, C1, is activated, it activates the next component, C2, and so on, in a cascade sequence of activation reactions. The five final components, C5 through C9, assemble into a large, doughnut-shaped protein complex, the **membrane attack complex (MAC),** which embeds itself in the surface membrane of nearby microorganisms, creating a large channel through the membrane (● Figure 11-17). In other words, the parts make a hole. This hole-punching technique makes the membrane extremely leaky; the resulting osmotic flux of water into the victim cell causes it to swell and burst. Such complement-induced lysis is the major means of directly killing microbes without phagocytizing them.

AUGMENTING INFLAMMATION Unlike the other cascade systems, in which the sole function of the various components leading up to the end step is activation of the next precursor in the sequence, several activated proteins in the complement cascade additionally act on their own to augment the inflammatory process by the following methods:

■ *Serving as chemotaxins,* which attract and guide professional phagocytes to the site of complement activation (that is, the site of microbial invasion)

■ *Acting as opsonins* by binding with microbes and thereby enhancing their phagocytosis

■ *Promoting vasodilation and increased vascular permeability,* thus increasing blood flow to the invaded areas

■ *Stimulating release of histamine* from mast cells in the vicinity, which in turn enhances the local vascular changes characteristic of inflammation

Several activated components in the cascade are very unstable. Because these unstable components can carry out the sequence only in the immediate area in which they are activated before they decompose, the complement attack is confined to the surface membrane of the microbe whose presence initiated activation of the system. Nearby host cells are thus spared from lytic attack.

We have now completed our discussion of innate immunity and turn our attention to adaptive immunity.

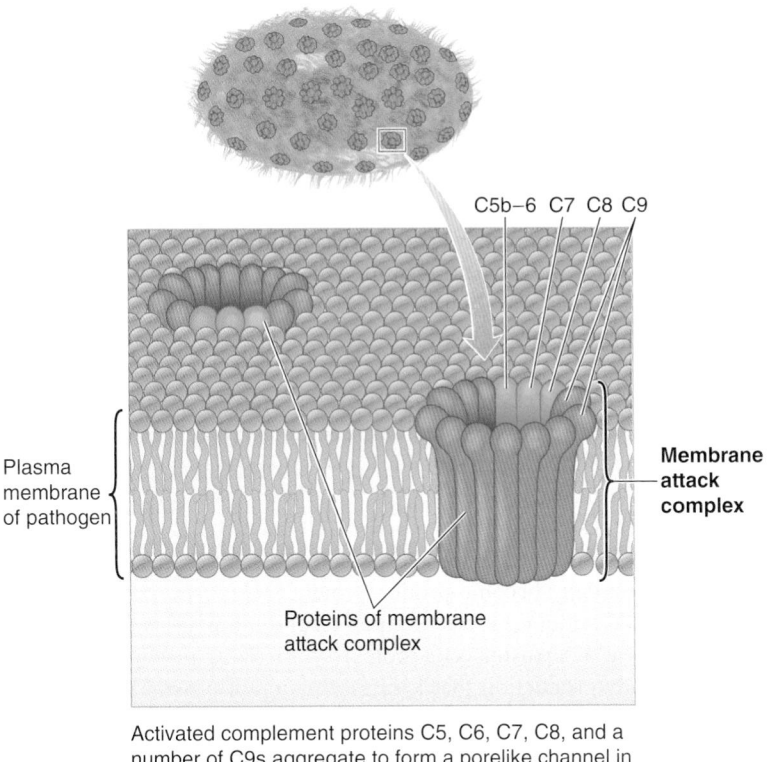

C5b–6 C7 C8 C9

Plasma
membrane
of pathogen

Membrane
attack
complex

Proteins of membrane
attack complex

Activated complement proteins C5, C6, C7, C8, and a
number of C9s aggregate to form a porelike channel in
the plasma membrane of the target cell. The resulting
leakage leads to destruction of the cell.

● FIGURE 11-17 **Membrane attack complex of the complement system.**

Adaptive Immunity: General Concepts

A specific adaptive immune response is a selective attack aimed at limiting or destroying a particular offending target for which the body has been specially prepared after exposure to it.

Adaptive immune responses include antibody-mediated immunity and cell-mediated immunity.

There are two classes of adaptive immune responses: **antibody-mediated,** or **humoral, immunity,** involving production of antibodies by B lymphocyte derivatives known as *plasma cells,* and **cell-mediated immunity,** involving production of *activated T lymphocytes,* which directly attack unwanted cells. Because antibodies are blood borne, antibody-mediated immunity is sometimes known as humoral immunity, in reference to the ancient Greek use of the term *humors* for the various body fluids (see p. 283).

Lymphocytes can specifically recognize and selectively respond to an almost limitless variety of foreign agents, as well as cancer cells. The recognition and response processes are different in B and in T cells. In general, B cells recognize free-existing foreign invaders such as bacteria, which they combat by secreting antibodies specific for the invaders. T cells specialize in recognizing and destroying body cells gone awry, including virus-infected cells and cancer cells. We examine each of these processes in de-

tail in the upcoming sections. For now, we explore the different life histories of B and T cells.

ORIGINS OF B AND T CELLS Both types of lymphocytes, like all blood cells, are derived from common stem cells in the bone marrow (see p. 332). Whether a lymphocyte and all its progeny are destined to be B or T cells depends on the site of final differentiation and maturation of the original cell in the lineage (● Figure 11-18). B cells differentiate and mature in the bone marrow. As for T cells, during fetal life and early childhood, some immature lymphocytes from the bone marrow migrate through the blood to the thymus, where they undergo further processing to become T lymphocytes (named for their site of maturation). The **thymus** is a lymphoid tissue located midline within the chest cavity above the heart in the space between the lungs (see ● Figure 11-12, p. 331).

On being released into the blood from either the bone marrow or the thymus, mature B and T cells take up residence and establish lymphocyte colonies in the peripheral lymphoid tissues. Here, on appropriate stimulation, they undergo cell division to produce new generations of either B or T cells, depending on their ancestry. After early childhood, most new lymphocytes are derived from these peripheral lymphocyte colonies rather than from the bone marrow.

Each of us has an estimated 2 trillion lymphocytes, which, if aggregated in a mass, would be about the size of the brain. At any one time, most of these lymphocytes are concentrated in the various strategically located lymphoid tissues, but both B and T cells continually circulate among the lymph, blood, and body tissues, where they remain on constant surveillance.

ROLE OF THYMOSIN Because most of the migration and differentiation of T cells occurs early in development, the thymus gradually atrophies and becomes less important as the person matures. It does, however, continue to produce **thymosin,** a hormone important in maintaining the T-cell lineage. Thymosin enhances proliferation of new T cells within the peripheral lymphoid tissues and augments the immune capabilities of existing T cells.

Let us now see how lymphocytes detect their selected target.

An antigen induces an immune response against itself.

Both B and T cells must be able to specifically recognize unwanted cells and other material to be destroyed as being distinct from the body's own normal cells. The presence of antigens enables lymphocytes to make this distinction. Recall that an antigen is a large, unique molecule that triggers a specific immune response against itself, such as generation of antibodies that lead to its destruction, when it gains entry into the body (*antigen* means *anti*body *gen*erator, although some antigens trigger cell-mediated immune responses instead of antibody production). In general, the more complex a molecule is, the

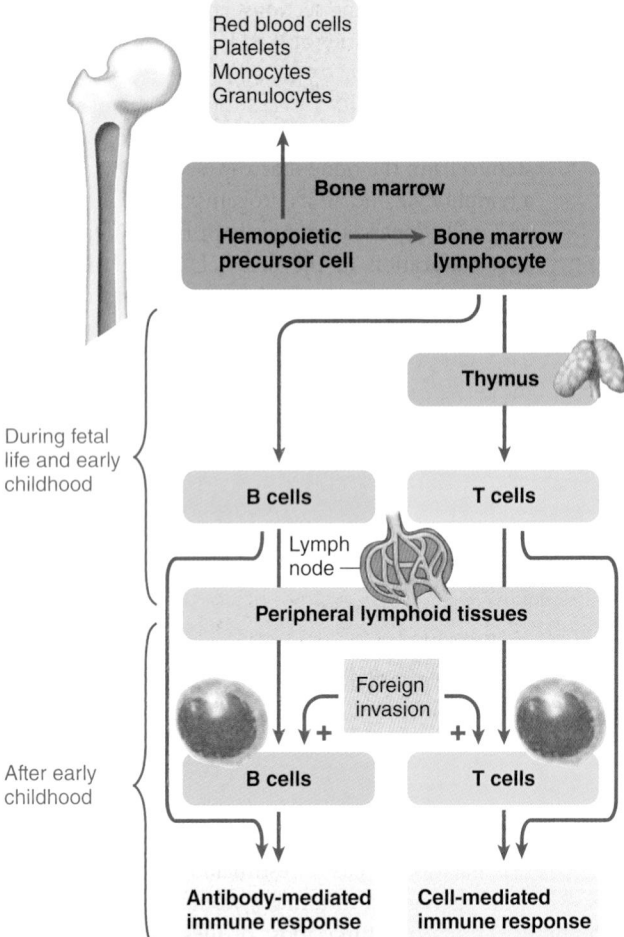

Red blood cells
Platelets
Monocytes
Granulocytes

Bone marrow

Hemopoietic ⟶ **Bone marrow**
precursor cell   **lymphocyte**

Thymus

During fetal
life and early
childhood

B cells   **T cells**

Lymph
node

Peripheral lymphoid tissues

Foreign
invasion

After early
childhood

B cells   **T cells**

Antibody-mediated   **Cell-mediated**
immune response   **immune response**

● **FIGURE 11-18 Origins of B and T cells.** B cells are derived from lymphocytes that matured and differentiated in the bone marrow, whereas T cells are derived from lymphocytes that originated in the bone marrow but matured and differentiated in the thymus. After early childhood, new B and T cells are produced primarily by colonies of B and T cells established in peripheral lymphoid tissues during fetal life and early childhood.

greater its antigenicity. Foreign proteins are the most common antigens because of their size and structural complexity. Antigens may exist as isolated molecules, such as bacterial toxins, or they may be an integral part of a multimolecular structure, as when they are on the surface of an invading foreign microbe.

We first see how B cells respond to their targeted antigen, after which we look at T cells' response to their antigen.

B Lymphocytes: Antibody-Mediated Immunity

Each B and T cell has receptors—**B-cell receptors (BCRs)** and **T-cell receptors (TCRs)**—on its surface for binding with one particular type of the multitude of possible antigens (● Figure 11-19). These receptors are the "eyes of the adaptive immune system," although a given lymphocyte can "see" only one unique antigen. This is in contrast to the TLRs of the innate effector

cells, which recognize generic "trademarks" characteristic of all microbial invaders.

Antigens stimulate B cells to convert into plasma cells that produce antibodies.

When B-cell receptors bind with an antigen, most B cells differentiate into active *plasma cells* while others become dormant *memory cells.* We first examine the role of plasma cells and their antibodies and then later in the chapter turn our attention to memory cells.

PLASMA CELLS A **plasma cell** produces antibodies that can combine with the specific type of antigen that stimulated activation of the plasma cell. During differentiation into a plasma cell, a B cell swells as the rough endoplasmic reticulum (the site for synthesis of proteins to be exported; see p. 23) greatly expands (● Figure 11-20). Because antibodies are proteins, plasma cells essentially become prolific protein factories, producing up to 2000 antibody molecules per second. So great is the commitment of a plasma cell's protein-synthesizing machinery to antibody production that it cannot maintain protein synthesis for its own viability and growth. Consequently, it dies after a brief (5- to 7-day), highly productive life span.

ANTIBODY SUBCLASSES Antibodies (immunoglobulins) are grouped into five subclasses based on differences in their biological activity. For example, **IgG** antibodies produce most specific immune responses against bacterial invaders and a few types of viruses, whereas **IgE** is the antibody mediator for common allergic responses, such as hay fever, asthma, and hives, and helps protect against parasitic worms. Note that this classification is based on different ways in which antibodies function. It does not imply that there are only five different antibodies. Within each functional subclass are millions of different antibodies, each able to bind only with a specific antigen.

Antibodies are Y shaped and classified according to properties of their tail portion.

Antibodies of all five subclasses are arranged in the shape of a Y (● Figure 11-21). Characteristics of the arm regions of the Y determine the *specificity* of the antibody (that is, with what antigen the antibody can bind). Properties of the tail portion of the antibody determine the *functional properties* of the antibody (what the antibody does once it binds with an antigen).

An antibody has two identical antigen-binding sites, one at the tip of each arm. These **antigen-binding fragments (Fab)** are unique for each antibody, so each antibody can interact only with an antigen that specifically matches it, much like a lock and key. The tremendous variation in the fragments of different antibodies leads to the extremely large number of unique antibodies that can bind specifically with millions of different antigens.

In contrast to these variable Fab regions at the arm tips, the tail portion of every antibody within each immunoglobulin subclass is identical. The tail, the antibody's **constant (Fc) region,** contains binding sites for particular mediators of

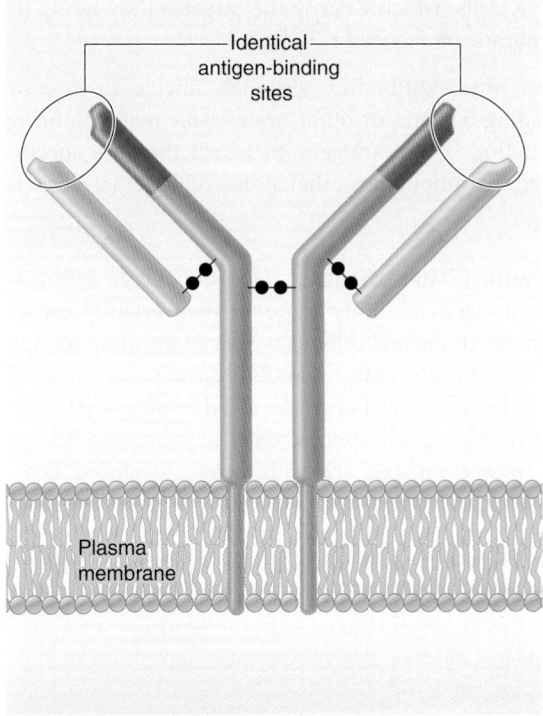

Identical antigen-binding sites

Plasma membrane

(a) B-cell receptor (BCR)

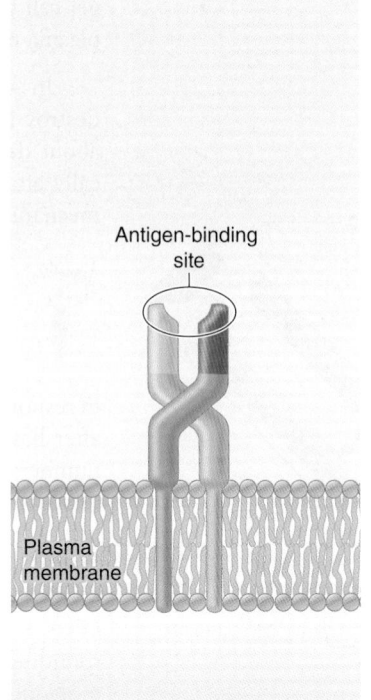

Antigen-binding site

Plasma membrane

(b) T-cell receptor (TCR)

● **FIGURE 11-19 B- and T-cell receptors.**

antibody-induced activities, which vary among the subclasses. In fact, differences in the constant region are the basis for distinguishing among the immunoglobulin subclasses. For example, the constant tail region of IgG antibodies, when activated by antigen binding in the Fab region, binds with phagocytic cells and serves as an opsonin to enhance phagocytosis. In comparison, the constant tail region of IgE antibodies attaches to mast cells and basophils, even in the absence of antigens. When the appropriate antigen gains entry to the body and binds with the attached antibodies, this triggers the release of histamine

● **FIGURE 11-20 Comparison of an unactivated B cell and a plasma cell.** Electron micrographs at the same magnification of (a) an unactivated B cell, or small lymphocyte, and (b) a plasma cell. A plasma cell is an activated B cell. It is filled with an abundance of rough endoplasmic reticulum distended with antibody molecules.

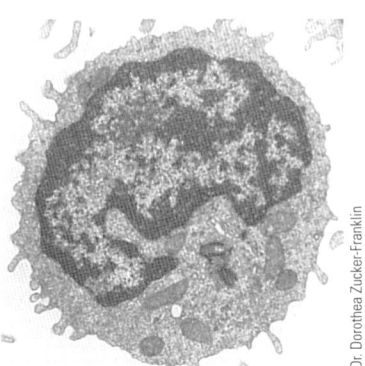

(a) Unactivated B cell

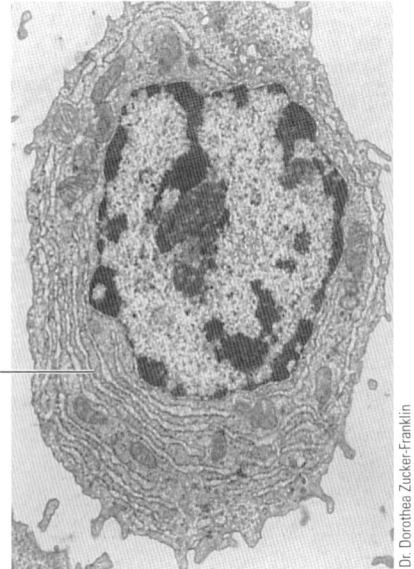

Endoplasmic reticulum

(b) Plasma cell

from the affected mast cells and basophils. Histamine, in turn, induces the allergic manifestations that follow.

Antibodies largely amplify innate immune responses to promote antigen destruction.

Antibodies cannot directly destroy foreign organisms or other unwanted materials on binding with antigens on their surfaces. Instead, they exert their protective influence by physically hindering antigens or, more commonly, by amplifying innate immune responses (● Figure 11-22).

PHYSICAL HINDRANCE OF AN ANTIGEN Agglutination is an example of how antibodies can physically hinder some antigens from exerting their detrimental effects. In **agglutination,** multiple antibody molecules cross-link numerous antigen molecules into chains or lattices of antigen–antibody complexes (● Figure 11-22a). Through this means, foreign cells, such as bacteria or mismatched transfused red blood cells, bind together in a clump. When linked antigen–antibody complexes involve soluble antigens, such as tetanus toxin, the lattice can become so large that it precipitates out of solution. (**Precipitation** is the process in which a substance separates from a solution.)

Within the body, these physical hindrance mechanisms play only a minor protective role against invading agents. However, the tendency for certain antigens to agglutinate or precipitate on forming large complexes with antibodies specific for them is useful for detecting the presence of particular antigens or antibodies. Pregnancy diagnosis tests, for example, use this principle to detect, in urine, the presence of a hormone secreted soon after conception.

AMPLIFICATION OF INNATE IMMUNE RESPONSES The most important function of antibodies by far is to profoundly augment the innate immune responses already initiated by the invaders. Antibodies mark foreign material as targets for actual destruction by the complement system, phagocytes, or natural killer cells while enhancing the activity of these other defense systems by the following methods:

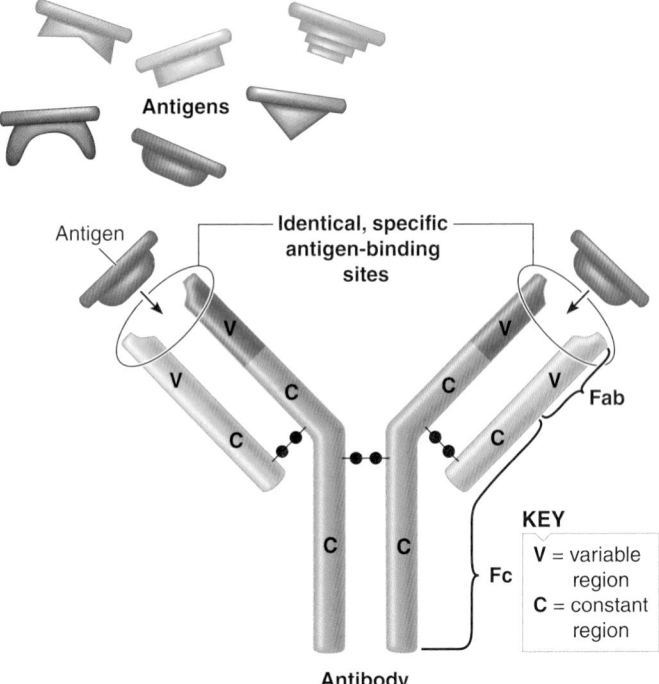

● FIGURE 11-21 **Antibody structure.** An antibody is a Y-shaped molecule. It is able to bind only with the specific antigen that "fits" its antigen-binding sites (Fab) on the arm tips. The tail region (Fc) binds with particular mediators of antibody-induced activities.

1. *Activating the complement system.* When an appropriate antigen binds with an antibody, receptors on the tail portion of the antibody bind with and activate C1, the first component of the complement system. This sets off the cascade of events leading to formation of the membrane attack complex, which is specifically directed at the membrane of the invading cell that bears the antigen that initiated the activation process (● Figure 11-22b). Antibodies are the most powerful activators of the complement system. The biochemical attack subsequently unleashed against the invader's membrane is the most important mechanism by which antibodies exert their protective influence. Furthermore, various activated complement components enhance virtually every aspect of the inflammatory process. The same complement system is activated by an antigen–antibody complex regardless of the type of antigen. Although the binding of antigen to antibody is highly specific, the outcome, which is determined by the antibody's constant tail region, is identical for all activated antibodies within a given subclass; for example, all IgG antibodies activate the same complement system.

2. *Enhancing phagocytosis.* Antibodies, especially IgG, act as opsonins. The tail portion of an antigen-bound IgG antibody binds with a receptor on the surface of a phagocyte and subsequently promotes phagocytosis of the antigen-containing victim attached to the antibody (● Figure 11-22c).

3. *Stimulating natural killer (NK) cells.* The binding of antibody to antigen also induces attack of the antigen-bearing target cell by NK cells. NK cells have receptors for the constant tail portion of antibodies. In this case, when the target cell is coated with antibodies, the tail portions of the antibodies link the tar-

get cell to NK cells, which destroy the target cell by lysing its plasma membrane (● Figure 11-22d).

In these ways, antibodies, although unable to directly destroy invading bacteria or other undesirable material, bring about destruction of the antigens to which they are specifically attached, by amplifying other nonspecific lethal defense mechanisms.

Clinical Note **IMMUNE COMPLEX DISEASE** Occasionally, an overzealous antigen–antibody response inadvertently causes damage to normal cells, as well as to invading foreign cells. Typically, antigen–antibody complexes, formed in response to foreign invasion, are removed by phagocytic cells after having revved up nonspecific defense strategies. If large numbers of these complexes are continuously produced, however, the phagocytes cannot clear away all the immune complexes formed. Antigen–antibody complexes that are not removed continue to activate the complement system, among other things. Excessive amounts of activated complement and other inflammatory agents may "spill over," damaging the surrounding normal cells, as well as the unwanted cells. Furthermore, destruction is not necessarily restricted to the initial site of inflammation. Antigen–antibody complexes may circulate freely and become trapped in the kidneys, joints, brain, small vessels of the skin, and elsewhere, causing widespread inflammation and tissue damage. Such damage produced by immune complexes is referred to as an **immune complex disease,** which can be a complicating outcome of bacterial, viral, or parasitic infection.

More insidiously, immune complex disease can stem from overzealous inflammatory activity prompted by immune complexes formed by "self-antigens" (proteins synthesized by the person's own body) and antibodies erroneously produced against them. *Rheumatoid arthritis* develops in this way.

Clonal selection accounts for the specificity of antibody production.

Consider the diversity of foreign molecules a person can potentially encounter during a lifetime. Despite this, each B cell is preprogrammed to respond to only 1 of probably more than 100 million different antigens. Other antigens cannot combine with the same B cell and induce it to secrete different antibodies. The astonishing implication is that each of us is equipped with about 100 million kinds of preformed B lymphocytes, at least one B lymphocyte for every possible antigen that we might ever encounter. The clonal selection theory proposes how a "matching" B cell responds to its antigen.

Early researchers in immunologic theory believed antibodies were "made to order" whenever a foreign antigen gained entry to the body. In contrast, the currently accepted **clonal selection theory** proposes that diverse B lymphocytes are produced during fetal development, each capable of synthesizing an antibody against a particular antigen before ever being exposed to it. All offspring of a particular ancestral B lymphocyte form a family of identical cells, or a **clone,** that is committed to producing the same specific antibody. B cells

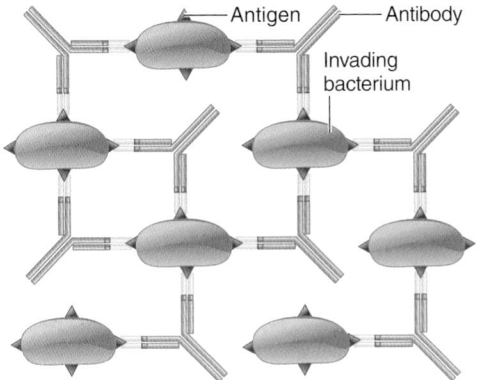

(a) **Agglutination** (clumping of antigenic cells) and **precipitation** (if soluble antigen–antibody complex is too large to stay in solution)

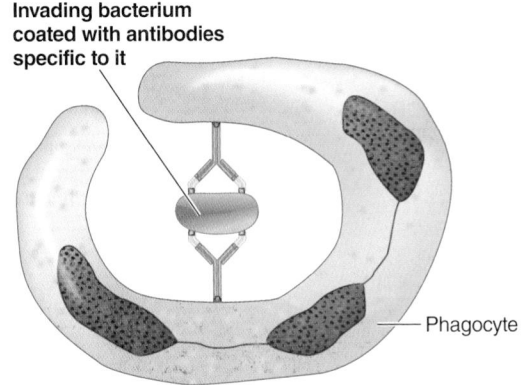

(c) Enhancement of phagocytosis (opsonization)

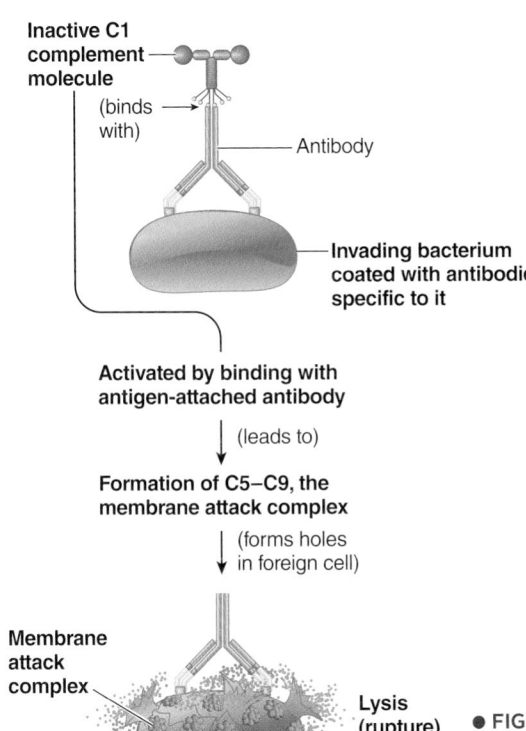

(b) Activation of complement system

(d) Stimulation of natural killer (NK) cells

Structures are not drawn to scale.

● FIGURE 11-22 **How antibodies help eliminate invading microbes.** Antibodies may physically hinder antigens, such as through agglutination (a). More commonly, antibodies amplify innate immune responses by (b) activating the complement system, (c) enhancing phagocytosis by acting as opsonins, and (d) stimulating natural killer cells.

remain dormant, not actually secreting their particular antibody product nor undergoing rapid division until (or unless) they come into contact with the appropriate antigen. When an antigen gains entry to the body, the particular clone of B cells that bear receptors (BCRs) on their surface uniquely specific for that antigen is activated or "selected" by the antigen binding with the BCRs, hence the term *clonal selection theory* (● Figure 11-23).

The first antibodies produced by a newly formed B cell are inserted into the cell's plasma membrane rather than secreted. Here they serve as BCRs for binding with a specific kind of antigen, almost like "advertisements" for the kind of antibody that the cell can produce. Binding of the appropriate antigen to

a B cell amounts to "placing an order" for the manufacture and secretion of large quantities of that particular antibody.

Selected clones differentiate into active plasma cells and dormant memory cells.

Antigen binding causes the activated B-cell clone to multiply and differentiate into two cell types—the previously described plasma cells and memory cells, which we focus on next. Most progeny are transformed into active plasma cells, which are prolific producers of customized antibodies that contain the same antigen-binding sites as the surface receptors. In the blood, the secreted antibodies combine with the invading, free-

Population of unactivated B cells, each a member of a different B-cell clone that makes a specific receptor, which is displayed on the membrane surface as a BCR

Antigen

BCR

B cell specific to antigen

Binding of antigen and interaction with helper T cell stimulates the matching B cells to divide and expand the clone of selected cells.

Plasma cells

Memory B cells

Rough ER

Antibodies

Most of the new B cells differentiate into plasma cells, which secrete antibodies.

A few of the new B cells differentiate into memory B cells, which respond to a later encounter with the same antigen.

● FIGURE 11-23 **Clonal selection theory.** The B-cell clone specific to the antigen proliferates and differentiates into plasma cells and memory cells. Plasma cells secrete antibodies that bind with a free antigen not attached to B cells. Memory cells are primed and ready for subsequent exposure to the same antigen.

existing antigen, marking it for destruction by the complement system, phagocytic ingestion, or NK cells.

MEMORY CELLS Not all new B lymphocytes produced by the specifically activated clone differentiate into antibody-secreting plasma cells. A small proportion become **memory cells,** which do not participate in the current immune attack against the antigen but instead remain dormant and expand this specific clone. If the person is ever reexposed to the same antigen, these memory cells are primed and ready for even more immediate action than the original lymphocytes in the clone were.

Even though each of us has essentially the same original pool of different B-cell clones, the

pool gradually becomes appropriately biased to respond most efficiently to each person's particular antigenic environment. Those clones specific for antigens to which a person is never exposed remain dormant for life, whereas those specific for antigens in the individual's environment typically become expanded and enhanced by forming highly responsive memory cells.

PRIMARY AND SECONDARY RESPONSES During initial contact with a microbial antigen, the antibody response is delayed for several days until plasma cells are formed and does not reach its peak for a couple of weeks. This response is known as the **primary response** (● Figure 11-24a). Meanwhile, symptoms characteristic of the particular microbial invasion persist until either the invader succumbs to the mounting specific immune attack against it or the infected person dies. After reaching the peak, the antibody levels gradually decline over time. If the same antigen ever reappears, the long-lived memory cells launch a more rapid, more potent, and longer-lasting **secondary response** than occurred during the primary response (● Figure 11-24b). This swifter, more powerful immune attack is frequently adequate to prevent or minimize overt infection on subsequent exposures to the same microbe, forming the basis of long-term immunity against a specific disease.

Clinical Note The original antigenic exposure that induces the formation of memory cells can occur through the person either having the disease or being vaccinated. **Vaccination (immunization)** deliberately exposes the person to a pathogen that has been stripped of its disease-inducing capability but that can still induce antibody forma-

● FIGURE 11-24 **Primary and secondary immune responses.** (a) Primary response on first exposure to a microbial antigen. (b) Secondary response on subsequent exposure to the same microbial antigen. The primary response does not peak for a couple of weeks, whereas the secondary response peaks in a week. The magnitude of the secondary response is 100 times that of the primary response. (The relative antibody response is in the logarithmic scale.)

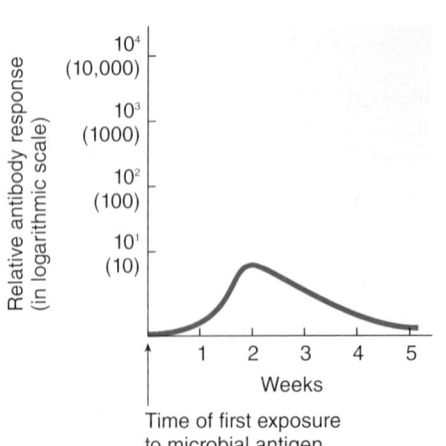

(a) **Primary immune response**

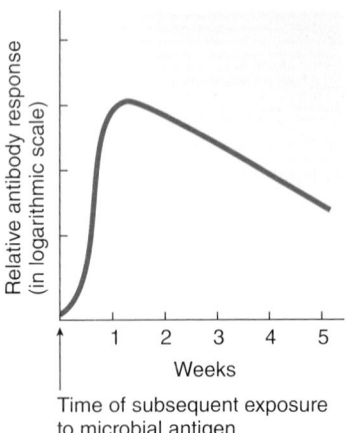

(b) **Secondary immune response**

Vaccination: A Victory Over Many Dreaded Diseases

Modern society has come to hope and even expect that vaccines can be developed to protect us from almost any dreaded infectious disease. This expectation has been brought into sharp focus by our current frustration over the inability to date to develop a successful vaccine against HIV, the virus that causes AIDS.

Nearly 2500 years ago, our ancestors were aware of the existence of immune protection. Writing about a plague that struck Athens in 430 BC, Thucydides observed that the same person was never attacked twice by this disease. However, the ancients did not understand the basis of this protection, so they could not manipulate it to their advantage.

Early attempts to deliberately acquire lifelong protection against smallpox, a dreaded disease that was highly infectious and frequently fatal (up to 40% of the sick died), consisted of intentionally exposing oneself by coming into direct contact with a person suffering from a milder form of the disease. The hope was to protect against a future fatal bout of smallpox by deliberately inducing a mild case of the disease. By the beginning of the 17th century, this technique had evolved into using a needle to extract small amounts of pus from active smallpox pustules (the fluid-filled bumps on the skin, which leave a characteristic depressed scar or "pock" mark after healing) and introducing this infectious material into healthy individuals. This inoculation process was done by applying the pus directly to slight cuts in the skin or by inhaling dried pus.

Edward Jenner, an English physician, was the first to demonstrate that immunity against cowpox, a disease similar to but less serious than smallpox, could also protect humans against smallpox. Having observed that milkmaids who got cowpox seemed to be protected from smallpox, Jenner in 1796 inoculated a healthy boy with pus he had extracted from cowpox boils (*vacca,* as in *vaccination,* means "cow"). After the boy recovered, Jenner (not being restricted by modern ethical standards of research on human subjects) deliberately inoculated him with what was considered a normally fatal dose of smallpox infectious material. The boy survived.

Jenner's results were not taken seriously, however, until a century later when, in the 1880s, Louis Pasteur, the first great experimental immunologist, extended Jenner's technique. Pasteur demonstrated that the disease-inducing capability of organisms could be greatly reduced (attenuated) so that they could no longer produce disease but would still induce antibody formation when introduced into the body—the basic principle of modern vaccines. His first vaccine was against anthrax, a deadly disease of sheep and cows. Pasteur isolated and heated anthrax bacteria and then injected these attenuated organisms into a group of healthy sheep. A few weeks later, at a gathering of fellow scientists, Pasteur injected these vaccinated sheep, as well as a group of unvaccinated sheep, with fully potent anthrax bacteria. The result was dramatic—all the vaccinated sheep survived, but all the unvaccinated sheep died. Pasteur's notorious public demonstrations such as this, coupled with his charismatic personality, caught the attention of physicians and scientists of the time, sparking the development of modern immunology.

---

tion against itself. (For the early history of vaccination development, see the accompanying boxed feature, ❯ Beyond the Basics.)

We now turn our attention to T cells.

T Lymphocytes: Cell-Mediated Immunity

As important as B lymphocytes and their antibody products are in specific defense against invading bacteria and other foreign material, they represent only half of the body's specific immune defenses. The T lymphocytes are equally important in defense against most viral infections and also play an important regulatory role in immune mechanisms.

T cells bind directly with their targets.

Whereas B cells and antibodies defend against conspicuous invaders in the ECF, T cells defend against covert invaders that hide inside cells where antibodies and the complement system cannot reach them. Unlike B cells, which secrete antibodies that can attack antigens at long distances, T cells do not secrete antibodies. Instead, they must directly contact their targets, a process known as *cell-mediated immunity.* T cells of the killer type release chemicals that destroy the targeted cells they contact, such as virus-infected cells and cancer cells.

Like B cells, T cells are clonal and exquisitely antigen specific. On its plasma membrane, each T cell bears unique receptor proteins called *T-cell receptors (TCRs),* similar although not identical to the surface receptors on B cells (see ● Figure 11-19b, p. 341). Immature lymphocytes acquire their TCRs in the thymus during their differentiation into T cells. Unlike B cells, T cells are activated by a foreign antigen only when it is on the surface of a cell that also carries a marker of the individual's own identity; that is, both foreign antigens and **self-antigens** must be on a cell's surface before a T cell can bind with it. During thymic education, T cells learn to recognize foreign antigens only in combination with the person's own tissue antigens—a lesson passed on to all T cells' future progeny. The importance of this dual antigen requirement and the nature of the self-antigens are described shortly.

A delay of a few days generally follows exposure to the appropriate antigen before **activated T cells** are prepared to launch a cell-mediated immune attack. When exposed to a specific antigen combination, cells of the complementary T-cell clone proliferate and differentiate for several days, yielding large numbers of activated effector T cells that carry out various cell-mediated responses. Like B cells, T cells form a memory pool and display both primary and secondary responses.

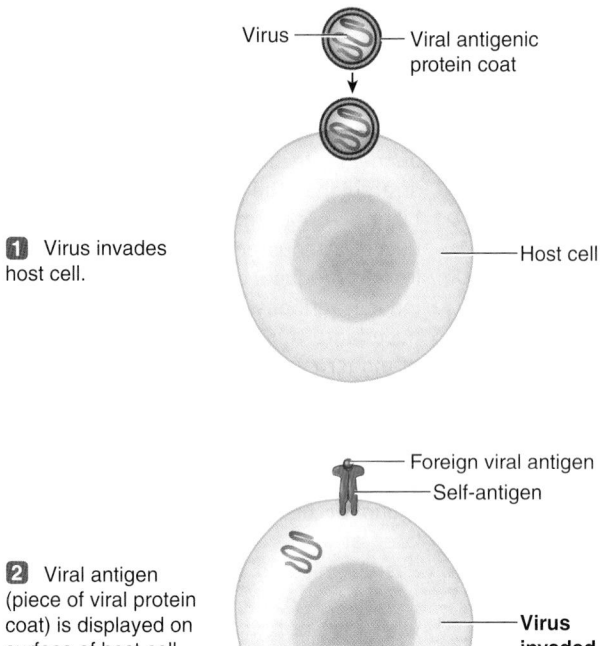

1 Virus invades host cell.

Virus — Viral antigenic protein coat

Host cell

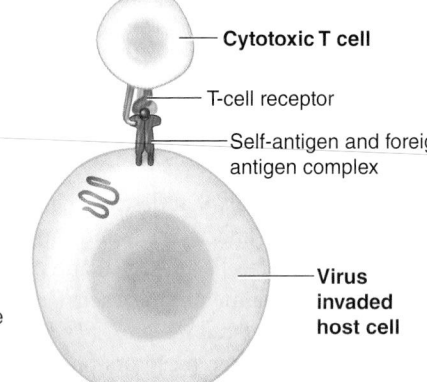

2 Viral antigen (piece of viral protein coat) is displayed on surface of host cell alongside the cell's self-antigen.

Foreign viral antigen
Self-antigen

Virus invaded host cell

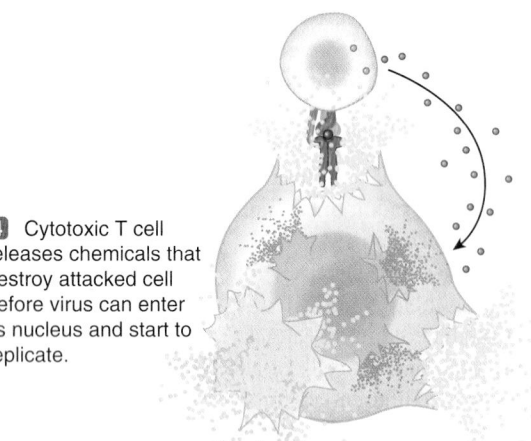

3 Cytotoxic T cell recognizes and binds with a specific foreign antigen (viral antigen) in association with the self-antigen.

Cytotoxic T cell

T-cell receptor

Self-antigen and foreign antigen complex

Virus invaded host cell

4 Cytotoxic T cell releases chemicals that destroy attacked cell before virus can enter its nucleus and start to replicate.

● **FIGURE 11-25 A cytotoxic T cell lysing a virus-invaded cell.**

The three types of T cells are cytotoxic, helper, and regulatory.

There are three subpopulations of T cells, depending on their roles when activated by an antigen:

■ **Cytotoxic,** or **killer, T cells** destroy host cells harboring anything foreign and thus bearing a foreign antigen, such as body cells invaded by viruses, cancer cells that have mutated proteins resulting from malignant transformations, and transplanted cells.

■ **Helper T cells** do not directly participate in immune destruction of invading pathogens. Instead, they modulate activities of other immune cells. Because of the important role they play in "turning on" the full power of all the other activated lymphocytes and macrophages, helper T cells constitute the immune system's "master switch." Helper T cells are by far the most numerous T cells, making up 60% to 80% of circulating T cells.

■ **Regulatory T cells,** originally called **suppressor T cells,** are a recently identified small subset of T cells that suppress immune responses. They keep the rest of the immune system under tight control. Regulatory T cells are specialized to inhibit both innate and adaptive immune responses in a check-and-balance fashion to minimize harmful immune pathology.

We now examine the functions of the two most abundant and best-known T cells, cytotoxic T cells and helper T cells, in further detail.

Cytotoxic T cells secrete chemicals that destroy target cells.

Cytotoxic T cells are microscopic "hit men." The targets of these destructive cells most frequently are host cells infected with viruses. When a virus invades a body cell, as it must to survive, the cell breaks down the envelope of proteins surrounding the virus and loads a fragment of this viral antigen piggyback onto a newly synthesized self-antigen. This self-antigen–viral antigen complex is inserted into the host cell's surface membrane, where it serves as a red flag indicating the cell is harboring the invader (● Figure 11-25, steps **1** and **2**). To attack the intracellular virus, cytotoxic T cells must destroy the infected host cell in the process. Cytotoxic T cells of the clone specific for this particular virus recognize and bind to the viral antigen and self-antigen on the surface of an infected cell (step **3**). Thus activated by the viral antigen, a cytotoxic T cell can kill the infected cell by either direct or indirect means, depending on the type of lethal chemicals the activated T cell releases. Let us elaborate.

■ An activated cytotoxic T cell may directly kill the victim cell by releasing chemicals that lyse the attacked cell before viral replication can begin (step **4**). Specifically, cytotoxic T cells, as well as NK cells, destroy a targeted cell by releasing **perforin** molecules, which penetrate the target cell's surface membrane and join to form porelike channels (● Figure 11-26). This technique of killing a cell by punching holes in its membrane is similar to the method employed by the membrane attack complex of the complement cascade.

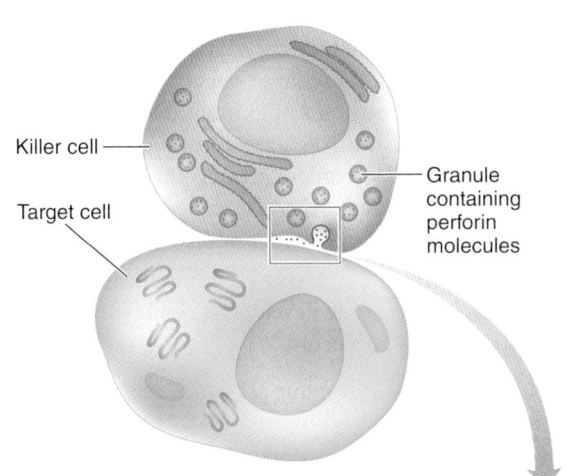

Killer cell

Target cell

Granule containing perforin molecules

1 Killer cell binds to its target.

2 As a result of binding, killer cell's perforin-containing granules fuse with plasma membrane.

3 Granules disgorge their perforin by exocytosis into a small pocket of intercellular space between killer cell and its target.

4 On exposure to Ca^{2+} in this space, individual perforin molecules change from spherical to cylindrical shape.

5 Remodeled perforin molecules bind to target cell membrane and insert into it.

6 Individual perforin molecules group together like staves of a barrel to form pores.

7 Pores admit salt and H_2O, causing target cell to swell and burst.

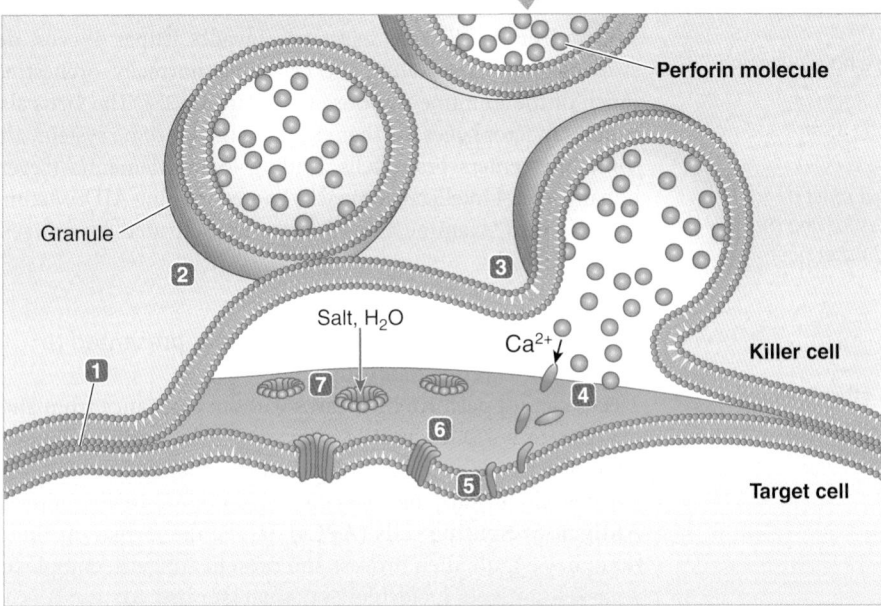

(a) Details of the killing process for cytotoxic T cells and NK cells

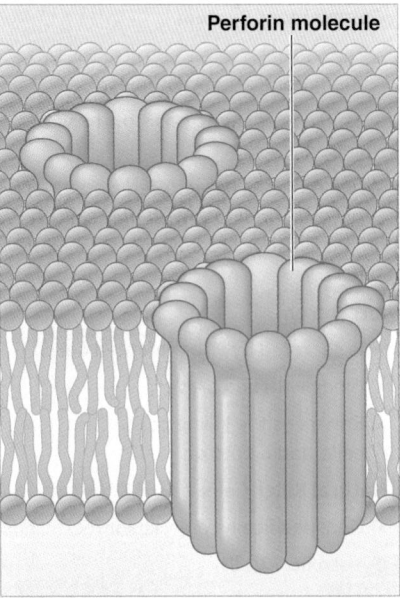

(b) Enlargement of perforin-formed pores in a target cell

● **FIGURE 11-26 Mechanism of killing by killer cells.** Note the similarity of the perforin-formed pores in a target cell to the membrane attack complex formed by complement molecules (see Figure 11-17, p. 339).
(*Source:* Adapted from the illustration by Dana Burns-Pizer in "How Killer Cells Kill," by John Ding-E Young and Zanvil A. Cohn, in *Scientific America,* 1988.)

■ A cytotoxic T cell can also indirectly bring about death of an infected host cell by releasing **granzymes,** which are enzymes similar to digestive enzymes. Granzymes enter the target cell through the perforin channels. Once inside, these chemicals trigger the virus-infected cell to self-destruct through apoptosis (cell suicide; see p. 104).

The virus released on destruction of the host cell by either of these methods is directly destroyed in the ECF by phagocytic cells and the complement system. Meanwhile, the cytotoxic T cell, which has not been harmed in the process, can move on to kill other infected host cells.

The surrounding healthy cells replace the lost cells by means of cell division. Usually, to halt a viral infection, only some of the host cells must be destroyed. If the virus has had a chance to multiply, however, with replicated virus leaving the original cell and spreading to other host cells, the cytotoxic T-cell defense mechanism may sacrifice so many of the host cells that serious malfunction may ensue.

Recall that other nonspecific defense mechanisms come into play to combat viral infections, most notably NK cells, interferon, macrophages, and the complement system. As usual, an intricate web of interplay exists among the immune defenses that are launched against viral invaders (▲ Table 11-3).

Helper T cells secrete chemicals that amplify the activity of other immune cells.

In contrast to cytotoxic T cells, helper T cells are not killer cells. Instead, helper T cells secrete cytokines that "help," or augment, nearly all aspects of the immune response. The following are among the best known of helper T-cell cytokines:

▲ Table 11-3 Defenses against Viral Invasion

When the virus is free in the ECF,

Macrophages

- Destroy the free virus by phagocytosis.
- Process and present the viral antigen to helper T cells.
- Secrete interleukin 1, which activates B- and T-cell clones specific to the viral antigen.

Plasma Cells Derived from B Cells Specific to the Viral Antigen Secrete Antibodies That

- Act as opsonins to enhance phagocytosis of the virus
- Activate the lethal complement system as part of adaptive immunity

Complement System

- Directly destroys the free virus by forming a hole-punching membrane attack complex.
- Enhances phagocytosis of the virus by acting as an opsonin.

When the virus has entered a host cell (which it must do to survive and multiply, with the replicated viruses leaving the original host cell to enter the ECF in search of other host cells),

Interferon

- Is secreted by virus-infected cells.
- Binds with and prevents viral replication in other host cells.
- Enhances the killing power of macrophages, natural killer cells, and cytotoxic T cells.

Natural Killer Cells

- Nonspecifically lyse virus-infected host cells.

Cytotoxic T Cells

- Are specifically activated by the viral antigen and lyse the infected host cells before the virus has a chance to replicate.

Helper T Cells

- Secrete cytokines, which enhance cytotoxic T-cell activity and B-cell antibody production.

When a virus-infected cell is destroyed, the free virus is released into the ECF, where it is attacked directly by macrophages, antibodies, and the activated complement components.

1. Helper T cells secrete *B-cell growth factor,* which contributes to B-cell function in concert with IL-1 secreted by macrophages. Antibody secretion is greatly reduced or absent without the assistance of helper T cells.

2. Helper T cells similarly secrete *T-cell growth factor,* which augments the activity of cytotoxic T cells and even of other helper T cells responsive to the invading antigen.

3. Some chemicals secreted by T cells act as *chemotaxins* to lure more neutrophils and macrophages-to-be to the invaded area.

4. Once macrophages are attracted to the area, *macrophage-migration inhibition factor,* another important cytokine released from helper T cells, keeps these large phagocytic cells in the region by inhibiting their outward migration. As a result, many chemotactically attracted macrophages accumulate in the infected area. This factor also confers greater phagocytic power on the gathered macrophages. These so-called **angry macrophages** have more powerful destructive ability.

5. One cytokine secreted by helper T cells activates eosinophils, and another promotes the development of IgE antibodies for defense against parasitic worms.

 Clinical Note This variety of immune activities helped by helper T cells is why **acquired immunodeficiency syndrome (AIDS),** caused by the **human immunodeficiency virus (HIV),** is so devastating to the immune defense system. The AIDS virus selectively invades helper T cells, destroying or incapacitating the cells that normally orchestrate much of the immune response (● Figure 11-27). The virus also invades macrophages, further crippling the immune system, and sometimes enters brain cells, leading to the dementia (severe impairment of intellectual capacity) noted in some AIDS victims.

We next examine how T cells are activated by antigen-presenting cells.

T lymphocytes respond only to antigens presented to them by antigen-presenting cells.

T cells cannot perform their tasks without assistance from antigen-presenting cells. That is, relevant T cells cannot recognize "raw" foreign antigens entering the body; before reacting to it, a T-cell clone must be formally "introduced" to the antigen. **Antigen-presenting cells (APCs)** handle the formal introduction; they engulf, then process and present antigens, complexed with self-antigen molecules, on their surface to the T cells. Once displayed at the cell surface, the combined presence of

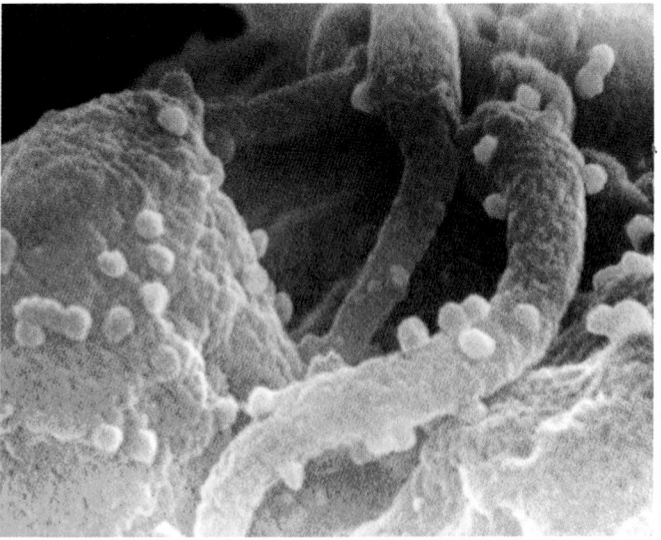

● **FIGURE 11-27 AIDS virus.** Human immunodeficiency virus (HIV) *(in small purple spheres),* the AIDS-causing virus, is shown on a portion of a helper T lymphocyte, HIV's primary target.

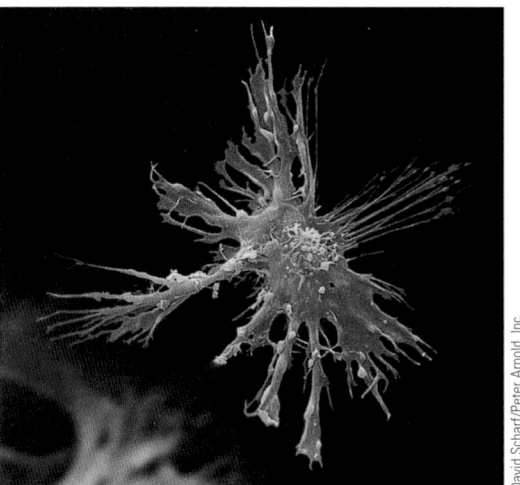

● **FIGURE 11-28 Dendritic cell.**

these self- and non-self-antigens alerts the immune system to the presence of an undesirable agent within the cell.

APCs include macrophages and closely related dendritic cells, both of which not only are phagocytic effector cells of the innate defense system but also play a key role in activating cell-mediated adaptive immunity. You are already familiar with macrophages. **Dendritic cells** are specialized APCs that act as sentinels in almost every tissue. They are so named because they have many surface projections, or branches, that resemble the dendrites of neurons (*dendros* means "tree") (● Figure 11-28). Dendritic cells are especially abundant in the skin and mucosal linings of the lungs and digestive tract—strategic locations where microbes are likely to enter the body.

To be activated, T cells must bind with foreign antigens presented on the surface of APCs and complexed with self-antigens. What is the nature of the self-antigens that the immune system learns to recognize as markers of a person's own cells? That is the topic of the next section.

The major histocompatibility complex is the code for self-antigens.

Self-antigens are plasma membrane–bound glycoproteins (proteins with sugar attached) known as **MHC molecules** because their synthesis is directed by a group of genes called the **major histocompatibility complex,** or **MHC.** The MHC genes are the most variable ones in humans. More than 100 different MHC molecules have been identified in human tissue, but each individual has a code for only 3 to 6 of these possible antigens. Because of the tremendous number of combinations possible, the exact pattern of MHC molecules varies from one individual to another, much like a "biochemical fingerprint" or "molecular identification card."

The major histocompatibility complex (*histo* means "tissue"; *compatibility* means "ability to get along") was so named because these genes and the self-antigens they encode were first discerned in relation to tissue typing (similar to blood typing), which is done to obtain the most compatible matches for tissue grafting and transplantation. However, the transfer of tissue from one individual to another does not normally occur in nature. The natural function of MHC antigens lies in their ability to direct the responses of T cells, not in their artificial role in rejecting transplanted tissue.

CLASS I AND CLASS II MHC MOLECULES T cells become active only when they match a given MHC–foreign antigen combination. In addition to having to fit a specific foreign antigen, the T-cell receptor must match the appropriate MHC molecule. Each person has two main classes of MHC-encoded molecules that are differentially recognized by cytotoxic and helper T cells—class I and class II MHC molecules, respectively (● Figure 11-29). The class I and II markers serve as signposts to guide cytotoxic and helper T cells to the precise cellular locations where their immune capabilities can be most effective. The **coreceptors** on the T cells bind with the MHC molecules on the target molecule, linking the two cells together.

Cytotoxic T cells can respond to foreign antigens only in association with **class I MHC glycoproteins,** which are found on the surface of all nucleated body cells. This binding specificity occurs because the cytotoxic T cell's **CD8 coreceptor** can interact only with class I MHC molecules. To carry out their role of dealing with pathogens that have invaded host cells, it is appropriate that cytotoxic T cells (also known as *CD8+ cells,* because of their coreceptor) bind only with body cells that viruses have infected—that is, with foreign antigens in association with self-antigens. Furthermore, these deadly T cells can link up with any cancerous body cell, because class I MHC molecules also display mutated (and thus "foreign" appearing) cellular proteins characteristic of these abnormal cells. Because any nucleated body cell can be invaded by viruses or become cancerous, essentially all cells display class I MHC glycoproteins, enabling cytotoxic T cells to attack any virus-invaded host cell or any cancer cell. In the case of cytotoxic T cells, the outcome of this binding is destruction of the infected body cell. Because cytotoxic T cells do not bind to MHC self-antigens in the absence of foreign antigens, normal body cells are protected from lethal immune attack.

In contrast, **class II MHC glycoproteins,** which are recognized by helper T cells, are restricted to the surface of a few special types of immune cells. The **CD4 coreceptor** associated with these helper T cells (also known as *CD4+ cells*) can interact only with class II MHC molecules. Thus, the specific binding requirements for cytotoxic and helper T cells ensure the appropriate T-cell responses. A helper T cell can bind with a foreign antigen only when it is found on the surfaces of immune cells with which the helper T cell directly interacts—*macrophages, dendritic cells,* and *B cells.* Class II MHC molecules are found on macrophages and dendritic cells, which present antigens to helper T cells, as well as on B cells, whose activities are enhanced by cytokines secreted by helper T cells. Binding of the antigen-bearing B cell with the matching helper T cell causes the T cell to secrete cytokines that activate this specific B cell, leading to clonal expansion and conversion of this B-cell clone into antibody-producing plasma cells and memory cells (● Figure 11-30 on pp. 352–353). The capabilities of helper T cells

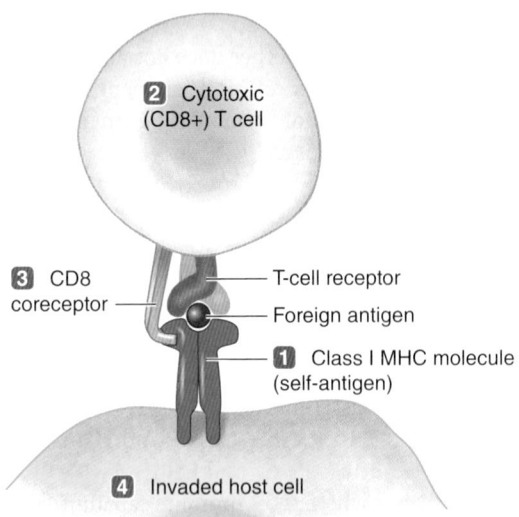

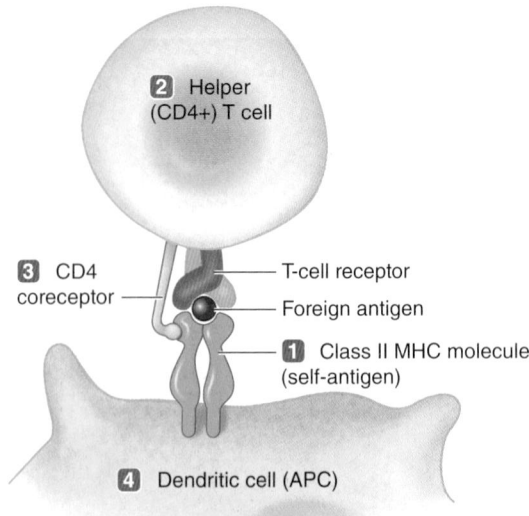

1 Cytotoxic (CD8+) T cell

3 CD8 coreceptor

T-cell receptor

Foreign antigen

1 Class I MHC molecule (self-antigen)

4 Invaded host cell

2 Helper (CD4+) T cell

3 CD4 coreceptor

T-cell receptor

Foreign antigen

1 Class II MHC molecule (self-antigen)

4 Dendritic cell (APC)

1 Class I MHC molecules are found on surface of all cells.

2 They are recognized only by cytotoxic (CD8+) T cells.

3 CD8 coreceptor links the two cells together.

4 Linked in this way, cytotoxic T cells can destroy body cells if invaded by foreign (viral) antigen.

1 Class II MHC molecules are found on the surface of immune cells with which helper T cells interact: dendritic cells, macrophages, and B cells.

2 They are recognized only by helper (CD4+) T cells.

3 CD4 coreceptor links the two cells together.

4 To be activated, helper T cells must bind with a class II MHC–bearing APC (dendritic cell or macrophage). To activate B cells, helper T cell must bind with a class II MHC–bearing B cell with displayed foreign antigen.

(a) Class I MHC self-antigens

(b) Class II MHC self-antigens

● **FIGURE 11-29 Distinctions between class I and class II major histocompatibility complex (MHC) glycoproteins.** Specific binding requirements for the two types of T cells ensure that these cells bind only with the target cells with which they can interact. Cytotoxic T cells can recognize and bind with a foreign antigen only when the antigen is in association with class I MHC glycoproteins, which are found on the surface of all body cells. This requirement is met when a virus invades a body cell, whereupon the cell is destroyed by the cytotoxic T cells. Helper T cells, which interact exclusively with dendritic cells, macrophages, and B cells, can recognize and bind with a foreign antigen only when it is in association with class II MHC glycoproteins, which are found only on the surface of these other immune cells.

would be squandered if these cells were able to bind with body cells other than these special APC and B immune cells. This is the primary pathway by which the adaptive immune system fights bacteria. ▲ Table 11-4 summarizes the innate and adaptive immune strategies that defend against bacterial invasion.

 TRANSPLANT REJECTION T cells bind with MHC antigens present on the surface of transplanted cells in the absence of a foreign viral antigen. The ensuing destruction of the transplanted cells triggers the rejection of transplanted or grafted tissues. Presumably, some of the recipient's T cells "mistake" the MHC antigens of the donor cells for a closely resembling combination of a conventional viral foreign antigen complexed with the recipient's MHC self-antigens.

To minimize the rejection phenomenon, technicians match the tissues of donor and recipient according to MHC antigens as closely as possible. Therapeutic procedures to suppress the immune system then follow.

What factors normally prevent the adaptive immune system from unleashing its powerful defense capabilities against the body's own self-antigens? We examine this issue next.

The immune system is normally tolerant of self-antigens.

The term **tolerance** in this context refers to preventing the immune system from attacking the person's own tissues. During embryonic development, some B and T cells are by chance formed that could react against the body's own tissue antigens.

If these lymphocyte clones were allowed to function, they would destroy the individual's own body. Fortunately, the immune system normally does not produce antibodies or activated T cells against the body's own self-antigens.

Multiple mechanisms are involved in tolerance. The following are examples:

1. *Clonal deletion.* In response to continuous exposure to body antigens early in development, B and T lymphocyte clones specifically capable of attacking these self-antigens in most cases are permanently destroyed within the thymus. This **clonal deletion** is accomplished by triggering apoptosis of immature cells that would react with the body's own proteins. This physical elimination is the major mechanism by which tolerance is developed.

2. *Clonal anergy.* The premise of clonal anergy is that a T lymphocyte must receive two specific simultaneous signals to be activated ("turned on"), one from its compatible antigen and a stimulatory cosignal found only on the surface of an APC. These dual signals—antigen plus cosignal—never are present for self-antigens because these antigens are not handled by cosignal-bearing APCs. The first exposure to a single signal from a self-antigen "turns off" the compatible T cell, rendering the cell unresponsive to further exposure to the antigen. This reaction is referred to as **clonal anergy** (*anergy* means "lack of energy") because T cells are inactivated (that is, "become lazy") rather than activated by their antigens. Anergized T lymphocyte clones survive, but they can't function.

▲ Table 11-4 Innate and Adaptive Immune Responses to Bacterial Invasion

Innate Immune Mechanisms	Adaptive Immune Mechanisms
Inflammation Resident tissue macrophages engulf invading bacteria. Histamine-induced vascular responses increase blood flow to the area, bringing in additional immune-effector cells and plasma proteins. Neutrophils and monocytes–macrophages migrate from the blood to the area to engulf and destroy foreign invaders and to remove cell debris. Phagocytic cells secrete cytokines, which enhance both innate and adaptive immune responses and induce local and systemic symptoms associated with an infection. **Nonspecific Activation of the Complement System** Complement components form a hole-punching membrane attack complex that lyses bacterial cells. Complement components enhance many steps of inflammation, such as serving as chemotaxins and acting as opsonins	B cells specific to an antigen present the antigen to helper T cells. On binding with the B cells, helper T cells activate the B cells. The activated B-cell clone proliferates and differentiates into plasma cells and memory cells. Plasma cells secrete customized antibodies, which specifically bind to invading bacteria. Plasma-cell activity is enhanced by: • Interleukin 1 secreted by macrophages. • Helper T cells, which have been activated by the same bacterial antigen processed and presented to them by macrophages or dendritic cells. Antibodies bind to invading bacteria and enhance innate mechanisms that lead to the bacteria's destruction. Specifically, antibodies: • Act as opsonins to enhance phagocytic activity. • Activate the lethal complement system. • Stimulate killer cells, which directly lyse bacteria. Memory cells persist that are capable of responding more rapidly and more forcefully should the same bacteria be encountered again.

Activation of helper T cells by antigen presentation

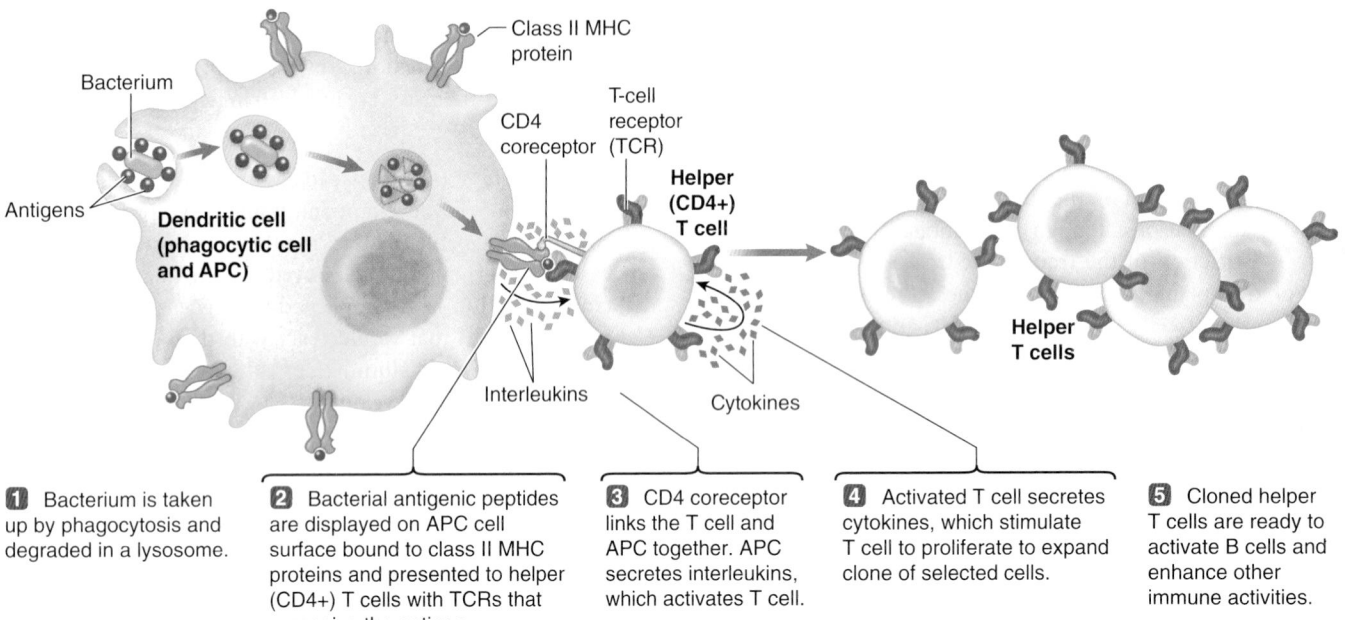

1 Bacterium is taken up by phagocytosis and degraded in a lysosome.	**2** Bacterial antigenic peptides are displayed on APC cell surface bound to class II MHC proteins and presented to helper (CD4+) T cells with TCRs that recognize the antigen.	**3** CD4 coreceptor links the T cell and APC together. APC secretes interleukins, which activates T cell.	**4** Activated T cell secretes cytokines, which stimulate T cell to proliferate to expand clone of selected cells.	**5** Cloned helper T cells are ready to activate B cells and enhance other immune activities.

● **FIGURE 11-30** **Interactions among large phagocytic cells (APCs), helper T cells, and B cells.**

3. *Receptor editing.* With **receptor editing,** once a B cell that bears a receptor for one of the body's own antigens encounters the self-antigen, the B cell escapes death by swiftly changing its antigen receptor to a nonself version. In this way, an originally self-reactive B cell survives but is "rehabilitated" so that it will never target the body's own tissues again.

4. *Active suppression by regulatory T cells.* Regulatory T cells play a role in tolerance by inhibiting throughout life some lymphocyte clones specific for the body's own tissues.

 Occasionally, the immune system fails to distinguish between self-antigens and foreign antigens and unleashes its deadly powers against one or more of the body's own tissues. A condition in which the immune system fails to recognize and tolerate self-antigens associated with particular tissues is known as an **autoimmune disease** (*auto* means "self"). Autoimmune diseases arise from a combination of genetic predisposition and environmental insults that lead to failure of the immune system's tolerance mechanisms. Autoimmunity underlies more than 80 diseases, many of which are well known. Examples include *multiple sclerosis, rheumatoid arthritis, Type 1 diabetes mellitus,* and *psoriasis.* About 50 million Americans suffer from some type of autoimmune disease.

Let us now look in more detail at the role of T cells in defending against cancer.

Immune surveillance against cancer cells involves an interplay among immune cells and interferon.

Besides destroying virus-infected host cells, an important function of the T-cell system is recognizing and destroying newly arisen, potentially cancerous tumor cells before they have a chance to multiply and spread, a process known as **immune surveillance.** At least once a day, on average, your immune system destroys a mutated cell that could potentially become cancerous. Any normal cell may be transformed into a cancer cell if mutations occur within its genes that govern cell division and growth. Such mutations may occur by chance alone or, more frequently, by exposure to **carcinogenic** (cancer-causing) factors such as ionizing radiation, certain environmental chemicals, or physical irritants. Alternatively, a few cancers are caused by tumor viruses, which turn the cells they invade into cancer cells, an example being the *human papillomavirus* that causes cervical cancer. The immune system recognizes cancer cells because they bear new and different surface antigens alongside the cell's normal self-antigens because of either genetic mutation or invasion by a tumor virus.

 BENIGN AND MALIGNANT TUMORS Cell multiplication and growth are normally under strict control, but the regulatory mechanisms are largely unknown. Cell multiplication in an adult is generally restricted to replacing lost cells. Furthermore, cells normally respect their own place and space in the body's society of cells. If a cell that has transformed into a tumor cell manages to escape immune destruction, however, it defies the normal controls on its proliferation and position. Unrestricted multiplication of a single tumor cell results in a **tumor** that consists of a clone of cells identical to the original mutated cell.

If the mass is slow growing, stays put in its original location, and does not infiltrate the surrounding tissue, it is considered a **benign tumor.** In contrast, the transformed cell may multiply rapidly and form an invasive mass that lacks the "altruistic" behavior characteristic of normal cells. Such invasive tu-

Activation of B cells responsive to antigen

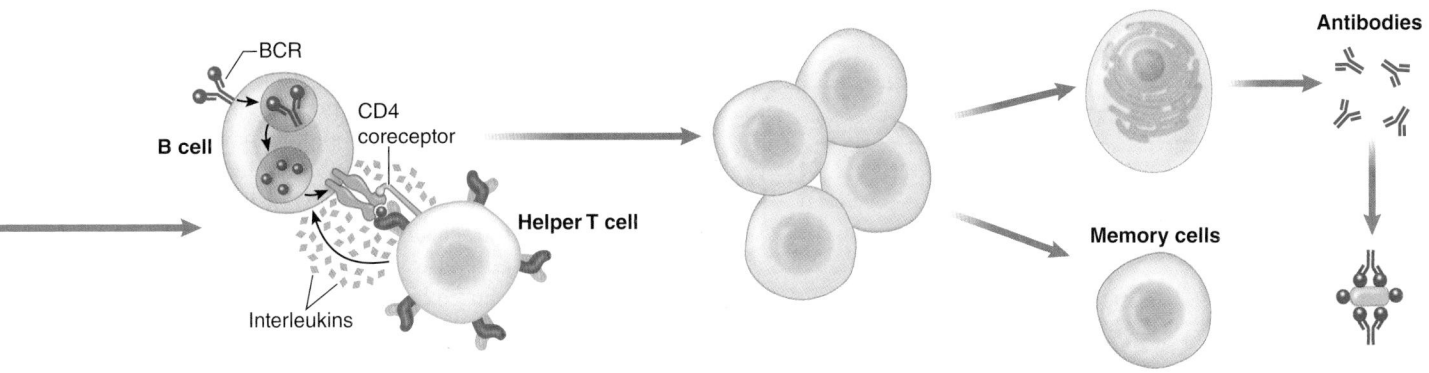

6 BCR binds to antigen. Antigen is internalized by receptor-mediated endocytosis and its macromolecules degraded. Antigenic peptides produced are displayed on cell surface bound to class II MHC proteins.

7 TCR of a helper T cell recognizes specific antigen on B cell, and CD4 coreceptor links the two cells together.

8 Helper T cell secretes interleukins, which stimulate B cell proliferation to produce clone of selected cells.

9 Some cloned B cells differentiate into plasma cells, which secrete antibodies specific for the antigen, while a few differentiate into memory B cells.

10 Antibodies bind with antigen, targeting antigenic invader for destruction by the innate immune system.

mors are **malignant tumors,** or **cancer.** Malignant tumor cells usually do not adhere well to the neighboring normal cells, so often some of the cancer cells break away from the parent tumor. These "emigrant" cancer cells are transported through the blood to new territories, where they continue to proliferate, forming multiple malignant tumors. The term **metastasis** is applied to this spreading of cancer to other parts of the body.

If a malignant tumor is detected early, before it has metastasized, it can be removed surgically. Once cancer cells have dispersed and seeded multiple cancerous sites, surgical elimination of the malignancy is impossible. In this case, agents that interfere with rapidly dividing and growing cells, such as certain chemotherapeutic drugs, are used in an attempt to destroy the malignant cells. Unfortunately, these agents also harm normal body cells, especially rapidly proliferating cells such as blood cells and the cells lining the digestive tract.

Untreated cancer is eventually fatal in most cases, for several interrelated reasons. The uncontrollably growing malignant mass crowds out normal cells by vigorously competing with them for space and nutrients, yet the cancer cells cannot take over the functions of the cells they are destroying. Cancer cells typically remain immature and do not become specialized, often resembling embryonic cells instead (● Figure 11-31). Such poorly differentiated malignant cells lack the ability to perform the specialized functions of the normal cell type from which they mutated. Affected organs gradually become disrupted to the point that they can no longer perform their life-sustaining functions, and the person dies.

EFFECTORS OF IMMUNE SURVEILLANCE Immune surveillance against cancer depends on an interplay among three types of immune cells—*cytotoxic T cells, NK cells,* and *macrophages*—as

well as *interferon.* These three immune cell types not only can attack and destroy cancer cells directly but also secrete interferon. Interferon, in turn, inhibits multiplication of cancer cells and increases the killing ability of the immune cells (● Figure 11-32).

Still, cancer does sometimes occur because cancer cells occasionally escape these immune mechanisms. Some cancer cells

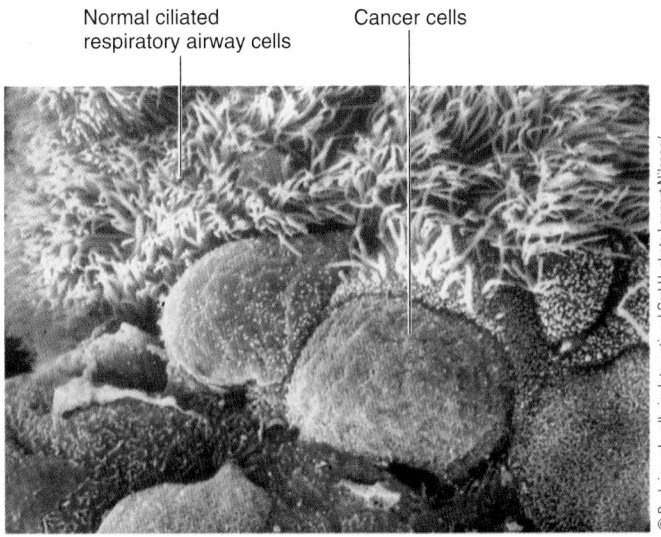

● **FIGURE 11-31 Comparison of normal and cancerous cells in the large respiratory airways.** The normal cells display specialized cilia, which constantly contract in a whiplike motion to sweep debris and microorganisms from the respiratory airways so that they do not gain entrance to the deeper portions of the lungs. The cancerous cells are not ciliated, so they are unable to perform this specialized defense task.

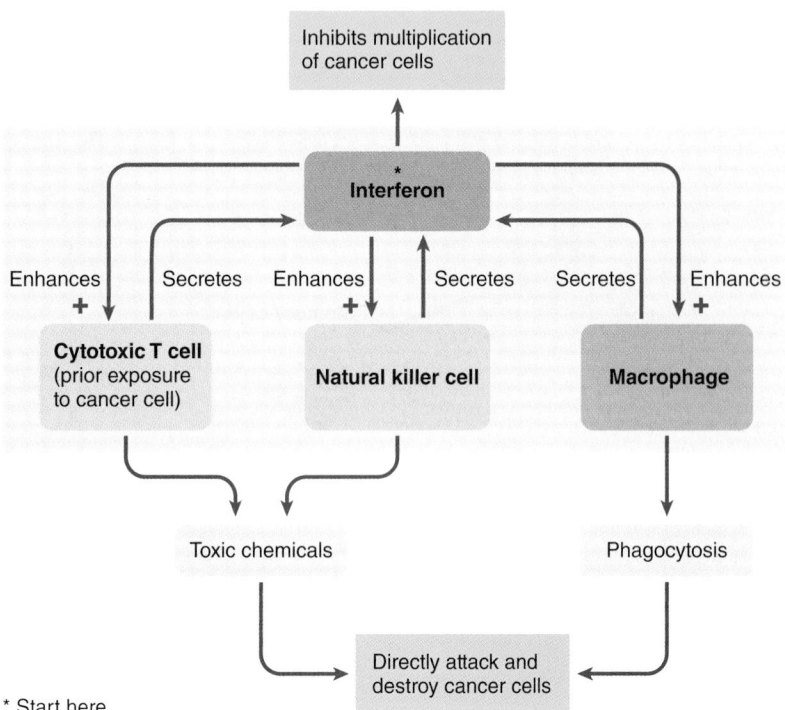

Inhibits multiplication
of cancer cells

Interferon *

Enhances + — Secretes — Enhances + — Secretes — Secretes — Enhances +

Cytotoxic T cell
(prior exposure
to cancer cell)

Natural killer cell

Macrophage

Toxic chemicals

Phagocytosis

Directly attack and
destroy cancer cells

* Start here

● **FIGURE 11-32 Immune surveillance against cancer.** Anticancer
interactions of cytotoxic T cells, natural killer cells, macrophages,
and interferon.

are believed to survive by evading immune detection—for example, by failing to display identifying antigens on their surface or by being surrounded by counterproductive **blocking antibodies** that interfere with T-cell function. Although B cells and antibodies are not believed to play a direct role in cancer defense, B cells, on viewing a mutant cancer cell as an alien to "normal self," may produce antibodies against it. These antibodies, for unknown reasons, do not activate the complement system, which could destroy the cancer cells. Instead, the antibodies bind with the antigenic sites on the cancer cell, "hiding" these sites from recognition by cytotoxic T cells. The coating of a tumor cell, by blocking antibodies, thus protects the harmful cell from attack by deadly T cells. Still other successful cancer cells thwart immune attack by turning on their pursuers. They induce the cytotoxic T cells that bind with them to commit suicide. In addition, some cancer cells secrete large amounts of a specific chemical messenger that recruits regulatory T cells and programs them to suppress cytotoxic T cells.

We have completed our discussion of the B and T cells. ▲ Table 11-5 compares the properties of these two adaptive effector cells.

Immune Diseases

Abnormal functioning of the immune system can lead to immune diseases in two general ways: *immunodeficiency diseases* (too little immune response) and *inappropriate immune attacks* (too much or mistargeted immune response).

 **Immunodeficiency diseases result from insufficient immune responses.** **Immunodeficiency diseases** occur when the immune system fails to respond adequately to foreign invasion. The condition may be congenital (present at birth) or acquired (nonhereditary), and it may specifically involve impairment of antibody-mediated immunity, cell-mediated immunity, or both. The most recent and tragically the most common immunodeficiency disease is AIDS, which, as described earlier, is caused by HIV, a virus that invades and incapacitates the critical helper T cells.

Let us now look at inappropriate immune attacks.

Allergies are inappropriate immune attacks against harmless environmental substances.

 **Inappropriate immune attacks** cause reactions harmful to the body. These include (1) *autoimmune diseases,* in which the immune system turns against one of the body's own tissues (see p. 352); (2) *immune complex diseases,* which involve overexuberant antibody responses that "spill over" and damage normal tissue (see p. 342); and (3) allergies. The first two conditions have been described earlier in this chapter, so we now concentrate on allergies.

An **allergy** is the acquisition of an inappropriate specific immune reactivity, or **hypersensitivity,** to a normally harmless environmental substance, such as dust or pollen. The offending agent is known as an **allergen.** Subsequent reexposure of a sensitized individual to the same allergen elicits an immune attack, which may vary from a mild, annoying reaction to a severe, body-damaging reaction that may even be fatal.

Allergic responses are classified into two categories: immediate hypersensitivity and delayed hypersensitivity. In **immediate hypersensitivity,** the allergic response appears within about 20 minutes after a sensitized person is exposed to an allergen. In **delayed hypersensitivity,** the reaction does not generally show up until a day or so following exposure. The difference in timing is the result of the different mediators involved. A particular allergen may activate either a B- or a T-cell response. Immediate allergic reactions involve B cells and are elicited by antibody interactions with an allergen; delayed reactions involve T cells and the more slowly responding process of cell-mediated immunity against the allergen. Let us examine the causes and consequences of each of these reactions in more detail.

TRIGGERS FOR IMMEDIATE HYPERSENSITIVITY In immediate hypersensitivity, the antibodies involved and the events that ensue on exposure to an allergen differ from the typical antibody-mediated response to bacteria. The most common allergens that provoke immediate hypersensitivities are pollen grains, bee stings, penicillin, certain foods, molds, dust, feathers, and ani-

Characteristic	B Lymphocytes	T Lymphocytes
Ancestral Origin	Bone marrow	Bone marrow
Site of Maturational Processing	Bone marrow	Thymus
Receptors for an Antigen	Known as B-cell receptors or BCRs, are antibodies inserted in the plasma membrane; highly specific	Known as T-cell receptors or TCRs, are present in the plasma membrane but are not the same as antibodies; highly specific
Bind with	Extracellular antigens such as bacteria	Foreign antigens in association with self-antigens, such as virus-infected cells
Types of Active Cells	Plasma cells	Cytotoxic, helper, and regulatory T cells
Formation of Memory Cells	Yes	Yes
Type of Immunity	Antibody-mediated immunity	Cell-mediated immunity
Secretory Product	Antibodies	Cytokines
Functions	Help eliminate free foreign invaders by enhancing innate immune responses against them; provide immunity against most bacteria and a few viruses	Lyse virus-infected cells and cancer cells; provide immunity against most viruses and a few bacteria; aid B cells in antibody production; modulate immune responses
Life Span	Short	Long

mal fur. (Actually, people allergic to cats are not allergic to the fur itself. The true allergen is in the cat's saliva, which is deposited on the fur during licking.) For unclear reasons, these allergens bind to and elicit the synthesis of IgE antibodies rather than the IgG antibodies associated with bacterial antigens. IgE antibodies are the least plentiful immunoglobulin, but their presence spells trouble. Without IgE antibodies, there would be no immediate hypersensitivity. When a person with an allergic tendency is first exposed to a particular allergen, compatible helper T cells secrete a cytokine that prods compatible B cells to synthesize IgE antibodies specific for the allergen. During this initial **sensitization period,** no symptoms are evoked, but memory cells form that are primed for a more powerful response on subsequent reexposure to the same allergen.

In contrast to the antibody-mediated response elicited by bacterial antigens, IgE antibodies do not freely circulate. Instead, their tail portions attach to mast cells and basophils, both of which produce and store an arsenal of potent inflammatory chemicals, such as histamine, in preformed granules. Mast cells are most plentiful in regions that come into contact with the external environment, such as the skin, the outer surface of the eyes, and the linings of the respiratory system and digestive tract. Binding of an appropriate allergen with the outreached arm regions of the IgE antibodies that are lodged tail-first in a mast cell or basophil triggers the rupture of the cell's granules. As a result, histamine and other chemical mediators spew forth into the surrounding tissue.

A single mast cell (or basophil) may be coated with several different IgE antibodies, each able to bind with a different allergen. Thus, the mast cell can be triggered to release its chemical products by any one of several allergens (● Figure 11-33).

CHEMICAL MEDIATORS OF IMMEDIATE HYPERSENSITIVITY The chemicals released by the mast cell cause the reactions that characterize immediate hypersensitivity. The following are among the most important chemicals released during immediate allergic reactions:

1. *Histamine,* which brings about vasodilation and increased capillary permeability, as well as increased mucus production.

2. **Slow-reactive substance of anaphylaxis (SRS-A),** which induces prolonged and profound contraction of smooth muscle, especially of the small respiratory airways. SRS-A is a collection of three related leukotrienes, locally acting mediators similar to prostaglandins (see p. 592).

3. **Eosinophil chemotactic factor,** which specifically attracts eosinophils to the area. Interestingly, eosinophils release enzymes that inactivate SRS-A and may inhibit histamine, perhaps serving as an "off switch" to limit the allergic response.

SYMPTOMS OF IMMEDIATE HYPERSENSITIVITY Symptoms of immediate hypersensitivity vary depending on the site, allergen, and mediators involved. Most frequently, the reaction is localized to the body site in which the IgE-bearing cells first come into contact with the allergen. If the reaction is limited to the upper respiratory passages after a person inhales an allergen such as ragweed pollen, the released chemicals bring about the symptoms characteristic of **hay fever**—for example, nasal congestion caused by histamine-induced localized edema and sneezing and runny nose caused by increased mucus secretion. If the reaction is concentrated primarily within the bronchioles (the small respiratory airways that lead to the tiny air sacs within the lungs), **asthma** results. Contraction of the smooth

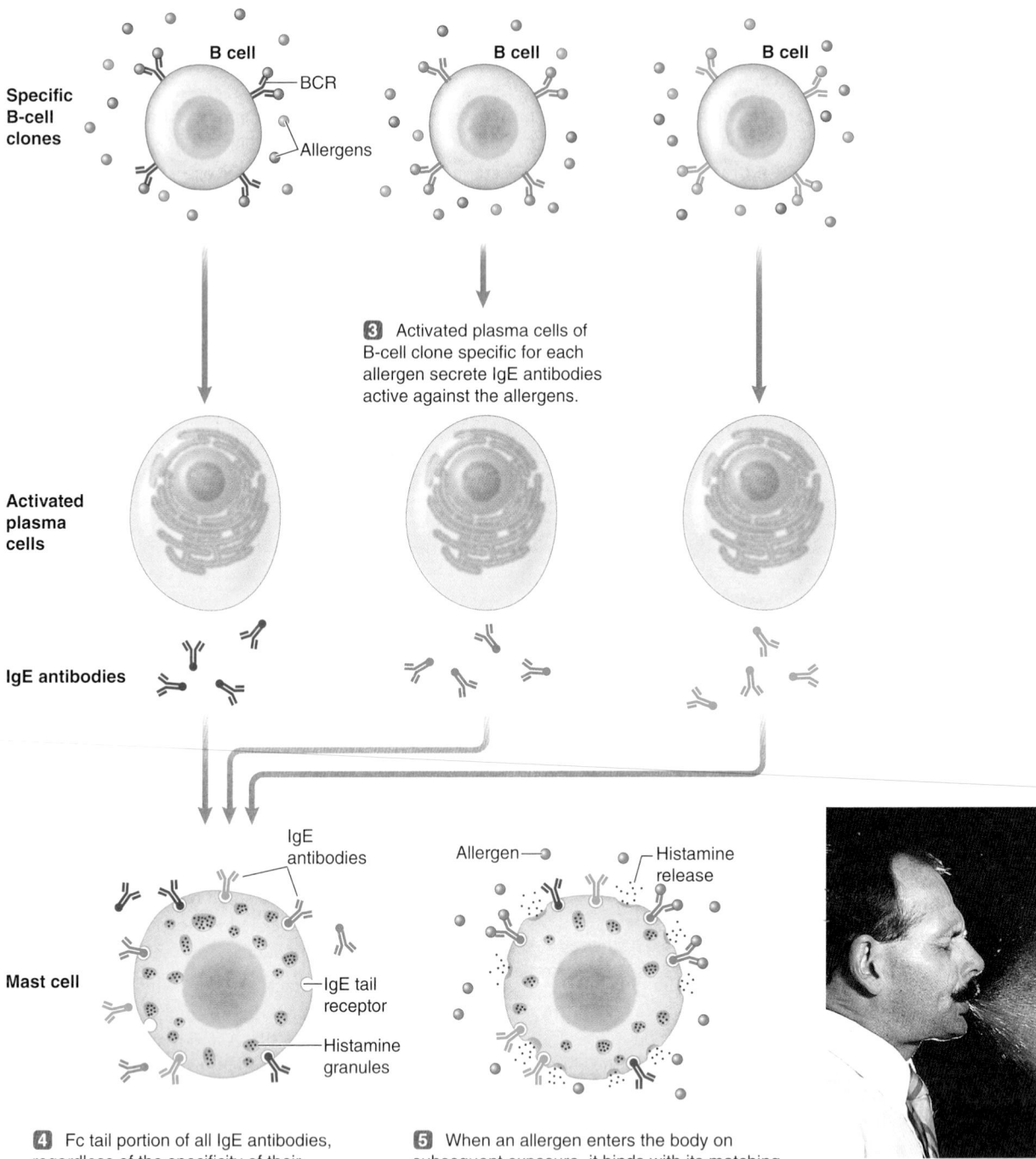

1 Allergens (antigens) enter the body for the first time.

2 Allergens bind to matching BCRs; B cells now process the allergens and, with stimulation by helper T cells (not shown), proceed through the steps leading to clonal expansion of activated plasma cells.

Specific B-cell clones

B cell

BCR

Allergens

B cell

B cell

3 Activated plasma cells of B-cell clone specific for each allergen secrete IgE antibodies active against the allergens.

Activated plasma cells

IgE antibodies

Mast cell

IgE antibodies

IgE tail receptor

Histamine granules

Allergen

Histamine release

4 Fc tail portion of all IgE antibodies, regardless of the specificity of their Fab arm regions, binds to IgE tail receptors on mast cells and basophils. Unlike B cells, each mast cell can have a variety of antibody surface receptors for binding different allergens.

5 When an allergen enters the body on subsequent exposure, it binds with its matching IgE antibodies on mast cells; binding stimulates mast cell to release histamine and other substances by exocytosis. Any allergen for which preformed, matching IgE are attached to the mast cell can trigger histamine release.

6 Histamine and other released chemicals elicit the allergic response.

● **FIGURE 11-33 Role of IgE antibodies and mast cells in immediate hypersensitivity.** B-cell clones are converted into plasma cells, which secrete IgE antibodies on contact with the allergen for which they are specific. All IgE antibodies, regardless of their antigen specificity, bind to mast cells or basophils. When an allergen combines with the IgE receptor specific for it on the surface of a mast cell, the mast cell releases histamine and other chemicals by exocytosis. These chemicals elicit the allergic response.

muscle in the walls of the bronchioles in response to SRS-A narrows or constricts these passageways, making breathing difficult. Localized swelling in the skin because of allergy-induced histamine release causes **hives.** An allergic reaction in the digestive tract in response to an ingested allergen can lead to diarrhea.

TREATMENT OF IMMEDIATE HYPERSENSITIVITY Treatment of localized immediate allergic reactions with antihistamines often offers only partial relief of the symptoms because some manifestations are invoked by other chemical mediators not blocked by these drugs. For example, antihistamines are not particularly effective in treating asthma, the most serious symptoms of which are invoked by SRS-A. Adrenergic drugs (which mimic the sympathetic nervous system; see p. 197) are helpful through their vasoconstrictor–bronchodilator actions in counteracting the effects of both histamine and SRS-A. Anti-inflammatory drugs such as cortisol derivatives are often used as the primary treatment for ongoing allergen-induced inflammation, such as that associated with asthma. Newer drugs such as Singulair that inhibit leukotrienes, including SRS-A, have been added to the arsenal for combating immediate allergies.

ANAPHYLACTIC SHOCK A life-threatening systemic reaction can occur if the allergen becomes blood borne or if very large amounts of chemicals are released from the localized site into the circulation. When large amounts of these chemical mediators gain access to the blood, the extremely serious systemic (involving the entire body) reaction known as **anaphylactic shock** occurs. Severe hypotension that can lead to circulatory shock (see p. 312) results from widespread vasodilation and a massive shift of plasma fluid into the interstitial spaces as a result of a generalized increase in capillary permeability. Concurrently, pronounced bronchiolar constriction occurs and can lead to respiratory failure. The person may suffocate from an inability to move air through the narrowed airways. Unless countermeasures, such as injecting a vasoconstrictor–bronchodilator drug, are undertaken immediately, anaphylactic shock is often fatal. This reaction is the reason even a single bee sting or eating a peanut can be so dangerous in people sensitized to these allergens.

DELAYED HYPERSENSITIVITY Some allergens invoke delayed hypersensitivity, a T-cell-mediated immune response, rather than an immediate, B cell–IgE antibody response. Among these allergens are poison ivy toxin and certain chemicals to which the skin is frequently exposed, such as cosmetics and household cleaning agents. Most commonly, the response is characterized by a delayed skin eruption that reaches its peak intensity 1 to 3 days after contact with an allergen to which the T-cell system has previously been sensitized. To illustrate, poison ivy toxin does not harm the skin on contact, but it activates T cells specific for the toxin, including formation of a memory component. On subsequent exposure to the toxin, activated T cells diffuse into the skin within a day or two, combining with the poison ivy toxin that is present. The resulting interaction gives rise to the tissue damage and discomfort typical of the condition. The best relief is obtained from application of anti-inflammatory preparations, such as those containing cortisol derivatives.

▲ Table 11-6 summarizes the distinctions between immediate and delayed hypersensitivities. This completes our discussion of the internal immune defense system. We now turn to external defenses that thwart entry of foreign invaders as a first line of defense.

External Defenses

The body's defenses against foreign microbes are not limited to the intricate, interrelated immune mechanisms that destroy microorganisms that have actually invaded the body. In addition to the internal immune defense system, the body is equipped with external defense mechanisms designed to prevent microbial penetration wherever body tissues are exposed to the external environment. The most obvious external defense is the **skin,** or **integument,** which covers the outside of the body (*integere* means "to cover").

▲ Table 11-6 **Immediate versus Delayed Hypersensitivity Reactions**

Characteristic	Immediate Hypersensitivity Reaction	Delayed Hypersensitivity Reaction
Time of Onset of Symptoms After Exposure to the Allergen	Within 20 minutes	Within 1 to 3 days
Type of Immune Response	Antibody-mediated immunity against the allergen	Cell-mediated immunity against the allergen
Immune Effectors Involved	B cells, IgE antibodies, mast cells, basophils, histamine, slow-reactive substance of anaphylaxis, and eosinophil chemotactic factor	T cells
Allergies Commonly Involved	Hay fever, asthma, hives, and, in extreme cases, anaphylactic shock	Contact allergies, such as allergies to poison ivy, cosmetics, and household cleaning agents

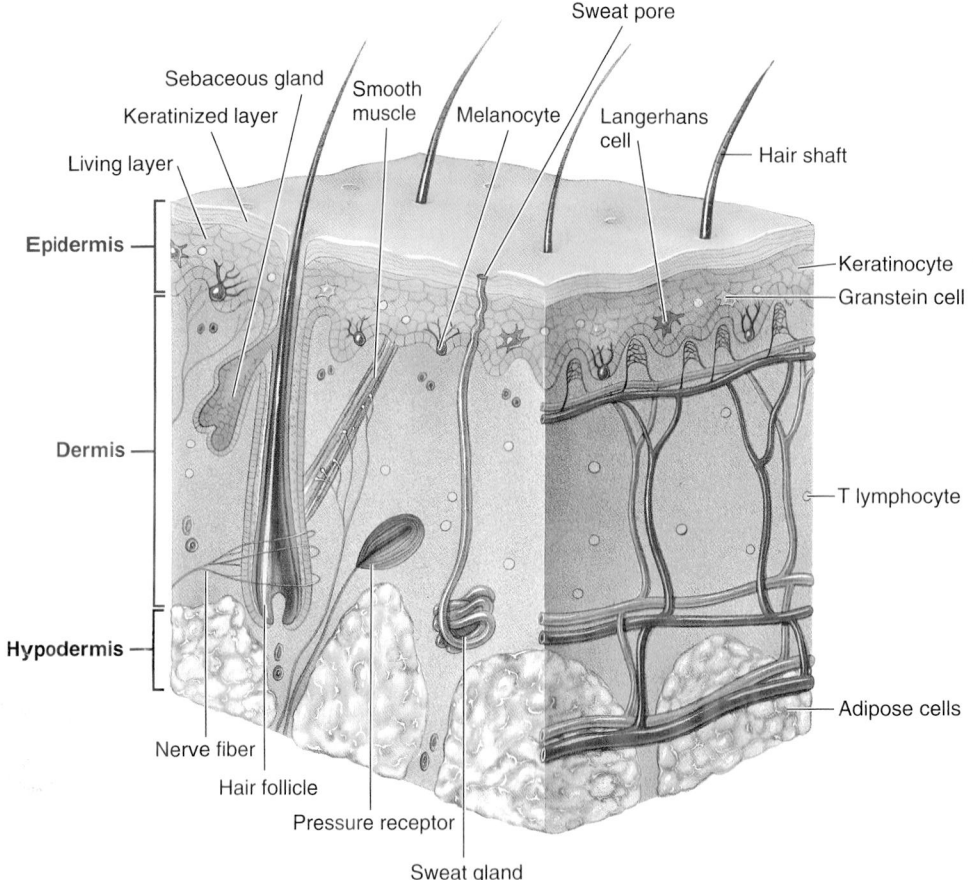

Sebaceous gland
Keratinized layer
Living layer
Epidermis
Dermis
Hypodermis
Nerve fiber
Hair follicle
Pressure receptor
Sweat gland
Smooth muscle
Sweat pore
Melanocyte
Langerhans cell
Hair shaft
Keratinocyte
Granstein cell
T lymphocyte
Adipose cells

● **FIGURE 11-34 Anatomy of the skin.** The skin consists of two layers, a keratinized outer epidermis and a richly vascularized inner connective tissue dermis. Special infoldings of the epidermis form the sweat glands, sebaceous glands, and hair follicles. The epidermis contains four types of cells: keratinocytes, melanocytes, Langerhans cells, and Granstein cells. The skin is anchored to underlying muscle or bone by the hypodermis, a loose, fat-containing layer of connective tissue.

The skin consists of an outer protective epidermis and an inner, connective tissue dermis.

The skin, which is the largest organ of the body, not only is a mechanical barrier between the external environment and the underlying tissues but is dynamically involved in defense mechanisms and other important functions as well. The skin in an average adult weighs 9 pounds and covers a surface area of 21 square feet. Its deeper layer contains an abundance of blood vessels, which if laid end to end would extend more than 11 miles. The skin consists of two layers, an outer *epidermis* and an inner *dermis* (● Figure 11-34).

EPIDERMIS The **epidermis** consists of numerous layers of epithelial cells. On average, the epidermis replaces itself about every 2.5 months. The inner epidermal layers are composed of cube-shaped cells that are living and rapidly dividing, whereas the cells in the outer layers are dead and flattened. The epidermis has no direct blood supply. Its cells are nourished only by diffusion of nutrients from a rich vascular network in the underlying dermis. The newly forming cells in the inner layers constantly push the older cells closer to the surface and ever farther from their nutrient supply. This, coupled with the continuous subjection of the outer layers to pressure and "wear and tear," causes these older cells to die and become flattened. Epidermal cells are riveted tightly together by desmosomes (see p. 52), which interconnect with intracellular keratin filaments (see p. 41) to form a strong, cohesive covering. During maturation of a keratin-producing cell, keratin filaments progressively accumulate and cross-link with one another within the cytosol. As the outer cells die, this fibrous keratin core remains, forming flattened, hardened scales that provide a tough, protective **keratinized layer.** As the scales of the outermost keratinized layer slough or flake off through abrasion, they are continuously replaced by means of cell division in the deeper epidermal layers. The keratinized layer is airtight, fairly waterproof, and impervious to most substances. It resists anything passing in either direction between the body and the external environment. For example, it minimizes loss of water and other vital constituents from the body and prevents most foreign material from penetrating into the body.

This protective layer's value in holding in body fluids becomes obvious after severe burns. Bacterial infections can occur in the unprotected underlying tissue, but even more serious are the systemic consequences of loss of body water and plasma proteins, which escape from the exposed, burned surface. The resulting circulatory disturbances can be life threatening.

DERMIS Under the epidermis is the **dermis,** a connective tissue layer that contains many elastin fibers (for stretch) and collagen fibers (for strength), as well as an abundance of blood vessels and specialized nerve endings. The dermal blood vessels not only supply both the dermis and the epidermis but also play a major role in temperature regulation. The caliber of these vessels, and hence the volume of blood flowing through them, is subject to control to vary the amount of heat exchange between these skin surface vessels and the external environment (see Chapter 16). Receptors at the peripheral endings of afferent nerve fibers in the dermis detect pressure, temperature, pain, and other somatosensory input. Efferent nerve endings in the dermis control blood vessel caliber, hair erection, and secretion by the skin's exocrine glands.

SKIN'S EXOCRINE GLANDS AND HAIR FOLLICLES Special infoldings of the epidermis into the underlying dermis form the skin's exocrine glands—the sweat glands and the sebaceous glands—as well as the hair follicles. **Sweat glands,** which are distributed over most of the body, release a dilute salt solution through small openings, the sweat pores, onto the skin surface (● Figure 11-34). Evaporation of this sweat cools the skin and is important in regulating temperature.

The cells of the **sebaceous glands** produce an oily secretion released into adjacent hair follicles. From there sebum flows to the skin surface, oiling both the hairs and the outer keratinized layers of the skin, helping to waterproof them and prevent them from drying and cracking. Chapped hands or lips indicate insufficient protection by sebum. The sebaceous glands are particularly active during adolescence, causing the oily skin common among teenagers.

Each **hair follicle** is lined by special keratin-producing cells, which secrete keratin and other proteins that form the hair shaft. Hairs increase the sensitivity of the skin's surface to tactile (touch) stimuli. In some other species, this function is more finely tuned. For example, the whiskers on a cat are exquisitely sensitive in this regard. An even more important role of hair in hairier species is heat conservation, but this function is not significant in us relatively hairless humans.

HYPODERMIS The skin is anchored to the underlying tissue (muscle or bone) by the **hypodermis** (*hypo* means "below"), also known as **subcutaneous tissue** (*sub* means "under"; *cutaneous* means "skin"), a loose layer of connective tissue. Most fat cells are housed within the hypodermis. These fat deposits throughout the body are collectively referred to as **adipose tissue.**

Specialized cells in the epidermis produce keratin and melanin and participate in immune defense.

The epidermis contains four distinct resident cell types—*melanocytes, keratinocytes, Langerhans cells,* and *Granstein cells*—plus transient T lymphocytes that are scattered throughout the epidermis and dermis. Each of these resident cell types performs specialized functions.

MELANOCYTES **Melanocytes** produce the pigment **melanin,** which they disperse to surrounding skin cells. The amount and type of melanin, which can vary among black, brown, yellow, and red pigments, are responsible for the shades of skin color of the various races. Fair-skinned people have about the same number of melanocytes as dark-skinned people; the difference in skin color depends on the amount of melanin produced by each melanocyte. In addition to hereditary determination of melanin content, the amount of this pigment can be increased transiently in response to exposure to ultraviolet (UV) light rays from the sun. This additional melanin, the outward appearance of which constitutes a "tan," performs the protective function of absorbing harmful UV rays.

KERATINOCYTES The most abundant epidermal cells are the **keratinocytes,** which, as the name implies, are specialists in keratin production. As they die, they form the outer protective keratinized layer. They also generate hair and nails. A surprising, recently discovered function is that keratinocytes are also important immunologically. They secrete a cytokine that influences the maturation of T cells that tend to localize in the skin.

OTHER IMMUNE CELLS OF THE SKIN The two other epidermal cell types play a role in immunity. **Langerhans cells** are dendritic cells that serve as antigen-presenting cells. Thus, the skin not only is a mechanical barrier but actually alerts lymphocytes if the barrier is breached by invading microorganisms. In contrast, **Granstein cells** seem to act as a "brake" on skin-activated immune responses. These cells are the most recently discovered and least understood of the skin's immune cells. Significantly, Langerhans cells are more susceptible to damage by UV radiation (as from the sun) than Granstein cells are, leaving the skin more vulnerable to microbial invasion and cancer cells.

Protective measures within body cavities discourage pathogen invasion into the body.

The human body's defense system must guard against entry of potential pathogens not only through the outer surface of the body but also through the internal cavities that communicate directly with the external environment—namely, the digestive system, the urogenital (urinary and reproductive) system, and the respiratory system. These systems use various tactics to destroy microorganisms entering through these routes.

DEFENSES OF THE DIGESTIVE SYSTEM Saliva secreted into the mouth at the entrance of the digestive system contains an enzyme that lyses certain ingested bacteria. "Friendly" bacteria that live on the back of the tongue convert food-derived nitrate into nitrite, which is swallowed. Acidification of nitrite on reaching the highly acidic stomach generates nitric oxide, which is toxic to a variety of microorganisms. Furthermore, many of the surviving bacteria that are swallowed are killed directly by the strongly acidic gastric juice in the stomach. Farther down the tract, the intestinal lining is endowed with gut-associated lymphoid tissue. These defensive mechanisms are not 100% effective, however. Some bacteria do manage to survive and reach the large intestine (the last portion of the digestive tract), where they continue to flourish. Surprisingly, this normal microbial population provides a natural barrier against infection within the lower intestine. These harmless resident microbes competitively suppress the growth of potential pathogens that have managed to escape the antimicrobial measures of earlier parts of the digestive tract.

 Occasionally, orally administered antibiotic therapy against an infection elsewhere within the body may induce an intestinal infection. By knocking out some normal intestinal bacteria, an antibiotic may permit an antibiotic-resistant pathogenic species to overgrow in the intestine.

DEFENSES OF THE UROGENITAL SYSTEM Within the urogenital system, would-be invaders encounter hostile conditions in the acidic urine and acidic vaginal secretions. The urogenital organs also produce a sticky mucus, which, like flypaper, entraps small invading particles. Subsequently, the particles are either engulfed by phagocytes or are swept out as the organ empties (for example, they are flushed out with urine flow).

DEFENSES OF THE RESPIRATORY SYSTEM The respiratory system is likewise equipped with several important defense mechanisms against inhaled particulate matter. The respiratory system is the largest surface of the body that comes into direct contact with the increasingly polluted external environment. The surface area of the respiratory system exposed to the air is 30 times that of the skin. Larger airborne particles are filtered out of the inhaled air by hairs at the entrance of the nasal passages. Lymphoid tissues, the *tonsils* and *adenoids,* provide immunological protection against inhaled pathogens near the beginning of the respiratory system. Farther down in the respiratory airways, millions of tiny hairlike projections known as *cilia* constantly beat in an outward direction (see p. 38). The respiratory airways are coated with a layer of thick, sticky mucus secreted by epithelial cells within the airway lining. This mucus sheet, laden with any inspired particulate debris (such as dust) that adheres to it, is constantly moved upward to the throat by ciliary action. This moving "staircase" of mucus is known as the **mucus escalator.** The dirty mucus is either spit out or, in most cases, is swallowed without the person even being aware of it; any indigestible foreign particulate matter is later eliminated in the feces. Besides keeping the lungs clean, this mechanism is an important defense against bacterial infection, because many bacteria enter the body on dust particles. Also contributing to defense against respiratory infections are antibodies secreted in the mucus. In addition, an abundance of phagocytic specialists called **alveolar macrophages** scavenge within the air sacs (alveoli) of the lungs. Further respiratory defenses include coughs and sneezes. These commonly experienced reflex mechanisms involve forceful outward expulsion of material in an attempt to remove irritants from the trachea *(coughs)* or nose *(sneezes).*

 Clinical Note Cigarette smoking suppresses these normal respiratory defenses. The smoke from a single cigarette can paralyze the cilia for several hours, with repeated exposure eventually leading to ciliary destruction. Failure of ciliary activity to sweep out a constant stream of particulate-laden mucus enables inhaled carcinogens to remain in contact with the respiratory airways for prolonged periods. Furthermore, cigarette smoke incapacitates alveolar macrophages. In addition, noxious agents in tobacco smoke irritate the mucous linings of the respiratory tract, resulting in excess mucus production, which may partially obstruct the airways. "Smoker's cough" is an attempt to dislodge this excess stationary mucus. These and other direct toxic effects on lung tissue lead to the increased incidence of lung cancer and chronic respiratory diseases associated with cigarette smoking.

We examine the respiratory system in greater detail in the next chapter.

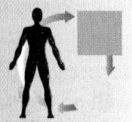
Blood contributes to homeostasis in various ways. First, the composition of interstitial fluid, the true internal environment that surrounds and directly exchanges materials with the cells, depends on the composition of blood plasma. Because of the thorough exchange that occurs between the interstitial and the vascular compartments, interstitial fluid has the same composition as plasma with the exception of plasma proteins, which cannot escape through the capillary walls. Thus, blood is the vehicle for rapid, long-distance, mass transport of materials to and from the cells, and interstitial fluid is the go-between.

Homeostasis depends on the blood carrying materials such as O_2 and nutrients to the cells as rapidly as the cells consume these supplies and carrying materials such as metabolic wastes away from the cells as rapidly as the cells produce these products. It also depends on the blood carrying hormonal messengers from their site of production to their distant site of action. Once a substance enters the blood, it can be transported throughout the body within seconds, whereas diffusion of the substance over long distances in a large multicellular organism such as a human would take months to years—a situation incompatible with life. Diffusion can, however, effectively accomplish short local exchanges of materials between blood and surrounding cells through the intervening interstitial fluid.

Blood has special transport capabilities that enable it to move its cargo efficiently throughout the body. For example, life-sustaining O_2 is poorly soluble in water, but blood is equipped with O_2-carrying specialists, the erythrocytes (red blood cells), which are stuffed full of hemoglobin, a complex molecule that transports O_2. Likewise, homeostatically important water-insoluble hormonal messengers are shuttled in the blood by plasma protein carriers.

Specific components of the blood perform the following additional homeostatic activities that are unrelated to blood's transport function:

- Blood helps maintain the proper pH in the internal environment by buffering changes in the body's acid–base load.
- Blood helps maintain body temperature by absorbing heat produced by heat-generating tissues, such as contracting skeletal muscles, and distributing it throughout the body. Excess heat is carried by the blood to the body surface for elimination to the external environment.
- Electrolytes in the plasma are important in membrane excitability, which is critical for nerve and muscle function.
- Electrolytes in the plasma are important in osmotic distribution of fluid between the extracellular and intracellular fluid. Plasma proteins play a critical role in distributing extracellular fluid between the plasma and interstitial fluid.
- Through their hemostatic functions, the platelets and clotting factors minimize the loss of life-sustaining blood after vessel injury.

The leukocytes (white blood cells), their secretory products, and certain types of plasma proteins, such as antibodies, constitute the immune defense system. This system defends the body against invading disease-causing agents, destroys cancer cells, and paves the way for wound healing and tissue repair by clearing away debris from dead or injured cells. These actions indirectly contribute to homeostasis by helping the organs that directly maintain homeostasis stay healthy. We could not survive beyond early infancy were it not for the body's defense mechanisms.

The skin contributes indirectly to homeostasis by serving as a protective barrier between the external environment and the rest of the body cells. It helps prevent harmful foreign agents such as pathogens and toxic chemicals from entering the body and helps prevent the loss of precious internal fluids from the body. The skin also contributes directly to homeostasis by helping maintain body temperature by means of the sweat glands and adjustments in skin blood flow. The amount of heat carried to the body surface for dissipation to the external environment is determined by the volume of warmed blood flowing through the skin.

Other systems that have internal cavities in contact with the external environment, such as the digestive, urogenital, and respiratory systems, also have defense capabilities to prevent harmful external agents from entering the body through these avenues.

REVIEW EXERCISES

Objective Questions (Answers on p. A-45)

1. Hemoglobin can carry only O_2. (True or false?)
2. Erythrocytes originate from the same undifferentiated pluripotent stem cells as leukocytes and platelets do. (True or false?)
3. White blood cells spend the majority of their time in the blood. (True or false?)
4. The complement system can be activated only by antibodies. (True or false?)
5. Specific adaptive immune responses are accomplished by neutrophils. (True or false?)
6. Active immunity against a particular disease can be acquired only by actually having the disease. (True or false?)
7. A secondary response has a more rapid onset, is more potent, and has a longer duration than a primary response. (True or false?)
8. _____ are receptors on the plasma membrane of phagocytes that recognize and bind with telltale molecular patterns present on the surface of microorganisms but absent from human cells.
9. A chemical that enhances phagocytosis by serving as a link between a microbe and the phagocytic cell is known as a(n) _____.
10. _____, collectively, are all the chemical messengers other than antibodies secreted by lymphocytes.
11. Which of the following is not a function served by the plasma proteins?
    a. facilitating retention of fluid in the blood vessels
    b. playing an important role in blood clotting
    c. binding and transporting certain hormones in the blood
    d. transporting O_2 in the blood
    e. serving as antibodies
    f. contributing to the buffering capacity of the blood

12. Which of the following is not directly triggered by exposed collagen in an injured vessel?
    a. initial vascular spasm
    b. platelet aggregation
    c. activation of the clotting cascade
    d. activation of plasminogen
13. Which of the following statements concerning leukocytes is (are) incorrect? (Indicate all incorrect answers.)
    a. Monocytes are transformed into macrophages.
    b. T lymphocytes are transformed into plasma cells that secrete antibodies.
    c. Neutrophils are highly mobile phagocytic specialists.
    d. Basophils release histamine.
    e. Lymphocytes arise largely from lymphoid tissues.
14. Match the following blood abnormalities with their causes:
    ___ 1. deficiency of intrinsic factor
    ___ 2. insufficient amount of iron to synthesize adequate hemoglobin
    ___ 3. destruction of bone marrow
    ___ 4. abnormal loss of blood
    ___ 5. tumorlike condition of bone marrow
    ___ 6. inadequate erythropoietin secretion
    ___ 7. excessive rupture of circulating erythrocytes
    ___ 8. consequence of living at high altitudes

    (a) hemolytic anemia
    (b) aplastic anemia
    (c) nutritional anemia
    (d) hemorrhagic anemia
    (e) pernicious anemia
    (f) renal anemia
    (g) primary polycythemia
    (h) secondary polycythemia

15. Match the following:
    ____ 1. a protein that nonspecifically defends against viral infection
    ____ 2. a response to tissue injury in which neutrophils and macrophages play a major role
    ____ 3. a group of plasma proteins that, when activated, bring about destruction of foreign cells by attacking their plasma membranes
    ____ 4. lymphocyte-like cells that spontaneously lyse tumor cells and virus-infected host cells

    (a) complement system
    (b) natural killer cells
    (c) interferon
    (d) inflammation

16. Using the answer code on the right, indicate whether the numbered characteristics of the adaptive immune system apply to antibody-mediated immunity, cell-mediated immunity, or both:
    ____ 1. involves secretion of antibodies
    ____ 2. is mediated by B cells
    ____ 3. is mediated by T cells
    ____ 4. is accomplished by thymus-educated lymphocytes
    ____ 5. is triggered by the binding of specific antigens to complementary lymphocyte receptors
    ____ 6. involves formation of memory cells in response to initial exposure to an antigen
    ____ 7. is primarily aimed against virus-infected host cells
    ____ 8. protects primarily against bacterial invaders
    ____ 9. directly destroys targeted cells
    ____ 10. is involved in rejection of transplanted tissue
    ____ 11. requires binding of a lymphocyte to a free extracellular antigen
    ____ 12. requires dual binding of a lymphocyte with both foreign antigens and self-antigens present on the surface of a host cell

    (a) antibody-mediated immunity
    (b) cell-mediated immunity
    (c) both antibody-mediated and cell-mediated immunity

Essay Questions

1. What is the average blood volume in women and in men?
2. What is the normal percentage of blood occupied by erythrocytes and by plasma? What is the hematocrit? What is the buffy coat?
3. What is the composition of plasma?
4. Describe the structure and functions of erythrocytes.
5. Why can erythrocytes survive for only about 120 days?
6. Describe the process and control of erythropoiesis.
7. Discuss the derivation of platelets.
8. Describe the three steps of hemostasis, including a comparison of the intrinsic and extrinsic pathways by which the clotting cascade is triggered.
9. Compare the structure and functions of the five types of leukocytes.
10. Distinguish between bacteria and viruses.
11. Distinguish between innate and adaptive immune responses.
12. Compare the life histories of B and T cells.
13. What is an antigen?
14. Describe the structure of an antibody. In what ways do antibodies exert their effect?
15. Describe the clonal selection theory.
16. Compare the functions of B and T cells. What are the roles of the three types of T cells?
17. Describe four mechanisms involved in tolerance.
18. What is the importance of class I and class II MHC molecules?
19. Describe the factors that contribute to immune surveillance against cancer cells.
20. Distinguish among immunodeficiency disease, autoimmune disease, immune complex disease, immediate hypersensitivity, and delayed hypersensitivity.
21. What are the immune functions of the skin?

POINTS TO PONDER

(Explanations on p. A-45)

1. There are different forms of hemoglobin. *Hemoglobin A* is normal adult hemoglobin. The abnormal form *hemoglobin S* causes RBCs to warp into fragile, sickle-shaped cells. Fetal RBCs contain *hemoglobin F*, the production of which stops soon after birth. Now researchers are trying to goad the genes that direct hemoglobin F synthesis back into action as a means of treating sickle cell anemia. Explain how turning on these fetal genes could be a useful remedy. (Indeed, the first effective drug therapy approved for treating sickle cell anemia, *hydroxyurea*, acts on the bone marrow to boost production of fetal hemoglobin.)
2. Low on the list of popular animals are vampire bats, leeches, and ticks, yet these animals may someday

indirectly save your life. Scientists are currently examining the "saliva" of these blood-sucking creatures in search of new chemicals that might limit cardiac muscle damage in heart attack victims. What do you suspect the nature of these sought-after chemicals is?
3. What impact would failure of the thymus to develop embryonically have on the immune system after birth?
4. Medical researchers are currently working on ways to "teach" the immune system to view foreign tissue as "self." What useful clinical application will the technique have?
5. When someone looks at you, are the cells of your body that person is viewing dead or alive?

(Explanation on p. A-46)

Heather L., who has Rh-negative blood, has just given birth to her first child, who has Rh-positive blood. Both mother and baby are fine, but the doctor administers an Rh immunoglobulin preparation so that any future Rh-positive babies Heather has will not suffer from erythroblastosis fetalis (hemolytic disease of the newborn) (see p. 323). During gestation (pregnancy), fetal and maternal blood do not mix. Instead, materials are exchanged between these two circulatory systems across the placenta, a special organ that develops during gestation from both maternal and fetal structures (see p. 612). Red blood cells are unable to cross the placenta, but antibodies can cross. During the birthing process, a small amount of the infant's blood may enter the maternal circulation.

1. Why did Heather's first-born child not have erythroblastosis fetalis; that is, why didn't maternal antibodies against the Rh factor attack the fetal Rh-positive red blood cells during gestation?

2. Why would any subsequent Rh-positive babies Heather might carry be likely to develop erythroblastosis fetalis if she were not treated with Rh immunoglobulin?

3. How would administering Rh immunoglobulin immediately following Heather's first pregnancy with an Rh-positive child prevent erythroblastosis fetalis in a later pregnancy with another Rh-positive child? Similarly, why must Rh immunoglobulin be given to Heather after the birth of each Rh-positive child she bears?

4. Suppose Heather were not treated with Rh immunoglobulin after the birth of her first Rh-positive child, and a second Rh-positive child developed erythroblastosis fetalis. Would administering Rh immunoglobulin to Heather immediately after the second birth prevent this condition in a third Rh-positive child? Why or why not?

Plasma (pp. 317–319)

■ Blood consists of three types of cellular elements—erythrocytes (red blood cells), leukocytes (white blood cells), and platelets (thrombocytes)—suspended in the liquid plasma. (*Review Figure 11-1 and Table 11-1.*)

■ The 5.5-liter volume of blood in an adult male consists of 45% erythrocytes, less than 1% leukocytes and platelets, and 55% plasma. The percentage of whole-blood volume occupied by erythrocytes is the hematocrit. (*Review Figure 11-1.*)

■ Plasma is a complex liquid consisting of 90% water that is a transport medium for substances being carried in the blood. All plasma constituents are freely diffusible across the capillary walls except the plasma proteins, which perform various important functions. (*Review Table 11-1.*)

Erythrocytes (pp. 319–324)

■ Erythrocytes are specialized for their primary function of O_2 transport in the blood. Their biconcave shape maximizes the surface area available for diffusion of O_2 into cells of this volume. They do not contain a nucleus or organelles but instead are packed full of hemoglobin, an iron-containing molecule carry four O_2 molecules. (*Review Figures 11-1 and 11-2.*)

■ Unable to replace cell components, erythrocytes are destined to a short life span of about 120 days. Undifferentiated pluripotent stem cells in the red bone marrow give rise to all cellular elements of the blood. Erythrocyte production (erythropoiesis) by the marrow normally keeps pace with the rate of erythrocyte loss, keeping the red cell count constant. Erythropoiesis is stimulated by erythropoietin, a hormone secreted by the kidneys on reduced O_2 delivery. (*Review Figures 11-3 and 11-13.*)

Platelets and Hemostasis (pp. 324–329)

■ Platelets, cell fragments derived from large megakaryocytes in the bone marrow, play a role in hemostasis, the arrest of bleeding from an injured vessel. The three main steps in hemostasis are (1) vascular spasm, (2) platelet plugging, and (3) clot formation. (*Review Figures 11-6, 11-7, 11-11, and 11-13.*)

■ Most factors necessary for clotting are always present in the plasma in inactive precursor form. When a vessel is damaged, exposed collagen initiates a cascade of reactions involving successive activation of these clotting factors, ultimately converting fibrinogen into fibrin via the intrinsic clotting pathway. Blood that has escaped into the tissues clots on exposure to tissue thromboplastin, which sets the extrinsic clotting pathway into motion. Fibrin, an insoluble threadlike molecule, is laid down as the meshwork of the clot; the meshwork in turn entangles blood cellular elements to complete clot formation. (*Review Figures 11-8 and 11-9.*)

■ Clots form quickly. When no longer needed, they are slowly dissolved by plasmin, a fibrinolytic factor also activated by exposed collagen. (*Review Figure 11-10.*)

Leukocytes (pp. 329–333)

■ Leukocytes are the defense corps of the body. They attack foreign invaders (bacteria and viruses), destroy cancer cells that arise in the body, and clean up cellular debris. Leukocytes, as well as certain plasma proteins, make up the immune system.

■ Each type of leukocytes has a different task: (1) Neutrophils, the phagocytic specialists, engulf bacteria and debris. (2) Eosinophils attack parasitic worms and play a role in allergic responses. (3) Basophils release histamine, which is also important in allergic responses, and heparin, which helps clear fat particles from the blood. (4) Monocytes, on leaving the blood, set up residence in the tissues and greatly enlarge to become macrophages, large tissue phagocytes. (5) Lymphocytes provide immune defense against bacteria, viruses, and other targets for which they are specifically programmed. Microscopically, neutrophils, eosinophils, and basophils are polymorphonuclear granulocytes; monocytes and lymphocytes are mononuclear agranulocytes. (*Review Figure 11-11 and Table 11-1.*)

■ Leukocytes are present in the blood only while in transit from their site of production and storage to their site of action. At any given time, most leukocytes are out in the tissues on surveillance or performing actual combat missions.

Innate Immunity (pp. 333–339)

■ Immunity, the body's ability to resist or eliminate potentially harmful foreign invaders and newly arisen mutant cells, includes both innate and adaptive immune responses. Innate immune responses are nonspecific responses that nonselectively defend against foreign material even on initial exposure to it. Innate immune responses include inflammation, interferon, natural killer cells, and the complement system. Adaptive immune responses are specific responses that selectively target particular invaders for which the body has been specially prepared after a prior exposure.

■ Inflammation is a nonspecific response to foreign invasion or tissue damage mediated largely by the professional phagocytes (neutrophils and monocytes turned macrophages). These cells destroy foreign and damaged cells both by phagocytosis and by release of lethal chemicals. Phagocytes secrete a variety of cytokines (any chemical other than antibodies that are secreted by leukocytes) that also augment inflammation, induce systemic manifestations such as fever, and enhance adaptive immune responses. Histamine-induced vasodilation and increased permeability of local capillaries at the site permit delivery of more phagocytes and also produce the observable local manifestations of inflammation—swelling, redness, heat, and pain. *(Review Figures 11-14 and 11-15.)*

■ Interferon is nonspecifically released by virus-infected cells and transiently inhibits viral multiplication in other cells to which it binds. *(Review Figure 11-16.)*

■ Natural killer (NK) cells nonspecifically lyse and destroy virus-infected and cancer cells on first exposure to them. *(Review Figure 11-22.)*

■ On being activated by microbes or by antibodies produced against the microbes, the complement system directly destroys the foreign invaders by forming a hole-punching membrane attack complex that causes osmotic rupture of the victim cell. Activated complement components also act as chemotaxins (that attract phagocytes) and opsonins (that link microbes to phagocytes). *(Review Figures 11-17 and 11-22.)*

Adaptive Immunity: General Concepts (pp. 339–340)

■ Lymphocytes, the effector cells of adaptive immunity, can distinguish among millions of foreign molecules because each is uniquely equipped with surface membrane receptors that can bind with only one specific complex foreign molecule, or antigen.

■ The two classes of adaptive immune responses are anti-body-mediated immunity accomplished by plasma cells derived from B lymphocytes (B cells) and cell-mediated immunity accomplished by T lymphocytes (T cells). B cells develop from lymphocytes that originally matured within the bone marrow. T-cells come from lymphocytes that migrated from the bone marrow to the thymus to complete their maturation. New B and T cells arise from lymphocyte colonies in lymphoid tissues. *(Review Figures 11-12 and 11-18 and Table 11-5, p. 354.)*

B Lymphocytes: Antibody-Mediated Immunity (pp. 340–345)

■ Each B cell recognizes a specific free extracellular antigen, such as that found on the surface of bacteria. After being activated by binding of its receptor (a B-cell receptor, or BCR) with its specific antigen, a B cell rapidly proliferates, producing a clone of its own kind that can specifically wage battle against the invader. Most lymphocytes in the expanded B-cell clone become antibody-secreting plasma cells that participate in the primary response against the invader. Some new lymphocytes do not participate in the attack but become memory cells that lie in wait, ready to launch a swifter and more forceful secondary response should the same foreigner ever invade the body again. *(Review Figures 11-19, 11-20, 11-23, and 11-24.)*

■ Antibodies (immunoglobulins) are Y-shaped molecules. The antigen-binding sites on the tips of each arm of the antibody determine with what specific antigen the antibody can bind. Properties of the antibody's tail portion determine what the antibody does once it binds with an antigen. *(Review Figure 11-21.)*

■ Antibodies do not directly destroy antigenic material; they intensify lethal innate immune responses already called into play by the foreign invasion. Antibodies act as opsonins to enhance phagocytosis, activate the complement system, and stimulate NK cells. *(Review Figure 11-22 and Table 11-4, p. 351.)*

T Lymphocytes: Cell-Mediated Immunity (pp. 345–354)

■ T cells accomplish cell-mediated immunity by being in direct contact with their targets and by releasing cytokines.

■ There are three types of T cells: (1) Cytotoxic T cells destroy virally invaded and cancer cells by releasing perforin molecules that form a lethal hole-punching complex that inserts into the membrane of the victim cell or by releasing granzymes that trigger the victim cell to undergo apoptosis. (2) Helper T cells bind with other immune cells and release cytokines that augment the activity of these other cells. (3) Regulatory T cells secrete cytokines that suppress other immune cells, "putting the brakes" on immune responses in a check-and-balance fashion. *(Review Figures 11-25, 11-26, and 11-30 and Table 11-3.)*

■ Like B cells, T cells bear receptors (T-cell receptors, or TCRs) that are antigen specific *(review Figure 11-19),* undergo clonal selection, exert primary and secondary responses, and form memory pools for long-lasting immunity against targets to which they have already been exposed. T cells have a dual binding requirement of foreign antigens in association with self-antigens on the surface of one of the body's own cells. The self-antigens are class I or class II MHC molecules, which are unique for each individual. *(Review Figures 11-29 and 11-30.)*

■ Helper T cells can recognize and bind with an antigen only when it has been processed and presented to them by antigen-presenting cells (APCs), such as macrophages and dendritic cells. *(Review Figures 11-28 and 11-30.)*

■ In the process of immune surveillance, natural killer cells, cytotoxic T cells, and macrophages and the interferon they collectively secrete normally eradicate newly arisen cancer cells before they have a chance to spread. *(Review Figure 11-32.)*

Immune Diseases (pp. 354–357)

■ Immune diseases are of two types: immunodeficiency diseases (insufficient immune responses) or inappropriate immune attacks (excessive or mistargeted immune responses).

■ Inappropriate attacks include autoimmune diseases, immune complex diseases, and allergies (hypersensitivities), of which there are two types: B-cell mediated immediate hypersensitivities and T-cell mediated delayed hypersensitivities. *(Review Figure 11-33 and Table 11-6.)*

External Defenses (pp. 357–360)

■ Body surfaces exposed to the outside environment—both the skin and the linings of internal cavities that communicate with the outside—not only serve as mechanical barriers to deter would-be pathogenic invaders but also play an active role in thwarting entry of bacteria and other unwanted materials.

■ The skin consists of an outer, keratinized epidermis and an inner, connective tissue dermis. The epidermis contains four cell types: pigment-producing melanocytes, keratin-producing keratinocytes, antigen-presenting Langerhans cells, and immune-suppressive Granstein cells. *(Review Figure 11-34.)*

Respiratory System

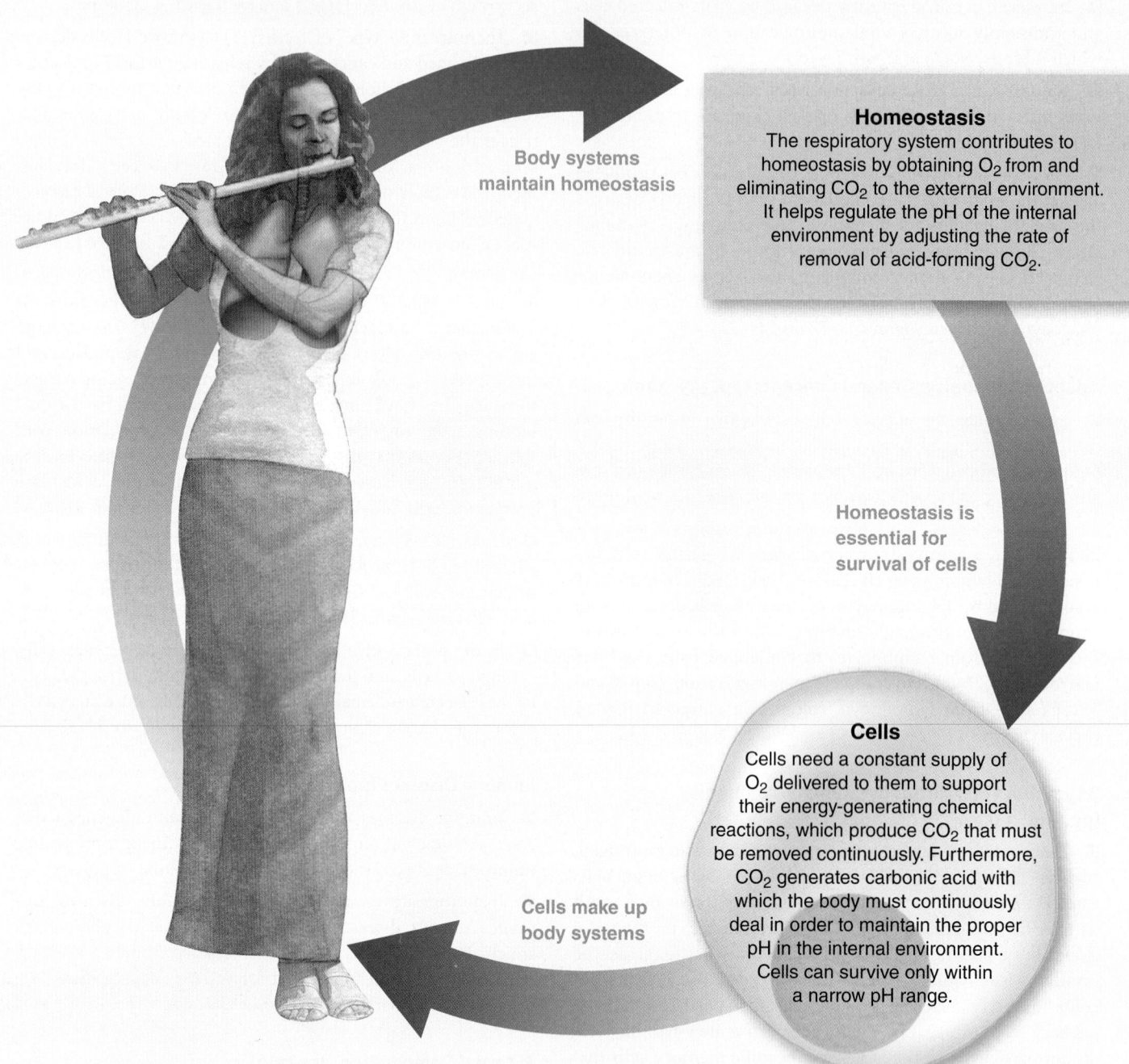

Body systems maintain homeostasis

Homeostasis
The respiratory system contributes to homeostasis by obtaining O_2 from and eliminating CO_2 to the external environment. It helps regulate the pH of the internal environment by adjusting the rate of removal of acid-forming CO_2.

Homeostasis is essential for survival of cells

Cells
Cells need a constant supply of O_2 delivered to them to support their energy-generating chemical reactions, which produce CO_2 that must be removed continuously. Furthermore, CO_2 generates carbonic acid with which the body must continuously deal in order to maintain the proper pH in the internal environment. Cells can survive only within a narrow pH range.

Cells make up body systems

Energy is essential for sustaining life-supporting cellular activities, such as protein synthesis and active transport across plasma membranes. The cells of the body need a continuous supply of O_2 to support their energy-generating chemical reactions. The CO_2 produced during these reactions must be eliminated from the body at the same rate as it is produced to prevent dangerous fluctuations in pH (that is, to maintain acid–base balance), because CO_2 generates carbonic acid.

Respiration involves the sum of the processes that accomplish ongoing passive movement of O_2 from the atmosphere to the tissues to support cell metabolism, as well as the continual passive movement of metabolically produced CO_2 from the tissues to the atmosphere. The **respiratory system** contributes to homeostasis by exchanging O_2 and CO_2 between the atmosphere and the blood. The blood transports O_2 and CO_2 between the respiratory system and the tissues.

The Respiratory System

CHAPTER AT A GLANCE

Respiratory Anatomy
Cellular and external respiration
Anatomy of the respiratory system, thorax, and pleura

Respiratory Mechanics
Pressure considerations
Respiratory cycle
Airway resistance
Elastic behavior of the lungs
Lung volumes and capacities
Pulmonary and alveolar ventilation

Gas Exchange
Concept of partial pressure
Gas exchange across the pulmonary and systemic capillaries

Gas Transport
Oxygen transport
Carbon dioxide transport
Abnormalities in blood-gas content

Control of Respiration
Respiratory control centers in the brain stem
Generation of respiratory rhythm
Chemical inputs affecting the magnitude of ventilation

Respiratory Anatomy

The primary function of respiration is to obtain O_2 for use by the body cells and to eliminate the CO_2 the cells produce.

The respiratory system does not participate in all steps of respiration.
Most people think of respiration as the process of breathing in and breathing out. In physiology, however, respiration has a broader meaning. Respiration encompasses two separate but related processes: cellular respiration and external respiration.

CELLULAR RESPIRATION The term **cellular respiration** refers to the intracellular metabolic processes carried out within the mitochondria, which use O_2 and produce CO_2 while deriving energy from nutrient molecules (see p. 29). The term **external respiration** refers to the entire sequence of events in the exchange of O_2 and CO_2 between the external environment and the tissue cells. External respiration, the topic of this chapter, encompasses four steps (● Figure 12-1):

1. Air is alternately moved into and out of the lungs so that air can be exchanged between the atmosphere (external environment) and the air sacs *(alveoli)* of the lungs. This exchange is accomplished by the mechanical act of **breathing,** or **ventilation.** The rate of ventilation is regulated to adjust the flow of air between the atmosphere and the alveoli according to the body's metabolic needs for O_2 uptake and CO_2 removal.

2. Oxygen and CO_2 are exchanged between air in the alveoli and the blood within the pulmonary *(pulmonary* means "lung") capillaries by the process of diffusion.

3. The blood transports O_2 and CO_2 between the lungs and the tissues.

4. Oxygen and CO_2 are exchanged between the tissue cells and the blood by the process of diffusion across the systemic (tissue) capillaries.

The respiratory system does not accomplish all the steps of respiration; it is involved only with ventilation and the exchange of O_2 and CO_2 between the lungs and the blood (steps **1** and **2**). The circulatory system carries out the remaining steps.

NONRESPIRATORY FUNCTIONS OF THE RESPIRATORY SYSTEM The respiratory system also fills these nonrespiratory functions:

■ It is a route for water loss and heat elimination. Inspired (inhaled) atmospheric air is humidified and warmed by the respiratory airways before it is expired. Moistening of inspired air is essential to prevent the alveolar linings from drying out. Oxygen and CO_2 cannot diffuse through dry membranes.

■ It enhances venous return (see the "respiratory pump," p. 305).

■ It helps maintain normal acid–base balance by altering the amount of H^+-generating CO_2 exhaled (see p. 457).

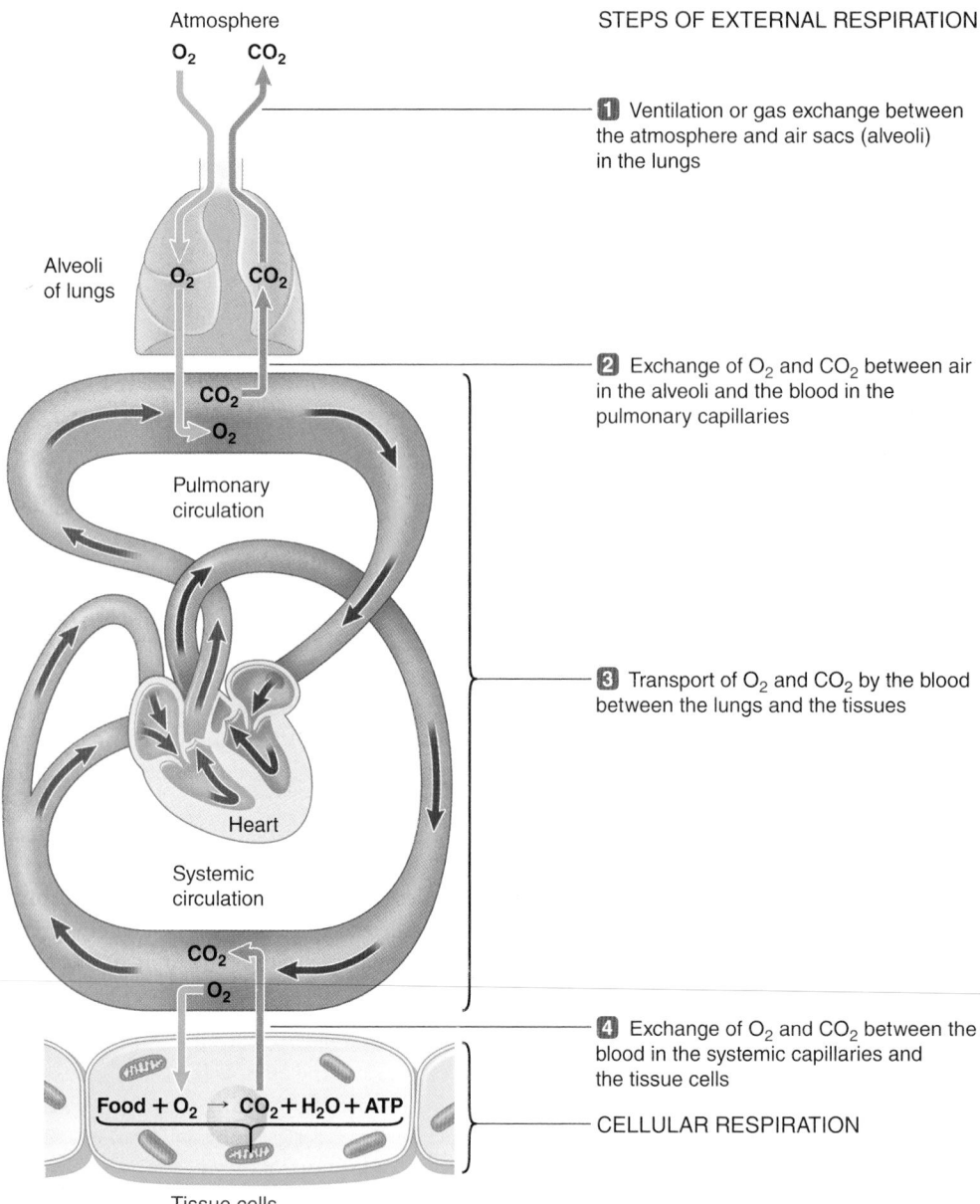

STEPS OF EXTERNAL RESPIRATION

1 Ventilation or gas exchange between the atmosphere and air sacs (alveoli) in the lungs

2 Exchange of O_2 and CO_2 between air in the alveoli and the blood in the pulmonary capillaries

3 Transport of O_2 and CO_2 by the blood between the lungs and the tissues

4 Exchange of O_2 and CO_2 between the blood in the systemic capillaries and the tissue cells

CELLULAR RESPIRATION

Atmosphere
O_2 CO_2

Alveoli of lungs

CO_2
O_2
Pulmonary circulation

Heart

Systemic circulation

CO_2
O_2

$Food + O_2 \rightarrow CO_2 + H_2O + ATP$

Tissue cells

● **FIGURE 12-1 External and cellular respiration.** External respiration encompasses the steps involved in the exchange of O_2 and CO_2 between the external environment and the tissue cells (steps 1 through 4). Cellular respiration encompasses the intracellular metabolic reactions involving the use of O_2 to derive energy (ATP) from food, producing CO_2 as a by-product.

■ It enables speech, singing, and other vocalization.

■ It defends against inhaled foreign matter (see p. 360).

■ It removes, modifies, activates, or inactivates various materials passing through the pulmonary circulation. All blood returning to the heart from the tissues must pass through the lungs before being returned to the systemic circulation. The lungs, therefore, are uniquely situated to act on specific materials that have been added to the blood at the tissue level before they have a chance to reach other parts of the body by means of the arterial system. For example, prostaglandins, a collection of chemical messengers released in many tissues to mediate particular local responses (see p. 592), may spill into the blood, but they are inactivated during passage through the lungs so

that they cannot exert systemic effects.

■ The nose, a part of the respiratory system, is the organ of smell (see p. 183).

The respiratory airways conduct air between the atmosphere and the alveoli.

The **respiratory system** includes the respiratory airways leading into the lungs, the lungs themselves, and the respiratory muscles of the thorax (chest) and abdomen involved in producing movement of air through the airways into and out of the lungs. The **respiratory airways** are tubes that carry air between the atmosphere and the air sacs, the latter being the only site where gases can be exchanged between air and blood. The airways begin with the **nasal passages (nose)** (● Figure 12-2a). The nasal passages open into the **pharynx (throat),** which serves as a common passageway for both the respiratory and the digestive systems. Two tubes lead from the pharynx—the **trachea (windpipe),** through which air is conducted to the lungs, and the **esophagus,** the tube through which food passes to the stomach. Air normally enters the pharynx through the nose, but it can enter by the mouth as well when the nasal passages are congested; that is, you can breathe through your mouth when you have a cold. Because the pharynx serves as a common passageway for food and air, reflex mechanisms close off the trachea during swallowing so that food enters the esophagus and not the airways. The esophagus stays closed except during swallowing to keep air from entering the stomach during breathing.

The **larynx,** or **voice box,** is located at the entrance of the trachea. The anterior protrusion of the larynx forms the "Adam's apple." The **vocal folds,** two bands of elastic tissue that lie across the opening of the larynx, can be stretched and positioned in different shapes by laryngeal muscles (● Figure 12-3a). Air passes into the larynx through the space between the vocal folds. This laryngeal opening is known as the **glottis.** As air

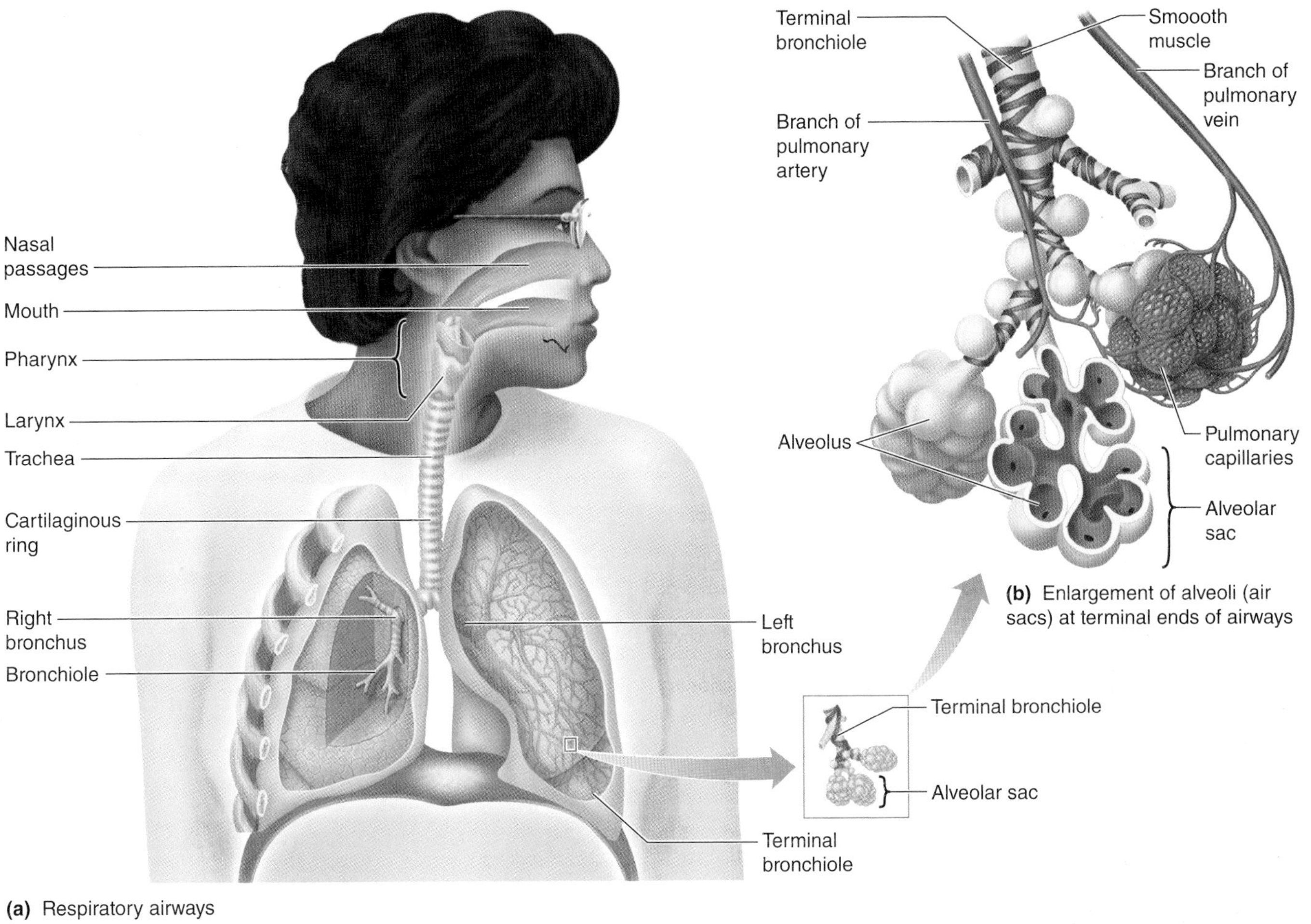

Terminal bronchiole

Branch of pulmonary artery

Smoooth muscle

Branch of pulmonary vein

Alveolus

Pulmonary capillaries

Alveolar sac

(b) Enlargement of alveoli (air sacs) at terminal ends of airways

Nasal passages

Mouth

Pharynx

Larynx

Trachea

Cartilaginous ring

Right bronchus

Bronchiole

Left bronchus

Terminal bronchiole

Alveolar sac

Terminal bronchiole

(a) Respiratory airways

● **FIGURE 12-2 Anatomy of the respiratory system.** (a) The respiratory airways include the nasal passages, pharynx, larynx, trachea, bronchi, and bronchioles. (b) Most alveoli (air sacs) are clustered in grapelike arrangements at the end of the terminal bronchioles.

moves through the open glottis past the variably positioned, taut vocal folds, they vibrate to produce the many sounds of speech. The lips and tongue modify the sounds into recognizable sound patterns. During swallowing, the vocal folds assume a function not related to speech: They close the glottis. That is, laryngeal muscles bring the vocal folds into tight apposition to each other to close off the entrance to the trachea so that food does not get into the airways (● Figure 12-3b).

Beyond the larynx, the trachea divides into two main branches, the right and left **bronchi,** which enter the right and left lungs, respectively. Within each lung, the bronchus continues to branch into progressively narrower, shorter, and more numerous airways, much like the branching of a tree. The smaller branches are known as **bronchioles.** Clustered at the ends of the terminal bronchioles are the **alveoli,** the tiny air sacs where gases are exchanged between air and blood (see ● Figure 12-2b).

The gas-exchanging alveoli are thin-walled, inflatable air sacs encircled by pulmonary capillaries.

The lungs are ideally structured for gas exchange. According to Fick's law of diffusion, the shorter the distance through which

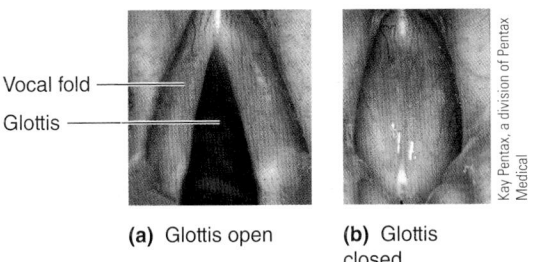

Vocal fold

Glottis

(a) Glottis open

(b) Glottis closed

Kay Pentax, a division of Pentax Medical

● **FIGURE 12-3 Vocal folds.** Photographs of the vocal folds as viewed from above at the laryngeal opening, showing the vocal folds (a) positioned apart when the glottis is open and (b) in tight apposition when the glottis is closed.

diffusion must take place, the greater the rate of diffusion. Also, the greater the surface area across which diffusion can take place, the greater the rate of diffusion (see p. 55).

The alveoli are clusters of thin-walled, inflatable, grapelike sacs at the terminal branches of the conducting airways. The alveolar walls consist of a single layer of flattened, **Type I alveolar cells** (● Figure 12-4a). Each alveolus is surrounded by a network of pulmonary capillaries, the walls of which are also

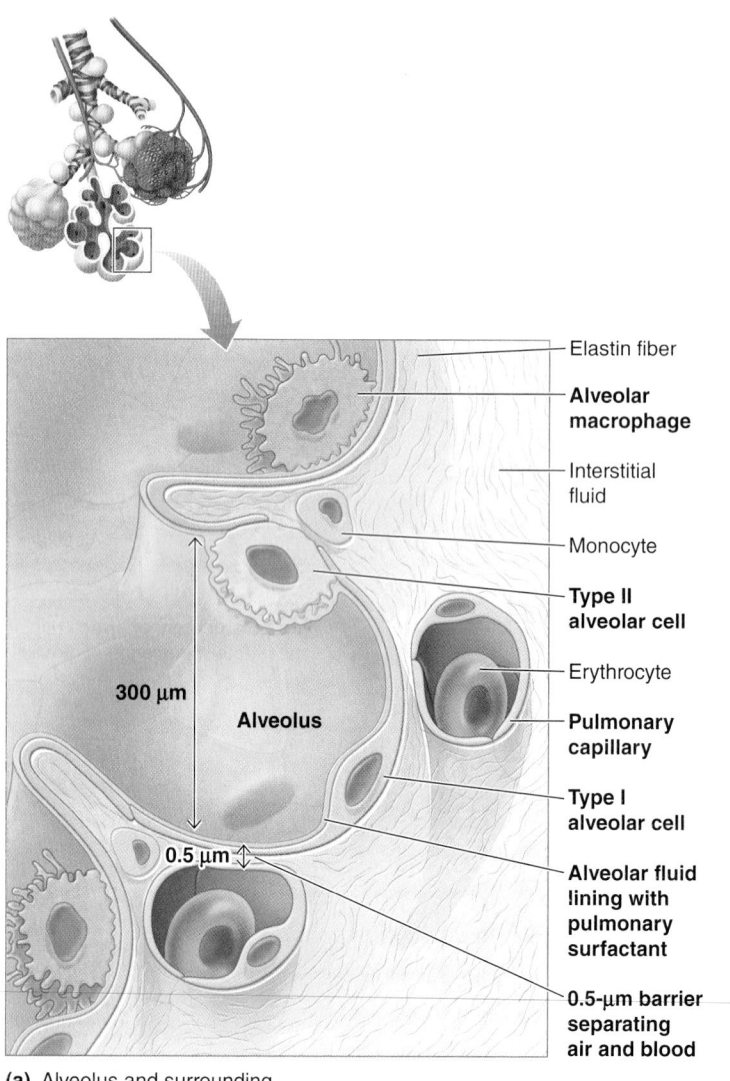

Elastin fiber

Alveolar macrophage

Interstitial fluid

Monocyte

Type II alveolar cell

Erythrocyte

Pulmonary capillary

Type I alveolar cell

Alveolar fluid lining with pulmonary surfactant

0.5-μm barrier separating air and blood

300 μm

Alveolus

0.5 μm

(a) Alveolus and surrounding pulmonary capillaries

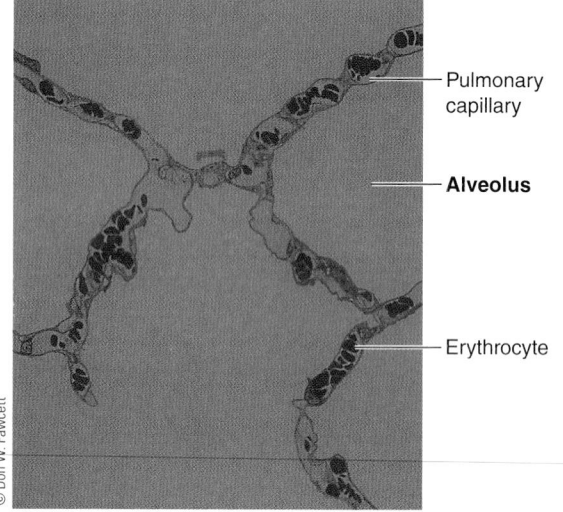

Alveolus surrounded by pulmonary capillaries

Pulmonary capillary networks

Alveolus with capillary cut away

(b) Scanning electron micrograph of alveoli and surrounding pulmonary capillaries

Dr. Richard Kessel and Dr. Randy Kardon, Tissues and Organs, Visuals Unlimited, Inc.

Pulmonary capillary

Alveolus

Erythrocyte

© Don W. Fawcett

(c) Transmission electron micrograph of several alveoli and surrounding pulmonary capillaries

● FIGURE 12-4 **Alveolus and associated pulmonary capillaries.** (a) A single layer of flattened Type I alveolar cells forms the alveolar walls. Type II alveolar cells embedded within the alveolar wall secrete pulmonary surfactant. Wandering alveolar macrophages are found within the alveolar lumen. The size of the cells and respiratory membrane is exaggerated compared to the size of the alveolar and pulmonary capillary lumens. The diameter of an alveolus is actually about 600 times larger (300 μm) than the intervening space between air and blood (0.5 μm). (b) Each alveolus is encircled with a dense network of pulmonary capillaries. (c) Note that each alveolus is surrounded by an almost continuous sheet of blood.

only one cell thick (● Figure 12-4b). The interstitial space between an alveolus and the surrounding capillary network forms an extremely thin barrier, with only 0.5 μm separating air in the alveoli from blood in the pulmonary capillaries. (A sheet of tracing paper is about 50 times thicker than this air-to-blood barrier.) The thinness of this barrier facilitates gas exchange.

Furthermore, the alveolar air–blood interface presents a tremendous surface area for exchange. The lungs contain about 500 million alveoli, each about 300 μm in diameter. So dense are the pulmonary capillary networks that each alveolus is encircled by an almost continuous sheet of blood (● Figure

12-4c). The total surface area thus exposed between alveolar air and pulmonary capillary blood is about 75 m² (about the size of a tennis court). In contrast, if the lungs consisted of a single hollow chamber of the same dimensions instead of being divided into a multitude of alveolar units, the total surface area would be only about 0.01 m².

In addition to the thin, wall-forming Type I cells, 5% of the alveolar surface epithelium is covered by **Type II alveolar cells** (● Figure 12-4a). These cells secrete *pulmonary surfactant,* a chemical complex that facilitates lung expansion (described later). Furthermore, defensive alveolar macrophages stand guard within the lumen of the air sacs (see p. 359).

The lungs occupy much of the thoracic cavity. There are two **lungs,** each divided into several lobes and each supplied by one of the bronchi. The lung tissue itself consists of the series of highly branched airways, the alveoli, the pulmonary blood vessels, and large quantities of elastic connective tissue. The only muscle within the lungs is the smooth muscle in the walls of the arterioles and the walls of the bronchioles, both of which are subject to control. No muscle is present within the alveolar walls to cause them to inflate and deflate during the breathing process. Instead, changes in lung volume (and accompanying changes in alveolar volume) are brought about through changes in the dimensions of the thoracic (chest) cavity. You will learn about this mechanism after we complete our discussion of respiratory anatomy.

The lungs occupy most of the volume of the **thoracic (chest) cavity,** the only other structures in the chest being the heart and associated vessels, the esophagus, the thymus, and some nerves. The outer chest wall **(thorax)** is formed by 12 pairs of curved **ribs,** which join the **sternum** (breastbone) anteriorly and the **thoracic vertebrae** (backbone) posteriorly. The rib cage provides bony protection for the lungs and heart. Skeletal muscles connect these bony structures and enclose the thoracic cavity. The **diaphragm,** which forms the floor of the thoracic cavity, is a large, dome-shaped sheet of skeletal muscle that separates the thoracic cavity from the abdominal cavity. It is penetrated only by the esophagus and blood vessels traversing the thoracic and abdominal cavities. The only communication between the atmosphere and the thoracic cavity is through the respiratory airways into the alveoli.

A pleural sac separates each lung from the thoracic wall.

A double-walled, closed sac called the **pleural sac** separates each lung from the thoracic wall and other surrounding structures (● Figure 12-5). The interior of the pleural sac is known as the **pleural cavity.** In the illustration, the dimensions of the pleural cavity are greatly exaggerated to aid visualization; in reality, the layers of the pleural sac are in close contact with one another. The surfaces of the pleura secrete a thin **intrapleural fluid** (*intra* means "within"), which lubricates the pleural surfaces as they slide past each other during respiratory movements.

Pleurisy, an inflammation of the pleural sac, is accompanied by painful breathing, because each inflation and each deflation of the lungs cause a "friction rub."

Respiratory Mechanics

Air tends to move from a region of higher pressure to a region of lower pressure, that is, down a **pressure gradient.**

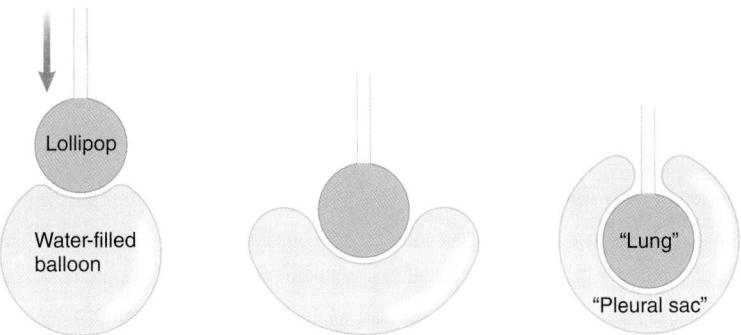

(a) Analogy of relationship between lung and pleural sac

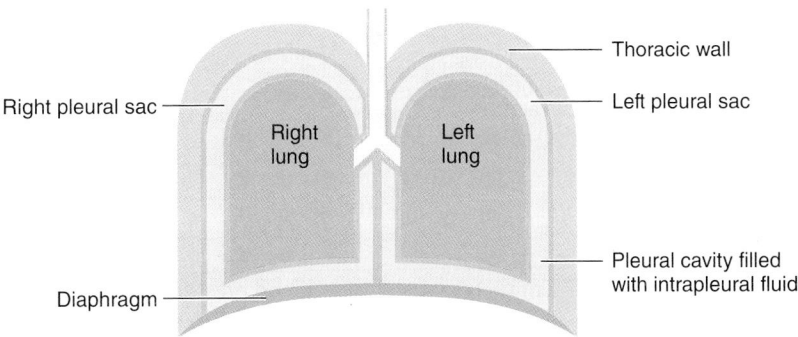

(b) Relationship of lungs to pleural sacs, thoracic wall, and diaphragm

● **FIGURE 12-5 Pleural sac.** (a) Pushing a lollipop into a small water-filled balloon produces a relationship analogous to that between each double-walled, closed pleural sac and the lung that it surrounds and separates from the thoracic wall. (b) One layer of the pleural sac closely adheres to the surface of the lung and then reflects back on itself to form another layer that lines the interior surface of the thoracic wall. The relative size of the pleural cavity between these two layers is grossly exaggerated for the purpose of visualization.

Interrelationships among pressures inside and outside the lungs are important in ventilation.

Air flows into and out of the lungs during the act of breathing by moving down alternately reversing pressure gradients established between the alveoli and the atmosphere by cyclic respiratory muscle activity. Three pressure considerations are important in ventilation (● Figure 12-6):

1. **Atmospheric (barometric) pressure** is the pressure exerted by the weight of the air in the atmosphere on objects on Earth's surface. At sea level, it equals 760 mm Hg (● Figure 12-7). Atmospheric pressure diminishes with increasing altitude above sea level as the layer of air above Earth's surface correspondingly decreases in thickness. Minor fluctuations in atmospheric pressure occur at any height because of changing weather conditions (that is, when barometric pressure is rising or falling).

2. **Intra-alveolar pressure** is the pressure within the alveoli. Because the alveoli communicate with the atmosphere through the conducting airways, air quickly flows down its pressure gradient any time intra-alveolar pressure differs from atmospheric pressure; air flow continues until the two pressures equilibrate (become equal).

3. **Intrapleural pressure** is the pressure within the pleural sac. It is the pressure exerted outside the lungs within the thoracic cavity. The intrapleural pressure is usually less than atmospheric

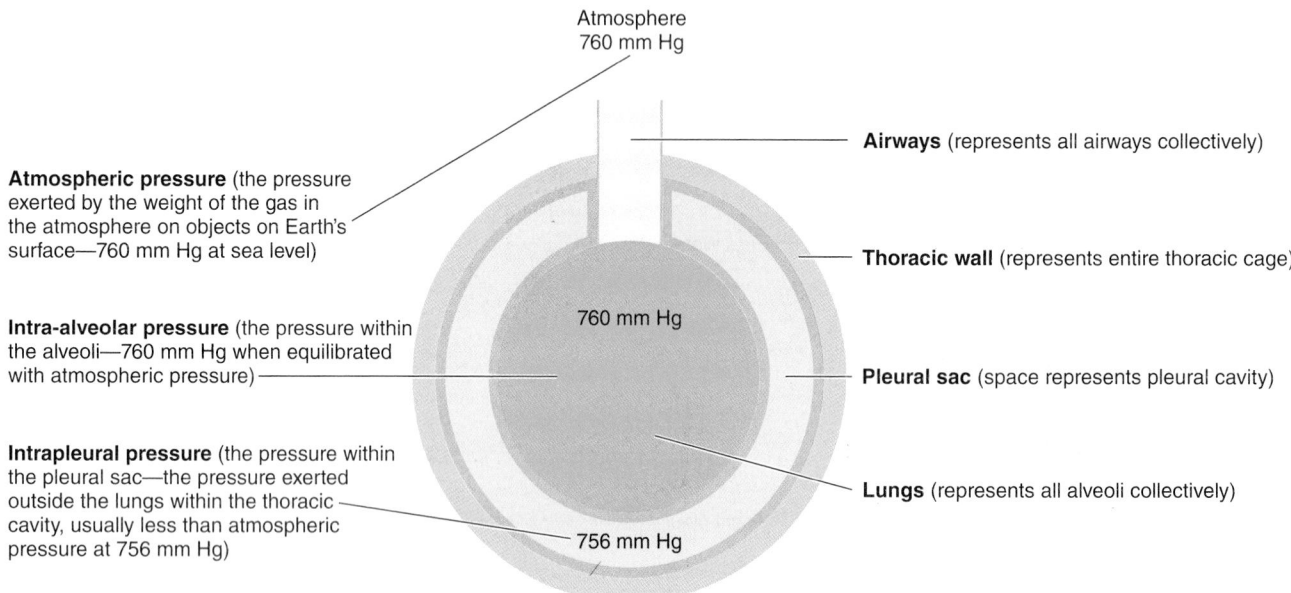

Atmospheric pressure (the pressure exerted by the weight of the gas in the atmosphere on objects on Earth's surface—760 mm Hg at sea level)

Intra-alveolar pressure (the pressure within the alveoli—760 mm Hg when equilibrated with atmospheric pressure)

Intrapleural pressure (the pressure within the pleural sac—the pressure exerted outside the lungs within the thoracic cavity, usually less than atmospheric pressure at 756 mm Hg)

Atmosphere
760 mm Hg

Airways (represents all airways collectively)

Thoracic wall (represents entire thoracic cage)

760 mm Hg

Pleural sac (space represents pleural cavity)

Lungs (represents all alveoli collectively)

756 mm Hg

● **FIGURE 12-6 Pressures important in ventilation.**

pressure, averaging 756 mm Hg at rest. Just as blood pressure is recorded using atmospheric pressure as a reference point (that is, a systolic blood pressure of 120 mm Hg is 120 mm Hg greater than the atmospheric pressure of 760 mm Hg or, in reality, 880 mm Hg), 756 mm Hg is sometimes referred to as a pressure of −4 mm Hg. However, there is really no such thing as an absolute negative pressure. A pressure of −4 mm Hg is just negative when compared with the normal atmospheric pressure of 760 mm Hg. To avoid confusion, we use absolute positive values throughout our discussion of respiration.

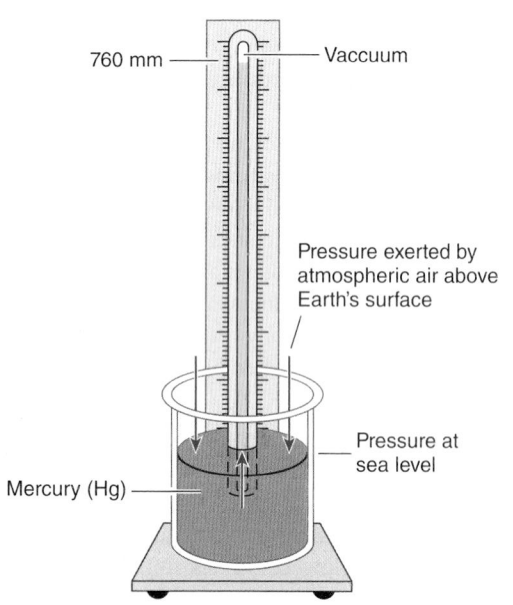

760 mm — Vaccuum

Pressure exerted by atmospheric air above Earth's surface

Pressure at sea level

Mercury (Hg)

● **FIGURE 12-7 Atmospheric pressure.** The pressure exerted on objects by the atmospheric air above Earth's surface at sea level can push a column of mercury to a height of 760 mm. Therefore, atmospheric pressure at sea level is 760 mm Hg.

Intrapleural pressure does not equilibrate with atmospheric or intra-alveolar pressure because the pleural sac is a closed sac with no openings, so air cannot enter or leave despite any pressure gradients that might exist between the pleural cavity and the atmosphere or lungs.

The transmural pressure gradient normally stretches the lungs to fill the larger thoracic cavity.

The thoracic cavity is larger than the unstretched lungs because the thoracic wall grows more rapidly than the lungs during development. However, a *transmural pressure gradient* across the lung wall holds the lungs and thoracic wall in close apposition, stretching the lungs to fill the larger thoracic cavity. Let us examine the significance of this gradient and how it arises.

TRANSMURAL PRESSURE GRADIENT The intra-alveolar pressure, equilibrated with atmospheric pressure at 760 mm Hg, is greater than the intrapleural pressure of 756 mm Hg, so a greater pressure is pushing outward than is pushing inward across the lung wall. This net outward pressure differential, the **transmural pressure gradient,** pushes out on the lungs, stretching, or distending, them (*trans* means "across"; *mural* means "wall") (● Figure 12-8). Because of this pressure gradient, the lungs are always forced to expand to fill the thoracic cavity, no matter its size. As the thoracic cavity enlarges, the lungs enlarge; that is, the lungs follow the movements of the chest wall.

WHY THE INTRAPLEURAL PRESSURE IS SUBATMOSPHERIC Because of the lungs' elasticity, they try to pull inward away from the thoracic wall as they are stretched to fill the larger thoracic cavity. The transmural pressure gradient, however, prevents the lungs from pulling away except to the slightest degree. The resultant ever-so-slight expansion of the pleural cavity is sufficient to drop the pressure in this cavity by 4 mm Hg, bringing the intrapleural pressure to the subatmospheric

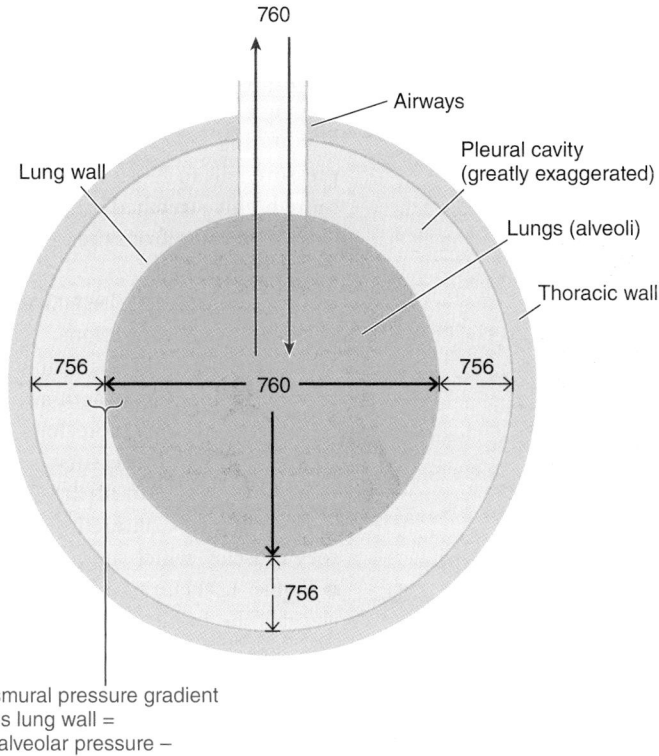

Transmural pressure gradient
across lung wall =
intra-alveolar pressure –
intrapleural pressure

Numbers are mm Hg pressure.

● **FIGURE 12-8 Transmural pressure gradient.** Across the lung wall, the intra-alveolar pressure of 760 mm Hg pushes outward, while the intrapleural pressure of 756 mm Hg pushes inward. This 4 mm Hg difference in pressure constitutes a transmural pressure gradient that pushes out on the lungs, stretching them to fill the larger thoracic cavity.

level of 756 mm Hg. This pressure drop occurs because the pleural cavity is filled with fluid, which cannot expand to fill the slightly larger volume. Therefore, a vacuum exists in the infinitesimal space in the slightly expanded pleural cavity not occupied by intrapleural fluid, producing a small drop in intrapleural pressure below atmospheric pressure.

Note the interrelationship between the transmural pressure gradient and the subatmospheric intrapleural pressure. The lungs are stretched by the transmural pressure gradient that exists across their walls because the intrapleural pressure is less than atmospheric pressure. The intrapleural pressure, in turn, is subatmospheric because the stretched lungs tend to pull away from the larger thoracic wall, slightly expanding the pleural cavity and dropping the intrapleural pressure below atmospheric pressure.

PNEUMOTHORAX Normally, air does not enter the pleural cavity, because there is no communication between the cavity and either the atmosphere or the alveoli. However, if the chest wall is punctured (for example, by a stab wound or a broken rib), air flows down its pressure gradient from the higher atmospheric pressure and rushes into the pleural space (● Figure 12-9a). The abnormal condition of air entering the pleural cavity is known as **pneumothorax** ("air in the chest"). Intrapleural and intra-alveolar

pressure are now both equilibrated with atmospheric pressure, so a transmural pressure gradient no longer exists across the lung wall. With no force present to stretch the lung, it collapses to its unstretched size (● Figure 12-9b). Similarly, pneumothorax and lung collapse can occur if air enters the pleural cavity through a hole in the lung produced, for example, by a disease process (● Figure 12-9c).

Flow of air into and out of the lungs occurs because of cyclic changes in intra-alveolar pressure.

Because air flows down a pressure gradient, the intra-alveolar pressure must be less than atmospheric pressure for air to flow into the lungs during inspiration. Similarly, the intra-alveolar pressure must be greater than atmospheric pressure for air to flow out of the lungs during expiration. Intra-alveolar pressure can be changed by altering the volume of the lungs, in accordance with Boyle's law. **Boyle's law** states that, at any constant temperature, the pressure exerted by a gas in a closed container varies inversely with the volume of the gas (● Figure 12-10); that is, as the volume of a gas increases, the pressure exerted by the gas decreases proportionately. Conversely, the pressure increases proportionately as the volume decreases. Changes in lung volume, and accordingly intra-alveolar pressure, are brought about indirectly by respiratory muscle activity.

The respiratory muscles that accomplish breathing do not act directly on the lungs to change their volume. Instead, these muscles change the volume of the thoracic cavity, causing a corresponding change in lung volume because the thoracic wall and lungs are linked by the transmural pressure gradient.

Let us follow the changes that occur during one respiratory cycle—that is, one breath in (**inspiration**) and out (**expiration**).

ONSET OF INSPIRATION: CONTRACTION OF INSPIRATORY MUSCLES The major **inspiratory muscles**—the muscles that contract to accomplish an inspiration during quiet breathing—include the *diaphragm* and *external intercostal muscles* (● Figure 12-11). Before the beginning of inspiration, all respiratory muscles are relaxed (● Figure 12-12a). At the onset of inspiration, the inspiratory muscles are stimulated to contract, enlarging the thoracic cavity. The major inspiratory muscle is the diaphragm. The relaxed diaphragm has a dome shape that protrudes upward into the thoracic cavity. When the diaphragm contracts, it descends downward, enlarging the volume of the thoracic cavity by increasing its vertical (top-to-bottom) dimension (● Figure 12-12b). During quiet breathing, the diaphragm descends about 1 cm during inspiration, but during heavy breathing, it may descend as much as 10 cm. The abdominal wall, if relaxed, bulges outward during inspiration as the descending diaphragm pushes the abdominal contents downward and forward. Seventy-five percent of the enlargement of the thoracic cavity during quiet inspiration is accomplished by contraction of the diaphragm.

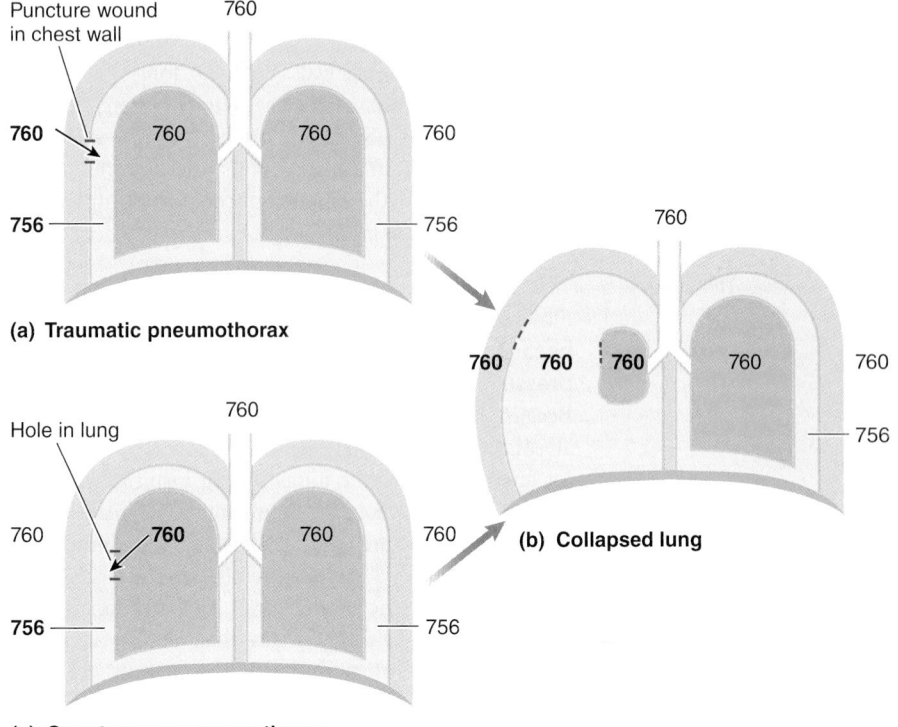

(a) Traumatic pneumothorax

(b) Collapsed lung

(c) Spontaneous pneumothorax

Numbers are mm Hg pressure.

● **FIGURE 12-9 Pneumothorax.** (a) In *traumatic pneumothorax,* a puncture in the chest wall permits air from the atmosphere to flow down its pressure gradient and enter the pleural cavity, abolishing the transmural pressure gradient. (b) When the transmural pressure gradient is abolished, the lung collapses to its unstretched size. (c) In *spontaneous pneumothorax,* a hole in the lung wall permits air to move down its pressure gradient and enter the pleural cavity from the lungs, abolishing the transmural pressure gradient. As with traumatic pneumothorax, the lung collapses to its unstretched size.

Two sets of **intercostal muscles** lie between the ribs (*inter* means "between"; *costa* means "rib"). The *external intercostal muscles* lie on top of the *internal intercostal muscles.* Contraction of the **external intercostal muscles,** whose fibers run downward and forward between adjacent ribs, enlarges the thoracic cavity in both the lateral (side-to-side) and the anteroposterior (front-to-back) dimensions. When the external intercostals contract, they elevate the ribs and subsequently the sternum upward and outward (● Figure 12-12b).

Before inspiration, at the end of the preceding expiration, intra-alveolar pressure is equal to atmospheric pressure, so no air is flowing into or out of the lungs (● Figure 12-13a). As the thoracic cavity enlarges during inspiration on contraction of the diaphragm and external intercostals, the lungs are also forced to expand to fill the larger thoracic cavity. As the lungs enlarge, the intra-alveolar pressure drops because the same number of air molecules now occupy a larger lung volume. In a typical inspiratory excursion, the intra-alveolar pressure drops 1 mm Hg to 759 mm Hg (● Figure 12-13b). Because the intra-alveolar pressure is now less than atmospheric pressure, air flows into the lungs down the pressure gradient from higher to lower pressure. Air continues to enter the lungs until no further gradient exists—that is, until intra-alveolar pressure equals atmospheric pressure. Thus, lung expansion is not caused by

movement of air into the lungs; instead, air flows into the lungs because of the fall in intra-alveolar pressure brought about by lung expansion.

During inspiration, the intrapleural pressure falls to 754 mm Hg because the more highly stretched lungs tend to pull away a bit more from the thoracic wall.

ROLE OF ACCESSORY INSPIRATORY MUSCLES Deeper inspirations (more air breathed in) can be accomplished by contracting the diaphragm and external intercostal muscles more forcefully and by bringing the **accessory inspiratory muscles** into play to further enlarge the thoracic cavity. Contracting these accessory muscles, which are in the neck (see ● Figure 12-11), raises the sternum and elevates the first two ribs, enlarging the upper portion of the thoracic cavity. As the thoracic cavity increases even further in volume than under resting conditions, the lungs likewise expand more, dropping the intra-alveolar pressure further. Consequently, a larger inward flow of air occurs before equilibration with atmospheric pressure is achieved; that is, a deeper breath occurs.

ONSET OF EXPIRATION: RELAXATION OF INSPIRATORY MUSCLES At the end of inspiration, the inspiratory muscles relax. The diaphragm assumes its original dome-shaped position when it relaxes. The elevated rib cage falls because of gravity when the external intercostals relax (see ● Figure 12-12c). With no forces expanding the chest wall (and accordingly, expanding the lungs), the chest wall and stretched lungs recoil to their preinspiratory size because of their elastic properties, much as a stretched balloon would on release. As the lungs recoil and become smaller in volume, the intra-alveolar pressure rises, because the greater number of air molecules contained within the larger lung volume at the end of inspiration are now compressed into a smaller volume. In a resting expiration, the intra-alveolar pressure increases about 1 mm Hg above atmospheric level to 761 mm Hg (● Figure 12-13c). Air now leaves the lungs down its pressure gradient from higher intra-alveolar pressure to lower atmospheric pressure. Outward flow of air ceases when intra-alveolar pressure becomes equal to atmospheric pressure and a pressure gradient no longer exists. ● Figure 12-14 summarizes the intra-alveolar and intrapleural pressure changes that take place during one respiratory cycle.

FORCED EXPIRATION: CONTRACTION OF EXPIRATORY MUSCLES
During quiet breathing, expiration is normally a passive process because it is accomplished by elastic recoil of the lungs on relaxation of the inspiratory muscles, with no muscular exertion or

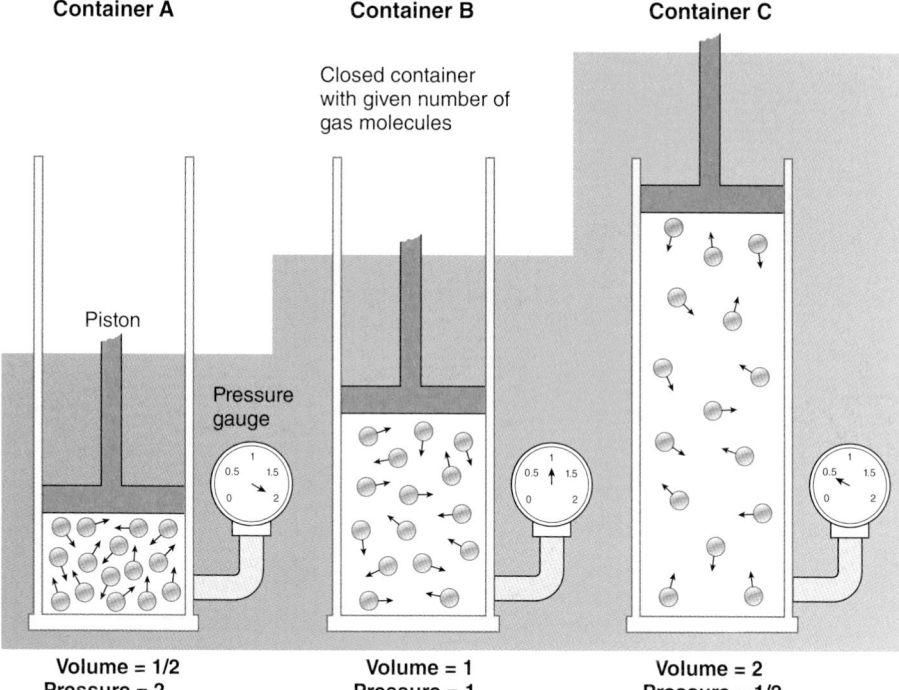

Container A

Piston

Pressure gauge

Volume = 1/2
Pressure = 2

Container B

Closed container with given number of gas molecules

Volume = 1
Pressure = 1

Container C

Volume = 2
Pressure = 1/2

● **FIGURE 12-10 Boyle's law.** Each closed container has the same number of gas molecules. Given the random motion of gas molecules, the likelihood of a gas molecule striking the interior wall of the container and exerting pressure varies inversely with the volume of the container at any constant temperature. The gas in container B exerts more pressure than the same gas in larger container C but less pressure than the same gas in smaller container A. This relationship is stated as Boyle's law: $P_1V_1 = P_2V_2$. As the volume of a gas increases, the pressure of the gas decreases proportionately; conversely, the pressure increases proportionately as the volume decreases.

stretched as much to fill the smaller thoracic cavity; that is, they are permitted to recoil to an even smaller volume. The intra-alveolar pressure increases further as the air in the lungs is confined within this smaller volume. The differential between intra-alveolar and atmospheric pressure is even greater now than during passive expiration, so more air leaves down the pressure gradient before equilibration is achieved. In this way, the lungs are emptied more completely during forceful, active expiration than during quiet passive expiration.

Airway resistance influences airflow rates.

Thus far, we have discussed airflow in and out of the lungs as a function of the magnitude of the pressure gradient between the alveoli and the atmosphere. However, just as flow of blood through the blood vessels depends not only on the pressure gradient but also on the resistance to the flow offered by the vessels, so it is with airflow:

$$F = \frac{\Delta P}{R}$$

energy expenditure required. In contrast, inspiration is *always* active, because it is brought about only by contraction of inspiratory muscles at the expense of energy use. Expiration does become active to empty the lungs more completely and more rapidly than is accomplished during quiet breathing, as during the deeper breaths accompanying exercise. To force more air out, the intra-alveolar pressure must be increased even further above atmospheric pressure than can be accomplished by simple relaxation of the inspiratory muscles and elastic recoil of the lungs. To produce such a **forced,** or **active, expiration,** expiratory muscles must contract to further reduce the volume of the thoracic cavity and lungs (see ● Figures 12-11 and 12-12d). The most important **expiratory muscles** are (unbelievable as it may seem at first) the *muscles of the abdominal wall*. As the abdominal muscles contract, the resultant increase in intra-abdominal pressure exerts an upward force on the diaphragm, pushing it farther up into the thoracic cavity than its relaxed position, thus decreasing the vertical dimension of the thoracic cavity even more. The other expiratory muscles are the **internal intercostal muscles,** whose contraction pulls the ribs downward and inward, flattening the chest wall and further decreasing the size of the thoracic cavity; this action is just the opposite of that of the external intercostal muscles.

As active contraction of the expiratory muscles further reduces the volume of the thoracic cavity, the lungs also become further reduced in volume because they do not have to be

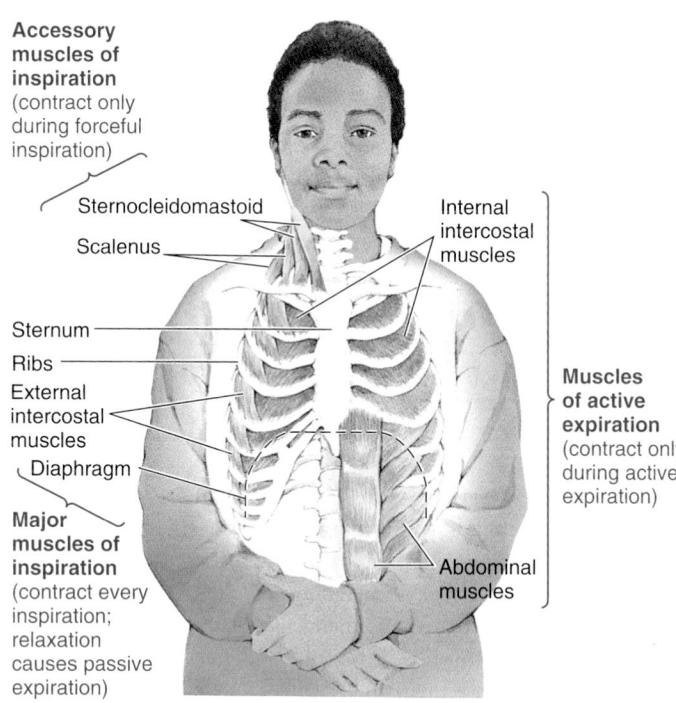

Accessory muscles of inspiration (contract only during forceful inspiration)

Sternocleidomastoid

Scalenus

Sternum

Ribs

External intercostal muscles

Diaphragm

Major muscles of inspiration (contract every inspiration; relaxation causes passive expiration)

Internal intercostal muscles

Muscles of active expiration (contract only during active expiration)

Abdominal muscles

● **FIGURE 12-11 Anatomy of the respiratory muscles.**

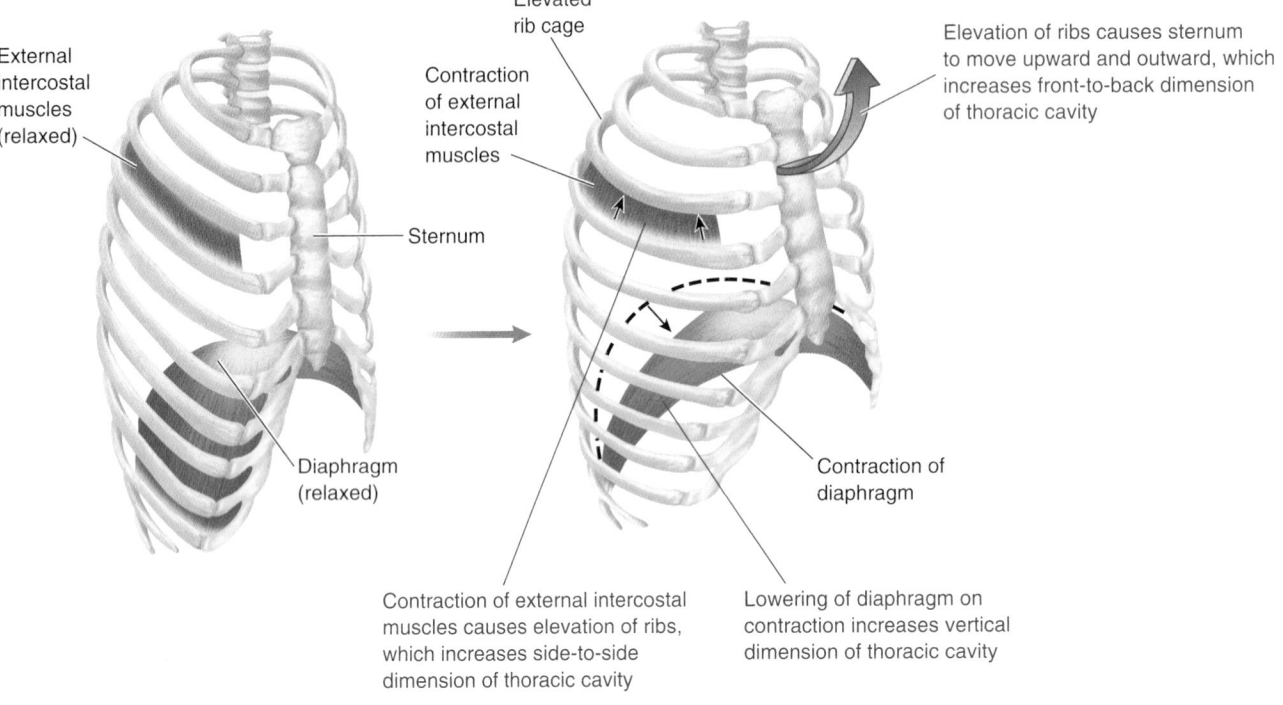

External intercostal muscles (relaxed)

Elevated rib cage

Contraction of external intercostal muscles

Sternum

Diaphragm (relaxed)

Elevation of ribs causes sternum to move upward and outward, which increases front-to-back dimension of thoracic cavity

Contraction of diaphragm

Contraction of external intercostal muscles causes elevation of ribs, which increases side-to-side dimension of thoracic cavity

Lowering of diaphragm on contraction increases vertical dimension of thoracic cavity

(a) Before inspiration

(b) Inspiration

● **FIGURE 12-12 Respiratory muscle activity during inspiration and expiration.** (a) Before inspiration, all respiratory muscles are relaxed. (b) During inspiration, the diaphragm descends on contraction, increasing the vertical dimension of the thoracic cavity. Contraction of the external intercostal muscles elevates the ribs and subsequently the sternum to enlarge the thoracic cavity from front to back and from side to side.

where

$$F = \text{airflow rate}$$

ΔP = difference between atmospheric and intra-alveolar pressure (pressure gradient)

R = resistance of airways, determined by their radius

The primary determinant of resistance to airflow is the radius of the conducting airways. We ignored airway resistance in our preceding discussion of pressure gradient–induced airflow rates because, in a healthy respiratory system, the radius of the conducting system is large enough that resistance remains extremely low. Therefore, the pressure gradient between the alveoli and the atmosphere is usually the primary factor determining the airflow rate. Indeed, the airways normally offer such low resistance that only small pressure gradients of 1 to 2 mm Hg are needed to achieve adequate rates of airflow into and out of the lungs. (By comparison, it would take a pressure gradient 250 times greater to move air through a smoker's pipe than through the respiratory airways at the same flow rate.)

Normally, modest adjustments in airway size can be accomplished by autonomic nervous system regulation to suit the body's needs. Parasympathetic stimulation, which occurs in quiet, relaxed situations when the demand for airflow is low, promotes bronchiolar smooth muscle contraction, which increases airway resistance by producing **bronchoconstriction** (a decrease in the radius of bronchioles). In contrast, sympathetic stimulation and to

a greater extent its associated hormone, epinephrine, bring about **bronchodilation** (an increase in bronchiolar radius) and decreased airway resistance by promoting bronchiolar smooth muscle relaxation. Thus, during periods of sympathetic domination, when increased demands for O_2 uptake are actually or potentially placed on the body, bronchodilation ensures that the pressure gradients established by respiratory muscle activity can achieve maximum airflow rates with minimum resistance. Because of this bronchodilator action, epinephrine or related drugs such as albuterol are useful therapeutic tools to counteract airway constriction in patients with bronchial spasms.

Resistance becomes an extremely important impediment to airflow when airway lumens become abnormally narrowed by disease. We have all transiently experienced the effect that increased airway resistance has on breathing when we have a cold. We know how difficult it is to produce an adequate airflow rate through a "stuffy nose" when the nasal passages are narrowed by swelling and mucus accumulation. More serious is chronic obstructive pulmonary disease, to which we now turn our attention.

Airway resistance is abnormally increased with chronic obstructive pulmonary disease.

 Clinical Note **Chronic obstructive pulmonary disease (COPD)** is a group of lung diseases characterized by increased airway resistance resulting from narrowing of the lumen of the lower airways. When airway resistance

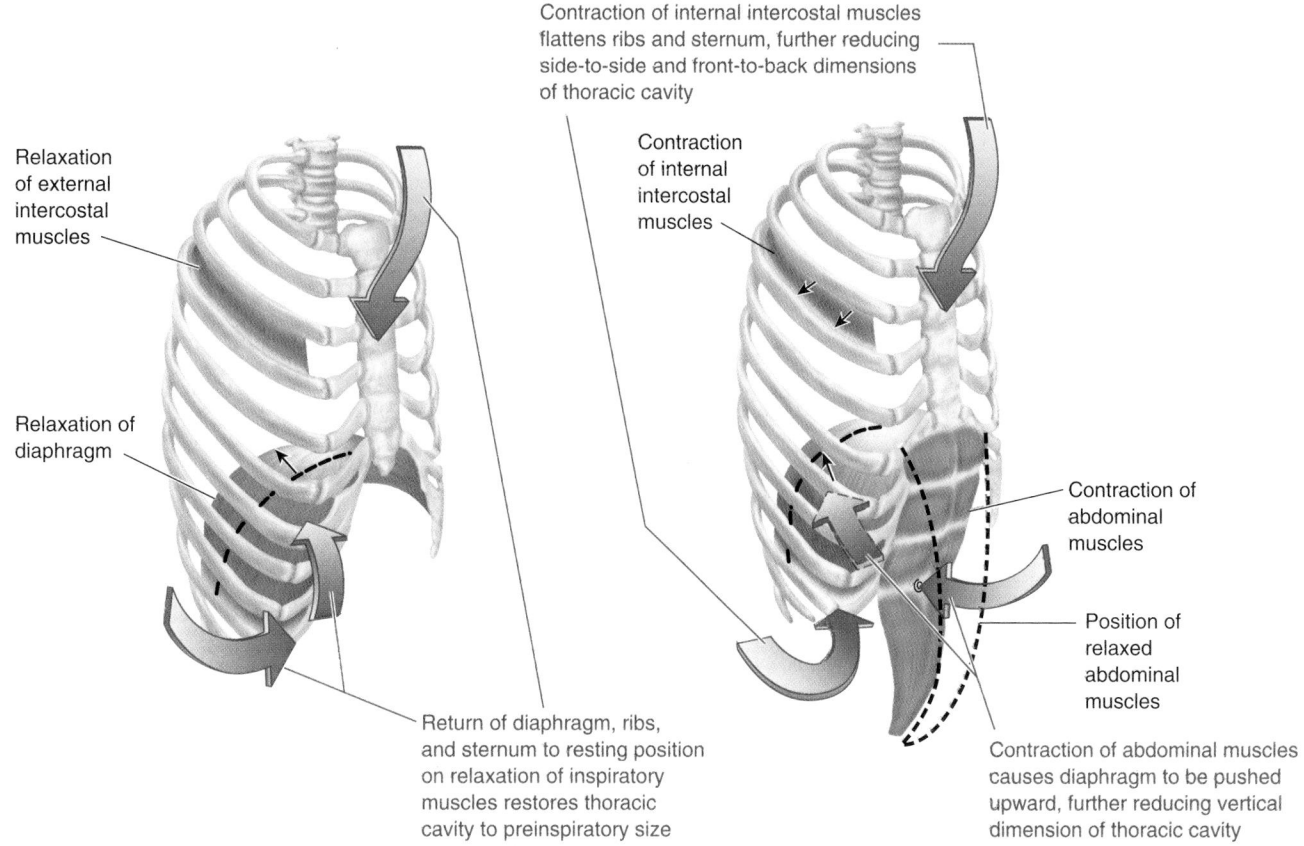

Contraction of internal intercostal muscles flattens ribs and sternum, further reducing side-to-side and front-to-back dimensions of thoracic cavity

Relaxation of external intercostal muscles

Contraction of internal intercostal muscles

Relaxation of diaphragm

Contraction of abdominal muscles

Position of relaxed abdominal muscles

Return of diaphragm, ribs, and sternum to resting position on relaxation of inspiratory muscles restores thoracic cavity to preinspiratory size

Contraction of abdominal muscles causes diaphragm to be pushed upward, further reducing vertical dimension of thoracic cavity

(c) Passive expiration

(d) Active expiration

● **FIGURE 12-12** *(continued)* **(c)** During quiet passive expiration, the diaphragm relaxes, reducing the volume of the thoracic cavity from its peak inspiratory size. As the external intercostal muscles relax, the elevated rib cage falls because of gravity. This also reduces the volume of the thoracic cavity. **(d)** During active expiration, contraction of the abdominal muscles increases the intra-abdominal pressure, exerting an upward force on the diaphragm. This reduces the vertical dimension of the thoracic cavity further than it is reduced during quiet passive expiration. Contraction of the internal intercostal muscles decreases the front-to-back and side-to-side dimensions by flattening the ribs and sternum.

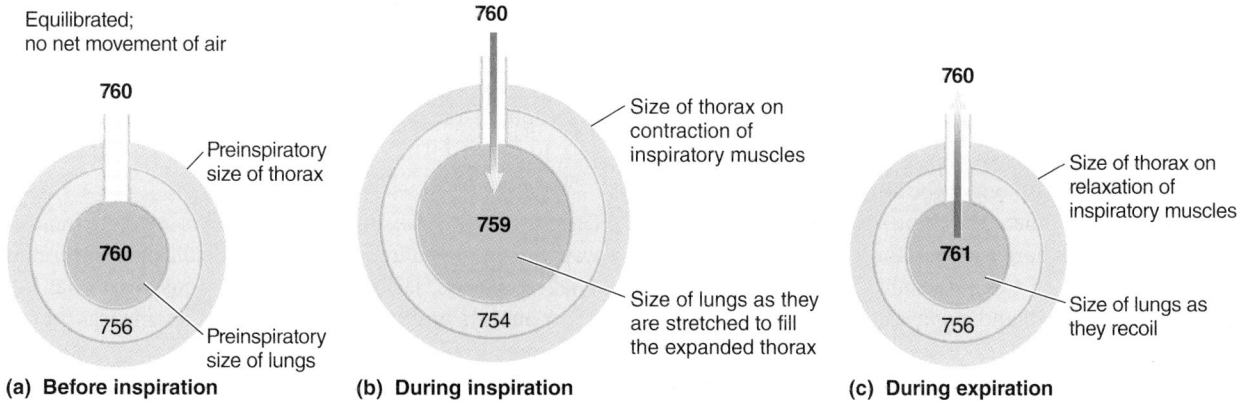

Equilibrated;
no net movement of air

760

760

756

Preinspiratory size of thorax

Preinspiratory size of lungs

760

759

754

Size of thorax on contraction of inspiratory muscles

Size of lungs as they are stretched to fill the expanded thorax

760

761

756

Size of thorax on relaxation of inspiratory muscles

Size of lungs as they recoil

(a) Before inspiration

(b) During inspiration

(c) During expiration

Numbers are mm Hg pressure.

● **FIGURE 12-13 Changes in lung volume and intra-alveolar pressure during inspiration and expiration.** (a) Before inspiration, at the end of the preceding expiration, intra-alveolar pressure is equilibrated with atmospheric pressure, and no air is flowing. (b) As the thorax (and thoracic cavity) and accordingly the lungs increase in volume during inspiration, the intra-alveolar pressure decreases, establishing a pressure gradient that favors the flow of air into the alveoli from the atmosphere; that is, an inspiration occurs. (c) As the lungs recoil to their preinspiratory size on relaxation of the inspiratory muscles, the intra-alveolar pressure increases, establishing a pressure gradient that favors the flow of air out of the alveoli into the atmosphere; that is, an expiration occurs.

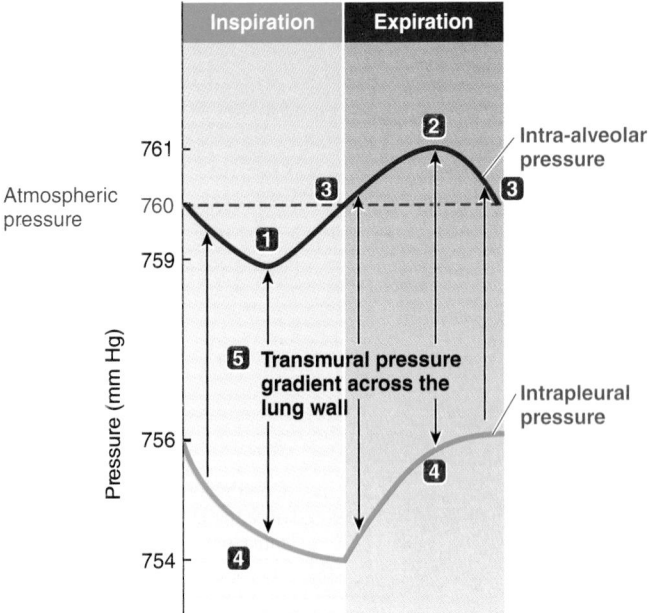

1 During inspiration, intra-alveolar pressure is less than atmospheric pressure.

2 During expiration, intra-alveolar pressure is greater than atmospheric pressure.

3 At the end of both inspiration and expiration, intra-alveolar pressure is equal to atmospheric pressure because the alveoli are in direct communication with the atmosphere, and air continues to flow down its pressure gradient until the two pressures equilibrate.

4 Throughout the respiratory cycle, intrapleural pressure is less than intra-alveolar pressure.

5 Thus, a transmural pressure gradient always exists, and the lung is always stretched to some degree, even during expiration.

● **FIGURE 12-14 Intra-alveolar and intrapleural pressure changes throughout the respiratory cycle.**

increases, a larger pressure gradient must be established to maintain even a normal airflow rate. For example, if resistance is doubled by narrowing of airway lumens, ΔP must be doubled through increased respiratory muscle exertion to induce the same flow rate of air in and out of the lungs as a healthy person accomplishes during quiet breathing. Accordingly, patients with COPD must work harder to breathe.

COPD encompasses three chronic (long-term) diseases: *chronic bronchitis, asthma,* and *emphysema.*

CHRONIC BRONCHITIS **Chronic bronchitis** is a long-term inflammatory condition of the lower respiratory airways, generally triggered by frequent exposure to irritating cigarette smoke, polluted air, or allergens. In response to the chronic irritation, the airways become narrowed by prolonged edematous thickening of the airway linings, coupled with overproduction of thick mucus. Despite frequent coughing associated with the chronic irritation, the plugged mucus often cannot be satisfactorily removed, especially because the irritants immobilize the ciliary mucus escalator (see p. 359). Pulmonary bacterial infec-

tions frequently occur because the accumulated mucus is an excellent medium for bacterial growth.

ASTHMA In **asthma,** airway obstruction is the result of (1) thickening of airway walls, brought about by inflammation and histamine-induced edema (see p. 301 and p. 333); (2) plugging of the airways by excessive secretion of thick mucus; and (3) airway hyperresponsiveness, characterized by profound constriction of the smaller airways caused by trigger-induced spasm of the smooth muscle in the walls of these airways (see p. 355). Triggers that lead to these inflammatory changes, the exaggerated bronchoconstrictor response, or both include repeated exposure to allergens (such as dust mites or pollen), irritants (as in cigarette smoke), respiratory infections, and vigorous exercise. In severe asthmatic attacks, pronounced clogging and narrowing of the airways can cut off all airflow, leading to death. An estimated 15 million people in the United States have asthma, with the number steadily climbing. Asthma is the most common chronic childhood disease.

EMPHYSEMA **Emphysema** is characterized by (1) collapse of the smaller airways and (2) breakdown of alveolar walls. This irreversible condition can arise in two ways. Most commonly, emphysema results from excessive release of protein-digesting enzymes such as *trypsin* from alveolar macrophages as a defense mechanism in response to chronic exposure to inhaled cigarette smoke or other irritants. The lungs are normally protected from damage by these enzymes by α_1-*antitrypsin,* a protein that inhibits trypsin. Excessive secretion of these destructive enzymes in response to chronic irritation, however, can overwhelm the protective capability of α_1-antitrypsin so that these enzymes destroy not only foreign materials but lung tissue as well. Loss of lung tissue leads to the breakdown of alveolar walls and collapse of small airways, which characterize emphysema.

Less frequently, emphysema arises from a genetic inability to produce α_1-antitrypsin so that the lung tissue has no protection from trypsin. The unprotected lung tissue gradually disintegrates under the influence of even small amounts of macrophage-released enzymes, in the absence of chronic exposure to inhaled irritants.

DIFFICULTY IN EXPIRING When COPD of any type increases airway resistance, expiration is more difficult than inspiration. The smaller airways, lacking the cartilaginous rings that hold the larger airways open, are kept open by the same transmural pressure gradient that distends the alveoli. Expansion of the thoracic cavity during inspiration indirectly dilates the airways even further than their expiratory dimensions, like alveolar expansion, so airway resistance is lower during inspiration than during expiration. In a healthy individual, the airway resistance is always so low that the slight variation between inspiration and expiration is not noticeable. When airway resistance has substantially increased, however, as during an asthmatic attack, the difference is quite noticeable. Thus, a person with asthma has more difficulty expiring than inspiring, giving rise to the characteristic "wheeze" as air is forced out through the narrowed airways.

Elastic behavior of the lungs is a result of elastic connective tissue and alveolar surface tension.

During the respiratory cycle, the lungs alternately expand during inspiration and recoil during expiration. What properties of the lungs enable them to behave like balloons, being stretchable and then snapping back to their resting position when the stretching forces are removed? Two interrelated concepts are involved in pulmonary elasticity: compliance and elastic recoil.

The term **compliance** refers to how much effort is required to stretch or distend the lungs and is analogous to how easy or hard it is to blow up a balloon. (By comparison, 100 times more distending pressure is required to inflate a toy balloon than to inflate the lungs.) Specifically, compliance is a measure of how much change in lung volume results from a given change in the transmural pressure gradient, the force that stretches the lungs. A highly compliant lung stretches further for a given increase in the pressure difference than a less compliant lung does. Stated another way, the lower the compliance of the lungs, the larger the transmural pressure gradient that must be created during inspiration to produce normal lung expansion. In turn, a greater-than-normal transmural pressure gradient during inspiration can be achieved only by making the intrapleural pressure more subatmospheric than usual. This is accomplished by greater expansion of the thoracic cavity through more vigorous contraction of the inspiratory muscles. Therefore, the less compliant the lungs are, the more work is required to produce a given degree of inflation. A poorly compliant lung is referred to as a "stiff" lung because it lacks normal stretchability.

 Respiratory compliance can be decreased by several factors, as in *pulmonary fibrosis,* where normal lung tissue is replaced with scar-forming fibrous connective tissue as a result of chronically breathing in asbestos fibers or similar irritants.

The term **elastic recoil** refers to how readily the lungs rebound after having been stretched. It is responsible for the lungs returning to their preinspiratory volume when the inspiratory muscles relax at the end of inspiration.

Pulmonary elastic behavior depends mainly on two factors: *highly elastic connective tissue* in the lungs and *alveolar surface tension.* Pulmonary connective tissue contains large quantities of stretchy elastin fibers (see ● Figure 12-4a, p. 370; also see p. 52). An even more important factor influencing elastic behavior of the lungs is the **alveolar surface tension** displayed by the thin liquid film that lines each alveolus. At an air–water interface, the water molecules at the surface are more strongly attracted to other surrounding water molecules than to the air above the surface. This unequal attraction produces a force known as *surface tension* at the surface of the liquid. Surface tension has a twofold effect. First, the liquid layer resists any force that increases its surface area; that is, it opposes expansion of the alveolus because the surface water molecules oppose being pulled apart. Accordingly, the greater the surface tension, the less compliant the lungs. Second, the liquid surface area tends to shrink as small as possible because the surface water molecules, being preferentially attracted to one another, try to get as close together as possible. Thus, the

surface tension of the liquid lining an alveolus tends to reduce alveolus size, squeezing in on the air inside. This property, along with the rebound of the stretched elastin fibers, produces the lungs' elastic recoil back to their preinspiratory size when inspiration is over.

Pulmonary surfactant decreases surface tension and contributes to lung stability.

The cohesive forces between water molecules are so strong that if the alveoli were lined with water alone, surface tension would be so great that the lungs would collapse. The recoil force attributable to the elastin fibers and high surface tension would exceed the opposing stretching force of the transmural pressure gradient. Furthermore, the lungs would be poorly compliant, so exhausting muscular efforts would be required to accomplish stretching and inflation of the alveoli. The tremendous surface tension of pure water is normally counteracted by pulmonary surfactant.

PULMONARY SURFACTANT **Pulmonary surfactant** is a complex mixture of lipids and proteins secreted by the Type II alveolar cells (see ● Figure 12-4a, p. 370). It intersperses between the water molecules in the fluid lining the alveoli and lowers alveolar surface tension, because the cohesive force between a water molecule and an adjacent pulmonary surfactant molecule is very low. By lowering alveolar surface tension, pulmonary surfactant provides two important benefits: (1) it increases pulmonary compliance, reducing the work of inflating the lungs, and (2) it reduces the lungs' tendency to recoil so that they do not collapse as readily.

The opposing forces acting on the lung (that is, the forces keeping the alveoli open and the countering forces that promote alveolar collapse) are summarized in ▲ Table 12-1.

 NEWBORN RESPIRATORY DISTRESS SYNDROME Developing fetal lungs normally cannot synthesize pulmonary surfactant until late in pregnancy. Especially in an infant born prematurely, not enough pulmonary surfactant may be produced to reduce the alveolar surface tension to manageable levels. The resulting collection of symptoms is termed **newborn respiratory distress syndrome.** The infant must make strenuous inspiratory efforts to overcome the high surface tension in an attempt to inflate the poorly compliant

▲ Table 12-1 Opposing Forces Acting on the Lung

Forces Keeping the Alveoli Open	Forces Promoting Alveolar Collapse
Transmural pressure gradient	Elasticity of stretched pulmonary elastin connective tissue fibers
Pulmonary surfactant (which opposes alveolar surface tension)	Alveolar surface tension

lungs. Moreover, the work of breathing is further increased because the alveoli, in the absence of surfactant, tend to collapse almost completely during each expiration. It is more difficult (requires a greater transmural pressure differential) to expand a collapsed alveolus by a given volume than to increase an already partially expanded alveolus by the same volume. The situation is analogous to blowing up a new balloon. It takes more effort to blow in that first breath of air when starting to blow up a new balloon than to blow additional breaths into the already partially expanded balloon. With newborn respiratory distress syndrome, it is as though with every breath the infant must start blowing up a new balloon. Lung expansion may require transmural pressure gradients of 20 to 30 mm Hg (compared to the normal 4 to 6 mm Hg) to overcome the tendency of surfactant-deprived alveoli to collapse. Worse yet, the newborn's muscles are still weak. The respiratory distress from surfactant deficiency may soon lead to death if breathing efforts become exhausting or inadequate to support sufficient gas exchange.

This life-threatening condition affects 30,000 to 50,000 newborns, primarily premature infants, each year in the United States. Until the surfactant-secreting cells mature sufficiently, the condition is treated by surfactant replacement. In addition, drugs can hasten the maturation process.

The lungs normally operate about "half full."

On average, in healthy young adults, the maximum air that the lungs can hold is about 5.7 liters in males (4.2 liters in females). Anatomic build, age, the distensibility of the lungs, and the presence or absence of respiratory disease affect this total lung capacity. Normally, during quiet breathing, the lungs are nowhere near maximally inflated, nor are they deflated to their minimum volume. Thus, the lungs normally remain moderately inflated throughout the respiratory cycle. At the end of a normal quiet expiration, the lungs still contain about 2200 ml of air. During each typical breath under resting conditions, about 500 ml of air are inspired and the same quantity is expired, so during quiet breathing the lung volume varies from 2200 ml at the end of expiration to 2700 ml at the end of inspiration (● Figure 12-15a). During maximal expiration, lung volume can decrease to 1200 ml in males (1000 ml in females), but the lungs can never be completely deflated because the small airways collapse during forced expirations at low lung volumes, blocking further outflow.

A beneficial outcome of not being able to empty the lungs completely is that even during maximal expiratory efforts gas exchange can continue between the blood flowing through the lungs and the remaining alveolar air. As a result, the gas content of the blood leaving the lungs for delivery to the tissues normally remains remarkably constant throughout the respiratory cycle. By contrast, if the lungs completely filled and emptied with each breath, the amount of O_2 taken up and CO_2 dumped off by the blood would fluctuate widely. Another advantage of the lungs not completely emptying with each breath is the reduced work of breathing. Recall that it takes less effort to inflate a partially inflated alveolus than a totally collapsed one.

The changes in lung volume that occur with different respiratory efforts can be determined by a spirometer. A traditional wet **spirometer** consists of an air-filled drum floating in a water-filled chamber. As the person breathes air in and out of the drum through a tube connecting the mouth to the air chamber, the drum rises and falls in the water chamber. This rise and fall can be recorded as a **spirogram**, which is calibrated to volume changes. Inspiration is recorded as an upward deflection and expiration as a downward deflection. Today, less cumbersome computerized spirometers have replaced the wet spirometer for clinical use, but the principles of the lung volumes and capacities determined by the older instrument are the same, as follows:

Lung Volumes and Capacities ● Figure 12-15b is a hypothetical example of a spirogram in a healthy young adult male. Generally, the values are lower for females. The following lung volumes and lung capacities (a lung capacity is the sum of two or more lung volumes) can be determined:

■ **Tidal volume (TV).** The volume of air entering or leaving the lungs during a single breath. Average value under resting conditions = 500 ml.

■ **Inspiratory reserve volume (IRV).** The extra volume of air that can be maximally inspired over and above the typical resting tidal volume. The IRV is accomplished by maximal contraction of the diaphragm, external intercostal muscles, and accessory inspiratory muscles. Average value = 3000 ml.

■ **Inspiratory capacity (IC).** The maximum volume of air that can be inspired at the end of a normal quiet expiration (IC = IRV + TV). Average value = 3500 ml.

■ **Expiratory reserve volume (ERV).** The extra volume of air that can be actively expired by maximally contracting the expiratory muscles beyond that normally passively expired at the end of a typical resting tidal volume. Average value = 1000 ml.

■ **Residual volume (RV).** The minimum volume of air remaining in the lungs even after a maximal expiration. Average value = 1200 ml. The residual volume cannot be measured directly with a spirometer, because this volume of air does not move into and out of the lungs. It can be determined indirectly, however, through gas-dilution techniques involving inspiration of a known quantity of a harmless tracer gas such as helium.

■ **Functional residual capacity (FRC).** The volume of air in the lungs at the end of a normal passive expiration (FRC = ERV + RV). Average value = 2200 ml.

■ **Vital capacity (VC).** The maximum volume of air that can be moved out during a single breath following a maximal inspiration. The subject first inspires maximally and then expires maximally (VC = IRV + TV + ERV). The VC represents the maximum volume change possible within the lungs. It is rarely used, because the maximal muscle contractions involved become exhausting, but it is valuable in determining the functional capacity of the lungs. Average value = 4500 ml.

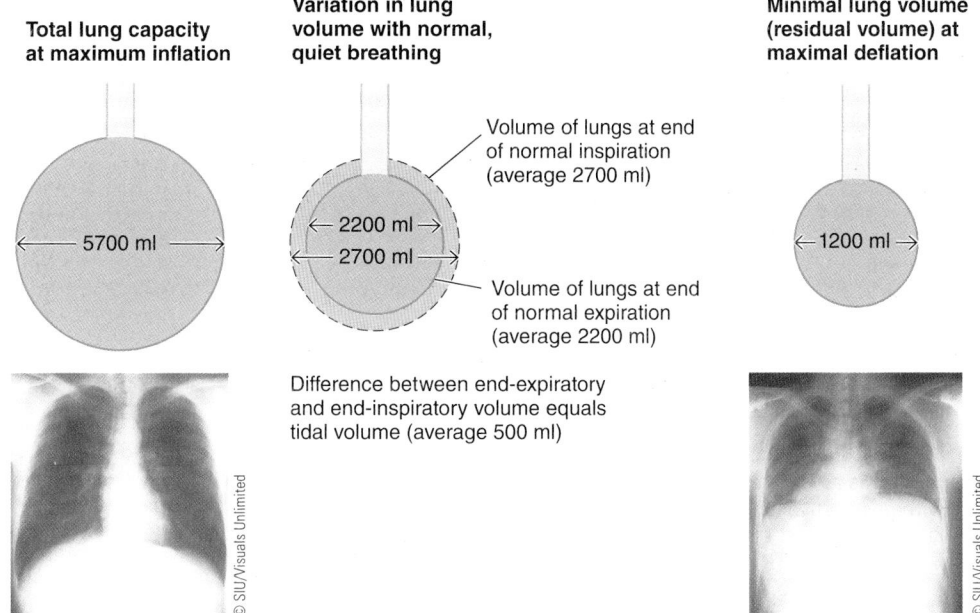

Total lung capacity at maximum inflation

5700 ml

Variation in lung volume with normal, quiet breathing

Volume of lungs at end of normal inspiration (average 2700 ml)

2200 ml
2700 ml

Volume of lungs at end of normal expiration (average 2200 ml)

Difference between end-expiratory and end-inspiratory volume equals tidal volume (average 500 ml)

Minimal lung volume (residual volume) at maximal deflation

1200 ml

© SIU/Visuals Unlimited

© SIU/Visuals Unlimited

(a) Normal range and extremes of lung volume in a healthy young adult male

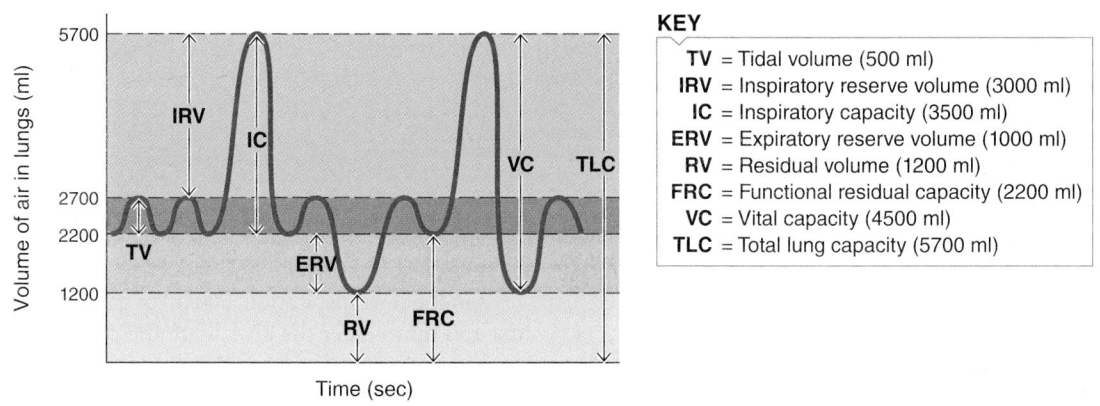

KEY

TV	= Tidal volume (500 ml)
IRV	= Inspiratory reserve volume (3000 ml)
IC	= Inspiratory capacity (3500 ml)
ERV	= Expiratory reserve volume (1000 ml)
RV	= Residual volume (1200 ml)
FRC	= Functional residual capacity (2200 ml)
VC	= Vital capacity (4500 ml)
TLC	= Total lung capacity (5700 ml)

(b) Normal spirogram of a healthy young adult male

● **FIGURE 12-15 Variations in lung volume in a healthy young adult male.** Values for females are somewhat lower. (Note that residual volume cannot be measured with a spirometer but must be determined by another means.)

■ **Total lung capacity (TLC).** The maximum volume of air that the lungs can hold (TLC = VC + RV). Average value = 5700 ml.

■ **Forced expiratory volume in 1 second (FEV$_1$).** The volume of air that can be expired during the first second of expiration in a VC determination. Usually, FEV$_1$ is about 80% of VC; that is, normally 80% of the air that can be forcibly expired from maximally inflated lungs can be expired within 1 second. This measurement indicates the maximal airflow rate possible from the lungs.

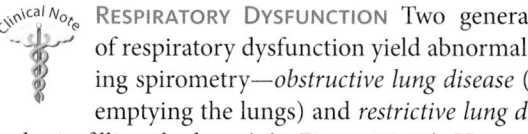

RESPIRATORY DYSFUNCTION Two general categories of respiratory dysfunction yield abnormal results during spirometry—*obstructive lung disease* (difficulty in emptying the lungs) and *restrictive lung disease* (difficulty in filling the lungs) (● Figure 12-16). However, these are not the only categories of respiratory dysfunction, nor is spirometry the only pulmonary function test. Other conditions affecting respiratory function include (1) diseases impairing diffusion of O_2 and CO_2 across the pulmonary membranes; (2) reduced ventilation because of mechanical failure, as with neuromuscular disorders affecting the respiratory muscles; (3) inadequate perfusion (failure of adequate pulmonary blood flow); or (4) ventilation–perfusion imbalances involving a poor matching of air and blood so that efficient gas exchange cannot occur. Some lung diseases are actually a complex mixture of different types of functional disturbances. To determine what abnormalities are present, the diagnostician relies on a variety of pulmonary function tests in addition to spirometry, including X-ray examination, blood-gas determinations, and tests to measure the diffusion capacity of the alveolar capillary membrane.

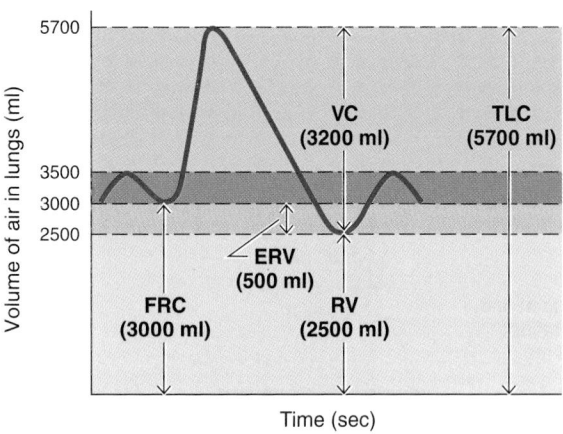

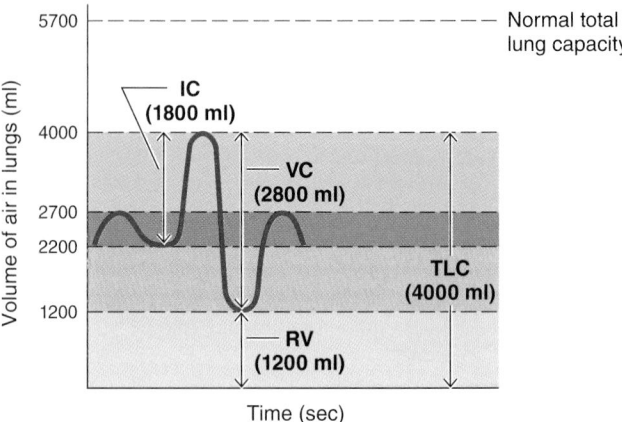

(a) Spirogram in obstructive lung disease

(b) Spirogram in restrictive lung disease

● FIGURE 12-16 **Abnormal spirograms associated with obstructive and restrictive lung diseases.** (a) Because a patient with obstructive lung disease has more difficulty emptying the lungs than filling them, the total lung capacity (TLC) is essentially normal, but the functional residual capacity (FRC) and the residual volume (RV) are elevated due to additional air trapped in the lungs following expiration. Another common finding is a markedly reduced forced expiratory volume in 1 second (FEV_1) because the airflow rate is reduced by the airway obstruction. (b) In restrictive lung disease, the lungs are less compliant than normal. TLC, inspiratory capacity (IC) and vital capacity (VC) are reduced because the lungs cannot be expanded as normal.

Alveolar ventilation is less than pulmonary ventilation because of dead space.

Various changes in lung volume represent only one factor in determining **pulmonary ventilation,** which is the volume of air breathed in and out in 1 minute. The other important factor is **respiratory rate,** which averages 12 breaths per minute:

Pulmonary ventilation = tidal volume × respiratory rate

(ml/min)   (ml/breath)   (breaths/min)

At an average tidal volume of 500 ml/breath and a respiratory rate of 12 breaths/min, pulmonary ventilation is 6000 ml, or 6 L, of air breathed in and out in 1 minute under resting conditions. For a brief period, a healthy young adult male can voluntarily increase his total pulmonary ventilation 25-fold, to 150 L/min. To increase pulmonary ventilation, both tidal volume and respiratory rate increase, but depth of breathing increases more than frequency of breathing. It is usually more advantageous to have a greater increase in tidal volume than in respiratory rate because of anatomic dead space, discussed next.

ANATOMIC DEAD SPACE Not all the inspired air gets down to the site of gas exchange in the alveoli. Part remains in the conducting airways, where it is not available for gas exchange. The volume of the conducting passages in an adult averages about 150 ml. This volume is considered **anatomic dead space** because air within these conducting airways is useless for exchange. Anatomic dead space greatly affects the efficiency of pulmonary ventilation. In effect, even though 500 ml of air are moved in and out with each breath, only 350 ml are actually exchanged between the atmosphere and the alveoli because of the 150 ml occupying the anatomic dead space.

Looking at ● Figure 12-17, note that at the end of inspiration the respiratory airways are filled with 150 ml of fresh atmospheric

air from the inspiration. During the subsequent expiration, 500 ml of air are expired to the atmosphere. The first 150 ml expired are the fresh air that was retained in the airways and never used. The remaining 350 ml expired are "old" alveolar air that has participated in gas exchange with the blood. During the same expiration, 500 ml of gas also leave the alveoli. The first 350 ml are expired to the atmosphere; the other 150 ml of old alveolar air never reach the outside but remain in the conducting airways.

On the next inspiration, 500 ml of gas enter the alveoli. The first 150 ml to enter the alveoli are the old alveolar air that remained in the dead space during the preceding expiration. The other 350 ml entering the alveoli are fresh air inspired from the atmosphere. Simultaneously, 500 ml of air enter from the atmosphere. The first 350 ml of atmospheric air reach the alveoli; the other 150 ml remain in the conducting airways to be expired without benefit of being exchanged with the blood, as the cycle repeats itself.

ALVEOLAR VENTILATION Because the amount of atmospheric air that reaches the alveoli and is actually available for exchange with blood is more important than the total amount breathed in and out, **alveolar ventilation**—the volume of air exchanged between the atmosphere and the alveoli per minute—is more important than pulmonary ventilation. In determining alveolar ventilation, the amount of wasted air moved in and out through the anatomic dead space must be taken into account, as follows:

Alveolar ventilation = (tidal volume − dead space volume) × respiratory rate

With average resting values,

Alveolar ventilation = (500 ml/breath − 150 ml dead space volume) × 12 breaths/min

= 4200 ml/min

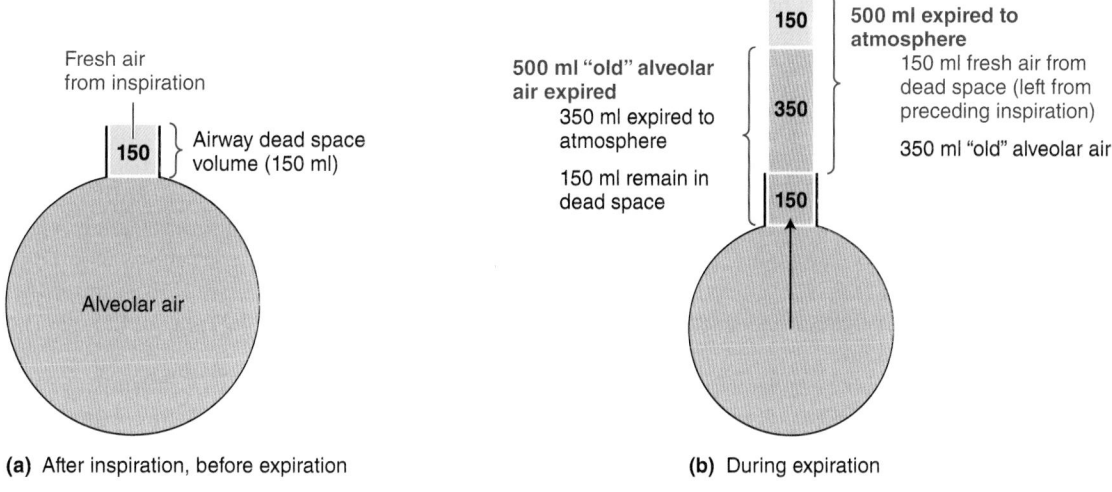

(a) After inspiration, before expiration

(b) During expiration

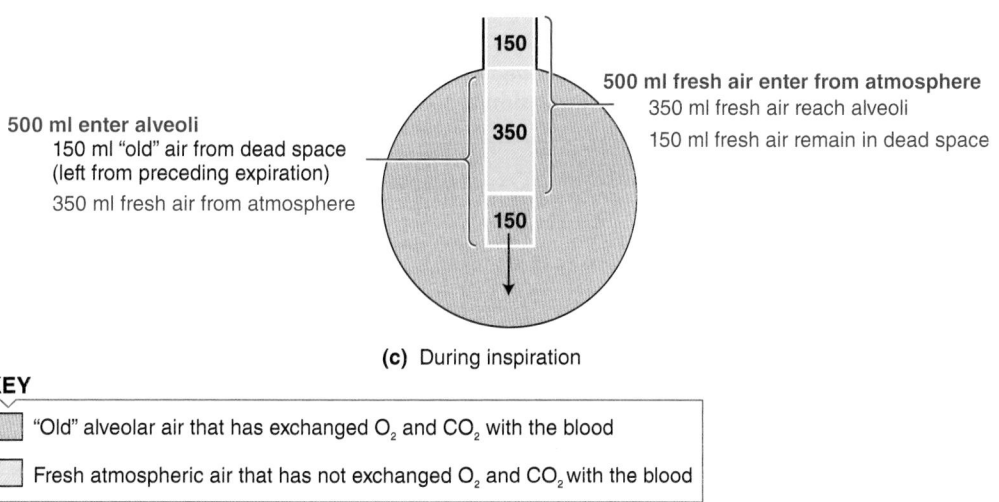

(c) During inspiration

KEY

	"Old" alveolar air that has exchanged O_2 and CO_2 with the blood
	Fresh atmospheric air that has not exchanged O_2 and CO_2 with the blood

● **FIGURE 12-17 Effect of dead space volume on exchange of tidal volume between the atmosphere and the alveoli.** Even though 500 ml of air move in and out between the atmosphere and the respiratory system and 500 ml move in and out of the alveoli with each breath, only 350 ml are actually exchanged between the atmosphere and the alveoli because of the anatomic dead space (the volume of air in the respiratory airways).

▲ Table 12-2   Effect of Different Breathing Patterns on Alveolar Ventilation

Breathing Pattern	Tidal Volume (ml/breath)	Respiratory Rate (breaths/min)	Dead Space Volume (ml)	Pulmonary Ventilation (ml/min)*	Alveolar Ventilation (ml/min)**
Quiet breathing at rest	500	12	150	6000	4200
Deep, slow breathing	1200	5	150	6000	5250
Shallow, rapid breathing	150	40	150	6000	0

*Equals tidal volume × respiratory rate.
**Equals (tidal volume − dead space volume) × respiratory rate.

Thus, with quiet breathing, alveolar ventilation is 4200 ml/min, whereas pulmonary ventilation is 6000 ml/min.

EFFECT OF BREATHING PATTERNS ON ALVEOLAR VENTILATION
To understand how important dead space volume is in deter-

mining the magnitude of alveolar ventilation, examine the effect of various breathing patterns on alveolar ventilation, as shown in ▲ Table 12-2. If a person deliberately breathes deeply (for example, a tidal volume of 1200 ml) and slowly (for example, a respiratory rate of 5 breaths/min), pulmonary ventilation is 6000 ml/min, the same as during quiet breathing at rest, but alveolar ventilation increases to 5250 ml/min compared to the resting rate of 4200 ml/min. In contrast, if a person deliberately breathes shallowly (for example, a tidal volume of 150 ml) and rapidly (a frequency of 40 breaths/min), pulmonary ventilation would still be 6000 ml/min; however, alveolar ventilation would be 0 ml/min. In effect, the person would only be drawing air in and out of the anatomic dead space without any atmospheric air being exchanged with the alveoli, where it could be useful. The individual could voluntarily maintain such a breathing pattern for only a few minutes before losing consciousness, at which time normal breathing would resume.

The value of reflexly bringing about a larger increase in depth of breathing than in rate of breathing when pulmonary ventilation increases during exercise should now be apparent. It is the most efficient means of elevating alveolar ventilation. When tidal volume increases, the entire increase goes toward elevating alveolar ventilation, whereas an increase in respiratory rate does not go entirely toward increasing alveolar ventilation. When respiratory rate increases, the frequency with which air is wasted in the dead space also increases, because a portion of *each breath* must move in and out of the dead space. As needs vary, ventilation is normally adjusted to a tidal volume and respiratory rate that meet those needs most efficiently in terms of energy cost.

We have now completed our discussion of respiratory mechanics—all the factors involved in ventilation. We next examine gas exchange between the alveolar air and the blood and then between the blood and the systemic tissues.

Gas Exchange

The purpose of breathing is to provide a continual supply of fresh O_2 for pickup by the blood and to constantly remove CO_2 unloaded from the blood. Blood acts as a transport system for O_2 and CO_2 between the lungs and the tissues, with the tissue cells extracting O_2 from the blood and eliminating CO_2 into it.

Gases move down partial pressure gradients.

Gas exchange at both the pulmonary capillary and the tissue capillary levels involves simple passive diffusion of O_2 and CO_2 down *partial pressure gradients*. No active transport mechanisms exist for these gases. Let us see what partial pressure gradients are and how they are established.

PARTIAL PRESSURES Atmospheric air is a mixture of gases; typical dry air contains about 79% nitrogen (N_2) and 21% O_2, with almost negligible percentages of CO_2, H_2O vapor, other gases, and pollutants. Altogether, these gases exert a total atmospheric pressure of 760 mm Hg at sea level. This total pressure is equal to the sum of the pressures that each gas in the mixture partially contributes. The pressure exerted by a particular gas is directly proportional to the percentage of that gas in the total air mixture. Every gas molecule, no matter what its size, exerts the same amount of pressure; for example, a N_2 molecule exerts the same pressure as an O_2 molecule. Because 79% of the air consists of N_2 molecules, 79% of the 760 mm Hg atmospheric pressure, or

600 mm Hg, is exerted by the N_2 molecules. Similarly, because O_2 represents 21% of the atmosphere, 21% of the 760 mm Hg atmospheric pressure, or 160 mm Hg, is exerted by O_2 (● Figure 12-18). The individual pressure exerted independently by a particular gas within a mixture of gases is known as its **partial pressure,** designated by P_{gas}. Thus, the partial pressure of O_2 in atmospheric air, P_{O_2}, is normally 160 mm Hg. The atmospheric partial pressure of CO_2, P_{CO_2}, is negligible at 0.23 mm Hg.

Gases dissolved in a liquid such as blood or another body fluid also exert a partial pressure. The greater the partial pressure of a gas in a liquid is, the more of that gas is dissolved.

PARTIAL PRESSURE GRADIENTS A difference in partial pressure between the capillary blood and the surrounding structures is known as a **partial pressure gradient.** Partial pressure gradients exist between the alveolar air and the pulmonary capillary blood. Similarly, partial pressure gradients exist between the systemic capillary blood and the surrounding tissues. A gas always diffuses down its partial pressure gradient from the area of higher partial pressure to the area of lower partial pressure, similar to diffusion down a concentration gradient.

Oxygen enters and CO_2 leaves the blood in the lungs passively down partial pressure gradients.

We first consider the magnitude of alveolar P_{O_2} and P_{CO_2} and then look at the partial pressure gradients that move these two gases between the alveoli and the incoming pulmonary capillary blood.

ALVEOLAR P_{O_2} AND P_{CO_2} Alveolar air is not of the same composition as inspired atmospheric air, for two reasons. First, as soon as atmospheric air enters the respiratory passages, exposure to

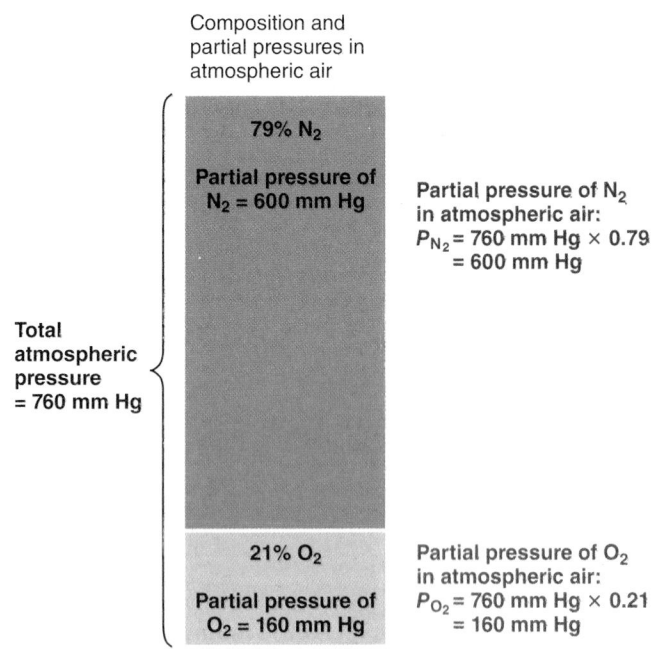

● **FIGURE 12-18 Concept of partial pressures.** The partial pressure exerted by each gas in a mixture equals the total pressure times the fractional composition of the gas in the mixture.

the moist airways saturates it with H_2O. Like any other gas, water vapor exerts a partial pressure. Humidification of inspired air in effect "dilutes" the partial pressure of the inspired gases, because the sum of the partial pressures must total the atmospheric pressure. Second, alveolar P_{O_2} is also lower than atmospheric P_{O_2} because fresh inspired air (average volume equals 350 ml out of the tidal volume of 500 ml) is mixed with the large volume of old air that remained in the lungs at the end of the preceding expiration (average volume equals 2200 ml; the functional residual capacity). At the end of inspiration, only about 13% of the air in the alveoli is fresh air. As a result of humidification and the small turnover of alveolar air, the average alveolar P_{O_2} is 100 mm Hg, compared to the atmospheric P_{O_2} of 160 mm Hg.

It is logical to think that alveolar P_{O_2} would increase during inspiration with the arrival of fresh air and would decrease during expiration. Only small fluctuations occur, however, for two reasons. First, only a small proportion of the total alveolar air is exchanged with each breath. The relatively small volume of inspired, high-P_{O_2} air is quickly mixed with the larger volume of retained alveolar air, which has a lower P_{O_2}. Thus, the O_2 in the inspired air can only slightly elevate the level of the total alveolar P_{O_2}. Even this potentially small elevation of P_{O_2} is diminished for another reason. Oxygen is continually moving by passive diffusion down its partial pressure gradient from the alveoli into the blood. The O_2 arriving in the alveoli in the newly inspired air simply replaces the O_2 diffusing out of the alveoli into the pulmonary capillaries. Therefore, alveolar P_{O_2} remains relatively constant around 100 mm Hg throughout the respiratory cycle. Because pulmonary blood P_{O_2} equilibrates with alveolar P_{O_2}, the P_{O_2} of the blood leaving the lungs likewise remains fairly constant at this same value. Accordingly, the amount of O_2 in the blood available to the tissues varies only slightly during the respiratory cycle.

A similar situation exists in reverse for CO_2. Carbon dioxide, which is continuously produced by the body tissues as a metabolic waste product, is constantly added to the blood at the level of the systemic capillaries. In the pulmonary capillaries, CO_2 diffuses down its partial pressure gradient from the blood into the alveoli and is subsequently removed from the body during expiration. As with O_2, alveolar P_{CO_2} remains fairly constant throughout the respiratory cycle but at a lower value of 40 mm Hg.

P_{O_2} AND P_{CO_2} GRADIENTS ACROSS THE PULMONARY CAPILLARIES
As blood passes through the lungs, it picks up O_2 and gives up CO_2 simply by diffusion down partial pressure gradients between blood and alveoli. Ventilation constantly replenishes alveolar O_2 and removes CO_2, thus maintaining the appropriate gradients to ensure this diffusion. Blood entering the pulmonary capillaries is systemic venous blood pumped to the lungs through the pulmonary arteries. This blood, having just returned from the body tissues, is relatively low in O_2, with a P_{O_2} of 40 mm Hg, and is relatively high in CO_2, with a P_{CO_2} of 46 mm Hg. As this blood flows through the pulmonary capillaries, it is exposed to alveolar air (● Figure 12-19). Because the alveolar P_{O_2} at 100 mm Hg is higher than the P_{O_2} of 40 mm Hg

in the blood entering the lungs, O_2 diffuses down its partial pressure gradient from the alveoli into the blood until no further gradient exists. As blood leaves the pulmonary capillaries, it has a P_{O_2} equal to alveolar P_{O_2} at 100 mm Hg.

The partial pressure gradient for CO_2 is in the opposite direction. Blood entering the pulmonary capillaries has a P_{CO_2} of 46 mm Hg, whereas alveolar P_{CO_2} is only 40 mm Hg. Carbon dioxide diffuses from the blood into the alveoli until blood P_{CO_2} equilibrates with alveolar P_{CO_2}. Thus, blood leaving the pulmonary capillaries has a P_{CO_2} of 40 mm Hg. After leaving the lungs, the blood, which now has a P_{O_2} of 100 mm Hg and a P_{CO_2} of 40 mm Hg, is returned to the heart and then pumped out to the body tissues as systemic arterial blood.

Note that blood returning to the lungs from the tissues still contains O_2 (P_{O_2} of systemic venous blood = 40 mm Hg) and that blood leaving the lungs still contains CO_2 (P_{CO_2} of systemic arterial blood = 40 mm Hg). The extra O_2 carried in the blood beyond that normally given up to the tissues represents an immediately available O_2 reserve that can be tapped by the tissue cells whenever their O_2 demands increase. The CO_2 remaining in the blood even after passage through the lungs plays an important role in the acid–base balance of the body, because CO_2 generates carbonic acid. Furthermore, arterial P_{CO_2} is important in driving respiration. This mechanism is described later.

The amount of O_2 picked up in the lungs matches the amount extracted and used by the tissues. When the tissues metabolize more actively (for example, during exercise), they extract more O_2 from the blood, reducing the systemic venous P_{O_2} even lower than 40 mm Hg—for example, to a P_{O_2} of 30 mm Hg. When this blood returns to the lungs, a larger-than-normal P_{O_2} gradient exists between the newly entering blood and the alveolar air. The difference in P_{O_2} between alveoli and blood is now 70 mm Hg (alveolar P_{O_2} of 100 mm Hg and blood P_{O_2} of 30 mm Hg), compared to the normal P_{O_2} gradient of 60 mm Hg (alveolar P_{O_2} of 100 mm Hg and blood P_{O_2} of 40 mm Hg). Therefore, more O_2 diffuses from the alveoli into the blood down the larger partial pressure gradient before blood P_{O_2} equals alveolar P_{O_2}. This additional transfer of O_2 into the blood replaces the increased amount of O_2 consumed, so O_2 uptake matches O_2 use even when O_2 consumption increases. As more O_2 is diffusing from the alveoli into the blood because of the increased partial pressure gradient, ventilation is stimulated so that O_2 enters the alveoli more rapidly from the atmosphere to replace the O_2 diffusing into the blood. Similarly, the amount of CO_2 given up to the alveoli from the blood matches the amount of CO_2 picked up at the tissues.

Factors other than the partial pressure gradient influence the rate of gas transfer.

We have been discussing diffusion of O_2 and CO_2 between alveoli and blood as if these gases' partial pressure gradients were the sole determinants of their rates of diffusion. According to Fick's law of diffusion, the diffusion rate of a gas through a sheet of tissue also depends on the surface area and thickness of the membrane through which the gas is diffusing, with the rate of diffusion decreasing as surface area decreases or thickness in-

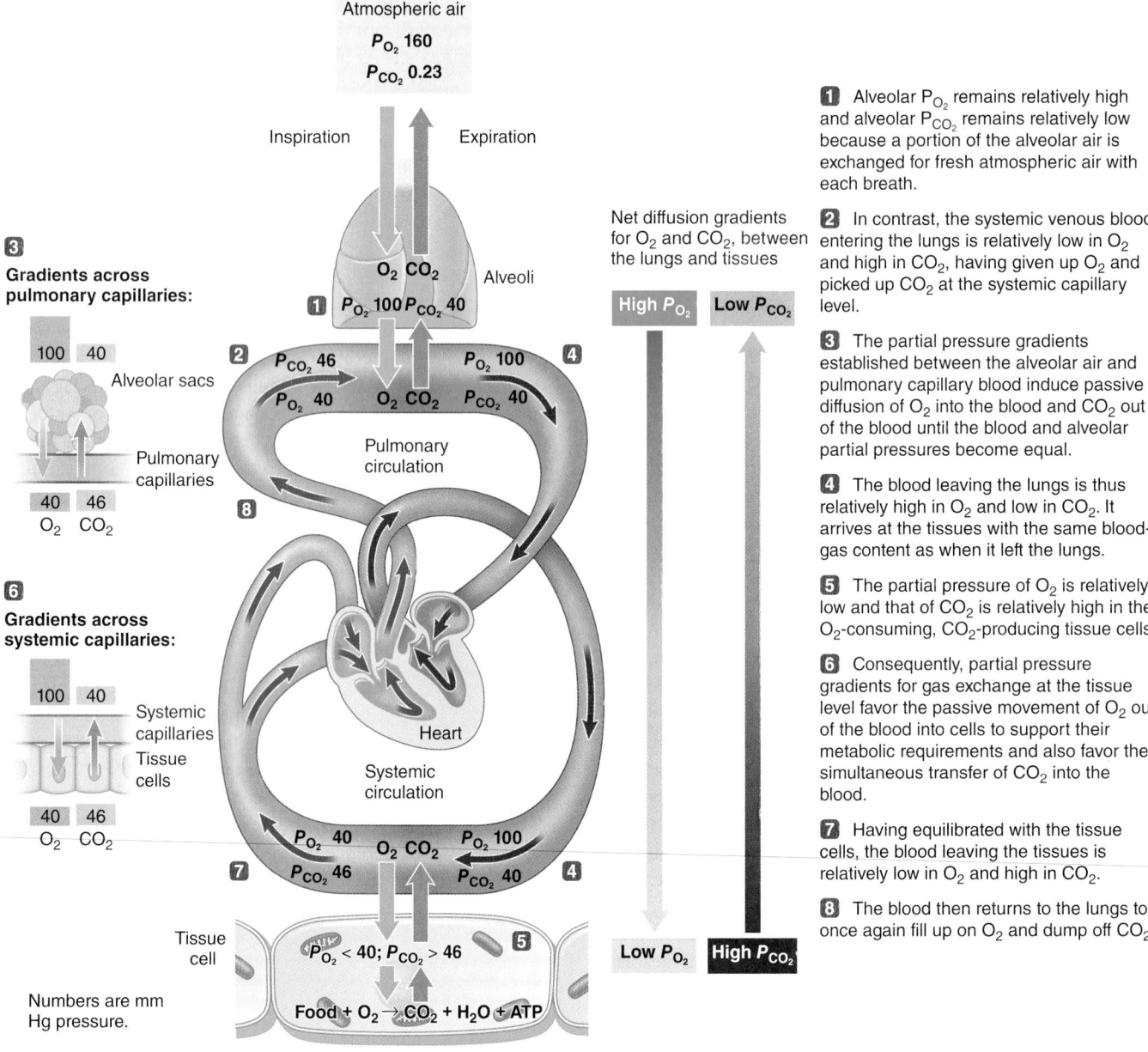

Atmospheric air
P_{O_2} 160
P_{CO_2} 0.23

Inspiration   Expiration

3

Gradients across
pulmonary capillaries:

100   40

Alveolar sacs

40   46
O_2 CO_2

Pulmonary
capillaries

6

Gradients across
systemic capillaries:

100   40

Systemic
capillaries

Tissue
cells

40   46
O_2 CO_2

Numbers are mm
Hg pressure.

Alveoli

1 P_{O_2} 100 P_{CO_2} 40

2 P_{CO_2} 46 ... P_{O_2} 100 **4**

P_{O_2} 40 O_2 CO_2 P_{CO_2} 40

Pulmonary
circulation

8

Heart

Systemic
circulation

P_{O_2} 40 O_2 CO_2 P_{O_2} 100

7 P_{CO_2} 46 ... P_{CO_2} 40 **4**

5 $P_{O_2} < 40;\ P_{CO_2} > 46$

Tissue
cell

Food + $O_2 \rightarrow CO_2 + H_2O$ + ATP

Net diffusion gradients
for O_2 and CO_2, between
the lungs and tissues

High P_{O_2} Low P_{CO_2}

Low P_{O_2} High P_{CO_2}

1 Alveolar P_{O_2} remains relatively high and alveolar P_{CO_2} remains relatively low because a portion of the alveolar air is exchanged for fresh atmospheric air with each breath.

2 In contrast, the systemic venous blood entering the lungs is relatively low in O_2 and high in CO_2, having given up O_2 and picked up CO_2 at the systemic capillary level.

3 The partial pressure gradients established between the alveolar air and pulmonary capillary blood induce passive diffusion of O_2 into the blood and CO_2 out of the blood until the blood and alveolar partial pressures become equal.

4 The blood leaving the lungs is thus relatively high in O_2 and low in CO_2. It arrives at the tissues with the same blood-gas content as when it left the lungs.

5 The partial pressure of O_2 is relatively low and that of CO_2 is relatively high in the O_2-consuming, CO_2-producing tissue cells.

6 Consequently, partial pressure gradients for gas exchange at the tissue level favor the passive movement of O_2 out of the blood into cells to support their metabolic requirements and also favor the simultaneous transfer of CO_2 into the blood.

7 Having equilibrated with the tissue cells, the blood leaving the tissues is relatively low in O_2 and high in CO_2.

8 The blood then returns to the lungs to once again fill up on O_2 and dump off CO_2.

● **FIGURE 12-19 Oxygen and CO_2 exchange across pulmonary and systemic capillaries caused by partial pressure gradients.**

creases. Because these other factors are relatively constant under resting conditions in a healthy lung, changes in the rate of gas exchange normally are determined primarily by changes in partial pressure gradients between blood and alveoli.

Clinical Note However, several pathological conditions can markedly reduce pulmonary surface area and, in turn, decrease the rate of gas exchange. Most notably, in *emphysema* surface area is reduced because many alveolar walls are lost, resulting in larger but fewer chambers (● Figure 12-20).

Inadequate gas exchange can also occur when the thickness of the barrier separating the air and blood is pathologically increased. Thickness increases in (1) *pulmonary edema,* an excess accumulation of interstitial fluid between the alveoli and the pulmonary capillaries caused by pulmonary inflammation or

left-sided congestive heart failure (see p. 268); (2) *pulmonary fibrosis,* involving replacement of delicate lung tissue with thick, fibrous tissue in response to certain chronic irritants; and (3) *pneumonia,* which is characterized by inflammatory fluid accumulation within or around the alveoli.

Gas exchange across the systemic capillaries also occurs down partial pressure gradients.

Just as they do at the pulmonary capillaries, O_2 and CO_2 move between the systemic capillary blood and the tissue cells by simple passive diffusion down partial pressure gradients. Refer again to ● Figure 12-19. The arterial blood that reaches the systemic capillaries is essentially the same blood that left the lungs by means of the pulmonary veins, because the only two

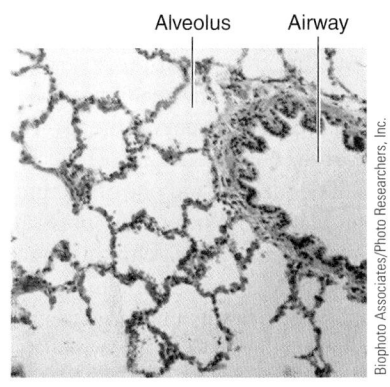

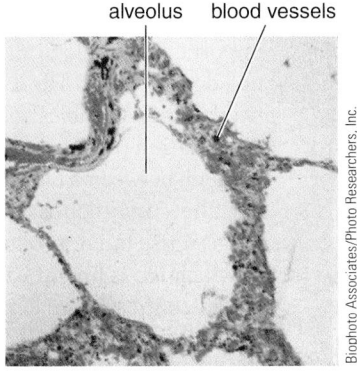

(a) Normal lung tissue   **(b)** Lung tissue in emphysema

● **FIGURE 12-20 Comparison of normal and emphysematous lung tissue.** (a) Each of the smallest clear spaces is an alveolar lumen in normal lung tissue. (b) Note the loss of alveolar walls in the emphysematous lung tissue, resulting in larger but fewer alveolar chambers.

places in the entire circulatory system at which gas exchange can take place are the pulmonary capillaries and the systemic capillaries. The arterial P_{O_2} is 100 mm Hg, and the arterial P_{CO_2} is 40 mm Hg, the same as alveolar P_{O_2} and P_{CO_2}.

P_{O_2} AND P_{CO_2} GRADIENTS ACROSS THE SYSTEMIC CAPILLARIES Cells constantly consume O_2 and produce CO_2 through oxidative metabolism. Cellular P_{O_2} averages about 40 mm Hg and P_{CO_2} about 46 mm Hg, although these values are highly variable, depending on the level of cellular metabolic activity. Oxygen moves by diffusion down its partial pressure gradient from the entering systemic capillary blood (P_{O_2} = 100 mm Hg) into the adjacent cells (P_{O_2} = 40 mm Hg) until equilibrium is reached. Therefore, the P_{O_2} of venous blood leaving the systemic capillaries is equal to the tissue P_{O_2} at an average of 40 mm Hg.

The reverse situation exists for CO_2. Carbon dioxide rapidly diffuses out of the cells (P_{CO_2} = 46 mm Hg) into the entering capillary blood (P_{CO_2} = 40 mm Hg) down the partial pressure gradient created by the ongoing production of CO_2. Transfer of CO_2 continues until blood P_{CO_2} equilibrates with tissue P_{CO_2}.[1] Accordingly, blood leaving the systemic capillaries has an average P_{CO_2} of 46 mm Hg. This systemic venous blood, which is relatively low in O_2 (P_{CO_2} = 40 mm Hg) and relatively high in CO_2 (P_{CO_2} = 46 mm Hg), returns to the heart and is subsequently pumped to the lungs as the cycle repeats itself.

The more actively a tissue is metabolizing, the lower the cellular P_{O_2} falls and the higher the cellular P_{CO_2} rises. As a consequence of the larger blood-to-cell partial pressure gradients, more O_2 diffuses from the blood into the cells, and more CO_2 moves in the opposite direction before blood P_{O_2} and P_{CO_2} achieve equilibrium with the surrounding cells. Thus, the

---

[1]Actually, the partial pressures of the systemic blood gases never completely equilibrate with tissue P_{O_2} and P_{CO_2}. Because the cells are constantly consuming O_2 and producing CO_2, the tissue P_{O_2} is always slightly less than the P_{O_2} of the blood leaving the systemic capillaries, and the tissue P_{CO_2} always slightly exceeds the systemic venous P_{CO_2}.

amount of O_2 transferred to the cells and the amount of CO_2 carried away from the cells both depend on the rate of cellular metabolism.

NET DIFFUSION OF O_2 AND CO_2 BETWEEN ALVEOLI AND TISSUES Net diffusion of O_2 occurs first between alveoli and blood and then between blood and tissues because of the O_2 partial pressure gradients created by continuous replenishment of fresh alveolar O_2 provided by alveolar ventilation and continuous use of O_2 in the cells. Net diffusion of CO_2 occurs in the reverse direction, first between tissues and blood and then between blood and alveoli because of the CO_2 partial pressure gradients created by continuous production of CO_2 in the cells and continuous removal of alveolar CO_2 through the process of alveolar ventilation (see ● Figure 12-19).

Now let us see how O_2 and CO_2 are transported in the blood between alveoli and tissues.

Gas Transport

Oxygen picked up by the blood at the lungs must be transported to the tissues for cell use. Conversely, CO_2 produced at the cell level must be transported to the lungs for elimination.

Most O_2 in the blood is transported bound to hemoglobin.

Oxygen is present in the blood in two forms: physically dissolved and chemically bound to hemoglobin (▲ Table 12-3).

PHYSICALLY DISSOLVED O_2 Little O_2 physically dissolves in plasma water, because O_2 is poorly soluble in body fluids. The amount dissolved is directly proportional to the P_{O_2} of the blood: the higher the P_{O_2}, the more O_2 dissolved. At a normal arterial P_{O_2} of 100 mm Hg, only 3 ml of O_2 can dissolve in 1 liter of blood. Thus, only 15 ml of O_2 can dissolve per minute in the normal pulmonary blood flow of 5 liters/min (the resting cardiac output). Even under resting conditions, the cells consume 250 ml of O_2 per minute, and consumption may increase up to 25-fold during strenuous exercise. To deliver the O_2 needed by the tissues even at rest, the cardiac output would have to be

▲ Table 12-3 **Methods of Gas Transport in the Blood**

Gas	Method of Transport in Blood	Percentage Carried in This Form
O_2	Physically dissolved	1.5
	Bound to hemoglobin	98.5
CO_2	Physically dissolved	10
	Bound to hemoglobin	30
	As bicarbonate (HCO_3^-)	60

83.3 liters/min if O_2 could only be transported in dissolved form. Obviously, there must be an additional mechanism for transporting O_2 to the tissues. This mechanism is *hemoglobin (Hb)*. Only 1.5% of the O_2 in the blood is dissolved; the remaining 98.5% is transported in combination with Hb. *The O_2 bound to Hb does not contribute to the P_{O_2} of the blood;* thus, blood P_{O_2} is not a measure of the total O_2 content of the blood but only of the dissolved portion of O_2.

OXYGEN BOUND TO HEMOGLOBIN Hemoglobin, an iron-bearing protein molecule contained within the red blood cells, can form a loose, easily reversible combination with O_2 (see p. 319). When not combined with O_2, Hb is referred to as **reduced hemoglobin,** or **deoxyhemoglobin;** when combined with O_2, it is called **oxyhemoglobin (HbO$_2$):**

$$Hb + O_2 \rightleftharpoons HbO_2$$

$$\text{reduced hemoglobin} \qquad \text{oxyhemoglobin}$$

We need to answer several questions about the role of Hb in O_2 transport. What determines whether O_2 and Hb are combined or dissociated (separated)? Why does Hb combine with O_2 in the lungs and release O_2 at the tissues? How can a variable amount of O_2 be released at the tissues, depending on the level of tissue activity? How can we talk about O_2 transfer between blood and surrounding tissues in terms of O_2 partial pressure gradients when 98.5% of the O_2 is bound to Hb and thus does not contribute to the P_{O_2} of the blood?

The P_{O_2} is the primary factor determining the percent hemoglobin saturation.

Each of the four atoms of iron within the heme portions of a hemoglobin molecule can combine with an O_2 molecule, so each Hb molecule can carry up to four molecules of O_2. Hemoglobin is considered *fully saturated* when all the Hb present is carrying its maximum O_2 load. The **percent hemoglobin (% Hb) saturation,** a measure of the extent to which the Hb present is combined with O_2, can vary from 0% to 100%.

The most important factor determining the % Hb saturation is the P_{O_2} of the blood, which in turn is related to the concentration of O_2 physically dissolved in the blood. According to the **law of mass action,** if the concentration of one substance involved in a reversible reaction is increased, the reaction is driven toward the opposite side. Conversely, if the concentration of one substance is decreased, the reaction is driven toward that side. Applying this law to the reversible reaction involving Hb and O_2 (Hb + $O_2 \rightleftharpoons$ HbO$_2$), when blood P_{O_2} increases, as in the pulmonary capillaries, the reaction is driven toward the right side of the equation, increasing formation of HbO$_2$ (increased % Hb saturation). When blood P_{O_2} decreases, as in the systemic capillaries, the reaction is driven toward the left side of the equation and oxygen is released from Hb as HbO$_2$ dissociates (decreased % Hb saturation). Thus, because of the difference in P_{O_2} at the lungs and other tissues, Hb automatically "loads up" on O_2 in the lungs, where ventilation is continually providing fresh supplies of O_2, and "unloads" it in the tissues, which are constantly using up O_2.

O_2–Hb DISSOCIATION CURVE The relationship between blood P_{O_2} and % Hb saturation is not linear, however, a point that is important physiologically. Doubling the partial pressure does not double the % Hb saturation. Rather, the relationship between these variables follows an S-shaped curve, the **O_2–Hb dissociation** (or **saturation) curve** (● Figure 12-21). At the upper end, between a blood P_{O_2} of 60 mm Hg and one of 100 mm Hg, the curve flattens off, or plateaus. Within this pressure range, a rise in P_{O_2} produces only a small increase in the extent to which Hb is bound with O_2. In the P_{O_2} range of 0 to 60 mm Hg, in contrast, a small change in P_{O_2} results in a large change in the extent to which Hb is combined with O_2, as shown by the steep lower part of the curve. Both the upper plateau and the lower steep portion of the curve have physiological significance.

SIGNIFICANCE OF THE PLATEAU PORTION OF THE O_2–Hb CURVE The plateau portion of the curve is in the blood P_{O_2} range at the pulmonary capillaries where O_2 is being loaded onto Hb. The

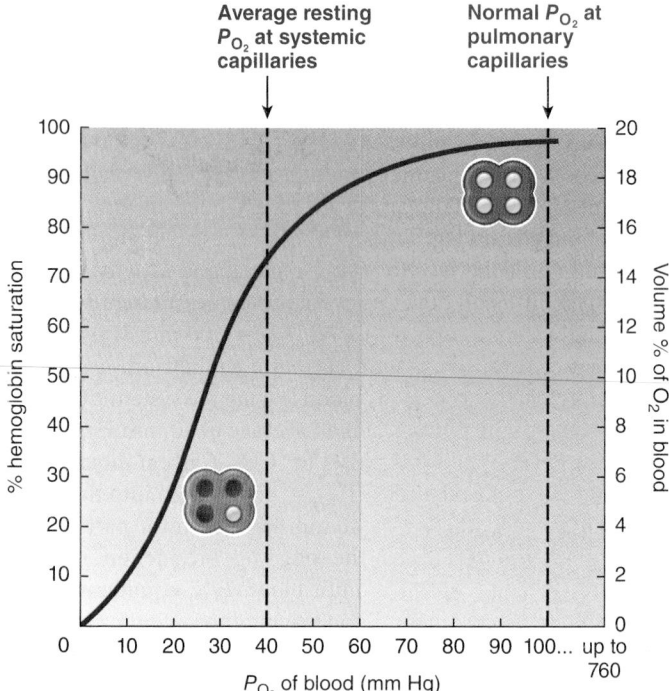

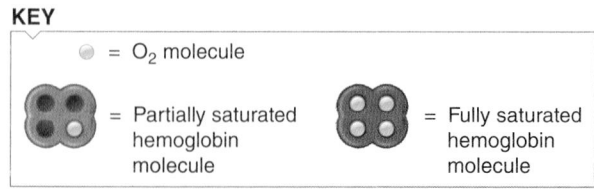

KEY

● = O_2 molecule

= Partially saturated hemoglobin molecule

= Fully saturated hemoglobin molecule

● **FIGURE 12-21 Oxygen–hemoglobin (O_2–Hb) dissociation (saturation) curve.** The % hemoglobin saturation (the scale on the left side of the graph) depends on the P_{O_2} of the blood. The relationship between these two variables is depicted by an S-shaped curve with a plateau region between a blood P_{O_2} of 60 mm Hg and one of 100 mm Hg and a steep portion between 0 and 60 mm Hg. Another way of expressing the effect of blood P_{O_2} on the amount of O_2 bound with hemoglobin is the volume % of O_2 in the blood (number of milliliters of O_2 bound with hemoglobin in each 100 ml of blood). That relationship is represented by the scale on the right side of the graph.

systemic arterial blood leaving the lungs, having equilibrated with alveolar P_{O_2}, normally has a P_{O_2} of 100 mm Hg. Looking at the O_2–Hb curve, note that at a blood P_{O_2} of 100 mm Hg, Hb is 97.5% saturated. Therefore, Hb in the systemic arterial blood normally is almost fully saturated.

If the alveolar P_{O_2} and, consequently, the arterial P_{O_2} fall below normal, there is little reduction in the total amount of O_2 transported by the blood until the P_{O_2} falls below 60 mm Hg. This is because of the plateau region of the curve. If the arterial P_{O_2} falls 40%, from 100 to 60 mm Hg, the concentration of dissolved O_2 as reflected by the P_{O_2} is likewise reduced 40%. At a blood P_{O_2} of 60 mm Hg, however, the % Hb saturation is still remarkably high, at 90%. Accordingly, the total O_2 content of the blood is only slightly decreased despite the 40% reduction in P_{O_2}, because Hb is still carrying an almost full load of O_2, and, as mentioned before, the vast majority of O_2 is transported by Hb rather than dissolved. However, even if the blood P_{O_2} is greatly increased—say, to 600 mm Hg—by breathing pure O_2, little additional O_2 is added to the blood. A small extra amount of O_2 dissolves, but the % Hb saturation can be maximally increased by only another 2.5%, to 100% saturation. Therefore, in the P_{O_2} range between 60 and 600 mm Hg or even higher, there is only a 10% difference in the amount of O_2 carried by Hb. Thus, the plateau portion of the O_2–Hb curve provides a good margin of safety in O_2-carrying capacity of the blood.

 Clinical Note Arterial P_{O_2} may be reduced by pulmonary diseases accompanied by inadequate ventilation or defective gas exchange or by circulatory disorders that result in inadequate blood flow to the lungs. It may also fall in healthy people under two circumstances: (1) at high altitudes, where total atmospheric pressure and hence the P_{O_2} of the inspired air are reduced, or (2) in O_2-deprived environments at sea level, such as if someone were accidentally locked in a vault. Unless the arterial P_{O_2} becomes markedly reduced (falls below 60 mm Hg) in either pathological conditions or abnormal circumstances, near-normal amounts of O_2 can still be carried to the tissues.

SIGNIFICANCE OF THE STEEP PORTION OF THE O_2–Hb CURVE
The steep portion of the curve between 0 and 60 mm Hg is in the blood P_{O_2} range at the systemic capillaries, where O_2 is unloaded from Hb. In the systemic capillaries, the blood equilibrates with the surrounding tissue cells at an average P_{O_2} of 40 mm Hg. Note in ● Figure 12-21 that at a P_{O_2} of 40 mm Hg the % Hb saturation is 75%. The blood arrives in the tissue capillaries at a P_{O_2} of 100 mm Hg with 97.5% Hb saturation. Because Hb can only be 75% saturated at the P_{O_2} of 40 mm Hg in the systemic capillaries, nearly 25% of the HbO_2 must dissociate, yielding reduced Hb and O_2. This released O_2 is free to diffuse down its partial pressure gradient from the red blood cells through the plasma and the interstitial fluid into the tissue cells.

The Hb in the venous blood returning to the lungs is still normally 75% saturated. If the tissue cells are metabolizing more actively, the P_{O_2} of the systemic capillary blood falls (for example, from 40 to 20 mm Hg) because the cells are consuming O_2 more rapidly. Note on the curve that this drop of 20 mm Hg in decreases the % Hb saturation from 75% to 30%; that is,

about 45% more of the total HbO_2 than normal gives up its O_2 for tissue use. The normal 60 mm Hg drop in P_{O_2} from 100 to 40 mm Hg in the systemic capillaries causes about 25% of the total HbO_2 to unload its O_2. In comparison, a further drop in P_{O_2} of only 20 mm Hg results in an additional 45% of the total HbO_2 unloading its O_2 because the O_2 partial pressures in this range are operating in the steep portion of the curve. In this range, only a small drop in systemic capillary P_{O_2} can automatically make large amounts of O_2 immediately available to meet the O_2 needs of more actively metabolizing tissues. As much as 85% of the Hb may give up its O_2 to actively metabolizing cells during strenuous exercise. In addition to this more thorough withdrawal of O_2 from the blood, even more O_2 is made available to actively metabolizing cells, such as exercising muscles, by circulatory and respiratory adjustments that increase the flow rate of oxygenated blood through the active tissues.

Hemoglobin promotes the net transfer of O_2 at both the alveolar and the tissue levels.

We still have not really clarified the role of Hb in gas exchange. Because blood P_{O_2} depends entirely on the concentration of *dissolved* O_2, we could ignore the O_2 bound to Hb in our earlier discussion of O_2 being driven from the alveoli to the blood by a P_{O_2} gradient. However, Hb does play a crucial role in permitting the transfer of large quantities of O_2 before blood P_{O_2} equilibrates with the surrounding tissues (● Figure 12-22).

ROLE OF HEMOGLOBIN AT THE ALVEOLAR LEVEL Hemoglobin acts as a "storage depot" for O_2, removing O_2 from solution as soon as it enters the blood from the alveoli. Because only dissolved O_2 contributes to P_{O_2}, the O_2 stored in Hb cannot contribute to blood P_{O_2}. When systemic venous blood enters the pulmonary capillaries, its P_{O_2} is considerably lower than alveolar P_{O_2}, so O_2 immediately diffuses into the blood, raising blood P_{O_2}. As soon as the blood P_{O_2} increases, the percentage of Hb that can bind with O_2 likewise increases, as indicated by the O_2–Hb curve. Consequently, most of the O_2 that has diffused into the blood combines with Hb and no longer contributes to blood P_{O_2}. As O_2 is removed from solution by combining with Hb, blood P_{O_2} falls to about the same level it was when the blood entered the lungs, even though the total quantity of O_2 in the blood actually has increased. Because blood P_{O_2} is again considerably below alveolar P_{O_2}, more O_2 diffuses from the alveoli into the blood, only to be soaked up by Hb again.

Even though we have considered this process stepwise for clarity, net diffusion of O_2 from alveoli to blood occurs continuously until Hb becomes as saturated with O_2 as it can be at that particular P_{O_2}. At a normal P_{O_2} of 100 mm Hg, Hb is 97.5% saturated. Thus, by soaking up O_2, Hb keeps blood P_{O_2} low and prolongs the existence of a partial pressure gradient so that a large net transfer of O_2 into the blood can take place. Not until Hb can store no more O_2 (that is, Hb is maximally saturated for that P_{O_2}) does all the O_2 transferred into the blood remain dissolved and directly contribute to the P_{O_2}. Only now does blood P_{O_2} rapidly equilibrate with alveolar P_{O_2} and bring further O_2

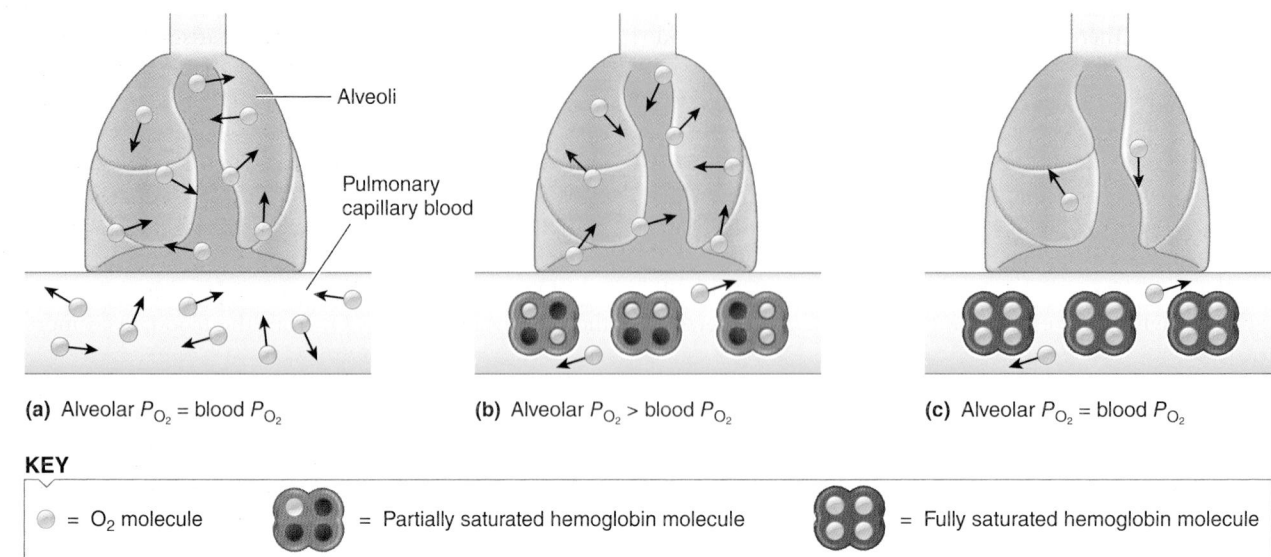

(a) Alveolar P_{O_2} = blood P_{O_2} **(b)** Alveolar P_{O_2} > blood P_{O_2} **(c)** Alveolar P_{O_2} = blood P_{O_2}

KEY

⬤ = O_2 molecule   🔲 = Partially saturated hemoglobin molecule   🔲 = Fully saturated hemoglobin molecule

⬤ **FIGURE 12-22 Hemoglobin facilitating a large net transfer of O_2 by acting as a storage depot to keep P_{O_2} low.** (a) In the hypothetical situation in which no hemoglobin is present in the blood, the alveolar P_{O_2} and the pulmonary capillary blood P_{O_2} are at equilibrium. (b) Hemoglobin has been added to the pulmonary capillary blood. As the Hb starts to bind with O_2, it removes O_2 from solution. Because only dissolved O_2 contributes to blood P_{O_2}, the blood P_{O_2} falls below that of the alveoli, even though the same number of O_2 molecules are present in the blood as in part (a). By "soaking up" some of the dissolved O_2, Hb favors the net diffusion of more O_2 down its partial pressure gradient from the alveoli to the blood. (c) Hemoglobin is fully saturated with O_2, and the alveolar and blood P_{O_2} are at equilibrium again. The blood P_{O_2} resulting from dissolved O_2 is equal to the alveolar P_{O_2}, despite the total O_2 content in the blood being greater than in part (a), when blood P_{O_2} was equal to alveolar P_{O_2} in the absence of Hb.

transfer to a halt, but this point is not reached until Hb is already loaded to the maximum extent possible. Once blood P_{O_2} equilibrates with alveolar P_{O_2}, no further O_2 transfer can take place, no matter how little or how much total O_2 has already been transferred.

ROLE OF HEMOGLOBIN AT THE TISSUE LEVEL The reverse situation occurs at the tissue level. Because the P_{O_2} of blood entering the systemic capillaries is considerably higher than the P_{O_2} of the surrounding tissue, O_2 immediately diffuses from the blood into the tissues, lowering blood P_{O_2}. When blood P_{O_2} falls, Hb must unload some stored O_2 because the % Hb saturation is reduced. As the O_2 released from Hb dissolves in the blood, blood P_{O_2} increases and again exceeds the P_{O_2} of the surrounding tissues. This favors further movement of O_2 out of the blood, although the total quantity of O_2 in the blood has already fallen. Only when Hb can no longer release any more O_2 into solution (when Hb is unloaded to the greatest extent possible for the P_{O_2} existing at the systemic capillaries) can blood P_{O_2} fall as low as in surrounding tissue. At this time, further transfer of O_2 stops. Hemoglobin, because it stores a large quantity of O_2 that can be freed by a slight reduction in P_{O_2} at the systemic capillary level, permits the transfer of tremendously more O_2 from the blood into the cells than would be possible in its absence.

Thus, Hb plays an important role in the *total quantity* of O_2 that the blood can pick up in the lungs and drop off in the tis-

sues. If Hb levels fall to one half of normal, as in a severely anemic patient (see p. 321), the O_2-carrying capacity of the blood falls by 50% even though the arterial P_{O_2} is the normal 100 mm Hg with 97.5% Hb saturation. Only half as much Hb is available to be saturated, emphasizing again how critical Hb is in determining how much O_2 can be picked up at the lungs and made available to tissues.

Factors at the tissue level promote the unloading of O_2 from hemoglobin.

Even though the main factor determining the % Hb saturation is the P_{O_2} of the blood, other factors can affect the affinity, or bond strength, between Hb and O_2 and, accordingly, can shift the O_2–Hb curve (that is, change the % Hb saturation at a given P_{O_2}). These other factors are CO_2, acidity, temperature, and 2,3-bisphosphoglycerate, which we examine separately. The O_2–Hb dissociation curve with which you are already familiar (see ⬤ Figure 12-21) is a typical curve at normal arterial CO_2 and acidity levels, normal body temperature, and normal 2,3-bisphosphoglycerate concentration.

EFFECT OF CO_2 ON % Hb SATURATION An increase in P_{CO_2} shifts the O_2–Hb curve to the right (⬤ Figure 12-23). The % Hb saturation still depends on the P_{O_2}, but for any given P_{O_2} less O_2 and Hb can be combined. This effect is important, because the P_{CO_2}

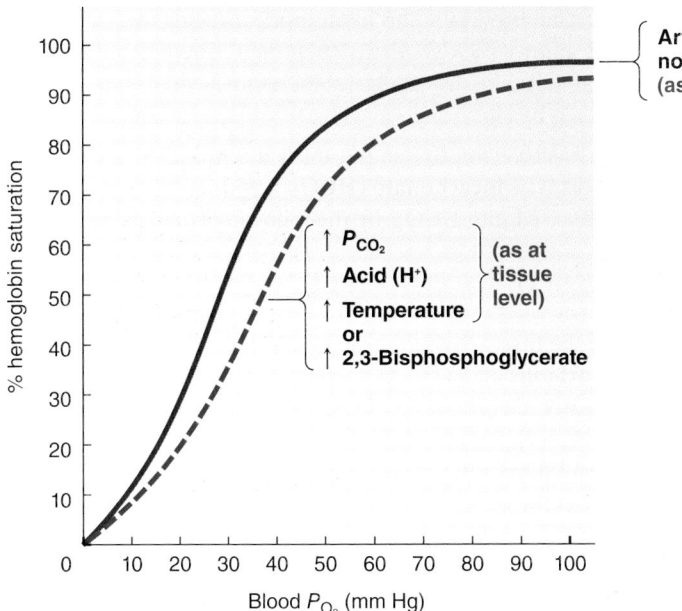

● FIGURE 12-23 **Effect of increased P_{CO_2}, H⁺, temperature, and 2,3-bisphosphoglycerate on the O₂–Hb curve.** Increased P_{CO_2}, acid, and temperature, as found at the tissue level, shift the O₂–Hb curve to the right. As a result, less O₂ and Hb can be combined at a given P_{O_2} so that more O₂ is unloaded from Hb for use by the tissues. Similarly, 2,3-bisphosphoglycerate, whose production is increased in red blood cells when arterial HbO₂ is chronically below normal, shifts the O₂–Hb curve to the right, making more of the limited O₂ available at the tissue level.

of the blood increases in the systemic capillaries as CO_2 diffuses down its gradient from the cells into the blood. The presence of this additional CO_2 in the blood in effect decreases the affinity of Hb for O₂, so Hb unloads even more O₂ at the tissue level than it would if the reduction in P_{O_2} in the systemic capillaries were the only factor affecting % Hb saturation.

EFFECT OF ACID ON % Hb SATURATION An increase in acidity also shifts the curve to the right. Because CO_2 generates carbonic acid, the blood becomes more acidic at the systemic capillary level as it picks up CO_2 from the tissues. The resulting reduction in Hb affinity for O₂ in the presence of increased acidity aids in releasing even more O₂ at the tissue level for a given P_{O_2}. In actively metabolizing cells, such as exercising muscles, not only is more carbonic acid–generating CO_2 produced, but lactate (lactic acid) also may be produced if the cells resort to anaerobic metabolism (see pp. 32 and 224). The resultant local elevation of acid in the working muscles facilitates further unloading of O₂ in the very tissues that need the most O₂.

EFFECT OF TEMPERATURE ON % Hb SATURATION In a similar manner, a rise in temperature shifts the O₂–Hb curve to the right, resulting in more unloading of O₂ at a given P_{O_2}. An exercising muscle or other actively metabolizing cell produces heat. The resulting local rise in temperature enhances O₂ release from Hb for use by more active tissues.

COMPARISON OF THESE FACTORS AT THE TISSUE AND PULMONARY LEVELS As you just learned, increases in CO_2, acidity, and temperature at the tissue level, all of which are associated with

increased cellular metabolism and increased O₂ consumption, enhance the effect of a drop in P_{O_2} in facilitating the release of O₂ from Hb. These effects are largely reversed at the pulmonary level, where the extra acid-forming CO_2 is blown off and the local aerated environment is cooler. Appropriately, therefore, Hb has a higher affinity for O₂ in the pulmonary capillary environment, enhancing the effect of raised P_{O_2} in loading O₂ onto Hb.

EFFECT OF 2,3-BISPHOSPHOGLYCERATE ON % Hb SATURATION The preceding changes take place in the *environment* of the red blood cells, but a factor *inside* the red blood cells can also affect the degree of O₂–Hb binding: **2,3-bisphosphoglycerate (BPG).** This erythrocyte constituent, which is produced during red blood cell metabolism, can bind reversibly with Hb and reduce its affinity for O₂, just as CO_2 and H⁺ do. Thus, an increased level of BPG, like the other factors, shifts the O₂–Hb curve to the right, enhancing O₂ unloading as the blood flows through the tissues.

BPG production by red blood cells gradually increases whenever Hb in the arterial blood is chronically undersaturated—that is, when arterial HbO₂ is below normal. This condition may occur in people living at high altitudes or in those suffering from certain types of circulatory or respiratory diseases or anemia. By helping unload O₂ from Hb at the tissue level, increased BPG helps maintain O₂ availability for tissue use even though arterial O₂ supply is chronically reduced.

Hemoglobin has a much higher affinity for carbon monoxide than for O₂.

Clinical Note **Carbon monoxide (CO)** and O₂ compete for the same binding sites on Hb, but Hb's affinity for CO is 240 times that of its affinity for O₂. The combination of CO and Hb is known as **carboxyhemoglobin (HbCO).** Because Hb preferentially latches onto CO, even small amounts of CO can tie up a disproportionately large share of Hb, making Hb unavailable for O₂ transport. Even though the Hb concentration and P_{O_2} are normal, the O₂ content of the blood is seriously reduced.

Fortunately, CO is not a normal constituent of inspired air. It is a poisonous gas produced during the incomplete combustion (burning) of carbon products such as automobile gasoline, coal, wood, and tobacco. Carbon monoxide is especially dangerous because it is so insidious. If CO is being produced in a closed environment so that its concentration continues to increase (for example, in a parked car with the motor running and windows closed), it can reach lethal levels without the victim ever being aware of the danger. Because it is odorless, colorless, tasteless, and nonirritating, CO is not detectable. Furthermore, for reasons described later, the victim has no sensation of breathlessness and makes no attempt to increase ventilation, even though the cells are O_2 starved.

Most CO_2 is transported in the blood as bicarbonate.

When arterial blood flows through the tissue capillaries, CO_2 diffuses down its partial pressure gradient from the tissue cells into the blood. Carbon dioxide is transported in the blood in three ways (as described in the following list and shown with corresponding numbers in ● Figure 12-24; see also ▲ Table 12-3, p. 387):

1. *Physically dissolved.* As with dissolved O_2, the amount of CO_2 physically dissolved in the blood depends on the P_{CO_2}. Because CO_2 is more soluble than O_2 in plasma water, a greater proportion of the total CO_2 than of O_2 in the blood is physically dissolved. Even so, only 10% of the blood's total CO_2 content is carried this way at the normal systemic venous P_{CO_2} level.

2. *Bound to hemoglobin.* Another 30% of the CO_2 combines with Hb to form **carbamino hemoglobin (HbCO$_2$).** Carbon dioxide binds with the globin portion of Hb, in contrast to O_2,

which combines with the heme portions. Reduced Hb has a greater affinity for CO_2 than HbO_2 does. The unloading of O_2 from Hb in the tissue capillaries therefore facilitates the picking up of CO_2 by Hb.

3. *As bicarbonate.* By far the most important means of CO_2 transport is as **bicarbonate (HCO$_3^-$),** with 60% of the CO_2 being converted into HCO_3^- by the following chemical reaction:

$$CO_2 + H_2O \rightleftharpoons H_2CO_3 \rightleftharpoons H + HCO_3^-$$

In the first step of the reaction, CO_2 combines with H_2O to form **carbonic acid (H$_2$CO$_3$).** As is characteristic of acids, some of the carbonic acid molecules spontaneously dissociate into hydrogen ions (H^+) and bicarbonate ions (HCO_3^-). The one carbon and two oxygen atoms of the original CO_2 molecule are thus present in the blood as an integral part of HCO_3^-. This is beneficial because HCO_3^- is more soluble in the blood than CO_2 is.

This reaction takes place slowly in the plasma, but it proceeds swiftly within the red blood cells because of the presence of the erythrocyte enzyme **carbonic anhydrase,** which catalyzes (speeds up) the reaction. In fact, under the influence of carbonic anhydrase, the reaction proceeds directly from CO_2 + H_2O to H^+ + HCO_3^- without the intervening H_2CO_3 step:

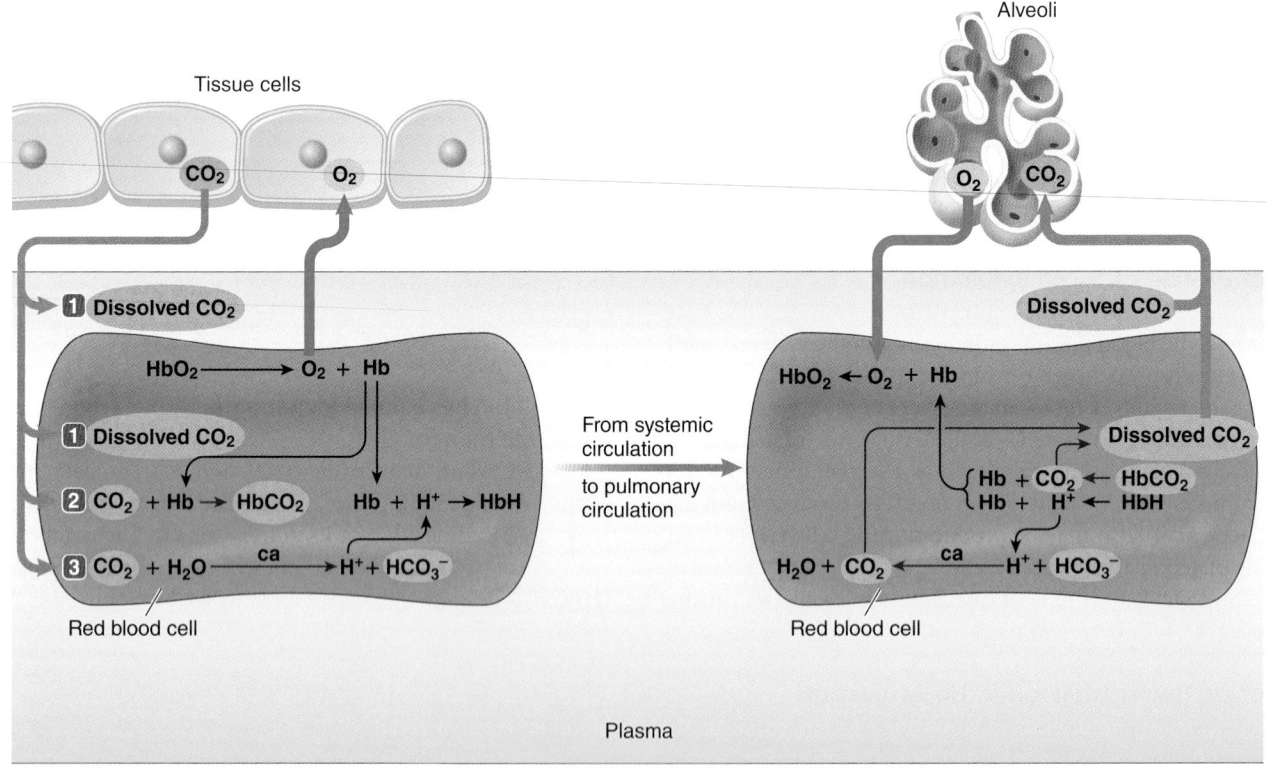

ca = Carbonic anhydrase

● **FIGURE 12-24 Carbon dioxide transport in the blood.** Carbon dioxide (CO_2) picked up at the tissue level is transported in the blood to the lungs in three ways: (1) physically dissolved, (2) bound to hemoglobin (Hb), and (3) as bicarbonate ion (HCO_3^-). Hemoglobin is present only in the red blood cells, as is carbonic anhydrase, the enzyme that catalyzes the production of HCO_3^-. The H^+ generated during the production of HCO_3^- also binds to Hb. The reactions that occur at the tissue level are reversed at the pulmonary level, where CO_2 diffuses out of the blood to enter the alveoli.

$$\text{CO}_2 + \text{H}_2\text{O} \xrightarrow{\text{carbonic anhydrase}} \text{H}^+ + \text{HCO3}^-$$

Hemoglobin binds with most of the H^+ formed within the erythrocytes. As with CO_2, reduced Hb has a greater affinity for H^+ than HbO_2 does. Therefore, unloading O_2 facilitates Hb pickup of CO_2-generated H^+. Because only free, dissolved H^+ contributes to the acidity of a solution, venous blood would be considerably more acidic than arterial blood if Hb did not mop up most of the H^+ generated at the tissue level.

Note how hemoglobin's unloading of O_2 and its uptake of CO_2 and CO_2-generated H^+ at the tissue level work in synchrony. Increased CO_2 and H^+ cause increased O_2 release from Hb, and increased O_2 release from Hb in turn causes increased CO_2 and H^+ uptake by Hb. The entire process is efficient. Reduced Hb must be carried back to the lungs to refill on O_2 anyway. After O_2 is released, Hb picks up new passengers—CO_2 and H^+—that are going in the same direction to the lungs.

The reactions at the tissue level as CO_2 enters the blood from the tissues are reversed once the blood reaches the lungs and CO_2 leaves the blood to enter the alveoli (● Figure 12-24).

Various respiratory states are characterized by abnormal blood-gas levels.

▲ Table 12-4 is a glossary of terms used to describe various states associated with respiratory abnormalities, most of which

▲ Table 12-4 Miniglossary of Clinically Important Respiratory States

Apnea   Transient cessation of breathing

Asphyxia O_2 starvation of tissues, caused by a lack of O_2 in the air, respiratory impairment, or inability of the tissues to use O_2

Cyanosis   Blueness of the skin resulting from insufficiently oxygenated blood in the arteries

Dyspnea   Subjective sensation of shortness of breath, often accompanying labored or difficult breathing

Eupnea   Normal breathing

Hypercapnia   Excess CO_2 in the arterial blood

Hyperpnea   Increased pulmonary ventilation that matches increased metabolic demands, as in exercise

Hyperventilation   Increased pulmonary ventilation in excess of metabolic requirements, resulting in decreased P_{CO_2} and respiratory alkalosis

Hypocapnia   Below-normal CO_2 in the arterial blood

Hypoventilation   Underventilation in relation to metabolic requirements, resulting in increased P_{CO_2} and respiratory acidosis

Hypoxia   Insufficient O_2 at the cellular level

Respiratory arrest   Permanent cessation of breathing (unless clinically corrected)

Suffocation O_2 deprivation as a result of an inability to breathe oxygenated air

are discussed in more detail here and in the final section of this chapter.

ABNORMALITIES IN ARTERIAL P_{O_2} The term **hypoxia** refers to the condition of having insufficient O_2 at the cell level. There are four general categories of hypoxia:

1. *Hypoxic hypoxia* is characterized by a low arterial blood P_{O_2} accompanied by inadequate Hb saturation. It is caused by (a) a respiratory malfunction involving inadequate gas exchange, typified by a normal alveolar P_{O_2} but a reduced arterial P_{O_2}, or (b) exposure to high altitude or to a suffocating environment where atmospheric P_{O_2} is reduced so that alveolar and arterial P_{O_2} are likewise reduced.

2. *Anemic hypoxia* is a reduced O_2-carrying capacity of the blood. It can result from (a) a decrease in circulating red blood cells, (b) an inadequate amount of Hb within the red blood cells, or (c) CO poisoning. In all cases of anemic hypoxia, arterial P_{O_2} is normal but the O_2 content of the arterial blood is lower than normal because of inadequate available Hb.

3. *Circulatory hypoxia* arises when too little oxygenated blood is delivered to the tissues. Circulatory hypoxia can be restricted to a limited area by a local vascular blockage. Or the body may experience circulatory hypoxia in general from congestive heart failure or circulatory shock. Arterial P_{O_2} and O_2 content are typically normal, but too little oxygenated blood reaches the cells.

4. In *histotoxic hypoxia*, O_2 delivery to the tissues is normal, but the cells cannot use the O_2 available to them. The classic example is *cyanide poisoning*. Cyanide blocks enzymes essential for cellular respiration (enzymes in the electron transport system; see p. 32).

Hyperoxia, an above-normal arterial P_{O_2}, cannot occur when a person is breathing atmospheric air at sea level. However, breathing supplemental O_2 can increase alveolar and consequently, arterial P_{O_2}. Because more of the inspired air is O_2, more of the total pressure of the inspired air is attributable to the O_2 partial pressure, so more O_2 dissolves in the blood before arterial P_{O_2} equilibrates with alveolar P_{O_2}. Even though arterial P_{O_2} increases, the total blood O_2 content does not significantly increase because Hb is nearly fully saturated at the normal arterial P_{O_2}. In certain pulmonary diseases associated with a reduced arterial P_{O_2}, however, breathing supplemental O_2 can help establish a larger alveoli-to-blood driving gradient, improving arterial P_{O_2}. Far from being advantageous, a markedly elevated arterial P_{O_2} can be dangerous. If arterial P_{O_2} is too high, **oxygen toxicity** can occur. Even though the total O_2 content of the blood is only slightly increased, exposure to a high P_{O_2} can cause brain damage and blindness-causing damage to the retina. Therefore, O_2 therapy must be administered cautiously.

ABNORMALITIES IN ARTERIAL P_{CO_2} The term **hypercapnia** refers to the condition of having excess CO_2 in arterial blood; it is caused by **hypoventilation** (ventilation inadequate to meet metabolic needs for O_2

Effects of Heights and Depths on the Body

Our bodies are optimally equipped for existence at normal atmospheric pressure. Ascent into mountains high above sea level or descent into the depths of the ocean can have adverse effects on the body.

Effects of High Altitude on the Body

Atmospheric pressure progressively declines as altitude increases. At 18,000 feet above sea level, atmospheric pressure is only 380 mm Hg—half of its normal sea-level value. Because the proportion of O_2 and N_2 in the air remains the same, the P_{O_2} of inspired air at this altitude is 21% of 380 mm Hg, or 80 mm Hg, with alveolar P_{O_2} being even lower at 45 mm Hg. At any altitude above 10,000 feet, the arterial P_{O_2} falls into the steep portion of the O_2–Hb curve, below the safety range of the plateau region. As a result, the % Hb saturation in arterial blood declines precipitously with further increases in altitude.

People who rapidly ascend to altitudes of 10,000 feet or more experience symptoms of **acute mountain sickness** attributable to hypoxic hypoxia and the resultant hypocapnia-induced alkalosis. The increased ventilatory drive to obtain more O_2 causes respiratory alkalosis, because acid-forming CO_2 is blown off more rapidly than it is produced. Symp-

toms of mountain sickness include fatigue, nausea, loss of appetite, labored breathing, rapid heart rate (triggered by hypoxia as a compensatory measure to increase circulatory delivery of available O_2 to the tissues), and nerve dysfunction characterized by poor judgment, dizziness, and incoordination.

Despite these acute responses to high altitude, millions of people live at elevations above 10,000 feet, with some villagers even residing in the Andes at altitudes higher than 16,000 feet. How do they live and function normally? They do so through the process of **acclimatization.** When a person remains at high altitude, the acute compensatory responses of increased ventilation and increased cardiac output are gradually replaced over a period of days by more slowly developing compensatory measures that permit adequate oxygenation of the tissues and restoration of normal acid–base balance. Red blood cell (RBC) production increases, stimulated by erythropoietin in response to reduced O_2 delivery to the kidneys (see p. 320). The rise in the number of RBCs increases the O_2-carrying capacity of the blood. Hypoxia also promotes the synthesis of BPG within the RBCs so that O_2 is unloaded from Hb more easily at the tissues (see p. 391). The number of capillaries within the tissues increases, reducing the distance that O_2 must diffuse from the blood to reach the cells. Also, the high-altitude inhabitants' endothelial cells release up to 10 times more nitric oxide (NO) than is released in those dwelling

---

delivery and CO_2 removal). With most lung diseases, CO_2 accumulates in arterial blood concurrently with an O_2 deficit.

Hypocapnia, below-normal arterial P_{CO_2} levels, is brought about by hyperventilation. **Hyperventilation** occurs when a person "overbreathes," that is, when the rate of ventilation exceeds the body's metabolic needs for CO_2 removal. As a result, CO_2 is blown off to the atmosphere more rapidly than it is produced in the tissues, and arterial P_{CO_2} falls. Hyperventilation can be triggered by anxiety states, fever, and aspirin poisoning.

Hyperventilation significantly affects CO_2 levels in the body but has little effect on the body's O_2 content. Even though extra fresh O_2 is inspired during hyperventilation and alveolar and arterial P_{O_2} subsequently increase, little additional O_2 is added to the blood, because Hb is almost fully saturated at the normal arterial P_{O_2}. Except for the small extra amount of dissolved O_2, blood O_2 content remains essentially unchanged during hyperventilation.

Increased ventilation is not synonymous with hyperventilation. Increased ventilation that matches an increased metabolic demand, such as the increased need for O_2 delivery and

CO_2 elimination during exercise, is termed **hyperpnea.** During exercise, alveolar and arterial P_{O_2} and P_{CO_2} remain constant, with the increased atmospheric exchange just keeping pace with the increased O_2 consumption and CO_2 production.

CONSEQUENCES OF ABNORMALITIES IN ARTERIAL BLOOD GASES The consequences of reduced O_2 availability to the tissues during hypoxia are apparent. The cells need adequate O_2 to sustain energy-generating metabolic activities. The consequences of abnormal blood CO_2 levels are less obvious. Changes in blood CO_2 concentration primarily affect acid–base balance. Hypercapnia elevates production of CO_2-generated H^+. The subsequent generation of excess H^+ produces an acidic condition termed *respiratory acidosis.* Conversely, less-than-normal amounts of H^+ are generated from CO_2 in conjunction with hypocapnia. The resultant alkalotic (less acidic than normal) condition is called *respiratory alkalosis* (see Chapter 14). (To learn about the effects of mountain climbing and deep sea diving on blood gases, see the accompanying boxed feature, ❱ Beyond the Basics.)

near sea level. This extra NO more than doubles blood flow in the acclimatized individuals (see p. 290). Furthermore, acclimatized cells are able to use O_2 more efficiently through an increase in the number of mitochondria, the energy organelles (see p. 28). The kidneys restore arterial pH to nearly normal by conserving acid that normally would have been lost in the urine (see p. 458).

These compensatory measures come with undesirable trade-offs. For example, the greater number of RBCs increases blood viscosity (makes the blood "thicker"), thereby increasing resistance to blood flow (see p. 281). As a result, the heart has to work harder to pump blood through the vessels.

Effects of Deep-Sea Diving on the Body

When a deep-sea diver, with the help of a self-contained underwater breathing apparatus (scuba), descends underwater, the body is exposed to greater than atmospheric pressure. Pressure rapidly increases with sea depth as a result of the weight of the water. Pressure is already doubled about 30 feet below sea level. The air provided by scuba equipment is delivered to the lungs at these high pressures. Recall that (1) the amount of a gas in solution is directly proportional to the partial pressure of the gas and (2) air is

composed of 79% N_2. Nitrogen is poorly soluble in body tissues, but the high P_{N_2} that occurs during deep-sea diving causes more of this gas than normal to dissolve in the body tissues. The small amount of N_2 dissolved in the tissues at sea level has no known effect, but as more N_2 dissolves at greater depths, **nitrogen narcosis, or "rapture of the deep,"** develops. Nitrogen narcosis is be-

lieved to result from a reduction in the excitability of neurons when the highly lipid-soluble N_2 dissolves in their lipid membranes. At 150 feet underwater, divers experience a feeling of euphoria and become drowsy, similar to the effect of having a few cocktails. At lower depths, divers become weak and clumsy, and at 350 to 400 feet, they lose consciousness. Oxygen toxicity resulting from the high P_{O_2} is another possible detrimental effect of descending deep underwater.

Another problem associated with deep-sea diving occurs during ascent. If a diver who has been submerged long enough for a significant amount of N_2 to dissolve in the tissues suddenly ascends to the surface, the rapid reduction in P_{N_2} causes N_2 to quickly come out of solution and form bubbles of gaseous N_2 in the body, much as bubbles of gaseous CO_2 form in a bottle of champagne when the cork is popped. The consequences depend on the amount and location of N_2 bubble formation in the body. This condition is called **decompression sickness** or **"the bends"** because the victim often bends over in pain. Decompression sickness can be prevented by ascending slowly to the surface or by decompressing gradually in a decompression tank so that the excess N_2 can slowly escape through the lungs without bubble formation.

Control of Respiration

Like the heartbeat, breathing must occur in a continuous, cyclic pattern to sustain life processes. Cardiac muscle must rhythmically contract and relax to alternately empty blood from the heart and fill it again. Similarly, inspiratory muscles must rhythmically contract and relax to alternately fill the lungs with air and empty them. Both of these activities are accomplished automatically, without conscious effort. However, the underlying mechanisms and control of these two systems are remarkably different.

Respiratory centers in the brain stem establish a rhythmic breathing pattern.

Whereas the heart can generate its own rhythm by means of its intrinsic pacemaker activity, the respiratory muscles, being skeletal muscles, contract only when stimulated by their nerve supply. The rhythmic pattern of breathing is established by cyclic neural activity to the respiratory muscles. In other words,

the pacemaker activity that establishes breathing rhythm resides in the respiratory control centers in the brain, not in the lungs or respiratory muscles themselves. The nerve supply to the heart, not being needed to initiate the heartbeat, only modifies the rate and strength of cardiac contraction. In contrast, the nerve supply to the respiratory system is essential in maintaining breathing and in reflexly adjusting the level of ventilation to match changing needs for O_2 uptake and CO_2 removal. Furthermore, unlike cardiac activity, which is not subject to voluntary control, respiratory activity can be voluntarily modified to accomplish speaking, singing, whistling, playing a wind instrument, or holding one's breath while swimming.

COMPONENTS OF NEURAL CONTROL OF RESPIRATION Neural control of respiration involves three distinct components: (1) factors that generate the alternating inspiration–expiration rhythm, (2) factors that regulate the magnitude of ventilation (that is, the rate and depth of breathing) to match body needs, and (3) factors that modify respiratory activity to serve other purposes. The latter modifications may be either voluntary, as in the breath control required for speech, or involuntary, as in the respiratory maneuvers involved in a cough or sneeze.

Respiratory control centers housed in the brain stem generate the rhythmic pattern of breathing. The primary respiratory control center, the *medullary respiratory center,* consists of several aggregations of neuronal cell bodies within the medulla that provide output to the respiratory muscles. In addition, two other respiratory centers lie higher in the brain stem in the pons—the *pneumotaxic center* and the *apneustic center.* These pontine centers influence output from the medullary respiratory center (● Figure 12-25). Here is a description of how these various regions interact to establish respiratory rhythmicity.

Inspiratory and Expiratory Neurons in the Medullary Center

We rhythmically breathe in and out during quiet breathing because of alternate contraction and relaxation of the inspiratory muscles, namely, the diaphragm and external intercostal muscles. Contraction and relaxation of these muscles in turn is commanded by the medullary respiratory center, which sends impulses to the motor neurons supplying these muscles.

The **medullary respiratory center** consists of two neuronal clusters known as the *dorsal respiratory group* and the *ventral respiratory group* (● Figure 12-25):

■ The **dorsal respiratory group (DRG)** consists mostly of *inspiratory neurons* whose descending fibers terminate on the motor neurons that supply the inspiratory muscles. When the DRG inspiratory neurons fire, inspiration takes place; when they cease firing, expiration occurs. Expiration is brought to an end as the inspiratory neurons fire again. The DRG has important interconnections with the ventral respiratory group.

■ The **ventral respiratory group (VRG)** is composed of *inspiratory neurons* and *expiratory neurons,* both of which remain inactive during normal quiet breathing. This region is called into play by the DRG as an "overdrive" mechanism during periods when demands for ventilation are increased. It is especially important in active expiration. No impulses are generated in the descending pathways from the expiratory neurons during quiet breathing. Only during active expiration do the expiratory neurons stimulate the motor neurons supplying the expiratory muscles (the abdominal and internal intercostal muscles). Furthermore, the VRG inspiratory neurons, when stimulated by the DRG, rev up inspiratory activity when demands for ventilation are high.

Generation of Respiratory Rhythm

Until recently, the DRG was generally thought to generate the basic rhythm of ventilation. However, generation of respiratory rhythm is now widely believed to lie in the **pre-Bötzinger complex,** a region located near the upper (head) end of the medullary respiratory center (● Figure 12-25). A network of neurons in this region display pacemaker activity, undergoing self-induced action potentials similar to those of the SA node of the heart. Scientists believe the rate at which the DRG inspiratory neurons rhythmically fire is driven by synaptic input from this complex.

Influences from the Pneumotaxic and Apneustic Centers

The respiratory centers in the pons exert "fine-tuning" influences over the medullary center to help produce normal, smooth inspirations and expirations. The **pneumotaxic center** sends impulses to the DRG that help "switch off" the inspiratory neurons, limiting the duration of inspiration. In contrast, the **apneustic center** prevents the inspiratory neurons from being switched off, thus providing an extra boost to the inspiratory drive. In this check-and-balance system, the pneumotaxic center dominates over the apneustic center, helping halt inspiration and letting expiration occur normally. Without the pneumotaxic brakes, the breathing pattern consists of prolonged inspiratory gasps abruptly interrupted by brief expirations. This abnormal breathing pattern is known as **apneusis;** hence, the center that promotes this type of breathing is the apneustic center. Apneusis occurs in certain types of severe brain damage.

Hering–Breuer Reflex

When the tidal volume is large (greater than 1 liter), as during exercise, the **Hering–Breuer reflex** is triggered to prevent overinflation of the lungs. **Pulmonary stretch receptors** within the smooth muscle layer of the airways are activated by stretching of the lungs at large tidal volumes. Action potentials from these stretch receptors travel through afferent nerve fibers to the medullary center and inhibit the inspiratory neurons. This negative feedback from the highly stretched lungs helps cut inspiration short before the lungs become overinflated.

The magnitude of ventilation is adjusted in response to three chemical factors: P_{O_2}, P_{CO_2}, and H^+.

No matter how much O_2 is extracted from the blood or how much CO_2 is added to it at the tissue level, the P_{O_2} and P_{CO_2} of the systemic arterial blood leaving the lungs are normally held

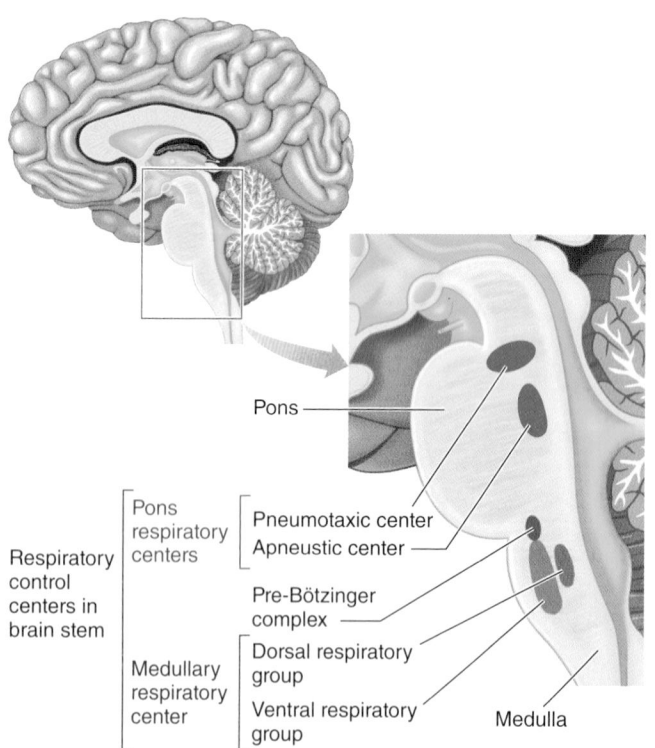

● **FIGURE 12-25 Respiratory control centers in the brain stem.**

remarkably constant, indicating that arterial blood-gas content is precisely regulated. Arterial blood gases are maintained within the normal range by varying the magnitude of ventilation (rate and depth of breathing) to match the body's needs for O_2 uptake and CO_2 removal. If more O_2 is extracted from the alveoli and more CO_2 is dropped off by the blood because the tissues are metabolizing more actively, ventilation increases correspondingly to bring in more fresh O_2 and blow off more CO_2.

The medullary respiratory center receives inputs that provide information about the body's needs for gas exchange. It responds by sending appropriate signals to the motor neurons supplying the respiratory muscles, to adjust the rate and depth of ventilation to meet those needs. The two most obvious signals to increase ventilation are a decreased arterial P_{O_2} or an increased arterial P_{CO_2}. These two factors do indeed influence the magnitude of ventilation, but not to the same degree nor through the same pathway. Also, a third chemical factor, H^+, notably influences the level of respiratory activity. We examine the role of each of these important chemical factors in the control of ventilation (▲ Table 12-5).

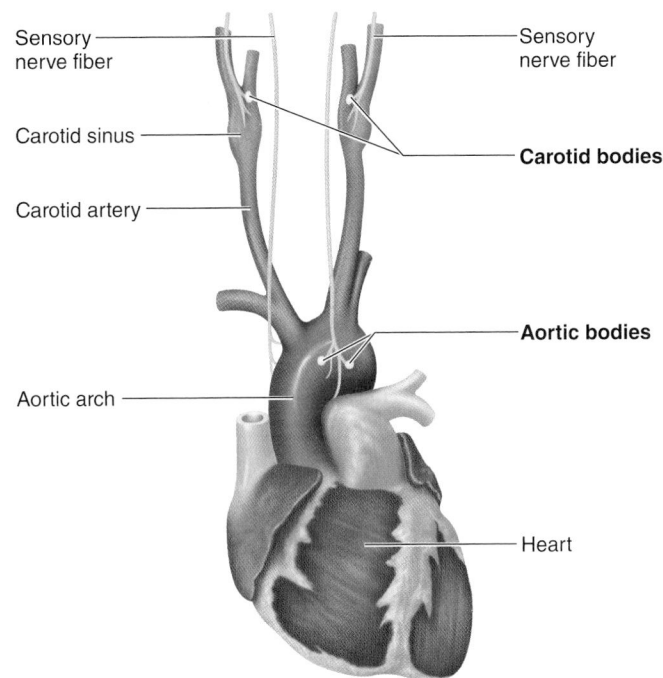

● FIGURE 12-26 **Location of the peripheral chemoreceptors.** The carotid bodies are located in the carotid sinus, and the aortic bodies are located in the aortic arch.

Decreased arterial P_{O_2} increases ventilation only as an emergency mechanism.

Arterial P_{O_2} is monitored by **peripheral chemoreceptors** known as the **carotid bodies** and **aortic bodies,** which lie at the fork of the common carotid arteries (that supply the brain) on both the right and the left sides and in the arch of the aorta, respectively (● Figure 12-26). These chemoreceptors respond to specific changes in the chemical content of the arterial blood that bathes them. They are distinctly different from the carotid sinus and aortic arch baroreceptors located in the same vicinity. The latter monitor pressure changes rather than chemical changes and are important in regulating systemic arterial blood pressure (see p. 307).

EFFECT OF A LARGE DECREASE IN P_{O_2} ON THE PERIPHERAL CHEMORECEPTORS The peripheral chemoreceptors are not sensitive to modest reductions in arterial P_{O_2}. Arterial P_{O_2} must fall below 60 mm Hg (>40% reduction) before the peripheral chemoreceptors respond by sending afferent impulses to the medul-

lary inspiratory neurons, thereby reflexly increasing ventilation. Because arterial P_{O_2} falls below 60 mm Hg only in the unusual circumstances of severe pulmonary disease or reduced atmospheric P_{O_2}, it does not play a role in the normal ongoing regulation of respiration. This fact may seem surprising at first because a primary function of ventilation is to provide enough O_2 for uptake by the blood. However, there is no need to increase ventilation until arterial P_{O_2} falls below 60 mm Hg, because of the safety margin in % Hb saturation afforded by the plateau portion of the O_2–Hb curve. Hemoglobin is still 90% saturated at an arterial P_{O_2} of 60 mm Hg, but the % Hb saturation drops precipitously when P_{O_2} falls below this level. Therefore, reflex stimulation of respiration by the peripheral chemoreceptors is an important emergency mechanism in dangerously low arterial P_{O_2} states.

▲ Table 12-5 Influence of Chemical Factors on Respiration

Chemical Factor	Effect on the Peripheral Chemoreceptors	Effect on the Central Chemoreceptors
↓ P_{O_2} in the Arterial Blood	Stimulates only when the arterial P_{O_2} has fallen to the point of being life threatening (<60 mm Hg); is an emergency mechanism	Directly depresses the central chemoreceptors and the respiratory center itself when < 60 mm Hg
↑ P_{CO_2} in the Arterial Blood (↑ H^+ in the Brain ECF)	Weakly stimulates	Strongly stimulates; is the dominant control of ventilation (Levels > 70–80 mm Hg directly depress the respiratory center and central chemoreceptors)
↑ H^+ in the Arterial Blood	Stimulates; is important in acid–base balance	Does not affect; cannot penetrate the blood–brain barrier

DIRECT EFFECT OF A LARGE DECREASE IN P_{O_2} ON THE RESPIRATORY CENTER The reflex increase in ventilation brought about by the peripheral chemoreceptors when arterial P_{O_2} falls below 60 mm Hg is a lifesaver because a low arterial P_{O_2} tends to directly depress the respiratory center, as it does all the rest of the brain. Were it not for stimulatory intervention of the peripheral chemoreceptors when arterial P_{O_2} falls threateningly low, a vicious cycle ending in cessation of breathing would develop. Direct depression of the respiratory center by the markedly low arterial P_{O_2} would further reduce ventilation, leading to an even greater fall in arterial P_{O_2}, which would even further depress the respiratory center until ventilation ceased and death occurred.

Clinical Note Because the peripheral chemoreceptors respond to the P_{O_2} of the blood, *not* the total O_2 content of the blood, O_2 content in the arterial blood can fall to dangerously low or even fatal levels without the peripheral chemoreceptors ever responding to reflexly stimulate respiration. Remember that only physically dissolved O_2 contributes to blood P_{O_2}. The total O_2 content in the arterial blood can be reduced in anemic states, in which O_2-carrying Hb is reduced, or in CO poisoning, when Hb preferentially binds to this molecule rather than to O_2. In both cases, arterial P_{O_2} is normal, so respiration is not stimulated, even though O_2 delivery to the tissues may be so reduced that the person dies from cellular O_2 deprivation.

Carbon dioxide–generated H^+ in the brain is normally the main regulator of ventilation.

In contrast to arterial P_{O_2}, which does not contribute to the minute-to-minute regulation of respiration, arterial P_{CO_2} is the most important input regulating the magnitude of ventilation under resting conditions. This role is appropriate, because changes in alveolar ventilation have an immediate and pronounced effect on arterial P_{CO_2}. By contrast, changes in ventilation have little effect on % Hb saturation and O_2 availability to the tissues until arterial P_{O_2} falls by more than 40%. Even slight alterations from normal in arterial P_{CO_2} bring about a significant reflex effect on ventilation. An increase in arterial P_{CO_2} reflexly stimulates the respiratory center, with the resultant increase in ventilation promoting elimination of the excess CO_2 to the atmosphere. Conversely, a fall in arterial P_{CO_2} reflexly reduces the respiratory drive. The subsequent decrease in ventilation lets metabolically produced CO_2 accumulate so that P_{CO_2} can be returned to normal.

EFFECT OF INCREASED P_{CO_2} ON THE CENTRAL CHEMORECEPTORS Surprisingly, given the key role of arterial P_{CO_2} in regulating respiration, no important receptors monitor arterial P_{CO_2} per se. The carotid and aortic bodies are only weakly responsive to changes in arterial P_{CO_2}, so they play only a minor role in reflexly stimulating ventilation in response to an elevation in arterial P_{CO_2}. More important in linking changes in arterial P_{CO_2} to compensatory adjustments in ventilation are the **central chemoreceptors**, located in the medulla near the respiratory center. These central chemoreceptors do not monitor CO_2 itself; however, they are sensitive to changes in CO_2-induced H^+ concentration in the brain extracellular fluid (ECF) that bathes them.

Movement of materials across the brain capillaries is restricted by the blood–brain barrier (see p. 120). Because this barrier is readily permeable to CO_2, any increase in arterial P_{CO_2} causes a similar rise in brain-ECF P_{CO_2} as CO_2 diffuses down its pressure gradient from the cerebral blood vessels into the brain ECF. Under the influence of carbonic anhydrase, the increased P_{CO_2} within the brain ECF correspondingly raises the concentration of H^+ according to the law of mass action as it applies to this reaction: $CO_2 + H_2O \rightleftharpoons H^+ + HCO_3^-$. An elevation in H^+ concentration in the brain ECF directly stimulates the central chemoreceptors, which in turn increase ventilation by stimulating the respiratory center through synaptic connections (● Figure 12-27). As the excess CO_2 is subsequently blown off, arterial P_{CO_2} and brain-ECF P_{CO_2} and H^+ concentration return to normal. Conversely, a decline in arterial P_{CO_2} below normal is paralleled by a fall in P_{CO_2} and H^+ in the brain ECF, the result of which is a central chemoreceptor–mediated decrease in ventilation. As CO_2 produced by cell metabolism is consequently allowed to accumulate, arterial P_{CO_2} and brain-ECF P_{CO_2} and H^+ are restored toward normal.

Unlike CO_2, H^+ cannot readily permeate the blood–brain barrier, so H^+ in the plasma cannot gain access to the central chemoreceptors. Accordingly, the central chemoreceptors respond only to H^+ generated within the brain ECF itself as a result of CO_2 entry. Thus, the major mechanism controlling ventilation under resting conditions is specifically aimed at regulating the brain-ECF H^+ concentration, which in turn directly reflects the arterial P_{CO_2}. Unless there are extenuating circumstances such as reduced availability of O_2 in the inspired air, arterial P_{O_2} is coincidentally also maintained at its normal value by the brain-ECF H^+ ventilatory driving mechanism.

The powerful influence of the central chemoreceptors on the respiratory center is responsible for your inability to deliberately hold your breath for more than about a minute. While you hold your breath, metabolically produced CO_2 continues to accumulate in your blood and then to build up the H^+ concentration in your brain ECF. Finally, the increased P_{CO_2}–H^+ stimulant to respiration becomes so powerful that central chemoreceptor excitatory input overrides voluntary inhibitory input to respiration, so breathing resumes despite deliberate attempts to prevent it. Breathing resumes long before arterial P_{O_2} falls to the threateningly low levels that trigger the peripheral chemoreceptors. Therefore, you cannot deliberately hold your breath long enough to create a dangerously high level of CO_2 or low level of O_2 in the arterial blood.

DIRECT EFFECT OF A LARGE INCREASE IN P_{CO_2} ON THE RESPIRATORY CENTER In contrast to the normal reflex stimulatory effect of the increased P_{CO_2}–H^+ mechanism on respiratory activity, very high levels of CO_2 directly depress the entire brain, including the respiratory center, just as very low levels of O_2 do. Up to a P_{CO_2} of 70 to 80 mm Hg, progressively higher P_{CO_2} levels promote correspondingly more vigorous respiratory efforts in an attempt to blow off the excess CO_2. A further increase in P_{CO_2} beyond 70 to 80 mm Hg, however, does not further increase

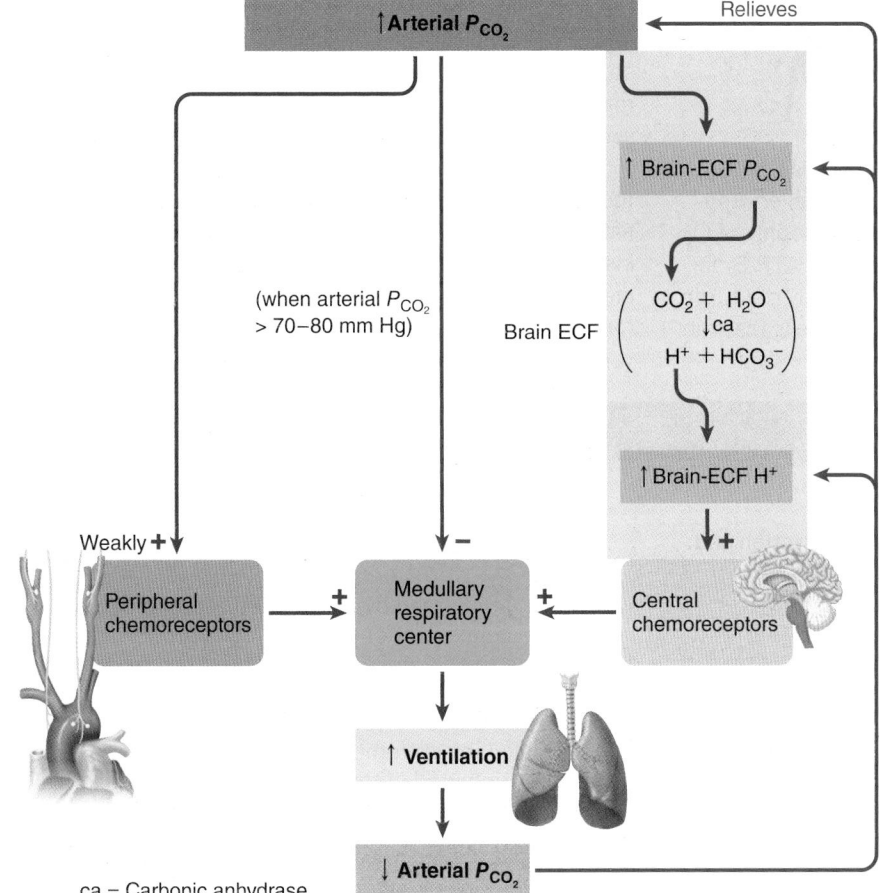

(when arterial P_{CO_2} > 70–80 mm Hg)

Brain ECF

$$\begin{pmatrix} CO_2 + H_2O \\ \downarrow ca \\ H^+ + HCO_3^- \end{pmatrix}$$

ca = Carbonic anhydrase

● **FIGURE 12-27 Effect of increased arterial P_{CO_2} on ventilation.**

ventilation but actually depresses the respiratory neurons. For this reason, CO_2 must be removed and O_2 supplied in closed environments such as closed-system anesthesia machines, submarines, or space capsules. Otherwise, CO_2 could reach lethal levels, not only because it depresses respiration but also because it produces severe respiratory acidosis.

Adjustments in ventilation in response to changes in arterial H^+ are important in acid–base balance.

Changes in arterial H^+ concentration cannot influence the central chemoreceptors because H^+ does not readily cross the blood–brain barrier. However, the aortic and carotid body peripheral chemoreceptors are highly responsive to fluctuations in arterial H^+ concentration, in contrast to their weak sensitivity to deviations in arterial P_{CO_2} and their unresponsiveness to arterial P_{O_2} until it falls 40% below normal. In many situations, even though P_{CO_2} is normal, arterial H^+ concentration is changed by the addition or loss of non-CO_2-generated acid from the body. For example, arterial H^+ concentration increases during diabetes mellitus because excess H^+-generating keto acids are abnormally produced and added to the blood. A rise in arterial H^+ concentration reflexly stimulates ventilation by means of the peripheral chemoreceptors. Conversely, the peripheral chemoreceptors reflexly suppress respiratory activity in response to a fall in arterial H^+

concentration resulting from nonrespiratory causes. Changes in ventilation by this mechanism are extremely important in regulating the body's acid–base balance. Changing the magnitude of ventilation can vary the amount of H^+-generating CO_2 eliminated. The resulting adjustment in the amount of H^+ added to the blood from CO_2 can compensate for the nonrespiratory-induced abnormality in arterial H^+ concentration that first elicited the respiratory response. (See Chapter 14 for further details.)

During apnea, a person "forgets to breathe."

Apnea is the transient interruption of ventilation, with breathing resuming spontaneously. If breathing does not resume, the condition is called **respiratory arrest.** Because ventilation is normally decreased and the central chemoreceptors are less sensitive to the arterial P_{CO_2} drive during sleep, apnea is most likely to occur during this time. Victims of **sleep apnea** may stop breathing for a few seconds or up to 1 or 2 minutes as many as 500 times a night. Mild sleep apnea is not dangerous unless the sufferer has pulmonary or circulatory disease, which can be worsened by recurrent bouts of apnea.

 SUDDEN INFANT DEATH SYNDROME In exaggerated cases of sleep apnea, the victim may be unable to recover from an apneic period, and death results. This is the case in **sudden infant death syndrome (SIDS),** or "crib death," the leading cause of death in the first year of life. With this tragic form of sleep apnea, a previously healthy 2- to 4-month-old infant is found dead in his or her crib for no apparent reason. The underlying cause of SIDS is the subject of intense investigation. Most evidence suggests that the baby "forgets to breathe" because the respiratory control mechanisms are immature, either in the brain stem or in the chemoreceptors that monitor the body's respiratory status. Abnormal lung development has been suggested as being responsible for at least some cases.

Whatever the underlying cause, certain risk factors make babies more vulnerable to SIDS. Among them are sleeping position (an almost 40% higher incidence of SIDS is associated with sleeping on the abdomen rather than on the back or side) and exposure to nicotine during fetal life or after birth. Infants whose mothers smoked during pregnancy or who breathe cigarette smoke in the home are three times more likely to die of SIDS than those not exposed to smoke.

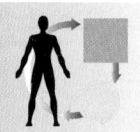

Chapter in Perspective: Focus on Homeostasis

The respiratory system contributes to homeostasis by obtaining O_2 from and eliminating CO_2 to the external environment. All body cells ultimately need an adequate supply of O_2 to use in oxidizing nutrient molecules to generate ATP. Brain cells, which especially depend on a continual supply of O_2, die if deprived of O_2 for more than 4 minutes. Even cells that can

resort to anaerobic ("without O_2") metabolism for energy production, such as strenuously exercising muscles, can do so only transiently by incurring an O_2 deficit that must be made up during the period of excess postexercise O_2 consumption (see p. 225).

As a result of these energy-yielding metabolic reactions, the body produces large quantities of CO_2 that must be eliminated. Because CO_2 and H_2O form carbonic acid, adjustments in the rate of CO_2 elimination by the respiratory system are important in regulating acid–base balance in the internal environment. Cells can survive only within a narrow pH range.

REVIEW EXERCISES

Objective Questions (Answers on p. A-46)

1. Breathing is accomplished by alternate contraction and relaxation of muscles within the lung tissue. (True or false?)
2. Normally, the alveoli empty completely during maximal expiratory efforts. (True or false?)
3. Alveolar ventilation does not always increase when pulmonary ventilation increases. (True or false?)
4. Hemoglobin has a higher affinity for O_2 than for any other substance. (True or false?)
5. Rhythmicity of breathing is brought about by pacemaker activity displayed by the respiratory muscles. (True or false?)
6. The expiratory neurons send impulses to the motor neurons controlling the expiratory muscles during normal quiet breathing. (True or false?)
7. The two forces that tend to keep the alveoli open are _____ and _____.
8. The two forces that promote alveolar collapse are _____ and _____.
9. _____ is a measure of the magnitude of change in lung volume accomplished by a given change in the transmural pressure gradient.
10. ___ is the phenomenon of the lungs snapping back to their resting size after having been stretched.
11. ___ is the erythrocytic enzyme that catalyzes the conversion of CO_2 into HCO_3^-.
12. Which of the following reactions take(s) place at the pulmonary capillaries?
    a. $Hb + O_2 \rightarrow HbO_2$
    b. $CO_2 + H_2O \rightarrow H^+ + HCO_3^-$
    c. $Hb + CO_2 \rightarrow HbCO_2$
    d. $Hb + H^+ \rightarrow HbH$
13. Using the answer code on the right, indicate which chemoreceptors are being described:
    ___ 1. stimulated by an arterial P_{O_2} of 80 mm Hg
    ___ 2. stimulated by an arterial P_{O_2} of 55 mm Hg
    ___ 3. directly depressed by an arterial P_{O_2} of 55 mm Hg
    ___ 4. weakly stimulated by an elevated arterial P_{CO_2}

    (a) peripheral chemo-receptors
    (b) central chemoreceptors
    (c) both peripheral and central chemoreceptors
    (d) neither peripheral nor central chemoreceptors

    ___ 5. strongly stimulated by an elevated brain-ECF H^+ concentration induced by an elevated arterial P_{CO_2}
    ___ 6. stimulated by an elevated arterial H^+ concentration
14. Indicate the O_2 and CO_2 partial pressure relationships important in gas exchange by circling > (greater than), < (less than), or = (equal to) as appropriate in each of the following statements:
    a. P_{O_2} in blood entering the pulmonary capillaries is (>, <, or =) P_{O_2} in the alveoli.
    b. P_{CO_2} in blood entering the pulmonary capillaries is (>, <, or =) P_{CO_2} in the alveoli.
    c. P_{O_2} in the alveoli is (>, <, or =) P_{O_2} in blood leaving the pulmonary capillaries.
    d. P_{CO_2} in the alveoli is (>, <, or =) P_{CO_2} in blood leaving the pulmonary capillaries.
    e. P_{O_2} in blood leaving the pulmonary capillaries is (>, <, or =) P_{O_2} in blood entering the systemic capillaries.
    f. P_{CO_2} in blood leaving the pulmonary capillaries is (>, <, or =) P_{CO_2} in blood entering the systemic capillaries.
    g. P_{O_2} in blood entering the systemic capillaries is (>, <, or =) P_{O_2} in the tissue cells.
    h. P_{CO_2} in blood entering the systemic capillaries is (>, <, or =) P_{CO_2} in the tissue cells.
    i. P_{O_2} in the tissue cells is (>, <, or approximately =) P_{O_2} in blood leaving the systemic capillaries.
    j. P_{CO_2} in the tissue cells is (>, <, or approximately =) P_{CO_2} in blood leaving the systemic capillaries.
    k. P_{O_2} in blood leaving the systemic capillaries is (>, <, or =) P_{O_2} in blood entering the pulmonary capillaries.
    l. P_{CO_2} in blood leaving the systemic capillaries is (>, <, or =) P_{CO_2} in blood entering the pulmonary capillaries.

Essay Questions

1. Distinguish between cellular and external respiration. List the steps in external respiration.
2. Describe the components of the respiratory system. What is the site of gas exchange?
3. Compare atmospheric, intra-alveolar, and intrapleural pressures.

4. Why are the lungs normally stretched even during expiration?
5. Explain why air enters the lungs during inspiration and leaves during expiration.
6. Why is inspiration normally active and expiration normally passive?
7. Why does airway resistance become an important determinant of airflow rates in chronic obstructive pulmonary disease?
8. Explain pulmonary elasticity in terms of compliance and elastic recoil.
9. State the source and function of pulmonary surfactant.
10. Define the various lung volumes and capacities.
11. Compare pulmonary and alveolar ventilation. What is the consequence of anatomic dead space?
12. What determines the partial pressures of a gas in air and in blood?
13. List the methods of O_2 and CO_2 transport in the blood.
14. What is the primary factor that determines the percent hemoglobin saturation? What are the significances of the plateau and the steep portions of the O_2–Hb dissociation curve?
15. How does hemoglobin promote the net transfer of O_2 from the alveoli to the blood?
16. Define the following: hypoxic hypoxia, anemic hypoxia, circulatory hypoxia, histotoxic hypoxia, hypercapnia, hypocapnia, hyperventilation, hypoventilation, hyperpnea, and apnea.
17. What are the locations and functions of the three respiratory control centers? Distinguish between the dorsal respiratory group (DRG) and the ventral respiratory group (VRG).
18. What brain region establishes the rhythmicity of breathing?

POINTS TO PONDER

(Explanations on p. A-46)

1. Why is it important that airplane interiors are pressurized (that is, the pressure is maintained at sea-level atmospheric pressure even though the atmospheric pressure surrounding the plane is substantially lower)? Explain the physiological value of using O_2 masks if the pressure in the airplane interior cannot be maintained.
2. Would hypercapnia accompany the hypoxia produced in each of the following situations? Why or why not?
   a. cyanide poisoning
   b. pulmonary edema
   c. restrictive lung disease
   d. high altitude
   e. severe anemia
   f. congestive heart failure
   g. obstructive lung disease
3. At body temperature, the partial pressure of water vapor is 47 mm Hg. If a person lives 1 mile above sea level in Denver, Colorado, where the atmospheric pressure is 630 mm Hg, what would the P_{O_2} of the inspired air be once it is humidified in the respiratory airways before it reaches the alveoli?
4. Based on what you know about the control of respiration, explain why it is dangerous to voluntarily hyperventilate to lower the arterial P_{CO_2} before going underwater. The purpose of the hyperventilation is to stay under longer before P_{CO_2} rises above normal and drives the swimmer to surface for a breath of air.
5. If a person whose alveolar membranes are thickened by disease has an alveolar P_{O_2} of 100 mm Hg and an alveolar P_{CO_2} of 40 mm Hg, which of the following values of systemic arterial blood gases are most likely to exist?
   a. $P_{O_2} = 105$ mm Hg, $P_{CO_2} = 35$ mm Hg
   b. $P_{O_2} = 100$ mm Hg, $P_{CO_2} = 40$ mm Hg
   c. $P_{O_2} = 90$ mm Hg, $P_{CO_2} = 45$ mm Hg
   If the person is administered 100% O_2, will the arterial P_{O_2} increase, decrease, or remain the same? Will the arterial P_{CO_2} increase, decrease, or remain the same?

CLINICAL CONSIDERATION

(Explanation on p. A-47)

Keith M., a former heavy cigarette smoker, has severe emphysema. How does this condition affect his airway resistance? How does this change in airway resistance influence Keith's inspiratory and expiratory efforts? Describe how his respiratory muscle activity and intra-alveolar pressure changes compare to normal to accomplish a normal tidal volume. How would his spirogram compare to normal? What influence would Keith's condition have on gas exchange in his lungs? What blood gas abnormalities are likely to be present? Some patients like Keith who have severe chronic lung disease lose their sensitivity to an elevated arterial P_{CO_2}. In a prolonged increase in H⁺ generation in the brain ECF, from long-standing CO_2 retention, enough HCO_3^- may cross the blood–brain barrier to buffer, or "neutralize," the excess H⁺. The additional HCO_3^- combines with the excess H⁺, removing it from solution so that it no longer contributes to free H⁺ concentration. When brain-ECF HCO_3^- concentration rises, brain-ECF H⁺ concentration returns to normal, although arterial P_{CO_2} and brain-ECF P_{CO_2} remain high. The central chemoreceptors are no longer aware of the elevated P_{CO_2}, because brain-ECF H⁺ is normal. Because the central chemoreceptors no longer reflexly stimulate the respiratory center in response to the elevated P_{CO_2}, the drive to eliminate CO_2 is blunted in such patients; that is, their level of ventilation is abnormally low considering their high arterial P_{CO_2}. In these patients, the hypoxic drive to ventilation becomes their primary respiratory stimulus, in contrast to normal individuals, in whom arterial P_{CO_2} level is the dominant factor governing the magnitude of ventilation. Given this situation, would it be appropriate to administer O_2 to Keith to relieve his hypoxic condition?

Chapter 12

Respiratory Anatomy (pp. 367–371)

■ *Cellular respiration* refers to the intracellular metabolic reactions that use O_2 and produce CO_2 during energy-yielding oxidation of nutrients. *External respiration* refers to the transfer of O_2 and CO_2 between the external environment and the tissue cells. The respiratory and circulatory systems together accomplish external respiration. *(Review Figure 12-1.)*

■ The respiratory system exchanges air between the atmosphere and the lungs. The airways conduct air from the atmosphere to the alveoli, across which O_2 and CO_2 are exchanged between air in these air sacs and blood in the surrounding pulmonary capillaries. The extremely thin alveolar walls are formed by Type I alveolar cells. Type II alveolar cells secrete pulmonary surfactant. *(Review Figures 12-2 and 12-4.)*

■ The lungs are in the thoracic cavity, a closed compartment of the thorax (chest), the volume of which can be changed by contractile activity of surrounding respiratory muscles.

■ Each lung is surrounded by a double-walled, closed sac, the pleural sac. *(Review Figure 12-5.)*

Respiratory Mechanics (pp. 371–384)

■ Ventilation, or breathing, is the process of cyclically moving air in and out of the lungs so that old alveolar air that has given up O_2 and picked up CO_2 can be exchanged for fresh air.

■ Ventilation is accomplished by alternately shifting the direction of the pressure gradient for airflow between the atmosphere and the alveoli through the cyclic expansion and recoil of the lungs. When intra-alveolar pressure decreases as a result of lung expansion during inspiration, air flows into the lungs from the higher atmospheric pressure. When intra-alveolar pressure increases as a result of lung recoil during expiration, air flows out of the lungs toward the lower atmospheric pressure. The larger the gradient between the alveoli and the atmosphere in either direction, the larger the airflow rate, because air flows until intra-alveolar pressure equilibrates with atmospheric pressure. *(Review Figures 12-6, 12-7, 12-10, 12-13, and 12-14.)*

■ Alternate contraction and relaxation of the inspiratory muscles (primarily the diaphragm and to a lesser extent the external intercostal muscles) indirectly produce periodic inflation and deflation of the lungs by cyclically expanding and compressing the thoracic cavity, with the lungs passively following its movements. *(Review Figures 12-11 and 12-12.)*

■ The lungs follow the movements of the thoracic cavity because the transmural pressure gradient across the lung wall (with the subatmospheric intrapleural pressure being less than the intra-alveolar pressure) stretches the lungs to fill the larger thoracic cavity. *(Review Figures 12-8 and 12-14.)*

■ Because energy is required for contracting the inspiratory muscles, inspiration is an active process, but expiration is passive during quiet breathing because it is accomplished by elastic recoil of the lungs on relaxing inspiratory muscles, at no energy expense. *(Review Figure 12-12a through 12-12c.)*

■ For more forceful active expiration, contraction of the expiratory muscles (primarily the abdominal muscles and to a lesser extent the internal intercostal muscles) further decreases the size of the thoracic cavity and lungs, which further increases the pressure gradient between the alveoli and atmosphere. *(Review Figures 12-11 and 12-12d.)*

■ For more forceful inspiration, the accessory inspiratory muscles in the neck contract to make the thoracic cavity and lungs even larger and drop the intra-alveolar pressure even further than during quiet breathing, thus accomplishing a greater inspiration before equilibration is reached.

■ Besides being directly proportional to the pressure gradient, airflow rate is inversely proportional to airway resistance. Because airway resistance, which depends on the caliber of the conducting airways, is normally very low, airflow rate usually depends primarily on the pressure gradient between the alveoli and the atmosphere. Airway resistance is abnormally increased with obstructive lung disease.

■ The lungs can stretch to varying degrees during inspiration and then recoil to their preinspiratory size during expiration because of their elastic behavior. *Pulmonary compliance* refers to the distensibility of the lungs—how much they stretch in response to a given change in the transmural pressure gradient. *Elastic recoil* refers to the snapping back of the lungs to their resting position during expiration.

■ Pulmonary elastic behavior depends on the elastic connective tissue within the lungs and on alveolar surface tension–pulmonary surfactant interaction. Alveolar surface tension, which is the result of attractive forces between the surface water molecules lining each alveolus, tends to resist the alveolus being stretched on inflation (decreases compliance) and tends to return it back to a smaller surface area during deflation (increases lung rebound). *(Review Table 12-1.)*

■ If the alveoli were lined by water alone, the surface tension would be so great that the lungs would be poorly compliant and would tend to collapse. Pulmonary surfactant intersperses between the water molecules and lowers alveolar surface tension, thereby increasing compliance and counteracting the tendency for alveoli to collapse. *(Review Table 12-1.)*

■ The lungs can be filled to about 5700 ml on maximal inspiration or emptied to about 1200 ml on maximal expiration in an adult male (lower values in females). Normally, the lungs operate "half full." Lung volume typically varies from about 2200 ml to 2700 ml as an average tidal volume of 500 ml of air is moved in and out with each breath. *(Review Figure 12-15.)*

■ The amount of air moved in and out of the lungs in 1 minute is the pulmonary ventilation. Pulmonary ventilation = tidal volume × respiratory rate.

Not all the air moved in and out is available for gas exchange with the blood, because part occupies the conducting airways (*anatomic dead space*). Alveolar ventilation, the volume of air exchanged between the atmosphere and the alveoli in 1 minute, is a measure of the air actually available for gas exchange with the blood. Alveolar ventilation = (tidal volume − dead space volume) × respiratory rate. (*Review Figure 12-17 and Table 12-2.*)

Gas Exchange (pp. 384–387)

Oxygen and CO_2 move across body membranes by passive diffusion down partial pressure gradients. The partial pressure of a gas in air is that portion of the total atmospheric pressure contributed by this individual gas, which in turn is directly proportional to the percentage of this gas in the air. The partial pressure of a gas in blood depends on the amount of this gas dissolved in the blood. (*Review Figure 12-18.*)

Net diffusion of O_2 occurs first between alveoli and blood and then between blood and tissues, as a result of O_2 partial pressure gradients created by the cells' continuous use of O_2 and ongoing replenishment of fresh alveolar O_2 provided by ventilation. Net diffusion of CO_2 occurs in the reverse direction, first between tissues and blood and then between blood and alveoli, as a result of CO_2 partial pressure gradients created by the cells' continuous production of CO_2 and ongoing removal of alveolar CO_2 through ventilation. (*Review Figure 12-19.*)

Other factors that influence the rate of gas exchange include surface area and thickness of the membrane across which the gas is diffusing (Fick's law of diffusion).

Gas Transport (pp. 387–394)

Because O_2 and CO_2 are not very soluble in blood, they must be transported primarily by mechanisms other than simply being physically dissolved. (*Review Table 12-3.*)

Only 1.5% of the O_2 is physically dissolved in the blood, with 98.5% chemically bound to hemoglobin (Hb).

The primary factor that determines the extent to which Hb and O_2 are combined (the % Hb saturation) is the P_{O_2} of the blood, depicted by an S-shaped curve known as the O_2–Hb dissociation curve. In the P_{O_2} range of the pulmonary capillaries (the plateau portion of the curve), Hb is still almost fully saturated even if the blood P_{O_2} falls as much as 40%. This provides a margin of safety by ensuring near-normal O_2 delivery to the tissues despite a substantial reduction in arterial P_{O_2}. In the P_{O_2} range in the systemic capillaries (the steep portion of the curve), Hb unloading increases greatly in response to a small local decline in blood P_{O_2} associated with increased cellular metabolism. In this way, more O_2 is provided to match the increased tissue needs. (*Review Figure 12-21.*)

Increased P_{CO_2}, increased acid, and increased temperature at the tissue level shift the O_2–Hb curve to the right, facilitating the unloading of O_2 from Hb for tissue use. (*Review Figure 12-23.*)

Hemoglobin facilitates a large net transfer of O_2 between alveoli and blood and between blood and tissue cells by acting as a storage depot to keep P_{O_2} (that is, dissolved O_2 concentration) low, despite a considerable increase in the total O_2 content of the blood. (*Review Figure 12-22.*)

Carbon dioxide picked up at the systemic capillaries is transported in the blood by three methods: (1) 10% is physically dissolved, (2) 30% is bound to Hb, and (3) 60% takes the form of bicarbonate (HCO_3^-). The erythrocyte enzyme carbonic anhydrase catalyzes conversion of CO_2 to HCO_3^- according to the reaction $CO_2 + H_2O \rightleftharpoons H^+ + HCO_3^-$. These reactions are all reversed in the lungs as CO_2 is eliminated to the alveoli. (*Review Table 12-3 and Figure 12-24.*)

Control of Respiration (pp. 395–399)

Ventilation involves two aspects, both subject to neural control: (1) rhythmic cycling between inspiration and expiration and (2) regulation of ventilation magnitude, which depends on control of respiratory rate and depth of tidal volume.

Respiratory rhythm is established by the pre-Bötzinger complex, which displays pacemaker activity and drives the inspiratory neurons in the dorsal respiratory group (DRG) of the medullary respiratory control center. When these neurons fire, impulses ultimately reach the inspiratory muscles to bring about inspiration during quiet breathing (*Review Figure 12-25.*)

When the inspiratory neurons stop firing, the inspiratory muscles relax and passive expiration takes place. For active expiration, the expiratory muscles are activated by expiratory neurons in the ventral respiratory group (VRG) of the medullary respiratory control center. Inspiratory neurons in the VRG can also be called into play for more vigorous inspirations.

This basic rhythm is smoothed out by the apneustic and pneumotaxic centers located in the pons. The apneustic center prolongs inspiration; the more powerful pneumotaxic center limits inspiration. (*Review Figure 12-25.*)

Three chemical factors play a role in determining the magnitude of ventilation: P_{CO_2}, P_{O_2}, and H^+ concentration of the arterial blood. (*Review Table 12-5.*)

The dominant factor in the ongoing regulation of ventilation is arterial P_{CO_2}, an increase of which is the most potent chemical stimulus for increasing ventilation. Changes in arterial P_{CO_2} alter ventilation by bringing about corresponding changes in the brain-ECF H^+ concentration, to which the central chemoreceptors are very sensitive. (*Review Figure 12-27.*)

The peripheral chemoreceptors are responsive to an increase in arterial H^+ concentration, which likewise reflexly brings about increased ventilation. The resulting adjustment in arterial H^+-generating CO_2 is important in maintaining the acid–base balance of the body. (*Review Figure 12-26.*)

The peripheral chemoreceptors also reflexly increase ventilation in response to a marked reduction in arterial P_{O_2} (60 mm Hg), serving as an emergency mechanism to increase respiration when arterial P_{O_2} levels fall below the safety range provided by the plateau portion of the O_2–Hb curve.

Respiration activity can also be voluntarily modified.

Urinary System

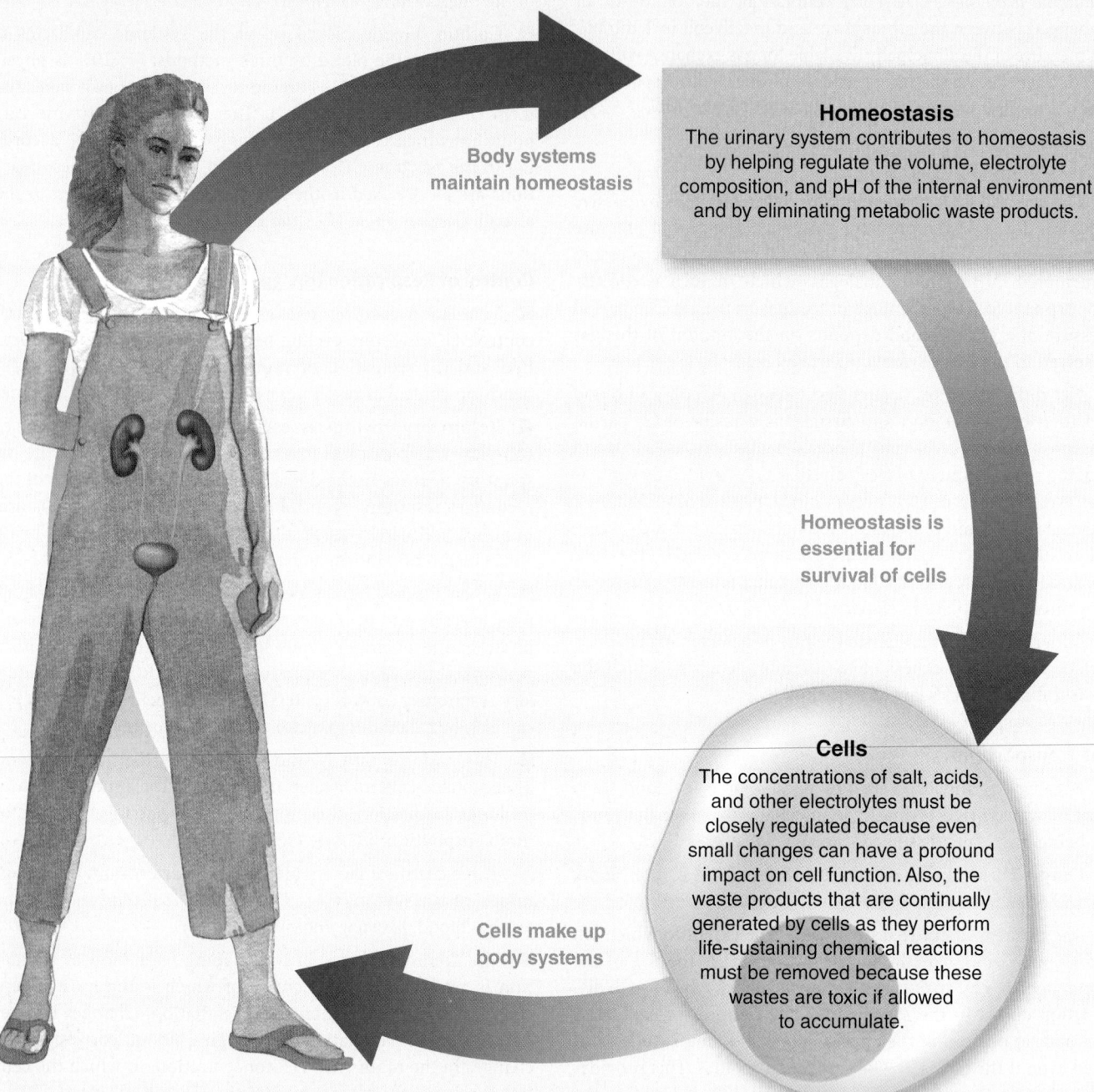

Homeostasis
The urinary system contributes to homeostasis by helping regulate the volume, electrolyte composition, and pH of the internal environment and by eliminating metabolic waste products.

Body systems maintain homeostasis

Homeostasis is essential for survival of cells

Cells
The concentrations of salt, acids, and other electrolytes must be closely regulated because even small changes can have a profound impact on cell function. Also, the waste products that are continually generated by cells as they perform life-sustaining chemical reactions must be removed because these wastes are toxic if allowed to accumulate.

Cells make up body systems

The survival and proper functioning of cells depend on maintaining stable concentrations of salt, acids, and other electrolytes in the internal fluid environment. Cell survival also depends on continuous removal of toxic metabolic wastes that cells produce as they perform life-sustaining chemical reactions. The kidneys play a major role in maintaining homeostasis by regulating the concentration of many plasma constituents, especially electrolytes and water, and by eliminating all metabolic wastes (except CO_2, which is removed by the lungs). As plasma repeatedly filters through the kidneys, they retain constituents of value for the body and eliminate undesirable or excess materials in the urine. Of special importance is the kidneys' ability to regulate the volume and osmolarity (solute concentration) of the internal fluid environment by controlling salt and water balance. Also crucial is their ability to help regulate pH by controlling elimination of acid and base in the urine.

The Urinary System

CHAPTER AT A GLANCE

Kidneys: Functions, Anatomy, and Basic Processes
Functions of the kidneys
Anatomic considerations
Basic renal processes

Glomerular Filtration
Forces responsible for glomerular filtration
Magnitude and regulation of the GFR
Renal blood flow; filtration fraction

Tubular Reabsorption
Transepithelial transport
Active versus passive reabsorption
Process and control of active Na^+ reabsorption
Secondary active reabsorption of glucose and amino acids
Tubular maximum; renal threshold
Regulated reabsorption of PO_4^{3-} and Ca^{2+}
Passive reabsorption of Cl^-, H_2O, and urea

Tubular Secretion
Hydrogen ion secretion
Potassium ion secretion
Organic ion secretion

Urine Excretion and Plasma Clearance
Urine excretion rate
Plasma clearance
Excretion of urine of varying concentrations; medullary countercurrent system
Vasopressin-controlled H_2O reabsorption
Renal failure
Micturition

Kidneys: Functions, Anatomy, and Basic Processes

The composition of the fluid bathing all the cells could be notably altered by exchanges between the cells and this internal fluid environment if mechanisms did not exist to keep the extracellular fluid (ECF) stable.

The kidneys perform a variety of functions aimed at maintaining homeostasis. The kidneys, in concert with hormonal and neural inputs that control their function, are the organs primarily responsible for maintaining the stability of ECF volume, electrolyte composition, and osmolarity (solute concentration). By adjusting the quantity of water and various plasma constituents that are either conserved for the body or eliminated in the urine, the kidneys can maintain water and electrolyte balance within the narrow range compatible with life, despite a wide range of intake and losses of these constituents through other avenues. The kidneys not only adjust for variations in ingestion of water (H_2O), salt, and other electrolytes but also adjust urinary output of these ECF constituents to compensate for abnormal losses through heavy sweating, vomiting, diarrhea, or hemorrhage. Thus, as the kidneys do what they can to maintain homeostasis, urine composition varies greatly.

When the ECF has a surplus of H_2O or a particular electrolyte such as salt (NaCl), the kidneys can eliminate the excess in the urine. If a deficit exists, the kidneys cannot provide additional quantities of the depleted constituent, but they can limit urinary losses of the material in short supply and thus conserve it until the person can take in more of the depleted substance. Accordingly, the kidneys can compensate more efficiently for excesses than for deficits. In fact, in some instances the kidneys cannot halt the loss of a valuable substance in the urine, even though the substance may be in short supply. A prime example is a H_2O deficit. Even if a person is not consuming any H_2O, the kidneys must put out about half a liter of H_2O in the urine each day to fill another major role as the body's "cleaners."

In addition to the kidneys' important regulatory role in maintaining fluid and electrolyte balance, they are the main route for eliminating potentially toxic metabolic wastes and foreign compounds from the body. These wastes cannot be eliminated as solids; they must be excreted in solution, thus obligating the kidneys to produce a minimum volume of around 500 ml of waste-filled urine per day. Because H_2O eliminated in the urine is derived from the blood plasma, a person stranded without H_2O eventually urinates to death: The plasma volume falls to a fatal level as H_2O is unavoidably removed to accompany the wastes.

OVERVIEW OF KIDNEY FUNCTIONS The kidneys perform the following specific functions, most of which help preserve the constancy of the internal fluid environment:

1. *Maintaining H_2O balance in the body* (see Chapter 14).

2. *Maintaining the proper osmolarity of body fluids, primarily through regulating H_2O balance.* This function is important to prevent osmotic fluxes into or out of the cells,

which could lead to detrimental swelling or shrinking of the cells, respectively (see Chapter 14).

3. *Regulating the quantity and concentration of most ECF ions,* including sodium (Na^+), chloride (Cl^-), potassium (K^+), calcium (Ca^{2+}), hydrogen ion (H^+), bicarbonate (HCO_3^-), phosphate (PO_4^{3-}), sulfate (SO_4^{2-}), and magnesium (Mg^{2+}). Even minor fluctuations in the ECF concentrations of some of these electrolytes can have profound influences. For example, changes in the ECF concentration of K^+ can potentially lead to fatal cardiac dysfunction.

4. *Maintaining proper plasma volume,* which is important in the long-term regulation of arterial blood pressure. This function is accomplished through the kidneys' regulatory role in salt (Na^+ and Cl^-) and H_2O balance (see Chapter 14).

5. *Helping maintain the proper acid–base balance* of the body by adjusting urinary output of H^+ and HCO_3^- (see Chapter 14).

6. *Excreting (eliminating) the end products (wastes) of bodily metabolism,* such as urea (from proteins), uric acid (from nucleic acids), creatinine (from muscle creatine), bilirubin (from hemoglobin), and hormone metabolites. If allowed to accumulate, many of these wastes are toxic, especially to the brain.

7. *Excreting many foreign compounds,* such as drugs, food additives, pesticides, and other exogenous nonnutritive materials that have entered the body.

8. *Producing erythropoietin,* a hormone that stimulates red blood cell production (see Chapter 11).

9. *Producing renin,* an enzymatic hormone that triggers a chain reaction important in salt conservation by the kidneys.

10. *Converting vitamin D into its active form* (see Chapter 17).

The kidneys form the urine; the rest of the urinary system carries the urine to the outside.

The **urinary system** consists of the urine-forming organs—the **kidneys**—and the structures that carry the urine from the kidneys to the outside for elimination from the body (● Figure 13-1a). The kidneys are a pair of bean-shaped organs about 4 to 5 in. long that lie behind the abdominal cavity (between the abdominal cavity and the back muscles), one on each side of the vertebral column, slightly above the waistline. Each kidney is supplied by a **renal artery** and a **renal vein,** which, respectively, enters and leaves the kidney at the medial indentation that gives this organ its beanlike form. The kidney acts on the plasma flowing through it to produce urine, conserving materials to be retained in the body and eliminating unwanted materials into the urine.

After urine is formed, it drains into a central collecting cavity, the **renal pelvis,** located at the medial inner core of each kidney (● Figure 13-1b). From there urine is channeled into the **ureter,** a smooth muscle–walled duct that exits at the medial border close to the renal artery and vein. There are two ureters, one carrying urine from each kidney to the single urinary bladder.

The **urinary bladder,** which temporarily stores urine, is a hollow, distensible, smooth muscle–walled sac. Periodically, urine is emptied from the bladder to the outside through an-

other tube, the **urethra,** as a result of bladder contraction. The urethra in females is straight and short, passing directly from the neck of the bladder to the outside (see ● Figure 18-2, p. 582). In males, the urethra is longer and follows a curving course from the bladder to the outside, passing through both the prostate gland and the penis (● Figure 13-1a; see also ● Figure 18-1, p. 581). The male urethra serves the dual function of providing both a route for eliminating urine from the bladder and a passageway for semen from the reproductive organs. The prostate gland lies below the neck of the bladder and completely encircles the urethra.

 Prostatic enlargement, which often occurs during middle to older age, can partially or completely occlude the urethra, impeding the flow of urine.

The parts of the urinary system beyond the kidneys merely serve as "ductwork" to transport urine to the outside. Once formed by the kidneys, urine is not altered in composition or volume as it moves downstream through the rest of the tract.

The nephron is the functional unit of the kidney.

Each kidney consists of about 1 million microscopic functional units known as **nephrons,** which are bound together by connective tissue (● Figure 13-1c). Recall that a functional unit is the smallest unit within an organ capable of performing all of that organ's functions. Because the main function of the kidneys is to produce urine and, in so doing, maintain constancy in the ECF composition, a nephron is the smallest unit capable of forming urine.

The arrangement of nephrons within the kidneys gives rise to two distinct regions—an outer region called the **renal cortex,** which looks granular, and an inner region, the **renal medulla,** which is made up of striated triangles, the **renal pyramids** (● Figure 13-1b and c).

Knowledge of the structural arrangement of an individual nephron is essential for understanding the distinction between the cortical and the medullary regions of the kidney and, more important, for understanding renal function. Each nephron consists of a *vascular component* and a *tubular component,* both of which are intimately related structurally and functionally (● Figure 13-2).

VASCULAR COMPONENT OF THE NEPHRON The dominant part of the nephron's vascular component is the **glomerulus,** a ball-like tuft of capillaries through which part of the water and solutes is filtered from blood passing through. This filtered fluid, which is almost identical in composition to plasma, then passes through the nephron's tubular component, where various transport processes convert it into urine.

On entering the kidney, the renal artery subdivides to ultimately form many small vessels known as **afferent arterioles,** one of which supplies each nephron. The afferent arteriole delivers blood to the glomerulus. The glomerular capillaries rejoin to form another arteriole, the **efferent arteriole,** through which blood that was not filtered into the tubular component leaves the glomerulus (● Figures 13-2 and 13-3). The efferent arterioles are the only arterioles in the body that drain from capillar-

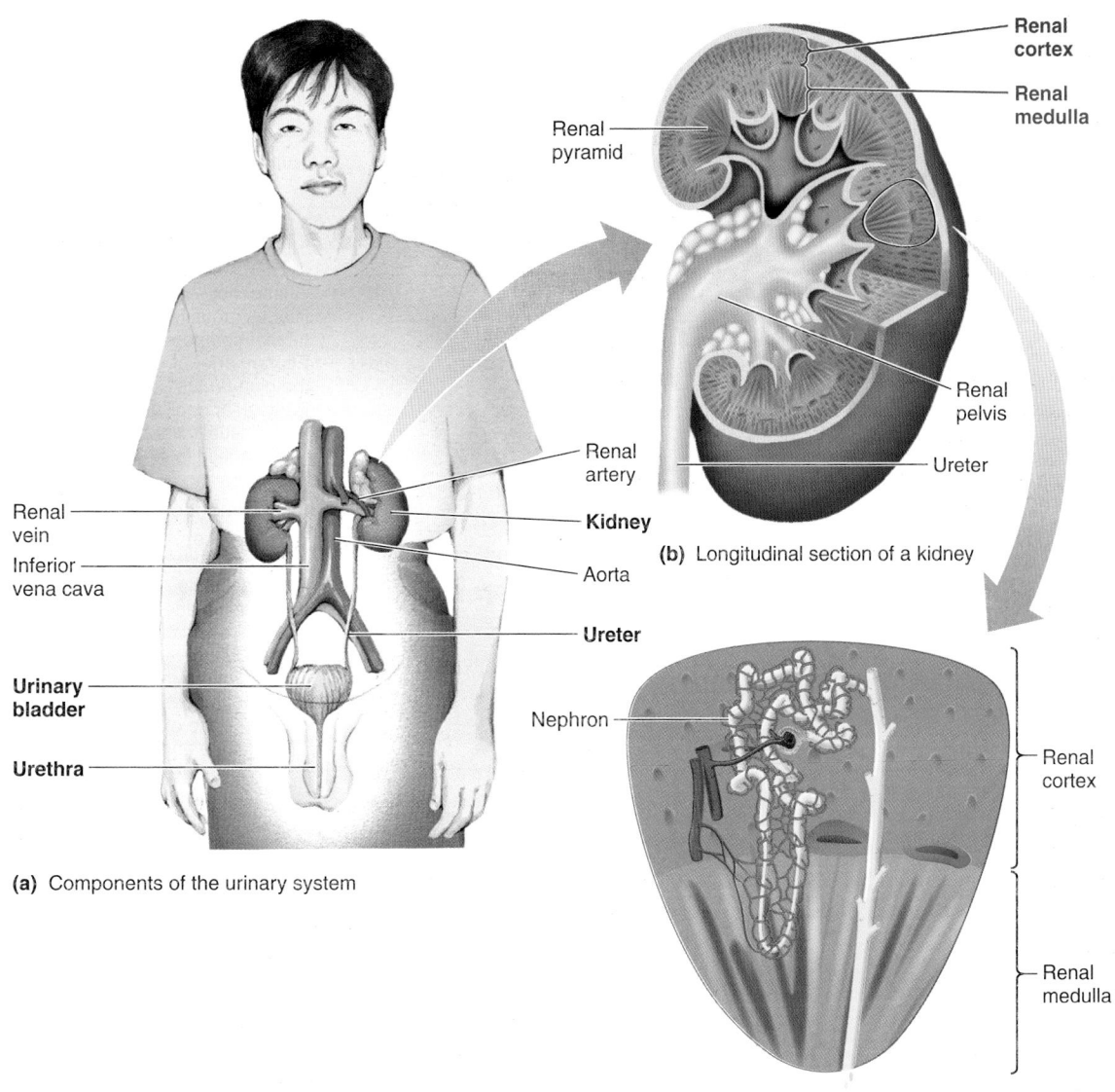

Renal cortex

Renal medulla

Renal pyramid

Renal pelvis

Ureter

(b) Longitudinal section of a kidney

Renal artery

Kidney

Aorta

Ureter

Renal vein

Inferior vena cava

Urinary bladder

Urethra

(a) Components of the urinary system

Nephron

Renal cortex

Renal medulla

(c) A greatly exaggerated nephron

● **FIGURE 13-1 The urinary system.** (a) The pair of kidneys produce urine, which the ureters carry to the urinary bladder. Urine is stored in the bladder and periodically emptied to the exterior through the urethra. (b) The kidney consists of an outer, granular-appearing renal cortex and an inner, striated-appearing renal medulla. The renal pelvis at the medial inner core of the kidney collects urine after it is formed. (c) Each kidney has a million nephrons. One of these microscopic functional units is shown here, greatly exaggerated, in a medullary renal pyramid capped by a section of renal cortex.

ies. Typically, arterioles break up into capillaries that rejoin to form venules. At the glomerular capillaries, no O_2 or nutrients are extracted from the blood for use by the kidney tissues, nor are waste products picked up from the surrounding tissue. Thus, arterial blood enters the glomerular capillaries through the afferent arteriole, and arterial blood leaves the glomerulus through the efferent arteriole.

The efferent arteriole quickly subdivides into a second set of capillaries, the **peritubular capillaries,** which supply the renal tissue with blood and are important in exchanges between the tubular system and the blood during conversion of the filtered fluid into urine. These peritubular capillaries, as their name implies, are intertwined around the tubular system (*peri*

means "around"). The peritubular capillaries rejoin to form venules that ultimately drain into the renal vein, by which blood leaves the kidney.

TUBULAR COMPONENT OF THE NEPHRON The nephron's tubular component is a hollow, fluid-filled tube formed by a single layer of epithelial cells. Even though the tubule is continuous from its beginning near the glomerulus to its ending at the renal pelvis, it is arbitrarily divided into various segments based on differences in structure and function along its length (● Figure 13-2). The tubular component begins with **Bowman's capsule,** an expanded, double-walled "cup" that surrounds the glomerulus to collect fluid filtered from the glomerular capillaries. The

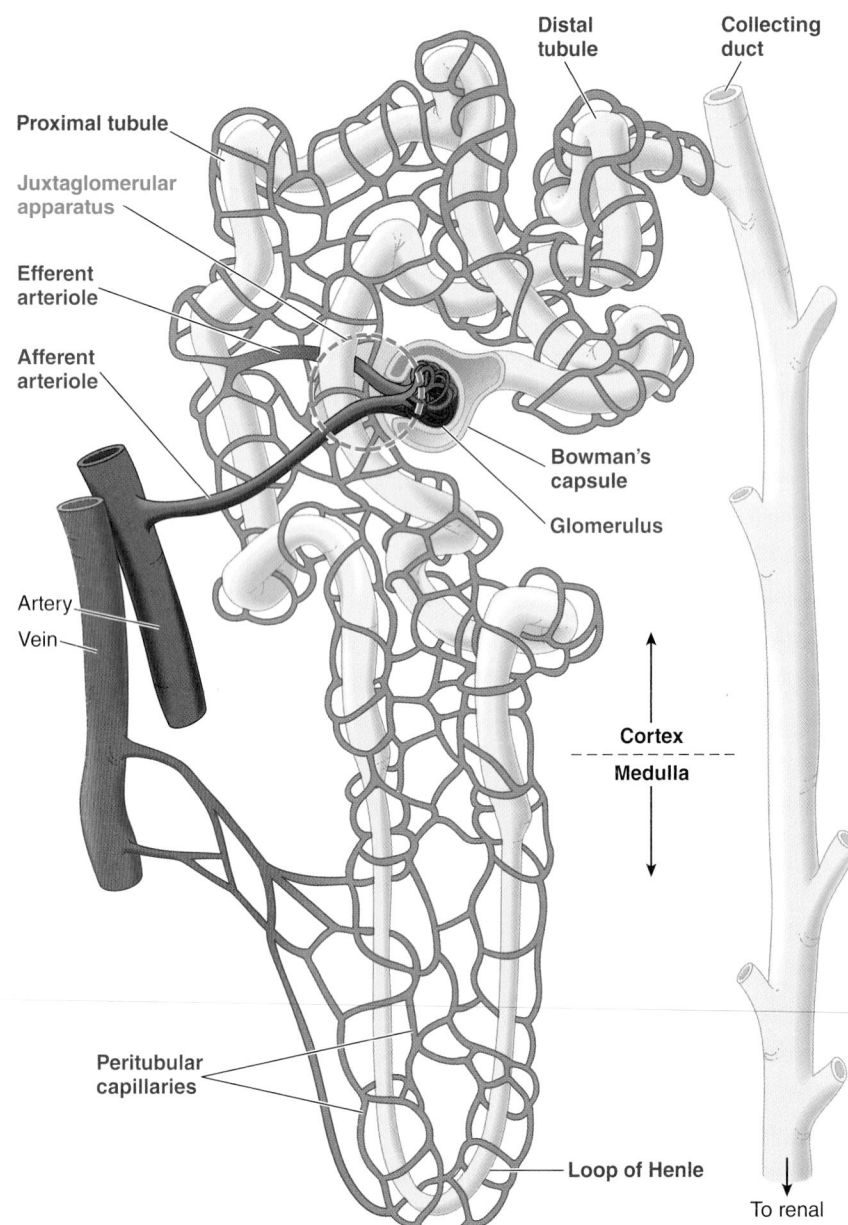

Distal tubule

Collecting duct

Proximal tubule

Juxtaglomerular apparatus

Efferent arteriole

Afferent arteriole

Bowman's capsule

Glomerulus

Artery

Vein

Cortex

Medulla

Peritubular capillaries

Loop of Henle

To renal pelvis

Overview of Functions of Parts of a Nephron

Vascular component
- Afferent arteriole—carries blood to the glomerulus
- Glomerulus—a tuft of capillaries that filters a protein-free plasma into the tubular component
- Efferent arteriole—carries blood from the glomerulus
- Peritubular capillaries—supply the renal tissue; involved in exchanges with the fluid in the tubular lumen

Tubular component
- Bowman's capsule—collects the glomerular filtrate
- Proximal tubule—uncontrolled reabsorption and secretion of selected substances occur here
- Loop of Henle—establishes an osmotic gradient in the renal medulla that is important in the kidney's ability to produce urine of varying concentration
- Distal tubule and collecting duct—variable, controlled reabsorption of Na^+ and H_2O and secretion of K^+ and H^+ occur here; fluid leaving the collecting duct is urine, which enters the renal pelvis

Combined vascular/tubular component
- Juxtaglomerular apparatus—produces substances involved in the control of kidney function

● **FIGURE 13-2 A nephron.**

presence of all glomeruli and associated Bowman's capsules in the cortex produces this region's granular appearance.

From Bowman's capsule, the filtered fluid passes into the **proximal tubule,** which lies entirely within the cortex and is highly coiled or convoluted throughout much of its course. The next segment, the **loop of Henle,** forms a sharp U-shaped or hairpin loop that dips into the renal medulla. The *descending limb* of the loop of Henle plunges from the cortex into the medulla; the *ascending limb* traverses back up into the cortex. The ascending limb returns to the glomerular region of its own nephron, where it passes through the fork formed by the afferent and efferent arterioles. Both the tubular and the vascular cells at this point are specialized to form the **juxtaglomerular apparatus,** a structure that lies next to the glomerulus (*juxta* means "next to"). This specialized region plays an important role in regulating kidney function. Beyond the juxtaglomerular

apparatus, the tubule again coils tightly to form the **distal tubule,** which also lies entirely within the cortex. The distal tubule empties into a **collecting duct** or **tubule,** with each collecting duct draining fluid from up to eight separate nephrons. Each collecting duct plunges down through the medulla to empty its fluid contents (now converted into urine) into the renal pelvis. The parallel arrangement of long loops of Henle and collecting ducts in the medulla creates this region's striated appearance.

The three basic renal processes are glomerular filtration, tubular reabsorption, and tubular secretion.

Three basic processes are involved in forming urine: *glomerular filtration, tubular reabsorption,* and *tubular secretion.* To aid in visualizing the relationships among these renal processes, it is useful to unwind the nephron schematically, as in ● Figure 13-4.

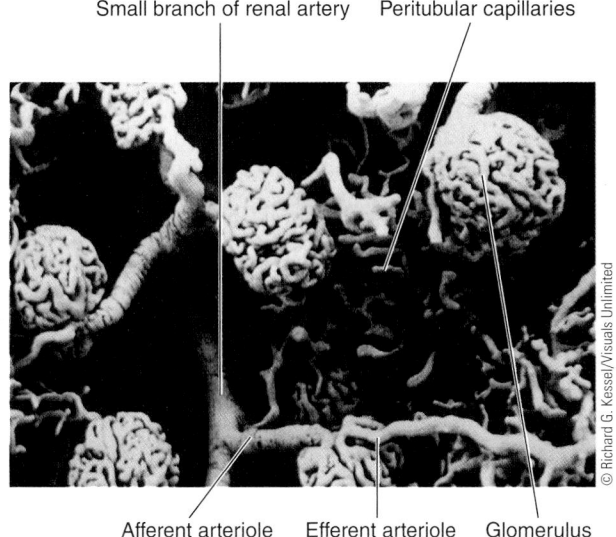

Small branch of renal artery   Peritubular capillaries

© Richard G. Kessel/Visuals Unlimited

Afferent arteriole   Efferent arteriole   Glomerulus

● FIGURE 13-3 **Scanning electron micrograph of glomeruli and associated arterioles.**

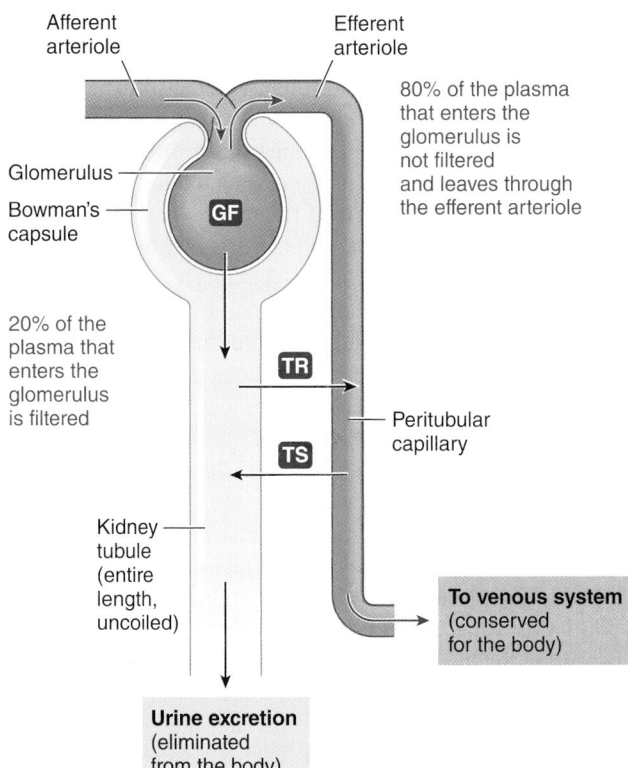

Afferent arteriole

Efferent arteriole

80% of the plasma that enters the glomerulus is not filtered and leaves through the efferent arteriole

Glomerulus

Bowman's capsule

GF

20% of the plasma that enters the glomerulus is filtered

TR

TS

Peritubular capillary

Kidney tubule (entire length, uncoiled)

To venous system (conserved for the body)

Urine excretion (eliminated from the body)

GF = **Glomerular filtration**—nondiscriminant filtration of a protein-free plasma from the glomerulus into Bowman's capsule

TR = **Tubular reabsorption**—selective movement of filtered substances from the tubular lumen into the peritubular capillaries

TS = **Tubular secretion**—selective movement of nonfiltered substances from the peritubular capillaries into the tubular lumen

● FIGURE 13-4 **Basic renal processes.** Anything filtered or secreted but not reabsorbed is excreted in the urine and lost from the body. Anything filtered and subsequently reabsorbed, or not filtered at all, enters the venous blood and is saved for the body.

GLOMERULAR FILTRATION As blood flows through the glomerulus, protein-free plasma filters through the glomerular capillaries into Bowman's capsule. Normally, about 20% of the plasma that enters the glomerulus is filtered. This process, known as **glomerular filtration,** is the first step in urine formation. On average, 125 ml of glomerular filtrate (filtered fluid) are formed collectively through all the glomeruli each minute. This amounts to 180 liters (about 47.5 gallons) each day. Considering that the average plasma volume in an adult is 2.75 liters, this means that the kidneys filter the entire plasma volume about 65 times per day. If everything filtered passed out in the urine, the total plasma volume would be urinated in less than half an hour! This does not happen, however, because the kidney tubules and peritubular capillaries are intimately related throughout their lengths so that materials can be transferred between the fluid inside the tubules and the blood within the peritubular capillaries.

TUBULAR REABSORPTION As the filtrate flows through the tubules, substances of value to the body are returned to the peritubular capillary plasma. This selective movement of substances from inside the tubule (the tubular lumen) into the blood is called **tubular reabsorption.** Reabsorbed substances are not lost from the body in the urine but instead are carried by the peritubular capillaries to the venous system and then to the heart to be recirculated. Of the 180 liters of plasma filtered per day, 178.5 liters, on average, are reabsorbed. The remaining 1.5 liters left in the tubules pass into the renal pelvis to be eliminated as urine. In general, substances the body needs to conserve are selectively reabsorbed, whereas unwanted substances that must be eliminated stay in the urine.

TUBULAR SECRETION The third renal process, **tubular secretion,** is the selective transfer of substances from the peritubular capillary blood into the tubular lumen. It provides a second route for substances to enter the renal tubules from the blood,

the first being by glomerular filtration. Only about 20% of the plasma flowing through the glomerular capillaries is filtered into Bowman's capsule; the remaining 80% flows on through the efferent arteriole into the peritubular capillaries. Tubular secretion provides a mechanism for more rapidly eliminating selected substances from the plasma by extracting an additional quantity of a particular substance from the 80% of unfiltered plasma in the peritubular capillaries and adding it to the quantity of the substance already present in the tubule as a result of filtration.

URINE EXCRETION **Urine excretion** is the elimination of substances from the body in the urine. It is not a separate process but the result of the first three processes. All plasma constituents filtered or secreted but not reabsorbed remain in the tubules and pass into the renal pelvis to be excreted as urine and eliminated from the body (● Figure 13-4). (Do not confuse excretion with secretion.) Note that anything filtered and subsequently reabsorbed, or not filtered at all, enters the venous blood from the peritubular capillaries and thus is conserved for the body instead of being excreted in urine, despite passing through the kidneys.

THE BIG PICTURE OF THE BASIC RENAL PROCESSES Glomerular filtration is largely an indiscriminate process. With the exception of blood cells and plasma proteins, all constituents within the blood—H₂O, nutrients, electrolytes, wastes, and so on— nonselectively enter the tubular lumen as a bulk unit during filtration. That is, of the 20% of the plasma filtered at the glomerulus, everything in that part of the plasma enters Bowman's capsule except for the plasma proteins. The highly discriminating tubular processes then work on the filtrate to return to the blood a fluid of the composition and volume necessary to maintain constancy of the internal fluid environment. The unwanted filtered material is left behind in the tubular fluid to be excreted as urine. Glomerular filtration can be thought of as pushing a part of the plasma, with all its essential components, as well as those that need to be eliminated from the body, onto a tubular "conveyor belt" that terminates at the renal pelvis, which is the collecting point for urine within the kidney. All plasma constituents that enter this conveyor belt and are not subsequently returned to the plasma by the end of the line are spilled out of the kidney as urine. It is up to the tubular system to salvage by reabsorption the filtered materials that need to be preserved for the body while leaving behind substances that must be excreted. In addition, some substances not only are filtered but also are secreted onto the tubular conveyor belt, so the amounts of these substances excreted in the urine are greater than the amounts that were filtered. For many substances, these renal processes are subject to physiologic control. Thus, the kidneys handle each constituent in the plasma by a particular combination of filtration, reabsorption, and secretion.

The kidneys act only on the plasma, yet the ECF consists of both the plasma and the interstitial fluid. The interstitial fluid is the true internal fluid environment of the body, because it is the only component of the ECF that comes into direct contact with the cells. However, because of the free exchange between the plasma and the interstitial fluid across the capillary walls (with the exception of plasma proteins), interstitial fluid composition reflects the composition of plasma. Thus, by performing their regulatory and excretory roles on plasma, the kidneys maintain the proper interstitial fluid environment for optimal cell function. Most of the rest of this chapter is devoted to considering how the basic renal processes are accomplished and the mechanisms by which they are carefully regulated to help maintain homeostasis.

Glomerular Filtration

Fluid filtered from the glomerulus into Bowman's capsule must pass through the three layers that make up the **glomerular membrane** (● Figure 13-5):

1. The *glomerular capillary wall* consists of a single layer of flattened endothelial cells. It is perforated by many large pores

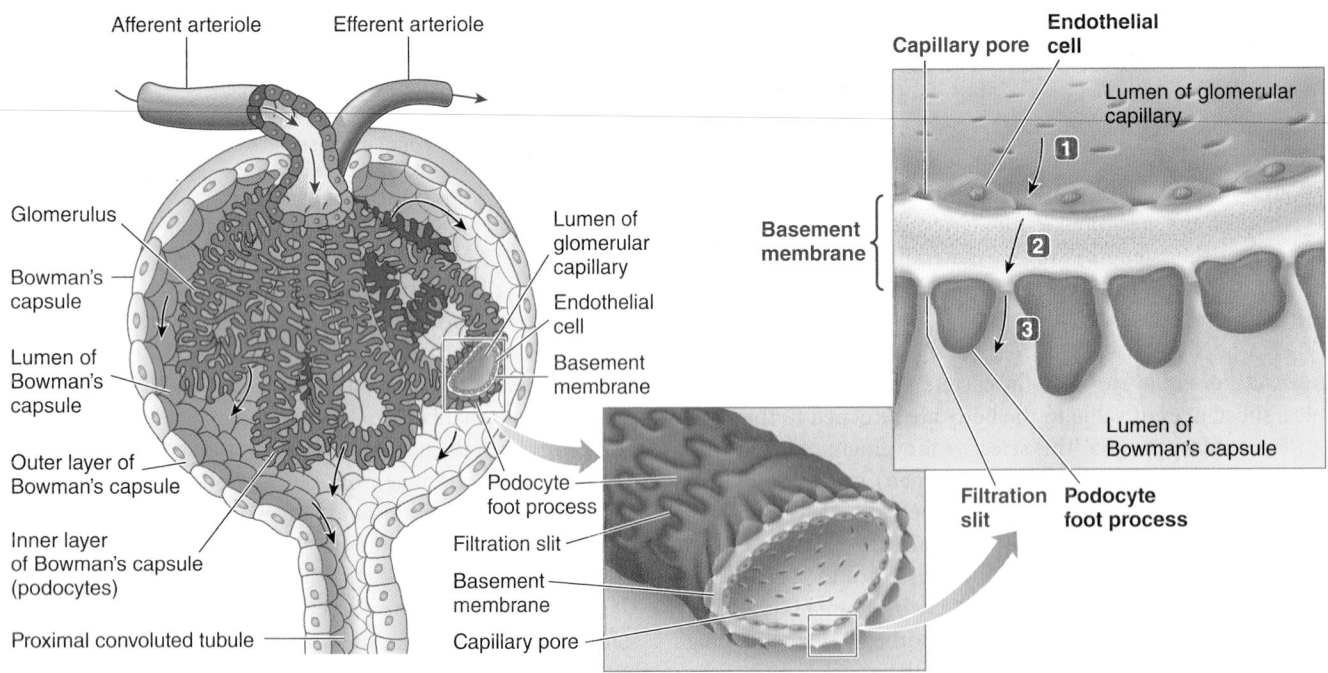

To be filtered, a substance must pass through

1 the pores between the endothelial cells of the glomerular capillary

2 an acellular basement membrane

3 the filtration slits between the foot processes of the podocytes in the inner layer of Bowman's capsule

● **FIGURE 13-5 Layers of the glomerular membrane.**

(or fenestrations; see p. 295) that make it more than 100 times more permeable to H_2O and solutes than capillaries elsewhere in the body.

2. The *basement membrane* is an acellular (lacking cells) gelatinous layer sandwiched between the glomerulus and Bowman's capsule.

3. The *inner layer of Bowman's capsule* consists of **podocytes,** octopus-like cells that encircle the glomerular tuft. Each podocyte bears many elongated foot processes (*podo* means "foot"; a *process* is a projection or appendage) that interdigitate with foot processes of adjacent podocytes, much as you interlace your fingers between each other when you cup your hands around a ball (● Figure 13-6). The narrow slits between adjacent foot processes, known as **filtration slits,** provide a pathway through which fluid leaving the glomerular capillaries can enter the lumen of Bowman's capsule.

Thus, the route that filtered substances take across the glomerular membrane is completely extracellular—first through capillary pores, then through the acellular basement membrane, and finally through capsular filtration slits (see ● Figure 13-5). Collectively, these layers function as a fine molecular sieve that retains the blood cells and plasma proteins but permits H_2O and solutes to filter through.

Glomerular capillary blood pressure is the major force that causes glomerular filtration.

To accomplish glomerular filtration, a force must drive a part of the plasma in the glomerulus through the openings in the glomerular membrane. No active transport mechanisms or local energy expenditures are involved in moving fluid from the plasma across the glomerular membrane into Bowman's capsule. Passive physical forces similar to those acting across capillaries elsewhere accomplish glomerular filtration. Because the glomerulus is a tuft of capillaries, the same principles of fluid

Cell body of podocyte

Foot processes   Filtration slits

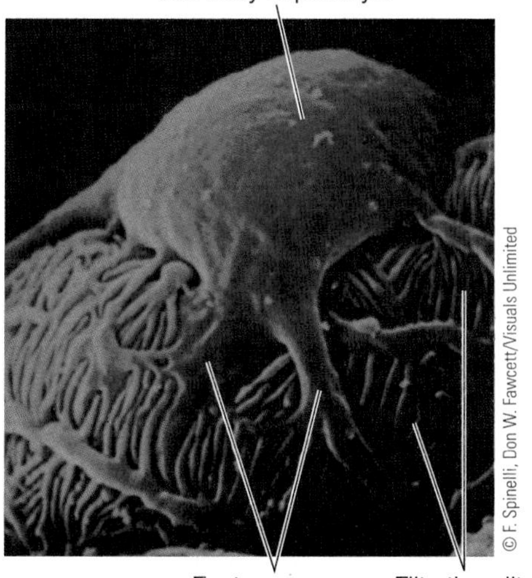

● **FIGURE 13-6 Bowman's capsule podocytes with foot processes and filtration slits.** Note the filtration slits between adjacent foot processes on this scanning electron micrograph. The podocytes and their foot processes encircle the glomerular capillaries.

© F. Spinelli, Don W. Fawcett/Visuals Unlimited

dynamics apply here that cause ultrafiltration across other capillaries (see p. 297), except for two important differences: (1) The glomerular capillaries are more permeable than capillaries elsewhere, so more fluid is filtered for a given filtration pressure, and (2) the balance of forces across the glomerular membrane is such that filtration occurs the entire length of the capillaries. In contrast, the balance of forces in other capillaries shifts so that filtration occurs in the beginning part of the vessel but reabsorption occurs toward the vessel's end (see ● Figure 10-18, p. 298).

FORCES INVOLVED IN GLOMERULAR FILTRATION Three physical forces are involved in glomerular filtration (▲ Table 13-1): glomerular capillary blood pressure, plasma-colloid osmotic pressure, and Bowman's capsule hydrostatic pressure. Let us examine the role of each.

1. *Glomerular capillary blood pressure* is the fluid (hydrostatic) pressure exerted by the blood within the glomerular capillaries. It ultimately depends on contraction of the heart (the source of energy that produces glomerular filtration) and the resistance to blood flow offered by the afferent and efferent arterioles. Glomerular capillary blood pressure, at an estimated average value of 55 mm Hg, is higher than capillary blood pressure elsewhere. The reason for the higher pressure is the larger diameter of the afferent arteriole compared to that of the efferent

▲ Table 13-1 Forces Involved in Glomerular Filtration

Force	Effect	Magnitude (mm Hg)
Glomerular Capillary Blood Pressure	Favors filtration	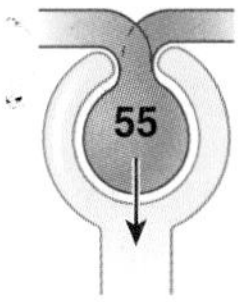 55
Plasma-Colloid Osmotic Pressure	Opposes filtration	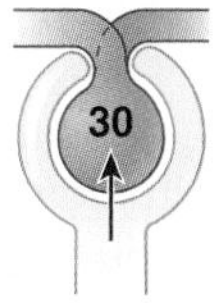 30
Bowman's Capsule Hydrostatic Pressure	Opposes filtration	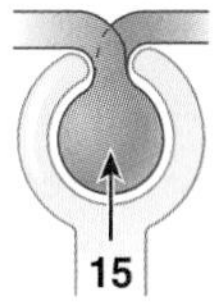 15
Net Filtration Pressure (difference between force favoring and forces opposing filtration)	Favors filtration	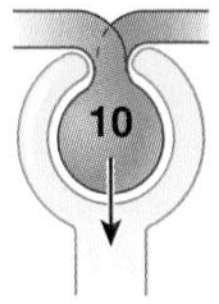 10 55 − (30 + 15) = 10

arteriole. Because blood can flow more rapidly into the glomerulus through the wide afferent arteriole than it can leave through the narrower efferent arteriole, glomerular capillary blood pressure is maintained high as a result of blood damming up in the glomerular capillaries. Also, because of the high resistance offered by the efferent arterioles, blood pressure does not have the same tendency to fall along the length of the glomerular capillaries as it does along other capillaries. This elevated, nondecremental glomerular blood pressure tends to push fluid out of the glomerulus into Bowman's capsule along the glomerular capillaries' entire length, and it is the major force producing glomerular filtration.

Whereas glomerular capillary blood pressure *favors* filtration, the two other forces acting across the glomerular membrane (plasma-colloid osmotic pressure and Bowman's capsule hydrostatic pressure) *oppose* filtration.

2. *Plasma-colloid osmotic pressure* is caused by the unequal distribution of plasma proteins across the glomerular membrane. Because plasma proteins cannot be filtered, they are in the glomerular capillaries but not in Bowman's capsule. Accordingly, the concentration of H_2O is higher in Bowman's capsule than in the glomerular capillaries. The resulting tendency for H_2O to move by osmosis down its own concentration gradient from Bowman's capsule into the glomerulus opposes glomerular filtration. This opposing osmotic force averages 30 mm Hg, which is slightly higher than across other capillaries. It is higher because more H_2O is filtered out of the glomerular blood, so the concentration of plasma proteins is higher than elsewhere.

3. *Bowman's capsule hydrostatic pressure,* the pressure exerted by the fluid in this initial part of the tubule, is estimated to be about 15 mm Hg. This pressure, which tends to push fluid out of Bowman's capsule, opposes the filtration of fluid from the glomerulus into Bowman's capsule.

GLOMERULAR FILTRATION RATE As can be seen in ▲ Table 13-1, the forces acting across the glomerular membrane are not in balance. The total force favoring filtration is the glomerular capillary blood pressure at 55 mm Hg. The total of the two forces opposing filtration is 45 mm Hg. The net difference favoring filtration (10 mm Hg of pressure) is called the **net filtration pressure.** This modest pressure forces large volumes of fluid from the blood through the highly permeable glomerular membrane.

Normally, about 20% of the plasma that enters the glomerulus is filtered at the net filtration pressure of 10 mm Hg, producing collectively through all glomeruli 180 liters of glomerular filtrate each day for an average **glomerular filtration rate (GFR)** of 125 ml/min in males (160 liters of filtrate per day for an average GFR of 115 ml/min in females).

Changes in the GFR result primarily from changes in glomerular capillary blood pressure.

Because the net filtration pressure that accomplishes glomerular filtration is simply the result of an imbalance of opposing physical forces between the glomerular capillary plasma and Bowman's capsule fluid, alterations in any of these physical forces can affect the GFR. We now examine the effect that changes in each of these physical forces have on the GFR.

UNREGULATED INFLUENCES ON THE GFR Plasma-colloid osmotic pressure and Bowman's capsule hydrostatic pressure are not subject to regulation and, under normal conditions, do not vary much.

However, they can change pathologically and thus inadvertently affect the GFR. Because plasma-colloid osmotic pressure opposes filtration, a decrease in plasma protein concentration, by reducing this pressure, leads to an increase in the GFR. An uncontrollable reduction in plasma protein concentration might occur, for example, in severely burned patients who lose a large quantity of protein-rich, plasma-derived fluid through the exposed burned surface of their skin. Conversely, when plasma-colloid osmotic pressure is elevated, such as in cases of dehydrating diarrhea, the GFR is reduced.

Bowman's capsule hydrostatic pressure can become uncontrollably elevated, and filtration subsequently can decrease, given a urinary tract obstruction, such as a kidney stone or enlarged prostate. The damming up of fluid behind the obstruction elevates capsular hydrostatic pressure.

CONTROLLED ADJUSTMENTS IN THE GFR Unlike plasma-colloid osmotic pressure and Bowman's capsule hydrostatic pressure—which may be uncontrollably altered in various disease states and thereby may inappropriately alter the GFR—glomerular capillary blood pressure can be controlled to adjust the GFR to suit the body's needs. Assuming that all other factors stay constant, as the glomerular capillary blood pressure goes up, the net filtration pressure increases and the GFR increases correspondingly. The magnitude of the glomerular capillary blood pressure depends on the rate of blood flow within each of the glomeruli. The amount of blood flowing into a glomerulus per minute is determined largely by the resistance offered by the afferent arterioles. If resistance increases in the afferent arteriole, less blood flows into the glomerulus, decreasing the GFR. Controlled changes in the GFR are brought about by the sympathetic nervous system, which adjusts glomerular blood flow by regulating the caliber of the afferent arterioles. The parasympathetic nervous system does not have any influence on the kidneys.

Sympathetic control of the GFR is aimed at long-term regulation of arterial blood pressure. If plasma volume is decreased—for example, by hemorrhage—the resulting fall in arterial blood pressure is detected by the arterial carotid sinus and aortic arch baroreceptors, which initiate neural reflexes to raise blood pressure toward normal (see p. 307). These reflex responses are coordinated by the cardiovascular control center in the brain stem and are mediated primarily through increased sympathetic activity to the heart and blood vessels. Although the resulting increase in both cardiac output and total peripheral resistance helps raise blood pressure toward normal in the short term, plasma volume is still reduced. In the long term, plasma volume must be restored to normal. One compensation for a depleted plasma volume is reduced urine output so that more fluid than normal is conserved for the body. Urine output is reduced in part by reducing the GFR; if less fluid is filtered, less is available to excrete.

ROLE OF THE BARORECEPTOR REFLEX IN EXTRINSIC CONTROL OF THE GFR No new mechanism is needed to decrease the GFR. It is reduced by the baroreceptor reflex response to a fall in blood pressure (● Figure 13-7). During this reflex, sympathetically induced vasoconstriction occurs in most arterioles throughout the body (including the afferent arterioles) as a compensatory mechanism to increase total peripheral resistance. When the afferent arterioles carrying blood to the glomeruli constrict from increased sympathetic activity, less blood flows into the glomeruli than normal, lowering glomerular capillary blood pressure (● Figure 13-8a). The resulting decrease in GFR, in turn, reduces urine volume. In this way, some of the H_2O and salt that would otherwise have been lost in the urine are saved for the body, helping restore plasma volume to normal in the long term so that short-term cardiovascular adjustments that have been made are no longer necessary. Other mechanisms, such as increased tubular reabsorption of H_2O and salt, as well as increased thirst (described more thoroughly elsewhere), also contribute to long-term maintenance of blood pressure, despite a loss of plasma volume, by helping restore plasma volume.

Conversely, if blood pressure is elevated (for example, because of an expansion of plasma volume following ingestion of excessive fluid), the opposite responses occur. When the baroreceptors detect a rise in blood pressure, sympathetic vasoconstrictor activity to the arterioles, including the renal afferent arterioles, is reflexly reduced, allowing afferent arteriolar vasodilation to occur. As more blood enters the glomeruli through the dilated afferent arterioles, glomerular capillary blood pressure rises, increasing the GFR (● Figure 13-8b). As more fluid is filtered, more fluid is available to be eliminated in the urine. A hormonally adjusted reduction in the tubular reabsorption of H_2O and salt also contributes to the increase in urine volume. These two renal mechanisms—increased glomerular filtration and decreased tubular reabsorption of H_2O and salt—increase urine volume and eliminate the excess fluid from the body. Reduced thirst and fluid intake also help restore an elevated blood pressure to normal in the long term.

Before turning to the process of tubular reabsorption, we examine the percentage of cardiac output that goes to the kidneys. This further reinforces the concept of how much blood flows through the kidneys and how much of that fluid is filtered and subsequently acted on by the tubules.

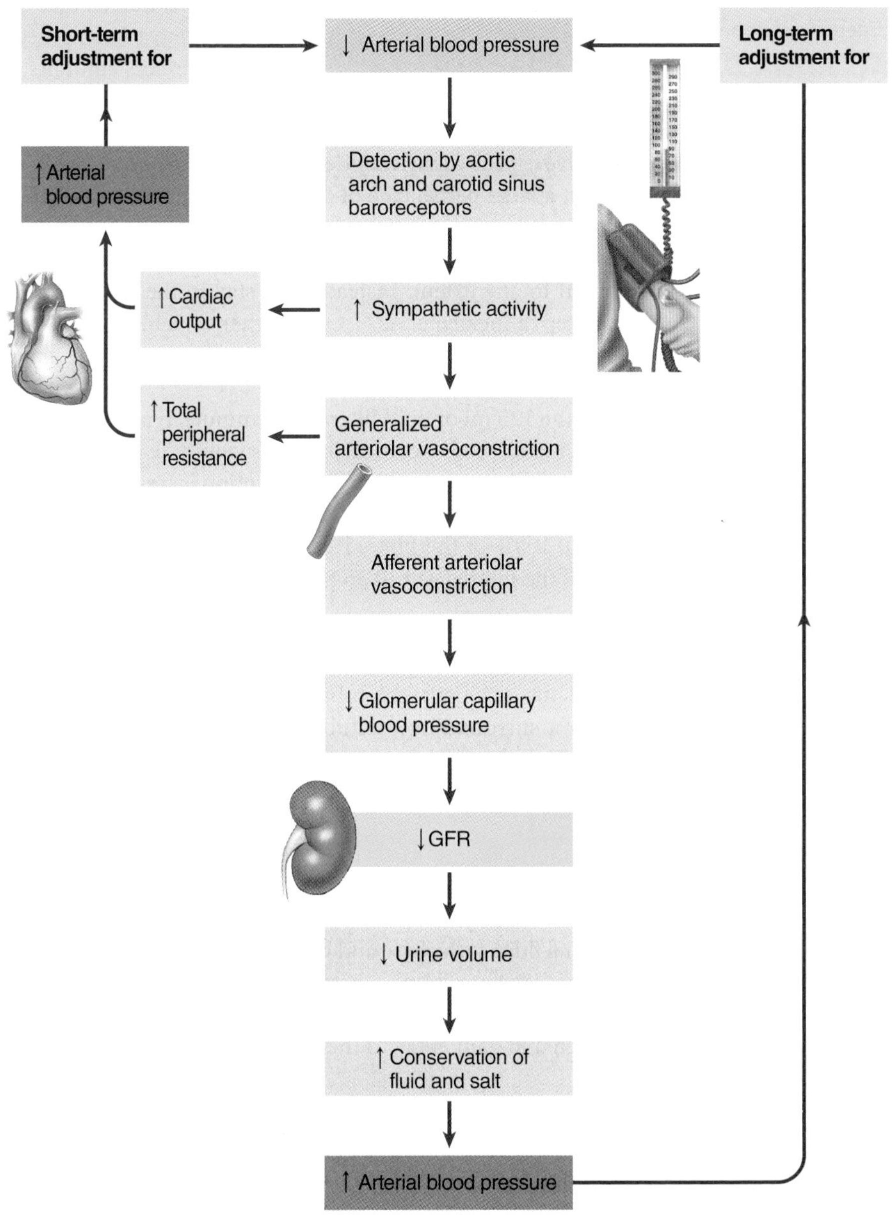

The kidneys normally receive 20% to 25% of the cardiac output.

At the average net filtration pressure, 20% of the plasma that enters the kidneys is converted into glomerular filtrate. That means at an average GFR of 125 ml/min, the total renal plasma flow must average about 625 ml/min. Because 55% of whole blood consists of plasma (that is, hematocrit = 45; see p. 317), the total flow of blood through the kidneys averages 1140 ml/min. This quantity is about 22% of the total cardiac output of

● FIGURE 13-7 Baroreceptor reflex influence on the GFR in long-term regulation of arterial blood pressure.

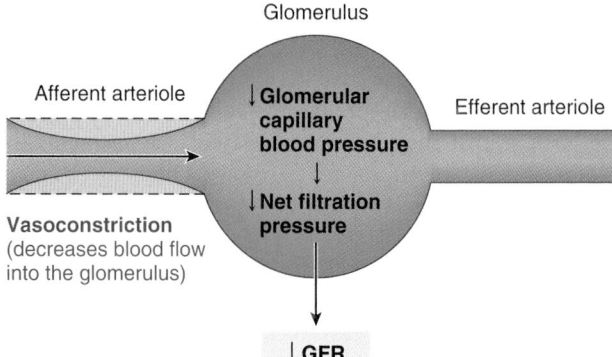

(a) Arteriolar vasoconstriction decreases the GFR

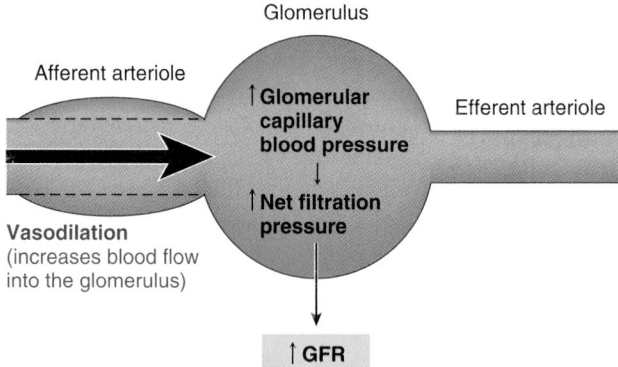

(b) Arteriolar vasodilation increases the GFR

● **FIGURE 13-8 Adjustments of afferent arteriole caliber to alter the GFR.**

5 L/min (5000 ml/min), although the kidneys compose less than 1% of total body weight.

The kidneys receive such a seemingly disproportionate share of the cardiac output because they must continuously perform their regulatory and excretory functions on the huge volumes of plasma delivered to them to maintain stability in the internal fluid environment. Most of the blood goes to the kidneys not to supply the renal tissue but to be adjusted and purified by the kidneys. On average, 20% to 25% of the blood pumped out by the heart each minute "goes to the cleaners" instead of serving its normal purpose of exchanging materials with the tissues. Only by continuously processing such a large proportion of the blood can the kidneys precisely regulate the volume and electrolyte composition of the internal environment and adequately eliminate the large quantities of metabolic waste products that are constantly produced.

Tubular Reabsorption

All plasma constituents except the plasma proteins are indiscriminately filtered together through the glomerular capillaries. In addition to waste products and excess materials that the body must eliminate, the filtered fluid contains nutrients, electrolytes, and other substances that the body cannot afford to lose in the urine. Indeed, through ongoing glomerular filtra-

tion, greater quantities of these materials are filtered per day than are even present in the entire body. The essential materials that are filtered are returned to the blood by *tubular reabsorption,* the discrete transfer of substances from the tubular lumen into the peritubular capillaries.

Tubular reabsorption is tremendous, highly selective, and variable.

Tubular reabsorption is a highly selective process. All constituents except plasma proteins are at the same concentration in the glomerular filtrate as in plasma. In most cases, the quantity reabsorbed of each substance is the amount required to maintain the proper composition and volume of the internal fluid environment. In general, the tubules have a high reabsorptive capacity for substances needed by the body and little or no reabsorptive capacity for substances of no value. Accordingly, only a small percentage, if any, of filtered plasma constituents that are useful to the body are present in the urine, most having been reabsorbed and returned to the blood. Only excess amounts of essential materials such as electrolytes are excreted in the urine. For the essential plasma constituents regulated by the kidneys, absorptive capacity may vary depending on the body's needs. In contrast, a large percentage of filtered waste products are present in the urine. These wastes, which are useless or even potentially harmful to the body if allowed to accumulate, are not reabsorbed to any extent. Instead, they stay in the tubules to be eliminated in the urine. As H_2O and other valuable constituents are reabsorbed, the waste products remaining in the tubular fluid become highly concentrated.

Of the 125 ml of fluid filtered per minute, typically 124 ml/min are reabsorbed. Considering the magnitude of glomerular filtration, the extent of tubular reabsorption is tremendous: The tubules typically reabsorb 99% of the filtered water (47 gallons per day), 100% of the filtered sugar (2.5 pounds per day), and 99.5% of the filtered salt (0.36 pounds per day).

Tubular reabsorption involves transepithelial transport.

Throughout its length, the tubule wall is one cell thick and is close to a surrounding peritubular capillary (● Figure 13-9). Adjacent tubular cells do not come into contact with each other except where they are joined by tight junctions (see p. 52) at their lateral edges near their *luminal membranes,* which face the tubular lumen. The interstitial fluid lies in the gaps between adjacent cells—the **lateral spaces**—as well as between the tubules and the capillaries. The *basolateral membrane* faces the interstitial fluid at the base and lateral edges of the cell. The tight junctions largely prevent substances from moving *between* the cells, so materials must pass *through* the cells to leave the tubular lumen and gain entry to the blood.

TRANSEPITHELIAL TRANSPORT To be reabsorbed, a substance must go across five distinct barriers (the following numbers correspond to the numbered barriers in ● Figure 13-9):

1. It must leave the tubular fluid by crossing the luminal membrane of the tubular cell.

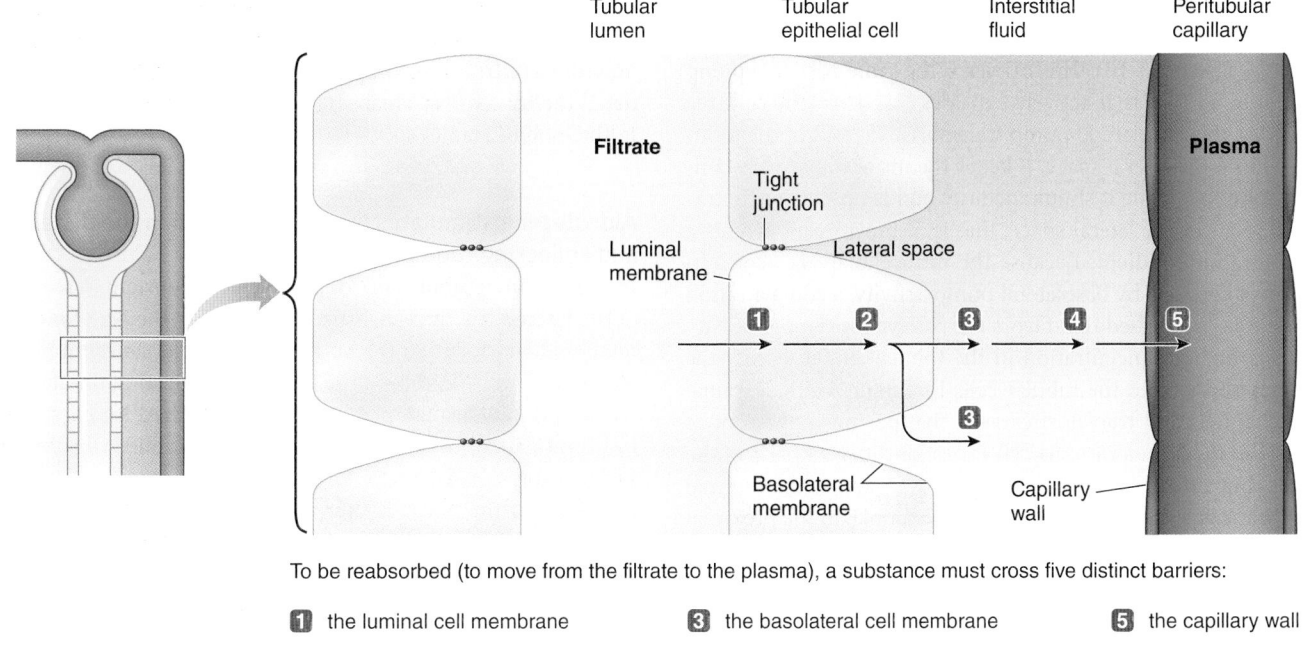

To be reabsorbed (to move from the filtrate to the plasma), a substance must cross five distinct barriers:

1 the luminal cell membrane   3 the basolateral cell membrane   5 the capillary wall

2 the cytosol   4 the interstital fluid

● FIGURE 13-9 **Steps of transepithelial transport.**

2. It must pass through the cytosol from one side of the tubular cell to the other.

3. It must cross the basolateral membrane of the tubular cell to enter the interstitial fluid.

4. It must diffuse through the interstitial fluid.

5. It must penetrate the capillary wall to enter the blood plasma.

This entire sequence of steps is known as **transepithelial transport** (*transepithelial* means "across the epithelium").

PASSIVE VERSUS ACTIVE REABSORPTION The two types of tubular reabsorption—passive and active—depend on whether local energy expenditure is needed for reabsorbing a particular substance. In *passive reabsorption,* all steps in the transepithelial transport of a substance from the tubular lumen to the plasma are passive; that is, no energy is spent for the substance's net movement, which occurs down electrochemical or osmotic gradients (see p. 56). In contrast, *active reabsorption* takes place if any step in the transepithelial transport of a substance requires energy, even if the four other steps are passive. With active reabsorption, net movement of the substance from the tubular lumen to the plasma occurs *against* an electrochemical gradient. Substances that are actively reabsorbed are of particular importance to the body, such as glucose, amino acids, and other organic nutrients, as well as Na^+ and other electrolytes, such as PO_4^{3-}. Rather than specifically describing the reabsorptive process for each of the many filtered substances returned to the plasma, we provide illustrative examples of the general mechanisms involved, after first highlighting the unique and important case of Na^+ reabsorption.

An active Na^+–K^+ ATPase pump in the basolateral membrane is essential for Na^+ reabsorption.

Sodium reabsorption is unique and complex. Of the total energy spent by the kidneys, 80% is used for Na^+ transport, indicating the importance of this process. Unlike most filtered solutes, Na^+ is reabsorbed throughout most of the tubule, but this occurs to varying extents in different regions. Of the Na^+ filtered, 99.5% is normally reabsorbed. Of the Na^+ reabsorbed, on average 67% is reabsorbed in the proximal tubule, 25% in the loop of Henle, and 8% in the distal and collecting tubules. Sodium reabsorption plays different important roles in each of these segments, as will become apparent as our discussion continues. Here is a preview of these roles:

■ Sodium reabsorption in the *proximal tubule* plays a pivotal role in reabsorbing glucose, amino acids, H_2O, Cl^-, and urea.

■ Sodium reabsorption in the ascending limb of the *loop of Henle,* along with Cl^- reabsorption, plays a critical role in the kidneys' ability to produce urine of varying concentrations and volumes, depending on the body's need to conserve or eliminate H_2O.

■ Sodium reabsorption in the *distal* and *collecting tubules* is variable and subject to hormonal control. It plays a key role in regulating ECF volume, which is important in long-term control of arterial blood pressure, and is also linked in part to K^+ secretion.

Sodium is reabsorbed throughout the tubule with the exception of the descending limb of the loop of Henle. You will learn about the significance of this exception later. Throughout all Na^+-reabsorbing segments of the tubule, the active step in

Na^+ reabsorption involves the energy-dependent Na^+–K^+ ATPase carrier located in the tubular cell's basolateral membrane (● Figure 13-10). This carrier is the same Na^+–K^+ pump present in all cells that actively extrudes Na^+ from the cell (see p. 63). As this basolateral pump transports Na^+ out of the tubular cell into the lateral space, it keeps the intracellular Na^+ concentration low while it simultaneously builds up the concentration of Na^+ in the lateral space; that is, it moves Na^+ against a concentration gradient. Because the intracellular Na^+ concentration is kept low by basolateral pump activity, a concentration gradient is established that favors the passive movement of Na^+ from its higher concentration in the tubular lumen across the luminal border into the tubular cell. The nature of the luminal Na^+ channels and transport carriers that permit movement of Na^+ from the lumen into the cell varies for different parts of the tubule, but in each case, movement of Na^+ across the luminal membrane is always a passive step. For example, in the proximal tubule, Na^+ crosses the luminal border by a symport carrier that simultaneously moves Na^+ and an organic nutrient such as glucose from the lumen into the cell. You will learn more about this cotransport process shortly. By contrast, in the collecting duct, Na^+ crosses the luminal border through a Na^+ leak channel (see p. 49). Once Na^+ enters the cell across the luminal border by whatever means, it is actively extruded to the lateral space by the basolateral Na^+–K^+ pump. This step is the same throughout the tubule. Sodium continues to diffuse down a concentration gradient from its high concentration in the lateral space into the surrounding interstitial fluid and finally into the peritubular capillary blood. Thus, net transport of Na^+ from the tubular lumen into the blood occurs at the expense of energy.

First, let us consider the importance of regulating Na^+ reabsorption in the distal portion of the nephron and examine how this control is accomplished. Later, we explore in further detail the roles of Na^+ reabsorption in the proximal tubule and in the loop of Henle.

Aldosterone stimulates Na^+ reabsorption in the distal and collecting tubules.

In the proximal tubule and loop of Henle, a constant percentage of the filtered Na^+ is reabsorbed regardless of the **Na^+ load** (*the total amount* of Na^+ in the body fluids, *not the concentration* of Na^+ in the body fluids). In the distal and collecting tubules, the reabsorption of a small percentage of the filtered Na^+ is subject to hormonal control. The extent of this controlled, discretionary reabsorption is inversely related to the magnitude of the Na^+ load in the body. If there is too much Na^+, little of this controlled Na^+ is reabsorbed; instead, it is lost in the urine, thereby removing excess Na^+ from the body. If Na^+ is depleted, most or all of this controlled Na^+ is reabsorbed, conserving for the body Na^+ that otherwise would be lost in the urine.

The Na^+ load in the body is reflected by the ECF volume. Sodium and its accompanying anion Cl^- account for more than 90% of the ECF's osmotic activity. Whenever we speak of Na^+ load, we tacitly mean salt load, too, because Cl^- goes along with Na^+. (NaCl is common table salt.) The Na^+ load is subject to regulation; Cl^- passively follows along. Recall that osmotic pressure can be thought of loosely as a "pulling" force that attracts and holds H_2O (see p. 57). When the Na^+ load is above normal and the ECF's osmotic activity is therefore increased, the extra Na^+ "holds" extra H_2O, expanding the ECF volume. Conversely, when the Na^+ load is below normal, thereby decreasing ECF osmotic activity, less H_2O than normal can be held in the ECF, so the ECF volume is reduced. Because plasma is part of the ECF, the most important result of a change in ECF volume is the matching change in blood pressure with expansion (increased blood pressure) or reduction (decreased blood pressure) of the plasma volume. Thus, long-term control of arterial blood pressure ultimately depends on Na^+-regulating mechanisms. We now turn our attention to these mechanisms.

ACTIVATION OF THE RENIN–ANGIOTENSIN–ALDOSTERONE SYSTEM The most important and best-known hormonal system involved in regulating Na^+ is the **renin–angiotensin-aldosterone system (RAAS)**. This system is initiated by the *juxtaglomerular apparatus,* the specialized combination of tubular and vascular cells where the tubule, after having bent back on itself, passes through the angle formed by the afferent and efferent arterioles as they join the glomerulus (● Figure 13-11). The juxtaglomerular apparatus secretes an enzymatic

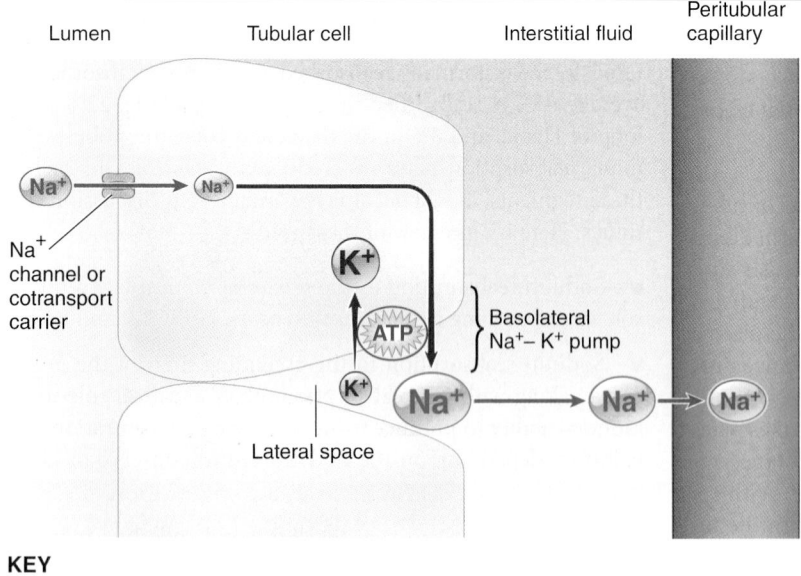

KEY

→ = Active transport of ion against concentration gradient

→ = Passive movement of ion down concentration gradient

● **FIGURE 13-10 Sodium reabsorption.** The basolateral Na^+–K^+ pump actively transports Na^+ from the tubular cell into the interstitial fluid within the lateral space. This process establishes a concentration gradient for passive movement of Na^+ from the lumen into the tubular cell and from the lateral space into the peritubular capillary, accomplishing net transport of Na^+ from the tubular lumen into the blood at the expense of energy.

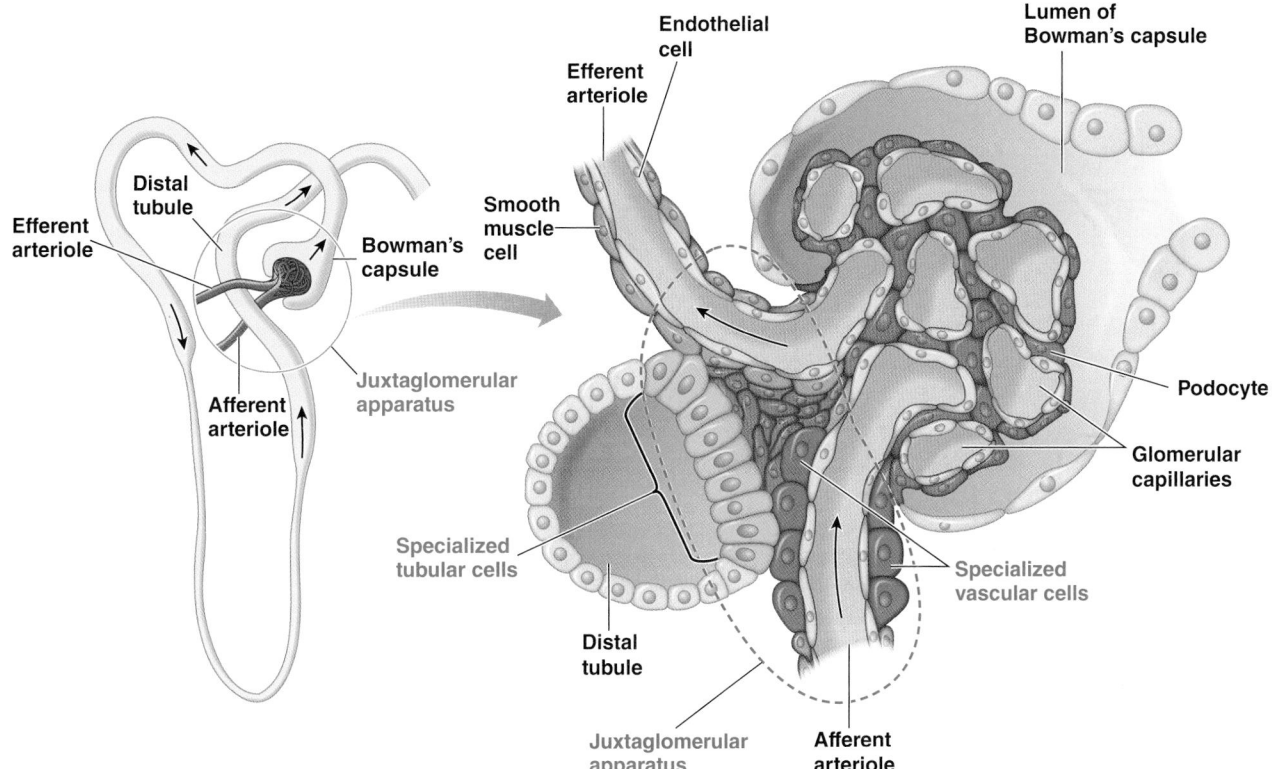

● **FIGURE 13-11 The juxtaglomerular apparatus.** The juxtaglomerular apparatus consists of specialized vascular cells and specialized tubular cells at a point where the distal tubule passes through the fork formed by the afferent and efferent arterioles of the same nephron.

hormone, **renin,** into the blood in response to a fall in NaCl, ECF volume, and arterial blood pressure. These interrelated signals for increased renin secretion all indicate the need to expand the plasma volume to increase the arterial pressure to normal in the long term. Through a complex series of events involving the RAAS, increased renin secretion brings about increased Na^+ reabsorption by the distal and collecting tubules (with Cl^- passively following Na^+'s active movement). The ultimate benefit of this salt retention is osmotically induced H_2O retention, which helps restore the plasma volume.

Let us examine in further detail the RAAS mechanism that ultimately leads to increased Na^+ reabsorption (● Figure 13-12). Once secreted into the blood, renin acts as an enzyme to activate **angiotensinogen** into **angiotensin I.** Angiotensinogen is a plasma protein synthesized by the liver and always present in the plasma in high concentration. On passing through the lungs via the pulmonary circulation, angiotensin I is converted into **angiotensin II** by **angiotensin-converting enzyme (ACE),** which is abundant in the pulmonary capillaries. Angiotensin II is the main stimulus for secretion of the hormone *aldosterone* from the adrenal cortex. The *adrenal cortex* is an endocrine gland that produces several hormones, each secreted in response to different stimuli.

FUNCTIONS OF THE RENIN–ANGIOTENSIN–ALDOSTERONE SYSTEM Among its actions, **aldosterone** increases Na^+ reabsorption by the distal and collecting tubules. It does so by promoting the insertion of additional Na^+ leak channels into the luminal membranes and additional Na^+–K^+ pumps into the basolateral membranes of the distal and collecting tubular cells. The net result is greater passive movement of Na^+ into the tubular cells from the lumen and increased active pumping of Na^+ out of the cells into the plasma—that is, an increase in Na^+ reabsorption, with Cl^- following passively. RAAS thus promotes salt retention and a resulting H_2O retention and rise in arterial blood pressure. Acting in a negative-feedback fashion, this system alleviates the factors that triggered the initial release of renin—namely, salt depletion, plasma volume reduction, and decreased arterial blood pressure.

In addition to stimulating aldosterone secretion, angiotensin II is a potent constrictor of the systemic arterioles, directly increasing blood pressure by increasing total peripheral resistance (see p. 291).

The opposite situation exists when the Na^+ load, ECF and plasma volume, and arterial blood pressure are above normal. Under these circumstances, renin secretion is inhibited. Therefore, because angiotensinogen is not activated to angiotensin I and II, aldosterone secretion is not stimulated. Without aldosterone, the small aldosterone-dependent part of Na^+ reabsorption in the distal segments of the tubule does not occur. Instead, this nonreabsorbed Na^+ is lost in the urine. In the absence of aldosterone, the ongoing loss of this small percentage of filtered Na^+ can rapidly remove excess Na^+ from the body. Even though only about 8% of the filtered Na^+ depends on aldoste-

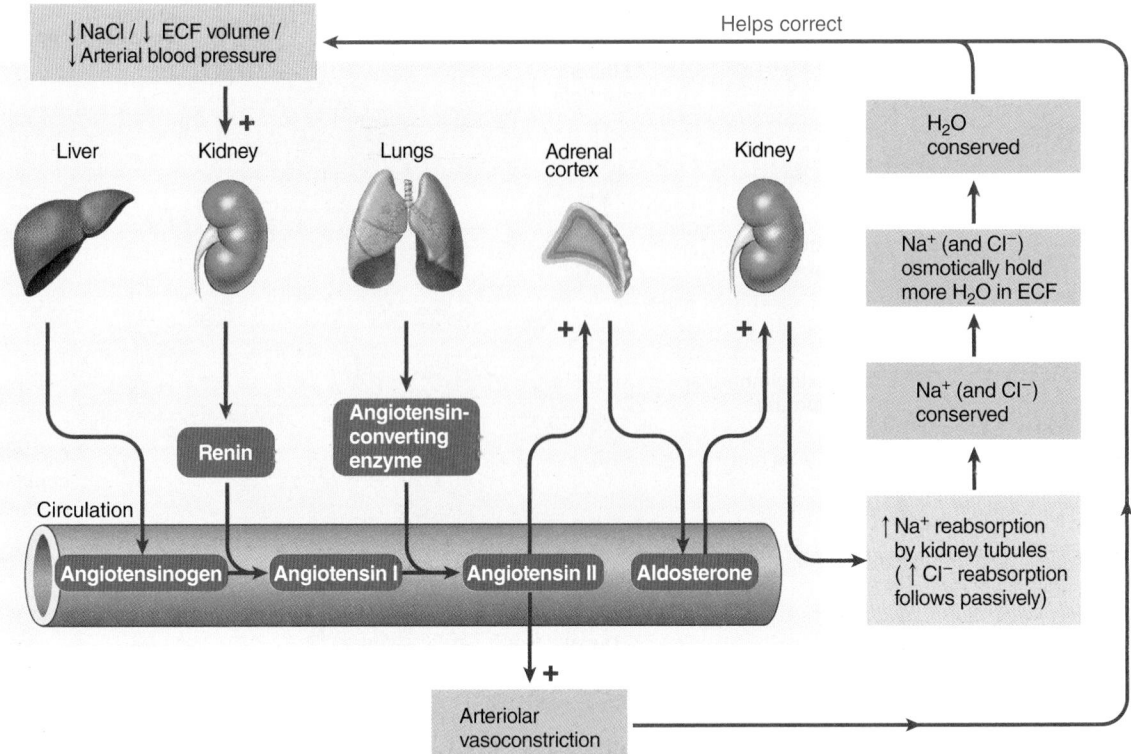

● **FIGURE 13-12 Renin–angiotensin–aldosterone system (RAAS).** The kidneys secrete the enzymatic hormone renin in response to reduced NaCl, ECF volume, and arterial blood pressure. Renin activates angiotensinogen, a plasma protein produced by the liver, into angiotensin I. Angiotensin I is converted into angiotensin II by angiotensin-converting enzyme (ACE) produced in the lungs. Angiotensin II stimulates the adrenal cortex to secrete the hormone aldosterone, which stimulates Na^+ reabsorption by the kidneys. The resulting retention of Na^+ exerts an osmotic effect that holds more H_2O in the ECF. Together, the conserved Na^+ and H_2O help correct the original stimuli that activated this hormonal system. Angiotensin II also exerts other effects that help rectify the original stimuli, such as by promoting arteriolar vasoconstriction.

rone for reabsorption, this small loss, multiplied many times as the entire plasma volume is filtered through the kidneys many times per day, can lead to a sizable loss of Na^+.

In the complete absence of aldosterone, 20 g of salt may be excreted per day. With maximum aldosterone secretion, all the filtered Na^+ (and, accordingly, all the filtered Cl^-) is reabsorbed, so salt excretion in the urine is zero. The amount of aldosterone secreted, and consequently the relative amount of salt conserved versus salt excreted, usually varies between these extremes, depending on the body's needs. For example, an average salt consumer typically excretes about 10 g of salt per day in the urine, a heavy salt consumer excretes more, and someone who has lost considerable salt during heavy sweating excretes less urinary salt. By varying the amount of renin and aldosterone secreted in accordance with the salt-determined fluid load in the body, the kidneys can finely adjust the amount of salt conserved or eliminated. In doing so, they maintain the salt load, ECF volume, and arterial blood pressure at a relatively constant level despite wide variations in salt consumption and abnormal losses of salt-laden fluid. It should not be surprising that some cases of hypertension (high blood pressure) are due to abnormal increases in RAAS activity.

 Many **diuretics,** therapeutic agents that cause *diuresis* (increased urinary output) and thus promote loss of fluid from the body, function by inhibiting tubular reabsorption of Na^+. As more Na^+ is excreted, more H_2O is also lost from the body, helping remove excess ECF. Diuretics are often beneficial in treating congestive heart failure (see p. 268), as well as certain cases of hypertension.

ACE inhibitor drugs, which block the action of angiotensin-converting enzyme (ACE), and **aldosterone receptor blockers,** are both also beneficial in treating these conditions. By blocking the generation of angiotensin II and by blocking the binding of aldosterone with its renal receptors, respectively, these two classes of drugs halt the ultimate salt- and fluid-conserving actions and arteriolar constrictor effects of RAAS.

Atrial natriuretic peptide inhibits Na^+ reabsorption.

Whereas RAAS exerts the most powerful influence on the renal handling of Na^+, this Na^+-retaining, blood pressure–raising system is opposed by a Na^+-losing, blood pressure–lowering system that involves the hormone **atrial natriuretic peptide (ANP)** (*natriuretic* means "inducing excretion of large amounts of sodium in the urine"). The heart, in addition to its pump action, produces ANP, which is stored in specialized cardiac atrial muscle cells and is released when the heart muscle cells are mechanically stretched by an expansion of the circulating plasma volume when the ECF volume is increased. This expansion, which occurs as a result of Na^+ and H_2O retention, increases arterial blood pressure. In turn, the main action of ANP is to inhibit Na^+ reabsorption in the distal parts of the nephron, thus increasing Na^+ excretion and thereby promoting accompanying osmotic H_2O excretion in the urine. This natriuresis and accompanying diuresis indirectly lower blood pressure by reducing the Na^+ load and hence the fluid load in the body. In addition, ANP directly lowers blood pressure by decreasing the cardiac output and reducing peripheral vascular resistance by inhibiting sympathetic nervous activity to the heart and blood vessels.

The relative contributions of ANP in maintaining salt and H_2O balance and blood pressure regulation are presently being intensively investigated. Recent studies suggest that a deficiency of the counterbalancing natriuretic system may underlie some cases of long-term hypertension by leaving the powerful Na^+-conserving system unopposed. The resulting salt retention, especially in association with high salt intake, could expand ECF volume and elevate blood pressure.

We now shift our attention to the reabsorption of other filtered solutes. Nevertheless, we continue to discuss Na^+ reabsorption, because the reabsorption of many other solutes is linked in some way to Na^+ reabsorption.

Glucose and amino acids are reabsorbed by Na^+-dependent secondary active transport.

Large quantities of nutritionally important organic molecules such as glucose and amino acids are filtered each day. Because these substances normally are completely reabsorbed into the blood by energy- and Na^+-dependent mechanisms located in the proximal tubule, none of these materials are usually excreted in the urine. This rapid and thorough reabsorption early in the tubules protects against the loss of these important organic nutrients.

Reabsorption of glucose and amino acids involves **secondary active transport**. With this process, specialized *symport carriers,* such as the *sodium and glucose cotransporter (SGLT),* located only in the proximal tubule, simultaneously transfer both Na^+ and the specific organic molecule from the lumen into the cell (see p. 64). This luminal cotransport carrier is the means by which Na^+ passively crosses the luminal membrane in the proximal tubule. The lumen-to-cell Na^+ concentration gradient maintained by the energy-consuming basolateral Na^+–K^+ pump drives this cotransport system and pulls the organic molecule against its concentration gradient into the tubular cell without the direct expenditure of energy. Because the overall process of glucose and amino acid reabsorption depends on the use of energy, these organic molecules are considered to be actively reabsorbed, even though energy is not used directly to transport them across the luminal membrane into the cell. In essence, glucose and amino acids get a "free ride" at the expense of energy already used in the reabsorption of Na^+. Once transported into the tubular cell, glucose and amino acids passively diffuse down their concentration gradients across the basolateral membrane into the plasma, facilitated by a carrier, such as the *glucose transporter (GLUT),* which does not depend on energy (see p. 562; also see ● Figure 3-17, p. 65).

In general, actively reabsorbed substances exhibit a tubular maximum.

All actively reabsorbed substances bind with plasma membrane carriers that transfer them across the membrane against a concentration gradient. Each carrier is specific for the types of substances it can transport; for example, SGLT can transport glucose but not amino acids. Because a limited number of each carrier type is present in the tubular cells, there is an upper limit on how much of a particular substance can be actively transported from the tubular fluid in a given period. The maximum reabsorption rate is reached when all of the carriers specific for a particular substance are fully occupied or saturated so that they cannot handle additional passengers at that time (see p. 60). This maximum reabsorption rate is designated as the **tubular maximum**, or T_m.[1] Any quantity of a substance filtered beyond its T_m is not reabsorbed and escapes instead into the urine. With the exception of Na^+, all actively reabsorbed substances have a T_m. (Even though individual Na^+ transport carriers can become saturated, the tubules as a whole do not display a T_m for Na^+, because aldosterone promotes the insertion of more active Na^+–K^+ carriers in the distal and collecting tubular cells as needed.)

The plasma concentrations of some substances that display carrier-limited reabsorption are regulated by the kidneys. How can the kidneys regulate some actively reabsorbed substances but not others, when the renal tubules limit the quantity of each of these substances that can be reabsorbed and returned to the plasma? We compare glucose, a substance that has a T_m but *is not regulated* by the kidneys, with phosphate, a T_m-limited substance that *is regulated* by the kidneys.

Glucose is an example of an actively reabsorbed substance that is not regulated by the kidneys.

The normal plasma concentration of glucose is 100 mg of glucose for every 100 ml of plasma. Because glucose is freely filterable at the glomerulus, it passes into Bowman's capsule at the same concentration it has in the plasma. Accordingly, 100 mg of glucose are present in every 100 ml of plasma filtered. With 125 ml of plasma normally being filtered each minute (average GFR = 125 ml/min), 125 mg of glucose pass into Bowman's

---

[1] For clarification, although both are designated as T_m, *transport maximum* refers to the upper limit on transport of a particular substance across a cell's plasma membrane that occurs when all of the carriers specific for the substance are saturated (see p. 60), whereas *tubular maximum* refers to the upper limit on transepithelial transport across the kidney tubules when all of the carriers specific for the substance are saturated.

capsule with this filtrate every minute. The quantity of any substance filtered per minute, known as its **filtered load,** can be calculated as follows:

$$\text{Filtered load of a substance} = \text{plasma concentration} \times \text{GFR of the substance}$$

$$\begin{aligned}\text{Filtered load of glucose} &= 100 \text{ mg/100 ml} \times 125 \text{ ml/min} \\ &= 125 \text{ mg/min}\end{aligned}$$

At a constant GFR, the filtered load of glucose is directly proportional to the plasma glucose concentration. Doubling the plasma glucose concentration to 200 mg/100 ml doubles the filtered load of glucose to 250 mg/min, and so on (● Figure 13-13).

TUBULAR MAXIMUM FOR GLUCOSE The T_m for glucose averages 375 mg/min; that is, the glucose carrier mechanism is capable of actively reabsorbing up to 375 mg of glucose per minute before it reaches its maximum transport capacity. At a normal plasma glucose concentration of 100 mg/100 ml, the 125 mg of glucose filtered per minute can readily be reabsorbed by the glucose carrier mechanism, because the filtered load is well below the T_m for glucose. Ordinarily, therefore, no glucose appears in the urine. Not until the filtered load of glucose exceeds 375 mg/min is the T_m reached. When more glucose is filtered per minute than can be reabsorbed because the T_m has been exceeded, the maximum amount is reabsorbed, while the rest stays in the filtrate to be excreted. Accordingly, the plasma glucose concentration must be greater than 300 mg/100 ml—more than three times normal—before the amount filtered exceeds 375 mg/min and glucose starts spilling into the urine.

RENAL THRESHOLD FOR GLUCOSE The plasma concentration at which the T_m of a particular substance is reached and the substance first starts appearing in the urine is called the **renal threshold.** At the average T_m of 375 mg/min and GFR of 125 ml/min, the renal threshold for glucose is 300 mg/100 ml.[2] Beyond the T_m, reabsorption stays constant at its maximum rate, and any further increase in the filtered load leads to a directly proportional increase in the amount of the substance excreted. For example, at a plasma glucose concentration of 400 mg/100 ml, the filtered load of glucose is 500 mg/min, 375 mg/min of which can be reabsorbed (a T_m worth) and 125 mg/min of which are excreted in the urine. At a plasma glucose concentration of 500 mg/100 ml, the filtered load is 625 mg/min, still only 375 mg/min can be reabsorbed, and 250 mg/min spill into the urine (● Figure 13-13).

 The plasma glucose concentration can become extremely high in *diabetes mellitus,* an endocrine disorder involving inadequate insulin action. Insulin is a pancreatic hormone that facilitates transport of glucose into many body cells. When cellular glucose uptake is impaired, glucose that cannot gain entry into cells stays in the plasma, elevating the plasma glucose concentration. Consequently, although glucose does not normally appear in urine, it is found in the urine of people with untreated diabetes when the plasma glucose concentration exceeds the renal threshold, even though renal function has not changed.

What happens when plasma glucose concentration falls below normal? The renal tubules reabsorb all filtered glucose, because the glucose reabsorptive capacity is far from being exceeded. The kidneys cannot do anything to raise a low plasma glucose level to normal. They simply return all filtered glucose to the plasma.

WHY THE KIDNEYS DO NOT REGULATE GLUCOSE The kidneys do not influence plasma glucose concentration over a range of values, from abnormally low levels up to three times the normal level. Because the T_m for glucose is well above the normal filtered load, the kidneys usually conserve all the glucose, thereby protecting against loss of this important nutrient in the urine. The kidneys do not regulate glucose, because they do not maintain glucose at some specific plasma concentration. Instead, this concentration is normally regulated by endocrine and liver mechanisms, with the kidneys merely maintaining whatever plasma glucose concentration is set by these other mechanisms (except when excessively high levels overwhelm the kidneys'

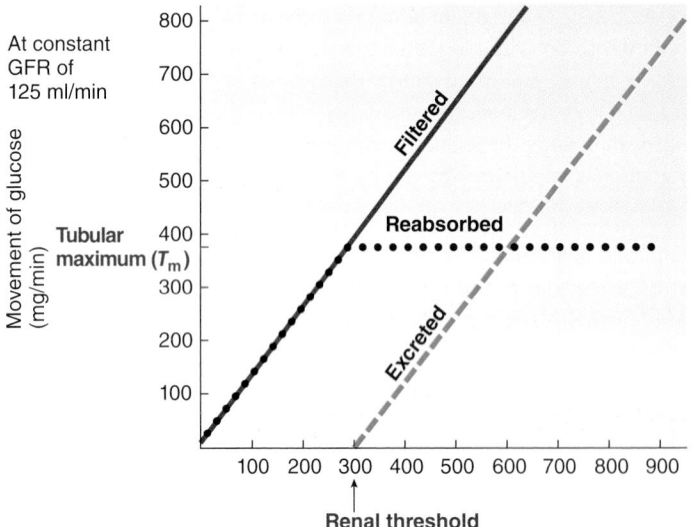

● FIGURE 13-13 Renal handling of glucose as a function of plasma glucose concentration. At a constant GFR, the quantity of glucose filtered per minute is directly proportional to the plasma concentration of glucose. All the filtered glucose can be reabsorbed up to the tubular maximum (T_m). If the amount of glucose filtered per minute exceeds the T_m, the maximum amount of glucose is reabsorbed (a T_m worth) and the rest stays in the filtrate to be excreted in the urine. The renal threshold is the plasma concentration at which the T_m is reached and glucose first starts appearing in the urine.

[2]This is an idealized situation. In reality, glucose often starts spilling into the urine at glucose concentrations of 180 mg/100 ml and above. Glucose is often excreted before the average renal threshold of 300 mg/100 ml is reached for two reasons. First, not all nephrons have the same T_m, so some nephrons may have exceeded their T_m and may be excreting glucose while others have not yet reached their T_m. Second, the efficiency of the glucose cotransport carrier may not be working at its maximum capacity at elevated values less than the true T_m, so some of the filtered glucose may fail to be reabsorbed and spill into the urine even though the average renal threshold has not been reached.

reabsorptive capacity). The same principle holds true for other organic plasma nutrients, such as amino acids and water-soluble vitamins.

Phosphate is an example of an actively reabsorbed substance that is regulated by the kidneys.

The kidneys do directly contribute to the regulation of many electrolytes, such as phosphate (PO_4^{3-}) and calcium (Ca^{2+}), because the renal thresholds of these inorganic ions equal their normal plasma concentrations. We can use PO_4^{3-} as an example. Our diets are generally rich in PO_4^{3-}, but because the tubules can reabsorb up to the normal plasma concentration's worth of PO_4^{3-} and no more, the excess ingested PO_4^{3-} is quickly spilled into the urine, restoring the plasma concentration to normal. The greater the amount of PO_4^{3-} ingested beyond the body's needs, the greater the amount excreted. In this way, the kidneys maintain the desired plasma PO_4^{3-} concentration while eliminating any excess PO_4^{3-} ingested.

Unlike the reabsorption of organic nutrients, the reabsorption of PO_4^{3-} and Ca^{2+} is also subject to hormonal control. Parathyroid hormone can alter the renal thresholds for PO_4^{3-} and Ca^{2+}, thus adjusting the quantity of these electrolytes conserved, depending on the body's momentary needs (see Chapter 17).

Active Na^+ reabsorption is responsible for the passive reabsorption of Cl^-, H_2O, and urea.

Not only is secondary active reabsorption of glucose and amino acids linked to the basolateral Na^+–K^+ pump, but passive reabsorption of Cl^-, H_2O, and urea also depends on this active Na^+ reabsorption mechanism.

CHLORIDE REABSORPTION The negatively charged chloride ions are passively reabsorbed down the electrical gradient created by the active reabsorption of the positively charged sodium ions. For the most part, chloride ions pass between, not through, the tubular cells (through "leaky" tight junctions). The amount of Cl^- reabsorbed is determined by the rate of active Na^+ reabsorption instead of being directly controlled by the kidneys.

WATER REABSORPTION Water is passively reabsorbed throughout the length of the tubule as H_2O osmotically follows Na^+ that is actively reabsorbed. Of the H_2O filtered, 65%—117 L per day—is passively reabsorbed by the end of the proximal tubule. Another 15% of the filtered H_2O is obligatorily reabsorbed from the loop of Henle. This 80% of the filtered H_2O is reabsorbed in the proximal tubule and Henle's loop regardless of the H_2O load in the body and is not subject to regulation. Variable amounts of the remaining 20% are reabsorbed in the distal portions of the tubule; the extent of reabsorption in the distal and collecting tubules is under direct hormonal control, depending on the body's state of hydration. No part of the tubule directly requires energy for this tremendous reabsorption of H_2O.

During reabsorption, H_2O passes primarily through **aquaporins,** or **water channels,** formed by specific plasma membrane proteins in the tubular cells. Different types of water channels are present in various parts of the nephron. The water channels in the proximal tubule are always open, accounting for the high H_2O permeability of this region. The channels in the distal parts of the nephron, in contrast, are regulated by the hormone *vasopressin,* accounting for the variable H_2O reabsorption in this region. The mechanisms of H_2O reabsorption beyond the proximal tubule are described later.

UREA REABSORPTION Passive reabsorption of urea, in addition to Cl^- and H_2O, is indirectly linked to active Na^+ reabsorption. **Urea** is a waste product from the breakdown of protein. The osmotically induced reabsorption of H_2O in the proximal tubule secondary to active Na^+ reabsorption produces a concentration gradient for urea that favors passive reabsorption of this waste, as follows (● Figure 13-14): Extensive reabsorption of H_2O in the proximal tubule gradually reduces the original 125 ml/min of filtrate until only 44 ml/min of fluid remain in

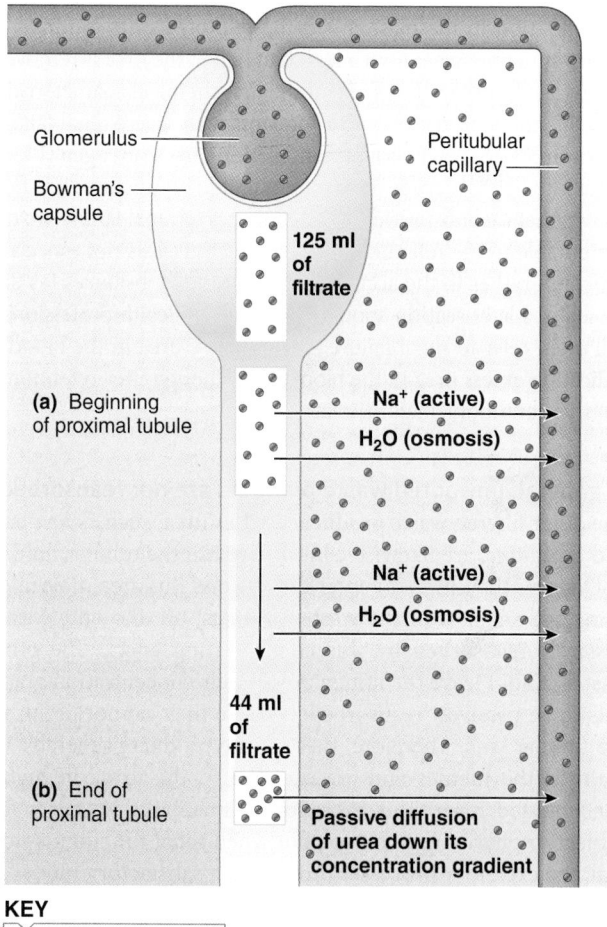

KEY

🝰 = Urea molecules

● **FIGURE 13-14 Passive reabsorption of urea at the end of the proximal tubule.** (a) In Bowman's capsule and at the beginning of the proximal tubule, urea is at the same concentration as in the plasma and the surrounding interstitial fluid. (b) By the end of the proximal tubule, 65% of the original filtrate has been reabsorbed, concentrating the filtered urea in the remaining filtrate. This establishes a concentration gradient favoring passive reabsorption of urea.

the lumen by the end of the proximal tubule (65% of the H_2O in the original filtrate, or 81 ml/min, has been reabsorbed). Substances that have been filtered but not reabsorbed become progressively more concentrated in the tubular fluid as H_2O is reabsorbed while they are left behind. Urea is one such substance.

Urea's concentration as it is filtered at the glomerulus is identical to its concentration in the plasma entering the peritubular capillaries. The quantity of urea present in the 125 ml of filtered fluid at the beginning of the proximal tubule, however, is concentrated almost threefold in the 44 ml left at the end of the proximal tubule. As a result, the urea concentration within the tubular fluid becomes greater than the urea concentration in the adjacent capillaries. Therefore, a concentration gradient is created for urea to passively diffuse from the tubular lumen into the peritubular capillary plasma. Because the walls of the proximal tubules are only somewhat permeable to urea, only about 50% of the filtered urea is passively reabsorbed by this means.

 Even though only half of the filtered urea is eliminated from the plasma with each pass through the nephrons, this removal rate is adequate. The urea concentration in the plasma becomes elevated only in impaired kidney function, when much less than half of the urea is removed. An elevated urea level was one of the first chemical characteristics to be identified in the plasma of patients with severe renal failure. Accordingly, clinical measurement of **blood urea nitrogen (BUN)** came into use as a crude assessment of kidney function. It is now known that the most serious consequences of renal failure are not attributable to the retention of urea, which itself is not especially toxic, but rather to the accumulation of other substances (as discussed in a later section about renal failure). Health professionals still often refer to renal failure as "uremia" ("urea in the blood"), indicating excess urea in the blood, even though urea retention is not this condition's major threat.

In general, unwanted waste products are not reabsorbed.

The other filtered waste products besides urea, such as *uric acid* and *creatinine,* are likewise concentrated in the tubular fluid as H_2O leaves the filtrate to enter the plasma. But urea molecules, being the smallest of the waste products, are the only wastes passively reabsorbed by this concentrating effect. The other wastes cannot leave the lumen down their concentration gradients to be passively reabsorbed, because they cannot permeate the tubular wall. Therefore, these waste products generally remain in the tubules and are excreted in the urine in highly concentrated form. This excretion of metabolic wastes is not subject to physiologic control, but when renal function is normal, the excretory processes proceed at a satisfactory rate.

We have now completed discussion of tubular reabsorption and are going to shift to the other basic renal process carried out by the tubules—tubular secretion.

Tubular Secretion

Like tubular reabsorption, tubular secretion involves transepithelial transport, but now the steps are reversed. By providing a second route of entry into the tubules for selected substances,

tubular secretion, the discrete transfer of substances from the peritubular capillaries into the tubular lumen, is a supplemental mechanism that hastens elimination of these compounds from the body. Anything that gains entry to the tubular fluid, whether by glomerular filtration or tubular secretion, and fails to be reabsorbed is eliminated in the urine.

The most important substances secreted by the tubules are *hydrogen ion (H^+)*, potassium ion (K^+), and *organic anions and cations,* many of which are compounds foreign to the body.

Hydrogen ion secretion is important in acid–base balance.

Renal H^+ secretion is extremely important in regulating acid–base balance in the body. Hydrogen ion secreted into the tubular fluid is eliminated from the body in the urine. Hydrogen ion can be secreted by the proximal, distal, and collecting tubules, with the extent of H^+ secretion depending on the acidity of the body fluids. When the body fluids are too acidic, H^+ secretion increases. Conversely, H^+ secretion is reduced when the H^+ concentration in the body fluids is too low. (See Chapter 14 for further details.)

Potassium ion secretion is controlled by aldosterone.

Potassium is one of the most abundant cations in the body, but about 98% of the K^+ is in the intracellular fluid, because the Na^+–K^+ pump actively transports K^+ into the cells. Because only a relatively small amount of K^+ is in the ECF, even slight changes in the ECF K^+ load can have a pronounced effect on the plasma K^+ concentration. Changes in the plasma K^+ concentration have a marked influence on membrane excitability. Therefore, plasma K^+ concentrations are tightly controlled, primarily by the kidneys.

Potassium ion is selectively moved in opposite directions in different parts of the tubule; it is actively reabsorbed in the proximal tubule and actively secreted in the distal and collecting tubules. Early in the tubule, K^+ is constantly reabsorbed without regulation, whereas K^+ secretion later in the tubule is variable and subject to regulation.

During K^+ depletion, K^+ secretion in the distal parts of the nephron is reduced to a minimum, so only the small percentage of filtered K^+ that escapes reabsorption in the proximal tubule is excreted in the urine. In this way, K^+ that normally would have been lost in urine is conserved for the body. Conversely, when plasma K^+ levels are elevated, K^+ secretion is adjusted so that just enough K^+ is added to the filtrate for elimination to reduce the plasma K^+ concentration to normal. Thus, K^+ secretion, not the filtration or reabsorption of K^+, is varied in a controlled fashion to regulate the rate of K^+ excretion and maintain the desired plasma K^+ concentration.

MECHANISM OF K^+ SECRETION Potassium ion secretion in the distal and collecting tubules is coupled to Na^+ reabsorption by the energy-dependent basolateral Na^+–K^+ pump (● Figure 13-15). This pump not only moves Na^+ out of the cell into the lateral space but also transports K^+ from the lateral space into the tubular cells. The resulting high intracellular K^+ concentration favors net movement of K^+ from the cells into the tubular lumen. Movement across the luminal membrane occurs passively through the large number of K^+ leak channels in this barrier in the distal and collecting tubules. By keeping the interstitial fluid concentration of K^+ low as it transports K^+ into the tubular cells from the surrounding interstitial fluid, the basolateral pump encourages passive movement of K^+ out of the peritubular capillary plasma into the interstitial fluid. A potassium ion leaving the plasma in this manner is later pumped into the cells, from which it passively moves into the lumen. In this way, the basolateral pump actively induces the net secretion of K^+ from the peritubular capillary plasma into the tubular lumen in the distal parts of the nephron.

Because K^+ secretion is linked with Na^+ reabsorption by the Na^+–K^+ pump, why isn't K^+ secreted throughout the Na^+-reabsorbing segments of the tubule instead of taking place only in the distal parts of the nephron? The answer lies in the location of the passive K^+ leak channels. In the distal and collecting tubules, the K^+ channels are concentrated in the luminal membrane, providing a route for K^+ pumped into the cell to exit into the lumen, thus being secreted. In the other tubular segments, the K^+ leak channels are located primarily in the basolateral membrane. As a result, K^+ pumped into the cell from the lateral space by the Na^+–K^+ pump simply moves back out into the lateral space through these channels. This K^+ recycling permits the ongoing operation of the Na^+–K^+ pump to accomplish Na^+ reabsorption with no local net effect on K^+.

CONTROL OF K^+ SECRETION Several factors can alter the rate of K^+ secretion, the most important being aldosterone. This hormone stimulates K^+ secretion by the tubular cells late in the nephron while simultaneously enhancing these cells' reabsorp-

tion of Na^+. A rise in plasma K^+ concentration directly stimulates the adrenal cortex to increase its output of aldosterone, which in turn promotes the secretion and ultimate urinary excretion and elimination of excess K^+. Conversely, a decline in plasma K^+ concentration causes a reduction in aldosterone secretion and a corresponding decrease in aldosterone-stimulated renal K^+ secretion.

Note that a rise in plasma K^+ concentration *directly* stimulates aldosterone secretion by the adrenal cortex, whereas a fall in plasma Na^+ concentration stimulates aldosterone secretion by means of the complex RAAS pathway. Thus, aldosterone secretion can be stimulated by two separate pathways (● Figure 13-16).

The kidneys usually exert a fine degree of control over plasma K^+ concentration. This is extremely important because even minor fluctuations in plasma K^+ concentration can detrimentally influence the membrane electrical activity of excitable tissues, adversely affecting their performance. For example, a change in ECF K^+ concentration in either direction causes cardiac malfunction, which can lead to fatal cardiac arrhythmias.

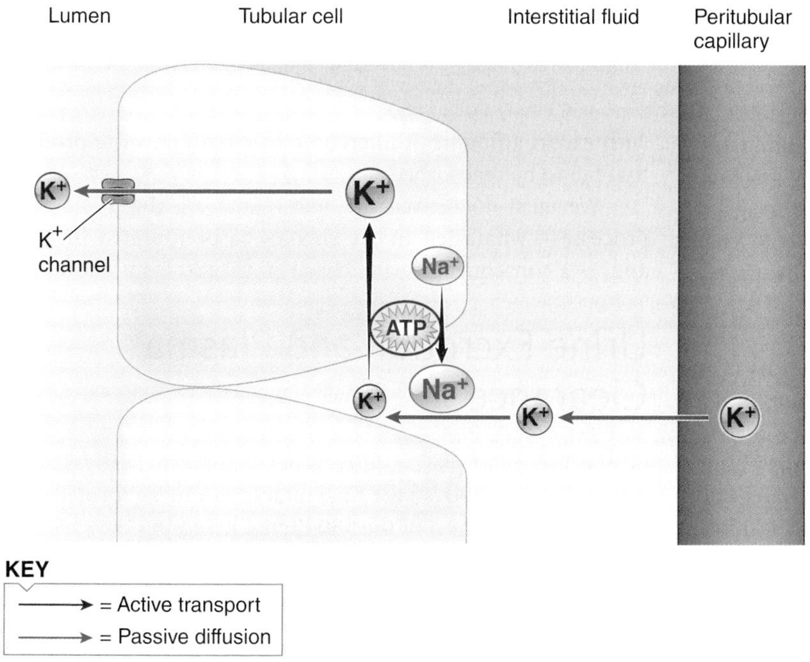

Organic anion and cation secretion helps efficiently eliminate foreign compounds from the body.

The proximal tubule contains two distinct types of secretory carriers, one for the secretion of organic anions and a separate system for secretion of organic cations.

FUNCTIONS OF ORGANIC ION SECRETORY SYSTEMS The organic ion secretory systems serve two major functions:

1. By adding more of a particular type of organic ion to the quantity that has already gained entry to the tubular fluid by glomerular filtration, the organic secretory pathways facilitate excretion of these substances. Included among these organic ions are certain blood-borne chemical messengers such as prostaglandins and epinephrine, which, having served their purpose, must be rapidly removed from the blood so that their biological activity is not unduly prolonged.

2. The proximal tubule organic ion secretory systems play a key role in eliminating many foreign compounds from the body. These systems can secrete a large number of different organic ions, both those produced within the body and those foreign organic ions that have gained access to the body fluids. This nonselectivity permits the organic ion secretory systems to hasten removal of many foreign organic chemicals, including food additives, environmental pollutants (for example, pesticides), drugs, and other nonnutritive organic substances that have entered the body. Even though this mechanism helps rid the body of potentially harmful foreign compounds, it is not

KEY

→ = Active transport

→ = Passive diffusion

● FIGURE 13-15 **Potassium ion secretion.** The basolateral pump simultaneously transports Na^+ into the lateral space and K^+ into the tubular cell. In the parts of the tubule that secrete K^+, this ion leaves the cell through leak channels located in the luminal border, thus being secreted. (In the parts of the tubule that do not secrete K^+, the K^+ pumped into the cell during Na^+ reabsorption leaves the cell through leak channels located in the basolateral border, thus being retained in the body.)

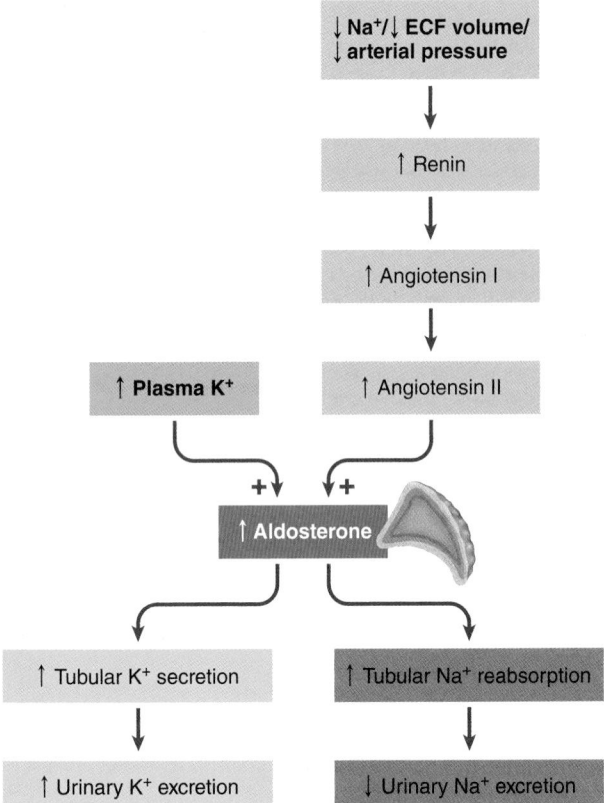

Figure content:

↓ Na⁺/↓ ECF volume/
↓ arterial pressure

↓

↑ Renin

↓

↑ Angiotensin I

↓

↑ Angiotensin II

↑ Plasma K⁺

+   +

↑ Aldosterone

↑ Tubular K⁺ secretion   ↑ Tubular Na⁺ reabsorption

↓   ↓

↑ Urinary K⁺ excretion   ↓ Urinary Na⁺ excretion

● FIGURE 13-16 Dual control of aldosterone secretion by K⁺ and Na⁺.

Table 13-2 Summary of Transport Across Proximal and Distal Portions of the Nephron

PROXIMAL TUBULE

Reabsorption	Secretion
67% of filtered Na^+ actively reabsorbed, not subject to control; Cl^- follows passively	Variable H^+ secretion, depending on acid–base status of body
All filtered glucose and amino acids reabsorbed by secondary active transport; not subject to control	Organic ion secretion; not subject to control
Variable amounts of filtered PO_4^{3-} and other electrolytes reabsorbed; subject to control	
65% of filtered H_2O osmotically reabsorbed; not subject to control	
50% of filtered urea passively reabsorbed; not subject to control	
Almost all filtered K^+ reabsorbed; not subject to control	

DISTAL TUBULE AND COLLECTING DUCT

Reabsorption	Secretion
Variable Na^+ reabsorption, controlled by aldosterone; Cl^- follows passively	Variable H^+ secretion, depending on acid–base status of body
Variable H_2O reabsorption, controlled by vasopressin	Variable K^+ secretion, controlled by aldosterone

subject to physiologic adjustments. The carriers cannot pick up their secretory pace when confronting an elevated load of these organic ions.

Many drugs, such as penicillin and nonsteroidal anti-inflammatory drugs (NSAIDs), are eliminated from the body by the organic ion secretory systems. To keep the plasma concentration of these drugs at effective levels, the dosage must be repeated frequently to keep pace with the rapid removal of these compounds in the urine.

SUMMARY OF REABSORPTIVE AND SECRETORY PROCESSES This completes our discussion of the reabsorptive and secretory processes that occur across the proximal and distal portions of the nephron. These processes are summarized in ▲ Table 13-2. To generalize, the proximal tubule does most of the reabsorbing. This mass reabsorber transfers much of the filtered water and needed solutes back into the blood in unregulated fashion. Similarly, the proximal tubule is the major site of secretion, with the exception of K^+ secretion. The distal and collecting tubules then determine the final amounts of H_2O, Na^+, K^+, and H^+ excreted in the urine and thus eliminated from the body. They do so by fine-tuning the amount of Na^+ and H_2O reabsorbed and the amount of K^+ and H^+ secreted. These processes in the distal part of the nephron are all subject to control, depending on the body's momentary needs. The unwanted filtered waste products are left behind to be eliminated in the urine, along

with excess amounts of filtered or secreted nonwaste products that fail to be reabsorbed.

We next focus on the end result of the basic renal processes—what's left in the tubules to be excreted in urine, and, as a consequence, what has been cleared from plasma.

Urine Excretion and Plasma Clearance

Of the 125 ml of plasma filtered per minute, typically 124 ml/min are reabsorbed, so the final quantity of urine formed averages 1 ml/min. Thus, of the 180 liters filtered per day, 1.5 liters of urine are excreted.

Urine contains high concentrations of various waste products plus variable amounts of the substances regulated by the kidneys, with any excess quantities having spilled into the urine. Useful substances are conserved by reabsorption, so they do not appear in the urine.

A relatively small change in the quantity of filtrate reabsorbed can bring about a large change in the volume of urine formed. For example, a reduction of less than 1% in the total reabsorption rate, from 124 to 123 ml/min, increases the urinary excretion rate by 100%, from 1 to 2 ml/min.

Plasma clearance is the volume of plasma cleared of a particular substance per minute.

Compared to plasma entering the kidneys through the renal arteries, plasma leaving the kidneys through the renal veins lacks the materials that were left behind to be eliminated in the urine. By excreting substances in the urine, the kidneys clean or "clear" the plasma flowing through them of these substances. The **plasma clearance** of any substance is defined as the volume of plasma completely cleared of that substance by the kidneys per minute.[3] It refers not to the *amount of the substance* removed but to the *volume of plasma* from which that amount was removed. Plasma clearance is actually a more useful measure than urine excretion; it is more important to know what effect urine excretion has on removing materials from body fluids than to know the volume and composition of discarded urine. Plasma clearance expresses the kidneys' effectiveness in removing various substances from the internal fluid environment.

Plasma clearance can be calculated for any plasma constituent as follows:

$$\text{Clearance rate of a substance (ml/min)} = \frac{\begin{array}{c}\text{urine concentration of the substance (quantity/ml urine)}\end{array} \times \begin{array}{c}\text{urine flow rate (ml/min)}\end{array}}{\begin{array}{c}\text{plasma concentration of the substance (quantity/ml plasma)}\end{array}}$$

The plasma clearance rate varies for different substances, depending on how the kidneys handle each substance.

If a substance is filtered but not reabsorbed or secreted, its plasma clearance rate equals the GFR.

Assume that a plasma constituent, substance X, is freely filterable at the glomerulus but is not reabsorbed or secreted. As 125 ml/min of plasma are filtered and subsequently reabsorbed, the quantity of substance X originally contained within the 125 ml is left behind in the tubules to be excreted. Thus, 125 ml of plasma are cleared of substance X each minute (● Figure 13-17a). (Of the 125 ml/min of plasma filtered, 124 ml/min of the filtered fluid are returned, through reabsorption, to the plasma minus substance X, thus clearing this 124 ml/min of substance X. In addition, the 1 ml/min of fluid lost in urine is eventually replaced by an equivalent volume of ingested H_2O

---

[3]Actually, plasma clearance is an artificial concept, because when a particular substance is excreted in the urine, that substance's concentration in the plasma as a whole is uniformly decreased as a result of thorough mixing in the circulatory system. However, it is useful for comparative purposes to consider clearance in effect as the volume of plasma that would have contained the total quantity of the substance (at the substance's concentration prior to excretion) that the kidneys excreted in 1 minute—that is, the hypothetical volume of plasma completely cleared of that substance per minute.

that is already clear of substance X. Therefore, 125 ml of plasma cleared of substance X are, in effect, returned to the plasma for every 125 ml of plasma filtered per minute.)

No normally occurring chemical in the body has the characteristics of substance X. All substances naturally present in the plasma, even wastes, are reabsorbed or secreted to some extent. However, **inulin** (do not confuse with insulin), a harmless foreign carbohydrate, is freely filtered and not reabsorbed or secreted—an ideal substance X. Inulin can be injected and its plasma clearance determined as a clinical means of finding out the GFR. Because all glomerular filtrate formed is cleared of inulin, the volume of plasma cleared of inulin per minute equals the volume of plasma filtered per minute—that is, the GFR.

If a substance is filtered and reabsorbed but not secreted, its plasma clearance rate is always less than the GFR.

Some or all of a reabsorbable substance that has been filtered is returned to the plasma. Because less than the filtered volume of plasma will have been cleared of the substance, the plasma clearance rate of a reabsorbable substance is always less than the GFR. For example, the plasma clearance for glucose is normally zero. All the filtered glucose is reabsorbed with the rest of the returning filtrate, so none of the plasma is cleared of glucose (● Figure 13-17b).

For a substance that is partially reabsorbed, such as urea, only part of the filtered plasma is cleared of that substance. With about 50% of the filtered urea being passively reabsorbed, only half of the filtered plasma, or 62.5 ml, is cleared of urea each minute (● Figure 13-17c).

If a substance is filtered and secreted but not reabsorbed, its plasma clearance rate is always greater than the GFR.

Tubular secretion allows the kidneys to clear certain materials from the plasma more efficiently. Only 20% of the plasma entering the kidneys is filtered. The remaining 80% passes unfiltered into the peritubular capillaries. The only means by which this unfiltered plasma can be cleared of any substance during the trip through the kidneys before being returned to the general circulation is by secretion. An example is H^+. Not only is filtered plasma cleared of nonreabsorbable H^+, but the plasma from which H^+ is secreted is also cleared of H^+. For example, if the quantity of H^+ secreted is equivalent to the quantity of H^+ present in 25 ml of plasma, the clearance rate for H^+ will be 150 ml/min at the normal GFR of 125 ml/min. Every minute 125 ml of plasma will lose its H^+ through filtration and failure of reabsorption, and an additional 25 ml of plasma will lose its H^+ through secretion. The plasma clearance for a secreted substance is always greater than the GFR (● Figure 13-17d).

Just as inulin can be used clinically to determine the GFR, plasma clearance of another foreign compound, the organic anion **para-aminohippuric acid (PAH),** can be used to measure renal plasma flow. Like inulin, PAH is freely filterable and nonreabsorbable. It differs, however, in that all the PAH in the plasma that escapes filtration is secreted from the peritubular capillaries by the

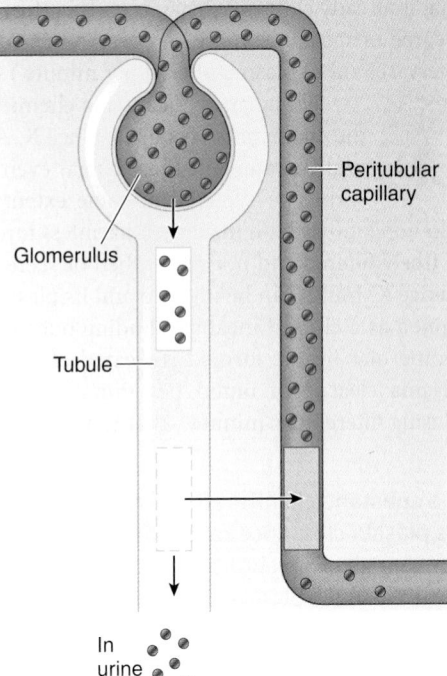

Peritubular
capillary

Glomerulus

Tubule

In
urine

(a) For a substance filtered and not reabsorbed or secreted, such as inulin, all of the filtered plasma is cleared of the substance.

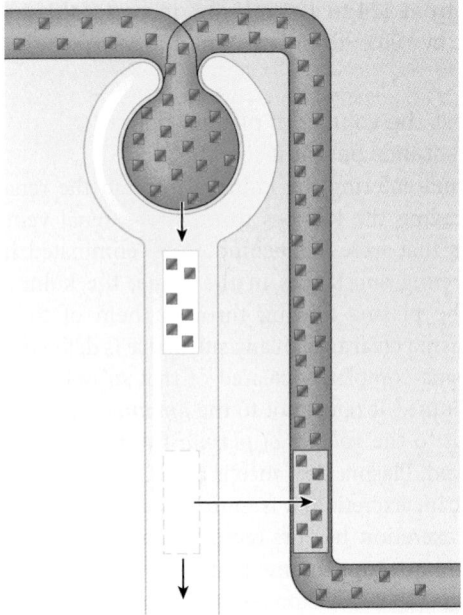

(b) For a substance filtered, not secreted, and completely reabsorbed, such as glucose, none of the filtered plasma is cleared of the substance.

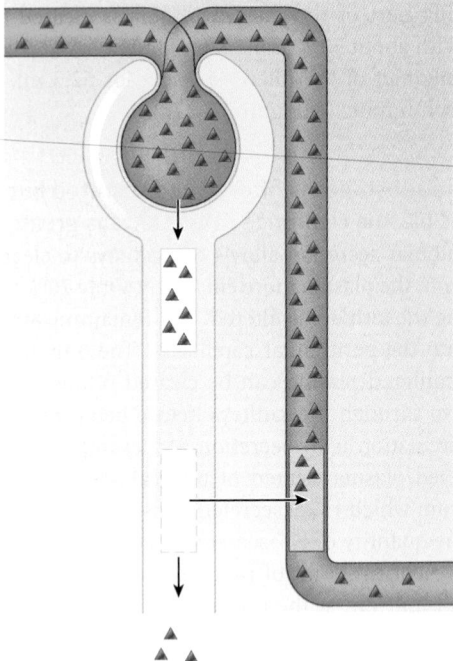

(c) For a substance filtered, not secreted, and partially reabsorbed, such as urea, only a portion of the filtered plasma is cleared of the substance.

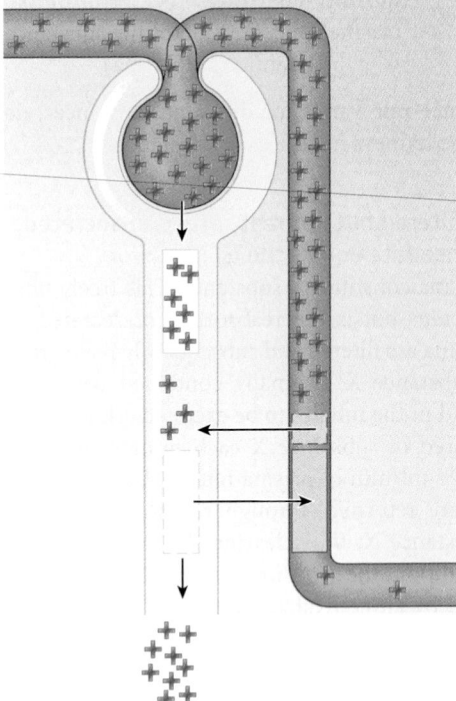

(d) For a substance filtered and secreted but not reabsorbed, such as hydrogen ion, all of the filtered plasma is cleared of the substance, and the peritubular plasma from which the substance is secreted is also cleared.

● FIGURE 13-17 Plasma clearance for substances handled in different ways by the kidneys.

organic anion secretory pathway in the proximal tubule. Thus, PAH is removed from all the plasma that flows through the kidneys—both from plasma that is filtered and subsequently reabsorbed without its PAH and from unfiltered plasma that continues on in the peritubular capillaries and loses its PAH by active secretion into the tubules. Because all the plasma that flows through the kidneys is cleared of PAH, the plasma clearance for PAH is a reasonable estimate of the rate of plasma flow through the kidneys. Typically, renal plasma flow averages 625 ml/min, for a renal blood flow (plasma plus blood cells) of 1140 ml/min—more than 20% of the cardiac output.

FILTRATION FRACTION If you know PAH clearance (renal plasma flow) and inulin clearance (GFR), you can easily determine the **filtration fraction,** the fraction of plasma flowing through the glomeruli that is filtered into the tubules:

$$\text{Filtration fraction} = \frac{\text{GFR (plasma inulin clearance)}}{\text{renal plasma flow (plasma PAH clearance)}}$$

$$= \frac{125 \text{ ml/min}}{625 \text{ ml/min}} = 20\%$$

Thus, 20% of the plasma that enters the glomeruli is typically filtered.

The kidneys can excrete urine of varying concentrations depending on the body's state of hydration.

Having considered how the kidneys deal with a variety of solutes in the plasma, we now concentrate on renal handling of plasma H_2O. The ECF osmolarity (solute concentration) depends on the relative amount of H_2O compared to solute. At normal fluid balance and solute concentration, the body fluids are **isotonic** at an osmolarity of 300 milliosmols per liter (mOsm) (see pp. 59 and A-9). If too much H_2O is present relative to the solute load, the body fluids are **hypotonic,** which means they are too dilute at an osmolarity less than 300 mOsm. However, if a H_2O deficit exists relative to the solute load, the body fluids are too concentrated or are **hypertonic,** having an osmolarity greater than 300 mOsm.

Knowing that the driving force for H_2O reabsorption the entire length of the tubules is an osmotic gradient between the tubular lumen and the surrounding interstitial fluid, you would expect, given osmotic considerations, that the kidneys could not excrete urine more or less concentrated than the body fluids. Indeed, this would be the case if the interstitial fluid surrounding the tubules in the kidneys were identical in osmolarity to the rest of the body fluids. Water reabsorption would proceed only until the tubular fluid equilibrated osmotically with the interstitial fluid, and the body would have no way to eliminate excess H_2O when the body fluids were hypotonic or to conserve H_2O in the presence of hypertonicity.

Fortunately, a large **vertical osmotic gradient** is uniquely maintained in the interstitial fluid of the medulla of each kidney. The concentration of the interstitial fluid progressively increases from the cortical boundary down through the depth of the renal medulla until it reaches a maximum of 1200 mOsm in humans at the junction with the renal pelvis (Figure 13-18).

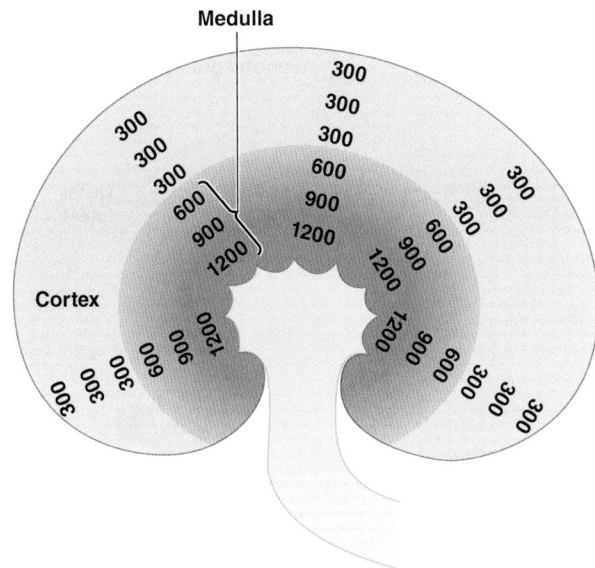

 FIGURE 13-18 Vertical osmotic gradient in the renal medulla. Schematic representation of the kidney rotated 90° from its normal position in an upright person for better visualization of the vertical osmotic gradient in the renal medulla. All values are in mOsm. The osmolarity of the interstitial fluid throughout the renal cortex is isotonic at 300 mOsm, but the osmolarity of the interstitial fluid in the renal medulla increases progressively from 300 mOsm at the boundary with the cortex to a maximum of 1200 mOsm at the junction with the renal pelvis.

By a mechanism described shortly, this gradient enables the kidneys to produce urine that ranges in concentration from 100 to 1200 mOsm, depending on the body's state of hydration. When the body is in ideal fluid balance, 1 ml/min of isotonic urine is formed. When the body is overhydrated (too much H_2O), the kidneys can produce a large volume of dilute urine (up to 25 ml/min and hypotonic at 100 mOsm), eliminating the excess H_2O in the urine. Conversely, the kidneys can put out a small volume of concentrated urine (down to 0.3 ml/min and hypertonic at 1200 mOsm) when the body is dehydrated (too little H_2O), conserving H_2O for the body.

Unique anatomic arrangements and complex functional interactions among the various nephron components in the renal medulla establish and use the vertical osmotic gradient. In most nephrons the hairpin loop of Henle dips only slightly into the medulla, but in about 20% of nephrons the loop plunges through the entire depth of the medulla so that the tip of the loop lies near the renal pelvis (Figure 13-19). Flow in the long loop of Henle is considered *countercurrent* because the flow in the two closely adjacent limbs of the loop moves in opposite directions. Also running through the medulla in the descending direction only, on their way to the renal pelvis, are the collecting ducts that serve both types of nephrons. This arrangement, coupled with the permeability and transport characteristics of these tubular segments, plays a key role in the kidneys' ability to produce urine of varying concentrations, depending on the body's needs for water conservation or elimination. Briefly, the long loops of Henle *establish* the vertical osmotic gradient and the collecting ducts of all nephrons *use*

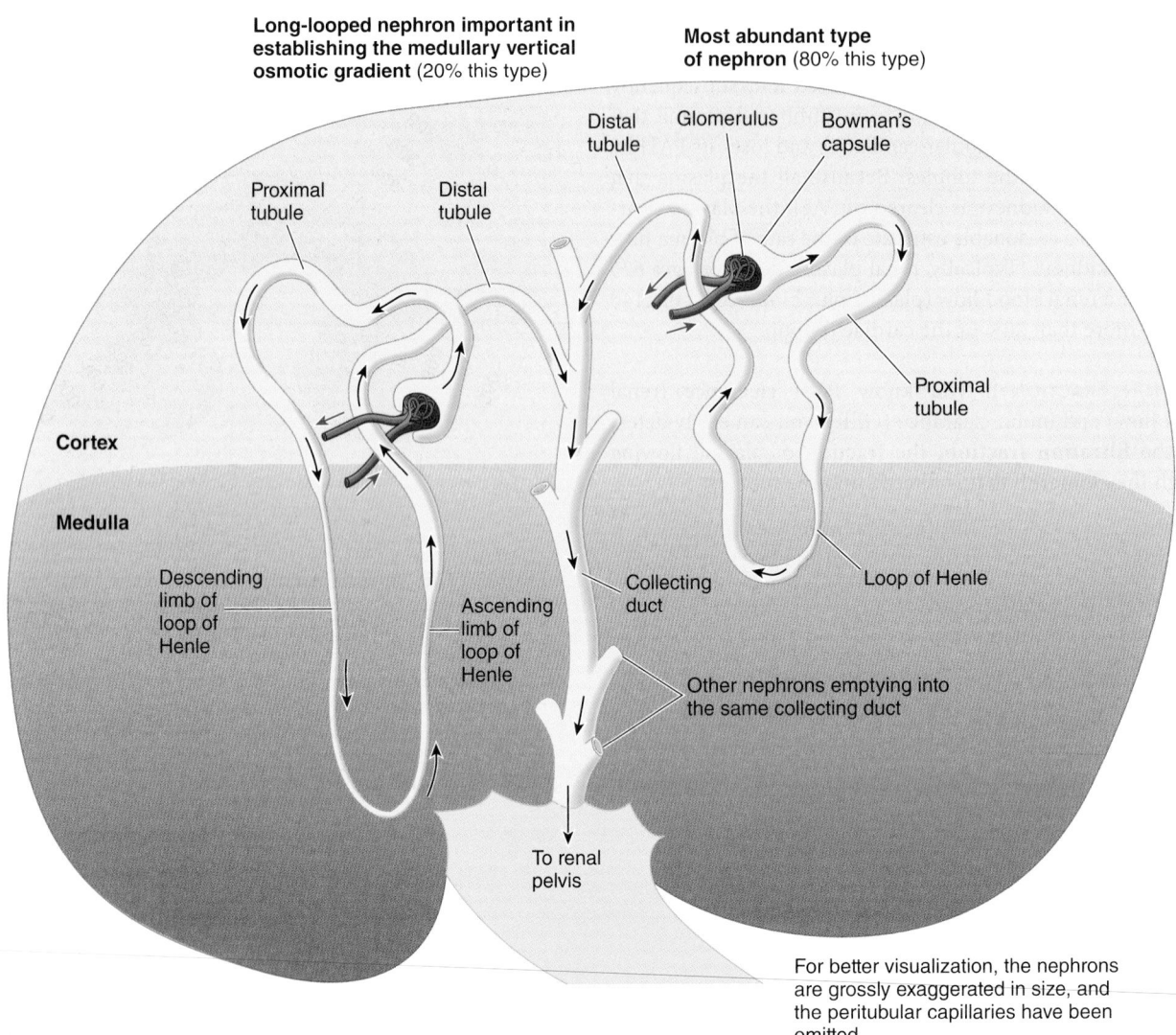

Long-looped nephron important in establishing the medullary vertical osmotic gradient (20% this type)

Most abundant type of nephron (80% this type)

Distal tubule

Glomerulus

Bowman's capsule

Proximal tubule

Distal tubule

Proximal tubule

Cortex

Medulla

Descending limb of loop of Henle

Ascending limb of loop of Henle

Collecting duct

Loop of Henle

Other nephrons emptying into the same collecting duct

To renal pelvis

For better visualization, the nephrons are grossly exaggerated in size, and the peritubular capillaries have been omitted.

● **FIGURE 13-19 Schematic representation of the two types of nephrons.** Note that the loop of Henle of long-looped nephrons plunges deep into the medulla.

the gradient, in conjunction with the hormone vasopressin, to produce urine of varying concentrations. Collectively, this entire functional organization is known as the **medullary countercurrent system.** We next examine each of its facets in greater detail.

The medullary vertical osmotic gradient is established by countercurrent multiplication.

We now follow the filtrate through a long-looped nephron to see how this structure establishes a vertical osmotic gradient in the medulla. Immediately after the filtrate is formed, uncontrolled osmotic reabsorption of filtered H_2O occurs in the proximal tubule secondary to active Na^+ reabsorption. As a result, by the end of the proximal tubule, about 65% of the filtrate has been reabsorbed, but the 35% remaining in the tubular lumen still has the same osmolarity as the body fluids. Therefore, the fluid entering the loop of Henle is still isotonic. An additional 15% of the filtered H_2O is obligatorily reabsorbed

from the loop of Henle during the establishment and maintenance of the vertical osmotic gradient, with the osmolarity of the tubular fluid being altered in the process.

PROPERTIES OF THE DESCENDING AND ASCENDING LIMBS OF A LONG HENLE'S LOOP The following functional distinctions between the descending limb of a long Henle's loop (which carries fluid from the proximal tubule down into the depths of the medulla) and the ascending limb (which carries fluid up and out of the medulla into the distal tubule) are crucial for establishing the incremental osmotic gradient in the medullary interstitial fluid.

The *descending limb*

1. is highly permeable to H_2O (via abundant, always-open water channels).

2. does not actively extrude Na^+. (That is, it does not reabsorb Na^+. It is the only segment of the entire tubule that does not do so.)

The *ascending limb*

1. actively transports NaCl out of the tubular lumen into the surrounding interstitial fluid.
2. is always impermeable to H_2O, so salt leaves the tubular fluid without H_2O osmotically following along.

MECHANISM OF COUNTERCURRENT MULTIPLICATION The proximity and countercurrent flow of the two limbs allow important interactions between them. Even though the flow of fluids is continuous through the loop of Henle, we can visualize what happens step by step, much like an animated film run so slowly that each frame can be viewed.

Initially, before the vertical osmotic gradient is established, the medullary interstitial fluid concentration is uniformly 300 mOsm, as are the rest of the body fluids (● Figure 13-20).

The active salt pump in the ascending limb can transport NaCl out of the lumen until the surrounding interstitial fluid is 200 mOsm more concentrated than the tubular fluid in this limb. When the ascending limb pump starts actively extruding NaCl, the medullary interstitial fluid becomes hypertonic. Water cannot follow osmotically from the ascending limb, because this limb is impermeable to H_2O. However, net diffusion of H_2O does occur from the descending limb into the interstitial fluid. The tubular fluid entering the descending limb from the proximal tubule is isotonic. Because the descending limb is highly permeable to H_2O, net diffusion of H_2O occurs by osmosis out of the descending limb into the more concentrated interstitial fluid. The passive movement of H_2O out of the descending limb continues until the osmolarities of the fluid in the descending limb and the interstitial fluid become equilibrated. Thus, the tubular fluid entering the loop of Henle immediately starts to become more concentrated as it loses H_2O. At equilibrium, the osmolarity of the ascending limb fluid is 200 mOsm and the osmolarities of the interstitial fluid and descending limb fluid are equal at 400 mOsm (● Figure 13-20, step **1**).

If we now advance the entire column of fluid in the loop of Henle several frames (step **2**), a mass of 200 mOsm fluid exits from the top of the ascending limb into the distal tubule, and a new mass of isotonic fluid at 300 mOsm enters the top of the descending limb from the proximal tubule. At the bottom of the loop, a comparable mass of 400 mOsm fluid from the descending limb moves forward around the tip into the ascending limb, placing it opposite a 400 mOsm region in the descending limb. Note that the 200 mOsm concentration difference has been lost at both the top and the bottom of the loop.

The ascending limb pump again transports NaCl out while H_2O passively leaves the descending limb until a 200 mOsm difference is reestablished between the ascending limb and both the interstitial fluid and the descending limb at each horizontal level (step **3**). Note, however, that the concentration of tubular fluid is progressively increasing in the descending limb and progressively decreasing in the ascending limb.

As the tubular fluid is advanced still farther (step **4**), the 200 mOsm concentration gradient is disrupted again at all horizontal levels. Again, active extrusion of NaCl from the ascending limb, coupled with the net diffusion of H_2O out of the

descending limb, reestablishes the 200 mOsm gradient at each horizontal level (step **5**).

As the fluid flows slightly forward again and this stepwise process continues (step **6**), the fluid in the descending limb becomes progressively more hypertonic until it reaches a maximum concentration of 1200 mOsm at the bottom of the loop, four times the normal concentration of body fluids. Because the interstitial fluid always achieves equilibrium with the descending limb, an incremental vertical concentration gradient ranging from 300 to 1200 mOsm is likewise established in the medullary interstitial fluid. In contrast, the concentration of the tubular fluid progressively decreases in the ascending limb as NaCl is pumped out but H_2O is unable to follow. In fact, the tubular fluid even becomes hypotonic before leaving the ascending limb to enter the distal tubule at a concentration of 100 mOsm, one third the normal concentration of body fluids.

Note that although a gradient of only 200 mOsm exists between the ascending limb and the surrounding fluids at each medullary horizontal level, a larger vertical gradient exists from the top to the bottom of the medulla. Even though the ascending limb pump can generate a gradient of only 200 mOsm, this effect is multiplied into a large vertical gradient because of the countercurrent flow within the loop. This concentrating mechanism accomplished by the loop of Henle is known as **countercurrent multiplication.**

We have artificially described countercurrent multiplication in a stop-and-flow, stepwise fashion to facilitate understanding. It is important to realize that once the incremental medullary gradient is established, it stays constant because of the continuous flow of fluid, coupled with the ongoing ascending limb active transport and the accompanying descending limb passive fluxes.

BENEFITS OF COUNTERCURRENT MULTIPLICATION If you consider only what happens to the tubular fluid as it flows through the loop of Henle, the whole process seems an exercise in futility. The isotonic fluid that enters the loop becomes progressively more concentrated as it flows down the descending limb, achieving a maximum concentration of 1200 mOsm, only to become progressively more diluted as it flows up the ascending limb, finally leaving the loop at a minimum concentration of 100 mOsm. What is the point of concentrating the fluid fourfold and then turning around and diluting it until it leaves at one third the concentration at which it entered? Such a mechanism offers two benefits. First, it establishes a vertical osmotic gradient in the medullary interstitial fluid. This gradient, in turn, is used by the collecting ducts to concentrate the tubular fluid so that a urine *more concentrated* than normal body fluids can be excreted. Second, because the fluid is hypotonic as it enters the distal parts of the tubule, the kidneys can excrete a urine *more dilute* than normal body fluids. Let us see how.

Vasopressin-controlled, variable H_2O reabsorption occurs in the final tubular segments.

After obligatory H_2O reabsorption from the proximal tubule (65% of the filtered H_2O) and loop of Henle (15% of the filtered H_2O), 20% of the filtered H_2O remains in the lumen to enter the distal and collecting tubules for variable reabsorption under

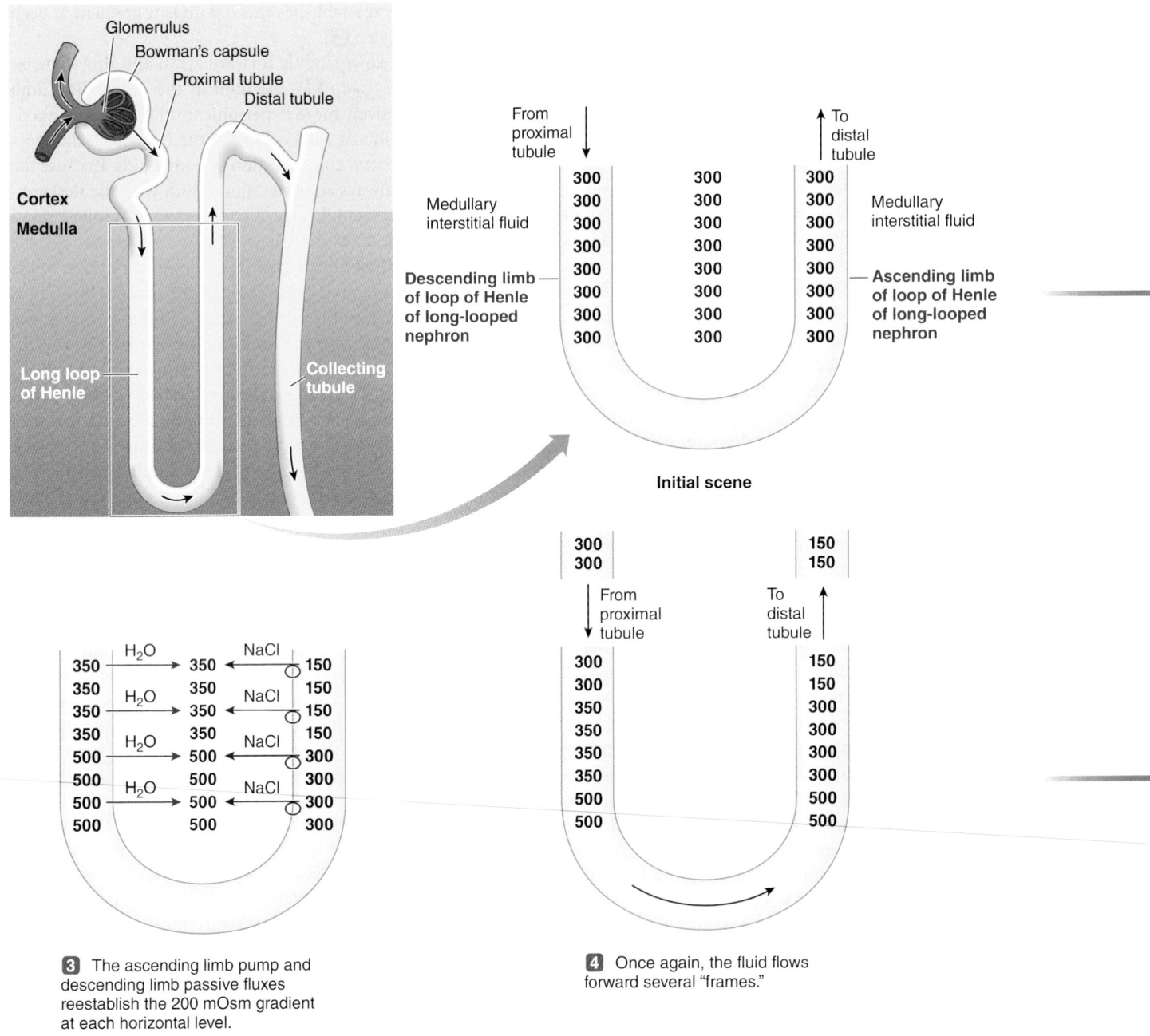

3 The ascending limb pump and descending limb passive fluxes reestablish the 200 mOsm gradient at each horizontal level.

4 Once again, the fluid flows forward several "frames."

● **FIGURE 13-20 Countercurrent multiplication in the renal medulla.** All values are in mOsm.

hormonal control. This is still a large volume of filtered H_2O subject to regulated reabsorption; 20% × GFR (180 L per day) = 36 L per day to be reabsorbed to varying extents, depending on the body's state of hydration. This is more than 13 times the amount of plasma H_2O in the entire circulatory system.

The fluid leaving the loop of Henle enters the distal tubule at 100 mOsm, so it is hypotonic to the surrounding isotonic (300 mOsm) interstitial fluid of the renal cortex through which the distal tubule passes. The distal tubule then empties into the collecting duct, which is bathed by progressively increasing concentrations (300 to 1200 mOsm) of the surrounding interstitial fluid as it descends through the medulla.

ROLE OF VASOPRESSIN For H_2O absorption to occur across a segment of the tubule, two criteria must be met: (1) an osmotic gradient must exist across the tubule, and (2) the tubular segment must be permeable to H_2O. The distal and collecting tubules are *impermeable* to H_2O except in the presence of **vasopressin,** also known as **antidiuretic hormone** (*anti* means "against"; *diuretic* means "increased urine output"),[4] which increases their perme-

---

[4]Even though textbooks traditionally tend to use the name *antidiuretic hormone* for this hormone, especially when discussing its actions on the kidney, investigators in the field now prefer *vasopressin*.

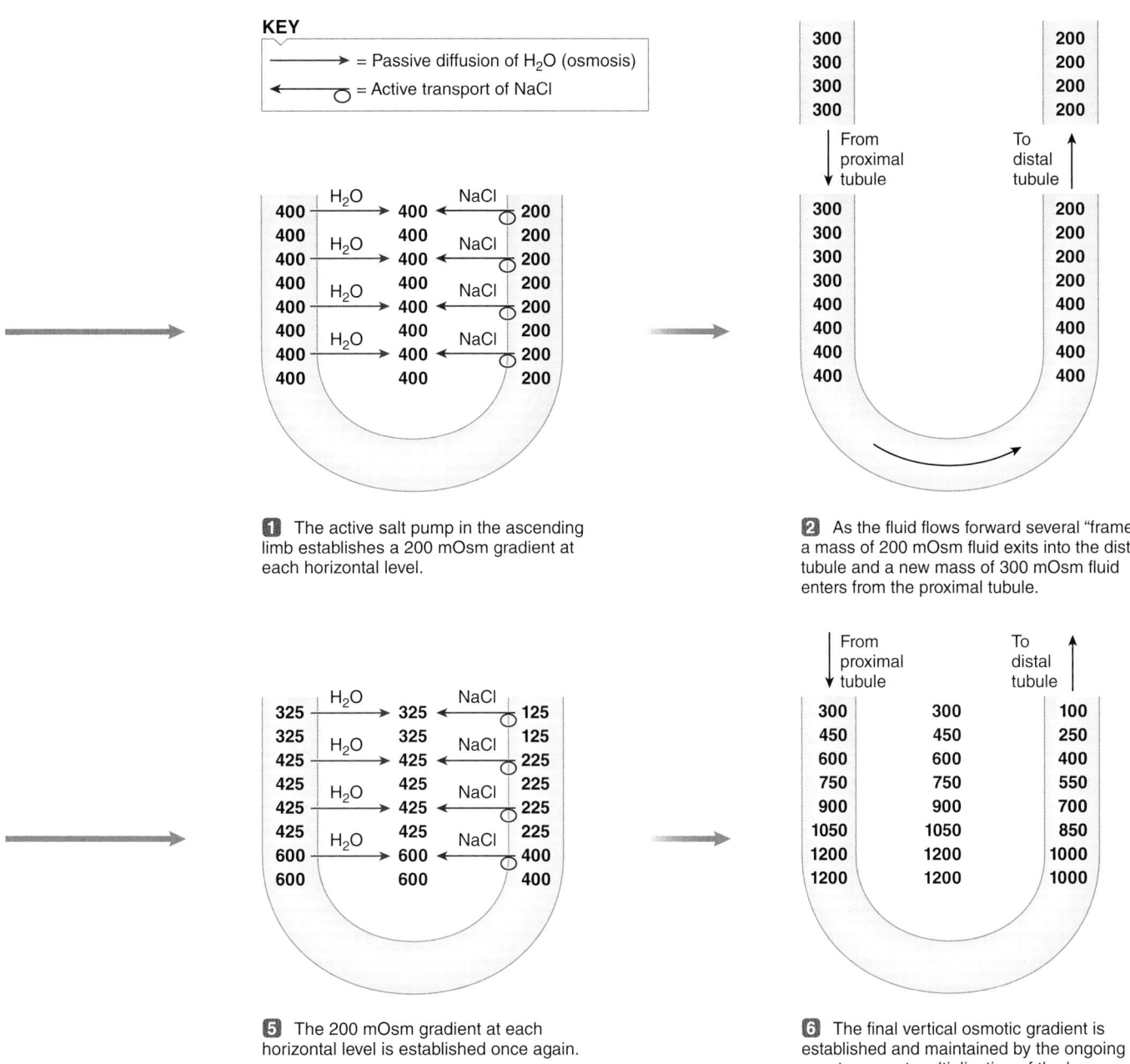

KEY

⟶ = Passive diffusion of H_2O (osmosis)

⟵○ = Active transport of NaCl

1 The active salt pump in the ascending limb establishes a 200 mOsm gradient at each horizontal level.

2 As the fluid flows forward several "frames," a mass of 200 mOsm fluid exits into the distal tubule and a new mass of 300 mOsm fluid enters from the proximal tubule.

5 The 200 mOsm gradient at each horizontal level is established once again.

6 The final vertical osmotic gradient is established and maintained by the ongoing countercurrent multiplication of the long loops of Henle.

ability to H_2O. Vasopressin is produced by several specific neuronal cell bodies in the *hypothalamus* and then stored in the *posterior pituitary gland,* which is attached to the hypothalamus by a thin stalk (see ● Figure 17-4, p. 534). The hypothalamus controls release of vasopressin from the posterior pituitary into the blood. In a negative-feedback fashion, vasopressin secretion is stimulated by a H_2O deficit when the ECF is too concentrated (that is, hypertonic) and H_2O must be conserved for the body, and it is inhibited by a H_2O excess when the ECF is too dilute (that is, hypotonic) and surplus H_2O must be eliminated in urine.

Vasopressin reaches the basolateral membrane of the tubular cells lining the distal and collecting tubules through the circulatory system. Here, it binds with receptors specific for it (● Figure 13-21). This binding activates the cyclic AMP (cAMP) second-messenger system within these tubular cells

(see p. 102). This binding ultimately increases permeability of the opposite luminal membrane to H_2O by promoting insertion of vasopressin-regulated water channels in this membrane by means of exocytosis. Without these water channels, the luminal membrane is impermeable to H_2O. Once H_2O enters the tubular cells from the filtrate through these vasopressin-regulated luminal water channels, it passively leaves the cells down the osmotic gradient across the cells' basolateral membrane to enter the interstitial fluid. The water channels in the basolateral membrane of the distal and collecting tubule are always present and open, so this membrane is always permeable to H_2O. By permitting more H_2O to permeate from the lumen into the tubular cells, the additional vasopressin-regulated luminal channels thus increase H_2O reabsorption from the filtrate into the interstitial fluid. The tubular response to vasopressin is graded: The

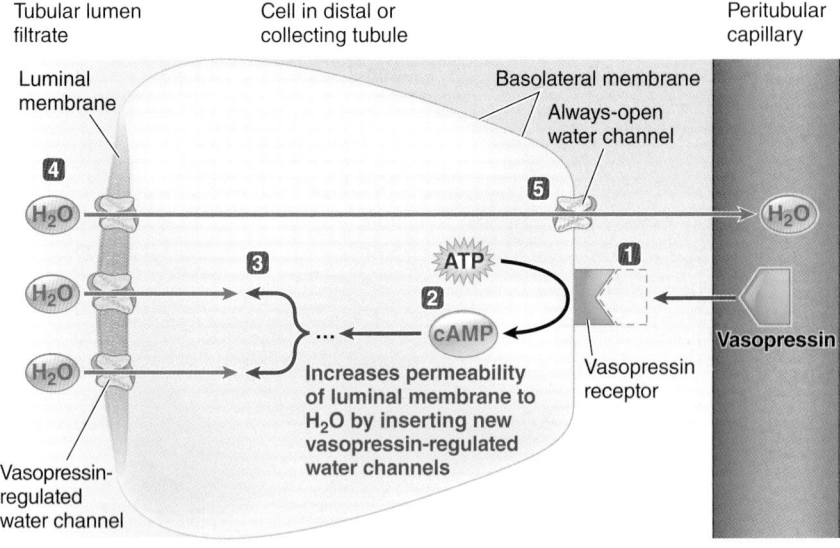

Tubular lumen filtrate | Cell in distal or collecting tubule | Peritubular capillary

Luminal membrane

Basolateral membrane
Always-open water channel

Vasopressin-regulated water channel

Increases permeability of luminal membrane to H_2O by inserting new vasopressin-regulated water channels

Vasopressin receptor

Vasopressin

1 Blood-borne vasopressin binds with its receptor sites on the basolateral membrane of a cell in the distal or collecting tubule.

2 This binding activates the cyclic AMP (cAMP) second-messenger system within the cell.

3 Cyclic AMP increases the opposite luminal membrane's permeability to H_2O by promoting the insertion of vasopressin-regulated water channels into the membrane. This membrane is impermeable to water in the absence of vasopressin.

4 Water enters the tubular cell from the tubular lumen through the inserted water channels.

5 Water exits the cell through a different, always-open water channel permanently positioned at the basolateral border, and then enters the blood, in this way being reabsorbed.

● **FIGURE 13-21 Mechanism of action of vasopressin.**

more vasopressin present, the more luminal water channels inserted, and the greater the permeability of the distal and collecting tubules to H_2O. The increase in luminal membrane water channels is not permanent, however. The channels are retrieved by endocytosis when vasopressin secretion decreases and cAMP activity is similarly decreased. Accordingly, H_2O permeability is reduced when vasopressin secretion decreases. These H_2O channels are stored in the internalized vesicles ready for reinsertion the next time vasopressin secretion increases. This shuttling of regulated water channels into and out of the luminal membrane under vasopressin command provides a means of rapidly controlling H_2O permeability of the distal and collecting tubules, depending on the body's momentary needs.

Vasopressin influences H_2O permeability only in the distal and collecting tubules. It has no influence over the 80% of the filtered H_2O that is obligatorily reabsorbed without control in the proximal tubule and loop of Henle. The ascending limb of Henle's loop is always impermeable to H_2O, even in the presence of vasopressin.

REGULATION OF H_2O REABSORPTION IN RESPONSE TO A H_2O DEFICIT When vasopressin secretion increases in response to a H_2O deficit and the permeability of the distal and collecting tubules to H_2O accordingly increases, the hypotonic tubular fluid entering the distal part of the nephron can lose progressively more H_2O by osmosis into the interstitial fluid as the tu-

bular fluid first flows through the isotonic cortex and then is exposed to the ever-increasing osmolarity of the medullary interstitial fluid as it plunges toward the renal pelvis (● Figure 13-22a). As the 100 mOsm tubular fluid enters the distal tubule and is exposed to a surrounding interstitial fluid of 300 mOsm, H_2O leaves the tubular fluid by osmosis across the now-permeable tubular cells until the tubular fluid reaches a maximum concentration of 300 mOsm by the end of the distal tubule. As this 300 mOsm tubular fluid progresses farther into the collecting duct, it is exposed to even higher osmolarity in the surrounding medullary interstitial fluid. Consequently, the tubular fluid loses more H_2O by osmosis and becomes further concentrated; only to move farther forward, be exposed to an even higher interstitial fluid osmolarity, and lose even more H_2O; and so on.

Under the influence of maximum levels of vasopressin, the tubular fluid can be concentrated up to 1200 mOsm by the end of the collecting ducts. The fluid is not modified any further beyond the collecting duct, so what remains in the tubules at this point is urine. As a result of this extensive vasopressin-promoted reabsorption of H_2O in the late segments of the tubule, a small volume of urine concentrated up to 1200 mOsm can be excreted. As little as 0.3 ml of urine may be formed each minute, less than one third the normal urine flow rate of 1 ml/min. The reabsorbed H_2O entering the medullary interstitial fluid is picked up by the peritubular capillaries and returned to the general circulation, thus being conserved for the body.

Although vasopressin promotes H_2O conservation by the body, it cannot halt urine production, even when a person is not taking in any H_2O, because a minimum volume of H_2O must be excreted with the solute wastes. Collectively, the waste products and other constituents eliminated in the urine average 600 milliosmols each day. Because the maximum urine concentration is 1200 mOsm (milliosmols per liter), the minimum volume of urine required to excrete these wastes is 500 ml per day (600 milliosmols of wastes per day ÷ 1200 milliosmols per liter of urine = 0.5 L, (500 ml) per day, or 0.3 ml/min). Thus, under maximal vasopressin influence, 99.7% of the 180 L of plasma H_2O filtered per day is returned to the blood, with an obligatory H_2O loss of 0.5 L.

The kidneys' ability to tremendously concentrate urine to minimize H_2O loss when necessary is possible only because of the presence of the vertical osmotic gradient in the medulla. If this gradient did not exist, the kidneys could not produce a urine more concentrated than the body fluids no matter how much vasopressin was secreted, because the only driving force for H_2O reabsorption is a concentration differential between the tubular fluid and the interstitial fluid.

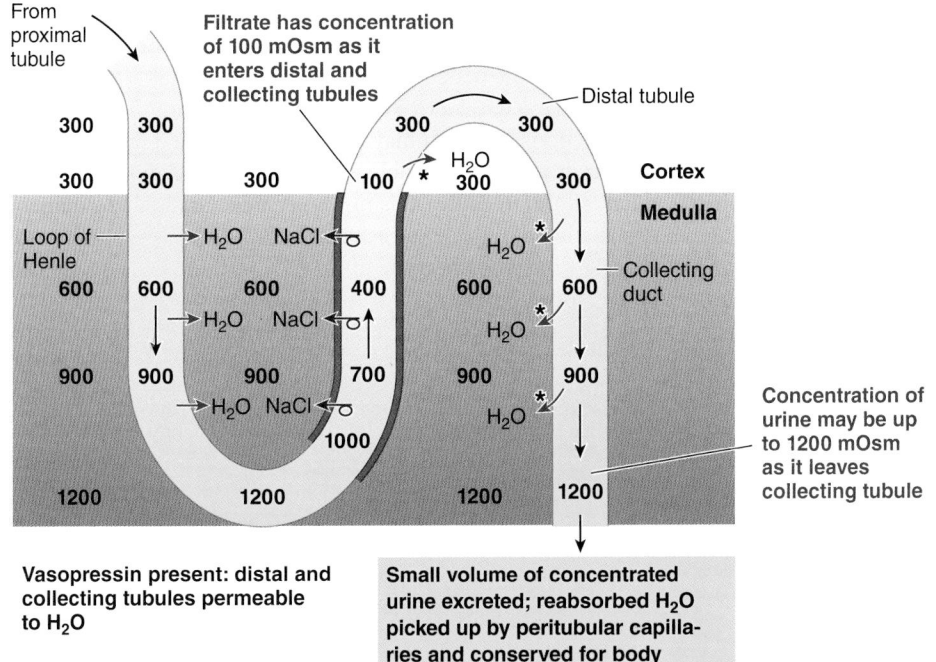

Filtrate has concentration of 100 mOsm as it enters distal and collecting tubules

From proximal tubule

Distal tubule

300   300   300   300

H₂O

300   300   300   100   *   300   300   **Cortex**

Medulla

Loop of Henle   → H₂O   NaCl ←   H₂O *   Collecting duct

600   600   600   400   600   600

→ H₂O   NaCl ←   H₂O *

900   900   900   700   900   900

→ H₂O   NaCl ←   H₂O *

1000

Concentration of urine may be up to 1200 mOsm as it leaves collecting tubule

1200   1200   1200   1200

Vasopressin present: distal and collecting tubules permeable to H₂O

Small volume of concentrated urine excreted; reabsorbed H₂O picked up by peritubular capillaries and conserved for body

(a) In the face of a water deficit

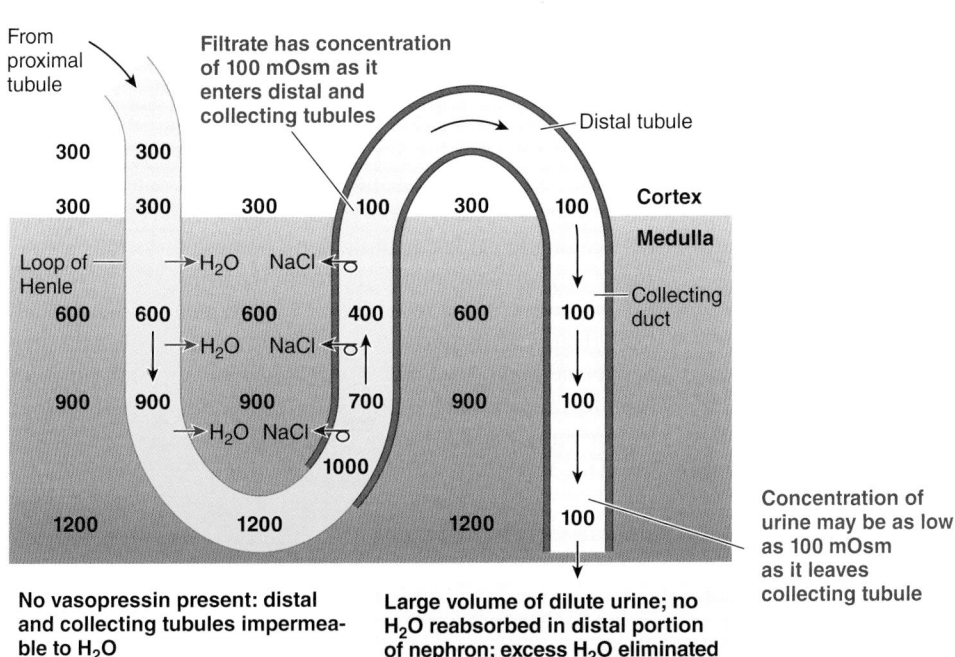

Filtrate has concentration of 100 mOsm as it enters distal and collecting tubules

From proximal tubule

Distal tubule

300   300

300   300   300   100   300   100   **Cortex**

Medulla

Loop of Henle   → H₂O   NaCl ←

600   600   600   400   600   100   Collecting duct

→ H₂O   NaCl ←

900   900   900   700   900   100

→ H₂O   NaCl ←

1000

Concentration of urine may be as low as 100 mOsm as it leaves collecting tubule

1200   1200   1200   100

No vasopressin present: distal and collecting tubules impermeable to H₂O

Large volume of dilute urine; no H₂O reabsorbed in distal portion of nephron; excess H₂O eliminated

(b) In the face of a water excess

KEY

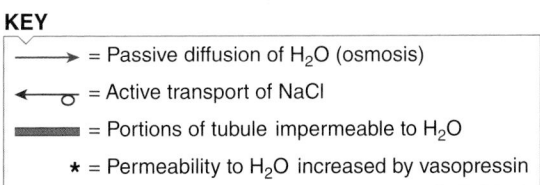

    → = Passive diffusion of H₂O (osmosis)

    ← = Active transport of NaCl

    ▬ = Portions of tubule impermeable to H₂O

    ★ = Permeability to H₂O increased by vasopressin

● **FIGURE 13-22 Excretion of urine of varying concentration depending on the body's needs.** All values are in mOsm.

REGULATION OF H₂O REABSORPTION IN RESPONSE TO A H₂O EXCESS Conversely, when a person consumes large quantities of H_2O, the excess H_2O must be removed from the body without simultaneously losing solutes that are critical for maintaining homeostasis. Under these circumstances, no vasopressin is secreted, so the distal and collecting tubules remain impermeable to H_2O. The tubular fluid entering the distal tubule is hypotonic (100 mOsm), having lost salt without an accompanying loss of H_2O in the ascending limb of Henle's loop. As this hypotonic fluid passes through the distal and collecting tubules (● Figure 13-22b), the medullary osmotic gradient cannot exert any influence because the late tubule is impermeable to H_2O. In other words, none of the H_2O remaining in the tubules can leave the lumen to be reabsorbed, even though the tubular fluid is less concentrated than the surrounding interstitial fluid. Thus, in the absence of vasopressin, the 20% of the filtered fluid that reaches the distal tubule is not reabsorbed. Meanwhile, excretion of wastes and other urinary solutes remains constant. The net result is a large volume of dilute urine, which helps rid the body of excess H_2O. Urine osmolarity may be as low as 100 mOsm, the same as in the fluid entering the distal tubule. Urine flow may be increased up to 25 ml/min in the absence of vasopressin, compared to the normal urine production of 1 ml/min.

The ability to produce urine less concentrated than the body fluids depends on the tubular fluid being hypotonic as it enters the distal part of the nephron. This dilution is accomplished in the ascending limb, as NaCl is actively extruded but H_2O cannot follow. Therefore, the loop of Henle, by simultaneously establishing the medullary osmotic gradient and diluting the tubular fluid before it enters the distal segments, plays a key role in allowing the kidneys to excrete urine that ranges in concentration from 100 to 1200 mOsm.

Note that through the combined effects of the medullary vertical osmotic gradient and vasopressin-controlled variability in permeability to H_2O in the distal parts of the nephron, the body is able to retain or lose **free H₂O** (that is, H_2O not accompanied by solutes.) Thus, free H_2O can be reabsorbed without comparable solute reabsorption to correct for hypertonicity of the body fluids. Conversely, a large quantity of free H_2O can be excreted unaccompanied by comparable solute excretion to rid the body of excess pure H_2O, thus correcting for hypotonicity of the body fluids.

The kidneys inappropriately lose too much H_2O following alcohol ingestion because alcohol inhibits vasopressin secretion. Typically, more fluid is lost in the urine than is consumed in the alcoholic beverage, so the body becomes dehydrated despite substantial fluid ingestion.

Renal failure has wide-ranging consequences.

Urine excretion and the resulting clearance of wastes and excess electrolytes from the plasma are crucial for maintaining homeostasis. When the functions of both kidneys are so disrupted that they cannot perform their regulatory and excretory functions sufficiently to maintain homeostasis, **renal failure** has set in. Renal failure can manifest itself either as *acute renal failure,*

characterized by a sudden onset with rapidly reduced urine formation until less than the essential minimum of around 500 ml of urine is being produced per day, or as *chronic renal failure,* characterized by slow, progressive, insidious loss of renal function. A person may die from acute renal failure, or the condition may be reversible and lead to full recovery. Chronic renal failure, in contrast, is not reversible. Gradual, permanent destruction of renal tissue eventually proves fatal. Chronic renal failure is insidious because up to 75% of the kidney tissue can be destroyed before the loss of kidney function is even noticeable. Because of the abundant reserve of kidney function, only 25% of kidney tissue is needed to adequately maintain all the essential renal excretory and regulatory functions. With less than 25% of functional kidney tissue remaining, however, renal insufficiency becomes apparent. *End-stage renal failure* results when 90% of kidney function has been lost. More than 20 million people in the United States have some extent of kidney disease, which leads to more than 80,000 deaths per year.

We will not sort out the stages and symptoms associated with various renal disorders, but ▲ Table 13-3, which summarizes the potential consequences of renal failure, gives you an idea of the broad effects that kidney impairment can have. The extent of these effects should not be surprising, considering the central role the kidneys play in maintaining homeostasis. When the kidneys cannot maintain a normal internal environment, widespread disruption of cell activities can bring about abnormal function in other organ systems as well. By the time end-stage renal failure occurs, literally every body system has become impaired to some extent. The most life-threatening consequences of renal failure are retention of H^+ (causing metabolic acidosis) and K^+ (leading to cardiac malfunction), because these ions are not adequately secreted and eliminated in the urine.

Because chronic renal failure is irreversible and eventually fatal, treatment is aimed at maintaining renal function by alternative methods, such as dialysis and kidney transplantation. (For further explanation of these procedures, see the boxed feature on p. 436, ◗ Beyond the Basics.)

This finishes our discussion of kidney function. For the remainder of the chapter, we focus on the plumbing that stores and carries the urine formed by the kidneys to the outside.

Urine is temporarily stored in the bladder, from which it is emptied by micturition.

Once urine has been formed by the kidneys, it is transmitted through the ureters to the urinary bladder. Urine does not flow through the ureters by gravitational pull alone. Peristaltic (forward-pushing) contractions of the smooth muscle within the ureteral wall propel the urine forward from the kidneys to the bladder.

ROLE OF THE BLADDER The bladder can accommodate large fluctuations in urine volume. The bladder wall consists of smooth muscle, which can stretch tremendously without building up bladder wall tension (see p. 238). In addition, the highly folded bladder wall flattens out during filling to increase bladder storage capacity. Because the kidneys continuously form

▲ Table 13-3   Potential Ramifications of Renal Failure

Uremic toxicity caused by retention of waste products

- Nausea, vomiting, diarrhea, and ulcers caused by a toxic effect on the digestive system
- Bleeding tendency arising from a toxic effect on platelet function
- Mental changes—such as reduced alertness, insomnia, and shortened attention span, progressing to convulsions and coma— caused by toxic effects on the central nervous system
- Abnormal sensory and motor activity caused by a toxic effect on the peripheral nerves

Metabolic acidosis caused by the inability of the kidneys to adequately secrete H^+ that is continually being added to the body fluids as a result of metabolic activity *(among most life-threatening consequences of renal failure)*

- Altered enzyme activity caused by the action of too much acid on enzymes
- Depression of the central nervous system caused by the action of too much acid interfering with neuronal excitability

Potassium retention resulting from inadequate tubular secretion of K^+ *(among most life-threatening consequences of renal failure)*

- Altered cardiac and neural excitability as a result of changing the resting membrane potential of excitable cells

Sodium imbalances caused by the inability of the kidneys to adjust Na^+ excretion to balance changes in Na^+ consumption

- Elevated blood pressure, generalized edema, and congestive heart failure if too much Na^+ is consumed
- Hypotension and, if severe enough, circulatory shock if too little Na^+ is consumed

Phosphate and calcium imbalances arising from impaired reabsorption of these electrolytes

- Disturbances in skeletal structures caused by abnormalities in deposition of calcium phosphate crystals, which harden bone

Loss of plasma proteins as a result of increased "leakiness" of the glomerular membrane

- Edema caused by a reduction in plasma-colloid osmotic pressure

Inability to vary urine concentration as a result of impairment of the countercurrent system

- Hypotonicity of body fluids if too much H_2O is ingested
- Hypertonicity of body fluids if too little H_2O is ingested

Hypertension arising from the combined effects of salt and fluid retention and vasoconstrictor action of excess angiotensin II

Anemia caused by inadequate erythropoietin production

Depression of the immune system, most likely caused by toxic levels of wastes and acids

- Increased susceptibility to infections

---

urine, the bladder must have enough storage capacity to preclude the need to continuously get rid of the urine.

The bladder smooth muscle is richly supplied by parasympathetic fibers, stimulation of which causes bladder contraction. If the passageway through the urethra to the outside is open, bladder contraction empties urine from the bladder. The exit from the bladder, however, is guarded by two sphincters, the *internal urethral sphincter* and the *external urethral sphincter*.

ROLE OF THE URETHRAL SPHINCTERS A *sphincter* is a ring of muscle that can variably close off or permit passage through an opening. The **internal urethral sphincter** is smooth muscle and, accordingly, under involuntary control. It is not really a separate muscle but instead consists of the last part of the bladder. When the bladder is relaxed, the anatomic arrangement of the internal urethral sphincter region closes the outlet of the bladder.

Farther down the passageway, the urethra is encircled by a layer of skeletal muscle, the **external urethral sphincter.** The motor neuron that supplies the external sphincter fires continuously at a moderate rate unless it is inhibited, keeping this muscle tonically contracted so that it prevents urine from escaping through the urethra. Normally, when the bladder is relaxed and filling, both the internal and the external urethral sphincters are closed to keep urine from dribbling out. Furthermore, because the external sphincter is skeletal muscle and thus under voluntary control, the person can deliberately tighten it to prevent urination from occurring even when the bladder is contracting and the internal sphincter is open.

MICTURITION REFLEX **Micturition,** or **urination,** the process of bladder emptying, is governed by two mechanisms: the micturition reflex and voluntary control. The **micturition reflex** is initiated when stretch receptors within the bladder wall are stimulated (● Figure 13-23). The bladder in an adult can accommodate 250 to 400 ml of urine before the tension within its walls begins to rise sufficiently to activate the stretch receptors. The greater the distension beyond this, the greater is the extent of receptor activation. Afferent fibers from the stretch receptors carry impulses into the spinal cord and eventually, via interneurons, stimulate the parasympathetic supply to the bladder and inhibit the motor-neuron supply to the external sphincter. Parasympathetic stimulation of the bladder causes it to contract. No special mechanism is required to open the internal sphincter;

THE URINARY SYSTEM   **435**

Beyond the Basics

Dialysis: Cellophane Tubing or Abdominal Lining as an Artificial Kidney

Because chronic renal failure is irreversible and eventually fatal, treatment is aimed at maintaining renal function by alternative methods, such as dialysis and kidney transplantation. More than 300,000 people in the United States are currently on dialysis, and this number is expected to climb as the population ages and the incidence of diabetes mellitus, one of the leading causes of kidney failure, continues to rise. End-stage renal failure (less than 10% kidney function) caused by diabetes mellitus is increasing at a rate of more than 11% annually.

The process of dialysis bypasses the kidneys to maintain normal fluid and electrolyte balance and remove wastes artificially. In the original method of dialysis, **hemodialysis,** a patient's blood is pumped through cellophane tubing that is surrounded by a large volume of fluid similar in composition to normal plasma. After dialysis, the blood is returned to the patient's circulatory system. During hemodialysis, about 250 ml of blood is outside of the body at any given time.

Like capillaries, cellophane is highly permeable to most plasma constituents but is impermeable to plasma proteins. As blood flows through the tubing, solutes move across the cellophane down their individual concentration gradients; plasma proteins, however, stay in the blood. Urea and other wastes, which are absent in the dialysis fluid, diffuse out of the plasma into the surrounding fluid, cleaning the blood of these wastes. Plasma constituents that are not regulated by the kidneys and are at normal concentration, such as glucose, do not move across the cellophane into the dialysis fluid, because there is no driving force to produce their movement. (The dialysis fluid's glucose concentration is the same as normal plasma glucose concentration.) Electrolytes, such as K^+ and PO_4^{3-}, which are higher than their normal plasma concentrations because the diseased kidneys cannot eliminate excess quantities of these substances, move out of the plasma until equilibrium is achieved between the plasma and the dialysis fluid.

Because the dialysis fluid's solute concentrations are maintained at normal plasma values, the solute concentration of the blood returned to the patient after dialysis is essentially normal. Hemodialysis is repeated as often as necessary to maintain the plasma composition within an acceptable level. Conventionally, it is done three times per week for several hours at each session at a treatment center or at home, but newer, more user-friendly, at-home methods dialyze the blood up to six times per week during the day or at night while the person is sleeping. The more frequent methods maintain better stability in plasma constituents than the less frequent methods do.

Another method of dialysis, **continuous ambulatory peritoneal dialysis (CAPD),** uses the peritoneal membrane (the lining of the abdominal cavity) as the dialysis membrane. With this method, 2 liters of dialysis fluid are inserted into the patient's abdominal cavity through a permanently implanted catheter. Urea, K^+, and other wastes and excess electrolytes diffuse from the plasma across the peritoneal membrane into the dialysis fluid, which is drained off and replaced several times a day. The CAPD method offers several advantages: The patient can self-administer it, the patient's blood is continuously purified and adjusted, and the patient can engage in normal activities while dialysis is being accomplished. One drawback is the increased risk of peritoneal infections.

Although dialysis can remove metabolic wastes and foreign compounds and help maintain fluid and electrolyte balance within acceptable limits, this plasma-cleansing technique cannot make up for the failing kidneys' reduced ability to produce hormones (erythropoietin and renin) and to activate vitamin D. One new experimental technique incorporates living kidney cells derived from pigs within a dialysis-like machine. Standard ultrafiltration technology like that used in

hemodialysis purifies and adjusts the plasma as usual. Importantly, the living cells not only help maintain even better control of plasma constituents, especially K^+, but also add the deficient renal hormones to the plasma passing through the machine and activate vitamin D. This promising new technology has not yet been tested in large-scale clinical trials.

For now, transplanting a healthy kidney from a donor is another option for treating chronic renal failure. A kidney is one of the few transplants that can be provided by a living donor. Because 25% of the total kidney tissue can maintain the body, both the donor and the recipient have ample renal function with only one kidney each. The biggest problem with transplants is the possibility that the patient's immune system will reject the organ. Risk of rejection can be minimized by matching the tissue types of the donor and the recipient as closely as possible (the best donor choice is usually a close relative), coupled with immunosuppressive drugs. More than 15,000 kidney transplants are performed in the United States each year, with 60,000 more people on waiting lists for a donor kidney.

Another new technique on the horizon for treating end-stage renal failure is a continuously functioning artificial kidney that mimics natural renal function. Using nanotechnology (very small-scale devices), researchers are working on a device that contains two membranes, the first for filtering blood like the glomerulus does and the second for mimicking the renal tubules by selectively altering the filtrate. The device, which will directly process the blood on an ongoing basis without using dialysis fluid, will return important substances to the body while discharging unneeded substances to a discardable bag that will serve as an external bladder. Scientists have developed computer models for such a device and thus far have created the filtering membrane.

---

changes in the shape of the bladder during contraction mechanically pull the internal sphincter open. Simultaneously, the external sphincter relaxes as its motor neuron supply is inhibited. Now both sphincters are open, and urine is expelled through the urethra by the force of bladder contraction. This micturition reflex, which is entirely a spinal reflex, governs

bladder emptying in infants. As soon as the bladder fills enough to trigger the reflex, the baby automatically wets.

VOLUNTARY CONTROL OF MICTURITION In addition to triggering the micturition reflex, bladder filling gives rise to the conscious urge to urinate. The perception of bladder fullness

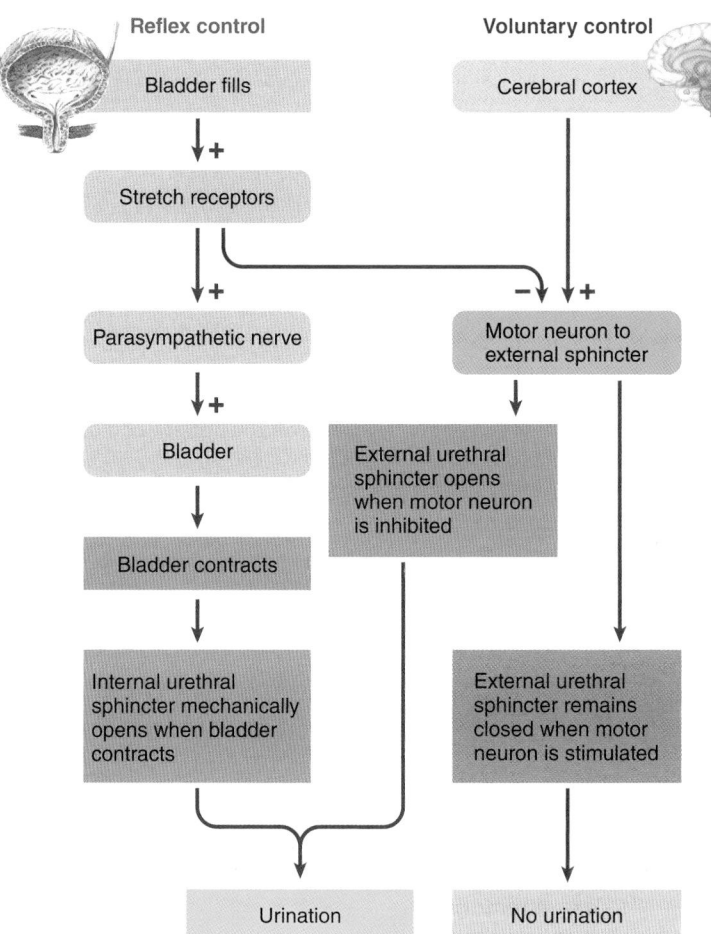

Reflex control

Bladder fills

↓ +

Stretch receptors

↓ +

Parasympathetic nerve

↓ +

Bladder

↓

Bladder contracts

↓

Internal urethral sphincter mechanically opens when bladder contracts

Voluntary control

Cerebral cortex

− +

Motor neuron to external sphincter

↓

External urethral sphincter opens when motor neuron is inhibited

External urethral sphincter remains closed when motor neuron is stimulated

Urination

No urination

● **FIGURE 13-23 Reflex and voluntary control of micturition.**

appears before the external sphincter reflexly relaxes, warning that micturition is imminent. As a result, voluntary control of micturition, learned during toilet training in early childhood, can override the micturition reflex so that bladder emptying can take place at the person's convenience rather than when bladder filling first activates the stretch receptors. If the time when the micturition reflex is initiated is inopportune for urination, the person can voluntarily prevent bladder emptying by deliberately tightening the external sphincter. Voluntary excitatory impulses from the cerebral cortex override the reflex inhibitory input from the stretch receptors to the involved motor neurons (the relative balance of EPSPs and IPSPs), keeping these muscles contracted so that no urine is expelled (see p. 95).

Urination cannot be delayed indefinitely. As the bladder continues to fill, reflex input from the stretch receptors increases with time. Finally, reflex inhibitory input to the external sphincter motor neuron becomes so powerful that it can no longer be overridden by voluntary excitatory input, so the sphincter relaxes and the bladder uncontrollably empties.

Micturition can also be deliberately initiated, even though the bladder is not distended, by voluntarily relaxing the external sphincter. Lowering of the pelvic floor allows the bladder to drop downward, which simultaneously pulls open the internal

urethral sphincter and stretches the bladder wall. The subsequent activation of the stretch receptors brings about bladder contraction by the micturition reflex. Voluntary bladder emptying may be further assisted by contracting the abdominal wall and respiratory diaphragm. The resulting increase in intra-abdominal pressure squeezes down on the bladder to facilitate its emptying.

URINARY INCONTINENCE Urinary incontinence, or inability to prevent discharge of urine, occurs when descending pathways in the spinal cord that mediate voluntary control of the external sphincter are disrupted, as in spinal-cord injury. Because the components of the micturition reflex arc are still intact in the lower spinal cord, bladder emptying is governed by an uncontrollable spinal reflex, as in infants. A lesser degree of incontinence characterized by urine escaping when bladder pressure suddenly increases transiently, such as during coughing or sneezing, can result from impaired sphincter function. This is common in women who have borne children or in men whose sphincters have been injured during prostate surgery.

Chapter in Perspective: Focus on Homeostasis

The kidneys contribute to homeostasis more extensively than any other single organ. They regulate the electrolyte composition, volume, osmolarity, and pH of the internal environment and eliminate all the waste products of bodily metabolism except for respiration-removed CO_2. They accomplish these regulatory functions by eliminating in the urine substances the body doesn't need, such as metabolic wastes and excess quantities of ingested salt or water, while conserving useful substances. The kidneys can maintain the plasma constituents they regulate within the narrow range compatible with life, despite wide variations in intake and losses of these substances through other avenues. Illustrating the magnitude of the kidneys' task, about a quarter of the blood pumped into the systemic circulation goes to the kidneys to be adjusted and purified, with only three quarters of the blood being used to supply all the other tissues.

The kidneys contribute to homeostasis in the following specific ways.

Regulatory Functions

- The kidneys regulate the quantity and concentration of most ECF electrolytes, including those important in maintaining proper neuromuscular excitability.

- They help maintain proper pH by eliminating excess H^+ (acid) or HCO_3^- (base) in the urine.
- They help maintain proper plasma volume, which is important in long-term regulation of arterial blood pressure, by controlling salt balance in the body. The ECF volume, including plasma volume, reflects total salt load in the ECF, because Na^+ and its attendant anion, Cl^-, are responsible for more than 90% of the ECF's osmotic (water-holding) activity.
- The kidneys maintain water balance in the body, which is important in maintaining proper ECF osmolarity (concentration of solutes). This role is important in maintaining stability of cell volume by keeping water from osmotically moving into or out of the cells, thus preventing them from swelling or shrinking, respectively.

Excretory Functions
- The kidneys excrete the end products of metabolism in the urine. If allowed to accumulate, these wastes are toxic to cells.
- The kidneys also excrete many foreign compounds that enter the body.

Hormonal Functions
- The kidneys produce erythropoietin, the hormone that stimulates the bone marrow to produce red blood cells. This action contributes to homeostasis by helping maintain the optimal O_2 content of blood. More than 98% of O_2 in the blood is bound to hemoglobin within red blood cells.
- They also produce renin, the hormone that initiates the renin–angiotensin–aldosterone pathway for controlling renal tubular Na^+ reabsorption, which is important in long-term maintenance of plasma volume and arterial blood pressure.

Metabolic Functions
- The kidneys help convert vitamin D into its active form. Vitamin D is essential for Ca^{2+} absorption from the digestive tract. Calcium, in turn, exerts a variety of homeostatic functions.

REVIEW EXERCISES

Objective Questions (Answers on p. A-48)

1. Part of the kidneys' energy supply is used to accomplish glomerular filtration. *(True or false?)*
2. Sodium reabsorption is under hormonal control throughout the length of the tubule. *(True or false?)*
3. Glucose and amino acids are reabsorbed by secondary active transport. *(True or false?)*
4. Water excretion can occur without comparable solute excretion. *(True or false?)*
5. The functional unit of the kidneys is the _____.
6. _____ is the only ion actively reabsorbed in the proximal tubule and actively secreted in the distal and collecting tubules.
7. The daily minimum volume of obligatory H_2O loss that must accompany excretion of wastes is _____ ml.
8. Which of the following filtered substances is normally *not* present in the urine?
   a. Na^+
   b. PO_4^{3-}
   c. H^+
   d. glucose
   e. urea
9. Reabsorption of which of the following substances is *not* linked in some way to active Na^+ reabsorption?
   a. glucose
   b. PO_4^{3-}
   c. H_2O
   d. urea
   e. Cl^-

   In Questions 10 through 12, indicate, by writing the identifying letters in the proper order in the blanks, the proper sequence through which fluid flows as it traverses the structures in question.
10. ___ ___ ___ ___ ___
    a. ureter
    b. kidney

    c. urethra
    d. bladder
    e. renal pelvis
11. ___ ___ ___ ___ ___ ___
    a. efferent arteriole
    b. peritubular capillaries
    c. renal artery
    d. glomerulus
    e. afferent arteriole
    f. renal vein
12. ___ ___ ___ ___ ___ ___ ___
    a. loop of Henle
    b. collecting duct
    c. Bowman's capsule
    d. proximal tubule
    e. renal pelvis
    f. distal tubule
    g. glomerulus
13. Using the answer code on the right, indicate what the osmolarity of the tubular fluid is at each of the designated points in a nephron:
    ___ 1. Bowman's capsule   (a) isotonic (300 mOsm)
    ___ 2. end of the proximal tubule   (b) hypotonic (100 mOsm)
    ___ 3. tip of Henle's loop of a long-looped nephron (at the bottom of the U-turn)   (c) hypertonic (1200 mOsm)
    ___ 4. end of Henle's loop of a long-looped nephron (before entry into distal tubule)   (d) ranging from hypotonic to hypertonic (100 to 1200 mOsm)
    ___ 5. end of the collecting duct

Essay Questions

1. List the functions of the kidneys.
2. Describe the anatomy of the urinary system. Describe the components of a nephron.
3. Describe the three basic renal processes; indicate how they relate to urine excretion.
4. Distinguish between *secretion* and *excretion.*
5. Discuss the forces involved in glomerular filtration. What is the average GFR?
6. How is GFR regulated as part of the baroreceptor reflex?
7. Why do the kidneys receive a seemingly disproportionate share of the cardiac output? What percentage of renal blood flow is normally filtered?
8. List the steps in transepithelial transport.
9. Distinguish between active and passive reabsorption.
10. Describe all the tubular transport processes that are linked to the basolateral Na^+–K^+ ATPase carrier.
11. Describe the renin–angiotensin–aldosterone system (RAAS). What are the functions of aldosterone and angiotensin II? Discuss the source and function of atrial natriuretic peptide (ANP).
12. To what do the terms *tubular maximum (T_m)* and *renal threshold* refer? Compare two substances that display a T_m, one substance that *is* and one that *is not* regulated by the kidneys.
13. What is the importance of tubular secretion? What are the most important secretory processes?
14. What is the average rate of urine formation?
15. Define *plasma clearance.*
16. What establishes a vertical osmotic gradient in the medullary interstitial fluid? Of what importance is this gradient?
17. Discuss the source, function, and mechanism of action of vasopressin.
18. Describe the transfer of urine to, the storage of urine in, and the emptying of urine from the bladder.

POINTS TO PONDER

(Explanations on p. A-48)

1. The long-looped nephrons of animals adapted to survive with minimal water consumption, such as desert rats, have relatively longer loops of Henle than humans have. Of what benefit would these longer loops be?
2. Using the data provided, indicate the rate of filtration, reabsorption, and excretion for hypothetical substance X. (a) If the plasma concentration of substance X is 200 mg/100 ml and the GFR is 125 ml/min, what is the filtered load of this substance? (b) If the T_m for substance X is 200 mg/min, how much of the substance will be reabsorbed at a plasma concentration of 200 mg/100 ml and a GFR of 125 ml/min? (c) How much of substance X will be excreted?
3. *Conn's syndrome* is an endocrine disorder brought about by a tumor of the adrenal cortex that secretes excessive aldosterone in uncontrolled fashion. Given what you know about the functions of aldosterone, describe what the most prominent features of this condition would be.
4. Because of a mutation, a child was born with an ascending limb of Henle that was water permeable. What would be the minimum and maximum urine osmolarities (in units of mOsm) the child could produce?
   a. 100/300
   b. 300/1200
   c. 100/100
   d. 1200/1200
   e. 300/300
5. An accident victim suffers permanent damage of the lower spinal cord and is paralyzed from the waist down. Describe what governs bladder emptying in this individual.

CLINICAL CONSIDERATION

(Explanation on p. A-48)

Marcus T. has noted a gradual decrease in his urine flow rate and is now experiencing difficulty in initiating micturition. He needs to urinate frequently, and often he feels as if his bladder is not empty even though he has just urinated. Analysis of Marcus's urine reveals no abnormalities. Are his urinary tract symptoms most likely caused by kidney disease, a bladder infection, or prostate enlargement?

Chapter 13

Kidneys: Anatomy, Functions, and Basic Processes (pp. 405–410)

■ Each of the pair of kidneys consists of an outer renal cortex and inner renal medulla. The kidneys form urine. They eliminate unwanted plasma constituents in the urine while conserving materials of value to the body. Urine from each kidney is collected in the renal pelvis and then transmitted from both kidneys through the pair of ureters to the single urinary bladder, where urine is stored until emptied through the urethra to the outside. (*Review Figure 13-1.*)

■ The urine-forming functional unit of the kidneys, the nephron, is composed of interrelated vascular and tubular components. The vascular component consists of two capillary networks in series, the first being the glomerulus, a tuft of capillaries that filters large volumes of protein-free plasma into the tubular component. Blood enters the glomerulus through the afferent arteriole and leaves through the efferent arteriole, which breaks up into the second capillary network, the peritubular capillaries. The peritubular capillaries, which wrap around the tubules, nourish the renal tissue and participate in exchanges between the tubular fluid and the plasma. (*Review Figures 13-2 and 13-3.*)

■ The tubular component begins with Bowman's capsule, which cups around the glomerulus to catch the filtrate, and then continues a specific tortuous course through the proximal tubule, loop of Henle, distal tubule, and collecting duct to ultimately empty into the renal pelvis. (*Review Figure 13-2.*) As the filtrate passes through various regions of the tubule, cells lining the tubules modify it, returning to the plasma only those materials necessary for maintaining proper ECF composition and volume. What is left behind in the tubules is excreted as urine.

■ The kidneys perform three basic processes: (1) glomerular filtration, the nondiscriminating movement of protein-free plasma from the blood into the tubules; (2) tubular reabsorption, the selective transfer of specific constituents in the filtrate back into the blood of the peritubular capillaries; and (3) tubular secretion, the highly specific movement of selected substances from peritubular capillary blood into the tubular fluid. Everything filtered or secreted but not reabsorbed is excreted as urine. (*Review Figure 13-4.*)

Glomerular Filtration (pp. 410–414)

■ Glomerular filtrate is produced when part of the plasma flowing through each glomerulus is passively forced under pressure through the sievelike glomerular membrane into the underlying Bowman's capsule. The net filtration pressure results from a high glomerular capillary blood pressure that favors filtration, outweighing the combined opposing forces of plasma-colloid osmotic pressure and Bowman's capsule hydrostatic pressure. (*Review Figures 13-5 and 13-6 and Table 13-1.*)

■ On average, 20% to 25% of the cardiac output is delivered to the kidneys to be acted on by renal regulatory and excretory processes. Of the plasma flowing through the kidneys, normally 20% is filtered through the glomeruli, for an average glomerular filtration rate (GFR) of 125 ml/min.

■ The GFR can be deliberately altered by changing the glomerular capillary blood pressure via sympathetic influence on the afferent arterioles as part of the baroreceptor reflex response that compensates for changes in arterial blood pressure. When blood pressure falls too low, sympathetically induced afferent arteriolar vasoconstriction lowers glomerular blood pressure and GFR. When blood pressure rises too high, reduced sympathetic activity causes afferent arteriolar vasodilation, leading to a rise in GFR. As the GFR is altered, the amount of fluid lost in urine changes correspondingly, adjusting plasma volume as needed to help restore blood pressure to normal over the long term. (*Review Figures 13-7 and 13-8.*)

Tubular Reabsorption (pp. 414–422)

■ After the filtrate is formed, the tubules handle each filtered substance discretely, so even though the initial glomerular filtrate is identical to plasma (with the exception of plasma proteins), the concentrations of different constituents are variously altered as the filtered fluid flows through the tubular system. (*Review Table 13-2, p. 424.*)

■ The reabsorptive capacity of the tubular system is tremendous. More than 99% of the filtered plasma is returned to the blood through reabsorption. On average, 124 ml out of the 125 ml filtered per minute are reabsorbed.

■ Tubular reabsorption involves transepithelial transport from the tubular lumen into the peritubular capillary plasma. This process may be active (requiring energy) or passive (using no energy). (*Review Figure 13-9.*)

■ The pivotal event to which most reabsorptive processes are linked is the active reabsorption of Na^+, driven by the energy-dependent Na^+–K^+ pump in the basolateral membrane of the tubular cells. The transport of Na^+ out of the cells into the lateral spaces between adjacent cells by this carrier induces the net reabsorption of Na^+ from the tubular lumen to the peritubular capillary plasma. (*Review Figure 13-10.*)

■ Most Na^+ reabsorption takes place early and constantly in the nephron without regulation, but in the distal and collecting tubules, the reabsorption of a small percentage of the filtered Na^+ is variable and controlled, primarily by the renin–angiotensin–aldosterone system (RAAS).

■ Because Na^+ and its attendant anion, Cl^-, are the major osmotically active ions in the ECF, the ECF volume is determined by the Na^+ load in the body. (The Na^+ load is the total *amount* of Na^+, not the *concentration* of Na^+, in the body fluids.) In turn, the plasma volume, which reflects the total ECF volume, is important in the long-term determination of arterial blood pressure. Whenever the Na^+ load, ECF volume, and arterial blood pressure are below normal, the juxtaglomerular apparatus secretes renin, an enzymatic hormone that triggers a series of events ultimately leading to increased aldosterone secretion by the adrenal cortex. Aldosterone increases Na^+ reabsorption from the distal portions of the tubule, thus correcting for the original reduction in Na^+, ECF volume, and blood pressure. (*Review Figures 13-11 and 13-12.*)

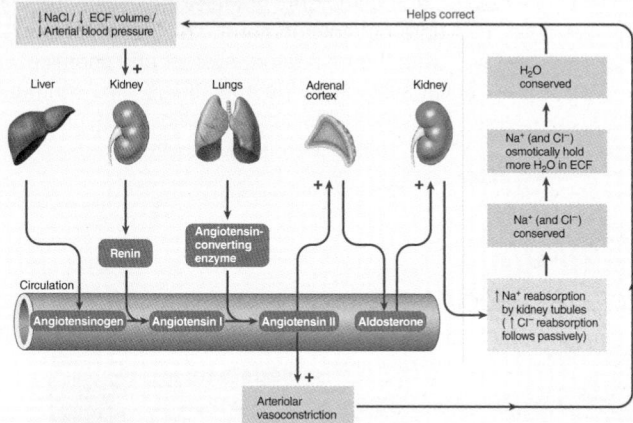

■ By contrast, Na^+ reabsorption is inhibited by atrial natriuretic peptide (ANP), a hormone released from the cardiac atria in response to expansion of the ECF volume and a subsequent increase in blood pressure.

■ In addition to driving Na^+ reabsorption, the energy used by the Na^+–K^+ pump is ultimately responsible for the reabsorption of organic nutrients (glucose or amino acids) from the proximal tubule by secondary active transport. (*Review Figure 3-17, p. 65.*)

■ Other electrolytes actively reabsorbed by the tubules, such as PO_4^{3-} and Ca^{2+}, have their own independently functioning carrier systems within the proximal tubule.

■ Because the electrolyte and nutrient carriers can become saturated, each exhibits a maximal carrier-limited transport capacity (T_m). Once the filtered load of an actively reabsorbed substance exceeds the T_m, reabsorption proceeds at a constant maximal rate, and any additional filtered quantity of the substance is excreted in the urine. (*Review Figure 13-13.*)

■ Active Na^+ reabsorption also drives the passive reabsorption of Cl^- (via an electrical gradient), H_2O (by osmosis), and urea (down a urea concentration gradient created as a result of extensive osmotic-driven H_2O reabsorption). Of the H_2O filtered, 65% is osmotically reabsorbed without regulation from the proximal tubule. Reabsorption of H_2O increases the concentration of other substances remaining in the tubular fluid, most of which are filtered waste products. The small urea molecules are the only waste products that can passively permeate the tubular membranes, so urea is the only waste product partially (50%) reabsorbed as a result of being concentrated. (*Review Figure 13-14.*)

■ The other waste products, which are not reabsorbed, remain in the urine in highly concentrated form.

Tubular Secretion (pp. 422–424)

■ Tubular secretion involves transepithelial transport from the peritubular capillary plasma into the tubular lumen. Via tubular secretion, the kidney tubules can selectively add some substances to the quantity already filtered. Secretion of substances hastens their excretion in the urine.

■ The most important secretory systems are for (1) H^+, which helps regulate acid–base balance; (2) K^+, which keeps the plasma K^+ concentration at the level needed to maintain normal membrane excitability in the heart, other muscles, and nerves; and (3) organic ions, which helps eliminate foreign organic compounds from the body more efficiently. Hydrogen ion is secreted in the proximal, distal, and collecting tubules. Potassium ion is secreted only in the distal and collecting tubules under control of aldosterone. Organic ions are secreted only in the proximal tubule. (*Review Figures 13-15 and 13-16 and Table 13-2.*)

Urine Excretion and Plasma Clearance (pp. 424–437)

■ Of the 125 ml/min of glomerular filtrate formed, normally only 1 ml/min remains in the tubules to be excreted as urine. Only wastes and excess electrolytes not wanted by the body are left behind, dissolved in a given volume of H_2O to be eliminated in the urine.

■ Because the excreted material is removed or "cleared" from the plasma, the term *plasma clearance* refers to the volume of plasma cleared of a particular substance each minute by renal activity. (*Review Figure 13-17.*)

■ The kidneys can excrete urine of varying volumes and concentrations to either conserve or eliminate H_2O, depending on whether the body has a H_2O deficit or excess, respectively. The kidneys can produce urine ranging from 0.3 ml/min at 1200 mOsm to 25 ml/min at 100 mOsm by reabsorbing variable amounts of H_2O from the distal portions of the nephron.

■ This variable reabsorption is made possible by a vertical osmotic gradient in the medullary interstitial fluid, established by the long loops of Henle via countercurrent multiplication. (*Review Figures 13-18 through 13-20.*) This vertical osmotic gradient, to which the hypotonic (100 mOsm) tubular fluid is exposed as it passes through the distal portions of the nephron, establishes a passive driving force for progressive reabsorption of H_2O from the tubular fluid, but the actual extent of H_2O reabsorption depends on the amount of vasopressin (antidiuretic hormone) secreted. (*Review Figure 13-22.*)

■ Vasopressin increases the permeability of the distal and collecting tubules to H_2O; they are impermeable to H_2O in its absence. (*Review Figure 13-21.*) Vasopressin secretion increases in response to a H_2O deficit, increasing H_2O reabsorption. Its secretion is inhibited in response to a H_2O excess, reducing H_2O reabsorption. Thus, vasopressin-controlled H_2O reabsorption helps correct any fluid imbalances.

■ Once formed, urine is propelled by peristaltic contractions through the ureters from the kidneys to the urinary bladder for temporary storage.

■ The bladder can accommodate 250 to 400 ml of urine before stretch receptors within its wall initiate the micturition reflex. This reflex causes involuntary emptying of the bladder by simultaneous bladder contraction and opening of both the internal and the external urethral sphincters. Micturition can be transiently prevented by voluntarily tightening the external sphincter. (*Review Figure 13-23.*)

Systems of Major Importance in Maintaining Fluid and Acid-Base Balance

Body systems maintain homeostasis

Homeostasis
The kidneys, in conjunction with hormones involved in salt and water balance, are responsible for maintaining the volume and osmolarity of the extracellular fluid (internal environment). The kidneys, along with the respiratory system and chemical buffer systems in the body fluids, also contribute to homeostasis by maintaining the proper pH in the internal environment.

$$CO_2 + H_2O \rightleftharpoons H_2CO_3 \rightleftharpoons H^+ + HCO_3^-$$
Chemical buffer systems in body fluids

Homeostasis is essential for survival of cells

Cells
The volume of circulating blood must be maintained to help ensure adequate pressure to drive life-sustaining blood to the cells. The osmolarity of fluid surrounding the cells must be closely regulated to prevent detrimental osmotic movement of water between the cells and ECF. The pH of the internal environment must remain stable because pH changes alter neuromuscular excitability and enzyme activity, among other serious consequences.

Cells make up body systems

Homeostasis depends on maintaining a balance between the input and the output of all constituents in the internal fluid environment. Regulation of **fluid balance** involves two separate components: *control of extracellular fluid (ECF) volume*, of which circulating plasma volume is a part, and *control of ECF osmolarity* (solute concentration). The kidneys control ECF volume by maintaining **salt balance** and control ECF osmolarity by maintaining **water balance.** The kidneys maintain this balance by adjusting the output of salt and water in the urine as needed to compensate for variable input and abnormal losses of these constituents.

Similarly, the kidneys help maintain **acid–base balance** by adjusting the urinary output of hydrogen ion (acid) and bicarbonate ion (base) as needed. Also contributing to acid-base balance are the buffer systems in the body fluids, which chemically compensate for changes in hydrogen ion concentration, and the lungs, which can adjust the rate at which they excrete hydrogen ion–generating CO_2.

Fluid and Acid–Base Balance

CHAPTER AT A GLANCE

Balance Concept
Internal pool of a substance
Balance of input and output

Fluid Balance
Body-fluid compartments
Importance of regulating ECF volume
Control of ECF volume by regulating salt balance
Importance of regulating ECF osmolarity
Control of ECF osmolarity by regulating water balance

Acid–Base Balance
Acid–base chemistry; pH
Consequences of changes in [H$^+$]
Sources of H$^+$
Lines of defense against changes in [H$^+$]
Chemical buffer systems
Respiratory control of pH
Renal control of pH
Acid–base imbalances

Balance Concept

The cells of complex multicellular organisms are able to survive and function only within a narrow range of composition of the extracellular fluid (ECF), the internal fluid environment that bathes them.

The internal pool of a substance is the amount of that substance in the ECF.
The quantity of any particular substance in the ECF is a readily available internal **pool.** The amount of the substance in the pool may be increased either by transferring more in from the external environment (most commonly by ingestion) or by metabolically producing it within the body (● Figure 14-1). Substances may be removed from the body by being excreted to the outside or by being used up in a metabolic reaction. If the quantity of a substance is to remain stable within the body, its **input** through ingestion or metabolic production must be balanced by an equal **output** through excretion or metabolic consumption. This relationship, known as the **balance concept,** is extremely important in maintaining homeostasis. Not all input and output pathways are applicable for every body-fluid constituent. For example, salt is not synthesized or consumed by the body, so the stability of salt concentration in the body fluids depends entirely on a balance between salt ingestion and salt excretion.

The ECF pool can further be altered by transferring a particular ECF constituent into storage within the body. If the body as a whole has a surplus or deficit of a particular stored substance, the storage site can be expanded or partially depleted to maintain the ECF concentration of the substance within homeostatically prescribed limits. For example, after absorption of a meal, when more glucose is entering the plasma than is being consumed by the cells, the extra glucose can be temporarily stored, in the form of glycogen, in muscle and liver cells. This storage depot can then be tapped between meals as needed to maintain the plasma glucose level when no new nutrients are being added to the blood by eating.

To maintain stable balance of an ECF constituent, its input must equal its output.
When total body input of a particular substance equals its total body output, a **stable balance** exists. When the gains via input for a substance exceed its losses via output, a **positive balance** exists. The result is an increase in the total amount of the substance in the body. In contrast, when losses for a substance exceed its gains, a **negative balance** exists and the total amount of the substance in the body decreases.

Changing the magnitude of any of the input or output pathways for a given substance can alter its plasma concentration. To maintain homeostasis, any change in input must be balanced by a corresponding change in output (for example, increased salt intake must be matched by a corresponding increase in salt output in the urine), and

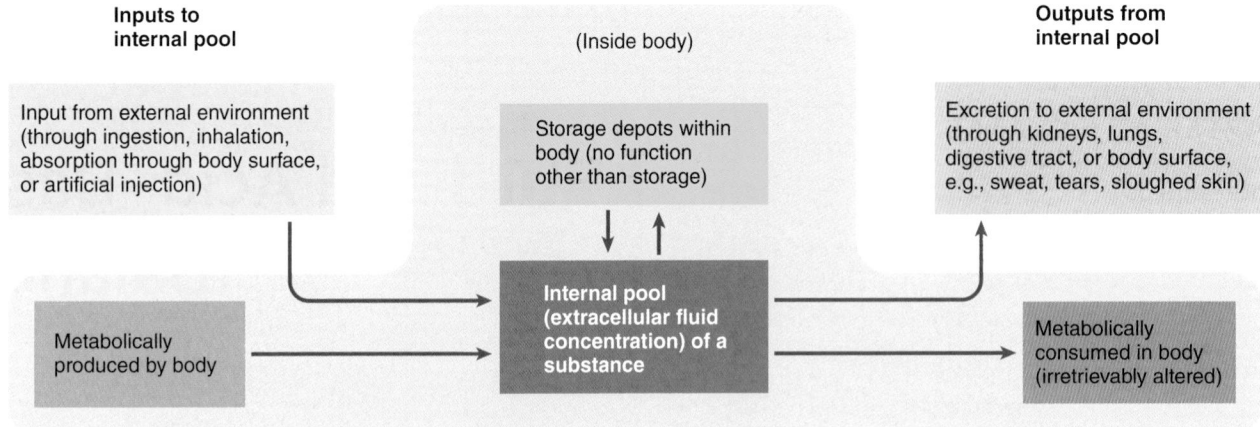

● FIGURE 14-1 Inputs to and outputs from the internal pool of a body constituent.

conversely, increased losses must be compensated for by increased intake. Thus, maintaining a stable balance requires control. The rest of this chapter is devoted to discussing the regulation of fluid balance (maintaining salt and H_2O balance) and acid–base balance (maintaining H^+ balance).

Fluid Balance

Water is by far the most abundant component of the human body, constituting 60% of body weight on average. The H_2O content of an individual remains fairly constant, largely because the kidneys efficiently regulate H_2O balance.

Body water is distributed between the ICF and the ECF compartments.

Body H_2O is distributed between two major fluid compartments: fluid within the cells, or **intracellular fluid (ICF)**, and fluid surrounding the cells, or **extracellular fluid (ECF)** (▲ Table 14-1). (The terms *water (H₂O)* and *fluid* are commonly used interchangeably. Although this usage is not entirely accurate, because it ignores the solutes in body fluids, it is acceptable

▲ Table 14-1 Classification of Body Fluid

Compartment	Volume of Fluid (in liters)	Percentage of Body Fluid	Percentage of Body Weight
Total Body Fluid	42	100	60
Intracellular fluid (ICF)	28	67	40
Extracellular fluid (ECF)	14	33	20
Plasma	2.8	6.6 (20% of ECF)	4
Interstitial fluid	11.2	26.4 (80% of ECF)	16

when discussing total volume of fluids because the major proportion of these fluids consists of H_2O.)

The ICF compartment composes about two thirds of the total body H_2O. Even though each cell contains a unique mixture of constituents, these trillions of minute fluid compartments are similar enough to be considered collectively as one large fluid compartment.

The remaining third of the body H_2O found in the ECF compartment is further subdivided into plasma and interstitial fluid. The **plasma,** which makes up about a fifth of the ECF volume, is the fluid portion of blood. The **interstitial fluid,** which represents the other four fifths of the ECF compartment, is the fluid in the spaces between cells. It bathes and makes exchanges with tissue cells.

The plasma and interstitial fluid are similar in composition, but the ECF and ICF differ markedly.

Several barriers separate the body-fluid compartments, limiting the movement of H_2O and solutes among the various compartments to differing degrees.

THE BARRIER BETWEEN PLASMA AND INTERSTITIAL FLUID: BLOOD VESSEL WALLS The two components of the ECF—plasma and interstitial fluid—are separated by the walls of the blood vessels. However, H_2O and all plasma constituents except for plasma proteins are continuously and freely exchanged between plasma and interstitial fluid by passive means across the thin, pore-lined capillary walls. Accordingly, plasma and interstitial fluid are nearly identical in composition, except that interstitial fluid lacks plasma proteins. Any change in one of these ECF compartments is quickly reflected in the other compartment because they are constantly mixing.

THE BARRIER BETWEEN THE ECF AND THE ICF: CELLULAR PLASMA MEMBRANES In contrast to the similar composition of plasma and interstitial fluid compartments, the composition of the ECF differs considerably from that of the ICF (● Figure 14-2). Each cell is surrounded by a highly selective plasma membrane that permits passage of certain materials while excluding others. Movement through the membrane barrier occurs by both passive and active means and may be highly discriminating (see Table

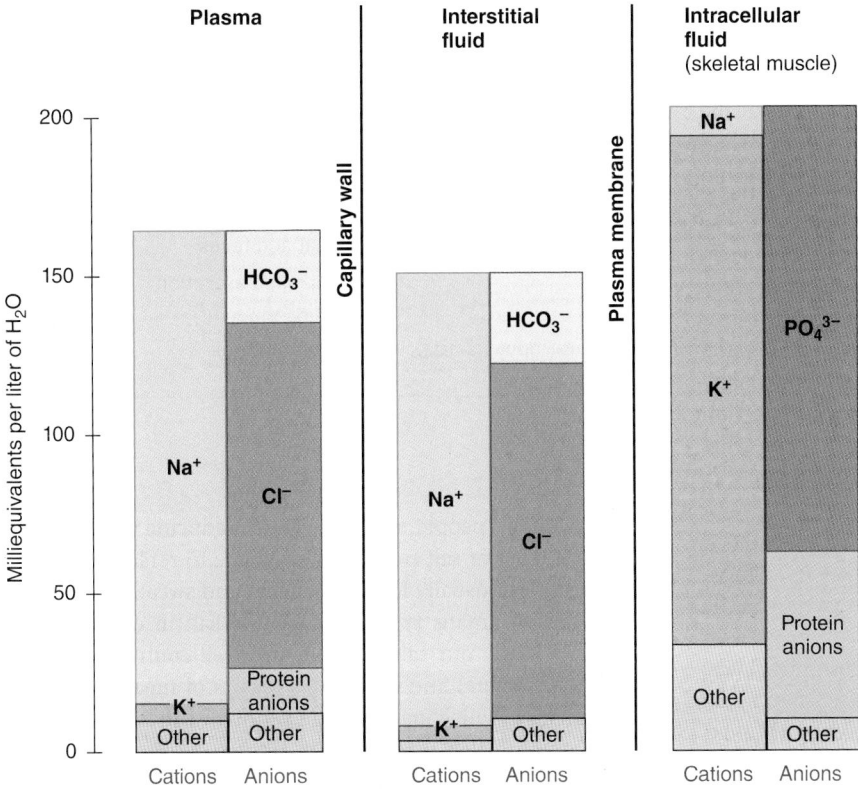

Plasma | Interstitial fluid | Intracellular fluid (skeletal muscle)

Milliequivalents per liter of H_2O

200 —

150 —

100 —

50 —

0 —

Capillary wall

Plasma membrane

HCO_3^-

Na^+

Cl^-

K^+
Other

Protein anions
Other

HCO_3^-

Na^+

Cl^-

K^+
Other

Na^+

K^+

PO_4^{3-}

Other

Protein anions
Other

Cations Anions | Cations Anions | Cations Anions

● **FIGURE 14-2 Ionic composition of the major body-fluid compartments.**

3-2, p. 67). Among the major differences between the ECF and the ICF are (1) the presence of cell proteins in the ICF that cannot permeate the enveloping membranes to leave the cells and (2) the unequal distribution of Na^+ and K^+ and their attendant anions as a result of the action of the membrane-bound Na^+–K^+ pump present in all cells. Because this pump actively transports Na^+ out of and K^+ into cells, Na^+ is the primary ECF cation and K^+ is the primary ICF cation (see p. 63, also see ▲ Table 3-3, p. 68).

Except for the extremely small, electrically unbalanced portion of the total intracellular and extracellular ions involved in membrane potential, most ECF and ICF ions are electrically balanced. In the ECF, Na^+ is accompanied primarily by the anion chloride (Cl^-) and to a lesser extent by bicarbonate (HCO_3^-). The major intracellular anions are phosphate (PO_4^{3-}) and the negatively charged proteins trapped within the cell.

The movement of H_2O between plasma and interstitial fluid across capillary walls is governed by relative imbalances between capillary blood pressure (a fluid, or hydrostatic, pressure) and colloid osmotic pressure (see p. 297). The net transfer of H_2O between the interstitial fluid and the ICF across the cellular plasma membranes occurs as a result of osmotic effects alone (see p. 58). The hydrostatic pressures of the interstitial fluid and ICF are both extremely low and fairly constant.

Fluid balance is maintained by regulating ECF volume and osmolarity.

Extracellular fluid serves as an intermediary between the cells and the external environment. All exchanges of H_2O and other constituents between the ICF and the external world must oc-

cur through the ECF. Water added to the body fluids always enters the ECF compartment first, and fluid always leaves the body via the ECF.

Plasma is the only fluid that can be acted on directly to control its volume and composition. This fluid circulates through all the reconditioning organs that perform homeostatic adjustments (see p. 279). However, because of the free exchange across the capillary walls, if the volume and composition of the plasma are regulated, the volume and composition of the interstitial fluid bathing the cells are likewise regulated. Thus, any control mechanism that operates on plasma in effect regulates the entire ECF. The ICF in turn is influenced by changes in the ECF to the extent permitted by the permeability of membrane barriers surrounding the cells.

Two factors are regulated to maintain **fluid balance** in the body: ECF volume and ECF osmolarity. Although regulation of these two factors is interrelated, both depending on the relative NaCl and H_2O load in the body, the reasons why and the mechanisms by which they are controlled are significantly different:

1. *ECF volume* must be closely regulated to help *maintain blood pressure*. Maintaining *salt balance* is of primary importance in the long-term regulation of ECF volume.

2. *ECF osmolarity* must be closely regulated to *prevent swelling or shrinking of cells*. Maintaining *water balance* is of primary importance in regulating ECF osmolarity.

Control of ECF volume is important in the long-term regulation of blood pressure.

A reduction in ECF volume causes a fall in arterial blood pressure by decreasing plasma volume. Conversely, expanding ECF volume raises arterial blood pressure by increasing plasma volume. Two compensatory measures come into play to transiently adjust blood pressure until the ECF volume can be restored to normal. Let us review them.

SHORT-TERM CONTROL MEASURES TO MAINTAIN BLOOD PRESSURE

1. *The baroreceptor reflex alters both cardiac output and total peripheral resistance* to adjust blood pressure in the proper direction through autonomic nervous system effects on the heart and blood vessels (see p. 307). Cardiac output and total peripheral resistance are both increased to raise blood pressure when it falls too low, and conversely, both are decreased to reduce blood pressure when it rises too high.

2. *Fluid shifts occur temporarily and automatically between plasma and interstitial fluid* as a result of changes in the balance of hydrostatic and osmotic forces acting across the capillary

walls that arise when plasma volume deviates from normal (see p. 298). A reduction in plasma volume is partially compensated for by a shift of fluid out of the interstitial compartment into the blood vessels, expanding the circulating plasma volume at the expense of the interstitial compartment. Conversely, when plasma volume is too large, much of the excess fluid shifts into the interstitial compartment.

These two measures provide temporary relief to help keep blood pressure fairly constant, but they are not long-term solutions. Furthermore, these short-term compensatory measures have a limited ability to minimize a change in blood pressure. For example, if plasma volume is too inadequate, blood pressure remains too low no matter how vigorous the pump action of the heart, how constricted the resistance vessels, or what proportion of interstitial fluid shifts into the blood vessels.

LONG-TERM CONTROL MEASURES TO MAINTAIN BLOOD PRESSURE It is important, therefore, that other compensatory measures come into play in the long run to restore the ECF volume to normal. Long-term regulation of blood pressure rests with the kidneys and the thirst mechanism, which control urinary output and fluid intake, respectively. In so doing, they make needed fluid exchanges between the ECF and the external environment to regulate the body's total fluid volume. Accordingly, they have an important long-term influence on arterial blood pressure. Of these measures, control of urinary output by the kidneys is the most crucial for maintaining blood pressure. You will see why as we discuss these long-term mechanisms in more detail.

Control of salt balance is primarily important in regulating ECF volume.

By way of review, sodium and its attendant anions account for more than 90% of the ECF osmotic activity. As the kidneys conserve salt, they automatically conserve H_2O because H_2O follows Na^+ osmotically. This retained salt solution is isotonic (see p. 59). The more salt there is in the ECF, the more H_2O there is in the ECF. The concentration of salt is not changed by changing the amount of salt in the body, because H_2O always follows salt to maintain osmotic equilibrium—that is, to maintain the normal concentration of salt. A reduced salt load leads to decreased H_2O retention, so the ECF remains isotonic but reduced in volume. The total mass of Na^+ salts in the ECF—that is, the *Na+ load*—therefore determines the ECF volume, and appropriately, regulation of ECF volume depends primarily on controlling salt balance.

To maintain salt balance at a set level, salt input must equal salt output, thus preventing salt accumulation or deficit in the body. We now look at the avenues and control of salt input and output.

POOR CONTROL OF SALT INTAKE The only avenue for salt input is ingestion, which typically is well in excess of the body's need for replacing obligatory salt losses. In our example of a typical daily salt balance (▲ Table 14-2) salt intake is 10.5 g per day. (The average American salt intake is about 10 to 15 g per day,

▲ Table 14-2 Daily Salt Balance

SALT INPUT		SALT OUTPUT	
Avenue	Amount (g/day)	Avenue	Amount (g/day)
Ingestion	10.5	Obligatory loss in sweat and feces	0.5
		Controlled excretion in urine	10.0
Total input	10.5	Total output	10.5

although many people are consciously reducing their salt intake.) Yet 0.5 g of salt per day is adequate to replace the small amounts of salt usually lost in the feces and sweat.

Because humans typically consume salt in excess of our needs, obviously our salt intake is not well controlled. Carnivores (meat eaters) and omnivores (eaters of meat and plants, like humans), which naturally get enough salt in fresh meat (meat contains an abundance of salt-rich ECF), normally do not display a physiologic appetite to seek additional salt. In contrast, herbivores (plant eaters), which lack salt naturally in their diets, develop salt hunger and will travel miles to a salt lick. Humans generally have a hedonistic (pleasure-seeking) rather than a regulatory appetite for salt; we consume salt because we like it rather than because we have a physiologic need, except in the unusual circumstance of severe salt depletion caused by a deficiency of aldosterone, the salt-conserving hormone.

PRECISE CONTROL OF SALT OUTPUT IN THE URINE To maintain salt balance, excess ingested salt must be excreted in the urine. The three avenues for salt output are obligatory loss of salt in *sweat* and *feces* and controlled excretion of salt in *urine* (▲ Table 14-2). The total amount of sweat produced is unrelated to salt balance, being determined instead by factors that control body temperature. The small salt loss in feces is not subject to control. Except when sweating heavily or during diarrhea, the body uncontrollably loses only about 0.5 g of salt per day. This amount is the only salt that normally needs to be replaced by salt intake.

Because salt consumption is typically far more than the meager amount needed to compensate for uncontrolled losses, the kidneys precisely excrete the excess salt in the urine to maintain salt balance. In our example, 10 g of salt are eliminated in the urine per day so that total salt output exactly equals salt input. By regulating the rate of urinary salt excretion (that is, by regulating the rate of Na^+ excretion, with Cl^- following along), the kidneys normally keep the total Na^+ mass in the ECF constant despite any notable changes in dietary intake of salt or unusual losses through sweating or diarrhea. As a reflection of keeping the total Na^+ mass (tacitly including the total Cl^- mass) in the ECF constant, the ECF volume, in turn, is maintained within the narrowly prescribed limits essential for normal circulatory function.

Deviations in the ECF volume accompanying changes in the salt load trigger renal compensatory responses that quickly bring the Na^+ load and ECF volume back into line. Sodium is freely filtered at the glomerulus and actively reabsorbed, but it is not secreted by the tubules, so the amount of Na^+ excreted in the urine represents the amount of Na^+ filtered but not subsequently reabsorbed:

$$Na^+ \text{ excreted} = Na^+ \text{ filtered} - Na^+ \text{ reabsorbed}$$

The kidneys accordingly adjust the amount of salt excreted by controlling two processes: (1) the glomerular filtration rate (GFR) and (2) more important, the tubular reabsorption of Na^+. You have already learned about these regulatory mechanisms, but we are pulling them together here as they relate to the long-term control of ECF volume and blood pressure.

■ *The amount of Na^+ filtered is controlled by regulating the GFR.* The amount of Na^+ filtered is equal to the plasma Na^+ concentration times the GFR. At any given plasma Na^+ concentration, any change in the GFR correspondingly changes the amount of Na^+ and accompanying fluid that are filtered. Thus, control of the GFR can adjust the amount of Na^+ filtered each minute. Recall that the GFR is deliberately changed to alter the amount of salt and fluid filtered, as part of the general baroreceptor reflex response to a change in blood pressure (see ● Figure 13-7, p. 413). Changes in Na^+ load in the body are not sensed as such; instead,

they are monitored indirectly through the effect that the Na^+ load ultimately has on blood pressure. Fittingly, baroreceptors that monitor fluctuations in blood pressure bring about adjustments in the amounts of Na^+ filtered and eventually excreted.

■ *The amount of Na^+ reabsorbed is controlled through the renin–angiotensin–aldosterone system.* The amount of Na^+ reabsorbed also depends on regulatory systems that play an important role in controlling blood pressure. Although Na^+ is reabsorbed throughout most of the tubule's length, only its reabsorption in the late parts of the tubule is subject to control. The main factor controlling the extent of Na^+ reabsorption in the distal and collecting tubules is the powerful renin–angiotensin–aldosterone system (RAAS), which promotes Na^+ reabsorption and thereby Na^+ retention. Sodium retention, in turn, promotes osmotic retention of H_2O and subsequent expansion of plasma volume and elevation of arterial blood pressure. Appropriately, this Na^+-conserving system is activated by a reduction in NaCl, ECF volume, and arterial blood pressure (see ● Figure 13-12, p. 418).

Thus, control of GFR and Na^+ reabsorption are interrelated, and both are intimately tied in with long-term regulation of ECF volume as reflected by blood pressure. For example, a fall in arterial blood pressure brings about (1) a reflex reduction in the GFR to decrease the amount of Na^+ filtered and (2) a hormonally adjusted increase in the amount of Na^+ reabsorbed (● Figure 14-3). Together, these effects reduce the amount of Na^+ excreted, thereby conserving for the body the Na^+ and accompanying H_2O needed to compensate for the fall in arterial pressure. (To look at how exercising muscles and cooling mechanisms compete for an inadequate plasma volume, see the boxed feature on p. 448, ❱ Beyond the Basics.)

Controlling ECF osmolarity prevents changes in ICF volume.

Maintaining fluid balance depends on regulating both ECF volume and ECF osmolarity. Whereas regulating ECF volume is important in long-term control of blood pressure, regulating ECF osmolarity is important in preventing changes in cell volume. The **osmolarity** of a fluid is a measure of the concentration of the individual solute particles dissolved in it. The higher the osmolarity, the higher the concentration of solutes or, to look at it differently, the lower the concentration of H_2O. Recall that water tends to move by osmosis down its own concentration gradient from an area of lower solute (higher H_2O) concentration to an area of higher solute (lower H_2O) concentration (see p. 57).

IONS RESPONSIBLE FOR ECF AND ICF OSMOLARITY Osmosis occurs across the cellular plasma membranes only when a

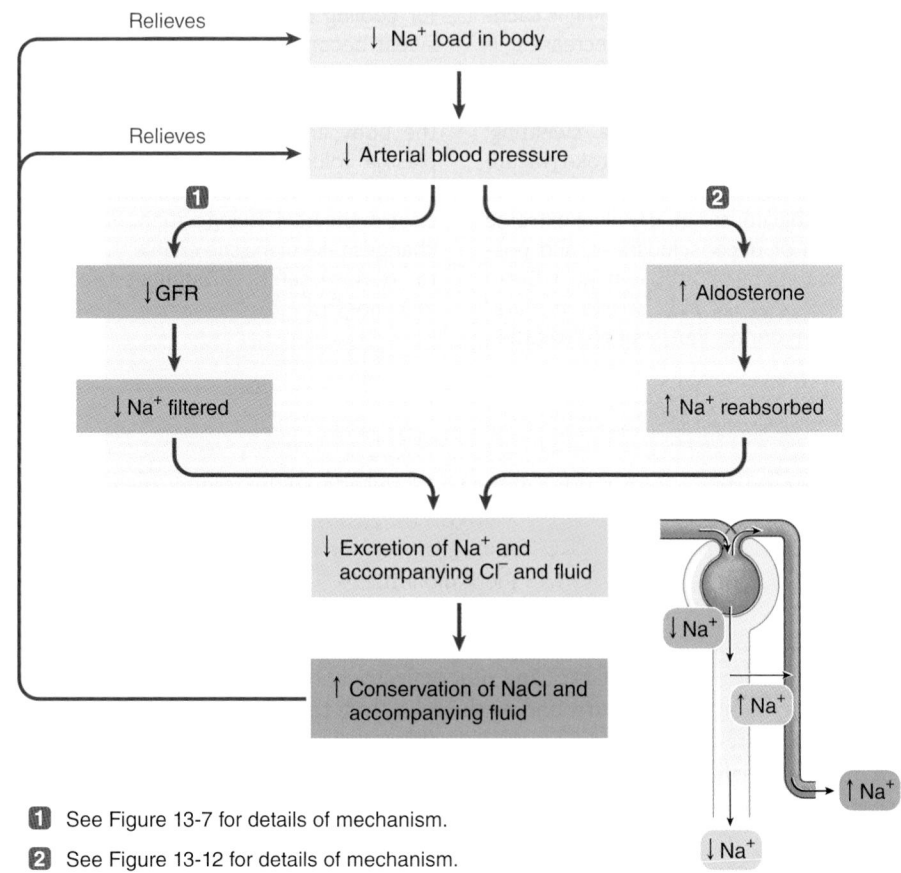

1 See Figure 13-7 for details of mechanism.

2 See Figure 13-12 for details of mechanism.

● **FIGURE 14-3 Dual effect of a fall in arterial blood pressure on renal handling of Na^+.**

A Potentially Fatal Clash: When Exercising Muscles and Cooling Mechanisms Compete for an Inadequate Plasma Volume

An increasing number of people of all ages are participating in walking or jogging programs to improve their level of physical fitness and decrease their risk of cardiovascular disease. For people living in environments that undergo seasonal temperature changes, fluid loss can make exercising outdoors dangerous during the transition from the cool days of spring to the hot, humid days of summer. If exercise intensity is not modified until the participant gradually adjusts to the hotter environmental conditions, dehydration and salt loss can indirectly lead to heat cramps, heat exhaustion, or ultimately heat stroke and death.

The term **acclimatization** refers to the gradual adaptations the body makes to maintain long-term homeostasis in response to a prolonged physical change in the surrounding environment, such as a change in temperature. When a person exercises in the heat without gradually adapting to the hotter environment, the body faces a terrible dilemma. During exercise, large amounts of blood must be delivered to the muscles to supply O_2 and nutrients and to remove the wastes that accumulate from their high rate of activity. Exercising muscles also produce heat. To maintain body temperature in the face of this extra heat, blood flow to the skin is increased so that heat from the warmed blood can be lost through the skin to the surrounding environment. If the environmental temperature is hotter than the body temperature, heat cannot be lost from the blood to the surrounding environment despite maximal skin vasodilation. Instead, the body gains heat from its warmer surroundings, further adding to the dilemma. Because extra blood is diverted to both the muscles and the skin when a person exercises in the heat, less blood is returned to the heart, and the heart pumps less blood per beat in accordance with the Frank–Starling mechanism (see p. 265). Therefore, the heart must beat faster than it would in a cool environment to deliver the same amount of blood per minute. The increased rate of cardiac pumping further contributes to heat production.

The sweat rate also increases so that evaporative cooling can take place to help maintain the body temperature during periods of excessive heat gain. In an unacclimatized person, maximal sweat rate is about 1.5 liters per hour. During sweating, water-retaining salt, as well as water, is lost. The resulting loss of plasma volume through sweating further depletes the blood supply available for muscular exercise and for cooling through skin vasodilation.

The heart has a maximum rate at which it can pump. If exercise continues at a high intensity and this maximal rate is reached, the exercising muscles win the contest for blood supply. Cooling is sacrificed as skin blood flow decreases. If exercise continues, body heat continues to rise, and heat exhaustion (rapid, weak pulse; hypotension; profuse sweating; and disorientation) or heat stroke (failure of the temperature control center in the hypothalamus; hot, dry skin; extreme confusion or unconsciousness; and possibly death) can occur (see p. 521). Every year people die of heat stroke in marathons run during hot, humid weather.

(Some people make matters worse by adding a caffeine-containing energy drink to their workout or competition. Caffeine may provide a jolt of energy, but it also acts as a diuretic and can lead to performance-reducing dehydration, the opposite effect of what the people might think they are accomplishing by drinking these beverages.)

By contrast, if a person exercises in the heat 2 weeks at reduced, safe intensities, the body makes the following adaptations so that after acclimatization the person can do the same amount of work as was possible in a cool environment: (1) The plasma volume is increased by as much as 12%. Expansion of the plasma volume provides enough blood to both supply the exercising muscles and direct blood to the skin for cooling. (2) The person begins sweating at a lower temperature so that the body does not get so hot before cooling begins. (3) The maximal sweat rate increases nearly three times, to 4 liters per hour, with a more even distribution over the body. This increase in evaporative cooling reduces the need for cooling by skin vasodilation. (4) The sweat becomes more dilute so that less salt is lost in the sweat. The retained salt exerts an osmotic effect to hold water in the body and help maintain circulating plasma volume. These adaptations take 14 days and occur only if the person exercises in the heat. Being patient until these changes take place can enable the person to exercise safely throughout the summer months.

---

difference in concentration of nonpenetrating solutes exists between the ECF and the ICF. Solutes that can penetrate a barrier separating two fluid compartments quickly become equally distributed between the two compartments and thus do not contribute to osmotic differences.

Sodium and its attendant anions, being by far the most abundant solutes in the ECF in terms of numbers of particles, account for the vast majority of the ECF osmotic activity. In contrast, K^+ and its accompanying intracellular anions are responsible for the ICF osmotic activity. Even though small amounts of Na^+ and K^+ passively diffuse across the plasma membrane all the time, these ions behave as if they were nonpenetrating because of Na^+–K^+ pump activity. Any Na^+ that passively diffuses down its electrochemical gradient into the cell is promptly pumped back outside, so the result is the same as if Na^+ were barred from the cells. In reverse, K^+ in effect remains trapped within the cells.

Normally, the osmolarities of the ECF and ICF are the same, because the total concentration of K^+ and other effectively nonpenetrating solutes inside the cells is equal to the total concentration of Na^+ and other effectively nonpenetrating solutes in the fluid surrounding the cells. Even though nonpenetrating solutes in the ECF and ICF differ, their concentrations are normally identical, and the number (not the nature) of the unequally distributed particles per volume determines the fluid's osmolarity. Because the osmolarities of the ECF and ICF are normally equal, no net movement of H_2O usually occurs into or out of the cells. Therefore, cell volume normally remains constant.

IMPORTANCE OF REGULATING ECF OSMOLARITY Any circumstance that results in a loss or gain of *free H_2O* (that is, loss or gain of H_2O that is not accompanied by comparable solute deficit or excess) leads to changes in ECF osmolarity. If there is a deficit of free H_2O in the ECF, the solutes become too concentrated and ECF osmolarity becomes abnormally high; that is, it becomes *hypertonic* (see p. 59). If there is excess free H_2O in the ECF, the solutes become too dilute and ECF osmolarity becomes abnormally low; that is, it becomes *hypotonic*. When ECF osmolarity changes with respect to ICF osmolarity, osmosis takes place, with H_2O either leaving or entering the cells, depending on whether the ECF is more concentrated or less concentrated, respectively, than the ICF.

The osmolarity of the ECF must therefore be regulated to prevent these undesirable shifts of H_2O out of or into the cells. As far as the ECF itself is concerned, the concentration of its solutes does not really matter. However, it is crucial that ECF osmolarity be maintained within narrow limits to prevent the cells from shrinking or swelling.

Let us examine the fluid shifts that occur between the ECF and the ICF when ECF osmolarity becomes hypertonic or hypotonic relative to the ICF. Then we consider how water balance and consequently ECF osmolarity are normally maintained to minimize harmful changes in cell volume.

During ECF hypertonicity, the cells shrink as H_2O leaves them.

Hypertonicity of the ECF, the excessive concentration of ECF solutes, is usually associated with **dehydration,** or a negative free H_2O balance.

CAUSES OF HYPERTONICITY (DEHYDRATION) Dehydration with accompanying hypertonicity can be brought about in three major ways:

1. *Insufficient H_2O intake,* such as might occur during desert travel or might accompany difficulty in swallowing

2. *Excessive H_2O loss,* such as might occur during heavy sweating, vomiting, or diarrhea

 3. **Diabetes insipidus,** a disease characterized by a deficiency of vasopressin

Vasopressin (antidiuretic hormone) increases the permeability of the distal and collecting tubules to H_2O and thus enhances water conservation by reducing urinary output of water (see p. 430). Without adequate vasopressin, the kidneys cannot conserve H_2O because they cannot reabsorb H_2O from the distal parts of the nephron. Such patients typically produce up to 20 liters of very dilute urine daily, compared to the normal average of 1.5 liters per day. Unless H_2O intake keeps pace with this tremendous loss of H_2O in the urine, the person quickly dehydrates. Such patients complain that they spend an extraordinary amount of time day and night going to the bathroom and getting drinks. Fortunately, they can be treated with replacement vasopressin administered by nasal spray.

Clinical Note **DIRECTION AND RESULTING SYMPTOMS OF WATER MOVEMENT DURING HYPERTONICITY** Whenever the ECF compartment becomes hypertonic, H_2O moves out of the cells by osmosis into the more concentrated ECF until the ICF osmolarity equilibrates with the ECF. As H_2O leaves them, the cells shrink. Of particular concern is that considerable shrinking of brain neurons disturbs brain function, which can be manifested as mental confusion and irrationality in moderate cases and as possible delirium, convulsions, or coma in more severe hypertonic conditions.

Rivaling the neural symptoms in seriousness are circulatory disturbances that arise from a reduction in plasma volume in association with dehydration. Circulatory problems may range from a slight lowering of blood pressure to circulatory shock and death.

Other more common symptoms become apparent even in mild cases of dehydration. For example, dry skin and sunken eyeballs indicate loss of H_2O from the underlying soft tissues, and the tongue becomes dry and parched because salivary secretion is suppressed.

During ECF hypotonicity, the cells swell as H_2O enters them.

Hypotonicity of the ECF is usually associated with **overhydration;** that is, excess free H_2O. When a positive free H_2O balance exists, the ECF is less concentrated (more dilute) than normal.

CAUSES OF HYPOTONICITY (OVERHYDRATION) Usually, any surplus free H_2O is promptly excreted in the urine, so hypotonicity generally does not occur. However, hypotonicity can arise in three ways:

1. Patients with *renal failure* who cannot excrete a dilute urine become hypotonic when they consume relatively more H_2O than solutes.

2. Hypotonicity can occur transiently in healthy people if *H_2O is rapidly ingested* to such an excess that the kidneys cannot respond quickly enough to eliminate the extra H_2O.

3. Hypotonicity can occur when excess H_2O without solute is retained in the body as a result of the *syndrome of inappropriate vasopressin secretion.*

Vasopressin is normally secreted in response to a H_2O deficit, which is relieved by increasing H_2O reabsorption in the distal part of the nephrons. However, vasopressin secretion, and therefore hormonally controlled tubular H_2O reabsorption, can be increased in response to pain, trauma, and other stressful situations, even when the body has no H_2O deficit. The increased vasopressin secretion and resulting H_2O retention elicited by stress are appropriate in anticipation of potential blood loss in the stressful situation. The extra retained H_2O could minimize the effect a loss of blood volume would have on blood pressure. However, because modern-day stressful situations generally do not involve blood loss, the increased vasopressin secretion is inappropriate as far as the body's fluid balance is concerned. The reabsorption and retention of too much H_2O dilute the body's solutes.

DIRECTION AND RESULTING SYMPTOMS OF WATER MOVEMENT DURING HYPOTONICITY Excess free H_2O retention first dilutes the ECF compartment, making it hypotonic. The resulting difference in osmotic activity between the ECF and the ICF causes H_2O to move by osmosis from the more dilute ECF into the cells, with the cells swelling as H_2O moves into them. Like the shrinking of cerebral neurons, pronounced swelling of brain cells also leads to brain dysfunction. Symptoms include confusion, irritability, lethargy, headache, dizziness, vomiting, drowsiness, and in severe cases, convulsions, coma, and death.

Nonneural symptoms of overhydration include weakness caused by swelling of muscle cells and circulatory disturbances, including hypertension and edema, caused by expansion of plasma volume.

Let us now contrast the situations of hypertonicity and hypotonicity with what happens as a result of isotonic fluid gain or loss.

No water moves into or out of cells during an ECF isotonic fluid gain or loss.

An example of an isotonic fluid gain is therapeutic intravenous administration of an isotonic solution, such as isotonic saline. When isotonic fluid is injected into the ECF compartment, ECF volume increases, but the concentration of ECF solutes remains unchanged; in other words, the ECF is still isotonic. Because the ECF osmolarity has not changed, the ECF and ICF are still in osmotic equilibrium, so no net fluid shift occurs between the two compartments. The ECF compartment has increased in volume without shifting H_2O into the cells.

Similarly, in an isotonic fluid loss such as hemorrhage, the loss is confined to the ECF, with no corresponding loss of fluid from the ICF. Fluid does not shift out of the cells, because the ECF remaining within the body is still isotonic, so no osmotic gradient draws H_2O out of the cells. Many other mechanisms counteract loss of blood, but the ICF compartment is not directly affected by the loss.

We now look at how free H_2O balance is normally maintained.

Control of water balance by means of vasopressin is important in regulating ECF osmolarity.

Control of free H_2O balance is crucial for regulating ECF osmolarity. Because increases in free H_2O cause the ECF to become too dilute and deficits of free H_2O cause the ECF to become too concentrated, the osmolarity of the ECF must be immediately corrected by restoring stable free H_2O balance to avoid harmful osmotic fluid shifts into or out of the cells.

To maintain a stable H_2O balance, H_2O input must equal H_2O output.

SOURCES OF H_2O INPUT

■ In a person's typical daily H_2O balance (▲ Table 14-3), a little more than a liter of H_2O is added to the body by *drinking liquids.*

▲ **Table 14-3** Daily Water Balance

WATER INPUT		WATER OUTPUT	
Avenue	Quantity (ml/day)	Avenue	Quantity (ml/day)
Fluid intake	1250	Insensible loss (from lungs and nonsweating skin)	900
H_2O in food intake	1000	Sweat	100
Metabolically produced H_2O	350	Feces	100
		Urine	1500
Total input	2600	Total output	2600

■ Surprisingly, an amount almost equal to that is obtained from *eating solid food.* Muscles consist of about 75% H_2O; meat (animal muscle) is 75% H_2O. Fruits and vegetables consist of 60% to 90% H_2O. Therefore, people normally get almost as much H_2O from solid foods as from the liquids they drink.

■ The third source of H_2O input is *metabolically produced H_2O.* Chemical reactions within the cells convert food and O_2 into energy, producing CO_2 and H_2O in the process. This **metabolic H_2O** produced during cell metabolism and released into the ECF averages about 350 ml per day.

The average H_2O intake from these three sources totals 2600 ml per day.

SOURCES OF H_2O OUTPUT

■ On the output side of the H_2O balance tally, the body loses nearly a liter of H_2O daily without being aware of it. This **insensible loss** (loss of which the person has no sensory awareness) occurs from the *lungs* and *nonsweating skin.* During respiration, inspired air becomes saturated with H_2O within the airways. This H_2O is lost when the moistened air is subsequently expired (see p. 367). Normally, we are not aware of this H_2O loss, but we can recognize it on cold days, when H_2O vapor condenses so that we can "see our breath." The other insensible loss is continual loss of H_2O from the skin even in the absence of sweating. Water molecules can diffuse through skin cells and evaporate without being noticed. Fortunately, the skin is fairly waterproofed by its keratinized exterior layer, which protects against a greater loss of H_2O by this avenue (see p. 357).

■ Sensible loss (loss of which the person is aware) of H_2O from the skin occurs through *sweating,* which represents another avenue of H_2O output. At an air temperature of 68°F, an average of 100 ml of H_2O is lost daily through sweating. Loss of water from sweating can vary substantially, depending on the environmental temperature and humidity and the degree of physical activity; it may range from zero up to as much as several liters per hour in very hot weather.

■ Another passageway for H_2O loss from the body is through the *feces*. Normally, only about 100 ml of H_2O are lost this way each day. During fecal formation in the large intestine, most H_2O is absorbed out of the digestive tract lumen into the blood, thereby conserving fluid and solidifying the digestive tract's contents for elimination. Additional H_2O can be lost from the digestive tract through vomiting or diarrhea.

■ By far the most important output mechanism is *urine excretion*, with 1500 ml (1.5 L) of urine being produced daily on average.

The total H_2O output is 2600 ml per day, the same as the volume of H_2O input in our example. This balance is not by chance. Normally, H_2O input matches H_2O output so that the H_2O in the body remains in balance.

FACTORS REGULATED TO MAINTAIN WATER BALANCE Of the many sources of H_2O input and output, only two can be regulated to maintain H_2O balance. On the intake side, thirst influences the amount of fluid ingested; and on the output side, the kidneys can adjust how much urine is formed. Controlling H_2O output in the urine is the most important mechanism in controlling H_2O balance.

Some of the other factors are regulated, but not for maintaining H_2O balance. Food intake is subject to regulation to maintain energy balance, and control of sweating is important in maintaining body temperature. Metabolic H_2O production and insensible losses are unregulated.

CONTROL OF WATER OUTPUT IN THE URINE BY VASOPRESSIN Fluctuations in ECF osmolarity caused by imbalances between H_2O input and H_2O output are quickly compensated for by adjusting urinary excretion of H_2O without changing the usual excretion of salt. That is, H_2O reabsorption and excretion are partially dissociated from solute reabsorption and excretion, so the amount of free H_2O retained or eliminated can be varied to quickly restore ECF osmolarity to normal. Free H_2O reabsorption and excretion are adjusted through changes in vasopressin secretion (see ● Figure 13-22, p. 433). Throughout most of the nephron, H_2O reabsorption is important in regulating ECF volume because salt reabsorption is accompanied by comparable H_2O reabsorption. In the distal and collecting tubules, however, variable free H_2O reabsorption can take place without comparable salt reabsorption because of the vertical osmotic gradient in the renal medulla to which this part of the tubule is exposed. Vasopressin increases the permeability of this late part of the tubule to H_2O. Depending on the amount of vasopressin present, the amount of free H_2O reabsorbed can be adjusted as necessary to restore ECF osmolarity to normal.

CONTROL OF WATER INPUT BY THIRST **Thirst** is the subjective sensation that drives you to ingest H_2O. The **thirst center** is located in the hypothalamus close to the vasopressin-secreting cells.

We now elaborate on the mechanisms that regulate vasopressin secretion and thirst.

Vasopressin secretion and thirst are largely triggered simultaneously.

The hypothalamic control centers that regulate vasopressin secretion (and thus urinary output) and thirst (and thus drinking) act in concert. Vasopressin secretion and thirst are both stimulated by a free H_2O deficit and suppressed by a free H_2O excess. Thus, appropriately, the same circumstances that call for reducing urinary output to conserve body H_2O give rise to the sensation of thirst to replenish body H_2O.

ROLE OF HYPOTHALAMIC OSMORECEPTORS The predominant excitatory input for both vasopressin secretion and thirst comes from **hypothalamic osmoreceptors** located near the vasopressin-secreting cells and thirst center. These osmoreceptors monitor the osmolarity of fluid surrounding them, which in turn reflects the concentration of the entire internal fluid environment. As the osmolarity increases (too little H_2O) and the need for H_2O conservation increases, vasopressin secretion and thirst are both stimulated (● Figure 14-4). As a result, reabsorption of H_2O in the distal and collecting tubules is increased so that urinary output is reduced and H_2O is conserved, while H_2O intake is simultaneously encouraged. These actions restore depleted H_2O stores, thus relieving the hypertonic condition by diluting the solutes to normal concentration. In contrast, H_2O excess, manifested by reduced ECF osmolarity, prompts increased urinary output (through decreased vasopressin release) and suppresses thirst, which together reduce the water load in the body.

ROLE OF LEFT ATRIAL VOLUME RECEPTORS Even though the major stimulus for vasopressin secretion and thirst is an increase in ECF osmolarity, the vasopressin-secreting cells and thirst center are both influenced to a moderate extent by changes in ECF volume mediated by input from the **left atrial volume receptors.** Located in the left atrium, these volume receptors respond to pressure-induced stretch caused by blood flowing through, which reflects the ECF volume. That is, they monitor the "fullness" of the vascular system. In contrast, the aortic arch and carotid sinus baroreceptors monitor the mean driving pressure in the vascular system (see p. 307). In response to a major reduction in ECF volume, and accordingly in arterial pressure, as during hemorrhage, the left atrial volume receptors reflexly stimulate both vasopressin secretion and thirst. Outpouring of vasopressin and increased thirst lead to decreased urine output and increased fluid intake, respectively. Furthermore, vasopressin, at the circulating levels elicited by a large decline in ECF volume and arterial pressure, exerts a potent vasoconstrictor (that is, a "vaso" "pressor") effect on arterioles (thus giving rise to its name; see p. 292). Both by helping expand the ECF and plasma volume and by increasing total peripheral resistance, vasopressin helps relieve the low blood pressure that elicited vasopressin secretion. Simultaneously, the low blood pressure is detected by the aortic arch and carotid sinus baroreceptors, which help raise the pressure by increasing sympathetic activity to the heart and blood vessels (see ● Figure 10-33, p. 309).

Conversely, vasopressin and thirst are both inhibited when ECF volume (and, accordingly, plasma volume) and arterial

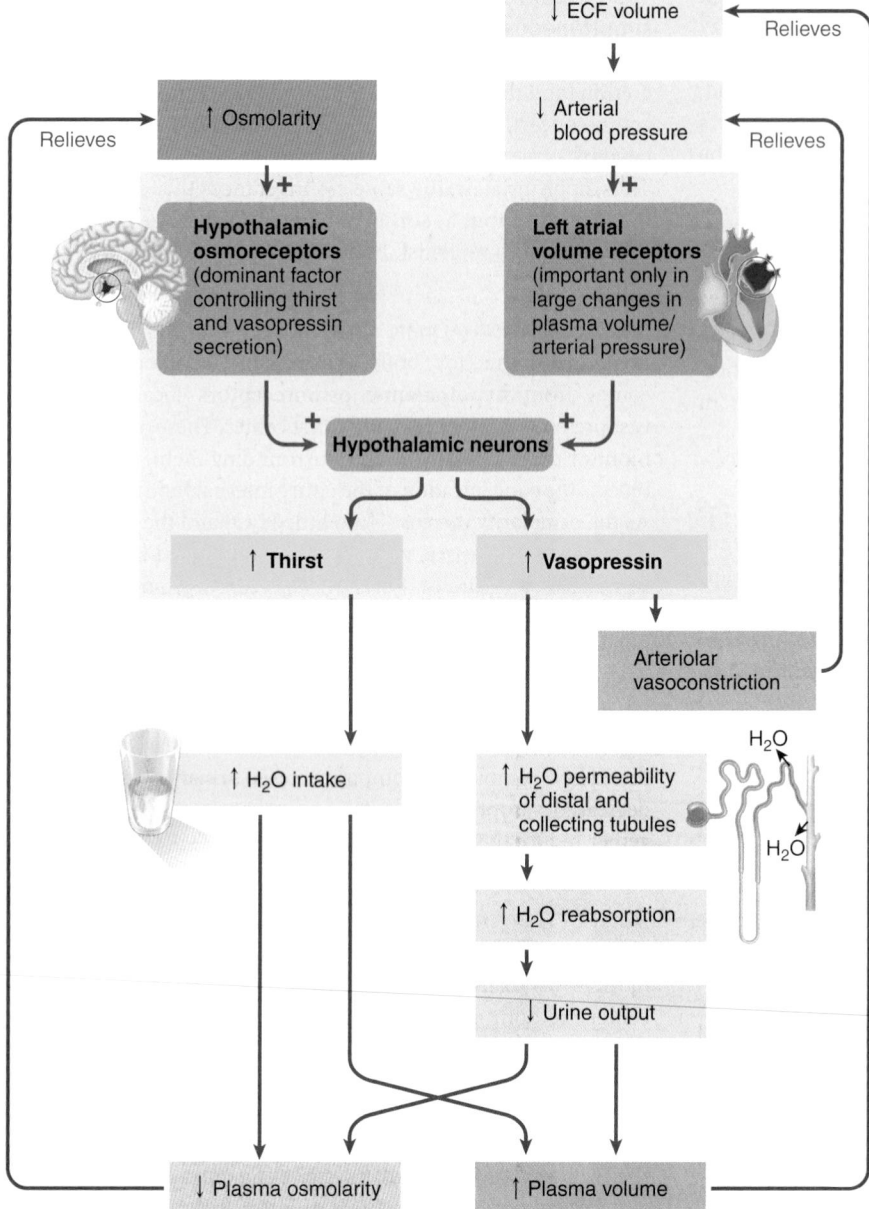

● FIGURE 14-4 **Control of increased vasopressin secretion and thirst during a H$_2$O deficit.**

ciological factors than by the need to regulate H$_2$O balance. Thus, even though H$_2$O intake is critical in maintaining fluid balance, it is not precisely controlled in humans, who err especially on the side of excess H$_2$O consumption. We usually drink when we are thirsty, but we often drink even when we are not thirsty because, for example, we are on a coffee break.

With H$_2$O intake being inadequately controlled and indeed even contributing to H$_2$O imbalances in the body, the primary factor involved in maintaining H$_2$O balance is urinary output regulated by the kidneys. Accordingly, *vasopressin-controlled H$_2$O reabsorption is of primary importance in regulating ECF osmolarity.*

Before we shift our attention to acid–base balance, examine ▲ Table 14-4, which summarizes the regulation of ECF volume and osmolarity, the two factors important in maintaining fluid balance.

Acid–Base Balance

Note: *The scope of this topic has been limited to what can be understood by students with no college chemistry background. Students who have the background and need a more chemistry-oriented coverage of acid–base balance should refer to Appendix D, pp. A-30–A-37, which covers the chemistry in more detail.*

The term **acid–base balance** refers to the precise regulation of **free** (that is, unbound) **hydrogen ion (H$^+$) concentration** in the body fluids. To indicate the concentration of a chemical, its symbol is enclosed in square brackets. Thus, [H$^+$] designates H$^+$ concentration.

blood pressure are elevated. The resultant suppression of H$_2$O intake, coupled with elimination of excess ECF and plasma volume in the urine, helps restore blood pressure to normal.

Recall that low ECF and plasma volume and low arterial blood pressure also reflexly increase aldosterone secretion via RAAS. The resulting increase in Na$^+$ reabsorption leads to osmotic retention of H$_2$O, expansion of ECF volume, and an increase in arterial blood pressure. Aldosterone-controlled Na$^+$ reabsorption is the most important factor in regulating ECF volume, with the vasopressin and thirst mechanism playing only a supportive role.

NONPHYSIOLOGIC INFLUENCES ON FLUID INTAKE Even though the thirst mechanism exists to control H$_2$O intake, fluid consumption by humans is often influenced more by habit and so-

Acids liberate free hydrogen ions, whereas bases accept them.

Acids are a special group of hydrogen-containing substances that *dissociate,* or separate, when in solution to liberate free H$^+$ and anions (negatively charged ions). Many other substances (for example, carbohydrates) also contain hydrogen, but they are not classified as acids, because the hydrogen is tightly bound within their molecular structure and is never liberated as free H$^+$.

A strong acid has a greater tendency to dissociate in solution than a weak acid does; that is, a greater percentage of a strong acid's molecules separate into free H$^+$ and anions. Hydrochloric acid (HCl) is an example of a strong acid; every HCl molecule dissociates into free H$^+$ and chloride (Cl$^-$) when dissolved in H$_2$O. With a weaker acid such as carbonic acid

▲ Table 14-4 Summary of the Regulation of ECF Volume and Osmolarity

Regulated Variable	Importance of Regulating the Variable	Outcomes of Abnormal Variable	Regulation Mechanism
ECF Volume	For long-term control of arterial blood pressure	↓ ECF volume → ↓ arterial blood pressure ↑ ECF volume → ↑ arterial blood pressure	Maintenance of salt balance (salt osmotically "holds" H_2O, so the Na^+ load determines the ECF volume), accomplished primarily by aldosterone-controlled adjustments in urinary Na^+ excretion
ECF Osmolarity	For prevention of detrimental osmotic movement of H_2O between the ECF and the ICF	↓ ECF osmolarity (hypotonicity) → H_2O enters the cells → cells swell ↑ ECF osmolarity (hypertonicity) → H_2O leaves the cells → cells shrink	Maintenance of free H_2O balance, accomplished primarily by vasopressin-controlled adjustments in excretion of H_2O in the urine

(H_2CO_3), only a portion of the molecules dissociate in solution into H^+ and bicarbonate anions (HCO_3^-). The remaining H_2CO_3 molecules remain intact. Because only free H^+ contributes to the acidity of a solution, H_2CO_3 is a weaker acid than HCl because H_2CO_3 does not yield as many free H^+ per number of acid molecules present in solution (● Figure 14-5).

A **base** is a substance that can combine with a free H^+ and thus remove it from solution. A strong base can bind H^+ more readily than a weak base can.

The pH designation is used to express [H⁺].

The concept of pH was developed to express the low value of $[H^+]$ more conveniently. Specifically, **pH** equals the logarithm (log) to the base 10 of the reciprocal of $[H^+]$.

$$pH = \log\frac{1}{[H^+]}$$

This formula may seem intimidating, but you only need to glean one important point from it: Because $[H^+]$ is in the denominator, *a high $[H^+]$ corresponds to a low pH, and a low $[H^+]$ corresponds to a high pH.* The greater the $[H^+]$, the larger the number by which 1 must be divided, and the lower the pH. You do not need to know what a log is to recognize this relationship.

ACIDIC AND BASIC SOLUTIONS IN CHEMISTRY The pH of pure H_2O is 7.0, which is considered chemically neutral. An extremely small proportion of H_2O molecules dissociate into H^+ and hydroxyl (OH^-) ions. Because an equal number of acidic H^+ and basic OH^- are formed, H_2O is neutral, being neither acidic nor basic. Solutions having a pH less than 7.0 contain a higher $[H^+]$ than pure H_2O and are considered acidic. Conversely, solutions having a pH value greater than 7.0 have a lower $[H^+]$ and are considered **basic,** or **alkaline** (● Figure 14-6a). ● Figure 14-7 compares the pH values of common solutions.

ACIDOSIS AND ALKALOSIS IN THE BODY The pH of arterial blood is normally 7.45 and the pH of venous blood is 7.35, for an average blood pH of 7.4. The pH of venous blood is slightly lower (more acidic) than that of arterial blood because H^+ is gener-

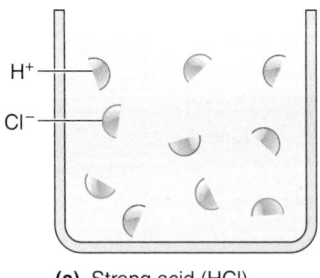

(a) Strong acid (HCl)

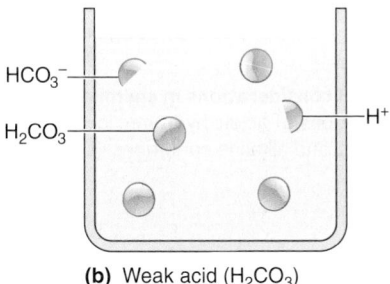

(b) Weak acid (H_2CO_3)

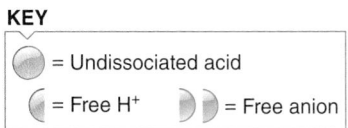

KEY

○ = Undissociated acid

◖ = Free H⁺   ◗◗ = Free anion

● **FIGURE 14-5 Comparison of a strong and a weak acid.** (a) Five molecules of a strong acid. A strong acid such as hydrochloric acid (HCl) completely dissociates into free H^+ and anions in solution. (b) Five molecules of a weak acid. A weak acid such as carbonic acid (H_2CO_3) only partially dissociates into free H^+ and anions in solution.

ated by the formation of H_2CO_3 from CO_2 picked up at the tissue capillaries. **Acidosis** exists whenever blood pH falls below 7.35, whereas **alkalosis** occurs when blood pH is above 7.45 (see ● Figure 14-6b). Note that the reference point for determining the body's acid–base status is not the chemically neutral pH of 7.0 but the normal blood pH of 7.4. Thus, a blood pH of 7.2 is considered acidotic even though in chemistry a pH of 7.2 is considered basic.

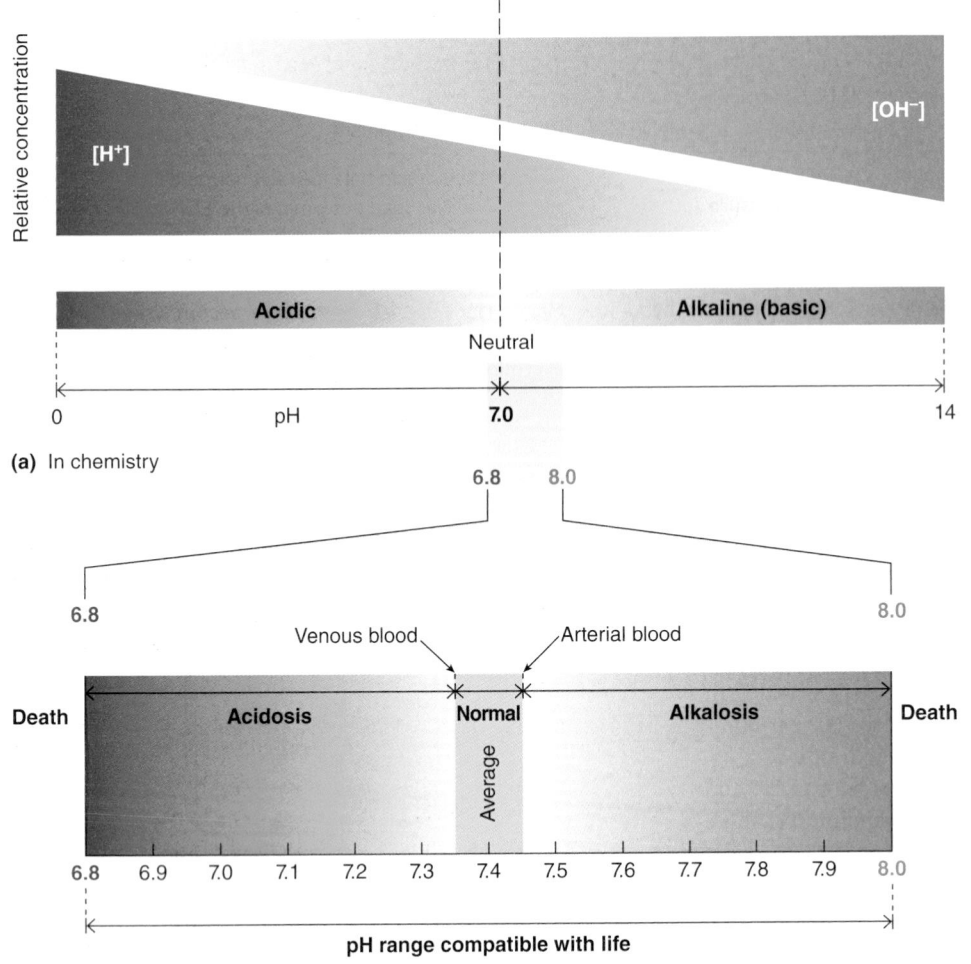

(a) In chemistry

(b) In the body

● **FIGURE 14-6 pH considerations in chemistry and physiology.** (a) Relationship of pH to the relative concentrations of acidic hydrogen ion (H⁺) and basic hydroxyl ion (OH⁻) under chemically neutral, acidic, and alkaline conditions. (b) Blood pH range under normal, acidotic, and alkalotic conditions.

nerves become so excitable that they fire even in the absence of normal stimuli. Such overexcitability of the afferent (sensory) nerves gives rise to abnormal "pins-and-needles" tingling sensations. Overexcitability of efferent (motor) nerves brings about muscle twitches and, in more pronounced cases, severe muscle spasms. Death may occur in extreme alkalosis because spasm of the respiratory muscles seriously impairs breathing. Alternatively, severely alkalotic patients may die of convulsions resulting from overexcitability of the CNS. In less serious situations, CNS overexcitability is manifested as extreme nervousness.

2. *Hydrogen ion concentration exerts a marked influence on enzyme activity.* Even slight deviations in [H⁺] alter the shape and activity of protein molecules. Because enzymes are proteins, a shift in the body's acid–base balance disturbs the normal pattern of metabolic activity catalyzed by these enzymes.

3. *Changes in [H⁺] influence K⁺ levels in the body.* When reabsorbing Na⁺ from the filtrate, the renal tubular cells secrete either K⁺ or H⁺ in exchange. Normally, they secrete a preponderance of K⁺ compared to H⁺. Because of the intimate relationship between secretion of H⁺ and that of K⁺ by the kidneys, when H⁺ secretion increases to compensate for acidosis, less K⁺ than usual can be secreted; conversely, when H⁺ secretion is reduced during alkalosis, more K⁺ is secreted than normal. The resulting changes in ECF [K⁺] can lead to cardiac abnormalities, among other detrimental consequences (see p. 423).

An arterial pH of less than 6.8 or greater than 8.0 is not compatible with life. Because death occurs if arterial pH falls outside the range of 6.8 to 8.0 for more than a few seconds, [H⁺] in the body fluids must be carefully regulated.

Fluctuations in [H⁺] alter nerve, enzyme, and K⁺ activity.

Only a narrow pH range is compatible with life, because even small changes in [H⁺] have dramatic effects on normal cell function, as the following consequences indicate:

1. *Changes in excitability of nerve and muscle cells are among the major clinical manifestations of pH abnormalities.*

- The major clinical effect of increased [H⁺] (acidosis) is depression of the central nervous system (CNS). Acidotic patients become disoriented and, in more severe cases, eventually die in a state of coma.

- In contrast, the major clinical effect of decreased [H⁺] (alkalosis) is overexcitability of the nervous system, first the peripheral nervous system and later the CNS. Peripheral

Hydrogen ions are continually added to the body fluids as a result of metabolic activities.

As with any other constituent, input of hydrogen ions must be balanced by an equal output to maintain a constant [H⁺] in the body fluids. On the input side, only a small amount of acid capable of dissociating to release H⁺ is taken in with food, such as the weak citric acid found in oranges. Most H⁺ in the body fluids is generated internally from metabolic activities.

SOURCES OF H⁺ IN THE BODY Normally, H⁺ is continuously being added to the body fluids from the three following sources:

1. *Carbonic acid formation.* The major source of H⁺ is from metabolically produced CO_2. Cellular oxidation of nutrients

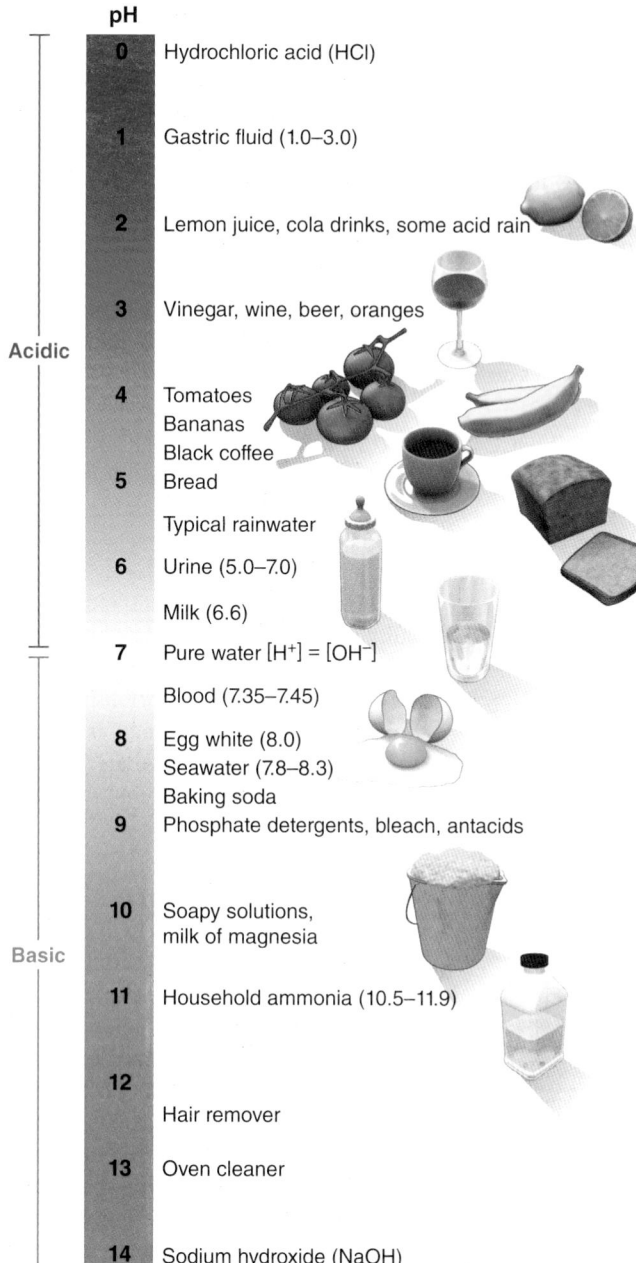

pH	
0	Hydrochloric acid (HCl)
1	Gastric fluid (1.0–3.0)
2	Lemon juice, cola drinks, some acid rain
3	Vinegar, wine, beer, oranges
4	Tomatoes
	Bananas
	Black coffee
5	Bread
	Typical rainwater
6	Urine (5.0–7.0)
	Milk (6.6)
7	Pure water [H$^+$] = [OH$^-$]
	Blood (7.35–7.45)
8	Egg white (8.0)
	Seawater (7.8–8.3)
	Baking soda
9	Phosphate detergents, bleach, antacids
10	Soapy solutions, milk of magnesia
11	Household ammonia (10.5–11.9)
12	
	Hair remover
13	Oven cleaner
14	Sodium hydroxide (NaOH)

Acidic

Basic

● **FIGURE 14-7 Comparison of pH values of common solutions.**

yields energy, with CO_2 and H_2O as end products. Without catalyst influence, CO_2 and H_2O slowly form H_2CO_3, which then rapidly partially dissociates to liberate free H$^+$ and HCO$_3^-$:

$$CO_2 + H_2O \underset{\text{slow}}{\rightleftharpoons} H_2CO_3 \underset{\text{fast}}{\rightleftharpoons} H^+ + HCO_3^-$$

The slow first reaction is the rate-limiting step in the plasma, but the hydration (combination with H_2O) of CO_2 is greatly accelerated by the enzyme *carbonic anhydrase,* which is abundant in red blood cells (see p. 392). Under the influence of carbonic anhydrase (represented by *ca* in the next equation), these cells directly convert CO_2 and H_2O into H$^+$ and HCO$_3^-$ (with no intervening production of H_2CO_3) as follows:

$$CO_2 + H_2O \underset{}{\overset{ca}{\rightleftharpoons}} H^+ + HCO_3^-$$

These reactions are reversible because they can proceed in either direction, depending on the concentrations of the substances involved as dictated by the *law of mass action* (see p. 388). Within the systemic capillaries, the CO_2 level in the blood increases as metabolically produced CO_2 enters from the tissues. This drives the reaction (with or without carbonic anhydrase) to the H$^+$ side. In the lungs, the reaction is reversed: CO_2 diffuses from the blood flowing through the pulmonary capillaries into the alveoli (air sacs), from which it is expired to the atmosphere. The resultant reduction in blood CO_2 drives the reaction toward the CO_2 side. Hydrogen ion and HCO$_3^-$ form CO_2 and H_2O again. The CO_2 is exhaled while the hydrogen ions generated at the tissue level are incorporated into H_2O molecules.

When the respiratory system can keep pace with the rate of metabolism, there is no net gain or loss of H$^+$ in the body fluids from metabolically produced CO_2. When the rate of CO_2 removal by the lungs does not match the rate of CO_2 production at the tissue level, however, the resulting accumulation or deficit of CO_2 leads to an excess or shortage, respectively, of free H$^+$ in the body fluids.

2. *Inorganic acids produced during breakdown of nutrients.* Dietary proteins found abundantly in meat contain a large quantity of sulfur and phosphorus. When these nutrient molecules are broken down, sulfuric acid and phosphoric acid are produced as by-products. Being moderately strong acids, these two inorganic acids largely dissociate, liberating free H$^+$ into the body fluids.

3. *Organic acids resulting from intermediary metabolism.* Numerous organic acids are produced during normal intermediary metabolism. For example, fatty acids are produced during fat metabolism, and lactic acid (lactate) is produced by muscles during heavy exercise (see p. 225). These acids partially dissociate to yield free H$^+$.

Hydrogen ion generation therefore normally goes on continuously, as a result of ongoing metabolic activities. In certain disease states, additional acids may be produced that further contribute to the total body pool of H$^+$. For example, in diabetes mellitus, large quantities of keto acids may be produced by abnormal fat metabolism (see p. 564). Thus, input of H$^+$ is unceasing, highly variable, and essentially unregulated.

THREE LINES OF DEFENSE AGAINST CHANGES IN [H$^+$] The key to H$^+$ balance is maintaining normal alkalinity of the ECF (pH 7.4) despite this constant onslaught of acid. The generated free H$^+$ must be largely removed from solution while in the body and ultimately must be eliminated so that the pH of body fluids can remain within the narrow range compatible with life. Mechanisms must also exist to compensate rapidly for the occasional situation in which the ECF becomes too alkaline.

Three lines of defense against changes in [H$^+$] operate to maintain [H$^+$] of body fluids at a nearly constant level despite unregulated input: (1) the *chemical buffer systems,* (2) the *respiratory mechanism of pH control,* and (3) the *renal mechanism of pH control.* We now look at each of these methods.

Chemical buffer systems minimize changes in pH by binding with or yielding free H⁺.

A **chemical buffer system** is a mixture in a solution of two chemical compounds that minimize pH changes when either an acid or a base is added to or removed from the solution. A buffer system consists of a pair of substances involved in a reversible reaction—one substance that can yield free H^+ as the $[H^+]$ starts to fall and another that can bind with free H^+ (thus removing it from solution) when $[H^+]$ starts to rise.

An important example of such a buffer system is the carbonic acid–bicarbonate ($H_2CO_3:HCO_3^-$) buffer pair, which is involved in the following reversible reaction:

$$H_2CO_3 \rightleftharpoons H^+ + HCO_3^-$$

When a strong acid such as HCl is added to an unbuffered solution, all the dissociated H^+ remains free in the solution (● Figure 14-8a). In contrast, when HCl is added to a solution containing the $H_2CO_3:HCO_3^-$ buffer pair, the HCO_3^- immediately binds with the free H^+ to form H_2CO_3 (● Figure 14-8b). This weak H_2CO_3 dissociates only slightly compared to the marked reduction in pH that occurred when the buffer system was not present and the additional H^+ remained unbound. In the opposite case, when the pH of the solution starts to rise from the addition of base or loss of acid, the H^+-yielding member of the buffer pair, H_2CO_3, releases H^+ to minimize the rise in pH.

The body has four buffer systems: (1) the $H_2CO_3:HCO_3^-$ buffer system, (2) the protein buffer system, (3) the hemoglobin buffer system, and (4) the phosphate buffer system. Each buffer system serves an important role, as described next.

THE $H_2CO_3:HCO_3^-$ BUFFER SYSTEM The $H_2CO_3:HCO_3^-$ buffer pair is the primary ECF buffer for noncarbonic acids. It is the most important buffer system in the ECF for buffering pH changes brought about by causes other than fluctuations in CO_2-generated H_2CO_3. It is an effective ECF buffer system for two reasons. First, H_2CO_3 and HCO_3^- are abundant in the ECF, so this system is readily available to resist changes in pH. Second, and more importantly, each component of this buffer pair is closely regulated. The kidneys regulate HCO_3^-, and the respiratory system regulates CO_2, which generates H_2CO_3.

THE PROTEIN BUFFER SYSTEM The protein buffer system is primarily important intracellularly. The most plentiful buffers of the body fluids are the proteins, including the intracellular proteins and the plasma proteins. Proteins are excellent buffers, because they contain both acidic and basic groups that can give up or take up H^+. Quantitatively, the protein system is most important in buffering changes in $[H^+]$ in the ICF because of the sheer abundance of the intracellular proteins. The more limited number of plasma proteins reinforces the $H_2CO_3:HCO_3^-$ system in extracellular buffering.

THE HEMOGLOBIN BUFFER SYSTEM Hemoglobin (Hb) buffers the H^+ generated from metabolically produced CO_2 in transit between the tissues and the lungs. At the systemic capillary level, CO_2 continuously diffuses into the blood from the tissue cells where it is being produced. The greatest percentage of this CO_2, along with H_2O, forms H^+ and HCO_3^- under the influence of carbonic anhydrase within the red blood cells. Most H^+ generated from CO_2 at the tissue level becomes bound to reduced Hb

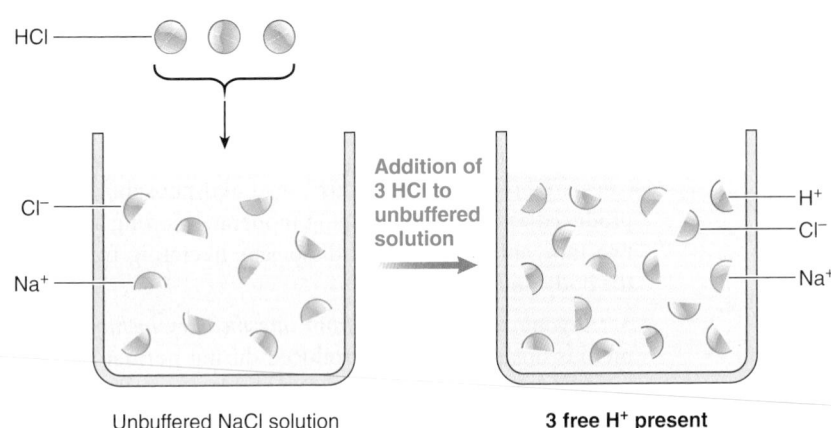

(a) Addition of HCl to an unbuffered solution

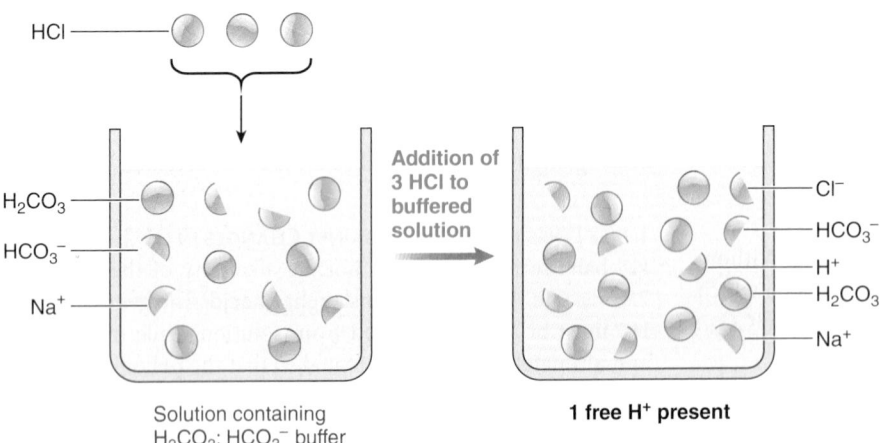

(b) Addition of HCl to a buffered solution

● **FIGURE 14-8 Action of chemical buffers.** (a) Addition of HCl to an unbuffered solution. All the added hydrogen ions (H^+) remain free and contribute to the acidity of the solution. (b) Addition of HCl to a buffered solution. Bicarbonate ions (HCO_3^-), the basic member of the buffer pair, bind with some of the added H^+ and remove them from solution so that they do not contribute to its acidity.

and no longer contributes to acidity of body fluids (see p. 393). Were it not for Hb, blood would become too acidic after picking up CO_2 at the tissues. With the tremendous buffering capacity of the Hb system, venous blood is only slightly more acidic than arterial blood despite the large volume of H^+-generating CO_2 carried in venous blood. At the lungs, the reactions are reversed and the resulting CO_2 is exhaled.

THE PHOSPHATE BUFFER SYSTEM The phosphate buffer system is an important urinary buffer. It consists of an acid phosphate salt that can donate a free H^+ when the $[H^+]$ falls and a basic phosphate salt that can accept a free H^+ when the $[H^+]$ rises. Even though the phosphate pair is a good buffer, its concentration in the ECF is rather low, so it is not very important as an ECF buffer. Because phosphates are most abundant within the cells, this system contributes significantly to intracellular buffering, being rivaled only by the more plentiful intracellular proteins.

Even more important, the phosphate system serves as an excellent urinary buffer. Humans normally consume more phosphate than needed. The excess phosphate filtered through the kidneys is not reabsorbed but remains in the tubular fluid to be excreted (because the renal threshold for phosphate is exceeded; see p. 420). This excreted phosphate buffers urine as it is being formed by removing from solution the H^+ secreted into the tubular fluid. None of the other body-fluid buffer systems are present in the tubular fluid to play a role in buffering urine during its formation. Most or all of the filtered HCO_3^- and CO_2 (alias H_2CO_3) are reabsorbed, whereas Hb and plasma proteins are not even filtered.

Chemical buffer systems act as the first line of defense against changes in $[H^+]$.

All chemical buffer systems act immediately, within fractions of a second, to minimize changes in pH. When $[H^+]$ is altered, the reversible chemical reactions of the involved buffer systems shift at once (by the law of mass action) to compensate for the change in $[H^+]$. Accordingly, the buffer systems are the *first line of defense* against changes in $[H^+]$ because they are the first mechanism to respond.

Through the mechanism of buffering, most hydrogen ions seem to disappear from the body fluids between the times of their generation and those of their elimination. It must be emphasized, however, that none of the chemical buffer systems actually eliminate H^+ from the body. These ions are merely removed from solution by being incorporated within one member of the buffer pair, thus preventing them from contributing to body-fluid acidity. Because each buffer system has a limited capacity to soak up H^+, the H^+ that is unceasingly produced must ultimately be removed from the body. If H^+ were not eventually eliminated, soon all the body-fluid buffers would already be bound with H^+ and there would be no further buffering ability.

The respiratory and renal mechanisms of pH control actually eliminate acid from the body instead of merely suppressing it, but they respond more slowly than chemical buffer systems. We now turn to these other defenses against changes in acid–base balance.

The respiratory system regulates $[H^+]$ by controlling the rate of CO_2 removal.

The respiratory system plays an important role in acid–base balance through its ability to alter pulmonary ventilation and consequently to alter excretion of H^+-generating CO_2. The level of respiratory activity is governed in part by arterial $[H^+]$, as follows (▲ Table 14-5):

■ When arterial $[H^+]$ increases as the result of a *nonrespiratory* (or *metabolic*) cause, the respiratory center in the brain stem is reflexly stimulated to increase pulmonary ventilation (the rate at which gas is exchanged between the lungs and the atmosphere; see p. 399). As the rate and depth of breathing increase, more CO_2 than usual is blown off. Because hydration of CO_2 generates H^+, removal of CO_2 in essence removes acid from this source from the body, offsetting extra H^+ present from a nonrespiratory source.

■ Conversely, when arterial $[H^+]$ falls, pulmonary ventilation is reduced. As a result of slower, shallower breathing, metabolically produced CO_2 diffuses from the cells into the blood faster than it is removed from the blood by the lungs, so higher-than-usual amounts of acid-forming CO_2 accumulate in the blood, thus restoring $[H^+]$ toward normal.

The respiratory system serves as the second line of defense against changes in $[H^+]$.

Respiratory regulation acts at a moderate speed, coming into play only when chemical buffer systems alone cannot minimize $[H^+]$ changes. When deviations in $[H^+]$ occur, the buffer sys-

▲ Table 14-5 Respiratory Adjustments to Acidosis and Alkalosis Induced by Nonrespiratory Causes

	ACID–BASE STATUS		
Respiratory Compensations	Normal (pH 7.4)	Nonrespiratory (metabolic) Acidosis (pH 7.1)	Nonrespiratory (metabolic) Alkalosis (pH 7.7)
Ventilation	Normal	↑	↓
Rate of CO_2 Removal	Normal	↑	↓
Rate of H^+ Generation from CO_2	Normal	↓	↑

tems respond immediately, whereas adjustments in ventilation require a few minutes to be initiated. If a deviation in $[H^+]$ is not swiftly and completely corrected by the buffer systems, the respiratory system comes into action a few minutes later, thus serving as the *second line of defense* against changes in $[H^+]$.

When changes in $[H^+]$ stem from $[CO_2]$ fluctuations that arise from respiratory abnormalities, the respiratory mechanism cannot contribute to pH control. For example, if acidosis exists because of CO_2 accumulation caused by lung disease, the impaired lungs cannot possibly compensate for acidosis by increasing the rate of CO_2 removal. The buffer systems (other than the $H_2CO_3:HCO_3^-$ pair) plus renal regulation are the only mechanisms available for defending against respiratory-induced acid–base abnormalities.

Let us now see how the kidneys help maintain acid–base balance.

The kidneys help maintain acid–base balance by adjusting their rate of H^+ excretion, HCO_3^- excretion, and NH_3 secretion.

The kidneys control the pH of body fluids by adjusting three interrelated factors: (1) H^+ excretion, (2) HCO_3^- excretion, and (3) ammonia (NH_3) secretion. We examine each of these mechanisms in further detail.

RENAL H^+ EXCRETION Acids are continuously being added to body fluids as a result of metabolic activities, yet the generated H^+ must not be allowed to accumulate. Although the body's buffer systems can resist changes in pH by removing H^+ from solution, the persistent production of acidic metabolic products would eventually overwhelm the limits of this buffering capacity. Therefore, the constantly generated H^+ must ultimately be eliminated from the body. The lungs can remove only CO_2-generated H^+ by eliminating CO_2. The task of eliminating H^+ derived from sulfuric, phosphoric, lactic, and other acids rests with the kidneys. Furthermore, the kidneys can eliminate extra H^+ derived from CO_2.

All the filtered H^+ is excreted, but most of the excreted H^+ enters the urine via secretion (see p. 422). Energy-dependent carriers in the membrane of the tubular cells secrete the extra H^+ from the peritubular capillary plasma into the tubular fluid. The proximal, distal, and collecting tubules all secrete H^+. Because the kidneys normally excrete H^+, urine is usually acidic, having an average pH of 6.0.

The magnitude of H^+ secretion depends primarily on a direct effect of the plasma's acid–base status on the kidneys' tubular cells (● Figure 14-9). No neural or hormonal control is involved.

■ When the $[H^+]$ of the plasma passing through the peritubular capillaries is elevated above normal, the tubular cells respond by secreting greater-than-usual amounts of H^+ from the plasma into the tubular fluid to be excreted in the urine.

■ Conversely, when plasma $[H^+]$ is lower than normal, the kidneys conserve H^+ by reducing its secretion and subsequent excretion in the urine.

RENAL HCO_3^- EXCRETION Before being eliminated by the kidneys, H^+ generated from noncarbonic acids is buffered to a large extent by plasma HCO_3^-. Appropriately, therefore, renal handling of acid–base balance also involves adjustment of HCO_3^- excretion, depending on the H^+ load in the plasma (● Figure 14-9).

■ When plasma $[H^+]$ is higher than normal, the kidneys reabsorb more HCO_3^- than usual, making it available to help buffer the extra H^+ load in the body, rather than excreting it in the urine.

■ When plasma $[H^+]$ is below normal, a smaller proportion of the HCO_3^- pool than usual is tied up buffering H^+, so plasma $[HCO_3^-]$ is elevated above normal. The kidneys compensate by reabsorbing less HCO_3^-, thus excreting more HCO_3^- in the urine and removing the excess, unused HCO_3^- from the plasma.

Note that to compensate for acidosis, the kidneys acidify urine (by getting rid of extra H^+) and alkalinize plasma (by conserving HCO_3^-) to bring plasma pH to normal. In the opposite case—alkalosis—the kidneys make urine alkaline (by eliminating excess HCO_3^-) while acidifying plasma (by conserving H^+) (▲ Table 14-6).

RENAL NH_3 SECRETION The energy-dependent H^+ carriers in the tubular cells can secrete H^+ against a concentration gradient until the tubular fluid (urine) becomes 800 times more acidic than the plasma. At this point, further H^+ secretion stops because the gradient becomes too great for the secretory process to continue. The kidneys cannot acidify urine beyond a gradient-limited urinary pH of 4.5. If left unbuffered as free H^+, only about 1% of the excess H^+ typically excreted daily would produce a urinary pH of this magnitude at normal urine flow rates, and elimination of the other 99% of the usually secreted H^+ load would be prevented—a situation that would be intolerable. For H^+ secretion to proceed, most secreted H^+ must be buffered in the tubular fluid so that it does not exist as free H^+ and, accordingly, does not contribute to tubular acidity.

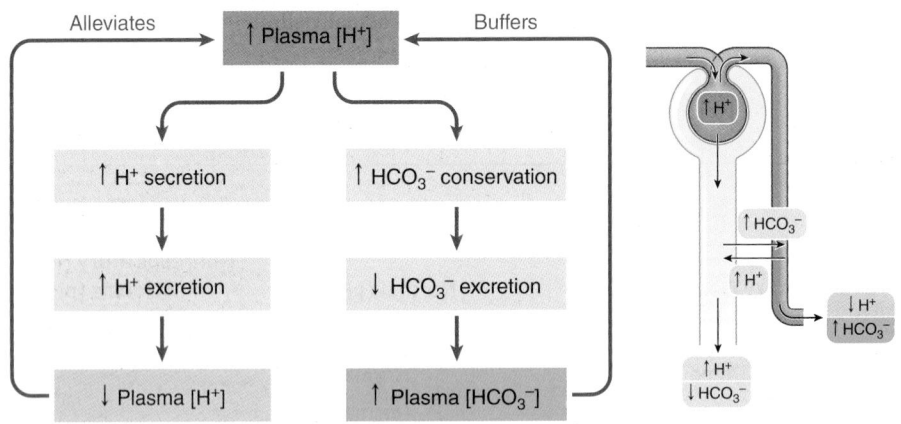

● FIGURE 14-9 **Control of the rate of tubular H^+ secretion and HCO_3^- reabsorption.**

Acid–Base Abnormality	H⁺ Secretion	H⁺ Excretion	HCO_3^- Reabsorption	HCO_3^- Excretion	pH of Urine	Compensatory Change in Plasma pH
Acidosis	↑	↑	↑	↓	Acidic	Alkalinization toward normal
Alkalosis	↓	↓	↓	↑	Alkaline	Acidification toward normal

Bicarbonate cannot buffer urinary H⁺ as it does H⁺ in the ECF, because HCO_3^- is not excreted in the urine simultaneously with H⁺. (Whichever of these substances is in excess in the plasma is excreted in the urine.) There are, however, two important urinary buffers: (1) filtered phosphate buffers and (2) secreted ammonia.

■ *Filtered phosphate as a urinary buffer.* Normally, secreted H⁺ is first buffered by the phosphate buffer system, which is in the tubular fluid because excess ingested phosphate has been filtered but not reabsorbed. When H⁺ secretion is high, the buffering capacity of urinary phosphates is exceeded, but the kidneys cannot respond by excreting more basic phosphate. Only the quantity of phosphate reabsorbed, not the quantity excreted, is subject to control. As soon as all basic phosphate ions that are coincidentally excreted have soaked up H⁺, the acidity of the tubular fluid quickly rises as more H⁺ ions are secreted. Without additional buffering capacity from another source, H⁺ secretion would soon halt abruptly as the free [H⁺] in the tubular fluid quickly rose to the critical limiting level.

■ *Secreted NH₃ as a urinary buffer.* When acidosis exists, the tubular cells secrete **ammonia (NH₃)** into the tubular fluid once the normal urinary phosphate buffers are saturated. This NH₃ enables the kidneys to continue secreting additional H⁺ ions because NH₃ combines with free H⁺ in the tubular fluid to form **ammonium ion (NH₄⁺)** as follows:

$$NH_3 + H^+ \rightleftharpoons NH_4^+$$

The tubular membranes are not very permeable to NH₄⁺, so the ammonium ions remain in the tubular fluid and are lost in the urine, each one taking a H⁺ with it. Thus, NH₃ secreted during acidosis buffers excess H⁺ in the tubular fluid so that large amounts of H⁺ can be secreted into the urine before the pH falls to the limiting value of 4.5. Were it not for NH₃ secretion, the extent of H⁺ secretion would be limited to whatever phosphate-buffering capacity coincidentally happened to be present as a result of dietary excess.

The kidneys are a powerful third line of defense against changes in [H⁺].

The kidneys require hours to days to compensate for changes in body-fluid pH, compared to the immediate responses of the buffer systems and the few minutes of delay before the respiratory system responds. Therefore, they are the *third line of defense* against [H⁺] changes in body fluids. However, the kidneys are the most potent acid–base regulatory mechanism; they can not only vary removal of H⁺ from any source but also can variably conserve or eliminate HCO_3^- depending on the acid–base status of the body. By simultaneously removing acid (H⁺) from and adding base (HCO_3^-) to body fluids, the kidneys are able to restore the pH toward normal more effectively than the lungs, which can adjust only the amount of H⁺-forming CO_2 in the body.

Acid–base imbalances can arise from either respiratory dysfunction or metabolic disturbances.

 Deviations from normal acid–base status are divided into four categories, depending on the source and direction of the abnormal change in [H⁺]. These categories are *respiratory acidosis, respiratory alkalosis, metabolic acidosis,* and *metabolic alkalosis.* An acid–base imbalance that has a respiratory cause is associated with an abnormal [CO_2]. A deviation in pH resulting from any cause other than an abnormal [CO_2] is considered a metabolic (or nonrespiratory) acid–base imbalance.

RESPIRATORY ACIDOSIS **Respiratory acidosis** is the result of abnormal CO_2 retention arising from *hypoventilation* (see p. 393). As less-than-normal amounts of CO_2 are lost through the lungs, the resulting increase in CO_2 generates more H⁺ from this source. Possible causes include lung disease, depression of the respiratory center by drugs or disease, nerve or muscle disorders that reduce respiratory muscle ability, or (transiently) even the simple act of holding one's breath.

RESPIRATORY ALKALOSIS Respiratory alkalosis occurs when excessive CO_2 is lost from the body as a result of *hyperventilation* (see p. 394). When pulmonary ventilation increases out of proportion to the rate of CO_2 production, too much CO_2 is blown off. Consequently, less [H⁺] is formed from this source. Possible causes of respiratory alkalosis include fever, anxiety, and aspirin poisoning, all of which excessively stimulate ventilation without regard to the status of O_2, CO_2, or H⁺ in the body fluids. Respiratory alkalosis also occurs as a result of physiological mechanisms at high altitude. When the low concentration of O_2 in arterial blood reflexly stimulates ventilation to obtain more O_2, too much CO_2 is blown off, inadvertently leading to an alkalotic state (see p. 394).

METABOLIC ACIDOSIS **Metabolic (or nonrespiratory) acidosis** encompasses all types of acidosis besides that caused by excess CO_2 in body fluids. Metabolic acidosis is the type of acid–base disorder most frequently encountered. Here are its most common causes:

1. *Severe diarrhea.* During digestion, a HCO_3^--rich digestive juice is normally secreted into the digestive tract by the pancreas and is later reabsorbed back into the plasma when digestion is completed. During diarrhea, this HCO_3^- is lost from the body rather than reabsorbed. Because of the loss of HCO_3^-, less HCO_3^- is available to buffer H^+, leading to more free H^+ in the body fluids.

2. *Diabetes mellitus.* Abnormal fat metabolism resulting from the inability of cells to preferentially use glucose because of inadequate insulin action leads to formation of excess keto acids whose dissociation increases plasma $[H^+]$.

3. *Strenuous exercise.* When muscles resort to anaerobic glycolysis during strenuous exercise, excess lactic acid (lactate) is produced, raising plasma $[H^+]$.

4. *Uremic acidosis.* In severe renal failure (uremia), the kidneys cannot rid the body of even the normal amounts of H^+ generated from noncarbonic acids formed by ongoing metabolic processes, so H^+ starts to accumulate in the body fluids. Also, the kidneys cannot conserve an adequate amount of HCO_3^- for buffering the normal acid load.

METABOLIC ALKALOSIS **Metabolic (or nonrespiratory) alkalosis** is a reduction in plasma $[H^+]$ caused by a relative deficiency of noncarbonic acids. This condition arises most commonly from the following:

1. *Vomiting* causes abnormal loss of H^+ from the body as a result of lost acidic gastric juices. Hydrochloric acid is secreted into the stomach lumen during digestion and is usually later reabsorbed back into the plasma.

2. *Ingestion of alkaline drugs* can produce alkalosis, such as when baking soda ($NaHCO_3$, which dissociates in solution into Na^+ and HCO_3^-) is used as a self-administered remedy for treating gastric hyperacidity. By neutralizing excess acid in the stomach, HCO_3^- relieves the symptoms of stomach irritation and heartburn; but when more HCO_3^- than needed is ingested, the extra HCO_3^- is absorbed from the digestive tract and increases plasma $[HCO_3^-]$. The extra HCO_3^- binds with some of the free H^+ normally present in plasma from noncarbonic acid sources, reducing free $[H^+]$. (In contrast, commercial alkaline products for treating gastric hyperacidity are not absorbed from the digestive tract to any extent and therefore do not alter the body's acid–base status.)

Chapter in Perspective: Focus on Homeostasis

Homeostasis depends on maintaining a balance between the input and the output of all constituents present in the internal fluid environment. Regulation of fluid balance involves two separate components: control of salt balance and control of H_2O balance. Control of salt balance is primarily important in the long-term regulation of arterial blood pressure because the body's salt load osmotically holds H_2O, thereby determining the ECF volume, of which plasma volume is a part. An increased salt load in the ECF leads to an expansion in ECF volume, including plasma volume, which in turn causes a rise in blood pressure. Conversely, a reduction in the ECF salt load brings about a fall in blood pressure. Salt balance is maintained by constantly adjusting salt output in the urine to match unregulated, variable salt intake.

Control of H_2O balance is important in preventing changes in ECF osmolarity, which would induce detrimental osmotic shifts of H_2O between the cells and the ECF. Such shifts of H_2O into or out of the cells would cause the cells to swell or shrink, respectively. Cells, especially brain neurons, do not function normally when swollen or shrunken. Water balance is largely maintained by controlling the volume of free H_2O (H_2O not accompanied by solute) lost in the urine to compensate for uncontrolled losses of variable volumes of H_2O from other avenues, such as through sweating or diarrhea, and for poorly regulated H_2O intake. Even though a thirst mechanism exists to control H_2O intake based on need, the amount a person drinks is often influenced by social custom and habit instead of thirst alone.

A balance between input and output of H^+ is critical to maintaining the body's acid–base balance within the narrow limits compatible with life. Deviations in the internal fluid environment's pH lead to altered neuromuscular excitability, to changes in enzymatically controlled metabolic activity, and to K^+ imbalances, which can cause cardiac arrhythmias. These effects are fatal if the pH falls outside the range of 6.8 to 8.0.

Hydrogen ions are uncontrollably and continuously added to the body fluids as a result of ongoing metabolic activities, yet the ECF pH must be kept constant at a slightly alkaline level of 7.4 for optimal body function. Like salt and H_2O balance, control of H^+ output by the kidneys is the main regulatory factor in achieving H^+ balance. The lungs, which can adjust their rate of excretion of H^+-generating CO_2, also help eliminate H^+ from the body. Furthermore, chemical buffer systems can take up or liberate H^+, transiently keeping its concentration constant within the body until its output can be brought into line with its input. Such a mechanism is not available for salt or H_2O balance.

REVIEW EXERCISES

Objective Questions (Answers on p. A-48)

1. The only avenue by which materials can be exchanged between the cells and the external environment is the ECF. (*True or false?*)
2. Water is driven into the cells when the ECF volume is expanded by an isotonic fluid gain. (*True or false?*)
3. Salt balance in humans is poorly regulated because of our hedonistic salt appetite. (*True or false?*)
4. The largest body-fluid compartment is the _____.
5. Of the two members of the H_2CO_3:HCO_3^- buffer system, _____ is regulated by the lungs and _____ is regulated by the kidneys.
6. Which of the following factors does *not* increase vasopressin secretion?
   a. ECF hypertonicity
   b. an ECF volume deficit following hemorrhage
   c. an increase in arterial blood pressure
   d. stressful situations
7. Indicate all correct answers:
   a. pH equals log $1/[H^+]$.
   b. pH is high in acidosis.
   c. pH falls as $[H^+]$ increases.
8. Indicate all correct answers:
   a. Acidosis causes overexcitability of the nervous system.
   b. Acidosis exists when the plasma pH falls below 7.35.
   c. Acidosis occurs when CO_2 is blown off more rapidly than it is being produced by metabolic activities.
   d. Acidosis occurs when excessive HCO_3^- is lost from the body, as in diarrhea.
9. Indicate all correct answers that complete the following sentence: The kidney tubular cells secrete NH_3
   a. when the urinary pH becomes too high.
   b. when the body is in a state of alkalosis.
   c. to enable further renal secretion of H^+ to occur.
   d. to buffer excess filtered HCO_3^-.
   e. when there is excess NH_3 in the body fluids
10. Match each acid–base imbalance with a possible cause:
   ___ 1. respiratory acidosis   (a) vomiting
   ___ 2. respiratory alkalosis   (b) diabetes mellitus
   ___ 3. metabolic acidosis   (c) pneumonia
   ___ 4. metabolic alkalosis   (d) aspirin poisoning

Essay Questions

1. Explain the balance concept.
2. Outline the distribution of body H_2O.
3. Compare the ionic composition of plasma, interstitial fluid, and intracellular fluid.
4. What factors are regulated to maintain the body's fluid balance?
5. Why is regulation of ECF volume important? How is it regulated?
6. Why is regulation of ECF osmolarity important? How is it regulated? What are the causes and consequences of ECF hypertonicity and ECF hypotonicity?
7. Outline the sources of input and output in a daily salt balance and a daily H_2O balance. Which are subject to control to maintain the body's fluid balance?
8. Distinguish between an acid and a base.
9. What is the relationship between $[H^+]$ and pH?
10. What is the normal pH of body fluids? How does this compare to the pH of H_2O? Define acidosis and alkalosis.
11. What are the consequences of fluctuations in $[H^+]$?
12. What are the body's sources of H^+?
13. Describe the three lines of defense against changes in $[H^+]$ in terms of their mechanisms and speed of action.
14. List and indicate the functions of each of the body's chemical buffer systems.
15. What are the causes of the four categories of acid–base imbalances?

POINTS TO PONDER

(Explanations on p. A-48)

1. Alcoholic beverages inhibit vasopressin secretion. Given this fact, predict the effect of alcohol on the rate of urine formation. Predict the actions of alcohol on ECF osmolarity. Explain why a person still feels thirsty after excessive consumption of alcoholic beverages.
2. If a person loses 1500 ml of salt-rich sweat and drinks 1000 ml of water during the same period, what will happen to vasopressin secretion? Why is it important to replace both the water and the salt?
3. If a solute that can penetrate the plasma membrane, such as dextrose (a type of sugar), is dissolved in sterile water at a concentration equal to that of normal body fluids and then is injected intravenously, what is the impact on the body's fluid balance?
4. Explain why a buffer system cannot buffer itself. For example, why can't the H_2CO_3:HCO_3^- buffer system compensate for increased plasma $[H^+]$ arising from CO_2 retention as a result of a respiratory problem?

CLINICAL CONSIDERATION

(Explanation on p. A-49)

Marilyn Y. has had pronounced diarrhea for more than a week as a result of having acquired salmonellosis, a bacterial intestinal infection, from improperly handled food. What impact has this prolonged diarrhea had on her fluid and acid–base balance? In what ways has Marilyn's body been trying to compensate for these imbalances?

Chapter 14

Study Card

Balance Concept (pp. 443–444)

■ The internal pool of a substance is the quantity of that substance in the ECF. The inputs to the pool are by way of ingestion or metabolic production of the substance. The outputs from the pool are by way of excretion or metabolic consumption of the substance. (*Review Figure 14-1.*)

■ Input must equal output to maintain a stable balance of the substance.

Fluid Balance (pp. 444–452)

■ On average, body fluids compose 60% of total body weight. Two thirds of the body H_2O is in the ICF. The remaining third, in the ECF, is distributed between plasma (20% of ECF) and interstitial fluid (80% of ECF). (*Review Table 14-1.*)

■ Because all plasma constituents are freely exchanged across the capillary walls, the plasma and interstitial fluid are nearly identical in composition, except for the lack of plasma proteins in the interstitial fluid. In contrast, the ECF and the ICF have markedly different compositions, because the plasma membrane barriers are highly selective as to what materials are transported into or out of the cells. (*Review Figure 14-2.*)

■ The essential components of fluid balance are control of ECF volume by maintaining salt balance and control of ECF osmolarity by maintaining water balance. (*Review Tables 14-2 through 14-4.*)

■ Because of the osmotic holding power of Na^+, the major ECF cation, a change in the body's total Na content, or load, causes a corresponding change in ECF volume, including plasma volume, which alters arterial blood pressure in the same direction. Appropriately, in the long run, Na^+-regulating mechanisms compensate for changes in ECF volume and arterial blood pressure. (*Review Table 14-4.*)

■ Salt intake is poorly controlled by the human body, but control of salt output in the urine is closely regulated to maintain salt balance. Blood pressure–regulating mechanisms (the baroreceptor reflex) can vary the GFR, and thus the amount of Na^+ filtered, by adjusting the radius of the afferent arterioles supplying the glomeruli. Blood pressure–regulating mechanisms (the renin–angiotensin–aldosterone system; RAAS) can also vary aldosterone secretion to adjust Na^+ reabsorption by the renal tubules. Varying Na^+ filtration and Na^+ reabsorption can adjust how much Na^+ is excreted in the urine to regulate plasma volume and thus arterial blood pressure in the long term. (*Review Figure 14-3.*)

■ ECF osmolarity must be closely regulated to prevent osmotic shifts of H_2O between the ECF and the ICF, because cell swelling or shrinking is harmful, especially to brain neurons. Excess free H_2O in the ECF dilutes ECF solutes; the resulting ECF hypotonicity drives H_2O into the cells. An ECF free H_2O

deficit, by contrast, concentrates ECF solutes, so H_2O leaves the cells to enter the hypertonic ECF. (*Review Table 14-4.*)

■ To prevent these harmful fluxes, changes in ECF osmolarity are primarily detected and corrected by the systems that maintain free H_2O balance (H_2O without accompanying solute). Free H_2O balance is regulated largely by vasopressin and, to a lesser degree, by thirst. Both of these factors are governed primarily by hypothalamic osmoreceptors, which monitor ECF osmolarity, and to a lesser extent by left atrial volume receptors, which monitor vascular "fullness." The amount of vasopressin secreted determines the extent of free H_2O reabsorption by the distal and collecting tubules of the nephrons, thereby determining the volume of urinary output. (*Review Figure 14-4.*)

■ Simultaneously, intensity of thirst controls volume of fluid intake. However, because the volume of fluid drunk is often not directly correlated with the intensity of thirst, control of urinary output by vasopressin is the most important regulatory mechanism for maintaining H_2O balance.

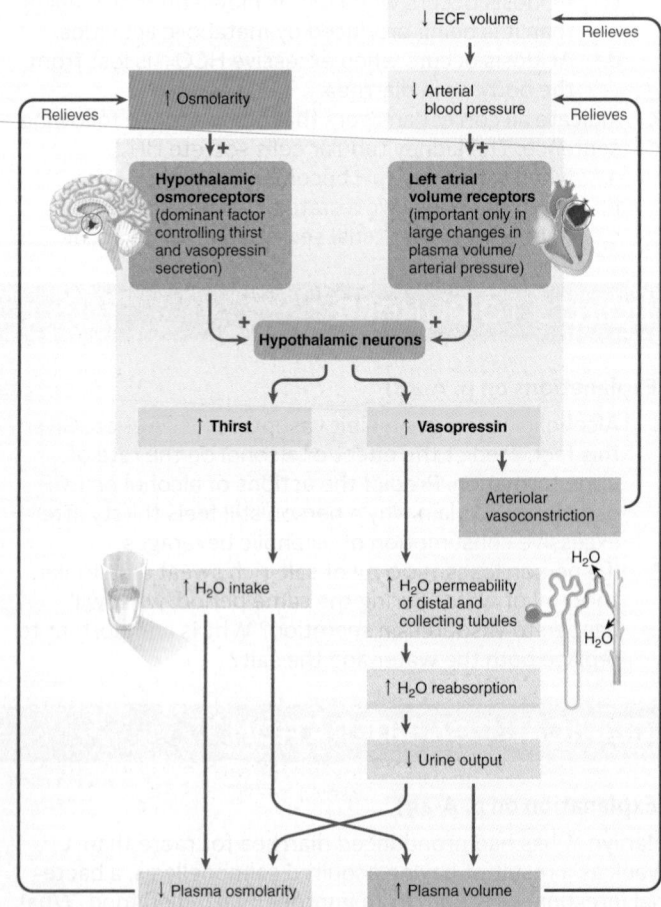

462

Acid–Base Balance (pp. 452–460)

■ Acids liberate free hydrogen ions (H^+) into solution; bases bind with and remove free H^+ from solution. *(Review Figure 14-5.)*

■ Acid–base balance refers to regulation of H^+ concentration, designated by $[H^+]$, in the body fluids. To precisely maintain $[H^+]$, input of H^+ by metabolic production of acids within the body must continually be matched with H^+ output by urinary excretion of H^+ and by respiratory removal of H^+-generating CO_2. Furthermore, between the time of this generation and its elimination, H^+ must be buffered within the body to prevent marked fluctuations in $[H^+]$.

■ Hydrogen ion concentration is often expressed in terms of pH, which is the logarithm of $1/[H^+]$.

■ The normal pH of the plasma is 7.4, slightly alkaline compared to neutral H_2O, which has a pH of 7.0. A pH lower than normal ($[H^+]$ higher than normal) indicates a state of acidosis. A pH higher than normal ($[H^+]$ lower than normal) characterizes a state of alkalosis. *(Review Figure 14-6.)*

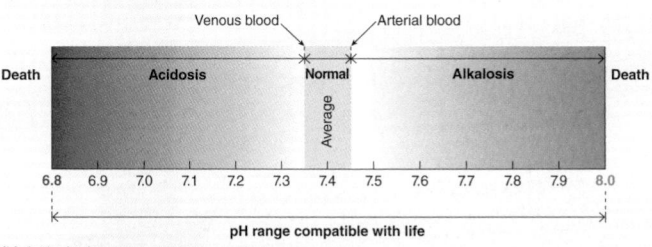

(b) In the body

■ Fluctuations in $[H^+]$ have profound effects, most notably (1) changes in neuromuscular excitability, with acidosis depressing excitability, especially in the CNS, and alkalosis producing overexcitability of both the PNS and the CNS; (2) disruption of normal metabolic reactions by altering the structure and function of all enzymes; and (3) alterations in plasma $[K^+]$ (which affect cardiac function) brought about by H^+-induced changes in the rate of K^+ elimination by the kidneys.

■ The primary challenge in controlling acid–base balance is maintaining normal plasma alkalinity despite continual addition of H^+ to the plasma from ongoing metabolic activity. The major source of H^+ is from CO_2-generated H^+.

■ The three lines of defense for resisting changes in $[H^+]$ are (1) the chemical buffer systems, (2) respiratory control of pH, and (3) renal control of pH.

■ Chemical buffer systems each consist of a pair of chemicals involved in a reversible reaction, one that can liberate H^+ and the other that can bind H^+. By acting according to the law of mass action, a buffer pair acts immediately to minimize any changes in pH. The four chemical buffers are (1) $H_2CO_3:HCO_3^-$ (primary ECF buffer against noncarbonic acid changes), (2) proteins (primary ICF buffer), (3) hemoglobin (primary buffer against carbonic acid changes), and (4) phosphate (primary urinary buffer). *(Review Figure 14-8.)*

■ The respiratory system normally eliminates metabolically produced CO_2 so that CO_2-generated H^+ does not accumulate in the body fluids.

■ When chemical buffers alone have been unable to immediately minimize a pH change, the respiratory system responds within a few minutes by altering its rate of CO_2 removal. An increase in $[H^+]$ from sources other than CO_2 stimulates respiration so that more H^+-forming CO_2 is blown off, compensating for acidosis by reducing generation of CO_2-associated H^+. Conversely, a fall in $[H^+]$ depresses respiratory activity so that CO_2 and thus H^+ generated from this source can accumulate in the body fluids to compensate for alkalosis. *(Review Table 14-5.)*

■ The kidneys are the most powerful line of defense. They require hours to days to compensate for a deviation in body-fluid pH. Not only can they eliminate the normal amount of H^+ produced from non-CO_2 sources, but they can also alter their rate of H^+ removal in response to changes in both non-CO_2- and CO_2-generated acids. In contrast, the lungs can adjust only H^+ generated from CO_2. Furthermore, the kidneys can regulate $[HCO_3^-]$ in body fluids.

■ The kidneys compensate for acidosis by secreting the excess H^+ in the urine while adding new HCO_3^- to the plasma to expand the HCO_3^- buffer pool. During alkalosis, the kidneys conserve H^+ by reducing its secretion in urine. They also eliminate HCO_3^-, which is in excess because less HCO_3^- than usual is tied up buffering H^+ when H^+ is in short supply. *(Review Figure 14-9 and Table 14-6.)*

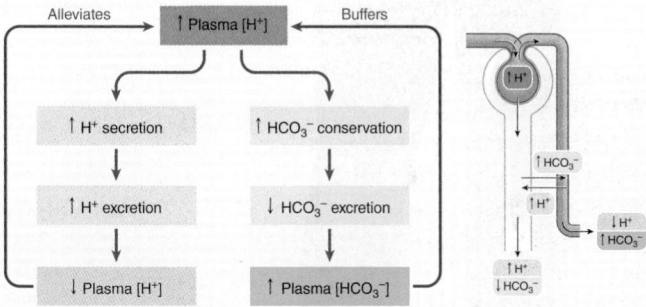

■ Secreted H^+ must be buffered in the tubular fluid to prevent the concentration gradient for H^+ from becoming so great that it blocks further H^+ secretion. Normally, H^+ is buffered by the urinary phosphate buffer pair, which is abundant in the tubular fluid because excess dietary phosphate spills into the urine to be excreted from the body.

■ In acidosis, when all the phosphate buffer is already used up in buffering the extra secreted H^+, the kidneys secrete NH_3 into the tubular fluid to serve as a buffer so that H^+ secretion can continue.

■ The four types of acid–base imbalances are respiratory acidosis, respiratory alkalosis, metabolic acidosis, and metabolic alkalosis. Respiratory acid–base disorders stem from deviations from normal $[CO_2]$, whereas metabolic (nonrespiratory) acid–base imbalances include all deviations in pH other than those caused by abnormal $[CO_2]$.

Digestive System

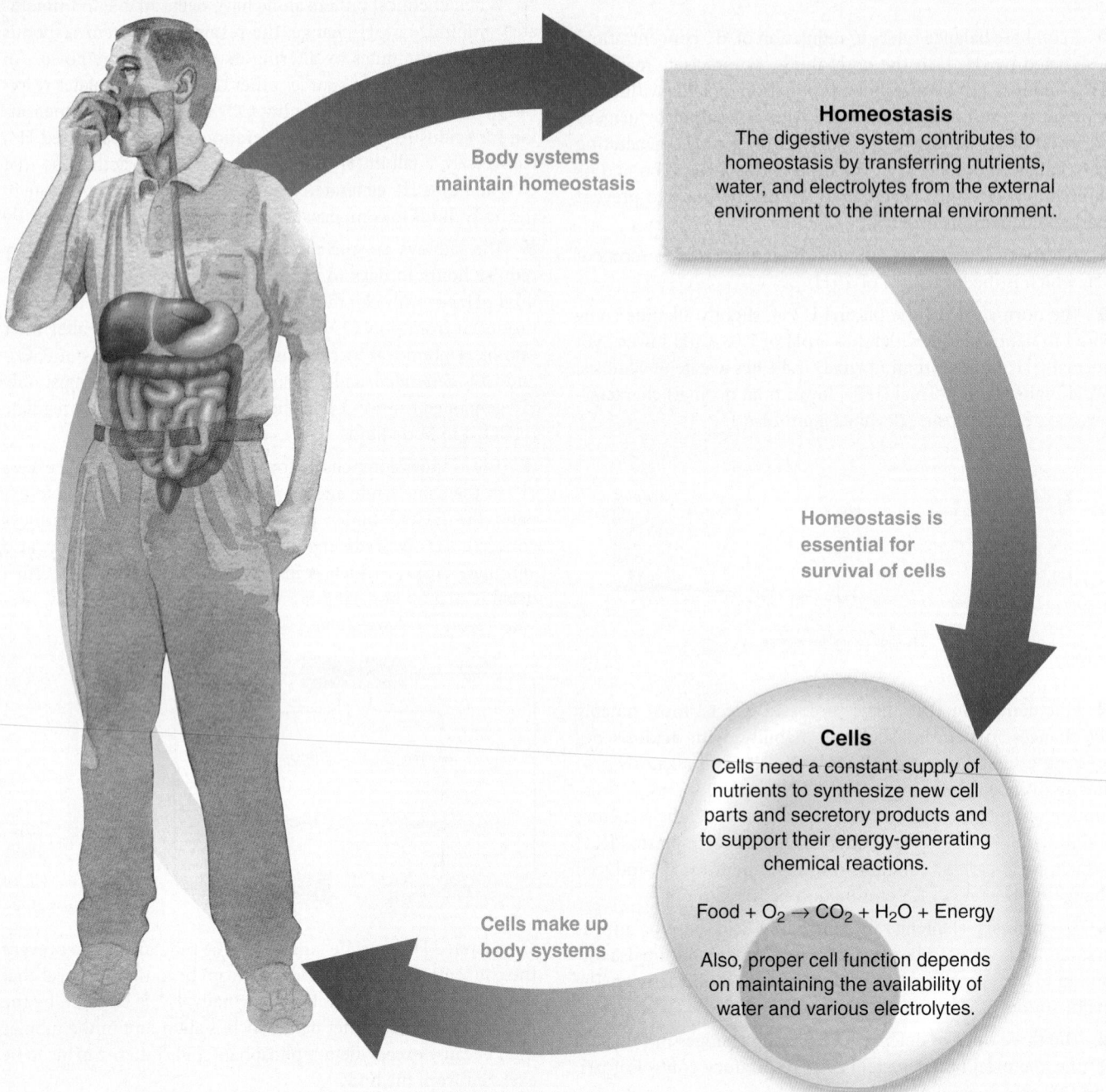

Body systems maintain homeostasis

Homeostasis
The digestive system contributes to homeostasis by transferring nutrients, water, and electrolytes from the external environment to the internal environment.

Homeostasis is essential for survival of cells

Cells
Cells need a constant supply of nutrients to synthesize new cell parts and secretory products and to support their energy-generating chemical reactions.

$$Food + O_2 \rightarrow CO_2 + H_2O + Energy$$

Also, proper cell function depends on maintaining the availability of water and various electrolytes.

Cells make up body systems

To maintain homeostasis, nutrient molecules used for energy production must continually be replaced by new, energy-rich nutrients. Also, nutrient molecules, especially proteins, are needed for ongoing synthesis of new cells and cell parts in the course of growth and tissue turnover. Similarly, water and electrolytes constantly lost in urine and sweat and through other avenues must be replenished regularly. The **digestive system** contributes to homeostasis by transferring nutrients, water, and electrolytes from the external environment to the internal environment. The digestive system does not directly regulate the concentration of any of these constituents in the internal environment. It does not vary nutrient, water, or electrolyte uptake based on body needs (with few exceptions); rather, it optimizes conditions for digesting and absorbing what is ingested.

15

The Digestive System

CHAPTER AT A GLANCE

General Aspects of Digestion
Basic digestive processes
Components of the digestive system
General mechanisms of regulating
  digestive function

Mouth
Chewing
Salivary secretion

Pharynx and Esophagus
Swallowing

Stomach
Gastric motility
Gastric secretion
Digestion in the stomach
Absorption by the stomach

Pancreatic and Biliary Secretions
Exocrine pancreas
Liver and biliary system

Small Intestine
Small-intestine motility
Small-intestine secretion
Digestion in the small intestine
Absorption by the small intestine

Large Intestine
Large-intestine motility
Large-intestine secretion
Colonic bacteria
Absorption by the large intestine
Composition and elimination of feces

Overview of the Gastrointestinal
Hormones

General Aspects of Digestion

The primary function of the digestive system is to transfer nutrients, water, and electrolytes from the food we eat into the body's internal environment. Ingested food is essential as an energy source, or fuel, from which the cells can generate adenosine triphosphate (ATP) to carry out their particular energy-dependent activities, such as active transport, contraction, synthesis, and secretion. Food is also a source of building supplies for the renewal and addition of body tissues.

The act of eating does not automatically make the preformed organic molecules in food available to the body cells. The food first must be digested, or biochemically broken down, into small, simple molecules that can be absorbed from the digestive tract into the circulatory system for distribution to the cells. Normally, about 95% of the ingested food is made available for the body's use.

We provide an overview of the digestive system, examining the common features of the various components of the system, before we begin a detailed tour of the tract from beginning to end.

The digestive system performs four basic digestive processes.

There are four basic digestive processes: *motility, secretion, digestion,* and *absorption.*

MOTILITY The term **motility** refers to the digestive tract's muscular contractions, of which there are two basic types: propulsive movements and mixing movements. *Propulsive movements* propel or push the contents forward through the digestive tract, with the rate of propulsion varying depending on the functions accomplished by the different regions. For example, transit of food through the esophagus is rapid, which is appropriate because this structure merely serves as a passageway from the mouth to the stomach. In comparison, in the small intestine—the main site of digestion and absorption—the contents are moved forward slowly, allowing time for the breakdown and absorption of food.

Mixing movements have a twofold function. First, by mixing food with the digestive juices, these movements promote digestion of the food. Second, they facilitate absorption by exposing all parts of the intestinal contents to the absorbing surfaces of the digestive tract.

Contraction of the smooth muscle within the walls of the digestive organs accomplishes movement of material through most of the digestive tract. The exceptions are at the ends of the tract—the mouth through the early part of the esophagus at the beginning and the external anal sphincter at the end—where motility involves skeletal muscle rather than smooth muscle activity. Accordingly, the acts of chewing, swallowing, and defecation have voluntary components, because skeletal muscle is under voluntary control. By contrast, motility accomplished by smooth muscle throughout the rest of the tract is controlled by complex involuntary mechanisms.

SECRETION A number of digestive juices are secreted into the digestive tract lumen by exocrine glands (see p. 4) along the route, each with a specific secretory product. Each **digestive secretion** consists of water, electrolytes, and specific organic constituents important in the digestive process, such as enzymes, bile salts, or mucus. The secretory cells extract from the plasma large volumes of water and the raw materials necessary to produce their particular secretion. Secretion of all digestive juices requires energy, both for active transport of some of the raw materials into the cell (others diffuse in passively) and for synthesis of secretory products by the endoplasmic reticulum. On appropriate neural or hormonal stimulation, the secretions are released into the digestive tract lumen. Normally, the digestive secretions are reabsorbed in one form or another back into the blood after their participation in digestion. Failure to do so (because of vomiting or diarrhea, for example) results in loss of this fluid that has been "borrowed" from the plasma.

DIGESTION Humans consume three categories of energy-rich foodstuffs: *carbohydrates, proteins,* and *fats.* These large molecules cannot cross plasma membranes intact to be absorbed from the lumen of the digestive tract into the blood or lymph. The term **digestion** refers to the biochemical breakdown of the structurally complex foodstuffs of the diet into smaller, absorbable units by the digestive enzymes as follows:

1. The simplest **carbohydrates** are the simple sugars or **monosaccharides** ("one-sugar" molecules), such as **glucose, fructose,** and **galactose,** few of which are normally found in the diet (see p. A-11). Most ingested carbohydrates are in the form of **polysaccharides** ("many-sugar" molecules), which consist of chains of interconnected glucose molecules. The most commonly consumed polysaccharide is **starch** derived from plant sources. In addition, meat contains **glycogen,** the polysaccharide storage form of glucose in muscle. **Cellulose,** another dietary polysaccharide, found in plant walls, cannot be digested into its constituent monosaccharides by the digestive juices humans secrete; thus, it represents the indigestible *fiber* or "bulk" of our diets. Besides polysaccharides, a lesser source of dietary carbohydrate is in the form of **disaccharides** ("two-sugar" molecules), including **sucrose** (table sugar, which consists of one glucose and one fructose molecule) and **lactose** (milk sugar made up of one glucose and one galactose molecule). Through the process of digestion, starch, glycogen, and disaccharides are converted into their constituent monosaccharides, principally glucose with small amounts of fructose and galactose. These monosaccharides are the absorbable units for carbohydrates.

2. Dietary **proteins** consist of various combinations of **amino acids** held together by peptide bonds (see p. A-14). Through the process of digestion, proteins are degraded into their constituent amino acids, which are the absorbable units for protein.

3. Most dietary **fats** are in the form of **triglycerides,** which are neutral fats, each consisting of a glycerol with three **fatty acid** molecules attached (*tri* means "three"; see p. A-12). During digestion, two of the fatty acid molecules are split off, leaving a **monoglyceride,** a glycerol molecule with one fatty acid molecule attached (*mono* means "one"). Thus, the end products of fat digestion are monoglycerides and free fatty acids, which are the absorbable units of fat.

Digestion is accomplished by enzymatic **hydrolysis** (breakdown by water; see p. A-16). By adding H_2O at the bond site, enzymes in the digestive secretions break down the bonds that hold the small molecular subunits within the nutrient molecules together, thus setting the small molecules free (● Figure 15-1). Removal of H_2O at the bond sites originally joined these small subunits to form nutrient molecules. Hydrolysis replaces the H_2O and frees the small absorbable units. Digestive enzymes are specific in the bonds they can hydrolyze. As food moves through the digestive tract, it is subjected to various enzymes, each of which breaks down the food molecules even further. In this way, large food molecules are converted to simple absorbable units in a progressive, stepwise fashion, like an assembly line in reverse, as the digestive tract contents are propelled forward.

ABSORPTION In the small intestine, digestion is completed and most absorption occurs. Through the process of **absorption,** the small absorbable units that result from digestion, along with water, vitamins, and electrolytes, are transferred from the digestive tract lumen into the blood or lymph.

As we examine the digestive tract from beginning to end, we discuss the four processes of motility, secretion, digestion, and absorption as they take place within each digestive organ (▲ Table 15-1).

The digestive tract and accessory digestive organs make up the digestive system.

The digestive system consists of the *digestive* (or *gastrointestinal*) *tract* plus the accessory digestive organs (*gastro* means "stomach"). The accessory digestive organs include the *salivary glands,* the *exocrine pancreas,* and the *biliary system,* which is composed of the *liver* and *gallbladder.* These exocrine organs lie outside the digestive tract and empty their secretions through ducts into the digestive tract lumen.

● **FIGURE 15-1 An example of hydrolysis.** In this example, the disaccharide maltose (the intermediate breakdown product of polysaccharides) is broken down into two glucose molecules by the addition of H_2O at the bond site.

The digestive tract is essentially a tube about 4.5 m (15 feet) in length in its normal contractile state.[1] Running through the middle of the body, the digestive tract includes the following organs (▲ Table 15-1): *mouth, pharynx* (throat), *esophagus, stomach, small intestine* (consisting of the *duodenum, jejunum,* and *ileum*), *large intestine* (the *cecum, appendix, colon,* and *rectum*), and *anus.* Although these organs are continuous with one another, they are considered as separate entities because of their regional modifications, which allow them to specialize in particular digestive activities.

Because the digestive tract is continuous from the mouth to the anus, the lumen of this tube, like the lumen of a straw, is continuous with the external environment. As a result, the contents within the lumen of the digestive tract are technically outside the body, just as the soda you suck through a straw is not a part of the straw. Only after a substance has been absorbed from the lumen across the digestive tract wall is it considered part of the body. This is important, because conditions essential to the digestive process can be tolerated in the digestive tract lumen that could not be tolerated in the body proper. Consider the following examples:

■ The pH of the stomach contents falls as low as 2.0 as a result of gastric secretion of hydrochloric acid (HCl), yet in the body fluids the pH range compatible with life is 6.8 to 8.0.

■ The digestive enzymes that hydrolyze the protein in food could also destroy the body's own tissues that produce them. (Protein is the main structural component of cells.) Therefore, once these enzymes are synthesized in inactive form, they are not activated until they reach the lumen, where they actually attack the food outside the body (that is, within the lumen), thereby protecting the body tissues against self-digestion.

■ Quadrillions of microorganisms live in the large intestine, where they are normally harmless and even beneficial, yet if these same microorganisms enter the body proper (as may happen with a ruptured appendix), they may be extremely harmful or even lethal.

■ Foodstuffs are complex foreign particles that would be attacked by the immune system if they were in contact with the body proper. However, the foodstuffs are digested within the lumen into absorbable units such as glucose, amino acids, and fatty acids that are indistinguishable from these simple energy-rich molecules already present in the body.

The digestive tract wall has four layers.

The digestive tract wall has the same general structure throughout most of its length from the esophagus to the anus, with some local variations characteristic for each region. A cross section of the digestive tube reveals four major tissue layers

---

[1]Because the uncontracted digestive tract in a cadaver is about twice as long as the contracted tract in a living person, anatomy texts indicate that the digestive tract is 30 feet long compared to the length of 15 feet indicated in physiology texts.

(● Figure 15-2). From the innermost layer outward they are the *mucosa,* the *submucosa,* the *muscularis externa,* and the *serosa.*

MUCOSA The **mucosa** lines the luminal surface of the digestive tract. The primary component of the mucosa is a **mucous membrane,** an inner epithelial layer that serves as a protective surface. The mucous membrane is also modified in particular areas for secretion and absorption: It contains *exocrine gland cells* for secretion of digestive juices, *endocrine gland cells* for secretion of blood-borne gastrointestinal hormones, and *epithelial cells* specialized for absorbing digested nutrients.

SUBMUCOSA The **submucosa** ("under the mucosa") is a thick layer of connective tissue that provides the digestive tract with its distensibility and elasticity. It contains the larger blood and lymph vessels, both of which send branches inward to the mucosal layer and outward to the surrounding thick muscle layer. Also, a nerve network known as the *submucosal plexus* lies within the submucosa (*plexus* means "network").

MUSCULARIS EXTERNA The **muscularis externa,** the major smooth muscle coat of the digestive tube, surrounds the submucosa. In most parts of the tract, the muscularis externa consists of two layers: an *inner circular layer* and an *outer longitudinal layer.* The fibers of the inner smooth muscle layer (adjacent to the submucosa) run circularly around the tube. Contraction of these circular fibers decreases the diameter of the lumen, constricting the tube at the point of contraction. Contraction of the fibers in the outer layer, which run longitudinally along the length of the tube, shortens the tube. Together, contractile activity of these smooth muscle layers produces the propulsive and mixing movements. Another nerve network, the *myenteric plexus,* lies between the two muscle layers (*myo* means "muscle"; *enteric* means "intestine"). Together, the submucosal and myenteric plexuses, along with hormones and local chemical mediators, help regulate local gut activity.

SEROSA The outer connective tissue covering of the digestive tract is the **serosa,** which secretes a watery, slippery fluid that lubricates and prevents friction between the digestive organs and the surrounding viscera.

Regulation of digestive function is complex and synergistic.

Digestive motility and secretion are carefully regulated to maximize digestion and absorption of ingested food. Four factors are involved in regulating digestive system function: (1) autonomous smooth muscle function, (2) intrinsic nerve plexuses, (3) extrinsic nerves, and (4) gastrointestinal hormones.

AUTONOMOUS SMOOTH MUSCLE FUNCTION Like self-excitable cardiac muscle cells, some specialized cells in digestive smooth muscle are pacemaker cells that display rhythmic, spontaneous variations in membrane potential. The prominent type of self-induced electrical activity in digestive smooth muscle is **slow-wave potentials** (see p. 236), alternatively referred to as the

▲Table 15-1 Anatomy and Functions of Components of the Digestive System

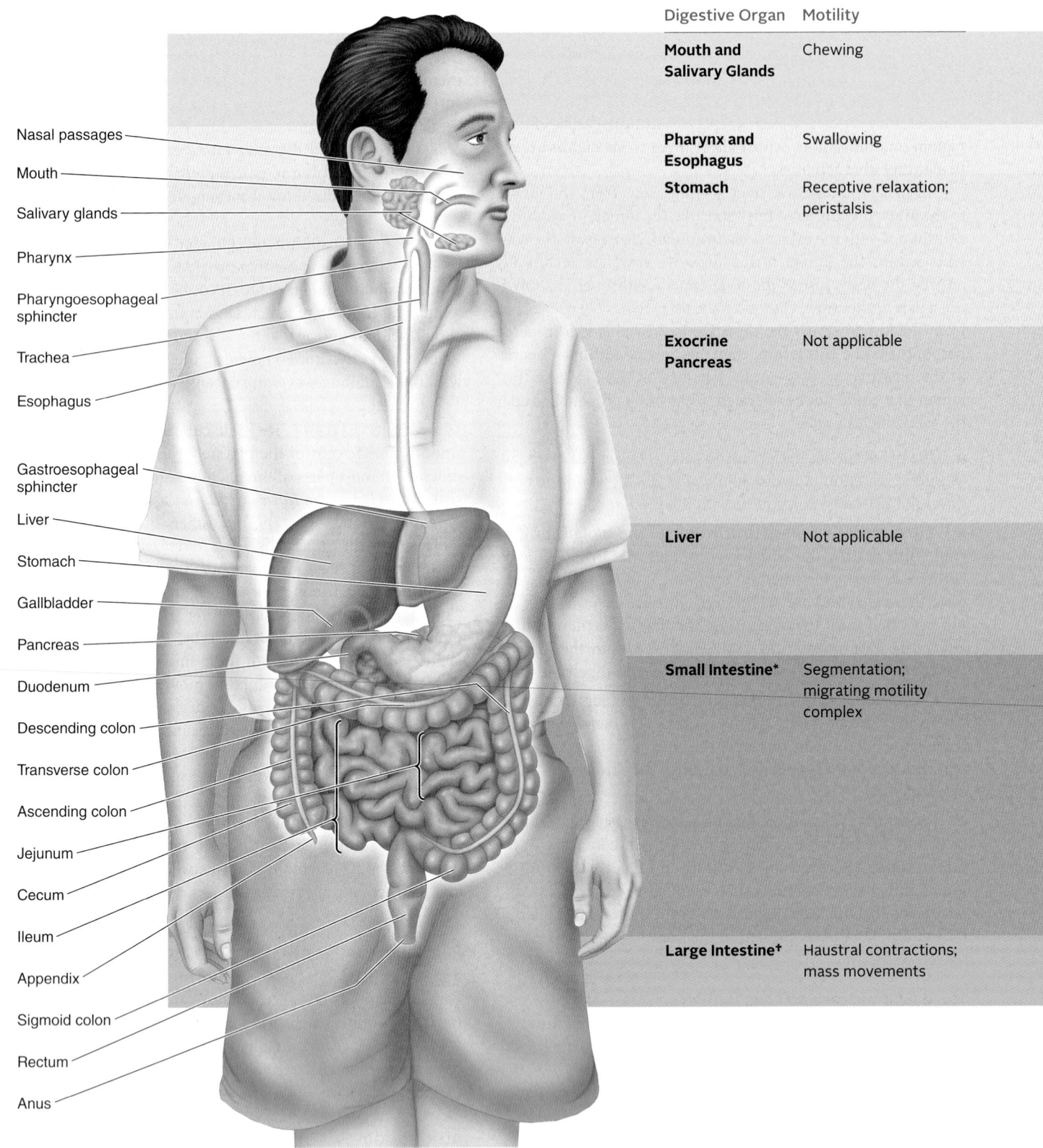

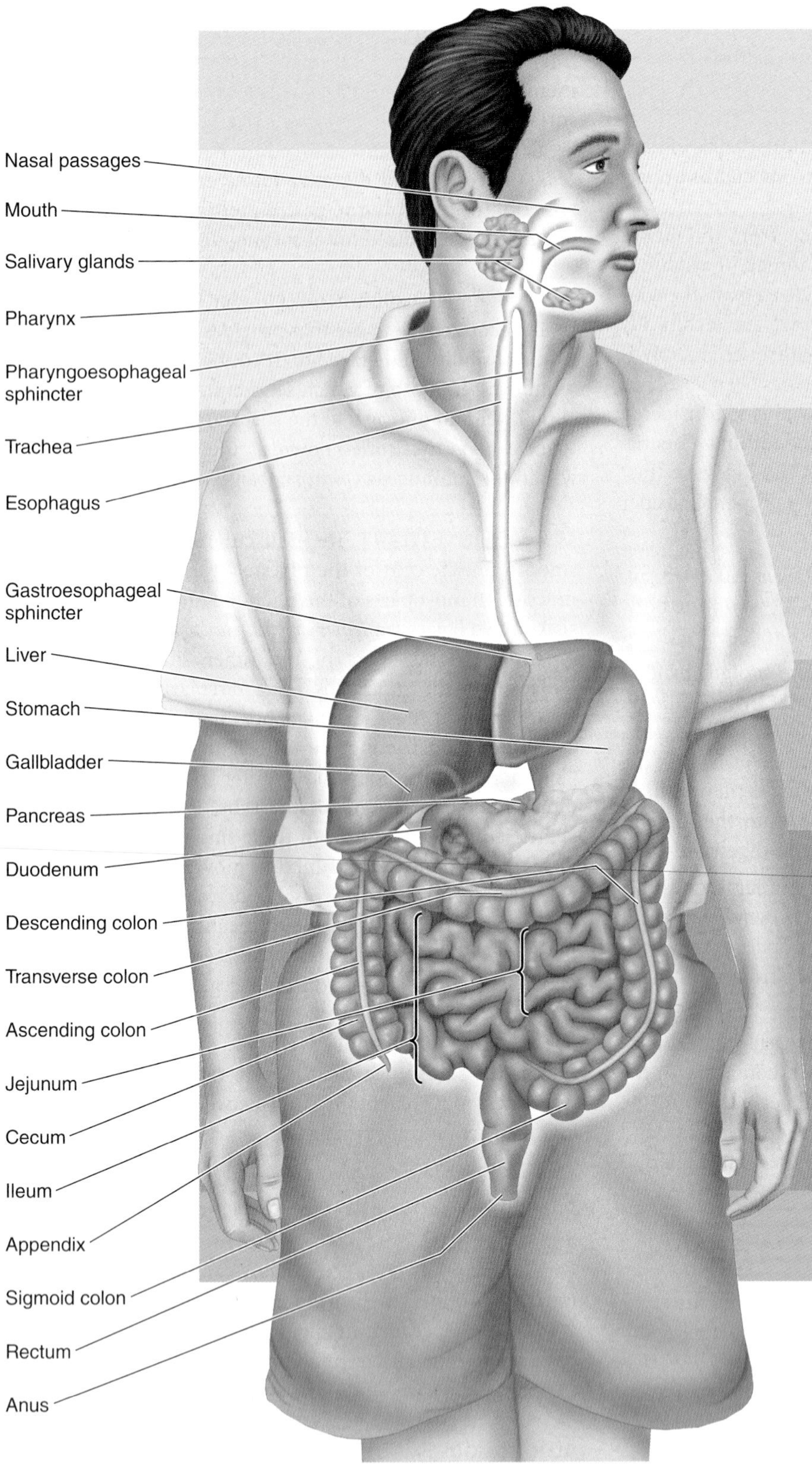
Nasal passages
Mouth
Salivary glands
Pharynx
Pharyngoesophageal sphincter
Trachea
Esophagus
Gastroesophageal sphincter
Liver
Stomach
Gallbladder
Pancreas
Duodenum
Descending colon
Transverse colon
Ascending colon
Jejunum
Cecum
Ileum
Appendix
Sigmoid colon
Rectum
Anus

Digestive Organ	Motility
Mouth and Salivary Glands	Chewing
Pharynx and Esophagus	Swallowing
Stomach	Receptive relaxation; peristalsis
Exocrine Pancreas	Not applicable
Liver	Not applicable
Small Intestine*	Segmentation; migrating motility complex
Large Intestine†	Haustral contractions; mass movements

*The small intestine includes the duodenum, the jejunum, and the ileum.
†The large intestine includes the cecum, appendix, ascending colon, transverse colon, descending colon, sigmoid colon, and rectum.

Secretion	Digestion	Absorption
Saliva • Amylase • Mucus • Lysozyme	Carbohydrate digestion begins.	No foodstuffs; a few medications (e.g., nitroglycerin)
Mucus	None	None
Gastric juice • HCl • Pepsin • Mucus • Intrinsic factor	Carbohydrate digestion continues in the body of the stomach; protein digestion begins in the antrum of the stomach.	No foodstuffs; a few lipid-soluble substances (e.g., alcohol, aspirin)
Pancreatic digestive enzymes • Trypsin, chymotrypsin, carboxypeptidase • Amylase • Lipase Pancreatic aqueous NaHCO$_3$ secretion	These pancreatic enzymes accomplish digestion in the duodenal lumen.	Not applicable
Bile • Bile salts • Alkaline secretion • Bilirubin	Bile does not digest anything, but bile salts facilitate fat digestion and absorption in the duodenal lumen.	Not applicable
Intestinal juice • Mucus • Salt (Small intestine enzymes—disaccharidases and aminopeptidases—are not secreted but function intracellularly in the brush border)	In the lumen, under the influence of pancreatic enzymes and bile, carbohydrate and protein digestion continues and fat digestion is completely accomplished; in the brush border, carbohydrate and protein digestion is completed.	All nutrients, most electrolytes, and water
Mucus	None	Salt and water, converting the contents to feces

digestive tract's **basic electrical rhythm (BER).** The pacemaker cells, which are noncontractile cells known as the **interstitial cells of Cajal,** lie at the boundary between the longitudinal and the circular smooth muscle layers. These pacemaker cells are connected with surrounding smooth muscle cells by gap junctions through which charge-carrying ions can flow (see p. 53). Thus, once electrical activity is initiated by a pacemaker cell it spreads to the adjacent contractile cells. Slow waves are not action potentials and do not directly induce muscle contraction; they are rhythmic, wavelike fluctuations in membrane potential that cyclically bring the membrane closer to or further from threshold potential. If these waves reach threshold at the peaks of depolarization, a volley of action potentials is triggered at each peak, resulting in rhythmic cycles of muscle contraction.

Like cardiac muscle, sheets of digestive smooth muscle cells are connected by gap junctions so that the whole muscle sheet behaves like a functional syncytium, becoming excited and contracting as a unit when threshold is reached (see p. 236). If threshold is not achieved, the oscillating slow-wave electrical activity continues to sweep across the muscle sheet without being accompanied by contractile activity.

Whether threshold is reached depends on the effect of various mechanical, neural, and hormonal factors that influence the starting point around which the slow-wave rhythm oscillates. If the starting point is nearer the threshold level, as it is when food is present in the digestive tract, the depolarizing slow-wave peak reaches threshold, so action potential frequency and its accompanying contractile activity increase. Conversely, if the starting point is further from threshold, as when no food is present, there is less likelihood of reaching threshold, so action potential frequency and contractile activity are reduced.

Self-induced rhythmic digestive contractile activities include *peristalsis* in the stomach, *segmentation* in the small intestine, and *haustral contractions* in the large intestine. Specific details about these rhythmic contractions are discussed when we examine the organs involved.

INTRINSIC NERVE PLEXUSES The **intrinsic nerve plexuses** are the two major networks of nerve fibers—the **submucosal plexus** and the **myenteric plexus**—that lie entirely within the digestive tract wall and run its entire length. Thus, unlike any other body system, the digestive tract has its own intramural ("within-wall") nervous system, which contains as many neurons as the spinal cord (about 100 million neurons) and endows the tract with a considerable degree of self-regulation. Together, these two plexuses are often termed the **enteric nervous system** (see p. 116).

The intrinsic plexuses influence all facets of digestive tract activity. Various types of neurons are present in the intrinsic plexuses. Some are sensory neurons, which have receptors that respond to specific local stimuli in the digestive tract, such as the presence of ingested protein. Other local neurons innervate the smooth muscle cells and exocrine and endocrine cells of the digestive tract to directly affect digestive tract motility, secretion of digestive juices, and secretion of gastrointestinal hormones. As with the central nervous system, these input and output neurons of the enteric nervous system are linked by interneurons. Some of the output neurons are excitatory, and some are inhibitory. These

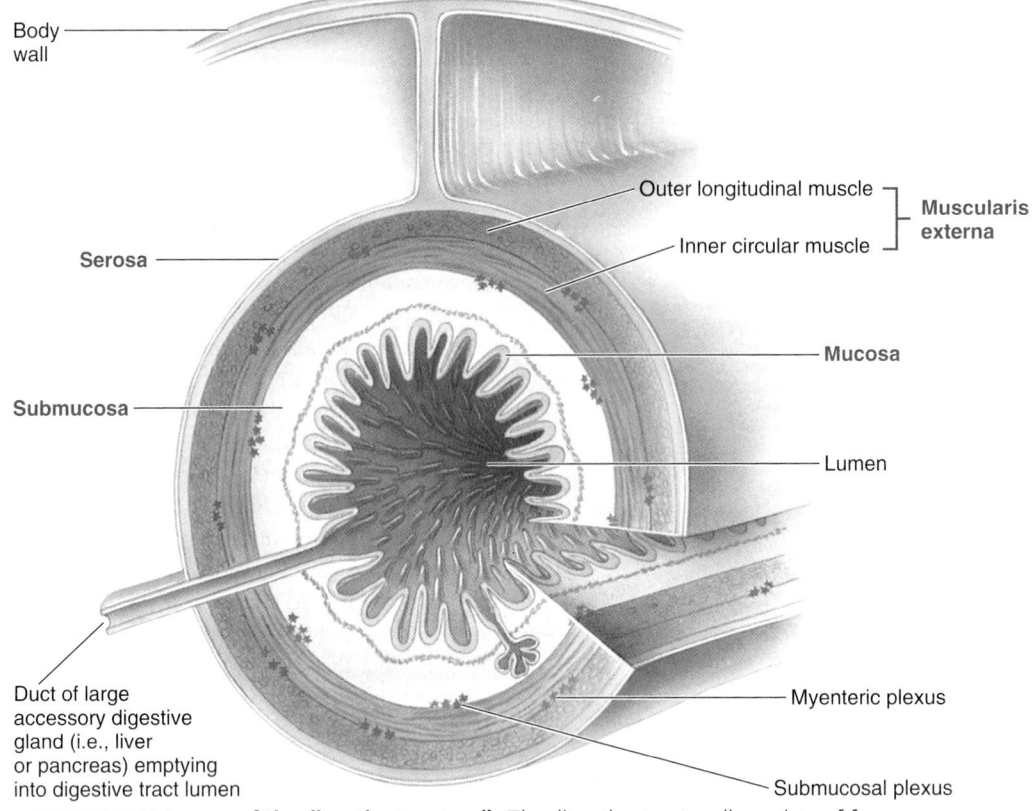

Body wall

Outer longitudinal muscle ⎤ **Muscularis externa** ⎦

Inner circular muscle

Serosa

Mucosa

Submucosa

Lumen

Duct of large accessory digestive gland (i.e., liver or pancreas) emptying into digestive tract lumen

Myenteric plexus

Submucosal plexus

● FIGURE 15-2 **Layers of the digestive tract wall.** The digestive tract wall consists of four major layers: from the innermost outward, they are the mucosa, submucosa, muscularis externa, and serosa.

intrinsic nerve networks primarily coordinate local activity within the digestive tract. To illustrate, if a large piece of food gets stuck in the esophagus, the intrinsic plexuses coordinate local responses to push the food forward. Adding to the complexity of control and accomplishing extensive coordination throughout the digestive tract, intrinsic nerve activity can be influenced by a vast array of endocrine, paracrine, and extrinsic nerve signals.

EXTRINSIC NERVES The **extrinsic nerves** are the nerve fibers from both branches of the autonomic nervous system that originate outside the digestive tract and innervate the various digestive organs. The autonomic nerves influence digestive tract motility and secretion either by modifying ongoing activity in the intrinsic plexuses, altering the level of gastrointestinal hormone secretion, or, in some instances, by acting directly on the smooth muscle and glands.

Recall that, in general, the sympathetic and parasympathetic nerves supplying any given tissue exert opposing actions on that tissue. The sympathetic system, which dominates in "fight-or-flight" situations, tends to inhibit or slow digestive tract contraction and secretion. This action is appropriate, considering that digestive processes are not of highest priority when the body faces an emergency. The parasympathetic nervous system, by contrast, dominates in quiet, "rest-and-digest" situations, when maintenance types of activities such as digestion can proceed optimally. Accordingly, the parasympathetic nerve fibers supplying the digestive tract, which arrive primarily by way of the vagus

nerve (see p. 138), tend to increase smooth muscle motility and promote secretion of digestive enzymes and hormones.

In addition to being called into play during generalized sympathetic or parasympathetic discharge, the autonomic nerves, especially the vagus nerve, can be discretely activated to modify only digestive activity. One of the major purposes of specific activation of extrinsic innervation is to coordinate activity among different regions of the digestive system. For example, the act of chewing food reflexly increases not only salivary secretion but also stomach, pancreatic, and liver secretion via vagal reflexes in anticipation of the arrival of food.

GASTROINTESTINAL HORMONES Tucked within the mucosa of certain regions of the digestive tract are endocrine gland cells that, on appropriate stimulation, release hormones into the blood. These **gastrointestinal hormones** are carried through the blood to other areas of the digestive tract, where they exert either excitatory or inhibitory influences on smooth muscle and exocrine gland cells.

Receptor activation alters digestive activity through neural reflexes and hormonal pathways.

The digestive tract wall contains three types of sensory receptors that respond to local changes in the digestive tract: (1) *chemoreceptors* sensitive to chemical components within the lumen, (2) *mechanoreceptors* (pressure receptors) sensitive to stretch or tension within the wall, and (3) *osmoreceptors* sensitive to the osmolarity of the luminal contents.

Stimulation of these receptors elicits neural reflexes or secretion of hormones, both of which alter the level of activity in the digestive system's effector cells. These effector cells include smooth muscle cells (for modifying motility), exocrine gland cells (for controlling secretion of digestive juices), and endocrine gland cells (for varying secretion of gastrointestinal hormones (● Figure 15-3).

From this overview, you can see that regulation of gastrointestinal function is complex, being influenced by many synergistic, interrelated pathways designed to ensure that the appropriate responses occur to digest and absorb the ingested food. Nowhere else in the body is so much overlapping control exercised.

We are now going to take a "tour" of the digestive tract, beginning with the mouth and ending with the anus. We examine the four basic digestive processes of motility, secretion, digestion, and absorption at each digestive organ along the way. Again, ▲ Table 15-1 summarizes these activities and serves as a useful reference throughout the rest of the chapter.

Mouth

The oral cavity is the entrance to the digestive tract.
Entry to the digestive tract is through the **mouth** or **oral cavity.** The opening is formed by the muscular **lips,** which help procure, guide, and contain the food in the mouth. The lips also have nondigestive functions; they are important in speech (articulation of many sounds depends on a particular lip formation) and as a sensory receptor in interpersonal relationships (for example, as in kissing).

The **palate,** which forms the arched roof of the oral cavity, separates the mouth from the nasal passages. Its presence allows breathing and chewing or sucking to take place simultaneously. Hanging from the palate in the rear of the throat is a dangling projection, the **uvula,** which plays an important role in sealing off the nasal passages during swallowing. (The uvula is the structure you elevate when you say "ahhh" so that the physician can better see your throat.)

The **tongue,** which forms the floor of the oral cavity, is composed of voluntarily controlled skeletal muscle. Movements of the tongue are important in guiding food within the mouth during chewing and swallowing, and they play an important role in speech. Furthermore, the major **taste buds** are located on the tongue (see p. 181).

The **pharynx** is the cavity at the rear of the throat. It acts as a common passageway for both the digestive system (by serving as the link between the mouth and the esophagus, for food) and the respiratory system (by providing access between the nasal passages and the trachea, for air). This arrangement necessitates mechanisms (to be described shortly) to guide food and air into the proper passageways beyond the pharynx. Housed within the side walls of the pharynx are the **tonsils,** lymphoid tissues that are part of the body's defense team (see p. 331).

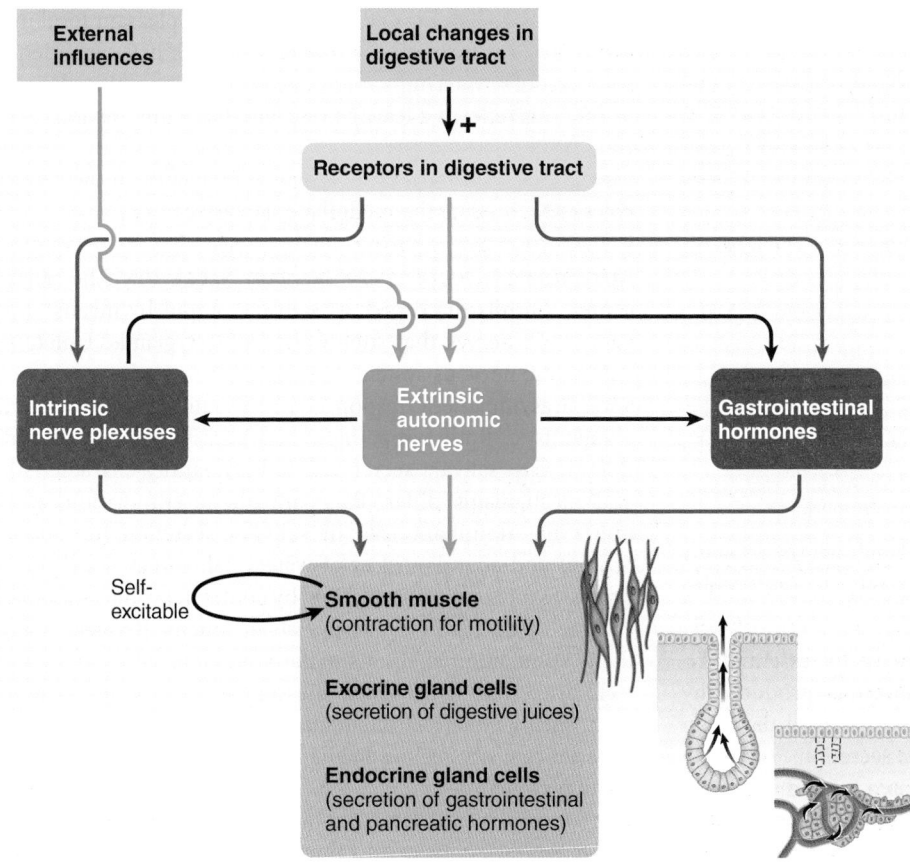

● **FIGURE 15-3 Summary of pathways controlling digestive system activities.**

The teeth are responsible for chewing.
The first step in the digestive process is **mastication,** or **chewing,** the motility of the mouth that involves the slicing, tearing, grinding, and mixing of ingested food by the **teeth.** The teeth are firmly embedded in and protrude from the jawbones. The exposed part of a tooth is covered by **enamel,** the hardest structure of the body. Enamel forms before the tooth's eruption by special cells that are lost as the tooth erupts.

Clinical Note Because enamel cannot be regenerated after the tooth has erupted, any defects (**dental caries,** or "cavities") that develop in the enamel must be patched by artificial fillings, or else the surface will continue to erode into the underlying living pulp.

The functions of chewing are (1) to grind and break food into smaller pieces to facilitate swallowing and to increase the food surface area on which salivary enzymes will act, (2) to mix food with saliva, and (3) to stimulate the taste buds. The third function not only gives rise to the pleasurable subjective sensation of taste but also reflexly increases salivary, gastric, pancreatic, and bile secretion to prepare for the arrival of food.

Saliva begins carbohydrate digestion, is important in oral hygiene, and facilitates speech.

Saliva, the secretion associated with the mouth, is produced largely by three major pairs of salivary glands that lie outside the oral cavity and discharge saliva through short ducts into the mouth.

Saliva is about 99.5% H_2O and 0.5% electrolytes and protein. The salivary salt (NaCl) concentration is only one seventh of that in the plasma, which is important in perceiving salty tastes. Similarly, discrimination of sweet tastes is enhanced by the absence of glucose in the saliva. The most important salivary proteins are *amylase, mucus,* and *lysozyme.* They contribute to the functions of saliva, which are as follows:

1. Saliva begins digestion of carbohydrate in the mouth through action of **salivary amylase,** an enzyme that breaks polysaccharides down into **maltose,** a disaccharide consisting of two glucose molecules (see ● Figure 15-1).

2. Saliva facilitates swallowing by moistening food particles, thereby holding them together, and by providing lubrication through the presence of **mucus,** which is thick and slippery.

3. Saliva exerts some antibacterial action by a twofold effect— first by **lysozyme,** an enzyme that lyses, or destroys, certain bacteria by breaking down their cell walls, and second by rinsing away material that may be a food source for bacteria.

4. Saliva serves as a solvent for molecules that stimulate the taste buds. Only molecules in solution can react with taste bud receptors. You can demonstrate this for yourself: Dry your tongue and then drop some sugar on it—you cannot taste the sugar until it is moistened.

5. Saliva aids speech by facilitating movements of the lips and tongue. It is difficult to talk when your mouth feels dry.

6. Saliva plays an important role in oral hygiene by helping keep the mouth and teeth clean. The constant flow of saliva helps flush away food residues, foreign particles, and old epithelial cells that have shed from the oral mucosa. Saliva's contribution in this regard is apparent to anyone who has experienced a foul taste in the mouth when salivation is suppressed for a while, such as during a fever or states of prolonged anxiety.

7. Saliva is rich in bicarbonate buffers, which neutralize acids in food, as well as acids produced by bacteria in the mouth, thereby helping prevent dental caries.

Despite these many functions, saliva is not essential for digesting and absorbing foods, because enzymes produced by the pancreas and small intestine can complete food digestion even in the absence of salivary and gastric secretion.

 The main problems associated with diminished salivary secretion, a condition known as **xerostomia,** are difficulty in chewing and swallowing, inarticulate speech unless frequent sips of water are taken when talking, and a rampant increase in dental caries unless special precautions are taken.

Salivary secretion is continuous and can be reflexly increased.

On average, about 1 to 2 liters of saliva are secreted per day, ranging from a continuous spontaneous basal rate of 0.5 ml/min to a maximum flow rate of about 5 ml/min in response to a potent stimulus such as sucking on a lemon. The continuous basal secretion of saliva in the absence of apparent stimuli is brought about by constant low-level stimulation by the parasympathetic nerve endings that terminate in the salivary glands. This basal secretion is important in keeping the mouth and throat moist at all times. In addition to this continuous, low-level secretion, salivary secretion may be increased by two types of salivary reflexes, simple and conditioned (● Figure 15-4).

SIMPLE AND CONDITIONED SALIVARY REFLEXES The **simple salivary reflex** occurs when chemoreceptors and pressure receptors within the oral cavity respond to the presence of food. On activation, these receptors initiate impulses in afferent nerve fibers that carry the information to the **salivary center,** which is located in the medulla of the brain stem, as are all the brain centers that control digestive activities. The salivary center, in turn, sends impulses via the extrinsic autonomic nerves to the salivary glands to promote increased salivation.

With the **conditioned,** or **acquired, salivary reflex,** salivation occurs without oral stimulation. Just thinking about, seeing, smelling, or hearing the preparation of pleasant food initiates salivation through this reflex. All of us have experienced such "mouth watering" in anticipation of something delicious to eat. This reflex is a learned response based on previous experience. Inputs that arise outside the mouth and are mentally associated with the pleasure of eating, act through the cerebral cortex to stimulate the medullary salivary center.

AUTONOMIC INFLUENCE ON SALIVARY SECRETION The salivary center controls the degree of salivary output by means of the autonomic nerves that supply the salivary glands. Unlike the autonomic nervous system elsewhere in the body, sympathetic and parasympathetic responses in the salivary glands are not antagonistic. Both sympathetic and parasympathetic stimulation increase salivary secretion, but the quantity, characteristics, and mechanisms differ. Parasympathetic stimulation, which exerts the dominant role in salivary secretion, produces a prompt and abundant flow of watery saliva that is rich in enzymes. Sympathetic stimulation, by contrast, produces a smaller volume of thick saliva that is rich in mucus. Because sympathetic stimulation elicits a smaller volume of saliva, the mouth feels drier than usual when the sympathetic system is dominant, such as in stressful situations. For example, people often experience a dry feeling in the mouth when they are nervous about giving a speech.

Salivary secretion is the only digestive secretion entirely under neural control. All other digestive secretions are regulated by both nervous system reflexes and hormones.

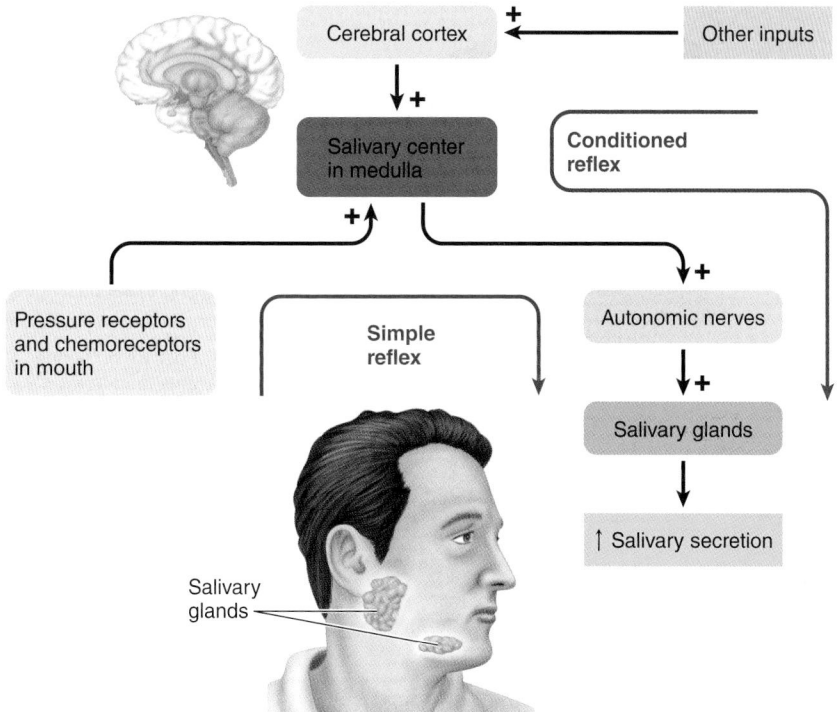

● **FIGURE 15-4 Control of salivary secretion.**

Digestion in the mouth is minimal; no absorption of nutrients occurs.

Digestion in the mouth involves the hydrolysis of polysaccharides into disaccharides by amylase. However, most digestion by this enzyme is accomplished in the body of the stomach after the food mass and saliva have been swallowed. Acid inactivates amylase, but in the center of the food mass, where stomach acid has not yet reached, this salivary enzyme continues to function for several more hours.

No absorption of foodstuff occurs from the mouth. Importantly, some drugs can be absorbed by the oral mucosa, a prime example being *nitroglycerin,* a vasodilator drug sometimes used by cardiac patients to relieve anginal attacks (see p. 270) associated with myocardial ischemia (see p. 259).

Pharynx and Esophagus

The motility associated with the pharynx and esophagus is **swallowing.** Most of us think of swallowing as the limited act of moving food out of the mouth into the esophagus. However, swallowing actually is the entire process of moving food from the mouth through the esophagus into the stomach.

Swallowing is a sequentially programmed all-or-none reflex.

Swallowing is initiated when a **bolus,** or ball of chewed or liquid food, is voluntarily forced by the tongue to the rear of the mouth and into the pharynx. The pressure of the bolus stimulates pharyngeal pressure receptors, which send afferent impulses to the **swallowing center** located in the medulla of the brain stem. The swallowing center then reflexly activates in the appropriate se-

quence the muscles involved in swallowing. Swallowing is the most complex reflex in the body. Multiple highly coordinated responses are triggered in a specific all-or-none pattern over a period of time to accomplish the act of swallowing. Swallowing is initiated voluntarily, but once begun it cannot be stopped. Perhaps you have experienced this when a large piece of hard candy inadvertently slipped to the rear of your throat, triggering an unintentional swallow.

Next we describe the two stages of swallowing: the *oropharyngeal stage* and the *esophageal stage.*

During the oropharyngeal stage of swallowing, food is prevented from entering the wrong passageways.

The **oropharyngeal stage** lasts about 1 second and consists of moving the bolus from the mouth through the pharynx and into the esophagus. When the bolus enters the pharynx, it must be directed into the esophagus and prevented from entering the other openings that communicate with the pharynx. In other words, food must be kept from reentering the mouth and from entering the nasal passages and trachea. All of this is managed by the following coordinated activities (● Figure 15-5):

■ The position of the tongue against the hard palate keeps food from reentering the mouth during swallowing.

■ The uvula is elevated and lodges against the back of the throat, sealing off the nasal passage from the pharynx so that food does not enter the nose.

■ Food is prevented from entering the trachea primarily by elevation of the larynx and tight closure of the vocal folds across the laryngeal opening, or **glottis.** The first part of the trachea is the *larynx,* or *voice box,* across which the *vocal folds* are stretched. During swallowing, the vocal folds serve a purpose unrelated to speech. Contraction of laryngeal muscles aligns the vocal folds in tight apposition to each other, thus sealing the glottis entrance (see ● Figure 12-3, p. 369). Also, the bolus tilts a small flap of cartilaginous tissue, the **epiglottis** (*epi* means "upon"), backward down over the closed glottis as further protection from food entering the respiratory airways.

■ The person does not attempt futile respiratory efforts when the respiratory passages are temporarily sealed off during swallowing, because the swallowing center briefly inhibits the nearby respiratory center.

■ With the larynx and trachea sealed off, pharyngeal muscles contract to force the bolus into the esophagus.

The pharyngoesophageal sphincter keeps air from entering the digestive tract during breathing.

The esophagus is a fairly straight muscular tube that extends between the pharynx and the stomach (see ▲ Table 15-1, p. 468). Lying mostly in the thoracic cavity, it penetrates the

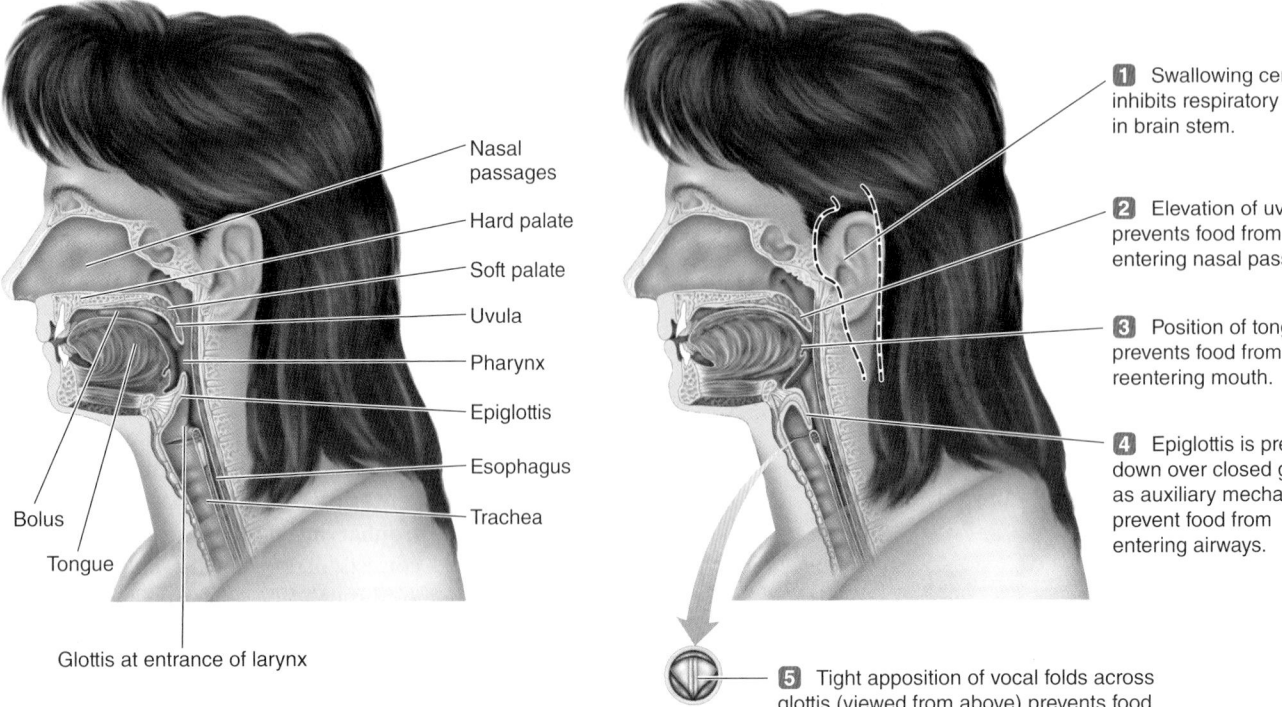

Nasal passages
Hard palate
Soft palate
Uvula
Pharynx
Epiglottis
Esophagus
Trachea

Bolus
Tongue

Glottis at entrance of larynx

1. Swallowing center inhibits respiratory center in brain stem.

2. Elevation of uvula prevents food from entering nasal passages.

3. Position of tongue prevents food from reentering mouth.

4. Epiglottis is pressed down over closed glottis as auxiliary mechanism to prevent food from entering airways.

5. Tight apposition of vocal folds across glottis (viewed from above) prevents food from entering respiratory airways.

(a) Position of the oropharyngeal structures at rest

(b) Changes during the oropharyngeal stage of swallowing to prevent food from entering the wrong passageways

● **FIGURE 15-5 Oropharyngeal stage of swallowing.**

diaphragm and joins the stomach in the abdominal cavity a few centimeters below the diaphragm.

The esophagus is guarded at both ends by sphincters. A sphincter is a ringlike muscular structure that, when closed, prevents passage through the tube it guards. The upper esophageal sphincter is the *pharyngoesophageal sphincter,* and the lower esophageal sphincter is the *gastroesophageal sphincter.* We first discuss the role of the pharyngoesophageal sphincter, then the process of esophageal transit of food, and finally the importance of the gastroesophageal sphincter.

Except during a swallow, the **pharyngoesophageal sphincter** keeps the entrance to the esophagus closed to prevent large volumes of air from entering the esophagus and stomach during breathing. Instead, air is directed only into the respiratory airways. Otherwise, the digestive tract would be subjected to large volumes of gas, which would lead to excessive burping. During swallowing, this sphincter opens and allows the bolus to pass into the esophagus. Once the bolus has entered the esophagus, the pharyngoesophageal sphincter closes, the respiratory airways are opened, and breathing resumes. The oropharyngeal stage is complete, and about 1 second has passed since the swallow was first initiated.

Peristaltic waves push food through the esophagus.

The **esophageal stage** of the swallow now begins. The swallowing center triggers a **primary peristaltic wave** that sweeps from the beginning to the end of the esophagus, forcing the bolus

ahead of it through the esophagus to the stomach. The term **peristalsis** refers to ringlike contractions of the circular smooth muscle that move progressively forward, pushing the bolus into a relaxed area ahead of the contraction (● Figure 15-6). The peristaltic wave takes about 5 to 9 seconds to reach the lower end of the esophagus.

If a large or sticky swallowed bolus, such as a bite of peanut butter sandwich, fails to be carried along to the stomach by the primary peristaltic wave, the lodged bolus distends the esophagus, stimulating pressure receptors within its walls. As a result, a second, more forceful peristaltic wave is initiated, mediated by the intrinsic nerve plexuses at the level of the distension. These **secondary peristaltic waves** do not involve the swallowing center, nor is the person aware of their occurrence. Distension of the esophagus also reflexly increases salivary secretion. The trapped bolus is eventually dislodged and moved forward through the combination of lubrication by the extra swallowed saliva and the forceful secondary peristaltic waves.

The gastroesophageal sphincter prevents reflux of gastric contents.

Except during swallowing, the **gastroesophageal sphincter** stays contracted to keep a barrier between the stomach and the esophagus, reducing the chance of reflux of acidic gastric contents into the esophagus. If gastric contents do flow backward despite the sphincter, the acidity of these contents irritates the

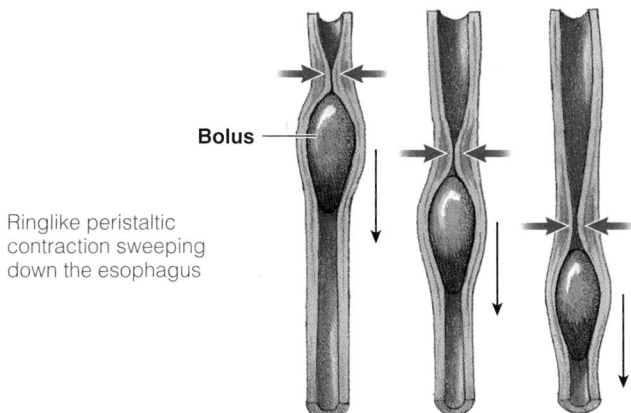

● **FIGURE 15-6 Peristalsis in the esophagus.** As the wave of peristaltic contraction sweeps down the esophagus, it pushes the bolus into the relaxed area ahead of it, propelling the bolus toward the stomach.

esophagus, causing the esophageal discomfort known as **heartburn.** (The heart itself is not involved.)

As the peristaltic wave sweeps down the esophagus, the gastroesophageal sphincter relaxes so that the bolus can pass into the stomach. After the bolus has entered the stomach, the swallow is complete and this lower esophageal sphincter again contracts.

Esophageal secretion is entirely protective.

Esophageal secretion is entirely mucus. In fact, mucus is secreted throughout the length of the digestive tract by mucus-secreting gland cells in the mucosa. By lubricating the passage of food, esophageal mucus lessens the likelihood that the esophagus will be damaged by any sharp edges in the newly entering food. Furthermore, it protects the esophageal wall from acid and enzymes in gastric juice if gastric reflux occurs.

The entire transit time in the pharynx and esophagus averages a mere 6 to 10 seconds, too short a time for any digestion or absorption in this region. We now move on to our next stop, the stomach.

Stomach

The **stomach** is a J-shaped saclike chamber lying between the esophagus and the small intestine. It is divided into three sections based on structural and functional distinctions (● Figure 15-7). The **fundus** is the part of the stomach that lies above the esophageal opening. The middle or main part of the stomach is the **body.** The smooth muscle layers in the fundus and body are relatively thin, but the lower part of the stomach, the **antrum,** has heavier musculature. This difference in muscle thickness plays an important role in gastric motility in these two regions, as you will see shortly. There are also glandular differences in the mucosa of these regions, as described later. The end part of the stomach is the **pyloric sphincter,** which acts as a barrier between the stomach and the upper part of the small intestine, the duodenum.

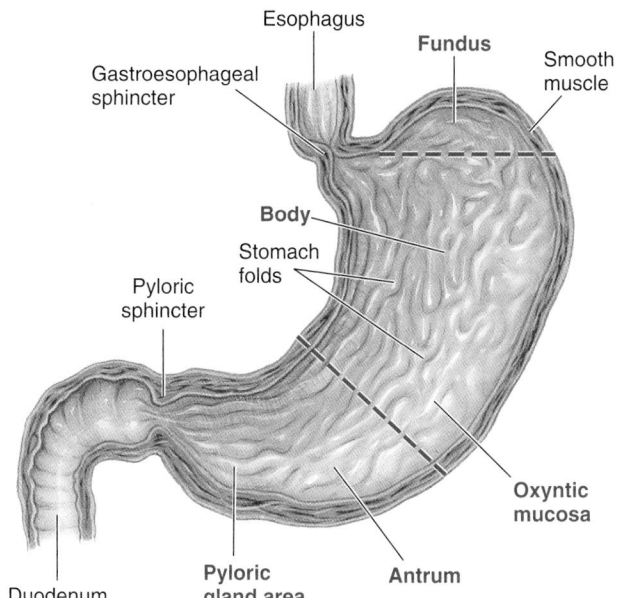

● **FIGURE 15-7 Anatomy of the stomach.** The stomach is divided into three sections based on structural and functional distinctions—the fundus, body, and antrum. The mucosal lining of the stomach is divided into the oxyntic mucosa and the pyloric gland area based on differences in glandular secretion.

The stomach stores food and begins protein digestion.

The stomach performs three main functions:

1. The stomach's most important function is to store ingested food until it can be emptied into the small intestine at a rate appropriate for optimal digestion and absorption. It takes hours to digest and absorb a meal that was consumed in only a matter of minutes. Because the small intestine is the primary site for this digestion and absorption, it is important that the stomach store the food and meter it into the duodenum at a rate that does not exceed the small intestine's capacities.

2. The stomach secretes hydrochloric acid (HCl) and enzymes that begin protein digestion.

3. Through the stomach's mixing movements, the ingested food is pulverized and mixed with gastric secretions to produce a thick liquid mixture known as **chyme.** The stomach contents must be converted to chyme before they can be emptied into the duodenum.

Next we discuss how the stomach accomplishes these functions as we examine the four basic digestive processes—motility, secretion, digestion, and absorption—as they relate to the stomach. Starting with motility, gastric motility is complex and subject to multiple regulatory inputs.

The four aspects of gastric motility are (1) filling, (2) storage, (3) mixing, and (4) emptying. We begin with gastric filling.

Gastric filling involves receptive relaxation.

When empty, the stomach has a volume of about 50 ml, but it can expand to a capacity of about 1 liter (1000 ml) during a meal. The stomach can accommodate such a 20-fold change in volume with little change in tension in its walls and little rise in intragastric pressure through the following mechanism: The interior of the stomach is thrown into deep folds. During a meal, the folds get smaller and nearly flatten out as the stomach relaxes slightly with each mouthful, much like the gradual expansion of a collapsed ice bag as it is being filled. This reflex relaxation of the stomach as it is receiving food is called **receptive relaxation;** it allows the stomach to accommodate the meal with little rise in pressure. If more than a liter of food is consumed, however, the stomach becomes overdistended and the person experiences discomfort. Receptive relaxation is triggered by the act of eating and is mediated by the vagus nerve.

Gastric storage takes place in the body of the stomach.

A group of pacemaker cells located in the upper fundus region of the stomach generate slow-wave potentials that sweep down the length of the stomach toward the pyloric sphincter at a rate of three per minute. This rhythmic pattern of spontaneous depolarizations—the basic electrical rhythm, or BER, of the stomach—occurs continuously and may or may not be accompanied by contraction of the stomach's circular smooth muscle layer. Depending on the level of excitability in the smooth muscle, it may be brought to threshold by this flow of current and undergo action potentials, which in turn initiate peristaltic waves that sweep over the stomach in pace with the BER at a rate of three per minute.

Once initiated, the peristaltic wave spreads over the fundus and body to the antrum and pyloric sphincter. Because the muscle layers are thin in the fundus and body, the peristaltic contractions in this region are weak. When the waves reach the antrum, they become stronger and more vigorous, because the muscle there is thicker.

Because only feeble mixing movements occur in the body and fundus, food delivered to the stomach from the esophagus is stored in the relatively quiet body without being mixed. The fundic area usually does not store food but contains only a pocket of gas. Food is gradually fed from the body into the antrum, where mixing does take place.

Gastric mixing takes place in the antrum of the stomach.

The strong antral peristaltic contractions mix the food with gastric secretions to produce chyme. Each antral peristaltic wave propels chyme forward toward the pyloric sphincter (● Figure 15-8). Tonic contraction (see p. 238) of the pyloric sphincter normally keeps it almost, but not completely, closed. The opening is large enough for water and other fluids to pass through with ease but too small for the thicker chyme to pass through except when a strong antral peristaltic contraction pushes it through. Even then, of the 30 ml of chyme that the antrum can hold, usually only a few milliliters of antral contents are pushed into the duodenum with each peristaltic wave. Before more chyme can be squeezed out, the peristaltic wave reaches the pyloric sphincter and causes it to contract more forcefully, sealing off the exit and blocking further passage into the duodenum. The bulk of the antral chyme that was being propelled forward but failed to be pushed into the duodenum is abruptly halted at the closed sphincter and is tumbled back into the antrum, only to be propelled forward and tumbled back again as the new peristaltic wave advances. This tossing back and forth thoroughly mixes the chyme in the antrum.

Gastric emptying is controlled by factors in the duodenum.

In addition to mixing gastric contents, the antral peristaltic contractions are the driving force for gastric emptying (● Figure 15-8). The amount of chyme that escapes into the duodenum with each peristaltic wave before the pyloric sphincter tightly closes depends largely on the strength of antral peristalsis. The intensity of antral peristalsis can vary markedly under the influence of various signals from the duodenum.

The duodenum must be ready to receive the chyme and can delay gastric emptying by reducing the strength of antral peristalsis until the duodenum is ready to accommodate more chyme. The four most important duodenal factors that influence gastric emptying are *fat, acid, hypertonicity,* and *distension.* The presence of one or more of these stimuli in the duodenum activates appropriate duodenal receptors, triggering either a neural or a hormonal response that puts brakes on antral peristaltic activity, thereby slowing the rate of gastric emptying:

■ The *neural response* is mediated through both the intrinsic nerve plexuses and the autonomic nerves. Collectively, these reflexes are called the **enterogastric reflex.**

■ The *hormonal response* involves the release from the small-intestine mucosa of several hormones collectively known as **enterogastrones.** The blood carries these hormones to the stomach, where they inhibit antral contractions to reduce gastric emptying. The two most important enterogastrones are **secretin** and **cholecystokinin (CCK).** Secretin was the first hormone discovered (in 1902). Because it was a secretory product that entered the blood, it was termed *secretin.* The name *cholecystokinin* derives from this same hormone also causing contraction of the bile-containing gallbladder (*chole* means "bile"; *cysto* means "bladder"; and *kinin* means "contraction"). Secretin and CCK are major gastrointestinal hormones that perform other important functions, in addition to serving as enterogastrones.

Let us examine why it is important that each of these stimuli in the duodenum (fat, acid, hypertonicity, and distension) delays gastric emptying:

■ *Fat.* Fat is digested and absorbed more slowly than the other nutrients. Furthermore, fat digestion and absorption take place only within the lumen of the small intestine. Therefore, when fat is already in the duodenum, further gastric emptying of more fatty stomach contents into the duodenum is prevented until the small intestine has processed the fat already there. Fat is the most potent stimulus for inhibition of gastric motility. This is evident when you compare the rate of emptying of a high-fat meal (after 6 hours, some of a bacon-and-eggs meal may still be in the stomach) with that of a protein and carbohydrate meal (a meal of lean meat and potatoes may empty in 3 hours).

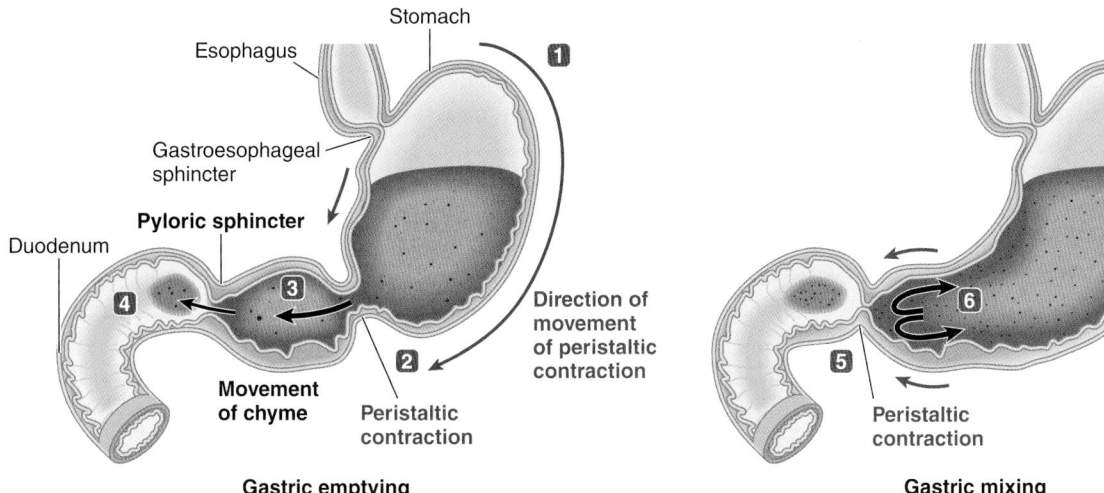

Gastric emptying

1 A peristaltic contraction originates in the upper fundus and sweeps down toward the pyloric sphincter.

2 The contraction becomes more vigorous as it reaches the thick-muscled antrum.

3 The strong antral peristaltic contraction propels the chyme forward.

4 A small portion of chyme is pushed through the partially open sphincter into the duodenum. The stronger the antral contraction, the more chyme is emptied with each contractile wave.

Gastric mixing

5 When the peristaltic contraction reaches the pyloric sphincter, the sphincter is tightly closed and no further emptying takes place.

6 When chyme that was being propelled forward hits the closed sphincter, it is tossed back into the antrum. Mixing of chyme is accomplished as chyme is propelled forward and tossed back into the antrum with each peristaltic contraction.

● **FIGURE 15-8 Gastric emptying and mixing as a result of antral peristaltic contractions.**

■ *Acid.* Because the stomach secretes HCl, highly acidic chyme is emptied into the duodenum, where it is neutralized by sodium bicarbonate ($NaHCO_3$) secreted into the duodenal lumen primarily from the pancreas. Unneutralized acid irritates the duodenal mucosa and inactivates the pancreatic digestive enzymes that are secreted into the duodenal lumen. Appropriately, therefore, unneutralized acid in the duodenum inhibits further emptying of acidic gastric contents until complete neutralization can be accomplished.

■ *Hypertonicity.* As molecules of protein and starch are digested in the duodenal lumen, large numbers of amino acid and glucose molecules are released. If absorption of these amino acid and glucose molecules does not keep pace with the rate at which protein and carbohydrate digestion proceeds, these large numbers of molecules remain in the chyme and increase the osmolarity of the duodenal contents. Osmolarity depends on the number of molecules present, not on their size, and one protein molecule may be split into several hundred amino acid molecules, each of which has the same osmotic activity as the original protein molecule. The same holds true for one large starch molecule, which yields many smaller but equally osmotically active glucose molecules. Because water is freely diffusible across the duodenal wall, it enters the duodenal lumen from the plasma as the duodenal osmolarity rises. Large volumes of water entering the intestine from the plasma lead to intestinal distension, and more important, circulatory disturbances result because of the reduction in plasma volume. To prevent these effects, gastric emptying is reflexly inhibited when the osmolarity of the duodenal contents starts to rise. Thus, the amount of food entering the duodenum for further digestion into a multitude of additional osmotically active particles is reduced until absorption processes have had an opportunity to catch up.

■ *Distension.* Too much chyme in the duodenum inhibits the emptying of even more gastric contents, giving the distended duodenum time to cope with the excess volume of chyme it already contains before it gets any more.

Emotions can influence gastric motility.

Other factors unrelated to digestion, such as emotions, can alter gastric motility by acting through the autonomic nerves to influence the degree of gastric smooth muscle excitability. Even though the effect of emotions on gastric motility varies from one person to another and is not always predictable, sadness and fear generally tend to decrease motility, whereas anger and aggression tend to increase it. In addition to emotional influences, intense pain from any part of the body tends to inhibit motility, not just in the stomach but throughout the digestive tract. This response is brought about by increased sympathetic activity.

The stomach does not actively participate in vomiting.

Clinical Note

Vomiting, or **emesis,** the forceful expulsion of gastric contents out through the mouth, is not accomplished by reverse peristalsis in the stomach, as might be predicted. Actually, the stomach, the esophagus, and associated sphincters are all relaxed during vomiting. The major force for expulsion comes, surprisingly, from contraction of the respiratory muscles—namely, the diaphragm (the major inspiratory muscle) and the abdominal muscles (the muscles of active expiration) (see ● Figure 12-12, pp. 376 and 377).

The complex act of vomiting is coordinated by a **vomiting center** in the medulla of the brain stem. Vomiting begins with a deep inspiration and closure of the glottis. The contracting diaphragm descends downward on the stomach while simultaneous contraction of the abdominal muscles compresses the abdominal cavity, increasing the intra-abdominal pressure and forcing the abdominal viscera upward. As the flaccid stomach is squeezed between the diaphragm from above and the compressed abdominal cavity from below, the gastric contents are forced upward through the relaxed sphincters and esophagus and out through the mouth. The glottis is closed, so vomited material does not enter the respiratory airways. Also, the uvula is raised to close off the nasal cavity. The vomiting cycle may be repeated several times until the stomach is emptied. Vomiting is usually preceded by profuse salivation, sweating, rapid heart rate, and sensation of nausea, all of which are characteristic of a generalized discharge of the autonomic nervous system.

CAUSES OF VOMITING Vomiting can be initiated by afferent input to the vomiting center from a number of receptors throughout the body. The causes of vomiting include the following:

■ Tactile (touch) stimulation of the back of the throat, which is one of the most potent stimuli. For example, sticking a finger in the back of the throat or even the presence of a tongue depressor or dental instrument in the back of the mouth is enough stimulation to cause gagging and even vomiting in some people.

■ Irritation or distension of the stomach and duodenum.

■ Elevated intracranial pressure, such as that caused by cerebral hemorrhage. Thus, vomiting after a head injury is considered a bad sign; it suggests swelling or bleeding within the cranial cavity.

■ Rotation or acceleration of the head producing dizziness, such as in motion sickness.

■ Chemical agents, including drugs or noxious substances that initiate vomiting (that is, **emetics**) either by acting in the upper parts of the gastrointestinal tract or by stimulating chemoreceptors in a specialized **chemoreceptor trigger zone** next to the vomiting center in the brain. Activation of this zone triggers the vomiting reflex. For example, chemotherapeutic agents used in treating cancer often cause vomiting by acting on the chemoreceptor trigger zone.

■ Psychogenic vomiting induced by emotional factors, including those accompanying nauseating sights and odors and anxiety, as before taking an examination or in other stressful situations.

EFFECTS OF VOMITING With excessive vomiting, the body experiences large losses of secreted fluids and acids that normally would be reabsorbed. The resulting reduction in plasma volume can lead to dehydration and circulatory problems, and the loss

of acid from the stomach can lead to metabolic alkalosis (see p. 460).

We have completed our discussion of gastric motility and now shift to gastric secretion.

Gastric digestive juice is secreted by glands located at the base of gastric pits.

Each day, the stomach secretes about 2 liters of gastric juice. The cells that secrete gastric juice are in the lining of the stomach, the gastric mucosa, which is divided into two distinct areas: (1) the **oxyntic mucosa,** which lines the body and fundus, and (2) the **pyloric gland area (PGA),** which lines the antrum. The luminal surface of the stomach is pitted with deep pockets formed by infoldings of the gastric mucosa. The first parts of these invaginations are called **gastric pits,** at the base of which lie the **gastric glands.** A variety of secretory cells line these invaginations, some exocrine and some endocrine or paracrine (▲ Table 15-2). Let us look at the gastric exocrine secretory cells first.

Three types of gastric exocrine secretory cells are found in the walls of the pits and glands in the oxyntic mucosa.

■ **Mucous cells** line the gastric pits and the entrance of the glands. They secrete a thin, watery *mucus.* (*Mucous* is the adjective; *mucus* is the noun.)

■ The deeper parts of the gastric glands are lined by chief and parietal cells. The more numerous **chief cells** secrete the enzyme precursor *pepsinogen.*

■ The **parietal cells** in the oxyntic mucosa secrete *HCl* and *intrinsic factor* (*oxyntic* means "sharp," a reference to these cells' potent HCl secretory product).

These exocrine secretions are all released into the gastric lumen. Collectively, they make up the gastric digestive juice.

A few **stem cells** are also found in the gastric pits. These cells rapidly divide and are the parent cells of all new cells of the gastric mucosa. The daughter cells that result from cell division either migrate out of the pit to become surface epithelial cells or migrate deeper to the gastric glands, where they differentiate into chief or parietal cells. Through this activity, the entire stomach mucosa is replaced about every 3 days. This frequent turnover is important, because the harsh acidic stomach contents expose the mucosal cells to lots of wear and tear.

Between the gastric pits, the gastric mucosa is covered by **surface epithelial cells,** which secrete a thick, viscous, alkaline mucus that forms a visible layer several millimeters thick over the surface of the mucosa.

The gastric glands of the PGA primarily secrete mucus and a small amount of pepsinogen; no acid is secreted in this area, in contrast to the oxyntic mucosa.

Let us consider these exocrine products and their roles in digestion in further detail.

Hydrochloric acid activates pepsinogen.

The parietal cells actively secrete HCl into the lumen of the gastric pits, which in turn empty into the lumen of the stomach. As a result of this HCl secretion, the pH of the luminal contents falls as low as 2.0. Hydrogen ion (H^+) and chloride ion (Cl^-) are

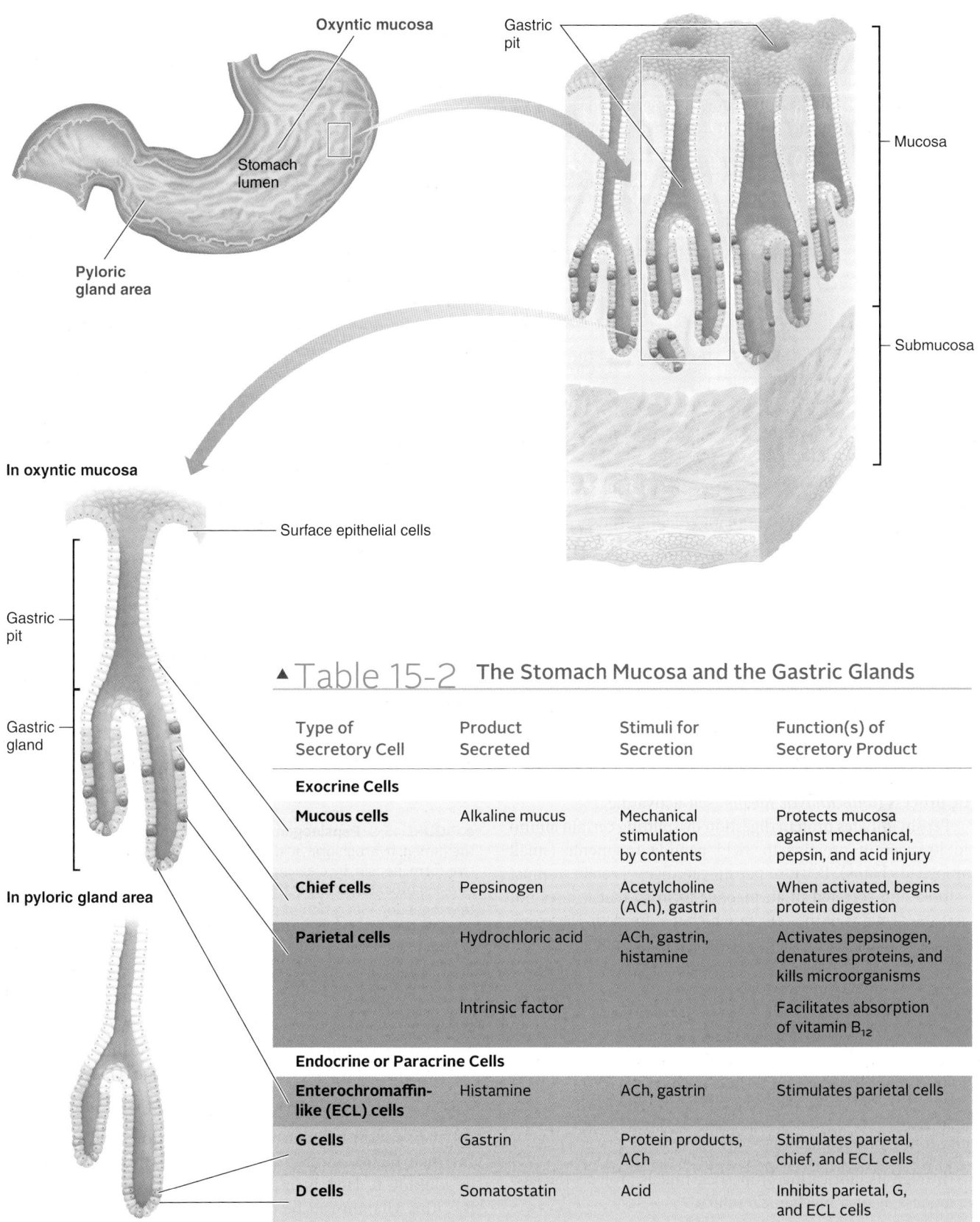

Oxyntic mucosa

Gastric pit

Stomach lumen

Pyloric gland area

Mucosa

Submucosa

In oxyntic mucosa

Surface epithelial cells

Gastric pit

Gastric gland

In pyloric gland area

▲ Table 15-2   The Stomach Mucosa and the Gastric Glands

Type of Secretory Cell	Product Secreted	Stimuli for Secretion	Function(s) of Secretory Product
Exocrine Cells			
Mucous cells	Alkaline mucus	Mechanical stimulation by contents	Protects mucosa against mechanical, pepsin, and acid injury
Chief cells	Pepsinogen	Acetylcholine (ACh), gastrin	When activated, begins protein digestion
Parietal cells	Hydrochloric acid	ACh, gastrin, histamine	Activates pepsinogen, denatures proteins, and kills microorganisms
	Intrinsic factor		Facilitates absorption of vitamin B_{12}
Endocrine or Paracrine Cells			
Enterochromaffin-like (ECL) cells	Histamine	ACh, gastrin	Stimulates parietal cells
G cells	Gastrin	Protein products, ACh	Stimulates parietal, chief, and ECL cells
D cells	Somatostatin	Acid	Inhibits parietal, G, and ECL cells

actively transported by separate pumps in the parietal cells' plasma membrane. Hydrogen ion is actively transported against a tremendous concentration gradient, with the H^+ concentration being as much as 3 million times greater in the lumen than in the blood. Chloride is secreted by a secondary active-transport mechanism against a much smaller concentration gradient of only 1.5 times (see p. 64).

Although HCl does not actually digest anything (that is, it does not break apart nutrient chemical bonds), it performs these specific functions that aid digestion:

1. HCl activates the enzyme precursor pepsinogen to an active enzyme, pepsin, and provides an acid environment optimal for pepsin action.

2. It denatures protein; that is, it uncoils proteins from their highly folded final form, thus exposing more of the peptide bonds for enzymatic attack (see p. A-16).

3. Along with salivary lysozyme, HCl kills most of the microorganisms ingested with food, although some escape and then grow and multiply in the large intestine.

Pepsinogen is activated to pepsin, which initiates protein digestion.

The major digestive constituent of gastric secretion is **pepsinogen,** an inactive enzymatic molecule produced by the chief cells. Pepsinogen, once activated, begins protein digestion. It is stored in the chief cells' cytoplasm within secretory vesicles, from which it is released by exocytosis on appropriate stimulation (see p. 26). When pepsinogen is secreted into the gastric lumen, HCl cleaves off a small fragment of the molecule, converting it to the active form of the enzyme **pepsin** (● Figure 15-9). Once formed, pepsin acts on other pepsinogen molecules to produce more pepsin, a mechanism called an **autocatalytic process** (*autocatalytic* means "self-activating").

Pepsin initiates protein digestion by splitting certain amino acid linkages in proteins to yield peptide fragments (small amino acid chains). Because pepsin can digest protein, it must be stored and secreted in an inactive form so that it does not digest the proteins of the cells in which it is formed. Therefore, pepsin is maintained in the inactive form of pepsinogen until it reaches the gastric lumen, where it is activated by HCl secreted into the lumen by a different cell type.

Mucus is protective.

The surface of the gastric mucosa is covered by a layer of mucus derived from the surface epithelial cells and mucous cells. This mucus is a protective barrier against several forms of potential injury to the gastric mucosa:

■ Through its lubricating properties, mucus protects the gastric mucosa against mechanical injury.

■ It helps protect the stomach wall from self-digestion because pepsin is inhibited when it comes in contact with the layer of mucus coating the stomach lining. (However, mucus does not affect pepsin activity in the lumen, where digestion of dietary protein proceeds without interference.)

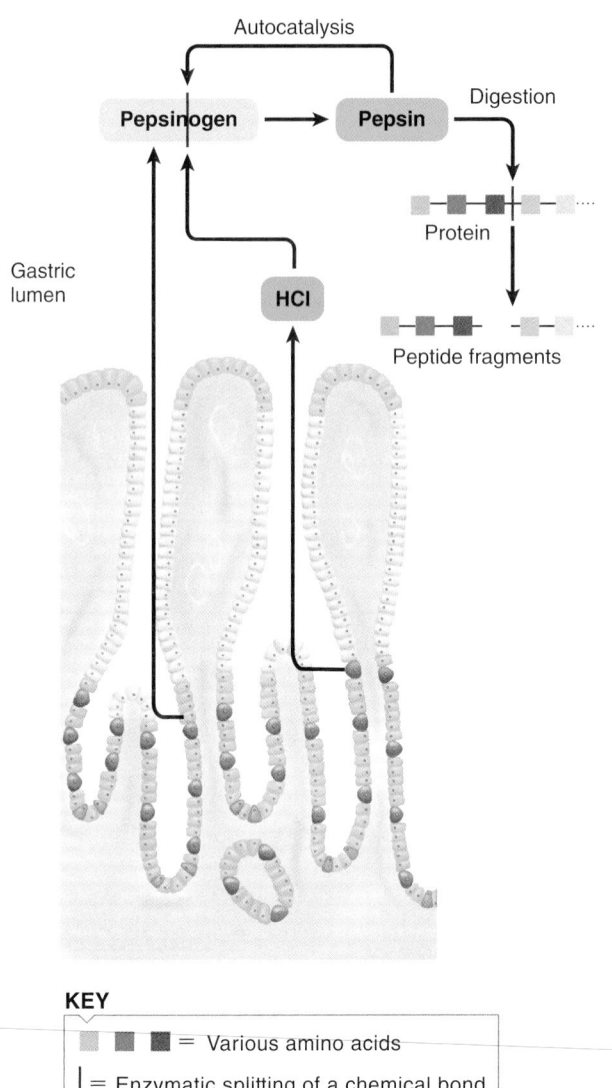

KEY

▨ ▨ ▨	= Various amino acids
|	= Enzymatic splitting of a chemical bond

● **FIGURE 15-9 Pepsinogen activation in the stomach lumen.** In the lumen, hydrochloric acid (HCl) activates pepsinogen to its active form, pepsin, by cleaving off a small fragment. Once activated, pepsin autocatalytically activates more pepsinogen and begins protein digestion. Secretion of pepsinogen in the inactive form prevents it from digesting the protein structures of the cells in which it is produced.

■ Being alkaline, mucus helps protect against acid injury by neutralizing HCl in the vicinity of the gastric lining, but it does not interfere with the function of HCl in the lumen.

Intrinsic factor is essential for absorption of vitamin B_{12}.

Intrinsic factor, another secretory product of the parietal cells in addition to HCl, is important in the absorption of vitamin B_{12}. This vitamin can be absorbed only when combined with intrinsic factor. Binding of intrinsic factor with vitamin B_{12} triggers the receptor-mediated endocytosis of this complex in the terminal ileum, the last part of the small intestine (see p. 26).

Vitamin B_{12} is essential for the normal formation of red blood cells. In the absence of intrinsic factor, vitamin B_{12} is not absorbed, so erythrocyte production is defective and *pernicious anemia* results (see p. 321).

Multiple regulatory pathways influence the parietal and chief cells.

In addition to the gastric exocrine secretory cells, other secretory cells in the gastric glands release endocrine and paracrine regulatory factors instead of products involved in the digestion of nutrients in the gastric lumen (see p. 98). These other secretory cells are also shown in ▲ Table 15-2:

■ Endocrine cells known as **G cells,** found in the gastric pits only in the PGA, secrete the hormone *gastrin* into the blood.

■ **Enterochromaffin-like (ECL) cells,** dispersed among the parietal and chief cells in the gastric glands of the oxyntic mucosa, secrete the paracrine *histamine.*

■ **D cells,** which are scattered in glands near the pylorus but are more numerous in the duodenum, secrete the paracrine *somatostatin.*

These three regulatory factors from the gastric pits, along with the neurotransmitter *acetylcholine (ACh),* primarily control the secretion of gastric digestive juices. Parietal cells have separate receptors for each of these chemical messengers. Three of them—ACh, gastrin, and histamine—stimulate HCl secretion. The fourth regulatory agent—somatostatin—inhibits HCl secretion. ACh and gastrin also increase pepsinogen secretion through their stimulatory effect on the chief cells. We now consider each of these chemical messengers in further detail.

■ **Acetylcholine** is a neurotransmitter released from the intrinsic nerve plexuses in response to both local reflexes and vagal stimulation. ACh stimulates both the parietal and the chief cells, as well as the G cells and the ECL cells.

■ The G cells secrete the hormone **gastrin** into the blood in response to protein products in the stomach lumen and in response to ACh. Like secretin and CCK, gastrin is a major gastrointestinal hormone. After being carried by the blood back to the body and fundus of the stomach, gastrin stimulates the parietal and chief cells, promoting secretion of a highly acidic gastric juice. In addition to directly stimulating the parietal cells, gastrin indirectly promotes HCl secretion by stimulating the ECL cells to release histamine, which also stimulates the parietal cells. Gastrin is the main factor that brings about increased HCl secretion during meal digestion.

■ **Histamine,** a paracrine, is released from the ECL cells in response to ACh and gastrin. Histamine acts locally on nearby parietal cells to speed up HCl secretion.

■ **Somatostatin** is released from the D cells in response to acid. It acts locally as a paracrine in negative-feedback fashion to inhibit secretion by the parietal cells, G cells, and ECL cells, thus turning off the HCl-secreting cells and their most potent stimulatory pathway.

From this list, it is obvious not only that multiple chemical messengers influence the parietal and chief cells but also that these chemicals influence one another. As we examine the phases of gastric secretion, you will see under what circumstances each of these regulatory agents is released.

Control of gastric secretion involves three phases.

The rate of gastric secretion can be influenced by (1) factors arising before food ever reaches the stomach, (2) factors resulting from the presence of food in the stomach, and (3) factors in the duodenum after food has left the stomach. Accordingly, gastric secretion is divided into three phases: cephalic, gastric, and intestinal.

CEPHALIC PHASE OF GASTRIC SECRETION The cephalic phase of gastric secretion refers to the increased secretion of HCl and pepsinogen that occurs in anticipatory fashion in response to stimuli acting in the head even before food reaches the stomach (*cephalic* means "head"). Thinking about, seeing, smelling, tasting, chewing, and swallowing food increases gastric secretion by vagal nerve activity in two ways. First, vagal stimulation of the intrinsic plexuses promotes increased secretion of ACh, which leads to increased secretion of HCl and pepsinogen by the secretory cells. Second, vagal stimulation of the G cells within the PGA causes the release of gastrin, which further enhances secretion of HCl and pepsinogen, with the effect on HCl being potentiated (made stronger) by gastrin promoting the release of histamine (▲ Table 15-3).

GASTRIC PHASE OF GASTRIC SECRETION The gastric phase of gastric secretion begins when food actually reaches the stomach. Stimuli acting in the stomach—namely, *protein, distension, caffeine,* and *alcohol*—increase gastric secretion by overlapping efferent pathways. For example, protein in the stomach, the most potent stimulus, stimulates chemoreceptors that activate the intrinsic nerve plexuses, which in turn stimulate the secretory cells. Furthermore, protein brings about activation of the extrinsic vagal fibers to the stomach. Vagal activity further enhances intrinsic nerve stimulation of the secretory cells and triggers the release of gastrin. Protein also directly stimulates the release of gastrin. Gastrin, in turn, is a powerful stimulus for further HCl and pepsinogen secretion and calls forth release of histamine, which also increases HCl secretion. Through these synergistic and overlapping pathways, protein promotes the secretion of a highly acidic, pepsin-rich gastric juice, which continues digestion of the protein that first initiated the process (▲ Table 15-3).

When the stomach is distended with protein-rich food that needs to be digested, these secretory responses are appropriate. Caffeine and, to lesser extent, alcohol also stimulate the secretion of a highly acidic gastric juice, even when no food is present. This unnecessary acid can irritate the linings of the stomach and duodenum. For this reason, people with ulcers or gastric hyperacidity should avoid caffeinated and alcoholic beverages.

INTESTINAL PHASE OF GASTRIC SECRETION The intestinal phase of gastric secretion encompasses the factors originating in the small intestine that influence gastric secretion. Whereas the

▲ Table 15-3 Stimulation of Gastric Secretion

Phase	Stimuli	Excitatory Mechanism for Enhancing Gastric Secretion
Cephalic Phase of Gastric Secretion	In the head— seeing, smelling, tasting, chewing, swallowing food	
Gastric Phase of Gastric Secretion	In the stomach— protein, distension, caffeine, alcohol	

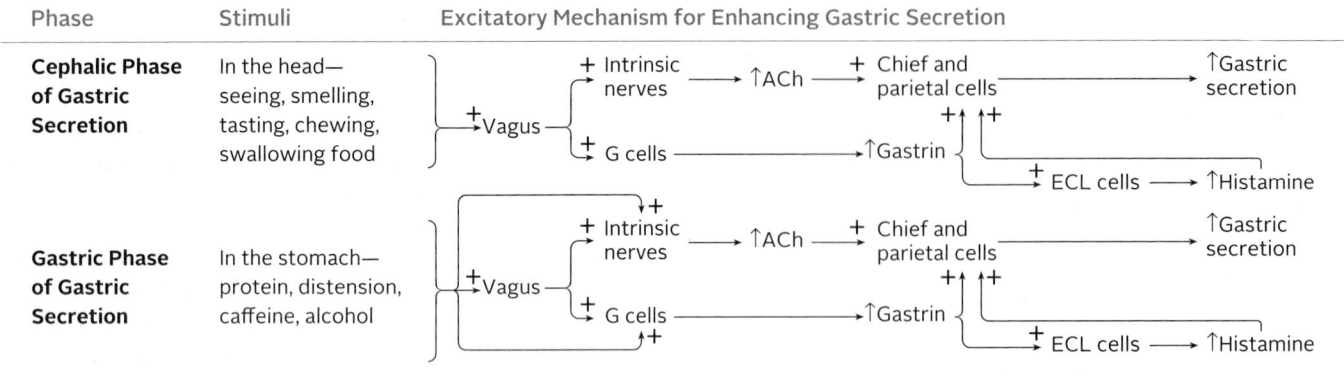

other phases are excitatory, this phase is inhibitory. The intestinal phase is important in helping shut off the flow of gastric juices as chyme begins to be emptied into the small intestine, a topic to which we now turn.

Gastric secretion gradually decreases as food empties from the stomach into the intestine.

You now know what factors turn on gastric secretion before and during a meal, but how is the flow of gastric juices shut off when they are no longer needed? Gastric secretion is gradually reduced in three ways as the stomach empties (▲ Table 15-4):

1. As the meal is gradually emptied into the duodenum, the major stimulus for enhanced gastric secretion—the presence of protein in the stomach—is withdrawn.

2. After foods leave the stomach and gastric juices accumulate to such an extent that gastric pH falls to a very low point, somatostatin is released. As a result of somatostatin's inhibitory effects, gastric secretion declines.

3. The same stimuli that inhibit gastric motility (fat, acid, hypertonicity, or distension in the duodenum brought about by emptying of stomach contents into the duodenum) inhibit gastric secretion as well. The enterogastric reflex and the enterogastrones suppress the gastric secretory cells while they simultaneously reduce the strength of antral peristalsis. This inhibitory response is the intestinal phase of gastric secretion.

The gastric mucosal barrier protects the stomach lining from gastric secretions.

How can the stomach contain strong acid contents and proteolytic enzymes without destroying itself? You already learned that mucus provides a protective physical coating. Furthermore, the surface mucus-secreting cells secrete HCO_3^- that is trapped in the mucus and neutralizes acid in the vicinity. Other barriers to mucosal acid damage are provided by the mucosal lining itself. First, the luminal membranes of the gastric mucosal cells are almost impermeable to H^+, so acid cannot penetrate into the cells and damage them. Second, the lateral edges

▲ Table 15-4 Inhibition of Gastric Secretion

Region	Stimuli	Inhibitory Mechanism for Reducing Gastric Secretion
Body and Antrum	Removal of protein and distension as the stomach empties	
Antrum and Duodenum	Accumulation of acid	
Duodenum (Intestinal Phase of Gastric Secretion)	Fat Acid Hypertonicity Distension	

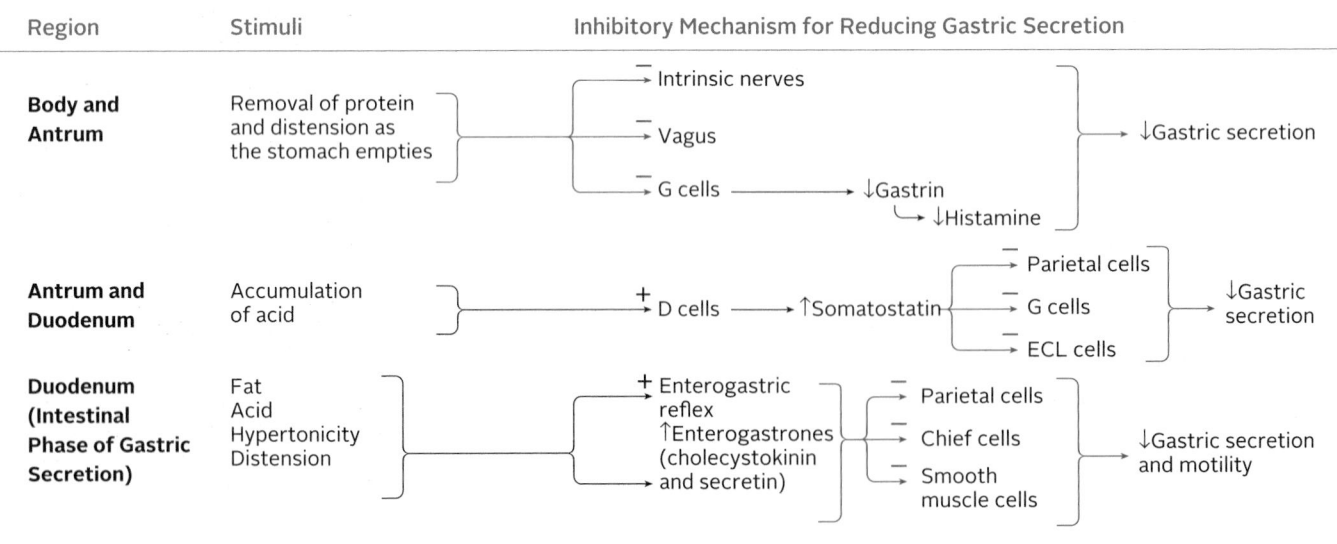

of these cells are joined near their luminal borders by tight junctions, so acid cannot diffuse between the cells from the lumen into the underlying submucosa (see p. 52). The properties of the gastric mucosa that enable the stomach to contain acid without injuring itself constitute the **gastric mucosal barrier** (● Figure 15-10). These protective mechanisms are further enhanced by replacement of the entire stomach lining every 3 days. Because of rapid mucosal turnover, cells are usually replaced before they are exposed to the wear and tear of harsh gastric conditions long enough to suffer damage.

The gastric mucosal barrier occasionally is broken and the gastric wall is injured by its acidic and enzymatic contents. When this occurs, an erosion, or **peptic ulcer,** of the stomach wall results. Excessive gastric reflux into the esophagus and dumping of excessive acidic gastric contents into the duodenum can lead to peptic ulcers in these locations as well. (For a further discussion of ulcers, see the boxed feature on p. 484, ❱ Beyond the Basics.)

We now turn to the remaining two digestive processes in the stomach, gastric digestion and absorption.

Carbohydrate digestion continues in the body of the stomach; protein digestion begins in the antrum.

Two separate digestive processes take place within the stomach. In the body of the stomach, food remains in a semisolid mass because peristaltic contractions in this region are too weak for mixing to occur. Because food is not mixed with gastric secretions in the body of the stomach, little protein digestion occurs here. In the interior of the mass, however, carbohydrate digestion continues under the influence of salivary amylase. Even though acid inactivates salivary amylase, the unmixed interior of the food mass is free of acid. Food is not mixed with HCl until the gastric contents reach the antrum.

Digestion by the gastric juice itself is accomplished in the antrum of the stomach, where the food is thoroughly mixed with HCl and pepsin, beginning protein digestion.

The stomach absorbs alcohol and aspirin but no food.

No food or water is absorbed into the blood through the stomach mucosa. However, two noteworthy nonnutrient substances are absorbed directly by the stomach—*ethyl alcohol* and *aspirin.* Alcohol is somewhat lipid soluble, so it can diffuse through the lipid membranes of the epithelial cells that line the stomach and can enter the blood through the submucosal capillaries. Although alcohol can be absorbed by the gastric mucosa, it can be absorbed even more rapidly by the small-intestine mucosa because the surface area for absorption in the small intestine is greater than in the stomach. Thus, alcohol absorption occurs more slowly if gastric emptying is delayed so that the alcohol remains in the more slowly absorbing stomach longer. Because fat is the most potent duodenal stimulus for inhibiting gastric motility, consuming fat-rich foods (for example, whole milk, pizza, or nuts) before or during alcohol ingestion delays gastric emptying and prevents the alcohol from producing its effects as rapidly.

Another category of substances absorbed by the gastric mucosa includes weak acids, most notably *acetylsalicylic acid* (aspirin). In the highly acidic environment of the stomach lumen, weak acids are lipid soluble, so they can be absorbed quickly by crossing the plasma membranes of the epithelial cells that line the stomach. Most other drugs are not absorbed until they reach the small intestine, so they do not begin to take effect as quickly.

Having completed our coverage of the stomach, we move to the next part of the digestive tract, the small intestine and the accessory digestive organs that release their secretions into the small-intestine lumen.

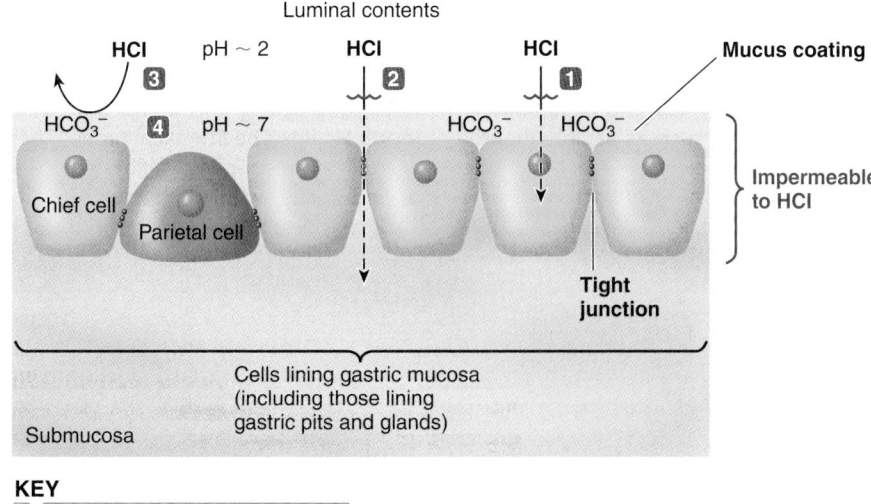

The components of the gastric mucosal barrier enable the stomach to contain acid without injuring itself:

1 The luminal membranes of the gastric mucosal cells are impermeable to H^+ so that HCl cannot penetrate into the cells.

2 The cells are joined by tight junctions that prevent HCl from penetrating between them.

3 A mucus coating over the gastric mucosa serves as a physical barrier to acid penetration.

4 The HCO_3^--rich mucus also serves as a chemical barrier that neutralizes acid in the vicinity of the mucosa. Even when luminal pH is 2, the mucus pH is 7.

KEY

⊢{⊣ --▸ = Passage prevented

● **FIGURE 15-10 Gastric mucosal barrier.**

Beyond the Basics

Ulcers: When Bugs Break the Barrier

Peptic ulcers are erosions that typically begin in the mucosal lining of the stomach and may penetrate into the deeper layers of the stomach wall. They occur when the gastric mucosal barrier is disrupted; thus, pepsin and HCl act on the stomach wall instead of food in the lumen. Frequent backflow of acidic gastric juices into the esophagus or excess unneutralized acid from the stomach in the duodenum can lead to peptic ulcers in these sites as well.

In a surprising discovery in the early 1990s, the bacterium *Helicobacter pylori* was pinpointed as the cause of more than 80% of all peptic ulcers. In the United States, 30% of the population harbors *H. pylori*. Those who have this slow bacterium have a risk of developing an ulcer within 10 to 20 years of acquiring the infection that is 3 to 12 times greater than the risk for those without the bacterium. They are also at increased risk of developing stomach cancer.

For years, scientists had overlooked the possibility that ulcers could be triggered by an infectious agent, because bacteria typically cannot survive in a strongly acidic environment such as the stomach lumen. As an exception, *H. pylori* exploits several strategies to survive in this hostile environment. First, these organisms are motile, being equipped with four to six flagella (whiplike appendages; see the accompanying figure), which enable them to tunnel through and take up residence under the stomach's thick layer of alkaline mucus. Here, they are protected from the highly acidic gastric contents. Second, *H. pylori* preferentially settles in the antrum, which has no acid-producing parietal cells, although HCl from the upper parts of the stomach does reach the antrum. Third, these bacteria produce *urease,* an enzyme that breaks down urea, an end product of protein metabolism, into ammonia (NH_3) and CO_2. Ammonia serves as a buffer (see p. 459) that neutralizes stomach acid locally in the vicinity of the *H. pylori.*

H. pylori contributes to ulcer formation in part by secreting toxins that cause

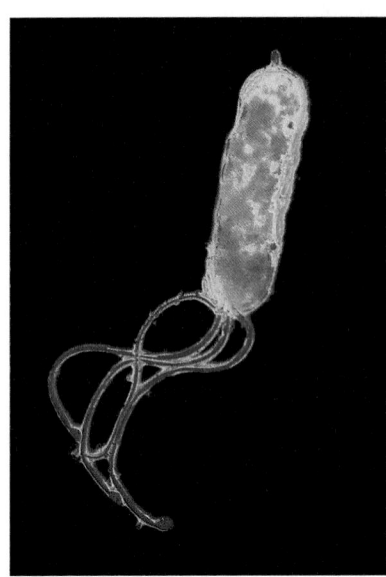

Helicobacter pylori. *Helicobacter pylori,* the bacterium responsible for most cases of peptic ulcers, has flagella that enable it to tunnel beneath the protective layer of mucus that coats the stomach lining, protecting it from the harsh luminal contents.

a persistent inflammation, or *chronic superficial gastritis,* at the site it colonizes. *H. pylori* further weakens the gastric mucosal barrier by disrupting the tight junctions between the gastric epithelial cells, thereby making the gastric mucosa leakier than normal.

Alone or in conjunction with this infectious culprit, other factors are known to contribute to ulcer formation. Frequent exposure to some chemicals can break the gastric mucosal barrier; the most important of these are ethyl alcohol and nonsteroidal anti-inflammatory drugs (NSAIDs), such as aspirin, ibuprofen, or more potent medications for the treatment of arthritis or other chronic inflammatory processes. The barrier frequently breaks in patients with preexisting debilitating conditions, such as severe injuries or infections. Persistent stressful

situations are often associated with ulcer formation, presumably because emotional response to stress can stimulate excessive gastric secretion.

When the gastric mucosal barrier is broken, acid and pepsin diffuse into the mucosa and underlying submucosa, with serious pathophysiological consequences. The surface erosion, or ulcer, progressively enlarges as increasing levels of acid and pepsin continue to damage the stomach wall. Two of the most serious consequences of ulcers are (1) hemorrhage resulting from damage to submucosal capillaries and (2) perforation, or complete erosion through the stomach wall, resulting in the escape of potent gastric contents into the abdominal cavity.

Treatment of ulcers includes antibiotics, H-2 histamine receptor blockers, and proton-pump inhibitors. With the discovery of the infectious component of most ulcers, antibiotics are now a treatment of choice. The other drugs are also used alone or in combination with antibiotics.

Two decades before the discovery of *H. pylori,* researchers discovered an antihistamine *(cimetidine)* that specifically blocks H-2 receptors, the type of receptors that bind histamine released from the stomach. These receptors differ from H-1 receptors, which bind the histamine involved in allergic respiratory disorders. Accordingly, traditional antihistamines used for respiratory allergies (such as hay fever and asthma) are not effective against ulcers, nor is cimetidine useful for respiratory problems.

Another recent class of drugs used in treating ulcers inhibits acid secretion by directly blocking the pump that transports H^+ into the stomach lumen. These so-called proton-pump inhibitors (H^+ is a naked proton without its electron) help reduce the corrosive effect of HCl on the exposed tissue.

Pancreatic and Biliary Secretions

When gastric contents are emptied into the small intestine, they are mixed not only with juice secreted by the small-intestine mucosa but also with the secretions of the exocrine pancreas and liver that are released into the duodenal lumen. We discuss the roles of each of these accessory digestive organs before we examine the contributions of the small intestine itself.

The pancreas is a mixture of exocrine and endocrine tissue.

The **pancreas** is an elongated gland that lies behind and below the stomach, above the first loop of the duodenum (● Figure 15-11). This mixed gland contains both exocrine and endocrine tissue. The predominant exocrine part consists of grapelike clusters of secretory cells that form sacs known as **acini,** which connect to ducts that eventually empty into the duodenum. The smaller endocrine part consists of isolated islands of endocrine tissue, the **islets of Langerhans,** which are dispersed throughout the pancreas. The most important hormones secreted by the islet cells are insulin and glucagon (see Chapter 17).

The exocrine pancreas secretes digestive enzymes and an aqueous alkaline fluid.

The **exocrine pancreas** secretes a pancreatic juice consisting of two components: (1) *pancreatic enzymes* actively secreted by the *acinar cells* that form the acini and (2) an *aqueous alkaline solution* actively secreted by the *duct cells* that line the pancreatic ducts. The aqueous (watery) alkaline component is rich in sodium bicarbonate ($NaHCO_3$).

Like pepsinogen, pancreatic enzymes are stored within secretory vesicles after being produced and then are released by

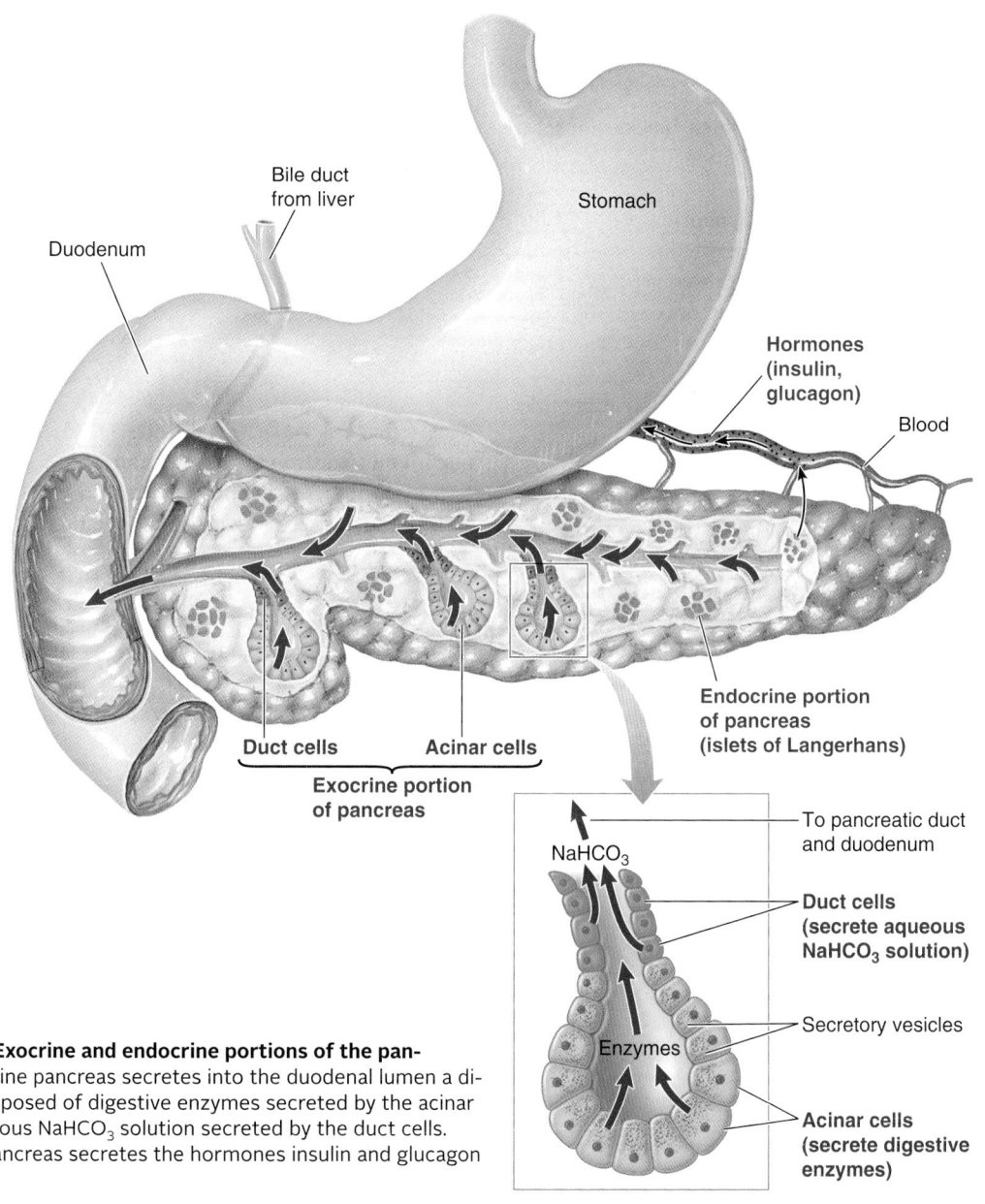

● **FIGURE 15-11 Exocrine and endocrine portions of the pancreas.** The exocrine pancreas secretes into the duodenal lumen a digestive juice composed of digestive enzymes secreted by the acinar cells and an aqueous $NaHCO_3$ solution secreted by the duct cells. The endocrine pancreas secretes the hormones insulin and glucagon into the blood.

exocytosis as needed. These pancreatic enzymes are important because they can almost completely digest food in the absence of all other digestive secretions. The acinar cells secrete three types of pancreatic enzymes capable of digesting all three categories of foodstuffs: (1) *proteolytic enzymes* for protein digestion, (2) *pancreatic amylase* for carbohydrate digestion, and (3) *pancreatic lipase* for fat digestion.

PANCREATIC PROTEOLYTIC ENZYMES The three major pancreatic **proteolytic enzymes** are *trypsinogen, chymotrypsinogen,* and *procarboxypeptidase,* each of which is secreted in an inactive form. When **trypsinogen** is secreted into the duodenal lumen, it is activated to its active enzyme form, **trypsin,** by **enterokinase,** an enzyme embedded in the luminal membrane of the cells that line the duodenal mucosa. Trypsin then autocatalytically activates more trypsinogen. Like pepsinogen, trypsinogen must remain inactive within the pancreas to prevent this proteolytic enzyme from digesting the proteins of the cells in which it is formed. Trypsinogen remains inactive, therefore, until it reaches the duodenal lumen, where enterokinase triggers the activation process, which then proceeds autocatalytically. As further protection, the pancreas also produces a chemical known as **trypsin inhibitor,** which blocks trypsin's actions if spontaneous activation of trypsinogen inadvertently occurs within the pancreas.

Chymotrypsinogen and **procarboxypeptidase,** the other pancreatic proteolytic enzymes, are converted by trypsin to their active forms, **chymotrypsin** and **carboxypeptidase,** respectively, within the duodenal lumen. Thus, once enterokinase has activated some of the trypsin, trypsin carries out the rest of the activation process.

Each of these proteolytic enzymes attacks different peptide linkages. The end products that result from this action are a mixture of small peptide chains and amino acids. Mucus secreted by the intestinal cells protects against digestion of the small-intestine wall by the activated proteolytic enzymes.

PANCREATIC AMYLASE Like salivary amylase, **pancreatic amylase** contributes to carbohydrate digestion by converting polysaccharides into the disaccharide maltose. Amylase is secreted in the pancreatic juice in an active form because active amylase does not endanger the secretory cells. These cells do not contain any polysaccharides.

PANCREATIC LIPASE **Pancreatic lipase** is extremely important because it is the only enzyme secreted throughout the entire digestive system that can digest fat. (In humans, insignificant amounts of lipase are secreted in the saliva and gastric juice.) Pancreatic lipase hydrolyzes dietary triglycerides into monoglycerides and free fatty acids, which are the absorbable units of fat. Like amylase, lipase is secreted in its active form because there is no risk of pancreatic self-digestion by lipase. Triglycerides are not a structural component of pancreatic cells.

 PANCREATIC INSUFFICIENCY When pancreatic enzymes are deficient, digestion of food is incomplete. Because the pancreas is the only significant source of lipase, pancreatic enzyme deficiency results in serious maldigestion of fats. The main clinical manifestation of pancreatic exocrine insufficiency is **steatorrhea,** or excessive undigested fat in the feces. Digestion of protein and carbohydrates is impaired to a lesser degree because salivary, gastric, and small-intestinal enzymes contribute to the digestion of these two foodstuffs.

PANCREATIC AQUEOUS ALKALINE SECRETION Pancreatic enzymes function best in a neutral or slightly alkaline environment, yet the highly acidic gastric contents are emptied into the duodenal lumen in the vicinity of pancreatic enzyme entry into the duodenum. This acidic chyme must be neutralized quickly in the duodenal lumen, not only to allow optimal functioning of the pancreatic enzymes but also to prevent acid damage to the duodenal mucosa. The alkaline ($NaHCO_3$-rich) fluid secreted by the pancreatic duct cells into the duodenal lumen serves the important function of neutralizing the acidic chyme as the latter is emptied into the duodenum from the stomach. This aqueous $NaHCO_3$ secretion is by far the largest component of pancreatic secretion. The volume of pancreatic secretion ranges between 1 and 2 liters per day, depending on the type and degree of stimulation.

Pancreatic exocrine secretion is regulated by secretin and CCK.

Pancreatic exocrine secretion is regulated primarily by hormonal mechanisms. A small amount of parasympathetically induced pancreatic secretion occurs during the cephalic phase of digestion. However, the predominant stimulation of pancreatic secretion occurs during the intestinal phase of digestion when chyme is in the small intestine. The release of the two major enterogastrones, secretin and cholecystokinin (CCK), in response to chyme in the duodenum plays the central role in controlling pancreatic secretion (● Figure 15-12).

ROLE OF SECRETIN IN PANCREATIC SECRETION Of the factors that stimulate enterogastrone release (fat, acid, hypertonicity, and distension), the primary stimulus specifically for secretin release is acid in the duodenum. Secretin, in turn, is carried by the blood to the pancreas, where it stimulates the duct cells to markedly increase their secretion of a $NaHCO_3$-rich aqueous fluid into the duodenum. Even though other stimuli may cause the release of secretin, it is appropriate that the most potent stimulus is acid, because secretin promotes the alkaline pancreatic secretion that neutralizes the acid. This mechanism provides a control system for maintaining neutrality of the chyme in the intestine.

ROLE OF CCK IN PANCREATIC SECRETION Cholecystokinin is important in regulating pancreatic digestive enzyme secretion. The main stimulus for release of CCK from the duodenal mucosa is the presence of fat and, to a lesser extent, protein products. The circulatory system transports CCK to the pancreas, where it stimulates the pancreatic acinar cells to increase digestive enzyme secretion. Among these enzymes are lipase and the

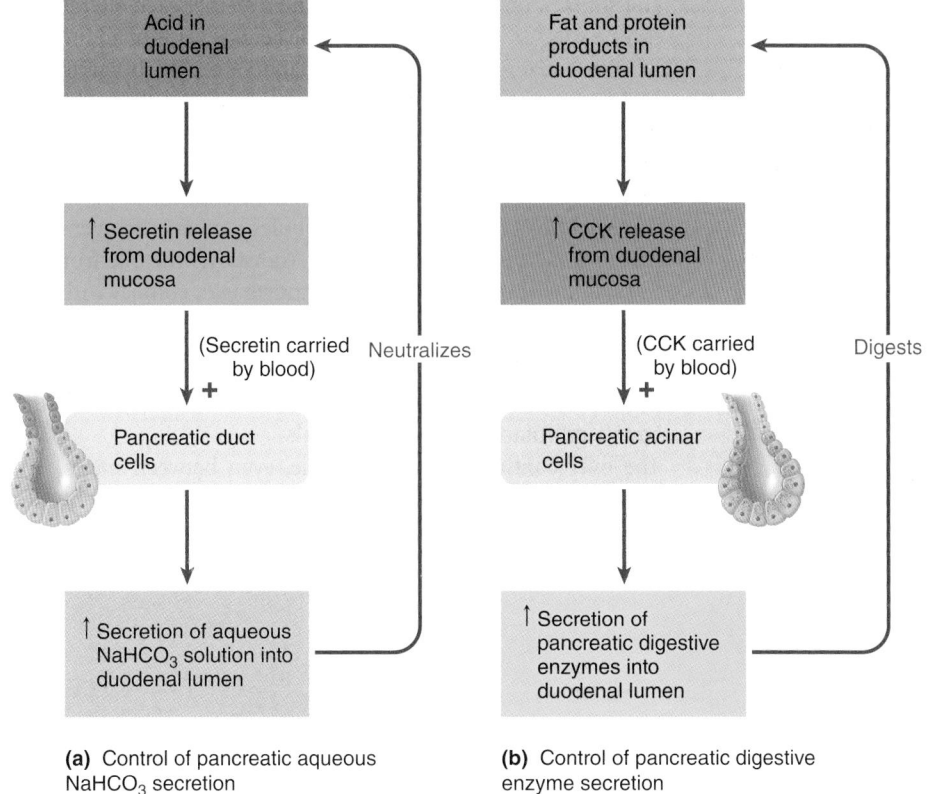

(a) Control of pancreatic aqueous NaHCO$_3$ secretion

(b) Control of pancreatic digestive enzyme secretion

● **FIGURE 15-12 Hormonal control of pancreatic exocrine secretion.**

proteolytic enzymes, which appropriately further digest the fat and protein that initiated the response and help digest carbohydrate. In contrast to fat and protein, carbohydrate does not directly influence pancreatic digestive enzyme secretion.

We now look at the contributions of the remaining accessory digestive unit, the liver and gallbladder.

The liver performs various important functions, including bile production.

Besides pancreatic juice, the other secretory product emptied into the duodenal lumen is **bile.** The **biliary system** includes the *liver,* the *gallbladder,* and associated ducts.

LIVER FUNCTIONS The **liver** is the largest and most important metabolic organ in the body; it can be viewed as the body's major biochemical factory. Its importance to the digestive system is its secretion of *bile salts,* which aid fat digestion and absorption. The liver also performs a variety of functions not related to digestion, including the following:

1. Metabolic processing of the major categories of nutrients (carbohydrates, proteins, and lipids) after their absorption from the digestive tract (see p. 499)

2. Detoxifying or degrading body wastes and hormones, as well as drugs and other foreign compounds

3. Synthesizing plasma proteins, including those needed for blood clotting (see p. 326), those that transport steroid and thyroid hormones and cholesterol in the blood (see pp. 102 and 272), and angiotensinogen important in the salt-conserving

renin–angiotensin–aldosterone system (see p. 417)

4. Storing glycogen, fats, iron, copper, and many vitamins (see p. 37)

5. Activating vitamin D, which the liver does in conjunction with the kidneys (see p. 571)

6. Removing bacteria and worn-out red blood cells, thanks to its resident macrophages (see p. 330)

7. Secreting the hormones thrombopoietin (stimulates platelet production; see p. 324) and insulin-like growth factor (stimulates growth; see p. 539)

8. Excreting cholesterol and bilirubin, the latter being a breakdown product derived from the destruction of worn-out red blood cells (see pp. 24 and 320).

Given this range of complex functions, there is amazingly little specialization among cells within the liver. Each liver cell, or **hepatocyte,** performs the same wide variety of metabolic and secretory tasks (*hepato* means "liver"; *cyte* means "cell"). The specialization comes from the highly developed organelles within each hepatocyte. The only liver function not accomplished by the hepatocytes is the phagocytic activity carried out by the resident macrophages.

LIVER BLOOD FLOW To carry out these wide-ranging tasks, the anatomic organization of the liver permits each hepatocyte to be in direct contact with blood from two sources: arterial blood coming from the aorta and venous blood coming directly from the digestive tract. Like other cells, the hepatocytes receive fresh arterial blood via the hepatic artery, which supplies their oxygen and delivers blood-borne metabolites for hepatic processing. Venous blood also enters the liver by the **hepatic portal system,** a unique and complex vascular connection between the digestive tract and the liver (● Figure 15-13). The veins draining the digestive tract do not directly join the inferior vena cava, the large vein that returns blood to the heart. Instead, the veins from the stomach and intestine enter the *hepatic portal vein,* which carries the products absorbed from the digestive tract directly to the liver for processing, storage, or detoxification before they gain access to the general circulation. Within the liver, the portal vein again breaks up into a capillary network (the liver *sinusoids*) to permit exchange between the blood and the hepatocytes before draining into the hepatic vein, which joins the inferior vena cava.

LIVER ORGANIZATION The liver is organized into functional units known as **lobules,** which are hexagonal arrangements of tissue surrounding a central vein and delineated by vascular sinusoids in plates two cell layers thick so that each lateral edge faces a sinusoidal pool of blood. The central veins of all the liver lobules converge to form the hepatic vein, which carries the blood away from the liver. The thin bile-carrying channel, a **bile canaliculus,** runs between the cells within each hepatic plate. Hepatocytes continuously secrete bile into these thin channels, which carry the bile to a bile duct at the periphery of the lobule. The bile ducts from the various lobules converge to eventually form the *common bile duct,* which transports the bile from the liver to the duodenum. Each hepatocyte is in contact with a sinusoid on one side and a bile canaliculus on the other side.

Bile is continuously secreted by the liver and is diverted to the gallbladder between meals.

The liver continuously secretes bile, even between meals. The opening of the bile duct into the duodenum is guarded by the **sphincter of Oddi,** which prevents bile from entering the duodenum except during digestion of meals (● Figure 15-15). When this sphincter is closed, bile secreted by the liver hits the closed sphincter and is diverted back up into the **gallbladder,** a small, saclike structure tucked beneath but not directly connected to the liver. Thus, bile is not transported directly from the liver to the gallbladder. Bile is subsequently stored and concentrated in the gallbladder between meals. After a meal, bile enters the duodenum as a result of the combined effects of relaxation of the sphincter of Oddi, gallbladder contraction, and increased bile secretion by the liver. The amount of bile secreted per day ranges from 250 ml to 1 liter, depending on the degree of stimulation.

 Because the gallbladder stores concentrated bile, it is the primary site for precipitation of concentrated bile constituents into **gallstones.** Fortunately, the gallbladder does not play an essential digestive role, so its removal as a treatment for gallstones or other gallbladder disease presents no particular problem. After gallbladder removal, the bile secreted between meals is stored instead in the common bile duct, which becomes dilated.

Bile salts are recycled through the enterohepatic circulation.

Bile contains several organic constituents, namely, *bile salts, cholesterol, lecithin* (a phospholipid), and *bilirubin* (all derived from hepatocyte activity) in an *aqueous alkaline fluid* (added by the duct cells). Even though bile does not contain any digestive enzymes, it is important for the digestion and absorption of fats, primarily through the activity of bile salts.

Bile salts are derivatives of cholesterol. They are actively secreted into the bile and eventually enter the duodenum, along with the other biliary constituents. Following their participation in fat digestion and absorption, most bile salts are reabsorbed into the blood by special active-transport mechanisms located only in the terminal ileum. From here, bile salts are returned by the hepatic portal system to the liver, which resecretes them into the bile. This recycling of bile salts between the small intestine and the liver is called the **enterohepatic circulation** (*entero* means "intestine"; *hepatic* means "liver") (● Figure 15-15).

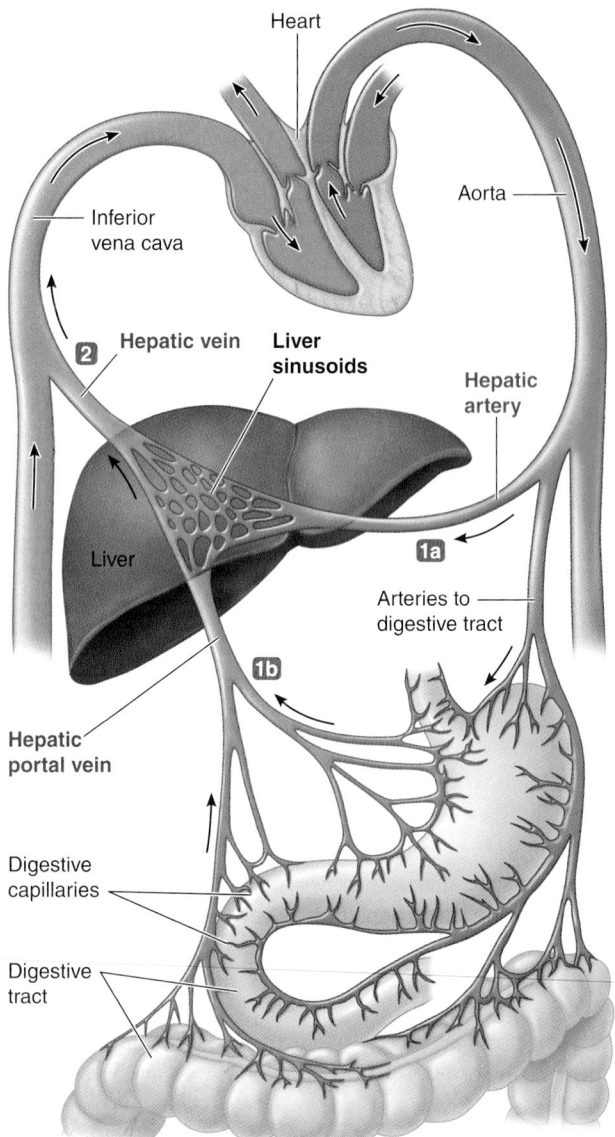

The liver receives blood from two sources:

1a Arterial blood, which provides the liver's O_2 supply and carries blood-borne metabolites for hepatic processing, is delivered by the **hepatic artery**.

1b Venous blood draining the digestive tract is carried by the **hepatic portal vein** to the liver for processing and storage of newly absorbed nutrients.

2 Blood leaves the liver via the **hepatic vein**.

● **FIGURE 15-13 Schematic representation of liver blood flow.**

and bile channels (● Figure 15-14a). At each of the six outer corners of the lobule are three vessels: a branch of the hepatic artery, a branch of the hepatic portal vein, and a bile duct. Blood from the branches of both the hepatic artery and the portal vein flows from the periphery of the lobule into large, expanded capillary spaces called **sinusoids,** which run between rows of liver cells to the central vein like spokes on a bicycle wheel (● Figure 15-14b). The hepatocytes are arranged between the

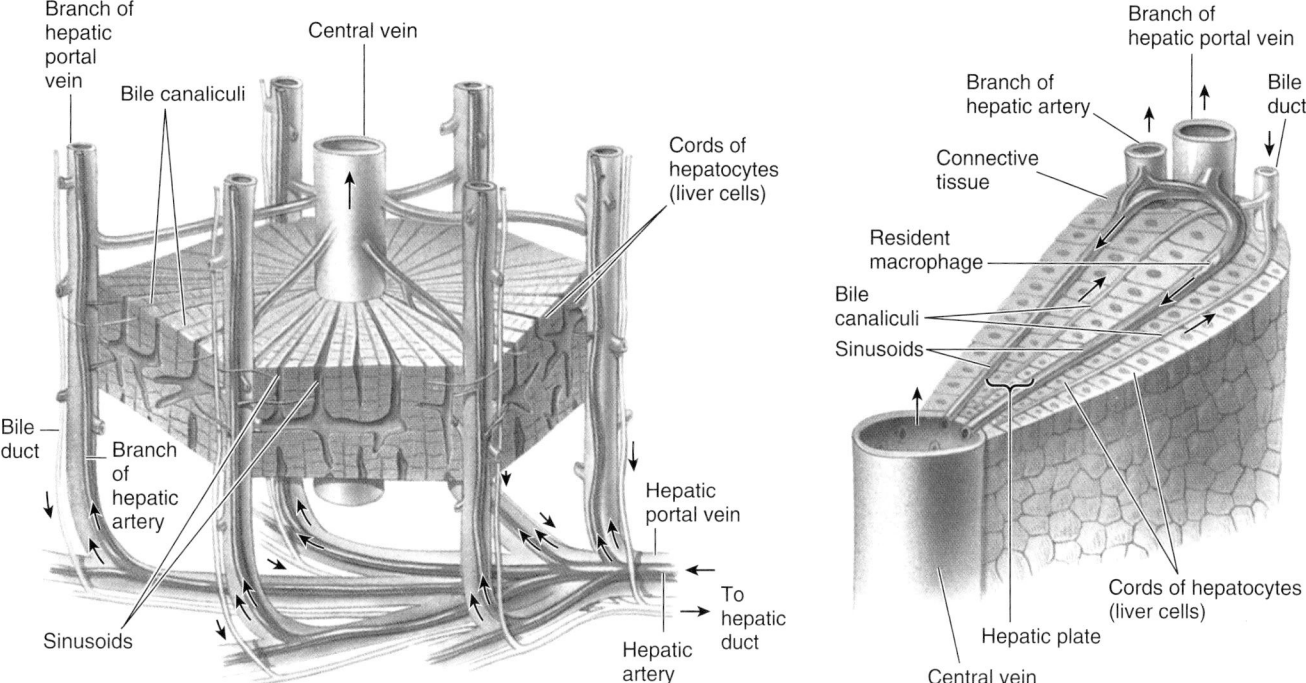

Branch of hepatic portal vein

Bile canaliculi

Central vein

Cords of hepatocytes (liver cells)

Bile duct

Branch of hepatic artery

Sinusoids

Hepatic portal vein

To hepatic duct

Hepatic artery

(a) Hepatic lobule

Branch of hepatic portal vein

Branch of hepatic artery

Bile duct

Connective tissue

Resident macrophage

Bile canaliculi

Sinusoids

Cords of hepatocytes (liver cells)

Hepatic plate

Central vein

(b) Wedge of a hepatic lobule

● FIGURE 15-14 **Anatomy of the liver.**

The total amount of bile salts in the body averages about 3 to 4 g, yet 3 to 15 g of bile salts may be emptied into the duodenum in a single meal. On average, bile salts cycle between the liver and the small intestine twice during the digestion of a typical meal. Usually, only about 5% of the secreted bile escapes into the feces daily. These lost bile salts are replaced by new bile salts synthesized by the liver; thus, the size of the pool of bile salts is kept constant.

Bile salts aid fat digestion and absorption.

Bile salts aid fat digestion through their detergent action (emulsification) and facilitate fat absorption by participating in the formation of micelles. Both functions are related to the structure of bile salts. Let us see how.

DETERGENT ACTION OF BILE SALTS The term **detergent action** refers to bile salts' ability to convert large fat globules into a **lipid emulsion** consisting of many small fat droplets suspended in the aqueous chyme, thus increasing the surface area available for attack by pancreatic lipase. Fat globules, no matter their size, are made up primarily of undigested triglyceride molecules. To digest fat, lipase must come into direct contact with the triglyceride molecule. Because triglycerides are not soluble in water, they tend to aggregate into large droplets in the watery environment of the small-intestine lumen. If bile salts did not emulsify these large droplets, lipase could act on the triglyceride molecules only at the surface of the large droplets, and fat digestion would be greatly prolonged.

Bile salts exert a detergent action similar to that of the detergent you use to break up grease when you wash dishes. A bile salt molecule contains a lipid-soluble part (a steroid derived

from cholesterol) plus a negatively charged, water-soluble part. Bile salts *adsorb* on the surface of a fat droplet; that is, the lipid-soluble part of the bile salt dissolves in the fat droplet, leaving the charged water-soluble part projecting from the surface of the droplet (● Figure 15-16a). Intestinal mixing movements break up large fat droplets into smaller ones. These small droplets would quickly recoalesce were it not for bile salts adsorbing on the surface of each droplet and creating a shell of water-soluble negative charges. Because like charges repel, these negatively charged groups on the droplet surfaces cause the fat droplets to repel one another (● Figure 15-16b). This electrical repulsion prevents the small droplets from recoalescing into large fat droplets and thus produces a lipid emulsion that increases the surface area available for lipase action.

MICELLAR FORMATION Bile salts—along with cholesterol and lecithin, which are also constituents of bile—play an important role in facilitating fat absorption through micellar formation. Like bile salts, lecithin (a phospholipid similar to the ones in the lipid bilayer of the plasma membrane) has both a lipid-soluble and a water-soluble part, whereas cholesterol is almost insoluble in water. In a micelle, the bile salts and lecithin aggregate in small clusters with their fat-soluble parts huddled together in the middle to form a hydrophobic ("water-fearing") core, while their water-soluble parts form an outer hydrophilic ("water-loving") shell (● Figure 15-17). A micelle is 3 to 10 nm in diameter, compared to an average diameter of 1000 nm for an emulsified lipid droplet. Micelles are water soluble because of their hydrophilic shells, but they can dissolve water-insoluble (and hence lipid-soluble) substances in their lipid-soluble cores. Micelles thus provide a handy vehicle for carrying water-insoluble substances through the watery luminal contents. The most im-

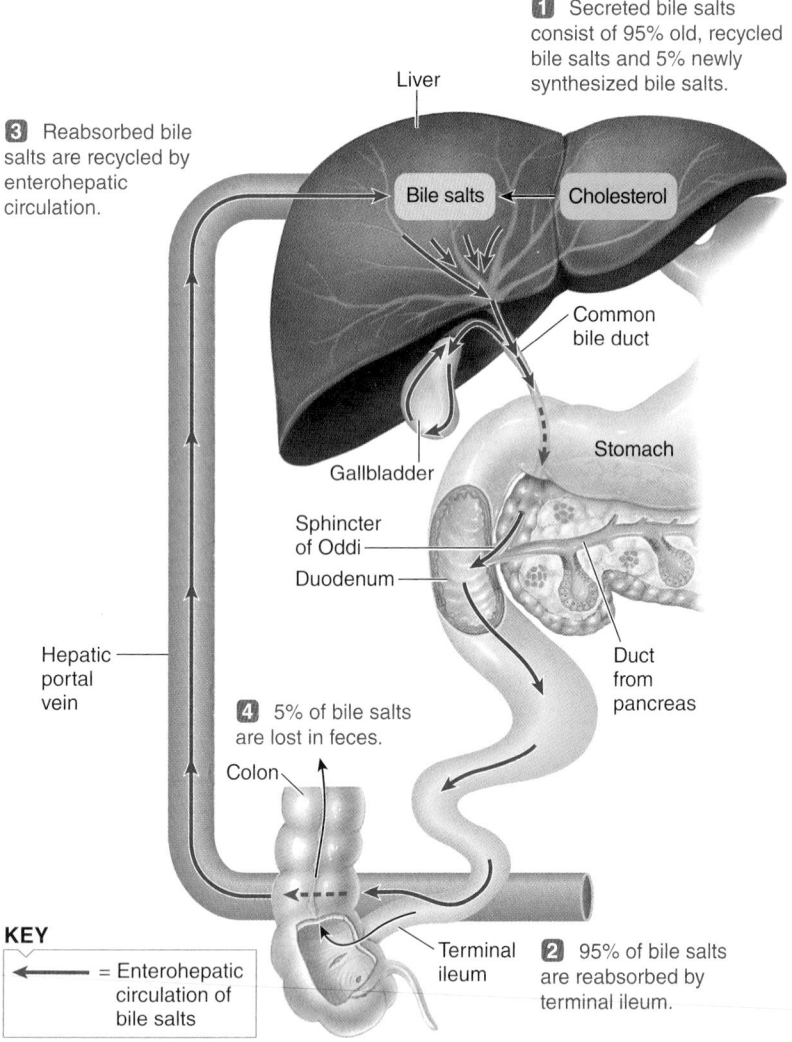

1 Secreted bile salts consist of 95% old, recycled bile salts and 5% newly synthesized bile salts.

Liver

3 Reabsorbed bile salts are recycled by enterohepatic circulation.

Bile salts ← Cholesterol

Common bile duct

Stomach

Gallbladder

Sphincter of Oddi

Duodenum

Duct from pancreas

Hepatic portal vein

4 5% of bile salts are lost in feces.

Colon

KEY

← = Enterohepatic circulation of bile salts

Terminal ileum

2 95% of bile salts are reabsorbed by terminal ileum.

● **FIGURE 15-15 Enterohepatic circulation of bile salts.** The majority of bile salts are recycled between the liver and the small intestine through the enterohepatic circulation (blue arrows). After participating in fat digestion and absorption, most bile salts are reabsorbed by active transport in the terminal ileum and returned through the hepatic portal vein to the liver, which resecretes them in the bile.

portant lipid-soluble substances carried within micelles are the products of fat digestion (monoglycerides and free fatty acids), as well as fat-soluble vitamins, which are all transported to their sites of absorption by this means. If they did not hitch a ride in the water-soluble micelles, these nutrients would float on the surface of the aqueous chyme (just as oil floats on top of water), never reaching the absorptive surfaces of the small intestine.

In addition, cholesterol, a highly water-insoluble substance, dissolves in the micelle's hydrophobic core. This mechanism is important in cholesterol homeostasis.

Bile salts are the most potent stimulus for increased bile secretion; CCK promotes gallbladder emptying.

Bile secretion by the liver may be increased by chemical, hormonal, and neural mechanisms:

■ *Chemical mechanism (bile salts).* Any substance that increases bile secretion is called a **choleretic.** The most potent

choleretic is bile salts themselves. Between meals bile is stored in the gallbladder, but during a meal bile is emptied into the duodenum as the gallbladder contracts. After bile salts participate in fat digestion and absorption, they are reabsorbed and returned by the enterohepatic circulation to the liver, where they act as potent choleretics to stimulate further bile secretion. Therefore, during a meal, when bile salts are needed and being used, bile secretion by the liver is enhanced.

■ *Hormonal mechanism (secretin).* Besides increasing the aqueous $NaHCO_3$ secretion by the pancreas, secretin stimulates an aqueous alkaline bile secretion by the liver ducts without any corresponding increase in bile salts.

■ *Neural mechanism (vagus nerve).* Vagal stimulation of the liver plays a minor role in bile secretion during the cephalic phase of digestion, promoting an increase in liver bile flow before food ever reaches the stomach or intestine.

During digestion of a meal, when chyme reaches the small intestine, the presence of food, especially fat products, in the duodenal lumen triggers the release of CCK. This hormone stimulates relaxation of the sphincter of Oddi and contraction of the gallbladder, so bile is discharged into the duodenum, where it appropriately aids in the digestion and absorption of the fat that initiated the release of CCK.

Bilirubin is a waste product excreted in the bile.

Bilirubin, the other major constituent of bile, does not play a role in digestion but instead is a waste product excreted in the bile. Bilirubin is the primary bile pigment derived from the breakdown of worn-out red blood cells. The typical life span of a red blood cell in the circulatory system is 120 days. Worn-out red blood cells are removed from the blood by the macrophages that line the liver sinusoids and reside in other areas in the body. Bilirubin is the end product from degradation of the heme (iron-containing) part of the hemoglobin contained within these old red blood cells (see p. 319). This bilirubin is extracted from the blood by the hepatocytes and is actively excreted into the bile.

Bilirubin is a yellow pigment that gives bile its color. Within the intestinal tract, this pigment is modified by bacterial enzymes, giving rise to the characteristic brown color of feces. When bile secretion does not occur, as when the bile duct is completely obstructed by a gallstone, the feces are grayish white. A small amount of bilirubin is normally reabsorbed by the intestine back into the blood, and when it is eventually excreted in the urine, it is largely responsible for the urine's yellow color. The kidneys cannot excrete bilirubin until after it has been modified during its passage through the liver and intestine.

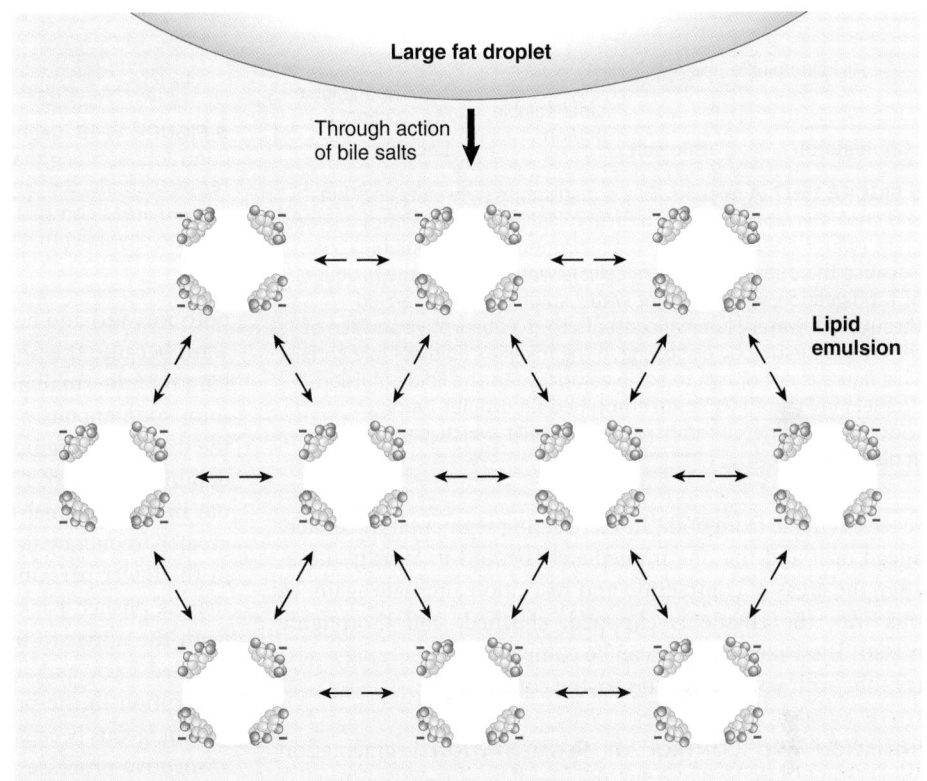

Clinical Note If bilirubin is formed more rapidly than it can be excreted, it accumulates in the body and causes **jaundice.** Patients with this condition appear yellowish, with this color being seen most easily in the whites of their eyes. Jaundice can be brought about in three ways:

1. *Prehepatic* (the problem occurs "before the liver"), or *hemolytic, jaundice* arises from excessive breakdown (hemolysis) of red blood cells, which results in the liver being presented with more bilirubin than it is capable of excreting.

2. *Hepatic* (the problem is the "liver") *jaundice* occurs when the liver is diseased and cannot deal with even the normal load of bilirubin.

3. *Posthepatic* (the problem occurs "after the liver"), or *obstructive, jaundice* occurs when the bile duct is obstructed, such as by a gallstone, so that bilirubin cannot be eliminated in the feces.

Having looked at the accessory digestive organs that empty their exocrine products into the small-intestine lumen, we now examine the contributions of the small intestine itself.

Small Intestine

The **small intestine** is the site where most digestion and absorption take place. No further digestion is accomplished after the luminal contents pass beyond the small intestine, and no further absorption of ingested nutrients occurs, although the large intestine does absorb small amounts of salt and water. The small intestine lies coiled within the abdominal cavity, extending between the stomach and the large intestine. It is arbitrarily divided into three segments—the **duodenum,** the **jejunum,** and the **ileum.**

As usual, we examine motility, secretion, digestion, and absorption in the small intestine, in that order. Small-intestine motility includes *segmentation* and the *migrating motility complex.*

Segmentation contractions mix and slowly propel the chyme.

Segmentation, the small intestine's primary method of motility during digestion of a meal, both mixes and slowly propels the chyme. Segmentation consists of oscillating, ringlike contrac-

(a) Structure of bile salts and their adsorption on the surface of a small lipid droplet

(b) Formation of a lipid emulsion through the action of bile salts

● **FIGURE 15-16 Schematic structure and function of bile salts.** (a) A bile salt consists of a lipid-soluble part that dissolves in the fat droplet and a negatively charged, water-soluble part that projects from the surface of the droplet. (b) When a large fat droplet is broken up into smaller fat droplets by intestinal contractions, bile salts adsorb on the surface of the small droplets, creating shells of negatively charged, water-soluble bile salt components that cause the fat droplets to repel one another. This emulsifying action holds the fat droplets apart and prevents them from recoalescing, increasing the surface area of exposed fat available for digestion by pancreatic lipase.

tions of the circular smooth muscle along the small intestine's length; between the contracted segments are relaxed areas containing a small bolus of chyme. The contractile rings occur every few centimeters, dividing the small intestine into segments like a chain of sausages. These contractile rings do not sweep along the length of the intestine as peristaltic waves do. Rather, after a brief period, the contracted segments relax, and ringlike contractions appear in the previously relaxed areas (● Figure 15-18). The new contraction forces the chyme in a previously relaxed segment to move in both directions into the now relaxed adjacent segments. A newly relaxed segment therefore

Within figure (a): "Negatively charged water-soluble portion— hydrophilic (polar) groups, all located on one side of molecule)"; "Lipid-soluble portion— derived from hydrophobic (nonpolar) cholesterol"; "Water (polar)"; "Small lipid droplet (nonpolar) with bile salt molecules adsorbed on its surface".

Within figure (b): "Large fat droplet"; "Through action of bile salts"; "Lipid emulsion".

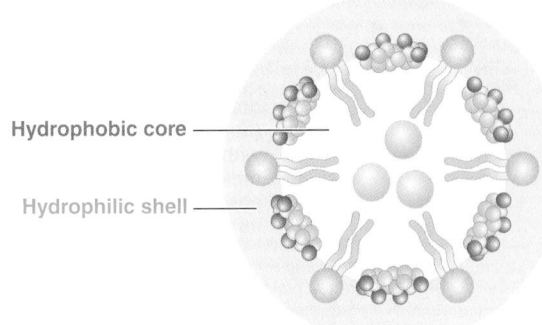

Hydrophobic core ⎯

Hydrophilic shell ⎯

KEY

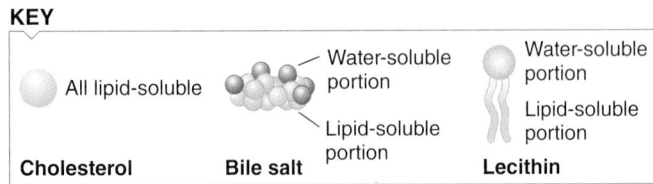

◯ All lipid-soluble	Water-soluble portion / Lipid-soluble portion	Water-soluble portion / Lipid-soluble portion
Cholesterol	**Bile salt**	**Lecithin**

● **FIGURE 15-17 A micelle.** Bile constituents (bile salts, lecithin, and cholesterol) aggregate to form micelles that consist of a hydrophilic (water-soluble) shell and a hydrophobic (lipid-soluble) core. Because the outer shell of a micelle is water soluble, the products of fat digestion, which are not water soluble, can be carried through the watery luminal contents to the absorptive surface of the small intestine by dissolving in the micelle's lipid-soluble core. This figure is not drawn to scale compared to the lipid emulsion droplets in Figure 15-16b. An emulsified fat droplet averages 1000 nm in diameter compared to a micelle, which is 3 to 10 nm in diameter.

receives chyme from both the contracting segment immediately ahead of it and the one immediately behind it. Shortly thereafter, the areas of contraction and relaxation alternate again. In this way, the chyme is chopped, churned, and thoroughly mixed. These contractions can be compared to squeezing a pastry tube with your hands to mix the contents.

INITIATION AND CONTROL OF SEGMENTATION Segmentation contractions are initiated by the small intestine's pacemaker cells, which produce a BER similar to the gastric BER that governs peristalsis in the stomach. If the small-intestine BER brings the circular smooth muscle layer to threshold, segmentation contractions are induced, with the frequency of segmentation following the frequency of the BER.

Segmentation is slight or absent between meals but becomes vigorous immediately after a meal. Both the duodenum and the ileum start to segment simultaneously when the meal first enters the small intestine. The duodenum starts to segment primarily in response to local distension caused by the presence of chyme. Segmentation of the empty ileum, in contrast, is brought about by gastrin secreted in response to the presence of chyme in the stomach, a mechanism known as the **gastroileal reflex.** Extrinsic nerves can modify the strength of these contractions. Parasympathetic stimulation enhances segmentation, whereas sympathetic stimulation depresses segmental activity.

FUNCTIONS OF SEGMENTATION Segmentation not only mixes but also slowly moves chyme through the small intestine. How can this be, when each segmental contraction propels chyme

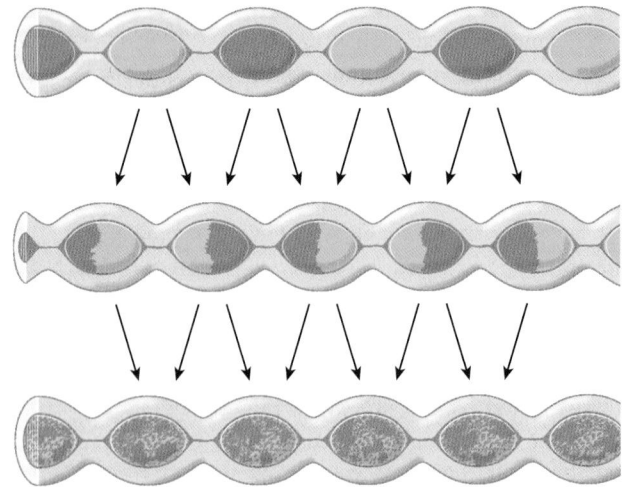

● **FIGURE 15-18 Segmentation.** Segmentation consists of ringlike contractions along the length of the small intestine. Within a matter of seconds, the contracted segments relax and the previously relaxed areas contract. These oscillating contractions thoroughly mix the chyme within the small-intestine lumen.

both forward and backward? The chyme slowly progresses forward because the frequency of segmentation declines along the length of the small intestine. The pacemaker cells in the duodenum spontaneously depolarize faster than those farther down the tract, with segmentation contractions occurring in the duodenum at a rate of 12 per minute, compared to only 9 per minute in the terminal ileum. Because segmentation occurs with greater frequency in the upper part of the small intestine than in the lower part, more chyme, on average, is pushed forward than is pushed backward. As a result, chyme is moved slowly from the upper to the lower part of the small intestine, being shuffled back and forth to accomplish thorough mixing and absorption in the process. This slow propulsive mechanism is advantageous because it allows ample time for the digestive and absorptive processes to take place. The contents usually take 3 to 5 hours to move through the small intestine.

The migrating motility complex sweeps the intestine clean between meals.

When most of the meal has been absorbed, segmentation contractions cease and are replaced between meals by the **migrating motility complex,** or **"intestinal housekeeper."** This between-meal motility consists of weak, repetitive peristaltic waves that move a short distance down the intestine before dying out. The waves start at the stomach and migrate down the intestine; that is, each new peristaltic wave is initiated at a site a little farther down the small intestine. These short peristaltic waves take about 100 to 150 minutes to gradually migrate from the stomach to the end of the small intestine, with each contraction sweeping any remnants of the preceding meal plus mucosal debris and bacteria forward toward the colon, just like a good "intestinal housekeeper." After the end of the small intestine is reached, the cycle begins again and continues to repeat itself until the next meal. The migrating motility complex is regulated between meals by the hormone *motilin,* which is secreted during the unfed state by endocrine cells of the small-intestine mucosa. When the next meal arrives, segmental activity is triggered again, and the migrating motility complex ceases. Motilin release is inhibited by feeding.

The ileocecal juncture prevents contamination of the small intestine by colonic bacteria.

At the juncture between the small and the large intestines, the last part of the ileum empties into the cecum (● Figure 15-19). Two factors contribute to this region's ability to act as a barrier between the small and the large intestines. First, the anatomic arrangement is such that valvelike folds of tissue protrude from the ileum into the lumen of the cecum. When the ileal contents are pushed forward, this **ileocecal valve** is easily pushed open, but the folds of tissue are forcibly closed when the cecal contents attempt to move backward. Second, the smooth muscle within the last several centimeters of the ileal wall is thickened, forming a sphincter that is under neural and hormonal control. Most of the time, this **ileocecal sphincter** remains at least mildly constricted. Pressure on the cecal side of the sphincter causes it to contract more forcibly; distension of the ileal side causes the sphincter to relax, a reaction mediated by the intrinsic plexuses in the area. In this way, the ileocecal juncture prevents the bacteria-laden contents of the large intestine from contaminating the small intestine yet lets the ileal contents pass into the colon. If the colonic bacteria gained access to the nutrient-rich small intestine, they would multiply rapidly. Relaxation of the sphincter is enhanced by release of gastrin at the onset of a meal, when increased gastric activity is taking place. This relaxation allows the undigested fibers and unabsorbed solutes from the preceding meal to be moved forward as the new meal enters the tract.

Small-intestine secretions do not contain any digestive enzymes.

Each day, the exocrine gland cells in the small-intestine mucosa secrete into the lumen about 1.5 liters of an aqueous salt and mucus solution. Secretion increases after a meal in response to local stimulation of the small-intestine mucosa by the presence of chyme.

The mucus in the secretion provides protection and lubrication. Furthermore, this aqueous secretion provides plenty of H_2O to participate in the enzymatic digestion of food. Recall that digestion involves hydrolysis—bond breakage by reaction with H_2O—which proceeds most efficiently when all the reactants are in solution.

No digestive enzymes are secreted into this intestinal juice. The small intestine does synthesize digestive enzymes, but they act intracellularly within the borders of the epithelial cells that line the lumen instead of being secreted directly into the lumen.

The small-intestine enzymes complete digestion within the brush-border membrane.

Digestion within the small-intestine lumen is accomplished by the pancreatic enzymes, with fat digestion being enhanced by bile secretion. As a result of pancreatic enzymatic activity, fats are completely reduced to their absorbable units of monoglycerides and free fatty acids, proteins are broken down into small peptide fragments and some amino acids, and carbohydrates are reduced to disaccharides and some monosaccharides. Thus, fat digestion is completed within the small-intestine lumen, but carbohydrate and protein digestion have not been brought to completion.

Special hairlike projections on the luminal surface of the small-intestine epithelial cells, the **microvilli,** form the **brush border** (see p. 40). The brush-border plasma membrane contains three categories of membrane-bound enzymes:

1. **Enterokinase,** which activates the pancreatic proteolytic enzyme trypsinogen

2. The **disaccharidases (maltase, sucrase,** and **lactase),** which complete carbohydrate digestion by hydrolyzing the remaining disaccharides (maltose, sucrose, and lactose, respectively) into their constituent monosaccharides

3. The **aminopeptidases,** which hydrolyze the small peptide fragments into their amino acid components, thereby completing protein digestion

Thus, carbohydrate and protein digestion are completed within the confines of the brush border. (▲ Table 15-5 provides a summary of the digestive processes for the three major categories of nutrients.)

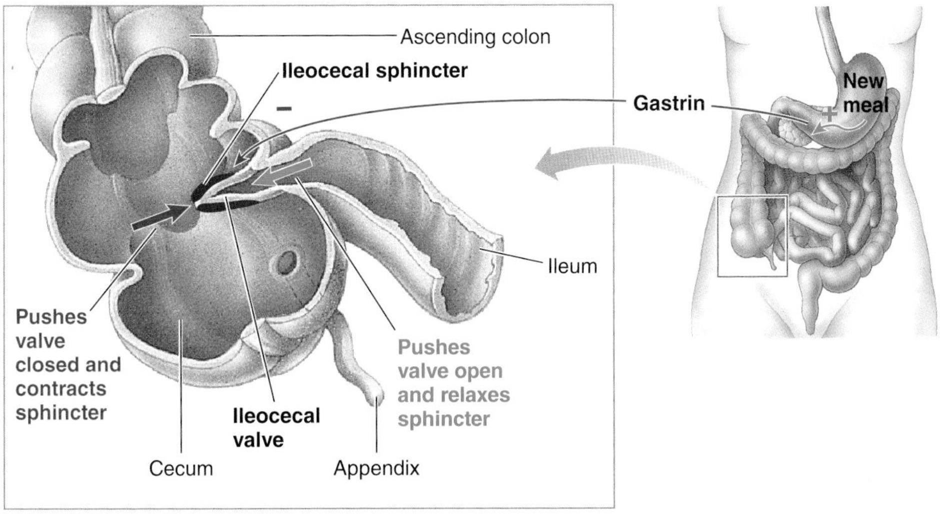

● **FIGURE 15-19 Control of the ileocecal valve and sphincter.** The juncture between the ileum and the large intestine is the ileocecal valve, which is surrounded by thickened smooth muscle, the ileocecal sphincter. Pressure on the cecal side pushes the valve closed and contracts the sphincter, preventing the bacteria-laden colonic contents from contaminating the nutrient-rich small intestine. The valve–sphincter opens and allows ileal contents to enter the large intestine in response to pressure on the ileal side of the valve and to the hormone gastrin secreted as a new meal enters the stomach.

▲ Table 15-5 Digestive Processes for the Three Major Categories of Nutrients

Nutrients	Enzymes for Digesting the Nutrients	Source of Enzymes	Site of Action of Enzymes	Action of Enzymes	Absorbable Units of the Nutrients
Carbohydrates	Amylase	Salivary glands	Mouth and (mostly) body of stomach	Hydrolyzes polysaccharides to disaccharides (maltose)	
		Exocrine pancreas	Small-intestine lumen		
	Disaccharidases (maltase, sucrase, lactase)	Small-intestine epithelial cells	Small-intestine brush border	Hydrolyze disaccharides to monosaccharides	Monosaccharides, especially glucose
Proteins	Pepsin	Stomach chief cells	Stomach antrum	Hydrolyzes protein to peptide fragments	
	Trypsin, chymotrypsin, carboxypeptidase	Exocrine pancreas	Small-intestine lumen	Attack different peptide fragments	
	Aminopeptidases	Small-intestine epithelial cells	Small-intestine brush border	Hydrolyze peptide fragments to amino acids	Amino acids
Fats	Lipase	Exocrine pancreas	Small-intestine lumen	Hydrolyzes triglycerides to fatty acids and monoglycerides	Fatty acids and monoglycerides
	Bile salts (not an enzyme)	Liver	Small-intestine lumen	Emulsify large fat globules for attack by pancreatic lipase	

A fairly common disorder, **lactose intolerance,** involves a deficiency of lactase, the disaccharidase specific for the digestion of lactose, or milk sugar. Most children under 4 years of age have adequate lactase, but this may be gradually lost so that, in many adults, lactase activity is diminished or absent. When lactose-rich milk or dairy products are consumed by a person with lactase deficiency, the undigested lactose remains in the lumen and has several related consequences. First, accumulation of undigested lactose creates an osmotic gradient that draws H_2O into the intestinal lumen. Second, bacteria living in the large intestine have lactose-splitting ability, so they eagerly attack the lactose as an energy source, producing large quantities of CO_2 and methane gas in the process. Distension of the intestine by both fluid and gas produces pain (cramping) and diarrhea. Infants with lactose intolerance may also suffer from malnutrition.

Finally, we are ready to discuss absorption of nutrients. Up to this point, no food, water, or electrolytes have been absorbed.

The small intestine is remarkably well adapted for its primary role in absorption.

All products of carbohydrate, protein, and fat digestion, as well as most of the ingested electrolytes, vitamins, and water, are normally absorbed by the small intestine indiscriminately. Usually, only the absorption of calcium and iron is adjusted to the body's needs. Thus, the more food consumed, the more that will be digested and absorbed, as people who are trying to control their weight are all too painfully aware.

The mucous lining of the small intestine is remarkably well adapted for its special absorptive function for two reasons: (1) it has a large surface area, and (2) the epithelial cells in this lining have a variety of specialized transport mechanisms.

ADAPTATIONS THAT INCREASE THE SMALL INTESTINE'S SURFACE AREA The following special modifications of the small-intestine mucosa greatly increase the surface area available for absorption (● Figure 15-20):

■ The inner surface of the small intestine is thrown into permanent circular folds that are visible to the naked eye and increase the surface area threefold.

■ Extending from this folded surface are microscopic, fingerlike projections known as **villi,** which give the lining a velvety appearance and increase the surface area another 10 times (● Figure 15-21). The surface of each villus is covered by epithelial cells interspersed occasionally with mucous cells.

■ Even smaller hairlike projections, the *brush border* or *microvilli,* arise from the luminal surface of these epithelial cells, increasing the surface area another 20-fold. Each epithelial cell has as many as 3000 to 6000 of these microvilli, which are visible only with an electron microscope. The small-intestine enzymes perform their functions within the membrane of this brush border.

Altogether, the folds, villi, and microvilli provide the small intestine with a luminal surface area 600 times greater than if it were a tube of the same length and diameter lined by a flat sur-

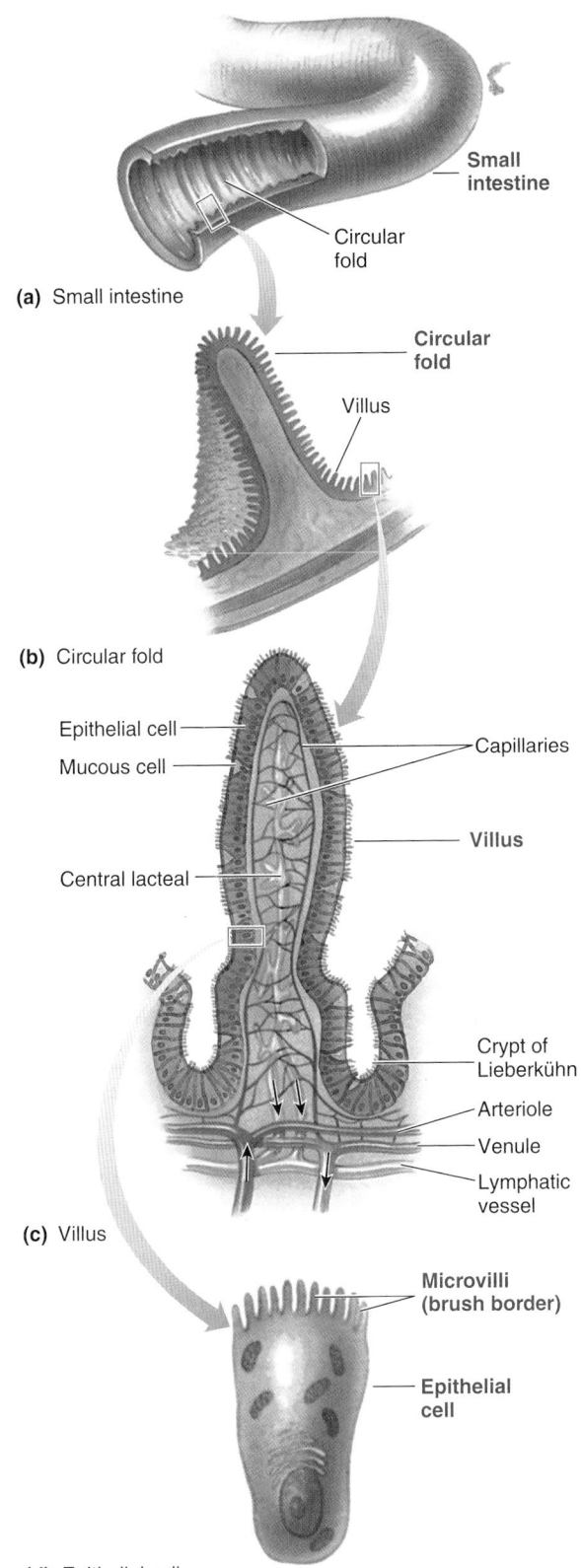

(a) Small intestine

Small intestine

Circular fold

(b) Circular fold

Circular fold

Villus

(c) Villus

Epithelial cell

Mucous cell

Central lacteal

Capillaries

Villus

Crypt of Lieberkühn

Arteriole

Venule

Lymphatic vessel

(d) Epithelial cell

Microvilli (brush border)

Epithelial cell

● **FIGURE 15-20 Small-intestine absorptive surface.** (a) Gross structure of the small intestine. (b) The circular folds of the small-intestine mucosa collectively increase the absorptive surface area threefold. (c) Microscopic, fingerlike projections known as villi collectively increase the surface area another 10-fold. (d) Each epithelial cell on a villus has microvilli on its luminal border; the microvilli increase the surface area another 20-fold. Together, these surface modifications increase the small intestine's absorptive surface area 600-fold.

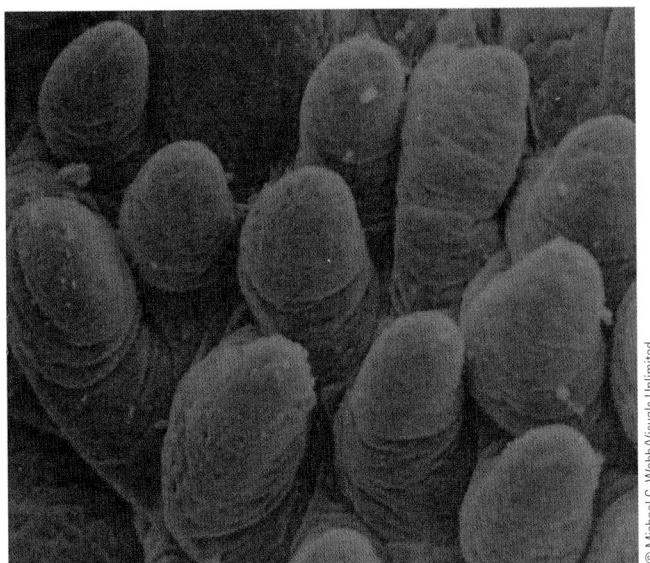

● **FIGURE 15-21 Scanning electron micrograph of villi projecting from the small-intestine mucosa.**

face. If the surface area of the small intestine were spread out flat, it would cover an entire tennis court.

Clinical Note **Malabsorption** (impairment of absorption) may be caused by damage to or reduction of the surface area of the small intestine. One of the most common causes is **gluten enteropathy,** also known as **celiac disease.** In this condition, the person's small intestine is abnormally sensitive to *gluten,* a protein constituent of wheat, barley, and rye. These grain products are widely prevalent in processed foods. This condition is a complex immunological disorder in which exposure to gluten erroneously activates a T-cell response (see p. 345) that damages the intestinal villi: The normally luxuriant array of villi is reduced, the mucosa becomes flattened, and the brush border becomes short and stubby (● Figure 15-22). Because this loss of villi decreases the surface area available for absorption, absorption of all nutrients is impaired. The condition is treated by eliminating gluten from the diet.

STRUCTURE OF A VILLUS Absorption across the digestive tract wall involves transepithelial transport similar to movement of material across the kidney tubules (see p. 415). Each villus has the following major components (see ● Figure 15-20c):

■ *Epithelial cells that cover the surface of the villus.* The epithelial cells are joined at their lateral borders by tight junctions, which limit passage of luminal contents between the cells, although the tight junctions in the small intestine are leakier than those in the stomach. Within their luminal brush borders, these epithelial cells have carriers for absorption of specific nutrients and electrolytes from the lumen, as well as the membrane-bound digestive enzymes that complete carbohydrate and protein digestion.

■ *A connective tissue core*

■ *A capillary network.* Each villus is supplied by an arteriole that breaks up into a capillary network within the villus core.

THE DIGESTIVE SYSTEM　　**495**

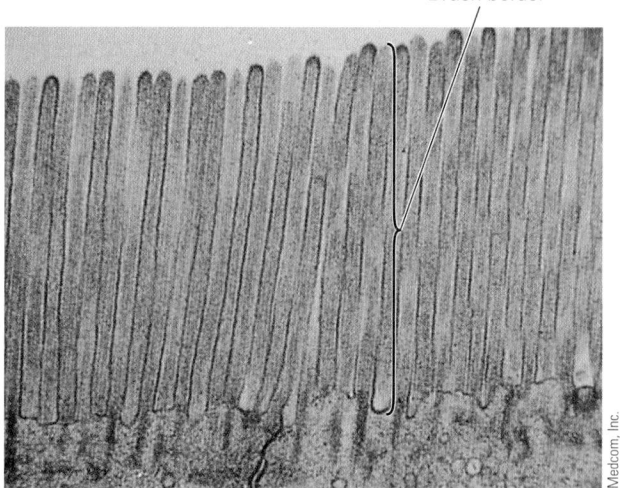

Brush border

(a) Normal

Medcom, Inc.

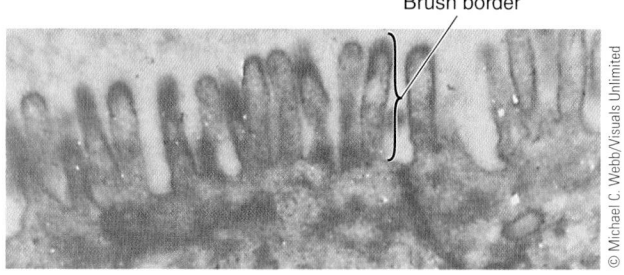

Brush border

(b) Gluten enteropathy

© Michael C. Webb/Visuals Unlimited

● **FIGURE 15-22 Reduction in the brush border with gluten enteropathy.** (a) Electron micrograph of the brush border of a small-intestine epithelial cell in a normal individual. (b) Electron micrograph of the short, stubby brush border of a small-intestine epithelial cell in a patient with gluten enteropathy.

(*Source:* Thomas W. Sheehy, M.D.; Robert L. Slaughter, M.D.: *The Malabsorption Syndrome* by Medcom, Inc. Reproduced by permission of Medcom, Inc.)

The capillaries rejoin to form a venule that drains away from the villus.

■ *A terminal lymphatic vessel.* Each villus is supplied by a single blind-ended lymphatic vessel known as the **central lacteal,** which occupies the center of the villus core.

During the process of absorption, digested substances enter the capillary network or the central lacteal. To be absorbed, a substance must pass completely through the epithelial cell, diffuse through the interstitial fluid within the connective tissue core of the villus, and then cross the wall of a capillary or lymph vessel. Like renal transport, intestinal absorption may be active or passive, with active absorption involving energy expenditure during at least one of the transepithelial transport steps.

The mucosal lining experiences rapid turnover.

Dipping down into the mucosal surface between the villi are shallow invaginations known as the **crypts of Lieberkühn** (see ● Figure 15-20c). Unlike the gastric pits, these intestinal crypts do not secrete digestive enzymes, but they do secrete water and salt, which, along with the mucus secreted by the cells on the villus surface, constitute the intestinal juice.

Furthermore, the crypts function as nurseries. The epithelial cells lining the small intestine slough off and are replaced at a rapid rate as a result of high mitotic activity of *stem cells* in the crypts. New cells that are continually being produced in the crypts migrate up the villi and, in the process, push off the older cells at the tips of the villi into the lumen. In this manner, more than 100 million intestinal cells are shed per minute. The entire trip from crypt to tip averages about 3 days, so the epithelial lining of the small intestine is replaced approximately every 3 days. Because of this high rate of cell division, the crypt stem cells are very sensitive to damage by radiation and anticancer drugs, both of which may inhibit cell division.

The new cells undergo several changes as they migrate up the villus. The concentration of brush-border enzymes increases and the capacity for absorption improves, so the cells at the tip of the villus have the greatest digestive and absorptive capability. Just at their peak, these cells are pushed off by the newly migrating cells. Thus, the luminal contents are constantly exposed to cells that are optimally equipped to complete the digestive and absorptive functions efficiently. Furthermore, just as in the stomach, the rapid turnover of cells in the small intestine is essential because of the harsh luminal conditions. Cells exposed to the abrasive and corrosive luminal contents are easily damaged and cannot live for long, so they must be continually replaced by a fresh supply of newborn cells.

The old cells sloughed off into the lumen are not entirely lost to the body. These cells are digested, with the cell constituents being absorbed into the blood and reclaimed for synthesis of new cells, among other things.

In addition to stem cells, *defensive cells* are found in the crypts. These cells produce lysozyme and other chemicals that thwart bacteria.

We now turn our attention to the ways in which the epithelial lining of the small intestine is specialized to accomplish absorption of luminal contents and the mechanisms through which the specific dietary constituents are normally absorbed.

Energy-dependent Na$^+$ absorption drives passive H$_2$O absorption.

Sodium may be absorbed both passively and actively. When the electrochemical gradient favors movement of Na$^+$ from the lumen to the blood, passive diffusion of Na$^+$ can occur *between* the intestinal epithelial cells through the "leaky" tight junctions into the interstitial fluid within the villus. Movement of Na$^+$ *through* the cells is energy dependent, being driven by the Na$^+$–K$^+$ pumps located at the cells' basolateral borders, similar to the process of Na$^+$ reabsorption across the kidney tubules (see p. 414).

As with the renal tubules in the early part of the nephron, the absorption of Cl$^-$, H$_2$O, glucose, and amino acids from the small intestine is linked to this energy-dependent Na$^+$ absorption. Chloride passively follows down the electrical gradient created by Na$^+$ absorption and can be actively absorbed if needed. Water is reabsorbed passively down the osmotic gradient produced by active reabsorption of Na$^+$.

Digested carbohydrates and proteins are both absorbed by secondary active transport and enter the blood.

Absorption of the digestion end products of both carbohydrates and proteins is accomplished by Na$^+$- and energy-dependent secondary active transport (see p. 64), and both categories of end products are absorbed into the blood.

CARBOHYDRATE ABSORPTION Dietary carbohydrates are presented to the small intestine for absorption mainly in the forms of the disaccharides maltose (the product of polysaccharide digestion), sucrose, and lactose. The disaccharidases located in the brush-border membrane of the small intestine cells further reduce these disaccharides into the absorbable monosaccharide units of glucose (mostly), galactose, and fructose.

Glucose and galactose are both absorbed by secondary active transport, in which symport carriers, such as the *sodium and glucose cotransporter (SGLT;* see ● Figure 3-17, p. 65) on the luminal membrane transport both the monosaccharide and Na$^+$ from the lumen into the interior of the intestinal cell. Glucose (or galactose), having been concentrated in the cell by these symporters, leaves the cell down its concentration gradient by facilitated diffusion to enter the capillary network within the villus. Fructose is absorbed into the blood solely by facilitated diffusion.

PROTEIN ABSORPTION Both ingested proteins and endogenous (within the body) proteins that have entered the digestive tract lumen from the following sources are digested and absorbed:

- Digestive enzymes, all of which are proteins, that have been secreted into the lumen
- Proteins within the cells that are pushed off from the villi into the lumen during the process of mucosal turnover

About 20 to 40 g of endogenous proteins enter the lumen each day from these sources. This quantity can amount to more than the quantity of proteins in ingested food. All endogenous proteins must be digested and absorbed, along with the dietary proteins, to prevent depletion of the body's protein stores. The amino acids absorbed from both food and endogenous proteins are used primarily to synthesize new proteins in the body.

The proteins presented to the small intestine for absorption are in the form of amino acids. Amino acids are absorbed into the intestinal cells by symporters, similar to glucose and galactose absorption. Like monosaccharides, amino acids leave the intestinal cells by facilitated diffusion and enter the capillary network within the villus.

Digested fat is absorbed passively and enters the lymph.

Fat absorption is quite different from carbohydrate and protein absorption because the insolubility of fat in water presents a special problem. Fat must be transferred from the watery chyme through the watery body fluids, even though fat is not water soluble. Therefore, fat must undergo a series of physical and chemical transformations to circumvent this problem during its digestion and absorption (● Figure 15-23).

A REVIEW OF FAT EMULSIFICATION AND DIGESTION When the stomach contents are emptied into the duodenum, the ingested fat is aggregated into large, oily triglyceride droplets that float in the chyme. Recall that through the bile salts' detergent action in the small-intestine lumen, the large droplets are dispersed into a lipid emulsification of small droplets, exposing a greater surface area of fat for digestion by pancreatic lipase (● Figure 15-23, step **1**). The products of lipase digestion (monoglycerides and free fatty acids; step **2**) are also not very water soluble, so little of these end products of fat digestion can diffuse through the aqueous chyme to reach the absorptive lining. However, biliary components facilitate absorption of these fatty end products by forming micelles.

FAT ABSORPTION Remember that micelles are water-soluble particles that can carry the end products of fat digestion within their lipid-soluble interiors (● Figure 15-23, step **3**). Once these micelles reach the luminal membranes of the epithelial cells, the monoglycerides and free fatty acids passively diffuse from the micelles through the lipid component of the epithelial cell membranes to enter the interior of these cells (step **4**). As these fat products leave the micelles and are absorbed across the epithelial cell membranes, the micelles can pick up more monoglycerides and free fatty acids, which have been produced from digestion of other triglyceride molecules in the fat emulsion.

Bile salts continuously repeat their fat-solubilizing function down the length of the small intestine until all fat is absorbed. Then the bile salts themselves are reabsorbed in the terminal ileum by special active transport. This is an efficient process because relatively small amounts of bile salts can facilitate digestion and absorption of large amounts of fat, with each bile salt performing its ferrying function repeatedly before it is reabsorbed.

Once within the interior of the epithelial cells, the monoglycerides and free fatty acids are resynthesized into triglycerides (step **5**). These triglycerides conglomerate into droplets and are coated with a layer of lipoprotein (synthesized by the endoplasmic reticulum of the epithelial cell), which makes the fat droplets water soluble (step **6**). The large, coated fat droplets, known as **chylomicrons,** are extruded by exocytosis from the epithelial cells into the interstitial fluid within the villus (step **7**). Chylomicrons are 75 to 500 nm in diameter, compared to micelles, which are 3 to 10 nm in diameter. The chylomicrons subsequently enter the central lacteals rather than the capillaries because of the structural differences between these two vessels (step **8**). Capillaries have a basement membrane (an outer layer of polysaccharides) that prevents the chylomicrons from entering, but the lymph vessels do not have this barrier. Thus, fat can be absorbed into the lymphatics but not directly into the blood.

The actual absorption of monoglycerides and free fatty acids from the chyme across the luminal membrane of the small-intestinal epithelial cells is a passive process because the lipid-soluble fatty end products merely dissolve in and pass through the lipid part of the membrane. However, the overall sequence of events needed for fat absorption requires energy. For example, bile salts are actively secreted by the liver, the resynthesis of triglycerides and formation of chylomicrons within the epithelial cells are active processes, and the exocytosis of chylomicrons requires energy.

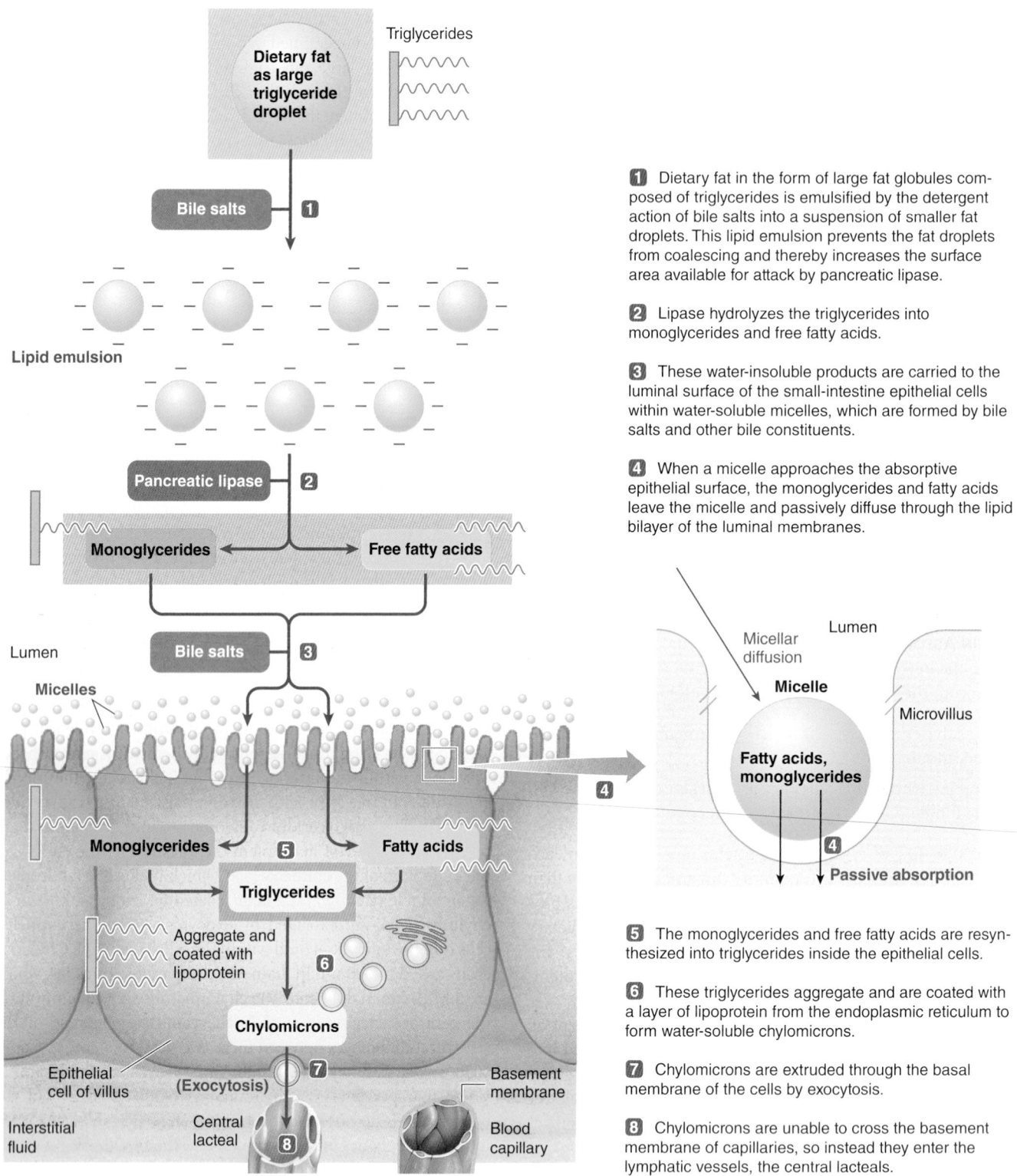

1 Dietary fat in the form of large fat globules composed of triglycerides is emulsified by the detergent action of bile salts into a suspension of smaller fat droplets. This lipid emulsion prevents the fat droplets from coalescing and thereby increases the surface area available for attack by pancreatic lipase.

2 Lipase hydrolyzes the triglycerides into monoglycerides and free fatty acids.

3 These water-insoluble products are carried to the luminal surface of the small-intestine epithelial cells within water-soluble micelles, which are formed by bile salts and other bile constituents.

4 When a micelle approaches the absorptive epithelial surface, the monoglycerides and fatty acids leave the micelle and passively diffuse through the lipid bilayer of the luminal membranes.

5 The monoglycerides and free fatty acids are resynthesized into triglycerides inside the epithelial cells.

6 These triglycerides aggregate and are coated with a layer of lipoprotein from the endoplasmic reticulum to form water-soluble chylomicrons.

7 Chylomicrons are extruded through the basal membrane of the cells by exocytosis.

8 Chylomicrons are unable to cross the basement membrane of capillaries, so instead they enter the lymphatic vessels, the central lacteals.

● **FIGURE 15-23 Fat digestion and absorption.** Because fat is not soluble in water, it must undergo a series of transformations to be digested and absorbed.

Vitamin absorption is largely passive.

Water-soluble vitamins are primarily absorbed passively with water, whereas fat-soluble vitamins are carried in the micelles and absorbed passively with the end products of fat digestion. Some of the vitamins can also be absorbed by carriers, if necessary. Vitamin B_{12} is unique in that it must be in combination with gastric intrinsic factor for absorption by receptor-mediated endocytosis in the terminal ileum.

Iron and calcium absorption is regulated.

In contrast to the almost complete, unregulated absorption of other ingested electrolytes, dietary iron and calcium may not be absorbed completely because their absorption is subject to regulation, depending on the body's needs for these electrolytes. Normally, only enough iron and calcium are actively absorbed into the blood to maintain the homeostasis of these electrolytes, with excess ingested quantities being lost in the feces.

Most absorbed nutrients immediately pass through the liver for processing.

The venules that leave the small-intestine villi, along with those from the rest of the digestive tract, empty into the hepatic portal vein, which carries the blood to the liver. Consequently, anything absorbed into the digestive capillaries first must pass through the hepatic biochemical factory before entering the general circulation. Thus, the products of carbohydrate and protein digestion are channeled into the liver, where many of these energy-rich products are subjected to immediate metabolic processing. Furthermore, harmful substances that may have been absorbed are detoxified by the liver before gaining access to the general circulation. After passing through the portal circulation, the venous blood from the digestive system empties into the vena cava and returns to the heart to be distributed throughout the body, carrying glucose and amino acids for use by the tissues.

Fat, which cannot penetrate the intestinal capillaries, is picked up by the central lacteal and enters the lymphatic system instead. Contractions of the villi periodically compress the central lacteal and "milk" the lymph out of this vessel. The smaller lymph vessels converge and eventually form a large lymph duct that empties into the venous system within the chest. In this way, fat gains access to the blood for distribution throughout the body.

Extensive absorption by the small intestine keeps pace with secretion.

The small intestine normally absorbs about 9 L of fluid per day in the form of H_2O and solutes, including the absorbable units of nutrients, vitamins, and electrolytes. How can that be, when humans normally ingest only about 1250 ml of fluid and consume 1250 g of solid food (80% of which is H_2O) per day (see p. 450)? ▲ Table 15-6 illustrates the tremendous daily absorption performed by the small intestine. Each day, about 9500 ml of H_2O and solutes enter the small intestine. Note that of this 9500 ml, only 2500 ml are ingested from the external environ-

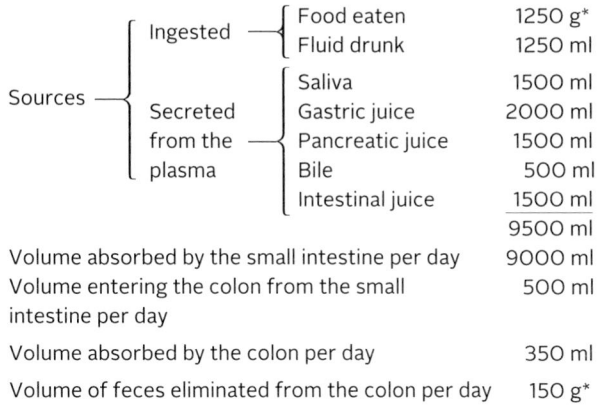

▲ Table 15-6 Volumes Absorbed by the Small and Large Intestine per Day

Volume entering the small intestine per day			
Sources	Ingested	Food eaten	1250 g*
		Fluid drunk	1250 ml
	Secreted from the plasma	Saliva	1500 ml
		Gastric juice	2000 ml
		Pancreatic juice	1500 ml
		Bile	500 ml
		Intestinal juice	1500 ml
			9500 ml
Volume absorbed by the small intestine per day			9000 ml
Volume entering the colon from the small intestine per day			500 ml
Volume absorbed by the colon per day			350 ml
Volume of feces eliminated from the colon per day			150 g*

*One milliliter of H_2O weighs 1 g. Therefore, because a high percentage of food and feces is H_2O, we can roughly equate grams of food or feces with milliliters of fluid.

ment. The remaining 7000 ml (7 L) of fluid are digestive juices derived from the plasma. Recall that plasma is the ultimate source of digestive secretions because the secretory cells extract from the plasma the necessary raw materials for their secretory product. Considering that the entire plasma volume is only about 2.75 liters, absorption must closely parallel secretion to keep the plasma volume from falling sharply.

Of the 9500 ml of fluid entering the small-intestine lumen per day, about 95%, or 9000 ml of fluid, is normally absorbed by the small intestine back into the plasma, with only 500 ml of the small-intestine contents passing on into the colon. Thus, the body normally does not lose the digestive juices. After the constituents of the juices are secreted into the digestive tract lumen and perform their function, they are returned to the plasma. The only secretory product that escapes from the body is bilirubin, a waste product that must be eliminated.

Diarrhea results in loss of fluid and electrolytes.

Diarrhea is characterized by passage of a highly fluid fecal matter, often with increased frequency of defecation. The abnormal fluidity of the feces usually occurs because the small intestine is unable to absorb fluid as extensively as normal. This extra unabsorbed fluid passes out in the feces. The most common cause of diarrhea is excessive small-intestinal motility, which arises either from local irritation of the gut wall by bacterial or viral infection of the small intestine or from emotional stress. Rapid transit of the small-intestine contents does not allow enough time for adequate absorption of fluid to occur. Not only are some of the ingested materials lost, but some of the secreted materials that normally would have been reabsorbed are lost as well. Excessive loss of intestinal contents causes dehydration, loss of unabsorbed nutrients, and metabolic acidosis resulting from the loss of HCO_3^- (see p. 460).

Large Intestine

The **large intestine** consists of the colon, cecum, appendix, and rectum (● Figure 15-24). The **cecum** forms a blind-ended pouch below the junction of the small and large intestines at the ileocecal valve. The small, fingerlike projection at the bottom of the cecum is the **appendix,** a lymphoid tissue that houses lymphocytes (see p. 331). The **colon,** which makes up most of the large intestine, is not coiled like the small intestine but consists of three relatively straight parts—the *ascending colon,* the *transverse colon,* and the *descending colon.* The end part of the descending colon becomes S shaped, forming the *sigmoid colon* (*sigmoid* means "S shaped"), and then straightens out to form the **rectum** (meaning "straight").

The large intestine is primarily a drying and storage organ.

The colon normally receives about 500 ml of chyme from the small intestine each day. Because most digestion and absorption have been accomplished in the small intestine, the contents delivered to the colon consist of indigestible food residues (such as cellulose), unabsorbed biliary components, and the remaining fluid. The colon extracts more H_2O and salt from the contents. What remains to be eliminated is known as **feces.** The primary function of the large intestine is to store feces before defecation. Cellulose and other indigestible substances in the diet provide bulk and help maintain regular bowel movements by contributing to the volume of the colonic contents.

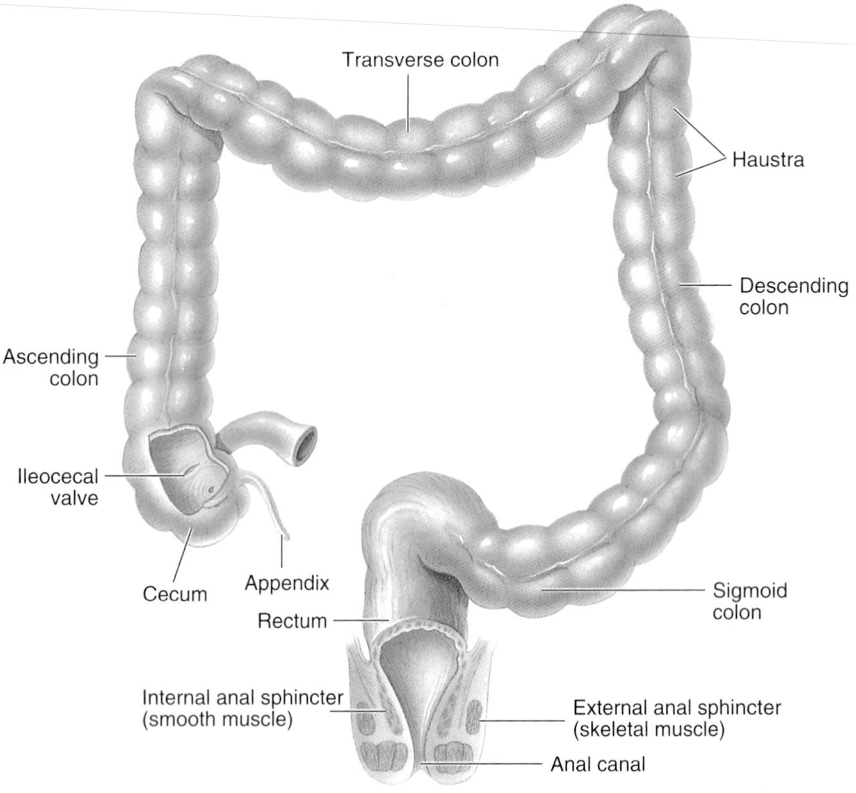

Haustral contractions slowly shuffle the colonic contents back and forth.

Most of the time, movements of the large intestine are slow and nonpropulsive, as is appropriate for its absorptive and storage functions. The colon's main motility is **haustral contractions** initiated by the autonomous rhythmicity (BER) of colonic smooth muscle cells. These contractions, which throw the large intestine into pouches or sacs called **haustra,** are similar to small-intestine segmentations but occur less frequently. Thirty minutes may elapse between haustral contractions, whereas segmentation contractions in the small intestine occur at rates of between 9 and 12 per minute. The location of the haustral sacs gradually changes as a relaxed segment that has formed a sac slowly contracts while a previously contracted area simultaneously relaxes to form a new sac. These movements are nonpropulsive; they slowly shuffle the contents in a back-and-forth mixing movement that exposes the colonic contents to the absorptive mucosa. Haustral contractions are largely controlled by locally mediated reflexes involving the intrinsic plexuses.

Mass movements propel feces long distances.

Three to four times a day, generally after meals, a marked increase in motility takes place during which large segments of the ascending and transverse colon contract simultaneously, driving the feces one third to three fourths of the length of the colon in a few seconds. These massive contractions, appropriately called **mass movements,** drive the colonic contents into the distal part of the large intestine, where material is stored until defecation occurs.

When food enters the stomach, mass movements are triggered in the colon primarily by the **gastrocolic reflex,** which is mediated from the stomach to the colon by gastrin and by the extrinsic autonomic nerves. In many people, this reflex is most evident after the first meal of the day and is often followed by the urge to defecate. Thus, when a new meal enters the digestive tract, reflexes are initiated to move the existing contents farther along the tract to make way for the incoming food. The gastroileal reflex moves the remaining small-intestine contents into the large intestine, and the gastrocolic reflex pushes the colonic contents into the rectum, triggering the defecation reflex.

Feces are eliminated by the defecation reflex.

When mass movements of the colon move feces into the rectum, the resultant distension of the rectum stimulates stretch receptors in the rectal wall, initiating the **defecation reflex.** This reflex causes the **internal anal sphincter** (which is smooth muscle) to relax and the rectum and sigmoid colon to contract more vigorously. If the **external**

● **FIGURE 15-24 Anatomy of the large intestine.**

Transverse colon

Haustra

Descending colon

Ascending colon

Ileocecal valve

Cecum

Appendix

Rectum

Internal anal sphincter (smooth muscle)

External anal sphincter (skeletal muscle)

Anal canal

Sigmoid colon

anal sphincter (which is skeletal muscle) is also relaxed, defecation occurs. Being skeletal muscle, the external anal sphincter is under voluntary control. The initial distension of the rectal wall is accompanied by the conscious urge to defecate. If circumstances are unfavorable for defecation, voluntary tightening of the external anal sphincter can prevent defecation despite the defecation reflex. If defecation is delayed, the distended rectal wall gradually relaxes, and the urge to defecate subsides until the next mass movement propels more feces into the rectum, again distending the rectum and triggering the defecation reflex. During periods of inactivity, both anal sphincters remain contracted to ensure fecal continence.

When defecation does occur, it is usually assisted by voluntary straining movements that involve simultaneous contraction of the abdominal muscles and a forcible expiration against a closed glottis. This maneuver greatly increases intra-abdominal pressure, which helps expel the feces.

Constipation occurs when the feces become too dry.

If defecation is delayed too long, **constipation** may result. When colonic contents are retained for longer periods than normal, more than the usual amount of H_2O is absorbed from the feces, so they become hard and dry. Possible causes for delayed defecation that might lead to constipation include (1) ignoring the urge to defecate; (2) decreased colon motility accompanying aging, emotion, or a low-bulk diet; (3) obstruction of fecal movement in the large bowel caused by a local tumor or colonic spasm; and (4) impairment of the defecation reflex, such as through injury of the nerve pathways involved.

 If hardened fecal material becomes lodged in the appendix, it may obstruct normal circulation and mucus secretion in this narrow, blind-ended appendage. This blockage leads to **appendicitis.** The inflamed appendix often becomes swollen and filled with pus, and the tissue may die as a result of local circulatory interference. If not surgically removed, the diseased appendix may rupture, spewing its infectious contents into the abdominal cavity.

Large-intestine secretion is entirely protective.

The large intestine does not secrete any digestive enzymes. None are needed, because digestion is completed before chyme ever reaches the colon. Colonic secretion consists of an alkaline ($NaHCO_3$) mucus solution, whose function is to protect the large-intestine mucosa from mechanical and chemical injury. The mucus provides lubrication to facilitate passage of feces, whereas the $NaHCO_3$ neutralizes irritating acids produced by local bacterial fermentation.

No digestion takes place within the large intestine because there are no digestive enzymes. However, the colonic bacteria do digest some of the cellulose for their use.

The colon contains myriad beneficial bacteria.

Because of slow colonic movement, bacteria have time to grow and accumulate in the large intestine. In contrast, in the small intestine the contents are moved through too rapidly for bacterial growth to occur. Furthermore, the mouth, stomach, and small intestine secrete antibacterial agents, but the colon does not. Not all ingested bacteria are destroyed by lysozyme and HCl, however. The surviving bacteria continue to thrive in the large intestine. About 10 times more bacteria live in the human colon than the human body has cells. An estimated 500 to 1000 species of bacteria typically live in the colon. These colonic microorganisms not only are typically harmless but actually are beneficial. Indigenous bacteria (1) enhance intestinal immunity by competing with potentially pathogenic microbes for nutrients and space (see p. 359), (2) promote colonic motility, (3) help maintain colonic mucosal integrity, and (4) make nutritional contributions. For example, bacteria synthesize absorbable vitamin K and raise colonic acidity, thereby promoting the absorption of calcium, magnesium, and zinc.

The large intestine absorbs salt and water, converting the luminal contents into feces.

Some absorption takes place within the colon, but not to the same extent as in the small intestine. Because the luminal surface of the colon is fairly smooth, it has considerably less absorptive surface area than the small intestine. Furthermore, the colon is not equipped with extensive specialized transport mechanisms as the small intestine is. When excessive small-intestine motility delivers the contents to the colon before absorption of nutrients has been completed, the colon cannot absorb most of these materials and they are lost in diarrhea.

The colon normally absorbs salt and H_2O. Sodium is actively absorbed, Cl^- follows passively down the electrical gradient, and H_2O follows osmotically. The colon absorbs token amounts of other electrolytes, as well as vitamin K synthesized by colonic bacteria.

Through absorption of salt and H_2O, a firm fecal mass is formed. Of the 500 ml of material entering the colon per day from the small intestine, the colon normally absorbs about 350 ml, leaving 150 g of feces to be eliminated from the body each day (see ▲ Table 15-6). This fecal material normally consists of 100 g of H_2O and 50 g of solid, including undigested cellulose, bilirubin, bacteria, and small amounts of salt. Thus, contrary to popular thinking, the digestive tract is not a major excretory passageway for eliminating wastes from the body. The main waste product excreted in the feces is bilirubin. The other fecal constituents are unabsorbed food residues and bacteria, which were never actually a part of the body. Bacteria account for nearly one third the dry weight of feces.

Intestinal gases are absorbed or expelled.

Occasionally, instead of feces passing from the anus, intestinal gas, or **flatus,** passes out. Most gas in the colon is due to bacterial activity, with the quantity and nature of the gas depending on the type of food eaten and the characteristics of the colonic bacteria. Some foods, such as beans, contain types of carbohydrates that humans cannot digest but that can be attacked by gas-producing bacteria. Much of the gas is absorbed through the intestinal mucosa. The rest is expelled through the anus.

To selectively expel gas when feces are also present in the rectum, the person voluntarily contracts the abdominal muscles and external anal sphincter at the same time. When abdominal contraction raises the pressure against the contracted anal sphincter sufficiently, the pressure gradient forces air out at a high velocity through a slitlike anal opening that is too narrow for solid feces to escape through. This passage of air at high velocity causes the edges of the anal opening to vibrate, giving rise to the characteristic low-pitched sound accompanying passage of gas.

Overview of the Gastrointestinal Hormones

Throughout our discussion of digestion, we have repeatedly mentioned different functions of the three major gastrointestinal hormones: gastrin, secretin, and CCK. Let us now fit all of these functions together so that you can appreciate the overall adaptive importance of these interactions. Furthermore, we introduce a more recently identified gastrointestinal hormone, GIP.

GASTRIN Protein in the stomach stimulates the release of gastrin, which performs the following functions:

1. It acts in multiple ways to increase secretion of HCl and pepsinogen, two substances of primary importance in initiating digestion of the protein that promoted their secretion.

2. It enhances gastric motility, stimulates ileal motility, relaxes the ileocecal sphincter, and induces mass movements in the colon—all functions aimed at keeping the contents moving through the tract on arrival of a new meal.

Predictably, gastrin secretion is inhibited by an accumulation of acid in the stomach and by the presence in the duodenal lumen of acid and other constituents that necessitate a delay in gastric secretion.

SECRETIN As the stomach empties into the duodenum, the presence of acid in the duodenum stimulates the release of secretin, which performs the following interrelated functions:

1. It inhibits gastric emptying to prevent further acid from entering the duodenum until the acid already present is neutralized.

2. It inhibits gastric secretion to reduce the amount of acid being produced.

3. It stimulates the pancreatic duct cells to produce a large volume of aqueous $NaHCO_3$ secretion, which is emptied into the duodenum to neutralize the acid. Neutralization of the acidic chyme in the duodenum helps prevent damage to the duodenal walls and provides a suitable environment for optimal functioning of the pancreatic digestive enzymes, which are inhibited by acid.

4. It stimulates secretion by the liver of a $NaHCO_3$-rich bile, which likewise is emptied into the duodenum to assist in the neutralization process.

CCK As chyme empties from the stomach, fat and other nutrients enter the duodenum. These nutrients, especially fat and, to a lesser extent, protein products, cause the release of CCK, which performs the following interrelated functions:

1. It inhibits gastric motility and secretion, thereby allowing adequate time for the nutrients already in the duodenum to be digested and absorbed.

2. It stimulates the pancreatic acinar cells to increase secretion of pancreatic enzymes, which continue the digestion of these nutrients in the duodenum (this action is especially important for fat digestion, because pancreatic lipase is the only enzyme that digests fat).

3. It causes contraction of the gallbladder and relaxation of the sphincter of Oddi so that bile is emptied into the duodenum to aid fat digestion and absorption. Bile salts' detergent action is particularly important in enabling pancreatic lipase to perform its digestive task. Again, the multiple effects of CCK are remarkably well adapted to dealing with the fat whose presence in the duodenum triggered this hormone's release.

4. Besides facilitating the digestion of ingested nutrients, CCK is an important regulator of food intake. It plays a key role in satiety, the sensation of having had enough to eat (see p. 514).

GIP A more recently recognized hormone released by the duodenum, GIP, helps promote metabolic processing of the nutrients once they are absorbed. This hormone was originally named *gastric inhibitory peptide (GIP)* for its presumed role as an enterogastrone. It was believed to inhibit gastric motility and secretion, similar to secretin and CCK. Its contribution in this regard is now considered minimal. Instead, this hormone stimulates insulin release by the pancreas, so it is now called **glucose-dependent insulinotropic peptide** (again, **GIP**). This action is remarkably adaptive. As soon as the meal is absorbed, the body has to shift its metabolic gears to use and store the newly arriving nutrients. The metabolic activities of this absorptive phase are largely under the control of insulin (see pp. 560 and 562). Stimulated by the presence of a meal, especially glucose, in the digestive tract, GIP initiates the release of insulin in anticipation of absorption of the meal. Insulin is especially important in promoting the uptake and storage of glucose.

This overview of the multiple, integrated, adaptive functions of the gastrointestinal hormones provides an excellent example of the remarkable efficiency of the human body.

Chapter in Perspective: Focus on Homeostasis

To maintain constancy in the internal environment, materials that are used up in the body (such as energy-rich nutrients and O_2) or uncontrollably lost from the body (such as evaporative H_2O loss from the airways or salt loss in sweat) must constantly be replaced by new supplies of these materials from the external environment. Fresh supplies of O_2 are transferred to the internal environment by the respiratory system, but all the nutrients, H_2O, and various electrolytes needed to maintain homeostasis are acquired through the digestive system. The large, complex food that is ingested is broken down by the digestive system into small absorbable units. These small energy-rich nutrient molecules are transferred across the small-intestine epithelium into the blood for delivery to the cells to replace the nutrients constantly used for ATP production and for repair and growth of body tissues. Likewise, ingested H_2O, salt, and other electrolytes are absorbed by the intestine into the blood.

Unlike regulation in most body systems, regulation of digestive system activities is not aimed at maintaining homeostasis. The quantity of nutrients and H_2O ingested is subject to control, but the quantity of ingested materials absorbed by the digestive tract is not subject to control, with few exceptions. The hunger mechanism governs food intake to help maintain energy balance (see Chapter 16), and the thirst mechanism controls H_2O intake to help maintain H_2O balance (see Chapter 14). However, we often do not heed these con-trol mechanisms, eating and drinking even when we are not hungry or thirsty. Once these materials are in the digestive tract, the digestive system does not vary its rate of nutrient, H_2O, or electrolyte uptake according to body needs (with the exception of iron and calcium); rather, it optimizes conditions for digesting and absorbing what is ingested. Truly, what you eat is what you get. The digestive system is subject to many regulatory processes, but these are not influenced by the nutritional or hydration state of the body. Instead, these control mechanisms are governed by the composition and volume of digestive tract contents so that the rate of motility and secretion of digestive juices are optimal for digestion and absorption of the ingested food.

If excess energy-rich nutrients are ingested and absorbed, the extra nutrients are placed in storage, such as in adipose tissue (fat), so that the blood level of nutrient molecules is kept at a constant level. Excess ingested H_2O and electrolytes are eliminated in the urine to homeostatically maintain the blood levels of these constituents.

REVIEW EXERCISES

Objective Questions (Answers on p. A-49)

1. The extent of nutrient uptake from the digestive tract depends on the body's needs. (True or false?)
2. The stomach is relaxed during vomiting. (True or false?)
3. Acid cannot normally penetrate into or between the cells lining the stomach, which enables the stomach to contain acid without injuring itself. (True or false?)
4. Protein is continually lost from the body through digestive secretions and sloughed epithelial cells, which pass out in the feces. (True or false?)
5. Foodstuffs not absorbed by the small intestine are absorbed by the large intestine. (True or false?)
6. The endocrine pancreas secretes secretin and CCK. (True or false?)
7. When food is mechanically broken down and mixed with gastric secretions, the resultant thick, liquid mixture is known as _____.
8. The entire lining of the small intestine is replaced approximately every _____ days.
9. The two substances absorbed by specialized transport mechanisms located only in the terminal ileum are _____ and _____.
10. The most potent choleretic is _____.
11. Which of the following is not a function of saliva?
    a. begins digestion of carbohydrate
    b. facilitates absorption of glucose across the oral mucosa
    c. facilitates speech
    d. exerts an antibacterial effect
    e. plays an important role in oral hygiene

12. Match the following:
    ___ 1. prevents reentry of food into the mouth during swallowing
    ___ 2. triggers the swallowing reflex
    ___ 3. seals off the nasal passages during swallowing
    ___ 4. prevents air from entering the esophagus during breathing
    ___ 5. closes off the respiratory airways during swallowing
    ___ 6. prevents gastric contents from backing up into the esophagus

    (a) closure of the pharyngoesophageal sphincter
    (b) elevation of the uvula
    (c) position of the tongue against the hard palate
    (d) closure of the gastroesophageal sphincter
    (e) bolus pushed to the rear of the mouth by the tongue
    (f) tight apposition of the vocal folds

13. Use the answer code on the right to identify the characteristics of the listed substances:
    ___ 1. activates pepsinogen
    ___ 2. inhibits amylase
    ___ 3. is essential for vitamin B_{12} absorption
    ___ 4. can act autocatalytically
    ___ 5. is a potent stimulant for acid secretion
    ___ 6. denatures protein
    ___ 7. begins protein digestion
    ___ 8. serves as a lubricant
    ___ 9. kills ingested bacteria
    ___ 10. is alkaline
    ___ 11. is deficient in pernicious anemia
    ___ 12. coats the gastric mucosa

    (a) pepsin
    (b) mucus
    (c) HCl
    (d) intrinsic factor
    (e) histamine

Essay Questions

1. Describe the four basic digestive processes.
2. List the three categories of energy-rich foodstuffs and the absorbable units of each.
3. List the components of the digestive system. Describe the cross-sectional anatomy of the digestive tract.
4. What four general factors are involved in regulating digestive system function? What is the role of each?
5. Describe the types of motility in each component of the digestive tract. What factors control each type of motility?
6. State the composition of the digestive juice secreted by each component of the digestive system. Describe the factors that control each digestive secretion.
7. List the enzymes involved in digesting each category of foodstuff. Indicate the source and control of secretion of each of the enzymes.
8. Why are some digestive enzymes secreted in inactive form? How are they activated?
9. What absorption processes take place within each component of the digestive tract? What special adaptations of the small intestine enhance its absorptive capacity?
10. Describe the absorptive mechanisms for salt, water, carbohydrate, protein, and fat.
11. What are the contributions of the accessory digestive organs? What are the nondigestive functions of the liver?
12. Summarize the functions of each of the three major gastrointestinal hormones. What is the role of GIP?
13. What waste product is excreted in the feces?
14. How is vomiting accomplished? What are the causes and consequences of vomiting and diarrhea?

POINTS TO PONDER

(Explanations on p. A-49)

1. Why do patients who have had a large part of their stomachs removed for treatment of stomach cancer or severe peptic ulcer disease have to eat small quantities of food frequently instead of consuming three meals a day?
2. The number of immune cells in the *gut-associated lymphoid tissue (GALT)* housed in the mucosa is estimated to be equal to the total number of these defense cells in the rest of the body. Speculate on the adaptive significance of this extensive defense capability of the digestive system.
3. How would defecation be accomplished in a patient paralyzed from the waist down by a lower spinal-cord injury?
4. After bilirubin is extracted from the blood by the liver, it is conjugated (combined) with glucuronic acid by the enzyme *glucuronyl transferase* within the liver. Only when conjugated can bilirubin be actively excreted into the bile. For the first few days of life, the liver does not make adequate quantities of glucuronyl transferase. Explain how this transient enzyme deficiency leads to the common condition of jaundice in newborns.
5. Explain why removal of either the stomach or the terminal ileum leads to pernicious anemia.

(Explanation on p. A-50)

Thomas W. experiences a sharp pain in his upper right abdomen after eating a high-fat meal. Also, he has noted that his feces are grayish white instead of brown. What is the most likely cause of his symptoms? Explain why each of these symptoms occurs with this condition.

Chapter 15

General Aspects of Digestion (pp. 465–471)

■ The four basic digestive processes are motility, secretion, digestion, and absorption.

■ The three classes of energy-rich nutrients are digested by hydrolysis into absorbable units as follows: (1) Dietary carbohydrates in the form of the polysaccharides starch and glycogen are digested into monosaccharides, mostly glucose. *(Review Figure 15-1.)* (2) Dietary proteins are digested into amino acids. (3) Dietary fats (triglycerides) are digested into monoglycerides and free fatty acids.

■ The digestive system consists of the digestive tract and accessory digestive organs (salivary glands, exocrine pancreas, and biliary system). *(Review Table 15-1.)*

■ The lumen of the digestive tract (a tube that runs from the mouth to the anus) is continuous with the external environment, so its contents are technically outside the body; this arrangement permits digestion of food without self-digestion occurring in the process.

■ The digestive tract wall has four layers: (from innermost outward) the mucosa, submucosa, muscularis externa, and serosa. The mucosa contains exocrine gland cells that secrete digestive juices into the lumen, endocrine gland cells that secrete gastrointestinal hormones into the blood, and epithelial cells specialized for absorbing digested nutrients. *(Review Figure 15-2.)*

■ Digestive activities are carefully regulated by synergistic autonomous, neural (both intrinsic and extrinsic), and hormonal mechanisms to ensure that ingested food is maximally made available to the body. The submucosal plexus and myenteric plexus constitute the intrinsic plexuses (enteric nervous system). Extrinsic control is by the parasympathetic system, which enhances digestive activity, and the sympathetic system, which slows digestive activity. *(Review Figure 15-3.)*

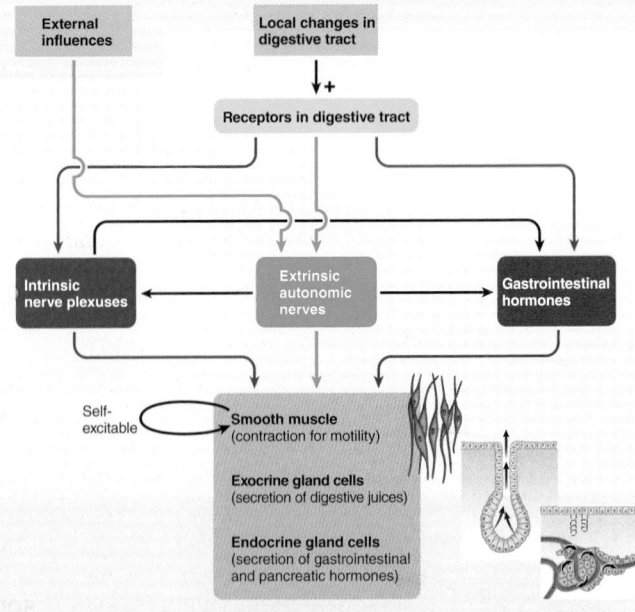

Mouth (pp. 471–473)

■ *Motility:* Food enters the digestive system through the mouth, where it is chewed and mixed with saliva.

■ *Secretion and digestion:* The salivary enzyme, amylase, begins to digest polysaccharides into the disaccharide maltose, a process that continues in the stomach after swallowing. Salivary secretion is controlled by a salivary center in the medulla, mediated by autonomic nerves to the salivary glands. *(Review Figures 15-1 and 15-4.)*

■ *Absorption:* No food is absorbed from the mouth.

Pharynx and Esophagus (pp. 473–475)

■ *Motility:* The tongue propels the bolus of food to the rear of the throat, which initiates the swallowing reflex. The swallowing center in the medulla coordinates a complex group of activities that result in closure of the respiratory passages and propulsion of food through the pharynx and esophagus into the stomach. *(Review Figures 15-5 and 15-6.)*

■ *Secretion, digestion, and absorption:* The esophageal secretion, mucus, is protective. No nutrient digestion or absorption occurs here.

Stomach (pp. 475–484)

■ *Motility:* Gastric motility includes filling, storage, mixing, and emptying. Gastric filling is facilitated by receptive relaxation of the stomach. Gastric storage takes place in the body of the stomach, where peristaltic contractions of the thin muscle walls are too weak to mix the contents. Gastric mixing in the thick-muscled antrum results from vigorous peristaltic contractions. *(Review Figures 15-7 and 15-8.)*

■ Fat, acid, hypertonicity, and distension in the duodenum delay gastric emptying until the duodenum is ready to process more chyme. These factors inhibit antral peristaltic activity and thus slow gastric emptying via the enterogastric reflex and the enterogastrones, secretin and cholecystokinin (CCK), which are secreted by the duodenal mucosa. *(Review Figure 15-8 and Table 15-4, p. 482)*

■ *Secretion:* Gastric secretions into the stomach lumen include (1) HCl (from the parietal cells), which activates pepsinogen; (2) pepsinogen (from the chief cells), which, once activated, initiates protein digestion; (3) mucus (from the mucous cells), which provides a protective coating; and (4) intrinsic factor (from the parietal cells), which is needed for vitamin B_{12} absorption. *(Review Table 15-2 and Figures 15-9 and 15-10.)*

■ The stomach also secretes the hormone gastrin, which plays a dominant role in stimulating gastric secretion, and the paracrines histamine and somatostatin, which stimulate and inhibit gastric secretion, respectively. *(Review Table 15-2.)*

■ Gastric secretion is increased before and during a meal via excitatory vagal and intrinsic nerve responses, along with the stimulatory actions of gastrin and histamine. After the meal empties, gastric secretion is reduced by withdrawal of stimulatory factors, release of inhibitory somatostatin, and inhibitory actions of the enterogastric reflex and enterogastrones. *(Review Tables 15-3 and 15-4.)*

■ *Digestion and absorption:* Carbohydrate digestion continues by swallowed salivary amylase in the body of the stomach. Protein digestion is initiated by pepsin in the antrum of the stomach, where vigorous peristaltic contractions mix the food with gastric secretions, converting it to a thick liquid mixture known as chyme. *(Review Table 15-5, p. 494.)* No nutrients are absorbed from the stomach.

Pancreatic and Biliary Secretions (pp. 485–491)

■ Pancreatic exocrine secretions and bile from the liver both enter the duodenal lumen.

■ Pancreatic secretions include (1) potent digestive enzymes from the acinar cells, which digest all three categories of foodstuff, and (2) an aqueous $NaHCO_3$ solution from the duct cells, which neutralizes the acidic contents emptied into the duodenum from the stomach. Secretin stimulates the pancreatic duct cells, and CCK stimulates the acinar cells. *(Review Figures 15-11 and 15-12.)*

■ The pancreatic digestive enzymes include (1) the proteolytic enzymes trypsinogen, chymotrypsinogen, and procarboxypeptidase, which are secreted in inactive form and are activated in the duodenal lumen on exposure to enterokinase and activated trypsin; (2) pancreatic amylase, which continues carbohydrate digestion; and (3) lipase, which accomplishes fat digestion. *(Review Table 15-5.)*

■ The liver, the body's largest and most important metabolic organ, performs many varied functions. Its contribution to digestion is the secretion of bile, which contains bile salts. Bile salts aid fat digestion through their detergent action (forming a lipid emulsion that increases the surface area of fat exposed to attack by pancreatic lipase) and facilitate fat absorption by forming water-soluble micelles that carry the water-insoluble products of fat digestion to their absorption site. *(Review Figures 15-14 through 15-17 and 15-23, p. 498)*

■ Between meals, bile is stored and concentrated in the gallbladder, which is stimulated by CCK to contract and empty into the duodenum during meal digestion. After participating in fat digestion and absorption, bile salts are reabsorbed and returned via the hepatic portal system to the liver, where they are resecreted and act as a potent choleretic to stimulate secretion of more bile. *(Review Figures 15-13 and 15-15.)*

■ Bile also contains bilirubin, a derivative of degraded hemoglobin, which is the major excretory product in the feces.

Small Intestine (pp. 491–499)

■ *Motility:* Segmentation, the small intestine's primary motility during digestion of a meal, thoroughly mixes the chyme with digestive juices to facilitate digestion; it also exposes the products of digestion to the absorptive surfaces. *(Review Figure 15-18.)* Between meals, the migrating motility complex sweeps the lumen clean.

■ *Secretion:* The juice secreted by the small intestine does not contain any digestive enzymes. The enzymes synthesized by the small intestine act within the brush-border membrane of the epithelial cells.

■ *Digestion:* The small intestine is the main site for digestion and absorption. Carbohydrate and protein digestion continues in the small-intestine lumen by the pancreatic enzymes and is completed by the small-intestine brush-border enzymes (disaccharidases and aminopeptidases, respectively). Fat is digested entirely in the small-intestine lumen, by pancreatic lipase. *(Review Table 15-5.)*

■ *Absorption:* The small-intestine lining is remarkably adapted to its digestive and absorptive function. Its folds bear a rich array of fingerlike projections, the villi, which have a multitude of even smaller hairlike protrusions, the microvilli (brush border). Together, these surface modifications tremendously increase the area available to house the membrane-bound enzymes and to accomplish absorption. *(Review Figures 15-20 through 15-22.)* This lining is replaced about every 3 days to ensure it is optimally healthy despite harsh lumen conditions.

■ The energy-dependent process of Na^+ absorption provides the driving force for Cl^-, water, glucose, and amino acid absorption. All of these absorbed products enter the blood.

■ Because they are not soluble in water, the products of fat digestion must undergo a series of transformations that enable them to be passively absorbed, eventually entering the lymph. *(Review Figure 15-23.)*

■ The small intestine absorbs almost everything presented to it, from ingested food to digestive secretions to sloughed epithelial cells. In contrast to the almost complete, unregulated absorption of ingested nutrients, water, and most electrolytes, the amount of iron and calcium absorbed is variable and subject to control. Only a small amount of fluid and indigestible food residue passes on to the large intestine. *(Review Table 15-6.)*

Large Intestine (pp. 500–502)

■ *Motility:* The colon *(review Figure 15-24)* concentrates and stores undigested food residues (fiber; that is, plant cellulose) and bilirubin until they can be eliminated in the feces. Haustral contractions slowly shuffle the colonic contents back and forth to mix and facilitate absorption of most of the remaining fluid. Mass movements several times a day, usually after meals, propel the feces long distances. Movement of feces into the rectum triggers the defecation reflex.

■ *Secretion, digestion, and absorption:* The alkaline mucus secretion is protective. No secretion of digestive enzymes or absorption of nutrients takes place in the colon. Absorption of some of the remaining salt and water converts the colonic contents into feces.

Overview of the Gastrointestinal Hormones (p. 502)

■ The three major gastrointestinal hormones are gastrin from the stomach mucosa and secretin and cholecystokinin from the duodenal mucosa. Gastrin is released primarily in response to protein in the stomach, and its effects promote digestion of protein. Secretin is released primarily in response to acid in the duodenum, and its effects neutralize the acid. Cholecystokinin is released primarily in response to fat in the duodenum, and its effects optimize conditions for digesting fat.

507

Components Important in Energy Balance and Temperature Regulation

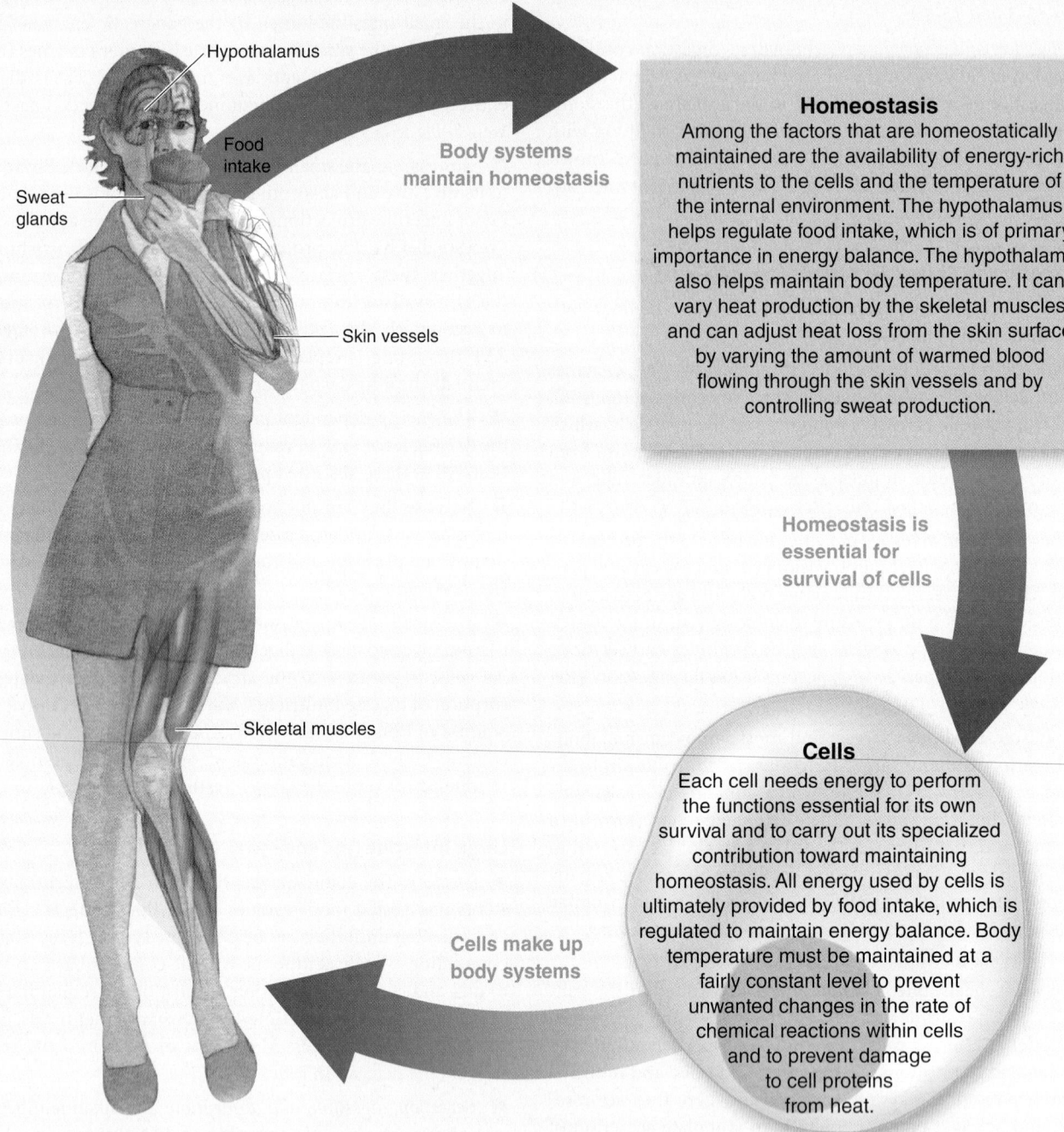

Hypothalamus

Food intake

Sweat glands

Skin vessels

Skeletal muscles

Body systems maintain homeostasis

Homeostasis
Among the factors that are homeostatically maintained are the availability of energy-rich nutrients to the cells and the temperature of the internal environment. The hypothalamus helps regulate food intake, which is of primary importance in energy balance. The hypothalamus also helps maintain body temperature. It can vary heat production by the skeletal muscles and can adjust heat loss from the skin surface by varying the amount of warmed blood flowing through the skin vessels and by controlling sweat production.

Homeostasis is essential for survival of cells

Cells
Each cell needs energy to perform the functions essential for its own survival and to carry out its specialized contribution toward maintaining homeostasis. All energy used by cells is ultimately provided by food intake, which is regulated to maintain energy balance. Body temperature must be maintained at a fairly constant level to prevent unwanted changes in the rate of chemical reactions within cells and to prevent damage to cell proteins from heat.

Cells make up body systems

Food intake is essential to power cell activities. For body weight to remain constant, the caloric value of food must equal total energy needs. **Energy balance** and thus body weight are maintained primarily by controlling food intake.

Energy expenditure generates heat, which is important in **temperature regulation.** Humans, usually in environments cooler than their bodies, must constantly generate heat to maintain their body temperatures. Also, they must have mechanisms to cool the body if it gains too much heat from heat-generating skeletal muscle activity or from a hot external environment. Body temperature must be regulated because the rate of cellular chemical reactions depends on temperature and because overheating damages cell proteins.

The hypothalamus is the major integrating center for maintaining both energy balance and body temperature.

Energy Balance and Temperature Regulation

CHAPTER AT A GLANCE

Energy Balance

Sources of energy input and output

Metabolic rate

Neutral, positive, and negative energy balance

Maintenance of energy balance and control of food intake

Temperature Regulation

Body temperature

Sources of heat gain and heat loss

Physical mechanisms of heat exchange

Sweating

The hypothalamus as a thermostat

Control of heat production; shivering

Control of heat loss; skin vasomotor activity

Integrated responses to cold and heat exposure

Fever

Energy Balance

Each cell in the body needs energy to perform the functions essential for the cell's own survival (such as active transport and cellular repair) and to carry out its specialized contributions toward maintaining homeostasis (such as gland secretion or muscle contraction). All energy used by cells is ultimately provided by food intake.

Most food energy is ultimately converted into heat in the body.

According to the **first law of thermodynamics,** energy can be neither created nor destroyed. Therefore, energy is subject to the same kind of input–output balance as are the chemical components of the body, such as H_2O and salt (see p. 443).

ENERGY INPUT AND OUTPUT The energy in ingested food constitutes *energy input* to the body. Chemical energy locked in the bonds that hold the atoms together in nutrient molecules is released when these molecules are broken down in the body. Cells capture a portion of this nutrient energy in the high-energy phosphate bonds of adenosine triphosphate (ATP; see pp. 29 and A-17). Energy harvested from biochemical processing of ingested nutrients is either used immediately to perform biological work or stored in the body for later use as needed during periods when food is not being digested and absorbed.

Energy output or *expenditure* by the body falls into two categories (● Figure 16-1): external work and internal work. **External work** is the energy expended when skeletal muscles contract to move external objects or to move the body in relation to the environment. **Internal work** constitutes all other forms of biological energy expenditure that do not accomplish mechanical work outside the body. Internal work encompasses two types of energy-dependent activities: (1) skeletal muscle activity used for purposes other than external work, such as the contractions associated with postural maintenance and shivering, and (2) all energy-expending activities that must go on all the time just to sustain life. The latter include the work of pumping blood and breathing, the energy required for active transport of critical materials across plasma membranes, and the energy used during synthetic reactions essential for the maintenance, repair, and growth of cellular structures—in short, the "metabolic cost of living."

CONVERSION OF NUTRIENT ENERGY TO HEAT Not all energy in nutrient molecules can be harnessed to perform biological work. Energy cannot be created or destroyed, but it can be converted from one form to another. The energy in nutrient molecules not used to energize work is transformed into **thermal energy,** or **heat.** During biochemical processing, only about 50% of the energy in nutrient molecules is transferred to ATP; the other 50% of nutrient energy is immediately lost as heat. When the cells expend ATP, another 25% of the energy derived from ingested food becomes heat.

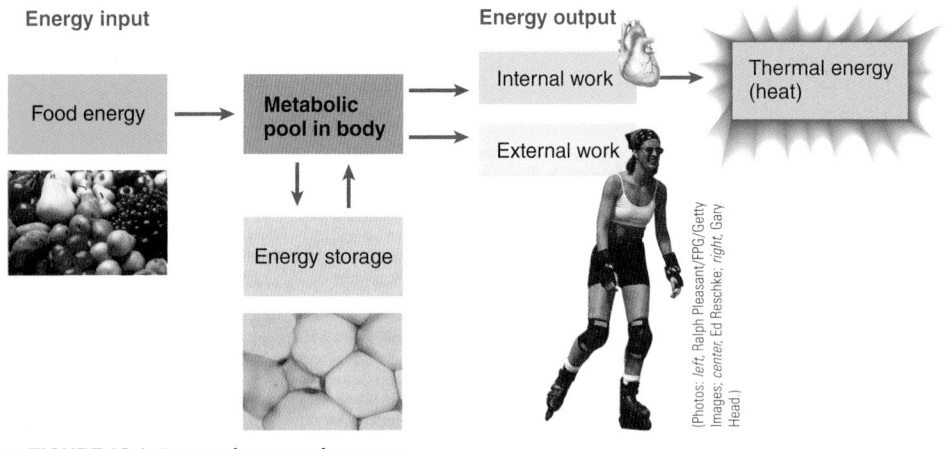

● FIGURE 16-1 Energy input and output.

(Photos: *left,* Ralph Pleasant/FPG/Getty Images; *center,* Ed Reschke; *right,* Gary Head.)

Because the body is not a heat engine, it cannot convert heat into work. Therefore, not more than 25% of nutrient energy is available for work, either external or internal. The remaining 75% is lost as heat during the sequential transfer of energy from nutrient molecules to ATP to cellular systems.

Furthermore, of the energy actually captured for use by the body, almost all expended energy eventually becomes heat. To exemplify, energy expended by the heart to pump blood is gradually changed into heat by friction as blood flows through the vessels. Likewise, energy used in synthesizing structural protein eventually appears as heat when that protein is degraded during the normal course of turnover of bodily constituents. Even in performing external work, skeletal muscles convert chemical energy into mechanical energy inefficiently; as much as 75% of the expended energy is lost as heat. Thus, all energy liberated from ingested food that is not directly used for moving external objects or stored in fat (adipose tissue) deposits (or, in the case of growth, as protein) eventually becomes body heat. This heat is not entirely wasted energy, however, because much of it is used to maintain body temperature.

The metabolic rate is the rate of energy use.

The rate at which energy is expended by the body during both external and internal work is known as the **metabolic rate:**

Metabolic rate = energy expenditure/unit of time

Because most of the body's energy expenditure eventually appears as heat, the metabolic rate is normally expressed in terms of the rate of heat production in kilocalories per hour. The basic unit of heat energy is the **calorie,** which is the amount of heat required to raise the temperature of 1 g of H_2O by 1°C. This unit is too small to be convenient when discussing the human body because of the magnitude of heat involved, so the **kilocalorie** or **Calorie,** which is equivalent to 1000 calories, is used. When nutritionists speak of "calories" in quantifying the energy content of various foods, they are actually referring to kilocalories or Calories. Four kilocalories of heat energy are released when 1 g of glucose is oxidized or "burned," whether the oxidation takes place inside or outside the body.

CONDITIONS FOR MEASURING THE BASAL METABOLIC RATE The metabolic rate and, consequently, the rate of heat production vary depending on several factors, such as exercise, anxiety, shivering, and food intake. Increased skeletal muscle activity is the factor that can increase metabolic rate to the greatest extent. Even slight increases in muscle tone notably elevate the metabolic rate, and various levels of physical activity markedly alter energy expenditure and heat production (▲ Table 16-1). For this reason, a person's metabolic rate is determined under standardized basal conditions established to control as many variables that can alter metabolic rate as possible. Specifically, the person should be at physical and mental rest at comfortable room temperature and should not have eaten within the last 12 hours. In this way, the metabolic activity necessary to maintain the basic body functions at rest can be determined. The **basal metabolic rate (BMR)** is a reflection of the body's "idling speed," or the minimal waking rate of internal energy expenditure.

METHODS OF MEASURING THE BASAL METABOLIC RATE The rate of heat production in BMR determinations can be measured directly or indirectly. To directly measure heat production, the

▲ Table 16-1 **Rate of Energy Expenditure for a 70-kg (154-Pound) Person during Different Activities**

Activity	Energy Expenditure (kcal/hr)
Sleeping	65
Awake, lying still	77
Sitting at rest	100
Standing relaxed	105
Getting dressed	118
Typing	140
Walking slowly on level ground (2.6 mi/hr)	200
Carpentry or painting a house	240
Sexual intercourse	280
Bicycling on level ground (5.5 mi/hr)	304
Shoveling snow or sawing wood	480
Swimming	500
Jogging (5.3 mi/hr)	570
Rowing (20 strokes/min)	828
Walking up stairs	1100

person sits in an insulated chamber with water circulating through the walls. The difference in the temperature of the water entering and leaving the chamber reflects the amount of heat liberated by the person and picked up by the water as it passes through the chamber. However, a more convenient method of indirectly determining the rate of heat production was developed for widespread use. With the indirect method, only the person's O_2 uptake per unit of time is measured, which is a simple task using minimal equipment. Recall that

$$\text{Food} + O_2 \rightarrow CO_2 + H_2O + \text{energy (mostly transformed into heat)}$$

Accordingly, a direct relationship exists between the volume of O_2 used and the quantity of heat produced. This relationship also depends on the type of food being oxidized. Although carbohydrates, proteins, and fats require different amounts of O_2 for their oxidation and yield different amounts of kilocalories when oxidized, an average estimate can be made of the quantity of heat produced per liter of O_2 consumed on a typical mixed American diet. This approximate value, known as the **energy equivalent of O_2,** is 4.8 kcal of energy liberated per liter of O_2 consumed. Using this method, the metabolic rate of a person consuming 15 L/hr of O_2 can be estimated as follows:

$$
\begin{array}{rl}
15 & \text{L/hr} = O_2 \text{ consumption} \\
\times\ 4.8 & \text{kcal/L} = \text{energy equivalent of } O_2 \\
\hline
72 & \text{kcal/hr} = \text{estimated metabolic rate}
\end{array}
$$

Once the rate of heat production is determined under the prescribed basal conditions, it must be compared with normal values for people of the same sex, age, height, and weight, because these factors all affect the basal rate of energy expenditure. For example, a large man has a higher rate of heat production than a smaller man, but expressed in terms of total surface area (which is a reflection of height and weight), the output in kilocalories per hour per square meter of surface area is normally about the same.

FACTORS INFLUENCING THE BASAL METABOLIC RATE Thyroid hormone is the primary but not sole determinant of the rate of basal metabolism. As thyroid hormone increases, the BMR increases correspondingly.

Surprisingly, the BMR is not the body's lowest metabolic rate. The rate of energy expenditure during sleep is 10% to 15% lower than the BMR, presumably because of the more complete muscle relaxation that occurs during the paradoxical stage of sleep (see p. 139).

Energy input must equal energy output to maintain a neutral energy balance.

Because energy cannot be created or destroyed, energy input must equal energy output, as follows:

$$\text{Energy input} = \text{energy output}$$

$$
\begin{array}{c}
\text{Energy in food} = \text{external} + \text{internal heat} \pm \text{stored} \\
\text{consumed} \qquad \text{work} \qquad \text{production} \qquad \text{energy}
\end{array}
$$

There are three possible states of energy balance:

- *Neutral energy balance.* If the amount of energy in food intake exactly equals the amount of energy expended by the muscles in performing external work plus the basal internal energy expenditure that eventually appears as body heat, then energy input and output are exactly in balance, and body weight remains constant.

- *Positive energy balance.* If the amount of energy in food intake is greater than the amount of energy expended by means of external work and internal functioning, the extra energy taken in but not used is stored in the body, primarily as adipose tissue, so body weight increases.

- *Negative energy balance.* Conversely, if the energy derived from food intake is less than the body's immediate energy requirements, the body must use stored energy to supply energy needs, and body weight decreases accordingly.

For a person to maintain a constant body weight (with the exception of minor fluctuations caused by changes in H_2O content), energy acquired through food intake must equal energy expenditure by the body. Because the average adult maintains a fairly constant weight over long periods, this implies that precise homeostatic mechanisms exist to maintain a long-term balance between energy intake and energy expenditure. Theoretically, total body energy content could be maintained at a constant level by regulating the magnitude of food intake, physical activity, or internal work and heat production. Control of food intake to match changing metabolic expenditures is the major means of maintaining a neutral energy balance. The level of physical activity is principally under voluntary control, and mechanisms that alter the degree of internal work and heat production are aimed primarily at regulating body temperature rather than total energy balance.

However, after several weeks of eating less or more than the body's desired amount, small counteracting changes in metabolism may occur. For example, a compensatory increase in the body's efficiency of energy use in response to underfeeding partially explains why some dieters become stuck at a plateau after having lost the first 10 or so pounds of weight fairly easily. Similarly, a compensatory reduction in the efficiency of energy use in response to overfeeding accounts in part for the difficulty experienced by very thin people who are deliberately trying to gain weight. Despite these modest compensatory changes in metabolism, regulation of food intake is the most important factor in the long-term maintenance of energy balance and body weight.

Food intake is controlled primarily by the hypothalamus.

Even though food intake is adjusted to balance changing energy expenditures over time, there are no calorie receptors per se to monitor energy input, energy output, or total body energy content. Instead, various blood-borne chemical factors that signal the body's nutritional state, such as how much fat is stored or the feeding status, are important in regulating food intake. Control of food intake does not depend on changes in a single signal but is determined by the integration of many inputs that provide information about the body's energy status. Multiple molecular signals together ensure that feeding behavior is synchronized with the body's immediate and long-term energy needs. Some information is used for short-term regulation of food intake, helping to control meal size and frequency. Even so, over a 24-hour period the energy in ingested food rarely matches energy expenditure for that day. The correlation between total caloric intake and total energy output is excellent, however, over long periods. As a result, the total energy content of the body—and, consequently, body weight—remains relatively constant long term. Thus, energy homeostasis, that is, energy balance, is carefully regulated.

ROLE OF THE ARCUATE NUCLEUS: NPY AND MELANOCORTINS

The **arcuate nucleus** of the hypothalamus plays a central role in both the long-term control of energy balance and body weight and the short-term control of food intake from meal to meal. The arcuate nucleus is an arc-shaped collection of neurons located adjacent to the floor of the third ventricle. Multiple, highly integrated, redundant pathways crisscross into and out of the arcuate nucleus, indicative of the complex systems involved in feeding and satiety. **Feeding,** or **appetite, signals** give rise to the sensation of **hunger,** driving us to eat. By contrast, **satiety** is the feeling of being full. **Satiety signals** tell us when we have had enough and suppress the desire to eat.

The arcuate nucleus has two subsets of neurons that function in an opposing manner. One subset releases *neuropeptide Y,* and the other releases *melanocortins* derived from proopiomelanocortin (POMC), a precursor molecule that can be cleaved in different ways to produce several hormone products (see p. 534).[1] **Neuropeptide Y (NPY),** one of the most potent appetite stimulators ever found, leads to increased food intake, thus promoting weight gain. **Melanocortins,** a group of hormones traditionally known to be important in varying the skin color for the purpose of camouflage in some species, have been shown to exert an unexpected role in energy homeostasis in humans. Melanocortins, most notably *melanocyte-stimulating hormone (MSH)* from the hypothalamus, suppress appetite, thus leading to reduced food intake and weight loss.

But NPY and melanocortins are not the final effectors in appetite control. These arcuate-nucleus chemical messengers, in turn, influence the release of neuropeptides in other parts of the brain that exert more direct control over food intake. Scientists are trying to unravel the other factors that act upstream and downstream from NPY and melanocortins to regulate appetite. Based on current evidence, the following regulatory inputs to the arcuate nucleus and beyond are important in the long-term maintenance of energy balance and the short-term control of food intake at meals (● Figure 16-2).

REGULATORY INPUTS TO THE ARCUATE NUCLEUS IN LONG-TERM MAINTENANCE OF ENERGY BALANCE: LEPTIN AND INSULIN

Scientists' notion of fat cells (**adipocytes**) in adipose tissue as merely storage space for triglyceride fat underwent a dramatic change late in the last century with the discovery of their active role in energy homeostasis. Adipocytes secrete several hormones, collectively termed **adipokines,** that play important roles in energy balance and metabolism. Thus, adipose tissue is now considered an endocrine gland. Some adipokines are released only from stored fat; *leptin,* for example, plays an important role in energy balance. Some, like inflammatory-related *tumor necrosis factor* and *interleukin 6,* are released from adipose tissue and immune cells and contribute to chronic, low-grade inflammation in excessive fat stores. Some, like *visfatin,* are released only from **visceral fat,** the deep, "bad" fat that surrounds the abdominal organs. Visceral fat is more likely to be chronically inflamed and is associated with increased heart disease, in contrast to the more superficial and less harmful **subcutaneous fat** that is deposited under the skin. (Subcutaneous fat is the fat you can pinch.)

One of the most important adipokines is **leptin,** a hormone essential for normal body-weight regulation (*leptin* means "thin"). The amount of leptin in the blood is an excellent indicator of the total amount of triglyceride fat stored in adipose tissue: The larger the fat stores, the more leptin released into the blood. This blood-borne signal, discovered in the mid-1990s, was the first molecular satiety signal identified. This finding touched off a flurry of research responsible for greatly expanding our knowledge in recent years of the complex interplay of chemical signals that regulate food intake and body size.

The arcuate nucleus is the major site for leptin action. Acting in negative-feedback fashion, increased leptin from burgeoning fat stores serves as a "trim-down" signal. Leptin suppresses appetite, thus decreasing food consumption and promoting weight loss, by inhibiting hypothalamic output of appetite-stimulating NPY and stimulating output of appetite-suppressing melanocortins. Conversely, a decrease in fat stores and the resultant decline in leptin secretion bring about an increase in appetite, leading to weight gain. The leptin signal is generally considered the dominant factor responsible for the long-term matching of food intake to energy expenditure so that total body energy content remains balanced and body weight remains constant.

Another blood-borne signal besides leptin that plays an important role in long-term control of body weight is **insulin.** Insulin, a hormone secreted by the pancreas in response to a rise in the concentration of glucose and other nutrients in the blood following a meal, stimulates cellular uptake, use, and storage of these nutrients (see p. 562). Thus, the increase in insulin secretion that accompanies nutrient abundance, use, and storage appropriately inhibits the NPY-secreting cells of the arcuate nucleus, thus suppressing further food intake.

---

[1]The two subsets of neurons in the arcuate nucleus are the **NPY/AgRP** population and the **POMC/CART** population. *AgRP* stands for *agouti-related protein.* Both NPY and AgRP stimulate appetite. *CART* stands for *cocaine- and amphetamine-related transcript.* Melanocortins and CART both suppress appetite. For simplicity's sake, we discuss only the role of NPY and melanocortins but recognize that other chemical signals released from the arcuate nucleus exert similar functions.

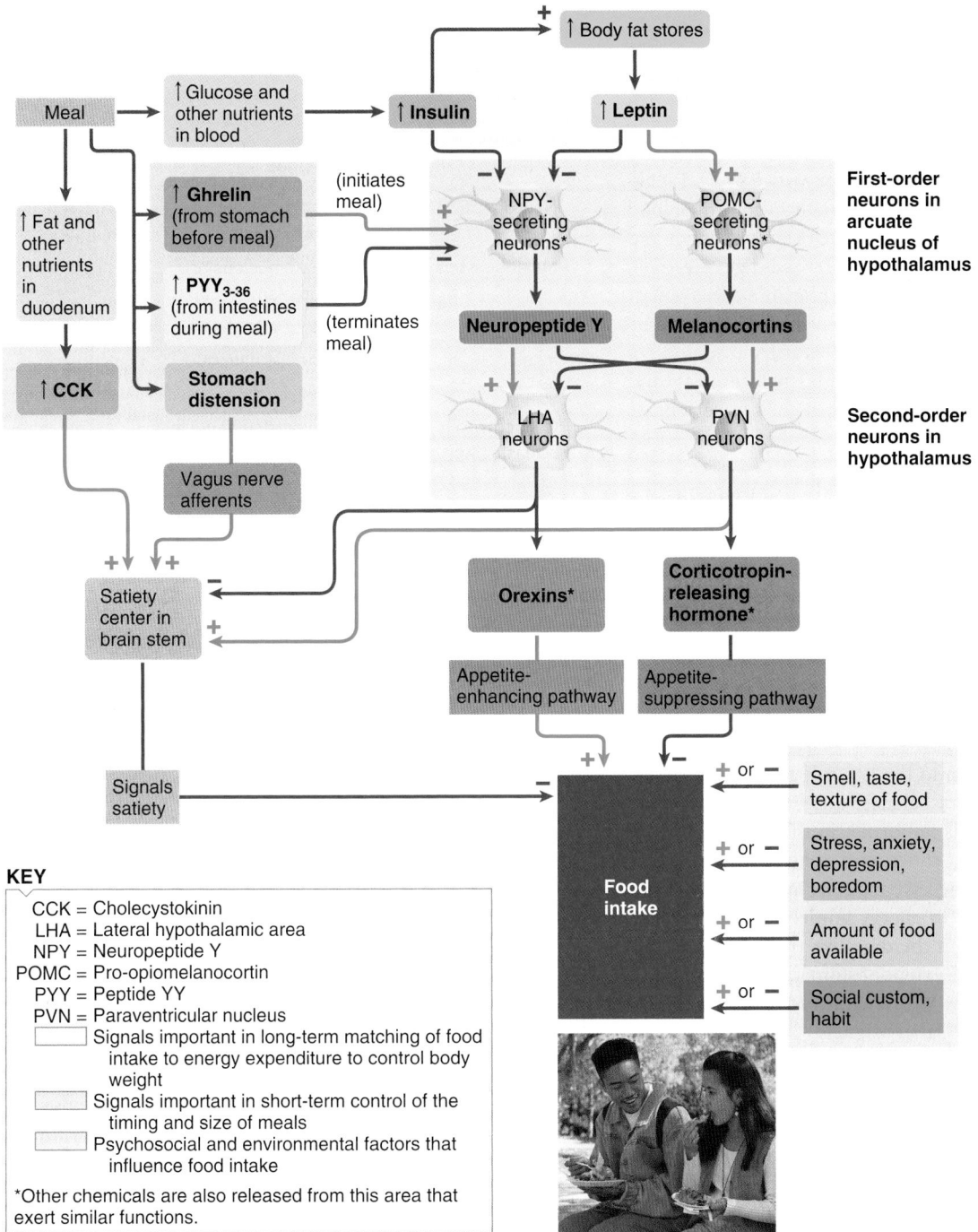

● **FIGURE 16-2 Factors that influence food intake.**

KEY

CCK = Cholecystokinin
LHA = Lateral hypothalamic area
NPY = Neuropeptide Y
POMC = Pro-opiomelanocortin
PYY = Peptide YY
PVN = Paraventricular nucleus

Signals important in long-term matching of food intake to energy expenditure to control body weight

Signals important in short-term control of the timing and size of meals

Psychosocial and environmental factors that influence food intake

*Other chemicals are also released from this area that exert similar functions.

BEYOND THE ARCUATE NUCLEUS: OREXINS AND OTHERS Two hypothalamic areas are richly supplied by axons from the NPY- and melanocortin-secreting neurons of the arcuate nucleus. These second-order neuronal areas involved in energy balance and food intake are the **lateral hypothalamic area (LHA)** and **paraventricular nucleus (PVN).** The LHA and PVN release chemical messengers in response to input from the arcuate nucleus neurons. These messengers act downstream from the NPY and melanocortin signals to regulate appetite. The LHA produces **orexins** (ore-EKS-ins), which are potent stimulators of food intake (*orexis* means "appetite"). NPY stimulates and melanocortins inhibit the release of appetite-enhancing orexins. By contrast, the PVN releases chemical messengers, for example, **corticotropin-releasing hormone,** that decrease appetite and food intake. (As its name implies, corticotropin-releasing hormone is better known for its role as a hormone; see p. 536.) Melanocortins stimulate and NPY inhibits the release of these appetite-suppressing chemicals.

In addition to these signals that are important in the long-term control of body weight, other factors play a role in controlling the timing and size of meals. Several blood-borne messengers from the digestive tract and pancreas are important in regulating how often and how much we eat in a given day.

SHORT-TERM EATING BEHAVIOR: GHRELIN AND PYY$_{3-36}$ SECRETION Two peptides important in the short-term control of food intake are *ghrelin* and *peptide YY$_{3-36}$*, which signify hunger and fullness, respectively. Both are secreted by the digestive tract. **Ghrelin** (GRELL-in), the so-called hunger hormone, is a potent appetite stimulator produced by the stomach and regulated by the feeding status (*ghrelin* is the Hindu word for "growth"). Secretion of this mealtime stimulator peaks before meals and makes people feel like eating, and then it falls once food is eaten. Ghrelin stimulates appetite by activating the hypothalamic NPY-secreting neurons.

Peptide YY$_{3-36}$ (PYY$_{3-36}$) is a counterpart of ghrelin. The secretion of PYY$_{3-36}$, which is produced by the small and large intestines, is at its lowest level before a meal but rises during meals and signals satiety. This peptide acts by inhibiting the appetite-stimulating NPY-secreting neurons in the arcuate nucleus. By thwarting appetite, PYY$_{3-36}$ is believed to be an important mealtime terminator.

The following other factors are also involved in signaling where the body is on the hunger–satiety scale.

SATIETY CENTER In addition to the key role the hypothalamus plays in maintaining energy balance, a **satiety center** in the brain stem processes signals important in the feeling of being full and thus contributes to short-term control of meals. Not only does the satiety center receive input from the higher hypothalamic neurons involved in energy homeostasis, but it also receives afferent inputs from the digestive tract (for example, afferent input indicating the extent of stomach distension) and elsewhere that signal satiety. We now turn to cholecystokinin, the most important of these satiety signals.

CHOLECYSTOKININ AS A SATIETY SIGNAL **Cholecystokinin (CCK),** one of the gastrointestinal hormones released from the duodenal mucosa during digestion of a meal, is an important satiety signal for regulating the size of meals. CCK is secreted in response to the presence of nutrients in the small intestine. Through multiple effects on the digestive system, CCK facilitates digestion and absorption of these nutrients (see p. 502). It is appropriate that this blood-borne signal, whose rate of secretion is correlated with the amount of nutrients ingested, contributes to the sense of being filled after a meal has been consumed but before it has been digested and absorbed. We feel satisfied when adequate food to replenish the stores is in the digestive tract even though the body's energy stores are still low. This explains why we stop eating before the ingested food is made available to meet the body's energy needs.

▲ Table 16-2 summarizes the effect of involuntary regulatory signals on appetite.

PSYCHOSOCIAL AND ENVIRONMENTAL INFLUENCES Thus far, we have described involuntary signals that automatically occur to control food intake. However, as with water intake, people's eating habits are also shaped by psychological, social, and environmental factors. Often our decision to eat or stop eating is not determined merely by whether we are hungry or full, respectively. Frequently, we eat out of habit (eating three meals a day on schedule no matter what our status on the hunger–satiety continuum) or because of social custom (food often plays a prime role in entertainment, leisure, and business activities). Even well-intentioned family pressure—"Clean your plate before you leave the table"—can affect the amount consumed.

Furthermore, the amount of pleasure derived from eating can reinforce feeding behavior. Eating foods with an enjoyable taste, smell, and texture can increase appetite and food intake. This has been demonstrated in an experiment in which rats were offered their choice of highly palatable human foods. They overate by as much as 70% to 80% and became obese. When the rats returned to eating their regular monotonous but nutritionally balanced rat chow, their obesity was rapidly reversed, as their food intake was controlled again by physiological drives rather than by hedonistic urges for the tastier offerings.

Stress, anxiety, depression, and boredom have also been shown to alter feeding behavior in ways unrelated to energy needs in both experimental animals and humans. People often eat to satisfy psychological needs rather than to satisfy hunger. Furthermore, environmental influences, such as the amount of food available, play an important role in determining the extent of food intake. Thus, any comprehensive explanation of how food intake is controlled must take into account these voluntary eating acts that can reinforce or override the internal signals governing feeding behavior.

▲ **Table 16-2** Effects of Involuntary Regulatory Signals on Appetite

Regulatory Signal	Source of Signal	Effect of Signal on Appetite
Neuropeptide Y	Arcuate nucleus of hypothalamus	↑
Melanocortins	Arcuate nucleus of hypothalamus	↓
Leptin	Adipose tissue	↓
Insulin	Endocrine pancreas	↓
Orexins	Lateral hypothalamus	↑
Corticotropin-releasing hormone	Paraventricular nucleus of hypothalamus	↓
Ghrelin	Stomach	↑
Peptide YY$_{3-36}$	Small and large intestines	↓
Stomach distension	Stomach	↓
Cholecystokinin	Small intestine	↓

Obesity occurs when more kilocalories are consumed than are burned up.

 Obesity is defined as excessive fat content in the adipose tissue stores; the arbitrary boundary for obesity is generally considered to be greater than 20% overweight compared to normal standards. More than two thirds of the adults in the United States are now clinically overweight, with one third being clinically obese. To make matters worse, obesity is on the rise. The number of obese adults in the United States is 75% higher now than it was 15 years ago. And much of the world is following the same trend, leading the World Health Organization to coin the word *globesity* to describe the worldwide situation.

Obesity occurs when, over time, more kilocalories are ingested in food than are used to support the body's energy needs, with the excessive energy being stored as triglycerides in adipose tissue. The causes of obesity are many, and some remain obscure.

POSSIBLE CAUSES OF OBESITY Some factors that may be involved in the development of obesity include the following:

■ *Disturbances in the leptin-signaling pathway.* Some cases of obesity have been linked to leptin resistance. Some investigators suggest that the hypothalamic centers involved in maintaining energy homeostasis are "set at a higher level" in obese people. For example, the problem may lie with faulty leptin receptors in the brain that do not respond appropriately to the high levels of circulating leptin from abundant adipose stores. Thus, the brain does not detect leptin as a signal to turn down appetite until a higher set point (and accordingly greater fat storage) is achieved. This could explain why overweight people tend to maintain their weight but at a heavier-than-normal level.

■ *Lack of exercise.* Numerous studies have shown that, on average, fat people do not eat more than thin people. One possible explanation is that overweight people do not overeat but underexercise—the "couch potato" syndrome. Low levels of physical activity typically are not accompanied by comparable reductions in food intake.

For this reason, modern technology is partly to blame for the current obesity epidemic. Our ancestors had to exert physical effort to eke out a subsistence. By comparison, we now have machines to replace much manual labor, remote controls to operate our machines with minimal effort, and computers that encourage long hours of sitting. We have to make a conscious effort to exercise.

■ *Differences in the "fidget factor."* **Nonexercise activity thermogenesis (NEAT),** or the "fidget factor," might explain some variation in fat storage among people. Those who engage in toe tapping or other types of repetitive, spontaneous physical activity expend a substantial number of kilocalories throughout the day without a conscious effort.

■ *Differences in extracting energy from food.* Another reason lean people and obese people may have dramatically different body weights despite consuming the same number of kilocalories may lie in the efficiency with which each extracts energy from food. Studies suggest that leaner individuals tend to derive less energy from the food they consume because they convert more of the food's energy into heat than into energy for immediate use or for storage.

■ *Hereditary tendencies.* Often, differences in the regulatory pathways for energy balance—either those governing food intake or those influencing energy expenditure—arise from genetic variations.

■ *Development of an excessive number of fat cells as a result of overfeeding.* One of the problems in fighting obesity is that once fat cells are created they do not disappear with dieting and weight loss. Even if a dieter loses a large portion of the triglyceride fat stored in these cells, the depleted cells remain, ready to refill. Therefore, rebound weight gain after losing weight is difficult to avoid and discouraging for the dieter.

■ *Certain endocrine disorders such as hypothyroidism.* Hypothyroidism involves a deficiency of thyroid hormone, the main factor that bumps up the BMR so that the body burns more calories in its idling state (see p. 548).

■ *Too little sleep.* Some studies suggest that decreased time sleeping may be a contributing factor in the recent rise of obesity. On average, people in the United States are sleeping 1 to 2 hours less per night now than they did 40 years ago. Researchers found that those who typically sleep 6 hours a night are 23% more likely to be obese, those who average 5 hours of sleep are 50% more likely to be obese, and those who sleep 4 hours nightly are 75% more likely to be obese than "traditional" sleepers who sleep for 7 to 8 hours. Studies have shown that levels of leptin (a signal to stop eating) are lower and levels of ghrelin (a signal to start eating) are higher in people who sleep less compared with those who sleep the traditional 8 hours.

■ *A possible virus link.* One intriguing proposal links a relatively common cold virus to a propensity to become overweight and may account for a portion of the current obesity epidemic.

■ *An abundance of convenient, highly palatable, energy-dense, relatively inexpensive foods.*

■ *Emotional disturbances in which overeating replaces other gratifications.*

Despite this rather lengthy list, our knowledge about the causes and control of obesity is still rather limited, as evidenced by the number of people who are constantly trying to stabilize their weight at a more desirable level. This is important from more than an aesthetic viewpoint. It is known that obesity, especially of the android type, can predispose an individual to illness and premature death from a multitude of diseases.

 ANDROID AND GYNOID OBESITY There are different ways to be fat, and one way is more dangerous than the other. Obese patients can be classified into two categories—*android,* a male-type of adipose tissue distribution, and *gynoid,* a female-type distribution—based on the anatomic distribution of adipose tissue measured as the ratio of

waist circumference to hip circumference. **Android obesity** is characterized by abdominal fat distribution (people shaped like "apples"), whereas **gynoid obesity** is characterized by fat distribution in the hips and thighs (people shaped like "pears"). Both sexes can display either android or gynoid obesity.

Android obesity is associated with a number of disorders, including insulin resistance, Type 2 (adult-onset) diabetes mellitus, excess blood lipid levels, high blood pressure, coronary heart disease, and stroke. "Apple" people have a greater proportion of visceral fat, which is more worrisome than accumulation of subcutaneous fat, because visceral fat releases more of the bad adipokines that promote insulin resistance and boost the low-level inflammation that underlies the development of atherosclerosis (see p. 269). Gynoid obesity is not associated with the high risk of these diseases.

People suffering from anorexia nervosa have a pathological fear of gaining weight.

Clinical Note The converse of obesity is generalized nutritional deficiency. The obvious causes for reduction of food intake below energy needs are lack of availability of food, interference with swallowing or digestion, and impairment of appetite.

One poorly understood disorder in which lack of appetite is a prominent feature is **anorexia nervosa.** Patients with this disorder, most commonly adolescent girls and young women, have a morbid fear of becoming fat. They have a distorted body image, tending to visualize themselves as being heavier than they actually are. Because they have an aversion to food, they eat little and consequently lose considerable weight, perhaps even starving themselves to death. Other characteristics of the condition include altered secretion of many hormones, absence of menstrual periods, and low body temperature. It is unclear whether these symptoms occur secondarily as a result of general malnutrition or arise independently of the eating disturbance as a part of a primary hypothalamic malfunction. Many investigators think the underlying problem may be psychological rather than biological. Some experts suspect that anorexics may suffer from addiction to endogenous opiates, self-produced morphinelike substances (see p. 156) thought to be released during prolonged starvation.

Temperature Regulation

Humans are usually in environments cooler than their bodies, but they constantly generate heat internally, which helps maintain body temperature. Heat production ultimately depends on the oxidation of metabolic fuel derived from food.

Changes in body temperature in either direction alter cell activity—an increase in temperature speeds up cellular chemical reactions, whereas a fall in temperature slows down these reactions. Because cell function is sensitive to fluctuations in internal temperature, humans homeostatically maintain body temperature at a level optimal for stable cellular metabolism. Overheating is more serious than cooling. Even moderate elevations of body temperature begin to cause nerve malfunction and irreversible

protein denaturation. Most people suffer convulsions when the internal body temperature reaches about 106°F (41°C); 110°F (43.3°C) is considered the upper limit compatible with life.

Clinical Note By contrast, most of the body's tissues can transiently withstand substantial cooling. This characteristic is useful during cardiac surgery when the heart must be stopped. For such surgery, the patient's body temperature is deliberately lowered; the cooled tissues need less nourishment than they do at normal body temperature because of their reduced metabolic activity. However, a pronounced, prolonged fall in body temperature slows metabolism to a fatal level.

Internal core temperature is homeostatically maintained at 100°F (37.8°C).

Normal body temperature taken orally (by mouth) has traditionally been considered 98.6°F (37°C). However, a recent study indicates that normal body temperature varies among individuals and varies throughout the day, ranging from 96.0°F (35.5°C) in the morning to 99.9°F (37.7°C) in the evening, with an overall average of 98.2°F (36.7°C). This variation is largely due to an innate biological rhythm or "biological clock."

Furthermore, there is no one body temperature because the temperature varies from organ to organ. From a thermoregulatory viewpoint, the body may conveniently be viewed as a *central core* surrounded by an *outer shell.* The temperature within the central core, which consists of the abdominal and thoracic organs, the central nervous system, and the skeletal muscles, generally remains fairly constant. This internal **core temperature** is subject to precise regulation to maintain its homeostatic constancy. The core tissues function best at a relatively constant temperature of around 100°F (37.8°C).

The skin and subcutaneous fat constitute the outer shell. In contrast to the constant high temperature in the core, the temperature within the shell is generally cooler and may vary substantially. For example, skin temperature may fluctuate between 68°F and 104°F (20°C and 40°C) without damage. As you will see, the temperature of the skin is deliberately varied as a control measure to help maintain the core's thermal constancy.

SITES FOR MONITORING BODY TEMPERATURE Several easily accessible sites are used for monitoring body temperature. The oral and axillary (under the armpit) temperatures are comparable, whereas rectal temperature averages about 1°F (0.56°C) higher. Also available is a temperature-monitoring instrument that scans the heat generated by the eardrum and converts this temperature into an oral equivalent. A more recent device is the temporal scanner that measures the temperature in the temporal artery. A computerized instrument is gently stroked from one side to the other across the forehead over the temporal artery, which lies less than 2 mm below the skin surface in this region. Temporal temperature is the best determinant of core temperature because it is nearly identical to the temperature of the blood exiting the heart. However, none of these measurements is an absolute indication of the internal core temperature, which is a bit higher, at 100°F, than the monitored sites.

Heat input must balance heat output to maintain a stable core temperature.

The core temperature is a reflection of the body's total heat content. Heat input to the body must balance heat output to maintain a constant total heat content and thus a stable core temperature (● Figure 16-3). *Heat input* occurs by way of heat gain from the external environment and internal heat production, the latter being the most important source of heat for the body. Recall that most of the body's energy expenditure ultimately appears as heat. This heat is important in maintaining core temperature. Usually, more heat is generated than required to maintain normal body temperature, so the excess heat must be eliminated. *Heat output* occurs by way of heat loss from exposed body surfaces to the external environment.

Balance between heat input and heat output is frequently disturbed by (1) changes in internal heat production for purposes unrelated to regulation of body temperature—most notably by exercise, which markedly increases heat production—and (2) changes in the external environmental temperature that influence the degree of heat gain or heat loss that occurs between the body and its surroundings. Compensatory adjustments must take place in heat-loss and heat-gain mechanisms to maintain body temperature within narrow limits, despite changes in metabolic heat production and changes in environmental temperature. We now elaborate how these adjustments are made.

Heat exchange takes place by radiation, conduction, convection, and evaporation.

All heat loss or heat gain between the body and the external environment must take place between the body surface and its surroundings. The same physical laws of nature that govern heat transfer between inanimate objects control the transfer of heat between the body surface and the environment. The temperature of an object is a measure of the concentration of heat within the object. Heat always moves down its concentration gradient—that is, down a **thermal gradient** from a warmer to a cooler region (*thermo* means "heat"). The body uses four mechanisms of heat transfer: *radiation, conduction, convection,* and *evaporation.*

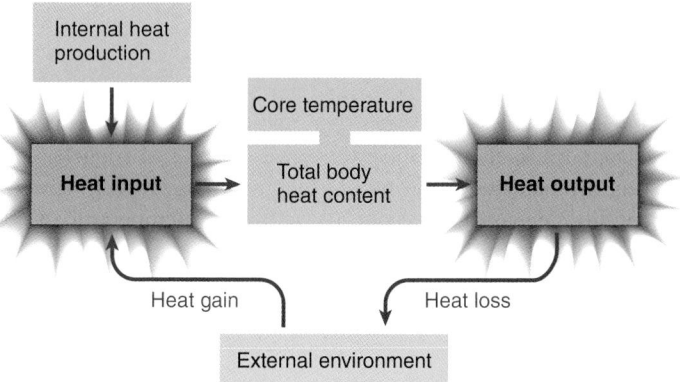

● **FIGURE 16-3 Heat input and output.**

RADIATION **Radiation** is the emission of heat energy from the surface of a warm body in the form of **electromagnetic waves,** or **heat waves,** which travel through space (● Figure 16-4a). When radiant energy strikes an object and is absorbed, the energy of the wave motion is transformed into heat within the object. The human body both emits (source of heat loss) and absorbs (source of heat gain) radiant energy. Whether the body loses or gains heat by radiation depends on the difference in temperature between the skin surface and the surfaces of other objects in the body's environment. Because net transfer of heat by radiation is always from warmer objects to cooler ones, the body gains heat by radiation from objects warmer than the skin surface, such as the sun, a radiator, or burning logs. By contrast, the body loses heat by radiation to objects in its environment whose surfaces are cooler than the surface of the skin, such as building walls, furniture, or trees. On average, humans lose close to half of their heat energy through radiation.

CONDUCTION **Conduction** is the transfer of heat between objects of differing temperatures that are in direct contact with each other, with heat moving down its thermal gradient from the warmer to the cooler object (● Figure 16-4b). When you hold a snowball, for example, your hand becomes cold because heat moves by conduction from your hand to the snowball. Conversely, when you apply a heating pad to a body part, the part is warmed up as heat is transferred directly from the pad to the body.

Similarly, you either lose or gain heat by conduction to the layer of air in direct contact with your body. The direction of heat transfer depends on whether the air is cooler or warmer, respectively, than your skin. Only a small percentage of total heat exchange between the skin and the environment takes place by conduction alone, however, because air is not a good conductor of heat. (For this reason, swimming pool water at 80°F (26.7°C) feels cooler than air at the same temperature; heat is conducted more rapidly from the body surface into the water, which is a good conductor, than into the air, which is a poor conductor.)

CONVECTION The term **convection** refers to the transfer of heat energy by *air* (or *water*) *currents.* As the body loses heat by conduction to the surrounding cooler air, the air in immediate contact with the skin is warmed. Because warm air is lighter (less dense) than cool air, the warmed air rises while cooler air moves in next to the skin to replace the vacating warm air. The process is then repeated (● Figure 16-4c). These air movements, known as *convection currents,* help carry heat away from the body. Without convection currents, no further heat could be dissipated from the skin by conduction once the temperature of the layer of air immediately around the body equilibrated with skin temperature.

The combined conduction–convection process of dissipating heat from the body is enhanced by forced movement of air across the body surface, either by external air movements, such as those caused by the wind or a fan, or by movement of the body through the air, as during bicycle riding. Because forced air movement sweeps away the air warmed by conduction and

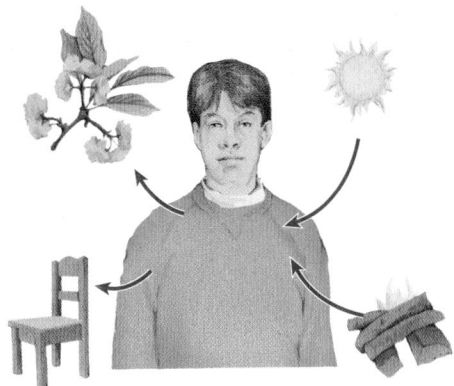

(a) Radiation—the transfer of heat energy from a warmer object to a cooler object in the form of electromagnetic waves ("heat waves"), which travel through space.

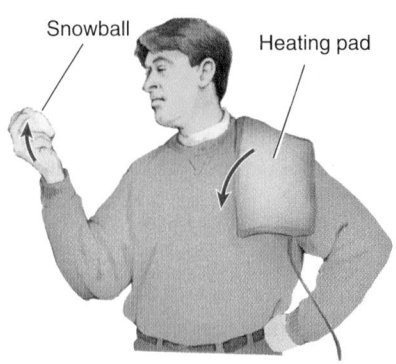

(b) Conduction—the transfer of heat from a warmer to a cooler object that is in direct contact with the warmer one. The heat is transferred through the movement of thermal energy from molecule to adjacent molecule.

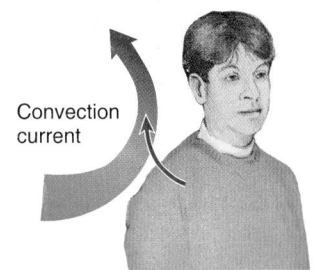

(c) Convection—the transfer of heat energy by air currents. Cool air warmed by the body through conduction rises and is replaced by more cool air. This process is enhanced by the forced movement of air across the body surface.

(d) Evaporation—conversion of a liquid such as sweat into a gaseous vapor, a process that requires heat (the heat of vaporization), which is absorbed from the skin.

● **FIGURE 16-4 Mechanisms of heat transfer.** The direction of the arrows depicts the direction of heat transfer.

replaces it with cooler air more rapidly, a greater total amount of heat can be carried away from the body over a given period. Thus, wind makes us feel cooler on hot days, and windy days in the winter are more chilling than calm days at the same cold temperature. For this reason, weather forecasters have developed the concept of *wind chill factor* (how cold it feels).

EVAPORATION During **evaporation** from the skin surface, the heat required to transform water from a liquid to a gaseous state is absorbed from the skin, thereby cooling the body (● Figure 16-4d). Evaporative heat loss makes you feel cooler when your bathing suit is wet than when it is dry. Evaporative heat loss occurs continually from the linings of the respiratory airways and from the surface of the skin. Heat is continuously lost in expired air as a result of the air being humidified (gaining water vapor) during its passage through the respiratory system (see p. 367). Similarly, because the skin is not completely waterproof, water molecules constantly diffuse through the skin and evaporate (see p. 450). This ongoing evaporation from the skin is unrelated to the sweat glands. These passive evaporative heat-loss processes are not subject to physiological control and go on even in very cold weather, when the problem is one of conserving body heat.

Sweating is a regulated evaporative heat-loss process.

Sweating is an active evaporative heat-loss process under sympathetic nervous control. The rate of evaporative heat loss can be deliberately adjusted by varying the extent of sweating, which is an important homeostatic mechanism to eliminate excess heat as needed. At normal temperature, an average of 100 ml of sweat is produced per day; this value increases to 1.5 liters during hot weather and climbs to 4 liters during heavy exercise.

Sweat is a dilute salt solution actively extruded to the surface of the skin by sweat glands dispersed all over the body. Sweat must be evaporated from the skin for heat loss to occur. If sweat merely drips from the surface of skin or is wiped away, no heat loss is accomplished. The most important factor determining the extent of evaporation of sweat is the *relative humidity* of the surrounding air (the percentage of H_2O vapor actually present in the air compared to the greatest amount that the air can possibly hold at that temperature; for example, a relative humidity of 70% means that the air contains 70% of the H_2O vapor it is capable of holding). When the relative humidity is high, the air is already almost fully saturated with H_2O, so it has limited ability to take up additional moisture from the skin. Thus, little evaporative heat loss can occur on hot, humid days. The sweat glands continue to secrete, but the sweat simply remains on the skin or drips off instead of evaporating and producing a cooling effect. As a measure of the discomfort associated with combined heat and high humidity, meteorologists have devised the *temperature–humidity index,* or *heat index* (how hot it feels).

The hypothalamus integrates a multitude of thermosensory inputs.

The hypothalamus is the body's thermostat. The home thermostat keeps track of the temperature in a room and triggers a heating mechanism (the furnace) or a cooling mechanism (the air conditioner) as necessary to maintain room temperature at the indicated setting. Similarly, the hypothalamus, as the body's thermoregulatory integrating center, receives afferent information about the temperature in various regions of the body and initiates extremely complex, coordinated adjustments in heat-gain and heat-loss mechanisms as necessary to correct any deviations in core temperature from normal. The hypothalamus is far more sensitive than your home thermostat. It can respond to changes in blood temperature as small as 0.01°C.

To appropriately adjust the delicate balance between the heat-loss mechanisms and the opposing heat-producing and heat-conserving mechanisms, the hypothalamus must be apprised continuously of both the core and the skin temperature by specialized temperature-sensitive receptors called **thermoreceptors.** The core temperature is monitored by *central thermoreceptors,* which are located in the hypothalamus itself, as well as in the abdominal organs and elsewhere. *Peripheral thermoreceptors* monitor skin temperature throughout the body.

Two centers for temperature regulation are in the hypothalamus. The *posterior region,* activated by cold, triggers reflexes that mediate heat production and heat conservation. The *anterior region,* activated by warmth, initiates reflexes that mediate heat loss. Let us examine the means by which the hypothalamus fulfills its thermoregulatory functions.

Shivering is the primary involuntary means of increasing heat production.

The body can gain heat as a result of internal heat production generated by metabolic activity or from the external environment if the latter is warmer than body temperature. Because body temperature usually is higher than environmental temperature, metabolic heat production is the primary source of body heat. In a resting person, most body heat is produced by the thoracic and abdominal organs as a result of ongoing, cost-of-living metabolic activities. Beyond this basal level, the rate of metabolic heat production can be variably increased primarily by changes in skeletal muscle activity or, to a lesser extent, by certain hormonal actions. Thus, changes in skeletal muscle activity constitute the major way heat gain is controlled for temperature regulation.

ADJUSTMENTS IN HEAT PRODUCTION BY SKELETAL MUSCLES In response to a fall in core temperature caused by exposure to cold, the hypothalamus takes advantage of increased skeletal muscle activity generating more heat. Acting through descending pathways that terminate on the motor neurons controlling the skeletal muscles, the hypothalamus first gradually increases skeletal muscle tone. (Muscle tone is the constant level of tension within the muscles.) Soon shivering begins. **Shivering** consists of rhythmic, oscillating skeletal muscle contractions that occur at a rapid rate of 10 to 20 per second. This mechanism is efficient and effective in increasing heat production; all energy liberated during these muscle tremors is converted to heat because no external work is accomplished. Within seconds to minutes, internal heat production may increase two- to five-fold as a result of shivering.

Frequently, these reflex changes in skeletal muscle activity are augmented by increased voluntary, heat-producing actions such as bouncing up and down or hand clapping. The hypothalamus influences these behavioral responses, as well as the involuntary physiological responses. As part of the limbic system, the hypothalamus is extensively involved with controlling motivated behavior (see p. 132).

In the opposite situation—a rise in core temperature caused by heat exposure—two mechanisms reduce heat-producing skeletal muscle activity: Muscle tone is reflexly decreased, and voluntary movement is curtailed. When the air becomes very warm, people often complain it is "too hot even to move."

NONSHIVERING THERMOGENESIS Although reflex and voluntary changes in muscle activity are the major means of increasing the rate of heat production, **nonshivering (chemical) thermogenesis** also plays a role in thermoregulation. In most experimental animals, chronic cold exposure brings about an increase in metabolic heat production independent of muscle contraction, instead being brought about by changes in heat-generating chemical activity. In humans, nonshivering thermogenesis is most important in newborns because they lack the ability to shiver. Nonshivering thermogenesis is mediated by the hormones epinephrine and thyroid hormone, both of which increase heat production by stimulating fat metabolism. Newborns have deposits of a special type of adipose tissue known as **brown fat,** which is especially capable of converting chemical energy into heat. The role of nonshivering thermogenesis in adults remains controversial.

Having examined the mechanisms for adjusting heat production, we now turn to the other side of the equation: adjustments in heat loss.

The magnitude of heat loss can be adjusted by varying the flow of blood through the skin.

Heat-loss mechanisms are subject to control, again largely by the hypothalamus. When we are hot, we need to increase heat loss to the environment; when we are cold, we need to decrease heat loss. The amount of heat lost to the environment by radiation and the conduction–convection process is largely determined by the temperature gradient between the skin and the external environment. To maintain a constant core temperature, the insulative capacity and temperature of the skin can be adjusted to vary the temperature gradient between the skin and the external environment, thereby influencing the extent of heat loss.

The insulative capacity of the skin can be varied by controlling the amount of blood flowing through. Skin blood flow serves two functions. First, it provides a nutritive blood supply to the skin. Second, most skin blood flow is for the function of temperature regulation; at normal room temperature, 20 to 30 times more blood flows through the skin than is needed for skin nutrition. In the process of thermoregulation, skin blood flow can vary tremendously, from 400 to 2500 ml/min. The more blood that reaches the skin from the warm core, the closer the skin's temperature is to the core temperature. The skin's blood vessels diminish the effectiveness of the skin as an insulator by carrying heat to the surface, where it can be lost from the body by radiation and the conduction–convection process. Accordingly, skin arteriolar vasodilation, which permits increased flow of heated blood through the skin, increases heat loss. Conversely, skin vasoconstriction, which reduces skin blood flow, decreases heat loss by keeping the warm blood in the central core, where it is insulated from the external environment. This response conserves heat that otherwise would have been lost.

These skin vasomotor responses are coordinated by the hypothalamus by means of sympathetic nervous system output. Increased sympathetic activity to the skin arterioles produces heat-conserving vasoconstriction in response to cold exposure, whereas decreased sympathetic activity produces heat-losing vasodilation of these vessels in response to heat exposure.

The hypothalamus simultaneously coordinates heat-production and heat-loss mechanisms.

Let us now pull together the coordinated adjustments in heat production and heat loss in response to exposure to either a cold or a hot environment (▲ Table 16-3). (For a discussion of the effects of extreme cold or heat exposure, see the accompanying boxed feature, ❱ Beyond the Basics.)

COORDINATED RESPONSES TO COLD EXPOSURE In response to cold exposure, the posterior region of the hypothalamus directs increased heat production, such as by shivering, while simultaneously decreasing heat loss (that is, conserving heat) by skin vasoconstriction and other measures.

Because there is a limit to the body's ability to reduce skin temperature through vasoconstriction, even maximum vasoconstriction is not sufficient to prevent excessive heat loss when the external temperature falls too low. Accordingly, other measures must be instituted to further reduce heat loss. In animals with dense fur or feathers, the hypothalamus, acting through the sympathetic nervous system, brings about contraction of the tiny muscles at the base of the hair or feather shafts to lift the hair or feathers off the skin surface. This puffing up traps a layer of poorly conductive air between the skin surface and the environment, thus increasing the insulating barrier between the core and the cold air and reducing heat loss. Even though the hair-shaft muscles contract in humans in response to cold exposure, this heat-retention mechanism is ineffective because of the low density and fine texture of most human body hair. The result instead is useless *goose bumps.*

After maximum skin vasoconstriction has been achieved as a result of exposure to cold, further heat dissipation in hu-

mans can be prevented only by behavioral adaptations, such as postural changes that reduce as much as possible the exposed surface area from which heat can escape. These postural changes include maneuvers such as hunching over, clasping the arms in front of the chest, or curling up in a ball.

Putting on warmer clothing further insulates the body from too much heat loss. Clothing entraps layers of poorly conductive air between the skin surface and the environment, thereby diminishing loss of heat by conduction from the skin to the cold external air and curtailing the flow of convection currents.

COORDINATED RESPONSES TO HEAT EXPOSURE Under the opposite circumstance—heat exposure—the anterior part of the hypothalamus reduces heat production by decreasing skeletal muscle activity and promotes increased heat loss by inducing skin vasodilation. When even maximal skin vasodilation is inadequate to rid the body of excess heat, sweating is brought into play to accomplish further heat loss through evaporation. If the air temperature rises above the temperature of maximally vasodilated skin, the temperature gradient reverses itself so that heat is gained from the environment. Sweating is the only means of heat loss under these conditions.

Humans also employ voluntary measures, such as using fans, wetting the body, drinking cold beverages, and wearing cool clothing, to further enhance heat loss. Contrary to popular belief, wearing light-colored, loose clothing is cooler than being nude. Naked skin absorbs almost all the radiant energy that strikes it, whereas light-colored clothing reflects almost all the radiant energy that falls on it. Thus, if light-colored clothing is loose and thin enough to permit convection currents and evaporative heat loss to occur, wearing it is actually cooler than going without any clothes.

During a fever, the hypothalamic thermostat is "reset" at an elevated temperature.

 The term **fever** refers to an elevation in body temperature as a result of infection or inflammation. In response to microbial invasion, certain phagocytic cells (macrophages) release chemicals that serve as an

▲ Table 16-3 Coordinated Adjustments in Response to Cold or Heat Exposure

RESPONSE TO COLD EXPOSURE (COORDINATED BY THE POSTERIOR HYPOTHALAMUS)		RESPONSE TO HEAT EXPOSURE (COORDINATED BY THE ANTERIOR HYPOTHALAMUS)	
Increased Heat Production	Decreased Heat Loss (Heat Conservation)	Decreased Heat Production	Increased Heat Loss
Increased muscle tone	Skin vasoconstriction	Decreased muscle tone	Skin vasodilation
Shivering	Postural changes to reduce exposed surface area (hunching shoulders, etc.)*	Decreased voluntary exercise*	Sweating
Increased voluntary exercise*	Warm clothing*		Cool clothing*
Nonshivering thermogenesis			

*Behavioral adaptations.

The Extremes of Cold and Heat Can Be Fatal

Prolonged exposure to temperature extremes in either direction can overtax the body's thermoregulatory mechanisms, leading to disorders and even death.

Cold-Related Disorders

The body can be harmed by cold exposure in two ways: frostbite and generalized hypothermia. **Frostbite** involves excessive cooling of a particular part of the body to the point at which tissue in that area is damaged. If exposed tissues actually freeze, tissue damage results from disruption of the cells by formation of ice crystals or by lack of liquid water.

Hypothermia, a fall in body temperature, occurs when generalized cooling of the body exceeds the ability of the normal heat-producing and heat-conserving regulatory mechanisms to match the excessive heat loss. As hypothermia sets in, the rate of all metabolic processes slows because of the declining temperature. Higher cerebral functions are the first affected by body cooling, leading to loss of judgment, apathy, disorientation, and tiredness, all of which diminish the cold victim's ability to initiate voluntary mechanisms to reverse the falling body temperature. As body temperature continues to plummet, depression of the respiratory center occurs, reducing the ventilatory drive so that breathing becomes slow and weak. Activity of the cardiovascular system also is gradually reduced. The heart is slowed, and cardiac output is decreased. Cardiac rhythm is disturbed, eventually leading to ventricular fibrillation and death.

Heat-Related Disorders

At the other extreme, two disorders related to excessive heat exposure are heat exhaustion and heat stroke. **Heat exhaustion** is a state of collapse, usually manifested by fainting, that is caused by reduced blood pressure brought about as a result of overtaxing the heat-loss mechanisms. Extensive sweating reduces cardiac output by depleting the plasma volume, and pronounced skin vasodilation causes a drop in total peripheral resistance. Because blood pressure is determined by cardiac output times total peripheral resistance, blood pressure falls, an insufficient amount of blood is delivered to the brain, and fainting takes place. Thus, heat exhaustion is a consequence of overactivity of the heat-loss mechanisms rather than a breakdown of these mechanisms. Because the heat-loss mechanisms have been very active, body temperature is only mildly elevated in heat exhaustion. By forcing cessation of activity when the heat-loss mechanisms are no longer able to cope with heat gain through exercise or a hot environment, heat exhaustion serves as a safety valve to help prevent the more serious consequences of heat stroke.

Heat stroke is an extremely dangerous situation that arises from the complete breakdown of the hypothalamic thermoregulatory systems. Heat exhaustion may progress into heat stroke if the heat-loss mechanisms continue to be overtaxed. Heat stroke is more likely to occur on overexertion during prolonged exposure to a hot, humid environment. The elderly, in whom thermoregulatory responses are generally slower and less efficient, are particularly vulnerable to heat stroke during prolonged, stifling heat waves. So too are individuals who are taking certain common tranquilizers, such as Valium, because these drugs interfere with the hypothalamic thermoregulatory centers' neurotransmitter activity.

The most striking feature of heat stroke is a lack of compensatory heat loss measures, such as sweating, in the face of a rapidly rising body temperature **(hyperthermia).** No sweating occurs, despite a markedly elevated body temperature, because the hypothalamic thermoregulatory control centers are not functioning properly and cannot initiate heat-loss mechanisms. During the development of heat stroke, body temperature starts to climb as the heat-loss mechanisms are eventually overwhelmed by prolonged, excessive heat gain. Once the core temperature reaches the point at which the hypothalamic temperature-control centers are damaged by the heat, body temperature rapidly rises even higher because of the complete shutdown of heat-loss mechanisms. Furthermore, as the body temperature increases, the rate of metabolism increases correspondingly, because higher temperatures speed up the rate of all chemical reactions; the result is even greater heat production. This positive-feedback state sends the temperature spiraling upward. Heat stroke is a dangerous situation that is rapidly fatal if untreated. Even with treatment to halt and reverse the rampant rise in body temperature, there is still a high rate of mortality. The rate of permanent disability in survivors is also high because of irreversible protein denaturation caused by the high internal heat.

---

endogenous pyrogen, which acts on the hypothalamic thermoregulatory center to raise the thermostat setting (● Figure 16-5; also see p. 336). The hypothalamus now maintains the temperature at the new set level instead of maintaining normal body temperature. If, for example, endogenous pyrogen raises the set point to 102°F (38.9°C), the hypothalamus senses that the normal prefever temperature is too cold, so it initiates the cold-response mechanisms to raise the temperature to 102°F. Specifically, it initiates shivering to rapidly increase heat production and promotes skin vasoconstriction to rapidly reduce heat loss, both of which drive the temperature upward. These events account for the sudden cold chills often experienced at the onset of a fever. Feeling cold, the person may voluntarily pile on more blankets to help raise body temperature by conserving body heat. Once the new temperature is achieved, body temperature is regulated as normal in response to cold and heat—but at a higher setting. Thus, fever production in response to an infection is a deliberate outcome and is not caused by a breakdown of thermoregulation. Although the physiological significance of a fever is still unclear, many medical experts believe that a rise in body temperature has a beneficial role in fighting infection. A fever augments the inflammatory response and may interfere with bacterial multiplication.

During fever production, endogenous pyrogen raises the set point of the hypothalamic thermostat by triggering the local release of *prostaglandins,* which are local chemical mediators that act directly on the hypothalamus. Aspirin reduces a fever by inhibiting the synthesis of prostaglandins. Aspirin does not

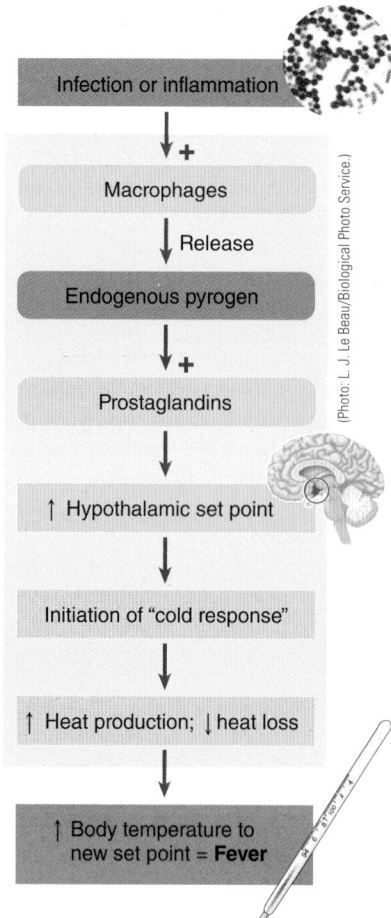

Infection or inflammation

+

Macrophages

Release

Endogenous pyrogen

+

Prostaglandins

↑ Hypothalamic set point

Initiation of "cold response"

↑ Heat production; ↓ heat loss

↑ Body temperature to new set point = **Fever**

● **FIGURE 16-5 Fever production.**

lower the temperature in a nonfebrile person, because in the absence of endogenous pyrogen, prostaglandins are not present in the hypothalamus in appreciable quantities.

The exact molecular cause of a fever "breaking" naturally is unknown, although it presumably results from reduced pyrogen release or decreased prostaglandin synthesis. When the hypothalamic set point is restored to normal, the temperature at 102°F (in this example) is too high. The heat-response mechanisms are instituted to cool the body. Skin vasodilation occurs, and sweating commences. The person feels hot and throws off extra covers. The gearing up of these heat-loss mechanisms by the hypothalamus reduces the temperature to normal.

Chapter in Perspective: Focus on Homeostasis

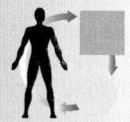

Because energy can be neither created nor destroyed, for body weight and body temperature to remain constant, input must equal output in the case of, respectively, the body's total energy balance and its heat energy balance. If total energy input exceeds total energy output, the extra energy is stored in the body and body weight increases. Similarly, if the input of heat energy exceeds its output, body temperature increases. Conversely, if output exceeds input, body weight decreases or body temperature falls. The hypothalamus is the major integrating center for maintaining both a constant total energy balance (and thus a constant body weight) and a constant heat energy balance (and thus a constant body temperature).

Body temperature, which is one of the homeostatically regulated factors of the internal environment, must be maintained within narrow limits, because the structure and reactivity of the chemicals that compose the body are temperature sensitive. Deviations in body temperature outside a limited range result in protein denaturation and death of the individual if the temperature rises too high or metabolic slowing and death if the temperature falls too low.

Body weight, in contrast, varies widely among individuals. Only the extremes of imbalances between total energy input and total energy output become incompatible with life. For example, in the face of insufficient energy input in the form of ingested food during prolonged starvation, the body resorts to breaking down muscle protein to meet its needs for energy expenditure once the adipose stores are depleted. Body weight dwindles because of this self-cannibalistic mechanism until death finally occurs as a result of loss of heart muscle, among other things. At the other extreme, when the food energy consumed greatly exceeds the energy expended, the extra energy input is stored as adipose tissue and body weight increases. The resultant gross obesity can also lead to heart failure. Not only must the heart work harder to pump blood to the excess adipose tissue, but obesity also predisposes the person to atherosclerosis and heart attacks (see p. 272).

REVIEW EXERCISES

Objective Questions (Answers on p. A-50)

1. If more food energy is consumed than is expended, the excess energy is lost as heat. (*True or false?*)
2. All energy within nutrient molecules can be harnessed to perform biological work. (*True or false?*)
3. Each liter of O_2 contains 4.8 kcal of heat energy. (*True or false?*)
4. A body temperature greater than 98.2°F is always indicative of a fever. (*True or false?*)
5. Core temperature is relatively constant, but skin temperature can vary markedly. (*True or false?*)
6. Sweat that drips off the body has no cooling effect. (*True or false?*)
7. Production of "goose bumps" has no value in regulating body temperature. (*True or false?*)
8. The posterior region of the hypothalamus triggers shivering and skin vasoconstriction. (*True or false?*)

9. The _____ of the hypothalamus contains two populations of neurons, one that secretes appetite-enhancing NPY and another that secretes appetite-suppressing melanocortins.
10. The primary means of involuntarily increasing heat production is _____.
11. Increased heat production independent of muscle contraction is known as _____.
12. The only means of heat loss when the environmental temperature exceeds the core temperature is _____.
13. Which of the following statements concerning heat exchange between the body and the external environment is *incorrect?*
    a. Heat gain is primarily by means of internal heat production.
    b. Radiation serves as a means of heat gain but not of heat loss.
    c. Heat energy always moves down its concentration gradient from warmer to cooler objects.
    d. The temperature gradient between the skin and the external air is subject to control.
    e. Little body heat is lost by conduction alone.
14. Which of the following statements concerning fever production is *incorrect?*
    a. Endogenous pyrogen is released by macrophages in response to microbial invasion.
    b. The hypothalamic set point is elevated.
    c. The hypothalamus initiates cold-response mechanisms to increase the body temperature.
    d. Prostaglandins mediate the effect.
    e. The hypothalamus is not effective in regulating body temperature during a fever.

15. Using the answer code on the right, indicate which mechanism of heat transfer is being described:
    ___ 1. sitting on a cold metal chair
    ___ 2. sunbathing on the beach
    ___ 3. being in a gentle breeze
    ___ 4. sitting in front of a fireplace
    ___ 5. sweating
    ___ 6. riding in a car with the windows open
    ___ 7. lying under an electric blanket
    ___ 8. sitting in a wet bathing suit
    ___ 9. fanning yourself
    ___ 10. immersing yourself in cold water

    (a) Radiation
    (b) Conduction
    (c) Convection
    (d) Evaporation

Essay Questions

1. Differentiate between external and internal work.
2. Define *metabolic rate* and *basal metabolic rate.* Explain the process of indirectly measuring metabolic rate.
3. Describe the three states of energy balance.
4. By what means is energy balance primarily maintained?
5. List the sources of heat input and output for the body.
6. Describe the source and role of the following in the long-term regulation of energy balance and the short-term control of the timing and size of meals: neuropeptide Y, melanocortins, leptin, insulin, orexins, corticotropin-releasing hormone, ghrelin, peptide YY_{3-36}, cholecystokinin (CCK), and stomach distension.
7. Discuss the compensatory measures that occur in response to a fall in core temperature as a result of cold exposure and in response to a rise in core temperature as a result of heat exposure.

POINTS TO PONDER

(Explanations on p. A-50)

1. Explain how drugs that selectively inhibit CCK increase feeding behavior in experimental animals.
2. What advice would you give an overweight friend who asks for your help in designing a safe, sensible, inexpensive program for losing weight?
3. Why is it dangerous to engage in heavy exercise on a hot, humid day?
4. Describe the avenues for heat loss in a person soaking in a hot bath.
5. Consider the difference between you and a fish in a local pond with regard to control of body temperature. Humans are *thermoregulators;* they can maintain a remarkably constant, rather high internal body temperature despite the body's exposure to a range of environ-

mental temperatures. To maintain thermal homeostasis, humans physiologically manipulate mechanisms within their bodies to adjust heat production, conservation, and loss. In contrast, fish are *thermoconformers;* their body temperatures conform to the temperature of their surroundings. Thus, their body temperatures vary capriciously with changes in the environmental temperature. Even though fish produce heat, they cannot physiologically regulate internal heat production, nor can they control heat exchange with their environment to maintain a constant body temperature when the temperature in their surroundings rises or falls. Knowing this, do you think fish run a fever when they have a systemic infection? Why or why not?

CLINICAL CONSIDERATION

(Explanation on p. A-51)

Michael F., a near-drowning victim, was pulled from the icy water by rescuers 15 minutes after he fell through thin ice when skating. Michael is now alert and recuperating in the hospital. How can you explain his "miraculous" survival even

though he was submerged without breathing air for 15 minutes, yet irreversible brain damage, soon followed by death, normally occurs if the brain is deprived of O_2 for more than 4 or 5 minutes?

Chapter 16 Study Card

Energy Balance (pp. 509–516)

■ Energy input to the body in the form of food energy must equal energy output, because energy cannot be created or destroyed. Energy output or expenditure includes (1) external work, performed by skeletal muscles to move an external object or move the body through the external environment, and (2) internal work, which consists of all energy-dependent activities that do not accomplish external work, including active transport, smooth and cardiac muscle contraction, glandular secretion, and protein synthesis. (*Review Figure 16-1.*)

■ Only about 25% of the chemical energy in food is harnessed to do biological work. The rest is immediately converted to heat. Furthermore, all the energy expended to accomplish internal work is eventually converted into heat, and 75% of the energy expended by working skeletal muscles is lost as heat. Therefore, most of the energy in food ultimately appears as body heat.

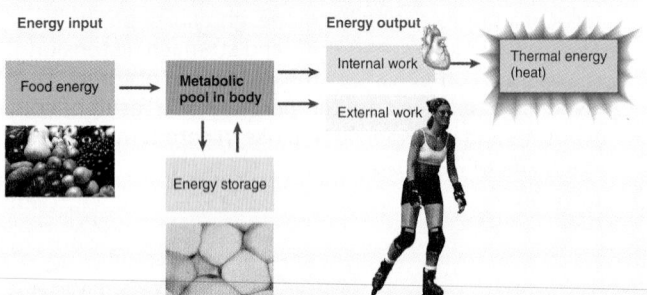

■ The metabolic rate (energy expenditure per unit of time) is measured in kilocalories of heat produced per hour.

■ The basal metabolic rate (BMR) is a measure of the body's minimal waking rate of internal energy expenditure.

■ For a neutral energy balance, the energy in ingested food must equal energy expended in performing external work and transformed into heat. If more energy is consumed than is expended, the extra energy is stored in the body, primarily as adipose tissue, so body weight increases. By contrast, if more energy is expended than is available in the food, body energy stores are used to support energy expenditure, so body weight decreases.

■ Usually, body weight remains fairly constant over a prolonged period (except during growth) because food intake is adjusted to match energy expenditure long term. Food intake is controlled primarily by the hypothalamus by means of complex regulatory mechanisms in which hunger and satiety are important components. Feeding or appetite signals give rise to the sensation of hunger and promote eating, whereas satiety signals lead to the sensation of fullness and suppress eating. (*Review Table 16-2.*)

■ The arcuate nucleus of the hypothalamus plays a key role in energy homeostasis through the two clusters of appetite-regulating neurons it contains: neurons that secrete neuropeptide Y (NPY), which increases appetite and food intake, and neurons that secrete melanocortins, which suppress appetite and food intake. (*Review Figure 16-2.*)

■ Adipocytes in fat stores secrete the hormone leptin, which reduces appetite and decreases food consumption by inhibiting the NPY-secreting neurons and stimulating the melanocortins-secreting neurons. This mechanism is important in the long-term matching of energy intake with energy output, thus maintaining body weight. (*Review Figure 16-2.*)

■ Insulin released by the endocrine pancreas in response to increased glucose and other nutrients in the blood also inhibits the NPY-secreting neurons and contributes to long-term control of energy balance and body weight.

■ NPY and melanocortins bring about their effects by acting on the lateral hypothalamic area (LHA) and paraventricular nucleus (PVN) to alter the release of chemical messengers from these areas. The LHA secretes orexins, which are potent stimulators of food intake, whereas the PVN releases neuropeptides such as corticotropin-releasing hormone, which decrease food intake. (*Review Figure 16-2.*)

■ Short-term control of the timing and size of meals is mediated primarily by the actions of two peptides secreted by the

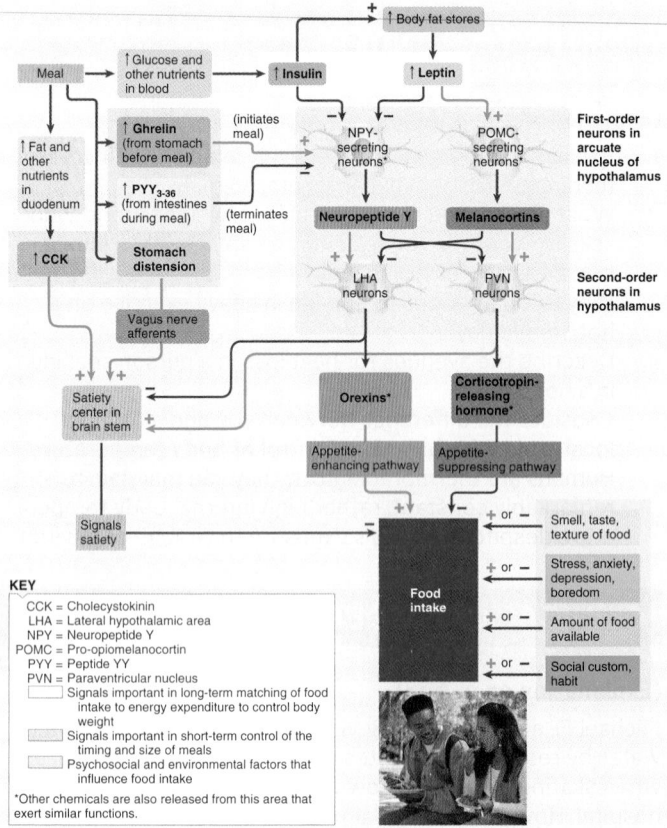

digestive tract. (1) Ghrelin, a mealtime initiator, is secreted by the stomach before a meal and signals hunger. Its secretion drops when food is consumed. Ghrelin stimulates appetite and promotes feeding behavior by stimulating the NPY-secreting neurons. (2) Peptide YY$_{3\text{-}36}$ (PYY$_{3\text{-}36}$), a mealtime terminator, is secreted by the small and large intestines during a meal and signals satiety. Its secretion is lowest before a meal. PYY$_{3\text{-}36}$ inhibits the NPY-secreting neurons. *(Review Figure 16-2.)*

■ The satiety center in the brain stem also plays a key role in short-term control of meals. The satiety center receives input from the higher hypothalamic areas concerned with control of energy balance and food intake, as well as input from the digestive tract and elsewhere. Satiety signals acting through the satiety center to inhibit further food intake include stomach distension and increased cholecystokinin (CCK), a hormone released from the duodenum in response to the presence of nutrients, especially fat, in the digestive tract lumen. *(Review Figure 16-2.)*

■ Psychosocial and environmental factors can also influence food intake beyond the internal signals that govern feeding behavior. *(Review Figure 16-2.)*

Temperature Regulation (pp. 516–522)

■ The body can be thought of as a heat-generating core (internal organs, central nervous system, and skeletal muscles) surrounded by a shell of variable insulating capacity (the skin).

■ The skin exchanges heat energy with the external environment, with the direction and amount of heat transfer depending on the environmental temperature and the momentary insulating capacity of the shell. The four physical means by which heat is exchanged are (1) radiation (net movement of heat energy via electromagnetic waves), (2) conduction (exchange of heat energy by direct contact), (3) convection (transfer of heat energy by means of air currents), and (4) evaporation (extraction of heat energy from the body by the heat-requiring conversion of liquid H_2O to H_2O vapor). Because heat energy moves from warmer to cooler objects, radiation, conduction, and convection can be channels for either heat loss or heat gain, depending on whether surrounding objects are cooler or warmer, respectively, than the body surface. Normally, they are avenues for heat loss, along with evaporation resulting from sweating. *(Review Figure 16-4.)*

■ To prevent serious cell malfunction, the core temperature must be held constant at about 100°F (equivalent to an average oral temperature of 98.2°F) by continuously balancing heat gain and heat loss despite changes in environmental temperature and variation in internal heat production. *(Review Figure 16-3.)*

■ This thermoregulatory balance is controlled by the hypothalamus. The hypothalamus is apprised of the skin temperature by peripheral thermoreceptors and of the core temperature by central thermoreceptors, which are located in the hypothalamus itself, as well as in abdominal organs and elsewhere.

■ The primary means of heat gain is heat production by metabolic activity, mostly skeletal muscle contraction.

■ Heat loss is adjusted by sweating and by controlling to the greatest extent possible the temperature gradient between the skin and the surrounding environment. The latter is accomplished by regulating the diameter of the skin's arterioles. (1) Skin vasoconstriction reduces the flow of warmed blood through the skin so that skin temperature falls. The layer of cool skin between the core and the environment increases the insulating barrier between the warm core and the external air. (2) Skin vasodilation brings more warmed blood through the skin so that skin temperature approaches the core temperature, thus reducing the insulative capacity of the skin.

■ On exposure to cool surroundings, the core temperature starts to fall as heat loss increases, because the skin-to-air temperature gradient is larger than normal. The posterior hypothalamus responds to reduce the heat loss by inducing skin vasoconstriction while simultaneously increasing heat production through heat-generating shivering. *(Review Table 16-3.)*

■ Conversely, in response to a rise in core temperature (resulting either from excessive internal heat production accompanying exercise or from excessive heat gain on exposure to a hot environment), the anterior hypothalamus triggers heat-loss mechanisms, such as skin vasodilation and sweating, while simultaneously decreasing heat production, such as by reducing muscle tone. *(Review Table 16-3.)*

■ In both cold and heat responses, voluntary behavioral actions help maintain thermal homeostasis.

■ A fever occurs when endogenous pyrogen released from macrophages in response to infection raises the hypothalamic set point. An elevated core temperature develops as the hypothalamus initiates cold-response mechanisms to raise the core temperature to the new set point. *(Review Figure 16-5.)*

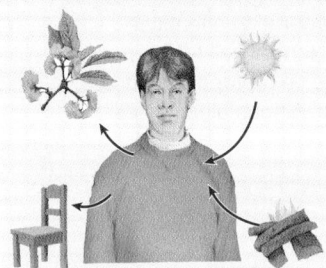

(a) Radiation—the transfer of heat energy from a warmer object to a cooler object in the form of electromagnetic waves ("heat waves"), which travel through space.

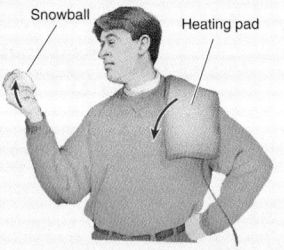

(b) Conduction—the transfer of heat from a warmer to a cooler object that is in direct contact with the warmer one. The heat is transferred through the movement of thermal energy from molecule to adjacent molecule.

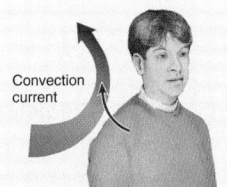

(c) Convection—the transfer of heat energy by air currents. Cool air warmed by the body through conduction rises and is replaced by more cool air. This process is enhanced by the forced movement of air across the body surface.

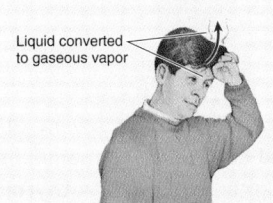

(d) Evaporation—conversion of a liquid such as sweat into a gaseous vapor, a process that requires heat (the heat of vaporization), which is absorbed from the skin.

Endocrine System

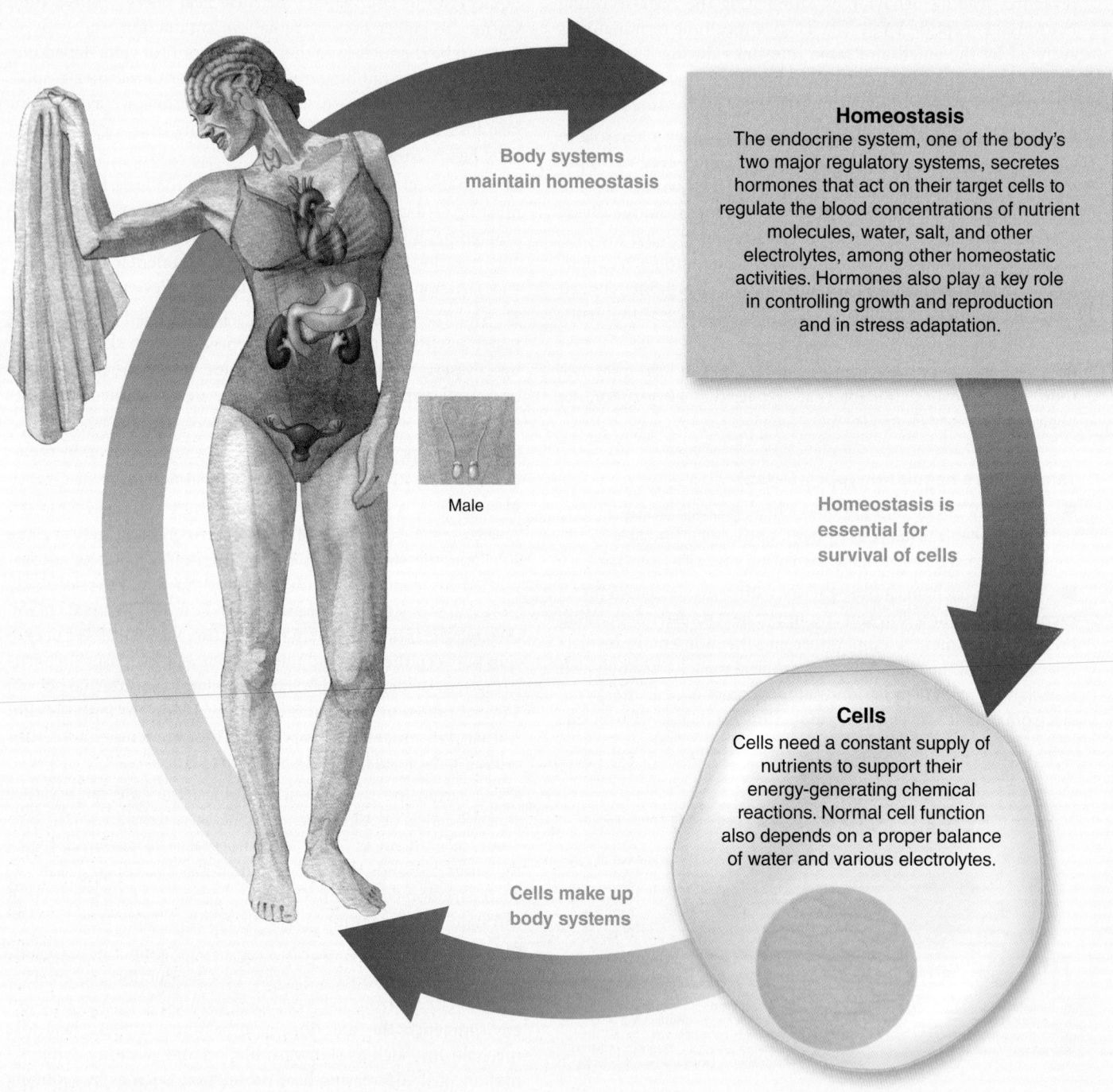

Body systems maintain homeostasis

Homeostasis
The endocrine system, one of the body's two major regulatory systems, secretes hormones that act on their target cells to regulate the blood concentrations of nutrient molecules, water, salt, and other electrolytes, among other homeostatic activities. Hormones also play a key role in controlling growth and reproduction and in stress adaptation.

Male

Homeostasis is essential for survival of cells

Cells
Cells need a constant supply of nutrients to support their energy-generating chemical reactions. Normal cell function also depends on a proper balance of water and various electrolytes.

Cells make up body systems

The **endocrine system,** by means of the blood-borne **hormones** it secretes, generally regulates activities that require duration rather than speed. Most target-cell activities under hormonal control are directed toward maintaining homeostasis. The **hypothalamus** (a part of the brain) and **posterior pituitary gland** act as a unit to release hormones essential for maintaining water balance and for giving birth and breast-feeding. The **anterior pituitary gland** secretes hormones that promote growth and control the hormonal output of several other endocrine glands. The **pineal gland** secretes a hormone important in establishing the body's biological rhythms. The **thyroid gland** controls the body's basal metabolic rate. The **adrenal glands** secrete hormones important in metabolizing nutrient molecules, in adapting to stress, and in maintaining salt balance. The **endocrine pancreas** secretes hormones important in metabolizing nutrient molecules. The **parathyroid glands** secrete a hormone important in Ca^{2+} metabolism.

17

The Endocrine System

CHAPTER AT A GLANCE

General Principles of Endocrinology

Hypothalamus and Pituitary

Hypothalamus–posterior pituitary relationship

Hypothalamus–anterior pituitary relationship

Anterior pituitary and hypophysiotropic hormones

Endocrine Control of Growth

Factors influencing growth

Functions and control of growth hormone

Pineal Gland and Circadian Rhythms

Suprachiasmatic nucleus as the master biological clock

Functions of melatonin

Thyroid Gland

Anatomy of the thyroid gland

Thyroid hormone

Adrenal Glands

Adrenocortical steroids

Adrenal medullary catecholamines

Integrated Stress Response

Hormonal and neural roles in the stress response

Endocrine Pancreas and Control of Fuel Metabolism

Metabolism, anabolism, catabolism

Absorptive and postabsorptive states

Endocrine pancreas: insulin and glucagon

Metabolic effects of other hormones

Parathyroid Gland and Control of Calcium Metabolism

Importance of free ECF calcium

Bone remodeling

Parathyroid hormone

Calcitonin

Vitamin D

General Principles of Endocrinology

The **endocrine system** consists of the ductless endocrine glands (see p. 4) scattered throughout the body (● Figure 17-1). Even though the endocrine glands for the most part are not connected anatomically, they constitute a system in a functional sense. They all accomplish their functions by secreting hormones into the blood, and many functional interactions take place among the various endocrine glands. Once secreted, a **hormone** travels in the blood to its distant target cells, where it regulates or directs a particular function (see p. 99). **Endocrinology** is the study of the homeostatic chemical adjustments and other activities that hormones accomplish. Even though the blood distributes hormones throughout the body, only specific **target cells** can respond to each hormone because only the target cells have receptors for binding with the particular hormone (see p. 107).

The binding of a hormone with its specific target-cell receptors initiates a chain of events within the target cells to bring about the hormone's final effect. Recall that the means by which a hormone brings about its ultimate physiologic effect depends on whether the hormone is hydrophilic (peptide hormones and catecholamines) or lipophilic (steroid hormones and thyroid hormone). *Peptide hormones,* the most abundant chemical category of hormone, are chains of amino acids of varying length. *Catecholamines,* produced by the adrenal medulla, are derived from the amino acid tyrosine. *Steroid hormones,* produced by the adrenal cortex and reproductive endocrine glands, are neutral lipids derived from cholesterol. *Thyroid hormone,* produced by the thyroid gland, is an iodinated tyrosine derivative. To review, hydrophilic hormones on binding with surface membrane receptors primarily act through second-messenger systems to alter the activity of preexisting proteins, such as enzymes, within the target cell to produce their physiologic response. Lipophilic steroid hormones and thyroid hormone, by contrast, activate genes on binding with receptors inside the cell, thus bringing about formation of new proteins in the target cell that carry out the desired response. Hydrophilic hormones circulate in the blood largely dissolved in the plasma, whereas lipophilic hormones are largely bound to plasma proteins. (See pp. 100–106 for further detail.)

Hormones exert a variety of regulatory effects throughout the body.

The endocrine system is one of the body's two major regulatory systems, the other being the nervous system, with which you are already familiar (Chapters 4 through 7). Recall that the endocrine and nervous systems are specialized for controlling different types of activities. In general, the nervous system coordinates rapid, precise responses and is especially important in mediating the body's interactions with the external environment. The endocrine system, by contrast, primarily controls activities that require duration rather than speed.

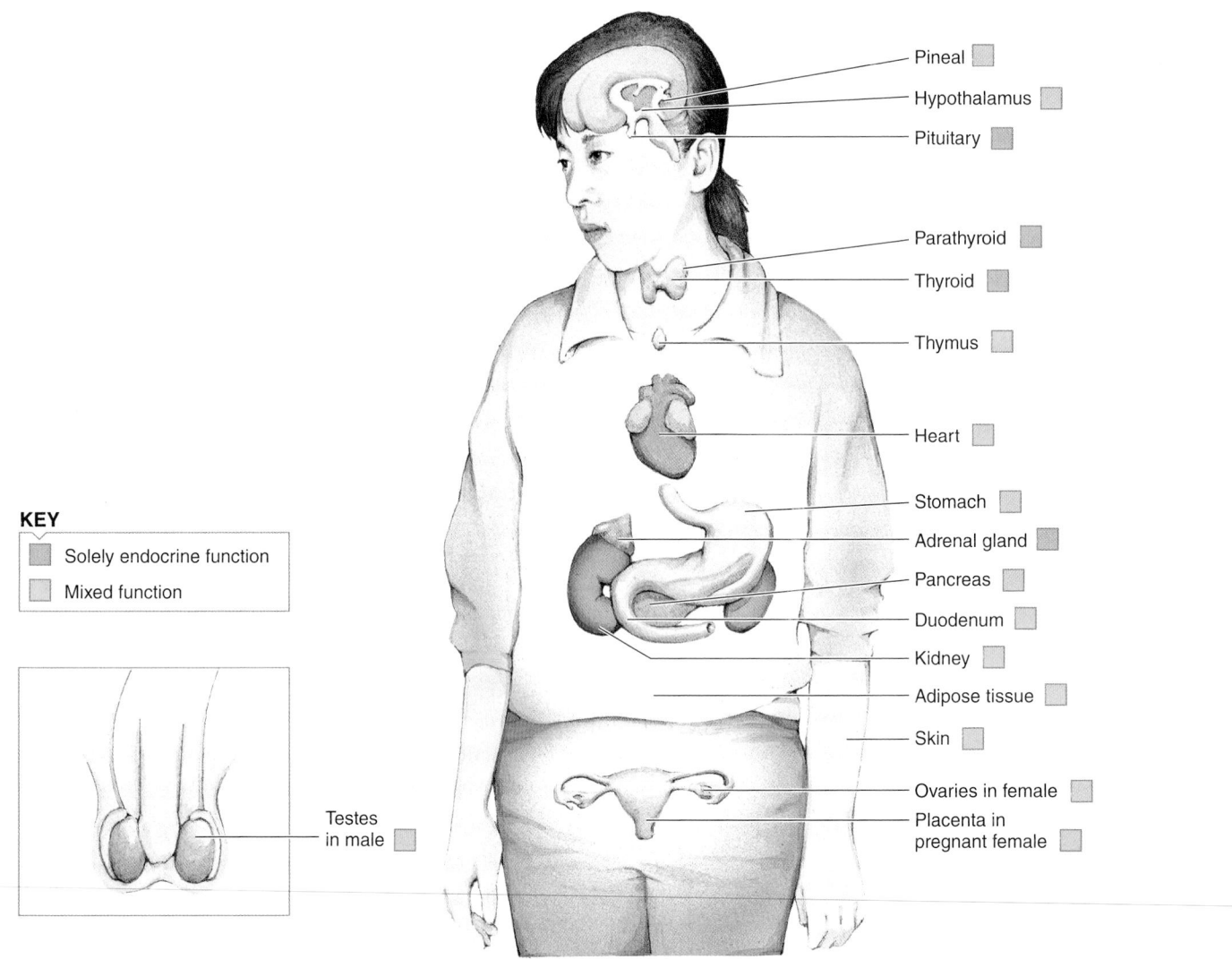

KEY

■	Solely endocrine function
▢	Mixed function

Pineal ▢
Hypothalamus ▢
Pituitary ▢
Parathyroid ▢
Thyroid ▢
Thymus ▢
Heart ▢
Stomach ▢
Adrenal gland ▢
Pancreas ▢
Duodenum ▢
Kidney ▢
Adipose tissue ▢
Skin ▢
Ovaries in female ▢
Placenta in pregnant female ▢

Testes in male ▢

● FIGURE 17-1 **The endocrine system.**

OVERALL FUNCTIONS OF THE ENDOCRINE SYSTEM In its regulatory role, the endocrine system exerts wide-ranging effects throughout the body, including the following:

1. Regulating nutrient metabolism and H_2O and electrolyte balance, which are important collectively in maintaining a constant internal environment
2. Inducing adaptive changes to help the body cope with stressful situations
3. Promoting smooth, sequential growth and development
4. Controlling reproduction
5. Regulating red blood cell production
6. Along with the autonomic nervous system, controlling and integrating activities of both the circulatory and the digestive systems

TROPIC HORMONES Some hormones regulate the production and secretion of another hormone. A hormone that has as its primary function the regulation of hormone secretion by another endocrine gland is classified functionally as a **tropic hormone**

(*tropic* means "nourishing" and is pronounced "trō-pik"). Tropic hormones stimulate and maintain their endocrine target tissues. For example, thyroid-stimulating hormone (TSH), a tropic hormone from the anterior pituitary, stimulates thyroid hormone secretion by the thyroid gland and maintains the structural integrity of this gland. In the absence of TSH, the thyroid gland atrophies (shrinks) and produces very low levels of its hormones.

MIXED FUNCTION GLANDS Some glands of the endocrine system are solely endocrine in function (they specialize in hormone secretion alone, the anterior pituitary being an example), whereas other endocrine organs perform nonendocrine functions, in addition to secreting hormones. For example, the testes produce sperm and secrete the male sex hormone testosterone.

The effective plasma concentration of a hormone is normally regulated by changes in its rate of secretion.
The primary function of most hormones is regulation of various homeostatic activities. Because hormones' effects are proportional to their concentrations in the plasma, these concentrations

are subject to control according to homeostatic need. Normally, the plasma concentration of a hormone is regulated by appropriate adjustments in the rate of its secretion. Endocrine glands do not secrete their hormones at a constant rate; the secretion rates of all hormones vary subject to control, often by a combination of several complex mechanisms. Furthermore, the magnitude of the hormonal response depends on the availability and sensitivity of the target cells' receptors for the hormone. We examine the factors that influence the plasma concentration of hormones before turning our attention to the target cells' responsiveness to hormones. The regulatory system for each hormone is considered in detail in later sections. For now, we address these general mechanisms of controlling secretion that are common to many hormones: negative-feedback control, neuroendocrine reflexes, and diurnal (circadian) rhythms.

NEGATIVE-FEEDBACK CONTROL Negative feedback is a prominent feature of hormonal control systems. Stated simply, *negative feedback exists when the output of a system counteracts a change in input,* maintaining a controlled variable within a narrow range around a set level (see p. 11). Negative feedback maintains the plasma concentration of a hormone at a given level, similar to the way in which a home heating system maintains the room temperature at a given set point. Control of hormonal secretion provides some classic physiologic examples of negative feedback. For example, when the plasma concentration of free circulating thyroid hormone falls below a given "set point," the anterior pituitary secretes TSH, which stimulates the thyroid to increase its secretion of thyroid hormone. Thyroid hormone in turn inhibits further secretion of TSH by the anterior pituitary. Negative feedback ensures that once thyroid gland secretion has been "turned on" by TSH, it will not continue unabated but instead will be "turned off" when the appropriate level of free circulating thyroid hormone has been achieved. The feedback loops often become quite complex.

NEUROENDOCRINE REFLEXES Many endocrine control systems involve neuroendocrine reflexes, which include neural, as well as hormonal, components. The purpose of such reflexes is to produce a sudden increase in hormone secretion (that is, "turn up the thermostat setting") in response to a specific stimulus, frequently a stimulus external to the body. Some endocrine control systems include both feedback control (which maintains a constant basal level of the hormone) and neuroendocrine reflexes (which cause sudden bursts in secretion in response to a sudden increased need for the hormone). An example is the increased secretion of cortisol, the "stress hormone," by the adrenal cortex during a stress response (see ● Figure 17-19, p. 552).

DIURNAL (CIRCADIAN) RHYTHM The secretion rates of many hormones rhythmically fluctuate up and down as a function of time. The most common endocrine rhythm is the **diurnal** ("day–night") or **circadian** ("around a day") **rhythm,** which is characterized by regular, repetitive oscillations in hormone levels that cycle once every 24 hours. Endocrine rhythms are locked on, or

entrained, to external cues such as the light–dark cycle. That is, the inherent 24-hour cycles of peak and ebb of hormone secretion are set to "march in step" with cycles of light and dark. For example, cortisol secretion rises during the night, reaching its peak secretion in the morning before a person gets up, and then falls throughout the day to its lowest level at bedtime (● Figure 17-2). Inherent hormonal rhythmicity and entrainment are not accomplished by the endocrine glands themselves but result from the central nervous system (CNS) changing the set point of these glands. We discuss in a later section the master biological clock responsible for this timing. Negative-feedback control mechanisms operate to maintain whatever set point is established for that time of day. Some endocrine cycles operate on time scales other than a circadian rhythm, a well-known example being the monthly menstrual cycle.

The plasma concentration of a hormone is influenced by its rate of excretion.

Even though the plasma concentration of a hormone is normally regulated by adjusting its rate of secretion, alterations in its rate of inactivation and excretion in the urine can also influence the hormone's plasma concentration, sometimes inappropriately. In contrast to the tight controls on hormone secretion, hormone inactivation and excretion are not regulated.

All hormones are eventually inactivated by enzymes in the liver, kidneys, blood, or target cells. The amount of time after a hormone is secreted before it is inactivated, and the means by which this takes place, differ among the classes of hormones. In general, the hydrophilic peptides and catecholamines are easy targets for blood and tissue enzymes, so they remain in the blood only briefly (a few minutes to a few hours) before being enzymatically inactivated. In contrast, binding of lipophilic hormones to plasma proteins makes them less vulnerable to metabolic inactivation and keeps them from escaping into the urine. Therefore, lipophilic hormones are removed from plasma more slowly: They may persist in the blood for hours (steroids) or up to a week (thyroid hormone). Lipophilic hormones typically undergo a series of reactions that reduce their biological activity and make them more water soluble so that they can be freed from their plasma protein carriers and be eliminated in the urine.

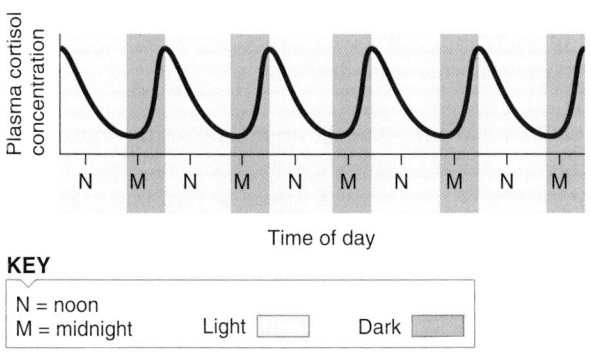

● FIGURE 17-2 **Diurnal rhythm of cortisol secretion.**
(*Source:* Adapted from George A. Hedge, Howard D. Colby, and Robert L. Goodman, *Clinical Endocrine Physiology,* Figure 1-13, p. 28. © 1987, with permission from Elsevier.)

Because the liver and kidneys are important in removing hormones from the plasma, patients with liver or kidney disease may suffer from excess activity of certain hormones solely because hormone inactivation and elimination are reduced.

When liver and kidney function are normal, measuring urinary concentrations of hormones and their metabolites provides a useful, noninvasive way to assess endocrine function because the rate of excretion of these products in the urine directly reflects their rate of secretion by the endocrine glands.

Endocrine disorders result from hormone excess or deficiency or decreased target-cell responsiveness.

Endocrine disorders most commonly result from abnormal plasma concentrations of a hormone caused by inappropriate rates of secretion—that is, too little hormone secreted (**hyposecretion**) or too much hormone secreted (**hypersecretion**). Occasionally, endocrine dysfunction arises because target-cell responsiveness to the hormone is abnormally low, even though plasma concentration of the hormone is normal. This unresponsiveness may be caused, for example, by an inborn lack of receptors for the hormone, as in **testicular feminization syndrome.** In this condition, receptors for testosterone, a masculinizing hormone produced by the male testes, are not produced because of a specific genetic defect. Although adequate testosterone is available, masculinization does not take place, just as if no testosterone were present. Abnormal responsiveness may also occur if the target cells for a particular hormone lack an enzyme essential to carrying out the response.

The responsiveness of a target cell can be varied by regulating the number of hormone-specific receptors.

In contrast to endocrine dysfunction caused by *unintentional* receptor abnormalities, the target-cell receptors for a particular hormone can be *deliberately altered* as a result of physiologic control mechanisms. A target cell's response to a hormone is correlated with the number of the cell's receptors occupied by molecules of that hormone, which in turn depends not only on the plasma concentration of the hormone but also on the number of receptors in the target cell for that hormone. Thus, the response of a target cell to a given plasma concentration can be fine-tuned up or down by varying the number of receptors available for hormone binding.

DOWN REGULATION As an illustration of this fine-tuning, when the plasma concentration of insulin is chronically elevated, the total number of target-cell receptors for insulin is gradually reduced as a direct result of the effect a sustained elevation of insulin has on the insulin receptors. This phenomenon, known as **down regulation,** constitutes an important locally acting negative-feedback mechanism that prevents the target cells from overreacting to a prolonged high concentration of insulin; that is, the target cells are *desensitized* to insulin, helping blunt the effect of insulin hypersecretion.

PERMISSIVENESS, SYNERGISM, AND ANTAGONISM A given hormone's effects are influenced not only by the concentration of the hormone itself but also by the concentrations of other hormones that interact with it. Because hormones are widely distributed through the blood, target cells may be exposed simultaneously to many different hormones, giving rise to numerous complex hormonal interactions on target cells. Hormones frequently alter the receptors for other kinds of hormones as part of their normal physiologic activity. A hormone can influence the activity of another hormone at a given target cell in one of three ways: permissiveness, synergism, and antagonism.

With **permissiveness,** one hormone must be present in adequate amounts for the full exertion of another hormone's effect. In essence, the first hormone, by enhancing a target cell's responsiveness to another hormone, "permits" this other hormone to exert its full effect. For example, thyroid hormone increases the number of receptors for epinephrine in epinephrine's target cells, increasing the effectiveness of epinephrine. In the absence of thyroid hormone, epinephrine is only marginally effective.

Synergism occurs when the actions of several hormones are complementary and their combined effect is greater than the sum of their separate effects. An example is the synergistic action of follicle-stimulating hormone and testosterone, both of which are needed to maintain the normal rate of sperm production. Synergism results from each hormone's influence on the number or affinity (attraction) of receptors for the other hormone.

Antagonism occurs when one hormone causes the loss of another hormone's receptors, reducing the effectiveness of the second hormone. To illustrate, progesterone (a hormone secreted during pregnancy that decreases contractions of the uterus) inhibits uterine responsiveness to estrogen (another hormone secreted during pregnancy that increases uterine contractions). By causing loss of estrogen receptors on uterine smooth muscle, progesterone prevents estrogen from exerting its excitatory effects during pregnancy and thus keeps the uterus as a quiet (noncontracting) environment suitable for the developing fetus.

Having completed our discussion of the general principles of endocrinology, we now begin to examine the individual endocrine glands and their hormones. ▲ Table 17-1 on pp. 532–533 summarizes the most important specific functions of the major hormones. Some of these hormones are presented in other chapters and not discussed further here; these are the renal hormones (erythropoietin in Chapter 11 and renin in Chapter 13), thrombopoietin from the liver (Chapter 11), thymosin from the thymus (Chapter 11), atrial natriuretic peptide from the heart (Chapter 13), the gastrointestinal hormones (Chapter 15), leptin and other adipokines from adipose tissue (Chapter 16), hunger and satiety signals from the digestive tract (Chapter 16), and the sex hormones from the gonads (Chapter 18). The remaining hormones are described in greater detail in this chapter. We start with those in or in close association with the brain—namely, the hypothalamus, the pituitary gland, and the pineal gland.

Hypothalamus and Pituitary

The **pituitary gland,** or **hypophysis,** is a small endocrine gland located in a bony cavity at the base of the brain just below the hypothalamus (● Figure 17-3). The pituitary is connected to the hypothalamus by a thin stalk. If you point one finger between your eyes and another finger toward one of your ears, the imaginary point where these lines would intersect is about where your pituitary is located.

The pituitary gland consists of anterior and posterior lobes.

The pituitary has two anatomically and functionally distinct lobes, the **posterior pituitary** and the **anterior pituitary.** The posterior pituitary is composed of nervous tissue and thus is also termed the **neurohypophysis.** The anterior pituitary consists of glandular epithelial tissue and accordingly is also called the **adenohypophysis** (*adeno* means "glandular"). The posterior and anterior pituitary lobes have only their location in common. They arise from different tissues embryonically, serve different functions, and are subject to different control mechanisms.

The release of hormones from both the posterior and the anterior pituitary is directly controlled by the hypothalamus, but the natures of these relationships are entirely different. The posterior pituitary connects to the hypothalamus by a neural pathway, whereas the anterior pituitary connects to the hypothalamus by a unique blood-vessel link. We look first at the posterior pituitary.

The hypothalamus and posterior pituitary act as a unit to secrete vasopressin and oxytocin.

The hypothalamus and posterior pituitary form a neuroendocrine system that consists of a population of neurosecretory neurons whose cell bodies lie in two well-defined clusters in the hypothalamus and whose axons pass down through the thin connecting stalk to terminate on capillaries in the posterior pituitary (● Figure 17-4). The posterior pituitary consists of these neuronal terminals plus glial-like supporting cells (see p. 117). Functionally as well as anatomically, the posterior pituitary is simply an extension of the hypothalamus.

The posterior pituitary does not produce any hormones. It simply stores and, on appropriate stimulation, releases into the blood two small peptide hormones, *vasopressin* and *oxytocin,* which are synthesized by the neuronal cell bodies in the hypothalamus. The synthesized hormones are packaged in secretory granules that are transported by molecular motors down the cytoplasm of the axon (see p. 38) and stored in the neuronal terminals within the posterior pituitary. Each terminal stores either vasopressin or oxytocin. Thus, these hormones can be released independently as needed. On stimulatory input to the hypothalamus, either vasopressin or oxytocin is released into the systemic blood from the posterior pituitary by exocytosis of the appropriate secretory granules. This hormonal release is triggered in response to action potentials that originate in the hypothalamic cell body and sweep down the axon to the neuronal terminal in the posterior pituitary. As in any other neuron, action potentials are generated in these neurosecretory neurons in response to synaptic input to their cell bodies.

The actions of vasopressin and oxytocin are briefly summarized here to make our endocrine story complete. They are described more thoroughly elsewhere—vasopressin in Chapter 13 and oxytocin in Chapter 18.

VASOPRESSIN **Vasopressin (antidiuretic hormone, ADH)** has two major effects that correspond to its two names: (1) it conserves H_2O during urine formation (an antidiuretic effect; *diuresis* means increased urine output) by the kidney nephrons (the functional units of the kidney), and (2) it causes contraction of smooth muscle in arterioles (a vessel pressor effect), the blood vessels whose caliber is an important determinant of blood pressure. The first effect has more physiologic importance. Under normal conditions, vasopressin is the primary endocrine factor that regulates urinary H_2O loss and overall H_2O balance. In contrast, typical levels of vasopressin play only a minor role in regulating blood pressure by means of the hormone's pressor (blood vessel–constricting) effect.

OXYTOCIN Oxytocin stimulates contraction of uterine smooth muscle to help expel the infant during childbirth, and it promotes ejection of milk from the mammary glands (breasts) during breast-feeding.

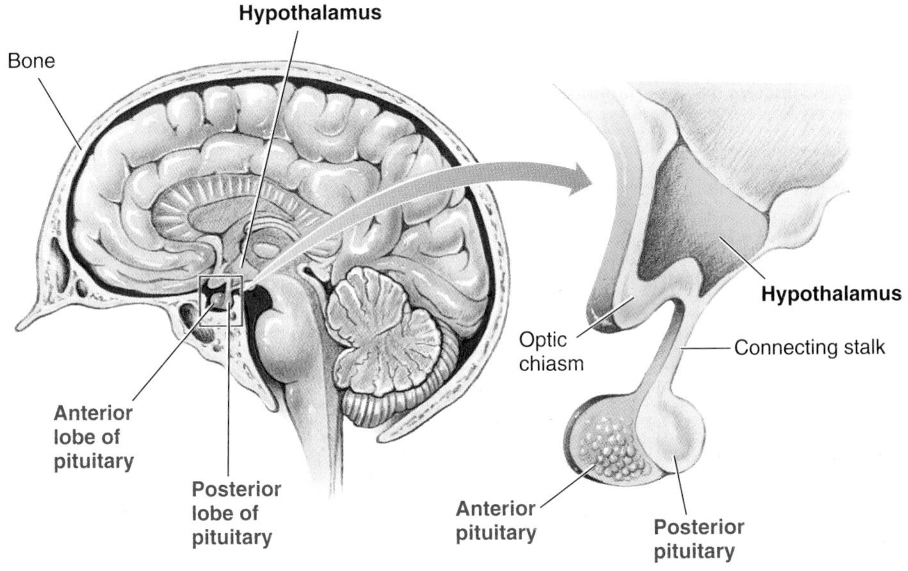

Hypothalamus

Bone

Anterior lobe of pituitary

Posterior lobe of pituitary

Optic chiasm

Hypothalamus

Connecting stalk

Anterior pituitary

Posterior pituitary

(a) Relation of pituitary gland to hypothalamus and rest of brain

(b) Enlargement of pituitary gland and its connection to hypothalamus

● FIGURE 17-3 **Anatomy of the pituitary gland.**

▲ Table 17-1 Summary of the Major Hormones

Endocrine Gland	Hormones	Target Cells	Major Hormone Functions
Hypothalamus	Releasing and inhibiting hormones (TRH, CRH, GnRH, GHRH, somatostatin, PRH, dopamine)	Anterior pituitary	Control release of anterior pituitary hormones
Posterior Pituitary (hormones stored in)	Vasopressin (antidiuretic hormone, ADH)	Kidney tubules	Increases H_2O reabsorption
		Arterioles	Produces vasoconstriction
	Oxytocin	Uterus	Increases contractility
		Mammary glands (breasts)	Causes milk ejection
Anterior Pituitary	Thyroid-stimulating hormone (TSH)	Thyroid follicular cells	Stimulates T_3 and T_4 secretion
	Adrenocorticotropic hormone (ACTH)	Zona fasciculata and zona reticularis of the adrenal cortex	Stimulates cortisol secretion
	Growth hormone (GH)	Bone and soft tissues	Is essential but not solely responsible for growth; by means of IGF, indirectly stimulates protein anabolism and growth of bones and soft tissues; direct metabolic effects include fat mobilization and glucose conservation
		Liver	Stimulates IGF secretion
	Follicle-stimulating hormone (FSH)	Females: Ovarian follicles	Promotes follicular growth and development; stimulates estrogen secretion
		Males: Seminiferous tubules in testes	Stimulates sperm production
	Luteinizing hormone (LH)	Females: Ovarian follicle and corpus luteum	Stimulates ovulation, corpus luteum development, and estrogen and progesterone secretion
		Males: Interstitial cells of Leydig in testes	Stimulates testosterone secretion
	Prolactin (PRL)	Females: Mammary glands	Promotes breast development; stimulates milk secretion
		Males	Uncertain
Pineal Gland	Melatonin	Brain, anterior pituitary, reproductive organs, immune system, and possibly others	Entrains body's biological rhythm with external cues; inhibits gonadotropins; its reduction likely initiates puberty; acts as an antioxidant; enhances immunity
Thyroid Gland Follicular Cells	Tetraiodothyronine (T_4 or thyroxine); triiodothyronine (T_3)	Most cells	Increases metabolic rate; is essential for normal growth and nerve development
Thyroid Gland C Cells	Calcitonin	Bone	Decreases plasma Ca^{2+} concentration
Adrenal Cortex			
Zona glomerulosa	Aldosterone (mineralocorticoid)	Kidney tubules	Increases Na^+ reabsorption and K^+ secretion
Zona fasciculata and zona reticularis	Cortisol (glucocorticoid)	Most cells	Increases blood glucose at the expense of protein and fat stores; contributes to stress adaptation
	Androgen (dehydroepiandrosterone)	Females: Bone and brain	Is responsible for pubertal growth spurt and sex drive
Adrenal medulla	Epinephrine and norepinephrine	Sympathetic receptor sites throughout the body	Reinforce sympathetic nervous system; contribute to stress adaptation and blood pressure regulation

Endocrine Gland	Hormones	Target Cells	Major Hormone Functions
Endocrine Pancreas (Islets of Langerhans)	Insulin (β cells)	Most cells	Promotes cellular uptake, use, and storage of absorbed nutrients
	Glucagon (α cells)	Most cells	Is important for maintaining nutrient levels in blood during the postabsorptive state
	Somatostatin (D cells)	Digestive system	Inhibits digestion and absorption of nutrients
Parathyroid Gland	Parathyroid hormone (PTH)	Bone, kidneys, and intestine	Increases plasma Ca^{2+} concentration; decreases plasma PO_4^{3-} concentration; stimulates vitamin D activation
Gonads			
Female: Ovaries	Estrogen	Female sex organs and body as a whole	Promotes follicular development; governs development of female secondary sexual characteristics; stimulates uterine and breast growth
		Bone	Promotes closure of the epiphyseal plate
	Progesterone	Uterus	Prepares for pregnancy
Male: Testes	Testosterone	Male sex organs and body as a whole	Stimulates sperm production; governs development of male secondary sexual characteristics; promotes sex drive
		Bone	Enhances pubertal growth spurt; promotes closure of the epiphyseal plate
Testes and ovaries	Inhibin	Anterior pituitary	Inhibits secretion of FSH
Placenta	Estrogen and progesterone	Female sex organs	Help maintain pregnancy; prepare breasts for lactation
	Human chorionic gonadotropin (hCG)	Ovarian corpus luteum	Maintains corpus luteum of pregnancy
Kidneys	Renin (by activating angiotensin)	Zona glomerulosa of the adrenal cortex (acted on by angiotensin, which is activated by renin)	Stimulates aldosterone secretion; angiotensin II is also a potent vasoconstrictor
	Erythropoietin	Bone marrow	Stimulates erythrocyte production
Stomach	Ghrelin	Hypothalamus	Signals hunger; stimulates appetite
	Gastrin	Digestive tract exocrine glands and smooth muscles, pancreas, liver, and gallbladder	Control motility and secretion to facilitate digestive and absorptive processes
Small Intestine	Secretin and cholecystokinin (CCK)		
	Glucose-dependent insulinotropic peptide (GIP)	Endocrine pancreas	Stimulates insulin secretion
	Peptide YY$_{3-36}$	Hypothalamus	Signals satiety; suppresses appetite
Liver	Insulin-like growth factor (IGF)	Bone and soft tissues	Promotes growth
	Thrombopoietin	Bone marrow	Stimulates platelet production
Skin	Vitamin D	Intestine	Increases absorption of ingested Ca^{2+} and PO_4^{3-}
Thymus	Thymosin	T lymphocytes	Enhances T lymphocyte proliferation and function
Heart	Atrial natriuretic peptide (ANP)	Kidney tubules	Inhibits Na^+ reabsorption
Adipose Tissue	Leptin	Hypothalamus	Suppresses appetite; is important in long-term control of body weight
	Other adipokines	Multiple sites	Play a role in metabolism and inflammation

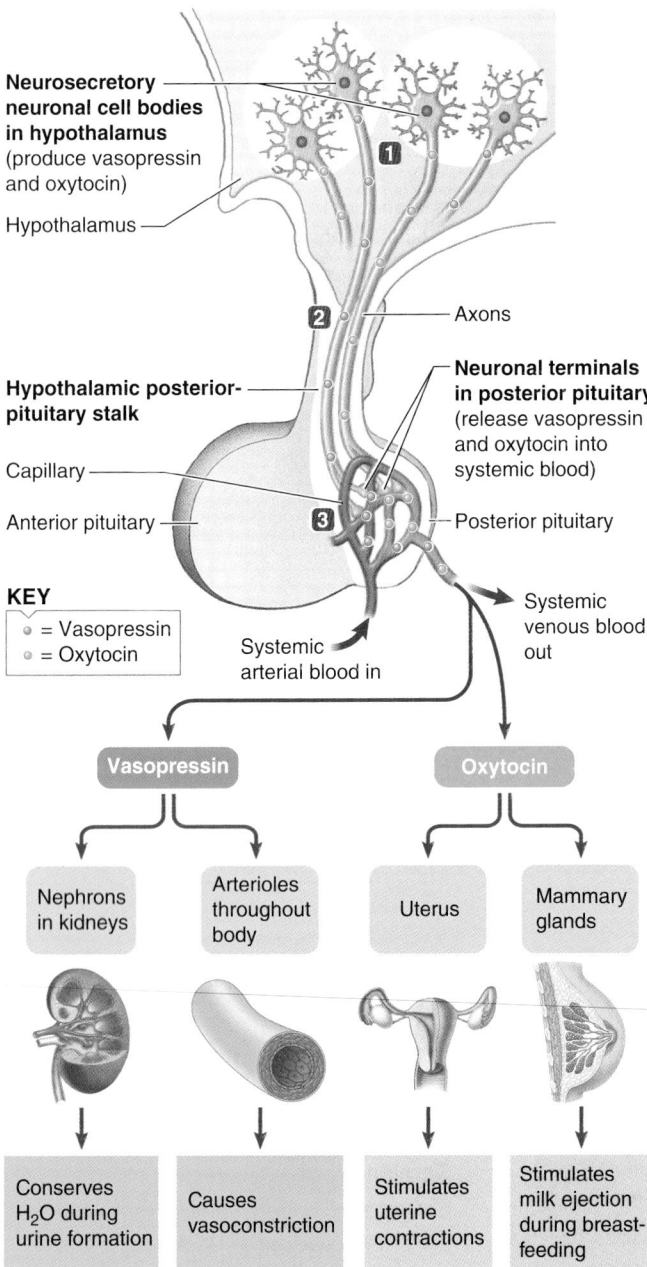

KEY
- ○ = Vasopressin
- ○ = Oxytocin

1 Two clusters of neurosecretory neuronal cell bodies in the hypothalamus produce either vasopressin or oxytocin depending on the neuron.

2 The hormone travels down the axon to be stored in the neuronal terminals within the posterior pituitary.

3 When the neuron is excited, the stored hormone is released from the terminals into the systemic blood for distribution throughout the body.

● **FIGURE 17-4** **Relationship of the hypothalamus and posterior pituitary.**

Most anterior pituitary hormones are tropic.

Unlike the posterior pituitary, which releases hormones synthesized by the hypothalamus, the anterior pituitary itself synthesizes the hormones it releases into the blood. Five different cell populations within the anterior pituitary secrete six major peptide hormones. The actions of each of these hormones are de-

scribed in detail in later sections. For now, this brief statement of their source and primary effects provides a rationale for their names (● Figure 17-5):

1. The anterior pituitary cells known as **somatotropes** secrete **growth hormone (GH, somatotropin),** the primary hormone responsible for regulating overall body growth (*somato* means "body"). GH also exerts important metabolic actions.

2. **Thyrotropes** secrete **thyroid-stimulating hormone (TSH, thyrotropin),** which stimulates secretion of thyroid hormone and growth of the thyroid gland.

3. **Corticotropes** produce and release **adrenocorticotropic hormone (ACTH, adrenocorticotropin),** the hormone that stimulates cortisol secretion by the adrenal cortex and promotes growth of the adrenal cortex.

4. **Gonadotropes** secrete two hormones that act on the gonads (reproductive organs, namely, the ovaries and testes)—follicle-stimulating hormone and luteinizing hormone. **Follicle-stimulating hormone (FSH)** helps regulate gamete (reproductive cells, namely, ova and sperm) production in both sexes. In females, it stimulates growth and development of ovarian follicles, within which the ova, or eggs, develop. It also promotes secretion of the hormone estrogen by the ovaries. In males, FSH is required for sperm production.

5. **Luteinizing hormone (LH)** helps control sex hormone secretion in both sexes, among other important actions in females. LH regulates ovarian secretion of the female sex hormones, estrogen and progesterone. In males, the same hormone stimulates the interstitial cells of Leydig in the testes to secrete the male sex hormone, testosterone. In females, LH is also responsible for ovulation (egg release) and luteinization (formation of a hormone-secreting corpus luteum in the ovary following ovulation). Note that both FSH and LH are named for their functions in females.

6. **Lactotropes** secrete **prolactin (PRL),** which enhances breast development and lactation (milk production) in females. Its reproductive function in males is uncertain. Recent studies suggest that PRL may enhance the immune system in both sexes.

Interestingly, ACTH is synthesized as part of a large precursor molecule known as **pro-opiomelancortin (POMC).** POMC can be cleaved into three active products: *ACTH, melanocyte-stimulating hormone (MSH),* and *endorphin.* Several diverse cell types produce POMC and slice it in unique ways, depending on the processing enzymes they possess, to yield different active products, along with peptide "scraps" that have no known function. For example, as their major active product from this same precursor molecule, corticotropes produce ACTH; in response to UV light from the sun, keratinocytes in the skin produce MSH, which promotes dispersal from nearby melanocytes of the pigment melanin to cause tanning (see p. 359); appetite-suppressing neurons in the hypothalamus secrete MSH to control food intake (see p. 512), and other

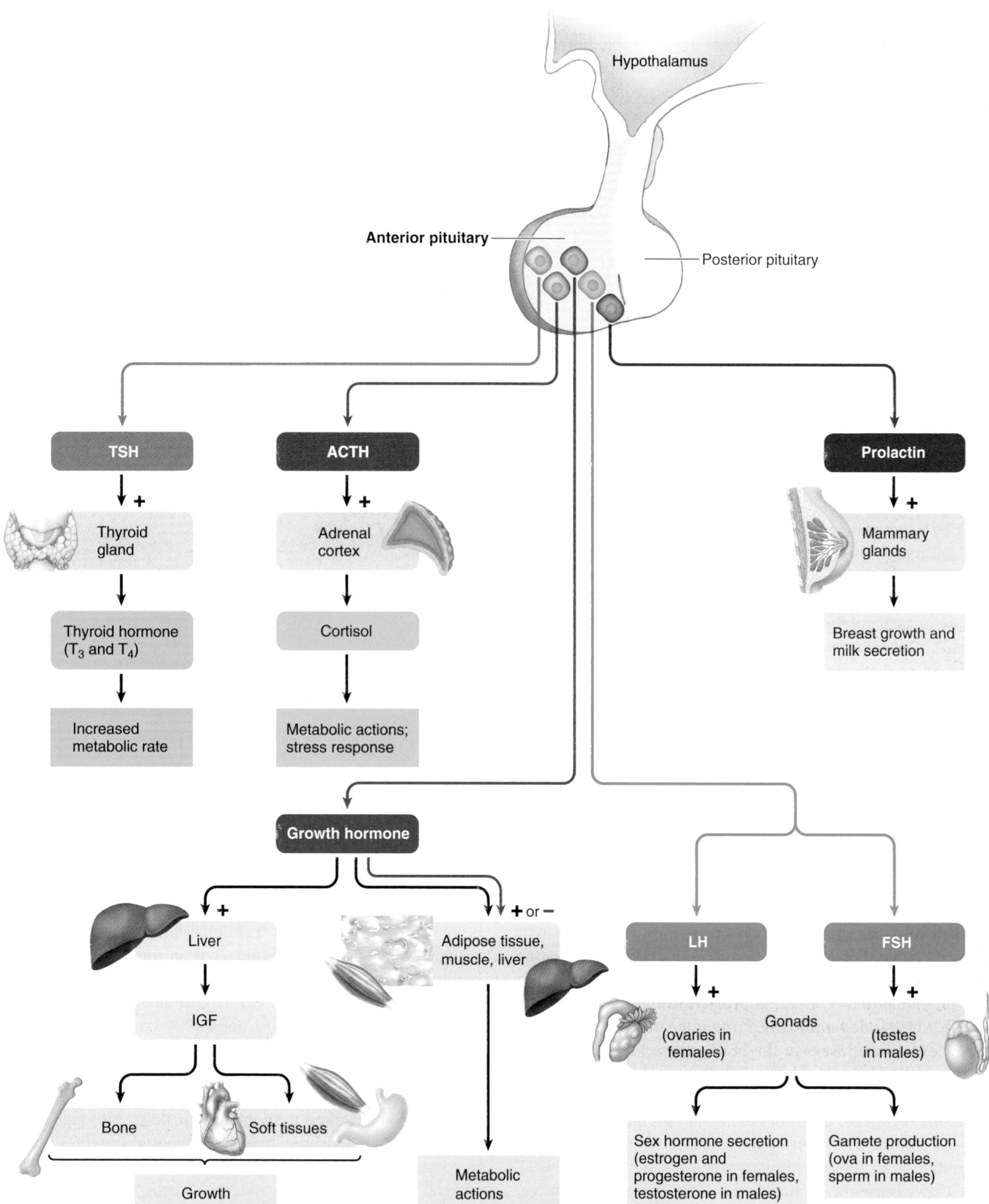

● FIGURE 17-5 **Functions of the anterior pituitary hormones.** Five different endocrine cell types produce the six anterior pituitary hormones—TSH, ACTH, growth hormone, LH and FSH (produced by the same cell type), and prolactin—which exert a range of effects throughout the body.

neurons in the CNS produce endorphin, an endogenous opiate that suppresses pain (see p. 156).

GH, TSH, ACTH, FSH, and LH are all tropic hormones because they each regulate secretion of another specific endocrine gland. FSH and LH are collectively referred to as **gonadotropins** because they control secretion of the sex hormones by the gonads. Because GH exerts its growth-promoting effects indirectly by stimulating the release of a liver hormone, *insulin-like growth factor (IGF)*, it too is a tropic hormone. Among the anterior pituitary hormones, PRL is the only one that does not stimulate secretion of another hormone. It acts directly on non-endocrine tissue to exert its effects. Of the tropic hormones, FSH, LH, and GH exert effects on nonendocrine target cells in addition to stimulating secretion of other hormones.

Hypothalamic releasing and inhibiting hormones help regulate anterior pituitary hormone secretion.

None of the anterior pituitary hormones are secreted at a constant rate. Even though each of these hormones has a unique control system, there are some common regulatory patterns. The two most important factors that regulate anterior pituitary hormone secretion are (1) hypothalamic hormones and (2) feedback by target-gland hormones.

Because the anterior pituitary secretes hormones that control the secretion of various other hormones, it long held the undeserved title of "master gland." Scientists now know that the release of each anterior pituitary hormone is largely controlled by still other hormones produced by the hypothalamus. The secretion of these regulatory neurohormones, in turn, is controlled by a variety of neural and hormonal inputs to the hypothalamic neurosecretory cells.

ROLE OF THE HYPOTHALAMIC RELEASING AND INHIBITING HORMONES The secretion of each anterior pituitary hormone is stimulated or inhibited by one or more of seven hypothalamic **hypophysiotropic hormones** (*hypophysis* means "pituitary"; *tropic* means "nourishing"). These small peptide hormones are listed in ▲ Table 17-2. Depending on their actions, these hormones are called **releasing hormones** or **inhibiting hormones.** In each case, the primary action of the hormone is apparent from its name. For example, **thyrotropin-releasing hormone (TRH)** stimulates the release of TSH (alias thyrotropin) from the anterior pituitary, whereas **prolactin-inhibiting hormone (PIH),** which is **dopamine** (the same as the neurotransmitter in the "pleasure" pathways in the brain; see p. 133), inhibits the release of PRL from the anterior pituitary. Note that hypophysiotropic hormones in most cases are involved in a three-hormone hierarchic chain of command (● Figure 17-6a): The hypothalamic hypophysiotropic hormone *(hormone 1)* controls the output of an anterior-pituitary tropic hormone *(hormone 2).* This tropic hormone, in turn, regulates secretion of the target endocrine gland's hormone *(hormone 3),* which exerts the final physiologic effect. This three-hormone sequence is called an **endocrine axis,** as in the hypothalamus–pituitary–thyroid axis.

Although endocrinologists originally speculated that there was one hypophysiotropic hormone for each anterior pituitary

▲ Table 17-2 Major Hypophysiotropic Hormones

Hormone	Effect on the Anterior Pituitary
Thyrotropin-Releasing Hormone (TRH)	Stimulates release of TSH (thyrotropin) and prolactin (PRL)
Corticotropin-Releasing Hormone (CRH)	Stimulates release of ACTH (corticotropin)
Gonadotropin-Releasing Hormone (GnRH)	Stimulates release of FSH and LH (gonadotropins)
Growth Hormone– Releasing Hormone (GHRH)	Stimulates release of growth hormone (GH)
Growth Hormone– Inhibiting Hormone (GHIH, Somatostatin)	Inhibits release of GH and TSH
Prolactin-Releasing Hormone (PRH)	Stimulates release of PRL
Prolactin-Inhibiting Hormone (PIH, Dopamine)	Inhibits release of PRL

hormone, many hypothalamic hormones have more than one effect, so their names indicate only the function first identified. Moreover, a single anterior pituitary hormone may be regulated by two or more hypophysiotropic hormones, which may even exert opposing effects. For example, **growth hormone–releasing hormone (GHRH)** stimulates growth hormone secretion, whereas **growth hormone–inhibiting hormone (GHIH),** also known as **somatostatin,** inhibits it.

ROLE OF THE HYPOTHALAMIC–HYPOPHYSEAL PORTAL SYSTEM The hypothalamic regulatory hormones reach the anterior pituitary by means of a unique vascular link. In contrast to the direct neural connection between the hypothalamus and the posterior pituitary, the anatomic and functional link between the hypothalamus and the anterior pituitary is an unusual capillary-to-capillary connection, the **hypothalamic–hypophyseal portal system.** A portal system is a vascular arrangement in which venous blood flows directly from one capillary bed through a connecting vessel to another capillary bed. The largest and best-known portal system is the hepatic portal system, which drains intestinal venous blood directly into the liver for immediate processing of absorbed nutrients (see p. 487). Although much smaller, the hypothalamic–hypophyseal portal system is no less important, because it provides a critical link between the brain and much of the endocrine system. It begins in the base of the hypothalamus with a group of capillaries that recombine into small portal vessels, which pass down through the connecting stalk into the anterior pituitary. Here, the portal vessels branch to form most of the anterior pituitary capillaries, which in turn drain into the systemic venous system (● Figure 17-7).

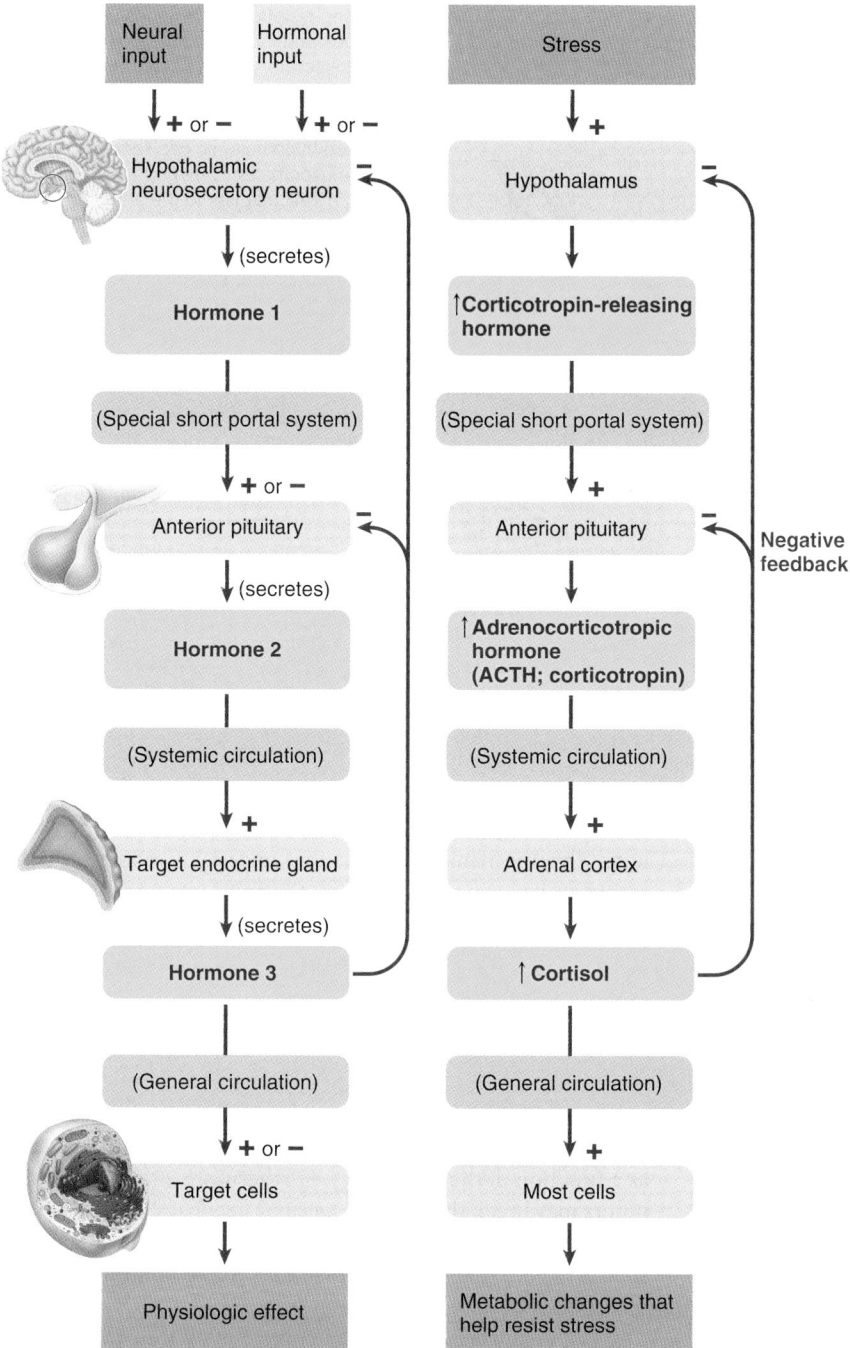

Neural input → + or − ↓
Hormonal input → + or − ↓

Hypothalamic neurosecretory neuron − ↑

↓ (secretes)

Hormone 1

↓

(Special short portal system)

↓ + or −

Anterior pituitary − ↑

↓ (secretes)

Hormone 2

↓

(Systemic circulation)

↓ +

Target endocrine gland

↓ (secretes)

Hormone 3

↓

(General circulation)

↓ + or −

Target cells

↓

Physiologic effect

Stress → + ↓

Hypothalamus − ↑

↓

↑**Corticotropin-releasing hormone**

↓

(Special short portal system)

↓ +

Anterior pituitary − ↑

↓

↑**Adrenocorticotropic hormone (ACTH; corticotropin)**

↓

(Systemic circulation)

↓ +

Adrenal cortex

↓ +

↑**Cortisol**

↓

(General circulation)

↓ +

Most cells

↓

Metabolic changes that help resist stress

Negative feedback

● **FIGURE 17-6 Hierarchic chain of command and negative feedback in endocrine control.** The general pathway involved in the hierarchic chain of command in the hypothalamus–anterior pituitary–peripheral target endocrine gland axis is depicted on the left. The pathway on the right leading to cortisol secretion provides a specific example of this endocrine chain of command. The hormone ultimately secreted by the target endocrine gland, such as cortisol, acts in negative-feedback fashion to reduce secretion of the regulatory hormones higher in the chain of command.

As a result, almost all blood supplied to the anterior pituitary must first pass through the hypothalamus. Because materials can be exchanged between blood and surrounding tissue only at the capillary level, the hypothalamic–hypophyseal portal system provides a "private" route through which releasing and inhibiting hormones can be picked up at the hypothalamus and delivered immediately and directly to the anterior pituitary

at relatively high concentrations, bypassing the general circulation. If the portal system did not exist, once the hypophysiotropic hormones were picked up in the hypothalamus, they would be returned to the heart by the systemic venous system. From here, they would travel to the lungs, move back to the heart through the pulmonary circulation, and finally enter the systemic arterial system for delivery throughout the body, including the anterior pituitary. Not only would this process take longer, but the hypophysiotropic hormones would also be considerably diluted by the much larger volume of blood flowing through this usual circulatory route.

The axons of the neurosecretory neurons that produce the hypothalamic regulatory hormones terminate on the capillaries at the origin of the portal system. These hypothalamic neurons secrete their hormones in the same way as the hypothalamic neurons that produce vasopressin and oxytocin. The hormone is synthesized in the cell body and then transported in vesicles by molecular motors to the axon terminal. It is stored there until its release by exocytosis into an adjacent capillary on appropriate stimulation. The major difference is that the hypophysiotropic hormones are released into the portal vessels, which deliver them to the anterior pituitary, where they control the release of anterior pituitary hormones into the general circulation. In contrast, the hypothalamic hormones stored in the posterior pituitary are themselves released into the general circulation.

Control of Hypothalamic Releasing and Inhibiting Hormones What regulates secretion of these hypophysiotropic hormones? Like other neurons, the neurons secreting these regulatory hormones receive abundant input of information (both neural and hormonal and both excitatory and inhibitory) that they must integrate. Studies are still in progress to unravel the complex neural input from many diverse areas of the brain to the hypophysiotropic secretory neurons. Some of these inputs carry information about a variety of environmental conditions. One example is the marked increase in secretion of corticotropin-releasing hormone (CRH) in response to stress (see ● Figure 17-6). Numerous neural connections also exist between the hypothalamus and the portions of the brain concerned with emotions (the limbic system; see p. 132). Thus, emotions greatly influence secretion of hypophysiotropic hormones. The

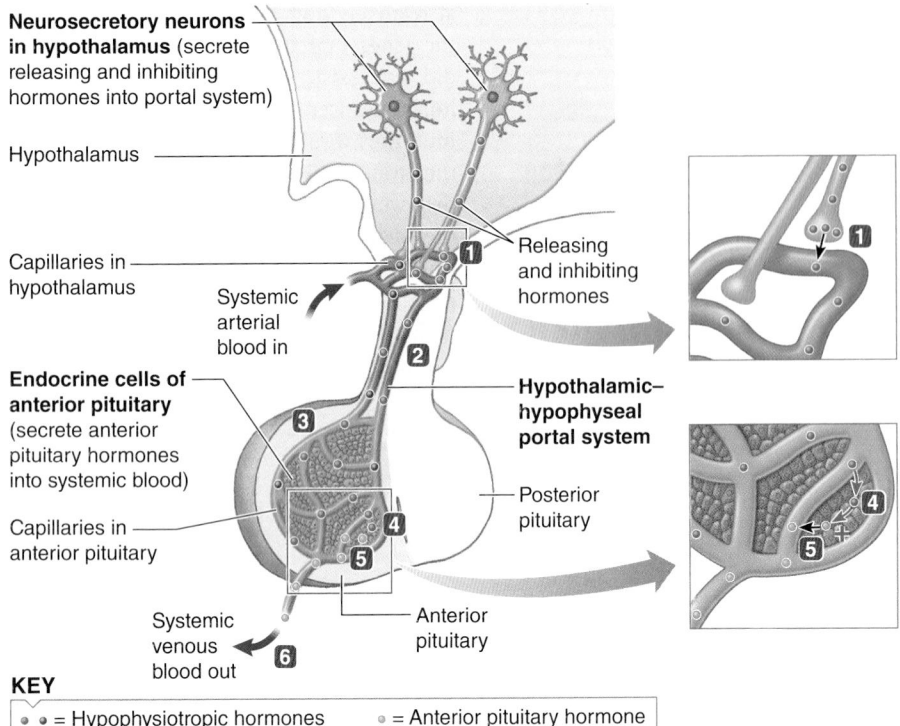

Neurosecretory neurons in hypothalamus (secrete releasing and inhibiting hormones into portal system)

Hypothalamus

Capillaries in hypothalamus

Systemic arterial blood in

Endocrine cells of anterior pituitary (secrete anterior pituitary hormones into systemic blood)

Capillaries in anterior pituitary

Systemic venous blood out

Releasing and inhibiting hormones

Hypothalamic–hypophyseal portal system

Posterior pituitary

Anterior pituitary

KEY

| ● ● = Hypophysiotropic hormones | ● = Anterior pituitary hormone |

1 Hypophysiotropic hormones (releasing hormones and inhibiting hormones) produced by neurosecretory neurons in the hypothalamus enter the hypothalamic capillaries.

2 These hypothalamic capillaries rejoin to form the hypothalamic–hypophyseal portal system, a vascular link to the anterior pituitary.

3 The portal system branches into the capillaries of the anterior pituitary.

4 The hypophysiotropic hormones, which leave the blood across the anterior pituitary capillaries, control the release of anterior pituitary hormones.

5 When stimulated by the appropriate hypothalamic releasing hormone, the anterior pituitary secretes a given hormone into these capillaries.

6 The anterior pituitary capillaries rejoin to form a vein, through which the anterior pituitary hormones leave for ultimate distribution throughout the body by the systemic circulation.

● **FIGURE 17-7 Vascular link between the hypothalamus and the anterior pituitary.**

menstrual irregularities sometimes experienced by women who are emotionally upset are a common manifestation of this relationship.

In addition to being regulated by different regions of the brain, the hypophysiotropic neurons are controlled by various chemical inputs that reach the hypothalamus through the blood. The most common blood-borne factors that influence hypothalamic neurosecretion are the negative-feedback effects of target-gland hormones, to which we now turn our attention.

Target-gland hormones inhibit hypothalamic and anterior pituitary hormone secretion via negative feedback.

Typically, in addition to producing its physiologic effects, the target-gland hormone suppresses secretion of the tropic hormone that is driving it. This negative feedback is accomplished by the target-gland hormone acting directly on the pituitary and on the release of hypothalamic hormones, which in turn regulate anterior pituitary function (see ● Figure 17-6). As an example, consider the CRH–ACTH–cortisol system. Hypothalamic CRH (corticotropin-releasing hormone) stimulates the anterior pituitary to secrete ACTH (adrenocorticotropic hormone, alias corticotropin), which in turn stimulates the adrenal cortex to secrete cortisol. The final hormone in the system, cortisol, inhibits the hypothalamus to reduce CRH secretion and acts directly on the corticotropes in the anterior pituitary to reduce ACTH secretion. Through this double-barreled approach, cortisol exerts negative-feedback control to stabilize its own plasma concentration. If plasma cortisol levels start to rise above a prescribed level, cortisol suppresses its own secretion by its inhibitory actions at the hypothalamus and anterior pitu-

itary. This mechanism ensures that once a hormonal system is activated its secretion does not continue unabated. If plasma cortisol levels fall below the desired set point, cortisol's inhibitory actions at the hypothalamus and anterior pituitary are reduced, so the driving forces for cortisol secretion (CRH–ACTH) increase accordingly. The other target-gland hormones act by similar negative-feedback loops to maintain their plasma levels relatively constant at the set point.

Diurnal rhythms are superimposed on this type of stabilizing negative-feedback regulation; that is, the set point changes as a function of the time of day. Furthermore, other controlling inputs may break through the negative-feedback control to alter hormone secretion (that is, change the set level) at times of special need. For example, stress raises the set point for cortisol secretion.

The detailed functions and control of all the anterior pituitary hormones except growth hormone are discussed elsewhere in conjunction with the target tissues that they influence; for example, thyroid-stimulating hormone is covered with the discussion of the thyroid gland. Accordingly, growth hormone is the only anterior pituitary hormone we elaborate on at this time.

Endocrine Control of Growth

In growing children, continuous net protein synthesis occurs under the influence of growth hormone (GH) as the body steadily gets larger. Weight gain alone is not synonymous with growth, because weight gain may occur from retaining excess H_2O or storing fat without true structural growth of tissues. Growth requires net synthesis of proteins and includes lengthening of the long bones (the bones of the extremities), as well as increases in the size and number of cells in the soft tissues.

Growth depends on GH but is influenced by other factors.

Although, as the name implies, growth hormone is essential for growth, it is not wholly responsible for determining the rate and final magnitude of growth in a given individual. The following factors affect growth:

- *Genetic determination* of an individual's maximum growth capacity. Attaining this full growth potential further depends on the other factors listed here.

- *Adequate diet,* including enough total protein and ample essential amino acids to accomplish the protein synthesis necessary for growth. Malnourished children never achieve their full growth potential. By contrast, a person cannot exceed his or her genetically determined maximum by eating a more-than-adequate diet. The excess food intake produces obesity instead of growth.

- *Freedom from chronic disease and stressful environmental conditions.* Stunted growth under adverse circumstances is largely a result of the prolonged stress-induced secretion of cortisol from the adrenal cortex. Cortisol exerts several potent antigrowth effects, such as promoting protein breakdown, inhibiting growth in the long bones, and blocking the secretion of GH.

- *Normal levels of growth-influencing hormones.* In addition to the essential GH, other hormones including thyroid hormone, insulin, and the sex hormones play secondary roles in promoting growth.

GH is essential for growth, but it also directly exerts metabolic effects not related to growth.

GH is the most abundant hormone produced by the anterior pituitary, even in adults in whom growth has already ceased, although GH secretion typically starts to decline after middle age. The continued high secretion of GH beyond the growing period implies that this hormone has important influences beyond its influence on growth, such as metabolic effects. We briefly describe GH's metabolic actions before turning to its growth-promoting actions.

To exert its metabolic effects, GH binds directly with its target organs, namely, adipose tissue, skeletal muscles, and liver. GH increases fatty acid levels in the blood by enhancing the breakdown of triglyceride fat stored in adipose tissue, and it increases blood glucose levels by decreasing glucose uptake by muscles and increasing glucose output by the liver. Muscles use the mobilized fatty acids instead of glucose as a metabolic fuel. Thus, the overall metabolic effect of GH is to mobilize fat stores as a major energy source while conserving glucose for glucose-dependent tissues such as the brain. The brain can use only glucose as its metabolic fuel, yet nervous tissue cannot store glycogen (stored glucose) to any extent. The metabolic pattern induced by GH is suitable for maintaining the body during

prolonged fasting or other situations when the body's energy needs exceed available glucose stores. GH also stimulates amino acid uptake and protein synthesis, but it does not act directly to accomplish these growth-promoting metabolic actions or any other growth-related actions. Before examining the means by which GH promotes growth, let us summarize its metabolic effects: It increases blood fatty acids, increases blood glucose and spares glucose for the brain, and stimulates protein synthesis (decreasing blood amino acids in the process).

GH exerts its growth-promoting effects indirectly by stimulating insulin-like growth factor.

GH does not act directly to bring about its growth-producing actions (increased cell division, enhanced protein synthesis, and bone growth). Instead, GH's growth-promoting actions are directly mediated by **insulin-like growth factor (IGF),** which acts on the target cells to cause growth of both soft tissues and bones.

The major source of circulating IGF is the liver, which releases this peptide product into the blood in response to GH stimulation. IGF is also produced by most other tissues, although they do not release it into the blood to any extent. Researchers propose that IGF produced locally in target tissues may act through paracrine means (see p. 98). Such a mechanism could explain why blood levels of GH are no higher, and indeed circulating levels are lower, during the first several years of life compared to adult values, even though growth is quite rapid during the postnatal (after birth) period. Local production of IGF in target tissues may be more important than delivery of blood-borne IGF during this time.

Production of IGF is controlled by a number of factors other than GH, including nutritional status, age, and tissue-specific factors. Thus, control of IGF production is complex and subject to a variety of systemic and local factors.

We now describe GH's growth-promoting effects, mediated by IGF.

GH, through IGF, promotes growth of soft tissues by stimulating hyperplasia and hypertrophy.

When tissues are responsive to its growth-promoting effects, GH (acting through IGF) stimulates growth of both the soft tissues and the skeleton. GH promotes growth of soft tissues by (1) increasing the number of cells (**hyperplasia)** and (2) increasing the size of cells (**hypertrophy).** GH increases the number of cells by stimulating cell division and by preventing apoptosis (programmed cell death; see p. 104). It increases the size of cells by favoring synthesis of proteins, the main structural component of cells. GH stimulates almost all aspects of protein synthesis while it simultaneously inhibits protein degradation. It promotes the uptake of amino acids (the raw materials for protein synthesis) by cells, decreasing blood amino acid levels in the process. Furthermore, it stimulates the cellular machinery responsible for accomplishing protein synthesis according to the cell's genetic code.

Growth of the long bones resulting in increased height is the most dramatic effect of GH. Before you can understand the means by which GH stimulates bone growth, you must become familiar with the structure of bone and how growth of bone is accomplished.

Bone grows in thickness and in length by different mechanisms, both stimulated by GH.

Bone is a living tissue. Being a form of connective tissue, it consists of cells and an extracellular organic matrix known as **osteoid** produced by the cells. The bone cells that produce the organic matrix are known as **osteoblasts** (*osteo* means "bone;" *blasts* means "formers"). Osteoid is composed of collagen fibers (see p. 52) in a semisolid gel. This organic matrix has a rubbery consistency and is responsible for bone's tensile strength (the resilience of bone to breakage when tension is applied). Bone is made hard by precipitation of *calcium phosphate crystals* within the osteoid. These inorganic crystals provide the bone with compressional strength (the ability of bone to hold its shape when squeezed or compressed). If bones consisted entirely of inorganic crystals, they would be brittle, like pieces of chalk. Bones have structural strength approaching that of reinforced concrete, yet they are not brittle and weigh much less because they have the structural blending of an organic scaffolding hardened by inorganic crystals. **Cartilage** is similar to bone, except that living cartilage is not calcified.

A long bone basically consists of a fairly uniform cylindrical shaft, the **diaphysis,** with a flared articulating knob at either end, an **epiphysis.** In a growing bone, the diaphysis is separated at each end from the epiphysis by a layer of cartilage known as the **epiphyseal plate** (● Figure 17-8). The central cavity of the bone is filled with bone marrow, the site of blood cell production (see p. 320).

MECHANISMS OF BONE GROWTH Growth in *thickness* of bone is achieved by adding new bone on top of the outer surface of existing bone. This growth is produced by osteoblasts within the connective tissue sheath that covers the outer bone. As osteoblast activity deposits new bone on the external surface, other cells within the bone, the **osteoclasts** ("bone breakers"), dissolve the bony tissue on the inner surface next to the marrow cavity. In this way, the marrow cavity enlarges to keep pace with the increased circumference of the bone shaft.

Growth in *length* of long bones is accomplished by a different mechanism. Bones lengthen as a result of activity of the cartilage cells in the epiphyseal plates. During growth, cartilage cells on the outer edge of the plate next to the epiphysis divide and multiply, temporarily widening the epiphyseal plate. As new cartilage cells are formed on the epiphyseal border, the older cartilage cells toward the diaphyseal border die and are replaced by osteoblasts, which swarm upward from the diaphysis, trailing their capillary supply with them. These new tenants lay down bone around the persisting remnants of disintegrating cartilage until bone entirely replaces the inner region of cartilage on the diaphyseal side of the plate. When this **ossification** ("bone formation") is complete, the bone on the diaphyseal side has lengthened and the epiphyseal plate has returned to its original thickness. The cartilage that bone has replaced on the diaphyseal end of the plate is as thick as the new cartilage on the epiphyseal end of the plate. Thus, bone growth is made possible by the growth and death of cartilage, which acts like a "spacer" to push the epiphysis farther out while it provides a framework for future bone formation on the end of the diaphysis.

MATURE, NONGROWING BONE As the extracellular matrix produced by an osteoblast calcifies, the osteoblast becomes entombed by the matrix it has deposited around itself. Osteoblasts trapped within a calcified matrix do not die, because they are supplied by nutrients transported to them through small canals that the osteoblasts themselves form by sending out cytoplasmic extensions around which the bony matrix is deposited. Thus, within the final bony product, a network of permeating tunnels radiates from each entrapped osteoblast, serving as a lifeline system for nutrient delivery and waste removal. The entrapped osteoblasts, now called **osteocytes,** retire from active bone-forming duty because their imprisonment prevents them from laying down new bone. However, they are involved in the hormonally regulated exchange of calcium between bone and blood. This exchange is under the control of parathyroid hormone (discussed later in the chapter), not GH.

GH CONTROL OF BONE GROWTH GH causes bones to grow both in length and in thickness. GH, via IGF, stimulates proliferation of epiphyseal cartilage, thereby making space for more bone formation, and stimulates osteoblast activity. It can promote lengthening of long bones as long as the epiphyseal plate remains cartilaginous, or is "open." At the end of adolescence, under the influence of the sex hormones, these plates completely ossify, or "close," so that the bones cannot lengthen any further despite the presence of GH. Thus, after the plates are closed, the individual does not grow any taller.

GH secretion is regulated by two hypophysiotropic hormones.

The control of GH secretion is complex, with two hypothalamic hypophysiotropic hormones playing a key role.

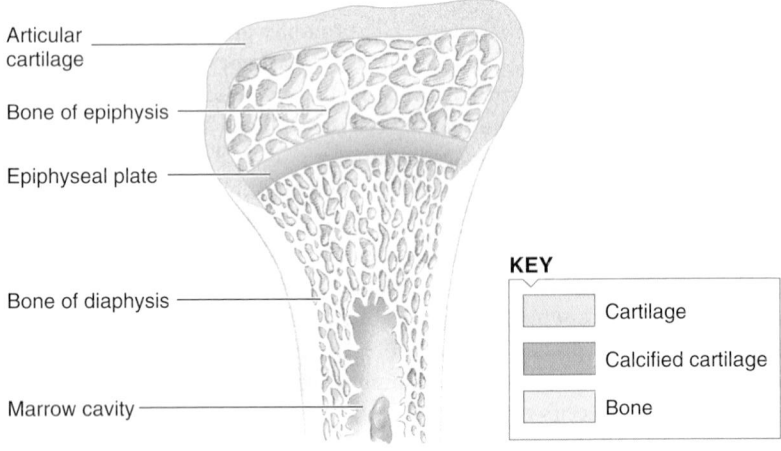

Articular cartilage

Bone of epiphysis

Epiphyseal plate

Bone of diaphysis

Marrow cavity

KEY

Cartilage

Calcified cartilage

Bone

● **FIGURE 17-8 Anatomy of long bones.**

GROWTH HORMONE–RELEASING AND GROWTH HORMONE–INHIBITING HORMONES Two antagonistic regulatory hormones from the hypothalamus are involved in controlling GH secretion: growth hormone–releasing hormone (GHRH), which is stimulatory and the dominant influence, and growth hormone–inhibiting hormone (GHIH, or somatostatin), which is inhibitory (● Figure 17-9).

As with control of other anterior pituitary hormones, negative-feedback loops participate in controlling GH secretion. Complicating the feedback loops for the hypothalamus–pituitary–liver axis is direct regulation of GH secretion by both stimulatory and inhibitory factors. Therefore, negative-feedback loops involve both inhibition of stimulatory factors and stimulation of inhibitory factors. GH stimulates IGF secretion by the liver, and IGF in turn is the primary inhibitor of GH secretion by the anterior pituitary. IGF inhibits the somatotropes in the pituitary directly and further decreases GH secretion by inhibiting GHRH-secreting cells and stimulating the somatostatin-secreting cells in the hypothalamus, thus decreasing hypothalamic stimulation of the somatotropes. Furthermore, GH itself inhibits hypothalamic GHRH secretion and stimulates somatostatin release.

FACTORS THAT INFLUENCE GH SECRETION A number of factors influence GH secretion by acting on the hypothalamus. GH secretion displays a well-characterized diurnal rhythm. Through most of the day, GH levels tend to be low and fairly constant. About an hour after the onset of deep sleep, however, GH secretion markedly increases up to five times the low daytime value.

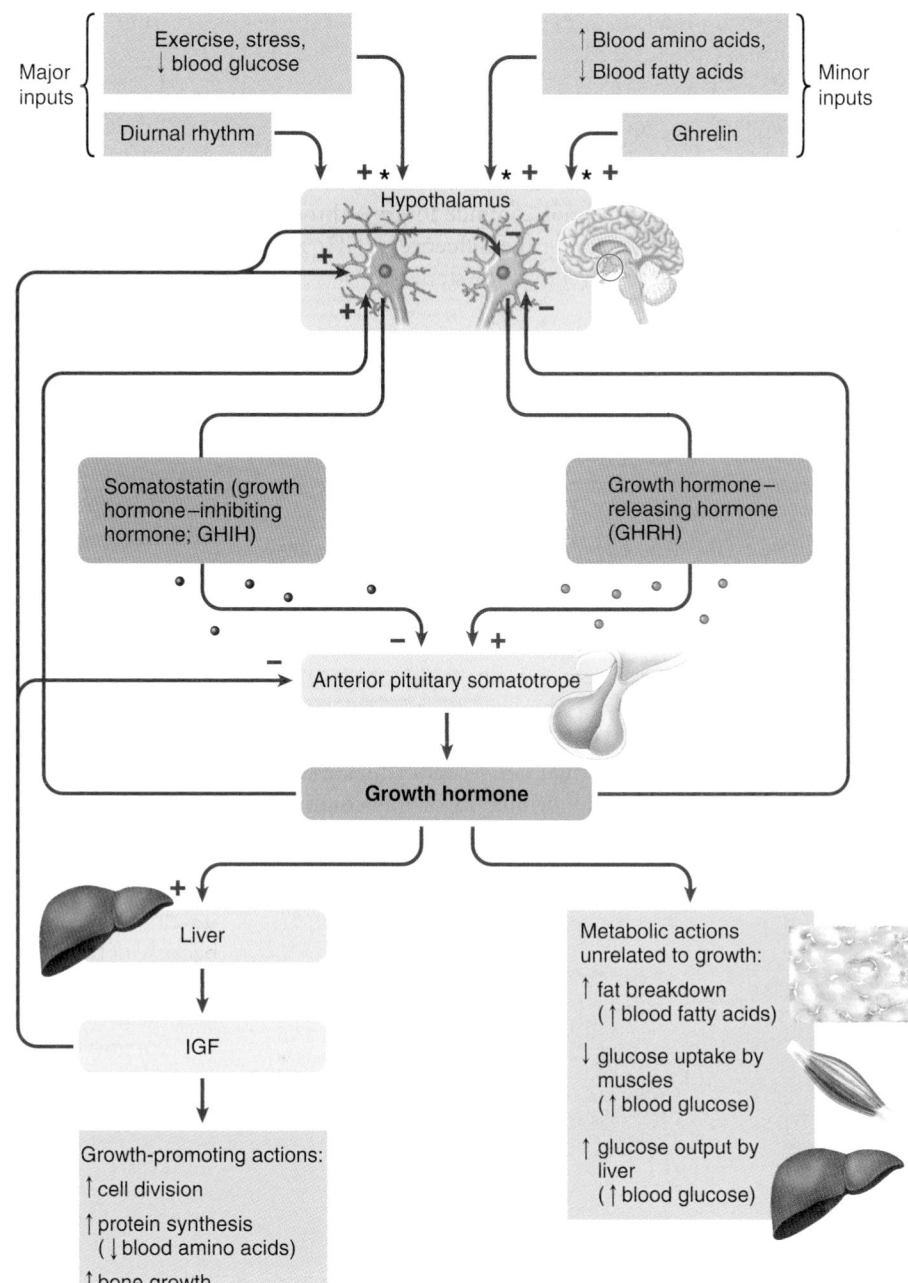

*These factors all increase growth hormone secretion, but it is unclear whether they do so by stimulating GHRH or inhibiting GHIH somatostatin, or both.

● **FIGURE 17-9 Control of growth hormone secretion.**

Superimposed on this diurnal fluctuation in GH secretion are further bursts in secretion that occur in response to exercise, stress, and low blood glucose, the major stimuli for increased secretion. The benefits of increased GH secretion during these situations when energy demands outstrip the body's glucose reserves are presumably that glucose is conserved for the brain and fatty acids are provided as an alternative energy source for muscle.

A rise in blood amino acids after a high-protein meal enhances GH secretion. In turn, GH promotes the use of these amino acids for protein synthesis. GH is also stimulated by a decline in blood fatty acids. Because GH mobilizes fat, such regulation helps maintain fairly constant blood fatty acid levels.

Finally, ghrelin, a potent appetite stimulator released from the stomach, also stimulates GH secretion (see p. 514). This "hunger hormone" may play a role in coordinating growth with nutrient acquisition.

Note that the known regulatory inputs for GH secretion are aimed at adjusting the levels of glucose, amino acids, and fatty acids in the blood. No known growth-related signals influence GH secretion. The whole issue of what really controls growth is complicated by GH levels during early childhood, a period of quite rapid growth in height, being similar to those in normal adults. As mentioned earlier, the poorly understood control of local IGF activity may be important in this regard. Another related question is, Why aren't adult tissues still responsive to GH's growth-promoting effects? We know we do not grow any taller after adolescence because the epiphyseal plates have closed, but why do soft tissues not continue to grow through hypertrophy and hyperplasia under the influence of GH? Further research is needed to unravel these mysteries.

Abnormal GH secretion results in aberrant growth patterns.

 Diseases related to both deficiencies and excesses of GH can occur. The effects on the pattern of growth are more pronounced than the metabolic consequences.

GH DEFICIENCY GH deficiency may be caused by a pituitary defect (lack of GH) or may occur secondary to hypothalamic dysfunctions (lack of GHRH). Hyposecretion of GH in a child is one cause of **dwarfism.** The predominant feature is short stature caused by retarded skeletal growth (● Figure 17-10).

In addition, growth may be thwarted because the tissues fail to respond normally to GH. An example is *Laron dwarfism,* which is characterized by abnormal GH receptors that are unresponsive to the hormone. The symptoms of this condition resemble those of severe GH deficiency even though blood levels of GH are actually high. In some instances, GH levels are

● **FIGURE 17-10 Examples of the effect of abnormalities in growth hormone secretion on growth.** The man at the right displays pituitary dwarfism resulting from underproduction of growth hormone in childhood. The man at the center of the photograph has gigantism caused by excessive growth hormone secretion in childhood. The man at the left is of average height.

adequate and target-cell responsiveness is normal, but IGF is lacking, as is the case with *African pygmies.*

The onset of GH deficiency in adulthood after growth is already complete produces relatively few symptoms. GH-deficient adults tend to have reduced skeletal muscle mass and strength (less muscle protein), as well as decreased bone density (less osteoblast activity during ongoing bone remodeling).

GH EXCESS Hypersecretion of GH is most often caused by a tumor of the GH-producing cells of the anterior pituitary. The symptoms depend on the age of the individual when the abnormal secretion begins. If overproduction of GH begins in childhood before the epiphyseal plates close, the principal manifestation is a rapid growth in height without distortion of body proportions. Appropriately, this condition is known as **gigantism** (● Figure 17-10). If not treated by removal of the tumor or by drugs that block the effect of GH, the person may reach a height of 8 feet or more. All the soft tissues grow correspondingly, so the body is still well proportioned.

If GH hypersecretion occurs after adolescence when the epiphyseal plates have already closed, further growth in height is prevented. Under the influence of excess GH, however, the bones become thicker and the soft tissues, especially connective tissue and skin, proliferate. This disproportionate growth pattern produces a disfiguring condition known as **acromegaly** (*acro* means "extremity"; *megaly* means "large"). Bone thickening is most obvious in the extremities and face. A marked coarsening of the features to an almost apelike appearance gradually develops as the jaws and cheekbones become more prominent because of thickening of the facial bones and the skin (● Figure 17-11). The hands and feet enlarge, and the fingers and toes become greatly thickened.

We now shift our attention to the other endocrine gland in the brain—the pineal gland.

Pineal Gland and Circadian Rhythms

The **pineal gland,** (PIN-ē-ul) a tiny, pinecone-shaped structure located in the center of the brain (see ● Figure 5-6b, p. 124, and ● Figure 17-1), secretes the hormone **melatonin.** (Do not confuse melatonin with the skin-darkening pigment, *melanin.*) Although melatonin was discovered in 1959, investigators have only recently begun to unravel its many functions. One of melatonin's most widely accepted roles is helping keep the body's inherent circadian rhythm in synchrony with the light–dark cycle. We examine circadian rhythm in general before looking at the role of melatonin in this regard and considering other functions of this hormone.

The suprachiasmatic nucleus is the master biological clock.

Hormone secretion rates are not the only factor in the body that fluctuates cyclically over a 24-hour period. Humans have similar biological clocks for many other bodily functions, ranging from

Age 13

Age 21

Age 35

● **FIGURE 17-11 Progressive development of acromegaly.** In this series of photos from childhood to the present, note how the patient's brow bones, cheekbones, and jawbones become progressively more prominent as a result of ongoing thickening of the bones and skin caused by excessive GH secretion.

gene expression, to physiologic processes such as temperature regulation (see p. 516), to behavior. The master biological clock that serves as the pacemaker for the body's circadian rhythm is the **suprachiasmatic nucleus (SCN).** It consists of a cluster of nerve cell bodies in the hypothalamus above the optic chiasm, the point at which part of the nerve fibers from each eye cross to the opposite half of the brain (*supra* means "above"; *chiasm* means "cross") (see ● Figures 17-3, p. 533, and 6-22, p. 169). The self-induced rhythmic firing of the SCN neurons plays a major role in establishing many of the body's inherent daily rhythms.

ROLE OF CLOCK PROTEINS Scientists have now unraveled the underlying molecular mechanisms responsible for the SCN's circadian oscillations. Specific self-starting genes within the nuclei of SCN neurons set in motion a series of events that brings about the synthesis of **clock proteins** in the cytosol surrounding the nucleus. As the day wears on, these clock proteins continue to accumulate, finally reaching a critical mass, at which time they are transported into the nucleus. Here, they block the genetic process responsible for their own production. The level of clock proteins gradually dwindles as they degrade within the nucleus, thus removing their inhibitory influence from the clock-protein genetic machinery. No longer being blocked, these genes again rev up the production of more clock proteins as the cycle repeats itself. Each cycle takes about a day. The fluctuating levels of clock proteins bring about cyclic changes in neural output from the SCN that, in turn, lead to cyclic changes in effector organs throughout the day. An example is the diurnal variation in cortisol secretion (see ● Figure 17-2, p. 529). In this way, internal timekeeping (circadian rhythm) is a self-sustaining mechanism built into the genetic makeup of the SCN neurons.

SYNCHRONIZATION OF THE BIOLOGICAL CLOCK WITH ENVIRONMENTAL CUES On its own, this biological clock generally cycles a bit slower than the 24-hour environmental cycle. Without any

external cues, the SCN sets up cycles that average about 25 hours. The cycles are consistent for a given individual but vary somewhat among different people. If this master clock were not continually adjusted to keep pace with the world outside, the body's circadian rhythm would become progressively out of sync with the cycles of light (periods of activity) and dark (periods of rest). Thus, the SCN must be reset daily by external cues so that biological rhythms are synchronized with the activity levels driven by the surrounding environment. The effect of not keeping the internal clock synchronized with the environment is well known by people who experience **jet lag** when their inherent rhythm is out of step with external cues. The SCN works with the pineal gland and its hormonal product melatonin to synchronize the circadian rhythm with the 24-hour day–night cycle. (For a discussion of problems associated with being out of sync with environmental cues, see the boxed feature on p. 544, ▶ Beyond the Basics.)

Melatonin helps keep the body's circadian rhythm in time with the light–dark cycle.

Daily changes in light intensity are the major environmental cue used to adjust the SCN master clock. Special photoreceptors in the eye contain **melanopsin,** a protein that responds to light to keep the body in tune with external time. These special photoreceptors, which are distinct from the rod and cone photoreceptors used to see light (that is, for vision; see p. 162), transmit their signals about the presence or absence of light along a specific neural pathway directly to the SCN. The SCN relays the message regarding light status to the pineal gland. This is the major way the internal clock is coordinated to a 24-hour day. Melatonin is the hormone of darkness. Melatonin secretion increases up to 10-fold during the darkness of night and then falls to low levels during the light of day. Fluctuations in melatonin secretion, in turn, help entrain the body's biological rhythms with the external light–dark cues.

Proposed roles of melatonin, besides regulating the body's biological clock, include the following:

■ Taken exogenously (in a pill), melatonin induces a natural sleep without the side effects that accompany hypnotic sedatives, so it may play a normal role in promoting sleep.

■ Melatonin is believed to inhibit the hormones that stimulate reproductive activity. Puberty may be initiated by a reduction in melatonin secretion.

Beyond the Basics

Tinkering with Our Biological Clocks

Research shows that the hectic pace of modern life, stress, noise, pollution, and the irregular schedules many workers follow can upset internal rhythms, illustrating how a healthy external environment affects our own internal environment—and our health.

Dr. Richard Restak, a neurologist and author, notes that the "usual rhythms of wakefulness and sleep . . . seem to exert a stabilizing effect on our physical and psychological health." The greatest disrupter of our natural circadian rhythms is the variable work schedule, surprisingly common in industrialized countries. Today, one out of every four working men and one out of every six working women has a variable work schedule—shifting frequently between day and night work. In many industries, to make optimal use of equipment and buildings, workers are on the job day and night. As a spin-off, more restaurants and stores stay open 24 hours a day and more health-care workers must be on duty at night to care for accident victims.

To spread the burden, many companies that maintain shifts round the clock alter their workers' schedules. One week, employees work the day shift. The next week, they move to the "graveyard shift" from midnight to 8 A.M. The next week, they work the night shift from 4 P.M. to midnight. Many shift workers feel tired most of the time and have trouble staying awake at the job. Work performance suffers because of the workers' fatigue. When workers arrive home for bed, they're exhausted but cannot sleep, because they are trying to doze off when the body is trying to wake them up. Unfortunately, the weekly changes in schedule never permit workers' internal alarm clocks to fully adjust. Most people require 4 to 14 days to adjust to a new schedule.

Workers on alternating shifts suffer more ulcers, insomnia, irritability, depression, and tension than workers on unchanging shifts. Their lives are never the same. To make matters worse, tired, irritable workers whose judgment is impaired by fatigue pose a threat to society. Consider two examples.

At 4 A.M. in the control room of the Three Mile Island nuclear reactor in Pennsylvania, three operators made the first mistake in a series of errors that led to the worst nuclear accident in U.S. history. The operators did not notice warning lights and failed to observe that a crucial valve had remained open. When the morning-shift operators entered the control room the next day, they quickly discovered the problems, but it was too late. Pipes in the system had burst, sending radioactive steam and water into the air and into two buildings. Ironically, this 1979 accident occurred 12 days after release of a popular movie, *The China Syndrome,* about a nuclear reactor accident, pumping up public awareness and alarm. Fortunately, no surrounding residents were immediately injured and no long-term studies have found a conclusive link between an increased incidence of cancer and the low level of radiation to which those living near the troubled reactor were exposed. Cleanup of the accident lasted from 1970 until 1993 and cost $975 million.

Late in April 1986, another nuclear power plant went amok. This accident, in Chernobyl in the former Soviet Union, was far more severe than the U.S. reactor incident. In the early hours of the morning, two engineers were testing the reactor. Violating standard operational protocol, they deactivated key safety systems. This single error in judgment (possibly caused by fatigue) led to the largest and most costly nuclear accident in world history. Steam built up inside the reactor and blew the roof off the containment building. A thick cloud of radiation rose skyward and then spread throughout Europe and the world. For 10 days the reactor burned, disgorging 400 times more radiation than was released from the atomic bomb dropped on Hiroshima in World War II. While workers battled to cover the molten radioactive core that spewed radiation into the sky, the world watched in horror.

The Chernobyl disaster, like the accident at Three Mile Island, may have been the result of workers operating at a time unsuitable for clear thinking. One has to wonder how many plane crashes, auto accidents, and acts of medical malpractice can be traced to judgment errors resulting from our insistence on working against inherent body rhythms.

Thanks to studies of biological rhythms, researchers are finding ways to reset biological clocks, which could help lessen the misery and suffering of shift workers and could improve the performance of the graveyard-shift workers. For instance, one simple measure is to put shift workers on 3-week cycles to give their clocks time to adjust. And instead of shifting workers from daytime to graveyard shifts, companies could transfer them forward rather than backward (for example, from a daytime to a nighttime shift). A forward transfer is an easier adjustment. Bright lights can also be used to reset the biological clock. It is a small price to pay for a healthy workforce and a safer society. Furthermore, use of supplemental melatonin, the hormone that sets the internal clock to march in step with environmental cycles, may prove useful in resetting the body's clock when that clock is out of sync with external cues.

■ Melatonin appears to be an effective **antioxidant,** a defense tool against biologically damaging free radicals. *Free radicals* are very unstable electron-deficient particles that are highly reactive and destructive. Free radicals have been implicated in several chronic diseases, such as coronary artery disease (see p. 270) and cancer, and are believed to contribute to the aging process.

■ Evidence suggests that melatonin may slow the aging process, perhaps by removing free radicals or by other means.

■ Melatonin appears to enhance immunity.

Clinical Note

Because of melatonin's many proposed roles, use of supplemental melatonin for a variety of conditions is promising. However, most researchers are cautious about recommending supplemental melatonin until its effectiveness as a drug is further substantiated. Meanwhile, many people are turning to melatonin as a health food supplement; as such, it is not regulated by the U.S. Food and Drug Administration (FDA) for safety and effectiveness. The two biggest self-prescribed uses of melatonin are as a prevention for jet lag and as a sleep aid.

Thyroid Gland

The **thyroid gland** consists of two lobes of endocrine tissue joined in the middle by a narrow portion of the gland, giving it a bow-tie shape (● Figure 17-12a). The gland is even located in the appropriate place for a bow tie, lying over the trachea in the neck.

The major cells that secrete thyroid hormone are organized into colloid-filled follicles.

The major thyroid secretory cells, known as **follicular cells,** are arranged into hollow spheres, each of which forms a functional unit called a **follicle.** On microscopic section (● Figure 17-12b), the follicles appear as rings consisting of a single layer of follicular cells enclosing an inner lumen filled with **colloid,** a substance that serves as an extracellular storage site for thyroid hormone. Note that the colloid within the follicular lumen is extracellular (that is, outside the thyroid cells), even though it is located within the interior of the follicle. Colloid is not in direct contact with the extracellular fluid (ECF) that surrounds the follicle, similar to an inland lake that is not in direct contact with the oceans that surround a continent.

The chief constituent of colloid is a large glycoprotein molecule known as **thyroglobulin (Tg),** within which are incorporated the thyroid hormones in their various stages of synthesis. The follicular cells produce two iodine-containing hormones derived from the amino acid tyrosine: **tetraiodothyronine (T_4, or thyroxine)** and **tri-iodothyronine (T_3).** The prefixes *tetra* and *tri* and the subscripts *4* and *3* denote the number of iodine atoms incorporated into each of these hormones. These two hormones, collectively referred to as **thyroid hormone,** are important regulators of overall basal metabolic rate.

Interspersed in the interstitial spaces between the follicles is another secretory cell type, the **C cells,** which secrete the peptide hormone **calcitonin.** Calcitonin plays a role in calcium metabolism and is not related to T_4 and T_3. We discuss T_4 and T_3 here and talk about calcitonin later in a section dealing with endocrine control of calcium balance.

Thyroid hormone is synthesized and stored on the thyroglobulin molecule.

The basic ingredients for thyroid hormone synthesis are tyrosine and iodine, both of which must be taken up from the blood by the follicular cells. Tyrosine, an amino acid, is synthesized in sufficient amounts by the body, so it is not essential to the diet. By contrast, the iodine needed for thyroid hormone synthesis must be obtained from dietary intake. Dietary iodine (I) is reduced to iodide (I⁻) prior to absorption by the small intestine. We now examine the steps involved in the synthesis, storage, secretion, and transport of thyroid hormone.

Most steps of thyroid hormone synthesis take place on the thyroglobulin molecules within the colloid. Thyroglobulin itself is produced by the endoplasmic reticulum–Golgi complex of the thyroid follicular cells. The amino acid tyrosine becomes incorporated in the much larger thyroglobulin molecules as the

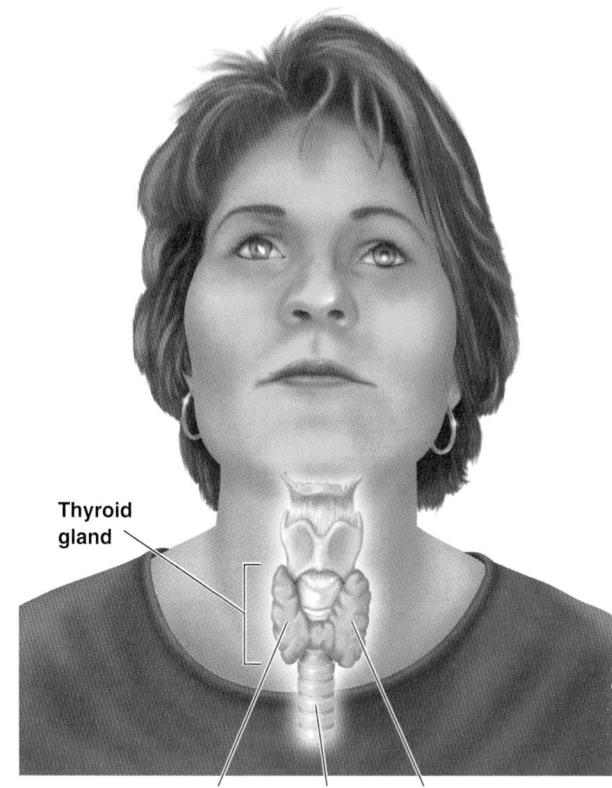

Thyroid gland

Right lobe   Trachea   Left lobe

(a) Gross anatomy of thyroid gland

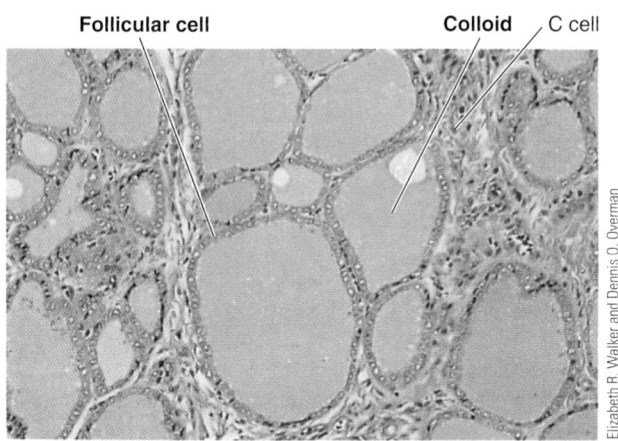

Follicular cell   Colloid   C cell

(b) Light-microscopic appearance of thyroid gland

● **FIGURE 17-12 Anatomy of the thyroid gland.** (a) Gross anatomy of the thyroid gland, anterior view. The thyroid gland lies over the trachea just below the larynx (voice box) and consists of two lobes connected by a thin strip. (b) Light-microscope appearance of the thyroid gland. The thyroid gland is composed primarily of colloid-filled spheres enclosed by a single layer of follicular cells.

latter are being produced. Once produced, tyrosine-containing thyroglobulin is exported in vesicles from the follicular cells into the colloid by exocytosis (● Figure 17-13, step **1**). The thyroid captures I⁻ from the blood and transfers it into the colloid by an *iodide pump*—the powerful, energy-requiring carrier proteins in the outer membranes of the follicular cells (step **2**). These carriers are secondary active transport symporters (see

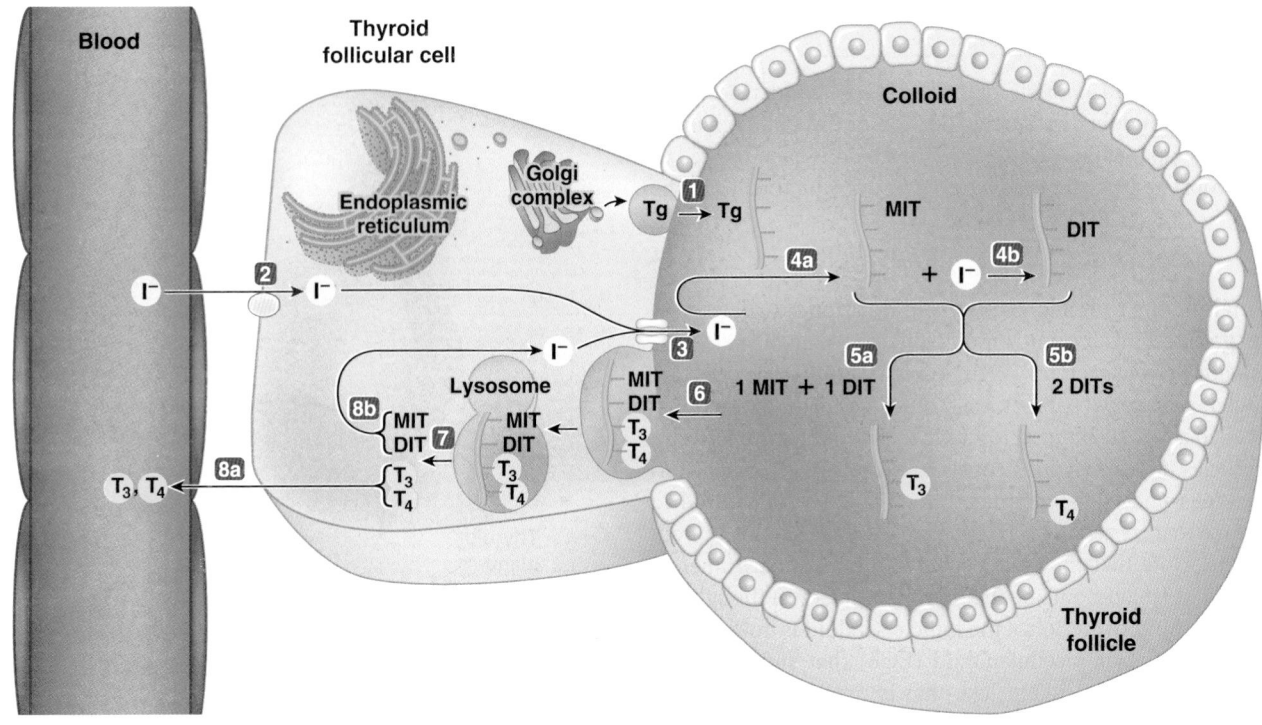

Colloid

Blood

Thyroid follicular cell

Golgi complex

Endoplasmic reticulum

MIT

DIT

Lysosome

Thyroid follicle

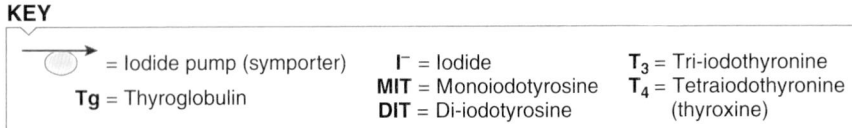

KEY

= Iodide pump (symporter)	I^- = Iodide	T_3 = Tri-iodothyronine
	MIT = Monoiodotyrosine	T_4 = Tetraiodothyronine
Tg = Thyroglobulin	**DIT** = Di-iodotyrosine	(thyroxine)

1. Tyrosine-containing Tg produced within the thyroid follicular cells by the endoplasmic reticulum–Golgi complex is transported by exocytosis into the colloid.

2 Iodide is carried by the energy-requiring iodide pump from the blood into the follicular cell across the basolateral membrane.

3 Iodide exits the cell through a luminal channel to enter the colloid.

4a Attachment of one iodide to tyrosine within the Tg molecule yields MIT.

4b Attachment of two iodides to tyrosine yields DIT.

5a Coupling of one MIT and one DIT yields T_3.

5b Coupling of two DITs yields T_4.

6 On appropriate stimulation, the thyroid follicular cells engulf a portion of Tg-containing colloid by phagocytosis.

7 Lysosomes attack the engulfed vesicle and split the iodinated products from Tg.

8a T_3 and T_4 diffuse into the blood (secretion).

8b MIT and DIT are deiodinated, and the freed iodide is recycled for synthesizing more hormone.

● **FIGURE 17-13 Synthesis, storage, and secretion of thyroid hormone.** Note that the organelles are not drawn to scale. The endoplasmic reticulum and Golgi complex are proportionally too small.

p. 64). Almost all iodide in the body is moved against its concentration gradient to become trapped in the thyroid for thyroid hormone synthesis. Iodide serves no other function in the body. Iodide exits the follicular cell through a channel in the luminal membrane to enter the colloid (step **3**).

Within the colloid, iodide is quickly attached to a tyrosine within the thyroglobulin molecule. Attachment of one iodide to tyrosine yields **monoiodotyrosine (MIT)** (step **4a**). Attachment of two iodides to tyrosine yields **di-iodotyrosine (DIT)** (step **4b**). After MIT and DIT are formed, a coupling process occurs within the thyroglobulin molecule between the iodin-

ated tyrosine molecules to form the thyroid hormones. Coupling of one MIT (with one iodide) and one DIT (with two iodides) yields **tri-iodothyronine,** or T_3 (with three iodides) (step **5a**). Coupling of two DITs (each bearing two iodides) yields **tetraiodothyronine (T_4, or thyroxine),** the four-iodide form of thyroid hormone (step **5b**). Coupling does not occur between two MIT molecules. All these products remain attached to thyroglobulin. Thyroid hormones remain stored in this form in the colloid until they are split off and secreted. Sufficient thyroid hormone is normally stored to supply the body's needs for several months.

To secrete thyroid hormone, the follicular cells phagocytize thyroglobulin-laden colloid.

The release of thyroid hormone into the systemic circulation is a rather complex process for two reasons. First, before their release, T_3 and T_4 are still bound within the thyroglobulin molecule. Second, these hormones are stored at an inland extracellular site, in the colloid in the follicular lumen, so they must be transported completely across the follicular cells to reach the capillaries that course through the interstitial spaces between the follicles.

The process of thyroid hormone secretion essentially involves the follicular cells "biting off" a piece of colloid, breaking the thyroglobulin molecule down into its component parts, and "spitting out" the freed T_3 and T_4 into the blood. On appropriate stimulation for thyroid hormone secretion, the follicular cells internalize a portion of the thyroglobulin-hormone complex by phagocytizing a piece of colloid (● Figure 17-13, step **6**). Within the cells, the membrane-enclosed droplets of colloid coalesce with lysosomes, whose enzymes split off the biologically active thyroid hormones, T_3 and T_4, as well as the inactive MIT and DIT (step **7**). The thyroid hormones, being very lipophilic, pass freely through the outer membranes of the follicular cells and into the blood (step **8a**).

MIT and DIT are of no endocrine value. The follicular cells contain an enzyme that swiftly removes the iodide from MIT and DIT, allowing the freed iodide to be recycled for synthesis of more hormone (step **8b**). This highly specific enzyme will remove iodide only from the worthless MIT and DIT, not the valuable T_3 or T_4.

Most of the secreted T_4 is converted into T_3 outside the thyroid.

About 90% of the secretory product released from the thyroid gland is in the form of T_4, yet T_3 is about 10 times more potent in its biological activity. However, most of the secreted T_4 is converted into T_3, or *activated*, by being stripped of one of its iodides outside the thyroid gland, primarily in the liver and kidneys. About 80% of the circulating T_3 is derived from secreted T_4 that has been peripherally stripped. Therefore, T_3 is the major biologically active form of thyroid hormone at the cellular level, even though the thyroid gland secretes mostly T_4.

Thyroid hormone is the main determinant of the basal metabolic rate and exerts other effects.

All body cells are affected either directly or indirectly by thyroid hormone. The effects of T_3 and T_4 can be grouped into several overlapping categories.

EFFECT ON METABOLIC RATE AND HEAT PRODUCTION Thyroid hormone increases the body's overall basal metabolic rate (BMR), or "idling speed" (see p. 510). It is the most important regulator of the body's rate of O_2 consumption and energy expenditure under resting conditions.

Closely related to thyroid hormone's overall metabolic effect is its **calorigenic effect** (*calorigenic* means "heat-producing"). Increased metabolic activity results in increased heat production.

SYMPATHOMIMETIC EFFECT Any action similar to one produced by the sympathetic nervous system is known as a **sympathomimetic effect** (*sympathomimetic* means "sympathetic-mimicking"). Thyroid hormone increases target-cell responsiveness to catecholamines (epinephrine and norepinephrine), the chemical messengers used by the sympathetic nervous system and its hormonal reinforcements from the adrenal medulla. Thyroid hormone accomplishes this permissive action by causing a proliferation of catecholamine target-cell receptors. Because of this action, many of the effects observed when thyroid hormone secretion is elevated are similar to those that accompany activation of the sympathetic nervous system.

EFFECT ON THE CARDIOVASCULAR SYSTEM Through its effect of increasing the heart's responsiveness to catecholamines, thyroid hormone increases heart rate and force of contraction, thus increasing cardiac output (see ● Figure 9-22, p. 267).

EFFECT ON GROWTH AND THE NERVOUS SYSTEM Thyroid hormone is essential for normal growth because of its effects on GH and IGF. Thyroid hormone not only stimulates GH secretion and increases production of IGF by the liver but also promotes the effects of GH and IGF on the synthesis of new structural proteins and on skeletal growth. Thyroid-deficient children have stunted growth that can be reversed by thyroid replacement therapy. Unlike excess GH, however, excess thyroid hormone does not produce excessive growth.

Thyroid hormone plays a crucial role in the normal development of the nervous system, especially the CNS, an effect impeded in children who have thyroid deficiency from birth. Thyroid hormone is also essential for normal CNS activity in adults.

Thyroid hormone is regulated by the hypothalamus–pituitary–thyroid axis.

Thyroid-stimulating hormone (TSH), the thyroid tropic hormone from the anterior pituitary, is the most important physiologic regulator of thyroid hormone secretion (● Figure 17-14). Almost every step of thyroid hormone synthesis and release is stimulated by TSH.

In addition to enhancing thyroid hormone secretion, TSH maintains the structural integrity of the thyroid gland. In the absence of TSH, the thyroid atrophies (decreases in size) and secretes its hormones at a very low rate. Conversely, it undergoes hypertrophy (increases the size of each follicular cell) and hyperplasia (increases the number of follicular cells) in response to excess TSH stimulation.

The hypothalamic **thyrotropin-releasing hormone (TRH),** in tropic fashion, "turns on" TSH secretion by the anterior pituitary, whereas thyroid hormone, in negative-feedback fashion, "turns off" TSH secretion by inhibiting the anterior pituitary and hypothalamus. Like other negative-feedback loops, the one between thyroid hormone and TSH tends to maintain a stable thyroid hormone output.

The only known factor that increases TRH secretion (and, accordingly, TSH and thyroid hormone secretion) is exposure

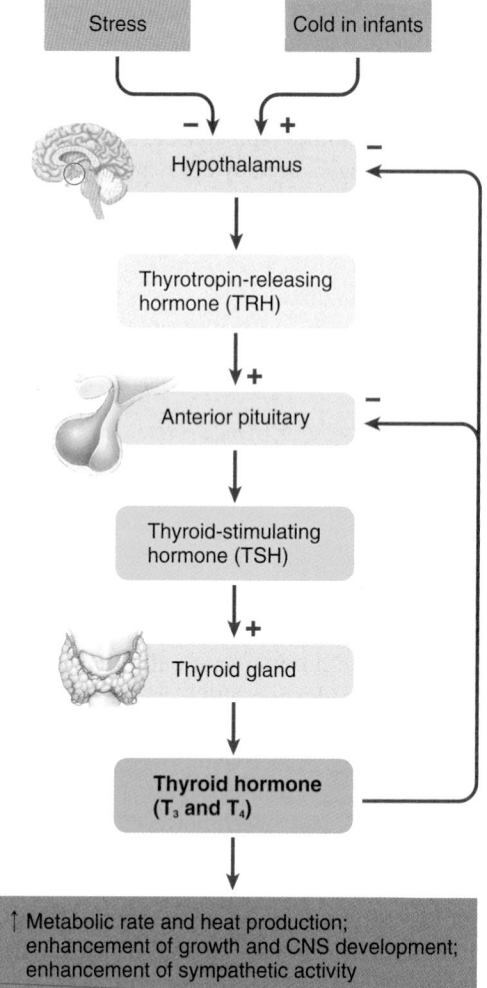

● **FIGURE 17-14 Regulation of thyroid hormone secretion.**

In the figure:

Stress → (−) Hypothalamus

Cold in infants → (+) Hypothalamus

Hypothalamus → Thyrotropin-releasing hormone (TRH)

TRH → (+) Anterior pituitary

Anterior pituitary → Thyroid-stimulating hormone (TSH)

TSH → (+) Thyroid gland

Thyroid gland → **Thyroid hormone (T₃ and T₄)**

Thyroid hormone → ↑ Metabolic rate and heat production; enhancement of growth and CNS development; enhancement of sympathetic activity

Negative feedback (−) from Thyroid hormone to Hypothalamus and Anterior pituitary.

---

to cold in newborn infants, a highly adaptive mechanism. Scientists think the dramatic increase in heat-producing thyroid hormone secretion helps maintain body temperature during the abrupt drop in surrounding temperature at birth as the infant passes from the mother's warm body to the cooler environmental air. A similar TSH response to cold exposure does not occur in adults, although it would make sense physiologically and does occur in many types of experimental animals.

Various types of stress, including physical stress, starvation, and infection, inhibit TSH and thyroid hormone secretion, presumably through neural influences on the hypothalamus, although the adaptive importance of this inhibition is unclear.

Abnormalities of thyroid function include both hypothyroidism and hyperthyroidism.

Abnormalities of thyroid function are among the most common endocrine disorders. They fall into two major categories—**hypothyroidism** and **hyperthyroidism**—reflecting deficient and excess thyroid hormone secretion, respectively. The consequences of too little or too much thyroid hormone secretion are largely predictable, given knowledge of the functions of thyroid hormone.

HYPOTHYROIDISM Hypothyroidism can result (1) from primary failure of the thyroid gland; (2) secondary to a deficiency of TRH, TSH, or both; or (3) from an inadequate dietary supply of iodine.

The symptoms of hypothyroidism are largely caused by a reduction in overall metabolic activity. Among other things, a patient with hypothyroidism has a reduced BMR (less energy expenditure at rest); displays poor tolerance of cold (lack of the calorigenic effect); has a tendency to gain excessive weight (not burning fuels at a normal rate); is easily fatigued (lower energy production); has a slow, weak pulse (caused by a reduction in the rate and strength of cardiac contraction and a lowered cardiac output); and exhibits slow reflexes and slow mental responsiveness (because of the effect on the nervous system). The mental effects are characterized by diminished alertness, slow speech, and poor memory.

Another notable characteristic is an edematous condition caused by infiltration of the skin with complex, water-retaining carbohydrate molecules, presumably as a result of altered metabolism. The resultant puffy appearance, primarily of the face, hands, and feet, is known as **myxedema.** If a person has hypothyroidism from birth, a condition known as **cretinism** develops. Because adequate levels of thyroid hormone are essential for normal growth and CNS development, cretinism is characterized by dwarfism and mental retardation, as well as general symptoms of thyroid deficiency. The mental retardation is preventable if replacement therapy is started promptly, but it is not reversible once it has developed for a few months after birth, even with later treatment with thyroid hormone.

HYPERTHYROIDISM The most common cause of hyperthyroidism is **Graves' disease.** This is an autoimmune disease in which the body erroneously produces **thyroid-stimulating immunoglobulin (TSI),** also known as **long-acting thyroid stimulator (LATS),** an antibody whose target is the TSH receptors on the thyroid cells. (An *autoimmune disease* is one in which the immune system produces antibodies for one of the body's own tissues.) TSI stimulates both secretion and growth of the thyroid in a manner similar to TSH. Unlike TSH, however, TSI is not subject to negative-feedback inhibition by thyroid hormone, so thyroid secretion and growth continue unchecked (● Figure 17-15). Less frequently, hyperthyroidism occurs secondary to excess TRH or TSH or in association with a hypersecreting thyroid tumor.

As expected, the hyperthyroid patient has an elevated BMR. The resultant increase in heat production leads to excessive perspiration and poor tolerance of heat. Body weight typically falls because the body is burning fuel at an abnormally rapid rate. Heart rate and strength of contraction may increase so much that the individual has palpitations (an unpleasant awareness of the heart's activity).

A prominent feature of Graves' disease but not of the other types of hyperthyroidism is **exophthalmos** (bulging eyes) (● Figure 17-16). Complex, water-retaining carbohydrates are deposited behind the eyes, although why this happens is still unclear. The resulting fluid retention pushes the eyeballs forward so that they bulge from their bony orbit.

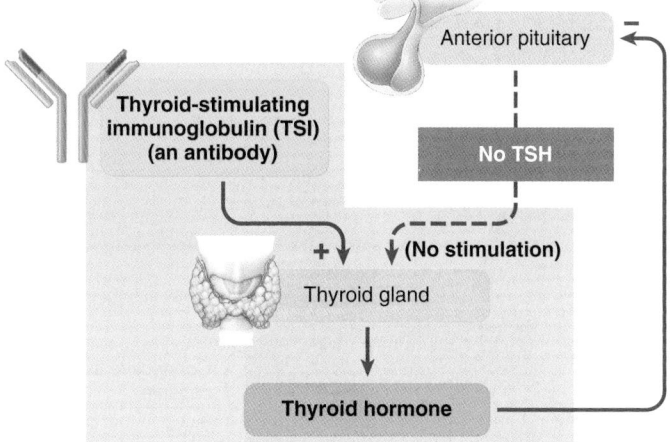

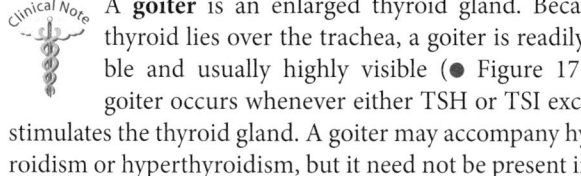

● FIGURE 17-15 **Role of thyroid-stimulating immunoglobulin in Graves' disease.** Thyroid-stimulating immunoglobulin (TSI), an antibody erroneously produced in the autoimmune condition of Graves' disease, binds with the TSH receptors on the thyroid gland and continuously stimulates thyroid hormone secretion outside the normal negative-feedback control system.

A goiter develops when the thyroid gland is overstimulated.

Clinical Note A **goiter** is an enlarged thyroid gland. Because the thyroid lies over the trachea, a goiter is readily palpable and usually highly visible (● Figure 17-17). A goiter occurs whenever either TSH or TSI excessively stimulates the thyroid gland. A goiter may accompany hypothyroidism or hyperthyroidism, but it need not be present in either condition. Knowing the axis and feedback control, we can predict which types of thyroid dysfunction will produce a goiter. Let us consider hypothyroidism first:

■ Hypothyroidism secondary to hypothalamic or anterior pituitary failure will not be accompanied by a goiter, because the thyroid gland is not being adequately stimulated, let alone excessively stimulated.

■ With hypothyroidism caused by thyroid gland failure or lack of iodine, a goiter does develop because the circulating level of thyroid hormone is so low that there is little negative-feedback inhibition on the anterior pituitary and hypothalamus; TSH secretion is therefore elevated. TSH acts on the thy-

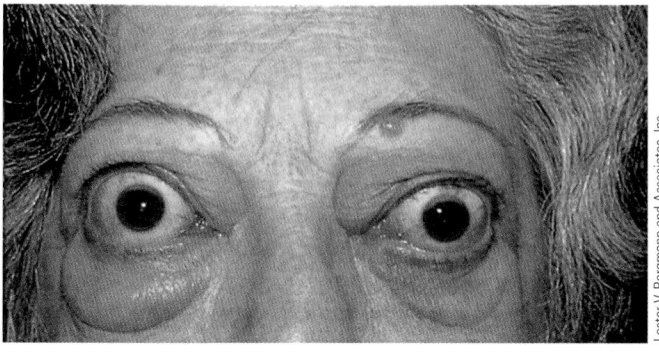

● FIGURE 17-16 **Patient displaying exophthalmos.** Abnormal fluid retention behind the eyeballs causes them to bulge forward.

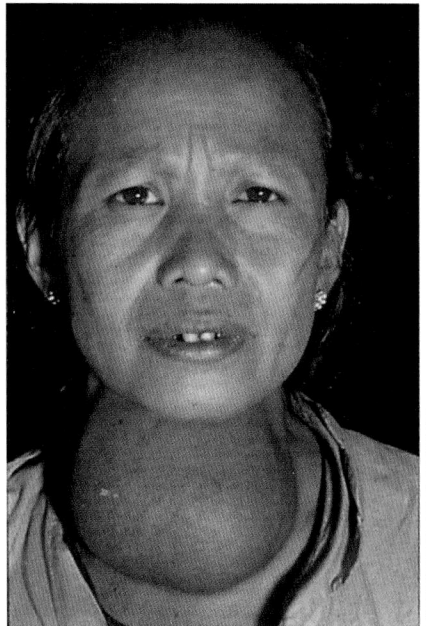

● FIGURE 17-17 **Patient with a goiter.**

roid to increase the size and number of follicular cells and to increase their rate of secretion. If the thyroid cells cannot secrete hormone because of a lack of a critical enzyme or lack of iodine, no amount of TSH will be able to induce these cells to secrete T_3 and T_4. However, TSH can still promote hypertrophy and hyperplasia of the thyroid, with a consequent paradoxical enlargement of the gland (that is, a goiter), even though the gland is still underproducing.

Similarly, a goiter may or may not accompany hyperthyroidism:

■ Excessive TSH secretion resulting from a hypothalamic or anterior pituitary defect would obviously be accompanied by a goiter and excess T_3 and T_4 secretion because of overstimulation of thyroid growth.

■ In Graves' disease, a hypersecreting goiter occurs because TSI promotes growth of the thyroid, as well as enhancing secretion of thyroid hormone. Because the high levels of circulating T_3 and T_4 inhibit the anterior pituitary, TSH secretion itself is low.

■ Hyperthyroidism resulting from overactivity of the thyroid in the absence of overstimulation, such as caused by an uncontrolled thyroid tumor, is not accompanied by a goiter. The spontaneous secretion of excessive amounts of T_3 and T_4 inhibits TSH, so there is no stimulatory input to promote growth of the thyroid. (Even though a goiter does not develop, a tumor may cause enlargement of the thyroid, depending on the nature or size of the tumor.)

Adrenal Glands

There are two **adrenal glands,** one embedded above each kidney in a capsule of fat (*ad* means "next to"; *renal* means "kidney") (● Figure 17-18a).

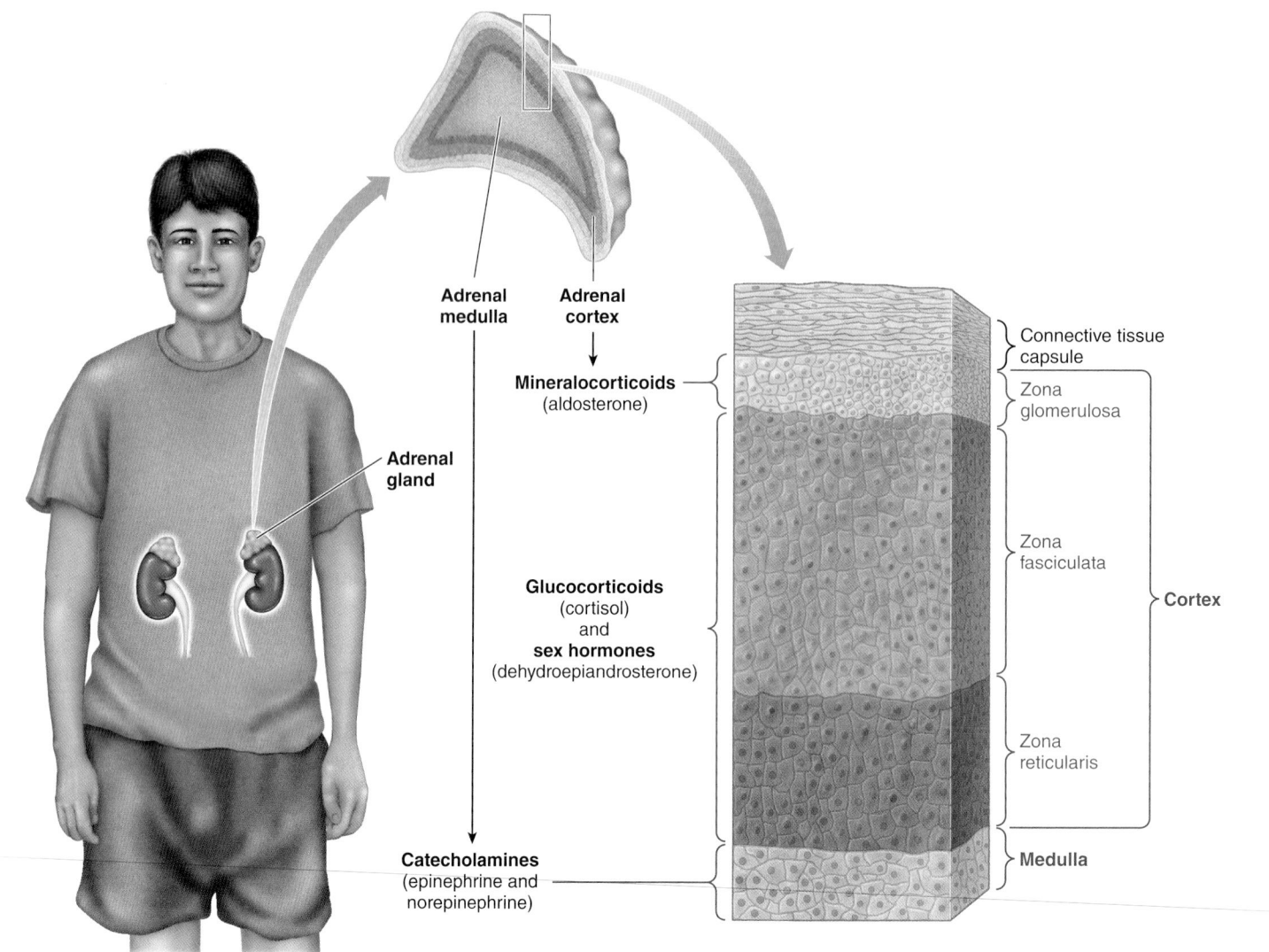

(a) Location and gross structure of adrenal glands

(b) Layers of adrenal cortex

● FIGURE 17-18 **Anatomy of and hormonal secretion by the adrenal glands.**

Each adrenal gland consists of a steroid-secreting cortex and a catecholamine-secreting medulla.

Each adrenal is composed of two endocrine glands, one surrounding the other. The outer layers composing the **adrenal cortex** secrete a variety of steroid hormones; the inner portion, the **adrenal medulla,** secretes catecholamines. We examine the adrenal cortex before turning to the adrenal medulla.

The adrenal cortex secretes mineralocorticoids, glucocorticoids, and sex hormones.

The adrenal cortex consists of three layers, or zones: the **zona glomerulosa,** the outermost layer; the **zona fasciculata,** the middle and largest portion; and the **zona reticularis,** the innermost zone (● Figure 17-18b). The adrenal cortex produces a number of different **adrenocortical hormones,** all of which are steroids. On the basis of their primary actions, the adrenal steroids can be divided into three categories:

1. **Mineralocorticoids,** mainly *aldosterone,* influence mineral (electrolyte) balance, specifically Na$^+$ and K$^+$ balance.

2. **Glucocorticoids,** primarily *cortisol,* play a major role in glucose metabolism, as well as in protein and lipid metabolism and in adaptation to stress.

3. **Sex hormones** are identical or similar to those produced by the gonads (testes in males, ovaries in females). The most abundant and physiologically important of the adrenocortical sex hormones is *dehydroepiandrosterone,* an androgen, or "male" sex hormone.

Of the two major adrenocortical hormones, aldosterone is produced exclusively in the zona glomerulosa, whereas cortisol synthesis is limited to the two inner layers of the cortex, with the zona fasciculata being the major source of this glucocorticoid (see ● Figure 17-18b). No other steroidogenic tissues have the capability of producing either mineralocorticoids or glucocorticoids. In contrast, the adrenal sex hormones, also produced by the two inner cortical zones, are produced in far greater abundance in the gonads.

The major effects of mineralocorticoids are on Na⁺ and K⁺ balance and blood pressure homeostasis.

The actions and regulation of the primary adrenocortical mineralocorticoid, **aldosterone,** are described thoroughly elsewhere (Chapter 13). Aldosterone promotes Na^+ retention and enhances K^+ elimination during the formation of urine. The promotion of Na^+ retention by aldosterone secondarily induces osmotic retention of H_2O, expanding the ECF volume (including the plasma volume), which is important in the long-term regulation of blood pressure.

Mineralocorticoids are *essential for life.* Without aldosterone, a person rapidly dies from circulatory shock because of the marked fall in plasma volume caused by excessive losses of H_2O-holding Na^+. With most other hormonal deficiencies, death is not imminent, even though a chronic hormonal deficiency may eventually lead to a premature death.

Aldosterone secretion is increased (1) by factors related to a reduction in Na^+ and a fall in blood pressure via the complex renin–angiotensin–aldosterone system (RAAS) (see ● Figure 13-12, p. 418), and (2) by direct stimulation of the adrenal cortex by a rise in plasma K^+ concentration (see ● Figure 13-16, p. 424). Adrenocorticotropic hormone (ACTH) from the anterior pituitary promotes the secretion of cortisol, not aldosterone. Thus, unlike cortisol regulation, the regulation of aldosterone secretion is independent of anterior pituitary control.

Glucocorticoids exert metabolic effects and play a key role in adaptation to stress.

Cortisol, the primary glucocorticoid, plays an important role in carbohydrate, protein, and fat metabolism; executes significant permissive actions for other hormonal activities; and helps people resist stress.

METABOLIC EFFECTS The overall effect of cortisol's metabolic actions is to increase the concentration of blood glucose at the expense of protein and fat stores. Specifically, cortisol performs the following functions:

- It stimulates hepatic **gluconeogenesis,** the conversion of noncarbohydrate sources (namely, amino acids) into carbohydrate within the liver (*gluco* means "glucose"; *neo* means "new"; *genesis* means "production"). Between meals or during periods of fasting, when no new nutrients are being absorbed into the blood for use and storage, the glycogen (stored glucose) in the liver tends to become depleted as it is broken down to release glucose into the blood. Gluconeogenesis is an important factor in replenishing hepatic glycogen stores and thus in maintaining normal blood glucose levels between meals. This is essential because the brain can use only glucose as its metabolic fuel, yet nervous tissue cannot store glycogen to any extent. The concentration of glucose in the blood must therefore be maintained at an appropriate level to adequately supply the glucose-dependent brain with nutrients.

- Cortisol inhibits glucose uptake and use by many tissues, but not the brain, thus sparing glucose for use by the brain, which requires it as a metabolic fuel. This action contributes to the increase in blood glucose concentration brought about by gluconeogenesis.

- It stimulates protein degradation in many tissues, especially muscle. By breaking down a portion of muscle proteins into their constituent amino acids, cortisol increases the blood amino acid concentration. These mobilized amino acids are available for use in gluconeogenesis or wherever else they are needed, such as for repair of damaged tissue or synthesis of new cellular structures.

- Cortisol facilitates lipolysis, the breakdown of lipid (fat) stores in adipose tissue, thus releasing free fatty acids into the blood (*lysis* means "breakdown"). The mobilized fatty acids are available as an alternative metabolic fuel for tissues that can use this energy source in lieu of glucose, thereby conserving glucose for the brain.

PERMISSIVE ACTIONS Cortisol is extremely important for its permissiveness. For example, cortisol must be present in adequate amounts to permit the catecholamines to induce vasoconstriction (blood vessel narrowing). A person lacking cortisol, if untreated, may go into circulatory shock in a stressful situation that demands immediate widespread vasoconstriction.

ROLE IN ADAPTATION TO STRESS Cortisol plays a key role in adaptation to stress. Stress of any kind is one of the major stimuli for increased cortisol secretion. Although cortisol's precise role in adapting to stress is not known, a speculative but plausible explanation might be as follows: A primitive human or an animal wounded or faced with a life-threatening situation must forgo eating. A cortisol-induced shift away from protein and fat stores in favor of expanded carbohydrate stores and increased availability of blood glucose would help protect the brain from malnutrition during the imposed fasting period. Also, the amino acids liberated by protein degradation would provide a readily available supply of building blocks for tissue repair if physical injury occurred. Thus, an increased pool of glucose, amino acids, and fatty acids is available for use as needed.

ANTI-INFLAMMATORY AND IMMUNOSUPPRESSIVE EFFECTS When stress is accompanied by tissue injury, inflammatory and immune responses accompany the stress response. Cortisol exerts *anti-inflammatory* and *immunosuppressive* effects to help hold these immune system responses in a check-and-balance fashion. An exaggerated inflammatory response has the potential of causing harm. Cortisol interferes with almost every step of inflammation. It inhibits immune responses by interfering with white blood cells that produce antibodies, among other actions.

 Synthetic glucocorticoids (drugs) have been developed that maximize the anti-inflammatory and immunosuppressive effects of these steroids while minimizing the metabolic effects (see p. 337). When

these drugs are administered therapeutically at pharmacologic levels (that is, at higher-than-physiologic concentrations), they are effective in treating conditions in which the inflammatory response itself has become destructive, such as *rheumatoid arthritis*. Glucocorticoids used in this manner do not affect the underlying disease process; they merely suppress the body's response to the disease. Because glucocorticoids also exert multiple inhibitory effects on the overall immune process, these agents have proved useful in managing various allergic disorders (inappropriate immune attacks) and in preventing organ transplant rejections (immune attack against foreign cells).

However, these steroids should be used only when warranted, and then only sparingly, for several important reasons. First, because these drugs suppress the normal inflammatory and immune responses that form the backbone of the body's defense system, a glucocorticoid-treated person has limited ability to resist infections. Second, troublesome side effects may occur with prolonged exposure to higher-than-normal concentrations of glucocorticoids. These effects include development of gastric ulcers, high blood pressure, atherosclerosis, menstrual irregularities, and bone thinning. Third, high levels of exogenous glucocorticoids act in negative-feedback fashion to suppress the hypothalamus–pituitary–adrenal axis that drives normal glucocorticoid secretion and maintains the integrity of the adrenal cortex. Prolonged suppression of this axis can lead to irreversible atrophy of the cortisol-secreting cells of the adrenal gland and thus to permanent inability of the body to produce its own cortisol. That is why *nonsteroidal anti-inflammatory drugs (NSAIDs),* such as aspirin and ibuprofen, are used as alternative anti-inflammatory therapy.

Cortisol secretion is regulated by the hypothalamus–pituitary–adrenal cortex axis.

Cortisol secretion by the adrenal cortex is regulated by a negative-feedback system involving the hypothalamus and anterior pituitary (● Figure 17-19). ACTH from the anterior pituitary stimulates the adrenal cortex to secrete cortisol. ACTH-producing cells, in turn, secrete only at the command of **corticotropin-releasing hormone (CRH)** from the hypothalamus. The feedback control loop is completed by cortisol's inhibitory actions on CRH and ACTH secretion by the hypothalamus and anterior pituitary, respectively.

The negative-feedback system for cortisol maintains the level of cortisol secretion relatively constant around the set point. Superimposed on the basic negative-feedback control system are two additional factors that influence plasma cortisol concentrations by changing the set point: *diurnal rhythm* and *stress,* both of which act on the hypothalamus to vary the secretion rate of CRH.

INFLUENCE OF DIURNAL RHYTHM ON CORTISOL SECRETION Recall that the plasma cortisol concentration displays a characteristic diurnal rhythm, with the highest level occurring in the morning and the lowest level at night (see ● Figure 17-2, p. 529). This diurnal rhythm, which is governed by the suprachiasmatic nucleus, is related primarily to the sleep–wake cycle. The peak and low levels are reversed in a person who works at night and sleeps during the day. The linking of cortisol secre-

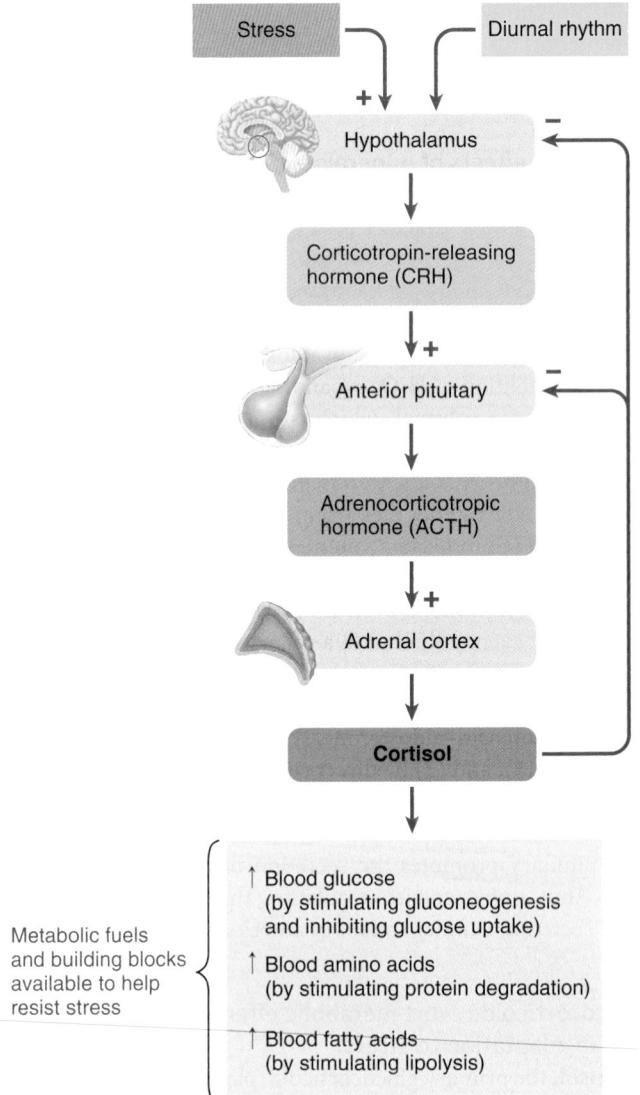

● **FIGURE 17-19 Control of cortisol secretion.**

tion to day–night activity patterns raises serious questions about the common practice of swing shifts at work (that is, constantly switching day and night shifts among employees).

INFLUENCE OF STRESS ON CORTISOL SECRETION The other major factor that is independent of, and can override, the stabilizing negative-feedback control of cortisol is stress. Dramatic increases in cortisol secretion, mediated by the CNS through enhanced activity of the CRH–ACTH–cortisol system, occur in response to all kinds of stressful situations. The magnitude of the increase in plasma cortisol concentration is generally proportional to the intensity of the stressful stimulation: A greater increase in cortisol levels takes place in response to severe stress than to mild stress.

The adrenal cortex secretes both male and female sex hormones in both sexes.

In both sexes, the adrenal cortex produces both *androgens,* or "male" sex hormones, and *estrogens,* or "female" sex hormones. The main site of production for the sex hormones is the gonads:

the testes for androgens and the ovaries for estrogens. Accordingly, males have a preponderance of circulating androgens, whereas in females estrogens predominate. However, no hormones are unique to either males or females (except those from the placenta during pregnancy), because the adrenal cortex in both sexes produces small amounts of the sex hormone of the opposite sex.

Under normal circumstances, the adrenal androgens and estrogens are not sufficiently abundant or powerful to induce masculinizing or feminizing effects, respectively. The only adrenal sex hormone that has any biological importance is the androgen **dehydroepiandrosterone (DHEA).** The testes' primary androgen product is the potent testosterone, but the most abundant adrenal androgen is the weaker DHEA. (Testosterone exerts about 100 times greater "androgenicity" than DHEA.) Adrenal DHEA is overpowered by testicular testosterone in males but is of physiologic significance in females, who otherwise have little androgens. DHEA governs androgen-dependent processes in the female such as growth of pubic and axillary (armpit) hair, enhancement of the pubertal growth spurt, and development and maintenance of the female sex drive.

In addition to controlling cortisol secretion, ACTH (not the pituitary gonadotropic hormones) controls adrenal androgen secretion. However, adrenal androgens feed back outside the hypothalamus–pituitary–adrenal axis. Instead of inhibiting CRH, DHEA inhibits the gonadotropin-releasing hormone, just as testicular androgens do.

A surge in DHEA secretion begins at puberty and peaks between the ages of 25 and 30. After 30, DHEA secretion slowly tapers off until, by the age of 60, the plasma DHEA concentration is less than 15% of its peak level.

 Some scientists suspect that the age-related decline of DHEA and other hormones such as GH and melatonin plays a role in some problems of aging. Early studies with DHEA replacement therapy demonstrated some physical improvement, such as an increase in lean muscle mass and a decrease in fat, but the most pronounced effect was a marked increase in psychological well-being and an improved ability to cope with stress. Advocates for DHEA replacement therapy do not suggest that maintaining youthful levels of this hormone is a fountain of youth (that is, it is not going to extend the life span), but they do propose that it may help people feel and act younger as they age. Other scientists caution that evidence supporting DHEA as an anti-aging therapy is still sparse. Also, they are concerned about DHEA supplementation until it has been thoroughly studied for possible harmful side effects. For example, some research suggests a potential increase in the risk of heart disease among women taking DHEA because of an observed reduction in high-density lipoproteins (HDL), the "good" cholesterol (see p. 272). Also, some experts fear that DHEA supplementation may raise the odds of acquiring ovarian or breast cancer in women and prostate cancer in men.

Ironically, although the FDA banned sales of DHEA as an over-the-counter drug in 1985 because of concerns about very real risks coupled with little proof of benefits, the product is widely available today as an unregulated food supplement. DHEA can be marketed as a dietary supplement without approval by the FDA as long as the product label makes no specific medical claims.

The adrenal cortex may secrete too much or too little of any of its hormones.

 Although uncommon, there are a number of different disorders of adrenocortical function. Excessive secretion may occur with any of the three categories of adrenocortical hormones: aldosterone hypersecretion, cortisol hypersecretion, and adrenal androgen hypersecretion.

ALDOSTERONE HYPERSECRETION Excess aldosterone secretion may be caused by (1) a hypersecreting adrenal tumor made up of aldosterone-secreting cells **(Conn's syndrome)** or (2) inappropriately high activity of RAAS (the primary aldosterone-stimulating mechanism). The symptoms are related to the exaggerated effects of aldosterone—namely, excessive Na$^+$ retention *(hypernatremia)* and K$^+$ depletion *(hypokalemia).* Also, high blood pressure (hypertension) is generally present, at least partially because of excessive Na$^+$ and fluid retention.

CORTISOL HYPERSECRETION Excessive cortisol secretion **(Cushing's syndrome)** can be caused by (1) overstimulation of the adrenal cortex by excessive amounts of CRH, ACTH, or both, or (2) adrenal tumors that uncontrollably secrete cortisol independent of ACTH. The prominent characteristics of this syndrome are related to the exaggerated effects of glucocorticoid, with the main symptoms caused by excessive gluconeogenesis. When too many amino acids are converted into glucose, the body suffers from combined glucose excess (high blood glucose) and protein shortage. For example, loss of structural protein within the walls of the small blood vessels leads to easy bruisability. For reasons that are unclear, some of the extra glucose is deposited as body fat in locations characteristic for this disease, typically in the abdomen, above the shoulder blades, and in the face. The abnormal fat distributions in the latter two locations are descriptively called a "buffalo hump" and a "moon face," respectively (● Figure 17-20). The appendages, in contrast, remain thin because of muscle breakdown.

ADRENAL ANDROGEN HYPERSECRETION Excess adrenal androgen secretion, a masculinizing condition, is more common than the extremely rare feminizing condition of excess adrenal estrogen secretion. Either condition is referred to as **adrenogenital syndrome,** emphasizing the pronounced effects that excessive adrenal sex hormones have on the genitalia and associated sexual characteristics. Adrenogenital syndrome is most commonly the result of an enzymatic defect that causes the cortisol-secreting cells to produce androgen instead of cortisol.

The symptoms that result from excess androgen secretion depend on the sex of the individual and the age at which the hyperactivity first begins.

■ *In adult females.* Because androgens exert masculinizing effects, a woman with this disease tends to develop a male pat-

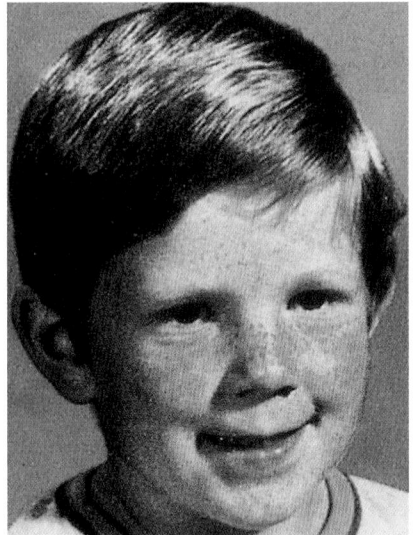

(a) Young boy prior to onset of the condition

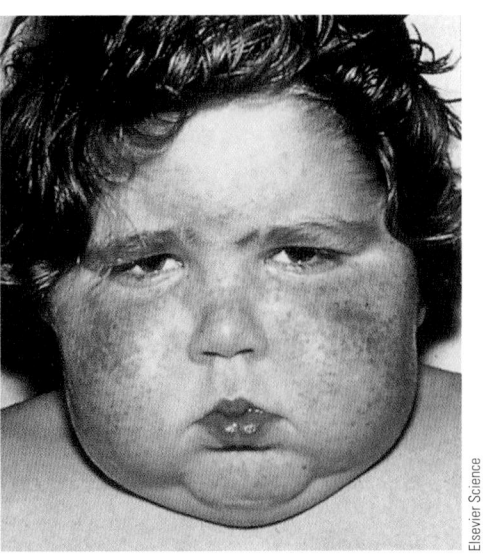

Elsevier Science

(b) Only four months later, the same boy displaying a "moon face" characteristic of Cushing's syndrome

● **FIGURE 17-20 Patient with Cushing's syndrome.**

tern of body hair, a condition referred to as **hirsutism.** She usually also acquires other male secondary sexual characteristics, such as deepening of the voice and more muscular arms and legs. The breasts become smaller, and menstruation may cease as a result of androgen suppression of the woman's hypothalamus–pituitary–ovarian axis for her own female sex-hormone secretion.

■ *In newborn females.* Female infants born with adrenogenital syndrome manifest male-type external genitalia because excessive androgen secretion occurs early enough during fetal life to induce development of their genitalia along male lines, similar to the development of males under the influence of testicular androgen (see p. 583). The clitoris, which is the female homologue of the male penis, enlarges under androgen influence and takes on a penile appearance, so in some cases it is difficult at first to determine the child's sex. Thus, this hormonal abnormality is one of the major causes of **female pseudohermaphroditism,** a condition in which female gonads (ovaries) are present but the external genitalia resemble those of a male. (A true hermaphrodite has the gonads of both sexes.)

■ *In prepubertal males.* Excessive adrenal androgen secretion in prepubertal boys causes them to prematurely develop male secondary sexual characteristics—for example, deep voice, beard, enlarged penis, and sex drive. This condition is referred to as **precocious pseudopuberty** to differentiate it from true puberty, which occurs as a result of increased testicular activity. In precocious pseudopuberty, the androgen secretion from the adrenal cortex is not accompanied by sperm production or any other gonadal activity, because the testes are still in their nonfunctional prepubertal state.

■ *In adult males.* Overactivity of adrenal androgens in adult males has no apparent effect, because any masculinizing effect induced by the weak DHEA, even when in excess, is unnoticeable in the face of the powerful masculinizing effects of the much more abundant and potent testosterone from the testes.

ADRENOCORTICAL INSUFFICIENCY If one adrenal gland is nonfunctional or removed, the other healthy organ can take over the function of both through hypertrophy and hyperplasia. Therefore, both glands must be affected before adrenocortical insufficiency occurs.

In **Addison's disease,** all layers of the adrenal cortex are undersecreting. This condition is most commonly caused by autoimmune destruction of the cortex by erroneous production of adrenal cortex–attacking antibodies, in which case both aldosterone and cortisol are deficient. Adrenocortical insufficiency may also occur because of a pituitary or hypothalamic abnormality, resulting in insufficient ACTH secretion. In this case, only cortisol is deficient because aldosterone secretion does not depend on ACTH stimulation.

The symptoms associated with aldosterone deficiency in Addison's disease are the most threatening. If severe enough, the condition is fatal because aldosterone is essential for life. However, the loss of adrenal function may develop slowly and insidiously so that aldosterone secretion may be subnormal but not totally lacking. Patients with aldosterone deficiency display K^+ retention *(hyperkalemia),* caused by reduced K^+ loss in the urine, and Na^+ depletion *(hyponatremia),* caused by excessive urinary loss of Na^+. The former disturbs cardiac rhythm. The latter reduces ECF volume, including circulating blood volume, which in turn lowers blood pressure (hypotension).

Symptoms of cortisol deficiency are as would be expected: poor response to stress, hypoglycemia (low blood glucose) caused by reduced gluconeogenic activity, and lack of permissive action for many metabolic activities.

Having completed discussion of the adrenal cortex, we now shift our attention to the adrenal medulla.

The adrenal medulla consists of modified sympathetic postganglionic neurons.

The adrenal medulla is actually a modified part of the sympathetic nervous system. A sympathetic pathway consists of two neurons in sequence. A preganglionic neuron originating in the CNS has an axonal fiber that terminates on a second peripherally located postganglionic neuron, which in turn terminates on the effector organ (see p. 191). The neurotransmitter released by sympathetic postganglionic fibers is norepinephrine.

The adrenal medulla consists of modified postganglionic sympathetic neurons. Unlike ordinary postganglionic sympathetic neurons, those in the adrenal medulla do not have axonal fibers that terminate on effector organs. Instead, on stimulation by the preganglionic fiber the ganglionic cell bodies within the adrenal medulla release their chemical transmitter directly into the blood (see ● Figure 7-2, p. 193). In this case, the transmitter qualifies as a hormone instead of a neurotransmitter. Like sympathetic fibers, the adrenal medulla does release norepinephrine, but its most abundant secretory output is a similar chemical messenger known as **epinephrine.** Both epinephrine and norepinephrine belong to the chemical class of catecholamines, which are derived from the amino acid tyrosine (see p. 100).

Epinephrine and norepinephrine are synthesized within the cytosol of the adrenomedullary secretory cells. Once produced, these catecholamines are stored in **chromaffin granules,** which are similar to the transmitter storage vesicles found in sympathetic nerve endings. Catecholamines are secreted into the blood by exocytosis of chromaffin granules.

Of the total adrenomedullary catecholamine output, epinephrine accounts for 80% and norepinephrine for 20%. Whereas epinephrine is produced exclusively by the adrenal medulla, the bulk of norepinephrine is produced by sympathetic postganglionic fibers. Adrenomedullary norepinephrine is generally secreted in quantities too small to exert significant effects on target cells. Therefore, for practical purposes we can assume that norepinephrine effects are predominantly mediated directly by the sympathetic nervous system and that epinephrine effects are brought about exclusively by the adrenal medulla.

Epinephrine reinforces the sympathetic nervous system and exerts additional metabolic effects.

Together, the sympathetic nervous system and adrenomedullary epinephrine mobilize the body's resources to support peak physical exertion in emergency or stressful situations. The sympathetic and epinephrine actions constitute a fight-or-flight response that prepares the person to combat an enemy or flee from danger (see p. 195). Epinephrine, by circulating in the blood, can reach catecholamine target cells that are not directly innervated by the sympathetic nervous system, such as the liver and adipose tissue. Accordingly, even though epinephrine and norepinephrine exert similar effects in many tissues, with epinephrine generally reinforcing sympathetic nervous activity, epinephrine can exert some unique effects because it gets into places not supplied by sympathetic fibers. For example, epinephrine prompts the mobilization of stored carbohydrate from the liver and stored fat from adipose tissue to provide immediately available energy for use as needed to fuel muscular work.

Realize, however, that epinephrine functions only at the bidding of the sympathetic nervous system, which is solely responsible for stimulating its secretion from the adrenal medulla. When the sympathetic system is activated under conditions of fear or stress, it simultaneously triggers a surge of adrenomedullary catecholamine release. The concentration of epinephrine in the blood may increase up to 300 times normal, with the amount of epinephrine released depending on the type and intensity of the stressful stimulus. Thus, sympathetic activity indirectly controls actions of epinephrine. By having the more versatile circulating epinephrine at its call, the sympathetic nervous system has a means of reinforcing its own neurotransmitter effects plus a way of executing additional actions on tissues that it does not directly innervate.

Because both components of the adrenal gland play an extensive role in responding to stress, this is an appropriate place to pull together the major factors involved in the stress response.

Integrated Stress Response

Stress is the generalized, nonspecific response of the body to any factor that overwhelms, or threatens to overwhelm, the body's compensatory abilities to maintain homeostasis. Contrary to popular usage, the agent inducing the response is correctly called a *stressor,* whereas *stress* refers to the state induced by the stressor. The following types of noxious stimuli illustrate the range of factors that can induce a stress response: *physical* (trauma, surgery, intense heat or cold); *chemical* (reduced O_2 supply, acid–base imbalance); *physiologic* (heavy exercise, hemorrhagic shock, pain); *psychological* or *emotional* (anxiety, fear, sorrow); and *social* (personal conflicts, change in lifestyle).

The stress response is a generalized pattern of reactions to any situation that threatens homeostasis.

Different stressors may produce some specific responses characteristic of that stressor; for example, the body's specific response to cold exposure is shivering and skin vasoconstriction, whereas the specific response to bacterial invasion includes increased phagocytic activity and antibody production. In addition to their specific response, however, all stressors produce a similar nonspecific, generalized response (● Figure 17-21). This set of responses common to all noxious stimuli is called the **general adaptation syndrome.** When a stressor is recognized, both nervous and hormonal responses bring about defensive measures to cope with the emergency. The result is a state of intense readiness and mobilization of biochemical resources.

To appreciate the value of the multifaceted stress response, imagine a primitive cave dweller who has just seen a large wild beast lurking in the shadows. We consider both the neural and the hormonal responses that would take place in this scenario. The body responds in the same way to modern-day stressors. We cover all these responses in further detail elsewhere. At this time, we are just examining how they work together.

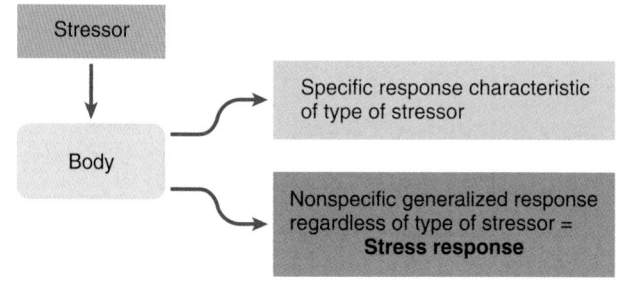

● **FIGURE 17-21 Action of a stressor on the body.**

ROLES OF THE SYMPATHETIC NERVOUS SYSTEM AND EPINEPHRINE IN STRESS The major neural response to such a stressful stimulus is generalized activation of the sympathetic nervous system. The resultant increase in cardiac output and breathing—as well as the diversion of blood from vasoconstricted regions of suppressed activity, such as the digestive tract and kidneys, to the more active vasodilated skeletal muscles and heart—prepares the body for a fight-or-flight response. Simultaneously, the sympathetic system calls forth hormonal reinforcements in the form of a massive outpouring of epinephrine from the adrenal medulla. Epinephrine strengthens sympathetic responses and mobilizes carbohydrate and fat stores.

ROLES OF THE CRH–ACTH–CORTISOL SYSTEM IN STRESS Besides epinephrine, a number of other hormones are involved in the overall stress response. The predominant hormonal response is activation of the CRH–ACTH–cortisol system. Recall that cortisol's role in helping the body cope with stress is presumed to be related to its metabolic effects. Cortisol breaks down fat and protein stores while expanding carbohydrate stores and increasing the availability of blood glucose. A logical assumption is that the increased pool of glucose, amino acids, and fatty acids is available for use as needed, such as to sustain nourishment to the brain and provide building blocks for repair of damaged tissues.

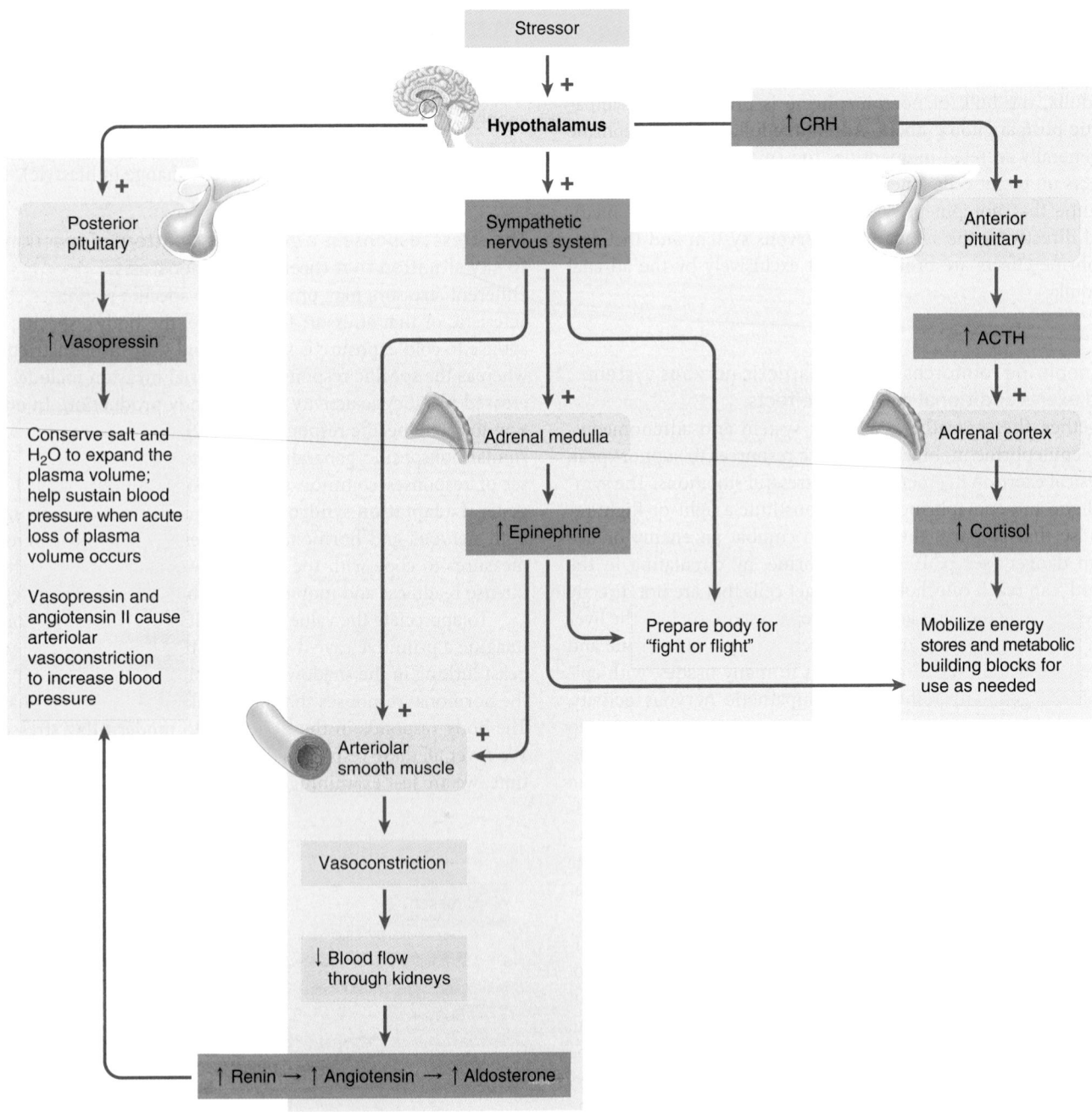

● **FIGURE 17-22 Integration of the stress response by the hypothalamus.**

ROLE OF BLOOD PRESSURE–SUSTAINING HORMONAL RESPONSES IN STRESS In addition to the hormonal changes that mobilize energy stores during stress, other hormones are simultaneously called into play to sustain plasma volume and blood pressure during the emergency. The sympathetic system and epinephrine play major roles in acting directly on the heart and blood vessels to improve circulatory function. In addition, the renin–angiotensin–aldosterone system is activated as a consequence of a sympathetically induced reduction of blood supply to the kidneys (see p. 417). Vasopressin secretion is also increased during stressful situations (see p. 449). Collectively, these hormones expand the plasma volume by promoting retention of salt and H_2O. Presumably, the enlarged plasma volume is a protective measure to help sustain blood pressure should acute loss of plasma fluid occur through hemorrhage or heavy sweating during the impending period of danger. Vasopressin and angiotensin also have direct vasopressor effects, which would be of benefit in maintaining an adequate blood pressure in the event of acute blood loss (see p. 292).

The multifaceted stress response is coordinated by the hypothalamus.

All the individual responses to stress just described are either directly or indirectly influenced by the hypothalamus (● Figure 17-22). The hypothalamus receives input concerning physical and emotional stressors from virtually all areas of the brain and from many receptors throughout the body. In response, the hypothalamus directly activates the sympathetic nervous system, secretes CRH to stimulate ACTH and cortisol release, and triggers the release of vasopressin. Sympathetic stimulation, in turn, brings about secretion of epinephrine. Furthermore, vasoconstriction of the renal afferent arterioles by the catecholamines triggers secretion of renin by reducing blood flow through the kidneys (a stimulus for renin secretion). Renin, in turn, sets in motion the renin–angiotensin–aldosterone system. In this way, the hypothalamus integrates the responses of both the sympathetic nervous system and the endocrine system during stress.

Activation of the stress response by chronic psychosocial stressors may be harmful.

Acceleration of cardiovascular and respiratory activity, retention of salt and H_2O, and mobilization of metabolic fuels and building blocks can be of benefit in response to a physical stressor, such as an athletic competition. Most of the stressors in our everyday lives are psychosocial in nature; however, they induce these same magnified responses. Stressors such as anxiety about an exam, conflicts with loved ones, or impatience while sitting in a traffic jam can elicit a stress response. Although the rapid mobilization of body resources is appropriate in the face of real or threatened physical injury, it is generally inappropriate in response to nonphysical stress. If no extra energy is demanded, no tissue is damaged, and no blood lost, body stores are being broken down and fluid retained needlessly, probably to the detriment of the emotionally stressed individual.

Endocrine Pancreas and Control of Fuel Metabolism

We have just discussed the metabolic changes elicited during the stress response. Now we concentrate on the metabolic patterns that occur in the absence of stress, including the hormonal factors that govern this normal metabolism.

Fuel metabolism includes anabolism, catabolism, and interconversions among energy-rich organic molecules.

The term **metabolism** refers to all the chemical reactions that occur within the cells of the body. Those reactions involving the degradation, synthesis, and transformation of the three classes of energy-rich organic molecules—protein, carbohydrate, and fat—are collectively known as **intermediary metabolism,** or **fuel metabolism** (▲ Table 17-3).

During the process of digestion, large nutrient molecules **(macromolecules)** are broken down into their smaller absorbable subunits as follows: Proteins are converted into amino

▲ Table 17-3 Summary of Reactions in Fuel Metabolism

Metabolic Process	Reaction	Consequence
Glycogenesis	Glucose → glycogen	↓ Blood glucose
Glycogenolysis	Glycogen → glucose	↑ Blood glucose
Gluconeogenesis	Amino acids → glucose	↑ Blood glucose
Protein Synthesis	Amino acids → protein	↓ Blood amino acids
Protein Degradation	Protein → amino acids	↑ Blood amino acids
Fat Synthesis (Lipogenesis, or Triglyceride Synthesis)	Fatty acids and glycerol → triglycerides	↓ Blood fatty acids
Fat Breakdown (Lipolysis, or Triglyceride Degradation)	Triglycerides → fatty acids and glycerol	↑ Blood fatty acids

acids, complex carbohydrates into monosaccharides (mainly glucose), and triglycerides (dietary fats) into monoglycerides and free fatty acids. These absorbable units are transferred from the digestive tract lumen into the blood, either directly or by way of the lymph (Chapter 15).

ANABOLISM AND CATABOLISM Once absorbed, the organic sub-units are constantly exchanged between the blood and the body cells. The chemical reactions in which these small organic molecules participate within the cells are categorized into two metabolic processes: anabolism and catabolism (● Figure 17-23). **Anabolism** is the buildup or synthesis of larger organic macromolecules from small organic molecular subunits. Anabolic reactions generally require energy input in the form of adenosine triphosphate (ATP). These reactions result in either (1) the manufacture of materials needed by the cell, such as cellular structural proteins or secretory products, or (2) the storage of excess ingested nutrients not immediately needed for energy production or as cellular building blocks. Storage is in the form of glycogen (the storage form of glucose) or fat reservoirs. **Catabolism** is the breakdown, or degradation, of large, energy-rich organic molecules within cells. Catabolism encompasses two levels of breakdown: (1) hydrolysis (see pp. 466 and A-16) of large cellular organic macromolecules into their smaller subunits, similar to the process of digestion except that the reactions take place within the body cells instead of within the digestive tract lumen (for example, release of glucose by the catabolism of stored glycogen), and (2) oxidation of the smaller subunits, such as glucose, to yield energy for ATP production (see p. 32).

As an alternative to energy production, the smaller, multi-potential organic subunits derived from intracellular hydrolysis may be released into the blood. These mobilized glucose, fatty acid, and amino acid molecules can then be used as needed for energy production or cellular synthesis elsewhere in the body.

In an adult, the rates of anabolism and catabolism are generally in balance, so the adult body remains in a dynamic steady state and appears unchanged even though the organic molecules that determine its structure and function are continuously being turned over. During growth, anabolism exceeds catabolism.

INTERCONVERSIONS AMONG ORGANIC MOLECULES In addition to being able to resynthesize catabolized organic molecules back into the same type of molecules, many cells of the body, especially liver cells, can convert most types of small organic molecules into other types—as in, for example, transforming amino acids into glucose or fatty acids. Because of these interconversions, adequate nourishment can be provided by a range of molecules present in different types of foods. There are limits, however. **Essential nutrients,** such as the essential amino acids and vitamins, cannot be formed in the body by conversion from another type of organic molecule.

The major fate of both ingested carbohydrates and ingested fats is catabolism to yield energy. Amino acids are predominantly used for protein synthesis but can be used to supply energy after being converted to carbohydrate or fat. Thus, all three categories of foodstuff can be used as fuel, and excesses of any foodstuff can be deposited as stored fuel, as you will see shortly.

At a superficial level, fuel metabolism appears relatively simple: The amount of nutrients in the diet must be sufficient to meet the body's needs for energy production and cellular synthesis. This apparently simple relationship is complicated, however, by two important considerations: (1) nutrients taken in at meals must be stored and then released between meals, and (2) the brain must be continuously supplied with glucose. Let us examine the implications of each.

Because food intake is intermittent, nutrients must be stored for use between meals.

Dietary fuel intake is intermittent, not continuous. As a result, excess energy must be absorbed during meals and stored for use during fasting periods between meals, when dietary sources of metabolic fuel are not available. Despite intermittent energy intake, the body cells' demand for energy is ever-present and fluctuating. That is, energy must constantly be available for cells to use as needed no matter what the status of food intake is. Stored energy fills in the gaps between meals. Energy storage takes three forms (▲ Table 17-4):

■ *Excess circulating glucose* is stored in the liver and muscle as *glycogen,* a large molecule consisting of interconnected glucose molecules. Because glycogen is a relatively small energy reservoir, less than a day's energy needs can be stored in this form. Once the liver and muscle glycogen stores are "filled up," additional glucose is transformed into fatty acids and glycerol, which are used to synthesize *triglycerides* (glycerol with three fatty acids attached), primarily in adipose tissue (fat).

■ *Excess circulating fatty acids* derived from dietary intake also become incorporated into triglycerides.

■ *Excess circulating amino acids* not needed for protein synthesis are not stored as extra protein but are converted to glucose and fatty acids, which ultimately end up being stored as triglycerides.

Thus, the major site of energy storage for excess nutrients of all three classes is adipose tissue. Normally, enough triglyceride is stored to provide energy for about 2 months, with more stored in an overweight person. Consequently, during any prolonged period of fasting, the fatty acids released from triglyceride catabolism are the primary source of energy for most tissues.

As a third energy reservoir, a substantial amount of energy is stored as *structural protein,* primarily in muscle, the most abundant protein mass in the body. Protein is not the first choice to tap as an energy source, however, because it serves other essential functions; in contrast, the glycogen and triglyceride reservoirs are solely energy depots.

The brain must be continuously supplied with glucose.

The second factor complicating fuel metabolism (besides intermittent nutrient intake and the resultant necessity of storing nutrients) is that the brain normally depends on delivery of adequate blood glucose as its sole source of energy. Consequently, the blood glucose concentration must be maintained above a critical level. The blood glucose concentration is typically 100 mg

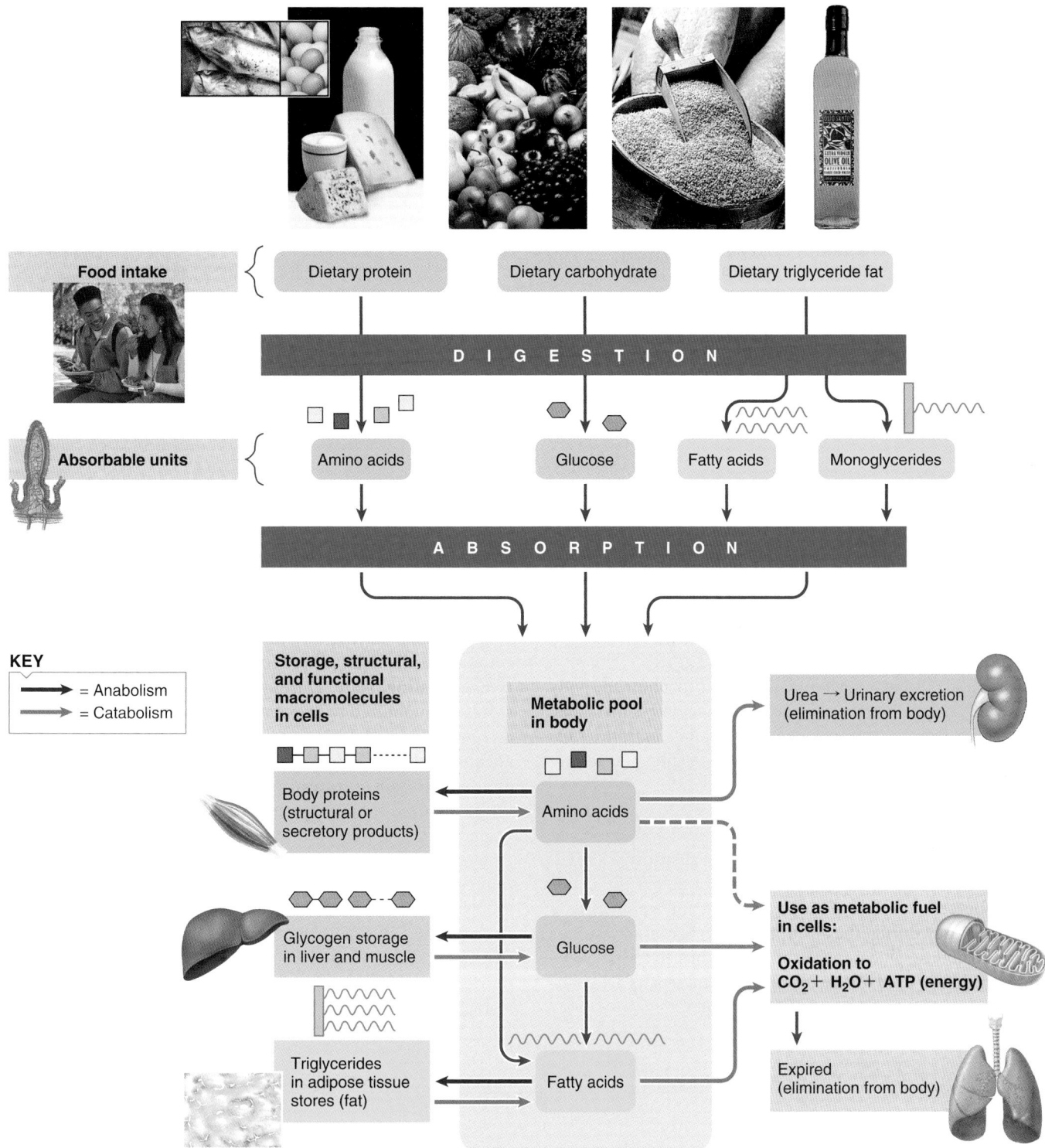

Food intake

Dietary protein   Dietary carbohydrate   Dietary triglyceride fat

D I G E S T I O N

Absorbable units

Amino acids   Glucose   Fatty acids   Monoglycerides

A B S O R P T I O N

KEY

→ = Anabolism
→ = Catabolism

Storage, structural, and functional macromolecules in cells

Metabolic pool in body

Urea → Urinary excretion (elimination from body)

Body proteins (structural or secretory products)

Amino acids

Use as metabolic fuel in cells:

Oxidation to $CO_2 + H_2O + ATP$ (energy)

Glycogen storage in liver and muscle

Glucose

Triglycerides in adipose tissue stores (fat)

Fatty acids

Expired (elimination from body)

● FIGURE 17-23 **Summary of the major pathways involving organic nutrient molecules.**

of glucose for every 100 ml of plasma and is normally kept within the narrow limits of 70 to 110 mg per 100 ml. Liver glycogen is an important reservoir for maintaining blood glucose levels during a short fast. However, liver glycogen is depleted relatively rapidly, so during a longer fast other mechanisms must meet the energy requirements of the glucose-dependent brain. First, when no new dietary glucose is entering the blood, tissues not obligated to use glucose shift their metabolic gears to burn fatty acids instead, sparing glucose for the brain. Fatty acids are made available by catabolism of triglyceride stores as an alternative energy source for tissues that are not glucose dependent. Second, amino acids can be converted to glucose by gluconeogenesis, whereas fatty acids cannot. Thus, once glycogen stores are depleted despite glucose sparing, new glucose supplies for the brain are

▲ Table 17-4 Stored Metabolic Fuel in the Body

▲ Table 17-4 Stored Metabolic Fuel in the Body

Metabolic Fuel	Circulating Form	Storage Form	Major Storage Site	Percentage of Total Energy Content (and Calories*)	Reservoir Capacity	Role
Carbohydrate	Glucose	Glyco-gen	Liver and muscle	1% (1500 Calories)	Less than a day's worth of energy	First energy source; essential for the brain
Fat	Free fatty acids	Triglyc-erides	Adipose tissue	77% (143,000 Calories)	About 2 months' worth of energy	Primary energy reservoir; energy source during a fast
Protein	Amino acids	Body proteins	Muscle	22% (41,000 Calories)	Death results long before capacity is fully used because of structural and functional impairment	Source of glucose for the brain during a fast; last resort to meet other energy needs

*Refers to kilocalories; see p. 510.

provided by the catabolism of body proteins and conversion of the freed amino acids into glucose.

Metabolic fuels are stored during the absorptive state and mobilized during the postabsorptive state.

The preceding discussion should make clear that how the body deals with organic molecules depends on the body's metabolic state. The two functional metabolic states—the *absorptive state* and the *postabsorptive state*—are related to eating and fasting cycles, respectively (▲ Table 17-5).

ABSORPTIVE STATE After a meal, ingested nutrients are being absorbed and entering the blood during the **absorptive, or fed, state.** During this time, glucose is plentiful and is the major energy source. Very little of the absorbed fat and amino acids is used for energy during the absorptive state, because most cells preferentially use glucose when it is available. Extra nutrients not immediately used for energy or structural repairs are channeled into storage as glycogen or triglycerides.

POSTABSORPTIVE STATE The average meal is completely absorbed in about 4 hours. Therefore, on a typical three-meals-a-day diet, no nutrients are being absorbed from the digestive tract during late morning and late afternoon and throughout the night. These times constitute the **postabsorptive, or fasting, state.** During this state, endogenous energy stores are mobilized to provide energy, whereas gluconeogenesis and glucose sparing maintain the blood glucose at an adequate level to nourish the brain. Synthesis of protein and fat is curtailed. Instead, stores of these organic molecules are catabolized for glucose formation and energy production, respectively. Carbohydrate synthesis does occur through gluconeogenesis, but the use of glucose for energy is greatly reduced.

Note that the blood concentration of nutrients does not fluctuate markedly between the absorptive and the postabsorptive states. During the absorptive state, the glut of absorbed nutrients is swiftly removed from the blood and placed into storage; during the postabsorptive state, these stores are catabo-

▲ Table 17-5 Comparison of Absorptive and Postabsorptive States

Metabolic Fuel	Absorptive State	Postabsorptive State
Carbohydrate	Glucose providing the major energy source	Glycogen degradation and depletion
	Glycogen synthesis and storage	Glucose sparing to conserve glucose for the brain
	Excess converted and stored as triglyceride fat	Production of new glucose through gluconeogenesis
Fat	Triglyceride synthesis and storage	Triglyceride catabolism
		Fatty acids providing the major energy source for non–glucose-dependent tissues
Protein	Protein synthesis	Protein catabolism
	Excess converted and stored as triglyceride fat	Amino acids used for gluconeogenesis

lized to maintain the blood concentrations at levels necessary to fill tissue energy demands.

ROLES OF KEY TISSUES IN METABOLIC STATES During these alternating metabolic states, various tissues play different roles, as summarized here:

■ The *liver* plays the primary role in maintaining normal blood glucose levels. It stores glycogen when excess glucose is available, releases glucose into the blood when needed, and is the principal site for metabolic interconversions such as gluconeogenesis.

■ *Adipose tissue* serves as the primary energy storage site and is important in regulating fatty acid levels in the blood.

■ *Muscle* is the primary site of amino acid storage and is the major energy user.

■ The *brain* normally can use only glucose as an energy source, yet it does not store glycogen, making it mandatory that adequate blood glucose levels be maintained.

The pancreatic hormones, insulin and glucagon, are most important in regulating fuel metabolism.

How does the body "know" when to shift its metabolic gears from a system of net anabolism and nutrient storage to one of net catabolism and glucose sparing? The flow of organic nutri-ents along metabolic pathways is influenced by a variety of hormones, including insulin, glucagon, epinephrine, cortisol, and GH. Under most circumstances, the pancreatic hormones, insulin and glucagon, are the dominant hormonal regulators that shift the metabolic pathways from net anabolism to net catabolism and glucose sparing, or vice versa, depending on whether the body is feasting or fasting, respectively.

ISLETS OF LANGERHANS The **pancreas** is an organ composed of both exocrine and endocrine tissues. The exocrine portion secretes a watery, alkaline solution and digestive enzymes through the pancreatic duct into the digestive tract lumen (see p. 485). Scattered throughout the pancreas between the exocrine cells are about a million clusters, or "islands," of endocrine cells known as the **islets of Langerhans** (● Figure 17-24a). The islets make up about 1% to 2% of the total pancreatic mass. The most abundant pancreatic endocrine cells are the **β (beta) cells,** which are the site of *insulin* synthesis and secretion and the **α (alpha) cells,** which produce *glucagon*. Less common the **D (delta) cells** are the pancreatic site of *somatostatin* synthesis. The β cells are concentrated centrally in the islets, with the other cells clustered around the periphery (● Figure 17-24b). We briefly highlight somatostatin now, and then we pay attention to insulin and glucagon, the most important hormones in the regulation of fuel metabolism.

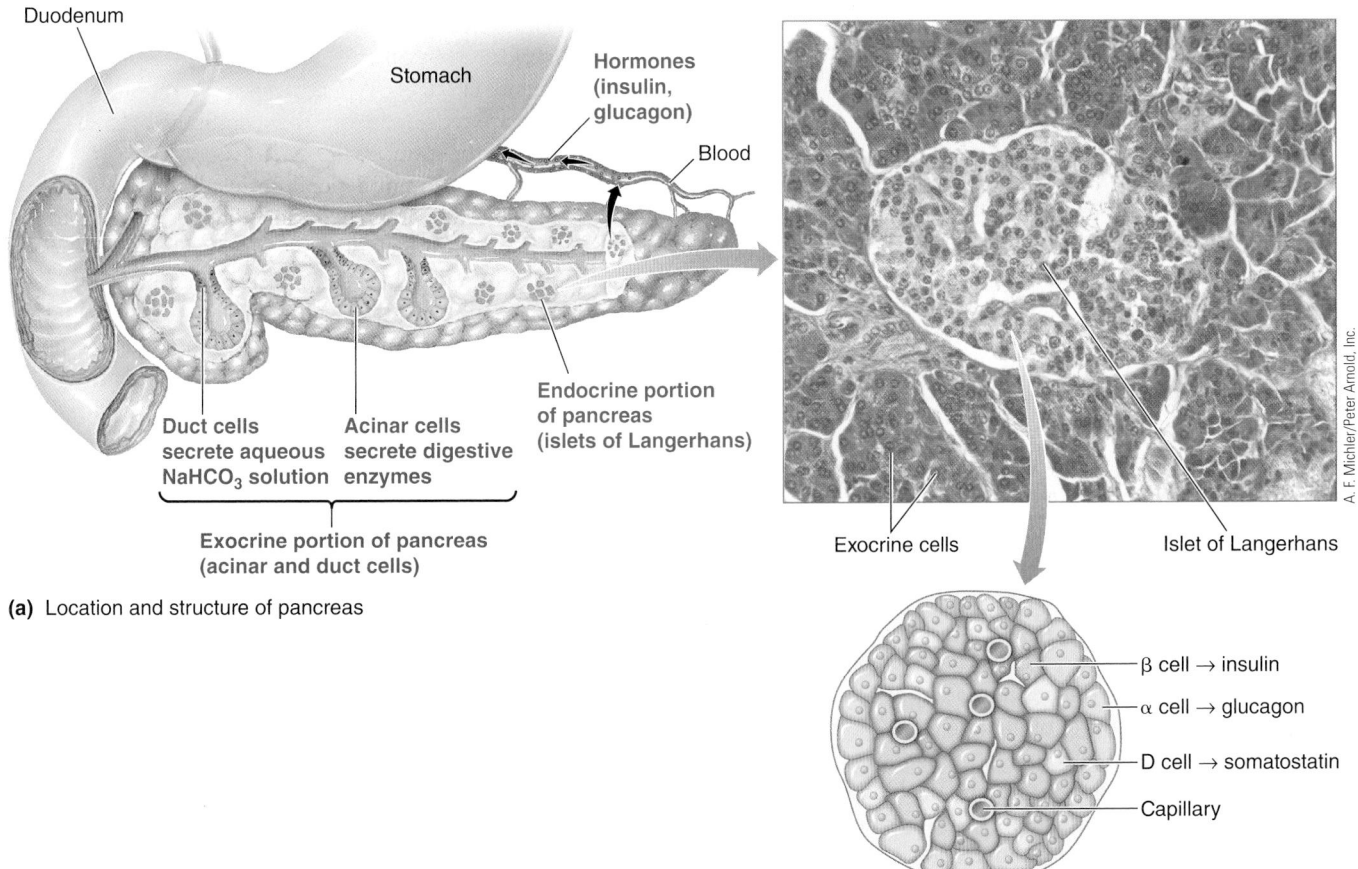

(a) Location and structure of pancreas

(b) Cell types in islet of Langerhans

● **FIGURE 17-24 Location and structure of the pancreas and cell types in the islets of Langerhans.**

SOMATOSTATIN Acting as a hormone, pancreatic **somatostatin** inhibits the digestive system in a variety of ways, the overall effects of which are to inhibit digestion of nutrients and to decrease nutrient absorption. Somatostatin is released from the pancreatic D cells in direct response to an increase in blood glucose and blood amino acids during absorption of a meal. By exerting its inhibitory effects, pancreatic somatostatin acts in negative-feedback fashion to put the brakes on the rate at which the meal is being digested and absorbed, thereby preventing excessive plasma levels of nutrients.

Somatostatin is also produced by cells lining the digestive tract, where it acts locally as a paracrine to inhibit most digestive processes (see p. 481). Furthermore, somatostatin (alias GHIH) is produced by the hypothalamus, where it inhibits the secretion of GH and TSH.

We next consider insulin and then glucagon, followed by a discussion of how insulin and glucagon function as an endocrine unit to shift metabolic gears between the absorptive and the postabsorptive states.

Insulin lowers blood glucose, fatty acid, and amino acid levels and promotes their storage.

Insulin has important effects on carbohydrate, fat, and protein metabolism. It lowers the blood levels of glucose, fatty acids, and amino acids and promotes their storage. As these nutrient molecules enter the blood during the absorptive state, insulin promotes their cellular uptake and conversion into glycogen, triglycerides, and protein, respectively. Insulin exerts its many effects by altering either transport of specific blood-borne nutrients into cells or activity of the enzymes involved in specific metabolic pathways.

ACTIONS ON CARBOHYDRATE Maintaining blood glucose homeostasis is a particularly important function of the pancreas. Insulin exerts four effects that lower blood glucose levels and promote carbohydrate storage:

1. Insulin facilitates glucose transport into most cells. (The mechanism of this increased glucose uptake is explained after insulin's other blood-glucose lowering effects are listed.)

2. Insulin stimulates **glycogenesis,** the production of glycogen from glucose, in both skeletal muscle and the liver.

3. Insulin inhibits **glycogenolysis,** the breakdown of glycogen into glucose.

4. Insulin inhibits gluconeogenesis, the conversion of amino acids into glucose in the liver.

Thus, insulin decreases the concentration of blood glucose by promoting the cells' uptake of glucose from the blood for use and storage while simultaneously blocking the two mechanisms by which the liver releases glucose into the blood (glycogenolysis and gluconeogenesis). Insulin is the only hormone capable of lowering blood glucose. Insulin promotes the uptake of glucose by most cells through glucose *transporter recruitment,* a topic to which we now turn.

Glucose transport between blood and cells is accomplished by means of a plasma membrane carrier known as a **glucose transporter (GLUT).** Fourteen forms of glucose transporters have been identified, named in the order they were discovered—GLUT-1, GLUT-2, and so on. All accomplish passive facilitated diffusion of glucose across the plasma membrane (see p. 62). Each member of the GLUT family performs slightly different functions. For example, *GLUT-1* transports glucose across the blood–brain barrier, and *GLUT-3* is the main transporter of glucose into neurons. The transporter responsible for the majority of glucose uptake by most body cells is *GLUT-4,* which operates only at the bidding of insulin. Glucose molecules cannot readily penetrate most cell membranes in the absence of insulin, making most tissues highly dependent on insulin for uptake of glucose from the blood and for its subsequent use. GLUT-4 is especially abundant in the tissues that account for the bulk of glucose uptake from the blood during the absorptive state, namely, resting skeletal muscle and adipose tissue cells.

GLUT-4 is the only type of transporter that responds to insulin. Unlike the other types of GLUT molecules, which are always present in the plasma membranes at the sites where they perform their functions, GLUT-4 is not present in the plasma membrane in the absence of insulin. Insulin promotes glucose uptake by **transporter recruitment.** Insulin-dependent cells maintain a pool of intracellular vesicles containing GLUT-4. Insulin induces these vesicles to move to the plasma membrane and fuse with it, thus inserting GLUT-4 molecules into the plasma membrane. In this way, increased insulin secretion promotes a rapid 10- to 30-fold increase in glucose uptake by insulin-dependent cells. When insulin secretion decreases, these GLUTs are retrieved from the membrane by endocytosis and returned to the intracellular pool.

Several tissues do not depend on insulin for their glucose uptake—namely, the brain, working muscles, and liver. The brain, which requires a constant supply of glucose for its minute-to-minute energy needs, is freely permeable to glucose at all times by means of GLUT-1 and GLUT-3 molecules. Skeletal muscle cells do not depend on insulin for their glucose uptake during exercise, even though they are dependent at rest. Muscle contraction triggers the insertion of GLUT-4 into the plasma membranes of exercising muscle cells in the absence of insulin. This fact is important in managing diabetes mellitus (insulin deficiency), as described later. The liver also does not depend on insulin for glucose uptake, because it does not use GLUT-4.

ACTIONS ON FAT Insulin exerts multiple effects to lower blood fatty acids and promote triglyceride storage:

1. It enhances the entry of fatty acids from the blood into adipose tissue cells.

2. It increases the transport of glucose into adipose tissue cells by means of GLUT-4 recruitment. Glucose serves as a precursor for the formation of fatty acids and glycerol, which are the raw materials for triglyceride synthesis.

3. It promotes chemical reactions that ultimately use fatty acids and glucose derivatives for triglyceride synthesis.

4. It inhibits lipolysis (fat breakdown), reducing the release of fatty acids from adipose tissue into the blood.

Collectively, these actions favor removal of fatty acids and glucose from the blood and promote their storage as triglycerides.

ACTIONS ON PROTEIN Insulin lowers blood amino acid levels and enhances protein synthesis through several effects:

1. It promotes the active transport of amino acids from the blood into muscles and other tissues. This effect decreases the circulating amino acid level and provides the building blocks for protein synthesis within the cells.

2. It increases the rate of amino acid incorporation into protein by stimulating the cells' protein-synthesizing machinery.

3. It inhibits protein degradation.

The collective result of these actions is a protein anabolic effect. For this reason, insulin is essential for normal growth.

SUMMARY OF INSULIN'S ACTIONS In short, insulin primarily exerts its effects by acting on the liver, adipose tissue, and non-working skeletal muscle. It stimulates biosynthetic pathways that lead to increased glucose use, increased carbohydrate and fat storage, and increased protein synthesis. In so doing, this hormone lowers the blood glucose, fatty acid, and amino acid levels. This metabolic pattern is characteristic of the absorptive state. Indeed, insulin secretion rises during this state and shifts metabolic pathways to net anabolism.

When insulin secretion is low, the opposite effects occur. The rate of glucose entry into cells is reduced, and net catabolism occurs rather than net synthesis of glycogen, triglycerides, and protein. This pattern is reminiscent of the postabsorptive state; indeed, insulin secretion is reduced during the postabsorptive state. However, the other major pancreatic hormone, glucagon, also plays an important role in shifting from absorptive to postabsorptive metabolic patterns, as described later.

The primary stimulus for increased insulin secretion is an increase in blood glucose concentration.

The primary control of insulin secretion is a direct negative-feedback system between the pancreatic β cells and the concentration of glucose in the blood flowing to them. An elevated blood glucose level, such as during absorption of a meal, directly stimulates the β cells to synthesize and release insulin. The increased insulin, in turn, reduces blood glucose to normal and promotes use and storage of this nutrient. Conversely, a fall in blood glucose below normal, such as during fasting, directly inhibits insulin secretion. Lowering the rate of insulin secretion shifts metabo-

lism from the absorptive to the postabsorptive pattern. Thus, this simple negative-feedback system can maintain a relatively constant supply of glucose to the tissues without requiring the participation of nerves or other hormones.

In addition to blood glucose concentration, which is the major controlling factor, other inputs are involved in regulating insulin secretion, as follows (● Figure 17-25):

■ An elevated blood amino acid level, such as after a high-protein meal, directly stimulates the β cells to increase insulin secretion. In negative-feedback fashion, the increased insulin enhances the entry of these amino acids into the cells, lowering the blood amino acid level while promoting protein synthesis.

■ Gastrointestinal hormones secreted by the digestive tract in response to the presence of food, especially glucose-dependent insulinotropic peptide (GIP) (see p. 502), stimulate pancreatic insulin secretion, in addition to having direct regulatory effects on the digestive system. Through this control, insulin secretion is increased in "feedforward," or anticipatory, fashion even before nutrient absorption increases the blood concentration of glucose and amino acids. Hormones released from the digestive tract that "notify" the pancreatic β cell of the impending rise in blood nutrients (primarily blood glucose) are termed **incretins.**

■ The autonomic nervous system also directly influences insulin secretion. The islets are richly innervated by both parasympathetic (vagal) and sympathetic nerve fibers. The increase in parasympathetic activity that occurs in response to food in the digestive tract stimulates insulin release. This, too, is a feedforward response in anticipation of nutrient absorption. In contrast, sympathetic stimulation and the concurrent increase in epinephrine both inhibit insulin secretion. The fall in insulin level allows the blood glucose level to rise, an appropriate re-

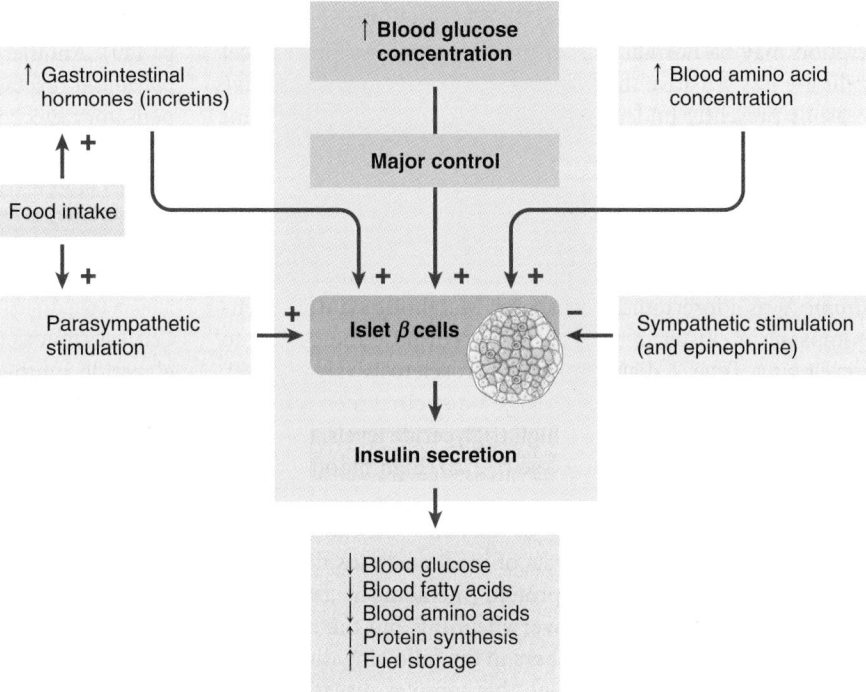

● **FIGURE 17-25** **Factors controlling insulin secretion.**

sponse to the circumstances under which generalized sympathetic activation occurs—namely, stress (fight-or-flight) and exercise. In both situations, extra fuel is needed for increased muscle activity.

The symptoms of diabetes mellitus are characteristic of an exaggerated postabsorptive state.

 Diabetes mellitus is by far the most common of all endocrine disorders. The acute symptoms of diabetes mellitus are attributable to inadequate insulin action. Because insulin is the only hormone capable of lowering blood glucose levels, one of the most prominent features of diabetes mellitus is elevated blood glucose levels, or *hyperglycemia*. *Diabetes* literally means "siphon" or "running through," a reference to the large urine volume accompanying this condition. A large urine volume occurs in both diabetes mellitus (a result of insulin insufficiency) and diabetes insipidus (a result of vasopressin deficiency; see p. 449). *Mellitus* means "sweet"; *insipidus* means "tasteless." The urine of patients with diabetes mellitus acquires its sweetness from excess blood glucose that spills into the urine, whereas the urine of patients with diabetes insipidus contains no sugar, so it is tasteless. (Aren't you glad you were not a health professional at the time when these two conditions were distinguished on the basis of the taste of the urine?)

TYPES OF DIABETES MELLITUS There are two distinct types of diabetes mellitus. **Type 1 (insulin-dependent, or juvenile-onset) diabetes mellitus,** which accounts for about 10% of all cases of diabetes, is characterized by a lack of insulin secretion because of erroneous autoimmune attack against the pancreatic β cells. Because their β cells secrete no insulin, Type 1 diabetics require exogenous insulin for survival. In **Type 2 (non-insulin-dependent, or maturity-onset) diabetes mellitus,** insulin secretion may be normal or even increased, but insulin's target cells are less sensitive than normal to this hormone for elusive reasons presently under intense investigation. Ninety percent of diabetics have the Type 2 form. Although either type can first be manifested at any age, Type 1 is more prevalent in children, whereas Type 2 more generally arises in adulthood, hence the age-related designations.

Many Type 2 diabetics have *metabolic syndrome,* or *syndrome X,* as a forerunner of diabetes. **Metabolic syndrome** encompasses a cluster of features that predispose the person to developing Type 2 diabetes and atherosclerosis (see p. 269). These features include obesity, large waist circumference (that is, "apple" shapes; see p. 516), high triglyceride levels, low HDL levels (the "good" cholesterol; see p. 272), high blood glucose, and high blood pressure.

The acute consequences of diabetes mellitus can be grouped according to the effects of inadequate insulin action on carbohydrate, fat, and protein metabolism (● Figure 17-26). The figure may look overwhelming, but the numbers, which correspond to the numbers in the following discussion, help you work your way through this complex disease step by step.

CONSEQUENCES RELATED TO EFFECTS ON CARBOHYDRATE METABOLISM Because the postabsorptive metabolic pattern is induced by low insulin activity, the changes that occur in diabetes mellitus are an exaggeration of this state, with the exception of hyperglycemia. In the usual fasting state, the blood glucose level is slightly below normal. Hyperglycemia, the hallmark of diabetes mellitus, arises from reduced glucose uptake by cells, coupled with increased output of glucose from the liver (● Figure 17-26, step **1**). As the glucose-yielding processes of glycogenolysis and gluconeogenesis proceed unchecked in the absence of insulin, hepatic output of glucose increases. Because many of the body's cells cannot use glucose without the help of insulin, an ironic extracellular glucose excess occurs coincident with an intracellular glucose deficiency—"starvation in the midst of plenty." Even though the non–insulin-dependent brain is adequately nourished during diabetes mellitus, further consequences of the disease lead to brain dysfunction, as you will see shortly.

When blood glucose rises to the level where the amount of glucose filtered by the kidney nephrons during urine formation exceeds their capacity for reabsorption (that is, when the T_m for glucose is exceeded; see p. 419), glucose appears in the urine (*glucosuria*) (step **2**). Glucose in the urine exerts an osmotic effect that draws H_2O with it, producing an osmotic diuresis characterized by *polyuria* (frequent urination) (step **3**). The excess fluid lost from the body leads to dehydration (step **4**), which in turn can lead to peripheral circulatory failure because of the marked reduction in blood volume (step **5**). Circulatory failure, if uncorrected, can lead to death because of low cerebral blood flow (step **6**) or secondary renal failure resulting from inadequate filtration pressure (step **7**). Furthermore, cells lose water as the body becomes dehydrated by an osmotic shift of water from the cells into the hypertonic (too concentrated) extracellular fluid (step **8**). Brain cells are especially sensitive to shrinking, so nervous system malfunction ensues (step **9**) (see p. 449). Another characteristic symptom of diabetes mellitus is *polydipsia* (excessive thirst) (step **10**), which is actually a compensatory mechanism to counteract the dehydration.

The story is not complete. In intracellular glucose deficiency, appetite is stimulated, leading to *polyphagia* (excessive food intake) (step **11**). Despite increased food intake, however, progressive weight loss occurs from the effects of insulin deficiency on fat and protein metabolism.

CONSEQUENCES RELATED TO EFFECTS ON FAT METABOLISM Triglyceride synthesis decreases while lipolysis increases, resulting in large-scale mobilization of fatty acids from triglyceride stores (step **12**). The increased blood fatty acids are largely used by the cells as an alternative energy source. Increased liver use of fatty acids results in the release of excessive ketone bodies into the blood, causing *ketosis* (step **13**). Ketone bodies include several different acids, such as acetoacetic acid, that result from incomplete breakdown of fat during hepatic energy production. Therefore, this developing ketosis leads to progressive metabolic acidosis (step **14**). Acidosis depresses the brain and, if severe enough, can lead to diabetic coma and death (step **15**).

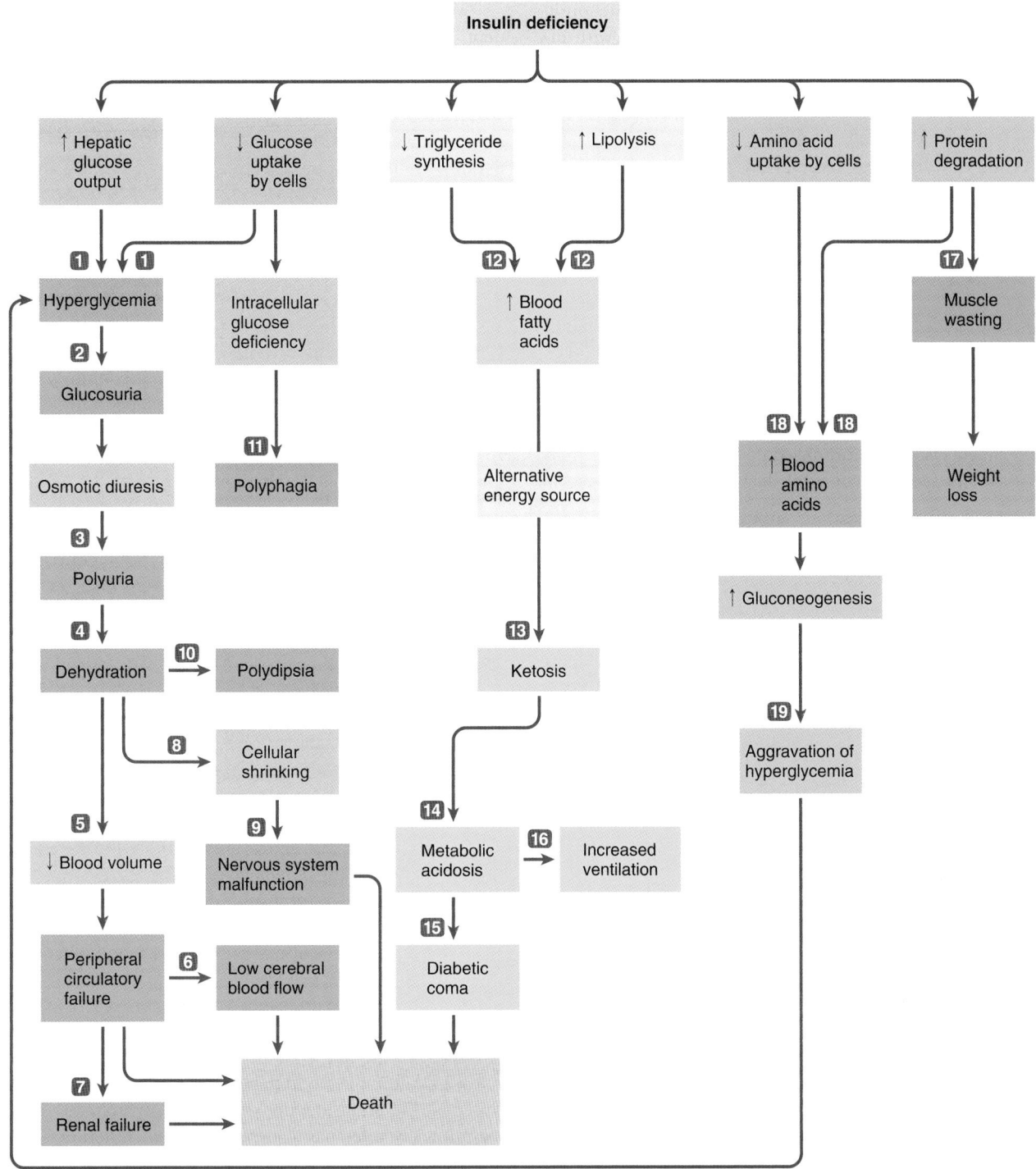

● FIGURE 17-26 **Acute effects of diabetes mellitus.** The acute consequences of diabetes mellitus can be grouped according to the effects of inadequate insulin action on carbohydrate, fat, and protein metabolism. These effects ultimately cause death through a variety of pathways. See pp. 564–566 for an explanation of the numbers.

A compensatory measure for metabolic acidosis is increased ventilation to blow off extra, acid-forming CO_2 (step **16**). Exhalation of one of the ketone bodies, acetone, causes a "fruity" breath odor that smells like a combination of Juicy Fruit gum and nail polish remover. Sometimes, because of this odor, passersby unfortunately mistake a patient collapsed in a diabetic coma for a "wino" passed out in a state of drunkenness. (This situation illustrates the

merits of medical alert identification tags.) People with Type 1 diabetes are more prone to develop ketosis than are Type 2 diabetics.

CONSEQUENCES RELATED TO EFFECTS ON PROTEIN METABOLISM
The effects of a lack of insulin on protein metabolism result in a net shift toward protein catabolism. The net breakdown of muscle proteins leads to muscle wasting and weakness, as well

as weight loss (step **17**) and, in child diabetics, a reduction in overall growth. Reduced amino acid uptake coupled with increased protein degradation results in excess amino acids in the blood (step **18**). The increased circulating amino acids can be used for additional gluconeogenesis, which further aggravates the hyperglycemia (step **19**).

As you can readily appreciate from this overview, diabetes mellitus is a complicated disease that can disturb both carbohydrate, fat, and protein metabolism and fluid and acid–base balance. It can also have repercussions on the circulatory system, kidneys, respiratory system, and nervous system.

LONG-TERM COMPLICATIONS In addition to these potential acute consequences of untreated diabetes, which can be explained on the basis of insulin's short-term metabolic effects, numerous long-range complications of this disease frequently occur after 15 to 20 years despite treatment to prevent the short-term effects. These chronic complications, which account for the shorter life expectancy of diabetics, primarily involve degenerative disorders of the blood vessels and nervous system. Cardiovascular lesions are the most common cause of premature death in diabetics. Heart disease and strokes occur with greater incidence than in nondiabetics. Because vascular lesions often develop in the kidneys and retinas of the eyes, diabetes is the leading cause of both kidney failure and blindness in the United States. Impaired delivery of blood to the extremities may cause these tissues to become gangrenous, and toes or even whole limbs may have to be amputated. In addition to circulatory problems, degenerative lesions in nerves lead to multiple neuropathies that result in dysfunction of the brain, spinal cord, and peripheral nerves. The latter is most often characterized by pain, numbness, and tingling, especially in the extremities.

Regular exposure of tissues to excess blood glucose over a prolonged time leads to tissue alterations responsible for the development of these long-range vascular and neural degenerative complications. Thus, the best management for diabetes mellitus is to continuously keep blood glucose levels within normal limits to diminish the incidence of these chronic abnormalities.

TREATMENT The treatment for Type 1 diabetes is a controlled balance of regular insulin injections timed around meals, management of the amounts and types of food consumed, and exercise. Insulin is injected because if it were swallowed, this peptide hormone would be digested by protein-digesting enzymes in the stomach and small intestine. Exercise is useful in managing both types of diabetes, because working muscles are not insulin dependent. Exercising muscles take up some of the excess glucose in the blood, reducing the overall need for insulin.

Several newer approaches are currently available for insulin-dependent diabetics that preclude the need for insulin injections. Implanted *insulin pumps* can deliver a prescribed amount of insulin regularly, but the recipient must time meals with care to match the automatic insulin delivery. *Pancreas transplants* are also being performed more widely now, with increasing success rates. On the downside, recipients of pancreas transplants must take immunosuppressive drugs for life to prevent rejection of their donated organs. Also, donor organs are in short supply.

Whereas Type 1 diabetics are permanently insulin dependent, dietary control and weight reduction may be all that is necessary to completely reverse the symptoms in Type 2 diabetics. Various blood-glucose lowering oral medications are available if needed for treating Type 2 diabetes in conjunction with a dietary and exercise regime. These pills help the patient's body use its own insulin more effectively by diverse mechanisms, for example by (1) stimulating the β cells to secrete more insulin than they do on their own *(sulfonylureas)*; (2) suppressing liver output of glucose *(metformin)*; (3) blocking enzymes that digest carbohydrates, thus slowing glucose absorption into the blood from the digestive tract and blunting the surge of glucose immediately after a meal *(α-glycosidase inhibitors)*; (4) making muscle and fat cells more receptive to insulin *(thiazolidinediones)*; (5) mimicking a naturally occurring incretin *(incretin mimetics)*; or (6) prolonging the action of a naturally occurring incretin *(DPP-4 inhibitors)*. Sometimes Type 2 diabetics eventually are no longer able to produce insulin, in which case they must be placed on insulin therapy.

Insulin excess causes brain-starving hypoglycemia.

Clinical Note Let us now look at the opposite of diabetes mellitus, insulin excess, which is characterized by *hypoglycemia* (low blood glucose) and can arise in two ways. First, insulin excess can occur in a diabetic patient when too much insulin has been injected for the person's caloric intake and exercise level, resulting in **insulin shock.** Second, blood insulin level may rise abnormally high in a nondiabetic individual whose β cells are overresponsive to glucose, a condition called **reactive hypoglycemia.** Such β cells "overshoot" and secrete more insulin than necessary in response to elevated blood glucose after a high-carbohydrate meal. The excess insulin drives too much glucose into the cells, resulting in hypoglycemia.

The consequences of insulin excess are primarily manifestations of the effects of hypoglycemia on the brain. Recall that the brain relies on a continuous supply of blood glucose for its nourishment and that glucose uptake by the brain does not depend on insulin. With insulin excess, more glucose than necessary is driven into the other insulin-dependent cells. The result is a lowering of the blood glucose level so that not enough glucose is left in the blood to be delivered to the brain. In hypoglycemia, the brain literally starves. The symptoms, therefore, are primarily referable to depressed brain function, which, if severe enough, may rapidly progress to unconsciousness and death. People with overresponsive β cells usually do not become sufficiently hypoglycemic to manifest these more serious consequences, but they do show milder symptoms of depressed CNS activity.

The treatment of hypoglycemia depends on the cause. At the first indication of a hypoglycemic attack with insulin overdose, the diabetic person should eat or drink something sugary. Prompt treatment of severe hypoglycemia is imperative to prevent brain damage.

Ironically, even though reactive hypoglycemia is characterized by a low blood glucose level, people with this disorder are treated by limiting their intake of sugar and other glucose-yielding carbohydrates to prevent their β cells from over-responding to a high glucose intake. Giving a symptomatic individual with reactive hypoglycemia something sugary temporarily alleviates the symptoms. The blood glucose level is transiently restored to normal so that the brain's energy needs are again satisfied. However, as soon as the extra glucose triggers further insulin release, the situation is merely aggravated.

Glucagon in general opposes the actions of insulin.

Even though insulin plays a central role in controlling metabolic adjustments between the absorptive and the postabsorptive states, the secretory product of the pancreatic islet α cells, **glucagon,** is also important. Many physiologists view the insulin-secreting β cells and the glucagon-secreting α cells as a coupled endocrine system whose combined secretory output is a major factor in regulating fuel metabolism.

Glucagon affects many of the same metabolic processes that insulin influences, but in most cases glucagon's actions are opposite to those of insulin. The major site of action of glucagon is the liver, where it exerts a variety of effects on carbohydrate, fat, and protein metabolism.

ACTIONS ON CARBOHYDRATE The overall effects of glucagon on carbohydrate metabolism result in an increase in hepatic glucose production and release and thus in an increase in blood glucose levels. Glucagon exerts its hyperglycemic effects by decreasing glycogen synthesis, promoting glycogenolysis, and stimulating gluconeogenesis.

ACTIONS ON FAT Glucagon also antagonizes the actions of insulin with regard to fat metabolism by promoting fat breakdown and inhibiting triglyceride synthesis. Thus, the blood levels of fatty acids increase under glucagon's influence.

ACTIONS ON PROTEIN Glucagon inhibits hepatic protein synthesis and promotes degradation of hepatic protein. Stimulation of gluconeogenesis further contributes to glucagon's catabolic effect on hepatic protein metabolism. Glucagon promotes protein catabolism in the liver, but it does not have any significant effect on blood amino acid levels because it does not affect muscle protein, the major protein store in the body.

Glucagon secretion is increased during the postabsorptive state.

Considering the catabolic effects of glucagon on energy stores, you would be correct in assuming that glucagon secretion increases during the postabsorptive state and decreases during the absorptive state, just the opposite of insulin secretion. In fact, insulin is sometimes referred to as a "hormone of feasting" and glucagon as a "hormone of fasting." Insulin tends to put nutrients in storage when their blood levels are high, such as after a meal, whereas glucagon promotes catabolism of nutrient stores between meals to keep up the blood nutrient levels, especially blood glucose.

As in insulin secretion, the major factor regulating glucagon secretion is a direct effect of the blood glucose concentration on the endocrine pancreas. In this case, the pancreatic α cells increase glucagon secretion in response to a fall in blood glucose. The hyperglycemic actions of this hormone tend to raise the blood glucose level back to normal. Conversely, an increase in blood glucose concentration, such as after a meal, inhibits glucagon secretion, which tends to drop the blood glucose level back to normal.

Insulin and glucagon work as a team to maintain blood glucose and fatty acid levels.

Thus, a direct negative-feedback relationship exists between blood glucose concentration and both β cells' and α cells' rates of secretion, but in opposite directions. An elevated blood glucose level stimulates insulin secretion but inhibits glucagon secretion, whereas a fall in blood glucose level leads to decreased insulin secretion and increased glucagon secretion (● Figure 17-27). Because insulin lowers and glucagon raises blood glucose, the changes in secretion of these pancreatic hormones in response to deviations in blood glucose work together homeostatically to restore blood glucose levels to normal.

Epinephrine, cortisol, and GH also exert direct metabolic effects.

The pancreatic hormones are the most important regulators of normal fuel metabolism. However, several other hormones exert direct metabolic effects, even though control of their secretion is keyed to factors other than transitions in metabolism between feasting and fasting states (▲ Table 17-6).

The stress hormones, epinephrine and cortisol, both increase blood levels of glucose and fatty acids through a variety of metabolic effects. In addition, cortisol mobilizes amino acids by

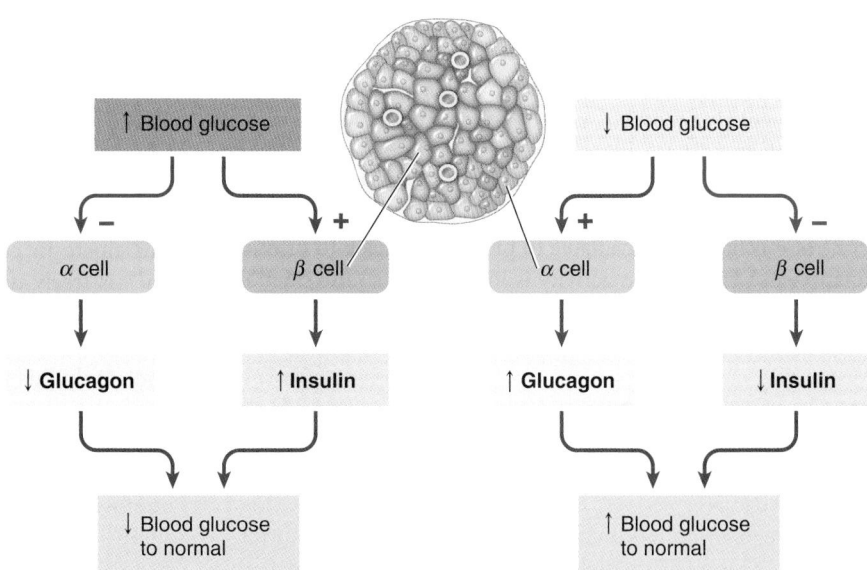

● **FIGURE 17-27 Complementary interactions of glucagon and insulin.**

Hormone	MAJOR METABOLIC EFFECTS				CONTROL OF SECRETION	
	Effect on Blood Glucose	Effect on Blood Fatty Acids	Effect on Blood Amino Acids	Effect on Muscle Protein	Major Stimuli for Secretion	Primary Role in Metabolism
Insulin	↓	↓	↓	↑	↑ Blood glucose	Primary regulator of absorptive and postabsorptive cycles
Glucagon	↑	↑	No effect	No effect	↓ Blood glucose	Regulation of absorptive and postabsorptive cycles in concert with insulin
Epinephrine	↑	↑	No effect	No effect	Sympathetic stimulation during stress	Provision of energy for emergencies
Cortisol	↑	↑	↑	↓	Stress	Mobilization of metabolic fuels and building blocks during adaptation to stress
Growth hormone	↑	↑	↓	↑	Deep sleep Exercise Stress ↓ Blood glucose	Promotion of growth; normally little role in metabolism; mobilization of fuels plus glucose sparing in extenuating circumstances

promoting protein catabolism. Neither hormone plays an important role in regulating fuel metabolism under resting conditions, but both are important for the metabolic responses to stress.

GH (acting through IGF) has protein anabolic effects in muscle. In fact, this is one of its growth-promoting features. Although GH can elevate the blood levels of glucose and fatty acids, it is normally of little importance to the overall regulation of fuel metabolism. Deep sleep (responsible for the marked nighttime diurnal increase in GH), exercise, stress, and severe hypoglycemia stimulate GH secretion, possibly to provide fatty acids as an energy source and spare glucose for the brain under these circumstances.

Note that, with the exception of the anabolic effects of GH on protein metabolism, all the metabolic actions of these other hormones are opposite to those of insulin. Insulin alone can reduce blood glucose and blood fatty acid levels, whereas glucagon, epinephrine, cortisol, and GH all increase blood levels of these nutrients. These other hormones are therefore considered **insulin antagonists.** Thus, the main reason diabetes mellitus has such devastating metabolic consequences is that no other control mechanism is available to pick up the slack to promote anabolism when insulin activity is insufficient, so the catabolic reactions promoted by other hormones proceed unchecked. The only exception is protein anabolism stimulated by GH.

Parathyroid Gland and Control of Calcium Metabolism

Besides regulating the concentration of organic nutrient molecules in the blood by manipulating anabolic and catabolic pathways, the endocrine system regulates the plasma concentration of a number of inorganic electrolytes. As you already know, aldosterone controls Na^+ and K^+ concentrations in the ECF. Three other hormones—*parathyroid hormone, calcitonin,* and *vitamin D*—control calcium (Ca^{2+}) and phosphate (PO_4^{3-}) metabolism. These hormonal agents concern themselves with regulating plasma Ca^{2+}; in the process, plasma PO_4^{3-} is maintained. Plasma Ca^{2+} concentration is one of the most tightly controlled variables in the body. The need for the precise regulation of plasma Ca^{2+} stems from its critical influence on so many body activities.

Plasma Ca^{2+} must be closely regulated to prevent changes in neuromuscular excitability.

About 99% of the Ca^{2+} in the body is in crystalline form within the skeleton and teeth. Of the remaining 1%, about 0.9% is found intracellularly within the soft tissues; less than 0.1% is present in the ECF. Approximately half of the ECF Ca^{2+} either is bound to plasma proteins and therefore restricted to the plasma or is complexed with PO_4^{3-} and therefore not free to participate in chemical reactions. The other half of the ECF Ca^{2+} is freely diffusible and can readily pass from the plasma into the interstitial fluid and interact with the cells. The free Ca^{2+} in the plasma and interstitial fluid is considered a single pool. Only this free ECF Ca^{2+} is biologically active and subject to regulation; it constitutes less than one thousandth of the total Ca^{2+} in the body.

This small, free fraction of ECF Ca^{2+} plays a vital role in a number of essential activities, including neuromuscular excitability, excitation–contraction coupling in smooth and cardiac muscle (see pp. 235 and 255), secretion of neurotransmitter and hydrophilic hormones (see p. 92), and blood clotting (see

p. 326). The most profound and immediate impact of even minor deviations from normal of ECF Ca^{2+} levels is the effect on neuromuscular excitability. A fall in free Ca^{2+} results in overexcitability of nerves and muscles; conversely, a rise in free Ca^{2+} depresses neuromuscular excitability. These effects result from the influence of Ca^{2+} on membrane permeability to Na^+. A decrease in free Ca^{2+} increases Na^+ permeability, with the resultant influx of Na^+ moving the resting potential closer to threshold. Consequently, in the presence of *hypocalcemia* (low blood Ca^{2+}) excitable tissues may be brought to threshold by normally ineffective physiologic stimuli so that skeletal muscles discharge and contract (go into spasm) "spontaneously" (in the absence of normal stimulation). If severe enough, spastic contraction of the respiratory muscles results in death by asphyxiation. *Hypercalcemia* (elevated blood Ca^{2+}) is also life threatening, because it causes cardiac arrhythmias and generalized depression of neuromuscular excitability.

Note that a *rise in cytosolic Ca^{2+}* within a muscle cell causes contraction (see p. 214), whereas an *increase in free ECF Ca^{2+}* decreases neuromuscular excitability and reduces the likelihood of contraction. Unless one keeps this point in mind, it is difficult to understand why low plasma Ca^{2+} levels cause muscle hyperactivity when Ca^{2+} is necessary to switch on the contractile apparatus. We are talking about two Ca^{2+} pools that exert different effects.

Because of the profound effects of deviations in free ECF Ca^{2+}, especially on neuromuscular excitability, the plasma concentration of this electrolyte is regulated with extraordinary precision via hormonal control of exchanges between the ECF and three other compartments: bone, kidneys, and intestine. Let us see how.

Parathyroid hormone raises free plasma Ca^{2+} levels by its effects on bone, kidneys, and intestine.

Parathyroid hormone (PTH), a peptide hormone secreted by the **parathyroid glands,** is the principal regulator of Ca^{2+} metabolism. The four rice grain–sized parathyroid glands are located on the back surface of the thyroid gland, one in each corner (see ● Figure 17-29, p. 571). Like aldosterone, PTH *is essential for life.* The overall effect of PTH is to increase the Ca^{2+} concentration of plasma (and, accordingly, of the entire ECF), thereby preventing hypocalcemia. In the complete absence of PTH, death ensues within a few days, usually because of asphyxiation caused by hypocalcemic spasm of respiratory muscles. By its actions on bone, kidneys, and intestine, PTH raises plasma Ca^{2+} concentration when it starts to fall, so hypocalcemia and its effects are normally avoided. This hormone also lowers plasma PO_4^{3-} concentration. We consider each of these mechanisms, beginning with an overview of bone remodeling and the actions of PTH on bone.

Bone continuously undergoes remodeling.

Recall that bone is a living tissue composed of an organic extracellular matrix (osteoid) made hard by precipitation of calcium phosphate—$Ca_3(PO_4)_2$—crystals, with 99% of the body's Ca^{2+} being found in the skeleton. By mobilizing some of these Ca^{2+} stores in bone, PTH raises plasma Ca^{2+} concentration when it starts to fall.

Despite the apparent inanimate nature of bone, its constituents are continually being turned over. **Bone deposition** (formation) and **bone resorption** (removal) normally go on concurrently so that bone is constantly being remodeled, much as people remodel buildings by tearing down walls and replacing them. Through remodeling, the adult human skeleton is completely regenerated an estimated every 10 years. Bone remodeling serves two purposes: (1) it keeps the skeleton appropriately "engineered" for maximum effectiveness in its mechanical uses, and (2) it helps maintain the plasma Ca^{2+} level. Let us examine in more detail the underlying mechanisms for each of these purposes.

Recall that three types of bone cells are present in bone. The *osteoblasts* secrete the extracellular organic matrix within which the $Ca_3(PO_4)_2$ crystals precipitate. The *osteocytes* are the retired osteoblasts imprisoned within the bony wall they have deposited around themselves. The *osteoclasts* resorb bone in their vicinity by releasing acids that dissolve the $Ca_3(PO_4)_2$ crystals and enzymes that break down the organic matrix. Thus, a constant cellular tug-of-war goes on in bone, with bone-forming osteoblasts countering the efforts of the bone-destroying osteoclasts. After it has created a cavity, an osteoclast moves on to an adjacent site to burrow another hole. Osteoblasts move into the cavity and secrete osteoid to fill in the hole. Subsequent mineralization of this organic matrix results in new bone to replace the bone dissolved by the osteoclast. These construction and demolition crews, working side by side, continuously remodel bone. At any given time, about a million microscopic-sized sites throughout the skeleton are undergoing resorption or deposition. Throughout most of adult life, the rates of bone formation and bone resorption are about equal, so total bone mass remains fairly constant during this period.

Mechanical stress favors bone deposition.

As a child grows, the bone builders keep ahead of the bone destroyers under the influence of GH and IGF. Mechanical stress also tips the balance in favor of bone deposition, causing bone mass to increase and the bones to strengthen. Mechanical factors adjust the strength of bone in response to the demands placed on it. The greater the physical stress and compression to which a bone is subjected, the greater the rate of bone deposition. For example, the bones of athletes are stronger and more massive than those of sedentary people.

By contrast, bone mass diminishes and the bones weaken when bone resorption gains a competitive edge over bone deposition in response to removal of mechanical stress. For example, bone mass decreases in people who undergo prolonged bed confinement or those in spaceflight. Early astronauts lost up to 20% of their bone mass during their time in orbit. Therapeutic exercise can limit or prevent such loss of bone.

 Bone mass also decreases as a person ages. Bone density peaks when a person is in the 30s and then starts to decline after age 40. By 50 to 60 years of age, bone resorption often exceeds bone formation. The

result is a reduction in bone mass known as **osteoporosis** (meaning "porous bones") (● Figure 17-28). This bone-thinning condition is characterized by a diminished laying down of organic matrix as a result of reduced osteoblast activity, increased osteoclast activity, or both rather than abnormal bone calcification. The underlying cause of osteoporosis is uncertain. Plasma Ca^{2+} and PO_4^{3-} levels are normal, as is PTH. Osteoporosis occurs with greatest frequency in postmenopausal women because of the associated withdrawal of bone-preserving estrogen (a female sex hormone). Osteoporosis is treated by regular weight-bearing exercise, a Ca^{2+}-rich diet and supplementation, and if needed, drugs that halt or reverse bone loss (for example, *Fosamax,* which blocks osteoclasts' bone-destroying actions).

PTH raises plasma Ca^{2+} by withdrawing Ca^{2+} from the bone bank.

In addition to the factors geared toward controlling the mechanical effectiveness of bone, throughout life PTH uses bone as a "bank" from which it withdraws Ca^{2+} as needed to maintain plasma Ca^{2+} level. PTH has two major effects on bone that raise plasma Ca^{2+} concentration:

1. As an immediate effect, PTH promotes rapid movement of Ca^{2+} into the plasma from Ca^{2+}-rich bone fluid. Recall that long cytoplasmic processes extend out from the entombed osteocytes into an extensive network of small canals in the bone to permit exchange of substances between the trapped osteocytes and the circulation. **Bone fluid** surrounds these cytoplasmic extensions within the canals. PTH accomplishes the fast exchange of Ca^{2+} between bone fluid and plasma by activating membrane-bound Ca^{2+} pumps located in the plasma membranes of these cytoplasmic extensions. These pumps promote movement of Ca^{2+} from the bone fluid into the osteocytes, from which the Ca^{2+} is transferred into the plasma circulating through the bone. Through this means, PTH draws Ca^{2+} out of the "quick-cash branch" of the bone bank and rapidly increases the plasma Ca^{2+} level without actually entering the bank (that is, without breaking down mineralized bone itself). Under normal conditions, this exchange is sufficient for maintaining plasma Ca^{2+} concentration.

2. Under conditions of chronic hypocalcemia, such as may occur with dietary Ca^{2+} deficiency, PTH stimulates actual localized dissolution of bone, promoting a slower transfer into the plasma of both Ca^{2+} and PO_4^{3-} from the minerals within the bone itself. It does so by stimulating osteoclasts to gobble up bone and transiently inhibiting the bone-forming activity of the osteoblasts. Bone contains so much Ca^{2+} compared to the plasma (more than 1000 times as much) that even when PTH promotes increased bone resorption, no immediate effects on the skeleton are discernible, because such a tiny amount of bone is affected. Yet the negligible amount of Ca^{2+} "borrowed" from the bone bank can be lifesaving in terms of restoring the free plasma Ca^{2+} level to normal. The borrowed Ca^{2+} is then redeposited in the bone at another time when Ca^{2+} supplies are more abundant. Meanwhile, the plasma Ca^{2+} level has been maintained without sacrificing bone integrity. However, prolonged excess PTH secretion over months or years eventually leads to the formation of holes throughout the skeleton, which are filled with very large, overstuffed osteoclasts.

When PTH promotes dissolution of the $Ca_3(PO_4)_2$ crystals in bone to harvest their Ca^{2+} content, both Ca^{2+} and PO_4^{3-} are released into the plasma. An elevation in plasma PO_4^{3-} is undesirable, but PTH deals with this dilemma by its actions on the kidneys.

PTH acts on the kidneys to conserve Ca^{2+} and eliminate PO_4^{3-}.

PTH promotes Ca^{2+} conservation and PO_4^{3-} elimination by the kidneys during urine formation. Under the influence of PTH, the kidneys can reabsorb more of the filtered Ca^{2+}, so less Ca^{2+} escapes into urine. This effect increases the plasma Ca^{2+} level and decreases urinary Ca^{2+} losses. (It would be counterproductive to dissolve bone to obtain more Ca^{2+} only to lose it in urine.) By contrast, PTH decreases PO_4^{3-} reabsorption, thus increasing urinary PO_4^{3-} excretion. As a result, PTH reduces plasma PO_4^{3-} levels at the same time it increases plasma Ca^{2+} concentrations.

This PTH-induced removal of extra PO_4^{3-} from the body fluids is essential for preventing reprecipitation of the Ca^{2+} freed from bone. Because PTH is secreted only when plasma Ca^{2+} falls below normal, the released Ca^{2+} is needed to restore plasma Ca^{2+} to normal, yet the released PO_4^{3-} tends to raise plasma PO_4^{3-} levels above normal. Because of the solubility characteristics of $Ca_3(PO_4)_2$ salt, if plasma PO_4^{3-} and plasma Ca^{2+} levels were allowed to increase simultaneously, some of the released Ca^{2+} would be forced back into bone through $Ca_3(PO_4)_2$ crystal formation. This self-defeating redeposition of Ca^{2+} would lower plasma Ca^{2+}, just the opposite of the needed effect. Therefore, PTH acts on the kidneys to decrease the reabsorption of PO_4^{3-} by

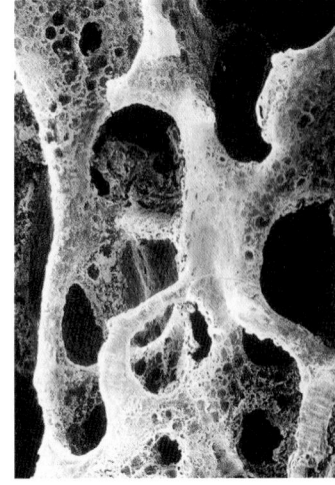

Normal bone   Osteoporotic bone

● **FIGURE 17-28 Comparison of normal and osteoporotic bone.**

the renal tubules. This action increases urinary excretion of PO_4^{3-} and lowers its plasma concentration, even though extra PO_4^{3-} is being released from bone into the plasma.

The third important action of PTH on the kidneys (besides increasing Ca^{2+} reabsorption and decreasing PO_4^{3-} reabsorption) is to enhance the activation of vitamin D by the kidneys.

PTH indirectly promotes absorption of Ca^{2+} and PO_4^{3-} by the intestine.

Although PTH has no direct effect on the intestine, it indirectly increases both Ca^{2+} and PO_4^{3-} absorption from the small intestine by helping activate vitamin D. This vitamin, in turn, directly increases intestinal absorption of Ca^{2+} and PO_4^{3-}, a topic we discuss more thoroughly shortly.

The primary regulator of PTH secretion is plasma concentration of free Ca^{2+}.

All the effects of PTH raise plasma Ca^{2+} levels. Appropriately, PTH secretion increases when plasma Ca^{2+} falls and decreases when plasma Ca^{2+} rises. The secretory cells of the parathyroid glands are directly and exquisitely sensitive to changes in free plasma Ca^{2+}. Because PTH regulates plasma Ca^{2+} concentration, this relationship forms a simple negative-feedback loop for controlling PTH secretion without involving any nervous or other hormonal intervention (● Figure 17-29).

Calcitonin lowers plasma Ca^{2+} concentration but is not important in the normal control of Ca^{2+} metabolism.

Calcitonin, the hormone produced by the C cells of the thyroid gland, also exerts an influence on plasma Ca^{2+} levels. Like PTH, calcitonin has two effects on bone, but in this case both effects *decrease* plasma Ca^{2+} levels: Short term, calcitonin decreases Ca^{2+} movement from the bone fluid into the plasma. Long term, calcitonin decreases bone resorption by inhibiting the activity of osteoclasts. The suppression of bone resorption low-

ers plasma PO_4^{3-} levels, as well as reducing plasma Ca^{2+} concentration. Calcitonin also inhibits Ca^{2+} and PO_4^{3-} reabsorption from the kidney tubules during urine formation, further reinforcing its hypocalcemic and hypophosphatemic effects. Calcitonin has no effect on the intestine.

As with PTH, the primary regulator of calcitonin release is free plasma Ca^{2+} concentration, but unlike with PTH, an increase in plasma Ca^{2+} stimulates calcitonin secretion and a fall in plasma Ca^{2+} inhibits calcitonin secretion (● Figure 17-29). Because calcitonin reduces plasma Ca^{2+} levels, this system constitutes a second simple negative-feedback control over plasma Ca^{2+} concentration, one opposed to the PTH system.

Most evidence suggests, however, that calcitonin plays little or no role in the normal control of Ca^{2+} or PO_4^{3-} metabolism. Although calcitonin protects against hypercalcemia, this condition rarely occurs under normal circumstances. Moreover, neither thyroid removal nor calcitonin-secreting tumors alter circulating levels of Ca^{2+} or PO_4^{3-}, implying that this hormone is not normally essential for maintaining Ca^{2+} or PO_4^{3-} homeostasis. Calcitonin may, however, play a role in protecting skeletal integrity when there is a large Ca^{2+} demand, such as during pregnancy or breast-feeding.

Vitamin D is actually a hormone that increases Ca^{2+} absorption in the intestine.

The final factor involved in regulating Ca^{2+} metabolism is **cholecalciferol,** or **vitamin D,** a steroidlike compound essential for Ca^{2+} absorption in the intestine. Strictly speaking, vitamin D should be considered a hormone because the body can produce it in the skin from a precursor related to cholesterol on exposure to sunlight. It is subsequently released into the blood to act at a distant target site, the intestine. The skin, therefore, is actually an endocrine gland and vitamin D is a hormone. Traditionally, however, this chemical messenger has been considered a vitamin for two reasons. First, it was originally discovered and isolated from a dietary source and tagged as a vitamin. Second, even though the skin would be an adequate source of vitamin D if it were exposed to sufficient sunlight, indoor dwelling and clothing in response to cold weather and social customs preclude significant exposure of the skin to sunlight in the United States and many other parts of the world most of the time. At least part of the essential vitamin D must therefore be derived from dietary sources.

ACTIVATION OF VITAMIN D Regardless of its source, vitamin D is biologically inactive when it first enters the blood from either the skin or the digestive tract. It must be activated by two sequential biochemical alterations. The first of these reactions occurs in the liver, and the second takes place in the kidneys. The kidney enzymes involved in the second step of vitamin D activation are stimulated by PTH in response to a fall in plasma Ca^{2+}. To a lesser extent, a fall in plasma PO_4^{3-} also enhances the activation process.

FUNCTIONS OF VITAMIN D The most dramatic effect of activated vitamin D is to increase Ca^{2+} absorption by the intestine. Un-

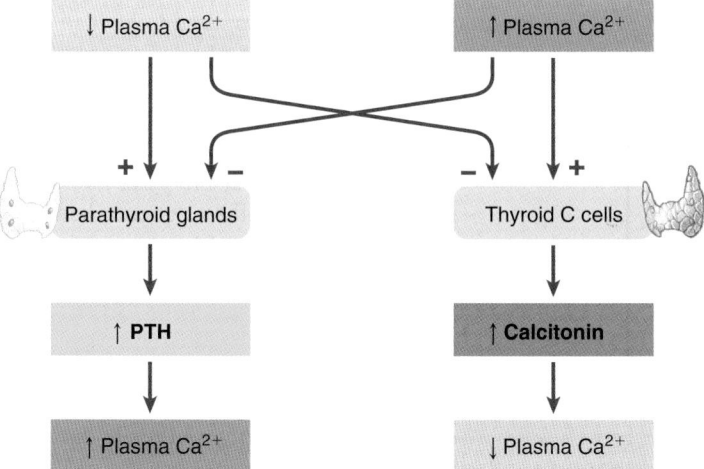

● **FIGURE 17-29 Negative-feedback loops controlling parathyroid hormone (PTH) and calcitonin secretion.**

like most dietary constituents, dietary Ca^{2+} is not indiscriminately absorbed by the digestive system. In fact, the majority of ingested Ca^{2+} is typically not absorbed but is lost in the feces. When needed, more dietary Ca^{2+} is absorbed into the plasma under the influence of vitamin D. Independently of its effects on Ca^{2+} transport, the active form of vitamin D increases intestinal PO_4^{3-} absorption. Furthermore, vitamin D increases the responsiveness of bone to PTH. Thus, vitamin D and PTH are closely interdependent (● Figure 17-30).

Recent research indicates that vitamin D's functions are more far reaching than its effects on uptake of ingested Ca^{2+} and PO_4^{3-}. Vitamin D, at higher blood concentrations than those sufficient to protect bone, appears to bolster muscle strength and is an important force in energy metabolism and immune health. It helps thwart development of diabetes mellitus, fights some types of cancer, and counters autoimmune diseases like multiple sclerosis by presently unknown mechanisms. Because of these newly found actions, scientists and dieticians are reevaluating the recommended daily allowance (RDA) for vitamin D in the diet, especially when sufficient sun exposure is not possible. The RDA will likely be bumped up, but the optimal value needs to be determined by further study.

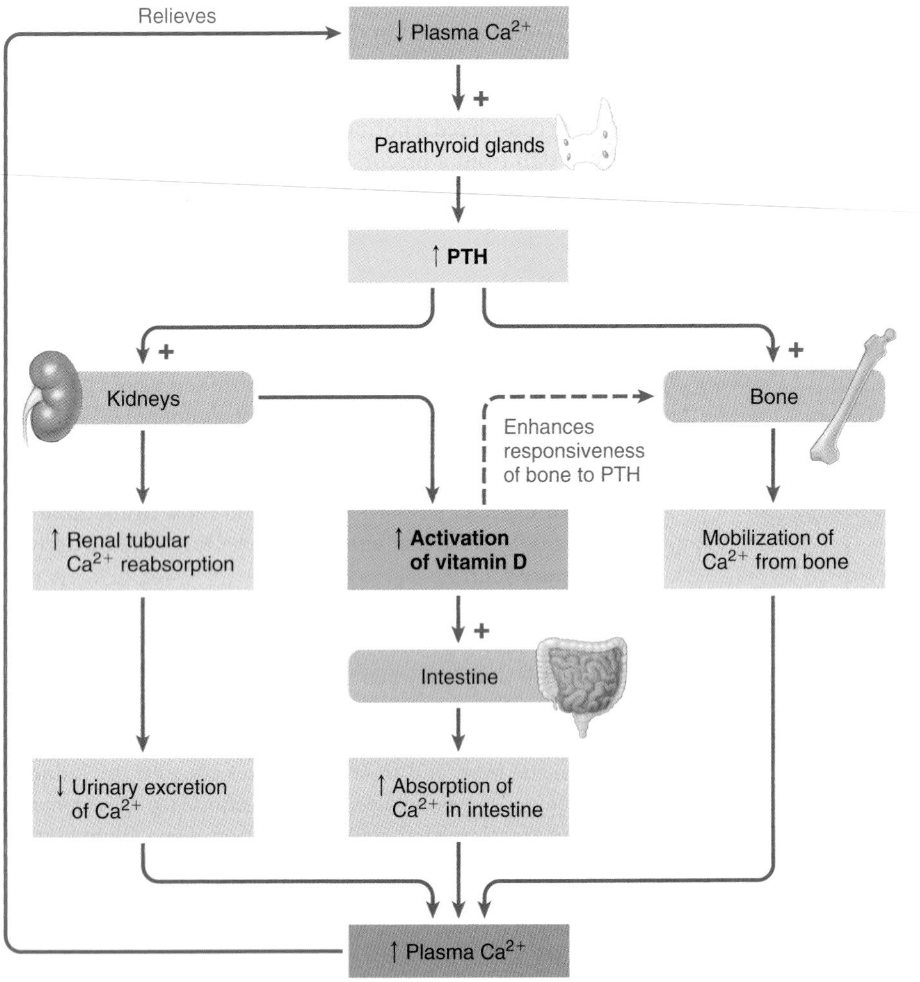

Disorders in Ca^{2+} metabolism may arise from abnormal levels of PTH or vitamin D.

 Clinical Note The primary disorders that affect Ca^{2+} metabolism are too much or too little PTH or a deficiency of vitamin D.

PTH HYPERSECRETION Excess PTH secretion, or **hyperparathyroidism,** which is usually caused by a hypersecreting tumor in one of the parathyroid glands, is characterized by hypercalcemia and hypophosphatemia. The affected individual can be asymptomatic or symptoms can be severe, depending on the magnitude of the problem. The following are among the possible consequences:

■ Hypercalcemia reduces the excitability of muscle and nervous tissue, leading to muscle weakness and neurologic disorders, including decreased alertness, poor memory, and depression. Cardiac disturbances may also occur.

■ Excessive mobilization of Ca^{2+} and PO_4^{3-} from skeletal stores leads to thinning of bone, which may result in skeletal deformities and increased incidence of fractures.

■ An increased incidence of Ca^{2+}-containing kidney stones occurs because the excess quantity of Ca^{2+} being filtered through the kidneys may precipitate and form stones. These stones may impair renal function. Passage of the stones through the ureters causes extreme pain. Because of these potential multiple consequences, hyperparathyroidism has been called a disease of "bones, stones, and abdominal groans."

■ To further account for the "abdominal groans," hypercalcemia can cause peptic ulcers, nausea, and constipation.

PTH HYPOSECRETION Because of the parathyroid glands' close anatomic relation to the thyroid, the most common cause of deficient PTH secretion, or **hypoparathyroidism,** used to be inadvertent removal of the parathyroid glands (before doctors knew about their existence) during surgical removal of the thyroid gland (to treat thyroid disease). If all the parathyroid tissue was removed, these patients died, of course, because PTH is essential for life. Physicians were puzzled why some patients died soon after thyroid removal but others did not. Now that the location and importance of the parathyroid glands are known, surgeons are careful to leave parathyroid tissue during thyroid removal.

Hypoparathyroidism leads to hypocalcemia and hyperphosphatemia.

● FIGURE 17-30 **Interactions between PTH and vitamin D in controlling plasma calcium.**

The symptoms are mainly caused by increased neuromuscular excitability from the reduced level of free plasma Ca^{2+}. In the complete absence of PTH, death is imminent. With a relative deficiency of PTH, milder symptoms of increased neuromuscular excitability become evident. Muscle cramps and twitches occur from spontaneous activity in the motor nerves, whereas tingling and pins-and-needles sensations result from spontaneous activity in the sensory nerves. Mental changes include irritability and paranoia.

VITAMIN D DEFICIENCY The major consequence of vitamin D deficiency is impaired intestinal absorption of Ca^{2+}. In the face of reduced Ca^{2+} uptake, PTH maintains the plasma Ca^{2+} level at the expense of the bones. As a result, the bone matrix is not properly mineralized, because Ca^{2+} salts are not available for deposition. The demineralized bones become soft and deformed, bowing under the pressures of weight bearing, especially in children. This condition is known as **rickets** in children and **osteomalacia** in adults (● Figure 17-31).

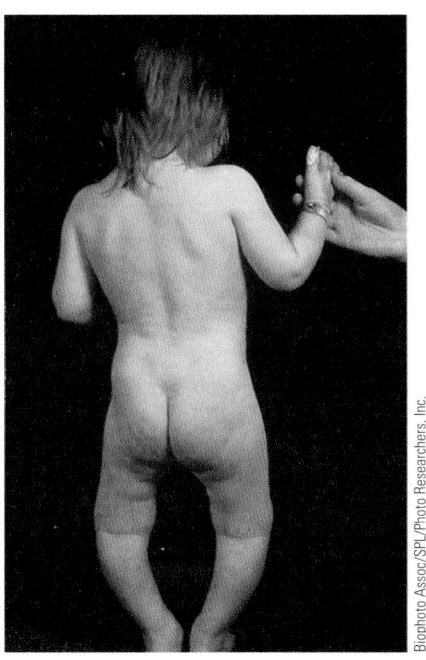

Biophoto Assoc/SPL/Photo Researchers, Inc.

● **FIGURE 17-31** **Rickets.**

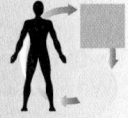

Chapter in Perspective: Focus on Homeostasis

The endocrine system is one of the body's two major regulatory systems, the other being the nervous system. Through its relatively slowly acting hormone messengers, the endocrine system generally regulates activities that require duration rather than speed. Endocrine glands secrete hormones in response to specific stimuli. The hormones, in turn, exert effects that act in negative-feedback fashion to resist the change that induced their secretion, thus maintaining stability in the internal environment. The specific contributions of the endocrine glands to homeostasis include the following:

- The hypothalamus–posterior pituitary unit secretes vasopressin, which acts on the kidneys to help maintain H_2O balance. Control of H_2O balance in turn is essential for maintaining ECF osmolarity and proper cell volume.
- For the most part, the hormones secreted by the anterior pituitary do not directly contribute to homeostasis. Instead, most are tropic; that is, they stimulate the secretion of other hormones.
- The pineal gland secretes melatonin, which helps entrain the body's circadian rhythm to the environmental cycle of light (period of activity) and dark (period of inactivity).
- Two closely related hormones secreted by the thyroid gland, tetraiodothyronine (T_4) and tri-iodothyronine (T_3), increase the overall basal metabolic rate. This action not only influences the rate at which cells use nutrient molecules and O_2 within the internal environment but also produces heat, which helps maintain body temperature.
- The adrenal cortex secretes three classes of hormones. Aldosterone, the primary mineralocorticoid, is essential for Na^+ and K^+ balance. Because of the osmotic effect of Na^+, its balance is critical to maintaining the proper ECF volume and arterial blood pressure. This action is essential for life. Without aldosterone's Na^+- and H_2O-conserving effect, so much plasma volume would be lost in the urine that death would quickly ensue. Maintaining K^+ balance is essential for homeostasis because changes in extracellular K^+ profoundly affect neuromuscular excitability, jeopardizing normal heart function, among other detrimental effects.
- Cortisol, the primary glucocorticoid secreted by the adrenal cortex, increases the plasma concentrations of glucose, fatty acids, and amino acids above normal. Although these actions destabilize the concentrations of these molecules in the internal environment, they indirectly contribute to homeostasis by making the molecules readily available as energy sources or building blocks for tissue repair to help the body adapt to stressful situations.
- The sex hormones secreted by the adrenal cortex do not contribute to homeostasis.
- The major hormone secreted by the adrenal medulla, epinephrine, generally reinforces activities of the sympathetic nervous system. It contributes to homeostasis directly by its role in blood pressure regulation. Epinephrine also contributes to homeostasis indirectly by helping prepare the body for peak physical responsiveness in fight-or-flight situations. This includes increasing the plasma concentrations of glucose and fatty acids above normal, which provides additional energy sources for increased physical activity.
- The two major hormones secreted by the endocrine pancreas, insulin and glucagon, are important in shifting metabolic pathways between the absorptive and the postabsorptive states, which maintains the appropriate plasma levels of nutrient molecules.
- Parathyroid hormone from the parathyroid glands is critical to maintaining plasma concentration of Ca^{2+}. PTH is essential for life because of the effect of Ca^{2+} on neuromuscular excitability. In the absence of PTH, death rapidly occurs from asphyxiation caused by pronounced spasms of the respiratory muscles.

Unrelated to homeostasis, hormones direct the growing process and control most aspects of the reproductive system.

Objective Questions (Answers on p. A-51)

1. All endocrine glands are exclusively endocrine in function. *(True or false?)*
2. Growth hormone levels in the blood are no higher during the early childhood growing years than during adulthood. *(True or false?)*
3. "Male" sex hormones are produced in both males and females by the adrenal cortex. *(True or false?)*
4. Excess glucose and amino acids, as well as fatty acids, can be stored as triglycerides. *(True or false?)*
5. Insulin is the only hormone that can lower blood glucose levels. *(True or false?)*
6. All ingested Ca^{2+} is indiscriminately absorbed in the intestine. *(True or false?)*
7. A hormone that has as its primary function the regulation of another endocrine gland is classified functionally as a _____ hormone.
8. The _____ in the hypothalamus is the body's master biological clock.
9. Activity within the cartilaginous layer of bone known as the _____ brings about lengthening of long bones.
10. The lumen of the thyroid follicle is filled with _____, the chief constituent of which is a large protein molecule known as _____.
11. _____ is the conversion of glucose into glycogen. _____ is the conversion of glycogen into glucose. _____ is the conversion of amino acids into glucose.
12. The three compartments with which ECF Ca^{2+} is exchanged are _____, _____, and _____.
13. Among the bone cells, _____ are bone builders, _____ are bone dissolvers, and _____ are entombed.
14. Indicate the relationships among the hormones in the hypothalamic–anterior pituitary–adrenal cortex system by using the following answer code to identify which hormone belongs in each blank:
    (a) cortisol
    (b) ACTH
    (c) CRH
    (1) _____ from the hypothalamus stimulates the secretion of (2) _____ from the anterior pituitary. (3) _____ in turn stimulates the secretion of (4) _____ from the adrenal cortex. In negative-feedback fashion, (5) _____ inhibits secretion of (6) _____ and (7) _____.

15. Indicate the primary circulating form and the storage form of each of the three classes of organic nutrients:

	Primary Circulating Form	Primary Storage Form
Carbohydrate	1. _____	2. _____
Fat	3. _____	4. _____
Protein	5. _____	6. _____

Essay Questions

1. List the overall functions of the endocrine system.
2. How is the plasma concentration of a hormone normally regulated?
3. List and briefly state the functions of the posterior pituitary hormones.
4. List and briefly state the functions of the anterior pituitary hormones.
5. Compare the relationship between the hypothalamus and the posterior pituitary with the relationship between the hypothalamus and the anterior pituitary. Describe the role of the hypothalamic–hypophyseal portal system and the hypothalamic releasing and inhibiting hormones.
6. Describe the metabolic actions of growth hormone (GH) that are unrelated to growth. What are GH's growth-promoting actions? What is the role of IGF?
7. Discuss the control of GH secretion.
8. Describe the steps of thyroid hormone synthesis.
9. What are the effects of T_3 and T_4? Which is the more potent? What is the source of most circulating T_3?
10. Describe the regulation of thyroid hormone.
11. What hormones are secreted by the adrenal cortex? What are the functions and control of each of these hormones?
12. What is the relationship of the adrenal medulla to the sympathetic nervous system? What are the functions of epinephrine? How is epinephrine release controlled?
13. Define stress. Describe the neural and hormonal responses to a stressor.
14. Define *fuel metabolism, anabolism,* and *catabolism.*
15. Distinguish between the absorptive and the postabsorptive states with regard to the handling of nutrient molecules.
16. Name the two major cell types of the islets of Langerhans, and indicate the hormonal product of each.
17. Compare the functions and control of insulin secretion with those of glucagon secretion.
18. Why must plasma Ca^{2+} be closely regulated?
19. Discuss the contributions of parathyroid hormone (PTH), calcitonin, and vitamin D to Ca^{2+} metabolism. Describe the source and control of each of these hormones.

(Explanations on p. A-51)

1. Why would males with testicular feminization syndrome be unusually tall?

2. Gigantism caused by a pituitary tumor is usually treated by surgically removing the pituitary gland. What hormonal replacement therapy would have to be instituted following this procedure?

3. Iodine is naturally present in saltwater and is abundant in soil along coastal regions. Fish and shellfish living in the ocean and plants grown in coastal soil take up iodine from their environment. Fresh water does not contain iodine, and the soil becomes more iron poor the farther inland it is. Knowing this, explain why the midwestern United States was once known as an endemic goiter belt. Why is this region no longer an endemic goiter belt even though the soil is still iodine poor?

4. Why would an infection tend to raise the blood glucose level of a diabetic individual?

5. Tapping the facial nerve at the angle of the jaw in a patient with moderate hyposecretion of a particular hormone elicits a characteristic grimace on that side of the face. What endocrine abnormality could give rise to this *Chvostek's sign*?

CLINICAL CONSIDERATION

(Explanation on p. A-51)

Najma G. sought medical attention after her menstrual periods ceased and she started growing excessive facial hair. Also, she had been thirstier than usual and urinated more frequently. A clinical evaluation revealed that Najma was hyperglycemic. Her physician told her that she had an endocrine disorder dubbed "diabetes of bearded ladies." Based on her symptoms and your knowledge of the endocrine system, what underlying defect do you think she has?

Chapter 17

Study Card

General Principles of Endocrinology (pp. 527–530)

■ The endocrine system is important in regulating organic metabolism, H_2O and electrolyte balance, growth, and reproduction and in stress adaptation. Some hormones are tropic, meaning their function is to stimulate and maintain other endocrine glands. *(Review Figure 17-1 and Table 17-1.)*

■ The effective plasma concentration of each hormone is normally controlled by regulated changes in the rate of hormone secretion via (1) neural input, which increases hormone secretion in response to a specific need and governs diurnal variations in secretion, and (2) input from another hormone, which involves either stimulatory input from a tropic hormone or inhibitory input from a target-cell hormone in negative-feedback fashion. *(Review Figures 17-2 and 17-6.)*

Hypothalamus and Pituitary (pp. 531–538)

■ The pituitary gland consists of two distinct lobes, the posterior pituitary and the anterior pituitary. *(Review Figure 17-3.)*

■ The posterior pituitary is a neural extension of the hypothalamus. Neuronal cell bodies in the hypothalamus synthesize two small peptide hormones, vasopressin and oxytocin, which pass down the axon to be stored in nerve terminals within the posterior pituitary, from which they are released into the blood on stimulation by the hypothalamus. *(Review Figure 17-4.)*

■ The anterior pituitary secretes six different peptide hormones that it produces itself: thyroid-stimulating hormone (TSH), adrenocorticotropic hormone (ACTH), follicle-stimulating hormone (FSH), luteinizing hormone (LH), growth hormone (GH), and prolactin (PRL). *(Review Figure 17-5.)*

■ The anterior pituitary releases its hormones into the blood at the bidding of hypophysiotropic releasing and inhibiting hormones carried from the hypothalamus to the anterior pituitary through the hypothalamic–hypophyseal portal system. Both the hypothalamus and the anterior pituitary are inhibited in negative-feedback fashion by the product of the target endocrine gland. *(Review Table 17-2 and Figures 17-6 and 17-7.)*

Endocrine Control of Growth (pp. 538–542)

■ GH promotes growth indirectly by stimulating liver production of insulin-like growth factor (IGF), which acts directly on soft tissues and bone to cause growth by stimulating protein synthesis, cell division, and lengthening and thickening of bones. Unrelated to growth, GH also conserves carbohydrates and mobilizes fat stores by its direct actions on skeletal muscle and adipose tissue *(Review Figures 17-8 and 17-9.)*

■ GH secretion by the anterior pituitary is regulated by two hypothalamic hormones, growth hormone–releasing hormone (GHRH) and growth hormone–inhibiting hormone (somatostatin). GH and IGF both inhibit GHRH and stimulate soma-tostatin. The primary signals for increased GH secretion (exercise, stress, and low blood glucose) are related to metabolic needs rather than growth. *(Review Figure 17-9.)*

Pineal Gland and Circadian Rhythms (pp. 542–544)

■ The suprachiasmatic nucleus (SCN) is the body's master biological clock. Cyclic variations in the concentration of SCN clock proteins drive the body's circadian (daily) rhythms.

■ Each day, the body's circadian rhythms must be entrained or adjusted to keep pace with environmental cues so that the internal rhythms are synchronized with the external light–dark cycle. Special light receptors in the eyes send input to the SCN. Acting through the SCN, the pineal gland's secretion of the hormone melatonin rhythmically decreases in the light and increases in the dark. Melatonin, in turn, synchronizes the body's natural circadian rhythms, such as diurnal (day–night) variations in hormone secretion and body temperature, with external cues such as the light–dark cycle.

Thyroid Gland (pp. 545–549)

■ The thyroid gland contains two types of endocrine secretory cells: (1) follicular cells, which produce the iodide-containing hormones, thyroxine or tetraiodothyronine (T_4) and tri-iodo-thyronine (T_3), collectively known as thyroid hormone, and (2) C cells, which synthesize a Ca^{2+}-regulating hormone, calcitonin. *(Review Figure 17-12.)*

■ Most steps of thyroid hormone synthesis take place on large thyroglobulin molecules within the colloid, an "inland" extracellular site within the interior of the spherical thyroid follicles. *(Review Figure 17-13.)*

■ Thyroid hormone is the primary determinant of the overall basal metabolic rate of the body. By accelerating metabolic rate, it increases heat production. It also enhances the actions of the sympathetic catecholamines and is essential for normal growth and for development and function of the nervous system.

■ Thyroid hormone secretion is regulated by a negative-feedback loop among hypothalamic TRH, anterior pituitary TSH, and thyroid gland T_3 and T_4. Cold exposure in newborn infants is the only input for increasing thyroid hormone secretion. *(Review Figure 17-14.)*

Adrenal Glands (pp. 549–555)

■ Each adrenal gland (of the pair) consists of two separate endocrine organs—an outer, steroid-secreting adrenal cortex and an inner, catecholamine-secreting adrenal medulla. *(Review Figure 17-18.)*

■ The adrenal cortex produces three categories of steroid hormones: mineralocorticoids (aldosterone), glucocorticoids (cortisol), and adrenal sex hormones (primarily the weak androgen, dehydroepiandrosterone). *(Review Figure 17-18.)*

■ Aldosterone regulates Na^+ and K^+ balance and is important for blood pressure homeostasis, which is achieved secondarily by the osmotic effect of Na^+ in maintaining the plasma volume, a lifesaving effect. Aldosterone is controlled by the renin–angiotensin–aldosterone system (RAAS) and by a direct effect of K^+ on the adrenal cortex. *(Review Figure 13-16, p. 424).*

■ Cortisol helps regulate fuel metabolism and is important in stress adaptation. It increases blood glucose, amino acids, and fatty acids and spares glucose for use by the glucose-dependent brain. The mobilized organic molecules are available for use as needed for energy or repair. Cortisol secretion is regulated by a negative-feedback loop involving hypothalamic CRH and pituitary ACTH. Stress is the most potent stimulus for cortisol secretion. *(Review Figures 17-2, 17-6, 17-19, and 17-22.)*

■ The adrenal medulla consists of modified sympathetic postganglionic neurons that secrete epinephrine into the blood in response to sympathetic stimulation. Epinephrine reinforces the sympathetic system in mounting fight-or-flight responses and in maintaining arterial blood pressure. It also increases blood glucose and blood fatty acids. *(Review Figures 7-2, p. 193 and 17-22.)*

Integrated Stress Response (pp. 555–557)

■ *Stress* is the body's generalized nonspecific response to any factor that threatens to overwhelm the ability to maintain homeostasis. A *stressor* is any noxious stimulus that elicits the stress response. *(Review Figure 17-21.)*

■ The stress response includes (1) increased sympathetic and epinephrine activity (prepares the body for fight-or-flight), (2) activation of the CRH–ACTH–cortisol axis (mobilizes metabolic resources), and (3) increased activity of RAAS and vasopressin (maintains blood volume and blood pressure), all coordinated by the hypothalamus. *(Review Figure 17-22.)*

Endocrine Pancreas and Control of Fuel Metabolism (pp. 557–568)

■ Intermediary or fuel metabolism is, collectively, the synthesis (anabolism), breakdown (catabolism), and transformations of the three classes of energy-rich organic nutrients—carbohydrates, fats, and proteins—within the body. Glucose and fatty acids derived from carbohydrates and fats, respectively, are primarily used as metabolic fuels; amino acids derived from proteins are primarily used for synthesis of structural and enzymatic proteins. *(Review Tables 17-3 and 17-4 and Figure 17-23.)*

■ During the *absorptive state* following a meal, excess absorbed nutrients not immediately needed for energy production or protein synthesis are stored to a limited extent as glycogen in the liver and muscle but mostly as triglycerides in adipose tissue. During the *postabsorptive state* between meals when no new nutrients are entering the blood, the glycogen and triglyceride stores are catabolized to release nutrient molecules into the blood. If necessary, body proteins are degraded to release amino acids for conversion into glucose (gluconeogenesis). The blood glucose concentration must be maintained above a critical level because the brain depends on blood-delivered glucose as its energy source. Tissues not dependent on glucose switch to fatty

acids as their metabolic fuel, sparing glucose for the brain. *(Review Table 17-5.)*

■ The shifts in metabolic pathways between the absorptive and the postabsorptive states are controlled by hormones, most importantly insulin. Insulin is secreted by the β cells of the islets of Langerhans in the endocrine pancreas. Insulin is an anabolic hormone; it promotes the cellular uptake of glucose, fatty acids, and amino acids and enhances their conversion into glycogen, triglycerides, and proteins, respectively. In so doing, it lowers the blood concentrations of these small organic molecules. Insulin secretion is increased during the absorptive state, primarily by a direct effect of elevated blood glucose on the β cells. *(Review Figures 17-24 through 17-27.)*

■ Glucagon, secreted by the pancreatic α cells, mobilizes the energy-rich molecules from their stores during the postabsorptive state. It is secreted in response to a direct effect of a fall in blood glucose on the α cells. *(Review Figures 17-24 and 17-27.)*

Parathyroid Glands and Control of Calcium Metabolism (pp. 568–573)

■ Changes in the concentration of free, diffusible (biologically active) plasma Ca^{2+} produce profound and life-threatening effects on neuromuscular excitability. Hypercalcemia reduces excitability, whereas hypocalcemia causes overexcitability of nerves and muscles. If the overexcitability is severe enough, fatal spastic contractions of respiratory muscles can occur.

■ Control of plasma Ca^{2+} depends on hormonally regulated exchanges between the ECF and three compartments—bone, kidneys, and intestine—by three hormones: parathyroid hormone (PTH), calcitonin, and vitamin D.

■ Bone consists of an organic extracellular matrix, the osteoid, which is hardened by via $Ca_3(PO_4)_2$ crystals. Bone constantly undergoes remodeling via bone-dissolving osteoclasts and bone-building osteoblasts. Entombed osteocytes are "retired" osteoblasts that have deposited bone around themselves.

■ PTH, whose secretion is directly increased by a fall in plasma Ca^{2+}, acts directly on bone and the kidneys and indirectly on the intestine to raise plasma Ca^{2+}. In so doing, it is essential for life by preventing the fatal consequences of hypocalcemia. PTH promotes Ca^{2+} movement from the bone fluid into the plasma in the short term and promotes localized dissolution of bone in the long term. *(Review Figure 17-29.)*

■ Dissolution of $Ca_3(PO_4)_2$ bone crystals releases PO_4^{3-}, as well as Ca^{2+}, into the plasma. PTH acts on the kidneys to conserve Ca^{2+} and eliminate PO_3^- during urine formation, which is important because a rise in plasma PO_4^{3-} would force the redeposition of some of the plasma Ca^{2+} back into the bone.

■ PTH facilitates activation of vitamin D (from the diet or made in the skin on sun exposure), which in turn stimulates Ca^{2+} and PO_4^{3-} absorption from the intestine. Vitamin D must be activated first by the liver and then by the kidneys (the site of PTH regulation of vitamin D activation) before it can exert its effect. *(Review Figure 17-27.)*

■ Calcitonin, a hormone produced by the thyroid C cells, is secreted in the rare instances when plasma Ca^{2+} is too high and acts on bone and kidneys to lower plasma Ca^{2+}. *(Review Figure 17-29.)*

577

Reproductive System

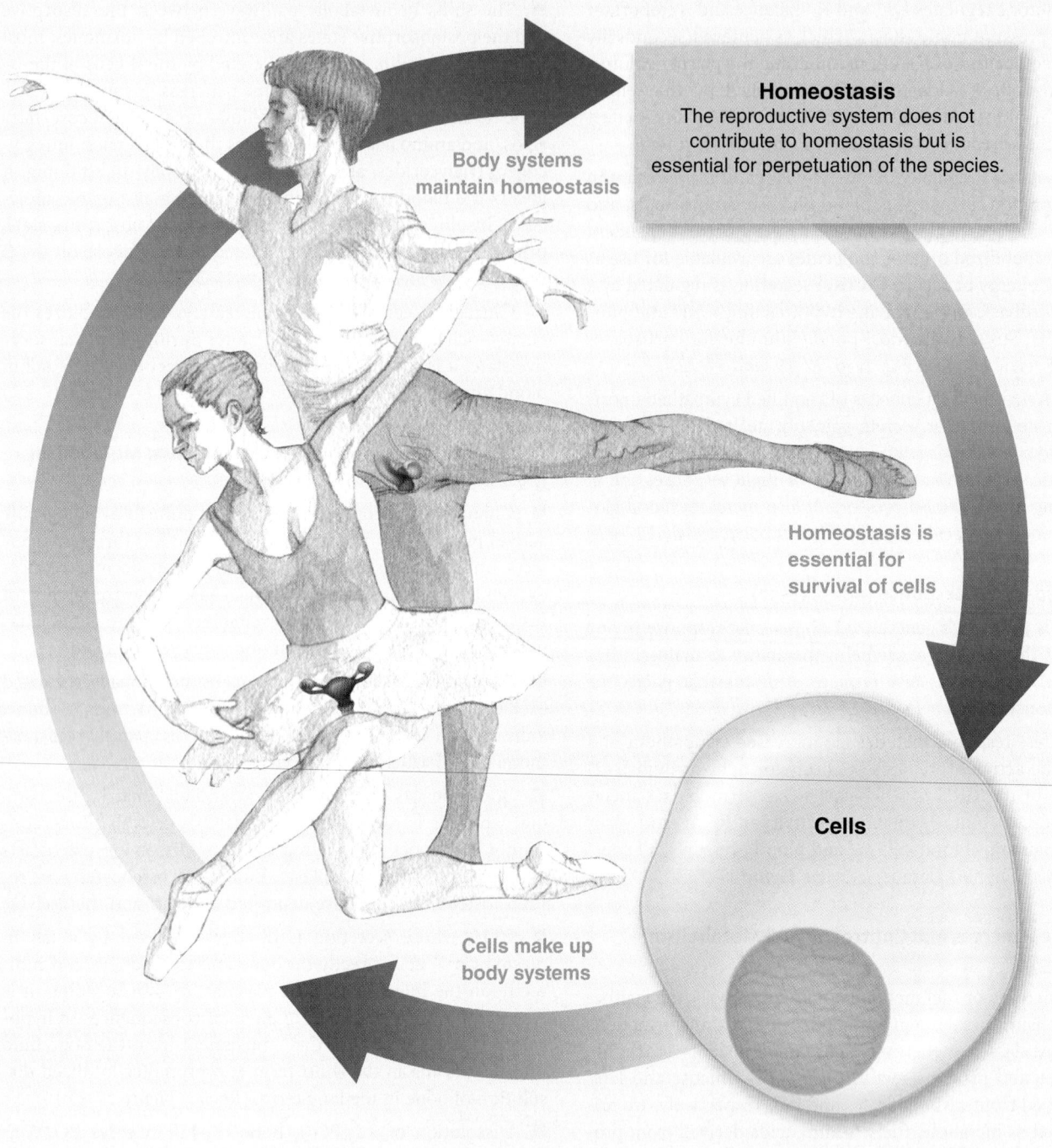

Body systems maintain homeostasis

Homeostasis
The reproductive system does not contribute to homeostasis but is essential for perpetuation of the species.

Homeostasis is essential for survival of cells

Cells

Cells make up body systems

Normal functioning of the **reproductive system** is not aimed at homeostasis and is not necessary for survival of an individual, but it is essential for survival of the species. Only through reproduc-

tion can the complex genetic blueprint of each species survive beyond the lives of individual members of the species.

The Reproductive System

CHAPTER AT A GLANCE

Uniqueness of the Reproductive System

Unique among body systems: no contribution to homeostasis

Unique anatomy of the reproductive systems between the sexes

Unique sex determination and sexual differentiation between males and females

Male Reproductive Physiology

Scrotal location of the testes

Testosterone secretion

Spermatogenesis

Puberty

Male reproductive tract

Male accessory sex glands

Prostaglandins

Sexual Intercourse between Males and Females

Male sex act

Female sex act

Female Reproductive Physiology

Ovarian function

Menstrual cycle

Puberty; menopause

Fertilization

Implantation; placentation

Gestation

Parturition

Lactation

Uniqueness of the Reproductive System

The central theme of this book has been the physiologic processes aimed at maintaining homeostasis to ensure survival of the individual. We are now going to leave this theme to discuss the reproductive system, which serves primarily the purpose of perpetuating the species.

Unique among body systems, the reproductive system does not contribute to homeostasis but exerts other important effects.

Even though the reproductive system does not contribute to homeostasis and is not essential for survival of an individual, it still plays an important role in a person's life. For example, the manner in which people relate as sexual beings contributes in significant ways to psychosocial behavior and has important influences on how people view themselves and how they interact with others. Reproductive function also has a profound effect on society. The universal organization of societies into family units provides a stable environment that is conducive for perpetuating our species.

Reproductive capability depends on intricate relationships among the hypothalamus, anterior pituitary, reproductive organs, and target cells of the sex hormones. In addition to these basic biological processes, sexual behavior and attitudes are deeply influenced by emotional factors and the sociocultural mores of the society in which the individual lives. We concentrate on the basic sexual and reproductive functions under nervous and hormonal control and do not examine the psychological and social ramifications of sexual behavior.

The reproductive system includes the gonads, reproductive tract, and accessory sex glands, all of which are different in males and females.

Reproduction depends on the union of male and female **gametes (reproductive, or germ, cells),** each with a half set of chromosomes, to form a new individual with a full, unique set of chromosomes. Unlike the other body systems, which are essentially identical in the two sexes, the reproductive systems of males and females are markedly different, befitting their different roles in the reproductive process. The **male** and **female reproductive systems** are designed to enable union of genetic material from the two sexual partners, and the female system is equipped to house and nourish the offspring to the developmental point at which it can survive independently in the external environment.

The **primary reproductive organs,** or **gonads,** consist of a pair of **testes** in the male and a pair of **ovaries** in the female. In both sexes, the mature gonads perform the dual function of (1) producing gametes **(gametogenesis),** that is, **spermatozoa (sperm)** in the male and **ova (eggs)** in the female, and (2) secreting sex hormones, specifically, **testosterone** in males and **estrogen** and **progesterone** in females.

In addition to the gonads, the reproductive system in each sex includes a **reproductive tract** encompassing a system of ducts specialized to transport or house the gametes after they are produced, plus **accessory sex glands** that empty their supportive secretions into these passageways. In females, the *breasts* are also considered accessory reproductive organs. The externally visible portions of the reproductive system are known as **external genitalia.**

SECONDARY SEXUAL CHARACTERISTICS The **secondary sexual characteristics** are the many external characteristics not directly involved in reproduction that distinguish males and females, such as body configuration and hair distribution. In humans, for example, males have broader shoulders, whereas females have curvier hips, and males have beards, whereas females do not. Testosterone in the male and estrogen in the female govern the development and maintenance of these characteristics. Progesterone has no influence on secondary sexual characteristics. Even though growth of axillary and pubic hair is promoted at puberty in both sexes by androgens—testosterone in males and adrenocortical dehydroepiandrosterone in females (see p. 553)—this hair growth is not a secondary sexual characteristic, because both sexes display this feature.

In some species, the secondary sexual characteristics are of great importance in courting and mating behavior; for example, the rooster's comb attracts the female's attention, and the stag's antlers are useful to ward off other males. In humans, the differentiating marks between males and females do attract the opposite sex, but attraction is also strongly influenced by the complexities of human society and cultural behavior.

OVERVIEW OF MALE REPRODUCTIVE FUNCTIONS AND ORGANS The essential reproductive functions of the male are as follows:

1. Production of sperm *(spermatogenesis)*

2. Delivery of sperm to the female

The sperm-producing organs, the testes, are suspended outside the abdominal cavity in a skin-covered sac, the **scrotum,** which lies within the angle between the legs. The male reproductive system is designed to deliver sperm to the female reproductive tract in a liquid vehicle, *semen,* which is conducive to sperm viability. The major **male accessory sex glands,** whose secretions provide the bulk of the semen, are the *seminal vesicles, prostate gland,* and *bulbourethral glands* (● Figure 18-1). The **penis** is the organ used to deposit semen in the female. Sperm exit each testis through the **male reproductive tract,** consisting on each side of an *epididymis* and *ductus (vas) deferens.* These pairs of reproductive tubes empty into a single *urethra,* the canal that runs the length of the penis and empties to the exterior. These parts of the male reproductive system are described more thoroughly when their functions are discussed.

OVERVIEW OF FEMALE REPRODUCTIVE FUNCTIONS AND ORGANS The female's role in reproduction is more complicated than the male's. The essential female reproductive functions include the following:

1. Production of ova *(oogenesis)*

2. Reception of sperm

3. Transport of the sperm and ovum to a common site for union *(fertilization,* or *conception)*

4. Maintenance of the developing fetus until it can survive in the outside world *(gestation,* or *pregnancy),* including formation of the *placenta,* the organ of exchange between mother and fetus

5. Giving birth to the baby *(parturition)*

6. Nourishing the infant after birth by milk production *(lactation)*

The product of fertilization is known as an **embryo** during the first 2 months of intrauterine development, when tissue differentiation is taking place. Beyond this time, the developing living being is recognizable as human and is known as a **fetus** during the remainder of gestation. Although no further tissue differentiation takes place during fetal life, it is a time of tremendous tissue growth and maturation.

The ovaries and female reproductive tract lie within the pelvic cavity. The female reproductive tract consists of the following components (● Figure 18-2a and b): Two **oviducts (uterine,** or **Fallopian tubes),** which are in close association with the two ovaries, pick up ova on ovulation (ovum release from an ovary) and serve as the site for fertilization. The thick-walled, hollow **uterus** is primarily responsible for maintaining the fetus during its development and expelling it at the end of pregnancy. The **vagina** is a muscular, expandable tube that connects the uterus to the external environment. The lowest portion of the uterus, the **cervix,** projects into the vagina and contains a single, small opening, the **cervical canal.** Sperm are deposited in the vagina by the penis during sexual intercourse. The cervical canal is a pathway for sperm through the uterus to the site of fertilization in the oviduct and, when greatly dilated during parturition, is the passageway for delivery of the baby from the uterus.

The vaginal opening is located in the **perineal region** between the urethral opening anteriorly and the anal opening posteriorly (● Figure 18-2c). It is partially covered by a thin mucous membrane, the **hymen,** which typically is physically disrupted by the first sexual intercourse. The vaginal and urethral openings are surrounded laterally by two pairs of skin folds, the **labia minora** and **labia majora.** The smaller labia minora are located medially to the more prominent labia majora. The **clitoris,** an erotic structure composed of tissue similar to that of the penis, lies at the anterior end of the folds of the labia minora. The female external genitalia are collectively referred to as the **vulva.**

Reproductive cells each contain a half set of chromosomes.

The deoxyribonucleic acid (DNA) molecules that carry the cell's genetic code are not randomly crammed into the nucleus but are precisely organized into **chromosomes** (see p. A-18). Each chromosome consists of a different DNA molecule that contains a unique set of genes. **Somatic cells** contain 46 chromosomes (the **diploid number**), which can be sorted into 23 pairs on the basis of various distinguishing features (*somatic* means "body"). Chromosomes composing a matched pair are termed **homologous chromosomes,** one member of each pair having

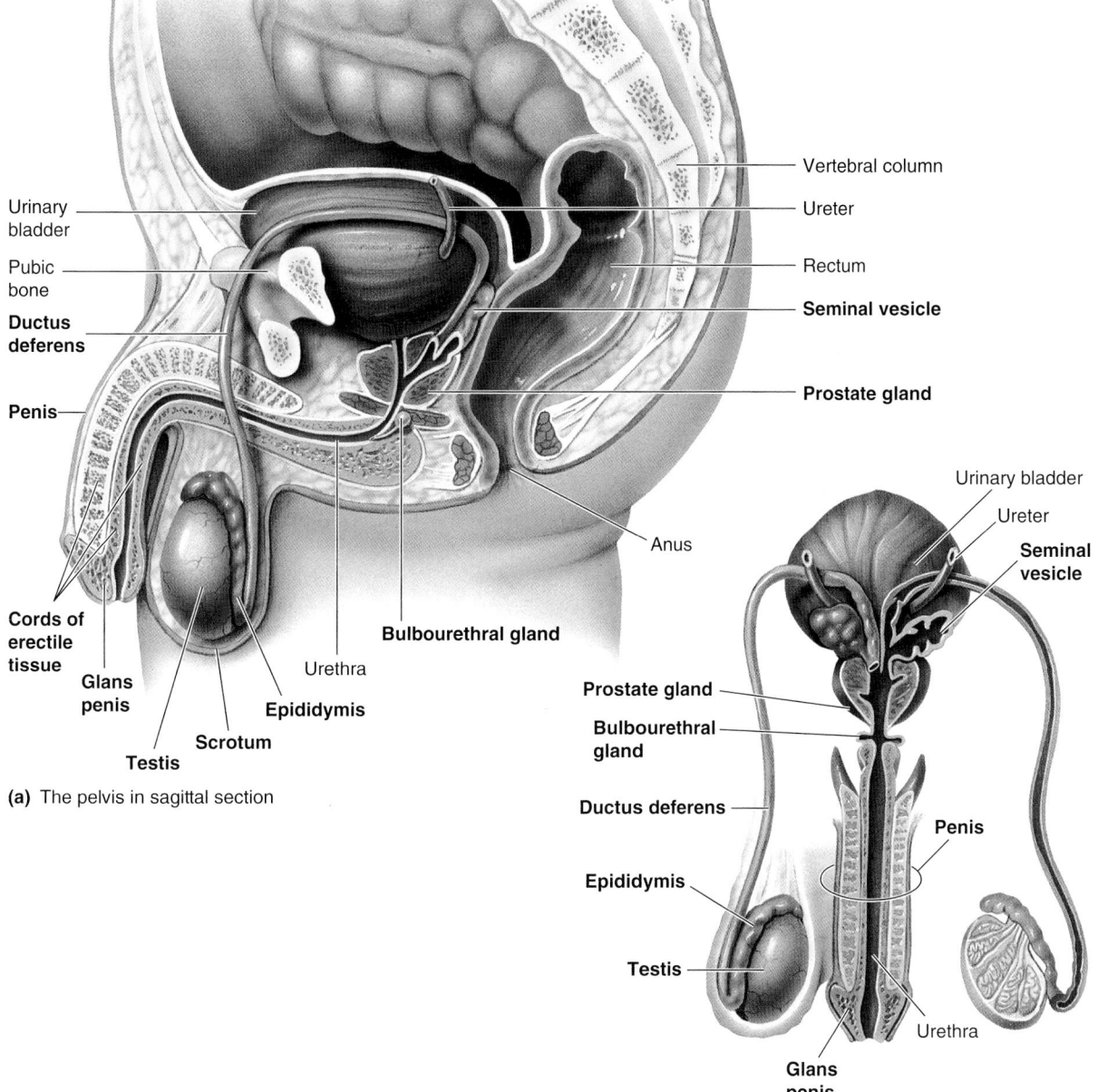

Urinary bladder

Pubic bone

Ductus deferens

Penis

Cords of erectile tissue

Glans penis

Testis

Scrotum

Epididymis

Urethra

Bulbourethral gland

Vertebral column

Ureter

Rectum

Seminal vesicle

Prostate gland

Anus

(a) The pelvis in sagittal section

Urinary bladder

Ureter

Seminal vesicle

Prostate gland

Bulbourethral gland

Ductus deferens

Epididymis

Penis

Testis

Urethra

Glans penis

● **FIGURE 18-1 The male reproductive system.**

(b) Posterior view of the reproductive organs

been derived from the individual's mother and the other member from the father. Gametes (that is, sperm and eggs) contain only one member of each homologous pair for a total of 23 chromosomes (the **haploid number**).

Gametogenesis is accomplished by meiosis, resulting in genetically unique sperm and ova.

Most cells in the human body have the ability to reproduce themselves, a process important in growth, replacement, and repair of tissues. Cell division involves two components: division of the nucleus and division of the cytoplasm. Nuclear division in somatic cells is accomplished by **mitosis.** In mitosis, the chromosomes replicate (make duplicate copies of themselves); then, the identical chromosomes are separated so that a complete set of genetic information (that is, a diploid number of

chromosomes) is distributed to each of the two new daughter cells. Nuclear division in the specialized case of gametes is accomplished by **meiosis,** in which only a half set of genetic information (that is, a haploid number of chromosomes) is distributed to each of four new daughter cells (see p. A-27).

During meiosis, a specialized diploid germ cell undergoes one chromosome replication followed by two nuclear divisions. In the first meiotic division, the replicated chromosomes do not separate into two individual, identical chromosomes but remain joined. The doubled chromosomes sort themselves into homologous pairs, and the pairs separate so that each of two daughter cells receives a half set of doubled chromosomes. During the second meiotic division, the doubled chromosomes within each of the two daughter cells separate and are distributed into two cells, yielding four daughter cells, each containing a half set of chromosomes, a single member of each pair. During this process,

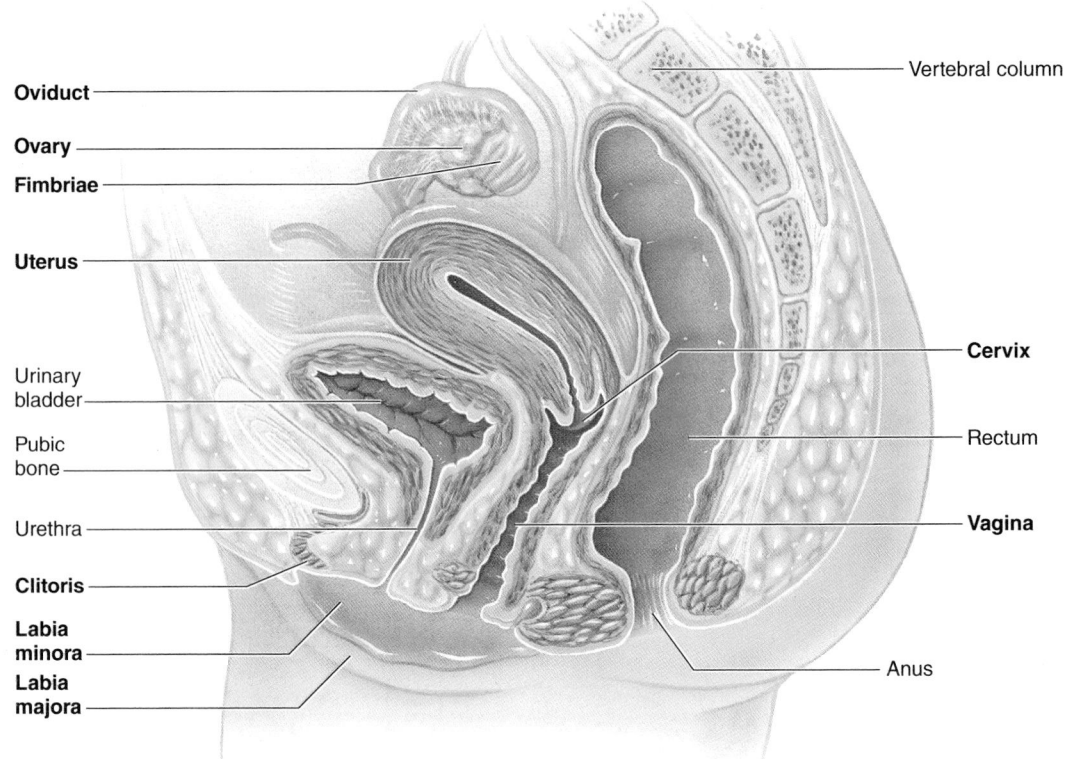

Oviduct

Ovary

Fimbriae

Uterus

Urinary bladder

Pubic bone

Urethra

Clitoris

Labia minora

Labia majora

Vertebral column

Cervix

Rectum

Vagina

Anus

(a) The pelvis in sagittal section

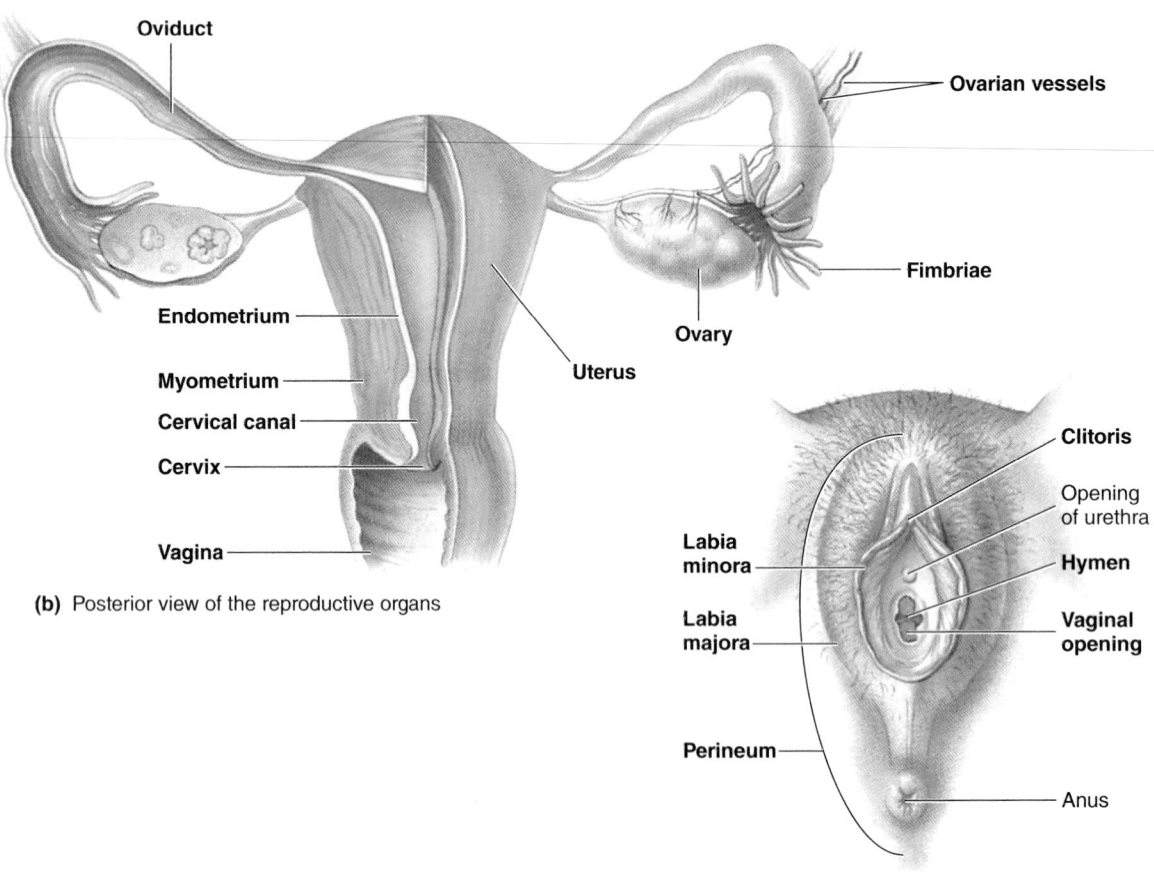

Oviduct

Ovarian vessels

Fimbriae

Ovary

Endometrium

Myometrium

Cervical canal

Cervix

Uterus

Vagina

(b) Posterior view of the reproductive organs

Clitoris

Opening of urethra

Hymen

Vaginal opening

Labia minora

Labia majora

Perineum

Anus

(c) Perineal view of the external genitalia

● FIGURE 18-2 **The female reproductive system.**

the maternally and paternally derived chromosomes of each homologous pair are distributed to the daughter cells in random assortments containing one member of each chromosome pair without regard for its original derivation. That is, not all of the mother-derived chromosomes go to one daughter cell and the father-derived chromosomes to the other cell. More than 8 million (2^{23}) mixtures of the 23 paternal and maternal chromosomes are possible. This genetic mixing provides novel combinations of chromosomes. Crossing-over contributes even further to genetic diversity. *Crossing-over* refers to the physical exchange of chromosome material between the homologous pairs prior to their separation during the first meiotic division (see p. A-27).

Thus, sperm and ova each have a unique haploid number of chromosomes. When fertilization takes place, a sperm and ovum fuse to form the start of a new individual with 46 chromosomes, one member of each chromosomal pair having been inherited from the mother and the other member from the father.

The sex of an individual is determined by the combination of sex chromosomes.

Whether individuals are destined to be males or females is a genetic phenomenon determined by the sex chromosomes they possess. As the 23 chromosome pairs are separated during meiosis, each sperm or ovum receives only one member of each chromosome pair. Of the chromosome pairs, 22 are **autosomal chromosomes** that code for general human characteristics, as well as for specific traits such as eye color. The remaining pair of chromosomes consists of the **sex chromosomes,** of which there are two genetically different types—a larger **X chromosome** and a smaller **Y chromosome.**

Sex determination depends on the combination of sex chromosomes: **Genetic males** have both an X and a Y sex chromosome; **genetic females** have two X sex chromosomes. Thus, the genetic difference responsible for all the anatomic and functional distinctions between males and females is the single Y chromosome. Males have it; females do not.

As a result of meiosis during gametogenesis, all chromosome pairs are separated so that each daughter cell contains only one member of each pair, including the sex chromosome pair. When the XY sex chromosome pair separates during sperm formation, half the sperm receive an X chromosome and the other half a Y chromosome. In contrast, during oogenesis, every ovum receives an X chromosome because separation of the XX sex chromosome pair yields only X chromosomes. During fertilization, combination of an X-bearing sperm with an X-bearing ovum produces a genetic female, XX, whereas union of a Y-bearing sperm with an X-bearing ovum results in a genetic male, XY. Thus, genetic sex is determined at the time of conception and depends on which type of sex chromosome is contained within the fertilizing sperm.

Sexual differentiation along male or female lines depends on the presence or absence of masculinizing determinants.

Differences between males and females exist at three sex levels: genetic, gonadal, and phenotypic (anatomic) (● Figure 18-3).

GENETIC AND GONADAL SEX **Genetic sex,** which depends on the combination of sex chromosomes at the time of conception, in turn determines **gonadal sex,** that is, whether testes or ovaries develop. The presence or absence of a Y chromosome determines gonadal differentiation. For the first month and a half of gestation, all embryos have the potential to differentiate along either male or female lines because the developing reproductive tissues of both sexes are identical and indifferent. Gonadal specificity appears during the seventh week of intrauterine life when the indifferent gonadal tissue of a genetic male begins to differentiate into testes under the influence of the **sex-determining region of the Y chromosome (SRY),** the single gene responsible for sex determination. This gene triggers a chain of reactions that leads to physical development of a male. SRY "masculinizes" the gonads by coding for production of **testis-determining factor (TDF)** within primitive gonadal cells. TDF directs a series of events that leads to differentiation of the gonads into testes. Because genetic females lack the SRY gene and consequently do not produce TDF, their gonadal cells never receive a signal for testes formation, so by default during the ninth week the undifferentiated gonadal tissue starts developing into ovaries instead.

PHENOTYPIC SEX **Phenotypic sex,** the apparent anatomic sex of an individual, is hormonally mediated and depends on the genetically determined gonadal sex. The term **sexual differentiation** refers to the embryonic development of the external genitalia and reproductive tract along either male or female lines. As with the undifferentiated gonads, embryos of both sexes have the potential to develop male or female external genitalia and reproductive tracts. For example, the same embryonic tissue can develop into either a penis or a clitoris. Differentiation into a male-type reproductive system is induced by androgens, which are masculinizing hormones secreted by the developing testes. Testosterone is the most potent androgen. The absence of these testicular hormones in female fetuses results in the development of a female-type reproductive system. By 10 to 12 weeks of gestation, the sexes can easily be distinguished by the anatomic appearance of the external genitalia.

Note that the undifferentiated embryonic reproductive tissue passively develops into a female structure unless actively acted on by masculinizing factors. In the absence of male testicular hormones, a female reproductive tract and external genitalia develop regardless of the genetic sex of the individual. For feminization of the fetal genital tissue, ovaries do not even need to be present. Such a control pattern for determining sexual differentiation is appropriate, considering that fetuses of both sexes are exposed to high concentrations of female sex hormones throughout gestation. If female sex hormones influenced the development of the reproductive tract and external genitalia, all fetuses would be feminized.

 ERRORS IN SEXUAL DIFFERENTIATION Genetic sex and phenotypic sex are usually compatible; that is, a genetic male anatomically appears to be a male and functions as a male, and the same compatibility holds true for females. Occasionally, however, discrepancies occur

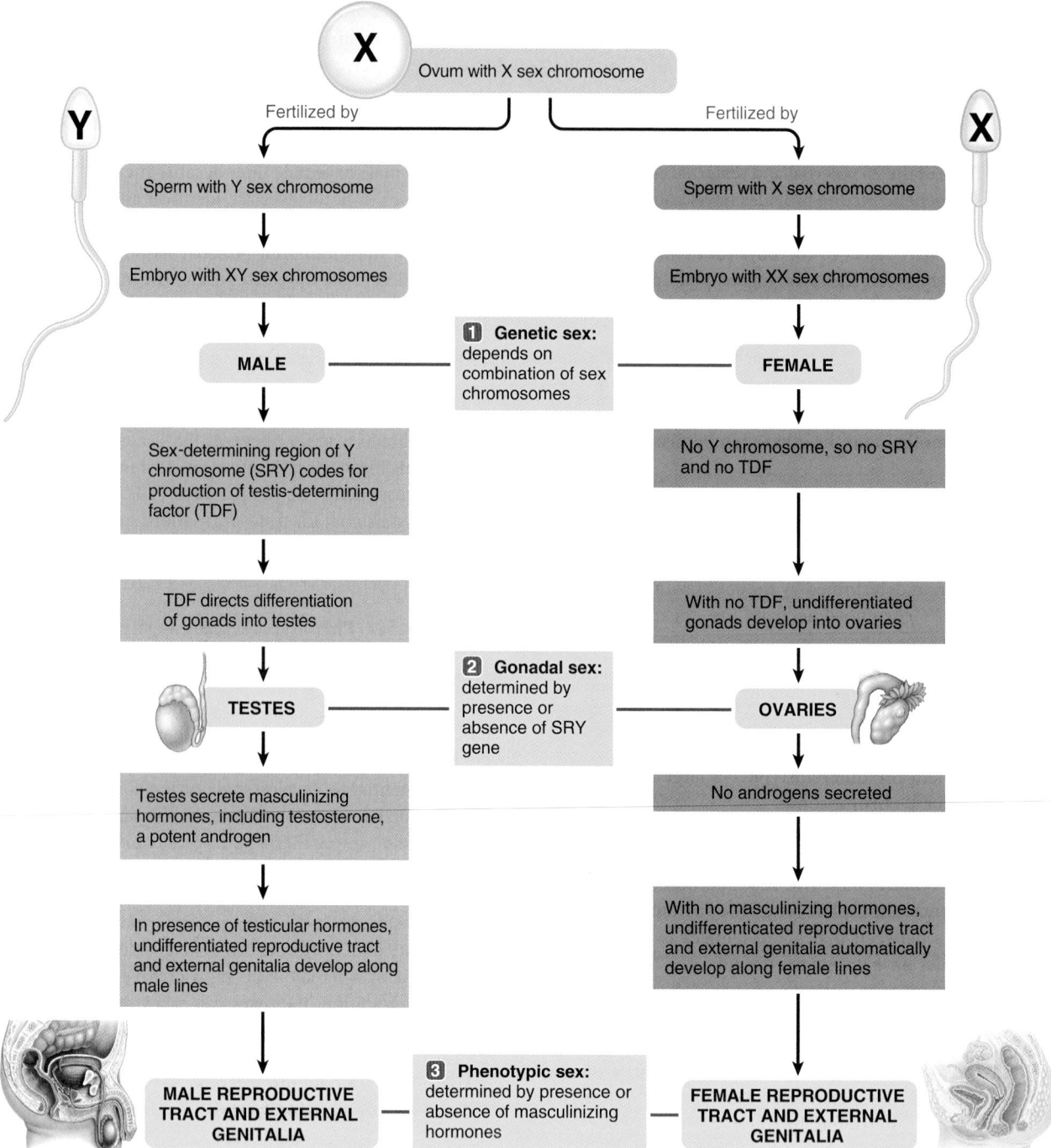

(a) Male sex determination and sexual differentiation

(b) Female sex determination and sexual differentiation

● FIGURE 18-3 **Sex determination and sexual differentiation.**

between genetic and anatomic sexes because of errors in sexual differentiation, as the following examples illustrate:

■ Genetic males whose target cells lack receptors for testosterone are feminized (develop into an apparent anatomic female), even though their testes secrete adequate testosterone (*testicular feminization syndrome;* see p. 530).

■ The adrenal gland normally secretes a weak androgen, *dehydroepiandrosterone (DHEA),* in insufficient quantities to masculinize females. However, pathologically excessive secretion of

this hormone in a genetically female fetus during critical developmental stages imposes differentiation of the reproductive tract and genitalia along male lines (*adrenogenital syndrome;* see p. 553).

Sometimes these discrepancies between genetic sex and apparent anatomic sex are not recognized until puberty, when the discovery produces a psychologically traumatic gender identity crisis. For example, a masculinized genetic female with ovaries but with male-type external genitalia may be reared as a boy until puberty, when breast enlargement (caused by estrogen secretion by the awakening ovaries) and lack of beard growth (caused by lack of testosterone secretion in the absence of testes) signal an apparent problem. Therefore, it is important to diagnose any problems in sexual differentiation in infancy. Once a sex has been assigned, it can be reinforced, if necessary, with surgical and hormonal treatment so that psychosexual development can proceed as normally as possible. Less dramatic cases of inappropriate sexual differentiation often appear as sterility problems.

Male Reproductive Physiology

In the embryo, the testes develop from the gonadal ridge located at the rear of the abdominal cavity. In the last months of fetal life, they begin a slow descent, passing out of the abdominal cavity through the **inguinal canal** into the scrotum, one testis dropping into each pocket of the scrotal sac. Testosterone from the fetal testes induces descent of the testes into the scrotum. Although the time varies somewhat, descent is usually complete by the seventh month of gestation. As a result, descent is complete in 98% of full-term baby boys.

 However, in a substantial percentage of premature male infants, the testes are still within the inguinal canal at birth. In most instances of retained testes, descent occurs naturally before puberty or can be encouraged with administration of testosterone. Rarely, a testis remains undescended into adulthood, a condition known as **cryptorchidism** (*crypt* means "hidden"; *orchid* means "testis").

The scrotal location of the testes provides a cooler environment essential for spermatogenesis.

The temperature within the scrotum averages several degrees Celsius less than normal body (core) temperature. Descent of the testes into this cooler environment is essential because spermatogenesis is temperature sensitive and cannot occur at normal body temperature. Therefore, a cryptorchid is unable to produce viable sperm.

The position of the scrotum in relation to the abdominal cavity can be varied by a spinal reflex mechanism that plays an important role in regulating testicular temperature. Reflex contraction of scrotal muscles on exposure to a cold environment raises the scrotal sac to bring the testes closer to the warmer abdomen. Conversely, relaxation of the muscles on exposure to heat permits the scrotal sac to become more pendulous, moving the testes farther from the warm core of the body.

The testicular Leydig cells secrete masculinizing testosterone.

The testes perform the dual function of producing sperm and secreting testosterone. About 80% of the testicular mass consists of highly coiled **seminiferous tubules,** within which spermatogenesis takes place (● Figure 18-4a). The endocrine cells that produce testosterone—the **Leydig,** or **interstitial, cells**—lie in the connective tissue (interstitial tissue) between the seminiferous tubules (● Figure 18-4b). Thus, the portions of the testes that produce sperm and secrete testosterone are structurally and functionally distinct.

Testosterone is a steroid hormone derived from a cholesterol precursor molecule, as are the female sex hormones, estrogen and progesterone. Once produced, some of the testosterone is secreted into the blood, where it is transported to its target sites of action. A substantial portion of the newly synthesized testosterone goes into the lumen of the seminiferous tubules, where it plays an important role in sperm production.

Most of testosterone's actions ultimately function to ensure delivery of sperm to the female. The effects of testosterone can be grouped into five categories: (1) effects on the reproductive system before birth, (2) effects on sex-specific tissues after birth, (3) other reproduction-related effects, (4) effects on secondary sexual characteristics, and (5) nonreproductive actions (▲ Table 18-1).

EFFECTS ON THE REPRODUCTIVE SYSTEM BEFORE BIRTH Before birth, testosterone secretion by the Leydig cells of the fetal testes masculinizes the reproductive tract and external genitalia and promotes descent of the testes into the scrotum, as already described. After birth, testosterone secretion ceases, and the testes and remainder of the reproductive system remain small and nonfunctional until puberty.

EFFECTS ON SEX-SPECIFIC TISSUES AFTER BIRTH **Puberty** is the period of arousal and maturation of the previously nonfunctional reproductive system, culminating in sexual maturity and the ability to reproduce. It usually begins sometime between the ages of 10 and 14; on average, it begins about 2 years earlier in females than in males. Usually lasting 3 to 5 years, puberty encompasses a complex sequence of endocrine, physical, and behavioral events. **Adolescence** is a broader concept that refers to the entire transition period between childhood and adulthood, not just to sexual maturation. In both sexes, the reproductive changes that take place during puberty are (1) enlargement and maturation of gonads, (2) development of secondary sexual characteristics, (3) achievement of fertility (gamete production), (4) growth and maturation of the reproductive tract, and (5) attainment of libido (sex drive).

At puberty in males, the Leydig cells start secreting testosterone again. Testosterone is responsible for growth and maturation of the entire male reproductive system. Under the influence of the pubertal surge in testosterone secretion, the testes enlarge and start producing sperm for the first time, the accessory sex glands enlarge and become secretory, and the penis and scrotum enlarge.

Ongoing testosterone secretion is essential for spermatogenesis and for maintaining a mature male reproductive tract throughout adulthood. Once initiated at puberty, testosterone secretion and spermatogenesis occur continuously throughout the male's life.

OTHER REPRODUCTION-RELATED EFFECTS Testosterone governs the development of sexual libido at puberty and helps maintain the sex drive in the adult male. Stimulation of this behavior by testosterone is important for facilitating delivery of sperm to

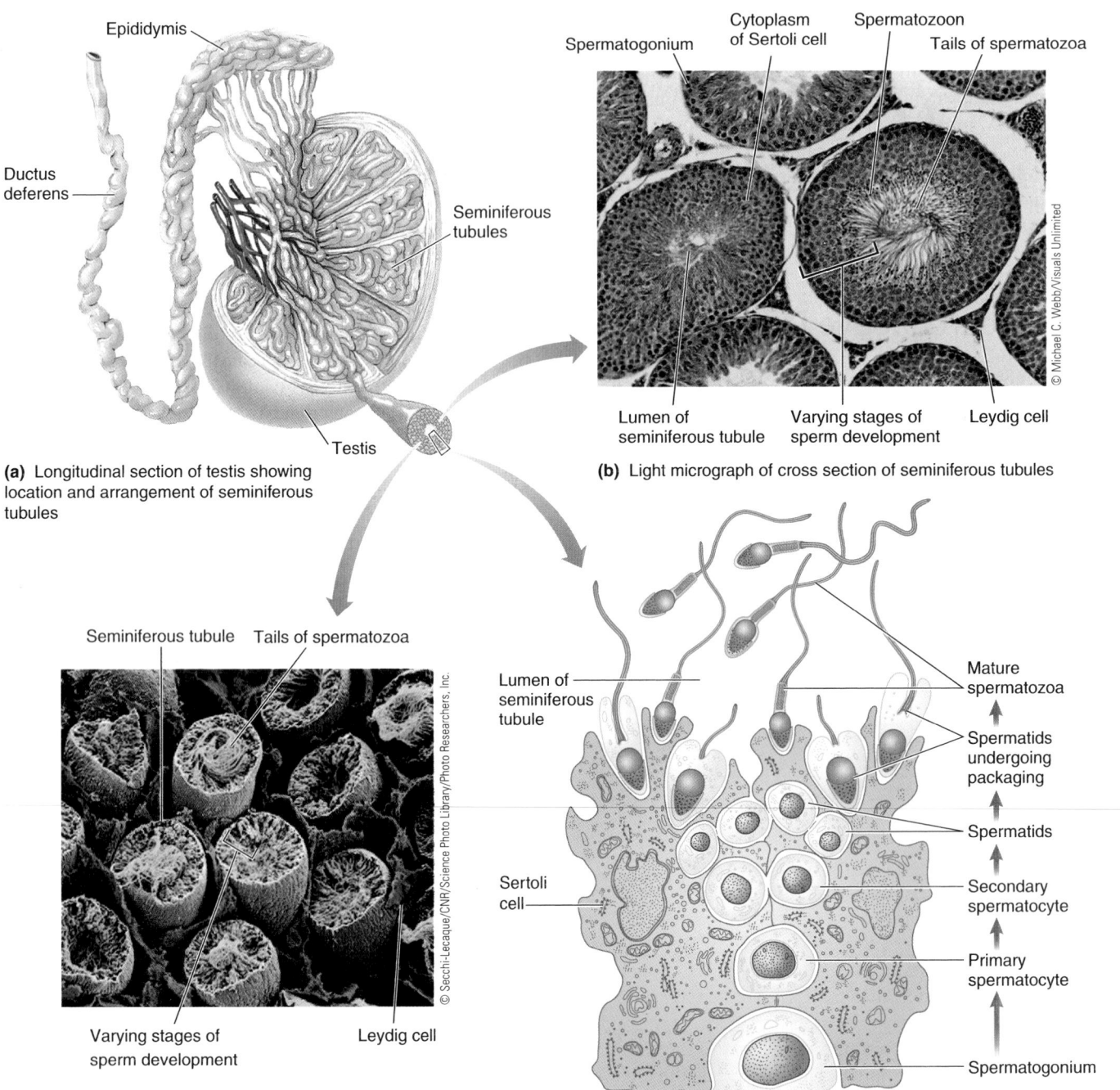

(a) Longitudinal section of testis showing location and arrangement of seminiferous tubules

(b) Light micrograph of cross section of seminiferous tubules

(c) Scanning electron micrograph of cross section of seminiferous tubules

(d) Relationship of Sertoli cells to developing sperm cells

● FIGURE 18-4 **Anatomy of testis depicting the site of spermatogenesis.** (a) The seminiferous tubules are the sperm-producing portion of the testis. (b) The undifferentiated germ cells (the spermatogonia) lie in the periphery of the tubule, and the differentiated spermatozoa are in the lumen, with the various stages of sperm development between. (c) Note the presence of the highly differentiated spermatozoa (recognizable by their tails) in the lumen of the seminiferous tubules. (d) Relationship of the Sertoli cells to the developing sperm cells.

females. In humans, libido is also influenced by many interacting social and emotional factors.

In another reproduction-related function, testosterone participates in the normal negative-feedback control of gonadotropin hormone secretion by the anterior pituitary, a topic covered more thoroughly later.

EFFECTS ON SECONDARY SEXUAL CHARACTERISTICS All male secondary sexual characteristics depend on testosterone for their development and maintenance. These nonreproductive male characteristics induced by testosterone include (1) the male pattern of hair growth (for example, beard and chest hair), (2) a deep voice caused by enlargement of the larynx and thick-

▲ Table 18-1 Effects of Testosterone

Effects before Birth

Masculinizes the reproductive tract and external genitalia

Promotes descent of the testes into the scrotum

Effects on Sex-Specific Tissues after Birth

Promotes growth and maturation of the reproductive system at puberty

Is essential for spermatogenesis

Maintains the reproductive tract throughout adulthood

Other Reproduction-Related Effects

Develops the sex drive at puberty

Controls gonadotropin hormone secretion

Effects on Secondary Sexual Characteristics

Induces the male pattern of hair growth (e.g., beard)

Causes the voice to deepen because vocal folds thicken

Promotes muscle growth responsible for the male body configuration

Nonreproductive Actions

Exerts a protein anabolic effect

Promotes bone growth at puberty

Closes the epiphyseal plates after being converted to estrogen by aromatase

May induce aggressive behavior

---

ening of the vocal folds, (3) thick skin, and (4) the male body configuration (for example, broad shoulders and heavy arm and leg musculature) as a result of protein deposition.

NONREPRODUCTIVE ACTIONS Testosterone exerts several important effects not related to reproduction. It has a general protein anabolic (synthesis) effect and promotes bone growth, thus contributing to the more muscular physique of males and to the pubertal growth spurt. Ironically, testosterone not only stimulates bone growth but also eventually prevents further growth by sealing the growing ends of the long bones (that is, ossifying, or "closing," the epiphyseal plates; see p. 540).

In animals, testosterone induces aggressive behavior, but whether it influences human behavior other than in the area of sexual behavior is an unresolved issue. Even though some athletes and bodybuilders who (illegally) take testosterone-like anabolic androgenic steroids to increase muscle mass have been observed to display more aggressive behavior (see p. 227), it is unclear to what extent general behavioral differences between the sexes are hormonally induced or result from social conditioning.

CONVERSION OF TESTOSTERONE TO ESTROGEN IN MALES Although testosterone is classically considered the male sex hormone and estrogen a female sex hormone, the distinctions are not as clear-cut as once thought. In addition to the small amount of estrogen produced by the adrenal cortex (see p. 552), a portion of the testosterone secreted by the testes is converted to estrogen

outside the testes by the enzyme **aromatase,** which is widely distributed but most abundant in adipose tissue. Because of this conversion, it is sometimes difficult to distinguish effects of testosterone itself and those of testosterone-turned-estrogen inside cells. For example, scientists recently learned that closure of the epiphyseal plates in males is induced not by testosterone per se but by testosterone turned into estrogen by aromatization. Estrogen receptors have been identified in the testes, prostate, bone, and elsewhere in males. The depth, breadth, and mechanisms of action of estrogen in males are only beginning to be explored. (Likewise, in addition to the weak androgenic hormone DHEA produced by the adrenal cortex in both sexes, the ovaries in females secrete a small amount of testosterone, the functions of which remain unclear.)

We now shift our attention from testosterone secretion to the other function of the testes—sperm production.

Spermatogenesis yields an abundance of highly specialized, mobile sperm.

About 250 m (800 ft) of sperm-producing seminiferous tubules are packed within the testes (● Figure 18-4a, b, and c). Two functionally important cell types are present in these tubules: *germ cells,* most of which are in various stages of sperm development, and *Sertoli cells,* which provide crucial support for spermatogenesis (● Figure 18-4b and d). **Spermatogenesis** is a complex process by which relatively undifferentiated primordial (primitive or initial) germ cells, the **spermatogonia** (each of which contains a diploid complement of 46 chromosomes), proliferate and are converted into extremely specialized, motile spermatozoa (sperm), each bearing a randomly distributed haploid set of 23 chromosomes.

Microscopic examination of a seminiferous tubule reveals layers of germ cells in an anatomic progression of sperm development, starting with the least differentiated in the outer layer and moving inward through various stages of division to the lumen, where the highly differentiated sperm are ready for exit from the testis (● Figure 18-4b, c, and d). Spermatogenesis takes 64 days for development from a spermatogonium to a mature sperm. Up to several hundred million sperm may reach maturity daily. Spermatogenesis encompasses three major stages: *mitotic proliferation, meiosis,* and *packaging* (● Figure 18-5).

MITOTIC PROLIFERATION Spermatogonia located in the outermost layer of the tubule continuously divide mitotically, with all new cells bearing the full complement of 46 chromosomes identical to those of the parent cell. Such proliferation provides a continual supply of new germ cells. Following mitotic division of a spermatogonium, one of the daughter cells remains at the outer edge of the tubule as an undifferentiated spermatogonium, thus maintaining the germ-cell line. The other daughter cell starts moving toward the lumen while undergoing the various steps required to form sperm, which will be released into the lumen. In humans, the sperm-forming daughter cell divides mitotically twice more to form four identical primary **spermatocytes.** After the last mitotic division, the primary

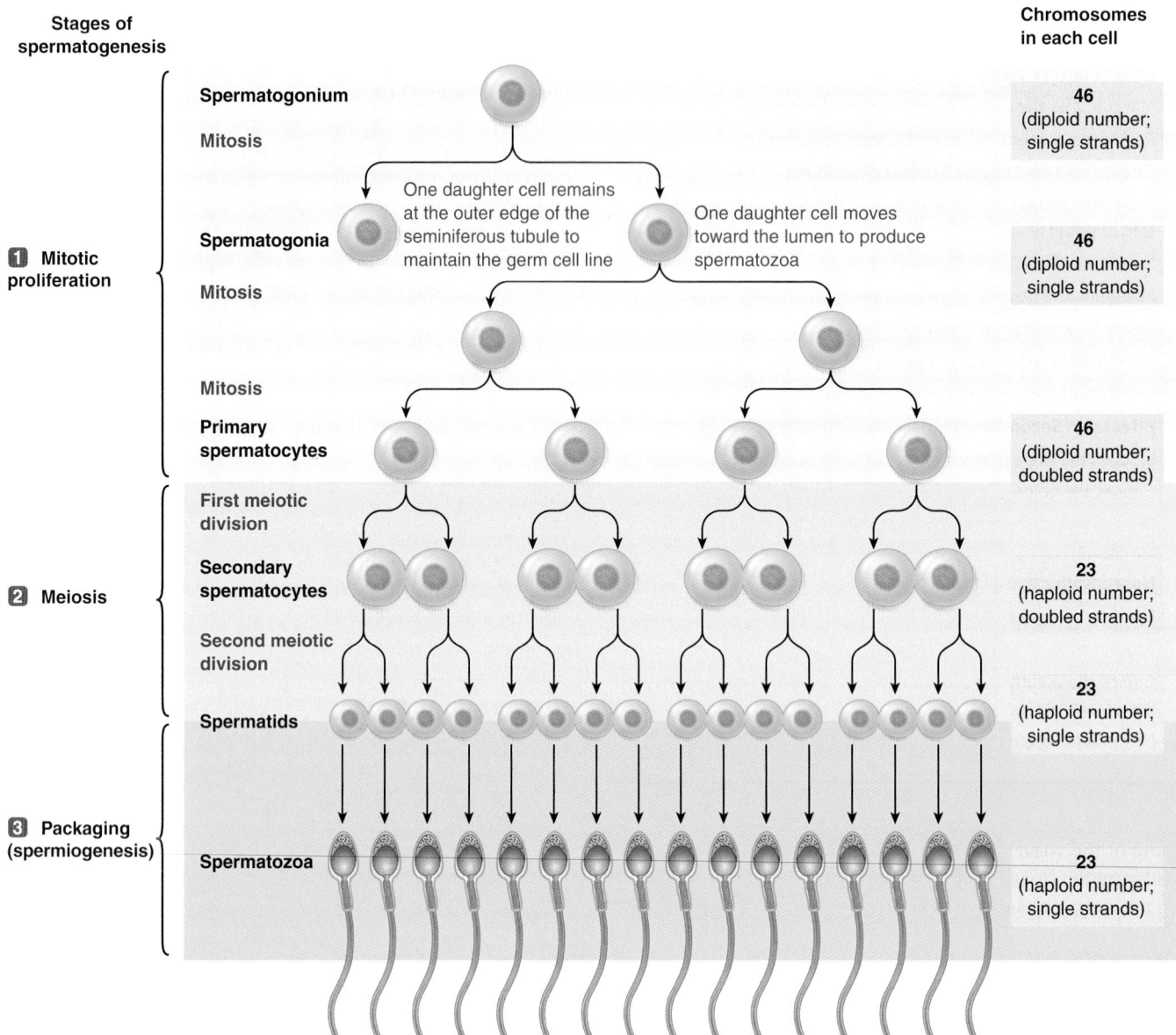

Spermatogonium

Mitosis

1 Mitotic proliferation

Spermatogonia

One daughter cell remains at the outer edge of the seminiferous tubule to maintain the germ cell line

One daughter cell moves toward the lumen to produce spermatozoa

Mitosis

Mitosis

Primary spermatocytes

First meiotic division

Secondary spermatocytes

2 Meiosis

Second meiotic division

Spermatids

3 Packaging (spermiogenesis)

Spermatozoa

46 (diploid number; single strands)

46 (diploid number; single strands)

46 (diploid number; doubled strands)

23 (haploid number; doubled strands)

23 (haploid number; single strands)

23 (haploid number; single strands)

● **FIGURE 18-5 Spermatogenesis.**

spermatocytes enter a resting phase during which the chromosomes are duplicated and the doubled strands remain together in preparation for the first meiotic division.

MEIOSIS During meiosis, each primary spermatocyte (with a diploid number of 46 doubled chromosomes) forms two **secondary spermatocytes** (each with a haploid number of 23 doubled chromosomes) during the first meiotic division, finally yielding four **spermatids** (each with 23 single chromosomes) as a result of the second meiotic division.

No further division takes place beyond this stage of spermatogenesis. Each spermatid is remodeled into a single spermatozoon. Because each sperm-producing spermatogonium mitotically produces four primary spermatocytes and each primary spermatocyte meiotically yields four spermatids (spermatozoa-to-be), the spermatogenic sequence in humans can theoretically produce 16 spermatozoa each time a spermatogonium initiates

this process. Usually, however, some cells are lost at various stages, so the efficiency of productivity is rarely this high.

PACKAGING Even after meiosis, spermatids still resemble undifferentiated spermatogonia structurally, except for their half complement of chromosomes. Production of extremely specialized, mobile spermatozoa from spermatids requires extensive remodeling, or **packaging,** of cell elements, a process alternatively known as **spermiogenesis.** Sperm are essentially "stripped-down" cells in which most of the cytosol and any organelles not needed for delivering the sperm's genetic information to an ovum have been extruded. Thus, sperm travel lightly, taking with them only the bare essentials to accomplish fertilization.

A **spermatozoon** has three parts (● Figure 18-6): a head capped with an acrosome, a midpiece, and a tail. The **head** consists primarily of the nucleus, which contains the sperm's complement of genetic information. The **acrosome,** an enzyme-

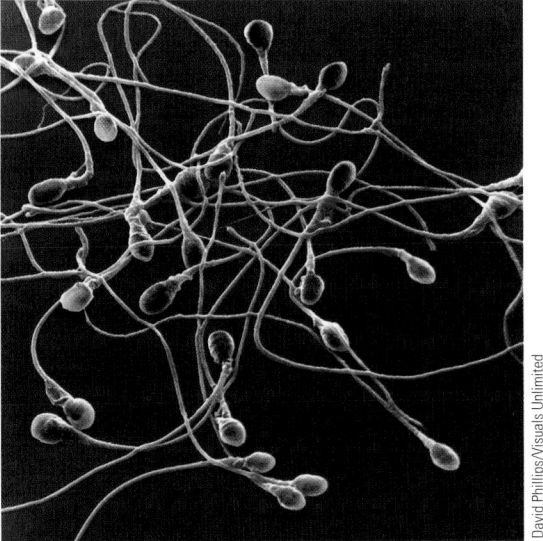

(a) Photomicrograph of human spermatozoa

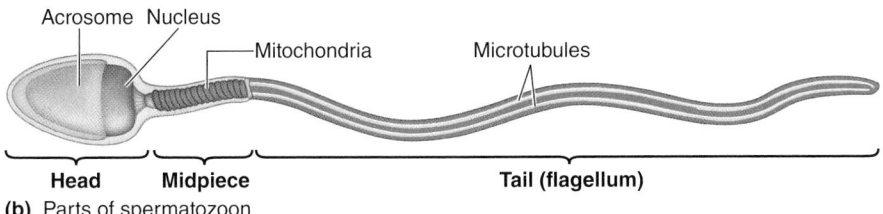

(b) Parts of spermatozoon

● **FIGURE 18-6 Anatomy of a spermatozoon.** (a) A phase-contrast photomicrograph of human spermatozoa. (b) A spermatozoon has three functional parts: a head with its acrosome "cap," a midpiece, and a tail.

filled vesicle that caps the tip of the head, is used as an "enzymatic drill" for penetrating the ovum. The acrosomal enzymes remain inactive until the sperm contacts an egg, at which time the enzymes are released. Mobility for the spermatozoon is provided by a long, whiplike **tail** (a flagellum; see p. 38), movement of which is powered by energy generated by the mitochondria concentrated within the **midpiece** of the sperm.

Throughout their development, sperm remain intimately associated with Sertoli cells.

The seminiferous tubules house the **Sertoli cells,** which are epithelial cells, in addition to the developing sperm cells. The Sertoli cells lie side by side and form a ring around the tubule lumen, with each Sertoli cell spanning the entire distance from the outer surface of the seminiferous tubule to the fluid-filled lumen. Developing sperm cells are tucked between adjacent Sertoli cells, with spermatogonia lying at the outer perimeter of the tubule (see ● Figure 18-4b and d). During spermatogenesis, developing sperm cells arising from spermatogonial mitotic activity migrate toward the lumen in close association with the adjacent Sertoli cells, undergoing their further divisions during this migration. The cytoplasm of the Sertoli cells envelops the migrating sperm cells, which remain buried within these cytoplasmic recesses throughout their development.

Sertoli cells perform the following functions essential for spermatogenesis:

1. The Sertoli cells form a **blood–testes barrier** that prevents blood-borne substances from passing between the cells to gain entry to the lumen of the seminiferous tubule. Because of this barrier, only selected molecules that can pass through the Sertoli cells reach the intratubular fluid. As a result, the composition of the intratubular fluid varies considerably from that of the blood. The unique composition of this fluid that bathes the germ cells is critical for later stages of sperm development. The blood–testes barrier also prevents the antibody-producing cells in the ECF from reaching the tubular sperm factory, thus preventing the formation of antibodies against the highly differentiated spermatozoa.

2. Because the secluded developing sperm cells do not have direct access to blood-borne nutrients, the "nurse" Sertoli cells provide nourishment for them.

3. The Sertoli cells have an important phagocytic function. They engulf the cytoplasm extruded from the spermatids during their remodeling, and they destroy defective germ cells that fail to successfully complete all stages of spermatogenesis.

4. The Sertoli cells secrete into the lumen **seminiferous tubule fluid,** which "flushes" the released sperm from the tubule into the epididymis for storage and further processing.

5. An important component of this Sertoli secretion is **androgen-binding protein.** As the name implies, this protein binds androgens (that is, testosterone), thus maintaining a very high level of this hormone within the seminiferous tubule lumen. Testosterone is 100 times more concentrated in the seminiferous tubule fluid than in the blood. This high local concentration of testosterone is essential for sustaining sperm production. Androgen-binding protein is necessary to retain testosterone within the lumen because this steroid hormone is lipid soluble and could easily diffuse across the plasma membranes and leave the lumen. Testosterone itself stimulates production of androgen-binding protein.

6. The Sertoli cells are the site of action for control of spermatogenesis by both testosterone and follicle-stimulating hormone (FSH). The Sertoli cells themselves release another hormone, *inhibin,* which acts in negative-feedback fashion to regulate FSH secretion.

LH and FSH from the anterior pituitary control testosterone secretion and spermatogenesis.

The testes are controlled by the two gonadotropic hormones secreted by the anterior pituitary, **luteinizing hormone (LH)** and **follicle-stimulating hormone (FSH),** which are named for their functions in females (see p. 534).

FEEDBACK CONTROL OF TESTICULAR FUNCTION LH and FSH act on separate components of the testes (● Figure 18-7). LH acts on the Leydig cells to regulate testosterone secretion. FSH acts on the Sertoli cells to enhance spermatogenesis. Secretion of both LH and FSH from the anterior pituitary is stimulated in turn by a single hypothalamic hormone, **gonadotropin-releasing hormone (GnRH)** (see p. 536). However, LH and FSH are segregated to a large extent into separate secretory vesicles in the gonadotrope and are not secreted in equal amounts because other regulatory factors influence how much of each gonadotropin is secreted.

Two factors—*testosterone* and *inhibin*—differentially influence the secretory rate of LH and FSH. Testosterone, the product of LH stimulation of the Leydig cells, acts in negative-feedback fashion to inhibit LH secretion in two ways. The predominant negative-feedback effect of testosterone is to decrease GnRH release by acting on the hypothalamus, thus indirectly decreasing both LH and FSH release by the anterior pituitary. In addition, testosterone acts directly on the anterior pituitary to selectively reduce LH secretion.

The testicular inhibitory signal specifically directed at controlling FSH secretion is the peptide hormone **inhibin,** which is secreted by the Sertoli cells. Inhibin acts directly on the anterior pituitary to selectively inhibit FSH secretion. This feedback inhibition of FSH by a Sertoli cell product is appropriate, because FSH stimulates spermatogenesis by acting on the Sertoli cells.

ROLES OF TESTOSTERONE AND FSH IN SPERMATOGENESIS Both testosterone and FSH play critical roles in controlling spermatogenesis, each exerting its effect by acting on the Sertoli cells. Testosterone is essential for both mitosis and meiosis of the germ cells, whereas FSH is needed for spermatid remodeling. Testosterone concentration is much higher in the testes than in the blood because a substantial portion of this hormone produced locally by the Leydig cells is retained in the intratubular fluid complexed with androgen-binding protein secreted by the Sertoli cells. Only this high concentration of testicular testosterone is adequate to sustain sperm production.

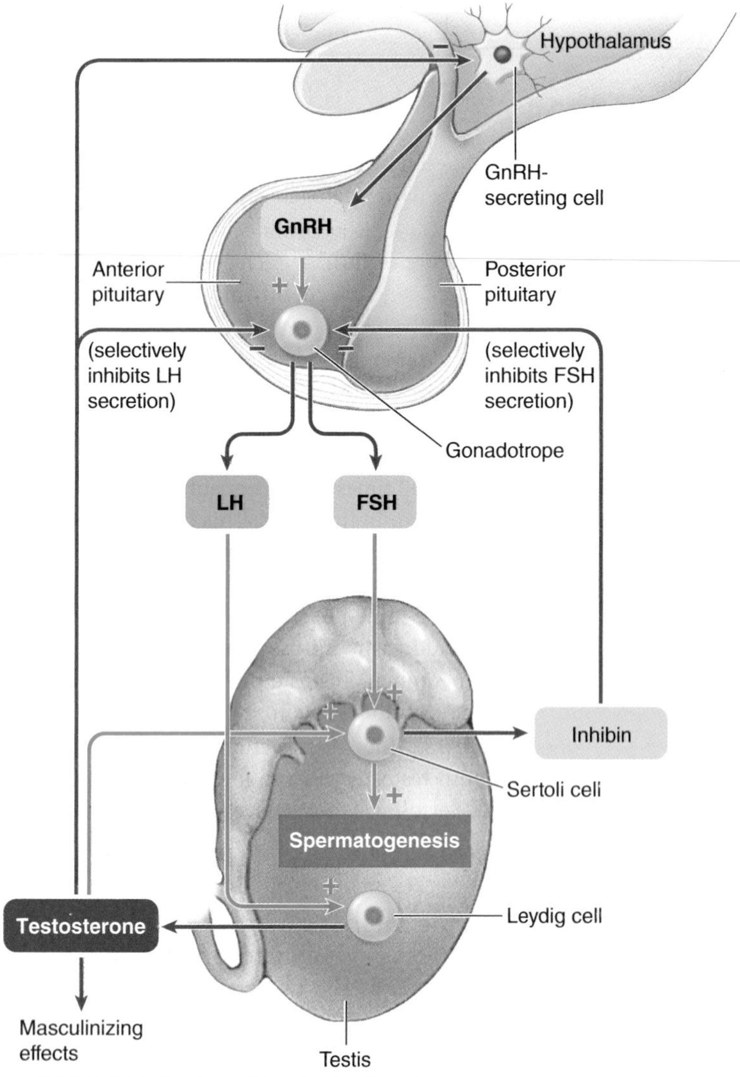

GnRH activity increases at puberty.

Even though the fetal testes secrete testosterone, which directs masculine development of the reproductive system, after birth the testes become dormant until puberty. During the prepubertal period, LH and FSH are not secreted at adequate levels to stimulate any significant testicular activity. The prepubertal delay in the onset of reproductive capability allows time for the individual to mature physically (although not necessarily psychologically) enough to handle child rearing. (This physical maturation is especially important in the female, whose body must support the developing fetus.)

During the prepubertal period, GnRH activity is inhibited. The pubertal process is initiated by an increase in GnRH activity sometime between 8 and 12 years of age. Early in puberty, GnRH secretion occurs only at night, causing a brief nocturnal increase in LH secretion and accordingly, testosterone secretion. The extent of GnRH secretion gradually increases as puberty progresses until the adult pattern of GnRH, FSH, LH, and testosterone secretion is established. Under the influence of the rising levels of testosterone during puberty, the physical changes that encompass the secondary sexual characteristics and reproductive maturation become evident.

The factors responsible for initiating puberty in humans remain unclear. The leading proposal focuses on a potential role for the hormone *melatonin,* which is secreted by the *pineal gland* within the brain (see p. 542). Melatonin, whose secretion decreases during exposure to the light and increases during exposure to the dark, has an antigonadotropic effect in many species. Light striking the eyes inhibits the nerve pathways that stimulate melatonin secretion. In many seasonally breeding species, the overall decrease in melatonin secretion in connec-

● **FIGURE 18-7 Control of testicular function.**

tion with longer days and shorter nights initiates the mating season. Some researchers suggest that an observed reduction in the overall rate of melatonin secretion at puberty in humans—particularly during the night, when the peaks in GnRH secretion first occur—is the trigger for the onset of puberty.

Having completed our discussion of testicular function, we now shift to the roles of the other components of the male reproductive system.

The reproductive tract stores and concentrates sperm and increases their fertility.

The remainder of the male reproductive system (besides the testes) is designed to deliver sperm to the female reproductive tract. Essentially, it consists of (1) a tortuous pathway of tubes (the reproductive tract), which transports sperm from the testes to outside the body; (2) several accessory sex glands, which contribute secretions important to the viability and motility of the sperm; and (3) the penis, which is designed to penetrate and deposit the sperm within the vagina of the female. We examine each of these parts in greater detail, beginning with the reproductive tract.

COMPONENTS OF THE MALE REPRODUCTIVE TRACT A comma-shaped **epididymis** is loosely attached to the rear surface of each testis (see ● Figures 18-1, p. 581, and 18-4a, p. 586). After sperm are produced in the seminiferous tubules, they are swept into the epididymis as a result of the pressure created by the continual secretion of tubular fluid by the Sertoli cells. The epididymal ducts from each testis converge to form a large, thick-walled, muscular duct called the **ductus (vas) deferens.** The ductus deferens from each testis passes up out of the scrotal sac and runs back through the inguinal canal into the abdominal cavity, where it eventually empties into the urethra at the neck of the bladder (see ● Figure 18-1). The urethra carries sperm out of the penis during ejaculation, the forceful expulsion of semen from the body.

FUNCTIONS OF THE EPIDIDYMIS AND DUCTUS DEFERENS These ducts perform several important functions. The epididymis and ductus deferens serve as the exit route for sperm from the testis. As they leave the testis, sperm are not capable of either moving or fertilizing. They gain both capabilities during their passage through the epididymis. This maturational process is stimulated by the testosterone retained within the tubular fluid bound to androgen-binding protein. The capacity of sperm to fertilize is further enhanced by exposure to secretions of the female reproductive tract. The epididymis also concentrates the sperm 100-fold by absorbing most of the fluid that enters from the seminiferous tubules. The maturing sperm are slowly moved through the epididymis into the ductus deferens by rhythmic contractions of the smooth muscle in the walls of these tubes.

The ductus deferens is an important site for sperm storage. Because the tightly packed sperm are relatively inactive and their metabolic needs are accordingly low, they can be stored in the ductus deferens for up to 2 months, even though they have no nutrient blood supply and are nourished only by simple sugars present in the tubular secretions.

 VASECTOMY In a **vasectomy,** a common sterilization procedure in males, a small segment of each ductus deferens (alias vas deferens, hence the term *vasectomy*) is surgically removed after it passes from the testis but before it enters the inguinal canal, thus blocking the exit of sperm from the testes. Sperm that build up behind the tied-off testicular end of the severed ductus are removed by phagocytosis. Although this procedure blocks sperm exit, it does not interfere with testosterone activity, because the Leydig cells secrete testosterone into the blood, not through the ductus deferens. Thus, testosterone-dependent masculinity or libido should not diminish after a vasectomy.

The accessory sex glands contribute the bulk of the semen.

Several accessory sex glands—the seminal vesicles and prostate—empty their secretions into the duct system before it joins the urethra (see ● Figure 18-1). A pair of saclike *seminal vesicles* empties into the last portion of the two ductus deferens, one on each side. The *prostate* is a large single gland that completely surrounds the urethra. Another pair of accessory sex glands, the *bulbourethral glands,* drains into the urethra after this canal has passed through the prostate and just before it enters the penis. Numerous mucus-secreting glands also lie along the length of the urethra.

 In a significant number of men, the prostate enlarges in middle to older age (a condition called **benign prostatic hypertrophy,** or **BPH).** Difficulty in urinating often occurs as the enlarging prostate impinges on the portion of the urethra that passes through the prostate.

SEMEN During ejaculation, the accessory sex glands contribute secretions that provide support for the continuing viability of sperm inside the female reproductive tract. These secretions constitute the bulk of the **semen,** which is a mixture of accessory sex gland secretions, sperm, and mucus. Sperm make up only a small percentage of the total ejaculated fluid.

FUNCTIONS OF THE MALE ACCESSORY SEX GLANDS Although the accessory sex gland secretions are not absolutely essential for fertilization, they do greatly facilitate the process.

■ The **seminal vesicles** (1) supply fructose, which is the primary energy source for ejaculated sperm; (2) secrete *prostaglandins,* which stimulate contractions of the smooth muscle in both the male and the female reproductive tracts, thereby helping transport sperm from their storage site in the male to the site of fertilization in the female oviduct; (3) provide about 60% of the semen volume, which helps wash the sperm into the urethra and dilutes the thick mass of sperm, enabling them to become mobile; and (4) secrete fibrinogen, a precursor of fibrin, which forms the meshwork of a clot (see p. 326).

■ The **prostate gland** (1) secretes an alkaline fluid that neutralizes the acidic vaginal secretions, an important function because sperm are more viable in a slightly alkaline environment; (2) provides clotting enzymes; and (3) releases **prostate-specific antigen (PSA).** The prostatic clotting enzymes act on fibrinogen from the seminal vesicles to produce fibrin, which "clots" the semen, thus helping keep the ejaculated sperm in the female reproductive tract during withdrawal of the penis. Shortly thereafter, the seminal clot is broken down by PSA, a fibrin-degrading enzyme from the prostate, thus releasing mobile sperm within the female tract.

 Because PSA is produced only in the prostate gland, measurement of PSA levels in the blood is used as one type of screening test for possible prostate cancer. Elevated levels of PSA in the blood are associated with prostate cancer, benign prostatic hypertrophy, or prostate infections.

■ During sexual arousal, the **bulbourethral glands** secrete a mucuslike substance that provides lubrication for sexual intercourse.

▲ Table 18-2 summarizes the locations and functions of the components of the male reproductive system.

Before turning to the act of delivering sperm to the female (sexual intercourse), we briefly digress to discuss the diverse roles of prostaglandins, which were first discovered in semen but are abundant throughout the body.

Prostaglandins are ubiquitous, locally acting chemical messengers.

Although **prostaglandins** were first identified in the semen and were believed to be of prostate gland origin (hence their name, even though they are actually secreted into the semen by the seminal vesicles), their production and actions are not limited to the reproductive system. These chemical messengers are found throughout the body, because they are produced in virtually all

tissues from arachidonic acid, a fatty acid constituent of the phospholipids within the plasma membrane. On appropriate stimulation, arachidonic acid is split from the plasma membrane by a membrane-bound enzyme and then is converted into the appropriate prostaglandin, which acts as a paracrine locally within or near its site of production (see p. 98). After prostaglandins act, they are rapidly inactivated by local enzymes before they gain access to the blood; if they do reach the circulatory system, they are swiftly degraded on their first pass through the lungs so that they are not dispersed through the systemic arterial system.

Prostaglandins and other closely related arachidonic-acid derivatives—namely, *prostacyclins, thromboxanes,* and *leukotrienes*—are collectively known as **eicosanoids** and are among the most biologically active compounds known. Prostaglandins exert a bewildering variety of effects. Not only are slight variations in prostaglandin structure accompanied by profound differences in biological action, but the same prostaglandin molecule may even exert opposite effects in different tissues. Besides enhancing sperm transport in semen, these abundant chemical messengers are known or suspected to exert other actions in the female reproductive system and in the respiratory, urinary, digestive, nervous, and endocrine systems, in addition to affecting platelet aggregation, fat metabolism, and inflammation (▲ Table 18-3).

 As prostaglandins' various actions are better understood, new ways of manipulating them therapeutically are becoming available. A classic example is the use of aspirin, which blocks the conversion of arachidonic acid into prostaglandins, for fever reduction and pain relief. Prostaglandin action is also therapeutically inhibited in the treatment of premenstrual symptoms and menstrual cramping. Furthermore, specific prostaglandins have been medically

▲ Table 18-2   Location and Functions of the Components of the Male Reproductive System

Component	Number and Location	Functions
Testis	Pair; located in the scrotum, a skin-covered sac suspended within the angle between the legs	Produces sperm
		Secretes testosterone
Epididymis and Ductus Deferens	Pair; one epididymis attached to the rear of each testis; one ductus deferens travels from each epididymis up out of the scrotal sac through the inguinal canal and empties into the urethra at the neck of the bladder	Serve as an exit route for sperm from the testis
		Serve as the site for maturation of sperm for motility and fertility
		Concentrate and store sperm
Seminal Vesicle	Pair; both empty into the last portion of the ductus deferens, one on each side	Supplies fructose to nourish ejaculated sperm
		Secretes prostaglandins that stimulate motility to help transport sperm within the male and female
		Provides the bulk of the semen
		Provides precursors for the clotting of semen
Prostate Gland	Single; completely surrounds the urethra at the neck of the bladder	Secretes an alkaline fluid that neutralizes the acidic vaginal secretions
		Triggers clotting of the semen to keep the sperm in the vagina during penis withdrawal
Bulbourethral Gland	Pair; both empty into the urethra, one on each side, just before the urethra enters the penis	Secretes mucus for lubrication

▲ Table 18-3 Actions of Prostaglandins

Body System Affected	Actions of Prostaglandins
Reproductive System	Promote sperm transport by action on smooth muscle in the male and female reproductive tracts
	Play a role in ovulation
	Play an important role in menstruation
	Contribute to preparation of the maternal portion of the placenta
	Contribute to parturition
Respiratory System	Some promote bronchodilation, others bronchoconstriction
Urinary System	Increase renal blood flow
	Increase excretion of water and salt
Digestive System	Inhibit HCl secretion by the stomach
	Stimulate intestinal motility
Nervous System	Influence neurotransmitter release and action
	Act at the hypothalamic "thermostat" to increase body temperature
	Intensify the sensation of pain
Endocrine System	Enhance cortisol secretion
	Influence tissue responsiveness to hormones in many instances
Circulatory System	Influence platelet aggregation
Fat Metabolism	Inhibit fat breakdown
Defense System	Promote many aspects of inflammation, including development of fever

administered in such diverse situations as inducing labor, treating asthma, and treating gastric ulcers.

Next, before considering the female in greater detail, we examine the means by which males and females come together to accomplish reproduction.

Sexual Intercourse Between Males and Females

Ultimately, union of male and female gametes to accomplish reproduction in humans requires delivery of sperm-laden semen into the female vagina through the **sex act,** also known as **sexual intercourse, coitus,** or **copulation.**

The male sex act is characterized by erection and ejaculation.

The *male sex act* involves two components: (1) **erection,** or hardening of the normally flaccid penis to permit its entry into the vagina, and (2) **ejaculation,** or forceful expulsion of semen into the urethra and out of the penis (▲ Table 18-4). In addition to these strictly reproduction-related components, the **sexual response cycle** encompasses broader physiologic responses that can be divided into four phases:

1. The *excitement phase* includes erection and heightened sexual awareness.

2. The *plateau phase* is characterized by intensification of these responses, plus more generalized body responses, such as steadily increasing heart rate, blood pressure, respiratory rate, and muscle tension.

3. The *orgasmic phase* includes ejaculation, as well as other responses that culminate the mounting sexual excitement and are collectively experienced as an intense physical pleasure.

4. The *resolution phase* returns the genitalia and body systems to their prearousal state.

The human sexual response is a multicomponent experience that, in addition to these physiologic phenomena, encompasses emotional, psychological, and sociological factors. We examine only the physiologic aspects of sex.

Erection is accomplished by penis vasocongestion.

Erection is accomplished by engorgement of the penis with blood. The penis consists almost entirely of **erectile tissue** made up of three columns of spongelike vascular spaces extending the length of the organ (see ● Figure 18-1, p. 581). In the absence

▲ Table 18-4 Components of the Male Sex Act

Components of the Male Sex Act	Definition	Accomplished by
Erection	Hardening of the normally flaccid penis to permit its entry into the vagina	Engorgement of the penis erectile tissue with blood as a result of marked parasympathetically induced vasodilation of the penile arterioles and mechanical compression of the veins
Ejaculation		
Emission Phase	Emptying of sperm and accessory sex-gland secretions (semen) into the urethra	Sympathetically induced contraction of the smooth muscle in the walls of the reproductive ducts and accessory sex glands
Expulsion Phase	Forceful expulsion of semen from the penis	Motor neuron–induced contraction of the skeletal muscles at the base of the penis

of sexual excitation, the erectile tissues contain little blood, because the arterioles that supply these vascular chambers are constricted. As a result, the penis remains small and flaccid. During sexual arousal, these arterioles reflexly dilate and the erectile tissue fills with blood, causing the penis to enlarge both in length and in width and to become more rigid. The veins that drain the erectile tissue are mechanically compressed by this engorgement and expansion of the vascular spaces, reducing venous outflow and thereby contributing even further to the buildup of blood, or *vasocongestion.* These local vascular responses transform the penis into a hardened, elongated organ capable of penetrating the vagina.

ERECTION REFLEX The erection reflex is a spinal reflex triggered by stimulation of highly sensitive mechanoreceptors located in the *glans penis,* which caps the tip of the penis. An **erection-generating center** lies in the lower spinal cord. Tactile stimulation of the glans reflexly triggers, by means of this center, increased parasympathetic vasodilator activity and decreased sympathetic vasoconstrictor activity to the penile arterioles. The result is rapid, pronounced vasodilation of these arterioles and an ensuing erection (● Figure 18-8). As long as this spinal reflex arc remains intact, erection is possible even in men paralyzed by a higher spinal-cord injury.

This parasympathetically induced vasodilation is the major instance of direct parasympathetic control over blood vessel diameter in the body. Parasympathetic stimulation brings about relaxation of penile arteriolar smooth muscle by nitric oxide, which causes arteriolar vasodilation in response to local tissue changes elsewhere in the body (see p. 292). Arterioles are typically supplied only by sympathetic nerves, with increased sympathetic activity producing vasoconstriction and decreased sympathetic activity resulting in vasodilation (see p. 291). Concurrent parasympathetic stimulation and sympathetic inhibition of penile arterioles accomplish vasodilation more rapidly and in greater magnitude than is possible in other arterioles supplied only by sympathetic nerves. Through this efficient means of rapidly increasing blood flow into the penis, the penis can become completely erect in as little as 5 seconds. At the same time, parasympathetic impulses promote secretion of lubricating mucus from the bulbourethral glands and the urethral glands in preparation for coitus.

A flurry of recent research has led to the discovery of numerous regions throughout the brain that can influence the male sexual response. The erection-influencing brain sites appear extensively interconnected and function as a unified network to either facilitate or inhibit the basic spinal erection reflex, depending on the momentary circumstances. As an example of facilitation, psychic stimuli, such as viewing something sexually exciting, can induce an erection in the absence of tactile stimulation of the penis. In contrast, failure to achieve an erection despite appropriate stimulation may result from inhibition of the erection reflex by higher brain centers. Let us examine erectile dysfunction in more detail.

Clinical Note ERECTILE DYSFUNCTION A pattern of failing to achieve or maintain an erection suitable for sexual intercourse—**erectile dysfunction (ED)** or **impotence**—may be attributable to psychological or physical factors. An occasional episode of a failed erection does not constitute impotence, but a man who becomes overly anxious about his ability to perform the sex act may well be on his way to chronic failure. Anxiety can lead to ED, which fuels the man's anxiety level and thus perpetuates the problem. Impotence may also arise from physical limitations, including nerve damage, certain medications that interfere with autonomic function, and problems with blood flow through the penis.

ED is widespread. More than 50% of men between ages 40 and 70 experience some impotence, climbing to nearly 70% by age 70. No wonder, then, that more prescriptions were written for the much-publicized drug *sildenafil (Viagra)* during its first year on the market after its approval in 1998 for treating

Thoughts about sex

Stimulation of mechanoreceptors in glans penis

Parasympathetic supply to bulbourethral glands and urethral glands

Parasympathetic supply to penile arterioles

Sympathetic supply to penile arterioles

Mucus

Lubrication

Penile arterioles dilate

Erection

Compresses veins

● FIGURE 18-8 **Erection reflex.**

ED than for any other new drug in history. Sildenafil does not produce an erection, but it amplifies and prolongs an erectile response triggered by usual means of stimulation. Here is how the drug works: Nitric oxide released in response to parasympathetic stimulation activates a membrane-bound enzyme, *guanylate cyclase,* within nearby arteriolar smooth muscle cells. This enzyme activates *cyclic guanosine monophosphate (cyclic GMP* or *cGMP),* an intracellular second messenger similar to cAMP. Cyclic GMP, in turn, leads to relaxation of the penile arteriolar smooth muscle, bringing about pronounced local vasodilation. Under normal circumstances, once cGMP is activated and brings about an erection, this second messenger is broken down by the intracellular enzyme *phosphodiesterase 5.* Sildenafil inhibits this enzyme. As a result, cGMP remains active longer so that penile arteriolar vasodilation continues and the erection is sustained long enough for a formerly impotent man to accomplish the sex act. Just as pushing a pedal on a piano will not cause a note to be played but will prolong a played note, sildenafil cannot cause the release of nitric oxide and subsequent activation of erection-producing cGMP, but it can prolong the triggered response. The drug has no benefit for those who do not have ED, but its success rate has been high among sufferers of the condition. Side effects have been limited because the drug concentrates in the penis, thus having more impact on this organ than elsewhere in the body.

Ejaculation includes emission and expulsion.

The second component of the male sex act is ejaculation. Like erection, ejaculation is a spinal reflex. The same types of tactile and psychic stimuli that induce erection cause ejaculation when the level of excitation intensifies to a critical peak. The overall ejaculatory response occurs in two phases: *emission* and *expulsion* (see ▲ Table 18-4).

EMISSION First, sympathetic impulses cause sequential contraction of smooth muscles in the prostate, reproductive ducts, and seminal vesicles. This contractile activity delivers prostatic fluid, then sperm, and finally seminal vesicle fluid (collectively, semen) into the urethra. This phase of the ejaculatory reflex is called **emission.** During this time, the sphincter at the neck of the bladder is tightly closed to prevent semen from entering the bladder and urine from being expelled, along with the ejaculate, through the urethra.

EXPULSION Second, filling of the urethra with semen triggers nerve impulses that activate skeletal muscles at the base of the penis. Rhythmic contractions of these muscles occur at 0.8-second intervals and increase the pressure within the penis, forcibly expelling the semen through the urethra to the exterior. This is the **expulsion** phase of ejaculation.

Orgasm and resolution complete the sexual response cycle.

Ejaculation is part of the sexual response cycle. The third phase of the cycle, orgasm, accompanies the expulsion part of the ejaculatory response and is followed by the resolution phase of the cycle.

ORGASM The rhythmic contractions that occur during semen expulsion are accompanied by involuntary rhythmic throbbing of pelvic muscles and peak intensity of the overall body responses that were climbing during the earlier phases. Heavy breathing, a heart rate of up to 180 beats per minute, marked generalized skeletal muscle contraction, and heightened emotions are characteristic. These pelvic and overall systemic responses that culminate the sex act are associated with an intense pleasure characterized by a feeling of release and complete gratification, an experience known as **orgasm.**

RESOLUTION During the resolution phase following orgasm, sympathetic vasoconstrictor impulses slow the inflow of blood into the penis, causing the erection to subside. A deep relaxation ensues, often accompanied by a feeling of fatigue. Muscle tone returns to normal, while the cardiovascular and respiratory systems return to their prearousal level of activity. Once ejaculation has occurred, a temporary refractory period of variable duration ensues before sexual stimulation can trigger another erection. Males therefore cannot experience multiple orgasms within a matter of minutes, as females sometimes do.

Volume and sperm content of the ejaculate vary.

The volume and sperm content of the ejaculate depend on the length of time between ejaculations. The average volume of semen is 2.75 ml, ranging from 2 to 6 ml, the higher volumes following periods of abstinence. An average human ejaculate contains about 165 million sperm (60 million/ml), but some ejaculates contain as many as 400 million sperm.

 Both quantity and quality of sperm are important determinants of fertility. A man is considered clinically infertile if his sperm concentration falls below 20 million/ml of semen. Even though only one spermatozoon actually fertilizes the ovum, large numbers of accompanying sperm are needed to provide sufficient acrosomal enzymes to break down the barriers surrounding the ovum until the victorious sperm penetrates into the ovum's cytoplasm. The quality of sperm also must be taken into account when assessing the fertility potential of a semen sample. The presence of substantial numbers of sperm with abnormal motility or structure, such as sperm with distorted tails, reduces the chances of fertilization. (For a discussion of how environmental estrogens may be decreasing sperm counts, as well as negatively affecting the male and female reproductive systems in other ways, see the boxed feature on pp. 596–597, ▶ Beyond the Basics.)

The female sexual cycle is similar to the male cycle.

Both sexes experience the same four phases of the sexual response cycle—excitement, plateau, orgasm, and resolution. Furthermore, the physiologic mechanisms responsible for orgasm are fundamentally the same in males and females.

The excitement phase in females can be initiated by either physical or psychological stimuli. Tactile stimulation of the clitoris and surrounding perineal area is an especially powerful sexual stimulus. These stimuli trigger spinal reflexes that bring about parasympathetically induced vasodilation of arte-

Beyond the Basics

Environmental "Estrogens": Bad News for the Reproductive System

Unknowingly, during the last 70 years we humans have been polluting our environment with synthetic endocrine-disrupting chemicals as an unintended side effect of industrialization. Known as **endocrine disrupters,** these hormone-like pollutants bind with the receptor sites normally reserved for the naturally occurring hormones. Depending on how they interact with the receptors, these disrupters can either mimic or block normal hormonal activity. Most endocrine disrupters exert feminizing effects. Many of these environmental contaminants mimic or alter the action of estrogen, the feminizing steroid hormone produced by the female ovaries. Although not yet conclusive, laboratory and field studies suggest that these estrogen disrupters might be responsible for some disturbing trends in reproductive health problems, such as falling sperm counts in males and an increased incidence of breast cancer in females.

Estrogenic pollutants are everywhere. They contaminate our food, drinking water, and air. Proved feminizing synthetic compounds include (1) certain weed killers and insecticides, (2) some detergent breakdown products, (3) petroleum by-products found in car exhaust, (4) a common food preservative used to retard rancidity, and (5) softeners that make plastics flexible. These plastic softeners are commonly found in food packaging and can readily leach into food with which they come in contact, especially during heating. They were also found to leach from some babies' plastic teething toys into the saliva. They are in numerous medical products, such as the bags in which blood is stored. Plastic softeners are among the most plentiful industrial contaminants in our environment.

Investigators are only beginning to identify and understand the implications for reproductive health of myriad synthetic chemicals that have become such an integral part of modern societies. An estimated 87,000 synthetic chemicals are already in our environment. Scientists suspect that the estrogen-mimicking chemicals among these may underlie a spectrum of reproductive disorders that have been rising in the past 70 years—the same period during which large amounts of these pollutants have been introduced into our environment. Here are examples of male reproductive dysfunctions that may be circumstantially linked to exposure to environmental **estrogen disrupters:**

- *Falling sperm counts.* The average sperm count has fallen from 113 million sperm per milliliter of semen in 1940 to 60 million/ml now. Making matters worse, the volume of a single ejaculate has declined from 3.40 to 2.75 ml. This means that men, on average, are now ejaculating less than half the number of sperm as men did 70 years ago—a drop from more than 380 million sperm to about 165 million sperm per ejaculate. Furthermore, the number of motile sperm has dipped. Importantly, the sperm count has not declined in the less polluted areas of the world during the same period.

- *Increased incidence of testicular and prostate cancer.* Cases of testicular cancer have tripled since 1940, and the rate continues to climb. Prostate cancer has also been on the rise over the same period.

- *Rising number of male reproductive tract abnormalities at birth.* The incidence of cryptorchidism (undescended testis) nearly doubled from the 1950s to the 1970s. The number of cases of hypospadia, a malformation of the penis, more than doubled between the mid-1960s and the mid-1990s.

- *Evidence of gender bending in animals.* Some fish and wild animal populations severely exposed to environmental estrogens—such as those living in or near water heavily polluted with hormone-mimicking chemical wastes—display a high rate of grossly impaired reproductive systems. Examples include male fish that are hermaphrodites (having both male and female reproductive parts) and male alligators with abnormally small penises. Similar reproductive abnormalities have been

---

rioles throughout the vagina and external genitalia, especially the clitoris. The resultant inflow of blood becomes evident as swelling of the labia and erection of the clitoris. The latter—like its male homologue (meaning of the same embryonic origin), the penis—is composed largely of erectile tissue. Vasocongestion of the vaginal capillaries forces fluid out of the vessels into the vaginal lumen. This fluid, which is the first positive indication of sexual arousal, is the primary lubricant for intercourse. Additional lubrication is provided by the mucus secretions from the male and by mucus released during sexual arousal from glands located at the outer opening of the vagina.

During the plateau phase, the changes initiated during the excitement phase intensify, while systemic responses similar to those in the male (such as increased heart rate, blood pressure, respiratory rate, and muscle tension) occur. Further vasocongestion of the lower third of the vagina during this time reduces its inner capacity so that it tightens around the thrusting penis, heightening tactile sensation for both the female and the male.

Simultaneously, the uterus raises upward, lifting the cervix and enlarging the upper two thirds of the vagina. This ballooning creates a space for ejaculate deposition.

If erotic stimulation continues, the sexual response culminates in orgasm as sympathetic impulses trigger rhythmic contractions of pelvic musculature at 0.8-second intervals, the same rate as in males. The contractions occur most intensely in the engorged lower third of the vaginal canal. Systemic responses identical to those of the male orgasm also occur. In fact, the orgasmic experience in females parallels that of males with two exceptions. First, there is no female counterpart to ejaculation. Second, females do not become refractory following an orgasm, so they can respond immediately to continued erotic stimulation and achieve multiple orgasms.

During resolution, pelvic vasocongestion and the systemic manifestations gradually subside. As with males, this is a time of great physical relaxation for females.

We now examine how females fulfill their part of the reproductive process.

identified in land mammals. Presumably, excessive estrogen exposure is emasculating these populations.

- *Decline in male births.* Many countries are reporting a slight decline in the ratio of baby boys to baby girls being born. In the United States, 17 fewer males were born per 10,000 births in 2007 compared to 1970, and Japan has seen an overall drop of 37 males per 10,000 births during the same period. Although several plausible explanations have been put forth, many researchers attribute this troubling trend to disruption of normal male fetal development by environmental estrogens. In one compelling piece of circumstantial evidence, people inadvertently exposed to the highest level of an endocrine-disrupting agent during an industrial accident have subsequently had all daughters and no sons, whereas those least exposed have had the normal ratio of girls and boys. Similarly, a 2004 study in the Russian Arctic found a remarkable ratio of 2.5 to 1 female-to-male births among women who had blood concentrations of 4 mg/L or greater of a known estrogen-mimicking pollutant.

Environmental estrogens are also implicated in the rising incidence of breast cancer in females. Breast cancer is 25% to 30% more prevalent now than in the 1940s. Many of the established risk factors for breast cancer, such as starting to menstruate earlier than usual and undergoing menopause later than usual, are associated with an elevation in the total lifetime exposure to estrogen. Because increased exposure to natural estrogen bumps up the risk for breast cancer, prolonged exposure to environmental estrogens may be contributing to the rising prevalence of this malignancy among women (and men).

In addition to the estrogen disrupters, scientists have recently identified a new class of chemical offenders—**androgen disrupters** that either mimic or suppress the action of male hormones. For example, studies suggest that bacteria in wastewater from pulp mills can convert the sterols in pine pulp into androgens. By contrast, anti-androgen compounds have been found in the fungicides commonly sprayed on vegetable and fruit crops. Yet another cause for concern comes from the androgens used by the livestock industry to enhance the production of muscle (that is, meat) in feedlot cattle. (Androgens have a protein anabolic effect.) These drugs do not end up in the meat, but they can get into drinking water and other food as hormone-laden feces contaminate rivers and streams.

In response to the growing evidence that has emerged circumstantially linking numerous environmental pollutants to disturbing reproductive abnormalities, the U.S. Congress legally mandated the Environmental Protection Agency (EPA) in 1996 to determine which synthetic chemicals might be endocrine disrupters. In response, the EPA formed an advisory committee, which in 1998 proposed an ambitious plan to begin comprehensive testing of manufactured compounds for their potential to disrupt hormones in humans and wildlife. Although eventually all the 87,000 existing synthetic compounds will be tested, the initial screening was narrowed to evaluating the endocrine-disrupting potential of 15,000 widely used chemicals. Declaring this a national health priority, the government has allocated millions of dollars for this research. Yet in this time-consuming process, only a few thousand chemicals were tested in the first 10 years of investigation as the EPA's *Toxic Release Inventory* slowly grows and other chemicals have been deemed safe. Complicating the situation further, scientists recently learned that individual chemicals present at harmless levels in the body may have synergistic effects and exert detrimental effects when they interact. Therefore, it might not be sufficient to evaluate the risk of synthetic chemicals one by one. Scientists and regulatory agencies might have to take into account the cumulative risk of mixtures of chemicals. Increasingly, environmental watchdogs are calling for increased measures to limit exposure to synthetic chemicals (such as switching from plastic to glass baby bottles) and better labeling from manufacturers so that consumers can make more informed decisions about products they use.

Female Reproductive Physiology

Female reproductive physiology is more complex than male reproductive physiology.

Complex cycling characterizes female reproductive physiology.

Unlike the continuous sperm production and essentially constant testosterone secretion characteristic of the male, release of ova is intermittent, and secretion of female sex hormones displays wide cyclic swings. The tissues influenced by these sex hormones also undergo cyclic changes, the most obvious of which is the monthly menstrual cycle (*menstruus* means "monthly"). During each cycle, the female reproductive tract is prepared for the fertilization and implantation of an ovum released from the ovary at ovulation. If fertilization does not occur, the cycle repeats. If fertilization does occur, the cycles are interrupted while the female system adapts to nurture and protect the newly conceived human until it has developed into an individual capable of living outside the maternal environment. Furthermore, the female continues her reproductive functions after birth by producing milk (lactation) for the baby's nourishment. Thus, the female reproductive system is characterized by complex cycles that are interrupted by even more complex changes should pregnancy occur.

The ovaries perform the dual function of producing ova (oogenesis) and secreting the female sex hormones, estrogen and progesterone. These hormones act together to promote fertilization of the ovum and to prepare the female reproductive system for pregnancy. Estrogen in the female governs many functions similar to those carried out by testosterone in the male, such as maturation and maintenance of the entire female reproductive system and establishment of female secondary sexual characteristics. In general, the actions of estrogen are important to preconception events. Estrogen is essential for ova maturation and release, development of physical characteristics that are sexually attractive to males, and transport of sperm from the vagina to the site of fertilization in the oviduct. Furthermore, estrogen contributes to breast development in anticipation of lactation. The other ovarian steroid, progesterone, is important in preparing a suitable environment for nourishing a developing embryo and then fetus and for contributing to the breasts' ability to produce milk.

As in males, reproductive capability begins at puberty in females, but unlike males, who have reproductive potential throughout life, female reproductive potential ceases during middle age at menopause.

The steps of gametogenesis are the same in both sexes, but the timing and outcome differ sharply.

Oogenesis contrasts sharply with spermatogenesis in several important aspects, even though the identical steps of chromosome replication and division take place during gamete production in both sexes. The undifferentiated primordial germ cells in the fetal ovaries, the **oogonia** (comparable to the spermatogonia), divide mitotically to give rise to 6 million to 7 million oogonia by the fifth month of gestation, when mitotic proliferation ceases.

FORMATION OF PRIMARY OOCYTES AND PRIMARY FOLLICLES

During the last part of fetal life, the oogonia begin the early steps of the first meiotic division but do not complete it. Known now as **primary oocytes,** they contain the diploid number of 46 replicated chromosomes, which are gathered into homologous pairs but do not separate. The primary oocytes remain in this state of **meiotic arrest** for years until they are prepared for ovulation.

Before birth, each primary oocyte is surrounded by a single layer of connective tissue–derived **granulosa cells.** Together, an oocyte and surrounding granulosa cells make up a **primary follicle.** Oocytes that are not incorporated into follicles self-destruct by apoptosis (cell suicide). At birth, only about 2 million primary follicles remain, each containing a single primary oocyte capable of producing a single ovum. No new oocytes or follicles appear after birth, with the follicles already present in the ovaries at birth serving as a reservoir from which all ova throughout the reproductive life of a female arise. The follicular pool gradually dwindles away as a result of processes that "use up" the oocyte-containing follicles.

Even before puberty, the pool of primary follicles gives rise to an ongoing trickle of developing follicles, stimulated by poorly understood paracrine factors produced by both oocytes and granulosa cells. Once it starts to develop, a follicle is destined for one of two fates: It will reach maturity and ovulate, or it will degenerate to form scar tissue, a process known as **atresia.** Until puberty, all the follicles that start to develop undergo atresia in the early stages without ever ovulating. Of the original total pool of follicles at birth, about 300,000 remain at puberty, and only about 400 will mature and release ova, with the rest undergoing atresia at some stage of development. By menopause, which occurs on average in a woman's early 50s, few primary follicles remain, having either already ovulated or become atretic. From this point on, the woman's reproductive capacity ceases.

This limited gamete potential in females is in sharp contrast to the continual process of spermatogenesis in males, who have the potential to produce several hundred million sperm in a single day. Furthermore, considerable chromosome wastage occurs in oogenesis compared with spermatogenesis. Let us see how.

FORMATION OF SECONDARY OOCYTES

The primary oocyte within a primary follicle is still a diploid cell that contains 46 doubled chromosomes. From puberty until menopause, a portion of the developing follicles in the pool progress cyclically into more advanced follicles. The mechanisms determining which follicles in the pool will develop during a given cycle are unknown. Further development of a follicle is characterized by growth of the primary oocyte and by expansion and differentiation of the surrounding cell layers. The oocyte enlarges about a thousandfold. This oocyte enlargement is caused by a buildup of cytoplasmic materials that will be needed by the early embryo.

Just before ovulation, the primary oocyte, whose nucleus has been in meiotic arrest for years, completes its first meiotic division. This division yields two daughter cells, each receiving a haploid set of 23 doubled chromosomes, analogous to the formation of secondary spermatocytes (● Figure 18-9). However, almost all the cytoplasm remains with one of the daughter cells, now called the **secondary oocyte,** which is destined to become the ovum. The chromosomes of the other daughter cell, together with a small share of cytoplasm, form the **first polar body.** In this way, the ovum-to-be loses half of its chromosomes to form a haploid gamete but retains all of its nutrient-rich cytoplasm. The nutrient-poor polar body soon degenerates.

FORMATION OF A MATURE OVUM

Actually, the secondary oocyte, and not the mature ovum, is ovulated and fertilized, but common usage refers to the developing female gamete as an *ovum* even in its primary and secondary oocyte stages. Sperm entry into the secondary oocyte is needed to trigger the second meiotic division. Unfertilized secondary oocytes never complete this final division. During this division, a half set of chromosomes, along with a thin layer of cytoplasm, is extruded as the **second polar body.** The other half set of 23 unpaired chromosomes remains behind in what is now the **mature ovum** (sometimes called the *ootid,* comparable to the spermatid, until the polar bodies disintegrate and the mature ovum alone remains). These 23 maternal chromosomes unite with the 23 paternal chromosomes of the penetrating sperm to complete fertilization. If the first polar body has not already degenerated, it too undergoes the second meiotic division at the same time the fertilized secondary oocyte is dividing its chromosomes.

COMPARISON OF STEPS IN OOGENESIS AND SPERMATOGENESIS

The steps involved in chromosome distribution during oogenesis parallel those of spermatogenesis, except that the cytoplasmic distribution and time span for completion differ sharply (● Figure 18-10). Just as four haploid spermatids are produced by each primary spermatocyte, four haploid daughter cells are produced by each primary oocyte (if the first polar body does not degenerate before it completes the second meiotic division). In spermatogenesis, each daughter cell develops into a highly

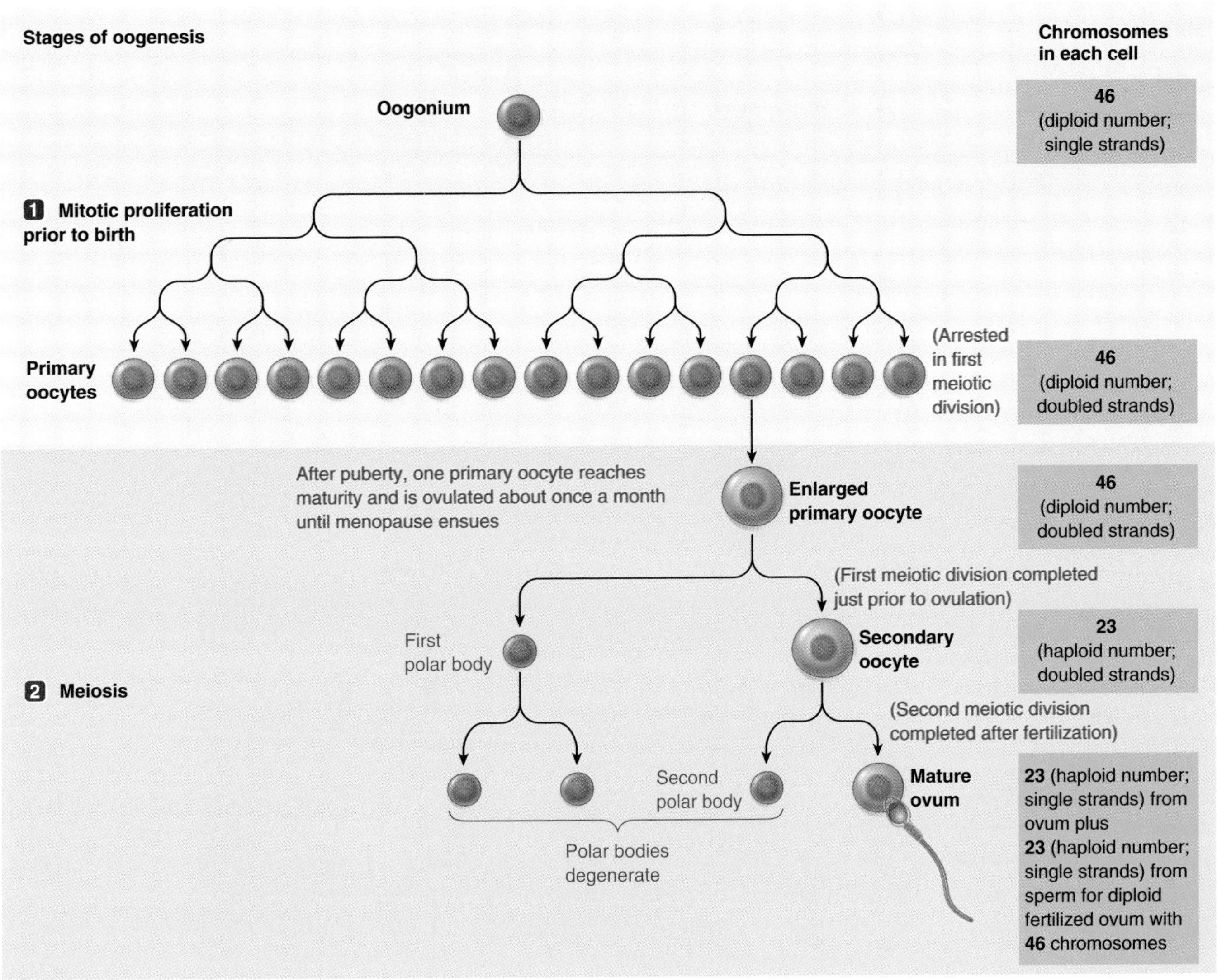

Stages of oogenesis

Chromosomes in each cell

Oogonium

46 (diploid number; single strands)

1 **Mitotic proliferation prior to birth**

Primary oocytes

(Arrested in first meiotic division)

46 (diploid number; doubled strands)

After puberty, one primary oocyte reaches maturity and is ovulated about once a month until menopause ensues

Enlarged primary oocyte

46 (diploid number; doubled strands)

(First meiotic division completed just prior to ovulation)

First polar body

Secondary oocyte

23 (haploid number; doubled strands)

2 **Meiosis**

(Second meiotic division completed after fertilization)

Second polar body

 Mature ovum

Polar bodies degenerate

23 (haploid number; single strands) from ovum plus **23** (haploid number; single strands) from sperm for diploid fertilized ovum with **46** chromosomes

● **FIGURE 18-9 Oogenesis.** Compare with Figure 18-5, p. 588, spermatogenesis.

specialized, motile spermatozoon unencumbered by unessential cytoplasm and organelles, its only destiny being to supply half of the genes for a new individual. In oogenesis, however, of the four daughter cells, only the one destined to become the mature ovum receives cytoplasm. This uneven distribution of cytoplasm is important because the ovum, in addition to providing half the genes, provides all of the cytoplasmic components needed to support early development of the fertilized ovum. The large, relatively undifferentiated ovum contains numerous nutrients, organelles, and structural and enzymatic proteins. The three other cytoplasm-scarce daughter cells, the polar bodies, rapidly degenerate, their chromosomes being deliberately wasted.

Note also the considerable difference in time to complete spermatogenesis and oogenesis. It takes about 2 months for a spermatogonium to develop into fully remodeled spermatozoa. In contrast, development of an oogonium (present before birth) to a mature ovum requires anywhere from 11 years (beginning of ovulation at onset of puberty) to 50 years (end of ovulation at onset of menopause). The actual length of the active steps in

meiosis is the same in both males and females, but in females the developing eggs remain in meiotic arrest for a variable number of years.

Clinical Note The older age of ova released by women in their late 30s and 40s is believed to account for the higher incidence of genetic abnormalities, such as Down syndrome, in children born to women in this age range.

The ovarian cycle consists of alternating follicular and luteal phases.

After the onset of puberty, the ovary constantly alternates between two phases: the **follicular phase,** which is dominated by the presence of *maturing follicles,* and the **luteal phase,** which is characterized by the presence of the *corpus luteum* (to be described shortly). Normally, this cycle is interrupted only if pregnancy occurs and is finally terminated by menopause. The average ovarian cycle lasts 28 days, but this varies among women and among cycles in any particular woman. The follicle operates in the first half of the cycle to produce a mature egg

Mitosis

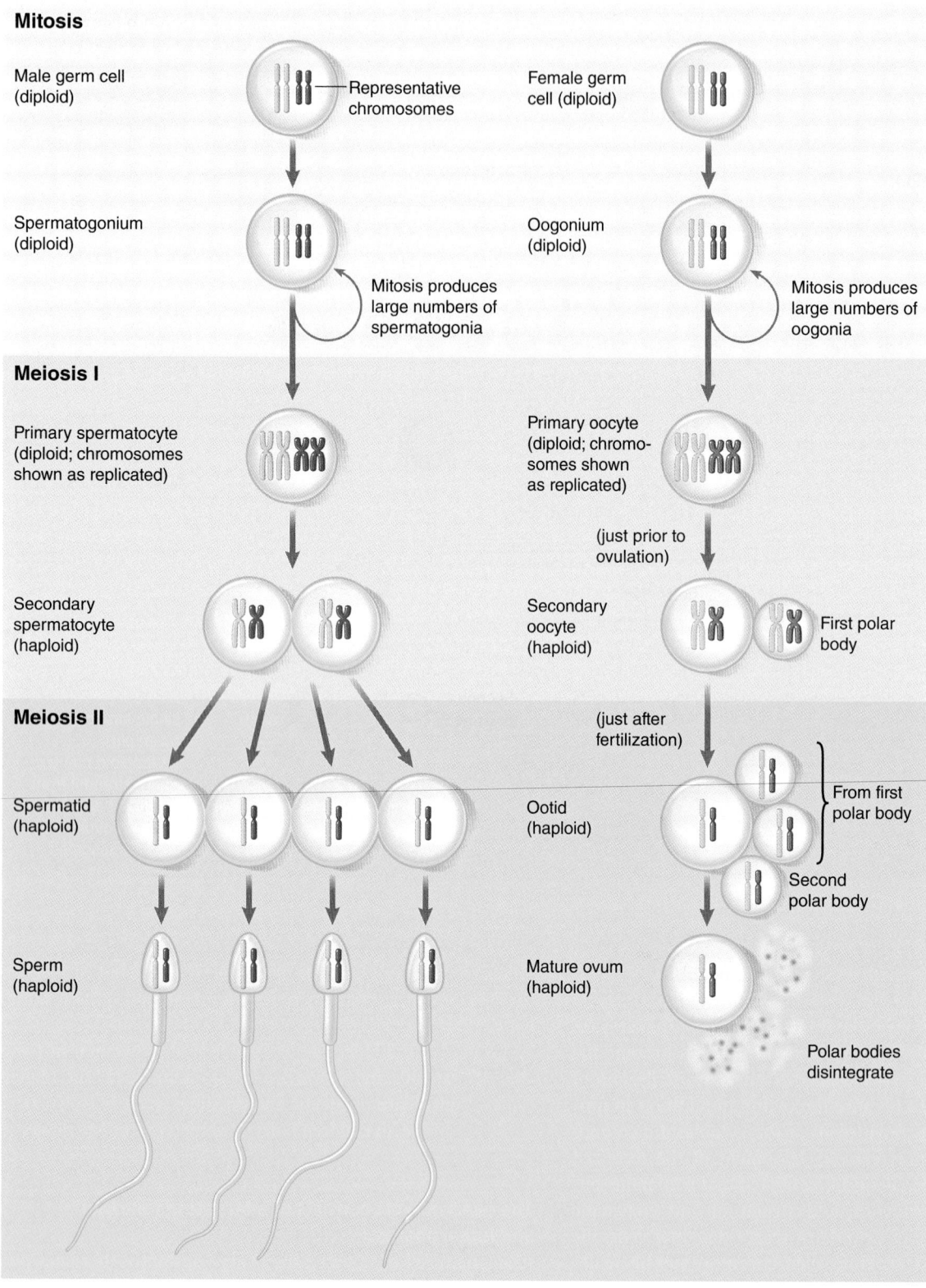

(a) Spermatogenesis

(b) Oogenesis

● FIGURE 18-10 Comparison of mitotic and meiotic divisions producing spermatozoa and eggs from germ cells.

ready for ovulation at midcycle. The corpus luteum takes over during the last half of the cycle to prepare the female reproductive tract for pregnancy in case fertilization of the released egg occurs.

The follicular phase is characterized by the development of maturing follicles.

At any given time throughout the cycle, a portion of the primary follicles is starting to develop (● Figure 18-11b, step **1**). However, only those that do so during the follicular phase, when the hormonal environment is right to promote their maturation, continue beyond the early stages of development. The others, lacking hormonal support, undergo atresia. During follicular development, as the primary oocyte is synthesizing and storing materials for future use if fertilized, important changes take place in the cells surrounding the reactivated oocyte in preparation for the egg's release from the ovary.

PROLIFERATION OF GRANULOSA CELLS AND FORMATION OF THE ZONA PELLUCIDA First, the single layer of granulosa cells in a primary follicle proliferates to form several layers that surround the oocyte. These granulosa cells secrete a thick, gel-like "rind" that covers the oocyte and separates it from the surrounding granulosa cells. This intervening membrane is known as the **zona pellucida** (step **2**).

PROLIFERATION OF THECAL CELLS; ESTROGEN SECRETION As the oocyte is enlarging and granulosa cells are proliferating, specialized ovarian connective tissue cells in contact with the expanding granulosa cells proliferate and differentiate to form an outer layer of **thecal cells** (step **3**). Thecal and granulosa cells, collectively known as **follicular cells,** function as a unit to secrete estrogen.

FORMATION OF THE ANTRUM The early stages of follicular development that occur without gonadotropin influence take about 2 months and are not part of the follicular phase of the ovarian cycle. Only follicles that have developed sufficiently to respond to FSH stimulation (now called **preantral follicles**) are "recruited" at the beginning of the follicular phase when FSH levels rise. Typically during each cycle, about 15 to 20 follicles are recruited. The hormonal environment of the follicular phase promotes rapid enlargement and development of the recruited follicular cells' secretory capacity, converting the preantral follicle into an **antral,** or **secondary, follicle** capable of estrogen secretion (step **4**). During this stage of follicular development, a fluid-filled cavity, or **antrum,** forms in the middle of the granulosa cells (● Figure 18-12). As the follicular cells start producing estrogen, some of this hormone is secreted into the blood for distribution throughout the body. However, a portion of the estrogen collects in the hormone-rich antral fluid.

The oocyte has reached full size by the time the antrum begins to form. The shift from a preantral follicle to an antral follicle initiates a period of rapid follicular growth (see ● Figure 18-11, step **5**). During this time, the follicle increases in size from a diameter of less than 1 mm to one of 12 to 16 mm shortly before ovulation. Part of the follicular growth is the result of continued proliferation of the granulosa and thecal cells, but most results from a dramatic expansion of the antrum. As the follicle grows, estrogen is produced in increasing quantities.

FORMATION OF A MATURE FOLLICLE One of the follicles, the "dominant" follicle, usually grows more rapidly than the others, developing into a **mature (preovulatory, tertiary,** or **Graafian) follicle** within about 14 days after the onset of follicular development (step **6**). The antrum occupies most of the space in a mature follicle. The oocyte, surrounded by the zona pellucida and a single layer of granulosa cells, is displaced asymmetrically at one side of the growing follicle, in a little mound that protrudes into the antrum.

OVULATION The greatly expanded mature follicle bulges on the ovarian surface, creating a thin area that ruptures to release the oocyte at ovulation (step **7**). Rupture of the follicle is facilitated by release from the follicular cells of enzymes (triggered by a burst in LH secretion, which is described later) that digest the connective tissue in the follicular wall. The bulging wall, thus weakened, balloons out even farther to the point that it can no longer contain the rapidly expanding follicular contents.

Just before ovulation, the oocyte completes its first meiotic division. The ovum (secondary oocyte), still surrounded by its tightly adhering zona pellucida and granulosa cells (now called the **corona radiata,** meaning "radiating crown"), is swept out of the ruptured follicle into the abdominal cavity by the leaking antral fluid (see ● Figure 18-11c). The released ovum is quickly drawn into the oviduct, where fertilization may or may not take place.

The other developing follicles that failed to reach maturation and ovulate undergo degeneration, never to be reactivated. Occasionally, two (or perhaps more) follicles reach maturation and ovulate around the same time. If both are fertilized, **fraternal twins** result. Because fraternal twins arise from separate ova fertilized by separate sperm, they share no more in common than any other two siblings except for the same birth date. **Identical twins,** in contrast, develop from a single fertilized ovum that completely divides into two separate, genetically identical embryos at an early stage of development.

Rupture of the follicle at ovulation signals the end of the follicular phase and ushers in the luteal phase.

The luteal phase is characterized by the presence of a corpus luteum.

The ruptured follicle left behind in the ovary after release of the ovum changes rapidly as the granulosa and thecal cells remaining in the remnant follicle undergo a dramatic structural and functional transformation.

FORMATION OF THE CORPUS LUTEUM; ESTROGEN AND PROGESTERONE SECRETION These old follicular cells form the **corpus luteum (CL)** (step **8**), a process called *luteinization.* The follicular-turned-luteal cells enlarge and are converted into very active steroid hormone–producing tissue. Abundant

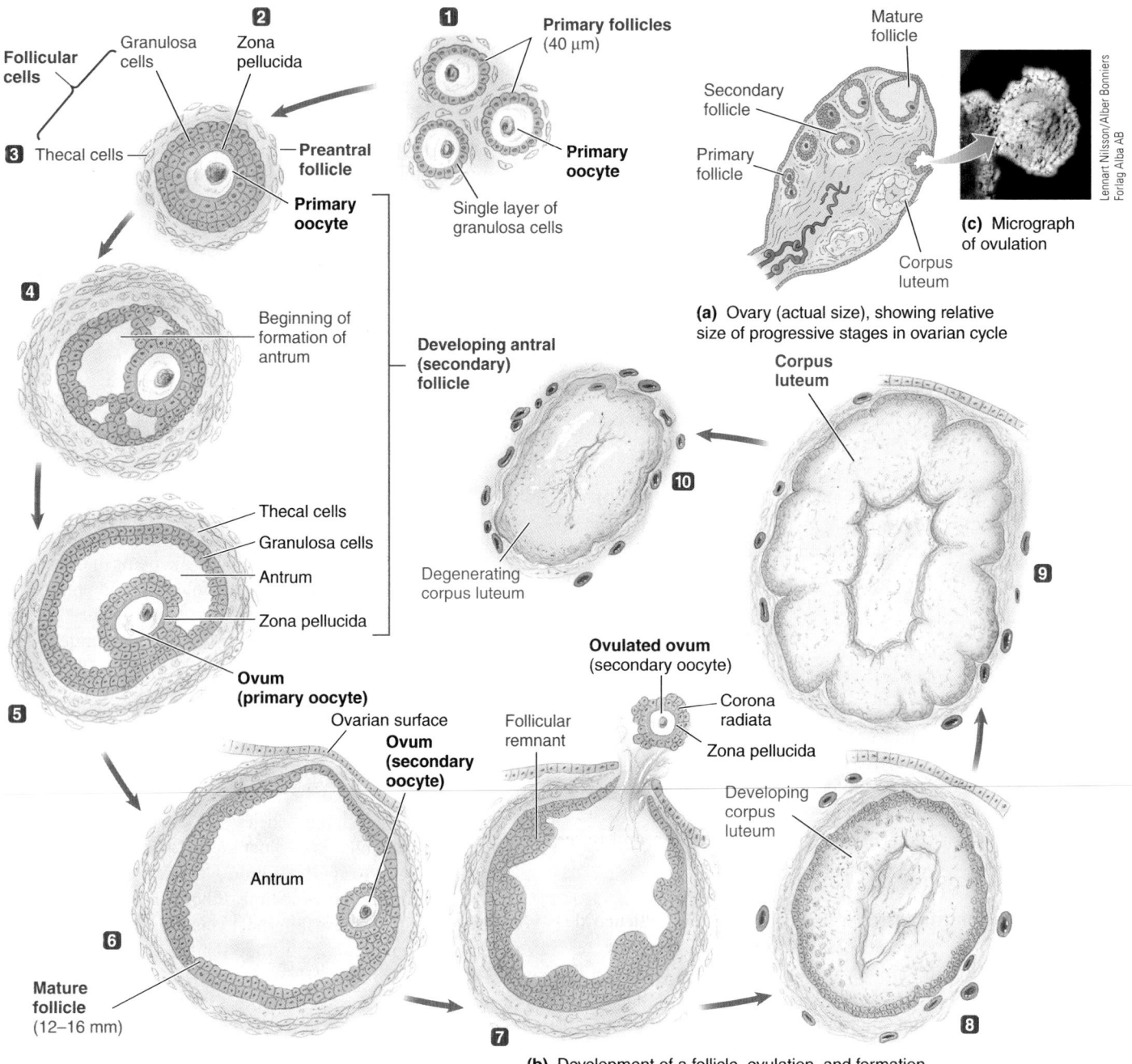

Follicular cells
Granulosa cells
Zona pellucida

3 Thecal cells

2

1 Primary follicles (40 μm)

Primary oocyte

Single layer of granulosa cells

Preantral follicle

Primary oocyte

4

Beginning of formation of antrum

Developing antral (secondary) follicle

Thecal cells
Granulosa cells
Antrum
Zona pellucida

Ovum (primary oocyte)

5

Ovarian surface

Ovum (secondary oocyte)

Antrum

6

Mature follicle (12–16 mm)

Follicular remnant

10

Degenerating corpus luteum

Ovulated ovum (secondary oocyte)

Corona radiata
Zona pellucida

Developing corpus luteum

7

8

Mature follicle
Secondary follicle
Primary follicle

Corpus luteum

Lennart Nilsson/Alber Bonniers Forlag Alba AB

(c) Micrograph of ovulation

(a) Ovary (actual size), showing relative size of progressive stages in ovarian cycle

Corpus luteum

9

(b) Development of a follicle, ovulation, and formation and degeneration of a corpus luteum

1 In a primary follicle, a primary oocyte is surrounded by a single layer of granulosa cells.

2 Under the influence of local paracrines, granulosa cells proliferate and form the zona pellucida around the oocyte.

3 Surrounding ovarian connective tissue differentiates into thecal cells, converting a primary follicle into a preantral follicle.

4 Follicles reaching the preantral stage are recruited for further development under the influence of FSH at the beginning of the follicular phase of the ovarian cycle. A recruited follicle develops into an antral, or secondary,

follicle as an estrogen-rich antrum starts to form.

5 The antrum continues to expand as the secondary follicle rapidly grows.

6 After about 2 weeks of rapid growth under the influence of FSH, the follicle has developed into a mature follicle, which has a greatly expanded antrum; the oocyte, which by now has developed into a secondary oocyte, is displaced to one side.

7 At midcycle, in response to a burst in LH secretion, the mature follicle, bulging on the ovarian surface, ruptures and releases the

oocyte, resulting in ovulation and ending the follicular phase.

8 Ushering in the luteal phase, the ruptured follicle develops into a corpus luteum under the influence of LH.

9 The corpus luteum continues to grow and secrete progesterone and estrogen that prepare the uterus for implantation of a fertilized ovum.

10 After 14 days, if a fertilized ovum does not implant in the uterus, the corpus luteum degenerates, the luteal phase ends, and a new follicular phase begins under the influence of a changing hormonal milieu.

● FIGURE 18-11 **Ovarian cycle.** (a) Ovary showing progressive stages in one ovarian cycle. All of these stages occur sequentially at one site, but the stages are represented in a loop in the periphery of the ovary so that all of the stages can be seen in progression simultaneously. (b) Enlarged view of the stages in one ovarian cycle. (c) Micrograph of a secondary oocyte being released (ovulation).

storage of cholesterol, the steroid precursor molecule, in lipid droplets within the corpus luteum gives this tissue a yellowish appearance, hence its name (*corpus* means "body"; *luteum* means "yellow").

The corpus luteum secretes into the blood abundant quantities of progesterone, along with smaller amounts of estrogen. Estrogen secretion in the follicular phase followed by progesterone secretion in the luteal phase is essential for preparing the uterus for implantation of a fertilized ovum. The CL becomes fully functional within 4 days after ovulation, but it continues to increase in size for another 4 or 5 days (step **9**).

DEGENERATION OF THE CORPUS LUTEUM If the released ovum is not fertilized and does not implant, the corpus luteum degenerates within about 14 days after its formation (step **10**). The luteal phase is now over, and one ovarian cycle is complete. A new wave of follicular development, which begins when degeneration of the old CL is completed, signals the onset of a new follicular phase.

CORPUS LUTEUM OF PREGNANCY If fertilization and implantation do occur, the corpus luteum continues to grow and produce increasing quantities of progesterone and estrogen instead of degenerating. Now called the *corpus luteum of pregnancy,* this ovarian structure persists until pregnancy ends. It provides the hormones essential for maintaining pregnancy until the developing placenta can take over this crucial function. You will learn more about the role of these structures later.

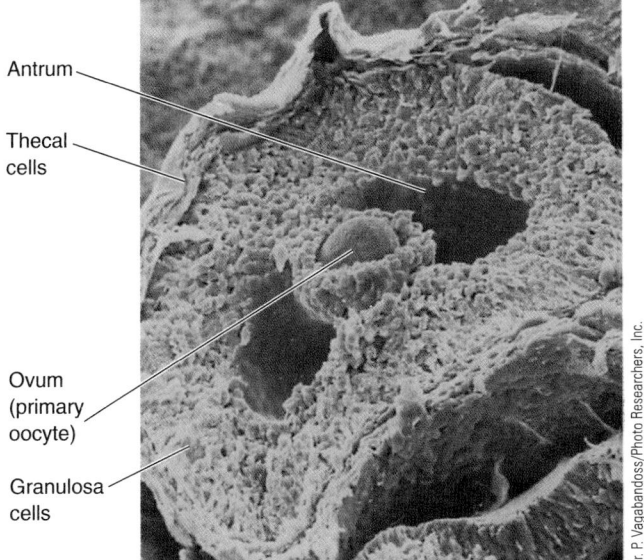

Antrum

Thecal cells

Ovum (primary oocyte)

Granulosa cells

Dr. P. Vagabandoss/Photo Researchers, Inc.

● FIGURE 18-12 **Scanning electron micrograph of a developing secondary follicle.**

The ovarian cycle is regulated by complex hormonal interactions.

The ovary has two related endocrine units: (1) the estrogen-secreting follicle during the first half of the cycle and (2) the corpus luteum, which secretes both progesterone and estrogen, during the last half of the cycle. These units are sequentially triggered by complex cyclic hormonal relationships among the hypothalamus, anterior pituitary, and these two ovarian endocrine units.

As in the male, gonadal function in the female is directly controlled by the anterior pituitary gonadotropic hormones, namely, follicle-stimulating hormone (FSH) and luteinizing hormone (LH). These hormones, in turn, are regulated by hypothalamic gonadotropin-releasing hormone (GnRH) and feedback actions of gonadal hormones. Unlike in the male, however, control of the female gonads is complicated by the cyclic nature of ovarian function. For example, the effects of FSH and LH on the ovaries depend on the stage of the ovarian cycle. Furthermore, as you will see, estrogen exerts negative-feedback effects during part of the cycle and positive-feedback effects during another part of the cycle, depending on the concentration of estrogen. Also in contrast to the male, FSH is not strictly responsible for gametogenesis, nor is LH solely responsible for gonadal hormone secretion. We consider control of follicular function, ovulation, and the corpus luteum separately, using ● Figure 18-13 as a means of integrating the various concurrent and sequential activities that take place throughout the cycle. To facilitate correlation between this rather intimidating figure and the accompanying text description of this complex cycle, the numbers in the figure and its legend correspond to the numbers in the text description.

CONTROL OF FOLLICULAR FUNCTION We begin with the follicular phase of the ovarian cycle (● Figure 18-13, step **1**). The early stages of preantral follicular growth and oocyte maturation do not require gonadotropic stimulation. Hormonal support is required, however, for further follicular development and antrum formation (step **2**) and for estrogen secretion (step **3**). Estrogen, FSH (step **4**), and LH (step **5**) are all needed. Antrum formation is induced by FSH. Both FSH and estrogen stimulate proliferation of the granulosa cells. Both LH and FSH are required for synthesis and secretion of estrogen by the follicle. LH stimulates the thecal cells to synthesize androgen, which diffuses into the adjacent granulosa cells. FSH stimulates the granulosa cells to convert this androgen into estrogen. Part of the estrogen produced by the growing follicle is secreted into the blood and is responsible for the steadily increasing plasma estrogen levels during the follicular phase (step **8**). The remainder of the estrogen remains within the follicle, contributing to the antral fluid and stimulating further granulosa cell proliferation.

The secreted estrogen, in addition to acting on sex-specific tissues such as the uterus, inhibits the hypothalamus and anterior pituitary in typical negative-feedback fashion (● Figure 18-14). The rising, moderate levels of estrogen characterizing the follicular phase act directly on the hypothalamus to inhibit GnRH secretion, thus suppressing GnRH-prompted release of

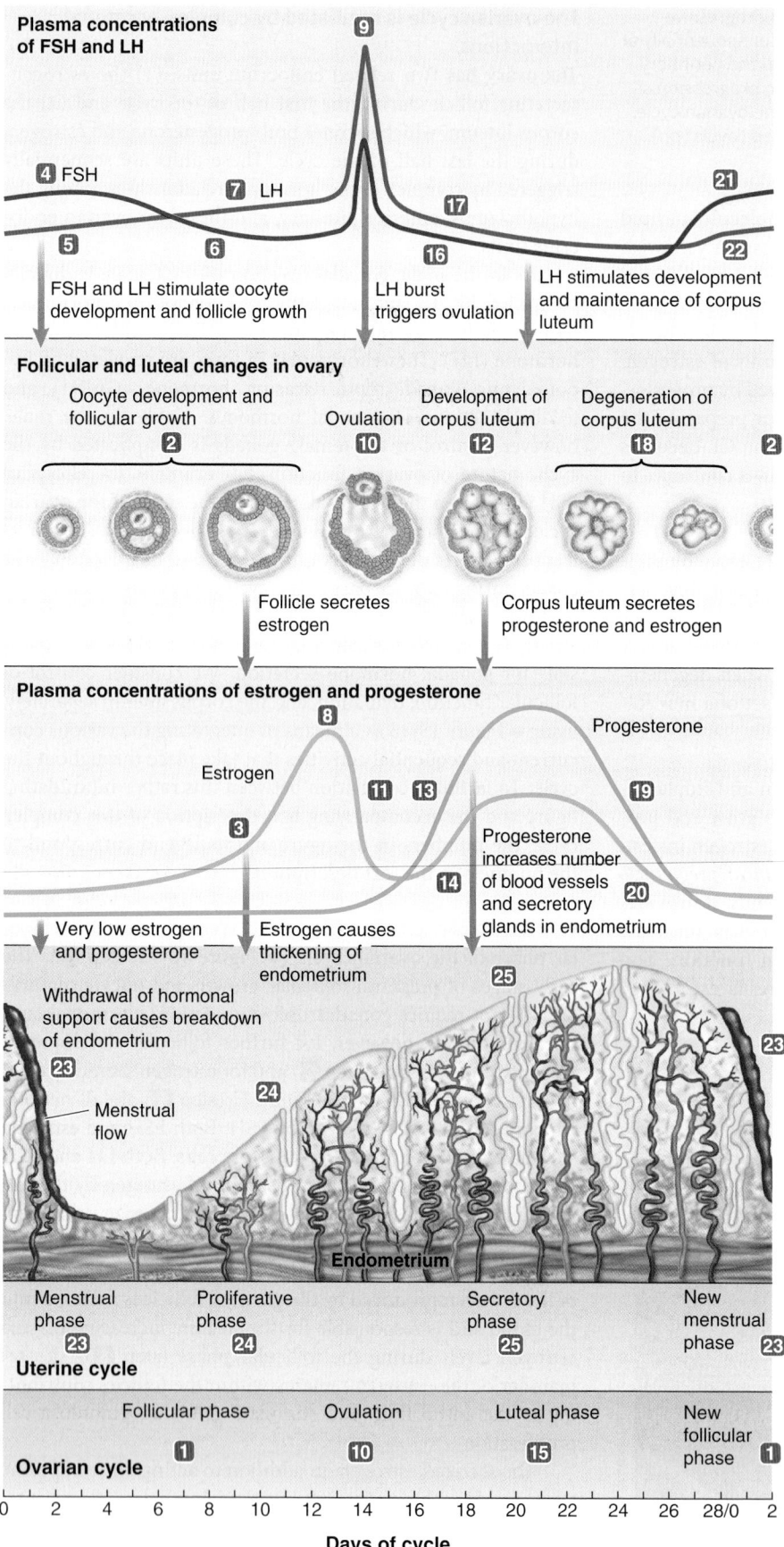

Plasma concentrations of FSH and LH

9

4 FSH

7 LH

21

5

6

17

16

22

FSH and LH stimulate oocyte development and follicle growth

LH burst triggers ovulation

LH stimulates development and maintenance of corpus luteum

Follicular and luteal changes in ovary

Oocyte development and follicular growth
2

Ovulation
10

Development of corpus luteum
12

Degeneration of corpus luteum
18

2

Follicle secretes estrogen

Corpus luteum secretes progesterone and estrogen

Plasma concentrations of estrogen and progesterone

8

Progesterone

Estrogen

11 13

19

3

Progesterone increases number of blood vessels and secretory glands in endometrium
14

20

Very low estrogen and progesterone

Estrogen causes thickening of endometrium

25

Withdrawal of hormonal support causes breakdown of endometrium
23

23

24

Menstrual flow

Endometrium

| Menstrual phase 23 | Proliferative phase 24 | Secretory phase 25 | New menstrual phase 23 |

Uterine cycle

| Follicular phase 1 | Ovulation 10 | Luteal phase 15 | New follicular phase 1 |

Ovarian cycle

Days of cycle: 0 2 4 6 8 10 12 14 16 18 20 22 24 26 28/0 2

Days of cycle

● **FIGURE 18-13 Correlation between hormonal levels and cyclic ovarian and uterine changes.** During the first half of the ovarian cycle, the follicular phase (step **1**), the ovarian follicle (step **2**) secretes estrogen (step **3**) under the influence of FSH (step **4**), LH (step **5**), and estrogen itself. The rising, moderate levels of estrogen inhibit FSH secretion, which declines (step **6**) during the last part of the follicular phase, and incompletely suppress tonic LH secretion, which continues to rise (step **7**) throughout the follicular phase. When the follicular output of estrogen reaches its peak (step **8**), the high levels of estrogen trigger a surge in LH secretion at midcycle (step **9**). This LH surge brings about ovulation of the mature follicle (step **10**). Estrogen secretion plummets (step **11**) when the follicle meets its demise at ovulation.

The old follicular cells are transformed into the corpus luteum (step **12**), which secretes progesterone (step **13**), as well as estrogen (step **14**), during the last half of the ovarian cycle, the luteal phase (step **15**). Progesterone strongly inhibits both FSH (step **16**) and LH (step **17**), which continue to decrease throughout the luteal phase. The corpus luteum degenerates (step **18**) in about 2 weeks if the released ovum has not been fertilized and implanted in the uterus. Progesterone (step **19**) and estrogen (step **20**) levels sharply decrease when the corpus luteum degenerates, removing the inhibitory influences on FSH and LH. As these anterior pituitary hormone levels start to rise again (steps **21** and **22**) when no longer inhibited, they stimulate the development of a new batch of follicles as a new follicular phase is ushered in (steps **1** and **2**).

Concurrent uterine phases reflect the influences of the ovarian hormones on the uterus. Early in the follicular phase, the highly vascularized, nutrient-rich endometrial lining is sloughed off (the uterine menstrual phase) (step **23**). This sloughing results from the withdrawal of estrogen and progesterone (steps **19** and **20**) when the old corpus luteum degenerated at the end of the preceding luteal phase (step **18**). Late in the follicular phase, the rising levels of estrogen (step **3**) cause the endometrium to thicken (the uterine proliferative phase) (step **24**). After ovulation (step **10**), progesterone from the corpus luteum (step **13**) brings about vascular and secretory changes in the estrogen-primed endometrium to produce a suitable environment for implantation (the uterine secretory, or progestational, phase) (step **25**). When the corpus luteum degenerates (step **18**), a new ovarian follicular phase (steps **1** and **2**) and uterine menstrual phase (step **23**) begin.

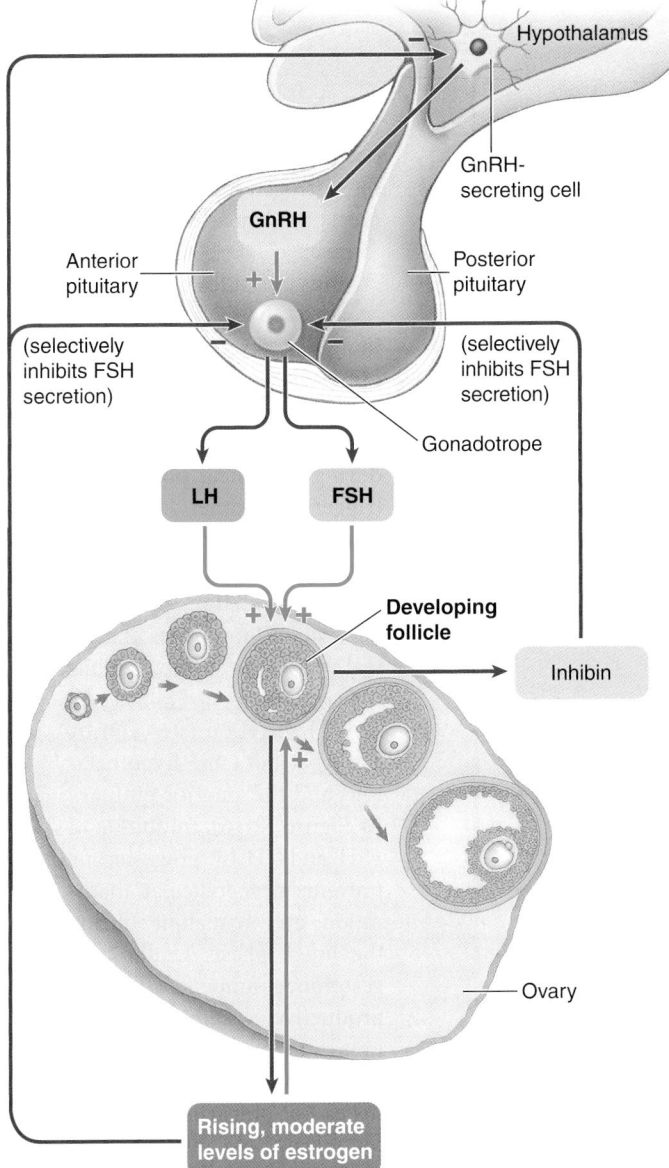

seeming paradox occurs because estrogen alone cannot completely suppress **tonic** (low-level, ongoing) **LH secretion;** to completely inhibit tonic LH secretion, both estrogen and progesterone are required. Because progesterone does not appear until the luteal phase of the cycle, the basal level of circulating LH slowly increases during the follicular phase under incomplete inhibition by estrogen alone.

CONTROL OF OVULATION Ovulation and subsequent luteinization of the ruptured follicle are triggered by an abrupt, massive increase in LH secretion (step **9**). This **LH surge** brings about four major changes in the follicle:

1. It halts estrogen synthesis by the follicular cells (step **11**).
2. It reinitiates meiosis in the mature follicle's oocyte, which had been in meiotic arrest since fetal development.
3. It triggers production of local prostaglandins, which induce ovulation by promoting vascular changes that cause rapid follicular swelling while inducing enzymatic digestion of the follicular wall. Together, these actions lead to rupture of the weakened wall that covers the bulging follicle (step **10**).
4. It causes differentiation of follicular cells into luteal cells. Because the LH surge triggers both ovulation and luteinization, formation of the corpus luteum automatically follows ovulation (step **12**). Thus, the midcycle burst in LH secretion is a dramatic point in the cycle; it terminates the follicular phase and initiates the luteal phase (step **15**).

The two modes of LH secretion—tonic LH secretion (step **7**) that promotes ovarian hormone secretion and the LH surge (step **9**) that causes ovulation—not only occur at different times and produce different effects but also are controlled by different mechanisms. Tonic LH secretion is partially suppressed by the inhibitory action of the rising, moderate levels of estrogen (step **3**) during the follicular phase and is completely suppressed (step **17**) by the increasing levels of progesterone during the luteal phase (step **13**). Because tonic LH secretion stimulates both estrogen and progesterone secretion, this is a typical negative-feedback effect.

In contrast, the LH surge is triggered by a *positive-feedback effect.* Whereas the rising, moderate level of estrogen early in the follicular phase *inhibits* LH secretion, the high level of estrogen that occurs during peak estrogen secretion late in the follicular phase (step **8**) *stimulates* LH secretion and initiates the LH surge (● Figure 18-15). Thus, LH enhances estrogen production by the follicle, and the resultant peak estrogen concentration stimulates LH secretion. The high plasma concentration of estrogen acts directly on the hypothalamus to increase GnRH, thereby increasing both LH and FSH secretion. It also acts directly on the anterior pituitary to specifically increase LH secretion by the gonadotropes. The latter effect largely accounts for the much greater surge in LH secretion compared to FSH secretion at midcycle (see ● Figure 18-13, step **9**). Also, continued inhibin secretion by the follicular cells preferentially inhibits FSH secretion, keeping the FSH levels from rising as high as the LH levels. There is no known role for the modest midcycle surge

● **FIGURE 18-14 Feedback control of FSH and tonic LH secretion during the follicular phase.**

FSH and LH from the anterior pituitary. However, estrogen's primary effect is directly on the pituitary. Estrogen selectively inhibits FSH secretion by the gonadotropes.

This differential secretion of FSH and LH by the gonadotropes induced by estrogen is in part responsible for the declining plasma FSH level, unlike the rising plasma LH concentration, during the follicular phase as the estrogen level rises (see ● Figure 18-13, step **6**). Another contributing factor to the fall in FSH during the follicular phase is secretion of *inhibin* by the follicular cells. Inhibin preferentially inhibits FSH secretion by acting at the anterior pituitary, just as it does in the male (● Figure 18-14). The decline in FSH secretion brings about atresia of all but the single dominant, most mature of the developing follicles.

In contrast to FSH, LH secretion continues to rise slowly during the follicular phase (see ● Figure 18-13, step **7**) despite inhibition of GnRH (and thus, indirectly, LH) secretion. This

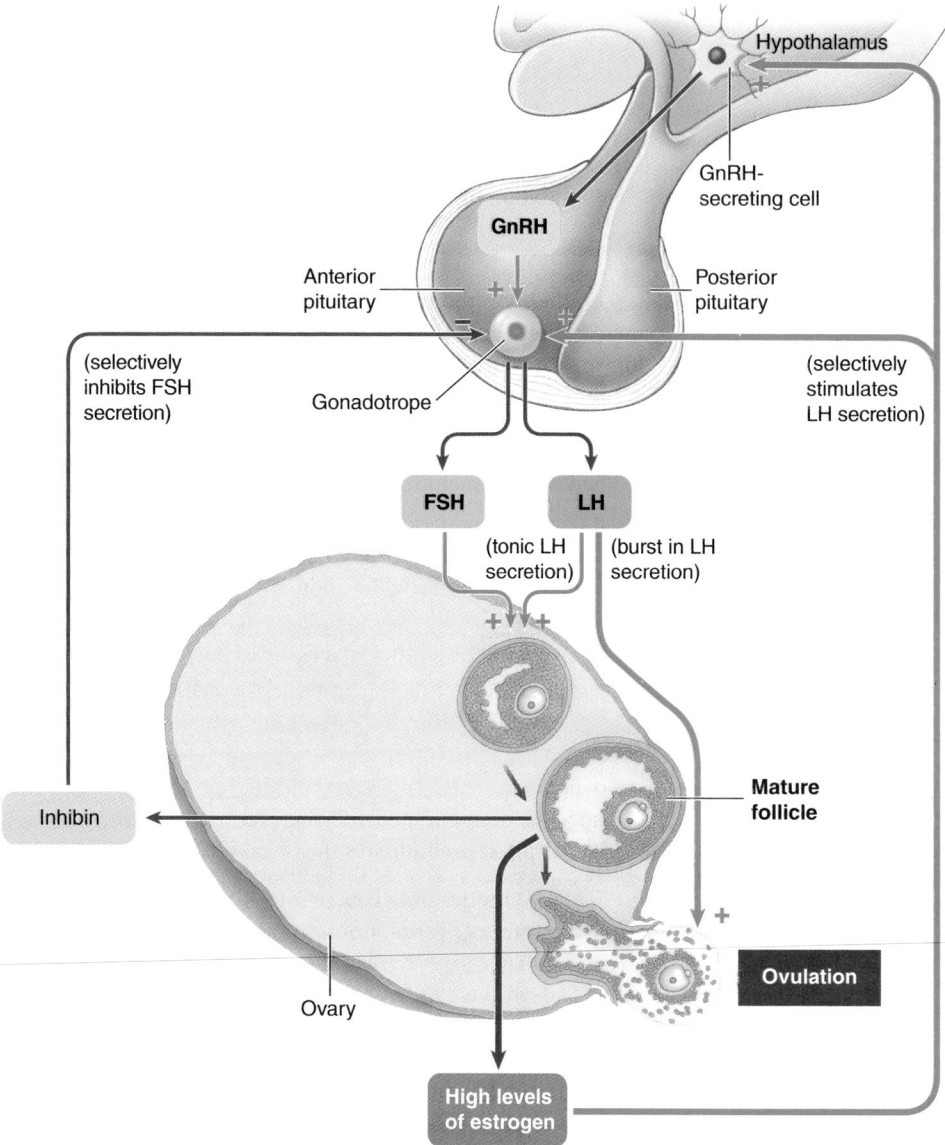

follicular phase is dominated by estrogen and the luteal phase by progesterone.

A transitory drop in the level of circulating estrogen occurs at midcycle (step **11**) as the estrogen-secreting follicle meets its demise at ovulation. The estrogen level climbs again during the luteal phase because of the CL's activity, although it does not reach the same peak as during the follicular phase. What keeps the modestly high estrogen level during the luteal phase from triggering another LH surge? Progesterone. Even though a high level of estrogen stimulates LH secretion, progesterone, which dominates the luteal phase, powerfully inhibits LH secretion (step **17**), as well as FSH secretion (step **16**) by acting at both the hypothalamus and the anterior pituitary (● Figure 18-16). Inhibition of FSH and LH by progesterone prevents new follicular maturation and ovulation during the luteal phase. Under progesterone's influence, the reproductive system is gearing up to support the just-released ovum, should it be fertilized, instead of preparing other ova for release. No inhibin is secreted by the luteal cells.

The corpus luteum functions for an average of 2 weeks and then degenerates if fertilization does not occur (see ● Figure 18-13, step **18**). The mechanisms that govern degeneration of the CL are not fully understood. The declining level of circulating LH (step **17**), driven down by inhibitory actions of progesterone, undoubtedly contributes to the CL's downfall. Prostaglandins and estrogen released by the luteal cells themselves may play a role. Demise of the CL terminates the luteal phase and sets the stage for a new follicular phase. As the CL degenerates, plasma progesterone (step **19**) and estrogen (step **20**) levels fall rapidly because these hormones are no longer being produced. Withdrawal of the inhibitory effects of these hormones on the hypothalamus allows FSH (step **21**) and tonic LH (step **22**) secretion to modestly increase again. Under the influence of these gonadotropic hormones, another batch of primary follicles (step **2**) is induced to mature as a new follicular phase begins (step **1**).

● FIGURE 18-15 **Control of the LH surge at ovulation.**

in FSH that accompanies the pronounced and pivotal LH surge. Because only a mature, preovulatory follicle, not follicles in earlier stages of development, can secrete high-enough levels of estrogen to trigger the LH surge, ovulation is not induced until a follicle has reached the proper size and degree of maturation. In a way, then, the follicle lets the hypothalamus know when it is ready to be stimulated to ovulate. The LH surge lasts for about a day at midcycle, just before ovulation.

CONTROL OF THE CORPUS LUTEUM LH "maintains" the corpus luteum; that is, after triggering development of the CL, LH stimulates ongoing steroid hormone secretion by this ovarian structure. Under the influence of LH, the CL secretes both progesterone (step **13**) and estrogen (step **14**), with progesterone being its most abundant hormonal product. The plasma progesterone level increases for the first time during the luteal phase. No progesterone is secreted during the follicular phase. Therefore, the

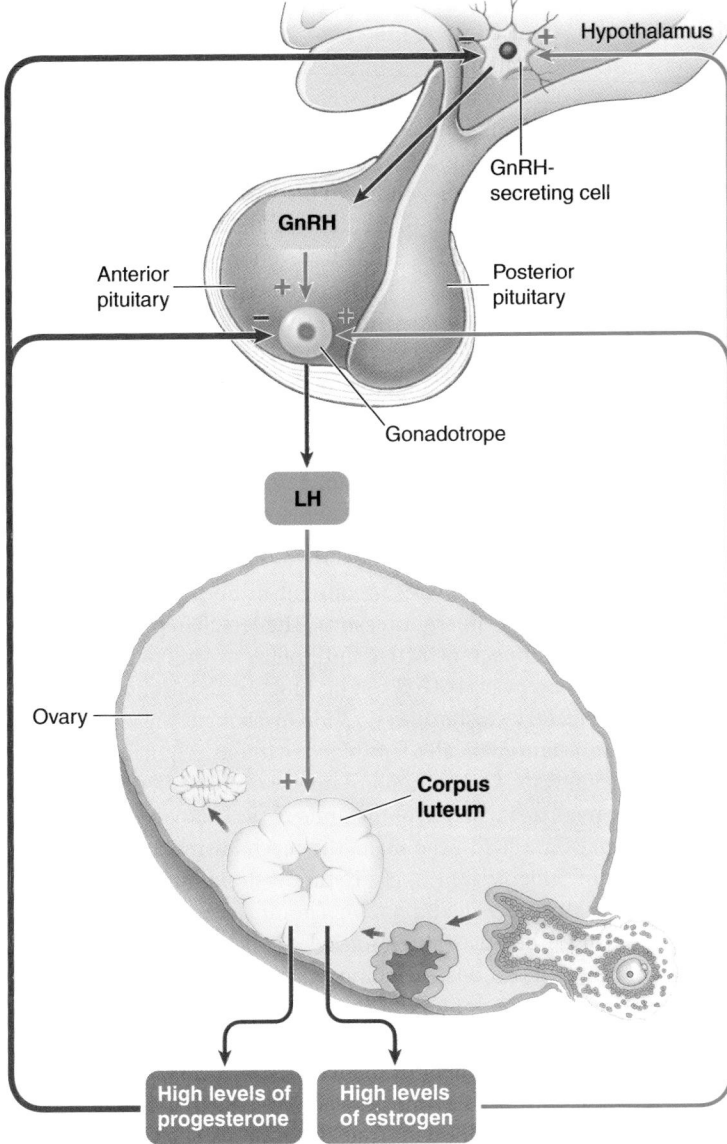

● **FIGURE 18-16 Feedback control during the luteal phase.**

We briefly examine the influences of estrogen and progesterone on the uterus and then consider the effects of cyclic fluctuations of these hormones on uterine structure and function.

INFLUENCES OF ESTROGEN AND PROGESTERONE ON THE UTERUS The uterus consists of two main layers: the **myometrium,** the outer smooth muscle layer, and the **endometrium,** the inner lining that contains numerous blood vessels and glands. Estrogen stimulates growth of both the myometrium and the endometrium. It also induces synthesis of progesterone receptors in the endometrium. Thus, progesterone can exert an effect on the endometrium only after it has been "primed" by estrogen. Progesterone acts on the estrogen-primed endometrium to convert it into a hospitable and nutritious lining suitable for implantation of a fertilized ovum. Under the influence of progesterone, the endometrial connective tissue becomes loose and edematous as a result of an accumulation of electrolytes and water, which facilitates implantation of the fertilized ovum. Progesterone further prepares the endometrium to sustain an early-developing embryo by stimulating the endometrial glands to secrete and store large quantities of glycogen (stored glucose) and by causing tremendous growth of the endometrial blood vessels. Progesterone also reduces the contractility of the uterus to provide a quiet environment for implantation and embryonic growth.

The menstrual cycle consists of three phases: the *menstrual phase,* the *proliferative phase,* and the *secretory,* or *progestational, phase.*

MENSTRUAL PHASE The **menstrual phase** is the most overt phase, characterized by discharge of blood and endometrial debris from the vagina (see ● Figure 18-13, step **23**). By convention, the first day of menstruation is considered the start of a new cycle. It coincides with the end of the ovarian luteal phase and onset of a new follicular phase. As the corpus luteum degenerates because fertilization and implantation of the ovum released during the preceding cycle did not take place (step **18**), circulating levels of progesterone and estrogen drop precipitously (steps **19** and **20**). Because the net effect of progesterone and estrogen is to prepare the endometrium for implantation of a fertilized ovum, withdrawal of these steroids deprives the highly vascular, nutrient-rich uterine lining of its hormonal support.

The fall in ovarian hormone levels also stimulates release of a uterine prostaglandin that causes vasoconstriction of the endometrial vessels, disrupting the blood supply to the endometrium. The subsequent reduction in O_2 delivery causes death of the endometrium, including its blood vessels. The resulting bleeding through the disintegrating vessels flushes the dying endometrial tissue into the uterine lumen. Most of the uterine lining sloughs during each menstrual period except for a deep,

Cyclic uterine changes are caused by hormonal changes during the ovarian cycle.

The fluctuations in circulating levels of estrogen and progesterone during the ovarian cycle induce profound changes in the uterus, giving rise to the **menstrual,** or **uterine, cycle.** Because it reflects hormonal changes during the ovarian cycle, the menstrual cycle averages 28 days, as does the ovarian cycle, although even normal adults vary considerably from this mean. The outward manifestation of the cyclic changes in the uterus is the menstrual bleeding once during each menstrual cycle (that is, once a month). Less obvious changes take place throughout the cycle, however, as the uterus is prepared for implantation, should a released ovum be fertilized, and then is stripped clean of its prepared lining (menstruation) if implantation does not occur, only to repair itself and start preparing for the ovum that will be released during the next cycle.

thin layer of epithelial cells and glands, from which the endometrium will regenerate. The same local uterine prostaglandin also stimulates mild rhythmic contractions of the uterine myometrium. These contractions help expel the blood and endometrial debris from the uterine cavity out through the vagina as **menstrual flow.** Excessive uterine contractions caused by prostaglandin overproduction produce the *menstrual cramps* some women experience.

The average blood loss during a single menstrual period is 50 to 150 ml. In addition to the blood and endometrial debris, large numbers of leukocytes are found in the menstrual flow. These white blood cells play an important defense role in helping the raw endometrium resist infection.

Menstruation typically lasts for about 5 to 7 days after degeneration of the CL, coinciding in time with the early portion of the ovarian follicular phase (steps 23 and 1). Withdrawal of progesterone and estrogen (steps 19 and 20) on degeneration of the CL leads simultaneously to sloughing of the endometrium (menstruation) (step 23) and development of new follicles in the ovary (steps 1 and 2) under the influence of rising gonadotropic hormone levels (steps 21 and 22). The drop in gonadal hormone secretion removes inhibitory influences from the hypothalamus and anterior pituitary, so FSH and LH secretion increases and a new follicular phase begins. After 5 to 7 days under the influence of FSH and LH, the newly growing follicles are secreting enough estrogen (step 3) to promote repair and growth of the endometrium.

PROLIFERATIVE PHASE Thus, menstrual flow ceases, and the **proliferative phase** of the uterine cycle begins concurrent with the last portion of the ovarian follicular phase as the endometrium starts to repair itself and proliferate (step 24) under the influence of estrogen from the newly growing follicles. When the menstrual flow ceases, a thin endometrial layer less than 1 mm thick remains. Estrogen stimulates proliferation of epithelial cells, glands, and blood vessels in the endometrium, increasing this lining to a thickness of 3 to 5 mm. The estrogen-dominant proliferative phase lasts from the end of menstruation to ovulation. Peak estrogen levels (step 8) trigger the LH surge (step 9) responsible for ovulation (step 10).

SECRETORY, OR PROGESTATIONAL, PHASE After ovulation, when a new corpus luteum is formed (step 12), the uterus enters the **secretory, or progestational, phase** (step 25), which coincides in time with the ovarian luteal phase (step 15). The CL secretes large amounts of progesterone (step 13) and estrogen (step 14). Progesterone converts the thickened, estrogen-primed endometrium to a richly vascularized, glycogen-filled tissue. This period is called either the *secretory phase,* because the endometrial glands are actively secreting glycogen into the uterine lumen for early nourishment of a developing embryo before it implants, or the *progestational* ("before pregnancy") *phase,* referring to the development of a lush endometrial lining capable of supporting an early embryo after implantation. If fertilization and implantation do not occur, the CL degenerates and a new follicular phase and menstrual phase begin again.

Oral contraceptives prevent ovulation.

 Oral contraceptives, or **birth control pills,** prevent ovulation and thus unwanted pregnancy primarily by suppressing gonadotropin secretion. These pills, which contain synthetic estrogen-like and progesterone-like steroids, are taken for 3 weeks, either in combination or in sequence, and then are withdrawn for 1 week. These steroids, like the natural steroids produced during the ovarian cycle, inhibit GnRH and thus FSH and LH secretion. As a result, follicle maturation and ovulation do not take place, so conception is impossible. The endometrium responds to the exogenous steroids by thickening and developing secretory capacity, just as it would respond to the natural hormones. When these synthetic steroids are withdrawn after 3 weeks, the endometrial lining sloughs and menstruation occurs, as it normally would on degeneration of the corpus luteum.

Pubertal changes in females are similar to those in males.

Regular menstrual cycles are absent in both young and aging females, but for different reasons. The female reproductive system does not become active until puberty. Unlike the fetal testes, the fetal ovaries need not be functional, because in the absence of fetal testosterone secretion in a female, the reproductive system is automatically feminized, without requiring the presence of female sex hormones. Puberty occurs in females around 12 years of age when hypothalamic GnRH activity increases for the first time. As in the male, the mechanisms that govern the onset of puberty are not clearly understood but are believed to involve the pineal gland and melatonin secretion.

GnRH begins stimulating release of anterior pituitary gonadotropic hormones, which in turn stimulate ovarian activity. The resulting secretion of estrogen by the activated ovaries induces growth and maturation of the female reproductive tract, as well as development of the female secondary sexual characteristics. Estrogen's prominent action in the latter regard is to promote fat deposition in strategic locations, such as the breasts, buttocks, and thighs, giving rise to the typical curvaceous female figure. Enlargement of the breasts at puberty is the result primarily of fat deposition in the breast tissue, not functional development of the mammary glands. The pubertal rise in estrogen also closes the epiphyseal plates, halting further growth in height, similar to the effect of testosterone-turned-estrogen in males. Three other pubertal changes in females—growth of axillary and pubic hair, the pubertal growth spurt, and development of libido—are attributable to a spurt in adrenal androgen secretion at puberty, not to estrogen.

Menopause is unique to females.

The cessation of a woman's menstrual cycles at menopause sometime between the ages of 45 and 55 has traditionally been attributed to the limited supply of ovarian follicles present at birth. According to this proposal, once this reservoir is depleted, ovarian cycles, and hence menstrual cycles, cease. Thus, the termination of reproductive potential in a middle-aged woman is "preprogrammed" at her own birth. Recent evidence suggests, however, that a midlife hypothalamic change instead of aging ovaries may trigger the onset of menopause. Evolutionarily, menopause may have developed as a mechanism that prevented pregnancy in women beyond the time that they could likely rear a child before their own death.

Menopause is preceded by a period of progressive ovarian failure characterized by increasingly irregular cycles and dwindling estrogen levels. In addition to the ending of ovarian and menstrual cycles, the loss of ovarian estrogen following menopause brings about many physical and emotional changes. These changes include vaginal dryness, which can cause discomfort during sex, and gradual atrophy of the genital organs. However, postmenopausal women still have a sex drive because of their adrenal androgens.

Males do not experience complete gonadal failure as females do, for two reasons. First, a male's germ cell supply is unlimited because mitotic activity of the spermatogonia continues. Second, gonadal hormone secretion in males is not inextricably dependent on gametogenesis, as it is in females. If female sex hormones were produced by separate tissues unrelated to those governing gametogenesis, as are male sex hormones, estrogen and progesterone secretion would not automatically stop when oogenesis stopped.

You have now learned about the events that take place if fertilization does not occur. Because the primary function of the reproductive system is, of course, reproduction, we next turn our attention to the sequence of events that take place when fertilization does occur.

The oviduct is the site of fertilization.

Fertilization, the union of male and female gametes, normally occurs in the upper third of the oviduct (● Figure 18-17). Thus, both the ovum and the sperm must be transported from their gonadal site of production to the upper oviduct.

OVUM TRANSPORT TO THE OVIDUCT   Unlike the male reproductive tract, which has a continuous lumen from the site of sperm production in the seminiferous tubules to exit of the sperm

from the urethra at ejaculation, the ovaries are not in direct contact with the reproductive tract. The ovum is released into the abdominal cavity at ovulation. Normally, however, the egg is quickly picked up by the oviduct. The dilated end of the oviduct cups around the ovary and contains **fimbriae,** fingerlike projections that contract in a sweeping motion to guide the released ovum into the oviduct (see ● Figures 18-2b, p. 582, and 18-17). Furthermore, the fimbriae are lined by cilia—fine, hairlike projections that beat in waves toward the interior of the oviduct—further assuring the ovum's passage into the oviduct (see p. 38).

Conception can take place during a limited time span in each cycle (the **fertile period**). If not fertilized, the ovum begins to disintegrate within 12 to 24 hours and is subsequently phagocytized by cells that line the reproductive tract. Fertilization must therefore occur within 24 hours after ovulation, when the ovum is still viable. Sperm typically survive about 48 hours but can survive up to 5 days in the female reproductive tract, so sperm deposited from 5 days before ovulation to 24 hours after ovulation may be able to fertilize the released ovum, although these times vary considerably.

SPERM TRANSPORT TO THE OVIDUCT   After sperm are deposited in the vagina at ejaculation, they must travel through the cervical canal, through the uterus, and then up to the egg in the upper third of the oviduct (● Figure 18-17). The first sperm arrive in the oviduct within half an hour after ejaculation. Even though sperm are mobile by means of whiplike contractions of their tails, 30 minutes is too soon for a sperm's own mobility to transport it to the site of fertilization. To make this formidable journey, sperm need the help of the female reproductive tract.

The first hurdle is passage through the cervical canal. Throughout most of the cycle, the cervical mucus is too thick to permit sperm penetration. The cervical mucus becomes thin and watery enough to permit sperm to penetrate only when estrogen levels are high, as in the presence of a mature follicle about to ovulate. Sperm migrate up the cervical canal under

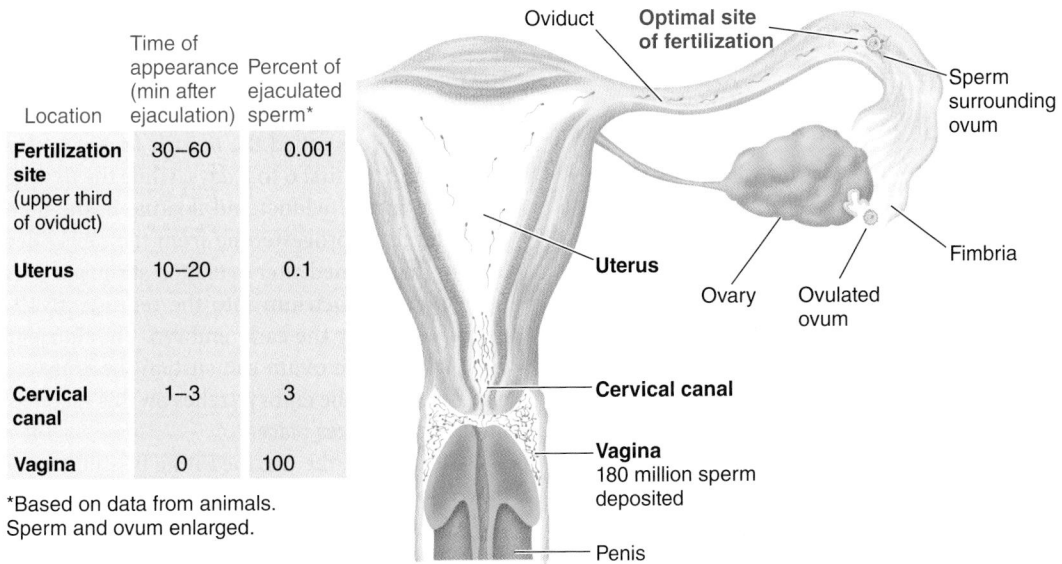

Location	Time of appearance (min after ejaculation)	Percent of ejaculated sperm*
Fertilization site (upper third of oviduct)	30–60	0.001
Uterus	10–20	0.1
Cervical canal	1–3	3
Vagina	0	100

*Based on data from animals.
Sperm and ovum enlarged.

● FIGURE 18-17 **Ovum and sperm transport to the site of fertilization.**

their own power. The canal remains penetrable for only 2 or 3 days during each cycle, around the time of ovulation.

Once sperm have entered the uterus, contractions of the myometrium churn them around in "washing-machine" fashion. This action quickly disperses sperm throughout the uterine cavity. When sperm reach the oviduct, they are propelled to the fertilization site in the upper end of the oviduct by upward contractions of the oviduct smooth muscle. These myometrial and oviduct contractions that facilitate sperm transport are induced by the high estrogen level just before ovulation, aided by seminal prostaglandins.

Even around ovulation time, when sperm can penetrate the cervical canal, of the 165 million sperm typically deposited in a single ejaculate, only a few thousand make it to the oviduct (● Figure 18-17). That only a very small percentage of the deposited sperm ever reach their destination is one reason sperm concentration must be so high (20 million/ml of semen) for a man to be fertile. The other reason is that the acrosomal enzymes of many sperm are needed to break down the barriers surrounding the ovum (● Figure 18-18).

FERTILIZATION The tail of the sperm is used to maneuver for final penetration of the ovum. To fertilize an ovum, a sperm must first pass through the corona radiata and zona pellucida surrounding it. The sperm penetrates the corona radiata by means of membrane-bound enzymes in the surface membrane that surrounds the head (● Figure 18-19a, step ❶). Sperm can penetrate the zona pellucida only after binding with specific **ZP3 receptors** on the surface of this layer. Only sperm of the same species can bind to these zona pellucida sites and pass through. Binding of sperm triggers the **acrosome reaction,** in which the acrosomal membrane disrupts and the acrosomal enzymes are released (step ❷). The acrosomal enzymes digest the zona pellucida, enabling the sperm, with its tail still beating, to tunnel a path through this protective barrier (step ❸). The first sperm to reach the ovum itself fuses with the plasma membrane of the ovum (actually a secondary oocyte), and its head (bearing its DNA) enters the ovum's cytoplasm (step ❹). The sperm's tail is frequently lost in this process, but the head carries the crucial genetic information. Sperm–egg fusion triggers the exocytosis of enzyme-filled **cortical granules** that are located in the outermost, or cortical, region of the egg into the space between the egg membrane and the zona pellucida (step ❺). These enzymes diffuse into the zona pellucida, where they inactivate the ZP3 receptors so that other sperm reaching the zona pellucida cannot bind with it. The enzymes also harden the zona pellucida and seal off tunnels in progress to keep other penetrating sperm from advancing. These chemical changes in the ovum's surrounding membrane makes this outer layer impenetrable to the entry of any more sperm, a phenomenon is known as **block to polyspermy** ("many sperm").

Sperm entry also triggers the second meiotic division of the egg, which is now ready to unite with the sperm to complete the fertilization process. Within an hour, the sperm and egg nuclei fuse, thanks to a molecular complex provided by the sperm that forms microtubules (see p. 37) to bring the male and female chromosome sets together for uniting. In addition to contributing its half of the chromosomes to the fertilized ovum, now called a **zygote,** the victorious sperm activates ovum enzymes essential for the early embryonic developmental program.

The blastocyst implants in the endometrium through the action of its trophoblastic enzymes.

During the first 3 to 4 days following fertilization, the zygote remains within the oviduct. Then it descends and floats freely within the uterine cavity for another 3 to 4 days before implanting.

THE BEGINNING STEPS The zygote is not idle during this time. It rapidly undergoes a number of mitotic cell divisions to form a solid ball of cells called the *morula* (● Figure 18-20).

During the first 6 to 8 days, while the developing embryo is in transit in the oviduct and floating in the uterine lumen, the rising levels of progesterone from the newly developed corpus luteum that formed after ovulation stimulate release of glycogen from the endometrium into the reproductive tract lumen for use as energy by the early embryo. The nutrients stored in the cytoplasm of the ovum can sustain the embryo for less than a day. After that, the embryo relies on this secreted glycogen until implantation takes place.

Meanwhile, the uterine lining is simultaneously being prepared for implantation under the influence of luteal-phase progesterone. During this time, the uterus is in its secretory, or progestational phase, storing up glycogen and becoming richly vascularized.

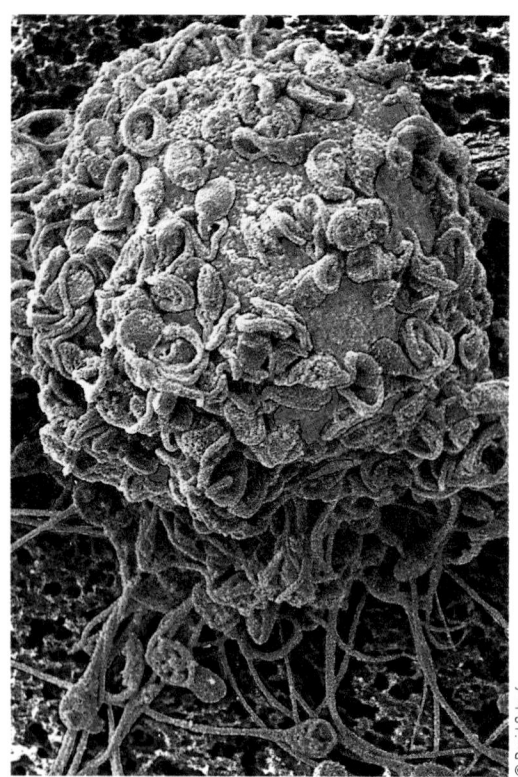

© David Scharf

● **FIGURE 18-18 Scanning electron micrograph of sperm amassed at the surface of an ovum.**

1 The fertilizing sperm penetrates the corona radiata via membrane-bound enzymes in the plasma membrane of its head and binds to ZP3 receptors on the zona pellucida.

2 Binding of sperm to these receptors triggers the acrosome reaction, in which hydrolytic enzymes in the acrosome are released onto the zona pellucida.

3 The acrosomal enzymes digest the zona pellucida, creating a pathway to the plasma membrane of the ovum. When the sperm reaches the ovum, the plasma membranes of the two cells fuse.

4 The sperm head with its DNA enters the ovum cytoplasm.

5 The sperm stimulates release of enzymes stored in cortical granules in the ovum, which in turn, inactivate ZP3 receptors and harden the zona pellucida, leading to the block to polyspermy.

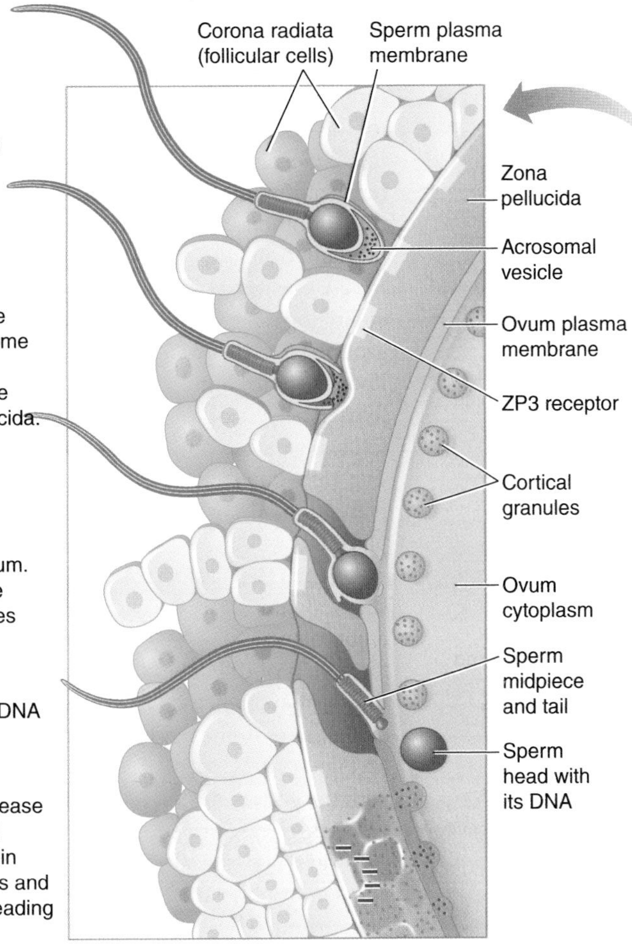

Corona radiata (follicular cells)
Sperm plasma membrane
Zona pellucida
Acrosomal vesicle
Ovum plasma membrane
ZP3 receptor
Cortical granules
Ovum cytoplasm
Sperm midpiece and tail
Sperm head with its DNA

(a) Sperm tunneling through the barriers surrounding an ovum

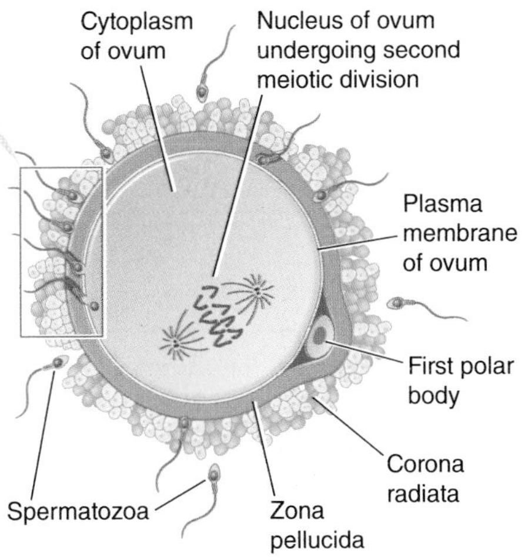

Cytoplasm of ovum
Nucleus of ovum undergoing second meiotic division
Plasma membrane of ovum
First polar body
Corona radiata
Zona pellucida
Spermatozoa

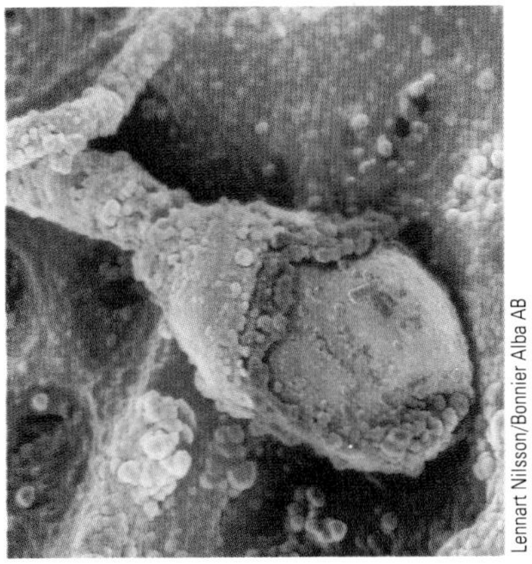

Lennart Nilsson/Bonnier Alba AB

(b) Scanning electron micrograph of spermatozoon with acrosomal enzymes (in red) exposed after acrosome reaction

● FIGURE 18-19 **Process of fertilization.**

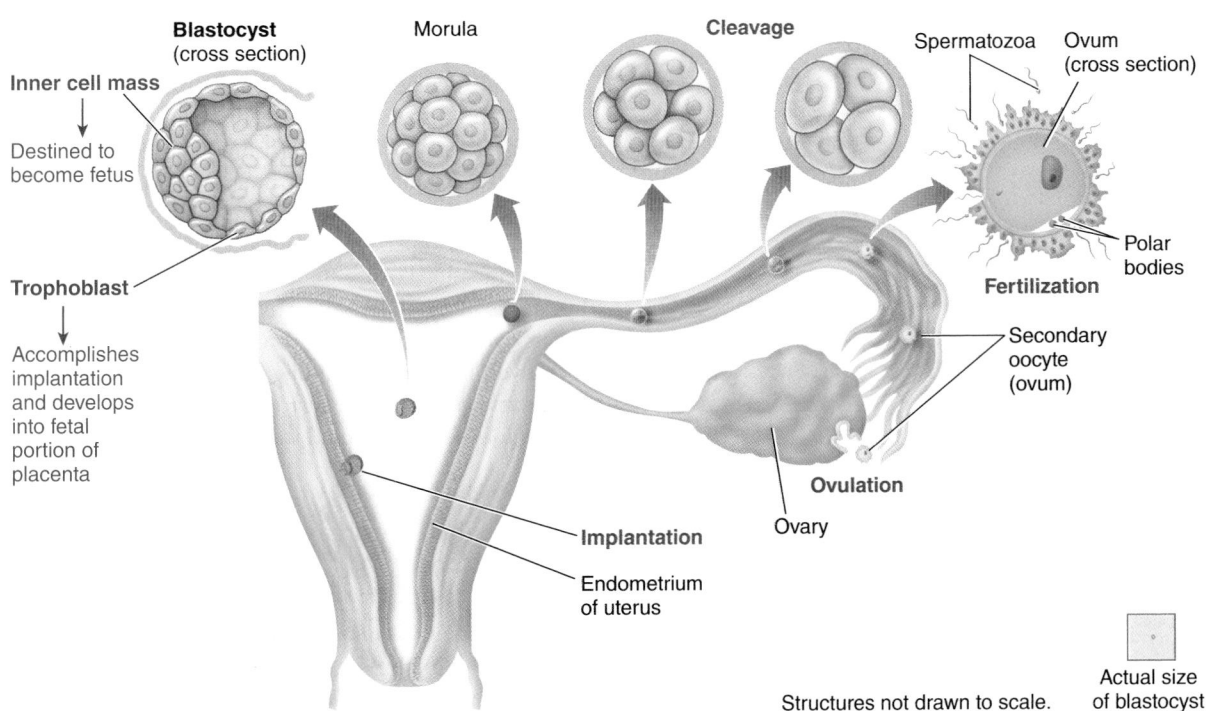

Blastocyst (cross section)
Inner cell mass
Destined to become fetus
Trophoblast
Accomplishes implantation and develops into fetal portion of placenta
Morula
Cleavage
Spermatozoa
Ovum (cross section)
Fertilization
Polar bodies
Secondary oocyte (ovum)
Ovulation
Ovary
Implantation
Endometrium of uterus
Structures not drawn to scale.
Actual size of blastocyst

● FIGURE 18-20 **Early stages of development from fertilization to implantation.** Note that the fertilized ovum progressively divides and differentiates into a blastocyst as it moves from the site of fertilization in the upper oviduct to the site of implantation in the uterus.

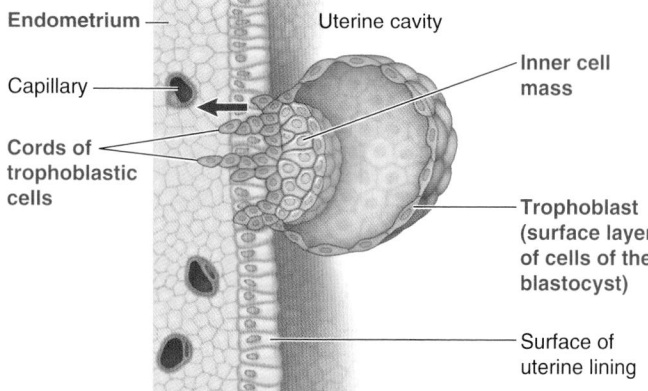

Endometrium — **Uterine cavity**

Capillary —

Cords of trophoblastic cells —

Inner cell mass

Trophoblast (surface layer of cells of the blastocyst)

Surface of uterine lining

1 When the free-floating blastocyst adheres to the endometrial lining, cords of trophoblastic cells begin to penetrate the endometrium.

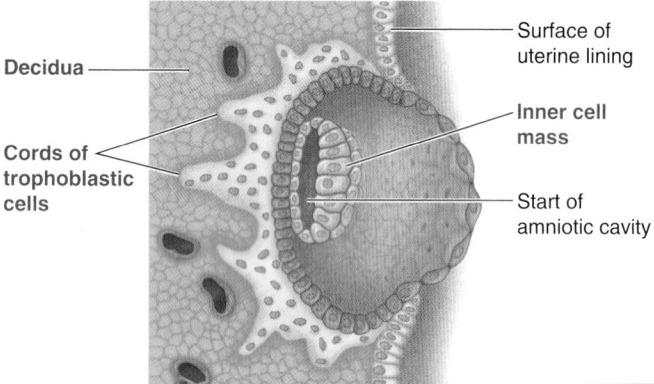

Decidua —

Cords of trophoblastic cells —

Surface of uterine lining

Inner cell mass

Start of amniotic cavity

2 Advancing cords of trophoblastic cells tunnel deeper into the endometrium, carving out a hole for the blastocyst. The boundaries between the cells in the advancing trophoblastic tissue disintegrate.

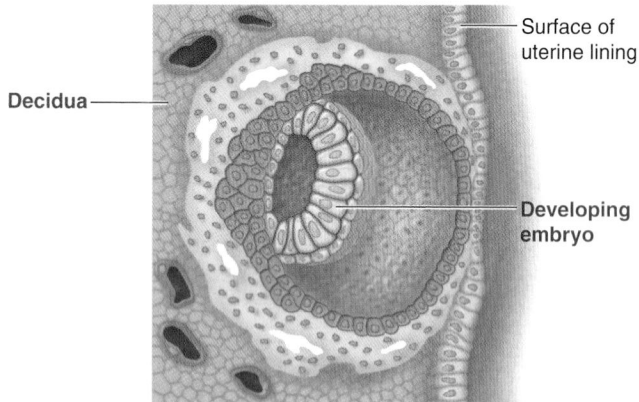

Decidua —

Surface of uterine lining

Developing embryo

3 When implantation is finished, the blastocyst is completely buried in the endometrium.

● **FIGURE 18-21 Implantation of the blastocyst.**

IMPLANTATION OF THE BLASTOCYST IN THE PREPARED ENDOMETRIUM By the time the endometrium is suitable for implantation (about a week after ovulation), the morula has descended to the uterus and continued to proliferate and differentiate into a *blastocyst* capable of implantation. The week's delay after fertilization and before implantation allows time for both the endometrium and the developing embryo to prepare for implantation.

A **blastocyst** is a single-layer hollow ball of about 50 cells encircling a fluid-filled cavity, with a dense mass of cells grouped together at one side (● Figure 18-20). This dense mass, known as the **inner cell mass,** becomes the embryo and then fetus. The rest of the blastocyst is never incorporated into the fetus, instead serving a supportive role during intrauterine life. The thin outermost layer, the **trophoblast,** accomplishes implantation, after which it develops into the fetal portion of the placenta.

When the blastocyst is ready to implant, its surface becomes sticky. By this time, the endometrium is ready to accept the early embryo and it too has become more adhesive through increased formation of cell adhesion molecules (CAMs) that help "Velcro" the blastocyst when it first contacts the uterine lining. The blastocyst adheres to the uterine lining on the side of its inner cell mass (● Figure 18-21, step **1**). **Implantation** begins when, on contact with the endometrium, the trophoblastic cells overlying the inner cell mass release protein-digesting enzymes. These enzymes digest pathways between the endometrial cells, permitting fingerlike cords of trophoblastic cells to penetrate into the depths of the endometrium, where they continue to digest uterine cells (step **2**). Through its cannibalistic actions, the trophoblast performs the dual functions of accomplishing implantation as it carves out a hole in the endometrium for the blastocyst and making metabolic fuel and raw materials available for the developing embryo as the advancing trophoblastic projections break down the nutrient-rich endometrial tissue. The plasma membranes of the advancing trophoblastic cells degenerate, forming a multinucleated syncytium that will eventually become the fetal portion of the placenta.

Stimulated by the invading trophoblast, the endometrial tissue at the contact site undergoes dramatic changes that enhance its ability to support the implanting embryo, such as increased vascularization and enhanced nutrient storage. The endometrial tissue so modified at the implantation site is called the **decidua.** It is into this super-rich decidual tissue that the blastocyst becomes embedded. After the blastocyst burrows into the decidua by means of trophoblastic activity, a layer of endometrial cells covers over the surface of the hole, completely burying the blastocyst within the uterine lining (step **3**). The trophoblastic layer continues to digest the surrounding decidual cells, providing energy for the embryo until the placenta develops.

The placenta is the organ of exchange between maternal and fetal blood.

The glycogen stores in the endometrium are sufficient to nourish the embryo only during its first few weeks. To sustain the growing embryo and then fetus for the duration of intrauterine life, the **placenta,** a specialized organ of exchange between ma-

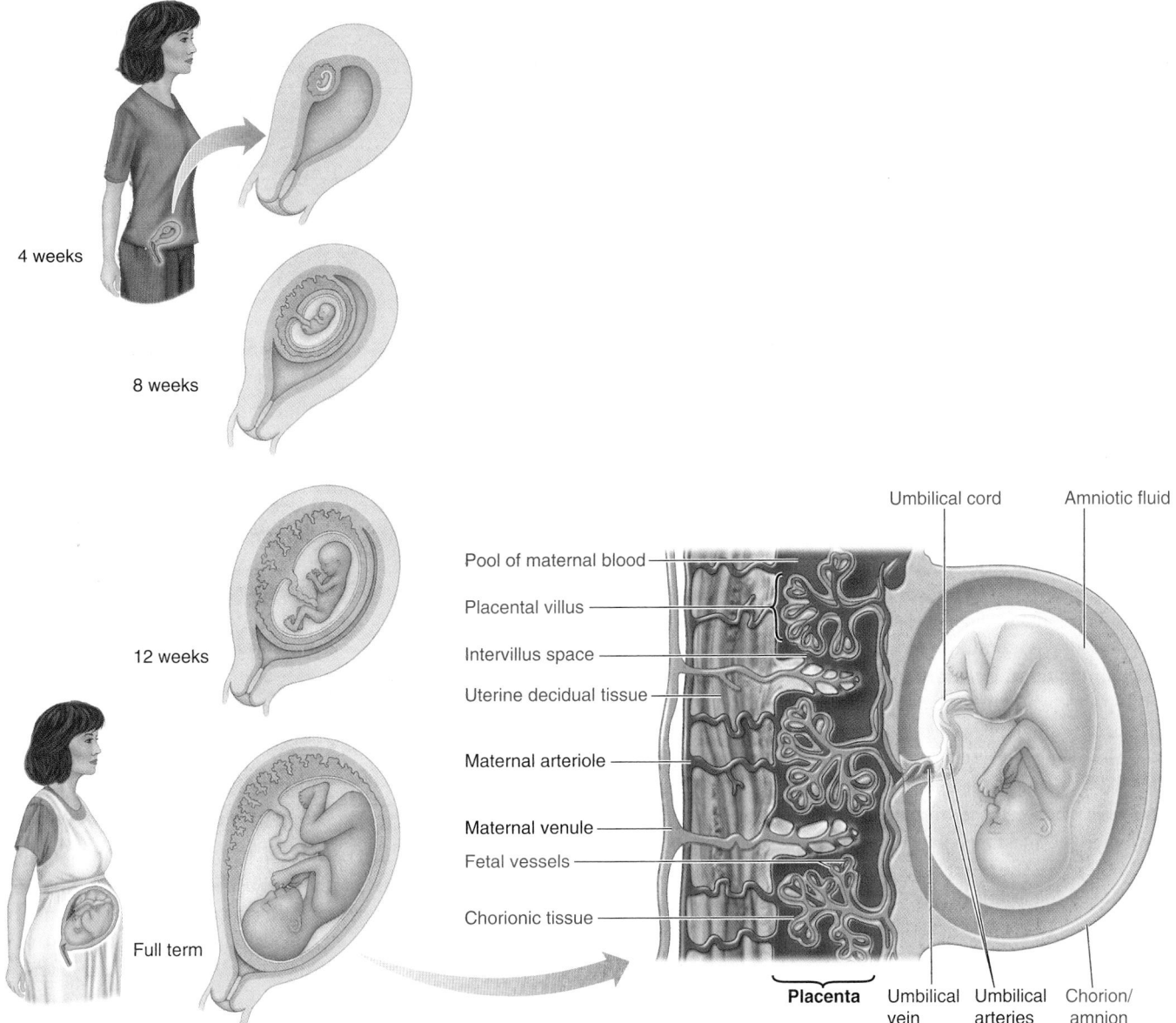

(a) Relationship between developing fetus and uterus as pregnancy progresses

(b) Representation of interlocking maternal and fetal structures that form the placenta

● **FIGURE 18-22 Placentation.** Fingerlike projections of chorionic (fetal) tissue form the placental villi, which protrude into a pool of maternal blood. Decidual (maternal) capillary walls are broken down by the expanding chorion so that maternal blood oozes through the spaces between the placental villi. Fetal placental capillaries branch off the umbilical arteries and project into the placental villi. Fetal blood flowing through these vessels is separated from the maternal blood by only the capillary wall and thin chorionic layer that forms the placental villi. Maternal blood enters through the maternal arterioles and then percolates through the pool of blood in the intervillous spaces. Here, exchanges are made between fetal and maternal blood before the fetal blood leaves through the umbilical vein and maternal blood exits through the maternal venules.

ternal and fetal blood, rapidly develops (● Figure 18-22). The placenta is derived from both trophoblastic and decidual tissue. It is an unusual organ because it is composed of tissues of two organisms: the embryo–fetus and the mother.

FORMATION OF THE PLACENTA AND AMNIOTIC SAC By day 12, the embryo is completely embedded in the decidua. By this time, the trophoblastic layer is two cell layers thick and is called

the **chorion.** As the chorion continues to release enzymes and expand, it forms an extensive network of cavities within the decidua. As the expanding chorion erodes decidual capillary walls, maternal blood leaks from the capillaries and fills these cavities. Fingerlike projections of chorionic tissue extend into the pools of maternal blood. Soon the developing embryo sends out capillaries into these chorionic projections to form **placental villi.**

Each placental villus contains embryonic (later fetal) capillaries surrounded by a thin layer of chorionic tissue, which separates the embryonic–fetal blood from the pools of maternal blood in the intervillous ("between villi") spaces. Maternal and fetal blood do not actually mingle, but the barrier between them is extremely thin. To visualize this relationship, think of your hands (the fetal capillary blood vessels) in rubber gloves (the chorionic tissue) immersed in water (the pool of maternal blood). Only the rubber gloves separate your hands from the water. In the same way, only the thin chorionic tissue (plus the capillary wall of the fetal vessels) separates the fetal and maternal blood. All exchanges between these two bloodstreams take place across this extremely thin barrier. This entire system of interlocking maternal (decidual) and fetal (chorionic) structures makes up the placenta.

Even though not fully developed, the placenta is well established and operational by 5 weeks after implantation. By this time, the heart of the developing embryo is pumping blood into the placental villi, as well as to the embryonic tissues. Throughout gestation, fetal blood continuously traverses between the placental villi and the circulatory system of the fetus by means of two **umbilical arteries** and one **umbilical vein,** which are wrapped within the **umbilical cord,** a lifeline between the fetus and the placenta (● Figure 18-22b). The maternal blood within the placenta is continuously replaced as fresh blood enters through the uterine arterioles; percolates through the intervillous spaces, where it exchanges substances with fetal blood in the surrounding villi; and then exits through the uterine vein.

Meanwhile, during the time of implantation and early placental development, the inner cell mass forms a fluid-filled **amniotic cavity** between the trophoblast–chorion and the portion of the inner cell mass destined to become the fetus (see ● Figure 18-21, step **2**). The epithelial layer that encloses the amniotic cavity is called the **amniotic sac, or amnion.** As it continues to develop, the amniotic sac eventually fuses with the chorion, forming a single combined membrane that surrounds the embryo–fetus. The fluid in the amniotic cavity, the **amniotic fluid,** which is similar in composition to normal ECF, surrounds and cushions the fetus throughout gestation (● Figures 18-22 and 18-23).

FUNCTIONS OF THE PLACENTA During intrauterine life, the placenta performs the functions of the digestive system, the respiratory system, and the kidneys for the "parasitic" fetus. The fetus has these organ systems, but within the uterine environment they cannot (and do not need to) function. Nutrients and O_2 move from the maternal blood across the thin placental barrier into the fetal blood, whereas CO_2 and other metabolic wastes simultaneously move from the fetal blood into the maternal blood. The nutrients and O_2 brought to the fetus in the maternal blood are acquired by the mother's digestive and respiratory systems, and the CO_2 and wastes transferred into the maternal blood are eliminated by the mother's lungs and kidneys, respectively. Thus, the mother's digestive tract, respiratory system, and kidneys serve the fetus's needs, as well as her own.

 Unfortunately, many drugs, environmental pollutants, other chemical agents, and microorganisms in the mother's bloodstream also can cross the placental barrier, and some of them may harm the developing

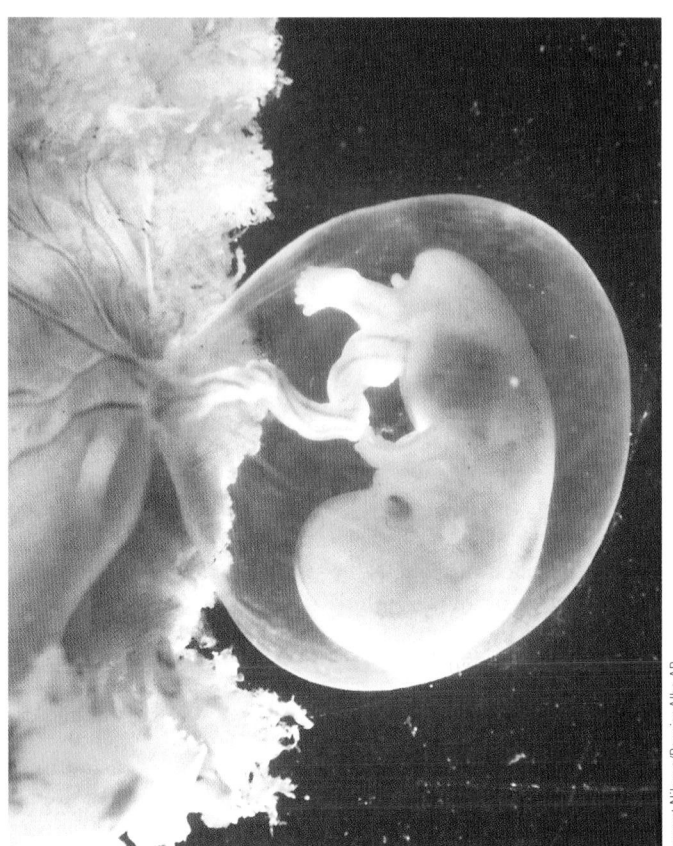

● **FIGURE 18-23 A human fetus surrounded by the amniotic sac.** The fetus is near the end of the first trimester of development.

fetus. For example, newborns who have become "addicted" during gestation by their mother's abuse of a drug such as heroin suffer withdrawal symptoms after birth. Even more common chemical agents such as aspirin, alcohol, and agents in cigarette smoke can reach the fetus and have adverse effects. Likewise, fetuses can acquire AIDS before birth if their mothers are infected with the virus. Pregnant women should therefore be cautious about potentially harmful exposure from any source.

The placenta has yet another important responsibility—it becomes a temporary endocrine organ during pregnancy, a topic to which we now turn. During pregnancy, three endocrine systems interact to support and enhance the growth and development of the fetus, to coordinate the timing of parturition, and to prepare the mammary glands for nourishing the baby after birth: placental hormones, maternal hormones, and fetal hormones.

Hormones secreted by the placenta play a critical role in maintaining pregnancy.

The fetally derived portion of the placenta has the remarkable capacity to secrete a number of peptide and steroid hormones essential for maintaining pregnancy. The most important are *human chorionic gonadotropin, estrogen,* and *progesterone.* Serving as the major endocrine organ of pregnancy, the placenta is unique among endocrine tissues in two regards. First, it is a transient tissue. Second, secretion of its hormones is not subject to extrinsic control, in contrast to the stringent, often complex mechanisms that regulate the secretion of other hormones. Instead, the type and rate of placental hormone secretion depend primarily on the stage of pregnancy.

SECRETION OF HUMAN CHORIONIC GONADOTROPIN One of the first endocrine events is secretion by the developing chorion of **human chorionic gonadotropin (hCG),** a peptide hormone that prolongs the life span of the corpus luteum. Recall that, during the ovarian cycle, the CL degenerates and the highly prepared, luteal-dependent uterine lining sloughs off if fertilization and implantation do not occur. When fertilization does occur, the implanted blastocyst saves itself from being flushed out in menstrual flow by producing hCG. This hormone, which is similar to LH and binds to the same receptor as LH, stimulates and maintains the corpus luteum so that it does not degenerate. Now called the **corpus luteum of pregnancy,** this ovarian endocrine unit grows even larger and produces increasingly greater amounts of estrogen and progesterone for an additional 10 weeks until the placenta takes over secretion of these steroid hormones. Because of the persistence of estrogen and progesterone, the thick, pulpy endometrial tissue is maintained instead of sloughing. Accordingly, menstruation ceases during pregnancy.

Stimulation by hCG is necessary to maintain the corpus luteum of pregnancy because LH, which maintains the corpus luteum during the normal luteal phase of the uterine cycle, is suppressed through feedback inhibition by the high levels of progesterone. Maintenance of a normal pregnancy depends on high concentrations of progesterone and estrogen. Thus, hCG production is critical during the first trimester to maintain ovarian output of these hormones.

The secretion rate of hCG increases rapidly during early pregnancy to save the corpus luteum from demise. Peak secretion of hCG occurs about 60 days after the end of the last menstrual period (● Figure 18-24). By the 10th week of pregnancy,

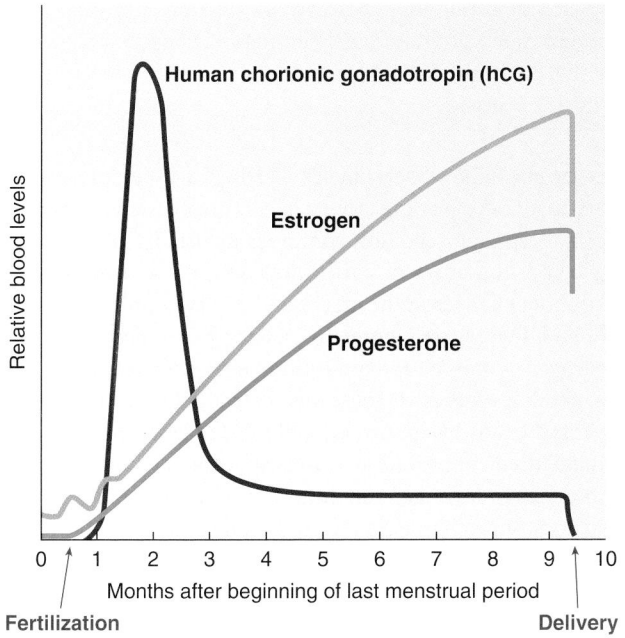

● FIGURE 18-24 **Secretion rates of placental hormones.**

hCG output declines to a low rate of secretion that is maintained for the duration of gestation. The fall in hCG occurs when the corpus luteum is no longer needed for its steroid hormone output because the placenta has begun to secrete substantial quantities of estrogen and progesterone.

 Human chorionic gonadotropin is eliminated from the body in the urine. Pregnancy diagnosis tests can detect hCG in urine as early as the first month of pregnancy, about 2 weeks after the first missed menstrual period. Because this is before the growing embryo can be detected by physical examination, the test permits early confirmation of pregnancy.

A frequent early clinical sign of pregnancy is **morning sickness,** a daily bout of nausea and vomiting that often occurs in the morning but can take place at any time of day. Because this condition usually appears shortly after implantation and coincides with the time of peak hCG production, scientists speculate that this early placental hormone may trigger the symptoms, perhaps by acting on the chemoreceptor trigger zone next to the vomiting center (see p. 478).

SECRETION OF ESTROGEN AND PROGESTERONE Why does the developing placenta not start producing estrogen and progesterone in the first place instead of secreting hCG, which in turn stimulates the corpus luteum to secrete these two critical hormones? The answer is that, for different reasons, the placenta cannot produce enough estrogen or progesterone in the first trimester of pregnancy. In the case of estrogen, the placenta does not have all the enzymes needed for complete synthesis of this hormone. Estrogen synthesis requires a complex interaction between the placenta and the fetus. The placenta converts the androgen hormone produced by the fetal adrenal cortex, dehydroepiandrosterone (DHEA), into estrogen. The placenta cannot produce estrogen until the fetus has developed to the point that its adrenal cortex is secreting DHEA into the blood. The placenta extracts DHEA from the fetal blood and converts it into estrogen, which it then secretes into the maternal blood.

 Estrogen comes in several variants. The primary estrogen synthesized by the placenta is **estriol,** in contrast to the main estrogen product of the ovaries, **estradiol.** Because estriol can only be synthesized from fetal DHEA, measurement of estriol levels in the maternal urine can be used clinically to assess the viability of the fetus.

In the case of progesterone, the placenta can synthesize this hormone soon after implantation. Even though the early placenta has the enzymes necessary to convert cholesterol extracted from the maternal blood into progesterone, it does not produce much of this hormone, because the amount of progesterone produced is proportional to placental weight. The placenta is simply too small in the first 10 weeks of pregnancy to produce enough progesterone to maintain the endometrial tissue. The notable increase in circulating progesterone in the last 7 months of gestation reflects placental growth during this period.

ROLES OF ESTROGEN AND PROGESTERONE DURING PREGNANCY As noted earlier, high concentrations of estrogen and progesterone are essential to maintain a normal pregnancy. Estrogen stimulates growth of the myometrium, which increases in size throughout pregnancy. The stronger uterine musculature is needed to expel the fetus during labor. Estrogen also promotes development of the ducts within the mammary glands, through which milk will be ejected during lactation.

Progesterone performs various roles throughout pregnancy. Its main function is to prevent miscarriage by suppressing contractions of the uterine myometrium. Progesterone also promotes formation of a thick mucus plug in the cervical canal to prevent vaginal contaminants from reaching the uterus. Finally, placental progesterone stimulates development of milk glands in the breasts in preparation for lactation.

Maternal body systems respond to the increased demands of gestation.

The period of **gestation (pregnancy)** is about 38 weeks from conception (40 weeks from the end of the last menstrual period). During gestation, the embryo–fetus develops and grows to the point of being able to leave its maternal life-support system. Meanwhile, a number of physical changes within the mother accommodate the demands of pregnancy. The most obvious change is uterine enlargement. The uterus expands and increases in weight more than 20 times, exclusive of its contents. The breasts enlarge and develop the ability to produce milk. Body systems other than the reproductive system also make needed adjustments. The volume of blood increases by 30%, and the cardiovascular system responds to the increasing demands of the growing placental mass. Weight gain during pregnancy is the result only in part of the weight of the fetus. The remainder is mostly from increased weight of the uterus, including the placenta, and increased blood volume. Respiratory activity increases by about 20% to handle the additional fetal requirements for O_2 use and CO_2 removal. Urinary output increases, and the kidneys excrete the additional wastes from the fetus.

The increased metabolic demands of the growing fetus increase nutritional requirements for the mother. In general, the fetus takes what it needs from the mother, even if this leaves the mother with a nutritional deficit. For example, the placenta produces a hormone similar to growth hormone that decreases maternal use of glucose and mobilizes fatty acids, making available greater quantities of these nutrients for shunting to the fetus. Also, if the mother does not consume enough Ca^{2+}, yet another placental hormone similar to parathyroid hormone mobilizes Ca^{2+} from the maternal bones to ensure adequate calcification of the fetal bones.

Changes during late gestation prepare for parturition.

Parturition (labor, delivery, or **birth)** requires (1) dilation of the cervical canal to accommodate passage of the fetus from the uterus through the vagina and to the outside and (2) contractions of the uterine myometrium that are sufficiently strong to expel the fetus.

Several changes take place during late gestation in preparation for the onset of parturition. During the first two trimesters of gestation, the uterus remains relatively quiet because of the inhibitory effect of the high levels of progesterone on the uterine muscle. During the last trimester, however, the uterus becomes progressively more excitable, so mild contractions (**Braxton–Hicks contractions**) are experienced with increasing strength and frequency. Sometimes these contractions become regular enough to be mistaken for the onset of labor, a phenomenon called "false labor."

Throughout gestation, the exit of the uterus remains sealed by the rigid, tightly closed cervix. As parturition approaches, the cervix begins to soften (or "ripen") as a result of the dissociation of its tough connective tissue (collagen) fibers. Because of this softening, the cervix becomes malleable so that it can gradually yield, dilating the exit, as the fetus is forcefully pushed against it during labor. This cervical softening is caused largely by **relaxin,** a peptide hormone produced by the corpus luteum of pregnancy and by the placenta. Other factors to be described shortly contribute to cervical softening. Relaxin also "relaxes" the birth canal by loosening the connective tissue between pelvic bones.

Meanwhile, the fetus shifts downward (the baby "drops") and is normally oriented so that the head is in contact with the cervix in preparation for exiting through the birth canal. In a **breech birth,** any part of the body other than the head approaches the birth canal first.

Scientists are closing in on the factors that trigger the onset of parturition.

Rhythmic, coordinated contractions, usually painless at first, begin at the onset of labor. As labor progresses, the contractions increase in frequency, intensity, and discomfort. These strong, rhythmic contractions force the fetus against the cervix, dilating the cervix. Then, after having dilated the cervix enough for the fetus to pass through, these contractions force the fetus out through the birth canal.

The exact factors triggering the increase in uterine contractility and thus initiating parturition are not fully established, although much progress has been made in recent years in unraveling the sequence of events. Let us look at what is known about this process.

ROLE OF HIGH ESTROGEN LEVELS During early gestation, maternal estrogen levels are relatively low, but as gestation proceeds, placental estrogen secretion continues to rise. In the immediate days before the onset of parturition, soaring levels of estrogen bring about changes in the uterus and cervix to prepare them for labor and delivery (● Figures 18-24 and 18-25). First, high levels of estrogen promote the synthesis of connexons within the uterine smooth muscle cells. These myometrial cells are not functionally linked to any extent throughout most of gestation. The newly manufactured connexons are inserted in the myometrial plasma membranes to form gap junctions that electrically link together the uterine smooth muscle cells so that they become able to contract as a coordinated unit (see p. 53).

Simultaneously, high levels of estrogen dramatically and progressively increase the concentration of myometrial receptors for oxytocin. Together, these myometrial changes collec-

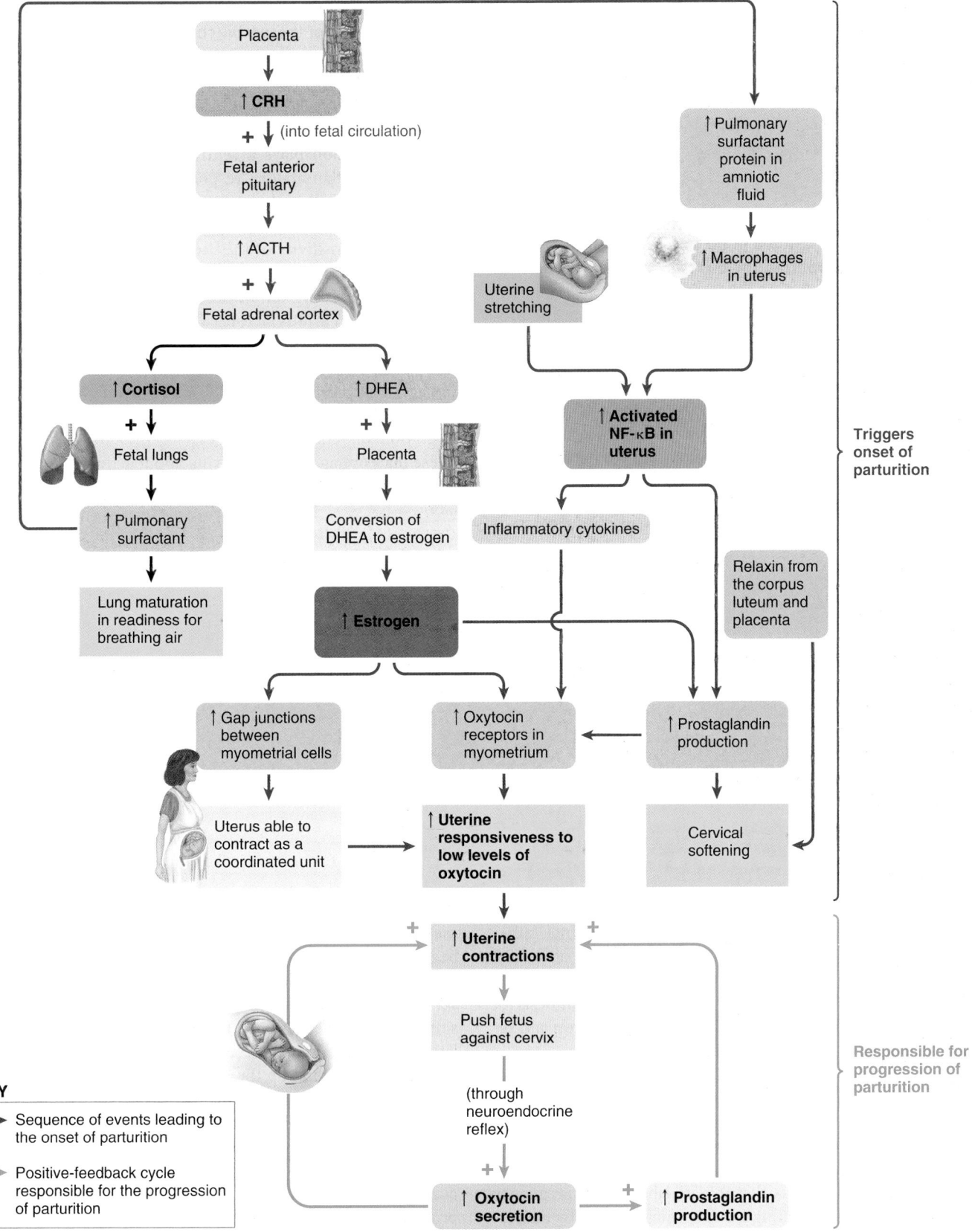

Placenta

↑ **CRH**

+ ↓ (into fetal circulation)

Fetal anterior pituitary

↑ ACTH

+ ↓

Fetal adrenal cortex

↑ **Cortisol**

+ ↓

Fetal lungs

↓

↑ Pulmonary surfactant

↓

Lung maturation in readiness for breathing air

↑ DHEA

+ ↓

Placenta

↓

Conversion of DHEA to estrogen

↓

↑ **Estrogen**

↑ Pulmonary surfactant protein in amniotic fluid

↓

↑ Macrophages in uterus

Uterine stretching

↑ **Activated NF-κB in uterus**

Inflammatory cytokines

Relaxin from the corpus luteum and placenta

↑ Gap junctions between myometrial cells

↓

Uterus able to contract as a coordinated unit

↑ Oxytocin receptors in myometrium

↑ Prostaglandin production

↓

Cervical softening

↑ **Uterine responsiveness to low levels of oxytocin**

↓

↑ **Uterine contractions**

↓

Push fetus against cervix

(through neuroendocrine reflex)

+ ↓

↑ **Oxytocin secretion**

+ →

↑ **Prostaglandin production**

Triggers onset of parturition

Responsible for progression of parturition

KEY

→ Sequence of events leading to the onset of parturition

→ Positive-feedback cycle responsible for the progression of parturition

● **FIGURE 18-25 Initiation and progression of parturition.**

tively bring about the increased uterine responsiveness to oxytocin that ultimately initiates labor.

In addition to preparing the uterus for labor, the increasing levels of estrogen promote production of local prostaglandins that contribute to cervical ripening by stimulating cervical enzymes that locally degrade collagen fibers. Furthermore, these prostaglandins themselves increase uterine responsiveness to oxytocin.

ROLE OF OXYTOCIN **Oxytocin** is a peptide hormone produced by the hypothalamus, stored in the posterior pituitary, and released into the blood from the posterior pituitary on nervous stimulation by the hypothalamus (see p. 533). A powerful uterine muscle stimulant, oxytocin plays the key role in the progression of labor. However, this hormone was once discounted as the trigger for parturition because the circulating levels of oxytocin remain constant prior to the onset of labor. The discovery that uterine responsiveness to oxytocin is 100 times greater at term than in nonpregnant women (because of the connexons and increased concentration of myometrial oxytocin receptors) led to the now widely accepted conclusion that labor begins when the myometrial responsiveness to oxytocin reaches a critical threshold that permits the onset of strong, coordinated contractions in response to ordinary levels of circulating oxytocin.

ROLE OF CORTICOTROPIN-RELEASING HORMONE Until recently, scientists were baffled by the factors that raise levels of placental estrogen secretion. Recent research has shed new light on the probable mechanism. Evidence suggests that *corticotropin-releasing hormone (CRH)* secreted by the fetal portion of the placenta into both the maternal and the fetal circulations not only drives the manufacture of placental estrogen, thus ultimately dictating the timing of the onset of labor, but also promotes changes in the fetal lungs needed for breathing air (● Figure 18-25). Recall that CRH is normally secreted by the hypothalamus and regulates the output of ACTH by the anterior pituitary (see pp. 536 and 552). In turn, ACTH stimulates production of both cortisol and DHEA by the adrenal cortex. In the fetus, much of the CRH comes from the placenta rather than solely from the fetal hypothalamus. The additional cortisol secretion summoned by the extra CRH promotes fetal lung maturation. Specifically, cortisol stimulates the synthesis of pulmonary surfactant, which facilitates lung expansion and reduces the work of breathing (see p. 379).

The bumped-up rate of DHEA secretion by the adrenal cortex in response to placental CRH leads to the rising levels of placental estrogen secretion, because the placenta converts DHEA from the fetal adrenal gland into estrogen, which enters the maternal bloodstream. When sufficiently high, this estrogen sets in motion the events that initiate labor. Thus, pregnancy duration and delivery timing are determined largely by the placenta's rate of CRH production. That is, a **"placental clock"** ticks out the length of time until parturition. When a critical level of placental CRH is reached, parturition is triggered. This critical CRH level ensures that when labor begins the infant is ready for life outside the womb. It does so by concurrently in-creasing the fetal cortisol needed for lung maturation and the estrogen needed for the uterine changes that bring on labor. The remaining unanswered puzzle regarding the placental clock is, What controls placental secretion of CRH?

ROLE OF INFLAMMATION Surprisingly, recent research suggests that inflammation plays a central role in the labor process. Key to this inflammatory response is activation of **nuclear factor κB (NF-κB)** in the uterus. NF-κB boosts production of inflammatory cytokines (see p. 336) and prostaglandins that increase the sensitivity of the uterus to contraction-inducing chemical messengers and help soften the cervix. What activates NF-κB, setting off an inflammatory cascade that helps prompt labor? Various factors can cause an upsurge in NF-κB. These include stretching of the uterine muscle and the presence of a specific pulmonary surfactant protein (stimulated by the action of CRH on the fetal lungs) in the amniotic fluid from the fetus. This pulmonary surfactant protein promotes migration of fetal macrophages (see p. 330) to the uterus. These macrophages, in turn, bring about activation of NF-κB. In this way, fetal lung maturation contributes to the onset of labor.

Clinical Note Bacterial infections and allergic reactions can lead to premature labor by activating NF-kB. Also, multiple-fetus pregnancies are at risk for premature labor, likely because the increased uterine stretching triggers earlier activation of NF-κB.

Parturition is accomplished by a positive-feedback cycle.

Once uterine responsiveness to oxytocin reaches a critical level and regular uterine contractions begin, myometrial contractions progressively increase in frequency, strength, and duration throughout labor until they expel the uterine contents. At the beginning of labor, contractions lasting 30 seconds or less occur about every 25 to 30 minutes; by the end, they last 60 to 90 seconds and occur every 2 to 3 minutes.

As labor progresses, a positive-feedback cycle involving oxytocin and prostaglandin ensues, incessantly increasing myometrial contractions (● Figure 18-25). Each uterine contraction begins at the top of the uterus and sweeps downward, forcing the fetus toward the cervix. Pressure of the fetus against the cervix does two things. First, the fetal head pushing against the softened cervix wedges open the cervical canal. Second, stimulation of receptors in the cervix in response to fetal pressure sends a neural signal up the spinal cord to the hypothalamus, which in turn triggers oxytocin release from the posterior pituitary. This additional oxytocin promotes more powerful uterine contractions. As a result, the fetus is pushed more forcefully against the cervix, stimulating the release of even more oxytocin, and so on. This cycle is reinforced as oxytocin stimulates prostaglandin production by the decidua. As a powerful myometrial stimulant, prostaglandin further enhances uterine contractions. Oxytocin secretion, prostaglandin production, and uterine contractions continue to increase in positive-feedback fashion throughout labor until delivery relieves the pressure on the cervix.

STAGES OF LABOR Labor is divided into three stages: (1) cervical dilation, (2) delivery of the baby, and (3) delivery of the placenta (● Figure 18-26). At the onset of labor or sometime during the first stage, the amniotic sac, or "bag of waters," ruptures. As amniotic fluid escapes out of the vagina, it helps lubricate the birth canal.

1. During the first stage, the cervix is forced to dilate to accommodate the diameter of the baby's head, usually to a maximum of 10 cm. This stage is the longest, lasting from several hours to as long as 24 hours in a first pregnancy. If another part of the fetus's body other than the head is oriented against the cervix, it is generally less effective than the head as a wedge. The head has the largest diameter of the baby's body. If the baby approaches the birth canal feet first, the feet may not dilate the cervix enough to let the head pass. In such a case, without medical intervention the baby's head would remain stuck behind the too-narrow cervical opening.

2. The second stage of labor, the actual birth of the baby, begins once cervical dilation is complete. When the infant begins to move through the cervix and vagina, stretch receptors in the vagina activate a neural reflex that triggers contractions of the abdominal wall in synchrony with the uterine contractions.

These abdominal contractions greatly increase the force pushing the baby through the birth canal. The mother can help deliver the infant by voluntarily contracting the abdominal muscles at this time in unison with each uterine contraction (that is, by "pushing" with each "labor pain"). Stage 2 is usually shorter than the first stage, lasting 30 to 90 minutes. The infant is still attached to the placenta by the umbilical cord at birth. The cord is tied and severed, with the stump shriveling up in a few days to form the **umbilicus (navel).**

3. Shortly after delivery of the baby, a second series of uterine contractions separates the placenta from the myometrium and expels it through the vagina. Delivery of the placenta, or **afterbirth,** constitutes the third stage of labor, typically the shortest stage, being completed within 15 to 30 minutes after the baby is born. After the placenta is expelled, continued contractions of the myometrium constrict the uterine blood vessels supplying the site of placental attachment to prevent hemorrhage.

UTERINE INVOLUTION After delivery, the uterus shrinks to its pregestational size, a process known as **involution,** which takes 4 to 6 weeks to complete. During involution, the remaining endometrial tissue not expelled with the placenta gradually

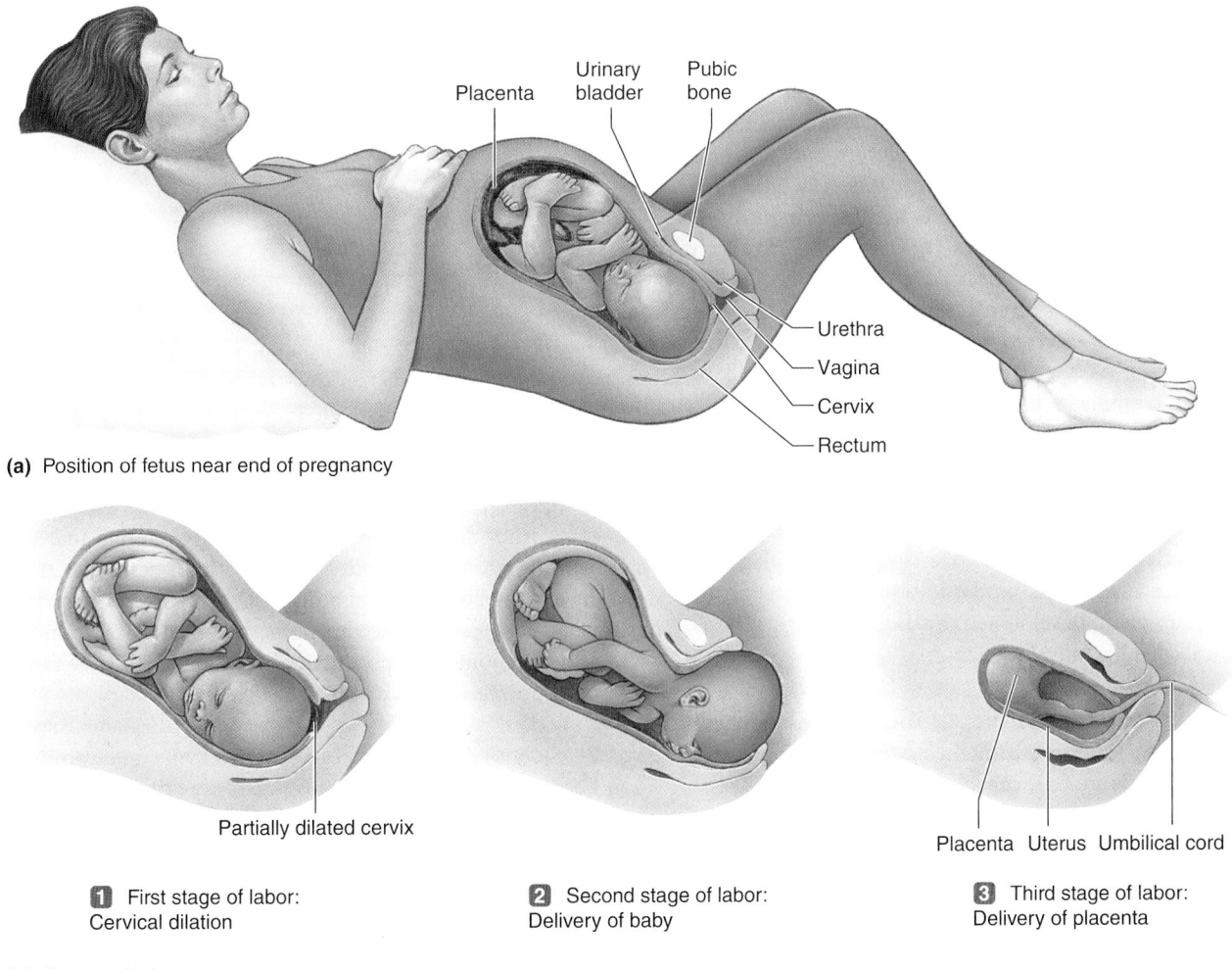

(a) Position of fetus near end of pregnancy

Placenta   Urinary   Pubic
            bladder   bone

Urethra
Vagina
Cervix
Rectum

Partially dilated cervix

Placenta Uterus Umbilical cord

1 First stage of labor:
Cervical dilation

2 Second stage of labor:
Delivery of baby

3 Third stage of labor:
Delivery of placenta

(b) Stages of labor
● FIGURE 18-26 **Stages of labor.**

disintegrates and sloughs off, producing a vaginal discharge that continues for 3 to 6 weeks following parturition. After this period, the endometrium is restored to its nonpregnant state.

Involution occurs largely because of the precipitous fall in circulating estrogen and progesterone when the placental source of these steroids is lost at delivery. The process is facilitated in mothers who breast-feed their infants because oxytocin is released in response to suckling. In addition to playing an important role in lactation, this periodic nursing-induced release of oxytocin promotes myometrial contractions that help maintain uterine muscle tone, enhancing involution. Involution is usually complete in about 4 weeks in nursing mothers but takes about 6 weeks in those who do not breast-feed.

Lactation requires multiple hormonal inputs.

The female reproductive system supports the new being from the moment of conception through gestation and continues to nourish it during its early life outside the supportive uterine environment. Milk (or its equivalent) is essential for survival of the newborn. Accordingly, during gestation the **mammary glands,** or **breasts,** are prepared for **lactation (milk production).**

The breasts in nonpregnant females consist mostly of adipose tissue and a rudimentary duct system. Breast size is determined by the amount of adipose tissue, which has nothing to do with the ability to produce milk.

PREPARATION OF THE BREASTS FOR LACTATION Under the hormonal environment present during pregnancy, the mammary glands develop the internal glandular structure and function necessary for milk production. A breast capable of lactating has a network of progressively smaller ducts that branch out from the nipple and terminate in lobules (● Figure 18-27a). Each lobule is made up of a cluster of saclike epithelial-lined, milk-producing glands known as **alveoli.** Milk is synthesized by the epithelial cells and then secreted into the alveolar lumen, which is drained by a milk-collecting duct that transports the milk to the surface of the nipple (● Figure 18-27b).

During pregnancy, the high concentration of *estrogen* promotes extensive duct development, whereas the high level of *progesterone* stimulates abundant alveolar–lobular formation. Elevated concentrations of *prolactin* (an anterior pituitary hormone stimulated by the rising levels of estrogen) and a placental hormone that has a structure similar to prolactin also contribute to mammary gland development by inducing the synthesis of enzymes needed for milk production.

PREVENTION OF LACTATION DURING GESTATION Most of these changes in the breasts occur during the first half of gestation, so the mammary glands are fully capable of producing milk by the middle of pregnancy. However, milk secretion does not occur until parturition. The high estrogen and progesterone concentrations during the last half of pregnancy prevent lactation by blocking prolactin's stimulatory action on milk secretion. Prolactin is the primary stimulant of milk secretion. Thus, even though the high levels of placental steroids promote development of the milk-producing machinery in the breasts, they

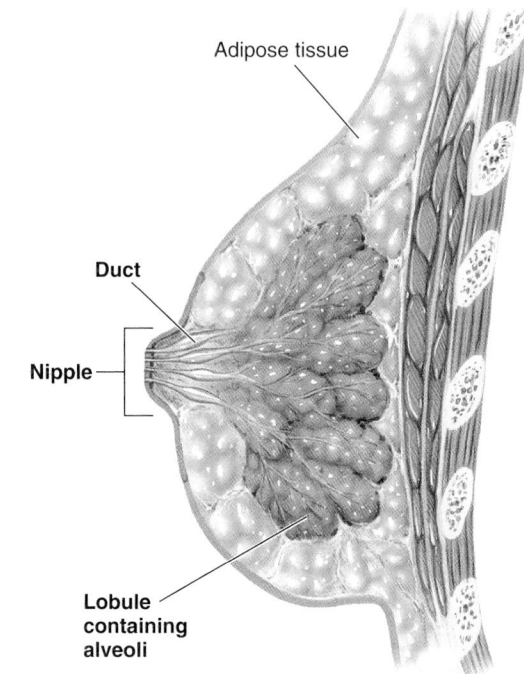

(a) Internal structure of mammary gland, lateral view

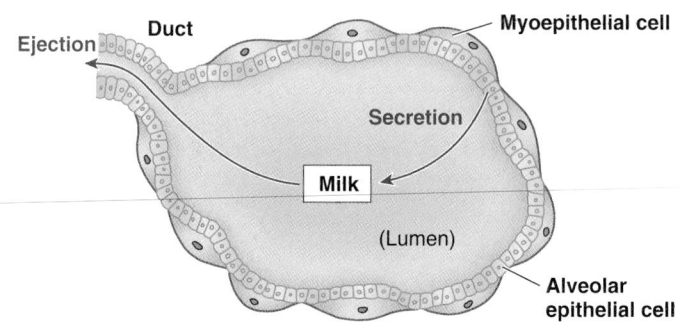

(b) Alveolus within mammary gland

● FIGURE 18-27 **Mammary gland anatomy.** The alveolar epithelial cells secrete milk into the lumen. Contraction of the surrounding myoepithelial cells ejects the secreted milk out through the duct.

prevent these glands from becoming operational until the baby is born and milk is needed.

The abrupt decline in estrogen and progesterone that occurs with loss of the placenta at parturition initiates lactation. (We have now completed our discussion of the functions of estrogen and progesterone during gestation and lactation, as well as throughout the reproductive life of females. These functions are summarized in ▲ Table 18-5.)

STIMULATION OF LACTATION VIA SUCKLING Once milk production begins after delivery, two hormones are critical for maintaining lactation: (1) *oxytocin,* which causes milk ejection, and (2) *prolactin,* which promotes milk secretion. **Milk ejection,** or **milk letdown,** refers to the forced expulsion of milk from the lumen of the alveoli out through the ducts. Release of both of these hormones is stimulated by suckling (● Figure 18-28). Let us examine each of these hormones, including control of their secretion and their roles in further detail.

▲ Table 18-5 Actions of Estrogen and Progesterone

Estrogen

Effects on sex-specific tissues

Is essential for egg maturation and release

Stimulates growth and maintenance of the entire female reproductive tract

Stimulates follicle maturation

Thins the cervical mucus to permit sperm penetration

Enhances transport of sperm to the oviduct by stimulating upward contractions of the uterus and oviduct

Stimulates growth of the endometrium and myometrium

Induces synthesis of endometrial progesterone receptors

Triggers onset of parturition by increasing uterine responsiveness to oxytocin during late gestation through a twofold effect: by inducing synthesis of myometrial oxytocin receptors and by increasing myometrial gap junctions so that the uterus can contract as a coordinated unit in response to oxytocin

Other reproductive effects

Promotes development of secondary sexual characteristics

Controls GnRH and gonadotropin secretion

    Inhibits secretion if at a low or moderate level

    Is responsible for triggering the LH surge if at a high level

Stimulates duct development in the breasts during gestation

Inhibits milk-secreting actions of prolactin during gestation

Nonreproductive effects

Promotes fat deposition

Increases bone density

Closes the epiphyseal plates

Progesterone

Prepares a suitable environment for nourishment of a developing embryo and then fetus

Causes a thick mucus plug to form in the cervical canal

Inhibits hypothalamic GnRH and gonadotropin secretion

Stimulates alveolar development in the breasts during gestation

Inhibits milk-secreting actions of prolactin during gestation

Inhibits uterine contractions during gestation

■ *Oxytocin release and milk ejection.* The infant cannot directly suck milk out of the alveolar lumen. Instead, milk must be actively squeezed out of the alveoli into the ducts, and hence toward the nipple, by contraction of specialized **myoepithelial cells** (musclelike epithelial cells) that surround each alveolus (see ● Figure 18-27b). The infant's suckling of the breast stimulates sensory nerve endings in the nipple, initiating action potentials that travel up the spinal cord to the hypothalamus. Thus activated, the hypothalamus triggers a burst of oxytocin release from the posterior pituitary. Oxytocin in turn stimulates contraction of the myoepithelial cells in the breasts to bring about

milk ejection. Milk letdown continues only as long as the infant continues to nurse. In this way, the milk ejection reflex ensures that the breasts release milk only when required and in the amount needed by the baby. Even though the alveoli may be full of milk, the milk cannot be released without oxytocin. The reflex can become conditioned to stimuli other than suckling, however. For example, the infant's cry can trigger milk letdown, causing a spurt of milk to leak from the nipples. In contrast, psychological stress, acting through the hypothalamus, can easily inhibit milk ejection. For this reason, a positive attitude toward breast-feeding and a relaxed environment are essential for successful breast-feeding.

■ *Prolactin release and milk secretion.* Suckling not only triggers oxytocin release but also stimulates prolactin secretion. Prolactin output by the anterior pituitary is controlled by two hypothalamic secretions: **prolactin-inhibiting hormone (PIH)** and **prolactin-releasing hormone (PRH)**. PIH is now known to be *dopamine,* which also serves as a neurotransmitter in the brain. The chemical nature of PRH has not been identified with certainty.

Throughout most of the female's life, PIH is the dominant influence, so prolactin concentrations normally remain low. During lactation, a burst in prolactin secretion occurs each time the infant suckles. Afferent impulses initiated in the nipple on suckling are carried by the spinal cord to the hypothalamus. This reflex ultimately leads to prolactin release by the anterior pituitary, although it is unclear whether this is from inhibition of PIH secretion, stimulation of PRH secretion, or both. Prolactin then acts on the alveolar epithelium to promote secretion of milk to replace the ejected milk (● Figure 18-28).

Concurrent stimulation by suckling of both milk ejection and milk production ensures that the rate of milk synthesis keeps pace with the baby's needs for milk. The more the infant nurses, the more milk is removed by letdown and the more milk is produced for the next feeding.

Breast-feeding is advantageous to both the infant and the mother.

Nutritionally, **milk** is composed of water, triglyceride fat, the carbohydrate lactose (milk sugar), a number of proteins, vitamins, and the minerals calcium and phosphate.

ADVANTAGES OF BREAST-FEEDING FOR THE INFANT In addition to nutrients, milk contains a host of immune cells, antibodies, and other chemicals that help protect the infant against infection until it can mount an effective immune response on its own a few months after birth. **Colostrum,** the milk produced for the first 5 days after delivery, contains lower concentrations of fat and lactose but higher concentrations of immunoprotective components. All human babies acquire some passive immunity during gestation by antibodies passing across the placenta from the mother to the fetus. These antibodies are short lived, however, and they often do not persist until the infant can fend for itself immunologically. Breast-fed babies gain additional protection during this vulnerable period.

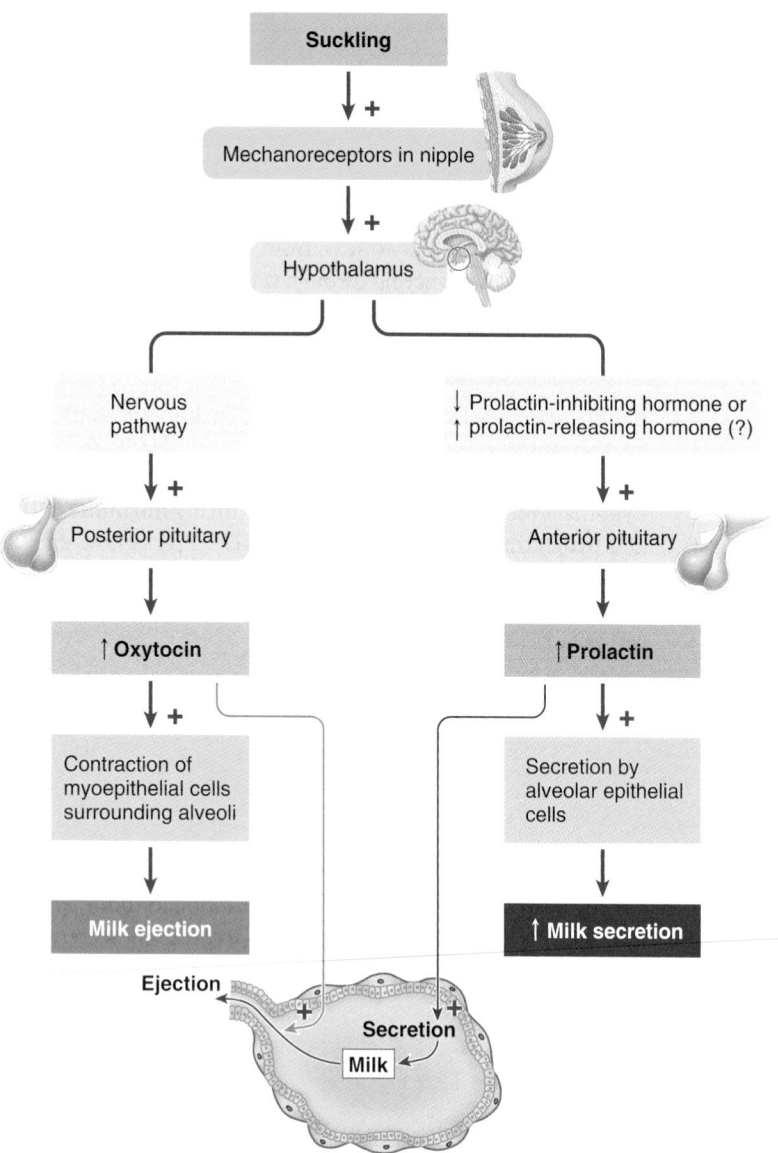

● FIGURE 18-28 **Suckling reflexes.**

Breast-feeding is also advantageous for the mother. Oxytocin release triggered by nursing hastens uterine involution. In addition, suckling suppresses the menstrual cycle because prolactin (sometimes termed "nature's contraceptive") inhibits GnRH, thereby suppressing FSH and LH secretion. Lactation, therefore, tends to prevent ovulation, decreasing the likelihood of another pregnancy (although it is not a reliable means of contraception). This mechanism permits all the mother's resources to be directed toward the newborn instead of being shared with a new embryo.

CESSATION OF MILK PRODUCTION AT WEANING When the infant is weaned, two mechanisms contribute to the cessation of milk production. First, without suckling, prolactin secretion is not stimulated, removing the main stimulus for continued milk synthesis and secretion. Also, in the absence of suckling, oxytocin is not released and milk letdown does not occur. Because milk production does not immediately shut down, milk accumulates in the alveoli, engorging the breasts. The resulting pressure buildup acts directly on the alveolar epithelial cells to suppress further milk production.

The end is a new beginning.

Reproduction is an appropriate way to end our discussion of physiology. The single cell resulting from the union of male and female gametes divides mitotically and differentiates into a multicellular individual made up of a number of body systems that interact cooperatively to maintain homeostasis (that is, stability in the internal environment). All the life-supporting homeostatic processes introduced throughout this book begin again at the start of a new life.

Chapter in Perspective: Focus on Homeostasis

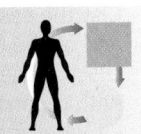

The reproductive system is unique in that it is not essential for homeostasis or for survival of the individual but is essential for sustaining the thread of life from generation to generation. Reproduction depends on the union of male and female gametes (reproductive cells), each with a half set of chromosomes, to form a new individual with a full, one-of-a kind set of chromosomes. Unlike the other body systems, which are essentially identical in the two sexes, the reproductive systems of males and females are remarkably different, befitting their different roles in the reproductive process.

The male system is designed to continuously produce huge numbers of mobile spermatozoa that are delivered to the female during the sex act. Male gametes must be produced in abundance for two reasons: (1) Only a small percentage of them survive the hazardous journey through the female reproductive tract to the site of fertilization, and (2) the cooperative effort of many spermatozoa is required to break down the barriers surrounding the female gamete (ovum or egg) to enable one spermatozoon to penetrate and unite with the ovum.

The female reproductive system undergoes complex changes on a cyclic monthly basis. During the first half of the cycle, a single nonmotile ovum is prepared for release. During the second half, the reproductive system is geared toward preparing a suitable environment for supporting the ovum if fertilization (union with a spermatozoon) occurs. If fertilization does not occur, the prepared supportive environment within the uterus sloughs off, and the cycle starts again as a new ovum is prepared for release. If fertilization occurs, the female reproductive system adjusts to support growth and development of the new individual until it can survive on its own on the outside.

There are three important parallels in the male and female reproductive systems, even though they differ considerably in structure and function. First, the same set of undifferentiated reproductive tissues in the embryo can develop into either a male or a female system, depending on the presence or absence, respectively, of male-determining factors. Second, the same hormones—namely, hypothalamic GnRH and anterior pituitary FSH and LH—control reproductive function in both sexes. In both cases, gonadal steroids and inhibin act in negative-feedback fashion to control hypothalamic and anterior pituitary output. Third, the same events take place in the developing gamete's nucleus during sperm formation and egg formation, although males produce millions of sperm in a day, whereas females produce only about 400 ova in a lifetime.

REVIEW EXERCISES

Objective Questions (Answers on p. A-51)

1. It is possible for a genetic male to have the anatomic appearance of a female. *(True or false?)*
2. Testosterone secretion essentially ceases from birth until puberty. *(True or false?)*
3. Prostaglandins are derived from arachidonic acid found in the plasma membrane. *(True or false?)*
4. Females do not experience erection. *(True or false?)*
5. Most of the lubrication for sexual intercourse is provided by the female. *(True or false?)*
6. If a follicle does not reach maturity during one ovarian cycle, it can finish maturing during the next cycle. *(True or false?)*
7. Rising, moderate levels of estrogen inhibit tonic LH secretion, whereas high levels of estrogen stimulate the LH surge. *(True or false?)*
8. Spermatogenesis takes place within the _____ of the testes, stimulated by the hormones _____ and _____.
9. The source of estrogen and progesterone during the first 10 weeks of gestation is the _____. The source of these hormones during the last two trimesters of gestation is the _____.
10. Detection of _____ in the urine is the basis of pregnancy diagnosis tests.
11. Which of the following statements concerning chromosomal distribution is *incorrect*?
    a. All human somatic cells contain 23 chromosomal pairs for a total diploid number of 46 chromosomes.
    b. Each gamete contains 23 chromosomes, one member of each chromosomal pair.
    c. During meiotic division, the members of the chromosome pairs regroup themselves into the original combinations derived from the individual's mother and father for separation into haploid gametes.
    d. Sex determination depends on the combination of sex chromosomes, an XY combination being a genetic male and XX a genetic female.
    e. The sex chromosome content of the fertilizing sperm determines the sex of the offspring.
12. When the corpus luteum degenerates,
    a. circulating levels of estrogen and progesterone rapidly decline.
    b. FSH and LH secretion start to rise as the inhibitory effects of the gonadal steroids are withdrawn.
    c. the endometrium sloughs off.
    d. both (a) and (b) occur.
    e. all of the above occur.

13. Match the following:
  ___ 1. secrete(s) prostaglandins
  ___ 2. increase(s) motility and fertility of sperm
  ___ 3. secrete(s) an alkaline fluid
  ___ 4. provide(s) fructose
  ___ 5. act(s) as the storage site for sperm
  ___ 6. concentrate(s) the sperm a hundredfold
  ___ 7. secrete(s) fibrinogen
  ___ 8. provide(s) clotting enzymes
  ___ 9. contain(s) erectile tissue

  (a) epididymis and ductus deferens
  (b) prostate gland
  (c) seminal vesicles
  (d) bulbourethral glands
  (e) penis

14. Using the following answer code, indicate when each event takes place during the ovarian cycle:
  (a) occurs during the follicular phase
  (b) occurs during the luteal phase
  (c) occurs during both the follicular and the luteal phases
  ___ 1. development of antral follicles
  ___ 2. secretion of estrogen
  ___ 3. secretion of progesterone
  ___ 4. menstruation
  ___ 5. repair and proliferation of the endometrium
  ___ 6. increased vascularization and glycogen storage in the endometrium

Essay Questions

1. What constitutes the primary reproductive organs, gametes, sex hormones, reproductive tract, accessory sex glands, external genitalia, and secondary sexual characteristics in males and in females?

2. List the essential reproductive functions of the male and of the female.

3. Discuss the differences between males and females with regard to genetic, gonadal, and phenotypic sex.

4. Of what functional significance is the scrotal location of the testes?

5. Discuss the source and functions of testosterone.

6. Describe the three major stages of spermatogenesis. Discuss the functions of each part of a spermatozoon. What are the roles of Sertoli cells?

7. Discuss the control of testicular function.

8. Compare the sex act in males and females.

9. Compare oogenesis with spermatogenesis.

10. Describe the events of the follicular and luteal phases of the ovarian cycle. Correlate the phases of the uterine cycle with those of the ovarian cycle.

11. How are the ovum and spermatozoa transported to the site of fertilization? Describe the process of fertilization.

12. Describe the process of implantation and placenta formation.

13. What are the functions of the placenta?

14. What is the role of human chorionic gonadotropin?

15. What factors contribute to the initiation of parturition? What are the stages of labor? What is the role of oxytocin?

16. Describe the hormonal factors that play a role in lactation.

17. Summarize the actions of estrogen and progesterone.

POINTS TO PONDER

(Explanations on p. A-52)

1. The hypothalamus releases GnRH in pulsatile bursts once every 2 to 3 hours, with no secretion occurring between bursts. The blood concentration of GnRH depends on the frequency of these bursts of secretion. A promising line of research for a new method of contraception involves administration of GnRH-like drugs. In what way could such drugs act as contraceptives when GnRH is the hypothalamic hormone that triggers the chain of events leading to ovulation? (Hint: The anterior pituitary is "programmed" to respond only to the normal pulsatile pattern of GnRH.)

2. Occasionally, testicular tumors composed of interstitial cells of Leydig may secrete up to 100 times the normal amount of testosterone. When such a tumor develops in young children, they grow up much shorter than their genetic potential. Explain why. What other symptoms would be present?

3. What type of sexual dysfunction might arise in men taking drugs that inhibit sympathetic nervous system activity as part of the treatment for high blood pressure?

4. Explain the physiologic basis for administering a posterior pituitary extract to induce or facilitate labor.

5. The symptoms of menopause are sometimes treated with supplemental estrogen and progesterone. Why wouldn't treatment with GnRH or FSH and LH also be effective?

CLINICAL CONSIDERATION

(Explanation on p. A-52)

Maria A., who is in her second month of gestation, has been experiencing severe abdominal cramping. Her physician has diagnosed her condition as a tubal pregnancy: The developing embryo is implanted in the oviduct instead of in the uterine endometrium. Why must this pregnancy be surgically terminated?

Chapter 18

Uniqueness of the Reproductive System (pp. 578–585)

■ Both sexes produce gametes (reproductive cells), sperm in males and ova (eggs) in females, each of which bears one member of each of the 23 pairs of chromosomes present in human cells. Union of a sperm and an ovum at fertilization results in the beginning of a new individual with 23 complete pairs of chromosomes, half from each parent.

■ The reproductive system is anatomically and functionally distinct in males and females. Males produce sperm and deliver them into the female. Females produce ova, accept sperm delivery, and provide a suitable environment for supporting development of a fertilized ovum until the new individual can survive on its own in the external world.

■ In both sexes, the reproductive system consists of (1) a pair of gonads, testes in males and ovaries in females, which are the primary reproductive organs that produce the gametes and secrete sex hormones; (2) a reproductive tract composed of a system of ducts that transport, house, or do both for the gametes after they are produced; and (3) accessory sex glands that provide supportive secretions for the gametes. The external genitalia are the externally visible parts of the reproductive system. (*Review Figures 18-1 and 18-2.*) Secondary sexual characteristics are the distinguishing features between males and females not directly related to reproduction.

■ *Sex determination* is a genetic phenomenon dependent on the combination of sex chromosomes at the time of fertilization: An XY combination is a genetic male, and an XX combination is a genetic female. *Sexual differentiation* refers to the embryonic development of the gonads, reproductive tract, and external genitalia along male or female lines, which gives rise to the apparent anatomic sex of the individual. In the presence of masculinizing factors, a male reproductive system develops; in their absence, a female system develops. (*Review Figure 18-3.*)

Male Reproductive Physiology (pp. 585–593)

■ The testes are located in the scrotum. The cooler temperature in the scrotum than in the abdominal cavity is essential for spermatogenesis (sperm production), which occurs in the testes' highly coiled seminiferous tubules. Leydig cells in the interstitial spaces between these tubules secrete the male sex hormone testosterone into the blood. (*Review Figures 18-4 and 18-5.*)

■ Testosterone is secreted before birth to masculinize the developing reproductive system; then its secretion ceases until puberty, at which time it begins again and continues throughout life. Testosterone is responsible for maturation and maintenance of the entire male reproductive tract, for development of secondary sexual characteristics, and for stimulating libido. (*Review Table 18-1.*)

■ The testes are regulated by the anterior pituitary gonadotropic hormones, luteinizing hormone (LH) and follicle-stimulating hormone (FSH), which are under control of hypothalamic gonadotropin-releasing hormone (GnRH). (*Review Figure 18-7.*)

■ Testosterone secretion is regulated by LH stimulation of the Leydig cells, and in negative-feedback fashion, testosterone inhibits LH secretion. (*Review Figure 18-7.*)

■ Spermatogenesis requires both testosterone and FSH. Testosterone stimulates the mitotic and meiotic divisions required to transform the undifferentiated diploid germ cells, the spermatogonia, into undifferentiated haploid spermatids. FSH stimulates the remodeling of spermatids into highly specialized motile spermatozoa. (*Review Figures 18-4, 18-5, and 18-7.*)

■ A spermatozoon consists only of a DNA-packed head bearing an enzyme-filled acrosome at its tip for penetrating the ovum, a midpiece containing the mitochondria for energy production, and a whiplike motile tail. (*Review Figure 18-6.*)

■ Also present in the seminiferous tubules are Sertoli cells, which protect, nurse, and enhance the germ cells throughout their development. Sertoli cells also secrete inhibin, a hormone that inhibits FSH secretion, completing the negative-feedback loop. (*Review Figures 18-4b, 18-4d, and 18-7.*)

■ The still-immature sperm are flushed out of the seminiferous tubules into the epididymis by fluid secreted by the Sertoli cells. The epididymis and ductus deferens store and concentrate the sperm and increase their motility and fertility prior to ejaculation. During ejaculation, the sperm are mixed with secretions released by the accessory glands. (*Review Figure 18-4 and Table 18-2.*)

■ The *seminal vesicles* supply fructose for energy and prostaglandins, which promote smooth muscle motility in both the male and the female reproductive tracts to enhance sperm transport. The seminal vesicles also contribute the bulk of the semen. The *prostate gland* contributes an alkaline fluid to neutralize the acidic vaginal secretions. The *bulbourethral glands* release lubricating mucus. (*Review Table 18-2.*)

Sexual Intercourse between Males and Females (pp. 593–597)

■ The male sex act consists of erection and ejaculation, which are part of a broader systemic sexual response cycle. (*Review Table 18-4.*)

■ Erection is a hardening of the normally flaccid penis that enables it to penetrate the female vagina. Erection is accomplished by marked vasocongestion of the penis brought about by reflexly induced vasodilation of the arterioles supplying the penile erectile tissue. (*Review Figure 18-8.*)

■ When sexual excitation reaches a critical peak, ejaculation occurs. It consists of two stages: (1) emission, the emptying of semen (sperm and accessory sex gland secretions) into the urethra, and (2) expulsion of semen from the penis. The latter is accompanied by a set of characteristic systemic responses and intense pleasure referred to as orgasm. (*Review Table 18-4.*)

■ Females experience a sexual response cycle similar to that of males, with both having excitation, plateau, orgasmic, and resolution phases. Like the penis, the highly vascular clitoris undergoes erection (but not ejaculation). During sexual response, the outer portion of the vagina constricts to grip the penis, and the inner part expands to create space for sperm deposition.

Female Reproductive Physiology (pp. 597–622)

■ In the nonpregnant state, female reproductive function is controlled by a complex, cyclic, negative-feedback control system among the hypothalamus (GnRH), the anterior pituitary (FSH and LH), and the ovaries (estrogen, progesterone, and inhibin). During pregnancy, placental hormones become the main controlling factors.

■ The ovaries perform the dual and interrelated functions of oogenesis (producing ova) and secretion of estrogen and progesterone. (Review Table 18-5, p. 621.) Two related ovarian endocrine units sequentially accomplish these functions: the follicle and the corpus luteum.

■ The same steps in chromosome replication and division take place in oogenesis as in spermatogenesis, but the timing and end result are markedly different. Spermatogenesis is accomplished within 2 months, but the similar steps in oogenesis take anywhere from 12 to 50 years to complete cyclically from the onset of puberty until menopause. A female is born with a limited, nonrenewable supply of germ cells, whereas postpubertal males can produce several hundred million sperm each day. Each primary oocyte yields only one cytoplasm-rich ovum along with three doomed cytoplasm-poor polar bodies that disintegrate, whereas each primary spermatocyte yields four equally viable spermatozoa. (Review Figures 18-9, 18-10, and Figure 18-5, p. 588.)

■ Oogenesis and estrogen secretion take place within an ovarian follicle during the first half of each reproductive cycle (the follicular phase) under the influence of FSH, LH, and estrogen. (Review Figures 18-11 through 18-14.)

■ At approximately midcycle, the maturing follicle releases a single ovum (ovulation). Ovulation is triggered by an LH surge brought about by the high level of estrogen produced by the mature follicle. (Review Figures 18-11, 18-13, and 18-15.)

■ LH converts the empty follicle into a corpus luteum (CL), which produces progesterone and estrogen during the last half of the cycle (the luteal phase). This endocrine unit prepares the uterus for implantation if the released ovum is fertilized. (Review Figures 18-11, 18-13, and 18-16.)

■ If fertilization and implantation do not occur, the CL degenerates, withdrawing hormonal support for the highly developed uterine lining. This causes the lining to disintegrate and slough, producing menstrual flow. Simultaneously, a new follicular phase is initiated. (Review Figures 18-11 and 18-13.)

■ Menstruation ceases and the uterine lining (endometrium) repairs itself under the influence of rising estrogen levels from the newly maturing follicle. (Review Figure 18-13.)

■ If fertilization does take place, it occurs in the oviduct as the released egg and sperm deposited in the vagina are both transported to this site. (Review Figures 18-17 through 18-19.)

■ The fertilized ovum begins to divide mitotically. Within a week, it grows and differentiates into a blastocyst capable of implantation. (Review Figure 18-20.)

■ Meanwhile, the endometrium has become richly vascularized and stocked with stored glycogen under the influence of luteal-phase progesterone. (Review Figure 18-13.) Into this especially prepared lining, the blastocyst implants by means of enzymes released by the trophoblast, which forms the blastocyst's outer layer. These enzymes digest the nutrient-rich endometrial tissue, accomplishing the dual function of carving a hole in the endometrium for implantation of the blastocyst while simultaneously releasing nutrients from the endometrial cells for use by the developing embryo. (Review Figure 18-21.)

■ After implantation, an interlocking combination of fetal and maternal tissues, the placenta, develops. The placenta is the organ of exchange between maternal and fetal blood and acts as a transient, complex endocrine organ that secretes a number of hormones essential for pregnancy. Human chorionic gonadotropin (hCG), estrogen, and progesterone are the most important of these hormones. hCG maintains the CL of pregnancy, which secretes estrogen and progesterone during the first trimester of gestation until the placenta takes over this function in the last two trimesters. High levels of estrogen and progesterone are essential for maintaining a normal pregnancy. (Review Figures 18-22 and 18-24 and Table 18-5.)

■ At parturition, rhythmic contractions of increasing strength, duration, and frequency accomplish the three stages of labor: dilation of the cervix, birth of the baby, and delivery of the placenta (afterbirth). (Review Figure 18-26.)

■ Parturition is initiated by a complex interplay of multiple maternal and fetal factors. Once the contractions are initiated at the onset of labor, a positive-feedback cycle is established that progressively increases their force. As contractions push the fetus against the cervix, secretion of oxytocin, a powerful uterine muscle stimulant, is reflexly increased. The extra oxytocin causes stronger contractions, giving rise to even more oxytocin release, and so on. This positive-feedback cycle progressively intensifies until cervical dilation and delivery are complete. (Review Figure 18-25.)

■ During gestation, the breasts are specially prepared for lactation. The elevated levels of placental estrogen and progesterone, respectively, promote development of the ducts and alveoli in the mammary glands. (Review Figure 18-27.)

■ Prolactin stimulates the synthesis of enzymes essential for milk production by the alveolar epithelial cells. However, the high gestational level of estrogen and progesterone prevents prolactin from promoting milk production. Withdrawal of the placental steroids at parturition initiates lactation.

■ Lactation is sustained by suckling, which triggers the release of oxytocin and prolactin. Oxytocin causes milk ejection (letdown) by stimulating the myoepithelial cells surrounding the alveoli to squeeze the secreted milk out through the ducts. Prolactin stimulates secretion of more milk to replace the milk the baby nurses. (Review Figures 18-27 and 18-28.)

Appendix A
The Metric System

▲ Table A-1 **Metric Measures and English Equivalents**

Unit	Measure	Symbol	English Equivalent
Linear Measure			
1 kilometer	= 1000 meters	10^3 m km	0.62137 mile
1 meter		10^0 m m	39.37 inches
1 decimeter	= 1/10 meter	10^{-1} m dm	3.937 inches
1 centimeter	= 1/100 meter	10^{-2} m cm	0.3937 inch
1 millimeter	= 1/1000 meter	10^{-3} m mm	Not used
1 micrometer (or micron)	= 1/1,000,000 meter	10^{-6} m μm (or μ)	Not used
1 nanometer	= 1/1,000,000,000 meter	10^{-9} m nm	Not used
Measures of Capacity (for fluids and gases)			
1 liter		L	1.0567 U.S. liquid quarts
1 milliliter	= 1/1000 liter = volume of 1 gram of water at stp*	ml	
Measures of Volume			
1 cubic meter		m^3	
1 cubic decimeter	= 1/1000 cubic meter = 1 liter	dm^3	
1 cubic centimeter	= 1/1,000,000 cubic meter = 1 milliliter	cm^3	
1 cubic millimeter	= 1/100,000,000 cubic meter	mm^3	
Measures of Mass			
1 kilogram	= 1000 grams	kg	2.2046 pounds
1 gram		g	15.432 grains
1 milligram	= 1/1000 gram	mg	0.01 grain (about)
1 microgram	= 1/1,000,000 gram	μg (or mcg)	

*stp = standard temperature and pressure.

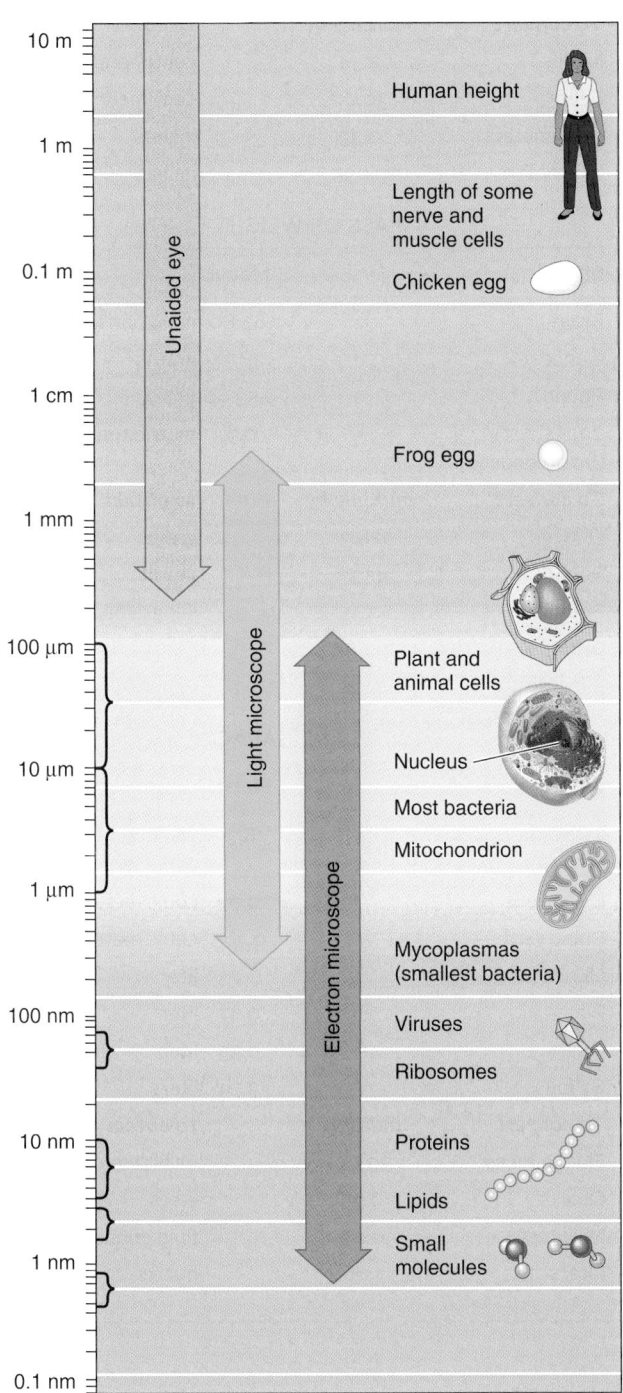

Comparison of human height in meters with the sizes of some biological and molecular structures.

▲ Table A-2 Metric–English Conversions

LENGTH

English		Metric	
Inch	=	2.54	centimeters
Foot	=	0.30	meter
Yard	=	0.91	meter
Mile (5280 feet)	=	1.61	kilometers
To convert	**multiply by**	**to obtain**	
Inches	2.54	centimeters	
Feet	30.00	centimeters	
Centimeters	0.39	inches	
Millimeters	0.039	inches	

MASS OR WEIGHT

English		Metric	
Grain	=	64.80	milligrams
Ounce	=	28.35	grams
Pound	=	453.60	grams
Ton (short) (2000 pounds)	=	0.91	metric ton
To convert	**multiply by**	**to obtain**	
Ounces	28.3	grams	
Pounds	453.6	grams	
Pounds	0.45	kilograms	
Grams	0.035	ounces	
Kilograms	2.2	pounds	

VOLUME AND CAPACITY

English		Metric	
Cubic inch	=	16.39	cubic centimeters
Cubic foot	=	0.03	cubic meter
Cubic yard	=	0.765	cubic meter
Ounce	=	0.03	liter
Pint	=	0.47	liter
Quart	=	0.95	liter
Gallon	=	3.79	liters
To convert	**multiply**	**to obtain**	
Fluid ounces	30.00	milliliters	
Quarts	0.95	liters	
Milliliters	0.03	fluid ounces	
Liters	1.06	quarts	

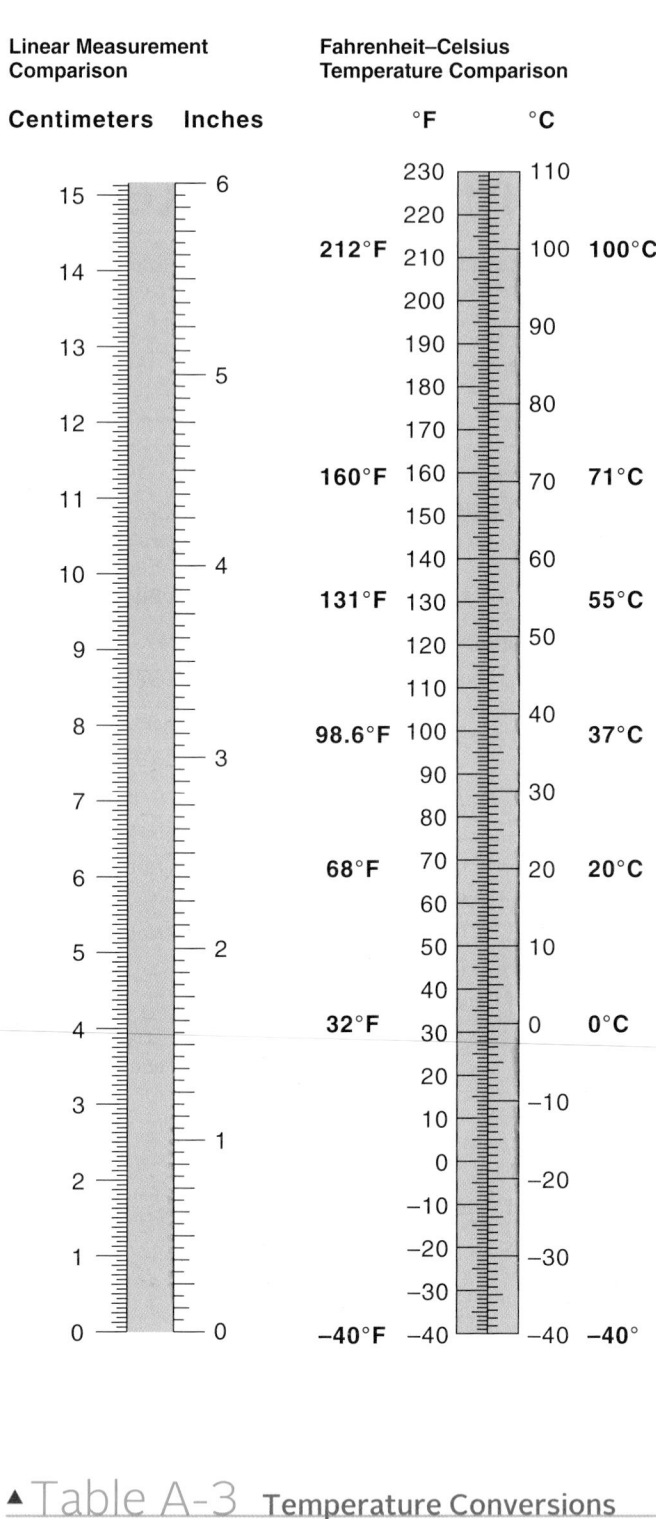

Linear Measurement Comparison

Centimeters   Inches

Fahrenheit–Celsius Temperature Comparison

°F   °C

▲ Table A-3 Temperature Conversions

To convert Fahrenheit to Celsius:

$Tc = (Tf - 32)/1.8$

To convert Celsius to Fahrenheit:

$Tf = (Tc \times 1.8) + 32$

Key
Tc = temperature in Celsius
Tf = temperature in Fahrenheit

Appendix B
A Review of Chemical Principles

By Spencer Seager, Weber State University, and Lauralee Sherwood

Chemical Level of Organization in the Body

Matter is anything that occupies space and has mass, including all living and nonliving things in the universe. **Mass** is the amount of matter in an object. **Weight,** in contrast, is the effect of gravity on that mass. The more gravity exerted on a mass, the greater the weight of the mass. An astronaut has the same mass whether on Earth or in space but is weightless in the zero gravity of space.

Atoms

All matter is made up of tiny particles called **atoms.** These particles are too small to be seen individually, even with the most powerful electron microscopes available today.

Even though extremely small, atoms consist of three types of even smaller subatomic particles. The types of atoms vary in the numbers of these subatomic particles they contain. **Protons** and **neutrons** are particles of nearly identical mass, with protons carrying a positive charge and neutrons having no charge. **Electrons** have a much smaller mass than protons and neutrons and are negatively charged. An atom consists of two regions—a dense, central *nucleus* made of protons and neutrons surrounded by a three-dimensional *electron cloud,* where electrons move rapidly around the nucleus in orbitals (● Figure B-1). The magnitude of the charge of a proton exactly matches that of an electron, but it is opposite in sign, being positive. In all atoms, the number of protons in the nucleus is equal to the number of electrons moving around the nucleus, so their charges balance and the atoms are neutral.

Elements and atomic symbols

A pure substance composed of only one type of atom is called an **element.** A pure sample of the element carbon contains only carbon atoms, even though the atoms might be arranged in the form of diamond or in the form of graphite (pencil "lead"). Each element is designated by an **atomic symbol,** a one- or two-letter chemical shorthand form of the element's name. Usually these symbols are easy to follow, because they are derived from the English name for the element. Thus, H stands for *hydrogen,* C for *carbon,* and O for *oxygen.* In a few cases, the atomic symbol is based on the element's Latin name—for

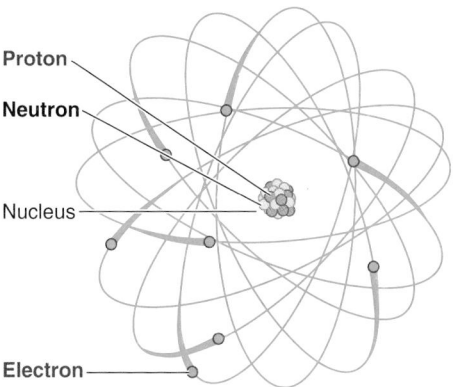

● **FIGURE B-1 The atom.** The atom consists of two regions. The central nucleus contains protons and neutrons and makes up 99.9% of the mass. Surrounding the nucleus is the electron cloud, where the electrons move rapidly around the nucleus. (Figure not drawn to scale.)

Labels: Proton, Neutron, Nucleus, Electron

example, Na for *sodium* (*natrium* in Latin) and K for *potassium* (*kalium*). Of the 109 known elements, 26 are normally found in the body. Four elements—hydrogen, carbon, oxygen, and nitrogen—compose 96% of the body's mass.

Compounds and molecules

Pure substances composed of more than one type of atom are known as **compounds.** Pure water, for example, is a compound that contains atoms of hydrogen and atoms of oxygen in a 2:1 ratio, regardless of whether the water is in the form of liquid, solid (ice), or vapor (steam). A **molecule** is the smallest unit of a pure substance that has the properties of that substance and is capable of a stable, independent existence. For example, a molecule of water consists of two atoms of hydrogen and one atom of oxygen, held together by chemical bonds.

Atomic number

Exactly what are we talking about when we refer to a "type" of atom? That is, what makes hydrogen, carbon, and oxygen atoms different? The answer is the number of protons in the nucleus. Regardless of where they are found, all hydrogen atoms have 1 proton in the nucleus, all carbon atoms have 6, and all oxygen atoms have 8. These numbers also represent the number of electrons moving around each nucleus, because the number of electrons and number of protons in an atom are equal. The

Name and Symbol	Number of Protons	Atomic Number	Atomic Weight (amu)
Hydrogen (H)	1	1	1.01
Carbon (C)	6	6	12.01
Nitrogen (N)	7	7	14.01
Oxygen (O)	8	8	16.00
Sodium (Na)	11	11	22.99
Magnesium (Mg)	12	12	24.31
Phosphorus (P)	15	15	30.97
Sulfur (S)	16	16	32.06
Chlorine (Cl)	17	17	35.45
Potassium (K)	19	19	39.10
Calcium (Ca)	20	20	40.08

number of protons in the nucleus of an atom of an element is called the **atomic number** of the element.

Atomic weight

As expected, tiny atoms have tiny masses. For example, the actual mass of a hydrogen atom is 1.67×10^{-24} g, that of a carbon atom is 1.99×10^{-23} g, and that of an oxygen atom is 2.66×10^{-23} g. These very small numbers are inconvenient to work with in calculations, so a system of relative masses has been developed. These relative masses simply compare the actual masses of the atoms with one another. Suppose the actual masses of two people were determined to be 45.50 and 113.75 kg. Their relative masses are determined by dividing each mass by the smaller mass of the two: $45.50/45.50 = 1.00$, and $113.75/45.50 = 2.50$. Thus, the relative masses of the two people are 1.00 and 2.50; these numbers simply express that the mass of the heavier person is 2.50 times that of the other person. The relative masses of atoms are called **atomic masses,** or **atomic weights,** and they are given in *atomic mass units (amu)*. In this system, hydrogen atoms, the least massive of all atoms, have an atomic weight of 1.01 amu. The atomic weight of carbon atoms is 12.01 amu, and that of oxygen atoms is 16.00 amu. Thus, oxygen atoms have a mass about 16 times that of hydrogen atoms. ▲ Table B-1 gives the atomic weights and some other characteristics of the elements that are most important physiologically.

Chemical Bonds

Because all matter is made up of atoms, atoms must somehow be held together to form matter. The forces holding atoms together are called *chemical bonds*. Not all chemical bonds are formed in the same way, but all involve the electrons of atoms. Whether one atom will bond with another depends on the number and arrangement of its electrons. An atom's elec-

trons are arranged in electron shells, to which we now turn our attention.

Electron shells

Electrons tend to move around the nucleus in a specific pattern. The orbitals, or pathways traveled by electrons around the nucleus, are arranged in an orderly series of concentric layers known as **electron shells,** which consecutively surround the nucleus. Each electron shell can hold a specific number of electrons. The first shell, closest to the nucleus (innermost), can contain a maximum of only 2 electrons, no matter what the element is. The second shell can hold a total of 8 more electrons. The third shell also can hold a maximum of 8 electrons. As the number of electrons increases with increasing atomic number, still more electrons occupy successive shells, each at a greater distance from the nucleus. Each successive shell from the nucleus has a higher **energy level.** Because the negatively charged electrons are attracted to the positively charged nucleus, it takes more energy for an electron to overcome the nuclear attraction and orbit farther from the nucleus. Thus, the first electron shell has the lowest energy level and the outermost shell of an atom has the highest energy level.

In general, electrons belong to the lowest energy shell possible, up to the maximum capacity of each shell. For example, hydrogen atoms have only 1 electron, so it is in the first shell. Helium atoms have 2 electrons, which are both in the first shell and fill it. Carbon atoms have 6 electrons, 2 in the first shell and 4 in the second shell, whereas the 8 electrons of oxygen are arranged with 2 in the first shell and 6 in the second shell.

Bonding characteristics of an atom and valence

Atoms tend to undergo processes that result in a filled outermost electron shell. Thus, the electrons of the outer or higher-energy shell determine the bonding characteristics of an atom and its ability to interact with other atoms. Atoms that have a vacancy in their outermost shell tend to give up, accept, or share electrons with other atoms (whichever is most favorable energetically) so that all participating atoms have filled outer shells. For example, an atom that has only 1 electron in its outermost shell may empty this shell so that its remaining shells are full. By contrast, another atom that lacks only 1 electron in its outer shell may acquire the deficient electron from the first atom to fill all its shells to the maximum. The number of electrons an atom loses, gains, or shares to achieve a filled outer shell is known as the atom's **valence.** A **chemical bond** is the force of attraction that holds participating atoms together as a result of an interaction between their outermost electrons.

Consider sodium atoms (Na) and chlorine atoms (Cl) (● Figure B-2). Sodium atoms have 11 electrons: 2 in the first shell, 8 in the second shell, and 1 in the third shell. Chlorine atoms have 17 electrons: 2 in the first shell, 8 in the second shell, and 7 in the third shell. Because 8 electrons are required to fill the second and third shells, sodium atoms have 1 electron more than is needed to provide a filled second shell, whereas chlorine atoms have 1 fewer electron than is needed to fill the third shell. Each sodium atom can lose an electron to a chlorine atom, leav-

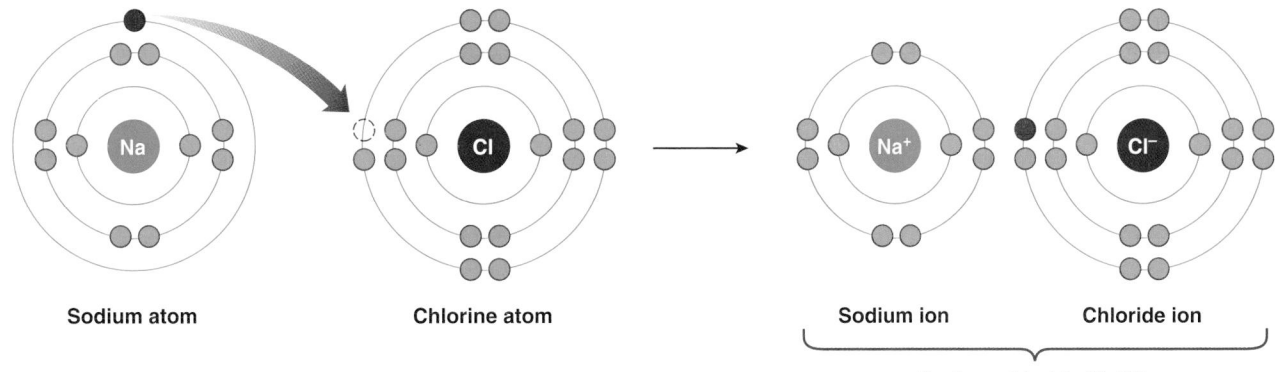

Sodium atom   Chlorine atom   Sodium ion   Chloride ion

Sodium chloride (NaCl)

● **FIGURE B-2 Ions and ionic bonds.** Sodium (Na) and chlorine (Cl) atoms both have partially filled outermost shells. Therefore, sodium tends to give up its lone electron in the outer shell to chlorine, filling chlorine's outer shell. As a result, sodium becomes a positively charged ion, and chlorine becomes a negatively charged ion known as chloride. The oppositely charged ions attract each other, forming an ionic bond.

ing each sodium atom with 10 electrons; 8 of these are in the second shell, which is full and is now the outer shell occupied by electrons. By accepting 1 electron, each chlorine atom now has a total of 18 electrons, with 8 of them in the third, or outer, shell, which is now full.

Ions; ionic bonds

Recall that atoms are electrically neutral because they have an identical number of positively charged protons and negatively charged electrons. By giving up and accepting electrons, the sodium atoms and chlorine atoms have achieved filled outer shells, but now each atom is unbalanced electrically. Although each sodium atom now has 10 electrons, it still has 11 protons in the nucleus and a net electrical charge, or valence, of +1. Similarly, each chlorine atom now has 18 electrons but only 17 protons. Thus, each chlorine atom has a −1 charge. Such charged atoms are called **ions.** Positively charged ions are called **cations;** negatively charged ions are called **anions.** As a helpful hint to keep these terms straight, imagine the "t" in *cation* as standing for a "+" sign and the first "n" in *anion* as standing for "negative."

Note that both a cation and an anion are formed whenever an electron is transferred from one atom to another. Because opposite charges attract, sodium ions (Na^+) and charged chlorine atoms, now called *chloride* ions (Cl^-), are attracted toward each other. This electrical attraction that holds cations and anions together is known as an **ionic bond.** Ionic bonds hold Na^+ and Cl^- together in the compound **sodium chloride, NaCl,** which is common table salt. A sample of sodium chloride actually contains sodium and chloride ions in a three-dimensional geometrical arrangement called a *crystal lattice*. The ions of opposite charge occupy alternate sites within the lattice (● Figure B-3).

Covalent bonds

It is not favorable, energywise, for an atom to give up or accept more than three electrons. Nevertheless, carbon atoms, which have four electrons in their outer shell, form compounds. They do so by another bonding mechanism, *covalent bonding*. Atoms that would have to lose or gain four or more electrons to achieve

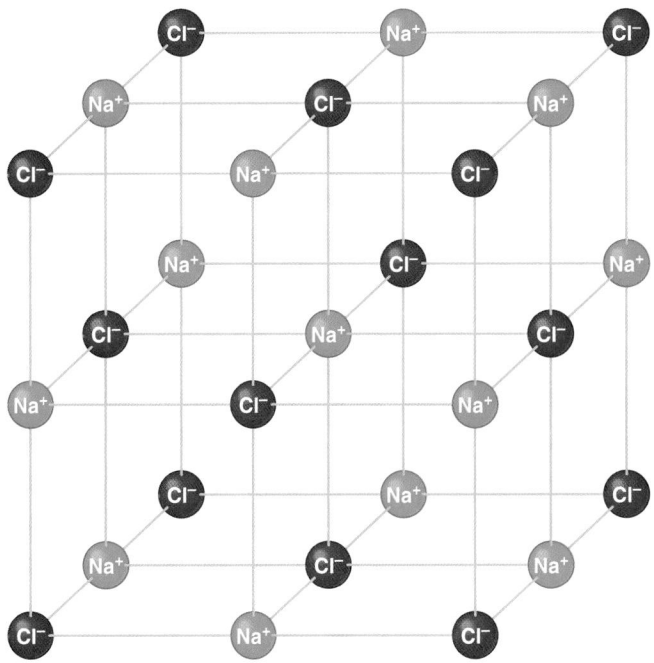

● **FIGURE B-3 Crystal lattice for sodium chloride (table salt).**

outer-shell stability usually bond by *sharing* electrons. Shared electrons actually orbit around *both* atoms. Thus, a carbon atom can share its 4 outer electrons with the 4 electrons of 4 hydrogen atoms, as shown in Equation B-1, where the outer-shell electrons are shown as dots around the symbol of each atom. (The resulting compound is methane, CH_4, a gas made up of individual CH_4 molecules.)

$$\cdot \overset{\cdot}{C} \cdot + 4 \cdot H \rightarrow H \! : \! \overset{\cdot\cdot}{\underset{H}{C}} \! : \! H \qquad \text{Eq. B-1}$$

Shared electron pairs

Shared electron pairs

Each electron that is shared by two atoms is counted toward the number of electrons needed to fill the outer shell of each atom.

Molecular formula	Atomic structure	Structural formula with covalent bond

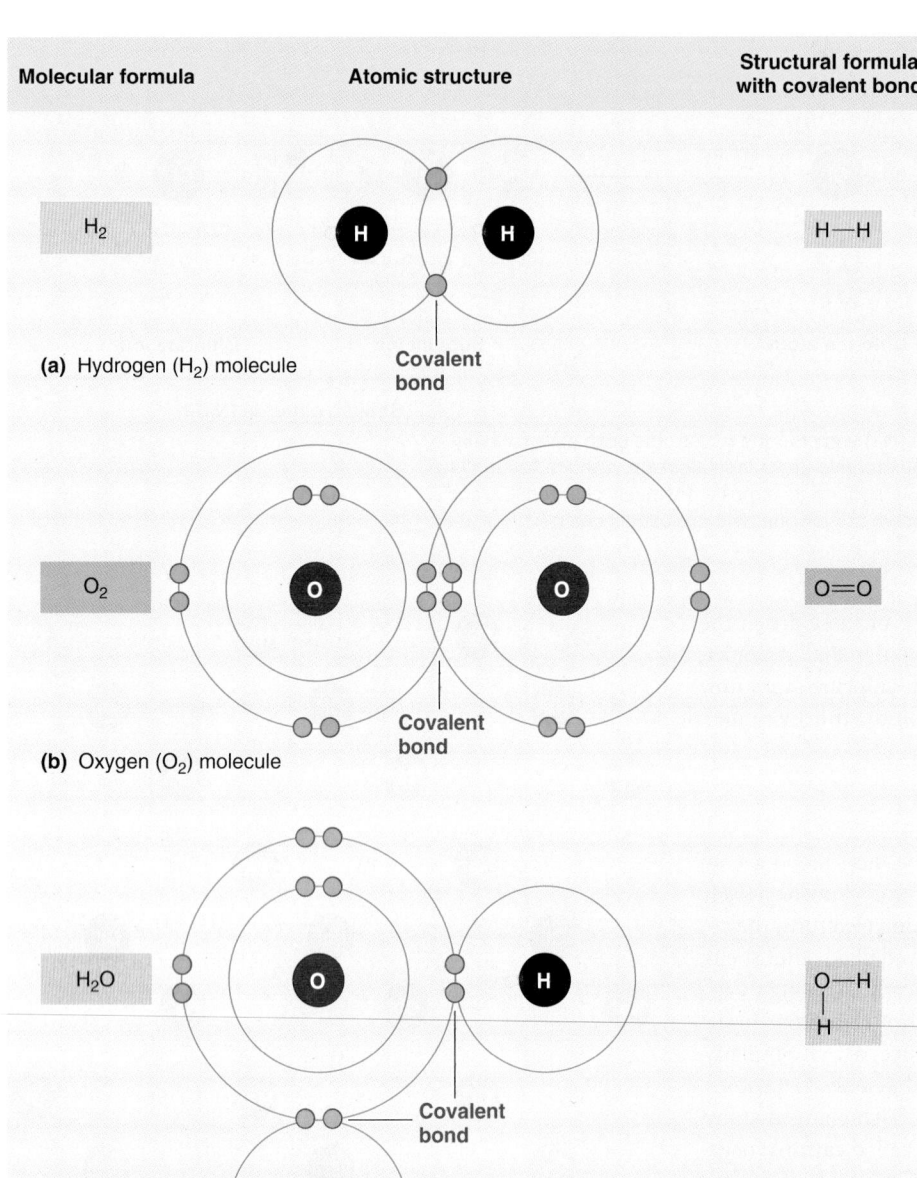

(a) Hydrogen (H_2) molecule — Covalent bond

(b) Oxygen (O_2) molecule — Covalent bond

(c) Water (H_2O) molecule — Covalent bond

● FIGURE B-4 **A covalent bond.** A covalent bond is formed when atoms that share a pair of electrons are both attracted toward the shared pair.

Thus, each carbon atom shares four pairs, or 8 electrons, and thus has 8 in its outer shell. Each hydrogen atom shares one pair, or 2 electrons, and thus has a filled outer shell. (Remember, hydrogen atoms need only two electrons to complete their outer shell, which is the first shell.) The sharing of a pair of electrons by atoms binds them together by means of a **covalent bond** (● Figure B-4). Covalent bonds are the strongest of chemical bonds; that is, they are the hardest to break.

Covalent bonds also form between some identical atoms. For example, two hydrogen atoms can complete their outer shells by sharing one electron pair made from the single electrons of each atom, as shown in Equation B-2:

Thus, hydrogen gas consists of individual H_2 molecules (● Figure B-4a). (A subscript following a chemical symbol indicates the number of that type of atom present in the molecule.) Several other nonmetallic elements also exist as molecules because covalent bonds form between identical atoms; oxygen (O_2) is an example (● Figure B-4b).

Often, an atom can form covalent bonds with more than one atom. One of the most familiar examples is water (H_2O), consisting of two hydrogen atoms each forming a single covalent bond with one oxygen atom (● Figure B-4c). Equation B-3 represents the formation of water's covalent bonds:

$$\begin{matrix} H\cdot \\ \\ H\cdot \end{matrix} + \cdot\ddot{\underset{\cdot}{O}}: \rightarrow H\!:\!\ddot{\underset{\overset{\cdot}{H}}{O}}: \qquad \text{Eq. B-3}$$

The water molecule is sometimes represented as

$$\begin{matrix} H - O \\ \quad | \\ \quad H \end{matrix}$$

where the nonshared electron pairs are not shown and the covalent bonds, or shared pairs, are represented by dashes.

Nonpolar and polar molecules

The electrons between two atoms in a covalent bond are not always shared equally. When the atoms sharing an electron pair are identical, such as two oxygen atoms, the electrons are attracted equally by both atoms and so are shared equally. The result is a **nonpolar molecule.** The term *nonpolar* implies no difference at the two ends (two "poles") of the bond. Because both atoms within the molecule exert the same pull on the shared electrons, each shared electron spends the same amount of time orbiting each atom. Thus, both atoms remain electrically neutral in a nonpolar molecule such as O_2.

When the sharing atoms are not identical, unequal sharing of electrons occurs because atoms of different elements do not exert the same pull on shared electrons. For example, an oxygen atom strongly attracts electrons when it is bonded to other atoms. A **polar molecule** results from the unequal sharing of electrons between different types of atoms covalently bonded together. The water molecule is a good example of a polar molecule. The oxygen atom pulls the shared electrons more strongly than do the hydrogen atoms within each of the two covalent bonds. Consequently, the electron of each hydrogen atom tends to spend more time away orbiting around the oxygen atom than at home around the hydrogen atom. Because of this nonuniform distribution of electrons, the oxygen side of the water molecule where the shared electrons spend more time is slightly negative, and the two hydrogens that are visited less frequently by the electrons are slightly more positive (● Figure B-5). Note that the entire water molecule has the same number of electrons as it has protons, so as a whole it has no net charge. This is unlike ions, which have an electron excess or deficit. Polar molecules have a balanced number of protons and electrons but an unequal distribution of the shared electrons among the atoms making up the molecule.

Hydrogen bonds

Polar molecules are attracted to other polar molecules. In water, for example, an attraction exists between the positive hydrogen ends of some molecules and the negative oxygen ends of others. Hydrogen is not a part of all polar molecules, but when it is covalently bonded to an atom that strongly attracts electrons to form a covalent molecule, the attraction of the positive (hydrogen) end of the polar molecule to the negative end of another polar molecule is called a **hydrogen bond** (● Figure B-6). Thus,

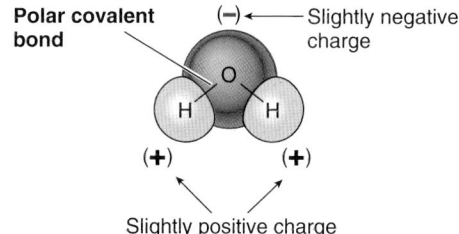

● **FIGURE B-5 A polar molecule.** A water molecule is an example of a polar molecule, in which the distribution of shared electrons is not uniform. Because the oxygen atom pulls the shared electrons more strongly than the hydrogen atoms do, the oxygen side of the molecule is slightly negatively charged and the hydrogen sides are slightly positively charged.

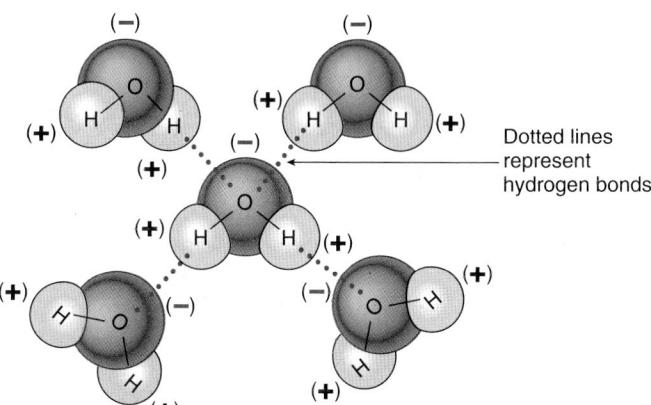

● **FIGURE B-6 A hydrogen bond.** A hydrogen bond is formed by the attraction of a positively charged hydrogen end of a polar molecule to the negatively charged end of another polar molecule.

the polar attractions of water molecules to each other are an example of hydrogen bonding.

Chemical Reactions

Processes in which chemical bonds are broken, formed, or both are called **chemical reactions.** Reactions are represented by equations in which the reacting substances (**reactants**) are typically written on the left, the newly produced substances (**products**) are written on the right, and an arrow meaning "yields" points from the reactants to the products. These conventions are illustrated in Equation B-4:

$$\underset{\text{Reactants}}{A + B} \rightarrow \underset{\text{Products}}{C + D} \qquad \text{Eq. B-4}$$

Balanced equations

A chemical equation is a "chemical bookkeeping" ledger that describes what happens in a reaction. By the **law of conservation of mass,** the total mass of all materials entering a reaction equals the total mass of all the products. Thus, the total number of atoms of each element must always be the same on the left and right sides of the equation, because no atoms are lost. Such equations in which the same number of atoms of each type appears on both sides are called **balanced equations.** When writing a balanced equation, the number *preceding* a chemical symbol designates the number of independent (unjoined) atoms, ions, or molecules of that type, whereas a number written as a subscript *following* a chemical symbol denotes the number of a particular atom within a molecule. The absence of a number indicates "one" of that particular chemical. Let us look at a specific example, the oxidation of glucose (the sugar that cells use as fuel), as shown in Equation B-5:

$$\underset{\text{glucose}}{C_6H_{12}O_6} + \underset{\text{oxygen}}{6\,O_2} \rightarrow \underset{\substack{\text{carbon}\\\text{dioxide}}}{6\,CO_2} + \underset{\text{water}}{6\,H_2O} \qquad \text{Eq. B-5}$$

According to this equation, 1 molecule of glucose reacts with 6 molecules of oxygen to produce 6 molecules of carbon dioxide and 6 molecules of water. Note the following balance in this reaction:

■ 6 carbon atoms on the left (in 1 glucose molecule) and 6 carbon atoms on the right (in 6 carbon dioxide molecules)

■ 12 hydrogen atoms on the left (in 1 glucose molecule) and 12 on the right (in 6 water molecules, each containing 2 hydrogen atoms)

■ 18 oxygen atoms on the left (6 in 1 glucose molecule plus 12 more in the 6 oxygen molecules) and 18 on the right (12 in 6 carbon dioxide molecules, each containing 2 oxygen atoms, and 6 more in the 6 water molecules, each containing 1 oxygen atom)

Reversible and irreversible reactions

Under appropriate conditions, the products of a reaction can be changed back to the reactants. For example, carbon dioxide gas dissolves in and reacts with water to form carbonic acid, H_2CO_3:

$$CO_2 + H_2O \rightarrow H_2CO_3 \qquad \text{Eq. B-6}$$

Carbonic acid is not very stable, however, and as soon as some is formed, part of it decomposes to give carbon dioxide and water:

$$H_2CO_3 \rightarrow CO_2 + H_2O \qquad \text{Eq. B-7}$$

Reactions that go in both directions are called **reversible reactions.** They are usually represented by double arrows pointing in both directions:

$$CO_2 + H_2O \rightleftharpoons H2CO_3 \qquad \text{Eq. B-8}$$

Theoretically, every reaction is reversible. Often, however, conditions are such that a reaction, for all practical purposes, goes in only one direction; such a reaction is called **irreversible.** For example, an irreversible reaction takes place when an explosion occurs, because the products do not remain in the vicinity of the reaction site to get together to react.

Catalysts; enzymes

The rates (speeds) of chemical reactions are influenced by a number of factors, of which catalysts are one of the most important. A **catalyst** is a "helper" molecule that speeds up a reaction without being used up in the reaction. Living organisms use catalysts known as **enzymes.** These enzymes exert amazing influence on the rates of chemical reactions that take place in the organisms. Reactions that take weeks or even months to occur under normal laboratory conditions take place in seconds under the influence of enzymes in the body. One of the fastest-acting enzymes is **carbonic anhydrase,** which catalyzes the reaction between carbon dioxide and water to form carbonic acid. This reaction is important in the transport of carbon dioxide from tissue cells, where it is produced metabolically, to the lungs, where it is excreted. The equation for the reaction was shown in Equation B-6.[1] Each molecule of carbonic anhydrase catalyzes the conversion of 36 million CO_2 molecules per minute! Enzymes are important in essentially every chemical reaction that takes place in living organisms.

Molecular and Formula Weight and the Mole

Because molecules are made up of atoms, the relative mass of a molecule is simply the sum of the relative masses (atomic weights) of the atoms found in the molecule. The relative masses of molecules are called **molecular masses** or **molecular weights.** The molecular weight of water, H_2O, is thus the sum of the atomic weights of two hydrogen atoms and one oxygen atom, or 1.01 amu + 1.01 amu + 16.00 amu = 18.02 amu.

Not all compounds exist in the form of molecules. Ionically bonded substances such as sodium chloride consist of three-

dimensional arrangements of sodium ions (Na^+) and chloride ions (Cl^-) in a 1:1 ratio. The formulas for ionic compounds reflect only the ratio of the ions in the compound and should not be interpreted in terms of molecules. Thus, the formula for sodium chloride, NaCl, indicates that the ions combine in a 1:1 ratio. It is convenient to apply the concept of relative masses to ionic compounds even though they do not exist as molecules. The **formula weight** for such compounds is defined as the sum of the atomic weights of the atoms found in the formula. Thus, the formula weight of NaCl is equal to the sum of the atomic weights of one sodium atom and one chlorine atom, or 22.99 amu + 35.45 amu = 58.44 amu.

As you have seen, chemical reactions can be represented by equations and discussed in terms of numbers of molecules, atoms, and ions reacting with one another. To carry out reactions in the laboratory, however, a scientist cannot count out numbers of reactant particles but instead must be able to weigh the correct amount of each reactant. Using the mole concept makes this task possible. A **mole** (abbreviated *mol*) of a pure element or compound is the amount of material contained in a sample of the pure substance that has a mass in grams equal to the substance's atomic weight (for elements) or the molecular weight or formula weight (for compounds). Thus, 1 mol of potassium, K, would be a sample of the element with a mass of 39.10 g. Similarly, 1 mol of H_2O would have a mass of 18.02 g, and 1 mol of NaCl would be a sample with a mass of 58.44 g.

Atomic weights, molecular weights, and formula weights are relative masses, which leads to a fundamental characteristic of moles. For example, 1 mol of oxygen atoms has a mass of 16.00 g, and 1 mol of hydrogen atoms has a mass of 1.01 g. Thus, the ratio of the masses of 1 mol of each element is 16.00 to 1.01, the same as the ratio of the atomic weights for the two elements. Recall that these atomic weights compare the relative masses of oxygen and hydrogen. Accordingly, the number of oxygen atoms present in 16 g of oxygen (1 mol of oxygen) is the same as the number of hydrogen atoms present in 1.01 g of hydrogen. Therefore, 1 mol of oxygen contains exactly the same number of oxygen atoms as the number of hydrogen atoms in 1 mol of hydrogen. Thus, it is possible and sometimes useful to think of a mole as a specific number of particles. This number, called **Avogadro's number,** is equal to 6.02×10^{23}.

Solutions, Colloids, and Suspensions

In contrast to a compound, a **mixture** consists of two or more types of elements or molecules physically blended together (intermixed) instead of being linked by chemical bonds. A compound has very different properties from the individual elements of which it is composed. For example, the solid, white NaCl (table salt) crystals you use to flavor your food are different from either sodium (a silvery white metal) or chlorine (a poisonous yellow–green gas found in bleach). By comparison, each component of a mixture retains its chemical properties. If you mix salt and sugar together, each retains a distinct taste and other individual properties. The constituents of a compound

---

[1] Carbonic anhydrase (ca) indirectly catalyzes this reaction by swiftly converting $CO_2 + H_2O$ directly to H^+ and HCO_3^-, which can combine to form H_2CO_3 (see p. 455). In the absence of ca, $CO_2 + H_2O$ slowly, directly form H_2CO_3. The reactions both with and without catalyst are commonly shown as in Equation B-6.

can only be separated by chemical means—bond breakage. By contrast, the components of a mixture can be separated by physical means, such as filtration or evaporation. The most common mixtures in the body are mixtures of water and various other substances. These mixtures are categorized as *solutions, colloids,* or *suspensions,* depending on the size and nature of the substance mixed with water.

Solutions

Most chemical reactions in the body take place between reactants that have dissolved to form solutions. **Solutions** are homogenous mixtures containing a relatively large amount of one substance called the **solvent** (the dissolving medium) and smaller amounts of one or more substances called **solutes** (the dissolved particles). Saltwater, for example, contains mostly water, which is thus the solvent, and a smaller amount of salt, which is the solute. Water is the solvent in most solutions found in the human body.

Electrolytes versus nonelectrolytes

When ionic solutes are dissolved in water to form solutions, the resulting solution will conduct electricity. This is not true for most covalently bonded solutes. For example, a salt–water solution conducts electricity, but a sugar–water solution does not. When salt dissolves in water, the solid lattice of Na^+ and Cl^- is broken down, and the individual ions are separated and distributed uniformly throughout the solution. These mobile, charged ions conduct electricity through the solution. Solutes that form ions in solution and conduct electricity are called **electrolytes.** When sugar dissolves, however, individual covalently bonded sugar molecules leave the solid and become uniformly distributed throughout the solution. These uncharged molecules cannot conduct a current. Solutes that do not form conductive solutions are called **nonelectrolytes.**

Measures of concentration

The amount of solute dissolved in a specific amount of solution can vary. For example, a salt–water solution might contain 1 g of salt in 100 ml of solution, or it could contain 10 g of salt in 100 ml of solution. Both solutions are salt–water solutions, but they have different concentrations of solute. The **concentration** of a solution indicates the relationship between the amount of solute and the amount of solution. Concentrations can be given in various units.

MOLARITY Concentrations given in terms of **molarity (M)** give the number of moles of solute in exactly 1 liter of solution. Thus, a half molar (0.5 M) solution of NaCl would contain 0.5 mol, or 29.22 g, of NaCl in each liter of solution.

NORMALITY When the solute is an electrolyte, it is sometimes useful to express the concentration of the solution in a unit that gives information about the amount of ionic charge in the solution. This is done by expressing concentration in terms of **normality (N).** The normality of a solution gives the number of

equivalents of solute in exactly 1 liter of solution. An **equivalent** of an electrolyte is the amount that produces 1 mole of positive (or negative) charges when it dissolves. The number of equivalents of an electrolyte can be calculated by multiplying the number of moles of electrolyte by the total number of positive charges produced when one formula unit of the electrolyte dissolves. Consider NaCl and calcium chloride ($CaCl_2$) as examples. The ionization reactions for one formula unit of each solute are

$$NaCl \rightarrow Na^+ + Cl^- \qquad \text{Eq. B-9}$$
$$CaCl_2 \rightarrow Ca^{2+} + 2\ Cl^- \qquad \text{Eq. B-10}$$

Thus, 1 mol of NaCl produces 1 mole of positive charges (Na^+) and so contains 1 equivalent:

$$(1 \text{ mol NaCl}) \times 1 = 1 \text{ equivalent}$$

where the number 1 used to multiply the 1 mol of NaCl came from the +1 charge on Na^+.

One mole of $CaCl_2$ produces 1 mol of Ca^{2+}, which is 2 moles of positive charge. Thus, 1 mol of $CaCl_2$ contains 2 equivalents:

$$(1 \text{ mol CaCl}_2) \times 2 = 2 \text{ equivalents}$$

where the number 2 used in the multiplication came from the +2 charge on Ca^{2+}.

If two solutions were made such that one contained 1 mol of NaCl per liter and the other contained 1 mol of $CaCl_2$ per liter, the NaCl solution would contain 1 equivalent of solute per liter and would be 1 normal (1 N). The $CaCl_2$ solution would contain 2 equivalents of solute per liter and would be 2 normal (2 N).

OSMOLARITY Another expression of concentration frequently used in physiology is osmolarity (Osm), which indicates the total *number* of solute particles in a liter of solution instead of the relative weights of the specific solutes. The osmolarity of a solution is the product of molarity (M) and *n,* where *n* is the number of moles of solute particles obtained when 1 mole of solute dissolves. Because nonelectrolytes such as glucose do not dissociate in solution, $n = 1$ and the osmolarity ($n \times M$) is equal to the molarity of the solution. For electrolyte solutions, the osmolarity exceeds the molarity by a factor equal to the number of ions produced on dissociation of each molecule in solution. For example, because a NaCl molecule dissociates into two ions, Na^+ and Cl^-, the osmolarity of a 1 M solution of NaCl is 2×1 M = 2 Osm.

Colloids and suspensions

In solutions, solute particles are ions or small molecules. By contrast, the particles in colloids and suspensions are much larger than ions or small molecules. In colloids and suspensions, these particles are known as **dispersed-phase particles** instead of *solutes.* When the dispersed-phase particles are no more than about 100 times the size of the largest solute particles found in a solution, the mixture is called a **colloid.** The dispersed-phase particles of colloids generally do not settle out.

All dispersed-phase particles of colloids carry electrical charges of the same sign. Thus, they repel each other. The constant buffeting from these collisions keeps the particles from settling. The most abundant colloids in the body are small functional proteins that are dispersed in the body fluids. An example is the colloidal dispersion of the plasma proteins in the blood (see p. 318).

When dispersed-phase particles are larger than those in colloids, if the mixture is left undisturbed the particles will settle out because of the force of gravity. Such mixtures are usually called **suspensions.** The major example of a suspension in the body is the mixture of blood cells suspended in the plasma. The constant movement of blood as it circulates through the blood vessels keeps the blood cells rather evenly dispersed within the plasma. However, if a blood sample is placed in a test tube and treated to prevent clotting, the heavier blood cells gradually settle to the bottom of the tube.

Inorganic and Organic Chemicals

Chemicals are commonly classified into two categories: inorganic and organic.

Distinction between inorganic and organic chemicals

The original criterion used for this classification was the origin of the chemicals. Those that came from living or once-living sources were *organic,* and those that came from other sources were *inorganic.* Today, the basis for classification is the element carbon. **Organic** chemicals are generally those that contain carbon. All others are classified as **inorganic.** A few carbon-containing chemicals are also classified as inorganic; the most common are pure carbon in the form of diamond and graphite, carbon dioxide (CO_2), carbon monoxide (CO), carbonates such as limestone ($CaCO_3$), and bicarbonates such as baking soda ($NaHCO_3$).

The unique ability of carbon atoms to bond to one another and form networks of carbon atoms results in an interesting fact. Even though organic chemicals all contain carbon, millions of these compounds have been identified. Some were isolated from natural plant or animal sources, and many have been synthesized in laboratories. Inorganic chemicals include all the other 108 elements and their compounds. The number of known inorganic chemicals made up of all these other elements is estimated to be about 250,000, compared to millions of organic compounds made up predominantly of carbon.

Monomers and polymers

Another result of carbon's ability to bond to itself is the large size of some organic molecules. Organic molecules range in size from methane (CH_4), a small, simple molecule with one carbon atom, to molecules such as DNA that contain as many as a million carbon atoms. Organic molecules that are essential for life are called **biological molecules,** or **biomolecules** for short. Some biomolecules are rather small organic compounds, including *simple sugars, fatty acids, amino acids,* and *nucleotides.*

These small, single units, known as **monomers** (meaning "single unit"), are building blocks for the synthesis of larger biomolecules, including *complex carbohydrates, lipids, proteins,* and *nucleic acids,* respectively. These larger organic molecules are called **polymers** (meaning "many units"), reflecting that they are made by the bonding together of a number of smaller monomers. For example, starch is formed by linking many glucose molecules together. Very large organic polymers are often referred to as **macromolecules,** reflecting their large size (*macro* means "large"). Macromolecules include many naturally occurring molecules, such as DNA and structural proteins, as well as many molecules that are synthetically produced, such as synthetic textiles (for example, nylon) and plastics.

Acids, Bases, and Salts

Acids, bases, and salts may be inorganic or organic compounds.

Acids and bases

Acids and bases are chemical opposites, and salts are produced when acids and bases react with each other. In 1887, Swedish chemist Svante Arrhenius proposed a theory defining acids and bases. He said that an *acid* is any substance that will dissociate, or break apart, when dissolved in water and in the process release a hydrogen ion (H^+). Similarly, *bases* are substances that dissociate when dissolved in water and in the process release a hydroxyl ion (OH^-). Hydrogen chloride (HCl) and sodium hydroxide (NaOH) are examples of Arrhenius acids and bases; their dissociations in water are represented in Equations B-11 and B-12, respectively:

$$HCl \rightarrow H^+ + Cl^- \qquad \text{Eq. B-11}$$
$$NaOH \rightarrow Na^+ + OH^- \qquad \text{Eq. B-12}$$

Note that the hydrogen ion is a bare proton, the nucleus of a hydrogen atom. Also note that both HCl and NaOH would behave as electrolytes.

Arrhenius did not know that free hydrogen ions cannot exist in water. They covalently bond to water molecules to form hydronium ions, as shown in Equation B-13:

$$H^+ + \overset{..}{\underset{|}{\text{O}}}{-}H \rightarrow \left[H{-}\overset{..}{\underset{|}{\text{O}}}{-}H \right]^+ \qquad \text{Eq. B-13}$$

In 1923, Johannes Brønsted in Denmark and Thomas Lowry in England proposed an acid–base theory that took this behavior into account. They defined an **acid** as any hydrogen-containing substance that donates a proton (hydrogen ion) to another substance (an acid is a *proton donor*) and a **base** as any substance that accepts a proton (a base is a *proton acceptor*). According to these definitions, the acidic behavior of HCl given in Equation B-11 is rewritten as shown in Equation B-14:

$$HCl + H_2O \rightleftharpoons H_3O^+ + Cl^- \qquad \text{Eq. B-14}$$

Note that this reaction is reversible, and the hydronium ion is represented as H_3O^+. In Equation B-14, the HCl acts as an acid in the forward (left-to-right) reaction, whereas water acts as a base. In the reverse reaction (right-to-left), the hydronium ion gives up a proton and thus is an acid, whereas the chloride ion, Cl^-, accepts the proton and so is a base. It is still a common practice to use equations such as Equation B-11 to simplify the representation of the dissociation of an acid, even though scientists recognize that equations like Equation B-14 are more correct.

Salts; neutralization reactions

At room temperature, **inorganic salts** are crystalline solids that contain the positive ion (cation) of an Arrhenius base such as NaOH and the negative ion (anion) of an acid such as HCl. Salts can be produced by mixing solutions of appropriate acids and bases, allowing a **neutralization reaction** to occur. In neutralization reactions, the acid and base react to form a salt and water. Most salts that form are water soluble and can be recovered by evaporating the water. Equation B-15 is a neutralization reaction:

$$HCl + NaOH \rightarrow NaCl + H_2O \qquad \text{Eq. B-15}$$

When acids or bases are used as solutes in solutions, the concentrations can be expressed as normalities just as they were earlier for salts. An equivalent of acid is the amount that gives up 1 mol of H^+ in solution. Thus, 1 mol of HCl is also 1 equivalent, but 1 mol of H_2SO_4 is 2 equivalents. Bases are described in a similar way, but an equivalent is the amount of base that gives 1 mol of OH^-.

See Chapter 14 and Appendix D for further discussion of acid–base balance in the body.

Functional Groups of Organic Molecules

Organic molecules consist of carbon and one or more additional elements covalently bonded to one another in "Tinker Toy" fashion. The simplest organic molecules, hydrocarbons (such as methane and petroleum products), have only hydrogen atoms attached to carbon backbones of varying lengths. All biomolecules always have elements besides hydrogen added to the carbon backbone. The carbon backbone forms the stable portion of most biomolecules. Other atoms covalently bonded to the carbon backbone, either alone or in clusters, form functional groups. **Functional groups** are specific combinations of atoms that generally react in the same way, regardless of the number of carbon atoms in the molecule to which they are attached. All organic compounds can be classified according to the functional group or groups they contain. For example, all *aldehydes* contain a functional group that includes one carbon atom, one oxygen atom, and one hydrogen atom covalently bonded in a specific way:

$$\overset{\displaystyle O}{\overset{\|}{(-C-H)}}$$

The carbon atom in an aldehyde group forms a single covalent bond with the hydrogen atom and a **double bond** (a bond in which two covalent bonds are formed between the same atoms, designated by a double line between the atoms) with the oxygen atom. The aldehyde group is attached to the rest of the molecule by a single covalent bond extending to the left of the carbon atom. Most aldehyde reactions are the same regardless of the size and nature of the rest of the molecule to which the aldehyde group is attached. Reactions of physiological importance often occur between two functional groups or between one functional group and a small molecule such as water.

Carbohydrates

Carbohydrates are organic compounds of tremendous biological and commercial importance. They are widely distributed in nature and include such familiar substances as starch, table sugar, and cellulose. Carbohydrates have five important functions in living organisms: They provide energy, serve as a stored form of chemical energy, provide dietary fiber, supply carbon atoms for the synthesis of cell components, and form part of the structural elements of cells.

Chemical composition of carbohydrates

Carbohydrates contain carbon, hydrogen, and oxygen. They acquired their name because most of them contain these three elements in an atomic ratio of one carbon to two hydrogens to one oxygen. This ratio suggests that the general formula is CH_2O and that the compounds are simply carbon hydrates ("watered" carbons), or carbohydrates. It is now known that they are not hydrates of carbon, but the name persists. All carbohydrates have a large number of functional groups per molecule. The most common functional groups in carbohydrates are *alcohol, ketone,* and *aldehyde*

$$(-OH), \quad \overset{\displaystyle O}{\overset{\|}{(-C-)}}, \quad \overset{\displaystyle O}{\overset{\|}{(-C-H)}}$$

$$\text{Alcohol} \qquad \text{Ketone} \qquad \text{Aldehyde}$$

or functional groups formed by reactions between pairs of these three.

Types of carbohydrates

The simplest carbohydrates are simple sugars, also called **monosaccharides.** As their name indicates, they consist of single, simple-sugar units called saccharides (*mono* means "one"). The molecular structure of glucose, an important monosaccharide, is shown in ● Figure B-7a. In solution, most glucose molecules assume the ring form shown in ● Figure B-7b. Other common monosaccharides are *fructose, galactose,* and *ribose.*

Disaccharides are sugars formed by linking two monosaccharide molecules together through a covalent bond (*di* means "two"). Some common examples of disaccharides are *sucrose* (common table sugar) and *lactose* (milk sugar). Sucrose molecules are formed from one glucose and one fructose molecule. Lactose molecules each contain one glucose and one galactose unit.

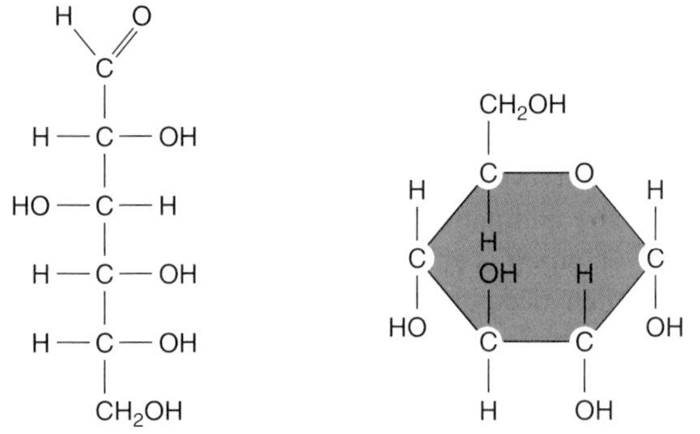

Forms of glucose figure

(a) Chain form of glucose   **(b)** Ring form of glucose

● FIGURE B-7 **Forms of glucose.**

Because of the many functional groups on carbohydrate molecules, large numbers of simple carbohydrate molecules are able to bond together and form long chains and branched networks. The resultant substances, **polysaccharides,** contain many saccharide units (*poly* means "many"). Three common polysaccharides made up entirely of glucose units are glycogen, starch, and cellulose:

■ *Glycogen* is a storage carbohydrate found in animals. It is a highly branched polysaccharide that averages a branch every 8 to 12 glucose units. The structure of glycogen is represented in ● Figure B-8, where each circle represents one glucose unit.

■ *Starch,* a storage carbohydrate of plants, consists of two fractions, amylose and amylopectin. Amylose consists of long, essentially unbranched chains of glucose units. Amylopectin is a highly branched network of glucose units averaging 24 to 30 glucose units per branch. Thus, it is less highly branched than glycogen.

■ *Cellulose,* a structural carbohydrate of plants, exists in the form of long, unbranched chains of glucose units. The bonding between the glucose units of cellulose is slightly different from the bonding between the glucose units of glycogen and starch. Humans have digestive enzymes that catalyze the breaking (hydrolysis) of the glucose-to-glucose bonds in starch but lack the necessary enzymes to hydrolyze cellulose glucose-to-glucose bonds. Thus, starch is a food for humans, but cellulose is not. Cellulose is the indigestible fiber in our diets.

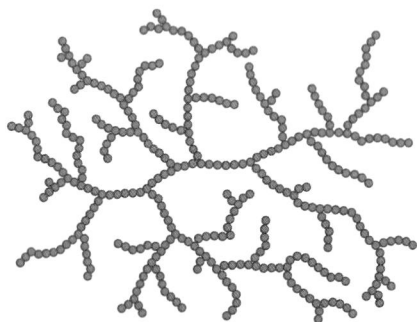

● FIGURE B-8 **A simplified representation of glycogen.** Each circle represents a glucose molecule.

Lipids

Lipids are a diverse group of organic molecules made up of substances with widely different compositions and molecular structures. Unlike carbohydrates, which are classified on the basis of their *molecular structure,* substances are classified as lipids on the basis of their *solubility.* **Lipids** are insoluble in water but soluble in nonpolar solvents such as alcohol.

Lipids are the waxy, greasy, or oily compounds found in plants and animals. These compounds repel water, a useful characteristic of the protective wax coatings found on some plants. Fats and oils are energy rich and have relatively low densities. These properties account for the use of fats and oils as stored energy in plants and animals. Still other lipids occur as structural components, especially in cellular membranes. The oily plasma membrane that surrounds each cell serves as a barrier that separates the intracellular contents from the surrounding extracellular fluid (see pp. 2, 22, and 47).

Simple lipids

Simple lipids contain just two types of components: fatty acids and alcohols. **Fatty acid molecules** consist of a hydrocarbon chain with a *carboxyl* functional group (—COOH) on the end. The hydrocarbon chain can be of variable length, but natural fatty acids always contain an even number of carbon atoms. The hydrocarbon chain can also contain one or more double bonds between carbon atoms. Fatty acids with no double bonds are called **saturated fatty acids,** whereas those with double bonds are called **unsaturated fatty acids.** The more double bonds present, the higher the degree of unsaturation. Saturated fatty acids predominate in dietary animal products (for example, meat, eggs, and dairy products), whereas unsaturated fatty acids are more prevalent in plant products (for example, grains, vegetables, and fruits). Consumption of a greater proportion of saturated than unsaturated fatty acids is linked with a higher incidence of cardiovascular disease (see p. 272).

The most common alcohol found in simple lipids is **glycerol** (glycerin), a three-carbon alcohol that has three alcohol functional groups (—OH).

Simple lipids called fats and oils are formed by a reaction between the carboxyl group of three fatty acids and the three alcohol groups of glycerol. The resulting lipid is an E-shaped molecule called a **triglyceride.** Such lipids are classified as fats or oils on the basis of their melting points. *Fats* are solids at room temperature, whereas *oils* are liquids. Their melting points depend on the degree of unsaturation of the fatty acids of the triglyceride. The melting point goes down with increasing degree of unsaturation. Thus, oils contain more unsaturated fatty acids than fats do. Examples of the components of fats and oils and a typical triglyceride molecule are shown in ● Figure B-9.

When triglycerides form, a molecule of water is released as each fatty acid reacts with glycerol. Adipose tissue in the body contains triglycerides. When the body uses adipose tissue as an energy source, the triglycerides react with water to release free fatty acids into the blood. The fatty acids can be used as an immediate energy source by many organs. In the liver, free fatty

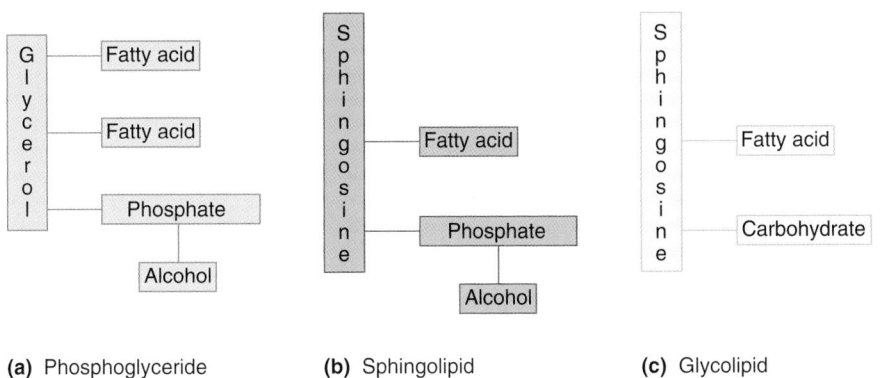

Fatty acid (saturated)

$$HO-C(=O)-(CH_2)_{14}CH_3$$

CH₂—OH
|
CH—OH
|
CH₂—OH

Glycerol

$$HO-C(=O)-(CH_2)_7CH=CH(CH_2)_7CH_3$$

Fatty acid (unsaturated)

$$CH_2-O-C(=O)-(CH_2)_7CH=CH(CH_2)_7CH_3$$
$$CH-O-C(=O)-(CH_2)_{14}CH_3$$
$$CH_2-O-C(=O)-(CH_2)_{16}CH_3$$

Triglyceride

● FIGURE B-9 **Triglyceride components and structure.**

G l y c e r o l		
— Fatty acid		
— Fatty acid		
— Phosphate		
— Alcohol		

(a) Phosphoglyceride

S p h i n g o s i n e		
— Fatty acid		
— Phosphate		
— Alcohol		

(b) Sphingolipid

S p h i n g o s i n e		
— Fatty acid		
— Carbohydrate		

(c) Glycolipid

● FIGURE B-10 **Examples of complex lipids.** In parts (b) and (c), sphingosine is an alcohol similar to glycerol.

acids are converted into compounds called **ketone bodies.** Two of the ketone bodies are acids, and one is the ketone called *acetone.* Excess ketone bodies are produced during diabetes mellitus, a condition in which most cells resort to using fatty acids as an energy source because the cells are unable to take up adequate amounts of glucose in the face of inadequate insulin action (see p. 564).

Complex lipids

Complex lipids have more than two types of components. The different complex lipids usually contain three or more of the following components: glycerol, fatty acids, a phosphate group, an alcohol other than glycerol, and a carbohydrate. Those that contain phosphate are called **phospholipids.** ● Figure B-10 contains representations of a few complex lipids; it emphasizes the components but does not give details of the molecular structures.

Steroids are lipids that have a unique structural feature consisting of a fused carbon ring system that contains three six-membered rings and a single five-membered ring (● Figure B-11). Different steroids possess this characteristic ring structure but have different functional groups and carbon chains attached.

Cholesterol, a steroidal alcohol, is the most abundant steroid in the human body. It is a component of cell membranes and is used by the body to produce other important steroids

that include bile salts, male and female sex hormones, and adrenocortical hormones. The structures of cholesterol and cortisol, an important adrenocortical hormone, are given in ● Figure B-12.

Proteins

The name *protein* is derived from the Greek word *proteios,* which means "of first importance." It is certainly an appropriate term for these important biological compounds. Proteins are indispensable components of all living things, where they play crucial roles in all biological processes. Proteins are the main structural component of cells, and all chemical reactions in the body are catalyzed by enzymes, all of which are proteins.

Chemical composition of proteins

Proteins are macromolecules made up of monomers called **amino acids.** Hundreds of different amino acids, both natural and synthetic, are known, but only 20 are commonly found in natural proteins. From this limited pool of 20 amino acids, cells build thousands of types of proteins, each with a distinct function, in much the same

(a) Detailed steroid ring system

(b) Simplified steroid ring system

● FIGURE B-11 **The steroid ring system.**

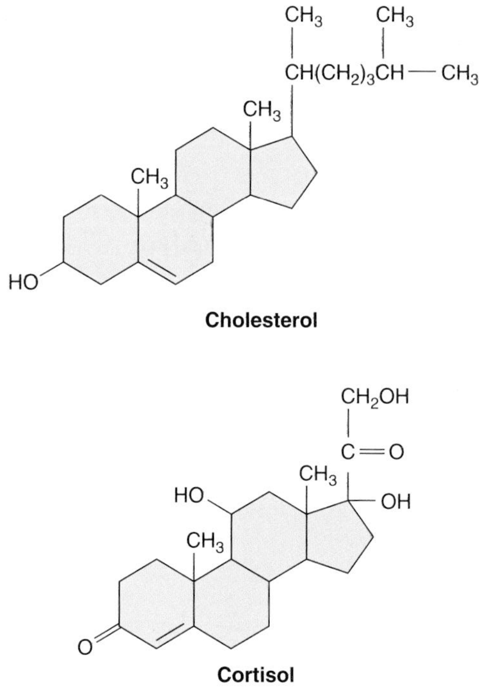

Cholesterol

Cortisol

● FIGURE B-12 **Examples of steroidal compounds.**

Side chain (different for each amino acid)
● FIGURE B-13 **The general structure of amino acids.**

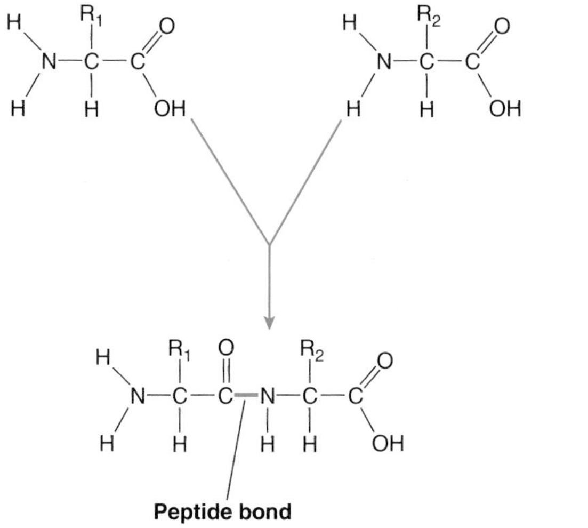

Peptide bond
● FIGURE B-14 **A peptide bond.** In forming a peptide bond, the carboxyl group of one amino acid reacts with the amino group of another amino acid.

way that composers create diverse music from a relatively small number of notes. Different proteins are constructed by varying the types and numbers of amino acids used and by varying the order in which they are linked together. However, proteins are not built haphazardly, by randomly linking together amino acids. Every protein in the body is deliberately and precisely synthesized under the direction of the blueprint laid down in the person's genes. Thus, amino acids are assembled in a specific pattern to produce a given protein that can accomplish a particular structural or functional task in the body. (More information about protein synthesis can be found in Appendix C.)

Peptide bonds
Each amino acid molecule has three important parts: an amino functional group ($-NH_2$), a carboxyl functional group ($-COOH$), and a characteristic side chain or R group. These components are shown in expanded form in ● Figure B-13. Amino acids form long chains as a result of reactions between the amino group of one amino acid and the carboxyl group of another amino acid. This reaction is illustrated in Equation B-16:

Eq. B-16

The covalent bond formed in the reaction is called a **peptide bond** (● Figure B-14). Notice that after the two molecules

react, the ends of the product still have an amino group and a carboxyl group that can react to extend the chain length.

On a molecular scale, proteins are immense molecules. Their size can be illustrated by comparing a glucose molecule to a molecule of hemoglobin, a protein. Glucose has a molecular weight of 180 amu and a molecular formula of $C_6H_{12}O_6$. Hemoglobin, a relatively small protein, has a molecular weight of 65,000 amu and a molecular formula of $C_{2952}H_{4664}O_{832}N_{812}S_8Fe_4$.

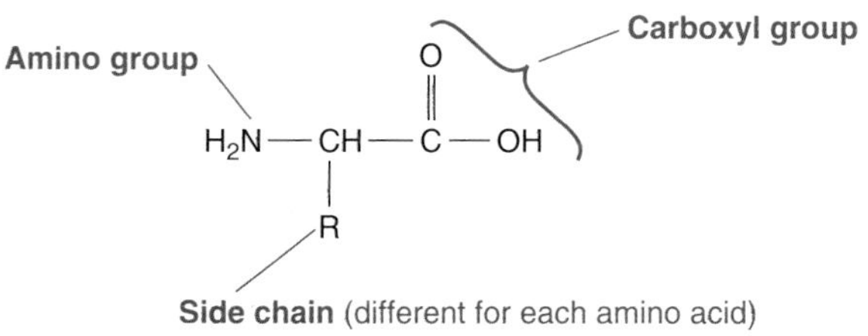

Levels of protein structure
The many atoms in a protein are not arranged randomly. In fact, proteins have a high degree of structural organization that plays an important role in their behavior in the body.

PRIMARY STRUCTURE The first level of protein structure is called the **primary structure.** It is simply the order in which amino acids are bonded together to form the protein chain. Amino acids are frequently represented by three-letter abbreviations, such as Gly for glycine and Arg for arginine. When this practice is followed, the primary structure of a protein can be represented as in ● Figure B-15, which shows part of the primary structure of human insulin, or as in ● Figure B-16a, which depicts a portion of the primary structure of hemoglobin.

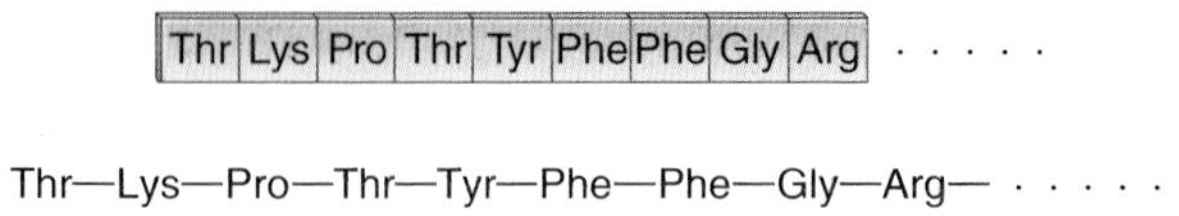

Thr—Lys—Pro—Thr—Tyr—Phe—Phe—Gly—Arg— · · · · ·
● FIGURE B-15 **A portion of the primary protein structure of human insulin.**

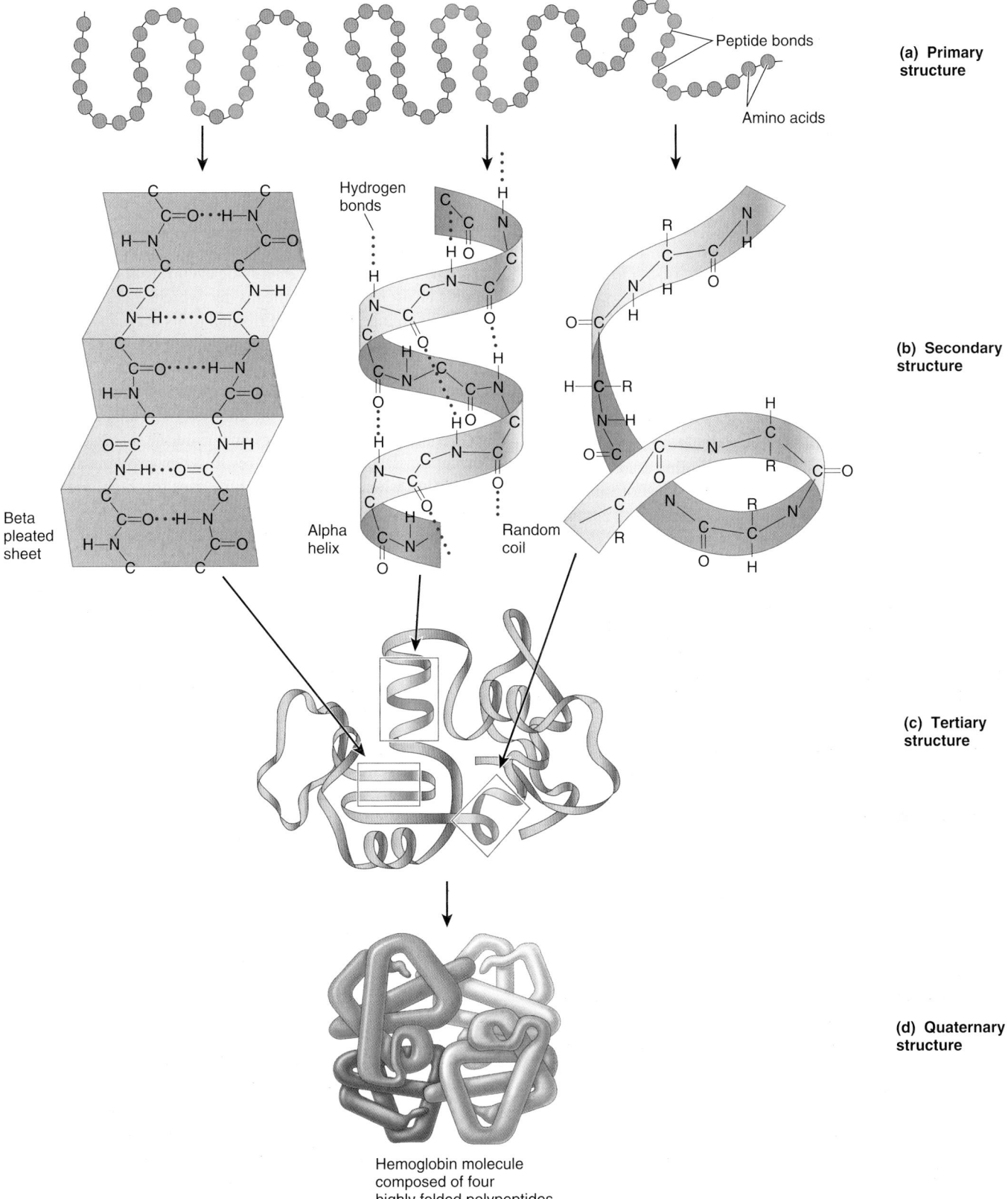

(a) Primary structure

Peptide bonds

Amino acids

Hydrogen bonds

(b) Secondary structure

Beta pleated sheet

Alpha helix

Random coil

(c) Tertiary structure

(d) Quaternary structure

Hemoglobin molecule composed of four highly folded polypeptides

● FIGURE B-16 **Levels of protein structure.** Proteins can have four levels of structure. (a) The primary structure is a particular sequence of amino acids bonded in a chain. (b) At the secondary level, hydrogen bonding occurs between various amino acids within the chain, causing the chain to assume a particular shape. The most common secondary protein structure in the body is the alpha helix. (c) The tertiary structure is formed by the folding of the secondary structure into a functional three-dimensional configuration. (d) Many proteins have a fourth level of structure composed of several polypeptides, as exemplified by hemoglobin.

SECONDARY STRUCTURE The second level of protein structure, called the **secondary structure,** results when hydrogen bonding occurs between the amino hydrogen of one amino acid and the carboxyl oxygen of another amino acid in the same chain:

$$\overset{\displaystyle O}{\underset{\displaystyle (-C-)}{\|}}$$

As a result of this hydrogen bonding, the involved portion of the chain typically assumes a coiled, helical shape called an *alpha (α) helix,* which is by far the most common secondary structure found in the body (● Figure B-16b). Other secondary structures such as *beta (β) pleated sheets* and *random coils* can also form, depending on the pattern of hydrogen bonding between amino acids located in different parts of the same chain.

TERTIARY AND QUATERNARY STRUCTURE The third level of structure in proteins is the **tertiary structure.** It results when functional groups of the side chains of amino acids in the protein chain react with each other. Several types of interactions are possible, as shown in ● Figure B-17. Tertiary structures can be visualized by letting a length of wire represent the chain of amino acids in the primary structure of a protein. Next imagine that the wire is wound around a pencil to form a helix, which represents the secondary structure. The pencil is removed, and the helical structure is now folded back on itself or carefully wadded into a ball. Such folded or spherical structures represent the tertiary structure of a protein (see ● Figure B-16c).

All functional proteins exist in at least a tertiary structure. Sometimes, several polypeptides interact with one another to form a fourth level of protein structure, the **quaternary structure.** For example, hemoglobin contains four highly folded polypeptide chains (the **globin** portion) (see ● Figure B-16d). Four iron-containing *heme* groups, one tucked within the interior of each of the folded polypeptide subunits, complete the quaternary structure of hemoglobin (see ● Figure 11-2, p. 319).

Hydrolysis and denaturation

In addition to serving as enzymes that catalyze the many essential chemical reactions of the body, proteins can undergo reactions themselves. Two of the most important are hydrolysis and denaturation.

HYDROLYSIS Notice that according to Equation B-16, the formation of peptide bonds releases water molecules. Under appropriate conditions, it is possible to reverse such reactions by adding water to the peptide bonds and breaking them. **Hydrolysis** ("breakdown by H_2O") reactions of this type convert large proteins into smaller fragments or even into individual amino acids. Hydrolysis is the means by which digestive enzymes break down ingested food into small units that can be absorbed from the digestive tract lumen into the blood.

DENATURATION **Denaturation** of proteins occurs when the bonds holding a protein in its characteristic shape are broken so that the protein chain takes on a random, disorganized conformation. Denaturation can result when proteins are heated (including when body temperature rises too high; see p. 516), subjected to extremes of pH (see p. 454), or treated with specific chemicals such as alcohol. In some instances, denaturation is accompanied by coagulation or precipitation, as illustrated by the changes that occur in the white of an egg as it is fried.

Nucleic Acids

Nucleic acids are high-molecular-weight macromolecules responsible for storing and using genetic information in living cells and passing it on to future generations. These important biomolecules are classified into two categories: **deoxyribonucleic acid (DNA)** and **ribonucleic acid (RNA).** DNA is found primarily in the cell's nucleus, and RNA is found primarily in the cytoplasm that surrounds the nucleus.

Both types of nucleic acid are made up of units called **nucleotides,** which in turn are composed of three simpler components: Each nucleotide contains an organic nitrogenous base, a sugar, and a phosphate group. The three components are chemically bonded together, with the sugar molecule lying between the base and the phosphate. In RNA the sugar is ribose, whereas in DNA it is deoxyribose. When nucleotides bond together to form nucleic acid chains, the bonding is between the phosphate of one nucleotide and the sugar of another. The resulting nucleic acids consist of chains of alternating phosphates and sugar molecules, with a base molecule extending out of the chain from each sugar molecule (see ● Figure C-1, p. A-19).

The chains of nucleic acids have structural features somewhat like those found in proteins. DNA takes the form of two chains that mutually coil around each other to form the well-known double helix. Some RNA occurs in essentially straight chains, whereas in other types the chain

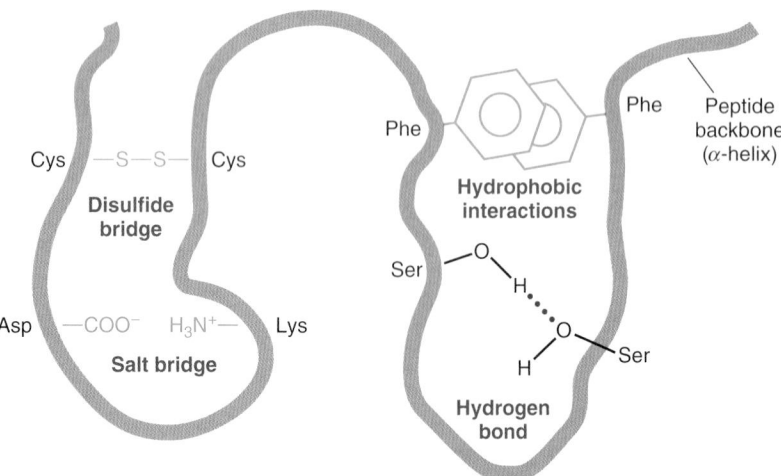

● FIGURE B-17 **Side chain interactions leading to the tertiary protein structure.**

forms specific loops or helices. See Appendix C for further details.

High-Energy Biomolecules

Not all nucleotides are used to construct nucleic acids. One important nucleotide—**adenosine triphosphate (ATP)**—is used as the body's primary energy carrier. Certain bonds in ATP temporarily store energy that is harnessed during the metabolism of foods and make it available to the parts of the cells where it is needed to do specific cellular work (see pp. 29–35). Let us see how ATP functions in this role. Structurally, ATP is a modified RNA (ribose-containing) nucleotide that has adenine as its base and two additional phosphates bonded in sequence to the original nucleotide phosphate. Thus, as its name implies, adenosine

triphosphate has three phosphates attached in a string to *adenosine,* the composite of ribose and adenine (● Figure B-18). Attaching these additional phosphates requires considerable energy input. The high-energy input used to create these **high-energy phosphate bonds** is "stored" in the bonds for later use. Most energy transfers in the body involve ATP's terminal phosphate bond. When energy is needed, the third phosphate is cleaved off by hydrolysis, yielding *adenosine diphosphate (ADP)* and an inorganic phosphate (P_i) and releasing energy in the process (Equation B-17):

$$ATP \rightarrow ADP + P_i + \text{energy for use by cell} \quad \text{Eq. B-17}$$

Why use ATP as an energy currency that cells can cash in by splitting the high-energy phosphate bonds as needed? Why not just directly use the energy released during the oxidation of nutrient molecules such as glucose? If all the chemical energy stored in glucose were to be released at once, most of the energy would be squandered because the cell could not capture much of the energy for immediate use. Instead, the energy trapped within the glucose bonds is gradually released and harnessed as cellular "bite-size pieces" in the form of the high-energy phosphate bonds of ATP.

Under the influence of an enzyme, ATP can be converted to a cyclic form of adenosine monophosphate (AMP), which contains only one phosphate group, the other two having been cleaved off. The resultant molecule, called **cyclic AMP** or **cAMP,** serves as an intracellular messenger, affecting the activities of a number of enzymes involved in important reactions in the body (see p. 102).

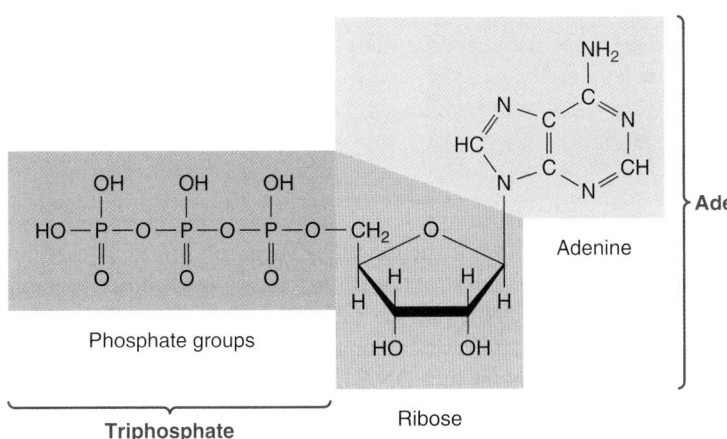

● FIGURE B-18 **The structure of ATP.**

Appendix C
Storage, Replication, and Expression of Genetic Information

Deoxyribonucleic Acid and Chromosomes

The nucleus of the cell houses **deoxyribonucleic acid (DNA),** the genetic blueprint that is unique for each individual.

Functions of DNA

As genetic material, DNA serves two essential functions. First, it contains "instructions" for assembling the structural and enzymatic proteins of the cell. Cellular enzymes in turn control the formation of other cellular structures and determine the functional activity of the cell by regulating the rate at which metabolic reactions proceed. The nucleus serves as the cell's control center by directly or indirectly controlling almost all cell activities through the role its DNA plays in governing protein synthesis. Because cells make up the body, the DNA code determines the structure and the function of the body as a whole. The DNA an organism has not only dictates whether the organism is a human, a toad, or a pea but also determines the unique physical and functional characteristics of that individual, all of which ultimately depend on the proteins produced under DNA control.

Second, by replicating (making copies of itself), DNA perpetuates the genetic blueprint within all new cells formed within the body and is responsible for passing on genetic information from parents to children. We first examine the structure of DNA and the coding mechanism it uses, and then we turn our attention to the means by which DNA replicates itself and controls protein synthesis.

Structure of DNA

DNA is a huge molecule, composed in humans of millions of nucleotides arranged into two long, paired strands that spiral around each other to form a double helix. Each **nucleotide** has three components: (1) a *nitrogenous base,* a ring-shaped organic molecule containing nitrogen; (2) a five-carbon ring-shaped sugar molecule, which in DNA is *deoxyribose;* and (3) a phosphate group. Nucleotides are joined end to end by linkages between the sugar of one nucleotide and the phosphate group of the adjacent nucleotide to form a long *polynucleotide* ("many nucleotide") strand with a sugar–phosphate backbone and bases projecting out one side (● Figure C-1). The four bases in DNA are the double-ringed bases **adenine (A)** and **guanine (G)** and the single-ringed bases **cytosine (C)** and **thymine (T).** The two polynucleotide strands within a DNA molecule are wrapped around each other so that their bases all project to the interior of the helix. The strands are held together by weak hydrogen bonds formed between the bases of adjoining strands (see ● Figure B-6, p. A-7). Base pairing is highly specific: Adenine pairs only with thymine, and guanine pairs only with cytosine (● Figure C-2).

Genes in DNA

The composition of the repetitive sugar–phosphate backbones that form the "sides" of the DNA "ladder" is identical for every molecule of DNA, but the sequence of the linked bases that form the "rungs" varies among DNA molecules. The particular sequence of bases in a DNA molecule serves as "instructions" or a "code," dictating the assembly of amino acids into a given order for the synthesis of specific **polypeptides** (chains of amino acids linked by peptide bonds; see p. A-14). A **gene** is a stretch of DNA that codes for the synthesis of a particular polypeptide. Polypeptides, in turn, are folded into a three-dimensional configuration to form a functional protein. Not all portions of a DNA molecule code for structural or enzymatic proteins. Some stretches of DNA code for proteins that regulate genes. Other segments appear important in organizing and packaging DNA within the nucleus. Still other regions are "nonsense" base sequences that have no apparent significance.

Packaging of DNA into chromosomes

The DNA molecules within each human cell, if lined up end to end, would extend more than 2 m (2,000,000 μm), yet these molecules are packed into a nucleus that is only 5 μm in diameter. These molecules are not randomly crammed into the nucleus but are precisely organized into **chromosomes.** Each chromosome consists of a different DNA molecule and contains a unique set of genes.

Somatic (body) **cells** contain 46 chromosomes (the **diploid number**), which can be sorted into 23 pairs on the basis of various distinguishing features. Chromosomes composing a matched pair are termed **homologous chromosomes,** one member of each pair having been derived from the individual's mother and the other member from the father. **Germ** (reproductive) **cells** (that is, sperm and eggs) contain only one mem-

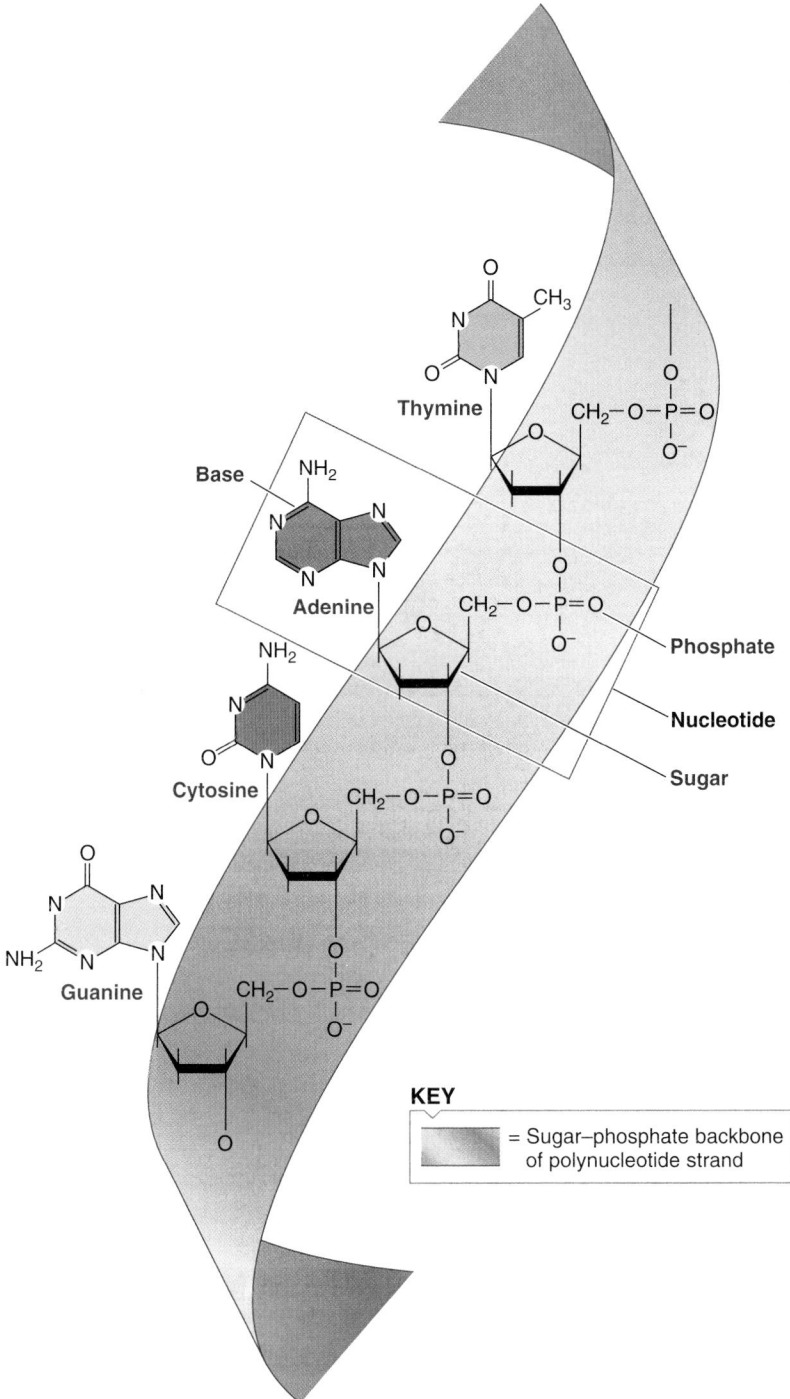

KEY

= Sugar–phosphate backbone of polynucleotide strand

● **FIGURE C-1 Polynucleotide strand.** Sugar–phosphate bonds link adjacent nucleotides together to form a polynucleotide strand with bases projecting to one side. The sugar–phosphate backbone is identical in all polynucleotides, but the sequence of the bases varies.

ber of each homologous pair for a total of 23 chromosomes (the **haploid number**). Union of a sperm and an egg results in a new diploid cell with 46 chromosomes, consisting of a set of 23 chromosomes from the mother and another set of 23 chromosomes from the father (see ● Figure 18-9, p. 599).

DNA molecules are packaged and compressed into discrete chromosomal units in part by nuclear proteins associated with DNA. Two classes of proteins—histone and nonhistone—bind with DNA. **Histones** form bead-shaped bodies that play a key role in packaging DNA into its chromosomal structure. The **nonhistones** are important in gene regulation. The complex formed between the DNA and its associated proteins is known as **chromatin.** The long threads of DNA within a chromosome are wound around histones at regular intervals, thus compressing a given DNA molecule to about one sixth of its fully extended length. This "beads-on-a-string" structure is folded and supercoiled into ever higher levels of organization to further condense DNA into rodlike chromosomes that are readily visible through a light microscope during cell division (● Figure C-3). When the cell is not dividing, the chromosomes partially "unravel" or decondense to a less compact form of chromatin that is indistinct under a light microscope but appears as thin strands and clumps with an electron microscope. The decondensed form of DNA is its working form; that is, it is the form used as a template for protein assembly. Let us turn our attention to this working form of DNA in operation.

Complementary Base Pairing, Replication, and Transcription

Complementary base pairing serves as the foundation for both the replication of DNA and the initial step of protein synthesis. We examine the mechanism and significance of complementary base pairing in each of these circumstances, starting with DNA replication.

DNA replication

During DNA replication, the two decondensed DNA strands "unzip" as the weak bonds between the paired bases are enzymatically broken. Then **complementary base pairing** takes place: New nucleotides present within the nucleus pair with the exposed bases from each unzipped strand (● Figure C-4). For example, new adenine-bearing nucleotides pair with exposed thymine-bearing nucleotides in an old strand, and new guanine-bearing nucleotides pair with exposed cytosine-bearing nucleotides in an old strand. This complementary base pairing is initiated at one end of the two old strands and proceeds in an orderly fashion to the other end. The new nucleotides attracted to and thus aligned in a prescribed order by the old nucleotides are sequentially joined by sugar–phosphate linkages to form two new strands that are complementary to each of the old strands. This replication process results in two complete double-stranded DNA molecules, one strand within each molecule having come

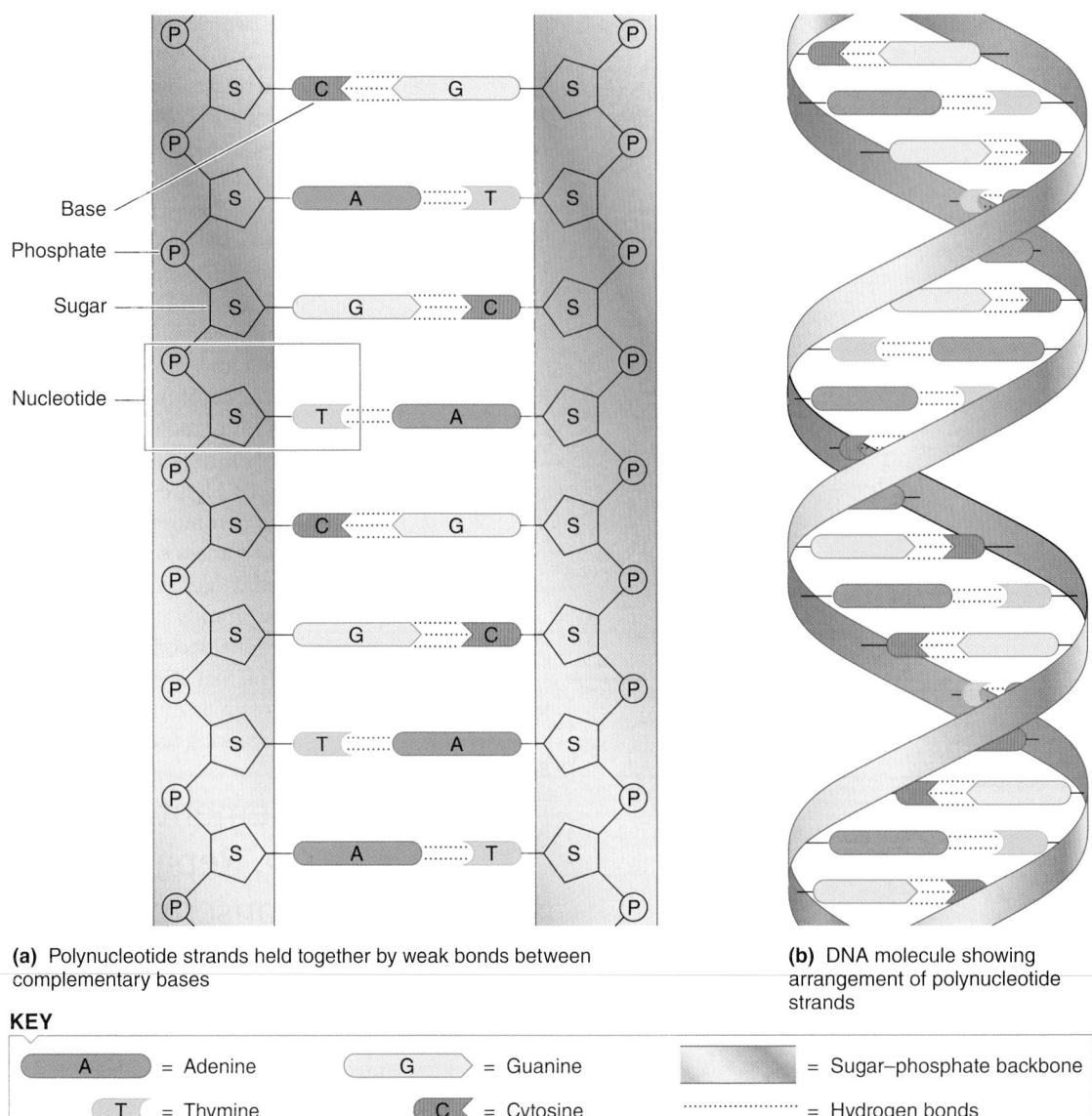

(a) Polynucleotide strands held together by weak bonds between complementary bases

(b) DNA molecule showing arrangement of polynucleotide strands

KEY

A	= Adenine	G	= Guanine		= Sugar–phosphate backbone
T	= Thymine	C	= Cytosine	....	= Hydrogen bonds

● **FIGURE C-2 Complementary base pairing in DNA.** (a) Two polynucleotide strands held together by weak hydrogen bonds formed between the bases of adjoining strands—adenine always paired with thymine and guanine always paired with cytosine. (b) Arrangement of the two bonded polynucleotide strands of a DNA molecule into a double helix.

from the original DNA molecule and one strand having been newly formed by complementary base pairing. These two DNA molecules are both identical to the original DNA molecule, with the "missing" strand in each of the original separated strands having been produced as a result of the imposed pattern of base pairing. This replication process, which occurs only during cell division, is essential for perpetuating the genetic code in both new daughter cells. The duplicate copies of DNA are separated and evenly distributed to the two halves of the cell before it divides. We cover the topic of cell division in more detail later.

DNA transcription and messenger ribonucleic acid

When DNA is not replicating in preparation for cell division, it serves as a blueprint for dictating cellular protein synthesis. How is this accomplished when DNA is confined to the nucleus and protein synthesis is carried out by ribosomes within the cytoplasm? Several types of another nucleic acid, **ribonucleic acid (RNA),** serve as the "go-betweens."

STRUCTURE OF RNA RNA differs structurally from DNA in three regards: (1) The five-carbon sugar in RNA is ribose instead of deoxyribose, the only difference between them being the presence in ribose of a single oxygen atom that is absent in deoxyribose; (2) RNA contains the closely related base **uracil** instead of thymine, with the three other bases being the same as in DNA; and (3) RNA is single stranded and not self-replicating.

All RNA molecules are produced in the nucleus using DNA as a template and then exit the nucleus through openings in the nuclear membrane, called *nuclear pores* (see p. 22), which are large enough for passage of RNA molecules but block the much larger DNA molecules.

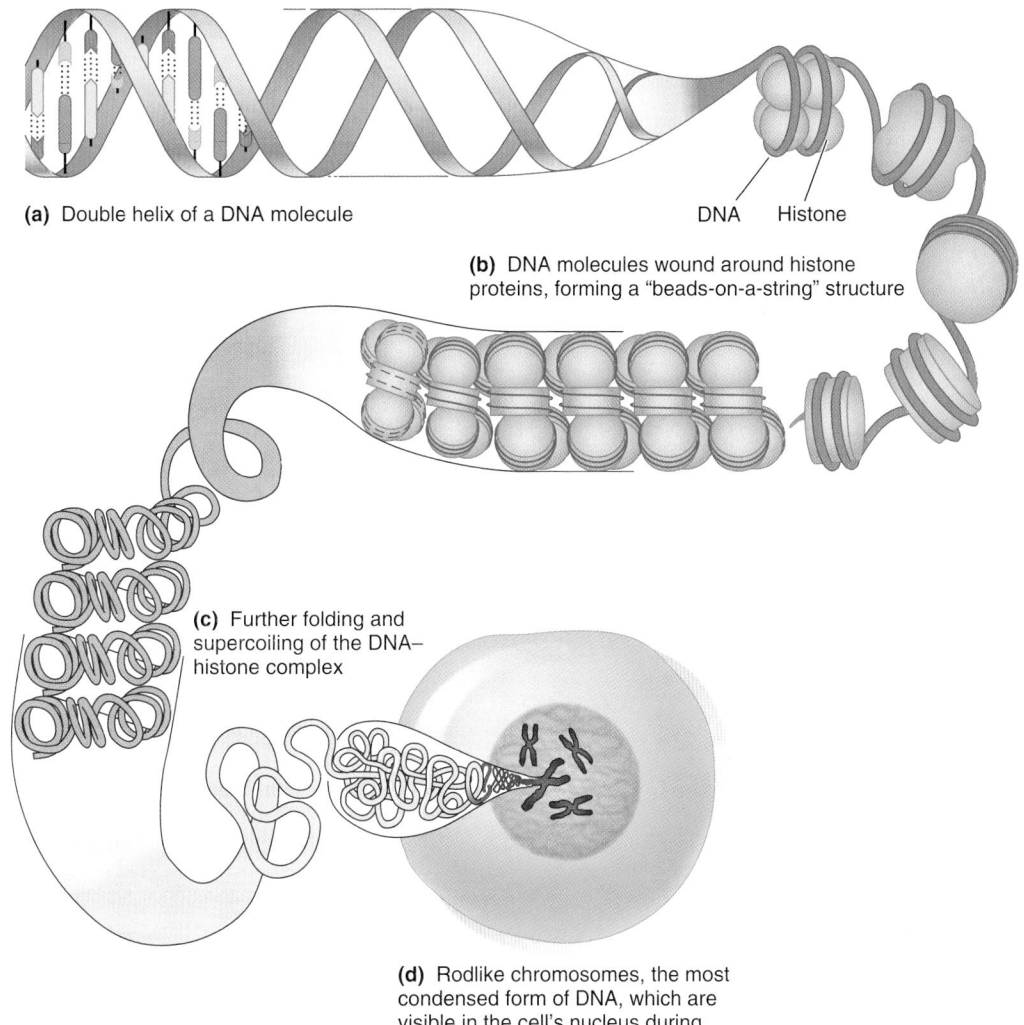

(a) Double helix of a DNA molecule

DNA   Histone

(b) DNA molecules wound around histone proteins, forming a "beads-on-a-string" structure

(c) Further folding and supercoiling of the DNA–histone complex

(d) Rodlike chromosomes, the most condensed form of DNA, which are visible in the cell's nucleus during cell division

● **FIGURE C-3 Levels of organization of DNA.**

The DNA instructions for assembling a particular protein coded in the base sequence of a given gene are "transcribed" into a molecule of **messenger RNA (mRNA).** The segment of the DNA molecule to be copied uncoils, and the base pairs separate to expose the particular sequence of bases in the gene. In any given gene, only one of the DNA strands is used as a template for transcribing RNA, with the copied strand varying for different genes along the same DNA molecule. The beginning and end of a gene within a DNA strand are designated by particular base sequences that serve as "start" and "stop" signals.

TRANSCRIPTION **Transcription** is accomplished by complementary base pairing of free RNA nucleotides with their DNA counterparts in the exposed gene (● Figure C-5). The same pairing rules apply except that uracil, the RNA nucleotide substitute for thymine, pairs with adenine in the exposed DNA nucleotides. As soon as the RNA nucleotides pair with their DNA counterparts, sugar–phosphate bonds are formed to join the nucleotides together into a single-stranded RNA molecule that is released from DNA once transcription is complete. The original conformation of DNA is then restored. The RNA strand is much shorter than a DNA strand because only a one-gene segment of DNA is transcribed into a single RNA molecule. The length of the finished RNA transcript varies, depending on the size of the gene. Within its nucleotide base sequence, this RNA transcript contains instructions for assembling a particular protein. Note that the message is coded in a base sequence that is *complementary to, not identical to,* the original DNA code.

The mRNA delivers the final coded message to the ribosomes for **translation** into a particular amino acid sequence to form a given protein. Thus, genetic information flows from DNA (which can replicate itself) through RNA to protein. This is accomplished first by *transcription* of the DNA code into a complementary RNA code, followed by *translation* of the RNA code into a specific protein (● Figure C-6). In the next section, you will learn more about the steps in translation. The structural and functional characteristics of the cell as determined by its protein composition can be varied, subject to control, depending on which genes are "switched on" to produce mRNA.

Free nucleotides present in the nucleus cannot be randomly joined together to form either DNA or RNA strands

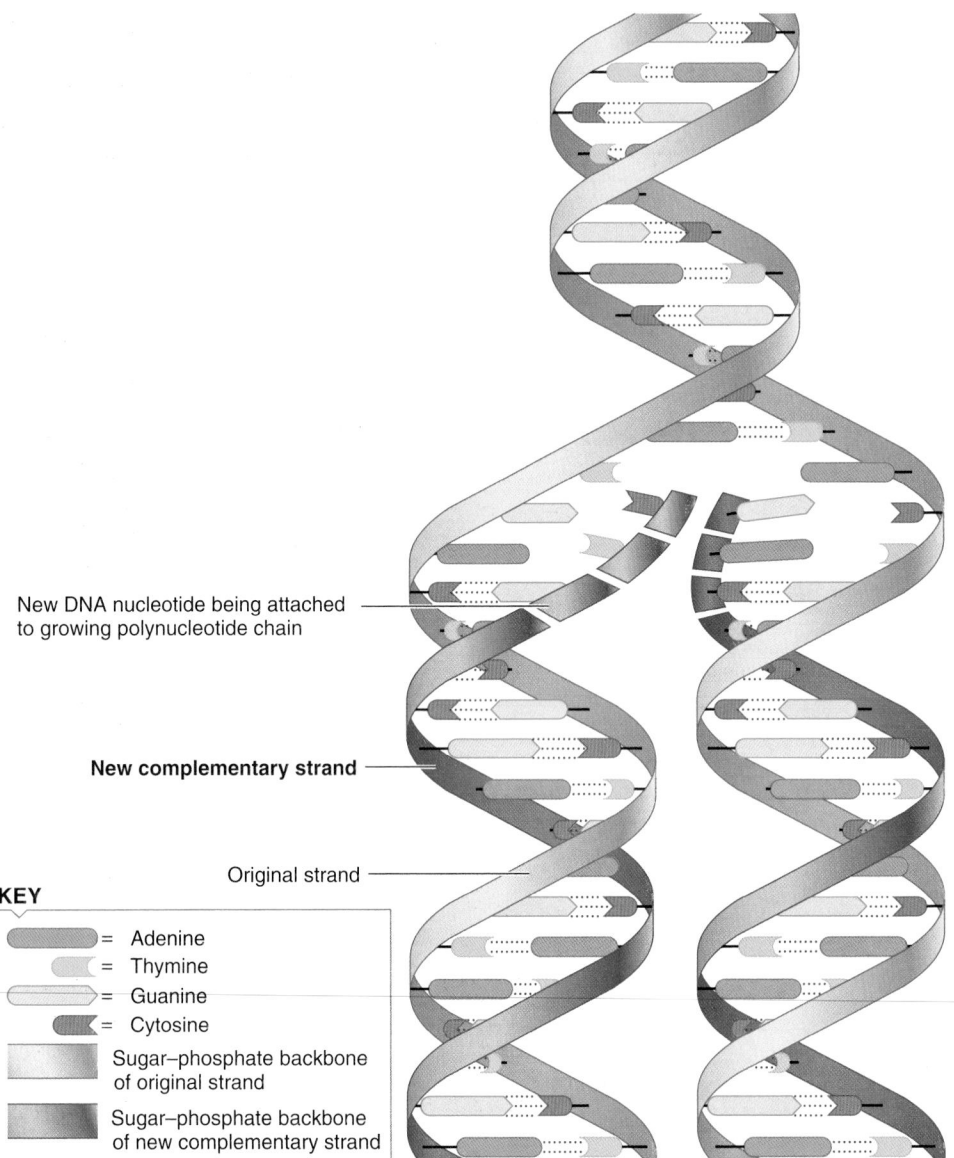

New DNA nucleotide being attached to growing polynucleotide chain

New complementary strand

Original strand

KEY

= Adenine
= Thymine
= Guanine
= Cytosine

Sugar–phosphate backbone of original strand

Sugar–phosphate backbone of new complementary strand

● **FIGURE C-4 Complementary base pairing during DNA replication.** During DNA replication, the DNA molecule is unzipped, and each old strand directs the formation of a new strand; the result is two identical double-helix DNA molecules.

because the enzymes required to link together the sugar and phosphate components of nucleotides are active only when bound to DNA. This ensures that DNA, mRNA, and protein assembly occur only according to genetic plan.

Translation and Protein Synthesis

Three forms of RNA participate in protein synthesis. Besides mRNA, two other forms of RNA are required for translation of the genetic message into cellular protein: ribosomal RNA and transfer RNA (see p. 22).

■ The mRNA carries the coded message from nuclear DNA to a cytoplasmic ribosome, where it directs the synthesis of a particular protein.

■ **Ribosomal RNA (rRNA)** is an essential component of *ribosomes,* the "workbenches" for protein synthesis (see p. 23). Ribosomes "read" the base sequence code of mRNA and translate it into the appropriate amino acid sequence during protein synthesis.

■ **Transfer RNA (tRNA)** transfers the appropriate amino acids in the cytosol to their designated site in the amino acid sequence of the protein under construction.

Triplet code; codon

Twenty amino acids are used to construct proteins, yet only four nucleotide bases are used to code for these amino acids. In the "genetic dictionary," each amino acid is specified by a **triplet code** that consists of a specific sequence of three bases in the DNA nucleotide chain. For example, the DNA sequence

ACA (adenine, cytosine, adenine) specifies the amino acid cysteine, whereas the sequence ATA specifies the amino acid tyrosine. Each DNA triplet code is transcribed into mRNA as a complementary code word, or **codon,** consisting of a sequenced order of the three bases that pair with the DNA triplet. For example, the DNA triplet code ATA is transcribed as UAU (uracil, adenine, uracil) in mRNA.

Sixty-four DNA triplet combinations (and, accordingly, 64 mRNA codon combinations) are possible using the four nucleotide bases (4^3). Of these possible combinations, 61 code for specific amino acids and the remaining 3 serve as "stop signals." A stop signal acts as a "period" at the end of a "sentence." The sentence consists of a series of triplet codes that specify the amino acid sequence in a particular protein. When the stop codon is reached, rRNA releases the finished polypeptide product. Because 61 triplet codes each specify a particular amino acid and there are 20 amino acids, a given amino acid may be specified by more than one base–triplet combination. For example, tyrosine is specified by the DNA sequence ATG, as well as by ATA. In addition, one DNA triplet code, TAC (mRNA codon sequence AUG) functions as a "start signal" in addition to specifying the amino acid methionine. This code marks the place on mRNA where translation is to begin so that the message is started at the correct end and thus reads in the right direction. Interestingly, the same genetic dictionary is used universally; a given three-base code stands for the same amino acid in all living things, including microorganisms, plants, and animals.

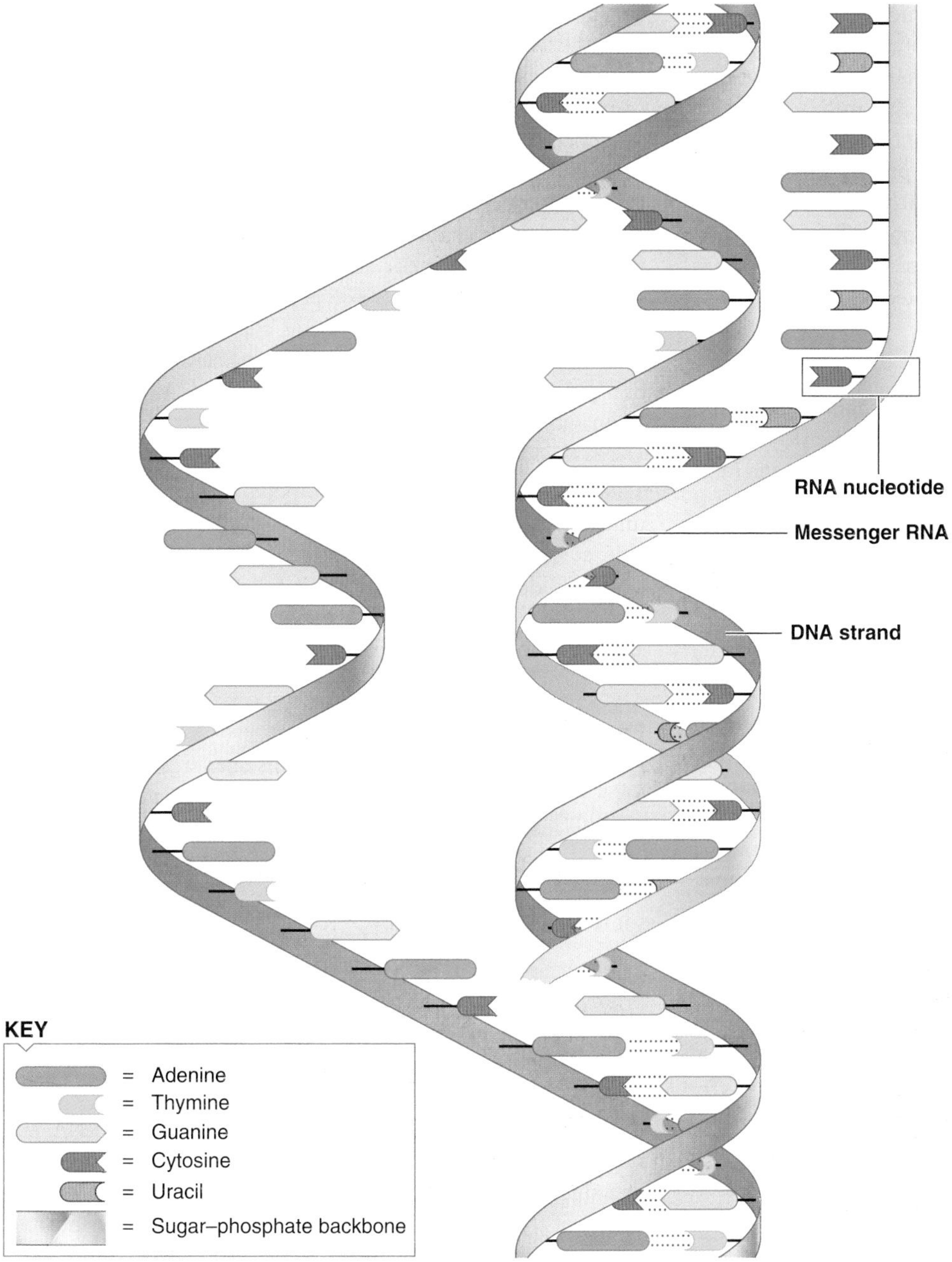

KEY

	=	Adenine
	=	Thymine
	=	Guanine
	=	Cytosine
	=	Uracil
	=	Sugar–phosphate backbone

RNA nucleotide

Messenger RNA

DNA strand

● FIGURE C-5 **Complementary base pairing during DNA transcription.** During DNA transcription, a messenger RNA molecule is formed as RNA nucleotides are assembled by complementary base pairing at a given segment of one strand of an unzipped DNA molecule (that is, a gene).

Ribosomes

A **ribosome** brings together all components that participate in protein synthesis—mRNA, tRNA, and amino acids—and provides the enzymes and energy required for linking the amino acids together. The nature of the protein synthesized by a given ribosome is determined by the mRNA message being translated. Each mRNA serves as a code for only one particular polypeptide.

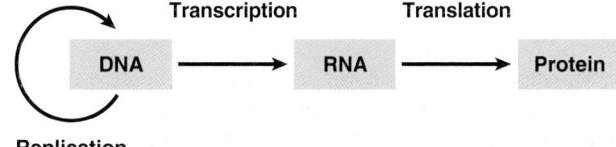

Transcription Translation

DNA → RNA → Protein

Replication

● FIGURE C-6 **Flow of genetic information from DNA through RNA to protein by transcription and translation.**

A ribosome is an rRNA–protein structure organized into two subunits of unequal size. These subunits are brought together only when a protein is being synthesized (● Figure C-7, step **1**). During assembly of a ribosome, an mRNA molecule attaches to the smaller of the ribosomal subunits by means of a *leader sequence,* a section of mRNA that precedes the start codon. The small subunit with mRNA attached then binds to a large subunit to form a complete, functional ribosome. When the two subunits unite, a groove is formed that accommodates the mRNA molecule as it is being translated.

tRNA and anticodons

Free amino acids in the cytosol cannot "recognize" and bind directly with their specific codons in mRNA. The tRNA must bring the appropriate amino acid to its proper codon. Even though tRNA is single stranded, as are all RNA molecules, it is folded back onto itself into a T shape with looped ends (● Figure C-8). The open-ended stem portion recognizes and binds to a specific amino acid. There are at least 20 varieties of tRNA, each able to bind with only one of the 20 kinds of amino acids. A tRNA is said to be "charged" when it is carrying its passenger amino acid. The loop end of a tRNA opposite the amino acid binding site contains a sequence of three exposed bases, known as the **anticodon,** which is complementary to the mRNA codon that specifies the amino acid being carried. Through complementary base pairing, a tRNA can bind with mRNA and insert its amino acid into the protein under construction only at the site designated by the codon for the amino acid. For example, the tRNA molecule that binds with tyrosine bears the anticodon AUA, and this can pair only with the mRNA codon UAU, which specifies tyrosine. This dual binding function of tRNA molecules ensures that the correct amino acids are delivered to mRNA for assembly in the order specified by the genetic code. The tRNA can only bind with mRNA at a ribosome, so protein assembly does not occur except in the confines of a ribosome.

Steps of protein synthesis

The three steps of protein synthesis are initiation, elongation, and termination.

INITIATION Protein synthesis is initiated when a charged tRNA molecule bearing the anticodon specific for the start codon binds at this site on mRNA (see ● Figure C-7, step **2**).

ELONGATION A second charged tRNA bearing the anticodon specific for the next codon in the mRNA sequence then occupies the site next to the first tRNA (step **3**). At any given time, a ribosome can accommodate only two tRNA molecules bound to adjacent codons. Through enzymatic action, a peptide bond is formed between the two amino acids that are linked to the stems of the adjacent tRNA molecules (step **4**). The linkage is subsequently broken between the first tRNA and its amino acid passenger, leaving the second tRNA with a chain of two amino acids. The uncharged tRNA molecule (the one minus its amino acid passenger) is released from mRNA (step **5**). The ribosome then moves along the mRNA molecule by precisely three bases,

a distance of one codon (step **6**), so that the tRNA bearing the chain of two amino acids is moved into the number one ribosomal site for tRNA. Then, an incoming charged tRNA with a complementary anticodon for the third codon in the mRNA sequence occupies the number two ribosomal site that was vacated by the second tRNA (step **7**). The chain of two amino acids subsequently binds with and is transferred to the third tRNA to form a chain of three amino acids (step **8**). Through repetition of this process, amino acids are subsequently added one at a time to a growing polypeptide chain in the order designated by the codon sequence as the ribosomal translation machinery moves stepwise along the mRNA molecule one codon at a time (step **9**). This process is rapid. As many as 10 to 15 amino acids can be added per second.

TERMINATION Elongation of the polypeptide chain continues until the ribosome reaches a stop codon in the mRNA molecule, at which time the polypeptide is released. The polypeptide is then folded and modified into a full-fledged protein. The ribosomal subunits dissociate and are free to reassemble into another ribosome for translation of other mRNA molecules.

Energy cost of protein synthesis

Protein synthesis is expensive in terms of energy. Attachment of each new amino acid to the growing polypeptide chain requires a total investment of splitting four high-energy phosphate bonds—two to charge tRNA with its amino acid, one to bind tRNA to the rRNA–mRNA complex, and one to move the ribosome forward one codon.

Polyribosomes

A number of copies of a given protein can be produced from a single mRNA molecule before the latter is chemically degraded. As one ribosome moves forward along the mRNA molecule, a new ribosome attaches at the starting point on mRNA and starts translating the message. Attachment of many ribosomes to a single mRNA molecule results in a *polyribosome.* Multiple copies of the identical protein are produced as each ribosome moves along and translates the same message (● Figure C-9). The released proteins are used within the cytosol, except for the few that move into the nucleus through the nuclear pores.

In contrast to the cytosolic polyribosomes, ribosomes directed to bind with the rough endoplasmic reticulum (ER) feed their growing polypeptide chains into the ER lumen (see ● Figure 2-3, p. 25). The resultant proteins are subsequently packaged for export out of the cell or for new cellular membrane.

Control of gene activity and protein transcription

Because each somatic cell in the body has the identical DNA blueprint, you might assume that they would all produce the same proteins. This is not the case, however, because different cell types are able to transcribe different sets of genes and thus synthesize different sets of structural and enzymatic proteins. For example, only red blood cells can synthesize hemoglobin, even though all body cells carry the DNA instructions for

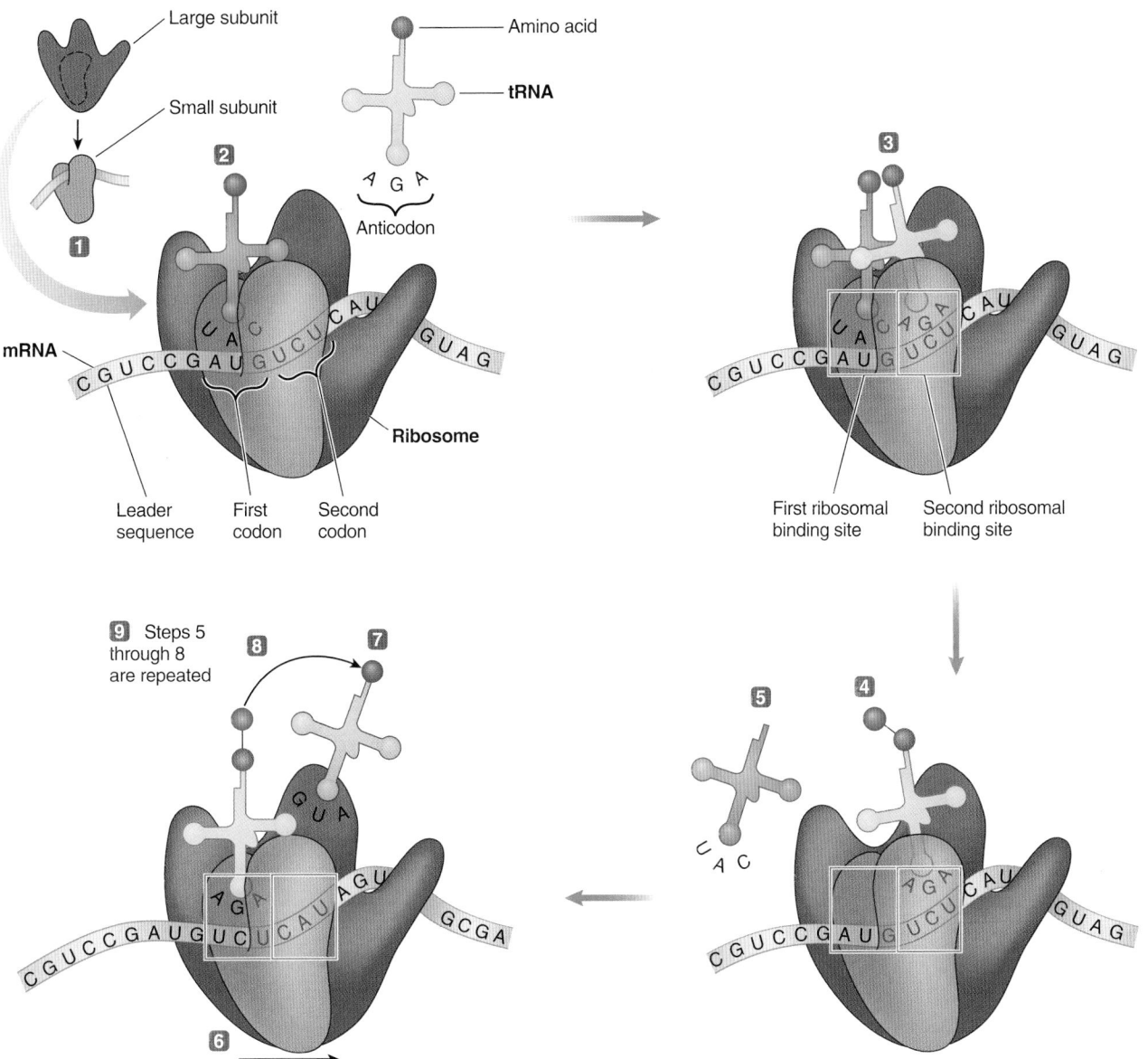

1. On binding with a messenger RNA (mRNA) molecule, the small ribosomal subunit joins with the large subunit to form a functional ribosome.

2. A transfer RNA (tRNA), charged with its specific amino acid passenger, binds to mNRA by means of complementary base pairing between the tRNA anticodon and the first mRNA codon positioned in the first ribosomal binding site.

3. Another tRNA molecule attaches to the next codon on mRNA positioned in the second ribosomal binding site.

4. The amino acid from the first tRNA is linked to the amino acid on the second tRNA.

5. The first tRNA detaches.

6. The ribosome shifts forward one codon (a distance of a three-base sequence) along the mRNA molecule.

7. Another charged tRNA moves in to attach with the next codon on mRNA, which has now moved into the second ribosomal binding site.

8. The amino acids from the tRNA in the first ribosomal site are linked with the amino acid in the second site.

9. This process continues (that is, steps 5 through 8 are repeated), with the polypeptide chain continuing to grow, until a stop codon is reached and the polypeptide chain is released.

● FIGURE C-7 Ribosomal assembly and protein translation.

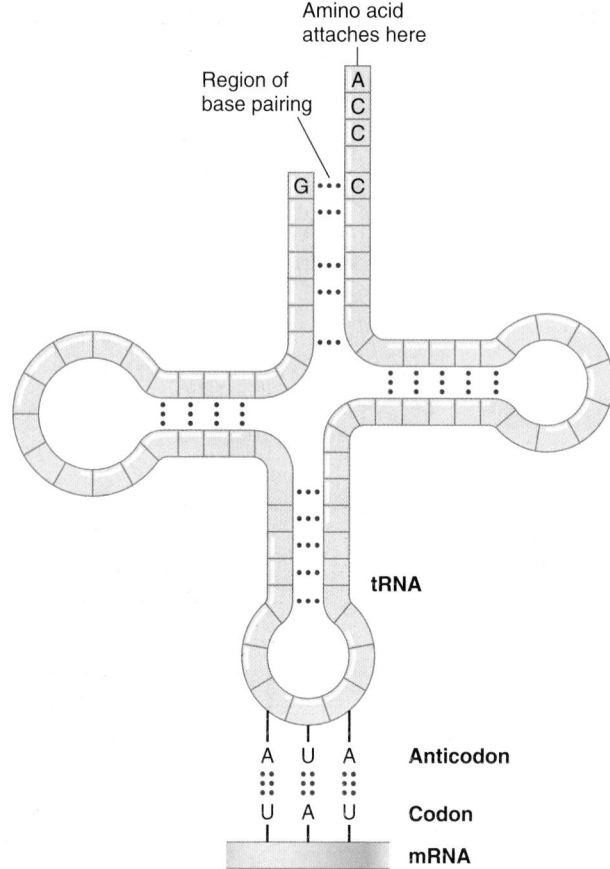

● FIGURE C-8 **Structure of a tRNA molecule.** The open end of a tRNA molecule attaches to free amino acids. The anticodon loop of the tRNA molecule attaches to a complementary mRNA codon.

Labels in figure: Amino acid attaches here; Region of base pairing; A C C; G ··· C; tRNA; A U A Anticodon; U A U Codon; mRNA

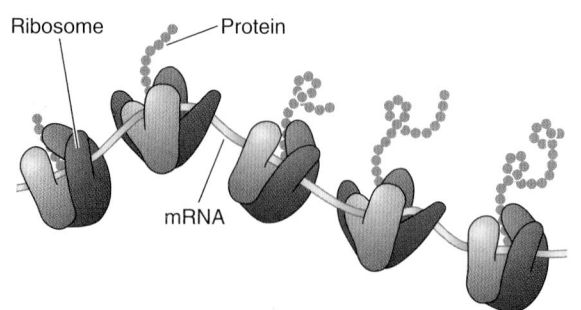

● FIGURE C-9 **A polyribosome.** A polyribosome is formed by numerous ribosomes simultaneously translating mRNA.

Labels in figure: Ribosome; Protein; mRNA

hemoglobin synthesis. Only about 7% of the DNA sequences in a typical cell are ever transcribed into mRNA for ultimate expression as specific proteins.

Control of gene expression involves gene regulatory proteins that activate ("switch on") or repress ("switch off") the genes that code for specific proteins within a given cell. Various DNA segments that do not code for structural and enzymatic proteins code for synthesis of these regulatory proteins. The molecular mechanisms by which these regulatory genes in turn are controlled in human cells are only beginning to be understood. In some instances, regulatory proteins are controlled by **gene-signaling factors** that bring about differential gene activity among various cells to accomplish specialized tasks. Hormones are the largest group of known gene-signaling factors in humans. Some hormones exert their homeostatic effect by selectively altering the transcription rate of the genes that code for enzymes, which are in turn responsible for catalyzing the reaction or reactions regulated by the hormone. For example, the hormone cortisol promotes the breakdown of fat stores by stimulating synthesis of the enzyme that catalyzes the conversion of stored fat into its component fatty acids. In other cases, gene action is time specific; that is, certain genes are expressed only at a certain developmental stage in the individual. This is especially important during embryonic development.

Cell Division

Most cells in the human body can reproduce themselves, a process important in growth, replacement, and repair of tissues. The rate at which cells divide is highly variable. Cells within the deeper layers of the intestinal lining divide every few days to replace cells that are continually sloughed off the surface of the lining into the digestive tract lumen. In this way, the entire intestinal lining is replaced about every three days (see p. 496). At the other extreme are nerve cells, which permanently lose the ability to divide beyond a certain period of fetal growth and development. Consequently, when nerve cells are lost through trauma or disease, they cannot be replaced (see p. 3). Between these two extremes are cells that divide infrequently except when needed to replace damaged or destroyed tissue. The factors that control the rate of cell division remain obscure.

Mitosis

Recall that cell division involves two components: nuclear division and cytoplasmic division *(cytokinesis)* (see p. 40). Nuclear division in somatic cells is accomplished by **mitosis,** in which a complete set of genetic information (that is, a diploid number of chromosomes) is distributed to each of two new daughter cells.

A cell capable of dividing alternates between periods of mitosis and those of nondivision. The interval of time between cell divisions is known as **interphase.** Because mitosis takes less than an hour to complete, the vast majority of cells in the body at any given time are in interphase.

Replication of DNA and growth of the cell take place during interphase in preparation for mitosis. Although mitosis is a continuous process, it displays four distinct phases: *prophase, metaphase, anaphase,* and *telophase* (● Figure C-10, top).

PROPHASE

1. Chromatin condenses and becomes microscopically visible as chromosomes. The condensed duplicate strands of DNA, known as *sister chromatids,* remain joined together within the chromosome at a point called the *centromere* (● Figure C-11).

2. Cells contain a pair of **centrioles,** short cylindrical structures that form the mitotic spindle during cell division (see ● Figure 2-1, p. 22). The centriole pair divides, and the daughter centrioles move to opposite ends of the cell, where

they assemble between them a mitotic spindle made up of microtubules (see p. 39).

3. The membrane surrounding the nucleus starts to break down.

METAPHASE

1. The nuclear membrane disappears.

2. The 46 chromosomes, each consisting of a pair of sister chromatids, align themselves at the midline, or equator, of the cell. Each chromosome becomes attached to the spindle by means of several spindle fibers that extend from the centriole to the centromere of the chromosome.

ANAPHASE

1. The centromeres split, converting each pair of sister chromatids into two identical chromosomes, which separate and move toward opposite poles of the spindle. Molecular motors pull the chromosomes along the spindle fibers toward the poles (see p. 38).

2. At the end of anaphase, an identical set of 46 chromosomes is present at each of the poles, for a transient total of 92 chromosomes in the soon-to-be-divided cell.

TELOPHASE

1. The cytoplasm divides through formation and gradual tightening of an actin contractile ring at the midline of the cell, thus forming two separate daughter cells, each with a full diploid set of chromosomes (see p. 40).

2. The spindle fibers disassemble.

3. The chromosomes uncoil to their decondensed chromatin form.

4. A nuclear membrane reforms in each new cell.

Cell division is complete with the end of telophase. Each of the new cells now enters interphase.

Meiosis

Nuclear division in the specialized case of germ cells is accomplished by **meiosis,** in which only half a set of genetic information (that is, a haploid number of chromosomes) is distributed to each daughter cell. Meiosis differs from mitosis in several important regards (see ● Figure C-10, bottom). Specialized diploid germ cells undergo one chromosome replication followed by two nuclear divisions to produce four haploid germ cells.

MEIOSIS I

1. During prophase of the first meiotic division (prophase I), the members of each homologous pair of chromosomes line up side by side to form a **tetrad,** which is a group of four sister chromatids with two identical chromatids within each member of the pair.

2. The process of crossing over occurs during this period, when the maternal copy and the paternal copy of each chromosome are paired. **Crossing over** involves a physical exchange of chromosome material between nonsister chromatids

within a tetrad (● Figure C-12). This process yields new chromosome combinations, thus contributing to genetic diversity.

3. During metaphase I, the 23 tetrads line up at the equator.

4. At anaphase I, homologous chromosomes, each consisting of a pair of sister chromatids joined at the centromere, separate and move toward opposite poles. Maternally and paternally derived chromosomes migrate to opposite poles in random assortments of one member of each chromosome pair without regard for its original derivation. This genetic mixing provides novel combinations of chromosomes.

5. During telophase I, the cell divides into two cells. Each cell contains 23 chromosomes consisting of two sister chromatids.

MEIOSIS II

1. Following a brief interphase in which no further replication occurs, the 23 unpaired chromosomes line up at the equator, the centromeres split, and the sister chromatids separate for the first time into independent chromosomes that move to opposite poles (prophase II–telophase II in ● Figure C-10).

2. During cytokinesis, each of the daughter cells derived from the first meiotic division forms two new daughter cells. The end result is four daughter cells, each containing a haploid set of chromosomes.

Union of a haploid sperm and haploid egg results in a zygote (fertilized egg) that contains the diploid number of chromosomes. Development of a new multicellular individual from the zygote is accomplished by mitosis and cell differentiation. Because DNA is normally faithfully replicated in its entirety during each mitotic division, all cells in the body possess an identical aggregate of DNA molecules. Structural and functional variations among cell types result from differential gene expression.

Mutations

An estimated 10^{16} cell divisions take place in the body during the course of a person's lifetime to accomplish growth, repair, and normal cell turnover. Because more than 3 billion nucleotides must be replicated during each cell division, it is no wonder that "copying errors" occasionally occur. Any change in the DNA sequence is known as a **point (gene) mutation.** A point mutation arises when a base is inadvertently substituted, added, or deleted during the replication process.

When a base is inserted in the wrong position during DNA replication, the mistake can often be corrected by a built-in "proofreading" system. Repair enzymes remove the newly replicated strand back to the defective segment, at which time normal base pairing resumes to resynthesize a corrected strand. Not all mistakes can be corrected, however.

Mutations can arise spontaneously by chance alone, or they can be induced by **mutagens,** which are factors that increase the rate at which mutations take place. Mutagens include various chemical agents, as well as ionizing radiation such as X-rays and atomic radiation. Mutagens promote mutations either by chemically altering the DNA base code through a variety of

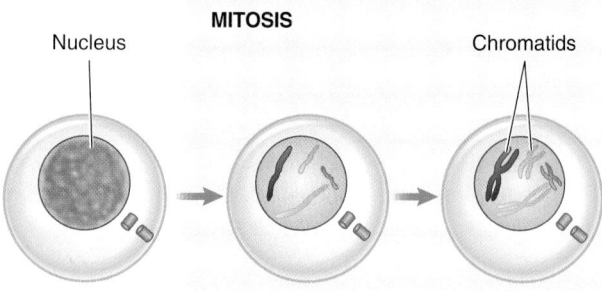

MITOSIS

Nucleus

Chromatids

Interphase

DNA replication

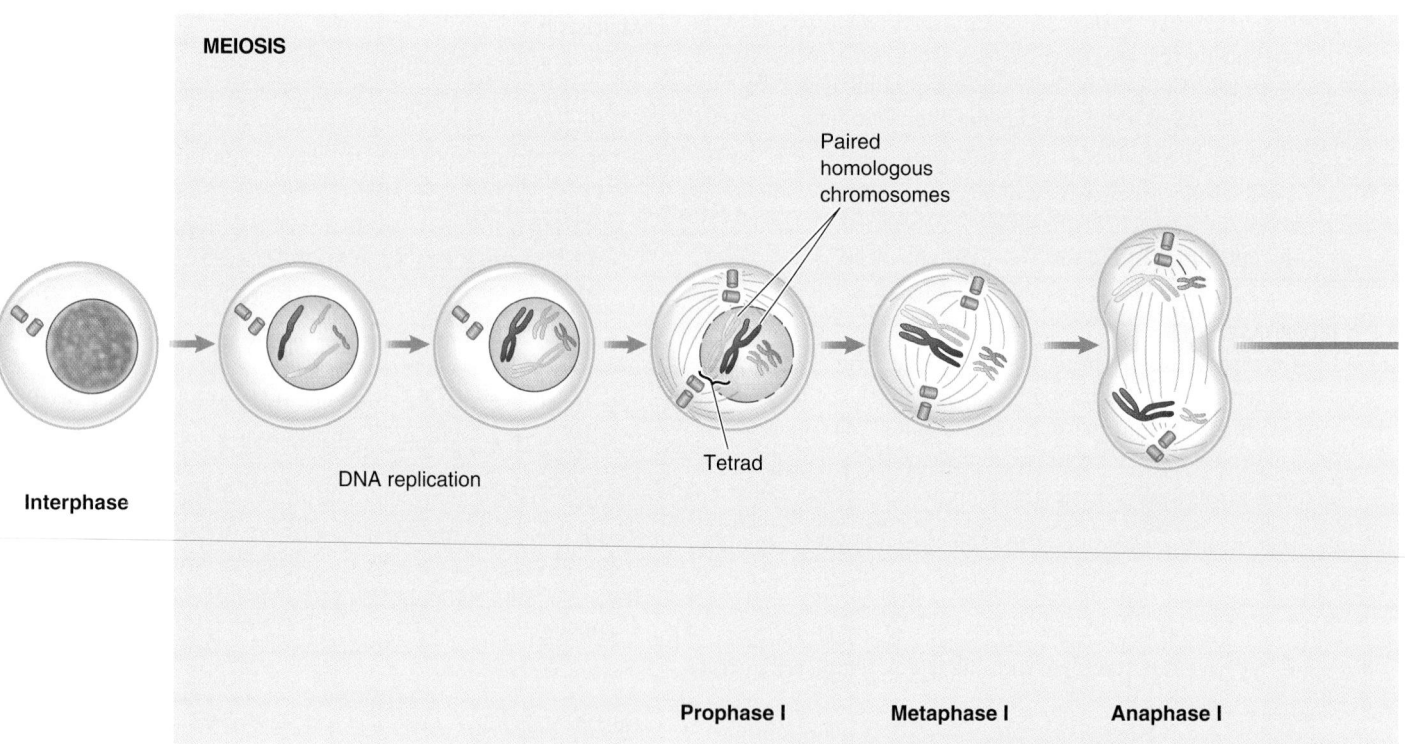

MEIOSIS

Paired homologous chromosomes

Interphase

DNA replication

Tetrad

Prophase I

Metaphase I

Anaphase I

● FIGURE C-10 **A comparison of events in mitosis and meiosis.**

mechanisms or by interfering with the repair enzymes so that abnormal base segments cannot be cut out.

Depending on the location and nature of a change in the genetic code, a given mutation may (1) have no noticeable effect if it does not alter a critical region of a cellular protein; (2) adversely alter cell function if it impairs the function of a crucial protein; (3) be incompatible with the life of the cell, in which case the cell dies and the mutation is lost with it; or (4) in rare cases, prove beneficial if a more efficient structural or enzymatic protein results. If a mutation occurs in a body cell (a **somatic mutation**), the outcome will be reflected as an alteration in all future copies of the cell in the affected individual, but it will not be perpetuated beyond

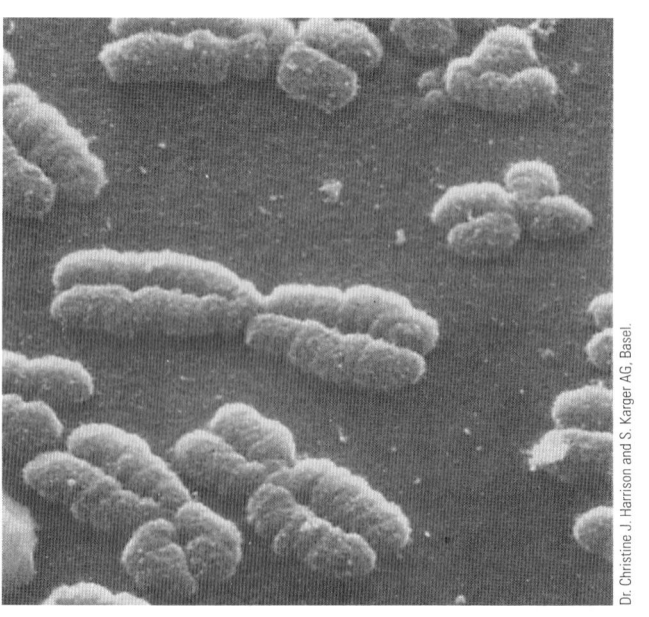

● FIGURE C-11 **A scanning electron micrograph of human chromosomes from a dividing cell.** The replicated chromosomes appear as double structures, with identical sister chromatids joined in the middle at a common centromere.

Dr. Christine J. Harrison and S. Karger AG, Basel.

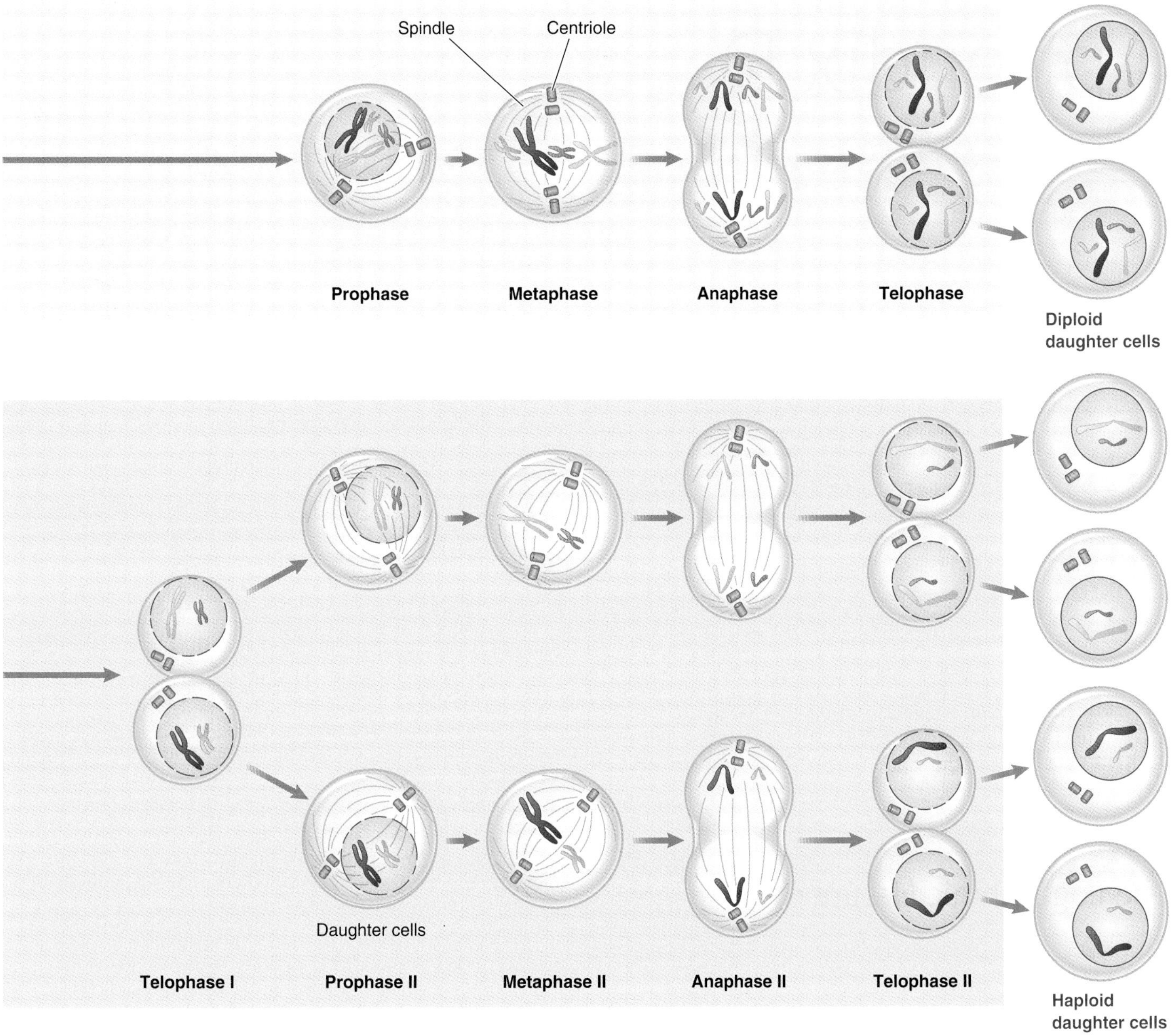

Spindle Centriole

Prophase **Metaphase** **Anaphase** **Telophase**

Diploid
daughter cells

Telophase I **Prophase II** **Metaphase II** **Anaphase II** **Telophase II**

Daughter cells

Haploid
daughter cells

the life of the individual. If, by contrast, a mutation occurs in a sperm- or egg-producing cell **(germ cell mutation),** the genetic alteration may be passed on to succeeding generations.

In most instances, **cancer** results from multiple somatic mutations that occur over time within DNA segments known as **proto-oncogenes.** Proto-oncogenes are normal genes whose coded products are important in the regulation of cell growth and division. These genes have the potential of becoming overzealous **oncogenes** ("cancer genes"), which induce the uncontrolled cell proliferation characteristic of cancer. Proto-oncogenes can become cancer producing as a result of several sequential mutations in the gene itself or changes in adjacent regions that regulate the proto-oncogenes. Less frequently, tumor viruses become incorporated in the DNA blueprint and act as oncogenes. Alternatively, cancer may arise from mutations that disable **tumor suppressor genes,** which normally restrain cell proliferation in check-and-balance fashion.

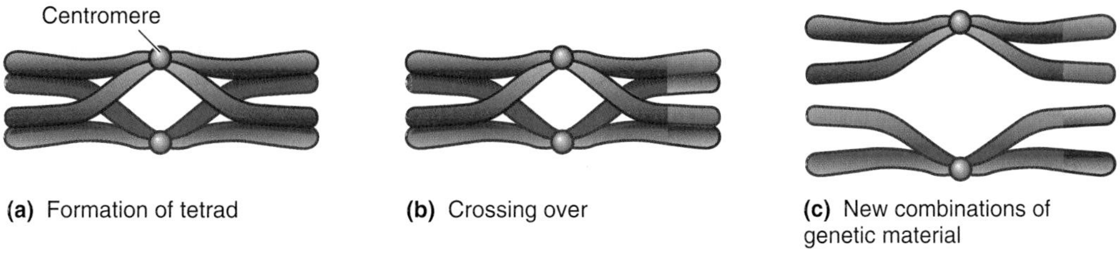

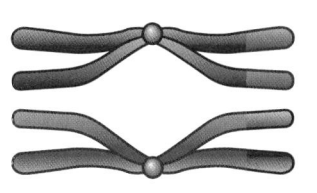

Centromere

(a) Formation of tetrad   **(b)** Crossing over   **(c)** New combinations of
genetic material

● **FIGURE C-12 Crossing over.** (a) During prophase I of meiosis, each homologous pair of chromosomes lines up side by side to form a tetrad. (b) Physical exchange of chromosome material occurs between nonsister chromatids. (c) As a result of this crossing over, new combinations of genetic material are formed within the chromosomes.

Appendix D
The Chemistry of Acid–Base Balance

Dissociation Constants for Acids

Acids are a special group of hydrogen-containing substances that dissociate, or separate, when in solution to liberate free H^+ and anions (negatively charged ions). The extent of dissociation for a given acid is always constant; that is, when in solution, the same proportion of a particular acid's molecules always separate to liberate free H^+, with the other portion always remaining intact. The constant degree of dissociation for a particular acid (in this example, H_2CO_3) is expressed by its dissociation constant (K) as follows:

$$[H^+] [HCO_3^-]/[H_2CO_3] = K$$

where

$[H^+] [HCO_3^-]$ represents the concentration of ions resulting from H_2CO_3 dissociation.

$[H_2CO_3]$ represents the concentration of intact (undissociated) H_2CO_3.

The dissociation constant varies for different acids.

The Logarithmic Nature of pH

Recall that **pH** equals the logarithm (log) to the base 10 of the reciprocal of the hydrogen ion concentration:

$$pH = \log 1/[H^+]$$

Every unit change in pH actually represents a 10-fold change in $[H^+]$ because of the logarithmic relationship. A log to the base 10 indicates how many times 10 must be multiplied to produce a given number. For example, the log of $10 = 1$, whereas the log of $100 = 2$, because 1 ten equals 10 and 2 tens multiplied together equals 100 ($10 \times 10 = 100$). Numbers less than 10 have logs less than 1. Numbers between 10 and 100 have logs between 1 and 2, and so on. Accordingly, each unit of change in pH indicates a 10-fold change in $[H^+]$. For example, a solution with a pH of 7 has a $[H^+]$ 10 times less than that of a solution with a pH of 6 (a 1-pH-unit difference) and 100 times less than that of a solution with a pH of 5 (a 2-pH-unit difference).

Chemical Buffer Systems

Recall that a chemical buffer system consists of a pair of substances involved in a reversible reaction—one substance that can yield free H^+ as the $[H^+]$ starts to fall and another that can bind with free H^+ (thus removing it from solution) when $[H^+]$ starts to rise. An important example of a buffer system is the **carbonic acid–bicarbonate (H_2CO_3:HCO_3^-) buffer system,** which is the primary ECF buffer for noncarbonic acids and is involved in the following reversible reaction:

$$H_2CO_3 \rightleftharpoons H^+ + HCO_3^-$$

Because CO_2 generates H_2CO_3, the H_2CO_3:HCO_3^- buffer system in the body involves CO_2 by means of the following reaction, with which you are already familiar:

$$CO_2 + H_2O \rightleftharpoons H_2CO_3 \rightleftharpoons H^+ + HCO_3^-$$

Chemical buffer systems function according to the law of mass action, which states that if the concentration of one of the substances involved in a reversible reaction is increased, the reaction is driven toward the opposite side; if the concentration of one of the substances is decreased, the reaction is driven toward that side.

Let us apply the law of mass action to the reversible reaction involving the H_2CO_3:HCO_3^- buffer system. When new H^+ is added to the plasma from any source other than CO_2 (for example, through lactic acid released into the ECF from exercising muscles), the preceding reaction is driven toward the left side of the equation. As the extra H^+ binds with HCO_3^-, it no longer contributes to the acidity of body fluids, so the rise in $[H^+]$ declines. In the converse situation, when the plasma $[H^+]$ occasionally falls below normal for some reason other than a change in CO_2 (such as the loss of plasma-derived HCl in the gastric juices during vomiting), the reaction is driven toward the right side of the equation. Dissolved CO_2 and H_2O in the plasma form H_2CO_3, which generates additional H^+ to make up for the H^+ deficit. In so doing, the H_2CO_3:HCO_3^- buffer system resists the fall in $[H^+]$.

This system cannot buffer changes in pH induced by fluctuations in H_2CO_3. A buffer system cannot buffer itself. Consider, for example, the situation in which the plasma $[H^+]$ is elevated by CO_2 retention from a respiratory problem. The rise in CO_2 drives the reaction to the right according to the law of mass action, elevating $[H^+]$. The increase in $[H^+]$ occurs as a result of the reaction being driven to the *right* by an increase in CO_2, so the elevated $[H^+]$ cannot drive the reaction to the *left* to buffer the increase in $[H^+]$. Only if the increase in $[H^+]$ is brought about by some mechanism other than CO_2 accumulation can this buffer system be shifted to the CO_2 side of the equation and effectively reduce $[H^+]$. Likewise, in the opposite situation, the H_2CO_3:HCO_3^- buffer system cannot compensate for a reduction in $[H^+]$ from a deficit of CO_2 by generating more H^+-yielding H_2CO_3 when the problem in the first place is a shortage of H_2CO_3-forming CO_2.

The **hemoglobin buffer system** resists fluctuations in pH caused by changes in CO_2 levels. At the systemic capillary level, CO_2 continuously diffuses into the blood from the tissue cells where it is produced. The greatest percentage of this CO_2 in the plasma forms H_2CO_3, which partially dissociates into H^+ and HCO_3^-. This process is hastened within the red blood cells by the erythrocytic enzyme *carbonic anhydrase,* which catalyzes the conversion of CO_2 and H_2O directly to H^+ and HCO_3^- (see p. 392). Simultaneously, some oxyhemoglobin (HbO_2) releases O_2, which diffuses into the tissues. Reduced (unoxygenated) Hb has a greater affinity for H^+ than HbO_2 does. Therefore, most H^+ generated from CO_2 at the tissue level becomes bound to reduced Hb and no longer contributes to the acidity of body fluids:

$$H^+ + Hb \rightleftharpoons HHb$$

At the lungs, the reactions are reversed. As Hb picks up O_2 diffusing from the alveoli (air sacs) into the red blood cells, the affinity of Hb for H^+ is decreased, so H^+ is released. This liberated H^+ combines with HCO_3^- to generate CO_2 and H_2O (with or without carbonic anhydrase). CO_2 is exhaled, and the hydrogen ion has been reincorporated into a neutral H_2O molecule.

The intracellular proteins and plasma proteins constitute the protein buffer system. Their acidic and basic side groups enable them to give up and take up H^+, respectively.

The **phosphate buffer system** consists of an acidic phosphate salt (NaH_2PO_4) that can donate a free H^+ when the $[H^+]$ falls and a basic phosphate salt (Na_2HPO_4) that can accept a free H^+ when the $[H^+]$ rises. Basically, this buffer pair can alternately switch a H^+ for a Na^+ as demanded by the $[H^+]$.

$$Na_2HPO_4 + H^+ \rightleftharpoons NaH_2PO_4 + Na^+$$

Henderson–Hasselbalch Equation

The relationship between the $[H^+]$ and the members of a buffer pair can be expressed according to the **Henderson–Hasselbalch equation,** which, for the H_2CO_3:HCO_3^- buffer system is as follows:

$$pH = pK + \log [HCO_3^-]/[H_2CO_3]$$

Although you do not need to know the mathematical manipulations involved, it is helpful to understand how this formula is derived. Recall that the dissociation constant K for H_2CO_3 is

$$[H^+] [HCO_3^-]/[H_2CO_3] = K$$

and that the relationship between pH and $[H^+]$ is

$$pH = \log 1/[H^+]$$

Then, by solving the dissociation constant formula for $[H^+]$ (that is, $[H^+] = K \times [H_2CO_3]/[HCO_3^-]$) and replacing this value for $[H^+]$ in the pH formula, you come up with the Henderson–Hasselbalch equation.

Practically, $[H_2CO_3]$ directly reflects the concentration of dissolved CO_2, henceforth referred to as $[CO_2]$, because most of the CO_2 in the plasma is converted into H_2CO_3. (The dissolved CO_2 concentration is equivalent to P_{CO_2}, as described in Chapter 12.)

$$pH = pK + \log [HCO_3^-]/[CO_2]$$

The pK is the log of l/K and, like K, remains a constant for any given acid. For H_2CO_3, the pK is 6.1. Because the pK is always a constant, changes in pH are associated with changes in the ratio between $[HCO_3^-]$ and $[CO_2]$.

Normally, the ratio between $[HCO_3^-]$ and $[CO_2]$ in the ECF is 20 to 1; that is, there is 20 times more HCO_3^- than CO_2. Plugging this ratio into the formula,

$$pH = pK + \log [HCO_3^-]/[CO_2]$$
$$= 6.1 + \log 20/1$$

The log of 20 is 1.3. Therefore, pH = 6.1 + 1.3 = 7.4, which is the normal pH of plasma.

■ When the ratio of $[HCO_3^-]$ to $[CO_2]$ increases above 20/1, the pH increases. Accordingly, either a rise in $[HCO_3^-]$ or a fall in $[CO_2]$, both of which increase the $[HCO_3^-]/[CO_2]$ ratio if the other component remains constant, shifts the acid–base balance toward the alkaline side.

■ In contrast, when the $[HCO_3^-]/[CO_2]$ ratio decreases below 20/1, the pH decreases toward the acid side. This can occur either if the $[HCO_3^-]$ decreases or if the $[CO_2]$ increases while the other component remains constant.

Because $[HCO_3^-]$ is regulated by the kidneys and $[CO_2]$ by the lungs, plasma pH can be shifted up and down by kidney and lung influences. The kidneys and lungs regulate pH (and thus free $[H^+]$) largely by controlling plasma $[HCO_3^-]$ and $[CO_2]$, respectively, to restore their ratio to normal. Accordingly,

$$pH = \frac{[HCO_3^-] \text{ controlled by kidney function}}{[CO_2] \text{ controlled by respiratory function}}$$

Because of this relationship, not only do both the kidneys and the lungs normally participate in pH control, but renal or respiratory dysfunction can also induce acid–base imbalances by altering the $[HCO_3^-]/[CO_2]$ ratio.

Respiratory Regulation of Hydrogen Ion Concentration

The major source of H^+ in the body fluids is from metabolically produced CO_2. Cellular oxidation of nutrients yields energy, with CO_2 and H_2O as end products. Without catalyst influence, CO_2 and H_2O slowly form H_2CO_3, which then rapidly dissociates to liberate free H^+ and HCO_3^-.

$$CO_2 + H_2O \overset{\text{slow}}{\rightleftharpoons} H_2CO_3 \overset{\text{fast}}{\rightleftharpoons} H^+ + HCO_3^-$$

The enzyme carbonic anhydrase (ca) is abundant in red blood cells and kidney tubular cells, among a few other specialized cell types. Under the influence of carbonic anhydrase, these cells directly convert CO_2 and H_2O into H^+ and HCO_3^- with no intervening production of H_2CO_3.

$$CO_2 + H_2O \overset{ca}{\rightleftharpoons} H^+ + HCO_3^-$$

Within the systemic capillaries, the CO_2 level in the blood increases as metabolically produced CO_2 enters from the tissues. This drives the reaction to the acid side (with or without carbonic anhydrase), generating H^+, as well as HCO_3^-, in the process. In the lungs, the reaction is reversed: CO_2 diffuses from the blood flowing through the pulmonary capillaries into the alveoli, from which it is expired to the atmosphere. The resultant reduction in blood CO_2 drives the reaction toward the CO_2 side. Hydrogen ion and HCO_3^- generate CO_2 and H_2O again. The CO_2 is exhaled while the hydrogen ions generated at the tissue level are incorporated into H_2O molecules.

The lungs are extremely important in maintaining the $[H^+]$ of plasma. Every day, they remove from body fluids what amounts to 100 times more H^+ derived from CO_2 than the kidneys remove from sources other than CO_2–H^+. When the respiratory system can keep pace with the rate of metabolism, there is no net gain or loss of H^+ in the body fluids from metabolically produced CO_2. When the rate of CO_2 removal by the lungs does not match the rate of CO_2 production at the tissue level, however, the resulting accumulation or deficit of CO_2 leads to an excess or shortage, respectively, of free H^+ from this source. Therefore, respiratory abnormalities can lead to acid–base imbalances.

On the other hand, the respiratory system, through its ability to regulate arterial $[CO_2]$, can adjust the amount of H^+ added to body fluids from this source as needed to restore pH toward normal when fluctuations occur in $[H^+]$ from sources other than CO_2-H^+.

However, the respiratory system alone can return the pH to only 50% to 75% of the way toward normal. Two reasons contribute to the respiratory system's inability to fully compensate for a non-respiratory-induced acid–base imbalance. First, during respiratory compensation for a deviation in pH, the peripheral chemoreceptors, which increase ventilation in response to an elevated arterial $[H^+]$ (see p. 399), and the central chemoreceptors, which increase ventilation in response to a rise in $[CO_2]$ (by monitoring CO_2-generated H^+ in brain ECF; see p. 398), work at odds. Consider what happens in response to an acidosis arising from a nonrespiratory cause. When the peripheral chemoreceptors detect an increase in arterial $[H^+]$, they reflexly *stimulate* the respiratory center to step up ventilation, causing more acid-forming CO_2 to be blown off. In response to the resultant fall in CO_2, however, the central chemoreceptors start to *inhibit* the respiratory center. By opposing the action of the peripheral chemoreceptors, the central chemoreceptors stop the compensatory increase in ventilation short of restoring pH all the way to normal.

Second, the driving force for the compensatory increase in ventilation is diminished as the pH moves toward normal. Ventilation is increased by the peripheral chemoreceptors in response to a rise in arterial $[H^+]$, but as the $[H^+]$ is gradually reduced by stepped-up removal of H^+-forming CO_2, the enhanced ventilatory response is also gradually reduced.

Renal Regulation of Hydrogen Ion Concentration

Renal control of $[H^+]$ is the most potent acid–base regulatory mechanism; the kidneys not only can vary H^+ removal but can also variably conserve or eliminate HCO_3^-, depending on the acid–base status of the body. For example, during renal compensation for acidosis, not only is extra H^+ excreted in urine, but extra HCO_3^- also is added to the plasma to buffer (by means of the H_2CO_3:HCO_3^- system) more H^+ that remains in body fluids. By simultaneously removing acid (H^+) from and adding base (HCO_3^-) to body fluids, the kidneys can restore the pH toward normal more effectively than the lungs, which can adjust only the amount of H^+-forming CO_2 in the body.

Also contributing to the kidneys' acid–base regulatory potency is their ability to return pH almost exactly to normal. In contrast to the respiratory system's inability to fully compensate for a pH abnormality, the kidneys can continue to respond to a change in pH until compensation is essentially complete.

The kidneys control pH of body fluids by adjusting three interrelated factors: (1) H^+ excretion, (2) HCO_3^- excretion, and (3) ammonia (NH_3) secretion. We examine each of these mechanisms in further detail.

RENAL H^+ EXCRETION Almost all excreted H^+ enters the urine via secretion. Recall that the filtration rate of H^+ equals plasma $[H^+]$ times GFR. Because plasma $[H^+]$ is extremely low (less than in pure H_2O except during extreme acidosis, when pH falls below 7.0), the filtration rate of H^+ is likewise extremely low. This minute amount of filtered H^+ is excreted in urine. However, most excreted H^+ gains entry into tubular fluid by being actively secreted.

The H^+ secretory process begins in the tubular cells with CO_2 from three sources: CO_2 diffused into the tubular cells from (1) the plasma or (2) the tubular fluid, or (3) the CO_2 metabolically produced within the tubular cells, with CO_2 and H_2O ultimately yielding H^+ and HCO_3^-. To secrete H^+, an energy-dependent carrier in the luminal membrane then transports H^+ out of the cell into the tubular lumen.

The magnitude of H^+ secretion depends primarily on a direct effect of the plasma's acid–base status on the kidneys' tubular cells. No neural or hormonal control is involved.

■ When the $[H^+]$ of plasma passing through the peritubular capillaries is elevated above normal, the tubular cells respond by secreting greater-than-usual amounts of H^+ from the plasma into the tubular fluid to be excreted in urine.

■ Conversely, when plasma $[H^+]$ is lower than normal, the kidneys conserve H^+ by reducing its secretion and subsequent excretion in urine.

Because chemical reactions for H^+ secretion begin with CO_2, the rate at which they proceed is also influenced by $[CO_2]$:

■ When plasma $[CO_2]$ increases, the rate of H^+ secretion speeds up.

■ Conversely, the rate of H^+ secretion slows when plasma $[CO_2]$ falls below normal.

These responses are especially important in renal compensations for acid–base abnormalities involving a change in H_2CO_3 caused by respiratory dysfunction. The kidneys can therefore adjust H^+ excretion to compensate for changes in both carbonic and noncarbonic acids.

RENAL HANDLING OF HCO_3^- The kidneys regulate plasma $[HCO_3^-]$ by two interrelated mechanisms: (1) variable reabsorption of filtered HCO_3^- back into the plasma and (2) variable addition of new HCO_3^- to the plasma. both mechanisms are inextricably linked with H^+ secretion by the kidney tubules. Every time a H^+ is secreted into the tubular fluid, a HCO_3^- is simultaneously transferred into the peritubular capillary plasma. Whether a filtered HCO_3^- is reabsorbed or a new HCO_3^- is added to the plasma in accompaniment with H^+ secretion depends on whether filtered HCO_3^- is present in the tubular fluid to react with the secreted H^+ as follows:

■ *H^+ secretion coupled with HCO_3^- absorption.* Bicarbonate is freely filtered, but because the luminal membranes of tubular cells are impermeable to filtered HCO_3^-, it cannot diffuse into these cells. Therefore, reabsorption of HCO_3^- must occur indirectly (● Figure D-1). Under the influence of carbonic anhydrase, which is present on the surface of the luminal membrane, H^+ secreted into the tubular fluid reacts with filtered HCO_3^- to form CO_2 and H_2O within the filtrate. Unlike HCO_3^-, CO_2 can easily penetrate tubular cell membranes. Within the cells, CO_2 and H_2O, under the influence of intracellular carbonic anhydrase, form H^+ and HCO_3^-. Because HCO_3^- can permeate the tubular cells' basolateral membrane by secondary active trans-

port (see p. 64), it leaves the cells and enters the peritubular capillary plasma. Meanwhile, the generated H^+ is actively secreted. Because the disappearance of a HCO_3^- from the tubular fluid is coupled with the appearance of another HCO_3^- in the plasma, a HCO_3^- has, in effect, been "reabsorbed." Even though the HCO_3^- entering the plasma is not the same HCO_3^- that was filtered, the net result is the same as if HCO_3^- were directly reabsorbed.

Normally, slightly more hydrogen ions are secreted into the tubular fluid than bicarbonate ions are filtered. Accordingly, all the filtered HCO_3^- is usually absorbed, because secreted H^+ is available in the tubular fluid to combine with it to form highly reabsorbable CO_2. The vast majority of the secreted H^+ combines with HCO_3^- and is not excreted, because it is "used up" in HCO_3^- reabsorption. However, the slight excess of secreted H^+ that is not matched by filtered HCO_3^- is excreted in the urine. This normal H^+ excretion rate keeps pace with the normal rate of noncarbonic-acid H^+ production.

■ *H^+ secretion and excretion coupled with addition of new HCO_3^- to the plasma.* Secretion of H^+ that is excreted is coupled with the addition of new HCO_3^- to the plasma, in contrast to the secreted H^+ that is coupled with HCO_3^- reabsorption and is not excreted, instead being incorporated into reabsorbable H_2O molecules. When all the filtered HCO_3^- has been reabsorbed and additional secreted H^+ is generated from CO_2 and H_2O, the HCO_3^- produced by this reaction enters the plasma by secondary active transport as a "new" HCO_3^-. It is "new" because its appearance in plasma is not associated with reabsorption of filtered HCO_3^- (● Figure D-2). Meanwhile, the secreted H^+

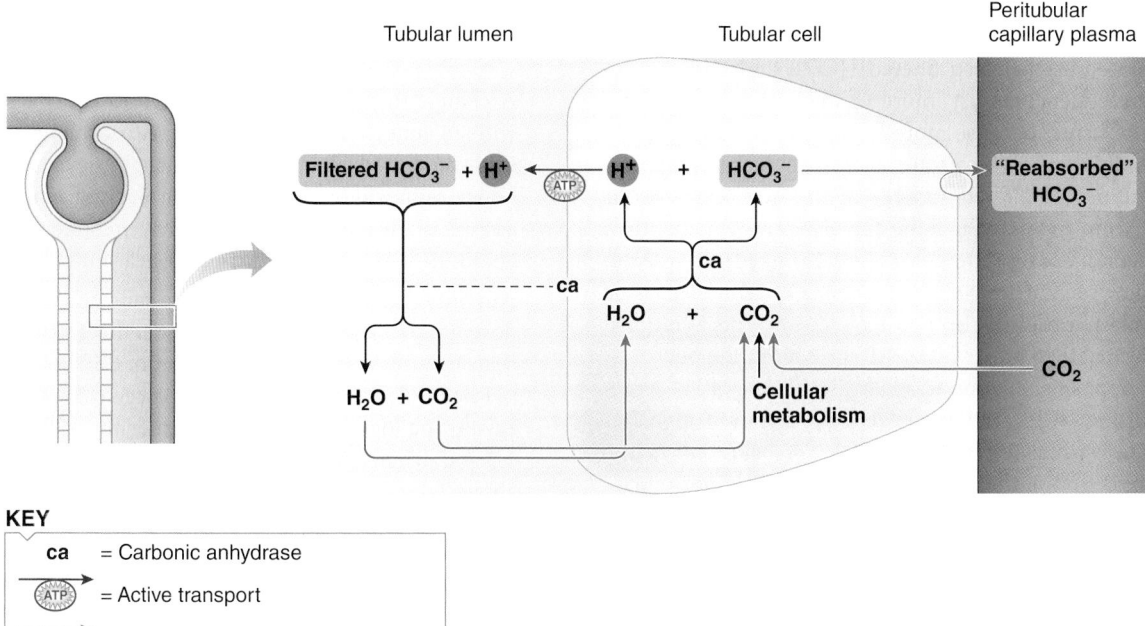

KEY

ca = Carbonic anhydrase

(ATP) = Active transport

= Secondary active transport

——→ = Passive diffusion

——→ = Chemical reaction

------ = Catalyzed by membrane-bound ca

● FIGURE D-1 **Hydrogen ion secretion coupled with bicarbonate reabsorption.** Because the disappearance of a filtered HCO_3^- from the tubular fluid is coupled with the appearance of another HCO_3^- in the plasma, HCO_3^- is considered to have been "reabsorbed."

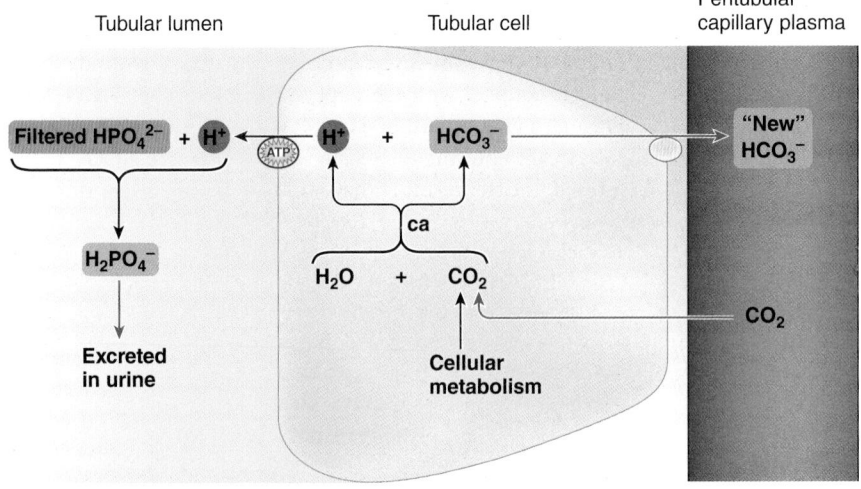

Tubular lumen   Tubular cell   Peritubular capillary plasma

● **FIGURE D-2 Hydrogen ion secretion and excretion coupled with the addition of new HCO_3^- to the plasma.** Secreted H^+ does not combine with filtered HPO_4^{2-} and is not subsequently excreted until all the filtered HCO_3^- has been "reabsorbed," as depicted in Figure D-1. Once all the filtered HCO_3^- has combined with secreted H^+, further secreted H^+ is excreted in the urine, primarily in association with urinary buffers such as basic phosphate. Excretion of H^+ is coupled with the appearance of new HCO_3^- in the plasma. The "new" HCO_3^- represents a net gain rather than merely a replacement for filtered HCO_3^-.

combines with urinary buffers, especially basic phosphate (HPO_4^{2-}), and is excreted.

RENAL HANDLING OF H^+ AND HCO_3^- DURING ACIDOSIS AND ALKALOSIS When plasma $[H^+]$ is elevated during acidosis, more H^+ is secreted than normal. At the same time, less HCO_3^- is filtered than normal because more of the plasma HCO_3^- is used up in buffering the excess H^+ in the ECF. This greater-than-usual inequity between filtered HCO_3^- and secreted H^+ has two consequences. First, more of the secreted H^+ is excreted in the urine, because more hydrogen ions are entering the tubular fluid when fewer are needed to reabsorb the reduced quantities of filtered HCO_3^-. In this way, extra H^+ is eliminated from the body, making the urine more acidic than normal. Second, because excretion of H^+ is linked with the addition of new HCO_3^- to the plasma, more HCO_3^- than usual enters the plasma passing through the kidneys. This additional HCO_3^- is available to buffer excess H^+ present in the body.

In the opposite situation of alkalosis, the rate of H^+ secretion diminishes, while the rate of HCO_3^- filtration increases compared to normal. When plasma $[H^+]$ is below normal, a smaller proportion of the HCO_3^- pool is tied up buffering H^+, so plasma $[HCO_3^-]$ is elevated above normal. As a result, the rate of HCO_3^- filtration correspondingly increases. Not all the filtered HCO_3^- is reabsorbed, because bicarbonate ions are in excess of secreted hydrogen ions in the tubular fluid and HCO_3^- cannot be reabsorbed without first reacting with H^+. Excess HCO_3^- is left in the tubular fluid to be excreted in the urine, thus reducing plasma $[HCO_3^-]$ while making the urine alkaline.

SECRETED NH_3 AS A URINARY BUFFER In contrast to the phosphate buffers, which are in the tubular fluid because they have been filtered but not reabsorbed, NH_3 is deliberately synthe-

sized from the amino acid *glutamine* within the tubular cells. Once synthesized, NH_3 readily diffuses passively down its concentration gradient into the tubular fluid; that is, it is secreted. The rate of NH_3 secretion is controlled by a direct effect on the tubular cells of the amount of excess H^+ to be transported in the urine. When someone has been acidotic for more than two or three days, the rate of NH_3 production increases substantially. This extra NH_3 provides additional buffering capacity to allow H^+ secretion to continue after the normal phosphate-buffering capacity is overwhelmed during renal compensation for acidosis.

Acid–Base Imbalances

Because of the relationship between the $[H^+]$ and the concentrations of the members of a buffer pair, changes in $[H^+]$ are reflected by changes in the ratio of $[HCO_3^-]$ to $[CO_2]$. Recall that the normal ratio is 20/1. Using the Henderson–Hasselbalch equation and with pK being 6.1 and the log of 20 being 1.3, normal pH = 6.1 + 1.3 = 7.4. Determinations of $[HCO_3^-]$ and $[CO_2]$ provide more meaningful information about the underlying factors responsible for a particular acid–base status than do direct measurements of $[H^+]$ alone. The following rules of thumb apply when examining acid–base imbalances *before any compensations take place*:

1. A change in pH that has a respiratory cause is associated with an abnormal $[CO_2]$, giving rise to a change in carbonic acid–generated H^+. In contrast, a pH deviation of metabolic origin will be associated with an abnormal $[HCO_3^-]$ as a result of the participation of HCO_3^- in buffering abnormal amounts of H^+ generated from noncarbonic acids.

2. Anytime the $[HCO_3^-]/[CO_2]$ ratio falls below 20/1, an acidosis exists. The log of any number lower than 20 is less than 1.3 and, when added to the pK of 6.1, yields an acidotic pH below 7.4. Anytime the ratio exceeds 20/1, an alkalosis exists. The log of any number greater than 20 is more than 1.3 and, when added to the pK of 6.1, yields an alkalotic pH above 7.4.

Putting these two points together, we can note the following:

■ *Respiratory acidosis* has a ratio of less than 20/1 arising from an increase in $[CO_2]$.

■ *Respiratory alkalosis* has a ratio greater than 20/1 because of a decrease in $[CO_2]$.

■ *Metabolic acidosis* has a ratio of less than 20/1 associated with a fall in $[HCO_3^-]$.

■ *Metabolic alkalosis* has a ratio greater than 20/1 arising from an elevation in $[HCO_3^-]$.

We examine each of these categories separately in more detail, paying particular attention to possible causes and the compensations that occur. The "balance beam" concept, presented in ● Figure D-3, in conjunction with the Henderson–Hasselbalch equation, will help you better visualize the contributions of the lungs and kidneys to the causes of and compensations for various acid–base disorders. The normal situation is represented in ● Figure D-3a.

RESPIRATORY ACIDOSIS In uncompensated respiratory acidosis (● Figure D-3b, left), $[CO_2]$ is elevated because of hypoventilation (in our example, it is doubled) whereas $[HCO_3^-]$ is normal, so the ratio is 20/2 (10/1) and pH is reduced. Let us clarify a potentially confusing point. You might wonder why when $[CO_2]$ is elevated and drives the reaction $CO_2 + H_2O \rightleftharpoons H^+ + HCO_3^-$ to the right, we say that $[H^+]$ becomes elevated but $[HCO_3^-]$ remains normal, although the same quantities of H^+ and HCO_3^- are produced by this reaction. The answer depends on the $[HCO_3^-]$ normally being 600,000 times the $[H^+]$. For every one hydrogen ion and 600,000 bicarbonate ions present in the ECF, the generation of one additional H^+ and one HCO_3^- doubles the $[H^+]$ (a 100% increase) but only increases the $[HCO_3^-]$ 0.00017% (from 600,000 to 600,001 ions). Therefore, an elevation in $[CO_2]$ brings about a pronounced increase in $[H^+]$, but $[HCO_3^-]$ remains essentially normal.

Compensatory measures act to restore pH to normal:

■ The chemical buffer systems immediately take up additional H^+.

■ The respiratory mechanism usually cannot respond with compensatory increased ventilation, because impaired respiration is the problem initially.

■ Thus, the kidneys are most important in compensating for respiratory acidosis. They conserve all the filtered HCO_3^- and add new HCO_3^- to the plasma while simultaneously secreting and, accordingly, excreting more H^+.

As a result, HCO_3^- stores in the body become elevated. In our example (● Figure D-3b, right), the plasma $[HCO_3^-]$ is doubled, so the $[HCO_3^-]/[CO_2]$ ratio is 40/2 rather than 20/2, as it was in the uncompensated state. A ratio of 40/2 is equivalent to a normal 20/1 ratio, so pH is again the normal 7.4. Enhanced renal conservation of HCO_3^- has fully compensated for CO_2 accumulation, thus restoring pH to normal, although both $[CO_2]$ and $[HCO_3^-]$ are now distorted. Note that maintaining normal pH depends on preserving a normal ratio between $[HCO_3^-]$ and $[CO_2]$, no matter what the absolute values of each of these buffer components are. (Compensation is never fully complete because pH can be restored close to but not precisely to normal. In our examples, however, we assume full compensation, for ease in mathematical calculations. Also bear in mind that the values used are only representative. Deviations in pH actually occur over a range, and the degree to which compensation can be accomplished varies.)

RESPIRATORY ALKALOSIS Looking at the biochemical abnormalities in uncompensated respiratory alkalosis (● Figure D-3c, left), the increase in pH reflects a reduction in $[CO_2]$ (half the normal value in our example) as a result of hyperventilation, whereas the $[HCO_3^-]$ remains normal. This yields an alkalotic ratio of 20/0.5, which is comparable to 40/1.

Compensatory measures act to shift pH back toward normal:

■ The chemical buffer systems liberate H^+ to diminish the severity of the alkalosis.

■ As plasma $[CO_2]$ and $[H^+]$ fall below normal because of excessive ventilation, two of the normally potent stimuli for driving ventilation are removed. This effect tends to "put the brakes" on the extent to which some nonrespiratory factor such as fever or anxiety can overdrive ventilation. Therefore, hyperventilation does not continue completely unabated.

■ If the situation continues for a few days, the kidneys compensate by conserving H^+ and excreting more HCO_3^-.

If, as in our example (● Figure D-3c, right), the HCO_3^- stores are reduced by half because of loss of HCO_3^- in the urine, the $[HCO_3^-]/[CO_2]$ ratio becomes 10/0.5, equivalent to the normal 20/1. Therefore, the pH is restored to normal by reducing the HCO_3^- load to compensate for the CO_2 loss.

METABOLIC ACIDOSIS Uncompensated metabolic acidosis (● Figure D-3d, left), is always characterized by a reduction in plasma $[HCO_3^-]$ (in our example, it is halved), whereas $[CO_2]$ remains normal, producing an acidotic ratio of 10/1. The problem may arise from excessive loss of HCO_3^--rich fluids from the body (as in diarrhea) or from an accumulation of noncarbonic acids (as in diabetes mellitus or uremic acidosis). In the case of accumulation of noncarbonic acids, plasma HCO_3^- is used up in buffering the additional H^+.

Except in uremic acidosis, metabolic acidosis is compensated for by both respiratory and renal mechanisms, as well as by chemical buffers:

■ The chemical buffer systems take up extra H^+.

■ The lungs blow off additional H^+-generating CO_2.

■ The kidneys excrete more H^+ and conserve more HCO_3^-.

In our example (● Figure D-3d, right), these compensatory measures restore the ratio to normal by reducing $[CO_2]$ to 75% of normal and by raising $[HCO_3^-]$ halfway back toward normal (up from 50% to 75% of the normal value). This brings the ratio to 15/0.75 (equivalent to 20/1).

Note that in compensating for metabolic acidosis, the lungs deliberately displace $[CO_2]$ from normal in an attempt to restore $[H^+]$ toward normal. Whereas in respiratory-induced acid–base disorders an abnormal $[CO_2]$ is the *cause* of the $[H^+]$ imbalance, in metabolic acid–base disorders $[CO_2]$ is intentionally shifted from normal as an important *compensation* for the $[H^+]$ imbalance.

When kidney disease causes metabolic acidosis, complete compensation is not possible because the renal mechanism is not available for pH regulation. Recall that the respiratory system can compensate only up to 75% of the way toward normal. Uremic acidosis is very serious, because the kidneys cannot help restore pH all the way to normal.

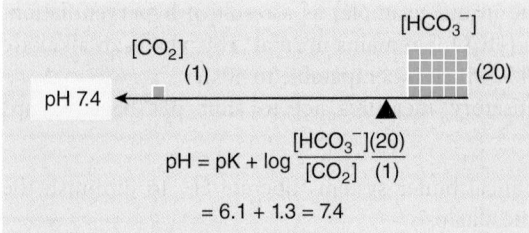

(a) Normal acid–base balance

Uncompensated acid–base disorders   Compensated acid–base disorders

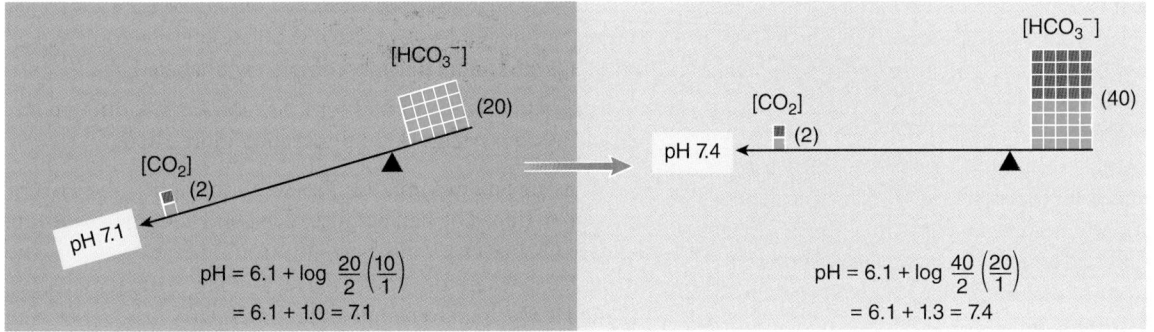

(b) Respiratory acidosis

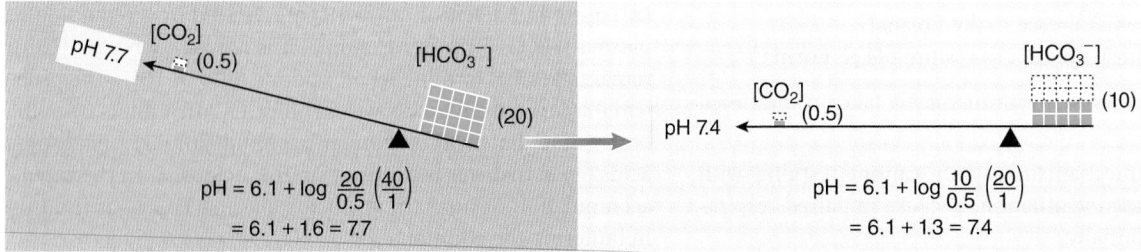

(c) Respiratory alkalosis

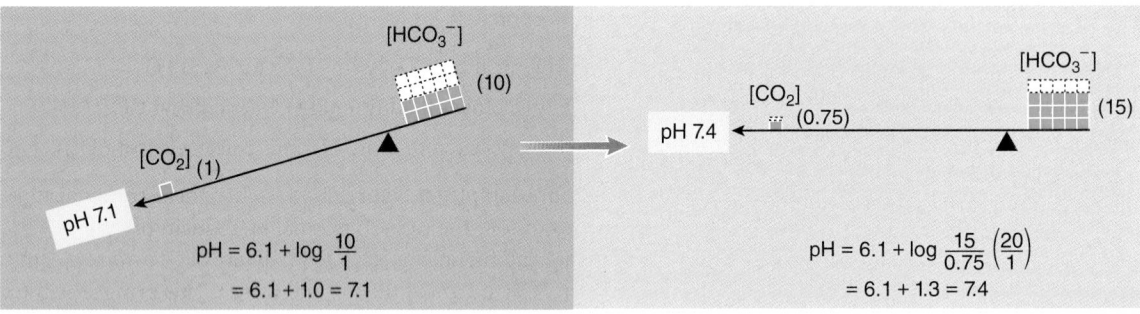

(d) Metabolic acidosis

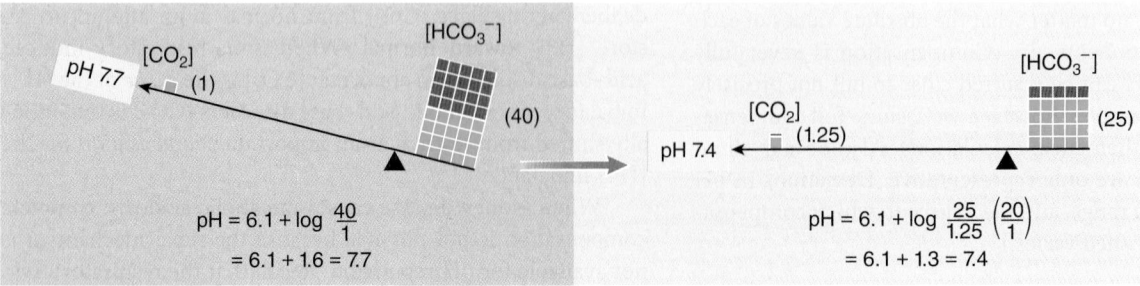

(e) Metabolic alkalosis

● **FIGURE D-3 Relationship of [HCO$_3^-$] and [CO$_2$] to pH in various acid–base statuses, shown visually as a balance beam and mathematically as a solution to the Henderson–Hasselbalch equation.** Note that the lengths of the arms of the balance beams are not to scale. (a) When acid–base balance is normal, the [HCO$_3^-$]/[CO$_2$] ratio is 20/1. Each of the four types of acid–base disorders has an uncompensated state and a compensated state. (b) In uncompensated respiratory acidosis, the [HCO$_3^-$]/[CO$_2$] ratio is reduced (20/2), because CO$_2$ has accumulated. In compensated respiratory acidosis, HCO$_3^-$ is retained to balance the CO$_2$ accumulation, which restores the [HCO$_3^-$]/[CO$_2$] ratio to a normal equivalent (40/2). (c) In uncompensated respiratory alkalosis, the [HCO$_3^-$]/[CO$_2$] ratio is increased (20/0.5) by a reduction in CO$_2$. In compensated respiratory alkalosis, HCO$_3^-$ is eliminated to balance the CO$_2$ deficit, which restores the [HCO$_3^-$]/[CO$_2$] ratio to a normal equivalent (10/0.5). (d) In uncompensated metabolic acidosis, the [HCO$_3^-$]/[CO$_2$] ratio is reduced (10/1) by a HCO$_3^-$ deficit. In compensated metabolic acidosis, HCO$_3^-$ is conserved, which partially makes up for the HCO$_3^-$ deficit, and CO$_2$ is reduced; these changes restore the [HCO$_3^-$]/[CO$_2$] ratio to a normal equivalent (15/0.75). (e) In uncompensated metabolic alkalosis, the [HCO$_3^-$]/[CO$_2$] ratio is increased (40/1) by excess HCO$_3^-$. In compensated metabolic alkalosis, some of the extra HCO$_3^-$ is eliminated, and CO$_2$ is increased; these changes restore the [HCO$_3^-$]/[CO$_2$] ratio to a normal equivalent (25/1.25).

METABOLIC ALKALOSIS Uncompensated metabolic alkalosis is associated with an increase in [HCO$_3^-$], which, in the uncompensated state, is not accompanied by a change in [CO$_2$]. In our example (● Figure D-3d, left), [HCO$_3^-$] is doubled, producing an alkalotic ratio of 40/1.

This condition arises most commonly from excess ingestion of alkaline drugs, such as when baking soda (NaHCO$_3$) is used as a self-administered remedy for the treatment of gastric hyperacidity, or from excessive vomiting of acidic gastric juices. Hydrochloric acid is secreted into the stomach lumen during digestion. Bicarbonate is added to the plasma during gastric HCl secretion. This HCO$_3^-$ is neutralized by H$^+$ as the gastric secretions are eventually reabsorbed back into the plasma, so normally there is no net addition of HCO$_3^-$ to the plasma from this source. However, when this acid is lost from the body during vomiting not only is plasma [H$^+$] decreased, but reabsorbed H$^+$ is also no longer available to neutralize the extra HCO$_3^-$ added to the plasma during gastric HCl secretion. Thus, loss of HCl in effect increases plasma [HCO$_3^-$].

The following compensatory measures come into play to restore the pH toward normal:

■ The chemical buffer systems immediately liberate H$^+$.

■ Ventilation is reduced so that extra H$^+$-generating CO$_2$ is retained in the body fluids.

■ If the condition persists for several days, the kidneys conserve H$^+$ and excrete the excess HCO$_3^-$ in the urine.

The resultant compensatory increase in [CO$_2$] (up 25% in our example; ● Figure D-3e, right) and the partial reduction in [HCO$_3^-$] (75% of the way back down toward normal in our example) together restore the [HCO$_3^-$]/[CO$_2$] ratio back to the equivalent of 20/1 at 25/1.25.

Thus, an individual's acid–base status cannot be assessed on the basis of pH alone. Even though the pH is essentially normal, determinations of [HCO$_3^-$] and [CO$_2$] can reveal compensated acid–base disorders.

Appendix E
Answers to End-of-Chapter Objective Questions, Points to Ponder, and Clinical Considerations

Chapter 1 Introduction to Physiology and Homeostasis

(Questions on p. 15.)

1. e
2. b
3. F
4. T
5. muscle tissue, nervous tissue, epithelial tissue, connective tissue
6. secretion
7. exocrine, endocrine, hormones
8. intrinsic, extrinsic
9. 1. d, 2. g, 3. a, 4. e, 5. b, 6. j, 7. h, 8. i, 9. c, 10. f

(Questions on p. 16.)

1. The respiratory system eliminates internally produced CO_2 to the external environment. A decrease in CO_2 in the internal environment brings about a reduction in respiratory activity (that is, slower, shallower breathing) so that CO_2 produced within the body accumulates instead of being blown off as rapidly as normal to the external environment. The extra CO_2 retained in the body increases the CO_2 levels in the internal environment to normal.
2. b, c, b
3. b
4. immune defense system
5. When a person is engaged in strenuous exercise, the temperature-regulating center in the brain brings about widening of the blood vessels of the skin. The resultant increased blood flow through the skin carries the extra heat generated by the contracting muscles to the body surface, where it can be lost to the surrounding environment.

(Question on p. 17.)

Loss of fluids threatens the maintenance of proper plasma volume and blood pressure. Loss of acidic digestive juices threatens maintenance of the proper pH in the internal fluid environment. The urinary system helps restore the proper plasma volume and pH by reducing the amount of water and acid eliminated in the urine. The respiratory system helps restore the pH by adjusting the rate of removal of acid-forming CO_2. Adjustments are made in the circulatory system to help maintain blood pressure despite fluid loss. Increased thirst encourages increased fluid intake to help restore plasma volume. These compensatory changes in the urinary, respiratory, and circulatory systems, as well as the sensation of thirst, are all controlled by the two regulatory systems, the nervous and endocrine systems. Furthermore, the endocrine system makes internal adjustments to help maintain the concentration of nutrients in the internal environment even though no new nutrients are being absorbed from the digestive system.

Chapter 2 Cell Physiology

(Questions on p. 42.)

1. plasma membrane
2. deoxyribonucleic acid (DNA), nucleus
3. organelles, cytosol, cytoskeleton
4. endoplasmic reticulum, Golgi complex
5. oxidative
6. adenosine triphosphate (ATP)
7. F
8. F
9. 1. b, 2. a, 3. b
10. 1. b, 2. c, 3. c, 4. a, 5. b, 6. c, 7. a, 8. c, 9. c

(Questions on p. 43.)

1.   24 moles O_2/day $\times$ 6 moles ATP/mole O_2
                = 144 moles ATP/day
   144 moles ATP/day $\times$ 507 g ATP/mole = 73,000 g ATP/day
           1000 g/2.2 lb = 73,000 g/x lb
                1000x = 160,600
                x = approximately 160 lb

2. The chief cells have an extensive rough endoplasmic reticulum, with this organelle being responsible for synthesizing these cells' protein secretory product, namely, pepsinogen. Because the parietal cells do not secrete a protein product to the cells' exterior, they do not need an extensive rough endoplasmic reticulum.

3. With cyanide poisoning, cell activities that depend on ATP expenditure could not continue, such as synthesis of new chemical compounds, membrane transport, and mechanical work. The resultant inability of the heart to pump blood and failure of the respiratory muscles to accomplish breathing would lead to imminent death.

4. ATP is required for muscle contraction. Muscles can store limited supplies of nutrient fuel for use in generating ATP. During anaerobic exercise, muscles generate ATP from these nutrient stores by means of glycolysis, which yields two molecules of ATP per glucose molecule processed. During aerobic exercise, muscles can generate ATP by oxidative phosphorylation, which yields 32 molecules of ATP per glucose molecule processed. Because glycolysis inefficiently generates ATP from nutrient fuels, it rapidly depletes the muscle's limited stores of fuel, and ATP can no longer be produced to sustain the muscle's contractile activity. Aerobic exercise, in contrast, can be sustained for prolonged periods. Not only does oxidative phosphorylation use far less nutrient fuel to generate ATP, but it can be supported by nutrients delivered to the muscle by the blood instead of relying on fuel stored in the muscle. Intense anaerobic exercise outpaces the ability to deliver supplies to the muscle by the blood, so the muscle must rely on stored fuel and inefficient glycolysis, thus limiting anaerobic exercise to brief periods before energy sources are depleted.

5. skin. The mutant keratin weakens the skin cells of patients with epidermolysis bullosa so that the skin blisters in response to even a light touch.

CLINICAL CONSIDERATION

(Question on p. 43.)

Some hereditary forms of male sterility involving nonmotile sperm have been traced to defects in the cytoskeletal components of the sperm's flagella. These same individuals usually also have long histories of recurrent respiratory tract disease because the same types of defects are present in their respiratory cilia, which are unable to clear mucus and inhaled particles from the respiratory system.

Chapter 3 The Plasma Membrane and Membrane Potential

OBJECTIVE QUESTIONS

(Questions on p. 72.)

1. T
2. T
3. T
4. F
5. negative, positive
6. 1. b, 2. a, 3. b, 4. a, 5. c, 6. b, 7. a, 8. b
7. 1. a, 2. a, 3. b, 4. a, 5. b, 6. a, 7. b
8. 1. c, 2. b, 3. a, 4. a, 5. c, 6. b, 7. c, 8. a, 9. b

POINTS TO PONDER

(Questions on p. 73.)

1. Osmolarity refers to the concentration of all particles in a solution, both penetrating and nonpenetrating, yet only nonpenetrating solutes contribute to the tonicity of a solution. Therefore, a solution with a mixture of penetrating and nonpenetrating solutes may have an osmolarity of 300 mOsm, the same as in the ICF, but be hypotonic to the cells because the solution's concentration of nonpenetrating solutes is less than the concentration of nonpenetrating solutes inside the cells. The entire osmolarity of the ICF at 300 mOsm is attributable to nonpenetrating solutes.

2. c. As Na^+ moves from side 1 to side 2 down its concentration gradient, Cl^- remains on side 1, unable to permeate the membrane. The resultant separation of charges produces a membrane potential, negative on side 1 because of unbalanced chloride ions and positive on side 2 because of unbalanced sodium ions. Sodium does not continue to move to side 2 until its concentration gradient is dissipated because an opposing electrical gradient is developed.

3. More positive. Because the electrochemical gradient for Na^+ is inward, the membrane potential would become more positive as a result of an increased influx of Na^+ into the cell if the membrane were more permeable to Na^+ than to K^+. (Indeed, this is what happens during the rising phase of an action potential once threshold potential is reached—see Chapter 4).

4. d. active transport. Leveling off of the curve designates saturation of a carrier molecule, so carrier-mediated transport is involved. The graph indicates that active transport is being used instead of facilitated diffusion, because the concentration of the substance in the intracellular fluid is greater than the concentration in the extracellular fluid at all points until after the transport maximum is reached. Thus, the substance is being moved *against* a concentration gradient, so active transport must be the transport method used.

5. vesicular transport. The maternal antibodies in the infant's digestive tract lumen are taken up by the intestinal cells by pinocytosis and are extruded on the opposite side of the cell into the interstitial fluid by

exocytosis. The antibodies are picked up from the intestinal interstitial fluid by the blood supply to the region.

(Question on p. 73.)

As Cl⁻ is secreted by the intestinal cells into the intestinal tract lumen, Na⁺ follows passively along the established electrical gradient. Water passively accompanies this salt (Na⁺ and Cl⁻) secretion by osmosis. Increased secretion of Cl⁻ and the subsequent passively induced secretion of Na⁺ and water are responsible for the severe diarrhea that characterizes cholera.

Chapter 4   Principles of Neural and Hormonal Communication

OBJECTIVE QUESTIONS

(Questions on p. 109.)

1. T
2. F
3. F
4. F
5. T
6. F
7. refractory period
8. axon hillock
9. synapse
10. convergence, divergence
11. G protein
12. 1. b, 2. a, 3. a, 4. b, 5. b, 6. a
13. 1. a, 2. b, 3. a, 4. b, 5. d, 6. b, 7. b, 8. b, 9. a, 10. b, 11. a, 12. c

POINTS TO PONDER

(Questions on p. 110.)

1. c. The action potentials would stop as they met in the middle. As the two action potentials moving toward each other both reached the middle of the axon, the two adjacent patches of membrane in the middle would be in a refractory period, so further propagation of either action potential would be impossible.

2. The hand could be pulled away from the hot stove by flexion of the elbow accomplished by summation of EPSPs at the cell bodies of the neurons controlling the biceps muscle, thus bringing these neurons to threshold. The subsequent action potentials generated in these neurons would stimulate contraction of the biceps. Simultaneous contraction of the triceps muscle, which would oppose the desired flexion of the elbow, could be prevented by generation of IPSPs at the cell bodies of the neurons controlling this muscle. These IPSPs would keep the triceps neurons from reaching threshold and firing so that the triceps would not be stimulated to contract.

The arm could deliberately be extended despite a painful finger prick by voluntarily generating EPSPs to override the reflex IPSPs at the neuronal cell bodies controlling the triceps while simultaneously generating IPSPs to override the reflex EPSPs at the neuronal cell bodies controlling the biceps.

3. A subthreshold stimulus would transiently depolarize the membrane but not sufficiently to bring the membrane to threshold, so no action potential would occur. Because a threshold stimulus would bring the membrane to threshold, an action potential would occur. An action potential of the same magnitude and duration would occur in response to a suprathreshold stimulus as to a threshold stimulus. Because of the all-or-none law, a stimulus larger than that necessary to bring the membrane to threshold would not produce a larger action potential. (The magnitude of the stimulus is coded in the *frequency* of action potentials generated in the neuron, not the *size* of the action potentials.)

4. An EPSP, being a graded potential, spreads decrementally from its site of initiation in the postsynaptic neuron. If presynaptic neuron A (near the axon hillock of the postsynaptic cell) and presynaptic neuron B (on the opposite side of the postsynaptic cell body) both initiate EPSPs of the same magnitude and frequency, the EPSPs from presynaptic neuron A will be of greater strength when they reach the axon hillock than will the EPSPs from presynaptic neuron B. An EPSP from presynaptic neuron B will decrease more in magnitude as it travels farther before reaching the axon hillock, the region of lowest threshold and thus the site of action potential initiation. Temporal summation of the larger EPSPs from presynaptic neuron A may bring the axon hillock to threshold and initiate an action potential in the postsynaptic neuron, whereas temporal summation of the weaker EPSPs from presynaptic neuron B at the axon hillock may not be sufficient to bring this region to threshold. Thus, the proximity of a presynaptic neuron to the axon hillock can bias its influence on the postsynaptic cell.

5. (1) Angiotensin receptor blockers decrease blood pressure by reducing the load of osmotically active (water holding) salt in the body, thereby decreasing the volume of circulating plasma. The greater the plasma volume, and accordingly the blood volume, the higher the blood pressure, all other factors being equal.
(2) β₁-Adrenergic receptor blockers suppress the action of epinephrine on the heart, thereby reducing the rate and strength of contraction of the heart. The more rapidly and more forcefully the heart beats, the more blood pumped into the blood vessels per minute and the greater the pressure exerted by the blood on the vessel walls, all other factors being equal.

CLINICAL CONSIDERATION

(Question on p. 111.)

Initiation and propagation of action potentials would not occur in nerve fibers acted on by local anesthetic because blockage of Na⁺ channels by the local anesthetic would prevent the massive opening of voltage-gated Na⁺ channels at threshold potential. As a result, pain impulses (action potentials in nerve fibers that carry pain signals) would not be initiated and propagated to the brain and reach the level of conscious awareness.

Chapter 5 The Central Nervous System

(Questions on p. 145.)

1. F
2. F
3. F
4. T
5. F
6. consolidation
7. dorsal, ventral
8. 1. d, 2. c, 3. f, 4. e, 5. a, 6. b
9. 1. a, 2. c, 3. a and b, 4. b, 5. a, 6. c, 7. c

POINTS TO PONDER

(Questions on p. 146.)

1. Only the left hemisphere has language ability. When sharing of information between the two hemispheres is prevented as a result of severance of the corpus callosum, visual information presented only to the right hemisphere cannot be verbally identified by the left hemisphere, because the left hemisphere is unaware of the information. However, the information can be recognized by nonverbal means, of which the right hemisphere is capable.
2. c. A severe blow to the back of the head is most likely to traumatize the visual cortex in the occipital lobe.
3. Insulin excess drives too much glucose into insulin-dependent cells so that the blood glucose falls below normal and insufficient glucose is delivered to the non–insulin-dependent brain. Therefore, the brain, which depends on glucose as its energy source, does not receive adequate nourishment.
4. Salivation when seeing or smelling food, striking the appropriate letter on the keyboard when typing, playing the correct note on a musical instrument, and many of the actions involved in driving a car are conditioned reflexes. You undoubtedly will have many other examples.
5. Strokes occur when a portion of the brain is deprived of its vital O_2 and glucose supply because the cerebral blood vessel supplying the area either is blocked by a clot or has ruptured. Although a clot-dissolving drug could be helpful in restoring blood flow through a cerebral vessel blocked by a clot, such a drug would be detrimental in the case of a ruptured cerebral vessel sealed by a clot. Dissolution of a clot sealing a ruptured vessel would lead to renewed hemorrhage through the vessel and make the problem worse.

CLINICAL CONSIDERATION

(Question on p. 147.)

The deficits following the stroke—numbness and partial paralysis on the upper right side of the body and inability to speak—are indicative of damage to the left somatosensory cortex and left primary motor cortex in the regions devoted to the upper part of the body, as well as damage to Broca's area.

Chapter 6 The Peripheral Nervous System: Afferent Division and Special Senses

OBJECTIVE QUESTIONS

(Questions on p. 186.)

1. transduction
2. adequate stimulus
3. F
4. T
5. T
6. F
7. T
8. F
9. F
10. 1. d, 2. f, 3. i, 4. g, 5. c, 6. a, 7. h, 8. e, 9. b
11. 1. a, 2. b, 3. c, 4. c, 5. c, 6. a, 7. b, 8. b

POINTS TO PONDER

(Questions on p. 187.)

1. Pain is a conscious warning that tissue damage is occurring or is about to occur. A patient unable to feel pain because of a nerve disorder does not consciously take measures to withdraw from painful stimuli and thus prevent more serious tissue damage.
2. Pupillary dilation (mydriasis) can be deliberately induced by ophthalmic instillation (eye drops) of either an adrenergic drug (one that mimics sympathetic action, such as epinephrine or related compounds) or a cholinergic blocking drug (one that blocks parasympathetic action, such as atropine or related compounds). Adrenergic drugs produce mydriasis by causing contraction of the sympathetically supplied dilator muscle of the iris. Cholinergic blocking drugs cause pupillary dilation by blocking parasympathetic activity to the constrictor muscle of the iris so that action of the sympathetically controlled dilator muscle of the iris is unopposed.
3. The defect would be in the left optic tract or optic radiation.
4. Fluid accumulation in the middle ear in accompaniment with middle ear infections impedes the normal movement of the tympanic membrane, ossicles, and oval window in response to sound. All these structures

vibrate less vigorously in the presence of fluid, causing temporary hearing impairment. Chronic fluid accumulation in the middle ear is sometimes relieved by surgical implantation of drainage tubes in the eardrum. Hearing is restored to normal as the fluid drains to the exterior. Usually, the tube "falls out" as the eardrum heals and pushes out the foreign object.

5. The sense of smell is reduced when you have a cold, even though the cold virus does not directly adversely affect the olfactory receptor cells, because odorants do not reach the receptor cells as readily when the mucous membranes lining the nasal passageways are swollen and excess mucus is present.

CLINICAL CONSIDERATION

(Question on p. 187.)

Syncope most frequently occurs as a result of inadequate delivery of blood carrying sufficient oxygen and glucose supplies to the brain. Possible causes include circulatory disorders such as impaired pumping of the heart or low blood pressure; respiratory disorders resulting in poorly oxygenated blood; anemia, in which the oxygen-carrying capacity of the blood is reduced; or low blood glucose from improper endocrine management of blood glucose levels. Vertigo, in contrast, typically results from a dysfunction of the vestibular apparatus, arising, for example, from viral infection or trauma, or abnormal neural processing of vestibular information, as, for example, with a brain tumor.

Chapter 7 The Peripheral Nervous System: Efferent Division

OBJECTIVE QUESTIONS

(Questions on p. 204.)

1. T
2. F
3. c
4. c
5. sympathetic, parasympathetic
6. adrenal medulla
7. 1. a, 2. b, 3. a, 4. b, 5. a, 6. a, 7. b
8. 1. b, 2. b, 3. a, 4. a, 5. b, 6. b, 7. a

POINTS TO PONDER

(Questions on p. 205.)

1. By promoting arteriolar constriction, epinephrine administered in conjunction with local anesthetics reduces blood flow to the region and thus helps the anesthetic stay in the region instead of being carried away by the blood.
2. No. Atropine blocks the effect of acetylcholine at muscarinic receptors but does not affect nicotinic receptors. Nicotinic receptors are present on the motor end plates of skeletal muscle fibers.

3. The voluntarily controlled external urethral sphincter is composed of skeletal muscle and supplied by the somatic nervous system.
4. By interfering with normal acetylcholine activity at the neuromuscular junction, α-bungarotoxin leads to skeletal muscle paralysis, with death ultimately occurring as a result of an inability to contract the diaphragm and breathe.
5. If the motor neurons that control the respiratory muscles, especially the diaphragm, are destroyed by poliovirus or amyotrophic lateral sclerosis, the person is unable to breathe and dies (unless breathing is assisted by artificial means).

CLINICAL CONSIDERATION

(Question on p. 205.)

Drugs that block β_1 receptors are useful for prolonged treatment of angina pectoris because they interfere with sympathetic stimulation of the heart during exercise or emotionally stressful situations. By preventing increased cardiac metabolism and thus an increased need for oxygen delivery to the cardiac muscle during these situations, β blockers can reduce the frequency and severity of angina attacks.

Chapter 8 Muscle Physiology

OBJECTIVE QUESTIONS

(Questions on p. 240.)

1. F
2. F
3. F
4. T
5. F
6. T
7. concentric, eccentric
8. alpha, gamma
9. a, b, e
10. b
11. 1. f, 2. d, 3. c, 4. e, 5. b, 6. g, 7. a
12. 1. a, 2. a, 3. a, 4. b, 5. b, 6. b

POINTS TO PONDER

(Questions on p. 241.)

1. By placing increased demands on the heart to sustain increased delivery of O_2 and nutrients to working skeletal muscles, regular aerobic exercise induces changes in cardiac muscle that enable it to use O_2 more efficiently, such as increasing the number of capillaries supplying blood to the heart muscle. Intense exercise of short duration, such as weight training, in contrast, does not induce cardiac efficiency. Because this type of exercise relies on anaerobic glycolysis for ATP formation, no demands are placed on the heart for increased delivery of blood to the working muscles.

2. The length of the thin filaments is represented by the distance between a Z line and the edge of the adjacent H zone. This distance remains the same in a relaxed and contracted myofibril, leading to the conclusion that the thin filaments do not change in length during muscle contraction.

3. Regular bouts of anaerobic, short-duration, high-intensity resistance training would be recommended for competitive downhill skiing. By promoting hypertrophy of the fast glycolytic fibers, such exercise better adapts the muscles to activities that require intense strength for brief periods, such as a swift, powerful descent downhill. In contrast, regular aerobic exercise would be more beneficial for competitive cross-country skiers. Aerobic exercise induces metabolic changes within the oxidative fibers that enable the muscles to use O_2 more efficiently. These changes, which include an increase in mitochondria and capillaries within the oxidative fibers, adapt the muscles to better endure the prolonged activity of cross-country skiing without fatiguing.

4. Because the site of voluntary control to overcome the micturition reflex is at the external urethral sphincter and not the bladder, the external urethral sphincter must be skeletal muscle, which is innervated by the voluntarily controlled somatic nervous system, and the bladder must be smooth muscle, which is innervated by the involuntarily controlled autonomic nervous system. The only other type of involuntarily controlled muscle besides smooth muscle is cardiac muscle, which is found only in the heart. Therefore, the bladder must be smooth, not cardiac, muscle.

5.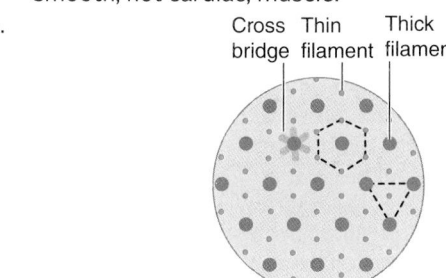

Cross Thin Thick
bridge filament filament

Schematic representation of the geometrical relationships among thick and thin filaments and cross bridges.

CLINICAL CONSIDERATION

(Question on p. 241.)

The muscles in the immobilized leg have undergone disuse atrophy. The physician or physical therapist can prescribe regular resistance-type exercises that specifically use the atrophied muscles to help restore them to their normal size.

Chapter 9   Cardiac Physiology

OBJECTIVE QUESTIONS

(Questions on p. 274.)

1. intercalated discs, desmosomes, gap junctions
2. F

3. F
4. T
5. d
6. d
7. e
8. 1. e, 2. a, 3. d, 4. b, 5. f, 6. c
9. AV, systole, semilunar, diastole
10. less than, greater than, less than, greater than, less than

POINTS TO PONDER

(Questions on p. 275.)

1. Because, at a given heart rate, the interval between a premature beat and the next normal beat is longer than the interval between two normal beats, the heart fills for a longer period following a premature beat before the next period of contraction and emptying begins. Because of the longer filling time, the end-diastolic volume is larger. According to the Frank–Starling law of the heart, the subsequent stroke volume will also be correspondingly larger.

2. Trained athletes' hearts are stronger and can pump blood more efficiently so that the resting stroke volume is larger than it is in an untrained person. For example, if the resting stroke volume of a strong-hearted athlete is 100 ml, a resting heart rate of only 50 beats per minute produces a normal resting cardiac output of 5000 ml per minute. An untrained individual with a resting stroke volume of 70 ml, in contrast, must have a heart rate of about 70 beats per minute to produce a comparable resting cardiac output.

3. In the fetus, blood is shunted from the pulmonary artery into the aorta through the ductus arteriosus, thus bypassing the nonfunctional lungs. Blood flows in this direction down its pressure gradient, with pulmonary artery pressure in the collapsed lungs being greater than aortic pressure during fetal life.

   The direction of flow through a patent ductus arteriosus is the reverse of the flow that occurs through this vascular connection during fetal life. With a patent ductus arteriosus, some of the blood present in the aorta is shunted through the still-open ductus arteriosus into the pulmonary artery because, after birth, the aortic pressure is greater than the pulmonary artery pressure.

   As a result of this abnormal shunting, only some of the blood pumped out by the left ventricle goes into the systemic circulation, and excessive blood enters the pulmonary circulation. If the condition is not corrected by tying off the patent ductus arteriosus, the left ventricle compensates by hypertrophying (enlarging and becoming stronger) so that it can pump out even more blood. This extra output provides adequate systemic circulation, even through part of the left ventricular output is diverted to the pulmonary circulation. The right ventricle also hypertrophies, enabling it to pump against the elevated pulmonary arterial pressure, which is increased due to the excess volume of blood shunted into the pulmonary circulation. If the condition is not corrected, this extra workload on the heart eventually leads to heart failure and premature death.

4. A transplanted heart that does not have any innervation adjusts the cardiac output to meet the body's changing needs by means of both intrinsic control (the Frank–Starling mechanism) and extrinsic hormonal influences (such as the effect of epinephrine on the rate and strength of cardiac contraction).
5. In left bundle-branch block, the right ventricle becomes completely depolarized more rapidly than the left ventricle. As a result, the right ventricle contracts before the left ventricle, and the right AV valve is forced closed prior to closure of the left AV valve. Because the two AV valves do not close in unison, the first heart sound is "split"; that is, two distinct sounds in close succession can be detected as closure of the left valve lags behind closure of the right valve.

CLINICAL CONSIDERATION

(Question on p. 275.)

The most likely diagnosis is atrial fibrillation. This condition is characterized by rapid, irregular, uncoordinated depolarizations of the atria. Many of these depolarizations reach the AV node when it is not in its refractory period, thus bringing about frequent ventricular depolarizations and a rapid heartbeat. However, because impulses reach the AV node erratically, the ventricular rhythm and thus the heartbeat are irregular, as well as rapid.

Ventricular filling is only slightly reduced despite the fibrillating atria being unable to pump blood, because most ventricular filling occurs during diastole prior to atrial contraction. Because of the erratic heartbeat, variable lengths of time are available between ventricular beats for ventricular filling. However, the majority of ventricular filling occurs early in ventricular diastole after the AV valves first open, so even though the filling period may be shortened, the extent of filling may be near normal. Only when the ventricular filling period is very short is ventricular filling substantially reduced.

Cardiac output, which depends on stroke volume and heart rate, usually is not seriously impaired with atrial fibrillation. Because ventricular filling is only slightly reduced during most cardiac cycles, stroke volume, as determined by the Frank–Starling mechanism, is likewise only slightly reduced. Only when the ventricular filling period is very short and the cardiac muscle fibers are operating on the lower end of their length–tension curve is the resultant ventricular contraction weak. When the ventricular contraction becomes too weak, the ventricles eject a small or no stroke volume. During most cardiac cycles, however, the slight reduction in stroke volume is often offset by the increased heart rate, so cardiac output is usually near normal. Furthermore, if the mean arterial blood pressure falls because the cardiac output does decrease, increased sympathetic stimulation of the heart brought about by the baroreceptor reflex helps restore cardiac output to normal by shifting the Frank–Starling curve to the left.

On those cycles when ventricular contractions are too weak to eject enough blood to produce a palpable wrist pulse, if the heart rate is determined directly, either by the apex beat or via the ECG, and the pulse rate is taken concurrently at the wrist, the heart rate will exceed the pulse rate, producing a pulse deficit.

Chapter 10 The Blood Vessels and Blood Pressure

OBJECTIVE QUESTIONS

(Questions on p. 312.)

1. T
2. F
3. T
4. T
5. F
6. T
7. a, c, d, e, f
8. 1. a, 2. a, 3. b, 4. a, 5. b
9. 1. b, 2. a, 3. b, 4. a, 5. a, 6. a, 7. b, 8. a, 9. b, 10. a, 11. b, 12. a, 13. a

POINTS TO PONDER

(Questions on p. 313.)

1. An elastic support stocking increases external pressure on the remaining veins in the limb to produce a favorable pressure gradient that promotes venous return to the heart and minimizes swelling that would result from fluid retention in the extremity.
2. a. 125 mm Hg
   b. 77 mm Hg
   c. 48 mm Hg; that is, 125 mm Hg − 77 mm Hg = 48 mm Hg
   d. 93 mm Hg; that is, 77 mm Hg + (1/3)48 mm Hg = 77 mm Hg + 16 mm Hg = 93 mm Hg
   e. no. No blood would be able to get through the brachial artery, so no sound would be heard.
   f. yes. Blood would flow through the brachial artery when the arterial pressure was between 118 and 125 mm Hg and would not flow through when the arterial pressure fell below 118 mm Hg. The turbulence created by this intermittent blood flow would produce sounds.
   g. no. Blood would flow continuously through the brachial artery in smooth, laminar fashion, so no sound would be heard.
3. The classmate has apparently fainted because of insufficient blood flow to the brain as a result of pooling of blood in the lower extremities brought about by standing still for a prolonged time during the laboratory experiment. When the person faints and assumes a horizontal position, the pooled blood will quickly be returned to the heart, improving cardiac output and blood flow to his brain. Trying to get the person up would be counterproductive, so the classmate trying to get him up should be advised to let him remain lying down until he recovers on his own.
4. The drug is apparently causing the arteriolar smooth muscle to relax by causing the release of a local vasoactive chemical mediator from the endothelial cells that induces relaxation of the underlying smooth muscle.
5. a. Because activation of α_1-adrenergic receptors in vascular smooth muscle brings about vasoconstric-

tion, blockage of α_1-adrenergic receptors reduces vasoconstrictor activity, thereby lowering the total peripheral resistance and arterial blood pressure.

b. Because activation of β_1-adrenergic receptors, which are found primarily in the heart, increases the rate and strength of cardiac contraction, drugs that block β_1-adrenergic receptors reduce cardiac output and thus arterial blood pressure by decreasing the rate and strength of the heart beat.

c. Drugs that directly relax arteriolar smooth muscle lower arterial blood pressure by promoting arteriolar vasodilation and reducing total peripheral resistance.

d. Diuretic drugs reduce the plasma volume, thereby lowering arterial blood pressure, by increasing urinary output. Salt and water that normally would have been retained in the plasma are excreted in the urine.

e. Because sympathetic activity promotes generalized arteriolar vasoconstriction, thereby increasing total peripheral resistance and arterial blood pressure, drugs that block the release of norepinephrine from sympathetic endings lower blood pressure by preventing this sympathetic vasoconstrictor effect.

f. Similarly, drugs that act on the brain to reduce sympathetic output lower blood pressure by preventing the effect of sympathetic activity on promoting arteriolar vasoconstriction and the resultant increase in total peripheral resistance and arterial blood pressure.

g. Drugs that block Ca^{2+} channels reduce the entry of Ca^{2+} into the vascular smooth-muscle cells from the ECF in response to excitatory input. Because the level of contractile activity in vascular smooth-muscle cells depends on their cytosolic Ca^{2+} concentration, drugs that block Ca^{2+} channels reduce the contractile activity of these cells by reducing Ca^{2+} entry and lowering their cytosolic Ca^{2+} concentration. Total peripheral resistance and, accordingly, arterial blood pressure are decreased as a result of reduced arteriolar contractile activity.

h. Drugs that interfere with the production of angiotensin II block activation of the hormonal pathway that promotes salt and water conservation (the renin–angiotensin–aldosterone system). As a result, more salt and water are lost in the urine, and less fluid is retained in the plasma. The resultant reduction in plasma volume lowers the arterial blood pressure.

i. Drugs that block angiotensin receptors prevent angiotensin II from causing arteriolar vasoconstriction, thereby decreasing total peripheral resistance, and reduce the action of the salt- and water-conserving renin–angiotensin–aldosterone system, thereby decreasing plasma volume. Together, these effects lower arterial blood pressure.

CLINICAL CONSIDERATION

(Question on p. 313.)

The abnormally elevated levels of epinephrine found with a pheochromocytoma bring about secondary hypertension by (1) increasing the heart rate; (2) increasing cardiac contrac-

tility, which increases stroke volume; (3) causing venous vasoconstriction, which increases venous return and subsequently stroke volume by means of the Frank–Starling mechanism; and (4) causing arteriolar vasoconstriction, which increases total peripheral resistance. Increased heart rate and stroke volume both lead to increased cardiac output. Increased cardiac output and increased total peripheral resistance both lead to increased arterial blood pressure.

Chapter 11 The Blood and Body Defenses

OBJECTIVE QUESTIONS

(Questions on p. 361.)

1. F
2. T
3. F
4. F
5. F
6. F
7. T
8. toll-like receptors
9. opsonin
10. cytokines
11. d
12. a
13. b
14. 1. e, 2. c, 3. b, 4. d, 5. g, 6. f, 7. a, 8. h
15. 1. c, 2. d, 3. a, 4. b
16. 1. a, 2. a, 3. b, 4. b, 5. c, 6. c, 7. b, 8. a, 9. b, 10. b, 11. a, 12. b

POINTS TO PONDER

(Questions on p. 362.)

1. If the genes that direct fetal hemoglobin F synthesis could be reactivated in a patient with sickle cell anemia, a portion of the abnormal hemoglobin S that causes the erythrocytes to warp into defective sickle-shaped cells would be replaced by "healthy" hemoglobin F, thus sparing a portion of the RBCs from premature rupture. Hemoglobin F would not completely replace hemoglobin S because the gene for synthesis of hemoglobin S would still be active.

2. Most heart-attack deaths are attributable to the formation of abnormal clots that prevent normal blood flow. The sought-after chemicals in the "saliva" of blood-sucking creatures are agents that break up or prevent the formation of these abnormal clots.

    Although genetically engineered tissue–plasminogen activator (tPA) is already being used as a clot-busting drug, this agent brings about degradation of fibrinogen, as well as fibrin. Thus, even though the life-threatening clot in the coronary circulation is dissolved, the fibrinogen supplies in the blood are depleted for up to 24 hours until new fibrinogen is synthesized by the liver. If the patient sustains a ruptured vessel in the interim, insufficient fibrinogen might be available to form a blood-staunching clot. For example, many patients treated with tPA suffer hemorrhagic strokes within 24 hours of treatment due to incomplete sealing of a ruptured cerebral vessel. Therefore, scientists are searching for better alternatives to combat abnormal clot formation by examining the naturally occurring chemicals produced by blood-sucking creatures that permit them to suck a victim's blood without the blood clotting.

3. Failure of the thymus to develop embryonically would lead to an absence of T lymphocytes and no cell-mediated immunity after birth. This outcome would seriously compromise the individual's ability to defend against viral invasion and cancer.

4. Researchers are working on ways to "teach" the immune system to view foreign tissue as "self" as a means of preventing the immune systems of organ transplant patients from rejecting the foreign tissue while leaving the patients' immune defense capabilities fully intact. The immunosuppressive drugs currently being used to prevent transplant rejection cripple the recipients' immune defense systems, leaving the patients more vulnerable to microbial invasion.

5. The skin cells visible on the body surface are all dead.

CLINICAL CONSIDERATION

(Question on p. 363.)

1. Heather's firstborn Rh-positive child did not have hemolytic disease of the newborn, because the fetal and maternal blood did not mix during gestation. Consequently, Heather did not produce any maternal antibodies against the fetus's Rh factor during gestation.

2. Because a small amount of the infant's blood likely entered the maternal circulation during the birthing process, Heather would produce antibodies against the Rh factor as she was first exposed to it at that time. During any subsequent pregnancies with Rh-positive fetuses, Heather's maternal antibodies against the Rh factor could cross the placental barrier and bring about destruction of fetal erythrocytes.

3. If any Rh factor that accidentally mixed with the maternal blood during the birthing process were immediately tied up by Rh immunoglobulin administered to the mother, the Rh factor would not be available to induce maternal antibody production. Thus, no anti-Rh antibodies would be present in the maternal blood to threaten the RBCs of an Rh-positive fetus in a subsequent pregnancy. (The exogenously administered Rh immunoglobulin, being a passive form of immunity, is short lived. In contrast, the active immunity that would result if Heather were exposed to Rh factor would be long lived because of the formation of memory cells.)

4. Rh immunoglobulin must be administered following the birth of every Rh-positive child Heather bears to sop up any Rh factor before it can induce antibody production. Once an immune attack against Rh factor is launched, subsequent treatment with Rh immunoglobulin will not reverse the situation. Thus, if Heather were not treated

with Rh immunoglobulin following the birth of a first Rh-positive child, and a second Rh-positive child developed hemolytic disease of the newborn, administration of Rh immunoglobulin following the second birth would not prevent the condition in a third Rh-positive child. Nothing could be done to eliminate the maternal antibodies already present.

Chapter 12   The Respiratory System

OBJECTIVE QUESTIONS

(Questions on p. 400.)

1. F
2. F
3. T
4. F
5. F
6. F
7. transmural pressure gradient, pulmonary surfactant action
8. pulmonary elasticity, alveolar surface tension
9. compliance
10. elastic recoil
11. carbonic anhydrase
12. a
13. 1. d, 2. a, 3. b, 4. a, 5. b, 6. a
14. a. $<$, b. $>$, c. $=$, d. $=$, e. $=$, f. $=$, g. $>$, h., $<$, i. approximately $=$, j. approximately $=$, k. $=$, l. $=$

POINTS TO PONDER

(Questions on p. 401.)

1. Total atmospheric pressure decreases with increasing altitude, yet the percentage of O_2 in the air remains the same. At an altitude of 30,000 feet, the atmospheric pressure is only 226 mm Hg. Because 21% of atmospheric air consists of O_2, the P_{O_2} of inspired air at 30,000 feet is only 47.5 mm Hg, and alveolar P_{O_2} is even lower: around 20 mm Hg. At this low P_{O_2}, hemoglobin is only about 30% saturated with O_2—much too low to sustain tissue needs for O_2.

  The P_{O_2} of inspired air can be increased by two means when flying at high altitude. First, by pressurizing the plane's interior to a pressure comparable to that of atmospheric pressure at sea level, the P_{O_2} of inspired air within the plane is 21% of 760 mm Hg, or the normal 160 mm Hg. Accordingly, alveolar and arterial P_{O_2} and percent hemoglobin saturation are likewise normal. In the emergency situation of failure to maintain internal cabin pressure, breathing pure O_2 can raise the P_{O_2} considerably above that accomplished by breathing normal air. When a person is breathing pure O_2, the entire pressure of inspired air is attributable to O_2. For example, with a total atmospheric pressure of 226 mm Hg at an altitude of 30,000 feet, the P_{O_2} of inspired pure O_2 is 226 mm Hg, which is more than adequate to maintain normal arterial hemoglobin saturation.

2. a. Hypercapnia would not accompany the hypoxia associated with cyanide poisoning. In fact, CO_2 levels decline, because oxidative metabolism is blocked by the tissue poisons so that CO_2 is not being produced.

    b. Hypercapnia could but may not accompany the hypoxia associated with pulmonary edema. Pulmonary diffusing capacity is reduced in pulmonary edema, but O_2 transfer suffers more than CO_2 transfer because CO_2 is more soluble than O_2 in the body fluids; thus, CO_2 diffuses more rapidly than O_2. Therefore, the blood is more likely to have equilibrated with alveolar P_{CO_2} than with alveolar P_{O_2} by the end of the pulmonary capillaries. As a result, hypoxia occurs more readily than hypercapnia in these circumstances.

    c. Hypercapnia would accompany the hypoxia associated with restrictive lung disease because ventilation is inadequate to meet the metabolic needs for both O_2 delivery and CO_2 removal. The O_2 and CO_2 exchange between the lungs and the atmosphere are equally affected.

    d. Hypercapnia would not accompany the hypoxia associated with high altitude. In fact, arterial P_{CO_2} levels actually decrease. One of the compensatory responses in acclimatization to high altitudes is reflex stimulation of ventilation as a result of the reduction in arterial P_{O_2}. This compensatory hyperventilation to obtain more O_2 blows off too much CO_2 in the process, so arterial P_{CO_2} levels decline below normal.

    e. Hypercapnia would not accompany the hypoxia associated with severe anemia. Reduced O_2-carrying capacity of the blood has no influence on blood CO_2 content, so arterial P_{CO_2} levels are normal.

    f. Hypercapnia would exist in accompaniment with circulatory hypoxia associated with congestive heart failure. Just as the diminished blood flow fails to deliver adequate O_2 to the tissues, it also fails to remove sufficient CO_2.

    g. Hypercapnia would accompany the hypoxic hypoxia associated with obstructive lung disease because ventilation would be inadequate to meet the metabolic needs for both O_2 delivery and CO_2 removal. The O_2 and CO_2 exchange between the lungs and the atmosphere would be equally affected.

3. $P_{O_2} = 122$ mm Hg
    0.21(atmospheric pressure − partial pressure of H_2O)
    $$= 0.21(630 \text{ mm Hg} - 47 \text{ mm Hg})$$
    $$= 0.21(583 \text{ mm Hg})$$
    $$= 122 \text{ mm Hg}$$

4. Voluntarily hyperventilating before going underwater lowers the arterial P_{CO_2} but does not increase the O_2 content in the blood. Because the P_{CO_2} is below normal, the person can hold his or her breath longer than usual before the arterial P_{CO_2} increases to the point that the swimmer is driven to surface for a breath. Therefore, the person can stay underwater longer. The risk, however, is that the O_2 content of the blood, which was normal, not increased, before going underwater, continues to fall. Therefore, the O_2 level in the blood can fall dangerously low before the CO_2 level builds to the point of driving the person to take a breath. Low arterial P_{O_2} does not stimulate respiratory activity until it has plummeted to 60 mm Hg. Meanwhile, the person may lose consciousness and drown due to inadequate O_2 delivery to the brain. If the person does not hyperventilate so that both the arterial P_{CO_2} and the O_2 content are normal before going underwater, the buildup of CO_2 will drive the person to the surface for a breath before the O_2 levels fall to a dangerous point.

5. c. The arterial P_{O_2} will be less than the alveolar P_{CO_2}, and the arterial P_{CO_2} will be greater than the alveolar P_{CO_2}. Because pulmonary diffusing capacity is reduced, arterial P_{O_2} and P_{CO_2} do not equilibrate with alveolar P_{O_2} and P_{CO_2}.

    If the person is administered 100% O_2, the alveolar P_{O_2} will increase; the arterial P_{O_2} will increase accordingly. Even though arterial P_{O_2} will not equilibrate with alveolar P_{O_2}, it will be higher than when the person is breathing atmospheric air.

    The arterial P_{CO_2} will remain the same whether the person is administered 100% O_2 or is breathing atmospheric air. The alveolar P_{CO_2} and thus the blood-to-alveolar P_{CO_2} gradient are not changed by breathing 100% O_2 because the P_{CO_2} in atmospheric air and 100% O_2 are both essentially zero (P_{CO_2} in atmospheric air = 0.23 mm Hg).

CLINICAL CONSIDERATION

(Question on p. 401.)

Emphysema is characterized by a collapse of smaller respiratory airways and a breakdown of alveolar walls. Because of the collapse of smaller airways, airway resistance is increased with emphysema. As with other chronic obstructive pulmonary diseases, expiration is impaired to a greater extent than inspiration because airways are naturally dilated slightly more during inspiration than during expiration as a result of the greater transmural pressure gradient during inspiration. Because airway resistance is increased, a patient with emphysema must produce larger-than-normal intra-alveolar pressure changes to accomplish a normal tidal volume. Unlike quiet breathing in a normal person, the accessory inspiratory muscles (neck muscles) and the muscles of active expiration (abdominal muscles and internal intercostal muscles) must be brought into play to inspire and expire a normal tidal volume of air.

The spirogram would be characteristic of chronic obstructive pulmonary disease. Because the patient experiences more difficulty emptying the lungs than filling them, the total lung capacity would be essentially normal, but the functional residual capacity and the residual volume would be elevated as a result of the additional air trapped in the lungs following expiration. Because the residual volume is increased, the inspiratory capacity and vital capacity will be reduced. Also, the FEV_1 will be markedly reduced because the airflow rate is decreased by the airway obstruction.

Because of the reduced surface area for exchange as a result of a breakdown of alveolar walls, gas exchange would be impaired. Therefore, arterial P_{CO_2} would be elevated and arterial P_{O_2} would be reduced compared to normal.

Ironically, administering O_2 to this patient to relieve his hypoxic condition would markedly depress his drive to breathe by elevating the arterial P_{O_2} and removing the primary driving stimulus for respiration. Because of this danger, O_2 therapy either should not be administered or should be administered extremely cautiously.

Chapter 13 The Urinary System

OBJECTIVE QUESTIONS

(Questions on p. 438.)

1. F
2. F
3. T
4. T
5. nephron
6. potassium
7. 500
8. d
9. b
10. b, e, a, d, c
11. c, e, d, a, b, f
12. g, c, d, a, f, b, e
13. 1. a, 2. a, 3. c, 4. b, 5. d

POINTS TO PONDER

(Questions on p. 439.)

1. The longer loops of Henle in desert rats (known as *kangaroo rats*) permit a greater magnitude of countercurrent multiplication and thus a larger medullary vertical osmotic gradient. As a result, these rodents can produce urine that is concentrated up to an osmolarity of almost 6000 mOsm, which is five times more concentrated than maximally concentrated human urine at 1200 mOsm. Because of this tremendous concentrating ability, kangaroo rats never have to drink; the H_2O produced metabolically within their cells during oxidation of foodstuff (food + $O_2 \rightarrow CO_2$ + H_2O + energy) is sufficient for their needs.

2. a. 250 mg/min filtered

   filtered load of substance = plasma concentration of substance $\times$ GFR

   = 200 mg/100 ml $\times$ 125 ml/min

   = 250 mg/min

   b. 200 mg/min reabsorbed. A T_m worth of the substance will be reabsorbed.

   c. 50 mg/min excreted

   amount of substance excreted = amount of substance filtered – amount of substance reabsorbed

   = 250 mg/min - 200 mg/min

   = 50 mg/min

3. Aldosterone stimulates Na^+ reabsorption and K^+ secretion by the renal tubules. Therefore, the most prominent features of Conn's syndrome (hypersecretion of aldosterone) are hypernatremia (elevated Na^+ levels in the blood) caused by excessive Na^+ reabsorption, hypophosphatemia (below-normal K^+ levels in the

blood) caused by excessive K^+ secretion, and hypertension (elevated blood pressure) caused by excessive salt and water retention.

4. e. 300/300. If the ascending limb were permeable to water, it would not be possible to establish a vertical osmotic gradient in the medullary interstitial fluid, nor would the ascending-limb fluid become hypotonic before entering the distal tubule. As the ascending limb pumped NaCl into the interstitial fluid, water would osmotically follow, so both the interstitial fluid and the ascending limb would remain isotonic at 300 mOsm. With the tubular fluid entering the distal tubule being 300 mOsm instead of the normal 100 mOsm, it would not be possible to produce urine with an osmolarity less than 300 mOsm. Likewise, in the absence of the medullary vertical osmotic gradient, it would not be possible to produce urine more concentrated than 300 mOsm, no matter how much vasopressin was present.

5. Because the descending pathways between the brain and the motor neurons supplying the external urethral sphincter and pelvic diaphragm are no longer intact, the accident victim can no longer voluntarily control micturition. Therefore, bladder emptying in this individual will be governed entirely by the micturition reflex.

CLINICAL CONSIDERATION

(Question on p. 439.)

prostate enlargement

Chapter 14 Fluid and Acid–Base Balance

OBJECTIVE QUESTIONS

(Questions on p. 461.)

1. T
2. F
3. F
4. intracellular fluid
5. $[H_2CO_3]$, $[HCO_3^-]$
6. c
7. a, c
8. b, d
9. c
10. 1. c, 2. d, 3. b, 4. a

POINTS TO PONDER

(Questions on p. 461.)

1. The rate of urine formation increases when alcohol inhibits vasopressin secretion and the kidneys are unable to reabsorb water from the distal and collecting tubules. Because extra free water that normally would have been reabsorbed from the distal parts of the tubule is lost from the body in the urine, the body becomes dehydrated and the ECF osmolarity increases following alcohol consumption. That is, more fluid is lost

in the urine than is consumed in the alcoholic beverage as a result of alcohol's action on vasopressin. Thus, the imbibing person experiences a water deficit and still feels thirsty, despite the recent fluid consumption.

2. If a person loses 1500 ml of salt-rich sweat and drinks 1000 ml of water without replacing the salt during the same period, there will still be a volume deficit of 500 ml, and the body fluids will have become hypotonic (the remaining salt in the body will be diluted by the ingestion of 1000 ml of free H_2O). As a result, the hypothalamic osmoreceptors (the dominant input) will signal the vasopressin-secreting cells to *decrease* vasopressin secretion and thus increase urinary excretion of the extra free water that is making the body fluids too dilute. Simultaneously, the left atrial volume receptors will signal the vasopressin-secreting cells to *increase* vasopressin secretion to conserve water during urine formation and thus help relieve the volume deficit. These two conflicting inputs to the vasopressin-secreting cells are counterproductive. This is why it is important to replace both water and salt following heavy sweating or abnormal loss of other salt-rich fluids. If salt is replaced along with water intake, the ECF osmolarity remains close to normal, and the vasopressin-secreting cells receive signals only to increase vasopressin secretion to help restore the ECF volume to normal.

3. When a dextrose solution equal in concentration to that of normal body fluids is injected intravenously, the ECF volume is expanded but the ECF and ICF are still osmotically equal. Therefore, no net movement of water occurs between the ECF and the ICF. When the dextrose enters the cell and is metabolized, however, the ECF becomes hypotonic as this solute leaves the plasma. If the excess free water is not excreted in the urine rapidly enough, water will move into the cells by osmosis.

4. A buffer system cannot buffer itself. Consider, for example, the H_2CO_3:HCO_3^- buffer system in the situation in which the plasma [H^+] is elevated by CO_2 retention from a respiratory problem. This rise in CO_2 drives the reaction $CO_2 + H_2O \rightleftharpoons H_2CO_3 \rightleftharpoons H^+ + HCO_3^-$ to the right according to the law of mass action, elevating H^+. Thus, the increase in [H^+] occurs as a result of the reaction being driven to the *right* by an increase in CO_2, so the elevated [H^+] cannot drive the reaction to the *left* to buffer the increase in [H^+]. Only if the increase in [H^+] is brought about by some mechanism other than CO_2 accumulation can this buffer system be shifted to the CO_2 side of the equation and effectively reduce [H^+]. Likewise, in the opposite situation, the H_2CO_3:HCO_3^- buffer system cannot compensate for a reduction in [H^+] from a deficit of CO_2 by generating more H^+-yielding H_2CO_3 when the problem in the first place is a shortage of H_2CO_3-forming CO_2.

CLINICAL CONSIDERATION

(Question on p. 461.)

The resultant prolonged diarrhea will lead to dehydration and metabolic acidosis due to excessive loss in the feces of fluid and $NaHCO_3$, respectively, that normally would have been absorbed into the blood.

Compensatory measures for dehydration have included increased vasopressin secretion, resulting in increased water reabsorption by the distal and collecting tubules and a subsequent reduction in urine output. Simultaneously, fluid intake has been encouraged by increased thirst. The metabolic acidosis has been combated by removal of excess H^+ from the ECF by the HCO_3^- member of the H_2CO_3:HCO_3^- buffer system, by increased ventilation to reduce the amount of acid-forming CO_2 in the body fluids, and by the kidneys excreting extra H^+ and conserving HCO_3^-.

Chapter 15 The Digestive System

OBJECTIVE QUESTIONS

(Questions on p. 503.)

1. F
2. T
3. T
4. F
5. F
6. F
7. chyme
8. three
9. vitamin B_{12}, bile salts
10. bile salts
11. b
12. 1. c, 2. e, 3. b, 4. a, 5. f, 6. d
13. 1. c, 2. c, 3. d, 4. a, 5. e, 6. c, 7. a, 8. b, 9. c, 10. b, 11. d, 12. b

POINTS TO PONDER

(Questions on p. 504.)

1. Patients who have had their stomachs removed must eat small quantities of food frequently instead of consuming the typical three meals a day because they have lost the ability to store food in the stomach and meter it into the small intestine at an optimal rate. If a person without a stomach consumed a large meal that entered the small intestine all at once, the luminal contents would quickly become too hypertonic, as digestion of the large nutrient molecules into a multitude of small, osmotically active, absorbable units outpaced the more slowly acting process of absorption of these units. As a consequence of this increased luminal osmolarity, water would enter the small intestine lumen from the plasma by osmosis, resulting in circulatory disturbances, as well as intestinal distension. To prevent this "dumping syndrome" from occurring, the patient must "feed" the small intestine only small amounts of food at a time so that absorption of the digestive end products can keep pace with their rate of production. The person has to consciously take over metering the delivery of food into the small intestine because the stomach is no longer present to assume this responsibility.

2. The gut-associated lymphoid tissue launches an immune attack against any pathogenic (disease-causing) microorganisms that enter the readily acces-

sible digestive tract and escape destruction by salivary lysozyme or gastric HCl. This action defends against entry of these potential pathogens into the body proper. The large number of immune cells in this tissue is adaptive as a first line of defense against foreign invasion when considering that the surface area of the digestive tract lining represents the largest interface between the body proper and the external environment.

3. Defecation would be accomplished entirely by the defecation reflex in a patient paralyzed from the waist down because of lower spinal cord injury. Voluntary control of the external anal sphincter would be impossible because of interruption in the descending pathway between the primary motor cortex and the motor neuron supplying this sphincter.

4. When insufficient glucuronyl transferase is available in the neonate to conjugate all of the bilirubin produced during erythrocyte degradation with glucuronic acid, the extra unconjugated bilirubin cannot be excreted into the bile. Therefore, this extra bilirubin remains in the body, giving rise to mild jaundice in the newborn.

5. Removal of the stomach leads to pernicious anemia because of the resultant lack of intrinsic factor, which is necessary for absorption of vitamin B_{12}. Removal of the terminal ileum leads to pernicious anemia because this is the only site where vitamin B_{12} can be absorbed.

CLINICAL CONSIDERATION

(Question on p. 505.)

A person whose bile duct is blocked by a gallstone experiences a painful "gallbladder attack" after eating a high-fat meal because the ingested fat triggers the release of cholecystokinin (CCK), which stimulates gallbladder contraction. As the gallbladder contracts and bile is squeezed into the blocked bile duct, the duct becomes distended prior to the blockage. This distension is painful.

The feces are grayish white because no bilirubin-containing bile enters the digestive tract when the bile duct is blocked. Bilirubin, when acted on by bacterial enzymes, produces the brown color of feces, which are grayish white in its absence.

Chapter 16 Energy Balance and Temperature Regulation

OBJECTIVE QUESTIONS

(Questions on p. 522.)

1. F
2. F
3. F
4. F
5. T
6. T
7. T
8. T
9. arcuate nucleus
10. shivering
11. nonshivering thermogenesis
12. sweating
13. b
14. e
15. 1. b, 2. a, 3. c, 4. a, 5. d, 6. c, 7. b, 8. d, 9. c, 10. b

POINTS TO PONDER

(Questions on p. 523.)

1. Cholecystokinin (CCK), a hormone released from the duodenal mucosa during digestion of a meal, serves as a satiety signal. That is, it serves as a signal to stop eating when enough food has been consumed to meet the body's energy needs, even though the food is still in the digestive tract. Therefore, when drugs that inhibit CCK release are administered to experimental animals, the animals overeat because this satiety signal is not released.

2. Don't go on a "crash diet." Be sure to eat a nutritionally balanced diet that provides all essential nutrients, but reduce total caloric intake, especially by cutting down on high-fat foods. Spread out consumption of the food throughout the day instead of just eating several large meals. Avoid bedtime snacks. Burn more calories through a regular exercise program.

3. Engaging in heavy exercise on a hot day is dangerous because of problems arising from trying to eliminate the extra heat generated by the exercising muscles. First, there will be conflicting demands for distribution of the cardiac output—temperature-regulating mechanisms will trigger skin vasodilation to promote heat loss from the skin surface, whereas metabolic changes within the exercising muscles will induce local vasodilation in the muscles to match the increased metabolic needs with increased blood flow. Further exacerbating the problem of conflicting demands for blood flow is the loss of effective circulating plasma volume resulting from the loss of a large volume of fluid through another important cooling mechanism, sweating. Therefore, it is difficult to maintain an effective plasma volume and blood pressure and simultaneously keep the body from overheating when engaging in heavy exercise in the heat, so heat exhaustion is likely to ensue.

4. When a person is soaking in a hot bath, loss of heat by radiation, conduction, convection, and evaporation is limited to the small surface area of the body exposed to the cooler air. Heat is being gained by conduction at the larger skin surface area exposed to the hotter water.

5. The thermoconforming fish would not run a fever when it has a systemic infection because it has no mechanisms for regulating internal heat production or for controlling heat exchange with its environment. The fish's body temperature varies capriciously with the external environment whether it has a systemic infection or not. It cannot maintain body temperature at a "normal" set point or an elevated set point (i.e., a fever).

(Question on p. 523.)

Cooled tissues need less nourishment than they do at normal body temperature because of their pronounced reduction in metabolic activity. The lower O_2 need of cooled tissues accounts for the occasional survival of drowning victims who have been submerged in icy water considerably longer than they could normally survive without O_2.

Chapter 17 The Endocrine System

OBJECTIVE QUESTIONS

(Questions on p. 574.)

1. F
2. T
3. T
4. T
5. T
6. F
7. tropic
8. suprachiasmatic nucleus
9. epiphyseal plate
10. colloid, thyroglobulin
11. glycogenesis, glycogenolysis, gluconeogenesis
12. bone, kidneys, digestive tract
13. osteoblasts, osteoclasts, osteocytes
14. 1. c, 2. b, 3. b, 4. a, 5. a, 6. c, 7. b
15. 1. glucose, 2. glycogen, 3. free fatty acids, 4. triglycerides, 5. amino acids, 6. body proteins

POINTS TO PONDER

(Questions on p. 575.)

1. Males with testicular feminization syndrome would be unusually tall because of the inability of testosterone to promote closure of the epiphyseal plates of the long bones in the absence of testosterone receptors.
2. Hormonal replacement therapy following pituitary gland removal should include thyroid hormone (the thyroid gland will not produce sufficient thyroid hormone in the absence of TSH) and glucocorticoid (because of the absence of ACTH), especially in stress situations. If indicated, male or female sex hormones can be replaced, even though these hormones are not essential for survival. For example, testosterone in males plays an important role in libido. Growth hormone and prolactin need not be replaced, because their absence will produce no serious consequences in this individual. Vasopressin may have to be replaced if the blood picks up insufficient quantities of this hormone at the hypothalamus in the absence of the posterior pituitary.
3. Because the soil in the midwestern United States is iodine poor, this region was once considered an endemic goiter belt because of the propensity of its residents to develop goiters as a result of consuming too little iodine to produce sufficient thyroid hormone. *Endemic* means peculiar to a particular locality. The Midwest is no longer an endemic goiter belt even though the soil is still iodine poor, because individuals living in this region obtain iodine from iodine-supplemented nutrients, such as iodinated salt, and from seafood and other naturally iodine-rich foods shipped from coastal regions.
4. An infection elicits the stress response, which brings about increased secretion of cortisol and epinephrine, both of which increase the blood glucose level. This can become a problem in managing the blood glucose level of a diabetic patient. When the blood glucose is elevated too high, the patient can reduce it by injecting additional insulin or, preferably, by reducing carbohydrate intake, exercising to use up some of the extra blood glucose, or both. In a normal individual, the check-and-balance system between insulin and other hormones that oppose insulin's actions helps maintain the blood glucose within reasonable limits during the stress response.
5. The presence of Chvostek's sign results from increased neuromuscular excitability caused by moderate hyposecretion of parathyroid hormone.

(Question on p. 575.)

"Diabetes of bearded ladies" is descriptive of both excess cortisol and excess adrenal androgen secretion. Excess cortisol secretion causes hyperglycemia and glucosuria. Glucosuria promotes osmotic diuresis, which leads to dehydration and a compensatory increased sensation of thirst. All these symptoms—hyperglycemia, glucosuria, polyuria, and polydipsia—mimic diabetes mellitus. Excess adrenal androgen secretion in females promotes masculinizing characteristics, such as beard growth. Simultaneous hypersecretion of both cortisol and adrenal androgen most likely occurs secondary to excess CRH or ACTH secretion, because ACTH stimulates both cortisol and androgen production by the adrenal cortex.

Chapter 18 The Reproductive System

OBJECTIVE QUESTIONS

(Questions on p. 623.)

1. T
2. T
3. T
4. F
5. T
6. F
7. T
8. seminiferous tubules, FSH, testosterone
9. corpus luteum of pregnancy, placenta
10. human chorionic gonadotropin
11. c

12. e
13. 1. c, 2. a, 3. b, 4. c, 5. a, 6. a, 7. c, 8. b, 9. e
14. 1. a, 2. c, 3. b, 4. a, 5. a, 6. b

POINTS TO PONDER

(Questions on p. 624.)

1. The anterior pituitary responds only to the normal pulsatile pattern of GnRH and does not secrete gonado-tropins in response to continuous exposure to GnRH. In the absence of FSH and LH secretion, ovulation and other events of the ovarian cycle do not ensue, so continuous GnRH administration may find use as a contraceptive technique.

2. Testosterone hypersecretion in a young boy causes premature closure of the epiphyseal plates so that he stops growing before he reaches his genetic potential for height. The child would also display signs of preco-cious pseudopuberty, characterized by premature development of secondary sexual characteristics, such as deep voice, beard, enlarged penis, and sex drive.

3. A potentially troublesome side effect of drugs that inhibit sympathetic nervous system activity as part of the treatment for high blood pressure is males' inability to carry out the sex act. Both divisions of the autonomic nervous system are required for the male sex act. Parasympathetic activity is essential for accomplishing erection, and sympathetic activity is important for ejaculation.

4. Posterior pituitary extract contains an abundance of stored oxytocin, which can be administered to induce or facilitate labor by increasing uterine contractility. Exogenous oxytocin is most successful in inducing labor if the woman is near term, presumably because of the increasing concentration of myometrial oxytocin receptors at that time.

5. GnRH or FSH and LH are not effective in treating the symptoms of menopause because the ovaries are no longer responsive to the gonadotropins. Thus, treat-ment with these hormones would not cause estrogen and progesterone secretion. In fact, GnRH, FSH, and LH levels are already elevated in postmenopausal women because of lack of negative feedback by the ovarian hormones.

CLINICAL CONSIDERATION

(Question on p. 624.)

The first warning of a tubal pregnancy is pain caused by stretching of the oviduct by the growing embryo. A tubal pregnancy must be surgically terminated because the ovi-duct cannot expand as the uterus does to accommodate the growing embryo. If not removed, the enlarging embryo will rupture the oviduct, causing possibly lethal hemorrhage.

Glossary

A band One of the dark bands that alternate with light (I) bands to create a striated appearance in a skeletal or cardiac muscle fiber when these fibers are viewed with a light microscope

absorption The transfer of digested nutrients and ingested liquids from the digestive tract lumen into the blood or lymph

absorptive state The metabolic state following a meal when nutrients are being absorbed and stored; fed state

accessory digestive organs Exocrine organs outside the wall of the digestive tract that empty their secretions through ducts into the digestive tract lumen

accessory sex glands Glands that empty their secretions into the reproductive tract

accommodation The ability to adjust the strength of the lens in the eye so that both near and far sources can be focused on the retina

acetylcholine (ACh) (as´-uh-teal-KŌ –lēn) The neurotransmitter released from all autonomic preganglionic fibers, parasympathetic postganglionic fibers, and motor neurons

acetylcholinesterase (AChE) (as´-uh-teal-kō-luh-NES-tuh-rās) An enzyme present in the motor end-plate membrane of a skeletal muscle fiber that inactivates acetylcholine

ACh See *acetylcholine*

AChE See *acetylcholinesterase*

acid A hydrogen-containing substance that yields a free hydrogen ion and anion on dissociation

acidosis (as-i-DŌ-sus) Blood pH of less than 7.35

acini (ĀS-i-nī) The secretory component of saclike exocrine glands, such as digestive enzyme–producing pancreatic glands or milk-producing mammary glands

acquired immune responses Responses that are selectively targeted against particular foreign material to which the body has previously been exposed; see also *antibody-mediated immunity* and *cell-mediated immunity*

ACTH See *adrenocorticotropic hormone*

actin The contractile protein forming the backbone of the thin filaments in muscle fibers

action potential A brief, rapid, large change in membrane potential that serves as a long-distance electrical signal in an excitable cell

active expiration Emptying of the lungs more completely than when at rest by contracting the expiratory muscles; also called *forced expiration*

active force A force that requires expenditure of cellular energy (ATP) in the transport of a substance across the plasma membrane

active reabsorption When any one of the five steps in the transepithelial transport of a substance reabsorbed across the kidney tubules requires energy expenditure

active transport Active carrier-mediated transport involving transport of a substance against its concentration gradient across the plasma membrane

acuity Discriminative ability; the ability to discern between two different points of stimulation

adaptation A reduction in receptor potential despite sustained stimulation of the same magnitude

adenosine diphosphate (ADP) (uh-DEN-uh-sēn) The two-phosphate product formed from the splitting of ATP to yield energy for the cell's use

adenosine triphosphate (ATP) The body's common energy "currency," which consists of an adenosine with three phosphate groups attached; splitting of the high-energy, terminal phosphate bond provides energy to power cellular activities

adenylyl cyclase (ah-DEN-il-il sī-klās) The membrane-bound enzyme activated by a G protein intermediary in response to binding of an extracellular messenger with a surface membrane receptor that, in turn, activates cyclic AMP, an intracellular second messenger

adequate stimulus The type of stimulus to which a specific receptor type responds, such as a photoreceptor responding to light

ADH See *vasopressin*

adipocytes Fat cells in adipose tissue; store triglyceride fat and secrete hormones termed *adipokines*

adipokines Hormones secreted by adipose tissue that play important roles in energy balance and metabolism

adipose tissue The tissue specialized for storage of triglyceride fat; found under the skin in the hypodermis

ADP See *adenosine diphosphate*

adrenal cortex (uh-DRĚ-nul) The outer portion of the adrenal gland; secretes three classes of steroid hormones: glucocorticoids, mineralocorticoids, and sex hormones

adrenal medulla (muh-DUL-uh) The inner portion of the adrenal gland; secretes the hormones epinephrine and norepinephrine into the blood in response to sympathetic stimulation

adrenergic fibers (ad´-ruh-NUR-jik) Nerve fibers that release norepinephrine as their neurotransmitter

adrenocorticotropic hormone (ACTH) (ad-rē´-nō-kor´-tuh-kō-TRŌP-ik) An anterior pituitary hormone that stimulates cortisol secretion by the adrenal cortex and promotes growth of the adrenal cortex

aerobic Referring to a condition in which oxygen is available

aerobic exercise Exercise that can be supported by ATP formation accomplished by oxidative phosphorylation because adequate O_2 is available to support the muscle's modest energy demands; also called *endurance-type exercise*

afferent arteriole (AF-er-ent ar-TIR-ē-ōl) The vessel that carries blood into the glomerulus of the kidney's nephron

afferent division The portion of the peripheral nervous system that carries information from the periphery to the central nervous system

afferent neuron Neuron that possesses a sensory receptor at its peripheral ending and carries information to the central nervous system

after hyperpolarization (hī´-pur-pō-luh-ruh-ZĀ-shun) A slight, transient hyperpolarization that sometimes occurs at the end of an action potential

agonist A substance that binds to a neurotransmitter's receptors and mimics the neurotransmitter's response

agranulocytes (ā-GRAN-yuh-lō-sīts´) Leukocytes that do not contain granules, including lymphocytes and monocytes

albumin (al-BEW-min) The smallest and most abundant plasma proteins; binds and transports many water-insoluble substances in the blood; contributes extensively to plasma-colloid osmotic pressure

aldosterone (al-dō-steer-OWN) or (al-DOS-tuh-rōn) The adrenocortical hormone that stimulates Na^+ reabsorption by the distal and collecting tubules of the kidney's nephron during urine formation

alkalosis (al´-kuh-LŌ-sus) Blood pH of greater than 7.45

allergy Acquisition of an inappropriate specific immune reactivity to a normally harmless environmental substance

all-or-none law An excitable membrane either responds to a stimulus with a maximal action potential that spreads nondecrementally throughout the membrane or does not respond with an action potential at all

alpha (α) cells The endocrine pancreatic cells that secrete the hormone glucagon

alpha motor neuron A motor neuron that innervates ordinary skeletal muscle fibers

alveolar surface tension (al-VĚ-ō-lur) The surface tension of the fluid lining the alveoli in the lungs; see *surface tension*

alveolar ventilation The volume of air exchanged between the atmosphere and alveoli per minute; alveolar ventilation = (tidal volume − dead space volume) × respiratory rate

alveoli (al-VĚ-ō-lī) The air sacs across which O_2 and CO_2 are exchanged between the blood and air in the lungs

amines (AH-mēnz) Hormones derived from the amino acid tyrosine, including thyroid hormone and catecholamines

amoeboid movement (uh-MĚ-boid) "Crawling" movement of white blood cells, similar to the means by which amoebas move

anabolism (ah-NAB-ō-li-zum) The buildup, or synthesis, of larger organic molecules from small organic molecular subunits

anaerobic (an´-uh-RŌ-bik) Referring to a condition in which oxygen is not present

anaerobic exercise High-intensity exercise that can be supported by ATP formation accomplished by anaerobic glycolysis for brief periods of time when O_2 delivery to a muscle is inadequate to support oxidative phosphorylation

analgesic (an-al-JĒ-zic) Pain relieving

anatomy The study of body structure

androgen A masculinizing "male" sex hormone; includes testosterone from the testes and dehydro-epiandrosterone from the adrenal cortex

anemia A reduction below normal in O_2-carrying capacity of the blood

anion (AN-ī-on) Negatively charged ion that has gained one or more electrons in its outer shell

ANP See *atrial natriuretic peptide*

antagonism Actions opposing each other; in the case of hormones, when one hormone causes the loss of another hormone's receptors, reducing the effectiveness of the second hormone

antagonist A substance that blocks a neurotransmitter's receptor, thus preventing the neurotransmitter from binding and producing a response

anterior pituitary The glandular portion of the pituitary that synthesizes, stores, and secretes growth hormone, TSH, ACTH, FSH, LH, and prolactin

antibody An immunoglobulin produced by a specific activated B lymphocyte (plasma cell) against a particular antigen; binds with the specific antigen against which it is produced and promotes the antigenic invader's destruction by augmenting nonspecific immune responses already initiated against the antigen

antibody-mediated immunity A specific immune response accomplished by antibody production by B cells

antidiuretic hormone (ADH) (an´-ti-dī´-yū-RET-ik) See *vasopressin*

antigen A large, complex molecule that triggers a specific immune response against itself when it gains entry into the body

antioxidant A substance that helps inactivate biologically damaging free radicals

antiport The form of secondary active transport in which the driving ion and transported solute move in opposite directions across the plasma membrane; also called *countertransport* or *exchange*

antrum (of ovary) The fluid-filled cavity formed within a developing ovarian follicle

antrum (of stomach) The lower portion of the stomach

aorta (a-OR-tah) The large vessel that carries blood from the left ventricle

aortic valve A one-way valve that permits the flow of blood from the left ventricle into the aorta during ventricular emptying but prevents the backflow of blood from the aorta into the left ventricle during ventricular relaxation

apoptosis (ā-pop-TŌ-sis) Programmed cell death; deliberate self-destruction of a cell.

aquaporin Water channel

aqueous humor (Ā-kwē-us) The clear, watery fluid in the anterior chamber of the eye; provides nourishment for the cornea and lens

arcuate nucleus (ARE-kyou-it´) The subcortical brain region housing neurons that secrete appetite-enhancing neuropeptide Y and those that secrete appetite-suppressing melanocortins

aromatase An enzyme that converts testosterone to estrogen outside of the testes

arterioles (ar-TIR-ē-ōlz) The highly muscular, high-resistance vessels that branch from arteries, the caliber of which can be changed to regulate the amount of blood distributed to the various tissues

artery A vessel that carries blood away from the heart

ascending tract A bundle of nerve fibers of similar function that travels up the spinal cord to transmit signals derived from afferent input to the brain

astrocyte A type of glial cell in the brain; major functions include holding the neurons together in proper spatial relationship, inducing the brain capillaries to form tight junctions important in the blood–brain barrier, and enhancing synaptic activity

atmospheric pressure The pressure exerted by the weight of the air in the atmosphere on objects on Earth's surface; equals 760 mm Hg at sea level

ATP See *adenosine triphosphate*

ATPase An enzyme that can split ATP

ATP synthase The mitochondrial enzyme that catalyzes the synthesis of ATP from ADP and inorganic phosphate

atrial natriuretic peptide (ANP) (Ā-trē-al NĀ-tree-ur-eh´tik) A peptide hormone released from the cardiac atria that promotes urinary loss of Na^+

atrioventricular (AV) node (ā´-trē-ō-ven-TRIK-yuh-lur) A small bundle of specialized cardiac cells at the junction of the atria and ventricles that is the only site of electrical contact between the atria and ventricles

atrioventricular (AV) valve A one-way valve that permits the flow of blood from the atrium to the ventricle during filling of the heart but prevents the backflow of blood from the ventricle to the atrium during emptying of the heart

atrium (atria, plural) (Ā-tree-um) An upper chamber of the heart that receives blood from the veins and transfers it to the ventricle

atrophy (AH-truh-fē) Decrease in mass of an organ

autoimmune disease Disease characterized by erroneous production of antibodies against one of the body's own tissues

autonomic nervous system The portion of the efferent division of the peripheral nervous system that innervates smooth and cardiac muscle and exocrine glands; subdivided into the sympathetic and the parasympathetic nervous systems

autoregulation The ability of an organ to adjust its own rate of blood flow despite changes in the driving mean arterial blood pressure

autorhythmicity The ability of an excitable cell to rhythmically initiate its own action potentials

AV nodal delay The delay in impulse transmission between the atria and ventricles at the AV node, which allows enough time for the atria to become completely depolarized and contract, emptying their contents into the ventricles, before ventricular depolarization and contraction occur

AV valve See *atrioventricular valve*

axon A single, elongated tubular extension of a neuron that conducts action potentials away from the cell body; also known as a *nerve fiber*

axon hillock The first portion of a neuronal axon plus the region of the cell body from which the axon leaves; the site of action-potential initiation in most neurons

axon terminals The branched endings of a neuronal axon, which release a neurotransmitter that influences target cells in close association with the axon terminals

balance concept The balance between input of a substance through ingestion or metabolic production and its output through excretion or metabolic consumption

baroreceptor reflex An autonomically mediated reflex response that influences the heart and blood vessels to oppose a change in mean arterial blood pressure

baroreceptors Receptors located within the circulatory system that monitor blood pressure

basal ganglia See *basal nuclei*

basal metabolic rate (BĀ-sul) The minimal waking rate of internal energy expenditure; the body's "idling speed"

basal nuclei Several masses of gray matter located deep within the white matter of the cerebrum of the brain; play an important inhibitory role in motor control

base A substance that can combine with a free hydrogen ion and remove it from solution

basic electrical rhythm (BER) Self-induced electrical activity of the digestive-tract smooth muscle

basilar membrane (BAS-ih-lar) The membrane that forms the floor of the middle compartment of the cochlea and bears the organ of Corti, the sense organ for hearing

basophils (BĀY-sō-fills) White blood cells that synthesize, store, and release histamine, which is important in allergic responses, and heparin, which hastens the removal of fat particles from the blood

BER See *basic electrical rhythm*

beta (β) cells The endocrine pancreatic cells that secrete the hormone insulin

bicarbonate (HCO_3^-) The anion resulting from dissociation of carbonic acid, H_2CO_3

bile An alkaline solution containing bile salts and bilirubin secreted by the liver, stored in the gallbladder, and emptied into the small intestine lumen

bile salts Cholesterol derivatives secreted in the bile that facilitate fat digestion through their detergent action and facilitate fat absorption through their micellar formation

biliary system (BIL-ē-air´-ē) The bile-producing system, consisting of the liver, gallbladder, and associated ducts

bilirubin (bill-eh-RŪ-bin) A bile pigment, which is a waste product derived from the degradation of hemoglobin during the breakdown of old red blood cells

blastocyst The developmental stage of the fertilized ovum by the time it is ready to implant; consists of a single-layered sphere of cells encircling a fluid-filled cavity

blood–brain barrier (BBB) Special structural and functional features of the brain capillaries that limit access of materials from the blood into the brain tissue

B lymphocytes (B cells) White blood cells that produce antibodies against specific targets to which they have been exposed

body of the stomach The main, or middle, part of the stomach

body system A collection of organs that perform related functions and interact to accomplish a common activity that is essential for survival of the whole body; for example, the digestive system

bone marrow The soft, highly cellular tissue that fills the internal cavities of bones and is the source of most blood cells

Bowman's capsule The beginning of the tubular component of the kidney's nephron that cups around the glomerulus and collects the glomerular filtrate as it is formed

Boyle's law (boils) At any constant temperature, the pressure exerted by a gas varies inversely with the volume of the gas

brain stem The portion of the brain that is continuous with the spinal cord, serves as an integrating link between the spinal cord and higher brain levels, and controls many life-sustaining processes, such as breathing, circulation, and digestion

bronchioles (BRONG-kē-ōlz) The small, branching airways within the lungs

bronchoconstriction Narrowing of the respiratory airways

bronchodilation Widening of the respiratory airways

brush border The collection of microvilli projecting from the luminal border of epithelial cells lining the digestive tract and kidney tubules

buffer See *chemical buffer system*

bulbourethral glands (bul-bō-you-RĒTH-ral) Male accessory sex glands that secrete mucus for lubrication

bulk flow Movement in bulk of a protein-free plasma across the capillary walls between the blood and surrounding interstitial fluid; encompasses ultrafiltration and reabsorption

bundle of His (hiss) A tract of specialized cardiac cells that rapidly transmits an action potential down the interventricular septum of the heart

calcitonin (kal´-suh-TŌ-nun) A hormone secreted by the thyroid C cells that lowers plasma Ca^{2+} levels

calcium-induced calcium release When in cardiac and smooth muscle cells the excitation-induced entry of a small amount of Ca^{2+} from the ECF through voltage-gated surface membrane receptors triggers the opening of Ca^{2+}-release channels in the sarcoplasmic reticulum, causing a much larger release of Ca^{2+} into the cytosol from this intracellular store

calmodulin (kal´-MA-jew-lin) An intracellular Ca^{2+} binding protein that, on activation by Ca^{2+}, induces a change in structure and function of another intracellular protein; especially important in smooth-muscle excitation–contraction coupling

cAMP See *cyclic adenosine monophosphate*

CAMs See *cell adhesion molecules*

capillaries The thin-walled, pore-lined smallest of blood vessels, across which exchange between the blood and surrounding tissues takes place

carbonic anhydrase (an-HĪ-drās) The enzyme found in erythrocytes, kidney tubular cells, and a few other specialized cells that catalyzes the conversion of CO_2 and H_2O into H^+ and HCO_3^-

cardiac cycle One period of systole and diastole

cardiac muscle The specialized muscle found only in the heart

cardiac output (CO) The volume of blood pumped by each ventricle each minute; equals stroke volume times heart rate

cardiovascular control center The integrating center located in the medulla of the brain stem that controls mean arterial blood pressure

carrier-mediated transport Transport of a substance across the plasma membrane facilitated by a carrier molecule

carrier molecules Membrane proteins that, by undergoing reversible changes in shape so that specific binding sites are alternately exposed at either side of the membrane, can bind with and transfer particular substances unable to cross the plasma membrane on their own

cascade A series of sequential reactions that culminates in a final product, such as a clot

catabolism (kuh-TAB-ō-li-zum) The breakdown, or degradation, of large, energy-rich molecules within cells

catecholamines (kat´-uh-KŌ-luh-means) Amine hormones derived from tyrosine and secreted largely by the adrenal medulla

cations (KAT-ī-onz) Positively charged ions that have lost one or more electrons from their outer shell

C cells The thyroid cells that secrete calcitonin

CCK See *cholecystokinin*

cell The smallest unit capable of carrying out the processes associated with life; the basic unit of both structure and function in living organisms

cell adhesion molecules (CAMs) Proteins that protrude from the surface of the plasma membrane and form loops or other appendages that the cells use to grip one another and the surrounding connective tissue fibers

cell body The portion of a neuron that houses the nucleus and organelles

cell-mediated immunity A specific immune response accomplished by activated T lymphocytes, which directly attack unwanted cells

cellular respiration The entire series of chemical reactions involving the intracellular breakdown of nutrient-rich molecules to yield energy, using O_2 and producing CO_2 in the process

center A functional collection of cell bodies within the central nervous system

central chemoreceptors (kē-mō-rē-SEP-turz) Receptors located in the medulla near the respiratory center that respond to changes in ECF H^+ concentration resulting from changes in arterial P_{CO_2} and adjust respiration accordingly

central lacteal (LAK-tē-ul) The initial lymphatic vessel that supplies each of the small-intestinal villi

central nervous system (CNS) The brain and spinal cord

central sulcus (SUL-kus) A deep infolding of the brain surface that runs roughly down the middle of the lateral surface of each cerebral hemisphere and separates the parietal and frontal lobes

centrioles (SEN-trē-ōlz) A pair of short, cylindrical structures within a cell that form the mitotic spindle during cell division

cerebellum (ser´-uh-BEL-um) The part of the brain attached at the rear of the brain stem and concerned with maintaining proper position of the body in space and subconscious coordination of motor activity

cerebral cortex The outer shell of gray matter in the cerebrum; site of initiation of all voluntary motor output and final perceptual processing of all sensory input as well as integration of most higher neural activity

cerebral hemispheres The cerebrum's two halves, which are connected by a thick band of neuronal axons

cerebrospinal fluid (CSF) (ser´-uh-brō-SPĪ-nul) or (sah-REE-brō-SPĪ-nul) A special cushioning fluid that is produced by, surrounds, and flows through the central nervous system

cerebrum (SER-uh-brum) or (sah-REE-brum) The division of the brain that consists of the basal nuclei and cerebral cortex

channels Small, water-filled passageways through the plasma membrane; formed by membrane proteins that span the membrane and provide highly selective passage for small water-soluble substances such as ions

chemical bonds The forces holding atoms together

chemical buffer system A mixture in a solution of two or more chemical compounds that minimize pH changes when either an acid or a base is added to or removed from the solution

chemically gated channels Channels in the plasma membrane that open or close in response to the binding of a specific chemical messenger with a membrane receptor site that is in close association with the channel

chemical mediator A chemical that is secreted by a cell and that influences an activity outside the cell

chemiosmosis (kē-ma-OS-mō-sis) ATP production in mitochondria catalyzed by ATP synthase, which is activated by flow of H^+ down a concentration gradient established by the electron transport system

chemoreceptor (kē-mō-rē-sep´-tur) A sensory receptor sensitive to specific chemicals

chemotaxin (kē-mō-TAK-sin) A chemical released at an inflammatory site that attracts phagocytes to the area

chief cells The cells in the gastric pits that secrete pepsinogen

cholecystokinin (CCK) (kō´-luh-sis-tuh-kī-nun) A hormone released from the duodenal mucosa primarily in response to the presence of fat; inhibits gastric motility and secretion, stimulates pancreatic enzyme secretion, stimulates gallbladder contraction, and acts as a satiety signal

cholesterol A type of fat molecule that serves as a precursor for steroid hormones and bile salts and is a stabilizing component of the plasma membrane

cholinergic fibers (kō´-lin-ER-jik) Nerve fibers that release acetylcholine as their neurotransmitter

chromaffin granules The granules that store catecholamines in adrenomedullary cells

chyme (kīm) A thick liquid mixture of food and digestive juices

cilia (SILL-ē-ah) Motile, hairlike protrusions from the surface of cells lining the respiratory airways and the oviducts

ciliary body The portion of the eye that produces aqueous humor and contains the ciliary muscle

ciliary muscle A circular ring of smooth muscle within the eye whose contraction increases the strength of the lens to accommodate for near vision

circadian rhythm (sir-KĀ-dē-un) Repetitive oscillations in the set point of various body activities, such as hormone levels and body temperature, that are very regular and have a frequency of one cycle every 24 hours, usually linked to light–dark cycles; diurnal rhythm; biological rhythm

circulatory shock When mean arterial blood pressure falls so low that adequate blood flow to the tissues can no longer be maintained

citric acid cycle A cyclic series of biochemical reactions that processes the intermediate breakdown products of nutrient molecules, generating carbon dioxide and preparing hydrogen carrier molecules for entry into the high-energy-yielding electron transport system

CNS See *central nervous system*

cochlea (KOK-lē-uh) The snail-shaped portion of the inner ear that houses the receptors for sound

collecting tubule The last portion of tubule in the kidney's nephron that empties into the renal pelvis

colloid (KOL-oid) The thyroglobulin-containing substance enclosed within the thyroid follicles

colloid osmotic pressure The osmotic force across the capillary wall resulting from the uneven colloidal dispersion of plasma proteins between the blood and interstitial fluid

competition When several closely related substances compete for the same carrier binding sites

complement system A collection of plasma proteins that are activated in cascade fashion on exposure to invading microorganisms, ultimately producing a membrane attack complex that destroys the invaders

compliance The distensibility of a hollow, elastic structure, such as a blood vessel or the lungs; a measure of how easily the structure can be stretched

concave surface Curved in, as a surface of a lens that diverges light rays

concentration gradient A difference in concentration of a particular substance between two adjacent areas

conduction The transfer of heat between objects of differing temperature that are in direct contact

cones The eye's photoreceptors used for color vision in the light

connective tissue Tissue that serves to connect, support, and anchor various body parts; distinguished by relatively few cells dispersed within an abundance of extracellular material

contiguous conduction The means by which an action potential is propagated throughout a non-myelinated nerve fiber; local current flow between an active and adjacent inactive area brings the inactive area to threshold, triggering an action potential in a previously inactive area

contractility (of heart) The strength of contraction of the heart at any given end-diastolic volume

control center See *integrator*

controlled variable Some factor that can vary but is held within a narrow range by a control system

convection Transfer of heat energy by air or water currents

convergence The converging of many presynaptic terminals from thousands of other neurons on a single neuronal cell body and its dendrites so that activity in the single neuron is influenced by the activity of many other neurons

convex surface Curved out, as a surface in a lens that converges light rays

core temperature The temperature within the inner core of the body (abdominal and thoracic organs, central nervous system, and skeletal muscles) that is homeostatically maintained at about 100°F

cornea (KOR-nē-ah) The clear, anteriormost outer layer of the eye through which light rays pass to the interior of the eye

coronary circulation The blood vessels that supply the heart muscle

corpus callosum (ka-LŌ-sum) The thick band of nerve fibers that connects the two cerebral hemispheres structurally and functionally

corpus luteum (LOO-tē-um) The ovarian structure that develops from a ruptured follicle after ovulation

corticotropes Anterior pituitary cells that secrete adrenocorticotropic hormone

cortisol (KORT-uh-sol) The adrenocortical hormone that plays an important role in carbohydrate, protein, and fat metabolism and helps the body resist stress

cotransport See *symport*

countercurrent multiplication The means by which long loops of Henle establish the vertical osmotic gradient in the renal medulla, making it possible to put out urine of variable concentration depending on the body's needs

countertransport See *antiport*

cranial nerves The 12 pairs of peripheral nerves, the majority of which arise from the brain stem

cross bridges The myosin molecules' globular heads that protrude from a thick filament within a muscle fiber and interact with the actin molecules in the thin filaments to bring about shortening of the muscle fiber during contraction

CSF See *cerebrospinal fluid*

current The flow of electrical charge, such as by movement of positive charges toward a more negatively charged area

cyclic adenosine monophosphate (cyclic AMP or cAMP) An intracellular second messenger derived from ATP

cyclic AMP See *cyclic adenosine monophosphate*

cytokines All chemicals other than antibodies that are secreted by lymphocytes

cytoplasm (SĪ-tō-plaz´-um) The portion of the cell interior not occupied by the nucleus

cytoskeleton The complex intracellular protein network that acts as the "bone and muscle" of the cell

cytosol (SĪ-tuh-sol´) The semiliquid portion of the cytoplasm not occupied by organelles

cytotoxic T cells (sī-tō-TOK-sik) The population of T cells that destroys host cells bearing foreign antigen, such as body cells invaded by viruses or cancer cells

dead-space volume The volume of air that occupies the respiratory airways as air is moved in and out and that is not available to participate in exchange of O_2 and CO_2 between the alveoli and atmosphere

dehydration A water deficit in the body

dehydroepiandrosterone (DHEA) (dē-HĪ-drō-epi-and-ro-steer-own) The androgen secreted by the adrenal cortex in both sexes

dendrites Projections from the surface of a neuron's cell body that carry signals toward the cell body

deoxyribonucleic acid (DNA) (dē-OK-sē-rī-bō-new-klā-ik) The cell's genetic material, which is found within the nucleus and which provides codes for protein synthesis and serves as a blueprint for cell replication

depolarization (de´-pō-luh-ruh-ZĀ-shun) A reduction in membrane potential from resting potential; movement of the potential from resting toward 0 mV

dermis The connective tissue layer that lies under the epidermis in the skin; contains the skin's blood vessels and nerves

descending tract A bundle of nerve fibers of similar function that travels down the spinal cord to relay messages from the brain to efferent neurons

desmosome (dez´-muh-sōm) An adhering junction between two adjacent but nontouching cells formed by the extension of filaments between the cells' plasma membranes; most abundant in tissues that are subject to considerable stretching

DHEA See *dehydroepiandrosterone*

diaphragm (DIE-uh-fram) A dome-shaped sheet of skeletal muscle that forms the floor of the thoracic cavity; the major inspiratory muscle

diastole (dī-AS-tō-lē) The period of cardiac relaxation and filling

diencephalon (dī´-un-SEF-uh-lan) The division of the brain that consists of the thalamus and hypothalamus

differentiation The process of each type of cell becoming specialized during development of a multicellular organism to carry out a particular function

diffusion Random collisions and intermingling of molecules as a result of their continuous thermally induced random motion

digestion The process by which the structurally complex foodstuffs of the diet are broken down into smaller absorbable units by the enzymes produced within the digestive system

diploid number (DIP-loid) A complete set of 46 chromosomes (23 pairs), as found in all human somatic cells

discriminative ability See *acuity*

distal tubule A highly convoluted tubule that extends between the loop of Henle and the collecting duct in the kidney's nephron

diurnal rhythm (dī-URN´-ul) Repetitive oscillations in hormone levels that are very regular and have a frequency of one cycle every 24 hours, usually linked to the light–dark cycle; circadian rhythm; biological rhythm

divergence The diverging, or branching, of a neuron's axon terminals so that activity in this single neuron influences the many other cells with which its terminals synapse

DNA See *deoxyribonucleic acid*

dorsal root ganglion A cluster of afferent neuronal cell bodies located adjacent to the spinal cord

down regulation A reduction in the number of receptors for (and thereby the target cell's sensitivity to) a particular hormone as a direct result of the effect that an elevated level of the hormone has on its own receptors

dynein (DĪ-neen) The molecular motor that "walks" along microtubular "highways" toward the cell center, such as in transporting debris from the axon terminal to the cell body for destruction by lysosomes

ECG See *electrocardiogram*

ECM See *extracellular matrix*

edema (i-DĒ-muh) Swelling of tissues as a result of excess interstitial fluid

EDV See *end-diastolic volume*

EEG See *electroencephalogram*

effector The component of a control system that accomplishes the output commanded by the integrator

effector organs The muscles or glands innervated by the nervous system that carry out the nervous system's orders to bring about a desired effect, such as a particular movement or secretion

efferent division (EF-er-ent) The portion of the peripheral nervous system that carries instructions from the central nervous system to effector organs

efferent neuron Neuron that carries information from the central nervous system to an effector organ

efflux (Ē-flux) Movement out of the cell

eicosanoids (ī-KŌ-sa-noydz) Derivatives of arachidonic acid in the phospholipid tails of the plasma membrane including the prostaglandins, prostacyclins, thromboxanes, and leukotrienes, that act as paracrines near their site of production throughout the body

elastic recoil Rebound of the lungs after having been stretched

electrical gradient A difference in charge between two adjacent areas

electrocardiogram (ECG) The graphic record of the electrical activity that reaches the surface of the body as a result of cardiac depolarization and repolarization

electrochemical gradient The simultaneous existence of an electrical gradient and concentration (chemical) gradient for a particular ion

electroencephalogram (EEG) (i-lek´-trō-in-SEF-uh-luh-gram´) A graphic record of the collective postsynaptic potential activity in the cell bodies and dendrites located in the cortical layers of the brain under a recording electrode

electrolytes Solutes that form ions in solution and conduct electricity

electron transport system The series of electron carriers in the mitochondrial inner membrane that transfer electrons from higher to lower energy levels, with the released energy being used to establish the H^+ concentration gradient in the mitochondria that powers ATP synthesis

embolus (EM-bō-lus) A freely floating clot

embryonic stem cells (ESCs) Undifferentiated cells resulting from the early divisions of a fertilized egg that ultimately give rise to all the mature, specialized cells of the body while at the same time renewing themselves

end-diastolic volume (EDV) The volume of blood in the ventricle at the end of diastole, when filling is complete

endocrine axis A three-hormone sequence consisting of (1) a hypothalamic hypophysiotropic hormone that controls the output of (2) an anterior pituitary tropic hormone that regulates secretion of (3) a target endocrine gland hormone, which exerts the final physiologic effect

endocrine glands Ductless glands that secrete hormones into the blood

endocytic vesicle A small, intracellular, membrane-enclosed vesicle in which extracellular material is trapped

endocytosis (en´-dō-sī-TŌ-sis) Internalization of extracellular material within a cell as a result of the plasma membrane forming a pouch that contains the extracellular material, then sealing at the surface of the pouch to form an endocytic vesicle

endogenous opiates (en-DAJ´-eh-nus Ō´-pē-āts) Endorphins and enkephalins, which bind with opiate receptors and are important in the body's natural analgesic system

endogenous pyrogen (pī´-ruh-jun) A chemical released from macrophages during inflammation that acts by means of local prostaglandins to raise the set point of the hypothalamic thermostat to produce a fever

endometrium (en´-dō-MĒ-trē-um) The lining of the uterus

endoplasmic reticulum (ER) (en´-dō-PLAZ-mik-ri-TIK-yuh-lum) An organelle consisting of a continuous membranous network of fluid-filled tubules (smooth ER) and flattened sacs, partially studded with ribosomes (rough ER); synthesizes proteins and lipids for formation of new cell membrane and manufactures products for secretion

endothelium (en´-dō-THĒ-lē-um) The thin, single-celled layer of epithelial cells lining the entire circulatory system

end-plate potential (EPP) The graded receptor potential that occurs at the motor end plate of a skeletal muscle fiber in response to binding with acetylcholine

end-systolic volume (ESV) The volume of blood in the ventricle at the end of systole, when emptying is complete

endurance-type exercise See *aerobic exercise*

energy balance The balance between energy input by means of food intake and energy output by means of external work and internal work

enteric nervous system The extensive network of nerve fibers consisting of the myenteric plexus and submucous plexus within the digestive tract wall that endows the tract with considerable self-regulation

enterogastrones (ent´-uh-rō-GAS-trōnz) Hormones secreted by the duodenal mucosa that inhibit gastric motility and secretion; include secretin and cholecystokinin

enterohepatic circulation (en´-tur-ō-hi-PAT-ik) The recycling of bile salts and other bile constituents between the small intestine and liver by means of the hepatic portal vein

enzyme A special protein molecule that speeds up a particular chemical reaction in the body

eosinophils (ē´-uh-SIN-uh-fils) White blood cells that are important in allergic responses and in combating internal parasite infestations

ependymal cells (eh-PEN-dim-ul) The glial cells lining the ventricles of the brain, which serve as neural stem cells

epidermis (ep´-uh-DER-mus) The outer layer of the skin, consisting of numerous layers of epithelial cells, with the outermost layers being dead and flattened

epididymis The male accessory reproductive organ that stores sperm and increases their motility and fertility prior to ejaculation

epinephrine (ep´-uh-NEF-rin) The primary hormone secreted by the adrenal medulla; important in preparing the body for "fight-or-flight" responses and in regulating arterial blood pressure; adrenaline

epiphyseal plate (eh-pif-i-SĒ-al) A layer of cartilage that separates the diaphysis (shaft) of a long bone from the epiphysis (flared end); the site at which bones grow longer before the cartilage ossifies (turns into bone)

epithelial tissue (ep´-uh-THĒ-lē-ul) A functional grouping of cells specialized in the exchange of materials between the cell and its environment; lines and covers various body surfaces and cavities and forms secretory glands

EPSP See *excitatory postsynaptic potential*

equilibrium potential (E_x) The potential that exists when the concentration gradient and opposing electrical gradient for a given ion exactly counterbalance each other so that there is no net movement of the ion

erythrocytes (i-RITH-ruh-sīts) Red blood cells, which are plasma membrane–enclosed bags of hemoglobin that transport O_2 and, to a lesser extent, CO_2 and H^+ in the blood

erythropoiesis (i-rith´-rō-poi-Ē-sus) Erythrocyte production by the bone marrow

erythropoietin The hormone released from the kidneys in response to a reduction in O_2 delivery to the kidneys; stimulates the bone marrow to increase erythrocyte production

ESCs See *embryonic stem cells*

esophagus (i-SOF-uh-gus) A straight muscular tube that extends between the pharynx and stomach

estrogen Feminizing "female" sex hormone

ESV See *end-systolic volume*

evaporation The transfer of heat from the body surface by the transformation of water from a liquid to a gaseous state

exchange See *antiport*

excitable tissue Tissue capable of producing electrical signals when excited; includes nervous and muscle tissue

excitation–contraction coupling The series of events linking muscle excitation (the presence of an action potential) to muscle contraction (filament sliding and sarcomere shortening)

excitatory postsynaptic potential (EPSP) (pōst´-si-NAP-tik) A small depolarization of the postsynaptic membrane in response to neurotransmitter binding, bringing the membrane closer to threshold

excitatory synapse (SIN-aps´) Synapse in which the postsynaptic neuron's response to neurotransmitter release is a small depolarization of the postsynaptic membrane, bringing the membrane closer to threshold

exocrine glands Glands that secrete through ducts to the outside of the body or into a cavity that communicates with the outside

exocytosis (eks´-Ō-sī-TŌ-sis) Fusion of a membrane-enclosed intracellular vesicle with the plasma membrane, followed by the opening of the vesicle and the emptying of its contents to the outside

expiration A breath out

expiratory muscles The skeletal muscles whose contraction reduces the size of the thoracic cavity and lets the lungs recoil to a smaller size, bringing about movement of air from the lungs to the atmosphere

external environment The environment surrounding the body

external genitalia The externally visible portions of the reproductive system

external intercostal muscles Inspiratory muscles whose contraction elevates the ribs, thereby enlarging the thoracic cavity

external work Energy expended by contracting skeletal muscles to move external objects or to move the body in relation to the environment

extracellular fluid (ECF) All the fluid outside the cells of the body; consists of interstitial fluid and plasma

extracellular matrix (ECM) An intricate meshwork of fibrous proteins embedded in the interstitial fluid secreted by local cells

extrinsic controls Regulatory mechanisms initiated outside an organ that alter the activity of the organ; accomplished by the nervous and endocrine systems

extrinsic nerves The nerves originating outside the digestive tract that innervate the various digestive organs

facilitated diffusion Passive carrier-mediated transport involving transport of a substance down its concentration gradient across the plasma membrane

fatigue Inability to maintain muscle tension at a given level despite sustained stimulation

feedback A response that occurs after a change has been detected; may be *negative feedback* or *positive feedback*

feedforward mechanism A response designed to prevent an anticipated change in a controlled variable

feeding signals Appetite signals that give rise to the sensation of hunger and promote the desire to eat

fibrinogen (fī-BRIN-uh-jun) A large, soluble plasma protein that when converted into an insoluble, threadlike molecule forms the meshwork of a clot during blood coagulation

Fick's law of diffusion The rate of net diffusion of a substance across a membrane is directly proportional to the substance's concentration gradient, the lipid solubility of the substance, and the surface area of the membrane and inversely proportional to the substance's molecular weight and the diffusion distance

fight-or-flight response The changes in activity of the various organs innervated by the autonomic nervous system in response to sympathetic stimulation, which collectively prepare the body for strenuous physical activity in the face of an emergency or stressful situation, such as a physical threat from the outside environment

firing When an excitable cell undergoes an action potential

first messenger An extracellular messenger, such as a hormone, that binds with a surface membrane receptor and activates an intracellular second messenger to carry out the desired cellular response

flagellum (fluh-JEL-um) The single, long, whip-like appendage that serves as the tail of a spermatozoon

flow rate (of blood or air) The volume of blood or air passing through a blood vessel or airway, respectively, per unit of time

fluid balance Maintenance of ECF volume (for long-term control of blood pressure) and ECF osmolarity (for maintaining normal cell volume)

follicle (of ovary) A developing ovum and the surrounding specialized cells

follicle-stimulating hormone (FSH) An anterior pituitary hormone that stimulates ovarian follicular development and estrogen secretion in females and stimulates sperm production in males

follicular cells (of ovary) (fah-LIK-you-lar) Collectively, the granulosa and thecal cells

follicular cells (of thyroid gland) The cells that form the walls of the colloid-filled follicles in the thyroid gland and secrete thyroid hormone

follicular phase The phase of the ovarian cycle dominated by the presence of maturing follicles prior to ovulation

Frank–Starling law of the heart Intrinsic control of the heart such that increased venous return resulting in increased end-diastolic volume leads to an increased strength of contraction and increased stroke volume; that is, the heart normally pumps out all the blood returned to it

free radicals Very unstable electron-deficient particles that are highly reactive and destructive

frontal lobes The lobes of the cerebral cortex at the top of the brain in front of the central sulcus, which are responsible for voluntary motor output, speaking ability, and elaboration of thought

FSH See *follicle-stimulating hormone*

fuel metabolism See *intermediary metabolism*

functional syncytium (sin-sish´-ē-um) A group of smooth or cardiac muscle cells that are interconnected by gap junctions and function electrically and mechanically as a single unit

functional unit The smallest component of an organ that can perform all the functions of the organ

gametes (GAM-ētz) Reproductive, or germ, cells, each containing a haploid set of chromosomes; sperm and ova

gamma motor neuron A motor neuron that innervates the fibers of a muscle–spindle receptor

ganglion (GAN-glē-un) A collection of neuronal cell bodies located outside the central nervous system

ganglion cells The nerve cells in the outermost layer of the retina whose axons form the optic nerve

gap junction A communicating junction formed between adjacent cells by small connecting tunnels that permit passage of charge-carrying ions between the cells so that electrical activity in one cell is spread to the adjacent cell

gastrin A hormone secreted by the pyloric gland area of the stomach that stimulates the parietal and chief cells to secrete a highly acidic gastric juice

gastrointestinal hormone Hormones secreted into the blood by the endocrine cells in the digestive tract mucosa that control motility and secretion in other parts of the digestive system

gestation Pregnancy

ghrelin (GRELL-in) The "hunger" hormone, a potent appetite stimulator secreted by the empty stomach

glands Epithelial tissue derivatives that are specialized for secretion

glial cells (glē-ul) Connective tissue cells of the CNS, which support the neurons both physically and metabolically, including astrocytes, oligodendrocytes, ependymal cells, and microglia

glomerular filtration (glow-MAIR-yū-lur) Filtration of a protein-free plasma from the glomerular capillaries into the tubular component of the kidney's nephron as the first step in urine formation

glomerular filtration rate (GFR) The rate at which glomerular filtrate is formed

glomerulus (in kidney) (glow-MAIR-yū-lus) A ball-like tuft of capillaries in the kidney's nephron that filters water and solute from the blood as the first step in urine formation

glomerulus (in olfactory bulb) A ball-like neural junction within the olfactory bulb that serves as a "smell file" sorting different scent components

glucagon (GLOO-kuh-gon) The pancreatic hormone that raises blood glucose and blood fatty-acid levels

glucocorticoids (gloo´-kō-KOR-ti-koidz) Adrenocortical hormones that are important in intermediary metabolism and in helping the body resist stress; primarily cortisol

gluconeogenesis (gloo´-kō-nē-ō-JEN-uh-sus) The conversion of amino acids into glucose

glycogen (GLĪ-kō-jen) The storage form of glucose in the liver and muscle

glycogenesis (glī´-kō-JEN-i-sus) The conversion of glucose into glycogen

glycogenolysis (glī´-kō-juh-NOL-i-sus) The conversion of glycogen to glucose

glycolysis (glī-KOL-uh-sus) A biochemical process taking place in the cell's cytosol that breaks down glucose into pyruvate molecules

GnRH See *gonadotropin-releasing hormone*

Golgi complex (GOL-jē) An organelle consisting of sets of stacked, flattened membranous sacs; processes raw materials transported to it from the endoplasmic reticulum into finished products and sorts and directs the finished products to their final destination

gonadotropes Anterior pituitary cells that secrete gonadotropin-releasing hormone

gonadotropin-releasing hormone (GnRH) (gō-nad´-uh-TRŌ-pin) The hypothalamic hormone that stimulates the release of FSH and LH from the anterior pituitary

gonadotropins FSH and LH; hormones that control secretion of the sex hormones by the gonads

gonads (GŌ-nadz) The primary reproductive organs, which produce the gametes and secrete the sex hormones; testes and ovaries

G protein A membrane-bound intermediary, which, when activated on binding of an extracellular first messenger to a surface receptor, activates effector proteins on the intracellular side of the membrane in the cAMP second-messenger system

G-protein coupled receptor A type of receptor that activates the associated G protein on binding with an extracellular chemical messenger

gradation of contraction Variable magnitudes of tension produced in a single whole muscle

graded potential A local change in membrane potential that occurs in varying grades of magnitude; serves as a short-distance signal in excitable tissues

grand postsynaptic potential (GPSP) The total composite potential in a postsynaptic neuron resulting from the sum of all EPSPs and IPSPs occurring at the same time

granulocytes (gran´-yuh-lō-sīts) Leukocytes that contain granules, including neutrophils, eosinophils, and basophils

granulosa cells (gran´-yuh-LŌ-suh) The layer of cells immediately surrounding a developing oocyte within an ovarian follicle

gray matter The portion of the central nervous system composed primarily of densely packaged neuronal cell bodies and dendrites

growth hormone (GH) An anterior pituitary hormone that is primarily responsible for regulating overall body growth and is also important in intermediary metabolism; somatotropin

H^+ See *hydrogen ion*

haploid number (HAP-loid) The number of chromosomes found in gametes; a half set of chromosomes, one member of each pair, for a total of 23 chromosomes in humans

Hb See *hemoglobin*

hCG See *human chorionic gonadotropin*

helper T cells The population of T cells that enhances the activity of other immune-response effector cells

hematocrit (hi-MAT´-uh-krit) The percentage of blood volume occupied by erythrocytes as they are packed down in a centrifuged blood sample

hemoglobin (HĒ-muh-glō´-bun) **(Hb)** A large iron-bearing protein molecule in erythrocytes that binds with and transports most O_2 in the blood; also carries some of the CO_2 and H^+ in the blood

hemolysis (hē-MOL-uh-sus) Rupture of red blood cells

hemostasis (hē´-mō-STĀ-sus) The stopping of bleeding from an injured vessel

hepatic portal system (hi-PAT-ik) A complex vascular connection between the digestive tract and liver such that venous blood from the digestive system drains into the liver for processing of absorbed nutrients before being returned to the heart

hippocampus (hip-ō-CAM-pus) The elongated, medial portion of the temporal lobe that is a part of the limbic system and is especially crucial for forming long-term memories

histamine A chemical released from mast cells or basophils that brings about vasodilation and increased capillary permeability; important in allergic responses and inflammation

homeostasis (hō´-mē-ō-STĀ-sus) Maintenance by the highly coordinated, regulated actions of the body systems of relatively stable chemical and physical conditions in the internal fluid environment that bathes the body cells

homeostatic control system A regulatory system that includes a sensor, integrator, and effectors that work together to bring about a corrective adjustment that opposes an original deviation from a normal set point

hormone A long-distance chemical mediator that is secreted by an endocrine gland into the blood, which transports it to its target cells

hormone response element (HRE) The specific attachment site on DNA for a given steroid hormone and its nuclear receptor

host cell A body cell infected by a virus

HRE See *hormone response element*

human chorionic gonadotropin (hCG) (kō-rē-ON-ik gō-nad´-uh-TRŌ-pin) A hormone secreted by the developing placenta that stimulates and maintains the corpus luteum of pregnancy

hydrogen ion (H^+) The cationic portion of a dissociated acid

hydrolysis (hī-DROL-uh-sis) The digestion of a nutrient molecule by the addition of water at a bond site

hydrostatic (fluid) pressure (hī-drō-STAT-ik) The pressure exerted by fluid on the walls that contain it

hyperglycemia (hī´-pur-glī-SĒ-mē-uh) Elevated blood glucose concentration

hyperplasia (hī-pur-PLĀ-zē-uh) An increase in the number of cells

hyperpolarization An increase in membrane potential from resting potential; potential becomes even more negative than at resting potential

hypersecretion Too much of a particular hormone secreted

hypertension (hī´-pur-TEN-chun) Sustained, above-normal mean arterial blood pressure

hypertonic solution (hī´-pur-TON-ik) A solution with osmolarity greater than that of normal body fluids; more concentrated than normal

hypertrophy (hī-PUR-truh-fē) Increase in the size of an organ as a result of an increase in the size of its cells

hyperventilation Overbreathing; when the rate of ventilation is in excess of the body's metabolic needs for CO_2 removal

hypophysiotropic hormones (hi-PŌ-fiz-ē-ō-TRŌ-pik) Hormones secreted by the hypothalamus that regulate the secretion of anterior pituitary hormones; see also *releasing hormone* and *inhibiting hormone*

hyposecretion Too little of a particular hormone secreted

hypotension (hī-pō-TEN-chun) Sustained, below-normal mean arterial blood pressure

hypothalamic-hypophyseal portal system (hī-pō-thuh-LAM-ik hī-pō-FIZ-ē-ul) The vascular connection between the hypothalamus and anterior pituitary gland used for the pickup and delivery of hypophysiotropic hormones

hypothalamus (hī´-pō-THAL-uh-mus) The brain region beneath the thalamus that regulates many aspects of the internal fluid environment, such as water and salt balance and food intake; serves as an important link between the autonomic nervous system and endocrine system

hypotonic solution (hī´-pō-TON-ik) A solution with osmolarity less than that of normal body fluids; more dilute than normal

hypoventilation Underbreathing; ventilation inadequate to meet the metabolic needs for O_2 delivery and CO_2 removal

hypoxia (hī-POK-sē-uh) Insufficient O_2 at the cellular level

I band One of the light bands that alternate with dark (A) bands to create a striated appearance in a skeletal or cardiac muscle fiber when these fibers are viewed with a light microscope

ICF See *intracellular fluid*

IGF See *insulin-like growth factor*

immune surveillance Recognition and destruction of newly arisen cancer cells by the immune system

immunity The body's ability to resist or eliminate potentially harmful foreign materials or abnormal cells

immunoglobulins (im´-ū-nō-GLOB-yū-lunz) Antibodies; gamma globulins

impermeable Prohibiting passage of a particular substance through the plasma membrane

implantation The burrowing of a blastocyst into the endometrial lining

inclusion A nonpermanent mass of stored material, such as glygogen or triglycerides (fat), in a cell

incretin A hormone released by the digestive tract that stimulates insulin secretion by the pancreas

inflammation An innate, nonspecific series of highly interrelated events, especially involving neutrophils, macrophages, and local vascular changes, that are set into motion in response to foreign invasion or tissue damage

influx Movement into the cell

inhibin (in-HIB-un) A hormone secreted by the Sertoli cells of the testes or by the ovarian follicles that inhibits FSH secretion

inhibiting hormone A hypothalamic hormone that inhibits the secretion of a particular anterior pituitary hormone

inhibitory postsynaptic potential (IPSP) (pōst´-si-NAP-tik) A small hyperpolarization of the postsynaptic membrane in response to neurotransmitter binding, thereby moving the membrane farther from threshold

inhibitory synapse (SIN-aps´) Synapse in which the postsynaptic neuron's response to neurotransmitter release is a small hyperpolarization of the postsynaptic membrane, moving the membrane farther from threshold

innate immune responses Inherent defense responses that nonselectively defend against foreign or abnormal material, even on initial exposure to it; see also *inflammation, interferon, natural killer cells,* and *complement system*

inorganic Referring to substances that do not contain carbon; from nonliving sources

insensible loss Loss of water of which the person is not aware from the lungs or nonsweating skin

inspiration A breath in

inspiratory muscles The skeletal muscles whose contraction enlarges the thoracic cavity, bringing about lung expansion and movement of air into the lungs from the atmosphere

insulin (IN-suh-lin) The pancreatic hormone that lowers blood levels of glucose, fatty acids, and amino acids and promotes their storage

insulin-like growth factor (IGF) Synonymous with *somatomedin;* hormone secreted by the liver into the blood on stimulation by growth hormone that acts directly on target cells to promote growth, with other tissues producing IGF that acts locally as a paracrine to promote growth

integrator A region that determines efferent output based on processing of afferent input; also called a *control center*

integument (in-TEG-yuh-munt) The skin and underlying connective tissue

intercostal muscles (int-ur-KOS-tul) The muscles that lie between the ribs; see also *external intercostal muscles* and *internal intercostal muscles*

interferon (in´-tur-FĒR-on) A chemical released from virus-invaded cells that provides nonspecific resistance to viral infections by transiently interfering with replication of the same or unrelated viruses in other host cells

intermediary metabolism The collective set of intracellular chemical reactions that involve the degradation, synthesis, and transformation of small nutrient molecules; also known as *fuel metabolism*

intermediate filaments Threadlike cytoskeletal elements that play a structural role in parts of the cells subject to mechanical stress

internal environment The body's aqueous extracellular environment, which consists of the plasma and interstitial fluid and which must be homeostatically maintained for the cells to make life-sustaining exchanges with it

internal intercostal muscles Expiratory muscles whose contraction pulls the ribs downward and inward, thereby reducing the size of the thoracic cavity

internal respiration The intracellular metabolic processes carried out within the mitochondria that use O_2 and produce CO_2 during the derivation of energy from nutrient molecules

internal work All forms of biological energy expenditure that do not accomplish mechanical work outside the body

interneuron Neuron that lies entirely within the central nervous system and is important for integrating peripheral responses to peripheral information as well as for the abstract phenomena associated with the "mind"

interstitial fluid (in´-tur-STISH-ul) The portion of the extracellular fluid that surrounds and bathes all the body cells

intra-alveolar pressure (in´-truh-al-VĒ-uh-lur) The pressure within the alveoli

intracellular fluid (ICF) The fluid collectively contained within all the body cells

intrapleural pressure (in´-truh-PLOOR-ul) The pressure within the pleural sac

intrinsic controls Local control mechanisms inherent to an organ

intrinsic factor A special substance secreted by the parietal cells of the stomach that must be combined with vitamin B_{12} for this vitamin to be absorbed by the intestine; deficiency produces pernicious anemia

intrinsic nerve plexuses Interconnecting networks of nerve fibers within the digestive tract wall

involuntary muscle Muscle innervated by the autonomic nervous system and not subject to voluntary control; cardiac and smooth muscle

ion An atom that has gained or lost one or more of its electrons, so it is not electrically balanced

IPSP See *inhibitory postsynaptic potential*

iris A pigmented smooth muscle that forms the colored portion of the eye and controls pupillary size

islets of Langerhans (LAHNG-er-honz) The endocrine portion of the pancreas that secretes the hormones insulin and glucagon into the blood

isometric contraction (ī´-sō-MET-rik) A muscle contraction in which muscle tension develops at constant muscle length

isotonic contraction A muscle contraction in which muscle tension remains constant as the muscle fiber changes length

isotonic solution (ī´-sō-TON-ik) A solution with osmolarity equal to that of normal body fluids

juxtaglomerular apparatus (juks´-tuh-glō-MAIR-ū-lur) A cluster of specialized vascular and tubular cells at a point where the ascending limb of the loop of Henle passes through the fork formed by the afferent and efferent arterioles of the same nephron in the kidney

keratin (CARE-uh-tin) The protein found in the intermediate filaments in skin cells that give the skin strength and help form a waterproof outer layer

killer (K) cells Cells that destroy a target cell that has been coated with antibodies by lysing its membrane

kinesin (kī-NĒ´-sin) The molecular motor that transports secretory vesicles along the microtubular highway within neuronal axons by "walking" along the microtubule to the end of the axon

lactate (lactic acid) An end product formed from pyruvate (pyruvic acid) during the anaerobic process of glycolysis

lactation Milk production by the mammary glands

larynx (LARE-inks) The "voice box" at the entrance of the trachea; contains the vocal cords

lateral sacs The expanded saclike regions of a muscle fiber's sarcoplasmic reticulum; store and release calcium, which plays a key role in triggering muscle contraction

law of mass action If the concentration of one of the substances involved in a reversible reaction is increased, the reaction is driven toward the opposite side, and if the concentration of one of the substances is decreased, the reaction is driven toward that side

leak channels Unregulated, ungated channels that are open all the time

left ventricle The heart chamber that pumps blood into the systemic circulation

length–tension relationship The relationship between the length of a muscle fiber at the onset of contraction and the tension the fiber can achieve on a subsequent tetanic contraction

lens A transparent, biconvex structure of the eye that refracts (bends) light rays and whose strength can be adjusted to accommodate for vision at different distances

leptin A hormone released from adipose tissue that plays a key role in long-term regulation of body weight by acting on the hypothalamus to suppress appetite

leukocytes (LOO-kuh-sīts) White blood cells, which are the immune system's mobile defense units

leukotrienes (loo-ko-TRĪ-eenz) Local chemical mediators derived from the plasma membrane that are especially important in development of asthma

Leydig cells (LĪ-dig) The interstitial cells of the testes that secrete testosterone

LH See *luteinizing hormone*

LH surge The burst in LH secretion that occurs at midcycle of the ovarian cycle and triggers ovulation

limbic system (LIM-bik) A functionally interconnected ring of forebrain structures that surrounds the brain stem and is concerned with emotions, basic survival and sociosexual behavioral patterns, motivation, and learning

lipase (LĪ-payz) An enzyme secreted primarily by pancreatic acinar cells that digests dietary fat

lipid emulsion A suspension of small fat droplets held apart as a result of adsorption of bile salts on their surface

loop of Henle (HEN-lē) A hairpin loop that extends between the proximal and distal tubule of the kidney's nephron

lumen (LOO-men) The interior space of a hollow organ or tube

luteal phase (LOO-tē-ul) The phase of the ovarian cycle dominated by the presence of a corpus luteum

luteinization (loot´-ē-un-uh-ZĀ-shun) Formation of a postovulatory corpus luteum in the ovary

luteinizing hormone (LH) An anterior pituitary hormone that stimulates ovulation, luteinization, and secretion of estrogen and progesterone in females and testosterone secretion in males

lymph Interstitial fluid that is picked up by the lymphatic vessels and returned to the venous system, meanwhile passing through the lymph nodes for defense purposes

lymphocytes White blood cells that provide immune defense against targets for which they are specifically programmed

lymphoid tissues Tissues that produce and store lymphocytes, such as lymph nodes and tonsils

lysosomes (LĪ-sō-sōmz) Organelles consisting of membrane-enclosed sacs containing powerful hydrolytic enzymes that destroy unwanted material within the cell, such as internalized foreign material or cellular debris

macrophages (MAK-ruh-fājs) Large, tissue-bound phagocytes

mast cells Cells located within connective tissue that synthesize, store, and release histamine, as during allergic responses

mean arterial blood pressure The average pressure responsible for driving blood forward through the arteries into the tissues throughout the cardiac cycle; mean arterial blood pressure = cardiac output × total peripheral resistance

mechanically gated channels Channels that open or close in response to stretching or other mechanical deformation

mechanoreceptor (meh-CAN-ō-rē-SEP-tur) or (mek´-uh-nō-rē-SEP-tur) A sensory receptor sensitive to mechanical energy, such as stretching or bending

medullary respiratory center (MED-you-LAIR-ē) Several aggregations of neuronal cell bodies within the medulla that provide output to the respiratory muscles and receive input important for regulating the magnitude of ventilation

megakaryocyte A large bone-marrow bound cell that sheds off blood-borne platelets from its outer edges

meiosis (mī-ō-sis) Cell division in which the chromosomes replicate followed by two nuclear divisions so that only a half set of chromosomes is distributed to each of four new daughter cells

melanocyte-stimulating hormone (MSH) (mel-AH-nō-sīt) A hormone produced by the pituitary in lower vertebrates that regulates skin coloration for camouflage in these species; in humans, is secreted as a paracrine by the hypothalamus for control of food intake and by keratinocytes in the skin to control dispersion of melanin granules from melanocytes during tanning

melatonin (mel-uh-TŌ-nin) A hormone secreted by the pineal gland during darkness that helps entrain the body's biological rhythms with the external light and dark cues

membrane attack complex A collection of the five final activated components of the complement system that aggregate to form a porelike channel in the plasma membrane of an invading microorganism, with the resultant leakage leading to destruction of the invader

membrane potential A separation of charges across the membrane; a slight excess of negative charges lined up along the inside of the plasma membrane and separated from a slight excess of positive charges on the outside

memory cells B or T cells that are newly produced in response to a microbial invader but that do not participate in the current immune response against the invader; instead, they remain dormant, ready to launch a swift, powerful attack should the same microorganism invade again in the future

meninges (men-IN-geez) Three membranes that wrap the brain and spinal cord

menstrual cycle (men´-stroo-ul) The cyclic changes in the uterus that accompany the hormonal changes in the ovarian cycle

menstrual phase The phase of the menstrual cycle characterized by sloughing of endometrial debris and blood out through the vagina

messenger RNA (mRNA) Carries the transcribed genetic blueprint for synthesis of a particular protein from nuclear DNA to the cytoplasmic ribosomes where the protein is synthesized

metabolic acidosis (met-uh-bol´-ik) Acidosis resulting from any cause other than excess accumulation of carbonic acid in the body

metabolic alkalosis (al´-kuh-LŌ-sus) Alkalosis caused by a relative deficiency of noncarbonic acid

metabolic rate Energy expenditure per unit of time

metabolism All chemical reactions that occur within the body cells

micelle (mī-SEL) A water-soluble aggregation of bile salts, lecithin, and cholesterol that has a hydrophilic shell and a hydrophobic core; carries the water-insoluble products of fat digestion to their site of absorption

microfilaments Cytoskeletal elements made of actin molecules (and myosin molecules in muscle cells); play a major role in various cellular contractile systems and serve as a mechanical stiffener for microvilli

microglia The type of glial cells that serve as the immune defense cells of the CNS

microtubules Cytoskeletal elements made of tubulin molecules arranged into long, slender, unbranched tubes that help maintain asymmetric cell shapes and coordinate complex cell movements

microvilli (mī´-krō-VIL-ī) Actin-stiffened, nonmotile, hairlike projections from the luminal surface of epithelial cells lining the digestive tract and kidney tubules; tremendously increase the surface area of the cell exposed to the lumen

micturition (mik-too-RISH-un) or (mik-chuh-RISH-un) The process of bladder emptying; urination

milk ejection The squeezing out of milk produced and stored in the alveoli of the breasts by means of contraction of the myoepithelial cells that surround each alveolus

mineralocorticoids (min-uh-rul-ō-KOR-ti-koidz) The adrenocortical hormones that are important in Na^+ and K^+ balance; primarily aldosterone

mitochondria (mī-tō-KON-drē-uh) The energy organelles, which contain the enzymes for oxidative phosphorylation

mitosis (mī-TŌ-sis) Cell division in which the chromosomes replicate before nuclear division so that each of the two daughter cells receives a full set of chromosomes

mitotic spindle The system of microtubules assembled during mitosis along which the replicated chromosomes are moved away from each other toward opposite sides of the cell prior to cell division

modality The energy form to which sensory receptors respond, such as heat, light, pressure, and chemical changes

molecular motor Specialized protein molecule with "feet" that can be alternately swung forward enabling the molecule to "walk" along a microtubular highway, carrying cargo from one part of the cell to another

molecule A chemical substance formed by the linking of atoms; the smallest unit of a given chemical substance

monocytes (MAH-nō-sīts) White blood cells that emigrate from the blood, enlarge, and become macrophages

monosaccharides (mah´-nō-SAK-uh-rīdz) Simple sugars, such as glucose; the absorbable unit of digested carbohydrates

motility Muscular contractions of the digestive tract wall that mix and propel forward the luminal contents

motor activity Movement of the body accomplished by contraction of skeletal muscles

motor end plate The specialized portion of a skeletal muscle fiber that lies immediately underneath the terminal button of the motor neuron and possesses receptor sites for binding acetylcholine released from the terminal button

motor neurons The neurons that innervate skeletal muscle and whose axons constitute the somatic nervous system

motor unit One motor neuron plus all the muscle fibers it innervates

motor unit recruitment The progressive activation of a muscle fiber's motor units to accomplish increasing gradations of contractile strength

mucosa (mew-KŌ-sah) The innermost layer of the digestive tract that lines the lumen

multiunit smooth muscle A smooth muscle mass consisting of multiple discrete units that function independently of one another and that must be separately stimulated by autonomic nerves to contract

muscarinic receptor (MUS-ka-rin´-ik) Type of cholinergic receptor found at the effector organs of all parasympathetic postganglionic fibers

muscle fiber A single muscle cell, which is relatively long and cylindrical in shape

muscle tension See *tension*

muscle tissue A functional grouping of cells specialized for contraction and force generation

myelin (MĪ-uh-lun) An insulative lipid covering that surrounds myelinated nerve fibers at regular intervals along the axon's length; each patch of myelin is formed by a separate myelin-forming cell that wraps itself jelly-roll fashion around the neuronal axon

myelinated fibers Neuronal axons covered at regular intervals with insulative myelin

myocardial ischemia (mī-ō-KAR-dē-ul is-KĒ-mē-uh) Inadequate blood supply to the heart tissue

myocardium (mī´-ō-KAR-dē-um) The cardiac muscle within the heart wall

myofibril (mī´-ō-FĪB-rul) A specialized intracellular structure of muscle cells that contains the contractile apparatus

myogenic activity Muscle-produced, nerve-independent contractile activity

myometrium (mī´-ō-mē-TRĒ-um) The smooth muscle layer of the uterus

myosin (MĪ-uh-sun) The protein forming the thick filaments in muscle fibers

Na^+–K^+ pump A carrier that actively transports Na^+ out of the cell and K^+ into the cell

Na^+ load See *sodium (Na^+) load*

natural killer cells Naturally occurring, lymphocyte-like cells that nonspecifically destroy virus-infected cells and cancer cells by directly lysing their membranes on first exposure to them

negative balance Situation in which the losses for a substance exceed its gains so that the total amount of the substance in the body decreases

negative feedback A regulatory mechanism in which a change in a controlled variable triggers a response that opposes the change, thus maintaining a relatively steady set point for the regulated factor

nephron (NEF-ron´) The functional unit of the kidney; consisting of an interrelated vascular and tubular component, it is the smallest unit that can form urine

nerve A bundle of peripheral neuronal axons, some afferent and some efferent, enclosed by a connective tissue covering and following the same pathway

nerve fiber See *axon*

nervous system One of the two major regulatory systems of the body; in general, coordinates rapid activities of the body, especially those involving interactions with the external environment

nervous tissue A functional grouping of cells specialized for initiation and transmission of electrical signals

net diffusion The difference between the opposing movements of two types of molecules in a solution

net filtration pressure The net difference in the hydrostatic and osmotic forces acting across the glomerular membrane that favors the filtration of a protein-free plasma into Bowman's capsule

neurogenic activity Contractile activity in muscle cells initiated by nerves

neuroglia See *glial cells*

neurohormones Hormones released into the blood by neurosecretory neurons

neuromodulators (ner´-ō-MA-jew-lā´-torz) Chemical messengers that bind to neuronal receptors at nonsynaptic sites and bring about long-term changes that subtly depress or enhance synaptic effectiveness

neuromuscular junction The juncture between a motor neuron and a skeletal muscle fiber

neuron (NER-on) A nerve cell specialized to initiate, propagate, and transmit electrical signals, typically consisting of a cell body, dendrites, and an axon

neuropeptides Large, slowly acting peptide molecules released from axon terminals along with classical neurotransmitters; most neuropeptides function as neuromodulators

neuropeptide Y (NPY) A potent appetite stimulator secreted by the hypothalamic arcuate nucleus

neurotransmitter The chemical messenger released from the axon terminal of a neuron in response to an action potential that influences another neuron or an effector with which the neuron is anatomically linked

neutrophils (new´-truh-filz) White blood cells that are phagocytic specialists and important in inflammatory responses and defense against bacterial invasion

nicotinic receptor (nick´-ō-TIN-ik) Type of cholinergic receptor found at all autonomic ganglia and the motor end plates of skeletal muscle fibers

nitric oxide A local chemical mediator released from endothelial cells and other tissues; its effects range from causing local arteriolar vasodilation to acting as a toxic agent against foreign invaders to serving as a unique type of neurotransmitter

nociceptor (nō-sē-SEP-tur) A pain receptor, sensitive to tissue damage

nodes of Ranvier (RAN-vē-ā) The portions of a myelinated neuronal axon between the segments of insulative myelin; the axonal regions where the axonal membrane is exposed to the ECF and membrane potential exists

norepinephrine (nor´-ep-uh-NEF-run) The neurotransmitter released from sympathetic postganglionic fibers; noradrenaline

NPY See *neuropeptide Y*

nucleus (of brain) (NŪ-klē-us) A functional aggregation of neuronal cell bodies within the brain

nucleus (of cells) A distinct spherical or oval structure, usually located near the center of a cell, that contains the cell's genetic material, deoxyribonucleic acid (DNA)

occipital lobes (ok-SIP´-ut-ul) The posterior lobes of the cerebral cortex, which initially process visual input

O₂–Hb dissociation curve A graphic depiction of the relationship between arterial P_{O_2} and percent hemoglobin saturation

oligodendrocytes (ol-i-gō´-DEN-drō-sitz) The myelin-forming cells of the central nervous system

oogenesis (ō´-ō-JEN-uh-sus) Egg production

opsonin (OP´-suh-nun) Body-produced chemical that links bacteria to macrophages, thereby making the bacteria more susceptible to phagocytosis

optic nerve The bundle of nerve fibers leaving the retina that relay information about visual input

optimal length The length before the onset of contraction of a muscle fiber at which maximal force can be developed on a subsequent tetanic contraction

organ A distinct structural unit composed of two or more types of primary tissue organized to perform one or more particular functions; for example, the stomach

organelles (or´-gan-ELZ) Distinct, highly organized, membrane-bound intracellular compartments, each containing a specific set of chemicals for carrying out a particular cellular function

organic Referring to substances that contain carbon; originally from living or once-living sources

organism A living entity, whether unicellular or multicellular

organ of Corti (KOR-tē) The sense organ of hearing within the inner ear that contains hair cells whose hairs are bent in response to sound waves, setting up action potentials in the auditory nerve

osmolarity (oz´-mo-LAIR-ut-ē) A measure of the concentration of a solution given in terms of milliosmoles/liter (mOsm), the number of millimoles of solute particles in a liter of solution

osmosis (os-MŌ-sis) Movement of water across a membrane down its own concentration gradient toward the area of higher solute concentration

osmotic pressure (os-MAH-tic) A measure of the tendency for osmotic flow of water into a solution resulting from its relative concentration of nonpenetrating solutes and water

osteoblasts (OS-tē-ō-blasts´) Bone cells that produce the organic matrix of bone

osteoclasts Bone cells that dissolve bone in their vicinity

osteocytes Retired osteoblasts entombed within the bone that they have laid down around themselves that continue to participate in calcium and phosphate exchange between the bone fluid and plasma

otolith organs (ŌT´-ul-ith) Sense organs in the inner ear that provide information about rota-

tional changes in head movement; include the utricle and saccule

oval window The membrane-covered opening that separates the air-filled middle ear from the upper compartment of the fluid-filled cochlea in the inner ear

overhydration Water excess in the body

ovulation (ov´-yuh-LĀ-shun) Release of an ovum from a mature ovarian follicle

oxidative phosphorylation (fos´-for-i-LĀ-shun) The entire sequence of mitochondrial biochemical reactions that uses oxygen to extract energy from the nutrients in food and transforms it into ATP, producing CO_2 and H_2O in the process; includes the electron transport system and chemiosmosis

oxyhemoglobin (ok-si-HĒ-muh-glō-bun) Hemoglobin combined with O_2

oxyntic mucosa (ok-SIN-tic) The mucosa lining the body and fundus of the stomach, which contains gastric pits that lead to the gastric glands lined by mucous neck cells, parietal cells, and chief cells

oxytocin (ok´-sē-TŌ-sun) A hypothalamic hormone stored in the posterior pituitary that stimulates uterine contraction and milk ejection

pacemaker activity Self-excitable activity of an excitable cell in which its membrane potential gradually depolarizes to threshold on its own

pacemaker potential A self-induced slow depolarization to threshold occurring in a pacemaker cell as a result of shifts in passive ionic fluxes across the membrane accompanying automatic changes in channel permeability

pancreas (PAN-krē-us) A mixed gland composed of an exocrine portion that secretes digestive enzymes and an aqueous alkaline secretion into the duodenal lumen and an endocrine portion that secretes the hormones insulin and glucagon into the blood

paracrine (PEAR-uh-krin) A local chemical messenger whose effect is exerted only on neighboring cells in the immediate vicinity of its site of secretion

parasympathetic nervous system (pear´-uh-simpuh-THET-ik) The subdivision of the autonomic nervous system that dominates in quiet, relaxed situations and promotes body maintenance activities such as digestion and emptying of the urinary bladder

parathyroid glands (pear´-uh-THĪ-roid) Four small glands located on the posterior surface of the thyroid gland that secrete parathyroid hormone

parathyroid hormone (PTH) A hormone that raises plasma Ca^{2+} levels

parietal cells (puh-RĪ-ut-ul) The stomach cells that secrete hydrochloric acid and intrinsic factor

parietal lobes The lobes of the cerebral cortex that lie at the top of the brain behind the central sulcus, which contain the somatosensory cortex

partial pressure The individual pressure exerted independently by a particular gas within a mixture of gases

partial pressure gradient A difference in the partial pressure of a gas between two regions that promotes the movement of the gas from the region of higher partial pressure to the region of lower partial pressure

parturition (par´-too-RISH-un) Delivery of a baby

passive expiration Expiration accomplished during quiet breathing as a result of elastic recoil of the lungs on relaxation of the inspiratory muscles, with no energy expenditure required

passive force A force that does not require expenditure of cellular energy to accomplish transport of a substance across the plasma membrane

passive reabsorption Reabsorption when none of the steps in the transepithelial transport of a substance across the kidney tubules requires energy expenditure

pathogens (PATH-uh-junz) Disease-causing microorganisms, such as bacteria or viruses

pathophysiology (path´-ō-fiz-ē-OL-ō-gē) Abnormal functioning of the body associated with disease

pepsin; pepsinogen (pep-SIN-uh-jun) An enzyme secreted in inactive form by the stomach that, once activated, begins protein digestion

peptide hormones Hormones that consist of a chain of specific amino acids of varying length

peptide YY$_{3-36}$ A satiety signal secreted by the small and large intestines that inhibits appetite and serves as a mealtime terminator

percent hemoglobin saturation A measure of the extent to which the hemoglobin present is combined with O_2

perception The conscious interpretation of the external world as created by the brain from a pattern of nerve impulses delivered to it from sensory receptors

peripheral chemoreceptors (kē´-mō-rē-SEP-turz) The carotid and aortic bodies, which respond to changes in arterial P_{O_2}, P_{CO_2}, and H^+ and adjust respiration accordingly

peripheral nervous system (PNS) Nerve fibers that carry information between the central nervous system and other parts of the body

peristalsis (per´-uh-STOL-sus) Ringlike contractions of the circular smooth muscle of a tubular organ that move progressively forward with a stripping motion, pushing the contents of the organ ahead of the contraction

peritubular capillaries (per´-i-TŪ-bū-lur) Capillaries that intertwine around the tubules of the kidney's nephron; they supply the renal tissue and participate in exchanges between the tubular fluid and blood during the formation of urine

permeable Permitting passage of a particular substance

permissiveness When one hormone must be present in adequate amounts for the full exertion of another hormone's effect

peroxisomes (puh-ROK´-suh-sōmz) Sac-like organelles containing powerful oxidative enzymes that detoxify various wastes produced within the cell or foreign compounds that have entered the cell

pH The logarithm to the base 10 of the reciprocal of the hydrogen ion concentration; pH = log 1/[H^+]

phagocytosis (fag´-ō-sī-TŌ-sus) A type of endocytosis in which large, multimolecular, solid particles are engulfed by a cell

pharynx (FARE-inks) The back of the throat, which serves as a common passageway for the digestive and respiratory systems

phosphorylation (fos´-for-i-LĀ-shun) Addition of a phosphate group to a molecule

photoreceptor A sensory receptor responsive to light

phototransduction The mechanism of converting light stimuli into electrical activity by the rods and cones of the eye

physiology (fiz-ē-OL-ō-gē) The study of body functions

pineal gland (PIN-ē-ul) A small endocrine gland located in the center of the brain that secretes the hormone melatonin

pinocytosis (pin-ō-cī-TŌ-sus) A type of endocytosis in which the cell internalizes fluid

pitch The tone of a sound, determined by the frequency of vibrations (that is, whether a sound is a C or G note)

pituitary gland (pih-TWO-ih-tair-ee) A small endocrine gland connected by a stalk to the hypothalamus; consists of the anterior pituitary and posterior pituitary

placenta (plah-SEN-tah) The organ of exchange between the maternal and fetal blood; also secretes hormones that support the pregnancy

plaque A deposit of cholesterol and other lipids, perhaps calcified, in thickened, abnormal smooth-muscle cells within blood vessels as a result of atherosclerosis

plasma The liquid portion of the blood

plasma cell An antibody-producing derivative of an activated B lymphocyte

plasma clearance The volume of plasma that is completely cleared of a given substance by the kidneys per minute

plasma-colloid osmotic pressure (KOL-oid os-MOT-ik) The force caused by the unequal distribution of plasma proteins between the blood and surrounding fluid that encourages fluid movement into the capillaries

plasma membrane A protein-studded lipid bilayer that encloses each cell, separating it from the extracellular fluid

plasma proteins The proteins in the plasma, which perform a number of important functions; include albumins, globulins, and fibrinogen

plasticity (plas-TIS-uh-tē) The ability of portions of the brain to assume new responsibilities in response to the demands placed on it

platelets (PLĀT-lets) Specialized cell fragments in the blood that participate in hemostasis by forming a plug at a vessel defect

pleural sac (PLOOR-ul) A double-walled, closed sac that separates each lung from the thoracic wall

pluripotent stem cells Precursor cells, for example those that reside in the bone marrow and continuously divide and differentiate to give rise to each of the types of blood cells

polarization The state of having membrane potential

polycythemia (pol-ē-sī-THĒ-mē-uh) Excess circulating erythrocytes, accompanied by an elevated hematocrit

polysaccharides (pol´-ē-SAK-uh-rīdz) Complex carbohydrates, consisting of chains of interconnected glucose molecules

pool (of a substance) Total quantity of any particular substance in the ECF

positive balance Situation in which the gains via input for a substance exceed its losses via output, so that the total amount of the substance in the body increases

positive feedback A regulatory mechanism in which the input and the output in a control system continue to enhance each other so that the controlled variable is progressively moved farther from a steady state

postabsorptive state The metabolic state after a meal is absorbed during which endogenous energy stores must be mobilized and glucose must be spared for the glucose-dependent brain; fasting state

posterior pituitary The neural portion of the pituitary that stores and releases into the blood on hypothalamic stimulation two hormones produced by the hypothalamus, vasopressin and oxytocin

postganglionic fiber (pōst´-gan-glē-ON-ik) The second neuron in the two-neuron autonomic nerve pathway; originates in an autonomic ganglion and terminates on an effector organ

postsynaptic neuron (pōst´-si-NAP-tik) The neuron that conducts its action potentials away from a synapse

power stroke The ATP-powered cross-bridge binding and bending that pulls the thin filaments in closer together between the thick filaments during contraction of a muscle fiber

preganglionic fiber The first neuron in the two-neuron autonomic nerve pathway; originates in the central nervous system and terminates on an autonomic ganglion

pressure gradient A difference in pressure between two regions that drives the movement of blood or air from the region of higher pressure to the region of lower pressure

presynaptic neuron (prē-si-NAP-tik) The neuron that conducts its action potentials toward a synapse

primary active transport A carrier-mediated transport system in which energy is directly required to operate the carrier and move the transported substance against its concentration gradient

primary follicle A primary oocyte surrounded by a single layer of granulosa cells in the ovary

primary motor cortex The portion of the cerebral cortex that lies anterior to the central sulcus and is responsible for voluntary motor output

progestational phase See *secretory phase*

prolactin (PRL) (prō-LAK-tun) An anterior pituitary hormone that stimulates breast development and milk production in females

proliferative phase The phase of the menstrual cycle during which the endometrium repairs itself and thickens following menstruation; lasts from the end of the menstrual phase until ovulation

pro-opiomelanocortin (prō-ōp´-Ē-ō-ma-LAN-ō-kor´-tin) A large precursor molecule that can be variably cleaved into adrenocorticotropic hormone, melanocyte-stimulating hormone, and endorphin

proprioception (prō´-prē-ō-SEP-shun) Awareness of position of body parts in relation to one another and to surroundings

prostaglandins (pros´-tuh-GLAN-dins) Local chemical mediators that are derived from a component of the plasma membrane, arachidonic acid

prostate gland A male accessory sex gland that secretes an alkaline fluid, which neutralizes acidic vaginal secretions

protein kinase (KĪ-nase) An enzyme that phosphorylates and thereby induces a change in the shape and function of a particular intracellular protein

proteolytic enzymes (prōt´-ē-uh-LIT-ik) Enzymes that digest protein

proximal tubule (PROKS-uh-mul) A highly convoluted tubule that extends between Bowman's capsule and the loop of Henle in the kidney's nephron

PTH See *parathyroid hormone*

pulmonary artery (PULL-mah-nair-ē) The large vessel that carries blood from the right ventricle to the lungs

pulmonary circulation The closed loop of blood vessels carrying blood between the heart and lungs

pulmonary surfactant (sur-FAK-tunt) A phospholipoprotein complex secreted by the Type II alveolar cells that intersperses between the water molecules that line the alveoli, thereby lowering the surface tension within the lungs

pulmonary valve A one-way valve that permits the flow of blood from the right ventricle into the pulmonary artery during ventricular emptying but prevents the backflow of blood from the pulmonary artery into the right ventricle during ventricular relaxation

pulmonary veins The large vessels that carry blood from the lungs to the heart

pulmonary ventilation The volume of air breathed in and out in one minute; pulmonary ventilation = tidal volume × respiratory rate

pupil An adjustable round opening in the center of the iris through which light passes to the interior portions of the eye

Purkinje fibers (pur-KIN-jē) Small terminal fibers that extend from the bundle of His and rapidly transmit an action potential throughout the ventricular myocardium

pyloric gland area (PGA) (pī-LŌR-ik) The specialized region of the mucosa in the antrum of the stomach that secretes gastrin

pyloric sphincter (pī-LŌR-ik SFINGK-tur) The juncture between the stomach and duodenum

RAAS See *renin-angiotensin-aldosterone system*

radiation Emission of heat energy from the surface of a warm body in the form of electromagnetic waves

reabsorption The net movement of interstitial fluid into the capillary

receptive field The circumscribed region surrounding a sensory neuron within which the neuron responds to stimulus information

receptor See *sensory receptor* or *receptor (in membrane)*

receptor-channel A type of receptor that is an integral part of a channel that opens (or closes) on binding with an extracellular messenger

receptor (in membrane) Membrane protein that binds with a specific extracellular chemical messenger, bringing about membrane and intracellular events that alter the activity of the particular cell

receptor-mediated endocytosis Import of a particular large molecule from the ECF into a cell by formation and pinching off of an endocytic pouch in response to binding of the molecule to a surface membrane receptor specific for it

receptor potential The graded potential change that occurs in a sensory receptor in response to a stimulus; generates action potentials in the afferent neuron fiber

reduced hemoglobin Hemoglobin that is not combined with O_2

reflex Any response that occurs automatically without conscious effort; the components of a reflex arc include a receptor, afferent pathway, integrating center, efferent pathway, and effector

refraction Bending of a light ray

refractory period (rē-FRAK-tuh-rē) The time period when a recently activated patch of membrane is refractory (unresponsive) to further stimulation, which prevents the action potential from spreading backward into the area through which it has just passed and ensures the unidirectional propagation of the action potential away from the initial site of activation

regulatory T cells A class of T lymphocytes that suppresses the activity of other lymphocytes

releasing hormone A hypothalamic hormone that stimulates the secretion of a particular anterior pituitary hormone

renal cortex An outer granular-appearing region of the kidney

renal medulla (RĒ-nul muh-DUL-uh) An inner striated-appearing region of the kidney

renal threshold The plasma concentration at which the T_m of a particular substance is reached and the substance first starts appearing in the urine

renin (RĒ-nin) An enzymatic hormone released from the kidneys in response to a decrease in NaCl or ECF volume or arterial blood pressure; activates angiotensinogen

renin–angiotensin–aldosterone system (RAAS) (an´jē-ō-TEN-sun al-dō-steer-OWN) The salt-conserving system triggered by the release of renin from the kidneys, which activates angiotensin, stimulating aldosterone secretion and Na^+ reabsorption by the kidney tubules during the formation of urine

repolarization (rē´-pō-luh-ruh-ZĀ-shun) Return of membrane potential to resting potential following a depolarization

reproductive tract The system of ducts specialized to transport or house the gametes after they are produced

residual volume The minimum volume of air remaining in the lungs even after a maximal expiration

resistance Hindrance of blood or air flow through a blood vessel or respiratory airway, respectively

respiration The sum of processes that accomplish ongoing passive movement of O_2 from the atmosphere to the tissues, as well as the continual passive movement of metabolically produced CO_2 from the tissues to the atmosphere

respiratory acidosis (as-i-DŌ-sus) Acidosis resulting from abnormal retention of CO_2 arising from hypoventilation

respiratory airways The system of tubes that conducts air between the atmosphere and the alveoli of the lungs

respiratory alkalosis (al´-kuh-LŌ-sus) Alkalosis caused by excessive loss of CO_2 from the body as a result of hyperventilation

respiratory rate Breaths per minute

resting membrane potential The membrane potential that exists when an excitable cell is not displaying an electrical signal

reticular activating system (RAS) (ri-TIK-ū-lur) Ascending fibers that originate in the reticular formation and carry signals upward to arouse and activate the cerebral cortex

reticular formation A network of interconnected neurons that runs throughout the brain stem and initially receives and integrates all synaptic input to the brain

retina The innermost layer in the posterior region of the eye that contains the eye's photoreceptors (rods and cones)

ribonucleic acid (RNA) (rī-bō-new-KLĀ-ik) A nucleic acid that exists in three forms (messenger RNA, ribosomal RNA, and transfer RNA), which participate in gene transcription and protein synthesis

ribosomes (RĪ-bō-sōmz) Special ribosomal RNA-protein complexes that synthesize proteins under the direction of nuclear DNA

right atrium (Ā-trē´-um) The heart chamber that receives venous blood from the systemic circulation

right ventricle The heart chamber that pumps blood into the pulmonary circulation

RNA See *ribonucleic acid*

rods The eye's photoreceptors used for night vision

rough ER The flattened, ribosome-studded sacs of the endoplasmic reticulum that synthesize proteins for export or for use in membrane construction

round window The membrane-covered opening that separates the lower chamber of the cochlea in the inner ear from the middle ear

salivary amylase (AM-uh-lās´) An enzyme produced by the salivary glands that begins carbohydrate digestion in the mouth and continues it in the stomach after the food and saliva have been swallowed

saltatory conduction (SAL-tuh-tōr´-ē) The means by which an action potential is propagated throughout a myelinated fiber, with the impulse jumping over the myelinated regions from one node of Ranvier to the next

salt balance Balance between salt intake and salt output; important in controlling ECF volume

SA node See *sinoatrial node*

sarcomere (SAR-kō-mir) The functional unit of skeletal muscle; the area between two Z lines within a myofibril

sarcoplasmic reticulum (ri-TIK-yuh-lum) A fine meshwork of interconnected tubules that surrounds a muscle fiber's myofibrils; contains expanded lateral sacs, which store calcium that is released into the cytosol in response to a local action potential

satiety signals (suh-TĪ-ut-ē) Signals that lead to the sensation of fullness and suppress the desire to eat

saturation The condition in which all binding sites on a carrier molecule are occupied

Schwann cells (shwahn) The myelin-forming cells of the peripheral nervous system

sclera The visible, white, outer layer of the eye

secondary active transport A transport mechanism in which a carrier molecule for glucose or an amino acid is driven by a Na^+ concentration gradient established by the energy-dependent Na^+ pump to transfer the glucose or amino acid uphill without directly expending energy to operate the carrier

secondary follicle A developing ovarian follicle that is secreting estrogen and forming an antrum

secondary sexual characteristics The many external characteristics that are not directly involved in reproduction but that distinguish males and females

second messenger An intracellular chemical that is activated by binding of an extracellular first messenger to a surface receptor site, triggering a preprogrammed series of biochemical events that alter activity of intracellular proteins controlling a particular cellular activity

secretin (si-KRĒT-′n) A hormone released from the duodenal mucosa primarily in response to the presence of acid; inhibits gastric motility and secretion and stimulates secretion of $NaHCO_3$ solution from the pancreas and liver

secretion Release to a cell's exterior, on appropriate stimulation, of substances produced by the cell

secretory phase The phase of the menstrual cycle characterized by the development of a lush endometrial lining capable of supporting a fertilized ovum; also known as the *progestational phase*

secretory vesicles (VES-i-kuls) Membrane-enclosed sacs containing proteins that have been synthesized and processed by the endoplasmic reticulum and Golgi complex of the cell and which will be released to the cell's exterior by exocytosis on appropriate stimulation

segmentation The small intestine's primary method of motility; consists of oscillating, ringlike contractions of the circular smooth muscle along the small intestine's length

selectively permeable membrane A membrane that permits some particles to pass through while excluding others

self-antigens Antigens that are characteristic of a person's own cells

semen (SĒ-men) A mixture of accessory sex gland secretions and sperm

semicircular canal Sense organ in the inner ear that detects rotational or angular acceleration or deceleration of the head

semilunar valves (sem′-i-LEW-nur) The aortic and pulmonary valves

seminal vesicles (VES-i-kuls) Male accessory sex glands that supply fructose to ejaculated sperm and secrete prostaglandins

seminiferous tubules (sem′-uh-NIF-uh-rus) The highly coiled tubules within the testes that produce spermatozoa

sensor The component of a control system that monitors the magnitude of the controlled variable

sensory afferent Pathway into the central nervous system carrying information that reaches the level of consciousness

sensory input Input from somatic sensation and special senses

sensory receptor An afferent neuron's peripheral ending, which is specialized to respond to a particular stimulus in its environment

sensory transduction The conversion of stimulus energy into a receptor potential

Sertoli cells (sur-TŌL-lē) Cells located in the seminiferous tubules that support spermatozoa during their development

serum Plasma minus fibrinogen and other clotting precursors

set point The desired level at which homeostatic control mechanisms maintain a controlled variable

sex hormones The steroid hormones responsible for the development of masculine and feminine characteristics; testosterone in males and estrogens in females

signal molecule An extracellular chemical messenger that initiates signal transduction in a cell

signal transduction The sequence of events in which incoming signals from extracellular chemical messengers are conveyed into a target cell where they are transformed into the dictated cellular response

single-unit smooth muscle The most abundant type of smooth muscle; made up of muscle fibers interconnected by gap junctions so that they become excited and contract as a unit; also known as *visceral smooth muscle*

sinoatrial (SA) node (sī-nō-Ā-trē-ul) A small specialized autorhythmic region in the right atrial wall of the heart that has the fastest rate of spontaneous depolarizations and serves as the normal pacemaker of the heart

skeletal muscle Striated muscle, which is attached to the skeleton and is responsible for movement of the bones in purposeful relation to one another; innervated by the somatic nervous system and under voluntary control

slow-wave potentials Self-excitable activity of an excitable cell in which its membrane potential undergoes gradually alternating depolarizing and hyperpolarizing swings

smooth ER The tubules of the endoplasmic reticulum that package newly synthesized proteins in transport vesicles

smooth muscle Involuntary muscle in the walls of hollow organs and tubes innervated by the autonomic nervous system

sodium (Na^+) load The total amount of Na^+ in the body, which determines the ECF volume through its osmotic effect

somatic cells (sō-MAT-ik) Body cells, as contrasted with reproductive cells

somatic nervous system The portion of the efferent division of the peripheral nervous system that innervates skeletal muscles; consists of the axonal fibers of the alpha motor neurons

somatic sensation Sensory information arising from the body surface, including somesthetic sensation and proprioception

somatomedin (sō′-mat-uh-MĒ-din) See *insulin-like growth factor*

somatosensory cortex The region of the parietal lobe immediately behind the central sulcus; the site of initial processing of somesthetic and proprioceptive input

somatotropes Anterior pituitary cells that secrete growth hormone

somesthetic sensations (SŌ-mes-THEH-tik) Awareness of sensory input such as touch, pressure, temperature, and pain from the body's surface

sound waves Traveling vibrations of air in which regions of high pressure caused by compression of air molecules alternate with regions of low pressure caused by rarefaction of the molecules

spatial summation The summing of several postsynaptic potentials arising from the simultaneous activation of several excitatory (or several inhibitory) synapses

special senses Vision, hearing, equilibrium, taste, and smell

specificity Ability of carrier molecules to transport only specific substances across the plasma membrane

spermatogenesis (spur′-mat-uh-JEN-uh-sus) Sperm production

sphincter (sfink-tur) A voluntarily controlled ring of skeletal muscle that controls passage of contents through an opening into or out of a hollow organ or tube

spinal reflex A reflex that is integrated by the spinal cord

spleen A lymphoid tissue in the upper left part of the abdomen that stores lymphocytes and platelets and destroys old red blood cells

state of equilibrium State of a system in which no net change is occurring

stem cells Relatively undifferentiated cells that can give rise to highly differentiated, specialized cells while at the same time making new stem cells

steroids (STEER-oidz) Hormones derived from cholesterol

stimulus A detectable physical or chemical change in the environment of a sensory receptor

stress The generalized, nonspecific response of the body to any factor that overwhelms, or threatens to overwhelm, the body's compensatory abilities to maintain homeostasis

stretch reflex A monosynaptic reflex in which an afferent neuron originating at a stretch-detecting receptor in a skeletal muscle terminates directly on the efferent neuron supplying the same muscle to cause it to contract and counteract the stretch

stroke volume (SV) The volume of blood pumped out of each ventricle with each contraction, or beat, of the heart

subcortical regions The brain regions that lie under the cerebral cortex, including the basal nuclei, thalamus, and hypothalamus

submucosa The connective tissue layer of the digestive tract that lies under the mucosa and contains the larger blood and lymph vessels and a nerve network

substance P The neurotransmitter released from pain fibers

subsynaptic membrane (sub-sih-NAP-tik) The portion of the postsynaptic cell membrane that lies immediately underneath a synapse and contains receptor sites for the synapse's neurotransmitter

suprachiasmatic nucleus (soup´-ra-kī-as-MAT-ik) A cluster of nerve cell bodies in the hypothalamus that serves as the master biological clock, acting as the pacemaker establishing many of the body's circadian rhythms

surface tension The force at the liquid surface of an air–water interface resulting from the greater attraction of water molecules to the surrounding water molecules than to the air above the surface; a force that tends to decrease the area of a liquid surface and resists stretching of the surface

sympathetic nervous system The subdivision of the autonomic nervous system that dominates in emergency ("fight-or-flight") or stressful situations and prepares the body for strenuous physical activity

symport The form of secondary active transport in which the driving ion and transported solute move in the same direction across the plasma membrane; also called *cotransport*

synapse (SIN-aps´) The specialized junction between two neurons where an action potential in the presynaptic neuron influences the membrane potential of the postsynaptic neuron, typically by releasing a chemical messenger that diffuses across the small cleft between the neurons

synergism (SIN-er-jiz´-um) The result of several complementary actions in which the combined effect is greater than the sum of the separate effects

systemic circulation (sis-TEM-ik) The closed loop of blood vessels carrying blood between the heart and body systems

systole (SIS-tō-lē) The period of cardiac contraction and emptying

T_3 See *tri-iodothyronine*

T_4 See *thyroxine*

T_m See *transport maximum* and *tubular maximum*

tactile (TACK-til) Referring to touch

target-cell receptors Receptors located on a target cell that are specific for a particular chemical mediator

target cells The cells that a particular extracellular chemical messenger, such as a hormone or a neurotransmitter, influences

temporal lobes The lateral lobes of the cerebral cortex, which initially process auditory input

temporal summation The summing of several postsynaptic potentials that occur very close together in time because of successive firing of a single presynaptic neuron

tension The force produced during muscle contraction by shortening of the sarcomeres, resulting in stretching and tightening of the muscle's elastic connective tissue and tendon, which transmit the tension to the bone to which the muscle is attached

terminal button A motor neuron's enlarged knob-like ending that terminates near a skeletal muscle fiber and releases acetylcholine in response to an action potential in the neuron

testosterone (tes-TOS-tuh-rōn) The male sex hormone, secreted by the Leydig cells of the testes

tetanus (TET´-n-us) A smooth, maximal muscle contraction that occurs when the fiber is stimulated so rapidly that it does not have a chance to relax at all between stimuli

tetraiodothyronine See *thyroxine*

thalamus (THAL-uh-mus) The brain region that serves as a synaptic integrating center for preliminary processing of all sensory input on its way to the cerebral cortex

thecal cells (THĀY-kel) The outer layer of specialized ovarian connective tissue cells in a maturing follicle

thermoreceptor (thur´-mō-rē-SEP-tur) A sensory receptor sensitive to heat and cold

thick filaments Specialized cytoskeletal structures within skeletal muscle that are made up of myosin molecules and interact with the thin filaments to shorten the fiber during muscle contraction

thin filaments Specialized cytoskeletal structures within skeletal muscle that are made up of actin, tropomyosin, and troponin molecules and interact with the thick filaments to shorten the fiber during muscle contraction

thoracic cavity (thō-RAS-ik) Chest cavity

threshold potential The critical potential that must be reached before an action potential is initiated in an excitable cell

thrombus An abnormal clot attached to the inner lining of a blood vessel

thymus (THĪ-mus) A lymphoid gland located midline in the chest cavity that processes T lymphocytes and produces the hormone thymosin, which maintains the T-cell lineage

thyroglobulin (thī´-rō-GLOB-yuh-lun) A large, complex molecule on which all steps of thyroid hormone synthesis and storage take place

thyroid gland A bilobed endocrine gland that lies over the trachea and secretes the hormones thyroxine and tri-iodothyronine, which regulate overall basal metabolic rate, and calcitonin, which contributes to control of calcium balance

thyroid hormone Collectively, the hormones secreted by the thyroid follicular cells, namely, thyroxine and tri-iodothyronine

thyroid-stimulating hormone (TSH) An anterior pituitary hormone that stimulates secretion of thyroid hormone and promotes growth of the thyroid gland; thyrotropin

thyrotropes Anterior pituitary cells that secrete thyroid-stimulating hormone

thyroxine (thī-ROCKS-in) The most abundant hormone secreted by the thyroid gland; important in the regulation of overall metabolic rate; also known as *tetraiodothyronine* or T_4

tidal volume The volume of air entering or leaving the lungs during a single breath

tight junction An impermeable junction between two adjacent epithelial cells formed by the sealing together of the cells' lateral edges near their luminal borders; prevents passage of substances between the cells

tissue (1) A functional aggregation of cells of a single specialized type, such as nerve cells forming nervous tissue; (2) the aggregate of various cellular and extracellular components that make up a particular organ, such as lung tissue

tissue-specific stem cells Partially differentiated cells that can generate the highly differentiated, specialized cell types composing a particular tissue

T lymphocytes (T cells) White blood cells that accomplish cell-mediated immune responses against targets to which they have been previously exposed; see also *cytotoxic T cells, helper T cells,* and *regulatory T cells*

tone The ongoing baseline of activity in a given system or structure, as in muscle tone, sympathetic tone, or vascular tone

tonicity A measure of the effect a solution has on cell volume when the solution surrounds the cell

total peripheral resistance The resistance offered by all the peripheral blood vessels, with arteriolar resistance contributing most extensively

trachea (TRĀ-kē-uh) The "windpipe"; the conducting airway that extends from the pharynx and branches into two bronchi, each entering a lung

tract A bundle of nerve fibers (axons of long interneurons) with a similar function within the spinal cord

transduction Conversion of stimuli into action potentials by sensory receptors

transepithelial transport (tranz-ep-i-THĒ-lē-al) The entire sequence of steps involved in the transfer of a substance across the epithelium between either the renal tubular lumen or digestive tract lumen and the blood

transmural pressure gradient The pressure difference across the lung wall (intra-alveolar pressure is greater than intrapleural pressure) that stretches the lungs to fill the thoracic cavity, which is larger than the unstretched lungs

transporter recruitment The phenomenon of inserting additional transporters (carriers) for a particular substance into the plasma membrane, thereby increasing membrane permeability to the substance, in response to an appropriate stimulus

transport maximum *(T_m)* The maximum rate of a substance's carrier-mediated transport across the membrane when the carrier is saturated; known as *tubular maximum* in transepithelial transport across the kidney tubules

transport vesicle Membranous sac enclosing newly synthesized proteins that buds off the smooth endoplasmic reticulum and moves the proteins to the Golgi complex for further processing and packaging for their final destination

transverse tubule (T tubule) A perpendicular infolding of the surface membrane of a muscle fiber; rapidly spreads surface electric activity into the central portions of the muscle fiber

triglycerides (trī-GLIS-uh-rīdz) Neutral fats composed of one glycerol molecule with three fatty acid molecules attached

tri-iodothyronine (T_3) (trī-ī-ō-dō-THĪ-ro-nēn) The most potent hormone secreted by the thyroid follicular cells; important in the regulation of overall metabolic rate

trophoblast (TRŌF-uh-blast´) The outer layer of cells in a blastocyst that is responsible for accomplishing implantation and developing the fetal portion of the placenta

tropic hormone (TRŌ-pik) A hormone that regulates the secretion of another hormone

tropomyosin (trōp´-uh-MĪ-uh-sun) One of the regulatory proteins in the thin filaments of muscle fibers

troponin (trō-PŌ-nun) One of the regulatory proteins in the thin filaments of muscle fibers

TSH See *thyroid-stimulating hormone*

T tubule See *transverse tubule*

tubular maximum *(T_m)* The maximum amount of a substance that the renal tubular cells can actively transport within a given time period; the kidney cells' equivalent of transport maximum

tubular reabsorption The selective transfer of substances from tubular fluid into peritubular capillaries during urine formation

tubular secretion The selective transfer of substances from peritubular capillaries into the tubular lumen during urine formation

twitch A brief, weak contraction that occurs in response to a single action potential in a muscle fiber

twitch summation The addition of two or more muscle twitches as a result of rapidly repetitive stimulation, resulting in greater tension in the fiber than that produced by a single action potential

tympanic membrane (tim-PAN-ik) The eardrum, which is stretched across the entrance to the middle ear and which vibrates when struck by sound waves funneled down the external ear canal

Type I alveolar cells (al-VĒ-ō-lur) The single layer of flattened epithelial cells that forms the wall of the alveoli within the lungs

Type II alveolar cells The cells within the alveolar walls that secrete pulmonary surfactant

ultrafiltration The net movement of a protein-free plasma out of the capillary into the surrounding interstitial fluid

umami A meaty or savory taste

ureter (yū-RĒ-tur) A duct that transmits urine from the kidney to the bladder

urethra (yū-RĒ-thruh) A tube that carries urine from the bladder out of the body

urine excretion The elimination of substances from the body in the urine; anything filtered or secreted and not reabsorbed is excreted

vagus nerve (VĀ-gus) The tenth cranial nerve, which serves as the major parasympathetic nerve

varicosities Swellings in autonomic postganglionic fibers that simultaneously release neurotransmitter over a large area of an innervated organ

vascular tone The state of partial constriction of arteriolar smooth muscle that establishes a baseline of arteriolar resistance

vasoconstriction (vă´-zō-kun-STRIK-shun) The narrowing of a blood vessel lumen as a result of contraction of the vascular circular smooth muscle

vasodilation The enlargement of a blood vessel lumen as a result of relaxation of the vascular circular smooth muscle

vasopressin (vă-zō-PRES-sin) A hormone secreted by the hypothalamus, then stored and released from the posterior pituitary; increases the permeability of the distal and collecting tubules of the kidneys to water and promotes arteriolar vasoconstriction; also known as *antidiuretic hormone (ADH)*

vein A vessel that carries blood toward the heart

vena cava (venae cavae, plural) (VĒ-nah CĀV-ah; VĒ-nē cāv-ē) A large vein that empties blood into the right atrium

venous return (VĒ-nus) The volume of blood returned to each atrium per minute from the veins

ventilation The mechanical act of moving air in and out of the lungs; breathing

ventricle (VEN-tri-kul) **(of brain)** One of four interconnected chambers within the brain through which cerebrospinal fluid flows

ventricle (of heart) A lower chamber of the heart that pumps blood into the arteries

vertical osmotic gradient A progressive increase in the concentration of the interstitial fluid in the renal medulla from the cortical boundary down to the renal pelvis; important in the ability of the kidneys to put out urine of variable concentration, depending on the body's needs

vesicle (VES-i-kul) A small, intracellular, fluid-filled, membrane-enclosed sac

vesicular transport Movement of large molecules or multimolecular materials into or out of the cell within a vesicle, as in endocytosis or exocytosis

vestibular apparatus (veh-STIB-yuh-lur) The component of the inner ear that provides information essential for the sense of equilibrium and for coordinating head movements with eye and postural movements; consists of the semicircular canals, utricle, and saccule

villus (villi, plural) (VIL-us) Microscopic finger-like projections from the inner surface of the small intestine

virulence (VIR-you-lentz) The disease-producing power of a pathogen

visceral afferent A pathway into the central nervous system that carries subconscious information derived from the internal viscera

visceral smooth muscle (VIS-uh-rul) See *single-unit smooth muscle*

viscosity (vis-KOS-i-tē) The friction developed between molecules of a fluid as they slide over each other during flow of the fluid; the greater the viscosity, the greater the resistance to flow

visible light The portion of the electromagnetic spectrum to which the eyes' photoreceptors are responsive (wavelengths between 400 and 700 nanometers)

vital capacity The maximum volume of air that can be moved out during a single breath following a maximal inspiration

vitreous humor The jelly-like substance in the posterior cavity of the eye between the lens and retina

voltage-gated channels Channels in the plasma membrane that open or close in response to changes in membrane potential

voluntary muscle Muscle innervated by the somatic nervous system and subject to voluntary control; skeletal muscle

water balance The balance between water intake and water output; important in controlling ECF osmolarity

white matter The portion of the central nervous system composed of myelinated nerve fibers

Z line A flattened disclike cytoskeletal protein that connects the thin filaments of two adjoining sarcomeres

zona fasciculata (zō-nah fa-SIK-ū-lah-ta) The middle and largest layer of the adrenal cortex; major source of cortisol

zona glomerulosa (glō-MAIR-yū-lō-sah) The outermost layer of the adrenal cortex; sole source of aldosterone

zona reticularis (ri-TIK-yuh-lair-us) The innermost layer of the adrenal cortex; produces cortisol, along with the zona fasciculata

Index

2,3-bisphosphoglycerate (BPG) and percent hemoglobin saturation, 391

A band of skeletal muscle, 210
ABO blood group system, 322–323
Absolute refractory period and action potential, 88
Absorption, digestive, 466
Absorptive state (metabolic), 560
Acclimatization
  defined, 448
  process, 394
Accommodation, visual, 160–161
ACE inhibitor drugs and sodium reabsorption, 418
Acetylcholine (ACh)
  digestion and, 481
  nerve pathway and, 192
  neuromuscular junctions and, 198–200
Acetylcholinesterase (AChE), 200
Acid (chemical)
  defined, 452–453, A–10
  dissociation constants, A–30
  effect on percent hemoglobin saturation, 391
  gastric emptying and, 476–477
  hydrogen generation and, 455
Acid-base balance
  buffer systems and, 456–457
  chemistry, A–30–A–37
  diagram, A–36–A–37
  disruptions, 459–460
  hydrogen ion secretion and, 422
  kidneys and, 442, 458–459
  overview, 452–460
  respiratory regulation of, 457–458
Acid–base imbalance
  diagram, A–36–A–37
  rules of thumb, A–34
Acidic solution, 453
Acidosis
  defined, 453
  effects on the body, 454
  renal responses, A–34, 459
  respiratory adjustments to, 457
Acini, 485
Acquired salivary reflex, 472
Acromegaly, 542, 543
Acrosome, 588–589
Acrosome reaction, 610
Actin
  cell contractile systems and, 40
  defined, 39
  smooth muscles and, 234
Actin of skeletal muscle, 210
Action potential
  all-or-none law, 89
  cardiac contractile cells, 254
  compared to graded potential, 87
  contiguous conduction, 86
  defined, 80
  frequency in afferent fibers, 153
  initiation in excitable tissues, 237
  initiation sites, 152
  ion movement and, 81–84
  membrane permeability and, 81–84
  membrane potential changes and, 81
  myelination and, 89
  Na+–K+ pump and, 84
  nerve fibers and, 86

neuromuscular junctions and, 199
normal rate of discharge in heart, 252
propagation, 84–86
refractory period, 87–88
sensory receptor potential and, 152
skeletal muscle, 214
skeleton muscle fiber and, 218
stimulus strength and, 89
Activated T cell and immunity, 345
Active hyperemia, 289
Active transport, 62–64
Acupuncture analgesia (AA), 157
Acupuncture endorphin hypothesis, 157
Acute mountain sickness, 394
Acute myocardial infarction
  defined, 259
  possible outcomes, 271
Adaptive immunity
  bacterial infection and, 351
  function, 332, 333
  general concepts, 339–340
Addiction, steroidal, 227
Addison's disease, 554
Adenine (A) and DNA, A–18
Adenohypophysis, 533
Adenosine diphosphate (ADP)
  ATP generation and, 29
  energy cycle, 35
Adenosine triphosphate (ATP). See ATP
Adenylyl cyclase and cAMP second-messenger pathways, 103
Adhesion, cell to cell, 51
Adipocyte, 512
Adipokine, 512
Adipose tissue
  defined, 358
  hormonal function, 532
  metabolic states and, 561
  stored nutrients in, 36, 37
Adolescence and testosterone, 585
ADP
  ATP generation and, 29
  energy cycle, 35
Adrenal androgen hypersecretion, 553–554
Adrenal cortex
  function, 531, 550
  sex hormone secretion and, 552–554
Adrenal gland
  anatomy, 550
  function, 526
  hormonal function, 550
  overview, 549–555
Adrenal medulla
  anatomy, 554–555
  function, 196, 550
Adrenaline source, 196
Adrenergic fiber, 192
Adrenergic receptor, 196
Adrenocortical hormone and adrenal cortex, 550
Adrenocortical insufficiency, 554
Adrenocorticotropic hormone (ACTH)
  adrenal androgen secretion and, 553
  function, 534–536
Adrenocorticotropin, 534
Adrenogenital syndrome, 553–554, 584
Aerobic, defined, 32
Aerobic exercise
  defined, 224
  discussion, 36

Afferent arteriole
  function, 406–407
  GFR control and, 414
Afferent fiber
  action potential frequency in, 153
  pain processing, 155–156
  visceral, 153–154
Afferent neuron
  action potential and, 152
  action potential initiation, 237
  defined, 117
  features, 200
  sensory receptors on, 151
Afferent pathway and reflex arc, 142
Afferent fiber and spinal nerve, 141
After hyperpolarization, 81
Afterbirth, 619
Agglutination, 341
Agranulocyte, 330
Airflow and airway resistance, 375–377
Aldosterone
  deficiency, 554
  function, 550–551
  hypersecretion, 553
  potassium ion secretion and, 422
  sodium reabsorption and, 417–418
  tubular reabsorption and, 416–418
Aldosterone receptor blocker, 418
Alkaline mucus and digestion, 479
Alkaline solution, 453
Alkalosis
  defined, 453
  effects on the body, 454
  renal responses, 459, A–34
  respiratory adjustments to, 457
Allergen, 354
Allergy, 354
All-or-none law and action potential, 89
Alpha cell, 561
Alpha motor neuron, 229–230
Alpha receptor, 196
Altitude effects on the body, 393–394
Alveolar air, 384–385
Alveolar macrophage, 359
Alveolar surface tension and lungs, 379
Alveolar ventilation
  anatomic dead space and, 382–383
  breathing pattern effects, 383–384
Alveolus
  function, 620
  hemoglobin and, 389
  hemoglobular gas exchange and, 389–390
  net diffusion of gasses, 387
  overview, 369–370
  pulmonary capillaries and, 370
Alzheimer's disease (AD) and hippocampus, 136
Amblyopia, 115
Amine, 100
Amino acid
  digestion and, 466
  GH secretion and, 541
  insulin and, 562, 563
  kidney function and, 419
  proteins and, A–13–A–14
Aminopeptidase, 493
Ammonia secretion, 458–459, A–34
Ammonium ion formation, 459
Amnesia, 135
Amnion, 614

Amniotic fluid, 614
Amniotic sac
  parturition and, 619
  pregnancy and, 614
Amoeboid movement, 40
Amygdala and emotion, 132
Amylase, salivary, 472
Amyotrophic lateral sclerosis (ALS), 198
Anabolic, defined, 227
Anabolic androgenic steroid, 227
Anabolism, 558
Anaerobic, 32, 224
Anaerobic exercise
  defined, 224
  discussion, 36
Anal sphincter, 500–501
Analgesic, 155
Anaphase
  meiotic, A–27
  mitotic, A–26, A–27
Anaphylactic shock, 355, 357
Anatomic dead space and ventilation, 382–383
Anatomy, 1
Androgen
  defined, 552
  hypersecretion, 553–554
  sexual differentiation and, 583
Androgen disrupter, 597
Androgen-binding protein, 589
Androgenic, 227
Android obesity, 515–516
Anemia
  causes, 321–322
  renal failure and, 435
Anemic hypoxia, 393
Angina pectoris and atherosclerosis, 270
Angiogenesis and VEGF, 290
Angiotensin I and sodium reabsorption, 417
Angiotensin II and sodium reabsorption, 417
Angiotensin-converting enzyme (ACE), 417–418
Angiotensinogen and sodium reabsorption, 417
Anion, 56, A–5
Anorexia nervosa, 516
Antagonism (hormonal), 530
Anterior pituitary gland
  defined, 533
  function, 534
  hypothalamus and, 536, 538
Anterior pituitary hormones, 536
Anterograde amnesia, 135
Antibody
  constant (Fc) region, 340–341
  function, 322, 341
  microbe elimination process, 343
  production, 342–344
  structure, 342
  subclasses, 340–341
Antibody-mediated immunity
  B lymphocytes and, 340–344
  defined, 339
Anticodon and tRNA, A–24
Antidiuretic hormone, 430–431
Antidiuretic hormone (ADH), 533
Antigen
  adaptive immunity and, 339–340
  antibodies and, 341
  defined, 322
Antigen-binding fragment (Fab), 340
Antigen-presenting cell (APC)
  interactions, 351
  T lymphocytes and, 348
Antioxidant, 544
Antiport
  carrier-mediated transport and, 64
  characteristics, 67

Antral follicle, 601
Antrum
  defined, 475
  formation, 601
Aorta, 248
Aortic arch baroreceptor, 307
Aortic body and blood gas, 397
Aortic valve, 249
Aphasia, 128
Aplastic anemia, 321
Apnea, 393, 399
Apneusis, 396
Apneustic center, 396
Apoptosis, 104–105
Appendicitis, 501
Appendix, 500
Appetite signal
  defined, 512
  effects of involuntary, 514
Aquaporin, 56, 421
Aqueous humor
  formation and drainage, 158
  function, 157, 170
Arcuate nucleus and energy balance, 512
Aristotle, 283
Aromatase, 587
Arousal system and sleep, 140
Arrhenius, Svante, A–10
Arterial baroreceptor, 308
Arteriolar radius
  cardiac output and, 289
  extrinsic sympathetic control of, 291
  factors affecting, 293
  metabolic influences on, 289
Arteriole
  contributions to homeostasis, 278
  features, 284
  function, 287
  kidney, 406–407
  location, 282
  parasympathetic innervation and, 292
  response to stretch, 290–291
  temperature application effects, 291
Artery
  contributions to homeostasis, 278
  defined, 246
  features, 284
  location, 282
  as pressure reservoir, 282, 284, 285
Artificial pacemaker, 252
Asphyxia, 393
Aspirin
  peptic ulcers and, 484
  stomach and, 483
Asthma, 355, 378
Astigmatism, 160
Astrocyte, 117–119
Atherosclerosis
  C-reactive protein and, 273
  discussion, 272
  homocysteine and, 273
  process, 269–270
Atherosclerotic plaque, 269
Atmospheric air, 384
Atmospheric pressure and ventilation, 371, 372
Atom
  bonding characteristics, A–4–A–5
  defined, 2
  types, A–3
Atomic mass, A–4
Atomic mass unit (amu), A–4
Atomic number, A–3
Atomic symbol, A–3
Atomic valence bonding characteristics, A–4–A–5
Atomic weight, A–4

ATP
  cross-bridge cycling power, 215, 217
  energy cycle, 35
  energy uses, 35
  function, A–17
  mitochondria and production, 29–35
  muscle contraction speed and, 225
  muscle motion and, 224
  production process, 34
  structure, A–17
ATP synthase, 32
Atresia, 598
Atria, 246
Atrial excitation, 254
Atrial natriuretic peptide (ANP) and sodium re-
  absorption, 418–419
Atrial volume receptor, 451
Atrioventricular (AV) node, 251
Atrioventricular (AV) valve, 248
Atrophy, 226
Auditory cortex, 175
Auditory hair cell, 175
Auditory nerve, 175
Autocatalytic process and digestion, 480
Autoimmune, 203
Autoimmune disease, 352, 548
Autonomic agonist, 197
Autonomic antagonist, 197
Autonomic nerve pathway, 191–192
Autonomic nervous system
  defined, 190
  diagram, 193
  effects, 195
  features, 199
  insulin secretion and, 563–564
  overview, 191–197
  parasympathetic division, 116
  smooth muscle activity modification, 238
  sympathetic division, 116
Autonomic neurotransmitter receptor types,
  196–197
Autonomic receptor types, 196
Autonomous smooth muscle function, 467,
  469
Autoregulation, 290
Autorhythmic cell, 250, 251
Autorhythmicity, 250
Autosomal chromosome, 583
AV nodal delay, 254
Avogadro's number, A–8
Axon
  defined, 85
  efferent, 117
Axon hillock, 84–86
Axon terminal, 84–86
Axonal transport
  example, 37
  process, 39

B cell. See B lymphocyte; specializations
B lymphocyte
  adaptive immunity and, 339
  antibody-mediated immunity and, 340
  characteristics, 354
  defined, 331
  interactions, 351
  as memory cells, 344
  origins, 340
  unactivated, 341
Backbone, 245
Bacteria
  colonic, 501
  immune system and, 329
Balance beam concept and acid-base status,
  A–36–A–37

Balance concept, 443
Balanced equation, A–7
Barometric pressure and ventilation, 371
Baroreceptor
    See also specific types
    adaptation during hypertension, 310
    function, 307
Baroreceptor reflex
    blood pressure and, 445
    diagram, 309
    function, 307
    GFR control and, 413, 414
Basal ganglia, 130
Basal metabolic rate (BMR)
    factors influencing, 511
    measuring, 510–511
    thyroid hormone and, 547
Basal nuclei
    diagram, 130
    location, 122
    motor control and, 131
    overview, 130
Base (chemical), 453, A–10
Basement membrane, 411
Basic electrical rhythm (BER) and digestive regu-
    lation, 469
Basic solution, 453
Basilar membrane
    deflection, 175, 177
    description, 175
    function, 182
Basophil, 330
B-cell receptor (BCR)
    diagram, 341
    function, 340
Behavior
    higher cortex and, 132
    limbic system and, 132
    neurotransmitters and, 133
    patterns during sleep, 139
    steroids and, 227
Bends, 395
Benign prostatic hypertrophy (BPH), 591
Benign tumor, 353
Beta amyloid and Alzheimer's disease, 136
Beta cell, 561
Beta receptor, 196
Beyond the Basics
    acupuncture, 157
    aerobic exercise, 36
    altitude effects on the body, 393–394
    atherosclerosis, 272
    biological clock, 544
    botulinum toxin's reputation, 204
    circulation history, 283
    cystic fibrosis, 50
    dialysis, 436
    environmental "estrogens", 596–597
    extreme temperatures, 521
    immunization, 345
    plasma volume, 448
    programmed cell suicide, 104
    stem cell science and tissue engineering, 7
    steroids, 227
    strokes, 121
    ulcers, 484
    vaccination, 345
Bicarbonate
    carbon dioxide transport and, 392–393
    regulating reabsorption, 458
    renal excretion, 459
    renal regulation of, A–33–A–34
Bicuspid valve, 248
Bile, 487, 488
Bile canaliculus, 488

Bile salts
    diagram, 491
    fat absorption and, 497–498
    function, 488–490
Bile secretion, stimulating, 490
Biliary secretion, 487–491
Bilirubin, 490–491
Binocular, 169
Biological clock, 543–544
Biological molecule, A–10
Biomolecule
    defined, A–10
    high-energy, A–17
Bipolar cell
    function, 166–167, 170
    retinal, 162
Birth. See Parturition
Birth control pill, 608
Birth decline and endocrine disrupters, 597
Bitter taste perception, 183
Black widow spider venom and neuromuscular
    junctions, 201
Bladder, 406, 434–435
Blastocyst implantation, 610–612
Blepharospasm, 204
Blind spot
    defined, 162
    diagram, 164
    function, 170
Block to polyspermy, 610
Blood
    cellular elements, 330
    circulation circuit, 246–248
    coagulation (See Clot formation)
    components, 316, 317
    constituent functions, 318
    contributions to homeostasis, 316
    defined, 245
    gas transports, 387–395
    reconditioning, 279
    reconditioning organs, 279–280
    storage percentages, 302
Blood cell
    production, 332
    types, 318
    typical human count, 330
    white, 40
Blood donor, universal, 323
Blood flow
    blood vessel radius and, 281
    capillaries and, 292–294
    coronary, 268–269
    dependencies, 280
    laminar, 262
    liver, 487–488
    patterns, 278
    physics, 278–287
    pressure gradient and, 281
    through the heart, 247
    turbulent, 262
Blood gas. See Gas exchange; Gas transport;
    specific types
Blood glucose
    diabetes and, 564
    insulin and, 562, 563
    insulin and glucagon and, 567
Blood pressure
    See also specific types
    cardiovascular control center and. 292
    defined, 284
    discussion, 305–311
    ECF volume and, 445–446
    fluctuations, 284–285
    glomerular capillary, 411
    mean arterial, 287

    measuring, 285–286
    regulating, 291–292
    renal handling of sodium and, 447
    stress and, 557
    systemic, 287
Blood recipient, universal, 323
Blood reservoir. veins as, 301–302
Blood type, 322–324
Blood vessel
    contributions to homeostasis, 278
    defined, 245
    features, 284
    flow and radius, 281
    repair, 328
    resistance and radius, 281
    walls as barriers, 444
Blood–brain barrier (BBB), 120
Blood-testes barrier, 589
Body
    cell components, A–18–A–19
    cellular level, 2
    chemical level, 2
    levels of organization, 1–5
    organ level, 4
    organism level, 5
    system level, 5
    tissue level, 3
Body fluid, 444
    See also specific types
Body system
    See also specific systems
    components, 6
    contributions to homeostasis, 10, 11
    defined, 5
    homeostasis and, 8, 13
    interdependencies, 9, 20
Body temperature, 516–522
Body water
    distribution, 444
    insensible loss, 450
    movement, 445
    sensible loss, 450
Bone
    anatomy, 540
    deposition, 569–570
    mature, 540
    nongrowing, 540
    plasma calcium and, 569
    resorption, 569
    structure, 570
Bone fluid, 570
Bone growth
    growth hormone and, 539–540
    growth hormone control, 540
    mechanisms, 540
    testosterone and, 587
Bone marrow and erythrocytes, 320
Botox, 204
Botulinum toxin, 204
Botulinum toxin and neuromuscular junctions,
    201
Bowman's capsule
    defined, 407–408
    hydrostatic pressure, 411, 412
    inner layer, 411
Boyle's law, 373, 375
Bradycardia, 259
Brain
    analgesic system, 156
    component functions, 123
    diagram, 124
    frontal lobes, 123
    frontal section, 130
    glucose and, 558–560
    lobe location, 124

Brain (Continued)
  metabolic states and, 561
  motor neuron influence from, 228
  nourishing, 120
  occipital lobes, 123
  parietal lobes, 123
  protecting, 119–120
  structure, 122
  subcortical regions, 130
  temporal lobes, 123
  ventricles, 119
Brain death, 129
Brain stem
  diagram, 124
  function, 121, 138
  location, 125
  respiratory centers, 395–396
Braxton–Hicks contraction, 616
Breast and lactation, 620
Breastbone
  defined, 245
  respiration and, 371
Breast-feeding advantages, 621–622
Breathing
  See also Respiration; Ventilation
  defined, 367
  gas exchange and, 384–387
Breech birth, 616
Broca's area
  diagram, 125
  location, 128
Bronchiole, 369
Bronchitis, chronic, 378
Bronchoconstriction, 376
Bronchodilation, 376
Bronchus, 369
Brønsted, Johannes, A–10
Brown fat, 519
Brush border
  defined, 493
  function, 494–495
  gluten enteropathy and, 496
Bulbourethral gland
  defined, 580
  function, 591–592
  location, 592
Bulk flow
  defined, 297
  forces influencing, 297
  function, 298
Bundle of His, 251

C cell and thyroid, 545
Ca2+-dependent phosphorylation, 234
Ca2+-induced Ca2+ release, 255
Calcitonin
  function, 571
  thyroid and, 545
Calcium (Ca)
  absorption in small intestine, 499
  characteristics, A–4
  imbalance and renal failure, 435
  metabolic control, 568–571
  metabolic disorders, 572
  muscle contraction and, 236
  muscle cross bridges and, 214
Calmodulin, 234
Calorie, 510
Calorigenic effect of thyroid hormone, 547
CAM
  function, 612
  plasma membrane and, 51
cAMP
  function, A–17
  hydrophilic hormone effects and, 102–105

Cancer
  cell, 352–353
  defined, 353, A–29
  endocrine disrupters and, 596, 597
  immune surveillance against, 353
  interferon and, 337
  T cells and, 352–354
Cancer gene, A–29
Capacitance vessel, 301
Capacity metric-English conversions, A–2
Capillary
  alveoli and, 370
  blood flow and, 292–294
  contributions to homeostasis, 278
  features, 284
  location, 282
  material exchange and, 295–296
  net fluid exchange, 298
  as sites of exchange, 292–294
Capillary blood pressure, 297
Capillary permeability
  diffusion and, 295
  inflammation and, 333–334
Capillary pore, 295
Capsaicin, 156
Carbamino hemoglobin, 392
Carbohydrate
  absorption, 497
  cells and, 48
  digestion and, 466, 497
  digestive process, 483, 494
  glucagon and, 567
  insulin and, 562
  metabolism and diabetes, 564
  overview, A–11–A–12
Carbon (C) characteristics, A–4
Carbon dioxide
  alveolar, 384–385
  effect on percent hemoglobin saturation, 390–391
  hydrogen ion regulation and, 457
  partial pressure of, 384
  transport, 392–393
Carbon monoxide and hemoglobin, 391–392
Carbonic acid
  carbon dioxide transport and, 392
  hydrogen ions and, 454–455
Carbonic acid/bicarbonate buffer system
  function, A–30–A–31
  hydrogen ions and, 456
Carbonic anhydrase
  carbon dioxide transport and, 392
  function, A–8
  hemoglobin buffer system and, A–31
  hydrogen ion regulation and, A–31–A–32
Carboxyhemoglobin (HbCO), 391
Carcinogenic, 352
Cardiac cycle, 259–263
Cardiac excitation
  coordination, 252–254
  diagram of spread, 251
Cardiac length–tension relationship, 265–276
Cardiac muscle
  action potential in contractile cells, 254–255
  action potential initiation, 237
  characteristics, 232–233
  defined, 208
  fiber interconnectivity, 249–250
  fiber organization, 250
  overview, 239
Cardiac myopathy, 259
Cardiac output (CO), 263–268
  arteriolar radius and, 289
  at rest, 280
  summary of factors affecting, 266–267
Cardiopulmonary resuscitation (CPR), 246

Cardiovascular control center, 292
  blood pressure and, 307
Cardiovascular system
  contributions to homeostasis, 278
  organization, 282
  steroids and, 227
  thyroid hormone and, 547
Carotid body and blood gas, 397
Carotid sinus, 307
Carotid sinus baroreceptor, 308
Carrier molecule
  carrier-mediated transport and, 60–64
  plasma membrane and, 50
Carrier-mediated transport, 60–62, 67
Cartilage, 540
Cascade as cellular response, 100
Caspase, 104
Catabolism, 558
Catalyst, A–8
Cataract, 162
Catecholamine
  adrenal medulla and, 555
  defined, 527
Catecholamine hormone
  adrenal glands and, 550
  properties, 101
  receptor location, 102
Catecholamine target-cell receptor, 547
Cation, 56, A–5
Cavity (dental), 471
CD4 coreceptor, 349
CD8 coreceptor, 349
Cecum, 500
Celiac disease, 495
Cell
  See also specific types
  activities requiring energy expenditure, 35
  basic functions, 3
  cholesterol uptake, 272
  components, 20
  crenated, 59
  defined, 2
  diagram, 20, 22
  differentiation, 3
  energy generation, 28–35
  energy generation conditions, 32, 35
  homeostatic needs, 13
  homeostatically regulated factors, 9
  interdependencies, 9, 20
  intermediate filaments and, 41
  mechanical support of, 40
  membrane carbohydrates and, 51
  membrane potential, 46
  membrane proteins and, 49–51
  movement, 40
  net diffusion of gasses, 387
  neuron, 84
  overview, 21
  specialized functions, 3
  specialized junctions, 52, 53, 54
  structure, 21–29, 35–41
  tissue cohesion, 52
  virus invaded and T, 346
Cell adhesion molecule (CAM)
  function, 612
  plasma membrane and, 51
Cell contractile system, 40
Cell culture, 7
Cell division, A–26–A–29
Cell-mediated immunity, 339, 345
Cell-to-cell adhesion, 51–54
Cellular respiration
  defined, 29, 367
  diagram, 368
  stages, 30

Cellulose
    defined, A-12
    digestion and, 466
Celsius to Fahrenheit comparison, A-2
Celsius to Fahrenheit conversion formula, A-2
Centimeters to inches comparison, A-2
Central chemoreceptor, 397, 398
Central lacteal, 496
Central nervous system (CNS)
    autonomic activity control, 197
    contributions to homeostasis, 150
    homeostasis and, 114
    motor neurons and, 197-198
    nucleus in, 130
    organization, 116
    overview, 115, 120-122
    protecting, 120
Central sulcus, 123, 125
Centriole
    microtubule formation and, 39
    mitosis and, A-26-A-27
Centromere, A-26
Cephalic phase of gastric secretion, 481
Cerebellum
    diagram, 136-137
    function, 121
    location, 125, 131
    overview, 136-137
    procedural memories and, 136
    voluntary movement and, 136-137
Cerebral cortex
    association areas, 128
    function, 122
    functional areas, 125
    language control, 127-128
    overview, 122-130
Cerebral dysfunction, 129
Cerebral hemisphere
    description, 122
    specializations, 129
Cerebrocerebellum, 137
Cerebrovascular accident (CVA), 121
Cerebrum, 122
Cervical canal, 580
Cervix
    defined, 580
    parturition and, 618, 619
    pregnancy and, 616
Channel
    See also specific types
    blockers, 49
    ion movement and, 78
    lipid bilayer and, 49
    osmosis and, 60
    positive-feedback cycle, 82
Chemical bond
    See also specific types
    defined, A-4
    overview, A-4-A-7
Chemical buffer system
    function, A-30-A-31
    hydrogen ions and, 456-457
Chemical categories, A-10
Chemical equation, A-7
Chemical gradient
    defined, 54
    ion movement and, 56
Chemical principle review, A-3
Chemical reaction, A-7-A-8
Chemical thermogenesis, 519
Chemically gated channel and ion
    movement, 78
Chemically gated receptor-channel and extracel-
    lular chemical messengers, 99
Chemosmosis, 32

Chemoreceptor
    defined, 152
    digestive regulation and, 470-471
Chemoreceptor trigger zone and vomiting, 478
Chemotaxin, 335
Chernobyl, 544
Chest. See Thoracic cavity
Chewing, 471-472
Chief cell, 478, 479
Chloride channel and cystic fibrosis, 50
Chloride reabsorption and kidney function, 421
Chlorine (Cl) characteristics, A-4
Cholecalciferol, 571-572
Cholecystokinin (CCK)
    food intake and, 514
    functions, 502
    gastric motility and, 476
    pancreatic secretion and, 486-487
Choleretic, 490
Cholesterol
    defined, A-13
    plasma membrane and, 48
    sources, 272
    steroid hormone processing and, 101
    types, 272
Cholinergic fiber, 192
Cholinergic receptor, 196
Chordae tendineae, 248
Chorion, 613
Choroid, 156, 170
Chromaffin granule, 555
Chromatin, A-19
Chromosome
    See also specific types
    defined, 580
    diagram, A-28
    DNA and, A-18-A-19
    homologous, 580-581
Chronic bronchitis, 378
Chronic obstructive pulmonary disease (COPD),
    376, 377
Chronic superficial gastritis, 484
Chylomicron, 497
Chyme
    defined, 475
    gastric motility and, 476
    small intestine motility and, 492
Chymotrypsin, 486
Chymotrypsinogen, 486
Cigarettes and immunity, 360
Cilia
    movement, 38
    in the respiratory tract, 40
Ciliary body
    defined, 157
    function, 170
Ciliary muscle, 160-161, 170
Cilium
    movement, 38
    in the respiratory tract, 40
Cimetidine, 484
Circadian rhythm
    defined, 529, 543
    resetting, 544
Circulation
    complete circuit, 246-248
    history, 283
Circulatory hypoxia, 393
Circulatory shock and blood pressure, 310-311
Circulatory system
    components, 6, 245
    contributions to homeostasis, 10, 12, 244, 278
Citric acid cycle, 30-31
Clitoris, 580
Clock protein, 543

Clonal anergy, 352
Clonal deletion, 352
Clonal selection theory, 342-344
Clostridium botulinum, 204
Clot
    dissolution, 328
    pathway, 326-327
    retraction, 327-328
Clot formation
    hemostasis and, 326
    preventing inappropriate, 328
Clotting cascade, 326-327
Coactivation of gamma and alpha motor neu-
    trons, 230
Cocaine and synaptic transmission, 96
Cochlea
    function, 182
    structure, 174-175
Cochlear duct
    description, 175
    function, 182
Cochlear nerve, 175
Codon, A-23
Cognition, 120
Coitus, 593
Cold exposure
    responses to, 520
    thyroid hormone and, 548
Cold-related disorders, 521
Collagen and ECM, 52
Collecting duct
    defined, 408
    transport across, 424
Collecting tubule
    defined, 408
    transport across, 424
Colloid, 545, A-9-A-10
Colon, 500, 501
Color blindness, 168
Color vision, 167-168
Colostrum, 621
Compensated heart failure, 267-268
Complement system
    activating, 342
    immunity and, 337-339
    inflammation and, 338
    nonspecific activation, 351
Complementary base pairing
    during DNA replication, A-22
    during DNA transcription, A-23
    process, A-19-A-20
Complete heart block, 252
Complex lipid, A-13
Compliance and respiration, 379
Compound, A-3
Concave surface, 160
Concentration (solution), A-9
Concentration gradient, 54, 56
Concentration of solution, 54, 56
Concentric isotonic contraction, 220
Conditioned salivary reflex, 472
Conduction and body heat exchange, 517, 518
Conductive deafness, 178
Cone (retinal)
    See also Photoreceptor
    function, 156, 167, 170
    structure, 162
    vision properties, 167
Congestive heart failure, 268
Connective tissue, 4
Connexin, 53
Connexon, 53
Conn's syndrome, 553
Consciousness, 138
Consolidation and memory, 134

Constipation, 501
Continuous ambulatory peritoneal dialysis (CAPD), 436
Contractile activity, 223
Contractile cell (heart), 250
Contractility, 266
Contractility and heart failure, 267
Contraction
    See also specific types
    calcium and, 236
    cardiac muscle, 250
    heart cycle and, 260
    heart muscle, 252–253
    muscle banding patterns during, 214
    muscle metabolism and, 224–225
    process, 219
    skeletal muscle, 212–218
    smooth muscle speed, 239
    strength of muscle, 220–221
Control center and negative feedback, 11
Controlled variable, 11
Convection and body heat exchange, 517, 518
Convergence, neuronal, 97
Convex surface, 159, 160
Copulation, 593
Core temperature, 516, 517
Coreceptor, T cell, 349
Cornea, 156, 160, 170
Corona radiata, 601
Coronary artery disease (CAD), 269
Coronary circulation, 268–269
Corpus callosum, 122
Corpus luteum (CL)
    controlling, 606
    degeneration, 603
    formation, 601, 603
    menstruation and, 608
    of pregnancy, 603, 615
Cortical granule, 610
Cortical gustatory area, 183
Cortical lobe, 124
Corticospinal motor system, 228
Corticotrope, 534
Corticotropin-releasing hormone (CRH), 513, 618
Cortisol
    deficiency, 554
    diurnal rhythm of secretion, 529
    function, 550, 551
    hypersecretion, 553
    metabolic effects of, 567–568
    secretion regulation, 552
    stress and, 556
Cotransport and carrier-mediated transport, 64
Countercurrent multiplication
    benefits, 429
    mechanism, 429, 430, 431
    vertical osmotic gradient and, 428–429
Countertransport and carrier-mediated transport, 64
Covalent bond, A–5–A–6
Cranial nerve, 138
Cranium as CNS protection, 120
C-reactive protein and atherosclerosis, 273
Creatine phosphate and muscle contractile activity, 224
Creatinine and kidney function, 422
Cretinism, 548
CRH–ACTH–cortisol system, 556
Cristae, 29
Cross bridge
    ATP-powered, 215
    calcium and, 214
    cycle activity, 215
    cycle diagram, 217
    of skeletal muscle, 210

Crossing-over (genetic)
    defined, 583, A–27
    diagram, A–29
Crypt of Lieberkühn, 496
Cryptorchidism, 585
Crystal lattice, A–5
Cupula, 178
Curare and neuromuscular junctions, 201–202
Current (electrical) and graded potential, 79
Cushing's syndrome, 553, 554
Cyanosis, 393
Cyclic adenosine monophosphate (cAMP)
    function, A–17
    hydrophilic hormone effects and, 102–105
Cystic fibrosis (CF), 50
Cystic fibrosis transmembrane conductance regulator (CFTR), 50
Cytokine and inflammation, 336
Cytokinesis
    defined, 39
    meiotic, A–27
    process, 40
Cytoplasm
    component summaries, 38
    defined, 20, 21
    overview, 23
Cytosine (C) and DNA, A–18
Cytoskeletal element, 210
Cytoskeleton
    components, 37
    defined, 20, 23
    overview, 37–41
Cytosol
    defined, 20, 23
    function, 38
    glycolysis in, 29, 30
    intermediary metabolism and, 36
    nutrient storage and, 36
    overview, 35–37
    ribosomal protein synthesis and, 36
    structure, 38
Cytosolic Ca2+, twitch summation and, 222
Cytotoxic T cell
    function, 346
    lysing diagram, 346
    mechanism of killing, 347

D cell, 479, 481
Dark adaptation (visual), 168
Dark current, 166
Daughter cell, 598–600
Deafness, 177–178
Decibel (dB), 172
Decidua, 612
Declarative memory and hippocampus, 136
Decompensated heart failure, 268
Decompression sickness, 395
Deep-sea diving, effects on the body, 395
Defecation reflex, 500–501
Defensin and cystic fibrosis, 50
Defensive cell and gastric mucosa, 496
Dehydration, 449
Dehydroepiandrosterone (DHEA)
    defined, 553
    function, 550
    pregnancy and, 615, 618
Delayed hypersensitivity
    characteristics, 357
    defined, 354
    overview, 357
Delivery (pregnancy). *See* Parturition
Delta cell, 561
Denaturation, A–16

Dendrite
    neuron, 84
    synaptic input to, 91
Dendritic cell, 349
Dense body in smooth muscle, 234
Dental caries, 471
Deoxyhemoglobin, 388
Deoxyribonucleic acid (DNA)
    See also DNA
    defined, 580
    structure, A–16
Depolarization
    membrane potential and, 78
    smooth muscles and, 236
Depolarization block, 201
Depression and limbic system, 133
Depth perception, 169–170
Dermis, 358
Desmosome
    cell junctions and, 52
    defined, 249
Detergent action of bile salts, 489
Diabetes insipidus and dehydration, 449
Diabetes mellitus
    acute effects of, 564–566
    defined, 564
    long-term complications of, 566
    treatments, 566
Dialysis, 436
Diaphragm and respiration, 371
Diaphysis, 540
Diarrhea, 499
Diastole
    defined, 260
    heart nourishment during, 268–269
Diastolic murmur, 263
Diastolic pressure, 285
Diencephalon, 121, 131
Diffusion
    capillaries and, 292–296
    carrier-mediated transport and, 61
    characteristics, 67
    membrane transport and, 54
    process, 54
Digestion
    basic processes, 465–466
    carbohydrate, 472, 483, 493, 494
    defined, 466
    fat, 483, 494
    general aspects, 465–471
    in the mouth, 473
    processes, 494
    protein, 483, 493, 494
Digestive motility
    defined, 465
    regulating, 467, 469–471
Digestive organ, accessory, 466
Digestive secretion
    absorption and, 499
    defined, 466
Digestive system
    anatomy and functions, 468–469
    components, 6, 466–467
    contributions to homeostasis, 10, 12, 464
    defenses of, 359
    function, 465–466
    pathways controlling, 471
    regulating, 467, 469–471
Digestive tract
    description, 467
    digestive system and, 466–467
    wall layers, 467, 470
Di-iodotyrosine (DIT), 546
Diploid number, 580
Direct intercellular communication, 97–98

Disaccharidase, 493
Disaccharide
    defined, A–11
    digestion and, 466
Dispersed-phase particle, A–9–A–10
Distal tubule
    defined, 408
    transport across, 424
Distension, gastric emptying and, 476–477
Diurnal rhythm
    cortisol secretion and, 552
    defined, 529
    GH secretion and, 541
Divergence, neuronal, 97
DNA
    chromosomes and, A–18–A–19
    defined, 22
    functions, A–18
    levels of organization, A–21
    molecule diagram, A–20
    replication process, A–19–A–22
    structure, A–16, A–18
DNA transcription
    mRNA and, A–20–A–21
    process, A–21–A–22, A–23
DNA translation
    mRNA and, A–21, A–23
    protein synthesis and, A–22–A–26
Docking marker acceptor and plasma membrane, 51
Dopamine
    function, 536
    milk secretion and, 621
Dorsal respiratory group (DRG), 396
Dorsal root, 141
Dorsal root ganglion, 141
Double bond, A–11
Down regulation (hormonal), 530
Dual innervation
    advantages, 195
    defined, 192
Ductus deferens, 580, 591–592
Duodenum
    defined, 491
    gastric motility and, 476
Dwarfism, 542
Dynein, 38
Dynorphin, 156
Dyslexia, causes, 128
Dyspnea, 393, 400
Dystonia, 204

Ear
    See also External ear; Inner ear; Middle ear
    function, 173, 182
    major components functions, 182
    structure, 171
Ear canal
    defined, 173
    function, 182
Eardrum, 173, 182
Eccentric isotonic contraction, 220
ECF. See Extracellular fluid (ECF)
ECG. See Electrocardiogram (ECG)
Ectopic focus, 252
Edema
    causes, 300–301
    defined, 300
    localized, immune system and, 334
Effector
    digestive regulation and, 470–471
    immune surveillance, 353–354
    negative feedback and, 11
    reflex arc and, 142
Effector organ, 116

Effector protein, 100
Efferent arteriole, 406–407
Efferent axon, 117
Efferent fiber, 141
Efferent nervous system, 116
Efferent neuron
    action potential and, 152
    action potential initiation, 237
    defined, 117
    features, 200
Efferent pathway and reflex arc, 142
Eicosanoid, 592
Ejaculate, 595
Ejaculation
    defined, 593
    phases, 595
EKG. See Electrocardiogram (ECG)
Elastic recoil, 379
Elastin
    ECM and, 52
    function, 4
Electrical gradient and ion movement, 56
Electrocardiogram (ECG)
    baseline points, 258–259
    function, 256
    leads, 256–257
    uses, 259
    waveforms, 257–258
Electrochemical gradient and ion movement, 56
Electroencephalogram (EEG)
    overview, 129
    sleep patterns, 139
Electrolyte
    defined, A–9
    equivalent, A–9
Electromagnetic wave
    body heat exchange and, 517
    properties, 158–159
Electron, A–3
Electron cloud, A–3
Electron shell, A–4
Electron transport system and oxidative phosphorylation, 32
Element
    characteristics of selected, A–4
    defined, A–3
Elephantiasis, 301
Embolus, 328
Embryo, 580
Embryonic stem cells (ESCs), 7
Emesis, stomach and, 477–478
Emetic, 478
Emission (ejaculatory), 595
Emmetropia
    defined, 162
    diagram, 163
Emotion
    higher cortex and, 132
    limbic system and, 132
    neurotransmitters and, 133
Emphysema, 378, 387
Enamel (dental), 471
End-diastolic volume (EDV), 260
    stroke volume and, 265
Endocrine axis, 536
Endocrine cell, 479
Endocrine disorder
    defined, 530
    obesity and, 515
Endocrine disrupter, 596–597
Endocrine gland
    diagram, 4
    functions, 531
Endocrine gland cell in digestive tract wall, 467

Endocrine pancreas, 526, 532
    See also Pancreas
Endocrine rhythm, 529
Endocrine specificity and receptor specialization, 107
Endocrine system
    components, 6
    contributions to homeostasis, 10, 13, 522
    functions, 527–528
    growth control and, 538–542
    homeostasis and, 76
    nervous system and, 106–108
    properties, 107
    specializations, 108
Endocrinology
    defined, 100
    general principals, 527
Endocytic vesicle, 26
Endocytosis
    characteristics, 67
    defined, 26, 66
    diagram, 27
    forms, 28
    receptor-mediated, 26, 28
Endogenous opiate, 156
Endogenous pyrogen and fever, 521
Endogenous pyrogen (EP), 336
Endometrium, 607
Endoplasmic reticulum (ER)
    See also Rough ER; Smooth ER
    diagram, 24
    overview, 23–24
    protein synthesis, 25
Endorphin, 156, 536
Endothelin and arteriolar smooth muscle contraction, 290
Endothelium, 249, 269
End-plate potential (EPP)
    defined, 199
    initiating action potentials in excitable tissues, 237
End systolic volume (ESV), 260
Endurance exercise, 224
Energy balance
    See also Food intake
    hypothalamus and, 511–515
    overview, 509–516
    states, 511
Energy equivalent of oxygen, 511
Energy input
    defined, 509
    diagram, 510
Energy level of electron shell, A–4
Energy output
    defined, 509
    diagram, 510
    rates for different activities, 510
Energy storage forms, 558, 560
Energy yield (cell)
    anaerobic versus aerobic, 32, 35
    uses, 35
English-metric conversions, A–2
Enkephalin, 156
Enteric nervous system
    defined, 116
    digestive regulation and, 469
Enterochromaffin-like (ECL) cell, 479, 481
Enterogastric reflex, 476
Enterogastrone and gastric motility, 476
Enterohepatic circulation
    defined, 488
    diagram, 490
Enterokinase
    digestion and, 486
    function, 493

Entrainment, 529
Environmental "estrogen", 596–597
Enzyme
    defined, 3
    digestive, 493
    function, A–8
    hydrogen ions and, 454
    membrane-bound, 51
    oxidative, 27
Eosinophil, 330
Eosinophil chemotactic factor and allergic reactions, 355
Ependymal cell, 119
Epicardium, 249
Epidermis, 357–359
Epididymis
    defined, 580
    function, 591, 592
    location, 592
Epiglottis, 473
Epilepsy and EEGs, 129
Epinephrine
    function, 555
    metabolic effects of, 567–568
    source, 196
    stress and, 556
Epiphyseal plate, 540
Epiphysis, 540
Epithelial cell
    in digestive tract wall, 467
    in small intestine, 495–496
Epithelial sheet, 3
Epithelial tissue, 3
Equilibrium
    defined, 55, 178
    process, 178–181
Equilibrium potential for K+ and membrane potential, 69
Equilibrium potential for Na+ and membrane potential, 69–70
Equivalent electrolyte, A–9
Erasistratus, 283
Erectile dysfunction (ED), 594–595
Erectile tissue, 593
Erection
    defined, 593
    generating center, 594
    process, 593–594
    reflex, 594
Erythroblast, 324
Erythroblastosis fetalis, 323–324
Erythrocyte
    replacing, 320
    structure, 319–320
Erythropoiesis, 320–321
Erythropoietin, 320–321
ESC, 7
Esophageal secretion, 475
Esophageal swallowing stage, 474
Esophagus, 473–475
Essential hypertension, 308
Estradiol, 615
Estriol, 615
Estrogen
    actions, 621
    defined, 552, 579
    disrupter, 596–597
    effects on the uterus, 607
    follicular function control, 603–604
    functions, 597–598
    lactation and, 620
    ovarian cycle and, 601, 606
    as parturition trigger, 616, 618
    pregnancy and, 614–616
    testosterone and, 587

Estrogen secretion, 603
Estrogenic pollutant, 596–597
Ethyl alcohol
    peptic ulcers and, 484
    stomach and, 483
Eupnea, 393
Eustachian tube, 173
Evaporation and body heat exchange, 518
Excess postexercise oxygen consumption (EPOC), 225
Exchange, carrier-mediated transport and, 64
Excitable tissue
    membrane potential and, 66
    neural communication and, 77
Excitation–contraction coupling
    cardiac cell contraction and, 255
    diagram, 216
    skeletal muscle contraction and, 213–217
    smooth muscle contraction and, 234–235
Excitatory postsynaptic potential (EPSP)
    concurrent, 95
    defined, 93
    initiating action potentials in excitable tissues, 237
Excitatory synapse, 92
Excitotoxicity and stroke, 121
Exercise
    See also specific types
    oxygen consumption and, 225
Exocrine cell, 479
Exocrine gland
    defined, 358
    diagram, 4
Exocrine gland cell in digestive tract wall, 467
Exocrine pancreas, 485–486
Exocytosis
    characteristics, 67
    defined, 26, 66
    diagram, 27
    Golgi complex and, 25
Exophthalmos, 548, 549
Expiration (respiratory)
    active, 375
    defined, 373
    difficulties, 378
    forced, 375
    process, 374–375
Expiratory muscle
    activity during ventilation, 376, 377
    diagram, 375
    ventilation and, 374–375
Expiratory neuron and respiratory control, 396
Expiratory reserve volume (ERV), 380
Expulsion (ejaculatory), 595
Extension, 219
External anal sphincter, 500–501
External auditory meatus
    defined, 173
    function, 182
External ear
    defined, 171
    function, 182
    structure, 173
External environment
    defined, 5
    homeostasis and, 12–13
External genitalia, 579–580
External respiration, 367, 368
External work, 509
Extracellular chemical messenger types, 98
Extracellular fluid (ECF)
    See also Internal pool
    compartment separation, 444–445
    components, 9
    defined, 5, 443, 444

    fluid balance and, 450
    hypertonicity, 449
    hypotonicity, 449–450
    internal pool, 443
    ionic composition, 444–445
    negative balance, 443
    osmolarity regulation, 445, 447, 450, 453
    positive balance, 443
    separation from ICF, 444–445
    stable balance, 443
    volume and thirst, 451–452
    volume regulation, 445–447, 453
Extracellular matrix (ECM), 51
Extracellular messenger and signal transduction, 99
Extrafusal fiber, 229
Extrapyramidal motor system, 228
Extrinsic clot pathway, 326–327
Extrinsic homeostatic control, 11
Extrinsic nerve and digestive regulation, 470
Eye
    external muscle, 171
    function, 162
    light refraction, 158
    light sensitivity, 168
    major components functions, 170
    refractive structures, 160
    structure, 156, 158

Facilitated diffusion
    characteristics, 67
    diagram, 61
    process, 62
Factor XII, 326
Factor VI, 326
Factor X, 326
Fahrenheit to Celsius, A–2
Fallopian tubes, 580
Farsightedness
    defined, 162
    diagram, 163
Fast pain pathway, 155
Fasting state (metabolic), 560–561
Fat
    absorption, 497–498
    bile salts and, 489–490
    defined, A–12
    digestion, 466, 497–498
    digestive process, 494
    emulsification, 497
    gastric emptying and, 476
    glucagon and, 567
    insulin and, 562–563
    metabolism and diabetes, 564–565
    storage and cytosol, 36
    types, 512, 519
Fatigue, delaying, 221
Fatty acid
    digestion and, 466
    insulin and, 562–563
    insulin and glucagon and, 567
Fatty acid molecule, A–12
Feces, 500
Fed state (metabolic), 560
Feedback. See Negative feedback; Positive feedback
Feeding signal, 512
Female pseudohermaphroditism, 554
Fenestration, capillary, 295
Fertile period, 609
Fertilization, 609–612
Fetus
    defined, 580
    harmful influences, 614
Fever, 520–521, 522
Fibrillation, 253

Fibrin, 326
Fibrinogen, 326
Fibrinolytic plasmin, 328
Fibroblast
    atherosclerosis and, 270
    blood clotting and, 328
    defined, 40
    ECM and, 52
Fick's Law of Diffusion
    capillaries and, 292
    defined, 55
    factors, 56
Fidget factor and obesity, 515
Fight or flight response, 195
Filament
    composition of thin, 213
    skeletal muscle, 210
    sliding mechanism, 212–213
Filtration fraction, 427
Filtration slit, 411
Fimbriae, 609
Firing, membrane potential changes and, 81
First law of thermodynamics and energy balance,
    509
First messenger and signal transduction, 99
First polar body, 598
Flaccid paralysis, 228
Flagellum movement, 38
Flatus, 501
Flavine adenine dinucleotide (FAD) and citric
    acid cycle, 30
Flexion, 219
Flow rate (blood)
    blood velocity and, 294
    defined, 280
    resistance and, 289
Fluid balance
    blood pressure and, 445–446
    components, 442
    ECF and, 450
    maintaining, 445
    overview, 444–452
Fluid measures and English equivalents, A–1
Fluid mosaic model of membrane structure, 48, 49
Focal point (visual), 159
Follicle
    hair, 358
    reproductive, 598, 601
    thyroid, 545
Follicle-stimulating hormone (FSH)
    function, 534–536, 589–590
    function in ovarian cycles, 603–606
    menstruation and, 608
Follicular cell
    defined, 545, 601
    thyroid hormone secretion and, 547
Follicular phase (ovarian cycle)
    controlling, 603–605
    defined, 599, 601
Food intake
    See also Energy balance
    environmental influences, 514
    factors influencing, 513
    hypothalamus and, 511–515
    involuntary regulatory signals and, 514
    psychosocial influences, 514
Force and plasma membrane permeation, 54
Forced expiratory volume in 1 second (FEV$_1$), 381
Forgetting, 135
Formula weight function, A–8
Fovea, 162, 170
Frank-Starling curve
    heart failure and, 267, 268
    normal, 265–266
    sympathetic stimulation and, 266, 267

Frank-Starling law of the heart, 265
Fraternal twins, 601
Free hydrogen ion concentration, regulating. See
    Acid-base balance
Free lipophilic hormone and protein synthesis,
    106
Free radical, 544
Frontal lobe, 125
Frostbite, 521
Fructose, 466
Fuel metabolism
    defined, 557–558
    enzymatic regulation of, 36
    hormonal control, 567–568
    reactions, 557
Functional groups of organic molecules, A–11
Functional residual capacity (FRC), 380
Functional syncytium, 236
Functional unit, 210
Fundus, 475
Funny channel, 250

G cell, 479, 481
G protein
    defined, 100
    hydrophilic hormone effects and, 102
Galactose, 466
Galen and circulatory system, 283
Gallbladder, 488
Gamete, 579, 581
Gametogenesis
    comparison of types, 598–600
    defined, 579
    process, 581, 583, 598–599
Gamma motor neuron, 229–230
Ganglion cell
    function, 170
    retinal, 162
Gap junction
    cells and, 53
    intercellular communication and, 97
Gas exchange
    conditions reducing, 386
    hemoglobin and, 389–391
    partial pressure gradients and, 384
    rate factors, 385–386
    respiration and, 384–386
Gas measures and English equivalents, A–1
Gas transport, 387–395
Gastric gland, 478, 479
Gastric inhibitory peptide (GIP), 522
Gastric juice secretion, 478
Gastric motility, 475–477
Gastric mucosa, 478
Gastric mucosal barrier, 482–483
Gastric phase of gastric secretion, 481
Gastric pit
    defined, 478
    gastric juice secretion and, 481
Gastric secretion
    controlling, 481–482
    inhibiting, 482
    process, 478
    stimulating, 482
Gastrin
    digestion and, 479, 481
    functions, 502
Gastrocolic reflex, 500
Gastroesophageal sphincter, 474–475
Gastroileal reflex, 492
Gastrointestinal hormone
    digestive regulation and, 470
    insulin secretion and, 563
Gastrointestinal hormones, 502
Gastrointestinal tract. See Digestive tract

Gated channel
    ion movement and, 78
    lipid bilayer and, 49
Gender bending and endocrine disrupters, 596
Gene activation
    controlling, A–24, A–26
    protein synthesis and, 106
Gene doping, 227
Gene in DNA, A–18
Gene mutation, A–27
General adaptation syndrome, 555
Gene-signaling factor, A–26
Genetic sex, 583
Germ cell (reproductive)
    components, A–18–A–19
    mutation, A–29
    spermatogenesis and, 587
Gestation
    See also Pregnancy
    defined, 580, 615
    lactation prevention during, 620
Ghrelin
    food intake and, 514
    GH secretion and, 541
Gigantism, 542
Gland, 4
    See also specific types
Glans penis, 594
Glaucoma, 157
Glial cell
    diagram, 118
    interneurons and, 117
    types, 117–119
Globin, 319
glomerular capillary, 407
Glomerular capillary blood pressure, 411–412
Glomerular capillary wall, 410–411
Glomerular filtration
    forces involved, 411–412
    overview, 410–414
    process, 409
Glomerular filtration rate (GFR)
    changes, 411–412
    defined, 411
    plasma clearance and, 425
    salt output and, 447
Glomerular membrane, 410–411
Glomerulus
    diagram, 409
    function, 184, 406–407
Glottis
    defined, 368–369
    swallowing and, 473
Glucagon, 567–568
Glucocorticoid, 550, 551
Gluconeogenesis
    function, 551
    insulin and, 562
Glucose
    brain and, 558–560
    brain nourishment, 120
    digestion and, 466
    forms, A–12
    kidney function and, 419–421
    symport, 65
Glucose transporter (GLUT), 562
Glucose-dependent insulinotropic peptide
    (GIP)
    function, 522
    insulin secretion and, 563
Glucosuria, 564
Gluten, 495
Gluten enteropathy, 495
Glycerin, A–12
Glycerol, A–12

Glycogen
  defined, A–12
  digestion and, 466
  metabolism and, 558
  storage and cytosol, 36, 37
Glycogenesis, 562
Glycogenolysis, 562
Glycolysis
  ATP generation and, 224
  diagram, 30
  process, 29
Glycolytic muscle fiber, 225–226
Glycoprotein, 349
Goiter, 549
Golgi complex
  diagram, 26
  exocytosis and, 25
  functions, 24–25
  overview, 24–26
  secretory vesicles and, 25
  transport vesicles and, 24
Golgi tendon organ, 230–231
Gonad
  defined, 579
  function, 532
  sex hormone secretion and, 553
Gonadal failure in males compared to menopause,
    609
Gonadal sex, 583
Gonadotrope, 534
Gonadotropin
  function, 536
  human chorionic, 614–615
Gonadotropin-releasing hormone (GnRH),
    590–591, 603
Goose bumps, 520
G-protein-coupled receptor, 99–100
Graafian follicle, 601
Graded potential
  compared to action potential, 87
  membrane potential changes and, 78–80
Grand postsynaptic potential (GPSP), 94–95
Granstein cell and immunity, 359
Granulocyte
  colony–stimulating factor, 331
  defined, 330
Granulosa cell
  defined, 598
  proliferation, 601
Granzyme, 347
Graves' disease, 548–549
Gravity and venous return, 303–304
Gray matter, 123
  See also Basal nuclei
Growth
  factors affecting, 539
  thyroid hormone and, 547
Growth factor and immunity, 348
Growth hormone (GH)
  deficiency, 542
  excess, 542
  function, 534–536
  growth and, 538–542
  metabolic effects of, 539, 568
  secretion, 540–542
  thyroid hormone and, 547
Growth hormone–inhibiting hormone (GHIH),
    536, 541
Growth hormone–releasing hormone (GHRH),
    536, 541
Guanine (G), A–18
Gustation. See Taste
Gynoid obesity, 515–516

H zone of skeletal muscle, 210
Hageman factor, 326

Haploid number, 581, A–19
Harvey, William, 283
Haustra, 500
Haustral contraction
  digestive regulation and, 469
  in large intestine, 500
Hay fever, 355
Hearing, 171–178
Hearing loss, 177–178
Hearing threshold, 172
Heart
  complete block, 252
  conduction system, 251
  contributions to homeostasis, 244
  defined, 245
  ECG patterns, 259
  effect of parasympathetic stimulation, 264
  effect of sympathetic stimulation, 264
  electrical activity, 250–259
  excitation coordination, 252–253
  hormonal function, 532
  normal rate of action potential discharge, 252
  nourishing, 268–271
  position, 245–246
  pump action, 246–248
  sounds, 262
  structure, 246
Heart attack
  atherosclerosis and, 271
  defined, 259
  possible outcomes, 271
Heart failure, 267–268
Heart murmur, 262–263
Heart rate
  cardiac output and, 263
  controls, 264–265
  determinants, 263
Heart valve
  diagram, 249
  function, 248
  mechanism, 248
Heart wall structure, 249
Heartburn, 474–475
Heat, 519
Heat exchange, 517–518
Heat exhaustion, 521
Heat exposure, responses to, 520
Heat input, 517
Heat loss
  blood flow and, 519–520
  methods, 517–518
  responses to, 520
Heat output, 517
  See also Heat loss
Heat production
  increasing, 519
  rate factors, 510–511
Heat stroke, 521
Heat wave and body heat exchange, 517
Heat-related disorders, 521
Helicobacter pylori, 484
Helicotrema, 175
Helper T cell
  activating, 350
  function, 346, 347–348
  interactions, 351
Hematocrit
  defined, 317
  diagram, 318
Heme group, 319
Hemiplegia, 228
Hemodialysis, 436
Hemoglobin
  carbon monoxide and, 391–392
  effect of acid on percent saturation, 391
  effect of BPG on percent saturation, 391

effect of carbon dioxide on percent saturation,
    390–391
  effect of temperature on percent saturation, 391
  function, 319–320
  gas transport, 387–393
  as oxygen storage depot, 390
  transport capacity, 319
Hemoglobin buffer system
  function, A–31
  hydrogen ions and, 456–457
Hemolysis, 321
Hemolytic anemia, 321
Hemolytic disease of the newborn, 323–324
Hemolytic jaundice, 491
Hemophilia, 329
Hemorrhagic anemia, 321
Hemostasis, 324–328
Henderson–Hasselbalch equation
  acid-base status and, A–36–A–37
  defined, A–31
Hepatic jaundice, 491
Hepatic portal system, 487
Hepatic portal vein, 487
Hepatocyte, 487, 488
Hering–Breuer reflex, 396
High altitude, effects on the body, 394
High-density lipoproteins (HDL), 272
Higher cortex
  behavior and, 132
  learning and, 134
  memory and, 134
Higher motor area and motor control, 127
High-intensity exercise, 224
Hippocampus and declarative memories, 135–136
Hirsutism, 553–554
Histamine
  allergic reactions and, 355
  arteriolar dilation and, 290
  digestion and, 479, 481
  function, 99
Histone, A–19
Histotoxic hypoxia, 393
Hives, 355
Homeostasis
  acid-base balance and, 442
  blood and, 316
  blood vessels and, 278
  body system contributions, 10, 12–13
  cardiovascular system and, 278
  cells and, 13, 20
  central nervous system and, 114
  circulatory system and, 244, 278
  control system, 11–15
  defined, 8, 13
  digestive system and, 464
  disruptions, 15
  endocrine system and, 76, 522
  energy balance and, 508
  factors maintained, 13
  fluid balance and, 442
  immune system and, 316
  integumentary system and, 316
  interdependencies, 9
  introduction, 5
  kidneys and, 405
  muscular system and, 208
  nervous system and, 76
  peripheral nervous system and, 150, 190
  plasma membrane and, 46
  reproductive system and, 578
  respiratory system and, 366
  skin and, 316
  temperature regulation and, 508
  urinary system and, 404
Homeostatic control system, 11–15
Homeostatic drive, 133

Homocysteine and atherosclerosis, 273
Homologous chromosome, 580–581, A–18
Hormonal communication, 100–106
Hormonal plasma concentration regulation,
  528–530
Hormonal stress response, 557
Hormone
  See also specific types
  blood pressure and, 292
  defined, 4
  effect process, 102
  function, 99
  functions, 527–528
  hierarchic chain of command, 537, 538
  hydrophilic (See Hydrophilic hormone)
  hypothalamic inhibiting, 536
  hypothalamic releasing, 536
  lipophilic (See Lipophilic hormone)
  ovarian cycle and, 603–606, 607–608
  placental and pregnancy, 614–615
  summary of major, 531–532
  types, 100–101
Hormone response element (HRE), 106
Host cell and immune system, 329
Human chorionic gonadotropin (hCG), 614–615
Human height compared to other structures,
  A–1
Human immunodeficiency virus (HIV), 348
Humor (physical), 283
Humoral immunity, 339
Hydration and urine excretion, 427
Hydrochloric acid (HCl), 475, 478–480
Hydrogen bond, A–7
Hydrogen (H) characteristics, A–4
Hydrogen ion
  acid–base balance and secretion, 422
  acids and, 452
  defenses against changes in, 455–459
  fluctuations, 454
  renal excretion, 458
  renal regulation of, A–32–A–34
  respiratory regulation of, A–31–A–32
  sources, 454–455
Hydrolysis
  defined, 26, A–16
  digestion and, 466
Hydrolytic enzyme, 26
Hydrophilic hormone
  defined, 100
  function, 527
  means of action, 102
  processing, 100
  receptor location, 102
  second-messenger systems and, 102
  transport, 102
Hydrophilic peptide hormone. See Hydrophilic
  hormone
Hydrostatic pressure, 57
Hymen, 580
Hypercalcemia, effects on the body, 569
Hypercapnia, 393
Hyperglycemia, 564
Hyperopia
  defined, 162
  diagram, 163
Hyperoxia, 393
Hyperparathyroidism, 572
Hyperplasia, 539
Hyperpnea, 393, 394
Hyperpolarization
  after, 81
  membrane potential and, 78
Hypersecretion, 530
Hypersensitivity
  allergic, 354–355
  characteristics, 357

Hypertension
  baroreceptor adaptation during, 310
  complications, 310
  defined, 308
  renal failure and, 435
Hyperthermia, 521
Hyperthyroidism, 548–549
Hypertonic
  defined, 427
  ECF osmolarity, 449
Hypertonic solution and osmosis, 59
Hypertonicity
  causes, 449
  gastric emptying and, 476–477
Hypertrophy, 226, 539
Hyperventilation
  acid-base imbalance and, 459
  defined, 393, 394
Hypocalcemia
  effects on the body, 569
  PTH and, 570
Hypocapnia, 393, 394
Hypocapnia-induced alkalosis and acute moun-
  tain sickness, 394
Hypodermis, 358
Hypoglycemia, 566–567
Hypoparathyroidism, 572–573
Hypophysiotropic hormone
  function, 536
  GH secretion and, 540–542
  summary of major, 536
Hypophysis. See Pituitary gland
Hyposecretion, 530
Hypotension, 308, 310
Hypothalamic hypophysiotropic hormones,
  540–542
Hypothalamic inhibiting hormone, 536–538
Hypothalamic osmoreceptor and thirst, 451
Hypothalamic releasing hormone control, 536–538
Hypothalamic–hypophyseal portal system, 536
Hypothalamus
  anterior pituitary gland and, 536, 538
  body temperature and, 518–519
  diagram, 130
  fever and, 520–522
  food intake and, 511–515
  function, 121, 526, 531
  functions, 132
  location, 124, 131
  overview, 536–538
  posterior pituitary gland and, 533–534
  stress response and, 556–557
  temperature balance and, 520–522
Hypothalamus–pituitary–adrenal cortex axis and
  cortisol secretion, 552
Hypothalamus–pituitary–thyroid axis
  defined, 536
  thyroid hormone and, 547
Hypothermia, 521
Hypothyroidism, 548–549
Hypotonic
  defined, 427
  ECF osmolarity and, 449
Hypotonic solution and osmosis, 59
Hypotonicity, 449–450
Hypoventilation
  acid-base imbalance and, 459
  defined, 393
Hypoxia, 393
Hypoxic hypoxia, 393, 394

I band of skeletal muscle, 210
ICF. See Intracellular fluid (ICF)
Identical twins, 601
Idiopathic hypertension, 308
IgE antibody and immediate hypersensitivity, 356

Ileocecal juncture/valve/sphincter, 493
Ileum, 491
Immediate hypersensitivity
  antibodies and mast cells in, 356
  characteristics, 357
  chemical mediators, 355
  defined, 354
  symptoms, 355
  treatments, 355
  triggers, 355
Immune complex disease, 342
Immune disease, 354–357
Immune response
  activation, 341–342
  adaptive, 333, 339–351
  to bacterial invasion, 333–336, 351
  innate, 332, 333–338
  primary, 344
  secondary, 344
  to viral invasion, 346–347, 348
Immune surveillance
  against cancer, 353
  defined, 352
  effectors, 353–354
Immune system
  acquired, 332, 333, 339–340
  adaptive, 332, 333, 339–340
  components, 6
  contributions to homeostasis, 10, 13, 316
  depression in renal failure, 435
  external defenses, 357–360
  function, 329
  innate, 332–339
  tolerance of self-antigens, 352
Immunity, 329
Immunization, 344–345
Immunodeficiency disease, 354
Immunodeficiency syndrome (AIDS), 348
Immunosuppressive drugs, 7
Impermeable, 54
Implantation (reproductive), 610–612
Impotence, 594–595
Inappropriate immune attack, 354–357
Inches to centimeters comparison, A–2
Inclusions, stored nutrients as, 36
Incompetent valve, 262
Incretin, 563
Incus, 173
  function, 182
Indirect intercellular communication, 98–99
Induced pluripotent stem cells (iPSCs), 8
Inflammation
  bacterial infection and, 351
  chronic illnesses and, 336
  complement system and, 338
  drugs suppressing, 337
  manifestations, 335
  outcomes, 335
  as parturition trigger, 618
  process, 333–336
  steps producing, 334
Inguinal canal, 585
Inhibin
  FSH and, 590
  function, 605
Inhibiting hormone, 536
Inhibitory postsynaptic potential (IPSP), 93, 95
Inhibitory synapse, 93
Initial lymphatics, 299
Innate immunity
  bacterial infection and, 351
  defenses, 333–339
Inner cell mass (blastocyst), 612
Inner ear
  defined, 171
  function, 173–175, 182

Innervate, 91
Inorganic chemical, A–10
Inorganic salts, A–11
Inspiration (respiratory), 373–374
Inspiratory capacity (IC), 380
Inspiratory muscle
    activity during ventilation, 376, 377
    diagram, 375
    expiration and, 374
    ventilation and, 373
Inspiratory neuron and respiratory control, 396
Inspiratory reserve volume (IRV), 380
Insufficient valve, 262
Insulin
    body-weight regulation and, 512
    function, 562–564
    glucagon and, 567
    metabolic effects of, 568
    secretion stimuli, 563–564
Insulin antagonist, 568
Insulin excess, 566–567
Insulin shock, 566
Insulin-dependent diabetes mellitus
    defined, 564
    treatment, 566
Insulin-like growth factor (IGF)
    growth hormone and, 539
    thyroid hormone and, 547
Integrating center and reflex arc, 142
Integrator and negative feedback, 11
Integument. See Skin
Integumentary system
    components, 6
    contributions to homeostasis, 10, 13, 316
    defined, 316
Intensity (sound), 172–173
Intensity discrimination, 177
Interatrial pathway, 254
Intercalated disc, 249
Intercellular communication, 97–100
Intercostal muscle, 374
Interferon, 337
    effects, 338
Intermediary metabolism. See Fuel metabolism
Intermediate filament
    cells and, 41
    diagram, 37
Internal anal sphincter, 500
Internal core temperature
    defined, 516
    maintaining, 517
Internal environment
    defined, 5
    homeostatically regulated factors, 9
Internal pool
    defined, 443
    inputs, 444
    outputs, 444
Internal work, 509
Interneuron
    action potential and, 152
    action potential initiation, 237
    defined, 117
    features, 200
    glial cells and, 117
Internodal pathway, 254
Interphase in cell division, A–26
Interstitial cell, 585
Interstitial cells of Cajal, 469
Interstitial fluid
    defined, 5, 444
    material exchange and, 295
Interstitial fluid hydrostatic pressure and bulk flow, 297

Interstitial fluid–colloid osmotic pressure and bulk flow, 297
Intestinal gas and digestion, 501–502
Intestinal housekeeper, 492–493
Intestinal phase of gastric secretion, 481–482
Intra-alveolar pressure
    changes during respiration, 377, 378
    ventilation and, 371, 373
Intracellular fluid (ICF)
    defined, 5, 444
    ECF osmolarity and, 447–449
    ionic composition, 444–445
    separation from ECF, 444–445
Intrafusal fiber, 229
Intrapleural pressure
    changes during respiration, 378
    ventilation and, 371–372
Intrinsic clot pathway, 326–327
Intrinsic factor
    defined, 478
    digestion and, 479
    function, 480–481
Intrinsic homeostatic control, 11
Intrinsic nerve plexus, 469–470
Inulin, 425
Iodide pump, 545
Iodine, 545
Ion
    defined, A–5
    membrane potential and, 68
    plasma membrane permeation and, 56
Ion movement
    action potential and, 81, 82, 83
    membrane potential changes and, 78
Ionic bond, A–5
iPSC. See Induced pluripotent stem cells (iPSCs)
Iris, 157–158, 170
Iron absorption in small intestine, 499
Iron deficiency anemia, 321
Irreversible shock, 311
Islet of Langerhans
    cell types in, 561
    defined, 485
    function, 532, 561
Isometric contraction, 219–220
Isotonic, defined, 55, 427
Isotonic contraction, 220–221
Isotonic solution and osmosis, 59
Isovolumetric ventricular contraction, 260
Isovolumetric ventricular relaxation, 262

Jaundice, 491
Jejunum, 491
Jenner, Edward, 345
Jet lag, 543
Junction
    gap, 53–54
    tight, 52–53
Juvenile-onset diabetes mellitus
    defined, 564
    treatment, 566
Juxtaglomerular apparatus
    defined, 408
    sodium reabsorption and, 416–417

K+ level and hydrogen ions, 454
K+ movement and membrane potential, 70
Keratin
    diagram, 37
    as intermediate filaments, 41
Keratinized skin layer and immunity, 357–358
Keratinocyte, 359
Ketone body, A–12–A–13

Kidney
    See also Renal
    cardiac output and, 413–414
    function, 406
    glucose regulation, 420–421
    hormonal function, 532
    hormones and, 530
    hydrogen ion changes and, 459
    overview, 405
    plasma pH and, A–31
Kidney function
    acid-base balance and, 458–459
    heart failure and, 267
    overview, 405–406
    phosphate and, 421
    reabsorptive processes summary, 424
    salt output, 447
    secretory processes summary, 424
    urine concentration, 427, 433
Kilocalorie, 510
Kinesin
    description, 38
    movement, 39
Knee-jerk reflex
    diagram, 231
    process, 229–230
Krebs cycle. See Citric acid cycle

Labeled line, 154
Labia, 580
Labor (pregnancy). See Parturition
Lactase, 493
Lactate and muscle energy, 224–225
Lactation, 580
    defined, 620
Lactose and digestion, 466
Lactose intolerance, 494
Lactotrope, 534
Langerhans cell and immunity, 359
Language
    cortex control, 127
    cortical pathways for speaking, 128
Large intestine
    absorption and, 501
    anatomy, 500
    overview, 500–502
    secretion, 501
    volumes absorbed, 499
Laron dwarfism, 105
    defined, 542
Laryngeal opening, 473
Larynx
    defined, 368–369
    swallowing and, 473
Latch phenomenon, 239
Lateral hypothalamic area (LHA) and energy balance, 513
Lateral sac, 214
Lateral space and tubular reabsorption, 414
Law of conservation of mass, A–7
Law of mass action
    gas transport and, 388
    hydrogen ions and, 455
Leader sequence, A–24
Leak channel
    ion movement and, 78
    lipid bilayer and, 49
Leaky valve, 262
Learning
    higher cortex and, 134
    limbic system and, 134
Length English-metric conversions, A–2
Length Metric-English conversions, A–2
Length–tension relationship, 223

Lens (eye)
  defined, 157
  function, 170
  refraction and, 160
  structure, 162
Leptin, 512
Leptin-signaling pathway and obesity,
    515
Leukemia, immune system and, 332
Leukocyte
  See also White blood cell (WBC)
  bacteria destruction by, 335
  defined, 316, 329
  emigration, immune system and, 335
  function, 329
  production, 331
  production abnormalities, 331–332
  proliferation, immune system and, 335
  types, 329–331
Leukotriene, 592
Leydig cell
  function, 585
  LH and, 590
LH surge, 605–606
Light, 158–159
Light adaptation (visual), 168
Light chain, 234
Light ray
  defined, 159
  focusing, 159–160
  refraction and, 160
Limbic association cortex
  diagram, 125
  overview, 129
Limbic system
  diagram, 132
  functions, 132–133
  learning and, 134
  memory and, 134
  motivation and, 133
Linear measurement comparison, A–2
Linear measures and English equivalents,
    A–1
Lipid, A–12–A–13
Lipid bilayer
  channels, 49
  functions, 49
  in plasma membrane, 47
Lipid emulsion and bile salts, 489
Lipid-soluble substance and plasma membrane
    permeation, 54
Lipolysis, 551
  defined, 562–563
Lipophilic hormone
  defined, 100
  means of action, 102
  protein synthesis and, 106
  receptor location, 102
Lips, 471
Liver
  absorbed nutrients and, 499
  anatomy, 489
  blood flow, 487–488
  functions, 487
  hormonal function, 532
  hormones and, 530
  IGF and, 539
  metabolic states and, 561
  organization, 487–488
  steroids and, 227
Load and muscle movement, 219
Lobule, 487–488
Local homeostatic control, 11
Long-acting thyroid stimulator (LATS) and
    Graves' disease, 548

Long-term memory
  defined, 134
  molecular mechanisms, 135
  short-term memory and, 134–135
Loop of Henle
  defined, 408
  kidney function and, 427–428
  properties, 428–429
Lou Gehrig's disease, 198
Loudness
  defined, 172
  relative magnitudes, 173
Loudness discrimination, 177
Low-density lipoprotein (LDL), 270, 272
Low-level LH secretion suppression, 605
Lowry, Thomas, A–10
Lumen, 3
Lung
  capacity, 380–381
  defined, 371
  elastic behavior, 379
  elastic recoil, 379
  forces influencing, 379
  hydrogen ions and, A–32
  plasma pH and, A–31
  stability, 379–380
  volume, 380–381
  volume changes during respiration, 377
Luteal phase, 599, 601, 603
Luteinization, 601
  process, 603
Luteinizing hormone (LH)
  function, 534–536, 589–590
  function in ovarian cycles, 603–606
  menstruation and, 608
  secretion modes, 605
Lymph
  defined, 299
  flow of, 299
  pickup of, 299
Lymph node, 300
Lymph vessel, 299
Lymphatic system
  functions, 299–300
  interstitial fluid and, 299–301
Lymphocyte
  adaptive immunity and, 339
  function, 331
Lymphoid tissue, 331
Lysosome
  diagram, 27
  organelles and, 27
  overview, 26–27
Lysozyme, 472

M line of skeletal muscle, 210
Macromolecule, A–10
  defined, 557
Macrophage
  atherosclerosis and, 270
  defined, 330–331
  immunity and, 348
Macula lutea
  function, 170
  structure, 162
Macular degeneration, 162
Magnesium (Mg), A–4
Major histocompatibility complex (MHC), 349
Malabsorption, 495
Malignant tumor, 353
Malleus, 173, 182
Malpighi, Marcello, 283
Maltase, 493
Maltose and digestion, 472
Mammary gland, 620

Mass, A–3
Mass English-metric conversions, A–2
Mass measures and English equivalents, A–1
Mass Metric-English conversions, A–2
Mass movement and feces elimination, 500
Mast cell and immediate hypersensitivity, 356
Mastication, 471–472
Matrix, 29
Matter, A–3
Mature follicle, 601
Maturity-onset diabetes mellitus
  defined, 564
  treatment, 566
Mean arterial pressure
  calculating, 306
  carotid sinus baroreceptor and, 308
  defined, 287
  determinants, 306–307
  function, 305
  nervous system effects on, 309
  regulating, 306–308
  total peripheral resistance on, 291
Measures of capacity and English equivalents, A–1
Mechanical stress and bone deposition, 569–570
Mechanically gated channels and ion movement,
    78
Mechanoreceptor
  defined, 151
  digestive regulation and, 470–471
Medulla, 124
Medullary countercurrent system, 429–431
Medullary respiratory center, 396–397
Megakaryocyte, 324
Meiosis
  diagram, A–28–A–29
  process, A–27, 581, 583, 588
  reproductive system and, 600
Meiotic arrest, 598
Melanin, 359
Melanocortin, 512
Melanocyte, 359
Melanocyte-stimulating hormone (MSH), 512
  function, 536
Melanopsin, 171
  function, 543
Melatonin
  circadian rhythm and, 543–544
  function, 542–544
  puberty and, 590–591
Membrane
  See also Plasma membrane
Membrane attack complex (MAC) and comple-
    ment system, 337–339
Membrane permeability and action potential, 81
Membrane potential
  action potential and, 81
  changes in, 78
  defined, 46, 66
  Depolarization, 78
  determining, 68
  Hyperpolarization, 78
  ion characteristics, 68
  K+ And Na+ effects, 66–71
  overview, 66–71
  polarization, 77
  Repolarization, 78
  triggering event, 78
Memory
  cerebellum and, 136
  higher cortex and, 134
  hippocampus and, 135–136
  limbic system and, 134
  prefrontal cortex and, 136
  stages of, 134–135
  storage capacity, 135

Memory trace, 134
Menopause, 608–609
Menstrual cramp, 608
Menstrual cycle
  function, 597
  process, 607–608
Menstrual flow, 607–608
Menstrual phase, 607–608
Messenger RNA (mRNA)
  See also mRNA
  DNA transcription and, A–20–A–21
  protein synthesis and, A–22
Metabolic acidosis
  compensations, A–35
  defined, 460
  diagram, A–36–A–37
  ratio, A–34
  renal failure and, 435
Metabolic alkalosis
  compensations, A–37
  defined, 460
  diagram, A–36–A–37
  ratio, A–34
Metabolic fuel storage, 560
Metabolic rate, 510
  measuring basal, 510
Metabolic state
  comparison of types, 560–561
  roles of tissues in, 561
Metabolic syndrome, 564
Metabolic water, 450
Metabolism
  See also Fuel metabolism
  cortisol and, 551
  defined, 557
  epinephrine and, 555
  regulating, 561–562
  thyroid hormone and, 547
Metaphase
  meiotic, A–27
  mitotic, A–26, A–27
Metric measures and English equivalents, A–1
Metric-English conversions, A–2
MHC molecule, 349–350
Micellar formation and bile salts, 489–490
Micelle
  diagram, 492
  function, 489–490
Microcirculation, 282
Microfilament
  diagram, 37
  functions of, 40
  importance of, 39
Microglia, 119
Microtubule
  cilia and, 38
  diagram, 37
  flagella and, 38
  functions, 37
Microvilli
  defined, 40
  digestion and, 493
  function, 494–495
  in kidney, 41
  in small intestine, 41
Micturition, 435–437
Micturition reflex, 435–436
Midbrain, 124
Middle ear
  defined, 171
  diagram, 174
  function, 173, 182
Midventricular diastole, 260
Migrating motility complex and digestion,
    492–493

Milk
  composition, 621
  ejection, 620
  letdown, 620
  weaning and production, 622
Mineralocorticoid, 550–551
Mitochondria, 28–35
Mitochondrial inner membrane, oxidative phos-
    phorylation in, 32, 33
Mitochondrial matrix, citric acid cycle in, 30–31
Mitochondrion. See Mitochondria
Mitosis
  defined, 39, 581
  diagram, A–28–A–29
  phases, A–26–A–27
  process, 39
  reproductive system and, 600
Mitotic proliferation, 587–588
Mitotic spindle, 39
Mitral cell, 184
Mitral valve, 248
Mixed function gland, 528
Mixing movement and digestion, 465
Mixture (chemical), A–8
Molarity, A–9
Mole (chemical), A–8
Molecular mass, A–8
Molecular motor and vesicle transport, 38
Molecular weight, A–8
Molecule
  biological, A–10
  defined, 2, A–3
  nonpolar, A–6
  organic, A–11
  organic nutrient, 558, 559
  polar, A–6
Monocyte, 330–331
Monoglyceride and digestion, 466
Monoiodotyrosine (MIT), 546
Monomer, A–10
Mononuclear agranulocyte, 330
Monosaccharide
  defined, A–11–A–12
  digestion and, 466
Monosynaptic reflex, 143
Morning sickness, 615
Morula, 610
Motilin, 492–493
Motility, 465
Motion sickness, 180
Motivation, 133
Motor control
  abnormalities, 228–229
  higher motor areas, 127
  primary motor cortex, 125
Motor end plate, 198
Motor homunculus
  description, 125
  diagram, 126
  overview, 127
Motor movement control, 228–231
Motor neuron
  alpha, 229, 230
  function, 197
  gamma, 229, 230
  input for output control, 228
  muscle innervation, 220
  skeletal muscle cell innervation, 201
Motor program task coordination, 127
Motor unit
  defined, 220
  diagram, 221
  output influences, 228
Motor unit recruitment, 221
Mouth, 471–473

mRNA
  defined, 22
  rough ER and, 23
Mucosa
  digestive tract, 467
  gastric, 478
  small intestine, 494–495
  stomach, 479
Mucous cell, 478–479
Mucous membrane, 467
Mucus and digestion, 472
Multineuronal motor system, 228
Multiple sclerosis (MS), 90
Multiunit smooth muscle
  characteristics, 232–233
  properties, 235
Muscarinic receptor, 196
Muscle
  See also specific types
  action potential and twitch, 218
  atrophy, 226
  categories, 209–210
  characteristics, 209, 232–233
  contractile component, 219
  contraction strength, 220–221
  exercise and cooling mechanisms, 448
  function, 209
  hypertrophy, 226
  insertion, 219
  length–tension relationship, 223
  metabolic states and, 561
  optimal length, 223
  origin, 219
  relaxation, 218
  relaxation diagram, 216
  series-elastic component, 219
  structure, 218
  tension, 219, 220
  tension, maximal, 223
  tissue, 3
  types, 208, 209
Muscle cell and membrane potential, 71
Muscle fiber
  adaptation, 226
  ATP formation and, 224
  defined, 198
  genetic endowment of types, 226
  red, 225
  skeletal, 209–210
  skeletal characteristics, 226
  skeletal types, 225
  tension development, 221
  white, 226
Muscle length
  contractile activity and, 223
  limitations, 223–224
Muscle spindle
  function, 230
  structure, 229
Muscular system
  components, 6
  contributions to homeostasis, 10, 13, 208
Muscularis externa, 467
Mutagen, A–27–A–28
Mutation, cellular, A–27–A–29
Myasthenia gravis, 203
Myelinated fiber
  action potential and, 89
  diagram, 90
Myenteric plexus
  digestive regulation and, 469
  in digestive tract wall, 467
Myocardial infarction, acute, 259
Myocardial ischemia, 259
Myocardium, 249

Myoepithelial cell, 621
Myofibril, 209–210
Myoglobin, 225
Myometrium, 607
Myopia
  defined, 162
  diagram, 163
Myosin
  actin microfilaments and, 40
  diagram, 212
  muscle cells and, 40
  skeletal muscle and, 210
  smooth muscle cross bridge, 235
  smooth muscles and, 234
Myxedema, 548

Na+
  blood pressure and renal handling, 447
  osmosis in ECF and ICF and, 447–448
Na+ absorption in small intestine, 496
Na+ load, 416
Na+ movement and membrane potential, 69, 70
Na+ reabsorption
  kidney function and, 421–422
  RAAS and, 447
  urinary system and, 415–416
Na+-dependent secondary active transport and
    kidney function, 419
Na+–K+ ATPase pump
  action potential and, 84
  membrane potential and, 69
  process, 63
  tubular reabsorption and, 415–416
Nasal passage, 368
Natural killer (NK) cell
  function, 337
  stimulating, 342
Nearsightedness. See Myopia
Necrosis
  apoptosis compared with, 104
  heart muscle, 259
Negative feedback
  components, 14
  in endocrine control, 537
  in homeostatic control systems, 11
  process, 14
Negative-feedback control, hormonal, 529
Nephron
  defined, 406
  diagram, 408
  in renal medulla, 427–428
  transport across, 424
  tubular component, 407–408
  vascular component, 406–407
Nerve, 141
Nerve cell and membrane potential, 71
Nerve fiber, 85
Nervous system
  See also specializations
  components, 6
  contributions to homeostasis, 10, 12
  digestive, 469
  effects on blood pressure, 309
  endocrine system and, 106–108
  homeostasis and, 76
  organization, 115–119
  properties, 107
  specializations, 107
  thyroid hormone and, 547
Nervous tissue, 3
Net diffusion
  Fick's Law, 55, 56
  membrane transport and, 54
Net filtration pressure, 411
Neural presbycusis, 178

Neural respiratory control, 395–396
Neural specificity, 107
Neural system and sleep stage control, 140
Neural toxin and synaptic transmission, 97
Neuritic plaque, 136
Neuroendocrine reflex, 529
Neuroendocrine system, 533
Neurofibrillary tangle and Alzheimer's disease,
    136
Neurogenic, 235
Neuroglia. See Glial cell
Neurohormone, 99
Neurohypophysis, 533
Neuromodulator, 96
Neuromuscular excitability, 569
Neuromuscular junction
  compared to synapses, 203
  defined, 198
  drugs and diseases affecting, 210–212
  events diagram, 202
  overview, 198–201
  vulnerabilities, 201–203
Neuron
  See also specific types
  classes, 117
  comparison of types, 200
  hormones and, 108
  initial segment, 85
  labeled lines, 154
  neurosecretory, 99
  relationships, 97
  secretions, 96
  structure, 84–85
  termination, 91
Neuronal center, 138
Neuronal cluster, 138
Neuronal integration, 91–97
Neuropeptide and synapses, 96
Neuropeptide Y (NPY), 512
Neurotransmitter
  behavior and, 133
  common, 93
  emotions and, 133
  function, 99
  for neuromuscular junctions, 198
  rate of release, 153
  synaptic, 91, 92
  synaptic cleft and, 94
Neurotransmitter–receptor combination, 93
Neutralization reaction, A–11
Neutron, A–3
Neutrophil, 330
Newborn respiratory distress syndrome, 379–380
Nicotinamide adenine dinucleotide (NAD+) and
    citric acid cycle, 30
Nicotinic receptor, 196
Night blindness, 168
Nitric oxide
  arteriolar vasodilation and, 290
  atherosclerosis and, 270
  functions, 290
Nitrogen (N), A–4
Nitrogen narcosis, 395
Nociceptor
  defined, 152
  function, 155–156
Nodes of Ranvier and action potential, 89
Nonelectrolyte, A–9
Nonexercise activity thermogenesis (NEAT) and
    obesity, 515
Nonhistone, A–19
Non-insulin dependent diabetes mellitus
  defined, 564
  treatment, 566
Nonpolar molecule, A–6

Nonrespiratory acidosis, 460
Nonrespiratory alkalosis, 460
Nonshivering (chemical) thermogenesis, 519
Nonsteroidal anti-inflammatory drug (NSAID)
    and peptic ulcers, 484
Noradrenaline and nerve pathway, 192
Norepinephrine
  nerve pathway and, 192
  producing, 555
Normality (concentration), A–9
Nuclear envelope, 22
Nuclear factor kB (NF-kB) as parturition trigger,
    618
Nuclear pore, A–20, 22
Nucleic acid, A–16
Nucleotide, A–16
  structure, A–18
Nucleus
  in CNS, 130
  defined, 20, 21, A–3
  overview, 22
Nutrient energy
  conversion to heat, 509–510
  metabolism and, 558
Nutrient storage
  cytosol and, 36
  forms, 558, 560
Nutritional anemia, 321

O2–Hb dissociation (saturation) curve and gas
    transport, 388–389
Obesity, 515–516
Obstructive jaundice, 491
Occipital lobe, 125
Occludins and cell junctions, 52
Odor discrimination, 185
Odorant, 183
Off response, 153
Off-center cell, 166
Oil, A–12
Olfaction. See Smell
Olfactory bulb, 184–187
Olfactory cortex, primary, 185
Olfactory mucosa, 183
Olfactory nerve, 183
Olfactory receptor cell
  defined, 183
  diagram, 184
Olfactory system adaptation, 185
Oligodendrocyte
  action potential and, 89
  overview, 119
Oncogene, A–29
Ongoing LH secretion suppression, 605
Oocyte formation, 598
Oogenesis
  compared to spermatogenesis, 598–600
  defined, 580, 597
  diagram, 599
  process, 598–599
Oogonia, 598
Ootid, 598
Opiate receptor, 156
Opsin, 166
Opsonin and inflammation, 335
Optic chiasm, 169
Optic disc
  defined, 162
  function, 170
Optic nerve
  function, 170
  structure, 162
Optic radiation, 169
Optic tract, 169
Optimal length of muscle, 223

Oral cavity, 471–473
Oral contraceptive, 608
Orexin, 513
Organ, 4
Organ of Corti
    diagram, 174
    function, 175, 182
Organ printing, 7
Organelle
    defined, 20
    function, 38
    lysosomes and, 27
    overview, 23
    structure, 38
Organic chemical, A–10
Organic ion secretory system, 423–424
Organic molecule, A–11
Organism, 3
Organophosphate and neuromuscular junctions, 202
Orgasm, 595
Oropharyngeal swallowing stage, 473–474
Orthostatic hypotension, 310
Osmolarity
    defined, 57, 447, A–9
    regulating ECF, 449
Osmoreceptor
    defined, 152
    digestive regulation and, 470–471
Osmosis
    characteristics, 67
    defined, 56, 57
    ECF, 447–449
    ICF, 447–448
    nonpenetrating solute and, 57, 58, 59
    penetrating solute and, 58
    processes, 56–58
Osmotic movement and tonicity, 60
Osmotic pressure, 57
Ossicle, 173
Osteoblast
    defined, 540
    function, 569
Osteoclast
    defined, 540
    function, 569
Osteocyte
    defined, 540
    function, 569
Osteoid, 540
Osteomalacia, 573
Osteoporosis, 569–570
Otolith, 180
Otolith organ and equilibrium, 180–181
Ova, 579
Oval window, 173
    function, 182
Ovarian cycle
    diagram, 602, 604
    hormonal levels and, 603–606
    overview, 599, 601–606
    regulating, 603–606
Ovary
    defined, 579
    diagram, 602
    functions, 597–598
Overhydration, 449
Oviduct
    defined, 580
    fertilization and, 609–610
Ovulation
    controlling, 605–606
    preventing, 608
    process, 601

Ovum
    fertilization and, 610
    formation of mature, 598
    transport to the oviduct, 609
Oxidation, 32, 34
Oxidative capacity improvement, 226
Oxidative enzyme, 27
Oxidative muscle fiber, 225
Oxidative phosphorylation
    diagram, 33
    muscle contractile activity and, 224
    process, 32
Oxygen
    alveolar, 384–385
    blood transport of, 387–395
    bound to hemoglobin, 388
    brain nourishment, 120
    characteristics, A–4
    deficit and exercise, 225
    energy equivalent of, 511
    hemoglobin storage, 390
    partial pressure of, 384
    physically dissolved, 387–388
Oxyhemoglobin (HbO2), 388
Oxyntic mucosa, 478
Oxytocin
    function, 533
    milk ejection and, 620–621
    as parturition trigger, 617

P wave, 257
Pacemaker (artificial), 252
Pacemaker activity
    abnormal, 252
    analogy diagram, 253
    cardiac autorhythmic cells and, 250–252
    normal, 252
Pacemaker potential
    cardiac autorhythmic cells and, 250–251
    initiating action potentials in excitable tissues, 237
    smooth muscles and, 236–237
Packaging (reproductive), 588
Packed cell volume, 317
Pain
    defined, 155
    perceiving, 155–156
    referred, 141
Pain receptor. See Nociceptor
Palate, 471
Pancreas
    See also Endocrine pancreas; Exocrine pancreas
    anatomy, 485
    cystic fibrosis and, 50
    function, 561–562
    location and structure, 561
Pancreatic amylase, 486
Pancreatic aqueous alkaline secretion, 485–486
Pancreatic enzyme, 485–486
Pancreatic exocrine secretion regulation, 486–487
Pancreatic hormone and fuel metabolism, 561–562
Pancreatic insufficiency, 486
Pancreatic lipase, 486
Pancreatic secretion
    CCK and, 486–487
    digestion and, 485–487
    secretin and, 486
Papillary muscle, 248–249
Para-aminohippuric acid (PAH), 425–426
Paracrine, 98
Paracrine cell, 479
Paradoxical sleep, 139
Paradoxical sleep center, 140
Paraplegia, 228

Parasympathetic dominance
    defined, 192
    times of, 195
Parasympathetic innervation and arterioles, 292
Parasympathetic nervous system
    defined, 116, 191
    digestive regulation and, 470
    effects on blood pressure, 309
    features, 198
    function, 192
    salivary secretion and, 472
    structures innervated by, 194
Parasympathetic preganglionic fiber, 192
Parasympathetic stimulation, effect on heart, 264
Parasympathetic tone, 192
Parathyroid gland, 526, 532, 569
Parathyroid hormone (PTH)
    hypersecretion, 572
    hyposecretion, 572–573
    plasma calcium and, 569, 570–571
    plasma phosphate and, 570–571
    vitamin D and plasma calcium, 572
Paraventricular nucleus (PVN), 513
Parietal cell, 478, 479
Parietal lobe, 123–125
Parietal-temporal-occipital association cortex
    diagram, 125
    overview, 129
Parkinson's disease (PD) and basal nuclei, 131
Partial pressure (gas)
    abnormalities in arterial, 393–394
    consequences of abnormalities in arterial, 394–395
    defined, 384
    percent hemoglobin saturation and, 388
    respiration and, 384–385
    ventilation and, 397
Partial pressure gradient, 384–387
Parturition
    defined, 580
    process diagram, 617
    requirements, 616
    stages, 619
    triggers, 616, 618
Passive current flow and graded potential, 79, 80
Passive diffusion and plasma membrane permeation, 54
Pasteur, Louis, 345
Patellar tendon reflex
    diagram, 231
    process, 229–230
Pathogen, 329
Pathophysiology, 15
Penis, 580
Penis vasocongestion, 593–594
Pepsin and digestion, 480
Pepsinogen
    digestion and, 479, 480
    gastric gland and, 478
Peptic ulcer, 483–484
Peptide, 100
Peptide bond, A–14
Peptide hormone
    defined, 527
    processing, 100
    properties, 101
Peptide YY$_{3-36}$ and food intake, 514
Percent hemoglobin saturation
    acid and, 391
    BPG and, 391
    carbon dioxide and, 390–391
    defined, 388
    temperature and, 391
Perception, 155
Perforin and immunity, 346

Perineal region, 580
Peripheral chemoreceptor
    blood gas and, 397
    chemical factor influences, 397
Peripheral nervous system (PNS)
    afferent division, 116
    contributions to homeostasis, 190
    defined, 116, 150
    efferent division, 116
Peripheral resistance and mean arterial pressure, 291
Peristalsis
    defined, 474, 475
    digestive regulation and, 469
Peristaltic wave
    digestion and, 492–493
    swallowing and, 474
Peritubular capillary, 407
Permeable, defined, 54
Permissiveness (hormonal)
    cortisol and, 551
    defined, 530
Pernicious anemia cause, 321
Peroxisome, 27
pH designation
    hydrogen ions and, 453–454, 456
    logarithmic nature, A–30
    values of common solutions, 455
Phagocyte
    inflammation and, 336
    interactions, 351
Phagocytosis
    characteristics, 67
    enhancing, 342
    process, 26, 28
Pharyngoesophageal sphincter, 473–474
Pharynx
    defined, 173, 368
    function, 471
    overview, 473–475
Phasic receptor
    defined, 153
    diagram, 154
Phenotypic sex, 583
Phosphate
    kidney function and, 421
    metabolic control, 570–571
    as urinary buffer, 459
Phosphate buffer system
    function, A–31
    hydrogen ions and, 457
Phosphate imbalance and renal failure, 435
Phospholipid
    defined, A–13
    molecular structure, 48
    structure, 47
Phosphorus (P), A–4
Photopigment
    See also Photoreceptor
    description, 162
    structure, 166
Photoreceptor
    See also Cones; Rods
    defined, 151
    diagram, 165
    structure, 162
Phototransduction, 166
Physiology, 1
Pineal gland
    function, 526, 531
    location, 124
    overview, 542–544
Pinna
    See also External ear
    function, 173, 182

major components functions, 182
    structure, 171
Pinocytosis
    characteristics, 67
    diagram, 28
    process, 26
Pitch
    defined, 172
    discrimination, 175
Pituitary dwarfism, 542
Pituitary gland
    See also Anterior pituitary gland; Posterior pituitary gland
    function, 526, 531
    overview, 533–536
Placenta
    defined, 580, 612
    delivery, 619
    formation, 613
    functions, 523, 614
    hormone secretion and pregnancy, 614–615
Placental clock, 618
Placental hormone secretion rate, 615
Placental villi, 613–614
Placentation, 613
Plaque (cellular), 52
Plasma
    components, 317–318
    defined, 5, 444
    inadequate volume, 448
    ionic composition, 445
    overview, 317–319
Plasma calcium, regulating, 568–571
Plasma cell
    diagram, 341
    function, 340
Plasma clearance, 425–426
Plasma concentration
    endocrine system and, 568
    hormonal, 528–530
Plasma glucose concentration and kidney function, 420
Plasma membrane
    See also Membrane
    current loss, 80
    defined, 2, 20, 21
    diagram, 48
    diffusion of, 55
    dividing ECF and ICF, 444–445
    functions, 46, 49
    membrane potential changes and, 78
    overview, 22, 47
    permeability and action potential, 82, 83
    protein receptors in, 85, 92, 151
    proteins in, 46
    transport, 54
    trilaminar structure, 47
Plasma membrane carbohydrate
    cells and, 48
    as self-identity markers, 51
Plasma membrane protein
    functions, 49, 51
    plasma membrane and, 48
Plasma membrane transport
    assisted, 59–65
    carrier-mediated, 60–62
    pathway summaries, 67
    unassisted, 54–59
Plasma membrane-bound enzyme and cells, 51
Plasma phosphate, 568, 570–571
Plasma protein
    function, 318–319
    loss in renal failure, 435
Plasma water, 317

Plasma-colloid osmotic pressure
    bulk flow and, 297
    defined, 411, 412
Plasmin, 328
Plasminogen, 328
Platelet, 324
Platelet plug and hemostasis, 325–326
Platelet-activating factor (PAF), 269
Pleural cavity, 371
Pleural sac, 371
Pleurisy, 371
Plexus, 467
Pluripotent stem cell, 320
Pneumatic theory, circulatory system and, 283
Pneumotaxic center and respiratory control, 396
Pneumothorax
    defined, 373
    diagram, 374
Podocyte, 411
Point mutation, A–27
Polar molecule, A–6–A–7
Polarization and membrane potential, 77
Poliovirus, 198
Polycythemia, 322
Polydipsia, 564
Polymer, A–10
Polymorphonuclear granulocyte, 330
Polynucleotide
    defined, A–18
    diagram, A–19, A–20
Polypeptide and DNA, A–18
Polyphagia, 564
Polyribosome
    diagram, A–26
    mRNA and, A–24
Polysaccharide
    defined, A–12
    digestion and, 466
Polyspermy, block to, 610
Polysynaptic reflex, 143
Polyuria, 564
Pons, 124
Pore, capillary, 295
Positive feedback
    defined, 14
    Na+ channels and, 82
    ovulation and, 605
    parturition and, 618
Postabsorptive state (metabolic)
    glucagon and, 567
    process, 560–561
Posterior parietal cortex
    diagram, 125
    overview, 127
Posterior pituitary gland, 533–534
Postganglionic fiber, 191
Postganglionic nerve terminal and smooth muscle innervation, 238
Posthepatic jaundice, 491
Postsynaptic neuron
    defined, 91
    spatial summation and, 94
    temporal summation and, 94
Postsynaptic neuronal integration, 95
Postsynaptic potentials, 93
Postural hypotension, 310
Potassium (K) characteristics, A–4
Potassium ion secretion
    aldosterone and, 422–424
    controlling, 423
    mechanism, 422–423
Potassium level and hydrogen, 454
Potassium movement and membrane potential, 69
Potassium retention and renal failure, 435
Power stroke and muscle contraction, 213

PR segment, 258
Preantral follicle, 601
Pre-Bötzinger complex, 396
Precipitation, 341
Precocious pseudopuberty, 554
Prefrontal association cortex
    diagram, 125
    overview, 129
Prefrontal cortex and working memory, 136
Preganglionic fiber, 191
Pregnancy
    defined, 580
    effects on the body, 616
    fetal and uterine relationships, 613
    placental hormone secretion and, 614–616
Prehepatic jaundice, 491
Prehypertension, 310
Premature ventricular contraction (PVC), 252
Premotor cortex
    diagram, 125
    overview, 127
Preovulatory follicle, 601
Preprohormone processing, 101
Presbyopia, 162
Pressure gradient
    blood flow and, 281
    defined, 280
    respiration and, 371–373
    respiratory gas exchange and, 384
Pressure reservoir, arteries as, 282, 284, 285
Presynaptic neuron, 91
Primary active transport
    characteristics, 67
    process, 62–63
Primary auditory cortex, 125
Primary hypertension, 308
Primary motor cortex, 125
Primary olfactory cortex, 185
Primary polycythemia, 322
Primary visual cortex, 125
Procarboxypeptidase and digestion, 486
Product of chemical reaction, A–7
Progestational phase (menstrual cycle), 608
Progesterone
    actions, 621
    defined, 579
    effects on the uterus, 607
    lactation and, 620
    ovarian cycle and, 606
    pregnancy and, 614–616
Progesterone secretion and ovarian cycle, 601, 603
Programmed cell suicide, 94–95
Prolactin (PRL)
    function, 534–536
    lactation and, 620
    milk secretion and, 620–621
Prolactin-inhibiting hormone (PIH)
    function, 536
    milk secretion and, 621
Prolactin-releasing hormone (PRH) and milk
        secretion, 621
Proliferative phase (menstrual cycle), 608
Pro-opiomelanocortin (POMC), 534, 536
Prophase
    meiotic, A–27
    mitotic, A–26–A–27
Proprioception, 123
Propulsive movement and digestion, 465
Prostacyclin, 592
Prostaglandin, 521, 592–593
Prostate, 591
Prostate gland, 580, 592
Prostate-specific antigen (PSA), 591–592
Protein
    composition, A–13–A–14
    defined, A–13

digestion and, 466
digestive process, 473, 494, 497
glucagon and, 567
insulin and, 563
metabolism and diabetes, 565–566
primary structure, A–14
quaternary structure, A–16
secondary structure, A–16
structure levels, A–14–A–16
tertiary structure, A–16
testosterone and, 587
Protein absorption and digestion, 497
Protein buffer system and hydrogen ions, 456
Protein digestion, 483
Protein kinase A and cAMP second-messenger
        pathway, 103
Protein structure
    levels, A–15
Protein synthesis, A–22, A–24
Protein transcription control, A–24, A–26
Protein translation and ribosomal assembly, A–25
Proteolytic enzyme, 486
Prothrombin and blood clotting, 326
Proton, A–3
Proton-pump inhibitor and peptic ulcers, 484
Proto-oncogene, A–29
Proximal tubule
    defined, 408
    transport across, 424
Pseudomonas aeruginosa and cystic fibrosis, 50
Pseudopod
    cell movement and, 40
    defined, 26
Psychoactive drugs and emotions, 133
Puberty
    comparison of male and female, 608
    GnRH activity and, 590–591
    primary follicles at, 598
    testosterone and, 585
Pulmonary artery, 248
Pulmonary capillary and gas exchange, 385–386
Pulmonary circulation
    defined, 245
    heart and, 246
    organization, 282
Pulmonary stretch receptor, 396
Pulmonary surfactant, 379
Pulmonary valve, 249
Pulmonary vein, 248
Pulmonary ventilation, 382
Pulse pressure, 285
Pupil, 170
Pupil (eye), 158
Purkinje fiber, 251
Pyloric gland area (PGA), 478
Pyloric sphincter, 475
Pyramidal cell, 228
Pyramidal motor system, 228
Pyruvate and glycolysis, 224

QRS complex, 257
Quadriplegia, 228
Quality (sound), 173

Radiation and body heat exchange, 517, 518
Rapture of the deep, 395
Reabsorption of extracellular fluid, 297–298
Reactant, A–7
Reactive hypoglycemia, 566–567
Readiness potential and motor cortex, 127
Receptive relaxation, 475–476
Receptor
    See also Sensory receptor
    G-protein-coupled, 99–100
    malfunctioning and disease, 105
    plasma membrane and, 51

regulating, 105
    skeletal muscle control and, 229
    stimulus-sensitive sensory, 151
Receptor activation and digestive regulation,
        470–471
Receptor editing, 352
Receptor potential
    defined, 151
    initiating action potentials in excitable tissues,
        237
Receptor-channel
    defined, 92
    extracellular chemical messengers and, 99
Receptor-mediated endocytosis
    characteristics, 67
    diagram, 28
    process, 26
Reciprocal innervation and withdrawal reflex, 143
Rectum, 500
Red blood cell (RBC), 319–320
Red bone marrow, 320
Red muscle fiber, 225
Reduced hemoglobin, 388
Reflex, 141–144
Reflex arc components, 142
Refraction
    defined, 159
    diagram, 159
    lens, 160
    process, 159–160
Refractory period
    action potential and, 87–88
    cardiac muscle and, 256
Regulatory T cell
    active suppression, 352
    function, 346
Relative refractory period and action potential, 88
Relaxation
    heart cycle and, 260
    muscular, 218
Relaxin, 616
Releasing hormone, 536
REM sleep, 139
Remembering process, 135
Renal ammonia secretion regulation,
        458–459
Renal anemia, 321
Renal artery, 406
Renal bicarbonate excretion, 459
Renal cortex, 406
Renal failure consequences, 434, 435
Renal hydrogen ion excretion, 458
Renal medulla
    defined, 406
    vertical osmotic gradient, 427
Renal pelvis, 406
Renal process, 408–410
Renal pyramid, 406
Renal threshold, 420
Renal vein, 406
Renin and sodium reabsorption, 417
Renin–angiotensin–aldosterone system
        (RAAS)
    functions, 417–418
    salt reabsorption and, 447
    sodium reabsorption and, 416–417
Repolarization and membrane potential, 78
Reproduction
    fertilization, 610–611
    physical requirements, 579–580
    zygote implantation, 610–612
Reproductive cell
    components, A–18–A–19
    spermatogenesis and, A–18–A–19
Reproductive functions, 580
Reproductive organs, 580

Reproductive physiology
  female, 597–622
  male, 585–595
Reproductive system
  components, 6, 579–580
  components of male, 592
  contributions to homeostasis, 10, 12
  contributions to life, 578
  cycling in female, 597–598
  diagram of female, 582
  diagram of male, 581
  effect of testosterone before birth, 585
  steroids and, 227
  uniqueness, 579–585
Reproductive tract
  components of male, 591
  defined, 579, 580
  endocrine disrupters and, 596
Resident tissue macrophage and inflammation, 333
Residual volume (RV), 380
Resistance
  arterioles and, 287
  blood flow rate and, 280, 289
  blood vessel radius and, 281
  defined, 80
Resolution (sexual response cycle), 595
Respiration
  alveolar air and, 384–385
  chemical factor influences, 397
  controlling, 395–400
  defined, 366, 367
  mechanics of, 371–384
Respiratory acidosis
  compensations, A–35
  defined, 459
  diagram, A–36–A–37
  ratio, A–34
Respiratory activity and venous return, 305
Respiratory airway, 368
Respiratory alkalosis
  compensations, A–35
  defined, 459
  diagram, A–36–A–37
  ratio, A–34
Respiratory arrest, 393, 399
Respiratory compliance and lungs, 379
Respiratory control center
  blood gas and, 398
  function, 396
  peripheral chemoreceptors and, 398
Respiratory dysfunction, 381, 382
Respiratory muscle
  activity during ventilation, 376, 377
  anatomy, 375
  overview, 373–375
Respiratory pump and venous return, 305
Respiratory rate, 382
Respiratory rhythm, generating, 396
Respiratory state characteristics, 393–395
Respiratory system
  anatomy, 368–369
  components, 6
  contributions to homeostasis, 10, 12, 366
  defenses of, 359
  hydrogen ion regulation and, 457–458, A–32
  nonrespiratory functions, 367–368
Rest and digest response, 195
Restak, Richard, 544
Resting membrane potential
  balance of leaks and pumping, 70
  defined, 66, 77
Reticular activating system (RAS), 138
Reticular formation and brain stem, 138
Retina
  diagram, 164
  focus and, 161

function, 156, 170
  light stimulus response, 166
  structure, 162
Retinal, 166
Retrograde amnesia, 135
Reversible shock, 311
Rh blood group system, 323–324
Rh factor, 323–324
Rheumatoid arthritis
  defined, 342
  glucocorticoids and, 551–552
Rhodopsin, 166
Rib and respiration, 371
Ribonucleic acid (RNA)
  defined, 22
  structure, A–16
Ribosomal assembly and protein translation, A–25
Ribosomal protein synthesis and cytosol, 36
Ribosomal RNA (rRNA)
  defined, 22
  protein synthesis and, A–22
Ribosome
  defined, 22
  DNA translation and, A–23–A–24
  rough ER and, 23
Rickets, 573
Rigor mortis, 217–218
RNA
  defined, 22
  structure, A–16
Rod (retinal)
  See also Photoreceptor
  function, 156, 167, 170
  structure, 162
  vision properties, 167
Rough ER
  diagram, 24
  overview, 23
Round window (ear)
  description, 175
  function, 182

Saccule, 180–181, 182
Saliva, 472–473
Salivary amylase, 472
Salivary center, 472
Salivary reflex, 472
Salt balance
  daily requirements, 446
  ECF volume and, 445–446
  kidneys and, 442
Saltatory conduction and action potential, 89
Salts (chemical), A–11
Salty taste perception, 183
Sarcomere, 210
Sarcoplasmic reticulum
  defined, 24
  diagram, 215
  function, 214
Satiety, 512
Satiety center and food intake, 514
Satiety signal, 512
Saturated fatty acid, A–12
Scar tissue and inflammation, 336
Schwann cell and action potential, 89
Sclera
  defined, 156
  function, 170
Scrotum
  function, 585
  location, 580
Sebaceous gland, 358
Second messenger, 100
Second polar body, 598
Secondary active transport
  characteristics, 67
  process, 64, 419

Secondary follicle
  defined, 601
  diagram, 603
Secondary hypertension, 308
Secondary polycythemia, 322
Secondary spermatocyte, 588
Second-messenger pathway
  amplification by, 104
  extracellular chemical messengers and, 99
  hydrophilic hormone effects and, 102–103
Secretin
  bile secretion and, 490
  functions, 502
  gastric motility and, 476
  pancreatic secretion and, 486
Secretion
  defined, 4
  digestive, 466
Secretory phase (menstrual cycle), 608
Secretory vesicle
  defined, 25
  Golgi complex and, 25
  nutrient storage and cytosol, 36, 37
  transporting, 39
Segmentation
  digestive regulation and, 469
  small intestine motility and, 491–492
Selective serotonin reuptake inhibitor (SSRI), 94
Self-antigen
  defined, 345, 349
  immune system tolerance and, 352
Self-excitable smooth muscles, 236
Semen
  defined, 580
  makeup, 591
  volume, 595
Semicircular canal
  equilibrium and, 178
  function, 182
Semilunar valve, 249
Seminal vesicle
  defined, 580
  function, 591, 592
  location, 592
Seminiferous tubule, 585
Seminiferous tubule fluid, 589
senile dementia, 136
Senile plaque, 136
Sensitization period (allergic), 355
Sensor in negative feedback, 11
Sensorineural deafness, 178
Sensory afferent, 153–154
Sensory homunculus
  description, 123
  diagram, 126
Sensory information, 154
Sensory receptor
  afferent neuron, 117
  digestive regulation and, 470–471
  permeability and graded potential, 152
  potential and action potential, 152
  potential magnitude, 153
  reflex arc and, 142
  stimulation adaptation, 153
  types, 151–153
  uses, 152
Sensory transduction, 151
Septicemic shock, 329
Septum, 246
Serosa in digestive tract wall, 467
Sertoli cell
  FSH and, 590
  sperm and, 589
  spermatogenesis and, 587
Serum, 327–328
Set point in negative feedback, 11

Sex act, 593–595
Sex chromosome, 583
Sex determination, 583–584
Sex gland, accessory, 579–580
Sex hormone
    function, 550
    secretion, 552–554
Sex-determining region of the Y chromosome
    (SRY), 583
Sexual characteristics, secondary, 580, 586–587
Sexual differentiation, 583–585
Sexual intercourse, 593
Sexual libido and testosterone, 585–586
Sexual response cycle
    comparison of male and female, 595–596
    phases of male, 593
Shivering and body temperature, 519
Shock, circulatory, 310–311
Short-term memory
    defined, 134
    long-term memory and, 134–135
    molecular mechanisms, 135
Sickle cell disease, 321–322
Sight. See Vision
Signal molecule, 98
Signal transduction, 99–100
Signal transduction pathway, 104
Sildenafil, 594–595
Simple diffusion
    See also Diffusion
    characteristics, 67
    membrane transport and, 54
    process, 54
Simple lipid, A–12–A–13
Simple salivary reflex, 472
Single-unit smooth muscle
    characteristics, 232–233
    contraction gradation, 237
    properties, 236–237
Sinoatrial (SA) node, 251
Sinusoid and liver blood flow, 487
Sinusoid, liver, 488
Sister chromatid, A–26
Skeletal muscle
    action potential initiation, 237
    Ca2+ and movement, 213
    calcium-induced contraction, 236
    characteristics, 232–233
    components, 212
    counteracting gravity, 303–304
    defined, 208
    fiber activity, 218
    fibers, 209–210
    heat production and, 519
    levels of organization, 211
    mechanics, 218–224
    metabolism, 224–225
    molecular basis of contraction, 212–218
    motor neurons and, 197, 201
    structure, 208–212
    whole-muscle tension determinants, 228
Skeletal muscle pump and venous return, 303–304
Skeletal system
    See also Bone
    components, 6
    contributions to homeostasis, 10, 13
Skin
    anatomy, 358
    components, 357–358
    contributions to homeostasis, 316
    hormonal function, 532
    immunity and, 357–359
Skull as CNS protection, 120
Sleep
    behavior patterns during, 139
    defined, 138

EEG and, 130
EEG patterns, 139
function, 140
obesity and, 515
types, 139
Sleep apnea, 399
Sleep–wake cycle
    defined, 138
    neural systems controlling, 140
Slow pain pathway, 156
Slow-reactive substance of anaphylaxis (SRS-A),
    355
Slow-wave potential
    digestive regulation and, 469
    initiating action potentials in excitable tissues,
        237
    smooth muscles and, 236–237
Slow-wave sleep, 139
Slow-wave sleep center, 140
Small intestine
    absorptive surface, 495
    digestive enzymes and, 493
    hormonal function, 532
    motility, 491–493
    mucosa modifications, 494–495
    role in absorption, 494–499
    secretion, 493
    volumes absorbed, 499
Smell
    See also Olfactory
    process, 183–185
Smooth ER
    diagram, 24
    overview, 23
Smooth muscle
    See also specific types
    action potential initiation, 237
    arteriolar, 290–291
    calcium-induced contraction, 236
    characteristics, 232–233
    contraction speed, 239
    defined, 208
    external influences, 238
    filament arrangement diagram, 235
    overview, 231–239
    properties, 231, 234
    tension when stretched, 238–239
    tone, 238
Sodium (Na), A–4
Sodium and glucose cotransporter (SGLT), 64
Sodium imbalance and renal failure, 435
Soft tissue growth and growth hormone, 539
Solute
    capillary exchange and, 296
    defined, 54, A–9
    water concentration and, 56
Solution
    concentration, 56
    defined, 54
Solution (chemical), A–9
Solvent, A–9
    defined, 54
Somatic, 580
Somatic cell
    components, A–18–A–19
    defined, 580
Somatic mutation, A–28–A–29
Somatic nervous system
    defined, 116, 190
    features, 199
    overview, 197–198
Somatic sensation, 154
Somatosensory cortex
    diagram, 125
    function, 123, 124

Somatotopic maps, 126
Somatosensory pathway, 154
Somatosensory processing, 123–124
Somatostatin
    digestion and, 479, 481, 562
    growth hormone and, 536, 541
Somatotrope, 534
Somatotropin, 534
Somesthetic sensation, 123
Somesthetic sensory neuron, 154–155
Sound transduction, 175, 177
Sound wave
    defined, 171–172
    transmission, 175–176
Sour taste perception, 183
Spasmodic torticollis and botulinum toxin,
    204
Spastic paralysis, 228
Spatial summation
    diagram, 95
    postsynaptic neuron threshold and, 94
Special senses, 154
Speech impediment, 128
Sperm
    endocrine disrupters and, 596
    fertilization and, 610
    Sertoli cells and, 589
    transport to the oviduct, 609–610
Spermatid, 588
Spermatocyte
    defined, 587
    secondary, 588
Spermatogenesis
    compared to oogenesis, 598–600
    defined, 580
    diagram, 588
    FSH and, 590
    process, 587–589
    site, 586
    testosterone and, 590
Spermatogonia
    See also Germ cell (reproductive)
    defined, 587
Spermatozoa, 579
Spermatozoon, 588–589
Spermiogenesis, 588
Sphincter, 220
    See also specializations
Sphincter of Oddi, 488
Sphygmomanometer, 285–286
Spike, membrane potential changes and,
    81
Spinal cord
    cross-section, 143
    diagram, 141
    location, 125, 140
    overview, 140–144
    reflexes and, 141
    regions, 142
    white matter, 140
Spinal nerve
    afferent fibers and, 141
    defined, 140
    efferent fibers and, 141
    regions, 142
Spinal reflex, 143–144
Spinocerebellum, 136–137
Spirogram, 380
Spirometer, 380
Spleen and red blood cells, 320
ST segment, 259
Stapes, 173
    function, 182
Starch, A–12
Steatorrhea, 486

Stem cell
    discussion, 7–8
    gastric mucosa and, 478, 496
Stenotic valve, 262
Sternum
    defined, 245
    respiration and, 371
Steroid
    defined, A–13
    discussion, 227
    ring system, A–13
Steroid hormone
    See also Lipophilic hormone
    adrenal glands and, 550
    defined, 100
    function, 527
    processing, 101
    properties, 101
    transport, 102
Steroidal compound, A–14
Stimulation, frequency and tension, 221
Stimulus
    coding, 154
    defined, 151
    functions of strength, 153
    sensory receptors and, 152
Stomach
    anatomy, 475
    functions, 475
    hormonal function, 532
    overview, 475–484
    vomiting and, 477–478
Stress
    cortisol and, 551
    cortisol secretion and, 552
    integrated response, 555–557
    mechanical and bone deposition, 569–570
    overview, 555–557
    thyroid hormone and, 548
Stressor
    chronic psychosocial, 557
    effects on the body, 555
Stretch reflex
    overview, 143
    process, 229–230
Stroke, 121
Stroke volume (SV)
    controls, 265, 266
    defined, 260
    summary of factors affecting, 266–267
Subcutaneous fat, 512
Subcutaneous tissue, 358
Submucosa, 467
Submucosal plexus
    digestive regulation and, 469
    in digestive tract wall, 467
Substance P and pain processing, 156
Subsynaptic membrane, 92
Suckling
    lactation stimulation and, 620
    reflexes, 622
Sucrase, 493
Sucrose, 466
Sudden infant death syndrome (SIDS), 399
Suffocation, 393
Sulfur (S), A–4
Summation and postsynaptic neuron threshold, 94
Supplementary motor area
    diagram, 125
    overview, 127
Suppressor T cell, 346
Suprachiasmatic nucleus, 542–543
Surface epithelial cell and gastric mucosa, 478
Suspension (solution), A–10

Suspensory ligament, 161, 170
Swallowing, 473
Swallowing center, 473
Sweat, 518
Sweat gland, 358
Sweating and body heat exchange, 518
Sweet taste perception, 183
Sympathetic collateral ganglia, 191
Sympathetic dominance
    defined, 192
    times of, 195
Sympathetic ganglion chain, 191
Sympathetic nervous system
    defined, 116, 191
    digestive regulation and, 470
    effects on blood pressure, 309
    features, 198
    function, 192
    salivary secretion and, 472
    stress and, 556
    structures innervated by, 194
Sympathetic postganglionic fiber, 192
Sympathetic stimulation
    effect on heart, 264, 266
    effect on stroke volume, 266, 267
    heart failure and, 267
    venous return and, 303
Sympathetic tone, 192
Sympathetic vasoconstriction
    blood pressure and, 291
    overriding, 292
Sympathomimetic effect of thyroid hormone, 547
Symport
    carrier-mediated transport and, 64
    characteristics, 67
    diagram, 65
Synapse
    compared to neuromuscular junctions, 203
    defined, 91
    diseases and, 96
    drugs and, 96
    excitatory, 92
    function, 92
    inhibitory, 93
    structure, 92
Synaptic cleft, 91
Synaptic input, 91
Synaptic knob, 91
Synaptic vesicle, 91
Syndrome X, 564
Synergism (hormonal), 530
Systemic capillary and gas exchange, 386–387
Systemic circulation
    defined, 245
    heart and, 246
    organization, 282
Systemic homeostatic control, 11
Systole, 260
Systolic murmur, 263
Systolic pressure, 285

T cell. *See specializations*; T lymphocyte
T lymphocyte
    adaptive immunity and, 339
    antigens and, 348–349
    cancer and, 352–354
    characteristics, 354
    defined, 331
    origins, 340
    target binding, 345
    types, 346
T tubule. *See* Transverse tubule
T wave, 257
Tachycardia, 259

Target cell
    defined, 527
    responsiveness, 530
Target-gland hormone, 537
    function, 538
Tastant, 183
Taste, 181, 183
Taste bud
    location, 471
    structure, 181
Taste pore, 181
Taste receptor cell, 181
Tay-Sachs disease, 27
T-cell receptor (BCR)
    diagram, 341
    function, 340
T-cell receptor (TCR), 345
Tectorial membrane
    defined, 175
    function, 182
Teeth, 471
Telophase
    meiotic, A–27
    mitotic, A–26, A–27
Temperature balance importance, 517
Temperature comparison, A–2
Temperature conversions, A–2
Temperature, effect on percent hemoglobin saturation, 391
Temperature regulation, 516–522
Temporal lobe, 125
Temporal summation
    diagram, 95
    postsynaptic neuron threshold and, 94
Tendon, 218
Tension
    defined, 219
    in stretched smooth muscles, 238–239
Terminal button, 198
Terminal ganglia, 192
Tertiary follicle, 601
Testicular feminization syndrome, 530, 584
Testicular function, feedback control of, 590
Testis
    anatomy, 586
    defined, 579
    function, 585, 592
    location, 580, 592
Testis-determining factor (TDF), 583
Testosterone
    defined, 579
    effects, 585–587
    estrogen and, 587
    LH and, 590
    muscle fibers and, 226
    sexual differentiation and, 583
Tetanic contraction, 222
Tetanus (physiologic)
    cardiac muscle and, 256
    twitch summation and, 221–222
Tetanus toxin and synaptic transmission, 97
Tetrad, A–27
Tetraiodothyronine (T4)
    conversion into T3, 547
    defined, 545
    synthesis, 546
Thalamus
    diagram, 130
    function, 121
    location, 124, 131
    motor control and, 131
    sight and, 169
The China Syndrome, 544
Thecal cell proliferation, 601
Thermal energy, 509

Thermal gradient, 517
Thermally gated channel and ion movement, 78
Thermoreceptor, 152
    defined, 519
Thirst, 451–452
Thirst center, 451
Thoracic cavity
    defined, 245
    overview, 371
Thoracic vertebrae and respiration, 371
Thorax, 371
Three Mile Island, 544
Threshold potential and membrane potential
        changes, 81
Thrombin, 326
Thrombocytopenia purpura, 329
Thromboembolism
    atherosclerosis and, 270–271
    cause, 328–329
Thrombopoietin and blood production, 324
Thromboxane, 592
Thrombus, 328
Thymine (T), A–18
Thymosin, 339
Thymus
    adaptive immunity and, 339
    function, 532
Thyroglobulin (Tg), 545
Thyroglobulin molecule, 545
Thyroid gland
    anatomy, 545
    function, 526, 531
    functional abnormalities, 548
    overview, 545–549
Thyroid hormone
    See also Lipophilic hormone
    defined, 100
    effects on the body, 547
    function, 527
    properties, 101
    secretion, 546, 547
    secretion regulation, 548
    storage, 546
    synthesis, 545–546
    transport, 102
Thyroid-stimulating hormone (TSH)
    function, 534–536
    thyroid hormone and, 547–548
Thyroid-stimulating immunoglobulin (TSI) and
        Graves' disease, 548, 549
Thyrotrope, 534
Thyrotropin, 534
Thyrotropin-releasing hormone (TRH)
    function, 536
    thyroid hormone and, 547
Thyroxine
    defined, 545
    synthesis, 546
Tidal volume (TV)
    anatomic dead space and, 382–383
    defined, 380
Tight junction
    cells and, 52
    diagram, 53
Timbre, 173
Timbre discrimination, 177
Tissue
    See also specific types
    hemoglobular gas exchange and, 390–391
    types, 3, 4
Tissue engineering, 7
Tissue plasminogen activator (tPA) and blood
        clotting, 328
Tissue repair and inflammation, 336
Tissue thromboplastin, 327

Tissue-specific stem cells, 7
Titin of skeletal muscle, 210
Tolerance and immune system, 352
Toll-like receptor (TLR) and immune system,
        333–339
Tone, defined, 172
Tongue, 471
Tonic LH secretion, suppressing, 605
Tonic receptor
    defined, 153
    diagram, 154
Tonicity
    defined, 58
    osmotic water movement and, 60
Total lung capacity (TLC), 381
Total peripheral resistance
    factors affecting, 293
    mean arterial pressure and, 291
Toxic Release Inventory, 597
TP interval, 259
Trachea, 368
Tract, white matter, 140–141
Transducer, 99
Transepithelial transport
    tubular reabsorption and, 414–415
    tubular secretion and, 422–424
Transfer RNA (tRNA)
    anticodons and, A–24
    defined, 22
    protein synthesis and, A–22
Transfusion reaction, 323
Transmural pressure gradient and respiration,
        372–373
Transplant rejection, 351
Transport maximum (T_m), 60, 61
Transport molecule, 50
Transport vesicle, 24
Transporter recruitment, 562
Transverse tubule
    diagram, 215
    function, 214
Tricarboxylic acid cycle. See Citric acid cycle
Tricuspid valve, 248
Triglyceride
    defined, A–12–A–13
    digestion and, 466
Tri-iodothyronine (T3)
    activating, 547
    defined, 545
    synthesis, 546
Triplet code, A–22–A–23
tRNA, A–26
Trophoblast, 612
Tropic hormone, 528
Tropomyosin, 211–212
Troponin, 211–212
Trypsin, 486
Trypsin Inhibitor, 486
Trypsinogen, 486
Tubular maximum
    for glucose, 420
    kidney function and, 419
Tubular reabsorption
    process, 409, 414–422
    types, 415
Tubular secretion
    process, 409, 422–424
    regulating hydrogen ion, 458
Tubulin, 40
Tumor, 352–353
Tumor suppressor gene, A–29
Twitch
    defined, 220
    summation, 221–222
Two-point threshold-of-discrimination test, 155

Tympanic membrane, 173, 182
Type 1 diabetes mellitus
    defined, 564
    treatment, 566
Type 2 diabetes mellitus
    defined, 564
    treatment, 566
Tyrosine and thyroid, 545

Ulcer. See Peptic ulcer
Ultrafiltration, 297–298
Umami taste, 183
Umbilical artery, 614
Umbilical cord, 614
Umbilical vein, 614
Umbilicus, 619
Universal blood donor, 323
Universal blood recipient, 323
Unsaturated fatty acid, A–12
Uracil, A–20
Urea reabsorption, 421–422
Uremic toxicity and renal failure, 435
Ureter, 406
Urethra
    defined, 406, 580
    function, 591
Urethral sphincter, 435
Uric acid and kidney function, 422
Urinary bladder, 406
Urinary incontinence, 437
Urinary system
    components, 6, 406
    contributions to homeostasis, 10, 12, 404
    diagram, 407
    water absorption, 429–430
Urine
    bladder and, 434–437
    concentrations in renal failure, 435
    salt output, 446–447
    water loss and, 451
Urine excretion
    concentrations, 433
    overview, 424–437
    process, 409
Urogenital system defenses, 359
Uterine cycle. See Menstrual cycle
Uterine tubes, 580
Uterus
    defined, 580
    hormonal changes and, 607–608
    hormonal levels and, 603–604
    involution, 619–620
    pregnancy and, 616
Utricle, 180–181, 182
Uvula, 471

Vaccination, 344–345
Vagina, 580
Vagus nerve
    bile secretion and, 490
    digestive control and, 470
    heart control and, 263
    overview, 138
Valve. See specific types
Variable, controlled, 11
Varicose vein, 305
Varicosity, 192
Vas deferens
    function, 592
    location, 580, 591
Vascular endothelial growth factor (VEGF), 290
Vascular spasm
    defined, 269
    hemostasis and, 324–325
Vascular tone, 288

Vascular tree, 282
Vasectomy, 591
Vasoactive paracrine, 290
Vasoconstriction, 288
Vasodilation, 333
    function, 288
Vasopressin
    dehydration and, 449
    functions, 533
    kidney function and, 429–433
    secretion triggers, 451–452
    urinal water output and, 451
Vein
    contributions to homeostasis, 278
    defined, 246
    features, 284
    function, 301–302
    structure, 301
Velocity
    blood flow and, 294–295
    muscle movement and, 220
Venae cavae, 248
Venous capacity, 302
Venous pressure and gravity, 303–304
Venous return, 302–305
Venous valve, 305
Ventilation
    acid-base balance and, 399
    blood gas and, 399
    defined, 367
    magnitude adjustment, 396–397
    main regulator, 398
    pressures important in, 371–372
Ventral respiratory group (VRG), 396
Ventricle (brain), 119
Ventricle (heart), 246
Ventricular diastole, 260
Ventricular ejection, 260
Ventricular excitation, 254
Ventricular filling, 262
Ventricular repolarization, 260
Ventricular systole, 260
Venule, 282
Vertebrae, 245
Vertebral column
    CNS protection, 120
    spinal cord and, 141
Vertical osmotic gradient
    countercurrent multiplication and, 428–429
    defined, 427
Vesicle, 24
Vesicle transport
    characteristics, 67
    large particle, 64, 66
    process, 37, 39

Vestibular apparatus
    diagram, 179
    function, 178–180, 182
    location, 171, 182
Vestibular nerve, 180
Vestibular nuclei, 181
Vestibulocerebellum, 136
Viagra, 594–595
Villus in small intestine, 494–496
Virulence, 329
Virus
    AIDS, 348
    defenses against invasion of, 348
    immune system and, 329
    interferon and, 337, 338
Visceral afferent, 153–154
Visceral fat, 512
Visceral smooth muscle, 236
Viscosity, 281
Vision
    color perception, 167
    cortical process hierarchy, 170–171
    process, 156–171
Visual field, 168
Visual input, functions other than sight, 171
Visual pathway
    diagram, 166, 169
    interruption, 169
    retinal, 164
Vital capacity (VC), 380
Vitamin absorption in small intestine, 499
Vitamin D
    deficiency, 573
    function, 571–572
    PTH and plasma calcium, 572
Vitreous humor, 157, 170
Vocal fold
    defined, 368–369
    swallowing and, 473
Voice box
    defined, 368–369
    swallowing and, 473
Voltage-gated channel
    action potential and, 81
    diagram, 82
    ion movement and, 78
Volume English-metric conversions, A–2
Volume measures and English equivalents, A–1
Volume Metric-English conversions, A–2
Vomiting, 477–478
Vomiting center, 478
Vulva, 580

Water
    absorption in small intestine, 496
    body, 444
    concentration and solute, 56
Water balance
    daily requirements, 450
    ECF hypertonicity and, 449
    hypotonicity and, 450
    kidneys and, 442, 452
    nonphysiologic influences, 452
    regulated factors, 451
    sources, 450–451
    vasopressin control, 450
Water reabsorption
    kidney function and, 421, 429–434
    as response to water deficit, 432–433
    as response to water excess, 433–434
    water balance and, 452
Water-soluble substance and plasma membrane
        permeation, 54
Wavelength, 158
Weight, A–3
Weight English-metric conversions, A–2
Weight Metric-English conversions, A–2
Wernicke's area
    diagram, 125
    location, 128
White blood cell (WBC)
    See also Leukocyte
    count, 331
    defined, 316
White matter
    description, 123
    diagram, 130
    spinal cord tracts, 140
White muscle fiber, 225
Withdrawal reflex, 143–144
Working memory, 134

X chromosome, 583
Xerostomia, 472

Y chromosome, 583
Yellow bone marrow, 320

Z line of skeletal muscle, 210
Zona fasciculata, 550
Zona glomerulosa, 550
Zona pellucida, 601
Zona reticularis, 550
ZP3 receptor, 610
Zygote, 610

Anatomical Terms Used to Indicate Direction and Orientation

anterior	situated in front of or in the front part of
posterior	situated behind or toward the rear
ventral	toward the belly or front surface of the body; synonymous with anterior
dorsal	toward the back surface of the body; synonymous with posterior
medial	denoting a position nearer the midline of the body or a body structure
lateral	denoting a position toward the side or farther from the midline of the body or a body structure
superior	toward the head
inferior	away from the head
proximal	closer to a reference point
distal	farther from a reference point
sagittal section	a vertical plane that divides the body or a body structure into right and left sides
longitudinal section	a plane that lies parallel to the length of the body or a body structure
cross section	a plane that runs perpendicular to the length of the body or a body structure
frontal or coronal section	a plane parallel to and facing the front part of the body

Word Derivatives Commonly Used in Physiology

a; an-	absence or lack	*epi-*	above; over	*osteo-*	bone
ad-; af-	toward	*erythro-*	red	*oto-*	ear
adeno-	glandular	*gastr-*	stomach	*para-*	near
angi-	vessel	*-gen; -genic*	produce	*pariet-*	wall
anti-	against	*gluc-; glyc-*	sweet	*peri-*	around
archi-	old	*hemi-*	half	*phago-*	eat
-ase	splitter	*hemo-*	blood	*-pod*	footlike
auto-	self	*hepat-*	liver	*-poiesis*	formation
bi-	two; double	*homeo-*	sameness	*poly-*	many
-blast	former	*hyper-*	above; excess	*post-*	behind; after
brady-	slow	*hypo-*	below; deficient	*pre-*	ahead of; before
cardi-	heart	*inter-*	between	*pro-*	before
cephal-	head	*intra-*	within	*pseudo-*	false
cerebr-	brain	*kal-*	potassium	*pulmon-*	lung
chondr-	cartilage	*leuko-*	white	*rect-*	straight
-cide	kill; destroy	*lip-*	fat	*ren-*	kidney
contra-	against	*macro-*	large	*reticul-*	network
cost-	rib	*mamm-*	breast	*retro-*	backward
crani-	skull	*mening-*	membrane	*sacchar-*	sugar
-crine	secretion	*micro-*	small	*sarc-*	muscle
crypt-	hidden	*mono-*	single	*semi-*	half
cutan-	skin	*multi-*	many	*-some*	body
-cyte	cell	*myo-*	muscle	*sub-*	under
de-	lack of	*natr-*	sodium	*supra-*	upon; above
di-	two; double	*neo-*	new	*tachy-*	rapid
dys-	difficult; faulty	*nephr-*	kidney	*therm-*	temperature
ecto-; exo-; extra-	outside; away from	*neuro-*	nerve	*-tion*	act or process of
ef-	away from	*oculo-*	eye	*trans-*	across
-elle	tiny; miniature	*-oid*	resembling	*tri-*	three
-emia	blood	*ophthalmo-*	eye	*vaso-*	vessel
encephalo-	brain	*oral-*	mouth	*-uria*	urine
endo-	within; inside				

Contents

Introduction   iv

Unit 1 Promoting Quality Care
1.1 Attitudes and prejudices   3
1.2 Rights and responsibilities of service users and providers   15
1.3 Facilitation of access to services   38
1.4 Care values   44

Unit 2 Communication in Care Settings
2.1 Types of communication   58
2.2 Factors that support and inhibit communication   62
2.3 Communication skills   76
2.4 Theories relating to communication   85
2.5 Interaction with the service users   94

Unit 3 Promoting Good Health
3.1 Concepts and models of health and well-being   105
3.2 Preventative measures and job roles   117
3.3 Factors affecting health and well-being   131
3.4 Health promotion   146

Unit 4 Health and Safety in Care Settings
4.1 The influence of current legislation on safe practice in care settings   164
4.2 Safety and security   176
4.3 Safe moving and handling techniques   186
4.4 Contribution to infection control   193

Unit 5 Caring for People with Additional Needs
5.1 Common causes of physical disability, sensory impairment and learning difficulties   202
5.2 The care management process   205

5.3 Managing care for people with learning difficulties 219
5.4 Models and approaches 227

Unit 6 Working in Early Years Care and Education
6.1 Care and education provision for early years 242
6.2 Job roles and responsibilities within early years care and education 250
6.3 The values and principles of the early years sector 258
6.4 The ways in which children learn and develop and factors that affect performance 264
6.5 Planning activities 271

Unit 7 Health as a Lifestyle Choice
7.1 Nutritional value of food and the dietary function of nutrients 278
7.2 Current dietary guidelines to promote the health of individuals 286
7.3 Positive effects of exercise 294
7.4 Health and safety requirements when designing an exercise programme 301
7.5 How diet and exercise interrelate to affect health 309

Unit 8 Complementary Therapies
8.1 Complementary therapies: a definition 312
8.2 The history and development of CAMs 314
8.3 The use and provision of CAMs 324
8.4 Meeting physical, emotional and social needs 333
8.5 The value of CAMs 338

Unit 9 Caring for Older People
9.1 The physical effects of ageing on body systems 348
9.2 The social, emotional and economic aspects of ageing 356
9.3 Community care and support services for older service users 369
9.4 The role of professional care workers 376
9.5 The impact of law on provision of care for older people 383

Answers to assessment questions 389
Glossary 397
Index 404

GCE AS Level Double Award

AS Level for OCR

Health & Social Care

Series editor:
Neil Moonie

www.heinemann.co.uk
✓ Free online support
✓ Useful weblinks
✓ 24 hour online ordering

01865 888058

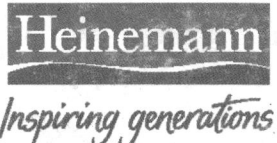

Heinemann

Inspiring generations

Heinemann Educational Publishers
Halley Court, Jordan Hill, Oxford OX2 8EJ
Part of Harcourt Education

Heinemann is a registered trademark of Harcourt Education Limited

Text © Neil Moonie, Jo Irvine, Dee Spencer-Perkins, Anne Bates, David Herne, Karen Hucker, Siân Lavers 2005

First published 2005

10 9 8 7 6 5 4 3 2 1
09 08 07 06 05

British Library Cataloguing in Publication Data is available
from the British Library on request.

10-digit ISBN: 0 435 45358 0
13-digit ISBN: 978 0 435453 58 9

Edited by Neil Moonie
Designed by Lorraine Inglis
Typeset by TechType

Original illustrations © Harcourt Education Limited, 2005

Illustrated by TechType

Cover design by Wooden Ark Studio

Printed by Edelvives

Cover photo © Getty Images

Acknowledgements
Every effort has been made to contact copyright holders of material reproduced in this book. Any omissions will be rectified in subsequent printings if notice is given to the publishers.

Dee Spencer-Perkins would like to thank Rob Dyson (Scope), Beth Tarlton (Norah Fry Research Centre), Clara Scammell, Karen Sharpe, Bernard Yu (Havering PCT), Adrian Coggins (Royston, Buntingford and Bishop's Stortford PCT), and also Richard Abbott, Barbara Brown, Emma Burnham, Roger Carruthers, Rosemary Cunningham, Violetta Etheridge, Gail Lincoln, Lynne Litton, Josephine O'Gorman, Shashi Sharma, Joannah Weightmann and Janet Wilkinson.

Photo acknowledgements
Alamy Images – pages 17, 29, 113, 118, 129, 254, 266, 339, 359; Alamy Images/Photofusion – pages 335, 357; John Birdsall Photo Library – pages 120, 194, 228, 232; Corbis – page 97; Digital Vision – page 110; Getty Images – pages 39, 229, 313, 315, 381; Harcourt Education Ltd/Gareth Boden – pages 191, 197, 221, 224, 261, 280, 304, 366; Harcourt Education Ltd/Trevor Clifford – page 279; Harcourt Education Ltd/Haddon Davies – page 256; Harcourt Education Ltd/Peter Evans – page 269; Harcourt Education Ltd/Jules Selmes – pages 210, 252, 265, 267; Harcourt Education Ltd/Tudor Photography – pages 108, 134, 271; PhotoLibrary.com – page 314; Science Photo Library – pages 132, 228, 324; Richard Smith – pages 58, 68, 78, 182, 197, 206, 216, 291.

Introduction

This book has been written to support students who are studying for the double award AS level GCE using the course structure designed by OCR. The book is designed to support the nine AS level units:

Unit 1   Promoting Quality Care
Unit 2   Communication in Care Settings
Unit 3   Promoting Good Health
Unit 4   Health and Safety in Care Settings
Unit 5   Caring for People with Additional Needs
Unit 6   Working in Early Years Care and Education
Unit 7   Health as a Lifestyle Choice
Unit 8   Complementary Therapies
Unit 9   Caring for Older People

This book has been organised to cover each of these units in detail. Headings are designed to make it easy to follow the content of each unit and to find the information needed to achieve a high grade. As well as providing information each unit is designed to stimulate the development of the thinking skills needed to achieve an advanced level award.

Assessment

Each unit will be assessed by coursework or by an external test set and marked by OCR. Detailed guidance for coursework assessment and external test requirements can be found in the unit specifications and at OCR's website. This book has been designed to support students to achieve high grades as set out in the guidance from OCR available during 2004/2005.

Special features of this book

Throughout the text, there are a number of features designed to encourage reflection and to help students make links between theory and practice. In particular, this book has been designed to encourage a depth of learning and understanding and to encourage students to go beyond a surface level of descriptive writing.

The special features of this book include:

Think it over   Think it over...

This feature provides thought-provoking questions that will encourage reflective thinking, or possibly reflection involving discussion with others.

Did you know?   ✳ DID YOU KNOW?

This feature highlights facts or snippets of information to encourage reflective thinking.

Scenario   SCENARIO

This feature presents scenarios throughout the units to help explain the significance of theoretical ideas within Health, Social Care and Early Years settings. The term 'Scenario' has been used in place of the more traditional term 'Case study' because the idea of people being perceived as 'cases' does not fit easily with the notion of empowerment – a key value highlighted by government policy.

Consider this

Consider this

This feature appears at the end of each section and presents a brief scenario followed by a series of questions. These questions are designed to encourage reflection and analysis of the issues covered within the section.

Key concept

Key concept

This feature identifies key concepts and offers a brief explanation of how these terms might be used. The development of analytical and evaluative skills requires the ability to use concepts.

Assessment guidance

At the end of each unit there is an assessment section that provides sample test material for externally assessed units or, for internally assessed units, outline guidance and ideas designed to help students achieve the highest grades when preparing coursework.

Glossary

This book contains a useful glossary to provide fast reference for key terms and concepts used within the units.

References

At the end of each unit there is a full list of references together with useful websites.

Author details

Neil Moonie, former Deputy Director of the Department of Social Services, Health and Education in a College of Further and Higher Education. Chartered Psychologist, part-time lecturer and contributor to a wide range of textbooks and learning resources in the field of health and social care. Editor of Heinemann's GNVQ Intermediate and Advanced textbooks on health and social care since 1993 and editor of the 2000 Standards AVCE textbook.

Jo Irvine has worked in health visiting and nursing and in further education for a number of years. She currently works as a consultant in health, social care and childcare.

Dee Spencer-Perkins began her social services career in research, moving on to become a trainer and then a training manager. She now works as an independent trainer, consultant and writer, and specialises in language and communication. Dee also has a keen interest in disability issues.

Anne Bates has worked in statutory social work since 1977 in a range of settings including child care, mental health, adult services and inspection and monitoring of day care services with under fives. Anne is currently working part-time as a social services team manager with a community dementia team and also as a lecturer and tutor on a social work degree programme in outer London.

David Herne works as a public health specialist for the Chorley and South Ribble Primary Care Trust.

Karen Hucker, an expert in early years care and education, currently works as Principal for a College of Further Education.

Siân Lavers is a lecturer at a College of Further Education, teaching on the Levels 2 and 3 Health and Social Care programmes, the BTEC National Diploma in Early Years and the CIEH Foundation Food Hygiene Certificate. She has also been a contributor to several textbooks on Health and Social Care, S/NVQ 3 Care and Key Skills.

UNIT 1

Promoting Quality Care

This unit contains the following sections:

1.1   Attitudes and prejudices

1.2   Rights and responsibilities of service users and providers

1.3   Facilitation of access to services

1.4   Care values

Introduction

This unit explores aspects of quality, and what this means in a care environment. Quality is an essential characteristic of care work, and refers to the standard of the services which are delivered. This unit begins by exploring issues concerning the values and attitudes of care workers towards vulnerable people. A fundamental principle of providing care is the recognition that everyone has rights as individuals and as human beings, and it is the responsibility of care workers to promote and protect the rights of those they care for. The rights and responsibilities of those using services and service providers are explored, as well as different ways in which individual rights can be promoted, and the interaction between rights and responsibilities. The values that apply to care work and work with children are also explored, together with the concept of safe working practices.

The range of health care provision includes preventive services, diagnostic services, general medical and surgical services, therapies, specialist services for adults, children, people with learning difficulties and mental ill health. These services are provided either in hospital (acute services) or in the community through Primary Health Trusts (preventive, long-term and rehabilitation services). Social care services support adults and children who are vulnerable due to life circumstances and unable to manage daily life without support of some kind, or who are at risk of harm or abuse. Such support may be offered at different times and be short- or long-term, depending on individual circumstances.

Children's services are concerned with the care, learning and development of all children, not just those who are ill or have special needs or those at risk of harm.

Children's services are delivered by a wide range of organisations, including private nurseries, childminders, playworkers, and classroom assistants.

When considering care services, there are two main aspects that it is helpful to take into account when examining quality, namely, what is delivered and how it is delivered.

What is delivered

Examples include specific services, treatments or interventions. Interventions are activities carried out by health or care workers.

How it is delivered

Service delivery may be focused on patient or user-centred care, which involves service users in decision-making, or task oriented care, in which the individual has little or no say in the arrangement or delivery of care and treatment.

How you will be assessed

The unit will be assessed through a 90-minute test.

Section 1: Attitudes and prejudices

Because care work involves working closely with people, it is important to develop trusting relationships between workers and service users. Therefore, the attitudes and values of care workers are of great importance. We all hold a range of attitudes that we may not have ever explored. Attitudes begin to develop from our earliest years, through values and beliefs that we pick up during the process of **socialisation** (see page 4), but it is important to note that socialisation is an active process that takes place throughout life and that attitudes can change as a result of experiences.

Attitudes

Attitudes involve beliefs and values. Beliefs and values concern issues which are considered to be of fundamental importance, such as the importance of family or religious beliefs, or the importance of independence or personal wealth. Every culture also has certain expectations of what is acceptable or unacceptable behaviour (**behavioural norms**), which reflect a particular culture's values. Attitudes and values provide the basis for all social interactions with other people, and the world around us.

Britain is a multicultural and diverse society in which there are many different customs and values. People from different cultures hold a variety of different views and beliefs, which can often be reflected in their behaviour. For example, in some social groups it is polite to shake hands on meeting, in other cultures a kiss on both cheeks is an acceptable greeting. Within a multicultural society it is important that a diversity of views and opinions is seen as a positive quality.

We all make unconscious judgments about people, based firstly on initial appearance, body language and expression. These initial opinions may be either confirmed or modified, once we begin to talk to others and get to know them better. We often instinctively prefer people similar to ourselves, because similar backgrounds and circumstances often lead to shared values and beliefs.

Prejudices

Prejudice means, literally, to pre-judge something or someone, and refers to preconceived opinions or attitudes held by individuals towards other people or groups. A prejudiced person may have a favorable attitude towards groups with whom they identify and a negative attitude or prejudice towards other groups, who are seen as different: such preconceived opinions are usually based on stereotypes.

> **✳ DID YOU KNOW?**
>
> The word *stereotypes* (stereo meaning two) originally referred to a printing stamp that was used to make multiple copies from a single model or mould.

Stereotyping

Stereotyping can be defined as a simplified or generalised image or idea, which is applied to individuals or groups. When applied to human beings, stereotyping is like 'stamping' a set of fixed and inflexible characteristics to a whole group of people, even though few members of the

FIGURE 1.1 *Stereotyped thinking can result in discriminatory behaviour*

group may have these characteristics. We all recognise stereotypes from the language used to describe them, which is often unflattering and has negative associations. Stereotypes are frequently based on limited and inaccurate information; they become embedded in cultural thinking and are difficult to eradicate. It has been said that stereotyping is a lazy way of thinking, because it requires both awareness and effort to ignore one's prejudices, suspend judgement and see others as individuals. When you hear someone talking about a particular group of people and they start a sentence with the words 'they all...', it often indicates stereotypical thinking.

> **Think it over...**
>
> Divide into two groups, or several smaller paired groups. One group should write out the name used to identify people or groups on cards or the board. The other group has to think of as many words to describe this group as possible. Here are some to start with:
>
> * Teenage mother   * Homeless person
>
> * Old woman   * Rapper
>
> * Youth
>
> 1. Do these words conjure up a mental image of the people named?
>
> 2. Do you think the descriptions are true of all people in these groups?
>
> 3. Think carefully about where your information has come from. Is it from personal experience? When discussing these issues, you need to be aware that people can have strong feelings about their values and beliefs, especially if they are challenged.

Primary socialisation

Socialisation is the process in which young children learn the cultural values and **norms** of the society into which they are born, primarily from their parents. Therefore **primary socialisation** refers to the child's growing understanding of the language, customs and practices of their particular family. Socialisation

> **Think it over...**
>
> 'Our government, politicians and the media sanction discrimination and disadvantage through perpetuating the belief that teenage mothers are at best, ignorant and at worst, irresponsible and incapable of being good parents.'
>
> Director, YWCA Charity, the *Guardian*: 8 September 2004
>
> This quote suggests that there is prejudice against teenage parents, particularly mothers.
>
> 1. Debate this statement in two groups, with one group supporting the statement and one group arguing against it. You will need to carry out research into the issues faced by teenage parents and young mothers in particular. You should find out about access to financial services, including benefits and banking facilities, housing options in your local area and the extent and availability of educational, health and social services.
>
> 2. Is access to services and facilities different for this group of people? If you consider that it is, explain in what ways?
>
> 3. What stereotypical assumptions are made about teenage mothers?

starts from birth, with the process known as bonding, and it is now understood that the infant is an active participant in this process.

Because infants and young children have little experience of the outside world, what they experience in the home environment, or care environment, is accepted as normal. In other words, young children expect that their experiences are the same as everyone else's. Children also learn about how to behave, i.e. find out what is acceptable and unacceptable behaviour, from how adults and children with whom they have regular contact behave towards each other, and from the rules that are in place in the home or care environment. Examples of these include: whether it is normal to eat together sitting around the table as a family; whether there are routines, for example, at bedtime; and saying, 'please' and 'thank you'. However, it is important to note that in addition to the parents' values and beliefs, any prejudices the parents may hold will also be transmitted to the children, and accepted as a given truth because young children do not have the experience to form their own views and opinions.

One example of primary socialisation is the way in which children learn what it means to be male or female, which starts with children using parents as **role models** for appropriate behaviour. This is known as **gender socialisation** and in order to understand this concept, it is important to recognise that sex is biologically determined and therefore fixed (except in the case of developmental abnormalities). Gender on the other hand, is socially determined with behaviour, which is based on sex differences. The concept of gender behaviour and characteristics can be thought of as a continuum along the line from male to female, with people (men and women) being located somewhere along the line.

FIGURE 1.2 *Concept of gender behaviour and characteristics*

For example, some men demonstrate what are often thought of as more 'feminine' qualities such as sympathy, kindness and sensitivity, whereas some women display more 'masculine' qualities,

Think it over...

Make two lists, one of masculine traits and behaviours and one of feminine, using the following words:

such as self-confidence, boldness and independence. Such behaviour can challenge assumptions about what is considered 'normal' behaviour for their gender, and people may experience prejudice and disapproval from others.

Sociologists such as Ann Oakley (1974), put forward the theory that gender roles are learned behaviour, because boys and girls are socialised differently according to adult views on what is acceptable and unacceptable social behaviour for different sexes. One of the first questions parents ask at the birth of their baby is whether it is a girl or boy. Oakley argues that, from then on boys and girls are treated differently according to the expectations of gender behaviour held by the parents, reflecting the cultural norms of masculine or feminine within their particular society. For example, the cries of baby boys may be described as 'lusty' or 'hearty', whereas girls may be expected to be quiet. This is regarded as 'good' behaviour and usually praised: in other words, children are conditioned to display gender appropriate behaviour. Boys may be expected to be active explorers of their environment: activities such as climbing on furniture are more likely to be tolerated in boys than girls.

Think it over...

1. Can you identify different ways in which adults may respond differently to boys and girls, starting from birth?

2. Think of examples of acceptable and unacceptable behaviour for girls. Does this differ from boys, and if so, in what way?

3. Listen to the way in which parents speak to their children or describe them to others – can you identify words or phrases that are more commonly associated with one sex or the other?

4. What conclusions can you draw about gender roles within society?

Research has now established that gender development is more complex and the stereotypical gender behaviour that young children demonstrate at around 2–3 years of age is thought to be a way of simplifying and making sense of complex social behaviour. (for more information see the Open University website supporting *Child of Our Time* which can be found at www.open2.net/childofourtime/2005)

The development of socialisation can be observed through the way in which young children play. Children's play gradually becomes more complex and formal, with defined sets of rules. This is true of play that is invented and initiated by the children themselves. Children are helped to understand the purpose of rules, and ideas about fair play through participation in team sports such as hockey and football.

Secondary socialisation

Secondary socialisation refers to the process in which the child comes to understand the social norms of a wider society. Although the parents or carers are the most enduring influence on a child's attitudes and behaviour, the child's assumption that everyone's family is the same, and that all families behave in the same way as their own is gradually challenged by contact with the wider world, and the different influences that they are exposed to. This process, which generally started at school age, now often starts earlier as increasingly more children go to nursery school and come into contact with different children and adults. It is particularly important therefore, that childcare workers and educationalists acknowledge, accept and positively value cultural diversity and understand different social customs and norms. Some of the key influences affecting secondary socialisation are discussed below.

Education

When children enter school, they encounter adults and children from other family backgrounds – teachers and other pupils – and learn what is expected from them in the school setting, in addition to the formal curriculum. These expectations are based on social and cultural values of the society and community in which the school operates: they may be similar to what children and young people are accustomed to at home, or they may be very different; this can cause conflict. The social and behavioural norms are transmitted through school rules, and

disobedience may be punished by sanctions, such as detention. In this way, children learn to behave in a socially acceptable way, with the school operating as a social institution. Sociologist Pierre Bourdieu (1977) referred to this as 'social reproduction'. This process of socialisation within the school is sometimes referred to as the 'hidden curriculum' because it is not concerned with formal school subjects. Schools are also involved in **gender socialisation**. Mairtin Mac an Ghaill in *The Making of Men* (1994) argues that schools are institutions in which such things as subject allocation, disciplinary procedures and student-teacher interaction serve to construct gender relations which reflect Western industrialised society and are based on traditional relationships and nuclear families, in which females tend to take a secondary or passive role. There is some evidence to suggest that this may be changing, reflecting the growing awareness of the importance of the contribution of educational institutions to socialisation.

Peers

A significant aspect of secondary socialisation concerns learning to understand and manage relationships with others, particularly peer-group relations. These relationships are different to those previously experienced within the family group, in that they are based on what each can do for the other, rather than the unconditional mutual loving relationships within the family. The child gradually realises that others have rights, wants and needs of their own, which may conflict with theirs. In addition, peers either reinforce or undermine the child's internal view of themselves through such social relations, for example, whether they are sporty and good at games, and whether they are popular. Children begin to measure their value as individuals through the way in which other children relate to them and the number of friends they consider themselves to have. In extreme cases, where the child experiences bullying, self-esteem can be cruelly damaged. Once the young person reaches adulthood, this process of socialisation continues in the workplace, through relationships with work colleagues.

The media

The television is an especially important influence in the process of secondary socialisation. Young children often have difficulty in differentiating between fact and fantasy in terms of what they see on television. Children may see TV characters as role models, and there has been much discussion on the influence that television has on children's behaviour, especially programmes which have violent or abusive content. The way in which families and different groups within society are portrayed on television also influences children's perceptions of the world around them, and their understanding of their own place within it. This can be particularly damaging to a child's developing self-esteem if he or she belongs to a group that is not represented accurately on television, not represented at all, or is portrayed in a negative light. In this way, the media can be responsible for perpetuating gender stereotypes, especially through marketing and advertisements. For example, adverts convey the relative power and social status of men and women by showing men as bigger and positioned physically higher than women. Similarly, whilst women are often shown averting their gaze from men, men only avert their gaze from a superior, such as their boss. Men are sometimes portrayed as inferior and incompetent when doing household or caring tasks, i.e. 'women's work'. Advertising sends out strong messages about the differences between boys and girls, men and women and the sort of behaviour that is acceptable; for example, adverts are likely to show boys as strong, independent, athletic and in control, whereas girls are shown as giggling, gentle, affectionate and concerned with their appearance.

Books and magazines are another influential source of information, especially when children are learning to read. The characters and illustrations in books can reinforce stereotypes or provide an alternative view of the world and other cultures.

Think it over...

1. Look carefully at both the programmes and adverts you see on TV for a week. Make a note of how the people in them are portrayed.

2. How many men on TV are like the men you know personally, for example, your father, friends, relations, and teachers?

3. Why does the perpetuation of traditional gender stereotypes disadvantage both men and women?

Religion

For some people, their religious beliefs are very important and their socialisation is directed by the behavioural codes found within their holy writings. Some religious practices, such as fasting or wearing special clothes, clearly identify members of a particular religious group, who may then become the focus for the prejudiced attitudes of others. Such religious intolerance is usually based on misinformation and stereotypical views. There are many different religions practised in Britain, and care workers should be familiar with the basic principles and practices of most of these in order to provide appropriate care.

It is through the process of socialisation that we develop beliefs about what is 'normal' within their society. These beliefs become 'internalised', i.e. they become subconscious and we do not even think about them. However, whether we are aware of them or not, they guide our behaviour and inform our attitudes to others. Adolescents and young adults often choose to break conventional social norms; this is a normal part of developing an individual identity. Adolescents who do things

FIGURE 1.3 *How many things linked to socialisation can you spot?*

1. In groups of two or three, select one religious or cultural group and carry out research into the cultural characteristics of the group. This must be a group *other* than the one with which you most identify.

2. Find out about:

   Festivals and celebrations
   Music, songs and dance
   Food and diet
   Personal hygiene
   Religious practices
   Clothes and fashion
   Family traditions
   Family roles
   Leisure and pastimes
   Death and dying.

3. Prepare a presentation for the rest of your group, using a range of images, handouts and visual aids.

socialisation is a process through which an individual comes to understand the social rules and normal expectations of behaviour in their society. Socialisation carries on throughout life as people are exposed to different circumstances and different cultures. It is important as it provides the basis for attitudes, values and beliefs which inform the way people behave towards others. It is important to remember that these attitudes, values and beliefs are internalised; however, they can be changed through experience.

continuing throughout life, such as, each time individuals come into contact with a new group of people, or when visiting different countries on business or on holiday, they will be exposed to a different set of social and cultural norms and values. Attitudes and beliefs will continue to change as we have new experiences.

differently may become the focus of disapproval because of the way they dress, or act.

An individual's identity and sense of self, including a sense of self-esteem is either made stronger or changed through feedback from others. So secondary socialisation can be seen as

Health and well-being

Human beings, all have a number of basic needs, which they need in order to stay healthy. Most people manage to meet their own needs through work, home life and leisure pursuits.

BASIC NEEDS OF A HUMAN BEING	
The need to give and receive attention.	Human beings are social creatures designed to live in groups and interact with each other, forming intimate relationships and social connections. This is why solitary confinement is seen as a punishment, and infants deprived of appropriate attention fail to thrive.
The need to take care of the body.	Includes the need to provide the body with healthy food to enable it to prevent disease, grow new cells and repair existing cells, also to maintain structures and functions through sufficient rest and exercise.
The need for stimulation and challenge.	This is constant throughout life, as the human brain needs exercise. If intellectual functions are insufficiently stimulated by external stimuli, such as new information, the brain will turn inwardly to the imagination in order to prevent boredom. However, even the imagination needs something to work on and without stimulation, mental health is at risk.
The need for meaning and purpose.	People need to have goals to aim for, in order to feel a sense of achievement. This sense of achievement is linked to feelings of value and self worth, particularly if these goals involve helping other people, i.e. they are outwardly directed.

FIGURE 1.4 *A summary of the basic needs of a human being*

These requirements can be summarised and are shown in Figure 1.4.

The effects of attitudes and prejudices on the health and well-being of service users when these needs are unmet can be profound. The effects of discriminatory actions are both physical and psychological. When prejudiced attitudes affect the way individuals behave towards other people, this is known as **discrimination**.

Discrimination

To discriminate means to show preference, or to choose. It is important to understand that discrimination can be in favour of someone or something as well as against. Care work is concerned with anti-discriminatory practice, which means not treating any person or group more favourably than another. Discrimination is defined by Giddens (2001) as 'activities [or actions] that deny to the members of a group resources or rewards which can be obtained by others'.

It is important to recognise that although prejudice is linked to discrimination, not everyone who is prejudiced behaves in a discriminatory way. In other words, people who discriminate are usually prejudiced, but not all prejudiced people discriminate.

Discrimination can occur because of the differences between people, as shown in Figure 1.5 overleaf.

Consider the following famous people, Christy Moore, author; Helen Keller, teacher; Stephen Hawking, scientist; Nelson Mandela, lawyer and activist; Amelia Earhart, aviator; Wayne Sleep, dancer. All these people have several things in common – they can be considered disadvantaged in some way. They belong to groups that are often discriminated against; they do not fit conventional stereotypical roles and, most importantly, they became famous because of their achievements, not because of their disadvantages and for the most part they regarded themselves as ordinary people.

Discriminatory actions include those shown in Figure 1.6 below.

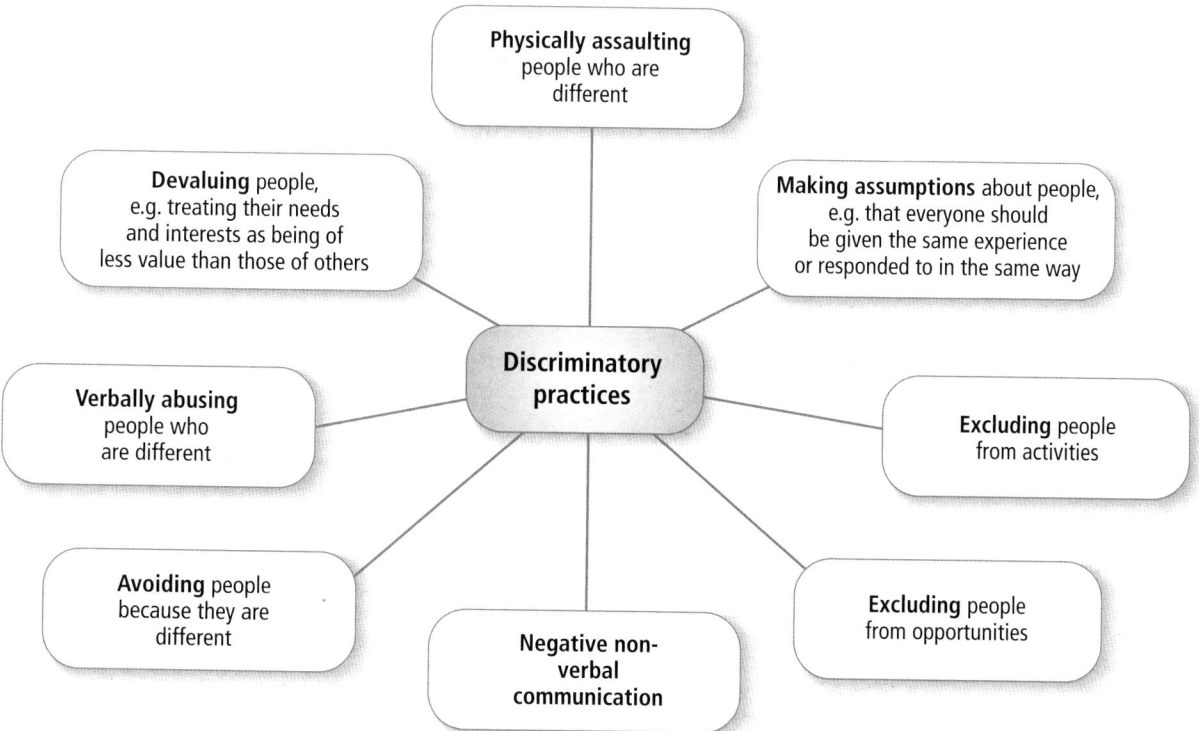

FIGURE 1.6 *Types of discrimination and abuse*

DIFFERENCES BETWEEN PEOPLE	
Ability	Individuals who have some form of physical or mental disability, e.g. wheelchair users, people with cerebral palsy, people with speech difficulties, people who talk to themselves, people with learning difficulties
Appearance	People with physical disfigurements, e.g. birthmarks, burns, unusual features including stature
Age	Older people or very young people can be prevented from participating in activities, sporting activities for example, based on assumptions about their competence and physical skills
Ethnicity or culture	People from different parts of the country or another country within the UK may be discriminated against because of the way they speak, for example
Gender	Women and men may be discriminated against if they do not conform to stereotypes of male or female role behaviour; some resources may be denied to individuals on the basis of gender or preferential treatment may be given to one sex over the other
Marital status	Within many societies, the expectation is that adults will marry in order to raise children. Certain financial advantages are therefore made available to married couples that are not available to single people, or single parents
Race	Racism is the term used to describe prejudice based on physical distinctions such as skin colour. Such a prejudice is based on the belief that some races are superior to others – usually white superior to others. There is a growing awareness of the extent to which racism is systemic within British society, that is, institutions within society such as the health and social services, the police and the education system promote policies, customs and practices that favour some groups more than others. The Macpherson report (1999) into the handling of the murder of black teenager Stephen Lawrence concluded that racism was institutionalised and there was a 'collective failure... to provide an appropriate and professional service to people because of their colour, culture or ethnic origin. It can be seen and detected in processes, attitudes and behaviour which amount to discrimination through unwitting prejudice, ignorance, thoughtlessness, and racist stereotyping which disadvantage minority ethnic people.' Following this report, the Race Relations Act was amended in 2001 (Section 19B) so that all public bodies now have a duty to prohibit race discrimination. Public bodies include the police, local government, mental hospitals, prisons and courts
Religion	Although many Western societies are secular and religion is of less importance to many people, some religious groups are returning to the fundamental principles of their religion in response to what they interpret as the declining moral values of Western society. For example, there are fundamentalist movements within both Christianity and Islam. In addition, there are differences between religious groups such as Protestants and Catholics, Muslims and Sikhs. Discrimination by one religious group against another is not uncommon, and has arguably been one of the most enduring causes of human warfare.

FIGURE 1.5 *Some of the differences between people that may give rise to discrimination*

Tariq is a young man aged 17 years, who, due to cerebral palsy affecting his legs, needs to use a wheelchair to get around outside. Tariq's other difficulties include occasional uncontrolled movements of his head and sometimes his speech can become difficult to understand, especially when he is angry or upset.

Tariq lives at home with his parents and older sister, but intends to move into independent living accommodation once he has finished his studies; he is currently studying business at college.

Tariq is making preparations for a party he intends to hold at a local hotel to celebrate his 18th birthday. He has arranged to go shopping for new clothes with two friends from college, Adam and Yousuf. In the local shopping mall, they go into a branch of a high street chain which sells fashionable clothes for young people. As they browse through the racks of clothes, they become aware that the assistants are watching them closely and talking quietly to each other.

With the help of Adam and Yousuf, who find the right size and reach up to fetch the clothes down from the rails, Tariq eventually chooses a shirt, trousers and jacket. However, when they go to the assistants to ask if Tariq can try them on, two of them walk away and one turns his back on the three boys and starts to price up some new stock. Undeterred, the they head towards the changing rooms to help Tariq out of his chair so he can try on the trousers, only to be approached by the senior assistant who tells them that only one person at a time is allowed in the changing rooms. He addresses his remarks to Adam.

When Tariq tells the assistant that he will manage by himself and call for assistance only if he gets into difficulties, the assistant turns to Adam and tells him that the changing rooms are unsuitable for wheelchairs due to access difficulties.

What legal rights protect people from this kind of discrimination nowadays?

1. **Read through the information above and identify the different ways you think Tariq is being discriminated against.**
2. **What would have been a non-discriminatory experience for Tariq?**
3. **How do you think this incident might affect Tariq?**

Prejudice can lead to discrimination and lack of respect for individuals, preventing them from having their needs met. In some cases, this can lead to bullying behaviour which culminates in abuse of vulnerable individuals, especially children and older people, by those who are in positions of power over them. In the care setting, this can result in the mistreatment of people, including elder and child abuse.

The effects of attitudes and prejudices are:

* prejudice
* discrimination
* disrespect
* bullying
* abuse.

In order to be an effective carer, workers need to examine their own attitudes honestly, work hard to overcome any prejudices and maintain respect for individuals as human beings with equal rights. This is called anti-discriminatory practice.

The effects off anti-discriminatory practice are:

* open mindedness
* fairness
* respect
* consideration
* care.

Abuse can take many forms, some of which are shown in Figure 1.7.

MISTREATMENT OF PEOPLE	
Physical abuse	Slapping, hitting, burning, scolding, pushing, inappropriate restraint, inappropriate use of medicine, withholding medicine as punishment, lack of consideration, roughness when handling or treating people, e.g. helping them to the toilet or when changing dressings. (An estimated 20 per cent of reported cases of elder abuse involve physical abuse.)
Psychological abuse	Shouting, swearing, frightening someone, threatening someone, withholding or damaging something with emotional importance to someone, and failing to deal with people with respect and dignity (35 per cent of reported cases)
Financial abuse	Stealing and fraud, especially from elderly people (20 per cent of reported cases)
Sexual abuse	Including inappropriate touching, unwanted sexual attention, making sexual remarks designed to make someone feel uncomfortable, and rape. (2 per cent of reported cases)
Neglect	Such as failure to provide food, heating, adequate care or attention to hygiene, such as helping with bathing; neglecting treatment, e.g. prevention of pressure sores (10 per cent of reported cases)

FIGURE 1.7 *Examples of some forms of abuse*

Source: House of Commons Health Committee Second Report on elder abuse, 2004

Note: Although the figures in brackets refer to elder abuse, these forms of abuse apply to all vulnerable individuals, including children.

Discriminatory and abusive practices damage individuals, both physically and psychologically as a result of the stress they cause. Stress has physical manifestations such as negative thoughts that affect sleep patterns, causing anxiety and depression. Associated physical symptoms include high blood pressure, comfort eating/drinking and other compulsive health-damaging behaviour. When a person faces a stressful situation, the body's response includes flooding the system with stress hormones such as adrenaline in preparation for what is known as 'flight or fight'. Normally, once the stressful situation has passed, physical exercise helps the body to excrete the stress hormones quickly. However, if individuals are unable to remove the stress hormones from the system, for example, if they occur in a working situation or a person is physically unable to exercise, the stress hormones continue to have a physical effect, keeping the body in readiness for action.

Physical injury and exclusion can affect access to economic resources and access to social opportunities, which results in the individual becoming isolated and financially vulnerable.

When individuals have been physically attacked, they may continue to feel unsafe because of the threat of attack, including intimidation and verbal abuse. Avoidance, devaluing and exclusion leads to people feeling that they do not belong and a predisposition to depression.

Self-esteem and empowerment

Discriminatory actions resulting from uninformed attitudes and prejudice have a significant impact on an individual's self-esteem. Self-esteem is concerned with the ability to have belief in oneself, confidence in one's abilities, a sense of self-assurance and self-respect – in other words, positive self-regard. Discriminatory actions undermine an individual's self-esteem. When individuals are suffering from low self-esteem they often feel that they have no control over their own life and cannot achieve anything. They have expectations of failure and stop trying to influence events in their lives. This blocks personal development and can lead to depression and in extreme cases, self-harming behaviour.

The negative effects on self-esteem and sense of empowerment for service users who are ill and experience prejudice and discrimination can delay the healing process because psychological health and well-being are an integral part of care. Service users are likely to feel a sense of helplessness and hopelessness, which will affect their ability to be independent and contribute to their own care; they may feel unable to ask for help for fear of recrimination, afraid of being perceived as a 'nuisance'. If they are not consulted about their care and treatment, they are likely to feel devalued.

> ### Key concept
>
> *empowerment* refers to the process through which individuals exercise choice and make decisions about their lives. Individuals can be disempowered by lack of information, lack of money, fear of consequences (e.g. bullying behaviour directed at them) or belonging to a group that is marginalised in society (e.g. homeless people). It is the responsibility of care workers to ensure that service users are empowered as equal partners in their care and treatment, for example by ensuring they have sufficient information on which to base a decision.

Direct and indirect discrimination

Direct discrimination

This occurs when it is obvious by the words or actions of individuals that they are deliberately disadvantaging another. For example, refusing to consider a black person or a woman for a job interview even though they have the required qualifications and experience would be discriminating on the basis of race or gender. Name calling and nicknames based on race, ethnicity, gender, age, and size, for example, are all forms of discrimination. Within care services, giving preferential treatment to some groups or denying appropriate treatment to other groups is discriminatory.

'Discrimination may be seen to occur where people are treated differently, and either do not receive the service, or it is delivered to them in an inappropriate way.

Unfair discrimination can occur on the grounds of age, class, caste, colour, creed, culture, gender, health status (e.g. HIV status), lifestyle, marital status, mental ability, mental health, offending background, physical ability, the place of origin, political beliefs, race, religion, responsibility for dependants, sensory ability, sexuality or other specific factors.'

(Tossell and Webb, 1994)

Indirect discrimination

This is much less obvious. It occurs when certain conditions are in place that demonstrates preference for some people over others. Examples could include not providing female toilets, and not providing toilet facilities that children or disabled people can use. As the Macpherson report (1999) concluded in relation to racism in the police and criminal justice system, the way in which health, care and childcare services are provided and delivered can contribute to indirect discriminatory practices. In 1992 the National Institute of Social Work's Race Equality Unit published a report entitled *A Home from Home – the Experiences of Black Residential Projects as a Focus of Good Practice*. The report stated that:

'On the one hand, those members of the black community who have received mainstream residential care have experienced prejudice and racism which has denied them their cultural reality, racial pride, self-dignity and black identity. On the other hand, myths and stereotypes of black families such as "they look after their own" and "residential care is not part of their culture" have worked against the interests and welfare of their members in need of residential care.'

The report concluded that health and social services agencies had not fulfilled their duty of care to black families and their communities because they had either not provided services, or provided poor quality services in which a discriminatory culture was present.

Summary

The way in which care workers treat the people they care for can have a marked effect on their health and well-being. A positive, respectful and considerate approach can improve the rate of recovery from illness and enable older people to maintain their mental alertness and enjoy a higher quality of life for longer. Negative attitudes and stereotypical thinking among care workers will be apparent to service users, whether or not these are consciously demonstrated, and will have a significant effect on the emotional and physical health of those they care for.

When working with children, care workers need to recognise that they become part of the process of socialisation and can influence the development of positive or negative attitudes, values or prejudices in the children they care for. Care workers therefore have a responsibility to examine their own views and be open-minded if they are to deliver high-quality, anti-discriminatory care.

Section 2: Rights and responsibilities of service users and providers

All members of our society have fundamental human rights that are grounded in moral, ethical and philosophical ideas, such as the principle that all people are of equal value and the sanctity of human life.

These universal rights are protected by laws (legislation) concerning human rights and the right to equal treatment; they are intended to protect individuals from physical and emotional harm and exploitation.

In addition to the laws protecting the rights of all individuals, there are also particular laws in Britain to safeguard those considered to be vulnerable or at risk.

Many of these laws were influenced by European Union Law, for example, Article 141 of the Treaty of Rome (1957): the founding document of the European Union, states:

'Each Member State shall ensure that the principle of equal pay for male and female workers for work of equal value is applied.'

After joining the European Union in 1973, legislation was passed outlawing discrimination against men or women on the grounds of sex: the Sex Discrimination Act 1975.

Sex Discrimination Act 1975

The Sex Discrimination Act (SDA) covers discrimination in the following areas;

* All areas of *employment*, including job advertisements, with some particular exemptions, such as where it would be detrimental to have a member of the opposite sex in a particular job, e.g. men being employed as counsellors for women survivors of rape or sexual assault. Any contract of employment, which contravenes the Act is invalid.

* All *educational establishments* designated by the Secretary of State for Education, except single-sex schools and colleges. Single-sex competitive sport is allowed, if women's physical strength would put them at a disadvantage. In practice, this is often been used to exclude girls from certain sports at school.

* A wide range of *goods, facilities and services* come under the Act, including clubs, cafes, restaurants, hotels, transport, banking, insurance, hire purchase, recreation and entertainment. However, there is also a wide range of exceptions, including private clubs, political parties, religious bodies, hospitals, prisons, hospitals and care homes, charities and non-profit making organisations that were set up to provide for one sex only.

* *Housing*, including renting, managing, sub-letting, or selling accommodation. Single-sex housing associations are exempt.

The Act makes the distinction between direct and indirect discrimination.

Direct sex discrimination

This occurs when a person is treated less favourably in the same circumstances than someone of the opposite sex, just because of their sex. For instance, charging women more than men for the same service, for example, mortgages or pensions, or offering an educational course in childcare to women only. Sexual harassment is also a form of direct discrimination. Sexual harassment, as defined by the European Commission code of practice is 'unwanted conduct of a sexual nature, or other conduct based on sex, affecting the dignity of women and men at work'. This includes unwelcome and repeated physical, verbal or non-verbal conduct, including ridicule, comments about appearance, requests for sexual favours and in extreme cases, physical assault. Both men and women can suffer from sexual harassment.

Indirect sex discrimination

This happens when, despite the same criteria, service or provision being applied to both sexes, far fewer members of one sex can take advantage of it. For example, if a Housing Association excluded single parents it may be indirectly discriminating against women, because the majority of single parents are women.

Indirect discrimination is against the law if it cannot be shown to be justified, irrespective of sex, and if the discrimination has caused disadvantage or distress to an individual.

The Sex Discrimination Act also protects people from being victimised by taking action under the Equal Pay Act or the Sex Discrimination Act; examples include making a complaint, or helping someone else to make a complaint, giving evidence at a court or tribunal, or accusing someone of breaking these laws. Indirect discrimination may occur, for example, where an employer refuses to give a reference on behalf of the employee, because he or she brought proceedings against him under the Act.

Strengths of the SDA

* The Act applies to both men and women, although in practice, women have probably benefited more, since they were discriminated against in more areas, particularly in relation to housing and financial services. For example, before the Act, women were not allowed to have a mortgage in their own right, denying their home ownership.

* The 'burden of proof' lies with the perpetrators not the victims; this means that although individuals have to demonstrate that their treatment appeared to be discriminatory, the employers or providers of services (perpetrator) have to prove that their action or omission was not intended to be discriminatory.

* The Act covers both actions and behaviour, such as, for example, harassment. It is unlawful for someone to assist, coerce or persuade someone else to carry out a discriminatory act. The law also protects people who have used the Act from victimisation by those who have been accused of breaking the law.

* In a significant development aimed at securing equal treatment for gay men, lesbians, bisexuals and **transgendered** people, the Act

has recently been amended to bring discrimination against **transsexuals** within the scope of the Act. Although there is no legal definition of transsexualism, the term 'gender re-assignment' is used to cover such situations.

* One important issue is that employers are liable for discriminatory acts (or omissions) carried out by their employees during the course of employment, whether they were aware of it or not. It is therefore the responsibility for employers to provide equality training for their staff and have an equal opportunities policy that is monitored regularly. The employers may escape prosecution providing they can demonstrate that they took reasonable steps to ensure their employees were offered appropriate training and took action such as ethnic monitoring of the workforce to ensure the employees were aware of the law.

Weaknesses of the SDA

* There are important areas not covered by the Act, such as income tax, social security benefits, immigration, and nationality, including asylum seekers.

* Although it is unlawful to discriminate against married people in the areas of employment and training, this does not apply to the other areas of the Act listed above.

* The status of single people is not covered by the Act in the same way, and discrimination against them because they are not married, is lawful.

* It is not a statutory requirement under the Act for local authorities to eliminate unlawful sex discrimination and promote equal opportunities.

* Although the law is reasonable and clear, legislation does not change deeply held attitudes and values of individuals; only time and experience can encourage people to reflect on their attitudes. The law may prevent the more open examples of discrimination, but to be truly effective individuals have to be prepared to use it. Sex discrimination does still occur, for example, around maternity rights.

However, women often fail to challenge employers because they are afraid of losing their jobs. Others are unaware of their rights and are not provided with information by their employers. In other cases, people have suspected discrimination but have been given other reasons for their treatment. For example, women who are passed over for promotion may be told they are not suitable, or their performance is not up to standard. Even where indirect discrimination is suspected, it can be difficult, time consuming and expensive to prove.

Equal Opportunities Commission

Compliance with the Sex Discrimination Act is currently overseen by the **Equal Opportunities Commission**, whose aims are shown in Figure 1.8.

1.
To work towards the elimination of sex discrimination.

2.
To promote equality of opportunity between men and women generally.

The Equal Opportunities Commission aim:

3.
To keep the Sex Discrimination Act and the Equal Pay Act under review and propose amendments to the Home Secretary.

FIGURE 1.8 *Aims of the Equal Opportunities Commission*

The Commission has the power to undertake formal investigations into discriminatory practices on behalf of individuals and provide financial support to individuals complaining about discrimination. The Commission publishes codes of practice on employment, which may be used as evidence in an employment tribunal. It is therefore important that employers are aware of such codes of practice and comply with them. The Commission undertakes research and keeps relevant government policy areas under review; social security, taxation and maternity rights, for example.

Individuals who believe they have been discriminated against, can contact the Commission directly for advice. (www.eoc.org.uk). Information is also available through local branches of the Citizens Advice Bureau, and other welfare rights organisations. Financial assistance with bringing a discrimination case may also be available in certain circumstances.

FIGURE 1.9 *The commission undertakes employment tribunals*

The Race Relations Act 1976 (amended 2001)

The Race Relations Act 1976 (RRA) shares many of the features of the Sex Discrimination Act in that it covers employment, education, goods, facilities and services as well as housing. The Act identifies, direct and indirect discrimination – the concept of treating someone less favourably because of their race. There are four types of discrimination covered by the Act:

* Direct discrimination   * Victimisation

* Indirect discrimination   * Harassment

Direct discrimination

Examples of direct discrimination include denying entry to a club, school or other establishment because of race, or operating quotas limiting the numbers of black and/or members of other racial groups. It is also direct discrimination to refuse employment to a person on the basis that customers will not like being attended to by a person of that race. For example, a nursing home manager who refused to employ a black care worker on the grounds that the residents would object would be breaking the law. The Race Relations Act also defines segregation as direct discrimination; for example, providing separate facilities or limiting the job roles of black or other ethnic minority employees to positions where they have no contact with the public, whilst allowing others a full range of job roles.

Indirect discrimination

Indirect racial discrimination is identified in a similar way to indirect sex discrimination; applying criteria which only some people can meet. For example, requiring employees to be clean shaven would disadvantage Sikhs and other groups, whose religious and cultural beliefs require that they wear beards. Special arrangements must be made to allow equal access to the full range of job opportunities. The Act also covers victimisation and harassment. The definition of victimisation is similar to the Sex Discrimination Act, protecting individuals who bring action under the Act; harassment, which was added as an amendment in 2003, is defined as 'unwanted conduct with the purpose or effect of violating dignity or creating a hostile, degrading, humiliating or offensive environment on the grounds of race or ethnic origin' (Race Relations Act (Amendment) 2003). The Act covers similar areas to the Sex Discrimination Act, namely, *employment; housing; education; the provision of goods, facilities and services; harassment and victimisation.*

* In the area of *employment* the Act covers training opportunities, promotion, hours of work and fringe benefits in both permanent and temporary jobs as well as apprentices and trainees, employment agencies and the police. There are exceptions, called 'genuine occupational requirements', such as in restaurants or for drama and theatre productions, or to provide personal care services to a particular racial group. Training organisations are allowed to practice 'positive

discrimination' in situations where there have been few people from different racial groups doing a particular job role during the previous 12 months; this includes specifically targeted training courses, for example. As with other equality legislation, employers are liable for the actions of their employees and need to ensure that they are aware of the law. Most organisations have an Equal Opportunities Policy which should be made available to staff and monitored.

* Following the amendment to the Act in 2000, it is unlawful for the government to discriminate on race grounds when appointing people to serve in public office or on committees. Similarly, trade unions and professional associations cannot refuse to let people join, provide different benefits, facilities or services (e.g. legal representation) or apply different terms of membership. These areas come under *goods, facilities and services.*

* Licensing bodies such as the Director General of Fair Trading (who licenses credit and hire purchase facilities), magistrates or the police cannot discriminate on the basis of race. They are also obliged to take into account any evidence about previous racist conduct on the part of the applicant when considering their character, such as refusal to serve ethnic minority customers.

* The Act covers discrimination between any racial group, including between different minority groups. In many parts of the world there are groups who have been at war with each other, often, but not always as a result of religious differences, for example, in former Yugoslavia, in India and Pakistan and between Greek and Turkish Cypriots. The law provides protection for all these different groups of citizens.

* The Race Relations Act applies to *education*; specifically to schools and colleges maintained by a local education authority, but also to independent and fee-paying schools, special schools and grant-maintained schools and universities. The only exception to this is overseas students, who are not British citizens and may not remain in Britain once they have

completed their course. This allows educational establishments to charge higher fees to overseas students.

* The Act applies to *housing*, including renting from landlords (public or private), buying and selling. For example, it is illegal to discriminate by making members of ethnic groups wait longer or pay different charges. The exceptions to this are small boarding houses or shared accommodation and private sales by owner-occupiers, unless they use the services of an estate agent, in which case the Act applies because this is a service provided by the agent and thus covered by the Act. As with the Sex Discrimination Act, charities acting for a particular group are allowed to provide exclusively for them.

Strengths of the RRA

* The Act is wide ranging in its application, covering most areas of life.

* Following the Macpherson report (1999) into the death of Stephen Lawrence, the Act was amended to extend to the police. This was a key recommendation; in 2000 it was further extended to cover all public bodies such as local government, mental hospitals, prisons and courts.

* The Act applies to all racial and ethnic groups, covering discrimination between minority groups as well as between majority and minority groups.

Weaknesses of the RRA

* The Act has made open racial discrimination socially unacceptable to most people; however, like sex discrimination it occurs in more hidden and indirect forms and can be difficult to prove.

* Legislation does not change deeply held attitudes; however, it can be effective in preventing unacceptable behaviour in the long term.

* Taking action (invoking) the Act requires individuals to know their rights and what options are available to them, including what action to take. Organisations such as Citizens Advice Bureau and other welfare rights organisations can assist individuals with such information and may be able to provide legal advice.

The Commission for Racial Equality

The Commission for Racial Equality (CRE) is the body responsible for monitoring and enforcing the Race Relations Act (RRA) and has wide ranging powers. The Commission's responsibilities are shown in Figure 1.10.

The CRE has similar powers to the Equal Opportunities Commission in terms of investigation,

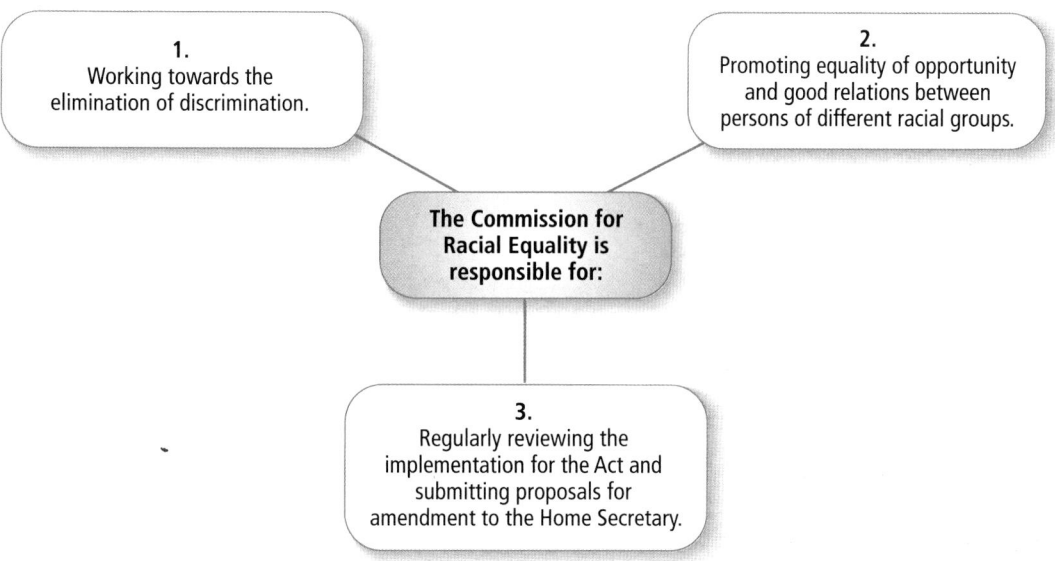

FIGURE 1.10 *Responsibilities of the Commission for Racial Equality*

alleged discriminatory practices and supporting individuals who are bringing action under the Act. It also provides codes of practice, which can be used as evidence in Employment Tribunals. The Commission can carry out a formal investigation into any area, but must give notice of such an intention and draw up the terms of reference, stating the nature and scope of the investigation. The organisation or person will then be required to produce information or evidence. In addition, in situations where it finds that discrimination has occurred, the Commission can issue non-discrimination notices requiring the organisation or individual to make changes, for example to procedures or policies, in order to comply. However, such notices are not legally binding, although they can be used in evidence in individual cases. The Commission is required to give notice to the organisation of its intentions to issue a notice and what they need to do in order to comply; they then have 28 days to make any changes or prepare an appeal, explaining why they cannot or should not need to comply.

The Commission can enforce a non-compliance order by applying to the court (County Court or High Court) to take out an injunction against the organisation or person. An **injunction** is a court order requiring the person or individual to comply; failure to do so is considered to be contempt of court, which can result in fines or imprisonment. It is important to recognise that the Commission has up to five years after the issuing of a non-compliance notice to apply for an injunction.

Consider this

Vincent is a 28-year-old Rastafarian, who has worked at a community home for people with learning disabilities for the last six years. He is the only black person working in the home, although there is a black male service user, aged 17 years, and an Asian girl of 14 years. Vincent gets on very well with his fellow workers, and occasionally goes out for a drink with them, after work.

The new line manager has recently been appointed, following the retirement of the previous post holder, who had been at the home for 10 years. The new manager seems to have taken a dislike to Vincent and has begun to follow him around whilst he undertakes his duties, making critical remarks about the quality of his work. He has been overheard making racist comments, particularly about Rastafarians, in the staffroom, and is critical of Vincent and his work in front of the other staff. He has suggested that Vincent should get his hair cut and remove his Rastafarian dreadlocks, even though he keeps them tied back whilst on duty.

The new manager has also introduced a new work rota, allocating Vincent most of the cleaning duties that are not undertaken by the housekeeper. None of the other staff have been given extra cleaning duties.

Recently, Vincent was late for work on two occasions due to his car breaking down, although his timekeeping is usually excellent – his colleagues rely on him to make the tea on the early shift and tease him about being unable to sleep. The manager gave Vincent a verbal warning on the first occasion and a written warning on the second. He has been informed that if he is one minute late for duty in future, he will be disciplined.

At the annual performance review, Vincent was given a particularly poor score and informed that he would not be getting a pay rise, although previously his reviews have been excellent, particularly in relation to his communication and relationships with the service users. All of the other staff received good reviews, and all have been awarded pay rises.

Using concepts can you identify?
1. What types of discrimination are evident in Vincent's treatment by the line manager?
2. What effect might this have upon Vincent?

Go further – can you analyse using theory?
3. What are the different ways in which the law protects Vincent's rights?
4. What action might Vincent take using the law?

Go further – can you evaluate, using a range of theory?
5. How might the line manager's attitude affect the residents, particularly the two non-white residents?

The Disability Discrimination Act 1995

The Disability Discrimination Act 1995 is concerned with the equal treatment of disabled people and outlaws discrimination against disabled people solely on the basis of their disability. In this respect it differs from the Sex Discrimination Act and The Race Relations Act, which apply to all people, and are general equality acts. There are proposed changes to the Act currently passing through the parliamentary process in the form of the Disability Discrimination Bill 2003.

The Act sets out the definition of a disabled person or person who has had a disability. There are four main criteria as set out in Figure 1.11.

✳ The Act covers similar areas to other equality legislation; *employment, trades unions and trade associations, goods, facilities and services, housing and education*. In addition, this Act includes *public transport*, because disabled people, as citizens, should have the same access to public spaces and transport as non-disabled people.

✳ Discrimination in *employment* applies to all job applicants, contract workers and employees. The Act covers appointments, contractual terms and conditions of employment, training opportunities, dismissal and redundancy. An employer is considered to have discriminated against a disabled person if he or she is treated less favourably than non-disabled people in the same employment, for reasons related to the disability, and they cannot demonstrate that such treatment is justified. In addition, employers are required to make 'reasonable adjustments' to the working environment to enable disabled people to work. This might include changes to the physical environment, or changes to policies and work practices, so that the disabled person is not placed at a disadvantage. The Act identifies the sort of things that might be considered reasonable adjustments, for example, allocating some of your duties to another person, altering working hours and permitting absences from work for rehabilitation, assessment and treatment. Importantly, it is not necessary for an employer to be aware that the employee is disabled, in order to be guilty of discriminating and failing to make reasonable adjustments. Many organisations now include a section in their job application forms that asks questions about disability in order to prevent such unintended discrimination. As with the other equality legislation, employers are held liable for acts of discrimination carried out by the employees in the course of their employment.

FOUR MAIN CRITERIA FOR DISABILITY	
Physical or mental impairment	Mental impairment includes suffering from mental illness, which is clinically well-recognised. Medical evidence may be required to show whether or not, there is impairment.
The ability to carry out daily activities	Impairment includes difficulties with any one of the following: mobility; manual dexterity; physical coordination; continence; ability to lift, carry or move everyday objects; speech, hearing or eyesight problems; memory or ability to concentrate, learn or understand; perception of risk and danger.
Substantial adverse effect	This means that the impairment must be more than minor, and may get worse over time.
Long term	The impairment must have lasted for at least one year. With progressive conditions such as cancer and HIV, the 1995 Act considers a person to be disabled as soon as the condition becomes symptomatic; however, under the proposed changes, such conditions would be considered a disability as soon as they were diagnosed. This is an important change, because individuals suffering from terminal or life-limiting diseases should not be subject to delays when seeking claims for discrimination under this Act.

FIGURE 1.11 *Definition of a person who has a disability*

* Trades unions and trade associations must be prepared to admit disabled people to their membership and existing disabled members should have the same rights and benefits as non-disabled members, including membership on the same terms.

* *Goods, facilities and services.* This includes services provided by public authorities, as well as private agencies and individuals, whether they are paid for or not. Areas included in the Act include: communications, information services, hotels and boarding houses, financial and insurance services, entertainment facilities, training, employment agencies and the use of public places. Education and transport facilities are dealt with separately. The proposed changes to the Act will also include private clubs, which at present are excluded, unless they provide services to the public, such as hiring rooms for private functions. Again, discrimination occurs when the service provider treats disabled people less favourably for reasons relating to their disability and the treatment cannot be justified under the provisions of the Disability Discrimination Act. They are also required to make reasonable adjustments, so that their services can be accessed by disabled people. Disabled people must be offered the same standard of service, delivered in the same manner, as non-disabled people. The service cannot be provided on less favorable terms to disabled people.

* Discrimination in the provision of *housing* services include refusing to provide premises to disabled people, offering the premises on less favorable terms or treating disabled people less favourably than non-disabled people requiring the same housing facilities. This is very similar to the provision of goods facilities and services in general. The proposed changes will require reasonable steps to be taken to provide aids, for example, handrails or ramps, where these would allow disabled persons to use the premises or facility.

* *Education.* From September 2002 new duties were imposed on schools, which were intended to provide greater support to disabled pupils in mainstream education. The Special Educational Needs and Disability Act 2001 amended the Disability Discrimination Act, preventing discrimination against disabled people in terms of access to education. This includes the duty not to discriminate in relation to admissions, for example by refusal to admit disabled pupils, or the terms in which admission is offered. The education or associated services that are provided for pupils should be equally available to disabled pupils. Local Education Authorities and schools are expected to improve access to education for disabled students, and they are expected to prepare access ability plans, including improvements in access to the curriculum, physical improvements, and the provision of information in a range of formats suitable for use by disabled students, for example, Braille. There have also been some changes to the Special Educational Needs framework which deals with the specific needs of individual children. In particular, the Special Educational Needs Tribunal, which oversees the decisions relating to children with special educational needs, can now decide whether schools or colleges have discriminated under the Disability Discrimination Act.

* *Transport.* The Act covers licensed taxi cabs, and the licensing authority will not be able to grant licenses to taxes, unless the vehicles comply with the accessibility provisions. The Disability Discrimination Act requires taxi drivers to carry disabled passengers while they remain in their wheelchairs without additional charge; to carry the wheelchair if the passenger chooses to sit in the passenger seat; and to ensure that the passenger is carried in safety and reasonable comfort. Taxi drivers are expected to give reasonable assistance to their disabled passengers, including those with guide dogs or hearing dogs. Public service vehicles such as buses and coaches carrying more than 22 passengers are also covered under the Disability Discrimination Act since the accessibility

regulations were brought into force in 2000. Small buses, private hire vehicles and minibuses are excluded, although the proposed changes will end this exemption, requiring all providers of transport services to comply with the regulations. Rail services are also included under the Disability Discrimination Act, as a result of the Rail Vehicle Accessibility Regulations 1998 which required all new vehicles to the accessible to people with disabilities. The Disability Discrimination Act does not state the timeframe in which vehicles will be required to be accessible, and the implementation of disabled facilities on all rail transport is likely to be sometime in future.

Consider this

Read the example of Tariq shopping for clothes on page 11.

Using concepts can you identify?
1. Which aspects of the Disability Discrimination Act apply to this situation?

Go further – can you analyse using theory?
2. What reasonable adjustments could the shop make to enable wheelchair users to access all the facilities?

Go further – can you evaluate using a range of theory?
3. What are the manager's responsibilities in relation to the staff attitudes towards Tariq?
4. What can be done to help staff fulfil their responsibilities under the Disability Discrimination Act?

Opportunities for redress

If any individual feels that they have been unfairly discriminated against, and they wish to rectify the situation or complain, this is known as 'seeking redress '. There are several ways in which this can be done; for example, if the complaint of discrimination relates to employment, individuals would usually use the organisation's policies and procedures and equal opportunity as a means of

changing their situation. Organisations are required to have an equal opportunities policy, which they should make available to all staff, for example through a staff handbook. Line managers and supervisors are responsible for implementing and monitoring equal opportunities for the staff they manage; however, senior managers have responsibility for ensuring the line managers and supervisors understand what is expected by making certain they are properly trained. Senior staff should monitor recruitment and retention to ensure that people are not leaving employment unnecessarily and expect to receive regular reports from managers and supervisors. An Equal Opportunities Policy should provide details on the recruitment, terms and conditions, training, promotion and the procedure for complaints, as set out below.

Recruitment

This will include information for managers and staff on the recruitment process, for example, the content of job advertisements, so that they do not contravene any of the equality Acts and details of any exemptions applicable to the particular job roles of the company.

Application forms should be designed so that the company does not ask for irrelevant information, which may be discriminatory, for example the age of the applicant. It is important, however, to monitor the ethnicity of applicants (ethnic monitoring) in order to highlight any possible inequalities, which can then be investigated and any disadvantage addressed; this will ensure that the composition of the workforce represents all sections of the local workforce. Benchmarks (comparisons) can be used to ensure fair representation, and to provide opportunities for increasing the number of employees from minority groups, for example by an agreed percentage. It is possible to discriminate positively in favour of under represented groups without contravening any law, and information from the Census can be used as a guide. In Scotland, information about ethnic minorities on the census returns is different.

And equal opportunities policy should also provide details of how to conduct recruitment interviews in order not to discriminate, for example by ensuring that all questions are asked of both men and women, and including questions about caring responsibilities. Many organisations now have standardised interview procedures in which the questions are agreed in advance of interviewing candidates.

Terms and conditions

Equal opportunities policies should provide information on the terms and conditions of employment, which will be included in the contract of employment, such as maternity rights, how pay is negotiated, holidays and paid leave, the rights to belong to a trade union, how performance is monitored and under what circumstances employees may be dismissed. This is to ensure that staff are fully aware of their rights and responsibilities and those of their employers before they sign the contract of employment. The policy should include under what circumstances the employee may be disciplined, and provide details of the disciplinary procedures. Employees are entitled to representation during disciplinary hearings, for example from a trade union representative or colleague, who can speak on their behalf and support them.

Training

An equal opportunities policy should state how opportunities for training are provided for all employees. This should include compulsory training, such as health and safety and diversity training. This is particularly important to the care sector, to ensure that employees are aware of their responsibilities not to discriminate. Training opportunities should be available to everyone, and based on individual learning needs, which should be identified from performance reviews.

Promotion

Equal opportunities policies should identify how and under what circumstances opportunities for promotion are provided for staff. It is good practice to ensure that people are encouraged to apply for promotion on the basis of their performance reviews, and that opportunities are offered to the existing workforce before advertising externally.

Complaints

The policy should give clear guidance to managers and staff on how employees can complain about their treatment, including discrimination, harassment, bullying and victimisation. This is sometimes called the grievance procedure, and often has a timescale within which the employee should apply for redress. It is important to recognise that the first step in a grievance procedure is often the individual's line manager, who may be the person that the employee wishes to complain about. The policy should clearly state what the employee should do in such situations.

The first step for employees who feel they have been a victim of discrimination should be to use the organisational procedures described above in order to rectify the situation. If the situation does not reach a satisfactory conclusion, employees may seek advice and guidance from the appropriate Commission, their trade union, the Citizens Advice Bureau or other welfare rights organisations such as the Low Pay Unit. Disputes relating to employment, which are not satisfactorily resolved between employer and employee may be taken to an Employment Tribunal, which will hear the evidence and make judgments. Employers who have been found guilty of discrimination will be obliged to change their procedures, reinstate the employee and sometimes pay compensation. If the employees are victimised on returning to work as a result of bringing such an action, they are entitled to redress for this as a separate case.

If the alleged discrimination relates to other areas covered by the relevant equality Acts, such as the provision of goods, facilities and services, individuals should contact the relevant Commission directly for advice and guidance. Other organisations may be able to provide assistance, for example, the Office of Fair Trading.

The Human Rights Act 1998

The Human Rights Act 1998 (HRA) is the most important significant piece of British legislation protecting human rights and freedoms, and has its origins in the European Convention on Human Rights, drafted after World War II. The countries that have signed up to the Convention make up the Council of Europe, which is separate from the European Union. The European Court of Human Rights is the international court set up to interpret and apply the Convention. The court is overseen by judges who are nominated by each of the countries that are members of the Council of Europe. The Human Rights Act enshrines the rights from the European Convention on Human Rights into a form of higher law in the UK.

The Convention is divided into 'articles ' which set out the rights that are protected, and new protocols giving additional rights have been incorporated over the years by the Council of Europe as circumstances have changed. Many of these are incorporated into the new Act. However, it is important to recognise that not all of the rights set out by the Convention and its protocols are incorporated into the Human Rights Act 1998.

The Rights
Article 2: The right to life
The right to life is protected by law, and there are only certain limited circumstances, where it is acceptable for the state to take away someone's life, such as a police officer acting in self-defence.

Article 3: The prohibition of torture
This covers the right of individuals not to be tortured or subjected to treatment or punishment, which is inhuman or degrading.

Article 4: The prohibition of slavery and forced labour
Individuals have the right not to be treated as a slave or forced to perform certain kinds of labour.

Article 5: The right to liberty and security
This means the right not to be deprived of one's liberty, for example 'arrested or detained', except in certain cases, such as where someone is suspected or convicted of committing a crime and this is justified by existing legal procedures.

Article 6: The right to a fair trial
Everyone has the right to a fair public hearing within a reasonable period of time. This covers criminal charges, civil rights and obligations. Hearings must be carried out by an independent and impartial tribunal, established by law. The public may be excluded from some hearings, if it is necessary, for example to protect national security or public order. Individuals accused of criminal charges are presumed innocent until proven guilty according to the law, and have the right to defend themselves.

Article 7: No punishment without law
This covers the protection of individuals who have committed actions that have since become criminal. It also protects people against later increases in sentences for an offence.

Article 8: The right to respect for private and family life
Everyone has the right of privacy and to have family life respected, including an individual's home and correspondence. This right can only be overridden in certain circumstances, for example in the interests of national security.

Article 9: Freedom of thought, conscience and religion
This enshrines the right of individuals to hold a broad range of views, beliefs and thoughts, including religious faiths.

Article 10: Freedom of expression
Everyone has the right to hold opinions and express their views, either individually or within groups. This includes unpopular or disturbing beliefs; however, it can be restricted in certain circumstances, for example incitement to religious hatred, or causing a breach of the peace.

Article 11: Freedom of assembly and association
This includes peaceful demonstrations, trade union membership and the right to associate with other people holding similar views. It can be restricted in a similar way to freedom of expression.

Article 12: The right to marry
Everyone has the right to marry and start a family; however, the national law still governs how and at what age this can take place.

Article 14: Prohibition of discrimination
This means that when the Convention rights are applied, individuals have the right not to be treated differently because of their race, religion,

sex, political views or any other status. This article ensures that the Convention applies to everyone.

Note: Article 13 is not included in the Human Right Act, since the government felt the existing legislation would be sufficient.

The protocols

These are later additions to the Convention.

Article 1 of protocol 1: The protection of property

This means that everyone has the right to enjoy their own possessions in peace. Public authorities are not allowed to interfere with things you own, or the way you use them, except in very limited circumstances, for example confiscation of property for noise pollution or from convicted drug dealers.

Article 2 of protocol 1: The right to education

Individuals must not be denied the right to the educational system.

Article 3 of protocol 1: The right to free elections

Elections for the members of any legislative body (law-making organisations such as Parliament) must be free and fair. They must take place by secret ballot, although qualifications may be imposed on those that are eligible to vote, such as a minimum age.

Article 1 and 2 of protocol 6: Abolition of the death penalty

This article formally abolishes the death penalty. There may be limited exceptions in times of war, but only in accordance with the law.

Compatability of new law and the Convention

It is important to recognise that as a result of the Human Rights Act, every time the government proposes a new law in Parliament, it has to ensure that the new law is compatible with the rights of the Convention. This is the reason that many of our existing equality Acts have recently been amended, particularly in respect of public bodies. The Human Rights Act states that all public authorities must pay attention to the rights of individuals when they are taking decisions that affect them. Public authorities include the government, civil servants, local authorities, health authorities, the police, the courts and private companies that carry out public functions.

Strengths of the HRA

1. Because the Human Rights Act is now enshrined in British law, individuals with human rights grievances will no longer have to go to the European Court of Human Rights in Strasbourg, but will be able to bring their case to court in the UK. However, it is still possible for individuals to make an application to the European Court of Human Rights under certain key requirements. For example, the individual must be a victim of a violation of one or more of the articles of the Convention, and he or she should generally have pursued any proceedings through the UK courts before making an application. Applications must be made within 6 months of the conclusion of any court proceedings in the UK.

2. Under the Human Rights Act, public bodies are no longer exempt from taking individual human rights into consideration when making decisions. This has considerable implications for the health and social care sector. For example, under Article 2 – The right to life – the State must safeguard life, as well as refraining from taking life. This means that, in theory, patients could challenge their local health authorities if certain drugs were unavailable in their area, but were available elsewhere. (**Postcode rationing**).

3. Some Acts of Parliament give the power to make detailed laws to a government minister. In such cases, known as secondary legislation, the law itself is often set out in regulations with orders. Much social security law is set out in such regulations rather than in Acts of Parliament. Where courts find that secondary legislation is incompatible with Convention rights, all courts have the power not to apply it.

Weaknesses of the HRA

1. The definition of public authorities remains unclear, and will be decided by the courts. For example, the status of a private day nursery remains unclear; even though it is subject to government regulation it provides a private service for which payment is made.

2. Many areas of the Act remain to be tested. For example, asylum seekers could challenge the restrictions introduced by the Home Secretary under the Immigration and Asylum Act 1999 , which leaves many asylum seekers without entitlement to help with accommodation costs.

3. If someone brings proceedings against a public authority for breach of their Convention rights, the authority may argue that it had no choice, because it was required to take action under an existing Act of Parliament. In such cases, the individual bringing the case can only hope for a declaration of incompatibility (this means that an existing Act of Parliament may breach the Convention rights – see page 25). Although the higher courts (the High Court, the Court of Appeal and the House of Lords) have the power to make such a declaration, which is meant to encourage Parliament to amend the law, the courts cannot force the government to amend the law if they do not want to.

The Home Office Human Rights Unit provides a range of guidance, explaining the Act for the public, for public authorities, for civil servants and for the private and voluntary sectors. These can be accessed through www.crimereduction.gov.uk

The Mental Health Act 1983

The Mental Health Act (MHA) is a complicated piece of legislation, because it deals with both the care and control of people suffering from mental illness. The circumstances under which an individual's rights can be overridden are detailed within the Act, which is wide-ranging. It also covers people who commit criminal acts as a result of their mental state.

The Act has 10 main sections:

* Part 1: Application
* Part 2: Compulsory admission to hospital and guardianship
* Part 3: Patients concerned in criminal proceedings while under sentence
* Part 4: Consent to treatment
* Part 5: Mental Health Review Tribunals
* Part 6: Removal and return of patients within the United Kingdom
* Part 7: Management of property and affairs of patients
* Part 8: Functions of local authorities and the Secretary of State
* Part 9: Offences
* Part 10: Miscellaneous provisions

The Act defines different types and degree of mental disorder, which are covered under the regulations. Definitions are as set out in Figure 1.12.

MENTAL HEALTH ACT 1983	
Mental disorder	Mental illness, arrested or incomplete development of mind, psychopathic disorder and any other disorder or disability of mind.
Mental impairment	A state of arrested or incomplete development of mind which includes significant impairment of intelligence and social functioning and is associated with abnormally aggressive or seriously irresponsible conduct on the part of the person concerned
Psychopathic disorder	A persistent disorder or disability of mind (whether or not including significant impairment of intelligence) which results in abnormally aggressive or seriously irresponsible conduct on the part of the person concerned

FIGURE 1.12 *Some definitions of types and degree of mental disorder*

Key points of the Mental Health Act 1983

1. Patients may be admitted to hospital against their will – '**sectioned**' – for assessment and/or treatment if they are suffering from a mental disorder that is considered to require medical treatment, because they may pose a danger to themselves or others. The request must be made on the written recommendations of two medical practitioners and a person can be detained for up to 28 days, unless a further order is made, or the individual has consented to remain in hospital. This is known as 'civil admission'.

2. In an emergency situation, where the individual poses as immediate threat to himself or others, an emergency application can be made either by an approved social worker, the police, or the nearest relative. In such situations, a person can be detained for up to 72 hours, unless a further application has been made. This is known as removing the person to a place of safety, which is usually a police station or a hospital.

3. Patients may be granted leave of absence, if authorised by a medical practitioner; this may be accompanied by a member of staff or unaccompanied.

4. In some circumstances, an application for guardianship may be made by the local authority social services department, or a person who is accepted by the local authority social services as a guardian if it is considered to be in the best interests of patient. The guardianship would be effective for the duration of patient's stay in hospital, but can only be made on behalf of patients over 16 years of age, and on the recommendation of two medical practitioners, as before. The person acting as guardian has to agree in writing to act as guardian.

5. If a person has committed an offence, and is either awaiting trial or has been convicted but not yet sentenced, the court can apply for admission to hospital for an assessment of the accused's mental condition (admission via the courts).

6. In certain circumstances, where individuals have committed a serious offence, they may be subjected to a '**restriction order**' by the courts. In such situations, the person will be detained in a secure unit instead of being sent to prison. The Crime (Sentences) Act 1997 provides the court with powers to specify the level of security in which the patient should be detained. The secure unit may be a locked psychiatric ward in a hospital, or a type of special 'medium secure' unit, or a special hospital, such as Rampton, Broadmoor or Ashworth. In such circumstances, only the Secretary of State can permit leave of absence, the transfer of patients, or the discharge of patients.

7. Patients can be treated without their consent if the responsible medical practitioner (usually a consultant psychiatrist) thinks it is appropriate. Exceptions to this include surgical treatment, and invasive procedures such as electro-convulsive therapy (this is not commonly used now).

8. A patient detained under the Mental Health Act, whether detained under civil proceedings or criminal proceedings, can apply to the Mental Health Tribunal to have the situation assessed. Tribunal provides an independent hearing and consists of a legal representative, a medical representative and one lay member. Patients are usually represented by a solicitor, although patients may choose to represent themselves. The Tribunal will decide whether the patient's condition continues to meet the legal and medical criteria for detention under the Mental Health Act, and may order the patient to be discharged.

9. The Mental Health Act requires steps to be taken to ensure that patients understand their rights as soon as possible after their detention has begun. The information must be given both orally and in writing, and includes the section under which the patient is detained, the effect of this section, and the patient's right to apply to the Mental Health Review Tribunal.

FIGURE 1.13 *The Mental Health Act requires that patients understand their rights*

Strengths of the Mental Health Act

1. The Act provides protection for people who might harm themselves or others, primarily through compulsory admission to hospital.

2. People detained under the Mental Health Act have the right to appeal to the Tribunal, which has the power to discharge them from detention in hospital.

3. Under the Act, individuals have the right to receive information, both orally and in writing, explaining why they have been detained and their right to appeal.

4. The Act makes provision for the aftercare and treatment of people who have been discharged into the community.

Weaknesses of the Mental Health Act

1. The Mental Health Act 1983 was put into place at a time when most patients with mental health problems were treated in psychiatric hospitals. Since then, there has been a concerted effort to treat people wherever possible within the community, in order to avoid 'institutionalisation'. People who have spent many years in institutions often lose the ability to live independent lives, because they have become dependent on others to take care of their needs. Therefore, this Act is now out of date, as it no longer meets the requirements of present-day modern mental health practice.

2. The Mental Health Act 1983 makes no provision for people suffering from 'severe personality disorder', who are considered to be untreatable, either with medication or through other methods. Sometimes such people pose a danger to others and this has raised concerns for public safety.

3. Compulsory detention in hospital poses issues for human rights, particularly in relation to consent to treatment. It can also delay recovery, due to its traumatic nature.

4. The Act does not address the stigma and discrimination suffered by people who have mental health problems. The Social Exclusion Unit has found that the biggest problem experienced by people suffering from mental health problems was stigma.

5. The Act makes no provision for people who are suffering from less severe mental illness, such as, for example, anxiety and depression. It has been suggested that patients need to be seriously ill before they are entitled to treatment and that this, in fact, diverts resources away from care in the community and towards hospital treatment.

6. It has been suggested that the Mental Health Act 1983 focuses more on control and containment of people with mental illness, rather than treatment, and therefore increases the perception of mentally ill people as dangerous, adding to their stigmatisation.

7. The current legislation does not adequately cover the needs of those suffering from 'dual diagnosis', such as those with substance abuse and mental illness.

Proposed reforms of the Mental Health Act

In response to the perceived weaknesses of the Mental Health Act 1983, the government has proposed to reform the legislation, and first put forward the Mental Health Bill in June 2002. This Bill was extremely controversial, particularly in its proposal to extend compulsory treatment of those being cared for in the community. This was overwhelmingly opposed by a wide range of people, including professionals, mental health campaigners, charities, service users and carers, who felt that this was both unnecessary and would reinforce the misconception that all people with mental health problems are dangerous.

The Bill was revised and a second draft is currently being consulted on; however, serious concerns remain. Campaigners argue that the new Bill over-emphasises the protection of the public at the expense of service users, that this will further stigmatise mental illness and continue to divert resources into compulsory care at the expense of those who voluntarily seek help. They argue that compulsion should be used as a last resort, and wherever possible people should be treated on a voluntary basis, fully consenting to their treatment. Campaigners maintain that the principles governing the care of people with mental illness should be the same as those for physical care, and argue for people to have a right to assessment and treatment if they feel that they are suffering from a mental disorder. There are concerns that removing the 'treatability' definitions of the existing 1983 Act in order to bring people with severe personality disorder under the legislation (in order to detain them in secure accommodation) means that people who are sexually deviant, or substance abusers would also be liable to compulsory detention, particularly since the definition of 'mental disorder' will be revised to cover 'a disturbance in the functioning of the mind or brain resulting from any disability or disorder of the mind or brain'. Examples of a mental disorder include **schizophrenia**, depression or a learning disability. The Bill is currently being examined by the Joint Scrutiny Committee, which has heard evidence from campaigners. It is likely that further changes will be made to this legislation before it finally becomes law.

The Human Rights Act can protect an individual's rights; for example, judgment has already been given in a case brought before the European Court of Human Rights, concerning a man with **autism** and learning disabilities, who was admitted to hospital treatment for his mental disorder. The man was not formally detained under the Mental Health Act 1983, because although he lacked the capacity to consent to treatment, he did not resist it. The court found that this person had been unlawfully deprived of his liberty under Article 5 of the Convention. The court however, made it clear that an individual's particular circumstances will need to be considered in any future judgments.

Consider this

Ryan is a 21-year-old man, who suffers from schizophrenia. He lives with his mother on a local housing estate and is currently unemployed.

Following a short spell in hospital, Ryan was discharged into his mother's care, and on medication. However, the medication made Ryan feel extremely ill, so he stopped taking it. Recently he has started to hear voices again, but is managing to cope with the help of a local support group for people with mental health problems. Ryan feels that he will eventually get better, and wants to get a job. However, his mother is very worried that he will relapse, and his behaviour will become more erratic and unpredictable.

Using concepts, can you identify?
1. Under which aspect of the Mental Health Act 1983, would Ryan have been admitted to hospital?

2. Can Ryan be forced to take his medication?

Go further – can you analyse using theory?
3. Examples of the type of circumstances under which Ryan's rights might be overridden?

Go further – can you evaluate using a range of theory?
4. How Ryan might be affected under the new proposals in the Mental Health Bill 2002?

The Mental Health Act Commission

The implementation of the Mental Health Act 1983 is overseen by the Mental Health Act Commission, which was established in 1983 and consists of some 100 members (Commissioners), including laypersons, lawyers, doctors, nurses, social workers, psychologists and other specialists. Its main functions are shown in Figure 1.14.

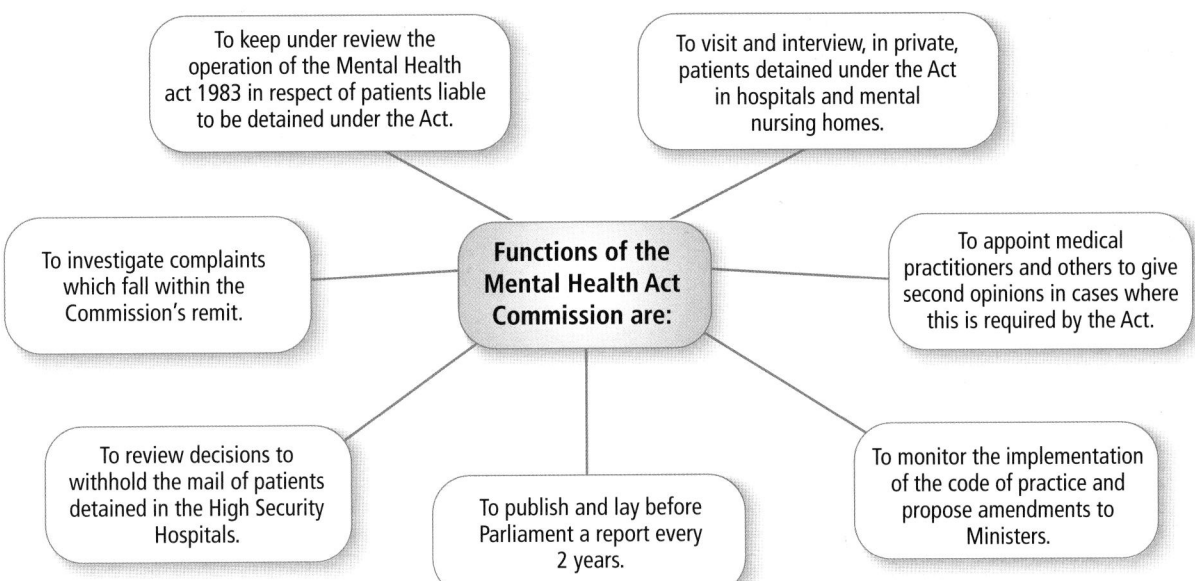

FIGURE 1.14 *Main functions of the Mental Health Act Commission*

In addition, the Commission advises government ministers on policy matters which can within its remit. More information can be found at: www.mhac.org.uk

The Children Act 1989

The Children Act 1989 is the primary legislation relating to the welfare of children. There are a number of very important principles contained in this legislation.

Key principles:

1. The welfare of the child is the paramount consideration when decisions are made by the courts or others in relation to the upbringing of the child. In practice, this means that the parent's wishes can be overridden if these are considered not been the best interests of the child. This is sometimes known as the **'paramountcy principle'**. Although the concept of welfare is not defined in the Children Act, there are a number of factors which are taken into consideration when the courts are making decisions (sometimes known as the 'welfare checklist').

2. Wherever possible, children should be brought up and cared for within their own families.

The welfare checklist

This includes that:

* the wishes or feelings of the child shall be ascertained in the light of his or her age and understanding

* the physical, emotional and education needs of the child shall be considered

* the likely effect of any change in the child's circumstances should be determined

* the age, sex, background in any other characteristics the court considers to be relevant, should be considered

* consideration should be given to any harm which the child has suffered, or is at risk of suffering

* the capability of the child's parents in meeting the child's needs should be taken into consideration

* the available powers of the court to take action should be determined.

---

3. Children in need and their parents should be supported in the upbringing of their child, by the local authority social services department. Local authorities have a duty to:

* safeguard and promote the welfare of children in need

* so far as is consistent with that duty, promote the upbringing of such children by their families.

Children are defined as being in need if they are:

* unlikely to achieve, or maintain, or have the opportunity of maintaining a reasonable standard of health for development without the provision of local authority services. Health includes physical or mental health; development includes physical, social, emotional, intellectual or behavioural development

* their health for development is likely to be significantly impaired, or further impaired without the provision of such services

* the child is disabled. Disabled includes the blind, deaf, dumb or suffering from mental disorder, or handicapped by illness, injury or congenital deformity or other disability as may be prescribed.

The help and assistance provided by the local authority should:

* be provided in partnership with the parents

* meet each child's identified needs

* be appropriate to the child's race, culture, religion and language

* allow for independent representations and complaints procedures

* be provided in effective partnerships with other agencies, including health, welfare and voluntary agencies.

4. Children should be kept safe to be protected by effective interventions, if they are in danger.

5. Courts should ensure that delays are avoided, and should only make on order if to do so is better than making no order at all.

6. Children should be kept informed about what happens to them, and should participate in decision-making, where it concerns their future.

7. Parents will continue to have parental responsibility for their children, even when they do not live with them. They should be kept informed about their children and participate in decisions made about the future.

Where children are involved in separation or divorce proceedings, parents are encouraged to agree about the child's welfare and the continuation of parental responsibility. It is important to recognise that Article 8 of the Convention – The right to respect for private and family life – may affect the decision-making process, in that the court must be aware of the parents' right to family life. However, the welfare principle continues to dominate the view of the courts and has not yet been challenged under the Human Rights Act.

Parental responsibility

Parental responsibility is defined within the Children Act as 'all the rights, duties, powers, responsibilities and authority, which, by law, the parent of the child has in relation to that child and his property'. It is important to recognise that mothers always have parental responsibility for their child. Where the parents are married, the father automatically has parental responsibility; where parents are unmarried, but the father's name is on the birth certificate, he also has parental responsibility. However, if the parents are unmarried and the father is not named on the birth certificate, he does not automatically have parental responsibility and can only acquire it: through marriage to the mother; by entering into an agreement with the mother; by obtaining a residence order (which states where the child shall live); or by order of the court. Other people who cannot obtain parental responsibility for a child include anyone granted a residence order, such as grandparents, or where a guardian is appointed by the court. When a child is taken into care, the local authority shares parental responsibility with the parents, unless the child has entered care voluntarily, in which case the parental responsibility remains with the parents.

As children get older, and gain maturity, they can make decisions about their own future. This is commonly known as the 'Gillick competence', following the decision by the House of Lords that a child under 16 years old, would consent to medical treatment, if he or she could understand what was involved in such treatment and was capable of expressing his or her views and wishes. In this case, the health authority was taken to court by the mother of a child for providing contraceptive services without the mother's consent.

Although there is no set age at which children are considered mature enough, the older the child, the more their views are considered. For example, according to the Gillick principles, a child is entitled to choose his or her own religion, and where there is a dispute between the child and parents, the child's welfare will prevail against resolving the conflict (paramountcy principle); it is unlikely that the child's wishes would be agreed, for example if they wished to become members of a religious cult that demanded isolation from the parents or the world in general.

Parents have the right to administer reasonable physical punishment. Although this was considered to be incompatible with the Convention rights, the government carried out a consultation exercise, following which guidelines were issued to assist the courts in defining the concept of reasonable chastisement. Corporal punishment is prohibited in all the circumstances, including in education, in care or in foster homes.

Child protection

Local authorities have a statutory duty to investigate, where a child is suspected of suffering from significant harm, in order to decide what action should be taken to safeguard the child's welfare. This usually means inter-agency enquiries regarding the child's education, health, general welfare and any particular issues which may have caused a child come to the attention of the local authority. Sometimes, the child protection conference is convened to ascertain any needs that the child may have requiring local authority action. A decision will be made following the conference about whether the child should be put on the child protection register as a precautionary measure. Children on the child protection register usually live with their parents, who are supported by social services in the upbringing of their children. In some cases, however, the local authority may decide that the child is at risk of significant harm and should be removed from the parents. It is at this point that care proceedings are initiated through the courts. Children are usually represented by the children's guardian (guardian *ad litem*), who is an approved social worker and will represent the child in care proceedings.

Emergency protection orders

In crisis situations, where the child needs immediate protection, social services can acquire parental responsibility by applying to the courts. This can be done without notice to the parents, although the parents to have a right to apply to the court for the order to be discharged. Children can also be removed into police protection for a period of up to 72 hours, if the police have reasonable cause to believe that they would otherwise suffer a significant harm. The police are required to ascertain the child's own views and inform parents at the earliest opportunity, as well as notifying the local authority to ensure that the child is taken into care.

Care orders

Following an emergency protection order, the local authority, usually applies for a care order, allowing them to share parental responsibility. Under such orders, the child is usually removed from home and placed with foster carers or with other members of the family. Care orders can only be made where the court is satisfied that the child is suffering, or is like to suffer significant harm as a result of the way the parents are caring for the child, or because the child is beyond parental control and poses a risk to him or herself and others. The introduction of the Human Rights Act (in 1998) means that the courts are now required to ensure that decisions about care orders must also consider the rights of parents, under Article 6 of the Convention – the right to a fair hearing. Parents are entitled to be consulted at all stages of the decision-making process and should be entitled to legal representation. The local authority is required to produce a care plan, giving details of the action it intends to take in relation to the child's future, such as where the child will be placed, what long-term proposals should be made, and details about contact with the family. Children who are received into care are known as 'looked after children'. It is important to understand that a care order automatically comes to an end when the child reaches 18 years of age; however, the local authority has an obligation to advise and assist the child and carry out an assessment of the child's needs. They must also prepare our 'pathway plan' for the child and appoint an adviser to help the child moving to independent living. Local authorities must take reasonable steps to keep in touch with the child until he or she is aged 21.

Education supervision orders

If a child of compulsory school-age is not being properly educated, because of poor school attendance, for example, he or she can be placed under supervision of the local education authority. The aim of this is to encourage parents to fulfil their responsibilities towards the child and, therefore, it is important that there is cooperation between representatives of the local education authority, school and the parents.

Strengths of the Children Act 1989

1. The Act clearly acknowledges the rights of children and protects their welfare, it was based on the United Nations Convention on the Rights of the Child, which was formalised by international agreement in order to protect the rights of children.

2. It enables children to have their views heard in matters that affect them, and provides equal treatment to all children.

3. The Act is very clear that children have rights and parents have responsibilities; it is clear about the role of parents in caring for the well-being of their children.

4. The Act provides details of circumstances under which children can be taken into local authority care, including the role of the courts, the police and other professionals concerned with the well-being of children, and that intervention should only take place as a last resort, or to provide support for parents in their parenting role.

Weaknesses of the Children Act 1989

1. Young offenders are not offered the same protection as other children under the Children Act 1989; children can be remanded to secure accommodation and are not protected by Article 5 – the right to liberty – because children can be detained for educational supervision, which has a very broad interpretation and includes education offered in such accommodation. Children can be charged with a criminal offence at the age of 10, below this they are considered incapable of committing such criminal offences; however, this is much lower than most other countries and has been criticised by the United Nations Committee.

2. Court proceedings under the Act are not open to the public in order to protect the identity of any children involved. However, there have been complaints that this prevents accountability and the basis on which decisions are made are not always clear.

Charlotte is 12 years old and is a pupil at the local comprehensive school. She is a bright and able pupil. Three years ago her mother, Sally, was diagnosed with multiple sclerosis and now uses a wheelchair. Charlotte's father left the family home 18 months ago and has moved to a different part of the country to take up a new job; he has had little contact with Charlotte and her mother since then. Charlotte has to help her mother get up and dressed in the morning and assist her downstairs; she also goes home at lunchtime to make sure her mother has lunch and helps her upstairs to the toilet. Both Charlotte and her mother are reluctant to ask Social Services for help because they fear that they will be separated; however Charlotte has been returning late from lunch and missing school. She is falling behind with her schoolwork and the school is concerned that their letters have not been answered. They have contacted the Educational Welfare Services.

Can you identify?
1. Which aspects of the Children Act might apply to Charlotte?

Go further – can you analyse, using theories of rights and responsibilities?
2. What rights Charlotte and her mother have under the law?

Go further – can you evaluate?
3. What needs Charlotte and her mother have and what actions could be taken to support them?

Children Act 2004

This Act has come into being, as a response to the Victoria Climbie Inquiry Report (2003) and the green paper *Every Child Matters* (2003), which proposed changes to policy and legislation in England, in order to maximise opportunities and minimise risks for all children and young people by focusing the services more effectively upon the needs of the children, young people and their families. One of the findings of the Victoria Climbie Inquiry was the failure of social services and other organisations involved in the care of this young child to work together effectively to protect her; in particular, information was not shared across services. The new arrangements under the Act will require much closer working between health, social services, education and child care organisations, including integrated planning, commissioning, joint funding and delivery of services for children and families.

Key points

* Children's Commissioner has been appointed to represent the views of children, in particular:

  * to seek views and identify the needs of children and young people

  * to look into any matter which relates to the interests and well-being of children and young people

  * to initiate inquiries on behalf of children and young people.

* In order to provide clear accountability for children's services, the Act will require local authorities in England to put in place a Director of Children's Services and a Lead Member for Children's Services in the governance arrangements.

* An information database is to be set up so that practitioners can more easily share information about children who are causing concern.

* The establishment of Local Safeguarding Children Boards to coordinate child protection procedures more effectively. These will replace the existing arrangements.

* Local authorities will be required to produce plans for children and young people.

* Children's services will be inspected and a new framework for integrated inspections will be put in place. Social services department will have their performance rated.

Part 1 of the Act, establishing a Commissioner, extends to the whole of the United Kingdom; Part 2, concerning the arrangements for the delivery of children's services and Local Safeguarding Children Boards, relates only to England. Part 3 concerns Wales, and Part 4 devolves functions to

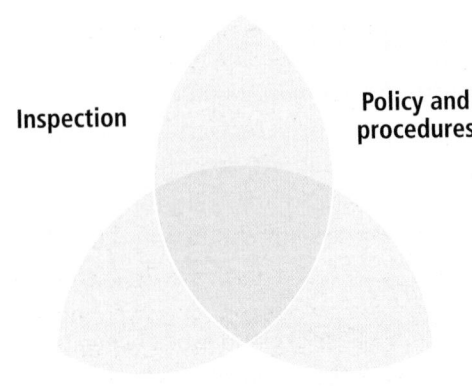

Inspection   Policy and procedures

Individual training and development

FIGURE 1.15 *The overlapping world of the individual and the legal and formal requirements in care environments*

Wales (The Welsh Assembly) that were previously carried out jointly across England and Wales. Other parts of the Act concern the application in Wales.

New legislation

With respect to laws that protect people from discrimination you should also be aware that new regulations now provide a legal right not to be discriminated against on the basis of sexual orientation and religious belief. These are the:

* Employment Equality (Sexual Orientation) Regulations 2003

* Employment Equality Regulations (Religion or Belief) Regulations 2003.

Northern Ireland

In Northern Ireland, health and social services operate jointly and services are managed through the Department of Health, Social Services and Public Safety. In order to meet the particular requirements of the population of Northern Ireland, some equality legislation has been amended; the implementation is monitored through the Equality Commission for Northern Ireland.

Equality (Disability, etc) (Northern Ireland) Order 2000 (EDO)

The Order extended the duties and powers of the Equality Commission Northern Ireland to include the requirement to:

* work towards the elimination of discrimination against disabled people

* promote the equalisation of opportunities for disabled people

* take steps to encourage good practice in the treatment of disabled people

* keep the Disability Discrimination Act 1995, and Part 2 of the EDO under review

* assist disabled people by offering information, advice and support in taking cases of discrimination forward

* provide information and advice to employers and service providers

* undertake formal investigations

* prepare statutory codes of practice, providing practical guidance on how to comply with the law

* arrange independent conciliation between service providers and disabled people in the area of access to goods, facilities and services.

Think it over...

Compare the powers and duties of the Equality Commission Northern Ireland with those of the Disability Rights Commission and identify any additional features.

Race Relations (Northern Ireland) Order 1997 (RRO)

Whilst this Order closely follows that of the Race Relations Act in the UK, it specifically outlawed discrimination against the Irish Traveller Community, which is identified as a racial group, against which racial discrimination is unlawful.

The Northern Ireland Act 1998

This Act places a statutory obligation and public authorities in Northern Ireland to carry out their functions relating to Northern Ireland with regard to the promotion of the equality of opportunity:

* between persons of different religious beliefs, political opinion, racial group, age, marital status or sexual orientation

* between men and women generally

* between people with the disability and people without

* between people with dependants and people without.

Public authorities must also promote good relations between persons of different religious belief, political opinion or racial group. This relates to the specific differences between the major communities within Northern Ireland.

The Employment Equality (Sexual Orientation) Regulations (NI) 2003

These regulations pre-empted the amendments to the Sex Discrimination Act 1975 in the UK by outlawing discrimination on grounds of sexual orientation in the areas of employment; vocational training, further and higher education.

The only explicitly stated exception in the regulations concerns employment for the purposes of organised religion. If the religious body or organisation does not wish to recruit people of the particular sexual orientation, they need to establish that this is in order to comply with that religious doctrine, or that the nature of the work and context in which it is carried out will cause conflict with significant number of followers with strongly held religious convictions.

Sex Discrimination (Northern Ireland) Order

The main differences here (the exceptions) concern:

* special treatment for women in connection with pregnancy and childbirth

* ministers of religion

* where the provision of goods, facilities and services may cause embarrassment/affront to decency/or physical contact.

In these areas, discriminatory treatment is allowed.

> ## Key concept
>
> *equality legislation* protects the right of all UK citizens to equal treatment. However, there is particular legislation to protect vulnerable people who cannot independently exercise their rights and these are of particular importance to workers in health, social care and childcare settings, as well as the organisations that provide such services. The law underpins philosophical ideas about equality that are a fundamental feature of the care services and which are reflected in the care values and principles.

Summary

As members of society we all have rights as well as responsibilities towards each other; this is a defining aspect of a civilised society. The purpose of the law is to uphold these rights and to allow individuals whose rights have been violated to seek redress.

While it is not possible for the law to prevent people from holding discriminatory views or expressing these, legislation can prevent individuals from acting upon these views and doing harm to others, either physically or emotionally. In the longer term, legislation can also help to promote a fairer society in which discriminatory attitudes and prejudices become socially unacceptable.

The main purpose of equality legislation is to promote equal treatment and to protect vulnerable people from those who would do them harm or take advantage of their inability to protect themselves. Care workers need to be aware of these laws in order to uphold them and to help to protect those they care for.

Section 3: Facilitation of access to services

Health, social care and child care service providers are required to ensure fair access to their services for all people. However, there are differences in the way the services are organised and delivered. It is important to recognise that not all services have 'open access'; individuals often have to be referred for consultation and treatment. There are three main types of referral as shown in Figure 1.16.

Physical barriers

It is extremely important that all buildings providing health, social care or childcare services are accessible to people with disabilities, including mobility problems and sensory difficulties, such a sight and hearing problems. Under the Disability Discrimination Act, all public services should be accessible. However, the level of accessibility tends to vary according to the focus of the services and the user groups for whom they are provided, as well as the limitations posed by financial constraints. For example, voluntary organisations that provide services may have relatively small budgets, which are only provided on a year-on-year basis, making long-term planning for capital projects such as altering premises very difficult. In contrast, statutory services (those which government funds) tend to have larger budgets and greater financial stability. Some examples of difficulties faced by particular types of provider are discussed below.

Hospitals

The historic development of hospital services means that many of them are housed in older buildings, which were often designed and built for a very different purpose, for example, those hospitals that were previously workhouses. Another problem faced by hospitals is that the range of services they now provide is much greater, and most hospitals have exceeded the capacity of their original buildings. This means that hospitals often do not have a consistent design or layout, with newer buildings being added over the years. In addition, modern medical technology requires much more equipment for both diagnosis and treatment; examples include Magnetic Resonance Imaging (MRI) scanners and mammography equipment, which require a lot of space. Most hospitals have made great efforts to make their buildings and

ACCESS TO SERVICES BY REFERRAL	
Self-referral	This is where individuals suspect that they have a health problem, or recognise that they need help with social problems. Individuals with health problems, access services through their GP, and anyone can make an appointment with the GP. It is also possible to self-refer to social services, by speaking to someone on the telephone, usually the duty social worker.
Professional referral	This is where individuals already have contact with health professionals, such as health visitors or midwives. If the professional suspects that there is an underlying health problem, the individual can be referred directly to the GP, social workers or the psychiatric services, for example. GPs also refer to specialists such as hospital consultants for treatments, following initial diagnosis.
Third-party referral	This is where a non-professional person such as a relative, friend or neighbour contacts the services on someone else's behalf. This may be because the person is unable to access the services for him or herself, for example in the case of an elderly housebound relative. In other cases, it may be because there are suspicions of child abuse or domestic violence. Sometimes the police will refer an individual to help for social services, following an incident, for example where there are suspected mental health problems. In such situations, the Mental Health

FIGURE 1.16 *Main types of referral*

FIGURE 1.17 *A Victorian workhouse/hospital*

services physically accessible to people with mobility problems. However, people with sensory difficulties may be less well-served. Blind people may have particular difficulties negotiating the physical environment in hospital, particularly where there has been additional building work and new buildings have been added. Where hospitals are brand-new, most of the accessibility problems have been overcome at the design stage, and although there is a programme of the new building underway in the NHS, it will be some time before all hospital buildings are fully accessible and usable by disabled people.

Health centres and GP surgeries

These buildings house primary care services and are used as the first port of call for anybody who wishes to access health care. If these buildings are physically inaccessible, access to basic forms of healthcare such as diagnosis becomes difficult and sometimes impossible. Many health centres are now housed in purpose-built buildings, which have been designed in order to ensure they are accessible to people with disabilities. However, some small outlying clinics are still housed in unsuitable premises. Although health centres often incorporate GP surgeries, some GPs still run what is known as the 'single-handed practice'. GPs offer their services to the NHS under contract, and are therefore not employees of the NHS in the same way that other professionals are. This means that when GPs manage their own surgery as a single-handed practice in the same way that people may run their own business, they will need their own premises. The Family Health Services Authority, which manages the GP contracts on behalf of the NHS has been helping such GPs to upgrade their premises in order to meet the requirements of the Disability Discrimination Act, as well as helping them move into purpose built premises, which may house other facilities.

Voluntary organisations

Many voluntary organisations are registered charities, which have very different governance and management arrangements than statutory services. Much of their income may be derived from charitable donations, for example, and there are often rules about how such money may be spent. Perhaps only a certain percentage of the income is allowed for administration, because as much as possible of the money raised is intended to go to the specific cause for which the charity provides. There are likely to be limited funds for capital building work. Voluntary and charitable organisations may be housed in older buildings or listed buildings which are difficult to make accessible.

Think it over...

Take a trip to your local health centre or hospital, starting from your home.

1. Imagine being a wheelchair user, what difficulties might you face in getting to the health centre or hospital?

2. When you get there, make a note of the facilities to enable access for people with disabilities; for example, can wheelchair users access the main entrance?

3. What facilities are there for people with hearing or sight difficulties?

4. Are their facilities for people with young children, for example, a play area or somewhere to leave a pram safely?

5. What sort of seating arrangements are there?

6. Compare your findings with others in your group. Discuss what improvements might be made to enable easier access. You might wish to rate your findings on a scale of 1 to 10, with one being fully accessible.

Psychological barriers

The extent to which people are likely to face psychological difficulties in accessing health services, depends on their attitude towards their own health and illness. For example, the Department of Health carried out research into men's health as part of a campaign to reduce the suicide rate in young men (Inequalities in Health, 1998; www.doh.gov.uk/ih) and found that:

* men are less likely to see a doctor and therefore the extent of their health problems, particularly mental health difficulties, is hidden
* doctors are less likely to diagnose men with mental health problems than a woman.

The Men's Health Forum, a registered charity (founded in 2001), found that young men were reluctant to use any kind of service and displayed stereotypical male attitudes towards help seeking. Services showed little understanding of young men or have to work with them effectively. The chair of the Men's Health Forum, Iain Banks, stated that:

'If you compare the major killers, such as heart disease and lung cancer, men easily come out best, from the undertaker's point of view'.

This illustrates that for many men illness is seen as weakness and incompatible with what it means to be male in our society, where maleness is associated with strength. These attitudes are formed as a result of gender socialisation.

People understand their health in different ways. For example, some individuals seek their body is a machine, which is liable to break down; this view is particularly common amongst men, and has resulted in various initiatives aimed at helping men take more responsibility for their health by providing information to dispel fear and myths about health and illness. One example is a men's health book, which has been put together in a similar format to a car manual, using humour and factual information to inform men about how their body works, the warning signs and symptoms of illness, and when to see a doctor. Women often have much more contact with health services as a result of pregnancy and childbirth. However, stereotypical attitudes amongst some male doctors can sometimes prevent women from accessing services. For example, women may feel that their concerns are minimised by a patronising attitude, which also undermines their self-esteem and prevents them from asking questions.

SCENARIO

Brenda is a 52-year-old woman who has recently attended for a routine mammography examination (breast screening). When the result arrives, the letter informs her that no cancer has been detected; however, the test shows some minor abnormalities.

Brenda is concerned, and wishes to find out more about the condition, such as the effects that the menopause may have on it. She makes an appointment to see her GP.

Brenda's young GP is very brisk during the consultation. He asks her to undress and examines her saying, 'You don't need a chaperone for this, do you? You look like a woman who can take care of herself and it will only take a minute'.

When the examination is finished, and as Brenda is getting dressed, the doctor tells her that her condition is not clinically significant. Brenda tries to express her concerns and explains that she has been experiencing a prickly sensation in her breast, which is extremely uncomfortable. The doctor repeats that her condition is not clinically significant, and shows her to the door.

1. **How do you think Brenda might feel, following this consultation?**
2. **Do you think this will influence any future decisions to consult the doctor with breast problems?**

Some individuals feel that their health is a matter of willpower and determination, dependent on choosing a healthy lifestyle. For these people, ill-health is also seen as weakness, primarily a lack of willpower. Such people may feel guilty if they become ill, or experience denial, attributing symptoms of ill-health to other things such as tiredness or stress. Attitudes to health and illness behaviour are shaped through socialisation, and many people lack knowledge and understanding of how their bodies work. Other people may feel that they have no control over whether they become ill or not; illness is seen as a matter of fate and they are not worried about long-term risks to health, often because of more pressing and immediate problems, such as financial hardship. For such people, the link between lifestyle choices and ill-health is denied or minimised because it may not be borne out by their own life experience, and they are resistant to health promotion and health education campaigns.

Some illnesses have a degree of stigma attached to them, particularly cancer, which is seen as life-threatening, and mental ill-health. Fear of confirming such illnesses, and the implications for individuals and their families may prevent people from accessing services, feeling they may be unable to cope with such serious illnesses. People with mental health difficulties may not recognise that they have a problem until there is a crisis.

Financial barriers

Although health and social services are free at the point of use, there are sometimes charges attached to certain types of treatment. For example, people need to pay for dental treatment, even though it is subsidised by the NHS. Many dentists only take private fee-paying patients, and access to NHS dentists varies considerably across the country. Access to dental treatment may be particularly difficult for elderly people with mobility problems, who find it difficult to visit the dentist's surgery. When older people have problems with their teeth, it affects their ability to eat, which can lead to long-term health problems as a result of chronic malnutrition.

In other cases, particularly in rural areas, the cost of travelling may be very high. Similarly, for people on low incomes, who are not eligible for free prescriptions, the cost of treatment may be considered to be too high. This may deter them from going to seek treatment in the first place, or prevent them from taking medication, and is a particular risk for people with complex conditions that require several different types of medication, or people with chronic conditions. Some conditions are exempt from prescription charges, and there is financial assistance for some people with chronic, and long-term conditions such as diabetes.

Childcare services, such as day nurseries or childminders, and residential care services for older people are usually run by private organisations, which charge for their services. For many people, these services are too expensive and beyond their means; however, the government does provide some assistance in the form of tax credits, particularly for working families requiring childcare.

It is important that individuals have access to information about the type of financial help that is available for health, social and childcare services. Leaflets are available through the Post Office, additional help is available through the Department of Health website and Citizens Advice Bureau or welfare rights organisations can also provide information. In terms of childcare services, the government proposes to set up Children's Centres in all areas which will provide information and access to local children's services.

Geographical barriers

Services are not distributed evenly through out the country, and this is particularly true of health services and childcare services. Although most areas have some provision, the number of GPs, for example, varies enormously across regions. There are more than twice as many GPs in Oxford than there are in Salford, for although GPs provide NHS services, they are not employed directly by the NHS and, therefore, are free to choose where they practice. Similarly, children's services are provided by private organisations and individuals and are therefore likely to be located in more affluent areas, where both parents work.

People living in rural areas often have trouble accessing services because of the geographical location; this is particularly the case, where they need to rely on public transport. Public transport tends to be more easily available, with more frequent services in areas with high-density populations. For example, it may not be considered cost-effective for companies to provide bus services, where there is likely to only be one or two passengers during the day. For low income families, the cost of public transport may be a barrier, whilst elderly people or those with mobility problems, who may not be able to use public transport, may need to make different travel arrangements, perhaps making use of taxi services. This will also add to the cost of travel.

Working people often have difficulty in accessing GP services, for example, because appointments are usually only made available during working hours. This means that people need to take time off work to visit their GP and may need to take annual leave, or may not be paid for time off work to attend appointments. It can also be difficult for women with small children to attend for appointments, as childcare arrangements may need to be made.

Where appointments are made centrally, as in the case of screening services, or outpatient appointments, people may be sent pre-arranged appointments, which may not be convenient.

Geographical aspects need to be taken into consideration when plans for services are made, and service providers should be aware of local bus services and other facilities such as 'Dial and Ride' or other voluntary services for people with mobility problems when planning new facilities. For those who can travel to hospital by car, parking is often difficult and limited. Many hospitals now charge for parking to prevent the public parking on hospital car parks when they are not using the services, so this can also add to the expense of accessing health care. It can be a particular problem if there are delays within the system and people are waiting to be seen for longer than planned.

Cultural and language barriers

Accessing services for people whose first language is not English can be a particular problem. In areas with high ethnic minority populations, information needs to be provided in more than one language. However, where several languages are spoken, it can be difficult for service providers to target the appropriate language. A good example of accessible information would be an invitation for breast screening, which contains information in English, together with the location and map, public transport information, and on the reverse the same information in eight different languages, as well as what to do if the individual is unable to keep the appointment. On health and social service premises, signs and directions are often only provided in English and receptionists and others who are sources of help and assistance may only be able to speak English. Many organisations now provide translation services; however, these often need to be arranged in advance, which can cause a problem for drop-in services and emergency provision. Some service providers allow family members who speak English to translate. It may be inappropriate in many cases, however, for an adult to be accompanied by children, particularly if sensitive or embarrassing issues need to be discussed. It can also be distressing for children and young people if they think that their parent is ill. Medical terms are often difficult to translate, causing problems with understanding, and this is why it is important to have specially trained translators available for people whose first language is not English.

Individuals from some cultures that have particularly strict gender roles may feel very uncomfortable in being seen or treated by health professionals of the opposite sex. It is therefore important that both male and female professionals are available to provide the required service. Other cultural issues include information about diet and nutrition. Unless a health professional is fully aware of the cultural and dietary requirements of a particular group, it may not be possible for the service user to make appropriate changes. Some services are particularly difficult for some cultures to access, such as family planning and sexual health services, because of religious beliefs relating to sex and sexuality. These issues can cause psychological as well as cultural barriers, and it is important for health and social care professionals to understand them and think about ways of providing culturally sensitive services.

Narinder is a 36-year-old mother of two who speaks little English. She has recently discovered a lump in her breast; however, she has told no one. Narinder lives in a block of flats in an inner-city council estate with her husband and mother-in-law. Her husband is a bus driver and works irregular hours.

Using theory, can you identify?

1. What are the barriers to access facing Narinder?

Go further – can you analyse theories?

2. Why Narinder has not told anyone about her problems?

Go further – can you evaluate?

3. The ways in which an accessible, sensitive and culturally appropriate service could be provided for Narinder?

Ways of facilitating access

There are several ways in which service providers can facilitate access for all of their service users. These include:

* adapting premises
* raising awareness and changing attitudes
* promoting self-advocacy
* identifying additional funding
* joint planning and funding for integrated services and effective care.

Summary

The barriers to services are related both to an individual's ability and to their motivation to access services. In order to overcome these barriers, action needs to be taken by government to ensure fair distribution of services; by service providers to ensure they have appropriate facilities that everyone can use and by providing widely available information to tell about the services available in their local area, so raising awareness.

Section 4: Care values

'Service users rights are rooted in the history of social Care, healthcare and social work; in theories and philosophies underpinning the practices of the welfare state.'

(Tossell and Webb, 1994)

All health and social care workers have a 'duty of care'; this means that workers in the sector have clear responsibilities to the users of their services, and are personally and professionally accountable for the service they deliver. This responsibility and accountability includes both service users, their relatives and carers and is defined within professional guidelines and legal frameworks. Where it can be proven that such a duty of care was not exercised, professionals can be disciplined and may be legally liable for acts or omissions that cause harm to those in their care, whether these were caused by themselves or by someone under their supervision.

Recent occupational standards for National Vocational Qualifications (NVQs) in care emphasised the three principles of promoting equality and diversity, promoting individual rights and beliefs and maintaining confidentiality. Proposed 2005 standards do not define principles as such, but do include these broad values within training standards.

Promoting equality and diversity

In order to promote equality and diversity within health and care services, the following key principle must be followed by all workers:

* everyone must be treated fairly and impartially when receiving care services; this is their right.

Promoting individual rights and beliefs

Health and social care workers often work with vulnerable people, who may not be in a position to exercise their rights independently. The following principles are intended to protect the rights of vulnerable service users and should be followed by all workers in health and social care:

* all people have a right to be consulted and involved in decisions that affect them

* people have a right to express their views and beliefs, including the right to refuse care or treatment

* these rights are protected by law (see the section on equality legislation on page 15).

It is important to recognise, however, that health and social care workers also need to protect individuals, and in some cases this may mean restricting their rights and freedoms. The situations in which individual rights may be restricted include:

* *when individuals are at risk of harming themselves*, for example, people with mental health problems, people in a disturbed emotional state, and people considering suicide or self-harm, such as cutting or substance abuse

* *when the individual poses a risk to others*, for example, people demonstrating challenging behaviour, violent or disturbed individuals who are threatening other people

* *when the individual is at risk from others*, for example, children or vulnerable adults, who may be at risk of abuse, including emotional and psychological abuse or bullying, physical abuse, sexual abuse and neglect

* *when the individual is intending to break the law*, or has broken the law, for example, theft of property, fraud, substance abuse.

However, it is not always easy for care workers to achieve a balance between promoting individual rights and providing appropriate physical, emotional and social care for individuals.

Ellen is a resident in Church House care home for older people. She is a quiet person who spends a lot of time in her room. She occasionally speaks to one or two of the other residents but has no close friends. Recently Ellen has been refusing to have a bath. She will not let anyone help her and she will not do it herself. She has told the staff that she believes she will catch cold if she has a bath. Ellen's personal hygiene is now causing the other residents to avoid her and the staff find it unpleasant to carry out personal care with Ellen.

Using concepts within the care values can you identify?
1. Ellen's rights?
2. The rights of the other residents?
3. The rights of the staff?

Go further – can you analyse using theories of equality?
4. How the staff could manage this situation to ensure equal treatment.

Go further – can you evaluate using a range of theory?
5. What the likely outcomes for Ellen's health and well-being will be if this behaviour continues?

Maintaining confidentiality

Health and care workers are responsible for personal and private information about service users, including details of their personal lives, families, care and treatment. It is crucial that they keep this information private, and exercise tact and diplomacy when they are asked questions by others about the people in their care. This is called maintaining confidentiality, and it is crucial to developing trust between service users and the people who are caring for them. If the service users do not believe that the person asking the questions will keep the information confidential, they are not likely to be honest in their answers, and this could compromise their care and treatment. This is particularly important in sensitive situations, for example where domestic violence is suspected; however, it is important in

all health and care situations. Confidentiality extends to all aspects of the service users' lives, including where they live. Maintaining confidentiality also demonstrates respect for service users, helping to promote trust, and helps them to feel valued and to maintain their self-esteem. It is important that clients are involved in discussions about confidentiality, and that those caring for them know what information they would prefer to be kept confidential. It is also important to let service users know in what situations practitioners are obliged to share information. For example, practitioners must be very careful not to promise to keep secrets and must make it clear to service users that they are acting on behalf of their organisation, and that any information given to them may need to be shared with others, in order to provide proper care for the individual. In such situations, it is important to reassure service users that only the information necessary for their care will be shared, and that any decisions will be discussed with them. Some service users may not want their families to know details of their medical condition, or their financial details.

Confidentiality is a basic human right, protected by law, through the Data Protection Act 1988, and the Freedom of Information Act 2000. Service users have a right to see records held about them, and it is important that practitioners write down clearly and concisely what they are told, and what they have observed without including their personal opinions or observations in the records. Health and care records are important documents that can be used in a court of law, for example, if service users have been unfairly treated or abused, whilst in the care of professionals, or the quality of care is being questioned.

Maintaining confidentiality does not mean that information about service users should never be shared. Services are often delivered by more than one professional and more than one organisation, and for effective continuous care, it is crucial that information is shared on a 'need to know' basis. This means that only information that is relevant to the care of the service user is passed on to others, usually other professionals. This is particularly important in relation to child

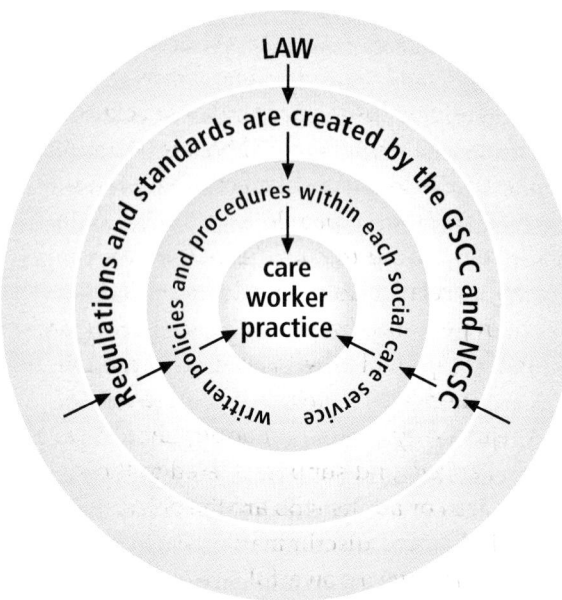

FIGURE 1.18 *Law, standards and policies influence practice*

protection, and the protection of vulnerable adults, who may not be in a position to speak for themselves. Please see Unit 2 for further discussion of confidentiality.

Principles and values for childcare workers

It is important to realise that the principles and values discussed above, relate to health and social care; the principles and values identified by the Early Years National Training Organisation for current NVQ qualifications are slightly different. These are set out below.

Principles:

The Underlying Principles of Early Years National Vocational Qualifications.
These principles draw on both the UN Convention on the Rights of the Child and the Children Act 1989, and also take into account the delivery of the School Curriculum and Assessment Authority (SCM) 'Desirable Outcomes for Children's Learning'. They are based on the premise that the earliest years of children's lives are a unique stage of human development, and that quality early years

provision benefits the wider society and it is an investment for the future.

1. **The welfare of the child**
   The welfare of the child is paramount [the most important thing]. All early years workers must give precedence [attend to first] the rights and well-being of the children they work with. Children should be listened to, and their opinions and concerns treated seriously. Management of children's behaviour should emphasise positive expectations for that behaviour, and responses to unwanted behaviour should be suited to the child's stage of development. A child must never be slapped, smacked, shaken or humiliated.

2. **Keeping children safe**
   Work practice should help prevent accidents to children and adults, and should protect their health. Emergency procedures of the work setting, including record keeping, must be adhered to. Every early years worker has a responsibility to contribute to the protection of children from abuse, according to her/his work role.

3. **Working in partnership with parents/ families**
   Parents and families occupy a central position in their children's lives, and early years workers must never try to take over that role inappropriately. Parents and families should be listened to as expert on their own child. Information about children's development and progress should be shared openly with parents. Respect must be shown for families' traditions and child care practices, and every effort made to comply with parent's wishes for their children.

4. **Children's learning and development**
   Children learn more and faster in their earliest years than at any other times in life. Development and learning in these earliest years lay the foundations for their abilities, characteristics and skills in later life. Learning begins at birth. The care and education of children are interwoven.

Children should be offered a range of experiences and activities which support all aspects of their development: social; physical; intellectual; communication; emotional. The choice of experiences and activities (the 'curriculum') should depend on accurate assessment of the stage of development reached by a child, following observation and discussion with families. Early years workers have varying responsibilities concerning the planning and implementation of the curriculum, according to their work role, but all contributions to such planning and implementation should set high expectations for children and build on their achievements and interests. Child – initiated play and activities should be valued and recognised, as well as the adult planned curriculum. Written records should be kept of children's progress, and these records should be shared with parents.

5. **Equality of opportunity**
Each child should be offered equality of access to opportunities to learn and develop, and so worked towards her/his potential. Each child is a unique individual; early years workers must respect this individuality; children should not be treated 'all the same'. In order to meet a child's needs, it is necessary to treat each child ' with equal concern': some children need more and/or different support in order to have equality of opportunity. It is essential to avoid stereotyping children on the basis of gender, racial origins, cultural or social background (including religion, language, class and family pattern), or disability: such stereotypes might act as barriers to equality of access to opportunity. Early years workers should demonstrate their valuing of children's racial and other personal characteristics in order to help them develop self-esteem.

These principles of equality of access to opportunity, and avoidance of stereotyping must also be applied to interactions with adult family members, colleagues and other professionals.

6. **Anti-discrimination**
Early years workers must not discriminate against any child, family or group in society on the grounds of gender, racial origins, cultural or social background (including religion, language, class and family pattern), disability or sexuality. They must acknowledge and address any personal beliefs or opinions which prevent them respecting the value systems of other people, and comply with legislation and the policies of their work setting relating to discrimination. Children learn prejudice from their earliest years, and must be provided with accurate information to help them avoid prejudice. Expressions of prejudice by children or adults should be challenged, and support offered to those children or adults who are the objects of prejudice and discrimination. Early years workers have a powerful role to play in ensuring greater harmony amongst various groups in our society for future generations.

7. **Celebrating diversity**
Britain is a multi-racial, multi-cultural society. The contributions made to this society by a variety of cultural groups should be viewed in a positive light, and information about varying traditions, customs and festivals should be presented as a source of pleasure and enjoyment to all children including those in areas where there are few members of minority ethnic groups. Children should be helped to develop a sense of their identity within their racial, cultural and social groups, as well as having the opportunity to learn about culture that is different from their own. No one culture should be represented as superior to any other: pride in one's own cultural and social background does not require condemnation of that of other people.

8. **Confidentiality**
Information about children and families must never be shared with others without the permission of the family, except in the interest of protecting children. Early years workers must adhere to the policy of their work setting concerning confidential information, including passing information to colleagues. Information about other workers must also be handled in a confidential manner.

9. **Working with other professionals**

Advice and support should be sought from other professionals in the best interests of children and families, and information shared with them, subject to the principle of confidentiality. Respect should be shown for the roles of other professionals.

10. **The reflective practitioner**

Early years workers should use any opportunity they are offered, or which arises, to reflect on their practice and principles, and make use of the conclusions from such reflection in developing and extending their practice. Seeking advice and support to help resolve queries or problems should be seen as a form of strength and professionalism. Opportunities for in-service training/ continuous professional development should be used to the maximum.

✳ DID YOU KNOW?

Under the new 2005 National Occupational Standards for Children's Care, Learning and Development, these values are expressed as follows:

✳ The needs, rights and views of the child are at the centre of all practice and provision

✳ Individuality, difference and diversity are valued and celebrated

✳ Equality of opportunity and anti-discriminatory practice are actively promoted

✳ Children's health and well-being are actively promoted

✳ Children's personal and physical safety is safe-guarded, whilst allowing for risk and challenge as appropriate to the capabilities of the child

✳ Self-esteem, resilience and a positive self-image are recognised as essential to every child's development

✳ Confidentiality and agreements about confidential information are respected as appropriate unless a child's protection and well-being are at stake

✳ Professional knowledge, skills and values are shared appropriately in order to enrich the experience of children more widely

✳ Best practice requires reflection and a continuous search for improvement

---

Consider this

Aaron is a 6-year-old boy whose family is in crisis and is currently being supported by a social worker. Aaron's father is an alcoholic with a violent temper when under the influence of alcohol. His mother is on anti-depressants and is a suspected victim of domestic violence. Both Aaron and his 2-year-old sister are on the child protection register as being 'at risk'.

Using the concepts of the paramountcy principle

Can you identify which of these people need to know that Aaron is on the child protection register?

His class teacher	His head teacher
The school nurse	The health visitor
The dinner lady	The caretaker
The family's neighbours	The GP

Go further – can you analyse using theory?

In the interests of confidentiality, which of the above need to know about:

Aaron's father's drink problem?
Aaron's mother being on anti-depressants?

Go further – can you evaluate using a range of theory?

Can you evaluate the impact of any breaches of confidentiality on:

Aaron	Aaron's mother
The social worker	Aaron's father?

As well as the care values defined within National Occupational Standards it is important to know that there is now a code of practice for social care workers and employers of social care workers published by the General Social Care Council (GSCC). This code of practice defines the principles that must guide working within health and social care. Further details of this code can be found in the next section of this unit.

Safe working

Safe working is concerned with the protection of the public, and this includes both workers and service users. There are two main groups of laws which concern people working in health, care and childcare services:

* laws that protect individuals at work and in employment
* laws that protect service users and vulnerable people.

In order to implement laws effectively, an organisation will need to have policies and procedures in place to raise awareness and explain what workers need to do in particular circumstances.

Laws protecting individuals at work

This is the equality legislation as described on page 15. In order to comply with the law, employers need to have policies and practices in place that enable the law to be implemented within the workplace and ensure that they do not discriminate against either their workers, or the people who use their services.

Organisations need to have an Equal Opportunities Policy, which should be based on the codes of practice produced by the Equal Opportunities Commission relating to equal pay and sex discrimination, and the code of practice produced by the Commission for Racial Equality. This will ensure that organisations do not inadvertently discriminate against individuals or groups. An Equal Opportunities Policy needs to be tailored to the specific requirements of any organisation and developed by the organisation itself, in consultation with recognised trade unions or representative bodies. It should cover the aspects outlined below.

A statement of policy

This should clearly describe the commitment of the organisation to the promotion of equality of opportunity, for example:

'It is our aim to provide employment equality to all. In particular, Cherry Trees Day Nursery is committed to promoting equal treatment irrespective of; age, sex, marital status, disability, sexual orientation, race, religion or ethnicity . We are opposed to all forms of unfair and

unlawful discrimination, and will ensure that all workers and applicants for jobs, whether full-time or part-time, will be treated fairly and equitably in selection for employment, promotion, training or any other benefits. All opportunities will be on the basis of aptitude and ability, and it is our aim to ensure that all workers are able to develop their full potential, in order to benefit themselves and ensure efficiency within the organisation. We are committed to:

* preventing direct or indirect discrimination or victimisation
* promoting equal opportunities for all
* promoting harmonious working environments in which our staff are treated with dignity and respect and in which no form of intimidation harassment or bullying will be tolerated
* fulfilling all legal obligations under the relevant legislation and associated codes of practice
* ensuring that our policy is monitored and action taken to redress any imbalances, including taking positive or affirmative action, and setting targets and timescales for achievement.'

Implementation

The policy should clearly state the responsibility of senior management in relation to implementing the policy, including details of specific responsibilities for each tier of management. This section of policy should clearly state how it will be communicated to all workers, for example, through induction training, management training, team briefings, information on noticeboards, and staff handbooks. Training in non-discriminatory assessment and interview skills is particularly important for staff who are involved in the recruitment and selection of workers. Details of special measures to recruit members of underrepresented groups should also be outlined in the policy, and particulars about the information systems that will be used to assist the effective implementation of the policy should be provided to staff.

Monitoring and review

This section of the policy should say how the implementation of an Equal Opportunities Policy will be monitored following implementation, including how frequently it will be reviewed, and in what way. For example, there should be a statement, similar to the following:

> 'Provision of equality of opportunity between all men and women will be monitored through the collection and analysis of statistical data on the sex, marital status, ethnic origin, disability and full or part-time status of workers and job applicants. Progress on the implementation of this policy will be reviewed annually in consultation with staff representatives, who will be part of a joint employer/employee working group.'

Complaints

The policy should clearly state how employees who feel that they have suffered from any form of discrimination can complain. Organisations should ensure that where there are regulations relating to the timescales for taking complaints to an industrial tribunal, their internal systems for managing complaints do not cause undue delay. Employees are entitled to pursue internal complaints at the same time as taking action under any relevant legislation (tribunal procedures).

Harassment and bullying

The protection from the Harassment Act 1997 makes it a criminal offence to harass another person. It is also possible to sue an employer if you claim that harassment or bullying has taken place at work. Because of this, most employers are likely to have a policy to prevent harassment or bullying in order to protect staff from this form of abuse.

Codes of practice and their function

Health, social care and childcare services are strictly regulated; this means that people who work in the services need to have the right training and qualifications. It also means that organisations providing health, care or childcare services have to meet certain standards, and the care or treatment that is provided must be both effective and of a high standard.

In order to operate effectively, organisations offering health, social care and childcare services have a range of policies and procedures that are used to implement the standards and regulations set by government, as well as legislation relating to health and safety for example.

Historical codes of good practice provided by the regulatory bodies for health and social care have now been consolidated into a regulatory framework, in order to ensure a consistently high standard of care is being delivered across the UK. The Care Standards Act of 2000 established the framework for regulating the care sector and the organisations that are responsible for carrying out these regulatory duties. Because government responsibilities have been devolved to the four countries of Great Britain, different organisations have the responsibility for regulation in each of four countries.

The regulatory framework consists of:

* the professional councils that regulate practitioners and agree codes of professional practice

* the regulation and inspection bodies that regulate providers of health, care and early years services

* the national standards that set out minimum levels of care and evidence-based practice against which the organisation is measured.

The professional councils

The professional councils are responsible for the registration and regulation of practitioners, the individuals who provide direct care in health, social care or childcare settings.

Regulation of social care practitioners is the responsibility of the General Social Care Council (England), the Northern Ireland Social Care Council, the Care Council for Wales, and the Scottish Social Services Council. These organisations have produced a code of practice identifying the standards of professional conduct for both social care workers and employers, including what qualifications and training they require.

Some details of the GSCC code of practice are set out opposite:

The GSCC code of practice for social care workers

An outline summary

The Social Care Register was launched in April 2003; everyone working in social care will have to register, and abide by the code of practice. The register is being developed in stages, starting with the registration of qualified social workers, followed by social work students, residential childcare workers and care home managers. When applying to register, individuals will have their qualifications, health and character checked, including an enhanced check by the Criminal Records Bureau. Once this is completed satisfactorily, individuals will have a license to practice. Registers will have to renew their registration on a three-yearly basis, which will be subject to proof of continuing professional development.

In health, the Nursing and Midwifery Council (NMC) is the regulatory body for nursing, which replaced the United Kingdom Central Council (UKCC) in April 2002, and manages the registration and regulation of qualified nurses, midwives and health visitors.

Healthcare workers such as nurses follow a code of professional conduct published by the Nursing and Midwifery Council. The code has similar principles to the GSCC code for social care. Full details of the code can be found at www.nmc-uk.org but a summary of the key principles is listed below:

In caring for patients and clients, you must:

* respect each service user as an individual

* obtain consent before you give any treatment or care

* protect confidential information

* cooperate with others in the team

* maintain your professional knowledge and competence

* be trustworthy

* act to identify and minimise risk to patients and clients.

Other regulatory bodies for health professionals include the General Medical Council (GMC),

which regulates doctors, and the Health Professions Council (HPC), which replaced the Council for Professions Supplementary to Medicine (CPSM). The HPC regulates around 13 professions including dieticians, speech therapists, chiropodists/podiatrists, orthoptists, operating department practitioners, paramedics, radiographers and physiotherapists among others. These regulatory bodies, as well as holding registers of qualified practitioners, are also responsible for maintaining professional standards and investigating any complaints against professionals.

Regulation and inspection bodies

It is important to recognise that all services provided for health, care and childcare are regulated and inspected against the standards set out by the government. The regulatory bodies monitor the standard of services provided for groups of patients and clients by the wide range of organisations that deliver health, care and childcare services, for example, the NHS, local authority social services, independent healthcare providers, voluntary and charitable organisations such as the National Society for the Prevention of Cruelty to Children (NSPCC) and providers of childcare services such as childminders and nurseries. The bodies responsible for this are outlined below.

The Commission for Social Care Inspection (CSCI)

This Commission, which was formed in April 2004, brings together the work previously undertaken by the Social Services Inspectorate and includes the social care functions of the National Care Standards Commission (NCSC). The Commission works on a local and national level, and in each local council area the CSCI carries out the following functions:

* registers private and voluntary care services to ensure they meet the national standards (see below)

* inspects, assesses and reviews all care services in a particular area, including private and

voluntary care services and local council social services departments

* provides the local council with details of the number and quality of private and voluntary care services in their local area

* deals with complaints about service providers

* reviews complaints about council social services departments.

The Healthcare Commission (Commission for Healthcare Audit and Inspection – CHAI)

This Commission undertakes all of the work previously carried out by the Commission for Health Improvement (CHI), the Mental Health Act Commission (MHAC) and the Audit Commission, as well as the independent healthcare work previously carried out by the National Care Standards Commission. It also monitors value for money in the NHS. The aims of the Commission are to:

* encourage improvement in the quality and effectiveness of care

* ensure that services are provided, economically and effectively

* inspect the management, provision and quality of healthcare services, including how effectively public resources are being used

* carry out investigations into serious service failures and report serious concerns about the quality of public services to the Secretary of State

* publish annual performance ratings for all NHS organisations (star rating)

* carry out an independent review function for NHS complaints

* collaborate with the Commission for Social Care Inspection (CSCI).

The government is currently planning to merge the Healthcare Commission and the Commission for Social Care Inspection to reflect the increasing collaboration between the health and social care sectors; it is anticipated that a new body will be in place by 2008.

Ofsted (Office for Standards in Education)

There are two main integrated aspects to pre-school childcare; the first is the provision of physical, social and emotional care for children and the second is promoting children's learning and development.

Unlike health and social care, which has separate bodies for registration and inspection, there is currently no register of childcare practitioners, and Ofsted is responsible for both inspection and regulation of pre-school provision such as childminders and nurseries, ensuring that individuals have appropriate qualifications and have been subjected to Criminal Records Bureau checks, for example.

Ofsted inspect childcare provision to ensure that providers are meeting the:

* Early Learning Goals, set by the Qualifications and Curriculum Authority, which identifies what children should be able to do and understand in the pre-school years, i.e. the expected learning and development

* National Standards for Under Eight's Day Care and Childminding, which are a set of outcomes introduced by the Department for Education and Skills, identifying the levels of provision needed for the effective physical, social and emotional care of children, such as ratios of staff to children. Local authorities are responsible for ensuring that the childcare provision in their area meets the required standards, against which they are inspected by Ofsted

* Ofsted is also responsible for inspecting:
    * all state and independent schools
    * local education authorities
    * teacher training institutions
    * youth work
    * further education colleges
    * 14–19 education and training in partnership with the Adult Learning Inspectorate.

It is expected that the children's social care function of the CSCI (those services provided by social services departments for children in need) will merge with Ofsted to create a single children's services inspectorate with a new inspection framework in the near future.

National Minimum Standards

The Care Standards Act 2000 identified National Minimum Standards for a range of care services, which all service providers must meet. The standards form the baseline against which services are inspected and registered. For example, if a residential home for older people fails to comply with the minimum standards, it could lose its registration and be forced to cease operating. There are minimum standards covering the following areas:

* care homes for older people

* care homes with adult placements

* care homes for adults aged 18–65

* adult placement schemes (foster-type care for adults with particular needs)

* domiciliary care (care in a person's own home)

* nurses' agencies

* children's homes

* adoption

* residential family centres

* fostering services

* boarding schools

* residential special schools

* accommodation of students under 18 by Further Education Colleges.

National minimum standards apply to issues such as staffing levels, qualifications and training of staff and standards relating to the care and treatment of the particular service-user group. For example, the National Minimum Standards for the Care of Older People has sections on:

* choice of home; including how the service user's needs are assessed, trial visits and contracts

* health and personal care standards; including privacy and dignity, dying and death, health care provision, medication and a service user

plan, which states the individual's preferences and personal details

* daily life and social activities: including meals and mealtimes, social contact and activities, community contact, autonomy and choice

* complaints and protection: including policies such as how to complain and service users' rights to complain

* environment: such as the type of premises and space requirements, shared facilities, washing and toilet facilities, adaptations and equipment, heating and lighting facilities, hygiene and infection control.

It is through the National Minimum Standards that the values and principles of care are delivered.

National Service Frameworks

The National Service Frameworks (NSF) apply to health care services. They describe the standards of treatment for particular conditions or service-user groups: they are based on evidence from research and are currently in development. Completed frameworks at the present time include those for:

* diabetes

* coronary heart disease

* cancer

* renal services

* mental health

* older people's services

* children, young people and maternity services.

It is important to recognise that the NSF for Children, Young People and Maternity Services are the standards for children's health and social services combined, and the framework also covers the interface with education to reflect the proposed integration of these services for children in all local authority areas over the next 10 years.

Organisational policies

Organisational policies are the mechanism through which legislation is delivered and implemented. Examples of policies that organisations are likely to include are outlined below.

Child protection policy

Such a policy enables organisations and individuals concerned with the care and welfare of children to fulfill their responsibilities under the Children Act 1989 and subsequent amendments. The policy will give details of reporting mechanisms, lines of accountability and procedures to be followed in cases of suspected child abuse. Each local authority area has a designated Area Child Protection Committee consisting of professional representatives, police and local authority representatives. Under new arrangements proposed, these will be superseded by Local Protecting Children Boards.

Bullying policy

This is often part of a protection from harassment policy that will also link with the organisation's equal opportunities policy in order to protect staff in the workplace and, as such, will provide details of how a complaint may be taken forward within an organisation. However, schools are also required to have anti-bullying policies, which detail the approach the school takes to manage bullying and protect children while at school.

Confidentiality

Whilst this is covered in the National Minimum Standards, it is still necessary to have a policy which explains what staff should do if they feel that confidentiality has been broken. Such a policy is also likely to state what protection the organisation offers to 'whistle blowers', i.e. those individuals who go public with information that may be confidential to an organisation – for example, systematic abuse within a care environment.

Summary

Care workers are members of the public and therefore have to obey the law, especially in relation to equality legislation to ensure that all service users are treated equally. In addition, the regulatory bodies and regulatory frameworks for health, social care and childcare services ensure that the services are delivered in a way that protects and promotes service users' rights, by inspecting the premises, policies and procedures that organisations have in place to implement the law. There are also regulations to ensure that care workers are appropriate people to undertake such responsibilities, and there are mechanisms in place to deal with care workers who have been found guilty of abusing their positions of trust. Service users' rights, health and well-being are protected by both national law and regulations relating to care premises, the way in which care is delivered and the people delivering it.

Useful websites

www.open2.net/childofourtime/2005/
www.crimereduction.gov.uk
www.mhac.org.uk
www.doh.gov.uk/ih

References

Oakley, A. (1974) *The Sociology of Housework* (Oxford: Martin Robertson) in Giddens, A. (2001) *Sociology* (4th edition) (Polity Press) p. 177
Tossell, D. and Webb, R. (1994) Inside the Caring Services (2nd edition) (Arnold Publishers)

Aaron is having an unhappy time at school and at home. His father is a violent alcoholic and his mother is on anti-depressant medication. Aaron and his sister have been placed on the child protection register.

Aaron often has to get himself ready for school and sometimes looks rather scruffy because he has no clean clothes. One of the boys in Aaron's class has found out about Aaron's home situation and has started teasing him and calling him names. Last week, this boy and his friends cornered Aaron in the school toilets and started calling his mother names, making Aaron angry. He lashed out at one of the boys, who ran into the corridor crying loudly and was asked by a passing teacher what had happened. The boy replied that Aaron had hit him and the teacher punished Aaron.

Using theory, can you identify?
The responsibilities of the school
The responsibilities of the family social worker

Go further – can you analyse issues using theory?
Two actions Aaron could take to help himself
Actions which those responsible for Aaron's health, safety and well-being could take to help Aaron resolve the situation in school

Go further – can you evaluate using theory?
Two ways in which anti-bullying strategies in school could prevent such a situation
Likely outcomes for the school if they fail to act

UNIT 1 ASSESSMENT

How you will be assessed

This unit is externally assessed. You will need to make sure you understand how care workers' attitudes and values affect service users and the key principles and features of each of the Equality Acts.

Test questions

1. Give two examples of primary socialisation.

2. Give three influences on secondary socialisation.

3. Explain the importance of the four basic needs of human beings.

4. Explain the link between an individual's identity, self-esteem (self-worth) and socialisation.

5. Describe three examples of discriminatory actions.

6. Describe five types of abuse.

7. Explain what is meant by direct and indirect discrimination.

8. What are the main duties and responsibilities of the Commission for Racial Equality?

9. What are the implications of the Human Rights Act on new laws proposed by Parliament?

10. Describe three strengths and three weaknesses of the Mental Health Act 1983.

11. Identify four of the seven key principles contained in the Children Act 1989.

12. Using examples, describe the five common barriers which can be experienced by different people when accessing services.

13. What are the key values of care?

14. Describe the three main aspects of the regulatory framework for care established by the Care Standards Act 2000.

15. Identify the key components of an organisation's equal opportunities policy.

16. Why is it important that care workers are trusted by service users?

17. Describe the purpose of the new Children Act 2004 and three key features of this.

18. Why is it important for childcare workers to work in partnership with parents? Explain what this means in practice.

19. Why is it important for childcare workers to offer a range of different experiences to children?

20. Why should childcare organisations have child protection policies? What information should such a policy contain?

Answers to these questions are provided on page 389.

UNIT
2

Communication in Care Settings

This unit covers the following sections:

2.1 Types of communication

2.2 Factors that support and inhibit communication

2.3 Communication skills

2.4 Theories relating to communication

2.5 Interaction with the service users

Introduction

This unit focuses on communication skills in detail. In doing so, it explores different types of communication, together with some of the factors that may support or inhibit communication. There is an emphasis throughout on the importance of using theory to analyse practice.

How you will be assessed

As part of your studies you are required to produce a range of evidence as set out in assessment objectives (AO), and a report as set out in the fourth objective (AO4). Your report should explore the effectiveness of your communication skills in an interaction with an individual service user, or care worker, or with a small group of service users or care workers; it should also include an analysis of your performance.

Section 1: Types of communication

Different types of communication used in care settings

There are many different ways in which people communicate with each other. These can include: oral communication, body language, signs and symbols, written and electronically transferred communication.

Oral communication

Tearesa Thompson (1986) writing about health work, argues that communication is important for two major reasons. Firstly, communication enables people to share information; but secondly, communication enables relationships between people. Thompson states that 'communication is the relationship' (1986). So speaking or signing is central to establishing relationships between people, and care workers need to have highly developed social skills, in order to work with the

FIGURE 2.1 *Communication enables people to share information*

wide range of emotional needs that service users will have. Face-to-face, oral (or mouth) communication involves using words and sentences (verbal communication) together with a range of body language messages (non-verbal communication). Section 3 of this unit explores these issues in detail.

Oral communication may be central to the kind of tasks listed in Figure 2.2.

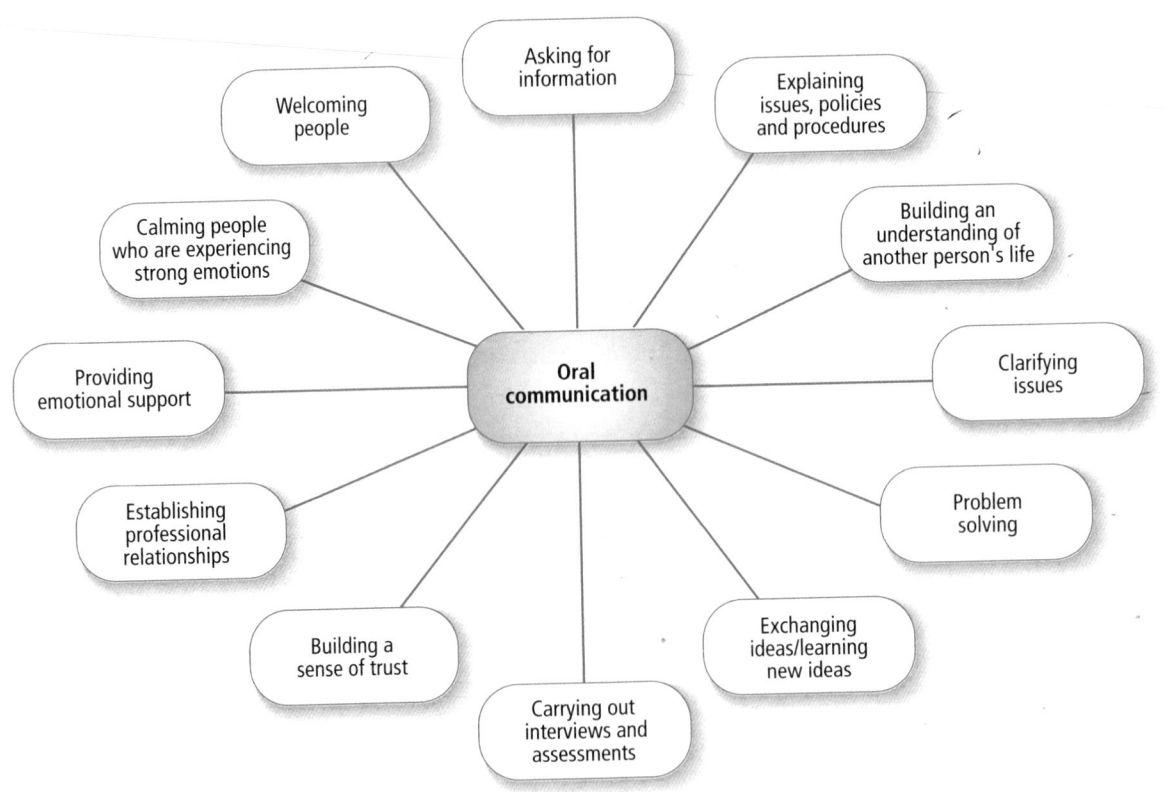

FIGURE 2.2 *Examples of tasks in which oral communication is key*

Written communication

There is an old saying in Chinese culture that 'the faintest ink is stronger than the strongest memory'. Written records are essential for communicating formal information that needs to be reviewed at a future date. When people remember conversations they have had, they will probably miss some details out, and also change some details. Written statements are much more permanent and if they are accurate when they are written they may be useful at a later date.

Some examples of important written documents are shown in Figure 2.3.

When an issue is recorded in writing it becomes formal. It is important that records of personal information are as factual and accurate as possible. You should describe only the facts or the events that happened, without giving your own interpretation or saying how you feel.

If written communication is inaccurate it could result in the following problems:

* serious delays in meeting people's needs
* inability to follow up enquiries
* making mistakes with arrangements for people's care
* missing meetings or important arrangements
* not providing a professional service for people
* inability to organise services for others properly
* other professional workers not having the right information to help them with decision-making.

Many organisations use printed forms to help staff to ask important questions and check that they have taken accurate information. Service users' personal records are likely to be written on forms that use headings. When writing information down it is a good idea to:

* check that the interviewee is giving you the information agrees with what you are writing
* check the spelling of names and repeat phone numbers back to interviewee in order to check that they are correct
* use a form or a prepared set of headings to

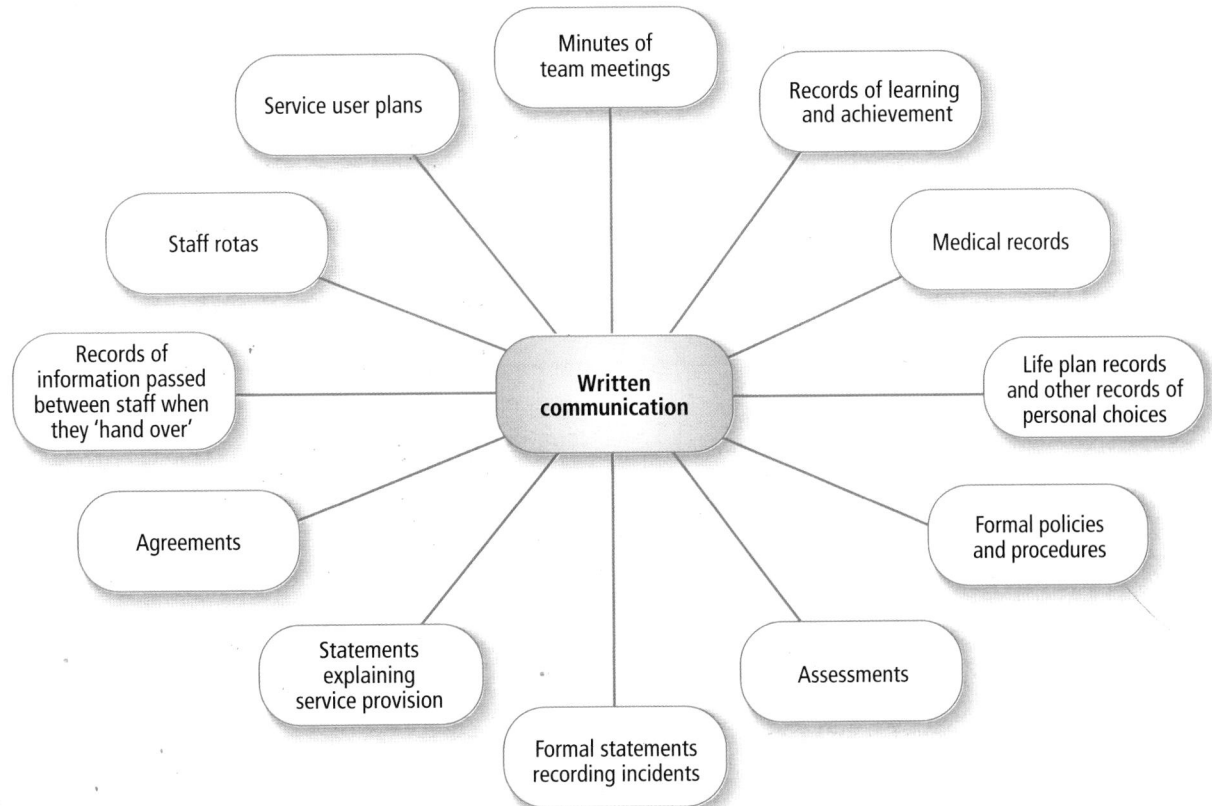

FIGURE 2.3 *Examples of important written communication*

help check that you are collecting the right information.

Computerised communication (Information and communication technology)

Nowadays, individuals can access a vast amount of information through the Internet. Email and text messages can reach people in a fraction of the time that paper-based written communication used to take. It is possible to network with a wide range of other professionals rapidly using electronically recorded messages. An important issue here is to consider the degree of formality involved. Some electronic communication, such as text messages between friends, can use short cuts to communicate. For example, everybody understands 'How R U?' But more complex informal systems of communication might confuse or exclude people in a work context.

Computerised records are very important in care work and should be treated with the same degree of formality as other written records. There will be a range of security measures designed to make sure the information stays confidential and is not lost or inappropriately altered. With electronic records it will be important to:

* keep a 'back-up copy' in case the system crashes

* use a password security check to ensure that only appropriate staff have access

* find out about the policy on the printing of details (similar to written records) so that hard copies do not get lost, or seen by others

* know the policy on who is authorised to update or change records. The recording system must prevent information being altered or lost by accident

* print out faxed documents in an appropriate confidential area and keep the documents in a safe system to prevent unauthorised people having access to confidential material.

Special methods

People who are Deaf may not use a spoken language system. The first (or main) language of many deaf people may be a signed language. People who are registered blind may use Braille, as opposed to English, in order to read information.

British Sign Language

The British Deaf Association states that British Sign Language (BSL) 'is the first or preferred language of nearly 70,000 Deaf people in the United Kingdom'. The British Deaf Association explains that BSL 'belongs to deaf people. It is not a communication system devised by hearing people. It is a real language which has evolved in the UK's Deaf community over hundreds of years.' The British Deaf Association campaign for the right of Deaf people to be educated in BSL and to access information and services through BSL, arguing that the Deaf community is a 'linguistic and cultural minority and is not measured in medical terms'.

Further details of BSL can be found at www.britishdeafassociation.org.uk. Details of signs and the finger spelling alphabet can be found at www.british-sign.co.uk and at www.royaldeaf.org.uk.

Makaton

Makaton is a system for developing language that uses speech, signs and symbols to help people with learning difficulties to communicate and to develop their language skills. People who communicate using Makaton may speak a word and perform a sign using hands and body language. There is a large range of symbols that may help people with learning difficulty to recognise an idea or to communicate with others. Further information on Makaton can be found at www.makaton.org.

Braille

Braille (a system of raised marks that can be felt with your fingers) provides a system of written communication, based on the sense of touch, for people who have limited vision. The communication system known as Braille was first published by Louis Braille, a blind 20-year-old, in 1829. The system is now widely adopted in the form of writing and reading and is used by people who cannot see written script.

Nowadays, computer software can translate written material into Braille, which can be printed out using special printers. Further details on Braille can be found at www.brailleplus.net.

Summary

There are many situations in care work, in which it is important to exchange information. Communication is also important because care work is about building, appropriate relationships and meeting social, emotional and intellectual needs, as well as the physical needs of service users. The quality of communication will establish the quality of relationships and the ability of carers to meet service users' needs.

Section 2: Factors that support and inhibit communication

In order to work supportively it is important to understand and work within a system of care values. Care values include understanding the importance of diversity and cultural variation, maintaining confidentiality and promoting the rights of service users.

Care values

Skilled caring does not result from just knowing the right skills and techniques. A carer also needs to 'value' the service users that he or she works with. The 1998 National Vocational Qualifications (NVQs) in Care Standards identified key values to 'Foster equality and diversity of people', 'maintain the confidentiality of information' and 'Foster people's rights and responsibilities'. The proposed standards for 2005 have been designed differently but still identify values that include: the promotion of equality and diversity; the ability to challenge discrimination; and an understanding of the rights and responsibilities of people involved in care settings.

> **Key concept**
>
> *care values* are occupational standards and codes of practice that identify a framework of values and moral rights of service users. In 2002 the General Social Care Council (GSCC) published a **'code of practice'** for both employees and employers. A summary of the code of practice for employees is set out in Unit 1 together with other codes of practice that provide a basis for care values.

Other codes of practice

Healthcare workers such as nurses follow a code of professional conduct published by the Nursing and Midwifery Council (NMC). The code has similar principles to the GSCC code for social care. Full details of the code can be found at www.nmc-uk.org. A summary of the key principles are listed below.

In caring for patients and service users, you must:

* respect each service user as an individual
* obtain consent before you give any treatment or care
* protect confidential information
* cooperate with others in the team
* maintain your professional knowledge and competence
* be trustworthy
* act to identify and minimise risk to patients and service users.

The majority of early years services are inspected by Ofsted and do not involve the GSCC code of practice. Instead Early Years National Vocational Qualifications have a set of 'underlying principles'; see Figure 2.4 for an outline specification.

UNDERLYING PRINCIPLES OF EARLY YEARS NVQS	
1	the welfare of the child is the most important issue
2	children must be kept safe
3	workers must work in partnership with parents and families
4	children's learning and development are centrally important
5	the principle of equality of opportunity is critically important
6	anti-discriminatory practice is vital
7	care practice must 'celebrate diversity'
8	the principle of confidentiality must be followed
9	workers must work with other professionals in the best interests of children and families
10	early years workers must learn to reflect on their practice and principles

FIGURE 2.4 *Outline specification of underlying principles of Early Years NVQs*

Promoting equality and diversity – diversity in individuals

You are special and no one is exactly the same as you. But you will be more like some people and less like others. We try to make ourselves individual; but we are also influenced by the 'groups' that we belong to. Some general differences between people (aspects of diversity) are listed in Figure 2.5.

DIFFERENCES BETWEEN PEOPLE	
Age	People may think of others as being children, teenagers, young adults, middle-aged or old. Discrimination can creep in to our thinking if we see some age groups as being 'the best' or if we make assumptions about the abilities of different age groups.
Gender	People are classified as male or female. In the past, men often had more rights and were seen as more important than women. Assumptions about gender still create discrimination.
Race	People may understand themselves as being black or white, as European, African or Asian. Many people have specific national identities such as Polish, Nigerian, English or Welsh. Assumptions about racial characteristics lead to discrimination.
Class	People differ in their upbringing, the kind of work they do and the money they receive. People also differ in the lifestyles they lead and the views and values that go with different levels of income and spending habits. People may discriminate against others because of their class or lifestyle.
Religion	People grow up in different traditions of religion. For some people, spiritual beliefs are at the centre of their understanding of life. For others, religion influences the cultural traditions that they celebrate; for example, many Europeans celebrate Christmas even though they might not see themselves as practising Christians. Discrimination can take place when people assume that their customs or beliefs should apply to everyone else.
Sexuality	Many people see their sexual orientation as very important to understanding who they are. Gay and lesbian relationships are often discriminated against. Heterosexual people sometimes judge other relationships as 'wrong' or abnormal.
Ability	People may make assumptions about what is 'normal'. People with physical disabilities or learning disabilities may become labelled or stereotyped.
Health	People who develop illnesses or mental health problems may feel that they are valued less by other people and discriminated against.
Relationships	People choose many different lifestyles and emotional commitments, such as: marriage, having children, living in a large family, living a single lifestyle but having sexual partners, being single and not sexually active. People live within different family and friendship groups. Discrimination can happen if people think that one lifestyle is 'right' or best.
Politics	People can develop different views as to how a government should act, how welfare provision should be organised, and so on. Disagreement and debate are necessary; but it is important not to discriminate against people because of their views.

FIGURE 2.5 *Some aspects of diversity*

Understanding diversity

Our own culture and life experience may lead us to make assumptions about what is right or normal. When we meet people who are different from ourselves it can be easy to see them as 'not right' or 'not normal'. People see the world in different ways. Our way of thinking may seem unusual to others. Look at Figure 2.6. Which is the 'normal front of the cube'?

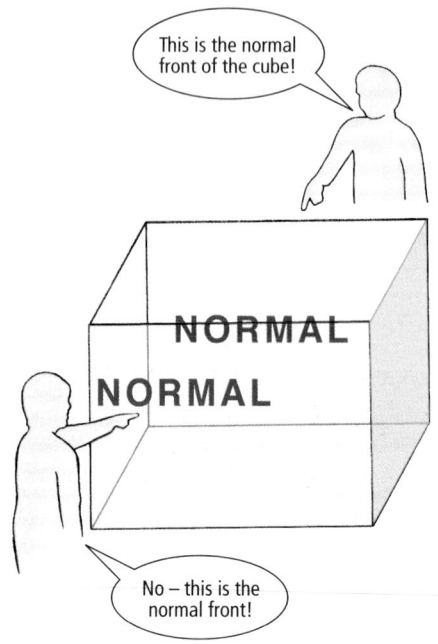

FIGURE 2.6 *Different individuals have different views*

If we were used to seeing the cube from only one direction we might be sure that our view is right. Our culture may lead us to think that some habits are more normal than others, but often there are many ways of looking at things. For instance, different cultures and different individuals have different views about what is right to eat or drink.

Think it over...

Do you think that it is appropriate for you to eat meat, insects, frogs, snakes? There is great diversity in what people believe is appropriate to eat. Culture, politics and religion play a role in influencing what people believe.

Skilled carers have to get to know the people that they work with in order to avoid making false assumptions. In getting to know an individual, carers will also need to understand the ways that class, race, age, gender and other social categories influence the person. A person's culture may include all social groups that he or she belongs to.

Knowledge of diverse characteristics

There are many different ethnic groups in the world, many different religions, cultural values, variations in gender role, and so on. Individuals

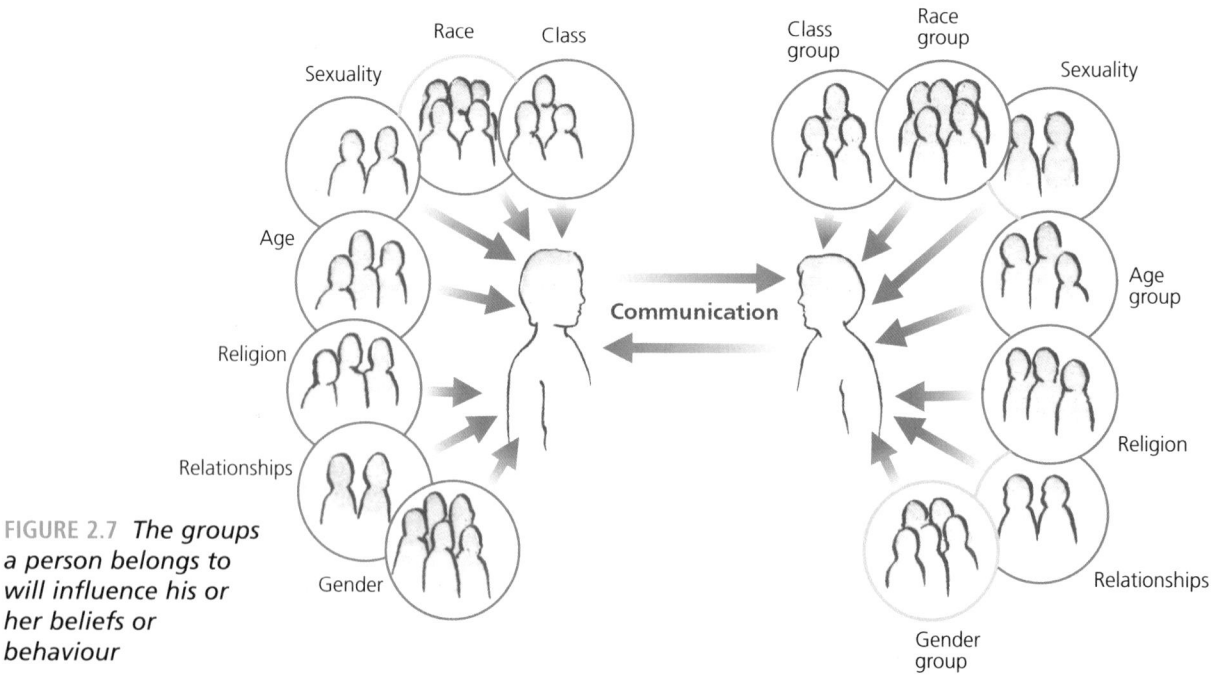

FIGURE 2.7 *The groups a person belongs to will influence his or her beliefs or behaviour*

may belong to the same ethnic group yet belong to different religions or class groups. Knowing someone's religion will not necessarily tell you all about his or her beliefs, or general culture.

You can pick up background knowledge on different ethnic and religious customs, but it is impossible to study and learn all the differences that can exist for individual service users. The best way to learn about diversity is to listen and communicate with people who lead very different lives.

Promoting equality and diversity in communication

It is important to be able to identify the different interpretations that words and body language have in different cultures. This is not a straightforward issue – words and signs can mean different things depending on their context. For example, the word 'wicked' can have different meanings. If older people were to use this phrase to describe their experience of World War II, it would mean 'horrific' or 'terrible'. In a TV comedy script written 15 years ago, the phrase would mean 'cool', i.e. something very desirable. In a religious context 'wicked' might relate to the concept of sin.

Making sense of spoken language requires knowledge of the context and intentions of the speaker. Understanding non-verbal communication involves exactly the same need to understand 'where the person is coming from', or, to put it more formally, what the circumstances and cultural context of the other person are.

Both spoken and non-verbal communication is influenced by culture. For example, in Britain the hand gesture with palm up and facing forward, means 'Stop, don't do that'. In Greece it can mean, 'You are dirt', and is a very rude gesture.

Why do the same physical movements have different meanings? One explanation for the hand signs is that the British version of the palm-and-fingers gesture means, 'I arrest you, you must not do it'; whereas the Greek interpretation goes back to medieval times when criminals had dirt rubbed in their faces to show how much people despised them.

Using care values means that carers must have respect for other people's culture. People learn different ways of communicating, and good carers

will try to understand the different ways in which people use non-verbal messages. For instance, past research in the USA suggests that white and black Americans might have used different non-verbal signals when they listened. It suggests that some black Americans may tend not to look much at the speaker. This can be interpreted as a mark of respect; by looking away it demonstrates that you are really thinking hard about the message. Unfortunately, not all white people understood this cultural difference in non-verbal communication. Some individuals misunderstood and assumed that this non-verbal behaviour meant exactly the same as if a white person had looked away from the speaker. That is, it would mean the individual was not listening.

> ### Key concept
>
> *cultural variation* describes the different special systems of meanings across different cultures. Cultures that are different from our own interpret body language differently: communication is influenced by these cultural systems of meaning.

There is an almost infinite variety of meanings that can be given to any type of eye contact, facial expression, posture or gesture. Every culture develops its own special system of meanings. Carers have to understand and show respect and value for all these different systems of sending messages. But how can you ever learn them all?

No one can learn every possible system of non-verbal message, but it is possible to learn the ones that people you are with are using. You may do this by first noticing and remembering what others do and which non-verbal messages they are sending. The next step is to make an intelligent guess about what messages the person is trying to give you. Finally, check your understanding (your guesses) with the person.

Skilled interpersonal interaction involves:

* watching other people
* remembering what they do
* guessing what words and actions mean and then checking your guesses with the person

* never relying on your own guesses, because these might turn into assumptions

* understanding that assumptions can lead to discrimination.

Using care values involves getting to understand people and not acting on unchecked assumptions. Non-verbal messages should never be relied on; they should always be checked.

Stereotyping

Sometimes people try to save mental energy and just make the assumption that groups of people are 'all the same'. Perhaps a younger person meets an 80-year-old, who has a problem with his or her memory, perhaps they have seen someone with a poor memory on TV – it is then easy to think that 'all old people are forgetful'. This would be a stereotype.

A stereotype is a fixed way of thinking. People may make assumptions based on stereotyped thinking. For example, a carer who works with older people might say 'I'll just go in and wash and dress this next one. I won't ask what she would like me to do because she's old. Old people don't remember, so it doesn't matter what I do'. Stereotyping is the opposite of valuing diversity.

Key concept

stereotyping is a fixed way of thinking involving generalisations and expectations about an issue or a group of people.

Maintaining confidentiality

Confidentiality is an important right for all service users. Confidentiality is important because:

* service users may not trust a carer if the carer does not keep information to him or herself

* service users may not feel valued or able to keep their self-esteem if their private details are shared with others.

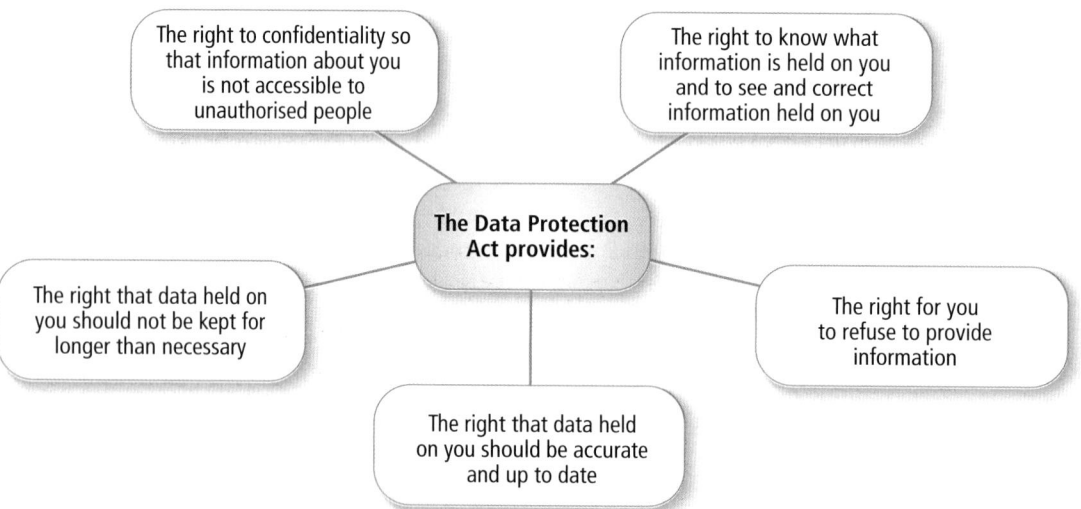

FIGURE 2.8 *Some rights provided under the Data Protection Act 1998*

* service users' safety may be put at risk if details of their property and habits are shared publicly

* a professional service which maintains respect for individuals must keep private information confidential

* there are legal requirements to keep personal records confidential.

The Data Protection Act 1998

The 1998 Data Protection Act establishes rights to confidentiality covering both paper and electronic records. This Act provides people with a range of rights including those shown in Figure 2.8.

> **Key concept**
>
> *confidentiality* involves keeping information safe and only passing it on where there is a clear right and a clear need to do so. Confidentiality is an important moral and legal right, promoting the safety and security of service users and their property. The maintenance of confidentiality is vital, in order to keep a sense of trust.

Service users have a right to confidentiality but also have a responsibility in relation to the rights of others. Confidentiality often has to be kept within boundaries, or broken where the rights of others have to balance with the service user's rights. An example of keeping confidentiality within boundaries would be a situation in which a carer tells his or her manager about something learned in confidence. As the information is not made public it is still partly confidential. Some of the situations in which information may need to be passed to managers are shown in Figure 2.9.

Confidentiality and the need to know

Good care practice involves asking service users if we can let other people know things. It would be wrong to pass on even the date of a person's birthday without asking him or her first. Some people might not want others to celebrate their birthday. Jehovah's Witnesses, for example, believe that it is wrong to celebrate birthdays. Whatever we know about a service user should be kept private unless the person tells us that it is all right to share the information. The exception to this rule is that information can be passed on when others have a right and a need to know it.

Some examples of people who have a need to know about work with service users are:

* the manager (he or she may need to help make decisions, which affect the service user)

* colleagues (these people may be working with the same person)

* other professionals (these people may also be working with the service user and need to be kept up to date with information).

SITUATION	EXAMPLE
Where there is a significant risk of harm to a service user	An older person in the community refuses to put her heating on in winter; she may be at risk of harm from the cold
When a service user might be abused	A person who explains that his son takes his money; he might be being financially abused
Where there is a significant risk of harm to others	A person who lives in a very dirty house with mice and rats; he or she may be creating a public health risk
Where there is a risk to the carer's health or well-being	A person is very aggressive; he or she is placing the carer at risk

FIGURE 2.9 *Examples of situations in which carers may need to pass on confidential information to managers*

FIGURE 2.10 *Service users have a right to know that information about them is recorded accurately*

When information is passed to other professionals it should be passed on with the understanding that they keep it confidential. It is important to check that other people are authentic. If you answer the telephone and the person speaking claims to be a social worker or other professional, you should explain that you must phone back before giving any information; this enables you to be sure that you are talking to an authorised person within an organisation. If you meet a person you don't know, you should ask for proof of identity before passing any information on.

Relatives will often say that they have a right to know about service users. Sometimes it is possible to ask relatives to discuss issues directly with the service user rather than giving information yourself, as shown in the illustration opposite, for example.

All services now have to have policies and procedures on the confidentiality of recorded information.

If service user records are not managed in accordance with the Data Protection Act and NCSC regulations, service users might suffer a range of damaging consequences, which might include those shown in Figure 2.11.

Values and moral rights

The table opposite lists key (value base principles) that might also be considered to be service users'

SCENARIO

Ethel is 88 years old and receives home care. One day she says 'Keep this confidential, but I don't take my tablets [pain killers for arthritis and tablets for blood pressure]. I'm saving them so that I can take them all at once and finish my life if my pain gets worse.' Ethel manages to say this before you can tell her that some things cannot be kept confidential.

Do you have to keep this information confidential? Ethel has a right to confidentiality but she also has a responsibility not to involve other people in any harm she may do to herself. Ethel does not have a right to involve you. The information about the tablets should be shared with managers and Ethel's GP, who can discuss the matter with her.

Ethel's neighbour stops you as you are leaving one day. The neighbour asks, 'How is Ethel, is she taking her tablets?'

Can you tell the neighbour of your worries? Before giving any information to anyone, carers have to ask the question, 'Does this person have a need to know?' A need to know is different from wanting to know. Ethel's neighbour might just be nosy, and it would be wrong to break the confidentiality without an important reason. If the GP knows Ethel does not take her tablets, she may be able to save her health or even her life. But the neighbour should not be told.

moral rights, together with other rights that are specified within the GSCC code of practice.

Other factors that support or inhibit communication

Communication can be supported or inhibited by both practical and emotional factors. This is because communication depends on receiving the message – a practical or physical issue – and on correctly interpreting the message – an emotional issue. So even if information is seen or heard, it can still be misunderstood because of other issues.

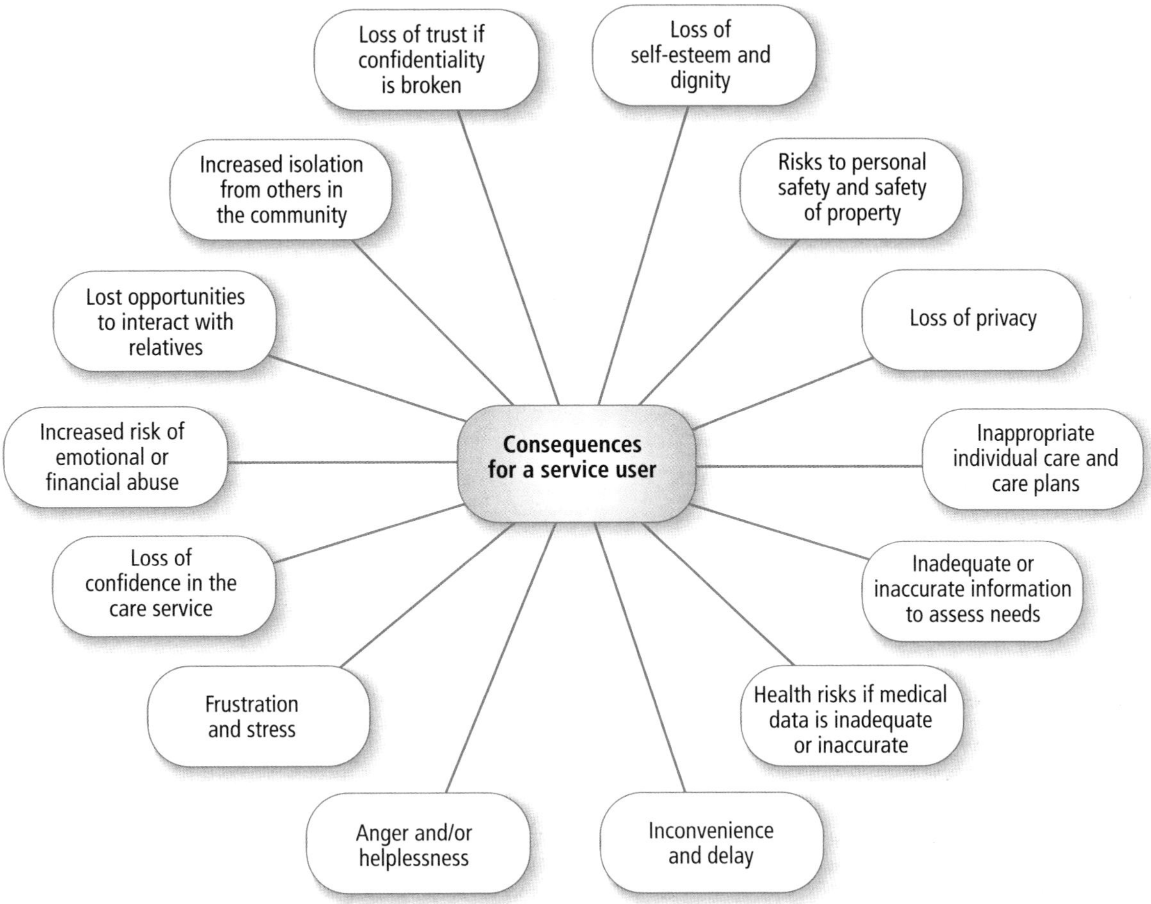

Loss of trust if confidentiality is broken

Loss of self-esteem and dignity

Increased isolation from others in the community

Risks to personal safety and safety of property

Lost opportunities to interact with relatives

Loss of privacy

Increased risk of emotional or financial abuse

Consequences for a service user

Inappropriate individual care and care plans

Loss of confidence in the care service

Inadequate or inaccurate information to assess needs

Frustration and stress

Health risks if medical data is inadequate or inaccurate

Anger and/or helplessness

Inconvenience and delay

FIGURE 2.11 *Some of the consequences for service users if their records are not managed in accordance with current legislation and regulations*

Positioning

Positioning can create both physical and emotional barriers that inhibit communication. If a person cannot see you this may inhibit communication. On an emotional level, leaning over somebody and looking down at them can send a message of dominance and power. Historically, courtrooms were designed so that the judge sat much higher than the defendant and also looked down on everyone else. The ability to look down shows how powerful you are. In care work it is very important not to look down on the people you care for. It is important that your eyes are at the same level as the person that you are communicating with.

It is important to consider positioning when working with people who have a hearing difficulty. Many people with partial hearing use lip-reading and this enables them to understand

FIGURE 2.12 *A carer moves to the same eye level as a service user*

what other people are saying. It is therefore important that you position yourself so that the person can see your face clearly. In this situation, therefore, it does make sense for a person who lip-reads to say, 'I'm sorry I can't hear you, I need to put my glasses on.'

Positioning is very important in group communication. Seating patterns can have a major influence on how a group works. In discussion groups it is very important that everyone can see and hear one another. Non-verbal communication will be important, and if people cannot see everybody's faces, this may not be possible. Usually, chairs are placed in a circle to enable all those taking part in a discussion to receive non-verbal messages from everyone in the group.

Organising a group to sit in a circle may suggest that everyone is equal and that everyone is expected to communicate with everyone else. This freedom to communicate is also linked with creating a feeling of belonging: 'We can all share together – this is our group.' (See Figure 2.13a).

Other patterns of seating will send different messages. Teachers might sit in the middle of a half-circle. This sends the message, 'We are all equal and we can all communicate with each other, but the teacher is going to do most of the communicating.' (See Figure 2.13b).

At a formal lecture, people sit in rows. This sends the message, 'The lecturer will talk to you. You can ask questions but you should not talk to one another.' (See Figure 2.13c).

Some less formal seating arrangements can create blocks. Sometimes a desk or table acts as a block. For example, in Figure 2.13d, the two people on their own might be sending the message, 'We are not sure we want to be with this

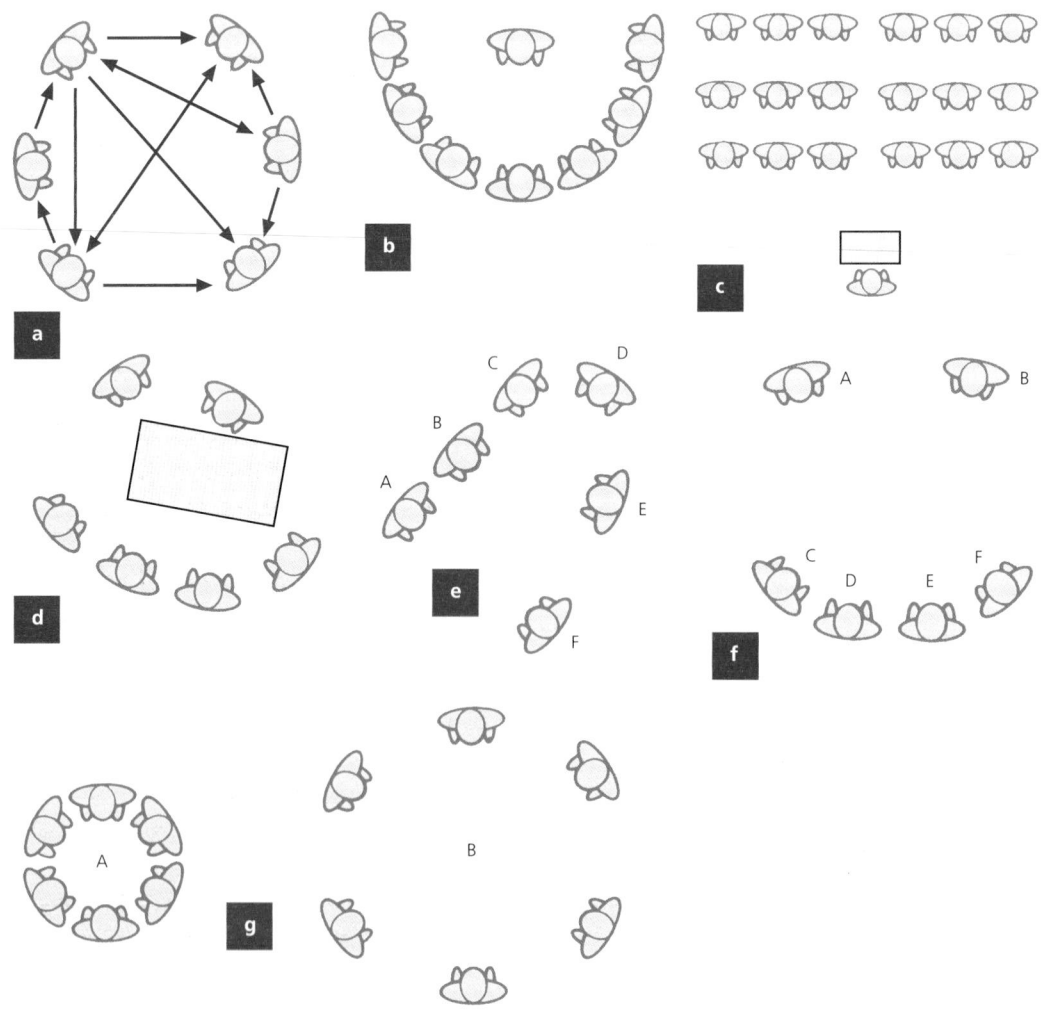

FIGURE 2.13 *Positioning is important in group communication*

group.' The table can make them feel separate: 'We'll join in only if we feel like it.'

Sometimes space can be used to create a gulf. In Figure 2.13e, person A cannot see person C properly; so the two of them are unable to exchange non-verbal messages. Person A sits 'square on' to person F. Perhaps A does not want to talk to C. Perhaps F and A do not trust each other. The layout of seats makes it look as though there could be tension or reluctance in this group.

Space can also signal social distance (see Figure 2.13f. A and B are keeping their distance from the rest of the group. There could be many reasons, but perhaps they are sending the message, 'We do not really belong with you four.'

Another consideration is whether a group of people is sitting close together or spaced apart. In Figure 2.13g, group A are huddled together, whereas group B are spaced further apart. There might be a number of reasons why people get closer or further apart in groups. For example, being close can signal that the environment is noisy and that the group has to get close to hear. It can suggest that the members like each other and are very interested in the discussion topic. Alternatively, it might be that group members feel unsafe and that being together gives each one more confidence that everyone will be supportive.

Proximity and personal space

The space between people can sometimes show how friendly or 'intimate' the conversation is. Different cultures have different assumptions about how close people should be (proximity) when they are talking.

In Britain, there are expectations or 'norms' as to how close you should be when you talk to others. When talking to strangers we may keep an arm's-length apart. The ritual of shaking hands indicates that you have been introduced and may come closer. When you are friendly with someone you may accept him or her being closer to you. Relatives and partners may not be restricted in how close they can come.

Personal space is a very important issue in care work. A care worker who assumes it is all right to enter a service user's personal space without asking or explaining, may be seen as being dominating or aggressive.

Another aspect of positioning is that of face to face. In many cultural contexts within the UK, standing or sitting eye to eye can send a message of being sincere, or it can mean formality, or it can mean confrontation and threat. A slight angle may create a more informal, relaxed and friendly feeling.

Emotion

Service users often have serious emotional needs; they are afraid or depressed because of the stresses they are experiencing. Sometimes service users may lack self-awareness or appear to be shy or aggressive. Listening involves learning about frightening and depressing situations. Carers sometimes avoid listening to avoid unpleasant emotional feelings. Emotion can create barriers because care workers:

* are tired – listening takes mental energy
* believe that they do not have sufficient time to communicate properly
* are emotionally stressed by the needs of service users
* react with negative emotions towards cultures that are different from their own
* make assumptions about others, or label or stereotype others.

When service users are depressed, angry or upset these emotions will influence their ability to understand what you are trying to communicate.

Emotion and quality of relationship

The ability to build a supportive relationship with service users will also greatly influence communication. People who trust you will be more inclined to share information. If you are attentive to people's needs they may respond to you with some gratitude. If you show respect to service users this may help to meet their self-esteem needs. If you are responsive to others they may be responsive to you. If you are good at listening then you may be able to build an understanding of the person you are communicating with and this, in time, may lead to empathy.

It will always be important to consider the emotional impact you have on other people and to try and adapt your communication to meet the emotional needs of others.

How do you know if another person sees you as being supportive? One of the key issues will be how the individual responds to you. If people treat you with respect perhaps it is because they perceive you as being respectful. If they try to please you perhaps it is because you meet their self-esteem needs.

Being assertive

Some people may seem shy and worried; they say little and avoid contact with people they do not know. Other people may want people to be afraid of them; they may try to dominate and control others. Fear and aggression are two of the basic emotions that we experience. It is easy to give in to our basic emotions and either become submissive or aggressive when we feel stressed. Assertion is an advanced skill that involves controlling the basic emotions involved in running away or fighting. Assertion involves a mental attitude of trying to negotiate, trying to solve problems rather than giving in to emotional impulses.

> **Key concept**
>
> *assertion* is different from both submission and aggression. Assertion involves being able to negotiate a solution to a problem.

Winning and losing

During an argument, people who are aggressive might demand that they are right and others are wrong. They will want to win while others lose. To be weak or submissive is the opposite of being aggressive. Submissive people accept that they will lose, get told off, or be put down. Assertive behaviour is different from both of these responses. In an argument an assertive person will try to reach a solution in which no one has to lose or be 'put down'. Assertion is a skill which facilitates 'win-win' situations – no one has to be the loser. For example, consider the situation illustrated in Figure 2.14 in which a service user is angry because of the carer's late arrival.

Assertive skills can help enable carers to cope

Aggresive response

Don't you talk to me like that – you're lucky I'm here at all. Don't you know how hard we work? There are other people to look after as well as you, you know!

The aggressive response meets the needs of the carer and not the service user. The service user is kept vulnerable: 'I win you lose.'

Angry service user

You're late again. I'm not putting up with it – I'm going to make a formal complaint about your behaviour.

Assertive response

I'm sorry that you're angry, but I really couldn't help it, please let me explain why I had to be late today.

The assertive response is aimed at meeting the needs of both the carer and the service user: 'We both win.'

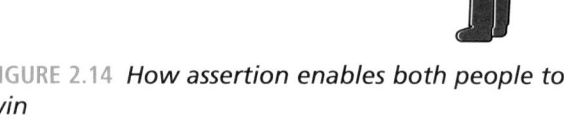

Submissive response

I'm terribly sorry, I promise I won't be late again.

The submissive response meets the needs of the service user and not the carer. The service user may dominate the carer: 'You win I lose.'

FIGURE 2.14 *How assertion enables both people to win*

with difficult and challenging situations. To be assertive a person usually has to:

* understand the situation – including the facts, details and other people's perceptions

* be able to control personal emotions and stay calm

* be able to act assertively using the right non-verbal behaviour

* be able to act assertively using the right words and statements.

Some verbal and non-verbal behaviours involved in assertion are summarised in Figure 2.15.

Aggressive behaviour	Assertive behaviour	Submissive behaviour
Main emotion: anger	*Main emotion*: staying in control of own actions	*Main emotion*: fear
Wanting your own way	Negotiating with others	Letting others win
Making demands	Trying to solve problems	Agreeing with others
Not listening to others	Aiming for no one to lose	Not putting your views across
Putting other people down	Listening to others	Looking afraid
Trying to win	Showing respect for others	Speaking quietly or not speaking at all
Shouting or talking very loudly	Keeping a clear, calm voice	
Threatening non-verbal behaviour including: fixed eye contact, tense muscles, waving or folding hands and arms, looking angry	**Normal non-verbal behaviour** including: varied eye contact, relaxed face muscles, looking 'in control', keeping hands and arms at your side	**Submissive non-verbal behaviour** including: looking down, not looking at others, looking frightened, tense muscles

FIGURE 2.15 *Aggressive, assertive and submissive behaviours*

Environmental conditions

It is very hard to hear what someone is saying if there is a great deal of background noise. It is also very difficult to make sense of other people's facial expressions if you cannot see their face properly due to poor lighting. A group of people might not see each other comfortably in rooms that have awkward seating positions. People sometimes feel uncomfortable if they are trying to communicate with a person who is too close or at a distance. A room that is too hot, or stuffy or cold may inhibit communication, if it makes people feel tired or stressed.

The environment also plays an important role in influencing the effectiveness of aids for communication. For instance, hearing aids will amplify background noise as well as the voice of the speaker. A noisy environment may therefore make the situation more difficult and unpleasant for someone who is using a hearing aid than for someone who does not use one. Good lighting will be critical for those who lip-read to support their understanding of speech, whereas the quality of lighting may not be quite as important for someone with good hearing.

Special situations and systems

Many service users will have specific communication needs. It may be important that service users employ an interpreter if they use a different language such as BSL. Some carers learn to use communication systems such as Makaton, in order to help them communicate with service users.

Hayman (1998) notes the following points for communicating with people with hearing impairments:

* make sure the person can see you clearly
* face both the light and the person at all times
* include the person in your conversation
* do not obscure your mouth
* speak clearly and slowly. Repeat if necessary, but you may need to rephrase your words
* do not shout into a person's ear or hearing aid
* minimise background noise
* use your eyes, facial expressions and hand gestures, where appropriate.

If people have limited vision it may be important that carers use language to describe issues that a sighted person might take for granted, such as non-verbal communication or the context of certain comments. Touch may be an important aspect of communication. Some registered blind people can work out what you look like if they touch your face (to build an understanding of your features).

It is always important to choose the right style of language when communicating with people from different language communities.

The content of communication

Unless you find yourself communicating in an emergency situation, most communication will involve some 'small talk' or relationship-building conversation at the beginning of an interaction. It is usually important to feel at ease and to put other people at ease during an interaction. When a lengthy conversation or interaction ends, it is usually important to leave on a positive emotional note; in most conversations this involves further 'small talk' or personal discussion that is not connected with the business of the conversation.

Some interactions are purely about social, emotional and relationship-building work.

When people meet together in family groups, or when friends meet in clubs, the purpose of communication may be to build emotional bonds or relationships. The whole content of the communication may be 'small talk' because it is the act of being together that is important, not the content of the communication.

Think it over...

Think about some instances when you have chatted to friends or relatives. If somebody had asked you 15 minutes later what you talked about, could you have remembered? Might you have said, 'I don't know we just talked – but it was enjoyable'?

Some communication is just about relationship building, but other communication is task-focused. When there is some business to resolve or a decision to be made, this is likely to form the 'serious' or task-focused content of communication. Task-focused communication should take place in-between social small talk if you are behaving in an unhurried and supportive way. Task-focused communication is likely to involve asking for information, giving information and using skills such as asking questions, and clarifying other people's answers.

Sometimes the content of communication will focus on major emotional issues. Service users might share their worries or feelings of anger or grief with you. When the content of communication focuses on issues that have great emotional significance for a service user it would be important to use advanced listening skills. Issues about self-esteem, trust and empathy will be very important when the content of communication focuses on emotional needs.

Some conversations are predictable. If you are going out with friends, for example, you might expect conversation to be mainly about relationship building. If you are attending a formal meeting with an agenda, on the other hand, then there will almost certainly be task-focused content to people's conversation. If you were working as a counsellor you might expect communication to address emotional issues. But sometimes in care settings, a service user might start with small talk or even task-focused discussion that then leads on to major emotional content. For example, an older service user might start a conversation by complimenting you on your appearance and then ask for your advice on some shopping that he or she wants, before reminiscing about the loss of a partner. You might need to change your style of response as the content of the conversation changes. It is not always possible to predict the content of an interaction in advance.

Summary

The foundation for conveying to others that you are a supportive care worker is to believe in, and work from, a set of values. It is vitally important that you value diversity and can identify the influence of cultural context on communication.

If you do not respect service users' rights, including their right to confidentiality, they are likely to feel threatened by your behaviour.

It is also important that you can identify the role of the following factors in influencing communication:

* emotion
* the importance of positioning
* environmental conditions
* special communication needs.

In order to earn extra pocket money, Zoe, who has never had any professional training, does some babysitting during the day with 10-month-old Mark. Zoe likes children but is 'addicted' to day-time TV 'soaps'. Zoe plays with Mark for a little while, but as soon as her favourite programme begins, she straps Mark into his pushchair in the hope that he will go to sleep if she ignores him.

Zana is a professional early years worker. Zana is focused on the need to work within a professional value system. When Mark makes sounds Zana will respond to him by speaking in a high-pitched tone, designed to attract his interest. Zana spends time smiling at Mark and talking to him to build a relationship with him.

Zana sees the purpose of her work as meeting Mark's needs, which include emotional and intellectual developmental needs. Mark has a right to appropriate communication and to be valued as an individual.

Using theory – can you identify?
Why Zoe does not understand the importance of responding to Mark and not ignoring him.

Using theory – can you explain?
Why Zana is a much better carer. Can you analyse how using care values might make her more responsive to Mark?

Using theory – can you evaluate?
Why it is important that care workers are sensitive to the rights of service users.

Section 3: Communication skills

Formal and informal communication in care

Speaking is about much more than just communicating information between people. For a start, many people may speak with different degrees of formality or informality. The degree of formality or informality is called the language 'register'.

For example, suppose you went into a hospital reception. You might expect the person on duty to greet you with a formal response such as, 'Good morning, how can I help you?' An informal greeting (typically used by white males in the South-east of England) might be 'Hello mate what's up then?' or 'How's it going?' It is possible that some people might prefer the informal greeting; this could put you at ease and make you feel that the receptionist is like you. But in many situations, the informal greeting might result in people feeling that they are not being respected.

The degree of formality or informality establishes a context. At a hospital reception you are unlikely to want to spend time making friends and chatting things over with the receptionist. You may be seeking urgent help. Your expectations of the situation might be that you want to be taken seriously and put in touch with professional services as soon as possible. You might see the situation as a very formal encounter.

If you are treated informally, you may interpret this as not being treated seriously, or in other words 'not being respected'.

Speech communities

Another issue is that informal speech is very likely to identify a specific speech community. Different localities, ethnic groups, professions and work cultures all have their own special words, phrases and speech patterns. An elderly middle-class woman is very unlikely to start a conversation with the words 'Hello mate'. Some service users may feel threatened or excluded by the kind of language they encounter. However, just using formal language will not solve this problem. The technical terminology used by social care workers may also create barriers for people who are not part of that 'speech community'.

Think it over...

Consider the following conversation.

Service user: I come about getting some help around the house, you know, 'cause it's getting 'ard' nowadays, what with me back an' everything.

Service worker: Well you need to speak to the Community Domiciliary Support Liaison Officer, who can arrange an assessment in accordance with our statutory obligations.

1. The two statements above use different levels of formality, but they also represent speech from different 'speech communities'. Can you work out what each person is saying?

2. How do you think the service user will feel given such a response? Will the service user feel respected and valued?

Professional relationships

People who are good at communication and assertive skills are likely to be good at building social relationships. Professional relationships may be regarded as different from ordinary social relationships and friendships because:

* professionals must work within a framework of values

* professional work always involves a duty of care for the welfare of service users (see Section 1.2 on rights)

* professional relationships involve establishing appropriate boundaries.

A boundary is a line that must not be crossed. In care work the metaphor of a boundary means that there are limits to the degree of emotional involvement and commitment within a relationship. Although professionals care about what happens to service users they do not form an emotional bond in the way that parents and children do.

Tone of voice

Tone involves the way our voice resonates as we speak. It is not just what we say, but the way that we say it. If we talk quickly in a loud voice with a fixed voice tone, people may perceive that we are angry. In most UK-contexts, a calm, slow voice with varying tone may send a message of being friendly. A sharp tone may be associated with angry or complaining behaviour. A flat tone might be associated with exhaustion or depression. A faint tone might be associated with submissive behaviour.

Pace of speech

Bostrom (1997) states that announcers (such as radio or TV presenters) speak at a rate of between 100 and 125 words per minute; this pace of speech might represent the ideal for explaining information. A great deal of speech is used to express emotional reaction rather than simply explaining issues to an audience. A faster pace of speech might indicate that the speaker is excited, anxious, agitated, nervous, angry or seeking to impress or dominate the listener. Alternatively, a fast pace of speech might simply mean that the speaker is in a hurry. Exactly what a fast pace of speech means can only be worked out by interpreting other non-verbal body language and the cultural context and situation of the speaker. Individuals who wave their arms, wide-eyed and smiling, talking rapidly about exam results might be interpreted as being excited at the news of having done well.

A slow pace of speech can indicate sadness or depression. Slow speech may sometimes be associated with impairment of thought processes, or might indicate tiredness or boredom. Slow emphasised speech might be used to convey dominance or hostility. Sometimes slow speech can indicate attraction, love and affection between individuals who know each other. Once again, this aspect of communication can only be interpreted once the non-verbal, social, cultural and practical context of the conversation have been understood.

In formal communication work – for example, if you were meeting people at an information desk or hospital reception – it might be important to maintain a normal pace of speech. This is because your work might focus on the formal exchange of information. Informal situations often involve a need to communicate emotions: for example, talking to a service user you know well. In this situation you might want to speak faster or slower to communicate your emotions clearly.

Eye contact

We can guess the feelings and thoughts that another person has by looking at their eyes. One poet called the eye 'the window of the soul'. We can sometimes understand the thoughts and feelings of another person by eye-to-eye contact. Our eyes get wider when we are excited, attracted to, or interested in someone else. A fixed stare may send the message that someone is angry. In European culture, looking away is often interpreted as being bored or not interested.

Body language

When we meet and talk with people, we will usually use two language systems: a verbal or spoken language and non-verbal or body language. Effective communication in care work requires care workers to be able to analyse their own and other people's non-verbal behaviour. Our body sends messages to other people – sometimes unconsciously. Some of the most important body areas that send messages are shown in Figure 2.16.

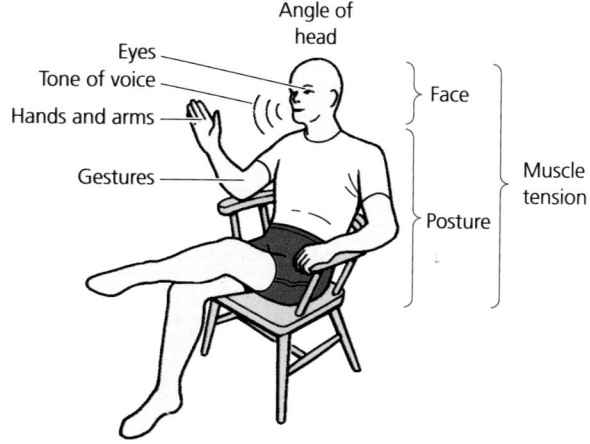

FIGURE 2.16 *Areas of the body that we use in communication*

body language is the way we use our bodies to communicate messages to other people. People communicate using words and also by using body language.

Facial expression represents a very important component of body language. The face can send very complex messages and we can read them easily – even in diagrammatic form.

FIGURE 2.17 *The face expresses emotion*

Our face often indicates our emotional state. When individuals are sad they may signal this emotion with eyes that look down; there may be tension in their face and their mouth will be closed. Their shoulder muscles are likely to be relaxed but their face and neck may show tension. A happy person will have 'wide eyes' that make contact with you and a smiling face. When people are excited they may move their arms and hands to signal their excitement.

The way we sit or stand can send messages. Body language includes the posture that a person takes. Sitting with crossed arms can mean 'I'm not taking any notice'. Leaning can send the message that you are relaxed or bored. Leaning forward

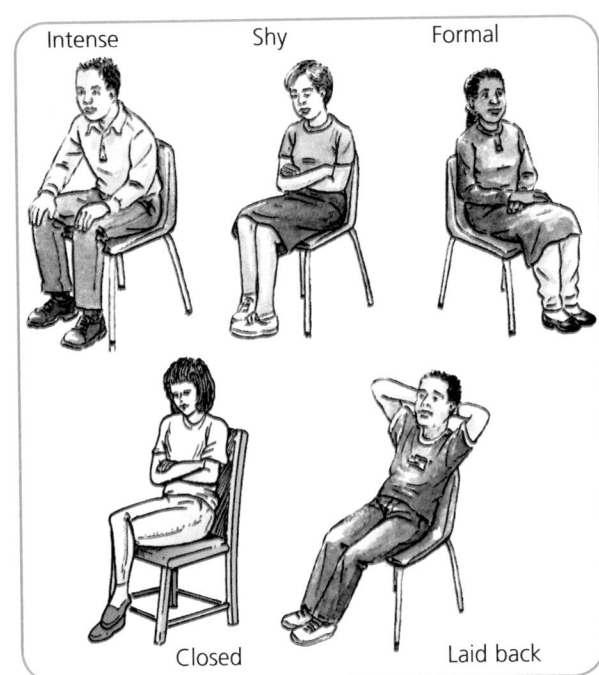

FIGURE 2.18 *Body postures that send out messages*

can show interest. See Figure 2.18 for illustrations of body postures and the messages they send.

Body language includes the movement of the body. The way we walk, move our head, sit, cross our legs and so on, send messages about whether we are tired, happy, sad or bored.

Muscle tension represents another aspect of body language. The tension in our feet, hands and fingers can tell others how relaxed or how tense we are. When we are very tense our shoulders might stiffen, our face muscles might tighten and we might sit or stand rigidly. Our mouths might be firmly closed and our lips and jaws tightly

FIGURE 2.19 *Gestures are important in communicating effectively*

clenched. A tense person might breathe quickly and become hot.

Our body also sends messages through gestures. Gestures are hand and arm movements that can help us to understand what a person is saying. Some gestures carry a meaning of their own.

The way in which we touch or avoid touching another person communicates important messages. Touching another person can send messages of care, affection, power over them, or sexual interest. The social setting and other body language usually help people to understand what touch might mean. Carers should not make assumptions about touch. Even holding someone's hand might be seen as trying to dominate them!

Clarifying

A central skill of all caring work is the ability to understand the thoughts and feelings of other people. An explanation of how to use the **communication cycle** to build an understanding is given in the next section. You may build an understanding of another person's thoughts by clarifying what he or she may have said. One way to seek clarification is to paraphrase or put what you think a person has said into your own words. Another way is to use open questions, probes or prompts in order to help build your understanding.

Some questions, which do not really encourage people to talk, or to clarify what they think, are called closed questions. For example, 'How old are you?' is a 'closed' question because there is only one, right, simple answer the person can give: 'I'm 84', and so on. Similarly, 'Do you like butter?' and 'Are you feeling well today?' are closed questions, as the person can only reply 'yes' or 'no.' Closed questions do not lead on to discussion.

Open questions are 'open' for discussion. Instead of giving a yes or no answer, the person is encouraged to think and discuss his or her thoughts and feelings. A question such as 'How do you feel about the food here?' means that the other person has to think about the food and then discuss it.

Open questions help to keep the conversation going. Sometimes closed questions can block a conversation and cause it to stop.

In some formal conversations it can be important to clarify a defined issue by asking direct closed questions; but the best way to ask closed questions is to ask open questions beforehand. There is an old saying that if you really want to find out what someone else thinks then, 'Every closed question should start life as an open one'. See Figure 2.20 for some examples of open and closed questions.

CLOSED QUESTION	OPEN QUESTION
Do you like your teacher?	What do you think about your teacher?
Is the food good in here?	What would you say the food is like here?
Do you like rock music?	What kind of music do you enjoy?
Do you sometimes feel lonely?	How do you feel about living on your own?
Do you enjoy drawing?	What are your favourite activities in school?

FIGURE 2.20 *Open and closed questions – some examples*

Probes and prompts

A probe is a very short question, such as 'Can you tell me more?' This kind of short question usually follows on from an answer that the other person has given. Probes are used to 'dig deeper' into the person's answer; they probe or investigate what the other person just said.

Prompts are short questions or words, which you offer to the other person in order to prompt them to answer. Questions such as 'So was it enjoyable or not?' or 'Would you do it again?' might prompt people to keep talking and clarify their thoughts. Sometimes a prompt might just be a suggested answer; for example, 'More than 50?' might be a prompt if you had just asked how many service users a carer worked with in a year and he or she seemed uncertain.

Probes and prompts are both useful techniques to help achieve a clearer understanding of another person's thoughts.

Some ideas that might help to clarify issues in a conversation include:

* use short periods of silence to prompt the other person to talk

* paraphrase or reflect back what the other person has said so that they will confirm that you have understood him or her

* ask open questions

* use probes and prompts to follow-up your questions.

Summarising

Summarising means to sum-up what has been said. It is a very important technique within group discussion, as creating a summary of what has been said may help to keep the group focused on their work. Summarising is also an important skill used in formal conversations, where information is to be written down; and it is important that people involved in the conversation agree about what is to be written. The ability to summarise requires a good memory and the ability to extract the important points in a conversation. Summarising is different from paraphrasing in that it results in a **synopsis** of a range of material rather than seeking to clarify a point.

Paraphrasing

Paraphrasing means to express the same meaning in other words. If you can use your own words to reflect back what another person has said then you are paraphrasing that individual's speech. It is very important to reflect back what another person has said, because this demonstrates that you have listened and built an understanding of their views. Paraphrasing is an important part of listening (see next section).

Empathising ✓

> **Key concept**
>
> *empathy* has been defined by Gerard Egan (1986) as 'the ability to enter into and understand the world of another person and communicate this understanding to him or her.'

At a deep level, empathy comes about within a relationship where one person has a deep understanding that involves both intellectual and emotional understanding of another person. Person-centred counsellors try to develop this deep level of empathy as a way of working, or indeed, a 'way of being' when they work with people.

Egan (1986) argues that the term 'empathy' can also be used to identify a communication skill – the skill of communicating an accurate understanding of the feelings and thoughts of another person. As a communication skill, empathy might involve a more superficial or short-term relationship than might be expected in professional counselling. Empathy as communication still involves the ability to understand the world of another person and the feelings that he or she has.

Empathising with another person is a skill based on **active listening**. Empathy may grow out of the ability to understand the thoughts and feelings of another person. But empathy is not a behavioural skill that can be defined in terms of a series of non-verbal and verbal components. Empathising identifies a caring attitude, where an individual person can see beyond his or her own assumptions about the world; and can imagine the thought and feelings of someone who is quite different. Many people have difficulty imagining the experiences of other people. The ability to empathise is the ability to see beyond assumptions that you have grown up with. Burnard and Morrison (1997) state 'caring and communicating are inseparably linked. You cannot hope to communicate effectively if you do not care about the person on the receiving end. You only have to study some of the 'professional communicators' whom we find in shops and offices to establish this point. The use of the term empathy might be used to identify the complex emotional and intellectual skill that lies at the heart of a genuine caring attitude.

Minimising communication barriers

Communication can become blocked if individual differences are not understood. There are three main ways that communication becomes blocked, as shown in Figure 2.21.

Examples of the first kind of block, where people do not receive the communication, include

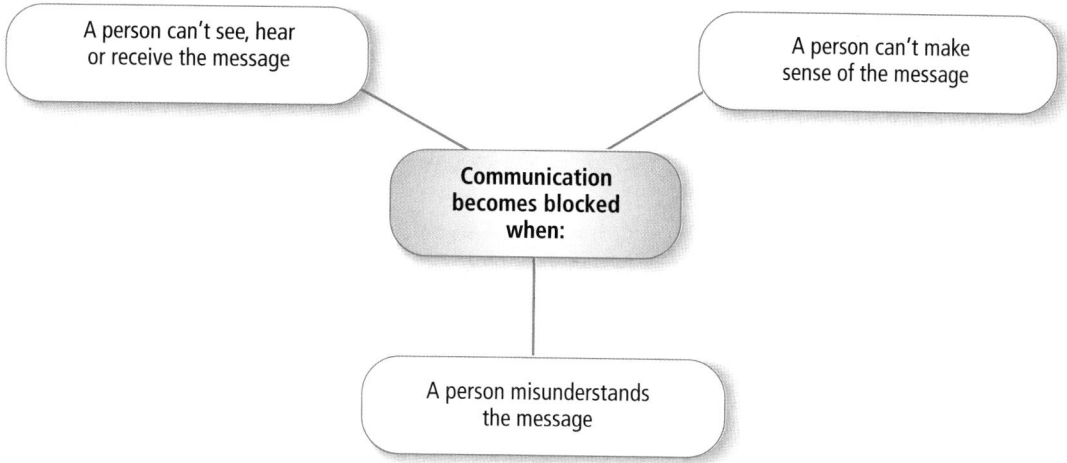

Communication becomes blocked when:

A person can't see, hear or receive the message

A person can't make sense of the message

A person misunderstands the message

FIGURE 2.21 *Ways in which communication is blocked*

visual disabilities, hearing disabilities, environmental problems such as poor lighting and noisy environments, and speaking from too far away. See Figure 2.22.

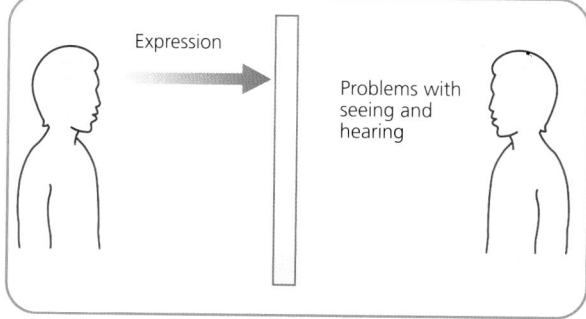

Expression

Problems with seeing and hearing

FIGURE 2.22 *Problems such as noise and poor light can create communication barriers*

Examples of situations in which people may not be able to make sense of the message include:

* the use of different languages, including signed languages

* the use of different terms in language, such as jargon (technical language), slang (different people using different terms), or dialect (people using different sounds to say the same words)

* physical and intellectual disabilities, such as dysphasia (difficulties with language expression or understanding), aphasia (an absence of language ability), being ill, or suffering memory loss or learning difficulty.

Reasons for misunderstanding a message include:

* cultural influences – cultures that are different from our own interpret non-verbal and verbal messages and humour, in different ways

* assumptions about people – race, gender, disability and other groupings

* labelling or stereotyping of others

* social context – statements and behaviour that are understood by friends and family may not be understood by strangers

* emotional barriers – a worker's own emotional needs may stop him or her wanting to know about others

* time pressures – mean that staff may withdraw from wanting to know about others

* emotional differences – these can sometimes be interpreted as personality clashes, or personality differences. Very angry, or very happy, or very shy people may misinterpret communication from others.

MINIMISING BARRIERS TO COMMUNICATION	
Visual disability	* Use language to describe things. * Assist people to touch things (e.g. touch your face to recognise you). * Explain details that sighted people might take for granted. * Check what people can see (many registered blind people can see shapes, or tell light from dark). * Explore technological aids such as information technology that can expand visual images. * Check glasses, other aids and equipment.
Hearing disability	* Do not shout, keep to normal clear speech and make sure your face is visible for people who can lip-read. * Show pictures, or write messages. * Learn to sign (for people who use signed languages). * Ask for help from, or employ a communicator or interpreter for signed languages. * Check that technological aids, such as hearing aids, are working.
Environmental constraints	* Check and improve lighting. * Reduce noise. * Move to a quieter or better-lit room. * Move to smaller groups to see and hear more easily. * Check seating arrangements.
Language differences	* Communicate using pictures, diagrams and non-verbal signs. * Use translators or interpreters. * Be careful not to make assumptions or stereotype. * Increase your knowledge of jargon, slang and dialects. * Re-word your messages – find different ways of saying things appropriate to the service user's 'speech community'. * Check your level of formality; speak in short, clear sentences if appropriate.
Intellectual disabilities	* Increase your knowledge of disabilities. * Use pictures and signs as well as clear, simple speech. * Be calm and patient. * Set up group meetings where people can share interests, experiences or reminiscences. * Check that people do not become isolated. * Use advocates – independent people who can spend time building an understanding of the needs of specific individuals to assist with communication work.
Preventing misunderstandings based on cultural differences	* Try to increase your knowledge of cultures and speech communities that are different from your own. * Watch out for differing cultural interpretations. * Avoid making assumptions about, or discriminating against, people who are different from yourself * Use active listening techniques to check that your understanding is correct. * Stay calm and try to create a calm atmosphere. * Be sensitive to different social settings and the form of communication that would be most appropriate in different contexts. * Check your work with advocates who will try to represent the best interests of the people that you are working with.

FIGURE 2.23 *How to minimise barriers to communication*

In order to minimise communication barriers it will be important to learn as much as possible about others. People may have 'preferred forms of interaction'. This may include a reliance on non-verbal messages, sign language, lip-reading, use of description, slang phrases, choice of room or location for a conversation, and so on. Everyone has communication needs of some kind.

Figure 2.23 lists some ideas for minimising barriers to communication.

Valuing people as individuals

The psychologist Abraham Maslow (1970) explained human needs in terms of five levels. Barriers to communication might block human need as shown in Figure 2.24.

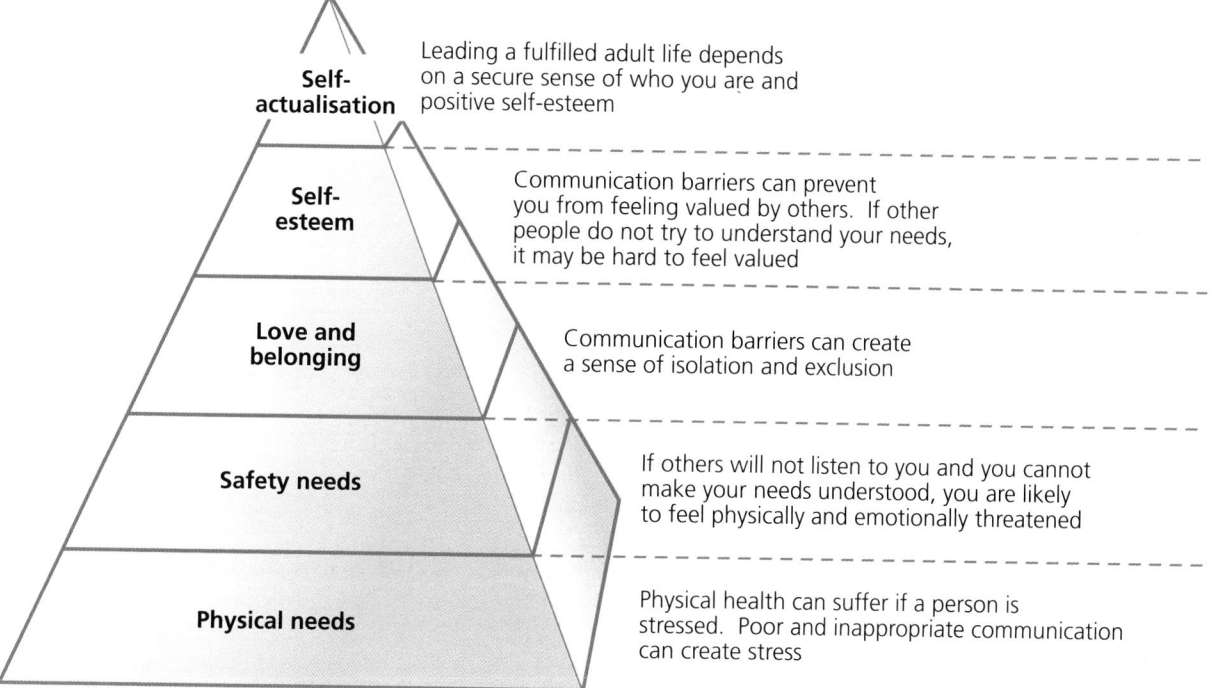

Self-actualisation Leading a fulfilled adult life depends on a secure sense of who you are and positive self-esteem

Self-esteem Communication barriers can prevent you from feeling valued by others. If other people do not try to understand your needs, it may be hard to feel valued

Love and belonging Communication barriers can create a sense of isolation and exclusion

Safety needs If others will not listen to you and you cannot make your needs understood, you are likely to feel physically and emotionally threatened

Physical needs Physical health can suffer if a person is stressed. Poor and inappropriate communication can create stress

FIGURE 2.24 *Communication barriers can damage a person's quality of life (Maslow, 1970)*

Summary

This section has explored a range of skills that include:

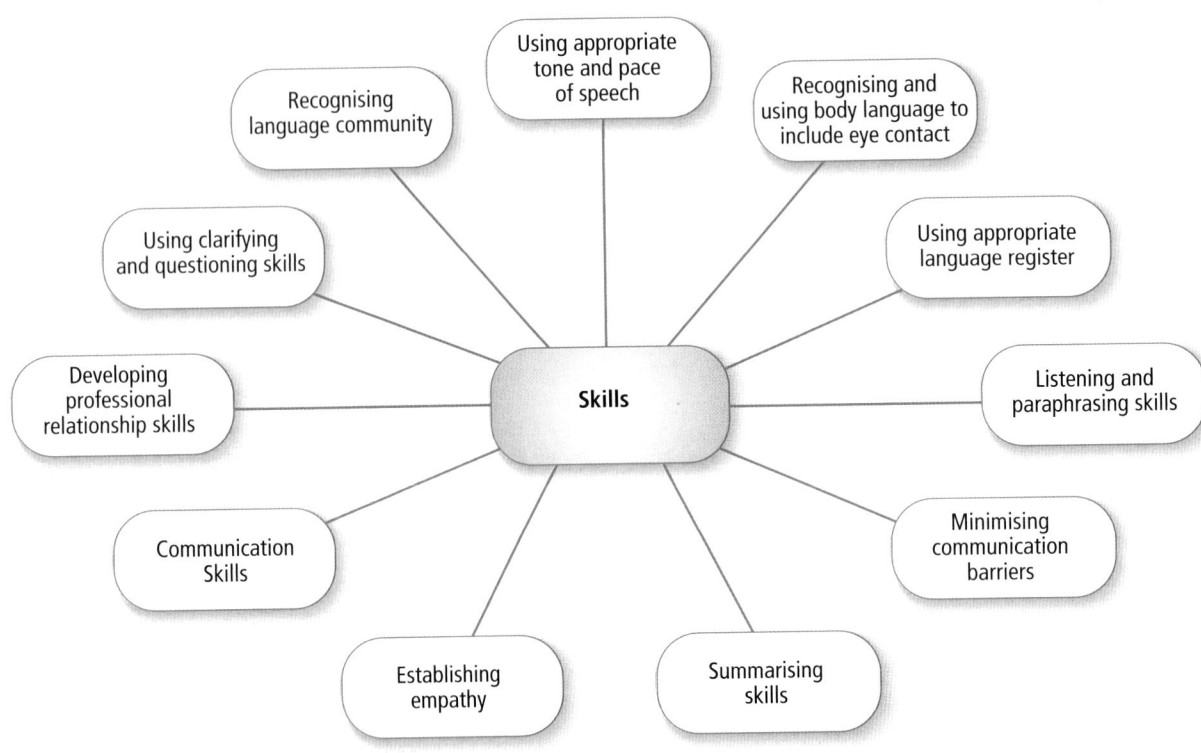

Consider this

Chloe works at a day nursery. Parents sometimes make an appointment to see the nursery and to talk to the staff in order to decide whether the nursery would be appropriate for their children. Chloe expects to meet some parents in order to show them around the nursery and talk about the work they do. These parents do not live locally, and are from different ethnic and age groups to Chloe. Both parents have well-paid professional jobs.

Using theory – can you identify?

1. What communication skills Chloe is likely to need in order to provide an appropriate welcome and to clearly explain the work of the nursery.

2. What barriers to communication Chloe should be prepared for as she takes the parents around the nursery.

Using theory – can you analyse?

How could Chloe know whether she was communicating clearly and effectively with the parents. How could Chloe know if she was successful at providing a warm and friendly welcome.

Can you evaluate – using a range of theory?

Chloe feels confident that she was highly skilled at holding the conversation with the parents. As she remembers how the conversation went, she can check what she did using the range of theory in this section. Can you imagine how you could use a range of concepts in order to judge the value of a conversation you have had.

Section 4: Theories relating to communication

The structure of interaction

When we talk to people we have to start the conversation off. Usually we start with a greeting or ask how someone is. Conversations have a beginning, a middle and an end. We have to create the right kind of atmosphere for a conversation at the beginning. We might need to help someone relax. We might need to show that we are friendly and relaxed. We then have the conversation. When we end the conversation we usually say something like 'See you soon'. When we end a conversation we have to leave the other person with the right feelings about what we have said. Figure 2.25 illustrates this structure.

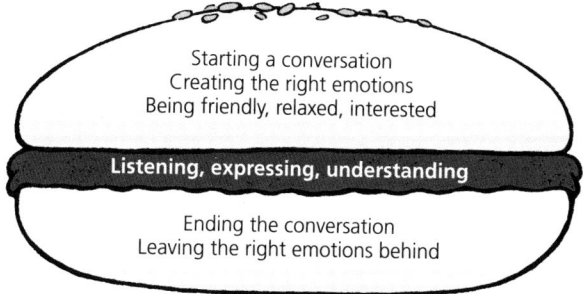

FIGURE 2.25 *The conversation sandwich: beginning, middle and end*

Listening skills and the communication cycle

When we communicate with other people we become involved in a process of expressing our own thoughts and interpreting the other person's understanding of what we are communicating. This process should usually involve the steps set out in figure 2.26.

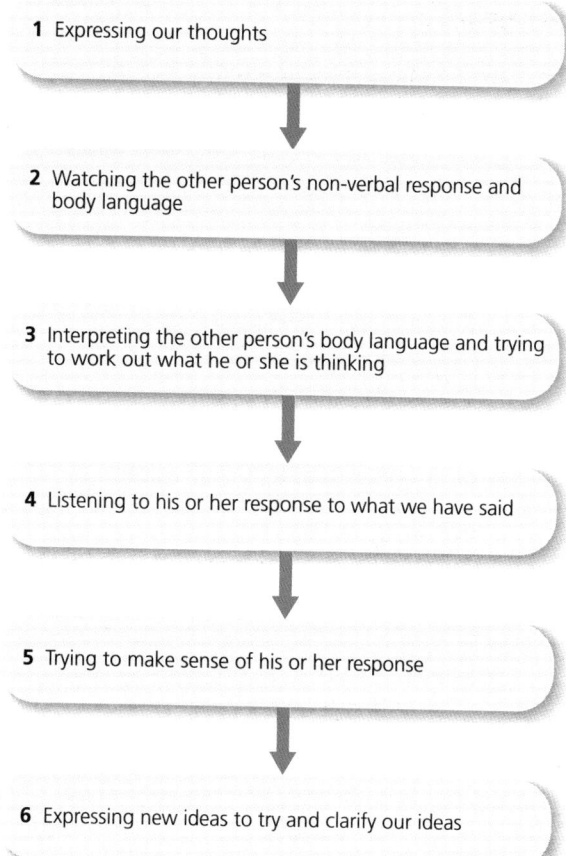

1 Expressing our thoughts

2 Watching the other person's non-verbal response and body language

3 Interpreting the other person's body language and trying to work out what he or she is thinking

4 Listening to his or her response to what we have said

5 Trying to make sense of his or her response

6 Expressing new ideas to try and clarify our ideas

FIGURE 2.27 *The process of expression and interpretation*

Communication needs to be a two-way process whereby each person attempts to understand the viewpoint of the other. The **communication cycle** requires professionals (at least) to have advanced listening skills and the ability to check their understanding of others' responses. See Figure 2.26.

Listening is not the same as hearing the sounds people make when they talk. Listening involves hearing another person's words, then thinking about what they mean, and then

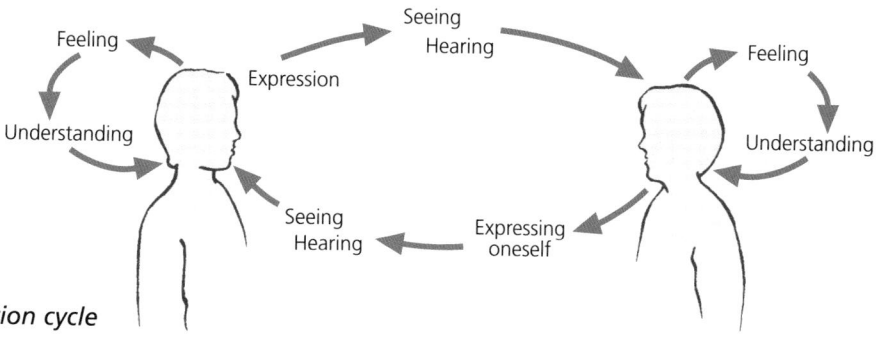

FIGURE 2.26 *The communication cycle*

thinking what to say back to the other person. Some people call this process **'active listening'**. As well as thinking carefully in remembering what someone has said, good listeners will also make sure their non-verbal communication demonstrates interest in the other person.

It is usually easier to understand people who are similar to ourselves. We can learn about different people by checking our understanding of what we have heard.

Checking our understanding involves hearing what the other person says and asking the other person questions. Another way to check our understanding is to put what a person has just said into our own words and to say this back to them. This technique is called paraphrasing; this enables us to find out whether or not we understood what another person said.

When we listen to complicated details of other people's lives, we often begin to form mental pictures based on what they are telling us. Listening skills involve checking these mental pictures to make sure that we understand correctly. It can be very difficult to remember

things accurately if we don't check how our ideas are developing.

Good listening involves thinking about what we hear while we are listening and checking our understanding as the conversation goes along. Sometimes this idea of checking our understanding is called 'reflection' because we reflect on the other person's ideas.

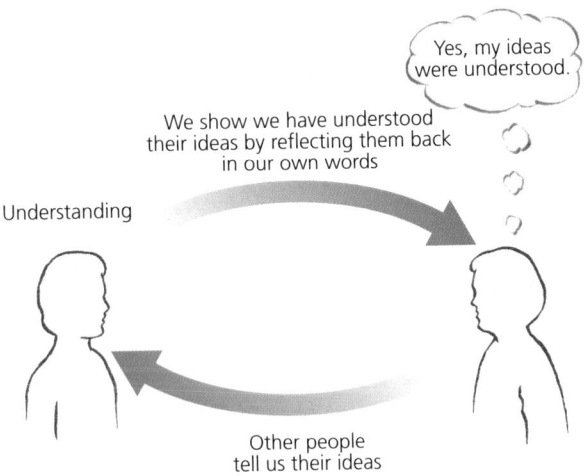

FIGURE 2.28 *Reflection is an important part of understanding*

SOLER principles

Egan (1986) argues that there are some basic **'micro skills'** that can help to create a sense of involvement or caring presence when working with another person. Egan defines these skills, as explained in Figure 2.29.

SOLER	
KEY IDEA	**EXPLANATION**
S: Face squarely	Egan states: 'In North American culture, facing another person squarely is often considered a basic posture of involvement… What is important is that the bodily orientation you adopt conveys the message that you are involved with the client. If, for any reason, facing a person squarely is too threatening, then an angled position may be called for. The point is the quality of your attention.' The key issue is that you have to face other people in a way that shows that you feel involved.
O: Keep an open posture	Egan says: 'In North American culture an open posture is generally seen as non defensive.' Crossed arms or legs might send a message that you do not feel involved with the person you're talking to. An open posture involves not crossing arms or legs (see Figure 2.18).
L: lean	Egan states: 'In North American culture a slight inclination towards a person is often interpreted as saying, I'm with you; I'm interested in you and what you have to say.' A degree of movement may help to convey interest in another person.
E: Use good eye contact	Egan argues that: 'Maintaining a good eye contact with a client is another way of saying I'm with you.' Steady but varied eye contact is associated with deep conversation within a North American cultural context.
R: Be relaxed	Egan argues that it is important not to fidget, and important to feel comfortable and relaxed with your own non-verbal behaviour.

FIGURE 2.29 *Skills that can help to create a sense of involvement or caring presence (Egan, 1986)*

Egan proposes the principles given in Figure 2.29 as guidelines to help with learning how to look like a caring person. He emphasised the importance of cultural context and that the SOLER rules should not be used rigidly. Egan states: 'These 'rules' should be followed cautiously. People differ both individually and culturally in the ways in which they show attentiveness.' The important issue is that your non-verbal behaviour comes across to another person as meaning that you are interested and involved with them.

Group structures

In everyday language, 'group' can mean a collection or set of things, so any collection of people could be counted as a group. For example, a group of people might be waiting to cross the road. They are a group in the everyday sense of the word but not in the special sense of 'group' that is often used in care work.

Think it over…

Can you remember back to the time you first joined the student group that you are doing this course with? How does it feel if you have to mix with new people? Did you feel stressed in any way if you had to work with people you had not met before?

What sort of experience is involved in communicating with new people and what does it feel like as people within a group get to know one another?

Use your memory of your own experience to interpret some of the theory below.

Working with a group is usually taken to imply that the individuals identify themselves as belonging to a group. Groups have a sense of belonging that gives the members a 'group feeling'. This could be described as a group identity.

Social scientists sometimes use the term 'primary group' and 'secondary group'. The term 'secondary group' is used when people simply have something in common with each other.

Primary groups usually share the following features:

* people know each other
* there is a 'feeling of belonging' shared by people in the group
* people have a common purpose or reason for coming together
* people share a set of beliefs or norms.

How do people get to know each other and develop a sense of belonging, common purpose and norms? Some researchers claim that there is a pattern to the way the communication develops in group formation.

Theories of group formation

Tuckman's sequential theory

The way in which people come together in a group can be understood as involving stages. Tuckman (1965) analysed around 50 studies on group development and concluded that groups generally go through a process of development that can be identified as four stages: Forming, Storming, Norming and Performing. In 1977 Tuckman and Jensen identified a fifth stage of Adjourning in order to describe the process of ending a group. Tuckman's stage (sequence) theory is one of the best known and most quoted theories. Johnson and Johnson (1997) state, 'Of all the sequential stage theories Tuckman's emphasis on forming, storming, norming, performing, and adjourning still seems the most useful and creates the most interest.'

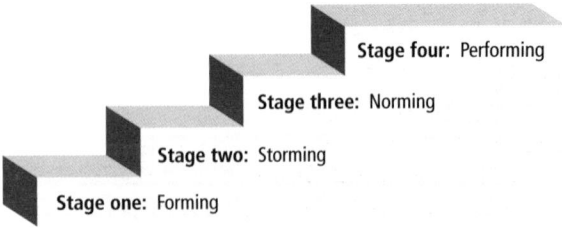

FIGURE 2.30 *Tuckman's four stages of group formation*

An outline explanation of group formation is given in Figure 2.31.

GROUP FORMATION	
Stage 1: Forming	When people first get together there is likely to be an introductory stage. People may be unsure about why they are attending a meeting. The purpose of the group may not be clear. People may have little commitment to the group and there may be no clear value system. Stereotyping and prejudice may be expressed.
Stage 2: Storming	There may be 'power struggles' within the group. Different individuals may contest each other for leadership of the group. There may be arguments about how the group should work, who should do tasks, and so on. Groups can fail at this stage and individuals can decide to drop out because they do not feel comfortable with other people in the group. Teams might split into sub-groups who refuse to communicate with each other if they become stuck in the storming stage.
Stage 3: Norming	At this stage group members develop a set of common beliefs and values. People are likely to begin to trust each other and develop clear roles. Norms are shared expectations which group members have of each other. Norms enable people to work together as a group.
Stage 4: Performing	Because people share the same values and norms the group can perform tasks effectively. People may feel that they are comfortable and belong in the group. There may be a sense of high **morale**.
Stage 5: Adjourning	The group has to conclude their activities and find an acceptable way for group members to part. The group has to complete and end the existence of the group's identity.

FIGURE 2.31 *An outline explanation of group formation (Tuckman, 1965 and 1977)*

Key concept

group norms For a group to perform effectively, group members will need to share a common system of beliefs, values or norms relevant to the purpose of the group. It may be very important to identify the extent to which a group does share a common set of beliefs and norms when observing a group or planning to run an activity.

Non-sequential theories

When people get together to create a group – such as a new student group – they may recognise Tuckman's stages described above. However, it may not always be the case that the stages are clear cut. If you were to join a group of carers or nurses working in health or social care you might not be aware of any stages. Some groups of people do not all come together at the same time. Some theorists identify general processes within a group rather than focusing on stage theories of group formation.

Bales (1970) put forward a theory of 'task and maintenance' activity within the group. Primary groups need to have a purpose; a student group, for example, might have the purpose of achieving their qualification. A group of nurses might have the purpose of providing quality health care. But working together with other people is a social activity. People cannot just concentrate on the work as if they were machines; they need to feel that they belong and that other people in the group respect them. Sometimes tensions need to be relieved with humour. Bales argued that there needs to be a balance between the practical work of achieving a task and the social needs of group members. Bales suggested that observers could understand and analyse what was happening in a group by using an **interaction analysis** of an individual member's behaviour. Such an analysis might enable the observer to understand how a group was moving between the focus on task activity and a focus on social activity. An interaction analysis involves classifying the way people behave using defined categories. Bales' categories are outlined in Figure 2.32.

PROCESSES WITHIN A GROUP	
Group task	* Gives suggestion (including taking the lead) * Gives opinion (including feelings and wishes) * Gives information (including clarifying and confirming) * Asks for information * Asks for opinion * Asks for suggestion
Group maintenance (called 'Social-emotional area' by Bales)	* Seems friendly * Dramatises * Agrees * Disagrees * Shows tension * Seems unfriendly

FIGURE 2.32 *Bales' 'task and maintenance' categories*

Think it over...

In a group of five or six people, take four matchsticks each and agree on a topic for group discussion. Next, agree the following rules for the discussion.

* Only one person may speak at a time.
* Whenever that person speaks, he or she must place a matchstick on the floor.
* When people run out of matchsticks they cannot say anything.
* No one may say anything unless others have finished.
* Non-verbal communication is allowed.
* People should not speak for more than one minute.

This exercise should emphasise the importance of group maintenance activity. The 'match stick game' can make people very focused on the task to the exclusion of much of the social maintenance activity. So being in the group might make you feel awkward or tense.

	1	2	3	4	5	6	7	8	9	10
Group task										
Starting discussion										
Giving information										
Asking for information										
Clarifying discussion										
Summarising discussion										
Group maintenance										
Humour										
Expressing group feelings										
Including others										
Being supportive										

FIGURE 2.33 *Grid to categorise the task and maintenance behaviours occurring in groups*

Using categories can be a useful way of gaining an insight into how an individual is influencing the work and the emotional maintenance or feeling involved in group communication. It is possible to design a grid that can be used 'minute by minute' to try to categorise the task and maintenance behaviours occurring in groups. An example is suggested in Figure 2.33.

Burnard's group dynamics

Burnard (1996) identifies the importance of Tuckman's theory of stages to explain group formation, but then points out the importance of identifying some of the processes that can happen as groups work together. A summary of the categories that Burnard identifies is set out in Figure 2.34.

Thompson's theory of defensive versus supportive communication

Thompson (1986) identified a range of issues that may result in people feeling that they are being attacked or being supported. These issues may be equally important in one-to-one communication, as in group settings. The value in exploring this theory is that it provides another way of monitoring the effect we may be having on others when we try to communicate. See Figure 2.35.

Think it over...

Do you ever watch 'reality TV', i.e. programmes in which a group of people are observed over a period of time? The people who are observed usually have to work with one another in order to perform certain tasks. Next time you watch such a programme, see if you can spot any of the group dynamics listed in Figure 2.34.

GROUP DYNAMIC	EXPLANATION
Pairing	Sometimes two people will choose to work together and ignore other members of the group. Sometimes people conduct a discussion with just one other person and other people are left out. These behaviours can disrupt a group and may create problems for group cohesion (feeling of belonging).
Scapegoating	A 'scapegoat' is someone who is 'picked-on' or 'attacked' by other people. When people feel threatened or unhappy they may 'take it out' on someone who appears to be an appropriate target. Again, this behaviour will disrupt group cohesion and will need to be challenged.
Projecting	Projecting occurs when a person places his or her own feelings on to the whole group. To quote Burnard's example, a person who is feeling anxious might say 'this is a very tense group' even though everyone else is relaxed. Another kind of projection occurs when the group projects their emotions onto an issue. Burnard describes an example of this as 'having a group moan' whereby the group describes how awful its problems are, but the issues are emotional rather than real.
Forming a 'league of gentlemen'	This term is used to describe a sub-group of 'hostile and often sarcastic' people 'whose aim is to make life in the group difficult'. It is important to understand this term as a metaphor; both men and women can form sub-groups that seek to wreck group cohesion and they are unlikely to be 'gentle'. Burnard points out that it is important to deal with such a sub-group as soon as possible.
Wrecking	This is when an individual person attempts to sabotage the group. Sometimes when people feel that they are being forced to attend a meeting they may 'take their emotions out' on the group.
Taking flight	When people's emotions create threat and stress, group members and sometimes the whole group try to avoid the issues. People may become silent or try to avoid the topic of discussion.
Shutting down	When individuals feel frightened they may become silent and withdraw.
Rescuing	Rescuing is where one or more members of the group always protects an individual. This can mean that the rescued individual does not need to take responsibility for his or her work within the group. Although 'rescuing' sounds caring, constant protection can disrupt group cohesion.
Introducing a hidden agenda	Groups usually have tasks to achieve as Bales identified. Many formal groups literally have a written agenda that defines the tasks of the meeting. A 'hidden agenda' may arise because of other issues of concern. For instance, people may have rivalries or emotional needs. This hidden agenda may strongly influence what happens in the group, although it may not be understandable to an observer.

FIGURE 2.34 *A summary of Burnard's categories*

ISSUE	EXPLANATION
Evaluation versus description	Thompson points out the importance of not making judgmental or evaluative comments about other people. If we simply stick to descriptive information then we are less likely to make other people feel that they are being attacked.
Control versus problem orientation	It is important not to manipulate and control other people if we wish to be supportive. Thompson recommends taking a problem-solving approach to encourage discussion amongst equals.
Strategy versus spontaneity	Sometimes people have prepared things that they wish to say. They use communication in order to make a speech. Thompson points out that when people follow their own strategy like this, then they are less likely to listen and use an appropriate communication cycle. Responding to other people and being spontaneous is a more supportive way of communicating.
Certainty versus provisionalism	Some people come across as being rigid and fixed in their ideas. These people are certain that they are right about issues. This kind of certainty will create defensiveness in other people. In order to be supportive it is important to appear open to other people's ideas. Thompson calls this openness 'provisionalism'.
Superiority and neutrality versus empathy	People who are fixed and rigid, often come across as being superior. Neutrality means a lack of concern for others. Thompson stressed the importance of empathy and trying to understand others as a key component of being supportive.

FIGURE 2.35 *Thompson's theory of defensive versus supportive communication*

Think it over...

One idea for studying group behaviour is to use the fish bowl method of observation.

The people in the middle are being watched; they probably feel like goldfish in a bowl. They will need to trust you if the observation is going to work. They discuss something important, while those outside only listen and watch. What

will you monitor? You might like to watch things such as:

* non-verbal messages, such as eye contact

* task behaviour – keeping people focused on the discussion

* maintenance behaviour – maintaining an appropriate emotional atmosphere in the group

* supportive behaviour.

After five minutes or so of listening and watching, the group should stop and people should share their ideas about what happened. Did the people in the group remember what the people outside reported? After discussing the exercise, the group on the inside of the goldfish bowl should change places with the observers.

Summary

This section has covered the following theories:

THEORY	DESCRIPTION
The structure of interaction	Interaction involves the stages of introduction, main content and winding down (beginning, middle and end)
The communication cycle	Communication involves reflection on the meaning of messages. You need to communicate that you have understood the content of another person's communication
Egan's theory of SOLER (1986)	A specific theory of non-verbal behaviour to communicate supportiveness
Group dynamics	Theories that explain people's behaviour within groups: Burnard (1996), Thompson (1986), Bales (1970) were explored
Group formation theories	Theories that explain how groups go through stages: Tuckman (1965) was described.

Consider this

Imagine you witnessed the following conversation taking place among a group of six early years workers.

Group member 1: I think it's our job to encourage the children to become as independent as possible; that's why I encourage them to play with the apparatus.

Group member 2: [angry tone] Well that's all right but safety comes first. I don't like to see too many children using the equipment at the same time. There will be an accident you know.

Group member 1: Children know what they can cope with; they will be all right.

Group member 2: So you think you know everything do you?

Group member 1: No, all I'm saying is that we can trust children more. It is important not to be over-controlling.

Group member 2: I think you want to put them at risk.

Group member 1: What do other people think?

Response of other four members:
long silence then one person says: 'don't know'.

There is not enough information here to be certain of what is happening, but there is enough information to guess at the basic assumptions that might be informing the group's behaviour. Interpret this interaction in terms of group dynamic theory. If this group is just getting together, what stage might they be at? Use any of the theories in this section.

Using theory – can you identify?
The basic assumptions associated with Bion's theory that might be operating in this group.

Using theory – can you analyse?
Some possible explanations for what is going on, using a range of theory on group dynamics.

Using theory – can you evaluate?
Can you explain a range of different interpretations of what is happening in this group? Can you use different theories of group formation and group dynamics in order to suggest a range of explanations? What is your preferred explanation, and why?

Section 5: Interaction with the service user

A systematic approach

Thompson (1996) emphasises the importance of 'being systematic' as an important skill in care work. Thompson summarises systematic practice as knowing:

1. What are you trying to achieve?
2. How are you going to achieve it?
3. How will you know when you have achieved it?

Thompson argues that vague, unfocused care work can result in poor quality care and also in stress for the care worker. Some benefits of planned, systematic work based on Thompson's analysis are shown in Figure 2.36.

For these reasons it is important to be able to imagine how you will communicate with service users before you start your work. It will be important to use your imagination in order to explain what you are hoping to achieve, what skills you will use and how you will be able to recognise whether or not you have been successful.

Applying Thompson's systematic practice:

1. In terms of studying your own interaction you might, for example, have the aim of establishing a degree of trust, with a service user.
2. You would not be able to plan a mechanical strategy to produce trust. Trust is an emotional feeling that might grow and develop within a caring relationship. But you could list some of the skills that you would be using in your communication work that would contribute to the development of a caring relationship.
3. You would have to have an understanding of relationships and trust in order to be able to explain the degree to which you have established a trusting relationship. You should use theory during the planning stage of your work in order to identify how you would know if you have achieved a trusting relationship.

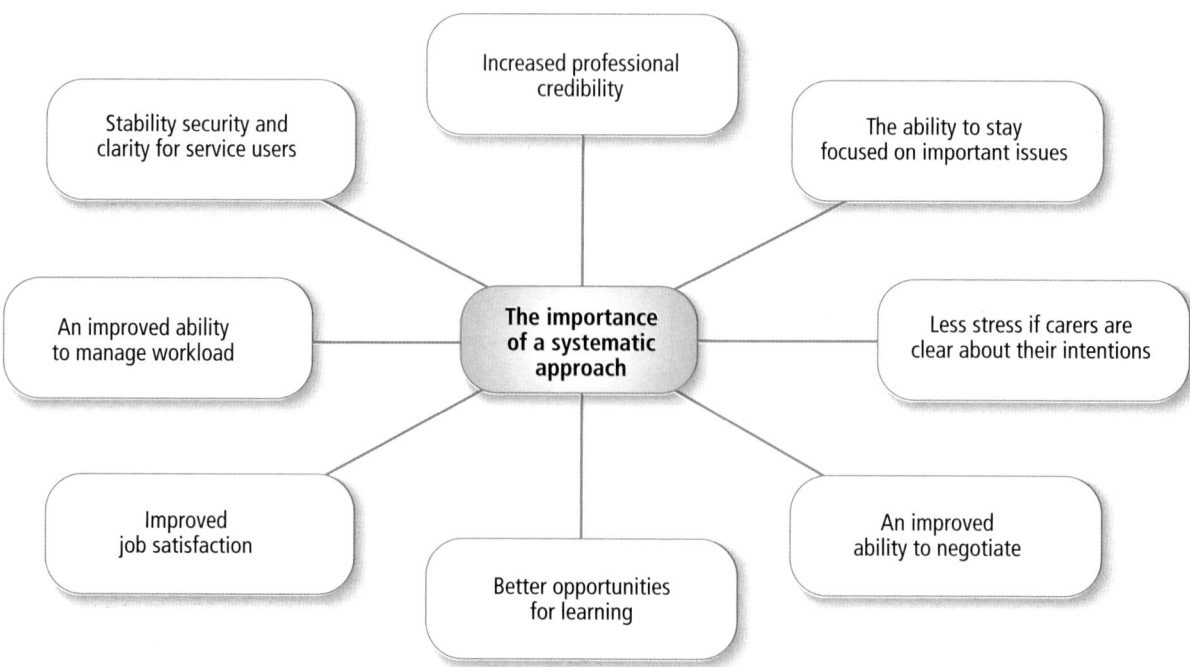

FIGURE 2.36 *Some benefits of planned, systematic work, based on Thompson's analysis (1996)*

Evaluating the effectiveness of an interaction

Planning

Your report must include records of your plans for interaction. The work that you plan may be simple. It could be that you plan just to talk to somebody about their likes and dislikes on a menu. It will be important to keep notes of how you prepared for your communication work. You will probably need to discuss your plans with a tutor and work out the aims and objectives you have for the practical work. It is vital that you do discuss your plans with a tutor, and/or with someone in the care setting before you undertake any practical communication work.

Detailed plans

Your plans should include the elements identified in Figure 2 .37.

PLANS FOR INTERACTION	
Introduction	You need to plan how you will start the interaction, or in other words what your introduction will involve
Main content	You need to think through the kind of content that the interaction is likely to involve.
Discussion	You need to be prepared to discuss issues that may arise during your interaction.
Reflection and winding up	You need to think through possible ways of finishing your interaction that will result in a positive emotional feeling at the conclusion of the work. You may also need to summarise issues at the end of the interaction in order to do this. Your summary will involve reflecting on the content of the interaction.

FIGURE 2.37 *Elements of a plan for your interaction*

Aims

Any communication work you do should aim to improve the quality of life for the people you are communicating with. Whatever happens, your communication work must not exploit others or make them more vulnerable. Following Thompson's (1996) advice it will be important to be systematic and to produce statements of your aims before you undertake any practical work. These statements should be checked with a tutor before the work is undertaken.

Your aims should also clarify whether the purpose of the interaction involved giving information, asking for information or exchanging ideas and opinions, perhaps as part of your supportive relationship-building work.

Skills

In order to evaluate your skills it will be important to identify the skills that you used during your communication work. The grid below might provide one way of starting to identify the quality of your verbal and non-verbal skills.

Communication rating scale:
How good were different aspects of non-verbal communication?

Eye contact	1	2	3	4	5
Facial expression	1	2	3	4	5
Angle of head	1	2	3	4	5
Tone of voice	1	2	3	4	5
Body language: hands and arms	1	2	3	4	5
Gestures	1	2	3	4	5
Posture	1	2	3	4	5
Muscle tension	1	2	3	4	5
Touch	1	2	3	4	5
Proximity	1	2	3	4	5

How to rate behaviour:

Place a circle around the number that fits your observation.

1 means: very effective and appropriate use of a skill.

2 means: some appropriate use of the skill.

3 means: the skill was not demonstrated or it does not seem appropriate to comment on the area.

4 means: some slightly ineffective or inappropriate behaviour in relation to the area.

5 means: very inappropriate or ineffective behaviour in relation to the area.

How good were verbal communication and listening skills?

Appropriate language: Speech community and register	1	2	3	4	5
Encouraging others to talk	1	2	3	4	5
Listening skill: Reflecting back what others have said	1	2	3	4	5
Clarifying: use of appropriate questions	1	2	3	4	5
Clarifying: use of prompts	1	2	3	4	5
Summarising	1	2	3	4	5
Paraphrasing	1	2	3	4	5
Pace of conversation	1	2	3	4	5
Tone of voice	1	2	3	4	5
Empathising	1	2	3	4	5

How to rate:

Place a circle around the number that fits your observation. Use the same rating as for non-verbal communication above.

This grid may help you to analyse and provide examples of your communication skills. In order to achieve the highest marks your report will need to go beyond a description of skills and you will need to provide comparisons and contrasts between different interactions. You will also need to explain some of the theory of that helps you to understand what is happening as you interact with others.

The barriers to communication grid
Barriers

In the environment

Lighting	1	2	3	4	5
Noise levels	1	2	3	4	5
Physical barriers to communication	1	2	3	4	5

Language differences

Appropriate use of language: (terminology and level of formality)	1	2	3	4	5
Your skills with different languages	1	2	3	4	5
Your skills with non-verbal communication	1	2	3	4	5
Availability of interpreters	1	2	3	4	5

Avoidance of assumptions/valuing diversity	1	2	3	4	5

Emotional barriers

Stress levels and tiredness	1	2	3	4	5
Being stressed by the emotional needs of others	1	2	3	4	5

Cultural barriers

Inappropriate assumptions made about others	1	2	3	4	5
Labelling or stereotyping present	1	2	3	4	5

Interpersonal skills

Degree of supportive non-verbal behaviour	1	2	3	4	5
Degree of supportive verbal behaviour	1	2	3	4	5
Appropriate use of listening skills	1	2	3	4	5
Appropriate maintenance of confidentiality	1	2	3	4	5

Rating Scale:

1 means: Good – there are no barriers.
2 means: Quite good – few barriers.
3 means: Not possible to decide or not applicable.
4 means: Poor – barriers identified.
5 means: Very poor – major barriers to communication.

Once you have identified potential barriers you need to research other people's perception of these issues. You might discuss your analysis of your interaction with a tutor or colleague. If possible, it would be ideal to discuss your work with a member of staff in the care setting where your interactions took place.

The views of service users are very important, and it might be possible for you to ask service users about issues such as the clarity of what you said, and whether or not there were any environmental barriers. It will be important to plan any questioning work carefully and to check your plans with a tutor before undertaking any research.

In order to achieve the highest marks you will need to take the initiative in obtaining feedback from others. You should analyse why people have responded in the way that they have. You will need to gain information from different sources and to provide an analysis of the issues you have identified.

Evaluation of your report

You must provide an evaluation of how well your interactions went and draw conclusions from the evidence you were able to gather. To achieve the highest marks you will need to evidence an in-depth evaluation of your own performance, identifying realistic and informed recommendations for improvement.

To achieve a good mark you will need to be able to show that you have fully understood what took place during your interactions and what impact you had on others. You will need to be able to give reasons for any conclusions you make and these conclusions will need to be supported with evidence.

Perspectives – getting feedback

You must evaluate the effectiveness of your interaction from the perspective of the service user, your own perspective, and the perspective of your assessor and/or your peers.

FIGURE 2.38 *Use three different perspectives to evaluate the effectiveness of your work*

Your own perspective

You should have been clear about your perspective before you started the work. Your aims might have involved clearly communicating information and will almost certainly have involved some aspect of relationship work – Thompson (1986). Issues to do with supportiveness, establishing a relationship, self disclosure and empathy may be important issues to consider from your own perspective.

The service user's perspective

The service user's perspective will be much harder to discover. You will have observed the response(s) to your communication. You will have observed any non-verbal behaviour, and you will probably have some idea whether the service user appeared to be comfortable, or whether he or she enjoyed interacting with you. Your observations will provide very important evidence, and you should record the non-verbal feedback you received from service users in order to help you evaluate your interaction.

The other main way you can get information and evidence is to ask service users what they experienced. Asking people what they thought of a conversation is not straightforward. People can be easily embarrassed when asked to give feedback and often avoid giving a detailed analysis by saying things like, 'Oh it was very good!' The quality of the information you obtain will be influenced by the quality of the questions that you ask. You must also be careful not to ask questions in a way that might make service users feel that they are being manipulated or exploited. For these reasons, it is important that you should check your plans for any questions with a tutor before you ask for feedback.

Your assessor's perspective

Other students can often give useful feedback on your work, so you may receive peer assessment or feedback to help you develop your skills. Assessors will have a range of questions that may include:

* Were your aims appropriate?
* Did you work within an appropriate value system for care work?
* How far did you succeed in meeting your aims?
* Did you establish an appropriate professional, supportive and/or empathetic relationship with the person or people you worked with?
* Did you communicate clearly? Were you aware of factors that may enhance, inhibit, or create barriers to communication?

* How effectively did you use theory in order to analyse what happened?

Try to guess what your assessor will be looking for, or better still, ask for this information directly.

The structure of an evaluation – why evaluation is important

Interpreting and explaining your interaction with others will not be a simple task. People have complex feelings and thoughts and each person is unique. Because people are different from one another, care work involves constant learning. If people were not complicated – if they were all the same – then it would only be necessary to learn a few simple rules and procedures in order to work effectively. It is the diversity and complexity of service users that makes the work interesting, as well as complicated to evaluate. Evaluation involves applying theory to practice.

Emotions and working with people

The great thing about working with people is that they are all so different and each person provides a new learning situation. Not evaluating your own performance saves emotional energy, but it can lead to a feeling that care work is boring. Emotions connected with boredom can make us want to give up and withdraw. Evaluation is important because it can help us to avoid thinking of service users as 'all the same' and the emotional feeling of boredom that can go with this.

Working with people creates emotional feelings. Working with interesting, attractive or kind people may make us feel good. But many service users will be worried or even depressed or upset; as such, they may not always be rewarding to work with. Our first emotional reaction may be to want to avoid them. When we have to work with a difficult child it is only natural to feel 'I don't want to. I'd rather do something else.'

If we are to work in a professional way then we have to be sure that we don't follow the emotional urge to withdraw, but instead we have to find ways of coping. Thinking a situation through can help us to solve problems. When

people have a problem to solve they sometimes go through a process like the one shown in Figure 2.39.

A theory of reflection and problem solving

Evaluation is sometimes understood as a process of actively **reflecting** on and developing our thoughts. Simply having experiences or simply reading about theories will not be enough on their own to develop the personal knowledge needed to guide skilled care work.

Kurt Lewin (as explained in Kolb, 1984) originally developed a theory of practical learning that could be used to improve problem-solving skills. Lewin's model argued that learning started with the concrete, practical experience that a carer might have, such as undertaking communication work. If workers carefully thought about their experiences they would be able to form ideas and generalisations that might help them to explain their experiences. The next step of the process would be to test the new ideas out in practice. Experimenting with new ideas would lead to new experiences.

David Kolb (1984) adapted Lewin's approach to problem solving and argued that effective learning depended on a '**learning cycle**' or a four-stage process, which might be summarised as in Figure 2.39.

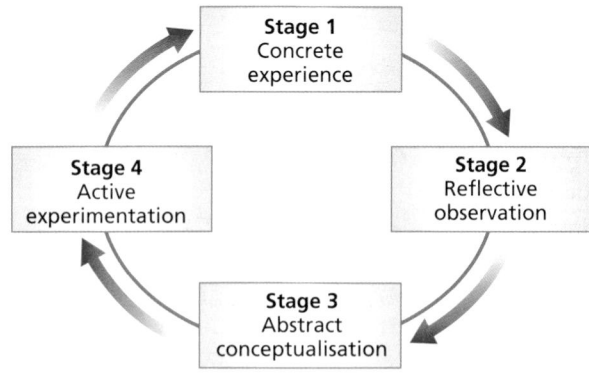

FIGURE 2.39 *Kolb's learning cycle: a four-stage process (1984)*

An example of this learning process might work something like the study opposite:

Imagine that you are working with a man with learning difficulty. It is the first time you have met him and you offer him a drink at lunchtime. You place a glass of orange squash in front of him. He immediately pushes the glass away and communicates with a facial expression that you assume means he is angry.

Within Kolb's four-stage learning cycle you have had a concrete experience.

STAGE 1

Stage 1 of the learning cycle about the individual needs of this service user is that he has rejected your provision of orange squash and communicated that he is angry. But why has he reacted this way?

STAGE 2

Stage 2 involves thinking through some possible reasons for the person's reaction. Perhaps he does not like orange squash? Perhaps he does not like the way you put it in front of him? Perhaps he does not like to take a drink with his meal? Could it be an issue to do with status? For example, could a cold drink symbolise being treated as a child for this individual? Does he see adult status as defined by having a hot drink? Reflection on the non-verbal behaviour of the service user may provide a range of starting points for interpreting his actions.

STAGE 3

Stage 3 involves trying to make sense of our reflections. What do we know about different cultural interpretations of non-verbal behaviour? What are the chances that the way we positioned ourselves when we placed the drink in front of the person have been construed as an attempt to control or dominate him? We did not intend to send this message, but the service user may have interpreted our behaviour as being unpleasant. The more we know about communication the more in-depth we can analyse the service user's reaction. We need to think through the most likely explanation for the service user's behaviour using everything we know about people.

STAGE 4

Stage 4 involves 'experimenting' or checking out ideas and assumptions that we may have made. The worker might attempt to modify his or her non-verbal behaviour to look supportive; the worker might show the service user a china cup and saucer to indicate the question, 'Is this what you would like?' If the service user responded with a positive non-verbal response then the worker would have been around the four stages of the cycle and would have solved the problem in a way which valued the individuality and diversity of the person he or she is working with.

Learning from experience

In real-life, workers might expect to have to go round this 'learning cycle' a number of times before they may correctly understand and interpret a service user's needs. (See Figure 2.40).

The important thing is to not just let things happen to you, but to think about your experiences and learn from them. It is easy to forget experiences if we don't think about them and discuss them.

Think about the reactions you get from service users. Try to imagine how they see you. What does a person's non-verbal behaviour toward you mean? What do service users say to you? How effective is your communication at meeting

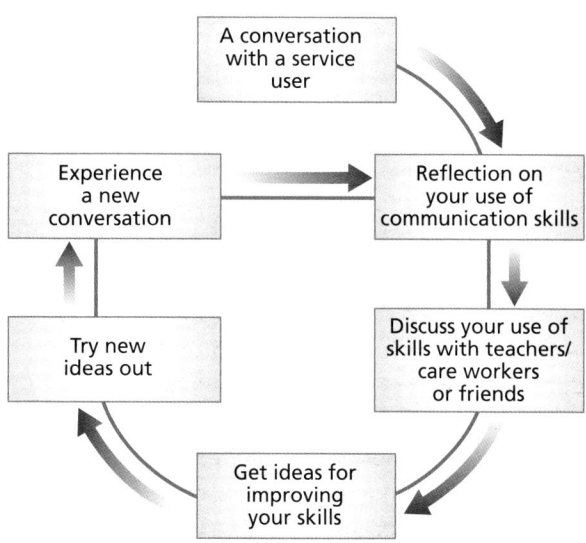

FIGURE 2.40 *The learning cycle in practice*

Reflection	Your evaluation should explain how you have thought things through and talked things through with other people, in order to reflect and develop your own understanding of the quality of your skills. Reflection is the second stage in Kolb's theory (1984).
Analysis	You must use theory to analyse the quality of your interaction. This is the third stage of the cycle identified by Kolb. Being able to explain issues using theory enables us to develop a deeper understanding of our experience.
Conclusions	You need to sum up what you have learned from reflection and from analysing your experience using theory. Your conclusions will emphasise the key things that you have learned.
Realistic improvements	The fourth stage in Kolb's theory is to be able to think of new ideas. Your reflection, analysis and conclusions should lead you to be able to suggest new ideas for developing and improving your interaction with service users. You could use Kolb's 'learning cycle' as a theory to explain how you intend to learn and develop your interaction skills.

FIGURE 2.41 *The four parts of an evaluation*

people's needs, including needs to belong and needs for self-esteem?

It is very difficult to check our own thoughts alone. A good way to check assumptions is to discuss practice with tutors or workplace supervisors. Skilled care workers may be able to help us question assumptions in our thinking and see new possibilities. If we get new ideas then they can be tried out in practice to see if they are right.

Summary

* It is important to be systematic and to plan and check your work before you undertake any practical interaction with service users.

* You must evaluate the effectiveness of your interactions from the perspective of the service user, your own perspective, and the perspective of assessors.

* Evaluation is an important skill because it can help us to make sense of our feelings, help us to avoid fixed thinking and develop a problem-solving attitude.

* The 'Kolb learning cycle' provides a theory for explaining the importance of reflection, analysis and ideas for improvement

* Your evaluation must include an explanation of your reflection, analysis, conclusions and realistic improvements.

Consider this

Caitlin undertook some conversational work with a 92-year-old woman. Caitlin reported that she spent over an hour listening and asking questions about the woman's past. Caitlin said 'I don't know where the time went. I guess I lost track of time. I was so interested.' The service user said she was very pleased to have a chance to talk about her life and that she thoroughly enjoyed talking to Caitlin.

Caitlin's aims included that of establishing a good relationship – perhaps involving empathy, using the communication cycle effectively and also being well organised.

Using theory – can you identify?
Any evidence that Caitlin may have established a good working relationship in this interaction.

Anything that might suggest effective use of the communication cycle.

Can you analyse – issues using theory?
Why might the conversation have become so enjoyable for both the people involved.

Can you evaluate – using theory?
If you were providing assessment feedback to Caitlin how would you balance the significance of losing track of time? Caitlin spent longer than she intended to in conversation, but she did establish a good relationship and perhaps a degree of empathy. How would you judge the relative importance of these issues.

UNIT 2 ASSESSMENT

How you will be assessed

You must produce evidence for the four assessment objectives shown below. Your report must evidence the following.

ASSESSMENT OBJECTIVE	DETAILS
AO1 An understanding of the different types of communication used in care settings and of the factors that support and inhibit communication, giving examples.	In order to achieve the highest marks you will need to show a comprehensive in-depth understanding of different kinds of communication and of the range of factors that support or inhibit communication.
AO2 An explanation of how care workers use four different communication skills in the care setting to value service users, giving examples.	In order to achieve the highest marks you will need to produce an in-depth analysis of how care workers apply different communication skills. You will need to provide examples of how care workers use skills in order to value others as individuals. Although you must clearly identify four skills it may be appropriate to discuss theories such as Thompson's theory of supportiveness (1986) when analysing skills.
AO3 Relevant research and analysis of two theories that provide guidance about the effects of communication on service users and/or care workers	In order to achieve the highest marks you should undertake research, using a range of sources, such as interviewing care workers, observing communication in care settings, reading, and researching information on Internet. Your analysis must provide guidance about the way in which two theories inform understanding of communication with service users.
AO4 The production of records to show the effectiveness of your communication skills in an interaction with an individual service user/care worker or a small group of service users/care workers, evaluating your own performance and making recommendations for improvements.	To achieve the highest marks your report must provide an in-depth evaluation of your own performance, making realistic and informed recommendations improvement.

(See Section 2.5 for more ideas on producing these records.)

References

Altman, I and Taylor, D. A. (1973) *Social Penetration: The Development of Interpersonal Relationships* (New York: Holt, Rinehart & Winston)

Bales, R. (1970) *Personality and Interpersonal Behaviour* (New York: Holt, Rinehart & Winston)

Benson, J. F. (2001) *Working more creatively with groups* 2nd edition (London & New York: Routledge)

Bion, W. R. (1961) *Experiences in Groups and Other Papers* (London: Tavistock Publications)

Bostrom, R. N. (1997) *The process of listening* in Hargie, O.D.W. (ed.) *The Handbook of Communication Skills* (2nd edition) (London and New York: Routledge)

Burnard, P. (1996) *Acquiring Interpersonal Skills* (2nd edition) (London: Chapman & Hall)

Burnard, P. and Morrison, P. (1997) *Caring and Communicating: Interpersonal Relationships in Nursing* (Basingstoke and London: Palgrave)

Egan, G. (1986) *The Skilled Helper* (Monterey, California: Brooks/Cole Publishing Company)

Garland, J., Jones, H. and Kolodny, K. (1965) *A model for stages in the development of social work groups*, in Bernstein, S. (ed) *Explorations in Group work* (London: Bookstall)

Hargie, C.T.C. and Tourish, D. (1997) *Relational Communication* in Hargie, O.D.W. (ed.) *The Handbook of Communication Skills* (2nd edition) (London and New York: Routledge)

Hayman, M. (1998) A *Protocol for People with Hearing Impairment* Nursing Times, October 28, Volume 94, No. 43.

Johnson D. and Johnson F. (1997) *Joining together: group theory and group skills* (6th edition) (Boston: Allyn & Bacon)

Kolb, D. (1984) *Experiential Learning: Experience as the Source of Learning and Development* (New Jersey: Prentice Hall)

Maslow, A. H. (1970) *Motivation and Personality* (2nd edition) (New York: Harper & Row)

Morgan, H. and Thomas, K. (1996) *A Psychodynamic Perspective on Group Process* in: Wetherell, M. (ed. *Identities, Groups and Social Issues* (London: Sage & Open University)

Morrison, P. and Burnard, P. (1997) *Caring and Communicating* (Basingstoke and London: Macmillan Press Ltd)

Pease, A. (1997) *Body Language* (London: Sheldon Press)

Schutz, W. (1979) *Profound Simplicity* (London: Turnstone Books)

Thompson, N. (1996) *People Skills* (Basingstoke and London: Macmillan)

Thompson, N. (2001) *Anti-Discriminatory Practice* 2nd edition (Basingstoke and London: Macmillan)

Thompson, T., L. (1986) *Communication for Health Professionals* (New York: Harper & Row)

Tuckman, B. (1965) *Development Sequence in Small Groups,* in Psychological Bulletin, Vol 63, No 6.

Tuckman, B. and Jensen, M. (1977) 'Stages of Small Group Development Revisited', *Group and Organisational Studies,* vol. 2, pp 419–27

Useful websites

www.britishdeafassociation.org.uk
More about British Sign Language (BSL) can be found at this website

www.british-sign.co.uk
Details of a sign and the finger spelling alphabet are outlined on this website

www.royaldeaf.org.uk
More information on special methods and alternative language methods are described here

www.makaton.org
Makaton is a language system that uses speech, signs and symbols

www.brailleplus.net
Braille is a communication system of raised marks that can be felt with the fingers and interpreted; it is used by people who cannot see print.

UNIT 3

Promoting Good Health

This unit covers the following sections:

3.1   Concepts and models of health and well-being

3.2   Preventative measures and job-roles

3.3   Factors affecting health and well-being

3.4   Health promotion

Introduction

This unit investigates the range of lifestyle choices and societal factors which influence health and well-being. You will investigate the ways in which ill health can be prevented in care settings and the health-promotion methods that are used by health-and-social-care practitioners. This unit has links with Unit 1: 'Promoting Quality Care'; Unit 7: 'Health as a Lifestyle Choice'; Unit 8: 'Complementary Therapies'; Unit 10: 'Care Practice and Provision'; and Unit 14: 'Mental Health Issues'.

In this unit you will learn about differing views and models of health and how these influence health-promotion activity, and key government policy initiatives to promote health. This unit also looks at health education, health protection and health promotion, and key people in the local community involved in health promotion. The range of factors affecting health and well-being including people's attitudes, lifestyle choices, social factors, environment, income and disability are discussed, along with varying approaches to health promotion and how to go about planning and carrying out a campaign.

The background to this unit is best summed up by the following passages from the recent government white paper *Choosing Health – Making Healthy Choices Easier* (DOH, 2004):

'There have been big improvements in health and life expectancy over the last century. On the most basic measure, people are living longer than ever before.

Boys born in 2004 can expect to live to the age of 76, compared with a life expectancy of 45 in 1900, and girls to 80, compared with 50 in 1900. A child born today is likely to live $9\frac{1}{2}$ years longer than a child born when the NHS was established in 1948.

Future progress on this dramatic scale cannot be taken for granted. England faces new challenges to ensure that as a society we continue to benefit from longer and healthier lives. Whilst the threat of childhood death from illness is falling and the big infectious killer diseases of the last century have been eradicated or largely controlled, the relative proportion of deaths from cancers, coronary heart disease (CHD) and stroke has risen. They now account for around two-thirds of all deaths. Cancer, stroke and heart disease not only kill, but are also major causes of ill health, preventing people from living their lives to the full and causing avoidable disability, pain and anxiety. And there are some worrying pointers for our future health:

* Smoking remains the single biggest preventable cause of ill health and there are still over 10 million smokers in the country.

* As many as one in 10 sexually active young women may be infected with chlamydia, which can cause infertility.

* Surveys carried out since 1974 show an increase in the mental health problems experienced by young people.

* Suicide remains the commonest cause of death in men under 35.

* Around one-third of all attendances to hospital Accident and Emergency departments are estimated to be alcohol related.'

Therefore, the government recognised that whilst we now live longer, and the major causes of premature death of the last century are largely under control, the same cannot be said for today's main killers. It is how we tackle these diseases of the modern day that is explored in this unit.

Section 1: Concepts and models of health and well-being

In this section you will explore the factors that can affect a person's health; the various concepts of health and ill health, which are used to try and understand how health is created and maintained; and the types of policy and strategy that governments have adopted to address these factors. The starting point is to consider what is important for your own health using this activity below:

Think it over...

		1	2	3
What does being healthy mean to you? In Column 1, tick any statements which seem to you to be important aspects of your health. In Column 2, tick the six statements which are the most important aspects of being healthy to you. In Column 3, rank these six in order of importance – put '1' by the most important, '2' by the next most important , and so on, down to '6'.				
1.	Enjoying being with my family and friends			
2.	Living to be a ripe old age			
3.	Feeling happy most of the time			
4.	Being able to run when I need to (e.g. for a bus) without getting out of breath			
5.	Having a job			
6.	Taking part in lots of sport			
7.	Being able to get down to making decisions			
8.	Hardly ever taking tablets or medicines			
9.	Being the ideal weight for my height			
10.	Feeling at peace with myself			
11.	Never smoking			
12.	Having clear skin, bright eyes and shiny hair			
13.	Never suffering from anything more serious than a mild cold, flu or stomach upset			
14.	Not getting things confused or out of proportion –- assessing situations realistically			
15.	Being able to adapt easily to changes in my life such as moving house, or changing jobs			
16.	Feeling glad to be alive			
17.	Drinking moderate amounts of alcohol or none at all			
18.	Enjoying my work without much stress or strain			
19.	Having all the parts of my body in good working order			
20.	Getting on well with other people most of the time			
21.	Eating the 'right' foods			
22.	Enjoying some form of relaxation/recreation			
23.	Hardly ever going to the doctor			

When you have finished the exercise ask yourself...

1. Was this what I expected to find?
2. Which of the lay perspectives from box 1 can I see in my own answers?
3. How might the outcome vary if I was were to complete this when I was 20 or 40 years older?
4. How might the responses from someone with a physical disability have differed from mine?
5. How might the responses from someone living on benefits have differed from mine?

Defining health

You may have found some surprising results from the activity on page 105: you will understand your responses better if you consider what a broad meaning the term 'health' has. It is derived from the Old English term *Hael* meaning 'whole', suggesting that health deals with the whole person, the entirety of their well-being. This brings together a range of facets of health, which together contribute to a person being healthy – as you will have discovered for yourself in carrying out the first activity in this unit.

A brief overview of facets of health is given in Figure 3.1.

FACET	DESCRIPTION
Physical health	the mechanical ability of the body
Mental Health	the ability to think clearly and coherently, strongly allied to emotional health
Emotional health	the ability to recognise emotions and express them appropriately. The ability to cope with potentially damaging aspects of emotional health, e.g. stress, depression, anxiety and tension
Social health	the ability to make and maintain relationships with others
Spiritual health	concerns personal creeds, principled behaviour, achieving peace of mind or religious beliefs and practices
Societal health	concerns wider societal impact on our own individual health, e.g. the impact of racism on people from a minority ethnic culture, the impact on women of living in a patriarchal society, and the impact of living under political oppression

FIGURE 3.1 *Facets of health*

In society today, 'health' is a term used most usually to express two aspects of well-being. It is used:

* as a negative expression, where health is viewed as the absence of disease or illness

* positively to express a state of well-being, perhaps most widely known through the 1948 World Health Organisation (WHO) definition shown below.

* DID YOU KNOW?

Definitions of 'health' include:

* 'A state of complete physical, psychological and social well-being and not merely the absence of disease and infirmity'
World Health Organisation, 1948

* 'A satisfactory adjustment of the individual to the environment'
Royal College of General Practitioners, 1972

* 'By health I mean the power to live a full adult, living, breathing life in close contact with what I love. I want to be all I am capable of becoming'
Katherine Mansfield

* 'The extent to which an individual or group is able on the one hand, to realise aspirations and satisfy needs and on the other hand, to change or cope with the environment. Health is therefore seen as a resource for everyday life, not the objective of living: it is a positive concept emphasising social and personal resources as well as physical capabilities'
World Health Organisation, 1984

Think it over...

If you examine the alternative definitions of health given above, can you identify which reflect either the positive or the negative use of the word health?

Defining health in terms of illness and disease

Illness, disease and ill health are terms often used interchangeably when in reality they have very different meanings. Disease is derived from the Middle English term *desaise* meaning discomfort, whilst illness is used to identify that a condition exists that causes a person harm or pain. Today, to be 'ill' usually requires the patient's condition to be classified according to current medical knowledge and practice: for example, by displaying a specific list of symptoms or by scientific testing. It is this focus on the scientific nature of diagnosis of illness, which emphasises the importance of the biomedical model in modern-day health care.

Illness is a subjective state, where the person may experience a range of symptoms but tests may not be able to identify a cause. For example, this can often be the case with **myalgic encephalopathy** (ME) where patients can experience a range of symptoms associated with the syndrome but medical testing may not be able to confirm the condition or identify a cause for the symptoms.

Disease and illness do not have to coexist. For example, a person may be diagnosed with a condition through routine screening prior to exhibiting any symptoms. This illustrates the reasoning behind screening programmes, i.e. to ensure that disease can be identified early enough to treat successfully. Therefore, the person may be defined as having the disease (for example, breast or cervical cancer) but not feel ill.

Personal responsibility and health

To the general public to be healthy is usually associated with not being ill: this is a negative perspective, one which is best summarised as not knowing what you had till you lost it. However, the way in which we view our health determines how we take responsibility for it. Stainton and Rogers (from Katz and Perberdy, 1997) summarise a variety of lay perspectives (held by members of the public) which illustrate that the ways in which people view their health will inevitably be reflected in their expression of taking responsibility for their own health. See Figure 3.2.

Therefore, people's notion of what being healthy means varies widely and is shaped by their experiences, knowledge, values and expectations, as well as what others expect of them. These differing attitudes to health influence their behaviour. For instance, a person who believes in the robust individualism model might well choose to smoke and take regular exercise, because these are both satisfying and that individual believes in the right to choose. This, however, would be a difficult position for someone who subscribes to the health promotion account or the will power model, both of which emphasise personal responsibility to maintain

---

✳ DID YOU KNOW?

- ✳ Myalgic encephalopathy (ME)
- ✳ Chronic fatigue syndrome (CFS)
- ✳ Post-viral fatigue syndrome (PVFS)
- ✳ Chronic fatigue immune dysfunction syndrome (CFIDS)

are all names for conditions of uncertain causes affecting many thousands of people. All types of people at all ages are affected. Common symptoms include severe and debilitating fatigue, painful muscles and joints, disordered sleep, gastric disturbances, and poor memory and concentration. In many cases, onset is linked to a viral infection. Other triggers may include an operation or an accident, although some people experience a slow onset.

In some the effects may be minimal, but in a large number, lives are changed drastically. For instance: in the young, schooling and higher education can be severely disrupted; in the working population, employment becomes impossible for many; for all, social life and family life become restricted and, in some cases, severely strained. People may be housebound or confined to bed for months or years.

Recovery is variable and unpredictable. Some people may recover completely, although it may take a number of months or years; in the majority, recovery is only partial and typically follows a slow course of variable improvement and relapse; a significant minority remain severely affected and may require a great deal of practical and social support.

WAYS IN WHICH PEOPLE VIEW THEIR HEALTH	
Body as machine	This has strong links to the medical model of health in that it sees illness as a matter of biological fact and scientific medicine as the natural type of treatment for any illness.
Inequality of access	This perspective is rooted in a reliance on modern medicine to cure illness but is less accepting than 'body as machine' because of awareness that there are great inequalities of access to treatment.
Health promotion account	This model emphasises the importance of a healthy lifestyle and personal responsibility: for example, if you are overweight it is simply a matter of your own choice of diet and lack of exercise that has led to this.
God's power	In this model health is viewed as part of spirituality, i.e. a feature of righteous living and spiritual wholeness. This might be seen as abstinence from alcohol consumption because it is an impure substance, which is not only unholy but also can lead to immoral activity.
Body under siege	This view perceives the world to be a sea of challenges to their health, be they communicable diseases such as colds and flu, or stress at work, and so on.
Cultural critique of medicine	This view sees science and the medical model on which healthcare is based as oppressive to certain groups (e.g. can take away their rights to self determination), e.g. the way health care manages pregnancy can be seen as an example of oppressive practice against women for the natural process of birth is routinely medicalised by health services
Robust individualism	A view best summarised as 'It's my life and I will do with it as I choose'.
Will power	This model considers that we all have a moral responsibility to remain healthy. This relies on strong will power to manage our health: for example, to eat the right things, take regular exercise and drink moderately.

FIGURE 3.2 *Lay perspectives of health*

health. In this situation that person's decision would appear to be contradictory. Therefore, it illustrates how our own attitudes to health define how we view our personal responsibilities for maintaining our own health.

The biomedical model of health

Central to our modern-day understanding of health is the biomedical model, which since the beginning of the 19th century has come to dominate all other models of health in the Western world. Its history lies in the developing understanding of how the various parts of the body might work together to ensure good health. Figure 3.4 summarises this scientific view of health and body functioning.

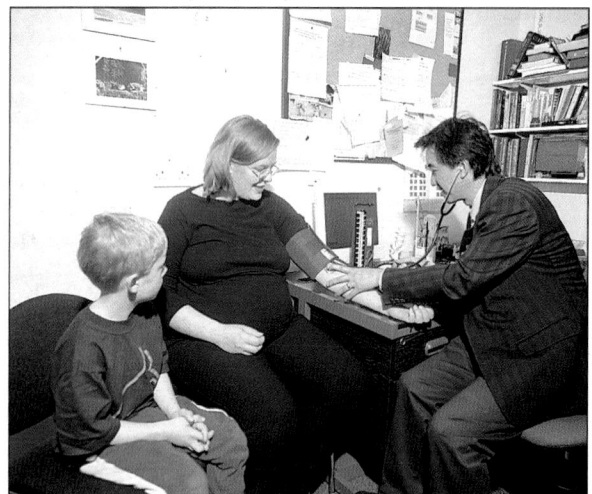

FIGURE 3.3 *A general practitioner focuses on cure rather than prevention*

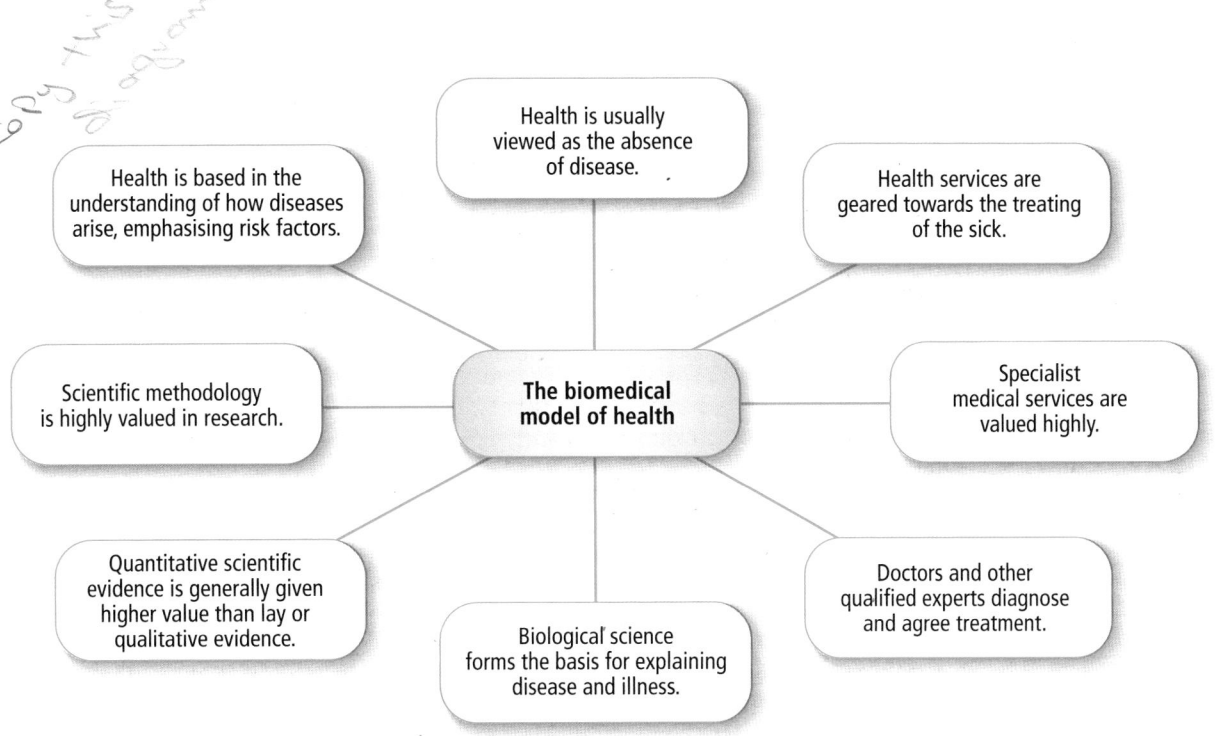

FIGURE 3.4 *Characteristics of the biomedical model of health*

This is the model of health most frequently used by members of the health care professions. In particular, it is the foundation of most medical science and therefore is central to the practice of medicine. As a result, it is the cure that doctors focus upon, their approach being founded in an impression of what is normal and what is abnormal in terms of bodily function. It is most effective with short-term or acute illness, where a cause is identified and the relevant treatment administered. The biomedical model is at its least

Think it over...

1. A diagnosis of ME is based on a collection of symptoms rather than a diagnostic test.

2. Looking at the type of symptoms outlined in this unit, what tensions might there be for a person with ME when they first visit their doctor with the symptoms?

3. Why might a doctor find it difficult to help a person with this condition?

4. As part of learning how to manage their condition, people with ME often learn a great deal about their condition. How might this challenge the usual doctor–patient relationship?

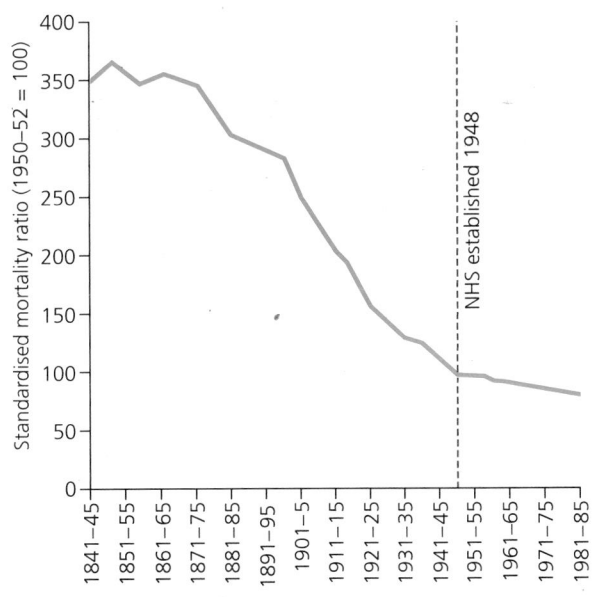

FIGURE 3.5 *Mortality rates (UK) 1841–1985*

effective with chronic illnesses, i.e. those which persist over longer periods of time and are managed rather than cured: examples include ME or Parkinson's disease, terminal care of the dying, and other aspects of health care (such as maternity care where the patient is not actually ill).

Think it over...

Look at the graph of Mortality rates (Figure 3.5).

1. What period saw the greatest decline in mortality?

2. Where does the introduction of the NHS fit in this time scale?

3. What impact has the introduction of the NHS had on mortality rates?

A social model of health

Although the biomedical model has contributed greatly to the increase in life expectancy during the 20th century, it is public health measures based on the social model of health that have contributed most to the decline in mortality.

A social model of health emphasises that in order to improve health it is necessary to address the origins of ill health, i.e. the social conditions that make ill health more prevalent in some groups than others. Its underlying philosophy is that the health differences between individuals and social groups are the result of a complex mixture of behavioural, structural, material and cultural factors, which together impact on health. The social model has strong links to the lay models of health because it recognises that people often have firmly held views about their own health, which are sometimes at odds with those of professionals. For example, the need to address damp conditions in housing and its link to childhood asthma might be prioritised by people living in those conditions, as opposed to the need to tackle parental smoking amongst those living in the same houses, as prioritised by health practitioners.

Think it over...

1. How have the environmental challenges facing humans changed in the last 100 years?

2. What local measures are you aware of that are being taken to improve the environment where you live?

3. What three things would you suggest as changes which would greatly improve the health of your local neighbourhood?

Health policy linked to national targets

Examples of health-promoting activity at the national level include:

* legislation such as the factory acts of the 19th century, which limited the hours that children, women and men could work

* public health legislation, which required towns to take steps to improve sanitary conditions

* the Clean Air Acts of the 1950s, which reduced city 'smogs' (pollution-laden fogs) considerably

* the Water (Fluoridation) Act of 1985, which enabled health authorities to ask water companies to add fluoride to drinking water to cut dental decay.

However, legislative action at the national level is strongly linked to political and ideological factors and evidence for a particular course of action. For example, it is widely accepted that tobacco kills more people than all the 'soft and hard drugs' that are often the cause of many media crusades. However, it can still be bought freely over the counter, the government generating enough revenue in the process to more than equal the expenditure on health care for people with smoking-related health conditions. Manufacturers spend millions of pounds advertising the product, particularly to recruit new young smokers. And yet

FIGURE 3.6 *Landfill sites cause public health concerns*

there remains considerable reluctance to legislate against tobacco. In the 2004 public health white paper *Choosing Health*, the government of the day shied away from introducing a total ban on smoking in public areas, choosing instead to adopt a partial ban with some pubs and clubs being able to continue to allow smoking on the premises: this measure was heavily criticised by health campaigning groups like ASH (Action on Smoking and Health) and doctors' representatives.

It was a concern over the public reception for this sort of measure that probably contributed to the reluctance to act. However, the public clearly supports government action in a range of fields, as is stated in the white paper (2004): 'The response to consultation suggests that government is expected (by the public) and trusted to act on inequalities and on wider issues that impact on society... Whilst people want to make their own health decisions they do expect the government to help by creating the right environment.'

National health strategy

This country's first ever health strategy (as opposed to health services) was published by the government in 1992 (with specific similar policy documents for both Wales and Scotland). Its stated aim was to ensure that 'action is taken whether through the NHS or otherwise, to improve and protect health'. It initiated action at three levels:

* through the Department of Health, which was given the lead role (viewed as a mistake by many as the department's role was in ill-health care)

* through some opportunities for the State but mainly focusing on the role of the individual

* and, for the first time, through a range of national health targets.

Independent inquiry into inequalities in health

In July 1997 Donald Acheson was invited by the Secretary of State for Health to review and summarise inequalities in health in England and to identify priority areas for the development of policies to reduce them. This followed in the wake of two renowned previous reports in this field: the report of Douglas Black in 1977 and the updated version from 1987. Both these reports suffered a degree of suppression at the time of their release because of their bleak picture of the widening health inequality in a developed country at the turn of the century, and the implications for the government of the day.

Acheson concluded his report (1998) with a list of 39 recommendations for addressing health inequality, 'judged on the scale of their potential impact on health inequalities and the weight of evidence'. The three areas identified as crucial to this process are:

* all policies likely to have an impact on health should be evaluated in terms of their impact on health inequality

* a high priority should be given to the health of families with children

* further steps should be taken to reduce income inequalities and improve the living standards of poor households.

Think it over...

Imagine you are the estates officer for a local Primary Care Trust. You are about to build a new health centre in the middle of the most deprived estate in your district. On paper this seems like an excellent opportunity to improve the health of this community. But what things might change for the better and the worse as a result of the health centre being built?

The 1992 health strategy was followed up in 1997 by the government publication *Saving Lives – Our Healthier Nation*. The revised strategy made clear links to the Acheson report, proposing to tackle the root causes of ill health: including air pollution, unemployment, low wages, crime and disorder and poor housing. It focused on prevention of the main killers: cancer, coronary heart disease and stroke, accidents and mental illness. It also included a wide range of service providers such as local councils, the NHS, and local voluntary bodies and businesses. Included within the strategy were specific health targets in key disease areas.

The main targets of the 1997 health strategy are:

Cancer	To reduce the death rate in under 75s by at least 20 per cent
Coronary heart disease and stroke	To reduce the death rate in under 75s by at least 40 per cent
Accidents	To reduce the death rate by at least 20 per cent and serious injury by at least 10 per cent
Mental illness	To reduce the death rate from suicide and undetermined injury by at least 20 per cent

The NHS plan (2000)

The NHS Plan (2000) is a government policy paper that outlines the modernisation of the NHS. It includes a stated intention to tackle the health inequalities that divide Britain and sets out national targets for tackling health inequalities with the relevant supporting investment such as:

✳ a £500 million expansion of 'Sure Start' projects

✳ a new Children's Fund for supporting services for children in the 5–13 age bracket: to improve educational achievement, reduce crime and improve attendance at schools, for example

✳ a more effective welfare foods programme with increased support for breast feeding

✳ a 15 per cent cut in teenage conception

✳ the number of smokers to be cut by at least 15 million by 2010

✳ every child in nursery and infant school aged 4–6 years to be entitled to a free piece of fruit each school day.

Health inequalities

In February 2001 the government announced two national health inequalities targets, one relating to infant mortality and the other to life expectancy. They complemented a range of other targets that had been set with an inequalities focus, in the areas of smoking and teenage pregnancy. The targets were:

✳ 'Starting with children under one year, by 2010 to reduce by at least 10 per cent the gap in mortality between manual groups and the population as a whole...

✳ Starting with health authorities, by 2010 to reduce by at least 10 per cent the gap between the quintile (fifth or 20 per cent) of areas with

Children's centres

The Children's Centre programme is based on the concept that providing integrated education, care, family support and health services are key factors for helping children and their parents to escape the poverty trap. Children's centres bring an integrated approach to service delivery in areas where it is most needed, as it is targeted into the top 20 per cent of deprived wards in the country. They will provide the following services to children under 5 years of age and their families:

✳ early education integrated with full day care, including early identification of and provision for children with special educational needs and disabilities

✳ parental outreach, e.g. to parents with additional needs

✳ family support, including support for parents with special needs

✳ health services, e.g. health visitors, mental health services

✳ a base for childminders, and a hub within the community for providers of childcare services

✳ effective links with Jobcentre Plus, local training providers and further and higher education institutions

✳ effective links with children's information services, neighbourhood nurseries, out of school clubs and extended schools

✳ management and workforce training for the services operating into the centre.

the lowest life expectancy at birth and the population as a whole.'

This announcement was followed up in 2003 by *A Programme for Action* (DOH) which set out plans to tackle health inequalities over the following three years. It established the foundations required to achieve the national targets. The different dimensions of health inequalities were set out in the document across four themes:

* *supporting families, mothers and children –* reflecting the high priority given to them in the Acheson report (1998)

* *engaging communities and individuals –* strengthening capacity to tackle local problems

* *preventing illness and providing effective treatment and care –* by tobacco policies, improving primary care and tackling the 'big killers' of coronary heart disease (CHD) and cancer

* *addressing the underlying determinants of health –* emphasising the need for concerted action across government at national and local level up to and beyond the 2010 target date.

'Choosing Health' (2004)

The public health white paper *Choosing health: making healthy choices easier* was published by the government in November 2004. It recognised that interest in health was increasing and recommended a new approach to public health that reflected the rapidly changing and increasingly technological society we live in. The document reviewed health and health inequalities and acknowledged the strong role for government in promoting social justice and tackling the wider causes of ill health and inequality, as well as recognising the need to support and empower individuals to make changes in their own lives:

The strategy set out in the document had three underpinning principles, outlined below.

1. Informed choice: although with two important qualifications –

   * protect children

   * do not allow one person's choice to adversely affect another, e.g. passive smoking

2. Personalisation: support tailored to the needs of individuals

3. Working together: real progress depends on effective partnerships across communities.

Its main priorities were to:

* reduce the number of people who smoke

* reduce obesity and improve diet and nutrition

* increase exercise

* encourage and support sensible drinking

* improve sexual health

* improve mental health.

The public health paper set out the areas for action shown in Figure 3.8.

FIGURE 3.7 *Walking to school is a health-promoting activity*

PROGRAMMES OF WORK	
Children and young people	✳ *Personal health plans* for children – to develop their own health goals with help from their parents or carers, school staff and health professionals. ✳ Healthy Start – a new scheme to provide disadvantaged pregnant women and mothers of young children with vouchers for fresh food and vegetables, milk and infant formula. ✳ Support and information for young people – e.g. a new magazine, *FIT,* to get health information across to young men aged 16 to 30 years. ✳ School travel – all schools in England should have active travel plans by 2010. ✳ Food in schools – all 4–6-year-olds in LEA maintained schools in England will be eligible for free fruit or vegetables.
Communities leading for health	✳ *Communities for Health* – to promote action on locally chosen priorities for health across the local voluntary sector, the NHS, local authorities, business and industry. ✳ Local authorities to work with the national transport charity Sustrans – to build over 7,000 miles of new cycle lanes and tracks. ✳ National and local organisations invited to develop their role as corporate citizens – by making their own pledges on improving health to their workforce and local community. ✳ All government departments and the NHS (subject to limited exceptions) – be smoke-free by 2006.
Health as a way of life	✳ Everyone who wants to will have the opportunity to use a Personal Health Kit to develop his or her own personal health guide. ✳ A personal health resource where NHS health trainers help people to make healthy choices and stick to them.
Health-promoting NHS	✳ All NHS staff will be trained to deliver key health messages effectively as part of their day-to-day work with patients. ✳ A national screening programme for chlamydia will cover all areas of England. ✳ Guidance and training to ensure all health professionals are able to identify alcohol problems early.
Work and health	✳ The NHS will become a model employer. ✳ New initiatives to challenge discrimination and improve access to work for people with mental illness.

FIGURE 3.8 *Areas for action set out in* Choosing Health *(2004)*

Local health strategy

The 1997 white paper *The New NHS – Modern and Dependable* created a responsibility for Primary Care Trusts to draw up a local health strategy and targets in a document called the *Health Improvement Programme* (HImP). These documents had to:

✳ give a clear description of how the national aims, priorities, targets and contracts can be tackled locally

✳ set out a range of locally determined targets

✳ show the action proposed is based on evidence of what is known to work

✳ show that measures of local progress will be used

✳ indicate which local organisations have been involved in compiling it

✳ ensure the plan is easy to understand and accessible

✳ be a vehicle for shaping future NHS strategy.

HImPs have now, largely, been subsumed within the community strategy, a partnership document which is drawn up through the district's Local Strategic Partnership (LSP). An LSP is a single body that:

* brings together, at a local level, the different parts of the public sector as well as the private, business, community and voluntary sectors so that different initiatives and services support each other and work together

* is a non-statutory, non-executive organisation

* operates at a level which enables strategic decisions to be taken and is close enough to individual neighbourhoods to allow actions to be determined at community level

* should be aligned with local authority boundaries.

The role of the LSP is to:

* prepare and implement a community strategy for the area, identify and deliver the most important things which need to be done, keep track of progress, and keep it up to date

* bring together local plans, partnerships and initiatives to provide a forum through which mainstream public service providers (local authorities, the police, health services, central government agencies, and so on) work effectively together to meet local needs and priorities

* develop and deliver a local neighbourhood renewal strategy to secure more jobs, better education, improved health, reduced crime, and better housing, closing the gap between deprived neighbourhoods and the rest, and contributing to the national targets to tackle deprivation.

From the list of responsibilities it is possible to see that the planning led by LSPs will be at the centre of improving local health and well-being; therefore, in most districts the HImP has been incorporated within the community strategy or no longer exists in any identifiable form. The community strategy is a local plan 'to improve the economic, social and environmental well-being of each area and its inhabitants, and contribute to the achievement of sustainable development in the UK' (*The New NHS – Modern and Dependable*, 1997).

It is the role of the Primary Care Trust to contribute to the process of drawing up a community strategy, informing the planners about local health patterns and to lead on planning local health services through the Local Development Plan (LDP), which is a five-year business plan for developing local health services drawn up by the PCTs.

Summary

* Health can be defined in many ways and has several aspects to it including physical, emotional, psychological, and so on

* Health can be defined both positively and negatively in terms of illness and disease

* People have their own perspectives on health, which influence their health behaviours

* The two dominant models of health are the biomedical model (on which modern medicine is based) and the social model

* Government has a major part to play in promoting health, as illustrated through the many policy initiatives such as *The Health of the Nation (1992)* through to the most recent, *Choosing Health (2004)*

* Local health strategy is defined in the health improvement plan (HImP) or increasingly in the community strategy.

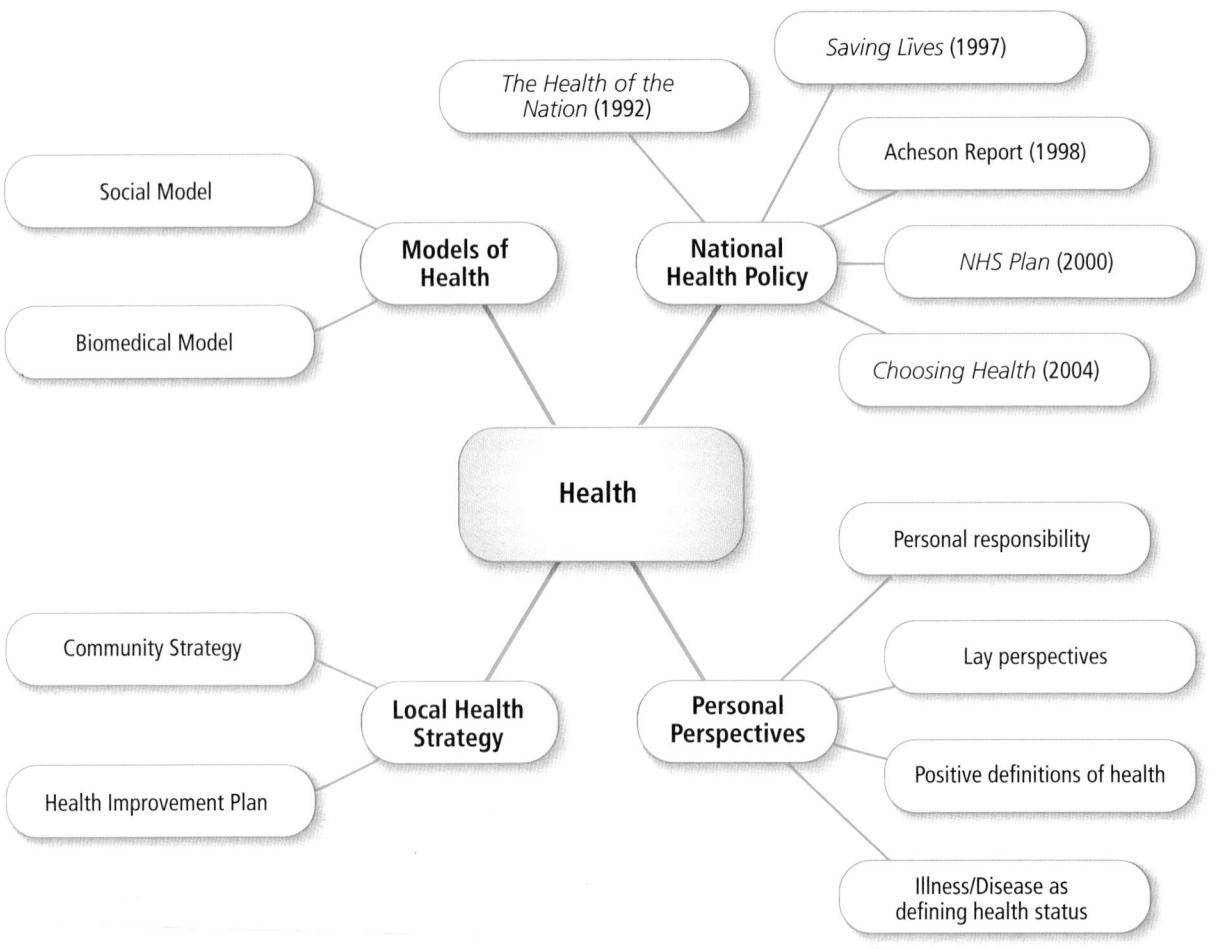

Consider this

1 Imagine you are a senior civil servant tasked by the Secretary of State for Health to draw up a discussion paper that will form the basis of a tobacco-control strategy for the country:

2 As a starting point you will need to review local action plans to see what is happening within local health districts. What actions are mentioned in your local community strategy or Primary Care Trust health plan?

3 You are approached by many pressure groups, some of which base their suggestions on a medical model of health. What types of actions might they be suggesting?

4 Other groups base their suggestions on a societal view of health. What actions might they be suggesting the government adopt?

5 One of your suggested actions is a campaign to alert people to the dangers of smoking. Pick three of the lay models of health and describe how you would tailor the message to meet the specific needs of people with that perspective.

6 Previous government action like that through taxation measures, for example, has been criticised for compounding health inequalities by encouraging wealthier groups to quit smoking with little impact on lower socio-economic groups. What steps could you suggest to counter the risk of adding to existing health inequalities?

Section 2: Preventive measures and job roles

Measures and models

Just as there are many models of health, so too there are many models of health promotion. One of the most widely accepted is that suggested by Tannahil (from Naidoo and Willis, 2000), who describes three overlapping and related areas of activity:

* **Health Education** – communication to improve health and prevent ill health by improving people's knowledge on health, and changing their attitudes to aspects of their health. The possibilities for health education to make a difference can be seen in the decline in smoking rates over the latter years of the last century.

* **Health Protection** – population measures to safeguard health, for example through legislation, financial or social means. This might include legislation to govern health and safety at work or food hygiene, and using taxation policy to reduce smoking levels or car use, by raising the price of cigarettes or petrol.

* **Prevention** – reducing or avoiding the risks of diseases and ill health primarily through medical 'interventions'.

There are several approaches and levels for health promotion activity to take place: these are dealt with in more detail in the next section.

Tannahil's model emphasises the breadth of activities that can be included in the term health promotion, and the way the various spheres of activity interconnect.

Figure 3.8 illustrates the wide variety of activities that can be classed as health promoting, from those which operate at an individual level to those which depend upon national government action.

Health education

This is usually defined as the process of giving information and advice and of facilitating the development of knowledge and skills in order to change behaviour. Health educators include a wide range of professions including teachers, social workers, practice nurses, health visitors, leisure centre staff, and so on. In some cases this is an acknowledged part of their role: for example, in health visiting and practice nursing it is accepted that part of the role is to work one to one with people to increase their knowledge and skills to enable them to improve their own health. However, in some cases the potential for a health promotion role may not be so easily recognised: for example, a community police officer walking the local streets will frequently come across groups of young people who might be smoking and/or intoxicated, which clearly presents a health promoting opportunity that the officer may not appreciate or be trained to deal with effectively.

There are also more developed models of health education, which see health education as

1	Preventive services	Immunisation, cervical screening, developmental surveillance
2	Preventive health education	Substance use education in schools
3	Preventive health protection	Fluoridation of water supplies
4	Health education for preventive health education	Lobbying for fluoridation or seatbelt legislation
5	Positive health education	Work with young people to develop positive self-esteem
6	Positive health protection	Smoking bans in public places
7	Health education aimed at positive health protection	Lobbying for a ban on tobacco advertising or smoking bans in pubs

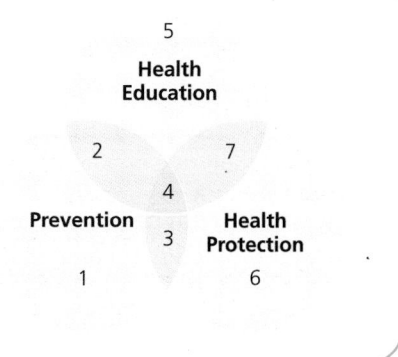

FIGURE 3.8 *Tannahil's model of health promotion*

raising critical consciousness (amongst key policy makers and members of the community), testing values and attitudes and empowering communities to address local health issues. In this model it also operates as a two-way process, informing policy makers as well (as members of the local community), raising their appreciation of the concerns of local people.

In this type of model, service users are not empty vessels waiting to be filled with the right health knowledge, i.e. people do not change their behaviour once they are in receipt of the right knowledge or skill. Health education is fraught with ethical considerations. Two of the most important issues here would be the right to self-determination of the service users and the need for the service providers to remain non-judgmental. Ethics plays an important part for health educators, as they draw out the needs of the service users and work with them towards an informed choice; this may turn out to be a health-damaging choice for the service users. Can the professionals now accept and respect that decision and not coerce or persuade them to adopt a different choice, when that would be neither effective nor ethical? Clearly health education can present serious challenges to the educators.

Think it over...

In a small group you might want to discuss:

* Should health educators tell people what is best for them?
* Do health educators fail if they accept the service user's health damaging behaviour?
* Who determines what is a healthy lifestyle, service user or educator?
* Should health behaviour be a matter of personal choice or is too important to leave to the individual?

The danger with health education activity is that health promoters become fixed on the goal of improved medical or physical health to the detriment of other aspects of holistic health. It is too easy for professionals to adopt a judgmental approach, deciding what is best for the individual to the exclusion of that person's right to self-

autonomy. It is important to remember that empowering people is an integral part of effective and ethical health-promotion work. To enable health promoters to make ethical judgments about the work they undertake, the following questions can be considered:

* Will service users be able to choose freely for themselves?
* Will I be respecting their decision, whether or not I approve of it?
* Will I be non discriminatory – respecting all people equally?
* Will I be serving the more basic needs before addressing other wants?
* Will I be doing good and preventing harm?
* Will I be telling the truth?
* Will I be minimising harm in the long term?
* Will I be able to honour promises and agreements I make?

These points are as equally applicable for a one-to-one service user/professional scenario, or a planner considering alterations to local roads in a housing estate. Here, for example they might be asking themselves whether they have adequately involved the local people in the decision-making process and if they have respected their input, not valuing it differently to that of other professionals.

Another example might be a midwife discussing smoking with a pregnant woman; here

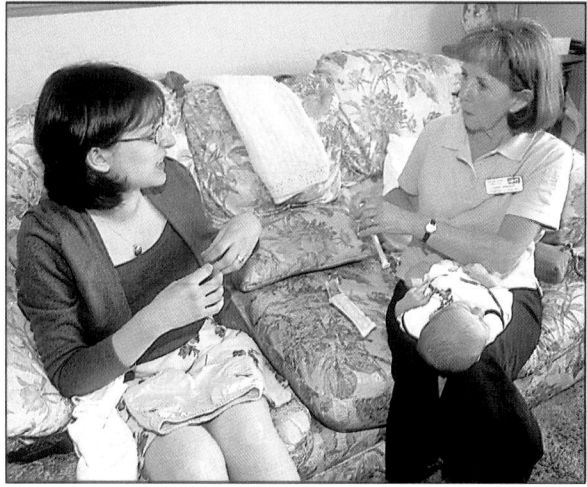

FIGURE 3.9 *Service providers respect the service user's right to choose*

the midwife has considerable knowledge about the potential damage to the unborn child and the possibility of further health damage if the mother continues to smoke after the birth. However, to be an ethical health promoter she must respect the service user's right to choose whether to continue smoking and not allow the decision to continue smoking (should that be the case) to change the relationship.

Midwives are not alone in facing this problem. Many women resume smoking after the birth, meaning that the health visitor may also face the challenge of how to sensitively discuss possible harm to the children without damaging the relationship she has with the mother. If you were that health visitor:

* Think of three things you would most wish to convey to the mother.

* What would you have to be mindful of when having this discussion?

* Would having this conversation in the mother's home present any difficulties/opportunities for you?

* Why is it appropriate for you to have this discussion with the mother?

This task is further complicated by the changing nature of health messages as the knowledge base for health education develops. This can lead to confusion within the general population: for example, the change in alcohol safe drinking limits, which recently moved from a weekly guidance to daily levels, to reflect the shift towards binge drinking patterns.

* DID YOU KNOW?

Currently the Department of Health advises that:

* men should not drink more than 3–4 units of alcohol <u>per day</u>

* women should drink no more than 2–3 units of alcohol <u>per day</u>.

Daily benchmarks apply whether you drink every day, once or twice a week, or occasionally.

Research has suggested that the majority of health professionals are not clear what advice to give people and are not aware of the change.

Think it over...

Review with a family member or friend an aspect of their health-related behaviour which they know is damaging to their health: for example, continuing to smoke or not taking sufficient exercise. Try to find out:

* The extent of their knowledge about that health issues. Do they know and understand the relevant health messages?

* Why they continue with that behaviour if they know it harms them?

* How they feel when people ask them about it, as you are doing?

* What their expectations of health professionals are. Do they expect to be asked about it each time they visit their GP, for example?

Prevention

It is all too easy to see health promotion as solely focusing on preventing people from becoming ill. This is, indeed, an important part of the span of health promotion, but it also includes two other categories of health-promoting activity which deal with people who are already ill in some way: these three tiers of health promotion activity are primary, secondary and tertiary prevention.

Primary prevention

This is an attempt to eliminate the possibility of getting a disease. The childhood immunisation programme is an example of a health protection activity under this heading. Other examples include smoking education as part of personal and social health education in schools, and leaflets and posters for use in promoting healthy eating.

Secondary prevention

This addresses those people identified as being in the early stages of a disease, usually through early detection of symptoms. Action focuses on addressing the underlying causes, in order to alleviate any further symptoms. Examples might include action to address raised blood pressure taken by a doctor, who identified those symptoms as part of a routine check-up for a patient. This action might be drug therapy but equally could be a referral onto a physical activity scheme for promoting regular exercise, in collaboration with the local leisure services departments (usually referred to as an 'exercise on prescription' scheme). This sort of scheme might also be used for people who are overweight, or for people with mild depression. Therefore, a range of secondary prevention issues can be addressed through one scheme. Alternatively, a 'stop smoking' group would be a secondary prevention initiative for someone who is already suffering from respiratory problems such as repeat infections, bronchitis and so on.

FIGURE 3.10 *Secondary prevention may include support groups*

* What do people gain from support groups that they cannot get from one-to-one counselling?

* What do one-to-one sessions provide that groups can not?

* How do you think the two can compliment each other?

Tertiary prevention

This refers to the control and reduction (as far as possible) of an already established disease. This is not easily distinguishable from medical care, but it is possible to consider issues such as increasing the capacity of individuals to manage their

condition and their own health. An example might be supporting and enabling people with a history of heart attacks to regain their confidence, enabling them to live a more fulfilling life and be in control of their own destiny, as far as is possible. It could also apply to someone suffering from Parkinson's disease being supported in learning about and managing his or her condition as independently as possible. A more common and less obvious example might be the provision of dentures to people who have had teeth extracted.

Think it over...

The following are examples of tertiary prevention services:

* an 'exercise on prescription' scheme
* a coronary rehabilitation scheme
* a stroke rehabilitation service
* a community drugs service.

1. Find out if you have any of these services operating in your area.

2. If you were a potential service user, how would you gain access to the service? What sources of information did you use to find out about them?

3. What do the services offer to the people using them?

Health protection – screening

Screening was defined by the American Commission on Chronic Illness in 1957 as 'the presumptive identification of unrecognised disease or defect by the application of tests, examinations and other procedures which can be applied rapidly. Screening tests sort out apparently well people who may have a disease from those who do not.'

However, screening a well population can be a contentious issue, with many attendant problems: for example, are we right to be medicalising a well population in this way? In almost all cases the majority of people screened will not be ill with the condition screened for. Also, screening for some conditions remains an imprecise science. To help with deciding if a screening programme is

1. The condition to be sought should be an important public health problem
2. There should be an acceptable intervention for a patient identified as having the condition
3. Effective facilities for diagnosis and treatment should be in place
4. There should be a period when early symptoms can be identified
5. There should be a suitable test or examination
6. The progress of the disease or defect should be understood
7. There should be an agreed definition for the condition so that a diagnosis can be made against clear criteria
8. Early treatment should have favourable results
9. The cost of screening should be favourable against treatment of people who develop the condition
10. Any repeat screening should be clearly justified

FIGURE 3.11 *Criteria for screening programmes*

Think it over...

Health workers sometimes use the two terms 'screening' and 'surveillance' interchangeably to talk about the same thing. Divide a page in two with a line: place one word on each side of the page and then quickly write down all the things that word makes you think about. Do not leave out things which do not appear to be about health. Try to capture all the feelings and thoughts that this word conjures up for you.

∗ Can you see any differences between the way in which you think about these two words?

∗ What messages might we be sending out to people through use of terms like screening and surveillance?

appropriate Wilson and Jungner (1968) set out a list of criteria against which screening programmes could be evaluated. See Figure 3.11.

Cervical screening

The NHS Cervical Screening Programme was set up in 1988. The programme screens almost four million women in England each year. Cervical screening – including the cost of treating cervical abnormalities – has been estimated to cost around £150 million a year in England, or about £37.50 per woman screened.

Cervical screening is not a test for cancer. It is a method of preventing cancer by detecting and treating early abnormalities that, if left untreated, could lead to cancer in a woman's cervix (the neck of the womb). The first stage in cervical screening is either a smear test or **liquid-based cytology** (LBC). A sample of cells is taken from the cervix for analysis. A doctor or nurse inserts an instrument (a speculum) to open the woman's vagina and uses a spatula to sweep around the cervix. The sample of cells is 'smeared' onto a slide, which is sent to a laboratory for examination under a microscope. Early detection and treatment can prevent 80–90 per cent of cancers developing, but like other screening tests, it is not perfect. It may not always detect early cell changes that could lead to cancer. The programme aims to reduce the number of women who develop invasive cervical cancer (incidence) and the number of women who die from it (mortality). It does this by regularly screening all women at risk so that conditions, which might otherwise develop into invasive cancer, can be identified and treated.

All women between the ages of 25 and 64 are eligible for a free cervical smear test every 3–5 years. In the light of new evidence, the NHS Cervical Screening Programme will now be implementing screening at different intervals depending on age.

AGE GROUP (YEARS)	FREQUENCY OF SCREENING
25	First invitation
25–49	3-yearly
50–64	5-yearly
65+	Only screen those who have not been screened since 50 years old or who have had recent abnormal tests

FIGURE 3.12 *The NHS Cervical Screening Programme*

The NHS call and recall system invites women who are registered with a GP. This also keeps track of any follow-up investigation, and, if all is well, recalls the woman for screening in 3–5 years time. Women who have not had a recent smear test may be offered one when they attend their GP or family planning clinic on another matter. Women should receive their first invitation for routine screening at 25. Women under 25 and women over 65 are not invited because cervical cancer is rare in women in these age groups. Also, young women may get an abnormal smear result purely because this is the time when the female body is still developing – particularly the cervix, where cell changes may be the result of growth. This could lead to unnecessary treatment so screening young women might do more harm than good.

Breast screening

The NHS Breast Screening Programme provides free breast screening every three years for all women in the UK aged 50 years and over. Around one-and-a-half million women are now screened in the UK each year. Women aged between 50–64 years are routinely invited for breast screening every three years, and work is being carried out to extend the programme to women up to and including the age of 70 by 2004.

Breast screening is a method of detecting breast cancer at a very early stage. The first step involves an X-ray of each breast – a **mammogram** – which is taken while carefully compressing the breast. The mammogram can detect small changes in breast tissue, which may indicate cancers that are too small to be felt either by the woman herself or by a doctor. There are over 90 breast screening units across the UK, each currently inviting an average population of around 45,000 women. Women are invited to a specialised screening unit, which can either be mobile, hospital based, or permanently based in a convenient location, such as a shopping centre.

The NHS Breast Screening Programme was the first of its kind in the world. It began inviting women for screening in 1990, and national coverage was achieved by the mid–1990s. The rate of cancers detected per 1,000 women screened and the standardised detection ratio has risen steadily. In 2001/2002, statistics showed that for every 1,000 women screened, 6.8 cancers were detected. In England, the budget for the Breast Screening Programme, including the actual cost of screening, is approximately £52 million. This works out at about £30 per woman invited, or £40 per woman screened.

Women under 50 years are not offered routine screening. Mammograms seem not to be as effective in pre-menopausal women, possibly because the density of the breast tissue makes it more difficult to detect problems and also because the incidence of breast cancer is lower. The average age of the menopause in the UK is 50 years. As women go through the menopause, the glandular tissue in the breast 'involutes' and the breast tissue is increasingly made up of only fat. This is clearer on the mammogram and makes interpretation of the X-ray more reliable. Breast cancer is also far more common in post-menopausal women and the risk continues to increase with rising age.

Infant screening

Some defects in young children are unlikely to be recognised by even the most astute of parents. In these situations, only a trained health professional may identify potential problems if specific screening tests are carried out. Good examples here would include: high frequency hearing loss, before an age when a child would normally be expected to start to talk; or congenital dislocation of the hip, before the age at which a child would normally walk. From the moment of birth, young children are routinely screened for specific conditions. A newborn baby will be screened for:

* height, weight and head circumference
* birthmarks
* heart defects
* congenital dislocation of the hips
* eye defects
* hearing
* a range of metabolic disorders.

Some or all of these tests are repeated at 2 weeks, 6–8 weeks, 3–4 months, 6–9 months, 18–24 months, 3–3$\frac{1}{2}$ years and at 5 years. This will involve a range of health personnel including the midwife, health visitor, family doctor and school nurse who must all liaise effectively to track the health record of the one child. This is usually through a 'patient held record', which is left with the parents or guardian.

Health protection – immunisation

Conquering infectious diseases has led to the most significant reductions in mortality. It is possible to make people immune to certain diseases by challenging their immune system with a weak or inactivated version of the disease organism to stimulate the person to create antibodies to the disease. This will enable their immune system to respond quickly should they contract the disease later on, resulting in no more than mild symptoms instead of experiencing the worst aspects of the disease.

The Immunisation Programme (see Figure 3.13) creates what is known as '**herd immunity**': that is, if enough people within the population are immunised the likelihood of any epidemic is greatly reduced. For this reason the government sets targets for immunisation rates for local health services to meet. Any regular fall below these levels signals a potential epidemic and becomes a serious cause of concern.

Routinely, children are immunised for diphtheria, typhoid, polio, measles, mumps and rubella. These last three are particularly contentious because some parents believe there

may be a link between the MMR (measles, mumps and rubella) vaccine and autism. Whilst there is, as yet, no strong supporting evidence it has undermined public confidence in the vaccine and reduced the uptake by parents. This in turn risks the herd immunity and consequently an epidemic of measles or rubella, for example.

WHEN TO IMMUNISE	WHAT IS GIVEN	HOW IT IS GIVEN
2, 3 and 4 months old	Diphtheria, tetanus, pertussis (whooping cough), polio and Hib	One injection
	Meningitis C	One injection
Around 13 months old	Measles, mumps and rubella (MMR)	One injection
3$\frac{1}{3}$–5 years old	Diphtheria, tetanus, pertussis (whooping cough) and polio	One injection
	Measles, mumps and rubella (MMR)	One injection
10–14 years old (and sometimes shortly after birth)	BCG (against tuberculosis)	Skin test, then, if needed, one injection
13–18 years old	Diphtheria, tetanus, polio	One injection

FIGURE 3.13 *The NHS Immunisation Programme*

Significant educators for health and well being

If you use a social model of health it is possible to see how the promotion of health will involve a wide range of possible interventions, which influence the so-called determinants of health. With this in mind it is possible to see that a wide range of people and agencies, therefore, have the potential to promote the health of the local population. See Figure 3.14.

It is possible to routinely screen for many other conditions: for example, there are many screening tools available to assess a person's alcohol use and identify those who are hazardous or harmful drinkers and at risk of damaging their health. However, it is not ethical to use population-screening approaches when the relevant treatment is not available, as in the case of alcohol use.

1. What reasons might lead to treatment not being available?

2. What challenges do you think this ethical dilemma might present for healthcare professionals who are not able to treat because of this situation?

3. How would you feel as a patient if this affected you?

FIGURE 3.14 *A local health-promoting network*

Health services

The health inequalities we see in society today can, to some extent, be explained by the wide variations in access to high quality health care. In the 1970s, a GP (Tudor Hart) coined the term the 'Inverse Care Law' to describe the way in which

the quality of health care provision was often directly inverse (opposite) to the local need. That is, services are usually poor in the areas with most sickness and death: for example, in these areas GPs often have larger lists, more work, less hospital support and poorer premises.

An understanding of the health care professional/patient relationship can help understand one aspect of the 'inverse care law', specifically the way in which people engage with local health services. Tudor Hart suggested that this relationship is often at its least effective in these disadvantaged communities. In 1994 Baldock and Ungerson attempted to summarise people's attitudes to community care services using a simple model which described four roles that people can adopt when services are made available to them in a free market format. This is illustrated in Figure 3.15.

This model is just that – a means of helping us understand how real world systems operate. It does not mean that people have to rigidly fit one role; they may move between roles depending upon their circumstances. However, it will explain why people will have different experiences of using the same health services.

The primary function of the NHS is to treat sick people. Although health promotion activity could and should be a feature of many health service roles, in practice this aspect of health activity is the poor relation to the primary goal of treating the sick. The recent government reorganisation of the NHS has emphasised its health improvement role, specifying that Primary Care Trusts have a primary function of 'improving the health of their local population'. There are key personnel within the NHS who can contribute to this end including those outlined opposite.

The public health department

This will usually now include both specialist public health practitioners and the health promotion service.

The public health team has a key role in assessing the patterns of ill health locally and identifying what types of health care provision and health promoting activities are required to

THE FOUR ROLES OF BALDOCK AND UNGERSON'S MODEL	
Consumers	People who expect nothing form the State and set out to arrange the necessary care by buying it themselves. They believe that using the market in this way gives them control and autonomy, much like buying a car or any other kind of consumer goods. These people know about the services but prefer to purchase their own care for a variety of reasons, including convenience and perceived quality.
Privatists	People who have learnt to manage alone. A group associated with the growth of home ownership and the increasing emphasis on home and family, as opposed to wider sociability. Adapting to being cared for in later life can mean leaving the family home and increased dependency, which they find hard to come to terms with because it means having to ask for help. They can become isolated and fail to access the necessary healthcare. Generally, they do least well of the four in accessing services.
Welfarists	People who believe in the Welfare State and their right to use it: they expect and demand their rights to relevant services. The attitudes that underpin this mode are based on a strong sense of citizenship and welfare rights. They have both the understanding and the know how to make sure they get the most from the system and use it effectively to access both public and voluntary provision.
Clientists	People who accept passively what they are offered without demanding or expecting more. Neither do they expect services to be flexible in being able to respond to their specific needs. This is commonly seen in older people and low income groups, explaining how people in disadvantaged communities will often accept the poor state of their local health services and not challenge and demand better provision.

FIGURE 3.15 *Roles that people adopt when services are made available to them in a free market format*

Source: Baldock and Ungerson (1994)

improve health locally. The activities provided through the public health team can be seen through the areas of competence which public health practitioners are able to demonstrate:

* surveillance and assessment of the population's health and well-being

* promoting and protecting the population's health and well-being

* risk management and evaluation of activity

* collaborative working for health and well-being

* developing health programmes and services and reducing inequalities

* policy and strategy development and implementation

* working with and for communities

* strategic leadership for health and well-being

* research and development

* ethical principles for health promotion and public health.

Specialist health promotion services

These are now usually located within, or alongside, the public health team. They are a small, specialised service which supports the development of the health promoting role of others, the development of new services and policies which can promote health locally. The role of these services has grown and developed over time, the flexibility to do this being largely due to the fact that it is not a profession governed by a professional body, thus enabling local teams to grow and develop into new areas of practice in response to local need. However, there is a national set of competencies for health promotion practice, which identifies the degree of overlap with public health practice, recognising that health promotion specialists are a part of the wider public health specialism. Their role is best illustrated by the example of the activities a service might offer in the school setting, as shown in Figure 3.16.

Improving health and preventing disease is also the responsibility of those working to provide health care – especially those with community-based roles (as opposed to hospital-based workers). Their health promotion role dates back to two key NHS papers, *Prevention and Health: Everybody's Business* (DHSS 1976) and the later *GP (family doctor) Contract* (1990), which emphasised the importance of risk factor reduction, screening and lifestyle advice in a primary health care setting.

Community nursing

Nurses are one professional group that has a long history of working in a primary and community care setting. Community nurses also contribute to public health practice, working with communities as well as providing care to individuals. The public health contribution of nurses, health visitors and midwives was outlined in *Making it Happen* (DOH 1995). This emphasised that nurses, midwives and health visitors were not only 'hands on'

HEALTH PROMOTION: CORE COMPETENCIES IN ACTION — THE SCHOOL SETTING	
Raising public awareness	Direct campaigning within schools, e.g. national days such as No Smoking Day or World Aids Day. The organisation of events such as sex education conferences or the supporting the school celebrations of achievements within the Healthy School Programme, linking with and involving the media in these types of events.
Advice and consultancy	The support by specialists offered to schools participating in the Healthy School Programme, facilitating training and policy development, advising on the submission and the particular topics the school is working on.
Service development	The 'health-promoting school award' provides a framework for schools to incorporate health issues into their development plans in terms of training, policy development, finance and so on. The extended schools programme also provides opportunities for developing school-based health services, e.g. School Nurse drop-in sessions. The health promotion specialists would provide a leading role for coordinating the development of these types of service-based initiatives.
Policy development	Supporting schools in the development of a wide range of specific policies including sex education, smoking, substance use, and nutrition.
Project planning	The management of specific projects, e.g. working with local parents on how to discuss difficult issues, such as sex and drugs.
Research	Undertaking research, e.g. health surveys to establish what young people's health behaviours are in the locality, or consulting young people about specific issues.
Training and education	Providing in-service training on health education, co-facilitating classes to offer models of good practice for health and health-related subjects.
Resources	Specialists both advise on purchases of new materials for the resource centre, and recommend resources and appropriate methods of use.
Challenging prejudice, and discrimination	Specialists encourage the development of policies and work practices that challenge the root causes of ill health, e.g. policies around equal opportunities, and ensuring that equal opportunities strategies are included in all policy documents and subsequent strategy initiatives.

FIGURE 3.16 *Example of a specialist health-promotion service in a school setting*

NURSE	TYPE OF ACTIVITIES
Community nurses	Carry out nursing care, e.g. bandaging and care of wounds in the patients' homes
Community midwives	Monitor and support expectant mothers, pre- and post-birth, outside the hospital; in some cases carry out home deliveries
Health visitors	Primary role is to monitor child development from first week after birth, carry out regular assessment tests and advise on parenting. However, they are also often referred to as public health nurses, able to respond to a diverse range of local community needs, such as establishing mother and toddler groups; providing a range of training and development groups for parents (e.g. on effective parenting, baby massage); or supporting local community activity such as food cooperatives.
School nurses	Carry out routine screening of school-age children and support administration of vaccination programme. They can also be involved in school-based PSHE programmes (personal and social health education).
Occupational health nurses	Provide nursing support on site for larger employers, which can include health-promoting activity, such as health check-ups and stop smoking advice.

FIGURE 3.17 *Diverse roles of nurses*

professionals, delivering care to individuals, but also had an important role to play in the development and implementation of local health improvement initiatives (see Figure 3.17).

Examples include:

* the school nursing role in supporting the implementation of the National Healthy School Standard, working with teachers, governors, parents and pupils to develop a healthy policy and practice in the school environment, across a range of issues.

* the role of the health visitor, profiling and then responding to local health needs, possibly by supporting groups of young parents, or volunteers trying to set up a food coop.

General practitioners (GPs)

GPs are independent practitioners; that is they are, in effect, small businesses that contract with the NHS in the shape of the local primary care trust to provide a range of services. GPs have a practice population, or list, which may be widely dispersed. This is because people who register with a GP may build up a relationship with them over many years and choose to remain with the

practice even when they move away from the area. GPs form the hub of a primary health care team that is itself the backbone of the local medical services. The World Health Organisation (WHO) defined primary health care in 1978 as being:

'Essential health care made universally accessible to individuals and families in the community… It forms an integral part of both the country's health system, of which it is the central function and main focus, and of the overall social and economic development of the community.'

Primary health care teams are the first point of contact for people who are unwell, and act as the gatekeeper to more specialised or secondary services in hospital settings. The operation of the GP services is governed by the new General Medical Services contract (nGMS contract)

The GMS contract aims to provide GPs with greater flexibility in determining the range of services they provide. It creates the possibility of opting-out of some provision, such as out-of-hours care, and providing others at a more enhanced or special interest level. The GMS contract is inspired by the government's NHS

SERVICES PROVIDED BY GPs	
Essential Services	All practices must provide a full range of essential services, covering the day-to-day work of general practice (for example, chronic disease management).
Additional Services	Most practices will offer a range of additional services like contraceptive services, maternity services, cervical screening and some minor surgery.
Enhanced Services	These are optional (other than Direct Enhanced Services which must be provided in every locality), and involve either the provision of essential or additional services to a higher standard, or more specialist interventions not provided by most GPs. Enhanced services can be negotiated at a local level, though for a small number of treatment areas there are national specifications and benchmark pricing.

FIGURE 3.18 *Clinical services provided by GPs under the GMS contract*

modernisation agenda, which has also informed the NHS Plan, the National Service Frameworks and the Priorities and Planning Frameworks.

The new contract will be between primary care organisations (PCOs) and practices, rather than GPs and health authorities. It compartmentalises clinical work into three service categories as shown in Figure 3.18.

Environmental health personnel

The environmental health service has a broad public health role covering housing, food safety, water supply, refuse disposal and pollution control. Increasingly, the emphasis on the key statutory duties of surveillance and enforcement, have frequently left little scope for developing a

SERVICES PROVIDED BY ENVIRONMENTAL HEALTH OFFFICERS	
Food safety	The food safety team is responsible for ensuring that all food produced or sold locally is safe. Complaints are investigated and food samples taken for examination. Diseases which could be food or water borne are also investigated.
Health and safety	The commercial safety team are responsible for enforcing health and safety legislation in the majority of work places including offices, shops, places of entertainment, consumer and leisure services. All premises allocated to the local authority for enforcement are regularly inspected and action taken, be it advice and education or formal enforcement action (including prosecution). It is a legal requirement that many workplace accidents are reported to the local authority and these are investigated to determine the cause and to prevent a repetition. Additional inspections are carried out at premises, which require special licences, including places of entertainment and skin piercers.
Environmental protection	The Environmental Health Department also has a role in investigating complaints from the public about a range of environmental nuisances which can affect people's health: this includes noise, smoke, fumes, odour and dust, all of which are investigated and minimised wherever possible.
Pest control/ Dog control	The pest control team treats rodent infestations in domestic and commercial premises throughout the district, as well as other public health pests, such as fleas, cockroaches and wasps. They also undertake an annual programme to control rats in the sewage system. The dog control team enforces the Dog Fouling Laws, provides advice and education on responsible dog ownership and removes stray dogs from the street.

FIGURE 3.19 *Some of the core statutory functions of Environmental Health Departments*

broader, comprehensive approach to the improvement of the public's health, such as the role it adopts in home safety promotion and food safety training. Environmental Health Departments have, therefore, tended to focus their activities around the core statutory functions which includes those listed in Figure 3.19.

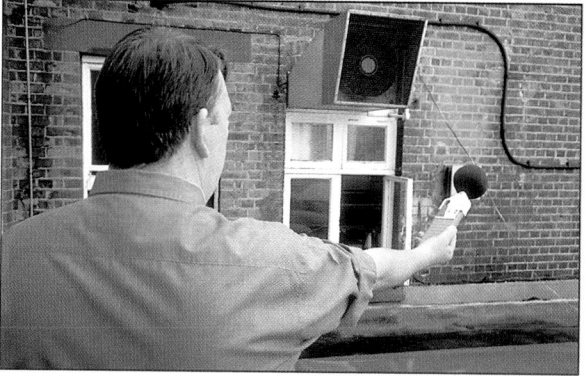

FIGURE 3.20 *Environmental Health Officer monitoring noise pollution*

Think it over...

Noise nuisance is the most common form of complaint in neighbourhood disputes.

* What types of noise pollution do you experience in the place where you live?
* How might you be contributing to the noise pollution in your neighbourhood?
* Contact your local Environmental Health Department and find out what constitutes a noise nuisance
* How can people complain and what steps can the department take to control that pollution?

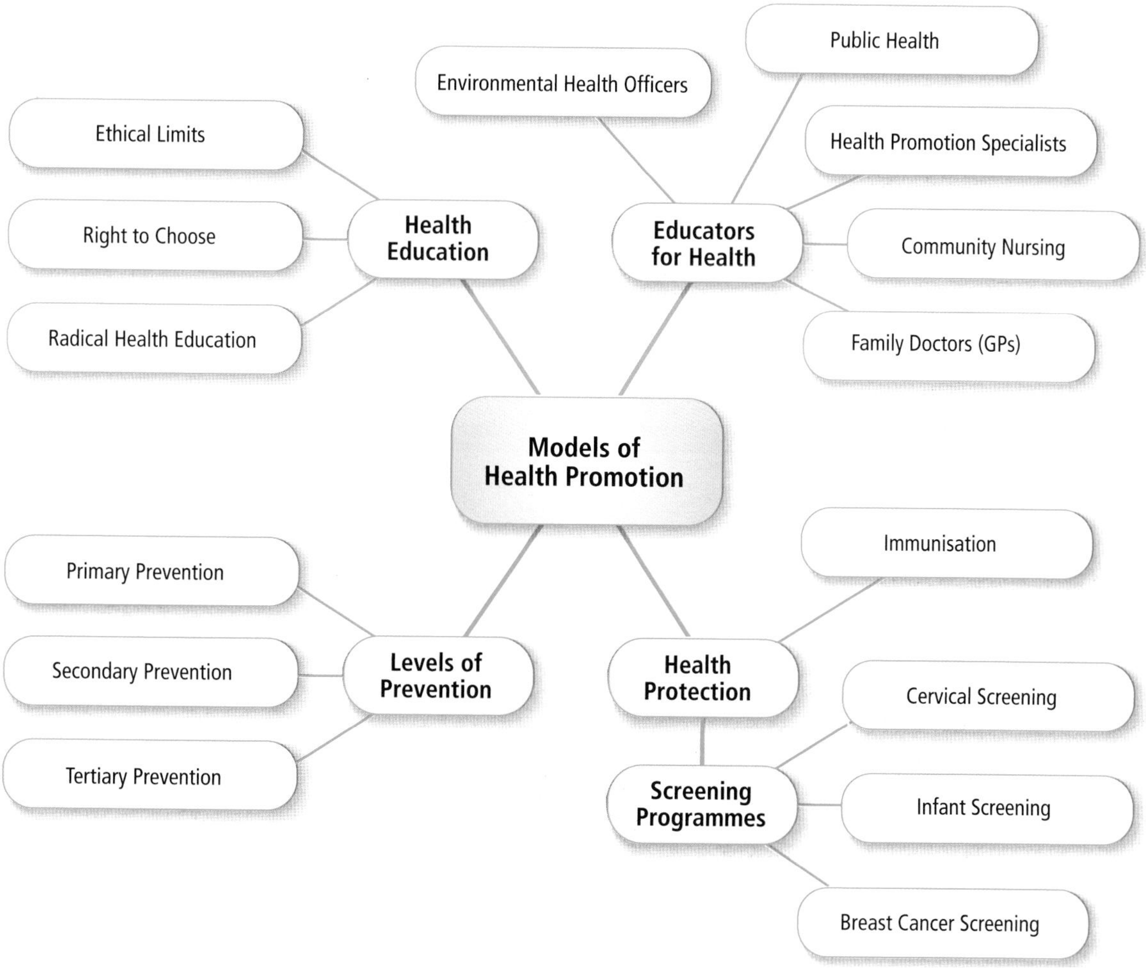

Models of Health Promotion
Health Education
Ethical Limits
Right to Choose
Radical Health Education
Educators for Health
Environmental Health Officers
Public Health
Health Promotion Specialists
Community Nursing
Family Doctors (GPs)
Levels of Prevention
Primary Prevention
Secondary Prevention
Tertiary Prevention
Health Protection
Immunisation
Screening Programmes
Cervical Screening
Infant Screening
Breast Cancer Screening

Summary

There are many models of health promotion but one of the most widely accepted is Tannahil's (Naidoo and Willis, 2000), which breaks health promotion into three areas of work:

* Health education – communication to improve health
  * Ethical behaviour is a challenge for health educators when considering the service user's right to choose

* Health protection – population measures to safeguard health
  * Prevention is split into three levels, primary secondary and tertiary prevention

* Prevention – reducing or avoiding the risks of disease
  * Health protection includes national screening programmes, such as those for breast cancer and cervical cancer, and immunisation programmes

Consider this

The role of the Environmental Health Department is described in this section.

1. What aspects of the service might be classified under the three aspects of health promotion: education, protection and prevention?

2. Think of an example of activities they might undertake which could be classed as primary and secondary prevention.

3. Of the other health educators described in this section, who could help you with your role in the Environmental Health Department and what activities would they contribute?

4. The incidence of food poisoning has been rising steadily in recent years. Find out what the position is in your district and what the likely causes are of this national problem

5. How could environmental health contribute to a radical health education approach to empower a local community? What types of issues might local people wish to work with this department to address? You might want to check with your local department to see what types of complaints they routinely deal with.

Section 3: Factors affecting health and well-being

Dahlgren and Whitehead (1995) mapped these fields as layers of influence, referring to them as the determinants of health, which can be modified to improve health expectancy:

Their work is now widely used to understand the broad range of influences on health, and more importantly how best to promote it. In this section we will look at a few of these factors from across their model including attitudes to health and their link to lifestyle choice, social factors including social class and culture income and disability.

Attitudes and prejudices

Lay perspectives can determine our attitudes to health and have a significant impact in determining how we respond to the challenge of managing our own health and well-being. However, of increasing importance has been the growing distrust by the general public of health professionals and the health advice they provide. This has been most graphically illustrated through the recent collapse of public confidence in the MMR vaccine as a result of one dissenting voice in the health establishment.

A research paper by Andrew Wakefield suggesting that MMR vaccination in young children might be linked to **autism** sparked a controversy, which was swept up by a media storm and went on to heavily influence the UK's Department of Health, the World Health Organization, and most broadcast and print media for several days either side of its publication. The ensuing media storm, in many cases adopting Wakefield's stance as a *cause célèbre*, flew in the face of all existing scientific evidence.

Findings from many other researchers provide no support for an MMR-associated form of autism. Despite this there has been significant damage to the public confidence in the vaccination, leading to a reduction in coverage and an increase in the associated deaths from these diseases. (Deaths from measles are common in some European countries, and this is directly related to poor vaccine coverage.) Measles has almost been eliminated in Britain, but high levels of population immunity (greater than 90 per cent) are needed to prevent the recurrence of epidemics.

This collapse in confidence might also be linked to the MMR vaccine becoming a victim of its own success. When disease elimination is close, attention inevitably shifts to the side-effects of the vaccine.

The latest findings from the Health Education Authority, which has been tracking a random sample of mothers with children aged 0–2 years since 1991, found that 8 per cent of mothers now consider that the MMR vaccine presents a greater risk than the diseases it protects against and that 20 per cent consider the vaccine to have a moderate or high risk of side-effects.

In October 1994, just before the national immunisation campaign against measles and rubella, 55 per cent of mothers considered measles to be a very serious illness; now only 20 per cent do so. This mirrors the problems experienced with the whooping cough vaccine, where a sustained, misinformed media campaign against the vaccine throughout the 1970s saw vaccine coverage drop from 81 per cent to 31 per cent.

Worryingly, 67 per cent of people knew that some scientists had linked the MMR vaccine with autism; however, they also thought that the

FIGURE 3.21 *The MMR vaccine is given at around 13 months of age*

evidence in favour of such a link was evenly balanced, or that the evidence even favoured a link. The long-term media coverage of controversy over the vaccine appears to have led the public to associate MMR and autism, despite the overwhelming evidence to the contrary. The public also thought the take-up of the MMR vaccine had fallen by more than 25 per cent since 1998, when, at the time of the survey, it was down by only 6 per cent.

The fears and concerns of parents are best seen through comments by one researcher who said: 'They [parents] wanted to trust their doctor and health visitor, but they felt they were being spun a political line', thus identifying the increasing politicisation of health practitioners and the erosion of public trust in their advice. Despite the huge amounts of scientific evidence to back up its policy, the government's medical advisors could not convince the public to simply accept their advice.

Lifestyle

As we have already seen it is too simplistic to see health as simply a matter of lifestyle choice as emphasized in this extract from *Choosing Health* (2004)...

'On paper, the answers can look deceptively simple – balance exercise and how much you eat, drink sensibly, practice safe sex, don't smoke. But knowing is not the same as doing. For individuals, motivation, opportunity and support all matter... Healthy choices are often difficult for anyone to make, but where people do not feel in control of their environment or their personal circumstances, the task can be more challenging. People who are disabled or suffer from mental ill health, stretched for money, out of work, poorly qualified, or who live in inadequate or temporary accommodation or in an area of high crime, are likely to experience less control over their lives than others.'

In a recent survey, 46 per cent of respondents agreed that there are too many factors outside of individual control to hold people responsible for their own health. Differences in responses for different groups suggest that people in lower socio-economic, socially excluded or black and minority ethnic groups may see health as being further beyond their individual control than others do.

The problem is not lack of information on what is good for you and what is not – people receive new 'facts' from all sides. The messages about health, however, are sometimes inconsistent or uncoordinated and out of step with the way people actually live their lives. It is a common assumption that lifestyle choices are simply a product of our attitudes to health. As a consequence, people routinely make judgements about the behaviours of others; statements such as 'that woman should not be smoking when she is pregnant' or 'that person who is overweight should go on a diet or take more exercise' might be typical examples of what is termed 'victim blaming' , i.e. lifestyle as a choice we all make. But there is now considerable evidence that choice is quite limited in many cases. For example, the vast majority of people who smoke are first recruited at a very young age, before they are mature enough to make an 'adult choice'. The complex nature of the environment and its impact on health choices is also important. For example, choosing healthy nutritious food is as much a feature of availability in the shops and access to the shops that provide it, as it is of personal choice. Therefore, it is unfair to make simple assumptions about people's health behaviours; lifestyle choice is often a more complex mix of issues. Several examples, including nutrition, smoking and substance use, are considered in more detail below.

Diet and nutrition

In the early parts of the 20th century the overwhelming focus of national food policy was that of securing enough food, as opposed to improving the diet of the population. This policy had its origins in the Boer War but became firmly established during the global conflicts of World War 1 and World War 11. Malnourishment, in terms of insufficient fat and protein in the diet, was widespread at this time and remained this way throughout the war years until the end of rationing. The current Western dietary problems are frequently traced back to this point as the origin of the range of choice and widespread availability of food, which we take for granted today. It is this shift to malnourishment in the form of over-consumption that now characterises the major dietary problems of the developed world.

Nutrition has recently become a high profile health issue, particularly in light of the way in which obesity has risen up the health agenda (as illustrated by its prominence in *Choosing Health*, 2004). This is particularly because of startling recent trends in young children, where among 3–4-year-olds there has been a 60 per cent increase in the prevalence of being overweight and a 70 per cent increase in rates of obesity. Most adults in England are now overweight and one in five (around 8 million) are obese (Body Mass Index in excess of 30) with 30,000 deaths a year linked to obesity and an estimated cost to the NHS of £500 million a year.

If trends continue obesity will become, if it is not already, a major public health concern contributing substantially to:

* type 2 diabetes
* coronary heart disease
* hypertension
* depression
* cancers
* high blood pressure
* stroke

As well as its role in tackling obesity, diet also has a major part to play in managing the current trends in cancers. Over the past 25 years the

* DID YOU KNOW?

The Body Mass Index (BMI) is a reliable indicator of total body fat, which is related to the risk of disease and death. BMI can be calculated using weight and height with the following equation:

$$BMI = \frac{\text{Weight in kilograms}}{\text{(Height in metres)} \times \text{(Height in metres)}}$$

The score is valid for both men and women but it does have limits. It may overestimate body fat in athletes and others who have a muscular build, and it may underestimate body fat in older persons and others who have lost muscle mass.

	BMI
Underweight	Below 18.5
Normal	18.5–24.9
Overweight	25.0–29.9
Obesity	30.0 and above

incidence of all cancers has risen by 8 per cent in men and 17 per cent in women. Up to 80 per cent of bowel and breast cancer may be preventable by dietary change. These trends in diet-related cancers and obesity have occurred, despite the main elements of the dietary message remaining the same for many years:

* eat plenty of fruit and vegetables

* eat plenty of cereal foods

* eat red meat and processed foods in moderation

* avoid high doses of vitamin supplements

* avoid highly salted foods

* drink alcohol in moderation.

If the message remains straightforward, why is it that 4 per cent of young people aged 4–18 years still eat no vegetables at all and an average 10-year-old will eat his or her own weight in chips over a 9-month period? One reason why people fail to act on this widely known information is that healthy eating messages carry too many negative and constricting associations. That is, the public view healthy eating as being part of a boring lifestyle, as the government states in the 2004 white paper: 'Alcohol and fast food are portrayed as offering excitement, escape and instant gratification.' Therefore, it raises a need to develop positive images of healthier lifestyles for people to aspire to.

It is all too easy to view public health issues, such as obesity, in simplistic ways; nutrition inequalities mirror those of other issues, for example:

* poorer groups eat the least quantities of fresh fruit and vegetables

* dental caries are more common in children from lower socio-economic groups – due to higher levels of sweet consumption

* households in the bottom 10 per cent of income distribution spend an average of 29 per cent of their disposable income on food, compared to 18 per cent for those in the top 10 per cent.

Assumptions about the buying patterns of the less well off are often flawed: people in the low socio-economic groups buy more efficiently than those in high income brackets, obtaining more grams of food per pound spent. However, that often requires spending more on high calorific value foods, such as those rich in sugar and fat and therefore little in the way of fruit and vegetables; this also leads to lack of choice and variety to avoid risking waste. The food budget is also liable to squeezing by other demands, which impacts less in higher income households, a particular issue when healthy baskets of food can cost more in disadvantaged areas than in affluent.

The advent of large scale out-of-town supermarkets has enabled these stores to drive down cost through bulk purchasing but, as a consequence, led to a reduction in availability of healthy nutritious food locally on some estates.

FIGURE 3.22 *Local traders cannot compete with prices at the out-of-town supermarkets*

This creates difficulties in terms of travel and additional expense for these families, leading to the creation of so called food deserts on some estates, described as being 'populated urban areas where residents do not have access to affordable healthy food'. The charity 'Sustain' identifies that only 14–46 per cent of households on a £60–150 income per week have a car, often making larger out-of-town supermarkets inaccessible. People in deprived areas have to travel at least one mile to be able to access shops with a wider stock range, often requiring an expense of £2–3 in fares, both facts being compounded by the frequent shopping patterns of these households because of limited cash flow and storage. The issue is made worse by the fact that stores that do remain in deprived areas are frequently high cost and often offer poorer quality produce.

Therefore, it is highly unlikely that simplistic messages to eat the recommended five portions of fruit and vegetables a day will succeed in reversing the steady increase in the numbers of people who are overweight and obese. This problem is clearly as much to do with planning of supermarket developments, travel plans, the length of the working day, cooking skills, and a whole host of other larger societal issues, as to do with individual choice.

Think it over...

Promoting better diet is clearly a complex issue.

Go back to the Dahlgren and Whitehead (1995) model of health inequalities; now break down the issue of nutrition using the layers this suggests. Use a single issue to consider it. For example, why are young children increasingly overweight and obese?

1 For each issue in each layer ask, how does this issue relate to the problem?

2 Write your observations down for each layer.

3 Now work back through the layers and try to suggest a couple of actions for each layer that would improve things

The result is what would be called a 'whole system' approach, one which starts with the individual and works its way out to include national and international actions.

Smoking

The link between smoking and ill health is now well documented. 'Smoking is the single most important modifiable risk factor for CHD in young and old.' (*Our Healthier Nation*, 1997) A lifetime non-smoker, is 60 per cent less likely to have CHD and 30 per cent less likely to have a stroke than a smoker. Smoking mirrors other patterns of ill health, in that the highest levels are in the lowest social groups. Although the proportion of young people who smoke is similar across all social groups, by their mid 30s, 50 per cent of young people from higher social classes have stopped, as opposed to only 25 per cent from the lowest income groups. The result is that about one third of the smokers in the population are concentrated in only the lowest 10 per cent of earners in the country.

✳ DID YOU KNOW?

✳ Tobacco smoking causes most lung cancers.

✳ It is implicated in a wide range of other cancers including those of the nose and throat but also cervical cancer.

✳ Overall, about one third of cancer deaths can be attributed to smoking.

✳ Smoking also contributes to CHD and stroke rates.

This reflects evidence that campaigning measures to reduce smoking levels have compounded this problem by encouraging those in higher social groups to quit, whilst having minimal effect on those in the lowest income brackets. Therefore, some health promotion campaigning can compound health inequality. In their response to the problem the government released a white paper, '*Smoking Kills*', in 1998. This outlined funding for a nationwide network of smoking cessation services to support smokers who wished to quit.

Substance use

In recent years there has been growing public concern over the levels of illegal drug use amongst young people. Data published by the Home Office (2002) shows that rates have been rising consistently over several decades and are now stabilising at an all-time high. Using the indicator of declared misuse, the percentage using any drug rises slightly from 23 per cent in 1994 to 25 per cent in 2000. Most of this use is **cannabis** (10 per cent using in the last year) or amphetamine (2 per cent). Much of this use is clearly not very regular because there is a significant difference between use in the last month (cannabis 14 per cent, amphetamine 2 per cent) and lifetime use (cannabis 44 per cent, amphetamine 22 per cent). Drug use rises to be most widespread in the 16–25 range before gradually declining, as illustrated by the 1998 figures for all drug use (See Figure 3.23).

Age range (in years)	11–15	16–25	16–29
Drug use in last year	11%	29%	25%

FIGURE 3.23 *Figures for all drug use*
Source: Home office (2002)

The cost to society of drug misuse is well documented. In the criminal justice system each crime costs on average £100 to record, (a cost of £2 million to the North West in 1998). On average, users spend £200 each week on drugs, amounting to an annual spend of £89 million per year in the North West. Approximately half this amount will be raised through acquisitive crime, burglary, shoplifting and muggings, where the depreciation in value of the stolen goods could mean a true figure for the goods stolen is nearer £134 million. Society also pays a high cost in terms of illness and deaths, with 2,117 drug-related deaths in 1997 alone, although this figure is widely acknowledged as being under-reported.

Recognising the growing concern about this widespread use of illegal substances the government of 1995 introduced the first national drugs strategy, *Tackling Drugs Together*, which set out three key aims:

＊ 'Increase the safety of communities from drug related crime

＊ Reduce the acceptability and availability of drugs to young people

＊ Reduce the health risks and other damage related to drug misuse.'

(HM Government, 1995)

This also created an infrastructure to drive forward the drugs strategy through a network of strategic Drug Action Teams (DATs) and their implementation counterparts, Drug Reference Groups. Multi-sectoral partnerships with key roles within these groups were taken up by criminal justice and treatment agencies such as the police force, probation service, prisons and the NHS.

Social factors

Social class has long been used as the method of measuring and monitoring health inequalities. Since the Black report of 1988, it has been clearly identified and acknowledged that those from the lowest social groupings experience the poorest health in society. Traditionally, inequalities reporting has used the following categories:

SOCIAL CLASS GROUPING		EXAMPLES
1	Professional	Doctors, engineers
11	Managerial/ technical	Managers, teachers
111N	Non manual (skilled)	Clerks, cashiers
111M	Non manual (unskilled)	Carpenters, van drivers
1V	Partly skilled	Warehouse workers, security guards
V	Unskilled	Labourers

However it has been accepted more recently that these groupings are no longer representative of the population. Therefore, for the 2001 census the Office of National Statistics (ONS) reclassified the population into eight layers as shown in Figure 3.24; specifically picking out the long-term unemployed as a separate group for the first time.

The unemployed are amongst the most socially disadvantaged and as a consequence experience significant inequalities in health. For a small minority, unemployment actually leads to an improvement in health, but for the vast majority being unemployed leads to significantly poorer health. The unemployed have higher

SOCIO-ECONOMIC CLASSIFICATION		
ANALYTIC CLASSES		**EXAMPLES**
1	Higher managerial and professional occupations	
1.1	Large employers and higher managerial occupations	Chief Executives of major organisations
1.2	Higher professional occupations	Doctors, lawyers
2	Lower managerial and professional occupations	Middle management in bigger organisations, departmental managers or customer services, teachers, physiotherapists
3	Intermediate occupations	lerks and bank workers
4	Small employers and own account workers	Painters and decorators, or small manufacturing company owners
5	Lower supervisory and technical occupations	Builders, joiners
6	Semi-routine occupations	Unskilled labouring jobs
7	Routine occupations	Assembly line workers
8	Never worked and long-term unemployed	

FIGURE 3.24 *Socio-economic Classification of the Office of National Statistics (2001)*

levels of depression, suicide and self-harm and a significantly increased risk of **morbidity** and **mortality** across all causes. Men unemployed at both census dates in 1971 and 1981 had mortality rates twice that of the rest of other men in that age range, and those men who were unemployed at one census date had an excess mortality of 27 per cent. Adverse effects associated with unemployment include:

* increased smoking at the onset of unemployment – the prevalence of smoking is considerably higher among those who are unemployed

* increased alcohol consumption with unemployment, especially in young men

* more weight gain for those who are unemployed

* reduced physical activity and exercise

* use of illicit drugs in the young who are without work

* increased sexual risk-taking among unemployed young men

* reduced psychological well-being, with a greater incidence of self-harm, depression and anxiety.

Race is also another factor to affect life expectancy, particularly because of the differences in culture this may bring. Black and minority ethnic groups have higher risks of mortality from a range of diseases such as diabetes, liver cancer, tuberculosis, stroke and heart disease. Infant mortality and mental illness have also been highlighted as problems amongst African-Caribbean men. However, establishing the cause of these variations has proved difficult. Medical interventions have tended to concentrate on cultural practices, but this does not acknowledge the compounding factors of poverty and low employment levels in these groups. However, racism must play a part in the experiences of minority ethnic communities in contact with health services and, as a causative factor, in leading to a higher than average experience of poverty and unemployment in these groups.

However we choose to classify the different social strata, most recent research suggests that it is the countries with the smallest income *differences* rather than the richest countries that have the best health status. Where income differences remain great, as in this country, health inequalities will persist; for example:

* children in the lowest social class are five times more likely to die from an accident than those in the top social class.

* someone in social Class 5 is three times more likely to experience a stroke than someone in Class 1

* infant mortality rates are highest amongst the lowest social groups

* the difference in life expectancy between a man from one of the most affluent areas in this country and a man living in Manchester is 6 years.

Environmental issues

The impact of the environment on health can be seen from two perspectives – the capacity to provide benefits to health and the capacity to do harm. Benefits to health are provided, for example, in that parks and recreational spaces can encourage us to participate in regular exercise or even just allow us the opportunity to experience time away from the stresses and strains of everyday life. On the other hand, the impact of the environment through pollution, or through poor housing which it is now well documented, can lead to chest illnesses such as asthma and bronchitis. There is also some argument as to whether landfill sites do have the potential to harm those people who live close to them and, of course, the argument still rages as to whether mobile phones and their masts have the potential, through the microwaves emitted, to cause cancer and possible brain damage in the people who use or live near them. Friends of the Earth (FOE) would argue that phone masts are often situated in built-up areas close to schools and on top of blocks of flats, thus having the potential to harm many people.

Pollution

Pollution can be said to have occurred when the environment is negatively affected in some way. It arises in many ways, from air pollution to land, water and aesthetic pollution (visual). Many of these forms of pollution have the potential to effect long-term damage on both the environment and human health and well-being on a global and national scale. It is argued that pollution should be monitored and measured to allow action to be taken to reduce the amount of all kinds of pollution.

Work environment

All companies in the UK with five or more employees have a legal duty to maintain and implement safe systems of work under the 1974 Health and Safety at Work Act. Occupational health services in the UK are an integral part of this process. They work within the spirit of the Act with the task of meeting the specific subordinate regulations relating to occupational health.

The Health and Safety at Work Act 1974 (HSWA) places a wide ranging duty on employers to protect the safety, health and welfare of their employees. Regulations made under the HSWA and other legislation place specific duties on employers relating to risk assessment, health surveillance, managing health, fitness for work, protecting the vulnerable and employing the disabled.

Home environment

The home environment links very closely with the local environment to the extent that, in some cases, they cannot be easily separated. For example, when we talk about the home we include all the internal and external factors, such as gardens, driveways and garages. The interior of the home usually consists of a number of rooms designed for specific purposes. Each room has the potential to create negative or positive effects on health. In fact, there are aspects of the entire house that could affect well-being. Think about the electricity supply, the wiring systems, electrical appliances, gas appliances, roof space and wall cavities. We also need to remember that in the home we often store cleaning materials that have the potential to harm our health and we also need to consider the environmental effects of food preparation, cooking and storage. Again, food safety forms an important part of our environment.

We can also include indoor air pollution in an exploration of the home environment; for example, inhaling other people's tobacco smoke (passive smoking) is clearly a risk to health. There is also a risk to health in some homes from **radon gas**, which is naturally occurring in many areas

Think it over...

Carry out an environmental audit of your own home or immediate locality.

Make a note of the factors that have the potential to affect health and well-being and then explain in what ways each could affect the health of a range of service-user groups, i.e. older people, children and adults.

Health practices

To understand what is meant by health practices it is probably best to consider some examples of specific activities that can protect our health. A good example might be to practice safe sex by using a condom. This practice protects both people not only from a range of sexually transmitted infections but also unplanned pregnancy. Another example might be to practice

safer injecting if you are an intravenous drug user (IDU). Intravenous (IV) drug users are at risk from a range of blood-borne viruses, most notably **HIV**, **hepatitis** C and B and a range of other diseases if they share needles, syringes or the paraphernalia associated with their drug use. Therefore intravenous drug users are encouraged to use safer injecting practices, such as, for example, not sharing paraphernalia (spoons, cotton wool, and so on.) and not sharing needles or syringes. This is known as a '**harm reduction'** approach since it acknowledges that the associated behaviour (IV drug use) is self-damaging but accepts that there is no need to compound the problem by adding additional risks through sharing needles. As part of this philosophy, most districts will have a needle/syringe exchange service, where IV drug users can exchange used needles and syringes for clean 'works'. This protects both the drug users and the rest of the population by reducing their risk of contracting a blood-borne virus. It takes their spent needles and syringes out of circulation safely, thereby reducing the numbers of discarded needles, and controlling the levels of blood-borne viruses in the population at large.

There are other simpler forms of health practice, which are equally important, such as, for example, simply washing your hands. This might seem like a basic practice but it is central to the government's recent initiative to reduce hospital-acquired infections. This recognises that basic hygiene practices must be maintained to prevent patients from acquiring infections like **MRSA** in hospital. MRSA is an antibiotic-resistant form of *Staphylococcus aureus*, a micro-organism which most people carry without symptoms. However, the resistance to antibiotic treatment can make this a potentially life-threatening condition, particularly for vulnerable people who are, by definition, already ill if they are admitted to hospital. If you observe nurses whilst they work today, it is highly likely that they will have a small bottle of cleansing solution attached to their uniform, which they use to wash their hands after dealing with a patient to avoid transferring any micro-organisms to another patient. This is supported by training in effective hand-washing techniques, strict cleaning rotas and promotional materials, urging people to remember to wash their hands and showing them how best to do it.

Recreation

What we do with our spare time in terms of recreation can have a significant influence on our health. Recreational pursuits can contribute to a wide range of health benefits such as promoting physically active lifestyles, weight management, stress release and promoting a sense of well-being, leading to improved mental health status. In 2004 the Health Development Agency published a review of how people use their leisure time, which found that:

* those who participate in sporting activities are also more likely to participate in cultural activities, and vice versa

* for both sport and culture, the biggest single groups were of people who tend to do very little of anything

* higher levels of household income, education and social class usually predicted higher rates of participation in most cultural and sporting activities

* after accounting for household income and social class, not having access to a vehicle was important in determining the amount of sporting and cultural activity that individuals are able to participate in

* there were no especially marked regional differences in participation in culture and sport.

ACTIVITY	PERCENTAGE OF RESPONDENTS WHO CARRIED OUT ACTIVITY IN PAST FOUR WEEKS	AVERAGE TIME SPENT ON ACTIVITY IN PAST FOUR WEEKS (MINUTES)
None	17	0
Walking or hiking (1 hour/2+ miles)	12	108
Swimming indoors	9	34
Keep-fit, aerobics, yoga, dance exercise	7	49
Cycling	7	26
Snooker, pool, billiards	6	26
Football outdoors	4	no data
Jogging, cross-country, road running	3	6
Weight training	3	no data
Golf	3	no data
Swimming outdoors	2	no data
Tenpin bowling	2	no data
Darts	2	no data
Football indoors	2	no data
Tennis	2	no data
Darts	2	no data
Badminton	2	no data

FIGURE 3.25 *Physical activities carried out in the past four weeks – all persons aged 8 years and over*

Source: ONS (2002)

In terms of participation in the last 12 months the five most popular sports, games or physical activities among adults were:

* walking (46 per cent)

* swimming (35 per cent)

* keep-fit/yoga – including aerobics and dance exercise (22 per cent) cycling (19 per cent)

* cue sports – billiards, snooker and pool (17 per cent).

Men were found to be more likely to participate in sports activities than women (either including or excluding walking). Active forms of recreation were found to be in decline. In 1996, 54 per cent of men and 38 per cent of women had participated in at least one activity, excluding walking, but by 2002 participation had fallen to just over half (51 per cent) of men and 36 per cent of women. Participation rates also decreased with age. In 2002, 72 per cent of young adults (aged 16 to 19 years) compared with 54 per cent of adults aged 30 to 44 years and 14 per cent of adults aged 70 years and over had participated in at least one activity (excluding walking) in the last four weeks before interview.

Whilst the levels of participation shown in Figure 3.25, at first glance, appear to be encouraging, it is important to reflect on the amount of time people spent on this activity in the last month. The longest average time spent was 108 minutes walking in a month, with most others being 20–30 minutes (where information was available). Therefore, this does little to dispel the concern that as a wealth of surveys now demonstrate we are becoming an increasingly sedentary (inactive) population that increasingly does not participate in active forms of recreation which would improve our heart health, or cultural activities which might benefit other aspects of health, such as our mental well-being.

Housing

Public health campaigners have been advocating for improvements in housing to better the public's health since the middle of the 19th century. For example, Edwin Chadwick's (an active campaigner on a number of public health issues, including poor housing), *Report on an inquiry into the sanitary conditions of the labouring population of Great Britain* (1842), resulted in the first national Public Health Act (1848).

The link between housing and health remains true to this day, the Office for National Statistics Longitudinal Study showing that between 1971 and 1981 age-standardised mortality rates for social tenants (those in rented accommodation) were 25 per cent higher than for owner-occupiers. Although death rates have declined since that time, the gap between these groups has widened. Owner-occupiers have seen greater reductions in death rates than those living in rented accommodation.

This link between housing tenure and health status is probably best explained by considering housing as an indicator for income deprivation, or social class. Those on low incomes are more likely to live in poor housing conditions, experience overcrowding, poor washing and cooking facilities, damp and disrepair. Children who live in such houses with damp are known to have higher than usual rates of respiratory conditions like asthma, and **communicable infections**, which are transmitted more easily in overcrowded conditions. Childhood accident rates are also highest in areas of high-density housing, where play facilities are limited and it is difficult for parents to supervise children at play outside.

The patterns of housing tenure are changing due to the introduction of the 'right-to-buy' scheme in the early 1980s, and the transfer of housing stock from local authorities to housing associations (or Registered Social Landlords [RSLs]), during the 1990s. The result has been an increase in home ownership from 49 per cent to 69 per cent, between 1971 and 2002, with most of the increase occurring in the 1980s, the increase levelling off since then.

Corresponding to this, the percentage of households which are rented council homes increased from 31 per cent in 1971 to 34 per cent in 1981, but then gradually declined during the 1980s to 24 per cent in 1991. The percentage continued to decrease so that by 2002 only 14 per cent of all households were rented from the council. The percentage of households renting from a housing association increased from 1 per cent in 1971 to 3 per cent in 1991, continuing throughout the 1990s to 7 per cent in 2002.

How these changes influence the health of the population is not yet apparent, but it may not be as simple as saying that the numbers of home owners has risen, therefore the health of those people will also improve. Right-to-buy schemes allowed people to purchase their home at heavily discounted rates, therefore it does not necessarily represent an increase in the income of those people. Indeed, the additional responsibilities of maintaining their own home may act as a drain on their limited resources in some cases, making them less well off with the attendant health problems this may bring.

Workplace health

Sickness absence costs employers at least £11 billion each year, a staggering 16 per cent of their total salary costs. Research has found that 90 per cent of employers believe sickness costs can be significantly reduced, yet very few employers monitor sickness absence or take active steps to reduce it. Indeed, 55 per cent of employers do not even measure the cost of sickness absence and only 49 per cent of employers have set targets to reduce sickness absence. However, despite this apparent indifference 60 per cent of employees do want their employers to take some responsibility for their health at work.

Two million people suffer an illness they believe has been caused by, or made worse by, their work. Forty million working days are lost each year to occupational ill health and injury, where stress-related conditions and **musculoskeletal** disorders are now the commonest reported causes of work-related sickness absence. Stress is commonly linked to long working hours; this country has the longest working week of any European country, with 3.74 million workers clocking up more than the 48-hour-limit under the Working Time Directive – 423,000 more than in 1992 when there was no protection against long working hours.

This illustrates the potential for improving health through the workplace and possible financial rewards for employers who are prepared to invest in their workforce's health. Reflecting on this information it should be apparent that workplace health promotion is not just about promoting healthy eating and physical activity it covers a wide range of issues, such as:

* health promotion policies for smoking, alcohol, transport and nutrition

* access to health care services, including occupational health

* good human resource approaches

* flexible working arrangements

* helping employees achieve a work life balance

* fostering good employer/employee relations

* staff benefits, e.g. discount arrangements with local shops or leisure providers.

Effective workplace programmes, which address these aspects, can provide real benefits for employers in terms of reduced absenteeism, increased productivity, improved staff attitude and morale and reduced staff turnover.

For example, the government introduced the Work–Life Balance Campaign in 2000. The campaign aims to help employers recognise the benefits of adopting policies and procedures that enable employees to adopt flexible working patterns. This helps their staff to become better motivated and more productive because they will be better able to balance their work and other aspects of their lives. There is now evidence that employers that offer flexibility in working arrangements are experiencing an increase in recruitment and retention, employee commitment and productivity, and a decrease in staff turnover and sickness absence. A report by the Institute for Employment Studies (IES) shows some small businesses save up to £250,000 on their budget, simply by using family-friendly work policies. One company claimed profitability was up by 37 per cent.

Family

Our family can play a significant part in determining our health status in a variety of ways.

The genes we inherit can determine our future health status; for example, the risk of developing coronary heart disease is linked to family history, as are certain types of breast and other cancers. These are aspects of our health that we have little control over (although the possibilities raised by genetic engineering may change this in the future).

The health behaviours of adults in key positions in the family can have a major impact on the health of young people. For example, an estimated 920,000 children are currently living in a home where one or both parents misuse alcohol, with 6.2 per cent of adults having grown up in a family where one or both of their parents drank excessively. Serious problems are experienced by children as a result of the drinking behaviour of their parents. An analysis of NSPCC helpline calls showed parental alcohol misuse to be a factor in 23 per cent of child neglect cases, and parental alcohol misuse was also reported in 13 per cent of calls about emotional abuse, 10 per cent of calls about physical abuse and 5 per cent of calls about sexual abuse. Children of problem drinkers have higher levels of behavioural difficulty, school-related problems and emotional disturbance than children of non-problem drinking parents, and higher levels of dysfunction than children whose parents have other mental or physical problems.

Another aspect of family life is the way in which we are socialised, i.e. the types of behaviours we are raised to accept as normal. This can involve our ethnicity, the region we live in, or our religious beliefs, for example. However, family health behaviours are also invloved; it is now well evidenced, for example, that young people are more likely to engage in sporting activity if their parents are also active.

We know that 42 per cent of British children live in a household where at least one person smokes. Smoking levels are often high amongst families and within friendship groups in the most income-deprived households. Here smoking is accepted as the norm; in these families many people started smoking regularly in their early teens, and there is considerable evidence that because smoking is very much the norm, parents are willing to accommodate their children's smoking (either actively or passively). In a recent piece of research by the Health Development Agency, a sample of young people from disadvantaged backgrounds were asked about their experiences of smoking and few said they encountered any pressure from parents or partners to quit smoking, usually because they themselves smoked.

This illustrates another aspect of family influence which is important – the link between family health and disadvantage. For example, people are more likely to smoke if:

* they have no educational qualifications/early school-leaving age

* live in rented accommodation

* do not having a car and/or phone

* the adults in the household are traditionally involved in manual labour

* they live off means-tested benefits (especially income support).

These are just some of the markers for predicting whether someone is more or less likely to smoke. No one chooses to be born into a disadvantaged family, but clearly the material wealth of the people in that family will play a major part in determining the health of its members. This fact is repeated through a range of the wider determinants of health. For example, the level of a mother's education correlates particularly strongly with her children's success at school.

In general, children from low-income households go on to leave full-time education much earlier, and with fewer formal qualifications than their more affluent counterparts. Of children born in 1970, for example, some 24 per cent failed to achieve any formal qualifications by the age of 30, whilst 23 per cent went on to get a degree. Among children from low-income households, however, only 11 per cent went on to get a degree and 38 per cent achieved no formal qualifications. Illustrating the cyclical nature of disadvantage, that once born into disadvantage, a person is likely to remain disadvantaged throughout life and consequently suffer poorer health.

Physical factors (disability as an example)

Disability is the consequence of impairment or other individual difference. The disability a person experiences is determined by the way in which other people respond to that difference. It can have serious social consequences, which in turn can harm that person's health. In the past, being left handed was considered a disability and left-handed people were banned from certain jobs. Today we are more accepting of that difference, but this does not apply for all such differences; for example, people with a disability are three times more likely to be unemployed with all the attendant health impacts described below. As a means of addressing some of these inequalities the Disability Discrimination Act 1995 (DDA) requires employers with 15 or more employees to treat disabled persons equally with non-disabled persons in all employment matters and make any reasonable changes to the premises, job design, and so on, that may be necessary to accommodate the needs of disabled employees.

Think it over...

Look at the Dahlgren/Whitehead diagram of the determinants of health. Using the categories in the layers of this diagram and the examples below, try to plot the issues which might impact on the health of the following two case studies.

But first consider all the factors which impact on your own health. Start at the centre with the issues that you can least influence and work outwards to think about issues like the work environment and local neighbourhood, before thinking about more national issues like our long working hours and high car dependency. Then you can begin to explore the case studies of people who might figure in socially excluded groups; for example:

* a woman aged 65 years, living alone and whose family has now moved abroad. She has arthritis and can only walk a short distance

* a gay man, living with his partner 'out' to close friends, but not 'out' to work

Summary

* People's attitudes to their own health and the advice of health professionals can significantly affect their behaviour.

* Lifestyle is both a product of our own lay beliefs about health and environmental influences; key lifestyle issues considered here include:

    * nutrition – and its links to rising obesity levels in all age ranges

    * substance use where young people's use (illicit substance use being predominantly an activity for under 25s) has stabilised in recent years

    * smoking – which is a major contributor to levels of cancers and coronary heart disease.

* Social factors are also an important contributor to health inequalities with the unemployed being amongst the least healthy people, as are other disadvantaged groups like ethnic minorities and those with a disability.

* Environment plays a both a negative and positive part in promoting health.

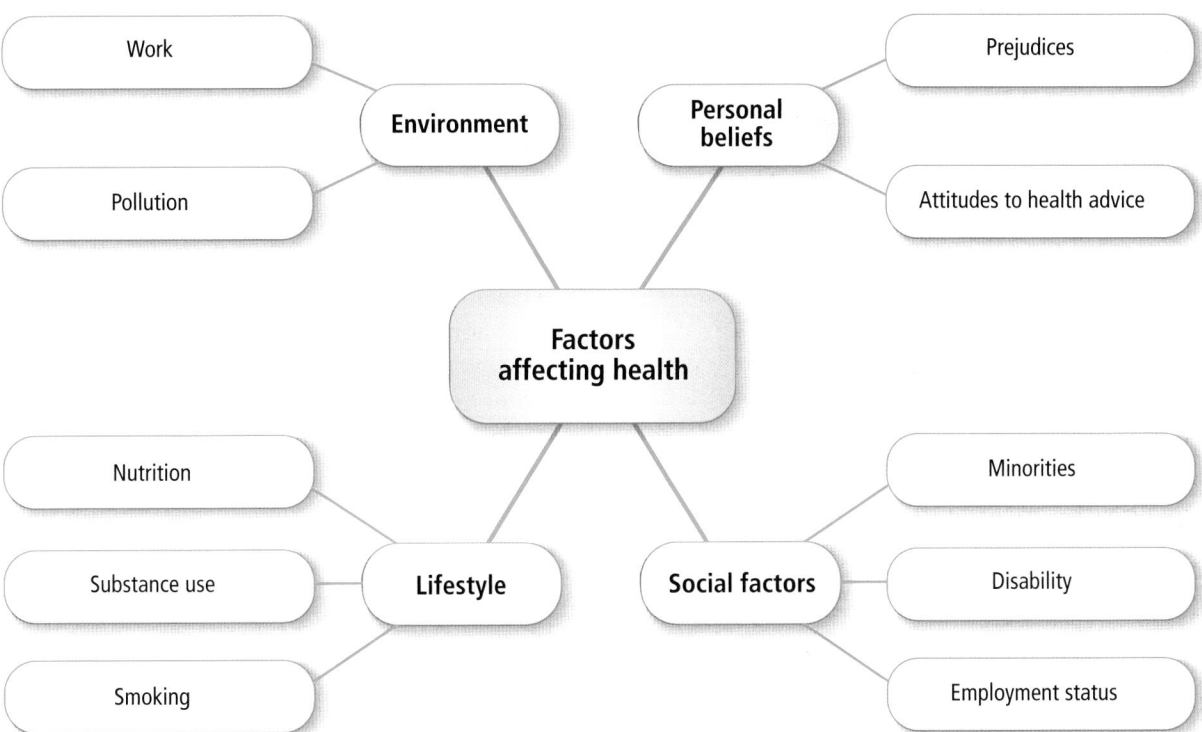

Young people are a key group for addressing many of the health issues dealt with in this chapter:

1 Research suggests that young people often over-estimate the numbers of people who smoke in the population. Make an educated guess about the proportion of people in college who smoke. Then design and carry out a piece of research to check how accurate your assessment was.

2 How would you have to change your research design if you were trying to do the same exercise for a range of illicit substances including cannabis, amphetamine and Ecstasy?

3 Does substance use mirror other health inequalities? I.e. Does it impact most on the poorest groups in society and, if not, why

not? If you are unsure, begin to find out by looking on the Home Office website, where this data is routinely published.

4 If you were planning a health education campaign to warn young people about the dangers of drug use, you need to know the age at which people start to experiment and the age that it becomes regular use? Which type of use is most dangerous and why? What messages would be appropriate for these two differing types of use?

5 How might public opinions and attitudes about drugs impact on the type of information you would like to get across to young people? How could it limit or moderate your ideas?

Section 4: Health promotion

Approaches to health promotion

The term health promotion covers a wide range of different activities, all of which have a part to play in promoting health. None of these differing approaches is essentially the right way; they are simply different aspects which complement each other. The balance between them is very much a choice based on personal perspective, influenced by our own life experience, personal standpoints and values, as illustrated in the wide range of differing lay perspectives on health. Health promotion is commonly characterised as having five differing approaches:

* the medical approach
* the behaviour change approach
* the educational approach
* the service-user-centred approach
* the societal change approach.

However, these are by no means the only approaches within this field of practice and, confusingly, people can refer to the same approach using differing terminology. Figure 3.26 identifies the most commonly identified five approaches and other terms used to describe those approaches. The issue of smoking is used to illustrate the varying aims and activities of each approach.

Approaches, methods and materials

There are many ways in which you can communicate health-promotion messages to your local community.

Interaction

It is hard to quantify the extent to which individual face-to-face interaction can contribute to health campaigning. However, it is clear that the general public hold certain groups within society in high regard and, therefore, respect the information they obtain from their doctors, nurses, teachers and environmental health officers; this creates considerable potential for promoting key health messages simply through the day-to-day routine of work. It might mean a doctor suggesting to people that they consider giving up smoking when they attend for a health check, or a district nurse suggesting that moderate activity is still possible and potentially beneficial for an older service user whilst visiting them at home. It is quite normal for key health campaigns to engage these health promoters in the communication of a key message: for example, National No Smoking Day, for which many health practitioners plan specific events to link with the national campaign and offer support to people wishing to quit smoking.

Leaflets

Leaflets are the backbone of health education activity. They can serve a wide variety of purposes such as informing people about local services, providing information about specific health conditions, giving advice about specific health-promotion issues or engaging people in thought about broader health considerations. In many cases leaflets are designed to support specific health campaigns such as those for immunisation and National No Smoking Day. However, it is important to remember that for many people a leaflet will not be a useful means of communication. It was identified in a 2003 national research study for the Department of Education and Science (DfES) that:

* 5.2 million adults in England could be described as lacking basic literacy (that is, they were at entry level 3 or below according to National Standards for Literacy and Numeracy)
* more than one third of people with poor or very poor health had literacy skills of entry level 3 or below
* low levels of literacy and numeracy were found to be associated with socio-economic deprivation
* 53 per cent of all adults surveyed had entry or lower level practical skills in using information and communication technology (ICT).

APPROACH	AIM	HEALTH-PROMOTION ACTIVITY
Medical model (Interventionist)	To be free from medically defined disease and disability	Using a medical treatment either to prevent or reduce the effects of ill health
E.g. smoking	To remain free from diseases associated with smoking, e.g. lung and heart diseases	Encouraging people to seek early detection and treatment of smoking-related disorders
Behaviourist (Preventive/ Persuasive)	To promote individual behaviours in the population which keep people free from disease	Encouraging adoption of 'healthier' lifestyle by changing attitude and therefore behaviour
E.g. smoking	To change people's smoking behaviour	Persuading people either not to start smoking or to stop smoking, and if they have already started, to stop
Educationalist (Informative)	To provide people with the necessary knowledge and skills to them to make well-informed decisions	Launching educational activity to disseminate information about health and maintenance of good health. Development of skills required for healthy living
E.g. smoking	To develop people's understanding of the effects of smoking on health and their decision-making skills	Giving information to service users about the effects of smoking. Developing their skills in quitting smoking or resisting enticement to start smoking
Service-user-centred (Empowerment)	To work on health issues on the service user's terms, not your own	Allowing the service user to identify health issues, choices and actions which they choose and thereby empowering the service user
E.g. smoking		Here the smoking issue would only arise if the service user selected it. Any further discussion would be led by the service user's willingness to address the topic
Working to change society	To change the physical and social environment to enable healthier lifestyles	Working within the political or social system to change the physical/social environment
E.g. smoking	To make smoking socially unacceptable, i.e. to change the way in which society as a whole views the behaviour – making it more difficult to smoke	Increasing the number of public spaces covered by no smoking policies, making non-smoking the norm in society, making cigarette sales to children more difficult, banning tobacco advertising and sports sponsorship
Fear	To frighten people into adopting a healthier lifestyle	Launching educational activity to disseminate information about the effects of unhealthy lifestyles
E.g. smoking	To make the effects of smoking so frightening as to prevent people taking up smoking or to encourage those who do smoke to quit	Using real-life patients talking about their experiences of lung cancer brought on by smoking

FIGURE 3.26 *Commonly used approaches to health-promoting activities*

Clearly many agencies still do little to take account of people's literacy levels. Another survey of the readability of patient information produced by hospices and palliative care units showed that 64 per cent of leaflets were readable only by an estimated 40 per cent of the population.

Therefore, a leaflet on first appearance is a relatively simple tool, but it is important to consider a range of questions when designing or using one:

✳ Who is this leaflet for? A drugs leaflet appropriate for secondary school children will not be appropriate for use in primary schools.

✳ Who produced the leaflet, will they have an interest in the information? If a commercial organisation, such as a drug company, produced the leaflet will this mean they have been selective in their reporting of the information?

✳ How long ago was it first produced? Is the information still relevant or accurate? For example, information on drug-related harm changes very rapidly.

✳ Is the language level used appropriate to the target audience? Is it too adult? Does it include abbreviations or technical terms?

✳ Is it well designed, i.e. will it grab the attention of the reader from amongst the other leaflets and posters? Will it connect specifically with the target audience?

✳ Are the key messages clearly identified, or are there too many other distractions?

✳ For the particular leaflet and target audience, where is the best place to display it?

Posters

Posters provide an excellent tool for catching the attention of the target audience and supporting the key broad messages you might then develop in more detail within a leaflet. The factors which draw attention to a poster can be divided into two groups – physical characteristics and motivational characteristics (see Figure 3.27). Clearly these summarise the key points of a poster: to be eye catching and big enough to attract attention. It will need to be in colour, or, if in black and white,

to use this for impact or dramatic effect. Wording should be minimal and very bold. Posters need to be placed carefully in positions where the target audience will see them, and routinely changed after a short period so the information is never out of date.

PHYSICAL CHARACTERISTICS	MOTIVATIONAL CHARACTERISTICS
Size: the whole of the poster as well as parts within it like key lettering	*Novelty:* unusual features or surprising objects
Intensity: bold headings	*Interest:* items of interest to the target audience
Colour: use of primary colours such reds, greens and orange	*Deeper motivations:* fashion and sex
Pictures: use of photographs and drawings	*Entertainment or humour:* i.e caricatures, cartoons

FIGURE 3.27 *Factors that draw people's attention to a poster*

The role of the mass media

Many people would view the use of the media as the most effective means of reaching the population to promote health, probably assuming that because it reaches a large number of people its effect will be correspondingly great. However, there are other considerations to take into account.

The success of a health message conveyed by the media will be dependent upon the attitudes

Think it over...

Consider the lay models of health. What types of message about moderating your drinking might appeal to the following lay perspectives:

✳ the robust individual account?

✳ the willpower account?

How different are these messages?

What does this tell you about the effectiveness of broad-based health messages in national campaigns?

and viewpoint of the individual receiving the message. Therefore, it is not surprising to find that many research studies have now shown that the direct persuasive power of the media is very limited. Expectations that the media alone will produce dramatic long-term changes in health behaviour are doomed to disappointment.

Realistic expectations of using mass media in health promotion work

Appropriate aims when using the media in health promotion work might include using it to:

* raise awareness of health and health issues – for example, to raise awareness about the link between over-exposure to the sun and the risk of skin cancer

* deliver a simple message – for example, that babies should sleep on their backs not their tummies; that there is a national advice line for young people wanting information about sexual health

* change behaviour if it is a simple one-off activity – for example, phone for a leaflet) which people are already motivated to do and which it is easy to do. (Phoning for a leaflet is more likely if you are at home with a phone than if you are at a friend's house or if the nearest phone is a broken public one a few streets away.)

The use of the media should be viewed as part of an overall strategy, which includes face-to-face discussion, and personal help, and attention to social and environmental factors that help or hinder change. For example, media publicity is just one strand in a long-term programme to combat smoking.

The media cannot be expected to:

* convey complex information (for example, about transmission routes of HIV)

* teach skills (for example, how to deal assertively with pressure to have sex without a condom or take drugs)

* shift people's attitudes or beliefs. If a message challenges a person's basic beliefs, he is more likely to dismiss the message than change his belief (for example, 'My grandad smoked sixty cigarettes a day till he died at 80, so saying I should stop smoking is rubbish')

* change people's behaviour unless it is a simple action, easy to do, and people are already motivated to do it (for example it will only encourage those people who are already motivated to be more active to start walking because this is an easy and accessible form of exercise, it will not do this for those who are not motivated to be more active).

Planning a campaign

To plan effectively requires a clear understanding of what you are trying to achieve. A health promoter should define clear aims and objectives before commencing any form of action. Planning should provide you with the answer to three questions:

* What am I trying to achieve?

* What am I going to do?

* How will I know whether I have succeeded?

Aims and objectives

Identifying the target audience for a campaign starts with the question, 'what is the health need which I should be addressing?' The need for a campaign will usually come from the types of sources discussed in Sections 1 and 2, where target setting for health and the collection of epidemiological data were covered. Having done this it is important to translate the idea of how to meet these needs into aims and objectives. It is important to start by differentiating between an aim and an objective.

Aim	A broad goal
Objective	Specific goal to be achieved

Any one *aim* may have several supplementary objectives within it, whilst *objectives* are usually defined as being SMART (see Figure 3.28). The objectives that do not fulfil the criteria cannot be effective aids to planning. They may be aims which require breaking down further into specific objectives. Without this level of detail an objective becomes immeasurable and therefore evaluation of the work is undermined.

Specific	Are defined in terms which is clear and not too vague
Measurable	When the work is finished we can see whether the objective has been achieved or not
Achievable	The target is realistic, i.e. within our power to change
Relevant	Is focused on addressing the issue within our broad aim
Timed	We have agreed a timescale by which we expect to have delivered this objective.

FIGURE 3.28 *SMART characteristics of objectives*

For a Theatre in Health Education project, for example, one objective might be:

'Engage young people in an accessible, fun but rigorous discussion about the legal, health, personal and social consequences of decisions made in relation to drugs, sex and crime.'

Identification of target audience

Identifying your target audience for a campaign starts with the question 'what is the health need which I should be addressing?' The need for a campaign will usually come from one of four sources as shown in Figure 3.29.

Think it over...

If you were to undertake a piece of health promotion activity locally, how would you start to identify local needs that would frame the aims and objectives of your work?

* List possible sources of useful information.
* What information might they provide for you?
* How would you decide whether this information is a reliable basis for your decision-making?
* What felt or expressed needs are you aware of within the student body of your college?

Therefore, as a health promoter the first action in undertaking any campaign is to identify the source of the need we are considering and this will identify who we are targeting.

Liaison with other agencies

Health promotion is rarely effective when the activity is focused within one organisation. The causes of ill health are so broad that it requires a wide-ranging response across agencies to influence health for the good. This is reflected in current government thinking through statutory duties to work in partnership on planning mechanisms such as the local community plan, HImP, community safety strategy, and so on. When working with other agencies it is important to know who you need at what stages of the

DIFFERING NEEDS FOR CAMPAIGNS	
Normative need	Defined by experts or professionals according to their own standards, where something falls short of this standard then a need is identified. For example, the percentage of people who are overweight or obese
Felt need	Needs which people feel, i.e. things we want. For example, people might want their food to be free of genetically modified products
Expressed need	A felt need which is voiced. For example, the felt need to have genetically modified free food becomes an issue of public debate with pressure groups focusing public debate on the issue
Comparative need	Arises from comparisons between similar groups of people, where one group is in receipt of health promotion activity and the other is not. Examples here might be one school having a well thought out and planned PSHE curriculum and another not

FIGURE 3.29 *Sources of campaigns*

work, to make sure you do not miss them out of your planning and then find that they are either unable or unwilling to support the work, or cannot fit in with your timescale.

Milestones

These are steps along the way to delivering the outcome or objective; they are useful for helping you to plan the work effectively. For example, the milestones towards an objective which involved recruiting people from local voluntary agencies, to participate in a focus group about support for carers, might include:

* design publicity materials including leaflets, posters and press adverts
* order sufficient stationary to support the mailing of these materials
* compile a circulation list for the mail
* arrange for materials to be printed
* mail to relevant people
* visit local community groups to raise awareness about the project.

Milestones can also contribute to the evaluation process for a piece of work; they can be documented as a series of process-related targets, which can be easily measured in terms of achievement – 'that milestone was met on time'.

Evaluation and outcome measures

Evaluation is something which we actively engage in on a daily basis. If evaluation is judging the worth of an activity, then questions to ask ourselves would be:

* Do I enjoy my job or should I apply for another one?
* Will I use that restaurant again?

Or on a professional footing:

* How did that session go?
* Did I achieve what I set out to do?
* Did that patient or service user really understand my explanation or was she just being polite when she said she did?

In the context of evaluating health-promoting activity we are probably considering something of a more formal approach to evaluation. An approach that is more public or open to scrutiny by an outsider and therefore capable of being made public. In this type of evaluation there are two key aspects:

* defining what we hope to achieve, i.e. aims and objectives
* gathering information to assess whether we have met these.

The question of when to evaluate is closely bound up with the purpose of the evaluation. Is it to be a final *summative* assessment of what has happened? Evaluation of this type, which seeks to establish the worth of work when it has reached its conclusion, is termed an *outcome* evaluation. Or is it an ongoing appraisal of the progress made? Evaluation that involves feedback during the course of a project, when things are still taking shape, is termed *formative* or an evaluation of *process*.

An outcome measure is the end point of the piece of work a health promoter undertakes. This can be a target as challenging as those seen in *Our Healthier Nation* (1997) which refer to reductions in disease but reflect national policy, and require coordinated action at that level to deliver them. Conversely, it could be something quite small-scale such as creating and improving the knowledge and skills of people from a specific geographical community about healthy cooking skills. There will be considerable overlap with objectives here, but it is important not to confuse the two.

Objectives refer to the work required to deliver the outcome. In this example, an objective might be to develop a model training programme for delivery to a group of women from the identified community. Outcomes refer to the product of the work; the health promoters will have to identify the desired outcomes in advance of the work, to ensure that they design into the process ways of measuring whether the product is delivered. That is, if the knowledge and skills were successfully developed in the community and people then went on to alter their diet and eating behaviours. It is not always possible to predict the outcome of a piece of work. It can create unintended or unexpected outcomes which are a bi-product of the work; for example, in this situation the bi-product might be better community relations due to the sustained programme of group activities during the cooking skills course, or the establishment of local community market gardening initiatives to grow local fresh produce.

For your assessment activity you need to ask yourself, how will I know that this has been a worthwhile activity? The key things to look at here are: what information will you need to enable you to state categorically that this has been achieved? You might want to scale down some of your objectives and outcomes when you begin to do this and realise how ambitious you have been!

Establishing clear objectives for your own work

If you have been working on your assessment activity you have probably tried to do this already as part of your original project proposal. For each

Objective
State your objective here (use a separate sheet for each objective).

Engage young people in an accessible, fun but rigorous discussion about the legal, health, personal and social consequences of decisions made in relation to drugs, sex and crime.

> One objective from a Theatre in Education project with Year 7–9 students.

Key tasks/activity
Briefly describe what service or activity you will be providing, and evaluating, that supports the achievement of this objective.

* Interactive theatre performances by a team of actors with groups of 60–90 students, lasting 90 minutes
* Students will receive preparatory and follow-up work in the school
* Some preparatory and follow-up work will be done with school staff

> Each Year group has a session on a different theme, watched by form tutors and other pastoral staff **Year 7: Bullying; Y8: Drugs; Y9: Sex and Relationships**

Results
What do you hope will change as a result of this activity?

* Students will show a greater repertoire of behaviours, enabling them to make informed and safe decisions
* Students and staff will feel more confident and informed when discussing the issues raised in the performances
* Staff will feel able and confident to follow up this work
* Students and staff will feel that the interactive theatre experience can make this learning enjoyable and memorable

Measures
How will you measure if the described change is occurring/has occurred?

* Access student attitudes before and after the performances
* Access staff attitudes and confidence before and after the performances
* Observe and evaluate the performances
* Follow up after 6 months to review progress

FIGURE 3.30 *An example of an Objective Sheet for a project*

objective, try and complete an Objective Sheet. The more carefully you describe your objectives and hoped-for outcomes, the easier it is to evaluate the effectiveness of your programme. An example of an Objective Sheet worked up in this way is shown in Figure 3.30.

Standard

Is it possible to define levels of success? It can be helpful to describe these at three levels (see Figure 3.31).

Changing behaviour

Activities in the health education arena focus on the need to motivate individuals to change their health-related behaviours, most commonly in areas such as increasing physical activity, quitting smoking, adopting a healthier diet, and adopting safe sex messages. It is not easy to monitor the changing behaviour of a group of people, possibly over many months, to assess how successful a health-promotion activity has been. This is exactly the problem faced by the smoking cessation services, set up with the support of government funding in each health district in 1999/2000. The services must report how many people referred to them: set a quit date; went on to quit smoking; were still not smoking after one month. To assess the effectiveness of the services in this way requires a considerable investment in administration to track the patients, collect the necessary information and collate it for the returns to the Department of Health.

In the case of behaviour change, outcome measures are often difficult to assess in a real-life situation, being time-consuming and expensive to observe systematically. In the case of provision of fruit to all schoolchildren the goal would be to increase their consumption of fruit and

What will be the best you could hope for?
(A great result!)

A highly enjoyable experience with high levels of satisfaction; students much more confident in discussion and feedback, staff very pleased, and happy to continue and develop the work; school uses some interactive techniques in its PSHE; we get to do more work with them!

What will you be happy with?
(A satisfactory result)

The students and staff enjoy the day; there is evidence of some change in student knowledge and attitudes, and some staff express interest in continuing the work. Some follow-up takes place in school and there is evidence of links to the PSHE curriculum.

What will you be unhappy with?
(A disappointing result)

Preparatory work is not done, or done badly; feedback from students and staff is only satisfactory; there is little evidence of increased knowledge or changed attitudes in the students. Staff don't attend the performances and show little interest in following up the work, or using or developing the techniques as part of their curriculum.

Start to think about what some of these mean in quantitative terms; for example, does 'high level of satisfaction' mean 100 per cent were very satisfied, or 90 per cent, or less?

FIGURE 3.31 *Levels of success*

vegetables, clearly not an easy outcome to monitor systematically. Therefore, instead of trying to observe the eating patterns of the children directly, an indirect indicator using the children's self reporting of changes to their own eating patterns might be used, or changes in purchasing patterns in local shops as a 'proxy indicator'.

Therefore self-reported change (i.e. change people perceive they have made and are willing to report) is a very popular measure in health-promotion evaluation, because it allows evaluation to take place without adding significantly to costs. Sometimes a project's aims and objectives are framed in terms of self-reported changes in knowledge, attitudes and behaviour. For instance, an HIV educational programme for young adults might aim to:

* increase knowledge
* generate positive attitudes towards condom use
* increase self-reported safer sexual practices involving condom use.

This illustrates a particular difficulty facing health promoters. It is difficult to see how information about sexual behaviour can be reported other than by those actually involved. (Routine observation of sexual activity is unlikely to be acceptable to subjects in the study!) Therefore, the health promoter is reliant upon the subject's honesty in self-reporting, an issue which is equally important in less private aspects of health-promoting activity.

FIGURE 3.32 *Collecting data on sexual behaviour*

If self-reported behaviour change is not considered a robust enough measure, then this must be externally verified in some way. In the Allied Dunbar Fitness survey of 1995 a large sample of the population were asked to self-assess their fitness. To gauge the accuracy of their assessment a smaller sub-sample were invited for a full fitness assessment and the results were compared against their self-reporting estimates. The results demonstrated that people routinely over-estimate both their level of activity and their level of fitness. This information became invaluable for informing the goals of future promotional activity.

An alternative to behaviour change is the use of knowledge and attitudes. However, it is not possible to bring about behaviour change directly through changes in knowledge or attitude change, since other factors can act to resist that change. A good example here is the fact that, at any time, over half the adult population who smoke would like to quit, but only a small proportion are ready to try at any one time. This reflects the fact that your health beliefs are also affected by other issues, such as moving house, getting divorced or being made unemployed, which would all act against a person's desire to quit smoking. However, changes in knowledge or attitude can mean that people are better informed and have attitudes that predispose them towards a particular line of action. A success here might be moving some one from the pre-contemplative phase (I am OK with my smoking) to contemplating quitting (thinking about quitting).

Cost effectiveness

Whilst much local health-promotion activity may be viewed as being relatively cheap in relation to the illness it seeks to prevent, it is also hard to measure the precise outcome of the work. Therefore, the investment of 2 or 3 hours of a practice nurse's time in helping someone to quit smoking is considerably less expensive than the cost of extensive treatment for lung cancer. However, it is impossible to state categorically that the nurse's time led to that individual quitting, since many other factors might have influenced the outcome; i.e. it is not an attributable outcome.

During recent years, questions about the relation between costs and effectiveness in the field of health promotion have become important. In a world of limited resources costs clearly have to be taken into account. If, for instance, a health education programme is entirely effective in changing the health behaviour of a small group of people but achieves this success through enormous financial and human resource investment, it is important to acknowledge that in the evaluation process. Without this information it is not possible to make comparisons between differing health-promotion activities, which achieve the same outcome, or health-promoting activities and medical interventions.

Cost-effectiveness analysis (CEA) compares the costs of similar interventions that achieve a specific objective (for example, the cost of the new smoking cessation services compared with GPs providing routine advice on giving up smoking). If different interventions meet with similar success then it becomes important to know which is cheaper. This is useful if the success is the same in each case but becomes difficult when there are differing degrees of success or costs are different. Therefore, the ability to measure the cost-effectiveness in health-promotion activity is fraught with difficulties, particularly when you take into account the range of issues it has to address, and the local flexibility to design individual responses to health challenges. It is precisely this problem which the HDA was set up to address by assessing the weight of evidence for specific interventions nationally and then informing local practitioners. This will be a work-in-progress because historically little investment has been made in assessing the cost-effectiveness of health promotion activity.

Deciding what will be an appropriate and feasible measure of effectiveness or change is a crucial step in planning and carrying out an evaluation. Where it is difficult to gather information directly about the outcome of an activity and where it is not possible to demonstrate a direct link between health promotion activities and the desired outcome, intermediate and indirect indicators are often used. For example, HIV/AIDS health promotion's ultimate aim is to reduce the incidence of infection, but trying to measure change along the way and, in particular, identifying changes that are directly linked with the activity being evaluated involve choosing intermediate and indirect indicators as well as lower-level outcome indicators. The choice of indicators will depend on the objectives of the activity as well as on an understanding of the relationship between health and factors influencing behaviour.

Disease reduction

It is virtually impossible to attribute the most important outcome (reduction of a specific disease) specifically to a health-promotion intervention. The range of other influences which impact on a person's life make this impossible. If we are not able to state categorically that smoking causes lung cancer (the appropriate terminology is that there is a very strong association between the two), how can we say that the 5 minutes spent with this person in counselling them on quitting smoking led to a reduction in lung cancer?

Therefore targets for disease reduction are usually set at national, regional or district level (as we have seen with the two national health strategies) but are rarely used as health-promotion success indicators. Even national health-promotion initiatives, such as the introduction of smoking cessation services, use short-term measures which are more easily attributable to the intervention; for example, the number of people setting a quit date, the numbers still stopped at one month, and the numbers stopped at 3 and 6 months.

It must also be recognised that some disease patterns can take several years to change even if the health promotion intervention succeeds. For example, the smoking cessation service can reduce the numbers of people smoking. For many people, however, their cancer may already be established but undiagnosed; therefore, it will take time for the impact of reducing smoking levels to take effect. Some health-promotion interventions can actually lead to a rise in the incidence of disease, screening campaigns being a particularly good example. Whenever campaigns are undertaken to encourage uptake of screening it is inevitable that the numbers of additional patients seen will lead to an increased number of diagnoses.

Imagine you are the project lead for the local stop smoking service. A variety of local practitioners refer people who wish to stop smoking to your service for one-to-one and group support.

* What measures could you use to show that the service was having the desired effect on the participants?
* What tests would you have to do to collect this information?
* How often would you need to collect it to monitor changes effectively?
* How practical is all of the above likely to be?
* What benefits, other than changes to physical health, might participants experience by being involved in the scheme?

Evaluating personal practice

An essential part of being an effective health promoter is to be a reflective practitioner, that is:

* to review your practice
* identify any areas of weakness or improvement
* to identify what would improve your practice in the future
* to build that into future work.

This is an essential part of adult learning as described by Kolb (1975).

The model of experiential learning

This model has four elements: concrete experience, observation and reflection, the formation of abstract concepts and testing in new situations. Kolb represented these in the experiential learning cycle. See Figure 3.33.

Kolb and Fry (1975) argue that the learning cycle can begin at any one of the four points – and that it should really be approached as a continuous spiral. However, it is suggested that

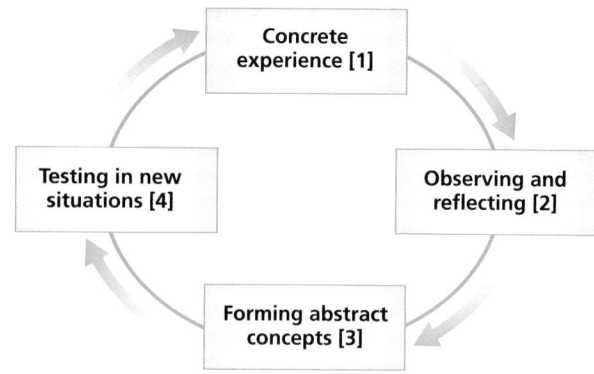

FIGURE 3.33 *Kolb's experiential learning cycle*

the learning process often begins with a person carrying out a particular action – in this case your health-promotion activity – and then seeing the effect of the action in this situation.

Following this, the second step is to understand these effects in the particular instance so that if the same action was taken in the same circumstances it would be possible to anticipate what would follow from the action.

In this pattern the third step would be to understand the general principle under which the particular instance falls. An educator who has learnt in this way may well have various rules of thumb or generalisations about what to do in different situations. So you will begin to develop both confidence and competence to deal with managing health-promotion activities (see Section 2 for detail about health promotion competencies).

When the general principle is understood, the last step is its application through action in a new circumstance within the range of generalisation. In some representations of experiential learning these steps, (or ones like them), are sometimes represented as a circular movement. In reality, if learning has taken place the process could be seen as a spiral.

Reflective practice is about taking time out to carry out steps 2 and 3 and using other people to discuss how you are performing within a role so you can begin to generalise about your future practice to change and improve it. This could cover any aspect of the areas of competence in health promotion in Section 2, be it acting ethically (e.g. not using inappropriately sponsored materials) managing projects (e.g. keeping to timescales in the milestone plan), or working in partnership (e.g. how well you maintain effective working relationships with your colleagues or other practitioners you are depending upon to get the job done).

Summary

The following key areas of theory have been covered in this section.

There are several different approaches to health promotion including the medical, behavioural, educational, service-user centered and societal change approaches

There are many methods and materials used within these approaches including one-to-one interaction, leaflets, posters and the media

There are many ways in which a health promotion project can be evaluated including its impact on health, or health behaviour, cost effectiveness and personal performance

PROMOTING GOOD HEALTH

The media has limitations in what it can achieve, for example it can get across simple messages like a phone number but not more complex information

Key to the planning process is defining clear aims, objectives and milestones against which progress and performance can be monitored

There is a systematic approach to planning any health promotion project

Consider this

Imagine you are a health promotion worker who has been asked to develop a local programme to raise awareness of HIV risk amongst older people. This request is based on recognition of the large number of older people who are leaving failed marriages without having the benefit of good health education on HIV risk, which many young people now receive in school. These people require some specifically targeted information that will meet the above criteria to help them manage their risk as they embark on life as a single person again.

1 First of all, describe an aim for the campaign.

2 Now establish 3–4 key objectives you could use to monitor the effectiveness of the programme. One of these should be to develop new leaflets and posters for the target group – but you will need to word that appropriately.

3 Now design a leaflet which would give the correct information, reach the target group specifically and be culturally appropriate for the group.

4 If people fail to take this advice they are likely to have to access their local genito-urinary medicine department (GUM clinic) to have their sexually transmitted infections treated. Find out where your nearest service is and when it operates. Think about the stigma which might be attached to attending this service – particularly for this age group. What actions could the service take to address them?

5 Write down a list of possible actions or activities which might form a part of your programme – to raise awareness of HIV with the target group. Next to each action, record any potential cost. Try to find out what the annual cost is for maintaining someone who is HIV positive on **combination therapy**. Prevention routinely has to compete with treatment for limited resources; this therapy is not cheap but can save someone's life. How would you argue for investment in this health promotion programme?

UNIT 3 ASSESSMENT

How you will be assessed

This unit is assessed through a portfolio of work, with the mark you gain for that assessment being your mark for the unit. As part of the portfolio you will be required to produce a report which describes the planning of, and your participation in, a small-scale campaign to promote good health in a care setting (or your own centre if you prefer).

Any materials you use for the campaign should be published by an existing agency, as opposed to produced by yourself. This will save you time, which can be spent more effectively on the other aspects of planning and delivering the campaign and documenting it accurately for your portfolio. There may be little time for them to produce posters and leaflets which are generally already available. Therefore, where possible, use existing campaigning materials, which for the most part, can be readily obtained from health-promotion departments, health centres, social services, and shops. Your evidence will include:

* Evidence that you understand the models and concepts of health and well-being, including ill health, and the implications of government initiatives
* Applying knowledge and showing understanding of the job roles of key workers who promote health, including information about two preventative measures
* Relevant research and analysis of two factors that can affect health and well-being, giving an analysis of their effects on service users
* Evidence of your own performance when planning, and participating in, a small health-promotion campaign, evaluating your own performance.

To help you understand how your work will be assessed, guidance on what you need to do to achieve the highest marks for each AO section have been included in the table at the end of the unit.

Key things to bear in mind

You will need to undertake some consultation activity with both service users and service providers about any planned activity which may affect them. Review your findings according to the theories of the social and medical models. Some of these people may be workers you cover in the course, such as health visitors, school nurses, community nurses, environmental health officers and GPs, so it will be important to either use opportunities with visiting speakers, or to go out to visit these workers to test out your ideas for the campaign and find out about their roles.

You can find information about government initiatives on most government department websites. Examples include the Department of Health (DOH) and Department for Education and Skills (DfES), whilst you can find information about the effectiveness of health-promotion activity on the (HDA) web site.

Both primary (your own) and secondary (review of other people's) research would be useful to enable you to develop an understanding of the different factors affecting health and well-being, and the effects of ill-health on service users in various settings. You will not be expected to give detailed information about substance abuse; the focus needs to be on how this can affect health and well-being.

In the assessment, you will be expected to provide an explanation of the health-promotion approach you have adopted in the planning and implementation of the campaign. It will be important to have a sound understanding of these approaches before you attempt any detailed planning, you will not be expected to have an in-depth knowledge of each approach that could be used, but to demonstrate a good understanding of the applied approach.

Most commonly, people use the educational approach which seeks to inform and educate to promote healthy practices, but the preventative approach is also frequently utilised. Increasing in popularity is the use of fear as an approach, particularly when used on television; for example, using vivid images of people suffering the consequences of unhealthy lifestyle choices, such as smoking, to instil fear into those who watch.

It is important to set clear aims and objectives in the plan for the campaign. These will vary with the intended outcomes. For example, improving health and well-being may be the aim of a campaign provided for people who are overweight and inactive and thus at risk of coronary heart disease. Alternatively, a campaign to promote safe sexual practices to young adults may have two aims, firstly to reduce the number of sufferers of sexually transmitted diseases, and secondly to reduce the number of unplanned pregnancies.

The objectives of the campaign will link directly to the different stages and tasks which need to be completed, to ensure the campaign takes place as efficiently as possible. You also need to consider the intended outcomes of the campaign so that effectiveness can be measured accurately. Try to identify the skills you use, such as, for example, practical skills, organisational skills and communication skills.

The evaluation needs to include evidence of reflective practice, where you make judgments about your performance and the success of the campaign against the pre-set criteria stated. Higher marks are dependent on demonstrating analytical skills and the ability to make reasoned judgments together with consideration of both the intended and unintended outcomes; for example, a campaign which encourages counselling may result in long waiting lists.

You may wish to work in groups to collect materials and when participating in the health-promotion campaign; however, for all other aspects of this unit, you are required to produce your own individual portfolio of evidence.

ASSESSMENT OBJECTIVE	MARK BAND 1	MARK BAND 2	MARK BAND 3
AO1 *evidence that you understand the models and concepts of health and well-being, including ill health and the implications of government initiatives*	You show a basic understanding of the concepts and models of health and wellbeing from **two** different perspectives, including the effects of ill health, and how they relate to service users, including the implications of **one** government initiative **[marks available 0–5]**	You show a sound understanding of the concepts and models of health and well-being from **two** different perspectives, including the effects of ill health, giving a detailed description of how they relate to service users, including the implications of **one** government initiative **[marks available 6–10]**	You show a comprehensive understanding of the concepts and models of health and well-being from **two** different perspectives, including the effects of ill-health, giving a detailed explanation of how they relate to service users, including the implications of **one** government initiative **[marks available 11–15]**
AO2 *applying knowledge and showing understanding of the job-roles of key workers who promote health, including information about two preventative measures*	You provide, with guidance, a basic account of the job roles of **two** key workers who are involved in promoting health, and you give a basic description of **two** preventative measures that they could apply; you write in a manner which is adequate to convey meaning, although it will be expressed in a non-specialist manner **[marks available 0–5]**	You provide a sound level of understanding of a range of job roles of **two** key workers who are involved in promoting health, and you describe thoroughly **two** preventative measures that they could apply; you write in a manner which conveys meaning, using specialist vocabulary with few errors/inaccuracies **[marks available 6–10]**	Working accurately and independently, you provide in-depth knowledge and understanding of a wide range of the job-roles of **two** key workers who are involved in promoting health, explaining **two** preventative measures that they could apply; you write in a manner which conveys appropriate meaning, using specialist vocabulary with accuracy – there will be no errors/inaccuracies **[marks available 11–15]**
AO3 *relevant research and analysis of two factors that can affect health and well-being, giving an analysis of their effects on service users*	You use limited sources of information to research and collect evidence about **two** factors that can affect health, giving a basic analysis of their effects on service users **[marks available 0–4]**	You use a range of sources of information to research **two** factors that can affect health, giving a detailed analysis of their effects on service users **[marks available 5–7]**	You undertake research using a range of techniques to explore **two** factors that can affect health, giving a comprehensive analysis of their effects on service users **[marks available 8–10]**
AO4 *evidence of your own performance when planning and participating in a small health-promotion campaign, evaluating your own performance*	You produce a plan for a small-scale health-promotion campaign and records to show how it was implemented, including a basic evaluation of your own performance **[marks available 0–4]**	You produce a plan for a small-scale health-promotion campaign and records to show how it was implemented, including an evaluation that draws valid conclusions about your own performance **[marks available 5–7]**	You produce a plan for a small-scale health-promotion campaign and records to show how it was implemented, including an evaluation that makes reasoned judgments about your own performance **[marks available 8–10]**

References

Acheson, D. (1998) *The Independent Inquiry into Inequalities in Health* (The Stationery Office)

Benzeval, M., Judge, K., Whitehead, M. (1995) *Tackling Inequalities in Health, an Agenda for Action* (Kings Fund Publishing)

Dawson, D. (1990) *Women's Cancers, The Treatment Options, Everything You Need to Know* (Piatkus Publishing)

Department of Health (1992) *Immunisation against Infectious Disease* (The Stationery Office)

Department of Health (2000) *The NHS Cancer Plan* (The Stationery Office)

Department of Health (2001) *The National Strategy for HIV and Sexual Health* (The Stationery Office)

Department of Health (2001) *Involving Patients and the Public in Healthcare* (The Stationery Office)

Downie, R. S., Tannahill, C., Tannahil, A. (1996) *Health Promotion Models and Values* (Oxford University Press, Oxford)

Draper, P. (1991) *Health Through Public Policy* (Green Print)

Ewles, L. and Simnett, I. (1999) *Promoting Health – A Practical Guide* (Bailliere Tindall, London)

Hall, D. (1996) *Health for all Children* (Oxford University Press, London)

HM Government (1992) *The Health Of the Nation* (The Stationery Office)

HM Government (1997) *The New NHS: Modern Dependable* (The Stationery Office)

HM Government (1997) *Saving Lives – Our Healthier Nation* (The Stationery Office)

HM Government (2004) *Choosing Health – Making Healthy Choices Easier* (The Stationery Office)

Jones, L. and Sidell, M. (1997) *The Challenge of Promoting Health – Exploration and Action* (Open University Press)

Jones, L. and Sidell, M. (1997) *Promoting Health – Knowledge and Practice* (Open University Press)

Moonie, N. (2000) *Advanced Health & Social Care* (Oxford, Heinemann)

Naidoo, J. and Wills, J. (2000) *Health Promotion – Foundations for Practice* (Bailliere Tindall, London)

Useful websites

http://www.cieh.org
The website of the Chartered Institute of Environmental Health Officers for information about their role and training to be one

www.quick.org.uk
Quality information checklist for young people to assess the quality of information they find on the Internet

http://www.hda.nhs.uk/index.asp
The home page of the Health Development Agency giving information about effective health promotion interventions

www.ohn.gov.uk
Gateway for the *Our Healthier Nation* website – original document, technical data and regular progress updates

www.wiredforhealth.gov.uk
Wired for Health provides teachers with access to relevant and appropriate health information

www.mindbodysoul.gov.uk
Provides accurate and up-to-date health information for young people

http://www.bhf.org.uk
Heart health information from the British Heart Foundation including information about activity and nutrition

http://www.homeoffice.gov.uk/drugs/index.html
Information about the National Drugs Strategy and links to information about current drug use trends and patterns

http://www.drugscope.org.uk
National Drugs Agency which provides advice to drugs treatment and prevention services, includes high quality information about patterns of use, information about specific drugs and advice on how to prevent use.

www.doh.gov.uk
Main Department of Health website – search here
for links to *Choosing Health* (public health white
paper) and health statistics

http://www.nhs.uk/england
This site connects you to local NHS services in
England and provides national information about
the NHS

www.givingupsmoking.co.uk
The NHS quit smoking website, information
about smoking, how to quit and where to access
local services

www.cancerscreening.nhs.uk
NHS screening programmes website, provides
good quality information about both Cervical and
Breast Cancer Screening programmes

www.nhlbisupport.com/bmi/bmicalc.htm
Calculate your own BMI using the information on
this site

www.who.int/en
The website of the World Health Organisation

http://www.surestart.gov.uk
The SureStart website for information about the
programme including its aims

http://www.immunisation.org.uk
Information about immunisation programmes

http://www.mmrthefacts.nhs.uk
Government website specifically set up to provide
quality information abut the MMR vaccine for
parents to counter the fall in public confidence in
the vaccine

Health and Safety in Care Settings

Sections that will be covered in this unit are:

4.1   The influence of current legislation on safe practice in care settings

4.2   Safety and security

4.3   Safe moving and handling techniques

4.4   Contribution to infection control

Introduction

This is an optional unit of the double award and is externally assessed. It is important to know about health and safety if you are working in care settings, both for your safety and for that of your colleagues and service users. Both employers and employees have responsibilities with regard to maintaining health and safety and it is important that legislation is understood and adhered to.

How you will be assessed

This unit is externally assessed through a 90-minute test.

Section 1: The influence of current legislation on safe practice in care settings

The Health and Safety at Work Act 1974

In the United Kingdom, the Health and Safety Executive (HSE) is the government body responsible for enforcing legislation and providing guidance on health and safety in the workplace. The Health and Safety at Work Act 1974 is the main piece of legislation that provides the legal framework for maintaining health and safety in workplaces. It is like an umbrella under which there are many other regulations designed to cover particular areas of risk.

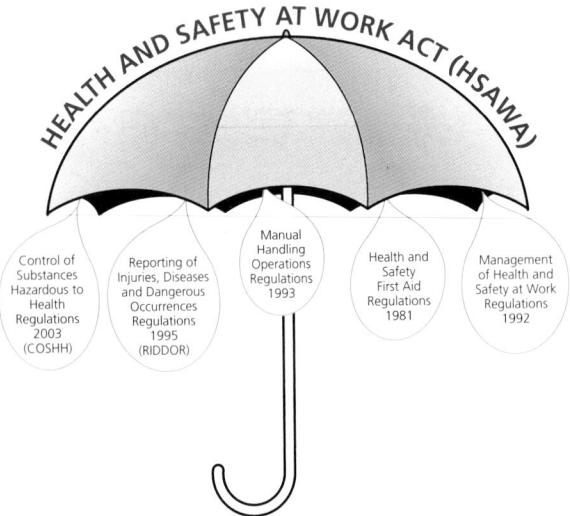

FIGURE 4.1 *The regulation under the HSAWA umbrella*

The responsibilities of employers and employees

Under the terms of the Act, both employers and employees have responsibilities to ensure that all work is carried out as safely as possible, without risks to other people.

The section of the Act that outlines the main responsibilities of the employer is shown below:

'It shall be the duty of every employer to ensure, so far as is reasonably practicable, the health, safety and welfare at work of all his employees.

Without prejudice to the generality of an employer's duty under the preceding subsection, the matters to which that duty extends include in particular:

A. the provision and maintenance of plant and systems of work that are, so far as is reasonably practicable, safe and without risks to health;

B. arrangements for ensuring, so far as is reasonably practicable, safety and absence of risks to health in connection with the use, handling, storage and transport of articles and substances;

C. the provision of such information, instruction, training and supervision as is necessary to ensure, so far as is reasonably practicable, the health and safety at work of his employees;

D. so far as is reasonably practicable as regards any place of work under the employer's control, the maintenance of it in a condition that is safe and without risks to health and the provision and maintenance of means of access to and egress from it that are safe and without such risks;

E. the provision and maintenance of a working environment for his employees that is, so far as is reasonably practicable, safe, without risks to health, and adequate as regards facilities and arrangements for their welfare at work.'

Employers also have to ensure that other people are protected as far as possible from harm. This is particularly important in a care setting as service users and their relatives and visitors must be protected while they are on the premises:

'It shall be the duty of every employer to conduct his undertaking in such a way as to ensure, so far as is reasonably practicable, that persons not in his employment who may be affected are not thereby exposed to risks to their health or safety.'

Although employees have every right to expect that their employer is doing his/her utmost to protect them while they are at work, they also have responsibilities regarding their conduct as shown below:

'It shall be the duty of every employee while at work:

* to take reasonable care for the health and safety of himself and of other persons who may be affected by his acts or omissions at work; and
* as regards any duty or requirement imposed on his employer or any other person by or under any of the relevant statutory provisions, to cooperate with him so far as is necessary to enable that duty or requirement to be performed or complied with.'

Consider this

Mary is a staff nurse who works on a busy surgical ward. Pilar is a newly arrived Spanish cleaner who speaks little English. This is her second week working on Mary's ward and she has had a basic induction period of three days. Pilar is washing the floor with a mop and bucket but has not put out signs to warn people that the floor is wet. Mary does not notice that the floor is wet and slips and falls, fracturing her wrist.

1. What are the employer's responsibilities in relation to this accident?

Think it over...

As a group discuss the meaning of the responsibilities of the employer and employees under the Health and Safety at Work Act 1974. What do you think they mean? Produce a leaflet or poster that explains them in more simple English.

✳ DID YOU KNOW?

Fatal injuries
There were 235 fatal injuries to workers in 2003/04, a rate of 0.81 per hundred thousand workers.

Other reported injuries
In 2002/03 employers reported 154,430 other injuries, a rate of 614.1 per hundred thousand employees.

Ill health
In 2001/02 an estimated 2.3 million people in Great Britain were suffering from an illness that they believed was caused or made worse by their current or past work.

Working days lost
In 2000/02 an estimated 40 million working days were lost overall, 33 million due to work-related ill health and 7 million due to workplace injury.

Source: www.hse.gov.uk

Management of Health and Safety at Work Regulations 1999

The Management of Health and Safety at Work Regulations first came into effect in 1992. Since then there have been several amendments, and the most recent came into effect on 29 December 1999. The reason for the modifications was the need for United Kingdom legislation to demonstrate full compliance with the European Framework Directive.

There are 30 regulations, which relate to how the Health and Safety at Work Act must be interpreted and acted upon. Prior to the implementation of the regulations, there was some flexibility in the way they could be interpreted, but it is now a legal requirement to ensure that they are adhered to. The regulations include requirements to:

* avoid risks and evaluate risks that cannot be avoided (carry out a risk assessment)
* ensure that as far as possible risks do not exist

* adapt work to the individual and to technical processes

* replace dangerous items, etc. with those that are less dangerous

* develop a coherent overall prevention policy, covering technology, organisation of work, working conditions etc.

* give collective protective measures priority over individual protective measures

* give appropriate instructions to employees.

Competent persons

A new requirement is that a competent person (one who possesses sufficient knowledge, training and expertise) in the employer's employment shall be appointed in preference to a competent person from outside the organisation, such as a consultant.

Contact with the external services

A new regulation stipulates that every employer must make any necessary contacts with external services, particularly in respect of first aid, emergency medical care and rescue work.

No defence

The new regulations make it explicit that it is not a defence for employers to claim that they were not able to meet their obligations because of any act or default on the part of any employee or competent person.

Fire legislation

The new regulations stipulate that, subject to certain exceptions, the Fire Precautions (Workplace) Regulations 1997 are now to be considered as health and safety legislation; this means they will be enforced by the health and safety enforcing authorities rather than by the fire services.

Revocations

The new regulations also consolidate earlier legislation relating to young people and new and expectant mothers, thus revoking the Health and Safety (Young Persons) Regulations 1997 and the Management of Health and Safety at Work (Amendment) Regulations 1994.

Think it over...

You have arranged a visit to your new work experience placement – a residential home for older people – that you have never been to before. You need to make sure that you will not be a risk to yourself or to staff or service users. What information would you find out from the manager about safeguarding yourself and others during your placement?

Reporting of Injuries, Diseases and Dangerous Occurrences Regulations (RIDDOR) 1995

RIDDOR – the Reporting of Injuries, Diseases and Dangerous Occurrences Regulations (1995) – came into effect on 1 April 1996. These enable the HSE and local authorities to identify where and how risks arise. The HSE and local authorities can then give employers advice on how to reduce injury, illness and accidents in the workplace.

When is it necessary to make a report?

It is a legal requirement that an employer or self-employed person reports some but not all work-related accidents, diseases and dangerous occurrences. Incidents that must be recorded are listed in Figure 4.3.

Record keeping

A record must be kept of any reportable injury, disease or dangerous occurrence for at least three years. This must include:

* the date and method of reporting

* the date, time and place of the event

* personal details of those involved

* a brief description of the nature of the event or disease.

See Figure 4.2 for an example of an accident report form.

Disease

If a doctor informs the employer that an employee has a reportable work-related disease, then the

INJURED PERSON	First Name(s)			Surname		Reference Number	
	Home Address			Parent/Next of Kin (If needed)		Employer's Name & Address	
	Home Phone			Telephone			
	Is Injured Person:-	Employee	Contractor	Trainee	Student	Member of Public	

LOCATION	Give full address of location where incident occurred		Precise location of incident, e.g. kitchen, stairs, workshop, laboratory, car park etc.
	Date of incident	Time of incident	

DETAILS OF INCIDENT	Describe injury or work-related illness (please state whether cut, fracture bruising etc. – indicate right or left as appropriate)
	What was person doing at the time of the incident?
	What was the incident and how did it happen? (If a fall state height of fall)
	Details of any follow-up action required as a result of this incident (continue on reverse if necessary)

ACTION TAKEN	None required	First aid	Returned to work	Sent home	Sent to doctor	Ambulance to hospital	Kept in hospital over 24 hrs	Next of kin informed

OTHER DETAILS	Name of first aider who treated casualty	1. Completed by: (print name)
	Duty Officer (name)	Signature
	Informed?	Date: Phone no:
	Witnesses' names (and addresses if NOT employees) 1. 2.	2. Received by designated person:
		Signature: Date:
	Post code Post code Phone: Phone:	3. RIDDOR Report Date: completed (if required)?

FIGURE 4.2 *An example of an accident report form*

DEATH OR INJURY

Type of incident:

* an employee or a self-employed person working on the premises is killed or has a major injury

* a member of the public is killed or needs to be taken to hospital.

The incident must be reported immediately, and within 10 days this must be followed up with a completed accident report form.

Examples of major injury include:

* fracture other than to fingers, thumbs or toes

* amputation

* dislocation of a major joint

* temporary or permanent loss of sight

* chemical or hot metal burn to the eye or any penetrating injury to the eye

* injury resulting from an electric shock or electrical burn leading to unconsciousness or requiring resuscitation or admittance to hospital for more than 24 hours

* any other injury leading to hypothermia, heat-reduced illness or unconsciousness or requiring admittance to hospital for more than 24 hours.

Over-three-day injury
An over-three-day injury results in the injured person being unable to carry out his or her normal duties for more than three days, not including the day the injury occurred. This type of injury is not considered to be major.

FIGURE 4.3 *Incidents that must be recorded*

employer must inform the local authority using a disease report form.

Dangerous occurrence

A dangerous occurrence is an incident that could have resulted in a reportable injury. This must be reported immediately to the local authority. Again, a completed accident report form must be sent to the HSE within 10 days of the incident.

Since April 2001 it has also been possible to report incidents to the Incident Contact Centre of the HSE by phone, fax, Internet, email or post. Alternatively the incident may be reported to the environmental health department of the relevant local authority.

Health and Safety (Signs and Signals) Regulations 1996

These regulations were produced in response to the European Community Safety Signs Directive, and came into force on 1 April 1996. The reason for producing these was to encourage the use of standardised safety signs in places of work within all the European Union member states. This means that safety signs will have the same meaning in every member country.

Under the regulations employers must provide specific safety signs wherever there is a risk that might cause an accident or incident and where there is no other means to control the risk. Requirements of the regulations include the regulation of road traffic by the use of road traffic signs. Employers must also:

* maintain the safety signs that they provide

* explain the signs to employees and provide instruction on what to do when they see a safety sign.

The regulations exclude signs and labels used in connection with the supply of substances, products and equipment or the transport of dangerous goods. Safety signs and signals include visible signs such as illuminated signs; hand and acoustic signals (e.g. fire alarms); spoken communication; and the marking of pipe work containing dangerous substances. These are in addition to traditional signboards such as prohibition and warning signs. Fire safety signs (i.e. signs for fire exits and fire-fighting equipment) are also covered.

Classification of signs

Safety signs are divided into categories according to what message they are designed to communicate. Each different category has a

specific format and set of colours. Some examples
of signs are shown in Figures 4.4 and 4.5.

Prohibition signs These signs are used to convey 'Do Not' commands, e.g. No Smoking or No Entry. These signs are round with a red border and a red diagonal line across them. The background is white with a pictogram of the forbidden activity in black.	  
Warning signs These signs should be used to alert people to a nearby danger. For example, a flammable liquid store or a laboratory where radioactive substances are in use should have an appropriate warning sign near the entrance. These signs are required by the Health and Safety (Signs and Signals) Regulations 1996 and in specific cases by the Dangerous Substances (Notification and Marking of Sites) Regulations 1990. These signs are triangular with a black border. The background is yellow with the pictogram of the type of hazard shown clearly in black.	  
Mandatory signs These signs are used to show that certain actions must be carried out in order to meet statutory requirements. These signs are normally written in white on a blue background and include a pictogram of the relevant hazard, or in the case of fire signs, an exclamation mark. (Fire hazard signs may contain a lot of written information and are often rectangular in shape).	   
Safe condition signs These signs should be used to indicate escape routes, emergency exits, first-aid equipment, emergency showers etc. Safe condition signs are made up of a green rectangle or square with the pictogram or text in white.	
Exit signs The requirements of the Building Regulations 1991 state that every doorway or other exit providing access to a means of escape should be marked with an exit sign. Exits that are used for normal entry and exits do not have to be signed unless they are also emergency exits. Employers have a duty to ensure that these signs are provided where the risk to the health and safety of employees cannot be entirely removed. In certain circumstances exit signs may not need to be used, for example in a single-storey building with a simple layout. However, for multiple-storey buildings with a complicated layout the signs should be used. Fire exit signs are normally rectangular and green with a pictogram and writing in white.	

FIGURE 4.4 *Safety signs*

Supplementary information signs

These are signs used to provide additional information. In the Health and Safety (Signs and Signals) Regulations 1996 these are confined to directional arrows. Supplementary signs consist of a square or rectangle in the appropriate colour with the pictogram or text positioned centrally.

The colours should be the same as that of the relevant main sign, i.e.:

* green where the information supplements a safe condition sign

* red where it supplements a fire equipment sign or

* yellow to supplement a warning sign.

FIGURE 4.5 *Safety signs providing additional information*

The role of the Health and Safety Executive

Britain's Health and Safety Commission (HSC) and the Health and Safety Executive (HSE) are responsible for the regulation of almost all the risks to health and safety arising from work activity in Britain. The Health and Safety Commission is sponsored by the Department of Work and Pensions and is accountable to the Minister of State for Work and Pensions. The HSE's job is to help the Health and Safety Commission ensure that risks to people's health and safety from work activities are properly controlled.

> 'Our mission is to protect people's health and safety by ensuring risks in the changing workplace are properly controlled.'
>
> (Source: www.hse.gov.uk)

The Health and Safety Executive state that:
The HSC believes that prevention is better than cure, and its key roles are:

* providing information and support to ensure that workplaces are safe

* ensuring health and safety legislation is adhered to

* prosecuting employers who fail in some way to safeguard the health and safety of people who use their premises.

* DID YOU KNOW?

The HSE's key enforcement figures, 2003/04:

* 982 cases were prosecuted.

* The total number of notices issued by HSE decreased from 13,324 to 11,295. There was a marked increase in the number of improvement notices issued in construction and agriculture. This was a result of the extra attention HSE inspectors were paying to these priority areas, and this has continued. This year's overall number of notices has returned to the levels seen in previous years. This is because fewer notices were issued in the services and manufacturing sectors.

* The average fine per case has increased from £8846 in 2002/03 to £13,947 in 2003/04

* Each case may involve prosecution for more than one offence. The average fine per offence prosecuted has risen from £6251 in 2002/03 to £9858 in 2003/04.

* 89 per cent of cases prosecuted lead to a conviction.

* HSE prosecuted a total of 17 directors and managers in 2003/04 and 11 of these were convicted.

* The largest fine in 2003/04 was £700,000 in a case where an explosion under a playing field could have endangered many lives. Fortunately, it occurred in the early hours of the morning, when the area wasn't being used.

(Source: www.hse.gov.uk)

Information for employees

Some health and safety information must be available to employees. It is the employees' responsibility to ensure that they know and understand the regulations that are in place to protect themselves and others from risk.

The Health and Safety Law poster

If an employer employs five or more people there is a legal requirement to display the Health and Safety Law poster or to provide employees with a leaflet containing the same information. The poster must be displayed where it can be seen clearly by all employees, and if it is dirty, illegible or torn it must be replaced immediately. The poster contains boxes for the names and locations of safety representatives to be inserted and for details of 'competent people appointed by the employer and their health and safety representatives'. The contact details of the local authority should also be included (see page 168).

First aid

The Health and Safety (First Aid) Regulations 1981 require employers to provide adequate and appropriate equipment, facilities and personnel to enable first aid to be given to employees if they are injured or become ill at work. These regulations apply to all workplaces including those with five or fewer employees and to the self-employed. Employers should assess what their first-aid needs are, as these will vary in different workplaces. The Health and Safety at Work Act 1974 does not require first-aid provision for members of the public, and employers are not obliged to provide first aid for anyone except their own employees, although many organisations do make provision for them.

The minimum requirements for first-aid provision at work are:

* a suitably stocked first-aid box
* an appointed person to take charge of first-aid arrangements
* a notice stating who the first aider is and where the first-aid box is situated

* first-aid provision that is available at all times when people are at work.

There is no standard list of items to put in a first-aid box, as needs will be different in each establishment. The employer would have to decide this in his or her assessment of risk. However, the Health and Safety Executive recommend the following list which can be used as a general guide for a workplace that does not have any particular special need:

* a leaflet giving general guidance on first aid e.g. HSE leaflet *Basic Advice on First Aid at Work*
* 20 individually wrapped sterile adhesive dressings (assorted sizes)
* two sterile eye pads
* four individually wrapped triangular bandages (preferably sterile)
* six safety pins
* six medium-sized (approximately 12 cm x 12 cm) individually wrapped sterile unmedicated wound dressings
* two large (approximately 18 cm x 18 cm) sterile individually wrapped unmedicated wound dressings
* one pair of disposable gloves.

Think it over...

As a group, consider the possible accidents that could occur at your school or college which would result in the need for first-aid to be administered. Make a list of the items that you would need to have in a first-aid box in order to provide basic first-aid treatment.

Think about your work placement. Do you think that the recommendations of the HSE about what should be in the first-aid box are sufficient? If not, what else would you consider adding?

Appointed persons and first aiders

Employers are required by law to ensure that there are adequate personnel available to give first aid to employees who become ill or are injured at work. They must also inform staff of the first-aid arrangements. This can be done by putting up notices stating who the first aiders are and where the first-aid box is situated. There will need to be special arrangements in place for employees who have language or reading difficulties to allow them to be fully aware of the first-aid arrangements. These might include signs in different languages or with pictorial representations, or employers may need to provide information in Braille for people with sight impairment. The suggested number of appointed persons and first aiders are given according to the category of risk (see Figure 4.6).

Appointed person

An appointed person is someone who can take charge if someone falls ill or requires first aid. He or she should not undertake any first-aid treatment that they have not been trained for but they can call an ambulance and take charge of first-aid equipment. An appointed person should always be available when there are employees on site, which might mean that an employer may need to nominate more than one. Short courses are available for appointed persons.

First aider

A first aider is someone who holds a valid certificate that has been approved by the Health and Safety Executive. Courses are usually held over 24 hours, and the certificate is valid for three years. Refresher courses are also available to ensure that first aiders can remain up to date. Additional courses such as how to use a defibrillator can also be taken to extend knowledge and skills.

Consider this

Appleton Drive Drop-in Centre is a centre run by social services where members of the public can go to get advice on health and social care and benefits. It also has an Internet café that people can use to access information independently. The centre employs six full-time and 15 part-time staff, and approximately 100 people access the services provided every day.

1. How many first aiders will be needed on the premises on any day?

2. Are there any particular issues that you would need to think about in relation to the provision of first aid to staff?

CATEGORY OF RISK	NUMBERS EMPLOYED AT ANY LOCATION	SUGGESTED NUMBER OF FIRST AID PERSONNEL
Lower risk, e.g. shops and offices, libraries	Fewer than 50	At least one appointed person
	50–100	At least one first aider
	More than 100	One additional first aider for every 100 employed
Medium risk, e.g. light engineering and assembly work, food processing, warehousing	Fewer than 20	At least one appointed person
	20–100	At least one first aider for every 50 employed
	More than 100	One additional first aider for every 100 employed
Higher risk, e.g. most construction, slaughterhouses, chemical manufacture, extensive work with dangerous machinery or sharp instruments	Fewer than five	At least one appointed person
	5–50	At least one first aider
	More than 50	One additional first aider for every 50 employed

FIGURE 4.6 *Suggested number of first-aid personnel according to risk*

The accident book

All staff should know the location of the accident book, which should be kept in a communal area. Since 31 December 2003, a new design of accident book has been in use for any business that employs 10 or more people. The new design was produced in order to meet the requirements of the Data Protection Act 1998, which states that all personal details of employees must be kept confidential. As a result, the pages are now perforated, which means that they can be removed from the book and stored in a separate and secure location.

Health and safety policy document

If an employer has five or more employees, it must have a written health and safety policy statement. This will set out how health and safety are managed in the workplace.

The policy must contain:

* a statement of intention to provide a safe workplace

* a list of any hazards identified by a risk assessment and how to deal with them

* a list of employees who might be at particular risk from any identified hazards

* the names of the people responsible for implementing the policy and of any individuals responsible for particular health and safety issues and when and how they carry out that responsibility

* procedures for reporting accidents at work

* details of how to evacuate the premises in an emergency.

An employer should discuss the details of the policy with his or her employees and should ensure that the policy is reviewed on a regular basis.

THE EIGHT STEPS TO COSHH	
Step 1	Work out what hazardous substances are used in your workplace and find out the risks to people's health from using these substances.
Step 2	Decide what precautions are needed before starting work with hazardous substances.
Step 3	Prevent people being exposed to hazardous substances, but where this is not reasonably practicable, control the exposure.
Step 4	Make sure control measures are used and maintained properly and that safety procedures are followed.
Step 5	If appropriate, monitor exposure of employees to hazardous substances.
Step 6	Carry out health surveillance where your assessment has shown that this is necessary or COSHH makes specific requirements.
Step 7	If appropriate, prepare plans and procedures to deal with accidents, incidents and emergencies.
Step 8	Make sure employees are properly informed, trained and supervised.

FIGURE 4.7 *The eight steps to COSHH*   (Source: www.hse.gov.uk)

FIGURE 4.8 *How many hazards can you spot in this kitchen?*

Control of Substances Hazardous to Health Regulations 2002 (COSHH)

What is COSHH?

The COSHH regulations (Control of Substances Hazardous to Health) were first introduced in 1988 but have been consolidated several times since. They require employers to control hazardous substances that employees and others may be exposed to during work activities.

What are hazardous substances?

Hazardous substances are any products used in the workplace that could consititute a risk to health if they are not controlled, for example by using ventilation. They can include glues, paints, cleaning agents, fumes, dust or bacteria. Warning labels on packaging will demonstrate whether the product is subject to COSHH Regulations. They will apply to certain substances that might be used for cleaning purposes in a health or social care setting, e.g. bleach. There are eight steps to COSHH set out by the HSE that employers must carry out (see Figure 4.7).

Responsibilities of employers and employees

Employers are required to take all reasonable steps to ensure that they use control measures properly and report defects. This may include providing protective equipment or clothing or total enclosure of an area where harmful substances are being used. Special requirements apply in relation to some substances such as those that are carcinogenic (potentially cancer-causing), although in most cases such substances are banned unless a suitable non-carcinogenic alternative can be found. An example of this is gluteraldehyde, a liquid used for cold sterilisation of instruments, particularly in an operating theatre. If it is used, it must be stored in a fume cabinet, but there are less harmful products available.

Summary

This section has covered a range of regulations that come under the Health and Safety at Work Act 1974, and has looked at how they affect care workers in everyday situations.

Consider this

1. What are the five main responsibilities of the employer under the Health and Safety at Work Act 1974?

2. What are the responsibilities of the employee under the Health and Safety at Work Act 1974?

3. Why were the Management of Health and Safety at Work Regulations amended in 1999?

4. What does RIDDOR stand for?

5. What is the role of the Health and Safety Executive?

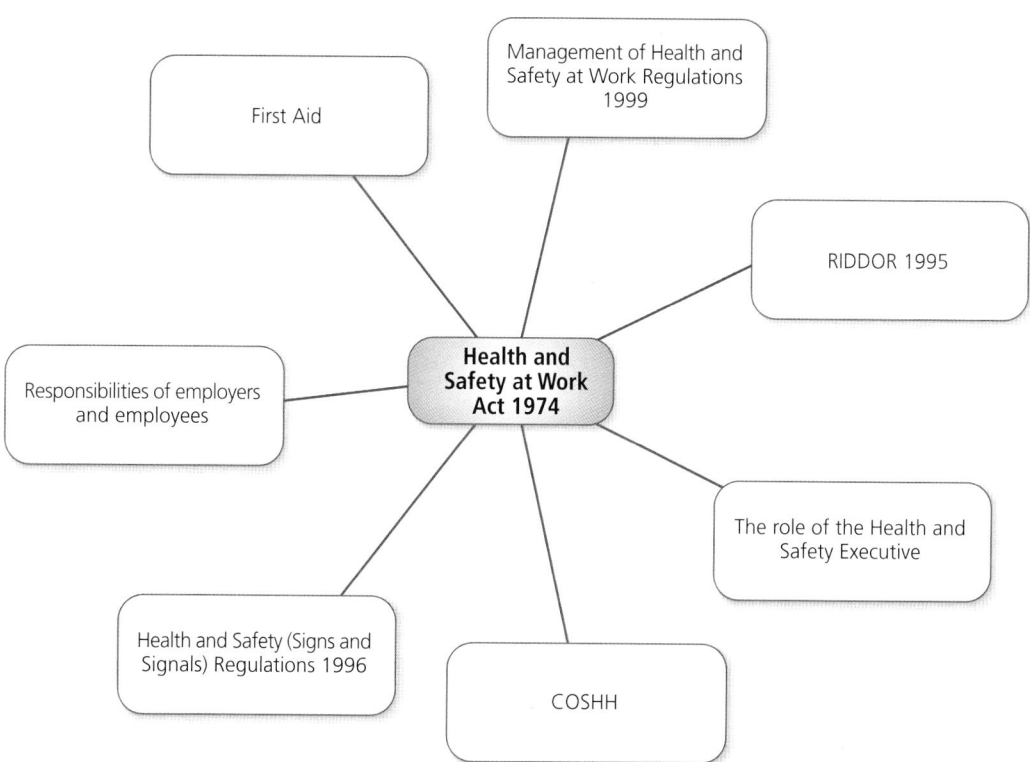

FIGURE 4.9 *Summary of the regulations covered by the HSAWA*

Section 2: Safety and security

Maintaining health, safety and security in a health and social care setting is a very important part of the role of workers. Often you will be working with clients who are vulnerable due to illness, age or social problems, and being at risk from accidents or breaches of security might add an extra burden to them, their visitors, you or your colleagues. It is your responsibility to ensure that all procedures are undertaken so as to minimise any risk.

Risk assessment

Risk assessment is designed for employers and self-employed people who are required by law to identify and assess risks in the workplace. This includes any situations where potential harm may be caused. There are many regulations that require risks to be assessed and some are covered by European Community directives. These include:

* Management of Health and Safety at Work Regulations 1999
* Manual Handling Operations Regulations 1992 (amended 2002)
* Personal Protective Equipment at Work Regulations 1992
* Health and Safety (Display Screen Equipment) Regulations 1992 (amended 2002)
* Noise at Work Regulations 1989
* Control of Substances Hazardous to Health Regulations 2002 (COSHH)
* Control of Asbestos at Work Regulations 2002
* Control of Lead at Work Regulations 2002.

There are other regulations that deal with very specialised risks, such as major hazards and ionising radiation. However, these are not considered to be common risks in most workplaces.

There are five key considerations in undertaking a risk assessment:
1. What is the purpose of the risk assessment?
2. Who has to assess the risk?
3. Whose risk should be assessed?
4. What should be assessed?
5. When should the risk be assessed?

The purpose of risk assessment

The purpose of carrying out risk assessment is to enable employers and self-employed people to make decisions about what might need to be done in the workplace to prevent people being harmed. Once a risk has been identified, measures must be put in place to comply with relevant health and safety legislation.

The Management of Health and Safety at Work Regulations 1999 is probably the most important piece of legislation as far as risk assessment is concerned, as it requires all risks to be assessed in the workplace. These will include anything that might cause harm to the employer, his or her employees and visitors. The employer then has a duty to ensure that precautions are put in place to minimise as far as possible the likelyhood of such risks occurring. The other regulations relate to specific risk-assessment provisions, and require employers to identify particular risks to particular groups of people. An example of this would be the use of asbestos and the risk of people breathing in its dust. In this situation, the employer would need to find out the type of asbestos being used and the level of risk to people of breathing in the dust. He or she would then decide what precautions would need to be in place to protect people from being harmed.

Who has to assess the risk?

Employers and self-employed people have the responsibility for ensuring that risks are assessed properly. This does not include Display Screen Regulations under which self-employed people do not have to carry out a risk assessment, but under the Management of Health and Safety at Work Regulations they do have to ensure that they are not at risk when working with display screens.

Employers do not have to carry out risk assessments themselves and can obtain help and advice from competent people. Often, the workforce knows from experience what risks and hazards there are and can contribute to the risk assessment process.

Whose risk should be assessed?

The Management Regulations state that employers must assess the risk to the health and safety of anyone who might be affected by their activities. However, the specific regulations will apply to particular risks or groups of people. An example of this would be assessing the risk to the employer or employees of moving and handling people or items, but not to the general public; though the Management Regulations state, that members of the public must not be harmed by any activities that might involve moving and handling.

What should be assessed?

Under the Management Regulations, anything in the workplace that may cause a potential risk to people must be assessed to ensure that all precautions have been taken or to identify whether further measures must be put in place. The specific regulations will provide further information about particular hazards – for example, the Manual Handling Operations Regulations, where the moving of loads must be considered.

When should risks be assessed?

There is no specific guidance for this in the Management Regulations, but in general risks should be assessed before any new work is started. Some of the specific regulations will give further guidance about when certain things have to be done.

Recording assessment

Some of the regulations, including the Management Regulations state, that significant findings of a risk assessment must be recorded in workplaces where five or more people are employed. However, there are certain regulations that state that recording must take place even if

---

Sunnydays Care Home
Long Lane
Smithtown
Westshire

Risk Assessment

Risk assessment for:	Fred Bloggs
Risk to be assessed:	Bathing using new hoist
Date:	7 September 2005
Assessment undertaken by:	Jane Smith (Staff nurse)
Assessment to be reviewed:	Every three weeks
Significant hazards:	Weight of Mr Bloggs, water temperature, water on the floor, training of staff using hoist, malfunction of hoist, possible injury to Mr Bloggs or staff
Who is at risk?	Mr Bloggs, carers

Existing controls in place to reduce risk: Hoist must always be used to bathe Mr Bloggs, hoist checked before each use and correct slings used, bath filled with cold water first then hot added, temperature checked before Mr Bloggs gets in, prevention of water splashing and floor mopped if any water spilt, staff trained in action to be taken if hoist breaks down.

Any risks not controlled and action to be taken: Insufficient training for staff in use of newly delivered battery operated hoists. All staff to be trained within next two weeks. Any untrained staff must be supervised until training has taken place.

FIGURE 4.10 *Example of a risk assessment record*

there are fewer than five employees. The assessment must be reviewed and revised whenever necessary. All the regulations state that if an employer suspects that this must take place if his or her 'assessment is no longer valid or there has been a significant change'. An example of this would be the installation of a new piece of equipment, or changes to the way a procedure is carried out. See Figure 4.10 for an example of a risk assessment carried out in a care home.

Reducing the risks

There are various procedures that can be followed to ensure that hazards in the workplace are minimised and that the workforce and others are protected from undue risk.

Training

The Health and Safety at Work Act 1974 states that the duty of employers is to ensure 'the provision of such information, instruction, training and supervision as is necessary to ensure, so far as is reasonably practicable, the health and safety at work of his or her employees'.

Knowledge and awareness of risks and how to deal with them help to maintain the health, safety and security of workers and other people who access working environments. An employer has a responsibility to provide free health and safety training for workers so that they know what hazards and risks they may face and how to deal with them. He or she must also obtain competent advice to help him or her to meet health and safety duties.

All employees must be given free health and safety induction training when they start work, which should cover basics such as first aid and fire safety. Job-specific health and safety training should also be given. When certain skills are not used frequently, there should be refresher training available.

Various courses are available for staff to attend. These include:

* First Aid – Appointed Persons
* First Aid at Work
* COSHH

* General Safety Awareness
* Manual Handling
* Basic, Intermediate and Advanced Food Hygiene Courses
* Risk Assessment
* Display Screen Equipment Assessors Course.

This is not an exhaustive list. Many companies will undertake their own training if they have the necessary trainers. Alternatively, there are many companies nationwide that provide health and safety training courses.

Early-warning systems

In order to maintain security, many care settings will use early-warning systems to protect property and the safety of employees and visitors. There are various methods that can be used.

Certain early warning systems will alert staff to potential problems that might cause a risk to health and safety. All refrigerators and freezers should have an external temperature gauge that will alert kitchen staff if they are not being maintained at the correct temperature. Food not properly stored can cause food poisoning, a grave risk for vulnerable groups such as babies and children, older people and people who are already ill or have compromised immune systems.

Intruder alarms

Intruder alarms can be installed to alert staff to the presence of intruders. They can be linked to a local police station, which should elicit a prompt response. However, these alarms can be set off accidentally and can cause a nuisance to neighbours. Alarms should be installed by qualified engineers and should be maintained regularly. They should have a cut-out to stop them ringing after a reasonable time, generally considered to be 20 minutes. It will then have to be reset. Alarms normally have keys, and key holders should be registered so that if an alarm goes off they can be contacted to switch off and reset the alarm.

Closed-circuit television cameras (CCTV)

Closed-circuit television is a system of cameras that are set up to provide an early-warning system against intruders. Generally the system consists of a series of cameras focused on locations that might allow a possible breach of security. The cameras are linked to monitors that will alert staff or a security company that there is a potential security problem on the premises. CCTV is increasingly being used as an early-warning system for hospitals and care homes.

'Statistics point to major reductions in the amount of crime being committed where there are cameras installed. An article in *New Scientist* magazine showed that simply installing a system can reduce crime, in the areas covered, by over 95 per cent.' Robyn Sones, www.cctv-information.co.uk

Although CCTV and intruder alarms are effective, there are many other precautions that can be taken to protect premises from intruders. There should be window locks with keys on all ground-floor windows, but the keys should be removed from the locks and kept out of sight of potential intruders. Doors should be fitted with alarms that can go off when opened, and some doors that are used only as emergency exits may only open from the inside.

Health and safety policies

It is very important that all health and social care settings have in place policies to safeguard staff, clients and visitors. The usual procedure is to maintain a policy book that contains all the relevant policies for that particular setting. Although many policies will be common to all settings, such as how to carry out a risk assessment or the fire policy, some specialised policies will need to be devised and included. Even common policies will contain some differences depending on the setting. These may be because particular risks have been identified that are unique to a setting, or they may relate especially to a certain client group, such as children or people who have mental-health problems.

Think it over...

At your work placement, ask to see the policy book. Make a note of the policies that are contained in it. As a group, discuss the differences in the types of policy held in different settings. Which are common to all the settings? Are there any that are unique to particular settings?

The use of safety and warning signs

The different safety and warning signs are described on page 169. It is the employer's responsibility to ensure that the correct signs are in place and that staff know what they mean. If you are concerned that a safety or warning sign is not being used properly or is missing, you have a responsibility to inform your supervisor. It is then their responsibility to ensure that this is put right.

Safety features

Many care settings will have in-built safety features designed to protect staff and service users. Such features might include smoke alarms, fire alarms and exit policies, all of which are covered separately in other sections of this chapter.

Personal protective equipment

The Personal Protective Equipment at Work Regulations 1992 state the responsibilities of employers regarding the provision of protective equipment for their employees. They are as follows:

✳ Every employer must ensure that personal protective equipment is provided to employees who may be exposed to a risk at work, except if the risk has been controlled by other means. This also applies to self-employed people who have to ensure that they have suitable personal protective equipment.

✳ Every employed or self-employed person must ensure that if he or she is required to wear an item of personal protective equipment, this is compatible and effective against risks.

* Employers and self-employed people must ensure that the personal protective equipment that is to be used is assessed and found suitable. This includes assessing any risks to health and safety and the characteristics that the equipment must have to ensure that it is effective against risks. The assessment will have to be reviewed if there are any changes that warrant this.

* Personal protective equipment is only considered to be suitable under the following conditions (as stated in the Regulations):

    a) it is appropriate for the risk or risks involved and the conditions at the place where exposure to the risk may occur

    b) it takes account of ergonomic requirements and the state of health of the person or persons who may wear it

    c) it is capable of fitting the wearer correctly, if necessary, after adjustments within the range for which it is designed

    d) so far as is practicable, it is effective to prevent or adequately control the risk or risks involved without increasing overall risk

    e) it complies with any enactment (whether in an Act or instrument) which implements in Great Britain any provision on design or manufacture with respect to health or safety, which is applicable to that item of personal protective equipment.

* Employers and self-employed people must ensure that all personal protective equipment is maintained properly and is in good repair and good working order.

* Appropriate accommodation must be provided for the storage of personal protective equipment when it is not in use.

* Employers must ensure that employees are given information, instruction and training in the use of personal protective equipment, which covers how risks will be avoided or limited, the purpose for which the personal portrait equipment is to be used and what the employee must do to ensure that it is kept in a good state of repair.

* Employers, employees and self-employed people all have a responsibility to ensure that the equipment provided is used properly and in accordance with training instructions.

* All personal protective equipment must be returned to its allocated storage place after use.

* Employees must report any loss or damage to the equipment to his or her employer.

Consider this

1. With reference to the information above about personal protective equipment, consider what types of protective equipment might be used in a care setting, and for what purposes. Create a table showing this information.

2. Obtain a copy of *A Short Guide to the Personal Protective Equipment at Work Regulations 1992* (www.hse.gov.uk). Find out the types of hazard that are included in this publication and what recommendations are made. Make another table showing this information.

3. Using your information, create a poster that could be used in a care setting to ensure that staff know what personal protective equipment they should use.

How does reducing risk affect service users and care workers?

The establishment and implementation of policies and procedures are important in helping to prevent accidents and injuries and the transmission of infection to service users and care workers. Service users have the right to be looked after safely and securely and care workers have a responsibility to ensure that this happens. People who work with children will have responsibilities under the Children Acts 1989 and 2004 to protect children in their care. The 2004 Act received Royal Assent on 15 November 2004, but only Section One came into effect on this date; the remainder of the Act will come into force on a date set by the Secretary of State.

The Criminal Records Bureau, which is an executive agency of the Home Office, was established to help make safe recruitment decisions in the public, private and voluntary sectors. Employers have wider access to criminal record information, which will make it possible to identify potential workers who may be unsuitable for care work, particularly for those wishing to work with children or vulnerable adults.

✱ DID YOU KNOW?

Fatal injuries – reported under RIDDOR

✱ Between 1996/97 and 2002/03 there were three fatal injuries to employees in the health services. One resulted from a low fall, one from being struck by a moving vehicle and one from slipping/tripping.

Major injuries – reported under RIDDOR

✱ There were 1238 reported major injuries to employees in the health services for 2002/03 (4 per cent of all reported major injuries in industry), a marginally smaller proportion than that for 2001/02 with 5 per cent (1267).

✱ The number of major injuries in the health services has been declining steadily since 1997/98. The number of injuries has fallen by 15 per cent and the rate of major injury by 25 per cent .

✱ Injuries as a result of slipping and tripping accounted for 54 per cent (667) of all the major injuries in the health services in 2002/03. Handling and assault/violence accounted for 12 per cent and 11 per cent respectively.

✱ In all industries combined, assault and violence account for 3 per cent of all major injuries and 14 per cent of over-three-day injuries.

Over-three-day injuries – reported under RIDDOR

✱ There were 9551 reported over-three-day injuries to employees in the health services for 2002/03 (8 per cent of all over-three-day injuries in industry), the same proportion as that for 2001/02 (10,077).

✱ Over the past five years, handling injuries have accounted for approximately 53 per cent of all over-three-day injuries in the health services. Slips and trips, assault/violence were the next most common kinds of accident resulting in over-three-day injuries in the health services.

✱ As with major injuries, the number of over-three-day injuries in the health services have been declining over recent years. The number of injuries has fallen by 16 per cent since 1997/98 and the rate of injury by 27 per cent since 1998/99.

Reporting levels

The average Labour Force Survey (LFS) rate of reportable injury allows us to estimate the level of reporting of non-fatal injuries. The estimate for the level of reporting of non-fatal injuries in health services in 2001/02 was 46 per cent compared with 51 per cent in 2000/01.

Revitalising health and safety target

The target across the whole economy is to reduce the indicator by 10 per cent in the 10-year period 1999/2000 to 2009/10, with an interim target of reducing the indicator by 5 per cent by the mid-point of this period, i.e. by 2004/05.

(Source: www.hse.gov.uk/statistics/pdf/rhshlth.pdf)

The Fire Precautions (Workplace) (Amendment) Regulations 1999

These regulations came into force on 1 December 1999 and amended the Fire Precautions (Workplace) Regulations 1997. They apply to workplaces where a fire certificate is in force or where a fire certificate is pending. The regulations were amended to comply with European Community directives.

The regulations place duties on employers, owners of commercial properties, anyone who has control of a workplace and anyone who is responsible for the maintenance or safety of a workplace.

The main duties under the regulations are:

* the provision of appropriate fire-fighting equipment, fire alarms and detectors
* the provision of a fire evacuation plan that protects employees and other people who may be on the site
* the appointment of designated employees who are equipped and trained
* consultation with emergency services about their needs regarding emergency rescue and fire fighting
* provision for manually operated fire fighting
* specific requirements for fire escape routes and emergency exits
* maintenance of the workplace and equipment
* risk assessment
* notification of offences and enforcement of regulations.

Fire safety

All workplaces must have procedures and policies that must be followed in the event of an emergency. Information must be displayed about the action to be taken if a fire breaks out. An example of such information is shown below:

FIRE SAFETY PROCEDURE

1. Raise the alarm
2. Inform the switchboard or dial 999
3. Ensure that everyone is safe or out of danger
4. Attack the fire with a fire extinguisher if it is safe to do so
5. Go to the fire assembly point (the location will be stated)
6. Do not return to the building for any reason until you are told that it is safe to do so.

Fire training for all staff must be provided by all employers every year. As an employee it is your responsibility to ensure that you are familiar with the fire procedure in your workplace. You should ensure that you know where all fire-fighting equipment is. This includes fire alarms, fire extinguishers and fire blankets. You must also know where the fire exits are.

Fire doors must never be propped open as this will enable a fire to spread. Lifts should never be used in the event of fire.

Fire extinguishers

All fire extinguishers are red and are clearly marked with instructions printed on them in

FIGURE 4.11 *An extinguisher for general fires and one for electrical and wiring fires*

different coloured labels depending on what type of fire they should be used for. You must be familiar with how to use them. You should only tackle a fire if you can do so safely. If not you must leave the fire and wait for the fire emergency service to arrive.

The colour labels for fire extinguishers are as follows:

* red – water, used for paper, wood and general fires

* cream – foam, used for liquid oil fires, fat, petrol, oil etc.

* blue – dry powder, used for fuel oil and can be used for electrical fires

* black – carbon dioxide, used for electrical and wiring fires.

Green extinguishers, used for electrical and most other fires, have now been phased out due to damage to health and the ozone layer.

Evacuation

You may be required to be involved in the evacuation of a building. It is important that you are aware that evacuation might not just be for a fire, but may also be for a bomb scare, a structurally unsafe building, an explosion or a chemical or fume leak.

Each workplace will have an evacuation plan that will have been drawn up according to the type and layout of the building. In general, most procedures will give similar instructions on how to react to an emergency that requires a building to be evacuated. Typical instructions are:

* stay calm; do not shout or run

* do not allow others to run

* organise people quickly without panic

* give directions to people who can move themselves

* help people who cannot move themselves

* use wheelchairs to move people quickly

* if necessary move a bed with a person in it.

Security

In general, most care settings are not locked as service users have the right to freedom of movement. However, establishments that provide care for people with dementia may have a locked-door policy to prevent clients from wandering out of the building and getting lost.

Security procedures should take into account different risks that may occur. These could include security against intruders and being abused, protection of property and safeguarding service users from unwanted visitors.

Large organisations such as NHS Trusts will provide all staff with photographic identity cards. Some of these may be swipe cards that must be used to access some areas. In smaller places visitors' badges may be issued to all visitors on arrival, and their time of arrival and departure will be logged in a visitors' book.

Some small establishments may just rely on the vigilance of staff to recognise regular visitors.

Although you should never attempt to challenge an intruder if you feel you are in a risky situation, there are steps you can take if you are suspicious:

* be vigilant: be aware of the people around you – do you recognise them?

* if you do not recognise them, challenge them – bogus visitors are likely to leave quickly if challenged

* make sure that your challenge is polite – they may be completely innocent and have a good reason for being on the premises

* if they ask for directions or to see a client by name, escort them and do not give directions

* raise the alarm if you are suspicious – do not tackle the intruder.

In the course of their work, care workers may look after people in their own homes. It is very important that they impress upon service users the need to take precautions to protect themselves and their property. If care workers are not sure about what is the best advice to give, the local neighbourhood watch scheme or the community police officer can advise about home security. This might include fitting window locks, door chains and bolts and burglar alarms. Sometimes local councils will provide grants for this type of work to be carried out.

Vulnerable individuals who are being cared for in their own homes must also be reminded not to allow access to anyone they do not know. They should always ask for identity, which genuine callers will have. If they are still not sure, they can telephone the company or organisation the caller says he or she is representing and ask for confirmation of identity. Some companies will operate a password scheme that will help provide this information.

Consider this

Contact your local utilities companies (gas, electric, water and telephone) and find out what security measures they use to reassure vulnerable customers that their employees are genuine. Make sure you state clearly why you want this information, as you do not want to arouse their suspicions!

You could also ask your tutor to arrange for a representative from the police or local neighbourhood watch scheme to give a talk about how to help protect vulnerable clients.

Security in early years settings and residential homes

Care settings where clients include children or vulnerable adults may have a policy stating that doors should be kept locked. In this instance, visitors will have to ring the door-bell to gain access and their identity should be checked by staff. All visitors should be asked to sign the visitors' book, marking the time of arrival and departure. As well as being a good method of monitoring security, a properly logged visitors' book will allow staff to know who is on the premises at any time in case of fire or other emergency that might require evacuation, so that everyone can be accounted for.

Sometimes service users may not wish to see

people who have come to visit them. This is their prerogative, and you should not try to persuade them otherwise or make excuses to unwanted visitors. It is possible that service users have in the past been victims of physical, sexual or financial abuse and they may have very good reason to decline visitors. Your job is to protect and care for your clients, and you must respect their wishes.

As a result of reported incidents of attempted and actual abductions of newborn babies, most maternity units now have locked doors, and visitors must ring a bell and identify themselves in order to gain access. Baby tagging is also in place in some hospitals, whereby a tag attached around a baby's ankle responds to sensor panels at hospital exits. This triggers an alarm to alert security staff. Further developments are in progress, which could result in tags being tracked after leaving the hospital grounds.

There must be a written procedure in early years settings for the collection of children, and all staff must know what the procedure states. In general, only a staff member who knows the parents and child can allow the child to leave. This is not always practical, especially in a crèche where a child may attend on an irregular or 'one-off' basis. In such a case, a system may be used where a password is chosen by the parent and recorded on the registration form. This has to be given to the staff before the child is allowed to leave. Normally, a nursery will have two contact names in case of emergency, and the second name must be someone the nursery staff is familiar with, such as a grandparent or a parent of another child. If the parents are in dispute and one does not wish the other to collect the child, this must be put in writing to the setting. If there are any specific issues relating to a child, such as the child being subject to a court order, the staff must be aware of any special procedures.

Valuable items owned by service users must be safeguarded. All valuable property and personal items should be listed in a property book, and you may be able to offer to store them in a safe place. Jewellery should be described by colour, for example 'yellow metal' rather than 'gold'. Clients should always be asked to sign for any valuables they are keeping and should be informed that they are liable for their loss. If you know that a client is in possession of a large quantity of money or valuables, you should inform your manager.

All service users are entitled to confidentiality, and this must never be breached by staff unless they feel that a client might come to harm by failing to disclose information. All workers must ensure that information is passed only to next of kin. If they are not sure about what details can be passed on they must refer to a senior member of staff. Some clients may have given instructions that they do not want any information to be given to anyone about their condition; this must be respected.

Unauthorised people should not have access to any information that is considered to be confidential, and for this reason paper records should be kept securely. In addition, computer screens should have screen savers and be password-protected. They should also be positioned in such a way that displayed information is concealed as far as possible.

Summary

This section has covered a range of issues that are concerned with maintaining the safety and security of vulnerable individuals and carers and professionals who work with them. It is important for each care worker to understand that they have individual responsibilities to protect and safeguard themselves and their clients, in addition to the responsibilities of their employer towards them.

Consider this

1. What are the five key considerations in undertaking a risk assessment?

2. Identify at least three courses that a manager could offer to his or her workers that would contribute to their health and safety and that of their clients.

3. What are the responsibilities of an employer regarding the Personal Protective Equipment at Work Regulations 1992?

4. Identify the four different types of fire extinguisher, and which type of fire each is used for.

5. What would you do if you were suspicious about a visitor to your work placement that you had never seen before?

Section 3: Safe moving and handling techniques

An employer has the responsibility to ensure that it examines and assesses all procedures that take place in the work environment and involve risk. One very important factor is moving and handling loads.

Manual Handling Operations Regulations 1992

The Manual Handling Operations Regulations 1992 (MHO) (revised 1999) came into force on 1 January 1993 under the Health and Safety at Work Act 1974, and enables UK legislation to implement a European Community directive on the manual handling of loads. It places duties on employers and employees to ensure that risks are minimised when lifting, moving or handling people or objects. There is no direct instruction in the regulations not to lift, but they do state that all personnel should 'avoid hazardous manual handling where reasonably practicable', and many organisations, particularly within the NHS and social services, do instruct their employees that they should not lift at all.

The employer's duties

Under the regulations, the duties of the employer include the following:

* to avoid the need for hazardous manual handling as far as is reasonably practicable
* to assess the risk of injury from any hazardous manual handling that cannot be avoided
* to reduce the risk of injury from hazardous manual handling as far as reasonably practicable.

The employee's duties

The HSE define 'manual handling' in the Manual Handling Operations Regulations 1992 as:

'Any transporting or supporting of a load (including the lifting, putting down, pushing, pulling, carrying or moving thereof) by hand or by bodily force.'

As with the Health and Safety at Work Act 1974, employees also have duties under the Manual Handling Operations Regulations 1992. These include:

* following appropriate systems of work laid down for their safety
* making proper use of any equipment provided to minimise the risk of injury
* cooperating with the employer on health and safety matters.

An example of this would be if a healthcare worker did not use a hoist or other moving equipment that had been provided and sustained an injury as a result. The employer would not be liable in this case.

Lifting Operations and Lifting Equipment Regulations 1992 (LOLER)

These regulations came into effect on 5 December 1998 and apply to all workplaces. An employee does not have any responsibilities under LOLER but under the Management of Health and Safety at Work Regulations, they do have a duty to ensure that they take reasonable care of themselves and others who may be affected by the actions they undertake.

Employers, however, do have duties under LOLER. They must ensure that all equipment provided for use at work is:

* sufficiently strong and stable for the particular use and marked to indicate safe working loads
* positioned and installed to minimise any risks
* used safely, i.e. the work is planned, organised and performed by competent people
* subject to ongoing thorough examination and, where appropriate, inspection by competent people.

In addition, employers must ensure that:

* lifting operations are planned, supervised and carried out in a safe way by competent people
* equipment for lifting people is safe

* lifting equipment and accessories are thoroughly examined

* a report is submitted by a competent person following a thorough examination or inspection.

Lifting equipment designed for lifting and moving loads must be inspected at least annually, but any equipment that is designed for the use of lifting and handling people must be inspected at least every six months. A nominated competent person may draw up an examination scheme for this purpose.

If employees provide their own lifting equipment, then this is covered by the regulations.

Risk assessment

As with any other potential hazardous procedure, a manual handling risk assessment must be carried out before attempting to move a service user. There are certain questions that should be asked. These are:

* What task is to be performed?

* Who is carrying out the task?

* What is being moved?

* In what environment is the manual handling operation being conducted?

* What equipment is being used?

These might be remembered more simply in the way illustrated in Figure 4.12.

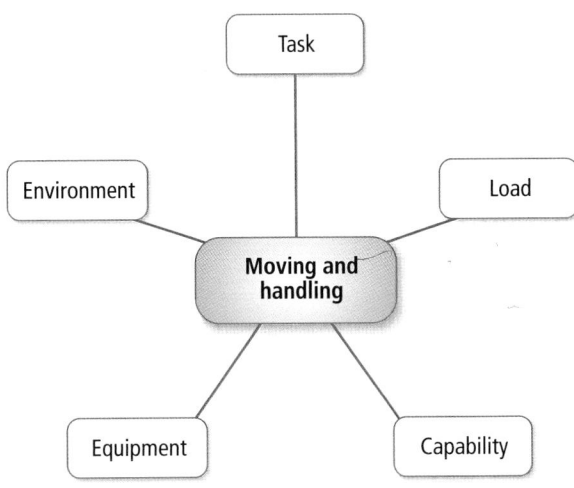

FIGURE 4.12 *Questions to consider when carrying out a manual handling risk assessment*

Consider this

Thursday October 17, 2002

Injured nurse wins £414,000 damages

CLARE DYER, LEGAL CORRESPONDENT

A nurse who suffered a crippling back injury as a result of lifting patients, which forced her to leave her job at the age of 36, won £414,335 damages in the High Court yesterday.

Angela Knott, 36, never returned to work after waking in agony in March 1998. She suffered a disc prolapse and neurological problems, including incontinence, diminished sexual function and weakness in her leg. She has been warned against having children.

Mrs Knott, of Berwick on Tweed, Northumberland, who became a nurse at 18, worked on a 28-bed ward at Newham hospital, east London, for acute medical cases. Her counsel, Colin McCaul, said that nursing levels on the ward could 'only be described as appalling'. One hoist was shared with another ward, so nurses had to lift patients weighing up to 75 kg (12 stone).

Mr Justice Simon ruled that Newham NHS Trust's arrangements for lifting were 'inadequate'. He found no real steps had been taken to reduce risk of injury to the lowest level reasonably practicable, and that the authority's breach of duty had caused, or contributed to, Mrs Knott's injury.

As a group discuss this case with reference to the appropriate legislation.

1. What do you think the responsibilities were of both the health authority and Mrs Knott?

2. Do you think this situation could have been avoided, and, if so, how?

It may be appropriate to produce a standard checklist like the one below that should be completed whenever a risk assessment is completed. This information should be kept in the client's care plan so that it is available for all staff to check before beginning to move or handle that service user. It is important to remember that such assessments must be reviewed regularly, as a service user's ability to participate in the planned move may change depending on whether they deteriorate or get better.

Checklist

1	Is individual capable of standing?	Yes	☐
		No	☐
2	Is individual unsteady?	Yes	☐
		No	☐
3	What is the general level of mobility?	Good	☐
		Poor	☐
3	(a) What is individual's weight?		
	(b) What is individual's height?		
	(c) How many people does this lift require?		
	[Work this out on the scale devised by your workplace]		
7	What lifting equipment is required?	Hoist	☐
		Sling	☐
		Trapeze	☐
		Transfer board	☐
8	Is equipment available?	Yes	☐
		No	☐
9	If not, is there a safe alternative?	Yes	☐
		No	☐
10	Are the required number of people available?	Yes	☐
		No	☐
11	What is the purpose of the move?		
12	Can this be achieved?	Yes	☐
		No	☐

FIGURE 4.13 *Example checklist for completing a risk assessment*

The Royal College of Nursing Advisory Panel on Back Pain in Nurses has produced a Code of Practice for Patient Handling. In 1996, the previous code recommended that there should be a 50 kg (8 stone) weight limit for a patient being lifted by two nurses. Conclusions from this version generated considerable debate, and it was suggested that fewer back injuries would be

ASSESSMENT FORM FOR PATIENTS WHO REQUIRE MANUAL HANDLING

Name: .... Weight: ....

Height: ....

Any relevant physical disabilities: _____

Patient's mental ability and comprehension:

_____

History of falls?   Yes   No
                      ☐   ☐

Any equipment to be used by patient ☐

Handling constraints
Skin
Pain
Infusions
Catheters etc.
Other

Abilities in following situations:

Walking
Standing
Toileting
Transferring in/out of bed
Transferring in/out of bath

TO BE COMPLETED WITHIN 24 HOURS OF ADMISSION AND THE RELEVANT INFORMATION WRITTEN INTO THE CARE PLAN. UPDATE THE ASSESSMENT FORM AND CARE PLAN AS NECESSARY

Assessor's signature: ....

Grade: ....

Date: ....

FIGURE 4.14 *Example assessment form for manual handling*

caused if all moving and handling operations were risk assessed before being undertaken. The code had the effect of excluding almost all manual lifting of patients by nurses.

The aim of using a safe handling policy is to stop hazardous manual handling in all situations unless they are exceptional or life-threatening. As far as possible, patients should be encouraged to assist in moving and handling operations, and aids must be used if these will minimise the risk of injury.

Factors that can contribute to back injury among nurses are:

* lifting patients

* working in awkward positions including bending forwards or sideways or twisting the body

* lifting loads at arm's length

* lifting with a starting position near the floor or overhead at arm's length

* lifting an uneven load with the weight mainly on one side

* handling an uncooperative or falling patient.

Source: RCN Code of Practice for Patient Handling

What factors do you need to take into account?

The following factors should be considered before moving a client:

* **Clothing** – Are you wearing appropriate clothing? Comfortable clothing such as a dress or tunic and trousers will allow for sufficient movement. Well-fitting flat shoes should be worn.

* **Environment** – Are there any hazards such as wet floors or equipment in the way that could result in a slip, trip or fall?

* **Equipment** – Is the equipment appropriate for the moving operation to be carried out, and is it in good working order?

* **Dignity** – Is the patient assured privacy during the move?

* **Competence** – Are you properly trained in the use of the equipment? Do you know what is the most appropriate equipment to use for the move you are about to carry out?

How to prepare individuals for moving and handling

It is very important that the individuals that you are helping to move are involved as much as possible. This is not only because they will know the methods of moving that best suit them, but also because it encourages them to maintain as much independence and dignity as possible. It will also help to prevent injury to the clients and to you. Therefore, before starting the move you must ensure that you explain what you are going to do and how the equipment works so that the clients understand and are prepared for what is going to happen.

Communication is extremely important when preparing and carrying out the move. Exchange of information between you and your clients will enable the move to be carried out smoothly and will allow the clients to maintain some control over what is happening to them. However, it is vital that all safety procedures are adhered to. You cannot be guided by what the client tells you if you feel that this poses a risk to either or both of you. In this situation you must explain to the client that there are certain health and safety rules that must be followed. Trying to save time by moving a client without the proper equipment could be catastrophic and should never be done. In addition, you should never move clients without their consent. If you experience any problems in respect of any of these issues, you must seek advice from a senior member of staff before attempting any moving or handling procedure.

How to prepare yourself for moving and handling

You must never attempt to move a service user unless you have been trained to do so. This includes training in the use of all the equipment you will use. Trained and non-trained clinical personnel in the National Health Service must complete a three-hour training course annually. Non-clinical staff such as receptionists and porters must receive at least one hour of training annually.

Before starting to move a service user you should ensure that you have all the equipment you will need to hand. Once the procedure is under way it is very difficult, if not impossible, to stop.

Your feet should be hip-width apart so that your body is balanced. One foot may be placed in front of the other and your body should be as close to the client as possible.

Your knees should be relaxed and flexed so that the back muscles do not tense, and your back should be kept straight so that the weight is taken by your legs.

FIGURE 4.15 *How to stand as you prepare to move a service user*

It is important that staff realise that most back and spinal pain is caused by continual bad lifting, twisting and stretching and not by injuries that occur as a result of a single incident.

Think it over...

At your work placement, find out the policy for moving and handling the service users. Are there any specific instructions regarding particular situations? Make notes on any information you find out.

As a group, compare your findings. Are most policies the same or similar? What are the differences?

How to use equipment

In most care settings there will be a variety of equipment available for use. What is used will depend on the clients and their abilities and preferences, and what is considered to be appropriate by a competent person.

Every piece of equipment will have an instruction manual that must be read before it is used. You must make sure you know how to use it, and you must receive mandatory training in moving and handling every year.

As with all equipment, moving and handling equipment must be kept in good condition and serviced regularly. It should also be cleaned and disinfected if it is going to be used for different clients to prevent cross infection.

Hoists and standards

Mobile hoists can be used to lift service users in a variety of ways, for example from bed to bathroom. They can be battery-operated or electric and mobile, or suspended overhead. All are used with slings, which are often colour coded according to the user's weight. It is very important to ensure that the correct sling is used for the correct weight of client, and that the user knows how to use the slings correctly. It is not generally necessary to lift the client very high – the hoist only needs to provide clearance from the piece of furniture that is being used.

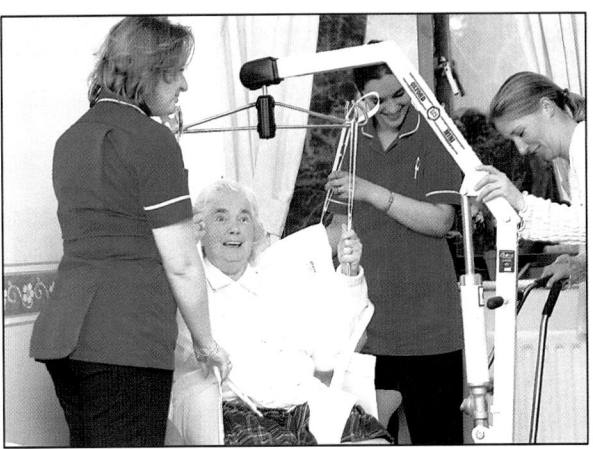

FIGURE 4.16 *Hoists are useful pieces of equipment*

Overhead hoists are attached to the ceiling and a track is used to move the client from one place to another, for example from bed into a bathroom.

A stand aid can be used to lift a client from a chair to a standing position as it has a footplate and padding for the knees. However, a client using this piece of equipment must be able to bear some weight. If he or she is not able to, then a hoist should be used.

Hoists are very useful pieces of equipment and work efficiently, but it must be remembered that they do require enough room to be used properly. Different sized hoists are available.

Transfer assist devices

Transfer assist devices are non-mechanical pieces of equipment that can help in moving clients

FIGURE 4.17 *Hand blocks help patients move up and down in bed*

more efficiently and safely. They include slide sheets, transfer belts, slide/transfer boards, patient hand blocks, turning discs and bed rope ladders. Used properly they can reduce the risk of injury to staff and can help service users to maintain as much independence and dignity as possible.

Slide sheet

Slide sheets are available in different sizes and are low-friction fabric tubes that will move easily to enable clients to be repositioned. They can be used to help move clients from bed to chair, to be moved to a more upright position in bed, and to turn clients with only one member of staff.

Support and transfer belts

These are used to help clients to perform various types of movement such as standing, walking or rotating using a turning disc. A support belt is made of strong material and is fastened securely but not too tightly round the waist of the person to be moved. The loops, which are situated at the back of the client, should be grasped firmly and the client helped to a standing position using a rocking motion. The hands should never be passed through the loops as this could cause injury. Support belts should only be used when the service user is able to support some of his or her own weight. If this is not the case, alternative equipment such as a hoist should be used. Transfer belts are adjustable and made of webbing. They are used to ensure that a care worker can grab at clothing and that he or she is close to the client during the movement.

Slide/transfer board

These are used for helping a service user to move from chair to bed or bed to commode with ease, where the two surfaces are level with each other. There should always be at least 10 cm of overlap to ensure that the board is secure, and the tapered edge of the board should be uppermost. Although the surface of these boards is usually very smooth, carers should ensure that as a service user shuffling along the length of the board suffers no friction on bare skin. Service users normally have to be able to balance well to be able to use this type of equipment.

Patient hand block

This is a relatively new piece of equipment that will allow clients to move themselves up and down the bed. Hand blocks are large plastic handles with a non-slip base and have the effect of lengthening the arms and preventing them from sinking into the mattress. Hand blocks are particularly good for use in moving up and down the bed and for providing an aid for using bedpans, although clients will need to have quite strong hands and arms in order to use them.

Turning disc

Turning discs are made of fabric and are placed on the floor. They are particularly useful for moving a service user from a chair to a commode or to the side of a bed, and help to prevent strain on joints and jerking movements that could be painful. Clients can be helped to stand using a transfer or support belt and then swivelled round to sit on another piece of furniture. The client's feet must fit properly onto the disc, and the disc must be removed after the procedure to prevent the risk of tripping.

Bed rope ladder

This is made from strong rope and plastic rungs and is attached to the legs of the bed. A client can then pull him or herself up in bed, working along the rungs, but he or she needs to have adequate upper body strength in order to do this.

Summary

This section has covered safe lifting and handling techniques and equipment that can be used to move individuals safely without injury to them or their carers. It includes employers' and employees' duties, LOLER and risk assessment for carrying out moving and handling. Key issues that care workers must understand are the need to plan and prepare for any moving and handling procedure, and the need to involve the individual to be moved as much as possible.

Consider this

The following clients all require help to move and change position. In pairs, using the information provided above, decide which equipment is the most appropriate for each person.

1. Dave is 20 years old and has broken his leg in a motorcycle accident. He is fit and strong but is unable to get out of bed until the fracture heals. He is very embarrassed because he has to use a bedpan until he is able to put any weight on his leg.

2. Mrs Jones is 80 years old and is recovering from a severe stroke, which has left her with a weakness down her left side. She finds it very difficult to stand and needs to be turned every two hours overnight to prevent pressure sores from forming. She likes to have a bath every day.

3. Meena is 18 years old and has cerebral palsy. She is a wheelchair user and is able to stand and bear weight for short periods of time. Occasionally, she likes to sit in an armchair in the lounge of her residential home.

4. Peter is 45 years old and is recovering from major abdominal surgery. He is normally fit and healthy, but has difficulty getting in and out of bed. Most of the time he is self-caring.

Section 4: Contribution to infection control

When working in care settings it is very important to take precautions to prevent the spread of infection. Although the prevention of infection is important for all clients, you may find yourself working with service users who are considered to be more vulnerable than others. This might include the very young, the very old and people who have conditions that make them more vulnerable to infection. Babies and young children have immature immune systems and older people have immune systems that are less efficient than when they were younger.

Infection is caused by micro-organisms that include bacteria and viruses. They can enter the body through the respiratory system, the digestive system or open wounds, and some can cross through the placenta from the mother to an unborn baby.

Cross-infection

Cross-infection is the term used to describe the passing of infection from one person to another. This can happen in a variety of ways:

* by touch – from the hands of a care worker working with a variety of service users

* by clothing – infection carried on the clothes and transmitted to clients

* by instruments or equipment – inadequate cleaning, disinfection or sterilisation of items between use by different clients

* by breathing in droplet or dust infection via the air

* by inadequate cleaning of bed linen or surfaces such as bed lockers, trolleys and floors.

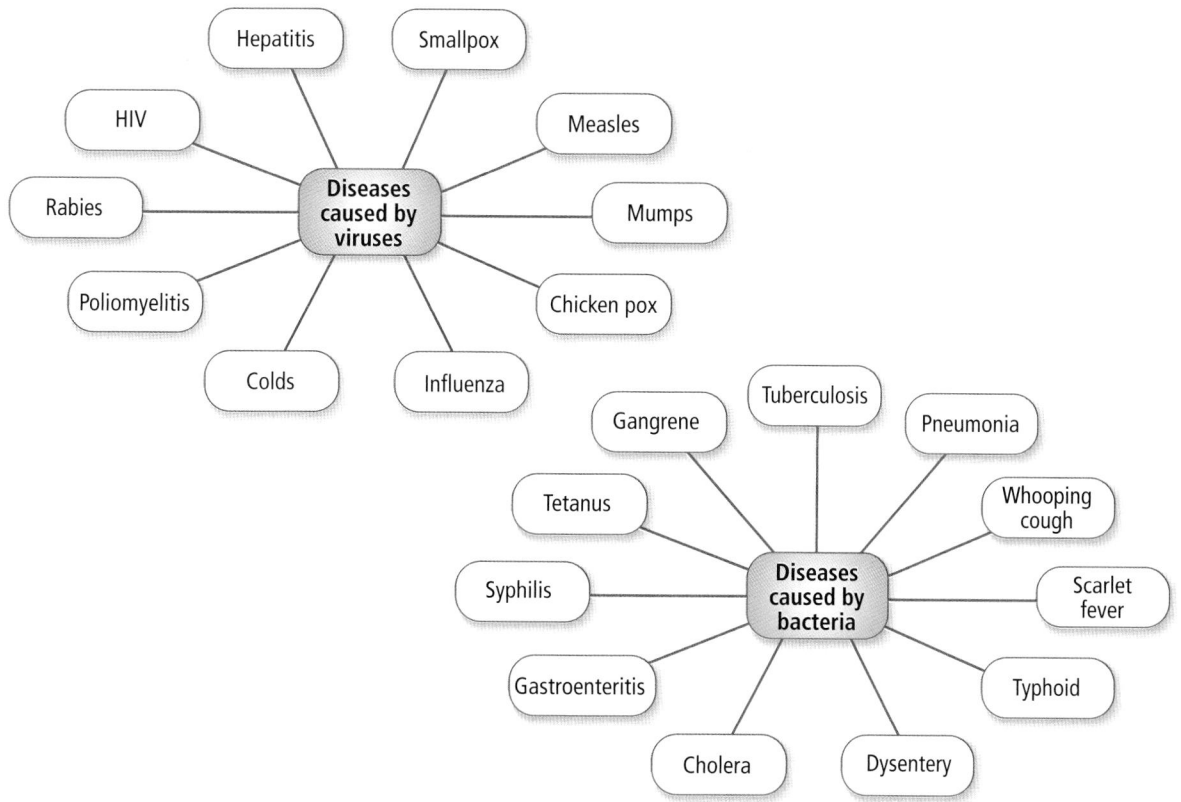

FIGURE 4.18 *Disease caused by viruses and bacteria*

The use of protective clothing

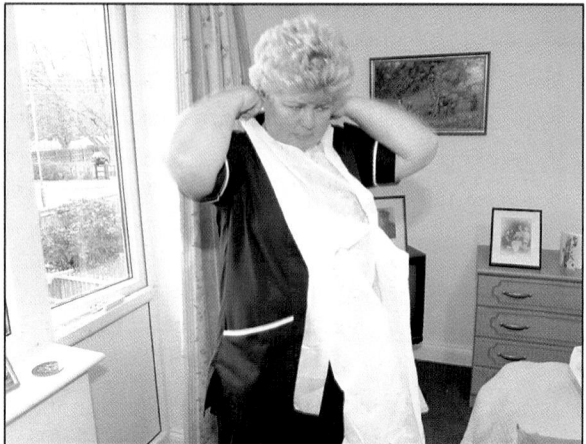

FIGURE 4.19 *Disposable plastic aprons prevent the spread of disease by cross-infection*

This section focuses on the importance of personal protective equipment when used for the prevention of cross-infection. Protective clothing for the protection of you and your clients includes: gloves, plastic aprons, masks, overshoes.

Gloves

Gloves should be worn whenever you are in contact with body fluids, mucous membranes and broken skin such as wounds. They are never a substitute for hand washing, and hands should always be washed before and after using them. Generally, gloves should be freely available for all staff. They are normally made of latex, but gloves made of other materials are available for those who are allergic to latex. You should always make sure that your gloves fit properly and they must always be changed if they are torn. Gloves must always be changed between working with different service users. There is little point in wearing them if you do not do this. They should be removed by pulling them from the cuff so that they turn inside out during removal. The second glove should be pulled off while you are holding the first so that the first is enclosed inside the second. They should then be disposed of in a clinical waste bin.

Plastic aprons

Plastic aprons should always be used when there is the possibility of clothing being splashed by body fluids, causing contamination. They should also be used if you know that a service user has an infection. They must be removed and disposed of carefully when you have completed a procedure.

Masks

These should be worn if there is a danger that your eyes, face or mouth might become splashed with body fluids, contaminated material or dangerous substances. They are particularly important if you are looking after someone who has an infection that is droplet-transmitted such as tuberculosis or severe acute respiratory syndrome (SARS). Most masks are designed to cover the mouth and nose, but some also have a clear visor attached to protect the eyes. Masks must be handled carefully and not handled too much after use as any contaminants could be transmitted to the hands. They should be handled by the strings only and disposed of in yellow clinical waste bags as soon as possible after use. They should be changed after each procedure or operation.

Overshoes

Overshoes are worn to prevent the transmission of infection via flooring. Most commonly they are used by staff entering a clean environment such as an operating theatre when escorting patients, or by operating theatre staff who have to leave the theatre area. This is necessary to prevent contamination of the floors. There may be other instances when overshoes need to be worn such as when clients are being treated in isolation.

Personal hygiene

Good personal hygiene is essential when working with people who could be at risk of infection. You should always make sure that you bathe or shower and wash your hair regularly and that you wear clean clothes. You should make sure that you launder uniforms regularly. Most uniforms are designed to be laundered at high temperatures to kill any pathogens on them.

Hand-washing is generally considered to be the single most important way of preventing infection. However, it is also acknowledged that many healthcare practitioners do not know or use the correct techniques for hand-washing. This means that certain areas of the hands are often missed.

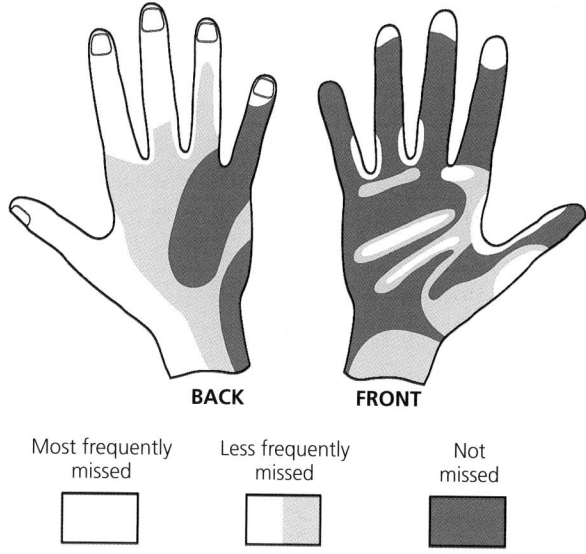

BACK   FRONT

Most frequently missed	Less frequently missed	Not missed

FIGURE 4.20 *The areas missed and not missed during hand-washing*

Hand-washing technique

Hands must be washed thoroughly on a regular basis, at least as often as between working with different clients. They must also be washed if in the course of your working day you are required to handle and serve food.

Hand-washing facilities should be available in patient areas, treatment rooms and sluices, and there should be adequate hot and cold water, liquid soap and paper hand towels available. Liquid soap is preferable to soap bars, as bars are likely to harbour bacteria. Taps should be lever operated so that they can be switched on and off with the forearms or elbows, and foot-operated waste bins should be used. These facilities enable a member of staff to avoid touching areas that might recontaminate their hands.

PROCEDURE FOR HAND-WASHING

1. Wet hands thoroughly with water at a comfortable temperature.
2. Apply liquid soap and rub hands palm to palm.
3. Rub right palm over back of left hand and left palm over back of right hand.
4. Rub hands palm to palm with fingers interlaced.
5. Lock fingers together and rub backs of fingers to opposing palms.
6. Rub both thumbs in opposing palms.
7. Rub clasped fingers of right hand in left palm and vice versa.
8. Rinse soap off thoroughly.
9. Dry with paper towel.

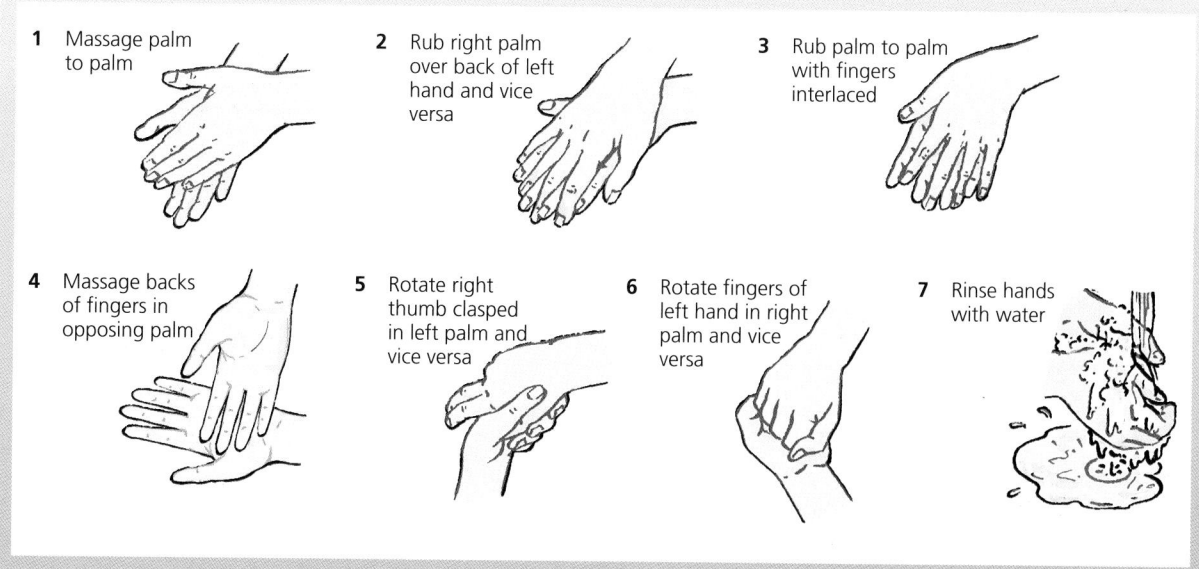

1. Massage palm to palm
2. Rub right palm over back of left hand and vice versa
3. Rub palm to palm with fingers interlaced
4. Massage backs of fingers in opposing palm
5. Rotate right thumb clasped in left palm and vice versa
6. Rotate fingers of left hand in right palm and vice versa
7. Rinse hands with water

FIGURE 4.21 *The correct procedure for hand-washing*

Alcohol hand rub

Alcohol hand rubs can be useful for use when hands are cleaned publicly and if you are not near a source of water. A small amount should be used and rubbed into the hands using the same technique as for washing with water. The hand rub should be rubbed in until the hands are completely dry.

Special precautions

Under certain circumstances special precautions may need to be taken in addition to standard practices to prevent cross-infection. These will include the treatment of clients suffering from infections such as HIV/AIDS, methicillin-resistant *Staphylococcus aureus* (MRSA), certain types of hepatitis and SARS. Local policy will determine the precautions that need to be taken, but these may include:

* use of an isolation room, keeping the door closed as much as possible

* screening of other clients, including contacts, admissions, discharges and transfers

* screening of any staff lesions and skin sites

* safe movement of temporary staff.

You will normally find that you are required by most organisations to be immunised against Hepatitis B, a virus that is blood-borne. Although it is normally transmitted by unprotected sexual contact, it is possible to contract it through a needle injury, such as, for example, pricking yourself with a used needle. If you work for an organisation that does not offer immunisation, you can request this from your GP.

Standard precautions

Usual precautions are now known as standard precautions, and are designed to protect both staff and service users from infection. It is important to apply these precautions for all service users at all times so that they become an automatic part of your practice and help to protect yourself, your clients and your colleagues. If in doubt you should treat every service user as though they have a potential infection that could be transmitted to others.

Standard precautions are:

* cover all cuts, abrasions and lesions with a waterproof dressing

* maintain hand hygiene

* maintain cleanliness of general environment, patient equipment and soft furnishings

* use disposable gloves when dealing with body fluids

* dispose of waste, including sharps, safely

* maintain a safe staff to patient ratio

* avoid overcrowding patients

* avoid unnecessary patient transfers between wards

* isolate patients with a known or suspected infection.

How to maintain personal safety

In addition to immunisation, there are other precautions you must take to ensure that you maintain your own personal safety, especially when dealing with clinical waste and instruments.

Safe disposal of clinical waste

Any waste that might be classified as clinical will include dressings and any disposable materials that may be contaminated with body fluids such as vomit, sputum, blood, urine and faeces. All of these have the potential to cause infection, and must be disposed of in the correct way. This waste must be placed in yellow clinical waste bags. These should not be overfilled and must be incinerated.

Safe disposal of sharps

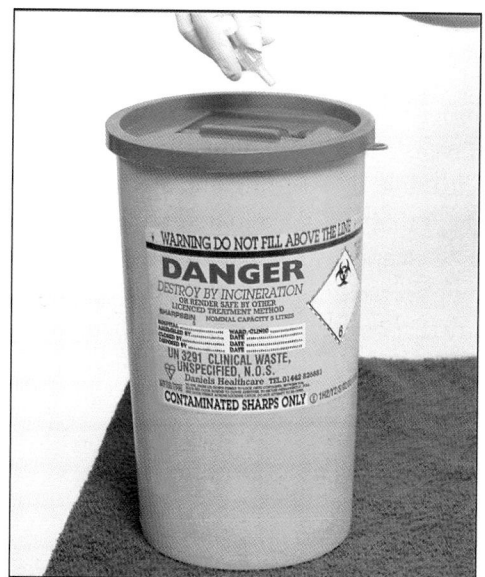

FIGURE 4.22 *Yellow container for disposal of sharps*

Blood-borne virus infections among healthcare workers were second only to back injuries between July 1997 and June 2002. It is for this reason that great care must be taken when handling and disposing of sharps such as syringes, needles and blades. All sharps must be disposed of in yellow rigid sharps containers which are incinerated. They should never be more than two thirds full. After use, needles should never be resheathed, removed from syringes or bent or snapped off. There are many products today that have been designed to ensure minimal handling of sharps. These include special sheathed needles for taking blood and needleless systems for setting up drips. Although they are more expensive, they offset the cost of treating sharps injuries.

Safe handling of equipment and instruments

Normally, soiled linen is disposed of in clear plastic bags or special linen bags, which are sent to the laundry. Contaminated linen should be removed from the bed and held at arm's length. It should be placed in special red plastic bags that are designed to disintegrate during the washing process, thus ensuring minimal handling.

Equipment can be cleaned, disinfected or sterilised, depending on the type of equipment involved.

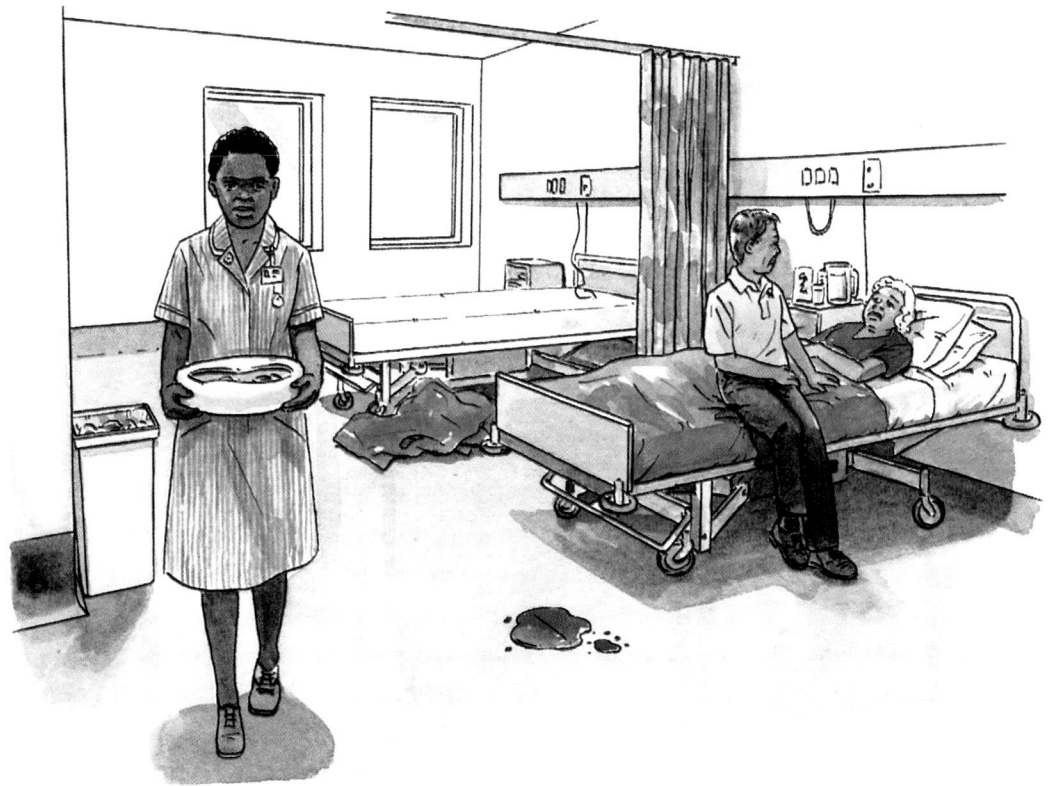

FIGURE 4.23 *How many hazards can you spot in this ward?*

Cleaning is the first stage of any process designed to reduce contamination. It is described as the removal of physical dirt from a surface. It is usually carried out using water and a detergent. For some areas or equipment this will be sufficient.

Disinfectant is used when there is a level of pathogens (disease-causing organisms) that need to be reduced to a safe level. This can be done using a chemical disinfectant or by using water at a temperature of 82°C or higher. If a chemical disinfectant is used, you must make sure that you use it correctly and leave it on for the correct contact time.

Instruments can be disinfected by being placed in boiling water for five minutes. Again, this will reduce the number of pathogens to a safe level. However, many instruments, especially those that are used for operations or invasive procedures, will need to be sterilised.

Sterilising is the complete removal of pathogens from equipment or instruments. There are many methods of doing this. Surgical instruments are generally sterilised in an autoclave, which uses a combination of steam and pressure. Other methods use heat, steam, hot air, gas, chemicals or radiation. The method used will depend on the type of equipment being sterilised.

In order to maintain personal safety you should ensure that you follow the correct policies when cleaning, disinfecting and sterilising. Any equipment that is contaminated with body fluids should be cleaned using gloves and aprons that should be correctly disposed of after use, along with any disposable cleaning equipment such as cloths. Dirty water should be disposed of in the sluice, and mops and buckets should be disinfected after use; there may be colour-coded mops and buckets used for different areas.

Summary

The control of infection is of vital importance, particularly when working with service users who may be vulnerable. Prevention of infection by 'superbugs' such as MRSA is proving to be a major problem for hospitals and care establishments nationally.

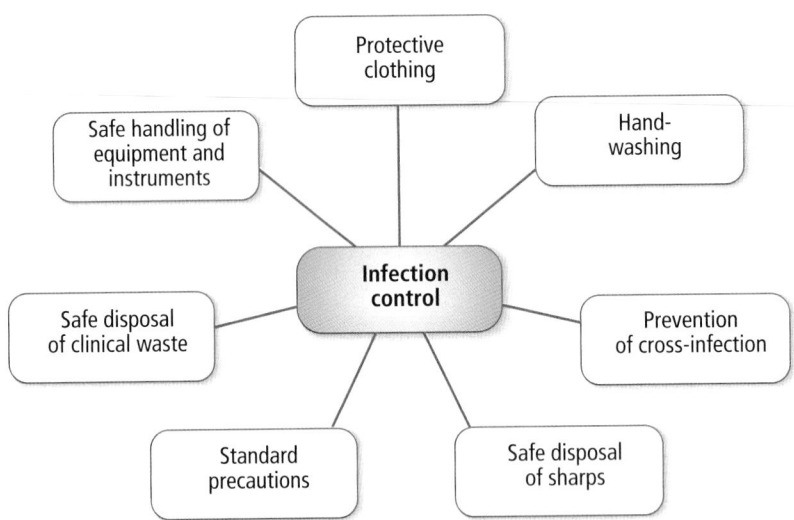

FIGURE 4.24 *Summary of the infection control methods*

Consider this

1. Which micro-organisms can cause infection?

2. What is cross-infection and how can it occur?

3. What special precautions may need to be taken for treating clients suffering from HIV/AIDS, MRSA or hepatitis?

4. What are standard precautions?

5. What methods can be used to disinfect and sterilise equipment and instruments?

UNIT 4 ASSESSMENT

How you will be assessed

You will need to show that you understand the issues involved in safe practices in care settings.

This unit is externally assessed.

Test questions

1. Give three responsibilities that the Health and Safety at Work Act places on employers.
2. What are the five key stages of risk assessment?
3. Explain the purpose of each of the five stages of risk assessment.
4. Why is it necessary to report and record accidents in the workplace?
5. What information should be recorded on an accident report form, and for how long by law must this information be kept?
6. Why has a new design of accident book been in place since 31 December 2003?
7. Identify two different types of safety sign, explain what they are used for and give two examples of each type.
8. What is the role of the Health and Safety Executive in maintaining health and safety in the workplace?
9. What information should be displayed on a Health and Safety Law poster?
10. What is the minimum requirement for first-aid provision at work?
11. What is the difference between an appointed person and a first aider?
12. Identify the four different types of fire extinguisher and explain what each is used for.
13. Give the name and date of the regulation that is used for moving and handling people safely.
14. What is LOLER?
15. Describe two different pieces of equipment that could be used for moving and handling service users safely, and evaluate the benefits of each.
16. Give two examples of security procedures that could be put in place in an early years setting to protect the children and staff, and evaluate how effective they might be.
17. What is meant by the term cross-infection?
18. Describe three situations in which cross-infection could occur.
19. What is the term used to describe the procedures for preventing the spread of infection in care settings, and what should you do to ensure you follow these procedures?
20. Explain the difference between disinfection and sterilisation.

Answers to these questions are provided on page 389.

References

Nazarko, L. (2000), *NVQs in Nursing and Residential Care Homes* (2nd edition) Oxford: Blackwell Science

Nolan, Y. (2001), *S/NVQ Care Level 3*. Oxford: Heinemann

Royal College of Nursing, (2003) *Code of Practice for Patient Handling*. London: Royal College of Nursing

Royal College of Nursing, (2004) *Methicillin Resistant Staphylococcus aureus, Guidance for Nursing Staff*. London: Royal College of Nursing

Useful websites

www.aduvent.co.uk
www.cctv-information.co.uk
www.firesafe.org.uk
www.hse.gov.uk
www.medesigns.co.uk
www.rcn.org.uk

UNIT 5

Caring for People with Additional Needs

This unit covers the following sections:

5.1 Common causes of physical disability, sensory impairment and learning difficulties

5.2 The care management process

5.3 Managing care for people with learning difficulties

5.4 Models and approaches

This unit explores caring for service users who have additional needs due to physical disability, sensory impairment, learning difficulty or because they have multiple additional needs.

In working through this unit you will learn about the common causes of physical disability, sensory impairment and learning difficulties and their effects on the body and mind. You will develop an understanding of the care management process, together with an appreciation of the different approaches used by care workers when providing specialist care or support to service users who have additional needs. You will also become aware of the attitudes and values of society experienced by service users with additional needs, and the barriers to inclusion that they can encounter.

You will also consider the models or approaches used by care workers, showing how this affects the way service users' needs are interpreted. In addition, you will research the ways in which people in society in general view those who have additional needs.

Finally, you will consider issues surrounding planning and conducting an interview with a service user in order to produce a profile of him or her for your portfolio.

How you will be assessed

The unit will be internally assessed through a portfolio in which you will include a profile of a service user and a guide to support a service provider.

Section 1: Common causes of physical disability, sensory impairment and learning difficulties

Categorising disabilities

Disabilities are usually considered in terms of three broad categories: physical disabilities, sensory disabilities and learning disabilities (also sometimes referred to as learning difficulties).

Physical disabilities are those that affect the body's main motor functions, i.e. the use of the large muscles of the arms and legs, head and neck and torso, and problems with some of the internal organs (for example, the bladder and bowel).

Sensory disabilities relate primarily to problems with the ears and eyes. Problems with the ears range from mild hearing impairment to profound deafness. Similarly, problems with the eyes range from visual impairments to complete blindness. There are also conditions that affect the senses of touch (anesthesia) and smell (anosmia).

Learning disabilities are those that affect a person's ability to interpret what is seen and heard, or to link information from different parts of the brain. This can lead to problems with spoken and written language, difficulty in coordinating limbs and body, limited attention span and hyperactivity, and sometimes the inability to make and sustain relationships with other people, even parents.

Of course, one person may have more than one disability (for example, someone who is deaf-blind), or disabilities from more than one of the broad categories (for example, a person with a learning difficulty who is also deaf).

It is also important to note that some conditions result in psychiatric or mental problems, that can be disabling, either physically or socially. Although this unit does not require you to be familiar with the causes and types of mental-health problems, it is important for you to be aware that for some people with additional needs, mental-health issues may also be important.

Figure 5.1 lists the main causes of disability, and gives just a few examples of medical conditions or diseases in each of these. Broadly speaking, the main causes of disability can be divided into pre-natal and post-natal groups. Beyond this, there are further sub-categories, as shown in Figure 5.1 below.

It must be stressed that some of the conditions listed in Figure 5.1 do not automatically lead to a disability. Some people recover fully from, for example, meningitis, and if diabetes is properly managed the symptoms of the condition can usually be kept to a minimum. Figure 5.1 is simply a guide to illustrate the range of potential causes of disability. You will need to do some further research with respect to the service user you are studying for this unit.

Some disabilities have their roots in pre-natal conditions. If a gene is faulty or is missing, for example, then conditions such as cystic fibrosis or muscular dystrophy may result. In cystic fibrosis, several glands in the body do not function properly, the pancreas does not produce enzymes and food is not properly absorbed; the glands in the bronchial tubes do not work effectively, and a sticky mucus clogs the person's airways; physiotherapy is often used to help with some aspects of cystic fibrosis. People with muscular dystrophy experience a gradual weakening and wasting of the muscles, beginning in childhood. Gradually it becomes harder to climb stairs to raise their arms above the head or to walk. People with this condition often need mobility aids, and sometimes adaptations to their homes to assist them in, for example, going upstairs or taking a bath.

Chromosomal disorders are different from genetic disorders in that blocks of genes are missing or are duplicated. The result is that a person has either too much or too little chromosomal information. People with Down's syndrome, for example, have an extra copy of Chromosome 21. Most people with Down's syndrome have learning difficulties, together with distinctive facial features and large tongues; they can sometimes also experience heart problems or early dementia.

UNDERLYING ORIGIN	CONDITION/DISEASE/ CIRCUMSTANCES	TYPE OF DISABILITY/ASSOCIATED PROBLEMS
PRE-NATAL		
Genetic problems	Cystic fibrosis Muscular dystrophy Sickle-cell anaemia Huntington's chorea Best's disease Gene mutation (linked to chromosomal information; different for men and women)	Physical Physical Physical Physical and mental Visual impairment (VI)/blindness Hearing impairment HI/deafness
Chromosomal disorders	Down's syndrome	Learning difficulties Physical problems (sometimes)
Damage before or during birth	Spina bifida Hydrocephalus Cerebral palsy Aniridia, coloboma Rubella during pregnancy	Physical Physical Physical VI/blindness VI/blindness in infant
POST-NATAL		
Disease and medical conditions	Multiple sclerosis Meningitis Glaucoma Diabetes Autism, Asperger's syndrome	Physical Sight or hearing loss/sometimes mental VI/blindness Physical/blindness Learning difficulties (often social)
Trauma (i.e. in an accident or during surgery)	Head injuries Spinal injury Broken limbs Shock Noise exposure	Physical Physical Physical Mental HI/deafness
Lifestyle	Excessive smoking/drinking Poor diet Noise exposure (e.g. to loud music)	Exacerbation of underlying condition, e.g. diabetes (can lead to VI/blindness) Exacerbation of underlying condition HI/deafness/tinnitus
Environmental	Exposure to toxic substance (e.g. radiation) Thalidomide drug (1960s)	Physical, sensory, mental Physical
The ageing process	Osteoarthritis Alzheimer's disease Stroke Failing senses	Physical Mental Physical/mental Hypothermia, loss of sight or hearing, dizziness

NOTE: VI = visual impairment; HI = hearing impairment

FIGURE 5.1 *Main causes of disabling conditions*

Sometimes, problems are caused for a baby during pregnancy, as a result of incomplete development of parts of its body. In the condition known as spina bifida, for example, part of the spine fails to develop properly, so that nerves can be left exposed (often in the lower spine). The result can be paralysis of the legs and also incontinence; the level of disability varies from one person to another.

After birth, there can be various events or situations leading to disability. Accident or trauma with other causes (such as surgery) can obviously lead to potentially disabling injuries to the head, spine or limbs. A self-abusing lifestyle involving drugs or excessive smoking and eating (especially the wrong things) can sometimes complicate existing medical conditions. Someone with diabetes, for example, should follow dietary guidelines and take regular medication in order to avoid complications such as blindness. Over-exposure to loud noise (for example, in nightclubs or in an industrial work setting) can lead to hearing problems or even deafness. Other environmental factors could include exposure to radiation or other toxic substances, often in the workplace, and particularly for people who were of working age before the protective legislation stemming from the 1974 Health and Safety at Work Act began to be introduced.

Finally, the ageing process itself can sometimes lead to disabling conditions. This is not to deny that many older people lead happy and healthy lifestyles. However, conditions such as stroke and Parkinson's disease can lead to physical problems; diseases such as Alzheimer's lead to gradual dementia; and failing senses can result in loss of sight or hearing.

Consider this

Choose an aspect of disability that interests you. Use the Resources section at the end of this unit as a starting point and collect further information on this particular disability.

You will find it useful to include:

* the disability's causes
* how the body is affected
* key problems and issues faced by people with this particular disability
* the names and contact details of relevant societies and support groups (both national and local).

You will probably need to repeat this process to research other kinds of disability as your portfolio grows.

Section 2: The care management process

The seven steps of care management

The process of assessing need in social and health care is currently very well defined in government policy and guidance. This guidance is associated with several key Acts of Parliament which give a framework to the help and services that people are entitled to receive.

Section 29 of the National Assistance Act 1948 states that local authorities have responsibilities and duties to promote the welfare of people who have sensory, physical or mental difficulties. Local authorities must do this by making accurate assessments of people's needs. The 1986 Disabled Persons Act stated that if a disabled person, or his or her representative, were to ask for an

assessment, the local authority has a duty to carry it out. This legislation was strengthened by the NHS and Community Care Act 1990, which says that if a person is disabled, he or she has an automatic right to an assessment and should be informed of this.

Both the law and associated guidance make it clear that the three areas to be assessed are need, risk and services. The resulting decisions are to be set out in the form of a **care plan**. Such care plans must record the objectives to be met for the service user, how this is going to be achieved (the implementation plan), what to do if things do not go according to plan (contingency arrangements) and how unmet needs will be identified and taken into account.

This system is dependent upon good-quality assessments of need and risk. Local authorities all have rules that set out how money and resources should be allocated to people with additional needs. Such rules are called **eligibility criteria**.

STEP	ACTION	
1	Publish information	Local authorities have legal requirements to publish information about services.
2	Assess the level of need	This may be simple or complex. The type of assessment offered will vary according to the apparent level of complexity of a person's situation.
3	Assessing need	Need, risk and services have to be taken into account using the local authority's eligibility criteria, with reference to the relevant legislation.
4	Care planning	A care plan should clearly identify the aims and objectives of an intervention, together with the services required. A record of unmet need and any areas of disagreement should also be recorded, together with contingency plans. The care plan should be signed and given to the service user being assessed.
5	Implementing the care plan	This will involve following each local authority's agreed funding procedures with agreed start dates and clearly identified tasks.
6	Monitoring the care plan	The care manager must check that services have started on the correct date, and that these services are meeting assessed needs.
7	Reviewing/evaluating	Any new package of care, whether in the social care setting or at home, must be reviewed within the first six weeks. Thereafter, there is flexibility to review, but there must be at least an annual review.

FIGURE 5.2 *Seven steps of care management*

Source: Moonie, Bates and Spencer-Perkins, 2004

care plan A formal document that sets out everything that is to be done to meet someone's needs. This document sets out the objectives or goals of the plan, together with the services that will be provided to meet these objectives.

eligibility criteria The rules that explain a person's entitlement to receive services. The greater a person's needs and threats to independence, the greater their entitlement to receive services.

FIGURE 5.3 *There are rules that set out how money and resources should be allocated to people with needs*

Basically, the more disabled a person is, the greater his or her entitlement is to receive all the services needed. In 2003, the government introduced Fair Access to Care Services, a system that sets out four categories of eligibility for services: critical, substantial, moderate and low.

The process of care management is, in fact, a cycle. Six weeks after service delivery has begun, the care manager must review the effect on the service user, to see if the goals of the plan are being met. If the service user's needs are not being met the plan will be changed. Local authorities are obliged to carry on reviewing services at least every 12 months. When such a review is carried out, the effects of service provision will be evaluated to check whether or not the planned intervention is working. **Evaluation** and the resetting of goals and plans are critical aspects of care management.

evaluation To evaluate something is to perform a systematic review of what has happened. For a care plan, an evaluation would consider whether the objectives had been met and whether the services given had been effective.

Consider the following scenario, in which an older person is at risk as a result of her physical disabilities.

SCENARIO

Help in taking a bath

Mrs Green is aged 68 years and lives with her husband. She has severe arthritis, which means that although she can manage to give herself a wash, she cannot get into the bath.

She is able to perform all other personal care tasks, but unless she receives some help she will have to give up taking baths. However, her hygiene and health are not at risk.

Although Mrs Green is fairly low risk in terms of the Fair Access to Care Services eligibility criteria, it is clear that she could be helped by the provision of specialist equipment. In her case, an assessment would be carried out (probably by an occupational therapist or a physiotherapist from an Older Persons' Team), and it is likely that a bath hoist would be ordered and installed. The assessment would also probably include Mrs Green's ability to perform household tasks, to walk and to travel (e.g. on public transport). After six weeks, the care manager allocated to support Mrs Green would check whether or not the hoist had been installed, and if Mrs Green was able to use it safely and with confidence.

If Mrs Green was found to have any further needs, these would then be built into a revised

TYPE OF SUPPORT	EXAMPLES
Adaptations to property	Provision of downstairs bathroom, toilet, shower etc. Provision of lift to aid transfer between lower and upper floors Hoist to help getting in and out of bath Grab rails in bathroom, top of stairs, other key places Ramps Widened door-frames
Aids to daily living and work	Wheelchair Walking frame/stick Dog to assist with daily tasks Easy-to-use kitchen equipment, e.g. tin openers Adapted Information and Communication Technology (ICT) equipment Adapted cars (hand controls)
Aids to vision	Large-print leaflets, books Documents in Braille Adapted ICT equipment Alarmed cooking utensils, e.g. kettle Guide dog
Aids to hearing	Hearing aids Cochlear implant/hearing aid device inserted into the ear surgically Hearing dog
Welfare benefits	Depends on severity of disability and personal circumstances

FIGURE 5.4 *Support for people with physical disabilities*

care plan. The local authority would keep an eye on Mrs Green at least every 12 months to see if either she or Mr Green had any further requirements. Other kinds of support offered to people with physical disabilities are set out in Figure 5.4.

There is a wide range of aids to assist people with physical disabilities, and they bear further investigation. The Department of Health publishes an extensive *Practical Guide for Disabled People* (DOH 2003). Many companies now specialise in providing such equipment, often displaying considerable imagination and creativity in their design. Mrs Green (in the scenario on page 206) currently needs help in taking a bath. However, as time goes by she might appreciate further assistance with other aspects of daily life, such as cooking. Her care manager may go on to suggest that the Greens consider what kind of practical tools and aids would be of use.

The assessment and planning process will be discussed further page 208.

Think it over...

Visit the Department of Health website and look up the eligibility criteria set out in the Fair Access to Care Services scheme.

Discuss the needs of the service user you will be profiling. Involve both the service user and his or her key worker. Determine whether the service user has critical, substantial, moderate or low risk to independence, for eligibility.

Different types of need

In the scenario on page 2006, Mrs Green has clear physical needs, but there are other types of need that lead to be met to enable an individual to lead a happy and fulfilled life. Consider the following scenario, which is also of an older person, but someone whose circumstances are very different from that of Mrs Green.

Esther lost her husband two years ago, and is very depressed. She misses him very much. Before he died, they both used to be active members of a local choir, but she lost confidence after his death and stopped going to choir practice.

In the last 12 months she has also developed visual problems and is reluctant to go out in the evenings. However, she still loves choral music. Esther has a large collection of recordings that she plays regularly, and she listens to concerts on the radio or TV.

1. What kinds of need does Esther appear to have?

2. What kinds of questions would you like to ask her to find out more about her situation?

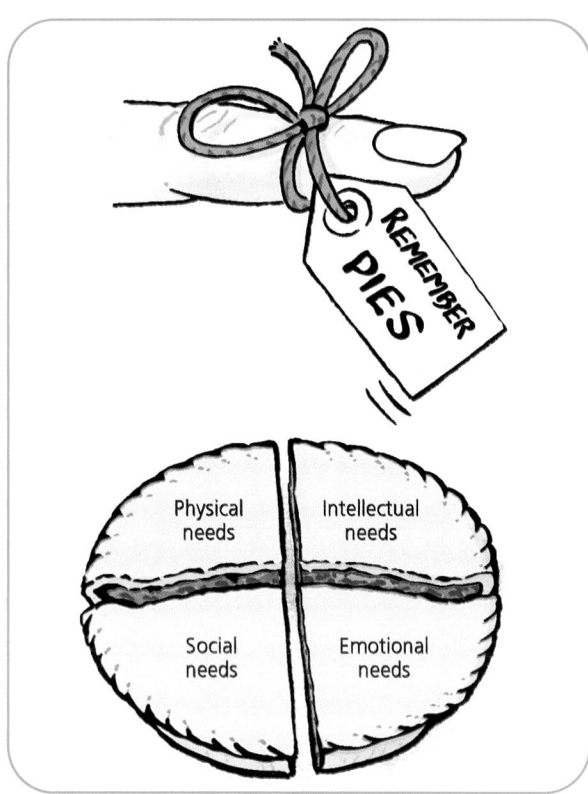

FIGURE 5.5 *P-I-E-S categories*

Esther appears to have a range of needs. Since she has developed visual problems, she has at least one area of physical difficulty that requires attention before she can do anything else. She has become depressed and may be missing the intellectual stimulation and social warmth that belonging to the choir gave her. She is certainly missing the emotional support and love that she received from her husband. The self-esteem and sense of personal creativity that she used to get from singing regularly with the choir (including public performances) is also lacking. Esther therefore has needs which are physical, intellectual, emotional and social.

These four broad categories can be usefully remembered with the acronym P-I-E-S. Any assessment of need should take all of these four areas into account.

Methods in care planning

Approaches to care planning

The Fair Access to Care Services Guidance explains that people should be entitled to services according to the level of risk to independence that they will suffer if their needs are not met. There are four bands of risk: as described above, critical, substantial, moderate and low.

It is the local council's responsibility to establish its own eligibility criteria, in order to work out how complex the assessment of need has to be. *The Fair Access to Care Services Guidance* (FACS) identifies four types of assessment, which are shown below:

FAIR ACCESS TO CARE SERVICES: TYPES OF ASSESSMENT

– Initial assessments

– Assessments to take stock of wider needs

– Specialist assessments

– Comprehensive assessments

Source: *Fair Access to Care Services* (DOH 2002)

In the case of Mrs Green (see page 206), her local council may have decided just to do a specialist assessment, focusing on her physical disabilities and the needs arising from these. However, Esther (see page 208) might have required a more comprehensive assessment (including specialist input on both her visual problems and her mental-health needs) taking everything into account in order to make a meaningful care plan.

The FACS Guidance also states that the purposes of assessment are:

* to gain a better understanding of a person's situation

* to identify the options available to that person to manage his or her own life

* to identify the desired outcomes from any help or service that is provided

* to understand the basis on which decisions are reached.

A meaningful care plan for Esther would take into account her physical needs (help to sort out her visual problems), her needs for emotional support and social inclusion (help to return to the choir) and also for intellectual stimulation (taking part in rehearsals and concert performances, and also enjoying talking about music with her friends).

Besides the FACS material, there is also government guidance on care planning for older people, for children and for people with learning difficulties. (Planning for people with learning difficulties is discussed on page 219).

The National Service Framework for Older People sets out a number of standards for providing NHS and social care to people in this age group. Standard Two describes the concept of **person-centred care**. This aims to ensure that older people are treated as individuals, and that they receive appropriate and timely packages of care which meet their needs as individuals, regardless of health and social services boundaries. Local authorities and health providers must work together to provide a **single assessment process** and 'joined-up' arrangements for getting services and equipment to people.

In practice, this would mean that Esther's care manager would make sure, firstly, that all the different assessments are booked and that Esther can get to the various appointments; secondly, he or she would ensure that all the information from the various assessments (for example, optical tests for her vision, a mental-health assessment, a comprehensive assessment of need by a social worker in the older persons' team) comes together and is kept in one place so that no information is lost. This single assessment process would ensure that any plan made for and with Esther took all her needs (physical, intellectual, emotional and social) into account.

The Framework for the Assessment of Children in Need and Their Families (Department of Health, 2000), although specific to children, contains some broad principles that are of relevance to work

KEY PRINCIPLES FOR ASSESSMENTS

Assessments should:

* be person centred

* see the person in the context of family, community and culture

* ensure equality of opportunity and respect diversity

* take into account the views and needs of carers and families

* build on strengths as well as identify difficulties

* take an inter-agency approach to assessment and service provision

* be a continuing process, not a single event

* be carried out in parallel with other action and services

* be grounded in **evidence-based** knowledge.

Adapted from: DOH (2000)

with all service users. Key aspects are set out above.

Focusing on the person is a critical aspect of social and care work. If the social worker sees Esther as simply another 'case' to be sorted out with medical or optical tests, then the system will have failed to see her as a person with complex and unique needs. Esther also needs to be seen as a member of her community – her choir membership is extremely important to her, as it provides her not only with social and emotional support, but also with a way to express her personal identity as a singer and performer. This means taking a person-centred approach that also maximises Esther's right to have the opportunity to take part in social events. Esther's views on what she wants are paramount in this respect.

Clearly, there are difficulties to be overcome, but focusing on the benefits to Esther and how they may be achieved gives the care plan a positive and developmental aspect (building on strengths). The care manager has to coordinate input from a number of agencies to make the assessment process work (an inter-agency approach); he or she must take the same approach to make sure that Esther receives the tests, visual equipment and transport that she needs to make the care plan work. As the care manager is carrying out the assessment, let us imagine that he or she discovers that someone from the local MIND Day Centre (a voluntary organisation) has already asked Esther if she would like to go to a coffee morning once a week, an invitation that Esther has accepted. The care manager is happy about this, and makes a note in the plan, so that anything the local authority does is in parallel with the MIND provision.

> ### Key concepts
>
> *evidence-based decision-making* This is decision-making that is fully informed by information. Social workers should not make plans based on guesswork.
>
> *objectivity* This refers to being open-minded and impartial when making decisions. An objective care plan will be based on evidence rather than on guesswork or on the personal preferences of the care manager.

Finally, the care manager has to be careful to take into account all the evidence available, including government guidance, information about what is available to support Esther, advice resulting from the optical and mental-health assessments, and so on. His or her decisions must be objective rather than subjective.

Making assessments: structured information

The FACS Guidance recognises a number of different types of assessment, including initial assessments, assessments to take stock of wider needs, specialist assessments and comprehensive assessments. Different authorities and service providers are likely to have a range of forms for collecting the information that is needed. Collecting data or information in this way is known as **structured data collection**, particularly when completion of the form requires ticking boxes or giving a rating scale to something.

FIGURE 5.6 *Collecting data on forms is known as structured data collection*

Such data or information might include the results of medical or health tests (for example, a GP's assessment of a person's medical condition), or the assessment of physical ability (such as tests by a physiotherapist to determine a person's level of mobility or their ability to perform certain physical tasks). For this kind of assessment, there are often recognised tests that a person has to undergo in order for a professional to establish his or her level of ability or need.

Structured forms or questionnaires might also include information about the levels of distress or disruption that a person experiences, and the kinds of problems that are encountered. Information about difficulties experienced both within and outside the person's home or care setting will also be recorded, and all four areas of need (physical, intellectual, emotional and social) should be taken into account.

The needs of the person's carer should also be recorded (see page 216).

Making assessments: working with people

Collecting information for the assessment process is more than simply assembling medical reports or ticking boxes on an assessment form. The information has to be obtained from people, and considerable communication skills are required to do this sensitively and meaningfully.

The *Framework for the Assessment of Children in Need and Their Families* (Department of Health, 2000) identifies five key steps that social workers should take when assessing the needs of children. It is such good advice that it is relevant to anyone who is assessing the needs of service users, whatever their age or the nature of their need. This guidance is set out in Figure 5.7.

Esther's care manager could not request the necessary medical and psychiatric tests without first seeing and observing her. It would be important for the care manager to listen to what Esther had to say, and to talk to her in order to develop a trusting relationship. In Esther's case, it might not have been possible to spend time with her in taking part in an activity or an intervention; however, later in the cycle, when Esther has started going to choir practice, it might

FIVE CRITICAL COMPONENTS OF COMMUNICATING WITH CHILDREN AND OTHER SERVICE USERS	
Seeing	You cannot make an assessment of a person's need without actually seeing him or her
Observing	You need to observe someone's responses to different events and activities
Engaging	It is important to develop a relationship with the person, in order to help him or her express thoughts, concerns and opinions as part of the process of making choices
Talking to children/other service users	This requires time, skill, confidence and careful preparation
Activities with children/other service users	Doing things with the service user can help to develop trust between you

FIGURE 5.7 *Communicating with children and others service users*

Adapted from: DOH (2000)

be appropriate for the care manager to go along to meet Esther there as part of the process of reviewing and evaluating the care plan. This not only shows that the care manager is interested in Esther, but also gives a chance to observe her interacting with her friends.

When you plan to do a profile of a service user, forming a trusting relationship with him or her will be a critical stage in the process. Your subject is not a 'case', but is a real person just like yourself, with needs for respect and the right to be recognised as an individual.

The *Framework for Assessment* also describes what children have said they value in social workers. Once again, this is so helpful that it could apply to service users and workers in many care settings, to all ages and to all types of need. This is set out below.

WHAT CHILDREN VALUE IN SOCIAL WORKERS
(could apply to all service users)

Children like workers who:

* **listen** – carefully and without trivialising or being dismissive of the issues raised
* are **available** and **accessible** – providing regular and predictable contact
* are **non-judgemental** and **non-directive** – accepting, explaining and suggesting options and choices
* have a **sense of humour** – which helps to build rapport
* are **straight talking** – with realism and reliability (children do not like false promises)
* can be **trusted** – i.e. to **maintain confidentiality** and also to **consult** before taking matters forward.

Adapted from: DOH (2000)

Making assessments: risk and need

A care manager has to make decisions about a person's eligibility to receive services based on the existing risks to their independence, including health risks. The service user, together with his or her carer or carers, should be involved in this process of decision-making, which should be 'person-centred'. This means that services and solutions to problems should be geared to the needs and wishes of the person rather than to what 'experts' think is appropriate or to the availability of services.

Key concept

person-centred A term used to describe a way of working that puts the service user at the centre of the care management process, involving him or her in all decisions that are made.

Service users should be helped to prepare for an assessment and also to express their own views and opinions. Sometimes, it will be necessary to use interpreters, advocates, translators or other supporting people to help in this process. The opinions of carers are also important.

SCENARIO
What would you do?

John is partially sighted, and has difficulty reading small print. He has recently applied to the council (with the help of a friend) to have his needs reassessed, as his visual problems have been getting worse. He really wants to know if he is entitled to any additional help, in particular an ICT package that will enable his computer to talk to him.

However, John does not have a lot of confidence, and he is very worried about the assessment process. He does not like talking to people he does not know.

How can John be helped through the process of being assessed?

An assessment should also be 'rounded'. This means that all aspects of a person's need should be taken into account. Besides health and social care needs, other issues such as housing should be considered.

Consider this

Jim has turned up at a mental health day centre looking for a place to get warm and have a cup of tea. He looks as if he has been living on the streets; he has no money and he is also extremely shaky.

1. What kinds of need do you think Jim might have?
2. What kinds of services or people might be involved in meeting those needs?

When assessing a person's need, the social worker will look at physical problems and the disruption they cause to everyday living, including the instability of such problems and whether or not they are likely to worsen.

Environmental factors, such as where the person is living, will also be taken into account, together with the social network that the person can rely on (for example, family, friends and work colleagues). The person's intellectual, emotional and social needs will also be taken into account.

Professional involvement

Often, a number of people from different services will work together to make sure that the needs and wishes of a service user are met. This will include the service user, health and social care professionals (such as district nurses, social workers), other council staff (e.g. from the housing department), the carer and/or the family of the service user, and service providers from the private and voluntary sector (e.g. staff and volunteers from MIND or Age Concern, or from a local private nursing home).

> **Key concept**
>
> *working in partnership* The involvement of all interested parties in the care management process. The service user, his or her carer, family and friends, health and social care professionals, other council staff and people from the private and voluntary sector may all be involved.

Figure 5.8 gives you an approximate guide to the kinds of professionals who may be consulted by the care manager when an assessment of need is made.

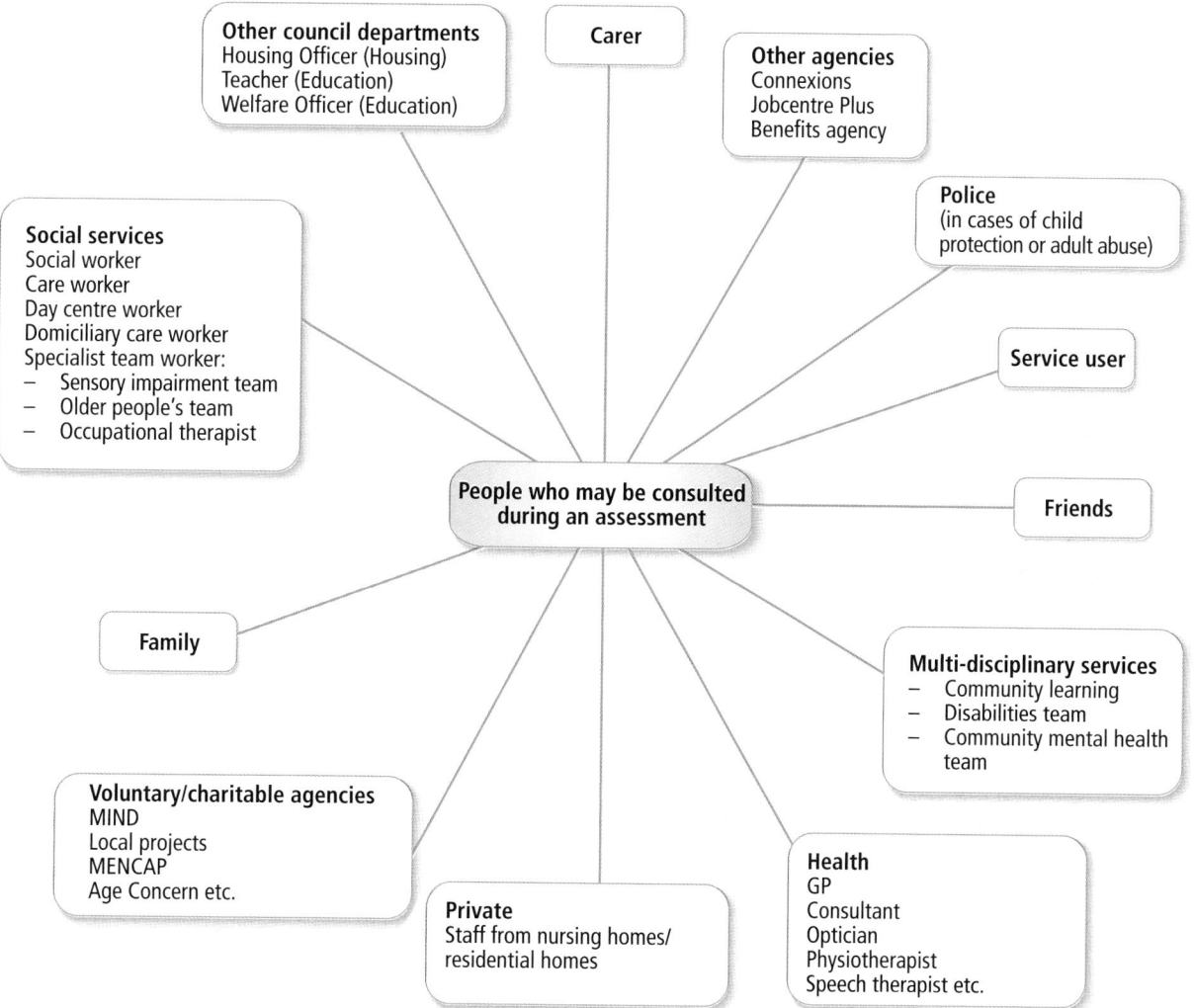

FIGURE 5.8 *Working in partnership: people who may be consulted by the care manager when an assessment of need is made*

(continued overleaf)

SERVICE PROVIDERS	KEY ROLES
Social worker	Assessment and planning Ensuring that services are provided according to the care plan Providing information and advice
Specialist social worker	As for a social worker but with particular focus on specific needs, e.g. sensory, psychiatric
Care worker	Providing daily physical care, often in a residential or day care setting Support for intellectual, emotional and/or social needs
Domiciliary care worker	Practical support for someone in his or her own home May include help with personal tasks such as washing, shaving or bathing
Day centre worker/support worker	Support to users of day units – such staff may have a range of job titles Support can be practical; can also include support with intellectual, emotional and social needs
Occupational therapist	Assessment and treatment of physical, psychological or social problems Using specific, purposeful activity to prevent disability and/or to promote independence in all aspects of daily life
Nursing staff	Can be hospital- or community-based Providing practical nursing support
GP, consultant	Giving medical advice in the context of the care planning process Recommending further treatment or medical input
Physiotherapist	Providing help and treatment to people of all ages with physical problems caused by illness, accident or ageing. Maximising movement potential through manual therapy, exercise and electro-physical treatments
Speech therapist	Assessing and treating people with speech, language and communication problems Also working with people who have eating or swallowing problems, learning disabilities, psychiatric disorders and a range of other conditions
Housing officer	Assessing and planning for a person's housing needs Providing housing information and advice
Teacher	Assessing a person's educational needs In a good position to comment on someone's emotional or social needs
Education welfare officer	As for a teacher but also making detailed assessments of a person's educational, social and emotional needs
Careers adviser	Providing information and advice on careers opportunities and how to get qualifications
Disability employment adviser (Jobcentre Plus)	Giving specific careers and qualifications advice to people with disabilities
Benefits adviser	Providing specialist advice on claiming benefits
Staff/volunteers in charitable or voluntary organisations	Giving social work type support as well as providing information, advice and counselling

FIGURE 5.8 *People who may be consulted by the care manager when an assessment is made*

Professionals who are consulted about a person's needs may come from social services (for example, a social worker, care worker or specialist team worker), or from other council departments such as education or education welfare. Others, such as GPs or physiotherapists, may be based in services provided by the health authority or the Primary Care Trust (PCT). However, some professionals are now based in multi-disciplinary teams with titles such as community learning disability team. As the name suggests, in such teams you would expect to find workers from a range of disciplines and with different job titles, such as challenging-behaviour nurse, or senior practitioner (care management).

You will need to access the websites of your local authority, PCT and health authority to find out exactly who is available and what services are provided in your area. Links to other service providers are often given on such websites. Alternatively, you could call in to the information desk of your Town Hall in order to obtain any printed material about local services.

Making care plans

Care plans need to be very precise and clear. The goals have to be clearly stated, together with all the services and people who will be involved in achieving those goals. If this is not done thoroughly, it will be impossible to evaluate and review the plan at a later stage. The *Fair Access to Care Services: Guidance* sets out what is to be included in a care plan (see below).

MAKING CARE PLANS: POINTS TO INCLUDE

* a note of eligible needs and associated risks
* the goals of the plan (i.e. what you want to achieve for the service user)
* the services to be provided
* contingency plans (in case something goes wrong or there is an emergency)
* a review date

Adapted from: DOH (2002)

The care plan will also include details of financial arrangements, such as any charges the service user has to pay, or benefits they may be entitled to. Help from a carer, or other people, will also be specified.

The recording of care plans is not a haphazard process, but is done within the guidance framework. It is essential for all workers who are involved in the process to be consistent, so that it does not matter which social worker actually wrote down the plan: all the necessary components will be there for anyone else to read and to see exactly what is required. All decisions in the care plan must be **evidence-based** – there must be no subjective judgements. Care plans for children may contain some additional information, particularly if there is a child protection issue involved. There are specially designed documents to record planning for children who are legally looked after by the local authority. The Social Services Inspectorate's booklet *Recording With Care* (DOH,1999) sets out Department of Health standards for the recording of care planning and management.

Finally, all notes and records must be securely kept. The Data Protection Act 1998 makes it a legal requirement to keep service user information confidential. The service user has the right to know what information is held and to make sure that it is correct. Information about the service user should not be disclosed to an unauthorised person, and it should be accurate and up to date. People keeping this information should have strict rules and procedures about storing the records, and about when it is acceptable to disclose details to someone else.

THE KEY PRINCIPLES OF RECORD-KEEPING

Keep thorough notes of what you observe and conversations you have had.

Make sure you store your notes securely.

Make sure your service user is not identified in these notes.

When making your profile of a service user, you will need to keep careful notes of what you see and of conversations you have, both with the service user and his or her carer, and of staff you meet during the process of your investigation. It will be important to store these notes carefully and not to disclose them to anyone other than your tutor. You will need to make it clear to the service user that this is what you intend to do, and to check out that he or she is happy with this.

It would also be a good idea to anonymise your notes, to give the service user increased protection. Remember, the service user has a right, under the Data Protection Act, to have his or her information treated as confidential.

FIGURE 5.10 *Carers have the right to be consulted throughout service delivery*

> **Key concept**
>
> *confidentiality* Normally, information about a service user should not be disclosed to another person without the knowledge and consent of that service user.

When writing up your profile of a service user, you will need to make sure that he or she is not identified anywhere in the report. You may also need to anonymise the service or establishment in which your study took place (e.g. by using made up names).

Carers have needs too

Sometimes, a person with significant needs may rely heavily on another person for his or her physical care. This person is often known as the carer, and he or she may also play a significant role in fulfilling the service user's emotional and social needs. The carer is often a close relative, sometimes a friend or neighbour. Even when carers are devoted to their relatives or friends, the stress put onto them can be very great. People with dementia, for example, may forget where they are, or even the names of the people close to them. They may ask the same questions repeatedly, or get lost when they go out.

In the last 10 years, carers from all over the UK have been working together to gain recognition and support for the work they do. In 1999, the government published a *National Strategy for Carers*, acknowledging their value and recognising their needs (Department of Health, 1999). Many authorities now have a Carers' Charter, setting out the rights that carers have. These rights include being consulted and involved at every stage of service delivery, and also to have their own needs addressed.

When an assessment is made, the needs and opinions of the carer should always be taken into account; the resulting care plan should also include their needs and wishes.

Monitoring the care plan

Whoever is responsible for the care management process must have arrangements in place to **monitor** the progress of each care plan. This could be as simple as checking that meetings do take place and that planned services go ahead according to the specifications in the care plan.

> **Key concept**
>
> *monitoring* To monitor something is to make regular checks on progress.

In the following scenario, Stella's care manager, Vikram, monitors the progress of her care plan.

At the start of a new care planning arrangement, the care manager will schedule a number of meetings or checks, to take place at regular intervals during the lifetime of the plan.

Evaluating the care plan

The Department of Health Practice Guidance says that a care plan must be reviewed within the first six weeks. Thereafter, a review or **evaluation** must be made at least every year, more frequently if necessary.

Evaluation involves reviewing the plan very thoroughly, including looking at the objectives, who was involved, the nature of the interventions and how well everything went. If the objectives have not been met, questions must be asked as to why this is the case. Perhaps the original objectives were not quite right, or maybe there has been a failure with respect to a particular service provision.

Key concept

evaluation To evaluate something is to assess it, in particular its worth, value or importance.

When evaluating a care plan it is vital that a balanced view is taken. In the above scenario, for example, after thinking it over and discussing it with others, including Stella, Vikram may decide that some things might have been done better, as well as identifying things that have gone very well. This process of critical thinking about something is also known as **reflection**. It is impossible to evaluate something without spending some time reflecting on it.

Key concept

reflection This is the act of thinking about something critically and calmly.

When Vikram spoke to Stella, and to the shop manager, he discovered that Stella was very worried about handling money, although the other shop assistants knew that she needed help with this, and she was never left alone to deal with payments. It was decided (with her agreement) that Stella would be given some additional money-skills training at the day unit. Until she felt more at ease about handling money, she would work mainly in the stockroom as she enjoyed cleaning and sorting the clothes and other goods, and felt very confident about doing this kind of work.

Implementing care plans is not a mechanical process, and just because something has been agreed does not mean that this is guaranteed to actually meet someone's needs. In practice, many unforeseen circumstances can arise. For this reason, regular evaluation is essential.

Summary

Care management addresses need, risk and service requirements. It is a cyclical process.

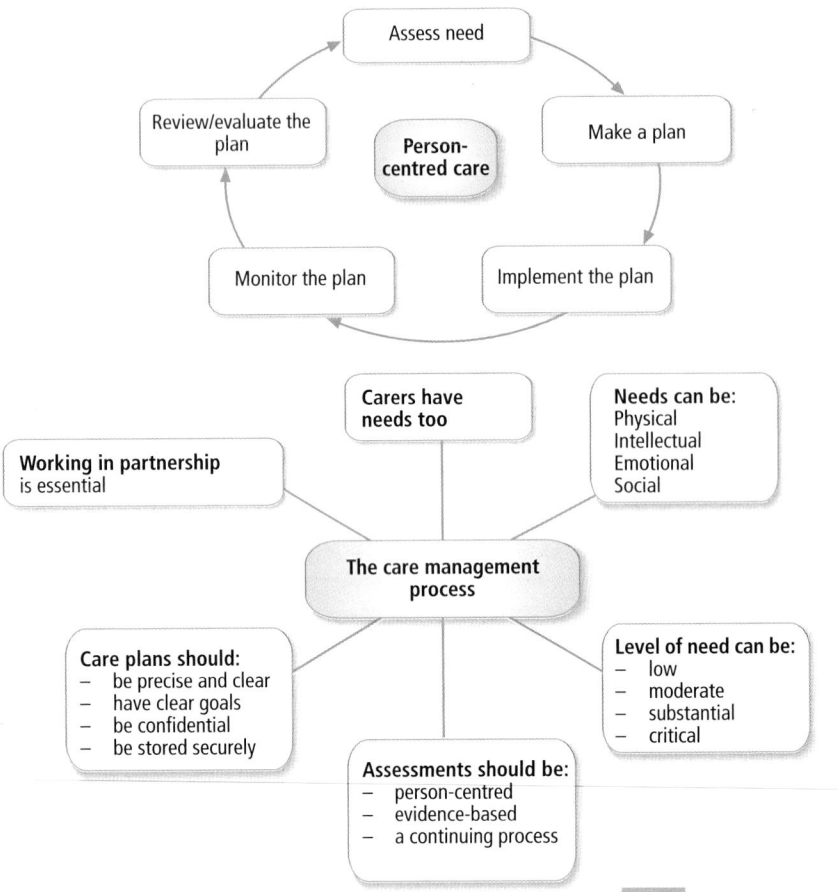

FIGURE 5.11 *The care management process*

Consider this

Rita has recently lost her sight as a result of having diabetes. She needs to work and wants to develop her ICT skills so that she can get a job. The local college is offering courses through the Learn Direct scheme, and she is keen to attend and gain a qualification.

She has a computer at home, but this has not been adapted for use by a non-sighted person.

1. What kinds of need does Rita have? (Use the Physical – Intellectual – Emotional – Social checklist.)

2. Which of these needs will have to be addressed first?

3. How can the care manager make sure that any solution to Rita's needs remains person-centred?

Section 3: Managing care for people with learning difficulties

Introduction

Care management for people with learning difficulties follows the same cyclical process as for other service users (i.e. assessment, implementation, monitoring and reviewing the plan and then making new decisions). However, the main difference is that people with learning difficulties have to be helped to make choices and to express their views about what they want. Sometimes, a person with learning difficulties may not know what choices are available, or may have difficulty in communicating. This means that care workers have to work out ways of making it possible for people with learning difficulties to take part in the assessment and planning process.

The Government initiative called *Valuing People* was launched in 2001 with a White Paper. This was followed by the publication of several guidance documents, and the setting up of a department called the Valuing People Support Team. *Valuing People* aims to improve planning and services for people with learning difficulties. This includes a system called **person-centred planning**, which is a way of working that directly includes not only people with learning difficulties, but also their families and carers, in the whole process of assessment and planning.

The guidance on person-centred planning (PCP) describes it in the following way: 'A process for continual listening and learning, focused on what is important for someone now and for the future, and acting upon this in alliance with family and friends' (DOH, 2002).

Like planning for other service users, it emphasises that that person should be at the very centre of all planning activity. However, it moves further than that in its emphasis on helping the person with a learning disability to make a contribution to and to have a place in the community and to get what he or she wants out of life. The five key features of person-centred planning are set out in Figure 5.12.

PCP is a positive and proactive approach that encourages creativity and active problem-solving. Rather than looking at what services already exist and then slotting people into them, PCP asks staff and service users to work together to find alternative solutions to meeting needs. The

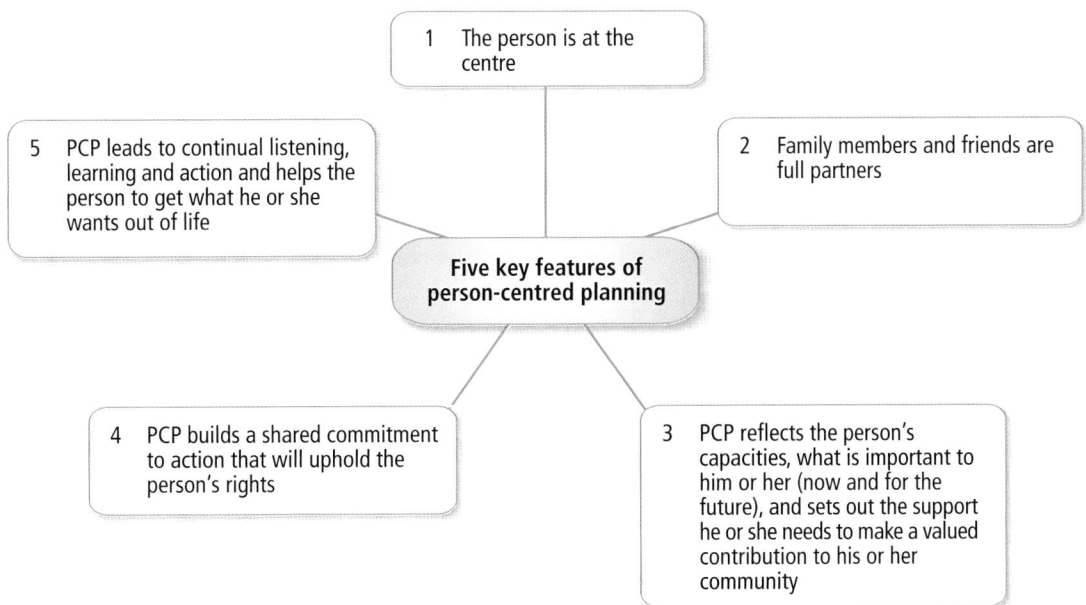

FIGURE 5.12 *Person-centred planning: five key features*

Source: DOH (2002/1)

following scenario demonstrates what this might mean in practice.

SCENARIO

We all need a break

Kevin has learning difficulties. He lives at home with his parents, Jim and Anne, who meet most of Kevin's needs for care. Every year, the council pays for Kevin to go away for a two-week holiday, to give Jim and Anne a break. This kind of service is called **respite care**.

Kevin goes to a respite care centre for these two weeks, but for the last few years he has been increasingly unhappy about going there. Person-centred planning has just been introduced by the council, and the care manager arranges some meetings to find out why Kevin is unhappy, and what can be done about it.

It turns out that Kevin does not like having to put his name on his clothes when he goes to the respite care centre (he says he feels like a baby); he does not like the noise and the fact that the centre can be very busy; he hates the lack of privacy (nobody knocks on his door before entering); and he hates the fact that his friends are not there with him.

Jim and Anne are quite upset that Kevin has been unhappy, and they are not sure what to do about it. The care manager asks them to make a list of all the other people who might help with providing a holiday for Kevin. It turns out that Kevin's uncle is very happy to take him away with him. They both love steam trains, so it is planned that Kevin and his uncle will make an extended visit to a steam railway together.

Because of the flexible funding that comes with PCP, the council will make available the money that would have been spent on the respite centre. Kevin (and his uncle) can have a holiday that he loves, and his parents can go away by themselves, happy in the knowledge that Kevin is doing what he wants, with someone that he trusts.

This story illustrates some of the key points about PCP. Kevin's needs and wishes are clearly at the heart of the process, but those of his parents are also part of the plan. A flexible and imaginative solution has been found by thinking laterally and involving other people (in this case, Kevin's uncle). The council has been flexible in its allocation of funding, and by not insisting that Kevin should go to the respite centre simply because this was what had always happened. It was not necessarily an easy process – several meetings were held and many telephone calls made before a solution was found. Time was spent with Kevin to make sure that he had fully expressed his feelings and wishes. However, the end result was a positive outcome that made everyone feel better, and did not cost any extra money. Everyone felt an 'ownership' of this plan, which had involved looking beyond what social services could offer to include people outside (in this case, Kevin's uncle). Everyone's contribution was valued in this process. The care manager had the role of facilitator, rather than of being an 'expert' problem-solver. (Many stories like this can be accessed on the *In Control* website, see below and also Resources section.)

What people with learning difficulties say

People with learning difficulties are now being helped to express their views on a number of issues that are important to them. The People First movement is an organisation that promotes **self-advocacy** by people with learning difficulties, setting up groups to help people express themselves, and publishing booklets to advise professionals about what people with learning difficulties want. A new national programme, In Control, which is sponsored by MENCAP, aims to promote the concept of self-directed support within social care for people with learning difficulties (and ultimately for all people with disabilities). At the heart of all initiatives like these is listening to what people have to say for themselves.

The magazine *Plain Facts* contains a great deal of information about what people with learning disabilities are actually saying. *Plain Facts* can be accessed via the Norah Fry Centre website at

Bristol University (www.bris.ac.uk). The box below contains some of the things that people have said (with help) about being in control of their lives and also on making decisions about health care.

Consider this: Making choices

Visit the Plain Facts website to find out what people with learning difficulties say about:

– housing
– receiving services
– shared care (respite care) and other issues.

Why do you think other people tend to make decisions for people with learning difficulties?

Sometimes, care workers might say that there is no point in asking people with learning difficulties what they want, because they don't know, or they are not able to say. If a person with a learning difficulty was invited to a meeting, for example, he or she might lose interest very quickly, or might not understand what is being said.

FIGURE 5.13 *People with learning difficulties want to make decisions about their own health care*

It is true that the ways in which health and social care workers speak and carry out their work is often hard to follow, even by people who

WHAT PEOPLE WITH LEARNING DIFFICULTIES SAY

People with learning difficulties have been consulted on a number of issues that are important to them.

Those consulted said the following about **being in control of their lives**:

– some people need support to help them have a say and choose things, such as where they live, their support workers who or what they do during the day, but some people do not get the support they need

– everyone should have a say in things that matter to them. If you need a lot of support, you should have the same choices and chances as everyone else.

On making decisions about health care they said:

– people with learning difficulties want to make decisions about their own health care, but healthcare workers usually ask parents and carers to make these decisions for them

– sometimes healthcare workers do not speak to them, but only to parents and carers. This makes people upset

– people with learning difficulties want more information about their health

– sometimes people need more time and help to make decisions on health care.

Source: *Plain Facts*, Numbers 23 and 15 (accessed through www.bris.ac.uk)

don't have a learning difficulty. However, by taking a different approach to working with service users, it is quite possible to include them in the assessment and planning processes (and this is true for people who do not have learning difficulties, too).

In the following section, some ways of involving and including people with learning difficulties are described.

Helping people to make choices

In the last few years, a number of different ways of including everyone in the planning process in a meaningful way have been developed. These include:

* advocacy
* self-advocacy
* facilitated decision-making
* providing mentors and/or other support for family members
* providing training for staff and family members.

The system of having a person to speak on behalf of another person is called **advocacy**. An advocate will go along with a person to a meeting, for example, and will make sure that his or her views are fully expressed. **Self-advocacy** involves empowering people to speak for themselves by building their confidence, self-esteem and communication skills.

Key concepts

advocacy The act of speaking on behalf of someone else, to make sure that his or her views and wishes are heard.

self-advocacy The act of speaking up for yourself.

self-directed support A process that involves the service user playing a key role in decision-making about the services he or she wants.

facilitator A person who helps to make something happen. This is often associated with decision-making or planning.

A key element in achieving person-centred planning is to have a **facilitator** to help people not only to say what they want, but also to know what is available. Consider the following scenario.

SCENARIO

Learning about what's available

Ellen has a learning difficulty, and regularly uses day services provided by her local social services department. Like many people with a learning difficulty, she is not used to being asked to say what she wants, and usually gives answers that she thinks the staff would like to hear. She also has a limited knowledge of what kinds of things are available to her.

Person-centred planning has recently been introduced by social services, and staff have come up with a way of finding out what each service user wants. One of the workers has been on a special training course to learn how to lead groups to do this, and there is now a weekly meeting at the Unit where people are helped to discover what they like.

This week, the subject is 'fruit'. Staff have brought in a very wide range of fruits for everyone to try. As each fruit is tasted, service users explain their reaction to it by pointing to a face-symbol: a smiley face for 'love it', a grumpy face for 'don't like it', and so on.

Ellen discovers that she loves fresh pineapple, something she's never tasted before, but she's not very keen on kiwi fruit.

Ellen keeps this information in her own box, which will eventually include details of the people who are important to her, music she likes, where she would like to live, who she would like to live with and where she wants to go on holiday. Everyone attending the meetings has one of these boxes that can be used for future decision-making.

In order to get people with learning difficulties to express themselves, it is vital for the facilitator to learn how to ask the right question, and how to adapt his or her listening style to suit the needs of the service user. Sometimes, this can be as simple (and as complex) as learning to observe (and correctly interpret) the non-verbal signals that a person gives. Non-verbal signals include movements such as those of the eye, hand, face, feet, body etc. Consider the following scenario.

SCENARIO

See what I'm saying

Tim is Kelly's father, and he has been learning how to find out more about Kelly's needs through working with her care manager (who has been trained on PCP techniques).

Kelly does not speak, and for years Tim and June (Kelly's Mother) thought that it was sufficient to make sure that she had enough to eat, was comfortable and had a safe home, together with sessions at the day unit.

Through the skilled facilitation of the care manager, the family began by sharing their stories about Kelly and experiences of being with her. Then they began to look carefully at Kelly's non-verbal signals, and found (to their surprise) that she had views and opinions about what was happening to her. By interpreting her signals, they found out that she did not like the day unit, but very much enjoyed listening to music and also going out to the shops.

They also found out how much Kelly valued having a cuddle in the morning before the day began. In fact, Kelly was able to explain that not having a cuddle could ruin her day.

By working very patiently with both Kelly and her family, the care manager was able to help them all to work out a plan for her that took into account what she actually wanted. Some of the things she told them took the family by surprise.

Adapted (with permission) from Sanderson et al (2002)

Skill is also required in listening to people speak, and can require the listener to adapt his or her listening style to suit the speaker. The following scenario describes the experience of a researcher collecting information from three men with learning difficulties, all of whom live in a residential establishment.

SCENARIO

Listen to me!

Asif is a researcher who is collecting information on what people with learning difficulties have to say. As part of the initial stage of his research, he spends some time just listening to people with learning difficulties, so that he can get to know them better and start to build a relationship with each person.

Peter, Max and Lee are three residents who live in the home in which Asif is doing his research. Asif discovers that just like people who do not have a learning difficulty, all three have very different approaches to being listened to.

Peter likes to talk without being interrupted. He also likes to walk about while he talks, even going outside into the garden. Asif just lets him talk, and will follow him outside so that he does not miss any of the story.

Max will only talk if he is asked questions, so Asif has to work out ways of asking the right sort of questions to encourage him to carry on talking.

Lee needs lots of positive feedback when he is talking, so Asif adapts yet again to let him know how much he is enjoying what he is saying.

1. How do you like to be listened to?

2. Do you like your listener to give you lots of feedback, or do you just like him or her to listen uncritically, giving you lots of positive noises of encouragement.

3. When you are listening to someone else, do you try to work out how they like to be listened to? Do you adapt your style to suit their needs?

4. Get a friend to assess your listening skills. (A checklist assessing your listening skills can be found on p. 225).

Adapted (with permission) from Croft (1999)

Helping people to make choices is a process that involves communication skills and sometimes facilitation skills (i.e. working with a group of people to bring about the desired outcome). Getting everybody to the point where person-centred planning can happen often involves people having training; it always requires proper preparation for everybody involved in the process – the service user, carers and staff – and sometimes other people, as Kevin's story on page 220 shows.

In the next section, ways of including people in the planning process are discussed.

Helping people to take part in planning

It is not good enough just to make sure that a service user attends a planning meeting. If he or she has not been adequately prepared, then they may just as well not be there. Often, staff use this as an excuse not to involve people with learning difficulties in meetings that affect them. However, a positive and creative approach can make all the difference.

FIGURE 5.14 *Listening involves adopting a style that suits the speaker*

The people from the Liverpool and Manchester *People First* scheme have produced a booklet about attending meetings. They have put forward some

very sensible ideas about how to include people with learning difficulties in meetings that affect them. See the box below to find out what they said.

INCLUDING PEOPLE WITH LEARNING DIFFICULTIES IN PLANNING

✳ Give them time and support to prepare.

✳ Let the people with learning difficulties choose who attends, the venue and the time of the meeting.

✳ Use video, pictures and photographs if you want to, instead of just talking.

✳ There is no point in having a meeting if nothing gets done.

Source: Liverpool and Manchester People First (1996)

Making a video about what someone likes and wants can be a very good way of helping them to express their needs to the right people, as the following scenario demonstrates.

SCENARIO

Going to the school of my choice

Martin was in mainstream primary school, but it was time for him to leave. His mother, Margaret, wanted him to go to a mainstream secondary school.

She knew that Martin's school reports were full of 'labels' (about what he could not do) and also about behaviour issues. She decided that she wanted the new school to see who Martin really was. So she sent the school a copy of Martin's person-centred plan and a video of him.

The head teacher told Margaret that if he had just seen the primary school's report, without the PCP and video, he would not have believed that Martin could go to mainstream school.

Source: Sanderson et al. (2002)

CHECK OUT YOUR LISTENING SKILLS

Ask a colleague to observe you listening to someone.

Get him or her to use this form to give you some feedback on how well you listened.
(Score 1 = low; 5 = high)

	Score 1	Score 2
Using acknowledgement responses to show that you are listening (e.g. 'mm')		
Not interrupting when someone is in the flow of talking		
Using reflective statements to show interest (e.g. 'I see', 'That must be difficult for you' etc.)		
Using appropriate questions to clarify what is being said		
Being sensitive to body language		
Being sensitive to tone of voice and facial expression		
Recognising that cultural difference can affect what is said and how		
Recognising that physical, sensory or learning disabilities can have an impact on communication		
Adapting conversational style to suit the situation		

FIGURE 5.15 *Listening skills checklist*

Staff also need to be fully involved in the planning process, as they have wishes and preferences too. The following scenario demonstrates why this is important.

SCENARIO

What everyone wants

In a small home for four men with learning difficulties, the residents are very bored and unfulfilled. All four have to take medication from time to time to help manage their aggression and behavioural problems.

As a result of a PCP programme, their personal likes, dislikes and fears have been identified.

Part of this process also involved finding out what the staff liked and what was important to them. As a result, they were not asked to do things they did not like. One person, for example, did not like swimming, so someone else started taking the men to the local pool.

One of the residents would get very anxious when he did not know what was going to happen on a daily basis, and who would be helping him. Consequently, a big daily plan was put up in the kitchen, setting out in pictures who would be doing what, together with a photograph of the staff member who would be helping with each activity.

Because the staff were feeling happier, the men began to feel more relaxed. The new programme meant that people were no longer feeling bored. One other result was that the men began to need less medication.

Source: Sanderson et al. (2002/1)

Summary

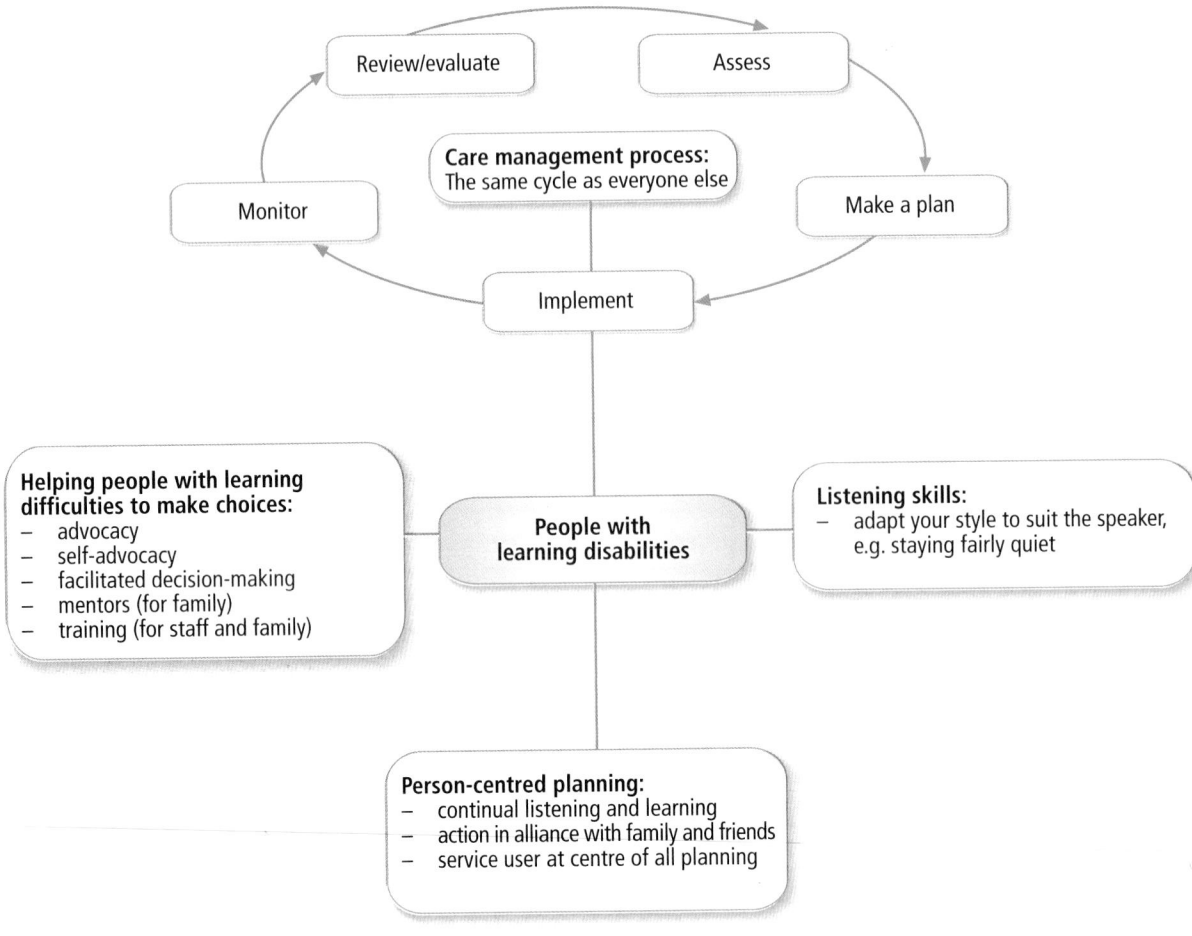

FIGURE 5.16 *Managing care for people with learning difficulties*

Consider this

John has mild learning difficulties. He is 45 years old and has lived with his parents all his life. His parents are now quite elderly and are beginning to worry about what will happen to John when they are no longer able to care for him.

1. Who is likely to be involved in the process of assessing John's future needs?

2. How could John's care manager use person-centred planning to find out what John would like to happen? (What techniques could be used to help him make choices and say what he wants?)

3. How should the care manager make sure that decisions about John's future are evidence-based?

Section 4: Models and approaches

Throughout history, societies have made decisions about how to regard people with disabilities, and this has often led to disabled people being treated very badly indeed. The Elizabethan Poor Law, for example (set up by an Act of Parliament in 1601), saw disabled people as a 'problem' that paid officials had to deal with. To some extent, this approach has survived into the 21st century, although there are now many people (both disabled and non-disabled) who are working hard to counteract this view of disability as a 'problem'.

The medical model of disability

This view is, in some respects, a hangover from the old view of disability as a 'problem'. From this perspective, people are disabled as a result of the physical or cognitive impairments they have. These impairments prevent them from functioning like the rest of society, who are, by definition, seen as 'normal'.

The medical solution to this is to intervene to cure people, or at any rate to rehabilitate them into society. This view sees disability as an individual problem, and it focuses on personal limitations. It is very much an 'impairment' view of disability. One consequence of this view is that if a disability cannot be 'cured', or if a person cannot successfully be rehabilitated, then he or she is seen as unable to play a full role as a member of society. He or she is thus devalued as a member of that society.

Consider the story of Nicholas in the following scenario.

The social model of disability

Disabled people have been challenging the social model of disability since the end of the 19th century. The British Deaf Association (BDA) and the National League of the Blind (NLB) were set up at this time, and the NLB actually registered as a trade union in 1899. Such organisations aimed to promote the rights of disabled people to have equal status with non-disabled people. In more recent years many such organisations have been founded (for example, the British Council of Disabled People in 1986, and Disabled Peoples' International in 1989).

The argument put forward by such organisations is that it is not the fact of having a disability, as such, that disables a person. Rather, it is the attitude of the rest of society towards that person that limits what he or she is able to do. This is a **social model of disability**.

If Nicholas had been born in the late 1990s, his life might have been quite different. His parents could have applied for equipment and adaptations to their home to allow him to live with them (for example, hoists, bathing aids, ramps and widened doors to accommodate a wheelchair). Other support might be available in the form of social work intervention, or home nursing. Adapted computer equipment is now available to help with intellectual and educational needs. Day care is available to support personal development, and it is no longer considered necessary for people with severe disabilities to be hidden away in institutions.

However, there is still some way to go before all barriers to the inclusion of disabled people in society are removed. Martin's story (on page 224)

SCENARIO

Out of sight, out of mind

Nicholas was born in the 1950s with cerebral palsy. He was considered by doctors at the time to be seriously impaired and incapable of enjoying a 'normal' life, or of making a meaningful contribution to society. He was put into a long-stay hospital, where he remained until he died 20 years later.

Sending Nicholas to a hospital was seen to solve a 'problem'. He could easily be fed and kept warm and clean by nursing staff, but he would not have to be a 'burden' to his family by living at home.

The problem of Nicholas's impairment was thus solved by applying a medical solution that sought to nurse him through his life.

FIGURE 5.17 *Empowerment of people with disabilities means they can take control of their own lives*

tells how he was allowed to go to mainstream school only after key decision-makers (including the headteacher) had been shown the video that Martin had made. In this video, Martin was able to present himself fully and in his own way, as someone with capabilities and who could make a contribution to the school. If he had not been helped to prove otherwise, a decision would have been made based on the forms and reports on Martin that said he should not have a place in a mainstream school. The educational system itself very nearly acted as a barrier to Martin's progress. This is what is meant by the social model of disability. It was not the case that Martin could not enjoy going to mainstream school: rather, the assumption was made automatically that this was not the right place for him, simply because he had a learning difficulty.

The many barriers that make it harder for disabled people to take control of their own lives and also to play a meaningful role within society will be considered below. The next section, another model of disability is considered – the empowerment model.

The empowerment model

Many people with disabilities (and their supporters) feel that there is still a lot of work to be done before they achieve anything like equality with non-disabled members of society. Such people are working towards the true empowerment of people with disabilities, whether these are physical, sensory or cognitive.

The *Valuing People* initiative seeks to put people with learning difficulties in control of their own lives. It involves helping them to know what choices they have, and giving them support to make these choices. It also involves an attitude shift on the part of the people who work to support those with learning difficulties. If you have been trained to assess problems and then to plan interventions, making decisions on behalf of the person with the disability (or with their families, but without consulting the service user), it takes a huge change in thinking to move to a point where control is shifted to the service user. This is why the *Valuing People* approach (together with person-centred planning) often requires intensive training (both for staff and families) if it is to be successfully implemented.

Deaf people have extended the social model of disability even further, in a very striking way. To understand this, it is first necessary to understand the limitations of the social model of disability. Although the social model stresses that people are disabled by society rather than the limiting conditions they suffer from, this model resembles

FIGURE 5.18 *Some deaf people see themselves as a distinct cultural group with its own language (sign) and its own values*

the medical model in that it assumes that there is something called 'normal', to which everybody within a society will aspire. However, some deaf people are currently challenging even the social model of deafness, and are promoting instead a linguistic and cultural model. This asserts that sign is a minority language, and that people who use it are a **linguistic minority** rather than disabled. Members of this group are proud to be **culturally Deaf** rather than simply **audiologically deaf**. People who see themselves as culturally Deaf (and they use the capital 'D' deliberately to express their distinctiveness as a social group) reject the deficit or medical model that says they are not 'normal'. Instead, they see themselves as a distinct cultural group with its own language (Sign), and its own values.

There are many sign-language systems currently in use throughout the world, and the observations in this section are based on research into British Sign Language (BSL). Some years ago, all sign language was regarded simply as a kind of 'picture writing', having no subtlety or precision, and capable of expressing only the simplest concepts. In fact, fully developed sign languages such as BSL are now regarded by some linguists as full languages rather than gestural codes. Problems arise only during the interface between sign and speech, when it is very easy for hearing people to exclude deaf people through failure to take steps such as facing the deaf person when speaking.

The history of the people in the island of Martha's Vineyard, in Massachsetts, USA, demonstrates very clearly how attitudes within society can either disable or empower people who have any kind of physical, sensory or cognitive problem. In this case, deaf and hearing people lived and worked together side by side very successfully. On Martha's Vineyard, between the 1690s and the early 20th century, there was a very high incidence of hereditary deafness. Consequently, everyone (hearing and deaf alike) learned to sign, and community members used both speech and sign in the same way as a bilingual person in a UK city might use, say, a variety of English and Gujerati, switching from one to the other as appropriate (Groce 1991; Sacks 1989). Furthermore, there were many advantages

to having two communication systems. Many of the vineyarders lived by fishing, and sign was often used between workers in boats up to 150 yards apart to facilitate the task in hand. People in houses some distance away from each other used to communicate by using their spyglasses in order to read their neighbours' sign language. There are also anecdotes about people signing to each other to tell funny stories in church. All residents on the island were genuinely bilingual, and this served to reinforce their identity – whether deaf or hearing. Socially, there were no distinctions made between deaf and hearing people – deafness was simply not an issue with respect to work, the formation of friendships or the setting up of social activities.

FIGURE 5.19 *In some communities the deaf and hearing learn to sign*

This picture of a totally integrated society of deaf and hearing people is in stark contrast to the ways in which deaf people (and indeed all people with disabilities) are largely excluded from the non-disabled world today. While deaf people have now begun to reject the label of 'disabled', and instead to assert a different identity – that of being culturally Deaf, other people with disabilities, while not necessarily asserting a different identity, now insist on their right to be fully included in society, and being enabled to do the things they want – including playing a part in (and being accepted by) their community. They are not just looking for better services: they also seek empowerment.

In the next section, barriers that prevent people with disabilities from being included within their communities are considered.

Barriers to inclusion

Environmental barriers

If you are reading this as a non-disabled person, please try the following exercises.

If you already have a disability of some kind, then it is likely that you have an understanding of the kinds of environmental barriers that people with physical and sensory difficulties experience on a daily basis.

In 1995, the Disability Discrimination Act (DDA) established that disabled people have rights of physical access to almost every kind of public service, such as hospitals and banks, for example. This means that businesses and public services are now legally obliged to make their premises and services accessible, by installing facilities such as ramps or power-operated doors, and loops for people with hearing problems.

However, the Act also says that businesses and service providers are expected to make 'reasonable adjustments,' with respect to the needs of disabled people. In practice, there are still many situations in which barriers to access have not yet been removed.

Sometimes, the removal of such barriers is simply a matter of better organisation, as the following example demonstrates.

In this example, the hospital where Kim is currently treated is very old, and is due to be replaced by a brand new building in the next four years. The new hospital is already under construction, and there will be 10 MRI scanners provided rather than just the two existing ones. Kim understands that the mobile scanner currently provides a much-needed service. She cannot appreciate, however, that no one has thought to put a note on her records that she cannot manage to climb steps. It might not be reasonable to expect the health authority to put a ramp up to the mobile scanner, given the tight space that it operates in; but it is certainly reasonable to insist that staff include notes about mobility and other physical problems on each person's record, so that mis-matches of this kind are avoided.

The following scenario provides another example of how forward planning and the allocation of a small amount of funding can improve access in a public setting.

SCENARIO

Is there a Mrs Jenkins here?

Mrs Jenkins is profoundly deaf. She has picked up an infection and because she is worried, she goes to her local Accident and Emergency Department for tests.

No one is available to go with her to help interpret, so she has to go by herself. There are rows of chairs facing one wall in the waiting area, but the door through which staff come and go to call each patient to see a doctor is positioned to the left-hand side of the rows of chairs. Consequently, if a patient is sitting down in one of the rows, this door is not visible.

The only way individuals know that it is their turn to see the doctor is when a staff member puts a head round the door and calls their name.

Mrs Jenkins does not know that this is the system; she also cannot hear her name called. Consequently, she misses her turn. As her daughter is soon due back from school, she leaves without being seen.

In this scenario, the system in the waiting area could have been improved by installing an electronic sign, warning people that their appointment was coming up. Blind people using the waiting area would also be helped by the installation of an associated audio system to make sure that people can hear their names. In fact, everyone would benefit from this kind of improvement.

Improving access and reducing environmental barriers require a positive and creative approach, as well as the allocation of funding. Managers and staff who do not have disabilities need to learn to look at their working environment differently in order to bring about meaningful and sensible changes. Consulting people with disabilities who use the service would be a good first step.

Think it over...

By now you should have been allocated a person with a disability who is happy to work with you to help you produce a profile.

Interview this person to find out what environmental barriers he or she has experienced.

Attitudinal barriers

Many people with disabilities will say that the attitudes of other people often act as barriers to prevent their being included in society. Negative attitudes can often prevent people with disabilities from securing jobs, because potential employers think that they are not capable of working reliably or of doing the job satisfactorily. Sometimes, disabled people are excluded from taking part in social or educational groups, because non-disabled people treat them differently. The following scenario shows how this can happen.

SCENARIO

Excluded from the group

Chris is an adult deaf student, studying for a social care qualification at a college of higher education. He has been allocated to a group for some of his project work, but has been excluded from the decision-making by his colleagues. The others have allocated Chris one of the simpler tasks, which they have decided should present him with fewer problems.

Chris is very angry, and, after making representations both to his colleagues and to his tutor, he has asserted his right to take part on an equal basis to the others, and has renegotiated his role in the project. However, this was a battle he could have done without, and it has left him feeling both annoyed and a little suspicious of the others.

Have you ever made a decision for someone else because you thought you were doing them a favour?

A number of things were going on here. Firstly, the group had made a number of assumptions about Chris, based solely on the fact that he was deaf. Thinking of Chris as deaf, rather than as a person who happens to be deaf, is known as **labelling**. The students had seen only his disability, and had made no attempt to find out about his abilities. This had led them to **stereotype** him as someone who, because of his deafness, could not do certain things. The following example shows how someone with a physical disability can be labelled.

SCENARIO

'Let the wheelchair through!'

Jo is an avid reader of science-fiction novels. A new book has just been published by her favourite author, and there is to be a book signing at the local bookstore.

As Jo uses an electric wheelchair and is very independent, she is able to go by herself into town, and is looking forward to meeting this famous writer.

When she arrives at the store, the book signing has already started and there is a big crowd in the shop. There does not seem to be a queue, and everyone is pushing and shoving. As Jo is deciding what to do, the store manager rushes forward and shouts: 'Stand back please! Let the wheelchair through!'

Jo has mixed feelings. She is glad to be allowed straight through, but she is also offended. She is not a 'wheelchair', but a person who happens to use a wheelchair.

What would you have said if you were the store manager?

The store manager is guilty of labelling Jo. He has seen only the wheelchair and not the person in it. He was right to help her with her access problem: the situation could have been dangerous for both Jo and the people around her if no one had attempted to manage the crowd. However, the manager's choice of language reveals that at a subconscious level he sees her as a wheelchair 'case' who is also a problem.

Think it over...

Write down all the words you have heard to refer to people with disabilities.

How many of these words are positive, and how many have negative connotations?

In practice, the attitudes of non-disabled people towards disability issues range from complete indifference through a continuum to the other end of the scale, which is pity and an overwhelming insistence on giving 'care' and sympathy. In fact, disabled people do not need sympathy; they need empathy, which is a very different quality.

Key concept

empathy not *sympathy* People with disabilities often resent being treated with overwhelming concern (sympathy). Rather, they appreciate it when others make an effort to understand their needs, do what is required and then allow them simply to get on with things. This understanding is known as empathy.

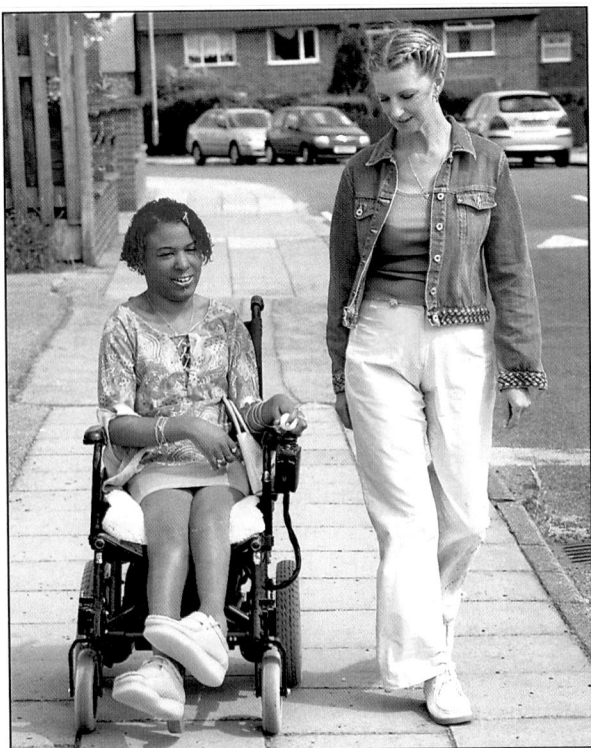

FIGURE 5.20 *People with disabilities appreciate empathy rather than sympathy*

The following scenario provides an example of empathy in action.

SCENARIO

Let me get on with it!

Jas has a physical problem that prevents her from standing for long periods. She loves singing and has enrolled at a local evening class, an amateur singing group.

Before the first session, she explains to the tutor that she cannot stand for long periods but that this is nothing to worry about. The tutor thus understands that Jas will have to sit down more frequently than the others in the group (they sing standing up). Accordingly, the tutor does not draw attention to Jas when she does have to sit down, and sometimes she designs short activities where everyone sits down for a while.

She leaves it to Jas to explain her disability to the others, should she choose to do so.

Jas feels very comfortable with this arrangement. The tutor understands her needs and lets her enjoy the class in her own way. This is practical empathy.

Achieving a position of empathy requires the ability to listen, and sometimes also an attitude shift. Try the following exercise, and answer the questions honestly.

Think it over...

Which of the following words best describe your attitude towards people with disabilities:

– pity   – sympathy
– fear   – disgust
– uncertainty   – understanding
– compassion   – empathy.

1. Are there any other attitudes or feelings that you have that have not been listed here?

2. Do you feel that you need to rethink the way you have viewed people with disabilities?

Economic barriers

There are a number of economic barriers to inclusion for people with disabilities. Sometimes, people are prevented from gaining paid work because of the attitudes of potential employers (see page 231). Employers may fear that disabled people cannot do the job, and may also be unaware that they can obtain financial assistance to adapt the workplace to meet the needs of disabled employees. In practice, it is perfectly possible for people with disabilities to make a great contribution to any business or organisation, given the right support and working arrangements.

Not all employers are as helpful as Wally's plumbing company, in that following scenario, and people with disabilities often have tremendous difficulty in finding employment.

SCENARIO

Tapping into talent

Wally had been a qualified plumber for over 30 years when an accident at work left him totally blind.

His employer did not want to lose his experience and expertise, however, and made it possible for him to carry on working with the help of an assistant.

Wally can diagnose some problems by listening, and visual clues are explained to him by his mate. Working as a pair, they give good service to the employer, who is glad not to have lost a valuable employee. Wally's assistant is also learning more about the trade by working alongside him.

Unemployed people with disabilities are entitled to benefits, but the benefits system can be very difficult to fathom. Many local authorities have Benefits Advisers to help people both to understand their entitlements and fill in forms. Being in receipt of benefits also restricts the amount of paid work that a person can take on.

Consequently, many disabled people are afraid to take on any sort of work for fear that their benefits will be adversely affected. There is also a fear that any employment may not work out, and that it will be a difficult and lengthy process to get back onto benefits once these have been given up. The whole issue of employment versus benefits is thus a very difficult area for many disabled people, who sometimes find themselves caught between a rock and a hard place.

Another barrier to inclusion is the eligibility system itself. The Fair Access to Care Services initiative is built around the concept of eligibility criteria. This means that the most disabled people are more likely to get services and resources allocated to them. Unfortunately, in practice, this can leave some people without the services that they would really like to have (because their disabilities are not classed as severe enough to qualify for help). However, as the person-centred planning initiative shows, sometimes it is possible to be very creative with what is available, rather than being restricted by the belief that tasks always have to be done in certain ways (see page 219).

Summary

Figure 5.21 summarises the models and approaches covered.

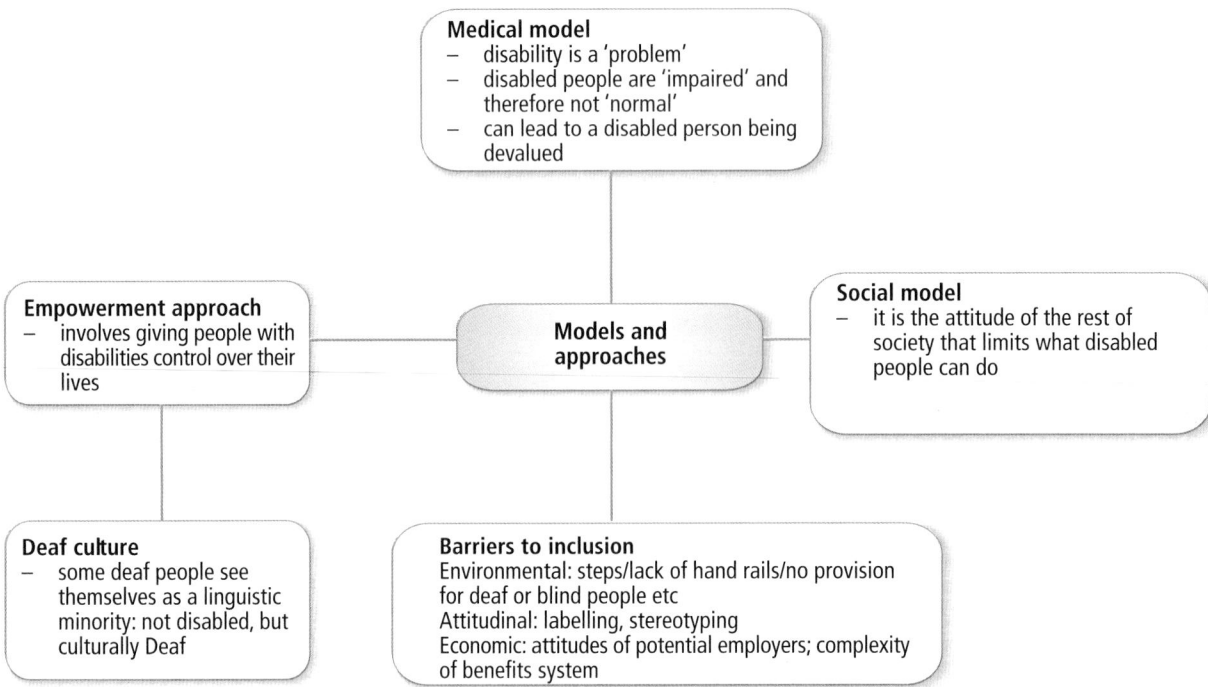

FIGURE 5.21 *Models and approaches*

A long-stay hospital for people with learning difficulties is in the process of closure. Patients are being moved out to smaller residential units in the community.

In one local authority, the Community Learning Disability Team is preparing to help 12 hospital residents to move back into the area from which they originated. The 12 people have been living in the hospital for between 15 and 20 years.

In the hospital, the residents did not go out much, so they had very little exercise. They also had a very bland diet, with little choice of food. Consequently, all 12 people had suffered with bowel problems for many years. In hospital, these problems were treated by regular use of enemas.

Once in their new residential settings (small homes for four or five people) life became very different. The Community Learning Disability Team began to encourage residents to go out every day for walks. A range of different foods was introduced, especially fresh fruit and vegetables. Within a month, only one of the 12 people still needed a daily enema, and everyone was starting to feel the benefit of the lifestyle and dietary changes.

Of course, there is still a lot of work to be done in order to help the residents to begin to explore their own potential, and to express themselves and their personal wants and preferences. However, it is clear that some very simple changes can make a big difference.

1. How does the Community Learning Disability Team's approach differ from that used in the long-stay hospital?

2. What are likely to be the difficulties for people who have been living in an institutional-style setting for a very long time?

3. How could person-centred planning be used to help residents start to make choices for themselves?

Producing a profile

Producing a profile of someone who has a disability is something you could try out in order to provide portfolio evidence. It will help you to imagine how you would help care for the person, identifying their needs and whether there are any particular aids or adaptions they should have.

aids (for people with disabilities) Any device that is used to assist a person with a disability is referred to as an aid. This may be a walking stick, a hearing aid, a device to open tins or a touch-pad type keyboard for a computer for instance.

adaptations Any alterations to a building to accommodate the needs of a disabled person are referred to as adaptation. This might include widening doors, building a ramp etc.

You should interview the service user to discuss these needs, following the guidelines listed.

* Adapt your listening skills to suit the service user.

* Adapt your style to work with any additional helper who may be present (e.g. signer, communicator, facilitator).

* Be sensitive to the needs of your interviewee at all times.

The steps for producing the profile after this interview are summarised in Figure 5.22.

The stages for producing a service user's profile

1 **Identify someone to work with:**
Approach the manager of a local service (e.g. care home)
Identify a friend or relative, explaining what you plan to do

2 **Make a plan:**
Consider practical matters (e.g. time, place, equipment, people)
Write a questionnaire

3 **Conduct the interview:**
Adapt your listening style
Use helpers if necessary (e.g. singer, interpreter)
Use supervision to give you feedback on your performance

4 **Pull everything together:**
Research aspects of the service user's disability further
Collate this with the information gained from the interview

5 **Evaluate:**
Reflect on all the information collected
Assess how you would care for the service user interviewed

FIGURE 5.22 *Steps in producing a profile*

Consider this

Record a TV documentary about someone who has a disability. Then imagine that you are going to produce a profile on this person for your portfolio. Study the TV programme carefully (you might want to replay it a couple of times).

Make a plan for the interview. Be sure to consider:

- time and place
- practical matters
- other people who might need to be there
- the questions you will ask
- who you might ask to supervise you.

UNIT 5 ASSESSMENT

How you will be assessed

In order to satisfy the requirements of this unit, you must produce a portfolio which will include a guide for care workers (which explores caring for service users with additional needs), and also a profile of a service user.

Assessment evidence

Your evidence will:

- demonstrate an understanding of the causes of additional needs and the effects of these needs on service users
- demonstrate an understanding of the care-management process and key roles of service providers who support service users with additional needs
- include research and analysis of the models or approaches used to support service users, recognising the attitudes of society towards service users with additional needs
- include a profile of a service user who has additional needs, including the barriers he or she has experienced; support, aids and adaptations used; and evaluating impact of these on the service user.

Information about real people (scenarios) will bring your portfolio to life (although you must be careful to anonymise the data and to observe confidentiality at all times). There are many useful websites (see the Resources section at the end of this unit) where you can access downloadable articles and other information.

Assessment guidance

Area AO1: The causes of additional needs

You will need to apply the knowledge gained from studying this section to any people that you study, whether in some of the scenarios in the text, scenarios given by your tutor, or people that you meet in the course of your research and investigations.

You may wish to seek out video or CD materials to supplement the information you gather. Local support groups, such as, for example, MENCAP, may also have information that you can access easily.

You will need to make sure that you understand exactly why a person is, for example, blind or deaf, or has a mobility problem.

Any information collected about real people is confidential and should be anonymised and stored securely.

Area AO2: The care management process

You will not have to make an assessment yourself, but you will need to show that you know how assessments are made, the kinds of question that are asked and the records that are kept.

You will need to show that you are aware of the key stages in the care management process: assessment, planning, implementation, monitoring and review/evaluation.

If you are able to show how the underlying causes of disability relate to a person's needs (P-I-E-S), this will earn higher marks.

If you show how the care plan can be linked to guidance such as the Fair Access to Care Services criteria or person-centred planning, this will also result in higher marks.

Area AO3: Medical and social models of disability

It will be important to show that you understand the difference between these two models. It would be helpful to collect examples of both approaches as they apply to real people. Whenever you consider a scenario (either hypothetical or real), consider which model is being applied in any plan that is proposed for a service user. You may, for instance, come across examples of the application of an empowerment model. If so, you will need to say clearly how this differs from the medical model, and how it develops the social model of disability.

One way to investigate barriers experienced by people with additional needs is to conduct a survey relating to access to health, social care, education and/or social activities. Use the guidance from Unit 16, Research Methods in Health and Social Care when planning your research.

Area AO4: Profile of a service user with additional needs

This can be based on someone you know, someone you have met on a work placement, or a case study.

Confidentiality must be maintained at all times, real names must not be used, and information must be gathered in a sensitive manner.

Your profile must show how the underlying causes of disability are linked to a service user's needs.

You should show how any care plan aims to meet a person's physical, intellectual, emotional and/or social needs.

A pass-level portfolio will include evidence to show that you appreciate the causes of additional needs for a service user, and how the medical and social models can lead to different solutions.

A good portfolio will contain all of these plus more detailed information about the causes of additional needs, how these affect daily living, and how they contribute to the barriers a person may experience.

Good use will be made of specialist vocabulary, for example:

- care setting
- person-centred planning
- working in partnership.

An excellent portfolio will achieve all of the foregoing, plus good use of key concepts such as:

- diversity
- eligibility criteria
- evidence-based decision-making
- objectivity
- confidentiality
- the difference between empathy and sympathy
- use of evaluation to modify individual care plans
- empowerment
- self-advocacy.

References

Davis, K. (1996, updated 1998) *The Disabled People's Movement – Putting the Power in Empowerment* (accessed via www.leeds.ac.uk/disability)

DOH (1999) *Caring About Carers: A National Strategy for Carers*. London: Department of Health (access via DOH website)

DOH (2000) *Framework for the Assessment of Children in Need and Their Families*. London: The Stationery Office

DOH (2001) *National Service Framework for Older People*. London: HMSO

DOH (2001) *Valuing People: A New Strategy for Learning Disability for the 21st Century. Planning With People: Guidance for Partnership Boards*. London: Department of Health (accessed via www.valuingpeople.gov.uk)

DOH (2002) *Fair Access to Care Services: Guidance on Eligibility Criteria for Adult Social Care* London: Department of Health (accessed via www.dh.gov.uk)

DOH (2002/1) *Valuing People: A New Strategy for Learning Disability for the 21st Century: Planning With People; Towards a Person–Centred Approach; Guidance for Implementation Groups*. London: Department of Health.

DOH (2003) *A Practical Guide for Disabled People or Carers: Where to find Information, Services and Equipment*. London: Department of Health

Groce, N. (1991) 'Everyone here spoke sign language', in S. Gregory and G.M. Hartley (eds) *Constructing Deafness*, London and New York: Pinter and the Open University Press

Liverpool and Manchester People First (1996) *Our Plan for Planning* (available directly from People First on email peoplefirst@another.com)

Moonie, N, Bates, A. and Spencer-Perkins, D. (2004) *Diversity and Rights in Care*. Oxford: Heinemann

Sacks, O. (1989) *Seeing Voices*. London Basingstoke and Oxford: Picador

Sanderson, H. (2002) *Families and Person-Centred Planning* – Valuing People (accessed via www.valuingpeople.gov.uk)

Sanderson, H. Jones, E. and Brown, K. (2002/1) *Essential Lifestyle Planning and Active Support* (accessed via www.nwtdt.com North West Training and Development Team)

Useful websites

www.bris.ac.uk
University of Bristol. Follow the links for the Norah Fry Research Centre. *Plain Facts* can be accessed via this site.

www.carers.gov.uk
Government website on the needs of carers.

www.carers.uk
Carers' website: lots of information about research.

www.dh.gov.uk
Main Department of Health website. Many government guidance notes and key documents can be downloaded directly from here.

www.nwtdt.com
Website of the North West Training and Development Team. This is a not-for-profit training and development organisation that focuses on services for people with learning disabilities. Useful articles are available from this site.

www.paradigm-uk.org
Paradigm is a not-for-profit organisation offering training and consultancy on person-centred services. You can download useful articles from this site.

www.peoplefirst.org.uk
A good place to find out what people with learning disabilities, their advocates and their carers are saying.

www.selfdirectedsupport.org
To access the organisation *In Control*.

www.valuingpeople.gov.uk
The main *Valuing People* website set up by the government. An excellent resource for articles/research about work for and with people with learning disabilities.

UNIT
6

Working in Early Years Care and Education

This unit includes the following sections:

6.1 Care and education provision in early years settings

6.2 Job roles and responsibilities within early years care and education

6.3 The values and principles of the early years sector

6.4 The ways in which children learn and develop and factors that affect performance

6.5 Planning activities

Introduction

This unit looks at care and education in early year settings. It covers how children learn and activities that help children to learn. It also explores the different settings in which children may be cared for, the care values those settings hold, and the roles and responsibilities within those settings.

How you will be assessed

This unit is internally assessed through a portfolio. You need to produce a guide for early years care and education provision in your local area and explore the different ways in which children learn.

Section 1: Care and education provision in early years settings

There are many different types of care and education provision in Britain today. They have increased dramatically in the last 30 years as the number of women working outside the home has increased. This phenomenon is partly due to changes in the age structure of the population, and partly due to it now being much more widely accepted that mothers may choose to continue working once they have had children. In recent years, a range of legislation has been passed by Parliament to encourage and support working mothers. The National Childcare Strategy is aimed to ensure the provision of high-quality early years care and education and after-school facilities. The government has also provided free pre-school places for all children from the term following their third birthday, for a limited number of sessions per week, through the 'voucher scheme', in addition to offering tax incentives for working mothers.

✳ DID YOU KNOW?

The early years voucher scheme does not always cover the full cost of a session at an early years facility. Parents are offered $12\frac{1}{2}$ hours per week for 33 weeks of the year. Parents often have to pay a 'top up' fee to cover the care required. It certainly does not cover full-time care for a working parent but does provide some support in helping parents with the cost of childcare.

How national policies influence the provision of care and education in early years settings

National policies are produced by central government. Central government sets taxes and determines how much is spent on areas such as education and health. The government is divided into different departments, and the Department for Education and Science (DfES) is responsible for all aspects of education.

Many laws and Acts of Parliament have influenced the provision of early years care and education. One of the most important ones was the Children Act 1989.

The Children Act 1989

This Act of Parliament resulted in a number of changes in the way young children were cared for and protected. It covered care in the home, including parenthood issues and arrangements that took place if parents separated. It also covered services provided outside the home, for example child-protection care.

The Children Act 2004

The Children Act 2004 established a new Children's Commissioner for England, whose job is to raise awareness of issues relating to children and young people and to report annually to Parliament, through the Secretary of State, on his or her findings. The role is to look at how both public and private bodies listen to children and to report on improvements. It also calls for cooperation between key agencies to improve children's well-being. It places a duty on people working with children and young people to have systems in place that ensure they safeguard and promote the well-being of children through their work.

It also calls for a basic database to hold information on children to facilitate 'joined-up' work between agencies.

Local authorities are required to have a Directorate of Children's Services which brings together Education and Social Services.

Every Child Matters – What's next?

Every Child Matters: Change for Children outlines how the Children Act 2004 will be implemented. It covers all children, from birth to the age of 19 years; through the *National Service Framework for Children, Young People and Maternity Services* (NSF), which is an integral part of the programme, the government aims to support parents from pregnancy onwards. The vision is to create a joined-up system of health, family support, childcare and education services so that all children receive the best start possible in the vital early years. It is a shared programme of change to improve outcomes for all children and young people. It takes forward the government's vision of radical reform for children, young people and families.

In a survey children and young people identified five outcomes that are key to well-being in childhood and later life: being healthy, staying safe, enjoying and achieving, making a positive contribution and achieving economic well-being. The *Every Child Matters* programme aims to improve those outcomes for all children and to close the gap in outcomes between the disadvantaged and their peers.

In the decade between 2004 and 2014 the government aims to offer parents greater help with childcare, often located conveniently in schools and/or provided in partnership with the voluntary and private sector.

The DfES *Five-year Strategy for Children and Learners* sets an expectation that primary schools should, over time, offer childcare between 8.00 am–6.00 pm, 48 weeks per year. This builds on the extended school programme and could include arrangements made by groups or clusters of schools.

National Childcare Strategy

Another key government strategy that has influenced the provision of early years services is the National Childcare Strategy. The government has put major resources into this strategy, which aims to ensure provision of good-quality early years provision. It also aims to increase the availability of before- and after-school clubs, including homework clubs for 5–15 year olds. The strategy include plans to make childcare more affordable, which has had a direct influence on increasing the demand for early years provision and, as a consequence, the level of childcare facilities available.

Early years curriculum

The curriculum covered in many pre-school groups and reception classes reflects the National Curriculum. This is a curriculum, outlined by the DfES, and it sets out the knowledge and skills that must be covered. It also outlines the level that children are expected to achieve by a particular age. The way in which material is delivered is left to the individual provider. Ofsted (the Office for Standards in Education) monitors whether providers have an appropriate curriculum.

Any pre-school provider that accepts nursery vouchers has to deliver the Foundation Stage Curriculum. This is the first stage of the National Curriculum and it focuses on the distinct needs of children aged from three years until the end of the reception year of primary school. It is a broad, balanced and purposeful curriculum, delivered through planned play activities to help ensure that all children have the opportunity to reach their full potential and experience the best possible start to their education. This approach has greatly influenced the work that is carried out in all education settings.

Key concept

early learning goals These identify six areas of learning that must be included in the curriculum designed by a provider: language and literacy; mathematics; knowledge and understanding of the world; physical development; creative development; and personal, social and emotional development. Personal, social and emotional development is, in effect, a core theme running through every activity. Many activities will cover more than one of these areas.

Think it over...

Many early years settings uses 'circle time' as an opportunity for children to talk about something they have done. Imagine a situation in which a nursery key worker asks a group of children to talk about what they did at the weekend. Which early learning goals would be covered by this activity?

Types of care and education provision

It has long been accepted that children need both care and education. 'Care' means providing for physical needs or comfort, and 'education' is defined as the process of imparting knowledge. Modern approaches to early years care and education are based on integrating these two areas – learning cannot take place if a child's physical needs are not met. Maslow's Hierarchy of Human Need (1970) can help us to understand why care and education have to be integrated to provide the most effective support for children. Maslow identified physical, intellectual, social and emotional needs when he developed his hierarchy. He suggested that each 'layer of need' has to be met before the next can be achieved. Therefore, physical needs such as feeling warm and well-fed need to be met before a child's emotional needs can be satisfied: a child will find it difficult to concentrate when feeling hungry. The higher up the pyramid you go, the more satisfaction is linked to social and intellectual rather than physical needs. The pyramid puts education or intellectual needs near the top.

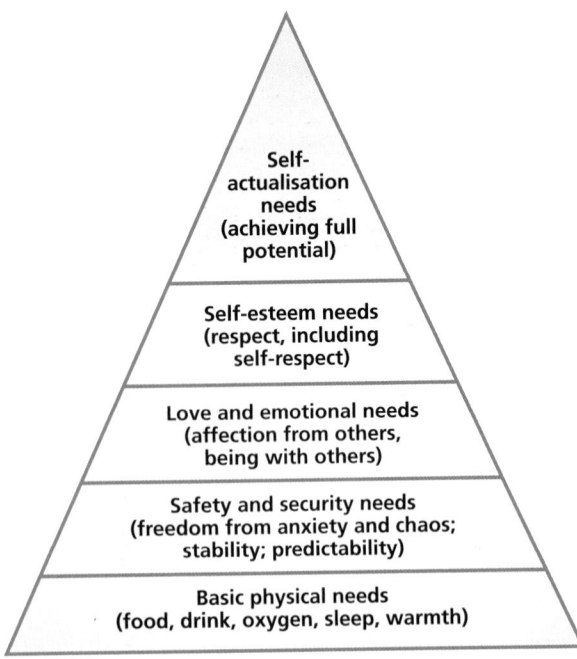

FIGURE 6.1 *Maslow's Hierarchy of Human Need*

Think it over...

With reference to Maslow's Hierachy of Human Need, think about the common needs in each classification for children. Why do you think children learn best when their physical or care needs are met?

Some of the first nursery schools that were founded at the beginning of the 20th century by early childcare theorists such as Maria Montessori (1869–1952), Rudolf Steiner (1861–1925) and, particularly, Margaret McMillian (1860–1931) worked on the principals of providing both care and education. These early theorists have had a great influence on the ethos of early years provision today. Figure 6.2 sets out some of the advantages and disadvantages of different early years provision.

✱ DID YOU KNOW?

Margaret McMillian (1860–1931)

McMillian was born in Britain in 1860. Initially, she designed her approach to the curriculum around toys that developed a child's fine and gross motor skills and manual dexterity. However, as her ideas developed, she saw the idea of children experiencing things for themselves or 'first hand' as increasingly important. Play became the way in which children applied what they knew and understood. Free play was seen as important.

Relationships and emotions were deemed to be as important as physical movement. Futhermore, McMillian created the first nursery school. She saw this very much as an extension to the home and placed great emphasis on working closely with parents. The outdoor environment was as important as the indoor, and McMillian recognised that children could learn a lot from the natural environment. She opened the first open-air nursery school in 1911.

Care and education, to McMillian's mind, went hand in hand. Critically she understood that children could not learn effectively if they were hungry, cold or ill. These needs had to be satisfied if learning was going to take place. Therefore, she promoted the provision of school meals and medical services to help ensure that all children could benefit from their education.

TYPE OF PROVISION	AGE RANGE	LENGTH OF PROVISION	STAFFING	WHAT IS IT?	ADVANTAGES	DISADVANTAGES
Childminders (private)	0–school age	Day care in carer's own home – hours to suit individual parents	A registered childminder must have a recognised early years qualification	Fee-paying care provision, often in the family's own home	Can build a relationship that will continue through the early years. Meets needs of working parents. Children are cared for in a home setting.	Parents have to take the child out of their home for care. Will not always provide the same play opportunities and stimulation that a nursery may provide
Private nursery/ pre-school care (private)	3 months – 5 years	Full day care	Supervisor/ manager must be trained to level 3 and 50% of staff must hold a childcare qualification	Fee-paying full day care provision or sessional provision. Some nurseries are open 52 weeks of the year; others operate term-time only	High child–staff ratios. Develops independence and social skills. Prepares the child for the routine of school. Children generally have a key worker who is their main carer and with whom they form a strong relationship	Expensive. Higher staff ratios can result in children finding it difficult to adapt to the lower ratios in schools. Some staff may not be qualified
Nannies (private)	0 +	Full-time care in the child's own home. Can be daytime only or both night and day	No stipulated qualifications but often a level 2 or 3 qualification in early years such as the Diploma in Childcare and Education is expected	Care in the child's own home that meets the needs of the parents. Often covers longer hours than those provided by a nursery	Child remains in his or her own home. More individual attention can be provided. One key carer for the child	Expensive. Parents may not be sure what the nanny is doing during the day

continued overleaf

FIGURE 6.2 *Early years provision: some advantages and disadvantages*

TYPE OF PROVISION	AGE RANGE	LENGTH OF PROVISION	STAFFING	WHAT IS IT?	ADVANTAGES	DISADVANTAGES
Local authority nursery school (statutory)	3.5–4.5 years	Often half days, term time only	Qualified teacher, plus nursery nurse	Often linked to primary/infant school. Limited availability often situated in priority areas. Ratios of 1 qualified teacher to up to 25	Good preparation for school. Develops independence. Encourages social skills. Activities provided are planned carefully to develop the skills of the child	Does not fit the needs of working parents. Low staff/child ratio
Local authority day nursery (statutory)	3 months – 5 years	Full day care	Qualified staff	Run by social services. Open for the working day, most days of the year. Parents may pay fees on a sliding scale	Meets needs of the working parent. It is often linked to a local authority workplace	Few of these nurseries exist
Family centres	0 +	Sessional support	Qualified staff including social workers and early years workers	Usually run by local authority social services departments, or by voluntary organisations such as NCH Action for Children. Aims to teach parenting and relationship skills to families experiencing difficulties	Family centres help support families to improve their parenting skills so that children have a better start in life	Not all areas have family centres. Parents may feel there is a stigma attached to attending a centre

continued overleaf

FIGURE 6.2 Early years provision: some advantages and disadvantages

TYPE OF PROVISION	AGE RANGE	LENGTH OF PROVISION	STAFFING	WHAT IS IT?	ADVANTAGES	DISADVANTAGES
Playgroups (voluntary and privately run)	2.5–4 years	Sessional care	Supervisor and deputy must be trained	Often run by committee. Do not have large budgets and often rely on fundraising. Lower fees than nursery	Valuable in the development of social skills. Develops links within a neighbourhood between the parents/carers of young children	May rely on untrained staff/parent help to meet ratio requirements. Often in premises that were not built to meet the needs of children. Mainly sessions – do not meet the needs of working parents
Parent and toddler groups (voluntary)	0 +	Sessional	Supervisor must be trained	Often run by committee. Parent remains for the session so it is an opportunity for parents to socialise with other parents. Do not have large budgets and often rely on fundraising	Good opportunity for young children to socialise with others before they move on to playgroup or nursery	Children can get used to parents being present and so find separation harder once they start pre-school
Crèches (private or voluntary)	0 +	Sessional	More popular in recent years in shopping centres and other places where care is needed for short periods of time	Short-term care which frees the parent to carry out certain tasks such as shopping	Located in appropriate areas	Child does not know the carer and relationship is difficult to build. Because the care provided is usually under 2 hours, the provision does not come under the regulations of the Children Act

continued overleaf

FIGURE 6.2 *Early years provision: some advantages and disadvantages*

TYPE OF PROVISION	AGE RANGE	LENGTH OF PROVISION	STAFFING	WHAT IS IT?	ADVANTAGES	DISADVANTAGES
Babysitters (informal)	0 +	As required by parents	Usually unqualified	Informal care of children often for short periods of time	Relatively cheap form of childcare which many parents rely on when going out	Inexperienced babysitters may not know what to do in an emergency
Reception classes (formal)	4–5 years	School day	Qualified teacher with teaching assistants	First stage of formal schooling. Children may start with a morning or afternoon session, depending on their birthday, and build up to a full day	Prepares children for the rigours of compulsory education	Additonal childcare may be needed after the end of the school day
Holiday play schemes (private or voluntary)	5–15 years	All day	Qualified staff	Organised provision for children during their holidays	Parents who work full time do not get school holidays and holiday clubs meets this need	
After-school provision (private)	5–15 years	Sessions 8.00-9.00 am and 3.00–6.00 pm	Qualified staff – play workers who are specifically trained for working with 5–15 year olds	Provides care for school-age children at the beginning and end of the day to enable parents to work. Fees are charged although there may be some subsidy through the National Childcare strategy	Provides regular care at each end of the school day. Generally reasonably priced. Children are often taken to and collected from school. Can include a homework club	After a day at school, many children prefer to go back to their own home

FIGURE 6.2 Early years provision: some advantages and disadvantages

Most services now aim to integrate these two important aspects of a child's development.

Care and education provision generally falls into four different categories. These are outlined below.

Private services

These are childcare services that are run for profit. The owner of the provision will see the service of whose as a business opportunity whose main aim will be to make money from the service provided. Many nurseries are privately owned. This category also includes private schools, many of which will have a pre-school section. Childminders also provide a private service. They are self-employed and work from home.

Statutory services

These are services that are required by law and are organised and run by local authorities. State-run nurseries are examples of statutory provision. These are usually attached to primary schools and provide term-time nursery classes for the year before the child reaches the age for entry to reception. Another example of a statutory service for children is family centres. These are often run by social services and provide support for children and their families.

Voluntary groups

These services are run by non-profit-making organisations and often provide services where the organisation believes that statutory and private provision are not meeting the needs in an area. Voluntary services are usually funded by grants, fundraising from the public and contributions from individuals. Voluntary services may be staffed by volunteers or may employ paid staff. An example of a voluntary service would be a church-run parent and toddler group.

Informal groups

Informal arrangements for childcare are common place. These are not covered by any statutory legislation. Many working parents cannot afford organised childcare and look for other solutions such as using friends or relatives to care for their children. This is often the case with after-school care when organised groups are not available in the area. This type of care also includes babysitting, which may be carried out by teenagers as a way of earning pocket money. This provision is unregulated.

Summary

Care and education provision can be summarised as:

* National policies
    - The Children Act (1989 & 2004)
    - The National Childcare Strategy
    - The early years curriculum

* Types of care
    - Private services, e.g. childminders, nurseries
    - Statutor services, e.g. state-run nurseries (usually attached to primary schools)
    - Voluntary groups, e.g. church-run toddler groups
    - Informal groups, e.g. after-school care by relatives

Consider this

Jane, a young mother, is about to return to full-time work. Her job requires her to be at work from 8.30 am until 5.30 pm. She has two children, Abigail, aged 4, and George, aged 6. Abigail is just about to start reception class but in the mornings only. The school allows children in at 8.45 am and finishes at 3.00 pm.

1. What factors would Jane need to consider when choosing childcare?

2. What choices are open to Jane for each of the children?

3. What are the advantages and disadvantages of each type of care?

4. What form of care would you recommend for Jane and why?

Section 2: Job roles and responsibilities within early years care and education

There is a wide range of jobs available in care and education settings, far too many to give full details of each one here. However, we will look at the main roles in early years care and education, including the responsibilities and day-to-day tasks each of these roles cover. For many of the roles in early years, there is a set of generic qualities that make a good early years worker. Obviously, you must enjoy working with children and want to work with them. Early years workers also need to be caring – this is a hard quality to

Think it over...

Devise a web diagram to show what you consider to be the main characteristics of a good early years worker. Share your ideas.

quantify, as it is something that is difficult to measure objectively. However, it is probably noticeable when an early years worker does not have that quality.

Main qualities of early years workers

The spidergram below shows the qualities needed by an early years worker. Figure 6.4 explains each of these in more detail.

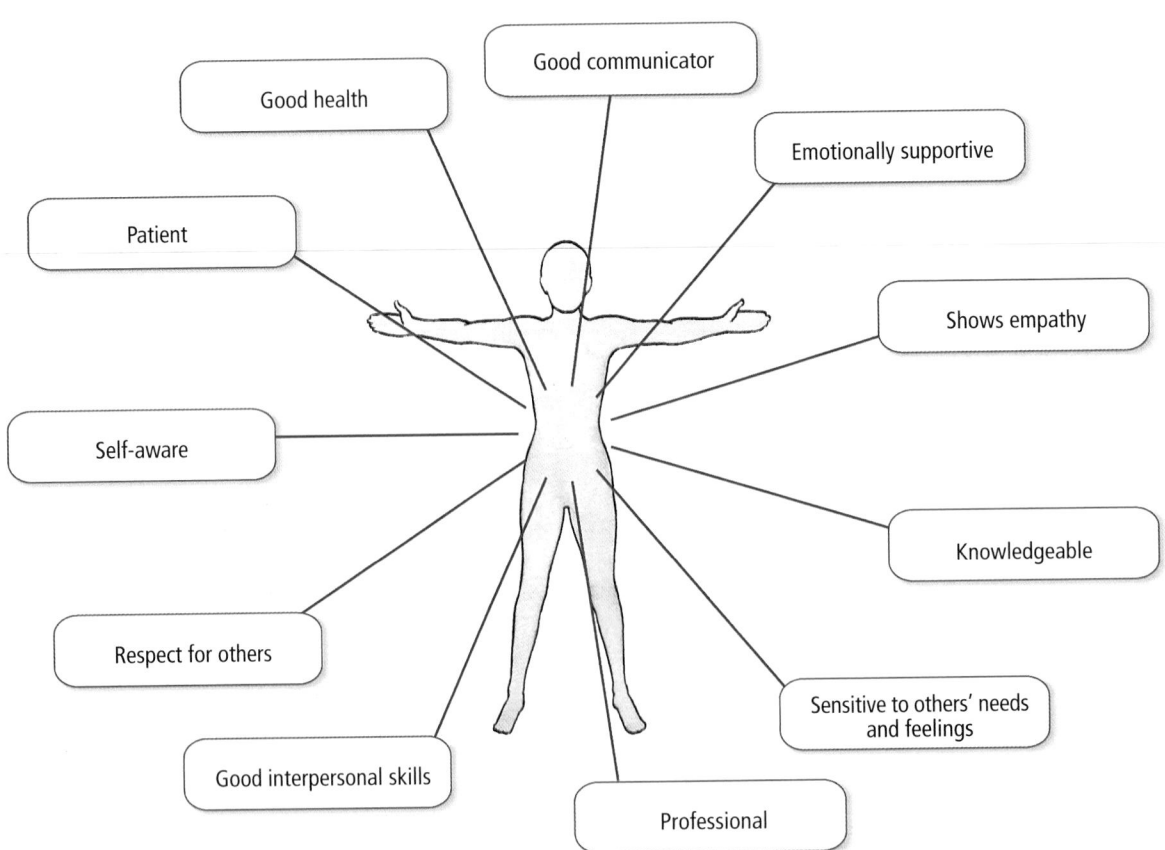

FIGURE 6.3 *The qualitites an early years worker needs*

CHARACTERISTIC	IMPORTANCE
Good communicator	Being a good communicator means being able to appreciate both verbal and non-verbal communication. The ability to listen to children and what they say and to react to their needs is an important skill. And being able to read their body language – as facial expressions, gestures and what is not said – is often as important
Patient	Working with children requires tolerance – different people deal with things in different ways and sometimes early years workers have to respect that fact, even if they would do things differently themselves
Helping young children to play	A good early years worker supports and encourages children in their play and to play themselves. ensures that children get the most out of their play experience. They do not join in with the play for their own gratification
Knowledgeable	The ability to support and develop children from one stage of their development to the next requires a detailed understanding of child development and how children learn. A good early years worker will develop these skills through formal education such as a BTEC National Diploma in Early Years, AVCE in Health and Social Care, CACHE Diploma or Certificate in Childcare and Education, NVQ in Early Years or other formal training. Some early years workers have built up skills and knowledge from working with children over a period of time; many of these are encouraged to obtain a formal qualification
Respect	Respect means being aware of children's personal rights, dignity and privacy. This should be shown in all aspects of an early years worker's work
Emotionally supportive	Children need emotional support. Often children feel anxious, particularly about new and unfamiliar situations. Sometimes children are distressed. A good childcare worker can provide the type of environment in which children feel safe and supported
Empathy	This means that an early years worker can appreciate a child's situation and offer meaningful support; this does not mean sympathy
Good interpersonal skills	An early years worker has to work with a range of different people, including parents, colleagues, other professionals and children. The skills of interpersonal interaction are likely to affect the quality of relationships with others. A wide range of abilities are needed, including verbal and non-verbal communication, listening skills and the ability to form and maintain relationships
Self-aware	An early years worker needs to be self-aware. Being self-aware means understanding how an individual's behaviour affects others around them. This helps them to become good team members
Good health	Working in early years is physically and mentally demanding. It can be a stressful situation to work in, as it is always busy and children will always make demands on your time. Therefore, being physically fit and having mechanisms for relaxation outside work are important in retaining a work–life balance
Professional	Professionalism is one of the most important characteristics an early years worker needs. It means being able to carry out the role effectively at all times. For example, early years workers should not bring personal difficulties into the workplace; they need to be able fully to support the children when in that role. Early years workers should also not allow their own personal views or opinions to affect the way they deal with different individuals – for example, they may not agree with a particular child-rearing technique that a parent may use but they need to be able to show respect for the choice made by the parent

FIGURE 6.4 *Main qualities of an early years worker*

Key roles and responsibilities available in care and education

Job roles can nominally be split between those that exist in the private, statutory and voluntary sectors; in practice, many roles can occur in each. For example, the role of a nursery nurse may exist in the private sector in a nursery, in the statutory sector in a hospital or school setting and in a playgroup run by a voluntary organisation.

Nursery nurse

Nursery nurses work in a wide range of early years settings including local authority and private nurseries, crèches, hospital wards and with individual families. The work generally involves taking care of young children and meeting their social, emotional, intellectual and physical needs.

Most nursery nurses would be responsible for the routine care of the children they are responsible for. This would include feeding, washing, dressing and other personal hygiene tasks. The level of this responsability would obviously differ according to the position – a nursery nurse working in a family setting, for example, is likely to spend more time on these tasks than a nursery nurse in a school setting. Within a nursery, those nursery nurses who work with babies and young children will spend more time on personal care tasks than those working with the older age groups.

Another key task will be planning, supporting and supervising children's play. In many settings, a nursery nurse would be involved in helping with early reading and number work, as well as providing activities that focus on simple learning.

Nursery nurses often have to plan the routine of the children's day. They may also be required to carry out observations and assessments, which take account of children's progress and identify how the setting may support the children and move them onto the next stage of their development. These assessments may cover health and general physical development as well as learning. Such roles will involve producing written reports and liasing with other professionals as necessary.

Nursery nurses also need to be able to carry out basic first aid when necessary.

Qualifications needed

Many nursery nurses have a formal qualification at Level 2 or Level 3 such as a CACHE Certificate or Diploma in Childcare and Education; a BTEC National Certificate or Diploma in Early Years, an NVQ in Early Years Care and Education, or a qualification in health and social care such as an Advanced Vocational Certificate or a Vocational AS/A level. Experience would also be gained from working in early years settings.

Pre-school leader

The term 'pre-school leader' covers a range of management roles in different settings, including nurseries, playgroups and crèches.

Managers or leaders carry the ultimate responsibility for the functioning of the organisation they are running. They have to establish the policies of the organisation, ensure they comply with any legal requirements and ensure that policies are carried out and are effective.

A leader is responsible for the safety and well-being of both children and staff in the setting. If anything goes wrong, they are answerable. They also have to manage the budget and may be responsible for fundraising to raise money to buy

FIGURE 6.5 *Pre-school leaders are responsible for the organisation they are running*

extra pieces of equipment. They also need to have an overview of the curriculum and ensure that the activities provided meet the needs of the children concerned, as well as covering external requirements such as the Foundation Stage where appropriate.

The manager is often the main contact for parents and has an important role in communicating information to both existing and prospective parents. This may include producing newsletters as well as producing marketing material for the group. Many groups also have parents' meetings, which the manager will often arrange.

There is a lot of paperwork involved. Managers will need to ensure effective records are kept on the children in their care, and this will include written records of assessments. They will also need to ensure they keep all other records on necessary records, such as accidents reports and other safety issues. Financial records will also need to be kept. This will include records of income and expenditure. A manager may have to issue bills to parents as well as writing bids for external grants. One of the most important aspects of paperwork is the registration with Ofsted and ensuring this is up to date.

In larger settings, there will be a number of staff, and this may involve levels of seniority. It will also mean that some tasks are delegated from the leader to other staff to carry out. This may include being responsible for a particular age group and producing the curriculum and routines for that group. The role of the leader in this situation would be to monitor the work that is carried out and ensure it meets the standard required.

Whatever the size of the setting there will be a number of staff, and the leader/manager will have to hold team meetings. These are important, as the effectiveness of the team is directly reflected in the effectiveness of the organisation. Team meetings are opportunities for the leader to outline the aims of the organisation and to ensure the whole team is working towards common goals. It is also an opportunity for the manager to offer encouragement and support to the team. Good managers will seek the views and ideas of their team members so that all feel involved in the development of the organisation. Such 'group ownership' creates loyalty in a team.

Some groups are overseen by a committee – this is particularly the case for groups run by voluntary organisations. The chair of the committee will often act as the direct line manager for the group leader. A key role for the leader/manager will be to liaise with the committee and ensure they are kept informed of what is happening in the group. This often occurs both informally through frequent conversations and formally via a regular written report produced by the manager for the committee.

Qualifications required

Leaders or managers of early years groups need to have a relevant qualification at Level 3 or above. This may include an NVQ 3 in Early Years Care and Education, a BTEC National Diploma in Early Years or a CACHE Diploma in Childcare and Education. Many managers have also gained management qualifications as well. All managers will have had significant experience working in the early years field.

Childminder

Childminding is one of the most widely used forms of full-time childcare for working parents. A childminder will often start out as a parent with young children who wants to work but not outside the home. Many continue to provide the service after their own children have grown up, as they are dedicated to looking after young children.

Childminders offer a flexible service, which can fit around the hours that working parents want. Some offer part-time care to more than one set of children to fit around part-time working. Many also offer an after-school collection service as well, so there can be continuity once a child starts school.

A childminder usually cares for no more than three children under the age of five and therefore children get a lot of individual attention. Childminders work from their own homes, and the atmosphere is usually more relaxed and less structured than in, say, a nursery. Daily household tasks such as washing or shopping may be performed as part of the normal day. Many childminders will encourage their children to mix with others by attending parent and toddler groups or playgroups with them. They will also offer play activities to engage the children.

Anyone who is paid to look after children for more than two hours per day is classed as a childminder and must conform to regulations. The childminder has to go through a registration process, which includes their home being visited; adaptations to the home may be necessary to make it safe for children. Childminders also have to take out insurance to cover their business, and have to keep records and registers. Parents usually visit a prospective childminder several times before choosing one, as they need to ensure the childminder has childrearing practices and a lifestyle that will reflect theirs.

Childminders usually live near the child's home and therefore long journeys are avoided. There needs to be very good communication between the childminder and the parents.

Qualifications required

Childminders have a wide range of educational backgrounds; however, before registering they should all attend an introductory course provided by the local authority through the Early Years Development and Childcare Partnership. This also allows them to access a small grant for start-up costs. Many childminders also follow an NVQ in Early Years at Level 2 or 3. A number of childminders will have followed other early years courses such as CACHE or BTEC.

Reception class teacher

Reception is the name given to the first year of compulsory schooling. Children in the reception class are aged 4–5 years. In a state school a reception class will have up to 30 children.

A reception class teacher is responsible for planning learning for all 30 children, taking into account their various individual needs and difficulties. The teacher has to assess the academic abilities of each child and then devise a curriculum that develops each child's knowledge and understanding. They have to plan activities that will extend and challenge children while

meeting their ability range. They have to design the timetable for each day, making sure that all aspects of the foundation curriculum are covered across the week.

The teacher controls discipline in the classroom. Many schools have a discipline policy, and it is the teacher's role to carry this out in their classroom. Good discipline is important in establishing an environment where learning can take place. A child who displays poor behaviour is disruptive to other children and can affect their work.

FIGURE 6.6 *Children in reception classes are aged 4–5 years*

A teaching role also involves a lot of paperwork. Teachers have to keep comprehensive records of their teaching as well as records on assessment. Records are kept on each child, assessing how they progress through their first year at school.

The reception teacher is also responsible for setting up an inviting, interesting, motivating classroom, which means teachers often have to be at work early to allow themselves to organise the classroom before the children arrive. Reception teachers are very creative and have to do practical/hands-on work as part of the job.

The teacher also has to deal with a broad range of issues connected to the area in which the school is situated. For example, in an inner-city school, it is possible that large numbers of children may not have English as their first language. Other social factors can also affect a child's ability to perform at school, such as quality of housing and family circumstances. These demands are challenging and time-consuming, sometimes frustrating, but most teachers find such challenges very rewarding.

Another important aspect of the teacher's role is forming relationships with parents. The link between home and school is seen as very important. Parents need to understand the work of the school and to support their child. One of the main times when teachers meet parents is at parent consultation events. At these meetings, the teacher needs to have a detailed knowledge of each child and be able to talk about his or her achievements in a positive, confident manner. They also have to point out any concerns such as poor behaviour, lack of interest in the work, problems in relating to other children or concerns about ability level.

A reception teacher also has to work with other people. There is often a classroom assistant in the reception class who works under the direction of the teacher. The teacher needs to make sure that the classroom assistant is fully aware of the work the children are doing and how the teacher wants them to be supported.

A reception teacher will also work as a member of the broader team within the school and take on responsibilities that involve other aspects of school life such as playground duty or running a school club. They will also have to attend staff meetings and possibly take part in school assemblies.

Qualifications required

A reception teacher will need to have a teaching qualification and a degree. Most teachers take Level 3 qualifications such as A levels, BTEC National Diplomas or other vocational qualifications before going to university to study at degree level. In order to teach, you must also have English, science and maths at GCSE grade C or above.

There are different routes into reception teaching, including:

- a subject-based degree followed by a PGCE in primary education
- a Bachelor of Education degree with qualified teacher status (QTS)
- the Graduate Teacher Training Scheme, which

is a school-based scheme for individuals with a degree who wish to train 'on the job'.

A degree with PGCE or BEd with QTS takes four years. The first year in post is a probationary year and teachers are 'Newly Qualified Teachers'. They take part in a programme to induct them into the full-time teaching role, which includes extra advice and support form experienced teachers. A teacher has to pass this year in order to be confirmed as qualified.

Classroom assistant

Many schools have classroom assistants as part of the team. Classroom assistants work under the direction of the teacher and they are usually allocated to a particular year group. They may support the whole class or be allocated to a particular child, or may supervise a small group for a particular activity.

A classroom assistant's role is to support the teacher in the delivery of the curriculum. They need to be fully aware of the activities planned for each day and the outcome that the teacher wants from them. Therefore, good communication with the teacher is extremely important. Often the teacher will meet the classroom assistant before or after school to ensure that they are fully aware of the work planned. The classroom assistant will support children doing their work: it is important that they resist the temptation to do the work for them.

Classroom assistants are often required to perform tasks related to preparing for activities and clearing up afterwards. This may range from preparing templates for children to use to setting out practical activities or washing up paintbrushes. They may also be required to put up displays of the children's work around the classroom.

They will have to manage children's behaviour and conform with the discipline policy of the school, although in difficult situations they will call on the teacher for support. Classroom assistants need to be aware of other policies and procedures in the school as they will need to conform with these in their role.

Classroom assistants may be required to attend meetings as part of the school team.

Qualifications required

At present, you do not need any formal qualifications to be a classroom assistant. However, the role of classroom assistant is becoming 'professionalised', and the government recommends that classroom assistants have a recognised early years qualification to at least Level 2 or equivalent, i.e. an NVQ 2 in Early Years Care and Education, a CACHE Certificate in Early Years Care and Education or a vocational GCSE. New qualifications are being developed such as an NVQ in Teaching Assistant and Higher Level Teaching Assistant's qualifications. This is in recognition of the new career structure that is being developed for teaching assistants. Teaching assistants will need to be qualified to at least Level 3 such as the A level Health and Social Care, NVQ 3 in Early Years Care and Education or BTEC National Diploma in Early Years plus a teaching assistant qualification.

Irrespective of the level of qualification, it is important that classroom assistants are literate and numerate, as they support children in these areas. Also, increasingly, they need to be IT literate, as many children are very familiar with IT and use it both in the classroom and at home.

Some classroom assistants are parents, especially mothers, who find the role fits in with school-age children. However, many are people who have chosen the role as a career.

Care assistant (children)

Care assistants who work with children may work in residential homes for children, or in a residential school where the care assistant works with the children outside of the school day and at weekends.

The role of a care assistant is to assist children with various everyday tasks such as getting up, washing and dressing. They may also be involved in providing food for children if there is no central food provision. The tasks will vary according to the needs of the children they are working with.

Some care assistants in the statutory sector work with children with special needs who may require more personal support with activities such as washing, bathing and using the toilet. They may also undertake domestic duties such as washing up, making beds, washing and ironing clothes, preparing meals, cooking and shopping. In some situations, they may support the children in learning new skills such as budgeting, cooking and shopping. They may also be required to provide social activities for the children they work with, as well as providing them with friendly support and being available to listen to them when necessary.

FIGURE 6.7 *The role of the care assistant involves assisting children with everyday tasks*

Often a care assistant will act as a 'key worker' for a number of children. This means they are the children's main carer, and they get to know them and their needs well. Care assistants often work shifts and may be required to work weekends, some may be required to live in.

Qualifications required

Care assistants who work with children are not required to have any formal qualifications, but increasingly employers are looking for staff who have relevant qualifications, such as a Level 2 in a care or early years-related area. Examples may include a Certificate in Childcare; a vocational GCSE in Health and Social Care or an NVQ 2 in Care or Early Years Care and Education. Many employers encourage unqualified staff to gain appropriate qualifications on the job, such as NVQs. Care assistants may also have Level 3 qualifications or higher.

Activities leader

Activities leaders may work in a range of settings such as an after-school club, weekend or evening activity clubs or holiday play schemes. Their role is to lead children in a wide range of both indoor and outdoor activities. They will need to have a good understanding of health and safety as well as a high level of knowledge of activities that will stimulate the interest of different aged children. They will also need to have a clear understanding of equal opportunities issues.

Activities leaders will have the responsibility for the group of children in their care, making sure that the activities provided suit their needs and that they are carried out in a safe manner. They will need to have some understanding of how to manage children's behaviour as this will be part of the role, not only in terms of maintaining discipline, but also in dealing with outbursts or aggressive behaviour. This will be particularly important if competitive activities are planned, as children can become angry and upset if they are not winning.

Qualifications required

Activity leaders may have qualifications from a range of different disciplines including early years, health and social care, sports science or leisure and tourism. These will generally be to at least Level 2. Some have a Community Sports Leader Award (CSLA) or Higher Sports Leader Award (HSLA) from the British Sports Council, which specifically teach the skills that needed to run sporting activities with young people – both disabled and able-bodied.

Babysitter

Babysitters offer an informal type of childcare. Traditionally, babysitters have been used by parents looking for short-term childcare, often for an evening out. Babysitters may be teenagers who carry out the role as a means of earning some pocket money.

Babysitters are usually left in sole charge of the children in their care. The role will vary according to the age of the children being cared for, and can therefore include all aspects of care, including feeding, personal care, entertaining children with activities such as games or reading to them and putting them to bed.

Parents usually leave a contact number so they can be reached if the babysitter is concerned about anything.

Some parents operate a babysitting circle where a group of parents get together and babysit for each other. Each time they babysit they are entitled to a babysitting session back. No money changes hands in this arrangement.

Qualifications required

Babysitters do not need to have any formal qualifications but they must be at least 13 years of age to be left in charge of young children. Parents look for mature, sensible young people to carry out this role. They need to be able to form relationships with young children and be confident in looking after them on their own. They may be young people they know or have been recommended to them – perhaps older sons or daughters of friends.

Consider this

You are looking for a holiday position working with young children while you finish your course. An opportunity is advertised for a holiday play scheme with 8 to 11 year olds. You decide to apply.

1. What sort of activities do you think might be covered in a holiday play scheme?
2. How would you present yourself for interview?
3. What skills and experience do you think the play-scheme manager will be looking for?
4. What skills and qualities would you bring to the role?
5. How could you make yourself stand out from the other candidates?

Section 3: Values and principles of the early years sector

Most professions have codes of practice, codes of conduct or value statements which underpin the way that professionals conduct themselves. They outline the way professionals are expected to behave when carrying out their roles and responsibilities.

Values are the viewpoints that form the foundation of the professional practice, and are a mix of knowledge and skills. They embrace areas of the profession that workers need to have knowledge of, but also link to skills, as they have a practical application in the decisions that are made by professionals. In early years work, these values and principles are important, as they underpin the way in which individuals working with children should operate. By working within these values, professionals enable children to develop and reach their full potential.

An individual's values and attitudes are shown through their behaviour, including verbal and non-verbal communication. It can be difficult to change values and attitudes, as many of these are acquired from an early age and influenced by family, friends and social situations.

> ### Think it over...
>
> Make a list of your own personal values. Think about how these values were acquired.
>
> Discuss the types of values you would want to underpin work with children.
>
> Early years care and education settings all work to a similar set of values. They focus on ensuring that they meet the intellectual, emotional, social and physical needs of the child and, in so doing, give all children the opportunity to reach their potential. The intention of the value base is to foster equality for all children. See Figure 6.8 for an outline of early years values.

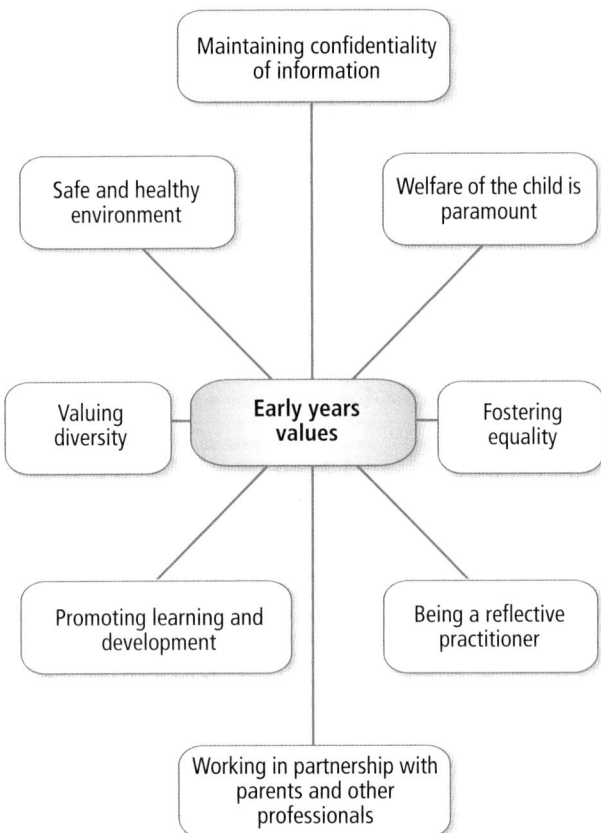

FIGURE 6.8 *Early years values*

Welfare of the child

In any early years setting the welfare of the child is central to the work being carried out. With every decision that is made, there should be consideration about how it will affect the child and whether it is in their best interests. The needs and rights of the child are paramount, and an early years worker must aim to meet these needs within the boundaries of their role.

Safe and healthy environment

It is important to provide a stimulating environment for young children. The environment should be well maintained and attractive. Children value seeing their own work on the walls, and this helps to develop their self-esteem.

It is important to provide a range of different areas within the environment for different types of activities such as wet play, quiet reading and a home corner for pretend play. If food is provided, a food-preparation area will be needed and should be kept extremely clean.

It is important that the care environment is as safe as possible. Children are vulnerable to accidents because they have little awareness of danger and are unable to control their environment. Children are naturally inquisitive and therefore explore the environment around them. An early years worker needs to be able to assess the area for any danger and minimise this risk. Accidents are the most common cause of death in children aged between 1 and 14 years.

As children get older, they begin to remember that certain actions will result in certain consequences – for example, cutting themselves with scissors hurts – and therefore they develop an element of self-protection.

Risk assessment is important. It is a straightforward process in which the early years worker assesses an area for potential risks to children in their care and makes adjustments to minimise that risk. Risk assessments are written down so that they can be seen and acted upon by others.

It is important that early years workers take safety seriously, as parents leave their children in their care 'in loco parentis'. They would expect early years workers to provide the same level of care as they would for their own children.

Working in partnership with parents and families

The relationship between parents and the care setting is seen as extremely important. The parent is the main carer of the child and therefore knows the child best. Early years settings should respect this knowledge and ensure that the partnership is effective. In the 1960s and 1970s, there was a tendency for parents to be kept 'at the school gates' and not welcomed into the learning environment.

However, nowadays there is a lot of emphasis on the importance of settings working with parents to support their child's learning. It has been shown that where parents and adults in the care and

FIGURE 6.9 *The days of parents being kept 'at the school gates' are in the past*

education setting work together, there are measurable and long-lasting positive effects on achievement; partnerships should therefore be developed as fully as possible. Whatever stage of education children are at, their experiences at home and the support they receive have a significant effect on their learning and achievements. Where possible, activities that take place in the setting, such as reading, should be continued and reinforced at home.

A positive relationship will ensure that information passes from the family to the staff and vice versa. A good setting will have a mechanism of regularly informing parents of all aspects of their child's progress. This can cover both physical and intellectual development. Many nurseries provide a daily record of food eaten, activities undertaken and rest taken, particularly if children attend all day.

Effective and supportive relationships are developed in a range of ways. Staff need to appreciate that every family is different and they need to be able to respect the different needs and traditions that arise from that diversity. Good settings are aware of the important role of the parent in the child's education, and they develop an open relationship based on mutual respect. By the time a child enters any early years setting, the parents have already played a significant role in the child's education and will continue to do so.

Many settings work hard to find ways in which parents can be involved – perhaps by working as a volunteer or coming in to talk about their own job.

Many setting have 'events' which parents are invited to, such as sports days. Many offer regular opportunities for parents to visit the setting, such as open evenings, meetings to discuss the curriculum, social events and parents' evenings.

Children like to feel their parents are interested in what they are doing. A parent who spends time looking at a child's work or discussing their child's day with the early years worker will be more aware of what their child is doing. That interest will show the child that what they do in the early years setting is important, and they are more likely to strive to do well.

Providing appropriate opportunities for learning and development

All children go through different stages of development, and a key role of the early years setting is to provide opportunities for learning and development that meet the child's developmental stage but also help move them forward in their learning. The types of activities provided will reflect the stage of development, both in the way children play and in their level of understanding. The stages of play are linked to ages; however, it should be remembered that children develop at different paces and some may take longer to go through a particular stage. Also, some children may need greater adult support to move from one stage to another, and this will be reflected in the activities planned. Much will depend on the child's experience. A child from a large family may find it easy to play cooperatively with other children in a nursery situation, whereas an only child may find settling in more difficult. Figure 6.10 shows the main stages of play.

The stages are not necessarily separated (i.e. one ends and another begins): a child who is able to play with other children may also like to play alone at times. Early years workers need to remember that not all children develop at the same rate; they must know the children they are working with and plan accordingly.

Valuing diversity, equal opportunities and anti-discriminatory practice

All individuals are different. The Children Act 1989 clearly stated that the needs of all children must be met regardless of age, gender, race, religion or ability. One way in which this is tackled is through equal opportunities and anti-discriminatory policies. These exist in many childcare settings as the staff try to ensure all children are included. This affects the play provision and the way in which staff encourage children to join in.

Many childcare providers aim to put equal opportunities into action through an anti-discriminatory policy. This encourages staff to

TYPE	AGE (IN YEARS)	EXPLANATION
Solitary	0–2	Children play alone. There is little interaction with other children
Spectator	2–2.5	Children will watch other children playing around them but do not join in
Parallel	2.5–3	Children play alongside each other but do not play together
Associative	3–4	Children begin to interact and cooperate with others in their play. There are signs of their beginning to develop friendship groups and a preference for playing with certain children. Play is usually in mixed sex groups
Cooperative	4 years +	Children play together and have shared goals for their play. Children are supportive towards others in their play. Their play can be quite complicated and they can sustain play for a longer period of time. As they reach school age, play is usually in single-sex groups

FIGURE 6.10 *The main stages of play*

look at their own ideals and values and adjust them to ensure that all children have equal access to opportunities provided by the service.

There are certain groups in society who tend to experience discrimination. These include females, members of ethnic minorities, people with disabilities and people from disadvantaged backgrounds. Often these groups are shown in a negative manner in the media. This can affect self-esteem, and therefore it is important that toys, games, posters, books and other equipment in the child-care setting are carefully chosen to avoid reinforcing such negative stereotypes.

FIGURE 6.11 *An anti-bias curriculum provides a good base for equal opportunities*

The promotion of an anti-bias curriculum is one of the hardest tasks that an early years setting has to achieve, as it is difficult to do this in a meaningful way. Early years workers must look at each activity they offer in an objective way to make sure that it is non-discriminatory.

Stereotyping is another way in which children can be disadvantaged. It is easy for staff to stereotype a child without realising it. Stereotyping occurs when staff assume that a child may behave in a particular way because they live, for example on a certain estate, or because their brother or sister behaved in a specific way. Staff may then convey to the child that they expect them to behave in a particular way. In doing this, staff can encourage a `self-

fulfilling prophecy': children find it hard to shake of such assumptions and can begin to act as the staff expect. It is important for children to be accepted as they are.

Despite the Sex Discrimination Acts of 1975 and 1986, women and girls are still treated differently to men and boys on occasion. This can start from when children are first born.

> ### Think it over...
>
> What picture does the rhyme below conjure up for boys and girls?
>
> What are little girls made of?
> Sugar and spice and all things nice,
> That's what little girls are made of.
> What are little boys made of?
> Snakes and snails and puppy dogs' tails,
> Thats what little boys are made of.
>
> How might you counteract such stereotypes in early years settings?

Maintaining confidentiality

Confidentiality means keeping any information secret that is disclosed in confidence about children and their families as a result of a professional relationship. It means not talking about it to anyone unless it is necessary to do so professionally. It is based on trust – a professional is told something in confidence and is expected to keep that confidence. Confidentiality is a complex issue, as sometimes it is important to pass on information – for example, a child who you feel is being abused may disclose information to you that you will need to pass on to other professionals, such as social services or doctors. It may be appropriate to talk about the situation within the setting, but the key is not to talk about confidential matters in a social situation.

Working with others

Working in any early years setting is very much about working with others – with colleagues, with parents and with other agencies that may support the child in some way. Integration and 'joined-up thinking' of services for the benefit of the child are central themes in government policy. The aim is to make the best use of resources in an efficient way and, in doing so, provide better services for children.

Think it over...

Make a list of all the different agencies you think early years workers may interact with in their role. Make sure you cover statutory, private and voluntary services.

Most early years settings require people to work in a team. The team works together to make sure there is a consistent atmosphere for the children and that the policies of the setting are put into practice. These teams are often 'multidisciplinary', which means they are made up of a range of people who bring different skills. For example, in a nursery setting the team may consist of the manager, qualified staff, unqualified staff, volunteers, students, parent helpers, cleaner and maybe a cook. Good teams do not just happen – it takes a lot of work on behalf of the team members to work well as a team. Often people have to learn to work together as they are brought together for organisational purposes and not by choice. A successful team will have common aims and objectives, share the same goal, and have the ability to manage relationships as well as to complete the tasks allocated to them. They will have good interpersonal skills.

Most early years teams will also have to work with other professionals who support the work they do. This wider team will include all the external agencies they work with, such as social services, education and health professionals. This wider group may, for example, contribute to a case conference on a child if this is needed.

Being a reflective practitioner

Being a reflective practitioner is part of being a professional. It means thinking about the role you are in and the work you are doing and self-assessing how effective that work is. A professional early years worker regularly reflects on the work they are carrying out and evaluates whether there is a better way of doing it. For example, after carrying out an activity with a group of children, a reflective practitioner would think about the activity and weigh up what went well and what perhaps could be changed the next time they perform that particular activity. In doing this, they are constantly improving what they are doing. One of the interesting aspects of working in early years is that you are working with people, and no two people are the same. An activity may work with one child, may not with another, and an early years worker needs to reflect on this and make adaptations to meet differing needs.

Reflective practitioners will also look for new ways of doing things. They will want to keep up to date through professional development or training opportunities, which will also help keep the work they are doing fresh.

The field of education and training is constantly changing. New theories or ways of doing things may be developed, and there will be the need to respond to new government initiatives. A reflective practitioner will be able to incorporate all these demands into their role and evolve.

The ability to accept that there are different ways of doing things, which may be better, and a willingness to take on new ideas are part of professional development and are key to being an effective early years worker.

Think it over...

Think about a specific early years setting, other than a nursery. List the team that might exist in your chosen setting.

Think about teams you know which you feel work well together.

What makes a good team? How do the members of the team work together? What are their characteristics?

What might be the consequences for an early years team that does not work well together?

Summary

By working with common values and principles the professionals enable children in the early years setting reach their full potential. Common values include:

* Welfare of the child
* Safe and healthy environment
* Fostering equality
* Valuing diversity
* Promoting hearing and development
* Maintaining confidentiality of information
* Working in partnership with parents and other professionals.

Consider this

You work in a nursery setting and have been asked to mentor a student who is on placement with you. This involves making sure that she knows about the values and principles of the nursery.

1. The student asks you to explain why values and principles are important to the nursery. What might you tell her?

2. Make a list of the values you feel are particularly important for a nursery and which you would explain to the student.

3. Identify the different ways in which a nursery can show it is promoting equality and diversity.

4. A parent complains about the behaviour of someone else's child in the nursery. You discover that the student has been unprofessional and has disclosed information about the child's background to that parent in an attempt to explain why the child behaves in a particular manner. How would you handle this?

Section 4: The ways in which children learn and factors that affect performance

Learning and development by direct experience through play

Children learn through play, and play therefore affects all aspect of a child's development. It is through play that children learn and understand many things about the world around them. Professionals who work with children need to understand the value of play and how it helps children to learn.

Play is considered to be one of the primary needs of the child. Play is often called a `child's work'. It is a common behaviour of children in all countries and cultures. Children naturally want to play, although children also learn to play. Therefore, both nature and nurture contribute to the development of skills needed to play effectively.

Think it over...

What is the difference between 'nature' and 'nurture' in the context of child development?

Providing opportunities for play that engage children's interest and are appropriate for their level of development takes time and effort. The key to successful play in the early years is the adult, both in the home and professional situation.

Play is a learning experience. Some theorists believe that it allows children to practise the roles they will need to take on in adulthood. Susan Issacs (1885) saw play as an integral part of child's life and the way by which children come to understand the world in which they live.

Figure 6.12 outlines how play contributes to a child's development.

Learning and development through indirect methods

A child can learn through experiences that are not strictly classed as play; however, in many ways they are central to modern society. These include

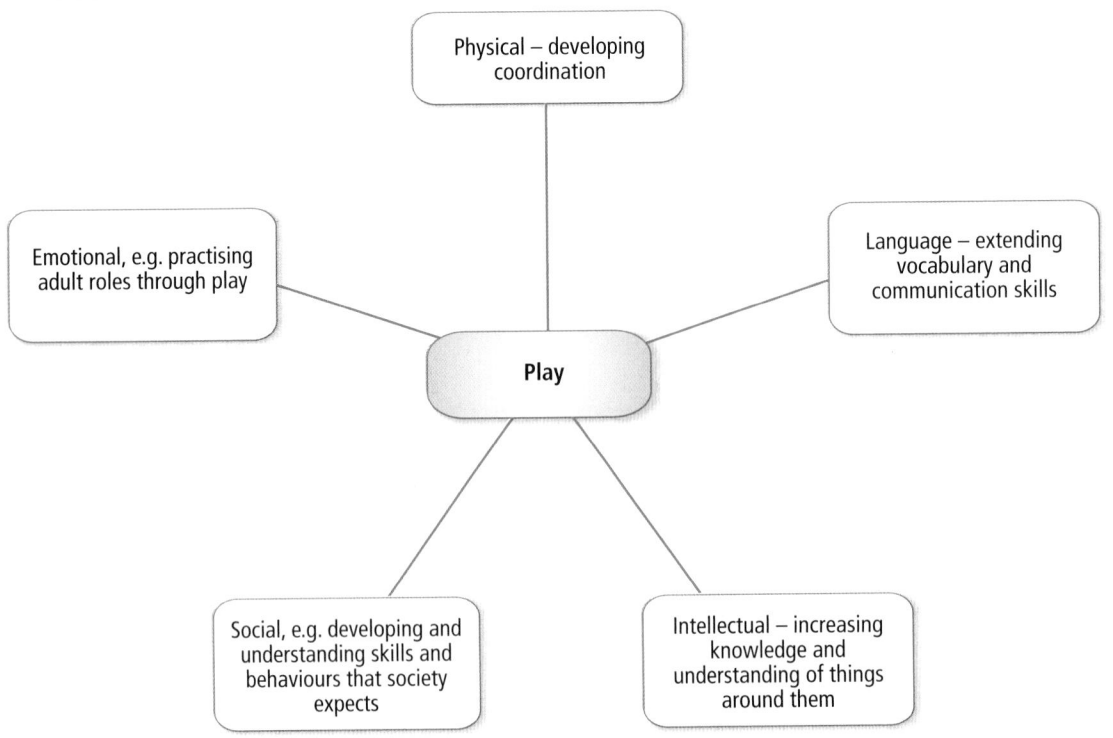

FIGURE 6.12 *The ways in which play contributes to a child's development*

learning from television and books, as well as learning that takes place when children are working with, and listening to, adults and other children.

Learning from adults

Adults have a key role in supporting children's learning. They do this in a range of ways, including supporting play, providing play activities and providing information about experiences that children have not yet had or things they need to know. The role of the adult in children's learning and play is one of finding the right balance between standing too far back and letting the children play alone and becoming too involved and taking control of the situation.

The adult has an important role in planning the environment and organising activities that will stimulate children's interests and promote learning. They need to make sure that both indoor and outdoor play areas are stimulating and that there are enough interesting materials and equipment for the children to play effectively. Materials and equipment should be presented in a manner that encourages children to explore them and discover their properties for themselves. This will encourage children to ask questions, and the adult then supports learning by clarifying ideas and correcting misunderstandings. Children learn through this direction and effective planning.

An adult may need to extend a child's play. If a child is unable to come up with his or her own ideas, the adult may offer ideas, which the child may take and develop further. In this situation,

FIGURE 6.13 *Adults can support children's learning through facilitating play*

the adult is **facilitating** the play, and through careful observation and listening to the play as it develops, is able to suggest ideas that make the activity more challenging.

An adult may also facilitate by helping children to remain in role or stay in their story in imaginative play. They may do this by providing props to help the pretend play, such as two pushchairs so that two children can play `Mummys'. They may offer ideas: for example, where children are playing `buses' by lining up chairs in a row, the adult may ask "Where is the bus taking you?" This may encourage the children to develop the activity, perhaps into a shopping trip.

Questions can be used to develop different skills. Figure 6.14 illustrates how questions can do this.

SKILL	QUESTION
Explaining	How are you going to use this?
Prediction	What do you think will happen if you put all those bricks in the bowl of water?
Recall	What did we see yesterday when we were digging the garden?
Recall a process	What did we need to do before we started cooking when we made biscuits?
Under-standing	How will you put together this train set?

FIGURE 6.14 *Using questions to develop skills*

Some children find it difficult to play. Adults may need to support children in their play and help them to join in any play activity that is going on. Shy children often need an adult with them in the initial stages of play until their confidence grows. Children may be encouraged to play alongside other children at first, rather than playing with them immediately, as a good way of moving into a group play situation. For example, an adult might encourage a child to play in the sandpit by asking them if they would like to make a sandcastle alongside another child. This may then develop into cooperative play.

Adults can provide information about experiences they have had or roles that they perform. Adults in well-known job roles such as police or fire crew may visit a nursery or school to talk about what they do. This helps children understand the world around them and the things that happen each day, and they may then incorporate these ideas into their play.

Adults may also need to pass on information that children need to know about but which is difficult to provide through direct experience such as 'stranger danger'.

FIGURE 6.15 *Adults can support children's learning through relating experiences and job roles*

Learning from books

Books are an important source of information. The ability to read and gain information from the written word is essential in modern society, as so much information is passed on in this way. Children's knowledge and creative thinking skills are developed through books. Children not only derive a lot of enjoyment from books, but they also contribute to emotional, intellectual,

language and social development. It is important that the early years setting introduces children to the joy of reading. This begins with adults sharing books with children, either by reading to children, or looking at picture books and talking about the images. This helps children to learn the structure of any written word – that pages go from front to back and that we read from left to right. It also helps them to understand that letters together make up words and helps to establish the building blocks of early writing.

Reading to children helps them to understand that reading is fun. Children should have plenty of opportunity to choose and share books. This may be on a one-to-one basis or in small groups. Children should be encouraged to handle books.

There is a wide range of books available for children that includes factual and fiction books on all sorts of subjects and most early years setting will have a book corner. A book can be the starting point for a theme or topic.

Think it over...

Make a list of the different categories of children's books. Think about how each may be used in an early years setting.

Books can be a way in which children can understand experiences they may not have had themselves. They can help them to understand things that may happen to them, such as the arrival of a new brother or sister.

Consider this

Choose a children's book that you particularly like and share it with your group. Explain why you like it and why you think it will appeal to children.

Learning from television

Television provides second-hand experiences, which means that it shows children different things although they do not experience those things for themselves. Television programmes can be educational, and children can acquire a lot of information from them; however, they cannot provide the same quality of learning as real-life experiences. Actual, first-hand or real-life experiences are richer and provide children with a wealth of information through which to develop their play.

For example, think of the seaside. Watching a seaside in the summer on the television does not provide the same experience as going to the beach, paddling in the sea, collecting shells and seeing the amusements. This first-hand experience gives children so much more to talk about, as well as providing the information they need to extend any ideas they use into all forms of play, including creative activities such as painting, or imaginative play such as role-playing going to the beach.

However, there is a place for television in the play routine. All children need quiet times in their day, and a period of quietly watching a suitable television programme or video can provide this. However, television should only be available for a limited amount of time, and there should also be active play to compliment it. If parents are paying for childcare, they would not expect their child to spend all day watching television.

Learning from other children

From an early age, children show interest in each other. One way in which they do this is by copying others. From as early as six months of age, babies will imitate other children – for example, doing hand-clapping or playing peek-a-boo; a one-year-old will try to walk or climb off a chair.

By the age of three or four years, children begin to become more influenced by other children and their actions. They will follow the lead of other children as well as sometimes taking the lead themselves. They learn to negotiate at their own level to satisfy their own needs and wants. Through other children they learn to be cooperative and positive and to care for others. Children can learn through arguments as well as situations that run smoothly.

The peer group becomes increasingly important as the child gets older. Children's desire to be accepted will influence their behaviour.

Think it over...

Make a list of the ways in which peer-group pressure might influence a child.

Children can also learn from each other about intellectual concepts. When children of different abilities work or play alongside each other this can result in shared learning, with one child beginning to understand a concept or idea that he or she had not previously quite grasped. Children watch each other when they are playing and often try to copy what they have seen.

Through chat and discussion, children will also learn about a range of social experiences from each other. All children have different life experiences, and these may offer learning opportunities. One example of this is 'circle time', where children are often encouraged to talk about an experience with the group. The teacher may then take this discussion and develop it into a learning experience.

FIGURE 6.16 *Children learn by watching and copying each other*

Factors that can affect learning and development

A child's ability to learn is influenced by a number of different external factors, which are often outside their control. From an early stage, these factors can have a significant effect on the child's life chances.

Social factors

The family unit is a small mirror image of the wider society. Through the family unit, children are introduced to the norms and values of the society in which they live. Children will initially believe that the way in which things are done in their own family is the way all families operate: the influence of the home on a child's development is huge and has long-lasting effects. The home determines the language that is learnt and the way language is used to express oneself. Bernstein (a researcher into language development) referred to two language codes – the elaborate and restricted codes. Children who could use the elaborate code were able to communicate more effectively in wider society and therefore make progress, whereas children who could only operate the restricted code could not progress, as they could not make themselves easily understood.

Equally, the family sets the norms for the type of language that is acceptable; therefore, if a child is brought up in a family in which swearing is the norm, the child will believe that this is the correct way to talk – until they meet other children, This will affect the perception of the child. Children find it hard to make changes which are against the norms of their family life.

The number of children in a family may also affect the child's experience. Children with older brothers or sisters may achieve things earlier as they copy their siblings. Their language skills may be more advanced for their age as they learn from the language used by their brothers and sisters. Equally, however, older children may speak for younger ones, and the latter may be less confident with their speech. In a large family, it may be expected that the older children 'look after' the younger children and provide activities for them.

The family will also influence attitudes to education. Some families value a good education and recognise it as a key to social success and economic stability in adult life. Such families would encourage learning as a positive experience and build this into the toys and games they provide for their children. They are also more likely to use early years provision as an opportunity for extending the child's learning and social skills; they would see this as an important preparation for school. Children from this background will have a stronger start at school. They are likely to be supported through their education as their parents show an interest in what they are doing.

Some families feel education is a waste of time. Research has shown that in some families where the parents have never worked education is not valued. Children from these backgrounds are less likely to attend pre-school education and, as a consequence, find themselves ill-prepared for the demands of school. This lack of grounding is difficult to catch up on. In areas with high levels of poverty, funding has been provided thorough schemes such as 'Education Action Zones' or 'Excellence Clusters' to provide additional support for children and help them to overcome these early barriers.

> **✳ DID YOU KNOW?**
>
> Education Action Zones were set up in areas of significant deprivation with the aim of giving additional support to both children in schools and in the family setting to raise aspirations and educational success. They are now known as 'Excellence Clusters'.

Environmental factors

The surroundings in which children live can affect their behaviour and the opportunities available to them. A child living in an urban area will have very different opportunities to a child living in a rural area. Families that live in urban areas, for example, are likely to have more access to early years care settings and have plenty of different learning opportunities for children, such as museums, playgrounds and other areas of interest. They are likely to have a better transport network, so parents can get children to their activities easily. Rural areas are often lacking in locally based activities and parents may need a car to be able to drive to the nearest playgroup/nursery. Often rural early years settings are based in local halls that are used by the community for a variety of purposes. These settings generally have to be arranged and taken down each day, and may therefore have different resources from those in a full-time, purpose-built nursery setting.

Think it over...

Investigate your area and the activities available for children. Compare your findings with a different area.

Urban areas, often have significant pockets of poverty. Living in an inner-city area can affect health, as many are now congested and polluted from vehicle exhausts and bi-products of industry. Many inner-city areas have poor housing conditions which also influence health. For example, children living in high-rise flats do not have access to a garden, limiting the opportunity to play outside.

FIGURE 6.7 *Living in a high-rise flat may limit the opportunities to play outside*

Statistics show that there are more one-parent families living in inner-city areas, and that these can have limited access to family support networks. People often feel socially isolated, even though they are living in an area of high population, as neighbourhoods in today's society

do not alway had used to. for interactio

The gover issues are ha and their life in significant SureStart sch access to goc

would not see this as ess
The wants and nee
influenced by the n
considered to be
would be ver
families in
struggli

DID YOU

Sure Start

Sure Start is the name given to a government programme that aims to achieve better outcomes for parents, children and communities by increasing the availability of childcare for all children; improving the health and emotional development of young children; and supporting parents to achieve their aims for employment. The programme focuses specifically on disadvantaged areas and provides financial support to help parents to afford childcare.

Economic factors

Family income has a significant effect on the opportunities a child may have. It will influence the area in which a child lives, the quality of the food they eat, the toys they have access to in the home and the learning opportunities they experience outside the home. A family with a high disposable income – that is, the income they have left to spend after the essentials of housing, utilities and food are paid for – will affect factors such as outings, holidays and membership of clubs. Most activities cost money, and therefore, giving children wider experiences such as swimming lessons, dancing or even attending cubs or brownies involves extra cost.

Parents need to make decisions about wants and needs. There are certain things that can be classed as needs and therefore have to be paid for, such as heating, food and housing. There is other expenditure that could be classed as wants – such as social activities, designer clothing, and money for alcohol or cigarettes. However, individuals will classify different things as needs – some individuals who smoke may feel that having money to buy cigarettes is a need, whereas others

...ntial expenditure. ...ds of any society are ...orms of that society; items ...essential by families in the West ...y different to those selected by ...third-world countries who are ...ng to survive.

Think it over...

Make a list of your own 'needs' and 'wants'. Compare your list with others. How many of your needs and wants are essential to survival, and how many are linked to a lifestyle choice?

Types of learning strategies

There has been a lot of research in recent years into learning styles and how children learn best. It is accepted that there are several different learning styles, and children may have a preference for one or for a mix of styles. The styles are visual, auditory or experiential/practical.

Experiential/practical

Practical or experiential learners learn best by doing. Carrying something out for themselves and seeing the results, by conducting an experiment or working out a maths problem, makes things easier to understand. Another way in which practical learners learn is by writing things out for themselves, in their own words.

Auditory learners

Auditory learners learn particularly well when someone explains concepts and ideas to them. They learn by talking about a new idea and then explaining it in their own words. Discussion is also an effective learning method for this type of learner. Being able to talk things through enables the auditory learner to verbalise the ideas to themselves and so develop understanding. This type of learner finds listening to information on tape far more effective than reading the written word. Reading information aloud is also an effective learning method, as is the use of questions and answers as a technique for consolidating learning.

Visual learners

Visual learners learn best by seeing information in print either in pictorial format or as the written word. The written word helps them to remember things better. Colour, diagrams and illustrations also help the learning process. Highlighting key words is a technique that promotes learning.

Consider this

Find out about your preferred learning style and how this can help you learn.

Summary

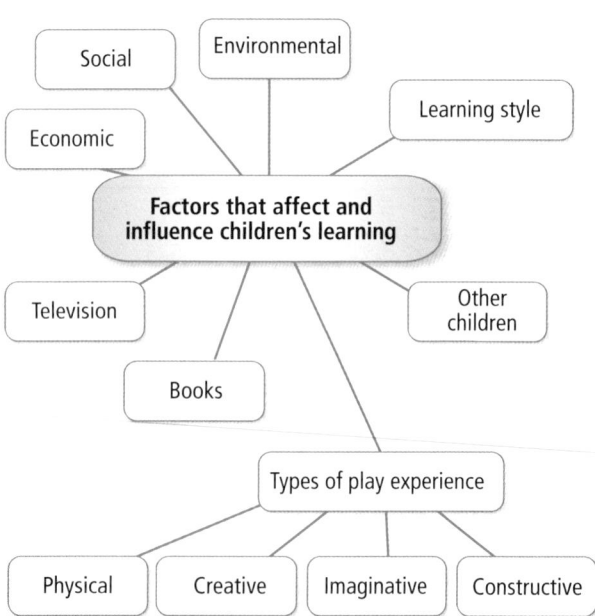

FIGURE 6.18 *Summary of factors affecting children's learning*

Consider this

Review a television programme and a book that have been designed for children.

1. Outline what the book and the programme are about.
2. Identify the ways in which you feel each one develops children's learning.
3. Explain how an adult could help to extend the learning experience.
4. Discuss the importance of the different ways in which children learn and how these can be included in early years settings.

Section 5: Planning activities

FIGURE 6.19 *It's important to plan for activities*

Plans for activities are also known as 'detailed plans'. Essentially, they set out exactly what the activity is, why it is being carried out and how it will be done. They also identify what materials or resources are needed and outline the stages the activity will go through. This helps to ensure that all aspects of an activity are thoroughly thought through before it is carried out; it helps to ensure that the activity goes smoothly. Plans are useful tools for others who may be involved in the activity to enable them to understand what is intended – this may include other staff in a setting, or volunteers. Settings may keep a file of activities so that ideas produced by a member of staff may be used again in the future.

Plans for activities should set out how different activities meet the developmental needs of children. Figure 6.20 outlines different types of activity and their developmental potential.

ACTIVITY	HOW IT HELPS A CHILD TO LEARN
Imaginative or pretend play, e.g. playing 'mums and dads' or 'schools'	Imaginative or pretend play develops self-expression as well as giving children the opportunity to explore experiences they have had. It helps children to come to terms with different aspects of their lives. Children also solve problems through imaginative play as they act out things that have happened or could happen. Imaginative play helps children to see things from others' point of view. It develops social skills, as children often play together for such activities, and fine and gross motor skills; for example, dressing-up will require children to use fine manipulative skills, whereas running around as a superhero will help to develop coordination and balance.
Constructive/ manipulative play, e.g. dough, cutting and sticking, junk modelling	This type of play involves putting things together. It can involve commercial products such as Lego, Duplo or jigsaw puzzles; or natural materials such as dough, sand and clay. It also includes junk modelling or using paper for cutting and sticking. There is usually an end product but for young children this is not the most important thing; they are more interested in what they are doing – the process – and often do not have an end product in mind when they start. This type of play helps to develop fine manipulative skills and problem-solving skills. It can be an individual or group activity so can develop cooperation between children. It is also a good opportunity for language development as children explain what they are trying to achieve.

FIGURE 6.20 *Activities and their development potential for children*

continued overleaf

ACTIVITY	HOW IT HELPS A CHILD TO LEARN
Creative play, e.g. painting, drawing, sand	Creative play is a term used to describe a wide range of activities including art and craft activities, such as drawing and painting, through to self-expression via music and dance. These activities can be offered at different levels to meet the child's stage of development and can be carried out alone or as part of a group. Through creative play, children learn about the properties of materials and what they can do – for example, the differences between wet and dry sand. Children will see pictures and patterns, shapes and symbols, which they interpret to mean different things, so developing imagination. They can also learn about different colours and textures, Creative play offers the opportunity for children to develop fine manipulative skills, as many activities such as drawing and colouring require precise, small movements.
Physical play, e.g. climbing frames, bicycles, running	Physical play can be indoors or outdoors. It develops both fine and gross motor skills as well as muscle control – as for example, with a toddler learning to ride a scooter. It helps children to develop spatial awareness, as well as offering them challenges, and develops an ability to risk-take. As a lot of outdoor play takes place with others it develops skills of cooperation. Physical play is also healthy for a child, as it helps them to eat and sleep well.

FIGURE 6.20 *Activities and their development potential for children*

Setting out an activity plan

There is no set layout for an activity plan; however, a good plan should have certain information in it. This should include:

* title or name of the activity

* number of children it is for (maximum and minimum may be given)

* age range the activity is aimed at

* time needed to prepare for the activity

* estimated time the activity will take to carry out

* rationale or reason for doing the activity – this may link to a theme that the setting is following or to skills or experience the setting wants the children to acquire. This may include aims and objectives: aims outline the broad intentions of the activity – what it hopes to achieve overall; the objectives should explain exactly how the activity will achieve its aims. For example, an aim might be to develop an appreciation of colour; the objective could therefore be to provide opportunity for mixing of primary colours

* learning opportunities that arise from the activity – this will cover a comment on developmental potential as well as how it will cover the early learning goals. A good detailed plan will include references to textbooks to highlight how the comments made about the learning benefits are backed up by theory

* resources and equipment required – this acts as a checklist and ensures that all equipment is available before the start of the activity

* implementation – this sets out a step-by-step approach to the activity. It may include timings of each stage as well as what the adult might be doing to support the children. This section is like a list of instructions

* extension possibilities – an activity plan may outline how the activity might be adapted to meet individual needs, for example, as a child with a disability or a child who is particularly gifted

* evaluation – good activity plans include an evaluation, in which the early years worker

* DID YOU KNOW?

Harvard method of referencing

Good referencing and a clear bibliography are useful as they allow the reader to check the source of a reference if they wish to. There are a number of different ways to reference; however, the Harvard system is most commonly used. If you are writing other authors' ideas in your own words, you must acknowledge this by giving their name and the date of the publication in which you have read their ideas. For example Smith (1999) suggested that . . .'

However, if you are directly quoting something that has appeared in another text, you must give author, date and page number. Directly quoted material usually appears indented in the text. For example:

As Smith states

'. . .' (1999, page 14)

References must be supported by a bibliography which lists all the texts you have used. The Harvard method has the following headings:

Author (Surname, initial) Date Title Publisher Place where published

Tassoni, P. and Hucker, K. (1999) *Planning Play and the Early Years,* Heinemann: Oxford

reflects on the success of the activity and whether it:

- was carried out effectively
- met the intended learning outcomes for the children

* references and bibliography – if you have referred to theorists in the plan, you should include a bibliography.

An example of a detailed plan

Detailed plans are the method by which activities are written out. There is no right or wrong way to do this, but good detailed plans will contain certain pieces of information, meaning that someone else can pick up the plan, follow it and carry out the activity. The plan below covers a cooking activity.

ACTIVITY	MAKING CORNFLAKE CAKES
Number of children	Group of 4
Age range	4-year-olds
Preparation time	10 minutes
Activity time	30 minutes
Rationale for activity	This activity links with the topic of 'Food' which the nursery is currently covering. The nursery is looking at how we can eat different food in different ways, so this shows how a breakfast cereal can be used in a cake.

FIGURE 6.21 *A detailed plan for a cooking activity*

continued overleaf

ACTIVITY	MAKING CORNFLAKE CAKES
Learning opportunities – links to early years curriculum cases	**Physical development**: The activity will develop fine manipulative skills though breaking up the chocolate and stirring the cornflakes into the melted chocolate. Hand–eye coordination will be used as the child spoons the mixture into the cake. **Mathematics**: Children will be able to weigh out the ingredients and use estimation to work out how many cakes they will each make. They will be able to count out items such as squares of chocolate and aprons. **Knowledge and understanding of the world**: Discovery of the fact that some materials can change appearance when treated in a particular way. They will also learn about heat and how you have to be careful with hot things to prevent burning. **Creative development**: Children will have the opportunity to discover that chocolate melts and has a different texture than when it is solid. They will be able to shape their cakes creatively. **Personal and social development**: The activity provides children with the opportunity to work as part of a group. They will have to share the scales so they will develop turn-taking skills. It will give them confidence as they should produce a finished item that looks good and is edible. **Language and literacy**: The activity will produce opportunitunities to talk about the food children like. They will also be able to develop descriptive skills as they describe the difference between solid and melted chocolate. They will be able to describe the texture differences between the cornflakes and the chocolate.
Equipment/ resources	Chocolate Cornflakes 4 aprons, 4 wooden spoons, 8 mixing bowls, 4 saucepans, 4 metal spoons, 2 sets of scales, cake cases, tray
Implement- ation	Talk to the children about hygiene and safety. Explain what they are going to do. Ask children to put on their aprons and wash their hands. Ask children to weigh out their chocolate – explain the markings on the scales. Ask children to break their chocolate into squares in their bowl (opportunity for counting). Melt the chocolate over a pan of hot water – show children half-way thorough the process; impress on them the importance of not touching – talk about the dangers of hot liquids. Pour chocolate into a cool bowl and pass to each child. Ask children to weigh out cornflakes, tip into another bowl of melted chocolate and stir. Ask children to spoon some of the mixture into each case with a metal spoon. Put in fridge to set. Children to help clear away. Children to taste cakes once finished and describe tastes textures.
Extension opportunities	For gifted children – more mathematical opportunities can be built, in e.g. adding together the total number of cakes. A wheelchair user will be able to take part with a specially adapted table.
Evaluation and comments	To be completed after the activity has finished.

FIGURE 6.21 *A detailed plan for a cooking activity*

UNIT 6 ASSESSMENT

How you will be assessed

This unit is assessed through a portfolio. You need to produce a guide for early years care and education provision in your local area and explore the different ways in which children learn.

Assessment evidence

To do this you must:

* provide information on different early years care and education services that are available in your local area. You must include two statutory, two private, two voluntary and two informal groups. You could compile a survey to find out what exists in your local area. To access mark band 3 you must show an in-depth understanding of the different types of provision.

Assessment guidance

Area A01

* You will need to explain the main purposes of each type of provision.

Area A02

* describe the roles and responsibilities of care workers in early years services and explore how they apply the care values to their day-to-day tasks. You must explain two job roles and the qualifications required from one early years setting. You need to include an outline of a typical day, including times. You may wish to obtain first-hand information about the roles you have chosen, perhaps through interviews or questionnaires.

  To access mark band 3, you must explore the roles independently and be able to explain, with examples, how the care values are applied.

Area A03

* provide information about the ways in which children in early years setting learn and develop, and show that you recognise the factors that affect learning and performance. You must cover two factors from each of the three main groups and also analyse two strategies which can aid learning.

  To access mark bank 3, you must use a range of sources to research information on the factors that affect learning and performance.

Area A04

* produce and implement an activity plan in an early years setting and evaluate its benefits to the children. You also need to evaluate how the activity could be improved. The activity should last at least 15 minutes.

  To access mark band 3, you must provide a detailed evaluation of the activity and have realistic recommendations for improvement.

To access the top mark bands, you must show a high standard of literacy. Your writing style must convey meaning and understanding. You must be able to use specialist language accurately and effectively. There should be no errors or inaccuracies.

References

Bruce, T., Meggitt, C. (2002) *Childcare and Education,* London: Hodder Arnold

Hucker, K. (2001) *Research Methods in Health Care and Early Years,* Oxford: Heinemann

Maslow, A.H. (1970) *Motivation and Personality* (2nd edition). New York: Harper & Row

O'Hagan, M., Smith, M. (1999) *Early Years Childcare and Education: Key Issues* London: Baillière Tindall

Tassoni, P., Hucker, K. (2000) *Planning Play and the Early Years,* Oxford: Heinemann

Useful websites

www.dfes.gov.uk
www.qca.gov.uk
www.surestart.gov.uk
www.underfives.co.uk

Health as a Lifestyle Choice

You will learn about:

7.1   Nutritional value of food and the dietary function of nutrients

7.2   Current dietary guidelines to promote the health of individuals

7.3   Positive effects of exercise

7.4   Health and safety requirements when designing an exercise programme

7.5   How diet and exercise interrelate to affect health

Introduction

This unit is about the physical aspects of health, in particular the links between nutrition, exercise, health and disease. People have different requirements depending on their age, gender and preferences, including those related to religion, culture and lifestyle.

How you will be assessed

This unit is internally assessed through a portfolio in which you will need to devise an individual exercise programme.

Section 1: Nutritional value of food and the dietary function of nutrients

The availability of food is something most people take for granted, especially in developed societies. Food provides nutrition, and is the basic building block of life: 'you are what you eat'. The matter making up the cells in your body comes from food in the digestive system. Adequate nutrition is necessary for normal functioning of the body in four main ways:

* to provide sufficient energy levels
* to maintain muscles, bones and soft tissues
* to maintain immunity, digestion and respiration
* to provide materials for growth, development and repair.

A person's nutritional needs depend on factors such as age, sex, type of work and body size and shape. Athletes need high levels of protein and energy to sustain performance and repair stress damage. People who work in cold environments may need higher levels of fat in their diets to maintain normal body temperature, whereas workers in sedentary occupations, such as office work, which do not require much physical activity, will need lower levels.

Children need a greater proportion of high energy food in their diet than adults, because they can only cope with small portions due to their body size. Women who are pregnant or breast–feeding require a higher calorie intake to meet the needs of their growing babies. Older people require less food in general, but the nutritional composition of their food needs to be carefully balanced, because their body systems are generally less efficient.

The energy value of food is measured in calories; a calorie is the unit of energy needed to raise the temperature of 1 gram of water by 1°C. Nutritional calories, called kilocalories, are written as **kcal**, that e.g. 149 kcal, which means, that the product, in the case of food, contains 149 dietary calories.

In order to ensure proper functioning of the body these calories must be obtained from nutritious food. There are a number of **essential nutrients** which the body cannot make: they must come from external sources. Essential nutrients include **vitamins**, **dietary minerals**, **essential fatty acids**, **phytochemicals** and **essential amino acids**. They are needed only in small quantities, and are stored and reused by the body as much as possible. The absence of essential nutrients leads to a deficiency disease or gradually to illness.

The main purpose of food is to build and maintain the body's structures and functions. It does this through a complex process known as **metabolism.**

✳ DID YOU KNOW?

The word 'metabolism' derives from the Greek word for change, and it is specific to living organisms. It describes the physical and chemical processes that break down food into their molecular parts (constituents) to form nutrients which can be absorbed into the body cells via the bloodstream. The molecules released by metabolism are rearranged and chemically combined to form new cells and tissues. The process starts with the ingestion and digestion of food and is accompanied by the release of energy in the form of heat and the production of waste products. The rate at which the body converts food into heat and energy when at rest is known as the basal metabolic rate. This rate is sufficient only to keep the body 'ticking over' like a car engine, sustaining basic functions such as heart rate. It is used as a baseline measurement of metabolic function.

MEN 19–50 YEARS	WOMEN 19–50 YEARS	BOYS 11–14 YEARS	GIRLS 11–14 YEARS	YOUNG MEN 15–18 YEARS	YOUNG WOMEN 15–18 YEARS
2500	2000	2200	1845	2755	2110

TABLE 7.1 *Calories needed each day by people of different ages*

Macro-nutrients

All main food groups contain different essential nutrients which the body needs for different processes. Certain nutrients appear in more than one food group but the body needs a balance of different foods to work effectively.

Food groups

Food is divided into five main groups:

1. Breads, cereals and potatoes
2. Fruit and vegetables
3. Meat, fish and alternatives
4. Beans, nuts and pulses
5. Milk and dairy products

Macro-nutrients are found in the five main food groups, and consist of:

* proteins
* fats
* carbohydrates.

Proteins

Protein (from food groups 3 and 4) provides a source of energy in the form of heat and is needed by every cell in the body for growth and repair of tissue. The two main types of protein are derived from plant and animal sources. Protein from animal sources (known as complete protein) is found in meat, fish, eggs, milk and dairy products. They contain all eight essential nutrients called amino-acids which are needed by humans. Amino-acids form part of DNA, they are needed in the body to produce other chemicals such as enzymes and neuro-transmitters. Enzymes break down and digest food; neurotransmitters are used to relay electrical signals for movement along the nerves and so are important for the functioning of the central nervous system. Complete proteins have a high biological value – that is, they contain some nutrients but not all that the body needs for growth and repair. It is also more difficult for the body to use and absorb the nutrients from low biological value food so they need to be combined to overcome both the absorption problem and the incomplete nutrient problem (see vegetarian diets, page 288).

FIGURE 7.1 *Foods containing protein*

Plant sources of protein include pulses (e.g. lentils, peas and beans), nuts, and 'novel' or synthesised protein such as tofu (soya bean curd) and quorn (myco-protein). Protein from plant sources is known as **incomplete protein** because although some sources contain some amino-acids, none contain all eight necessary to sustain life. These sources of protein have low biological value and need to be combined with other foods.

> ### ✳ DID YOU KNOW?
>
> Men need about 44 to 55 grams of protein each day, and women need about 36 to 45 grams. This should be about 15 per cent of total calorie intake per day. Children need protein for growth: those aged 4–6 years need 15–20 grams per day, children aged 7–10 need about 23–28 grams per day.

Fats

Although the body needs only small amounts of fats (from the food groups 3, 4 and 5), they contain essential fatty acids. These are needed for important functions such as brain and central nervous system function. They also help to regulate blood pressure and blood clotting and protect against coronary heart disease.

There are two main types of fat, **saturated** and **unsaturated**. Saturated fat comes mainly from animal sources and it is usually solid at room temperature. Dairy products such as butter, hard margarine, cheese, cream and ghee as well as meat, provide saturated fat; coconuts and palm oil also contain it. Too much saturated fat in the diet is believed to increase levels of blood cholesterol. This can contribute to cardiovascular disease by causing abnormal tissue growth on the lining of blood vessels, restricting blood flow, particularly to the heart and brain.

Unsaturated fat is usually liquid at room temperature. It comes mainly from plant sources and has two main forms: **polyunsaturated** fat and **monounsaturated** fat. The names refer to their different molecular structure. Foods containing monounsaturated fat include olive, rape seed, almond, hazelnut and peanut oils, as well as avocados, olives and nuts. Monounsaturated fats improve cholesterol levels by carrying cholesterol from the tissues to the liver for excretion.

Polyunsaturated fats contain essential fatty acids, particularly omega-3 which is essential for brain and central nervous system function, a healthy immune system, and normal growth and development in children. They are found in oily fish (e.g. mackerel, fresh tuna, salmon and trout), and in nuts and vegetable oils.

Fats called **trans-fats** are produced by hydrogenation, a process that makes the fat solid at room temperature, turning vegetable oils into products such as hard margarine or vegetable shortening (used extensively in the manufacture of biscuits and cakes). Trans-fats have no known nutritional value, although they raise blood cholesterol levels and are a risk factor in cardiovascular disease. On food labels they are called 'hydrogenated vegetable oil'. Some margarines contain unsaturated fat, but some low-fat spreads made from vegetable oils have been hydrogenated. You need to read food labels very carefully to identify the type of fat found in such spreads.

For adults, eating too much fat will cause any excess to be deposited under the skin, leading to obesity. Obese people have a much higher risk of heart disease, high blood pressure and diabetes, due to increased blood cholesterol. Babies and children need calorie-dense foods because they expend a lot of energy in relation to their size; they also need essential fatty acids to help their brain develop. However, from the age of five years, the total fat content of the diet should not

FIGURE 7.2 *High- and low-fat foods*

provide more than 35 per cent of total energy (or calories), and saturated fat should form no more than 10 per cent of this.

Carbohydrates (from food groups 1 and 2) provide a primary source of energy for the body. The body uses carbohydrates to store energy which it uses to maintain its functions and systems and to provide energy for movement. The two main types of carbohydrates are **starches** and **sugars**. Both contain carbon, hydrogen and oxygen molecules, but have slightly different molecular structures. Sugars are naturally occurring monosaccharides or disaccharides with a fairly simple structure ('mono'- means one, 'di'- two). They are found in fruits and vegetables. The common ones include fructose and glucose (monosaccharides), sucrose, lactose and maltose (disaccharides). Starches are polysaccharides or oligosaccharides ('poly'- or 'oligo'- meaning many), they have a much more complex structure and are sometimes known as '**complex carbohydrates**'.

The starches and sugars in carbohydrates are metabolised by the body and turned into glucose. This is stored in the liver and the skeletal muscles with water in the form of glycogen. The glycogen stored in the liver provides glucose, which is used by the rest of the body as fuel to maintain basic functions, including brain function. The glycogen stored in the muscles, in contrast, is not available to the rest of the body; it is used to provide an immediate reserve source of energy to propel the muscles, e.g. when running for a bus.

When carbohydrates are eaten, levels of glucose (known as blood sugar) in the blood rises. This triggers the secretion of the hormone insulin from the pancreas (an organ situated behind the stomach). Insulin stimulates other hormones, which turn glucose into glycogen for storage. When digestion is complete, the blood glucose level falls, insulin secretion reduces, and glycogen synthesis drops. When carbohydrate comes from sugars, the level of blood sugar rises very quickly (sometimes known as an energy rush), insulin is secreted in large quantities and the sugar is rapidly turned into glycogen.

In contrast, starches (complex carbohydrates) need to be turned into sugars before processing. They therefore have a much more gradual effect on blood sugar levels, insulin is released more slowly into the bloodstream, and conversion to glycogen takes place over a longer period. Carbohydrates in the form of starches provide the body with a steady supply of energy, in contrast to the quick burst provided through sugars.

Complex carbohydrates (starches) include potatoes, root vegetables, rice, pasta and bread; these should constitute about one third of the diet.

Micro-nutrients

Micro-nutrients are the vitamins, minerals and trace elements found in all food. They all have special properties and functions which interact with each other in complex ways. Because of the way they interact, it is difficult to identify what benefits supplements have for each particular individual: vitamins and minerals need to be synthesised and manufactured in ways that enable them to be properly absorbed by the body, and this will depend on individual metabolism. Vitamins and minerals from natural sources provide the right amounts of nutrients in forms that are compatible with individual needs.

It is important to recognise that the vitamins and minerals found in food can be lost during cooking and processing. At times of stress and during illness, when appetite may be poor, the body may need more vitamins and minerals to maintain health and bodily functions. And it is particulalry important to eat high-quality food during pregnancy.

Consider this

Keep a food diary for one week. Write down everything you eat and drink, including snacks.

Using concepts of healthy eating, can you identify:

* whether you ate foods from each of the main food groups every day

* what food group you ate most

* what food group you ate least.

Go further – can you analyse using the theory of nutritional balance:

* whether the amount of salt you consumed was within recommended limits

* the type and amount of fat you consumed

* how many calories you ate per day, on average?

Go further – can you evaluate:

* whether you are getting sufficient micro-nutrients (see below)

* whether you are drinking enough (6–8 glasses of water per day)

* whether your total daily calories, on average, were more or less than the recommended amount for your age and sex?

You can compare your findings with others in your group. Was your diet better or worse than you thought?

Vitamins

There are two main types of vitamins: those that are water-soluble and those that are fat-soluble. Water-soluble vitamins do not stay in the body and are needed daily. Fat-soluble vitamins are stored by the body and can be harmful if taken in excess.

Other essential micro-nutrients include **minerals** (sometimes known as macro-minerals because generally over 100 mg per day are needed) and **trace elements** (micro-minerals), which are needed in minute quantities. Minerals and trace elements are needed for **homeostasis.** Homeostasis is the body's ability to regulate its internal environment and maintain stability. Balance is achieved through adjusting the

VITAMIN	FOUND IN	PROPERTIES	DEFICIENCY CAUSES	WATER SOLUBLE	FAT SOLUBLE
A Retinol RDA 0.7 mg	Dairy products (milk, cheese, butter), eggs, chicken, oily fish (salmon, mackerel, trout) and liver	Essential for growth (thyroid function), healthy skin and hair, vision, immunity and healthy mucous membranes	Deficiency causes night blindness, excess can damage the liver, may damage growing foetus and may increase risk of fractures in older people		Y
Beta-carotene	A plant source converted to vitamin A by the body. Found in orange, yellow and green vegetables and fruits	Essential for growth (thyroid function), vision and immunity	Deficiency may result in lack of vitamin A in the body (useful source of vitamin A for vegetarians)		Y
B_1 Thiamine RDA 1.2 mg	Fish, meat, enriched breads and cereals, wholewheat grains, green leafy vegetables (e.g. spinach, broccoli), beans (e.g. butter beans, soya and kidney beans), peanuts and milk	Helps metabolism of carbohydrates and sugars	Beri-beri: symptoms include weight loss, impaired vision and hearing, weakness and irregular heartbeat. Can be fatal	Y	
B_2 Riboflavin RDA None UK; 6 mg EU	Milk, cheese, soya beans, almonds, leafy green vegetables, liver and yeast	Helps to metabolise fats, protein and carbohydrate, aids red blood-cell formation, respiration, antibody formation, regulates thyroid function (growth), promotes healthy skin, nails and hair	Eye disorders	Y	
B_3 Niacin RDA None UK; 8 mg EU	Meat, fish, eggs, leafy green vegetables (as above)	Needed for energy metabolism and regulates metabolic function and nervous system	Pellagra: symptoms include diarrhoea, weakness, dermatitis and dementia	Y	
B_5 Pantothenic acid RDA None UK; 6 mg EU	Cereals, pulses (lentils, beans and peas), eggs and meat	Promotes efficient immune-system function. Needed for healthy hair, skin etc. (as above)	Allergies, reduced adrenal gland function, rheumatoid arthritis	Y	
B_6 Pyridoxine RDA None UK; 2 mg EU	As above	Needed for metabolising amino-acids and glucose/glycogen and for a healthy nervous system	Deficiency in B_6 can trigger mental-health problems such as schizophrenia and depression in those who are genetically susceptible. It has also been identified in those suffering from ADHD and autism	Y	Y

FIGURE 7.3 *Micro-nutrients – their health benefits and RDA*

continued opposite

VITAMIN	FOUND IN	PROPERTIES	DEFICIENCY CAUSES	WATER SOLUBLE	FAT SOLUBLE
B_7 Biotin RDA None UK; 0.15 mg EU	As above	Important for synthesis of essential fatty acids and glucose metabolism	Symptoms include dry, scaly skin, fatigue, loss of appetite, nausea and depression	Y	
B_9 Folic acid RDA 2.0 mcg	Leafy green vegetables, cereals and grains, beans and peas	Nervous-system function	Diarrhoea, weight loss, sore tongue, palpitations, irritability and behavioural disorders. Also, low birth weight and spina bifida and hydrocephalus in the developing foetus	Y	
B_{12} Cyano-cobalamin RDA 1.0 mcg	Meat and dairy products, soya products	Needed for nerve cells, red blood cells and DNA	Anaemia, especially pernicious anaemia and nerve damage causing tingling and unsteady gait	Y but can be stored for short time	
C Ascorbic acid RDA 30 mg	Fruit and vegetables, especially citrus fruit	Needed for healthy tissues, e.g. skin, mucous membranes, teeth and bones; and for the production of neuro-transmitters (brain chemicals) and the transfer of energy into the cells	Scurvy: symptoms include loose teeth, fragile blood vessels and superficial bleeding, poor healing, compromised immunity and mild anaemia		Y
D Calciferol RDA 2.5 mcg	Milk and dairy products, eggs, oily fish, liver. Can be synthesised by the body in the presence of sunlight	Maintains normal levels of calcium and phosphorus and contributes to bone health	Osteoporosis (brittle bones) and rickets in children – a condition in which the bones do not form properly causing bowing of the legs. Dark-skinned people living in temperate climates can be at risk		Y
E Tocopherol RDA None UK; 10 mg EU	Avocados, tomatoes, blackberries, mangoes, sprouts, spinach, sweet potato and watercress. Oily fish and vegetable oils	Needed for cell maintenance, healthy heart and cardiovascular system. Helps to store vitamin A and assists vitamin K (see below) with blood clotting	People with disorders affecting fat absorption, such as Crohn's disease, as may be deficient, as may babies of very low birth weight (less than 1500 grams)		Y
K Naptho-quinone RDA none	Most green vegetables and wholegrain cereals. The body manufactures vitamin K from the bacteria in the intestine (gut flora)	Needed for blood-clotting processes and strong bones	Rare, but deficiency can impair blood coagulation (clotting) and cause bleeding		

FIGURE 7.3 *Micro-nutrients – their health benefits and RDA*

metabolic processes. The main features of homeostasis are:

* regulation of the amount of water and minerals in the body by the kidneys, through respiration and via the sweat glands in the skin

* removal of waste (excretion) through the kidneys, the bowels and the skin

* regulation of body temperature through the skin and blood vessels

* regulation of the blood glucose level through the production of insulin.

Important minerals

Calcium

Calcium is needed for strong bones and teeth. It is essential for blood clotting and regulates the contractions of muscles, including the heart muscle. Lack of calcium can cause cramp. Calcium is thought to aid in lowering high blood pressure, and may protect against cancer. Vitamin D is needed to absorb calcium. Calcium is found in milk, cheese, okra, leafy green vegetables (except spinach), fortified flour and fish bones. RDA (recommended daily allowance) is 500 mg per day.

Iron

Iron is a very important mineral. It is needed to form haemoglobin in the red blood cells that carry oxygen around body. To make red blood cells, the body also needs vitamin B_{12} and folic acid. Iron exists in food in two different forms:

* **haem iron** (from animal sources such as meat)

* **non-haem iron** (from plant sources such as green vegetables, pulses and wholegrain cereals).

The absorption of non-haem iron is increased if vitamin C is taken at the same time. This is important for vegetarians, and is why we tend to eat meat with vegetables. The absorption of iron is reduced by the caffeine and tannins in tea and coffee. RDA is 12 mg per day.

Magnesium

Magnesium is essential for general metabolism, particularly of carbohydrates. Magnesium helps the function of the parathyroid glands, which produce the hormones needed for bone health (calcium and phosphorus). It occurs in green leafy vegetables, nuts, bread, fish, meat and dairy products. RDA is 300 mg per day for men and 270 mg per day for women.

Phosphorus

Phosphorus is essential for healthy bones and teeth and plays a role with phosphorus and calcium in metabolism. Phosphorus is found in red meat, fish, bread, dairy products and poultry. RDA is 550 mg per day.

Sodium

Sodium is important for the central nervous system functions, particularly the transmission of electrical signals or nerve impulses that regulate movement. It is known as an electrolyte. Sodium is found in sodium chloride, or common salt and is present in many foods. Most people eat too much salt: the RDA is 6 g, but, most people eat more than 9 g per day.

Chlorine

Chlorine is an oxidising agent and aids the immune system function. It is usually taken internally as salt (see above). With sodium and potassium, it is one of the main electrolytes in the body.

Potassium

Potassium helps to regulate fluid balance and is important in homeostasis. It is found in fruit (particularly bananas), vegetables, pulses, nuts and seeds, meat, shellfish, poultry and bread. RDA is 3500 mg (3.5 g) per day

Trace elements

Trace elements work together with vitamins to maintain the body's processes and normal functions. Trace elements include cobalt, chromium, copper, iodine, manganese, molybdenum, selenium (important for the immune system function) and zinc.

> *** DID YOU KNOW?**
>
> British sailors were called 'limeys' by the Australians because they were provided with limes to prevent scurvy on long sea crossings. They also put limes in their rum rations – the basis of modern cocktails!

Food additives

Food additives are chemicals and other substances used in the manufacture and processing of food products. They preserve food, prolong shelf life and enhance appearance or taste. Additives are carefully regulated and mostly harmless, although some people can have an allergic reaction to one or more chemicals in processed food. Additives in food must, by law, be identified on the label, but unfortunately their names are so complex that most people do not understand them. In order to simplify matters, all additives in Britain have been given a code or 'E number' to show approval for use throughout the European Union. The full list can be found at http://www.food.gov.uk/safereating/additives branch/enumberlist

Different types of additives serve different purposes.

Food colourings

These are used to mask natural variations in colour or to enhance the natural colour of food. They provide identity to food – for example custard is yellow. Colourings also protect flavours and vitamins, and prevent colour loss during storage. They can be natural dyes, such as:

* caramel (brown), sfound in Coca-Cola

* annatto (yellow), which comes from a tropical seed

* chlorella (green), which comes from seaweed

* cochineal (red), which comes from insects.

Spices such as turmeric, paprika and saffron are also used as colourings. Artificial colours are dyes:

* tartrazine (E102 yellow), which comes from coal-tar

* sunset yellow (E110).

Both are often used in orange drinks.

Preservatives

There are many non-chemical ways of preserving food, including freezing, drying and curing (e.g. bacon and ham), canning, vacuum-packing and pasteurising. Some methods, however, use a range of chemicals, common ones include: E200 sorbic acid, E202 potassium sorbate, E210 benzoic acid and E220 sulphur dioxide.

Antioxidants

These are often either vitamins or derived from vitamins and are described on food labels by their names, e.g. E300 ascorbic acid is vitamin C, E306 tocopherol is vitamin E. They prevent natural oxidisation so food stays fresher for longer.

Sweeteners

Sweeteners can improve taste, provide fewer calories and can be better for teeth. They may be natural sugar or manufactured. They include: E420 sorbitol, E421 mannitol, E950 acesulfame, E951 aspartame and E954 saccharin. Natural sugars without E numbers found on food labels include fructose (fruit sugar), lactose (milk sugar) and glucose.

Emulsifiers

This group of additives includes thickening agents, gelling agents and stabilisers. They improve the texture of food and prevent the separation of oil and water during storage, e.g. in salad dressings. Common names include: E322 lecithin (emulsifier), E401 sodium alginate, E406 agar and E407 (thickeners), E440 pectin (a natural gelling agent present in fruit skins and used in jams), and E465 ethyl methyl cellulose.

Others

Other additives include acidity regulators, used in fruit-based products; anti-caking agents added to flour; bulking agents; anti-foaming agents and propellants (e.g. as used in aerosol dairy cream); flavour enhancers such as E621 monosodium glutamate; and modified starches.

Diet-related disorders

Most diseases and disorders result from many different and interrelated factors, both genetic and environmental. However, diet clearly plays a major role in preventing the onset of disease. In developed societies, diseases and ill health are often caused by an unbalanced diet, particularly over-consumption of certain types of food, rather than deficiencies in the availability of food or food nutrients. Diets that are high in saturated fat, refined flour and sugar products lead not only to obesity (with its increased risk of heart disease, stroke and diabetes), but also to a lack of essential nutrients.

Cancer and heart disease account for 60 per cent of all deaths before the age of 75 years. About 1 in 4 deaths from cancer and 1 in 3 deaths from coronary heart disease are estimated to be diet-related (*Choosing Health* resource pack, DOH 2005). Levels of obesity are increasing in both adults and children; rates have trebled since the 1980s with 22 per cent of men and 23.5 per cent of women now classed as overweight or obese; almost 17 per cent of children aged between 2 and 15 years are also obese. Being obese reduces life expectancy by an average of nine years.

Consider this

As a group, collect a variety of food labels from tins, packets and jars of common ready-prepared foods.

Using the concept of food labelling, can you:

* identify the three most common additives?

Go further, using theories of food additives, and deduce:

* the reason for the additives being present

* estimate the proportion of daily nutritional intake in a portion of each food.

Section 2: Current dietary guidelines to promote the health of individuals

In the UK, the Committee on Medical Aspects of Food and Nutrition Policy (COMA) advised the government on dietary requirements. It examined scientific evidence and estimated the nutritional requirements (called Dietary Reference Values or DRVs) of different groups of people within the UK population. This work was carried out in the 1990s, and it is likely that these values will be reviewed soon to take account of changing lifestyles and population differences. COMA has

been superseded by the Scientific Advisory Committee on Nutrition (SACN). DRVs are estimates of the requirements for groups of people, not individuals.

Dietary reference values (DRVs)

DRVs are:

Estimated Average Requirements (EAR)
EAR is the average requirement for a particular nutrient (protein, carbohydrates, vitamins etc). This means that of a group of people, half will require less and half will require more than the average.

Reference Nutrient Intake (RNI)
RNI is the amount of a particular nutrient that is sufficient to meet the needs of a particular group. However, many people will need less, depending on lifestyle and exercise, for example.

Lower Reference Nutrient Intake (LRNI)
LRNI is the amount of a nutrient that is enough for a small number of people with particularly low requirements. It is rarely used, because most people will require more.

Energy requirements
Energy requirements are based on the average activity levels and lifestyles of the general population. They are a very rough average, as energy requirements are related to age, gender, body size and level of activity. Growing children have higher energy requirements than adults, and boys generally have higher requirements than girls. By about 50 years of age, energy requirements are lower, due to a reduction in the basal metabolic rate (see page 292) and a general reduction in physical activity. The basal metabolic rate can increase because of illness, particularly infection, as the body needs energy to power the immune response system.

There are also specific requirements for micro-nutrients such as vitamins and minerals (see Figure 7.3) because too many or too few can affect the body in different ways. DRVs have replaced the Recommended Daily Allowance (RDA), but the latter term can still be found on food labels, particularly on manufactured vitamins and minerals.

Specific needs

Different groups of people have special dietary needs at different times in their lives.

Pregnancy

Lifelong health consequences for children can result from what happens during development within the womb. Diet is particularly important for the developing foetus in the first three months when the main organs, including the brain and central nervous system, develop. Iron and folic acid are especially important: iron supports the increase in blood supply to the foetus, and folic acid prevents neural tube defects such as spina bifida. There is an increased need for omega-3 fatty acids, which affect brain development and cognitive function. These compounds could be particularly important during the third trimester (last three months) of pregnancy and the first three months of life, when the baby's brain experiences a growth spurt. Some sources of oily fish (a good source of omega-3 fatty acids) contain high levels of mercury, which can damage the foetus, so no more than two portions per week are recommended. A low-protein diet during pregnancy could affect kidney development. Mineral requirements remain the same. Pregnant women need approximately 2500 calories per day. They should have less than 300 mg of caffeine a day, because it interferes with the absorption of essential nutrients; 300 mg is approximately:

* 3 mugs of instant coffee (100 mg each) or 4 cups of instant coffee (75 mg each)
* 3 cups of brewed coffee (100 mg each)
* 6 cups of tea (50 mg each)
* 8 cans of cola (up to 40 mg each)
* 4 cans of 'energy' drink (up to 80 mg each)
* 8 (50 g) bars of chocolate (up to 50 mg each)

Lactation

During breast feeding the requirement for energy, protein, most vitamins, calcium, phosphorus, magnesium, zinc, copper and selenium increases. Calorie requirements are approximately 3000 per day.

Infants

Breast milk is the recommended food for the first six months, because it contains all the essential nutrients required. The Department of Health recommends exclusive breast feeding until six months of age. Babies can draw upon iron stores they have accumulated before birth. Solid food should not be given before 17 weeks of age as the baby's digestive system is too immature to metabolise nutrients efficiently. The weaning diet (gradual introduction of solid food), must contain enough iron, protein, thiamin, niacin, B_6, B_{12}, magnesium, zinc, sodium and chloride. These are all necessary for growth and brain development. Additional salt and salty food should not be given as it can cause kidney damage.

Children aged 4 to 6 years

Young children are very active and their energy requirements increase with age. They need more protein and vitamins (except C and D), and minerals except iron. Young children need between 1500 and 2000 calories per day to meet their energy requirements.

Children aged 7 to 14 years

There is a continued increase in energy and protein requirements needed for growth. From 11 to 14 years, protein requirements increase by 50 per cent. Vitamin and mineral requirements, except for C and D, increase. At puberty, girls have a much higher iron requirement than boys due to menstruation. Calorie requirements are approximately 2200 for boys and 1845 for girls, depending on activity levels.

Adolescents aged 15 to 18 years

Energy and protein requirements continue to increase as children undergo another growth spurt. Vitamin and mineral requirements also rise, particularly for thiamine, riboflavin, niacin, B_6, B_{12}, C and A. Magnesium, potassium, zinc, copper, selenium and iodine support brain development. Bone development is rapid so the need for calcium increases. Calorie requirements are around 2750 for boys and 2110 for girls with average activity levels.

Adults aged 19 to 50 years

By the time individuals reach adulthood, their

energy requirements decrease. Women require increased magnesium, and men more iron. Requirements for calcium and phosphorus in both sexes reduce since bone growth is complete. Calorie requirements are around 2500 for men and 2000 for women.

Over 50s

Energy requirements begin to decrease as individuals age and become less active. Although protein requirements decrease in men, they continue to increase slightly for women. Vitamin and mineral requirements remain unchanged except for women's requirement for iron, which reduces after the menopause. Because energy needs are reduced, the diet needs to be high in nutrients to compensate for the reduced appetite.

Respecting religious beliefs and lifestyle choices

Dietary preferences vary because of cultural, religious or personal reasons. Because humans are very adaptable, such differences do not necessarily affect the health of individuals, if people have enough knowledge about combining foods to ensure sufficient essential nutrient intake. Traditional dishes from most cultures are well-balanced and ensure proper nutrition. In Britain it is common to eat meat and vegetables at the same time, balancing protein, vitamins and minerals, fibre and fat intake. It is particularly important for care workers to be familiar with the dietary preferences and customs they may find in the populations they care for.

Common diets

Vegetarian

People may choose to be vegetarian for ethical or religious reasons. There are different types of vegetarian diet:

* some vegetarians eat eggs and dairy products but no meat or fish

* other vegetarians eat fish but no meat – this is not considered strictly vegetarian

* vegans eat no meat, fish or dairy produce.

Maintaining health on a vegetarian diet is not difficult providing certain key principles are followed. Studies have shown that there is generally a lower incidence of heart disease, osteoporosis and cancer (particularly bowel cancer) among vegetarians. This is because the diet is high in vitamins, minerals and anti-oxidants, and higher in dietary fibre than that of meat eaters. However, only meat provides the eight essential amino-acids that the body cannot manufacture, although they are all present to some degree in nuts, seeds and plant foods. The key is to eat a wide variety of foods and to combine foods so that all eight amino-acids are present in a meal. Examples are combining grains e.g. rice with pulses e.g. peas or beans – such as beans on wholemeal toast or the traditional rice and peas dish common in Caribbean cultures.

Vitamin B_{12} deficiencies can occur in vegans (B12 is present in eggs and dairy products). Yeast extracts such as Marmite and fortified products such as soya milk (a vegan alternative to cow's milk) will provide this. Other soya products such as tofu (soya-bean curd) and textured vegetable protein (TVP) are often used as meat alternatives and provide B12. The body has a reserve 'pool' of amino-acids so it is not absolutely necessary to combine foods at every meal.

Since most vegetarians do not eat fish, it is harder to get the omega-3 essential fatty acids required. Most vegetables have some of these fatty acids in small quantities and the body can convert some types into others; 'however, it is advisable to supplement the diet with flax seeds, flax oil, walnuts or tofu. Flax seeds must be crushed and added near to the end of cooking to ensure maximum effect. If olive oil is used instead of sunflower or other polyunsaturated oils, the body's ability to metabolise essential fatty acids is not disrupted.

Another issue for vegetarians concerns the use of rennet in cheese making. Rennet is an enzyme traditionally extracted from the stomachs of calves. It causes milk to coagulate and separate so that the solids can be made into cheese. Vegetarian cheese uses plant alternatives from fungal or bacterial sources; more recently, genetically engineered rennet, identical to the live source, has become available.

Muslim

Muslims follow dietary principles as part of their religious observances. Food must be pure (halal) and no alcohol or other stimulants are allowed. Although Muslims eat meat, they are forbidden to eat pork or pork products as the pig is considered unclean. Meat must be verified as halal by a cleric and cheese must be made with vegetarian rennet. Animal gelatine is forbidden (gelatine is used to thicken products and causes jelly to set). Separate utensils are used for the preparation of meat.

Failure to observe these principles affects a Muslim's ability to worship. Muslims undergo a period of fasting during the month of Ramadan with no food or drink (other than water) during daylight hours; this is a form of ritual cleansing. There are exceptions to this rule for expectant mothers and young children.

Hindu

The Hindu faith opposes injury to animals so the diet is vegetarian. Hindus do not eat eggs or animal by-products such as rennet or gelatine. No alcohol is permitted, and some Hindus refrain from foods considered stimulating such as onions and garlic.

Buddhist

Buddhists are usually strict vegetarians, sharing similar views to Hindus on the sacredness of life. Food preparation and eating are often part of community life. Some Buddhists regard seafood as acceptable. It is always important to check individual interpretations of a faith.

Rastafarian

The Rastafarian movement began in Jamaica in the 1930s and is linked with anti-racism, non-conformism and world peace. Rastafarians believe that the Emperor Haile Selassie of Ethiopia represented god's form on earth. They believe in a natural way of life, and their food must not be artificially preserved, coloured, flavoured or chemically altered. Many, but not all, are vegetarian. Those who are not do not eat pork. Their approved food is called I-tal.

Jewish

Approved Jewish food is called kosher, which means that it has been prepared according to strict guidelines (like halal food). Jews do not eat pork or any pork products, but they do eat other meat. Kosher meats come from other animals with cloven hooves (cattle, goats and sheep) and poultry (chicken, goose, turkey and duck). The meat must be slaughtered by a professional slaughterer according to strict guidelines so as to minimise suffering and ensure that blood is removed and does not contaminate the meat. The carcass is examined for abnormalities and rejected if any are found, because it must be pure. Milk and dairy produce from kosher animals is permitted, but Jews must not mix meat and milk at the same meal or during preparation and cooking. Therefore, separate utensils are used for the preparation of meat and milk. Fruit and vegetables are 'pareve' and can be freely consumed. Wine is considered kosher only if it has been produced by Jews and according to Jewish law. During the festival of Passover, no wheat, barley, rye or oats can be eaten, and bread must be unleavened (not fermented, yeast free). Levels of orthodoxy differ as in other religions, so it is always best to ask.

Think it over...

Devise a weekly menu for a vegetarian family, ensuring it meets dietry requirements.

Consider this

Mr and Mrs Iqbal are Muslims. They have a 2-month-old baby and a 7-year-old son, Mohammed, who has just been chosen for the school football team.

Using the concept of culturally appropriate diets can you identify:

1. the key issues for the family when shopping for food?

Go further – using the theory of Dietary Reference Values:

2. Devise a menu for three days to meet the nutritional requirements of each member.

Go further – can you evaluate:

3. The long- and short-term health implications for Mrs Iqbal if these nutritional requirements are not met?

Diet-related diseases

Diabetes

Diabetes is on the increase and can be diet-related. It is an incurable, chronic and progressive metabolic disease affecting all age groups. Once diagnosed diabetes is a lifelong condition, needing careful monitoring and regular treatment to prevent complications.

Diabetes is caused by irregularities in the metabolism of carbohydrates, and is related to the production and regulation of the hormone insulin. Insulin is produced by special cells in the pancreas (b-cells) and is the main fuel-regulating hormone acting on carbohydrates. Following digestion, levels of glucose in the bloodstream rise. Insulin is released into the blood to move the glucose into the cells. Diabetes occurs when insufficient insulin is available for the body to use the glucose to provide energy.

There are two main types of diabetes, **Type 1** and **Type 2**, both characterised by raised blood glucose levels or **hyperglycaemia**, which causes drowsiness and confusion, followed eventually by loss of consciousness. This is sometimes known as diabetic coma; it can be fatal if left untreated.

In Type 1 diabetes, the insulin-producing cells no longer work or have been destroyed by the body's immune system. Without insulin, the body tries to expel the excess glucose in the blood into the urine, eventually damaging the kidneys. Type 1 diabetes more commonly affects children, young people and young adults, and makes up approximately 15 per cent of all cases. Its incidence is increasing in children, especially those under five years of age.

In Type 2 diabetes (diabetes mellitus), the pancreas cannot produce enough insulin to meet the body's needs. This may be complicated in the event that the body's cells are unable to respond properly to the insulin that is produced. Type 2 diabetes accounts for around 85 per cent of cases and is more common in older people, although it is increasing across all age groups. Certain people are more at risk than others, especially:

* people who are overweight or obese

* people of Chinese or South Asian, African, African-Caribbean or Middle Eastern descent

* older people: 1 in 20 (50 per 1000) people over

65 years and 1 in 5 (200 per 1000) people over 85 years have diabetes

* poor people: the most deprived (20 per cent of the British population) are one and a half times more likely to have diabetes at any age.

The illness is six times more common in people of South Asian descent compared with white populations, and three times more common in those from African or African-Caribbean backgrounds.

Symptoms of diabetes

Classic symptoms include:

* weight loss, despite increased appetite, demonstrating the body's inability to use food

* tiredness and blurred vision

* excessive passing of urine as the body tries to excrete the excess glucose, then extreme thirst as the body attempts to prevent dehydration

* high blood glucose levels (normal range is 70–100 mg glucose per 100 ml blood, or 4.5–5.6 mmol per litre)

* ketones in the urine (sometimes called acetone and caused by the body's failure to metabolise fats properly).

Treatment of diabetes

The key to treating diabetes is to maintain the balance between food consumption, particularly carbohydrates and sugars, and the amount of insulin needed to process the food. The better the balance, the more stable the diabetes and the less likelihood of complications.

In Type 1 diabetes, the principle treatment is daily injections of insulin and controlled diet. The levels of nutrition and insulin needed to maintain stability can be affected by lifestyle factors, e.g. the amount of physical exercise taken. Failure to maintain the balance between diet, activity levels and the dosage of insulin usually leads to **hypoglycaemia** (very low blood glucose) and **ketoacidosis** (where by-products of fat metabolism remain in the blood, causing it to become acidic). Insulin therapy can be tailored to individual needs. There are several types: some act quickly, others are slow-release. All insulin needs to be given by injection; an insulin pump can deliver a continuous supply under the skin.

It is often possible to treat Type 2 diabetes by

regulating diet alone. Otherwise a combination of diet and medication, usually tablets, can increase production of insulin; people with Type 2 diabetes may also need insulin injections.

High blood pressure

High blood pressure (hypertension) means the pressure in the blood vessels, particularly the arteries, is too high. Many people have high blood pressure without realising it because there are few symptoms. It is estimated that 25 per cent of middle-aged adults and 50 per cent of people over 65 will have high blood pressure. It is more common in certain groups of people, in particular African-Caribbean people and those of Indian or Pakistani origin. Often the cause is unknown, and it is generally referred to as 'essential hypertension'. One common factor is narrowing of the arteries through gradual accumulation of fatty deposits (arteriosclerosis), referred to as 'hardening of the arteries'. Damage to the kidneys or hormone problems can lead to hypertension because the balance of the body (homeostasis) is disrupted. Other contributory factors include:

* smoking
* lack of exercise
* poor diet, high in unsaturated fat
* too much alcohol – regularly drinking over the recommended limits
* obesity
* high cholesterol levels which contribute to arteriosclerosis
* family history of heart disease and stroke
* being male – female hormones have a protective factor
* diabetes, which affects the blood vessels
* ethnic group (see above).

The more of these factors a person has, the greater the risk. So, for example, a diabetic who smokes and is of African-Caribbean descent may be at greater risk than someone who does not smoke but is overweight.

Blood pressure (BP) is stated in millimetres of mercury (mmHg). Two figures are measured: the first is the **systolic** pressure (the pressure in the arteries when the heart contracts). This is usually the higher number as the pressure is greater during contraction. The **diastolic** pressure is measured when the heart is resting between beats. Blood pressure varies with time of day and other factors such as stress levels.

Blood-pressure measurements are written like this: 135/90 mmHg. Normal blood pressure varies with age and general health. The average for a healthy adult is less than 140/90. Moderately high BP is above 140/90 but below 160/100. Severely raised BP is higher than this. It is possible for only one figure to be raised, or both may be high.

Blood pressure is measured using a **sphygmomanometer**, which is an inflatable cuff placed on the upper arm and connected to a mercury measuring device. When the cuff is inflated, it squeezes the blood out of the arm and lets it back in slowly as the cuff is deflated. A stethoscope over the artery on the inner side of the elbow allows the person taking the reading to hear the distinct, and different, sounds of the heartbeat during contraction and rest. The mercury level is noted at each sound. Nowadays, more accurate electronic instruments are used for measuring BP.

High BP can weaken the heart muscle over time, or cause it to thicken and become less efficient. This can slow the blood flow, which can lead to blood clots. Clots can lodge in the coronary arteries, block the supply of blood and oxygen to the heart muscle, causing a heart attack or coronary thrombosis (a thrombosis is a clot). If blood clots occur in the vessels supplying the brain, a stroke can result.

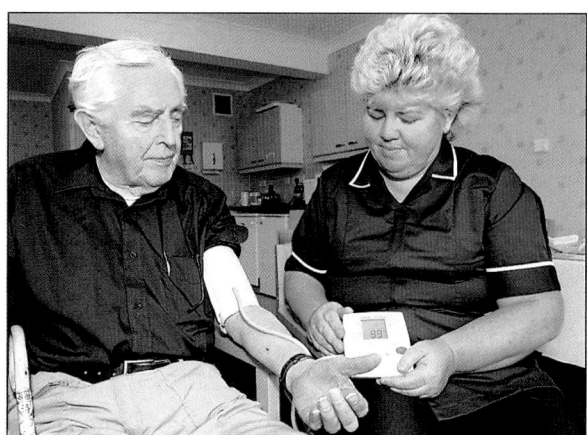

FIGURE 7.4 *Taking a blood-pressure reading*

Osteoporosis

In osteoporosis the bones lose mass and density – commonly referred to as 'thinning of the bones' ('osteo' means bone). Bone is living tissue: it constantly renews itself and also produces bone marrow, which makes blood cells. It comprises collagen (tough elastic fibres) and minerals (calcium and phosphorus). Loss of bone density occurs during ageing, but the amount lost varies. Women lose bone density about three times faster than men after the menopause because the hormone oestrogen, which provides a protective factor, falls following menopause. By the age of 70, some women will have lost up to 30 per cent of bone mass. This can cause bones to break (or fracture) more easily.

Risk factors include:

* diet deficient in vitamin D and calcium

* long periods of dieting or eating disorders (e.g. anorexia nervosa, bulimia)

* excessive alcohol intake (inhibits absorption of calcium)

* interrupted, infrequent menstrual cycle

* menopause, especially early menopause or as a result of hysterectomy

* family history

* medication (e.g. steroids) or medical conditions (e.g. overactive thyroid)

* lack of exercise – weight-bearing exercise causes bone density to increase

* previous fracture.

Bone mass can be measured using special X-rays. The first symptoms may be a stress fracture, particularly of the wrist, spine or hip. Dietary supplements can help to slow down bone loss, and in women, Hormone Replacement Therapy (with oestrogen and progesterone hormones) can also help. A good diet throughout life will reduce the risk of developing osteoporosis.

Obesity and being overweight

Weight alone is not an accurate guide to health because of differences in body size, shape and composition. Therefore, assessment of the body mass index (BMI) is a more accurate guide. This compares weight and height and estimates how much of your body is made up of fat. The body mass index is calculated by dividing weight by height (squared) – for example:

Weight = 70 kg
Height = 1.7 metres
BMI = 70 ÷ 1.75 x 1.75 = 22.9

BMI	CLASSIFIED WEIGHT	HEALTH RISK
Less than 18.5	Underweight	Some health risk
18.5–24.9	Ideal	Normal
25–29	Overweight	Moderate health risk
30–39	Obese	High health risk
40 and over	Very obese/ morbidly obese	Significant health risk

FIGURE 7.5 *Body mass index*

Consider this

Susan is a 34-year-old mother of two children, Thomas aged 4 years and Charlotte aged 18 months. When she was pregnant with Thomas, she put on extra weight. She failed to lose this following the birth. She returned to work when he was 2 years old. Susan feels that she would have lost more weight had she breastfed Thomas, because she has heard that breastfeeding helps you return to pre-pregnancy weight.

After Charlotte was born Susan became even heavier. She now weighs 72 kg; her height is 1.57 metres.

Using the concept of body mass index:

1. calculate Susan's body mass index and assess the level of health risk.

Go further – using the theory of calorie intake:

2. Devise a diet and exercise plan to help Susan lose weight, taking into consideration the principles of nutrition.

Go further – can you evaluate:

3. How likely is it that Susan would have lost more weight had she breastfed her children?

Irritable bowel syndrome

Irritable bowel syndrome (IBS) is a disorder of the bowel or gut. Its cause is unknown. It affects younger people more than older people, and women more than men. It does not lead to any other disease and life expectancy is normal. Symptoms include diarrhoea and/or constipation, bloating, abdominal pain and/or nausea, urgent need to pass stools, bloating and wind. Sometimes mucus is passed along with stools and some people feel that they have not properly emptied their bowels after having gone to the toilet. IBS is thought to be due to over-activity of the gut. In some cases it begins after an episode of gastro-enteritis, which is thought to leave the bowel over-sensitised. Sometimes a course of antibiotics can interfere with normal bowel function by destroying the bacteria in the gut that help to digest food.

Food allergies or food intolerance (particularly to wheat) can lead to IBS. In many cases, it is associated with stress because of the complex interaction between nervous-system function and bowel evacuation. In stressful situations, the brain sends urgent signals to the bowel to empty as part of the 'fight or flight' response.

Treatments vary according to the causes and symptoms, and a process of trial and error may be needed before IBS can be brought under control. Effective management may include relaxation techniques for stress, coupled with an elimination diet to identify any intolerance. Other measures include anti-spasmodic drugs to reduce pain or anti-diarrhoea treatments, dietary changes to reduce constipation and so on. Anti-depressants may be used to treat pain and diarrhoea.

Government initiatives

Britain has a work culture in which long hours are considered normal. This leaves little time for domestic responsibilities, particularly food preparation and cooking. In the 1980s the average time for meal preparation was an hour, it is now 20 minutes. There has been an increased consumption of ready meals, fast food and take-away meals. Many of these are nutritionally unbalanced and contain high proportions of saturated fats, sugar and salts. There is also a tendency to eat small, quick meals or snacks instead of three balanced meals, which have been shown to regulate metabolism and, in particular, blood sugar levels.

Other factors include changes to the National Curriculum in schools. Food Technology has replaced traditional Domestic Science, where cooking skills were taught. When school meals were tendered out to commercial contractors, nutritional standards were abolished, resulting in poorer quality meals with an emphasis on pre-prepared food and a tendency to provide popular items (often high in fat, sugar and salt).

Government initiatives to encourage healthy eating have had minimal effect because of these lifestyle changes. The government is putting into practise a comprehensive Food and Health Action Plan (*Choosing Health*, 2004), and new initiatives include:

* encouraging women to breastfeed for six months; increases in maternity benefits and maternity leave; getting workplaces to make provision for breastfeeding mothers

* reform of the Welfare Food Scheme to provide more milk and vitamins than before

* Food in Schools Programme to encourage a 'whole school' approach to healthy eating

* working with the food industry (through the Food Standards Agency) to address levels of fat, salt and added sugar in products

* a national scheme to differentiate between healthy and unhealthy foods on labels.

These initiatives, together with DRVs and RDAs, aim to raise the awareness and encourage people to adopt healthier lifestyles.

> **Key concept**
>
> *diet* Diet can reduce the risk of the onset of disease. Government guidelines are insufficient to prevent diet-related disease, and individuals must take action to improve their diet by learning about the consequences of poor eating.

Section 3: Positive effects of exercise

Exercise has been shown to benefit overall health in many different ways.

Physical health

Exercise improves cardiac output and strength, increasing lung capacity so that oxygen circulates round the body more effectively. This supports metabolic processes and improves cell and inter-cell nourishment. Exercise reduces cholesterol levels, increases blood supply to the muscles and reduces body fat, which is utilised during energetic activities. Bone strength and flexibility are improved by weight-bearing activity. Improvements in blood supply to the heart and brain can reduce the risk of coronary heart disease and stroke. Exercise increases the ability to remove toxins and waste products, and improves immune system function, reducing the likelihood of illness.

Mental health

Exercise improves the sense of well-being and mental health for two reasons: it improves blood supply to the brain and it provides oxygen. The brain responds by releasing 'feel-good' chemicals (endorphins) which enhance mood and counteract the effects of stress. Mental alertness is increased as the brain receives more blood rich in oxygen and nutrients.

Mental alertness is the ability to concentrate for extended periods on complex tasks, and includes cognitive functions (e.g. problem-solving, memory, awareness and quick thinking). Mentally alert people are more likely to predict and assess risks and respond appropriately. Doctors are encouraged to prescribe exercise programmes as a first-line treatment for mild depression instead of medication; they also prescribe exercise for obese patients. Exercise can also enhance self-esteem and confidence: low self-esteem is a factor in poor mental health.

Social benefits

There are social benefits to exercise, particularly through team sports. Friendship networks are developed, reducing the loneliness and isolation that can lead to depression. Exercise can also increase self-confidence through weight loss, improved posture and physique, and better skin and hair. These effects can motivate individuals to socialise more and widen their circle of friends.

Motivation – the conscious or unconscious reasons why people do things – is an important concept in relation to health behaviour. Without motivation, changes to lifestyle or diet do not occur.

Physical fitness

Physical fitness embraces a combination of physical attributes. Fitness levels measure an individual's ability to carry out daily activities without feeling exhausted, regardless of age, gender or sporting ability. Daily activities include regular physical movement, e.g. walking, going upstairs, running for the bus, carrying heavy loads, housework etc. Care work requires a reasonable level of fitness as it involves quite a lot of moving around, and lifting and carrying are often required.

Overall fitness
Strength and muscular endurance
Strength and endurance are important for everyone, not just sportspeople. Strength is the ability of the muscles to exert force using one single muscle contraction to overcome resistance, e.g. the amount of force needed to move a heavy object or lift a shopping bag. Strength is important for posture, since contraction and relaxation of specific muscle groups, e.g. those in the back, keep us upright. Muscular endurance is the ability to perform repeated muscle contractions over a period of time, e.g. walking or running. Everyday and sporting activities require muscular endurance.

Aerobic capacity and endurance
Aerobic capacity and endurance depend on the volume of air taken into the lungs to supply the muscles with oxygen via the blood stream. The

vessels supplying the muscles dilate, increasing blood flow and therefore the supply of oxygen. The more air the lungs can take in, the greater the oxygen supply will be. Aerobic endurance, sometimes described as **VO$_2$ max**, refers to the amount of oxygen extracted from the inhaled air that the body can use.

Aerobic endurance forms the basis of fitness for sporting activities and is vitally important for everyone. Someone with reduced aerobic endurance is likely become breathless with exertion and is less likely to exercise, thus decreasing their lung capacity. Good aerobic endurance can improve health by increasing the body's efficiency through increased blood and oxygen supply to vital organs. The more efficiently the body is functioning, the better it can, for example remove waste products and toxins. Better blood supply to the brain leads to more efficient production of brain chemicals that affect the mood and central nervous system, counteracting the effects of stress.

Flexibility

Flexibility concerns the ability of the joints to reach their full range of movement. If the full range of joint movements is not used on a regular basis, the joints become stiff and less flexible. People who are sitting for most of the working day can develop reduced movement in the hips. The ageing processes lead to lower flexibility as the normal joint lubrication mechanisms become less efficient. This, with general 'wear and tear' on the joints, can result in stiffness and associated loss of muscle tone, and can affect balance.

Body composition

Body composition is the ratio of fat to lean body tissue. Overall weight is not a good measurement of body composition, because lean body tissue also contributes to weight. Body mass index (BMI) is more commonly used to assess body composition. It measures weight in relation to height, but it does not distinguish between fat and fat-free mass. To measure body composition accurately, BMI needs to be used with other measures, e.g. skinfold measurements. This measures the amount of fat below the skin (subcutaneous fat) using callipers on various parts of the body. The percentage is calculated using tables calibrated for age.

Fat is weight that cannot be used, therefore the more fat a person is carrying, the less fit they will be. Weight is gained when calorie intake exceeds requirements. Increasing exercise a little and decreasing calorie intake will result in weight loss. Many people who try to lose weight reduce food intake without increasing exercise, resulting in the metabolism slowing as the body tries to conserve energy, so no weight is lost.

Consider this

Barry is a 34-year-old computer professional. He lives alone with his dog, within a mile of his workplace. Barry mainly eats ready meals heated in the microwave; he is particularly fond of pasta dishes such as macaroni cheese. He dislikes most vegetables and rarely eats fruit. He drinks eight cups of coffee per day on average. Barry exercises his dog every evening after work before settling down to watch TV. He rarely goes out and is feeling miserable. Recently he has become concerned about his weight, as he weighs 112 kg and is 1.75 metres tall. His waist measurement is 102 centimetres.

Using the concept of physical fitness, can you identify:

1. two actions that Barry could take to increase his fitness levels

2. two actions that Barry could take to improve his diet?

Go further – using the theories and principles of exercise can you analyse:

3. what conditions Barry may be at risk of developing

4. two types of exercise that would be most useful to Barry

5. how these would benefit Barry in the short, medium and long term?

Go further – using theories and principles of exercise, can you evaluate:

6. what goals Barry should aim for in order to reach total fitness

7. how long might this take

8. how Barry could be motivated to change his lifestyle?

To understand how exercise affects physical health, some basic understanding of the biological structures and functions of the cardiovascular (heart and blood vessels), circulatory (blood flow), musculoskeletal (muscles and bones) and respiratory systems (lungs) is needed.

Respiratory system

There are two main types of respiration: aerobic and anaerobic. In aerobic respiration oxygen is taken into the body via the lungs to contribute to the chemical reactions and metabolic processes involved in releasing energy from food. The by-products of this process are carbon dioxide and water, which are excreted via the lungs during exhalation.

Anaerobic respiration occurs when the body is working so hard that insufficient oxygen is taken in to manage metabolism; other chemicals have to be substituted for oxygen in order to release energy. It is less efficient than aerobic respiration and causes more waste products, e.g. lactic acid, which are excreted via the kidneys and skin in urine and sweat.

Oxygen enters the lungs through the mouth and nose during breathing. This happens through the coordinated efforts of the inter-costal muscles (between the ribs) and the diaphragm (the large muscle forming the 'floor' of the chest cavity and sealing it off from the rest of the body). Breathing occurs when the chest expands, causing negative pressure in the chest and causing the lungs to expand and fill with air drawn in from the environment. Breathing is controlled by the respiratory centre in the brain.

Cardiovascular system

This system consists of the heart and blood vessels throughout the body. The heart can be compared to the engine of a car: it pumps the nutrient-rich blood to every part of the body.

The heart is a muscular structure within the chest cavity. It has four sections (chambers): the two upper chambers are called **atria** (singular = atrium), the two larger lower chambers are called **ventricles**. The chambers are separated by valves that allow the blood to flow through the heart in one direction only. The ventricles are separated from each other by a muscular wall called a **septum**.

Blood returns to the heart from the body depleted of oxygen and nutrients. It enters the

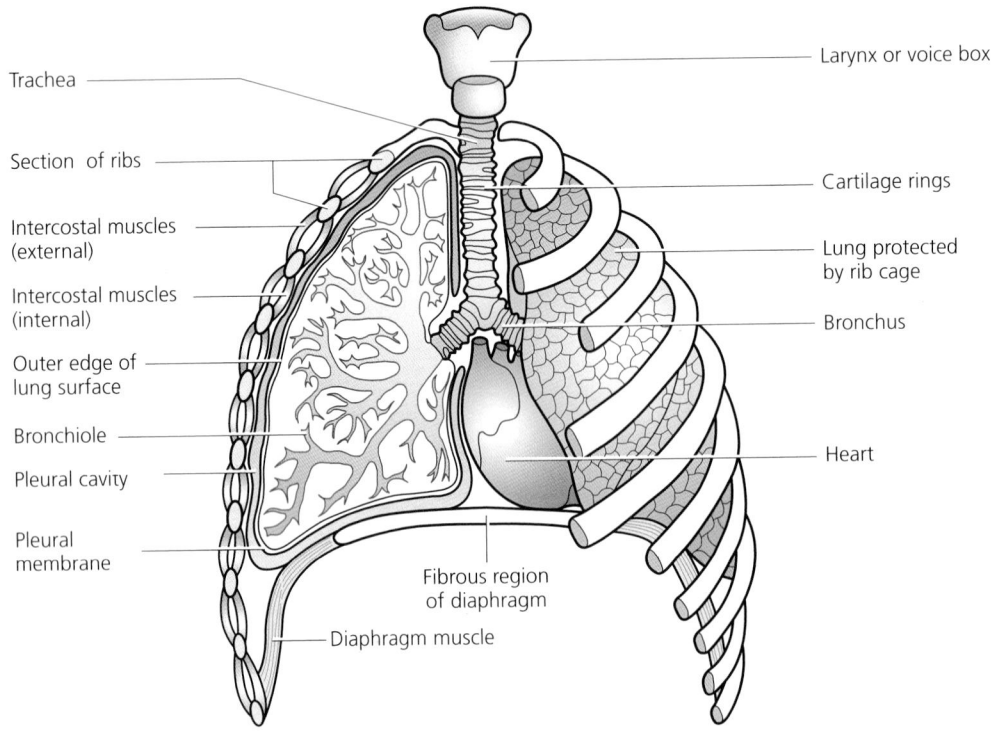

Trachea

Section of ribs

Intercostal muscles (external)

Intercostal muscles (internal)

Outer edge of lung surface

Bronchiole

Pleural cavity

Pleural membrane

Larynx or voice box

Cartilage rings

Lung protected by rib cage

Bronchus

Heart

Fibrous region of diaphragm

Diaphragm muscle

FIGURE 7.6 *Section through the thorax*

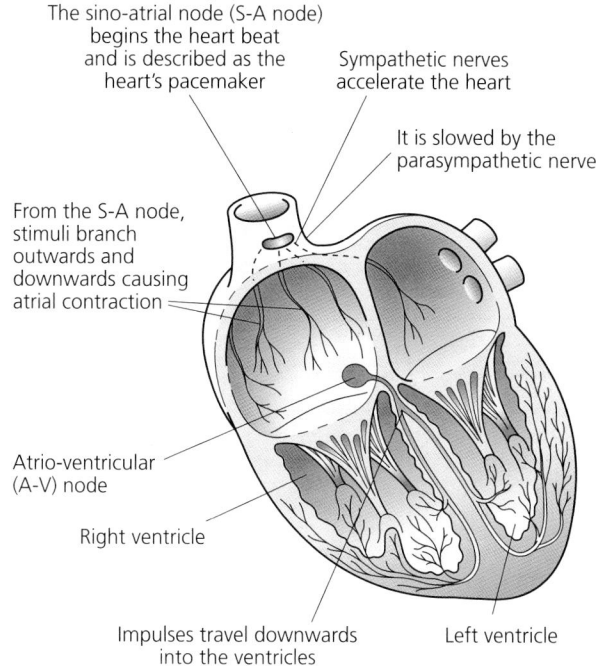

The sino-atrial node (S-A node) begins the heart beat and is described as the heart's pacemaker

Sympathetic nerves accelerate the heart

It is slowed by the parasympathetic nerve

From the S-A node, stimuli branch outwards and downwards causing atrial contraction

Atrio-ventricular (A-V) node

Right ventricle

Impulses travel downwards into the ventricles

Left ventricle

FIGURE 7.7 *Cross-section of the heart*

right atrium through two large veins: the superior vena cava, which brings blood from the upper body, and the inferior vena cava, which returns blood from the lower body. The right atrium contracts and squeezes the blood through the tricuspid valve (a one-way valve which prevents any backflow) and into the right ventricle. The right ventricle then contracts, sending the depleted blood to the lungs via the pulmonary artery. Here, waste carbon dioxide is removed and the blood is replenished with oxygen. The revitalised blood returns to the left atrium via the pulmonary veins. Here it is squeezed through the mitral valve as the left atrium contracts, into the left ventricle.

The left ventricle pumps the blood out of the heart into the main blood vessel, the aorta. The aorta carries the blood round the body; branching and dividing into smaller vessels as it gets further away from the heart. The left ventricle has to contract strongly in order to ensure the blood reaches the furthest parts of the body, it has a much thicker muscle wall than the right ventricle. The blood that nourishes the heart is supplied by the coronary arteries. These can become blocked,

either partly or fully, during a heart attack (coronary thrombosis). Restricted supply due to arteriosclerosis causes angina; complete blockage due to thrombosis (blood clot) causes death within minutes.

The actions described above happen with every heartbeat and are known as the cardiac cycle. The heart muscle contractions are controlled by the central nervous system, which sends electrical nerve stimuli to bundles of nerve fibres situated in the heart itself, causing the muscles to contract.

Circulatory system

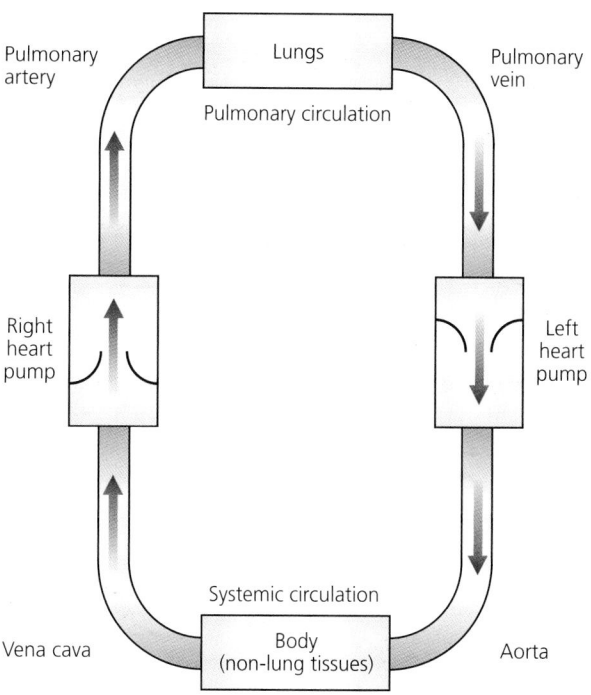

Pulmonary artery

Lungs

Pulmonary vein

Pulmonary circulation

Right heart pump

Left heart pump

Systemic circulation

Vena cava

Body (non-lung tissues)

Aorta

FIGURE 7.8 *Blood flow through the heart*

This is the network of blood vessels that transport blood around the body and to and from the heart. There are two main types of vessels: arterial and venous. Generally, arterial blood vessels carry blood from the heart around the body; veins carry blood back to the heart. The exceptions to this are the pulmonary vein and the pulmonary artery (see above).

Blood vessels differ in size and diameter, depending on their function. They also differ slightly in their structure, with arteries having a thicker muscle layer than veins. The inside of both arteries and veins is very smooth to assist blood flow.

Arteries

To withstand the pressure exerted by the force of the blood being pumped out of the heart, the arteries have elastic, muscular walls. These muscles can expand (vasodilation) and contract (vasoconstriction) in response to substances such as hormones, and blood pressure is affected. Contraction of the arteries will increase blood pressure, relaxation will decrease it.

The largest artery, the **aorta**, has many branches to different parts of the body. These are often named with reference to the organs they are supplying, e.g. the **renal artery** is a branch of the aorta that supplies the kidneys (renal = kidney).

Arterioles

These are smaller branches of arteries. They have thicker, muscular walls and contract and expand to control the rate of blood supply to the capillaries (see Figure 7.9).

Veins

Veins are collecting vessels which return blood to the heart. They carry blood against gravity, so they have valves to prevent the blood from flowing backwards or stagnating and clotting in the vessels. Varicose veins occur when the valves do not work properly and the vessel walls become dilated with blood. Like arteries, veins are named after the organs from which they collect blood, e.g. the portal vein carries blood from the liver (portal = liver). Veins are used for giving injections of medication or additional fluid directly into the circulation for fast action.

Venules

Venules are small blood vessels which collect blood from the capillaries and empty it into the veins. They have thinner walls than arterioles.

Capillaries

Capillaries are the smallest vessels of all, with walls of a single layer of cells. Molecules of oxygen and nutrients diffuse through them to enter the tissues. Waste products such as carbon dioxide diffuse back into the blood to be carried

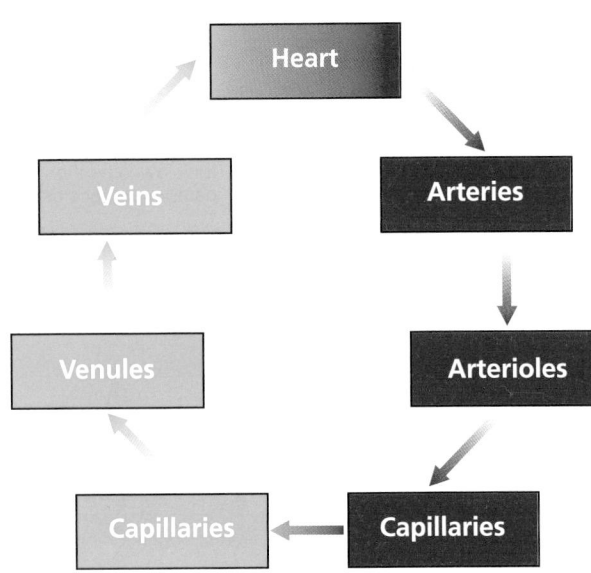

FIGURE 7.9 *Circulation of blood in the heart*

away and removed. The total length of capillaries in humans is around 40,000 kilometres (25,000 miles).

The musculoskeletal system

This system is the arrangement of bones, muscles and joints that support the body, provide the mechanics of movement, and protect the organs. The human skeleton consists of around 206 bones. It is useful to picture the skeleton in sections, all 'hanging' off the spine (the main upright support), with the skull on top.

* the **shoulder girdle**: collar bones (clavicle), shoulder blades (scapulae), shoulder joint, upper arm bone (humerus), lower arm bones (radius and ulna), wrist bones (carpals) and finger bones (metacarpals)

* the **thorax** (chest): rib bones (costal bones) and breastbone (sternum)

* the **pelvic girdle**: pelvis, **ilium** (hip bones), acetabulum (hip joint)

* the leg bones: femur (thigh bone), kneecap (patella), tibia, fibula, ankle bones (tarsals) and toes (metatarsals).

Bones consist of a hard shell (cortex) with a hard, meshed, honeycomb structure inside to give strength. Bone formation continues throughout life, although most growth takes place during childhood; growth occurs in children at the bone ends (epiphyses). In the womb, the early foetal skeleton is made up of cartilage, which is gradually replaced by bone. A particular type of cartilage lines the bones inside joints: this is called hyaline cartilage (from the Greek word for glass, because it is so smooth), and it prevents damage to the bone ends from friction during movement.

Joints

Joints occur where two bones come together. They assist with movement, in coordination with the muscles. Joints permit a range of movements, e.g. flexing (bending as in elbow or knee), adduction (bringing towards the middle, e.g. when crossing the legs) and rotation (e.g. when turning the hand palm upwards). Each joint is surrounded by a capsule made from fibrous tissue which produces lubricating fluid called synovial fluid.

The main types of joints are:

* **hinge joints**: the elbow (between the humerus and the ulna, upper and lower bones) and knee, which allow flexion

* **pivot joints**: the elbow (between the radius and ulna, the two lower bones), which allow rotation

* **condyloid joints**: the knee, which allows rotation when bent (flexed), but not when straight (extended)

* **ball and socket joints**: the hip, which allows a wide range of movement.

The spine is a column of bones (vertebrae) which vary in size and shape. They can be described as joints, as they allow movement; however, the most movement is in the head and neck region (the skull is attached to the spine with a special type of ball and socket joint), and the lower back or lumbar region, which allows flexion and rotation.

Muscles

Muscles also have different structures depending on their purpose. The muscles concerned with physical movement alter as a result of exercise. The main types of muscles are:

* **striated** (striped) muscles: skeletal (voluntary) muscles used in movement and the heart muscle. This type of muscle is used for short bursts of activity

* **smooth** muscle (involuntary): in the intestines, throat and blood vessels. Used when longer contraction is required, e.g. moving food through the gut over time.

Skeletal muscle is made up of special cells, or fibres, in bundles grouped together to form muscles. Receptors, called spindles, receive sensory information from the central nervous system at special points in the muscle. Muscles are connected to the bones with strong fibrous extensions called tendons.

Some muscle fibres (type 1) are more capable of supporting endurance activities that don't require maximum strength, because they are rich in oxygen and respond to aerobic metabolism. The other main type of muscle fibres (type 2) are better at generating short bursts of power and respond to anaerobic metabolism. These fibres are used when a task requires more than 25 per cent of your strength. Some type 2 fibres are big and strong but cannot sustain effort for more than a few seconds. They are known as 'couch potato' fibres because people who are sedentary and do not exercise have more of these. Other type 2 fibres can sustain effort for longer.

Regular exercise, particularly aerobic exercise, e.g. running, swimming and cycling, encourages 'couch potato' fibres to modify into the type that can sustain effort longer. They are a key feature of fitness improvement. With exercise over time, the muscles develop and the number of both types of fibres increases. For such adaptations to occur, exercise needs to regular over time and to increase in intensity.

Because the heart is a muscular organ and has striated muscles, the benefits of improved muscle performance, strength and endurance also apply. Increased heart performance can lower blood pressure and resting heart rate. Exercise will alter the ratio of fat to lean body mass, as the fat will be converted to energy once initial reserves have been exhausted. This will reduce the likelihood of cardiovascular disease by lowering cholesterol levels.

In diabetes, exercise helps control blood glucose levels and reduce the long-term effects of diabetes. Regular weight-bearing exercise (walking or jogging) can increase bone density.

Asthmatics benefit from regular exercise; indeed, many top class athletes are asthma sufferers. Care must be taken, however, because exercise can worsen symptoms and trigger an asthma attack. In asthma the air passages narrow and become clogged with mucus; sufferers wheeze and have difficulty exhaling. Cold, dry air and dusty atmospheres can trigger attacks. Regular exercise can increase the capacity of the lungs and encourage efficient gaseous exchange, benefiting asthma sufferers in the long term.

Consider this

Peter is a 12-year-old insulin-dependent diabetic. He is keen to improve his fitness and is an accomplished swimmer.

Using theories of Dietary Reference Values (DRVs), can you identify:

1. the appropriate calorie/energy intake for a boy of Peter's age?

Go further – using the theory of diabetes, can you analyse:

2. factors you need to consider when designing a training programme for Peter?

Go further – can you evaluate:

3. potential benefits and risks for Peter of undertaking exercise, including physical, social and emotional risks and benefits?

Key concept

exercise Exercise can benefit the physical, emotional and social well-being of individuals and reduce the risk of disease. However, the long-term effects of exercise depend on the body's ability to adapt to the increased effort required. Biological adaptation only occurs following sustained effort over a period of time, and so the frequency and consistency of exercise is crucial to initiating and maintaining health benefits. Motivation is an important aspect of this because it is a crucial factor in both initiating and sustaining changes in lifestyle that are likely to benefit health. Motivation is affected by conscious and unconscious reasoning, as well as individual values and beliefs.

Section 4: Health and safety considerations when designing an exercise programme

Programmes must take account of the individual's health status, the purpose of the exercise, the level of motivation and the end goals through:

* health-related fitness: based on fitness assessment scores; good scores mean the individual has a lower than average chance of developing health problems

* motor fitness: level of fitness that allows the individual to perform a particular activity, task or sport

* total fitness: fitness relating to quality of life; includes physical, social and spiritual well-being.

Everyone can benefit from exercise; however, there are certain groups of people who need special consideration when designing exercise programmes:

* children and young people, who have higher nutritional needs because they are still growing

* people over 50, whose strength, endurance and flexibility are generally decreasing

* disabled people, who need exercises tailored to accommodate their physical limitations

* pregnant women, who should not over-exert themselves but who benefit from exercise – a good level of general fitness helps in labour.

It is important to recognise cultural aspects related to exercise, such as dress codes for women and the gender of the assistant; however, this should not present insurmountable problems if discussed with the individual.

Principles of training

Any fitness and exercise programme must be based on the key principles of training in order to be effective.

Individuality
The programme must be tailored to the individual's needs and requirements including age, gender, and previous and current activity levels. Incorporate an element of choice wherever possible to initiate motivation. Include short-, medium- and long-term goals. Lifestyle factors will influence the ability to follow the programme, e.g. the availability of nearby facilities and equipment, access, cost and time factors.

Overload
Unless the body's capacity is repeatedly challenged (overloaded), long-term changes through biological adaptation do not occur. Overload involves increasing the frequency, intensity and duration of exercise, usually over a specific time period. It can take from six weeks to several months for lasting changes to occur.

Progression
Steadily increasing overload leads to an improvement in fitness over time. Known as progression, the body gradually adapts to steady overload and improves its efficiency. Progression is linked to motivation, and lack of noticeable improvement can demotivate individuals. Excessive overload can also lead to a lack of motivation and contribute to exercise-related injury.

Specificity
Specificity is important: it involves training muscles or muscle groups engaged in the chosen sport or activity. More generally, specificity refers to choosing particular activities to improve areas of weakness and meet goals. Increases in strength, flexibility or aerobic capacity and endurance may require different training programmes.

Reversibility
It is essential that the programme allows for rest and repair between sessions, but it is important that sessions are regular and at a steady pace. Lapses or marked decreases in overload will decrease any fitness gains made. There may be many reasons for interrupted or reduced sessions – for example, injury, illness, a decrease in motivation, irregular working hours or changes in responsibilities.

Testing is important to assess fitness levels, to set goals and to motivate the individual. Factors affecting the success or failure of a programme include:

* motivation and freely chosen participation
* choice of methods
* physical state, e.g. shortage of sleep
* nutritional state
* weight
* smoking
* medical conditions.

Assessment of fitness level

The first stage in designing a programme is an assessment of general health and current fitness levels, to identify any existing or previous condition that would prevent safe exercise. Thorough fitness testing measures the physiological processes, e.g. muscle strength, aerobic capacity, flexibility and joint function, balance, cardiac output and efficiency. Test results are compared with the average, or normal values. Programmes are designed to improve either overall levels of fitness or specific aspects, depending on an individual's strengths and weaknesses. It is usual to complete a questionnaire with participants: a face-to-face discussion will provide a clearer picture of any limitations and help you assess the level of motivation. If individuals have been prescribed exercise by the GP, they may not be convinced of its value. A health questionnaire needs to cover the following issues:

* medical conditions, e.g. asthma, diabetes, high blood pressure, angina, epilepsy
* previous surgery
* medication and drugs
* smoking and drinking
* allergies
* headaches, dizzy spells, fits or fainting attacks
* diet.

If possible, participants should complete a diet log for one week before starting the programme so that diet can be assessed and changes incorporated if needed. For insurance reasons the participant must make a declaration to state that they use any equipment and undertake exercise at their own risk. If you are assisting someone to undertake an exercise programme, you must ensure that they are given a full explanation of what it entails and check their understanding before they sign a declaration.

Following a questionnaire, the participant usually carries out a series of assessment activities. It is good practice to take a blood-pressure reading (see page 291) and resting pulse rate before any activity commences. The pulse can be felt wherever an artery is sufficiently near the surface to be detected; common sites include the inside of the wrist between the wrist bone (radius) and the tendons (**radial pulse**) – usually one or two finger-widths from the wrist bone at the base of the thumb. Other sites include the **carotid** pulse, at either side of the windpipe in the neck, about half way up. The **brachial** pulse, located inside the elbow, is a common site for intra-venous injections; to detect this pulse, the subject must extend the arm and the pulse is usually located about three finger-widths from the edge nearest the body.

When taking a pulse, you need a watch with a second hand to count the beats in one minute. Use your fingers, not your thumb, as you can sometimes feel your own pulse through the thumb. Average resting heartbeat is around 70

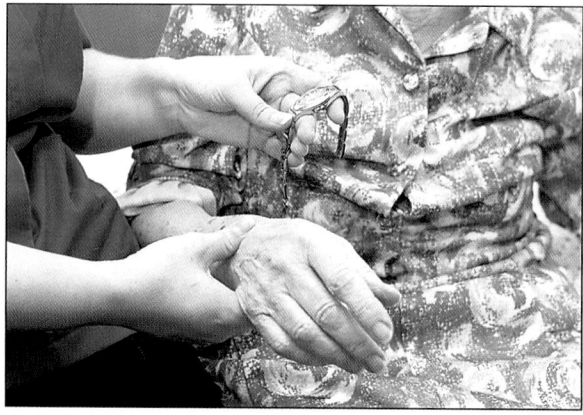

FIGURE 7.10 *Taking a radial pulse*

beats per minute (bpm) for men. Normal is considered to be 60 to 90 bpm, although this can vary depending on age and anxiety levels.

Following this, the participant should be weighed and measured and the BMI calculated.

Fitness assessment

There are different assessments for different components of fitness, e.g. strength, flexibility, cardiac output and aerobic capacity. Each test should measure one aspect of fitness only and should require no technical competence on the part of the participant. It is important to provide clear instructions and to carry out tests at the same time of day and under the same conditions to standardise testing and ensure accuracy over time.

There are different levels of tests:

✳ maximal tests: these stress the body by exercising to capacity; assess aerobic and anaerobic capacity

✳ sub-maximal tests: less demanding, less accurate, and only assess aerobic capacity.

It is important to find the reasons why an individual is participating in exercise. Maximal tests should not be taken on someone with a heart condition unless under medical supervision and with resuscitation equipment available. Some tests are general assessments of different components of fitness. Others are more suitable for sportspeople and athletes and usually assess a particular characteristic such as speed, agility or power in the legs or arms. Speed and agility are necessary for rugby and football, but rugby involves more physical contact so more strength is required. Sprinters need velocity, while long-distance runners need endurance and stamina.

Common tests

Sit-and-reach

A test for flexibility of hip and trunk. The individual sits on the floor with the back and head against a wall. The legs are stretched out in front with the feet flat against a sit-and-reach box. The client stretches the arms forward, keeping the back against the wall, and the distance from the fingertips to the box edge is measured. This is the starting point, or 0 (zero). The client slowly bends

and reaches forward as far as possible while sliding the fingers against the ruler, holding for two seconds. The reach is measured to the nearest tenth of an inch. The results can be used as a baseline measure to assess improvement with reassessment at intervals during training and on evaluation at the end.

RATING	MEN	WOMEN
Excellent	>17.9	>17.9
Good	17.0–17.9	16.7–17.9
Average	15.8–16.9	16.2–16.6
Fair	15.0–15.7	15.8–16.1
Poor	<15.0	<15.4

FIGURE 7.11 *Sit-and-reach performance for those aged under 36 years*

RATING	MEN	WOMEN
Excellent	>16.1	>17.4
Good	14.6–16.1	16.2–17.4
Average	13.9–14.5	15.2–16.1
Fair	13.4–13.8	14.5–15.1
Poor	<13.4	<14.5

FIGURE 7.12 *Sit-and-reach performance for those aged 36–39 years*

Multi-stage fitness test

This is a maximal endurance test of cardiovascular and aerobic fitness, sometimes known as the bleep/beep test or 20-metre shuttle run. It involves continuous running in time to recorded bleeps between two lines of shuttles (marking cones) set 20 metres apart. The time between bleeps decreases each minute until the person being tested is unable to keep up with them. The initial running speed is usually about 8.5 km/hour. The test score is the level and number of shuttles reached before they couldn't keep up with the tape recording. The score can be converted to a VO_2 max (maximal oxygen consumption) using published tables or calculators. There are numerous variations on this test, e.g. running for a set time such as 9, 10 or 12 minutes, or over a set distance. Either the distance covered (in the first instance) or the time taken (in the second instance) is the score. For adults the test last at least 10 minutes.

Maximal Oxygen Consumption Test (VO$_2$ max)

This maximal test actually measures oxygen consumption rather than estimating it. Aerobic and anaerobic fitness can be measured using this test. To perform the test, exercise is taken using a treadmill or cycle (this type of equipment is called an ergometer). The subject wears a mask (a Douglas bag) which collects the expired air. The volume and carbon dioxide concentrations are measured using special equipment. The workload gradually increases to maximum intensity with measurements taken near the end of the test. Maximum heart rate can also be measured during this test.

You may have seen these tests being used on TV to assess athletes or footballers. Maximum heart rate for an individual can be estimated by subtracting their age from 220. For example, maximum heart rate for a person aged 54 would be $220 - 54 = 166 \pm 10$ bpm (beats per minute).

Cycle ergometer test

This sub-maximal test estimates cardiovascular and aerobic fitness (VO$_2$ max and heart rate). The subject pedals an exercise cycle at a constant workload for seven minutes. Heart rate is measured every minute, and the steady–state heart rate (not fluctuating) is measured against published tables to estimate V0$_2$ max.

Harvard step test

This is another sub-maximal test which is not too demanding; it is suitable for older people, very unfit people or those with medical conditions that will benefit from exercise. It involves stepping up and down on a bench or step approximately 41.3 cm high, in time to a beat, for five minutes. Males should do 24 steps per minute and females 22. The heart rate is recorded for 15 seconds on completion, multiplied by four to calculate bpm. The heart rate can be used to calculate the individual's VO$_2$ max.

Skinfold measurements

These are a method of assessing body mass or body mass composition and refer to the ratio of fat to lean tissue (muscle, bone skin, etc.). Fat is not metabolically active; fat cells increase in size, not number, to accommodate excess calories – they are, in effect, a storage facility. Aerobic exercise decreases the amount of body fat because fat is converted to glucose to provide energy, strength training increases muscle mass and tone. Special callipers are used to measure the thickness of the fat layer just under the skin (subcutaneous fat). Several measurements are taken by a trained person at different points on the body. The results are calculated using equations to assess the ratio of fat to lean tissue. This test should be carried out several times – three is usual – in order to get an accurate figure. The average body fat of men is 15 to 18 per cent and for women 22 to 25 per cent. Too little body fat can affect health: women may cease menstruating, and they are at greater risk of osteoporosis in later life. Fat levels above 25 per cent for men and 32 per cent for women are also dangerous to health.

Grip

This assesses strength and is usually carried out using a special instrument called a dynamometer, calibrated to provide resistance. The subject grips a bar and squeezes as hard as possible, holding for 2–3 seconds before releasing. The result is measured in kilograms and is shown on the instrument.

RATING	MEN	WOMEN
Excellent	>64kg	>38 kg
Very good	56–64 kg	34–38 kg
Above average	52–56 kg	30–34 kg
Average	48–52 kg	26–30 kg
Below average	44–48 kg	22–26 kg
Poor	40–44 kg	20–22 kg
Very poor	<40 kg	<20 kg

FIGURE 7.13 *Average grip scores*

Monitoring techniques

It is important to record information for monitoring purposes at the start of each session, e.g general feelings, tiredness, health and composure, physiological data such as weight, resting heart rate and BP. Details of the programme should also be recorded, including what has been achieved, e.g. distance and time, repetitions (a set number of repeated actions such as sit-ups or weights) and recovery rate. As fitness improves, the heart rate returns to normal quicker, and it should be checked at the end of every strenuous activity. Sometimes it is useful to repeat a test throughout the programme, e.g. at the beginning of the session and after warm-up.

The results of the monitoring and evaluation should be discussed with the participant and any changes agreed.

Evaluation

Following any programme it is important to evaluate both progress during the programme and results at the end. The key features of effective evaluation include:

* what is being measured – the physical characteristics and improvements
* the method and suitability of the programme
* data collection, analysis and interpretation
* assessment of the programme based on data to make informed decisions about effectiveness
* adaptation of the plan and setting of new goals and targets as required.

Safe environments

Safety considerations are very important to the continued motivation and enjoyment of exercise programmes. If someone is cold, uncomfortable or finds the environment unpleasant, they won't want to work hard and benefits will be lost.

Indoor environments should be:

* well lit
* warm

* air conditioned or suitably ventilated to assist cooling down
* provided with fluids to drink.

Running or jogging outdoors:

* should be done with a partner for personal safety
* someone should be informed of the route and likely time of return
* run facing oncoming traffic
* vary your route so that it is not predictable
* only run in well-lit areas.

Exercising outdoors:

* wear several light layers of clothing to allow for changeable weather
* in the dark wear reflective clothing
* leave valuables at home
* use personal stereos discreetly
* hide mobile phones from view.

If team sports are played, it is important that the pitch is in good repair, i.e. not waterlogged, muddy or slippery. Artificial turf may be used to prevent such problems and allow play all year round; it also saves on maintenance costs, although it is expensive to install.

Correct equipment

Equipment should be fit for the intended purpose and should be adjustable. Users should be shown how to adjust the equipment and how to use it safely, and should be supervised on first-time use. Exercise machines should be well spaced out and in good repair.

Loose equipment such as mats and free weights should be stored safely in racks or cupboards. One person should have responsibility for reporting faulty equipment, and should know the measures be taken to ensure equipment is not used by mistake.

Flooring should be appropriate – for example, gymnastics requires a sprung floor. The surface should be smooth and non-slip. Electrical wires should be hidden beneath the floor or in conduits.

It is important that the right equipment is provided when taking part in sports. Footwear should fit properly, e.g. football boots with studs and hockey boots with ankle protectors. Goal-keeping gloves, helmets and shin pads should be the user's personal equipment. Ensure you know what equipment will be needed. In some cases it is possible to hire equipment.

Clothing

Clothing for exercise should be comfortable and appropriate. A wide variety of sportswear is available, some designed for the fashion market rather than for serious exercise. Clothing should be tried on to ensure a good fit. Tracksuit bottoms, stretch shorts and snugly fitting stretch tops are all suitable. Natural fibres absorb sweat, but there are also manmade materials that fulfil this function, although they can be more expensive.

Footwear should be chosen carefully. There are many types of trainer, some suitable for certain activities more than others. You should ensure that the trainers are large enough to accommodate absorbent socks, and provide sufficient support, especially around the instep and outer side of the foot. If your primary activity is likely to be jogging or running, they should have shock-absorbent, flexible soles. Always ask what purpose the trainers were designed for and go to a reputable sports shop for proper advice.

Long hair should be tied back – it is more comfortable and less likely to get in the way. Sweatbands are optional. In racquet sports (tennis or squash) absorbent wrist bands can keep sweat off the hands to prevent the racquet slipping.

Women must wear properly fitting sports bras to provide appropriate support, particularly if they are larger bosomed. Poor support can cause discomfort, chafing and soreness and decrease motivation. It also increases stress on the supporting muscles of the chest, shoulders and upper arms.

Suitability of exercise for intended purpose

The exercise programme must be tailored to individual requirements. Following initial assessment, discuss what the person hopes to achieve by undertaking this commitment. Goals should be realistic and incremental or staged. A short-term goal may be moderate weight loss and general improved fitness. Medium-term goals should aim for significant improvements, e.g. in cardiovascular efficiency and aerobic capacity, whereas long-term goals should aim for maintenance. A six-week programme will accommodate only short- to medium-term goals, though improvements will be noticeable and should increase motivation. Special commitments should be taken into consideration, e.g. business trips, celebrations, holidays. Contingency plans should be made so that the individual can continue some exercise during these times to prevent reversibility.

Types of training

Different types of training work on different aspects of physiological health. They include:

Interval training

The basic principle of interval training is an exercise bout, followed by a rest period, then another exercise. It can improve aerobic and anaerobic fitness, depending on the regime, e.g. by varying the intensity and length of exercise bouts and shortening or changing the resting period. Anaerobic fitness requires short bursts of maximum intensity – for example, running for two minutes at 60 per cent VO_2 (calculated at initial assessment to ascertain optimum speed), resting for 30 seconds and so on.

Steady-state training

Also known as continuous training, this involves maintaining a steady state over a long distance or interval. The intensity should be moderate to high (e.g. 60 per cent to 80 per cent of VO_2 max) over a long distance or time. This is ideal for people just starting structured exercise, children or older people. To achieve overload, increase the time or the distance.

Fartlek training

This involves running outdoors and improves aerobic fitness. The intensity is changed by varying the type of ground, e.g. grass, sand, hills, wooded areas and gentle undulations. Increasing the intensity by using different terrain, will improve aerobic and anaerobic fitness.

Circuit training

Circuit training is usually done on a running track. Several different activities are arranged at intervals around the track, and the participant completes each activity in a specified time, with rest periods between. Circuits can be designed for aerobic fitness, muscular endurance, strength etc. The activities should ensure the individual uses different muscle groups, e.g. lower body and legs, or upper body. Progression and overload can be increased as for interval training, e.g. by decreasing rest periods, increasing the number of circuits or decreasing the time for each activity. Circuit training is more suitable for people who undertake sporting activities, rather than fitness for health.

Resistance training

This improves muscle strength and endurance. Repeated actions using a specific muscle group increase muscular endurance. There are several ways in which resistance can be provided:

* resistance machines: usually found in fitness centres, these allow variable loads or weights to be used. They cater for specialist exercises such a bench or leg press, where a person pushes a fixed weight with legs or arms.

* free weights, bar-bells or dumb-bells allow an increased range of movement and can be combined with other exercises. Heavier weights need supervised use because of the risk of injury.

The number of repetitions is an important consideration in resistance training. A repetition is equal to one movement, e.g. one leg press. Repetitions are grouped into sets: for example one set may equal 10 repetitions (reps). The intensity can be varied and overload achieved by increasing the number of reps in each set, or increasing the number of sets per session. A general concept is low reps and a high load, with the load increasing gradually. It is usual to do five sets per session of 10 reps, or six reps at increased load, building up to 10. Rests between sets avoid a build-up of lactic acid in the muscles; massage

is helpful to assist toxin elimination. It is not advisable to undertake aerobic exercise at the same session as strength training. Three sessions per week with a rest day in between are required for optimal improvement.

Flexibility training

This refers to the amount of movement in and around the joints. A vital part of most sports, it is also beneficial to general heath and well-being because it makes daily activities easier to undertake. Flexibility is improved by overloading a specific muscle group through stretching beyond the normal range. Stretching should not exceed the tolerance level of the tissue: this can lead to injury such as tearing or ruptured tendons. Flexibility training should aim to increase the duration of the stretch and the number of repetitions.

There are different methods of stretching:

* static stretching: is controlled and slow and can be either passive or active.
Static active stretches are where the individual stretches and remains in that position for a given number of seconds, then applies internal force to overload the muscle, stretching it beyond its normal range. This should be smoothly applied as jerky movements can cause damage. Active stretches are achieved by the individual alone; this type of stretch is used in yoga
Static passive stretches require assistance from another person who applies external force, such as gentle, controlled pressure to encourage stretch. It is important that this is done in dialogue with the subject to avoid applying too much force. This type of stretch is also used in yoga; some forms of yoga use belts or blocks to help achieve stretch (as in Iyengar yoga)

* ballistic stretches use quick, jerky movements such as bouncing or bobbing through the full range of movement.

Acceleration exercises such as parachute sprinting, bounds, plyometrics or stair drills are used to improve speed and agility. It is important to differentiate between training for health fitness and training for sport, which is much more specialised and at a generally higher level, although the principles remain the same.

Correct preparation

Whatever exercise programmes are used, it is vitally important that individuals warm up properly first. More injuries are caused by failure to warm up sufficiently than by anything else. The aim of warm-up exercises is to raise the body temperature by one or two degrees, usually through gentle cardiovascular work. Exercise follows immediately in order to prevent cooling down and losing the benefit.

Warm-up exercises have the following advantages:

* they increase cardiac output and blood flow to the muscles

* they enhance the release of energy (glucose) from the muscles

* warm muscles stretch and contract more easily, reducing injury risk

* they increase the quantity or lubricating fluid in the joints

* they prepare the individual psychologically for exercise.

Warm-up exercises consist of loosening exercises, gentle aerobic activity and stretches. For particular sports, specific muscle groups used in the sport should be targeted. A programme should take around 15 minutes to perform.

After exercise, the cool-down period is equally important. It assists the removal of waste products from the muscles, prevents muscle stiffness and stabilises heart rate and blood pressure.

Section 5: How diet and exercise interrelate to affect health

For optimal health we need to achieve a balance between energy expended and energy consumed. This is sometimes described as the 'balance of good health'. If too many food calories are consumed and too little energy expended, weight gain will occur. The reverse will happen if too much exercise is combined with a restricted diet.

It is important to recognise that diet alone does not necessarily achieve long term weight loss. On the contrary, restricting calorie intake without increasing energy expenditure causes the body to adopt 'starvation mode'. When this happens, the body slows down the metabolic rate to conserve energy, so weight remains stable or slightly reduce even though calorie intake is restricted. Signs of this are increasing sensitivity to cold, tiredness and lethargy. For women, in extreme cases, periods will become irregular or cease altogether. Dieting without exercise can lead to weight fluctuations, because when normal eating resumes, the appetite centre in the brain has been disrupted and is out of balance, so appetite control may be impaired. Many diets are not nutritionally balanced, so essential vitamins, minerals and trace elements needed to support metabolic processes and brain function may be deficient. Signs of this include dull, unhealthy hair, breaking fingernails, and poor skin colour and texture. Digestive imbalance can also cause bad breath (halitosis). Mild depression is a side effect of nutritionally deficient dieting. All these symptoms are present in people suffering from eating disorders such as anorexia nervosa and bulimia.

Humans have not evolved to lead sedentary lives: our ancestors expended a great deal of energy in finding food and basic survival. It could be argued that the diseases of excess we see today are, in fact, maladaptions as our bodies seek to achieve a natural balance. The main benefits from exercise are:

* improved circulation
* more efficient transport of nutrients
* improved digestion
* more efficient metabolism
* a more efficient heart
* improved immunity to disease
* increased brain function
* efficient elimination of toxins and waste.

The benefits from exercise are diminished, however, if the food we eat is not nutritionally balanced. Many of today's diseases and conditions do not occur until later life because of the body's efforts to achieve stability and balance. Increasingly, diseases such as diabetes and those caused by obesity are appearing in the population at an earlier age because of poor diet originating before birth, and they are compounded by a lack of exercise. While it is difficult to change habits and motivate people in the short term, care workers are in a unique position to demonstrate the benefits of a healthy diet and exercise.

UNIT 7 ASSESSMENT

How you will be assessed

This unit is internally assessed through portfolio work. You will need to devise an individual exercise programme.

Assessment Task

Donna is a 26-year-old staff nurse on a busy surgical ward at the local general hospital. She works shifts on a regular pattern; however, she sometimes has to cover for colleagues who are ill. In two weeks' time, Donna will be going on temporary night duty for four weeks to cover absence.

Devise an exercise programme for Donna for three weeks. You should include details of the following:

* preliminary fitness assessment tests you will undertake, and why you undertake them
* details of your warm-up routine
* the aims and goals of your programme
* details of chosen activities and a rationale for these
* how these are to be carried out according to the principles of training
* what monitoring activities you will undertake and why
* a cool-down routine
* expected achievements, including time taken to reach goals
* factors influencing your design
* how you will accommodate Donna's spell of night duty
* what steps you could take to maintain Donna's motivation.

References

Fullick, A. *(1998) AVCE Sports Science.* Oxford: Heinemann

National Statistics Office (2003) *National Diet and Nutrition Survey 2003.* London: National Statistics Office

Useful websites

www.food.gov.uk
Food Standards Agency

http://en.wikipedia.org
Wikipedia on-line encyclopaedia

www.dh.gov.uk
Department of Health, *Choosing Health: making healthy choices easier* resource pack (2004)

www.sacn.gov.uk
Scientific Advisory Committee on Nutrition

UNIT 8

Complementary Therapies

This unit covers the following sections:

8.1   Complementary therapies: a definition

8.2   The history and development of CAMs

8.3   The use and provision of CAMs

8.4   Meeting physical, emotional and social needs

8.5   The value of CAMs

Introduction

In this unit, you will learn about a range of different complementary therapies and the ways in which they are used. There is a vast range of information available on this subject. Therefore, you will not find an exhaustive description of each of the therapies within this unit. Rather, you will be given pointers to help you in further research about the therapies you choose to study.

This unit also examines the ways in which complementary therapies are regarded by different sectors of society. This includes established health organisations such as the British Medical Association, consultants, GPs and other health professionals, practitioners of complementary therapies and their own organisations, and members of the public who choose to use complementary therapies.

You also need to be aware that the field of complementary therapies is constantly changing, and you should always take care to check out the situation that is current at the time you are studying.

How you will be assessed

The unit will be internally assessed through a portfolio of work.

Section 1: Complementary therapies: a definition

There is actually no single agreed definition of complementary therapies. The British Medical Association historically uses the term 'non-conventional therapies' (House of Lords 2000), and the term tends to be used to cover treatments and therapies that are not encompassed by conventional or 'allopathic' medicine.

A distinction has been made between those therapies that usually complement conventional medicine (hence the term 'complementary') and those that are seen to provide 'alternative' solutions, both in terms of diagnosis and the nature of the interventions offered. The House of Lords Select Committee on Science and Technology, in its report on complementary therapies, made this distinction, as shown in Figure 8.1.

In practice, the two terms 'complementary' and 'alternative' tend to be used interchangeably, and the abbreviation CAM or CAMs is now found extensively in books and articles on the subject. Indeed, it can be difficult to make a strict distinction between complementary and alternative uses of CAMs. For example, osteopathy is sometimes offered as part of an integrated musculoskeletal service within the NHS (together with physiotherapy and chiropractic).

The term 'CAM' will be used throughout this unit to refer to those therapies and approaches that generally fall outside the allopathic tradition, both in terms of treatment types and in their approach to patients.

Novey (2000) has summarised six key aspects of complementary therapies that distinguish them from allopathic medicine. These are set out in Figure 8.2.

ALTERNATIVE THERAPIES	COMPLEMENTARY THERAPIES
Osteopathy	Aromatherapy
Chiropractic	Alexander technique
Acupuncture	Bach and other flower
Herbal medicine	remedies
Homeopathy	Body work therapies
	(including massage)
	Counselling stress therapy
	Hypnotherapy
	Meditation
	Reflexology
	Shiatsu
	Healing
	Ayurvedic medicine
	Nutritional medicine
	Yoga

FIGURE 8.1 *Distinction between alternative and complementary therapies*
Source: House of Lords, Science & Technology Committee 2000

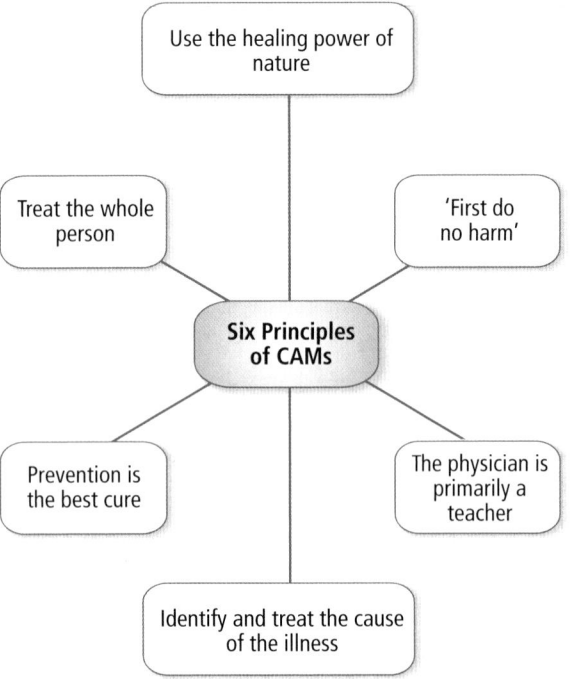

Source: Novey (2000)

FIGURE 8.2 *The six principles of CAMs*

These naturopathic principles work on the premise that the body has its own in-built mechanisms for maintaining health. CAMs, therefore, seek to work with these mechanisms as far as possible, removing blocks to health and enhancing a healthy human organism. Treating the whole person acknowledges the complex nature of each. Many factors combine to create health (or illness), including physical, emotional and social aspects (to name but three). A complementary practitioner is careful to take all aspects of a person's life into consideration. 'First Do No Harm' means that the CAMs practitioner should not attack symptoms without attempting to remove underlying causes. This is because suppressing symptoms without addressing the reasons for those symptoms can actually cause more harm in the long run. The main aim of practitioners should therefore be to identify and treat the actual cause of the problem, and they will always be more interested in the root cause than in the symptoms themselves. Most CAMs

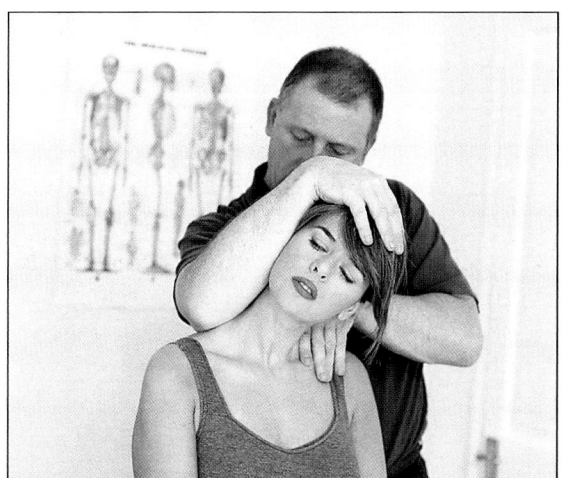

FIGURE 8.3 *Osteopathy is sometimes provided by the NHS as part of an integrated musculo-skeletal service*

take this holistic approach, as the following scenario demonstrates.

SCENARIO

A pain in the neck

Gemma works in an office, using a computer for several hours a day. She has recently developed RSI (repetitive strain injury), which affects both her hands. She also has neck pain.

The doctor has given her some painkillers and a neck brace. At work, her manager has advised her to follow health and safety rules, taking regular breaks away from the computer screen. He has also given Gemma a new fully adjustable chair.

However, she still has pain, and decides to visit an osteopath. After a long discussion (during which acupuncture is suggested for the pain), the osteopath discovers that Gemma is having some relationship problems. He suggests to Gemma that her personal difficulties may be causing additional stress. This in turn may be making her musculo-skeletal problems worse. Until Gemma tackles her other problems, she may not be able to overcome her physical difficulties.

In making this diagnosis, the osteopath takes a holistic approach to Gemma's problems. He looks for the root cause of her physical symptoms, and finds that these may not result solely from the ergonomic factors in her workplace (although these undoubtedly play a part). Instead, he finds that emotional difficulties may not only be making physical problems worse, but may actually be a main cause of Gemma's injuries.

Key concept

holistic approach this approach to illness treats the whole person, rather then just the disease or condition itself.

Section 2: The history and development of CAMs

Ancient systems and practices

Many CAMs in use today have their origins in ancient practices, and some are modern-day expressions of complete medical and philosophical systems that are several thousand years old.

Ayurveda

Ayurveda (pronounced Ai-yur-vey-dah) developed on the Indian subcontinent between 3000 and 5000 years ago. It is more than a medical system, having both a spiritual and a healing dimension. It was devised by the same teachers who developed astrology, yoga and meditation; the health of body, mind and soul are inextricably linked within this system.

FIGURE 8.4 *Ayurveda – an ancient healing system linked to philosophical and spiritual teachings*

Ayurveda works on the principle that there are three doshas (combinations of the five elements: ether, air, fire, water and earth) within the human body. These doshas are Vatha, Pitta and Kapha, and imbalance between them can lead to ill health. The training to become an Ayurvedic practitioner is long and complex, and today many practitioners are also trained in conventional medicine.

Traditional Chinese medicine

This is another ancient and complex system of healing. As with Ayurveda, it perceives both body and mind as integral components of a healthy bodily system, combining this with the concept of balance. The human body has vital energy, called Qi ('chee') which, if blocked, can lead to illness. It is vital for the yin and yang forces within the body to be in harmony, and also for each person to be in harmony with the external environment.

Diagnosis in Chinese medicine is very different from that of allopathic practitioners, and can include close examination of the state of the tongue and the nature of the pulse. Treatment will include a combination of therapies including **acupuncture**, **herbal medicine**, nutrition and **Qigong** (movements used to stimulate the Qi energy through the meridians of the body).

Massage

The use of **massage** to alleviate pain and other conditions also has a long history. The term 'massage' covers a broad range of interventions (see below, Classification of CAMs, page 319), and is used here to encompass manual therapy of all kinds. For example, '**Reflexology**', (the practice of stimulating reflex points on the hands and feet) is known to have been used in China about 5000

FIGURE 8.5 *Reflexology is still widely used today*

years ago as well as in ancient Egypt and in India. Ayurveda, for example, has its own massage technique, linked to the Ayurvedic diagnostic system. (Reflexology was subsequently developed in the 20th century by Dr William Fitzgerald, in about 1913, and later by Eunice Ingham in the 1930s.) Another version of Ayurvedic massage is Chavutti Thirumal. This was developed in southern India with the particular aim of stimulating the digestion, the circulation and the lymphatic system. It was found especially useful by traditional dancers and martial arts exponents. Thai massage is another longstanding practice that combines elements of both the Chinese and the Ayurvedic systems.

Herbal medicine

This has been practised by many societies for thousands of years. Traditional Chinese medicine (see page 314) uses herbal remedies in a system that can be dated back to the 3rd century BC. Many tribespeople have traditional remedies derived from plants. In such societies, there is also often a close link between food and medicine, as indeed there is in traditional Chinese medicine. In Egypt, a Theban papyrus dating from 1500 BC provides an inventory of herbs commonly used for healing; preparations derived from plants were also commonly used in ancient Greece and Rome. Of course, modern pharmaceutical products are also derived from plants, but the active ingredients are used in a highly refined form. In contrast, herbal preparations tend to use the whole plant or parts of it.

In Europe in the Middle Ages, monasteries had herb or 'physic' gardens, and recipes for herbal preparations would often be kept in monastic libraries.

More recently, some herbalists have welcomed a scientific approach to validating their practices, and the word **phytotherapy** is now sometimes used to refer to the practice of medical herbalism.

The 19th century

A number of CAMs have their origins in the late 18th or 19th centuries.

Homeopathy

This was developed by Samuel Hahnemann, a German doctor, who in 1796 developed a system of healing based on the principle that 'like cures like', otherwise known as the 'simile principle'. The simile principle says that an illness is best cured by giving a remedy that would produce symptoms very similar to those already experienced by the patient.

An allopethic practitioner would treat insomnia, for example, by giving sleeping tablets; in contrast, a homeopath might prescribe a very small dose of coffee, a substance that would normally induce sleeplessness if given in large doses.

Homeopathic remedies are diluted and shaken, then rediluted to the point where conventional medical science no longer recognises them as having any active ingredient at all. However, homeopaths believe that the more dilute the substance, the more powerful the active ingredient.

Homeopathy is now regulated in the UK by the Society of Homeopaths. It has been available on the NHS since 1948 and is practiced at five homeopathic hospitals.

During the 19th century, there were also developments in the ancient practice of massage.

There had been some earlier famous European practitioners, for example Ambroise Pare. In the 16th century Pare had adapted older techniques to incorporate physiological and anatomical considerations into the practice. In early 19th-century Sweden, Per Henrik Ling devised a new system (incorporating gymnastics), which is now known as Swedish Massage. This type of massage is very firm, with a range of movement types designed to work on both deep and superficial muscles. Swedish massage is popular with present-day practitioners and in many respects now represents a 'standard' for current western practice.

Chiropractic

This was developed in the late 19th century by Daniel Palmer. Palmer was concerned with the causes of illness, but he was also interested in comparing how different cultures and societies regarded the treatment and diagnosis of disease. A fascination with the spinal manipulation practised in ancient Egypt led him to evolve his own methods to correct misalignment of the spinal column. Chiropractic's underpinning theory is that problems with the spinal column can cause disease by damaging nerves. Although Palmer claimed that his system was a cure for all diseases (a 'single cause approach to disease'), modern chiropractors now limit their focus to musculoskeletal problems. In the UK, chiropractic is now monitored and controlled by the British Chiropractic Association (BCA).

The 20th century

In the early years of the 20th century, Rudolf Steiner developed the philosophy of **anthroposophical medicine** (AM). His approach was not conceived as an alternative system but was designed to complement conventional medicine as practised at that time. His system is holistic – that is, it regards everything about a patient's body and lifestyle to be significant. The system follows seven principles, including the belief that art is essential to human beings. For this reason, a number of other disciplines have developed from AM, including **art** and **music therapies**. Practitioners of AM are also qualified doctors, who use modern drugs and technology

when necessary. In this sense, AM was the forerunner of **integrated medicine** (see below), an approach taken by a some present-day physicians who want to embrace the best of both worlds in working to heal their patients.

Bach flower remedies

Bach flower remedies were developed by Edward Bach in the 1930s. Bach was both a homeopath and a bacteriologist. He believed that disease resulted from emotional or mental imbalance, and that the energy properties of plants could be used to help restore a natural balance within the body and the mind. The flower remedies use the homeopathic principle of potentisation (see page 315), and are made by boiling plants in spring water, or by letting them infuse into the spring water naturally. The resulting product is then preserved in brandy.

Bach identified seven negative emotional categories, which are themselves subdivided into 38 negative feelings. A practitioner will usually ask the patient to identify which flowers (from a selection of photographs) appeal most to him or her at that moment in time. The flowers chosen form the basis of the remedy, which is individually prepared. There are also off-the-shelf remedies available.

Cognitive and behavioural therapies

In the 20th century, developments in the study of psychology led to practical applications in the form of **cognitive** and **behavioural therapies**. This approach is widely recognised by doctors as providing a helpful alternative for treating many problems of a personal and emotional nature. Many counselling services use one or more of these approaches, including those dealing with substance abuse, relationship problems, post-traumatic stress disorder and bereavement, to name but a few. The underlying premise is that in order to solve a person's problem, his or her beliefs about him or herself and about life may have to be challenged, as the problem may have its roots in a damaging belief system.

Types of therapies include brief solution-focused therapy, cognitive-analytical therapy, cognitive-behavioural therapy, reality therapy and personal construct therapy.

Massage

Massage techniques continued to be developed throughout the 20th century. Many variations evolved, including Aston patterning (developed by Judith Aston), Hellerwork (Joseph Heller), sports massage and zero balancing (Fritz Smith) to name but a few.

Recent developments

The late 20th and early 21st centuries have witnessed a tremendous upsurge of interest in CAMs of all kinds. There are a number of reasons for this. First, some people are no longer satisfied with the relationship they have with their GP. The family doctor used to have a relatively intimate relationship with his or her patients, but now that intimacy is rare. Consultations are very short, and patients often feel they do not have the time to say what they want, or that they are not listened to. Secondly modern pharmaceutical preparations are very powerful, and can have some unwanted side-effects. Thirdly the increasing 'fragmentation' of treatment (for example, by several different specialists) can lead to a feeling of being a small cog in a huge, impersonal medical machine. Furthermore, many people feel they have lost control of their situation and their illness once they become 'patients'. Consulting a CAM practitioner can restore the feeling of being a person rather than a patient, and of being someone who is in control of the situation. Attitudes towards CAMs are considered further in Section 5 (see page 338).

The increasing popular interest in CAMs led to the commissioning of a House of Lords Select Committee Report (by the Science and Technology Committee), which was published in November 2000. This report states that CAMs deserve investigation, as it is important for the government to know how they should be regulated by public health policy.

Legislation in 2001 set up the new Health Professions Council (HPC), whose job is to regulate the standards and qualifications of a number of complementary professions. Thirteen groups of professionals are currently subject to this new regulation, and are shown in Figure 8.6.

It is possible that the HPC may regulate other professions in the future.

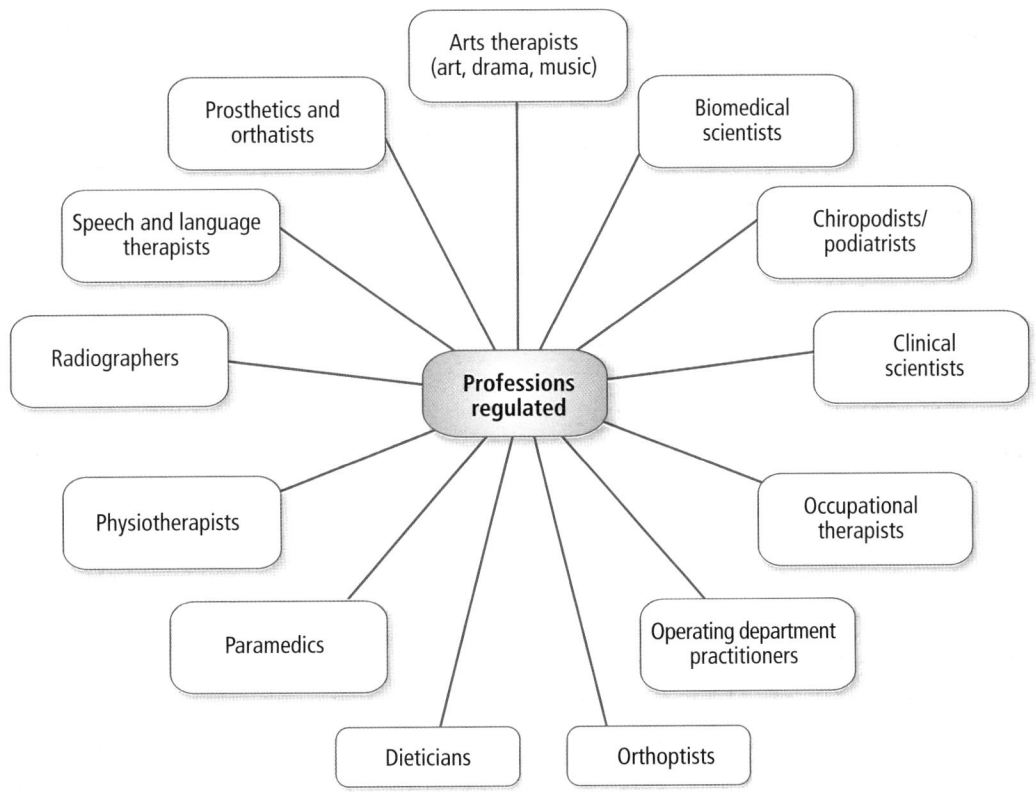

FIGURE 8.6 *Professions regulated by the Health Professions Council (2005)*

The establishment of this organisation is a recognition by government of the growing importance and use of many CAMs, not only by NHS practitioners but also by members of the public who are increasingly turning to such practitioners for help. Alongside this growing public interest is a developing tendency towards the self-regulation of CAMs, together with the development of agreed standards for practice. This trend is discussed in greater detail below (Training and Qualifications, page 328).

The growing interest in CAMs on the part of some members of the medical profession is evident in the development of the practice of **integrated medicine**. Practitioners are medically qualified, but are aware of, and sometimes practise, treatments and procedures that are either complementary or alternative to mainstream medical practice. In 2001 the *British Medical Journal* gave significant consideration to the benefits of taking a more integrated approach to CAMs by medical practitioners.

Although not universally welcomed by doctors, and despite the qualms of medical scientists about the unscientific nature of many therapies, the use of CAMs in the UK is now significant.

Categories of CAMs

Because they act holistically, it is hard to allocate CAMs to rigid categories.

Music therapy, for example, which might be said to be an expressive therapy, could also be considered to act on the senses (the sense of hearing), and also on the subtle relationship between the mind and the body. Music therapy is used to treat a range of conditions and situations, including pain relief (for example, after operations), anxiety, stress and depression. It is also used to help people with disorders such as autism.

This is in contrast to the medical model, where interventions are often categorised according to the kind of conditions they are used to treat. Thus in hospitals there are many departments such as Neurology (which deals with disorders of the nervous system), Cardiology (which specialises in heart conditions) or Oncology (which provides treatment to people with cancer). Of course, there will be similarities between procedures used across these different disciplines, but conventional medicine remains strictly divided into specialisms.

It is possible to attempt a very broad classification of CAMs, and one such classification system is presented here. However, you need to be aware that some of the therapies listed here fall into more than one of the categories.

The classification used in this unit allocates CAMs to five categories.

Sensory

First, there are sensory CAMs that work primarily with the five senses of touch, taste, smell, hearing and sight. An example of this would be aromatherapy, which uses primarily both smell and touch.

Cognitive

Cognitive CAMs work on the relationship between the mind and the body to promote healing. Hypnotherapy would fall into this category.

Expressive

Expressive CAMs use the expression of individual thoughts, feelings and ideas to enable people identify and work out their problems. Art, drama or music therapies would be classified in this way.

Physical

Physical CAMs work on the body's physiological systems to bring about the release of beneficial chemicals such as **endorphins**, or to promote circulatory systems. Massage would fall into this category. Also in this category would be CAMs that promote the flow of energy that is considered by some complementary medical systems to be essential to good health. (Traditional Chinese medicine calls this energy flow Qi, while Ayurvedic medicine refers to it as Prana). Reiki falls into this category, as it aims to maximise energy flow within the human body – as does acupuncture.

Medical systems

Finally, there are some CAMs that comprise complete medical systems in themselves. They have their own rationale and philosophies, and use distinctive diagnostic techniques. Traditional Chinese medicine (TCM), Ayurvedic medicine and homeopathy belong to this category. Such systems use a range of healing techniques that might also fall into one of the preceding four groups. Ayurveda, for example, uses meditation (a cognitive technique), diet (physical), massage (physical), herbal remedies (physical) and aromatherapy (physical and sensory). Furthermore, some CAMs that have their origins in such systems are now practised as separate disciplines. Acupuncture (part of the TCM group of healing techniques) is one such CAM.

Classification of CAMs

Figure 8.7 attempts to allocate some of the most commonly used CAMs to these five categories. Some clearly fall into more than one category and are marked with an asterisk.

CLASSIFICATION OF CAMs THERAPIES	
Sensory	Aromatherapy Bach flowers Colour therapy Music therapy*
Cognitive	Hypnotherapy Cognitive and behavioural therapies* Meditation
Expressive	Art therapy Drama therapy Music therapy* Cognitive and behavioural therapies*
Physical	*Manual Therapy:* Chiropractic Osteopathy Massage (e.g. Swedish, Reflexology, Acupressure) Bodywork (eg. Feldenkrais, Alexander Technique, Aromatherapy, Rolfing) *Energy Healing:* Reiki Therapeutic touch (Spiritual healing) *Nutrition Therapy* *Herbal Medicine* *Exercise systems* Qigong Yoga
Medical systems	Anthroposophical medicine Ayurveda Homeopathy Traditional Chinese Medicine Naturopathy

FIGURE 8.7 *A classification of some commonly used CAMs*

This is by no means a fully comprehensive list of complementary therapies. The Complementary Healthcare Information Service (www.chisuk.org.uk) lists 70 CAMs, and even this list is not exhaustive. There are other organisations and websites that give basic information about a number of CAMs, and some that are exclusively devoted to particular systems or therapies. There are also a number of basic textbooks that describe how CAMs work (see Resources and References section at the end of this unit). The following exercise will give you an overview of the range of CAMs, and also some practise at categorising them.

Think it over...

Research three CAMs from the list below, or alternatively, using the Internet or written resources.

For each of the CAMs you choose, decide which category or categories they belong to, using Figure 8.8 (e.g. sensory, cognitive, expressive, physical, medical systems).

Aura soma	Kanpo
Autogenic training	Kinesiology
Bates method	Life-coaching
Biochemic tissue salts	Manual lymph drainage
Biofeedback	McTimoney chiropractic
Bowen technique	Medau movement
Buteyko	Metabolic typing
Colonic irrigation	Metamorphic technique
Colour therapy	
Cranial osteopathy	NLP
Cranio-sacral therapy	Pilates
Do in	Polarity therapy
Ear acupuncture	Psychotherapy
Emotional freedom technique	Radionics
Holographic repatterning	Seichem
Hopi ear candles	Shiatsu
Indian head massage	Thai yoga massage
Iridology	The journey
Johrei	Thought field therapy
Kahuna bodywork	Toyohari
	Zero balancing

Source: *Complementary Healthcare Information Service* (www.chisuk.org.uk)

You may have found some additional CAMs not listed here. Whichever you chose, it is likely that you may have experienced some difficulty in allocating them to one category alone. The holistic nature of complementary therapies means that they seldom work purely on one aspect of a person's situation or condition.

The following scenario describes how the use of a CAM treatment for a physical injury led to other benefits.

SCENARIO

Extra benefits

Rick is having a bad time at work. Jobs are piling up, and he is afraid to tell his manager in case she thinks he is incompetent. Not only this, one of his colleagues has stopped speaking to him, and there is a terrible atmosphere in the office.

A friend suggests they have a game of squash to help take his mind off things and to get rid of some of Rick's negative energy. However, Rick sprains his elbow during the game, and needs to have a couple of days off work.

Another friend, Sue, is a Reiki healer, and she offers to give him a Reiki session to help speed up the healing process. Although Rick is sceptical, he agrees.

To his surprise, not only does the pain begin to ease, but he starts to feel much more relaxed, less stressed and more positive. He takes some time to think about the situation at work, and when he goes back he has a meeting with his manager to explain his difficulties, and she agrees to take some of the pressure off him.

He still hasn't sorted out the problem with his colleague, but he feels confident that by being assertive and open, he can find a way to discuss things and move towards a solution. He also decides to carry on with the Reiki session.

We have already seen how the Ayurvedic system comprises elements of healing that can be categorised as cognitive, physical and sensory (see page 318). Similarly, TCM – (traditional Chinese medicine) uses a variety of methods that may also be classified as 'physical'. Within TCM, acupuncture is used to restore energy flows (Qi) by stimulating nerves through the insertion of needles at key points on a number of bodily meridians. Acupuncture would be classed as a physical therapy using the system of classification described in this unit. Similarly, herbal medicine, nutrition and Qigong, the other key components of TCM, can all be classed as physical CAMs.

Another medical system that encompasses a range of types of CAM is **naturopathy**. This system was developed in the late 19th century, and declared itself to be a separate system in 1900. Naturopaths believe that the body wants to heal itself, and that disease is caused by imbalance as a result of poor environment, bad nutrition and/or harmful ways of living. Naturopaths will offer one or more well-respected

✳ DID YOU KNOW?

Reiki

Reiki is a Japanese therapy developed by Mikao Usui in (1865–1926), although its origins lie in Buddhist philosophy. The Japanese word ki (chi in Chinese) means 'energy', and rei means 'life'. The Reiki practitioner thus aims to stimulate a person's own 'life energy' by channelling Ki into his or her body. This in turn enhances the body's ability to heal itself.

This enhanced energy flow can have beneficial effects on the mind as well as the body, as Rick's story illustrates. However, Reiki is arguably not a cognitive therapy as such, because psychological benefits might be said to be a by-product of the enhanced physical energy flows. On the other hand, you might want to argue that Reiki should also be classified as a medical 'system', in that it has a complex underpinning philosophy that embraces ethics, behaviour towards others, and taking personal responsibility not only for health (including that of others) but also for living harmoniously and acting positively.

Reiki is not as complex as TCM or Ayurvedic medicine, however, both of these are clearly sophisticated systems that include not only an underpinning philosophy: but also a wide range of treatment types, together with specific diagnostic techniques.

CAMs, including acupuncture, chiropractic, biofeedback or autogenic training, meditation, herbal medicine and nutrition therapy, homeopathy, reflexology and physiotherapy. Naturopathy thus encompasses both physical and cognitive types of CAM.

Some of the CAMs that form part of wider medical systems (both ancient and more modern) are now sometimes practised as disciplines in their own right. Chinese herbal medicine and acupuncture, for example, are sometimes offered as individual therapies. Some practitioners may combine CAMs that have their origins in different medical systems, as the following scenario shows.

In following her interests, Sheila has acquired a range of CAMs skills, together with knowledge of several underpinning philosophies and systems. She first studied Swedish massage, which was developed in the 19th century, but then began to learn more about older traditions when she went on to study reflexology. Finally, in studying the Bowen technique, she added an additional perspective to her work. Sheila now offers a range of treatments that reflects her own personal interests and development as a CAM therapist.

CAMs and orthodox medicine

A naturopathic practitioner will always recommend that a client should see another specialist (including an allopathic doctor) if he or she feels that this would be best. This is true of many CAMs practitioners.

The House of Lords research (2000) distinguished between CAMs that offer diagnoses and those that do not. Included in the first group are osteopaths and chiropractors, acupuncturists, herbal medicine practitioners and homeopaths. However, many of these practitioners will aim to complement treatment that is being given by a conventional doctor.

The House of Lords report also identified a second group of CAMs that generally aim to complement conventional medicine and do not offer diagnoses to clients. These include Alexander technique, bodywork therapies including massage, counselling, stress therapy, hypnotherapy, reflexology, meditation and healing (House of Lords Report, 2000). Many practitioners of these CAMs will always refer a person to a conventional doctor or another specialist if they feel they cannot offer effective help.

The attitude of doctors towards CAMs varies considerably. Some GPs will refer their patients to CAMs practitioners if they feel this is appropriate. Of course, this depends on an individual GP's knowledge and experience of CAMs. Some allopathically trained doctors are now seeking to integrate complementary therapies into their own practice, and the concept of integrated medicine is now fairly well established. For example, the British Association for Allergy, Environmental and Nutritional Medicine (BAAENM) aims to raise the profile of CAMs among medical students, and even to establish postgraduate training in the use of CAMs for qualified doctors.

Recently, the National Institute for Clinical Excellence (NICE) issued guidelines to NHS practitioners on the care of people with multiple sclerosis (MS), a chronic medical condition for which there is still no cure. These guidelines give very cautious approval to the use of certain CAMs with respect to MS, including reflexology and massage, massage plus bodywork, the use of fish oils, magnetic field therapy, neural therapy and T'ai Chi (NICE, 2004). However, this section is a very short part of a document that is devoted

mainly to clinical techniques, and the advice to doctors is simply that they should suggest to patients that some of the CAMs listed might be useful. The guidance makes it clear that the cost of complementary treatments should be met by the patient and not by the NHS.

Indeed, many conventionally trained doctors remain sceptical about the use of CAMs, seeing them as, at best, therapies that work psychologically to make a patient feel better and, at worst, as techniques that do nothing to heal and that can even be dangerous (for example in cases where a patient rejects conventional treatments such as chemotherapy in favour of non-invasive healing methods such as meditation). The problem is that there is a lack of large-scale scientific research of the kind that would convince most medically trained practitioners (such as randomised clinical trials). It is certainly true that a great deal of research has been done into the effectiveness of CAMs, but until relatively recently this was small-scale and often used different methodologies, making it hard to compare the results from different studies. There is now a Professor of Complementary Medicine at the University of Exeter, and the aim of his staff team is to subject a range of CAMs to rigorous scientific study (see Resources section at the end of this unit). However, the funding for this post is from a private source, and it is by no means certain that it will continue indefinitely (Donnellan, 2004). Research into the effectiveness of CAMs has still not gained wholehearted support from orthodox practitioners. More positively, however, the Research Council for Complementary Medicine has recently received government funding (2003) to look at 12 CAMs in four NHS priority areas – cancer, coronary heart disease, mental health and chronic medical conditions (Donnellan, 2004). Furthermore, doctors who consciously practise **evidence-based medicine** seek to combine clinical expertise with external evidence that is relevant to individual patients. In practice, this means doctors may seek to establish what is best for a particular person.

The world of CAMs is in a constant state of change, and students should check the current situation at the time they conduct their research. The merging of older CAMs organisations is a current trend, and new bodies are being formed at an astonishing rate. In January 2005, for example, the Reflexology Society merged with the Association of Reflexologists; the Aromatherapy Council (in the process of being established at the time of writing) will eventually supersede the older Aromatherapy Organisations Council and other older organisations for the practice of aromatherapy.

The ways in which CAMs are used alongside orthodox medicine are discussed in Section 3 below.

SUMMARY

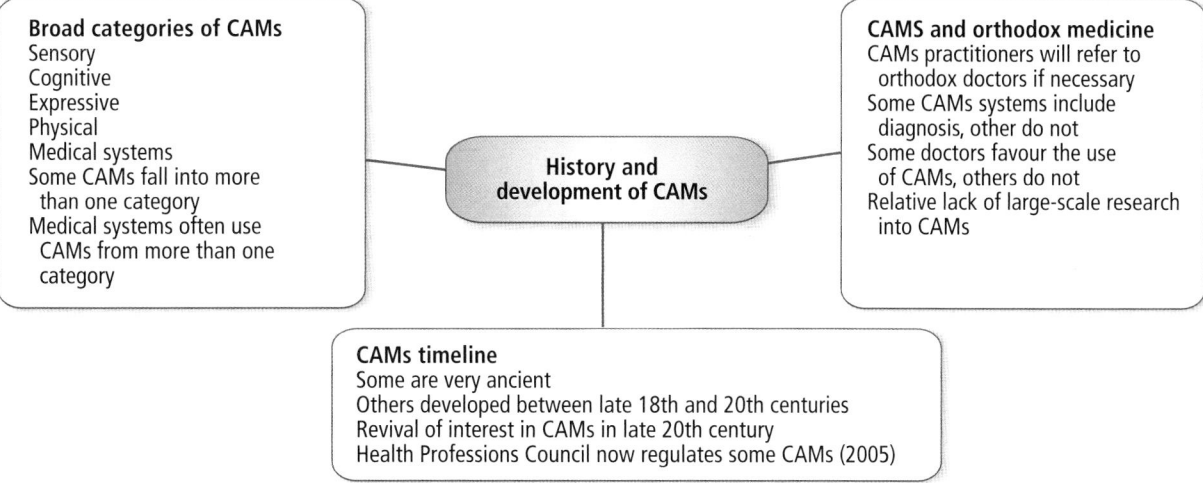

Broad categories of CAMs
Sensory
Cognitive
Expressive
Physical
Medical systems
Some CAMs fall into more than one category
Medical systems often use CAMs from more than one category

CAMS and orthodox medicine
CAMs practitioners will refer to orthodox doctors if necessary
Some CAMs systems include diagnosis, other do not
Some doctors favour the use of CAMs, others do not
Relative lack of large-scale research into CAMs

History and development of CAMs

CAMs timeline
Some are very ancient
Others developed between late 18th and 20th centuries
Revival of interest in CAMs in late 20th century
Health Professions Council now regulates some CAMs (2005)

FIGURE 8.8 *History and development of CAMs*

Consider this

Sue suffers badly from back pain and has been prescribed pain killers by her GP. These are not working, and she is now so desperate that she is seeking help from a naturopath.

During the initial consultation, the naturopath discovers that Sue is not sleeping well, and that she is suffering from low self-esteem. She is unhappy in her job, and dreads going to work on Monday mornings.

1. What options do you think the naturopath might consider for Sue?

2. What other specialists or CAMs therapists might the naturopath recommend?

Section 3: The use and provision of CAMs

How CAMs are used

CAMs are used in many ways in the UK today. Figure 8.9 sets out the main ways in which people can access and use CAMs.

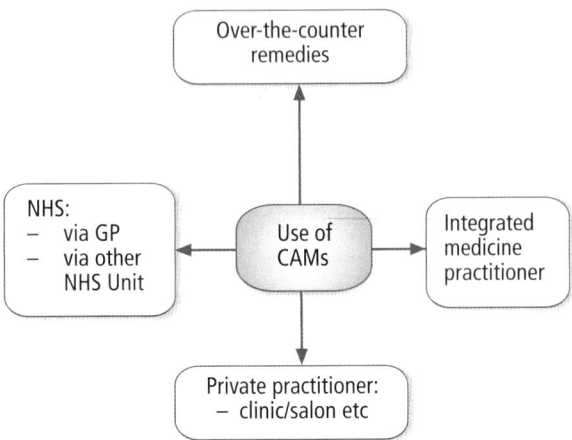

FIGURE 8.9 *Use of CAMs: some access routes*

FIGURE 8.10 *The amount of herbal remedies bought over the counter is rising*

Over-the-counter purchases and private practitioners

The Royal Pharmaceutical Society (RPS) estimated that in 1998 people in the UK spent about £93 million on herbal remedies, homeopathic preparations and aromatherapy oils (House of Lords Select Committee, 2000). The RPS also predicted that such sales would rise to £126 million by 2002. Many people are happy to take preparations that they have chosen and bought for themselves, based on information they obtain from magazines, books or the Internet.

Similarly, individuals often take the initiative in consulting CAMs practitioners privately. The reasons for this are complex, and are discussed in Section 5 below.

Research commissioned by the Prince of Wales' Foundation for Integrated Healthcare found that 28 per cent of NHS local plans (Primary Care Investment Plans) for 1999–2000 contained references to CAM services (Halpern 2001).

SCENARIO

Giving up smoking

Jen has been a heavy smoker for over 20 years. She has tried to give up on a number of occasions, but now feels she needs a bit more help.

She reads in a magazine that hypnotherapy sometimes helps people to stop smoking, so she goes on the Internet and finds the website of the Hypnotherapy Association. The website gives access to a list of registered acupuncture practitioners. She locates one close to her home, and books a course of six treatments. After the course, she has managed to reduce significantly her daily consumption of cigarettes.

In other words, of 135 local health plans for England and Scotland, 131 were offering some kind of CAM therapies to patients. Figure 8.11 sets out the therapies mentioned in these plans.

THERAPY	PERCENTAGE OF OF TOTAL
Acupuncture	32%
Osteopathy/chiropractic	24%
Homeopathy	14%
Hypnotherapy	4%
Aromatherapy/massage	4%
Reflexology	3%
Herbal/Chinese herbal	*
Yoga	*
Other	17%
* = less than 1%	

FIGURE 8.11 *CAMs offered by the NHS: 1999–2002*

Source: Halpern, 2001

SCENARIO

Comfort and pain relief

Gwen is 84 years old and has cancer. Doctors are reluctant to expose her to the risk of surgery, as she is very frail. However, she is in considerable pain from her tumour.

Gwen's consultant discusses her situation with the hospital Palliative Care Team. It is agreed that acupuncture may help with pain relief. After discussing this option with Gwen, treatment goes ahead with a private practitioner, paid on a sesional basis to treat her in hospital.

Think it over...

One GP surgery has adopted the use of acupuncture for carefully selected patients. As a result, the practice has noted an 80 per cent success rate, with a reduction in referrals to the physiotherapy department and in the cost of prescribing drugs.

The plan has been so successful that the PCT plans to develop acupuncture services throughout its area.

Source: Adapted from Halpern, 2001

Sometimes, the initiative for working in partnership with CAMs practitioners comes from outside the NHS. One such project is described in the following scenario.

SCENARIO

Working in partnership

A group of CAMs practitioners have approached the local primary care trust to see if there is any possibility of providing therapies to NHS patients. The health promotion manager is very interested, and he gives his support to the project.

After careful planning, and making a bid for PCT funding, Reiki is now being made available to people who use mental-health and substance-misuse services, and also to carers. Each person has to pay just £5 per Reiki session.

The effect these treatment sessions have on each person will be closely monitored, and the project will be evaluated after six months.

GPs and CAMs

Some GPs are very sympathetic to the use of CAMs by their patients – it was noted above that some allopathically trained practitioners are now positively seeking to integrate complementary techniques into their own practice. However, other GPs remain unsupportive and even suspicious of any therapy that is not wholly endorsed by NHS guidelines or recommendations. The situation varies locally.

A national survey of access to CAMs via GPs in England was conducted in 1995 and repeated in 2001, based on a target population of one in eight GP practices (Thomas, Coleman and Nicholl, 2003). The findings suggest that in 1995, about 39% of GP practices provided access to CAMs; by 2001, this had risen to about 50%. The researchers note that this rise was mainly due to GPs offering CAMs on-site (rather than to an increase in referrals to NHS provided CAMs). Over the same period, the financial contribution by patients towards CAMs services rose from 26% to 42%. In both 1995 and 2001, acupuncture and homeopathy were the CAMs most frequently provided via GPs.

However, in other areas, as a result of changes to the way in which GP practices are funded (changes that took place in 2000), some GPs are no longer able to afford to offer CAM therapies on site even if they want to.

Integrated medicine

The combining of the scientific method with the holistic approach of complementary systems and therapies is now being referred to as 'integrated medicine' by doctors who adopt this way of working. They often refer to this as a **biographical approach** to illness, as the focus is always on the whole person not just on the symptoms (Galland, 1998).

> ### Key concept
>
> *biographical approach* A term used by integrated-medicine practitioners to describe how they diagnose an illness.

Ayurvedic practitioners are often also conventionally trained. The work of Deepak Chopra (Chopra, 1990) provides a very clear explanation of how Ayurvedic practice can be combined with conventional medical techniques. The following scenario demonstrates how such a practitioner might work with a specific person.

> ### SCENARIO
>
> #### Chemotherapy and meditation
>
> Dr Suman Kohli practises in Nottingham. She has medical degrees from the University of London, and has also studied the Ayurvedic system of medicine.
>
> She is consulted by a patient who has cancer and who is troubled about embarking upon a course of chemotherapy. Dr Kohli advises her to accept the treatment, but also suggests some dietary changes that will help. She then recommends that she spend time each day meditating and visualising her tumour decreasing in size.
>
> Source: Adapted from Chopra, 1990

Outside the Ayurvedic tradition, Western-trained doctors are also seeing the advantages of combining the best of both conventional and complementary treatments. In the UK, the British Association for Allergy, Environmental and Nutritional Medicine (www.basaenm.free-online.co.uk) works to promote the study and practice of an integrated approach that looks particularly at the contribution of allergies, nutrition and environmental factors to poor health. The association runs courses, has a register of practitioners and also publishes a quarterly journal on relevant issues. The Prince of Wales' Foundation for integrated health (www.fihealth.org.uk) promotes research into integrated healthcare, and plays a key part in national developments such as the move towards the statutory regulation of CAMs. A web search based on the term 'integrated medicine' will result in a host of hits on UK and other organisations that exist to promote this practice.

Settings for complementary therapies

CAMs are practised in a wide range of settings, from the user's own home through to outpatient's departments in NHS hospitals. Figure 8.12 sets out information on a small sample of settings (together with the costs of treatment sessions), showing where CAMs could be accessed (as at the end of 2004).

As Figure 8.12 shows, a variety of settings. Some therapists will visit clients in their own homes, taking along all the necessary equipment, such as a massage couch and aromatherapy oils. Other practitioners will set up a treatment or consultation room, sometimes in their own homes, sometimes in rented premises such as shop units. Nutritional therapists use subsidised premises made available by a registered charity.

Leisure centres and health spas often offer CAMs as an additional service to customers, and many private gyms and health clubs now have treatment rooms on the premises. CAMs are also sometimes provided in NHS premises. Figure 8.12 lists two such examples (in a hospital outpatient department and in a community health centre),

SAMPLE OF CAMS: SETTINGS AND COSTS: (DECEMBER 2004)			
	SETTING	TYPE OF THERAPY	STATUS/SOURCE OF FUNDING	COST TO USER
A.	Hospital outpatient department	Reiki	NHS/Private	£5
B.	Own home	Massage	Private	£35
C.	Leisure centre	Massage Aromatherapy Reflexology	Private	£40–£50
D.	Workplace	On-site massage	Private	£10
E.	CAMs clinic	Osteopathy Chiropractic	Private	£35–40
F.	CAMs clinic	Nutrition therapy	Charity/Private	£35–£70
G.	Therapist's home	Massage Aromatherapy Reflexology	Private	£35–£40
H.	Community health centre	Homeopathy Osteopathy	Lottery funding/NHS	Free
I.	Health spa	Range of treatments	Private	From £229 per night
J.	Private clinic	Integrated-medicine practitioner	Private	£150

FIGURE 8.12 *A selection of CAMs, settings and typical costs*

and there are also instances of CAM clinics being established alongside GP surgeries.

Occasionally, short 'taster-sessions' of various therapies are on offer at workplaces. The fully clothed brief massage treatment known as on-site massage is popular, and reflexology, too, can be given fairly easily in this kind of environment.

The cost of complementary therapies

Research by White, Resch and Ernst (1997) found that, at that date, average fees for treatment ranged from £20 to £60 per hour. Figure 8.12 suggests that this is still broadly the case, although some practitioners are charging much higher fees.

The fee to the user very much depends on the status of the practitioner (i.e. whether he or she is working as a sole trader, in a partnership or for another business), and also whether or not the practice itself has external funding or is self-supporting. Some practitioners are actually employed directly by the establishment that offers the therapies.

Example A in Figure 8.12 is an example of collaboration between an NHS department and a group of Reiki practitioners. Special funding arrangements made it possible to lower the cost to users to £5 per person. Similarly, Example H was initially supported by Lottery funding. By creative management of resources, this health centre is able to offer free treatment sessions to users.

At the other end of the scale, private practitioners can sometimes command fees similar to those charged in private medical practice (Example J in Figure 8.12). In between is a range of practitioners who charge whatever is financially viable in relation to their circumstances. A massage therapist providing treatment at a local gym, for example, will have to pay rent for the use of the treatment room. A practitioner who rents shop premises will have to take into account the cost of the lease or rent, business rates and utilities (e.g. gas and electricity) when calculating the charge to the user. All therapists will have to have indemnity insurance (see below), and the cost of this must also be built into the final charge per session. Prestigious establishments such as some health spas charge higher fees, either to therapists renting their rooms or directly to the therapy users.

The training and qualifications of CAMs practitioners

Centralisation and standardisation

In the last 10 years there has been a move towards greater regulation by practitioners of some CAMs. This process has involved initiatives to standardise training courses and qualifications, as well as to establish codes of practice for the ways in which CAMs are delivered. **Standardisation** has been achieved, in several cases, by the establishment of new national bodies to supervise the new regulations, often by the merging of older organisations. However, not all CAMs are regulated in this way, and it is important for anyone considering complementary treatment of any kind to check out what training and qualifications a good practitioner should hold.

Key concept

standardisation A process whereby everything is made to conform to an agreed, common way of doing things – in this case training and qualifications.

Figure 8.14 gives details of some of the more highly regulated CAMs in UK (as at December 2004). It should be noted that the situation is changing constantly, and new organisations, qualifications and regulations will emerge in the next 10 years.

Osteopathy and chiropractic are currently regulated by Acts of Parliament, and this has been the case since before the House of Lords Select Committee Report in 2000. Statutory regulation

Key concept

regulation The control of something by establishing a set or rules that everything must conform to.

means that practitioners of these CAMs will be required by law to achieve approved qualifications and to adhere to certain standards and codes of practice. This is a safeguard both for clients using these practitioners (who are protected from unqualified practitioners, and can also seek redress if they feel that a registered practitioner has been negligent), and also for properly qualified CAMs therapists, who benefit from membership of a national organisation. The training of osteopaths is regulated by the General Osteopathic Council (GOSC), and that of chiropractors by the General Chiropractic Council (GCC).

There is currently (January 2005) a timetable for passing an Act to regulate medical herbalism. The European Herbal Practitioners Association, which represents therapists from Ayurveda, Tibetan herbal medicine, traditional herbal medicine and Western herbal medicine, is an umbrella organisation that sets standards for each of these areas of practice, and has also agreed a common core curriculum for the training of medical herbalists, with specialist curriculum areas for the different traditions noted above. Like osteopathy and chiropractic, the profession has a set of standards to which practitioners must adhere.

While not all CAMs are regulated by law, nevertheless there have been moves by a number of practitioners to achieve greater standardisation for their own therapies.

The regulation of aromatherapy, for example, is currently undergoing radical changes. The old Aromatherapy Organisations Council (AOC) has voluntarily dissolved itself in order to make way for a new group, called the Aromatherapy Consortium. In time, this will become the Aromatherapy Council. The Register of Qualified Aromatherapists, which was maintained by the old AOC, will be maintained by the new consortium. Aromatherapy already has a set of

THE TRAINING AND REGULATION OF CAMS (AS AT DECEMBER 2004)					
CAM/NATIONAL REGULATING BODY	STATUTORY REGULATION	ACCREDIT-ATION	CODES OF PRACTICE/ ETHICS, ETC.	NATIONAL OCCUPATIONAL STANDARDS	MINIMUM LENGTH OF TRAINING
Osteopathy General Osteopathy Council (GOsC)	x	x	x		4/5 years F/T
Chiropractic General Chiropractic Council (GCC)	x	x	x		4/5 years
Medical herbalism European Herbal Practitioners Association (EHPA)	In progress	x	x	x	
Acupuncture British Acupuncture Council	Under discussion	x	x		3 yrs F/T P/T equivalent
Aromatherapy Aromatherapy Consortium/Council		In progress		x	In progress
Homeopathy The Society of Homeopaths		x	x	x	3 yrs F/T 4 yrs P/T
Nutritional Therapy Nutrition Therapy Council (NTC) British Assocation of Nutritional Therapists (BANT)				x	3/4 yrs F/T
Reflexology Association of Reflexologists (from January 2005)		x	x	x	100 hours

FIGURE 8.13 *The training and regulation of CAMS*

national occupational standards (see page 323), and the new Aromatherapy Consortium is using these as the benchmark for all new qualifications in aromatherapy. A new core curriculum will be produced based on these standards, and there will be a single National Voluntary Register for Aromatherapists.

Aromatherapy is not the only CAM to have a set of National Occupational Standards (NOS) that set out how practitioners should deliver their service. In health and social care, the Skills for Health Initiative has been set up by the government to help professionals to define the standards that are required.

As at January 2005, nine CAMs had National Occupational Standards. As these are developed, they will give further impetus to the standardisation of CAMs practice in the UK (see below).

CAMS FOR WHICH THERE ARE NATIONAL OCCUPATIONAL STANDARDS (AS AT JANUARY 2005)
* Aromatherapy
* Complementary healthcare
* Herbal medicine
* Hypnotherapy
* Kinesiology
* Nutritional therapy
* Remedial and therapeutic massage
* Homeopathy
* Reflexology
Source: Skills for Health website (www.skillsforhealth.org.uk)

Another force for centralisation and standardisation for the practice of some CAMs is the establishment of the Health Professions Council (HPC), which was set up by the Health Professions Order in 2001. This body is now responsible for standards relating to training, performance and conduct for 13 health-related professions. See Figure 8.13 on page 329.

The HPC determines which courses are appropriate to each discipline, and also which colleges are accredited to offer these courses. It keeps a register of properly qualified practitioners in the professions listed.

Courses and colleges

Training courses are offered in a range of educational settings. There are degree courses in some CAMs (for example, homeopathy). For others, there is a variety of diplomas and certificates that have different status. The process of regulation described above will eventually result in greater clarity with respect to who is deemed to be qualified to practise.

Courses can be offered at universities, colleges, evening classes and in private training centres. The International Therapy Examination Council (ITEC) offers 17 qualifications that are accredited by the Qualifications and Curriculum Authority (QCA) on behalf of the Department for Education and Skills. Eight of these relate to CAMs professions, as shown below:

INTERNATIONAL THERAPY EXAMINATIONS COUNCIL: CAMs QUALIFICATIONS (AS AT DECEMBER 2004)

Level 3 Diplomas are offered in:

* Anatomy and Physiology
* Holistic Massage
* Aromatherapy
* Reflexology
* On Site Massage
* Lymphatic Drainage Massage
* Diet and Nutrition for Complementary Therapists
* Sports Massage

ITEC also maintains a register of professionals, which was merged with that of the Guild of Complementary Practitioners in April 2003 to form the International Guild of Professional Practitioners (IGPP).

Despite the trend towards standardisation, there is still a great deal of variation in the numbers of courses offered and the bodies that accredit them and award qualifications. The discussion in this unit has not included the multitude of short training courses and modules offered by private practitioners in some of the less well-regulated CAMs (for example, Bowen technique or crystal therapy). Many of these trainers may, indeed, be very well qualified in some other discipline and be quite competent to deliver training (for example, someone with a background as an NHS nurse who has specialised in a particular area of CAM). However, others will not be so well qualified. Anyone choosing or recommending a particular CAM is advised to do some homework into the therapy itself and into the qualifications of the practitioner. Careful research is needed into each of the CAMs chosen for study in this unit, to check on the latest status of qualifications and awarding bodies.

Health and safety

Law and regulations

In the UK, the practice of complementary therapies is regulated by legislation relating to Health and Safety at Work. Good training courses for CAMs practitioners will cover all aspects of this vital aspect of the work.

The Health and Safety at Work Act 1974 (HASAWA) provides the foundation for the way in which health and safety issues are managed. Since 1974, there have been numerous Acts of Parliament and guidance documents dealing with all aspects of safety, including manual handling (which includes the moving and lifting of people), managing hazardous substances, provision in case of fire and the use of equipment.

Under the HASAWA, both employer and employees have a 'duty of care' towards everyone on the premises, and both have clear responsibilities. Thus, in the case of a private sports centre, the management must make sure that the environment is safe; that any substances (particularly potentially dangerous ones) are stored, moved and handled safely; that systems of work, and equipment and access to and exit from the premises are safe; and that personal protective equipment is provided to employees. Management must also provide information, training and supervision on safety issues for staff, and must have a written safety policy. The protection of members of the public while on the premises is also the responsibility of management. Therapists working on the premises on a sessional basis are also covered by HASAWA, and are entitled to the same protection as those who are fully employed.

However, employees (including sessional therapists) also have a personal responsibility for health and safety issues. These are set out below:

> **HEALTH AND SAFETY AT WORK ACT 1974: STAFF RESPONSIBILITIES**
>
> Section 7 of this Act says that employees must:
>
> * take reasonable care for their own health and safety and that of others affected by their acts or omissions at work
> * cooperate with the employer
> * report any situation thought to be unsafe or unhealthy.

While on the premises of a care setting (whether a private club or public premises such as an NHS hospital or clinic) a therapist must behave in the same way as other staff members with respect to health and safety issues. They must follow the law and rules, and be prepared to take the responsibility (and the initiative) for making the environment safe for the client.

Practical considerations are also covered by the regulations. Dangers from electricity, gas and fire must be minimised by the proper maintenance of installations and equipment, and by staff training in fire and evacuation procedures. There should also be the correct number of trained first aiders on the premises (Health and Safety (First Aid) Regulations 1981).

Insurance

Both therapists and the owners of premises where therapies are delivered should be adequately insured. Some professional organisations (for example, ITEC and the Federation of Holistic Therapists) arrange access to insurance for practitioners who hold their recognised qualifications. Types of insurance include:

* public liability: to provide protection against bodily injury, and loss or damage to property
* third-party insurance: to cover the therapist against claims of negligence
* other types of insurance, relevant to owners of larger concerns are: premises and contents insurance, shopkeepers' liability insurance, and insurance against loss of takings or profit resulting from fire.

Membership of professional bodies

Many CAMs practitioners belong to professional bodies. This brings a number of benefits, both to practitioners themselves, and also to members of the public. Such benefits may include:

* professional status
* access to insurance
* credibility with customers/clients (especially with respect to the safe delivery of CAMs
* access to information and new techniques
* the prospect of a reasonable relationship with the medical profession
* public listing.

It is in the interests of both CAMs practitioners and their clients that therapists are seen to be well qualified, properly insured and safe to practise. Membership of professional bodies provides safeguards for both the practitioner and the client.

Codes of practice and standards

Many professional bodies and national CAMs organisations have codes of practice. From April 2005, those for 13 CAMs professions will be regulated by the Health Professions Council (HPC). The HPC sets standards for training, professional skills, behaviour and health, with the aim of ensuring the safety and well-being of anyone using an HPC-registered professional.

The Vocational Training Charitable Trust (VTCT) also has codes of practice governing standards of hygiene and behaviour in the salon or clinic. These guidelines cover the cleanliness of the therapist and equipment, ventilation and heating, and checking for contra-indications before the start of treatment.

Summary

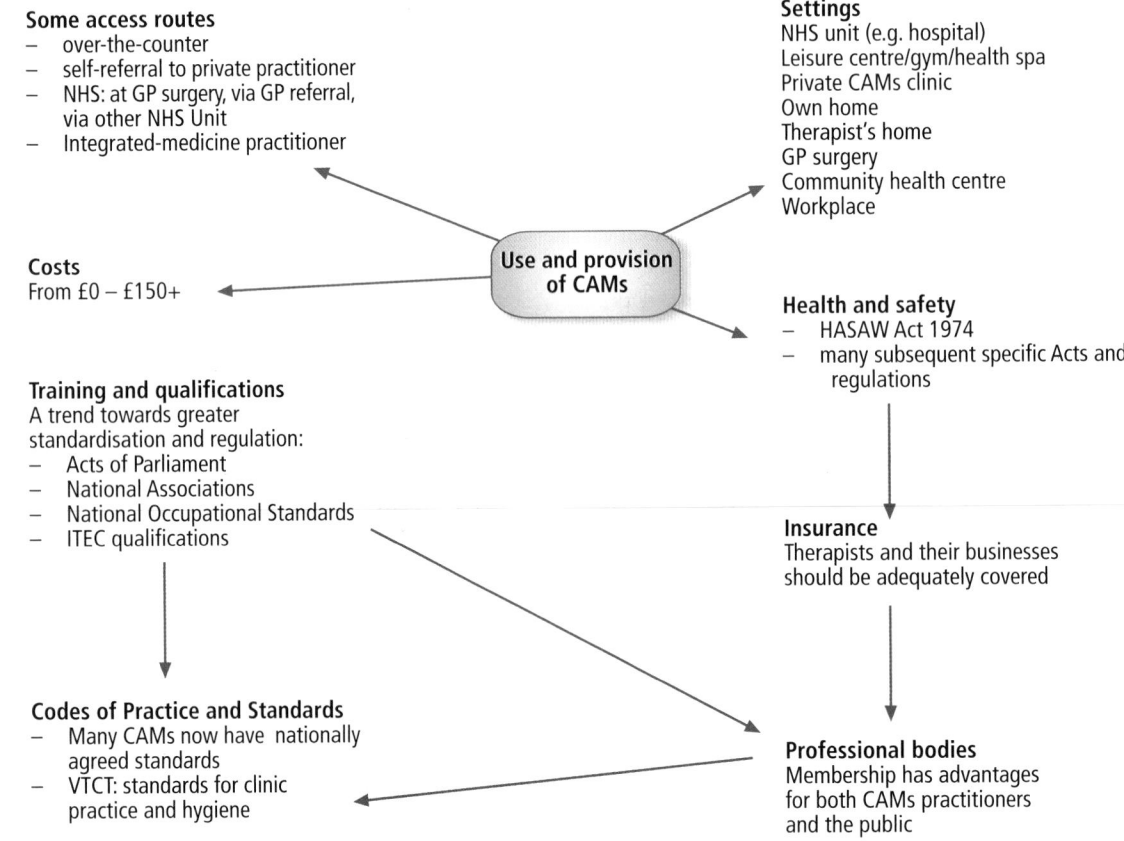

FIGURE 8.14 *The use and provision of complementary therapies*

Consider this

Jo is about to open her own practice as an acupuncturist and massage therapist. She has leased shop premises and is now decorating prior to installing furniture and equipment.

1. What insurance does she need?

2. How can she ensure that health and safety issues are addressed?

3. What national organisations does she need to register with?

Section 4: Meeting physical, emotional and social needs

The nature of need: physical, emotional and social

In this section, the ways in which CAMs can meet physical, emotional and social needs are considered. It must be remembered that human beings are very complex and their needs are interrelated. Emotional, social and physical problems can be closely linked, as the following scenario demonstrates.

Consider this

Jan has just come out of hospital after suffering serious facial disfigurement in a car accident. She is still taking daily medication to control the pain. She also feels ugly and unlovely, and has totally lost confidence socially.

Before her accident, Jan used to be an active member of a local drama group. Now she cannot bear seeing anyone, and is becoming quite depressed.

1. What types of need does Jan have?

2. What kinds of CAMs might be suggested to her to meet each kind of need? (You might want to use Figure 8.17 as a starting point.)

Clearly, as long as Jan still has pain she may not be able to move forward with her emotional recovery, and will also not be strong enough to start working on her social needs. It may be that a course of acupuncture will bring her some pain relief in the first instance, and some herbal preparations may enhance the healing process.

However, the emotional scars from her experience go very deep. Jan's self-image and sense of identity have been damaged as a result of the accident. Counselling may help her to begin to come to terms with her disfigurement. Finally, her interest in drama may help her to regain her social self. With support from friends and family, Jan may gradually regain the confidence to rejoin the drama group, and start to enjoy the intellectual stimulation and social therapy that this membership brings with it. Of course, CAMs can never be imposed on a person, and unless Jan is ready and willing to begin the process of reconstructing her life, any intervention is unlikely to be successful.

Matching CAMs to need

Figure 8.15 (below) lists some CAMs that may help with certain broad categories of need. It should be stressed that the list is neither exhaustive nor prescriptive. In reality, each person's needs are unique, and therefore CAMs (or combinations of CAMs) should be specifically chosen for each client.

You may be surprised by some of the entries in Figure 8.17. Why, for example, is art therapy listed as helping with some chronic conditions? In fact, art therapy is known to lower blood pressure, heart and respiratory rates (Lantin, 2004). It also helps with eye–hand coordination, which is why it is also listed under personal development (it can be useful for people recovering from injury, or for people with learning disabilities). Art therapy enhances an individual's sense of being in control, and also enables people to express difficult feelings; therefore, it is also listed as helping with mental-health problems.

Consider the following scenario.

SCENARIO

Depression and a taste for art

Tom has been suffering from depression for some time. He has been diagnosed by the doctor as clinically depressed.

He is allocated a psychiatric social worker (PSW) who works for the local social-services department, but is based at a psychiatric hospital.

The PSW suggests that Tom might benefit from a course of massage treatments, to which he agrees. During the massage, he starts to talk quite freely to the therapist, with whom he feels quite comfortable. During the conversation he discloses that he used to enjoy painting at school, but that he has not done any for some time. As a result, the PSW arranges for Tom to have art-therapy sessions at the hospital.

TYPE OF PROBLEM	SUGGESTED CAMs	
Acute pain	Acupuncture Aromatherapy Chiropractic	Hypnotherapy Music therapy
Chronic conditions (e.g.osteoarthritis, muscular dystrophy, multiple sclerosis, back pain etc.)	Acupuncture Alexander technique Art therapy Biofeedback Chiropractic Herbal medicine Hypnotherapy Massage	Meditation Music therapy Nutritional therapy Osteopathy QiGong Reflexology Yoga
Mental-health problems	Aromatherapy Art therapy Autogenic training Bach flower remedies Biofeedback Chiropractie Cognitive and behavioural therapies	Drama therapy Hypnotherapy Massage Meditation Music therapy QiGong Reflexology Yoga
Social isolation	Art therapy Bach flower remedies Drama therapy	Hypnotherapy Music therapy
Dietary disorders (including constipation and digestive problems)	Acupuncture Nutritional therapy Osteopathy	Reflexology Yoga
Habitual behaviour (e.g. fingernail-biting, thumb-sucking, and phobias)	Hypnotherapy Cognitive and behavioural therapies	
Addiction	Hypnotherapy Cognitive and behavioural therapies	
Social and personal development	Art therapy Drama therapy Music therapy	

FIGURE 8.15 *The uses of some complementary therapies*

Note: Treatment by practitioners of the large medical systems (Ayurveda, homeopathy, naturopathy, etc. may cover several of the above problem areas, and are not listed against individual problem types.

Needless to say, a person does not have to be a great artist to gain benefit from art therapy. Besides being used to give the sense of satisfaction that is gained from the act of creation, art therapy is also a means of communication between therapist and client. People can express complex emotional problems by means of pictures or symbols. This kind of therapy is often used to communicate with children who have been abused or who have suffered some other kind of trauma.

Music therapy is another CAM that has a wide range of uses. Besides meeting a person's emotional or social needs, music has also been found to assist in pain management after surgery (Good, 1995) and to enhance relaxation after surgery (Winter et al. 1994, Barnason et al. 1995). It has been used to enhance the cognitive development of children (Aldridge et al. 1995), and to reduce levels of depression in older people (Hanser and Thompson, 1994). Such studies indicate that further research into the benefits of music therapy would be helpful.

FIGURE 8.16 *Music therapy is helpful for many*

The following scenario describes how music is used in one setting for young people who have learning disabilities.

SCENARIO

The Music Man

A group of young people at a day facility for people with learning disabilities look forward to their weekly sessions with Asif, who is a music therapist. The young people call him the Music Man.

Asif encourages them to sing and to use a range of musical instruments. Songs are often memorised, which is good for concentration and cognitive development; using the instruments helps one or two of the group with their fine motor movements, while moving to the music is good for physical coordination.

As group members are from different cultures, Asif is careful to use different kinds of music, including Asian, British and Black British.

Asif's music sessions cater for a range of needs (physical and cognitive) while at the same time providing an important emotional outlet for the young people who attend. Friendships have been made at this group, and his concern to include music from a range of cultures has given group members the chance to see if they like other kinds of music.

A strategy for healing

Just as one kind of CAM may satisfy a range of different types of need, sometimes a specific need may require a strategy involving a number of CAMs in order to address it.

Many CAMs practitioners will suggest that a client should use other complementary or alternative therapies if need be, even if it means referral on to another person. Integrated-medicine practitioners are very likely to suggest a range of therapies to a patient. The way this might work has been described very thoroughly by Altshuler (2004). For example, for the treatment of chronic pain Altshuler suggests a range of options including dietary changes, exercise, meditation, acupuncture, counselling, bodywork such as the Feldenkrais method, Alexander technique or Rolfing, hypnosis, yoga and Chinese herbal medicine. If these methods fail to work, Altshuler will first suggest the patient should purchase an over-the-counter pharmaceutical painkiller. If this should fail, he will then prescribe painkillers of increasing strength.

He sometimes suggests counselling as a method of reducing pain because chronic pain can itself cause psychological problems (e.g. depression) which, in turn, can make the original pain worse. This recognition of the close relationship between the mind and the body is something recognised by most CAMs practitioners. It is also controversial, as sceptics often say that CAMs work simply because people believe they will. This aspect of the use of complementary therapies is considered briefly in the next section.

Lifestyle, beliefs and the power of the mind

Some critics of CAMs like to dismiss their effect as being 'all in the mind'. CAMs will only work, they say, if users believe they will be effective. On the one hand, this is a tempting explanation for the numbers of people who claim to have been cured or, at least, significantly helped by the use of complementary therapies.

There is a well-known phenomenon known as the 'placebo effect'. A placebo is a treatment that works simply because the patient has been told it will by the doctor. Such 'treatments' can take the form of sugar pills or injections of harmless, non-pharmaceutical solutions. Just as the mind can tell a person that he or she is ill (in the case of a 'psychosomatic' illness), the mind can also tell a person that a particular treatment will make them better. Research into placebos has gone so far as to show that they will work better when injected, and that pink tablets work better than white tablets in bringing about a 'cure' (Martin, 1997). While it is undoubtedly true that sometimes a person can convince him or herself of many things, research into the relationship between the brain and the body's physiological systems now shows that the mind–body relationship is extremely complex.

For many years, science has separated the study of the mind from that of the body. Thus, medicine has been practised as a totally separate discipline from psychology and psychiatry. Conventional medicine has been concerned with the physical causes of disease (with a treatment focus on physical factors). Equally, psychiatrists and psychologists have tended to see matters of the mind, emotions and behaviours as something quite distinct from physiological matters (Martin, 1997).

This has been gradually changing with the advent of a scientific discipline called **psychoneuroimmunology** (PNI). People who study PNI recognise that the mind–body relationship is very complex and is a two-way relationship: a person's state of mind can affect the body, and therefore its physical health; likewise, physical health can have an effect on the mind, emotions and behaviour. As Martin puts it, PNI 'is concerned with the complex inter-relationships between psychological and emotional factors, the brain, hormones, immunity and disease'.

Two examples will demonstrate how these processes can work. The first concerns a study of how stress can have an effect on the immune system.

Cohen's research (together with that of other researchers) shows that if someone is feeling low or experiencing negative emotions, then his or her resistance to infection can be lowered. This is particularly the case if that person has previously suffered a number of stressful life experiences (for example, bereavement). Similarly, the presence of a disease or a medical condition (or even the treatment process itself) can cause stress, as the following example illustrates.

SCENARIO

Chronic blues

Tim has multiple sclerosis, a chronic condition which he has had for over 20 years. He is normally cheerful, and has always concentrated on taking a positive approach to his condition – using different CAMs and doing all the things that he knows are good for him.

For the last few months, however, his fatigue levels have been very high, which has limited his ability to work, and also to go out with his friends.

In turn, this is making him feel depressed and fearful for the future.

Key concept

chronic A chronic condition is one that persists over a long period of time.

In Tim's case, the continued hard work of living with a medical condition has finally triggered negative emotions and resulted in depression. In this example, the state of the body has had an effect on the mind.

The study of PNI is beginning to throw light on this two-way process. An appreciation of the complexity of the mind–body relationship also underpins many CAMs. The practice of yoga, for example, has been shown to reduce respiration and heart–rate, to induce alpha waves in the brain (the state associated with meditation), and to reduce the body's metabolic rate (Chopra, 1990). It is possible to extend this 'hypometabolic state' by continued practice, to achieve one of deep inner calm and silence, and a feeling of 'knowingness'. The rishis of India referred to this as the 'fourth state', and they were profoundly aware of the complex relationship between the mind and the body. Indeed, Ayurvedic practitioners believe that 'without meditation the true potential of Ayurvedic medicine cannot be realised' (Gerson, 1993).

Whereas critics of CAMs like to dismiss their effectiveness as 'all in the mind', perhaps it is time to suggest another way of looking at the relationship between any form of treatment (whether allopathic or complementary) and the role of the mind. Perhaps it is time to accept that part of any healing process will be in the mind of the receiver – and quite rightly so. The researcher Jenny Cole has described how, while awaiting the final confirmation of a diagnosis of breast cancer, her enlightened NHS consultant said that he did not want to force her to undergo any treatment that she did not believe in, including chemotherapy. If she didn't believe in it, he said,

she would be fighting it all the time. Jenny was also advised to learn the technique of visualisation, to help her mind to fight the disease (Cole, 1995). Clearly, in this NHS unit practitioners acknowledge and use the power of the mind to enhance the effectiveness of conventional treatments.

Of course, a person's lifestyle will also have an impact on the effectiveness of both CAMs and orthodox treatments. Smoking, excessive drinking, drug taking and overeating all place a strain on the body's mechanisms. Similarly, failing to take enough exercise or to engage in recreational activities can impair the body's natural healing abilities. There is also a link between a person's state of mind and his or her lifestyle. Someone who is feeling low may not have enough drive to go out to the gym or local pool to do some exercise. Anxiety about a life event can cause people to turn to smoking, or to increase the number of cigarettes smoked per day. Even work can have an impact on health, as the following scenario shows.

SCENARIO

Work can damage your health

Rob has ME, and has been having reflexology sessions to see if he can overcome the severe fatigue that afflicts him.

Five sessions have had only a minimal impact on his energy levels, but long chats with the reflexologist have helped him to come to a decision.

He decides to give up his job at the Stock Exchange in the City of London and to take a less stressful post closer to home.

As a result, his energy levels have improved dramatically. He no longer has the same work stress, and he does not have to spend four hours a day travelling to and from work.

Section 5: The value of CAMs

Stereotypical images of CAMs

Despite the progress that has been made with respect to regulating many of the well-established CAMs, a number of stereotypical images of CAMs and their practitioners persist. These include the notion that CAMs are only for people with money, especially people who tend to be hypochondriacs (the 'worried well'), or that they are used by people with vague ailments – the 'heartsink' patients who frequent GPs' surgeries.

One of these is that of the 'Beauty-salon bimbo', a disrespectful attitude towards women who work in the beauty and CAM industries that dismisses them as being of little intelligence. Consider the following experience of one such woman.

> **Consider this**
>
> Kim, a massage therapist, is going out for the evening with friends to their local pub.
>
> Unfortunately, Kim has had a late appointment, and has not had time to change before meeting her friends. Consequently, she is still wearing her work ID, white tunic and dark blue trousers when they arrive at the pub.
>
> All evening, she is harassed by the unwanted attentions of men, who say things like 'You can give me a massage any day!'
>
> Kim is used to this, but it starts to wear a bit thin as the evening goes on. She is angry at being treated as a bit of a joke (at best) and as a sex object (at worst), rather than as an intelligent person who has studied hard to get where she is.
>
> Why do you think people reacted like this to Kim?

Another stereotypical image of CAMs practitioners is that of the 'New Age Weirdo'. This sees all CAMs as having no scientific basis or rationale, but rather as being rooted in certain mystical and spiritual beliefs, and consequently as being rather 'wacky'. It also regards those who use such CAMs as being the unquestioning followers of 'guru'-type individuals who dictate what needs to be done in order to regain health.

> **SCENARIO**
>
> **Bad for your health**
>
> Jim has suffered with backache for several months and finds only limited relief from the pain killers the doctor has given him. He does not want to take stronger tablets, and a friend has recommended that he see a spiritual healer.
>
> He arranges to visit the healer at her home. When he gets there, he is disturbed to find that the room set aside for the healing session is in almost complete darkness, even though it is midday. In the hallway he sees some strange symbols painted onto the walls, and there is an almost overpowering smell of incense in the healing room.
>
> He feels uncomfortable, especially when the healer tells him she is concerned about his aura. She feels that he is being troubled by a malign influence, but she will not tell him any more.
>
> Finally, she offers to sell him some powder that will boost his power to resist attacks from the spirit world.
>
> Jim decides that he does not want to hear anything further, and makes a quick exit.

It is certainly true that there are some unscrupulous people who will exploit the suffering of others. Anyone wishing to consult a CAMs practitioner should first check out whether or not the therapy on offer is regulated by a national body (in this case, the National Federation of Spiritual Healers), and should also check whether that practitioner has the qualifications endorsed by that body.

However, to some extent the image of the unqualified, exploitative 'quack' healer is often applied unquestioningly to all CAMs practitioners. Like all stereotypes, this view lacks precision and clarity. It is true that some CAMs are based in religious or spiritual teachings (e.g.

Ayurveda), but the view that people use CAMs without checking things out is itself questionable. While some people may follow specific religious teachings as part of their quest for health, much of the current research into the popularity of CAMs stresses the fact that people like to be in control of their health choices. Choosing to use CAMs (either as well as, or instead of, conventional medicine) gives people more autonomy over what happens to them. This is discussed further below.

Current public and medical opinions on CAMs

Public opinions

Research sponsored by the Prince of Wales' Foundation for Integrated Health (FIH) has highlighted several key reasons why many people in Britain today are turning to CAMs (Ong and Banks 2003). According to this study, patients expect:

* a comprehensive examination

* a satisfactory diagnosis

* effective treatment interventions

* freedom from unwanted side-effects.

The study also sets out both negative and positive reasons for the choice of CAMs as a preferred treatment option. These are set out in Figure 8.17.

This research indicates that people who are likely to use CAMs are those who want to have a choice and who want to take an active role in their own treatment. Such people reject the **medical model** of illness, which makes them into passive recipients of healthcare. They are more likely to take a holistic view of illness, in which a connection is made between illness, wellness and all other aspects of a person's life (for example, diet, lifestyle and beliefs).

> **Key concept**
>
> *medical model* The medical model of illness not only seeks to treat symptoms, but also maintains that the doctor ultimately knows what is best for the patient.

People who use CAMs are likely to expect a positive working relationship with the practitioner, and to make the final decisions regarding the treatment given to them.

Medical opinions

In summary, it can be said that medical opinion ranges, from that of the integrated-medicine Practitioner (who combines the use of specific CAMs into his or her medical practice) to that of doctors who are actively hostile to any therapy that has not been rigorously tested and demonstrated to work.

As we have seen, many NHS units now offer complementary therapies of some kind, and even

NEGATIVE REASONS	POSITIVE REASONS
Poor outcome from conventional treatment treatment	Good outcome from previous CAM
Adverse effects from pharmaceutical drugs	An active participant in healthcare
Negative experience of doctor–patient relationship	Positive experience of CAM practitioner–patient relationship
Health views not in line with conventional model	Health views in line with CAM model

FIGURE 8.17 *Reasons for choosing CAMs*

Source: Ong and Banks (2003)

FIGURE 8.18 *Doctors often lack information about CAMs*

the National Institute for Clinical Excellence gives cautious endorsement to the use of specified therapies for certain conditions (e.g. for multiple sclerosis, NICE (2003).

Yet, some medical practitioners are vitriolic in their opposition to CAMs, seeing them as 'pseudoscientific' health cures that lack a coherent, clearly defined explanatory theory that is internally consistent (Sampson, 2000). Clearly, there are some aspects of CAMs and their use that remain controversial, and in some respects medical concern is understandable, particularly when doctors lack information about the many different kinds of CAMs and the ways in which they are practised.

Some of these controversial aspects are examined below.

Controversial aspects

Because regulation of CAMs has been fairly lax in the past, unqualified or unlicensed practitioners have been able to trade freely in some areas. This has sometimes led to damage being caused by therapies that have gone wrong. In the UK, there has not been a single body to regulate the use of CAMs, (although this is changing). Furthermore, very high prices may be charged for treatments or products that at best may have no effect and at worst may even cause harm.

Claims are made for particular CAMs that are not backed up by thorough clinical research. There is certainly plenty of anecdotal evidence to support the use of complementary therapies (i.e. personal accounts describing their effects). But to satisfy the requirements of scientific medicine, more in-depth research, using a range of techniques, is necessary. Such techniques would include: detailed surveys of large samples of people, cohort studies, clinical trials and systematic reviews of the research literature. An excellent description of these rigorous research methods is described in a paper by the Research Council for Complementary Medicine (RCCM) (1999). There is currently a vast amount of research data on the use of particular CAMs, but many of these studies fall short of the requirements of rigorous scientific research. However, even those who promote the concept of

evidence-based medicine note that it has its weaknesses. They recognise that even the findings of scientific trials may be limited and do not always take into account people who may have several medical conditions. In some cases, therefore, those who promote this approach believe it may be appropriate to use different kinds of evidence when deciding on the best treatment for a particular person.

Some people might argue that by their very nature CAMs cannot be subject to such research techniques because they work in an individual way. As each person is a very complex organism, he or she will respond in a unique way to a particular therapy. Others reject this argument, believing that CAMs should, and can be, investigated using the same techniques as orthodox medicines.

Some doctors are concerned that the current popular interest in CAMs is having a negative effect on attitudes to conventional healthcare. One fear is that this may lead to a patient-driven approach in which resources are wasted on treatments that people want but which don't work (O'Mathuna, 2000).

There is also some concern that some CAMs may actually have a negative effect on health. In her survey of research into the use of QiGong among older adults, for example, Kemp notes that the number of cases of QIMD (QiGong-induced mental disorder) is increasing, particularly among members of the Chinese community (Kemp, 2004). Similarly, claims have been made that transcendental meditation (TM) can have harmful effects (O'Mathuna, 2000). However, it should be said that claims of negative effects should be subjected to the same rigorous evaluation as claims of positive effects. It is important to evaluate each piece of research in terms of its methodology, the size of the sample, and so on. The RCCM paper on research methods is very helpful in this respect

Finally, it should be noted that some people are opposed to the use of specific CAMs on the basis of their religious beliefs. Some evangelical fundamental Christians, for example, are deeply suspicious of practices that are embedded in different philosophical or religious systems.

Summary

The nature of need
Emotional, social and physical problems can be closely linked

Lifestyle, beliefs, power of the mind
Psychoneuroimmunology (PNI):
- the scientific study of the mind-body relationship
- a complex two-way process

Current public and medical opinions
- current popularity of CAMs
- people like:
  - holistic approach
  - being in control
  - good relationship with practitioner
  - having a choice

Matching CAMs to needs
- not a mechanistic process
- many CAMs meet a range of needs
- a strategy may work best: use more than one CAM or combine with conventional medicine

Stereotypical images of CAMs
'Beauty salon bimbo'
'New Age weirdo'

Controversial aspects
unsatisfactory research
unscrupulous/unqualified practitioners
some negative side-effects
some religious objections

FIGURE 8.19 *The value of CAMs*

Consider this

Someone has given Chris a gift voucher for a massage at a local beauty salon. She is very excited, as she has read a lot about the beneficial effects of massage. She has not been sleeping well lately, so is hoping the massage will help, and also that the practitioner can give her some further advice on health and staying well.

When she arrives at the salon she is shocked to find that the treatment room has not been cleaned after the previous session. The floor is dirty (talcum powder and cotton buds are lying around), and there are soiled towels on the massage couch.

The masseuse seems indifferent to Chris, and there is no in-depth questionnaire to be filled in about her current state of health or tablets she may be taking. The treatment is quite rough, and Chris is glad to get away. She decides that massage is not for her.

1. If Chris told you about this experience, what would your comments be?

2. Do you think that Chris should report this salon for poor standards? If so, who should she report it to?

3. How would you convince Chris that when done properly, massage can be very beneficial?

UNIT 8 ASSESSMENT

How you will be assessed

This unit is assessed through a portfolio of work.

Assessment evidence

To satisfy the requirements of this unit you will need to collect evidence from a range of sources. This will probably include printed reference books, websites, interviews with people who use CAMs or with CAMs practitioners, and information from other health practitioners (such as GPs or nursing staff).

Your study of a CAMs user can be based on someone you already know (e.g. a family member or friend). Alternatively, your tutor may be able to arrange for you to meet a suitable person, perhaps at a social services unit or a voluntary sector day centre. You should approach the meeting courteously, and make sure that the person is happy to help you with this project. You will need to explain the project clearly before you start. It may also help to prepare some questions in advance. Your meeting should take place in a venue that is acceptable to the CAMs user and you should make sure that your interview is private (as the person will be sharing personal information with you).

As you collect data, it is important to maintain a good filing system, so that you can find material easily when you come to present your evidence.

Personal information should be kept confidential, and for presentation it will be essential to anonymise the data (i.e. make it impossible for the person to be recognised). All this information should be stored securely.

Assessment guidance

AO1: Show an understanding of two complementary therapies, their development and purpose

A good starting point for this is the Complementary Health Information Service website (www.chisuk.org.uk), but you should go beyond this by exploring further information about your chosen therapies. Many established CAMs now have their own websites, and some of the research-based sites listed in the Resources section of this unit will allow you to take your enquiries further.

There are also a number of good basic descriptive guides to CAMs.

Higher marks will be gained if you demonstrate knowledge and good use of the following concepts:

- allopathic medicine
- the medical model
- holistic medicine
- the six principles of CAMs
- integrated medicine
- how your chosen CAMs work with respect to cognitive, physical, expressive and/or sensory factors
- evidence-based medicine

AO2: Show an understanding of why two complementary therapies are suitable for a particular service user, describing the role of the practitioners

It is important to remember the six principles of holistic therapies. They are person-centred, and therefore any CAMs that are suggested will have to be acceptable to the service user in every respect. CAMs are not 'prescribed' in the sense that allopathic medicines are.

Clear reasons should be given for the final choice of CAMs, together with the expected outcomes. Websites such as the Health Professions Council (www.hpc-uk.org), Connexions (www.connexions.gov.uk) or those of particular CAMs can help with information about the role of the practitioner. You may also want to interview personally the practitioners concerned.

Higher marks will be gained by:

- clearly stating the expected outcomes from the use of these two CAMs (including cognitive, physical, expressive or sensory benefits)
- describing how the service user will access these CAMs, and their cost
- describing the qualifications of the practitioners
- describing how these CAMs are regulated
- demonstrating an awareness of how the six principles of CAMs operate with respect to these chosen therapies and this particular service user
- demonstrating an awareness of how cultural issues might be important with respect to this service user
- use of specialist terms such as:
  - contra-indications
  - contra-actions.

AO3: Include relevant research and analysis on the value of a complementary therapy used by the service user to determine the view of members of the public and healthcare professionals

Good research websites are listed in the Resources section.

The Research Council for Complementary Medicine published a paper on the nature of research (RCCM 1999), which is available on the RCCM website (see Resources section at the end of this unit).

Higher marks will be achieved by:

- well-designed research
- setting clear objectives
- accurate recording of data
- thorough analysis of results
- clear statement of conclusions.

AO4: Evaluate how the service user had his or her needs met by complementary therapy and orthodox medicine

To evaluate something is to assess it, in particular its worth, value or importance. When evaluating something, it is important to give a balanced view.

You should refer back to the reasons for choosing these particular CAMs and the outcomes you were expecting. If unexpected outcomes were achieved, it is important to say so.

The views of the service user will be of great importance in this process. You might also like to include other people in the evaluative process, such as the service user's family and/or carer, the care worker and/or other people who are affected (for example, people who use the same care facility). It may be that some of the benefits could be extended to persons other than the service user for whom the CAMs were recommended.

You might like to distinguish between an evaluation of:

- the CAMs sessions
- the outcomes of the treatment.

For example, the service user might have a very positive experience during the session itself (e.g. a massage), but may have no positive outcomes with respect to the illness or condition that was being treated.

Higher marks will be achieved by:

- produce evidence that you have reflected on the data you have collected
- consultation of a wide range of people in assessing the outcomes
- use of technical terms in describing outcomes, e.g. contra-actions.

References

Aldridge, D., Gustoff, G. and Neugebauer, L. (1995) 'A pilot study of music therapy in the treatment of children with developmental delay, *Complementary Therapies in Medicine*, 3 (4), 197–205

Altshuler, L. (2004) *Balanced Healing*, Washington: Harbor Press

Barnason, S., Zimmerman, L. and Nieveen, J. (1995) 'The effects of music interventions on anxiety in the patient after coronary artery bypass grafting', Bryan Memorial Hospital, Lincoln, USA. *Heart Lung* (United States), 24 (2), 124–32

Barnett, H. (2002) *The Which? Guide to Complementary Therapies*, London: Which? Ltd.

Chopra, D. (1990) *Quantum Healing: Exploring the Frontiers of Mind–Body Medicine*, New York, Toronto, London, Sydney, Auckland: Bantam Books.

Cohen, S.(1993) *Ageless Body, Timeless Mind*, London, Sydney, Auckland, Johannesburg: Random House

Cohen, S. etal. (1991) 'Psychological stress and susceptibility to the common cold', *New England Journal of Medicine*, 325, 606

Cohen, S. (1993) 'Negative life events, perceived stress, negative affect, and susceptibility to the common cold', *Jnl Pers. Soc. Psychol.*, 64, 131

Cole, J. (1995) *Journeys (with a cancer)*, London: Pawprints

Donnellan, C (ed) (2004) 'Alternative Therapies', *Issues*, Vol. 81, Cambridge: Independence

Ernst, E. and White, A. (2000) 'The BBC survey of complementary medicine use in the UK'. *Complementary, Therapies in Medicine*, 8, 32–6

Galland, L. (1998) *Power Healing*, Random House

Gerson, S. (1993) *Ayurveda: The Ancient Indian Healing Art*. Shaftesbury: Element Books

Goldstein, M. (1999) *Alternative Health Care: Medicine, Miracle or Mirage?* Philadelphia: Temple University Press

Good, M. (1995) 'A comparison of the effects of jaw relaxation and music on postoperative pain', School of Nursing, Case Western Reserve University, Cleveland (1995). *Nursing Res.* (United States) 44 (1), 52–7

Halpern, S. (2001) *Points of Engagement: The Integration of Complementary and Alternative Medicine into NHS Primary Care*. London: The Foundation for Integrated Medicine, Occasional Paper 1

Hanser, S. and Thompson, L. (1994) 'Effects of music therapy strategy on depressed older adults', Stanford University School of Medicine. *Journal of Gerontology* (United States), 49 (6), 265–9

House of Lords Select Committee on Science and Technology (2000) *Complementary and Alternative Medicine*. London: The Stationery Office, HL Paper 123

Kemp, C. (2004) 'QiGong as a therapeutic intervention with older adults', *Journal of Holistic Nursing*, 22 (4), 351–73

Kurtz, Paul (2000) 'In Defense of Scientific Medicine' in Wallace Sampson and Lewis Vaughn (eds) *Science Meets Alternative Medicine: What the evidence says about unconventional treatments*, pp.13–19, New York: Prometheus Books

Lantin, B. (2004) 'Draw out fear and stress', www.telegraph.co.uk/health

Martin, P. (1997) *The Sickening Mind: Brain, Behaviour, Immunity and Disease*, London: Flamingo

National Institute for Clinical Excellence (NICE) (2003) *Multiple Sclerosis: Management of Multiple Sclerosis in Primary and Secondary Care*, Clinical Guideline 8. London: National Institute for Clinical Excellence

Novey, D. (2000) 'Basic Principles of Complementary/Alternative Therapies' in Donald W. Novey (ed) *Clinician's Complete Reference Guide to Complementary and Alternative Healthcare*, 5–7. St Louis, Philadelphia, London, Sydney, Toronto: Mosby

O'Mathuna, D. (2000) 'Therapeutic Touch: What Could Be the Harm?', in W. Sampson and L. Vaughn (eds), *Science Meets Alternative Medicine: What the Evidence Says About Unconventional Treatments*, 227–43. New York: Prometheus Books

Ong, C. and Banks, B.(2003) *Complementary and Alternative Medicine: the Consumer Perspective*, London: The Prince of Wales's Foundation for Integrated Health, Occasional Paper 2

Pinder, M. (ed) (2005) *Complementary Healthcare: a guide for patients*, London: The Prince of Wales.s Foundation for Integrated Health

Research Council for Complementary Medicine (1999) *An Introduction to Research*, access via www.rccm.org.uk

Sampson, W. and Vaughn, L. (2000) *Science Meets Alternative Medicine: What the Evidence Says About Unconventional Treatments*. New York: Prometheus Books

Thomas, K.J., Coleman, P., Nicholl, J.P. (2003) 'Trends in access to complementary or alternative medicines via primary care in England: 1995–2001.' *Family Practice* 20:5, 575

Tresidder, A. (2000) *Lazy Person's Guide to Emotional Healing*, Dublin: Newleaf

White, A., Resch, K. and Ernst, E. (1997) A Survey of Complementary Practitioners' Fees". *Complementary Ther. Med.*

Winter, M. Paskin, S. and Baker, T. (1994) 'Music Reduces Stress and Anxiety of Patients in the Surgical Holding Area', *Journal Post-Anesthetic Nursing* (United States), 9 (6), 340–43

Zollman, C. and Vickers, A. (2000) *ABC of Complementary Medicine*, London: BMJ Books

Useful websites

www.acupuncture.org.uk British Acupuncture Council. Information about acupuncture, including research articles

www.aocuk.net The Aromatherapy Organisations Council (AOC)

www.aor.org.uk Association of Reflexologists. This organisation absorbed the Reflexologists Society in January 2005

www.bant.org.uk British Association for Nutritional Therapy

www.chisuk.org.uk Complementary Healthcare Information Service. Basic information about 70 complementary therapies, their history and practice

www.connexions.gov.uk Information on careers and professions

www.fihealth.org.uk Website of the Prince of Wales' Foundation for Integrated Health. Many interesting papers and research information

www.homeopathy-soh The Society of Homeopaths website

www.hpc-uk.org Health Professions Council. The new (2005) regulatory body responsible for standards of professional training, performance and conduct of a number of healthcare professions.

www.internethealthlibrary.com Articles about current research projects

www.itecworld.co.uk International Therapy Examination Council (ITEC). Latest information about qualifications regulated by ITEC

www.nice.org.uk National Institute for Clinical Excellence. Information about latest guidelines for the clinical management of a number of conditions

www.nutritionalmed.co.uk Register of Nutritional Therapists

www.parliament.the-stationery-office.co.uk HMSO site. Many key government papers can be downloaded from here

www.rccm.org.uk Research Council for Complementary Medicine. Excellent source of information on research into CAMs.

www.skillsforhealth.org.uk Sector Skills Council for health. Information on the development of standards for health professions

www.ehpa European Herbal Practitioners Association

UNIT
9

Caring for Older People

This unit covers the following sections:

9.1 The physical effects of ageing on body systems

9.2 The social, emotional and economic aspects of ageing

9.3 Community care and support services for older service users

9.4 The role of professional care workers

9.5 The impact of law on provision of care for older people

Introduction

This unit will address the physical effects of ageing together with social, emotional and economic aspects of ageing. The risks of social isolation, poverty and poor health faced by some older people are explored. A small minority of older people may access health and social care services because of dementia or other mental disorders. This unit also looks at some of the issues associated with care services for older people. Service provision for older service users is explained and the role of professional care workers within community care is also explored.

How you will be assessed

This unit will be assessed through a 90 minute test that will be externally marked.

Section 1: The physical effects of ageing on body systems

Health is a major factor affecting quality of life at any age. The average life expectancy has increased considerably over the last 100 years but as people grow older a variety of physical changes begin to happen to the body. Its sensitivity to temperature changes may be reduced so that older people may not realise that their temperature has dropped and can be at risk of hypothermia; this is a condition in which the core temperature of the body falls to a dangerously low level. Older people cannot easily increase their body temperature and this explains why it is so important for them to stay warm. The amount of muscles and skeleton begin to reduce and the amount of fat in the body begins to increase. In addition, the way in which fat is stored in the body changes as people become older; it tends not to be stored under the skin but on the trunk of the body instead. Increasing amounts of water are lost from the body and the ways in which the body processes water also changes. This means that the ways older people react to drugs can be different from those of a younger person. Some changes in older age seem to be as a result of genetic information programmed into the body from birth. Other changes can be the result of disease processes. It is not always easy to identify which is which.

The heart, breathing and the circulatory system

The efficiency of the blood system is dependent on the efficiency of the lungs and other organs such as the kidneys and liver. The blood system provides a constant supply of oxygen and nutrients to the cells of the body and also carries away waste products (such as carbon dioxide) from the cells to the lungs and the liver. These organs process and eliminate waste products from the blood supply. The blood system also has other important functions such as transporting hormones, immune cells and materials essential for repair to areas of damage.

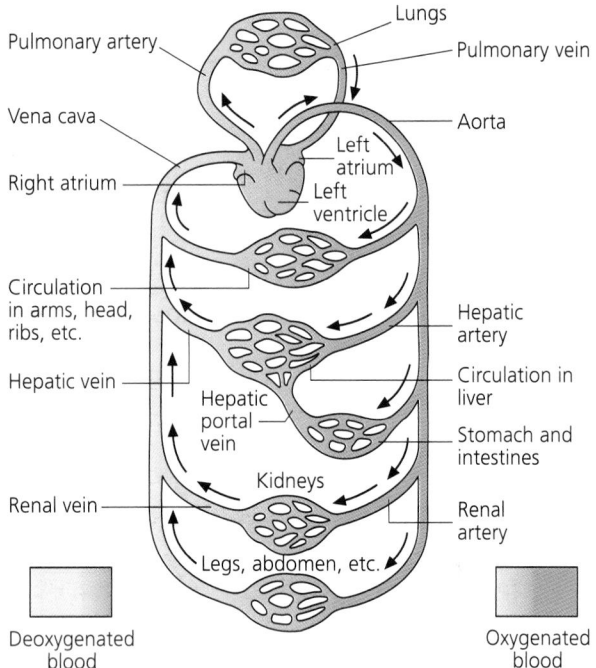

FIGURE 9.1 *The circulatory system*

> ✳ **DID YOU KNOW?**
>
> Blood pressure is the term describing the force of the blood in the veins and arteries against the blood vessel walls. Blood pressure readings have two levels such as 140 / 80. The first reading describes the pressure of the blood when the chambers (ventricles) of the heart contract and force blood through the system. This is the higher reading (systolic). The pressure of the blood when the heart muscles are relaxed is the lower (or diastolic) reading.
>
> In western societies, people's blood pressure tends to increase as they age but after the age of 70 years it tends to level off or decline. As older people process medication in a more complex way, the use of medication to lower blood pressure can have an effect on their health. Over one third of older people between the ages of 75–79 may have raised blood pressure. Older people in many non-western societies, however, do not experience an increase of blood pressure with increased age. This raises issues of diet, exercise and lifestyle playing a major role in the health of older people.

Heart disease

The circulatory system becomes less efficient with age, causing possible difficulties. For example, climbing stairs can be more difficult than in earlier years. Blood pressure is often higher as people age and this can increase the risk of a stroke or heart attack.

Disorders of the circulatory system include heart attack, heart disease, heart dysfunction and sclerosis.

The heart

The key function of the heart is to push blood through the circulatory system. The ability of the heart to do this is measured in terms of the amount of blood pumped through in one minute. This is called the cardiac output. It is estimated that up to three quarters of men over 60-years-of-age may have coronary artery disease. This causes a reduction in the flow of blood to the heart as the arteries become much narrower. Women are also affected but the equivalent level of damage occurs in women over 80 years.

As the elasticity in the walls of the blood vessels reduces, the heart has to work harder to

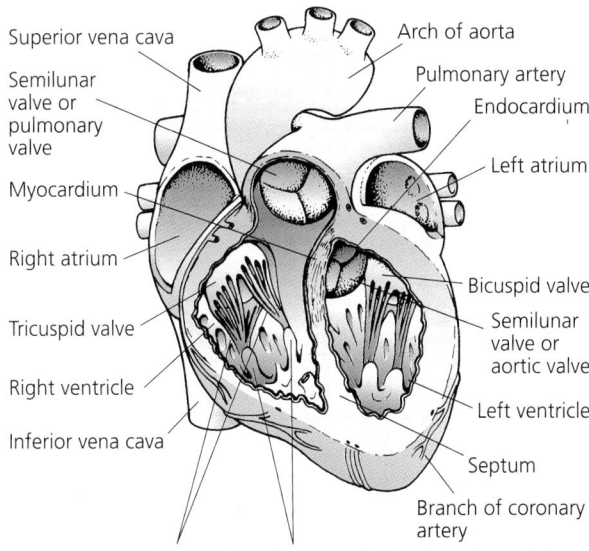

- Superior vena cava
- Semilunar valve or pulmonary valve
- Myocardium
- Right atrium
- Tricuspid valve
- Right ventricle
- Inferior vena cava
- Arch of aorta
- Pulmonary artery
- Endocardium
- Left atrium
- Bicuspid valve
- Semilunar valve or aortic valve
- Left ventricle
- Septum
- Branch of coronary artery

The valve tendons and papillary muscles tie the edges of the valves to the ventricular wall and stops the valve from turning inside out.

FIGURE 9.2 *Cross-section of the heart*

pump out the same amount of blood. This can result in an increase in the size of the heart and can also be shown by a rise in the blood pressure. The body therefore needs more oxygen and, in turn, the lungs may have to work harder.

Sclerosis

The amount of fats carried in the blood system also increases with age. Cholesterol is one example of this. These fats can be laid down in the walls of the blood vessels. This process is known as atherosclerosis.

Heart attack

A major blockage to an artery can prevent the flow of blood to the heart and this causes a heart attack (known in medical terminology as myocardial infarction). A heart attack can cause permanent damage to the heart and can be fatal.

Heart dysfunction

The heart muscles can deteriorate with age and the heart valves can also become less elastic. The rhythm of the heart can change and heart failure can occur when the blood is not efficiently pumped away from the heart. A reduced blood supply to the legs can cause ulcers or pain on exercise. Blockage of blood vessels to the brain can lead to a stroke. Heart failure can result from any problem that puts the heart muscle under excessive strain. Excessive blood pressure or a blockage or narrowing of the valves in the heart, or disorders with electrical rhythm of the heart, can result in a failure of the heart muscle to pump blood sufficiently.

Breathing

When blood is not being pumped round the system efficiently the burden placed on the lungs increases. This can cause lung congestion, which in turn may cause breathlessness. Diuretics (water tablets) are often prescribed to remove excess fluid from the blood system.

The strength of the chest muscles may also reduce with ageing and the efficiency of the lungs may deteriorate. Chronic disease such as bronchitis may occur and prove difficult to overcome. Bronchitis is the term used to describe the swelling and inflammation of the airways that connect the windpipe to the lungs. Breathing becomes more difficult and mucus is secreted, which may become infected. In some cases pneumonia may result. Pleurisy can also be caused (inflammation of the membrane surrounding the lungs and chest cavity).

Disorders of the respiratory system include emphysema and chronic obstructive and pulmonary disease (COP).

Emphysema

Emphysema is a disease in which the air sacs within the lungs (alveoli) are damaged. This causes shortness of breath and can result in respiratory or heart failure. It can be caused by smoking, which causes the air sacs in the lungs to produce chemicals that damage the walls of the alveoli. In time this results in a drop in the amount of oxygen in the blood.

Chronic Obstructive Pulmonary Disease (COPD)

When there is an airflow obstruction, perhaps due to emphysema or bronchitis, the resulting condition is described as chronic obstructive pulmonary disease (COPD). This condition can create a progressively worse disruption of airflow into the lungs. Some people increase their rate of breathing to cope, whereas others tend to have a bluish appearance and can appear bloated because of a deficiency in oxygen and a build up of fluid.

Lung cancer

According to NHS Direct (2005), lung cancer is uncommon before the age of 40 with only about one case in a hundred being diagnosed. The majority of people who develop lung cancer are over 60. Smoking directly damages the cells which line the lungs and smoking or breathing in other people's smoke represents a major cause of lung cancer. Exposure to certain other kinds of air pollution may also increase the risk of lung cancer.

Sensory impairment

Visual degeneration

After 45-years-of-age the ability of the eye to focus begins to weaken and by 65 years there is little focusing power left, making small print more difficult to read.

Older people may not process sugar as effectively due to diabetes; this can cause the lens of the eye to become opaque rather than clear. The resulting cataract interferes with clear vision. The majority of people aged 75 years or over have some degree of cataract formation.

Cataracts may start to form between the ages of 50 and 60 years and often take time to develop. Cataracts result from changes in the lens of the eye. As people grow older the lens can become hard and cloudy. This process stops the lens of the eye from being able to change shape or transmit light appropriately, resulting in symptoms such as blurred vision. Diabetes can also lead to the development of cataracts.

Another condition that can affect eyesight in older age is glaucoma (an increase of fluid pressure within the eye). Up to 50 per cent of people over 90-years-of-age may experience severe sight problems. Sight is crucial in maintaining independence and poor eyesight can be a major factor contributing to the increased chances of falling in older age. The loss of sight can be devastating for many older people but early detection can be very effective in reducing the rate of deterioration.

Hearing degeneration

The inner ear is the organ most frequently affected by changes from ageing. The sensitivity of the nerve cells to sound may decrease and there may also be a loss of nerve fibres, which affects the person's sense of balance. The sensory hair cells of the cochlea (inner ear) begin to degenerate. The amount of wax made by the ear may also increase and become harder, and this can affect the ability to hear clearly. High tones become more difficult to pick up and sound can become muffled. Trying to hear may be a great strain, and as the problems of hearing are less understood generally, they are therefore more likely to lead to mental distress, such as depression, than sight problems.

Musculoskeletal disorders

Disorders of the musculoskeletal system include osteoarthritis, osteoporosis, rheumatoid arthritis and rheumatism.

Where joints meet, the ends of the bones are protected by cartilage. A synovial membrane filled with fluid and covered by ligaments covers the space between the joints. Joints can either be a ball or socket (such as the hip) or a hinge joint (like the elbow). These joints can become damaged as people age. The cartilage can become thinner with age and may lose water, becoming less elastic. In osteoarthritis the bone ends can thicken and in the later stages form bony spurs, which restrict movement of the joint. The hips and the knees are most commonly affected and cause stiffness and pain, together with restricted movement.

Rheumatism

Rheumatism is a general name given to inflammation and pain in the joints or muscles of the body. Certain diseases such as rheumatic fever can cause problems with joints but these diseases are rare in the UK nowadays.

Rheumatoid arthritis

Rheumatoid arthritis is less common than osteoarthritis but is caused by swelling and inflammation of the synovial membrane. The swelling results in damage to the cartilage bone and soft tissue. The joints can degenerate and in the late stages can also cause deformation of the bones. Rheumatoid arthritis can happen at any age although NHS Direct states that it is more common in people over the age of 40. Rheumatoid arthritis is caused because of problems with the immune system attacking the joints of the body.

Osteoporosis

NHS Direct states that approximately 3 million people in the UK have osteoporosis and that there are over 200,000 fractured bones every year as a result of osteoporosis. Bone is part of our body and, like other body tissue, it needs to regenerate and rebuild itself. As people become older this ability to regenerate bone becomes less effective. The bones of older people often become thinner and more likely to break than when they were young. Women are more at risk of osteoporosis than men because bone strength is affected by sex hormones. Men continue to produce the male sex hormone testosterone throughout life, but women often experience a major decrease in the hormone oestrogen after the menopause. Some people are more at risk of developing osteoporosis because of genetics – it 'runs in their family'. People who live a lifestyle that involves little exercise may also be more at risk because exercise helps to strengthen bones.

Muscle

There are three types of muscle in the body:

* **Skeletal muscles**, which can be consciously controlled by nerves running from the brain.

* **Smooth muscles** are found in internal organs such as the stomach and the gut and the eyes.

* **Cardiac muscles**, which move involuntarily.

Most changes in older age affect the skeletal and cardiac muscles. There is a general reduction in the mass of the skeletal muscles due to shrinkage and loss of cells. This can also occur if there is a prolonged period of inactivity. The strength of muscles also reduces. The nerve cells (or neurons), which activate muscles, are also lost with age. One neuron will control a group of cells so the loss of one neuron will have a great effect. The amount of neurotransmitters (chemicals released by the nerves into muscles to cause a contraction) may also decrease with age. Exercise can help to maintain muscle mass and efficiency.

Skin

As people grow older the elasticity of the skin reduces under the skin. The amount of fat stored under the skin becomes less and the appearance of the skin becomes looser and develops wrinkles.

Bone

The mass and density of bone reduces as people get older. The rate differs between men and women. Excessive bone loss is called osteoporosis and occurs more commonly in women than men. This can increase the likelihood of bone fractures. A common cause of admission to hospital for older women is a fracture of the neck of the femur after a fall. Osteoporosis can also cause curvature of the spine. Men tend to have a higher level of bone density, which is in part due to the level of testosterone that men sustain. However, very old men do have increased rates of bone fractures and this is related to the decline in male hormones with extreme age.

Disorders of the nervous system

The nervous system can be divided into two parts:

* the *peripheral nervous system* (the nerves that connect the limbs and organs)

* the *central nervous system* (meaning the brain and the spinal cord).

Nerve cells accumulate extra material as they age, because they are unable to get rid of waste products as easily. Nerve cells communicate with each other through electrical impulses and, as people age, the messages about pain, touch and temperature slow down.

Disorders of the nervous system include strokes, Parkinson's disease and dementia.

Stroke

A stroke is caused by impairment in the flow of blood to the brain. This can be due to a blockage in the flow of blood or a bleed into the brain. The effect of the stroke depends on the area of brain affected, as each part of the brain has a specific function. Usually an interruption to the blood flow to the right-hand part of the brain will result in weakness and sensory disturbance in the left-hand side of the body. After heart problems, a stroke is the most major cause of death in older people. However, recovery from stroke is possible. Up to half of those people who survive a stroke will regain full independence; one quarter will need some help and one quarter will be dependent on a carer.

Parkinson's disease

Parkinson's disease is caused by problems with the production of a chemical messenger or 'neurotransmitter' essential for muscular movement. The absence of this chemical can cause muscular stiffness, weakness and slowness of movement.

Dementia

Dementia is a general term indicating that there is an ongoing disease process affecting the brain structure and function. The most common effects of dementia can be on memory, reasoning, orientation and judgement. There are many types of disease that can affect the brain but the most common type is Alzheimer's disease.

Those at highest risk of developing Alzheimer's are people over the age of 80 years; it is estimated that up to 20 per cent of people this age may be affected. It is thought that insoluble protein deposits build up within the brain. This process causes the brain cells to die at a much faster rate than normal. At present it is not known what causes this process to start. Alzheimer's disease is usually only confirmed by testing a sample of brain tissue, which is not possible to take while people are alive. Many other conditions have the same symptoms as Alzheimer's, such as diabetes or depression, and as a result many older people do not receive the medical treatment they need due to incorrect assumptions and diagnosis.

In recent years medication has been developed that helps to slow down the pace of Alzheimer's disease. This does not stop the process of protein deposition but does increase the level of a chemical messenger (acetylcholine) that is usually very low in people with Alzheimer's. There is much current research worldwide to find a cure for this disease, as in many western societies there are increasing proportions of older people and a rapid rise in the total number of people developing Alzheimer's.

Multiple sclerosis

Multiple sclerosis is not associated with the ageing process as such. NHS Direct explains that multiple sclerosis can occur at any age but it is rare for the illness to begin before puberty or after 60 years of age. The coating or protective sheath which surrounds nerve fibres becomes damaged, resulting in a wide range of problems to do with neurological functioning. These problems may include fatigue and feeling tired, problems with vision, numbness, tingling or other nervous sensations, bladder and bowel problems, problems with digestion, emotional and thinking difficulties, or problems with speech, bodily coordination and balance. The cause of multiple sclerosis is not known but it is likely that the body's immune system becomes triggered to attack its own tissue – perhaps by a virus.

Disorders of the digestive system

Serious disorders of the digestive system often occur in younger people, although older people can also develop these illnesses.

Irritable bowel syndrome

Irritable bowel syndrome involves a group of symptoms such as pain, excess gas, diarrhoea and constipation. Many people with irritable bowel syndrome experience alternating periods of diarrhoea and constipation. The nerves and muscles in the large intestine (bowel) become extra sensitive and the intestine does not work properly.

Ulcerative colitis

Ulcerative colitis is a much more serious condition, where the large intestine becomes inflamed and ulcerated. This condition usually causes diarrhoea, and people with this problem may experience fatigue, weight loss, loss of appetite and bleeding.

Crohn's disease

Crohn's disease is similar to ulcerative colitis in so far as it can cause similar symptoms and is

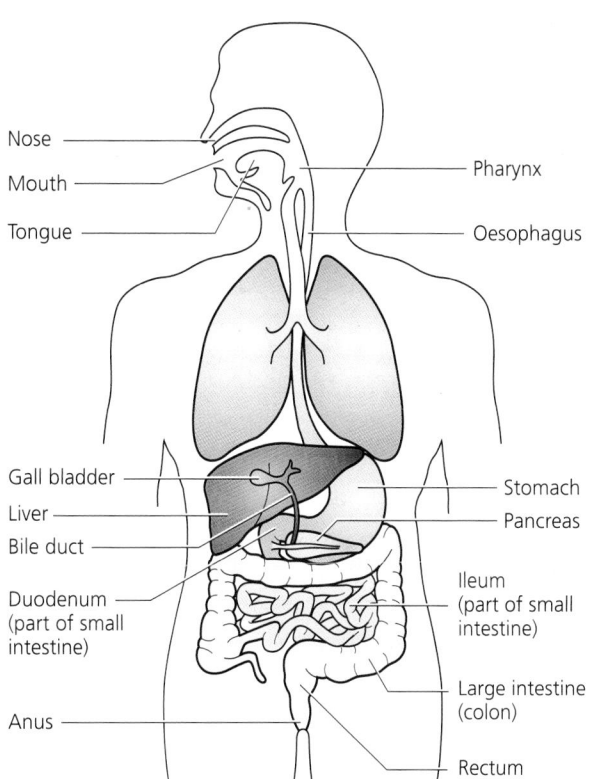

FIGURE 9.3 *The digestive system*

classified as an inflammatory bowel disease. Crohn's disease causes inflammation deeper within the intestine wall and also occurs in other areas of the digestive tract.

Chronic constipation

Constipation is a common problem that can result from insufficient exercise, lack of dietary fibre or insufficient liquid intake. Chronic or long-term constipation may be associated with more serious problems, such as those involving the nerves or muscles in the digestive tract.

Coping strategies

General health advice is to avoid cigarette smoke, eat a healthy diet, prevent obesity, take regular exercise and avoid excessive drinking of alcohol. This advice may help to delay or prevent the onset of some of the age-associated problems described above. Where people have begun to develop a problem, adopting a healthier lifestyle may still help. For example, older people can lower their risk of heart disease by eating a healthy diet that avoids saturated fats and by taking exercise. Smoking dramatically increases the risk of heart disease so stopping smoking may help. A healthy diet and regular exercise may help to prevent becoming overweight. Exercise, good diet and maintenance of a healthy body weight may all help to prevent atherosclerosis and the associated risks of high blood pressure heart disease and strokes.

Maintaining a healthy body weight may also help to reduce the symptoms of arthritis. Increased weight will place extra stress on joints. Exercise may help prevent osteoarthritis because it helps to strengthen muscles that support the joints. Regular exercise may also help to reduce the risk of osteoporosis as exercise is likely to strengthen bones. With respect to osteoporosis, a calcium rich diet may also help. As with so many diseases, smoking will increase the risk. Excessive drinking of alcohol may also contribute to problems associated with osteoporosis.

Older people may be able to reduce their risk of visual impairment by having regular eye tests in order to check visual needs and to detect the risk of eye disease. Much visual impairment associated with ageing can be corrected with appropriate prescribed lenses or glasses. Glaucoma can often be treated if detected early. It is thought that protecting the eyes from harmful ultraviolet sun rays may also help to reduce the risk of cataracts. Older people who experience difficulty with hearing may be able to reduce disability following medical assessment and manage hearing loss with the help of equipment such as hearing aids. People with disabilities may also benefit from organising their home environment in a way that is easy to manage. Occupational therapists can often provide an assessment of individual needs to include the organisation of domestic layout, routines and the use of assistive equipment to minimise disability.

Creating a safe and comfortable environment will be important for older people who have to cope with degenerative illness. For example, it will be important to eliminate trip hazards. If an older person with brittle bones trips over or falls, fractures can occur so much more easily than in a younger person with strong bones.

Whilst many degenerative illnesses cannot be cured, it is possible to do a great deal to manage and reduce the impact of these illnesses on a person's quality of life. Medical assessment is a vital step for coping with the problems associated with degenerative illness. For example, without assessment and treatment, incontinence can create a highly embarrassing problem that may greatly restrict the quality of life of an older person. However, a lot can be done to manage or treat a problem with urinary or faecial incontinence. Incontinence should not be regarded as an expected outcome of ageing. It is critically important that older people do not regard disability as inevitable, even if some problems are associated with an ageing process. It is not true that 'what cannot be cured must be endured'. GPs and hospitals may be able to provide treatment to manage pain and to increase the functioning of limbs or muscles affected by an illness. Part of the coping strategy to alleviate the effects of illnesses is to seek expert advice and support.

Advice might be gained from:

* general practitioners

* specialist organisations such as Age Concern or the Alzheimer's Society

* Social Services

* Internet research.

An individual may also improve his or her ability to cope through social support. The majority of older people enjoy good social support networks. Additional help with emotional and psychological problems may be available privately or from social services or counselling services associated with a GP's surgery.

Summary

The following key areas have been covered in this section.

Physical Ageing – at a glance

* Skin becomes thinner, less elastic and wrinkled

* Bones can become more brittle and more likely to fracture

* Joints can become stiffer and may become painful as the cartilage on the bone ends becomes worn away

* The ligaments which reinforce joints can become looser

* Height can be reduced because the cartilage that separates the vertebrae becomes compressed. The spine may also become more rounded

* Muscles become weaker

* Sense of balance can become impaired

* Taste and smell receptors deteriorate

* Vision can deteriorate because the lens of the eye starts to block light; cataracts can develop

* Hearing can deteriorate with a failure to hear high-pitched sounds

* Lack of skin sensitivity can lead to increased risk of hypothermia

* Muscles in the digestive tract become weaker – creating a risk of constipation

* The heart is less efficient at pumping blood

* Blood pressure becomes higher

* Nutrients from food are not absorbed as well as in earlier life

* Breathing is less efficient because respiratory muscles are weaker

* Gas exchange in the lungs becomes impaired as the elastic walls of the alveoli become damaged

* Body metabolism is reduced due to lowered performance of the endocrine glands

---

Consider this

Jenny is 80-years-old and has recently stopped going out to her social club, one that she has belonged to for many years. She says that she no longer enjoys going out because the walk is so difficult and that she finds it hard join in with what other people are doing and saying. She often makes statements such as 'They don't seem to make sense now, you never know what they're on about …' and 'Besides this, it is often very cold in there'.

Thinking about the physical issues involved in ageing, what physical changes may have contributed to Jenny losing interest in her club?

Section 2: Social, emotional and economic aspects of ageing

Lifestyle changes in later life

Life expectancy

In 1901 the average life expectancy for a newborn baby was only 49 years for a girl and 45 years for a boy. Many children died in the early years of their life and this resulted in a low figure for life expectancy. The Office for National Statistics (ONS) (2004) reports that by 2002, female life expectancy at birth was 81 years and male life expectancy at birth was 76 years.

Work patterns

According to the Office for National Statistics (2004) the great majority of older people who are beyond the state pension age do not work; 91 per cent of men and 90 per cent of women are classed as 'economically inactive'. Some people do continue to work; one per cent of men over the age of 65 and 2 per cent of women over the age of 60 remain in full-time employment. Some 3 per cent of men aged over 65 and 6 per cent of women aged over 60-years-of-age work part-time. Four per cent of men over retirement age are self-employed, but only one per cent of women over 60 are self-employed. It may be that in the future, an increasing number of older people will remain in employment, but at present it seems reasonable to describe the majority of women over 60 and men over 65 as being 'retired'. For many people, retirement represents a time of opportunity for relaxing and enjoying leisure pursuits. For some people retirement may involve a loss of earnings, loss of contact with work colleagues, and possibly a loss of the status and identity associated with work. For many people, retirement will be seen as a positive change, but for a few, retirement may result in significant stress.

Leisure

Older people often have more free time than younger people. Health and mobility problems can sometimes limit the activities older people may choose. The ONS reports an average time spent on the activities set out below by the over 65-year-old age group.

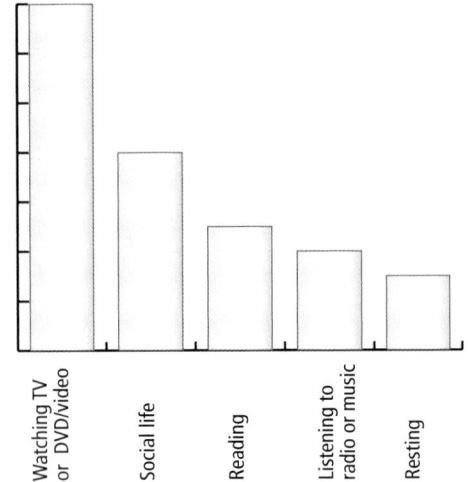

Source: Office for National Statistics, May 2004

FIGURE 9.4 *Average time spent on leisure activities by those over 65 years*

Income and decreased income

The over 65 year-old age group includes many people who are extremely well off and who enjoy high levels of saving and property ownership. For example, the ONS (2004) reports that in 2000, 61 per cent of people aged 65 and over owned their homes outright (they had paid off any mortgage). Social Trends (2004) reports that 16 per cent of one-person households and 30 per cent of two-person pensioner households have over £20,000 in savings. This compares with only 15 per cent of households across the age range.

On the other hand, the ONS reports that some 40 per cent of people aged 85 and over live in rented accommodation. Social Trends (2004) reports that 28 per cent of one-person pensioner households and 17 per cent of two-person pensioner households have no savings of any kind. Arber and Ginn (2004) report that some 21 per cent of people aged 65 years and above may be considered to live in poverty within the UK. This figure compares with 17 per cent of the population in general.

For some people old age can be a time of wealth and affluence but for others it can be a time of poverty. Writing about differences in income, Arbour and Ginn state: 'These differences in older

FIGURE 9.5 *For many people, later life represents an enjoyable and fulfilling experience*

people's incomes reflect mainly inequalities in their ability to build private (occupational or personal) pension entitlements during the working life. Arbour and Ginn point out that 'since 1980, the value of the basic state pension has declined relative to national earnings while those retiring with private occupational pensions received increasingly large amounts'. Although there is a range of benefits available to pensioners who would only otherwise receive the state pension, the possession of a large private pension may make a huge difference to quality of life.

Health

The 2001 National Census asked people about their experience of long-term illness and disability. The percentages in Figure 9.6 show the proportion of people who rated their general health as being good, fairly good or not good.

		GOOD HEALTH	FAIRLY GOOD HEALTH	NOT GOOD
Males	65 to 74 years	42 per cent	39 per cent	19 per cent
	75 years and over	31 per cent	43 per cent	26 per cent
Females	65 to 74 years	39 per cent	42 per cent	19 per cent
	75 years and over	28 per cent	44 per cent	29 per cent

FIGURE 9.6 *People's perceptions of their own health*

Source: Social Trends, 2004

As you can see, the majority of older people experience good or fairly good health. However, one in four men over the age of 75 and almost one in three women report that their health is not good.

Social contact and support

Many older people live alone. The 2001 census reported that 21.8 per cent of men and 43.5 per cent of women over the age of 65 live alone. Among the 85-year-old and older age group, 36.9 per cent of men and 54.5 per cent of women live alone.

The ONS (2004) reported that 79 per cent of people aged 65 and over saw a relative or friend at least once a week. Only a small minority – 2 per cent of over 65-year-old people – had no contact with friends or relatives. A further 19 per cent saw friends or relatives less than once a week.

Once again, as with the majority picture on health, the majority of older people appear to enjoy effective social networks only about one person in five may experience a degree of isolation, and only about 2 per cent of people are isolated from friends and relatives.

What does it take to be happy?

Seligman (2002) produced a textbook exploring what it takes to be happy. Although his research was not focused on older adults as such, his conclusions may still be worth noting. Seligman's research suggests that happiness mainly results from the way people apply their abilities in life, rather than on external circumstances. However, his research did suggest that being married, having a rich social network of friends and family, being religious and being good at avoiding negative experiences and emotions are associated with happiness for many people. Seligman did not find a meaningful link between wealth and happiness – although poverty may be associated with unhappiness. When it comes to health, the key issue seems to be whether you believe that you are healthy or not – he did not find a strong association between genuine health and happiness.

What is old age like?

From the brief evidence presented so far, it is fair to say that the majority of people over State retirement age experience reasonable health, a satisfactory social life and, in some cases, a high standard of material well-being. There is evidence that a minority of older people experience poor health, poverty and isolation. A small section of the older population may experience high levels of stress due to social and economic factors. Social care workers are more likely to come into contact with people with health, social or economic problems. However, it is important to guard against the assumption (or stereotype) that later life is a story of decline and misery for everyone.

In many ways old age will be like any other life stage. Whether or not an older person is leading a happy and fulfilled life will have a lot to do with his or her approach to it. Life satisfaction may not always be predictable from measurements of health, time spent with relatives, or money in the bank!

Risks faced by older people – increased isolation

Sixty years ago, many people lived in extended families, where grandparents, parents and children all lived together in the same building. Older people would not be isolated, because they lived with their adult children. Coleman and Salt (1992) report that in 1951, 15 per cent of households contained adult relatives. By 1990 only 4 per cent of households included adult relatives and today the figure is smaller still. Parents are increasingly less likely to live with their children when they become old.

Another factor is that people are geographically mobile – this means that people move away from the area where they were born a lot more than they may have done in the past. Older people often move home when they retire. Sometimes people move in order to 'downsize' and live in a smaller, cheaper property to save money. Sometimes, people move in order to live in what they consider to be a more desirable area. For example, over 30 per cent of the population of East Devon are over state retirement age. This geographical mobility may result in some older people losing touch with networks of family and friends. In addition to older people choosing to move, many find that their children have to relocate in order to take advantage of cheaper housing or better job opportunities. A lack of contact may result from people living long distances apart. It might be wrong to assume that isolation is caused by attitudes, i.e. because children no longer care about their parents.

Difficulties with travel

Older people may find it difficult to travel and to keep in contact with friends and family who do not live nearby. One factor that may increase isolation is lack of car ownership. The 2001 census reports that nearly 90 per cent of 50–54-year-olds have access to a car within their household. However, only 45 per cent of men and 25 per cent of women aged 85 and over have access to a car, according to Arber and Ginn (2004). Some older people may not be able to afford to run a car; others may give up driving for health reasons. Part of the reason that only a quarter of women over the age of 85 have access to a car is that historically women did not learn to drive, and instead relied on their husbands to own and drive a car. The loss or illness of a husband may therefore result in a loss of ability to travel for many women in this age group. If you cannot drive or cannot afford a car, you can of course use public transport. Arber and Ginn (2004) explain that many older people may be prevented from using public transport, because of frailty, disability or fear of crime. Public transport may be difficult to reach in many rural areas.

FIGURE 9.7 *Having access to a car may be an important factor in maintaining social contact*

Mobility problems

People have an increased risk of developing physical problems with movement as they grow older. Serious physical disability may include difficulties with walking and difficulties in transferring from a bed to a chair and so on. In the 2001 Health Survey for England a sample of people were interviewed about disabilities they experienced. Figure 9.8 reports the percentages of people in the survey who reported a serious disability with respect to body movement.

Figure 9.8 suggests that mobility problems increase dramatically with age. The survey detected very few people under the age of 24 with serious mobility problems. However, nearly one in three women over the age of 85 reported a serious disability in relation to body movement. Physical disability will limit the amount of travel that people can engage in. Some people may experience a sense of isolation because their physical health limits the amount of travelling they can do in order to meet with friends and family.

AGE GROUP	16–24	25–34	35–44	45–54	55–64	65–74	75–84	85+
Men	0 %	1 %	1 %	2 %	4 %	6 %	10 %	22 %
Women	0 %	1 %	1 %	2 %	5 %	6 %	16 %	32 %

FIGURE 9.8 *The percentage of adults in England with serious 'movement' or locomotor disability*

Source: Health Survey for England, 2001

Increased dependency

A significant number of older people experience long-term illnesses such as heart problems, arthritis and rheumatism. These illnesses may restrict daily living activities such as shopping, cooking and travel. The ONS (2004) suggest that approximately 70 per cent of people over the age of 85 experience a level of disability that restricts daily living activities. Interestingly, some people who experience disability may still report their health as being good.

Many people who have long-term illnesses are assessed for support, such as home care. Social Trends (2002) reported that nearly half of personal social services expenditure was spent on older people.

Many older people with disabilities become dependent on relatives. Data from the 2001 census suggests that 21 per cent of people in their fifties claimed to be providing some level of care for a relative. Much of the support provided by relatives involved 'keeping an eye on a person' or 'keeping them company', taking them out' or other practical help such as shopping. Smaller number of relatives provided physical help or personal care.

For some older people the thought of being dependent on others creates a threat to self-esteem. A mother who has always guided and advised her daughter may be unhappy about being dependent or indeed, a burden for that daughter. A father might worry about imposing on his children, who are still in full-time work. As well as threatening self-esteem, dependency might lower a person's satisfaction with life. If you can no longer cook for yourself you may not find 'meals on wheels' to be an adequate substitute. If you have to rely on someone else doing the shopping for you, you may become frustrated when they do not return with exactly what you would have chosen. Dependency can cause some people to give up trying to cope with their life. This can result in a process called learned helplessness (Seligman, 1975). According to Seligman, who developed the theory of learned helplessness, giving up and withdrawing from daily living activities can result in the onset of clinical depression.

Illness or disability can therefore start a process of feeling frustrated, followed by becoming withdrawn and losing **confidence** and the **motivation** to cope with daily living activities. A further issue is that many older people do not feel that they are useful or valued by others.

Many people are aware of a prejudiced attitude towards older people. Ageism as this prejudice is sometimes called, is often based on assumptions (or stereotypes) such as those shown in Figure 9.9.

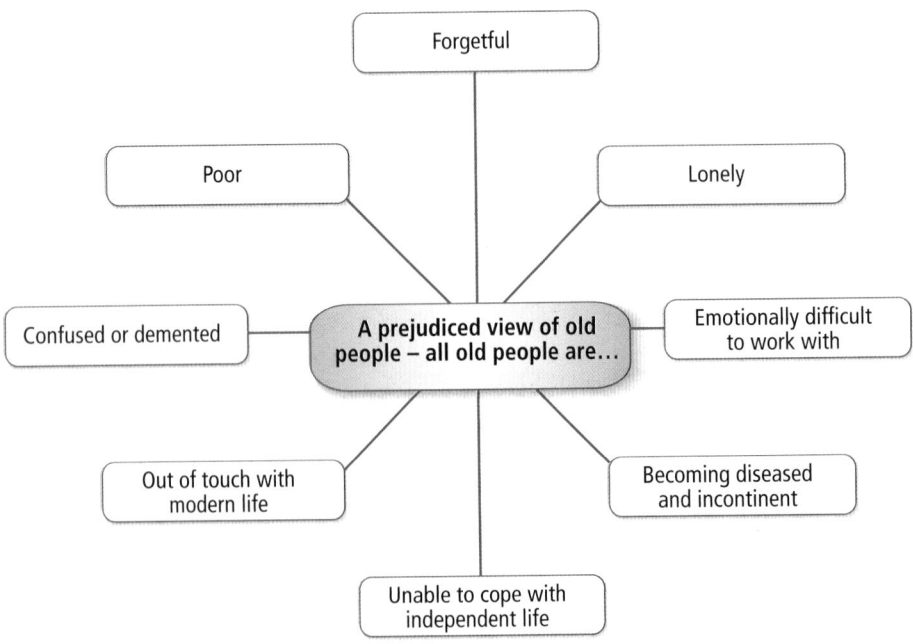

FIGURE 9.9 *Examples of some prejudiced attitudes towards old people*

Perhaps the most extreme danger of this kind of prejudice is that some older people may come to believe in this view of themselves; they may say things such as 'you can't expect much at my time of life'. When people have very limited expectations this may add to the risk of withdrawal and isolation that some people experience.

The impact of health problems

Describing and categorising mental health issues is not easy. Historically, the term neurosis was used to classify disorders involving distorted thinking. Neurosis included disorders such as depression and anxiety and irrational fear, called (phobia). More serious disorders involving a loss of rationality and seriously disordered thinking were classified as psychotic illness. Dementia was understood as a disorder with a physical cause and was understood as being different from neurosis or psychosis.

Nowadays, mental health problems are classified as 'disorders'. Many psychologists and psychiatrists use the classification system developed by the American Psychiatric Association, called the Diagnostic and Statistical Manual of Mental Disorders or DSM for short. The DSM is a complex system for interpreting disorders but the fourth version of the DSM includes the categories listed in Figure 9.10, within its interpretation of clinical disorders.

Mental health and income

Social Trends (2004) reports that among people aged 60–74 years the likelihood of having a neurotic mental illness such as depression, anxiety, obsessive compulsive disorder, panic or phobia increases with low income. Older women with a weekly household income of £500 or more in the year 2000 were three times less likely to experience a 'neurotic' mental illness than women living on a household income of under £200. It may be that the stress of living on a low income increases the risk of anxiety and depression.

Dementia

The Alzheimer's Society estimates that over one quarter of a million people in the UK are affected by dementia and that approximately 5 per cent of people over the age of 65 years have dementia.

DISORDER	BRIEF EXPLANATION
Delirium	Thinking and behaviour are disordered, perhaps due to a physical illness or perhaps due to the effects of drugs. Delirium results in 'confusion'. Many older people who are labelled confused are likely to be experiencing the effects of physical illness or drug 'side effects'
Dementia	A disorder resulting from a physical condition in the brain. There are different types of dementia
Schizophrenia	A serious disorder of thinking and emotion that can result in irrational beliefs about persecution and power, withdrawal from other people, disorganised thinking or even rigid, withdrawn body postures
Mood disorders: depression	A loss of ability to function effectively and to cope with practical and emotional issues in life
Anxiety disorders: panic disorder	An overwhelming emotional reaction that disables a person. Panic disorder may be associated with issues such as agoraphobia – a fear of open and usually public spaces, e.g. a fear of going out from home
Anxiety disorders: specific phobia	A specific fear which interferes with daily living, such as a fear of dogs, of spiders, or of looking down from tall buildings. A phobia may prevent an individual from leading a satisfactory life

FIGURE 9.10 *Classification of some clinical disorders*

The risk of developing dementia increases with age. The Alzheimer's Society estimates that as many as 20 per cent of people over the age of 80 are affected by dementia. This still means that dementia is not a normal part of ageing. Four out of five people who live to extreme old age will never experience dementia.

Dementia involves damage to the structure and chemistry of the brain. Because a person's brain becomes damaged, he or she is likely to experience problems with understanding, communicating, reasoning, becoming lost and remembering important recent events. It is wrong to assume that older people who cannot find their glasses are exhibiting the first symptoms of dementia. Dementia always involves a range of problems with mental functioning. Forgetfulness can be caused by a wide range of issues including physical illness and stress. Many older people report that they find it difficult to remember items of shopping and so on, but this type of forgetfulness is different from the problems associated with dementia.

There are many different kinds of dementia and research is constantly improving our understanding of the nature and potential causes of these illnesses. With respect to Alzheimer's disease, there is no straightforward explanation of

TYPE OF DEMENTIA	EXPLANATION
Alzheimer's disease	The Alzheimer's Society states that Alzheimer's disease is the most common form of dementia, making up 55 per cent of all cases. Alzheimer's disease involves problems with understanding, remembering and making sense of things. As the illness progresses people may lose the ability to make sense of their surroundings and recognise close friends and relatives. People with Alzheimer's become extremely dependent and lose the ability to speak clearly, to swallow and retain continence
Vascular disease	The blood supply to the cells of the brain becomes disrupted, so parts of the brain die. This type of dementia is also called multi-infarct dementia. An infarct is a dead area of tissue. Some people with this problem may experience mental decline in a series of steps, as if they were having multiple strokes. The disabilities experienced and the pattern of this illness may be different from Alzheimer's disease
Dementia, with Lewy bodies	Lewy bodies are microscopic deposits within the brain, which are associated with the death of nerve cells. The Alzheimer's Society states that more than half of people who have this type of dementia show symptoms of Parkinson's disease. This type of dementia is associated with visual hallucinations and difficulty in judging distances. Abilities can often fluctuate from day to day
Fronto-temporal dementia and Pick's disease	The front and side sections of the brain become damaged. The front of the brain (frontal lobes) is associated with the ability to control behaviour. People with this kind of dementia may show a loss of inhibition and may appear to have changed their personality. Some people who are affected by this disorder may be labelled as rude or aggressive by other people. Memory abilities may be relatively unaffected during the early stages of this kind of dementia
Rarer causes of dementia	There are many other kinds of dementia, including sub-cortical dementia, where the inner part of the brain appears to be more damaged than the outer part of the brain. A person with these problems may experience a wide range of physiological problems including difficulty staying awake

FIGURE 9.11 *Types of dementia*

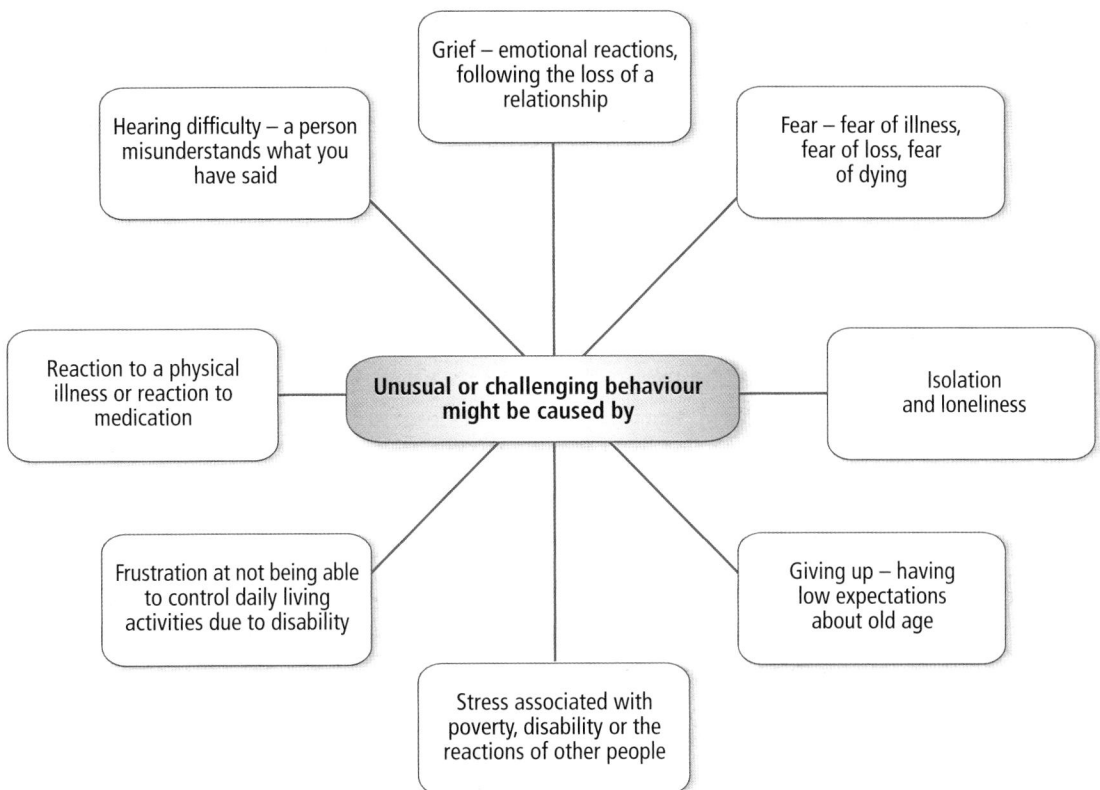

FIGURE 9.12 *Examples of issues that may cause unusual behaviour*

what causes this disorder even though there are many theories. There is no cure for Alzheimer's but there are a range of drug treatments that may help improve the mental abilities of people with the disease. Some of the main types of dementia as identified by the Alzheimer's Society are described in Figure 9.11.

Care workers should never attempt to diagnose psychiatric disorders. Even highly experienced professionals with extensive training will find difficulty in interpreting and understanding individual need. On the other hand, it is important that carers do not make assumptions about ageing and start to see all older people as suffering from dementia.

Unusual or challenging behaviour may result from a whole range of issues, and it is dangerous to assume that any unusual behaviour is a symptom of a mental disorder.

Some examples of issues that may cause unusual behaviour are listed in Figure 9.12.

Grief on losing a partner

As couples grow older the chances that one person will die increase. Bereavement causes a major change in people's lives. You might lose the main person that you talked to, the main person who helped you; you might lose your sexual partner, a person who you shared life with and a person who made you feel good. Living without a partner can involve great uncertainty. Your partner may have helped with sorting out household bills or with shopping or housework – now you have to do it all yourself. Bereavement can mean you have to learn to live a new life as a single person again. Coping on your own can take a lot of time and energy.

Colin Murray Parkes (1975) identified an outline theory of grief in his study of grieving individuals. Initially, many people experience shock and numbness when confronted with a loss – there is a tendency to block out or deny the loss. This phase may be followed by a reaction of

Consider the five short descriptions of people below. There is insufficient information for you to be able to be sure about the needs of any of these people. What would your best guess be as to the reasons for these people's problems?

Person A: this person spends a lot of time wandering outside his house or just standing indoors looking blankly into space. He rarely speaks; he has a poor appetite and is unable to explain why he wanders. He sometimes calls the name of his wife, who died six months ago, and he seems unable to accept that she is dead.

Person B: this person rarely gives a sensible answer when she is asked questions. She avoids talking with other people at the day centre she goes to and sometimes becomes agitated when other people try to communicate with her. She has moments of sitting and crying.

Person C: this person accuses care workers of spying on him and stealing his property. He says that his next door neighbour is trying to kill him by feeding poisonous gas under the door at night. This person has a problem with breathing and is at risk of developing pneumonia.

Person D: although this person used to be quite sociable, for the past week she has spent most of the day in total inactivity within the lounge of a care home. When this person is not actually asleep she will still have a vacant and detached expression. She is not responsive to care staff who try to talk to her. This person is incontinent of urine, and this problem has become worse in the last week.

Person E: this person lives in a sheltered housing complex, but has great difficulty in orientating herself and often becomes lost within the complex. This person often forgets whether her son has visited her and other details such as what she may have eaten for lunch. This person enjoys company and enjoys talking, but often repeats herself and sometimes seems insensitive to what other people are saying.

PERSON	BEST GUESS?
A	Bereavement, grief – appropriate social support may help
B	Hearing impairment – check communication aids
C	Fear or schizophrenia, or both. The person has an unreasonable belief that they are being attacked (paranoia). The person may be seriously stressed by their breathing problem. Clinical support may help and carers may be able to reduce stress by using effective communication
D	Delirium, perhaps due to urinary infection or possibly the effects of medication. Urgent medical attention is needed. The disorder could also be due to some other physical illness
E	Dementia – see theory on formal support in this section

searching for the lost person – a refusing to let go. A third phase involves trying to come to terms with the loss. Some people may experience emotions of self-blame or anger towards others as part of the emotional work that they need to go through. Parkes referred to this phase as 'mitigation'. Finally, people develop a new sense of self separate from the lost relationship and this phase might be called a phase of reconstruction.

Grief involves having to rebuild a sense of who you are. In general, this process may often start with denial followed by a period of struggle to come to terms with the need to change, followed by a period of rebuilding.

Increased likelihood of potential dangers to self or to others

Poor physical health or poor mental health might result in an increased likelihood of danger to self or others. Some potential dangers are listed in Figure 9.13.

Bereavement

Jack had been married for 22 years when his partner unexpectedly died of a heart attack. They had been very close. When Jack was first told about the death he made little reaction. Friends had to persuade Jack not to go into work the next day. Jack had said that it would give him something to do, take his mind off things.

Later, at the funeral, Jack said that he felt frozen inside and that he did not want to eat. It was some weeks later that Jack said he felt better because he could talk to his partner, sitting in a chair late at night.

Jack became angry and bitter about how badly everything had gone, saying that perhaps he was to blame for the illness or he should have noticed things earlier. Months later, Jack explained that he had sorted his life out a bit and would learn to cope alone.

After a year and half, Jack still misses his partner but he now says that the experience has made him stronger: "It's as if I understand more about life now. I feel – if I could cope with this – well, there isn't much I can't cope with". Jack has now become involved with the local voluntary support group for people who are bereaved. He says that helping others has helped him: 'It has given me new meaning and purpose in life. I had a good life before and now I've got a new life to lead.'

Jack has come through the experience in a positive way, even though he will always wish that his partner had never died. Bereavement can lead people to start what might feel like 'a new life'.

Can you identify a phase of shock, a phase of search, a phase of coming to terms with loss (mitigation) and a phase of reconstruction in Jack's story?

	RISK	WAYS IN WHICH INFORMAL CARERS CAN HELP
Risks from poor physical health	Hypothermia	Provide thermometers to help monitor temperature **in** the home – make regular visits
	Falls	Provide home alarm system
	Not taking medication as scheduled	Monitor medication – provide tablet boxes to help organise medication
	Self-neglect	Provide company or assistance
Risks from poor mental health	Security in the home	Make regular visits – try to organise a routine to check safety and security issues
	Memory problems	Provide orientation sheets – written details to remind a person what to do each day or what to do if there is a problem
	Withdrawal/depression	Provide company, try to interest the person in talking perhaps by discussing the past (reminiscence)
	Frustration and aggression	Try to stay calm and use conversational skills to calm the person
	Wondering and/or dangerous behaviour, such as turning gas taps on	Consult medical and social services for additional support

FIGURE 9.13 *Potential dangers faced by people in poor physical or mental health*

Communication problems

The theory on barriers to communication in Unit 2 will be relevant to all work with older people. There are special problems that may arise when working with people who are disorientated or who have memory problems. A 90-year-old service user might say things like 'my mother visited me yesterday'. On the surface, such a statement appears to be irrational. From a care perspective it is very important not to challenge the irrationality of what is being said. The most important thing is to make the older person feel valued and respected. People with memory disorders often substitute inappropriate words. The person has said that their mother visited, and perhaps you know that the visitor was in fact their daughter. The service user has simply used an incorrect word. They know what they meant, and perhaps you know what they meant – the technical inaccuracy is not important. It is much more important that the service user feels safe and respected.

In this scenario the service user is disorientated and has made statements about

SCENARIO

Encouragement through conversation

Service user: I must go home and get the tea ready for my children.

Carer: All right, shall we walk to your room then – you might want your coat.

Service user: Yes, that's right, you are so kind.

Carer [now in service user's room]: Is this a photograph of your son and daughter?

Service user: Yes, that's right.

Carer: They've both got married now – haven't they both grown up?

Service user: Yes, I'm very proud of them – they're coming to visit me tomorrow.

Carer: That's wonderful – why don't we go downstairs and have a cup of tea?

Service user: Yes that would be very nice – you are so kind to me.

needing to go home to look after her children. The carer has avoided arguing about logic, and has instead gently helped the service user to remember the age of her children now. Throughout the conversation, the carer has shown respect and value for the service user.

The role of other people in providing support

Family members, voluntary workers and members of the community can provide a great deal of support just by providing company. One of the main risks of old age is becoming lonely. Just sitting with somebody watching TV together can provide a feeling of support. Neighbours might help to make an older person feel valued just by asking if he or she is well. Voluntary workers can provide practical help, together with social support.

Changes in health and care needs

Informal support provided by family, friends, neighbours or voluntary workers can go a long way to reduce or prevent isolation and loneliness and to challenge the low expectations that some older people may have. Informal support may be vital to help people to cope with bereavement and grief. More formal support may be necessary when older people experience memory or disorientation problems associated with dementia.

> **Key concept**
>
> *personhood* The recognition and respect for the self-concept and self-esteem needs of service users.

Kitwood (1997) explains how in the past, people with dementia often experienced very poor quality care and were often understood in terms of 'no cure, no help, no hope' or 'the death that leaves the body behind'. The emphasises the importance of recognising the principle of 'personhood' when working with people with dementia. Carers need to establish a relationship involving recognition, respect and trust. The first task of care is to maintain a service user's sense of being a person.

NEED	EXPLANATION
Comfort	' ... the soothing of pain and sorrow, the calming of anxiety, the feeling of security which comes from being close to another. To comfort another person is to provide a kind of warmth and strength which might enable them to remain in one piece'
Attachment	'... without the reassurance that attachments provide it is difficult for any person, of whatever age, to function well'
Inclusion	All people need a distinct place in the 'shared life of a group'. Individual care plans may overlook the social needs of individuals
Occupation	People need a sense of purpose and need to be involved in personally significant activities that draw on their abilities
Identity	'To have an identity is to know who one is ... it means having a sense of continuity with the past, and hence a narrative, a story to present to others'

FIGURE 9.14 *The needs of people with dementia, based on Kitwood (1997)*

Kitwood argues that: 'The prime task of dementia care ... is to maintain personhood in the face of failing mental powers. Now it is possible to go further and suggest that this will occur through the sensitive meeting of this cluster of needs'. Kitwood's approach to maintaining personhood is summarised in Figure 9.14.

Kitwood's approach might be seen as arguing for person-centred relationships. A person-centred approach involves more than simply providing choice. Person-centred approaches place great value on the social, emotional and identity needs of each unique individual person.

SCENARIO

Compare two care settings

What evidence can you find of a person-centred approach in either of the two care settings below?

The Meadows is a modern purpose-built care home that accepts service users with dementia. The home is often short staffed, but residents are always well fed, and the home is clean and well equipped. Residents always have a choice of food, although communication difficulties often result in service users not understanding what they are being offered. The office keeps a 'service user plan' for each service user, but some care workers say they do not have time to use these plans.

Springfield Road has a specialist unit caring for people with dementia. There is a good ratio of care workers to service users and staff try to build a supportive relationship. All care workers understand the personal history and interests of the service users. Carers spend time listening to and reminiscing with service users, despite the fact that service users often repeat statements and say things that are not easy to follow. Care staff understand that people with dementia often have important emotional needs that may not be clearly expressed in verbal communication. Carers explain that 'you need to listen for the message behind the words – and not just for the words themselves'. Some care workers have learned basic aromatherapy and foot massage techniques, which are offered to service users. Carers explain that these approaches can help anxious people to relax and feel safe.

Although 'The Meadows' offers choice and a clean well equipped setting, there is little evidence of a person-centred approach here. 'Springfield Road' offers a feeling of personhood, outlined in Figure 9.15.

Comfort	Foot massage and aromatherapy
Attachment	Staff try to build supportive relationship
Inclusion	Staff listen – despite the difficulties
Occupation	Some reminiscence activity and foot massage and aromatherapy
Identity	Concern for service users' identities (staff learn their history)

FIGURE 9.15 *Fullfilling the needs of people with dementia*

Consider this

1. Make a list of the things you think you would need to go right for you in order for you to lead a happy and fulfilled old age. How far can you control the issues that you have listed?

2. Use the list of risks above and work out what you could do in theory to try to prevent these risks becoming a problem for you in later life.

3. Some risks, like dementia, might not be easy to avoid. In what ways can carers improve the quality of life for people with dementia?

Summary

The majority of older people are retired, with additional time to spend on leisure activities. The majority of older people perceive themselves to be in reasonable health, are not socially isolated and have adequate financial resources. A significant minority of older people, however, are at risk from the issues set out in Figure 9.16:

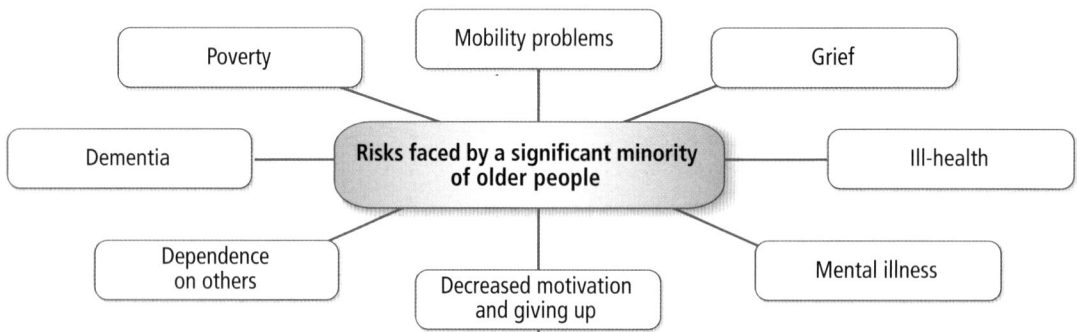

FIGURE 9.16 *The risks faced by most older people*

Section 3: Community care and support services for older service users

Service provision for older people

Services for older people are provided by a number of sources. These are set out in Figure 9.17.

FIGURE 9.17 *Services for older people: Who provides?*

Each of these providers and the types of service they provide will be discussed in much more detail below. Consider the following scenario, which gives an idea of how one person might receive services from a number of providers.

Background to current service provision

It is important to be aware that the political and social background to service provision changes over time. The information given in this section is based on the situation that is current at the time of writing (2005), and as part of your studies you should always check out details of current law, policy and guidelines for providing services.

At present, services are provided according to the *Fair Access to Care Services Guidance* (DOH, 2002). This is discussed in greater detail in Unit 5 (see page 201). This guidance states that people are

SCENARIO

Staying at home

Betty is 84 years old and has problems in walking due to arthritis. She can get around indoors, but has trouble with the stairs.

She has paid to have a stair-lift installed (by a private company), but social services have provided her with a commode to use downstairs. She has a home helper to do the cleaning and laundry once a week. The home helper works for a private company, but is paid for by social services. An NHS chiropodist (from the local health centre) treats Betty's feet every six weeks at home. Betty is well-known at the health centre, and can telephone for repeat prescriptions from her GP, which a neighbour takes to the chemist for her. She uses a personal alarm service run by the charity Age Concern.

The neighbour does Betty's shopping every week. Betty's support network is thus made up of a combination of health, social services, private, voluntary sector and informal support.

entitled to services according to the level of risk to independence that a person will suffer if his or her needs are not met. There are bands of need/risk, ranging from low to critical. Local councils have to work out their own eligibility criteria in order to determine how complex an assessment needs to be. Four types of assessment can be offered. These are set out in Figure 9.18.

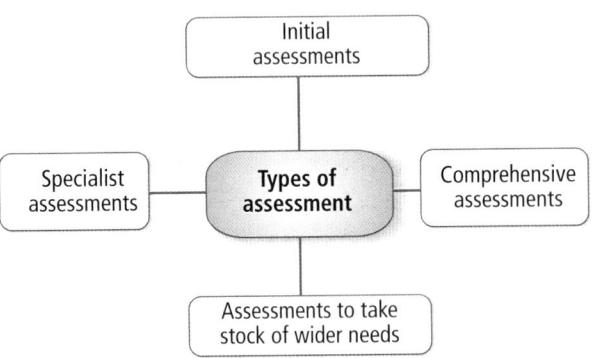

FIGURE 9.18 *Fair access to care services: types of assessment*
Source: DOH (2002)

These guidelines apply to all people in need of assessment. However, there are further guidelines on planning care for older people. The National Service Framework (NSF) issued by DOH (2001) sets out standards for the management of care for older people, together with the principles that should underpin the provision of care.

The NSF covers intermediate care, hospital care, strokes, falls and mental health issues. It also has sections on age discrimination, and the promotion of health and an active life. Most importantly, it promotes the concept of person centred care. This is summarised in the box below. Putting the person at the centre of care is one of the main ways to ensure that care values respect service user diversity, rights and beliefs.

A key concept in the implementation of services for older people is that of the single assessment process.

Consider this

Mrs Green has spent several weeks in hospital after breaking her hip in a fall. She is now ready to go home.

The hospital discharge team has been responsible for preparing a care plan to meet Mrs Green's needs. The care manager from the discharge team has coordinated information from a number of people. These have included the hospital consultant, the physiotherapist and the occupational therapist (who has done an assessment of Mrs Green's ability to perform a number of basic personal and domestic tasks for herself). Mrs Green lives alone as she is a widow, but she has a son and a daughter who live nearby.

The care manager has had to take all these facts into consideration when drawing up a plan for Mrs Green. Not least, she has to take into account Mrs Green's wishes for the kind of support she would like.

The resulting care plan includes support from a number of sources, including home care, and physical support from the district nursing team (to help Mrs Green get up and dressed in the morning, and to get to bed at night). Mrs Green lives in a flat, so she does not have the problem of getting up and down stairs. Her son and daughter will shop for her, and will call in every day to make sure she has had something to eat. Mrs Green has decided that she would also like to take the meals on wheels service.

The care manager has arranged for the situation to be re-assessed in a few weeks, as Mrs Green may not require intensive nursing support for longer than that.

Consider this case study about coming out of hospital. Is there anything you would do differently?

Person-centred care

Standard 2 of the National Service Framework for Older People says that:

Older people should be treated as individuals and receive appropriate and timely packages of care which meet their needs as individuals, regardless of health and social services boundaries.

Source: DOH (2001)

single assessment process a process by which everyone concerned (including the service user, his or her carer, health services, social services and any other providers) works together to make sure an individual gets exactly what is needed. This 'working together' begins at the assessment stage.

The kinds of services provided

Services provided by the National Health Service

The National Health Service (NHS) is responsible for a range of healthcare services. The NHS is itself divided up into a number of smaller organisations, some of which have a strategic or planning role, and others that deliver services. For example, in England there are 28 Strategic Health Authorities (SHAs) which are responsible for the quality of the services provided. Each SHA contains a number of Primary Care Trusts (PCTs), and NHS Trusts.

PCTs are responsible for commissioning and funding local healthcare services. NHS Trusts provide some services commissioned by the PCTs. The range of healthcare services is set out in Figure 9.19.

If the person's main need is for health care (i.e. related to his or her medical condition) then the responsibility for providing care rests with the health authority. This means that if, because of an existing medical condition or problem, someone needs continuing specialist nursing care, this

must be arranged by the health authority, even if this is in a care home (Age Concern, 2004).

Rehabilitation services are those that help a person regain a normal life. Such support may include physiotherapy (to help regain mobility or the ability to use the hands), speech therapy (to help with swallowing problems or speech difficulties) and occupational therapy to help a person perform basic tasks and assess the need for aids and/or adaptations in the home.

rehabilitation the process of helping a person to resume his or her normal life (after an illness or accident) by regaining physical skills and emotional confidence.

Palliative care is that provided to someone who has a life-threatening condition or disease and is not responding to treatment. Palliative care focuses on the care and comfort of the person, including pain-management, and the provision of emotional support both to the person with the condition and his or her family and carers.

palliative care nursing, practical and/or emotional support for people with life-threatening conditions or illnesses who are not responding to treatment. Such care often includes pain-management and help to improve quality of life.

HEALTH CARE SERVICES Commissioned by PCTs	
Community based services	GP; NHS walk-in centre; dentist; NHS Direct (telephone service); optician; chiropodist; district nursing service; mental health services
Hospital based services	Consultant; nursing care; physiotherapist
Continuing NHS health care services	Nursing care in a care home or other setting; rehabilitation and recovery services; palliative care; intermediate care; respite health care; specialist health care support; specialist health care equipment; specialist transport

Source: Age Concern (2004)

FIGURE 9.19 *The range of healthcare services commissioned by PCTs*

If the carer of a person with a medical condition or disability needs a break, then a short period of respite care can be arranged. This means that the person with the illness or medical condition can be given their care elsewhere, perhaps for a week or two, to allow the regular carer to take a rest.

Services provided by local authorities

Local authorities are responsible for providing a range of services to older people, including social care and housing. Figure 9.20 sets out some of the main kinds of service that local authorities may provide.

Figure 9.20 shows that the role of the local authority (in particular, social services) has been changing. All the services shown on the diagram used to be delivered directly by social services (or the housing service). However, the role of social services has become more involved in assessing need and purchasing the services that are required. Sometimes these services are bought from private businesses (e.g. companies that provide home care or frozen meal delivery) or from voluntary sector organisations (e.g. the

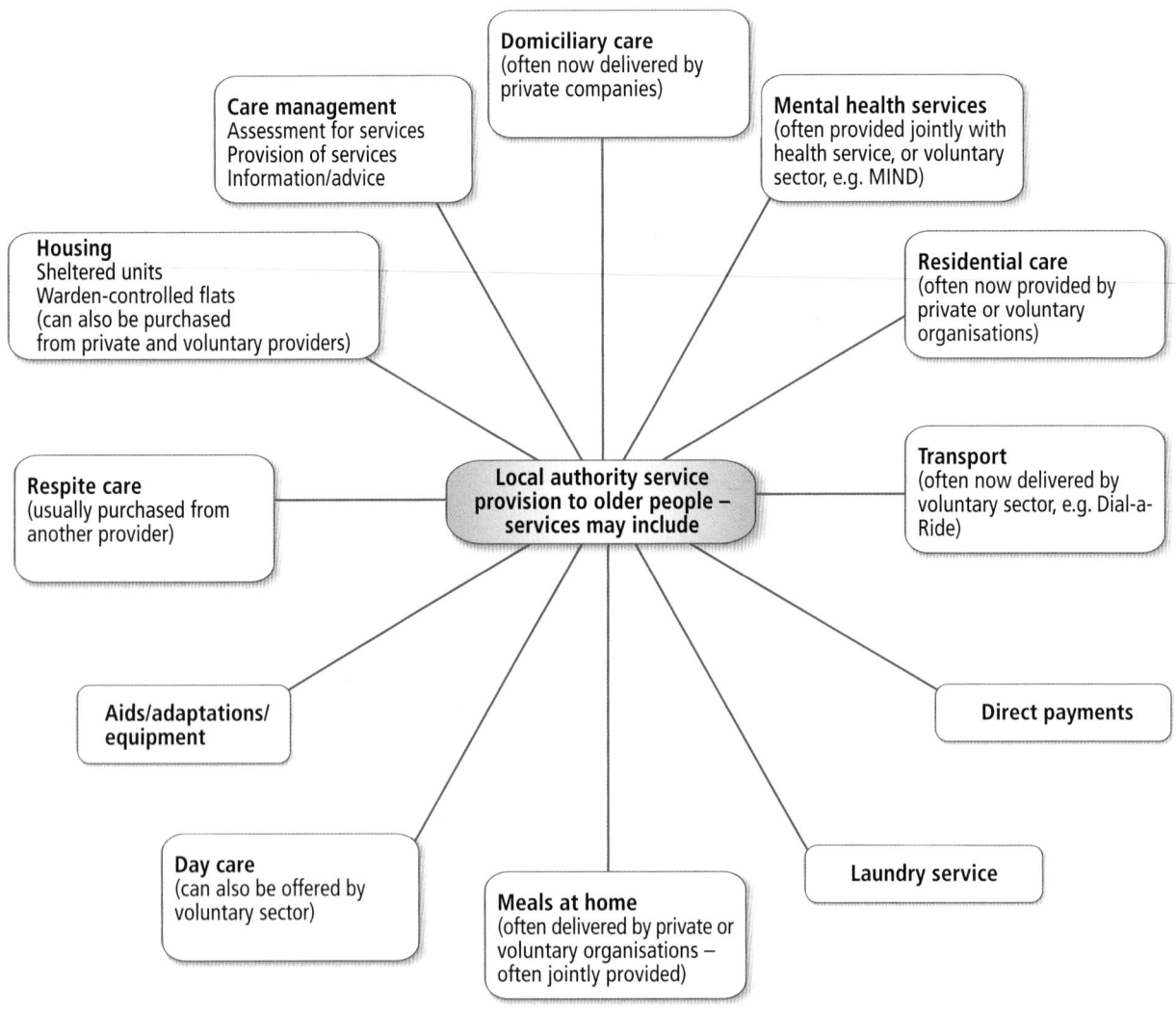

FIGURE 9.20 *Main kinds of services provided by local authorities*

provision of day care by Age Concern, or by mental health care from MIND). Local arrangements vary, and you should check out the arrangements for older people in your area.

Integrated service provision

Another important change to the way in which services are delivered is the provision of joint services, often in teams that contain staff from both health and social services, or from social services and the voluntary sector.

One example of this might be the hospital discharge team (see page 370). The care manager in this team may be provided by social services. His or her function will be to make assessments and to draw up care plans. However, within the team there may also be health service staff such as a nurse and an occupational therapist. The fact that these staff are part of the same team makes it easier for a care plan to be made, and makes service delivery more efficient.

Another example of joint working might be a day facility run by a voluntary or charitable organisation, but funded by social services with the addition of sessional support by, for example, Benefits Advisers or Housing Officers. There might also be sessions provided by an NHS chiropodist.

FIGURE 9.21 *Services provided by private companies for older people*

private medical care, just like anyone else who has the funds to do so. The provision of private hospital treatment has grown in recent years, with companies offering insurance schemes linked to treatment. Since the 1990 Care Act NHS and Community created the distinct concepts of **care purchasers** and **care providers**, the notion of a mixed economy of care has developed. It is now seen as quite normal for a care plan to be made up of services delivered by a combination of statutory, voluntary and private care suppliers.

Consider this

Contact your local authority to find out what services are available for older people in your area.

1. Find out who pays for and who provides each of these services.

2. Are there any jointly provided services (i.e. teams containing a mix of staff from health and social services, or from social services and the voluntary sector)?

Key concept

purchasers and providers the care purchaser is the organisation that controls the funding to buy care – usually the local authority or the PCT.

The care provider is any organisation that delivers a service; examples include a home meals delivery company and an NHS Trust.

Services provided by private companies

Figure 9.20 shows that many of the services formerly provided by social services are now often delivered by private companies, run on a profit-making basis.

An older person can, of course, opt to have

Key concept

mixed economy of care the notion that care can be provided by a range of different service providers, e.g. statutory agencies, private and voluntary organisations and informal carers.

Services provided by voluntary and charitable organisations

There are many voluntary organisations that provide a valuable service to people in need of care or support. Not all of these have charitable status (see page 381). Some of these organisations (e.g. Age Concern) are very large and cover the whole of the country, with local branches in each area. (Note that Scotland, Wales and Northern Ireland often have their own nationally based organisations.) Others are purely local and specific to particular groups and their needs. The kinds of service offered by such organisations are summarised below.

Services for older people
Provided by voluntary and charitable organisations

Such services might include:
- day care (e.g. social centres, lunch clubs)
- specialist support (e.g. for people with mental health problems)
- transport
- information/advice
- personal alarm service
- special deals on insurance products
- special deals on power supplies
- training for professionals working with older people.

Like private sector companies, the voluntary sector is now an important provider of services within the mixed economy of care.

Think it over...

Find out which local voluntary and charitable organisations provide services for older people in your area.

You might start with the local telephone book, and also contact your local council. There may be a Volunteer Bureau, or a branch of the Council for Voluntary Services in your area that has a list of such organisations.

Informal care

A very significant amount of care for older people (as for other groups) is provided informally by family, friends or neighbours. Anyone who plays a significant role in the care of an individual is known as a **carer**.

Key concept

carer anyone who looks after someone who is ill, disabled or otherwise unable to look after him or herself. This term usually refers to someone who provides informal (unpaid) care, rather than to a paid worker.

The carer could be a husband or wife, an adult son or daughter looking after a parent, any other relation, or even a friend or neighbour. The kinds of (unpaid) service that such carers provide are set out below.

Services for older people
Provided by informal carers

Support might include almost anything, but common tasks include:
- help in getting up in the morning and going to bed at night
- help with washing and dressing
- help with bathing or showering
- preparing snacks and meals
- cleaning and shopping
- help with taking medicines
- providing transport/escort support
- giving social and emotional support
- advocacy
- help with filling in forms.

Sometimes, an older person may greatly rely on the support given by an informal carer. Even when carers are very close to their relative or friend, they may be put under some degree of strain by the work they have to do. Looking after someone who is incontinent, for example, can be very physically and emotionally demanding.

There is now a *National Strategy for Carers* (1999), published by the government and acknowledging their value, as well as the fact that they have needs themselves.

The Carers (Recognition and Services) Act 1995 says that carers who provide, or intend to provide 'substantial and regular' care can also have their own needs assessed when a care assessment (or reassessment) takes place.

There are also several organisations that offer advice and support to carers (e.g. Carers UK and Crossroads – Caring for Carers). Details are listed in the References section at the end of the unit.

Many care packages for older people are likely to involve the services of an informal carer.

> ### Consider this:
>
> Mr Goldstein is 80 years old and a widower. He lives alone in a warden-controlled flat. For many years, he has enjoyed a lively social life. He attends a social centre run by a local voluntary organisation, taking lunch there once a week and spending time socialising with his friends. He is also a steam train enthusiast. He likes to attend the meetings of the local Steam Society, and going on outings with them at weekends to visit local steam railways and old stations.
>
> Unfortunately, Mr Goldstein has been experiencing problems with his sight. Because he dislikes what he calls 'making a fuss', he has not told anyone about this. However, it has now got to the point where he is reluctant to go out on his own. He finds it difficult to distinguish signs and numbers (e.g. on the front of the bus) and also cannot tell when it is time to get off the bus. He missed the last meeting of the Steam Society, and is quite upset about this.
>
> Finally, he confides in the social centre manager. With Mr Goldstein's permission, this manager contacts the care manager in the social services team for older people.
>
> 1. Who will be responsible for assessing Mr Goldstein's needs?
> 2. Who else might be involved in this process?
> 3. What kind of support and/or medical treatment might Mr Goldstein require?
> 4. How will the care manager ensure that Mr Goldstein receives person centred care?

Summary

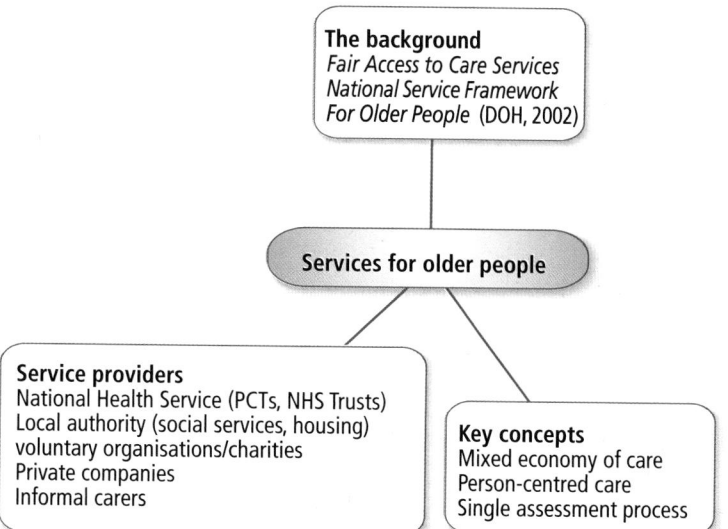

FIGURE 9.22 *Summary of services provided for older people*

Section 4: The role of professional care workers

Care workers must work in a way that shows value and respect for service users. Maintaining confidentiality, promoting equality and diversity, and promoting individual rights and beliefs are principles that all care workers should use in their work.

Ways of maintaining confidentiality

Often in situations of stress or need, personal information needs to be shared. In order to feel comfortable about discussing private concerns a person needs to have confidence that there is an emotional climate of safety in which to do so. Information is therefore entrusted to the care worker. A key principle in providing positive care environments requires that permission is needed before such information can be shared. Values of trust and confidence in the integrity of the worker are therefore essential. Information should be seen in terms of the property of the service user and violating confidentiality can cause considerable damage to people whose rights have been infringed.

An example might be an older female resident who tells a care worker that she was not married when she had children. The next day a lady in the next chair leans across and says, 'I hear you had your children when you weren't married'. The care worker has clearly broken the confidence for no good reason, and it is clear that the person whose confidence has been broken will be upset at the very least by this loss of trust.

Boundaries to confidentiality

The British Association of Social Workers states that confidentiality is in essence concerned with faith and trust and acknowledges a direct relationship between the principle of confidentiality and respect for people. However, confidentiality cannot be seen as an absolute right and might at times conflict with the equally valid rights of others to protection.

For instance, suppose that Ross, aged 84 years, says to his care worker that his son has hit him but he does not want any action to be taken. Ross does need protection, but the situation is not straightforward because an adult does have rights to choose what he or she wishes to do. There are difficult issues surrounding the limits of confidentiality and at times it is not easy to balance the right to confidentiality with the right of a vulnerable individual to protection from harm.

Service users have a right to confidentiality but a responsibility in relation to the rights of others. Confidentiality often has to be kept within boundaries, or broken where the rights of others have to balance with the service user's rights. Keeping confidentiality within boundaries occurs when carers tell their manager something that they learned in confidence. The information is not made public so it is still partly confidential.

For further information and ideas on confidentiality see the section on confidentiality in Unit 2 on pages 66–8.

Key concept

confidentiality this involves keeping information safe and only passing it on where there is a clear right and a clear need to do so. Confidentiality is an important moral and legal right, promoting safety and security of service users and their property. The maintenance of confidentiality is vital in order to maintain a sense of trust.

Equality and respect for difference

The UK is a multicultural, multiracial, and multi religion society. Caring for older people needs to reflect the diverse society in which we live. Consequently, caring for older people needs to be flexible and to value difference. Recognising and valuing the diversity in people's culture, religion, age, beliefs, sexuality and culture will add to the quality, richness and depth of working with older people.

All health or social care workers are required to work within codes of practice that emphasise the importance of promoting equality and diversity. Valuing diversity and equality involves being interested in and willing to learn about other cultures and belief systems. Promoting equality involves providing the same quality of service for everyone. If everybody were treated the same – if everyone were given the same dinner for instance – then some people would be discriminated against. Vegetarians might not get the food they need, for example. Equality is about everybody getting the same 'quality of service' – not 'exactly the same service'! Promoting equality and diversity involves preventing discrimination against people who are different from us.

> ### Key concept
>
> *discrimination* in care work, this means to treat some types of people less well than others. People are often discriminated against because of their race, beliefs, gender, religion, sexuality or age. Discrimination comes about because difference is seen as a problem rather than as something to positively value in people.

Ways of promoting diversity and equality

The first step is beginning to be aware of your own beliefs. This is important because your beliefs may lead you to judge other people, or to make inappropriate assumptions about them.

FIGURE 9.23 *Be aware of your own beliefs – think before you speak!*

In practice, one of the most important ways in which care workers and health staff can promote equality and diversity is for the staff to actively listen and build an understanding of the needs of individual service users. All service users will have their own identity and view of what is important in their life. Where dementia or mental health disorders make communication difficult, conversations with relatives or friends may help carers to understand the beliefs of the people they are working with.

Care workers need to think ahead and ensure that the rights of service users are being considered in a care setting. An example of this might be individual service users' religion. Does the home provide a diet that is in line with each individual's faith? Do service users have the opportunity to practise their faith on a daily and weekly basis? Do the staff understand about service users' religious festivals? Might there be particular newspapers or television channels they would like access to?

Ways of promoting individual rights and beliefs

Service users have a range of rights, established in Minimum National Standards for the relevant care service, and by the General Social Care Council's codes of practice.

These rights are shown in Figure 9.24.

FIGURE 9.24 *Service user rights*

One of the main ways in which professional care workers will promote individual rights is to adopt a person-centred approach when caring for people with dementia, or other mental health disorders. A person-centred approach puts 'the person' at the centre of the way services are delivered. It is not just people with dementia or mental health disorders who have rights. A person-centred approach values the individual uniqueness of every human being. Within a person-centred approach, staff will care about the emotional and self-esteem needs of people diagnosed as demented. Within a person centred approach carers will actively try to build an understanding of the needs and the beliefs of each person they work with. The person centred approach involves supporting people with dementia or mental disorders so they feel that they are valued as people. Because personhood comes first, carers will naturally respect the rights that are listed in Figure 9.24.

Kitwood (1997) argues that people with dementia are often seen as no longer human and no longer real people – they become de-personalised. He suggests that people with dementia are depersonalised because of a natural human tendency to protect ourselves from anxiety and fear. 'The anxieties seemed to be of two main kinds. First, and naturally enough, every human being is afraid of becoming frail and highly dependent; these fears are liable to be particularly strong in any society, where the sense of community is weak or non-existent. Added to that, there is the fear of a long drawn-out process of dying, and of death itself. Contact with those who are elderly, weak and vulnerable is liable to activate these fears and threaten our basic sense of security. Second, we carry fears about mental instability. The thought of being insane, deranged, lost forever in confusion, is terrifying.'

A failure to promote the individual rights and beliefs of people with dementia may have a lot to do with our own fear. One of the major skills required of a care worker is to find a way of not feeling threatened by the differences we experience in other people.

Think it over...

Can you think of at least two positive approaches that would help you to understand the behaviour and the emotional needs of a person with dementia?

Consider this

Gloria grew up on the island of St Kitts in the Caribbean. She has lived in the UK for the last 40 years. A year ago Gloria was diagnosed as having Alzheimer's disease and she now lives in a care home. Gloria appears restless and makes statements about needing to go out to the market in order to buy yams for the children.

Some care workers respond to her statements in a routine way, saying things like 'never mind all that, you live here now' and they talk to each other and say 'it's the dementia – she doesn't know what she is saying'. Olara is also a care worker, but she spends time sitting with Gloria, and listening to her. Olara will sometimes remind Gloria to look at a photograph of her daughter and grandchildren. Gloria will then discuss her early life in St.Kitts. Gloria recognises Olara and appears happier in her company.

Can you explain:
1. Why some care workers do not listen to Gloria – and just reject her as being demented?
2. Why Olara is concerned enough to spend time listening to Gloria?
3. Why Gloria is happier when Olara listens to her?

Healthcare workers

Older people may be supported by a very wide range of healthcare workers, some of whom will work within the NHS and others who will work for private organisations. Some of these workers (like ward nursing staff) may be generic, i.e. they do not necessarily specialise in the care of one particular patient group. Others (such as a consultant geriatrician) are specialists who work only with older people. Figure 9.25 lists some of the professionals you might expect to find working with older people.

Key concept

generic the opposite of specific or specialist worker. A generic social worker will serve a range of service users with many different

As the current situation is that of a mixed economy of care, healthcare professionals may be employed by a number of different organisations. Some are NHS-funded and managed; others may be in multi-disciplinary teams and be funded by the local authority. Some professionals, for example nursing staff, now work privately and are employed by nursing agencies. The situation is very complex and varies locally.

TITLE	ROLE	LOCATION
GP	Assessment, advice on and treatment of illness and medical conditions	Community
Consultant geriatrician	Assessment, advice on and treatment of illness and medical conditions	Hospital
Psycho-geriatrician	Assessment and treatment of psychiatric conditions in older people	Hospital
Community psychiatric nurse	Assessment and planning for people with mental health problems	Community
Nursing staff	General nursing care	Hospital
Nursing staff: district nurse, health visitor	General nursing care	Community (often in patient's own home)
Occupational therapist	Assessment/treatment of physical, psychological or social problems using specific, purposeful activity to prevent disability and/or promote independent function in daily life	Hospital, community
Speech therapist	Assessment/treatment for people with speech, language and communication problems (e.g. with patients who have suffered a stroke, or have Parkinson's disease)	Hospital, community, patient's own home
Continence adviser	Information and practical help for people with incontinence problems	Hospital, community
Optician	Advice and assessment on visual problems	Hospital, community
Dentist	Assessment and treatment of dental problems	Hospital, community
Chiropodist	Advice, treatment of problems relating to the feet	Hospital, community, own home
Complementary therapists	Therapy via art, drama, acupuncture, homeopathy, osteopathy, for example	Hospital, community

FIGURE 9.25 *Healthcare professionals (older people)*

Consider this

Bob has had a stroke, and now has trouble both in speaking and in swallowing.

A speech and language therapist, Liz, has been assigned to him as part of a rehabilitation package put together by the care manager at the hospital discharge team. Liz is based in an NHS community health centre, but she also carries out home visits.

Liz visits Bob regularly in his home to give him specialised sessions that will enable him to swallow properly, and also to begin to regain his speech.

Social care staff

As with healthcare professionals, the picture is now quite complex. Some staff are employed directly by local authorities, others may be privately funded or work for voluntary agencies and/or charities. Figure 9.26 gives information about the roles of some of these professionals, and where they might work. As with healthcare workers, some of these people will have a generic role, others will be more specialist in their remit.

Social workers may be employed directly by a local authority, but they may also work privately for social work agencies. Care workers, too, may work directly in a local authority facility, but this is becoming increasingly rare, because many residential homes are now run as private businesses. Day centre workers may work for local authorities, but are also just as likely to be employed by voluntary organisations such as MIND, or to be volunteers.

The following scenario describes the role of a care worker in a private residential home for older people.

TITLE	ROLE	LOCATION
Care manager	A social worker who has the designated role of assessing need and producing a care plan. The care manager will also ensure that services are provided according to the care plan, and will monitor and evaluate service provision and the effectiveness of the plan	Hospital, community
Social worker	Assessment of and planning to meet need	Hospital, community
Specialist social worker	As for social worker, but with a specialist responsibility (e.g. for older people)	Hospital, community
Care worker	Provides daily physical care, often in a residential or day care setting. Also gives support for intellectual, emotional and/or social needs	Residential or day care settings
Home help (domiciliary care worker)	Practical support to someone in his or her own home. May include help with personal tasks such as washing, shaving, bathing, etc.	Client's own home
Day centre worker/support worker	Support to users of day facilities. Such staff may have a range of job titles. Support can be practical; can also include support with intellectual, emotional and social needs	Community

FIGURE 9.26 *Social-care professionals and workers (older people)*

Home from home

Vikram works in a private residential care home for older people. He works shifts, and this week he is on 'earlies', starting his duties at 7.00 am. The first task is to help people to get up, washed and dressed. Some of the residents also need help in going to the toilet.

After this, the residents have breakfast in the communal dining room. Vikram helps to serve. Some people also need assistance with eating. After breakfast, residents like to listen to the radio or to watch TV. However, today a specialist reminiscence therapist is coming in to run a memory session with anyone who wishes to join in. Vikram makes sure that all the residents know about the session, and helps

people in settling down comfortably before it begins. The session is all about what the town centre looked like in the 1940s. The therapist has some photographs to start off the discussion, which becomes very lively.

Vikram sits in on the session and enjoys listening to the stories that people have to tell. He will use some of these at another time to encourage people to talk.

Later, he helps with lunch. He then gets the medicines trolley ready for the afternoon round.

His shift ends just after the residents have had afternoon tea.

Voluntary workers

Many people like to offer their services as voluntary workers. Their contribution to health and social care service provision is considerable. According to a report by the National Association of Hospital and Community Friends (NAHCF, 2005), 16 million people did some kind of voluntary work in 2003, and 39 per cent of adults

FIGURE 9.27 *Voluntary workers contribute greatly to health and social care service provision*

give time to a volunteering activity at least once a year (citing figures provided by the National Council for Volunteering Organisations). This report also finds that the contribution of volunteers in health settings not only enhances quality of life for patients, but also gives much-needed support to healthcare staff.

Voluntary workers can be found in many settings. They provide support in facilities run directly by voluntary organisations such as day or social centres run by MIND or Age Concern, in charity shops or by staffing telephone advice lines.

As the NAHCF report shows, volunteers also make a contribution in statutory settings such as hospitals. A recent Internet advertisement for a London hospital asked for volunteers to fulfil a number of roles including staffing advice and manning information desks, taking the tea or library trolleys around the wards, staffing the hospital shop, and simply befriending and talking to individual patients. However, volunteers can be involved in other, less traditional tasks. Other activities noted in the NAHCF report (not specifically in the healthcare sector) include website-building, boat-building and restoration work.

The NAHCF report stresses the benefits of voluntary arrangements. These include that of having diversity amongst volunteers, which ensures that support is available to meet the particular requirements of people from different religious and ethnic groups. Where joint training is given (to include both paid staff and volunteers), volunteer retention is improved, and some of these people go on to become professional health or social-care workers. The NAHCF report also finds that many hospital patients will talk more freely to volunteers than to professionals (who are often very busy). Patients value having attention from someone who sees them as individuals, rather than as people with particular symptoms or medical problems.

Volunteering can also offer older people the opportunity to have meaningful employment. Kitwood (1997) has stressed the importance of meaningful employment to the well-being of older people. Occupation, he says, contributes to the maintenance of personal abilities and skills, and also to a feeling of self-esteem. This does not have to be paid employment, and services given in a voluntary capacity will provide as much social, intellectual and emotional satisfaction as many well-paid and significant jobs. The following scenario demonstrates how regular volunteering enhanced Bill's retirement.

If you are considering a career in either health or social care, it would be a good idea to get some initial experience as a volunteer. The range of opportunities is immense, and there may also be some training and development opportunities, depending on where you gain your experience. The References section of this unit lists some of the major national organisations that give information and help to people wishing to work as volunteers.

SCENARIO

Life begins at 65

Bill retired 5 years ago, but he is very fit and does not like to stay indoors. He had a responsible job as fleet manager for a road haulage company, and when he first retired he greatly missed the stimulation of the job, and the friendship of his colleagues.

After a few months, he saw an advertisement in his local paper. A local charity (with a focus on people with disabilities) wanted people to help in their shop. They also wanted drivers to help in taking people to hospital, to day centres and to the shops. Bill volunteered for everything, and now works for three days a week, either in the shop or on driving duties.

He loves his new role, as it gives him plenty of time to talk to people (whether shop customers or the people he drives about). He has learned a lot about disability issues, benefits and other matters that concern people with disabilities. He is now on the committee of the organisation (which has charitable status).

Bill now wonders how he ever found the time to go to work.

Section 5: The impact of law on provision of care for older people

This section looks at the rights of older service users and how these are defined and protected in law. In the field of health and social care there are specific and general areas of law that affect people's rights and social care workers need to be familiar with these.

There are different ways that service user rights can be understood. These range from generalised human rights, protection from discrimination to the belief commonly held that individuals have an automatic right to services. Each approach has limitations and many of these approaches are the subject of misunderstanding by the general public. The ability to know the problems in the area of rights is essential in understanding how to promote a positive care environment.

NHS and Community Care Act 1990

The NHS and Community Care Act (NHSCCA) 1990 signified a major change to how local authorities should work with adults. The Act took away money previously given to the Department of Social Security and the NHS and gave it instead to local authorities. Long-term care in hospitals for older people was stopped and the aim of the NHS CCA was to enable people to stay at home for as long as possible. Admission to residential or nursing care was seen as the last resort under the Act. Prior to this, people did not receive an assessment of need before going into long-term care. The Act also introduced business ideas into social care services. Eighty-five per cent of a local authority's budget has to be spent in buying care services from private, voluntary and independent providers of care.

Before this Act the local authority was a major provider of services, whereas under the NHS CCA the key roles for local authorities are now:

* **assessment of need** – identifying what help a person needs

* **commissioning / purchasing of services** such as residential care and home care

* **monitoring of services** in terms of quality and value for money

* **arranging hospital discharges** – key role in ensuring quick hospital discharges

* **protecting** vulnerable adults from abuse.

Assessment of the needs of a disabled person

The NHS and Community Care Act gave people with a disability much clearer rights in terms of automatic entitlement to an assessment. It made clear that there are two situations in which someone is eligible for an assessment. These are:

* where the individual needs, or appears to need, community care services

* where someone who is disabled now has an automatic right to an assessment and should be informed of this.

The Act makes it clear that it should not be made difficult for an assessment to be made. Sometimes this goes wrong.

SCENARIO

Assessment as a first step

In one case a woman whose husband was due to have an operation on his brain phoned social services, asking for help with her mother who had Alzheimer's disease and was living with her.

Clearly, looking at the above Act, the woman's mother and husband should have been offered an assessment. Instead, social services asked how much money her mother had saved, as the worker was muddled between the rules for offering an assessment and for charging for services offered. No assessment was given and the only help the woman received was a booklet about private care homes.

The situation came to a crisis point some months later. An assessment was then made and a suitable place was eventually found for her mother, but this example shows how important it is for a social care worker to understand what the law says.

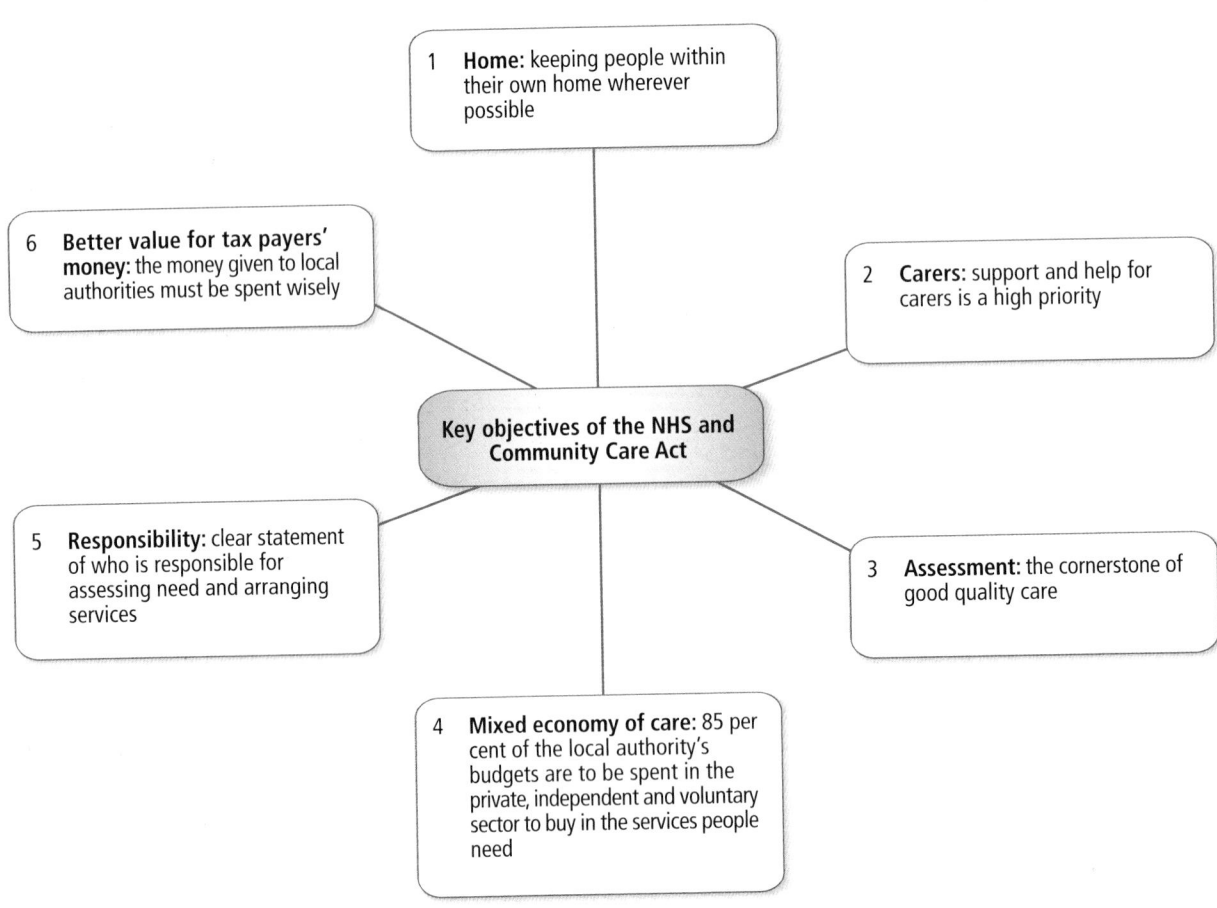

FIGURE 9.28 *The purpose of the NHS and Community Care Act (NHSCCA)*

The purpose of the NHS and Community Care Act 1990 has been set down as key objectives. These are shown in Figure 9.28.

The process by which assessments are carried out were also clearly set out. These are called the seven steps of care management, as shown below.

Step 1 Publish information: Local authorities have legal requirements to publish information about services.

Step 2 Assess the level of need: The person's needs may be simple or complicated. The type of assessment offered will vary according to the apparent level of difficulty the person is facing.

Step 3 Assessing need: The local authority is required to assess need and also to make a decision about providing services to meet those needs. In all cases a carer's assessment should be offered. A care manager carries out the assessment.

Step 4 Care planning: A care plan should be drawn up to identify the aims and objectives of the assessment. The plan should record the needs and risks to independence together with what services are going to be provided. A record of any unmet need should also be recorded as well as any areas of disagreement. Emergency plans should also be recorded, the care plan signed and given to the assessed person.

Step 5 Implementing the care plan: This will involve following each local authority, agreeing to the cost and purchasing the services on the care plan.

Step 6 Monitoring the care plan: This is the responsibility of the care manager to check that services have commenced on the correct date and are meeting the needs of the person concerned.

Step 7 Reviewing: Any new services must be reviewed and checked on within the first six weeks. Thereafter there must be at least an annual review.

Care Standards Act 2000

The Care Standards Act 2000 created a framework for defining and controlling quality within care work. The Act established the National Care Standards Commission (NCSC) and the General Social Care Council (GSCC). Both these organisations are part of the National Institutional Framework for Quality in Social Care. Both the NCSC and the GSCC developed standards and principles of good practice for social care work. The National Care Standards Commission started work in 2002. The NCSC produced a set of regulations and National Minimum Standards which care services must achieve. There are different sets of standards for different care services. The standards provide very detailed guidance on how services must be delivered. A new inspectorate called The Commission for Social Care Inspection (CSCI) now inspects care services, having taken over the inspection role of the NCSC.

The Carers (Recognition and Services) Act 1995

Carers have been recognised as the fundamental resource upon which care in the community depends. Until 2002 it was generally believed that older people as a group needed carers to look after them and their contribution as carers themselves was not recognised in the awarding of financial benefits. Increasingly, older people over 65 years are themselves caring for their parents who may be in their eighties or nineties.

The law has recognised that carers have their own needs and these also, should be assessed as well as the disabled person. The first recognition in law came under the Disabled Persons Act 1986 when local authorities were instructed to take into account the 'willingness' and 'ability' of a carer to continue to offer that care. The Carers (Recognition and Services) Act 1995 gave the right for carers to request an assessment their own needs. This assessment was tied to that of the disabled person, which meant that if the disabled person did not wish to be assessed under the NHS and Community Care Act 1990, the carer could not be assessed. This loophole was closed in the Carers and Disabled Children Act 2000 and now carers can have an assessment in their own right, even if the disabled person does not wish to be assessed. The results of the carer's assessment should be integrated into the services provided by the local authority. Carers can also now have direct payments in their own right. This means that instead of the local authority purchasing a service for a carer, the equivalent amount of money is given directly to the carer to purchase his or her own services. This gives much more power and control to the carer in arranging the care services they may need.

The Mental Health Act 1983

The Mental Health Act 1983 defines who is regarded as mentally disordered and sets out rules about when someone can be admitted to a hospital against their wishes.

The principles covering the Mental Health Act 1983 are defined by the Mental Health Act Code of Practice 1983, revised in 1999. Principles include:

* recognition of human rights
* respect for individuals and anti-discriminatory practice
* the need to be assessed
* treatment being the least controlling possible, taking into account risks to others
* care, promoting self-determination and personal responsibility
* discharging a person from compulsory sections as soon as possible safely.

Before someone can be compulsorily detained in hospital they have to be diagnosed as suffering from a mental disorder. This is defined in section 1 of the Mental Health Act 1983 as 'Mental illness, arrested or incomplete development of mind, psychopathic disorder and any other disorder or disability of mind'. The Act is due to be changed within the next two years, as parts of it do not meet the requirements of the Human Rights Act.

Health Act 1999

The Health Act 1999 enabled health and social services to work together with pooled budgets to purchase health and social care services.

One of the clearest lists of rights in law has been made by Brammer (2003).

The list includes:

* the right to an assessment for services under the NHSCCA 1990

* the right of carers to an assessment of their needs under Carer and Disabled Children Act 2000

* the right not to be discriminated against in specified circumstances, e.g. provision of goods and services on specified grounds, such as race, sex, disability, sexual orientation religion belief

* the right of a child (of sufficient understanding to make an informed choice to refuse a medical / psychiatric examination under the Child Care Act 1989 (Gillick Competence)

* the right of access to information held about you under the Data Protection Act 1998.

Summary

This section has looked at the important areas of law that affect health and social care. A positive care environment must take account of these laws and also understand how service users can complain if they are not followed. A clear understanding of the rights of service users is also essential together with the awareness that there are real limits to their rights.

Consider this

Saroshe lives with his wife who has just been diagnosed as having Alzheimer's disease. Saroshe is very worried that he will not be able to cope with caring for his wife as the illness progresses. What legal rights does Saroshe have with respect to getting help?

UNIT 9 ASSESSMENT

How you will be assessed

This unit will be assessed through a 90 minute test that will be externally marked.

Test questions

Some questions relevant to the theory in this unit are set out below.

Scenario 1:

Martha enjoyed a happy and fulfilled retirement with her husband until he died nine months ago. Martha used to be an active member of a walking group but can no longer drive to the walks and meetings. Martha has become very withdrawn. Her daughter is worried that she may have dementia.

1. How might the loss of a partner be expected to affect Martha?

2.. List three possible factors that may have caused Martha to have become withdrawn.

3. What assumptions or stereotypes might be made about an older person who has become withdrawn?

4. Describe four or five of the possible problems associated with Alzheimer's disease.

5. What services could Martha's daughter approach in order to seek help caring for her mother?

6. What legal rights does Martha have with respect to receiving assessment and services?

7. Explain what legal rights Martha's daughter might have for help in supporting her mother.

8. On an informal level, explain some types of support that Martha's daughter could provide.

Martha receives an assessment visit from a social worker.

9. Identify three major values issues that will inform the way the social worker works with Martha.

10. Explain why it is important for health and social care workers to work within the system of values.

Scenario 2:

Mr. Markan lives alone and has poor vision, due to cataracts, as well as serious osteoarthritis. Mr Markan has great difficulty coping with daily living activities such as shopping, cooking and cleaning. He appears to have lost the motivation to look after himself, and his son has arranged for an assessment of need with a view to arranging some formal support services.

1. Identify three problems that poor vision and arthritis might create for an older person.

2. Describe three different types of causes that could result in people losing the motivation to look after themselves.

3. What kind of formal help is Mr Markan likely to need?

4. Identify an appropriate service that may be able to support Mr Markan.

5. Mr Markan will receive an assessment of his needs, identify the law that creates a right to this assessment.

Scenario 3:

Tolu lived on her own until she was 84 years old. Tolu had become increasingly breathless and found it very difficult to go out of doors. She received informal care from her daughter until she became disorientated. Tolu may have dementia and is now cared for in a residential care setting that has adopted a person-centred approach to care.

1. What physical changes associated with ageing might result in breathlessness and mobility difficulties?

2. Explain some of the aids and support systems that might help people who have mobility difficulties.

3. Identify some of the needs that an older person with dementia might have within a care home.

4. Identify some of the ways in which care workers might provide formal care for Tolu.

5. What is meant by a person-centred approach?

Answers to these questions are provided on page 389.

References

Age Concern (2004) *Finding Help at Home,* Factsheet 6 London: Age Concern.

Age Concern (2004/1) *Continuing NHS Healthcare, NHS funded registered nursing care and intermediate care,* Factsheet 20 London: Age Concern.

Arber S. and Ginn J (2004) 'Ageing and Gender: Diversity and Change' in *Social Trends,* Vol. 34 (2004) London: HMSO

Coleman and Salt (1992) *The British Population* Oxford: Oxford University Press

Department of Health (2001) *National Service Framework for older people* (available at www.doh.gov.uk).

Department of Health (2002) *Fair Access to Care Services: Guidance on Eligibility Criteria for Adult Social Care.* London: Department of Health.

Kitwood, T. (1997) *Dementia Reconsidered* Buckingham UK and Bristol USA:Open University Press

Parkes, C.M. (1975) *Bereavement* Aylesbury: Pelican Books

Seligman, M. (1975) *Helplessness* San Francisco: W.H.Freeman and Co.

Seligman, M. (2002) *Authentic Happiness* London: Nicholas Brealey Publishing

Social Trends, Vol. 32 (2002) London: HMSO

Social Trends, Vol. 34 (2004) London: HMSO

Useful websites

The following websites may provide a source of updated information:

www.ageconcern.org.uk
Information, advice and a range of other services for older people in England. Scotland, Wales and northern Ireland have their own Age Concern organisations.

www.ageconcernni.org
As for England, but support to older people in Northern Ireland.

www.ageconcernscotand.org.uk
As for England, but support to older people in Scotland.

www.alzheimers.org.uk
Alzheimers Society

www.bgop.org.uk
Website of the Better Government for Older People network. Encourages older people to 'achieve participation and citizenship', and to bridge the gap between what policies say, and what actually happens in practice.

www.communitycare.co.uk
News on latest developments in social care, including policy and law, jobs, agencies, projects, funds and new initiatives.

www.csv.org.uk
Website of Community Service Volunteers. Information about volunteering and training opportunities.

www.gscc.org.uk
General Social Care Council

www.jrf.org
Joseph Rowntree Foundation. Research on social issues.

www.official-documents.co.uk/document/deps/doh/survey01/disa/disa07.htm
Health Survey for England 2001 – University College London: published by The Stationery Office.

www.nao.gov.uk
National Audit Office. Access to reports on current developments in services.

www.ncvo.org.uk
National Council for Voluntary Organisations. Umbrella body for the Voluntary Sector in England. (Scotland, Northern Ireland and Wales have their own VCO organisations.) Represents the views of the Voluntary Sector to policy makers and government. Consultation and research; telephone helpdesk, information, publications.

www.nelh.nhs.k
National Electronic Library for Health.

www.statistics.gov.uk
The Office for National Statistics.

www.nhscareers
NHS website giving full details of all jobs/professions within National Health Service.

www.nhsdirect.nhs.uk
Official website for the National Health Service. This offers a Health encyclopedia with up-to-date articles on many common diseases.

www.nicvo.org.uk
As for NCVO, but specifically for the VoluntarySector in Northern Ireland.

www.nursingolderpeople.co.uk
Online journal from RCN publishing.

www.scvo.org.uk
As for NCVO, but for the Voluntary Sector in Scotland.

www.socialworkcareers.co.uk
Department of Health website. Gives information on professions/jobs within social work. Relates to social work in England, but offers links to sites for Northern Ireland, Scotland and Wales. Also links to Jobcentre Plus.

www.wrvs.org.uk
Website of the Women's Royal Voluntary Service. Help and information about volunteering, especially to support older people and to keep them in their own homes. Useful case studies about volunteering.

Answers to assessment questions

Unit 1

1. Two from:

   * Gender socialisation/being a boy or girl
   * Language acquisition
   * Saying please and thank you/manners
   * Behaviour (e.g. hitting)
   * Eating habits.

2. Three from:

   * Peers
   * Media/TV
   * Education/teachers
   * Religion
   * Advertising.

3. Basic needs:

   * Giving and receiving attention – human beings are social animals designed to live in groups and have intimate relationships and social connections with others.
   * Care of the body/physical care – need for food, rest and exercise in sufficient amounts to maintain health.
   * Stimulation/challenge – human brain needs external stimuli to provide interest and prevent boredom or mental health is at risk.
   * Meaning and purpose – humans need to achieve things (aims and goals) and contribute to the group in order to feel valued as individuals.

4. An individual's identity and sense of self-esteem or self-worth is shaped through interaction with the wider world, therefore the more positive experiences an individual has, the higher their self-esteem is likely to be. If the individual belongs to a minority group which is under-represented and/or undervalued within society, this is likely to lead to low self esteem and feelings of marginalisation or *not belonging*.

5. Three from:

   * **Devaluing people** – treating other people's needs and interests as being of less value than those of others, including oneself.
   * **Making assumptions** – about people's needs, preferences and abilities, e.g. that it is acceptable to predict someone's needs without consulting them. Assuming that everyone should be treated the same, given the same experiences and responded to in the same way.
   * **Negative non-verbal communication** – such as not making eye contact when speaking to someone, walking away without waiting for a response or speaking to someone else, such as a colleague, whilst carrying out care activities with a client. All these actions make an individual feel invisible and unimportant, invalidating their existence.
   * **Avoiding people** – because they are different to you or what you are accustomed to, or because you do not know how to speak to them, or do not want to interact with them. This includes ignoring requests for help from clients, if you are a care worker.
   * **Excluding people from activities or opportunities** – for example, assuming someone does not want to join in an

activity, deliberately leaving someone out of the team or group exercise and failing to make appropriate arrangements, so that everyone can participate.

6. Types of abuse:

   * **Physical** – slapping, hitting, burning, scolding, pushing, inappropriate restraint, inappropriate use of medicine, withholding medicine as punishment, lack of consideration, roughness when handling or treating people, e.g. helping them to the toilet or when changing dressings.

   * **Psychological** – including shouting, swearing, frightening someone, threatening someone, withholding or damaging something with emotional importance to someone, and failing to deal with people with respect and dignity.

   * **Financial** – stealing and fraud, especially from elderly people.

   * **Sexual** – including inappropriate touching, unwanted sexual attention, making sexual remarks designed to make someone feel uncomfortable, and rape.

   * **Neglect** – such as failure to provide food, heating, adequate care or attention to hygiene, such as helping with bathing; neglecting treatment, e.g. prevention of pressure sores.

7. Direct discrimination is when a person is treated less favourably because of a certain characteristic (e.g. skin colour, age, marital status). Indirect discrimination is when criteria are applied that only some people can meet, preventing them from accessing the same opportunities as the majority. Direct discrimination is usually deliberate and intended; indirect discrimination is often unintentional.

8. The main duties of the CRE are:

   * to work towards the elimination of discrimination

   * to promote equality of opportunity and good relations between different racial groups

   * to review the implementation of the Race Relations Act and make proposals and recommendations for amendment to the Home Secretary (or government).

9. New laws proposed by parliament must ensure they are compatible with the articles in the European Convention on Human Rights detailed in the Human Rights Act 1998.

10. Three strengths from:

   * Provides protection for people who might harm themselves or others.

   * There is a right to appeal to a Mental Health Tribunal for a decision on discharge.

   * There is a right to receive information (orally and in writing) explaining why they have been detained and that they have a right to appeal.

   * The Act makes provision for aftercare services.

Three weaknesses from:

   * The Act is out of date and does not match present day mental health care practice

   * It does not make provision for those whose condition is untreatable, e.g. severe personality disorder.

Compulsory detention may be incompatible with the Human Rights Act

   * It does not address discrimination (stigma) against people who are or have been suffering from mental illness.

   * It makes no provision for the prevention or treatment of less severe mental ill health/mental health conditions such as anxiety/depression and diverts resources away from community treatment.

   * It may focus too much on control and containment of mentally ill people

instead of treatment, reinforcing the perception of all mentally ill people as dangerous.

 * It does not cover the needs of people with dual diagnosis – substance abuse and mental illness.

11. Four from:

 * The welfare of the child is paramount (the most important consideration).

 * Children should be cared for and brought up within their own families wherever possible.

 * Local Authority Social Services Departments have a duty to safeguard the welfare of children in need and support them and their parents.

 * Children should be protected and kept safe if they are in danger.

 * Courts should ensure that delays in the decision making process are kept to a minimum and should only make a care order if it is better for the child than not doing so (not making a care order).

 * Children should be kept informed about what is happening and should participate in the decisions affecting them.

 * Parents continue to have parental responsibility for their children even when they are not living with them and should therefore be informed and included in decision-making.

12. Physical barriers, e.g. stairs, narrow doorways, no disabled toilet. Geographical barriers, e.g. uneven distribution of services nationally, rural locations with poor transport. Psychological barriers e.g. stigma, fear, guilt. Financial barriers, e.g. childcare services and insufficient NHS dentists, prescription charges. Cultural and language barriers, e.g. no available translation service, health professionals of opposite gender, food and dietary requirements unable to be met.

13. The key values of care are:

 * promoting equality and diversity by treating everyone impartially and fairly

 * promoting individual rights and beliefs, especially for people who are vulnerable and unable to exercise their rights independently

 * maintaining confidentiality in relation to the personal and private information in order to promote trust and confidence between care workers and service users.

14. The regulatory framework consists of:

 * the professional councils responsible for registering and regulating practitioners and producing codes of professional practice, e.g. Nursing and Midwifery Council

 * the regulation and inspection bodies that monitor service providers, e.g. The Commission for Social Care Inspection

 * the National Minimum Standards for Care (NMS) and the National Service Frameworks (NSF) which set the basic standards of care (NMS)and evidence based treatment (NSF).

15. An Equal Opportunities Policy should contain:

 * a statement of the organisation's commitment to equality of opportunity

 * details of who is managerially responsible for implementing the policy

 * an explanation of how the policy will be monitored and reviewed

 * a list of the discriminatory treatment covered by the policy, e.g. harassment/bullying

 * guidelines for how to make a complaint or take out a grievance using the appropriate procedures.

16. If care workers are not trusted then service users are unlikely to share confidential information with them that may be important to their care and treatment.

17. The Children Act 2004 is intended to maximise opportunities and minimise the risks for all children by focusing services on the needs of children and young people. This means that health services, social services,

education services and child care organisations must work together to plan, commission, fund and deliver services for children and families. Three key features from the following:

* The appointment of a Children's Commissioner to represent children's views

* Local Authorities to appoint Director of Children's Services and Lead Member for Children's Services

* Information sharing across agencies

* Local Safeguarding Children Boards to be set up to coordinate child protection procedures

* Local authorities to produce plans for children and young people in their area

* New inspection arrangements across the integrated services.

18. Parents are experts on their own children and know them better than anyone else. They are central to children's well-being, so information on children's development, progress, behaviour and daily activities should be shared with parents.

19. Because childcare workers are part of the socialisation process, they can help to shape and expand the child's understanding of the world outside home, including differences and similarities between people.

20. Child protection policies enable childcare workers to fulfil their legal duty to protect children. The policy should outline the reporting procedures and lines of accountability within the organisation and externally between organisations concerned with child protection in cases of suspected abuse. The policy will detail how the different organisations work together and the responsibilities of each, including the Area Child Protection Committee (Local Protecting Children Boards).

Unit 4

1. Three responsibilities from:

* the provision and maintenance of plant and systems of work that are, so far as is reasonably practicable, safe and without risks to health

* arrangements for ensuring, so far as is reasonably practicable, safety and absence of risks to health in connection with the use, handling, storage and transport of articles and substances

* the provision of such information, instruction, training and supervision as is necessary to ensure, so far as is reasonably practicable, the health and safety at work of his employees

* so far as is reasonably practicable as regards any place of work under the employer's control, the maintenance of it in a condition that is safe and without risks to health and the provision and maintenance of means of access to and egress from it that are safe and without such risks

* the provision and maintenance of a working environment for his employees that is, so far as is reasonably practicable, safe, without risks to health, and adequate as regards facilities and arrangements for their welfare at work.

2–3. The five key stages and the purpose of each:

NO.	STAGE	PURPOSE
1	What is the purpose of the risk assessment?	To enable employers and self-employed people to make decisions about what might need to be done in the workplace.
2	Who has to assess the risk?	Employers and self-employed people have the responsibility for ensuring that risks are assessed properly.
3	Whose risk should be assessed?	The risk of health and safety to anyone who might be affected by their activities.

NO.	STAGE	PURPOSE
4	What should be assessed?	Anything in the workplace that may cause a potential risk to people must be assessed to ensure that all precautions have been taken or whether further measures must be put in place.
5	When should we be risk be assessed?	There is no specific guidance for this in the Management Regulations, but in general risks should be assessed before any new work is started.

4. It enables the HSE and local authorities to identify where and how risks arise. The HSE can then give employers advice on how to reduce injury, illness and accidents in the workplace.

5. A record must be kept of any reportable injury, disease or dangerous occurrence for at least three years. This must include:

   * the date and method of reporting

   * the date, time and place of the event

   * personal details of those involved

   * a brief description of the nature of the event or disease.

6. The new design was produced in order to meet the requirements of the Data Protection Act 1998, which states that all personal details of employees must be kept confidential. As a result, the pages are now perforated which means that they can be removed from the book and stored in a separate and secure location.

7. **Prohibition signs** – used to convey 'Do Not' commands. They are used for signs that indicate that a certain activity is not allowed (e.g. No Smoking or No Entry). These signs are round with a red border and a red diagonal line across them. The background is white with a pictogram of the forbidden activity in black. **Mandatory signs** – used to show that certain actions must be carried out in order to meet statutory requirements.

These signs are normally written in white on a blue background and include a pictogram of the relevant hazard, or in the case of fire signs, an exclamation mark. These signs are usually round and blue with white writing. However, fire hazard signs contain a lot of written information and are often rectangular in shape.

8. The HSE's job is to help the Health and Safety Commission ensure that risks to people's health and safety from work activities are properly controlled.

9. The names and locations of the safety representatives and for details of 'competent people appointed by the employer and their health and safety representatives'. The contact details of the local authority should also be included.

10. The minimum requirement for first aid provision at work is:

    * a suitably stocked first aid box

    * an appointed person must be identified to take charge of first aid arrangements

    * a notice stating who the first aider is and where the first aid box is situated.

First aid provision needs to be available at all times when people are at work.

11. An appointed person is someone who can take charge if someone falls ill or requires first aid. He or she should not undertake any first aid treatment that they have not been trained for but they can call an ambulance and take charge of first aid equipment. A first aider is someone who has taken a 24-hour course and holds a valid certificate that has been approved by the Health and Safety Executive.

12. The different types of fire extinguisher:

    * **Red** – water, used for paper, wood and general fires

    * **Cream** – foam, used for liquid oil fires, fat, petrol, oil etc

    * **Blue** – dry powder, used for fuel oil and can be used for electric fires

    * **Black** – carbon dioxide, used for electrical and wiring fires.

13. Manual Handling Operations Regulations 1992.

14. Lifting operations and Lifting Equipment Regulations 1992.

15. **Slide/transfer board** – used for helping a service user to move from chair to bed or bed to commode with ease, where the two surfaces are level with each other. There should always be at least 10 cm of overlap to ensure that the board is secure and the tapered edge of the board should be uppermost. Although the surface of these boards is usually very smooth, carers should ensure that as a service user is shuffling him or herself along the length of the board that there is not friction on bare skin. Service users normally have to be able to balance well to be able to use this type of equipment.

    Support and transfer belts – used to help clients to do various types of movement such as standing, walking or rotating using a turning disc. A support belt is made of strong material and is fastened securely but not too tightly round the waist of the person to be moved. The loops, which are situated at the back of the client, should be grasped firmly and the client helped to a standing position using a rocking motion. The hands should never be passed through the loops as this could cause injury. Support belts should only be used when the service user is able to support some of his or her own weight. If this is not the case, then alternative equipment such as a hoist should be used. Transfer belts are adjustable and made of webbing. They are used to ensure that a care worker can grab at clothing and that he or she is close to the client during the movement.

16. Due to reported incidents of attempted and actual abductions of new-born babies, most maternity units now have locked doors and visitors must ring a bell and identify themselves before they are given access. Baby tagging is also in place in some hospitals. A tag is attached around a baby's ankle which responds to sensor panels at hospital exits. This triggers an alarm and security staff are alerted. Further developments are in progress, which could result in the tags being tracked after leaving the hospital grounds. The reduction in the number of reported attempted abductions would seem to indicate that these measures are successful. There must be a written procedure in early years settings for the collection of children and all staff must know what the procedure states. In general, only a staff member who knows the parents and child can allow the child to leave. This is not always practical, especially in a crèche where a child may attend on an irregular or *one-off* basis. In a case such as this, a password system may be used where a password is chosen by the parent and recorded on the registration form. This has to be given to the staff before the child is allowed to leave. Normally a nursery will have two contact names in case of emergency, and the second name must be someone the nursery staff are familiar with, such as a grandparent or a parent of another child. If the parents are in dispute and one does not wish the other to collect the child, this must be put in writing to the setting. If there are any specific issues relating to a child, such as he or she is subject to a court order, then the staff must be aware of any special procedures. Staff training and parent awareness are the key to ensuring that these measures are successful.

17. Cross-infection is the term used to describe the passing of infection from one person to another.

18. For example:
    * **Home setting** – bacteria could be transmitted from one service user to another on a care worker's uniform.
    * **Hospital** – a care worker failing to wash their hands thoroughly between working with different service users.
    * **Day nursery** – Not disinfecting changing mats and nappy changing areas thoroughly.

19. The term is *standard precautions* and the procedure is:
    * cover all cuts, abrasions and lesions with a waterproof dressing
    * maintain hand hygiene
    * maintain cleanliness of general environment, patient equipment and soft furnishings

- ∗ use disposable gloves when dealing with body fluids
- ∗ dispose of waste including sharp safely
- ∗ maintain a safe staff to patient ratio
- ∗ avoid overcrowding patients
- ∗ avoid unnecessary patient transfers between wards
- ∗ isolate patients with a known or suspected infection.

20. Disinfection is used when there is a level of pathogens (disease causing organisms) that need to be reduced to a safe level. Sterilisation is the complete removal of pathogens from equipment or instruments.

Unit 9

Scenario 1

1. Practical issues: the loss of a person to talk to and plan activities with, the loss of the person who acted as a driver makes it more difficult to meet friends, less motivated to go out, more at risk of isolation.

   Emotional issues: shock, difficulty in adapting to a new lifestyle, difficulty rebuilding life and making sense of life following the loss.

2. Grief, ill-health – including heart problems osteoporosis and arthritis, depression, delirium associated with infections or medication side effects, learned helplessness, loss of motivation due to isolation.

3. The assumption that ageing involves dementia – that all old people experience problems with their brain, the assumption that withdrawal should be expected as part of the ageing process. The ageist assumption that all old people are diseased and incapable.

4. Problems with understanding, remembering and making sense of things, disorientation, inability to make sense of surroundings and recognise friends and relatives. Loss of mental function including the ability to speak and reason and eventually loss of the ability to swallow and retain continence.

5. Local authority social services, but referral might also be through her GP.

6. Martha has a legal right to receive an assessment under the NHS and Community Care Act 1990. Martha does not have a right specified in law to be provided with free care services following this assessment.

7. Martha's daughter has a legal right to receive an assessment under the Carers Act 1995.

8. Informal care often involves keeping an eye on a person – providing company, conversation, advice and emotional support. Informal care may also included practical help with tasks such as cooking and cleaning and shopping.

9. Key values include maintaining confidentiality, valuing equality and diversity, and individual people's rights and beliefs. Service user rights include the importance of promoting independence and choice.

10. A person's emotional needs or need for self-esteem will depend on being treated as a valued person. Respect for individual beliefs and rights and diversity will be central to creating a sense of value.

Scenario 2

1. Difficulty with mobility and maintaining social contact, difficulty with daily living activities such as cooking cleaning and shopping, difficulty with driving – the inability to drive may restrict social contact. Emotional problems, a lack of life satisfaction potentially leading to learned helplessness, depression or other psychiatric disorders.

2. Disability, the difficulties associated with physical impairment may make it very difficult to continue to cope. Learned helplessness and depression may result in a loss of motivation. A loss of social support or social role may reduce people's motivation.

3. Mr Markan is likely to need support with preparing food, cleaning the house, laundry, shopping and emotional support in order to cope with the loss of ability he is experiencing.

4. Care in the community home care services may be the most appropriate formal services to be recommended following an assessment.

5. The NHS and Community Care Act 1990.

Scenario 3

1. Vascular problems or heart disease.

2. Mobility aids such as walking sticks and frames, medical support – drugs to improve the functioning of the cardiovascular system, transport services such as dial-a-ride.

3. The need for support and comfort, for calming of anxiety, the need to feel a sense of belonging and part of a social network; social needs, the need to be occupied with something, the need for a sense of meaning or identity.

4. Care workers get to know the background, identity and beliefs of the people that they work with and spend time listening or reminiscing with older people. The provision of practical, comforting approaches such as foot massage or aromatherapy.

5. An approach that puts the individual person at the centre of the provision of care. An approach that focuses on valuing the individuality, diversity and rights of the individual.

Glossary

A

active listening: involves using the communication cycle and being able to demonstrate what you have understood when you listen to another person.

Acheson Report (1998): a major milestone report, which outlined the current state of health inequalities in the country and set out a programme to address them; this later influenced many areas of government policy.

acupuncture: an ancient Chinese procedure. Needles are inserted at key points in the body, and then manipulated to stimulate *chi (ki)* energy.

advocacy: a person or agency with a role in defending or promoting a cause or a person's rights and speaking on their behalf to ensure their views and wishes are heard.

African-Caribbean: people with ethnic origins in the African sub continent or the Caribbean Islands

aim: the 'aim', or outcome, is the broad goal for a piece of work. Usually a project has only one or two aims.

allopathic medicine: this kind of medicine treats medical conditions principally by attacking their symptoms, usually with pharmaceutical products or surgical interventions.

anthroposophical Medicine (AM): a holistic healing system designed to complement conventional medicine.

art therapy: the use of art as a form of psychotherapy.

arthritis: a condition that can result in pain and restriction of movement within the joints of the body.

assertion: this is different from both submission and aggression. Assertion involves being able to negotiate a solution to a problem.

attributable outcome: an outcome which can be directly related to a piece of health promotion activity, i.e. the cause and effect can be linked.

audiologically deaf: having a hearing impairment or profound hearing loss.

Alzheimer's disease: the most common form of dementia, involving problems with the way the nerve cells in the brain work.

Ayurveda: a system of medicine that has both a spiritual and a healing dimension. This system originates in India.

B

Bach Flower Remedies: remedies made by boiling or infusing plants in spring water. These work mainly on emotional problems.

behavioural therapy: a psychological system that aims to correct damaging behaviour patterns and attitudes.

biographical approach: that taken by integrated medicine practitioners towards making a diagnosis. The focus is on the whole person, his or her lifestyle and life history.

Black Report (1980): a milestone report which clearly described the health inequalities in Britain – viewed as too politically sensitive by the government of the day, the report was suppressed and its distribution strictly limited.

Braille: a system of raised marks that can be felt with fingers. It provides a system of written communication based on the sense of touch for people who have limited vision.

British Medical Association: the professional body for the medical profession, representing their interests at a national level, for example in negotiations with the government over changes in management of the medical profession.

British Sign Language: this is a real language in the same way that English or French is a language. BSL is not a signed version of the English language. BSL has evolved in the UK's Deaf community over hundreds of years.

bereavement: the loss of a loved person, such as a partner or other close relative who dies.

C

CAM/CAMs: acronym that implies all Complementary and Alternative systems of medicine and therapy.

carer: anyone who looks after someone who is ill, disabled or otherwise unable to look after him or herself. This term usually refers to someone who provides informal (unpaid) care, rather than to a paid worker.

care plan: a formal document that sets out everything that is to be done to meet someone's needs. This will include the objectives or goals of the Plan, together with the services that will be provided to meet these objectives.

care provider: any organisation that delivers a service, e.g. a home meals delivery company, an NHS Trust.

care purchaser: the organisation that controls the funding to buy care – usually the local authority or the PCT.

care values: occupational standards and codes of practice identify a framework of values and moral rights of service users that can be referred to as care values. These values include promoting equality and diversity, maintaining confidentiality, and promoting individual rights and beliefs.

cancer: a term which covers a wide variety of diseases caused by uncontrollable growth of a particular body tissue, for example, lung and bone cancer.

charity: any organisation that is officially registered as having charitable status.

chiropractic: a system that uses manipulation of the spinal column to ease musculo-skeletal problems.

chronic: a term used to describe a condition that persists over a long period of time.

cognitive therapies: a term used to refer to a number of psycho-analytical approaches.

community strategy: a planning document led by the local authority and owned by key partner agencies locally known as the Local Strategic Partnership. The plan sets out the way in which the partnership will work together to improve the local community across all issues, health, environment, crime, transport employment, housing, and so on.

comparative need: identified from comparisons between similar groups of people, where one group is identified as having poorer health as a consequence of an identified difference.

competent person: A person who possesses sufficient knowledge training and expertise.

confidentiality: the principle that information about a service user should not be disclosed to another person without the knowledge and consent of that person. It is an important moral and legal right, promoting safety and security of service users and their property. The maintenance of confidentiality is vital in order to maintain a sense of trust.

contra-actions: the possible negative side-effects of a complementary therapy treatment (e.g. bruising after a massage or mood-swings).

contra-indications: medical reasons why a treatment should not be given.

Council for Voluntary Services: an umbrella organisation for a wide variety of local voluntary sector organisations.

COSHH: Control of Substances Hazardous to Health. Regulations that require employers to control exposure to hazardous substances to prevent ill health.

culturally deaf: people who regard Sign as their first language and who are proud of being deaf are said to be Culturally Deaf. Such people do not see themselves as disabled.

cultural variation: communication is always influenced by cultural systems of meaning. Different cultures interpret systems of communication such as body language differently.

D

dental decay: usually recorded as DMF (decayed, missing filled teeth), the DMF ratio for an area is one of the best indicators of health inequality (high DMF = high levels of ill health).

disability: the consequence of impairment, or other individual difference. The disability a person experiences is determined by the way in which other people respond to that difference.

drug action team: a local partnership responsible for planning the local delivery of the government's drugs strategy.

drug prevention initiatives: a range of Initiatives which aim to discourage young people from using drugs.

Drug Reference Group: a local partnership which is tasked to deliver the DAT strategy.

dementia: a term used to identify a range of disorders, all of which involve a degeneration of the central nervous system.

Diagnostic and Statistical Manual of mental disorders: the DSM is a complex system for identifying and categorising mental disorders originally developed in the USA.

disinfection: the reduction of bacteria to safe levels by using hot water or chemicals.

discrimination: to treat some types of people less well than others. People are often discriminated against because of their race, beliefs, gender, religion, sexuality or age.

E

eligibility criteria: the rules that explain a person's entitlement to receive services. The greater a persons' needs and the risks to their independence, the greater is that person's entitlement to receive services.

empathy: Egan defines the term as: 'Empathy is the ability to enter into and understand the world of another person and communicate this understanding to him or her' (1986: 95).

emphysema: a disease in which the air sacs within the lungs (alveoli) are damaged. This can cause shortness of breath and result in respiratory or heart failure.

empowerment model: a view of disability that says with the right support, people with disabilities can (and have a right to) achieve their full potential as human beings, in the same way as non-disabled people.

endorphins: chemicals released into the body by the central nervous system in order to reduce pain and create a sense of well-being.

equity: the principle of social justice – directing resources to those who need them most.

ethics: acting in a principled fashion – to act ethically.

ethnic group: a group that shares a common origin, culture or language, as in black and minority ethnic groups.

European Framework Directive: Guidance from the European Parliament that has to be followed by every member country, although they have choice over how this is implemented. This guidance is intended to standardise some legislation in all the member states of the European Union.

evaluation: to evaluate something is to assess it, in particular its worth, value or importance.

evaluation of process: to establish the benefits delivered through the process of Implementing a piece of work, for example the new partnerships it creates.

evidence-based: a term used to describe decision-making in the care management process that uses reliable information.

evidence-based medicine: the combination of clinical expertise with external evidence in order to establish what is best for a particular patient.

evidence-based practice: to base your practice on evidence of what works best.

exercise on prescription: supervised series of exercise sessions usually based in a Leisure Centre provided to patients at a reduced rate, or free, in response to an identified condition such as high blood pressure or mild depression.

expressed need: a felt need that is voiced by a person or community.

F

facilitator: a person who helps to make something happen – often associated with decision-making or planning.

felt need: needs which people feel, i.e., things we *want*.

fluoride: an inert substance which when added to the water supply can reduce the level of tooth decay.

food deserts: populated urban areas where residents do not have access to affordable healthy food.

food safety: the practice of storing and preparing food safely.

formative evaluation: feedback during the course of a project, when things are still taking shape.

G

General Practitioner: the family doctor, who is an independent contractor funded through the NHS but not employed by it.

generic: the opposite of specific or specialist. A generic social worker will serve a range of service users with many different needs.

H

hazardous substances: any products used in the workplace that could provide a risk to health if they are not controlled.

Health and Safety Commission and Health and Safety Executive: Britain's Health and Safety Commission (HSC) and the Health and Safety Executive (HSE) are responsible for the regulation of almost all the risks to health and safety arising from work activity in Britain. Their mission is to protect people's health and safety by ensuring risks in the changing workplace are properly controlled.

health authorities: an arm of the health service whose role is to monitor the performance of PCTs, support public health practice and develop local health partnerships and networks.

Health Development Agency (HDA): a national health agency set up in 2000 to provide information about what works in terms of health promotion activity – to enable evidence-based practice in health promotion.

health education: an aspect of health promotion which largely relates to educating people about good health and how to develop and support it.

Health Education Authority (HEA): a special Health Authority which existed to co-ordinate national campaigns and provide government with specific advice about health promoting activity. This was replaced by the Health Development Agency (HDA) in 2000.

Health Improvement Programme (HimP): a local health document for each Primary Care Trust which sets out plans for meeting both national and local health targets in partnership with other local agencies Renamed the Health Improvement and Modernisation Plan as a result of the NHS Plan 2000.

health promotion outcome: the result of a piece of health promotion work – a reduction in a particular disorder or an uptake in screening, for example.

health protection: population measures to safeguard health, for example through legislation, financial or social means. This might include legislation like that to govern health and safety at work or food hygiene, and using taxation policy to reduce smoking levels or car use, by raising the price of cigarettes or petrol.

health visitors: a specific branch of the nursing profession with a key public health role in local communities, working at a neighbourhood level to identify local health need and support community activity to address those needs.

herbal medicine: the use of herbal preparations to treat diseases.

holistic approach: a view of illness that sees the one with the disease as a whole person, who is ultimately in control of any treatment or therapy that may be suggested. This approach sees the causes of disease as complex, and encompasses physical, intellectual, emotional and spiritual ways of healing.

holistic health: a holistic concept of health recognises that there are different dimensions of one health, physical, mental, emotional, social, spiritual and societal health which together build a holistic concept of health.

homeopathy: a system of healing based on the principle that 'like cures like'.

Human Immunodeficiency Virus (HIV): the virus which when acquired leads to the breakdown of the body's immune system, leading to the syndrome known as AIDS.

I

immunisation: the process of making people immune to certain diseases by challenging their immune system with a weak or inactivated version of the disease organism to stimulate the person to create antibodies to the disease.

In Control: an initiative sponsored by MENCAP to help people with learning disabilities take greater control over their lives, and over decisions that are made that will affect them.

intervention: to intervene or take action in order to effect a change, for example to intervene by helping someone quit smoking.

intermediate care: health care that is intended to promote recovery after a stay in hospital, or to prevent admission to hospital.

integrated medicine: an approach taken by physicians who want to use both conventional and complementary healing methods with their patients.

L

labelling: classifying someone in a fixed way that refers to only one aspect of that person, e.g. physical appearance, nationality, disability.

lay models of health: the term 'lay' refers to a non-professional viewpoint, i.e. the models of health held by the public at large as opposed to professionally or scientifically phrased perspectives.

lifestyle: How a person spends time and money to create a style of living.

Lifting Operations and Lifting Equipment Regulations (LOLER): Regulations to ensure that employees take reasonable care of themselves and others who may be affected by the actions that they undertake.

linguistic minority: those people within any society who use a different language from the majority.

local authorities: the local organisations responsible for environmental health, building control, leisure facilities, refuse collection, and street cleaning.

local strategic partnership: a local strategic partnership (LSP) is a single body that: brings together at a local level the different parts of the public sector as well as the private, business, community and voluntary sectors so that different initiatives and services support each other and work together is a non-statutory, non-executive organisation operates at a level which enables strategic decisions to be taken and is close enough to individual neighbourhoods to allow actions to be determined at community level; and should be aligned with local authority boundaries.

M

Makaton: a system for developing language that uses speech, signs and symbols to help people with learning difficulties to communicate and to develop their language skills.

massage: a bodywork therapy which uses stroking and kneading movements on the body's soft tissues.

mass media: an umbrella term for a range of media which convey information to the general population including radio, television, newspapers and magazines

medical model: probably the most widely known model of health and the one that has come to dominate all others in the Western world, this adopts a scientific view of health and body functioning (e.g. it views disability as a 'problem' because it physically prevents a person who is disabled from doing everything an able-bodied person can do).

Mental Health Act 1983: This Act defines mentally disorder and sets out rules about when someone can be admitted to a hospital against their wishes.

Methicillin Resistant Staphylococcus Aureus (MRSA): a bacterium that is resistant in differing degrees to antibiotics.

milestones: major points along a the course of a project by which its progress can be monitored.

mixed economy of care: the notion that care can be provided by a range of different service providers, e.g. statutory agencies, private and voluntary organisations and informal carers.

MMR vaccine: vaccination against measles, mumps and rubella.

monitoring: to monitor something is to make regular checks on its progress.

morbidity: the rate of illness caused by a particular condition.

mortality: deaths due to a particular condition.

music therapy: the use of music to allow emotional expression, to promote relaxation and to ease pain. Music can also be used to assist cognitive and personal development.

N

National Healthy School standard: a national initiative which uses an organisational approach to health promotion to provide schools with a framework within which they can work to develop their health promoting capacity.

National Service Frameworks: a mechanism for unifying standards of care within the NHS; these set out In quite practical terms what health districts must provide in key areas such as coronary heart disease, mental health, diabetes.

nGMS: the new contract negotiated by the government with family doctors to govern the delivery of General Medical Services.

NHS Plan (2000): government document which outlines a ten-year plan for modernising the NHS.

normative need: a need identified by an expert or professional according to their own standards; where something falls short of this standard then a need is identified.

norms: the expectations that people have of other people within a particular group or culture – what people regard as normal.

nutritional therapy: the treatment of disease by eliminating foods to which a person is allergic (or has an intolerance to), and by supplementing the diet with key nutrients.

O

obesity: a Body Mass Index in excess of 30.

objective: the specific goal to be achieved in delivering the stated aim or outcomes.

Office of Population Censuses and Surveys (OPCS): national body which compiles information on the UK population, responsible for carrying out the census every 10 years.

Ottawa Charter for Health Promotion (WHO 1986): defined the role of health promotion as being (Author query)

osteoporosis: a medical condition involving excessive loss of bone and weakness of the bones and joints.

outcome evaluation: seeks to establish the worth of work when it has reached its conclusion.

outcome measures: indicators of success for health-promotion activity.

P

palliative care: nursing, practical and/or emotional support to people with life-threatening conditions or illnesses that are not responding to treatment. Such care often includes pain-management, and help to improve quality of life.

pathogens: disease-causing organisms – may be bacteria, viruses or fungi.

paraphrase: to put what you think a person has said into your own words.

Parkinson's disease: a disorder caused by problems with the production of a chemical neurotransmitter essential for muscular movement. Parkinson's, disease, can result in serious problems with body movement and mobility.

People First: an organisation that promotes self-advocacy by people with learning difficulties.

Person centred: a term to describe a way of working with people that puts the individual at the centre of the care management process.

Person-centred care: care that places 'the person' at the centre of decision-making and activities. Care that seeks to value the individual 'personhood' of service users. It is an approach to care set out in Standard 2 of the National Service Framework for Older people, which says that older people should be treated as individuals and receive appropriate packages of care.

Person-centred planning: a way of working with people with learning disabilities that is promoted by the Government initiative called *Valuing People*. This includes the service user, his or her family, carer and friends in the care planning and management process, together with professionals from the relevant services.

personal protective equipment: equipment that must be provided by employers for employees who may be exposed to a risk at work.

personhood: recognition and respect for the self-concept and self-esteem needs of service users.

phytotherapy: the practice of medical herbalism.

poverty: where a person has a low income, i.e. worth 40 per cent less than the level of income enjoyed by the average person in the UK (60 per cent of median income) they may be understood as experiencing poverty.

prevalence: a measure of how many people are suffering from a particular condition or behaving in particular way at any one time.

prevention: reducing or avoiding the risks of diseases and ill health primarily through medical 'interventions'. There are several approaches and levels for health promotion activity to take place within.

Primary Care Trust (PCT): new NHS organisations, which have three key responsibilities: improve the health of their local population develop local primary health care services commission other local health services in line with local health needs.

primary health-care setting: usually a term used to refer to the GP surgery or health centre.

primary prevention: this is an attempt to eliminate the possibility of getting a disease.

private sector: this term refers to businesses that offer services, but that operate on a profit-making basis.

probes and prompts: a probe is a very short question that is used to 'dig deeper' or probe into a person's answer. Prompts are short questions or words, which you offer to the other person in order to prompt them to answer.

professional relationships: these are different from ordinary social relationships and friendships because: professionals must work within a defined framework of values; their work always involves a duty of care; and professional relationships involve working within appropriate boundaries.

psychoneuroimmunology (PNI): a scientific discipline that studies the relationship between the brain and the body.

public health specialism: workers with expertise in assessing the patterns of ill health locally and identifying what types of health care provision and health promoting activities are required to improve health.

Q

Qigong: a system of movements designed to stimulate the flow of *chi (ki)* within the body.

R

race: a large group of people with common ancestry and inherited physical characteristics.

racism: discrimination against people on the basis of their race background, usually based in the belief that some races are inherently superior to others.

reflection: the act of thinking about something critically and calmly.

reflexology: the practice of stimulating reflex points on the hands and feet.

regulation: the control of something by establishing a set of rules that everything must conform to.

regulations: Regulations are law, approved by Parliament. These are usually made under the Health and Safety at Work Act, following proposals from HSC. This applies to regulations based on EC Directives as well as 'home-grown' ones.

rehabilitation: the process of helping a person to resume his or her normal life (after an illness or accident) by regaining skills and emotional confidence.

Reporting of Injuries Diseases and Dangerous Occurrences Regulations (RIDDOR): the regulations that require injuries, diseases and dangerous occurrences to be reported. This enables local authorities and the Health and Safety Executive to identify where and how risks arise.

respite care: a short period of residential and/or nursing care given to someone to enable his or her usual carer to take a break.

risk assessment: a procedure carried out to identify any risks that may cause harm to people in the workplace.

S

school nurse: a specialist branch of community nursing, historically with a key role in screening programmes within schools, but increasingly they are involved with other health promoting activity ,such as drop-in sessions on school premises, offering advice about drug use, sexual health, for example.

screening: identification of unrecognised disease or defect by the application of tests, examinations and other procedures which can be applied rapidly. Screening tests sort out apparently well persons who may have a disease from those who do not.

secondary prevention: activity to improve the health of those people identified as being in the early stages of a disease.

self-advocacy: speaking up for yourself, to make sure that your views and wishes are heard.

self-directed support: a concept promoted by the In Control initiative, which involves the service playing a key role in decision-making about the service he or she wants.

settings-based approach: a way of organising health-promoting activity, a setting might be school, hospital, primary care, workplace, for example.

Severe Acute Respiratory Syndrome (SARS): Sars is a serious respiratory virus, which killed nearly 800 people worldwide in the months following its emergence in November 2002. Because it is a virus, it does not respond to antibiotics, although a combination of antivirals and antibiotics may be beneficial if caught early. Symptoms are similar to flu. There is no vaccine yet for this disease.

sexually transmitted disease: diseases which can only be passed by sexual activity.

single assessment process: a process by which everyone works together, starting at the assessment stage, to make sure that a person gets the services he or she needs. The process was set out in the *National Service Framework for Older People*, which states that all agencies should work in partnership to provide assessment and services to older people.

SMART: an acronym for effective objective setting; objectives should be Specific, Measurable, Achievable, Realistic, and Time specific.

social model: this model says that it is the attitude of society that disables people, preventing those with disabilities from doing what they want to.

social model of health: this emphasises that to improve health it is necessary to address the origins of ill health, which make it more prevalent in some groups than others.

societal change: attempts to elicit health improvement by radically changing society, for example by reducing tolerance to drink driving.

SOLER: an acronym formed from the words Squarely, Open, Lean, Eye Contact, Relaxed. These words are drawn from a theory of non-verbal supportive behaviour identified by Egan.

speech communities: a speech community might be based on people who live in a geographical area, a specific ethnic group, or different professions and work cultures. Speech communities are evidenced by their own special words, phrases and speech patterns.

specialist health promotion services: a small specialised service which supports the development of the health-promoting role of others, the development of new services and policies which can promote health locally.

standardisation: a process whereby everything is made to conform to an agreed, common way of doing things (e.g. the practice of a particular CAM).

standard precautions: formerly known as universal precautions, these are the safeguards that must be in place to protect staff and service users from infection.

statutory sector: this term refers to organisations set up to provide services that are required by law. It includes the NHS and local authorities.

stereotyping: a fixed way of thinking that involves generalisations and pre-formed expectations about an issue or a group of people.

sterilisation: the complete removal of pathogens from equipment or instruments by different methods.

structured data collection: a scientific method of collecting information using forms or questionnaires.

summative evaluation: an assessment of what has happened.

Sure Start/Sure Start Plus: local programmes concentrated in neighbourhoods where a high proportion of children are living in poverty and work with parents and parents-to-be to improve children's life chances through better access to, family support, advice on nurturing, health services and early learning.

T

Tackling Drugs Together: first national drugs strategy launched in 1993.

target audience: the group an activity is aimed at, be it research, marketing, or health education material, for example.

tertiary prevention: the control and reduction, as far as possible, of a disease or disability that is already established.

The Health of the Nation (1992): the country's first national health strategy.

Traditional Chinese Medicine (TCM): a traditional and complex system of medicine originating in China. It sees body and mind as integral components of a healthy body system.

transfer assist devices: non-mechanical pieces of equipment that can help in moving clients efficiently and safely.

V

vaccination: to challenge a person's immune system to produce antibodies by injecting a dead or weakened version of the disease organism.

value judgments: to judge someone or something from a standpoint based on your own values, for example because I don't smoke and believe it to be bad for you. I think that person who smokes is a bad person.

Valuing People: a government initiative set up in 2001 which aims to improve planning and services for people with learning difficulties.

victim blaming: people frequently simplify health choices by blaming the person who chooses to adopt an unhealthy behaviour for making that choice. In reality, things are rarely that simple; for example, people site lack of time due to work pressures as the major cause of taking too little exercise.

voluntary sector: agencies and organisations which obtain their funding from charitable giving, specific funding from public sector organisations such as PCTs or through the National Lottery. Voluntary sector organisations provide services to bridge gaps in statutory provision. These organizations, which sometimes provide services without charge, are non-profit-making.

W

Water (Fluoridation) Act 1985: an enabling act, i.e. it did not make all water companies fluoridate their water but enabled them to if they so chose.

World Health Organisation: established on 7 April 1948, it was a response to an international desire for a world free from disease, and since then 7 April has been celebrated each year as World Health Day.

Working in Partnership: way of working that includes everyone: the service user, his or her carer, family and friends, Health and Social Care professionals, other Council staff and people from the private and voluntary sector

Index

A

abuse 12
acceptable behaviour 3, 4
access to services
    cultural barriers 42–3
    facilitating 43
    financial barriers 41
    geographical barriers 41–2
    GPs (general practitioners)
        surgeries 39
    health centres 39
    hospitals 38–9
    language barriers 42–3
    physical barriers 38–9
    psychological barriers 40–1
    referral 38
    voluntary organisations 39
accident book 173
accident report form 167
Acheson, Donald 111
active listening 80
activities
    detailed (cooking) plan example
        273–4
    leader 257
    plan 272–4
    potential 271–2
acupuncture 320
ageing
    communication 366
    dependency on others 360–1,
        366–8
    grief 363–5
    happiness 358
    health 361
    isolation 358–61
    life satisfaction 358
    lifestyle changes 356–8
    mobility 359
    partner, losing 363–5
    physical 354
    potential dangers 365
    service provision 369–70
    social contact 358
    travel 359
aggressive people 72, 73
alcohol hand rub 196
allopathic medicine 312
alternative therapies see CAM
Alzheimer's disease 361–2
answers to assessment questions
    389–96
anthroposophical medicine 316
anti-discrimination practice 11
appointed person 171–2
Aromatherapy Council 328
ASH (Action on Smoking and
    Health) 111
assertive people 72, 73
assessments
    people consulted 213

    professional involvement 213–15
    risk and need 212–13
    structured information 210–11
    working with people 211–12
attitudes
    beliefs and values 3
    health 131
    health and lifestyle 40–1
audiologically deaf 229
autism 131–2
Ayurveda 314, 326

B

babysitter 248, 257
Bach flower remedies 316
Bales, R 89
bed rope ladder 192
behaviour
    acceptable 3, 4
    aggressive 72, 73
    assertive 72, 73
    gender appropriate 5
    norms 3
    submissive 72, 73
    unacceptable 3, 4
behavioural therapies 316
beliefs 335–7
beliefs, care values 44–5
biographical approach to illness 326
biomedical model of health 108–10
Black, Douglas 111
blood pressure 291, 348
body language 77–8
Body Mass Index (BMI) 133
Bourdieu, Pierre 6
breast screening 122
breathing 349–50
British Association for Allergy,
Environmental and Nutritional
Medicine 322
British Deaf Association 60
British Sign Language 60, 229
Buddhist dietary principles 289
bullying 6, 11, 50, 54
Burnard, P 90

C

CAM
    categories 318–19
    classification 319–21
    controversial aspects 340
    cost 327–8
    definition 312
    GPs 325–6
    healing strategy 335
    history and development 314,
        323
    image of 338–9
    medical opinions 339–40
    mind-body relationship 335–7

    National Occupational Standards
        329
    needs, meeting 333–5
    orthodox medicine 321–3
    over-the-counter purchases
        324–5
    practitioners' training 328–30
    private practitioners 324–5
    public opinion 339
    settings 326–7
    six principles 312–13
    use and provision summary 332
    uses 324–6, 334
    value 341
cardio vascular system 296–7
care assistant (children) 256–7
care management, seven steps 205–7
care orders 33–4
care plan 206
care planning
    approaches 208–10
    evaluation 217
    making care plans 215–16
    methods 208–10
    monitoring 216–17
    summary 218
care provision
    children's services 1–2
    fundamental principle 1
    range 1
Care Standards Act 2000: 50, 53
care values
    beliefs 44–5
    childcare workers 46–8
    communication 62
    confidentiality 45–6
    diversity 44
    duty of care 44
    equal opportunity policy 49–50
    equality 44
    individual rights 44–5
    legislation protecting workers 49
    safe working 48–9
    see also codes of practice
care workers
    confidentiality and boundaries of
        376
    difference, respect for 376–7
    diversity, promoting 377–8
    equality 376–7
    social care workers 380–1
    socialisation process 14
    titles and roles 378–80
    volunteers 381–2
Carers' Charter 216
carers' needs 216
CCTV (closed-circuit television
    cameras) 179
cervical screening 121–2
Chavutti Thirumal 315
child protection policy 54

childcare services 245
childminders 246, 253–4
children
    care orders 33–4
    care values 46–8
    collection of, from settings 184
    education supervision orders 34
    emergency protection orders 33
    'Gillick competence' 33
    local authorities 35
    paramountcy principle 31, 48
    play 6
    protection 33
    self-esteem 7
    'welfare checklist' 31–2
Children's Centre programme 112
Chinese medicine 314, 320, 321
chiropractic 316
Choosing Health – Making Healthy Choices Easier 103–4, 111, 113–14, 132, 133
chronic obstructive pulmonary disease 350
'circle time' 243, 267
circuit training 307
circulatory system 297–8, 348
classroom assistant 255–6
closed questions 79
closed-circuit television cameras (CCTV) 179
codes of practice
    Care Standards Act 2000: 50
    early years NVQs 62
    function 50
    General Social Care Council 48, 51, 62
    historical 50
    Nursing and Midwifery Council 51, 62
    professional councils 50
    regulatory framework 50
cognitive therapies 316
Commission for Racial Equality 19–20
Commission for Social Care Inspection 51–2
Committee on Medical Aspects of Food and Nutrition Policy 286
communicable infections 141
communication
    active listening 80, 86
    behaviour patterns 72–3
    blind people 60–1, 73
    body language 77–8
    braille 60–1
    care values 62
    clarifying 79–80
    computerised 60
    confidentiality 66–7
    content 74
    cycle 79, 85–6
    deaf people 60
    defensive 90, 92
    diversity 65
    empathising 80
    environmental conditions 73
    eye contact 65, 77
    facial expressions 78
    formal 76
    gestures 65, 78, 79
    group formation 88
    group structures 87–8
    hearing impairments 73

    informal 76
    inhibiting factors 62–74
    language 'register' 76
    learning difficulties 60
    limited vision 73
    listening skills 85–6
    minimising barriers 80–3
    misunderstanding, reasons 81
    non-verbal 65
    oral 58
    pace of speech 77
    paraphrasing 80
    positioning 69–71
    posture 78
    probes 79
    professional relationships 76–7
    prompts 79
    questions, open and closed 79
    reflection 86
    relationship building 74
    SOLER principles 86–7
    speech communities 76
    summarising 80
    supporting factors 62–74
    supportive 90, 92
    task-focussed 74
    tasks in which is key 59
    theories 85–93
    tone of voice 77
    types 58–61
    written 59–60
Complementary Healthcare Information Service 319
complementary therapies *see* CAM
computerised communication 60
confidentiality
    care values 45–6
    care workers 376
    children, information about 47
    communication 66–7
    Data Protection Act 1988: 45
    early years 261
    Freedom of Information Act 2000: 45
    information for managers 67
    'need to know' 67–8
    organisation policies 54
    paper records in settings 185
constipation 353
COSHH (Control of Substances Hazardous to Health Regulations 2002) 173–4, 176
Crohn's disease 353
cross-infection 193, 196
cultural barriers to accessing services 42–3
cultural diversity 65
cultural values 4
culturally deaf 229
cultures, respect for others 65
cycle ergometer test 304

D
deaf people 228–9
defensive communication 90, 92
dementia 352, 361–3
Desirable Outcomes for Children's Learning 46
diabetes 290–1
diet 133–5
diet and health 309
diet-related diseases 290–3
diet-related disorders 285–6

dietary needs by age 287–8
dietary reference values 286–8
digestive system 353
direct discrimination 13
direct race relations discrimination 17–18
direct sex discrimination 15
disabilities
    assessment 383–4
    attitudinal barriers 231–3
    barriers to inclusion 230–4
    categories 202–4
    deaf people 228–9
    definition and criteria 21
    different types of need 207–8
    economic barriers 233–4
    employment 143–4
    empowerment model 228–9
    environmental barriers 230–1
    labelling 232
    main causes 203
    medical model 227
    models summary 234
    profile of disabled person 235–6
    Rail Vehicle Accessibility Regulations (1998) 23
    social model 227–8
    Special Educational Needs and Disability Act 2001: 22
    support available 207
disciplinary hearings 24
discrimination
    anti-discrimination practice 11
    causes 10
    cerebral palsy 11
    Commission for Racial Equality 19–20
    direct 13
    direct race relations 17–18
    direct sex 15
    Disability Discrimination Act 1995: 21–2
    education 18–19, 22
    employment 18, 21, 23–4
    Equal Opportunities Commission 17
    housing 19, 22
    indirect 13
    indirect race relations 18
    indirect sex 15–16
    overview 9–12
    positive 23
    practices 9
    race relations 17–19
    Race Relations Act 1976, amended 2001: 17–19
    racism 10, 36
    Rail Vehicle Accessibility Regulations (1998) 23
    recruitment 23–4
    sex 15–17
    Special Educational Needs and Disability Act 2001: 22
    transport 22–3
    transsexuals 16
disease reduction 155–6
diseases 193
disinfectant 197–8
diversity
    aspects 63
    care values 44

characteristics 64–5
  communication 65
  understanding 64
drugs use 135–6, 139
duty of care 44

E
early learning goals 243
early years care and education
  anti-bias curriculum 261
  child welfare 258
  confidentiality 261
  curriculum 243
  environment 258–9
  job qualities 250–1
  key roles and responsibilities 252–7
  opportunities for development 260
  partnership with parents 259–60
  provision 244–9
  values and principles 258
  working in practice 261–2
Early Years National Vocational
  Qualifications 46–8, 62
early years voucher scheme 242
early-warning systems 178–9
economic factors 269–70
education 6
Education Action Zones 268
education supervision orders 34
Egan, Gerard 86–7
eligibility criteria 205–6
emergency protection orders 33
emotion 71
empathy not sympathy 232–3
emphysema 350
empowerment 12–13, 118
energy requirements 286
environmental factors 268–9
environmental health personnel 128–9
equal opportunities
  complaints 24
  employment 23–4
  policy 23, 49–50
  promotion 24
  recruitment 23–4
  training 24
Equal Opportunities Commission 17
equal pay 15
European Herbal Practitioners
  Association 328
evacuation of building 183
Every Child Matters: Change for
  Children 35, 242–3
evidence-based decision-making 210
evidence-based, definition 215
evidence-based medicine 322
Excellence Clusters 268
exercise
  benefits 294
  diet and health 309
  health and safety 301–2
  mental health 294
  physical fitness 294–300
  preparation 308
  social benefits 294
  suitability 306–8
  techniques 305–6
  training types 306–8
experimental learning cycle 156–7
eye contact 65, 77

F
facial expressions 78
Fair Access Guidance, The 208, 369
Fair Access to Care Services 206, 208
Family Health Services Authority 39
Fartlek training 306–7
fatigue 107
fats 279–81
fire extinguishers 182–3
fire safety 182–3
first aid 171–3
first aiders 171–2
fish bowl observation 92
fitness
  assessment 302–4
  tests 303–4
*Five-year Strategy for Children and
  Learners* 243
flexibility training 307–8
'flight or fight' 12
food additives 285
Food and Health Action Plan
  (Choosing Health 2004) 293
'food deserts' 134
food groups 279
formal communication 76
*Framework for the Assessment of
  Children in Need and Their Families*
  209–10, 211–12

G
gender socialisation 5, 6
General Chiropractic Council 328
General Medical Council 51
General Osteopathic Council 328
General Social Care Council 48, 51, 62
gestures 65, 78, 79
'Gillick competence' 33
glossary 397–403
gloves 194
GPs (general practitioners) 127–8
GPs (general practitioners) and CAM 325–6
GPs (general practitioners) surgeries 39
grip test 304
groups
  behaviour influence 64
  beliefs influence 64
  communication and positioning 70–1
  dynamics 90–1
  fish bowl observation 92
  formation 88
  formation theory 88–9
  identity 87
  'match stick game' 89
  non-sequential theories 89
  sequential theory 88–9
  structures 87–8
  'task and maintenance' activity 89–90

H
hand-washing technique 195–6
'harm reduction' approach 139
Hart, Tudor 124
Harvard referencing 273
Harvard step test 304
health
  attitudes 131
  attitudes towards 40–1

biomedical model 108–10
  campaigns 149–51
  community nursing 126–7
  current concerns 104
  definitions 106
  determinants 131, 144
  education 117–19
  environmental issues 138–9
  environmental personnel 128–9
  facets 106
  family 142–3
  fatigue 107
  GPs (general practitioners) 127–8
  housing 141–2
  illness and disease 106–7
  immunisation 123, 131–2
  inequalities reports 111
  inequalities targets 112–13
  infant mortality 112–13
  layers of influence 131
  life expectancy 112–13
  lifestyle 132–6
  maintaining 8–9
  myalgic encephalopathy 107
  National strategy 111–12
  national targets 110–11
  nurses 126–7
  personal responsibility 107–8
  perspective from lay view 108
  policy and targets 110–11
  practices 139–40
  prejudices 131
  promotion 117, 123–4
  promotion of core competencies 126
  promotion of specialist services 125–6
  protection 117, 120–3
  public health department 124–5
  recreation 140–1
  roles adopted when services available 125
  screening 121–3
  services 124–8
  smoking 104, 111, 119, 135, 146, 155
  social factors 136–8
  social model 110
  well-being concepts 105
  workplace 142
health and diet 309
health and safety
  employees' responsibilities 174–5
  employer's responsibilities 174–5
  exercise 301–2
  information for employees 171
  injury statistics 181
  policy book 179
  policy document 173
  poster 171
  statistics 165
  warning signs 168–70, 179
Health and Safety Commission 170
Health and Safety Executive 164, 170
health centres 39
Health Professions Council 51,
  317–18, 330, 331–2
health promotion
  approaches 146–7
  behavioural change 153–4
  campaign aims and objectives 149–50
  campaign planning 149–51

campaign target 150
cost effectiveness 154–6
evaluation 151–2
face-to-face 146
leaflets 146, 148
liaison between agencies 150–1
media 148–9
milestones 151
objectives for own work 152–3
posters 148
success levels 153–4
health-care services
charitable organisations 374
informal care 374–5
integrated service provision 373
local authorities 372–3
National Health Service 371–2
private companies 373
voluntary organisations 374
Healthcare Commission 52
hearing degeneration 350
heart disease 348–9
heart, the 296–7, 349
herbal medicine 315
'hidden curriculum' 6
hierarchy of human needs 83, 244
high blood pressure 291
Hindu dietary principles 289
hoists 190–1
holistic approach 313
home environment 139
*Home from Home, A – Experiences of
Black Residential Projects as a Focus of
Good Practice* 13
homeopathy 315–16
hospitals 38–9
HSAWA (Health and Safety at Work
Act 1974) 138, 164–5, 175, 178,
330–1

I
illness, coping strategies 353–4
immunisation 123, 131–2
In Control 220
indirect race relations discrimination
18
indirect sex discrimination 15–16
infant mortality 112–13
infant screening 122–3
infection control 193, 198
informal communication 76
integrated medicine 316, 318, 326
integrated society of deaf and
hearing people 229
International Guild of Professional
Practitioners 330
interval training 306
intruder alarms 178
'Inverse Care Law' 124
Irish Traveller community 36
irritable bowel syndrome 293, 353

J
Jewish dietary principles 289
judgments, unconscious 3

K
Kolb, David 98, 156

L
language 'register' 76
language barriers to accessing
services 42–3

learning cycles 98–9, 156–7
learning difficulties
care management 219–20, 226
decision making 222–4
help with choices 222–4
introduction 219–20
involvement in planning 224
'labels' 224
listening skills checklists 225
self-advocacy 220–2
learning, factors affecting 267–70
learning from adults 265
learning from books 266
learning from other children 267
learning from questions 265
learning from television 266–7
learning indirectly 264–5
learning strategies 270
learning through play 264
legislation
Care Standards Act 2000: 50, 53,
385
Carers (Recognition and Services)
Act 1995: 375, 385
Children Act 1989: 31–4, 46, 242,
260
Children Act 2004: 35–6, 242
Clean Air Acts 1950s 110
Control of Asbestos at Work
Regulations (2002) 176
Control of Lead at Work
Regulations (2002) 176
Control of Substances Hazardous
to Health Regulations (2002)
[COSHH] 173–4, 176
Crime (Sentences) Act 1997: 28
Data Protection Act 1988: 45
Data Protection Act 1998: 66,
67–8
Disability Discrimination Act
1995: 21–2, 230
Disabled Persons Act 1986: 205
Employment Equality (Religion
or Belief) Regulations (2003) 36
Employment Equality (Sexual
Orientation) Regulations (2003)
36
Equal Pay Act 1970: 15
European Convention of Human
Rights 24–5, 26
Fire Precautions (Workplace)
(Amendment) Regulations
(1999) 182
Fire Precautions (Workplace)
Regulations (1997) 166
Freedom of Information Act 2000:
45
Harassment Act 1997: 50
Health Act 1999: 386
Health and Safety (Display
Screen Equipment) Regulations
(1992 amended 2002) 176
Health and Safety (First Aid)
Regulations (1981) 171
Health and Safety (Signs and
Signals) Regulations (1996)
168–70
Health and Safety (Young
Persons Regulations (1997) 166
Health and Safety at Work Act
1974 [HSAWA] 138, 164–5, 175,
178, 330–1
Human Rights Act 1998: 24–7

Immigration and Asylum Act
1999: 27
Lifting Operations and Lifting
Equipment Regulations (1992)
[LOLER] 186–7
Management of Health and
Safety at Work (Amendment)
Regulations (1994) 166
Management of Health and
Safety at Work Regulations
(1999) 176
Manual Handling Operations
Regulations (1992 revised 1999
and 2002) 176, 186
Mental Health Act 1983 27–9, 385
Mental Health Act 1983, reforms
proposed 29–30
National Assistance Act 1948:
205
NHS and Community Care Act
1990: 205, 383–4
Noise at Work Regulations (1989)
176
Personal Protective Equipment at
Work Regulations (1992) 176,
179–80
Public Health Act 1848: 141
Race Relations Act 1976,
amended 2001: 17–19
Rail Vehicle Accessibility
Regulations (1998) 23
Reporting of Injuries, Diseases
and Dangerous Occurrences
Regulations (1995)[RIDDOR]
166–8
Sex Discrimination Act 1975:
15–17
Special Educational Needs and
Disability Act 2001: 22
Water (Fluoridation) Act 1985:
110
legislation strengths
Children Act 1989: 34
Human Rights Act 1998: 26
Mental Health Act 1983 29
Race Relations Act 1976,
amended 2001: 19
Sex Discrimination Act 1975: 16
legislation weaknesses
Children Act 1989: 34
Human Rights Act 1998: 27
Mental Health Act 1983 29
Race Relations Act 1976,
amended 2001: 19
Sex Discrimination Act 1975:
16–17
life expectancy 112–13
lifestyle
beliefs and the power of the mind
335–7
boring healthy eating 134
choices 288–9
diet 133–5
health 132–6
health, attitudes towards 40–1
less well off 134
nutrition 133–5
obesity 133
liquid-based cytology 121
listening skills 85–6
listening skills checklists 225
local health strategy 114–15
Local Strategic Partnership 115

LOLER (Lifting Operations and Lifting Equipment Regulations 1992) 186–7
lung cancer 350

M

Mac an Ghaill, Mairtin 6
Macpherson report 13
macro-nutrients 279–81
Makaton 60
malnourishment 133
manual handling
    assessment form 188
    factors when moving a client 189
    preparing individual 189
    preparing yourself 190
Martha's Vineyard 229
masks 194
Maslow, Abraham 83, 244
massage 314–15, 317
'match stick game' 89
maximal oxygen consumption test 304
McMillan, Margaret 244
Men's Health Forum 40
mental disorders
    autism 30
    restriction orders 28
    schizophrenia 30
    'sectioned' 28
    types and definitions 27
Mental Health Act Commission 30–1
mental health, exercise 294
metabolism 278
micro-nutrients 281–6
mind, power of the 335–7
minerals 284
MMR vaccine 131–2
mnemonic PIES 208
Montessori, Maria 244
moral rights 68
morbidity 137
mortality rates 109–10
moving and handling equipment 190
MRSA 139–40
multi-stage fitness test 303–4
multiple sclerosis 352
muscles 299–300, 351
musculo skeletal disorders 142, 350–1
musculo skeletal system 298–300
Muslim dietary principles 289
myalgic encephalopathy 107

N

Naidoo, J 117
nannies 246
National Association of Hospital and Community Friends 381
National Care Standards Commission 51
National Childcare Strategy 243
National health strategy 111–12
National Institute for Clinical Excellence 322
National Minimum Standards 53

National No Smoking Day 146
National Occupational Standards for Children's Care, Learning and Development 48
National Service Framework for Children, Young People and Maternity Services 242
National Service Framework for Older People 209, 370
National Service Frameworks 53
National Society for the Prevention of Cruelty to Children 51
National Strategy for Carers 216, 375
naturopathy 313, 320
'need to know' 67–8
needs, basic 8–9
needs, overview 333
nervous system 352
New NHS, The – Modern and Dependable 114
NHS Plan, The 112
non-verbal communication 65
Northern Ireland legislation
    Employment Equality (Sexual Orientation) Regulations (Northern Ireland) 2003: 37
    Equality (Disability etc) (Northern Ireland) Order 2000: 36
    Northern Ireland Act 1998: 37
    overview 36
    Race Relations (Northern Ireland) Order 1997: 36
    Sex Discrimination (Northern Ireland) Order 37
nursery nurse 252
nurses roles 127
Nursing and Midwifery Council 51, 62
nutrients 278
nutrition 133–5

O

Oakley, Ann 5
obesity 133, 292
Office for Standards in Education (Ofsted) 52–3
open questions 79
oral communication 58
organisation policies
    bullying policy 54
    child protection policy 54
    confidentiality 54
osteoporosis 292, 351
'over-three-day' injury 168
overshoes 194

P

pace of speech 77
palliative care 371
paramountcy principle 31, 48
paraphrasing 80
parents
    partnership with 259–60
    responsibility 32
    role models 5
    teenage 4
Parkinson's disease 352

patient hand block 192
person-centred care 209
person-centred, definition 212
person-centred planning 219
personal hygiene 194–5
personal protective equipment 179–80
personal safety 196–8
personal space 71
phytotherapy 315
PIES mnemonic 208
Plain Facts 221
Planning with People: Guidance for Implementation Groups 219
plastic aprons 194
play 260, 264
pollution 138
positive discrimination 23
'postcode rationing' 26
posture 78
Practical Guide for Disabled People 207
pre-school leader 252–3
pregnancy, dietary needs 287
prejudices 3, 5
preventative methods 117, 119–20
primary prevention 119
primary socialisation 4
professional relationships 76–7
Programme for Action, A 113
protective clothing 194
proteins 279
proximity 71

Q

Qigong 320
questions, open and closed 79

R

race relations
    Commission for Racial Equality 19–20
racism 10, 36
Rastafarian dietary principles 289
reception class teacher 248, 254–5
record keeping key principles 215
Recording with Care 215
recreation 140–1
recruitment 23–4
redress 23
references
    unit 1 Care values 54
    unit 2 Communication in Care Settings 102
    unit 3 Promoting Good Health 161
    unit 4 Health and Safety in Care Settings 199
    unit 5 Caring for People with Additional Needs 239
    unit 6 Working in Early Years Care and Education 275
    unit 7 Health as a Lifestyle Choice 310
    unit 8 Complementary Therapies 344–5
    unit 9 Caring for older people 387–8
referencing, Harvard method 273

reflective practitioner 156–7
reflexology 314–15
Reiki 320
relationship building communication 74
religion
    beliefs 288–9
    intolerance 7
    socialisation 7–8
resistance training 307
respiratory system 296
respite care 220, 372
restriction orders 28
rheumatism 351
RIDDOR (Reporting of Injuries, Diseases and Dangerous Occurrences Regulations 1995) 166–8
risk assessment
    checklist 188
    manual handling 187–9
    overview 176–8
    record example 177
risk reduction 178, 180–1
risk training 178
role models
    parents 5
    television characters 7

S
safety signs 168–70, 179
Saving Lives – Our Healthier Nation 111
scenarios and 'consider this' sections
    Alzheimer's sufferer, listening to 378
    babysitting 75
    bath, help in taking a 206–7
    bereavement 365
    care plan checking 217
    cerebral palsy 11
    Community Learning Disability Team 235
    deaf people not allowed for 231
    depressed widow 208
    dismissive GP 40
    employing talented blind person 233
    holistic approach by osteopath 313
    hospital, coming out of 370
    learning difficulties 99, 222–3, 224–5
    lifting patients 187
    mobility problems and health records 230
    multiple sclerosis 35
    'need to know' and confidentiality 68
    parents communication at day nursery 84
    partially sighted and lacking confidence 212
    person-centred approach 367–8
    professional value system 75
    raising HIV risk awareness 157
    Rastafarian worker 20
    respite care 220
    safety responsibilities 165
    tobacco control strategy 116
    young people and health issues 145

sclerosis 349
screening
    breast 122
    cervical 121–2
    infant 122–3
secondary prevention 119–20
'sectioned' 28
security
    early years settings 184–5
    residential homes 184–5
    settings in general 183–5
self-advocacy 220–2
self-esteem 12–13
sensory impairment 350
service providers' roles 214
service users, interaction with
    aims 95
    effectiveness 95
    evaluating effectiveness 99–100
    evaluation importance 98
    feedback 97
    learning from experience 99–100
    perspectives 97–8
    planning 95
    problem solving 98
    reflection 98
    skills evaluation 95–7
    skills identification 95–7
    systematic approach 94
seven steps of care management 205–7
shared learning 267
sharps disposal 197
sign-language systems 229
single assessment process 209, 371
'single-handed practice' 39
sit-and-reach test 303
skinfold measurements 304
slide sheet 191
slide/transfer board 191
smoking 104, 111, 119, 135, 146, 155
Social Care Register 51
social class grouping 136
social factors 268
socialisation
    attitudes 3
    attitudes to health 40–1
    care workers' part of process 14
    gender 5, 6
    key concept 8
    media 7
    peers 6
    primary 4
    religion 7–8
    secondary 6–8
    television 7
socio-economic classification 137
SOLER principles 86–7
speech communities 76
standard precautions 196
steady-state training 306
Steiner, Rudolf 244, 316
stereotypes 3–4, 66
sterilising 198
strokes 352
structured data collection 210–11
structured information 210–11
submissive people 72, 73
substance use 135–6, 139
summaries
    access and overcoming barriers to services 43
    attitudes and prejudices 14

care values 54
communication 61, 74, 93
communication skills 84
equality legislation 37
groups 93
health factors 144
health models 115
health promotion 130
rights and responsibilities 37
service users interaction 100
summarising 80
support belts 191
supportive communication 90, 92
SureStart 269

T
task-focussed communication 74
teenage parents 4
tertiary prevention 120
Thompson, N 94
Thompson, T L 90, 92
Thompson, Tearesa 58
tone of voice 77
training
    principles 301–2
    types 306–8
transfer assist devices 191
transfer belts 191
transsexuals 16
Tuckman, B 88
turning disc 192

U
ulcerative colitis 353
unacceptable behaviour 3, 4

V
Valuing People 219, 228
vegetarians 288
Victoria Climbe Inquiry report 35
visual degeneration 350
vitamins 281–3
Vocational Training Charitable Trust 332

W
waste (clinical) disposal 196
websites
    unit 1 Care values 54
    unit 2 Communication in Care Settings 102
    unit 3 Promoting Good Health 161–2
    unit 4 Health and Safety in Care Settings 199
    unit 5 Caring for People with Additional Needs 239
    unit 6 Working in Early Years Care and Education 275
    unit 7 Health as a Lifestyle Choice 310
    unit 8 Complementary Therapies 345
    unit 9 Caring for older people 388
'welfare checklist' 31–2
well-being 8–9
Willis, J 117
work environment 138–9
written communication 59–60